1976 BRITANNICA BOOK OF THE YEAR

ENCYCLOPÆDIA BRITANNICA, INC.

Chicago, Toronto, London, Geneva, Sydney, Tokyo, Manila, Johannesburg, Seoul

Library of Congress Catalog Card Number: 38–12082
International Standard Book Number: 0–85229–311–9

BRITANNICA BOOK OF THE YEAR

(*Trademark Reg. U.S. Pat. Off.*)
Printed in U.S.A.

THE UNIVERSITY OF CHICAGO

The Britannica Book of the Year is published with the editorial advice of the faculties of the University of Chicago.

Contents

Feature Articles

People of the Year

Chronology of Events

Book of the Year

Special Reports

WIDE WORLD

The Bicentennial of the United States

by Sam J. Ervin, Jr.

As we celebrate the bicentennial of the independence of our country, we ought to indulge in both retrospection and consecration.

The Uses of History. We cannot overmagnify the value of surveying with frequency things past. If a people deem history to be bunk or a dust heap, they lend credence to the disconsolate assertion of the German philosopher Hegel that people and governments never learn anything from history or act on principles deduced from it. The truth is that those who ignore the lessons history teaches are doomed to repeat the mistakes of the past.

History has the capacity to teach wisdom and patriotism. As Sir Walter Raleigh noted 350 years ago, "We may gather out of history a policy no less wise than eternal." In commenting on this concept, the British historian James Anthony Froude observed:

> History is a voice forever sounding across the centuries the laws of right and wrong. Opinions alter, manners change, creeds rise and fall, but the moral law is written on the tablets of eternity.

Surely nothing has greater potency to inspire love of our country as we celebrate its bicentennial than recurring to the historic truth that on its natal day 200 years ago the signers of the Declaration of Independence pledged their lives, their fortunes, and their sacred honour to make America free and independent.

When one reviews in detail the unjust actions of the king and the Parliament of Great Britain which provoked the American Colonies, Connecticut, Delaware, Georgia, Maryland, Massachusetts, New Hampshire, New Jersey, New York, North Carolina, Pennsylvania, Rhode Island, South Carolina, and Virginia, to revolt against British rule and become free and independent states, he is reminded that history is reputed to be prophecy in reverse, and that coming events are said to cast their shadows before them.

Settlement of the Colonies. Before detailing the unjust acts of king and Parliament, it is essential to describe the origins and characteristics of the men and women who established their homes in the 13 Colonies.

The predominating majority of them were English, Scots-Irish, and Lowland Scots. They made their mother tongue, the English language, the vernacular of their new land, and those of them who were of English ancestry gave the Colonies the common law of England and the colonists a pride in what they conceived to be their rights as subjects of Britain. The second most numerous group of colonists were Germans from the Rhineland-Palatinate, who had been much harassed by war and religious persecution and who located in Pennsylvania before spreading to other areas. They were preceded, or accompanied, or followed by lesser numbers of French Huguenots, Dutch, Highland Scots, Swiss, Swedes, and Welsh.

All of these people had one motive in common for coming to America. They desired to better their economic lot. Moreover, a substantial proportion of the original settlers had two additional motives for migrating to the Colonies. They dissented from the doctrines of the churches established by law in the lands of their origins, and for that reason were disabled by their laws from holding civil office. Hence, they came to America because they hoped to find in the New World the political and religious liberties denied them in the old.

The population of the Southern Colonies was augmented by black Africans involuntarily imported as slaves.

Causes of the Revolution. Let us enumerate briefly the grave injustices which king and Parliament visited on the Colonies.

By a series of Navigation Acts, which were adopted in 1660 and subsequent years and which were designed to secure a monopoly of colonial trade to English merchants and shippers, Parliament decreed that goods of any origin bound to England or to English colonies had to be transported in English ships; that the chief products of the Colonies, including cotton, sugar, and tobacco, could be exported only to England, where they were subjected to English customs duties; that all ships carrying goods of European manufacture to the Colonies had to pass through English ports and pay English customs duties on their cargoes; and that prosecutions for violations of the Navigation Acts were triable without juries in admiralty courts.

By 1760 the Colonies were divisible into five chartered colonies, which enjoyed limited powers of self-government under charters previously issued to them by the king with tacit parliamentary assent, and eight crown colonies, which were subject to all practical intents and purposes to the rule of the king acting through the agency of his Privy Council. To be sure, each colony had a legislative body, usually called the assembly, whose members were elected by their freeholders. But the acts of these assemblies had to be forwarded to England for approval or disapproval by the king-in-council before they could be operative. The repeated abuse by the king of his royal power to approve or disapprove the acts of colonial assemblies rightly generated complaints by the colonists that he refused his assent to laws demanded by "the public good" and neglected

---

Sam J. Ervin, Jr., was a U.S. senator from North Carolina for nearly 21 years and became a familiar figure in 1973 as chairman of the Senate Watergate committee. Renowned for his command of constitutional law, Ervin is a graduate of Harvard Law School. He served for 15 years on the North Carolina bench, six of them as associate justice of the state Supreme Court. In this article he provides a retrospective account of the meaning and promise of America, which is most appropriate in this bicentennial year.

to take any action whatever in respect to other "Laws of immediate and pressing importance."

The king delegated to the governors of crown colonies the royal authority to call, adjourn, and dissolve the assemblies chosen by the freeholders and to veto the legislation they adopted. Since the assemblies were the only representatives the colonists were permitted to choose, their members were the champions of the people, and the exercise of their drastic delegated powers by the governors kept them and the assemblies at constant loggerheads.

As a consequence, the inhabitants of crown colonies justifiably complained that royal governors vetoed acts adopted by assemblies for "the accommodation of large districts of people"; that they called the assemblies to meet "at places unusual, uncomfortable, and distant from the depository of their public Records, for the sole purpose of fatiguing them into compliance with" their wishes; that they dissolved assemblies "repeatedly, for opposing with manly firmness" their "invasions on the rights of the people"; and that they refused for long periods of time "after such dissolutions, to cause others to be elected."

Taxation Without Representation. The colonists entertained an abiding conviction that the unwritten English constitution prohibited any legislative body in which they were not represented from levying taxes on English subjects. As a consequence, they were sure that their basic rights as English subjects were flagrantly violated by Parliament when it enacted the Sugar Act of 1764, which imposed customs duties on molasses imported by New England Colonies from the non-British West Indies for the manufacture of rum, and the Stamp Act of 1765, which required that revenue stamps be affixed to all official documents and printed matter in the Colonies.

The Sugar Act was never really enforced.

The colonists were deeply incensed by the Stamp Act because it provided that prosecutions for its violation were triable without juries in admiralty courts. They deemed it offended both their right to trial by jury and their right to be taxed only by a legislative body in which they had representation. Opposition to the Stamp Act was characterized by an intensity of emotion among the colonists and widespread boycotting of English goods. Fearing loss of their American markets, English merchants persuaded Parliament to repeal the act a year after its enactment.

The ameliorating effect that the repeal of the Stamp Act would otherwise have had on the passions of the colonists was substantially diminished because Parliament simultaneously passed the Declaratory Act of 1766, which proclaimed that it possessed plenary power to legislate for the Colonies in respect to all matters. Parliament did not delay in exerting its asserted power.

Upon the recommendation of Charles Townshend, the British chancellor of the Exchequer, Parliament enacted during 1767 the acts which bear his name.

The first Townshend Act was directed against New York alone because its assembly had refused to obey the Mutiny Act of 1765, which required the Colonies to furnish barracks for British troops stationed in them and to provide certain free supplies, such as beer and rum, for such troops. The act suspended the New York assembly until it performed the obligations imposed by that act.

The second act, which was known as the Townshend Revenue Act, imposed customs duties on paper, glass, paint, lead, and the East India Company's tea, which the colonists imported from England.

The third Townshend Act reorganized the British customs system in America by increasing the number of its officers, requiring them to make every effort to collect all customs duties imposed on the Colonies by the Navigation Acts and the Townshend Revenue Act, and by authorizing them to employ in all Colonies in their efforts to perform their assignment hated writs of assistance, which empowered them to search homes, buildings, ships, and all other places for supposedly smuggled goods without obtaining specific warrants.

Rising Discontent. The Townshend Acts and the activities they sanctioned aroused indignation and opposition in all the Colonies. The reaction to them was particularly adverse in Massachusetts and Virginia. Since the king and his ministers had reached the conclusion that the popular leaders of the people in Massachusetts had already committed treason against the crown, they induced Parliament to revive the Statute of 35 Henry VIII, which authorized transportation to England for trial in English courts of persons charged with treason against the crown in areas outside England.

Parliament amended the Townshend Revenue Act in 1770 by eliminating all customs duties it imposed except that on tea. This event did not abate the dissatisfaction of the colonists. They established Committees of Correspondence in the various colonies to ban the importation of tea, which had become to them a symbol of British tyranny, and to consult with each other concerning other matters of mutual interest. Besides, other groups, known as the Sons of Liberty, were organized in the cities to engage, if need be, in more drastic action.

In May 1773 Parliament passed the Tea Act to aid the financially ailing East India Company. By this act, Parliament granted special concessions to the company in respect to the tea it shipped to the Colonies to enable it to undersell Dutch tea, which was being smuggled into the Colonies.

When ships carrying the East India Company's tea reached the chief ports of the Colonies in December, the Sons of Liberty managed to exclude it from commercial channels. At Charleston they had it impounded in a warehouse, and at Philadelphia and New York they induced the ships to turn back. At Boston members of the Sons of Liberty wearing disguises cast 342 chests of the tea into the harbour.

The last episode, which is known as the Boston Tea Party, goaded the king and his ministers into retaliatory measures. They increased the British garrison in Boston and induced Parliament to pass four acts which the colonists dubbed the Intolerable Acts of 1774.

The first act, the Boston Port Act, closed the port of Boston to commerce until Boston recompensed the owners of the tea that had been cast into its harbour and the king adjudged that obedience to law prevailed. The second, the Massachusetts Government Act, deprived that colony of substantial powers of self-rule it had enjoyed throughout its history. The third, the Administration of Justice Act, authorized the removal from Massachusetts to neighbouring colonies or even to Britain of the trials of persons charged with capital offenses allegedly committed in behalf of the government. The fourth, the Quartering Act, legalized the quartering of British soldiers in private homes without the consent of their owners.

Since they were so manifestly tyrannous, the Intolerable Acts raised the anger of the colonists to unprecedented heights. The First Continental Congress, which met at Philadelphia Sept. 5, 1774, denounced the Intolerable Acts and other recent parliamentary enactments as inimical to the rights of the colonists as British subjects, and proposed that colonial imports from Britain should cease after Dec. 1, 1774, and colonial exports to Britain should end after Sept. 10, 1775, unless the Intolerable Acts were sooner repealed. The terms of this proposal plainly indicated a desire to effect a peaceful reconciliation with Britain.

The Beginning of the Revolution. But this was not to be. On April 19, 1775, British soldiers, who were proceeding from Boston to Concord, 17 mi. distant, to seize colonial military stores, encountered Massachusetts minutemen at Lexington and Concord and engaged in bloody skirmishes with them.

News of these skirmishes, which marked the beginning of the American Revolution, spread like wildfire throughout the Colonies, which prepared to resist military subjugation by armed force. As the days passed, large numbers of colonial militia assembled at Boston, and powerful British military and naval forces converged nearby. On June 17, 1775, the British attacked American militia entrenched on Breed's Hill overlooking Charlestown, and a furious encounter, known to history as the Battle of Bunker Hill, ensued. After hard fighting, the British drove the Americans from their position but they suffered 1,000 casualties in so doing.

Two days previously the Second Continental Congress, which had convened at Philadelphia on May 10, had issued a commission as commanding general of American forces to George Washington, who assumed command at Boston in July and served in this post with great distinction throughout the Revolution. On Dec. 22, 1775, Parliament undertook to prevent the colonists from obtaining any outside aid by enacting a statute that prohibited all intercourse with them.

The Declaration of Independence. As hostilities expanded, the majority of Americans were reluctantly driven to the conclusion that independence from Britain offered the only solution to their problems.

On April 12, 1776, North Carolina became the first of the 13 Colonies to empower its delegates in the Continental Congress to vote for independence, and on May 15, 1776, Virginia became the first of the Colonies to instruct its delegates in that body to take affirmative action to accomplish that end.

On June 7, 1776, Richard Henry Lee, a delegate from Virginia, offered a resolution to the Congress declaring "that these United Colonies are, and of right ought to be, free and independent States." Congress forthwith named John Adams, Benjamin Franklin, Thomas Jefferson, Robert R. Livingston, and Roger Sherman as a committee to prepare a declaration conforming to Lee's resolution. The

"The Battle of Bunker's Hill," June 17, 1775. Painting by John Trumbull.

other committeemen delegated the actual drafting of the declaration to Thomas Jefferson, whose philosophy of government and facility of written expression ideally equipped him for the task.

On July 2, 1776, Congress passed Lee's resolution; on July 4, 1776, Congress adopted with slight modifications Jefferson's final draft of the Declaration of Independence and made it public; on July 19, 1776, Congress "resolved, that the Declaration passed on the 4th be fairly engrossed on parchment with the title and stile of 'The unanimous Declaration of the thirteen united States of America,' and that the same, when engrossed, be signed by every member of Congress"; and on Aug. 2, 1776, most of the 56 signers of the engrossed copy of the Declaration of Independence, which is now on display in the exhibition hall of the National Archives in Washington, D.C., affixed their signatures to that instrument, although a number of them did so subsequent to that day.

Of these four significant days, July 4, 1776, is universally accepted and celebrated as the birthday of the United States of America.

The Declaration of Independence, which is America's most eloquent and stirring political document, is divisible into a preamble and a resolution, and the preamble is, in turn, divisible into four sections.

The first section of the preamble asserts that when one people "dissolve the political bands which have connected them with another" and "assume among the powers of the earth" the station of a separate and independent nation, "a decent respect to the opinions of mankind requires that they should declare the causes which impel them to the separation."

The second section expounds these views:

> We hold these truths to be self-evident, that all men are created equal, that they are endowed by their Creator with certain inalienable Rights, that among these are Life, Liberty and the pursuit of Happiness.—That to secure these rights, Governments are instituted among Men, deriving their just powers from the consent of the governed,—That whenever any Form of Government becomes destructive of these ends, it is the Right of the People to alter or to abolish it, and to institute new Government, laying its foundation on such principles and organizing its powers in such form, as to them shall seem most likely to effect their Safety and Happiness.

After charging in general terms that king and Parliament had subjected the Colonies to repeated abuses, injuries, and usurpations to establish an absolute tyranny over them, the third section of the preamble undertakes to prove the truth of the charges to "a candid world" by specifying in vivid words the unjust acts of the king and Parliament.

The fourth section of the preamble recites that "In every stage of these Oppressions" the Colonies petitioned king and Parliament "for Redress in the most humble terms"; that their repeated petitions were "answered only by repeated injury." The fourth section further states that the Colonies appealed from time to time to their "British brethren" in the name of justice and kinship to disavow the attempts of Parliament "to extend an unwarrantable jurisdiction" over them; and that their "British brethren" were likewise "deaf to the voice of justice and of consanguinity." In the resolution, which concludes the Declaration, "the Representatives of the united States of America" declare:

> That these United Colonies are, and of Right ought to be Free and Independent States; that they are Absolved from all Allegiance to the British Crown, and that all political connection between them and the State of Great Britain, is and ought to be totally dissolved; and that as Free and Independent States, they have full Power to levy War, conclude Peace, contract Alliances, establish Commerce, and to do all other Acts and Things which Independent States may of right do.—And for the support of this Declaration, with a firm reliance on the Protection of Divine Providence, we mutually pledge to each other our Lives, our Fortunes and our sacred Honor.

Most of the hard fighting of the Revolution occurred in the North and the South and on the seas during the years following the Declaration of Independence. The fighting ceased Oct. 19, 1781, when Lord Cornwallis, the British commander in chief, surrendered to Washington at Yorktown, and the Revolution legally ended Sept. 3, 1783, with the formal signing of the Treaty of Paris, whereby Great Britain recognized the independence of the United States and ceded to them its claim to the territory lying north of the Ohio and south of Canada which it had won from France in the French and Indian War.

The Articles of Confederation. Although the 13 states adopted constitutions for themselves during the early days of the Revolution, efforts to unite them in a formal government suffered delays, and the Articles of Confederation, which the Continental Congress submitted to the states Nov. 15, 1777, were not made effective by the ratification of the last state, Maryland, until March 1, 1781.

There is more than a modicum of truth in the observation of James Madison that the Articles of Confederation were "nothing more than a treaty of amity and of alliance between independent and sovereign states."

The Articles converted the Continental Congress into the Congress of the Confederation; gave each state, regardless of population, one vote in that body; and provided that amendments to them had to be approved by all states. They vested in Congress the power to maintain an army and navy and to make war, to conduct foreign relations and negotiate treaties, to coin and borrow money, to establish a post office and standards of weights and measures, and to regulate dealings with the Indians. While they gave Congress the authority to create executive departments, they did not set up a federal judiciary.

Under the Articles, Congress was denied the power to levy taxes of any nature or to regulate commerce among the states or with foreign nations. It was forbidden to make any commercial treaty abridging the right of a state to collect customs duties, even on imports from other states. Moreover, Congress had no coercive powers and was compelled to depend for the payment of expenses and debts on moneys voluntarily supplied to it by the states in conformity with requisitions made by it on them.

With the coming of peace, the new nation was confronted by problems that demonstrated the insufficiency of the existing Articles of Confederation. The states failed to honour adequately congressional requisitions for money, and for that reason Congress became unable to make payments on the principal and interest of the debts it had incurred by borrowing. The enormous amounts of paper currency Congress and the states had issued to finance the Revolution became practically worthless and caused a high degree of inflation. Besides, some of the states made commercial war on others by imposing customs duties on im-

Congress adopts the Declaration of Independence. Painting by John Trumbull.

ports and by restricting the use of navigable waters by ships operated by nonresident owners.

At this sad juncture, Congress adopted a resolution inviting the 13 states to send delegates to a convention, which it called to meet at Philadelphia in May 1787, for the purpose of proposing revisions of the Articles of Confederation. All of the states except Rhode Island responded to the invitation by sending 55 delegates, who were much experienced in politics and government and deeply versed in history and political philosophy, to the convention which met in secret sessions in the Pennsylvania Statehouse, now Independence Hall, from May 25 to Sept. 17, 1787.

The Constitution. Instead of proposing revisions of the Articles of Confederation, the convention, which is known to history as the Constitutional Convention, prepared and reported to the Congress a plan in writing for a complete national government for the United States. Congress submitted the plan to the states for ratification or rejection by the people in specially called state conventions. Under the terms of the submission, the plan became effective as the Constitution of the United States on June 21, 1788, when the ninth state, New Hampshire, ratified it.

The Constitution consisted originally of seven articles. Since its adoption, 26 amendments have been added to it. Since the first ten amendments, which constitute the Bill of Rights, became effective Dec. 15, 1791, they are generally deemed to be a part of the original Constitution.

As its preamble recites, the people of the United States ordained and established the Constitution "to form a more perfect Union, establish Justice, insure domestic Tranquility, provide for the common defence, promote the general Welfare, and secure the Blessings of Liberty" to themselves and their posterity.

The Constitution is well adapted to these ends. Its chief characteristics are its diffusion of the power of government, its adoption of the principle that the just powers of government are derived from the people, its system of checks by which each of the departments resists the encroachments and excesses of the others, and its balancing of the authority which government must have in order to rule and the liberty which the individual must enjoy in order to pursue happiness.

The Constitution utilizes the doctrine of the separation of powers in a twofold way. First, the Constitution makes the United States a federal republic by delegating to it the powers which enable it to function as a national government for the states, the territories, and the people, and by reserving to the states the powers which enable them to regulate their internal and local affairs. Second, the Constitution divides the powers it delegates to the United States among its three departments by assigning the legislative power to the Congress, the executive power to the president, and the judicial power to the Supreme Court and the inferior federal courts.

Congress consists of the Senate, where each state is represented by two senators irrespective of its population, and the House of Representatives, where each state is represented by representatives whose numbers are proportional to its population.

Senators and representatives are chosen by the people whose qualifications for voting in each state must conform to those prescribed by state law for electors of the most numerous branch of its legislature, subject to the limitation that no state may base any qualification for voting in a federal or state election on race, or sex, or on age in respect to any persons who are 18 years or older, and subject to the further limitation that no state may base any qualification for voting in a federal election on the payment of any poll or other tax.

The only other elective officers of the United States are the president and the vice-president, who are chosen by electors acting for the states. The electors in each state are equal in number to its senators and representatives in Congress and are appointed in the manner its legislature directs. State legislatures universally provide nowadays that electors are to be elected by the people.

All principal officers of the United States are nominated by the president subject to confirmation by the Senate. A constitutional provision makes Supreme Court and other federal judges independent of the president, the Congress, and the people by giving them tenure during good behaviour and prescribing that the compensation for their services cannot be diminished during their continuance in office.

Time and space do not permit this article to analyze in detail the powers the Constitution confers on the United States, the powers the Constitution reserves to the states, the limitations the Constitution imposes on the states, and the limitations which the Constitution in general and the Bill of Rights in particular impose on the United States and the states to protect the people against governmental tyranny. It must suffice to say that the Constitution requires all laws, national and state, to operate in like manner on all persons similarly situated, and forbids the United States and the states to deprive any person of life, liberty, or property without due process of law.

Thomas Jefferson, third U.S. president and principal framer of the Declaration of Independence. Sketch by Benjamin Latrobe.

MARYLAND HISTORICAL SOCIETY

The First Amendment. More extended notice must be taken, however, of the First Amendment.

The wise men who added the First Amendment to the Constitution had two reasons for their action. As philosophers, they believed that a full and free flow of information and ideas is essential to free Americans from the worst sort of tyranny; *i.e.*, tyranny over the mind. As pragmatists, they recognized that a full and free flow of information and ideas is necessary to enable the people to make the institutions of government the Constitution creates operate with efficiency and without corruption.

The First Amendment condemns any governmental action "abridging the freedom of speech, or of the press." By so doing, it secures to every person within our borders freedom to think whatever he pleases and freedom to speak or publish whatever he wishes with impunity, provided what he says or publishes is not obscene and does not falsely defame another, or obstruct courts in their administration of justice, or impede legislative bodies in their discharge of their public functions, or create a clear and present danger that it will incite others to commit crimes.

The First Amendment condemns any governmental action "abridging . . . the right of the people peaceably to assemble, and to petition the Government for a redress of grievances." By so doing, it secures to every person within our borders freedom to associate with others of like mind to accomplish any lawful purpose, freedom to meet peaceably with others for consultation and protest, and freedom to petition those invested with powers of government for relief from any ills, real or imagined.

The First Amendment condemns any governmental action "respecting an establishment of religion, or prohibiting the free exercise thereof." By so doing, it secures to every person within our borders freedom to entertain such religious beliefs as appeal to his conscience, freedom to practice his religious beliefs in any form of worship not dangerous to himself or injurious to the rights of others, freedom to endeavour by peaceful persuasion to convert others to his religious beliefs, and freedom to be exempt from taxation to support any institution which teaches religion.

The United States Today. During the 200 years that have passed since the signing of the Declaration of Independence, America, which was composed at that time of the 13 states along the Atlantic seacoast, has become a mighty federal republic, whose 48 coterminous states and the State of Alaska in North America and the State of Hawaii in the mid-Pacific contain more than 3.6 million sq.mi., making it the fourth largest nation in area on Earth.

As a result of the birthrate among its vigorous people and the admission of upwards of 47 million immigrants from other lands, the population of the country has increased during the same period from about 3.5 million persons to more than 218 million, making it the world's fourth most populous country.

The Constitution guarantees to each of the inhabitants of America such precious liberties as the right to be free from arbitrary personal restraint or servitude; the right to equal treatment by the laws; the right to travel when and where he pleases; the right to be free in the enjoyment of his faculties and the acquisition of knowledge; the right to worship God according to the dictates of his own conscience; the right to pursue any lawful calling and acquire and own property; the right to marry, establish a home, and to rear children; the right to enjoy his home and privacies without unreasonable governmental intrusion; the right to speak freely and to associate with others for any lawful purpose; the right to petition government for a redress of grievances, actual or imaginary; and the right to do such other acts as he deems best for his own interests insofar as they are not inconsistent with the equal rights of others.

Moreover, the Constitution secures to those of America's inhabitants who possess the requisite qualifications the right to vote and to hold public office.

The energy of its people and the richness of its natural resources have made the United States the greatest agricultural, manufacturing, merchandising, trading, and investing nation of the world. Its combined economic power exceeds by a wide margin that of any other nation.

The Constitution makes these things possible because its commerce clause gives American business nationwide markets free from trade barriers, and the free enterprise system it supports inspires Americans to produce goods and services in abundance by allowing them to keep a fair share of the fruits of their labour for themselves, their families, and the causes they hold dear.

The present precarious state of mankind compels the United States to assume a position of leadership in the free world and to maintain potent armed forces to deter the threat of Communist aggression against itself and its allied nations.

Consecration. While they are of crucial importance to America and the free world at this critical stage of history, the vast domain, the economic power, the position of world leadership, and the military might of America do not constitute its most precious possession. America's most precious possession is the Constitution, which makes the United States a free republic.

The Constitution has enabled the United States to survive external and internal storms and has become the Earth's oldest continuing instrument of government.

Certainly the generation that witnessed the series of tragedies known collectively as the Watergate affair has ample reason to comprehend the value and vitality of the Constitution and its wise division of the powers it delegates to the national government among its three departments. When the president violated his constitutional obligation to take care that the laws be faithfully executed, the Senate, the House, and the judiciary remained steadfast to their constitutional trusts, and the president was driven from his high office for obstructing justice without disruption of the constitutional processes of the national government.

In addition, the Watergate affair teaches anew a lesson which the Supreme Court had previously recorded in these simple words in *United States* v. *Lee* (106 U.S. 196, 220):

> No man in this country is so high that he is above the law. No officer of the law may set that law at defiance with impunity. All of the officers of the law, from the highest to the lowest, are creatures of the law and are bound to obey it. It is the only supreme power in our system of government.

As Americans celebrate the bicentennial, it is proper to emphasize some inescapable truths.

Freedom is not free. Our freedom was bought for us by the blood, sweat, tears, and prayers of multitudes of men and women, great and small. Freedom is hard to win but easy to lose. The price of its keeping is eternal vigilance and an unceasing readiness to guard and defend it.

The Constitution, which consists of words on a piece of parchment, is not self-executing. It depends for its vitality on the love which men and women nourish for it in their hearts and the fidelity which public officers chosen by them manifest for it in performing their duties.

Strange as it may seem, the Constitution has covert enemies who appear to be unaware of their enmity for it. They do not seek to destroy it in one fell swoop. They undertake to nibble it away bit by bit.

All public officers love power, and many of them abuse it grossly. One department of government encroaches on the domains of the others. Some administrators and even some judges twist the words of the Constitution awry to effect constitutionally prohibited ends they deem just. Judicial activists succumb at times to the ever lurking temptation to misconstrue the Constitution and thus make it mean what it would have said if they instead of its framers had written it. Many public officers and individuals fear the exercise of constitutional liberties by persons whose ideas they hate and seek in devious ways to prevent or frustrate such exercise by them. Zealots undertake to nullify constitutional principles of inestimable value by annexing to them weasel-worded amendments expressing their own petty notions concerning insignificant or transitory problems. Many public officers and politically powerful groups seek to destroy the value of the United States as a federal republic by concentrating all powers in the national government and reducing the states to meaningless zeros on the nation's map.

These myriad endeavours put constitutional government and constitutional liberties in jeopardy and make it plain that a supreme obligation rests upon those Americans who really love the Constitution.

This obligation is to consecrate themselves during the bicentennial period and the after years to the task of preserving the Constitution for themselves and all succeeding generations of Americans.

If they will perform this task with vigilance and vigour, they will avert the calamity Daniel Webster feared when he uttered these true, but sad, words:

> Other misfortunes may be borne, or their effects overcome. If disastrous wars should sweep our commerce from the ocean, another generation may renew it; if it exhaust our treasury, future industry may replenish it; if it desolate and lay waste our fields, still, under a new cultivation, they will grow green again, and ripen to future harvests.
>
> It were but a trifle even if the walls of yonder Capitol were to crumble, if its lofty pillars should fall, and its gorgeous decorations be all covered by the dust of the valley. All of these may be rebuilt.
>
> But who shall reconstruct the fabric of demolished government?
>
> Who shall rear again the well-proportioned columns of constitutional liberty?
>
> Who shall frame together the skillful architecture which unites national sovereignty with State Rights, individual security, and public prosperity?
>
> No, if these columns fall, they will be raised not again. Like the Coliseum and the Parthenon, they will be destined to a mournful and melancholy immortality. Bitterer tears, however, will flow over them than ever were shed over the monuments of Roman or Grecian art; for they will be the monuments of a more glorious edifice than Greece or Rome ever saw—the edifice of constitutional American liberty.

Free Enterprise in America

by Robert Nozick

America has flourished under a system that includes large, but not unlimited, scope for free enterprise. Is this a coincidence, or is the large component of free enterprise a cause of America's flourishing? And have the limits placed on free enterprise been beneficial or detrimental?

Framework of the System. A system of free enterprise has several components: property rights, freedom of action, of exchange, of association, and of contract. There are private and transferable property rights. Each adult may contract to provide or purchase goods and services in the present or for the future. The markets in which such rights to means of production, goods, and services are transferred or exchanged are open. There are no regulations limiting any adult from buying or selling in the market and there are no regulations limiting the terms of any agreements made except, of course, that no agreement may be made to inflict violence on another or to defraud another. Within this same limitation, which sets forth the rights of others, individuals may associate as they choose with contractual commitments setting the terms of their association and fixing their obligations and liabilities to one another. Activities, enterprises, or projects take place when supported by private parties, voluntary groupings, customers, benefactors, or patrons and there are no government subsidies for particular activities. Under such a system there will be competition in diverse markets, but there is no need to look for some economist's abstract notion of "perfect competition."

The components of free enterprise are protected by a governmental structure. But it is important to notice that the relationship is reciprocal, that the U.S. structure itself rests to a large extent on free enterprise. It is difficult to see how freedom of the press, for example, can flourish in the absence of private owners of such resources as paper or printing presses who can help disseminate, if only to profit from, opinions that the general public or the government finds objectionable.

Within the framework of free enterprise are accomplished the tasks that any ongoing society must carry out. The tasks are accomplished without central direction and perhaps even without anyone noticing them. Three features of the human condition are that people are not omniscient, that they have separate interests, and that resources are not sufficient for everyone to have everything he desires. Any society, therefore, will have some way of determining what particular mix of consumer goods is to be produced, how many resources are to be held back from current consumption, and how much is to be invested to increase future production. Also, to effect these decisions the society will have to transmit information to the many people whose cooperation is needed for joint production.

The price system of an unhampered market in a free enterprise system provides people with a summary of far-flung information about the diverse uses of their labour and the material they control. They learn where its use is most wanted as compared with all other feasible uses. The retention of returns from performing these activities provides people with the requisite incentives to do them. In this way a market transmits knowledge of economic opportunities and coordinates the activities of people in an efficient manner, allowing people to spend their gained incentives for whatever purposes they choose.

Consumers pay for purchases with the results of their own previous economic activity, or with gifts received from the economic activity of others. Their desires for particular products are reflected back within the price system, ultimately to the owners of factors of production, who are eager to direct their resources so they will bring the highest return. Miscalculations about what consumers want or a lesser ability to serve these wants leads to losses rather than profits and so eventually to a redirection of these resources to more productive tasks. The risks of production for the market are borne, in a division of labour, by those who choose to carry them, by entrepreneurs who guarantee payment to factors of production including labour (even if their product, as it turns out, cannot profitably be sold) and who pay the producers before receiving returns from the sale of the final product. In organizing production of new products or new ways of producing old products the entrepreneur is ever alert, trying to outproduce or outfigure or outguess competitors to increase his profits. These profits (or losses) are the difference between what the entrepreneur must pay for the factors and labour utilized in production and the total payment for the final product.

Opportunities for profitable future use also lead people to hold back resources from current consumption and to turn them to the production of capital goods used for future production. Private and transferable property rights lead owners to take a long-term view of their resources and to forgo quick gains in order to realize future profits. With transferable rights future developments are capitalized into the present value of capital goods. In contrast, workers in a system of democratic workers' control, lacking transferable property rights, would downplay far-future benefits to be gotten from certain uses or preserving of current capital. It is precisely in activities where such property rights were lacking, for example in timbering on public lands, that future consequences were ignored. Allocation of goods over time is aided by speculators who

Robert Nozick, professor of philosophy at Harvard University, is the author of Anarchy, State, and Utopia *(1974), a widely acclaimed defense of private enterprise and critique of the welfare state which won the National Book Award in 1975.*

hold back goods from current consumption in anticipation of a higher future price. Time also enters in futures contracts, which enable the owner of a commodity to divest himself of the risk of fluctuations in its value.

Sometimes they are one and the same person but often they are not, and so savers who wish to invest and entrepreneurs who wish to organize factors of production must be brought together. This is done through private capital markets. The more developed a private capital market, the more sophisticated its money and credit instruments, the more intricate the enterprises it can sustain.

In a noncoercive fashion a system of free enterprise lures resources and people's activities into serving the desires of others and utilizes widely diverse information which no one person or central planning group does or can possess. Individuals, of course, may choose to pursue less lucrative activities; they may become artists rather than industrialists.

In theory a large number of different market forms are possible—each individual worker could act as an independent contractor, buying and selling intermediate products. But most production in the U.S. is carried on by business firms, wherein great economies are gained by specification and direction of labour. Corporations have come to the fore as vehicles allowing persons to invest and capitalize on increases in value without also having to manage the firm. Aided by transferable ownership shares and continuity through the death of owners, this division of tasks within the corporate form facilitates the raising of large amounts of capital.

Origins of Free Enterprise. U.S. history provides the prime example of how free enterprise operates. With the lifting of English mercantilist restrictions, the United States came to be an arena of largely free enterprise, at least as compared with other countries. The government was restricted to maintaining the peace within which economic activities could proceed and enforcing and making more precise laws of contracts and of property, including patent laws securing intellectual property. But there were some notable legal carry-overs from the English distrust of capitalism. America constituted a wide and open market with extensive division of labour and economies of scale. It was populated by persons desiring more goods and services who were willing to work, save, and bear risks for profit, and who were willing to learn and adapt to new situations and ideas. It contained large doses of entrepreneurial talent. Immigrants replenished its spirit of innovation and energy bringing scarce skills and a desire to work and advance into a situation that contained no established guilds, professional associations, restrictive trade unions, or government licensing. Anyone could market and benefit from the skills he had or could acquire. No land tenure system stopped enterprising persons from acquiring and utilizing more land, nor was there envy sufficient to exert strong social pressure against success.

Over a short period of time the U.S. equaled and then economically surpassed England, the home of the Industrial Revolution. There was an enormous increase in the population the U.S. supported, along with a great growth in per capita output, a widespread diffusion of material well-being, and high levels of health. Manufacturing thrived. There was large-scale utilization of technology in both industry and agriculture. Supporting, sustaining, and producing this was a high investment of capital per head, guided into diverse forms, areas, and uses by the opportunities for profit in the market. Without the market's wise and intricate detailing, specification, and continuous reshuffling and reorganization of capital, even a large amount of capital per head would avail little. From great entrepreneurs such as Andrew Carnegie and Henry Ford came an industry that was the wonder of the world. Fortunes were made and lost and much of investment came from the profits of industry reinvested. All were not equally well-off, but there was no serious attempt before the 20th century to redistribute wealth so as to inhibit capital formation or the exercise of special skills.

Economic Role of Natural Resources. We have spoken of free enterprise as a framework for entrepreneurship, saving, investment, and work and of an American population well fitted to utilize this framework. What role was played by the country's abundant natural resources and fertile land? These resources were not utilized to any great extent by the native Americans. To play an economic role, resources must be discovered and utilized and capital must be applied to them. Only in an appropriate economic context and environment do resources have economic value. Letting few opportunities for profit go unrealized, free enterprise encourages the efficient use of resources. Does the experience of the socialist countries show that free enterprise is unnecessary for economic prosperity and so cast doubt on its causal role in the U.S.? The hesitant and reluctant movements toward market forms in socialist bloc countries, driven by economic necessity, testify to the efficiency of allocation in a market and price system; but they will not reap its full benefits without private and transferable property rights.

Government Involvement. In what ways has the government aided the United States in achieving economic prosperity? The major governmental benefit was providing the framework of protection, specification of property, and enforcement of contract within which the voluntary and enterprising actions of persons caused the economy to flourish. Furthermore, there were government policies, from auctioning land to the homesteading act, that put land into private hands with the effect of aiding the cultivation and care of the land and long-term investment in it.

These government activities reinforced the system of free private enterprise by providing the framework within which it operated and extending its scope. But the U.S. did not have a completely free and unhampered enterprise system. There were government activities, national and local, which changed, diverted, or stopped certain market processes. Did these activities play a significant role in U.S. prosperity? Some examples of limits placed on free enterprise include the enslavement of blacks, whose liberty of activity and reward were severely limited with no adequate attempt at recompense. Another limit is government expansion of the credit supply (now through the Federal Reserve System), which brings malinvestment, an intensification of the trade cycle, inflation, and then depression, in which are eliminated the previous uneconomic investments induced by the distortion of price and interest rates caused by the credit expansion. In the 20th century there has been movement toward the cartelization of industry. Each of these deviations from a system of free enterprise has catastrophic results, some still occurring.

Government regulation of industries, supposedly to protect consumers, leads to industry-dominated regulatory bodies that act to restrict competition and to protect established firms from new competitors. This is not surprising because these regulatory bodies were favoured by the industries from the beginning as ways of securing their own positions. Antitrust regulation has acted to penalize efficient firms and keep prices up. Occupations are licensed, limiting entry and competition at a cost to the consumer. Prices, interest rates, rents, and wages are controlled, resulting in scarcities, unemployment, and misallocation of resources. Firms are subsidized by tax money and tariffs. Railroads received land grants and legal monopolistic positions and, secure from competition, proceeded to exploit their legally granted monopoly in the rates they charged farmers. It is generally true that the bad things attributed to free enterprise are effects of government interferences with free enterprise. These effects are then intensified by the further interventions made in an attempt to avoid or mitigate the unfortunate but predictable effects of the prior interferences.

The 19th-century governmental interventions most plausibly argued to be beneficial were those subsidies to transportation (turnpikes, canals, and some railroads) and education. Even with the most significant of these, the railroads, the 12.9% rate of return (according to a recent estimate) on private capital used in building railroads probably would have been sufficient to get them built. In education local government expenditure was high and education played a role in producing a literate labour force. But because in the absence of government provision there would have been more private expenditure it is difficult to know how much difference the government made.

Perhaps the actual government interventions were detrimental, but does not unlimited free enterprise have its own faults? Some of the most popular complaints are that it leads to monopolies, war and imperialism, capitalist bribing of government officials, pollution and nonconservation of resources, and to multinational corporations eroding national sovereignty. But these complaints do not hold up under scrutiny. It is the protection provided by the government regulatory agencies that has most aided monopolies and there is no indication that open markets over time will not erode any temporarily monopolistic position, especially with a well-developed capital market that will finance enterprise in areas with an especially high rate of return. International markets and free trade do not flourish under the rupture of wartime. Wars are made by nations who try to gain benefits by seizure rather than purchase. Pollution problems stem from imperfect enforcement and specification of the property rights of those polluted, while the future orientation of the market entrepreneur encourages conservation before any government might become alerted to its importance. Businessmen and others seek to influence government officials in order to gain special benefits from them. The solution is to eliminate or drastically restrict that illegitimate power to confer special benefits. Multinational corporations are new, but as a cement for international ties and peace they are promising. These and other objections to free enterprise can be met one by one, yet this has little effect. A puzzle whose satisfactory solution still evades us is why many persons, especially intellectuals, so desire there to be some conclusive objection to free enterprise.

If the economic activities of government beyond the maintenance of the free enterprise framework work out so badly, why are they allowed to continue? They work out badly for most of us, but they don't work out badly for each and every person. Those who specially and greatly benefit do so at the expense of the vast majority of others. The cost of one government intervention may be small to each person, but is great in total. The cost of all government intervention together is great to each person. Those benefiting greatly are willing to devote their energy and resources to inducing the government to intervene in their own behalf, whereas it is usually not sufficiently in any one other person's or consumer's interest to devote significant resources to opposing any particular governmental intervention and favouritism. Therefore a system that takes each case of intervention "on its own merits," allows, due to its dynamics, many harmful interventions strongly favoured by special interests. Only the adherence to a general prohibition of governmental interventions could prevent the pork barrel and because such a general prohibition is in everyone's interests, therein lies some hope.

Rights of the Individual. A system of free enterprise is productive and beneficial but is it just? Complaints sometimes are made against the distribution of wealth and the income that result. Some of the complaints about the actual distribution in the U.S. turn out, upon examination, to be about the effect of interference with free enterprise. If people gain what they have by legitimate market means, through voluntary transactions that others choose to enter, then they are entitled to what they have. A just distribution is one in which everyone is entitled to what he has and it would be unjust to forcibly impose some pattern of distribution by coercive government means. Nothing stops anyone who favours some alternative pattern not brought about by the total of previous voluntary choices from transferring some of his own holdings to others or convincing others to do this, so as to more nearly realize his preferred pattern. The liberty to engage in market transactions, unhampered, is itself a component of liberty. People have a moral right to engage in cooperative activities with others on mutually agreed on terms, including exchanges of goods, services, and labour. Governments have no moral right to prohibit capitalist acts between consenting adults.

The United States broke away from mercantilist England and stood, though imperfectly, for liberty (including economic liberty) and for property rights. These two ideals are right not only for their economic and productive fruits and for the allowing of new ideas to be tried out, picked up, imitated, and modified, important though these be, but also they are right, important, and valuable in themselves. If we fail to stop the drift away from these ideals, the drift in which England has preceded us, the apparent dismal fate of the country we broke away from will become our own.

The Meiji Restoration: American Democracy in Japan

by Frank Gibney

Meiji Tenno, emperor of Japan from 1867 to 1912.

SEKAI BUNKA PHOTO

> The oppression of the English king became more heavy every day and the American people suffered. At that point a man named Washington complained of the people's hardships. . . . He carried out an exclusion policy and expelled the barbarians. . . . —Nakaoka Shintaro [1866]

It was an era of battles, riots, and continuing appeals to pure reason and the "laws of nature"; of obstinate bureaucrats and "deliberative assemblies" making plans for future laws; of loyalists, revolutionaries, and violent impulses for freedom; the sort of time of which John Adams wrote in 1776 that "every post and every day rolls in upon us independence like a torrent." At home the teachings of old hierarchies were being questioned in the name of "people's rights." Embattled farmers were taking up arms and foundries were being built to cast guns for repelling invaders. Led by an extraordinary group of Founding Fathers—the oldest was only 43 at the time—a new system of government was to be based on principles of "justice and equity as they are universally recognized." People whose world had been bounded by provinces thought of themselves, for the first time, as citizens of one modern, united state. Education and discovery were the order of the day. "Civilization and Enlightenment" became the national slogan. Inspired, indeed, by the Enlightenment philosophers of the same Europe whose warships were bombarding the country's shores, a new breed of young philosophers pledged a commitment to pragmatic inquiry.

The foregoing description could almost have fit the American Colonies in 1776 and after. In fact, it summarizes the beginnings of Japan's Meiji Restoration in 1868. Reacting with extraordinary swiftness to the forcible "opening" of Japan by Commodore Matthew Perry's squadron—and the gathering pressure from the fleets and traders of European countries—a group of "reformers," most of them recruited from the lower ranks of the samurai nobility, turned Japan from a closed kingdom of feudal satrapies into a modern industrializing nation-state.

The parallel between the Philadelphia colonists and the Edo samurai is, of course, far from exact. American nationalism arose in protest against a tyrannical monarch; Japanese nationalism grew up in defense of a neglected one. Thus in America "loyalists" meant "traitorous" followers of King George III, and revolutionaries were the republican patriots who elected for independence. In Japan the loyalists and the revolutionaries were the same people. Loyal to the neglected figure of the emperor, they were in revolt against the feudalism of the Tokugawa shoguns who had governed Japan in isolation from the rest of the world since the early 17th century. Striking similarities remain, however. Each could justly be called a "conservative revolution." Yet of all the revolutions of modern history—including the Russian Revolution and the French—no two achieved the same extraordinary mixture of enlightenment and reform at home while building a nationalist ethos out

---

Frank Gibney, as president of TBS-Britannica in Tokyo, planned and edited the new Britannica International Encyclopædia *in Japanese. He speaks and reads Japanese and is an authority on that country's history and culture. A foreign correspondent, editor, and publisher, he has written a number of books on political affairs, of which his most recent is* Japan: The Fragile Superpower *(1975).*

SEKAI BUNKA PHOTO

An American sailing ship anchors in Yokohama Harbour.

of sectionalized populations. Each in its own way rejected, in the interests of unity, the class warfare and doctrinaire determinism which Marxism later made almost synonymous with the word revolution.

Two Democracies in the Making. The comparison of 1868 and 1776—differences as well as similarities—bears considerable study, and 1976 is a good year for the exercise. The Americans and the Japanese are connected by deeper associations than $20 billion in annual trade and one slightly used Mutual Security Pact. Although sharply different in their structure and their workings, the democracies of the United States and Japan have certain interesting common roots. Almost a hundred years before Gen. Douglas MacArthur flew from the Philippines to Tokyo with the idea of a "democratizing" occupation in his baggage, American education, American religion, and American political theory had started to influence the modernization of Japan.

Much of what America and the spirit of '76 had to teach Japan in the 1860s and '70s was rejected or stifled in later years. Thus foreigners visiting Japan during the militarist '30s, in the heyday of the artificial cult of "emperor worship," must have found it hard to believe that, half a century before the Greater East Asia Co-prosperity Sphere, Japan's great activist scholar, Fukuzawa Yukichi, could have written "Man is born free. The right to independence and freedom he receives from heaven cannot be bought or sold." Nonetheless, much of what the American Founding Fathers believed took hold in Japan. Over the past 150 years most of the world's revolutionaries, from Simón Bolívar to Ho Chi Minh, have variously pledged their sympathy with the American revolutionary tradition. But only in Japan, of all the non-European countries, did a nation, albeit at some cost, achieve the goals of modernization and popular rights by itself, without scrapping old traditions and institutions in the course of the effort.

The parallels between 1776 and 1868 suggest themselves from any reading of modern Japanese history. As with the story of the United States, we begin, a century ago, with a set of Founding Fathers, who in some respects were astonishingly like their American counterparts. Most of the young men who achieved Japan's modernization were, like most of the Americans, gentry. An astonishing proportion of them were at least part-time scholars.

Both groups owed a great debt to European thinkers, British and French, and the Japanese shared with the Americans a concern for putting ideas into practice that distinguished both from the Europeans. Fukuzawa Yukichi, perhaps the greatest of them all, founded a newspaper and a university and enjoyed a reputation as one of the finest writers of his time. Okuma Shigenobu holds with Jefferson the distinction of having founded both a university and a major political party. Of them and the other great Meiji figures, Okubo Toshimichi, Kido Koin, and Japan's constitution-maker, Ito Hirobumi, one could fairly apply the comment made by the American historian Henry Steele Commager about Jefferson and his fellows of the American Enlightenment: "The quality which distinguished [it] most sharply from the European [Enlightenment] was its constructive and consequential character . . . for the American *philosophes* . . . were not closet philosophers . . . they were working men."

The Coming of the West. When Commodore Perry opened Japan to foreign trade in 1854, he upended Pandora's box. The Tokugawa shoguns, ruling in the name of a secluded and powerless emperor, had kept power for two centuries by turning a military dictatorship into a complex bureaucratic oligarchy. At first a welcome respite from a century of civil war, Tokugawa rule came to stifle. As a reaction to the scare given the Japanese feudal rulers in the 16th century by the brushfire rise of Christianity as preached by Jesuit missionaries, the Tokugawa had enforced a rigid seclusion policy. All intercourse with the outside world was barred, except for the Dutch trading post at Deshima in Nagasaki Harbour.

Within the Japanese islands, however, creative society bubbled like a gas imprisoned in a bottle. A sophisticated merchant culture developed inside cities that were fully as metropolitan as the great centres of Europe. The trading houses of Ono and Mitsui, ancestor of the modern Mitsui multinational, were already prospering by the late 1700s. After decades of peace, the huge military caste (one of every 16 Japanese belonged) was reaching to new outlets for its energies. Samurai scholars, their researches confined within the stale air of the *sakoku* ("enclosed country"), tried to rethink the Heavenly Way of Confucianism —in a restricted sense an approximation of the Natural Law of the European schoolmen and the Enlightenment.

Even before 1854 European nations, interested in both

trade and colonies, had been knocking at Japan's closed doors. China had already been invaded in the first Opium War. British, French, and Russian warships now began to appear off the coasts of Japan. The first reaction of the samurai was one of arrogant hostility. But the bombardment of Shimonoseki and Kagoshima by European warships, among other things, made many Japanese aware that the modern science of Europe could not be overcome by warriors with swords and clumsy 17th-century fieldpieces.

In 1774 a man named Sugita Gempaku purchased and translated, at great personal risk, a Dutch textbook on anatomy and began the study of modern medicine in Japan. By the time Perry arrived on the scene, hundreds of *rangakusha* ("scholars of Dutch")—most of them samurai—had managed to learn Dutch and gain some access to the "new knowledge" of the West. A few bold spirits had been overseas and come back to tell what they had seen. In 1847 the "World Atlas" of Mitsukuri Seigo contained a detailed description of the United States, which excited great curiosity and some awe. Along with an order-of-battle listing of U.S. Navy frigates, Mitsukuri included a geography of the United States and a life of George Washington. He wrote:

> When the republican government was established in that country, the people were greatly exhausted, but in eight years in office Washington managed the affairs of state so well, that there was excellent military preparedness, the nation prospered, the people enjoyed peace and the country's renown encompassed the earth.
>
> . . . a dilapidated state was reborn as a newly risen nation. The national debt was no longer regarded as unpayable, every family prospered, men worked diligently, production greatly increased and the government's revenue grew and grew. The people were governed by law and not by individuals, their customs were benevolent and they behaved like persons of high birth.

The Reformers. There was no single George Washington in Japan. The Meiji Founding Fathers, in keeping with Japan's less individualistic society, acted in groups. The Emperor Meiji was barely 16 when restored to power. The Restoration's only real man on horseback, the Satsuma general Saigo Takamori, resigned from the government over an abortive plan to invade Korea and died in a brief rebellion of conservative samurai.

The origins of the Meiji reformers were modest. If they were all among the samurai gentry of their day, some were barely so. The brilliant Ito Hirobumi, who was only 27 in 1868, was a merchant's son from the southern clan of Choshu; he did not receive samurai status until 1863. Iwakura Tomomi, who led the critical fact-finding mission to the West in 1871, was a relatively minor noble from the emperor's diminished court in Kyoto. Okubo Toshimichi, probably the greatest single force in stabilizing the Meiji reforms, came from a low-ranking samurai family and had worked in the provincial administration for the daimyo of Satsuma. Yet, considered as a group, in their vitality and, ultimately, breadth of vision, the young samurai bear comparison to the planters, lawyers, and merchants who had forged the American republic.

The Meiji reformers had, furthermore, a far more bewildering world to contend with. Behind Jefferson's noble, carefully chosen phrases in the Declaration of Independence lay centuries of European political and philosophical evolution, from Aristotle to the Enlightenment. The philosophical and political milieu of the Japanese reformers, by contrast, had been virtually isolated from the rest of the world for centuries. The Meiji reformers had to reject their own history, in a sense, and find new models. As the often quoted remark of the young scholar to a German doctor in early Meiji Japan has it, "We have no history. Our history begins today."

The first reaction in Japan was one of defense. The Meiji reformers wanted to tear down the shogunate because it was incapable of fighting off the foreigners. Their grand design was to restore the emperor as the axis of Japanese society, and, thus proof against foreign ideological taint, use the foreigners' own weapons against them. Thus the early naive battlecry of *sonno-joi*—"Revere the Emperor! Drive out the Barbarians!" In 1855 Yoshida Shoin, as a standard-bearer of the new learning, wrote:

The first industrial exhibition of the Meiji period, held in Ueno in 1887.

SEKAI BUNKA PHOTO

In studying the learning of Europe and America to adore and idolize the barbarians . . . must be rejected absolutely. But the barbarians' artillery and shipbuilding, their knowledge of medicine and the physical sciences, can all be of use to us—these should properly be adopted. (As quoted in W. G. Beasley, *The Meiji Restoration*, Stanford University Press, 1972.)

Ideas from a Far Country. The more the young reforming samurai—the *shishi* ("men of spirit"), as they were called—read in the foreign books, however, and the more they thought about what they read, the more they realized that there was far more to Western learning than cannon and navigation instruments. Here was the irony of the Meiji Restoration, which has plagued Japanese thinking to this day. To many—probably most—who joined it, the Restoration was an almost religiously nationalistic movement. But behind this Japanese Junkerism the scholars were thinking. Translations of Montesquieu, Rousseau, Emerson, and Adam Smith provoked discussion about a "universal natural man." For the first time in the history of this most insular of peoples, a universalist philosophy was developing. Thus Sakuma Shozan, a teacher of Yoshida's, wrote in 1854:

When I was twenty I knew that men were linked together in one province,
When I was thirty I knew that they were linked together in one nation,
When I was forty I knew that they were linked together in one world of five continents.

His words were quoted fittingly by U.S. Pres. Gerald Ford when he visited Japan in 1974.

The brief time span in which Sakuma expressed his transformation was no figure of speech. Within two decades, or less, the Meiji reformers managed to overthrow centuries of fixed isolationist assumptions and put in their place a new and wildly eclectic set of plans and plots, theories and explications. Sakamoto Ryoma was an extreme case, but typical of his time. A talented, emotional samurai swordsman from the province of Tosa, and violently antiforeign, he came to the shogun's capital at the end of 1862 to assassinate a promising Tokugawa official named Katsu Rintaro, who was setting out with foreign help to build a Japanese navy. Katsu talked Sakamoto out of his plan, in what was even for that day a tense session, and persuaded him to work with, not against, Western learning. Within a few years he became a moving spirit in the Restoration's movement for "Civilization and Enlightenment." His draft plans for establishing representative assemblies and abolishing hereditary castes and privileges inspired post-restoration crusaders for constitutionalism and people's rights. In 1867, on the eve of success, he and his friend Nakaoka Shintaro were cut down by Tokugawa supporters who opposed their new progressivism. He was 32.

The very first Japanese embassy to a foreign power—eight years before the Meiji Restoration—was to the United States in 1860. Led by Shimmi Masaoki, the lord of Bizen, its members inspected factories, observatories, and made an intensive tour of the Philadelphia Mint (the shogunate in its last days was having problems with its coinage weights). In 1871, when the government selected several hundred students to study in the West, more than half were sent to the United States. In November 1871 Prince Iwakura's mission set out on its memorable two-year trip to the West, again starting in the U.S. and going on to Europe. The most influential foreign educators in Japan in the early Meiji period were Americans. David Murray was invited to Tokyo from Rutgers in 1872 to supervise the new nationwide system of public schools.

The Declaration of Independence, Washington's Farewell Address, and the Constitution were translated within the first Meiji decade. Fukuzawa's seminal book *Conditions in the West* included copious explanations of American society and government (although both Congress and the British Parliament confused him) and owed far more to John Locke than to Confucius. In his concern over Western progress and contempt for Japanese "knowledge," Fukuzawa was typical of the newly enlightened Meiji reformers. "No one would say," he wrote, "that our learning or business is on a par with that of the Western countries. All that Japan has to be proud of is its scenery."

In 1870 Kato Hiroyuki, a young reformer who went on to become one of the Meiji era's most successful bureaucrats, published a book called the *Outline of Practical Politics* (*Shinsei tai-i*), in which he expounded the idea of natural law, as it had been developed by John Locke and the American Founding Fathers, and a people's rights to life, basic freedoms, and property. Another scholar, Ueki Emori, went on from life and liberty to "the pursuit of happiness"—an idea with which Japan's Confucian-trained scholars had great difficulty. The *Federalist* papers were well known. When he was working on the Meiji constitution, Ito Hirobumi is said to have kept a copy constantly with him. In 1880 the charter of Japan's first political party, the Liberal (literally "Liberty") Party, held that "the preservation of liberty is man's greatest duty."

Cautious Borrowing. To a country literally coming out of feudalism, however, the drafts of American constitutional air were heady. By 1876 the Empress Meiji was writing a series of poems in praise of Benjamin Franklin's

Promulgation of the constitution at a ceremony within the palace, February 1889.

SEKAI BUNKA PHOTO

SEKAI BUNKA PHOTO

Deliberations in the Japanese Diet during the Meiji period.

famous maxims, but the roving Japanese ambassadors increasingly found Europe, with its kings and aristocracies, at least remotely similar to their own experience.

Thus the Japanese legal code was taken from France, as was the new system of centralized education. When Ito went to Europe in 1882, he found the atmosphere of imperial Germany even more congenial. In many ways the belated evolution of Germany into a united nation corresponded to that of Japan. There was the amalgamation of duchies and principalities into a new empire, a strong hereditary Junker nobility in Prussia with pretensions as hidebound as the Japanese daimyo, and an iron chancellor, Bismarck, whose ideas of popular rights were comfortably limited. The Japanese constitution of 1889, when finally drafted, reflected the imperial German constitution far more than the earlier American or British models.

The practical problems of simultaneously modernizing a society and arming and developing a new industrial state were almost insuperable. Bureaucrats trying to found national banking systems and build railroads grew impatient with the patriots and pamphleteers writing about "the rights of man" in the newspapers. Motoda Eifu, the Emperor Meiji's tutor, reflected his imperial pupil's concern when he called for a revival of Confucian moral training, based on a very strong central government. Kato himself, after further reading, obligingly discovered that he had gone overboard on the natural law; he retracted the ideas in his earlier book in favour of a modified "survival of the fittest" theory borrowed from the widely read Herbert Spencer. In Kato's case, the "fittest" meant the Emperor Meiji and his new ministers.

The American statesmen of that day, insofar as they considered the progress of Japan, were far from revolutionary in their appraisals. Kaneko Kentaro, Prince Ito's assistant in drafting the constitution, was himself a graduate of Harvard Law School. When he approached Oliver Wendell Holmes on the subject, he was gratified to find that Mr. Justice Holmes's approach was a gradualist one. It was well, Holmes felt, to keep popular participation in the affairs of government limited at first, until the people could be educated to their responsibilities. Former president Ulysses Grant, visiting Japan in 1879, echoed this advice. Indeed, it might be argued that the feeling of the Meiji statesmen that political parties were vaguely immoral was no different from the way George Washington had felt a century before, on the same matter. And Washington's America was not barely 20 years removed from feudalism.

Militarism and Beyond. By the early 1900s the Meiji Restoration had hardened into a mold. Although the trappings of a constitutional democracy were in place, Japan went into the 20th century run largely by bureaucrats and elder statesmen, with a leavening of party politicians. Japan's first minister of education, the extraordinary Mori Arinori, had written in 1870, "Progress can only be

SEKAI BUNKA PHOTO

The restoration of Imperial rule in Japan, January 1868.

achieved through revolutions and trials." But barely ten years later he was fastening a system of heavy indoctrination in nationalistic "morals" on the schools. For the first decade or so after the Restoration, the textbooks used in the national schools were astonishingly individualistic and liberal in tone—a great number of them were translations of American textbooks. The Imperial Rescript on education, drawn up in 1891, signaled a retreat from such uncritical borrowing of foreign ideas. Thereafter each generation of textbooks seemed to restate history more strongly in terms of emperors and Japanese national traditions.

The balls and parties continued at the Rokumeikan, Tokyo's club for the new Western-educated elite. The troops marched down the broad avenues in front of the imperial palace in their new Western uniforms. Factories proliferated, the railroad stretched past Yokohama to Osaka and beyond, and a formidable financial network was based on the Bank of Japan—a far cry from the time some four decades earlier when Japanese visitors' greatest interest had been in the precise weighing of coinage at the Philadelphia Mint. But the course of the next half century had been set.

Japan had become a democracy, in a sense, but a flawed one. The cautious and often brilliant compromising of Prince Ito and his constitution-makers provided loopholes to a later generation of militarists. The Meiji constitution had insufficient guarantees for basic individual rights. If government was to be *for* the people, it was not intended to be *by* them. The pursuit of happiness, insofar as it survived, was seen as a collective aspiration. Most dangerous of all was a system whereby ministers reported to the emperor rather than to the legislature, thus paving the way for a usurpation of power in the emperor's name.

Yet the victory of authority over dissent and independence was neither complete nor final in Japan. The Meiji reformers themselves were—many of them—sincere in their desire for popular liberty and constitutional government. The argument of some modern Japanese historians, influenced by a kind of high-buttoned-shoe Marxism, that the whole Meiji Restoration was merely a device to preserve authoritarianism is surely a form of second-guessing.

In the United States itself it proved a difficult task to translate the ideals of the Declaration of Independence into a stable, permanent democracy. Especially among the New England Federalists, democracy was feared as much as it was admired. "Your people," so the famous Hamiltonian comment runs, "your people, sir—it is a great beast." It is small exaggeration to note that Jefferson's election as president in 1800 saved the ideals of the Enlightenment in America. It was no small benefit to the United States, either, that the Founding Fathers enjoyed notably long lives and were able to guide the fortunes of the republic for half a century.

The Japanese reformers managed a similar continuity —enough to keep Japan something of a working democracy for six decades after 1868. Although some died young and died hard—Okubo was cut down by protesting samurai in 1878—others survived to become Japan's genro—"the elder statesmen." Ito was assassinated in 1909 at the age of 68 by a Korean revolutionary. But Matsukata Masayoshi, the man who had stabilized Japan's finances in the Meiji period, lived to the age of 90. Both Yamagata Aritomo, the Meiji conservative, and Okuma, who had been called the Japanese Jefferson, died in 1922, aged 84.

A Lasting Heritage. Despite the growing strength of the Japanese military and the limitations of Japan's political democracy, certain American examples continued to exercise their influence: Christianity and the private educational institutions allied with it and the labour movement, which kept alive the early Meiji tradition of dissent.

Christianity had not made wholesale conversions in the Meiji period, despite the initial attraction of its universalist doctrines. The Japanese found it hard to accept the idea of a transcendent God, and even many Japanese converts were bewildered by the fierce sectarianism and the no-smoke, no-drink puritanism which so many American missionaries confused with Christianity. The *example* of Christian missionaries was another matter. "Mission schools" like Doshisha University in Kyoto remained strongholds of Western learning, although they made relatively few converts. The Bible itself had a powerful attraction, and Japanese students continued to be moved by the ideals of world brotherhood implicit in the Christian message.

Led by tradition and what remained of Buddhist influence to think of all religions as rather nice but non-essential and susceptible to continual combinations, the intellectuals were reluctant to come to grips with personal Christianity, although people like Ito recognized it (with more clarity than most 19th-century Christians in the West) as something essential to Western culture. It remained both a propellant and an irritant in Japan's modernizing culture.

American teachers, missionaries included, continued to visit, live, and preach in Japan. In a curious way, their combination of idealism, informality, industry, and a pragmatic approach to problems found wide acceptance. Generations of Hokkaido University students marched out into the world with the classic slogan "Boys, be ambitious," given them by William Clark, the former president of the Massachusetts Agricultural College who had founded the university at Sapporo, on the invitation of the Japanese government, in 1876. Later, American teaching became more secular. Progressive schools like Tokyo's famous Jiyugakuen modeled themselves on American patterns. John Dewey and his followers were widely quoted. But the most abiding relationship, ambivalent though it became, was that between the eager Meiji learners and the optimistic missionary teachers. They shared a curious combination of rough competitiveness, narrow-minded dedication to goals, and a broad definition of learning (*i.e.*, anything that helped you get ahead). The samurai and the puritan elect were both of the hardy sort who felt that standing under cold showers is intrinsically a good thing.

The labour movement also had its roots in America. From Katayama Sen, Japan's first popular Socialist leader, to Nozaka Sanzo, still the chairman of Japan's Communist Party in 1975, several generations of aspiring Socialists visited and lived in the United States, to learn their ideas of dissent from a freer society. The first publication of the Japanese Socialists, the magazine *Kokumin no tomo* ("The People's Friend"), in the early 1900s, was modeled on the *Nation* in the U.S. Japan's first union manifesto, in 1897, was patterned on statements by the American Federation of Labor. Katayama, although he ultimately became a Communist (he was buried in the Kremlin Wall), began his career as a Christian settlement worker and acquired a master's degree in divinity from Yale.

The "Taisho democracy" which Japan experienced in the 1920s was far from a fiction. An increasingly urban, industrialized population was receptive to new ideas and looked for broader horizons. The labour movement gained strength, as the Marxism of post-World War I Europe joined (and fought with) the earlier strains of American socialism. The elite universities were small-scale ideological battlegrounds, where student dissent was a badge of temporary status. The American cultural impact continued strong as well. From serious lay preachers like John Dewey to Hollywood movies, jazz, and Harold Lloyd-style glasses, a kind of American irreverence and individualism, crude but vital, fascinated many Japanese.

In 1924 the Exclusion Acts in the United States, coming not long after the Allies had rejected the "racial equality" clause during the conference of Versailles, revived the worst fears of the Japanese about racial prejudice in the West. The same Japanese whose industry and intelligence had been so praised when they came to San Francisco 60 years before as visiting ambassadors were the objects of vicious discrimination when they appeared as immigrants. The predictions of right-wing nationalists about America were thus in a sense fulfilled. In the following year the notorious peace preservation laws of 1925 passed the Japanese Diet, and dissent in politics became a potentially dangerous exercise.

When the U.S. occupation came to Japan in 1945, defeat had brought the country once again to the point of "spiritual breakdown" of which Natsume Soseki wrote in the Meiji days. As in the beginnings of Meiji, there were many who said "We have no history. Our history begins today." They awaited the lessons that American *demokurashi* set out energetically to give. The MacArthur democratization program included a new constitution to replace that of the Meiji Founding Fathers. Modeled explicitly on that of the United States, it reduced the emperor to the status of a national symbol, made governments responsible to the legislative arm, strengthened the power of the judiciary, and made very concrete statements ensuring individual freedoms. With the zeal of clean-slate reformers, the young New Dealers of the U.S. occupation began their work in 1945 on the assumption that Japan was only then emerging from centuries of absolutism.

Yet the occupiers were not starting from scratch. The ideals of "natural man" had never been erased from the Japanese consciousness. The idea of individual freedoms had been buffeted, but it had survived—as had, indeed, a tradition of dissent. The Taisho democracy may have had its limitations, but it was a kind of democracy, based on the rising political consciousness of an industrializing society, in which some of the early freedoms of Meiji remained. Without this background, the U.S. occupation would never have achieved the success it had.

The Meiji reformers were cautious men, but so were most of America's Founding Fathers. The Japanese may have preferred Washington and Hamilton to Jefferson (singularly little known in Meiji Japan), but so did many early 19th-century Americans. They may have overstressed the Restoration's goals of *fukoku kyohei*—"a prosperous country and a strong army"—but we should not forget that a great many of the *Federalist* papers based their argument for union on the need for national defense. In one sense the men of Meiji lacked the universal transcendent vision of 1776. But their achievement in lowering the barriers between East and West and modernizing a feudal society was in its own way just as immense. After one hundred years of trying, no country has yet been able to equal or approach it.

PEOPLE OF THE YEAR

BIOGRAPHY

The following is a selected list of men and women who influenced events significantly in 1975.

Agostini, Giacomo

"I have no fear of death," Giacomo Agostini once said. "Why not? Because it doesn't help to win." And winning, it should be added, is just about all this daredevil has done. He races motorcycles for a living, and 15 world titles—a figure unmatched in the history of the sport—have enabled him to make an extremely good living, particularly when combined with the side ventures his success has made available to him.

Agostini was born in 1944 in Italy, a nation that has a history of producing great motorcyclists, including nine-time world champion Carlo Ubbiali. But Agostini has surpassed them all, not only in victories and in millions of dollars won but also in actual, on-bike performance. Ubbiali, for instance, won his titles in the slower 125- and 250-cc. (cubic centimetres of displacement) classes, whereas Agostini races in the heavier, faster, and more dangerous 350- and 500-cc. classes, hurtling around the treacherous courses at speeds of 150 mph.

He works hard for his victories, examining each racecourse on foot, by day and by night. He studies the bumps and curves as Jack Nicklaus would study a green while lining up a putt in the Masters golf tournament. There is ever present danger. "Only one unnoticed crack in the asphalt is enough to say 'Addio,'" he says in his broken English, quickly reiterating, "but I have no fear of death."

Agostini's name is hardly a household word in the United States, where only avid motorcycling fans are familiar with his deeds. But in Europe, where he does most of his racing on the World Motorcycling Championship circuit, he is a celebrity of the first magnitude. He is constantly sought for lucrative endorsements and has appeared in several motion pictures. Despite his short (5 ft. 3 in.) stature, his dark good looks have helped make him one of the continent's most eligible bachelors.

But Agostini, who began riding motorbikes when he was 12, has the ability to shut out all distractions when the money is on the line, and it has helped him become the undisputed ruler of world motorcycle racing. "I cannot think of my future without racing," he said. "I think I was born with gasoline in my veins."

(J. TIMOTHY WEIGEL)

Ahmed, Khandakar Mushtaque

Bangladesh's first president following the coup of August 1975, Khandakar Mushtaque Ahmed spent 2½ uneasy months in office before resigning on November 6. He left office after a three-day confrontation with a group of generals and was succeeded by Chief Justice Abu Sadat Mohammed Sayem. Ahmed's downfall was believed to have been precipitated by the execution of several high-ranking officials of the former government.

Ahmed had been a lifelong colleague and friend of his predecessor, Sheikh Mujibur Rahman (*see* OBITUARIES). During the last few years of the sheikh's regime, however, their ways seemed to have parted as Ahmed, a deeply religious and anti-Communist Bengali, resented the sheikh's pro-Soviet and pro-Indian policies. This cost Ahmed the post of foreign minister, and he was his country's minister for trade and commerce until August 15 when the sheikh was assassinated.

Born in 1918 in Daudkandi, in the Comilla district of East Bengal, Ahmed had his early education at Khidirpur Academy, Calcutta. He obtained his law degree from Dacca University and soon joined the independence movement against the British, who imprisoned him in 1946. After the establishment of Pakistan, Ahmed joined Sheikh Mujibur, first to revitalize the Bengali language movement and then to establish the autonomy-minded Awami League party in 1949. As joint secretary of the Awami League, Ahmed was in charge of the election campaign in the first by-election in Tangail, where he was arrested and detained by the Pakistan authorities. In 1954 he was elected a member of the East Pakistan Legislative Assembly, and he was again imprisoned for making anti-Pakistan speeches. On his release he served as chief whip of the United Front parliamentary party, but when martial law was imposed in 1958 he spent another spell in jail along with leaders of other banned political parties.

After the lifting of the ban on political activities in 1964, Ahmed played a leading role in reorganizing the Awami League. In the general election of 1970, he was elected a member of the National Assembly. He helped Sheikh Mujibur during the latter's difficult negotiations with former Pakistani president Agha Yahya Khan in early 1971. When the sheikh was detained in Pakistan, Ahmed remained in the vanguard of the independence struggle and was foreign minister and minister for law and parliamentary affairs of the provisional government set up in Mukibnagar in mid-1971, six months before Bangladesh attained independence.

(GOVINDAN UNNY)

Allin, The Rt. Rev. John

Should a woman serve in the Episcopal priesthood? "No," said the Rt. Rev. John Maury Allin, presiding bishop of the Episcopal Church, the U.S. branch of the Anglican Communion. "Yes," replied many of the church's 3.4 million members. The question might, or might not, be settled in 1976 when the House of Bishops and the House of Deputies (priests and laity) were scheduled to meet in the church's triennial General Convention.

As the chief executive of his church, John Allin seemed certain to be prominent in the 1976 convention debate over the ordination of women. Several outcomes of the debate were possible. The Episcopalians might continue, as they had in the past, to limit their priesthood to men. The convention might vote to accept the ordination of women anywhere in the United States. A local-option scheme in which each diocese decides the question locally might win adoption. Finally, a split or schism in the Episcopal Church, though desired by no one, was not unthinkable.

The Rt. Rev. John Allin

RAY ELLIS—RAPHO/PHOTO RESEARCHERS

John Allin was accustomed to controversy. A Southerner, he became important in his church during the 1960s, a time of severe racial unrest in the U.S. Born on April 22, 1921, in Helena, Ark., he received his divinity degree and was ordained to the ministry in 1945. Over the next 15 years, he served in Arkansas, Louisiana, and Mississippi. On Oct. 28, 1961, Allin was consecrated bishop coadjutor for the Mississippi diocese; five years later he succeeded to the post of diocesan bishop.

Much racial violence took place in Mississippi during Allin's tenure there. Many black churches were burned to the ground, and the murders of some civil rights advocates received international publicity. Though he could not be described as an activist, Allin did strive for reconciliation between the races and joined the Committee of Concern, a group that helped to rebuild black churches.

As Allin presided over his diocese in Mississippi, the national Episcopal Church moved sharply in the direction of innovation, endorsing programs and changes in procedure that antagonized many tradition-minded members. When the House of Bishops elected Allin to a 12-year term as presiding bishop in October 1973, he was considered the most conservative of the five nominees for that position. His election was interpreted in some quarters as a backlash and in others as the beginning of a period that would witness few changes in Episcopal practice.

After Allin was elected, some black Episcopalians and liberals denounced him as a Southern racist who had done as little as decency would allow to improve conditions in Mississippi. He responded to them in a conciliatory manner, however, and pointed to his record as a bishop. Eventually, most accepted Allin's leadership.

(VICTOR M. CASSIDY)

Altman, Robert

Whenever he released a new film, Robert Altman could be almost certain that the critics would praise or condemn it—extravagantly. Motion pictures directed by Altman rarely get mixed reviews. In his spare time, Altman liked to gamble at cards and on horse races. Considering his up-and-down career, such pastimes were quite in character.

Robert Altman celebrated his 50th birthday on Feb. 20, 1975. He was then working on *Nashville,* a motion picture that was released and very well received in June. An unconventional film, *Nashville* has no story line of the traditional sort. It proceeds instead in quasi-documentary fashion to depict incidents in the lives of 24 fictional characters, all of whom have some connection with U.S. "country and western" music. The film's focus of attention changes often and without warning. From this seeming chaos, a portrait of the popular music business in Nashville, Tenn., and a possible metaphor for American life emerge.

Altman began his film career in Kansas City, Mo., the city of his birth. After serving as a bomber pilot in World War II and attending college, he began during the 1950s to make industrial and documentary motion pictures. Twice during his years in Kansas City, Altman left jobs there and tried without success to find work with a major studio in Hollywood. In 1957 he got his first break. He had written, produced, and directed a drama called *The Delinquents.* United Artists bought this film, which received some fairly good reviews. Later that year, Altman directed *The James Dean Story,* a documentary about a movie star who had died in 1955 and had become a posthumous hero among young people. Though this picture was well received, Altman was not to make another for 11 years.

AUTHENTICATED NEWS INTERNATIONAL

Robert Altman

He worked instead in television. He wrote, produced, or directed more than 300 hours of programming for such well-known series as "Bonanza," "Combat," and "Suspense Theatre." By the mid-1960s Altman had become successful and prosperous. Then, at the peak of his television career, he abruptly quit. Dissatisfied with the limitations of that medium, he had begun to fear that his creative momentum might be lost.

After failing at the box office with two movies, Altman was offered the script for *M*A*S*H* (1970), a dark comedy about the lives of two U.S. Army surgeons during the Korean War. Fourteen directors before him had refused the project. Altman turned *M*A*S*H* into a huge critical and box-office success. Between *M*A*S*H* and *Nashville* his movies, which met with varying degrees of critical and popular acclaim, included *Brewster McCloud, McCabe and Mrs. Miller, Images, The Long Goodbye,* and *California Split.* (VICTOR M. CASSIDY)

Amin, Idi Dada Oumee

The self-styled Field Marshal Idi Amin, who took power in Uganda through a military coup in January 1971, became chairman of the Organization of African Unity (OAU) for 1975–76—a role that falls automatically to the leader of the country that plays host to the annual summit meeting of African heads of state. His chairmanship was strongly opposed by a number of member states. Zambia's foreign minister described him as "Africa's Hitler," while the Tanzanian government said that the OAU decision to use Uganda's capital as a venue for the summit was tantamount to condoning the brutal murders of Africans perpetrated by Amin. The Ugandan leader caused the British, French, U.S., and Israeli delegations to walk out of the UN General Assembly on Oct. 1, 1975, when he condemned the policies of the first three and called for the elimination of the state of Israel—a statement directly contradictory to OAU policy. He also became the centre of an international controversy when he threatened the public execution of a British lecturer and writer, Denis Hills, for describing Amin as a "village tyrant" in the manuscript of his book *The White Pumpkin.*

During the five years of his rule Amin proved himself to be a crafty politician—a mixture of tyrant and funny man who was both the source and the butt of humour that gained international currency. His ideas of government drove his rapidly changing and powerless ministers to despair. In 1974 his foreign minister, Elizabeth Bagaya (formerly Princess Elizabeth of Toro), was publicly humiliated and briefly detained before she succeeded in escaping from the country. In January 1975 his finance minister resigned and escaped into exile. Amin's power continued to lie with his skillfully recruited army, drawn mainly from a small number of trusted tribes and strongly reinforced by sophisticated weapons and training teams from the U.S.S.R. Despite this aid, the Soviet Union met with characteristic verbal abuse from Amin over its involvement in Angola, and suspended relations temporarily in November.

Born about 1925 in the village of Koboko, a devout Muslim from the small Kakwa tribe, Amin joined the British colonial army as a young man. He served in the Burma campaign in World War II and subsequently fought against the Mau Mau rebellion in Kenya. Most at ease with the rank and file of the army, Amin was for ten years heavyweight boxing champion of Uganda and was an enthusiastic rugby football player. (COLIN LEGUM)

Ashe, Arthur

As is his nature, Arthur Ashe once painstakingly documented one year of his professional tennis career in a diary. He precisely recorded that he had traveled 165,000 mi., occupied seats on 129 plane flights, and spent his nights in 71 different beds. "All this to play a game," Ashe wrote. "My life is one big game."

Still, his life is a game Ashe plays seriously. Always cool and unemotional, he has often been characterized as "aloof" by tennis players and observers. The antithesis of his archrival, Jimmy Connors, Ashe always appeared to be in complete control of his emotions, both on the tennis court and in his personal life.

But until 1975, Ashe had not been so successful in controlling his fortunes as a player. As a student at UCLA he won two national intercollegiate championships, and as an amateur he won the U.S. Open in 1968, becoming the first American to win at Forest Hills in 13 years. Thereafter, he quickly attained a reputation as a "choker," reaching the finals of a big tournament and then losing.

Just getting close to the top of the tennis world had involved a nearly impossible string of events. Ashe himself characterized his professional development as a "fluke, piled upon coincidence." Born in 1943 in Richmond, Va., Ashe later determined that his forebears had arrived in America in 1735 aboard a slave ship carrying 165 West Africans to Yorktown. He was introduced to tennis as a youngster of seven and was then aided by a Lynchburg, Va., physician, Rob-

RICHARD HOWARD—CAMERA 5

Arthur Ashe

ert Walter Johnson. Johnson sponsored Ashe, encouraging him to enter tournaments and, above all, teaching him to control his emotions.

Ashe learned that lesson well. Never was his control more dramatic than when his tennis career turned around in 1975. Ashe won the World Championship Tennis crown in May when he beat Sweden's Björn Borg. Then in July he dumped defending champion Jimmy Connors at Wimbledon. The Wimbledon match victory was intensified by a multimillion-dollar libel suit that Connors had filed against Ashe. Connors alleged that Ashe, as president of the players' association, had slandered Jimmy for his reluctance to play with the U.S. Davis Cup team.

If anyone felt added pressure because of the lawsuit, it appeared to be Connors. Playing with a meticulous strategy written on a scrap of paper and stuck in his racket cover for ready reference, Ashe forced the hard-hitting Connors into numerous errors and won the match, 6–1, 6–1, 5–7, 6–4. He casually dismissed references to his distinction as "the first black to win the Wimbledon men's singles." "It's no big deal," said Ashe. But, together with his nine other tournament victories during the year, it led to his replacing Connors as no. 1 in the U.S. Tennis Association rankings issued in December. (J. TIMOTHY WEIGEL)

Azevedo, José Batista Pinheiro de

On Aug. 29, 1975, the chief of staff of the Portuguese Navy, Adm. José Pinheiro de Azevedo, was appointed the nation's premier after a six-week political crisis during which widespread anti-Communist riots had taken place in northern Portugal, Oporto, and Lisbon. Growing opposition to the previous premier, Gen. Vasco dos Santos Gonçalves, from the Armed Forces Movement moderates and extreme left had made effective government impossible. Azevedo was a close and trusted friend of the president, Gen. Francisco da Costa Gomes, sharing with him a taste for mathematics.

Azevedo, a nationalist with socialist leanings, clearly was chosen by the president as a man who would not upset the nation's delicate political balance. He brought with him the support of the Navy for the new government, and his political and economic program allayed widespread fears of a Communist takeover in Portugal. Mutiny among extreme left-wing factions in the armed forces caused splits to reopen in the military over the direction of the revolution, and Azevedo therefore faced the task of redefining Portugal's social, political, and economic paths.

Azevedo was born on June 5, 1917, in Luanda (Angola), where his father was a government official. He entered the Naval Academy in Lisbon at 17. He rose slowly through the ranks, obtaining his first command, the destroyer "Almirante Schultz," in 1946. Between 1955 and 1963 he served as an instructor at the Naval Academy, and from 1963 to 1965 he commanded the sea defenses at the mouth of the Congo River in Angola.

From 1972 to 1974 Azevedo was the commander of the Marine Corps. Immediately after the coup on April 25, 1974, he was promoted to the rank of admiral and became a member of the ruling junta. He was credited with being the man mainly responsible for lining up the Navy behind the coup. (MICHAEL WOOLLER)

Barry, Rick

After leading his Golden State Warriors to the National Basketball Association championship in 1975, Rick Barry was considered by some basketball observers to have become the dominant player in his profession. Though others disagreed with this judgment, all concurred that Barry had established himself as one of the best businessmen in the game. His maneuvers between the NBA and the American Basketball Association were of great benefit to him financially.

Born in Elizabeth, N.J., on March 28, 1944, Barry played grade-school basketball for his father, "a strict disciplinarian" according to Barry. He enrolled at the University of Miami (Fla.), became an All-American basketball player, and obtained a degree in business in 1965.

That year he joined the San Francisco Warriors of the NBA and was named rookie of the year. In his second season, Barry led the NBA in scoring with an average of 35.6 points per game. Then he jumped to the American Basketball Association's Oakland Oaks, coached by his father-in-law. Because he was still under the option year of his contract with the Warriors, Barry had to sit out the 1967–68 season.

He joined the Oaks, but the club failed financially and was purchased by a Washington, D.C., businessman and moved to the nation's capital. Barry said that he did not want to go east, and so he signed a five-year, $1 million contract with his old San Francisco team. But court rulings ordered him to perform with Washington. Then, in 1970, the team was moved to Virginia and Barry balked again. His contract was sold to the New York Nets of the ABA and was renegotiated to bring Barry $165,000 a year.

But during the 1971–72 season, the Warriors filed suit to force Barry to honour the agreement he had signed with them a year earlier. Another court ruling determined that Barry did indeed belong back in San Francisco, where he returned after negotiating a lucrative contract.

The high point of Barry's career came in 1975 when he led his team to the NBA title. He was the top vote-getter on the NBA All-Star team and also established himself as the most accurate free-throw shooter in professional basketball history with his unorthodox, underhand style. (J. TIMOTHY WEIGEL)

Baryshnikov, Mikhail Nikolayevich

"It's a stupid comparison to make. We're very different people, different dancers. The only thing we have in common is that we come from the same school." This was the answer that Mikhail N. Baryshnikov, a Soviet ballet dancer who defected to the West in 1974, gave to those who compared him with his well-known predecessor, Rudolf Nureyev. Mistakenly or not, however, people continued to think of Nureyev and Baryshnikov together. Both men are superb dancers who became famous and prosperous in their homeland but left it to seek greater artistic freedom.

Baryshnikov began dancing rather late, at the age of 12, and just six years later was a soloist with one of the Soviet Union's leading ballet companies. Born in Riga, Latvia, on Jan. 27, 1948, he entered Riga's opera ballet school in 1960, largely as a favour to his mother. He had such a striking success as a schoolboy dancer, however, that he committed himself to that art at the age of 15.

In 1963, Baryshnikov applied for admission to the Vaganova Ballet School, the training institute for Leningrad's Kirov Ballet. At the Vaganova, he was instructed by Aleksandr Pushkin, the same man who had taught Nureyev. By 1966 Baryshnikov was ready to appear with the Kirov. But instead of beginning there, as most do, in the corps de ballet, he was made a soloist at once. During that same year, Baryshnikov entered an international competition in Varna, Bulg., and won a gold medal.

At the Kirov, Baryshnikov enjoyed one success after another. He had just celebrated his 20th birthday when he appeared in the leading role in *Gorianka,* a ballet that had been choreographed especially for him. One year later, in *Vestris,* another work created for him, Baryshnikov won the gold medal at an international dance competition in Moscow.

Though he lived as well as anyone in Leningrad, Baryshnikov began to feel unhappy with the official restrictions that were placed upon his freedom as an artist. The

MARTHA SWOPE

Mikhail Nikolayevich Baryshnikov

Soviet government permitted no foreign choreographers to work in that country and allowed no Soviet-born dance artists to tour with foreign companies. In late June 1974, while on tour in Toronto, Canada, Baryshnikov refused to enter the bus that was to carry his company back to their hotel. He walked instead to a waiting car that some friends had provided and was taken to a hiding place in a Toronto suburb. The Canadian government soon granted him asylum and, less than a month after his defection, Baryshnikov began a series of highly successful appearances before North American audiences. He was accepted with enthusiasm and was widely acclaimed for his flawless technique and stage presence. (VICTOR M. CASSIDY)

Barzun, Jacques (Martin)

It was the final class of the term at Columbia University. Prof. Jacques Barzun had completed his history lecture, and the students were filing out. Some paused at the desk to chat. At length, only two people stood in the room: Barzun and one of his students, a well-dressed adult who had spoken little during the semester. This man approached Barzun, praised his lectures, and handed him a business card. He said, "If you ever want anyone taken care of, Professor, just let me know." Barzun's student was a syndicate hit man. Though few others in Barzun's classes have entered such unusual professions, almost all have benefited from his teaching.

Barzun passed his entire professional career at Columbia University in New York City. He studied at Columbia College from 1923 to 1927, entered the department of history as an instructor two years later, and steadily advanced there, becoming a full professor in 1945. He later held various administrative posts and became one of three faculty members to receive the esteemed title of university professor. On June 17, 1975, Barzun retired.

Barzun had an unconventional childhood. His father Henri and his mother Anne Rosa were living in a commune of sorts for poets in Créteil, France, when Jacques was born on Nov. 30, 1907. They soon moved to Paris, where Guillaume Apollinaire, Marie Laurencin, and Marcel Duchamp were among the people who visited the Barzun household when Jacques was a boy. The experimental art and literature that shocked so many people during the years before and after World War I seemed normal to young Barzun. In 1920 Barzun and his family moved to the U.S.

In a recent account of Barzun's work and career, Richard F. Goldman distinguished four themes that dominate his writings: "the necessity of knowing history in order to understand the present; the establishment of an intelligent view and appreciation of Romanticism and 'the Romantic century'; the critical assessment of the 'crisis' in modern culture, including the situation of education; and, perhaps underlying all of these, restoration of respect for intellect and all its works."

Barzun expounded these ideas in such books as *Darwin, Marx, Wagner: Critique of a Heritage* (1941; rev. 1958), *Romanticism and the Modern Ego* (1943; rev. 1961), *The Energies of Art* (1956), *The House of Intellect* (1959), and *Science: The Glorious Entertainment* (1964). By his life and works, Barzun clearly influenced the best of his generation to respect and engage in the exercise of intellect. (VICTOR M. CASSIDY)

Beame, Abraham

Not since the epidemic of race riots swept across U.S. cities in the 1960s had a mayor faced a set of problems as intractable as those New York City's Abraham Beame faced in 1975. This time, however, the problem was not violence but money—or rather its absence. For all practical purposes, the city was broke, and it fell to Mayor Beame, former chief financial official before becoming mayor in 1974, to try to keep New York from defaulting on its obligations.

The problems of urban violence and city bankruptcy were not unrelated. Through three mayors and for more than a decade, the city overreached its financial limits in an attempt to provide services and relief for its population. Though its taxes were among the highest in the nation, the cost of its programs was even higher. Free tuition and open admission to the City University, a huge welfare burden and public hospital system, along with ever more generous city employee wage and benefit settlements and the severe national economic recession, finally drove the city over the brink.

Abraham Beame

WIDE WORLD

Beame spent the entire year trying to forestall default. He was forced to cut city payrolls, delay scheduled pay increases for the city's employees, raise subway fares, cut back the city's construction program, and finally, near the end, give up most of his constitutional authority over the city's affairs to a special, state-level board of overseers charged with bringing order to the city's fiscal chaos.

As the city's crisis worsened, Beame and other New York officials began regular pilgrimages to Washington seeking federal assistance. Both Congress and the Ford administration were at first less than eager to help. But when the state finally imposed $200 million in new taxes and postponed payments to the city's bondholders, the federal government granted a line of credit to the state to be used by the city. (*See* UNITED STATES: *Special Report*.)

Beame was born in London, England, on March 20, 1906. His parents brought him to the U.S. shortly after his birth, and he was raised in New York City. After graduating from City College of New York, Beame taught in city high schools from 1929 to 1945 and also was a public accountant. He entered city government in 1946, serving as assistant budget director until 1952, as budget director from 1952 to 1961, and as controller from 1962 to 1965.

Defeated by John V. Lindsay in the mayoral election of 1965, Beame left city government to become a financial consultant, bank director, and chairman of the board of Arrow Lock Corp. He became city controller again in 1970 and served until 1973, when he was elected mayor on the Democratic ticket. (JOHN F. STACKS)

Berlinguer, Enrico

The upsurge of the Communist Party in Italy's June 1975 local elections gave Enrico Berlinguer, party secretary-general since March 1972, an even more prominent position than he already held on the Italian political scene. The Communists had long been the country's second largest party; they were now capable of limiting, in part at least, the powers of the leading Christian Democrats and of their coalition government with the Republicans.

Berlinguer was born in Sassari, Sardinia, on May 25, 1922, into a middle-class family, his father being a socialist who became a deputy and later senator. The son became a Communist Party member in 1943 and was put in charge of Sassari's Young Communists. In 1944, during World War II, he took part in demonstrations against Italy's Fascist regime, was arrested, and spent four months in jail. After the war he continued as an organizer of Communist youth in Milan and then Rome, becoming a member of the party's Central Committee in 1945 and of the executive in 1948.

After a series of posts within the party, both in Rome and in Sardinia, Berlinguer became secretary for the Lazio region. In 1968 he was elected deputy to the Italian Parliament. The following year, on the occasion of the party's 12th national congress, he was elected assistant secretary, in support of the sick and aging secretary Luigi Longo. During the following three years Berlinguer gave proof of his main qualities; he was a hard worker if not a brilliant speaker, and a realistic rather than a flamboyant man. His ascendance came at a difficult moment in the development of Italian

SYGMA

Enrico Berlinguer

society. In a restless and uncertain country, his contribution to the strengthening of the Communist Party was undeniable; thus his election as secretary-general at the party's 13th congress in Milan, when Longo was given the newly created role of party president, was no surprise.

After becoming "opposition leader," Berlinguer frequently declared his readiness to take an active part in government in what he termed a "historic compromise" between Christian Democrats and Communists. Such offers were rejected, but the June 1975 local elections clearly indicated that the general election of 1977 might give him that opportunity, one that the Italian Communist Party had long been striving for.

(FABIO GALVANO)

Bhaktivedanta, A. C., Swami Prabhupāda

In the period from October 1968 to November 1975, his divine grace Abhay Charanaravinda Bhaktivedanta, Swami Prabhupāda, astonished academic and literary communities worldwide by writing and publishing 52 books on the ancient Vedic culture. These contained many original oil paintings reproduced in colour, translations from texts or *ślokas* printed in their original Sanskrit and Bengali alphabets, and detailed exegeses. His philosophical journal *Back to Godhead* had attained a monthly circulation of three million copies. These and other of his writings were being published throughout the world in 22 languages.

A. C. Bhaktivedanta, Swami Prabhupāda

BHAKTIVEDANTA BOOK TRUST

The International Society for Krishna Consciousness, which he had established in 1966, had expanded by the end of 1975 to 78 temples in five continents. By the late 1960s, as a direct result of his missionary activity, shaven-headed men and sari-clad women had become a familiar sight on the streets of the world's major cities as they performed *saṅkīrtana,* devotional chanting of and dancing to the mahāmantra: *Hare Kṛṣṇa Hare Kṛṣṇa Kṛṣṇa Kṛṣṇa Hare Hare, Hare Rāma Hare Rāma Rāma Rāma Hare Hare.*

A. C. Bhaktivedanta was 32nd in the spiritual succession, the *Gauḍīya Vaiṣṇava Sampradāya.* Twenty-second in the line was Śrī Caitanya Mahāprabhu, who began the Saṅkīrtana movement in 15th-century India. Śrīla Bhaktisiddhānta Sarasvatī Thākur, Bhaktivedanta's immediate predecessor and guru, had ordered him, as his foremost disciple, to disseminate Vedic literature in the English-speaking world. In 1965 Swami Prabhupāda sailed, with only 50 rupees, to Boston, Mass. His teachings were that the Vedic culture, when presented authoritatively and without personal motivation, would effect profound changes in the consciousness of a world afflicted with rampant materialism. Courses in Kṛṣṇa Consciousness were taught in institutions of higher education in many parts of the world, and the swami's books were in use as standard texts in numerous universities.

Born Abhay Charan De on Sept. 1, 1896, in Calcutta, India, A. C. Bhaktivedanta completed his B.A. studies at the University of Calcutta and in 1933 was formally initiated as a disciple of his spiritual master at Allahabad. (MUKUNDA DAS ADHIKARY)

Broadbent, (John) Edward

When David Lewis was defeated in a national election in July 1974, Ed Broadbent became interim parliamentary leader of the New Democratic Party in Canada's House of Commons. In January 1975 Broadbent announced that he would not seek the post of leader of the national NDP because it would not leave him enough time for himself and his family. Urging by important party officials and 10 of his 16 fellow NDP members of Parliament persuaded him, however, to run for the leadership post at the convention in Winnipeg in July 1975. Retiring leader Lewis, who had defeated Broadbent for the post at the 1971 convention, backed him, saying he "saw immense development in the man during the past year as parliamentary leader and given the opportunity he would make an effective leader."

At the convention Broadbent won on the fourth ballot, defeating Rosemary Brown who was supported by the feminist-socialist wing of the party. Backing by labour unions was important for his election. The New Democratic Party was formed in 1961 from the Co-operative Commonwealth Federation and the Canadian Labour Congress, and labour unions are entitled to almost half the votes at any convention. Broadbent, member of Parliament from the Oshawa-Whitby Riding in Ontario, a major auto centre, was backed by key Ontario unions.

John Edward Broadbent came from a working-class background. He was born in Oshawa, Ont., in 1936, the son of a clerk for General Motors Corp. His brother became an auto worker, but Ed attended the University of Toronto and received his Ph.D. from the London School of Economics and Political Science. In 1968 he was teaching political science at York University in Toronto when he was asked to run for Parliament. He won his first election by 15 votes and was reelected in 1972 and 1974.

A solid socialist, Broadbent hoped to develop a new economic plan for Canada by 1977, using socialist experts in government, the universities, and the NDP. It would focus on three major areas: housing, corporate power, and resources. Housing, he believed, should be removed from the private sector and a ceiling put on mortgage rates. He favoured selective nationalization of industry, *e.g.,* those dealing with natural resources, and believed that multinational companies should not have a voice in Canada's economic growth. What Broadbent wanted, he said, was an "independent Canada in which all men have the same say, direct or indirect, in running political and economic institutions. (DIANE LOIS WAY)

Brooks, Mel

For a funny man, Mel Brooks began to be taken very seriously in 1975. He was profiled in the prestigious *New York Times Magazine* and analyzed in a *Newsweek* cover story.

A onetime gag writer for Sid Caesar's television series "Your Show of Shows" and an occasional performer himself, Brooks was reveling in the success of his fourth film, *Young Frankenstein.* This parody of horror movies became the object of cultic adoration by young and antiestablishment fans. It followed closely on the roughshod heels of *Blazing Saddles,* a gamey and profitable satire that pricked the balloon of oncesacrosanct Westerns.

Brooks was born Melvin Kaminsky in Brooklyn in about 1926. "Look at Jewish history," he ordered one interviewer. "Unrelieved lamenting would be intolerable. So, for every ten Jews beating their breasts, God designated one to be crazy and amuse the breast-beaters. By the time I was five I knew I was that one."

At 17 he joined the Army and was sent to the Virginia Military Institute. "They had us ride horses and cut down flags on bamboo poles. I was trained to become a Confederate officer." Later, he fought in World War II in the Battle of the Bulge. The war's diversion from funny business over, he became a drummer in the Catskills, then filled in for a comic, and finally rose to the pinnacle of Borscht Circuit success as social director at Grossinger's resort.

Soon he was hired at $50 a week to write jokes for Sid Caesar, who went on to fame as a television comedian. Then Brooks teamed up with another writer in Caesar's stable, Carl Reiner, to invent "The 2,000-Year-Old Man," a jaded kosher sage who had seen everything and was never impressed.

Later, with Buck Henry, Brooks conceived "Get Smart," a television series that parodied the James Bond superspy films. He won an Academy Award for his first effort on film, a cartoon called *The Critic,* and then set out to write and direct a full-length comedy, *The Producers.* The screenplay for that movie brought him his second Oscar. His other film credit was *The Twelve Chairs,* a critical success but not a popular one. He had achieved his own goal in the view of many observers: "To be the funniest has always been my aim," says Brooks. "Not the most philosophical. Not the most profound, but the funniest." (PHILIP KOPPER)

ROBERT STINNETT—PHOTO TRENDS

Brown, Edmund G(erald), Jr.

California wasn't sure what it was getting when Edmund G. Brown, Jr., was elected to succeed Gov. Ronald Reagan in the 1974 election. But it was clear that he would be something different when a Buddhist choir chanted at his inaugural ceremony and he delivered a seven-minute address that concluded: "We have a lot to do, let's get to it."

Unpredictability, austerity, and economy became Jerry Brown's trademarks after he took the oath of office on Jan. 6, 1975. He pleasantly surprised some of his conservative Republican opponents, shocked some liberal Democratic supporters, irritated his party's leadership, but won at least temporary approval from an overwhelming majority of Californians. "I think American values need reassertion in terms of fundamental roots," he said on a "Meet the Press" TV program. "There has been an overemphasis on the ability of material comfort . . . to provide human happiness."

This streak of antimaterialism was a major force in Brown's efforts to reform state government. He slashed the state budget to bring it into line with a recession economy. The result of his ruthless poking into the bureaucracy was the elimination of some programs and jobs. He was criticized for failing to delegate authority—he personally reviewed every extradition paper that had to be signed—and for "out-Reaganing" his conservative predecessor in fiscal affairs. Educators were outraged when he blocked a cost-of-living increase. On the liberal side, he gained passage of a controversial bill granting the right of secret-ballot union elections to farm labourers.

Brown's own life-style was as austere as his governing style. He scorned the governor's mansion in favour of a modest apartment, refused to use a limousine, and insisted on traveling by commercial airline. He avoided the ceremonies of office and ignored politics. Born April 7, 1938, in San Francisco, he was the son of former governor Edmund G. ("Pat") Brown. He studied for the priesthood as a Jesuit, then left the seminary to attend the University of California at Berkeley and Yale University School of Law, graduating in 1964. He became involved in politics as an opponent of the Vietnam war and in 1970 won election as California's secretary of state.

(HAL BRUNO)

Burstyn, Ellen

Born in Detroit on Dec. 7, 1932, Edna Rae Gillooly was a cheerleader, acrobat, and president of her junior class at Cass Technical High School when she ran away to Dallas on a Greyhound bus. After starving for three days, she lied about her age to land a job as a model in a supermarket. When she went home again, she married a childhood boyfriend and settled down to live happily thereafter, as in the movie scripts of her time. But instead Edna Rae became a real movie star named Ellen Burstyn with three broken marriages behind her and a devoted following among both film audiences and the women's movement. In 1975 she scored a remarkable double triumph by winning an Academy Award for best actress in a motion picture and an Antoinette Perry Award for best actress in a stage play.

She won the Oscar as the title character in *Alice Doesn't Live Here Anymore,* a film about a young widow with a son to raise who sets out for California to become a nightclub singer but must seek other fulfillments when realities intervene. Burstyn was the prime mover behind this film. She discovered the script, revised it out of her personal experience and through improvisation sessions with other actors, and persuaded Warner Brothers to back the project with a $2.1 million budget. It was a critical and box-office success. Burstyn's Broadway triumph was in Bernard Slade's romantic comedy *Same Time, Next Year.*

Burstyn first reached New York in the early 1950s. One of her first jobs was as Miss Oven Crust, clad in only a chef's hat and apron. She drifted into television and did commercial lead-ins on "The Jackie Gleason Show." Taking a new name with almost every new step in her career, she was Keri Flynn as a dancer in Montreal, Erica Dean as an artist's model in New York, and Ellen McRae on Broadway in 1957. She entered psychoanalysis and studied at Lee Strasberg's famous Actors Studio.

After a number of unremembered movie and television soap opera roles she was cast opposite Rip Torn in *Tropic of Cancer* in 1969. She received critical acclaim for her performance in 1970 in *Alex in Wonderland.* This led to her pick of parts in *The Last Picture Show* (1971), for which she won two major critics' awards as well as her first Oscar nomination. Her second nomination was for the mother's role in *The Exorcist* in 1973.

The success of *Alice* . . . seemed to rest on the reality of the title character. Burstyn said "I wanted Alice to be a fully rounded mother, one who loves her kid and has a one-to-one relationship with him. And sometimes she makes a mistake. . . . That's what mothers do."

(PHILIP KOPPER)

Ellen Burstyn

WIDE WORLD

Buzo, Alexander

The new wave of indigenous Australian drama was best exemplified by 31-year-old Alexander Buzo, author of a spate of plays, both short and full-length, that made their mark in both Britain and the U.S., where they appeared in book form, and in his native Australia.

Buzo was a "typical product" of Sydney, where he was born in 1944, the son of an Albanian-born, American-educated civil engineer and an Australian mother. A liberal education, in Armindale, New South Wales, and at the International School of Geneva, in Switzerland, plus a degree from the University of New South Wales in 1965, underlay his passion for his native land and his fervent championship of the underdog.

After working as a clerk in the N.S.W. Education Department, as a waiter, and as an actor and stagehand in Sydney, he mounted a workshop production of his apprentice drama about conscription, *The Revolt,* in 1967. He made his professional playwriting debut with the one-act *Norm and Ahmed* in 1968. Like his subsequent plays, it exploited the exotic lingo of Australian vernacular and provoked several court actions. It was seen in London in 1973. *Rooted,* a black comedy, was staged on one day in Sydney and Canberra in 1969. A U.S. production in Hartford, Conn. (1972), and a British one in London (1973) were followed by a filmed version.

In 1969 Buzo wrote *The Back Room Boys,* "about the ritual and rhythms of office life," and the screenplay of the Mick Jagger film of *Ned Kelly.* The former, also published in West Germany, was performed throughout Australia, at the Perth Festival in 1970, and at the Royal Court Theatre, London, in 1971, and was scheduled for broadcasting by BBC Radio in 1976. Later plays were *The Greatest Game of All* (1970); the football play *The Roy Murphy Show* (1972); *MacQuarie* (1972), about a N.S.W. governor (1762–1824), financed by a Commonwealth Literary Grant; *Tom* (1972), a comedy, which was also staged in Washington in 1974 and, with its predecessor, won the 1972 Australian Literary Society's Gold Medal; *The Batman's Beachhead* (1973), based on Ibsen's *An Enemy of the People; Coralie Lansdowne Says No* (1974), about an unmarried art teacher; and *Martello Towers,* due for a first production in Sydney in March 1976.

Buzo also wrote a novel, *Mr. Ponsford and the Asian Cricketers,* the prizewinning short film *Rod* (1973), and its sister radio play, *File on Rod,* commissioned by the BBC.

(OSSIA TRILLING)

Cairns, James Ford

Australian Deputy Prime Minister Jim Cairns's fall from grace in July 1975 was a leading event in the prologue to the sensational fall of the Australian Labor Party (ALP) government in November. Cairns had provided the background of moral opposition to the Vietnam war, and when the ALP came to power he was seen as the personification of probity and concern for the underprivileged. The scandals that surrounded his dismissal from the Treasury, then from the Ministry for the Environment, and finally from the deputy prime ministership were shattering to Cairns's long-time supporters. His dismissal was the result of his unsuccessful attempt to obtain petrodollar loans from Middle East oil sources. In his search for funds he acted contrary to the advice of Treasury officials by encouraging unorthodox approaches to obtaining the money by private entrepreneurs.

Cairns had weathered attacks on his personal staff and deflected allegations of nepotism, but he was unable to avoid the invidious implications of the overseas loan negotiations. Early in June he misled Parliament by saying that at no stage had he offered a brokerage fee of 2½% to anyone. Subsequently, newspapers published copies of a letter in which he offered a commission, and Prime Minister Gough Whitlam called for an explanation. Cairns replied that he had answered the question in good faith, having no recollection of signing the letter.

Not satisfied with the excuse, Whitlam asked for Cairns's resignation. When Cairns declined to resign, Whitlam instructed the governor-general to dismiss him. Cairns responded with a bitter attack on the prime minister's lack of compassion. Opinion in the ALP was summed up by Jack Egerton, a senior party leader, who said that Cairns had "played like a mug, and deserved to be treated like a mug." Despite the magnitude of the loans scandal, Cairns commanded some grass-roots support. In the 88-member ALP parliamentary party caucus, 33 voted against the dismissal.

Born in Carlton, Victoria, on Oct. 4, 1914, Cairns was a police officer, an army education officer, and a university lecturer before election to Parliament in 1955. When the ALP took power in 1972, he became minister for overseas trade.

(A. R. G. GRIFFITHS)

Carter, William Beverly, Jr.

For W. Beverly Carter, Jr., U.S. ambassador to Tanzania since 1972, events took a sudden and dramatic turn the night of May 19, 1975, when a guerrilla band from neighbouring Zaire crossed Lake Tanganyika into western Tanzania and kidnapped four students—three American and one Dutch—working at a research centre for the study of primate behaviour.

The kidnappers were members of the People's Revolutionary Party (PRP), a Marxist group in rebellion against Zaire's president, Mobutu Sese Seko. Their original target was believed to have been British anthropologist Jane Goodall, director of the Gombe Stream Reserve, but they abducted the students when they could not find her. One of the Americans, Barbara Smuts, was released a week later with ransom notes addressed to Carter and Tanzanian Pres. Julius Nyerere, demanding £200,000 ($460,000), weapons, and the release of two PRP members who had been held in a Tanzanian jail. The kidnappers warned that the remaining hostages would be killed if their terms were not met within 60 days.

The Tanzanian government disclaimed any responsibility for the hostages, and Zaire offered no cooperation in searching for the rebel band. Carter was bound by a U.S. State Department policy banning negotiations with terrorists, but a month later, when two PRP representatives appeared at the U.S. embassy in Dar es Salaam, he permitted them to negotiate with the parents of the kidnap victims. Eventually, the parents paid a reported $40,000, and Carrie Jane Hunter and Emilie van Zinnick Bergmann were set free within a week.

WIDE WORLD

William Beverly Carter, Jr.

A radio operator from the U.S. embassy, sent to a remote border town to maintain communications with the parents, inadvertently was present when some of the ransom money was paid, thereby giving it the appearance of an official U.S. government action. This incurred the wrath of Secretary of State Henry Kissinger, but he was persuaded to defer any action until the last hostage, Kenneth Smith, was released on July 25. Carter, who was to have become U.S. ambassador to Denmark, was then recalled for "reassignment" to a less prestigious post.

Carter, who was born Feb. 1, 1921, in Coatesville, Pa., and had had a career as a newspaperman before entering the Foreign Service in 1965, was one of the highest-ranking black U.S. diplomats. The threat to end his career brought strong criticism from the families and associates of the kidnap victims, the Black Caucus in the U.S. Congress, and the press, who insisted that he should be praised rather than punished. Faced with these protests, Kissinger assured the Black Caucus leadership that nothing would be done to impede Carter's career.

(HAL BRUNO)

Carvalho, Otelo Saraiva de

On July 25, 1975, the ruling body of Portugal, the Armed Forces Movement, appointed a three-man Revolutionary Directorate as the state policymaking agency. Most controversial of the three was Gen. Otelo Saraiva de Carvalho, the commander of the 70,000-member internal security force, Copcon, who was identified with the leftist element of the military regime.

Carvalho also served for most of the year as military commander of the Lisbon region. But after several days of mass pro- and antigovernment demonstrations in Lisbon in November, the moderate government of Premier José Pinheiro de Azevedo (*q.v.*) asked for the removal of Carvalho from his command post.

Carvalho, who was 40 years of age in 1975, was born into a middle-class family in Lourenço Marques in Portugal's former African colony of Mozambique. He was graduated from officer cadet school in 1958, and in the 1960s served in the Portuguese African colonies of Angola and Guinea-Bissau. In the 1970s in Guinea-Bissau he was an intelligence officer on the staff of Gen. António de Spínola. In a much-quoted judgment, Spínola stated that Carvalho should never have been raised above the rank of sergeant. There is a kinder version, however, in which Spínola says that Otelo was a good battalion officer but unendowed for the responsibilities of a staff post.

In April 1974 Spínola led the coup that overthrew the government of Marcello Caetano and became president of Portugal. Three months later Carvalho was promoted to the rank of brigadier general, the youngest in the history of the Portuguese Army. It was the desertion of this new brigadier that sealed the downfall of General Spínola in September 1974.

The civil commotion and disorders of August and September 1975, the inability of Copcon to deal with the situation or identify completely with the sixth government and its new socialistic political program, led to the creation of a new security force on which the government felt better able to rely. Afterward, the role of Copcon and its head, Carvalho, remained ill-defined.

(MICHAEL WOOLLER)

Clarke, Bobby

There are really no logical explanations why Bobby Clarke is one of hockey's all-time greatest players. Clarke, the centre and captain of the 1974 and 1975 Stanley Cup winners, the Philadelphia Flyers, is not particularly fast or strong, and he skates and shoots just adequately. And, as a diabetic, Clarke must take daily insulin shots.

But Bobby Clarke adapted to the National Hockey League in the only way he knew how. "Hard work is the equalizer," he once said. "If everybody worked as hard as he could, then naturally the best players would

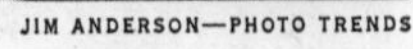

JIM ANDERSON—PHOTO TRENDS

Bobby Clarke

rise to the top. But not everyone is willing to work that hard. Each player has to make his contribution." Fred Shero, Clarke's coach at Philadelphia, called him "one of the best competitors I've ever seen."

Clarke was born Aug. 13, 1949, in Flin Flon, Man. He was the Flyers' second draft choice in 1969, after being bypassed by several teams because of his diabetes. Yet as of 1975 he had missed only two games in his NHL career.

In the 1969–70 season, Clarke was the NHL's West Division rookie of the year. After the 1971–72 season, he won the Bill Masterton Memorial Trophy as the player "who best exemplifies the qualities of perseverance, sportsmanship and dedication to hockey." Named as the Flyers' captain for the 1972–73 season, Clarke became the youngest captain (at 23) in NHL history.

In 1973 Clarke became the first player from the 1967–68 expansion teams to win the Hart Trophy as the league's most valuable player. All the while that Clarke was improving on the ice, he was also becoming his team's leader and spokesman off the ice, shedding the shy personality he brought with him from Flin Flon.

In May 1974 Clarke led the Flyers to their first Stanley Cup, as Philadelphia became the first expansion team to win the trophy. But Clarke had his finest season in 1974–75. The 5 ft. 10 in. 185-pounder scored 116 points, on 27 goals and 89 assists. His 89 assists were an NHL record for a centre. He also scored in 18 straight games, a Philadelphia club record. More important, Clarke led Philadelphia to its second consecutive Stanley Cup. The Flyers defeated the Buffalo Sabres 4–2 in the final round, and Clarke again won the Hart Trophy.

(J. TIMOTHY WEIGEL)

Cleese, John

One of the reasons that there was to be no more of the BBC television series "Monty Python's Flying Circus" was said to have been that John Cleese wanted to leave the team and try something different. It was a mark of the success both of the program, with its anarchic humour, and of Cleese within it that the matter seemed important —especially since the real popularity of the show had come with the repeats of earlier series, not the way hits are usually made. "Monty Python" was a hit, however, for at least two reasons: Terry Gilliam's animations and John Cleese himself. And it was a mark of Cleese's talents that he did do something else: in 1975 one of the critical successes of British television was "Fawlty Towers," a comedy series written by Cleese and his American actress wife, Connie Booth, which starred Cleese as Basil Fawlty, the manic proprietor of a small hotel.

John Cleese

B.B.C.

John Cleese was born in 1939, in the West Country seaside town of Weston-super-Mare. A tall lad (6 ft. before he entered his teens), he might have been destined for comedy on that basis alone, but was undoubtedly helped by reaching Cambridge University at a time when the Footlights dramatic society was enjoying a peak of esteem for humorous revue. Cleese, now 6 ft. 5 in. tall, starred in one, *Cambridge Circus,* which won a run in the West End of London and then—in the wake of *Beyond the Fringe*—transferred to New York City. It was there that he met Connie Booth. Back in England, Cleese was recruited for David Frost's "The Frost Report" series.

Part of Cleese's talent was physical, that of the clown, as seen in his creation of the Minister of Funny Walks for "Monty Python." But another archetype was the sober-suited man—a civil servant, or bank manager—who would suddenly explode with violence, seizing his client across the desk. The same sense of incipient loss of self-control was injected in many verbal jokes too. It nonetheless came as a surprise when, in 1975, with attention concentrated on the unexpected success of the "Monty Python" programs and feature films in the U.S., Cleese came up with a vehicle that exploited all these facets and more. Basil Fawlty, the hotel proprietor, was perfectly pitched: having to serve his guests, and doing so unctuously, but ever wanting to burst out and hit them. Throughout the half-hour Cleese and Connie Booth were consistently able to sustain farcical invention of a sort that a strong cast (Prunella Scales, Andrew Sachs) was able to make much of.

(PETER FIDDICK)

Colby, William Egan

The year 1975 began with the U.S. Central Intelligence Agency and its director, William E. Colby, under fire from all directions. It ended with Colby fired, but temporarily still on the job, while revelations of the CIA's alleged wrongdoings continued to make news.

Colby's dismissal by Pres. Gerald Ford came as no surprise. Rumours that his days at the CIA were numbered surfaced as soon as he began cooperating with congressional investigating committees earlier in the year. For the first time in the agency's 28-year history, its head man was answering questions about top secret matters, admitting past mistakes and even illegal activities. The most serious charges involved assassination plots against foreign leaders, intervention in other countries' political affairs, and domestic intelligence gathering in violation of the CIA's charter.

Colby answered most of the questions put to him by the inquiring senators and congressmen in executive sessions, while publicly defending the CIA in speeches and press conferences. While conceding the need for change, Colby's strategy was aimed at preserving the secrecy of current national security matters and preventing the CIA from being turned inside out by an angry Congress. Though his strategy might yet work, his tactics were not approved by President Ford and Secretary of State Henry Kissinger, who felt he gave too much too freely.

A lawyer by training and a master spy by career, Colby was an unlikely person to break the wall of secrecy that had surrounded the CIA for so long. He was born Jan. 4, 1920, in St. Paul, Minn., the son of an army officer, graduated from Princeton in 1940, joined the Office of Strategic Services (OSS) during World War II, and parachuted behind enemy lines in occupied France. After a postwar period of law practice, Colby served in several U.S. embassies, then became chief of the CIA's Far East division. In 1968 he was deputy director of the Civil Operations and Rural Development Support (CORDS) pacification program and the Phoenix intelligence campaign in South Vietnam. Pres. Richard Nixon named him CIA director in 1973.

WIDE WORLD

William Egan Colby

Colby was fired on Nov. 1, 1975, in a round of administration shuffles that became known as the "Halloween massacre." At President Ford's request, he agreed to remain at his post until his chosen replacement, diplomat George Bush, could be approved by the Senate—a confirmation that proved difficult because of Bush's background in domestic politics. (HAL BRUNO)

Coors, William

Without it, the United States might break down completely. The president might be unable to act. Other key leaders would falter. The situation in California, Texas, and the Rocky Mountain states could rapidly become chaotic.

Fortunately, none of this was likely to happen, for there was enough Coors Banquet Beer to go around—at least in the 11 states where it was sold. So, whenever Pres. Gerald Ford visited the West, he would be able to buy some there. Coors was served frequently in the White House. The Boston Red Sox baseball team also quaffed Coors, as did movie actor Paul Newman. So did millions of other less famous but equally thirsty people.

Coors tastes better, its admirers say, because it is not made like other U.S. beers. The brewery uses pure Rocky Mountain springwater treated with ozone to preserve its sweet flavour. California rice, Bavarian hops, and Colorado barley are the other ingredients. The entire brewing process takes 80 days, roughly four times longer than most other U.S. brewers spend on their product. Preservatives are never added, and because the beer is not pasteurized it must be kept cool or it will spoil in seven days.

The man responsible for the wonderful beverage was William Coors, president since

1970 of the Adolph Coors Co. This firm, largely family-owned, was established in Golden, Colo., in 1873 by Adolph Coors, a native of Germany. William, who was 58 years old in 1975, was one of six Coorses employed at the brewery. His brother Joseph gained prominence during the year when nominated to the board of the Corporation for Public Broadcasting—seen as a conflict of interest because of Joseph's ownership of Television News Inc., a broadcasting corporation that articulated his right-wing philosophy.

Even though William Coors did not want things that way, his beer might soon be available throughout the nation. In 1975 the U.S. Federal Trade Commission accused Coors of deliberately limiting distribution of its beer and of fixing prices in the areas where it was sold. Though the firm replied that the beer might spoil if it was sent to the East Coast, it lost its case and was compelled to sell in more states. For U.S. beer drinkers, that was very good news.

(VICTOR M. CASSIDY)

Crichton, (John) Michael

It should have come as no surprise to anyone—least of all to Michael Crichton—that his latest novel, *The Great Train Robbery,* was a runaway best-seller in 1975. An enormously popular writer, whose brashness was perhaps exceeded only by his height (6 ft. 9 in.), Crichton at 32 could already boast nine novels, two of which were sold to Universal Studios for over $500,000, the direction of several films, and the Mystery Writers of America Edgar award for the pro-abortion short story "A Case of Need."

Born in Chicago on Oct. 23, 1942, Crichton was raised in a family that stressed achievement motivation. His father, the executive editor of *Advertising Age,* often involved his four children in animated dinner discussions on the subject of writing. In high school, Michael became a star basketball player through sheer determination rather than by virtue of any natural ability. His career as a writer was launched at 14 when he sold an article to the *New York Times* travel section for $60.

Crichton graduated summa cum laude from Harvard in 1964, received his M.D. from the same institution in 1969, and became a post-doctoral fellow at the prestigious Salk Institute in La Jolla, Calif. But it became increasingly obvious that a career in medicine was not for him, and it was without serious qualms that he took off a week at a time from medical school to write detective stories.

Although Crichton had no literary pretensions—he once characterized the style of *The Andromeda Strain* as "arrant seventh-gradeism"—his novels enjoyed tremendous popularity for their pace, suspense, and magnificently constructed plot lines. Moreover, his years at Harvard did provide him with the intimate knowledge of medicine and science used to document such novels as *The Terminal Man.* To the "can't put it down" quality essential to popular literature, he added minute detail and careful research. In *The Andromeda Strain,* for example, he included computer printouts and attached a convincing—but mock—bibliography. *The Great Train Robbery* provides a cursory study of Victorian England while plunging the reader into the depths of its murky criminal underworld.

(CLAIRE SANDRA CHOW)

Cunhal, Alvaro Barreirinhas

The secretary-general of the Portuguese Communist Party, Alvaro Cunhal had been an active member of the party for 44 years, 14 of which he spent in prison. In exile after 1960, he returned to Portugal on April 30, 1974, after the coup that deposed the government of Marcello Caetano, to take command of what was then the only organized political party in Portugal.

Cunhal was born in 1914 at Ceia. In 1937, when he was first arrested and tortured, he was already a member of the Communist Party's Central Committee. From his cell he later won permission to sit for his final examinations in law, which he passed at the top of his class. On being released he became a schoolmaster and taught geography to the future leader of the Socialist Party, Mário Soares (*q.v.*).

In 1942 Cunhal became a secretary of the Portuguese Communist Party. Seven years later his active underground life in the Communist Party ended once more in arrest. There followed ten years of imprisonment, three-quarters of it in solitary confinement, till his spectacular escape from Peniche on Jan. 3, 1960. His years in exile were spent mostly in Eastern Europe and the Soviet Union.

During the third and fourth provisional governments in Portugal in 1975, Cunhal held ministerial status. There, he held solidly to the line of the ruling Armed Forces Movement. After the Communist Party's defeat in the April 1975 elections, power was maintained by a close identification with the Communist-dominated premier, Vasco dos Santos Gonçalves, and with the council of the Armed Forces Movement. After June, however, the alliance came under strain; the ability of the Communist Party to provide political support for Gonçalves became increasingly suspect with defeats in labour union elections and failed strikes. Violence and attacks on Communist Party personnel and property strained the alliance to the breaking point as it became clear that the government lacked the power to protect even its allies from the consequences of unpopular political actions.

When the Gonçalves government fell in August the Communist Party accepted a seat in the new government of José Pinheiro de Azevedo (*q.v.*), a moderate, but let it be known that the post was to be used for defending Communist gains and interests. Under Cunhal's leadership the party began exercising its strength by organizing strikes among peasants and steelworkers.

(MICHAEL WOOLLER)

Daly, Edward J.

The trauma and confusion of South Vietnam's collapse in the spring of 1975 were of such massive dimensions that individual decision and action seemed almost irrelevant. But while panic swept the small Asian country following a series of stunning victories by North Vietnamese troops, and while U.S. diplomats tried to use the appearance of normalcy to forestall even greater panic, one man's swashbuckling adventures captured the world's attention. Edward J. Daly, president and chairman of World Airways, Inc., was, briefly, the picture of all-American decisiveness in the midst of utter chaos.

Daly's charter airline, the largest of its kind in the U.S., with headquarters in Oakland, Calif., had for years been a mainstay of the U.S. government's airlift operations in Vietnam. When Saigon's troops began reeling backward, Daly rushed to the scene and took personal charge of World Airways' attempts to evacuate refugees.

WIDE WORLD

Edward J. Daly

Hacking away at red tape and often going completely outside government channels, Daly threw himself and his aircraft into the melee with typical abandon. Once, on a runway at Da Nang, he scuffled with mutinous South Vietnamese troops who were trying to shove aside civilian refugees and scramble aboard a World Airways jet. He also sent an angry cable to U.S. Secretary of State Henry Kissinger demanding quicker, bolder action in dealing with the refugees and orphans who were caught in the terrible confusion of South Vietnam's last days as a non-Communist state. Daly brushed aside criticisms of his actions. "The airlift was my own, personal decision," he said, "and I'm paying for it out of my own—not the corporate—pocket."

Daly was born in Chicago on Nov. 20, 1922. He majored in chemical engineering at the University of Illinois but did not graduate. After service as an enlisted man during World War II, he engaged in a series of business ventures that led to his acquisition of World Airways in 1950. In 1975 he owned more than 80% of the company's stock. Daly was a co-founder of the Aircoach Transportation Association, a predecessor of the National Air Carrier Association, of which he is a director. He emerged from Vietnam as an individual Americans could be proud of.

(STANLEY WILLS CLOUD)

Demirel, Suleyman

A "Western-style technocrat" who entered politics after a successful career in civil engineering, Suleyman Demirel in March 1975 became Turkey's prime minister for the second time. Previously he had held that office from 1965 until 1971, when he was ousted by the military.

When martial law was lifted in October 1973 and free elections were once again allowed, the Republican People's Party (RPP) had advanced to a leading position. Power passed to a coalition headed by RPP leader Bulent Ecevit, but when Ecevit tried to force fresh elections in 1974, following his popular military intervention in Cyprus, the coalition fell apart and Demirel set about reestablishing the unity of the right. In December 1974 he grouped his Justice Party (JP) and smaller right-wing parties into a Nationalist Front, which assumed power on March 31, 1975. In midterm Senate elections on October 12, he won back much of the support he had lost to his right-wing rivals. (The opposition RPP, however, did even better and increased its lead as the strongest single party.) Although Demirel's campaign had been staunchly anti-Communist in tone, his reception of Soviet Premier A. N. Kosygin in Ankara at year's end underlined an increasing rapprochement with the U.S.S.R. following the Cyprus affair and Turkey's subsequent alienation from the U.S.

Born in 1924 in the southwestern Turkish province of Isparta, Demirel majored in civil engineering in Istanbul. He specialized in the construction of dams, stayed twice in the U.S., and at 31 became director general of the Turkish State Hydrological Service at a time when the building of dams was a main ingredient of the development effort launched by Prime Minister Adnan Menderes. After Menderes fell victim to the military coup of May 27, 1960, Demirel went into private business, becoming a successful engineering contractor. He subsequently entered politics and in 1964 was elected leader of the JP, the main successor of Menderes' Democratic Party. On Feb. 19, 1965, he became deputy prime minister of a caretaker coalition government, and on October 27 won an absolute majority for his party in general elections and became prime minister. (ANDREW MANGO)

Drapeau, Jean

To make Montreal the world's first city by 1990 was the dream in 1975 of its mayor, Jean Drapeau. To this end he had since taking office in 1960 created a series of splendid and expensive projects. These included the city's network of underground shopping plazas, such as the Place Ville Marie; the subway system; and a downtown theatre complex, the Place des Arts.

From 1967 to 1971 Drapeau served as the senior Canadian representative at the International Bureau of Exhibitions in Paris, and in 1967 he brought a world's fair to Montreal, Expo 67. In the realm of sports, he brought major league baseball to Montreal with the National League team, the Expos.

"To be creative means to be ahead of others," said Drapeau. He received an award from the trade and industry departments of ten Canadian provinces for having contributed most to industrial development in Canada in 1965.

In 1970 Drapeau won the 1976 Olympic Games for Montreal. Involved in this project was a grand scheme to build an 80,000-seat stadium with an automatically retractable roof. Strikes hampered the building of the stadium, and the cost of the project doubled between 1970 and 1975, but Drapeau assured the government of Canada that the Olympics would not have a deficit. He blamed the federal government for part of the problem because it did not set up the financial machinery to deal with the Games until 1973.

Jean Drapeau

PACE/BLACK STAR

Drapeau became noted for his secrecy. His major plans were generally made in consultation with six members of the executive committee of the City Council. He stated that he believes in the Gaullist form of democracy, in which the populace drafts a leader and entrusts its fate to him.

Drapeau was born in Montreal in 1916 and received his law degree from the University of Montreal in 1941. In 1949 and 1950 he was the public prosecutor and looked into municipal corruption, and in 1954 was elected reform mayor of Montreal. Defeated in 1957, he formed his own political party, becoming mayor again in 1960. (DIANE LOIS WAY)

Edelin, Kenneth

The deliberations took longer than expected, and when the jurors returned to court on Feb. 15, 1975, the defendant, Kenneth Edelin, saw the verdict of "guilty" on their faces. The conviction of the Massachusetts physician for manslaughter in connection with an abortion astonished the United States and reopened the debate on that subject.

Kenneth Edelin, M.D., who was 36 years old at the time of his conviction, had since 1971 performed many abortions at Boston City Hospital. In October 1973 a 17-year-old woman, who had conceived more than 20 weeks earlier, requested an abortion. Because her pregnancy was so far advanced, Edelin employed a surgical technique known as hysterotomy, which involves opening the uterus, severing the connection between mother and fetus, and removing the fetus.

After Edelin completed this abortion, he took the dead fetus to the hospital laboratory where it was preserved for research purposes. A group of investigators from the Suffolk County district attorney's office were touring the hospital and saw the fetus. They charged that Edelin had committed manslaughter by not taking steps to preserve the life of the fetus after he had removed it from its mother.

Everyone agreed that Edelin broke no law in terminating his patient's pregnancy. The U.S. Supreme Court had legalized abortion in a 1973 decision, but it did not consider the possibility that an abortion might result in a fetus that was alive and possibly capable of surviving.

When Edelin's case came to trial in 1975, witnesses testified that the fetus could have survived, that it had taken a breath, and that Edelin had deliberately smothered it in the mother's uterus. Others contradicted this testimony, claiming that the fetus had never breathed and that it was not yet capable of living outside the womb. The judge in the case believed Edelin innocent, so charged the jury, and sentenced the physician to one year's probation after his conviction. This was a light punishment for manslaughter. Edelin planned to appeal the verdict and believed that his conviction would be struck down by a higher court. He maintained that he had followed good medical practice and did not break the law. (VICTOR M. CASSIDY)

Elizabeth, Queen (The Queen Mother)

The tributes that marked the 75th birthday of Queen Elizabeth, the queen mother, in August 1975 demonstrated her secure and almost archetypal position in British public life. Indeed, she was apparently the most dreamed-about member of the royal family.

NORMAN PARKINSON—CAMERA PRESS

Queen Elizabeth, the Queen Mother

On a more conscious level, even those who suspected that her influence might have contributed to what they considered the somewhat shabby treatment of the duke and duchess of Windsor would not deny the extent of the nation's debt to her.

Perhaps her greatest contribution was the unfailing support she gave to her husband, George VI, in the weighty burden of kingship that his brother's abdication thrust upon him. During World War II their steadfast refusal to leave London probably did as much to conserve public morale as the famous speeches of Winston Churchill. It would be understandable if she resented, consciously or unconsciously, the devolution to her delicate and much-loved husband of duties that almost certainly shortened his life.

Recently she had also lost those of her own family who were closest to her. But, sustained by Christian faith, affection for her children and grandchildren, and a strong sense of noblesse oblige, she continued a daunting program of public engagements and foreign tours that included, during 1975, a four-day visit to Iran and Cyprus in April and one to the Channel Islands in May. Her political acumen was recognized when she became the first queen dowager to be appointed a councillor of state; she had acted in that role during George VI's last illness, and regularly did so when her daughter, Queen Elizabeth II, was absent from Britain.

Elizabeth Angela Marguerite Bowes-Lyon was born on Aug. 4, 1900, in St. Paul's Waldenbury, Hertfordshire, England, a daughter of Claude George Bowes-Lyon (d. 1944) who in 1904 became 14th earl of Strathmore and Kinghorne. Educated privately, mainly at Glamis Castle, her family's Scottish seat in Angus, she married (April 26, 1923) Prince Albert, duke of York, who became King George VI on Dec. 11, 1936. She was interested in horse racing, fishing, and gardening, and kept Corgi dogs. In London she lived at Clarence House, spending weekends at Royal Lodge, Windsor. In Scotland she divided her time between her castle of Mey in Caithness and Birkhall, near Balmoral Castle. (STEPHANIE MULLINS)

Fahd ibn Abd al-Aziz Al Saud

When King Khalid succeeded to the throne of Saudi Arabia on March 25, 1975, he at once nominated his half brother Fahd, second deputy prime minister and minister of the interior, as his crown prince. It was assumed throughout Saudi Arabia that Crown Prince Fahd, with his strong personality and extensive political experience, would have the leading voice in the country's affairs, especially in view of King Khalid's well-known distaste for politics.

In the government reshuffle of October 13, Fahd dropped the post of minister of the interior while remaining first deputy prime minister. This did not imply any loss of power but allowed him to assume the real duties of the premiership, nominally in the hands of his brother the king. His political outlook was similar to that of King Faisal, although his anti-Zionism and anti-Communism were somewhat less vehement. Like most members of his family, he had no faith in representative government. In August 1975 he was quoted by an Egyptian journal as saying that an administrative consultative council would be formed, but it would be by selection rather than election because he did not believe that elections reflected true public opinion, judging from their results in the world at large.

Born in 1922, Fahd was one of the sons of the great King Ibn Saud by his influential wife Hassa bint Sudairi. His first position, in 1953, was that of minister of education. In 1962, two years before the deposition of King Saud, his eldest brother, Fahd was appointed minister of the interior, thus acquiring control over the police and domestic administration. Under King Faisal (*see* OBITUARIES), he was also made second deputy prime minister. Another key office he held was the chairmanship of the Supreme Petroleum Council, which formulates the guidelines for Saudi oil and investment policy. In January 1975 he represented King Faisal at the crucial conference of Organization of Petroleum Exporting Countries (OPEC) heads of state in Algiers, and he conducted many diplomatic missions to Arab and third world countries and also in the West, where his qualities as a reasonable and highly competent diplomat were widely appreciated. In June 1974 he signed an important Saudi-U.S. economic and military agreement in Washington. He was anglophile in his personal tastes and owned property in London. He had a reputation for enjoying life and was reported to be a well-known visitor to European gambling casinos.

(PETER MANSFIELD)

Fassbinder, Rainer Werner

Regarded by many critics as the best film director currently working in West Germany, Rainer Werner Fassbinder was certainly the most prolific, and in 1975 he directed three new feature films. Since his debut in 1969 he had directed 18, not including television productions. In the early days of his career success often alternated with total failure, but now everything he touched seemed to turn to gold.

Fassbinder was born May 31, 1945, in Bad Wörishofen, Bavaria, West Germany, the son of a doctor and a translator. While in a private acting school Fassbinder met the actress Hanna Schygulla, with whom he founded in 1968 his "Antitheatre" group. A television acting fee financed the group's first film, *Love Is Colder than Death,* which

DAVID ROBINSON

Rainer Werner Fassbinder

he wrote himself. His next film, *Katzelmacher,* together with his theatre productions in Munich and Dresden, established Fassbinder as the new *Wunderkind,* and inaugurated an output of films, stage productions, extended television series, and acting of bewildering variety.

The secret of Fassbinder's prolific output lay in part in his insistence upon surrounding himself with familiar and sympathetic co-workers, and in a precision and decisiveness of working method that enabled him to produce stylish work with financially limited resources.

His international reputation was secured in 1972–73 with *The Bitter Tears of Petra von Kant,* a brittle little chamberpiece; *Fear Eats the Soul* (1974), about an elderly German woman who encounters social humiliation when she marries a North African immigrant worker; and *Effi Briest* (1974), adapted from Theodor Fontane's 19th-century novel. His 1975 films were *Fox,* a fable about capitalist exploitation, set in a vividly realized homosexual milieu with the director playing the lead role; *Mother Küster's Journey to Heaven,* which greatly offended the left by showing how Marxists, too, are capable of the exploitation of others for political gain; and *Fear of Fear,* a television-produced study of the private obsessions of a woman who thinks she is losing her reason.

(DAVID ROBINSON)

Fodor, Eugene

A few decades ago nearly anyone traveling abroad would carry along one or two thick red guidebooks written by Karl Baedeker. These told the tourist which museums to visit, where to spend a night in comfort, and how to obtain a good dinner. They were so popular in their day that "Baedeker" became synonymous with "guidebook."

Today's best "Baedekers" are edited by Eugene Fodor, an author and publisher who heads firms in the United States and Britain that bear his name. In 1975 Fodor completed an eight-volume guidebook on the United States, which describes each geographic region. Containing the customary listings of hotels and monuments, it also attempts to characterize the unique aspects of each area.

Fodor first thought of writing a guidebook to the U.S. in 1930. He was then a 25-year-old native of Hungary who had studied economics and politics in Czechoslovakia, Paris, Hamburg, and London. Arriving in New York City as an interpreter on a French ship, Fodor persuaded a firm with transcontinental bus routes to give him a free pass in exchange for three travel articles about America. Fodor fell in love with the U.S., applied for citizenship, and ultimately served as a captain in the U.S. Army during World War II, winning six battle stars. While in Prague late in the war he met the woman who became his wife.

In 1949 he organized Fodor's Modern Guides, a firm which has since published more than 50 separate guidebooks in numerous editions. Most of these are routinely translated into French, German, Italian, Spanish, Dutch, Hungarian, and Japanese.

Fodor himself is a dedicated traveler who speaks six languages, reads four others, and has visited more than 100 countries. He passionately believes that travel is the most effective path to tolerance, understanding, and the recognition of the rights of others to their own values. Eugene Fodor has devoted his life to this end.

(VICTOR M. CASSIDY)

Ford, Betty

The politics surrounding the U.S. presidency are such that the chief executive normally weighs every word against possible negative reaction. And that caution is usually applied even more stringently to the first lady in the hope that the presidential wife will remain more an ornament than an issue.

Although a politician's wife most of her life, Betty Bloomer Ford has not followed this rule. Perhaps because her husband did not have to endure the ordeal of a presidential campaign, Mrs. Ford brought a delightful candour and brightness to the White House. During a television interview in midsummer, Mrs. Ford was asked about the politically hot issue of abortion and the Supreme Court's decision legalizing it. "A great, great decision," she said. On marijuana, another topic conservative Republicans such as her husband treat carefully, she opined that she would not be surprised had her four children sampled it and that were she younger she might try it herself.

Premarital sex was the next question, and Mrs. Ford, referring to her 18-year-old daughter, Susan, was again straightforward. "Well, I wouldn't be surprised. I think she's a perfectly normal human being like all young girls. If she wanted to continue, I would certainly counsel and advise her on the subject."

Many were aghast at Mrs. Ford's remarks. A Baptist bishop from Dallas said that she

Betty Ford

WIDE WORLD

had descended "to . . . a gutter type of mentality." But others were delighted she had spoken her mind. "At last, a real first lady," telegraphed one supporter to the White House.

The costs of her candour aside, it was not an easy year for Mrs. Ford. She was still under treatment for cancer that had forced a mastectomy in 1974. When President Ford journeyed twice to Europe in spring and summer, she was at his side, but painful arthritis forced her to curtail her schedule. Later she accompanied her husband to China.

Betty Ford was born in Chicago on April 8, 1918, and grew up in Grand Rapids, Mich. She studied at the Bennington School of the Dance and in 1939 joined a Martha Graham dance troupe. She modeled in fashion shows and worked as a fashion director for a Grand Rapids department store from 1943 to 1948. Her first marriage ended in divorce, and in 1948 she married Gerald Ford, then in the midst of his first campaign for Congress. (JOHN F. STACKS)

Foster, Brendan

Making a sensational 10,000-m. debut at the International Athletes Club meeting at London's Crystal Palace in August 1975, Britain's Brendan Foster (European 5,000-m. champion and world-record holder over 2 mi. and 3,000 m.) covered the 25 laps in 27 min. 45.4 sec.—the year's fastest time—to finish first in a field of top-class specialists at the distance. After narrowly beating U.S. Olympic marathon champion Frank Shorter in a wild last lap, Foster said: "I learned a lot from that race, but I'll have to decide later if I'll try it in the Olympics or not. It hurts like hell to run it hard."

In the three years since the 1972 Olympics in which he finished fifth in the 1,500 m., Foster had established himself as one of the three best 5,000-m. men in the world and there was speculation as to which distance he would concentrate on in the 1976 Olympics at Montreal. Earlier in the season he had lost only the second 5,000-m. race of his career when the formidable New Zealander Rod Dixon outpaced him over the last 500 m. The defeat led him to reevaluate his Olympic chances and to try the 10,000-m. distance seriously. After decisively winning the European Cup 5,000-m. semifinal and final races his confidence was partially restored. Nevertheless, many observers thought his best chance of a gold medal lay with the longer distance, for he undoubtedly had the speed to tack a sub-55-sec. lap onto the end of a fast race—very often a deciding factor in major championship races.

Born Jan. 12, 1948, in Hebburn, County Durham, Foster first showed promise as a schoolboy quarter miler, but on joining Gateshead Harriers and coming under the wing of coach Stan Long he turned to longer distances. He first made an impact on the British track scene in 1970 when he placed fourth in the intercounties mile final. In the Commonwealth Games that year he placed third in the 1,500 m. In 1973 he achieved his first world record, lowering Lasse Viren's 2-mi. time by one-fifth of a second to 8 min. 13.8 sec. His second world record came in August 1974 when he lowered Emiel Puttemans' 3,000-m. record to 7 min. 35.2 sec. before enthusiastic fans at Gateshead, where he was municipal director of sport and recreation. In Rome the following month he became European 5,000-m. champion with a time of 13 min. 17.2 sec. A courageous runner who held nothing back, Foster had proved to his opponents that they would have to run faster than ever before to beat him. (DAVID COCKSEDGE)

Fraser, John Malcolm

In 1975 Malcolm Fraser achieved two major ambitions. First, in March, he became leader of the Liberal-Country Party (LCP) opposition in the Australian Parliament, and then in December he became the nation's prime minister.

Fraser had been able to defeat the previous LCP leader, Billy Snedden, after the latter's attempt to bring down the Australian Labor Party (ALP) government failed. Together with the small Democratic Labor Party, the LCP had controlled the Senate, and Snedden had forced a midterm election by the expedient of threatening to deny the ALP supply (funds).

Although it was constitutional for the Senate to reject money bills, it had never been done in Australia's history. Faced with the prospect of having no money to govern the country, Prime Minister Gough Whitlam took up the challenge and was able to scrape home. But the ALP government still lacked a majority in the Senate. Fraser's dilemma was whether to force another election by refusing supply in the Senate. On the one hand, he had said as soon as he became opposition leader that he would not defeat supply legislation, except in very extraordinary circumstances. On the other, public opinion polls indicated that, with inflation and unemployment at their highest levels since 1945, the conservatives were bound to win a general election, and there were those who said it was a moral duty to throw the ALP out.

KEYSTONE

The shoe dropped in October, when the Senate refused the government budget. The election was precipitated by the dismissal of Whitlam as prime minister on November 11 by Sir John Kerr, the governor-general, on grounds that he had failed to obtain supply. In the election on December 13, the LCP coalition won a smashing victory.

Fraser was born on May 21, 1930. The son of a wealthy grazier at Nareen, Victoria, he went to Magdalen College, Oxford, and in 1955 entered the Australian Parliament as representative for the Liberal electorate of Wannon. He became a minister in the LCP government, holding the portfolios of the Army, education and science, and defense. It was while he was minister for defense that he caused his first political upheaval, resigning after making a stinging attack on the prime minister, J. G. Gorton. (A. R. G. GRIFFITHS)

THE CANADIAN PRESS

Geiger-Torel, Herman

He came to Toronto in 1948 to teach for three months at the Royal Conservatory of Music Opera School and to direct the newly formed Royal Conservatory Opera Company, but Herman Geiger-Torel stayed on for 27 years to make the building of the Canadian Opera Company from a student organization to a professional troupe his life's work. He began at the Royal Alexandra Theatre in Toronto with a cast of students and was paid $300 to stage three productions the first season. Bringing in singers from Vancouver and Montreal, he created in 1950 the Canadian Opera Company; by 1975 it boasted a cast of Canadian singers, conductors, stage directors, coaches, managers, and other experts. From the beginning of the company Geiger-Torel was its stage director and producer and after 1959 its general manager as well. In 1950 the company gave ten performances; in 1975, as Geiger-Torel retired from his active position with the company, it gave 32 performances of six operas at the O'Keefe Centre in Toronto.

Besides his work with the opera company, Geiger-Torel was the stage director of several operatic television programs in Toronto and the artistic adviser of the Canadian Broadcasting Corporation Opera Company, which did radio productions. For his work he was awarded the Service Medal of Canada and the Centennial Medal of Canada.

Geiger-Torel came to Toronto from a successful career in the opera houses of Europe and South America. From 1930 to 1937, he directed operas in the leading houses of Germany, Austria, Switzerland, and Czechoslovakia, and he was the stage director of the Salzburg Festival in 1930. He directed films in Paris (1937–38) before moving to South America, where he had a successful career for ten years as a stage director in Buenos Aires, Montevideo, and Rio de Janeiro.

Born in Frankfurt-am-Main, Germany, on July 13, 1907, Geiger-Torel was taught harmony and counterpoint by his mother. During his youth he was not interested in opera, and instead conducted symphony orchestras from age 16 to 23. His mother, however, encouraged him to pursue a career in opera, and so he studied with and assisted Lothar Wallenstein, the stage director of the Frankfurt Opera. At the same time he attended the Goethe University in Frankfurt, graduating as a teacher in dramatics in opera, theatre, and stage direction.

Geiger-Torel retired from the Canadian Opera Company in 1975, but would remain as its general director emeritus. He also intended to teach opera at the University of Toronto. (DIANE LOIS WAY)

Glistrup, Mogens

Founder of Denmark's Progress Party in 1972, during 1975 Mogens Glistrup stood trial on charges of tax evasion involving some $580,000. Meanwhile, in the January general election his party won 24 out of the 175 seats in the Folketing—a drop of 4 seats from the previous (December 1973) election, which nevertheless left it the third-largest parliamentary party after the Social Democrats and Liberals.

NORDISK PRESSEFOTO/PICTORIAL PARADE

Glistrup, a Copenhagen lawyer and tax consultant, had sprung into prominence as a result of a television interview in 1971 when he stated that although he was a krone millionaire he paid no income tax, that no one else need do so who did not wish to, and furthermore that the very concept of income tax was immoral and an outdated relic of feudal times. Not surprisingly, such notions met with a wide response and resulted in a rush of applicants who wanted to join the Glistrup "tax circus" as it came to be called. However, the complicated system of intercompany transactions which Glistrup claimed to be a legitimate means of avoiding tax was held by the authorities to be for the specific purpose of tax evasion. Consequently, following the lifting of Glistrup's parliamentary immunity by a vote in the Folketing, proceedings against him began in October 1974 and were expected to last for two to three years.

Glistrup was born in 1926 in Rønne, on the island of Bornholm. He went to Copenhagen University where he took a bachelor's degree in law, excelling particularly in tax law. A barrister from 1955, he taught as assistant professor at his old university. The Progress Party began to take shape following his 1971 television appearance; its program included not only abolition of personal income tax but also reduction of bureaucracy and simplification of the legal and electoral systems. Under the changes he proposed Denmark would become a single constituency with a parliament consisting of only 40 members, one to be elected every month. Bills passed by a majority of less than 60% would be subject to a national referendum, and ministers would have to be technically qualified. The party gained 13.6% of the votes cast in the 1975 election, and an opinion poll later in the year gave it 18.9%. (STENER AARSDAL)

Grasso, Ella

"The first lady governor who was not previously a governor's lady" was how Ella Tambussi Grasso described herself. On Jan. 8, 1975, she took the oath of office to become Connecticut's first woman governor and the first in the nation to be elected in her own right.

She had campaigned as an experienced political leader and continued to act as a skilled politician rather than a dedicated feminist. Mrs. Grasso learned politics from the precinct level up and achieved success long before the women's liberation movement. The wife of a retired school principal and mother of two grown children, she insisted that these roles had not handicapped her political career. "Being a woman," she said, "has never given me any special political problems."

Born May 10, 1919, in Windsor Locks, Conn., the daughter of immigrant parents from Italy, she earned scholarships to Mount Holyoke College, where she graduated in 1942 with a master's degree in economics and sociology. She became involved in politics with the Hartford Democratic organization, where her ability caught the attention of the late John Bailey, a powerful Connecticut party leader who became chairman of the Democratic National Committee. Elected to the Connecticut legislature in 1952, she became a floor leader in the General Assembly, then served 12 years as secretary of state and two terms in the U.S. Congress. She was elected governor by a plurality of 260,000 votes.

In a state faced with high unemployment, severe recession, and a $75 million deficit, Governor Grasso immediately drew up an austerity budget. She voluntarily took a $7,000 cut in her own salary and gave up riding in a chauffeured limousine in favour of a more modest state police car. She proposed replacing the Public Utilities Commission with a consumer-oriented agency but also worked to set aside an environmental law that she felt was unworkable.

Ella Grasso

WIDE WORLD

She outraged some feminists by her failure to name more women to posts in state government and her opposition to abortion (a sound position in a heavily Roman Catholic state). While supporting the objective of ending discrimination against women, she believed it could best be achieved "through law, moral persuasion and good work." (HAL BRUNO)

Greenspan, Alan

A Republican president looking for conservative economic advice could have found no more conservative, or competent, source of such counsel than economist Alan Greenspan, chairman of the Council of Economic Advisers. Appointed by Richard Nixon and retained in his post by Gerald Ford, Greenspan was an interesting mixture of firm ideological beliefs leavened with a growing sense of what is politically possible.

FRED WARD—BLACK STAR

Throughout 1975 Greenspan, more than any other economic adviser to the president, was the wellspring of ideas and policies pursued by the Ford administration through the worst recession since World War II. Like many other professional economists, Greenspan had been slow, in late 1974, to realize the depth of the recession that was to strike so hard the next year. He believed that unusual strength in orders for industrial goods might moderate the economic downturn. He was wrong, but when the new year came Greenspan accurately foresaw a midsummer bottoming out of the recession and correctly predicted a vigorous upturn late in the year.

Greenspan is widely respected even among liberal economists with whom he disagrees. Born in New York City on March 6, 1926, and educated at New York and Columbia universities, he achieved considerable success as a private consultant in New York before joining the Nixon administration in 1974. He helped fashion the Ford administration income-tax reduction plan offered in January as an antidote to the recession, and when the liberal Democratic Congress increased the size of the cuts and loaded benefits more heavily at the lower end of the income scale, he opposed other presidential advisers and urged Ford to sign the bill anyway.

Throughout 1975 Greenspan reinforced the president's inclination not to seek added tax-cut stimulus for the economy in 1976. But when it became obvious that the Congress would ignore that advice, he joined Ford in urging a bigger tax cut coupled with a drastic reduction in federal spending. The final result was a compromise bill that extended the 1975 tax cut coupled with a congressional promise to keep spending down. (JOHN F. STACKS)

Guise, Sir John

It was fitting that Papua New Guinea's National Constituent Assembly should elect the new country's constitutional head of state, and it was appropriate also that Sir John Guise should be chosen. Guise had been a principal architect of Papua New Guinea's progress toward independence. The strength of his commitment ensured that he would be no mere figurehead representative of Queen Elizabeth II.

Described by his friends as astute, crafty, and fiercely ambitious, before his election as governor-general Guise had worked as deputy to Michael Somare, the chief minister, and showed no reluctance to take the helm when Somare was absent from the country. The post-independence roles of Somare and Guise represented a division of power rather than a separation into political and ceremonial spheres of responsibility. It was not possible to kick Guise upstairs to the position of queen's viceroy, as was often done elsewhere in the Commonwealth.

Guise was born on Aug. 29, 1914, at Gedulalara in the Milne Bay District. Before World War II he was a messenger for the trading firm Burns Philp and worked on Samarai Island, Eastern Papua. During the war he served in the Australian New Guinea Administration Unit as a clerk. After the war Guise transferred to the police force and was a sergeant major when he left for a political career in 1961. Elected to the Legislative Council as the member for Eastern Papua, he played a major part in Papua New Guinea's moves toward independence. In 1967 he was chairman of the Select Committee on Political and Constitutional Development. Fighting attacks on his "mixed race" ancestry, he became speaker of the House of Assembly and was member for the open electorate of Alotau. In 1970 the University of Papua and New Guinea conferred the honorary degree of doctor of laws upon him, and in the queen's birthday honours list for 1975 he received a knighthood. (A. R. G. GRIFFITHS)

LONDON DAILY EXPRESS/PICTORIAL PARADE

EARL WILSON—PICTORIAL PARADE

Hackman, Gene

After winning the Academy Award for best actor in 1972 for his role in *The French Connection,* the exceptionally gifted Gene Hackman finally began to get appropriate rewards and notice. In 1975, when *French Connection II* was released just as the original made prime-time television, he was threatened with becoming an institution.

Hackman was born in San Bernardino, Calif., Jan. 30, 1931. Later, the family moved to Danville, Ill., where his father deserted them when the boy was 13. Gene dropped out of high school to join the Marines at 16, saw duty in the Far East, was promoted to corporal three times—and demoted as many. A civilian again, he tried college, radio school, the Art Students League in New York City, and acting classes at the Pasadena (Calif.) Playhouse. According to fellow student Dustin Hoffman, "The director graded us and the lowest anybody ever got before was 3, but Gene wound up with 1.4." His first Broadway job was as a doorman at the Times Square Howard Johnson restaurant. His old Marine captain passed it one night. "He never looked at me," Hackman recalled, "but he said out of the side of his mouth, 'Hackman, you're a sorry sonovabitch.' "

The barb was a goad. Hackman started working seriously at his acting, landed some off-Broadway roles, then appeared opposite Frances Sternhagen in a short-lived play. By 1963 he had a four-performance run on Broadway and won the Clarence Derwent Award as most promising young actor of the season. The next year he had a hit—*Any Wednesday* opposite Sandy Dennis. A Jean Kerr comedy followed, then a bit part in the film *Lilith* with Warren Beatty, who remembered him a few years later when casting *Bonnie and Clyde.*

Hackman won an Oscar nomination for his supporting role in that film and another for the sensitive *I Never Sang for My Father.* Suddenly he seemed omnipresent on the screen, in roles that ranged from Robert Redford's skiing coach in *Downhill Racer* to the conscience-stricken wire-tapper in *The Conversation.* His commonplace appeal helped him beat out Jackie Gleason and Steve McQueen for the lead role in *The French Connection,* a brutal thriller about Popeye, a detective who snares a narcotics ring only to mistakenly kill a colleague and let the criminal slip away. Critic Pauline Kael wrote in *The New Yorker,* "Unlike others who play mediocre men, Gene Hackman is such a consummate actor that he illuminates mediocrity." (PHILIP KOPPER)

Harper, Valerie

When Rhoda Morgenstern married a house-wrecker named Joe, more than half the people watching television in America that night were tuned in. The TV wedding, which attracted more than 50 million viewers, almost topped the record set when Lucille Ball delivered a baby off-camera in "I Love Lucy" two decades earlier.

The central character of "Rhoda" was born in September 1970 on the "Mary Tyler Moore Show" as the heroine's unquenchable bosom friend. The popularity of that program and the warm scriptwriting were two keys to "Rhoda's" success, but the sine qua non was Valerie Harper in the title role of an ex-bachelor girl New Yorker with a Jewish mother.

Surprisingly to many viewers, Harper was neither Jewish nor a New Yorker. She was born Aug. 22, 1940, in Suffern, N.Y., and as a child lived in Oregon, Massachusetts, New York, Michigan, California, and New Jersey. The one constant of her youth was dancing. She went on the professional stage at 16 as a member of the corps de ballet at New York City's Radio City Music Hall.

The next step was the chorus in *Li'l Abner.* Later she appeared on Broadway in *Take Me Along, Wildcat,* and *Subways Are for Sleeping,* studied acting with John Cassavetes, and helped support herself by selling magazine subscriptions, checking hats in a French restaurant, and playing in industrial shows—one role was that of stripper in a peanut butter production. Then came marriage to Richard Schaal, an actor in Chicago's famous "Second City" troupe. Valerie was also in "Second City" for a time, but when the couple moved to California, where Schaal headed a theatre workshop, his career went well and hers went into limbo. "I just sat in Laurel Canyon sobbing and eating Sara Lee cakes all day," she recalled. She got fat—and was considered the per-

Valerie Harper

WIDE WORLD

fect foil to Mary Tyler Moore's svelte career girl. Harper won three Emmy Awards for the role.

The fat girl jokes were eliminated from the script after she went from nearly 160 to 125 lb. with the help of a Weight Watchers diet. Then the spinster jokes were dropped. Finally, Rhoda became the heroine of her own weekly "sit-com." It was immediately popular, even denting the audience of the Monday night pro football telecast. "People identify with Rhoda because she's a born loser," said Harper. "But Rhoda is able to laugh it off. . . . She's a victorious loser." (PHILIP KOPPER)

Hart, Judith Constance Mary

One of the few casualties of a small reorganization of the British government after the European Economic Community referendum was Judith Hart, then minister of overseas development. She had opposed the government line favouring continued membership in the EEC, but it had been agreed that anti-EEC ministers could join in the referendum campaign. However, after the referendum Prime Minister Harold Wilson asked Hart to transfer to the Ministry of Transport, where she would have been one of a team of ministers linked to the Department of the Environment. At the same time Wilson decided to reincorporate the Ministry of Overseas Development with the Foreign and Commonwealth Office. Hart declined to remain in the government on these terms.

SYNDICATION INTERNATIONAL/PHOTO TRENDS

When she became minister of overseas development in March 1974 the department's status as an independent ministry was restored, which enabled her to pursue an independent policy. She had held the same post in the previous Labour government in 1969–70. Trained as a sociologist, she had an unusually well informed view of the problems of development in the third world.

At the time of her resignation she had almost completed a reorientation of British aid policy to give priority to the poorest of the poor countries, and to rural development in the villages. It seemed that this conflicted in some areas with Foreign and Commonwealth Office policy, which was more concerned with British interests.

Judith Hart had already won a considerable reputation for her part in the negotiation of the Lomé agreement between the EEC and 46 African, Caribbean, and Pacific countries to open European markets to their goods and to seek to guarantee their export earnings by stabilizing food and commodity prices. This breakthrough made her anti-EEC stand seem somewhat paradoxical.

Born in 1924 in Lancashire, Hart was elected to Parliament by the Scottish constituency of Lanark in 1959. Since 1969 she had been a member of the Labour Party's national executive committee. (HARFORD THOMAS)

Hawke, Robert James Lee

The leader of Australia's trade-union movement, Robert J. Hawke strode robustly over the crises that beset organized labour in 1975. His difficulties were compounded by dual roles. He was both federal president of the Australian Labor Party (ALP) and president of the Australian Council of Trade Unions (ACTU). Frequently, the ALP's political aims put it at odds with influential sections of Australia's workers.

Hawke's aggressive response to controversy was well illustrated by his reaction to the flow of baited questions concerning his capacity and willingness to supplant then prime minister Gough Whitlam. Answering an inquiry about his intention to leave industrial affairs and move into politics, Hawke retorted that "if I moved from this position into Parliament I feel I would have to entirely become an abstainer." Whitlam quipped that he realized that to hold his position he would have to turn over a new leaf and undertake a program of rigorous social drinking. Nevertheless, the ALP's rout in the December election made Hawke's replacement of Whitlam as party leader increasingly possible.

The variety of the problems Hawke faced left little time for relaxation. He played a pivotal role on the side of the Australian Jewish community in preventing representatives of the Palestine Liberation Organization from coming to the Commonwealth. He directed the employees' counsel in the national wage case and was successful in obtaining the court's agreement to a policy of wage indexation, linking wage increases to rises in the cost of living, although he lost the battle for tax indexation. He presided over the ACTU's biennial congress in Melbourne, which began on September 15. Hawke was also chairman of a company set up by the ACTU to market gasoline cheaply. The company, ACTU-Solo, failed when a royal commission found that it had deceived the minister for minerals and energy and the Australian government declined to give it any local crude oil. Although Hawke was absolved from blame, the troubles of ACTU-Solo were a blow to his plans to beat capitalism at its own game.

Born at Bordertown, South Australia, on Dec. 9, 1929, Hawke was Western Australian Rhodes scholar at Oxford University. He became president of the ACTU in 1970 after a distinguished career as an industrial advocate before the Conciliation and Arbitration Commission. He was elected federal president of the ALP in 1973. (A. R. G. GRIFFITHS)

Hellman, Lillian (Florence)

Having through the years been warmed in literary limelights and pilloried under political spotlights, Lillian Hellman was awarded the aura of a sage in her old age.

NICHOLAS SAPIEHA—CAMERA PRESS

Lillian Hellman

In 1975 the *Ladies' Home Journal* named her a Woman of the Year. As they had many times previously, however, some conservatives took her to task for her criticism of governmental misconduct while delivering a college commencement address.

In November Hellman was feted at a gathering at New York City's Circle in the Square theatre, which featured readings from her plays. The unusual event, attended by such diverse lights as Jacqueline Kennedy Onassis, Leonard Bernstein, and Mike Nichols, simultaneously honoured Hellman and benefited the Committee for Public Justice, a civil liberties organization she founded. It also heralded the coming publication of her third book of memoirs, *Scoundrel Time,* which recalls the horrors of the McCarthy era. During that period she refused to cooperate with the U.S. House of Representatives Committee on Un-American Activities, saying "I will not cut my conscience to fit this year's fashion."

Born in New Orleans, La., on June 20, 1905, Hellman attended New York and Columbia universities. She began her literary career as a book reviewer and playreader in New York and soon presented a script of her own to her employer. Herman Shumlin read it while she waited, saying "Swell" after finishing the first act, "I hope it keeps up" after the second, and, after the third, "I'll produce it." Staged on Broadway in 1934, *The Children's Hour* involved the ruin of two schoolteachers falsely accused of lesbian conduct by a student.

That celebrated play was followed by such works as *The Little Foxes, Watch on the Rhine, Another Part of the Forest,* and *Toys in the Attic.* She also adapted Jean Anouilh's *The Lark* and wrote the book for the musical version of Voltaire's *Candide.* Her previous volumes of memoirs are *An Unfinished Woman* and *Pentimento.* She won two New York Drama Critics' Circle awards, several honorary degrees, and a National Institute of Arts and Letters Gold Medal for distinguished achievement in the theatre. (PHILIP KOPPER)

Hersh, Seymour M.

Although the role of the press in the Watergate scandals returned investigative reporting to a place of honour among professional journalists, the current era of its popularity actually began earlier, largely with the work of Seymour Hersh. As a free-lance writer Hersh acted on a tip and interviewed some 45 participants in the My Lai massacre, producing a story that summed up the horror and futility of the U.S. involvement in Vietnam. He had great difficulty getting that story published, but an obscure news service finally sold it to 36 newspapers. After that Hersh had little trouble getting his work into print.

Although his employer, the *New York Times,* occasionally pressed him into service on the Watergate story, a key role in that exposé largely eluded him. His real contributions, as a Washington, D.C., correspondent for the *Times,* came through disclosure of the secret bombing of Cambodia, the Pentagon's use of a kind of informal spy to examine Henry Kissinger's working papers, and the CIA's involvement in the downfall of Pres. Salvador Allende of Chile.

At the end of 1974 Hersh set off another bomb with a 10,000-word *Times* piece charging illegal domestic surveillance of approximately 10,000 U.S. citizens by the CIA. The piece triggered official investigations of the spy agency's domestic activities by a commission headed by Vice-Pres. Nelson Rockefeller and later by both houses of Congress.

Hersh, 39, was born in Chicago, educated at the University of Chicago, and began his career in journalism in 1959. In 1972 he was hired by the *New York Times,* which had earlier turned him down. His abrasive manner and nearly boundless self-confidence made him a formidable interviewer and tracker of information. He left Washington in 1975 to live and work in New York City. (JOHN F. STACKS)

Husak, Gustav

On May 29, 1975, Gustav Husak, already secretary-general of the Czechoslovak Communist Party, was elected president of the republic, the first Slovak in the history of Czechoslovakia to become head of state. He succeeded Gen. Ludvik Svoboda, who had been recalled from office for reasons of health. Husak thus combined the three high offices (president, party leader, and chairman of the National Front) that Antonin Novotny had held before his downfall in 1968.

Husak's elevation came at a time when the political situation in Czechoslovakia had once again begun to show some movement. Several of the reformers of 1968, otherwise completely eliminated from public life, released protests about the existing stagnation in the country. Alexander Dubcek denounced Husak's policies in a letter to the Federal Assembly, made public in February 1975. This elicited a bitter personal

Gustav Husak

SPORT & GENERAL/PICTORIAL PARADE

attack by Husak, who told Dubcek that if he did not like matters in Czechoslovakia, he should emigrate to the West.

Despite his accumulation of offices, Husak did not command the kind of preponderance of power Novotny had enjoyed; he had to reckon with an influential hard-line-dogmatist faction within the party that blocked the more moderate policies he was thought to favour and represented a potential challenge to his power.

Born Jan. 10, 1913, in Bratislava to a well-to-do middle class family, Husak was trained as a lawyer. During World War II he was one of the leading figures in the Slovak national uprising of 1944, and after the war he was chairman of the Board of Commissioners in Slovakia. In this post, he helped prepare the ground for the 1948 Communist takeover. He was dismissed in 1950, however, and arrested and sentenced to life imprisonment in 1954 on charges of "bourgeois nationalism." Released in 1960, he was completely rehabilitated in 1963 and in 1968 became deputy premier in the federal government. Following the Soviet-led invasion in 1968 he became first secretary of the semi-autonomous Slovak Communist Party and gradually became one of the strongest protagonists of the pro-Soviet, antireform line. (GEORGE SCHÖPFLIN)

Ikeda, Daisaku

As third president of Soka-gakkai, a lay Buddhist organization in Japan, Daisaku Ikeda was a charismatic leader who commanded the fervent reverence of the organization's members. Soka-gakkai was formed by followers of the Nichiren-shoshu, a splinter denomination of the Nichiren sect. It purports to build a happy and peaceful society by disseminating the teachings of Nichiren throughout the world.

Ikeda became president in 1960, and his intensive missionary work was instrumental in the expansion of the organization. When he assumed the presidency the membership was 1,720,000 households. By 1975 this had grown to 7,650,000 households, drawn from all over the world.

Japan's Komeito, or Clean Government, party was founded as the political arm of Soka-gakkai, and as of October 1975 it had some 120,000 members and held 30 seats in the House of Representatives and 24 in the House of Councillors. It was known as a people's party that practiced middle-of-the-road politics and humanistic socialism. Because almost every member of Komeito belongs to Soka-gakkai, the 47-year-old Ikeda exerted considerable influence over the party.

In addition to being a religious leader, Ikeda is an educator. As Ikeda explains his belief: "My lifetime work is education. It is education which decides the future of a country, and accordingly, the future of mankind." In 1971 he founded Soka University as a "fortress to defend peace for mankind." In 1972 he made a global tour, visiting major universities in the U.S., the U.K., France, the Middle East, China, and the Soviet Union. In 1973 Ikeda proposed a "United Nations for Education," based on his belief that to secure peace the world needed a machinery for peaceful education that was not influenced by political powers.

His lifework, a book entitled *The Human Revolution,* was in process. In it he says: "War is barbarous and inhuman. Nothing is more cruel, nothing more tragic." Out of this, the core of his ideology, came his proposals to destroy all nuclear weapons, end the Vietnam war, and resume relations between Japan and China. At the bottom of these proposals was his perception of

WIDE WORLD

Daisaku Ikeda

interdependence among the people of the Earth and of the need for them to have a world government.

In December 1974 Ikeda held a secret meeting with Kenji Miyamoto, chairman of the Japan Communist Party, that led to a ten-year agreement of peaceful coexistence between Soka-gakkai and the Communists. The Communist Party agreed to recognize the freedom of faith and religious activities, and Soka-gakkai, in return, would not regard the Communist Party as an enemy; both would take action to oppose fascism on the basis of their own principles. The agreement, which was kept secret for seven months, had a traumatic effect on national politics. It also caused confusion within the Komeito Party, since even the Komeito leaders had been kept in the dark.

(IZUMI HOSOJIMA)

John, Elton

Can a nearsighted English boy, who could please his father only by playing Chopin, change his name and find happiness on the pop concert circuit behind 200 pairs of spectacles? The answer is yes, for Elton John seems to have done that while earning $7 million a year.

Elton John

CHRISTOPHER LITTLE—CAMERA 5

In 1975 he became the 24th performer in the Playboy Jazz and Pop Hall of Fame and filled London's Wembley Stadium with 75,000 ticket buyers for a single concert. With enormous numbers of devotees throughout the world, he was seen as the brightest constellation in the ever changing galaxy of rock stardom. "If I were not having a ball I would have quit a long time ago," said the composer who wears outlandish costumes and jumps on his piano when performing.

Reginald Kenneth Dwight was born in Pinner, Middlesex, England, on March 25, 1947. He took up the piano at 4 and won a Royal Academy of Music fellowship when he was 11. His father favoured flushing "all this pop nonsense out of his head," but his mother said the youth could play popular music in his spare time if he studied the classics seriously. At 17 he quit school to join a touring rhythm and blues band. Because his name "sounded like a cement mixer" he coined a new one, Elton John, by borrowing the first names of two fellow performers. Then he left the band for London.

Answering an ad in a trade paper, he sent some compositions to a record company. The firm teamed him with a lyricist named Bernie Taupin and then dropped them both. But the two stuck together, rented quarters in a north London slum, and began collaborating. The rest, as they say in show business, is history.

As Bernie Taupin describes it, "It's so simple. Bernie writes lyrics. Bernie gives lyrics to Elton. Elton writes a song." It generally takes them about two days to do an entire album, which they record in a studio in John's suburban London home.

The songs, plying the middle of the musical road between hard and soft rock, have been extraordinarily popular. More than one million copies of 12 different records have been sold in the U.S. alone, and John's concerts, in halls as large as New York's Madison Square Garden, have been sold out within hours of being announced. It might be said that 1975 was a record year for John. (PHILIP KOPPER)

Jones, Jack

Great Britain's biggest labour union, the Transport and General Workers' Union, had frequently produced leaders of great political weight and influence, and Jack Jones, general secretary of the TGWU since 1969, was in this tradition. Learning the role from his predecessor, Frank Cousins, with whom he worked as assistant general secretary, Jones had been a leader of union resistance to the Conservatives' industrial relations legislation during Edward Heath's government (1970–74), and then became a powerful ally of Harold Wilson's Labour government.

Adamantly opposed to statutory wage control, Jones was one of the chief architects of the "social contract" in 1974, and when this understanding with the unions to limit their wage claims broke down in 1975 he was instrumental in securing the unions' support for a £6 a week limit on increases for the next 12 months. He also took a leading part with ministers of the government in seeking to prevent damaging strikes, and although he could claim always to have been on the left of labour politics, this brought him into conflict with left-wing militants. He was shouted down by some of the dockworkers of his own union while urging them to end a strike, and was involved in a furious public row at the Labour Party conference in October with a left-wing member of Parliament, Ian Mikardo, who had accused the Trades Union Congress of failing to protect the interests of lower paid workers.

CAMERA PRESS/PHOTO TRENDS

Jack Jones

Born in Liverpool on March 29, 1913, James Larkin Jones became secretary of his constituency (ward) Labour Party at the age of 15 and was a Liverpool councillor at 23. He joined the International Brigade in Spain during the Spanish Civil War and was wounded in the Battle of the Ebro in 1938. During the next 25 years he moved up through a series of union posts in the automotive industry in the Midlands before going to the London headquarters. From 1964 to 1967 he served on the Labour Party's national executive committee.

Jones viewed the unions as an integral part of the labour movement, and argued that it was their responsibility to support a Labour government. He held that the unions exist not only to negotiate wages but also "to think in terms of the working community as a family" and "to make sure that big industry acts in a socially responsible way." (HARFORD THOMAS)

Jong, Erica Mann

Hailed by many as a champion of the woman's movement, but scorned by some as a second-rate fiction writer, Erica Jong was surrounded by controversy in 1975. Supporters viewed her as a talented author whose candid discussions of female sexuality focused attention on an emerging issue in feminist consciousness. But detractors contended that she not only failed to promote the cause of women's liberation but was simply whining in unliterary and often inelegant prose.

Jong first gained fame—or notoriety—with the 1973 appearance of *Fear of Flying*. She had previously published two volumes of poetry, *Fruits and Vegetables* (1971) and *Half Lives* (1973), which were well received but attracted no undue attention. *Fear of Flying,* however, recounted the adventures of a female Tom Jones and provoked widespread debate. The original typesetter was so offended by the book's scatology and foul language that he refused to work on it. Reviews ranged from vituperative indignation to enthusiastic praise, but few greeted the novel with apathy or disinterest. There was also much speculation about the book's autobiographical nature, and Jong noted that though the novel was not literally true, "it did convey the spirit of my childhood and upbringing."

Born in New York City on March 26, 1942, Erica—like the heroine of her story, Isadora Wing—was raised by prosperous Jewish parents who smothered her with opportunity. She attended New York's prestigious High School of Music and Art and then went on to Barnard College, where she started, but never completed, a dissertation in English literature. Like Isadora, she was twice married, once to a psychotic, who in the novel attempted to walk across Central Park Lake, and then to a Chinese-American child psychiatrist. Although the book left the fate of this second marriage in doubt, Jong's real-life divorce did not.

In terms of purely popular appeal, debate over Jong's work clearly was precluded. Sales of *Fear of Flying* were so promising that a movie version was planned and a volume of her poetry, *Loveroot* (1975), was selected as a Book-of-the-Month Club alternate. Whatever the relative merits of her work, as an art form or as a social document, one could agree with John Updike that Jong is a lady with "sass, class, brightness, and bite."

(CLAIRE SANDRA CHOW)

Jordan, Barbara

One of the two women on the 38-member House Judiciary Committee who voted in 1974 for the Articles of Impeachment against Pres. Richard Nixon, Texas Democrat Barbara Jordan impressed many with her eloquence and fervour during the impeachment debate: "When that document was completed on the 17th of September in 1787, I was not included in that 'We, the people.' I felt for many years that somehow George Washington and Alexander Hamilton left me out by mistake. But through the process of amendment, interpretation and court decision I have been included in 'We, the people.'"

Miss Jordan achieved many historic firsts. She was elected to the Texas State Senate in 1966, after two unsuccessful attempts, the only woman and the only black person among the 31 members. There she co-sponsored the state's first minimum wage bill, was chief sponsor of a workmen's

Barbara Jordan

CHESTER HIGGINS, JR.—RAPHO/PHOTO RESEARCHERS

compensation bill, and led the successful opposition to a bill meant to disfranchise blacks and Mexican-Americans by tightening voter registration. In 1972 she was elected to the U.S. House of Representatives, winning 81% of the votes in her Houston district; in her reelection in 1974 she gained the support of 85% of the voters.

Miss Jordan was born Feb. 21, 1936, in Houston, Texas. Her father was a Baptist minister who encouraged academic excellence and effective rhetoric. The victorious debate by the all-black Texas Southern University team led by Barbara Jordan against the Harvard University team in 1954 was a memorable event. After graduating magna cum laude from Texas Southern in 1956, she became the first black student admitted to Boston University Law School. She graduated in 1959, and then practiced law in her parents' dining room for three years until she could afford an office.

The representative from Houston arrived in Washington, D.C., in January 1973, aspiring to the powerful Judiciary Committee. "The Judiciary Committee dealt with the issues I was interested in. All civil rights legislation questions regarding the administration of justice and constitutional amendments are handled by the Judiciary Committee. I wanted to be on it." With help from her friend, former president Lyndon Johnson, Miss Jordan obtained the appointment. A skillful parliamentarian, she admits to a "total" and "complete" dedication to the Constitution. She also cheerfully acknowledges her patriotism: "I salute the flag and get goose pimples over the national anthem and 'God Bless America.' I don't apologize for it. I feel very keenly about the necessity for this country to survive on a republican form of government, having as its supreme law a Constitution which remains inviolate."

(JEANNETTE OATES)

Kain, Karen

A love of music and a desire to express it were the reasons Karen Kain wanted to become a dancer. In 1959 she decided on a career in ballet when she saw Celia Franca's performance of *Giselle* in Hamilton, Ont., the town where Karen was born on March 21, 1951. She began ballet lessons at age nine and two years later entered the National Ballet School in Toronto. Graduating at age 18, she joined the corps of the National Ballet of Canada in 1969. Six years later Clive Barnes, the *New York Times* critic, called her "one of the most talented ballerinas in the Western world."

Kain believes that everyone with talent has an opportunity to develop it at the National Ballet. Her opportunity came midway through her second season with the company when she was plucked from the corps, given one month to learn the role of the Swan Queen in *Swan Lake,* and made her debut as a principal dancer with the company on tour in Tempe, Ariz. She danced *Swan Lake* with Rudolf Nureyev in 1972, and has since become one of his favourite partners. Nureyev came along when she "needed inspiration" and was helpful to her with his critical advice.

Kain danced the role of Aurora in Nureyev's production of *The Sleeping Beauty* in New York, and in the summer of 1975 she danced the role with him with the London Festival Ballet in Australia. Earlier that summer she appeared with Nureyev, Dame Margot Fonteyn, and Paolo Bortoluzzi in Washington, D.C., where she danced *The Moor's Pavane* with Nureyev.

With the National Ballet, her principal partner was Frank Augustyn. In 1973 this pair represented Canada at the second International Ballet Competition in Moscow. They won the first prize in the pas de deux category, and Kain herself won the silver medal in the solo women's division. In Moscow she caught the attention of French choreographer Roland Petit. He created a new ballet for her based on Marcel Proust's *À la recherche du temps perdu.* She danced the role of Albertine at the ballet's premier in Monte Carlo in 1974. The next year she returned to France to dance with Petit's Ballet de Marseille in *Carmen* and to dance the role of Swanilda in his production of *Coppélia.*

Kain made her debut in *Giselle* in 1974, and it was hailed as a triumph. The next year she and Augustyn made a film version of this ballet for the Canadian Broadcasting Corporation.

It has been said that Karen has the perfect body for ballet, and her dancing has been described as "of such purity and clarity of utterance that the eye is constantly delighted." She is delighted as well, being a performer who dances for fun and is excited by an audience.

(DIANE LOIS WAY)

Kanetaka, Kaoru

Kaoru Kanetaka, world traveler, author, lecturer, critic, and television narrator, attended St. Hilda's School for Girls in Tokyo and the Los Angeles City College, where she majored in business administration. On returning to Japan from Los Angeles, she began a writing career, contributing articles to the *Japan Times* on life in foreign countries and interviewing international personalities.

In 1958, after seeing the movie *Around the World in Eighty Days,* she conceived and brought to fruition a plan to set a round-the-world commercial airplane flight record. Her record-breaking flight from Tokyo to Tokyo took 81 hours and stands as the fastest world-girdling time made on propeller-driven commercial aircraft. Her journalistic work led to a radio program called "Hopping Around the World" on the Tokyo Broadcasting System. From this her popular and prestigious "Around the World" television travel documentary series developed, with its premiere performance on Dec. 13, 1959. Kanetaka may well lay claim to traveling to more countries of the world than anyone else, having visited over 130. She was the first Japanese woman to visit the South Pole, which she did at the invitation of the U.S. Navy Department; the first Japanese woman to parachute jump, to take a balloon over the Alps, and to hang-glide. She was also the first to win the annual Mabuhay Award from the Philippines. She has won citations from the governments of the U.S., the United Kingdom, Australia, Hong Kong, and India. Her television program was the first to win the Japanese version of the U.S. Emmy, the award of the Radio and Television Writers Association for excellence in 1962.

Kanetaka has written four books on her travels and does a major part of the writing and editing for her program as well as directing the filming team in the field. Among the international personalities she has met and filmed are U.S. Presidents John F. Kennedy and Lyndon B. Johnson; King Faisal of Saudi Arabia; Archbishop Makarios of Cyprus; and the sultan of Zanzibar.

(KEIJI TAGA)

Karami, Rashid

Invited by Pres. Suleiman Franjieh of Lebanon to form a new Cabinet, on May 28, 1975, at a time of acute national crisis,

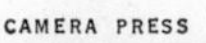
CAMERA PRESS

Rashid Karami

Rashid Karami became prime minister of his country for the eighth time since 1955. Although his premiership was supported by the left, he was regarded as a moderate who had consistently tried to prevent the various factions in Lebanese politics from taking extreme positions.

The polarization of Christian right and Muslim left in 1975 obliged him to appeal for both Syrian and Palestinian help in his efforts to calm the violence. He also questioned the basis of Lebanon's political system since independence by announcing, on July 27, that he intended to stand as a candidate for the presidency. By strong tradition, although not according to the constitution, this office was held by a Maronite Christian. Karami said he was convinced of the need to suppress confessionalism and for the president to be elected by national suffrage rather than by Parliament.

Karami was born in 1921 at Misriata, near Tripoli, into a prominent Sunni Muslim political family. His father was a leading figure in Lebanon's struggle for independence and subsequently was several times prime minister. Rashid received his secondary education in Lebanon, then went to Cairo University where he graduated in law in 1947. He was given his first ministerial post in 1951 and later held the portfolios of economy, finance, interior, defense, information, justice, and foreign affairs.

He was one of the leaders of the opposition to Pres. Camille Chamoun during the prolonged political troubles of 1958, but as head of a government of "national salvation" he became a close collaborator of Chamoun's successor, Pres. Fuad Chehab. As prime minister in 1969 and 1970 he had to handle the difficult situation caused by the presence of Palestinian guerrillas in the country. When Franjieh was narrowly elected president by Parliament in 1970, Karami was in the opposite camp, and it was only when the situation became unmanageable in 1975 that he was called in to head the government again. The six-man government he succeeded in forming after one month included, as the representative of right-wing Christian elements, his old enemy Chamoun, with whom he had not spoken since 1958.

(PETER MANSFIELD)

Khalid ibn Abd al-Aziz Al Saud

Within an hour of the death by assassination of King Faisal of Saudi Arabia on March 25, 1975, his half brother Khalid, crown prince and deputy prime minister,

ALAIN NOGUES

Khalid ibn Abd al-Aziz Al Saud

was proclaimed king. He received the allegiance of the royal princes, the heads of the armed services and tribes, and religious dignitaries on the following day when he was enthroned.

Born in 1913 in Riyadh, which was then a small desert town, Khalid became the closest supporter of his brothers Saud and Faisal, who preceded him on the throne. When he was 14, his father Ibn Saud, founder of the Saudi kingdom, sent him as his representative to the desert tribes to hear their grievances. In 1934 he took part in the Saudi expedition against Yemen led by his brother Faisal and since then he had been regarded as a "man of the desert," one more at home with desert pursuits than with politics or diplomacy.

In 1939 he left Arabia for the first time to take part in the abortive London conference on Palestine. He hastened to return and, unlike most of his brothers, he never pursued higher educational studies abroad. He concerned himself with the problems of the Bedouin and took a special interest in desert reclamation projects through the use of groundwater. When in Riyadh, he devoted himself to charitable work. His modest and self-effacing personality, coupled with his reputation for calm reason, made him the chief conciliator in the disputes that arose among the large family of royal princes. Such qualities led to his appointment as crown prince, in preference to his more forceful and ambitious brothers Fahd and Sultan, when King Saud was deposed in November 1964 and was succeeded by Faisal.

Khalid's popularity and lack of enemies were substantial assets, but his health was poor and he was known to have suffered at least one heart attack. His lack of ambition or taste for politics was interpreted to mean that the kingdom of Saudi Arabia would have more of a collective leadership under his reign than under his predecessor's. (PETER MANSFIELD)

Khieu Samphan

The triumph of pro-Communist forces in Indochina in 1975 touched off worldwide speculation about the real wielders of power in the newly constituted governments. All that was known was that those most in the limelight were not the same men who played decision-making roles. Even more than South Vietnam and Laos, Cambodia was shrouded in mystery. Was Khieu Samphan, the best known of Cambodian leaders, also the most important?

The Cambodian mystery had started with the ouster of Prince Norodom Sihanouk from power by Gen. Lon Nol and the outbreak of full-scale war in 1970. Overnight, Khieu Samphan became famous as deputy premier and defense minister of the ousted government as well as the principal guerrilla commander. At the war's end, he appeared to be the main government figure, but some questioned whether he was still alive.

Born in 1931, the son of a poor family in Kandal Province, Khieu Samphan went to France on a scholarship. He obtained a doctoral degree in economics from the University of Paris, but his real education was in left-wing student organizations.

Continuing his leftist activities on returning home, Khieu Samphan started a French-language newspaper that began harassing Sihanouk, at that time an absolute ruler. He also was a prime mover in founding Cambodian-Chinese friendship associations. In 1966 he won a National Assembly seat. Sihanouk took him into the Cabinet in the hope of silencing him, but the following year purged and publicly denounced him for alleged leadership of a powerful peasants' revolt that broke out in the rice-rich province of Battambang. The government was ruthless in suppressing the revolt, hundreds of peasants being tortured and killed, and Khieu Samphan went underground. Sihanouk's men claimed that he had been executed, but three years later, with Sihanouk in exile, Khieu was named a key figure in his Royal Government of National Union of Cambodia in Peking. Whether it was the real Khieu Samphan or, as some speculators still argued, a look-alike, the name and the slight, skinny frame, the boyish face, a ready grin, and the bookish manner that went with it dominated all discussions of the new Cambodia. (T. J. S. GEORGE)

Kitanoumi

Kitanoumi breaks sumo records in the same way that he eats and drinks—with gusto. He not only became the youngest wrestler in the long history of sumo to reach the top rank of *yokozuna* (grand champion), just two months after reaching 21, but set other age records along the way when he qualified as a *makuuchi* (major league wrestler) and as a *sanyaku* (wrestler in the top three categories below grand champion). He also came within two months of establishing a new age record for an *ozeki* (top rank below grand champion). Though twice demoted for tournament defeats, Kitanoumi quickly recovered and in 1975, still only 22, he was beyond question the man to beat in every major tournament.

Born Toshimitsu Ogata on May 16, 1953, in Hokkaido, Kitanoumi became a teenage giant. Several sumo masters who were barnstorming in northern Japan saw him and tried to induce his parents to let the boy join their other apprentices. It was Mihogaseki who finally took Kitanoumi under his wing and arranged his sumo debut in January 1967 when the boy was 13 years old. Following his master's instructions to indulge principally in eating, sleeping, and training, Kitanoumi gradually attained his present awesome proportions; he carries 331 lb. on a 5-ft. 11-in. frame. Despite his immense strength, childhood memories of being bitten by a dog cause him to start when a dog barks or suddenly comes into view. He likes comics and has promised to control a tendency toward wild spending and drinking.

During Kitanoumi's first year as the 55th *yokozuna* in history, he won 70 of 90 bouts, captured two tournaments, and finished second in two others. By the autumn of 1975 he had won four major tourneys and was runner-up four times. His overpowering offense is considered superior to his defense, but he is beyond doubt the master of superb techniques related to every aspect of sumo. Though he has shown some weakness under pressure, most observers think the problem will disappear in time. In fact, sumo fans are convinced that Kitanoumi has an excellent chance to win 70 straight bouts without a loss, thereby breaking still another record, which was set 36 years earlier by *yokozuna* Futabayama. (GYO HANI)

Kohl, Helmut

Minister president (prime minister) of the Rhineland-Palatinate, one of the ten *Länder* (states) of the Federal Republic of Germany, Helmut Kohl was chosen in June 1975 by the Christian Democratic Union (CDU) and its Bavarian wing, the Christian

Kitanoumi

THAYER PHOTO

SVEN SIMON/KATHERINE YOUNG

Helmut Kohl

Social Union (CSU), as their candidate for the chancellorship at the next federal election, due in 1976. The selection caused friction between the two parties, which together formed the opposition to the Social Democratic-Free Democratic governing coalition.

In May the national executive of the CDU voted unanimously in favour of Kohl, a move which the Bavarians criticized as premature, since they had insisted that the selection should be made jointly by both parties. Several weeks later—and a few days before the opening of the CDU's conference in Mannheim—the CSU gave its reluctant approval of Kohl. The extent of the rift between the parties was apparent in the communiqué issued after a day of grueling negotiations in the house of the Bavarian "mission" in Bonn. The CSU, according to the communiqué, took notice of the fact that, as the larger party, the Christian Democrats claimed that the chancellor candidate should be chosen from among their ranks. The CSU continued to regard its chairman, Franz Josef Strauss, as the suitable candidate but would support Kohl in the interests of unity.

Kohl was born on April 3, 1930, in Ludwigshafen. After attending high school, he studied law and history at the universities of Frankfurt and Heidelberg and afterward became an official of the Chemical Industry Federation in Ludwigshafen. He joined the CDU in 1947 and, after holding a number of offices in the Rhineland-Palatinate association of the party, was elected a member of the federal executive committee in 1964. He became minister president of the Rhineland Palatinate in 1969 and chairman of the Christian Democratic Union in 1973.

Kohl had not yet held federal office, but was regarded as a highly successful leader of a state government. He visited China and the Soviet Union in 1975, but in China he was not honoured by an audience with Chairman Mao Tse-tung as Strauss had been a few months earlier. Kohl had the reputation of being a firm advocate of a united Western Europe, while remaining skeptical of Soviet intentions. (NORMAN CROSSLAND)

Komer, Odessa

In 1975 Odessa Komer, one of the highest-ranking women in the U.S. labour movement, became the driving force behind her union's attempt to develop a demonstration project for the potential uses of solar and wind energy as alternatives to fossil fuels. A vice-president of the United Auto Workers union since 1974, Komer announced that the UAW's Family Education Camp near Onaway, Mich., had begun work on the project, assisted by the Rhode Island Research and Design Institute. She said she hoped the project would prove that the nation can "effectively harness solar and wind power."

Through the use of a solar hot-water collector on the copper roof of a gymnasium, the UAW camp's indoor Olympic-size swimming pool can be heated to 85° F. Hot water for showers is provided by a "flat-plate solar collector" located on a gazebo near Black Lake, adjacent to the camp. In addition, work was under way on an elaborate wind generator, mounted on an 85-ft. tower, to provide electrical power to the camp.

Komer's enthusiasm about the demonstration project was typical of her entire career in the union. Born June 29, 1925, in Kemper County, Mississippi, she moved at an early age to Michigan, where her father obtained a job with Ford Motor Co. at $5 a day. As an adult, his daughter, too, went to work for Ford as an assembler and joined UAW Local 228 on June 6, 1953. Her intense interest in union activities resulted in her becoming the first woman to be elected to office at the local level. In 1964, as a member of the local's bargaining committee, she was responsible for the negotiation of a new and historic clause in the union contract, making seniority a consideration in better job assignments.

On June 6, 1974, the day of her 21st anniversary with Local 228, Komer was elected a UAW vice-president at the union's 24th constitutional convention. In 1975 she was made head of the women's department. Other union departments she headed included those dealing with consumers, conservation and natural resources, and recreation and leisure time. She also directed the office of technical and professional services and continued to play an important role in the handling of grievances and negotiations for a number of corporations.

(STANLEY WILLS CLOUD)

Kurosawa, Akira

Akira Kurosawa's long-awaited 25th film, *Dersu Uzala,* released in May 1975, was acclaimed by the critics as one of his best works. The three-hour-long feature film won the Grand Prix Award at the 1975 Moscow Film Festival. The idea for the film about Vladimir Arsenyev's Siberian expeditions had been on Kurosawa's mind for 30 years. His dream came to be realized as a result of discussions between Kurosawa and Mosfilm when he attended the Moscow Film Festival in 1971.

When his plan was announced some expressed their doubts about the result because his last attempt at a joint production, the Japanese-U.S. film *Tora! Tora! Tora!,* had ended in fiasco and had left Kurosawa mentally exhausted. In 1971 he attempted suicide. He was able to complete *Dersu Uzala,* however, in satisfactory condition, with close cooperation between Mosfilm and Japanese producer Matsue.

The film's story depicts the struggle of men against nature and also a heartwarming friendship that grows between Arsenyev, an intelligent Slavic captain of a Siberian expedition, and Dersu Uzala, a solitary hunter who agrees to work as a guide for the expedition. From innocent and wise Uzala, Arsenyev learns the way to survive in wild and barren Siberia. The encounter of the two men can be interpreted as a dialogue between nature and civilization. When Arsenyev finds out that Uzala can no longer hunt, he takes Uzala to live with his family in Vladivostok. But Uzala fails to adapt himself to the urban life and eventually leaves for the forest where he is killed by a hunter. Kurosawa, an admirer of the late U.S. director John Ford, presented many breathtaking scenes—blood-red sun reflected on an ice field; foggy forest; a raft going down the torrents.

Kurosawa was born in 1910 and made his debut as a film director with *Sanshiro Sugata* in 1943. With his 11th film, *Rashomon,* he won the Grand Prix Award at the Venice Film Festival in 1951. He then successfully produced *Ikiru* (1952), *Seven Samurai* (1954), *The Throne of Blood* (adapted from Shakespeare's *Macbeth;* 1957), *Yojimbo* (1961), and *Red Beard* (1965), all of which secured him a position as a world-renowned film director with a superb directing technique. Kurosawa's deep understanding of and affection for Russian literature is well illustrated in his earlier adaptations—Dostoyevsky's *The Idiot* (1951) and Gorky's *The Lower Depths* (1957). (KIKUO YAMAMOTO)

Lafleur, Guy

The history of the Montreal Canadiens is rich in tradition. It is filled with some of the greatest names in professional ice hockey, such as Dickie Moore, "Boom-Boom" Geoffrion, Frank Mahovlich, Jean Beliveau, and, of course, Maurice "Rocket" Richard and his brother Henri.

But no Canadien ever had a greater season in the National Hockey League than did one who is afraid to fly in airplanes and whose nickname is "The Flower." In 1974–75 Guy Lafleur became the first Montreal player to score more than 100 points in a single season. His 53 goals were also a Canadien record.

Lafleur was born in Thurso, Que., on Sept. 20, 1951. He was Montreal's first draft choice and the first choice overall in the 1971 NHL draft. The expectations for Lafleur, thus, were always high, and they increased after the 1971–72 season, when he graduated to the Canadiens after scoring a record 130 goals in junior hockey with the Quebec Remparts.

Lafleur scored 29, 28, and 21 goals in his first three NHL seasons. Then in 1974–75 he achieved the greatness people had expected and demanded. Not since the 1960–61 season had a Canadien scored 50 goals in one season. Geoffrion did it then, matching Maurice Richard's 1944–45 total. But Lafleur, who missed ten games because of a fractured knuckle, scored 53 goals in 1974–75 for a new Canadiens single-season record, despite going scoreless in his first seven games of the season. With his 66 assists his points for the season totaled 119, breaking the mark of 96 set by Moore in 1958–59 and equaled by Mahovlich in 1971–72.

Lafleur finished second in the league to Phil Esposito of the Boston Bruins in goals scored in 1974–75. In Quebec it was duly noted that "The Flower" had finally bloomed. (J. TIMOTHY WEIGEL)

Laurence, Margaret

In 1975 *The Diviners* won the Canadian Governor General's Literary Award and was judged the best Canadian English-language novel of 1974. It also received the Molson Prize for outstanding contribution to the arts and humanities.

The life of the novel's author, Margaret Laurence, has been much like that of the heroine of *The Diviners,* Morag Gunn. Laurence was born Jean Margaret Wemyss in 1926 in Neepawa, Man. Her home town served as the model for the fictional Manawaka, the setting of five of her novels written between 1964 and 1974, including *The Diviners.* Another of the Manawaka novels, *A Jest of God,* won the Governor General's Literary Award in 1967 and was made into the film *Rachel, Rachel.*

Encouraged by her stepmother, Margaret Laurence began to write at age ten. *Pillars of the Nation,* written when Margaret was 12, won an honourable mention in the children's competition of the *Winnipeg Free Press.* She attended United College of the University of Manitoba, obtaining her B.A. in English in 1947. In 1967 this institution honoured her by making her the first woman fellow of the college. After graduation she worked as a reporter for the *Winnipeg Citizen.*

From 1950 to 1957 she and her husband lived in Africa. This experience gave Laurence the setting for her first books, published between 1960 and 1964. Her two years in British Somaliland produced *A Tree for Poverty,* a translation of local poems and prose, and her only travel book, *The Prophet's Camel Bell.* Five years in Ghana set the scene for a book of short stories, *The Tomorrow Tamer,* and her first novel, *This Side Jordan* (1960), which won the Beta Sigma Phi Award for a first novel by a Canadian.

Returning to Canada, she was named Canada's outstanding woman in literature and the arts in 1969 and became the first woman ever to hold office at Massey College, the University of Toronto, when she became its writer in residence. In 1972 she was made a Companion of the Order of Canada. (DIANE LOIS WAY)

Lazar, Gyorgy

Deputy premier since 1973, Gyorgy Lazar was appointed Hungary's premier by the Presidential Council on May 15, 1975. He took over from Jeno Fock, head of the government since 1967, who had resigned officially at his own request for reasons of health, but probably because he supported Rezso Nyers, principal architect of the New Economic Mechanism, who had been removed in March 1974 from the post of party secretary.

Lazar started his travels abroad with an official visit to Moscow (Oct. 21–23, 1975), where he had talks with Soviet leaders Leonid I. Brezhnev and Aleksey N. Kosygin. A long-term agreement was signed on Hungarian deliveries to the U.S.S.R. of agricultural products and livestock in the period up to 1990. Hungary's negotiating position was weakened by the fact that the country's Westward exports of these products were running below the 1974 levels, and that planned increases had not been achieved. According to the joint communiqué, Brezhnev and Lazar also discussed certain current problems of foreign policy and "the tasks of the struggle to expand and deepen the process of relaxation in international relations."

Gyorgy Lazar was born on Sept. 15, 1924, at Isaszeg, just outside Budapest, to working-class parents. He qualified as draftsman from a technical school in 1942 and worked in this capacity until 1948. He then moved to the National Planning Office, where he became a department head in 1953; he was appointed deputy president of the office in 1958. During this period he published a number of articles on questions of national and regional economic planning. In February 1970 he became minister of labour, a post which he held until June 1973, when he joined the government as deputy premier. At the same time he was appointed president of the National Planning Office. In May 1975 Istvan Huszar, a deputy premier, succeeded him as head of that office.

Lazar joined the Hungarian Socialist Workers' Party in 1945. In 1970 he was elected a member of the Central Committee and was chosen as a member of the Political Committee at the 11th party congress in March 1975. (K. M. SMOGORZEWSKI)

Levi, Edward Hirsch

No department of the U.S. federal government had been more buffeted by the Watergate scandal than the Department of Justice. Attorneys General John Mitchell and Richard Kleindienst were both tried and found guilty of charges stemming from the cover-up. Elliot Richardson resigned in protest rather than fire the special prosecutor of the Watergate case, as Pres. Richard Nixon had ordered. Thus, when Gerald Ford took over the presidency, no appointment was more important than the one he made early in 1975. He called on Edward H. Levi, president of the University of Chicago and former head of its law school, as his new attorney general.

Though opposed by conservatives, Levi's appointment was eagerly accepted by the Senate with no floor debate and merely a voice vote. Levi had been special assistant to the attorney general during the administration of Franklin Roosevelt, but he fit no easy political mold. During his confirmation hearings, he supported a limited use of the death penalty and upheld government surveillance and wiretapping in specific cases. On February 6 he was sworn in as the first Ford-nominated Cabinet member.

Unlike his immediate predecessor, William Saxbe, who was named ambassador to India, Levi maintained a low public profile in the Department of Justice. His two major policy initiatives involved an abortive attempt to resolve the gun-control issue and a more successful attempt to give the Department of Justice tighter control over the FBI. On the gun-control question, Levi attempted to counter the long-time opposition from rural hunters and sportsmen by limiting the ban to handguns in urban areas with violent crime rates significantly higher than the national average. He argued that "in crowded urban areas the handgun has become a medium of terror. . . . It makes an individual in a city too powerful for his environment." But like other proposals for gun control, his suggestion did not get very far.

Edward Hirsch Levi

DENNIS BRACK/BLACK STAR

Levi was born in Chicago on June 26, 1911. He received undergraduate and law degrees from the University of Chicago and taught at the law school there from 1936 to 1940 and again from 1945 to 1968, when he became president of the university. (JOHN F. STACKS)

Levine, James

James Levine would like to become all but invisible. Though this young man's wish was unlikely to be granted, it could be understood in the light of his particular work. In 1972 Levine was named to the highly visible post of principal conductor at the Metropolitan Opera in New York City. He believed that a conductor should "produce a performance as faithful to the composer's intention as possible." A perfectly literal reading of a score is likely to be dull. On the other hand, a showman-type conductor, whose personality intrudes between the music and the audience, often violates the composer's intentions. Levine sought a middle ground between these extremes, wishing to serve, almost unnoticed, as a knowledgeable intermediary between a dead composer and a living audience.

Born June 23, 1943, in Cincinnati, Ohio, Levine could sing and pick out melodies on the piano before he had acquired much speaking vocabulary. He began piano lessons at the age of four and not long after that learned how to follow a musical score. Soon acquiring a reputation as a child pianist, he made his public debut with the Cincinnati Symphony Orchestra at the age of ten. In the years that followed, he continued to appear occasionally with that orchestra.

Levine completed high school in 1961 and enrolled that autumn at the Juilliard School of Music in New York City, studying conducting with Jean Morel and piano with Mme Rosina Lhevinne. He completed the five-year course of instruction in 24 months. In 1962 he spent the summer at the Aspen Music Festival in Colorado, and there conducted his first opera, *The Pearl Fishers* by Georges Bizet. Two years later, Levine was a finalist in the Ford Foundation's American Conductors Project. After the competition ended, George Szell, who then led the Cleveland (Ohio) Symphony Orchestra, offered Levine a position as an apprentice conductor.

Levine left Cleveland in 1970 and began a series of guest appearances with orchestras in North America and Europe. During the next year, he made his debut at the Metropolitan Opera, conducting Puccini's *Tosca.* The Opera asked him to lead three productions during its 1972–73 season. Goeran Gentele, then director of the Metropolitan, was so impressed with Levine that he appointed him principal conductor on Feb. 16, 1972. (VICTOR M. CASSIDY)

Little, Joanne

In 1975, as often before in U.S. history, the South was the setting for a dramatic criminal trial that symbolized a clash between old and new social values and evolving patterns of legal justice. The defendant, a poor and obscure black woman named Joanne Little, was viewed as a heroine and a martyr

WIDE WORLD

Joanne Little

by feminists, civil rights organizations, and advocates of prison reform.

The 21-year-old Little was originally charged with first-degree murder when she admitted that she had fatally stabbed a white prison guard named Clarence Alligood with an ice pick in the Beaufort County Jail in Washington, N.C., on Aug. 27, 1974. At the time, Little was awaiting results of an appeal on her sentence of seven–ten years for breaking and entering. After stabbing Alligood, she fled the jail but surrendered to local authorities eight days later in the company of her attorney.

At Little's trial, prosecutor William Griffin argued that she had lured Alligood to her cell at 3 A.M. by promising him sex. Then she killed the jailer, stabbing him 11 times with the ice pick which, Griffin said, she had snatched earlier from Alligood's desk. According to the prosecutor, Little's motive was simply to escape.

Little's lawyers, whose fees were paid from a defense fund raised in nationwide appeals, did not deny that she killed Alligood. But they insisted, as Little testified, that she did so only after he had tried to rape her and that she fled only because of her fear that, as a woman and a black, she would have been unable to prove her innocence to a legal system dominated by males and whites. To bolster its case, the defense called three former female inmates of the jail, who testified that Alligood had made sexual advances toward them.

But the star witness for the defense was Little herself. Under cross-examination by Griffin, Little was asked why she had not "screamed, hollered, slapped, or run" when Alligood attacked her. She replied, "Mr. Griffin, if you had been a woman, you wouldn't have known what to do either." The jury agreed. After only one hour and 18 minutes of deliberations, Joanne Little was declared not guilty.

(STANLEY WILLS CLOUD)

López Rega, José

Until he was driven from his position of power and left Argentina for exile in Spain in July 1975, there was no stranger individual in any government than José López Rega. By reason of his influence over the late Pres. Juan Perón and Isabel Martínez de Perón, the widow who became "La Presidenta," this 59-year-old former police corporal was virtually the prime minister of the country.

The source of his influence was his position as personal secretary and manager of all the Peróns' affairs. But among the 24 million Argentines he was regarded as a man of nearly occult powers, a practicing astrologer who was the real power behind the presidencies of the former dictator and his widow.

In the records, López Rega was listed as minister of social welfare and private secretary to Isabelita, but he was much more than that. In effect he had ruled Argentina from the day in June 1973 when Perón returned after 18 years of exile. He was allegedly the mastermind behind right-wing strong-arm groups that took part in the round of political murders and kidnappings assailing Argentina. A probe begun after he left indicated that he may have enriched both himself and the widow-president at the public's expense.

López Rega's origins are obscure, except that he once served at low ranks in the Argentine police force. According to one story, he was Isabel Martínez' manager when she was dancing in Panamanian nightclubs, before meeting the former dictator whose third wife she eventually became. It is certain that he turned up in Spain in the mid-'60s and became Perón's private secretary. When Perón was elected president in 1973, at a time when Argentines were searching desperately for anyone who might bring order to their chaotic country, López Rega moved with him into the presidential residence at Los Olivos.

He personally supervised the somewhat mystic business of returning to Argentina the remains of Perón's second wife, Eva, who had played so charismatic a role in the days of Perón's glory. After Perón died on July 1, 1974, he contended that the president had asked him to take care of the widow. A Rasputin-like figure, he remained with her when she assumed the presidency. The skein ran out for López Rega in July when the military forced Isabel to fire him and he fled to Spain. At year's end, again under pressure from the military, she stripped him of the rank of ambassador extraordinary, conferred on him before he left the country, and an order was issued for his arrest. Even so, as Isabel's presidency tottered, it was said that he still influenced her from his Spanish exile. (JEREMIAH A. O'LEARY, JR.)

MacDonald, John D(ann)

Travis McGee, a "knight in slightly tarnished armor . . . a thinking man's Robin Hood," had by 1975 been the hero in 16 mystery-suspense novels by John D. MacDonald. Like its predecessors, the latest McGee novel, *The Dreadful Lemon Sky* (1975), became a best-seller.

McGee is both a cynic and a romantic, a moralist who inhabits a world filled with greed, corruption, and seediness. As MacDonald describes his creation: "I made him an iconoclast, a critic of the cheapening aspects of his culture, an unassimilated rebel in an increasingly structured society."

The McGee series began in 1964 with *The Deep Blue Good-By,* when MacDonald, overcoming his reluctance to tie himself to a set hero and a relatively set plot line, decided it was necessary to capture his share of the paperback market. MacDonald's earlier novels, while popular, had not made his name well known to the public. *Good-By* was followed quickly by *Nightmare in Pink* (1964), *A Purple Place for Dying* (1964), *The Quick Red Fox* (1964), and *A Deadly Shade of Gold* (1965).

The McGee novels are set in Florida (MacDonald himself lives in Sarasota), where the hero resides aboard a houseboat named "The Busted Flush." McGee is a quasi-retired salvage consultant extraordinaire, for whom women in trouble, large amounts of money, murder, illicit business practices, and con games are recurring themes. Good often wins a pyrrhic victory over evil in these books.

MacDonald was born on July 24, 1916, in Sharon, Pa. He studied business at the University of Pennsylvania and Syracuse University, and received a master's degree from the Harvard Graduate School of Business Administration in 1939. This training frequently shows up in MacDonald's novels, notably in the person of McGee's sidekick Meyer, an economist, and in the profit motive that is usually behind the murder.

MacDonald's career in business was interrupted by his service in the U.S. Army from 1940 to 1946. He wrote and sold his first short story in 1944. His first novel, *The Brass Cupcake,* appeared in 1950. By 1975 he had written more than 500 magazine stories, 2 nonfiction works, and 47 novels outside the Travis McGee series, some of them under pseudonyms. MacDonald had received critical praise, winning the Ben Franklin Award for the best American short story in 1955 and the Grand Prix de Littérature Policière in 1964 for the French edition of *A Key to the Suite.*

(JOAN NATALIE REIBSTEIN)

Malloum, Félix

Formerly commander in chief of the Chad Army, Brig. Gen. Félix Malloum became head of state in April 1975 following a military coup in which Pres. N'Garta Tombalbaye was killed (*see* OBITUARIES). Malloum, who had been in detention since 1973, claimed that the Army had acted to "put an end to the 15-year-long night imposed by Tombalbaye's dictatorship."

One strong point of disagreement between the new Chadian ruler and his predecessor was the conduct of the 11-year war against the rebel forces of the Chad National Liberation Front (Frolinat). Malloum favoured a policy of reconciliation, whereas Tombalbaye had insisted on showing no mercy. The coup was undoubtedly facilitated by the neutrality of the French Army, which maintained military bases in Chad; but in September Malloum peremptorily ordered the French forces to quit the country within a month following a dispute over attempts by the French government to negotiate directly with Frolinat for the release of a French ethnologist, Françoise Claustre, who was a hostage in their hands. Malloum claimed that the French, contrary to what they said, were prepared to provide Frolinat with weapons as part of a ransom deal.

A square-jawed soldier with deep-set eyes, Malloum was born on Sept. 10, 1932, at Ft. Archambault (renamed Sarh). Trained in French military academies and in the former French Congo, he served with the French forces in the colonial wars in Indochina and Algeria. He rose to the rank of colonel in 1968, when he became chief of President Tombalbaye's military Cabinet in charge of national defense and veterans' affairs. He was appointed chief of the general staff at the end of 1971 and commander in chief of the Chadian forces a year later. After he was arrested by Tombalbaye in July 1973, Frolinat actually asked for his release; but despite this apparent rapport his regime made no significant progress toward ending the rebellion. (COLIN LEGUM)

WIDE WORLD

Mansfield, Mike

Montana's Sen. Mike Mansfield continued in 1975 to establish a record by completing his 15th year as majority leader of the United States Senate. No one had ever held the post that long, the previous record being held by Alben Barkley.

As floor leader for the majority Democratic Party, the 72-year-old Mansfield was responsible for turning his party's program into legislative action. But with the opposition party's president in the White House, his role became more complicated as he strove for compromise to prevent the Senate from becoming bogged down in partisan political wrangling.

This was especially necessary in 1975, a year in which Congress often seemed paralyzed by political strife. The Democrats frequently were unsuccessful in attempts to override the vetoes of Republican Pres. Gerald Ford. This led to criticism that Mansfield and Carl Albert, the speaker of the House of Representatives, were failing to exert strong leadership. At the same time, Republicans were accusing the two men of playing partisan politics.

But arm twisting, bartering favours, and threatening revenge—the cloakroom techniques of some of his predecessors—were not Mansfield's style. Instead, he sought a consensus on divisive issues while ruling with common sense and a personal reputation for being honest and fair. The results were affection and respect for Mansfield from senators of both parties, and a record of more victories than defeats in votes on crucial issues. Despite the presidential vetoes, Mansfield and his Democratic majority were able to have their way, for example, on such major issues as the cut in federal income taxes and ending the U.S. involvement in the Vietnam war. Indeed, Mansfield called for a worldwide reassessment of United States foreign policy, declaring: "We are spread too far, too wide, too thin and have neither the resources nor the manpower to undertake the kind of foreign policy which has been the hallmark of all administrations, Democratic and Republican, since the end of World War II." It was a typically candid Mansfield statement in a city and profession where long-winded obfuscation is the accepted norm.

Mansfield first came to Congress from Montana in 1943, serving five terms in the House of Representatives before being elected to the Senate in 1952. Born March 16, 1903, in New York City, he joined the Navy at the age of 14 during World War I and then served in both the U.S. Army and the Marine Corps. He worked as a copper miner before resuming his education and had to be admitted to college by special examination because he had not completed grade school. Mansfield earned his master's degree from Montana State University in 1934 and was a professor of history at Montana State when he decided to enter politics.

(HAL BRUNO)

Mark, Sir Robert

The main responsibility for combating the wave of bombings, shootings, and other violent crime that threatened Londoners in 1975 fell to the head of the Metropolitan Police, which operates over an area of about 15 mi. radius from the centre of London. Since 1972 that post (officially, commissioner of police of the metropolis) had been held by Sir Robert Mark, who could congratulate himself and his force on two signal successes in 1975: the apprehension, without loss of life, of the three gunmen involved in the "Spaghetti House siege" in Knightsbridge in September–October and of the four Provisional IRA terrorists who held a middle-aged couple hostage in a flat in Balcombe Street in December.

Mark had established a reputation not only as a meticulous professional but also as a policeman-philosopher, with a propensity for speaking and writing and a readiness to engage in campaigning. Since the mid-1960s he had developed a formidable case against some aspects of the practice of criminal law. He claimed that the law operated against the police in the detection, prevention, and punishment of crime; that juries could be intimidated; that some lawyers abused court procedure by "forensic trickery" to secure acquittals and to blacken the reputation of police witnesses; and that some of the procedures to protect the accused, such as the police caution before questioning and the right of the accused to refuse to be cross-examined, made things too easy for the professional criminal. Lawyers objected to Mark's criticisms of the legal profession and court procedure as ill-founded. He had, however, achieved some results. He argued the case for majority verdicts as long ago as 1965, and this point was conceded in 1968, as was a requirement that defense lawyers disclose alibi pleas in advance of the trial.

Sir Robert Mark

WIDE WORLD

Born March 13, 1917, in Manchester, Mark joined the Manchester Police at the age of 20 and rose to be constable to chief superintendent before moving to Leicester in 1957 to be the youngest chief constable in the country and then to the Metropolitan Police as assistant commissioner in 1967. When he took over the London police the tasks he faced were to clean out some pockets of corruption; to integrate the Criminal Investigation Division (CID) more closely into the Metropolitan force as a whole; and to direct a drive against central London crime, notably in the Soho pornography and prostitution belt.

(HARFORD THOMAS)

Miki, Takeo

Assured of the post of prime minister of Japan at a meeting of Liberal-Democratic leaders on Dec. 2, 1974, Takeo Miki was not alone in expressing surprise. No one had expected Miki to be picked for the party presidency (which automatically brought him the post of prime minister) because he was only the leader of a small faction in the party.

The unusual decision reflected a serious party crisis that existed at that time, caused by mounting public criticism of excessive spending in the House of Councillors election and earlier financial scandals during the administration of former prime minister Kakuei Tanaka. Moreover, if either Takeo Fukuda or Masayoshi Ohira, two foremost contenders for the top party post, had been picked, it would have split the party. Under the circumstances, the choice was "clean" Miki, a man who would strongly promote a general reform of the party.

Miki had had an unusual career for a politician of his stature. Following graduation from Meiji University, he was elected to the House of Representatives at the age of 30 and was reelected 12 times in succession. A Dietman for 38 years, Miki called himself, with considerable pride, "the child of the Diet." Miki firmly resisted antidemocratic pressures at the outset of the Sino-Japanese War in 1937, and actively campaigned against war with the U.S. for three years before Pearl Harbor. Miki was therefore cordially treated by Gen. Douglas MacArthur when he became the supreme commander of Allied Powers in Japan after the end of World War II.

Sometimes termed a "Balkan politician" because he had long specialized in managing small parties or factions, Miki was obviously an artful leader with an instinct for survival. The foremost objectives of his administration were to restore public trust in national politics by living up to public expectations and to stabilize prices and enhance social fairness. Miki vowed to depend on dialogue and cooperation in dealing with his political opposition instead of confrontation by force. This idealistic approach, however, was thwarted time and again by pragmatic old-line conservatives within his own Liberal-Democratic Party. As an example of this problem, Miki had to retreat in the face of intraparty opposition to the bill to revise the Antimonopoly Law, despite his public pledge to tighten the antimonopoly regulations.

The Liberal-Democratic Party was considerably troubled by Miki. If the party should opt to force him out there was no suitable successor in sight. Moreover, party leaders feared that a political power play against him would damage the party's reputation. Thus, although Miki's leadership

AUTHENTICATED NEWS INTERNATIONAL

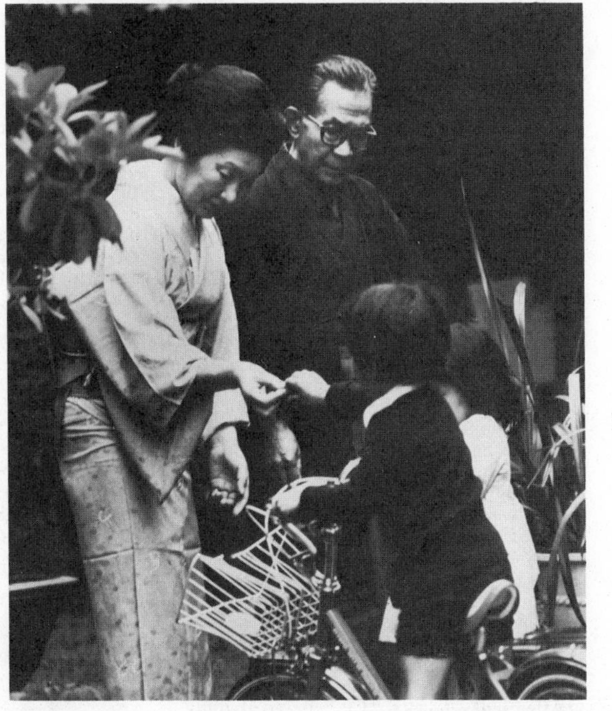

Takeo Miki

position sometimes appeared threatened, this longest-serving Dietman would likely perpetuate his regime into the future. How well he managed to meet the national expectation for reform, however, would determine his place in the political history of Japan. (IZUMI HOSOJIMA)

Mohammed, Murtala Ramat

Nigeria's new military leader, Brig. Murtala Mohammed, came to power on July 29, 1975, after a bloodless coup that took place while Gen. Yakubu Gowon, head of the provisional military government since 1966, was attending the Organization of African Unity summit meeting in Kampala, Uganda. By yielding gracefully to his deposition by his former commissioner (minister) of communications, Gowon eased the way for Nigeria's new leadership to assume power without rancour. Typical of his decisive and blunt style, Mohammed wielded a vigorous new broom, sweeping away many of the top leaders from the Army and the public service in a campaign for greater efficiency and against corruption.

A strong-willed Hausa soldier from the city of Kano in northern Nigeria, Mohammed first came into prominence during the July 1966 military coup that established Gowon as the supreme military leader. Mohammed at that time favoured the secession of the northern Hausa states, while Gowon insisted on maintaining the unity of Nigeria's federation. The civil war, precipitated by the Ibos' attempt to establish an independent Biafra in 1967, converted Mohammed to the idea of federal unity. He led a division against the Biafran forces and became renowned for his tough and stubborn military tactics.

Mohammed was born on Nov. 8, 1938. From 1959 to 1961 he attended the famous Royal Military Academy at Sandhurst, England, where he was commissioned as a second lieutenant before going to the School of Signals at Catterick, England. In 1962 he was posted to the Nigerian battalion serving with the UN peacekeeping forces in the Congolese Republic (Zaire), later returning to Catterick for an advanced course in telecommunications. He was appointed inspector of army signals in April 1966 with the rank of lieutenant colonel. He commanded a division in the civil war, but after pushing the rebel forces out of the Mid-Western State, he involved his troops in exceptionally heavy losses while trying to cross the Niger River. Opinions differed as to his personal responsibility, but he was relieved of his command and reappointed inspector of signals. (COLIN LEGUM)

Morales Bermúdez, Francisco

A member of Peru's ruling class, Gen. Francisco Morales Bermúdez seized control of the government of that South American nation in a bloodless coup d'etat on Aug. 29, 1975. The next day he was sworn in as president.

The 53-year-old Morales ousted his predecessor, Gen. Juan Velasco Alvarado, without a struggle just as Velasco had staged a bloodless coup in October 1968 against the constitutionally elected civilian president, Fernando Belaúnde Terry. Morales' motivation was regarded as more personal than ideological, although most authorities agreed that he was more moderate politically than the general he deposed.

Morales' rule, however, was not expected to deviate much from the socialist-minded principles that the armed forces espoused when they assumed power in 1968. The difference would be more apparent in style than in substance. Velasco had risen from the ranks and came from a family of modest circumstances, while Morales' grandfather was a president of Peru and his father was a famous general who was killed in an uprising of the populist APRA party.

There were no indications that Morales would restore democracy to Peru, but he did install a civilian in the Cabinet for the first time since the 1968 revolt. He also permitted newspapers that had been shut down by Velasco to open, and he announced that all political exiles could return. There was, however, still no Congress, and censorship still existed.

There had been considerable division among the Peruvian junta members over Velasco's policy of radical economics and close political association with the Soviet Union and Cuba. The coup might have been precipitated by sporadic unrest in the nation, by Velasco's ill health and his tendency to make decisions himself, and by changing international situations. Observers believed that the sophisticated members of the officer corps realized that Peru needed a massive infusion of international investment, which had slowed to a trickle when the Velasco regime began its wave of nationalization of property. Morales' accession also signaled an end to the hard-line anti-U.S. posture that Peru had maintained since 1968.

(JEREMIAH A. O'LEARY, JR.)

Morgan, Joe

The selection of Joe Morgan as the National League's most valuable player in 1975 was such a foregone conclusion that the only really interesting thing about it was his margin of victory, the largest in the 45-year history of the award. Morgan had done everything that should be done on a baseball field, and his team, the Cincinnati Reds, had won 108 regular-season games and the World Series. It was fitting that Morgan's single in the ninth inning of the last World Series game drove in the winning run. Earlier in the season, when the Reds were wrapping up their division with a record-setting 41 victories in 50 games, Morgan had 9 game-winning hits and 10 home runs.

Morgan stands 5 ft. 7 in., weighs 155 lb., and waits for a pitch by pumping his back elbow up and down like a turkey trying to fly, all of which gives pitchers who face him a misleading impression. His average of 20 home runs a season for his four years with the Reds, 17 of them in 1975, is more indicative of a hitter 40 or 50 lb. heavier. Morgan in 1975 also had a career high of 94 runs batted in, scored 107 runs, and continued to be considered one of baseball's best defensive second basemen. Between his .327 batting average (fourth in the National League) and 132 walks (first in the league), it was a rare game in which he did not reach base.

And Morgan has to be on base to do what he does best, which is steal the next base. Trying 78 times, Morgan stole 68 bases in 1975, a career high and second in the National League. He added four more against the Pittsburgh Pirates in three play-off games for the National League pennant.

Joseph Leonard Morgan was born Sept. 19, 1943, in Bonham, Texas. After attending small colleges in Oakland City, Ind., and Hayward, Calif., he returned to Texas as a Houston Astro. He was traded to Cincinnati after the 1971 season in a deal that has been called the best the Reds ever made. In four seasons with the Reds he never batted lower than .290, scored fewer than 107 runs, or stole fewer than 58 bases, and the Reds won in their division three of those four years. In 1973 he hit 26 home runs and stole 67 bases, becoming the first player in major league history to hit 25 or more home runs and steal 60 or more bases in the same season. (KEVIN M. LAMB)

Moynihan, Daniel Patrick

After serving first as a second-echelon domestic policy expert in Democratic administrations and later as a top-level adviser to Pres. Richard Nixon and an ambassador to India, the peripatetic Daniel Patrick Moynihan in 1975 was U.S. ambassador to the United Nations. As in previous posts, controversy followed Moynihan and his sharp tongue.

STEVE SCHAPIRO—BLACK STAR

Daniel Patrick Moynihan

Born March 16, 1927, in Tulsa, Okla., and educated at Tufts University and the Fletcher School of Law and Diplomacy, Moynihan first achieved national attention when he wrote, from a post in the U.S. Department of Labor, a study claiming that a central cause of problems in urban black neighbourhoods was the disintegration of the black family. As President Nixon's chief domestic policy adviser, he was a sort of house intellectual in the Republican administration, a counterpart to Henry Kissinger's early role in foreign policy.

In the early summer of 1975, largely under the sponsorship of Kissinger, Moynihan left a position as professor of government at Harvard University and entered federal service as U.S. representative to the UN. He arrived at the UN at a particularly difficult time. Partly encouraged by the success of the oil producers' cartel, the less developed nations of the world had taken a distinctly harder line toward the U.S. and its industrialized allies, demanding "a new economic order." One political result of that new stridency was a growing intolerance and opposition toward Israel.

Urbane, articulate, and often blunt, Moynihan became the centre of controversy in the fall after a visit to the UN General Assembly session by Ugandan Pres. Idi Amin. Amin infuriated the U.S. and Israeli delegations by calling for the extinction of Israel. In a speech two days later in San Francisco, Moynihan, borrowing a phrase from the *New York Times,* referred to Amin as a "racist murderer" and also suggested it was no accident that Amin was head of the Organization of African Unity. The latter remark aroused other African delegates to call Moynihan's remarks "a deliberate act of provocation." In November Moynihan severely criticized the General Assembly for adopting a resolution defining Zionism as "a form of racism and racial discrimination."

Despite these conflicts, Moynihan played an active role in the UN in formulating new approaches to world economic cooperation on such issues as commodity prices and foreign assistance. (JOHN F. STACKS)

Narayan, Jayaprakash

When Prime Minister Indira Gandhi's government declared a state of emergency throughout India on June 26, 1975, Jayaprakash Narayan, better known as "J.P." among his countrymen, was one of the first to be arrested by the police. A week earlier Narayan, at the age of 73, had assumed the leadership of a group of politically disparate opposition parties in their campaign to remove Mrs. Gandhi from power with a call for total revolution. Because of a chronic heart condition and other infirmities, Narayan after his arrest was kept under guard at the Medical College Hospital in Chandigarh, Punjab. On November 12 it was officially announced that he had been released on parole.

The third of six children of a minor court official, Narayan was born on Oct. 11, 1902, at Sitab Diyara village, Saran district, Bihar. At the age of 15, in response to the general appeal of Mahatma Gandhi, he interrupted his studies to join the anti-British struggle. In 1922 he went to the U.S. where he spent nearly seven years moving from one university to another, finally graduating in behavioural sciences from Ohio State University at Columbus. While in the U.S. he joined the Communist Party, but on returning to India and to the nationalist movement he became disenchanted with the Communist approach. In 1932, while in prison in Nasik, near Bombay, he and others established the Congress Socialist Party.

After independence "J.P." found it difficult to adjust to the realities of freedom. He was still suspicious of Commonwealth links. Along with his followers, he walked out of the ruling Congress Party in 1948 and tried to build up the Socialist Party as an alternative. But in the first general election the Socialists were routed. In 1954 Narayan announced his retirement from active politics, also renouncing his Marxist views, and joined Acharya Vinobha Bhave, another associate of Gandhi, in a campaign to persuade landlords to part with surplus holdings voluntarily for distribution among the landless.

Despite his "retirement" Narayan continued to be embroiled in political controversies. In 1974 he organized a campaign for the dissolution of the Bihar legislature, stating that the ruling Congress Party and its state government were corrupt. This brought him into confrontation with Mrs. Gandhi. His final showdown with the government came after he called for a program of agitation to paralyze the administration. (GOVINDAN UNNY)

Neto, (Antonio) Agostinho

Independence from Portuguese rule found Angola's territory divided among its three liberation movements. The central part of the country, including the capital, Luanda, was held by the Popular Movement for the Liberation of Angola (MPLA), however, and in a ceremony there, the MPLA's leader, Agostinho Neto, was proclaimed president of the People's Republic of Angola as from midnight Nov. 10–11, 1975.

Neto epitomized the assimilation of cultures that Portugal tried to achieve as an imperial power, but which produced only a tiny westernized elite of which Neto was an outstanding product. Born Sept. 17, 1922, in a small village 60 mi. from Luanda, where his father was a Methodist pastor, he proved himself a brilliant student at the Salvador Correia High School in Luanda and was chosen by the U.S. bishop the Rev. Ralph Dodge for a scholarship to pursue medicine at the universities of Lisbon and Coimbra in Portugal. While a student he wrote protest poetry, and although this got him into trouble with the authorities it also won him recognition as an exceptionally gifted Portuguese poet. He returned home as a doctor in 1959 but was arrested in the presence of his patients in June 1960 because of his militant opposition to the colonial authorities. When his patients protested his arrest the police opened fire, killing 30 and injuring 200.

Neto spent the next two years in detention in Cape Verde and in Portugal, where he produced a new volume of verse. Placed under house arrest in 1962, he managed to escape to Morocco where he joined the Angolan liberation movement in exile. At the end of 1962 he was elected president of the MPLA. Although a committed Marxist, Neto sought allies for the MPLA in Western as well as Eastern Europe, and in North America as well as in China. Despite strong Soviet support for the MPLA, Moscow's relations with Neto personally were never easy and they were suspended for a time but restored in 1974. His withdrawn manner made him seem remote and cold, yet he had considerable charm, though lacking the charisma of his rival Jonas Savimbi, leader of the National Union for the Total Independence of Angola, (UNITA), and the professional political manner of his other principal rival, Holden Roberto, leader of the National Front for the Liberation of Angola (FNLA). (COLIN LEGUM)

DANIEL TOPOLSKI—CAMERA PRESS

Agostinho Neto

Nishi, Noriko

It is remarkable enough that Noriko, a Chicago fashion designer, could gain national prominence in a world dominated by New York's Seventh Avenue. But perhaps more remarkable is her success story, which began with a fierce battle against centuries of Japanese tradition and became marked by the stamp of her indomitable will.

Noriko was born in Kashima, Japan, on Jan. 21, 1942. Judged by Japanese standards of beauty, she was a disappointment to herself and to her family. Wishing to compensate, she became obsessed with the idea of designing clothes but met with much resistance from her family. Tensions were rife, arguments pointless, and she ran away from home, returning only after her parents agreed to let her attend fashion school. In return she promised not to pursue fashion as a career.

Then came a lucky break—the man her parents had arranged for her to marry was

PHILIP GABRIEL RUFFOLO

Noriko Nishi

living in Chicago. She came to the U.S. in 1964 and for several years led the life of a model housewife. But her ambitions never diminished and so, with her husband's consent, she returned to school. Six months later she was on her own. Momentary disappointments were followed by triumphs, and one day the president of Blair Fashions decided she was exactly what the company needed in order to expand. Accepting his offer meant an almost certain, irrevocable break with her family, but she was too close to realizing her dreams for second thoughts.

Noriko fashions are carried exclusively by Saks Fifth Avenue, and Noriko was largely responsible for making Chicago a new centre of the fashion industry. Her designs are renowned for their simple elegance and individuality. Her small size—five feet tall and a mere 85 lb.—gave her a special interest in creating fashions for the petite woman as well as for the conventional model. And her success story had a happy ending—her parents attended the showing of her 1975 fall collection. (CLAIRE SANDRA CHOW)

Nkomo, Joshua Mqabuko Nyongolo

Veteran among black Rhodesian nationalist leaders, Joshua Nkomo emerged in 1975 as the key figure in negotiations that may have offered the last chance to achieve a peaceful settlement of the rebel British colony's ten-year-old crisis. His rival nationalist contenders in the African National Council (ANC) had gone into either voluntary or enforced exile, leaving the field at home clear for the burly Nkomo. He had spent 24 years of his life in politics, nine of them in a detention camp as a prisoner of the Ian Smith regime. After his release in 1974 it appeared that he had been eclipsed by younger rivals like the Rev. Ndabaningi Sithole and Bishop Abel Muzorewa; but he skillfully exploited their absence from the country to get himself elected as president-general of the ANC in October 1975 and began the long-delayed process of negotiating with Ian Smith about a future constitution for Rhodesia (renamed Zimbabwe by black nationalists).

Although Nkomo's reputation was that of a moderate in the ANC, he proved to be as militant as any of his rivals by insisting on immediate majority rule in a country with 5.9 million black and 274,000 white inhabitants. Like his rivals he also accepted the inevitability of an armed struggle if attempts at a negotiated settlement proved abortive.

"Josh" Nkomo was born June 19, 1917, the son of a cattle-owning teacher and lay preacher in Matabeleland. He was educated at the best black colleges in South Africa and obtained a B.A. degree. After serving as a social welfare worker he helped to organize the first African railway workers' union, which became the first stepping-stone in his political career. In 1957 he became president of the African National Congress. When it was banned he took over the leadership of its two successors, the National Democratic Party and the Zimbabwe African People's Union (ZAPU). A firm believer in the value of a multiracial society for Rhodesia, he denounced the all-white Rhodesian Front of Ian Smith, when it made its unilateral declaration of independence in 1965, as "a suicide squad." He was promptly arrested and confined in the remote and arid Gonakudzingwa detention camp until late 1974. A large, gentle-looking and slow-thinking man, he owed his survival and success to a cautious but sure instinct for political tactics. (COLIN LEGUM)

Obolensky, Alexis N.

The recent explosive growth in the popularity of the ancient game of backgammon can be traced in large part to the promotional efforts of Prince Alexis Obolensky, a descendant of Russian aristocrats, a socialite and member of the "jet set," and a successful entrepreneur. Obolensky learned backgammon as a child in Istanbul, Turkey, where his family had fled to escape the Russian Revolution. His varied career has included importing orchids and selling real estate in Palm Beach, Fla., but since the 1960s he has concentrated on running a large and steady publicity campaign to popularize backgammon, a game that had been largely a pastime of the very wealthy. His success can be measured by the millions of people who now play backgammon regularly and by the millions of dollars spent on it each year.

Obolensky has been promoting a game that has many appealing features: it is relatively easy to learn but difficult to master, success depends on both luck and skill, no two games are exactly alike, a tie is impossible, and the game is relatively fast. Backgammon also lends itself readily to gambling, particularly since the invention in the 1920s of the doubling cube, a device that allows the doubling and redoubling of the stakes.

Obolensky began his campaign a little more than a decade ago, when he decided that organizing an international backgammon tournament was a good way to bring members of the jet set to a new casino in the Bahamas. The first international tournament was held in Freeport in 1964, was attended by about 30 people, and offered about $40 in prize money. Tournaments have been held annually since then, with ever increasing attendance and publicity. Obolensky has played upon snob appeal, holding tournaments in such posh resort areas as Monte Carlo, Cannes (France), Las Vegas, and the Caribbean, and gaining such converts as Hugh Hefner and Jacqueline Onassis.

In his efforts to bring backgammon to a broader public, Obolensky has been helped by *Playboy* magazine and the Seagram Distillers Co. The latter became the first major firm to sponsor backgammon, underwriting tournaments that Obolensky organized as part of its liquor-promotion activities.

In 1973 Obolensky founded the World Backgammon Club and he helped to start several bars and clubs that feature the game. He is president of the American Backgammon Association and, with Ted James, wrote *Backgammon* (1969). His *Backgammon: Rules and Rulings* was published in 1974. (JOAN NATALIE REIBSTEIN)

Onassis, Christina

Aristotle Onassis may not have been the richest of Greek shipping magnates, but he was certainly the most celebrated—at least partly because of his much publicized affair with diva Maria Callas and his subsequent marriage to Jacqueline Kennedy, widow of a U.S. president. His death in Neuilly-sur-Seine, France, in March 1975 and the lopsided distribution of his billion-dollar estate left his sole surviving offspring a celebrity in her own right. She was, probably, the richest woman in the world.

Christina Onassis was born on Dec. 11, 1950, in New York City. Her mother has been described as "a pioneer jet-setter who was often indifferent" to the girl and her older brother, Alexander. Consequently, Christina was reared by servants during a lavish and peripatetic childhood in Paris, Athens, and the French Riviera. King Saud gave her purebred ponies; her favourite doll was dressed by Dior. She was educated at exclusive academies and a Swiss finishing school, followed by a few months at a London school.

At 20 she married a 47-year-old California realtor, but the marriage, of which

Christina Onassis

WIDE WORLD

her family disapproved, soon ended in divorce. This was perhaps the least traumatic event of the next three years: her brother was killed in a plane crash; her mother died under murky circumstances; and she tried to take her own life. Published reports suggest that she doted on her distant father, who in turn was devoted to his one son and heir. But Alexander's death led Aristotle to abandon his traditional male chauvinism and welcome his daughter into the corporate fold, grooming her to succeed him. She applied herself seriously to business and was soon described as a budding executive to be reckoned with.

By the terms of Onassis' will, all his business assets would remain intact under a holding company. Christina received 47.5% ownership of each of these assets, including a skyscraper under construction in New York, Olympic Airways (which was being ceded to the Greek government), and a fleet of ships and 15 supertankers. She also received 75% of her father's interests on the island of Skorpios and the yacht "Christina," plus an annual income of $250,000. In July, after a month-long acquaintance and a one-week engagement, she married Alexander Andreadis, a 30-year-old Greek banking heir. "Christina is a . . . serious woman," he said. "Ours is a serious marriage."

(PHILIP KOPPER)

Orfila, Alejandro

On May 17, 1975, Argentina's ambassador to the United States, Alejandro Orfila, was elected secretary-general of the Organization of American States. He gained the position largely because he was known and liked as a shrewd diplomat.

Orfila took over the OAS post from Ecuador's Galo Plaza Lasso and immediately began energetically reorganizing the hemispheric organization with the same vigour that he applied to his diplomatic, business, and social career. Although he was perhaps best known for his elegant parties, the ebullient Orfila was far more than a drawing-room dilettante. He had succeeded in everything he put his hand to, from the management of his family's properties in Argentina to the business ventures that made him a wealthy man and the diplomatic career that brought him near the top of the Argentine foreign service.

No one realized more than Orfila that the OAS needed a hard-driving businessman's approach, as well as diplomatic skill, in the secretary-general's chair. He quickly became involved in efforts to revivify the Western Hemisphere's version of the UN so as to make it something more than a debating society.

Orfila was born in Mendoza, Arg., on March 9, 1925, the son of a prosperous family of Catalan descent. His father was governor of the province and a great admirer of George Washington. (Orfila's first given name is Washington, but he never used it.) He received a law degree from the University of Buenos Aires and studied political science at Stanford University and foreign trade at Tulane University. Entering the Argentine diplomatic service in 1946, he was first assigned as secretary to the embassy in Moscow and consul in Warsaw between 1946 and 1948. Declared persona non grata in both capitals, he returned to the U.S. where between 1948 and 1952 he served as consul in San Francisco and New Orleans and secretary of the embassy in Washington, D.C.

WIDE WORLD

Alejandro Orfila

Orfila then resigned from the foreign service to manage his family's business, but later returned to serve five years as director of information at the OAS in Washington. After serving as Argentina's ambassador to Japan, he entered private business in Washington in 1962 and spent the next 11 years as a consultant and adviser in international trade and economic affairs. In November 1973 he became Argentine ambassador to the U.S.

(JEREMIAH A. O'LEARY, JR.)

Patrick, Ruth

The world's largest award in science, the $150,000 John and Alice Tyler Ecology Prize, administered by Pepperdine University in Los Angeles, was won in 1975 by Ruth Patrick for her ecological studies of rivers and streams. The award, which is larger than the Nobel Prize, was established in 1973 to honour the person or group making the greatest contribution to ecology by means of long-term research on a project that results in practical applications.

Patrick, a limnologist (scientist studying conditions in fresh waters) with a special interest in diatoms (microscopic algae), was concerned with water pollution long before that became a fashionable field of study. By 1975 she had worked with more than 100 industries and government agencies and had personally studied nearly 1,000 river sections throughout the world. She developed the basic theoretical principles for determining the condition of aquatic ecosystems. These are now applied throughout the world in environmental impact studies. Among her achievements were the design of a method of monitoring potentials for water pollution for the U.S. Atomic Energy Commission's hydrogen-bomb plant on the Savannah River and solutions to problems of Louisiana's oyster industry. From 1948 she served as a consultant on environmental issues for E. I. du Pont de Nemours and Co., and in 1975 she was elected a director of the company, the first woman and the first environmentalist to hold such a position.

As a member of the prestigious National Academy of Sciences, Patrick served on its Committee on Science and Public Policy. Her research achievements include a two-volume study, with Charles Reimer, entitled *The Diatoms of the United States* (1966 and in preparation); the invention of a device to measure diatom communities in streams as a means of assessing pollution; and a methodological advance in analyzing the effects of pollution.

Patrick was born in Topeka, Kan., Nov. 26, 1907. She studied at Coker College in South Carolina and then at the University of Virginia, where she received her doctorate in 1934. She began teaching at the Pennsylvania School of Horticulture, moving to the Academy of Natural Sciences in Philadelphia in 1945, where she has been credited with maintaining that institution's scientific reputation and financial viability. By 1975 she had become chairman of the board of the Academy as well as an adjunct professor at the University of Pennsylvania.

(JOAN NATALIE REIBSTEIN)

Pelé

One of the biggest names in the world of sports and acknowledged "king of soccer," Pelé signed a contract in 1975 that took him from his native Brazil to the United States. After 18 years as the leading soccer star of Latin America, Pelé moved to New York to play in the North American Soccer League.

Born in Três Corações, Brazil, on Oct. 23, 1940, with the name Edson Arantes do Nascimento, Pelé was for years little known in the U.S. As the star of the Brazilian national team and the Santos Football Club, he was recognized in most countries as the world's wealthiest and most celebrated athlete, his annual income at one time reaching $2 million. But this reputation meant little in the U.S., where soccer has been regarded as a second-rank sport.

Thus, in the U.S. Pelé did not establish himself on the same limelit pedestal with a Joe Namath or an Arnold Palmer until he

Pelé

MARC SADOUX—KATHERINE YOUNG

signed a reported $7 million contract with the New York Cosmos of the North American Soccer League in June 1975. The pact was ballyhooed as one of the most lucrative ever extended any athlete.

During his remarkable 18-year career in Brazil, Pelé averaged nearly a goal a game (1,216 goals for 1,253 games) before retiring in October 1974. He held the record for most goals scored by a professional player in a single match, collecting eight for Santos during a São Paulo State League game in 1964. In 1958, 1962, and 1970 he led Brazil to victory in the competition for soccer's highest honour, the World Cup.

When he came out of retirement to join the Cosmos in 1975, Pelé announced that his motivation was not primarily monetary. "I have enough money," he said. "Rather, my aim is to make soccer truly popular in the United States."

Pelé scored only a modest success during his first season of U.S. soccer, both as a player and as a promoter. The crowds in New York and other cities in the league were good but not great. And for one of the few times in his career, Pelé was slowed down on the field by injuries. But the Cosmos were confident that Pelé would soon help professional soccer attain the rank of a major U.S. sport. (J. TIMOTHY WEIGEL)

Petty, Richard Lee

Stock-car racing is not ancient, by any standard. The sport is believed to have evolved in the rural southeastern United States as an offshoot of the bootlegger's need to outrace federal agents across open fields and country roads. Eventually, the fastest cars would be matched up. Richard Petty, the greatest stock-car driver of them all, did not get his start that way. But he was born into a tradition. His father, Lee, won the National Association for Stock Car Auto Racing (NASCAR) Grand National championship three times before a serious crash ended his career in 1961.

Richard has carried on, to say the least. He is the only driver to win six Grand National titles, which are based on points won in NASCAR races within a given year. He was the first to win $1 million in a career, and in 1975 he became the second, after A. J. Foyt, ever to win $2 million.

Yet Richard Lee Petty has not disdained his roots. He was born on July 2, 1937, in Level Cross, N.C., 2 mi. S of Greensboro, and it is there that he and the other members of "the Petty clan" still do business. Petty Enterprises is a 50,000-sq.ft. complex where 35 full-time workers are employed, including 5 men whose entire time is devoted to Richard's cars.

"King Richard," as he is often called by his fans, has come a long way since he started out on a half-mile dirt track in Columbia, S.C., in 1958. So has his sport. "When we started runnin', they were strictly cars," said Petty. "I mean, they pulled 'em off the infield, pasted up the headlights and started racin' 'em. They found out the wheels broke, so they had to put on better wheels. Then when they got 'em to run fast, they started turnin' 'em over, so they put roller bars on 'em. It was like anything growin' to meet the need. We kept on improvin' the breed. You never stand still."

Petty certainly never does. He has won more stock-car races than anyone else, including the Daytona 500 five times. No one else has won it more than once. During the 1967 season he won 27 of 48 races, including 10 in a row.

Petty hit a slump in early 1974, NASCAR having altered its engine specifications so that the big-bore Chrysler power plants he had been running in his STP Dodge no longer were competitive. His crew then went to work on a round-the-clock, two-month, $75,000 program, restroking a new, 340-cu.in. standard Chrysler engine to 362 cu.in. Afterward, Petty went on to win 10 of 30 races and $299,175 en route to his fifth Grand National crown.

(J. TIMOTHY WEIGEL)

Pramoj, Kukrit

During 40 years of military dictatorship the name of Pramoj had remained in the forefront of the beleaguered civilian element in Thai politics. In 1975 it became the dominant name, for when the tortuously slow process of constitution-making finally led to general elections and a popular government, it was Seni Pramoj, leader of the Democrat Party, who found himself Thailand's prime minister. When he faltered, it was his younger brother Kukrit Pramoj, leader of the Social Action Party, who succeeded him. At the end of 1975 Kukrit was still in office, no mean achievement considering that the crises that beset him included a massed attack on his house by policemen.

Almost a Thai national institution, Kukrit Pramoj had been sometimes controversial, sometimes unpredictable, but always popular. This was hardly surprising for one whose record showed him to have worked as journalist, actor, classical dancer, economist, soldier, banker, and novelist. Although his party had only 18 seats in a 269-member house, his outstanding if unorthodox qualities were appreciated by Thais as they faced unprecedented problems.

Kukrit belonged to the Thai aristocracy, being the son of a prince and bearing the title Mom Rajawong. He was born on April 20, 1911, and went to school in Thailand and England. From Oxford he obtained a degree in politics, philosophy, and economics. Returning home, he joined the Ministry of Finance and then went into commercial banking. His irrepressible spirit then caused him to begin writing poems and stories, and he also followed tradition by becoming a Buddhist monk for 50 days. Emerging from the monastery, he founded the newspaper *Siam Rath,* which attacked the military rulers of the time and brought him a series of arrest warrants and fame. The fame skyrocketed when he appeared in the film *The Ugly American* opposite Marlon Brando playing an Asian head of government—a screen fiction that was to become fact. (T. J. S. GEORGE)

Kukrit Pramoj

WIDE WORLD

Prentice, Reginald Ernest

In an increasingly ferocious dispute between right and left wings in the British Labour Party, Reg Prentice, minister for overseas development in Harold Wilson's Cabinet, became the focal point of the controversy during 1975. In his London dockland constituency of Newham North-East, Prentice had an impregnable majority—so long as he remained the Labour candidate. Discontent among a new, younger generation of Labour activists came to a head in the summer of 1975 when the Newham general management committee, complaining of his "excessive moderation," successfully pressed home a resolution not to readopt him as their candidate at the next general election. This raised far-reaching issues of constitutional principle, as it could undermine the independence of elected MPs.

The Prentice counterattack was launched on September 11 at East Ham Town Hall where the home secretary, Roy Jenkins, was howled down by left-wing interrupters and bombarded with bags of flour by members of the right-wing National Front. In the speech he would have delivered Jenkins said, "I regard the Prentice case as of fundamental constitutional importance." Prentice' views, Jenkins said, were "well within what should be the mainstream of Labour Party tolerance." In November a party committee appointed the party's general secretary, Ron Hayward, to mediate the dispute between Prentice and his local party, but by year's end no reconciliation had been effected.

Born July 16, 1923, by 1975 Prentice had nearly 30 years' active experience in the Labour movement; as a trade union official after leaving the London School of Economics, which he attended after World War II, then as a Croydon borough councillor for six years, and as a member of Parliament since 1957, with a place in all the Wilson governments since 1964, joining the Cabinet as secretary of state for education and science in 1974 and succeeding Judith Hart (*q.v.*) as minister of overseas development in June 1975. He gained a reputation as an outspoken right-winger—although he insisted that he had been a loyal upholder of Labour Party manifesto policies, and in that sense an orthodox moderate. He provoked the wrath of the left wing by criticizing dock strikes in which dockers of his own constituency were involved, by questioning the conduct of violent strike pickets, and by saying that unions that pressed excessive wage claims were "welshing on the social contract" (an undiplomatic comment that drew a rebuke from Prime Minister Wilson). (HARFORD THOMAS)

Ratsiraka, Didier

The Malagasy Republic's new leader, Comdr. Didier Ratsiraka, pledged his regime to a policy of revolutionary socialism when he took power in June 1975 and dissolved the military directorate that had ruled the country since February. This leftward lurch in a traditionally agricultural society with pronounced class divisions promised a difficult ride for the militant naval engineer who now headed the government. While denying that his brand of

WIDE WORLD

Didier Ratsiraka

socialism implied Communism, he nevertheless added that "if Communism means struggling against social inequalities and working for the nation, then we are Communists." On his first day in office he announced the nationalization of the banks and insurance companies, and he followed this by taking a majority shareholding in a shipping line and in the island's leading insurance company. He also cut his own salary by 35% and ordered 12% cuts for the rest of the government. His presidency was approved by 95% of the voters in a December referendum.

Ratsiraka was born Nov. 4, 1936, at Vatomandry, Tamatave Province. From the lycée in Tananarive he went to France, earning a scholarship at the École Navale in Brest. He served with the French Navy as an engineer officer and was made a lieutenant commander after graduating from the École Supérieure de Guerre Navale. His strong political interests were sharpened by his experience as military attaché at the Malagasy embassy in Paris in the early 1970s.

He played a prominent role in the students' and workers' demonstrations that brought down the conservative government of Pres. Philibert Tsiranana in 1972. Brought into the new regime as foreign minister, he clashed with the French government in negotiations to revise the old colonial-type relationship with France, securing, among other concessions, evacuation by the French of their naval base at Diego Suarez. His enthusiasm for China after his visit to Peking in November 1972 was not approved by many of his government colleagues, and he was forced for the time being to tread a more careful line.

Ratsiraka was a huge, irrepressible figure with prominent eyebrows and bulging muscles under his eyes. His physical impact was as impressive as the daring of the revolutionary language he used at the large mass rallies he liked to address in his tours around the island. (COLIN LEGUM)

Ray, Dixy Lee

A 61-year-old nonconformist who had made the transition from academic life to government service in Washington, D.C., Dixy Lee Ray reversed her course in 1975 when she resigned as assistant secretary of state for oceans and international environmental scientific affairs. On announcing her intention to return to private life, she fired a broadside at her boss, Secretary of State Henry Kissinger. She charged that Kissinger and other ranking officials in the State Department had not consulted her when they made policy decisions regarding matters of concern to her office.

Outspokenness and controversy had been hallmarks of Ray's relatively brief career in Washington. She arrived in 1972 to serve as a member of the Atomic Energy Commission (AEC). The following year, Pres. Richard Nixon appointed her to be AEC chairman. In that office Ray moved quickly to change the commission's reputation as a secretive, unresponsive federal fief and to respond to widespread fears about nuclear power plants. She helped consumer affairs lobbyist Ralph Nader gain access to AEC reports on peaceful uses of the atom and was largely responsible for the commission's decision to ban construction of a nuclear power plant in New Jersey, arguing that it would have been too close to Trenton and Philadelphia for safety. Ray was not, however, opposed to the use of nuclear power for domestic purposes.

Ray's abrupt manner and new policies angered some of her colleagues at the AEC

AUTHENTICATED NEWS INTERNATIONAL

and in Congress, but others were delighted. In 1974 the AEC's functions were divided between two new agencies, the Energy Research and Development Administration and the Nuclear Regulatory Commission. As part of the reorganization, Ray was shifted from the AEC to the Department of State. But her tendency to speak her mind and her unusual life-style (she lived in a house trailer during her years in Washington) evidently made it difficult for her to adjust to professional life in the State Department.

Ray was born Sept. 3, 1914, in Tacoma, Wash. A marine biologist, she received her bachelor's degree from Mills College in Oakland, Calif., and her Ph.D. from Stanford University. From 1945 to 1972, she was on the zoology faculty at the University of Washington. (STANLEY WILLS CLOUD)

Rees, Merlyn

Perhaps the most taxing and frustrating job in British politics in the 1970s was that of secretary of state for Northern Ireland. When Labour returned to power in March 1974 it fell to Merlyn Rees, a quiet, thoughtful, kindly, and patient former teacher. Rees would probably have become a college head had he not gone into Parliament in 1963, filling the seat at South Leeds left vacant by the death of party leader Hugh Gaitskell.

His qualifications for the job were coincidental. Soon after entering Parliament he became parliamentary private secretary (a personal appointment) to James Callaghan. This led to junior ministerial posts in the Ministry of Defence and in 1968 to another junior post at the Home Office, where Callaghan had become home secretary and was about to become involved in the opening sequences of the Northern Ireland disturbances. This in turn led to Rees's becoming the chief Labour opposition spokesman on Northern Ireland, with a seat in the shadow cabinet from 1972 to 1974.

As Ulster secretary from March 1974, he had little option but to carry on as before. Terrorism continued, and Merlyn Rees repeated that the government would not be deterred by terrorists. He insisted that power sharing was the key to the future of Northern Ireland, but the concept was bitterly resisted by Protestant leaders who were able to stage a paralyzing strike in May 1974. In the end Protestant leaders agreed to talks, only to break away again in the late summer of 1975, when they rejected coalition government.

Meanwhile, Rees had patiently continued the phased release of Catholic detainees as a necessary step toward reconciliation with the Catholic community. This yielded an IRA truce in January 1975, but the IRA Provisionals resumed their bombing attacks later in the year after months of sectarian murders on both sides. The Protestants in Ulster and some Conservatives at Westminster were blaming Rees for secret deals with the IRA and for weakness in dealing with its leaders. By this time Rees himself was taking the view that violence in Northern Ireland could not be stopped, even with another ten battalions of troops.

Born in South Wales on Dec. 18, 1920, Rees had lived and worked in London ever since his family left Wales during the depression years between World Wars I and II. (HARFORD THOMAS)

Riccardo, John J.

In a year when Chrysler Corp. suffered massive losses and saw its share of the automotive market decline, it was probably inevitable that there would be a change in the top corporate leadership. The change occurred Oct. 1, 1975, when John Riccardo moved up from his position as president to become chairman and chief executive, replacing the retired Lynn A. Townsend.

The change did not appear to indicate a great deal of dissatisfaction with the way Chrysler had been run by Townsend; he was

John J. Riccardo

WIDE WORLD

understood virtually to have handpicked his successor, with whom he had been associated for years. Riccardo, a former accountant with a reputation as a cost cutter, promised to continue "working hard on returning to profitability," but he carefully refrained from predicting a quick recovery.

All U.S. automakers were seriously hurt by the general economic recession of 1974–75. Chrysler, however, was hit by the biggest slump of all, despite its extended use of cash rebates to its retail customers. For the first nine months of 1975, Chrysler lost $231.8 million, while General Motors and Ford posted net profits for the same period of $635 million and $152.8 million, respectively. Predictions for the fourth quarter were optimistic, and Chrysler pinned its hopes on the introduction of two "small luxury cars," the Plymouth Volaré and the Dodge Aspen. The future of the corporation's operations in Britain became a matter of political controversy there. Prime Minister Harold Wilson, faced with Riccardo's threat of a total shutdown failing massive state aid—and the consequent politically and socially unacceptable loss of some 25,000 jobs—accused Riccardo of "holding a pistol to the government's head."

In the campaign to improve Chrysler's competitive position, Riccardo and the man who succeeded him as president, Eugene A. Cafiero, were not expected to depart radically from Townsend's policies. Instead, the emphasis apparently would be on improving the marketability of Chrysler-made cars as well as on careful cost accounting.

Riccardo was born July 2, 1924, in Little Falls, N.Y., and attended the University of Michigan. After working for Touche Ross & Co., a public accounting firm, he joined Chrysler in 1959, where he became known as a protégé of Townsend (who had also come to Chrysler from Touche Ross). Riccardo rose quickly in the corporate structure and became president in 1970.

(STANLEY WILLS CLOUD)

Rivlin, Alice M.

Necessity is truly the mother of invention in politics. Thus, in 1974, when the heavily Democratic 93rd Congress found itself under telling attack from a Republican administration for its "spendthrift" record, it responded by creating an entirely new and more responsible method of dealing with each year's federal budget. Congress established a Congressional Budget Office (CBO) to provide senators and representatives with the kind of professional assistance that the executive branch receives from the Office of Management and Budget. With Alice Rivlin as director, the CBO's functions were tested for the first time in 1975.

Basically, Rivlin's job is to analyze the likely effects of various budgetary choices that Congress must make every fiscal year. In the past, appropriations bills were passed in a haphazard way. Little or no thought was given to the cumulative effect the bills might have on the budget. But by using information provided by Rivlin's office, members of Congress can know in advance whether or not their legislative decisions will create a deficit, a balanced budget, or a surplus. The CBO's projections also tell them whether or not total appropriations planned for the year will meet the spending goals Congress must set for itself. Although the system would not actually begin functioning until 1976, its "dry run" in 1975 was generally regarded as a success.

Rivlin's assignment is politically delicate. A liberal herself, she must steer a careful course between congressional conservatives, who favour the new budgetary process because it tends to hold down spending, and liberals, who like it because in effect it allows Congress to draw up its own budget rather than simply reacting each year to the president's budget.

Rivlin was born Alice Mitchell on March 4, 1931, in Philadelphia. She graduated from Bryn Mawr College in Pennsylvania in 1952 and received her Ph.D. in economics from Radcliffe (Cambridge, Mass.) in 1958. She was deputy assistant secretary of health, education, and welfare during the administration of Lyndon Johnson. Most recently, she was a senior fellow at the Brookings Institution in Washington, D.C.

(STANLEY WILLS CLOUD)

Rose, Pete

His nickname is Charley Hustle. He runs to first base on walks as if Doberman pinschers were chasing him. He was the captain of major league baseball's best team in 1975. But Pete Rose says that he has loafed in his 13-year career. Once. "It was back in 1966," Rose said. That was when his manager with the Cincinnati Reds told him to change positions because the Reds needed a third baseman, and Rose said, "I was just stubborn. I didn't give it my best shot."

That incident was especially hard to believe in 1975 because on May 2 another Reds manager, Sparky Anderson, asked—not told—Rose to change positions because the Reds needed a third baseman. Not only did Rose make the change eagerly, enabling a good young hitter to start at his left field position, but he also quickly became one of the best defensive third basemen in the National League. Anderson said that Rose's move made the Reds' World Series victory possible.

Rose had 210 hits in 1975, making it his seventh season with more than 200, one short of the National League record and two short of the major league record. He had his 2,500th hit on August 17 and finished the season with 174 more hits than Ty Cobb had after 13 seasons. Rose's .317 batting average in 1975 was over .300 for the tenth time in 11 years, and, although he has called himself "the first singles hitter to make $100,000 a year," he led the league in doubles with 48.

Rose played in his third World Series in six years in 1975 and became the most valuable player of the Series, which the Reds won over the Boston Red Sox. He led both teams with a .370 batting average, but his biggest play of the series may have been a slide in the last game that broke up a double play. That enabled the inning to continue long enough for a two-run home run to cut the Reds' deficit to 3–2, and they went on to win the game and the Series in the last inning.

Peter Edward Rose was born April 14, 1942, in Cincinnati, Ohio, and watched the Reds play a few miles from his home throughout his childhood. When he joined the team in 1963, he was the National League rookie of the year. He led the league in batting three times, his best average being .348 in 1969. In 1973 he was voted the league's most valuable player, and he was teammate Joe Morgan's runner-up for MVP in 1975. (KEVIN M. LAMB)

Rostropovich, Mstislav Leopoldovich

Highly praised cello and piano performances, a conducting debut in the U.S., and a self-imposed exile from his native Soviet Union in protest against its policy of stifling artistic freedom caused 1975 to be a significant year for Mstislav Rostropovich. The Soviet musician, who has been called the world's greatest living cellist, announced publicly that he and his wife, soprano Galina Vishnevskaya, would remain away from the U.S.S.R. so that they could fulfill their artistic goals.

INGER MCCABE—RAPHO/PHOTO RESEARCHERS

Mstislav Rostropovich

Rostropovich and Vishnevskaya had been granted a two-year travel visa by Soviet authorities in 1974, following a three-year travel ban imposed for their support of such Soviet dissidents as Andrey D. Sakharov and Aleksandr I. Solzhenitsyn. Rostropovich described his last five years in the Soviet Union as musically crippling, characterized by concerts canceled without his knowledge or consent, a deliberate policy of not advertising his or Vishnevskaya's name, the refusal of the best Soviet orchestras to allow him to conduct or play with them, and even the stopping of a recording session "literally in mid-note."

Rostropovich was born Aug. 12, 1927, in Baku, Azerbaijan S.S.R., into a family of musicians. He studied the cello under his father, Leopold, and the piano under his mother, Sofia. In 1931 the family moved to Moscow, where Rostropovich studied from 1934 to 1941 in a special Soviet elementary school for musically gifted students. By 1940 he had made his debut as a solo cellist.

Rostropovich was admitted to the Moscow Conservatory in 1943. He completed the postgraduate curriculum at the conservatory in 1948 and in 1953 became a teacher there. In 1946 he was first invited to perform as a soloist with the Moscow Philharmonic. He soon began winning international awards and made his Western debut in Florence, Italy, in 1951. He later performed in London, Paris, New York, and other Western musical centres as well as throughout the Soviet Union. After his marriage to Vishnevskaya in 1955, he appeared regularly as her accompanist. He received the Lenin Prize in 1964 and the Gold Medal of the London Royal Philharmonic Society in 1970. In 1960 he became an honorary professor at the Cuban National Conservatory, and in 1962 he was made an honorary member of the British Royal Academy of Music.

(JOAN NATALIE REIBSTEIN)

Ryan, Nolan

It might sound trite to say that Nolan Ryan stood at the crossroads of a brilliant pitching career as he approached the 1976 baseball season, but nonetheless it was true. The California Angels' flame-throwing righthander underwent surgery on Sept. 23, 1975, to remove bone chips from his pitching elbow. The threat of arm trouble is posed to every man who earns a living throwing baseballs, and in Ryan's case it would be particularly severe. At 29, he was considered to be in the prime years of a player's career.

Officially, if such a thing can be official, Ryan throws harder than any other man whose fastball has been clocked. On Aug. 20, 1974, the Angels employed a special machine to determine that Ryan threw one pitch 100.9 mph. He has used that speed well, to win 105 major league games, to pitch 4 no-hit games (tying Sandy Koufax' major league record), to strike out 383 batters in 1973 (a major league record), and to strike out 19 batters in one nine-inning game (a modern major league record).

Lynn Nolan Ryan, Jr., was born on Jan. 31, 1947, in Refugio, Texas, and grew up in Alvin, Texas, where he spends the off-season raising cattle. The New York Mets signed him after a distinguished high-school career during which he averaged 14 strikeouts a game. The price, cheap by 1975 standards, was a bonus in the neighbourhood of $14,000.

Ryan was brought up to the Mets initially in 1966. From 1968 to the end of 1971 he had won 29 and lost 38 and had 493 strikeouts in 510 innings. His pitches were fast, but they were also frequently misdirected. He walked 344. So, in need of a third baseman, the Mets reached to the Angels for Jim Fregosi on Dec. 10, 1971, giving up Ryan and three other players in return.

Even if Ryan never won another game after 1975, the trade was a steal for California. Although the Angels were among the game's weaker hitting clubs, Ryan managed seasons of 19–16, 21–16, 22–16, and 14–12. In 1975 he appeared headed for his greatest season. On June 1 he pitched his fourth career no-hitter, beating the Baltimore Orioles 1–0. That left him with a 9–3 record, a 2.44 earned run average and 96 strikeouts. He followed that with another shutout. But a pulled muscle suffered in spring training finally caught up with him. His condition deteriorated and finally the decision for surgery was made.

(J. TIMOTHY WEIGEL)

Ryder, Sydney Thomas Ryder, Baron

Don Ryder, who in 1975 became Lord Ryder, would appear in any short list of Britain's most successful businessmen. As chairman of the newly formed National Enterprise Board (NEB), set up by the 1975 Industry Act to enable the government to intervene widely in private industry, he became perhaps Britain's most powerful businessman. Although a notable exponent of private enterprise, he had been put in charge of the main instrument for extending the state interest in the private sector.

During the passage of the Industry Bill through Parliament, the NEB had been at the heart of some bitter controversy. The Labour government's intentions were viewed with deep suspicion by private industry. Ryder took a nonpolitical view. "In my mind politics don't come into it at all," he said. As he saw it, the NEB, with its powers to finance private industry, to plan agreements with individual companies, and to stimulate worker participation, would function as a catalyst for the regeneration of British industry.

Ryder's own career was a record of unbroken success. Born Sept. 16, 1916, in the London suburb of Ealing, he went straight from school into financial journalism. After World War II, in 1950, he became editor of the *Stock Exchange Gazette* and made it an outstanding success before it was taken over in 1960 by the International Publishing Corp. (IPC).

Ryder quickly advanced to the top rungs of the IPC. In 1963 he moved to the Reed Group Ltd., which in due course absorbed IPC into a new conglomerate company, Reed International Ltd., with wide-ranging interests, one of Britain's biggest industrial organizations. Ryder was chosen as chairman designate of the NEB before it officially came into being. During the interim, he masterminded the rescue and reorganization of British Leyland Motor Corp., the U.K.'s largest motor vehicle manufacturers, with the government buying up the equity capital. But he emphasized that he did not see his job as mounting rescue operations for ailing companies. He looked for the extension of public ownership into profitable industry. Ryder was knighted in 1972 and was made a life peer in 1975. (HARFORD THOMAS)

Schmücker, Toni

In February 1975, at a time when the firm was in considerable difficulty as a result of the world economic recession and a policy that had placed too much reliance on the success of the famous "Beetle" model, Toni Schmücker became chairman of the executive board of the West German Volkswagen concern. In 1974 the concern's losses had totaled DM. 807 million. Exports of the West German car industry as a whole fell by 22% in the first five months of 1975 as compared with January–May 1974.

During 1974 Volkswagenwerk AG reduced its labour force by 14,000 to 111,500, but soon after Schmücker took over the chairmanship he had to announce even more drastic economy measures. From Jan. 1, 1975, to the end of 1976 the number of workers was to be cut by an additional 25,000. Schmücker pointed out that Volkswagen had always been heavily dependent on the export market, especially sales to the U.S. These had slumped because of the high cost of importing, which was in turn caused by the decline in the exchange rate of the dollar against the mark.

Schmücker's predecessor, Rudolf Leiding, had supervised the introduction of such new models as the Passat, Scirocco, Golf, Audi 50, and Polo. The Golf became the best-selling West German car of 1975, and Schmücker said at the Frankfurt motor show in September that sales of Volkswagen cars in the first eight months of 1975 had increased by 5% over the corresponding period of the previous year. Home sales had gone up by 12% and exports to European countries by 12.5%.

Toni Schmücker

COURTESY, VOLKSWAGENWERK AG

Schmücker was born on April 23, 1921, at Frechen, near Cologne. He reached the medium grade at school and then took a course in salesmanship at the Ford works in Cologne. After serving in World War II, he went back to Ford and was appointed to the board in 1961. Seven years later he left Ford to join the board of the Rheinstahl steel firm and within a few months was its chairman. In October 1974 he became director of August Thyssen-Hütte AG, retaining his post with Rheinstahl. He joined Volkswagen five months later.

(NORMAN CROSSLAND)

Seaver, Tom

On Nov. 12, 1975, New York Mets' pitcher Tom Seaver capped a remarkable comeback year by becoming only the second player in major league history to win the Cy Young award three times (Sandy Koufax was the first). Seaver's 22–9 record and 2.38 earned run average gained him 15 first-place votes for the award out of a possible 24.

In 1974 Seaver had been troubled with a sciatic nerve condition in his hip and had struggled to an 11–11 record. His future in baseball was uncertain until a medical specialist diagnosed the problem and treated it successfully with hip manipulations.

Seaver was born Nov. 17, 1944, in Fresno, Calif. He began playing baseball in high school and in 1965 entered the University of Southern California on a baseball scholarship. In 1966 the Atlanta Braves signed him to a contract carrying a bonus estimated at $40,000, but William Eckert, commissioner of baseball, nullified it on the grounds that the Braves had violated the rule that prohibited them from drafting a player while the college season was in progress. Meanwhile, Seaver had been stripped of his amateur status, and Eckert then allowed any other team willing to match the Braves' bonus offer to sign him. Three teams offered to do so, and the Mets won his services in a lottery drawing.

During each of his first two seasons with the Mets Seaver won 16 games, and he was named rookie of the year in 1967. Then in 1969 he helped lead the team to its first National League pennant by winning 25 games; he also garnered a World Series triumph over Baltimore and his first Cy Young award. Seaver won 20 and 21 games in 1971 and 1972, and led the Mets to their second pennant in 1973 with 19 victories. That record sufficed to earn him his second Cy Young award. (DAVID R. CALHOUN)

Shawn, William

Eustace Tilley, the effete gentleman who first observed a butterfly through his monocle on the inaugural cover of *The New Yorker* in 1925, appeared as usual in 1975 on the February issue marking the magazine's anniversary. Like Tilley, *The New Yorker*'s typography and makeup had remained unaltered in the intervening 50 years, but the content had undergone substantial change. And much of the change could be traced to a man as unlike Eustace Tilley as could be imagined—a reticent and self-effacing editor named William Shawn.

Under Shawn, who succeeded Harold Ross, the magazine's founder, as editor in 1952, *The New Yorker* had shifted its emphasis from stylish, sophisticated fiction and humour done in a blithe and snobbish manner to analysis of serious public issues done from a strongly liberal point of view. While the old *New Yorker* had not entirely disappeared—humorist Woody Allen still had a place within its pages and glossy advertisements surrounded the articles on welfare mothers and pollution—the publication had become one of the most socially and politically active of major U.S. magazines.

Shawn denied that the responsibility for this was his alone. He attributed it to the changing concerns of the writers in concert with those of the editors. Nevertheless, Shawn himself approved everything the magazine published. As far back as 1946, Shawn, then managing editor, convinced Ross that John Hersey's "Hiroshima" should be published in its entirety in a single issue. The move toward greater seriousness accelerated in the 1960s, and for Shawn the 1970 Cambodian invasion marked a critical point in U.S. history, to which *The New Yorker* responded with articles on the abuse of political power.

Shawn was born in Chicago on Aug. 31, 1907, and studied at the University of Michigan. He worked briefly as a newspaper reporter and editor and for a while as a composer of theatrical music. He began his career at *The New Yorker* in 1933 as a freelance reporter for the "Talk of the Town" section, became an associate editor in 1935 and managing editor in 1939. Only one piece signed by Shawn has ever appeared in *The New Yorker:* a short fantasy entitled "The Catastrophe," published in 1936, that described the obliteration of New York City by a meteorite.

(JOAN NATALIE REIBSTEIN)

Simpson, O. J.

Another major record, that of most touchdowns scored in a single season, was added in 1975 to the collection of U.S. professional football's premier running back, O. J. Simpson. In the season's final game Simpson scored two touchdowns for the Buffalo Bills to bring his total to 23, one more than Gale Sayers scored in 1965. Simpson also led the league in yards rushing with 1,817, an outstanding performance but short of his 2,003-yd. league record in 1973.

Even with his 2,000-yd. season a fresh memory, Simpson's first five games in 1975 stretched the limits of imagination. He gained more than 100 yd. in all of them, and his per-game average projected to a season total of more than 2,300 yd. He did not achieve this, mainly because teams were willing to concentrate on defending against him even at the cost of weakening themselves against other parts of the Bills' offense. Simpson did manage to rush for his fourth 200-yd. game, tying Jim Brown's record.

O. J. Simpson

FOCUS ON SPORTS

One thing achieved by Simpson for the first time in 1975 was to win the Superstars competition, a television network promotion that involved professional athletes competing in ten different events for a $25,000 first prize. But that was an individual achievement, and Simpson contended all season that his only goal was for his team to win the National Football League championship. They failed, finishing with an 8–6 record.

Simpson is better known as "Orange Juice" than Orenthal James, the name given him when he was born July 9, 1947, in San Francisco, Calif. He first achieved recognition at the University of Southern California, where he averaged 164.4 yd. a game in his two seasons there. In 1968, his senior year, he won the Heisman Trophy as the nation's outstanding college football player. The year before that, he was a member of Southern California's world-record 440-yd. relay team.

In none of his first three seasons with Buffalo was Simpson allowed to carry the ball as many as 200 times. But he had nearly 300 carries in 1972, the year he began his streak of consecutive 1,000-yd. seasons.

Simpson is lavish in giving credit to his offensive line. In 1973 he refused to play in the league's post-season all-star game until one of the Buffalo linemen was added to the team.

(KEVIN M. LAMB)

Sinclair, Gordon Allan

Marking his 53rd year of reporting news to Toronto, Gordon Sinclair in 1975 was perhaps the most listened-to personality on Canadian radio and television and one of the ten best-known living Canadians. In August he opened the 97th Canadian National Exhibition at Toronto.

Sinclair began radio broadcasting in 1942 and in 1949 started a twice-daily news broadcast on radio station CFRB in Toronto, a station of which he became part-owner in 1944. Along with the news broadcasts, Sinclair had two five-minute programs each day. On "Gordon Sinclair's Show Biz" he discussed films he had seen during the week, and on "Let's Be Personal" he talked about himself and his views. One broadcast of the latter, in June 1973, made him famous in the U.S. when he praised Americans as "the most generous and possibly least appreciated people in all the Earth." This created such a response that he made a record of it, which sold more than two million copies. His share of the profits was donated to the American Red Cross.

Sinclair also became a well-known television personality across Canada, having been a panelist since 1957 on "Front Page Challenge," the longest-running program on Canadian network television. He was associated with television in Canada at its inception: he had been the host in 1938 of the first broadcast in the country.

Sinclair was born in Toronto on June 3, 1900. He started his career as a reporter at the *Toronto Daily Star* in 1923. From 1929 to 1940 he was a roving reporter for the paper, circling the globe four times and visiting 86 countries. Between 1932 and 1947 he published seven books, mostly travelogues about his adventures as a reporter. In 1966 he wrote his autobiography, *Will the Real Gordon Sinclair Please Stand Up,* and published a sequel in 1975, *Will the Real Gordon Sinclair Please Sit Down.* He was elected to the Canadian News Hall of Fame in 1972.

(DIANE LOIS WAY)

Siyad Barrah, Muhammad

President of Somalia's Supreme Revolutionary Council from Oct. 22, 1969, Maj. Gen. Muhammad Siyad Barrah came to power through a military coup pledged to eradicate tribalism, corruption, nepotism, and misrule. Although this powerfully built, energetic soldier campaigned vigorously to carry out his reforms against the stubborn clannishness of a largely peasant population, he had not by 1975 altogether succeeded in eliminating tribal policies. His strong Muslim faith—shared with virtually all Somalis—tempered his own Marxist beliefs to produce a political system that combined the economic ideas of Marx with the teachings of the prophet Muhammad.

When Siyad Barrah marked International Women's Year in 1975 by insisting on the complete equality of Somali men and women, some of his Muslim opponents claimed that this was against the teaching of the Koran and called for defiance of the regime. Ten were executed, probably the first time that opponents of women's liberation had paid with their lives for their opposition to sex equality. Yet far from being a despot, Siyad Barrah was generally considered an essentially humane and kindly leader, regarded, even by opponents, as the father figure of his nation. He showed particular concern for penal and social reform, and during 1975 released the last of his major political prisoners.

Heavily reliant on the U.S.S.R. for military support in his border disputes with Ethiopia, Kenya, and the French Territory of the Afars and Issas, Siyad Barrah clashed with the U.S. over charges that he was allowing a Soviet missile base to be established at Berbera; he strongly denied the accusation. Also controversial was Somalia's membership in the Arab League even though Somalis are not Arabs. But the most serious challenge he had to face during 1975 was the drought that left 800,000 Somalis facing starvation.

Siyad Barrah was born in 1919 into a Darod nomadic family in the Upper Juba region; both his parents died when he was ten. With the benefit of only elementary education, he joined the police during the period of British administration in World War II. When the Italians briefly returned to administer the country in 1950, he rose quickly to the highest permitted colonial police rank of chief inspector. After attending a military academy in Italy he transferred to the Somali Army as a lieutenant, becoming a colonel after independence in 1960 and commander in chief in 1965.

(COLIN LEGUM)

Soares, Mário

After two periods of exile imposed by the pre-revolutionary regime in Portugal, Mário Soares, secretary-general of the Portuguese Socialist Party (PSP), returned to Lisbon during the coup of April 1974. Foreign minister in the first three provisional governments after the coup, he was responsible for explaining to foreign heads of government much of what had been taking place in Portugal since the April revolution. On March 26, 1975, he became a minister without portfolio in the fourth provisional government, and at the same time organized his party and led the election campaign for the constituent assembly that brought about successes for himself and the PSP in April. These successes did not, however, bring power to the political parties, as they had earlier been forced to sign a five-year political settlement with the Armed Forces Movement (AFM).

In May a political crisis developed around Communist Party control of the media and their takeover of the Socialist newspaper *República,* and again in July around the AFM's new plans to establish a people's democracy in Portugal that would effectively exclude any political parties from power. On July 11 the Socialists resigned from the fourth government and went into opposition to the Communist-dominated fifth.

After conversations with Soares and the PSP, the president, Gen. Francisco da Costa Gomes, appointed a moderate, Adm. José Batista Pinheiro de Azevedo (*q.v.*), as the new premier. During these conversations agreements for pluralistic democracy, fixing a date for elections for legislative assemblies and municipal bodies, and the extinction of the armed militia were signed. On October 16 Soares took the seat he had won in the April elections and became leader of the PSP in the constituent assembly.

Born Dec. 7, 1924, in Lisbon, Soares graduated in arts from the University of Lisbon and in law from the Sorbonne in Paris. He was a founder member of the United Democratic Youth Movement and a member of its central executive from 1946 to 1948. After several key appointments in the opposition to the authoritarian government of António de Oliveira Salazar, he became a member of the campaign committee supporting the election of Gen. Humberto Delgado to the presidency in 1958. For these sympathies Soares was arrested and later exiled to São Tomé. In November 1968, soon after Marcello Caetano took over from the stricken Salazar, Soares was allowed to return to Lisbon. In 1970 he undertook a lecture tour of Europe and the U.S., during which he made speeches critical of the government. On his return to attend the funeral of his father, he was given the choice of leaving Portugal within 48 hours or being put under arrest without bail. Soares chose exile. (MICHAEL WOOLLER)

Starr, Bart

When the Green Bay Packers made Bart Starr their 1974 Christmas present to the city of Green Bay, fans of the National Football League team celebrated the arrival of its new coach with a fervour similar to that of the Wise Men 1,974 years earlier. Stickers reading "A Fresh Start With Bart" and "The Packers Need A Guiding Starr" appeared on the backs of automobiles. Packer fans, disappointed by two straight losing seasons and no championship for eight years, based their optimism on the memory that it was Starr who had quarterbacked the Packers to five NFL football championships between 1961 and 1967. The city that called itself "Titletown, USA" was ready for another title.

What it got was a team that won only one of its first eight games in 1975, a worse start than even the 1958 Packers had in their 1–10–1 season. The Packers finished with their worst record since that year (4–10) but they did improve in the course of the season, indicating that Starr might well have been making a reasonable request when he asked for a little patience. His only coaching experience had been as a Packer assistant in 1972, though this was the only year since 1967 when the team qualified for a postseason game.

"It's like going home and putting a fresh coat of paint on the farmhouse," Starr said. "I felt compelled to get a good new brush, a fresh bucket of paint, and jump right in. Confidence will be a big key for us."

Confidence in Starr as a quarterback had never been lacking, especially in postseason games. When the Packers were NFL champions in 1965, 1966, and 1967, they became the first team to win three straight league titles. Starr led the Packers to five victories in six championship games by completing 84 of 145 passes (57.9%) for 1,090 yd. and 11 touchdowns, and he threw only one interception. He was even better in football's first two Super Bowl games, after the 1966 and 1967 seasons, when he completed 29 of 47 passes (61.7%) for 452 yd. and three touchdowns with one interception.

The son of an Air Force master sergeant, Bryan Bartlett Starr was born in Montgomery, Ala., on Jan. 9, 1934. He was not chosen until the last round of the 1956 college draft because of his back injury two years earlier at the University of Alabama, but in 1959 he became the Packers' starter in their ninth game. He led them to victories in their last four games, giving them their first winning season in 12 years. The measure of the man is his adherence to a quotation of the late, great Packer coach Vince Lombardi, which Starr keeps in his office. It reads: "The quality of a man's life is in direct proportion to his commitment to excellence, regardless of his chosen field of endeavor." (KEVIN M. LAMB)

Stonehouse, John Thomson

Britain's vanishing member of Parliament, John Stonehouse, turned up in Australia on Christmas Eve 1974, more than a month after he had disappeared from a beach in Miami, Fla., apparently after having gone for a swim in the sea. The circumstances of his disappearance on Nov. 20, 1974, aroused some suspicion. Miami beach guards said it was impossible for him to have gone into the sea unnoticed. He was on a business trip, and it was known that some of his financial enterprises were in difficulties.

After he had been found living in Melbourne under an assumed name, he was reported to have said, "I had come to the end of my tether. Everything was going wrong." He asked to stay in Australia. Britain's Scotland Yard detectives and investigators from the Department of Trade began inquiries that lasted for many months. Finally, in July 1975, the Australian authorities conceded a British request for the extradition of Stonehouse. After he returned to London, criminal proceedings against him were commenced. He was held in prison for some weeks, but after a series of personal protests in court he was released on £30,000 bail on August 27. On November 5 he was committed for trial on 18 charges of fraud, theft, forgery, and conspiracy, bail being renewed. The charges involved some £170,000.

Meanwhile, pressure was put on Stonehouse to resign his seat as Labour MP for Walsall North, but this he declined to do. Some MPs argued that he should be expelled, but it was decided that any debate on his expulsion might prejudice the course of his trial, and he therefore remained an MP.

Stonehouse, who was born on July 28, 1925, entered Parliament in 1957 and held a number of posts in the Labour government between 1964 and 1970, ending up as minister of posts and telecommunications in 1969–70. In the three years from 1970 to 1974 when Labour was in opposition he established a number of financial and commercial companies. When Labour returned to power in 1974 he was not offered a place in the government. In November 1975 his autobiographical *Death of an Idealist* appeared, giving his version of the events that led to his committal for trial.

(HARFORD THOMAS)

LONDON DAILY EXPRESS/PICTORIAL PARADE

John Stonehouse

Tabei, Junko

On May 16, 1975, two spots moved slowly toward the peak of the highest mountain in the world. They were Junko Tabei, deputy leader of a Japanese women's expedition to Mt. Everest, and her Sherpa guide, Ang Tsering. Fourteen fellow alpinists were standing by at the base camp at a height of 5,350 m. and at the second camp at a height of 6,400 m., waiting excitedly for a transceiver report from "the point nearest to the eyes of heaven."

At 12:30 P.M. the first report from Mrs. Tabei reached the group informing them that she had just stood on the pinnacle of Mt. Everest. The 35-year-old alpinist, mother of a three-year-old daughter, said later that when she made her last step on the narrow, snow-capped pinnacle she felt only that she was worn out and would not try such a feat again. It was literally a dramatic moment of glory gained through hardships. In the predawn of May 4, the second camp was suddenly hit by a massive avalanche. All seven climbers in the camp,

Junko Tabei

WIDE WORLD

including Tabei, as well as six Sherpa guides, were injured. After having oxygen administered for two days Tabei recovered her health with difficulty, and though the accident made the conquest of Mt. Everest appear hopelessly difficult, she insisted on keeping up the assault.

Born in northern Fukushima Prefecture in 1939, Tabei started mountain climbing when she was nine years old. She had longed to climb high mountains in the Himalayan range since her graduation from Showa Women's University in Tokyo. In 1970 she joined the third Japanese women's Annapurna expedition, which succeeded in conquering the 7,577-m. peak. Tabei and Mrs. Eiko Hisano, the leader of the expedition to Mt. Everest, had planned to climb Everest in 1974, but the Nepalese government would not allow it until 1975.

Preparing for the Everest expedition was no easy task as the expedition team was comprised of housewives, schoolteachers, nurses, store clerks, and reporters. Fundraising was also a consideration. Tabei was fortunate because her husband, also a veteran alpinist, was fully sympathetic to her cause, supporting her financially and taking care of their daughter while she was away.

On May 30 both Tabei and Hisano received the decoration of Gorkha Dakshin Bahu from King Birendra of Nepal. Upon receiving it, Tabei said modestly that she would be happier if all the other members of the expedition could be decorated.

(YOSHINOBU EMOTO)

Teresa (of Calcutta), Mother

A nominee for the 1975 Nobel Peace Prize, Mother Teresa of Calcutta had already received many tributes to her outstanding work for the destitute, notably the first Pope John XXIII Peace Prize (1971). A Yugoslav peasant teaching in India with the Irish Loreto Sisters, she had felt a deeper call in 1946 and in 1948 was authorized to leave her convent in order to succour the poor and dying of Calcutta while sharing the conditions they endured. For her, religious poverty had to be total, involving the insecurity inevitable when not only the individual religious but the corporate order owned literally nothing. In 1952 she set up a home for the dying, her primary aim being to ease their suffering and passage with the "sight of a loving face"; she regarded being and feeling unwanted and unloved as "the most terrible disease of all."

Mother Teresa

SYMIL KUMAR DUTT—CAMERA PRESS/PICTORIAL PARADE

Mother Teresa was clearly a person of intense charisma; her simple message overwhelmed the most unlikely recipients, and people, upon seeing her, yearned to touch her. To her each individual she tended represented Christ, with whom, she said, her encounter in the persons of the poor was as direct as during the mass. In this intensely religious basis of her work (she abhorred the idea of becoming "only a social worker"), she seemed the direct antithesis of those who claim to find formal religious commitment a hindrance to effective service.

Teresa Boyaxhiu was born at Skopje, Yugos., on Aug. 27, 1910, one of three children of an Albanian grocer. She was briefly (1928) at Loreto Abbey near Dublin before sailing for India. On being released from her convent she donned the blue-bordered white sari that became her nun's habit and started her new work. The first of her recruits joined her in 1949; many were girls whom she had taught. Her Order of the Missionary Sisters of Charity was formally recognized in 1950 and became a pontifical congregation (subject only to the pope) in 1965; the Brothers of the Order were established in 1963. Although Calcutta remained the primary centre of the order's work, Mother Teresa founded houses in Ceylon, Tanzania, Jordan, Venezuela, Rome, Britain, and Australia.

(STEPHANIE MULLINS)

Thatcher, Margaret Hilda

The first woman to be chosen as leader of a major political party in Britain, Margaret Thatcher was elected to succeed Edward Heath as the Conservative Party's leader in February 1975. She had been a member of Parliament since 1959 but had relatively little experience in government, with three years as parliamentary secretary to the Ministry of Pensions and National Insurance (1961–64) and four as secretary of state for education and science, with a seat in the Cabinet (1970–74).

After losing two general elections in 1974 under Heath's leadership, the Conservatives were determined to find a new leader, but at first the betting odds were put at 50 to 1 against Margaret Thatcher. Yet in the first ballot of Conservative MPs on February 4 she eliminated Heath by 130 votes to 119, and a week later took over the leadership with 146 votes against party chairman William Whitelaw's 79. At first her leadership in Parliament was somewhat hesitant, but she quickly gained confidence and by October was able to win a triumphant endorsement from the annual party conference. Hitherto little known outside Britain, she visited Paris in May and later spent two weeks in the U.S. and Canada.

The secret of her success was elusive and much discussed. Her somewhat doll-like appearance and ladylike manner of speech were misleading. She was tough, there was a sharp edge to her politics, and she could be brutally outspoken. She did not hesitate to offend Heath by enlisting the support of those who, she said, felt "let down by their party" which they thought had become "just a pale version of the socialist party." She exploited the middle-class disgruntlement with inflation and high taxation. She attacked socialism as a spendthrift society, and took up the monetarist view on cutting government expenditure. She proclaimed the traditional Conservative faith in self-help. *The Times* of London said she was "the unabashed champion of inequality."

Born Oct. 13, 1925, in the small market town of Grantham, Lincolnshire, Thatcher was the daughter of a hard-working grocer who became mayor of Grantham. She went to local schools and then by scholarships to study chemistry at Oxford University, where she became president of the university Conservative association. After Oxford she worked as a research chemist, studying law in her spare time and specializing in taxation.

(HARFORD THOMAS)

RICHARD MELLOUL—SYGMA

Margaret Thatcher

Thoeni, Gustavo

Winner of the men's World Alpine Ski Cup an unprecedented four times in five years, Gustavo Thoeni, one-time Italian customs officer, owed his early successes entirely to outstanding performances in the slalom. Subsequently, he improved in the downhill event enough to be regarded as a true all-arounder. A brilliant slalom stylist with an exceptionally calm disposition, Thoeni won many major races without so much as touching any of the gate poles between which he had to descend.

Born at Trafoi, Italy, on Feb. 28, 1951, and initially coached by his father, Thoeni concentrated from the outset on gaining the maximum speed during turns between gates. After scoring the most giant slalom points in the 1970 World Cup series, his first of three successive overall World Cup victories came the following year. He finished third in the 1974 series but climaxed a great career in 1975 by recapturing the trophy in the final event, the first parallel slalom to be included. In 1972, Thoeni won an Olympic Games gold medal in the giant slalom and a silver in the slalom at Sapporo, Japan, where he also gained the world championship combined title, decided concurrently. In the 1974 world championships at St. Moritz, Switz., he was first in both the slalom and giant slalom, but his decision not to contest the downhill prevented any chance of retaining the combined title.

Thoeni was so good a slalomer that his first two World Cup overall victories were achieved without even competing in a downhill race. It was not until the rules for subsequent seasons were changed to encourage greater versatility that he took any serious interest in the downhill, with relatively modest success. Although approving the principle of testing all-around ability, he expressed regret that anyone's technique in slalom must suffer through having to devote more attention to downhill training, the two entailing appreciably different timing. Thoeni perhaps rightly regarded success in a World Cup series as more important than in a world championship, because the latter reflects ability in only one meet while the former demands consistency throughout a season. (HOWARD BASS)

Tiant, Luis Clemente

Although he was busy trying to protect a one-run lead with the bases loaded in the ninth inning of the fourth game in the 1975 World Series, Luis Tiant heard the noise. It was a cacophonic mixture of cowbells, bugles, and voices that was music to his ears, the sound of fans exhorting him to finish the inning safely so that his team, the Boston Red Sox, would tie the Cincinnati Reds in the Series for the major league baseball championship.

Tiant responded to the noise by pitching his way out of the jam to gain a 5–4 victory that was his second in four days. But no amount of noise or number of World Series victories could have been more important than knowing that his parents were in the stands sitting next to his wife.

When Luis Clemente Tiant was born Nov. 23, 1940, in Marianao, Cuba, there was no way of knowing that he would never see his father between 1960 and 1975. Tiant followed his father, who was one of Cuba's all-time greatest pitchers, into a baseball career and was unable to return home after Fidel Castro's rise to power. Neither of his parents saw their only child pitch in the major leagues until Aug. 19, 1975. The easing of tensions between the United States and Cuba and the efforts of Senators Edward Brooke (Rep., Mass.) and George McGovern (Dem., S.D.) made possible the reunion, which Tiant called the happiest day in his life.

The year was a big one on the field for Tiant. For much of the season he was Boston's only consistent pitcher. His record was 18–14 and his 4.05 earned run average was relatively high, but as one opposing manager said, "Tiant is the kind of guy who gives up seven or eight runs when he can afford to but doesn't give you a thing in a close game."

For the season to have a storybook ending, Tiant should have won the sixth game of the World Series, tying a Series record for three victories, and the Red Sox should have won their first World Series since 1918. But Tiant was knocked out of the sixth game before his team won it, and the Red Sox lost the Series in seven games.

It was, however, a storybook tale that Tiant pitched at all in 1975. After leading the league with a 1.60 earned run average and having a 21–9 record with Cleveland in 1968, he lost 20 games in 1969 and was discarded by two teams in 1971. But Boston picked him up and was rewarded with Tiant's 75–46 record and two 20-win seasons from 1972 through 1975.

(KEVIN M. LAMB)

Torrijos Herrera, Omar

The military strong man who took control of Panama in 1968, Brig. Gen. Omar Torrijos Herrera in 1975 entered the most critical year of his career. The fervour over the negotiations with the United States concerning future control of the Panama Canal made his nation a tinderbox of nationalist emotion. The 46-year-old commander of the Guardia Nacional, Panama's military and police force, was caught between his own rhetoric on when and how the U.S. would agree to a treaty turning over the isthmian waterway to his country and the political realities of this hot political issue.

All competent authorities agreed that miscalculations or excessive stubbornness by either side in the current negotiations could precipitate a repetition of the 1964 violence against the U.S. Torrijos well understood that the U.S. government was anxious to conclude a new treaty with Panama that would remove all vestiges of the 1903 treaty that is so odious to Panamanians, but he was also sophisticated enough to realize that there was a strong conservative sentiment in the U.S. and its Congress, especially in an election year, that opposed making any change in the status of the canal and the ten-mile-wide Canal Zone.

Torrijos' problem was to weigh the sentiment of his own people and determine whether it might be strong enough to force his hand into some precipitous action. An outbreak of patriotic rioting or an invasion of the unfenced Zone by fervent Panamanians, or even an attempt to sabotage the canal locks, would certainly force the U.S. to defend the Zone and perhaps to intervene with additional troops. Torrijos, thus, was a man on a tightrope.

Torrijos, a tough and charismatic dictator who preferred to let a civilian figurehead occupy the presidency, was born Feb. 13, 1929, in Santiago de Veraguas, about 115 mi. from Panama City. His parents were teachers, but he chose a military career. Entering Panama's Guardia Nacional as a sublieutenant in 1952, he had by 1966 risen to lieutenant colonel.

Torrijos came to power in a bloodless military coup in October 1968, as a sort of proconsul with another colonel, Boris Martínez, to replace the elected president, Arnulfo Arias. Within a year, Torrijos had ousted Martínez and assumed full control himself. (JEREMIAH A. O'LEARY, JR.)

Tsatsos, Konstantinos

Shortly after his electoral victory of Nov. 17, 1974, Greece's Prime Minister Konstantinos Karamanlis held a referendum on the restoration of the monarchy, which was rejected by a wide margin. A republican constitution was adopted by the Chamber of Deputies on June 7, 1975, and on June 19 the chamber elected Konstantinos Tsatsos president of the republic for five years.

The first democratically elected head of the Second Greek Republic (or *Dimokratia* as opposed to *Vasilevomeni Dimokratia,* or "monarchical democracy"), Tsatsos was a widely respected philosopher, lawyer, and man of letters. He was born in Athens on July 1, 1899, into a middle-class family. After law studies at the universities of Athens and Heidelberg, he practiced law in Athens from 1921. Nine years later he became lecturer on the philosophy of justice at Athens University and in 1932 was appointed professor there.

Tsatsos entered politics in April 1945 when he joined the government of Adm. Petros Voulgaris as minister of the interior. He then became minister for air in the short-lived government of Panayotis Kanellopoulos (Nov. 1–20, 1945). On March 31, 1946, Tsatsos was elected deputy in one of the Athens constituencies under the banner of National Union, an electoral formation led by Kanellopoulos. When Themistocles Sophoulis formed his second coalition government in January 1949, Tsatsos became minister of education, retaining this portfolio when Alexandros Diomedes succeeded Sophoulis (who died in June). Tsatsos failed at the general elections of March 1950, September 1951, and November 1952, but served as undersecretary of state for coordination in the Liberal government of Sophocles Venizelos (July–October 1951). He returned to the Vouli (Parliament) in February 1956 as a member of the National Radical Union of Karamanlis and from that date to June 1963 served as minister in the prime minister's office.

His many books include *Introduction to the Science of Justice* (1940) and *American Democracy* (1955). In 1961 he was elected a member of the Academy of Athens.

(K. M. SMOGORZEWSKI)

Tyler, Mary

Mary Tyler's account of her five years' imprisonment in India upon her return to Britain in July 1975 provided fresh evidence of the Indian government's current policies regarding human rights.

Tyler, a graduate teacher and translator who was born on July 11, 1943, at Tilbury, Essex, England, went to India for a six-month visit in January 1970. In Calcutta she met and married Amalendu Sen, an engineer with left-wing views whom she had first known in West Germany in 1966. In May 1970 she left Calcutta on a visit to some peasants in the country. She had, however, entered a disturbed area, where the Indian government suspected that Naxalites (Indian Maoists, their name taken from a district south of Darjeeling, where they had agitated for land reform) had set up a base. A police inspector's house was attacked on May 27, and as a result about 50 men were rounded up, as well as Tyler (allegedly arrested "in a jungle hideout and in possession of a sten gun and ammunition"). Later it was reported that the group, which included Sen but no one else known to her, had planned to blow up the uranium complex at Jadugoda, but no charge alleging this was in fact made.

At first Tyler expected a speedy release, but she was not committed for trial until August 1974, being moved for the hearing from the central jail at Hazaribagh to a prison in Jamshedpur. Her refusal to "confess," a course that might have secured swift release, probably forced the government to bring the accused men to trial. Her own trial finally began on June 23, 1975, before Sahdev Singh, known, for his incorruptibility, as "the English judge." Although the charges were soon withdrawn "for the sake of Commonwealth relations," Singh stated that the evidence brought was in any case insufficient to sustain them.

While in prison Tyler was at first confined alone but later mixed with other women prisoners. She wore Indian dress, chose to eat Indian food, and learned Hindi and Bengali. Back in England, she planned to write a book and worked for the release of her husband, still shackled in a Calcutta jail, and other political prisoners in India. (STEPHANIE MULLINS)

Vargas Llosa, Mario

One of Latin America's most respected novelists, Mario Vargas Llosa created an immediate sensation in 1962 with his first novel, *La ciudad y los perros* (*The Time of the Hero,* 1966, but literally "The City and the Dogs"). It was obvious to critics from the outset that this first work revealed a writer of natural power and assurance.

The background for Vargas' first book was his own vision of Peruvian society, the half-Indian, half-Spanish culture born of the merging of the Incas and the conquistadores. He displayed in this work the deep influence on his talent of Gustave

Flaubert and Victor Hugo and also Ernest Hemingway's gift for staccato dialogue.

In 1966 Vargas published his second novel, *La casa verde* (*The Green House,* 1968), which was acclaimed as better than the first. This chromatic tone poem propelled him to the forefront of Latin-American letters and certainly into first place among Peruvian writers. Critics have written that *La casa verde* is probably the most accomplished work of fiction ever to come out of Latin America. It is not easy reading because of its swirling, circular scope with overlapping scenes and shifting dimensions of time and identity. There is a similarity to the work of James Joyce.

Vargas was born March 28, 1936, in Arequipa. He studied in Bolivia and in Piura, Peru, before moving to Lima, where he attended the Leoncio Prado military college and studied literature at the National University of San Marcos. During this period he became a journalist and won a prize for articles written for the *Revue des Deux Mondes*.

Vargas lived in Madrid for a year before moving to Paris, where he continued to reside in 1975, teaching Spanish, working for French radio, and writing. During his brief stay in Madrid Vargas won the Leopoldo Alas Prize with a book of short stories, *Los jefes* ("The Chiefs"). Vargas' later works included *Los cachorros* in 1968 and a monumental two-volume work, *Conversación en la catedral,* published in 1969 and translated into English in 1975.

(JEREMIAH A. O'LEARY, JR.)

Veil, Simone

Minister of health from May 1974, when the new French government under Jacques Chirac was formed immediately after the election of Pres. Valéry Giscard d'Estaing, Simone Veil was the only woman to be given charge of a ministerial department at that time. Moreover, the ministry was an important one, with a budget considerably larger than that of the state itself; it was also a sensitive one, concerned not only with pressing problems of modernization and improvement of hospitals and medical care but also with fundamental questions of political and private morality—controversial matters (in a predominantly Roman Catholic country) such as contraception, abortion, and prostitution.

Simone Veil was the prime mover in major reforms that brought a liberalization of contraception policies and the passage of an act, which came into force in January 1975, legalizing abortion. She defended these measures on television and in Parliament and eventually secured their adoption by a combination of determination, common sense, and tact. Although the changes were already largely accepted by social custom and private morality, probably only a woman could have brought them onto the statute book; French law had until then treated abortion with extreme severity.

Simone Veil

ROBERT COHEN—AGIP/BLACK STAR

Born in Nice, France, in 1927, Simone Jacob was the daughter of an architect. Because of her Jewish ancestry she was deported to Germany in 1944, and many of her relations died in Nazi concentration camps. After the war she took a degree in law and studied at the Institut d'Études Politiques in Paris. Appointed to the Ministry of Justice in 1957, she was an assistant public prosecutor from 1959 to 1965. In 1969 she became a technical adviser to the keeper of the seals, René Pleven, and the following year was appointed secretary-general of the Higher Council of Judges, the body that assists the president of the republic in his role as supreme head of the judiciary; she was the first woman to hold that office. In the post of minister from 1974, her administrative experience, strength of personality, and natural authority earned her almost general admiration. Indeed, one opposition politician called her "the only real man in the government."

(PIERRE VIANSSON-PONTÉ)

Walker, John

On the evening of Aug. 12, 1975, John Walker stepped onto a track in Göteborg, Sweden, and made track-and-field history. Taking the lead on the third lap of the mile run, he ran away from the field to set a new world's record for the distance of 3 min. 49.4 sec. He was the first man to run the mile in under 3 min. 50 sec. and broke the previous record by a remarkable 1.6 sec.

Walker first burst onto the international track scene in 1974 when he finished second behind Tanzania's Filbert Bayi in the 1,500-m. run at the Commonwealth Games. Bayi set a world record of 3 min. 32.2 sec. in that race and then on May 17, 1975, set a world record of 3 min. 51.0 sec. in the mile. The second mark stood only three months, until Walker's effort at Göteborg.

Walker went to the starting line of the record-breaking race as a 23-year-old. He still lives in his home town of Manurewa, a suburb of Auckland, N.Z., and works as an advertising salesmen for a radio station in Auckland. At just over 6 ft. and weighing about 180 lb., he is large for a miler, one of the biggest middle-distance runners in the history of track and field. His size, however, appeared to give him the strength for endurance and for a finishing kick.

Until the Göteborg race, Walker's best mile time was 3 min. 52.2 sec., and he had never been able to beat Bayi. Three times he had finished second to the Tanzanian. Walker's record was an astounding ten seconds faster than that of Roger Bannister, who on May 6, 1954, became the first man to break the four-minute mile with a time of 3 min. 59.4 sec. (J. TIMOTHY WEIGEL)

Williamson, Malcolm Benjamin Graham Christopher

A leading composer in Britain since 1960, Australian-born Malcolm Williamson was appointed master of the queen's music in October 1975, in succession to Sir Arthur Bliss, who died earlier in the year (*see* OBITUARIES). The post, created in the reign of James I, entitled the holder to an annual stipend of £100 ($200). Because of Williamson's comparative youth—he was only 43 when appointed—the choice was surprising, but on reflection it seemed sensible: he was a fluent, accessible composer, who should have little difficulty in writing the pieces called for on royal occasions. His first test would probably come in the celebrations of the 25th anniversary of Queen Elizabeth II's accession to the throne, in 1977.

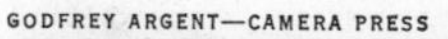

GODFREY ARGENT—CAMERA PRESS

Malcolm Williamson

Williamson was born on Nov. 21, 1931, in Sydney, New South Wales, where he was trained as a pianist and horn player and later as an organist. His first major success as a composer came in 1963 with the opera *Our Man in Havana,* and his dramatic gift became further evident in *The Violins of Saint-Jacques,* written for Sadler's Wells Opera in 1966, and in *Julius Caesar Jones, The Happy Prince,* and *The Red Sea,* written with children in mind.

Williamson also produced several attractive concertos, chamber pieces, and organ works. One of his most recent pieces, a commission for the London Promenade concerts in 1974, was entitled *Hammarskjöld Portrait,* a setting for soprano and orchestra of texts by the former UN secretary-general. He also proved to be adept at writing film and television scores and composed the music for the British Broadcasting Corporation's recent series "History of the English-Speaking Peoples," based on Winston Churchill's book of that name.

As a pianist he had appeared with most of the major orchestras in Britain and Australia, and he had lectured at several universities, including Princeton, where he was composer-in-residence at Westminster Choir College (1970–71). (ALAN BLYTH)

Wilson, (James) Harold

During 1975 Harold Wilson completed a total of more than seven years as Britain's prime minister, a period exceeded only by Herbert Asquith and Winston Churchill in the 20th century. Wilson had been leader of the Labour Party since 1963.

Wilson's adroitness in holding together a party of mixed economy social democrats on the right extending to declared Marxists on the left and relying on the support of the trade union movement was never more severely tested than in 1975. His party was deeply divided on British membership in the European Economic Community (EEC) and on inflation and incomes policy. By the

ULF ANDERSEN—NORMA/KATHERINE YOUNG

Harold Wilson

June referendum on EEC membership, Wilson was able not only to confirm the British role in Europe by an overwhelming majority, but also to end an acrimonious long-running quarrel inside the party. Confronted with inflation running at 25%, he was forced to abandon the "social contract" by which trade unions had undertaken to keep their wage claims voluntarily within certain limits and to substitute a flat rate ceiling for wage increases. Yet for this he won the support of a majority of unions. When the feud between the militant left wing and the centre-right of the party broke out in the autumn, Wilson intervened with a scathing rebuke for both extremes. By the end of the year, despite new dissension, mainly over the government decision to financially aid the Chrysler Corporation's U.K. operation, he seemed to be in as firm control of the party as ever. As some said, he had again proved himself the Houdini of British politics.

On the world scene Wilson was able to make decisive initiatives in EEC summit meetings. He was a pioneer of policies for stabilizing world trade in commodities, which he introduced at the Commonwealth heads of government conference in Jamaica in May. In Washington, D.C., and elsewhere he pressed on world leaders the need to avoid "beggar-my-neighbour" policies in tackling world inflation. In Moscow, Helsinki, and Bucharest he sought to promote détente between East and West.

Born March 11, 1916, in Huddersfield, Yorkshire, Wilson went as a scholarship boy to Oxford University, where he became a lecturer in economics before going into the civil service during World War II and then into Parliament in 1945. He became a Cabinet minister in Clement Attlee's government at the age of 31. (HARFORD THOMAS)

Wilson, Margaret Bush

For the first time in its 65-year history, the National Association for the Advancement of Colored People (NAACP) in 1975 chose as its national chairman a black woman, Margaret Bush Wilson. The only other woman ever to have held the post was Mary White Ovington, a white who served from 1917 to 1932.

An attorney who had been associated with civil rights throughout her adult life, Wilson was committed to the achievement of an integrated society. Her new position was a key one in terms of policymaking at the NAACP, with Executive Director Roy Wilkins serving under her. Although she foresaw no major changes in the orientation of the 400,000-member civil rights association, Wilson hoped to increase the participation of young blacks from the inner cities in the affairs of the NAACP.

Wilson grew up in a family active in the NAACP branch in St. Louis, Mo., where she was born on Jan. 30, 1919. She attended Talladega College in Alabama and Lincoln University School of Law in St. Louis. She worked for the Missouri Office of Urban Affairs from 1965 to 1967, established the Model Housing Corporation in St. Louis to get federal housing money for the black poor, served as deputy and then acting director of the St. Louis Model Cities program (1968–69), and was assistant director of St. Louis Lawyers for Housing (1969–72).

Wilson became active in the NAACP about 1956, when she helped in a campaign to urge local white businessmen to hire blacks. In 1958 she became the first woman to head the organization's St. Louis branch. After four years as president of the Missouri State Conference of Branches, which she

WIDE WORLD

had initiated, she was elected in 1963 to the national board of directors, where she became involved in fund raising and the internal affairs of the NAACP. In 1973 she was elected permanent chairman, or chief parliamentarian, of the national convention, a powerful and sought-after post. Wilson also served on the NAACP's task force on Pres. Lyndon Johnson's antipoverty and civil rights acts of 1964.

(JOAN NATALIE REIBSTEIN)

Wood, John

Playing the egregious Henry Carr in the Royal Shakespeare Company's coruscating production of Tom Stoppard's intellectual farce *Travesties,* British actor John Wood scored a resounding success on Broadway in 1975. A mock-biographical skit on literature and politics inspired by the coincidental presence in Zürich during World War I of Carr (a real-life British minor consular official) and Lenin, James Joyce, and the Dadaist Tristan Tzara, *Travesties* was written with Wood in mind for the leading role. The part was his second big success in the U.S. In 1974 he had starred in Washington, D.C., and on Broadway in the title role of the Royal Shakespeare's popular production of William Gillette's *Sherlock Holmes.* His performances in this and in *Travesties* won him the 1974 London *Evening Standard* and *Plays and Players* awards for best actor.

Wood was born in Harpenden, Hertfordshire, England, in 1930, and served in the Royal Horse Artillery as a lieutenant before going to Jesus College, Oxford, to study law. Like so many prominent actors before him, he began his stage career with OUDS (Oxford University Dramatic Society), of which he became president. At that time he directed and acted in a successful student production of *Richard III.* From Oxford he went to the Old Vic, where he stayed three years, playing anything from bit parts to a notable Richard II. In 1959 Peter Hall had cast him as Don Quixote in Tennessee Williams' *Camino Real* and as The Wali in Paul Tabori's *Brouhaha.* But Wood refused Hall's invitation to join the Royal Shakespeare, preferring television—with the notable exception of his performance in Stoppard's *Rosencrantz and Guildenstern Are Dead* on Broadway in 1967.

In 1969 Wood returned to the stage as Richard Rowan in Harold Pinter's revival of Joyce's *Exiles* at the Mermaid, winning the 1970 *Plays and Players* award for his performance. In 1971 he joined the Royal Shakespeare.

Wood's distinctive, angular appearance and vocal dexterity singled him out for such character roles as Yakov in Gorky's *Enemies,* Sir Fopling Flutter in Sir George Etherege's *The Man of Mode,* and Brutus in *Julius Caesar.* Among his films were *Nicholas and Alexandra* and *Slaughterhouse Five.* (OSSIA TRILLING)

Zaccagnini, Benigno

Elected national secretary of Italy's leading party, the Christian Democrats, on July 26, 1975, Benigno Zaccagnini was hailed as the party's "saviour." The former secretary, Amintore Fanfani, had resigned in the aftermath of the June 15–16 local elections, which had seen a sharp setback for the Christian Democrats and the upsurge of the Communists. In the struggle for power within the party that followed, Zaccagnini had remained on the sidelines; it was felt that as a "neutral" above party squabbles he was the right man to restore the Christian Democrats' image.

Zaccagnini was born on April 17, 1912, in Faenza, near Ravenna. He chose medicine as his profession and eventually became well known in medical circles as a consultant pediatrician. His political life started very early: a member of Azione Cattolica (Catholic Action) during the Mussolini years, he served as a medical officer in the Balkans during World War II. In 1943, after the armistice, he managed to reach the partisans of the Garibaldi Brigade, operating around Ravenna, and was later a member of the local Liberation Committee.

As political secretary of the Ravenna Christian Democrats, he was voted into the 1946 Constituent Assembly, which was to draft Italy's new constitution. In 1948, at the first postwar general elections, he became a deputy. After the 1953 elections, he was a member of the Labour and Social Services Committee. In 1954 he was elected to the party's National Committee. Four years later, after the 1958 elections, he became undersecretary for labour and social services in the Fanfani Cabinet. In the following Antonio Segni Cabinet, he was appointed minister. When Fanfani formed his third government, Zaccagnini became minister of public works and, soon afterward, chairman of the Christian Democrats' parliamentary group. After the 1968 elections he was nominated vice-chairman to the House of Deputies. On July 9, 1969, he became chairman of the party's National Committee. (FABIO GALVANO)

Some years the names of the Nobel Prize winners ring like notes plucked on a random musical scale. But in 1975 the 12 winners and their accomplishments struck many harmonious chords. The Prize for Economics, for instance, was shared by a Soviet and a U.S. scientist who had worked in identical problem areas of their respective nations' distinct economic systems. The Prizes for Physiology or Medicine, Physics, and Chemistry were all shared by scientists who had collaborated to some extent in their respective disciplines. In another area of relationships, one of the physicists, Aage Bohr, was the son of a previous Nobel laureate.

Regarding Andrey D. Sakharov, the first Soviet citizen ever to win the Prize for Peace, a U.S. news magazine wrote: "Of all the 72 recipients of the prize since 1901, probably none comes closer than Sakharov to the spirit of [Alfred] Nobel's bequest. The father of the Soviet hydrogen bomb, Sakharov went on to become an indefatigable fighter for thermonuclear disarmament and democracy in the U.S.S.R." The consonance between benefactor and honouree was particularly close here; Nobel, inventor of dynamite, dedicated the fortunes earned from his explosive product to the annual awards that bear his name.

Another form of harmony was seen in the kind of reception that the announcements received. With the notable exception of official Soviet diatribes against Sakharov's selection, there was little grumbling or criticism. This was in sharp contrast to some years and suggested that the recipients were widely regarded as worthy of the honours they received. In 1975 each prize, awarded on December 10, the 79th anniversary of Nobel's death, carried an honorarium of $143,000.

Prize for Peace

Andrey Dmitriyevich Sakharov, sole winner of the Prize for Peace, outspokenly advocated civil liberties and reform in the Soviet Union as well as rapprochement with non-Communist nations. Widely admired throughout the world for his courage and humanitarian beliefs, he was a prophet without honour in the eyes of his own nation's government.

In selecting him for the award, the Nobel Committee of the Norwegian Parliament said: "Uncompromisingly and forcefully, Sakharov has fought not only against the abuse of power and violations of human dignity in all its forms, but he has with equal vigour fought for the ideal of a state founded on the principle of justice for all. In a convincing fashion Sakharov has emphasized that the inviolable rights of man can serve as the only sure foundation for a genuine and long-lasting system of international cooperation. In this manner he has succeeded very effectively, and under trying conditions, in reinforcing respect for such values as all true friends of peace are anxious to support."

Andrey Dmitriyevich Sakharov, Peace

WIDE WORLD

Born in Moscow May 21, 1921, Sakharov followed his father's example and became a physicist. His exceptional scientific promise was recognized early. He won a doctorate at the age of 26 and was admitted as a full member of the Soviet Academy of Sciences at 32. By that time he had worked for several years as a theoretical physicist to develop the first hydrogen bomb, the most devastating weapon in the history of human warfare. As a preeminent and productive scientist, he was accorded luxuries and honours reserved for the favourites of the authoritarian government.

But in 1961 he went on record against Premier Nikita S. Khrushchev's plan to test a 100-megaton bomb in the atmosphere, fearing that the radioactive fallout from the test would have widespread ill effects. Three years later Sakharov got in political hot water by mobilizing opposition against a Khrushchev nominee to the Academy of Sciences. In 1968 he published a soon-to-be-famous plea for nuclear arms reduction by all nuclear powers. He also predicted and endorsed the eventual integration of Communist and capitalist systems, an idea supported by the selection of the 1975 economics prize winners (*see* below).

These actions and later writings put Sakharov at distinct odds with the Soviet government. Continuing to speak out against political repression at home and hostile relations abroad, he became the target of official censure, harassment, and humiliation. Many observers said that only his international stature saved him from worse punishment.

Predictably, the Soviet authorities swiftly announced that Sakharov would be prohibited from going to Norway to accept the peace prize. Their explanation was that he possessed scientific secrets, a rationale Sakharov considered nonsense because he had done no research since 1968. The refusal to let him go abroad echoed similar restrictions placed on two recent Soviet winners of the Prize for Literature, Boris L. Pasternak and Aleksandr I. Solzhenitsyn.

Prize for Literature

The Swedish Academy of Letters awarded the Prize for Literature to Eugenio Montale, the venerable and reclusive dean of Italian poetry. Named a senator for life in 1967, Montale had long been considered one of Italy's three major modern poets, along with Giuseppe Ungaretti and Salvatore Quasimodo, who won the literature prize in 1959. In awarding the 1975 prize, the Academy noted that Montale is now "being recognized more and more indisputably as one of the most important poets of the contemporary West."

Insiders believed that Montale had been promoted for some years by Anders Österling, the Academy's former secretary and a personal friend who had translated Montale into Swedish. He was known to have been favoured by the older Academy members.

The citation said that Montale's "distinctive poetry with great artistic sensitivity has interpreted human values under the sign of an outlook on life that has no illusions. . . . There is a negativism based not on misanthropy but on an indelible feeling for the value of life and the dignity of mankind. That is what gives Eugenio Montale's poetry its innate strength."

Montale was born on Oct. 12, 1896, in Genoa and trained to become a musician. He abandoned a promising career as a baritone for literature, helping to found the short-lived literary magazine *Primo Tempo* when he was 22.

As a young man he was a leader of the Hermetic School, which fostered modernistic structure, free rhyming, and innovative word combinations. One de facto purpose of the school was to let intellectuals express themselves more freely despite the growing Fascist restraints of the time. Montale worked as an editor and critic, serving as director of the Gabinetto Vieusseux Library in Florence for ten years until political pressure forced his removal in 1938. Also active as a translator, he interpreted such diverse writers in English as Herman Melville, Eugene O'Neill, Shakespeare, T. S. Eliot, and Gerard Manley Hopkins. Both Eliot and Robert Lowell translated his work into English.

Montale's literary style was generally crisp and terse, and his output slim. In 50 years he published only five books of poems, *The Occasions, The Storm and Other Things, Satura, Diary of '71 and '72,* and *Cuttlefish Bones.*

When he learned of the award, Montale had the telephone disconnected in his Milan apartment and went into seclusion after issuing a statement of thanks through his publisher. Asked what he wished to communicate, he said, "My poetry should not be understood as a message but as an invitation to hope."

Prize for Chemistry

John Warcup Cornforth of Britain and Vladimir Prelog of Switzerland shared the 1975 Prize for Chemistry. Both were recog-

John Warcup Cornforth, Chemistry

UPI COMPIX

nized for their work in stereochemistry, which deals with the three-dimensional arrangement of atoms within molecules.

Variations in molecular arrangements are of seminal importance to the behaviour and properties of biochemical substances. While a rose might be a rose under any circumstances, two molecules of identical composition can have different, mirror-image configurations (like a person's right and left hands). As a result their properties can be significantly different, as in the single substance that smells like spearmint or like caraway essence depending on its "right-handed" or "left-handed" configuration.

The Royal Swedish Academy of Sciences judged the work of both men to be "of fundamental importance to an understanding of biological processes." Their accomplishments also have vast applications extending far beyond the research laboratory, particularly in the fields of medicine, industry, and agriculture.

Cornforth was born in Sydney, Australia, in 1917. He studied at the university there and took a doctorate at Oxford University in 1941. During World War II he worked with Sir Robert Robinson, winner of the 1947 chemistry prize for discovering the structure of penicillin. Subsequently, Cornforth investigated enzymes, the proteins that catalyze changes in organic compounds by taking the place of hydrogen atoms in a substance's molecular chains and rings. The work was extraordinarily complex because it involved determining specifically which cluster of hydrogen atoms in a compound is replaced by an enzyme to cause a given effect. Cornforth developed techniques to pinpoint the specific hydrogen component by using the element's three isotopes. Because each isotope has a different reaction speed, copious experimentation and careful observation could reveal which hydrogen atom in a molecule was affected. In the course of his work Cornforth examined the minute alterations that occur at every point in the exceptionally complex cholesterol molecule.

The Academy noted that his work was "an outstanding intellectual achievement" —even by the particularly exacting standards of biochemistry. Cornforth's success in these demanding pursuits has been attributed to his unshakable concentration, a facility aided by what many people consider a tragic handicap: total deafness since young manhood. For him it has been at least a partial asset for, as his wife says, "He can't be interrupted easily."

Following World War II Cornforth joined the staff of Britain's Medical Research Council. In 1962 he became director of the Milstead Laboratory of Chemical Enzymology, a Shell Research facility in Kent, near London. Three years later he became an associate professor at the University of Warwick and six years after that a visiting professor at the University of Sussex, where in 1975 he was a Royal Society professor.

Prelog was born in Sarajevo, then in the Austro-Hungarian empire, in 1906 and was trained at the Technical University in Prague. He once studied with Leopold Ruzicka, who shared the chemistry prize in 1939. Prelog's early career was spent as an industrial chemist. In 1935 he joined the University of Zagreb faculty and then emigrated to Switzerland in 1941 after the Nazi takeover of Yugoslavia. He became a member of the faculty at the Federal Institute of Technology in Zürich, where Einstein had once taught.

Using X-ray techniques, Prelog determined the structures of several antibiotics. He also formulated systematic rules for identifying whether a molecule is right-handed or left-handed.

Prize for Physics

The physics prize was shared equally by Aage N. Bohr, Ben Roy Mottelson, and L. James Rainwater for work that fundamentally advanced atomic science nearly a quarter-century ago. Working in loose collaboration, the three achieved a deep understanding of the atomic nucleus that paved the way for nuclear fusion.

The Royal Swedish Academy of Sciences specified that the three were honoured for "the discovery of the connection between collective motion and particle motion in atomic nuclei and the development of the theory of the structure of the atomic nucleus based on this connection."

Scientists had first hypothesized that the nucleus of an atom was shaped like a drop of liquid. Exceptions to this rule led to the notion that the orbits of nuclear particles were arranged in concentric shells. Then further study suggested that these shells were not spherically symmetrical, a notion that was as unappealing as it was unexpected. Meeting with the press after the Nobel announcement, Rainwater recalled a seminar at Columbia University in 1949 when that idea was presented by Charles H. Townes, who was later to become a Nobel laureate himself. "It seemed obvious," Rainwater said, "that if nuclei weren't always perfectly spherical they might have radically asymmetrical shapes."

In April 1950 Rainwater wrote a paper in which he observed that the greater portion of nuclear particles form an inner nucleus while other particles form an outer nucleus. The shape of each set of particles, which are all in constant motion at tremendous velocities, affects the other set of particles. If some of the outer particles moved in similar orbits, he postulated, unequal centrifugal forces of enormous power would be created. These, in turn, could be strong enough to permanently deform the ideally symmetrical nucleus.

While Rainwater was wrestling with this explanation, his co-worker at Columbia was Aage Bohr, then a visiting professor. Struck by the promise of Rainwater's theory, Bohr worked out a more detailed explanation after returning to his native Denmark. In the next three years Bohr and Mottelson, his associate in Copenhagen, jointly published the results of experimental studies which provided data that confirmed the theoretical work.

Rainwater, born in Council, Idaho, on Dec. 9, 1917, received a physics degree from the California Institute of Technology in 1939. He then began his career-long association with Columbia University, where he received two advanced degrees. He remained there as an instructor, assistant professor, and associate professor, and was named to a full professorship in 1952. During two separate periods he served as director of the university's cyclotron, and he won the U.S. Atomic Energy Commission's E. O. Lawrence Memorial Award.

Bohr, born June 19, 1922, is the son of Niels Bohr, the founder of atomic theory who won the physics prize the year of his son's birth. During World War II both father and son worked on the Manhattan Project, which developed the first atomic bomb. After his father's death in 1962, Aage Bohr became director of the Nordic Institute for Theoretical Physics in Copenhagen, also known as the Niels Bohr Institute.

On receiving the award, he said, "I consider this a collective award and in a wider sense this is actually an international achievement thanks to cooperation and processes of development over a long time.

David Baltimore, Physiology or Medicine

WIDE WORLD

Renato Dulbecco, Physiology or Medicine

WIDE WORLD

Howard Temin, Physiology or Medicine

WIDE WORLD

Actually I feel that my father's institute has been given the prize."

Mottelson was born in Chicago on July 9, 1926. After earning a doctorate in theoretical physics at Harvard University, he won a fellowship at the Bohr Institute. There he and Aage Bohr discovered that they complemented each other perfectly. Subsequently, Mottelson took Danish citizenship.

Prize for Physiology or Medicine

When Renato Dulbecco was investigating animal viruses at California Institute of Technology in the late 1950s, one of his young assistants was Howard Temin. When Dulbecco studied cancer cell development at the Salk Institute for Biological Studies in La Jolla, Calif., in the late 1960s, David Baltimore assisted him for a time. All three subsequently shared the 1975 Nobel Prize for Physiology or Medicine for "discoveries concerning the interaction between tumour viruses and the genetic material of the cell."

The Nobel Committee of Sweden's Karolinska Institute noted that "viruses causing tumours in man have not been demonstrated except in the case of wart virus. The type of tumours caused by this virus are of a benign nature. It appears likely, however, that viruses will be found to be involved in the appearance of at least certain tumours of more serious nature to man. Technology to study such a possible relationship is available today and the conceptual foundation for an examination of this problem has been provided by the discoveries made by [these] Nobel Prize winners."

During their investigations the three scientists made some fundamental discoveries about the behaviour of normal cells, cancer cells, and enzymes. One specific discovery involved new information about the transferral of genetic information by ribonucleic acid (RNA) and deoxyribonucleic acid (DNA). In the late 1950s Dulbecco had questioned how viruses could make malignant changes in a normal cell. By 1967 he was able to clarify the fundamental aspects of the larger question and describe the difficulties in finding answers. As one science analyst described it, "A direct attack on the cancer problem was impossible . . . because in a cell several thousand genes made their products in the form of enzymes. . . . These products, in turn, gave rise to such an inextricable maze of biochemical pathways that it was impossible to identify the consequences of the primary cancer change in the jungle of gene effects."

The best approach, therefore, was to make educated guesses and test them by working backward. As Dulbecco described it, "We introduce into a cell a small number of viral genes whose functions can be known, and we determine, by a suitable exclusion procedure, which one is responsible for the cancerous change."

By that time scientists had accepted as dogma the notion that genetic change could only be caused by the master molecule DNA via the messenger molecule RNA. Temin, by then working at the University of Wisconsin, postulated that the accepted dogma was incorrect and predicted that a certain enzyme could be responsible for the reverse effect. Then he and Baltimore independently proved the existence of such an enzyme, dubbed "reverse transcriptase."

Dulbecco was born in Catanzaro, Italy, on Feb. 22, 1914, and earned a medical degree at the University of Turin in 1936. He has been awarded honorary degrees by the University of Glasgow and Yale University and won the Albert and Mary Lasker Basic Medical Research Award. A naturalized citizen of the U.S., he later moved to London to perform research at the Imperial Cancer Research Fund Laboratory.

Born in Philadelphia on Dec. 10, 1934, Temin obtained his doctorate at the California Institute of Technology, Pasadena. Formerly a U.S. Public Health Service fellow, he became professor of oncology (the study of tumours) at the University of Wisconsin in 1969.

Baltimore was born in New York City on March 7, 1938, and received his doctorate from Rockefeller Institute. He received the Eli Lilly Award administered by the American Association for the Advancement of Science, and in 1973 became a research professor at Massachusetts Institute of Technology.

Prize for Economics

Two theoreticians whose works were aimed at and applied to diametrically opposite economic systems shared the 1975 Prize for Economics. They were Leonid V. Kantorovich of the Soviet Institute of Economic Management and Tjalling C. Koopmans of Yale University. The two men were chosen by the Royal Swedish Academy of Sciences "for their contributions to the theory of optimum allocation of resources," a matter of basic practical importance to both collective and free-enterprise economic systems.

Their citation said, in part: "As they have formulated the problems and described the connection between production results and productive inputs in new ways, these two scholars have been able to achieve highly significant results. . . . Early in his research, Professor Kantorovich applied the analytical technique of linear programming to demonstrate how economic planning in his country could be improved. Professor Koopmans, for his part, has shown . . . that on the basis of certain efficiency criteria it is possible directly to make important deductions concerning optimum price systems."

Koopmans was born in The Netherlands on Aug. 28, 1910, studied mathematics and physics at the University of Utrecht, and earned a doctorate in economics from the University of Leiden in 1936. He taught at the University of Rotterdam and worked in the financial section of the League of Nations before coming to the U.S. in 1940 where he performed research at Princeton University and lectured at New York University.

The work that led to Koopmans' Nobel citation started with some elementary problem-solving during World War II when he "was in the humble role of statistician for the British Merchant Mission" in Washington, D.C. Working with the Allied Combined Shipping Adjustment Board, he sought "the best way to make the empty ships travel from where they shed their cargo to the next destination." In time he became an originator of econometrics, a discipline that attempts to measure economic developments and use mathematical models to simulate economic behaviour.

After World War II Koopmans joined the Cowles Commission for Research in Economics at the University of Chicago. In 1955 that institution relocated at Yale University, where he became professor of economics and a director of the then Cowles Foundation. Koopmans became a naturalized U.S. citizen in 1946.

Like his co-winner, Kantorovich made some early discoveries while working on a basic logistical problem, the most efficient use of transportation via the Siberian railroad. In 1939 he worked out a method of "linear programming" that helped policymakers reach goals such as maximum output in the face of problems like limited availability of materials. That work was ignored by the Soviet government because it contradicted the accepted economic ideology, which relied on subjective judgments by planners. According to one account, Kantorovich's theories were so unorthodox that associates thought he had taken leave of his senses. In later years Kantorovich jested that this appraisal might have been very fortunate since unorthodox thinking, when taken seriously during the Stalin era, was punished by persecution and imprisonment.

Born in St. Petersburg (later Leningrad) on Jan. 19, 1912, Kantorovich won a doctorate from the University of Leningrad when he was 18 and became a full professor there at 22. In time his theories won the approval of post-Stalin authorities. He was elected to full membership in the Soviet Academy of Sciences in 1964 and won the Lenin Prize.

For many years Kantorovich served as deputy director of the Mathematics Institute in Novosibirsk. In 1971 he became director of a mathematical economics laboratory established for him in Moscow's Institute of Economic Management.

(PHILIP KOPPER)

Leonid V. Kantorovich, Economics

WIDE WORLD

Tjalling C. Koopmans, Economics

WIDE WORLD

OBITUARIES

The following is a selected list of prominent men and women who died during 1975.

Adams, Sir Walter, British educator (b. Brighton, England, Dec. 16, 1906—d. Salisbury, Rhodesia, May 21, 1975), began a long, and often stormy, career in education as a lecturer in history (1926–34) at his alma mater, the University College of London University. Following his appointment in 1946 as first secretary of the Inter-University Council for Higher Education Overseas he established first-class British-type schools in Asia, Africa, Malta, and the West Indies. His years as head of the University College of Rhodesia and Nyasaland (1955–67) coincided with social and political unrest. Adams, who was sometimes criticized for his weak resistance to government policies and for insisting on standards that were deemed unrealistic for black graduates of poorly financed secondary schools, left the school and the country in 1967. He was then named director of the London School of Economics and Political Science, only to find himself in the midst of further turmoil. The havoc created by dissident students gradually subsided as they were allowed greater participation in academic and administrative decisions. Adams, who was knighted in 1970, retired in 1974.

Adderley, Julian Edwin ("Cannonball"), U.S. musician (b. Tampa, Fla., Sept. 15, 1928—d. Gary, Ind., Aug. 8, 1975), was a Florida high school band director and local jazzman when, during a 1955 visit to New York City, he volunteered to fill in for a tardy alto saxophonist at the Cafe Bohemia. He was such a hit that within days EmArcy Records signed him to an exclusive contract. During the next few years Adderley formed a quintet, joined the Miles Davis Sextet, toured with George Shearing, and rounded up a new quintet, whose "This Here" launched an era of social jazz. Adderley's popularity, during a period dominated by rock, was demonstrated by such hits as "Mercy, Mercy, Mercy" and numerous requests to appear on college campuses.

Alexanderson, Ernst Frederik Werner, Swedish-born electrical engineer (b. Uppsala, Sweden, Jan. 25, 1878—d. Schenectady, N.Y., May 14, 1975), revolutionized wireless communications by inventing (1906) a high frequency alternator that made possible the first radio transmission of speech and music. In addition to repeatedly upgrading the quality of his alternator, he significantly improved transmitting and receiving antennas, ship-propulsion and electric train systems, and telephone relays. His selective tuning device still forms part of modern radio systems. He also developed the amplidyne, an automatic control system; it was first used in factories to automate delicate manufacturing processes but its applications are virtually limitless. In 1927 he demonstrated television in his home and gave the first public exhibition in 1930. Alexanderson, who retired from the General Electric Co. in 1948 after 46 years of service, renewed an earlier association with RCA in 1952 and developed a colour television receiver that became his 321st patent.

Andric, Ivo, Yugoslav novelist and diplomat (b. Travnik, Bosnia, Oct. 10, 1892—d. Belgrade, Yugos., March 13, 1975), was awarded the Nobel Prize for Literature in 1961, mainly for two novels about Bosnia under Turkish rule: *Na Drini cuprija* (1945; *The Bridge on the Drina*) and *Travnicka hronika* (1945; *Bosnian Story*). Most of his fiction, including dozens of stories, was set in his native Bosnia. As a Serbian patriot opposed to Austrian rule he was imprisoned for three years after the 1914 assassination of Archduke Francis Ferdinand. During this period he produced his lyrical prose journal *Ex Ponto* (1918), which established his reputation, and studied the philosophical writings of Søren Kierkegaard, whose pessimism influenced Andric for years to come. After his release, he studied philosophy at the universities of Zagreb, Vienna, Krakow, and Graz. Following the creation of Yugoslavia Andric joined its diplomatic service and served successively in Rome, Bucharest, Madrid, Brussels, Geneva, and finally Berlin.

Arendt, Hannah, German-born political philosopher (b. Hanover, Germany, Oct. 14, 1906—d. New York, N.Y., Dec. 4, 1975), was highly regarded for her studies on totalitarianism and her critical writings on Jewish affairs. She was educated at the universities of Marburg, Freiberg, and Heidelberg, where she received her Ph.D. in 1928. When the Nazis came to power in Germany in 1933 she fled to Paris and later to New York City where she served as research director of the Conference on Jewish Relations (1944–46), chief editor of Schocken Books (1946–48), and executive director (1949–52) of Jewish Cultural Reconstruction, Inc., which sought to salvage Jewish writings dispersed by the Nazis. In her monumental *The Origins of Totalitarianism* (1951) Arendt related totalitarianism to 19th-century anti-Semitism and imperialism and saw its growth as the outcome of the disintegration of the traditional nation-state. Because of their pursuit of raw political power and neglect of material or utilitarian considerations, she argued, totalitarian regimes have revolutionized the social structure and made contemporary politics nearly unpredictable. *Origins* established her as a major political thinker. Her most controversial book was *Eichmann in Jerusalem* (1963), in which Jewish community leaders were accused of facilitating Nazi atrocities against the Jews during World War II.

Aron, Robert, French historian (b. Le Vésinet, Seine-et-Oise, France, May 25, 1898—d. Paris, France, April 19, 1975), published a monumental series of books on modern French history, including *Histoire de Vichy* (1954), *Histoire de la libération de la France* (1959), *De Gaulle* (1964), and *Histoire de l'épuration* (4 vol., 1967–75). He also published works on religion and on the history of Israel, including *Les Années obscures de Jésus* (1960) and *Le Dieu des origines des cavernes du Sinai* (1964). He was awarded the Prix Femina-Vacaresco in 1961 and was elected a member of the Académie Française shortly before his death.

Ashbridge, Sir Noel, British electrical engineer (b. Wanstead, Essex, England, Dec. 10, 1889—d. Speldhurst, Kent, England, June 4, 1975), spent virtually his entire professional career with the British Broadcasting Corporation (BBC). A graduate of London University, he was among the first to operate wireless equipment in the front lines during World War I. Then, after a stint with the Marconi Company (1920–26), he became assistant chief engineer (1926–29) at BBC. He was subsequently named controller of engineering (1929–48), deputy director general (1943–48), and director of technical services. Ashbridge's mastery of electrical engineering provided the BBC with the technology needed to meet the special demands of wartime broadcasting and the commercial use of such things as very-high-frequency radio transmissions and colour television. He was knighted in 1935.

Baker, Josephine, U.S.-born French entertainer (b. St. Louis, Mo., June 3, 1906—d. Paris, France, April 12, 1975), appeared on Broadway and in Harlem nightclubs as a teenager before going to Paris (1925) to dance in *La Revue Nègre* at the Théâtre des Champs-Elysées and later to star at the Folies-Bergère. Parisians, who loved the unencumbered exuberance of her acts, immediately took her to their hearts as a symbol of the beauty and vitality of Afro-American culture. Baker, whose flamboyant life-style also delighted her devotees, made her screen singing debut in 1934. Having become a French citizen in 1937, she worked with the Resistance during World War II and entertained troops in Africa and the Middle East. After the war she purchased Les Milandes, an estate in southwestern France, which from the early 1950s became a home for her "rainbow family"—12 orphans of various nationalities. To maintain the home, she came out of retirement in 1959 and gave one triumphant performance after another in such diverse places as Japan, Turkey, Mexico, Yugoslavia, Tunisia, and South Africa. She was also active in the civil rights movement in the U.S. in the 1960s. Baker collapsed at the Bobino in Paris during the third week of an elaborate revue celebrating the 50th anniversary of her Parisian debut. Her *Mémoires* appeared in 1949.

ROBERT COHEN—AGIP/PICTORIAL PARADE

Josephine Baker

Bando Mitsugoro VIII, Japanese Kabuki actor (b. Tokyo, Japan, Oct. 19, 1906—d. Kyoto, Japan, Jan. 16, 1975), made his debut on the classical Kabuki stage at the age of seven under the name Yososuke. He succeeded to the professional name of Bando Minosuke in 1928, gained considerable fame acting with such theatrical groups as the Osanai Kaoru Troupe, Toho Company, and Kansai Shochiku Company, and became headmaster of the Bando School of Japanese Dance. He then succeeded to the Mitsugoro name, borne by his illustrious father Mitsugoro VII. Considered by many to be Japan's greatest Kabuki actor in male roles (all female roles are also played by males), Mitsugoro was especially effective playing an old man or a villain. His numerous writings include theoretical works of great insight. In 1966 Mitsugoro received the Japan Art Academy Award and the Purple Ribbon Medal, and in 1973 he was designated a Living National Treasure by the Japanese government. Bando died after inadvertently eating the poisonous livers of several globefish.

CHIAKI YOSHIDA

Beaufré, André, French army general (b. Neuilly-sur-Seine, France, Jan. 25, 1902—d. Belgrade, Yugos., Feb. 12, 1975), was an outstanding military strategist and historian, and an articulate defender of Pres. Charles de Gaulle's plan for an independent nuclear force for France. Beaufré attended the military academy at Saint-Cyr, the École Supérieure de Guerre, and the École Libre des Sciences Politiques before being assigned to the army general staff. While serving (1940–41) as permanent secretary of national defense in Algeria, he was arrested by the pro-German French Vichy regime, but was released in 1942 and joined the Free French Army. After World War II he served in Indochina and Algeria, and commanded the landing force that tried to seize the Suez Canal in 1956. Beaufré later became chief of the general staff of SHAPE (Supreme Headquarters, Allied Powers in Europe) and was raised to the rank of general of the army while in Washington, D.C., as French representative to NATO. Beaufré's reputation as a military strategist was greatly enhanced by such books as *Introduction à la stratégie* (1963), *Dissuasion et stratégie* (1964), *L'O.T.A.N. et L'Europe* (1966; *NATO and Europe*), and *Mémoires, la nature des choses* (1969).

Bech, Joseph, Luxembourg statesman (b. Diekirch, Luxembourg, Feb. 17, 1887—d. Luxembourg, March 8, 1975), as prime minister (1953–58) and longtime foreign minister of the Grand Duchy was directly involved in international affairs for more than 30 years. He was a member of Luxembourg's Chamber of Deputies for 50 years and played an important part in negotiations that brought into existence such significant organizations as Benelux, the European Coal and Steel Community, NATO, and the European Economic Community (Common Market). Following his retirement he was awarded the Charlemagne and Robert Schuman prizes.

Benton, Thomas Hart, U.S. painter (b. Neosho, Mo., April 15, 1889—d. Kansas City, Mo., Jan. 19, 1975), was an American Regionalist, whose brilliant-coloured murals and paintings memorialized the ordinary lives of very ordinary people. Impatient with "modern French art," which he felt meant nothing to the general public, Benton roamed the nation and found inspiration in sharecroppers, riverboats, miners, prize fights, dance halls, hillbilly sweethearts, and folks at home. In his murals he developed an innovative technique by dividing one scene from another with arbitrary borders so that the changes in scale and the overlapping produced an effect not unlike photomontage. Examples of such murals are "Arts of the West" at the New Britain Museum of American Art in Connecticut and those at the New School for Social Research and at the Whitney Museum of American Art, both in New York.

Benton was educated at the Art Institute of Chicago and the Académie Julien in Paris. He taught at the Art Students League in New York, where Jackson Pollock was one of his pupils, and at the Kansas City Art Institute and School of Design in Missouri. His autobiography, *An Artist in America,* was published in 1937.

Billings, John Shaw, U.S. publishing executive (b. Beech Island, S.C., May 11, 1898—d. Augusta, Ga., Aug. 26, 1975), retired from Time, Inc., in 1955 after a remarkable 27-year career that involved a sudden switch from managing editor of *Time* to managing editor of *Life* just 17 days before the new magazine was scheduled for the presses. Billings took charge amid great confusion, met the deadline, and in virtually no time turned *Life* into the greatest magazine success of its day. In 1944, with some four million copies of *Life* selling each week, he became editorial director of Time, Inc., having already added a new dimension to news reporting with photojournalism.

Bjerknes, Jacob Aall Bonnevie, Norwegian-American meteorologist (b. Stockholm, Sweden, Nov. 2, 1897—d. Los Angeles, Calif., July 7, 1975), spent a lifetime studying the dynamics of the atmosphere, especially as an aid to forecasting weather, and was among the first to use photographs taken by high-altitude rockets for his meteorological research. During World War I he helped his father, Vilhelm F. K. Bjerknes, establish a network of Norwegian weather stations, which provided data for an understanding of polar fronts. One of his later major contributions was an analysis of the atmospheric dynamics that create cyclones. Bjerknes joined the faculty of the University of California at Los Angeles in 1940 and was awarded a gold medal by the World Meteorological Organization in 1959.

Bliss, Sir Arthur Edward Drummond, British composer (b. Barnes, London, England, Aug. 2, 1891—d. London, March 27, 1975), whose distinguished work led to his appointment as master of the queen's music in 1953, studied music at Pembroke College, Cambridge, and briefly at the Royal College of Music, London. He was encouraged in his music by Edward Elgar, Ralph Vaughan Williams, and Gustav Holst. His early works include *Conversations* and *A Colour Symphony*. From the mid-1920s his music became less experimental. Vocal compositions, the solemn choral symphony *Morning Heroes, Pastoral,* and *Serenade* followed. *Music for Strings*

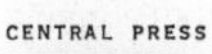
CENTRAL PRESS

was introduced at the 1935 Salzburg Festival. His dramatic music included scores for the films *Things to Come* (1934–35) and *Men of Two Worlds* (1945), the ballets *Checkmate* (1937), *Miracle in the Gorbals* (1944), and *Adam Zero* (1946), and the operas *The Olympians* (produced 1949, Covent Garden, London) and *Tobias and the Angel* (1960, designed for television). The sacred choral works *The Beatitudes* (1962) and *Mary of Magdala* (1963) were written for the Coventry and Worcester music festivals, respectively. Bliss was visiting professor at the University of California at Berkeley for a short time but returned to London to organize music services at the British Broadcasting Corporation (1941–44). He was knighted in 1950 and published his autobiography, *As I Remember,* in 1970.

Bronk, Detlev Wulf, U.S. scientist and educator (b. New York, N.Y., Aug. 13, 1897—d. New York, N.Y., Nov. 17, 1975), is generally considered to be the father of biophysics, the application of physics to living organisms. After obtaining his doctorate from the University of Michigan, Bronk taught physiology and biophysics and headed the Institute of Neurology at the University of Pennsylvania. He then became president of Johns Hopkins University (1949–53) and later president of Rockefeller Institute (1953–68), a medical research facility that became Rockefeller University in 1965. During these years Bronk also held such other important academic positions as head of the National Academy of Sciences (1950–62) and president of the American Association for the Advancement of Science. Throughout his career he had a powerful and innovative influence on research and scholarship.

Brundage, Avery, U.S. sports administrator (b. Detroit, Mich., Sept. 28, 1887—d. Garmisch-Partenkirchen, West Germany, May 8, 1975), was for 20 years the controversial and domineering president of the International Olympic Committee (IOC) and did more to set the tone of

UPI COMPIX

Avery Brundage

the modern Olympic Games than any other individual. So convinced was he of the need to preserve amateurism ("a sort of religion") in all its purity that he threatened or punished athletes for even relatively minor infractions of his stringent rules. In addition, he created a furor more than once by dismissing highly significant political events as unrelated to Olympic competition. In this spirit he overrode vociferous opposition during the 1972 Munich Olympics when he insisted that the Games must go on after 11 Israeli athletes were murdered by Palestinian guerrillas. Earlier he refused to boycott the 1936 Games in Nazi Germany.

Three years after participating in the pentathlon and decathlon at the Stockholm Olympics (1912), Brundage founded his own construction company with a few thousand dollars and eventually became a multimillionaire. His interest in amateur sports, however, never abated. He served seven years (1928–33, 1935) as president of the Amateur Athletic Union and was president of the U.S. Olympic Association and Committee (1929–53). In 1936 he was elected to the IOC. As its vice-president (1945–52) and president (1952–72) Brundage exemplified his principle of absolute noncommercialism in Olympic sports by devoting as much as six months a year to a post that paid no salary or personal expenses. Another of his major interests was Oriental art. Throughout the years he acquired some 8,000 items, one of the finest privately owned collections of its kind in the world, now displayed in the Asian Art Museum of San Francisco.

Buchman, Sidney, U.S. film producer and scenarist (b. Duluth, Minn., March 27, 1902—d. Cannes, France, Aug. 23, 1975), launched his writing career with a script for Cecil B. DeMille's *Sign of the Cross* (1932). His greatest success, *Mr. Smith Goes to Washington* (1939), was followed by such other well-known pictures as *Jolson Sings Again* (1949) and the adaptation of Mary McCarthy's *The Group* (1966), both of which Buchman produced. He was also one of the many writers hired to work on the extravaganza *Cleopatra* (1963).

Bulganin, Nikolay Aleksandrovich, Soviet statesman (b. Nizhny Novgorod, Russia, June 11, 1895—d. Moscow, U.S.S.R., Feb. 24, 1975), was an industrial and economic administrator and premier of the Soviet Union from 1955 to 1958. He began his career as a Cheka (secret police) officer in 1918, was transferred to the Supreme Council of National Economy in 1922, and five years later became manager of Moscow's leading electrical equipment factory. In 1931 he was made chairman of the Moscow Soviet and later became premier of the Russian Soviet Federated Socialist Republic (1937–38), chairman of the Soviet Union's state bank, deputy premier of the Soviet Union, and a full member of the Central Committee of the Communist Party (1939).

During World War II he served as the political officer on the councils of several military districts and earned the rank of general. In 1944 he was included in Stalin's elite war cabinet, the State Defense Committee. Later he resumed the

KEYSTONE

Nikolay Aleksandrovich Bulganin

post of deputy premier of the Soviet Union (1947), succeeded Stalin as minister of the armed forces (1947), and became a full member of the Politburo of the Central Committee (1948). After Stalin's death (March 1953) Bulganin became deputy premier and minister of defense in the government of Georgy Malenkov. During the power struggle between Malenkov and Nikita Khrushchev, Bulganin supported Khrushchev, and he was named to replace Malenkov as chairman of the Council of Ministers of the U.S.S.R. (premier) on Feb. 8, 1955.

For the next several years Bulganin accompanied Khrushchev on numerous state visits throughout the world. But when Malenkov, Vyacheslav Molotov, and Lazar Kaganovich formed the "antiparty group" that tried to oust Khrushchev as leader of the party (June 1957), Bulganin joined them. Although the antiparty group failed and its leaders were expelled from the Central Committee and its Presidium (July 1957), Bulganin remained premier until March 27, 1958, and a member of the Presidium until Sept. 5, 1958. Toward the end of 1958 he was given the obscure position of chairman of the economic council of Stavropol and in 1961 lost his membership on the Central Committee.

Cardus, Sir Neville, English journalist (b. Manchester, England, April 2, 1889—d. London, England, Feb. 28, 1975), was a music critic and sportswriter, whose cricket reports were unusually literate but no less technically sound. While assistant cricket coach at Shrewsbury School, he undertook a program of self-educative reading. After desultory music journalism, he obtained a position with *The Manchester Guardian* in 1917. Cardus became its cricket correspondent and set a new trend in imaginative sportswriting. Recognized as a sensitive interpreter of classical concert music, he was later appointed the paper's music critic. He spent 1941–47 in Australia with the *Sydney Morning Herald,* then returned to England to work on the *Sunday Times* (1948–49) before returning to *The Guardian* in 1951. Cardus wrote books on music and cricket and a final autobiography, *Full Score* (1970). He was knighted in 1967.

Georges Carpentier

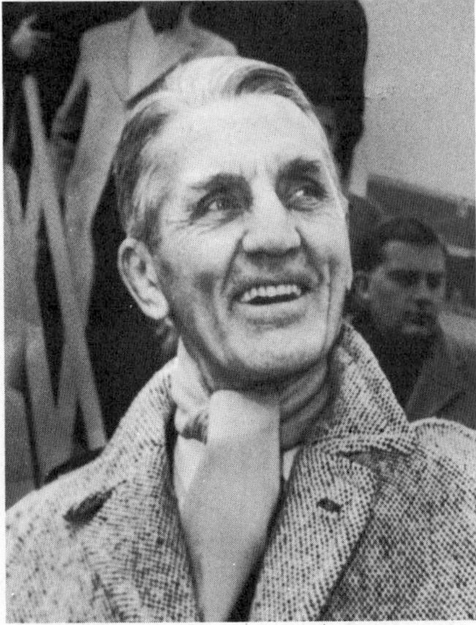

A.F.P./PICTORIAL PARADE

Carpentier, Georges, French boxer (b. Liévin, Pas-de-Calais, France, Jan. 12, 1894—d. Paris, France, Oct. 27, 1975), was world light-heavyweight champion from 1920 to 1922. His victories over British opponents—Joe Beckett, "Bombardier" Billy Wells, and Ted "Kid" Lewis—made him a legend in France. He became an international figure on July 2, 1921, when he fought Jack Dempsey in New Jersey for the world heavyweight championship and was knocked out in the fourth round. The event was boxing's first million-dollar gate. After retiring in 1927, he worked in films and cabaret, eventually becoming a fashionable restaurateur in Paris.

Cartier, Raymond Marcel Ernest, French journalist (b. Niort, Deux-Sèvres, France, June 14, 1904—d. Paris, France, Feb. 8, 1975), founder and editor in chief of the weekly *Paris-Match,* began his career on the daily *Écho de Paris* (1929–37), becoming after its closure editor in chief of the equally conservative daily *L'Époque* (1937–40). During the German occupation of northwestern France he moved to Lyons, where he contributed to the weekly *Sept Jours* (1940–43). During 1944–45 he served on the staff of Gen. Jean de Lattre de Tassigny and participated in the advance of the French 1st Army across the Rhine into Germany and Austria. After World War II he became special correspondent of *Samedi-Soir* and in 1949 founded *Paris-Match,* which was controlled financially by Jean Prouvost, a textile manufacturer. In 1968 he became a general director of *Paris-Match,* and from 1968 commented daily on world affairs from radio station RTL based in Luxembourg—an independent station also controlled by Prouvost.

Charles, Ezzard Mack, U.S. boxer (b. Lawrenceville, Ga., July 7, 1921—d. Chicago, Ill., May 28, 1975), went professional in 1940 after an undefeated amateur career, but had to win two major fights before becoming, in effect, heavyweight champion of the world. On the night of June 22, 1949, he outpointed Jersey Joe Walcott in Chicago and was recognized by the National Boxing Association as successor to the title vacated the previous March when Joe Louis retired undefeated. Then on Sept. 27, 1950, Charles got "the rest of the title" from the New York State Boxing Commission when he overwhelmed the aging Louis in 15 rounds and thoroughly shattered the "Brown Bomber's" hopes for a comeback. Charles was knocked out in Pittsburgh on July 18, 1951, by Walcott, whom Charles had decisioned just a few months earlier. In three unsuccessful attempts to regain the title, Charles lost once to Walcott and twice to Rocky Marciano. When he retired, he had won 96 of 122 professional fights and was a member of the Boxing Hall of Fame. In 1966 Charles was stricken with a muscle disease that confined him to a wheelchair until his death.

Chiang Kai-shek, Chinese general and head of state (b. Feng-hua, Chekiang Province, China, Oct. 31, 1887—d. Taipei, Taiwan, April 5, 1975), was, with Sun Yat-sen and Mao Tse-tung, one of the three most important men in modern Chinese history. While attending a military academy in Japan (1907–11), Chiang was converted to republicanism and actively supported Sun Yat-sen's revolution, which overthrew the Manchu (Ch'ing) dynasty in 1911. After a military mission to Moscow, Chiang founded the Whampoa Military Academy and as commandant directed the training of future Nationalist (Kuomintang) officers. When Sun died in 1925 Chiang took over the party leadership and launched a massive campaign against the warlords who still controlled sizable areas of the country. After capturing Peking in 1928, Chiang (who in December 1927 had taken Soong Meiling, sister-in-law of Sun Yat-sen, as his second wife) transferred the capital to Nanking.

The greatest threat to the government now came from the Communists, who had formed their own army and government and had withdrawn to rural strongholds. To give the nation greater moral cohesion Chiang revived Confucianism by launching the New Life Movement in 1934. That same year the hard-pressed Communists began their famous Long March from southeast China to Yen-an in the north. Sporadic fighting continued until 1937 when all-out war erupted with Japan, which had occupied Manchuria in 1931. Chiang then formed a fragile alliance with the Communists and fought Japan for four years until Allied help arrived late in 1941. In 1943 he visited Cairo for a conference with U.S. Pres. Franklin Roosevelt and British Prime Minister Winston Churchill and became, along with Joseph Stalin, one of the "Big Four" Allied statesmen.

WIDE WORLD

Chiang Kai-shek

By 1948 a full-scale civil war was raging with the Communists. As the Communist forces advanced southward Chiang's Nationalist troops were finally forced in 1949 to flee to the island province of Taiwan. With U.S. military support Chiang was able to prevent a Communist takeover, and he used U.S. economic aid to develop his island sanctuary into a prosperous exporting nation. With advancing age Chiang's strength ebbed, as did international support for his government. The People's Republic of China replaced Taiwan at the UN (1971) and U.S. Pres. Richard Nixon personally met with Chairman Mao in Peking (1972). Chiang died in the middle of his fifth six-year term as the first president of the Republic of China under the 1947 constitution.

Chipembere, Henry Blasius Masauko, African nationalist leader (b. Nyasaland [now Malawi], 1930?—d. Los Angeles, Calif., Sept. 24, 1975), played a prominent part in Malawi's struggle for independence. The son of an Anglican clergyman, Chipembere became minister of local government when Hastings Banda's Malawi Congress Party gained control of the Legislative Council in 1961 and, upon independence in 1964, minister of education. He was later dismissed and went into exile, first in Tanzania and then in the U.S., where he taught African history at California State University, Los Angeles.

Chitepo, Herbert Wiltshire Tfumaindini, Rhodesian nationalist (b. Bonda, Rhodesia, June 5, 1923—d. Lusaka, Zambia, March 18, 1975), was an outspoken opponent of compromise with the white government of Rhodesia, and the country's first black barrister. His law degree was awarded by Fort Hare University College in South Africa. In 1962 Chitepo went into voluntary exile in Tanganyika, where he was made the first African director of public prosecutions. Though not in Rhodesia, he became chairman of the country's militant Zimbabwe African National Union during Ndabaningi Sithole's presidency. He moved to Zambia in 1966 and opposed the British settlement proposals of 1971. When Pres. Kenneth Kaunda of Zambia coaxed the rival nationalist groups to cooperate with the African National Council's leadership for discussions (1974) with the Rhodesian government, Chitepo was made a senior official of the

ANC in Zambia. Chitepo was killed when his car was blown up by a bomb planted outside his home.

Considine, Robert Bernard, U.S. journalist (b. Washington, D.C., Nov. 4, 1906—d. New York, N.Y., Sept. 25, 1975), was a war correspondent, sportswriter, editor, syndicated columnist ("On the Line"), author or co-author of 25 books, movie scenarist, and news commentator on radio and television. A few months before his death, Considine was honoured in New York as one of the finest journalists in the nation. During nearly four decades with the Hearst publications, he filed stories on many of the great news events of the day, including Pres. Richard M. Nixon's

WIDE WORLD

visit to China in 1972. Among his books were *MacArthur the Magnificent* (1942); *The Babe Ruth Story* (1948), which was later rewritten as a film scenario; *It's All News to Me* (1967); and *Toots* (1969), the story of Toots Shor, the colourful restaurateur.

Cook, Sir James Wilfred, British scientist (b. London, England, Dec. 10, 1900—d. Devon, England, Oct. 21, 1975), graduated in chemistry at University College, London, and after a period of lecturing and research on coal-tar derivatives was invited by Sir Ernest Kennaway to join the Royal Cancer Hospital in London, later becoming regius professor of chemistry at both the University of London (1935–39) and the University of Glasgow (1939–54). While in London Cook demonstrated the relationship of coal-tar derivatives to carcinogenesis, a major step in cancer research, and in 1936 shared with Kennaway the prize of the International Union Against Cancer. In 1938 he was elected a fellow of the Royal Society. Cook began a second career in 1954 as principal of the University College of the South West which later became the University of Exeter. Soon after his retirement in 1965 he became vice-chancellor of the University of East Africa, Kampala, Uganda (1966–70), and then chairman of the Academic Advisory Committee of the New University of Ulster at Coleraine. Cook was knighted in 1963.

Coolidge, William David, U.S. physical chemist and inventor (b. Hudson, Mass., Oct. 23, 1873—d. Schenectady, N.Y., Feb. 3, 1975), graduated from Massachusetts Institute of Technology in 1896 before obtaining a Ph.D. (1899) from the University of Leipzig in Germany. In 1908, three years after joining General Electric Co. as a research scientist, he discovered a process that rendered tungsten ductile and therefore eminently suitable for use in incandescent light bulbs (earlier tungsten filaments were exceedingly brittle and short-lived). In 1916 he patented a revolutionary X-ray tube. Using a hot tungsten cathode in place of the traditional cold aluminum cathode, he made a high-vacuum X-ray tube producing highly predictable and accurate amounts of radiation. The Coolidge tube is still the prototype of tubes used in modern X-ray units.

Coolidge later developed portable X-ray units and devised techniques used in the construction of 1 million- and 2 million-volt X-ray machines for treatment of cancer and for quality control in industry. With Nobel laureate Irving Langmuir he also developed the first successful submarine-detection system. During World War II Coolidge extended his research to radar, rockets, antisubmarine devices, and the atomic bomb. He became director of GE's Research Laboratory in 1932 and vice-president and director of research in 1940. He retired in 1944 but remained a consultant and director emeritus.

Craig, (Elisabeth) May, U.S. newswoman (b. Coosaw, S.C., 1889?—d. Silver Spring, Md., July 15, 1975), gained national prominence as a Washington, D.C., correspondent (1926–65) for the Guy Gannett newspapers of Maine and as a regular interviewer (1949–65) on NBC's weekly television series "Meet the Press." Presidents Roosevelt, Truman, Eisenhower, Kennedy, and Johnson faced Craig at news conferences and (like guests on "Meet the Press") awaited her "dodge-proof" questions with ambivalent emotions. Craig, who fought relentlessly for equal rights with male reporters, was the only woman assigned to cover Pres. Harry S. Truman's visit to Brazil (1947). Even so, she was not permitted aboard the USS "Missouri" to complete her assignment when Truman returned home by sea. But two years later she stood on the deck of the "Midway" taking notes on sea-air maneuvers and became the first woman to file a story from a warship at sea.

Cross, Milton John, U.S. radio announcer (b. New York, N.Y., April 16, 1897—d. New York, Jan. 3, 1975), was for several generations of ordinary Americans only a name and a voice that taught them to appreciate and love the world's finest operas. For 43 years, beginning on Christmas Day 1931, Cross introduced the Saturday afternoon radiobroadcasts of the Metropolitan Opera to an unseen audience. He described each program, outlined the dramatic plot, and introduced the performing artists. The mellifluous "Voice of the Met" also described the costumes and the sets, which he carefully inspected during rehearsals to ensure that listeners could accurately visualize what they could not see. Cross sang tenor for a time after studying at the Institute of Musical Art (later part of Juilliard), but soon gave himself over to full-time broadcasting. Though his specialty was musical programs, he was called upon to handle a wide variety of broadcasts, including the inauguration of Pres. Herbert Hoover.

Dallapiccola, Luigi, Italian composer (b. Pisino, Istria, Austria-Hungary [now Pazin, Yugos.], Feb. 3, 1904—d. Florence, Italy, Feb. 19, 1975), was Italy's principal exponent of 12-tone, serial music, which he used to express a humanist's concern with man's fate. He completed his studies at Florence's Cherubini Conservatory and became Italian delegate to the International Society for Contemporary Music, for which he wrote an orchestral *Partita* (1930–32). *Volo di notte* (1937–39), his first success in opera, was based on Antoine de Saint-Exupéry's book *Vol de nuit*. Dallapiccola was eventually proscribed under Fascism for composing *Canti di prigionia* (1938–41; "Songs of Prison"). An important refinement in 12-tone technique is evident in his ballet *Marsia* (1942–43). *Il prigioniero* (1944–48; "The Prisoner"), an operatic requiem for the deported, was followed by instrumental and choral works, including *Canti di liberazione* (1952–55; "Songs of Liberation"), and by the opera *Ulisse* (1960–68), which reaffirmed the theme of human struggle against unknown odds while acknowledging the existence of a higher power.

Daubeny, Sir Peter Lauderdale, British theatrical director (b. Wiesbaden, Germany, April 16, 1921—d. London, England, Aug. 6, 1975), founded the World Theatre Season at the Aldwych Theatre, London, in 1964 and was its artistic director. He trained to be an actor, but turned to theatrical management after losing an arm in World War II. His interest in international theatre eventually led him to present foreign companies and personalities in London, including the Ballets des Champs-Élysées, the American National Ballet Company, Sacha Guitry, the Red Army Choir, Edwige Feuillère's company, the Chinese Classical Theatre from Taiwan, the Moscow Art Theatre, the Comédie Française, and the Malmö Municipal Theatre Company from Sweden. These were precursors of the annual seasons of World Theatre, backed by the Royal Shakespeare Company, which every year from 1964 to 1975 (1974 excepted) brought some of the best companies and plays from foreign countries to London for a brilliant short season. Daubeny was knighted in 1973 and was decorated by foreign governments. He published *Stage by Stage* (1952) and *My World of Theatre* (1971).

De Valera, Eamon, Irish statesman, prime minister, and president of Ireland (b. New York, N.Y., Oct. 14, 1882—d. Dublin, Ire., Aug. 29, 1975), was one of the founders of the Republic of Ireland and exercised a profound influence on its first half century of development. Born in New York City of an Irish mother and a Spanish father, he went to Ireland at the age of two and grew up during the period of the Celtic renaissance, increasingly committed to the independence of Ireland from Britain. He was the only revolutionary leader to survive the Easter Rising of 1916, and after imprisonment became president of the first parliament in Dublin. He split with his former colleagues over the treaty signed in 1921 and was on the losing side in the civil war that followed. After ten years of building up a new political party, Fianna Fail, he regained power in 1932 and was prime minister for the next 16 years. After three years in opposition, he returned to power in 1951, was out of office from 1954 to 1957, and then prime minister for two years before beginning a 14-year period as president. Altogether, he was actively involved in public life for more than 50 years.

De Valera's early contribution to the evolution of the Irish state was based on militant idealism. He was a forceful element in the leadership that forced the British to grant self-government to the greater part of Ireland. But when faced with the inevitability of partition, that same idealism led him to engage in the bitter and divisive civil war (1922–23), the scars of which remained in the sharp and nationwide antagonisms that continued to divide the two main political parties. His return to power in 1932 opened up a new era of statesmanship during which De Valera paved the way for the modern Irish state. He was responsible for the country's constitution—itself a model for many other states—and for the immensely difficult decision that kept Ireland neutral during World War II. During a singularly austere period in world history, his administrative and legislative programs confirmed the foundations of a small, independent democracy which he had, much earlier, done so much to create.

From the mid-1950s De Valera was virtually blind and increasingly the titular leader of the government, with more precise policy initiatives being taken by younger men in his Cabinet. His conservative and agrarian view of the Irish

Eamon De Valera

COLMAN DOYLE—CAMERA PRESS/PHOTO TRENDS

state, which was increasingly at odds with the drive toward development, nevertheless continued to act as a political counterbalance during the period of economic programming in the late 1950s and 1960s, when, as president, he reaped the rewards of his service to the country by becoming its natural and dignified elder statesman. Though the reunification of Ireland had always been his dearest wish, he maintained a prudent silence, both as president and after becoming a private citizen in 1973; during his final years he witnessed a hardening of attitudes and a sectarian bitterness worse than anything he had previously experienced.

(BRUCE ARNOLD)

Dobzhansky, Theodosius, Russian-born geneticist (b. Nemirov, Russia, Jan. 25, 1900—d. Davis, Calif., Dec. 18, 1975), won international renown for his work on evolution and genetics and their implications for modern man. After graduating from the State University in Kiev (1921), he taught for six years in Kiev and Leningrad before going to the U.S. (1927) as a Rockefeller Foundation fellow. From 1929 to 1940 Dobzhansky taught genetics at the California Institute of Technology and from 1940 to 1962 was professor of zoology at Columbia University in New York. His *Genetics and the Origin of Species* (1937) was the first substantial synthesis of Darwinian evolution and Mendelian genetics and established evolutionary genetics as an independent discipline. Other writings include *Mankind Evolving* (1962), a study of human evolution that has had great impact on anthropologists, *The Biological Basis of Human Freedom* (1956), *The Biology of Ultimate Concern* (1969), and *Genetics of the Evolutionary Process* (1970).

Doxiadis, Konstantinos Apostolos, Greek architect (b. Steinimachos, Bulg., May 14, 1913—d. Athens, Greece, June 30, 1975), was an urban planner whose vision of man-centred, rather than machine-dominated cities affected the lives of millions of persons all over the world. The science of human settlement that he developed—called "ekistics"—relies on the contributions of architects, engineers, and sociologists. Doxiadis studied at the Athens and Berlin polytechnic schools, graduating in 1936 as engineer-architect. The following year he was appointed director of town planning for the Athens-Piraeus area. After World War II he was director general of the Ministry of Reconstruction, planning adviser to various companies in Australia, consulting engineer on housing projects in the Middle East, and a teacher at Harvard University and the Massachusetts Institute of Technology. In 1968 the *Britannica Book of the Year* published a remarkable article by Doxiadis entitled "Ecumenopolis: Tomorrow's City."

Driver, Sir Godfrey Rolles, British scholar (b. Oxford, England, Aug. 20, 1892—d. Oxford, April 22, 1975), headed the group of Old Testament scholars who, after years of work, produced the New English Bible (1970). Driver, who brought to the task immense erudition and vast knowledge of ancient Semitic languages, was appointed (1965) joint director of the project along with C. H. Dodd. Educated at Winchester College and New College, Oxford, Driver became a fellow of Magdalen College, Oxford, was a reader in Semitic philology, then professor from 1938 to 1962. During this period he was chosen to do the final editing on *Aramaic Documents of the Fifth Century B.C.* (1954), a translation of the Dead Sea Scrolls.

Duclos, Jacques, French Communist leader (b. Louey, Hautes-Pyrénées, France, Oct. 2, 1896—d. Paris, France, April 25, 1975), joined the French Communist Party at its foundation in 1920 and remained a faithful "Muscovite" all his life. Short, stout, and bespectacled, he became a witty and fluent orator. A Politburo member since 1931, trusted by Stalin, he became in effect the latter's supervisor of Communist activities in Western Europe. After Hitler invaded the U.S.S.R. he organized the Communist resistance and emerged in 1945 as an influential figure. In the 1969 presidential race against Georges Pompidou, he received 21.3% of the votes. His published books include five volumes of memoirs.

Dunning, John Ray, U.S. physicist (b. Shelby, Neb., Sept. 24, 1907—d. Key Biscayne, Fla., Aug. 25, 1975), graduated from Columbia University with a Ph.D. in physics (1934), then visited many of Europe's greatest physicists before directing the construction of Columbia's first cyclotron. On Jan. 25, 1939, the cyclotron was used to confirm the possibility of controlled nuclear fission. Dunning subsequently directed a secret project that devised the gaseous diffusion process for isolating the isotope uranium-235. As a consequence, nuclear weapons could be built and enriched uranium could be produced for use in atomic reactors. While dean of Columbia's school of engineering (1950–69), Dunning was often consulted by Pres. Dwight D. Eisenhower and by Adm. Hyman G. Rickover on military uses of nuclear energy.

Ely, Paul Henri Romuald, French army general (b. Salonika, Turkey [now Thessaloniki, Greece], Dec. 17, 1897—d. Paris, France, Jan. 16, 1975), played a vital role in the French Resistance movement during World War II, making several dangerous trips from France to de Gaulle's London headquarters to deliver intelligence reports. After the war he served intermittently

ROBERT COHEN—AGIP/PICTORIAL PARADE

as chief of the general staff (1953–61). In 1954, after pleading in vain for massive U.S. military assistance in Indochina, Ely supervised the final withdrawal of all French troops. During the Algerian conflict, he resigned as chief of staff because of conflicting loyalties but later accepted the position of chief of staff of national defense during the presidency of de Gaulle.

Escrivá de Balaguer y Albás, Monsignor Josemaria, Spanish prelate of the Roman Catholic Church (b. Barbastro, Spain, Jan. 9, 1902—d. Rome, Italy, June 26, 1975), founded Opus Dei ("God's Work") in 1928, then devoted the rest of his life to this essentially lay organization whose members, numbering some 60,000 from 80 countries, strive to live Christian lives in whatever profession or vocation they choose to follow. Escrivá moved from Spain to Rome in 1946 and was named president-general of Opus Dei by Pope Pius XII who in 1950 gave the organization definitive approval. Escrivá oversaw the gradual establishment of vocational, trade, and agricultural centres, numerous high schools and schools of business administration, and the founding of the Universidad de Navarra, which many consider the finest university in Spain. Though Opus Dei makes a point of imposing no political ideology on any of its members, Opus Deistas were named to high government positions in Spain when Franco sought out highly trained technocrats to implement a program of economic development begun in 1956. The organization was thereafter attacked as political by its critics.

Evans, Walker, U.S. photographic artist (b. St. Louis, Mo., Nov. 3, 1903—d. New Haven, Conn., April 10, 1975), first focused his mind and camera on 19th-century architecture in New England, then began (1935) to record on film the effects of the Depression on rural Americans. He documented virtually every facet of their lives, as much through their artifacts and dwellings as through their faces, and published the collection in *American Photographs* (1938). His detached style and unique vision influenced the generation of photographers who followed him. Evans traveled to Alabama with James Agee in 1936 to document the lives of Southern sharecroppers. In *Let Us Now Praise Famous Men* (1941), Evans' photos, separated from Agee's text and without captions, produced a powerful complementary effect. He was an associate editor of *Fortune* magazine (1945–65), and then taught at the Yale University School of Art and Architecture. His most remarkable later work was a series of photographs of people taken in the mid-1940s in the New York City subway system. Out of courtesy to those his camera had so thoroughly revealed, the photos were not published until 1966.

Faisal ibn Abd al-Aziz, third king of Saudi Arabia (b. Riyadh, Saudi Arabia, 1905—d. Riyadh, March 25, 1975), was the fourth son of Ibn Saud, the desert king who conquered the province of Hejaz (and with it, Mecca) in 1926, then named Faisal its viceroy and his foreign minister. In October 1953 Faisal became Saudi Arabia's first prime minister. When King Ibn Saud died a month later, his eldest son, Saud, was proclaimed king. The new monarch immediately named his brother Faisal crown prince, prime minister, and commander in chief. In March 1964 Faisal was given all royal powers and on Nov. 2, 1964, became king after his brother was legally deposed by religious leaders, the ranking nobility, and the Council of Ministers. In October 1972 Faisal suggested an Arab-U.S. oil agreement which offered Washington favoured

ROBERT COHEN—AGIP/PICTORIAL PARADE

treatment in return for aid in industrial development and a pro-Arab shift in U.S. Middle East policies. When there was no response, he warned that production of Saudi Arabia's immense oil reserves might be curtailed. Faisal became an Arab hero overnight when the "oil weapon" was applied in the fall of 1973. He was inexplicably assassinated by a nephew on Muhammad's birthday during an audience accorded to the oil minister of neighbouring Kuwait. Faisal was succeeded by his brother Crown Prince Khalid (*see* BIOGRAPHY).

Felsenstein, Walter, Austrian theatre director (b. Vienna, Austria, May 30, 1901—d. East Berlin, Oct. 8, 1975), was the creator of East Berlin's Komische Oper, which he established in 1947 in the rebuilt Metropol Theatre in the Behrenstrasse, at the invitation of the Soviet military government. Music lovers who could make the pilgrimage to East Berlin, for no one, except Bertolt Brecht, lent the young German Democratic Republic such cultural prestige. A perfectionist, he sometimes rehearsed a new production for months and restricted his repertory to about 12 major works at any one time. Such rigour often produced spectacular results.

Feltin, Maurice Cardinal, French Roman Catholic prelate (b. Delle, near Belfort, France, May 15, 1883—d. near Paris, France, Sept. 27, 1975), became the youngest bishop in France when he was appointed to the Troyes see in December 1927. He was later appointed archbishop of Sens (1932–35), archbishop of Bordeaux (1935–49), and in 1949 archbishop of Paris. He was created a cardinal in 1953 and retired in 1966. Feltin was one of three French cardinals who went to Rome in 1953 to defend the controversial worker-priest movement, a revolutionary attempt to win back the working class. The movement was allowed to continue under new guidelines.

Fischer, (A)bram Louis, South African lawyer (b. Bloemfontein, South Africa, April 23, 1908—d. Bloemfontein, May 8, 1975), the son of prominent Afrikaner parents, attended Oxford University as a Rhodes scholar, then visited the U.S.S.R. before returning to South Africa (1937) to practice law in Johannesburg, where he became a king's counsel. In the late 1930s he joined the Communist Party and took over the national organization when the party was banned in South Africa in 1950. Fischer defended black nationalist leaders, including Nelson Mandela and Walter Sisulu, at the Rivonia sabotage trial in 1964 and was himself arrested. Temporarily released to plead a case before the Privy Council in London, he jumped bail but was recaptured in November 1965. The next year he was awarded a Lenin Peace Prize. A few weeks before his death, Fischer was released from prison suffering from terminal cancer.

Flanders, Michael Henry, British actor (b. London, England, March 1, 1922—d. North Wales, April 14, 1975), contracted poliomyelitis during World War II and was confined to a wheelchair for the rest of his life. Undaunted, he teamed up with an old schoolmate, Donald Swann, to produce two-man musical comedies that for 13 years played to packed audiences in England, Canada, and the U.S. Flanders supplied hilarious lyrics for songs played on the piano by Swann. It was their acting, however, that added additional substance to such wacky productions as *At the Drop of a Hat* (1956–59) and *At the Drop of Another Hat* (1963–64).

Fox, Nellie (Jacob Nelson Fox), U.S. baseball player (b. St. Thomas, Pa., Dec. 25, 1927—d. Baltimore, Md., Dec. 1, 1975), spent most of his career (1950–65) as a fiery, sure-hitting second baseman for the American League Chicago White Sox, and teamed up with shortstop Luis Aparicio to form one of the finest double-play combinations in the game. In the 1959 World Series he batted .375 against the Los Angeles Dodgers, who won the championship in six games. Fox led the league in singles for seven consecutive seasons and 13 times had the fewest strikeouts in the league while setting a record by batting 600 or more times in 12 different seasons.

Frachon, Benoît, French labour leader (b. Chambon-Feugerolles, Loire, France, May 13, 1893—d. Paris, France, Aug. 4, 1975), was secretary-general of the Confédération Générale du Travail (CGT) during 1936–39 and 1945–67. In 1920 he was a founder member of the French Communist Party and later, as a socialist trade unionist, became the CGT's secretary-general and leader of its Communist wing. At the height of his power, Frachon was able to command almost absolute allegiance from millions of French workers, but he retired in 1968 after strikers at the Renault auto plant in Boulogne-Billancourt vociferously repudiated a settlement negotiated by the CGT.

Franco Bahamonde, Francisco, Spanish head of state (b. El Ferrol, Galicia, Spain, Dec. 4, 1892—d. Madrid, Spain, Nov. 20, 1975), led the Nationalist forces to victory in the Spanish Civil War (1936–39), then ruled Spain with an iron hand for the next 36 years. He graduated from the Infantry Academy in Toledo in 1907, and served with conspicuous bravery in Morocco, to which he returned in 1920 as deputy commander of the Spanish Foreign Legion, becoming com-

WIDE WORLD

Francisco Franco Bahamonde

mander three years later. As Spain's youngest colonel he helped crush the 1925 Rif rebellion led by Abd el-Krim. Promoted brigadier general in 1926, he became director of the Military Academy in Saragossa a year later. The academy was closed when the Spanish Republic was proclaimed in April 1931 and Franco was transferred to the Balearic Islands.

Franco was not involved in the unsuccessful monarchist revolution of 1932 but played a leading role in suppressing the antirepublican Asturian miners' revolt of 1934. He was then created chief of staff but fell from grace after the electoral victory of the Popular Front in February 1936. Manuel Azaña, the second president of the republic, sent Franco into virtual retirement as governor of the Canary Islands. With violence and terror prevailing in the country, the secret Unión Militar Española decided to seize power. On July 17, 1936, the garrison of Melilla revolted. The same month Gen. José Sanjurjo, leader of the union, died in a plane crash, and Franco was chosen head of state and supreme commander (*caudillo y generalissimo*) on September 29. His first task was to unite the elements supporting the Movimiento Nacional: conservatives (landlords and businessmen), monarchists, and the Falange Española (a Fascist organization founded in 1933 by José Antonio Primo de Rivera). The republican camp, known as the Loyalists, consisted of liberals, radicals, socialists, anarchists, and Communists (both Stalinists and Trotskyists) as well as Catalan and Basque separatists and some soldiers of fortune from the U.S.; they lacked a genuine leader and were divided by political and regional rivalries. Franco won the Civil War, one of the bitterest in modern history: more than half a million Spaniards died in the conflict. Though Franco had accepted military aid from Italy and Germany and met with Hitler in October 1940, he did not involve Spain in World War II. After the war, however, the UN General Assembly recommended (Dec. 12, 1946), mainly under Soviet pressure, a diplomatic and economic boycott of Spain, a move that some believe significantly consolidated Franco's domestic power. Four years later the 1946 verdict was reversed and diplomatic normality restored. On Sept. 26, 1953, Franco agreed to the establishment of U.S. bases in Spain in return for economic and military aid; a month earlier a concordat between the Holy See and Spain was signed at the Vatican.

Franco gave Spain a long period of peace and political stability, but was repeatedly denounced, at home and abroad, for his rigorous authoritarian ways. During his rule Spain made such impressive economic progress that a new middle class was created that, toward the end of Franco's life, became increasingly vocal in demanding greater freedom. In 1947, with an eye to the future, Franco proclaimed Spain a monarchy, reserving for himself the power of regent. He groomed Don Juan Carlos, grandson of King Alfonso XIII, from a young age to be the future monarch, thus bypassing Juan Carlos' father, Don Juan, Conde de Barcelona, who was an opponent of Franco's regime. In 1969, at his formal investiture before the Cortes, Prince Juan Carlos swore loyalty to the principles of the Movimiento Nacional.

Fresnay, Pierre (Pierre Jules Laudenbach), French actor (b. Paris, France, April 4, 1897—d. Neuilly-sur-Seine, Jan. 9, 1975), was frequently rated the finest French actor of his time. After playing classical roles at the Comédie Française for more than a decade, he won a bitter legal battle and the right to perform elsewhere. He then turned to the Parisian commercial theatre to interpret the works of such playwrights as Sacha Guitry, Marcel Pagnol, Jean Anouilh, Marcel Achard, André Roussin, André Obey, and Noel Coward. Fresnay's great talents were equally evident in such films as *La Grande Illusion, Le Corbeau, Monsieur Vincent,* and in Pagnol's trilogy *Marius, Fanny,* and *César.*

Gabriel-Robinet, Louis, French journalist (b. Paris, France, Dec. 17, 1909—d. Paris, June 24, 1975), editor in chief (1948–65) and director of *Le Figaro,* Paris' conservative and most celebrated morning newspaper, turned to journalism soon after obtaining his degrees in law and letters at the University of Paris. After working for two years as a reporter for the *Écho de Paris,* he joined the editorial staff of *Le Figaro,* becoming political editor in 1944. After being named editor in chief in 1948, he continued to write the daily lead column. He was elected to the Académie des Sciences Morales et Politiques in 1971 and retired in 1974. His writings include *Histoire de la presse* (1960), *Journaux et journalistes hier et aujourd'hui* (1962), and *Je suis journaliste* (1961).

Gallimard, Gaston, French publisher (b. Paris, France, Jan. 18, 1881—d. Paris, Dec. 25, 1975), was the founder and president of Librairie Gallimard, one of the most influential publishing houses of the 20th century. In 1908, with André Gide and Jean Schlumberger, he started *La Nouvelle Revue Française,* a periodical of high intellectual standards. In 1911 Gallimard and his colleagues established a publishing house that in 1919 became Librairie Gallimard and eventually published some 250 titles each year, including works by André Malraux, Henry de Montherlant, Charles Péguy, Marcel Proust, and Paul Valéry. Through his authors he collected a record number of prizes: 25 Goncourts, 16 Féminas, and 12 Interalliés. A man with a sharp eye for business and an equally sharp one for talent, Gallimard built up an empire controlling five other houses besides his own. He also started *La Pléiade,* an edition of the classics of French literature.

Giancana, Sam, U.S. crime syndicate figure (b. Chicago, Ill., May 24, 1908—d. Oak Park, Ill., June 19, 1975), was a driver and triggerman for organized crime before serving four years in prison (1940–44) on moonshining charges. After his release, he engineered a violent takeover of the Chicago numbers racket and eventually ruled over an empire that extended into drugs, prostitution, gambling, and loansharking. Giancana was jailed again in 1965 for refusing to testify before a federal grand jury investigating organized crime; the case revolved around conversations that government agents had recorded from a microphone planted in Giancana's headquarters. He took refuge in Mexico after his release in 1966, but was summarily deported in 1974. Giancana was in virtual retirement when his gangland-style murder created national headlines and sparked animated speculation about possible motives and assailants.

Gibbons, Euell (Theophilus), U.S. naturalist (b. Clarksville, Texas, Sept. 8, 1911—d. Sunbury, Pa., Dec. 29, 1975), had a lifelong fascination with wild natural foods, which he effectively communicated to readers of his first book, *Stalking the Wild Asparagus* (1962). He subsequently made numerous appearances on television, sometimes in commercials, and published such sequels as *Stalking the Blue-Eyed Scallop* (1964), *Feast on a Diabetic Diet* (1969), and *Stalking the Good Life* (1971).

Gleason, Ralph Joseph, U.S. music critic (b. New York, N.Y., March 1, 1917—d. Berkeley, Calif., June 3, 1975), set a precedent by writing serious reviews of jazz, pop, and folk music for the *San Francisco Chronicle*. His later weekly newspaper articles on jazz were syndicated in the U.S. and Europe. Gleason co-founded *Jazz Information*, the first such American magazine, and was publisher of *Jazz*, neither of which survived. Far more successful was *Rolling Stone*, which he co-founded in 1967. He also produced jazz programs for television.

Gluckman, Max, British anthropologist (b. Johannesburg, South Africa, Jan. 26, 1911—d. Jerusalem, Israel, April 13, 1975), added a new chapter to social anthropology through his research on law as understood and practiced by African tribes. After studying at the University of Witwatersrand and Exeter College, Oxford, he did fieldwork in Zululand (1936–38) before joining the staff of the Rhodes-Livingstone Institute of Northern Rhodesia. While there he undertook field research in Barotseland (1939–41) that provided the basis for his studies of African jurisprudence. As director (1941–47) of the institute he laid the foundation for what was to become the Manchester School of Theory and Research in Social Anthropology. In time Gluckman and his associates expanded their studies to include India and the Middle East.

Goodbody, Mary Ann ("Buzz"), British theatrical director (b. London, England, June 25, 1946—d. London, April 11, 1975), was the Royal Shakespeare Company's first female director. At Sussex University she won a prize for her direction and adaptation of Dostoyevsky's *Notes from the Underground* during the 1966–67 National Students' Drama Festival. Spotted there by RSC director John Barton, she joined the company as his assistant, directed *As You Like It* in 1973, and assisted Trevor Nunn to direct his Roman plays in 1973-74. Made director of the RSC's smaller company, The Place, she manifested considerable creativity with productions of Trevor Griffiths' *Occupations* and of *Lear*.

Grandjany, Marcel Georges Lucien, French-born harpist (b. Paris, France, Sept. 3, 1891—d. New York, N.Y., Feb. 24, 1975), became a musical sensation in 1909 when, in his first professional performance, it became evident that the harp, as he played it, could become a solo instrument of unsuspected range and beauty. After studying at the Paris Conservatory and touring the concert halls of Europe, he made his U.S. debut in New York City in 1924. He joined the faculty of the Juilliard School of Music in 1938, where he remained until his death. He became a U.S. citizen in 1945.

Green, (William) Martyn, British actor (b. London, Eng., April 22, 1899—d. Hollywood, Calif., Feb. 8, 1975), sang, mugged, pantomimed, and danced his way to stardom in Gilbert and Sullivan operettas. In his famous encores, he could delight U.S. and European audiences by singing a single chorus a dozen different ways. In 1922 Green joined London's D'Oyly Carte Opera Company, which alone was permitted to use Sullivan's original orchestrations with Gilbert's personal stage notes. His first major role (1934) was that of Major General Stanley in *The Pirates of Penzance*. During the next 18 years he was unrivaled as an operatic comedian, singing such roles as Ko-Ko in *The Mikado*, the Lord Chancellor in *Iolanthe*, and Sir Joseph Porter in *H.M.S. Pinafore*. After leaving the D'Oyly Carte in 1951, Green revealed other facets of his talent in nonmusical productions. Memorable performances included the part of Brennan O' the Moor in Sean O'Casey's *Red Roses for Me* and that of the Captain in Eugene O'Neill's *The Iceman Cometh*.

Gregson, John, British actor (b. Liverpool, England, March 15, 1919—d. Porlock Weir, Somerset, England, Jan. 8, 1975), acquired considerable experience in the repertory theatre before turning to films in 1948. After appearing in such pictures as *Scott of the Antarctic, Whisky Galore!*, and *The Lavender Hill Mob*, he became an established star for his acting in *Genevieve* (1953). Among his later films were comedies and the war films *The Longest Day* and *The Night of the Generals*. Gregson also played in the long-running and popular television series "Gideon's Way" and in 1969 returned to the stage in *The Secretary Bird*.

Grove, Lefty (Robert Moses Grove), U.S. baseball player (b. Lonaconing, Md., March 6, 1900—d. Norwalk, Ohio, May 22, 1975), spent nine seasons as a pitcher with Connie Mack's Philadelphia Athletics (1925–33) before moving to the Boston Red Sox (1934–41). He had seven consecutive seasons of 20 or more wins (1927–33) and set an all-time two-season record (1930–31) with 59 wins and 9 defeats; during 1931 he posted 16 consecutive victories. Grove entered baseball's Hall of Fame in 1947 with a record of 300–141, an earned-run average of 3.06, and a total of 2,266 strikeouts. One of Grove's greatest triumphs came against the New York Yankees: they had the tying run on third in the ninth inning and he struck out Lou Gehrig, Babe Ruth, and Bob Meusel with a total of nine pitches.

Haile Selassie (Tafari Makonnen), emperor of Ethiopia (b. near Harar, Eth., July 23, 1892—d. Addis Ababa, Eth., Aug. 27, 1975), was the youngest son of Ras (Prince) Makonnen, a cousin and chief adviser to Emperor Menelik II. Tafari was educated at home by teachers of the French mission at Harar. Upon the death of his father in 1906, he became governor of Harar. When Emperor Menelik's daughter Zauditu became empress in 1916, Tafari was elected regent and heir to the throne. In 1928 he assumed the title of *negus* (king) and two years later, when Zauditu died, was crowned emperor with the name Haile Selassie ("Might of the Trinity"). Widely read, possessed of a powerful personality, and with enthusiasm for reform, he undertook the monumental task of modernizing Ethiopia.

After Fascist Italy invaded Ethiopia on Oct. 3, 1935, Haile Selassie fought heroically for seven months before circumstances compelled him to leave the country. His eloquent plea for help before the League of Nations on June 30, 1936, elicited wide sympathy but no concrete response. After British forces liberated Ethiopia, he returned in triumph to Addis Ababa in 1941 and began the huge task of reconstruction and rehabilitation.

Though grateful to the British, he was unwilling to lean too heavily on any one foreign power. At home his authority was virtually absolute. With advancing age, the emperor seemed to be removed more and more from the common people and less capable of carrying out necessary reforms. Though a 1960 coup by army officers was suppressed, widespread dissatisfaction was not extinguished. Ironically, it was education, which the emperor so keenly fostered, that eventually undermined the foundations of the old system. When, for example, the government tried to conceal the 1973 famine that took the lives of some 100,000 persons in the northern provinces, students directed foreign television teams to the scene. The following year young army officers backed student demands for a change of government with more concessions in the direction of democracy. A process of controlled change was thus unleashed, culminating in an attack on the entire ruling class, and finally on the emperor himself. He was accused by the armed forces of having exploited public funds for his own benefit and on Sept. 12, 1974, was deposed in favour of the ailing crown prince, who was himself deposed in March 1975 with the abolition of the monarchy. Haile Selassie, whose capital had become the headquarters of the Organization of African Unity, was ignominiously confined to a three-room mud hut in the army barracks before being allowed to return to the palace to die with dignity.

Haile Selassie

WIDE WORLD

Hansen, Alvin Harvey, U.S. economist (b. Viborg, S.D., Aug. 23, 1887—d. Alexandria, Va., June 6, 1975), had a long tenure at the University of Minnesota (1919–37) before occupying the prestigious Littauer chair of political economy at Harvard University. After reading John Maynard Keynes's *General Theory of Employment, Interest and Money* (1936), Hansen became a convinced Keynesian. He believed that national prosperity through high employment was directly related to demand for goods and services, and that this demand could and should be controlled by government spending and taxes. Deficits, moreover, and modest inflation were of no great consequence. Hansen's remarkable success in having these notions adopted as government policy was facilitated by his appointments as consultant to the U.S. Department of the Treasury, the Federal Reserve Board, and the National Resources Planning Board, and by his membership on numerous governmental commissions. He also played a role in establishing the Social Security system and the Council of Economic Advisers.

Hayward, Susan (Edythe Marrener), U.S. actress (b. Brooklyn, N.Y., June 30, 1919—d. Beverly Hills, Calif., March 14, 1975), became one of Hollywood's most marketable talents and one of the world's most popular screen stars in the course of receiving four Academy Award nominations and finally the Oscar itself in 1959. Some of her most effective acting was the portrayal of troubled or despairing women, scenarios that echoed private life agonies involving a court battle over custody of her children, divorce, attempted suicide, the sudden death of a second husband, and a brain tumour. Hayward's early career, by contrast, was a true-life version of a made-in-Hollywood fantasy. She was a young, poor, beautiful, stagestruck redhead; a famous director saw her photo and offered her the chance to play Scarlett O'Hara in *Gone with the Wind* but she failed the screen test; a bike accident caused a chance meeting with her future agent; pictures, publicity, disappointment, and discouragement followed. And then, finally, a 1939 role opposite Gary Cooper in *Beau Geste* led to stardom. Hayward's most memorable films were *Smash-Up* (1947), *My Foolish Heart* (1949), *With a Song in My Heart* (1952), *I'll Cry Tomorrow* (1955), and the award-winning *I Want to Live* (1958).

Heenan, John Carmel Cardinal, British prelate of the Roman Catholic Church (b. Ilford, Essex, England, Jan. 26, 1905—d. London, England, Nov. 7, 1975), as cardinal archbishop of Westminster was spiritual leader of four million Roman Catholics in England and Wales. The son of Irish parents, he entered a junior seminary in 1921, later studying at the English College in Rome (1923-30), from which he graduated with doctorates in philosophy and theology. After ordination in July 1930 he began a seven-year period as curate in the East End of London, during which time, under the guise of a student of engineering, he visited the Soviet Union. Ten years as parish priest at St. Stephen's in Manor Park, London, followed. During World War II he became a broadcaster and platform speaker and wrote several pastoral books. When the hierarchy decided to revive the Catholic Missionary Society he was selected as its superior. In 1951 he was appointed bishop of Leeds, in 1957 archbishop of Liverpool, and in 1963 archbishop of Westminster. On Feb. 22, 1965, he was created cardinal and primate of England.

Though skeptical of the value of doctrinal discussions as a road to unity among the Christian churches, he was on terms of quite remarkable intimacy and personal friendship with other Christian leaders. His autobiography was published in two volumes: *Not the Whole Truth* (1971) and *A Crown of Thorns* (1974).

Hepworth, Dame (Jocelyn) Barbara, English sculptress (b. Wakefield, Yorkshire, England, Jan. 10, 1903—d. St. Ives, Cornwall, England, May 20, 1975), created internationally acclaimed abstract forms which are often compared to and contrasted with those of Henry Moore, a lifelong friend and former contemporary at the Leeds College of Art and the Royal College of Art in London. Hepworth's early works were naturalistic and already showed an unusual sensitivity in the choice of materials. By the early 1930s, however, she had turned completely to abstract forms, an inclination reinforced by Ben Nicholson, her second husband and a leading abstract painter. With maturity, Hepworth concentrated on the counterplay between mass and space. Her sculptures became open, hollowed out, and perforated, so that interior space had as great an effect as the surrounding mass. Concave interiors were sometimes painted to produce a heightened effect and voids were strung with taut strings. Hepworth, who was made dame commander of the Order of the British Empire (1965), produced such major works as "Single Form" (1963) for the UN headquarters in New York City, "Meridian" for State House, Holborn, London, and the "Family of Man" designed for a Cornish hillside.

SYNDICATION INTERNATIONAL/PHOTO TRENDS

Hertz, Gustav Ludwig, German scientist (b. Hamburg, Germany, July 22, 1887—d. East Germany, Oct. 30, 1975), won the Nobel Prize for Physics with James Franck in 1925. He studied at the universities of Göttingen, Munich, and Berlin, and went to the physics department of Berlin University in 1913 where he worked with James Franck on atomic research, confirming by experiments that an atom can absorb only definite amounts of energy. Hertz was professor of physics at Halle University (1925–28) and at the Technische Hochschule in Berlin (1928). After the Soviet forces entered Berlin in 1945, he was taken to the Soviet Union but returned to East Germany, where he became professor of physics and director of the Physics Institute at Leipzig (1954–61).

Hill, Graham, British race car driver (b. London, England, Feb. 15, 1929—d. near Elstree, Hertfordshire, England, Nov. 29, 1975), who won the Grand Prix racing drivers' world championship in 1962 and 1968, met his death while trying to land his own aircraft in a fog. He studied engineering (1942–45) at Hendon Technical College near London before serving an engineering apprenticeship, then spent two years as an engine-room artificer in the Royal Navy. In answer to an advertisement, he became a motor racing mechanic and drove in his first race in 1954. Hill raced for Team Lotus (1950–59 and 1967–69) and for the British Racing Motor (1960–66), winning his first victory in world championship competition in the 1962 Dutch Grand Prix. Four years later he won the Indianapolis 500 in a Lola 90-Ford. After suffering severe leg injuries in a 150-mph crash in the U.S. Grand Prix in 1969, he ignored advice to retire and in 1972 won the Le Mans, France, 24-hour race. Hill won a total of 14 Grand Prix races and participated in a record 176 Grand Prix events. An articulate and thoughtful spokesman for motoring, he campaigned repeatedly for better highway driving and the banning of three-wheeled cars for invalids because of their inherent hazards.

RAY HAMILTON—CAMERA PRESS

Hogben, Lancelot Thomas, British scientist (b. Southsea, England, Dec. 9, 1895—d. Wrexham, Clwyd, Wales, Aug. 22, 1975), became widely known as a gifted popularizer of science through such best-selling books as *Mathematics for the Million* (1936) and *Science for the Citizen* (1938). A graduate of Trinity College, Cambridge, and an outstanding geneticist and physiologist, he also gave his name to the Hogben test for pregnancy. In 1936 he was elected a fellow of the Royal Society. After lecturing on zoology and physiology at London and Edinburgh universities, he accepted a series of professorial appointments (1925–47) in Great Britain, Canada, and South Africa. He then joined the University of Birmingham as a medical statistician (1947–61) and linguist (1961–64), devising an international language called "Interglossa." He concluded his career as vice-chancellor of the University of Guyana (1963–65). Hogben was also a contributing author to *Encyclopædia Britannica*.

Holford, William Graham Holford, 1st Baron, British architect and urban planner (b. Johannesburg, South Africa, March 22, 1907—d. London, England, Oct. 17, 1975), exerted a powerful influence on town planning in Britain and other parts of the world. After graduating in architecture from Liverpool University, he studied in Rome and visited the U.S. before entering private practice. He was appointed to the chair of civic design at Liverpool University in 1937 and was head (1948–70) of town planning at University College, London, succeeding Sir Patrick Abercrombie in both posts. In 1944 he became adviser to the new Ministry of Town and Country Planning and with the minister, Lewis (later Lord) Silkin, drew up the Town and Country Planning Act of 1947. Holford's most notable building was the Army Museum in London. He was also a consultant in Australia and South Africa and drew up plans for the precincts of St. Paul's Cathedral and Piccadilly Circus in London. His other responsibilities included the presidency of the Royal Institute of British Architects from 1960 to 1962 and membership in both the Royal Fine Arts Commission and the Historic Buildings Council.

Hurcomb, Cyril William Hurcomb, 1st Baron, British civil servant (b. Feb. 18, 1883—d. Sussex, England, Aug. 7, 1975), administered Britain's transport services during World War II as director general of the Ministry of Shipping (1939–41) and the Ministry of War Transport (1941–47). He also presided over such bodies as the Institute of Transport and the Electricity Commission (1938–47). In his World War II posts he controlled, in conjunction with his U.S. counterpart, all Allied merchant shipping and secured Britain's food supply. He was later named chairman of the British Transport Commission (1947–53) and effected the nationalization of transport during 1947–50. As a keen fisherman and ornithologist, he also served as vice-president (1954–60) of the International Union for the Conservation of Nature and Natural Resources. Hurcomb was knighted in 1938 and created a baron in 1950.

Huxley, Sir Julian Sorell, English biologist and philosopher of science (b. London, England, June 22, 1887—d. London, Feb. 14, 1975), was the eminent grandson of Thomas Henry Huxley, a noted biologist, and brother of Aldous Huxley, a widely read novelist. Julian's personal fame, both before and after he served as first director general (1946–48) of UNESCO, was due to a restlessly inquiring mind and a compelling desire to share his ideas with others. To this end he used radio, television, the classroom, the lecture platform, and the press. For the scientific community he produced highly regarded studies on such topics as the courtship of herons and grebes, the growth of animals, and the metamorphosis of the axolotl of Mexico. He was also biology editor of the 14th edition of the *Encyclopædia Britannica* and in 1937 won an Academy Award for a film entitled *The Private Life of the Gannets*.

Huxley's most widely discussed and perhaps most challenged theory, however, involved eugenic, behavioural, ethical, and religious principles. Called "evolutionary humanism," it reserved no place for God and postulated man as the sole arbiter of future evolutionary progress. To secure the fullest possible development for the greatest

Sir Julian Sorell Huxley

HORST TAPPE—PICTORIAL PARADE

number of individuals, human misery had to be wiped out by selective breeding and population control. Huxley, who studied at Oxford University and received a long list of distinguished honours during his lifetime, was knighted in 1958. Among his writings were *Religion Without Revelation* (1927); *Problems of Relative Growth* (1932); *Evolution: The Modern Synthesis,* which demonstrated his remarkable ability to interrelate the work of others (1942); *New Bottles for New Wine* (1957); and *Memories* (1970, 1972).

Ishizaka, Taizo, Japanese industrialist (b. Saitama Prefecture, Japan, June 3, 1886—d. Tokyo, Japan, March 5, 1975), graduated in law (1911) from Tokyo Imperial University, worked in the Ministry of Communications, and headed a successful insurance business before World War II. In 1949 he became top executive of the near-bankrupt Toshiba (Tokyo-Shibaura) Electric Co. Ltd., which under his tough management became a thriving concern. He also served as chairman of the Nippon Atomic Industry Group Co., Ltd. From 1956 to 1968 Ishizaka was virtual master of Japan's economy as president of the powerful Federation of Economic Organizations. At the age of 79, he agreed to build Expo 70 in Osaka and remain within the tight fiscal limits that had been set. But when he warned Prime Minister Eisaku Sato that the exposition would shame Japan, he quickly got an additional allocation. Though Ishizaka held hundreds of active and honorary posts, he was also an accomplished calligrapher and scholar who could mold pottery as beautifully as he could mold phrases into Japanese haiku.

Jewell, James Earl, U.S. radio scenarist and executive (b. Detroit, Mich., Feb. 20, 1906—d. Chicago, Ill., Aug. 5, 1975), was working for radio station WXYZ in Detroit when he wrote, produced, and directed the original "Lone Ranger" and the "Green Hornet" series (1933–38). Other credits as writer and director included the highly popular "Jack Armstrong, the All-American Boy." Jewell's administrative responsibilities included directing CBS radio in Chicago (1942–44) and managing Jewell Radio and Television Productions, which he established in 1944.

Jordan, Louis, U.S. musician (b. Brinkley, Ark., July 8, 1908—d. Los Angeles, Calif., Feb. 4, 1975), was an alto saxophonist and vocalist whose Tympany Five combo recorded several smash hits in the 1940s, including "I'm Gonna Move to the Outskirts of Town" and "Choo Choo Ch'Boogie," each of which sold more than a million copies. Jordan, who also recorded duets with Louis Armstrong, Ella Fitzgerald, and Bing Crosby, produced a rhythm-and-blues that many consider the forerunner of rock 'n' roll.

Judson, Arthur Leon, U.S. concert impresario (b. Dayton, Ohio, Feb. 17, 1881—d. Rye, N.Y., Jan. 28, 1975), struggled to support himself as a conductor, performer, teacher, writer, and promoter after abandoning hope of ever becoming "another Fritz Kreisler or Jascha Heifetz." In 1915 he happily became manager of the Philadelphia Orchestra and quickly established his own booking agency to promote new talent and appreciation of classical music. When he agreed in 1922 to extend his management to the Philharmonic Society of New York (now the New York Philharmonic-Symphony Orchestra), Judson was on the threshold of becoming the most powerful single figure in the history of American music. In 1926 the Judson Radio Program Corp. made history by inaugurating mass-media concerts, and in 1927, with two associates, Judson linked a group of private radio stations together for chain broadcasts; the following year the organization became the Columbia Broadcasting System. Over a period of years, by merging his management agencies with competing organizations, Judson created Columbia Concerts Corp. (now Columbia Records) in order to bring classical musical concerts to small-town music lovers throughout the U.S. and Canada. Among the artists Judson presented to American audiences for the first time were Vladimir Horowitz, Joseph Szigeti, and John Barbirolli. Among those he managed were Lucrezia Bori, Jascha Heifetz, and Rudolf Serkin.

Julian, Percy Lavon, U.S. chemist (b. Montgomery, Ala., April 11, 1899—d. Waukegan, Ill., April 19, 1975), taught at several universities and did graduate study at Harvard University (1922–26) before receiving his Ph.D. (1931) from the University of Vienna. His synthesis (1935) of physostigmine, used to treat glaucoma, led to his appointment as director of research in the soya products division of Glidden Co. in Chicago. He soon developed an inexpensive soya protein useful in paper manufacturing and in fire extinguishers. With his colleagues, Julian developed scores of soya derivatives. Steroids, derived or synthesized from a soya base, dramatically lowered the cost of treating arthritis and other diseases. In 1945 Julian was named director of research and management of fine chemicals at Glidden but left in 1953 to establish Julian Laboratories, Inc., with a branch in Mexico. From 1964 he served as president of Julian Associates Inc. and director of the Julian Research Institute. He was also active in the civil rights movement and donated generously to promote its goals.

Kamaraj, Kumaraswamy, Indian Tamil political leader (b. Madras Province, India, 1903—d. Madras, Oct. 2, 1975), was a member of the lower Nadar caste and a man with little formal education. He entered public life in 1921 during Mahatma Gandhi's campaign of noncooperation and subsequently spent nearly eight years in British jails. After India's independence he became an influential regional force in politics. In 1954 he was appointed chief minister of Madras and leader of the Tamil nationalist Dravida Munnetra Kazhagam party and in 1963 was elected president of the ruling Congress party. A powerful personality, Kamaraj relied on his instinctive grasp of political realities to help secure the prime ministership for Lal Bahadur Shastri after the death of Jawaharlal Nehru in May 1964. After Shastri's death in January 1966 Kamaraj successfully outmaneuvered Morarji Desai for a second time and Indira Gandhi became prime minister. In the general election of February 1971 he retired.

K'ang Sheng, Chinese Communist leader (b. Shantung, China, 1899—d. Peking, China, Dec. 16, 1975), joined the Chinese Communist Party (CCP) in the early 1920s, led uprisings in Shanghai in 1926, then went into hiding. Though arrested in 1930, he was released. From 1933 to 1937 he was in Moscow studying Soviet methods of security. By 1945 he had become a member of the Politburo of the seventh CCP Central Committee, which guaranteed him a place in the new Communist government of China. He supported Mao Tse-tung in the quarrel with the U.S.S.R., and during the crisis following the Cultural Revolution of 1966. K'ang was made third vice-chairman of the CCP in 1973.

Kay, George Marshall, U.S. geologist (b. Paisley, Ont., Canada, Nov. 10, 1904—d. Englewood, N.J., Sept. 3, 1975), made important discoveries in the field of Paleozoic stratigraphy and was an authority on geosynclines, large troughs in which sedimentary rocks accumulated during past geologic eras. Kay's studies on continental drift modified earlier geologic theories on the origin of North America and suggested that in time Japan would become part of the Asian mainland and Alaska part of Siberia. Kay, who was associated with Columbia University for nearly half a century, received the Penrose Medal of the Geological Society of America in 1971 and was the author of *North American Geosynclines* (1951) and *Stratigraphy and Life History* (1965).

Keating, Kenneth Barnard, U.S. politician and diplomat (b. Lima, N.Y., May 18, 1900—d. New York, N.Y., May 5, 1975), was a trial lawyer and six-term Republican congressman from New York before being elected (1958) to the Senate, where he served on the Judiciary Committee and on the Joint Congressional Committee on immigration. Politically, Keating shifted ground depending on the issues. He joined with liberals, for example, in supporting civil rights legislation, but lined up with conservatives in opposing Communism and the recognition of Mao Tse-tung's government in China. Keating was overwhelmed by Robert F. Kennedy in the 1964 Senate election, but returned to public life as ambassador to India (1969–72) and Israel (1973–75), where his hospitality and conviviality were proverbial.

Kellerman, Annette (Annette Kellerman Sullivan), Australian swimmer and entertainer (b. Sydney, Australia, July 6, 1888—d. Southport, Australia, Nov. 5, 1975), was a long-distance swimmer in Australia and Europe before launching a lucrative career as the "Million Dollar Mermaid" and "The Diving Venus." Before retiring in the 1930s, Kellerman—who was arrested in Boston in 1907 for wearing a skirtless one-piece bathing suit—became an international star in aquatic spectaculars, made movies on physical fitness, and lectured to women eager to learn how she preserved her fabled shapeliness.

Keres, Paul, Soviet chess grandmaster (b. Narva, Estonia, Russia [now Estonian S.S.R.], Jan. 7, 1916—d. Helsinki, Fin., June 5, 1975), was three times chess champion of the U.S.S.R., three times European champion, and the winner of four world chess Olympiads. As a youth he defeated such world masters as José Raúl Capablanca and Alexander Alekhine. Though he never captured the world championship, Keres

UPI COMPIX

won more than a score of international tournaments after World War II, defeating among others Mikhail Botvinnik, Tigran Petrosyan, and Boris Spassky, all world champions. His last book, *Practical Chess Endings,* was published in 1974.

Kisfaludi-Strobl, Zsigmond, Hungarian sculptor (b. Alsorajk, Zala County, Hung., 1884—d. Budapest, Hung., Aug. 14, 1975), studied in Budapest, Vienna, and Paris. During World War II he resided in London where he made busts of such prominent personalities as Princess Elizabeth (later Queen Elizabeth II), Neville Chamberlain, and Herbert Morrison. After the war he returned to Hungary where about 50 of his works were displayed in many cities, the best-known being the colossal Liberation Monument on Gellert Hill in Budapest.

Komissarov, Aleksandr, Soviet actor (b. Feb. 27, 1904—d. Moscow, U.S.S.R., Aug. 7, 1975), a leading comic actor of the Moscow Arts Theatre, studied under Konstantin Stanislavsky and remained with the Moscow Arts Theatre all his life. Noted for his lively interpretations of many roles, from Cherubino in *The Marriage of Figaro* by Pierre Beaumarchais to Mr. Winkle in *The Pickwick Club,* he appeared in London in Sir Peter Daubeny's first World Theatre Season in 1964. Komissarov was made a people's artist of the Soviet Union in 1948 and taught at the Moscow Art Theatre Drama School.

Kouwenhoven, William Bennett, U.S. electrical and biomedical engineer (b. New York, N.Y.,

Jan. 13, 1886—d. Baltimore, Md., Nov. 10, 1975), was responsible for developing heart resuscitating mechanisms and techniques that have since been used to save countless lives. His defibrillator imparts electrical shocks through the chest wall to suppress uncoordinated contractions of the heart so that its normal rhythm can be restored. Kouwenhoven, who spent some 60 years on the faculty of Johns Hopkins University, was also responsible for the worldwide use of external heart massage, an effective nonsurgical method for reversing cardiac arrest by applying brisk, repeated pressure on the breastbone.

Kriza, John, U.S. dancer (b. Berwyn, Ill., Jan. 15, 1919—d. Gulf of Mexico, Aug. 18, 1975), was a choreographer's delight, an inspiration to fledgling performers, and a premier danseur with the American Ballet Theatre of New York, which he joined at its inception in 1940. Before his accidental death by drowning, Kriza also displayed his vibrant style with such groups as the Chicago Civic Opera Ballet, staged ballets himself, and taught dance at Indiana University. Kriza appeared in *Swan Lake, Giselle, Don Quixote,* and numerous other classical ballets as well as in such modern productions as *Billy the Kid, Rodeo,* and *Fancy Free.*

Kuts, Vladimir, Soviet long-distance runner (b. Aleksino, Ukraine, U.S.S.R., 1927—d. Moscow, U.S.S.R., Aug. 16, 1975), became a celebrated athlete when in August 1954, at the European Games in Bern, Switz., he set his first world record running 5,000 m. in 13 min. 56.6 sec. Two months later, at White City in London, in a memorable 5,000-m. event, Christopher Chataway (U.K.) succeeded in clipping 5 sec. from Kuts's record. Ten days later, in Prague, Kuts beat Emil Zatopek (Czech.) and established a new record of 13 min. 51.2 sec. In 1956, at the XVI Olympic Games in Melbourne, Australia, Kuts achieved his greatest performances, winning both the 5,000- and 10,000-m. events. In Rome, on Oct. 13, 1957, he established a new 5,000-m. world record of 13 min. 35 sec., which stood for seven years.

Lacasse, Joseph, Belgian painter and sculptor (b. Tournai, Belgium, Aug. 6, 1894—d. Paris, France, Oct. 28?, 1975), was an early practitioner of abstract art who achieved recognition late in life. He studied in France and at the Royal Academy, Brussels, but subsisted as a manual labourer before settling in Paris in 1925. He worked as a Cubist before progressing to abstraction and figurative renditions of working-class life. During World War II he directed a rehabilitation centre for wounded soldiers at Stoke-on-Trent, England, where he also taught ceramic art. On his return to Paris in 1946 he resumed painting and sculpture. His work, which is displayed in museums of modern art, was exhibited in France, Belgium, Italy, Brazil, Chile, and the U.S.

Ladejinsky, Wolf Isaac, Russian-born expert on economics and agricultural programs (b. Ukraine, Russia, March 15, 1899—d. Washington, D.C., July 3, 1975), bettered the lot of millions of Asian farmers through land reform programs that permitted them to purchase land they formerly cultivated for the profit of landlords. Ladejinsky, who migrated to the U.S. as a penniless immigrant in 1922, obtained a master's degree in agricultural economics from Columbia University (1934) before joining the U.S. Department of Agriculture. Called to Japan by Gen. Douglas MacArthur in 1945, he formulated legislation that helped sweep away the foundations of the country's agrarian feudalism. Millions of tenant farmers profited from the redistribution of some 8,000 sq.mi. of land. He later provided the Chinese Nationalist government with blueprints for a similarly successful project in Taiwan. In India, South Vietnam, and elsewhere his success was minimal. In 1954 Ladejinsky became the central figure in a celebrated case involving security risks. He was recalled from Japan by order of Ezra Benson, the secretary of agriculture, but was cleared the following year. The affair moved the State Department to adopt new procedures to determine security reliability.

Lang, Jack (John Thomas Lang), Australian politician (b. Sydney, Australia, Dec. 21, 1876—d. Sydney, Sept. 27, 1975), was twice Labor prime minister of New South Wales (1925–27, 1930–32); his repudiation of Australian Labor Prime Minister James Henry Scullin's economic policies contributed to Scullin's defeat in 1931 and to the national decline of the Labor Party. After entering the New South Wales Parliament in 1913, Lang became party secretary and state treasurer, then prime minister and treasurer. During his first ministry he developed Australia's first child endowment plan and sponsored a widows' pension bill. In his successful 1930 campaign he opposed the deflationary policies of the federal Labor government. After refusing to pay New South Wales's interest payments on overseas loans in April 1931, Lang changed his position in exchange for federal payment of his government's expenses. In February 1932, however, he rejected the new federal statute requiring payment of state revenues to the Commonwealth and was dismissed by Gov. Philip Game. Lang's actions deepened the split in the national Labor Party and encouraged the development of the right-wing New Guard movement in opposition to Lang's policies. He served in Parliament (1943–49) as an independent after being expelled from the Labor Party in 1943. He was, however, reinstated three years before his death.

UPI COMPIX

Jack Lang

Laniel, Joseph, French politician (b. Vimoutiers, Orne, France, Oct. 12, 1889—d. Paris, France, April 9, 1975), was premier of France from June 1953 to June 1954. In 1940 he became undersecretary of state in the Ministry of Finance. Although Laniel was one of those who granted Marshal Philippe Pétain authority to promulgate a reactionary constitution in Vichy, he joined the National Council of Resistance in 1943. In 1945 he was reelected to the National Assembly and later served briefly as minister of state in the Cabinets of René Pleven and Edgar Faure. His brief tenure as premier ended with the disastrous French defeat at Dien Bien Phu in Indochina. His memoirs were published in 1971 as *Jours de gloire et jours cruels.*

Lapauri, Aleksandr, Soviet ballet dancer (b. June 15, 1926—d. U.S.S.R., Aug. 5, 1975), was one of the most celebrated members of Moscow's Bolshoi Ballet. He studied at the Bolshoi Ballet School before becoming a member of the company in 1944. He had already visited Britain with his ballerina wife, Raissa Struchkova, before he appeared in the full Bolshoi Ballet at Covent Garden, London, in 1956 with Galina Ulanova; his Hilarion in *Giselle* and Khan Girei in *The Fountain of Bakhchisarai* were enthusiastically acclaimed. He was also a teacher and choreographer, notably of *Lieutenant Kizhe,* performed by the Bolshoi in London in 1963.

Latife Hanim, Turkish feminist (b. Izmir, Turkey, 1898—d. Istanbul, Turkey, July 16, 1975), was for two years (1923–25) the wife of Kemal Ataturk, creator of the modern Turkish state. While traveling throughout the country as secretary to her husband, she shattered custom by discarding the woman's traditional face veil. Ataturk suddenly divorced her—perhaps because of her nagging criticism of his drinking habits—but shortly thereafter Turkey introduced civil divorce with equal rights for women.

Laver, James, British fashion historian (b. Liverpool, England, March 14, 1899—d. London, England, May 3, 1975), graduated from Oxford University and then joined (1922) London's Victoria and Albert Museum, where he remained until his retirement (1959). During these years Laver amassed an encyclopaedic knowledge of historical attire and became an expert on theatre art. In a score of books on the history of costume, he developed the thesis that fashions reflect the times and that a changing social milieu will lead to a subconscious transformation of the way people dress.

Laver also saw parallels between dress and architecture: stovepipe hats of Abraham Lincoln's day were copies of 19th-century chimneys, and pointed bishops' mitres mirrored medieval Gothic cathedral arches. Aside from such books as *The Changing Shape of Things: Dress* (1950) and *A Concise History of Costume* (1969), Laver also published poetry, a novel that was later dramatized, and books on art.

Legentilhomme, Paul, French army general (b. Valognes, Manche, France, March 26, 1884—d. Nice, France, May 23, 1975), was a member of the French Committee of National Liberation set up by Gen. Charles de Gaulle in Algiers in 1943 and one of de Gaulle's elite Companions of the Resistance. A graduate of the Saint-Cyr École Spéciale Militaire (1907) and of the École Supérieure de Guerre (1914), Legentilhomme was stationed in Indochina and in Madagascar after World War I. In 1938 he was transferred to Djibouti to organize the defense of French Somaliland; following the outbreak of World War II he was named commander in chief of the Franco-British forces of both Somalilands. After being dismissed from his command by Marshal Philippe Pétain in July 1940, he became the first army general to join the Free French forces of de Gaulle. In June 1941 he led the Anglo-French liberation of Syria and after the liberation of Paris by Allied troops was named military governor of the city.

Leider, Frida, German operatic soprano (b. Berlin, Germany, April 18, 1888—d. West Berlin, June 4, 1975), spent the major part of her career singing leading Wagnerian roles at the Berlin State Opera. After her professional debut (1915) at Halle singing Venus in *Tannhäuser,* she performed in many of the leading opera houses of Europe and the U.S. Though her most famous role was Isolde, she was also acclaimed for her Verdi and Mozart performances. After World War II she taught for a time in East Berlin, then at the West Berlin Conservatory (1948–58).

Lengyel, Jozsef, Hungarian novelist (b. Somogy Province, Hungary, 1896—d. Budapest, Hungary, July 14, 1975), began his literary and political careers as an Expressionist poet and a founder of the Hungarian Communist Party. When Bela Kun's Communist government fell in 1919 Lengyel went to Moscow where he edited a Hungarian newspaper. He was arrested in 1937 during a Stalinist purge and imprisoned for 18 years in various labour camps, an experience that he vividly described in such stories as *From Beginning to End* (translated 1966). Other translated works include *The Judge's Chair* (1968) and *Confrontation* (1973).

Levi, Carlo, Italian writer, painter, and political journalist (b. Turin, Italy, Nov. 29, 1902—d. Rome, Italy, Jan. 4, 1975), became an international literary sensation with his first documentary novel, *Cristo si è fermato a Eboli* (1945; *Christ Stopped at Eboli,* 1947), which depicted life in a malaria-ridden village in southern Italy. The book, which began a trend toward social realism in Italian literature, was followed by other notable works, including *L'Orologio* (1950; *The Watch*) and *Paura della libertà* (1947; *Of Fear and Freedom*). Levi, who was arrested several times during the period of the Mussolini regime for anti-Fascist views, was a physician and the director of a Florence periodical as well

KEYSTONE

Carlo Levi

as an accomplished painter. In 1963 and in 1968 he was elected to the Italian Senate as a left-wing independent.

Levy, Hyman, British mathematician (b. Edinburgh, Scotland, March 7, 1889—d. London, England, Feb. 27, 1975), joined the Imperial College of Science and Technology at the University of London, where he remained (1920–54) until his retirement. Though Levy's acknowledged expertise was in numerical methods and statistics, he wrote on such diverse topics as *Numerical Studies in Differential Equations* (1934), *Science, Curse or Blessing?* (1940), *Social Thinking* (1945), *Literature in an Age of Science* (1953), and *Finite Difference Equations* (1958). As a prominent member of the British Communist Party, he visited the U.S.S.R. in 1956 and was so appalled by the persecution of Jewish intellectuals and artists that he published *Jews and the National Question* (1957), which marked an end to his long-sustained sympathy for Marxism.

Lewis, Sir Aubrey Julian, Australian-born psychiatrist (b. Adelaide, Australia, Nov. 8, 1900—d. London, England, Jan. 21, 1975), was an independent-minded scholar who preferred eclecticism to dogmatism in regard to competing schools of psychiatry. He was deeply committed to advancing the academic frontiers of psychiatry and, though not a prolific writer, he produced studies on melancholia and obsessional illness that were widely read. Lewis has also been given generous credit for the rapid development of psychiatric epidemiology in Britain. In 1928 he began an enduring association with Maudsley Hospital in London. Serving as its clinical director from 1936 to 1948, he raised the institution to a position of world eminence as a centre for postgraduate teaching and research in psychiatry. At the University of London, he was professor of psychiatry from 1946 until his retirement in 1966. He was knighted in 1959.

Sir Aubrey Julian Lewis

GODFREY ARGENT—CAMERA PRESS

Li Fu-ch'un, Chinese Communist leader (b. Changsha, Hunan Province, China, 1900?—d. Peking, China, Jan. 9, 1975), was a student in France when he decided in 1922 to join the Communist Party of China. After returning home in 1925, he became deeply involved in Communist activities and with Mao Tse-tung, Chou En-lai, and his wife completed the 6,000-mi. Long March (1934–35) to Yen-an. In the years that followed, he proved his worth in various party posts before being named minister of heavy industry in the newly established (1949) People's Republic of China. As his government's top economist, he took part in negotiating (1953) for Soviet money and materials needed to launch and sustain the country's first five-year plan, and as head of the State Planning Commission he formulated and implemented the Great Leap Forward (1958–61) in industrial development, which had disastrous effects on agriculture.

Longwell, Chester Ray, U.S. geologist (b. Spalding, Mo., Oct. 15, 1887—d. Palo Alto, Calif., Dec. 15, 1975), was an expert on geologic history, who did extensive research on the western U.S. While a member of the Yale University faculty (1938–56), he directed a team of 16 geologists who completed the first tectonic map of the U.S. The seven-colour map, which measured 4 ft. by 6½ ft., took nine years to finish. Longwell was co-author of *Physical Geology* (1932) and *Introduction to Physical Geology* (1955).

Loomis, Alfred Lee, U.S. physicist (b. New York, N.Y., Nov. 4, 1887—d. East Hampton, N.Y., Aug. 11, 1975), graduated from Yale University (1909) and from Harvard Law School (1912), then established Loomis Laboratories (1928) and the Loomis Institute for Scientific Research (1930) while acquiring considerable wealth through investment banking. During the course of his career in science he was associated, in various capacities, with the Lawrence Radiation Laboratories, the Rand Corporation, the Carnegie Institution, and the Massachusetts Institute of Technology. Among his many accomplishments, Loomis played an important role in developing a device for measuring the velocity of projectiles, aided in the development of an electroencephalograph, directed research on radar during World War II, and helped devise the long-range navigational system called loran.

López, Eugenio, Sr., Philippine business tycoon (b. 1901?—d. San Francisco, Calif., July 6, 1975), was reputed to be the wealthiest man in the Philippines when he owned or had substantial interests in the Manila Electric Co., the nation's largest broadcasting network, the *Manila Chronicle,* banking, construction, and agriculture. López, whose severest critics questioned the propriety of some of his dealings, entered into a tenuous but mutually profitable alliance with Ferdinand E. Marcos. When Marcos was elected president in 1965 and 1969, Fernando López, Eugenio's brother, was elected vice-president on the same ticket. The uneasy relationship was sundered when Marcos proclaimed martial law in September 1972. Eugenio, who interpreted Marcos' move as a grab for permanent and absolute power, completed an overseas trip by settling in San Francisco. In short order his newspaper and broadcasting network were silenced and his son Geny (Eugenio, Jr.) was arrested with others on charges of participating in assassination plots against the president. Though López eventually signed away a large segment of his business interests, he bitterly complained that he acted under threats against his family. Marcos defended martial law as the only effective means for dealing with internal unrest, some of it Communist inspired, while his supporters argued that the disassembly of López' financial machinery was proof positive that Marcos was absolutely serious about establishing a new social order with a more equitable distribution of wealth. When López died, his son was still in prison and had not been formally charged or brought to trial.

Lopez, Vincent Joseph, U.S. bandleader and pianist (b. New York, N.Y., Dec. 30, 1894—d. North Miami, Fla., Sept. 20, 1975), retained his popularity for almost 60 years by interpreting popular tunes to appreciative audiences in night-clubs and hotels and through appearances on radio and television. After shuttling between engagements for nearly 20 years, he monopolized

UPI COMPIX

the spotlight at the Grill Room of New York's Hotel Taft from 1941 to 1966. Aside from his signature, "Hello, everybody—Lopez speaking," he was best known for "Nola." He also discovered such singers as Betty Hutton and counted Artie Shaw, Glenn Miller, and Xavier Cugat among his more famous sidemen.

Losch, Tilly (Ottilie Ethel Losch), Austrian-born dancer (b. Vienna, Austria, Nov. 15, 1907—d. New York, N.Y., Dec. 24, 1975), an international dancer of striking grace and beauty, appeared as a child dancer in the Vienna Opera House in 1912 and was a member of Max Reinhardt's company on its 1927 visit to the U.S. Under the London impresario Charles B. Cochran, she caught the imagination of London's West End in two reviews, *This Year of Grace* (1928) and *Wake Up and Dream* (1929). After visiting the U.S. she performed again in London with her own company, *Les Ballets* (1933). Losch also appeared in films and became a creditable painter.

Mabley, Moms (Jackie Mabley; Loretta Mary Aiken), U.S. comedienne (b. Brevard, N.C., March 19, 1897?—d. White Plains, N.Y., May 23, 1975), left home at 16 for a stage career, then worked her way up to bookings in such big-time night spots as the Cotton Club and Connie's Inn in Harlem and the Regal in Chicago. Her routines called for ragtag clothes, a raspy voice, and earthy lines, which were first munched to death by toothless gums. Mabley's first appearance on television, arranged by Harry Belafonte in 1967, led to numerous other engagements, including frequent spots on top-rated talk shows. The name "Moms" apparently came from struggling black actors, who appreciated her sympathy, encouragement, and motherly understanding.

McAuliffe, Anthony Clement, U.S. army general (b. Washington, D.C., July 2, 1898—d. Washington, D.C., Aug. 11, 1975), was acting commander of the U.S. 101st Airborne Division when

UPI COMPIX

Anthony Clement McAuliffe

the Germans launched a ferocious counterattack in the wooded Ardennes region of Belgium in December 1944. Rejecting a German ultimatum to surrender with a contemptuous "Nuts!" McAuliffe held Bastogne during the month-long Battle of the Bulge and became an instant legend. The battle was the last Nazi offensive on the Western Front. After World War II McAuliffe, who graduated from the U.S. Military Academy at West Point in 1919, held various command and staff appointments, ending his career as U.S. army commander in Europe (1955–56).

MacPhail, Larry (LELAND STANFORD MACPHAIL), U.S. sportsman (b. Cass City, Mich., Feb. 3, 1890—d. Miami, Fla., Oct. 1, 1975), at various times practiced law, headed a tool company, a department store, and an automobile agency, and was an army colonel, a football referee, and a breeder of Thoroughbred horses. But it was MacPhail's exploits in the world of baseball that will be remembered best of all. After becoming vice-president of the Cincinnati Reds, he upped attendance by hiring girl ushers, painted Crosley Field a brilliant orange, and introduced the major leagues' first night game in May 1935. He showed the same flair with the Brooklyn Dodgers, whose fans saw Johnny Vander Meer of the Reds pitch his second no-hitter in a row during the first night game in Brooklyn. After World War II MacPhail formed a partnership with Del Webb and Daniel Topping to buy the once mighty New York Yankees. When MacPhail sold his interests a few years later for a tidy profit, the Yankees had already gained the first of 15 pennants won over an 18-year stretch.

McWhirter, Ross, British sportswriter (b. London, England, Aug. 12, 1925—d. London, Nov. 27, 1975), was co-editor with his twin brother Norris of the perennial best-seller *Guinness Book of World Records.* He studied law at Trinity College, Oxford, where he and his brother were notable sprinters; both later became sportswriters and television personalities, and Ross the chairman of the Sports Writers' Association. He was also co-author of the official history of the Rugby Football Union and of *Get to Your Marks!* (1951), a historical and statistical survey of athletics.

McWhirter was a well-known champion of individual freedom and went to court many times to protest encroachments on personal liberty. His chief objects of criticism were bureaucratic governments, militant trade unions, and extremist organizations. As chairman of Self-Help, he offered £50,000 in rewards for information leading to the arrest of terrorists—several of whom gunned him down in the doorway of his home.

Maheu, René, French academic (b. Saint-Gaudens, France, March 28, 1905—d. Paris, France, Dec. 19, 1975), was director general of the UN Educational, Scientific and Cultural Organization (UNESCO) from 1962 to 1974. After graduating from the École Normale Supérieure, he taught philosophy in France, at the University of Cologne, and at the Institut Français in London. During World War II he taught at the Collège Franco-Musulman in Fez, Morocco, and from 1943 directed the Agence de Presse France-Afrique in Algiers. When UNESCO was set up in Paris in 1946, Maheu became a member of the secretariat and *chef de cabinet* of the director general, then assistant director general (1954) and acting director general in 1961. Maheu's great ambition was to eradicate illiteracy around the world. A decade later Maheu acknowledged that the number of illiterates had actually increased and lamented that the reasons for failure were "as much political as financial."

Main, Marjorie (MARY TOMLINSON KREBS), U.S. actress (b. Acton, Ind., Feb. 24, 1890—d. Los Angeles, Calif., April 10, 1975), brought joy and hilarity to thousands of devoted fans in nine "Ma and Pa Kettle" films, playing opposite Percy Kilbride. Though the first of the series set a record for the early 1950s by grossing about $3.5 million, the films were generally disregarded by the critics. Equally comfortable with serious dramatic parts, she played a wide variety of roles in some 100 films and enjoyed a successful Broadway career highlighted by her portrayal of the

WIDE WORLD

mother of a killer in *Dead End* (1935); she repeated the role in the screen version. Her last picture, *The Kettles on Old MacDonald's Farm,* was released in 1957.

Maisky, Ivan Mikhailovich, Soviet diplomat (b. near Nizhny-Novgorod, Russia, Jan. 19, 1884—d. Moscow, U.S.S.R., Sept. 3, 1975), the son of a Jewish army doctor, was an influential ambassador to the Court of St. James's (1932–43). He spent his early youth at Omsk, and attended the University of St. Petersburg, from which he was expelled for revolutionary activities as a Menshevik. He went to London in 1912 where he met Maksim Litvinov. In 1921 he converted to Bolshevism and joined the People's Commissariat for Foreign Affairs as a press officer. Maisky was appointed ambassador to London in October 1932. He succeeded in arranging the Eden-Stalin meeting in Moscow (March 29, 1935) and in 1941 signed a mutual assistance pact with Poland (July 30) and played a leading part in negotiating the Anglo-Soviet alliance treaty that was signed on May 26, 1942. In the summer of 1943 Maisky was recalled to Moscow to serve as deputy foreign minister and took part in the Yalta and Potsdam conferences. In later years he became an expert in Far Eastern history.

March, Fredric (FREDERICK MCINTYRE BICKEL), U.S. actor (b. Racine, Wis., Aug. 31, 1897—d. Los Angeles, Calif., April 14, 1975), displayed an amazingly versatile talent during a stage and film career that spanned more than 50 years. He received two Academy Awards, one for his role in *Dr. Jekyll and Mr. Hyde* (1932), the other for his portrayal of a war-weary veteran in *The Best Years of Our Lives* (1946). These superb performances were matched on Broadway in such dramas as *The Skin of Our Teeth* (1942), *A Bell for Adano* (1944), and *Long Day's Journey into Night* (1956). March had fixed his youthful hopes on a career in international finance, but

WIDE WORLD

Fredric March

he was also attracted to the stage and in 1920 made his debut. While playing summer stock in Denver in 1926, he met the leading lady, Florence Eldridge, who became his wife and inseparable professional partner. With the advent of talking pictures, he achieved instantaneous stardom because of his rich, sonorous voice and handsome features. At the height of his film career, he and his wife appeared in the New York play *Yr. Obedient Husband* (1938). Thereafter March alternated between stage and screen, feeling that each medium enhanced the other. His 69th and last film was O'Neill's *The Iceman Cometh* (1973).

Marshall, George E., U.S. movie director (b. Chicago, Ill., Dec. 29, 1891—d. Los Angeles, Calif., Feb. 17, 1975), made some 400 films during a career that lasted more than 60 years. Equally at ease with comedies, musicals, and Westerns, he directed such stars as W. C. Fields, Will Rogers, Alice Faye, Henry Fonda, Glenn Ford, Lucille Ball, and Bob Hope. Marshall was co-director of *How the West Was Won* (1962).

Maserati, Ernesto, Italian automobile manufacturer (b. Voghera, Italy, 1898—d. Bologna, Italy, Dec. 1, 1975), built and raced his own cars before devoting full time to the manufacture of high-performance vehicles. In 1930 the Maserati began to demonstrate its superb qualities by capturing most of the Grand Prix races. Though Maserati sold his interests before World War II, he remained as director of the company and planned the racing cars that later triumphed in the Indianapolis 500 and on the Grand Prix tours.

Mathieson, Muir, Scottish composer of film music (b. Stirling, Scotland, Jan. 24, 1911—d. Oxford, England, Aug. 2, 1975), was first associated, from 1934, with Alexander Korda's films, but a more significant contribution to film scores resulted when he teamed up with Arthur Bliss in the H. G. Wells film *Things to Come* (1935). Mathieson's effort to make a major contribution to motion pictures through music attracted such composers as William Walton, Benjamin Britten, and William Alwyn to write for films. Some of his later scores were used in documentaries and in films starring Noel Coward and Laurence Olivier.

Matthew, Sir Robert Hogg, British architect (b. Edinburgh, Scotland, Dec. 12, 1906—d. Keith Marischal Humbie, East Lothian, Scotland, June 21, 1975), as architect to the London County Council (LCC) from 1946 to 1953 was responsible for the Royal Festival Hall and later, in private practice, for the New Zealand House, both in London. Educated in Edinburgh and then a prizewinning student at the Royal Institute of British Architects (RIBA), Matthew became chief architect and planning officer of the Department of Health for Scotland in 1945, before moving to the LCC. From 1953 to 1968 he was

Forbes professor of architecture at Edinburgh University while practicing privately and serving as president of the International Union of Architects (1961–65) and of the Commonwealth Association of Architects (1965–68). He was knighted in 1962.

Medwick, Ducky (JOSEPH MICHAEL MEDWICK), U.S. baseball player (b. Carteret, N.J., Nov. 24, 1911—d. St. Petersburg, Fla., March 21, 1975), joined the flamboyant St. Louis Cardinals in 1932 as a hard-hitting, hot-tempered outfielder. During the seventh game of the 1934 World Series against Detroit, Medwick was spiked at third base and responded with flying fists. When he returned to the outfield, Detroit fans set off a near riot that reached dangerous proportions before Medwick agreed to leave the game. Following a contract dispute in 1940, Medwick was traded to the Brooklyn Dodgers and later played for several other teams. When he retired in 1948, his election to the Hall of Fame (1968) was assured: he had a career batting average of .324; his 64 doubles in one season (1936) was still a league record at the time of his death; and he was the last (1937) National League player to win the "triple crown" (best batting average, most home runs, most runs batted in).

Meouchi, Paul Pierre Cardinal, Lebanese prelate of the Roman Catholic Church (b. Jazzin, Lebanon, April 1, 1894—d. Bkirki, Lebanon, Jan. 11, 1975), became spiritual leader of all Maronite-rite Catholics when he was named patriarch of Antioch and all the East by Pope Pius XII in 1955. Ten years later he was raised to the cardinalate, the first Maronite so honoured. In Lebanon, where religious and political differences required a delicate balance, Meouchi was as widely respected by the Muslim minority as by his fellow Christians. Though a moderate by nature, he was capable of firm action as when he strongly opposed a second term for Pres. Camille Chamoun in 1958 and when he publicly endorsed the aspirations of the Palestinians for an independent country.

Mesta, Perle, U.S. hostess (b. Sturgis, Mich., Oct. 12, 1889—d. Oklahoma City, Okla., March 16, 1975), was for three decades the most publicized hostess in the nation's capital. Having abandoned earlier dreams of a career in classical music and possessing a sizable fortune inherited from her father (William B. Skirvin, an oil tycoon) and her husband (George Mesta, a steel industrialist), she settled in Washington, D.C., in 1941. Disregarding the *Social Register*, she sent party invitations to such "interesting persons" as heads of state, show people, and political enemies. All thoroughly enjoyed each other and the gaiety and informality that were sustained by the charming joviality of "the hostess with the mostes'." One of Mesta's favourite guests was Pres. Harry S. Truman, who unwittingly inspired the musical *Call Me Madam* by naming Mesta minister to the Grand Duchy of Luxembourg in grateful recognition of her support of his 1948 campaign. Though Mesta resumed her Washington entertaining in 1954, her parties lost much of their appeal during the Kennedy administration (she supported the Nixon campaign of 1960) and were never again quite so glamorous.

Perle Mesta

THE NEW YORK TIMES

Meynell, Sir Francis, British publisher (b. London, England, May 12, 1891—d. Lavenham, Suffolk, England, July 9, 1975), was especially known for his finely designed books, the most widely distributed of which were the series of English writers issued by the Nonesuch Press, which he founded in 1923. He was educated at Downside and Trinity College, Dublin, and in association with the typographer Stanley Morison became a book designer. Both worked for Burns & Oates and then at the Pelican Press, founded by Meynell in 1916. Meynell, a Socialist, wrote for the *Daily Herald* and was associated with Bertrand Russell's antiwar crusade. Meynell, who was knighted in 1946, was also an adviser to the Victoria and Albert Museum and the Royal Mint and served on the council of the Royal College of Art and the Council of Industrial Design. His graceful poetry was published in *Poems and Places* (1961).

Mindszenty, Jozsef Cardinal, Hungarian prelate of the Roman Catholic church (b. Csehimindszent, near Szombathely, Austria-Hungary, March 29, 1892—d. Vienna, Austria, May 6, 1975), became an international symbol of uncompromising opposition to human oppression—to many a hero, to others a stubborn and unreasonable man. His inflexibility eventually led to nearly eight years of imprisonment, punctuated with psychological and physical torture, and to 15 years of voluntary confinement in the U.S. embassy in Budapest.

CAMERA PRESS/PICTORIAL PARADE

Mindszenty, who had been imprisoned by the Nazis during the final months of World War II, became primate of Hungary in 1945 and a cardinal in February 1946. On Dec. 26, 1948, he was arrested by the Hungarian Communist government on charges of treason and espionage. After a mock trial he was sentenced (Feb. 8, 1949) to life imprisonment. On Oct. 30, 1956, he was released by Hungarian freedom fighters who brought him to his palace at Buda. But when Soviet armour moved in to suppress the insurrection, Mindszenty was given asylum in the U.S. embassy (Nov. 4, 1956). From 1963 the Vatican made many efforts to persuade him to leave the country in the interest of Hungarian Catholics, but the cardinal refused unless the government acknowledged his complete innocence. Finally, bowing to the pope's wishes, Mindszenty left Hungary in September 1971. He visited Rome, then took up residence in a priests' hostel in Vienna. Refusing to remain silent, he openly criticized the Vatican's policy of cautious détente with Communist Eastern Europe. In 1974 Pope Paul VI removed him as archbishop of Esztergom and primate of Hungary.

Mollet, Guy, French politician (b. Flers, Orne, France, Dec. 31, 1905—d. Paris, France, Oct. 3, 1975), was a teacher of English at the Arras lycée and a Resistance hero during World War II before being elected mayor of Arras (1945) and shortly afterward deputy for Pas-de-Calais. In 1946 he was elected secretary-general of the Socialist Party, a post he held for 22 years, resisting all moves for an alliance with the Communists. As premier of France from February 1956 to May 1957, he was responsible for sending conscripts to fight Algerian insurgents seeking independence and joined the British in a military expedition to Suez during the 1956 Arab-Israeli war. Of this decision he said: "I saved the state of Israel." During his tenure he also signed treaties establishing the Common Market and Euratom (European Atomic Energy Commission). In May 1958 he succeeded in defusing Socialist opposition to Gen. Charles de Gaulle as premier and joined de Gaulle's first government as minister of state. He remained mayor of Arras and a deputy until his death.

Muhammad, Elijah (ELIJAH POOLE), U.S. religious leader (b. Sandersville, Ga., Oct. 7, 1897—d. Chicago, Ill., Feb. 25, 1975), became Minister of the Nation of Islam (Black Muslims) following the mysterious disappearance of its founder, W. D. Fard, in 1934. During his tenure, Muhammad molded the Nation into an organization of considerable social, economic, and religious significance while preaching a message of black nationalism, self-knowledge, self-reliance, and the merits of a rigid morality that precluded alcohol, drugs, gambling, tobacco, and extramarital sex. For the most part, his followers steadfastly adhered to a code of behaviour more stringent than that which they had followed as Christians.

Muhammad's philosophy of black separatism derived from the belief that because triumph over the "white devils" would be divinely accomplished, blacks should not involve themselves in politics and civil rights movements. Although tens of thousands across the country responded to his call, Muhammad met with strong opposition, even from blacks who acknowledged his contribution to black social consciousness and pride and the success of Black Muslim mosques, schools, restaurants, grocery stores, a bank, a publishing house, and farmlands. Malcolm X, Muhammad's most influential disciple, became disenchanted with the Nation after vainly arguing for the acceptance of Caucasian Muslims and for black involvement in political and social struggles. In later years, however, Muhammad indicated a willingness to modify some of his more controversial positions.

PICTORIAL PARADE

Munakata, Shiko, Japanese woodblock artist (b. Aomori, Japan, Sept. 5, 1903—d. Tokyo, Japan, Sept. 13, 1975), was a prizewinning artist at the Imperial Art Academy before becoming totally engrossed in woodblock printing. Among his early masterpieces was "Ten Great Disciples of Buddha" (1938). Because he had lost one eye and was nearsighted in the other, Munakata worked hunched over, very close to his work, as he created roughly hewn Buddhist figures, Japanese subjects, and rustic settings that were exhibited all over the world and won countless prizes for their artistry. He was awarded the Japanese Medal of Honour with blue ribbon in 1963 and in 1970 the Order of Culture, the highest award conferred on an artist by the Japanese government.

Nelson, Ozzie (Oswald George Nelson), U.S. entertainer (b. Jersey City, N.J., March 20, 1907—d. Hollywood, Calif., June 3, 1975), graduated from Rutgers University in 1930 with a law degree, but to survive the Depression formed a dance band, which rapidly became one of the nation's favourites. The band's vocalist, Harriet Hilliard, became Nelson's wife in 1935. Their careers took a new turn in the early 1940s when audiences responded enthusiastically to their unsophisticated humour on the Red Skelton radio show. In 1944 Ozzie, as producer, director, and co-star, launched "The Adventures of Ozzie and Harriet," a situation comedy that had long runs on both radio (1944–58) and television (1952–66). The script eventually included parts for all the Nelson family: sons David and Eric (Ricky, the pop singer), their wives, and their children. In later years Nelson directed television shows, played summer stock, and with Harriet starred in the 1973 television series "Ozzie's Girls."

Nervo, Jimmy (James Holloway), British variety comedian (b. 1897?—d. London, England, Dec. 5, 1975), was especially associated with his partner Teddy Knox in the Crazy Gang shows from the 1930s to 1962. Nervo, who came from a family of circus clowns and acrobats, met Knox on a London street in 1918. George Black booked their show into the London Palladium, first for a week, then regularly for a "crazy month." During a long career, Nervo's comic falls earned him some fractured bones as well as rounds of wild applause.

Norfolk, Bernard Marmaduke Fitzalan-Howard, 16th Duke of, English peer (b. May 30, 1908—d. Arundel, Sussex, England, Jan. 30, 1975), was premier duke and earl marshal of England, whose hereditary duty of supervising state pageants began in 1936 with the obsequies of King George V. He later arranged such memorable events as the coronations of George VI and Elizabeth II, the investiture of Prince Charles as prince of Wales, the wedding of Princess Anne, and the state funeral of Sir Winston Churchill. In 1937 he married Lavinia Mary Strutt, only daughter of Lord Belper.

As a prominent English Roman Catholic, the duke became president of the Catholic Union of Great Britain and reported, after a private audience with Pope Paul VI, that he had informed the pontiff that recent changes in liturgy were unwelcome in Britain. He was also a keen cricketer and chairman of the Sussex County Cricket Club. As the queen's representative, he also organized the horse races at Royal Ascot for more than 25 years and in 1974 saw his own horse Ragstone win the Ascot Gold Cup.

Novotny, Antonin, Czechoslovak Communist leader (b. Letnany, Bohemia, Austria-Hungary, Dec. 10, 1904—d. Prague, Czech., Jan. 28, 1975), president of Czechoslovakia from 1957 to 1968, fought German occupation troops as an organizer of the Prague underground during World War II, but was arrested in 1941 and confined in the Mauthausen (Austria) concentration camp. In 1946 he was elected to the party's Central Committee and in February 1948 took a leading role in the Stalinist Communist takeover of the Czechoslovak government. He was admitted to the Politburo in 1951 and became first secretary of the Communist Party in 1953. After the death of Antonin Zapotocky (Nov. 13, 1957), he assumed the presidency and in 1964 was reelected to a five-year term. His close cooperation with Moscow, however, generated such severe criticism among the party's more nationalistic and less dogmatic factions that in January 1968 he was forced to resign the party leadership to Alexander Dubcek. Gen. Ludvik Svoboda became president in March and later in the year Novotny was deprived of his party offices and membership. At the party congress of May 1971, with the Moscow-oriented faction back in power, Novotny was reinstated in the party.

O'Daniel, John Wilson ("Iron Mike" O'Daniel), general (ret.), U.S. Army (b. Newark, Del., Feb. 15, 1894—d. San Diego, Calif., March 27, 1975), led the 3rd Infantry Division, 7th Army, during World War II after it landed at Anzio, 33 mi. S of Rome, finally broke through the German defenses, and entered Rome in June 1944. He next directed an assault on Saint-Tropez in southern France, then moved up the Rhône Valley and eastward to the Rhine River and Strasbourg. The following March his division spearheaded the 7th Army's drive on Nürnberg, capturing the Nazi stronghold after furious fighting on April 20, Hitler's birthday. Before the war ended, O'Daniel's forces also helped take Augsburg, Munich, and Berchtesgaden, Hitler's mountaintop retreat. After World War II O'Daniel headed (1945–48) the Infantry School at Ft. Benning, Georgia, served as military attaché (1948–50) in Moscow, led the I Corps in Korea, and in June 1952 assumed command of the Army in the Pacific. The appointment carried him to Vietnam where, at his urging, the U.S. made its first small commitments of help that eventually led to total U.S. involvement.

Onassis, Aristotle Socrates, Greek shipowner (b. Smyrna [now Izmir], Turkey, Jan. 15, 1906?—d. Neuilly-sur-Seine, France, March 15, 1975), made himself immensely rich through ownership of oil tankers and by pioneering supertanker

WALLACE LITWIN—PHOTO TRENDS

construction. The son of a Greek tobacco merchant who fled from Smyrna to Athens in 1922, Aristotle emigrated in 1923 to Buenos Aires, where he became a naturalized citizen of Argentina, a tobacco importer, and the Greek consul. In 1932, at a world-slump price, he bought six cargo ships, the nucleus of his future fleet. During World War II he leased his ships, which by that time included three oil tankers, to the Allies. After the war Onassis purchased 23 surplus Liberty ships cheaply from the U.S., which in 1953 indicted him on charges of fraud in the purchasing contract. Criminal and civil suits were dropped following a settlement of $7 million. In 1946 he married Athina ("Tina"), daughter of Stavros Livanos, the leading Greek shipowner. Onassis ventured into whaling in 1948 but came into conflict with Peru, Ecuador, and Chile over their claims to a 200-mi. territorial sea limit. Eight years later he sold off his whaling fleet to Japan, continued to build up his tanker fleet, and from the mid-1950s initiated construction of supertankers which in 1956 and again in 1967 reaped immense profits from the Cape of Good Hope route after the closing of the Suez Canal.

Onassis became well known in the 1950s, partly through well-publicized friendships with Winston Churchill and the volatile operatic soprano Maria Callas. He also made news as the rival of another Greek shipowner, Stavros Niarchos, whose first marriage to a Livanos daughter and later (1971) marriage to Onassis' ex-wife Tina intertwined their lives. Onassis married Jacqueline Kennedy in 1968 on the Greek island of Skorpios, which he had purchased in 1963. His other business operations, totaling about 100, included majority shares in Monte Carlo property and ownership by long-term concession of Olympic Airways, the Greek national airline.

Park, Sir Keith Rodney, New Zealand air chief marshal (b. Thames, N.Z., June 15, 1892—d. Auckland, N.Z., Feb. 5, 1975), commanded the Royal Air Force group that defended London and southeast England during the 1940 Battle of Britain. He was appointed air officer commanding Malta in 1942 and successfully defended the island against German and Italian strikes. In January 1944 Keith was named air officer commander in chief, Middle East, and a year later Allied air commander in chief, Southeast Asia command.

Parry-Williams, Sir Thomas Herbert, Welsh poet and scholar (b. Rhyd-ddu, Caernarvonshire [now Gwynedd], Wales, Sept. 21, 1887—d. Aberystwyth, Dyfed, Wales, March 3, 1975), was not only the first Welshman to win both the Crown and the Chair competitions at the National Eisteddfod but achieved this double twice, at Wrexham in 1912 and at Bangor in 1915. Educated at the University College of Wales, Aberystwyth, and at the universities of Oxford, Paris, and Freiburg, he became lecturer in Welsh language and literature in 1911 and was professor from 1920 to 1952 at the University College of Wales in Aberystwyth. His linguistic and literary research and his superb editing of Welsh poetry were matched by his own verse compositions, original in their use of living Welsh diction, his essays, and his translations into Welsh of well-known opera and choral librettos. He was knighted in 1958.

Pasolini, Pier Paolo, Italian film director and author (b. Bologna, Italy, March 5, 1922—d. near Rome, Italy, Nov. 2, 1975), made his reputation as an unorthodox, impassioned critic of society and as an impressive re-creator of erotic myth and story. His inspiration often came from the Roman slums, where he chose to live as a teacher and later as a director of films and a novelist. His first film, *Accattone* (1961), told the story of a Roman pimp. After the success of *Il Vangelo Secondo Matteo* (1964), he made two films reinterpreting classical myth, *Oedipus Rex* (1967) and *Medea* (1969), then ventured into medieval eroticism with *Il Decamerone* (1971) and *The Canterbury Tales* (1972), and into Eastern myth with *Il Fiore delle Mille e Una Notte* (1973). His last film, a reinterpretation of a work by the marquis de Sade, was called *Sado* or *The 120 Days of Sodoma,* and was set in Fascist Italy. Pasolini's novels *Ragazzi di vita* (1955) and *Una vita violenta* (1959) were realistic tales of slum life in Rome. Early in life he wrote poetry in the Friulian dialect and later published several volumes of poems and such critical writings as *Passione e ideologia* (1960) and *La poesia popolare italiana* (1960).

Pier Paolo Pasolini

LUTFI ÖZKÖK

BOOK OF THE YEAR

Payson, Joan Whitney, U.S. sports figure and civic leader (b. New York, N.Y., Feb. 5, 1903—d. New York, Oct. 4, 1975), was an ebullient multimillionaire who became a patron of the arts, a benefactor to the afflicted, and an exuberant sports fan. Though Payson took obvious pride in her Greentree racing stable in Kentucky, her abiding passion was baseball, especially after 1961 when she succeeded in purchasing a new National League expansion team, the New York Mets. Game after game she sat in her box seat watching the antics of one of the most inept teams in baseball history—they lost an incredible 737 games in seven seasons but somehow won the affection of countless fans who pushed through the turnstiles in astonishing numbers to cheer on their hapless heroes. Then suddenly in 1969, against seemingly insuperable odds, Payson's beloved Mets won the pennant and went on to defeat Baltimore in the World Series, 4–1.

Perkin, (Edwin) Graham, Australian editor (b. Hopetown, Victoria, Australia, Dec. 16, 1929—d. Melbourne, Australia, Oct. 16, 1975), whose editing of *The Age* in Melbourne made it one of Australia's most influential journals, was at first a reporter, then a subeditor and writer, deputy news editor, news editor, assistant editor, and finally editor (1966). He was also editor in chief with David Syme & Co., publishers of *The Age*. Perkin won a Kemsley scholarship in journalism in 1955 and a Walkley award for the best reporter in Australia in 1959. He also lectured in journalism at the University of Melbourne (1961–63) and was a director of both the Australian Associated Press and Reuters.

Perse, Saint-John (MARIE-RENÉ-AUGUSTE-ALEXIS LÉGER), French diplomat and poet (b. Saint-Léger-des-Feuilles, Guadeloupe, May 31, 1887—d. Presqu'île de Giens, Côte d'Azur, France, Sept. 20, 1975), was awarded the Nobel Prize for Literature in 1960. After graduation from Bordeaux University he moved to Paris where he began a friendship with Paul Claudel, also a diplomat and poet but 19 years older. His first poems under the pseudonym Saint-John Perse (*Images à Crusoe*) appeared in the *Nouvelle Revue Française* in 1909. Though he published only nine volumes of poetry, T. S. Eliot compared his literary influence with that of the great Irish writer James Joyce.

Léger entered the diplomatic service on Claudel's advice in 1914 and was sent to the French legation in Peking. In 1921 Aristide Briand, French foreign minister, chose him as his *chef de cabinet*. In 1933 Léger was appointed secretary-general at the Quai d'Orsay but was dismissed in 1940 and offered the post of ambassador to Washington, D.C., which he refused. His works were published in one volume in Paris in 1972.

Phillips, Alban William Housego, New Zealand economist (b. Dannevirke, N.Z., Nov. 18, 1914—d. Auckland, N.Z., March 4, 1975), gave his name to the "Phillips curve," which associates movements of wage rates and unemployment over an eight-year cycle (*see* INDUSTRIAL RELATIONS: *Special Report*). Phillips worked as an electrical engineer in a mining camp in Queensland, Australia, before traveling to England by way of the trans-Siberian railroad. While serving with the RAF in World War II, he was captured by the Japanese and learned Chinese from a fellow prisoner. After postwar studies at the London School of Economics, he progressed academically to become Tooke professor of economic science and statistics at London University (1958–67) and professor of economics at Australian National University (1967–70).

Powell, Lawrence Fitzroy, British scholar (b. Oxford, England, Aug. 9, 1881—d. Banbury, England, July 17, 1975), joined the staff of the Bodleian Library, Oxford, in 1895, worked on the *Oxford English Dictionary* (1902–16), served in the Admiralty, and from 1921 to 1949 was librarian of the Taylor Institution (modern languages, literature, and philology) of Oxford. In 1923 he began his revision of Birkbeck Hill's edition of Boswell's *Life of Johnson*, with the *Tour to the Hebrides* (vol. 5 and 6) and an *Index* volume (7 vol. in all), notable for its thorough scholarship.

Radhakrishnan, Sarvepalli, Indian philosopher and statesman (b. Tiruttani, near Madras, India, Sept. 5, 1888—d. Madras, April 17, 1975), second president of India, was a highly educated Brahmin who interpreted Hinduism to the West in numerous papers and books, most impressively in his two-volume *Indian Philosophy* (1923–27). Radhakrishnan was professor of philosophy at Madras, Mysore, and Calcutta universities, held lectureships at the universities of Oxford and Chicago, and in 1936 was appointed Spalding professor of Eastern religions and ethics at Oxford, becoming a fellow of All Souls College. He served as ambassador to Moscow and vice-president of India before being elected president in 1962. His five-year term encompassed a border conflict with China, war with Pakistan, the deaths of Jawaharlal Nehru (1964) and his successor Lal Bahadur Shastri (1966), and the accession to power of Indira Gandhi. He was knighted in 1931 and in 1975 became the first non-Christian to receive the Templeton Prize for Religion.

Rahman, Mujibur (SHEIKH MUJIB), president of Bangladesh (b. Tungipara, Faridpur district, India, March 17, 1920—d. Dacca, Bangladesh, Aug. 15, 1975), prime mover in establishing the new state of Bangladesh in December 1971, was assassinated with his family in an army coup. The son of a middle-class Bengali landowner, Mujib studied political science and law at the universities of Calcutta and Dacca. He founded the East Pakistan Muslim Students' League, which later played a major and often violent role in challenging Gen. Iskander Mirza's rule in Pakistan. His formal political career, however, began as co-founder (1949) and secretary (1953) of the Awami League, whose objective was autonomy for East Pakistan. When Gen. Mohammed Ayub Khan took power in Pakistan in October 1958, Mujib was arrested but refused to buy his release by pledging not to engage in politics for five years. His arrest in the late 1960s sparked mob violence that effectively eroded Ayub's authority in East Pakistan. In March 1969 Ayub was succeeded by Gen. Agha Mohammed Yahya Khan, who promised a new federal constitution. In the December 1970 elections, the Awami League secured 167 of 169 available seats in the projected Federal Assembly and 268 of 279 contested seats in the East Pakistan Provincial Assembly. Mujib's program called for complete internal self-government, with central government powers limited to defense and foreign affairs. When Mujib initiated a campaign (March 1971) of noncooperation in East Pakistan, Yahya imposed martial law and had Mujib arrested. Troops sent from West Pakistan to regain control of the eastern province were defeated with the help of the Indian Army. By December East Pakistan had become the independent republic of Bangladesh. On Jan. 12, 1972, Mujib took control of the government as prime minister, with Abu Sayeed Choudhury as president of the republic. Politically there was no alternative to the Awami League, which won 291 of 300 seats in the March 1973 election, but Choudhury resigned in December and was replaced by Mohammadullah, the speaker. Though Mujib himself had not entirely lost his prestige, several members of his family were accused of corruption. With unrest increasing, Mujib declared a state of emergency in December 1974 and in January assumed the presidency himself and abolished the multiparty system. Seven months later he was assassinated. (*See* BANGLADESH.)

Reid, James Scott Cumberland Reid, Baron, Scottish-born English judge (b. Drem, East Lothian, Scotland, July 30, 1890—d. London, England, March 29, 1975), was a lord of appeal in ordinary from 1948 until his retirement in 1975 and England's greatest judge since World War II. His was the voice that counted in most of the 600 appeals he sat on, cases that often influenced the direction of English law. He was educated at Edinburgh Academy and Jesus College, Cambridge, then studied Scots law at Edinburgh University. He was admitted to the Scottish bar in 1914 and became king's counsel in 1932. Reid sat in the House of Commons as Unionist member for Stirling and Falkirk burghs (1931–35) and for the Hillhead division of Glasgow (1934–48). He was also solicitor general for Scotland (1936–41) and lord advocate as dean of the Faculty of Advocates (1941–45). Reid reached the summit of the Scottish legal profession from 1945 until his appointment as an English law lord in 1948. From 1962 Lord Reid was the senior law lord, whose temperate judgments favoured individual freedom and opposed legal encroachments into Parliament's field of lawmaking. He was made a Companion of Honour in 1967.

Revson, Charles Haskell, U.S. business executive (b. Boston, Mass., Oct. 11, 1906—d. New York, N.Y., Aug. 24, 1975), began the Revlon cosmetic firm in 1932 in partnership with his brother Joseph and Charles Lachman; their total assets amounted to $300. Revson was chiefly responsible for giving the business its initial success by securing outlets in beauty parlours. In the following years he became a dynamic executive, demanding perfection before new products were put on the market, approving advertisements that often set new trends with their glamour and appeal, and branching out into such diverse industries as pharmaceuticals, health products, and clothing.

Riegel, Byron, U.S. chemist (b. Palmyra, Mo., June 17, 1906—d. Evanston, Ill., May 20, 1975), was an expert on drugs related to sex hormones, drugs for malaria and cancer, and an authority on the chemistry of vitamin K. He was on the faculty of Northwestern University, Evanston, Ill., from 1937 to 1951, then joined G. D. Searle & Co. in Chicago as director of chemical research and development. It was under Riegel's direction that the company's research section on steroid chemistry produced the first contraceptive pill publicly marketed in the U.S. (1960).

Robertson-Justice, James Norval Harald, Scottish film actor (b. northwest Scotland, June 15, 1905—d. Stockbridge, Hampshire, England, July 2, 1975), was a talented character actor—tall, grizzled, and bearded—who graduated from Marlborough College and Bonn University in Germany before becoming a teacher, salesman, manual worker, and writer. While acting as a music hall chairman he accepted a small part in Harry Watt's *Fiddlers Three* (1944) and launched a new career. In 1951 he went to Hollywood where he was cast as Sir Lancelot in *Doctor in the House* and other roles requiring a virile personality. Though Robertson-Justice was also rector of the University of Edinburgh twice (1957–60, 1963–66), he saw himself above all as an ornithologist and wildlife conservationist.

Robinson, Sir Robert, English organic chemist (b. Chesterfield, England, Sept. 13, 1886—d. Great Missenden, England, Feb. 8, 1975), was awarded the Nobel Prize for Chemistry in 1947 for research into the chemical constituents of plants. Long fascinated with the challenge of determining the sequence of chemical reactions through which alkaloids are formed in nature, he eventually synthesized the alkaloid tropinone by the interaction, in dilute aqueous solution at room temperature, of three simple compounds now known to be present in plants. His success in rationalizing the assembly of these organic compounds in terms of the electronic processes occurring during formation and disruption of chemical bonds was a vital step toward understanding all biosynthetic mechanisms. Robinson also contributed important researches on anthocyanin pigments of flowers and other vegetable colouring matters; he then proceeded to study the genetics of flower colour variations. Still other research centred on the synthesis of penicillin and of female hormones.

Robinson was educated at the Victoria University of Manchester and held the Waynflete chair of chemistry at the University of Oxford from 1930 until he retired in 1955. Elected to the Royal Society in 1920, he served as its president (1945–50) and was knighted in 1939.

Rojas Pinilla, Gustavo, Colombian politician (b. Tunja, Colombia, March 12, 1900—d. Malgar, Colombia, Jan. 17, 1975), came to power during a period of protracted political violence that took the lives of several hundred thousand persons. He assumed the presidency in 1953 after overthrowing Pres. Laureano Gómez, a Conservative, who had attempted to stamp out the Liberals and introduce a fascist state. On assuming office, Rojas promised peace, justice, and liberty. Instead, ruling by decree, he silenced the opposition press, perpetuated the secret police, repressed Protestant churches and schools, and embezzled government funds. Though forced into exile by Liberals and Conservatives acting together (May 1957), Rojas returned to Colombia (October 1958) and was impeached and deprived of his civil rights. Nonetheless, he ran for the presidency in 1962 and won 2.5% of the votes. Following a 1967 court ruling that restored his civil rights, Rojas ran for the presidency again in 1970 and narrowly lost in a hotly disputed election.

Rowell, Sir Sydney Fairbairn, Australian general (b. Locksley, Australia, Dec. 15, 1894—d. Melbourne, Australia, April 13, 1975), saw duty in Egypt and Gallipoli during World War I, became a major general and deputy chief of the Australian General Staff in 1941, and took command of the New Guinea Force in 1942. Transferred to the War Office in London, he helped plan the Allied invasion of Normandy in June 1944. Rowell retired as a lieutenant general after four years (1950–54) as chief of the Australian General Staff. He was knighted in 1953.

Sapir, Pinhas (PINHAS KOSLOWSKI), Israeli statesman (b. Suwalki, Poland, 1909—d. Nevatim, Negev, Israel, Aug. 12, 1975), went to Palestine at the age of 20, joined the Labour Party, organized demonstrations and strikes during the period of British rule, and was imprisoned for four months (1933). A member of Haganah, the Jewish underground military organization, he became its quartermaster in 1948 with the rank of lieutenant colonel. After Israel's independence he was appointed director general of the Ministry of Defense and then of the Ministry of Finance. From 1955 he was minister of trade and industry, and from 1963 minister of finance, trade, and industry. In 1974 he was elected chairman of the executive of the Jewish Agency for Israel and of the World Zionist Organization. Sapir became one of the most powerful men in Israeli politics through his ability to raise funds from overseas Jewish communities and through his success in obtaining military aid from the U.S. He was also influential in securing Golda Meir's succession to Levi Eshkol as prime minister in 1969 and the subsequent choice of Yitzhak Rabin as her successor.

Sastroamidjojo, Ali, Indonesian nationalist (b. Grabag, Java, Dutch East Indies, May 21, 1903—d. Jakarta, Indonesia, March 13, 1975), was first arrested as a student in The Netherlands for promoting the cause of independence for his homeland. After returning to Java to practice law, he cultivated the friendship of Sukarno and other political activists; in 1937 they founded the Gerindo party.

On Aug. 17, 1945, Sukarno unilaterally proclaimed Indonesian independence, realizing that the Dutch had lost control over their sprawling colony during the Japanese occupation. Ali was then appointed to a succession of government posts and was sent before the Security Council of the United Nations in 1948 to plead for formal recognition of Indonesia's independence. The following year he returned from The Hague with a signed declaration relinquishing all Dutch claims to Indonesia. He was also largely responsible, during his first term as Indonesia's prime minister (1953–55; also 1956–57), for organizing the Bandung Conference (April 1955), attended by representatives from 29 Asian and African countries. Ali was also ambassador to the U.S. (1950–53), Canada and Mexico (1953); was Indonesia's representative at the UN (1957–60); and served as vice-chairman of his nation's advisory parliament (1960–66). When Sukarno was ousted in 1967, Ali was arrested with other officials but released without trial.

Sato, Eisaku, Japanese politician (b. Tabuse, Japan, March 27, 1901—d. Tokyo, Japan, June 3, 1975), was Liberal-Democratic prime minister of Japan from November 1964 to July 1972. He was earlier chairman of the executive board of his party, minister of finance in the Cabinet of his brother, Nobusuke Kishi, and minister of international trade and industry in the Cabinet of Hayato Ikeda. Because of the close relationship that exists between business and government in Japan, Sato was immensely influential in raising Japan to the status of a world economic giant. In international affairs, he made little effort to better relations with China, but helped ease tensions in Asia by supporting the nonproliferation of nuclear weapons and guaranteeing that Japan would possess no nuclear arsenal of its own. His foreign policy was most closely allied to that of the U.S. Sato accordingly extended the U.S.-Japanese Security Treaty and cosponsored a U.S. resolution opposing Taiwan's expulsion from the UN. Ironically, it was Sato's closeness to the U.S. that eventually aggravated his problems at home. With the U.S. economy in difficulty, Pres. Richard Nixon insisted that Japan rectify a huge imbalance in its U.S. trade by severely cutting back its exports; Nixon also announced an import surcharge. These decisions had far-reaching effects on Japan's economy. In addition, Nixon's surprise announcement in July 1971 that he would visit China the next year stunned and embarrassed Sato because he had had no advance briefing on a major development affecting Japan's own foreign policy. With his popularity at an all-time low, Sato resigned. A few weeks earlier, however, one of his most cherished dreams was realized when the U.S. relinquished all control over the Ryukyu Islands. Sato was a joint recipient of the Nobel Peace Prize in 1974, but the honour was tarnished by reports that close friends had lobbied strenuously to influence the selection.

PICTORIAL PARADE

Eisaku Sato

Sauer, Carl Ortwin, U.S. geographer (b. Warrenton, Mo., Dec. 24, 1889—d. Berkeley, Calif., July 18, 1975), obtained his Ph.D. (1915) at the University of Chicago, then taught at the University of Michigan (1915–23) before serving as chairman of the department of geography (1923–54) at the University of California in Berkeley. For Sauer, geography was inseparable from human history inasmuch as the Earth, its resources, and its environment are profoundly affected by man. He thus found it quite natural to delve into anthropology, archaeology, and sociology as extensions of his geographic studies. From him students learned respect for the material world in which they live and the need to use it benignly. In his writings Sauer expressed a wide variety of views, including the contention that Irish monks visited America long before Leif Eriksson and that the New World was widely settled some 40,000 years ago.

Scoones, Sir Geoffry Allen Percival, British Army general (b. Quetta, India [now Pakistan], Jan. 25, 1893—d. England, Sept. 19, 1975), whose victory at Imphal, India, inflicted the first defeat on the Japanese Army in open battle in World War II. He commanded the 4th Corps, which met the full force of the Japanese March 1944 offensive and smashed it around Imphal. He was commander in chief, Central Command, India, 1945–46, and was principal staff officer, Commonwealth Relations Office, 1947–53, and U.K. high commissioner in New Zealand, 1953–57.

Serling, Rod, U.S. dramatist (b. Syracuse, N.Y., Dec. 25, 1924—d. Rochester, N.Y., June 28, 1975), achieved his first major television success with "Patterns," a story of intrigue involving top business executives that was featured on "Kraft Television Theatre" in January 1955 and won an Emmy Award. Thereafter, Serling won several other Emmy Awards and established himself as one of the country's finest television and motion-picture playwrights with such scripts as "The Rack," "A Town Has Turned to Dust," "Requiem for a Heavyweight," the "Twilight Zone" and "Night Gallery" series, and the motion picture *Planet of the Apes.*

Shafik, Doria, Egyptian journalist and reformer (b. Tanta, Egypt, Dec. 14, 1919—d. Cairo, Egypt, September 1975), campaigned for women's rights in Egypt and founded the Egyptian women's organization Bent el Nil (Daughters of the Nile) in 1948. In 1951 members of Bent el Nil interrupted a session of the Egyptian Parliament and demonstrated in Cairo, and in 1954 Mme Shafik went on a week's hunger strike with some of her followers. She later campaigned for the restoration of democracy.

Sheean, (James) Vincent, U.S. news reporter (b. Pana, Ill., Dec. 5, 1899—d. Arola, Italy, March 15, 1975), traveled the world covering such pivotal news events as Mussolini's march on Rome (1922), Chiang Kai-shek's break with the Communists (1927), the riots in Palestine (1929), the Spanish Civil War and Italy's invasion of Ethiopia (1930s), the signing of the United Nations Charter (1945), and the assassination of Mahatma Gandhi (1948). His 20 books and numerous articles had special importance in that they gave respectability to a subjective interpretation of the news which, in Sheean's case, was often sympathetic to leftist causes.

Sherriff, Robert Cedric, British author (b. Hampton Wick, Surrey, England, June 6, 1896—d. Kingston-on-Thames, England, Nov. 13, 1975), was best known for *Journey's End* (1929), a widely acclaimed play based on personal World War I experiences in the trenches. It had 595 performances in London and similar success in other parts of the world. None of his other plays met with such universal response, though *Home at Seven* (1950) was revived several times. At one time literary adviser to the film producer-director Alexander Korda, Sherriff also wrote notable film scripts, including *The Invisible Man* (1933) and *Goodbye, Mr. Chips* (1939).

Short, Luke (FREDERICK GLIDDEN), U.S. author (b. Kewanee, Ill., 1908—d. Aspen, Colo., Aug. 18, 1975), specialized in rough and tumble Westerns, many of which were first serialized in such magazines as *Argosy, Collier's,* and *The Saturday Evening Post.* Among the more than 50 stories that he wrote, successful film adaptations were made of *Ramrod, Ride the Man Down, Vengeance Valley, Station West,* and others.

Shostakovich, Dmitry Dmitrievich, Soviet composer (b. St. Petersburg, Russia, Sept. 25, 1906—d. Moscow, U.S.S.R., Aug. 9, 1975), was a pupil of Aleksandr Glazunov and a student at the conservatory in his home city from 1919 to 1925. Even before his early success as a pianist in the first International Chopin Competition in Warsaw in 1927, he manifested unique talents as a composer with the acclaimed First Symphony (1925). Though frequently castigated by Soviet authorities for the ideology expressed in his works, Shostakovich, a shy and withdrawn man, nonetheless continued to compose outstanding music. His opera *Lady Macbeth of the Mtsensk District* was withdrawn from production in 1936 because it offended "socialist realism." In 1948 his eighth and ninth symphonies were attacked as "formalistic"—a Communist synonym for "decadent." In 1963 his Thirteenth Symphony also fell into disfavour because it included a setting of Yevgeny Yevtushenko's poem *Babiy Yar,* which explicitly attacks Soviet anti-Semitism. Shostakovich taught at the Leningrad Conservatory and received numerous prizes, including the 1958 Lenin Prize for his Eleventh Symphony. He wrote 15 symphonies in all as well as string quartets, concertos, operas, and ballets.

Simon, Michel François, Franco-Swiss film actor (b. Geneva, Switz., April 9, 1895—d. Bry-sur-

GALA FILMS

Michel François Simon

Marne, near Paris, France, May 30, 1975), possessed a remarkable talent for portraying the inner depths of very ordinary, unattractive personalities. The mysterious quality of his acting, which embodied much more than a wide range of expressions and a gift for comedy, was especially evident in such films as *Port of Shadows* (1938) and *The Two of Us* (1967), in which he played the part of a rough, anti-Semitic peasant who develops great affection for a young Jewish boy in France during World War II. Simon made nearly 150 films, starred in 40 stage plays, and received numerous accolades during a long career that began in 1911 in a Paris music hall.

Singleton, Zutty (ARTHUR JAMES SINGLETON), U.S. jazz drummer (b. Bunkie, La., May 14, 1898—d. New York, N.Y., July 14, 1975), served his musical apprenticeship in the vibrant atmosphere of the New Orleans jazz clubs. In a career that spanned 50 years, he became one of New Orleans' greatest jazz drummers, playing with such greats as Louis Armstrong, Dizzy Gillespie, and Charlie ("Bird") Parker. Singleton also popularized the use of wire brushes and is often credited with originating drum solos integrated with an established melody.

Skorzeny, Otto, German SS officer (b. Vienna, Austria, 1908—d. Madrid, Spain, July 5, 1975), gained fame in 1943 for his daring rescue of Benito Mussolini from confinement at Campo Imperatore in the Abruzzi mountains where he had been imprisoned by Marshal Pietro Badoglio. Skorzeny joined the Nazi Party in 1933 and became a colonel in the Waffen SS during World War II. In 1944 he played a leading part in the roundup and torture of anti-Hitler conspirators after the failure of the July 20 assassination plot. On Oct. 17, 1944, he led an SS unit to the Budapest royal palace and arrested the Hungarian leader Adm. Miklos Horthy. In the course of the Germans' Ardennes offensive during Christmas week 1944, Skorzeny directed the infiltration of hundreds of English-speaking Germans clad in U.S. uniforms behind the Allied lines. After the war he was acquitted by the Allied War Crimes Tribunal (1947) on the testimony of a British officer who maintained that Skorzeny had done nothing that his Allied counterparts would not have attempted. While awaiting a denazification trial in 1949, he escaped from Darmstadt prison and spent his remaining years in Spain.

Otto Skorzeny

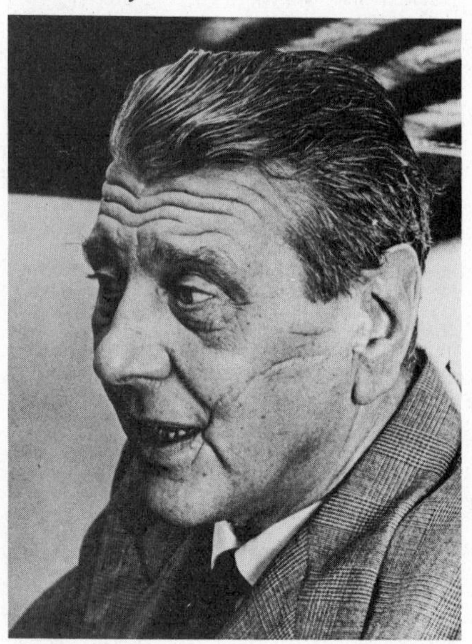

CAMERA PRESS

Sproul, Robert Gordon, U.S. university administrator (b. San Francisco, Calif., May 22, 1891—d. Berkeley, Calif., Sept. 10, 1975), graduated with a B.A. (1913) in civil engineering from the Berkeley campus of the University of California (UC) before working in the business office of his alma mater and serving as its comptroller for ten years. In 1930 he began an extraordinary 28-year career as president. During his administration he secured vast sums of money for the university from private individuals and from the state legislature, induced numerous Nobel laureates and other eminent scholars to join the faculty, expanded libraries, upgraded departments, gave hundreds of talks, forged a bond of unity between UC's widely scattered campuses, and weathered many crises. Though Sproul defended civil and academic freedoms, he denounced destructive groups and carried through, under protest, the loyalty oath imposed on faculty members in 1949 by the board of regents. His overall success and unusually long tenure were all the more remarkable because educational programs could be vetoed by the powerful Academic Senate and Sproul could be dismissed by a simple vote of the regents. When he retired in 1958, UC was not only educating some 100,000 students but was acknowledged to be one of the world's finest institutions.

Steen, Marguerite, British novelist (b. 1894—d. Newbury, England, Aug. 4, 1975), launched her writing career with *Gilt Cage* (1927), then produced nearly a book a year during the next four decades. Though she wrote a study of Hugh Walpole (1933), several biographies, two plays, and two volumes of autobiography, she secured a large and faithful following in Britain and the U.S. mainly because of the drama and action of her numerous novels. *Matador* (1934), a story about a retired bullfighter in Spain, became a Book Society selection in Britain and Book-of-the-Month Club selection in the U.S. *The Sun Is My Undoing* (1941), a 1,200-page historical novel about the Flood family of Bristol and the 18th-century slave trade, was among her most successful works.

Stehlin, Paul, French air force general (b. Hochfelden, Alsace, Aug. 11, 1907—d. Paris, France, June 22, 1975), fought with the Free French during World War II and held various staff appointments, including two years with the NATO Standing Group in Washington, D.C., before being named chief of staff of the French Air Force (1960). Gen. Charles de Gaulle then assigned him the task of building up a French *force de frappe* (strike force). Though Stehlin obeyed, he termed the plan a *force d'illusion*. Having retired from active duty in 1963, he entered politics and was twice (1968, 1973) elected to the National Assembly. Stehlin became the centre of a furious controversy when it was revealed that in September 1974 he sent a confidential letter to Pres. Valéry Giscard d'Estaing stating that the U.S. YF-16 and YF-17 aircraft were superior to their French competitor the Mirage F-1 and should replace NATO's Starfighters. It was later learned that Stehlin had been a paid consultant for the U.S. Northrop Corp., builder of the U.S. planes, since 1964.

Stengel, Casey (CHARLES DILLON STENGEL), U.S. baseball player and manager (b. Kansas City, Mo., July 30, 1890—d. Glendale, Calif., Sept. 29, 1975), was 84 years old when he mounted a Roman chariot dressed in a toga and gladiator's helmet and rode into Shea Stadium to celebrate Old-Timers' Day with the New York Mets. Such antics, and such inventive syntax as "I've always heard it couldn't be done, but sometimes it don't always work," delighted sportswriters, but tended to obscure the shrewdness and toughness of a man who knew baseball inside out. In a roller-coaster career as manager of four major league teams, "The Ol' Perfesser" was twice paid for not managing, but Stengel also led the New York Yankees to ten American League pennants and seven World Series championships between 1949 and 1960. "I couldn't have done it without the players," Casey explained. Stengel, who was inducted into baseball's Hall of Fame in 1966, was a left-handed outfielder on five major league teams, beginning with the Brooklyn Dodgers in 1912. During the 1923 season he hit .339 and gave the New York Giants two World Series victories with two home runs. But no one much remembered, for Babe Ruth blasted three home runs and the Yankees took the championship 4–2.

UPI COMPIX

Casey Stengel

Stevens, George Cooper, U.S. movie director (b. Oakland, Calif., Dec. 8, 1904?—d. Lancaster, Calif., March 8, 1975), achieved a high level of artistic and technical excellence in such films as *Shane* (1953), *A Place in the Sun* (1951), and *Giant* (1956)—the latter two winning Academy Awards. Like Stevens' *Gunga Din* (1939), these films are ranked as cinema classics. His early work included Laurel and Hardy comedy shorts and *Alice Adams* (1935) with Katharine Hepburn and Fred MacMurray.

Stirling, Matthew Williams, U.S. anthropologist (b. Salinas, Calif., Aug. 28, 1896—d. Washington, D.C., Jan. 23, 1975), was chief of the Bureau of American Ethnology at the Smithsonian Institution in Washington, D.C., from 1928 to 1947; thereafter he served as director until his retirement in 1958. Though Stirling led several important expeditions to Europe and the East Indies, Meso-America and South America provided him with his most rewarding discoveries. In southern Mexico a team under his leadership found remains of the long-extinct Olmec civilization. In Panama he identified the site of the region's oldest known village. And in Costa Rica he excavated 11 huge, perfectly formed, granite spheres, the function of which still baffles scholars. The Leyden Plate, which he uncovered in Tabasco, Mexico, in 1939, is a fragmented stone monument bearing a date corresponding to 291 B.C.; at the time, it was the oldest dated relic ever uncovered in the Americas.

Stocks, Mary Danvers, Baroness, British educator (b. London, England, July 25, 1891—d. London, July 6, 1975), an eloquent advocate of women's rights and a supporter of the Workers' Educational Association (WEA), became especially well known as a participant on the British Broadcasting Corporation's radio programs "Brains' Trust" and "Any Questions." She took her degree at the London School of Economics, lectured, then accompanied her husband to Manchester, where she served as a justice of the peace and as an extramural tutor at the university. From

1939 to 1951 she was principal of Westfield College, a London University women's college, meanwhile serving on such agencies as the Unemployment Insurance Statutory Committee. She was made a life peeress in 1966.

Stolz, Robert, Austrian composer and conductor (b. Graz, Austria, Aug. 25, 1880—d. West Berlin, June 27, 1975), composed more than 50 operettas, some 2,000 popular songs and piano pieces, and over 100 film scores, making him, in the eyes of some critics, the musical heir of "the Waltz King," Johann Strauss the Younger. Stolz began his career as a pianist at the age of 7, published his first musical composition at 11, and was a conductor at 17. For 12 years, beginning in 1905, he was principal conductor at the Theater-an-der-Wien in Vienna. Stolz won two Academy Awards: the first for "Waltzing in the Clouds" from the film *Spring Parade* (1940), the second for his music in *It Happened Tomorrow* (1944).

Stout, Rex Todhunter, U.S. writer (b. Noblesville, Ind., Dec. 1, 1886—d. Danbury, Conn., Oct. 27, 1975), introduced Nero Wolfe to a receptive audience in *Fer-de-Lance* (1934). Thereafter the massive and lethargic detective appeared in 45 other books, tending his orchids, eating with verve, and solving crimes with the help of Archie Goodwin, who did the legwork. Stout worked out his plots mentally while doing household chores, then gave himself 38 days to type the finished manuscript. Nero Wolfe's exploits entertained tens of millions of readers in over a score of languages and made Stout a wealthy man.

Tatum, Edward Lawrie, U.S. biochemist (b. Boulder, Colo., Dec. 14, 1909—d. New York, N.Y., Nov. 5, 1975), shared (with U.S. geneticists George Beadle and Joshua Lederberg) the 1958 Nobel Prize for Physiology or Medicine. While serving as research assistant at Stanford University in California (1937–41), Tatum, working with Beadle, confirmed that all biochemical processes are resolvable into a series of specific chemical reactions and that, when a genetic mutation can be shown to affect a specific chemical reaction, the enzyme catalyzing that reaction will be altered or missing. They thus demonstrated that each gene in some way determines the structure of a specific enzyme, creating the modern science of molecular genetics. At Yale, where he served as associate professor of botany (1945–46) and professor of microbiology (1946–48), Tatum worked with Lederberg. Their research was largely responsible for modern-day emphasis on bacteria as the primary source of information concerning the genetic control of biochemical processes in the cell. Tatum returned to Stanford (1948–57) before joining the faculty of New York's Rockefeller Institute (now Rockefeller University).

Taylor, Elizabeth, British author (b. Reading, Berkshire, England, July 3, 1912—d. Penn, Buckinghamshire, England, Nov. 19, 1975), had a Jane Austen-like gift for precise language and quiet wit, which she used in novels and short stories to describe life as seen from her home in Penn. Her first novel, *At Mrs. Lippincote's*, was published in 1945. Among those that followed were *A Wreath of Roses* (1949), *The Sleeping Beauty* (1953), *In a Summer Season* (1961), *Mrs. Palfrey at the Claremont* (1971), a study of lonely old age, and *A Dedicated Man,* which was adapted for U.S. television. Her short stories, many of which appeared in *The New Yorker*, were collected in *Hester Lilly* (1954), *The Blush* (1958), and *The Devastating Boys* (1972).

Taylor, Sir Geoffrey Ingram, British scientist (b. London, England, March 7, 1886—d. Cambridge, England, June 27, 1975), was a mathematician, physicist, and engineer whose creative insights led to significant advances in such wide-ranging fields as atmospheric and materials sciences, chemical and nuclear explosions, and engineering. After World War I, Taylor worked with Sir Ernest (later Lord) Rutherford at the Cavendish Laboratory at Cambridge and from 1923 to 1952 was also Yarrow research professor of the Royal Society, of which he had been made a fellow in 1919. Though his oral attempts to explain difficult matters in simple terms often amused his listeners, Taylor perceived an endless series of scientific principles at work in the most commonplace objects around him and used the principles in ingenious ways to perform experiments. He was knighted in 1944 and appointed to the Order of Merit in 1969.

Tertis, Lionel, British musician (b. West Hartlepool, England, Dec. 29, 1876—d. London, England, Feb. 22, 1975), established the viola as an instrument in its own right by his solo and ensemble playing. Having completed his training at the Royal Academy of Music, London, he played in (Sir) Henry Wood's Queen's Hall Orchestra (1897–1904), then embarked on a career as a solo viola player, whose command of his instrument inspired English composers to write for him. Tertis retired in 1936 after which he devoted himself to designing the now-standard viola and then a cello and violin. He made numerous arrangements of repertoire originally composed for other instruments.

Thompson, Sir (John) Eric Sidney, British archaeologist (b. Dec. 31, 1898—d. Cambridge, England, Sept. 9, 1975), was a leading authority on the ancient Mayan civilization. He fought with the Coldstream Guards in France in World War I, then worked as a gaucho on an Argentine cattle ranch before entering Cambridge University. He was an assistant curator at the Field Museum of Natural History in Chicago (1926–35) and played a major role in the British Museum's expedition to British Honduras under T. A. Joyce in 1927. His precise correlation of the complicated Mayan calendar with Western calendars became known as the Thompson Correlation. He joined the Carnegie Institution in 1935 and was knighted in 1975.

Thomson, Sir George Paget, British physicist (b. Cambridge, England, May 3, 1892—d. Cambridge, Sept. 10, 1975), shared the Nobel Prize for Physics in 1937 with Clinton J. Davisson for their independent discovery of electron diffraction. The son of Sir J. J. Thomson, who discovered the electron in 1897 and won the Nobel Prize in 1906, he attended Trinity College, Cambridge. In 1922 he became professor of natural philosophy at the University of Aberdeen, where he conducted experiments demonstrating that a beam of electrons is diffracted upon passage through a crystalline substance. This work confirmed the 1924 theoretical predictions of Louis de Broglie that electrons have wavelike properties as well as properties common to particles. Thomson was elected a fellow of the Royal Society in 1930 and was knighted in 1943.

Tidblad, Inga, Swedish stage actress (b. Stockholm, Sweden, May 1, 1901—d. Stockholm, Sept. 12, 1975), possessed a beauty and vitality matching those of the high-spirited Shakespearean women she played. She succeeded equally well in the drama of Strindberg, Ibsen, and Eugene O'Neill, in whose *Long Day's Journey into Night* and *More Stately Mansions* she scored outstanding successes. In the 1960s she took popular one-woman shows around Sweden, including portrayals of Shakespeare's heroines, and in the early 1970s was admired in *The Angel,* a television series written for her.

Tiltman, Alfred Hessell, British aircraft designer (b. London, England, March 17, 1891—d. Bognor Regis, Sussex, England, Oct. 28, 1975), studied engineering at London University, then worked in England and Canada before entering the aircraft industry in 1916. Five years later he joined the newly established De Havilland Aircraft Company as assistant designer. He worked with the author Nevil Shute (pen name of N. S. Norway, then working in aeronautics) on the airship R100, which unlike the government's R101 proved a success. When airship projects were abandoned, Tiltman and Shute formed Airspeed, a company that manufactured the Oxford Airspeed, a standard twin-engine trainer used in World War II, and the Horsa glider, which went into action on D-Day at Arnhem, Neth. The company also developed such features as retractable undercarriages, self-sealing gasoline tanks, and in-flight refueling. After the war Tiltman (Shute had already become a writer) left Airspeed to co-found Tiltman Langley, Ltd., of which he was technical director and chairman for six years.

Tolbert, Stephen, Liberian entrepreneur (b. Bensonville, Liberia, Feb. 16, 1922—d. in flying accident near Greenville, Liberia, April 28, 1975), a brother of Pres. William Tolbert, was Liberia's finance minister from 1972. Educated at the University of Michigan as a forester, he represented Liberia at the UN Food and Agriculture Organization in Rome. Tolbert, who amassed a huge personal fortune through the importation of fish and other business ventures, was remarkably successful as finance minister in eradicating corruption and attracting foreign investment. He also improved black-white political relations and served as intermediary in discussions between his brother and the prime minister of South Africa, B. J. Vorster.

Tolson, Clyde Anderson, U.S. law enforcement official (b. near Laredo, Mo., May 22, 1900—d. Washington, D.C., April 14, 1975), joined the FBI in 1928, four years after J. Edgar Hoover became its director. Tolson became assistant director in 1930, assistant to Hoover in 1938, and associate director of the bureau in 1947 with budgetary and administrative responsibilities. For decades Tolson and Hoover, both bachelors, dined together, vacationed together, visited the race track together, and apparently discussed top-level decisions only in each other's company. An enfeebled Tolson submitted his resignation from the FBI on May 3, 1972, the day after Hoover's death. A few weeks later a Washington court announced that Hoover had left the bulk of his estate, worth over half a million dollars, to his longtime associate.

Tombalbaye, N'Garta, first president of the republic of Chad (b. Bessada, French Equatorial Africa, June 15, 1918—d. N'Djamena, Chad, April 13, 1975), was a schoolteacher before entering politics in 1947 as co-founder of the Parti Progressiste Tchadien. In 1959 he was named premier, then became head of state when Chad gained independence from France in 1960. After merging the main opposition with his own party, he won the presidency in an uncontested election. Until recently, the most serious threat to his ruthless regime had come from northern Muslim tribes, whose rebellion was held at bay with the help of French troops sent at Tombalbaye's request. During Tombalbaye's 1973 campaign to "chadize" the country, he renounced his first name of François, adopted the tribal name of N'Garta ("chief"), and renamed Fort-Lamy, the capital, N'Djamena ("we are at peace"). Tombalbaye was assassinated during a military coup.

Toynbee, Arnold Joseph, British historian (b. London, England, April 14, 1889—d. York, England, Oct. 22, 1975), was one of the outstanding intellectual figures of his day. He attended Balliol College, Oxford, then joined the Political Intelligence Department of the Foreign Office. After participating in the Paris Peace Conference

Arnold Joseph Toynbee

UPI COMPIX

(1919) he was appointed professor of Byzantine and modern Greek studies at the University of London. From 1925 until retirement in 1955 he was director of studies at the Royal Institute of International Affairs (Chatham House) and research professor of international history at the London School of Economics. At Chatham House he began the annual *Survey of International Affairs* which was restarted, after an interruption in 1939, with a volume entitled *The World in March 1939.* Toynbee's fame, however, rests on his 12 vol. *A Study of History* (1934–61). In this monumental work he examined the rise and fall of 21 civilizations and concluded that they rose in response to external challenges and were guided by elite leaders whose abilities were renewed from time to time by a "withdrawal-and-return" process. Civilizations fell because of the sins of nationalism, militarism, and the tyranny of a dominant minority. Toynbee felt that Western civilization (the 21st in his series) had already reached the stage where only a universal state could save it. Toynbee's other works include *An Historian's Approach to Religion* (1956), *East to West: A Journey Round the World* (1958), and *Half the World* (1973), a cultural history of China and Japan. He was made a Companion of Honour in 1956.

Treacher, Arthur (Arthur Veary), British-born actor (b. Brighton, Eng., July 23, 1894—d. Manhasset, N.Y., Dec. 14, 1975), left England in 1926 and went to the U.S. where he continued to appear in relatively minor roles until the 1930s. He was then stereotyped as a polite butler disdainfully aware of the inferiority of the master he served. He appeared in such stage plays as *The School for Scandal* (1931) and *Androcles and the Lion* (1933), and could count among his 40-odd movie credits such films as *Thank You, Jeeves* (1936), *National Velvet* (1944), and

PICTORIAL PARADE

Mary Poppins (1964). He had no taste for television, and though he appeared in the 1960s as second fiddle on the Merv Griffin show he often remained passive while guests were interviewed.

Trilling, Lionel, U.S. literary critic (b. New York, N.Y., July 4, 1905—d. New York, Nov. 5, 1975), was internationally respected for his studies of Matthew Arnold (1939) and E. M. Forster (1943), for his writings on Sigmund Freud, and for his literary essays. During a teaching career of nearly 45 years at Columbia University in New York, Trilling came to view literature as essentially an author's view of society and invoked sociology, psychology, and philosophy in evaluating what he read. His collected essays include *The Liberal Imagination* (1950), *The Opposing Self* (1955), *Beyond Culture* (1965), and *Sincerity and Authenticity* (1973).

Tucker, Richard (Reuben Ticker), U.S. singer (b. New York, N.Y., Aug. 28, 1914?—d. Kalamazoo, Mich., Jan. 8, 1975), was one of the finest operatic tenors of modern times. Though not a great actor, Tucker had a powerful voice and exceptional precision of tone. His style and technique sometimes seemed to be patterned on those of the great Caruso, whom Tucker admired with undisguised enthusiasm. Tucker's serious interest in operatic singing did not commence until after his marriage to the sister of tenor Jan Peerce, whose reputation was already well established. After studying under Paul Althouse, Tucker made his Metropolitan Opera debut in January 1945, playing Enzo Grimaldo in *La Gioconda.* Four years later, when Arturo Toscanini planned his first nationwide opera telecast,

WIDE WORLD

he chose Tucker, by then a rising star, to sing Radames in *Aïda.* Tucker subsequently gave memorable performances as the clown Canio in *Pagliacci,* Eléazar in *La Juive,* and Rodolfo in *La Bohème.* He also sang occasionally in Europe, gave numerous recitals throughout the U.S., and was a well-known cantor.

Tung Pi-wu, Chinese Communist leader (b. Huangan, Hupeh Province, China, 1886—d. China, April 3, 1975), was considered the best educated among top-ranking Chinese Communist officials; he alone had an imperial degree in the Chinese classics as well as a law degree from Japan. Tung, whose early commitment to revolution was inspired by Sun Yat-sen, helped found (1921) the Chinese Communist Party in Shanghai with Mao Tse-tung. He entered the Kiangsi Province soviet in 1932, and after completing the Long March (1934–35) to Shensi Province in the north, opened a school in Yen-an to mold revolutionaries. When the People's Republic was established in 1949, Tung was named one of six vice-premiers and became acting head of state after the dismissal of Liu Shao-ch'i in 1968.

Tyler, Edward T(itlebaum), U.S. gynecologist (b. New York, N.Y., Feb. 26, 1913—d. Los Angeles, Calif., July 30, 1975), was one of the world's leading authorities on human fertility and among the first to undertake serious research on oral contraceptives and fertility drugs. He was associated with the University of California at Los Angeles, founded and directed the Tyler Clinic, and for 20 years headed the family planning centres in the Los Angeles area. Other jobs included a period (1942–44) as research director for the Ortho Pharmaceutical Corp. and six years (1948–54) as chief of a Los Angeles County endocrine clinic.

Um Kalthoum (Fatma el-Zahraa Ibrahim), Egyptian singer (b. Tamay az-Zahirah, Egypt, 1898—d. Cairo, Egypt, Feb. 3, 1975), mesmerized Arab audiences from the Persian Gulf to Morocco for half a century. Known as "the Star of the East" and "the Nightingale of the Nile," she was in private life the wife of a Cairo physician. Her immense repertoire, which included religious, nationalistic, and sentimental songs, was imbued with unique emotional qualities as she glided her plangent voice over quarter tones to produce hypnotic music against a traditionally simple or-

HENRI BUREAU—SYGMA

Um Kalthoum

chestral accompaniment. Her popularity was further enhanced by generous donations to Arab causes. News of her death provoked a spontaneous outpouring of hysterical grief on the same scale as that which marked the funeral of Egyptian president Gamal Abdel Nasser.

Ure, Mary Eileen, British actress (b. Glasgow, Scotland, Feb. 18, 1933—d. London, England, April 3, 1975), made her name as Alison Porter in John Osborne's *Look Back in Anger* (1956). Delicate-looking and fair, she succeeded in roles of passive suffering: as Amanda in Jean Anouilh's *Time Remembered,* as Abigail Williams in Arthur Miller's *The Crucible,* as Beatrice in *The Changeling,* and as Desdemona and Ophelia in Shakespeare. Shortly before her death she returned to the London stage in *The Exorcism.* Her films included *Sons and Lovers, Where Eagles Dare,* and *Reflections of Fear.*

Van Dusen, Henry Pitney, U.S. theologian (b. Philadelphia, Pa., Dec. 11, 1897—d. Belle Meade, N.J., Feb. 13, 1975), was graduated from Princeton University (1919) before entering Union Theological Seminary in New York City. Even though the Presbyterian General Assembly, disturbed by Van Dusen's "liberal views," withheld approval of his ordination for two years, Van Dusen became a member of the seminary faculty in 1926 and later served as its president (1945–63). During his tenure Roman Catholics lectured and nuns and priests attended classes. Though a man of deep religious convictions, Van Dusen was impatient with theological dogmatism and traveled the world to promote Protestant ecumenism. He was also largely responsible for the organization of the World Council of Churches in 1948.

Vionnet, Madeleine Marie Valentine, French couturiere (b. Chilleurs-aux-Bois, Loiret, France, June 22, 1876—d. Paris, France, March 2, 1975), invented the bias cut as a dressmaking technique and was the designer who most influenced fashions between 1919 and 1939. She set women free from the constriction of old-fashioned petticoats and corsets by shaping the dress to the body. Vionnet began sewing at the age of 11, was apprenticed to Kate Reilly in London (1896–1901), then worked in Paris fashion houses. She opened her own house in the rue de Rivoli in 1912, then moved to the Avenue Montaigne in 1922, where she reigned at this focus of elegance until it was closed in 1939.

Volkova, Vera, Russian ballet teacher (b. St. Petersburg, Russia, 1904—d. Copenhagen, Den., May 5, 1975), studied at the Imperial School of Ballet in St. Petersburg before dancing with Aleksandr Pushkin in the Maryinsky (later Kirov) Theatre Company, whose great star was Agrippina Vaganova. In later years Volkova gained fame as a teacher of the Vaganova method of dancing. With other Russians she went to Shanghai, China, to escape the Bolshevik Revolution. In the mid-1930s she made her way to Paris and opened a school in London in 1943, where Dame Margot Fonteyn was among her pupils. In 1950 she joined Milan's La Scala, but two years later accepted an invitation to become teacher and artistic adviser at the Royal Danish Ballet in Copenhagen.

Wahlöö, Per, Swedish novelist (b. Göteborg, Sweden, Aug. 5, 1926—d. Malmö, Sweden, June 23, 1975), wrote nine widely translated detective stories in collaboration with his wife, Maj Sjövall; *The Laughing Policeman* won the Mystery Writers of America's Edgar Allan Poe Award in 1971. In successive adventures Martin Beck, a fictional detective in the Stockholm police force, underwent an evolution of personality that mirrored changes in modern society and reflected Wahlöö's own left-wing political views.

Ward, Maisie (MARY JOSEPHINE WARD; MRS. FRANCIS J. SHEED), British author and publisher (b. Shanklin, Isle of Wight, England, Jan. 4, 1889—d. New York, N.Y., Jan. 28, 1975), devoted a large part of her life to the cause of Roman Catholicism as lecturer, biographer, and publisher. As a charter member of the Catholic Evidence Guild she was a regular speaker in Hyde Park, London, lectured widely in the U.S., wrote extensively on Catholic topics, and produced biographies of G. K. Chesterton and John Henry Cardinal Newman. Shortly after her marriage to Frank Sheed in 1926, the two established the London firm of Sheed & Ward and took special pride in publishing the writings of such "Catholic revolutionaries" as Hans Küng.

Weidman, Charles Edward, Jr., U.S. modern dance innovator (b. Lincoln, Neb., July 22, 1901—d. New York, N.Y., July 15, 1975), transformed modern American dance as a theorist, performer, choreographer, and teacher. The greatest influences on his early career at the Denishawn school of dance were Ruth St. Denis, Ted Shawn, and Doris Humphrey. Both Weidman and Humphrey became leading Denishawn dancers, but both were frustrated in their desires to choreograph and experiment. They finally left Denishawn to form their own school and company. The association lasted until 1945 and produced some of Weidman's finest works: "Kinetic Pantomime," "Atavisms" (which included the dynamic "Lynch Town"), "Flickers" (on silent films), and the musicals "As Thousands Cheer" and "School for Husbands." In 1945 Weidman established his own dance school and in 1948 the Theatre Dance Company. One of his most highly acclaimed works, "Fables for Our Time" (based on stories by James Thurber), belongs to this period. Among his many contributions to modern dance was masterfully executed nonrepresentational pantomime, which he integrated with dance and applied to comic, satirical, and sociological themes. He was also responsible for elevating male dancers from mediocrity and obscurity to positions of prominence as outstanding artists. His last creative ventures were a tribute to Ruth St. Denis and experimental pieces that blended the graphic and choreographic arts at his tiny Expression of Two Arts Theatre in New York City.

Weis-Fogh, Torkel, Danish physiologist (b. Århus, Denmark, March 25, 1922—d. Cambridge, England, Nov. 13, 1975), used a technique of electronprobe X-ray microanalysis in his studies of insect flight which led to important discoveries in biological fluid dynamics. As research assistant to the distinguished Danish physiologist August Krogh, Weis-Fogh became an authority on the muscles and flight mechanism of the desert locust. Later he was professor of zoophysiology and head of the Zoophysiological Laboratory at Copenhagen (1958–66). He was then elected professor of zoology at the University of Cambridge and a fellow of Christ's College. His studies revealed a new type of elastic protein at the locust's wing base, contractile material in protozoa, and discovered the mechanics of lift in very small insects.

Wellman, William Augustus, U.S. film director (b. Brookline, Mass., Feb. 29, 1896—d. Los Angeles, Calif., Dec. 9, 1975), directed more than 80 Hollywood movies, some of which he also produced and directed. *Wings* (1929), an early classic that won the first Academy Award and featured Gary Cooper in his first important role, was followed by such films as *Public Enemy* (1931) with James Cagney, the original *A Star Is Born* (1937), *Beau Geste* (1939), and *The Ox-Bow Incident* (1942), considered by many critics to be Wellman's best.

Wheeler, Earle Gilmore, U.S. general (b. Washington, D.C., Jan. 13, 1908—d. Frederick, Md., Dec. 18, 1975), was U.S. Army chief of staff (1962–64) and then chairman of the Joint Chiefs of Staff (1964–70). During World War II he was assigned the task of meeting the competing needs of the Army, Navy, Air Force, and Marine Corps. Wheeler, already retired, became the focus of attention in 1973 when it became known that B-52 bombers had made raids over Cambodia in 1969 and 1970 while he served as chairman of the Joint Chiefs of Staff. It was also revealed that false reports had been filed to conceal the attacks from the public, the Congress, and Pentagon officials. Wheeler denied knowledge of falsified reports but testified that the raids were launched on the personal orders of Pres. Richard M. Nixon.

Wheeler-Bennett, Sir John Wheeler, British historian (b. Keston, Kent, England, Oct. 13, 1902—d. London, England, Dec. 9, 1975), was a prolific writer on contemporary history who held a wide range of academic posts in Britain and the U.S. After World War I, he forsook a university education to become assistant to Gen. Sir Neill Malcolm, on whose staff he worked in the Far East and Berlin. After joining the Royal Institute of International Affairs (Malcolm was chairman) in 1924, Wheeler-Bennett founded its *Bulletin of International News,* editing it until 1932. From 1928 to 1936 he also edited *Documents on International Affairs,* supplementing A. J. Toynbee's annual *Survey of International Affairs.* In 1946 he was attached to the British prosecution team at the Nürnberg War Criminals Tribunal and was appointed British editor in chief of the captured archives of the German Foreign Ministry. Among the many books that established Wheeler-Bennett's reputation as a distinguished historian, four were outstanding: *Hindenburg: The Wooden Titan* (1936), *Brest-Litovsk: The Forgotten Peace* (1938), *Munich: Prologue to Tragedy* (1948), and *Nemesis of Power: The German Army in Politics, 1918–1945* (1953). He was knighted in 1959.

Wilder, Thornton Niven, U.S. author (b. Madison, Wis., April 17, 1897—d. Hamden, Conn., Dec. 7, 1975), graduated from Yale University (1920), studied archaeology in Rome, and taught high school French before winning a Pulitzer Prize for *The Bridge of San Luis Rey* (1927). The small novel, which begins with a statement that five persons died when a Peruvian bridge collapsed, was an instant success and foreshadowed Wilder's lifelong concern with human destiny and those universal experiences "that repeat and repeat in the lives of the millions." A natural-born teacher with extraordinary human rapport, Wilder moved to the University of Chicago, where he taught the classics and dramatic literature (1930–37). He also spent one year (1950–51) at Harvard University. Wilder's best-known play, *Our Town* (1938), was performed on a virtually bare stage and won for its author a second Pulitzer. Another play, *The Skin of Our Teeth* (1942), also received a Pulitzer. The characters appear in various locales and historical periods to show that human experience is much the same whatever the time or place. Though *The Matchmaker* (1954) created a lesser stir, it became a spectacularly successful musical as *Hello, Dolly!* and was made into a film.

Thornton Niven Wilder

RENATE PONSOLD—KEYSTONE

Winzer, Otto, East German politician (b. Berlin, Germany, April 3, 1902—d. Berlin, March 3, 1975), as foreign minister of the German Democratic Republic from 1965 took an active part in negotiations that led to the signing (Dec. 21, 1972) of the comprehensive treaty that normalized relations between the two German states and cleared the way for each to enter the United Nations in 1973. Winzer, a Communist from 1919, worked as a journalist on party newspapers. In 1933 he went underground, emigrating to France in 1935 and moving to the U.S.S.R. in 1939. With Walter Ulbricht he returned to Berlin in 1945 and was elected (1947) a member of the Central Committee of the Socialist Unity (Communist) Party. After a period as deputy editor in chief of *Neues Deutschland* he entered the Foreign Ministry, was appointed a deputy foreign minister (1956), and finally minister (1965) in place of Lothar Bolz.

Wodehouse, P(elham) G(renville), British-born humorist (b. Guildford, Surrey, England, Oct. 15, 1881—d. Long Island, N.Y., Feb. 14, 1975), wrote nearly 100 books and collaborated on dozens of plays, musical comedies, and film scripts. His best stories were irreverent farces that featured Bertie Wooster, a bachelor, and Jeeves, his effortlessly superior manservant. They first came to life in *The Man with Two Left Feet* (1917) and were still together, their ages unchanged, in *Much Obliged, Jeeves* (1971).

MARINA SCHINZ—CAMERA PRESS/PHOTO TRENDS

Wodehouse began writing humour in 1902 as a columnist for the London *Globe.* He became a widely published free-lance writer, living for long periods in the U.S. and France after 1909. Captured in France by the Germans in 1940, he was persuaded to make broadcasts to the U.S., which evoked long-lasting resentment in Britain. He became a U.S. citizen in 1956, but in a gesture of forgiveness was knighted by Queen Elizabeth II in January 1975.

Zacchini, Hugo, Italian-born circus performer (b. Italy—d. San Bernardino, Calif., Oct. 20, 1975), was serving with an Italian artillery unit in World War I when he conceived the idea for a circus act that later made him internationally famous. In 1922, while a member of his father's circus, he was shot out of a cannon and into a net. In time the human cannonball soared 75 ft. high and 200 ft. across the circus arena and was billed as one of the main attractions of the Ringling Brothers and Barnum & Bailey Circus. Zacchini, whose lifelong ambition was to paint a masterpiece, taught art at Caffey College, Alta Loma, Calif., after his retirement in 1961.

CHRONOLOGY OF EVENTS

JANUARY

1 *Communist drive in Cambodia*

Concentrating their attacks around the capital city of Phnom Penh, Communist-led Cambodian rebels began their annual dry-season offensive. The conflict between the Khmer Rouge rebels and Cambodian government forces had been going on since 1970 with neither side able to gain a decisive victory.

Jury convicts Watergate four

After more than 15 hours' deliberation over three days, a jury in Washington, D.C., convicted John N. Mitchell, H. R. Haldeman, John D. Ehrlichman, and Robert C. Mardian on all counts in the Watergate cover-up trial. All four faced prison terms ranging from 5 to 25 years and all were expected to appeal the verdict. Kenneth W. Parkinson, hired as counsel by the Committee for the Re-election of the President after the break-in, was acquitted.

2 *First woman premier in Africa*

Gen. Jean-Bédel Bokassa, president of the Central African Republic, named Elisabeth Domitien as the country's premier. She is the first woman to serve as premier of an African nation.

3 *Argentina's Perón grants powers to López Rega*

In a presidential decree, Pres. Isabel Perón gave Social Welfare Minister José López Rega control over her administrative assistants and her appointment calendar. The move made López Rega, whose power had been increasing ever since Perón became president in July 1974, the most powerful man in the Argentine government.

4 *U.K. Foreign Secretary on African tour*

U.K. Foreign Secretary James Callaghan and South African Prime Minister B. J. Vorster met in Port Elizabeth, South Africa, in what was described in the local press as the highest level of contact between the U.K. and South Africa since Harold Macmillan made his "wind of change" speech before the South African Parliament in 1960. Callaghan was visiting various African countries in an attempt to help settle the Rhodesian constitutional problem.

6 *Strike begins at South African gold mine*

Labour forces at South Africa's largest gold mine, the Vaal Reefs mine, went on strike to protest a government ruling that 60% of all earnings of Lesotho nationals must be deposited in a Lesotho bank and paid to the workers only when their contracts expire. The country of Lesotho is entirely surrounded by provinces of the Republic of South Africa.

7 *North Vietnamese troops capture Phuoc Binh*

After a week of intense fighting, North Vietnamese forces overran South Vietnamese troops and captured Phuoc Binh, the capital of Phuoc Long Province, 75 miles north of Saigon. This was the first provincial capital captured by the North Vietnamese since 1972, when they took Quang Tri.

8 *Judge Sirica frees three Watergate figures*

U.S. District Court Judge John J. Sirica ordered the immediate release of John W. Dean III, Herbert W. Kalmbach, and Jeb Stuart Magruder, reducing their sentences to time already served. All three had pleaded guilty to Watergate-related crimes and had served as witnesses for the prosecution in the Watergate cover-up trial.

12 *Pittsburgh wins Super Bowl*

The ninth annual Super Bowl contest was won by the Pittsburgh Steelers. Beating the Minnesota Vikings by a score of 16–6, the Steelers became National Football League champions for the first time in their 42-year history.

13 *U.S. warns of cease-fire violations*

The U.S. State Department sent a note to the eight countries that are guarantors of the 1973 Paris accords on Vietnam and to UN Secretary-General Kurt Waldheim charging North Vietnam with flagrant violations of the 1973 peace agreements.

14 *Kissinger announces Soviet-U.S. trade rift*

U.S. Secretary of State Henry Kissinger announced that the U.S.S.R. informed the U.S. that it could not accept a trading relationship based on the Trade Act signed by President Ford on January 3, which linked trade to free emigration. Kissinger said the U.S.S.R. and the U.S. had nullified their 1972 trade agreement.

15 *Economic travail in the U.S.*

Predicting shocking budget deficits in 1975 and 1976, U.S. Pres. Gerald Ford presented his economic plan to Congress in his state of the union address. He urged the Democratic-dominated Congress to enact his plan for stimulating the economy and to approve a sweeping program aimed at achieving energy independence.

India and Pakistan resume trade

India and Pakistan resumed shipping trade, which was halted ten years ago over the issue of Kashmir. The agreement between the two countries was signed in New Delhi.

16 *IRA cease-fire expires*

The Provisional wing of the Irish Republican Army announced in Dublin that it would not extend its 25-day cease-fire in Northern Ireland when it expired at mid-

Aftermath of London bombing by the IRA.

LONDON EXPRESS/PICTORIAL PARADE

night. The reason given was the "total lack of response" by the British government to IRA peace proposals.

19 *"The state applies the socialist principle: 'He who does not work, neither shall he eat' and 'from each according to his ability, to each according to his work.'"*

China published a new state constitution that embodies the basic ideas of Mao Tse-tung, chairman of the Central Committee of the Chinese Communist Party. Mao was not present at the fourth National People's Congress in Peking at which the constitution was finally approved. The constitution abolished the post of president, which had been vacant since it was formally stripped from Liu Shao-ch'i during the Cultural Revolution that began in 1966.

Papua New Guinea gets "interim government"

Simon Kaumi, a suspended civil servant, and Josephine Abaijah, the only female member of Papua New Guinea's 100-seat House of Assembly, declared a "Papua republic" with an interim government and pledged to seize control of the island from the Papua New Guinea government and Australia.

20 *GM offers rebate*

General Motors Corp., following the lead of Chrysler and Ford, offered cash rebates to purchasers of new cars in an attempt to lift the automobile industry out of one of the worst slumps since the 1940s. Rebates ranging from $200 to $500 were given to buyers of compact and subcompact cars.

23 *U.S. convoy reaches Phnom Penh*

Twenty U.S. ships carrying ammunition reached the besieged capital of Cambodia after several other convoys had failed to make the 60-mile journey up the Mekong River, which flows between the South Vietnamese border and Phnom Penh. The Cambodian rebels had cut all the land routes to the city and were closing in on Neak Luong, a naval base and ferry crossing on the river route to the city.

Britain to hold referendum on EEC membership

Prime Minister Harold Wilson announced that a nationwide referendum would be held in June to decide whether Britain should withdraw from the European Economic Community. Wilson stated that his government would make a recommendation to the people on how they should vote. The referendum fulfills a major plank in the Labour Party's October 1974 election platform.

25 *Bangladesh passes constitutional amendment*

The Bangladesh Parliament amended its constitution without debate or dissent, changing the form of government from a democracy to an authoritarian presidency. Prime Minister Sheikh Mujibur Rahman became president, with total executive power and authorization to establish the ruling Awami League as the country's only political party.

26 *Thais vote for new government*

In an election that was free from official constraint, the people of Thailand chose a new government. A total of 2,193 candidates from 42 different parties were vying for 269 seats in the new House of Representatives. A new prime minister will be chosen by that body.

29 *Agricultural export curbs relaxed in U.S.*

U.S. Agriculture Secretary Earl Butz announced that export quotas on wheat and soybeans, imposed by the government in October 1974 because of domestic shortages and rising food prices, would be relaxed. The announcement followed cancellation by the U.S.S.R. of orders for 3.7 million bushels of wheat with other cancellations under negotiation. China canceled an order for 22 million bushels of wheat on January 27.

Canada to increase price of oil exported to U.S.

Canadian Energy Minister Donald MacDonald announced that his government intended to institute a price increase for oil exported to the United States. On January 23, in a major foreign policy statement, Canada's Secretary of State for External Affairs, Allan J. MacEachen, said that Canada had reconsidered its relations with the U.S. and had decided to strengthen "the economy and other aspects of national life in order to secure independence."

31 *Transitional government takes control in Angola*

A three-party transitional government replaced Portugal as the ruling power in the African territory of Angola until independence on Nov. 11, 1975.

FEBRUARY

1–5 *Soviet Foreign Minister Gromyko visits the Middle East*

In what was generally viewed in Moscow as a substitute for the canceled tour of Leonid I. Brezhnev that was to have taken place in January, Soviet Foreign Minister Andrey A. Gromyko paid an official visit to Egypt and Syria. In Syria, Gromyko reaffirmed the commitment of the U.S.S.R. to "consolidate Syria's defense power," and in Cairo, a joint communiqué was issued calling for immediate resumption of the Geneva Middle East peace talks.

3 *Khmer Rouge rebels mine Mekong River*

The battle for control of the Mekong River, the only surface route for shipping supplies to the Cambodian capital of Phnom Penh, was intensified as Cambodian insurgents sank a number of empty supply vessels that were returning to South Vietnam. It was the first time the rebels had mined the river.

5 *U.S. ends military aid to Turkey*

Pursuant to a law passed by Congress in December 1974, the United States cut off military aid to Turkey because there had not been "substantial progress" toward a settlement of the Cyprus dispute. President Ford urged Congress to reconsider the matter, stating that ending aid might have damaging consequences for Western security in the eastern Mediterranean and that it was likely to impede negotiations over Cyprus.

5–6 *Police strike produces rioting in Lima*

Peruvian troops and tanks crushed a revolt in the capital city of Lima by policemen demanding wage increases. This move set off rioting by civilians, and the leftist military government declared a national state of emergency under which all constitutional guarantees were suspended. When calm returned to the city, deaths were estimated at more than 100.

8 *Bolivia and Chile resume diplomatic ties*

Bolivian Pres. Hugo Banzer Suárez and Chilean Pres. Augusto Pinochet Ugarte met in the Bolivian border town of Charaña and signed a declaration renewing diplomatic ties between their countries. The ties had been broken in 1962 over a Chilean decision to divert the waters of the Río Lauca, which then flowed into Bolivia. In the declaration Chile pledged to work to find an outlet to the Pacific Ocean for Bolivia.

11 *Tories elect Margaret Thatcher in U.K.*

Britain's Conservative Party chose Margaret Thatcher as its chief in the second round of party leadership elections. Mrs. Thatcher, who promised a blend of "continuity and change," succeeded former prime minister Edward Heath, who resigned after losing to her in the first round of voting on February 4.

FEBRUARY

IRA cease-fire

The British government announced the establishment of centres in Northern Ireland to maintain contact with IRA units and monitor the cease-fire that was announced by IRA provisionals on February 9. "Hostilities against crown forces" were suspended on February 10 and truce negotiations were begun between representatives of the IRA and the British.

President of Malagasy Republic assassinated

Col. Richard Ratsimandrava, president of the Malagasy Republic, was assassinated in the capital city of Tananarive. Ratsimandrava had assumed the presidency on February 5, when Gen. Gabriel Ramanantsoa stepped down as head of the ruling military junta. Ramanantsoa had been in power since 1972.

12 *U.S. doubles its airlift to Cambodia*

As Cambodian rebels intensified their blockade of the Mekong River, the United States doubled its arms and ammunition airlift to Phnom Penh. The operation, consisting of about 10 flights a day into Phnom Penh from Thailand, was to be increased to about 22 to 24 flights a day.

13 *Turkish Cypriots proclaim separate state*

Turkish Cypriots proclaimed the northern 40% of the island of Cyprus to be a separate state and offered to join with the Greek Cypriot community in a federation. Turkish Cypriot leader Rauf Denktash said it was "not a unilateral declaration of independence." Greek Cypriots and the government of Greece denounced the action and the Turkish government expressed its support.

New prime minister for Denmark

Anker Henrik Jørgensen, leader of Denmark's Social Democratic Party and prime minister 1972–73, was sworn in as prime minister of Denmark at the head of a minority Social Democratic Cabinet. Jørgensen succeeded Poul Hartling, whose Liberal Party government resigned on January 29 after losing a vote of confidence in the Folketing.

15 *South Korea to release political prisoners*

Park Chung Hee, president of South Korea, announced plans to release more than 200 political prisoners. The government of Park, and the constitution he had drawn up after imposing martial law in the country in 1972, had been approved in a referendum on February 12 by a reported 73% of the voters.

State of emergency in Eritrea

The government of Ethiopia declared a state of emergency in the northern province of Eritrea as fighting there continued. On February 6 it was reported that as many as 1,200 persons had been killed in Asmara, the Eritrean capital, since January 31, when Eritrean rebels attacked three military installations. The conflict between the Ethiopian government and Eritrean secessionists has been going on for 13 years.

WIDE WORLD

Arms and supplies for Eritrean rebel forces are transported by camels in Ethiopia.

17 *Italian art thefts*

The municipal Gallery of Modern Art in Milan was robbed of 28 paintings, including works of Cézanne, Gauguin, Renoir, and Van Gogh. The paintings were part of a collection donated to the city in 1955. On February 6 in Urbino, in the central part of the country, three valuable Renaissance paintings—one by Raphael and two by Piero della Francesca—were stolen from the National Gallery. A spokesman for the Italian government linked the Urbino thefts with the "industry of blackmail."

Prime Minister Vorster visits Liberia

South African Prime Minister B. J. Vorster confirmed a report first published in *The Times* of London that he had paid a visit to Liberia on February 11–12. This was the first time that a white South African head of government had acknowledged traveling to a black African country. Vorster's discussions with Liberian Pres. William R. Tolbert included frank exchanges on the situation in black Africa, on South Africa's relations with its neighbours, and on the future of South West Africa (Namibia) and Rhodesia.

18 *Soviets resume arms shipments to Egypt*

Egyptian Foreign Minister Ismail Fahmy confirmed that the U.S.S.R. had resumed shipment of advanced weapons systems to Egypt. Six MiG-23 fighter planes, the first of 50 aircraft, were delivered and tanks and surface-to-air missiles were promised. Syria received 45 MiG-23s from the Soviets and 40 were sent to Iraq.

21 *Ethiopian forces attack villages in Eritrea*

After several days of troop buildups, fighting broke out on a number of fronts in Eritrea, the northernmost province of Ethiopia. Ethiopian forces used fighter-bombers, armoured vehicles, artillery, and troops to attack villages and roads held by Eritrean secessionist guerrillas.

24 *Coup reported foiled in Greece*

The Greek government put troops in the Athens area on alert after thwarting what it called "conspiratorial movements" by followers of the right-wing military government that collapsed in July 1974. Thirty-seven officers were arrested.

25 *Insurgents gaining in Cambodia*

Two major government strongholds fell to Communist-led Cambodian insurgents: Oudong, 21 miles north of Phnom Penh, and Peam Reang, 37 miles southwest of Phnom Penh. In a letter to Carl Albert, speaker of the U.S. House of Representatives, President Ford said that the Cambodian government would fall to the rebels unless Congress approved the administration's $222 million supplemental aid request.

Right to life in West Germany

The Constitutional Court, the highest court of West Germany, struck down the law passed in June 1974 permitting abortion on request in the first three months of pregnancy. The court held 6–2 that the law violated the right to life for everyone. It did rule, however, that abortions could be performed in the first three months in cases of rape, danger to the mother's health, a possibility of deformity, or when the birth would cause "grave hardship."

26 *Arab boycott list*

The U.S. Senate Foreign Relations Subcommittee on Multinational Corporations published a list of 1,500 U.S. firms and organizations being boycotted by Saudi Arabia. A number of Arab governments had denied practicing racial or religious discrimination, saying they were only blacklisting companies that gave economic or military assistance to Israel. An international furor had been caused by reports that major European banking houses connected with Jewish families were being excluded from routine international financing operations involving Arabs.

28 *EEC and 46 less developed nations sign treaty*

A five-year trade and aid partnership linking the European Economic Community and 46 less developed nations in Africa, the Caribbean, and the Pacific was signed in Lomé, Togo. The agreement was completed in Brussels on February 1 after 18 months of negotiation. Preferential trade innovations included a stabilization fund against price fluctuations.

Argentine guerrillas slay U.S. diplomat

The body of John P. Egan, a U.S. honorary consul, was found on a road outside Córdoba, Arg., draped in the flag of the Montoneros, a leftist guerrilla group. The Montoneros had kidnapped Egan on February 26.

MARCH

1 *U.S. congressmen assess Indochina*

A fact-finding delegation of the U.S. Congress visited South Vietnam and Cambodia at President Ford's request to determine whether Saigon and Phnom Penh required additional military aid. One member of the delegation cited a report that Cambodian Pres. Lon Nol would resign if it would lead to a peace settlement in that country.

2 *Ethiopians celebrate Adowa victory*

Thousands of Ethiopians celebrated the victory of their nation over an Italian army 79 years ago, and vowed to achieve a similar triumph over the secessionist guerrillas in Eritrea. The victory at Adowa, in 1896, saved Ethiopia from becoming an Italian possession.

4 *Rhodesia arrests militant clergyman*

The government of Rhodesia arrested Methodist clergyman Ndabaningi Sithole, president of the militant Zimbabwe African National Union, on charges of plotting to murder black rivals. This represented a breakdown in progress toward racial peace in Rhodesia. Sithole, an outspoken black Rhodesian leader, had been involved in constitutional talks with Ian Smith's white minority government.

6 *Israeli Navy captures Arab commando ship*

An Israeli military spokesman announced that the Navy had captured a ship that had transported eight Palestinian guerrillas who had landed on the beach at Tel Aviv on March 5 and shot their way into the Savoy Hotel. The death toll was reported at 18 with 7 of the 8 Arabs dead. The major Palestinian guerrilla group al-Fatah claimed responsibility for the raid.

7 *Cambodian troops lose ground*

Cambodian government troops lost their last beachhead on the lower Mekong River, the vital waterway between the South Vietnamese border and Phnom Penh, Cambodia's capital. The entire garrison at the position, known as Sierra II, was evacuated by navy craft, which carried close to 1,000 men ten miles up the river to Neak Luong.

A refugee from Hue, South Vietnam, contemplates the changing tide of war.

WIDE WORLD

9 *Alaskan pipeline construction begins*

Work started on the 789-mi. Alaskan oil pipeline, the largest private construction project in the history of the United States. If the job proceeds on schedule, the first crude oil from the rich Prudhoe Bay oil field will begin flowing in the fall of 1978 at the rate of four miles an hour from the frozen Arctic tundra to the ice-free Alaskan port of Valdez, on the Gulf of Alaska.

11 *Coup attempt in Portugal*

A right-wing coup by followers of Gen. António de Spínola was crushed by troops loyal to the leftist provisional military government in Portugal. Sources said that the government remained in complete control. Spínola, who led the coup against the dictatorship in April 1974 but resigned as president of Portugal in September, fled to Spain.

13 *New Thai premier*

The National Assembly of Thailand elected Kukrit Pramoj as prime minister of Thailand. The government of Seni Pramoj, Kukrit's brother, was defeated on March 6 on a confidence vote, after serving for only eight days.

14 *Students protest in Mexico*

Several hundred leftist, antigovernment students shouted abuse and showered Mexican Pres. Luis Echeverría Álvarez with bottles and broken bricks when he tried to deliver an address opening the academic year at the National University in Mexico City. He was the first Mexican president to enter the campus since a student protest movement was crushed in 1968 with the loss of close to 300 lives.

14–15 *Nationalization in Portugal*

After its formation on March 12 to confirm leftist control, the High Council of the Revolution in Portugal seized the great bulk of the country's financial power. On March 14 it decreed the nationalization of almost all the country's banks, excepting those that were foreign-owned, and on March 15 it nationalized all of Portugal's 35 insurance companies.

UPI COMPIX

Refugee children are lifted by cargo net during the evacuation of Da Nang, South Vietnam, by ship.

18 *South Vietnamese flee the central highlands*

Sources in Saigon reported that about 100,000 refugees were fleeing down the last remaining road from South Vietnam's central highlands to the safety of the seacoast. The exodus began with the fall of Ban Me Thuot on March 13. The decision to abandon the highlands was made by the Saigon government because the region was considered to be militarily indefensible following 14 days of sharp reverses.

19 *CIA attempted salvage of Soviet vessel*

Unidentified high U.S. government officials released information indicating that the CIA had financed construction of a multimillion dollar deep-sea salvage vessel. It had been used in an unsuccessful attempt to recover nuclear-warhead missiles and codes from a Soviet submarine that sank in 1968 in the Pacific Ocean. The salvage vessel was reportedly built by industrialist Howard Hughes and was able to recover part of the submarine, but not the part containing the missiles.

22 *Kurdish leader declares rebellion's end*

Gen. Mustafa al-Barzani, leader of the Iraqi Kurdish rebellion, said that "the fighting is over," that his revolt had no foreign support, and that he was considering taking refuge in the U.S. Iran had withdrawn much of the support it had been giving the rebels, who sought independence from the Iraqi government. It was also reported that some members of Barzani's armed forces were fleeing to Iran. Iraqi armour and infantry units had pushed Kurdish rebels out of several militarily important mountain areas in the north in an offensive that began on March 7. The Iraqis captured most of two key areas in Kurdistan—Mount Serti and Mount Handran.

23 *Kissinger fails in the Middle East*

U.S. Secretary of State Henry Kissinger returned to Washington, D.C., after an 18-day peacemaking mission to the Middle East. Kissinger had announced in Jerusalem late on the evening of March 22 that he was suspending his efforts to achieve a new Egyptian-Israeli agreement on the Sinai Peninsula because of "irreconcilable" differences between the two sides.

Evacuation of Hue, South Vietnam

Reports from South Vietnam indicated that the Communists had cut off all overland routes from Hue, the capital of the province of Thua Thien, and refugees were streaming toward Da Nang, the second-largest city in South Vietnam. Thousands of refugees from Tam Ky and Quang Ngai were also headed for Da Nang.

24 *Cambodian airlift resumes*

U.S. officials in Phnom Penh, in what they conceded was a "calculated gamble," ordered the resumption of the U.S. airlift into Pochentong Airport, the last open supply link to the besieged Cambodian capital from the outside world. The airlift of food, fuel, and ammunition was stopped on March 22 when rebel fire hit two planes.

25 *Saudi Arabia's Faisal assassinated*

King Faisal of Saudi Arabia was assassinated in Riyadh by his nephew Prince Faisal ibn Musad ibn Abdul Aziz. Faisal's brother Crown Prince Khalid succeeded him on the throne. Another brother, Prince Fahd, who was minister of the interior under Faisal, was expected to be the real power in the country.

29 *Ford signs tax cut bill*

Stating that he had no choice but to "take it or leave it," U.S. Pres. Gerald Ford signed the $22.8 billion tax cut bill passed by the Congress on March 26. A tax rebate of $100 to $200 per family on 1974 income taxes and a small negative income tax were provided by the bill. The president expressed serious reservations about the $60 billion deficit it would help to create.

30 *North Vietnamese take Da Nang*

The North Vietnamese took over the city of Da Nang, South Vietnam, following the collapse of Saigon government resistance and the panicky exodus of thousands of refugees. The crisis in that coastal city came suddenly and mobs of people fought viciously to board any aircraft leaving Da Nang airport. It was estimated that the South Vietnamese had lost more than $1 billion in U.S. weapons and equipment in two weeks' time. The abandonment of artillery, trucks, planes, and tanks, coupled with the rapid retreat of army units, was viewed as a stunning and irreversible blow to the South Vietnamese cause.

APRIL

1 *Lon Nol leaves Cambodia*

General Lon Nol, leader of Cambodia since 1970 when his faction deposed Prince Norodom Sihanouk, departed Cambodia from Pochentong Airport under rocket and artillery fire. Lon Nol's removal had been long urged by the U.S. and Cabinet ministers in Cambodia as a possible step toward ending the conflict between the government and the Khmer Rouge rebels.

Communists take Qui Nhon

Qui Nhon, South Vietnam's third-largest city, was abandoned by government troops and taken by the North Vietnamese with little resistance. Meanwhile, opposition to South Vietnamese Pres. Nguyen Van Thieu was becoming widespread. Accusations were made that he no longer controlled the people, government, or armed forces of South Vietnam. Despite official denials from the U.S. embassy in Saigon, hundreds of Americans had begun evacuating the country.

4 *Disaster strikes airlift of Vietnamese orphans*

A Galaxy C-5A transport jet, the world's largest plane, crashed and burned five miles northeast of Saigon's Tan Son Nhut Airport. The plane was taking 243 Vietnamese orphans to new homes in the United States. More than 150 of the estimated 325 people aboard were killed when the plane apparently suffered a loss of pressure that blew out its rear door.

Rhodesia releases Sithole

Prime Minister Ian Smith of Rhodesia announced the release from detention of the Rev. Ndabaningi Sithole. This had been requested by the leader of the African National Council. Smith then invited Rhodesian black leaders to resume talks on the Rhodesian constitution.

5 *Chiang Kai-shek dies*

Chiang Kai-shek, president of the Republic of China (Nationalist China), died of a heart attack in Taipei. He was 87 years old and the last survivor of the "Big Four" Allied leaders of World War II. Chiang had been in exile on Taiwan since 1949, when his government was driven from mainland China by the Communists.

UPI COMPIX

Victorious Khmer Rouge troops enter the town of Poipet, Cambodia.

10 *President Ford requests $972 million for South Vietnam*

In an address to a joint session of Congress, President Ford asked for approval of nearly $1 billion in military and humanitarian aid for South Vietnam to give the country a chance to "save itself" and make possible large-scale evacuation of Americans and South Vietnamese "should the worst come to pass." The pending request for $222 million in aid for Cambodia was not reiterated and Ford stated that as far as Cambodia was concerned it might be "too late."

11–12 *Operation "Eagle Pull"*

U.S. Pres. Gerald Ford announced that because of the "seriously deteriorating military situation" in Cambodia, the United States was closing its embassy in Phnom Penh and evacuating several hundred people from the capital. A total of 276 persons, including Americans, Cambodians, and nationals from other countries, were evacuated from the city by helicopters from the carriers "Okinawa" and "Hancock." The U.S. ambassador to Cambodia, John Gunther Dean, was one of the last to leave.

12 *Sadat makes demands on U.S.*

Pres. Anwar as-Sadat of Egypt, in an interview held outside Cairo, stated, in effect, that U.S. mediation in the Middle East was no longer enough and the Ford administration must state clearly that it wanted Israel to withdraw to its 1967 borders. Sadat said that Israeli behaviour during U.S. Secretary of State Kissinger's mission in March had "humiliated the U.S."

13 *New Cambodian government vows to fight on*

The new military government in Cambodia, formed on April 12 under Premier Long Boret, vowed that despite a very serious military situation and the closing of the U.S. embassy it would refuse under any circumstances to surrender to the insurgents surrounding the capital.

President of Chad assassinated

N'Garta Tombalbaye was assassinated when soldiers stormed the presidential palace in N'Djamena, capital of Chad. Acting Army Chief of Staff Gen. Noël Odingar announced the takeover of the central African nation in a radio broadcast. Tombalbaye had ruled the country since it received its independence from France in 1960.

15 *Fighting in Lebanese capital*

After three days of bombings, rocket attacks, and gunfire, the unofficial death toll in the Beirut area was put at nearly 100 as Palestinian guerrillas and members of the Christian, right-wing Phalangist Party clashed. The survival of the coalition government of Rashid as-Solh was uncertain.

16 *Shelepin ousted in U.S.S.R.*

Tass, the official Soviet press agency, reported that Aleksandr N. Shelepin, once head of the secret police and a powerful party official, had been removed from the Communist Party's ruling Politburo. Shelepin's removal was the first change in Politburo membership since 1973.

17 *War in Cambodia ends*

The five-year-old Cambodian war came to an end as the government of Long Boret surrendered to insurgent forces and Khmer Rouge troops entered Phnom Penh. After a week of fighting around that city, the final victory for the insurgents came at 9:00 A.M. when troops seized the Information Ministry. A report filed by *New York Times* correspondent Sydney H. Schanberg after his safe transport to Bangkok, Thailand, indicated that shortly after the surrender the Communists began uprooting millions of Cambodian people. According to Schanberg's report, no one was excluded and even hospitals were emptied. The old, the sick, and the wounded were forced out of the city and into the countryside, where the new government said they would become peasants and till the soil.

19 *Celebration at Lexington and Concord*

The 200th anniversary of the battles that marked the beginning of the U.S. War for Independence was celebrated by more than 160,000 Americans at the scene of the first engagements at Lexington and Concord. On April 18, the 200th anniversary of Paul Revere's famous ride, President Ford initiated the American Revolution Bicentennial, a year-long, nationwide celebration.

Cambodian situation uncertain

The situation in Cambodia and its capital, Phnom Penh, was unknown because customary news channels to the outside world were blacked out. Since the fall of Phnom Penh on April 17, communications had been only in the form of confused refugee reports at the borders of the country, Communist radio broadcasts, and diplomatic assessments from other countries.

21 *South Vietnam's Thieu resigns*

Denouncing the United States as untrustworthy, South Vietnamese Pres. Nguyen Van Thieu resigned after ten years in office. He appointed his vice-president, Tran Van Huong, to replace him and said that President Huong would immediately press for an end to the war and a start to peace negotiations.

22 *Evacuation of Xuan Loc*

Xuan Loc, the northeastern anchor of Saigon's defense line, where South Vietnamese forces had held off Communist troops since April 9, was reported evacuated. The city was in ruins and the government troops were moving toward Saigon to defend that city's perimeters.

Coup in Honduras

A bloodless military coup d'etat ousted Honduran chief of state Gen. Oswaldo López Arellano. Earlier in April López was linked to a $1,250,000 bribe paid by the U.S. corporation United Brands. The Supreme Council of the Honduran Armed Forces announced that the new chief of state was Col. Juan Alberto Melgar Castro.

24 *Terrorist attack in Stockholm*

Terrorists attacked the West German embassy in Stockholm, killing the military attaché and taking 12 hostages. Their act was apparently a reprisal against the West German government, which refused to release 26 anarchists imprisoned in West Germany. The terrorists were believed to be part of the group that had kidnapped West Berlin mayoral candidate Peter Lorenz in March.

25 *Sihanouk named to head Cambodia*

In an announcement made by Phnom Penh radio during the second day of a three-day victory celebration in Cambodia, the Khmer Rouge's Royal Government of National Union of Cambodia (GRUNK) announced that Prince Norodom Sihanouk would be the country's chief of state for life. Since 1970 Sihanouk had been the head of a government-in-exile dedicated to overthrowing the Lon Nol regime.

Portuguese elections

In elections for the constituent assembly, held exactly one year after dissident army officers seized control of Portugal in a bloodless coup, Portugal's Communist Party made a poor showing behind the Socialists and the centrist Popular Democrats. The Socialists, with 38% of the vote, and the Popular Democrats, with 26%, had both campaigned on a platform of public freedoms and were identified as strong opponents of Communism and military dictatorship.

27 *Communists near Saigon*

With Communist forces located five miles from downtown Saigon and the highway between Saigon and Bien Hoa cut, the South Vietnamese National Assembly adopted a resolution to transfer all presidential power from Tran Van Huong to Gen. Duong Van Minh. In granting General Minh full power the Saigon government removed the last major obstacle to meeting initial Communist demands. Minh had led the coup that overthrew Pres. Ngo Dinh Diem in 1963.

WIDE WORLD

Reenactment of the 1775 confrontation at Concord Bridge.

29 *U.S. military involvement in Vietnam ends*

At 4:00 A.M. Communists launched a massive rocket and artillery attack on Tan Son Nhut Airport. It was estimated that more than 150 rockets struck the airport and two U.S. Marines were reported killed. The Marines were guarding thousands of Vietnamese and Americans waiting for evacuation from Saigon. In Washington, D.C., it was 4:00 P.M. April 28 when the shelling began and President Ford and his advisers made the decision to evacuate all remaining Americans. Helicopters evacuated 1,000 Americans and 5,500 South Vietnamese from Saigon—the last helicopter lifted off from the U.S. embassy at 7:52 P.M. Saigon time. Except for a few newsmen and missionaries, the American presence in Vietnam had come to an end.

30 *President Minh surrenders to the PRG*

At 10:02 A.M. Saigon time President Minh announced in a brief radio address that he was surrendering unconditionally to the Provisional Revolutionary Government of South Vietnam.

Saigon is renamed Ho Chi Minh City

At 12:15 P.M. the flag of the Provisional Revolutionary Government of South Vietnam was raised over the presidential palace in Saigon. Viet Cong forces announced over Saigon radio that "Saigon has been totally liberated. We accept the unconditional surrender of General Duong Van Minh, president of the former government." From Paris, Communist representatives announced that Saigon would be popularly known as Ho Chi Minh City, though the official name would remain the same.

MAY

1 *Communist victory in South Vietnam complete*

The new Communist rulers of South Vietnam announced that their forces had completed the takeover of all remaining areas of resistance after the surrender of Saigon. Identifying themselves as the "voice of liberated Saigon," the rulers said that their victory was now complete and they broadcast a series of decrees forbidding the publication of all newspapers, books, and other printed matter and banning prostitution, dance halls, and "acting like Americans."

Controversy over Vietnamese refugees

The U.S. House of Representatives overwhelmingly rejected a bill that would have authorized $327 million in aid for Vietnamese refugees. The arrival in the United States of the first thousands of refugees from South Vietnam brought a wave of hostility from a substantial number of citizens, most of whom objected to the economic impact the influx would have at a time when the unemployment rate in the U.S. was estimated at about 8.7%.

2 *Kurds' battle for autonomy ends*

In an interview with the Teheran newspaper *Kayhan International,* Gen. Mustafa al-Barzani, the former leader of the Kurdish rebels in their battle for autonomy in northern Iraq, said that the struggle was futile and would not be resumed.

3 *Cambodia releases embassy hostages*

Nearly 600 foreigners were permitted to leave Cambodia and cross the border into Thailand. Most of them had taken refuge in the French embassy in Phnom Penh when Communist-led insurgents began occupying the city in mid-April. Six journalists who were among the evacuees agreed not to discuss their ordeal until an additional 100 to 200 foreigners who remained restricted to the embassy compound were allowed to leave.

7 *Communications with Saigon restored*

The military committee ruling Saigon made its first public appearance. Gen. Tran Van Tra, head of the committee, stood on the balcony of the presidential palace, marking the emergence of the new authorities who have been returning the city's life to a peacetime routine. The rally, attended by about 30,000 persons, coincided with the end of the first week since Saigon's surrender and marked the 21st anniversary of the Communist victory over the French at Dien Bien Phu.

10 *South Korea prepares for possible aggression*

As concern increased over the Communist victories in Indochina, hundreds of thousands of South Koreans attended a rally in Seoul in support of Pres. Park Chung Hee's call for increased preparedness against possible aggression from North Korea. A resolution adopted at the rally included a call to the U.S. to honour its defense commitment to South Korea.

11 *Constitution Day in Vientiane*

Constitution Day was celebrated relatively quietly in Vientiane, the capital of Laos, after a week of political and military upheavals, demonstrations, and assassinations. The Laotian premier, Prince Souvanna Phouma, was working to stave off the collapse of his fragile coalition government and thus informed the nation by radio that "some important changes are about to take place."

12 *Cambodia seizes U.S. merchant ship*

The White House announced that a Cambodian naval ship had seized the "Mayaguez," an unarmed container ship, in what the U.S. called international waters off the coast of Cambodia. The ship was forced to anchor off Koh Tang, a tiny island in the Gulf of Thailand. Ron Nessen, White House press secretary, reported that President Ford considered the seizure "an act of piracy." First reports of the seizure, which came to the company that owns the ship at 5:30 A.M. New York time, said that the "Mayaguez" was being fired on and was being boarded by men from Cambodian gunboats.

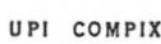

UPI COMPIX

American freighter "Mayaguez" after its release by Cambodian forces.

14 *U.S. forces recapture "Mayaguez"*

U.S. air, sea, and ground forces battled Cambodian troops and recaptured the seized "Mayaguez." The vessel and its 39 crew members were freed after operations that involved the sinking of three Cambodian gunboats by U.S. jet fighters, the landing of Marines on Koh Tang where they skirmished with Cambodian troops, and the bombing of Ream air base on the Cambodian mainland. The operation was apparently launched just after the Cambodian authorities announced that they would release the vessel.

15 *Anti-American demonstrations in Laos*

Laotian student demonstrators who seized three U.S. AID (Agency for International Development) officials on May 14 in Savannakhet allowed them to go to their homes under voluntary house arrest. Anti-American demonstrators had ransacked U.S. buildings in Luang Prabang and Savannakhet, and U.S. embassy officials in Vientiane, the capital, said the evacuation of Americans scheduled to leave this year would begin at once.

Lebanese prime minister resigns

Prime Minister Rashid as-Solh of Lebanon resigned because of the government's ineffectiveness in halting April's clashes between Palestinian guerrillas and the right-wing Phalangist Party's militia.

20 *International panel recommends changes in UN*

A panel consisting of one expert from each of 25 countries, including the U.S. and U.S.S.R., unanimously recommended drastic changes in the United Nations structure for dealing with economic issues. The revision would seek closer collaboration between rich and poor countries, instead of the usual confrontations and voting showdowns in which third world nations easily outnumber the industrial powers.

Communists advance in Laos

Communist-led Pathet Lao troops occupied the central Laotian city of Savannakhet, where student demonstrators had been holding U.S. AID officials and their dependents under house arrest. The Pathet Lao forces occupied virtually all major towns in the southern area of the country that had formerly been under rightist control. The takeover of Savannakhet came without violence.

21 *Casualty toll in "Mayaguez" incident*

The final toll of casualties directly related to the "Mayaguez" rescue was put at 15 killed, three missing, and 50 wounded. Spokesmen for the administration in Washington, D.C., disclosed that another 23 U.S. servicemen had been killed in a helicopter crash in Thailand. They were being transported from one air base to another for possible use in the rescue, but were not actually taking part in the operation, and so were not included in the casualty list.

23 *Souvanna Phouma tells troops not to resist*

Prince Souvanna Phouma, premier of Laos, said that in an effort to prevent a new civil war he had ordered right-wing government troops not to resist when Pathet Lao forces moved into their territory. At the same time, the U.S. began a large-scale evacuation of AID personnel and their dependents.

Kurdish rebels lay down their arms in return for amnesty promised by Iraq.

CAMERA PRESS/PHOTO TRENDS

Portuguese coalition weakened

The Armed Forces Council, Portugal's military rulers, met separately with leaders of the Socialist and Communist parties in an effort to maintain civilian political participation in the government. It was reported that the Armed Forces Council wanted to keep intact the four-party coalition but was not willing to make the concessions called for by the Socialist Party, which had threatened to resign if they were not forthcoming. Socialist Party leader Mário Soares had accused the council of discriminating in favour of the Communist Party.

27 *U.S. import tax on oil*

U.S. Pres. Gerald Ford announced that a second $1 a barrel tax on imported oil would begin on June 1 and that price controls on domestic oil supplies would start being phased out later in June. In his brief nationally televised address, the president accused Congress of wasting four months in unproductive debate on energy conservation and said that he was taking action because "the Congress cannot drift, dawdle, and debate forever with America's future."

28 *Karami designated new prime minister of Lebanon*

In an effort to form a government that could end the bloodshed and anarchy in Lebanon, Rashid Karami, a powerful Muslim political leader, was designated prime minister of Lebanon. Karami, who had the support of Palestine Liberation Organization leader Yasir Arafat, had been the prime minister of Lebanon seven times since 1955. In the sporadic fighting that began on April 13 when Phalangists machine-gunned a busload of Palestinians, killing 26 of them, the death toll reached 300.

29 *President Ford addresses NATO in Brussels*

Addressing a meeting of heads of state of the North Atlantic Treaty Organization in Brussels, Pres. Gerald Ford vigorously reconfirmed the United States commitment to NATO but warned that "partial membership or special arrangements" could endanger the alliance. The warning was directed in part at Portugal, which was viewed by the United States as tending to move toward Communism.

JUNE

1–2 *Ford and Sadat confer in Salzburg*

U.S. Pres. Gerald Ford and Egyptian Pres. Anwar as-Sadat held talks in Salzburg, Austria, that were described by Secretary of State Henry Kissinger as "very positive, very constructive." Ford praised Sadat for creating opportunities for peace and said that "the United States will not tolerate stagnation in our efforts for a negotiated settlement," a statement that was viewed by some as a rebuke to Israel.

Discord in Rhodesia

Fighting broke out between two factions of the African National Council in Salisbury, the capital of Rhodesia. The casualty toll was put at 13 blacks killed and 28 wounded. The incident began outside a hall where the executive committee of the council was meeting to consider Rhodesian Prime Minister Ian Smith's demand that it agree at once to attend a constitutional conference. The two factions in the council are the Zimbabwe African National Union, which favours continued guerrilla warfare against the white minority government, and the Zimbabwe African People's Union, which supports a negotiated settlement.

5 *Suez Canal reopened to shipping*

Exactly eight years after its closure during the 1967 Arab-Israeli war, the Suez Canal was reopened by Egypt's Pres. Anwar as-Sadat. He gave a formal address at Port Said and then boarded the Egyptian destroyer "Sixth of October" to lead a ceremonial convoy south through the canal. The destroyer was named for the day during the 1973 war when Egyptian forces crossed the canal and broke through the Israeli defense line.

Britons back EEC membership

In Great Britain's first national referendum, the people voted overwhelmingly to remain in the Common Market, ending a year-long political battle over the question of Britain's role in Europe. The final tally showed that 67.2% of the voters said "yes" to the EEC, with the other 32.8% voting to withdraw. The decision to remain in the EEC had been backed by Labour Prime Minister Harold Wilson.

8 *Turkish Cypriots approve constitution*

The Turkish community on Cyprus voted to approve a constitution for their autonomous state in northern Cyprus. The Turkish Federated State of Cyprus had been unilaterally proclaimed on February 13. On June 7 the second round of talks between Greek Cypriot leader Glafkos Clerides and Turkish Cypriot leader Rauf Denktash on the future of the government of Cyprus ended without concrete results. The two agreed to confer again in July.

9 *China and the Philippines establish diplomatic relations*

The People's Republic of China and the Republic of the Philippines announced that they had established diplomatic relations. The agreement was signed in Peking by Philippine Pres. Ferdinand Marcos and Chinese Premier Chou En-lai. Shortly afterward, the Chinese Nationalists on Taiwan announced the end of their relations with the Philippines. Taiwan now had diplomatic ties with only 26 nations, whereas the number of governments recognizing Peking totaled 100.

10 *Rockefeller Commission makes final report*

The Report to the President by the Commission on CIA Activities Within the United States was made public. Five months in preparation, the report stated

President Anwar as-Sadat, aboard the "Sixth of October," formally reopens the Suez Canal.

KEYSTONE

that the CIA had engaged in activities that were "plainly unlawful and constituted improper invasions upon the rights of Americans." The report said also, however, that the "great majority" of the CIA's domestic activities during its 28-year history had been in compliance with its statutory authority. The commission, headed by Vice-Pres. Nelson A. Rockefeller, also investigated reports of CIA assassination plots against foreign leaders. President Ford chose to withhold this information from the public because it was "incomplete" and "extremely sensitive."

New York State approves "Big Mac"

The New York State legislature passed an act approving the creation of a new state agency, the Municipal Assistance Corporation, designed to alleviate New York City's cash-flow crisis and oversee its long-range borrowing policies. The corporation, nicknamed "Big Mac," was empowered to offer long-term bonds to raise the money needed to retire the city's short-term debts.

11 *North Sea oil flow begins*

The first oil from Britain's North Sea fields was pumped from the Argyll field, located off the coast of Scotland. The crude was pumped into a tanker whose destination was a British Petroleum terminal in the Thames Estuary. The Argyll field, with a capacity of 40,000 barrels a day, was one of Britain's smaller ones.

12 *Belgian approval clinches jet deal*

The Belgian Parliament voted to accept a Cabinet proposal that Belgium purchase 102 F-16 jet fighters produced by General Dynamics Corp., a U.S. firm. The decision cleared the way for the purchase of a total of 306 of the aircraft, at a total cost of more than $2 billion, by a four-nation European consortium. The three other countries involved in the purchase, called the aviation deal of the century, were Denmark, Norway, and The Netherlands. General Dynamics had been competing chiefly with the French company Dassault for the contract.

Indira Gandhi convicted of election violations

The High Court of Allahabad, Indian Prime Minister Gandhi's home city, in the state of Uttar Pradesh, ruled that she had won her seat in Parliament illegally in 1971 and must give it up. With opposition parties demanding that she resign as prime minister, Mrs. Gandhi announced through an aide that she was appealing the verdict to the Supreme Court and that there was "no question of resignation."

15 *Malagasy Republic has new president*

Didier Ratsiraka, a naval officer and former foreign minister, was named head of the newly created Supreme Revolutionary Council and president of the Malagasy Republic. Ratsiraka succeeded Richard Ratsimandrava, who was assassinated on February 11. As foreign minister Ratsiraka reversed the pro-Western policies of former president Philibert Tsiranana, establishing relations with the Soviet bloc, quitting the French franc zone, and adopting a pro-Arab position in the Middle East.

15–16 *Communists gain in Italian elections*

The Communist Party made substantial advances in elections held in 15 of Italy's 20 regions. The party, under leader Enrico Berlinguer, also made gains in local and provincial elections held at the same time. The Socialist Party, which supported or joined the Communists in many local governments but backed the Christian Democrats in the national coalition government, also made gains in the voting.

18 *King Faisal's assassin executed*

Prince Faisal ibn Musad ibn Abdul Aziz was beheaded in Riyadh, Saudi Arabia, for the assassination of his uncle King Faisal on March 25. The execution, witnessed by a crowd of nearly 10,000, followed the prince's conviction by an Islamic court. The crowd was silent as the executioner swung the sword but then broke into chants of "God is great" and "Justice is done." Public beheading is the traditional form of execution for a convicted murderer in Saudi Arabia, where Islamic law prescribes a "soul for a soul."

21 *Liberation movements in Angola reach accord*

Angola's three rival liberation groups agreed to stop the violence that had brought Angola to the brink of civil war and to cooperate with one another to lead the Portuguese colony to independence in November. The talks were called by Kenyan Pres. Jomo Kenyatta, who had taken an active role in seeking to reconcile the three movements. They promised to integrate their armies into a national army, to release all prisoners, and to hold constituent assembly elections in October.

23 *Record Canadian budget*

The Canadian government introduced a record budget of nearly $36 billion, calling for increased personal income taxes in the upper brackets and higher prices for gasoline and home heating fuels, but no major policy changes. The second budget to be introduced in seven months, it reflected a reversal in the country's bright economic outlook at the end of 1974.

24 *Indian Supreme Court rules in favour of Mrs. Gandhi*

The Supreme Court of India ruled that Indira Gandhi could continue as prime minister for the near future, but could not vote in Parliament, pending the court's full review of her appeal of her conviction by a lower court on charges of election corruption. Gandhi's party, the Congress Party, urged her to remain in office, but opposition leaders said they would stage a nationwide campaign of passive resistance unless she stepped down.

25 *Mozambique gains full independence*

After 470 years of colonial rule, the area that was once known as Portuguese East Africa became the independent People's Republic of Mozambique. The nation is governed by the Front for the Liberation of Mozambique (Frelimo), which had staged the ten-year guerrilla war against the colonial government. Samora Moises Machel became the nation's first president.

26 *State of emergency in India*

Pres. Fakhruddin Ali Ahmed of India declared a nationwide emergency after hundreds of opposition leaders had been arrested in a crackdown against critics of Prime Minister Indira Gandhi. Government officials said the arrests were necessary to preserve the nation's safety and unity. Such an occurrence was unprecedented in the 28-year history of the Indian Republic. Press censorship was imposed and the government was authorized to conduct military operations to maintain

Jayaprakash Narayan, prominent opponent of Indira Gandhi, leads a demonstration in New Delhi.

J. P. LAFFONT—SYGMA

public order, pending formal parliamentary approval.

30 *Thousands of workers strike in Argentina*

Month-long protests in Argentina culminated when hundreds of thousands of workers went on strike in defiance of orders from Pres. Isabel Perón to return to their jobs and accept across-the-board wage increases of 50%. The June strikes throughout the country were in protest against the high cost of living and government austerity measures, including a rollback of previously negotiated wage increases. The trouble began on June 5 when the government announced an emergency program to deal with the estimated 100% annual inflation rate and other severe economic problems; the program included a 50% devaluation of the peso and a 38% ceiling on wage increases.

Karami forms new Lebanese Cabinet

Lebanese radio and television announced that premier-designate Rashid Karami had formed a Cabinet of prominent Muslims and Christians in an attempt to halt the factional fighting that had been going on in Lebanon since April. It was estimated that 800 people had been killed since the conflicts started. Meanwhile, violence continued, with heavy mortar fire reported between Muslims and Christians in Beirut.

JULY

2 *Women's year conference adopts plan*

The 1,300 official delegates to the UN International Women's Year World Conference in Mexico City unanimously adopted a ten-year World Plan of Action intended to improve the status of women. As the two-week conference ended, some saw it as the beginning of a new era while others warned that it would lead only to token gestures. A "Declaration of Mexico" against colonialism, Zionism, and apartheid was also approved, despite U.S. and Israeli opposition.

Australian relieved of Cabinet posts

Australian Prime Minister Gough Whitlam dismissed James F. Cairns as deputy prime minister and minister of the environment in connection with charges that he sought overseas loans for a real estate firm employing his stepson. In June Cairns had been demoted from Treasury minister to minister of the environment.

Delegates from throughout the world attended the UN International Women's Year World Conference in Mexico City.

PETER L. GOULD—KEYSTONE

3 *Truce in Beirut takes effect*

A truce aimed at ending the fighting between Christian and Muslim forces in Beirut took hold and the Lebanese capital was almost back to normal after fighting that began June 23. Palestinian police aided Lebanese security forces in keeping the peace in Shiyah, the predominantly Muslim area of Beirut where extremists had been hiding out since the proclamation of the cease-fire on July 1.

4 *Blast in Jerusalem kills 14*

A bomb concealed in an old refrigerator exploded in Jerusalem's Zion Square killing 14 Israelis and wounding nearly 80 persons. It was the bloodiest terrorist incident since the founding of Israel in 1948, and police rounded up hundreds of Arabs for questioning as well as to protect them from vengeful Israelis.

6 *Unilateral independence for Comoro Islands*

The Chamber of Deputies of the perfume-exporting Comoro Islands in the Indian Ocean unilaterally declared independence of French rule. The vote was 33–0 in favour of independence. Six members were absent, including five from the island of Mayotte, which had voted to remain French in a national referendum held in December 1974.

6–8 *Argentine Cabinet resigns; general strike held*

The entire Cabinet of Pres. Isabel Perón resigned the day before a scheduled general strike called by Argentine labour leaders. Eight Cabinet ministers, including strong man José López Rega, controversial minister of social welfare, stepped down on July 6 in order "to facilitate" Mrs. Perón's attempts to solve the political and economic crisis that brought her government close to downfall. The workers went ahead with the general strike on July 7 but called it off the next day after the government gave in to their wage demands.

7 *Canadian Socialists elect new leader*

The New Democratic Party, a socialist group that was third in strength in the Canadian Parliament, and which governs three of the country's ten provinces, elected John Edward Broadbent as its new leader. The party was thought to have turned further to the left than before. Broadbent, of Oshawa, Ont., had been a member of the House of Commons since 1966.

9–11 *Renewed fighting in Angola*

An estimated 200 people were killed when rival black liberation groups staged heavy attacks on each other's strongholds. The fighting was the worst since the three movements agreed in June to end hostilities. The clashes renewed a feud between the Soviet-backed Popular Movement for the Liberation of Angola and the National Front for the Liberation of Angola.

10 *Amin frees British lecturer*

Ugandan Pres. Idi Amin freed Denis Cecil Hills, whom he had twice threatened to execute by firing squad. Hills had been arrested on April 1 for referring to Amin in an unpublished manuscript as a "village tyrant." A military tribunal convicted Hills of treason and sentenced him to death by firing squad. The cancellation of the execution had been announced on July 1. Hills returned to London with British Foreign Secretary James Callaghan, who had met with Amin in Uganda.

11 *Socialists withdraw from Portuguese government*

Socialist leaders in Portugal's military government withdrew from that government in protest against the takeover by the military of the Socialist newspaper *República*. A long-smoldering conflict between the increasingly radicalized military rulers and moderate political groups became more serious after the armed forces announced a plan on July 9 to govern with the aid of popular assemblies that would exclude any political parties.

12 *São Tomé and Príncipe gain independence*

The tiny islands of São Tomé and Príncipe off the west coast of Africa became independent after nearly 500 years of Portuguese rule. Manuel Pinto da Costa was proclaimed the first president of the Democratic Republic of São Tomé and Príncipe, the fourth independent country to emerge from the decolonization of Portugal's African territories.

17 *Popular Democratic Party withdraws from Portuguese coalition*

The Popular Democratic Party withdrew from Portugal's coalition Cabinet—further widening the breach between the ruling Armed Forces Movement and the exponents of parliamentary democracy. Only the Communists and their ally, the Portuguese Democratic Movement, remained in the government.

17–19 *Apollo-Soyuz linkup*

The Soyuz spacecraft from the Soviet Union and the Apollo spacecraft from the United States linked together in space and, in what was publicized as a dramatic gesture of goodwill, astronauts from both nations shook hands 140 miles above the Earth. This event, on July 17, was the highlight of the Apollo/Soyuz Test Project; although several important joint and individual experiments took place, the linkup and its symbolism were considered the main mission.

21 *Soviets enter U.S. grain market*

For the second time in as many weeks, the Soviet Union purchased sizable quantities of grain from the United States, the U.S. Department of Agriculture reported. On July 16, 73 million bushels of wheat had been purchased by the U.S.S.R., supporting the rumours of a spring drought in that country. The latest transaction involved 177 million bushels of corn and 51 million bushels of barley.

22–23 *Indian Parliament approves emergency rule*

With most of the opposition party members absent from the sessions, the state of emergency imposed in India on June 26 was approved by the Rajya Sabha, the upper house of Parliament, by a vote of 136–33 and by the Lok Sabha, the lower house, by a vote of 336–59. The ratification authorized the government to maintain the emergency rule indefinitely.

24 *Astronauts splash down*

The three Apollo astronauts returned to Earth in the Pacific Ocean, successfully concluding the first international manned space flight and ending an age of U.S. space exploration that began in 1961. During reentry, the failure of the crew to throw two switches caused a series of problems, including the introduction of a poisonous rocket propellant, nitrogen tetroxide, into the space capsule. The astronauts were confined for tests, but were found to be in good health. No further manned space trips were planned by the U.S. until 1979 at the earliest.

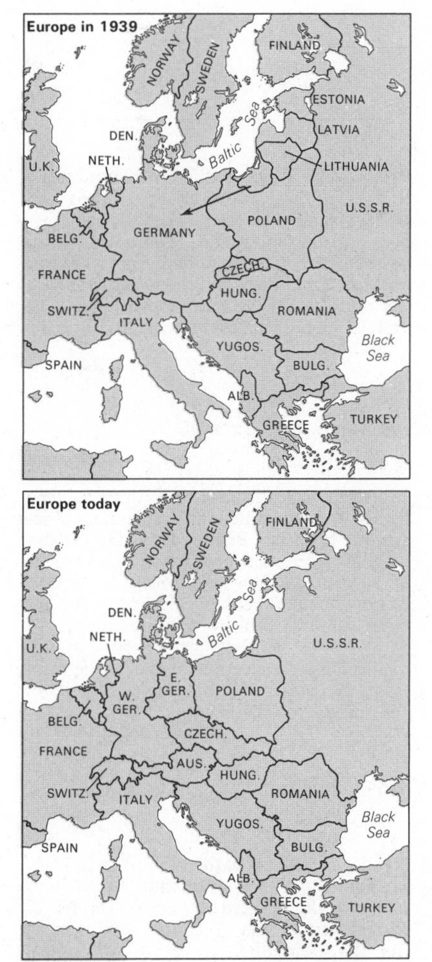

Final Act of the Conference on Security and Cooperation in Europe declared post-World War II boundaries "inviolable."

24–25 *No arms to Turkey; U.S. bases closed*

The U.S. House of Representatives rejected on July 24 a major effort by the Ford administration to lift the six-month-old ban on sales of arms to Turkey. The 223–206 vote was seen as a significant personal setback for President Ford. The next day the Turkish government announced that it would halt all activities on U.S. military installations in Turkey beginning July 26 because the existing joint defense agreements had "lost their legal validity." The base at Incirlik in southern Turkey was exempted from the order, but only defense activities on behalf of NATO would be allowed there.

26 *President Ford begins European tour*

U.S. Pres. Gerald Ford, accompanied by his wife and Secretary of State Henry Kissinger, flew to Bonn, West Germany, on the first leg of a ten-day diplomatic journey across Europe. In addition to Helsinki, Fin., where he would participate in the signing of the 35-nation charter at the Conference on Security and Cooperation in Europe, Ford was to visit Poland, Romania, and Yugoslavia.

29 *Nigerian chief of state overthrown*

Gen. Yakubu Gowon, head of Nigeria's provisional military government since 1966, was deposed in a bloodless coup while he was at a meeting of the Organization of African Unity in Kampala, Uganda. The posts of chief of state and commander in chief of the armed forces were given to Brig. Murtala Ramat Mohammed. Student and labour unrest had been increasing in Nigeria with demands for civilian rule.

OAS ends embargo on Cuba

The Organization of American States abolished the embargo placed on Cuba in 1964 for fostering Communist guerrilla activities in the hemisphere. The United States was one of 16 members at the meeting, held in San José, Costa Rica, that voted for the decision. Each OAS member was to decide separately how it wants to deal with the Castro government.

30 *Leaders of 35 nations meet in Helsinki*

The largest summit conference in the history of Europe convened in Helsinki, Fin., for the purpose of signing the Final Act of the Conference on Security and Cooperation in Europe. Attending the conference were the leaders of 33 European nations and the United States and Canada.

31 *Hoffa reported missing*

Former Teamsters union president James R. Hoffa was reported by his family to be missing. Hoffa was last seen publicly on July 30 outside a restaurant in Bloomfield Township, Mich., where he was supposed to have met several persons. He never returned to his home in nearby Lake Orion and his car was found in the restaurant parking lot.

Turkey rejects U.S. offer

Turkish Prime Minister Suleyman Demirel rejected a plea from U.S. Pres. Gerald Ford to reopen U.S. military bases in Turkey in exchange for $50 million in arms. The arms were offered under a provision of the Foreign Military Sales Act, which allows the president to provide up to $50 million a year in free arms by signing a waiver that such aid is essential to U.S. security. Demirel rejected the offer when he and Ford met in Helsinki because he objected in principle to the embargo of an ally.

Three-man military junta in Portugal

Portugal's Supreme Revolutionary Council approved the setting up of a three-man military junta to rule the country. On July 25 the country's Armed Forces Movement had put three generals in charge of the government and the military—Pres. Francisco da Costa Gomes, Premier Vasco dos Santos Gonçalves, and Otelo Saraiva de Carvalho, the head of the internal security forces.

AUGUST

1 *Summit meeting concludes in Helsinki*

The leaders of 33 European nations and the United States and Canada signed the Final Act of the Conference on Security and Cooperation in Europe, thus concluding a historic three-day meeting in Helsinki, Fin. The charter was intended to lay the foundations for peaceful cooperation among the signatories. It also represented formal acceptance of the European territorial changes wrought by World War II.

2 *Greek and Turkish Cypriots end refugee negotiations*

Greek Cypriot leader Glafkos Clerides and Turkish Cypriot leader Rauf Denktash concluded their third round of negotiations in Vienna. They issued a communiqué announcing their agreement to resettle nearly 20,000 refugees trapped in opposition territory on Cyprus. The talks were held under the auspices of UN Secretary-General Kurt Waldheim.

3 *Pro-French coup in Comoro Islands*

The National United Front, made up of four Comoro opposition parties, overthrew the government of Pres. Ahmed Abdallah in the capital city, Moroni, on Grande Comore island. Abdallah had issued a unilateral declaration of independence from France on July 6. The ouster was led by Ali Soilih, whose activities were supported by France.

5 *Israeli raids on Lebanon*

According to reports from Tyre, Lebanon, Israeli amphibious and air assaults against Palestinian and Lebanese targets in and around that city had killed 16 persons and wounded nearly 30. Israeli Chief of Staff Mordechai Gur said the Israeli air strike had hit a base north of Tyre which was shared by the Syrian-supported as-Saiqah guerrillas and the Popular Front for the Liberation of Palestine.

6 *Japanese terrorists release hostages*

Five members of the Japanese Red Army who had been holding hostages in the U.S. embassy in Kuala Lumpur, Malaysia, agreed on terms to release 15 hostages, take two Japanese and two Malaysian volunteers as hostages in their place, and fly to Libya on a Japanese airliner. On August 4 the terrorists had captured a total of 53 persons and gradually released all but the remaining 15.

9 *Ban on French arms to South Africa*

In a news conference in Kinshasa with Pres. Mobutu Sese Seko of Zaire, French Pres. Valéry Giscard d'Estaing announced that France was imposing a partial ban on French arms for South Africa. The suspension of arms sales would apply to weapons for the Army and Air Force but not to submarines or ships for use "on the open sea." The sale of other kinds of vessels would be examined on an individual basis.

10 *Mrs. Gandhi exempt from court charges*

Indian Pres. Fakhruddin Ali Ahmed signed into law a constitutional amendment designed to free Prime Minister Indira Gandhi from her conviction on charges of corrupt election practices. The legislation, which had been passed by the Parliament and ratified by a majority of the 22 state assemblies, prohibited lawsuits challenging the election of the prime minister, the president, the vice-president, or the speaker of the House.

11 *United States vetoes membership for two Vietnams*

The United States vetoed the proposed admission of North Vietnam and South Vietnam to the United Nations. Daniel P. Moynihan, the new U.S. representative to the UN, reminded the Security Council that this was the first time the U.S. had used its veto power to block an application for membership. Moynihan said that the U.S. would have voted for admission if the council had not on August 6 refused even to consider South Korea's application for admission.

14 *Portugal resumes control in Angola*

Portugal resumed control of the besieged territory of Angola, acting "in the absence of any functioning government." Two of Angola's three liberation groups had withdrawn from the government (the National Front for the Liberation of Angola [FNLA] on August 7 and the National Union for the Total Independence of Angola on August 9), leaving only the Portuguese and the Popular Movement for the Liberation of Angola (MPLA). Meanwhile, thousands of white residents were fleeing the territory in what was reported to be the largest exodus of whites from a black African country since the trouble in the former Belgian Congo in the early 1960s. The three liberation movements were fighting for the control of Angola, which was to be granted independence by Portugal on November 11.

15 *Bangladesh president slain in coup*

Sheikh Mujibur Rahman, whom the Bengalis called *Bangabandhu* ("Friend of Bengal"), was assassinated in an army coup that overthrew his government. Sheikh Mujib had been the founding president of Bangladesh when it became independent from Pakistan in 1972. The uprising was led by forces sympathetic to Khandakar Mushtaque Ahmed, commerce minister in Mujib's Cabinet. Mushtaque was sworn in as president of the civilian regime.

Joanne Little acquitted in Raleigh, N.C.

In a trial that became a cause célèbre among feminists and civil rights activists,

Anti-Communist demonstrators in Lisbon signal their defiance of an unpopular administration.

NORMA—KATHERINE YOUNG

21-year-old Joanne Little was acquitted of second degree murder in the death of her jailer, Clarence T. Alligood. Miss Little, who is black, had contended that she was defending herself from rape when she stabbed Alligood, who was white, with an ice pick in the Beaufort (N.C.) County jail on Aug. 27, 1974.

16 *Anti-Communist demonstrations in Portugal*

A mob of anti-Communist demonstrators using stones and gunfire broke up a Communist rally in Alcobaça, Portugal, as opponents of Premier Vasco dos Santos Gonçalves and the Communist Party continued to demonstrate throughout Portugal and to attack Communist Party headquarters in cities and towns. On August 5 a five-day siege of Communist Party headquarters in Vila Nova de Famalicão ended when thousands of townspeople broke through a line of troops and sacked the premises. The townspeople, angered by the accidental killing of two men by troops on August 3, said they were determined to show the people's hostility to a Communist dictatorship. At least 30 persons were injured in the northern town of Braga August 10–11 when hundreds of Roman Catholics and other anti-Communists rioted, burning down Communist headquarters.

17 *Seagram heir released by kidnappers*

Samuel Bronfman II, 21-year-old heir to the Seagram liquor fortune, was rescued without violence at 4:00 A.M., nine days after he was kidnapped from his mother's Purchase, N.Y., home. FBI agents and New York City policemen freed him when they surprised a captor in an apartment in the Flatbush section of Brooklyn. Two men were arrested and were charged initially with extortion by the use of the mails. The $2.3 million ransom paid by the family was recovered.

21 *U.S. lifts export ban on Cuba*

The United States lifted its 12-year-old ban on exports to Cuba by foreign subsidiaries of U.S. companies. The embargo on direct trade between Cuba and the United States remained in force, however. A Department of State spokesman said the action was related to the July 29 removal of trade sanctions against Cuba by the Organization of American States.

24 *Egypt-Israeli accord reported near*

Egypt and Israel were reported to have resolved virtually every major substantive issue that had been in the way of a new Sinai agreement. U.S. Secretary of State Henry Kissinger said he hoped to conclude the agreement within the week. One of the issues that was reported to have been resolved was the control of an early-warning system at strategic mountain passes that Israel would relinquish. U.S. technicians were to be assigned to points on the Giddi and Mitla passes.

25 *Greek Cabinet commutes death sentences*

The Greek Cabinet decided unanimously to spare the lives of the three men who led the military coup in 1967—former president Georgios Papadopoulos and the two officers who helped him to bring about the coup. Their death sentences, which had been handed down on August 23, were commuted to life imprisonment. The special criminal court also sentenced eight defendants, including former military strong man Brig. Gen. Demetrios Ioannidis, to life imprisonment for high treason in connection with the 1967 coup.

26 *Victoria Falls talks break down*

Talks at Victoria Falls between Rhodesia's white minority government led by Prime Minister Ian Smith and black nationalist leaders broke down, with each side blaming the other. An extraordinary effort was made at the meeting by South African Prime Minister B. J. Vorster and Pres. Kenneth Kaunda of Zambia to force Rhodesian leaders, black and white, to find a solution to their racial differences. The talks were held in a railway car in the middle of a bridge straddling the border between Zambia and Rhodesia on the Zambezi River.

27 *Selassie of Ethiopia dead at 83*

Former emperor Haile Selassie, ruler of Ethiopia for more than 50 years until deposed by a military coup in September 1974, died at Menelik Palace in Addis Ababa, apparently from the aftereffects of recent surgery.

29 *Gonçalves dismissed as premier in Portugal*

Gen. Vasco dos Santos Gonçalves, opposed for weeks by overwhelming military and political forces for attempting to promote Communist rule in Portugal, was dismissed from the post of premier by Portuguese Pres. Francisco da Costa Gomes. Gonçalves was replaced by Adm. José Pinheiro de Azevedo, chief of staff of the Navy. Continued conflict was envisioned, however, as General Gonçalves was appointed chief of staff of the armed forces, a move that his opponents resisted.

Peruvian president overthrown in bloodless coup

Gen. Juan Velasco Alvarado, the president of Peru, who had headed the leftist military government there for seven years, was overthrown in a bloodless coup. He was replaced by his premier, Gen. Francisco Morales Bermúdez, who was thought to be a more conservative and pragmatic leader.

SEPTEMBER

1 *Rightist coup attempt crushed in Ecuador*

Troops loyal to Pres. Guillermo Rodríguez Lara of Ecuador crushed a revolt by Gen. Raúl González Alvear, armed forces chief of staff. The government palace in Quito was initially seized, but those within were later surrounded and forced to surrender. It was estimated that 18 persons were killed and 80 wounded. González, who was taken prisoner, said that he moved against the president because of alleged mismanagement of the country's rich oil resources.

1–5 *30th annual meeting of IMF and World Bank*

H. Johannes Witteveen, managing director of the International Monetary Fund, closed the 30th annual meeting of the IMF and the World Bank by stating that the meeting was marked by the participants' "willingness to compromise and desire for cooperation." During the course of the meeting Robert S. McNamara, president of the World Bank, reported that the bank would direct more of its lending in the future toward solving the problem of urban poverty in less developed countries.

4 *Egypt and Israel initial accord in Geneva*

Representatives of Egypt and Israel, seated at separate tables, initialed the new U.S.-mediated interim peace agreement of September 1. Meanwhile, U.S. President Ford and Secretary of State Henry Kissinger asked Congress to approve the stationing of U.S. civilians in the Sinai, saying that prompt congressional action was necessary before Israel would sign the agreement. It was planned that 200 U.S. technicians would monitor the early warning system.

5 *Assassination attempt on President Ford*

A woman in Sacramento, Calif., pointed a .45-calibre automatic pistol at U.S. Pres. Gerald Ford from a distance of about two feet while he was shaking hands with the public. A Secret Service agent saw this and leaped to grasp the gun, which was discovered to have four bullets in it but none in the firing chamber. The woman subdued was identified as Lynette ("Squeaky") Fromme, 26, a follower of Charles Manson, leader of a cult convicted of killing seven persons in 1969. Manson was serving a life sentence in San Quentin prison.

Coup crushed in the Sudan

Rebel army officers seized the state radio station at Omdurman and announced the overthrow of the government of Pres. Gaafar Nimeiry. Within hours of the announcement, however, troops loyal to the government crushed the uprising in an assault on the station and in fighting around the presidential palace in Khartoum. It was reported to be the second such attempt since Nimeiry himself came to power through a coup in 1969.

Gonçalves gives up power in Portugal

Former premier Gen. Vasco dos Santos Gonçalves turned down his appointment as Portuguese armed forces chief of staff in the face of overwhelming opposition within the ruling Armed Forces Movement. Gonçalves was abandoned by Pres. Francisco da Costa Gomes, who felt that he would lose the presidency if he continued to support Gonçalves, and later by the Commúnist Party, which agreed to cooperate with more moderate civilian and military forces.

6 *Violent earthquake in eastern Turkey*

An earthquake occurred along the Anatolian fault in eastern Turkey, killing more than 2,000 people before the tremors finally ended. Rescue workers reported that the quake toppled buildings and touched off fires along the fault. The most serious damage was in the town of Lice, in which 1,000 lives were lost.

10 *Teachers' strikes and busing disrupt U.S. schools*

The reopening of schools for the fall term was marked in the U.S. by a rash of teachers' strikes and incidents of violence brought on by busing programs. In the first week of September it was estimated that nearly one million pupils in 12 states had been affected by strikes. By September 10, when New York City teachers went on strike, nearly two million pupils were said to be affected. In Louisville, Ky., the National Guard had been called in on September 6 after rioting broke out over busing in white working-class suburbs. On September 8 Boston's public schools had begun their court-ordered citywide busing program with only scattered incidents of violence.

Canadian finance minister resigns

Canadian Finance Minister John Turner resigned, reportedly in frustration over the handling of economic and fiscal affairs. His resignation came after federal statistics revealed that inflation and unemployment in Canada were continuing to rise. As of August the 12-month rate of inflation was 11.1%, and a jobless rate of 7.3% was reported.

11 *Cease-fire denied in Philippines*

An article in the *New York Times* reported that the deputy chairman of the Moro National Liberation Front, Abur Khair Alonto, had stated in a rare interview on September 4 that Muslim rebels in the southern Philippines had not accepted a cease-fire as was claimed in August by Pres. Ferdinand E. Marcos. Alonto and other leaders pledged that they would fight on until they achieved full autonomy.

UPI COMPIX

Secret Service agents surround President Ford moments after an assassination attempt by Sara Jane Moore in San Francisco.

13 *Perón begins leave of absence*

Argentine Pres. Isabel Perón began a leave of absence, ostensibly for health reasons. Senate Pres. Italo Luder took over as interim president. Perón had spent most of the month of August in bed, suffering from nervous and intestinal problems, and had spent little time on official duties since her closest adviser, José López Rega, was driven into exile in July.

14 *U.S.-born woman canonized in Rome*

In a colourful ceremony in St. Peter's Square, Rome, Pope Paul VI declared Mother Elizabeth Ann Bayley Seton a saint. Among the estimated 15,000 Americans who attended the mass was Carl Kalin, a 73-year-old New York man who attributed his recovery from brain disease 12 years earlier to the intercession of Mother Seton. This recovery was accepted by the Vatican as the final miracle required for the canonization of Mother Seton, who was born in New York in 1774.

16 *UN General Assembly opens 30th session*

The UN General Assembly opened its 30th session, electing Prime Minister Gaston Thorn of Luxembourg as president and admitting three countries to membership. The newly admitted states—Cape Verde, São Tomé and Príncipe, and Mozambique, all former Portuguese colonies—brought total UN membership to 141.

Papua New Guinea becomes independent

A fireworks display at midnight over Port Moresby, the capital, signaled the beginning of independence for Papua New Guinea, which had been a dependency of Australia since 1906. With the advent of independence Chief Minister Michael Somare became the country's first prime minister.

18 *Fugitive Patricia Hearst captured*

Patricia Hearst, who had been sought around the world since her alleged kidnapping on Feb. 4, 1974, was taken into custody by FBI agents in San Francisco, along with two of her companions in the Symbionese Liberation Army, William and Emily Harris, and Wendy Yoshimura. Miss Hearst, 21, was wanted for bank robbery, use of a firearm in the commission of a felony, and nearly 25 state charges, including assault with intent to kill and kidnapping.

19 *New Portuguese Cabinet*

A new coalition Cabinet, reflecting the relative strength of the parties in the April election, was sworn in in Portugal. The 15-member Cabinet, led by Adm. José Batista Pinheiro de Azevedo, a leftist career navy officer, as premier, included one Communist—the public works minister.

22 *Woman shoots at U.S. president*

A woman fired a shot from a .38-calibre pistol at President Ford as he walked out of the St. Francis Hotel in San Francisco, but a bystander deflected the weapon as it went off and Ford was not hit. Police officers reported that Oliver Sipple, a 33-year-old former Marine, had deflected the weapon and pounced on the assailant, who was later identified as Sara Jane Moore, a 45-year-old activist who had been questioned by the Secret Service on September 21 but not detained.

South Africa devalues rand

South Africa devalued the rand 17.9% against the U.S. dollar in an attempt to counteract the falling price of gold and worsening domestic recession. The country's economy had been hit by the plunging price of gold. Gold was responsible for 43% of the country's foreign exchange earnings and had fallen from a high of $200 an ounce in late 1974 to about $130 an ounce. The government was spending at a rate that presupposed the gold price would remain at about $180 an ounce.

27 *OPEC increases prices by 10%*

The Organization of Petroleum Exporting Countries ended four days of tense talks in Vienna with the announcement that there would be a 10% increase in the price of oil effective October 1. This represented a compromise between Iranian demands for a 40% increase and a Saudi Arabian bid for a maximum 5% increase in price. OPEC stated that it would freeze new prices for at least nine months as a gesture of goodwill.

Terrorists executed in Spain

Ignoring last-minute appeals for clemency and defying a rash of violent protests in cities throughout Europe, the government of Generalissimo Francisco Franco of Spain executed five political terrorists by firing squad. Death by firing squad, instead of garrote, traditionally used in Spain, was the only concession the government accorded the five men, who had been convicted of killing policemen or civil guards. Two of the executed men were members of the Basque separatist group ETA.

OCTOBER

1 *New Chilean currency devalued*

Chile devalued its currency by 4.48% as the cost of living and unemployment continued to rise and industrial production continued to fall. The peso, adopted as the new national currency on September 29, was worth 1,000 units of the old currency, the escudo, and was initially pegged at 6.4 to the U.S. dollar. The escudo was devalued 19 times in 1975.

2–3 *U.S. Congress eases arms embargo on Turkey*

In a major victory for the administration of Pres. Gerald Ford, the House of Representatives voted on October 2 to reverse itself and ease the eight-month arms embargo against Turkey. The next day, by voice vote, the Senate gave final approval to the bill that partly lifted the embargo against the shipment of U.S. arms to Turkey.

6 *UN delegates denounce Moynihan*

African and Arab delegates in the General Assembly denounced Daniel P. Moynihan, the chief United States delegate to the UN, for his use of the term "racist murderer" to describe Pres. Idi Amin of Uganda. Moynihan had been protesting a demand made by Amin for the extinction of Israel.

9 *Soviet awarded Nobel Peace Prize*

Andrey D. Sakharov, father of the Soviet hydrogen bomb, became the first Soviet citizen to win the Nobel Peace Prize. Sakharov had incurred the wrath of Soviet authorities by becoming the U.S.S.R.'s most outspoken advocate of civil liberties. In the citation the Nobel committee said "Uncompromisingly and forcefully, Sakharov has fought . . . against the abuse of power and violations of human dignity."

Contested areas in Beirut have become scenes of devastation and death.

CLAUDE SALHANI—SYGMA

9–10 *U.S. Congress approves Sinai technicians; Israel signs disengagement pact*

The Senate voted 70–18 to approve the stationing of 200 U.S. technicians to monitor the early warning system in the Sinai passes. In response to this vote of approval Israel formally signed the protocol of the disengagement agreement with Egypt in ceremonies in Jerusalem. The transfer of management of the Ras Sudr oil fields, one of 32 steps before Israeli withdrawal from some 1,900 sq.mi. of occupied Egyptian territory would be complete, was also effected. The important Abu Rudays fields were to be transferred in December.

13 *Trudeau announces Canadian austerity program*

Canadian Prime Minister Pierre Elliott Trudeau announced that he would ask Parliament on October 14 for authority to impose restraints on prices and wages. The program, he said in a national broadcast, was aimed at curtailing inflation and jobless rates. The plan would hold wage increases to a range of 8–10% and require that price increases be matched to rises in operating costs. If costs went down, prices must be reduced accordingly.

Emperor Hirohito ends U.S. tour

In a stop at Honolulu, Japanese Emperor Hirohito, accompanied by Empress Nagako, completed a two-week tour of the United States. The goodwill tour was the first by a reigning Japanese monarch and included stops in Washington, D.C., Cape Cod, Mass., New York City, Chicago, Los Angeles, and San Francisco.

15 *President Leone on Italy's state of the nation*

Pres. Giovanni Leone of Italy broke precedent by sending a message to Parliament that gave his own analysis of the crisis

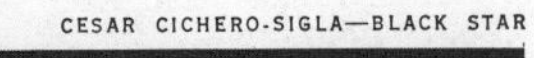
CESAR CICHERO-SIGLA—BLACK STAR

Pres. Isabel Perón addresses the nation following her return October 16.

facing Italy. It was reported that he broke the presidential silence that is traditional in Italy because of the urgency of national economic difficulties and associated administrative problems.

16 *Perón returns to office in Argentina*

Rejecting advice from military and political leaders, including the interim president, Italo Luder, Argentine Pres. Isabel Perón returned to office, ending her month-long leave of absence. A number of high government officials were advising her to prolong her leave or resign, in view of the nation's continuing political and economic troubles.

17 *Teachers' union saves New York City from default*

New York City escaped default by hours when Albert Shanker, president of the United Federation of Teachers, announced that the union would reverse its opposition to using its pension funds to purchase $150 million of Municipal Assistance Corporation bonds. The purchase was essential to completion of a $2.3 billion rescue program enacted by the state legislature in September. State appropriations of $250 million of a total of $750 million were due on this day and could not be turned over to the city unless there were sufficient proceeds from the sale of bonds to meet cash needs through November 30.

20 *U.S.-Soviet grain accord*

In a move that signaled the end of a two-month moratorium on grain sales to the U.S.S.R., the White House announced a five-year agreement for Soviet purchase of six million to eight million tons of U.S. grain a year. The White House also announced that a letter of intent was signed in Moscow to conclude an agreement for the U.S. to buy up to 200,000 barrels a day of Soviet oil and petroleum products.

24 *Military alert in Portugal*

A national alert for the armed forces was called by Portugal's leaders as fears of a coup heightened and minor bomb blasts occurred in the country. The explanation given for the alert was fear of sabotage and "armed actions by extreme right-wing groups." Lisbon remained calm with no evidence of military maneuvers.

28 *Violence in Beirut intensifies*

Gunmen in Parliament Square, Beirut, denounced Lebanon's political leaders and proceeded to shoot up the Chamber of Deputies, killing a member's bodyguard and wounding a gendarme. Lebanese Premier Rashid Karami had just announced a new initiative to end the fighting between the Christian right and Muslim left, which had resulted in the deaths of an estimated 3,000 persons since April and left the city in a shambles. Fighting was intense in the city's downtown hotel district and most foreigners had been evacuated. Beirut was once the principal focus for banks and large corporations in the Middle East, but several U.S., Japanese, British, French, and West German firms had relocated, primarily in Athens.

29 *Sadat visits U.S.*

On a ten-day tour of the United States, Pres. Anwar as-Sadat of Egypt formally asked the United Nations to help reconvene the Geneva conference to hasten a permanent peace in the Middle East. In a speech to the General Assembly Sadat appealed to Secretary-General Kurt Waldheim, the U.S., and the U.S.S.R. to start arrangements for a resumption of the talks. Sadat was the first Egyptian president to pay an official visit to the U.S.

Ford would veto federal aid to New York City

In an address before the National Press Club in Washington, D.C., U.S. Pres. Gerald Ford said he would veto any bill that would permit the federal government to rescue New York City from financial default. As an alternative he sent Congress legislation that would enable the city to file for bankruptcy while still carrying on essential services.

30 *Prince Juan Carlos to rule Spain*

Prince Juan Carlos de Borbón y Borbón, the designated successor to Generalissimo Francisco Franco, assumed the powers of Spain's chief of state. The transfer of power from the 82-year-old Franco, who was critically ill, marked the end of the 36-year-old Franco regime. Meanwhile, the new chief of state faced his first test as the situation in Spanish Sahara became more grave. Algeria warned of war if Morocco continued its efforts to annex the territory.

NOVEMBER

2 *Spain threatens to intervene in Spanish Sahara*

Spain's Prince Juan Carlos flew to Spanish Sahara where he told Spanish troops that the "legitimate rights" of the people of Spanish Sahara would be protected and "the honour and integrity of the Army will remain intact." His trip signified a stiffening of Spain's resistance toward Morocco's claims to the territory, a definite policy reversal. Both Algeria and the UN were pressuring Spain to cease negotiations with Morocco.

Ford dismisses Schlesinger and Colby

In a major administration reshuffle, U.S. President Ford dismissed Secretary of Defense James R. Schlesinger and Director of the Central Intelligence Agency William E. Colby. White House officials reported that Ford also asked Henry Kissinger to resign his post as national security adviser to the White House, but to stay on as secretary of state, and Kissinger agreed.

3–7 *Army takes power in Bangladesh*

A power struggle that began on November 3 with the slaying of four jailed supporters of former president Sheikh Mujibur Rahman led to the Army's seizure of government control and the November 6 resignation of Pres. Khandakar Mushtaque Ahmed. On November 7 Abu Sadat Mohammed Sayem, newly installed president, announced that he would remain chief martial law administrator but that he would be assisted by a three-man council of commanding officers. Mushtaque had become president in August.

5 *Prime Minister Wilson proposes a new program*

Britain's Prime Minister Harold Wilson proposed a new program for his economically depressed country that would revoke for at least five years the policies that successive governments since the end of World War II had endorsed. Priority would be given to aiding industry, and nationalized health care and subsidized housing would be given a back seat. The objective was "to transform a declining economy into a high output, high earnings economy."

6–7 *Moroccans march on Spanish Sahara*

Tens of thousands of Moroccans crossed the border into Spanish Sahara on the first day of the peaceful "Green March" that

SVEN SIMON/KATHERINE YOUNG

Juan Carlos I takes his oath as the new king of Spain before the Spanish Parliament in Madrid.

King Hassan II of Morocco had announced on October 16. The purpose of the march, Hassan claimed, was to regain the disputed territory and restore national integrity. The marchers, the first part of an estimated total of 350,000, departed from their base camp at Tarfaya but, fearing that the area might be mined, they halted their advance about seven miles inside the territory.

7 *Indian Supreme Court reverses Gandhi conviction*

The Indian Supreme Court unanimously reversed the lower court conviction of Prime Minister Indira Gandhi on June 12. The conviction was for two electoral offenses committed during her 1971 campaign for Parliament. The verdict of the Supreme Court was not based on any new interpretation of the law, but rather on the retroactive election law amendment adopted by Parliament in August, which in effect made her offenses legal.

9 *King Hassan ends the Spanish Sahara march*

Morocco's King Hassan declared an end to the peaceful march of Moroccans into Spanish Sahara. In a speech from his command post at Agadir he said that the takeover would have to be accomplished by other means and ordered the estimated 150,000 who had already crossed the border and entered Spanish Sahara to return to their base at Tarfaya, Morocco.

10–11 *UN General Assembly resolution equates Zionism and racism*

The United Nations General Assembly approved an Arab-sponsored resolution that classified Zionism as "a form of racism and racial discrimination." The vote was 72 to 35 with 32 abstentions. Opposition was widespread and in the U.S. both houses of Congress voted unanimously for a reassessment of the U.S. relationship to the international body.

Portuguese leave Angola

The departing high commissioner in Angola, Adm. Leonel Cardoso, lowered the Portuguese flag at Fort São Miguel in Luanda, symbol of Portugal's power over that colony since 1485. The colony was left in the hands of the Angolan people, who were in the process of fighting a civil war. On November 11 two distinct governments were proclaimed. The Soviet-backed Popular Movement for the Liberation of Angola (MPLA) proclaimed its leader, Agostinho Neto, president of the People's Republic of Angola. Later, in Huambo (known as Nova Lisboa since 1928), the joint formation of the People's Democratic Republic of Angola was announced by the National Front for the Liberation of Angola (FNLA) and the National Union for the Total Independence of Angola (UNITA).

11 *Australian prime minister dismissed*

Australian Governor-General Sir John Kerr dismissed Prime Minister Gough Whitlam and dissolved both houses of Parliament after a month-long political crisis that began when the opposition Liberal-Country Party Coalition used its majority in the Senate to block passage of the budget adopted by the Labor majority in the House. Malcolm Fraser was named caretaker prime minister and elections were scheduled for December 13.

12 *William O. Douglas steps down*

Ailing U.S. Supreme Court Justice William O. Douglas, a staunch and controversial defender of the rights of the individual, retired from the court after a record 36½ years of distinguished service. In his resignation letter to President Ford, the 77-year-old Douglas cited failing health as the reason for his departure from the high court bench.

17 *Six-nation economic meeting ends*

Leaders of the U.S., Japan, France, Italy, West Germany, and Britain ended a three-day meeting, at the Château de Rambouillet near Paris, after pledging to work together to "assure the recovery" of their economies and put them on a course of "growth that is steady and lasting." A compromise agreement was reached between the U.S. and France on a dispute over exchange rates. France favoured fixed exchange rates while the U.S. insisted upon retaining a modified floating exchange rate system.

20 *Franco succumbs*

Generalissimo Francisco Franco, ruler of Spain for 36 years, died in Madrid. The 82-year-old chief of state had led rightist military forces to victory in the Spanish Civil War.

22 *Juan Carlos installed as king of Spain*

Juan Carlos de Borbón y Borbón was proclaimed King Juan Carlos I of Spain one day before his predecessor as chief of state, Generalissimo Franco, was buried at a monument to Civil War veterans outside Madrid. In a ceremony in the Parliament building, Juan Carlos pledged fidelity to the present political regime. He would take possession of a throne that had been vacant since 1931, when his grandfather King Alfonso XIII abandoned his authority in favour of the Second Spanish Republic.

24 *Kissinger warns against intervention in Angola*

U.S. Secretary of State Henry Kissinger warned that "the United States cannot remain indifferent" to Soviet and Cuban military intervention in the civil war in Angola and stated that this could have severe consequences for East-West détente. It had been reported by U.S. officials on November 20 that Cuba had sent 3,000 fighting men and advisers to Angola, in addition to the large quantities of arms the Soviet Union had previously shipped to support the MPLA.

25 *Surinam attains independence*

The aluminum-producing South American territory of Surinam became independent following 308 years of Dutch colonial rule. At a ceremony in Paramaribo, the capital, Princess Beatrix of The Netherlands met with foreign dignitaries and the new prime minister of Surinam, Henk Arron.

25–27 *Rebellion crushed in Portugal*

Portuguese Pres. Francisco da Costa Gomes declared a state of emergency in the Lisbon military region when fighting broke out between loyal government troops and rebellious suporters of the Communist Party in Portugal. All civil rights were suspended and a curfew was imposed. On November 27 the president announced that the rebellion had been quashed by loyalist soldiers. Army Chief of Staff Gen. Carlos Fabião was dismissed and Gen. Otelo Saraiva de Carvalho was removed from his post as military security chief. Casualties were reported to be light.

26 *President Ford approves aid to New York City*

In a nationally televised press conference Pres. Gerald Ford asked Congress to approve legislation that would make up to $2.3 billion in direct federal loans available to New York City annually. Ford denied that this was a reversal of his stated position of late October, indicating that there had been a "concerted effort to put the finances of the city and the state on a sound basis."

27 *Physicians' strike endangers British health care*

Thousands of junior physicians staged a slowdown in Britain, forcing many hospitals in the country to refuse new patients and some to close. The junior doctors, equivalent to interns in the U.S., were demonstrating for higher pay and removal of what they considered to be inequities in the overtime pay system as laid down by the National Health Service. Thousands of senior physicians agreed to support them in their demands.

30 *Dahomey becomes Benin*

Lieut. Col Mathieu Kerekou, president of the West African republic of Dahomey, announced that the nation's name was changed to the People's Republic of Benin. The occasion of the announcement was a ceremony marking the first anniversary of Kerekou's proclamation of a society guided by Marxist-Leninist principles. Benin was the name of an African kingdom that reached its peak in the 17th century.

DECEMBER

1–5 *Ford visits China*

U.S. Pres. Gerald Ford, accompanied by his wife and daughter, Susan, and Secretary of State Henry Kissinger, visited the People's Republic of China as part of an Asian tour that included visits to Indonesia and the Philippines. Ford met with Chairman Mao Tse-tung and Deputy Premier Teng Hsiao-p'ing. Premier Chou En-lai, who was reported ailing, did not participate in any of the meetings.

2 *Israeli jets attack Lebanon*

In what was reported to be the most devastating Israeli raid of 1975, Israeli jets attacked Palestinian camps in northern and southern Lebanon. Newspaper accounts in Lebanon indicated the death toll was nearly 60. Spokesmen for Israel claimed the raids were aimed at purported terrorist concentrations and guerrilla bases where Israel had detected a military buildup.

8–9 *Chaos in Beirut*

Christian and Muslim gunmen were in control of much of the capital city of Beirut, Lebanon, and leftist Muslim troops laid siege to a number of hotels, including the Holiday Inn, which had Phalangist Christian gunmen trapped inside. The Lebanese government sent army commandos to separate the two factions, but it was estimated that over 100 persons were killed in battle or murdered during two days of fighting.

10 *Sakharov's wife accepts his Nobel Prize*

Yelena Bonner, wife of Andrey D. Sakharov, dissident Soviet physicist, accepted his Nobel Peace Prize in Oslo, Norway. She read his message that he shared the honour with "all prisoners of conscience in the Soviet Union and in other Eastern European countries as well as with those who fight for their liberation." Sakharov was refused Soviet permission to go to Oslo because he was familiar with "state and military secrets."

12 *Spanish Cabinet sworn in*

Spain's first Cabinet under the restored monarchy was sworn in and was expected to begin a program of cautious political reform. Prime Minister Carlos Arias Navarro was the major holdover from the Franco regime and 17 ministerial posts were taken by newcomers—most of them loyal Francoists, but favouring moderate political change.

13 *Fraser wins in Australia*

Malcolm Fraser's Liberal-Country Party alliance was elected in the largest parliamentary majority in the history of Australia. Nearly 54% of almost eight million voters took a sharp turn to the right in electing Fraser, who had been caretaker prime minister since Gough Whitlam was dismissed in an unprecedented action by the governor-general in November.

14 *U.S.S.R. outlines new five-year plan*

The Soviet Union outlined a modest five-year plan emphasizing a return to the country's traditional reliance on heavy industry. Previous efforts to establish an economy that would be more favourable to the consumer had apparently been abandoned. It was estimated that investment in agriculture would be increased by about one-third by the early 1980s. Early in the month information was released by officials in Moscow indicating that the 1975 grain crop was only 137 million tons, compared with the goal of 215 million tons.

15 *Anti-inflation legislation passed in Canada*

Setting strict wage and price controls and establishing an Anti-Inflation Board to enforce the measures, the Canadian govern-

Pres. Gerald Ford greeted these smiling youngsters during his first visit to Peking in December.

SYGMA

TED COWELL—BLACK STAR

Aftermath of horror in the TWA terminal area of La Guardia Airport in New York City.

ment's legislation setting up anti-inflation guidelines was passed into law in the Senate. The guidelines, first announced by Prime Minister Trudeau in October, would remain in effect for at least three years.

16 *Britain to aid Chrysler operation*

The House of Commons approved Prime Minister Harold Wilson's agreement to spend £162.5 million to aid the U.S.-based Chrysler group. The aid would be granted over a four-year period to assure the continued operation of Chrysler's automobile-manufacturing plants in Britain, which employed more than 25,000 workers.

17 *30th UN General Assembly adjourns*

The 30th session of the UN General Assembly ended after three months of what chief U.S. delegate Daniel P. Moynihan termed "profound, even alarming disappointment." In his closing address to the session Moynihan said the assembly had been "repeatedly the scene of acts which we regard as abominations." He was referring to the November 10 resolution equating Zionism with racism.

18 *Economic conference session ends*

The 27-nation Conference on International Economic Cooperation—a meeting of industrialized, less developed, and oil-producing states—ended its first (ministerial) session in Paris. Early in 1976 the world's problems in the areas of energy, raw materials, finance, and development were to be considered. Particular emphasis was to be placed on the desperate plight of the poorest states which had been severely affected by rising petroleum prices.

18–22 *Air Force revolt in Argentina fails*

Right-wing Argentine Air Force officers seized two air bases near Buenos Aires in an attempt to overthrow the government of Pres. Isabel Perón. On December 19 planes flew over Government House on the Plaza de Mayo dropping leaflets that denounced the Perón administration. Negotiations fell apart on December 20, and the Air Force commander then ordered Air Force jets to strafe Morón, one of the bases held. The rebels surrendered on December 22.

19 *Stevens inducted into Supreme Court*

In a brief ceremony U.S. Chief Justice Warren Burger administered the judicial oath to John Paul Stevens, who thus became an associate justice of the U.S. Supreme Court. Stevens, whose nomination was unanimously confirmed by the Senate on December 17, took the seat of retired justice William O. Douglas.

Terrorists release 25 in The Netherlands

Seven South Moluccan terrorists ended a siege that began on December 4 at the Indonesian consulate in Amsterdam. The rebels released 25 hostages, most of them Indonesian, without gaining any concessions. They had demanded that The Netherlands help them in their campaign for an independent homeland in the islands of the South Moluccas, which were incorporated into Indonesia when Dutch colonial rule ended there in 1950. Another group of Moluccan terrorists seized a train near Beilin in the north of The Netherlands on December 2, killing 2 and taking 50 people hostage. One hostage was killed attempting to escape. This ended on December 14 when the hijackers surrendered to police.

U.S. Senate votes to end aid to Angola

The U.S. Senate voted 54 to 22 to stop covert funding of military operations of two Angolan factions that were waging a civil war against the Soviet-backed MPLA. At issue was a relatively small sum of $37 million in aid, but the real struggle was between a group of liberal Democratic senators and the Ford administration, which had reportedly provided about $32 million in covert aid since the fighting began early in the year. The House would have an opportunity to reverse the Senate action when Congress reconvened in January 1976.

21–23 *Terrorists disrupt OPEC meeting*

Two persons were shot to death and at least 60 were taken hostage by pro-Palestinian terrorists who burst into a meeting of the Organization of Petroleum Exporting Countries in Vienna. Among the hostages were 11 delegates to the conference, including Saudi Arabia's minister of petroleum affairs. On December 22 the terrorists were allowed to fly out of Austria with 10 of the delegates. The latter were set free at various points, most of them in Algiers, where the kidnappers finally stopped. Austria demanded extradition, but Algeria indicated that political asylum would be granted to the terrorists.

23 *CIA man murdered in Greece*

Richard S. Welch, station chief of the U.S. Central Intelligence Agency in Greece, was shot and killed by unidentified gunmen outside his suburban Athens residence. Listed officially as a special assistant to the ambassador to Greece, Welch recently had been named as a CIA representative and his address listed in an English-language Athens daily newspaper.

29 *Bombing at New York's La Guardia*

One of the most lethal bombs ever exploded in New York City killed 11 people and injured 75 in a crowded locker area in the main terminal of La Guardia Airport. The terminal, jammed with holiday travelers and vacationers, was temporarily closed and authorities began a painstaking investigation of the incident.

Women's rights in Britain

The women's rights movement in Britain was advanced as two new laws became effective. One assured equal pay to women who hold the same type of job as men, and the other barred sex discrimination in employment, advertising, and other situations where British men traditionally have had preferred status.

Aerial Sports

1974 World Parachuting Championships

Event	Winner MEN	Winner WOMEN
Absolute team	Czechoslovakia	U.S.S.R.
Precision team	Austria	East Germany
Absolute individual	U.S.S.R.	U.S.S.R.
Precision individual	Poland	U.S.S.R.
Style individual	France	U.S.S.R.

Higher fuel costs and increased governmental regulation of powered-aircraft flight during 1975 did much to increase the popularity of three highly individualistic aerial sports, namely, gliding (soaring), ballooning, and sport parachuting.

Gliding. One of the year's major events took place when George Moffat of the U.S., the 1974 open-class champion, defeated Helmut Reichmann of West Germany by a solid 383 points at the fourth annual Smirnoff Sailplane Derby. By conquering the 1974 standard-class champion, Moffat became the unofficial champion of champions in gliding.

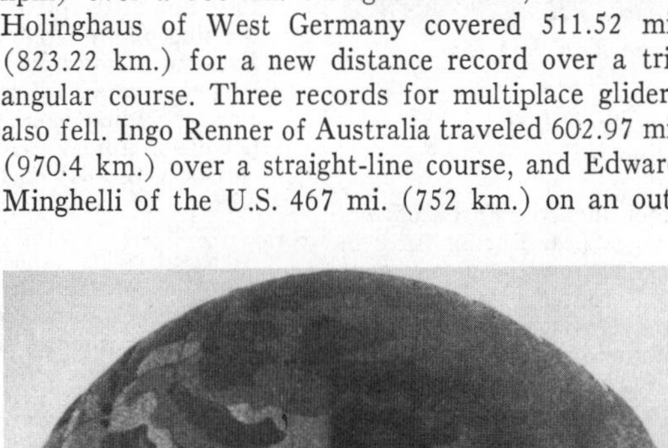

Three men flying single-place sailplanes set world records during the year. Georg Eckle of West Germany set a 750-km. triangular course speed mark of 76.28 mph (122.775 kph), Malcolm Jinks of Australia broke the speed record with 87.19 mph (140.33 kpm) over a 500-km. triangular course, and Klaus Holinghaus of West Germany covered 511.52 mi. (823.22 km.) for a new distance record over a triangular course. Three records for multiplace gliders also fell. Ingo Renner of Australia traveled 602.97 mi. (970.4 km.) over a straight-line course, and Edward Minghelli of the U.S. 467 mi. (752 km.) on an out-and-return flight. In the women's category, Babs Nutt of the U.S. set an altitude record of 35,463 ft. (10,809 m.).

Despite numerous accidents and some fatalities, resulting from the inherent instability of the craft when upset by sudden gusts of wind, hang gliding acquired new respectability during the year, with international competitions held in the U.S. and Austria. World championships recognized by the Fédération Aéronautique Internationale also came closer to realization. Mercury Aquarian of Hawaii claimed a time record in August after soaring over Oahu's Makapuu Cliffs for 13 hr. 5 min.

Ballooning. Donna Wiederkehr of the U.S. set five new records during the year. In the 200–400-cu.m. class, she stayed aloft for 2 hr. 40 min., covered a distance of 11.19 mi. (18.01 km.), and reached an altitude of 1,953 ft. (595 m.). In the 400–600-cu.m. class, she also set distance and duration records.

The balloon race has largely given way to the balloon task in international competition. The task involves flying over a given course and landing as close as possible to an official balloon which made the journey earlier. Changing winds tend to make this task a difficult one.

In marathon distance ballooning, two dramatic attempts were made to cross the Atlantic. When Bob Sparks of the U.S. attempted a solo crossing from Massachusetts, his crew chief clung to the ground line at launching and had to be hauled aboard. Both men were later rescued when the balloon developed a leak and plunged into the sea 145 mi. SE of Nantucket Island. Earlier in the year magazine publisher Malcolm Forbes and aerospace scientist Thomas Heinsheimer attempted a crossing from California in a 40-story-high balloon. Just prior to launching, a tether line snapped and the gondola was sent skidding across the ground. The two escaped death when the launch director leaped aboard the gondola and cut it free.

At the world hot-air balloon championships in October, David Schaffer of the United States won first place with 4,573.6 points for all five contest events, Janne Balkedal of Sweden won second place with 4,367.7 points, and Peter Vizzard of Australia was third with 3,867.6 total points.

Parachuting. A record held by 24 chutists was erased in May when 29 skydivers jumped near Tampa, Fla., then joined hands to form a ring. At the 1974 biennial parachuting championships in Hungary, Soviet chutists dominated the field by winning five of the ten championships. Soviet women captured all titles except the precision team championship. In the men's competition, Austria, Czechoslovakia, France, Poland, and the Soviet Union won one title each.

A handsomely decorated hot-air balloon rises above Washington, D.C., to publicize the world championship races, subsequently held in Albuquerque, New Mexico, in October.

WIDE WORLD

Aden:
see Yemen, People's Democratic Republic of

Advertising:
see Industrial Review

Two other chutists made headlines during the year, but for very different reasons. Owen Quinn jumped from atop the 110-story World Trade Center building in New York City in July and was arrested upon landing. And Allen Wooten survived a 4,500-ft. drop when trees and mud broke his fall after his main and reserve chutes failed to open. (MICHAEL D. KILIAN)

[452.B.4.d]

Afghanistan

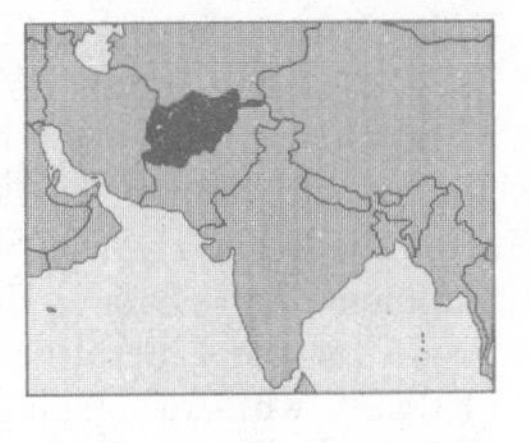

A republic in central Asia, Afghanistan is bordered by the U.S.S.R., China, Pakistan, and Iran. Area: 252,000 sq.mi. (652,000 sq.km.). Pop. (1975 est.): 19,250,000, including (1963 est.) Pashtoon 59%; Tadzhik 29%; Uzbek 5%; Hazara 3%. Cap. and largest city: Kabul (pop., 1974 est., 352,700). Language: Dari Persian and Pashto. Religion: Muslim. President in 1975, Sardar Mohammad Daud Khan.

Domestically, many of the economic difficulties of the previous year continued in 1975 in areas remote from the capital, with the result that the gap in living standards between Kabul and the more distant provinces widened. Under the energetic guidance of President Daud Khan, considerable external help was secured for the construction of oil refineries, fertilizer factories, and various agricultural projects envisaged in the current five-year plan, both China and the Soviet Union having contributed interest-free loans and technical aid.

There were no serious challenges to the president's authority, supported by a regular army equipped with Soviet weaponry, although some spasmodic discontent with the prevalent economic stringency found expression during the year.

DUNCAN, LIFE MAGAZINE © TIME, INC.

Pastoral life in the valleys bordering the great Hindu Kush range remains largely unchanged and unreflective of events in Kabul.

In foreign affairs, the government adhered firmly to the traditional policy of independence, accepting external aid but refusing entangling alliances. Improved terms were secured from the Soviet Union for the sale of Afghanistan's natural gas, but this did not prevent equally friendly relations with China. Pakistan's actions against insurgents in Baluchistan and the Northwest Frontier Province were bitterly criticized by the government and press in Kabul. The proscription by Pakistan of the National Awami Party, whose activities in Baluchistan and the Northwest Frontier Province were favoured by Afghanistan, further worsened relations between the two countries. President Daud Khan's efforts to mobilize international opinion against Pakistan's action met with a cool reception, however.

(L. F. RUSHBROOK WILLIAMS)

[978.C.2]

AFGHANISTAN

Education. (1973) Primary, pupils 620,576, teachers 16,022; secondary, pupils 160,895, teachers 7,317; vocational, pupils 8,124, teachers 608; teacher training, students 4,610, teachers 870; higher, students 8,292, teaching staff 888.

Finance. Monetary unit: afghani, with (Sept. 22, 1975) an official rate of 57.50 afghanis to U.S. $1 (free rate of 120 afghanis = £1 sterling). Gold, SDRs, and foreign exchange, central bank: (June 1975) U.S. $70,150,000; (June 1974) U.S. $61,590,000. Budget (1973–74 est.): revenue 7,892,000,000 afghanis; expenditure 8,517,000,000 afghanis. Money supply: (March 1975) 11,219,000,000 afghanis; (March 1974) 10,016,000,000 afghanis.

Foreign Trade. Imports (1973–74) U.S. $135 million; exports (1974–75) U.S. $213,650,000. Import sources (1972–73): U.S.S.R. 25%; Japan 15%; U.S. 11%; West Germany 9%; India 7%. Export destinations (1972–73): U.S.S.R. 29%; India 24%; U.K. 16%; West Germany 6%. Main exports (1974–75): fruits and nuts 40%; cotton 15%; natural gas 12%; carpets 9%; karakul (persian lamb) skins 6%.

Transport and Communications. Roads (1971) c. 6,000 km. all-weather. Motor vehicles in use (1971): passenger 38,400; commercial (including buses) 26,100. Air traffic (1973): 267 million passenger-km.; freight 1.2 million net ton-km. Telephones (Dec. 1972) 23,000. Radio receivers (Dec. 1973) c. 450,000.

Agriculture. Production (in 000; metric tons; 1974; 1973 in parentheses): corn c. 800 (c. 760); wheat c. 3,000 (c. 2,750); rice (1973) c. 360, (1972) 340; barley c. 400 (c. 360); cotton, lint c. 27 (c. 33); wool, clean c. 13, (1972) 13. Livestock (in 000; 1973): cattle c. 3,500; sheep c. 17,000; karakul sheep (1971) c. 6,800; horses c. 385; asses c. 1,225; goats c. 3,400; camels c. 300.

Industry. Production (in 000; metric tons; 1972–73): salt 31; cotton yarn (1971–72) 0.6; cotton fabrics (m.) 48,000; coal (1971–72) 135; cement 99; electricity (kw-hr.) 439,000.

African Affairs

The number of independent states in Africa rose by 5 to 49 during 1975. Four were former Portuguese colonies—Mozambique (June 25), Cape Verde Islands (July 5), São Tomé and Príncipe (July 12), and Angola (November 11). The fifth was the former French overseas territory in the Indian Ocean, the Comoro Islands, which unilaterally declared its independence on July 6. (*See* articles on these new states.) Britain promised independence for the Seychelles in 1976. However, hopes of reaching a peaceful settlement for the rebel British colony of Rhodesia were thwarted.

It was another disastrous year for the economy of most countries, suffering under the combined pressures of world inflation, inadequate food production, and generally lower commodity prices. Although the

Aerospace Industry: *see* Defense; Industrial Review; Space Exploration; Transportation

CAMERAPIX/CAMERA PRESS

President Idi Amin of Uganda (right) greets Zaire President Mobutu upon the latter's arrival in Kampala for the OAU conference.

severe drought was broken in the Sahel region, it persisted in other areas. The almost legendary former emperor of Ethiopia, Haile Selassie (*see* OBITUARIES), died a solitary figure in detention at the age of 83 on August 27.

The Organization of African Unity. The 12th annual summit conference of African heads of state was held in Kampala, Uganda, in July. Three (Tanzania, Botswana, and Zambia) of the 46 member states, which included the three newly independent former Portuguese colonies and the Comoro Islands, boycotted the summit to show their disapproval of Pres. Idi Amin (*see* BIOGRAPHY). As host, he automatically became chairman of the OAU for 1975–76. Some members had tried unsuccessfully to get the venue of the meeting changed.

Despite the influence of Arab member states, African leaders refused to commit the OAU to support for Israel's expulsion from the UN. Nevertheless, when President Amin spoke at the UN on October 1 as chairman of the OAU he called for the extinction of the state of Israel in contradiction to OAU policies on this question. Arab-African relations continued to be a source of some controversy within the OAU, especially the arrangements to distribute funds provided by Arab oil producers as compensation for oil price rises and the role of some Arab states in the Ethiopian-Eritrean dispute (*see* below).

The summit meeting endorsed a Strategy for the Liberation of Southern Africa, formulated by the African Liberation Committee (ALC), which pledged full support to the liberation movements engaged in an armed struggle in Rhodesia (Zimbabwe), South Africa, and Namibia (South West Africa). At the same time, it also endorsed the approach of the presidents of Zambia, Tanzania, Botswana, and Mozambique in working for a possible peaceful settlement of the Rhodesian and Namibian problems through negotiations with South Africa's prime minister (*see* below).

The OAU made unsuccessful attempts to avert a civil war in Angola and the secession of the oil-rich Angolan coastal enclave of Cabinda, geographically separated from Angola by Zaire. In June agreement was reached in Nakuru, Kenya, under Pres. Jomo Kenyatta's chairmanship, between the three rival movements—the Popular Movement for the Liberation of Angola (MPLA), the National Front for the Liberation of Angola (FNLA), and the National Union for the Total Independence of Angola (UNITA), but it was short-lived. A nine-nation mediation commission set up by the OAU to make a final effort to reconcile the rivals before independence also failed. The rivalries were fomented by some OAU members; Zaire backed the FNLA and the secessionist Front for the Liberation of the Enclave of Cabinda (FLEC), while others, including Mozambique, Congo, and Guinea, strongly supported the MPLA.

The OAU refused appeals by the Eritrean Liberation Front (ELF) to intervene in Ethiopia because its charter prevented interference in the domestic affairs of member states. However, the ELF attracted support from some member states, mainly Arab. The OAU succeeded in mediating between Upper Volta and Mali in their border conflict (*see* below).

The OAU's outstanding achievement was its success in maintaining unity among all African states in the negotiations that produced, in February 1975, the Lomé Convention between 46 African, Caribbean, and Pacific (ACP) countries and the European Economic Community (EEC). The new agreement, which replaced the Yaoundé and Arusha conventions, offered the ACP countries privileged access to the European market, economic development aid worth about $4,270,000,000 over five years, a price-stabilization fund for commodities, and a new basis for industrial cooperation.

The OAU budget for 1975–76 was fixed at $62 million, 12% larger than in the previous year.

Southern Africa. The continued diplomatic moves toward a peaceful settlement of the difficult racial and colonial problems of southern Africa led in late August to a dramatic meeting of Rhodesia's white and black leaders in a railway carriage on the Zambezi River bridge above Victoria Falls. Zambia's president, Kenneth Kaunda, and South Africa's prime minister, B. J. Vorster, were also present. The frontier on the Zambezi River was a most suitable meeting site because it symbolized the great divide between black-ruled and white-ruled Africa. Although the talks failed to achieve their immediate purpose of getting agreement on constitutional talks for an independent Rhodesia (renamed Zimbabwe by the black nationalists), they were nevertheless of historic importance, marking the changing realities of the struggle in southern Africa. The African side—led by the presidents of Zambia, Tanzania, Botswana, and Mozambique—was attempting to enlist South Africa's aid in preventing racial conflagration, and white South Africa was seeking to soften black African opposition to its separate development, or apartheid, system by contributing to a Rhodesian settlement.

The four African presidents were criticized by some OAU member states for their willingness to negotiate, but they managed to retain majority support. Vorster too was under pressure from the extremists in his white electorate, but his policy was welcomed by others because it had encouraged a dialogue with a few important African leaders that promised to lessen the republic's isolation inside the continent. Vorster had followed up his secret visit in September 1974 to Ivory Coast by visiting Liberia's president in February 1975. He also received delegations from Ivory Coast, Gabon, and the Central African Republic.

Wars and Coups. The armed struggle by the Zimbabwe liberation movement against the Ian Smith regime in Rhodesia continued, despite the efforts to obtain a cease-fire. South Africa withdrew all its security forces from the territory, leaving the white Rhodesian minority to face the threat of an intensified guerrilla war alone if the peace talks should finally fail. South Africa itself faced a stronger guerrilla challenge in Namibia from the South West African People's Organization (SWAPO).

The incipient civil war in Angola brought serious losses to the country and active international intervention in the power struggle between the MPLA, FNLA, and UNITA. The MPLA, led by Agostinho Neto (*see* BIOGRAPHY), succeeded in driving both its rivals out of the capital, Luanda, and extended its military control over a large area. Its initial military success was possible largely because of military and economic support from the Soviet Union and Cuba, as well as political backing from a dozen African countries, including Mozambique, Tanzania, and Algeria. China, South Africa, and the U.S. supported FNLA and UNITA, both of which also had the backing of a score or more of African states, notably Zaire.

The most serious war in the continent, however, was that waged in Eritrea between the Ethiopian Army and the ELF, which was determined to separate the region from the rest of Ethiopia. After more than a decade, the ELF appeared to have grown much stronger. The rift between two rival groups within the ELF was mended; substantial support was received from both moderate and radical Arab states; and, crucially, the influential leader of the Afar nomads, Sultan Ali Mirrah, entered the conflict in opposition to the Ethiopian Army. Armed uprisings also began to occur in other Ethiopian regions.

The indecisive struggle between the Chadian Army and the Chad National Liberation Front (Frolinat) was a precipitating factor in the military coup against Pres. N'Garta Tombalbaye in April, but the new military regime under Brig. Gen. Félix Malloum (*see* BIOGRAPHY) was no more successful in controlling the Chadian rebels. Dissension among the military leaders who had ruled Malagasy since the overthrow of Philibert Tsiranana in 1972 led to the installation of Comdr. Didier Ratsiraka (*see* BIOGRAPHY) as head of government in June.

Gen. Yakubu Gowon gracefully submitted in July to a bloodless coup in Nigeria led by Brig. Murtala Ramat Mohammed (*see* BIOGRAPHY). The unilateral declaration of independence in the French Overseas Territory of the Comoros in July by the president, Ahmed Abdallah, was followed by a military coup in August led by Ali Soilih, who was generally regarded as being francophile. Coups were attempted unsuccessfully in Zaire, Dahomey, Sudan, Libya, and, in December 1974, the Central African Republic.

Intra-African Relations. Libya's maverick leader, Col. Muammar al-Qaddafi, continued to involve his country in a series of conflicts in the continent. Bad relations with Egypt grew worse; Libya was accused by Sudan of having had a finger in an abortive coup against Pres. Gaafar Nimeiry in September; it was accused of annexing a large area of territory in neighbouring Chad; it actively supported the dissident ELF in Eritrea; and it helped to promote rebellion among the anti-Spanish forces in Spanish Sahara. The disputes over this latter territory led to serious difficulties among Morocco, Mauritania, and Algeria. In November Morocco and Mauritania reached agreement with Spain on the territory's future. Africa's other maverick leader, President Amin, brought Uganda into conflict with most of its neighbours.

The conflict in Eritrea kept tension high between Ethiopia and its old rival Somalia, as well as between it and the Arab states. The Tunisian embassy was expelled from Addis Ababa following Pres. Habib Bourguiba's advocacy of independence for Eritrea. The frontier conflict between Mali and Upper Volta was mediated with the signing of a peace treaty, while Nigeria and Cameroon finally reached agreement over their frontier problems. But the frontier conflict between Ghana and Togo over a demand for Ewe reunification remained unresolved.

South Africa's diplomatic moves toward détente with black Africa led to disagreements between the majority of OAU members and countries such as Ivory Coast, Gabon, and the Central African Republic which favoured closer ties with Pretoria as a means toward resolving the area's racial problems.

Relations between the three partners in the East African Community (Tanzania, Kenya, and Uganda) deteriorated during the year. Although the organization's breakup was freely predicted, the partners agreed to try to save the community by reviewing its operations. Undeterred by these internal regional disputes, 15 West African countries took the bold step of setting up, in May, an enlarged regional organization, the Economic Community of West African States (ECOWAS). It extended from Mauritania to Nigeria and was more broadly based than the former French Communauté Économique de l'Afrique de l'Ouest, which it absorbed. Two new regional organizations were an Economic Community of Great Lakes Countries (Zaire, Rwanda, and Burundi) and a Tanganyika-Kivu Lakes Basin Commission (Burundi, Rwanda, Tanzania, Zaire, and Zambia).

External Relations. On the economic plane, Africa's foreign relations concentrated on negotiations with the industrial countries to establish a "new international economic order"; an unexpected measure of understanding was reached at the special session of the UN General Assembly in September. Relations

CIFRA GRAFICA/PHOTO TRENDS

Residents of El Aiún, representing the Polisarian Front organization, welcome the UN investigating committee to the Spanish Sahara.

J.P. LAFFONT-SYGMA

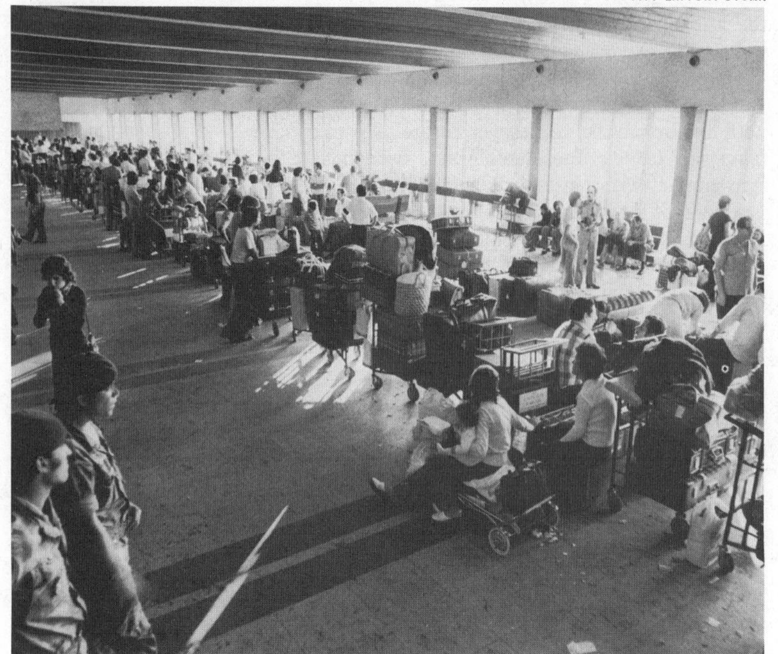

Scene at Luanda airport as thousands of Portuguese await flights to safety from war-torn Angola.

between Africa and the EEC were invigorated by the Lomé Convention. On the political plane, relations with the U.S. and the U.S.S.R. underwent important changes. While the ties between Egypt and the U.S.S.R. continued to weaken steadily, an unexpected rapprochement was achieved between the U.S.S.R. and Libya. Moscow also increased its military assistance to Uganda, but the relationship soured and in November Moscow broke off relations.

The U.S. came into conflict with the OAU over the appointment of Nathaniel Davis as the new U.S. assistant secretary of state for African affairs. The choice was criticized especially by Zaire, partly on the ground that he had no knowledge of Africa; subsequently Davis resigned because of disagreement with U.S. policy in Angola. Because U.S. implication in an abortive military coup against Pres. Mobutu Sese Seko in June was officially suspected, the U.S. ambassador in Kinshasa was asked to leave. In October, however, with Mobutu facing economic troubles at home and sharing a common interest with the U.S. over developments in Angola, relations improved.

The U.S. was also criticized for its proposal to develop a new Indian Ocean base on the island of Diego Garcia. The U.S. accused the U.S.S.R. of building a missile base at Berbera in Somalia, an allegation strongly denied by Moscow and the Somali government. Although the U.S. voted a $7 million military aid program for Ethiopia, over and above normal aid, Washington was reluctant to become involved in the conflicts inside Ethiopia, especially over Eritrea. A number of Arab states—including Saudi Arabia, Kuwait, Syria, Iraq, Yemen (Aden), and Libya—backed the ELF more strongly and more openly.

France experienced another troubled year in its relations with the French-speaking African countries, but it succeeded in reestablishing good relations with Guinea after a diplomatic rupture that had lasted for ten years. The French president visited Zaire, where he promised to end the sale of arms to South Africa other than for purposes of external defense. But French relations with Chad declined as the result of an attempt to rescue a French ethnologist, Françoise Claustre, held as a hostage by Frolinat. The Chad government ordered French troops withdrawn from their base in the country. This withdrawal, with that from Madagascan bases two years earlier, changed France's strategic role in Africa. France also faced the unilateral declaration of independence in the Comoro Islands. Spain clashed with Morocco over Spanish Sahara. Portugal, on the other hand, improved its relations with Africa by the manner in which it terminated its long era of colonialism.

Economy. The year brought no improvement in Africa's disappointing economic performance. The overall average rate of growth had been only 5% between 1970 and 1974. Only 27% of African countries achieved an average growth rate of 6% annually, 22% achieved between 4 and 6%, and the remaining 22 countries registered less than 4%. With population growing at rates of 2.6–2.8% annually, this meant that few countries experienced any real increase in wealth. Prices of Africa's exports continued to fall as the cost of imports, especially oil, soared, and since mid-1974 this reversal in terms of trade was estimated to have cost African countries, other than the eight fortunate oil exporters, a loss of about $3 billion in export earnings. The new executive secretary of the Economic Commission for Africa (ECA), Adebayo Adedeji, blamed this disappointing result on such factors as the deterioration in the continent's terms of trade and balance of payments, the world's cycle of inflation, the international trade recession, mounting unemployment, stagnation in agriculture, and famine due to drought in some countries.

Because Africa was the continent most dependent on raw materials exports, considerable emphasis was placed on the current efforts by the less developed countries to establish a new international economic order. Complementary to this strategy was the collective decision taken by ECA members to initiate action-oriented programs to explore and develop natural resources, encourage raw-materials producers' associations, establish centres to promote cooperation in the fields of industry, science and technology, transport, shipping, and the mass communications media, and to strengthen economic integration.

The drought that had devastated the Sahel states (Chad, Mauritania, Niger, Upper Volta, and Mali) for more than six years was finally broken in these regions in 1975, leaving a bitter legacy that would take years to remedy and that probably ended the traditional way of life of many of the nomad communities on the fringes of the Sahara. But the drought persisted in a number of countries, including Tunisia, Morocco, and Ethiopia. It became critical in Somalia, where 800,000 people had to be succoured.

Communications. The Tanzania-Zambia (Tanzam) railway line, built by the Chinese, became operational in October, almost a year ahead of schedule. Its final completion was scheduled for late 1976. Work continued on the two great continental road networks spanning the Sahara from west to east and from north to south. The planning for a pan-African telecommunications network was carried a stage further during the year. (COLIN LEGUM)

See also Dependent States; articles on the various political units.

[971.D.6; 978.D–E]

ENCYCLOPÆDIA BRITANNICA FILMS. *Boy of Botswana* (1970); *City Boy of the Ivory Coast* (1970); *A Family of Liberia* (1970); *Two Boys of Ethiopia* (1970); *Youth Builds a Nation in Tanzania* (1970); *Africa: Living in Two Worlds* (1971); *Elephant* (1971); *Giraffe* (1971); *Lion* (1971); *Zebra* (1971); *Cheetah* (1972); *Silent Safari* (1972); *The Pygmies: People of the Forest* (1975); *The Pygmies of the Ituri Forest* (1975).

Agriculture and Food Supplies

From a long-run point of view, not much encouragement can be drawn from developments in 1975, although that year's story is not without hopeful aspects. There is, of course, rarely an event in any one year that can be considered an unequivocal pointer to future conditions. Nor can a trend be firmly established, or confirmed, or refuted, on the basis of one year's record only.

Looking at the world picture as a whole, it can be said that nature was more bountiful in 1975, and it is gratifying that food production both in needy areas and in areas of great export potential has shown good increases. These results, from a global point of view, have overcompensated declines in Europe, and in the Soviet Union, where output was drastically curtailed by unfavourable growing conditions.

Economic recession and rising unemployment, coupled with continued increases in retail food prices, have curtailed consumption. Rates of inflation in the world at large, however, have declined, and general economic activity is beginning to expand. Prices received by farmers showed a varied picture in 1975, and important items have declined. On the other hand, the physical volume of output has risen and prices of important inputs have come down from the exorbitant heights to which they had risen in 1974. If farm incomes in developed economies have not increased, and even declined in some, food availabilities to subsistence farmers appear to have improved.

The consideration of prospects for world food supplies and requirements in the years to come and at a more distant time has received renewed and widespread attention since the harvesting and marketing season 1972–73. But what aroused concern was not only the great imbalance in that season between production and requirements for wheat and coarse grains, so spectacularly emphasized by the huge import purchases of the Soviet Union, and the depletion of world reserve stocks. Over the years a number of facts had accumulated, bearing upon the outlook within a wider framework: how wisely, or unwisely, the nations of the world were managing their natural and cultural heritage.

PRODUCTION

World grain production for the 1975–76 season appeared to be at a record high. Yields below those of 1973 were more than compensated by acreage expansion, much of it in the U.S. where the government had successfully urged farmers to increase plantings. U.S. harvests of both wheat and coarse grains achieved record levels. In Europe acreage had declined, and grain output there registered a decrease of about 6% from the 1974 record—the first decline in five years.

Grain production in the U.S.S.R. was reported to have fallen drastically, perhaps as much as 20% from the 1974 level, mainly because of prolonged hot, dry weather in important producing areas. Eastern Europe also saw a decline in the output of grain, especially wheat, largely as a result of flood damage in the south; in the north—East Germany and Poland—drought had reduced yields.

Crops and pastures in Asia and Africa benefited in 1975 from timely and abundant precipitation, but adverse weather over much of the growing season darkened the outlook in Australia. In China both wheat and rice production were reported at an all-time record. Rice production surpassed that of 1974 in most Asian countries.

Mixed conditions prevailed in South America. With acreage expanded, the outlook was for a sizable increase in wheat production in Argentina, despite unfavourable weather, but the corn crop was expected to be down by one-third as a result of rain damage. Brazilian farmers harvested record crops of corn and soybeans, greatly exceeding the results of 1974. Mexico on the whole was expected to profit from good

Table I. Indexes of Food and Agricultural Production
Average 1961–65 equals 100

Region	Total 1970	Total 1971	Total 1972	Total 1973	Total 1974*	Total % change 1973 to 1974	Per capita 1970	Per capita 1971	Per capita 1972	Per capita 1973	Per capita 1974*	Per capita % change 1973 to 1974
Food production												
Developed market economies†	116	123	122	126	128	+2	108	114	111	114	115	+1
Western Europe	117	121	119	125	130	+4	110	114	111	116	120	+3
North America	113	124	122	124	124	0	104	113	110	111	110	−1
Oceania	121	127	126	140	137	−2	106	109	107	117	113	−3
Eastern Europe and the U.S.S.R.	130	132	133	148	146	−1	121	122	122	135	132	−2
Total developed countries	121	126	126	134	135	+1	112	117	115	121	121	0
Less developed market economies†	124	125	125	129	131	+2	103	102	99	99	99	−1
Latin America	124	125	127	128	135	+5	102	100	98	97	99	+2
Far East	124	125	121	132	128	−3	104	102	97	103	97	−5
Near East	124	127	138	130	143	+10	102	101	107	98	105	+6
Africa	121	124	124	121	127	+5	102	101	99	94	96	+2
Asian centrally planned economies	122	125	124	130	133	+2	107	108	105	108	109	+1
Total less developed countries	123	125	125	129	132	+2	105	104	101	102	102	0
World	121	126	125	131	132	+1	106	108	105	108	107	−1
Agricultural production												
Developed market economies	113	120	119	122	124	+2	105	111	109	111	112	+1
Western Europe	116	121	119	125	130	+4	110	114	111	115	119	+3
North America	109	119	118	120	119	0	100	108	106	107	106	−1
Oceania	120	123	122	127	123	−3	106	107	104	107	102	−4
Eastern Europe and the U.S.S.R.	129	132	133	147	146	−1	121	122	122	134	132	−2
Total developed countries	119	124	124	131	132	+1	111	115	113	119	119	0
Less developed market economies	123	124	125	128	131	+2	103	101	99	99	98	−1
Latin America	122	122	125	126	132	+5	100	98	97	95	97	+2
Far East	124	124	122	132	129	−3	104	102	97	103	98	−5
Near East	124	127	138	130	143	+10	102	102	107	98	104	+6
Africa	121	123	124	121	127	+5	102	101	99	94	96	+3
Asian centrally planned economies	122	126	124	131	134	+2	108	109	106	109	110	+1
Total less developed countries	123	125	125	129	132	+2	104	103	101	102	102	0
World	120	125	124	130	131	+1	105	107	105	107	106	−1

*Preliminary. †Including countries in other regions not specified.
Source: Food and Agriculture Organization of the United Nations, *Monthly Bulletin of Agricultural Economics and Statistics* (July/August 1975).

crops, as were Chile and other South American countries. The Caribbean and Central America, on the other hand, reported losses from drought and large import requirements.

As a result of the 1974–75 inflation and recession in the industrial world, the long-term upward trend in the consumption of livestock products appeared to have been interrupted. Use of grains for feed in the U.S. for 1974–75 was estimated at 123 million metric tons, compared with 156 million in 1973–74. Canada, Japan, and the European Economic Community (EEC) also showed declines, while other parts of Western Europe registered moderate increases. It remained to be seen whether the hoped-for continuance of economic recovery in the world at large would restore the trend toward rising use of grain for livestock feed, thus putting additional upward pressure on all grain prices.

In its submission to the conference of the UN Food and Agriculture Organization (FAO) in November 1975, the secretariat estimated total world food production in 1975 at 2 to 3% above 1974. While the estimated increase for developed countries was only 1 to 2%, the gain in the less developed countries was tentatively placed at 4 to 5%, implying a per capita increase of from 1.5 to 2%. FAO's most striking finding related to the Far East, where total food output was assumed to have risen by 7 to 8% (excluding China, where the increase was placed at 3 to 4%). The generally good to excellent outturn of the rice crops, with records set in India and China, was of great importance. The rate of increase of food output in Africa was estimated at 1 to 2%.

Thus the food situation at the end of 1975, according to the FAO, contrasted favourably with the position in late 1974, following poor harvests in North America, the major grain exporter, and in the Far East, the major importer. The improvement in less developed countries found further striking expression in the FAO estimate of the number of countries suffering from serious food shortages: 7 in October 1975, as compared with 18 in October 1974.

The improvement in 1975, however, should not be permitted to distract attention from the unsatisfactory trends of recent years. In 1970–74 world grain output (including rice) increased by a yearly average of 2.5%, while grain output in less developed countries rose only 1.4%. World production of starchy roots and pulses, so important in the diets of many poorer countries, even declined.

New type of mechanized hay baler, in use from California to the Midwest during the year, promises to reduce costs and speed operations. The spool-shaped bales that are produced require no wire and can be left in the open field.

LUNSFORD—THE NEW YORK TIMES

Grains. Preliminary (October 1975) estimates of the 1975–76 world crop were around 360 million metric tons for wheat (350 for 1974–75), 230 million tons (milled basis) for rice (223), and 590 million tons for coarse grains (570). Thus there was some increase, particularly in rice and coarse grains. Wheat did not come up to the favourable results of 1973–74, though the U.S. produced an all-time record crop. The shortfall of wheat in the U.S.S.R. accounted for more than twice the world deficit as compared with 1973–74.

Fortunately, production of grains, including rice, in Southeast Asia was likely to have risen by a considerable margin. Rice stocks in most countries would probably increase, so that import requirements of the deficit areas should be reduced. Improved grain production was also reported from Latin America and the Near East. Africa, too, showed some improvement.

The year 1975–76 again demonstrated the extraordinary dependence of deficit areas on the U.S. Fully 50% of both wheat and total grain exports moving in international trade were provided by that country. This situation was particularly disquieting in light of the fact that the large reserve stocks the U.S. once held had been whittled down to very low levels. Furthermore, the 62 million ac. of set-aside cropland (20% of the total) that the U.S. held as a reserve three years earlier had by now dwindled to 2 million ac. Although 20 million ac. of the 60 million-ac. decline had gone into fallow or minor crops and could be largely recovered for cereal production, the conclusion was inescapable that grain reserves should be increased as soon as possible, with all important exporting and importing countries sharing the burden. This goal had been decided upon at the World Food Conference of November 1974, but as of 1975 international agreement on the subject was incomplete and largely theoretical. (See *Cereal Stocks and "World Food Security,"* below.)

An important factor in 1975 was the reappearance of the U.S.S.R. as a very large buyer of grain on the world market. The erratic and unpredictable nature of Soviet import demand was difficult to reconcile with the U.S.S.R.'s refusal to participate in the international plans for "food security" (emergency stocks of grains) or even the "early warning system" to provide prompt reports on crop estimates and other factors affecting the food outlook.

In a deliberate attempt to impress upon the Soviet government the need for a stocking policy that would tend to smooth out the effects of production cycles, the U.S. took the initiative of urging—and in the end concluded—a five-year agreement with the U.S.S.R. for the delivery of 30 million tons of grain (6 million per year). There were elasticities and escape clauses embodied in the agreement, however, and it remained to be seen how its actual implementation would work out.

In international circles the U.S.-Soviet agreement was received with mixed comment. The prevalent view seemed to be that arrangements of this kind must be built into a realistic framework of commodity agreements that could protect the interests of traditional importers as well as claimants of food aid and of exporters in general. It was also obvious that allocations of export supplies on a comprehensive scale should not be made to cover several years. Rather, the level of total supplies from year to year would have to be the basis for fair distribution of availabilities in relation to requirements, neither of which can be known years in advance. Meanwhile, efforts toward an international agreement on cereals made little progress.

Sugar. The history of sugar prices in recent years pointed up dramatically the enormous fluctuations to which an uncontrolled agricultural commodity with low elasticity of demand is subject on the international market.

Beginning with the sugar production-consumption year 1970–71, output could not keep pace with requirements. Hence stocks were drawn down continuously. At the end of the sugar year 1973–74 they had fallen to 19% of annual consumption, compared with a "usual" level of 25%. New York (spot) world contract no. 11 (no. 8 before May 1, 1970) averaged below two cents per pound in 1966–68 and above three cents in 1969 and 1970. Increases at the end of 1971 and 1972 doubled these prices, and by the end of 1973 the 12-cent level had been reached.

The International Sugar Agreement of 1968, which had attempted to stabilize prices at a reasonable level through a system of export quotas, broke down in 1972 under the pressure of the upsurge of the market; the U.S.S.R. changed from a net exporter to a large-scale net importer, and world consumption exceeded production by a considerable margin. By June 1974 the no. 11 spot price had risen to an average of almost 24 cents, only to more than double again by November 1974 to an average of 56 cents. By then the 1974–75 production and consumption outlook had again signaled a tight market situation.

The very nature of the primary causes of this upsurge—basic growth of demand and its low price elasticity—served to stimulate widespread speculation, resulting in a startling reinforcement of underlying market strength. Subsequently, when it became clear that acreages had been greatly expanded and world sugar production in 1975–76 would show a large increase, the fall in prices assumed proportions as extraordinary as those of the 1974 increase: at 14 cents in November 1975, the New York spot price for contract no. 11 was down to one-fourth of the 1974 high and below any month of 1974. As of late 1975, world output in 1975–76 was estimated at 84 million tons (79 million in 1974–75), or 2 million tons above prospective consumption. Both beet- and cane-sugar producers participated in the expansion.

The performance of the international sugar market demonstrated the need to conclude a new international agreement. Producer interests, responsible for the abrogation of the 1968 agreement, would now be favoured by a workable compact. The potential for the expansion of cane-sugar production was particularly great, not only through increases in acreage but also through the use of improved varieties and better growing, harvesting, and processing methods. Vast possibilities appeared to exist in Central and South America, especially in Brazil but also in Mexico, Cuba, and Argentina. Production reserves for sugar in Asia, Oceania, and Africa were also significant. Beet sugar production in Europe and North America was already being expanded.

Thus the stage was set for a considerable growth in world sugar output. On the other hand, consumption was likely to continue to rise. Product substitutions and physical restrictions on consumption, which some countries had introduced, might well be relaxed or abolished in the face of lower prices, and economic recovery should also contribute to greater utilization.

Dairy Products. As of late 1975, it appeared that the developed countries had experienced moderate changes in milk production during the year. There was some decline in the EEC, other Western European countries, the U.S.S.R., and Poland, while little change was reported from Canada and the U.S. Australia experienced a further drop of production, but it was much below the sharp decline of 1974 (11%). After a series of dry summers, New Zealand reported improved conditions and a sizable increase in output.

Market developments were uneven throughout 1975 and, on the whole, unsatisfactory. Intervention stocks of butter and especially skim milk rose. Skim milk in particular presented a great problem. In 1973–74 the U.S. had become a temporary importer of sizable quantities of butter, cheese, and skim milk. This was at a time when milk production was stagnating, prices of competing nondairy products were relatively high, and world consumption of butter and cheese was rising measurably. On the international market, prices of butter oil and skim milk powder rose to $1,000 per metric ton. Conditions began to deteriorate rapidly in the second half of 1974 and in 1975. Stocks of skim milk powder rose to over one million tons by July 1975 and toward the end of the year stood at 1.7 million tons. Prices fell to about half their 1974 high.

There was great uncertainty about future prospects for dairy products. Lower prices of competing products, including vegetable oils and meat, played a significant role. The need for national as well as international policy measures with respect to dairy products was well realized, but progress had been slow, and the parties were far from an agreement. There was a special problem with respect to skim milk powder. The minimum price of $350 per ton for skim

GARY SETTLE—THE NEW YORK TIMES

Organically grown corn on an experimental plot in Iowa dwarfs a farmer, suggesting that good yields can be obtained in the absence of chemical fertilizers and pesticides.

Table II. World Production and Trade of Principal Grains

In 000 metric tons

	Wheat			Barley			Oats			Rye			Corn (Maize)			Rice		
	Production		Imports− Exports+	Production		Imports− Exports+	Production		Imports− Exports+	Production		Imports− Exports+	Production		Imports− Exports+	Production		Imports− Exports+
	1961–65 average	1974	1971–74 average	1961–65 average	1974	1971–74 average	1961–65 average	1974	1971–74 average	1961–65 average	1974	1971–74 average	1961–65 average	1974	1971–74 average	1961–65 average	1974	1971–74 average
World total	254,399	359,660	−59,395* +62,048*	99,686	170,536	−12,369* +12,445*	47,813	53,503	−1,775* +1,794*	33,833	29,087	−1,192* +1,208*	215,583	290,672	−38,971* +39,261*	251,891	320,773	−9,344* +9,334*
EUROPE																		
Austria	704	1,102	−40 +18*	563	1,238	−66 +2*	322	290	−21	393	415	—	197	857	−62 +1*	—	—	−60* +1*
Belgium	826	c.1,000	−1,200† +289*†	485	c.702	−973† +166*†	389	c.240	−58† +7*†	120	c.50	−8*† +5*†	2	27	−1,4o2† +305†	—	—	−68† +23*†
Bulgaria	2,213	c.3,420	−78‡ +351*	694	c.1,400	−21* +18*	141	c.65	—	58	c.20	−3*	1,601	c.2,500	−34* +25*	37	c.61§	−2* +1*
Czechoslovakia	1,779	c.5,000	−982	1,556	c.2,950	−119 +47*	792	c.620	+2*	897	c.660	−86*	474	c.750	−422*	—	—	−73*
Denmark	535	597	−9 +118*	3,506	6,032	−119 +249	713	475	−36 +7	380	167	−13* +6*	—	—	−248 +1*	—	—	−13* +2*
Finland	448	536	−17 +77*	400	963	−13* +24*	828	1,216	+87*	141	175	−18	—	—	−54	—	—	−14* +1*
France	12,495	18,910	−252 +5,879	6,594	10,030	−6* +3,716	2,583	2,038	+169	367	308	−5* +60	2,760	c.8,900	−323 +3,714	120	60	−134 +5
Germany, East	1,357	c.3,250	−1,802*	1,291	c.3,250	−c.350*	850	c.840	—	1,741	c.1,900	−c.33*	3	c.35§	−1,029*	—	—	−44*
Germany, West	4,607	7,722	−2,297 +498*	3,462	7,047	−1,551 +367	2,185	3,448	−456 +31	3,031	2,543	−61 +232	55	534	−3,358 +247	—	—	−164 +31*
Greece	1,765	c.2,200	−2* +42*	248	c.980	−c.30* +6*	143	114	—	19	6§	—	241	600	−295*	88	c.93	−3* +7*
Hungary	2,020	4,860	−147* +463	970	c.840	−319* +70*	108	c.65	−23*	271	c.175	−44* +7*	3,350	c.5,900	−91* +269*	36	c.74	−14* +4*
Ireland	343	208	−168	575	835	−102 +20*	357	125	−14	1	c.1§	—	—	—	−222	—	—	−3*
Italy	8,857	9,590	−1,866 +48	276	552	−1,241 +15*	545	460	−189 +3*	87	37	−4*	3,633	5,193	−4,651 +13	612	988	−16* +372
Netherlands, The	606	746	−1,547 +491	390	315	−228 +151	421	163	−66 +74	312	78	−30 +34	c.1	c.14§	−3,379 +756*	—	—	−78 +24*
Norway	19	20§	−358	440	632	−133	126	370	−2* +8*	3	7§	−69	—	—	−93	—	—	−6*
Poland	2,988	c.6,150	−1,640	1,368	c.3,740	−966 +80	2,641	c.3,100	−55* +24*	7,466	c.7,620	−83* +135*	20	c.15§	−452*	—	—	−65
Portugal	550	505	−225	61	55§	−93*	87	94	—	177	156	−22*	560	c.500	−775	167	c.143	−13*
Romania	4,321	4,970	+376*	415	911	−c.140* +c.157*	154	91	—	95	c.40	—	5,853	c.7,500	−c.100* +404*	40	c.55	−40*
Spain	4,365	4,443	−64* +50*	1,959	5,404	−89	447	559	−1*	385	254	—	1,101	1,961	−2,815 +1*	386	384	+48
Sweden	909	1,443	−17 +369	1,167	2,040	−13* +284*	1,304	1,446	−7* +279	142	361	−1* +93	—	—	−59	—	—	−16*
Switzerland	355	355	−405	102	198	−473	40	42	−169	52	40	−37	14	130§	−243	—	—	−19*
U.S.S.R.	64,207	83,800	−8,533* +5,238*	20,318	c.54,800	−c.1,510* +421*	6,052	c.18,000	−217* +12*	15,093	12,000	−467* +69*	13,122	12,100	−3,460* +258*	390	1,900	+61*
United Kingdom	3,520	6,017	−3,861 +10*	6,668	9,017	−732 +139	1,531	976	−20 +19*	21	c.16	−38* +1*	—	—	−3,191 +11*	—	—	−137 +2*
Yugoslavia	3,599	6,284	−416* +1*	557	794	−95‡	343	353	−22*	169	120	—	5,618	8,000	−363* +155	23	31§	−13* +1*
ASIA																		
Bangladesh	37	91§	−1,432*	16	16§	—	—	—	—	—	—	—	4	c.2§	—	15,034	17,527	−309‖
Burma	38	36§	—	—	—	—	—	—	—	—	—	—	58	32§	+11*	7,786	c.8,350	+419
China	c.22,200	c.37,000	−5,162*	14,700	c.20,000	−c.350*	c.1,690	c.3,000	—	—	—	—	c.22,720	31,000	−c.1,800*	c.83,200	113,000	+c.2,640*
India	11,191	22,073	−1,482* +224*	2,590	2,327	—	—	—	—	—	—	—	4,593	c.5,000	−3*	52,733	c.60,000	−187 +14*
Indonesia	—	—	−510*	—	—	—	—	—	—	—	—	—	2,804	2,760	−76* +143*	12,393	22,800	−962*
Iran	2,873	4,100	−851*	792	826	−89*	—	—	—	—	—	—	16	c.27§	−93*	851	1,357	−125*
Iraq	849	1,339	−390* +57*	851	533	−124‡ +18‡	—	—	—	—	—	—	2	19§	−6*	138	c.200	−131*
Japan	1,332	232	−5,196	1,380	233	−1,152	145	51	−170	2	c.1§	−127	96	19	−6,692	16,444	15,826	−26 +545*
Korea, South	277	c.280	−1,914	1,419	1,881	−293*	—	—	—	37	c.16	—	26	61§	−429*	4,809	6,067	−724*
Malaysia	—	—	−349* +1*	—	—	−4*	—	—	−4*	—	—	—	8	13§	−196* +1*	1,140	c.1,957§	−264* +20*
Pakistan	4,152	7,631	−965 +4*	118	140	+6*	—	—	—	—	—	—	513	c.675	−3* +1*	1,824	3,225	−18‖ +584‖
Philippines	—	—	−571	—	—	−9*	—	—	−4*	—	—	−6*	1,305	c.2,350	−110*	3,957	5,720	−388* +1*
Syria	1,093	1,381	−245 +134*	649	714	−28* +11	2	c.2§	—	—	—	—	7	16§	−3*	1	—	−52*
Thailand	—	—	−74*	—	—	—	—	—	—	—	—	—	816	c.2,300	−3* +1,682*	11,267	13,274	+1,404
Turkey	8,585	11,082	−251* +197*	3,447	3,330	−6* +25‡	495	380	—	734	560	+4*	950	1,100	−2*	222	265§	−23*
AFRICA																		
Algeria	1,254	c.700	−c.800*	476	c.500	−c.50*	28	c.30	—	—	—	—	4	c.5§	−14*	7	c.6§	−11*
Egypt	1,459	c.1,850	−1,764	137	c.100	—	—	—	—	—	—	—	1,913	c.2,600	−64*	1,845	c.2,500	+351
Kenya	122	c.172§	−41* +44*	15	c.21§	−1*	2	c.4§	—	—	—	—	1,110	c.1,400	−10*	14	c.36§	−5* +1*
Morocco	1,336	3,048	−689	1,316	2,062	−c.19*	18	20	—	2	c.2§	—	352	323	−12*	20	c.13§	+2*
Nigeria	16	c.5§	−350*	—	—	—	—	—	—	—	—	—	1,040	c.1,000	−3*	205	c.550§	−2*
South Africa	840	1,547	−25* +116*	37	30§	−11*	117	107	+1*	11	5	−2*	5,229	11,035	−1* +2,031*	2	c.3§	−91 +1*
NORTH AMERICA																		
Canada	15,364	14,221	+12,278	3,860	8,585	+3,526	6,075	3,929	−5* +132	319	481	−1* +196	1,073	2,589	−629 +14*	—	—	−64*
Mexico	1,549	2,764	−512* +37*	175	310	−20* +7*	76	22	−11*	—	—	—	7,369	8,000	−359* +242*	314	c.400	−13* +8*
United States	33,040	48,807	−23 +24,973¶	8,676	6,708	−268 +1,380	13,848	9,007	−25 +377	828	490	−2* +291	95,561	118,145	−36 +24,586¶	3,084	5,175	−30* +1,718
SOUTH AMERICA																		
Argentina	7,541	4,800	+1,807*	679	386	+107*	676	316	+142*	422	310	+33*	4,984	9,900	+4,486*	193	316	+49*
Bolivia	48	53§	−c.25*	61	72§	—	4	c.5§	—	—	—	—	254	305§	—	43	69§	—
Brazil	574	2,305	−2,033	26	c.18§	−27	20	c.39	−27*	17	c.17	−1*	10,112	16,065	−3* +649	6,123	7,329	−5* +60
Chile	1,082	c.1,122	−627	74	c.179	+10*	89	c.142	+2*	7	14	—	204	367	−291*	85	55§	−37*
Colombia	118	c.91§	−370*	106	c.110	−45*	—	—	−6*	—	—	—	826	c.870	−57*	576	c.1,540	+c.3*
Peru	150	117	−687*	185	c.170	−19*	4	c.1§	—	1	c.1§	—	490	473	−c.107*	324	361	+22*
Uruguay	465	c.500	−132* +27*	30	c.32§	+c.10*	66	c.72	−1*	—	—	—	148	225	−3*	67	137§	+58*
Venezuela	1	1§	−604*	—	—	—	—	—	−10*	—	—	—	477	c.450	−73*	136	c.300	−3* +2*
OCEANIA																		
Australia	8,222	c.11,500	+6,738	978	2,500	+1,220	1,172	940	+285	11	c.20	—	169	157	−1* +23*	136	409	+146*
New Zealand	248	248	−29*	98	290	−18* +4*	34	59	—	—	—	—	16	119§	—	—	—	−5*

Note: (—) indicates quantity nil or negligible. (c.) indicates provisional or estimated.
*1971–73 average. †Belgium-Luxembourg economic union. ‡1971–72 average. §1973. ‖1972–74 average. ¶Including foreign aid shipments.
Sources: FAO *Monthly Bulletin of Agricultural Economics and Statistics;* FAO *Production Yearbook 1973;* FAO *Trade Yearbook 1973.*

(M. C. MacDONALD)

milk powder, established under the General Agreement on Tariffs and Trade (GATT) arrangement which had been in force for 12 years, was so low as to be unrealistic after the inflation of recent years.

Meat. The calendar year 1974 had been characterized by increases in production in North America, Europe, and some countries in South America and by lowered output in Oceania. Purchases by the main importing countries were considerably curtailed. They themselves had also increased their output, and some of them experienced a decline in consumer demand as recession and inflation gathered momentum. The decline of world trade in meat and livestock was further intensified by special import restrictions imposed by the EEC and Japan, as well as Greece. Israel, Spain, and Switzerland. Increased domestic price supports in the EEC were an additional factor.

As a result, price developments through 1974 and well into 1975 were unfavourable to producers, though this trend was partly counteracted by domestic support schemes (price supports, intervention purchases, producer credit guarantees). Producers in the main exporting countries were the most seriously affected. Producer prices for beef, mutton, and lamb fell drastically in Australia, New Zealand, and Argentina—by anywhere from 40 to 70%.

The cost-price squeeze produced an interesting development in cattle feeding in the U.S. in the form of a shift away from concentrates (including grain) and toward grass. Normally 70% of the beef produced in the U.S. was accounted for by grain-fed cattle, but more than 50% of the total beef supply in the past two years had been provided by the leaner grass-fed cattle.

More recently, cattle-feed price relationships had begun to turn around. A greater proportion of cattle were moving into feedlots, and experts expected the share of the beef supply from feedlots in the first quarter of 1976 to rise to something like 55%. The interesting aspect of these alternations was the flexibility they implied. They showed that, in the short term, larger supplies of grain could be freed for direct human consumption without seriously affecting the supply of meat, at least in the U.S.

Oilseeds and Oils. World production of oilseeds in 1975–76 might exceed offtake, making for a considerable accumulation of stocks. This was especially true in the U.S., where soybean supplies, so important in the total picture, were at a record level. U.S. production was estimated at more than 41 million metric tons, fully 23% above the 33.6 million tons produced in 1974 and almost up to the record harvest of 1973. At 47 million metric tons, total U.S. soybean supplies for 1975–76, including production and carry-over, represented an all-time record. A further substantial increase in carry-over supplies at the end of the 1975–76 marketing season was expected.

Brazil also looked forward to a sizable increase in the crop to be harvested early in 1976. With the exception of sunflower seed and cottonseed, most oilseeds in other parts of the world promised larger supplies as well. Production of sunflower seed in the Soviet Union and southeastern Europe had shown declines, and cottonseed was down because of much smaller cotton crops in the U.S. and the Soviet Union. There was also some uncertainty about the rapeseed crop in Western Europe. Peanut (groundnut) production in Africa and peanut and coconut production in India and Pakistan were reported to be satisfactory.

AID/AUTHENTICATED NEWS INTERNATIONAL

Accurate scales have replaced visual estimates as a method of weighing rice on cooperative farms in Ecuador.

Although demand for oils and protein feeds was expected to pick up as world economic recovery proceeded, and increased import purchases by the traditional deficit countries and the Soviet Union would lessen the pressure of a large supply, the latter was still likely to exert a bearish influence on price levels in 1975–76. The longer-term outlook for the supply/demand balance was much more uncertain.

Natural Fibres. In recent years the demand for jute had been considerably reduced as a result of the increasing utilization of synthetic substitutes in the production of bags, sacks, industrial textiles, and carpet backing. A similar situation prevailed, after 1974, for sisal and allied fibres. Price supports in Brazil added to the buildup of stocks.

With wool textile activity severely curtailed since the middle of 1974, wool prices experienced sharp

Table III. Estimated Total Carry-over Stocks of Cereals at the End of Respective Crop Years*†
In 000,000 metric tons

Item	Crop year ending in 1970	1971	1972	1973	1974	1975‡
Wheat stocks held by	80	64	67	44	39	42
main exporters	65	50	49	29	26	26
main importers	8	9	11	8	7	8
others	7	5	7	7	6	8
Rice stocks held by	25	24	21	13	14	13
selected exporters	10	9	6	4	4	4
selected importers	8	9	8	5	6	6
others	7	6	7	4	4	3
Coarse grain stocks held by	73	57	74	59	48	45
main exporters	54	39	54	39	28	23
main importers	10	10	11	11	12	14
others	9	8	9	9	8	8
Total cereals†	178	145	162	116	101	100
As % of consumption†	23	17	19	13	12	11

Note: This series has been adjusted to reflect stock positions on an end of season basis.
*Stock data are based on an aggregate of national carry-over levels at the end of national crop years and should not be construed as representing world stock levels at a fixed point of time.
†Excluding the U.S.S.R. and China, for which no data were available.
‡Estimated as of November 1975.
Source: Food and Agriculture Organization of the United Nations.

Table IV. Annual Changes in World Food and Agricultural Production
Percent

Region	1971–72	1972–73	1973–74	1974–75*	Annual average 1961–74
Food production					
Developed market economies†	−1.3	+ 3.2	+2.3	+1 to +2	+2.3
Western Europe	−1.7	+ 4.8	+4.3	−2 to −1	+2.3
North America	−1.9	+ 2.1	+0.7	+5 to +6	+2.2
Oceania	−0.5	+10.5	−5.2	0 to +1	+2.8
Eastern Europe and the U.S.S.R.	+0.5	+11.8	−1.5	0 to +1	+3.7
Total developed countries	−0.6	+ 6.5	+0.8	+1 to +2	+2.8
Less developed market economies	+0.2	+ 3.0	+2.0	+5 to +6	+2.7
Latin America	+1.2	+ 1.0	+5.7	+3 to +4	+2.8
Far East‡	−2.7	+ 8.8	−2.9	+7 to +8	+2.6
Near East§	+8.9	− 5.5	+9.9	+5 to +6	+3.2
Africa‖	+0.6	− 2.9	+5.2	+1 to +2	+2.4
Asian centrally planned economies	−1.2	+ 4.6	+2.5	+2 to +3	+2.7
Total less developed countries	−0.3	+ 3.5	+2.2	+4 to +5	+2.7
World	−0.5	+ 5.3	+1.3	+2 to +3	+2.7
Agricultural production					
Developed market economies†	−0.6	+ 2.6	+2.0	+1 to +2	+2.1
Western Europe	−1.6	+ 4.7	+4.2	−2 to −1	+2.3
North America	−0.6	+ 1.7	+0.5	+4 to +5	+1.8
Oceania	−0.8	+ 3.6	−5.2	+3 to +4	+2.3
Eastern Europe and the U.S.S.R.	+0.5	+11.3	−1.1	0 to +1	+3.5
Total developed countries	−0.2	+ 5.9	+0.7	+1 to +2	+2.6
Less developed market economies	+0.6	+ 2.8	+2.1	+4 to +5	+2.6
Latin America	+1.8	+ 0.8	+5.6	+2 to +3	+2.6
Far East‡	−2.2	+ 8.5	−2.8	+7 to +8	+2.6
Near East§	+8.5	− 5.8	+9.9	+3 to +4	+3.2
Africa‖	+0.8	− 2.9	+5.5	+1 to +2	+2.4
Asian centrally planned economies	−1.2	+ 5.1	+2.4	+2 to +3	+2.8
Total less developed countries	0	+ 3.5	+2.2	+3 to +4	+2.7
World	−0.1	+ 4.9	+1.3	+2 to +3	+2.6

Note: Data for total agricultural production and for food production are based on net production, with deductions for seed and feed, except for Eastern Europe and the U.S.S.R., for which no deductions have been made. Data for cereals and livestock (Table V) are based on total production, without any deduction.
*Preliminary. †Including Japan, Israel, and South Africa. ‡Excluding Japan. §Excluding Israel. ‖Excluding South Africa.
Source: Food and Agriculture Organization of the United Nations.

declines in early 1975. By October, however, prices had recovered to some extent and reached a level measurably above a year earlier. More pronounced improvement of industry activity could not be expected until economic recovery in the industrial countries had made more substantial progress.

World cotton consumption in 1974–75 fell by 5% as compared with the preceding season. The resultant decline in prices, as well as a further escalation of production costs almost everywhere, led to a sizable curtailment of cotton output for the consumption year 1975–76. This prospect for much reduced supplies finally halted the long decline in prices. There was even a good recovery in the second half of the year, and October prices were well above the depressed level of a year earlier. There was hope for a more balanced supply-consumption picture in 1975–76. The influence of large carry-over stocks had been neutralized by a pickup in cotton textile activity following a year in which operations had been greatly depressed.

Bemborough Solomon, a splendid brown bull and representative of a 100-year-old type of Gloucester cattle, is being used to provide semen for a deep freeze bank in an effort to prevent extinction of his kind.

KEYSTONE

Miscellaneous Products. After falling throughout 1974 and early 1975, coffee prices rebounded as news of severe frost damage to coffee trees in Brazil in July reached the market. The increases were extraordinary; by December New York March futures stood at 80 cents per pound, compared with the season's low of 50 cents. The 1975–76 world crop was estimated at 71 million bags (of 132.3 lb. each), compared with 79 million in 1974–75. The reduction of exportable supplies was estimated at 10% (53 million bags, compared with 58 million), and this, if consumption was maintained, would cause a lowering of world stocks. A new international coffee agreement, concluded in early December and providing funds to promote coffee consumption, was to take effect on Oct. 1, 1976. Production quotas would not be imposed unless the price dropped considerably (which was unlikely for a few years because of tree damage in Brazil and the civil war in Angola).

Favourable growing conditions for cocoa in various areas foreshadowed a record world crop in 1975–76, perhaps 6% above 1974–75 or 2% over the previous record of 1,570,000 metric tons in 1971–72. Prices in late November 1975 were still 35% above the season's low of 40 cents per pound (March 1976 futures). The futures discount for forward months was considerable, however, thus confirming the production outlook; September 1976, at 50 cents, was quoted 15% below December 1975 or 10% below March 1976.

Tea production, consumption, and price movements had not shown any remarkable changes in the recent past. It was notable, however, that the steady increase in prices during 1974 was maintained well into 1975. Average prices at the London auctions in the first half of 1975 stood at 62 pence per kilogram, compared with 59.9 pence, the annual average for 1974, and 43 pence for 1973. Growth in both world production and demand had been slow. There was some activity on the part of the International Tea Council to promote tea consumption. Although no international tea agreement existed, an FAO intergovernmental group had arranged for informal export quotas in order to help stabilize prices at fair levels.

Continued action by the government of Malaysia to limit market supplies of rubber succeeded in holding prices fairly stable. The New York spot quotations for smoked sheets in late November 1975 were above the year before. Malaysia's purpose was to regain some of the elastomer market lost to synthetics by holding natural rubber prices at competitive levels. At present, natural rubber accounted for only one-third of total world rubber consumption, but there were some hopeful developments. Considerable success had been achieved in the development of high-yielding varieties, notably by the Rubber Research Institute in Malaysia, where 90% of the rubber area was already in high-yielding stock. Other countries as well, such as Sri Lanka, India, and Thailand, had high proportions of their rubber acreage (30 to 50%) under such varieties. On the consumption side, the U.S. had increased the share of natural rubber in total consumption (57% in 1950) from 22% in 1971 to 24% in 1974, largely because of the shift to radial tires, which use more natural rubber. (*See* INDUSTRIAL REVIEW: *Rubber*.)

Prices, Incomes, and Inputs. Statistics were not available to permit a world review of prices received by farmers, prices paid for inputs, and farm incomes. For countries that do compile national information of this type, results were available only for periods predating 1975.

Some tentative estimates for 1975, however, were given for the U.S. at the National Agricultural Outlook Conference held in Washington, D.C., Nov. 17–20, 1975. A small gain in gross farm income was presumed to have taken place in 1975, but it was more than offset by increases in farm production expenses. Realized net farm income may have been as much as 8% below 1974. Since this estimate was in nominal terms, not discounting for inflation, the decline in real terms was even greater. With price improvements and increased farm production forecast for 1975–76, U.S. farm income was expected to increase, despite further rises in production expenses.

Although there were considerable declines in fertilizer prices during 1975, they were still at a high level since they had tripled in 1974. Accordingly consumption in most countries declined; fertilizer-crop price ratios were unfavourable, and weather developments also had an adverse effect on fertilizer consumption, at least in Western Europe and the U.S. Stocks had been building up, new production capacity came into operation in a number of countries, and further easing of prices was expected.

Spot shortages of pesticides and delivery delays continued, even though factories were operating at capacity. As a result, prices remained high. Farmers in the less developed countries were especially hard hit, particularly since prices of the "cheaper" products had risen most spectacularly. There was little prospect of relief until major additions to existing capacity became operational in 1977. In the meantime, the shortages could even intensify, posing a real threat to the higher-yielding crop varieties. Finally, the prices of gasoline and diesel fuel rose further.

POLICY ORIENTATION

The concerns about the prospects for food supply and requirements, voiced so vociferously at the World Food Conference of November 1974, had by no means stirred governments into early action. Nevertheless, some advances were made.

The World Food Council, recommended by the conference and duly set up by the UN General Assembly, held its first constitutive meeting in Rome in late June 1975. No firm decisions on concrete measures resulted, however, and the prevailing impression was one of uncertainty as to exactly what role the council should play, what its true authority was to be, and to what extent it could call for agreement on action. A clear-cut definition of the functions of the council and its relationship to the FAO seemed imperative.

Another recommendation of the conference, later adopted by the General Assembly, was the establishment of an International Fund for Agricultural Development to augment external resources for agricultural development by $1.2 billion. A number of meetings on the subject were held in 1975; adoption of rules, pledging of contributions, and agreement on operating procedures were planned for February 1976. Various consultative groups were also established, one on Food Production and Investment and another on International Agricultural Research (both with offices at the World Bank).

The FAO on its part pressed forward with two

KEYSTONE

A French decision to curb Italian wine imports prompted this demonstration by irate wine producers in Rome.

initiatives (also endorsed by the World Food Conference) that tended to prod governments into more earnest consideration of rational policies for international coordination. The first was the call for security reserves of grains; the second, the call for obligatory contributions of up-to-date reports to an early warning system, under which FAO would assemble pertinent information on developments in the outlook for production, consumption, trade, and other basic conditions affecting food supplies.

Unfortunately, despite an overwhelmingly favourable disposition toward these initiatives, there was as yet no prospect that 1975–76 would see the accumulation of grain reserves measurably exceeding the bare

Table V. Annual Changes in World Cereal and Livestock Production
Percent

Region	1971–72	1972–73	1973–74	1974–75*	Annual average 1961–74
Cereal production					
Developed market economies†	− 2.9	+ 3.7	− 3.7	+ 6 to + 7	+2.7
Western Europe	− 0.2	+ 1.5	+ 6.0	− 8 to − 7	+3.4
North America	− 4.4	+ 4.6	−12.3	+20 to +21	+2.7
Oceania	−25.4	+57.7	− 3.7	−10 to − 9	+2.9
Eastern Europe and the U.S.S.R.	− 3.5	+22.5	− 9.0	−11 to −10	+4.2
Total developed countries	− 3.1	+10.6	− 5.8	0	+3.3
Less developed market economies	− 2.5	+ 6.1	− 1.3	+ 8 to + 9	+2.7
Latin America	− 5.5	+ 8.2	+ 4.7	+ 5 to + 6	+3.3
Far East‡	− 4.6	+12.3	− 6.2	+10 to +11	+2.8
Near East§	+ 7.5	−13.4	+11.3	+13 to +14	+2.3
Africa‖	+ 4.5	−13.3	+12.6	− 6 to − 5	+1.9
Asian centrally planned economies	− 1.9	+ 5.5	+ 2.8	+ 3 to + 4	+3.1
Total less developed countries	− 2.3	+ 5.8	+ 0.3	+ 6 to + 7	+2.9
World	− 2.7	+ 8.3	− 2.9	+ 3 to + 4	+3.1
Livestock production					
Developed market economies†	+ 0.4	− 1.2	+ 3.5	0	+2.0
Western Europe	+ 0.2	+ 2.0	+ 5.3	0 to + 1	+2.4
North America	− 0.2	− 4.3	+ 3.9	− 2 to − 1	+1.4
Oceania	+ 2.4	− 2.9	− 7.0	+ 5 to + 6	+1.7
Eastern Europe and the U.S.S.R.	+ 3.8	+ 3.2	+ 6.2	+ 6 to + 7	+3.8
Total developed countries	+ 1.4	+ 0.2	+ 4.4	+ 1 to + 2	+2.5
Less developed market economies	+ 3.3	+ 1.2	+ 2.6	+ 3 to + 4	+2.7
Latin America	+ 5.0	0	+ 2.9	+ 4 to + 5	+2.9
Far East‡	+ 3.7	+ 4.1	+ 2.0	+ 2 to + 3	+2.8
Near East§	+ 2.5	+ 1.3	+ 3.5	+ 2 to + 3	+2.7
Africa‖	− 1.8	− 1.2	+ 1.8	+ 2 to + 3	+2.0
Asian centrally planned economies	+ 2.9	+ 2.4	+ 2.0	+ 1 to + 2	+2.4
Total less developed countries	+ 3.2	+ 1.6	+ 2.4	+ 2 to + 3	+2.6
World	+ 1.8	+ 0.6	+ 3.9	+ 2 to + 3	+2.6

Note: Data for total agricultural production and for food production (Table IV) are based on net production, with deductions for seed and feed, except for Eastern Europe and the U.S.S.R., for which no deductions have been made. Data for cereals and livestock are based on total production, without any deduction.

*Preliminary. †Including Japan, Israel, and South Africa. ‡Excluding Japan. §Excluding Israel. ‖Excluding South Africa.

Source: Food and Agriculture Organization of the United Nations.

Table VI. Statistical Summary of World Agricultural Production*

In 000,000 metric tons

Commodity	World			Developed market economies			North America			Western Europe			Oceania		
	1972	1973	1974	1972	1973	1974	1972	1973	1974	1972	1973	1974	1972	1973	1974
Cereals	1,278.74	1,376.02	1,333.24	451.93	465.80	442.38	263.72	274.96	235.96	148.10	150.64	158.60	11.51	17.93	17.55
Wheat	346.82	377.27	360.14	121.79	133.24	139.15	56.56	62.87	63.03	56.07	55.57	62.58	6.82	12.49	11.45
Rice, paddy	295.61	324.47	323.17	20.93	22.03	23.20	3.88	4.21	5.18	1.41	1.79	1.71	0.25	0.31	0.41
Corn	305.39	310.39	291.43	179.53	179.54	158.63	144.10	146.24	120.73	25.43	28.86	26.58	0.33	0.24	0.24
Barley	153.31	169.25	171.85	67.18	67.30	66.00	20.51	19.40	15.29	44.22	44.97	47.26	2.06	2.66	3.13
Root crops	535.10	575.24	558.62	80.28	79.33	81.72	16.00	16.33	18.48	56.09	56.05	57.01	1.07	0.94	0.91
Potatoes	280.74	315.73	292.47	76.82	76.76	79.30	15.43	15.76	17.87	56.01	55.98	56.94	1.06	0.93	0.90
Pulses	43.54	44.25	44.13	3.59	3.41	3.91	1.14	1.04	1.33	1.96	1.91	2.03	0.13	0.15	0.21
Vegetables and melons	268.92	281.52	283.90	83.96	87.99	89.64	23.47	24.40	25.36	43.74	45.91	46.37	1.20	1.39	1.42
Fruit	228.81	250.69	250.01	89.51	105.16	100.71	20.34	24.03	23.75	55.58	67.80	63.44	2.52	2.26	2.20
Grapes	50.51	63.28	61.76	32.89	43.23	40.94	2.39	3.86	3.88	28.21	37.34	35.00	0.85	0.61	0.63
Citrus fruit	41.23	43.14	43.91	24.16	25.65	25.35	11.03	12.61	12.15	6.46	6.47	6.46	0.44	0.38	0.41
Bananas	34.82	35.52	35.84	0.68	0.78	0.72	—	—	—	0.44	0.51	0.44	0.12	0.13	0.12
Apples†	19.44	22.37	21.37	13.87	16.66	14.94	3.06	3.21	3.31	9.03	11.59	9.85	0.51	0.57	0.51
Nuts	2.92	3.14	3.38	1.36	1.48	1.52	0.32	0.42	0.38	0.98	1.00	1.08	—	—	—
Vegetable oils‡	36.27	39.44	38.89	11.15	12.57	10.84	8.61	9.93	8.24	2.14	2.31	2.13	0.11	0.09	0.08
Sugar (centrifugal, raw)	74.25	78.34	78.76	22.92	22.48	21.67	5.90	5.33	5.14	11.61	12.21	11.07	2.84	2.53	2.85
Cocoa beans	1.45	1.35	1.47	—	—	—	—	—	—	—	—	—	—	—	—
Coffee	4.69	4.10	4.91	—	—	—	—	—	—	—	—	—	—	—	—
Tea	1.52	1.57	1.60	0.09	0.10	0.10	—	—	—	—	—	—	—	—	—
Vegetable fibres	19.74	20.29	19.93	3.47	3.28	3.05	2.98	2.83	2.55	0.27	0.25	0.27	0.05	0.04	0.04
Cotton	13.30	13.40	13.67	3.28	3.09	2.85	2.98	2.82	2.55	0.19	0.18	0.19	0.04	0.03	0.03
Jute and substitutes	3.70	4.21	3.45	—	—	—	—	—	—	—	—	—	—	—	—
Tobacco	4.94	4.96	5.22	1.41	1.47	1.51	0.88	0.91	1.01	0.33	0.35	0.32	0.02	0.02	0.02
Natural rubber	3.05	3.44	3.49	—	—	—	—	—	—	—	—	—	—	—	—
Meat§	109.64	110.31	115.25	53.69	53.32	55.93	25.51	24.46	25.78	21.81	22.26	23.93	3.55	3.63	3.15
Milk	407.66	414.13	424.43	205.47	204.69	207.14	62.41	60.00	59.92	121.47	123.28	126.08	13.20	13.05	12.53
Hen eggs	22.24	22.43	22.80	11.47	11.29	11.15	4.44	4.24	4.21	4.75	4.77	4.81	0.25	0.26	0.26
Wool (greasy)	2.72	2.56	2.55	1.56	1.39	1.33	0.08	0.07	0.07	0.16	0.16	0.16	1.20	1.04	0.99

Commodity	Other developed market economies			Less developed market economies			Africa			Latin America			Near East		
	1972	1973	1974	1972	1973	1974	1972	1973	1974	1972	1973	1974	1972	1973	1974
Cereals	28.60	22.94	30.27	368.58	387.59	386.96	44.99	38.66	43.92	67.80	73.92	76.84	47.76	41.18	45.49
Wheat	2.33	2.32	2.10	78.43	71.03	72.00	6.14	4.82	4.64	12.31	12.10	12.99	26.03	21.36	24.09
Rice, paddy	15.39	15.72	15.91	160.26	181.13	174.91	4.45	4.55	5.19	10.97	11.78	11.85	4.59	4.49	4.76
Corn	9.67	4.20	11.08	66.06	68.26	71.39	12.82	11.06	13.16	35.18	37.51	38.86	4.33	4.53	4.63
Barley	0.39	0.27	0.33	18.87	14.55	16.64	5.05	3.40	4.57	1.80	1.60	1.32	7.32	5.24	6.36
Root crops	7.12	6.01	5.32	166.79	164.21	169.75	71.06	72.83	76.58	49.58	44.29	48.19	5.60	5.85	5.98
Potatoes	4.32	4.10	3.59	21.09	20.80	21.48	1.79	1.92	1.84	8.62	8.30	8.83	3.79	4.05	4.13
Pulses	0.36	0.31	0.35	23.55	23.07	22.07	4.74	4.24	4.32	4.28	4.63	4.65	1.81	1.52	1.74
Vegetables and melons	15.55	16.29	16.49	93.94	93.86	96.64	9.19	9.03	9.40	11.06	11.51	11.57	24.16	22.98	24.43
Fruit	11.08	11.07	11.33	113.86	114.80	118.51	22.79	23.41	23.37	46.59	45.88	49.02	13.92	13.70	13.88
Grapes	1.45	1.41	1.43	11.63	11.15	12.13	1.56	1.42	1.45	4.54	4.40	5.40	5.24	5.03	4.98
Citrus fruit	6.24	6.19	6.34	15.92	16.28	17.26	2.22	2.30	2.36	8.83	8.87	9.85	2.73	2.86	2.82
Bananas	0.12	0.14	0.16	33.38	33.89	34.28	3.71	3.88	4.00	19.92	19.95	19.87	0.19	0.18	0.18
Apples†	1.27	1.29	1.27	2.84	2.57	3.24	0.04	0.04	0.04	0.96	0.71	1.30	1.28	1.22	1.29
Nuts	0.06	0.06	0.06	1.48	1.54	1.75	0.51	0.51	0.52	0.17	0.20	0.20	0.54	0.57	0.77
Vegetable oils‡	0.29	0.25	0.39	16.76	17.15	18.36	3.58	3.48	3.75	3.29	3.55	4.14	1.55	1.29	1.60
Sugar (centrifugal, raw)	2.58	2.41	2.62	34.62	38.06	40.45	2.83	3.05	2.99	21.44	23.73	25.37	2.24	2.19	2.35
Cocoa beans	—	—	—	1.45	1.35	1.47	1.02	0.94	1.03	0.38	0.37	0.39	—	—	—
Coffee	—	—	—	4.68	4.09	4.90	1.33	1.37	1.39	2.99	2.35	3.12	0.01	0.01	0.01
Tea	0.09	0.10	0.10	1.06	1.09	1.10	0.15	0.15	0.15	0.04	0.04	0.03	0.07	0.07	0.07
Vegetable fibres	0.17	0.17	0.20	10.68	10.91	10.49	0.96	0.92	1.04	2.25	2.30	2.46	1.75	1.63	1.71
Cotton	0.06	0.06	0.08	5.86	5.66	5.94	0.57	0.54	0.60	1.66	1.66	1.76	1.72	1.61	1.68
Jute and substitutes	—	—	—	3.00	3.45	2.66	0.02	0.02	0.02	0.08	0.09	0.09	—	—	—
Tobacco	0.18	0.19	0.17	2.02	1.87	2.06	0.19	0.18	0.21	0.59	0.57	0.61	0.24	0.18	0.26
Natural rubber	—	—	—	3.05	3.43	3.49	0.22	0.24	0.25	0.03	0.03	0.03	—	—	—
Meat§	2.83	2.97	3.07	19.77	20.05	20.43	3.19	3.17	3.19	10.56	10.65	10.86	2.18	2.22	2.28
Milk	8.39	8.35	8.61	76.55	77.28	79.73	6.26	6.05	6.27	26.23	26.05	27.37	12.22	12.18	12.51
Hen eggs	2.02	2.03	1.88	3.28	3.37	3.49	0.41	0.41	0.43	1.65	1.69	1.75	0.35	0.37	0.39
Wool (greasy)	0.12	0.11	0.12	0.57	0.56	0.58	0.05	0.05	0.05	0.31	0.30	0.30	0.15	0.14	0.17

Commodity	Far East			Other less developed market economies			Centrally planned economies			Asia			Europe and U.S.S.R.		
	1972	1973	1974	1972	1973	1974	1972	1973	1974	1972	1973	1974	1972	1973	1974
Cereals	208.02	233.79	220.68	0.03	0.03	0.03	458.23	522.63	503.91	222.94	235.02	241.48	235.29	287.61	262.43
Wheat	33.94	32.75	30.29	—	—	—	146.61	173.00	148.99	34.80	36.47	37.40	111.81	136.53	111.59
Rice, paddy	140.23	160.29	153.09	0.02	0.02	0.02	114.42	121.31	125.06	112.60	119.35	122.98	1.83	1.96	2.09
Corn	13.72	15.16	14.74	0.01	0.01	0.01	59.80	62.59	61.41	30.63	32.47	33.34	29.17	30.12	28.08
Barley	4.70	4.32	4.39	—	—	—	67.26	87.39	89.21	19.38	20.40	20.89	47.89	66.99	68.32
Root crops	39.10	39.74	37.46	1.46	1.50	1.54	288.03	331.70	307.15	138.29	150.65	154.62	149.75	181.05	152.53
Potatoes	6.88	6.53	6.68	0.01	0.01	0.01	182.83	218.16	191.69	33.08	37.12	39.16	149.75	181.05	152.53
Pulses	12.70	12.65	11.34	0.02	0.02	0.02	16.39	17.77	18.15	8.60	8.68	8.74	7.79	9.09	9.41
Vegetables and melons	49.29	50.09	50.97	0.25	0.26	0.26	91.02	99.66	97.62	55.16	56.97	57.47	35.86	42.69	40.16
Fruit	29.53	30.76	31.16	1.03	1.05	1.08	25.44	30.73	30.78	7.17	7.55	7.67	18.27	23.18	23.11
Grapes	0.29	0.30	0.31	—	—	—	5.99	8.90	8.69	0.16	0.16	0.17	5.83	8.73	8.53
Citrus fruit	2.14	2.24	2.22	0.01	0.01	0.01	1.14	1.21	1.30	1.08	1.15	1.17	0.06	0.06	0.14
Bananas	8.69	8.99	9.32	0.88	0.89	0.91	0.76	0.84	0.84	0.76	0.84	0.84	—	—	—
Apples†	0.56	0.60	0.61	—	—	—	2.74	3.15	3.20	0.51	0.54	0.55	2.22	2.61	2.64
Nuts	0.26	0.26	0.26	—	—	—	0.09	0.12	0.11	0.01	0.01	0.01	0.08	0.11	0.10
Vegetable oils‡	8.08	8.59	8.61	0.26	0.25	0.27	8.37	9.72	9.69	4.27	4.58	4.62	4.10	5.14	5.07
Sugar (centrifugal, raw)	7.81	8.77	9.47	0.30	0.32	0.28	16.71	17.81	16.64	4.04	4.12	4.30	12.67	13.69	12.34
Cocoa beans	0.01	0.02	0.02	0.03	0.03	0.03	—	—	—	—	—	—	—	—	—
Coffee	0.32	0.33	0.35	0.04	0.04	0.04	0.01	0.01	0.01	0.01	0.01	0.01	—	—	—
Tea	0.80	0.83	0.85	—	—	—	0.37	0.39	0.40	0.29	0.31	0.32	0.07	0.07	0.08
Vegetable fibres	5.72	6.06	5.28	—	—	—	5.59	6.10	6.39	2.45	2.89	2.91	3.15	3.21	3.48
Cotton	1.91	1.86	1.90	—	—	—	4.16	4.65	4.88	1.78	2.15	2.15	2.38	2.49	2.73
Jute and substitutes	2.90	3.33	2.54	—	—	—	0.69	0.75	0.79	0.63	0.71	0.73	0.06	0.05	0.06
Tobacco	0.99	0.93	0.99	—	—	—	1.51	1.63	1.65	0.90	1.01	1.03	0.61	0.61	0.62
Natural rubber	2.79	3.16	3.20	0.01	0.01	0.01	—	—	—	—	—	—	—	—	—
Meat§	3.79	3.95	4.03	0.06	0.06	0.06	36.18	36.95	38.89	15.29	15.70	15.97	20.89	21.26	22.92
Milk	31.79	32.94	33.53	0.06	0.06	0.06	125.63	132.16	137.55	5.38	5.43	5.49	120.26	126.73	132.06
Hen eggs	0.86	0.89	0.91	0.01	0.01	0.01	7.49	7.77	8.16	3.51	3.56	3.71	3.98	4.20	4.45
Wool (greasy)	0.06	0.06	0.06	—	—	—	0.59	0.61	0.64	0.08	0.08	0.08	0.51	0.53	0.56

*1974 forecast. †Excluding data for U.S.S.R.

‡These data represent the total production of oilseeds, oil nuts, and other oil crops harvested in the years indicated and expressed in terms of oil equivalent. That is to say, these figures do not relate to the actual production of vegetable oils but to the potential production. However, the data are useful as they provide a valid indication of year-to-year changes in the size of total oil crop production. The actual production of vegetable oils in the world is about 80% of the production reported here.

§Total meat production from animals slaughtered in the countries, irrespective of their origin.

Source: Food and Agriculture Organization of the United Nations, *Monthly Bulletin of Agricultural Economics and Statistics* (July/August 1975).

minimum carry-over held at the beginning of the season. Moreover, the U.S.S.R. and China, as well as some other countries, rejected the publicity and international coordination required for stocks and production programs. They even refused to contribute information on their countries to the early warning system. This attitude was especially disturbing since it was precisely the erratic buying of these two countries on international markets that had contributed most to the current insecure stocks situation. Despite these handicaps, the FAO secretariat made a good beginning with the collection and prompt dissemination to government members of information and analyses that served the purposes of the early warning system.

In a more general sense, pressures from the less developed countries for even more far-reaching consideration of their economic interests intensified. Some of these countries were very seriously affected by the inflation of import prices for food and other commodities and, especially, by the enormous increase in the price of crude oil and its effects upon the industrial economy and upon the supply and availability of such agricultural inputs as motor fuel, fertilizer, and pesticides. As in the industrial world, the severity of these effects was due as much to the suddenness of the price rise as to its extent. It could only be hoped that this very calamity would save the less developed countries from the industrial world's folly of basing economic development and even much of the evolution of social structure on the availability of cheap energy.

It was no accident that the need for a rethinking of prospects for economic development in the less developed areas was becoming more generally recognized. Special research on suitable technologies for less developed countries, in part emphasizing labour power rather than mechanical power, was being carried forward more vigorously, and the mere transplantation of Western achievements and methods—always suspect in the eyes of the true expert—was no longer uncritically attempted or accepted. The 21st general conference of the International Federation of Agricultural Producers debated these matters extensively in November 1975. The prospects of the so-called Green Revolution with its high-cost, capital-intensive, and energy-intensive inputs were also being evaluated more soberly.

The pressures for greater international recognition of the aspirations of less developed countries were given vigorous expression at the seventh special session of the UN General Assembly in September, where previous calls for a "new international economic order" were strongly supported. In contrast to the situation at the sixth special session, in 1974, there was a more conciliatory effort on the part of both less developed and developed countries to discuss the issues. The session ended with the adoption of a resolution on "development and international economic co-operation," which was extraordinary in the enormous scope of its demands for action to benefit less developed countries. Not all of the specific undertakings spelled out in the resolution were accepted by the U.S. and other developed countries, though most associated themselves with the resolution's larger objective: to promote and increase resource transfers to the less developed countries.

Among the measures endorsed by the resolution were integrated commodity programs, substantial expansion of existing facilities for compensatory financing of export shortfalls, preferential treatment of less developed countries' trade, effective increases in development assistance, additional assistance through a link with the Special Drawing Rights of the International Monetary Fund (IMF), and rescheduling of the less developed countries' existing debts. It remained to be seen how many of these proposals would progress toward programs of action. Plans for multicommodity agreements with joint financing of buffer stocks and indexation of commodity prices by linking them with inflation in the industrialized world were likely to give way to commodity-by-commodity approaches with price provisions that would encourage stabilization at reasonable levels.

The idea of a "development security fund" was buttressed by special U.S. proposals for helping poor nations through the IMF and the World Bank. What was involved was the expansion of the existing IMF "compensatory financing facility" through a more generous and more effective security fund. Furthermore, there would be grants for development purposes (in addition to loans) to come out of gold sales by the IMF. Major expansion of International Finance Corporation activities to facilitate larger private investments in the less developed countries was also suggested.

With respect to food and agriculture, the resolution of the seventh special session exhorted the less developed countries to do their utmost to increase food production and to curtail post-harvest losses. It urged the developed countries to expand technological assistance; to extend more generous aid in assuring adequate provision of fertilizer and other agricultural inputs; and to contribute generously to the proposed International Fund for Agricultural Development. The resolution also urged compliance with the World Food Conference's minimum target of ten million tons of food grains for aid during 1975–76 and an increase in the grant component of such aid. Pending the establishment of a world food-grain reserve, stocks should be earmarked for emergency purposes and placed at the disposal of the World Food Program (WFP) as a special reserve of no less than 500,000 tons.

The UN Conference on Trade and Development (UNCTAD) also emphasized the theme of a new economic order in which a $3 billion fund for stabilizing prices and earnings and the management of buffer

The use of oxen to till the soil is one of a number of methods advocated by agronomists of the Lake Chad Basin Commission to improve yields in the Sahel region.

THOMAS A. JOHNSON—THE NEW YORK TIMES

Table VII. Wheat: Import Requirements and Export Availabilities*
In 000,000 metric tons

Region	Imports 1973–74	Imports 1974–75 prelim.	Import requirements 1975–76 forecast	Countries	Exports 1973–74	Exports 1974–75 prelim.	Export availabilities 1975–76 forecast
Far East	24.0	26.9	22.1–24.6	U.S.	31.3	28.3	34.7–36.2†
Near East in Asia	4.0	6.0	4.0–4.5	Canada	11.7	11.0	12.2
South America	6.5	5.1	5.0	Australia	5.5	8.4	7.5–8.5
Africa	8.5	8.6	9.2	Argentina	1.1	2.2	2.0–2.5
Western Europe	7.8	6.4	6.3	EEC‡	5.3	6.7	6.0–8.0
EEC‡	(5.5)	(5.3)	(5.2)				
Eastern Europe	4.7	4.0	5.2	Total above	54.9	56.6	62.4–67.4
U.S.S.R	4.4	2.5	11.0–13.0				
North and Central				U.S.S.R.	5.0	4.0	2.0
America	2.6	2.6	2.6	Others	3.1	1.8	1.6
Others	0.6	0.3	0.6	World total	63.0	62.4	66.0–71.0
World total	63.1	62.4	66.0–71.0				

*July–June season.
†As residual supplier. In its "Agricultural Supply and Demand Estimates" released on Oct. 14, 1975, the U.S. Department of Agriculture officially projected U.S. exports in 1975–76 at between 31.3 million and 36.7 million metric tons. The range does not derive from supply uncertainties (as in the case of the other exporting countries) but from an assessment of market prospects.
‡Excluding intra-EEC trade.
Source: Food and Agriculture Organization of the United Nations.

stocks in multicommodity compacts would be important elements. The danger here was that insistence on such comprehensive and partly unrealistic approaches might well kill the more promising initiatives for international agreements on individual commodities.

A more realistic example in this field was set by the EEC and 46 less developed partner countries in Africa, the Caribbean, and the Pacific (ACP) when they concluded, in February 1975, the so-called Lomé Convention. Following upon the expiration of similar, but less comprehensive, agreements, the convention provided for free access to the EEC without reciprocity for many ACP exports (excepting certain agricultural products); compensatory financing for ACP receipts from exports to the EEC in the case of principal basic products under specified conditions; and special financial aid to the ACP countries, as well as industrial and technological cooperation. The convention was to last for five years from March 1, 1975.

The products for which the EEC would not grant free and unlimited access were those included in its common agricultural policy (CAP), mainly cereals, including millet and sorghum, rice, processed cereals, and rice products, fresh and processed fruits and vegetables, tobacco, beef, and veal. However, some preference would be given to imports of these products. Under a separate agreement on sugar, the EEC undertook to buy from the ACP countries, under agreed suballocation to the individual countries, an annual total of 1.4 million metric tons, with a minimum price guarantee at least equal to the prices guaranteed to European producers. The large quantity was partly explained by the inclusion in ACP of the countries and territories that previously benefited from the United Kingdom's Commonwealth Sugar Agreement.

Under terms of the Trade Act of 1974, the U.S., from Jan. 1, 1976, would also eliminate tariffs on a wide range of manufactured goods and agricultural products from less developed countries and territories, primarily in Asia, Latin America, and Africa.

Cereal Stocks and "World Food Security." According to the FAO, world stocks of cereals at the end of the 1974–75 marketing season (excluding the U.S.S.R. and China) were provisionally estimated at 100 million tons, representing a further, if slight, decline from the 101 million tons held at the end of 1973–74. This is a very low level. (At the beginning of 1970, these stocks were 180 million tons.) The decline in coarse grains was pronounced as stocks held by exporting countries were substantially reduced. Rice stocks also declined slightly. Wheat stocks showed a fair increase but remained far below safe limits.

At these levels, the FAO stated, cereal stocks continued to be below the minimum working levels necessary to assure a smooth and uninterrupted flow of supplies. It was unlikely that there would be a significant replenishment by the end of 1975–76, and the expected output from 1975 harvests would do little more than satisfy consumption requirements. If any rebuilding of world stocks occurred, it would result primarily from the increased corn harvest in the U.S.

World carry-over stocks of wheat were estimated at 42 million tons, compared with 39 million tons a year earlier. Wheat stocks held by the major exporters were at the lowest level in a quarter of a century. They now represented about 20% of domestic and export disappearances of the countries concerned.

Rice stocks were estimated at 13 million tons at the end of 1974–75—slightly below 1973–74. The outcome of the year-end harvest of the 1975 paddy crops in the Far East would largely determine the situation at the end of the 1975–76 marketing year. There might be a slight increase despite rising consumption requirements.

The FAO estimate of world coarse grains stocks (corn, sorghum, millet, barley, and rye) for the end of 1974–75 was 45 million tons, 3 million tons below a year earlier. A significant rebuilding of stocks in 1975–76 was not very probable.

One estimate of the minimum "safe" global level of cereal stocks was prepared by the FAO secretariat in 1974 for use by the FAO Council. According to this estimate, the world (excluding the U.S.S.R. and China, for which neither stock data nor reliable and comparable consumption estimates were available) needs to hold 17–18% of its annual cereal consumption requirement in stock at the start of the season. On the basis of average world consumption in 1972–73 to 1974–75, this would be equivalent to world cereal

ROBERT TRUMBULL—THE NEW YORK TIMES

India hopes to increase tea production on plantations such as this near Coonoor in order to increase exports and thus bolster its general economy.

stocks of 150 million to 160 million metric tons. Of this total, 45 million tons should be considered as constituting the minimum global "reserve" (*i.e.*, an extra quantity additional to "normal working stocks") to be available to meet unexpected deficits in current world supplies due to crop shortfalls, emergency food shortages, and other contingencies. Normal working stocks would thus amount to 105 million–115 million tons.

From these assumptions, the FAO concluded that the current global cereal stock level of 100 million metric tons did not provide for any reserve element of world food security. It was therefore imperative that, as soon as crop results allowed, each country should make the best effort it could to rebuild and hold reserves with proper coordination under international guidance. A Committee on World Food Security was established by the FAO conference in November 1975 as a standing committee of the FAO Council, in accordance with the World Food Conference Resolution XXII and subsequent recommendations by the FAO Council.

Food Aid. The minimum target of ten million metric tons of grains for world food aid in 1975–76, adopted by the World Food Conference in 1974, might not be fully reached, although U.S. shipments of cereals (and some other commodities) in 1975–76 would be increased to about six million metric tons under an allocation of $1.3 billion voted by Congress. In 1974–75 the U.S. shipped 4.7 million tons, or 50% more than in 1973–74. Canada expected to ship 1 million tons in 1975–76 (about double its 1974–75 contribution), Australia 350,000 tons, Sweden 75,000 tons, and the EEC 1,640,000 tons. In 1974–75 total food aid shipments reached only eight million tons—less than had been estimated earlier.

In October 1975 the Intergovernmental Committee of the World Food Program set a $750 million target for pledges in food, cash, and services to assist less developed countries during the 1977–78 biennium. For the 1975–76 biennium, WFP resources stood at $598 million, compared with the original target of $440 million.

REFLECTIONS ON THE LONGER TERM

The orientation of policies as they developed or continued in 1975 emphasized the need for action on segments of a comprehensive problem. The neglect of other segments in the promulgation or advocacy of policies appears to indicate lack of international consensus—or simply pessimism about the possibilities of overcoming the political and technical obstacles to putting a desirable policy into operation.

One such segment is growth. Population and economic growth, with its explosive technology, demands on natural resources, repercussions on the general balance of nature, and problems of waste disposal, have many direct and indirect effects upon agriculture, food supplies, and food requirements. A number of these effects are additional to developments in agriculture itself. Conversely, developments in agriculture contribute to the general problem of how to cope with and coordinate the growing demands of a growing world population on humanity's natural and cultural assets.

With respect to population, there is nothing that could encourage the expectation of an early drastic decline of growth so urgently needed over wide regions. On the contrary, an increase from the current 4,000,000,000 to 6,500,000,000 or even 7,000,000,000 people by the end of the 20th century is already a certainty, unless some cataclysmic event—including widespread famine or epidemics—occurs. While birthrates in the Western world and Japan have come down and total population in these regions will in time tend toward stability or even decline, growth in the South Asian, African, and Latin American population continues at high rates. These are, of course, just the areas that cannot even now provide sufficient food for themselves from their own resources. (*See* POPULATIONS AND AREAS.)

With respect to food production, a factor bearing upon the outlook in both the near and the more distant future has recently been receiving increased emphasis: climatic changes, especially deviations or shifts in rain-bearing winds. A southward shift of

Table VIII. Coarse Grains: Import Requirements and Export Availabilities*
In 000,000 metric tons

Region	Imports 1973–74	Imports 1974–75 prelim.	Import requirements 1975–76 forecast	Region	Exports 1973–74	Exports 1974–75 prelim.	Export availabilities 1975–76 forecast
Western Europe†	24.6	23.4	21.5	Western Europe†	3.8	2.4	1.7
Eastern Europe‡	2.5	4.5	6.8	Eastern Europe‡	0.2	0.7	0.2
U.S.S.R.	5.9	2.5	13.0§	North America	47.4	37.6	49.8
North America	1.4	1.5	1.2	of which, U.S.A.	(44.5)	(34.6)	(46.0)‖
Latin America	4.1	5.6	4.9	Latin America	8.9	10.0	8.7
Asia	22.8	19.9	19.6	Asia	2.6	2.6	3.0
Africa	1.9	1.7	2.0	Africa	0.8	3.9	4.0
Unspecified	2.4	0.9	—	Oceania	1.9	2.8	1.6
World total	65.6	60.0	69.0	World total	65.6	60.0	69.0

*July–June season.
†Excluding intra-EEC trade.
‡Excluding trade between countries with centrally planned economies.
§Estimated imports.
‖As residual supplier. In its "Agricultural Supply and Demand Estimates" released on Oct. 14, 1975, the U.S. Department of Agriculture officially projected U.S. exports in 1975–76 at between 39.9 million and 46.8 million metric tons.
Source: Food and Agriculture Organization of the United Nations.

WALLACE TURNER—THE NEW YORK TIMES

Papayas are knocked from trees by a plantation worker near Hilo, Hawaii. New methods have yielded a smaller variety of this fruit on trees that mature within one year.

Aircraft:
see Aerial Sports; Defense; Industrial Review; Transportation

Air Forces:
see Defense

wind patterns is believed to have caused the catastrophic drought in the African Sahel belt, where rainfall had been far below average for six consecutive years, and which has only recently been relieved. If a cooling trend in the Northern Hemisphere should in fact be established—meteorological science is still divided on the question—it could give rise to a more permanent southward shift of the Afro-Asian monsoon rains, with calamitous consequences.

It should also be noted that the U.S. in recent years has benefited from a remarkable run of near-normal—or even unusually favourable—weather. The grain yields of these years were due to an extraordinary sequence of favourable growing seasons, which the U.S. National Oceanic and Atmospheric Administration does not expect to persist. Considering the great importance of the U.S. as an agricultural exporter, a reduction in its productivity would be serious indeed.

Energy problems are also a source of concern. Petroleum today is a prime necessity for transportation, and transportation is a prime necessity for the food supply of the world as it is to economic activity in general. It has also been said, with much justification, that for food the world largely depends on U.S. agriculture and that U.S. agriculture largely depends on petroleum. With relative prices of energy rising and with the future of safely produceable supplies in doubt, the use of energy on the farm, both direct and indirect, will be affected. In high-energy farming it will have to be curtailed, and countries where agriculture currently consumes little energy may not be able to expand its use.

Aside from the direct use of fuel and electricity, such input items as fertilizer, pesticides, and herbicides require large amounts of energy in their production. Various metals and machinery used in agriculture also embody much energy. Tractors and equipment for the application of agricultural chemicals are voracious energy consumers, surpassed in energy consumption only by irrigation. This is a particularly serious matter in less developed areas where the high-yielding grain varieties have replaced, on a substantial scale, native strains that do not require irrigation. The new high-yielding varieties, the pride of the Green Revolution, require large amounts of water, fertilizer, and chemicals for disease and insect control. (The consequent need for large-scale capital investments is in itself a great social problem since such outlays are not within the reach of the small farmer.)

There is another aspect of the Green Revolution that may have serious consequences for the future. It is the threat to the genetic resources of crop plants that may result from the inroads made by new varieties on the reservoirs of genetic diversity and natural selection for survival. As Sir Otto Frankel has lucidly explained (*World Agriculture,* July 1970), the new high-yielding varieties were now spreading precisely in those areas where the ancient stock, adapted to environmental extremes, resistant to pests and diseases, and with competitive ability to combat weeds, had hitherto remained undisturbed. The loss of these reservoirs would have dire implications for the future food supply.

Among the factors that have come to command increasing attention in the past decade or so also is the continuing and persistent shift of demand toward higher-priced, higher-quality foodstuffs whose production requires much more original energy from the soil. The expansion of the demand for meat is not confined to a few affluent countries, but has spread to the middle-income groups in both the less developed market economies and the centrally planned economies. The utilization of increasing amounts of acreage to produce grains for feed restricts the availability of grains for human use and tends to raise their price.

It is unrealistic, however, to maintain that a simplification of diets in the affluent countries could quickly help in supplying food to the poor. There are formidable obstacles, for example, to the movement of large quantities of grain from the genuine surplus areas to the areas of great need. The large volume of trade in 1972–73 already overstrained the world's logistical system. And it is an even greater problem to get imported supplies in needy areas to the ultimate consumers. Internal distribution, handicapped by the sheer physical shortage of transport facilities—not to mention poor administration and corruption—can be improved only gradually. For the foreseeable future much of the less developed world will have to rely basically on its own capacity to provide food for its peoples. For the most part, outside help can reach only the accessible fringes of distress.

Considering the full range of the problems with which mankind will have to struggle in the decades ahead, it is clear that questions about the prospective balance between food supplies and population have lost their simple meaning. No longer is it possible to isolate food prospects from questions of general resource adequacy and of the effects of population numbers, urbanization, and technology on the environment in general. If population, material growth, and the aggressive type of technology are not brought under control within a generation, the food issue as such will pale into insignificance.

(J. H. RICHTER-ALTSCHAFFER)

See also Environment; Fisheries; Food Processing; Gardening; Industrial Review: *Alcoholic Beverages; Textiles; Tobacco.*

[451.B.1.c; 534.E; 731; 10/37.C]

ENCYCLOPÆDIA BRITANNICA FILMS. *Problems of Conservation: Soil* (1969); *Problems of Conservation: Our Natural Resources* (1970); *The Farmer in a Changing America* (1973).

Albania

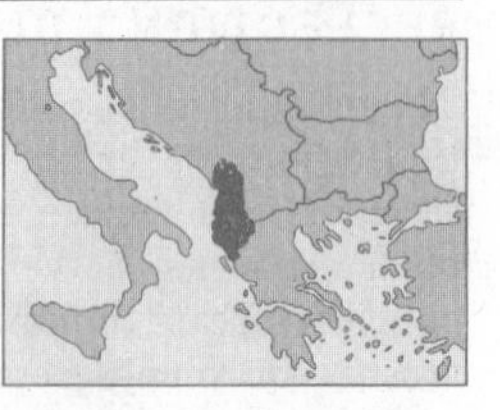

A people's republic in the western Balkan Peninsula, Albania is on the Adriatic Sea, bordered by Greece and Yugoslavia. Area: 11,100 sq.mi. (28,748 sq.km.). Pop. (1975 est.): 2,377,600. Cap. and largest city: Tirana (pop., 1971 est., 174,-800). Language: Albanian. Religion: Muslim, Orthodox, Roman Catholic. First secretary of the Albanian (Communist) Party of Labour in 1975, Enver Hoxha; president of the Presidium of the People's Assembly, Haxhi Leshi; chairman of the Council of Ministers (premier), Mehmet Shehu.

Continuing its policy of isolation, Albania was the only European country that did not sign the Final Act of the Conference on Security and Cooperation in Europe at Helsinki, Fin., in July 1975. China remained Albania's protector and principal trading partner, accounting for two-thirds of Albania's foreign trade.

Toward the end of 1974, three ministers—Col. Gen. Beqir Balluku (defense), Aleko Verli (finance), and Milo Quirko (communications)—had been dismissed

CAMERA PRESS/PHOTO TRENDS

Workers parade through the streets of Tirana to celebrate the 30th anniversary of Albanian liberation from Nazi rule.

after they criticized Hoxha for considering the U.S. as much of a danger to Albanian sovereignty as the U.S.S.R. This led to speculation that the next few years might see Albania emerge from its self-imposed isolation—as it already had moved toward Yugoslavia in 1975 (*see* YUGOSLAVIA).

Scores of senior officials were purged in September 1975, including two Politburo members: Abdyl Kellezi, deputy premier and chairman of the State Planning Commission, and Koco Theodhosi, minister of industry and mining. Kellezi was replaced by Petro Dode, former party secretary at Vlore, and Theodhosi by Pali Miska. On November 20 Hoxha headed a 51-man commission to draft a new constitution.

(K. M. SMOGORZEWSKI)

[972.B.3]

ALBANIA

Education. (1971–72) Primary, pupils 579,759, teachers 20,555; secondary, pupils 33,584, teachers 1,318; vocational and teacher training, pupils 62,212, teachers 1,712; higher (including Tirana University), students 26,668, teachers 1,157.

Finance. Monetary unit: lek, with (Sept. 22, 1975) an official exchange rate of 4.10 leks to U.S. $1 (free rate of 10.10 leks = £1 sterling) and a noncommercial (tourist) rate of 10.25 leks to U.S. $1 (free rate of 23.25 leks = £1 sterling). Budget (1971 est.): revenue 5,750,000,000 leks; expenditure 5,463,000,000 leks.

Foreign Trade. (1964) Imports 490.6 million leks; exports 299,620,000 leks. Import sources: China 63%; Czechoslovakia 10%; Poland 8%. Export destinations: China 40%; Czechoslovakia 19%; East Germany 10%; Poland 10%. Main exports: fuels, minerals, and metals (including bitumen, crude oil, chrome ore, iron ore, and copper) 54%; foodstuffs (including vegetables, wine, and fruit) 23%; raw materials (including tobacco and wool) 17%.

Transport and Communications. Roads (1969) 4,827 km. Motor vehicles in use (1970): passenger *c.* 3,500; commercial (including buses) *c.* 11,200. Railways: (1972) 302 km.; traffic (1971) 291.4 million passenger-km., freight 187.6 million net ton-km. Shipping (1974): merchant vessels 100 gross tons and over 20; gross tonnage 57,368. Shipping traffic (1970): goods loaded *c.* 2.1 million metric tons, unloaded *c.* 670,000 metric tons. Telephones (Dec. 1963) 10,150. Radio receivers (Dec. 1973) 172,000. Television receivers (Dec. 1973) 4,000.

Agriculture. Production (in 000; metric tons; 1973; 1972 in parentheses): corn *c.* 250 (*c.* 300); wheat *c.* 200 (*c.* 250); oats *c.* 16 (*c.* 16); cotton, lint *c.* 5.3 (*c.* 5.3); sugar, raw value *c.* 19 (*c.* 19); potatoes *c.* 120 (*c.* 120); grapes *c.* 61 (*c.* 58); tobacco *c.* 13 (*c.* 13). Livestock (in 000; Dec. 1973): sheep *c.* 1,165; cattle *c.* 400; pigs *c.* 117; goats (1972) *c.* 726; poultry *c.* 2,176.

Industry. Production (in 000; metric tons; 1973): crude oil 2,137; lignite (1971) 675; petroleum products (1971) 1,264; chrome ore (oxide content) 281; iron ore (1970) *c.* 540; copper ore (metal content) 7; cement 360; electricity (kw-hr.; 1972) *c.* 1,250,000.

Algeria

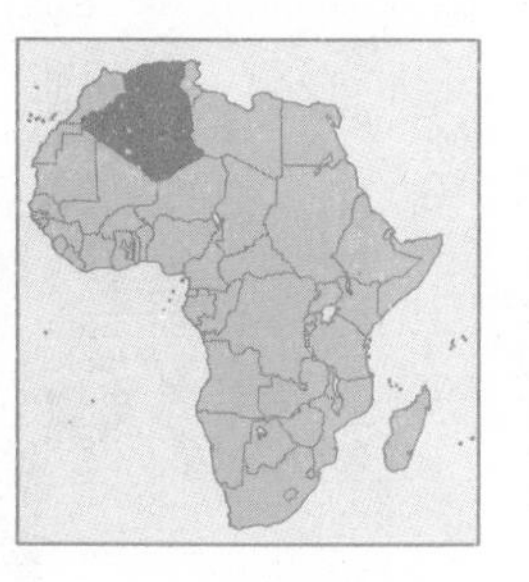

A republic on the north coast of Africa, Algeria is bounded by Morocco, Spanish Sahara, Mauritania, Mali, Niger, Libya, and Tunisia. Area: 896,593 sq.mi. (2,322,164 sq.km.). Pop. (1974 est.): 16,275,000. Cap. and largest city: Algiers (département pop., 1970 est., 1,839,000). Language: Arabic, Berber, French. Religion: Muslim. President in 1975, Col. Houari Boumédienne.

Algeria maintained its economic momentum in 1975, although crude-oil production at midyear was down to two-thirds of the average 1974 level. Price reductions from $12.50 a barrel to $11.75 proved insufficient to attract buyers. In October the price was raised by $1 a barrel to conform with the decisions of the Organization of Petroleum Exporting Countries (OPEC). The prospects for sales of Algerian natural gas were brighter, however.

President Boumédienne maintained his determination to industrialize Algeria. The large number of new projects made Algeria a borrower both in the Eurocurrency market and from the Persian Gulf states, where a bond issue was floated in Kuwait. The third phase of the agrarian reform program went ahead, but Boumédienne warned the farming cooperatives that they must pay their way.

The agrarian reform program was also the cause of unrest at Algiers and Constantine universities, where conservative students opposed the program as being contrary to Islamic principles and demanded that more attention be given to arabization of education and the administration. There were also rumbles of opposition from Algerian exiles abroad. The "Soldiers of the Algerian Opposition" claimed responsibility for placing bombs at Algerian embassies in Bonn, London, and Rome in August (only the bomb at Rome went off, causing some structural damage but no casualties). The *harkis,* Algerian soldiers who had fought with the French and been denied return home after independence, staged protests, including kidnappings, in France.

The death of Interior Minister Ahmed Medeghri in December 1974 and the dismissal of Sharif Belgassem, minister of state and former head of the National Liberation Front (FLN), in July left Boumédienne in the position of virtually unrivaled ruler. Greater popular participation in government at the lower levels was achieved by elections to 691 local councils

Alcoholic Beverages: *see* Industrial Review

Alcoholism: *see* Drug Abuse

ALGERIA

Education. (1974–75) Primary, pupils 2,435,365, teachers 60,179; secondary, pupils 406,565, teachers 15,340; vocational, pupils 15,499, teachers 589; teacher training, students 7,955, teachers 727; higher (including 3 universities), students 35,887, teaching staff 4,041.

Finance. Monetary unit: dinar, with (Sept. 22, 1975) a free rate of 3.97 dinars to U.S. $1 (8.21 dinars = £1 sterling). Gold, SDRs, and foreign exchange: (June 1975) U.S. $1,072,000,000; (June 1974) U.S. $1,839,000,000. Budget (1974 est.) balanced at 7,673,-000,000 dinars. Money supply: (Feb. 1975) 24,405,-000,000 dinars; (Feb. 1974) 20,668,000,000 dinars.

Foreign Trade. (1974) Imports 15,527,000,000 dinars; exports 23,474,000,000 dinars. Import sources (1973): France 32%; West Germany 14%; U.S. 8%; Italy 8%; Spain 5%; Belgium-Luxembourg 5%. Export destinations (1973): France 22%; West Germany 22%; Italy 10%; Spain 9%; U.S. 6%; U.K. 6%. Main exports: crude oil 88%; petroleum products 5%.

Transport and Communications. Roads (1973) 78,408 km. Motor vehicles in use (1973): passenger 176,900; commercial (including buses) 96,676. Railways (1973): 3,951 km.; traffic 943 million passenger km., freight 1,577,000,000 net ton-km. Air traffic (1973): 760 million passenger-km.; freight 5.3 million net ton-km. Shipping (1974): merchant vessels 100 gross tons and over 75; gross tonnage 239,815. Shipping traffic (1971): goods loaded *c.* 33,472,000 metric tons, unloaded *c.* 4 million metric tons. Telephones (Dec. 1973) 221,000. Radio receivers (Dec. 1973) 725,000. Television receivers (Dec. 1973) 260,-000.

Agriculture. Production (in 000; metric tons; 1974; 1973 in parentheses): wheat *c.* 700 (*c.* 1,100); barley *c.* 500 (*c.* 450); oats *c.* 30 (*c.* 30); potatoes *c.* 310 (*c.* 300); dates (1973) *c.* 170, (1972) *c.* 110; figs (1973) *c.* 58, (1972) *c.* 65; oranges (1973) *c.* 380, (1972) *c.* 380; mandarin oranges and tangerines (1973) *c.* 132, (1972) *c.* 130; tomatoes *c.* 132 (*c.* 130); onions *c.* 42 (*c.* 40); watermelons (1973) *c.* 204, (1972) *c.* 202; tobacco (1973) *c.* 6, (1972) *c.* 6; olives *c.* 150 (*c.* 150); wine (1973) *c.* 870, (1972) 570. Livestock (in 000; Nov. 1973): sheep *c.* 8,100; goats *c.* 2,300; cattle *c.* 1,029; asses *c.* 320; horses *c.* 150; camels *c.* 185.

Industry. Production (in 000; metric tons; 1973): iron ore (53–55% metal content) 3,130; phosphate rock 608; crude oil (1974) 48,100; natural gas (cu.m.) 4,745,000; electricity (kw-hr.; 1972) 2,325,000.

in March. There was a reported turnout of 79% in the elections, although candidature was restricted to members of the FLN. In June Boumédienne promised that elections for a National Assembly would be held within a year. In November he set up a commission to approve a national charter.

Algeria was host to OPEC oil, foreign, and finance ministers in January, and a conference of heads of state of less developed nations was held in Algiers in February. In April Pres. Valéry Giscard d'Estaing of France paid the first visit to Algeria by a French head of state since independence.

Algeria's relations with Morocco deteriorated over the Spanish Sahara. Algeria supported self-determination for the territory's inhabitants. (PETER KILNER)

[978.D.2.d]

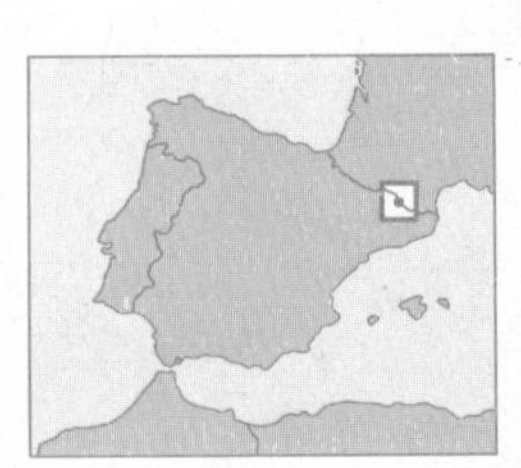

Andorra

An autonomous principality of Europe, Andorra is in the Pyrenees Mountains between Spain and France. Area: 179 sq.mi. (464 sq.km.). Pop. (1975): 26,560. Cap.: Andorra la Vella (commune pop., 1975, 10,930). Language: Catalan (official), French, Spanish. Religion: predominantly Roman Catholic. Co-princes: the president of the French Republic and the bishop of Urgel, Spain, represented by their *veguers* (provosts) and *batlles* (prosecutors). An elected Council General of 24 members elects the first syndic; in 1975, Julià Reig-Ribó.

On March 21, 1975, the Spanish government revoked two decrees that the Council General had considered damaging to the Andorran economy. The first, published in September 1974, required the holders of French identity cards entering Spain from Andorra to produce passports. The second, of November 1974, directed that Spaniards visiting Andorra could take with them only 3,000 pesetas (about $53). The first decree was an indirect protest against the French official position that diplomatic responsibility for the principality rested with the president of the French Republic, and that only religious and ecclesiastical control was vested in the bishop of Urgel. The second decree was a sanction against an anti-Franco demonstration organized on Nov. 2, 1974, at Andorra la Vella by a group of visiting Spaniards, presumably Catalans.

On Nov. 15, 1974, the Council General had published a declaration maintaining that irresponsible groups were seeking to exploit Andorra's traditional neutrality by using the country as a springboard for political propaganda. The Spanish decree of March 21, 1975, increased the amount of Spanish currency that visiting Spaniards could bring to the principality to 10,000 pesetas (about $176).

(K. M. SMOGORZEWSKI)

Angola

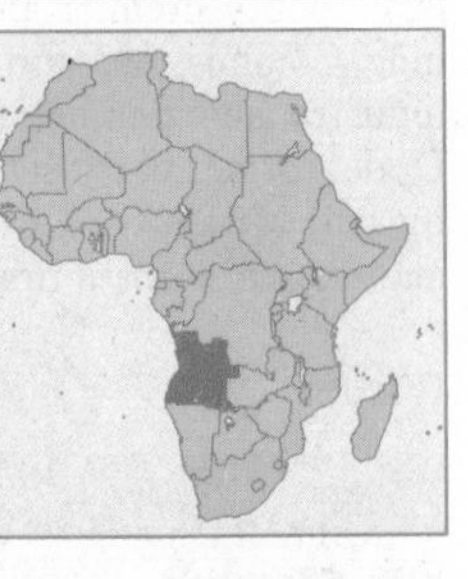

Located on the west coast of southern Africa, the state of Angola is bounded by Zaire, Zambia, South West Africa (Namibia), and the Atlantic Ocean. The small exclave of Cabinda, a district of Angola, is bounded by the Congo and Zaire. Area: 481,350 sq.mi. (1,246,-700 sq.km.). Pop. (1972 est.): 5,798,000. Cap. and largest city: Luanda (pop., 1970, 480,600). Language: Bantu languages (predominant), Portuguese, and some Khoisan dialects. Religion: traditional beliefs about 50%, Roman Catholicism about 38%, and Protestantism 12%. When independence was granted on Nov. 11, 1975, two rival governments were declared—the People's Republic of Angola, with Agostinho Neto as president; and the People's Democratic Republic of Angola, with Johnny Eduardo and José N'dele as prime ministers alternating each month.

At a meeting in Mombasa, Kenya, early in 1975, the leaders of the three rival liberation groups in the Portuguese territory of Angola, Agostinho Neto (*see* BIOGRAPHY) of the Popular Movement for the Liberation of Angola (MPLA), Holden Roberto of the National Front for the Liberation of Angola (FNLA), and Jonas Savimbi of the National Union for the Total Independence of Angola (UNITA), agreed that they would adopt a common political platform and achieve independence jointly, and that Cabinda was an integral and unalienable part of Angola. The agreement, signed on January 5, was the first between the rebel groups in 14 years of guerrilla warfare, and with their differences resolved it was expected that independence talks with Portugal would proceed smoothly. Ten days later, after talks in Portimão, Port., the Portuguese government agreed to grant independence to Angola on November 11, at which time the Portuguese high commissioner and a presidential council comprising the leaders of the three liberation groups would govern through a jointly controlled executive. The agreement also provided for a ten-month transitional government effective January 31.

The scheme did not work, and in February street fighting broke out in Luanda when MPLA troops attacked a group seeking Cabinda's independence, followed by more fighting between the MPLA and FNLA. In March the skirmishes were temporarily checked when a pact, negotiated by Portuguese officials, was agreed upon by the three liberation group leaders. In May, urged by the heads of neighbouring African states, Portugal imposed virtual military rule, but the fighting spread. A further meeting between Neto, Roberto, and Savimbi was held at Nakuru, Kenya, in mid-June. Kenyan Pres. Jomo Kenyatta mediated the talks aimed at preventing all-out civil war. On June 19 it was announced that the leaders had agreed to unite their armed forces in a single army and that measures to strengthen the transitional government had been decided upon.

The unity afforded by the peace accord was short-lived, however. Three days after its signing on June 21 fighting was reported again. Intense battles erupted and on July 15 Portugal dispatched troops to Luanda in an attempt to quell the widespread MPLA-FNLA skirmishes.

On August 7 FNLA withdrew from the transitional coalition government and UNITA followed suit two days later, leaving Angola virtually ungoverned. Meanwhile, reports from the capital said the situation there was confused with services practically at a standstill. A flood of refugees, both black and white, sought refuge in South West Africa as MPLA forces, armed by the U.S.S.R., struggled with FNLA's Zaire-backed troops. UNITA was drawn into the conflict against the MPLA, and FNLA and UNITA forces were evacuated from Luanda on August 11. Heavy fighting continued elsewhere in the territory, mostly to the north and east of Luanda. On August 14 Portugal resumed administrative control of the territory "in the absence of any functioning government."

In September it was reported that millions of dollars were being covertly poured into the territory by both East and West. By the end of the year there were several thousand Cuban militiamen fighting for the MPLA and large quantities of arms and supplies had been provided by the Soviet Union. Officials in Washington, D.C., conceded that as much as $25 million worth of military supplies had been sent by the U.S. to Angola to aid the FNLA-UNITA coalition, and that another $25 million had been allocated for this purpose. U.S. aid was transmitted primarily through Zaire, which was critically concerned because of its economic dependence on the Benguela Railroad

KEYSTONE

Leaders of the principal rival factions in Angola met in Kenya in what proved to be a futile attempt to make common cause and prevent civil war. From left to right are Agostinho Neto (MPLA), Holden Roberto (FNLA), and Jonas Savimbi (UNITA).

ANGOLA

Education. (1972–73) Primary, pupils 536,599, teachers 13,230; secondary and vocational, pupils 74,720, teachers 4,167; teacher training, students 334, teachers 47; higher (university only), students 2,942, teaching staff 274.

Finance and Trade. Monetary unit: Angola escudo, at par with the Portuguese escudo and with (Sept. 22, 1975) a free rate of 27.35 escudos to U.S. $1 (56.65 escudos = £1 sterling). Budget (1973 est.): revenue 13,707,000,000 escudos; expenditure 13,107,000,000 escudos. Foreign trade (1973): imports 13,710,600,000 escudos; exports 19.6 billion escudos. Import sources: Portugal 26%; West Germany 13%; U.S. 10%; U.K. 8%; France 7%; South Africa 6%; Japan 6%. Export destinations: U.S. 28%; Portugal 25%; Canada 10%; Japan 9%; West Germany 5%. Main exports: crude oil 29%; coffee 26%; diamonds 10%; iron ore 6%.

Transport and Communications. Roads (1973) 72,323 km. Motor vehicles in use (1973): passenger 127,271; commercial 24,123. Railways (1973): 2,966 km.; traffic 315.7 million passenger-km., freight 6.1 billion net ton-km. Ships entered (1972): vessels totaling 9,910,000 net registered tons; goods loaded (1973) 16,120,000 metric tons, unloaded 2,510,000 metric tons. Telephones (Jan. 1974) 38,000. Radio licenses (Dec. 1973) 115,000.

Agriculture. Production (in 000; metric tons; 1974; 1973 in parentheses): corn *c.* 500 (*c.* 450); millet *c.* 80 (*c.* 78); cassava (1973) *c.* 1,630, (1972) *c.* 1,620; dry beans *c.* 72 (*c.* 72); sugar, raw value *c.* 80 (*c.* 82); bananas (1973) *c.* 300, (1972) *c.* 250; palm kernels *c.* 12 (*c.* 12); palm oil *c.* 72 (*c.* 71); coffee *c.* 216 (*c.* 210); cotton, lint *c.* 35 (*c.* 33); sisal (1973) *c.* 62, (1972) *c.* 80; fish catch (1973) 470, (1972) 599. Livestock (in 000; Dec. 1973): cattle *c.* 2,900; sheep *c.* 195; goats *c.* 880; pigs *c.* 350.

Industry. Production (in 000; metric tons; 1973): cement 768; iron ore (metal content) 3,752; manganese ore (metal content) 1.9; diamonds (metric carats) 2,125; crude oil (1974) 8,705; salt (1972) 125; fish meal 96; electricity (81% hydroelectric in 1972; kw-hr.) 984,000.

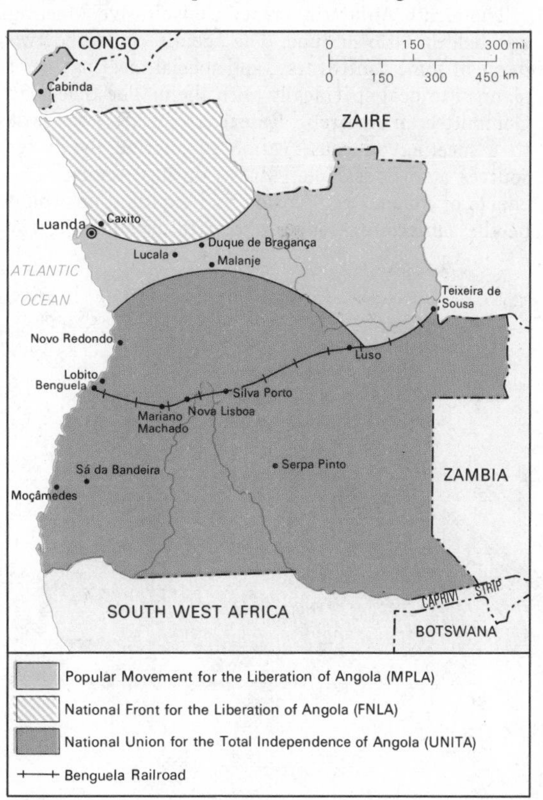

Aluminum: *see* Mining and Quarrying

American Literature: *see* Literature

Anglican Communion: *see* Religion

(*see* map). South Africa also was actively engaged in behalf of the FNLA-UNITA coalition.

Independence came as scheduled on November 11, and the three liberation groups fighting for control of Angola immediately set up rival republics. Neto declared the establishment of the People's Republic of Angola in Luanda, while Roberto and Savimbi jointly announced that they had formed the People's Democratic Republic of Angola with a temporary capital at Huambo (formerly Nova Lisboa). By year's end the civil war had become a global concern as nations took sides to protect their own interests.

(KENNETH INGHAM)

[978.E.8.b.iv]

Antarctica

In 1975 Norway rejoined the ten nations (Argentina, Australia, Chile, France, Japan, New Zealand, South Africa, the U.K., the U.S.S.R., and the U.S.) that had been conducting research on the Antarctic continent and in the surrounding seas. The U.S. officially dedicated a new Amundsen-Scott South Pole Station in January. The old station was slowly being crushed by about ten metres of snow, the accumulation of 17 years. The new station consisted of a geodesic dome housing the living and science buildings and an attached corrugated steel arch containing support elements. The U.S.S.R. announced plans to construct a new summer-only station on the edge of the Filchner Ice Shelf north of Berkner Island.

As costs continued to rise, there was an increasing effort by all nations toward cooperation in moving materials and personnel to and around the continent. The U.S. and New Zealand provided joint support to their bases on Ross Island; the French parties utilized U.S. air support; and in the Antarctic Peninsula area all countries utilized ships as they were available for resupply and research.

The eighth Antarctic Treaty Consultative Meeting was held in Oslo in June. The agenda contained two items of some controversy, and special meetings were planned to deal specifically with them. The Scientific Committee on Antarctic Research (SCAR) was host to a meeting on conservation of marine living resources at Woods Hole, Mass., during August. The effects of mineral exploration and exploitation would be the subject of a special preparatory meeting for the ninth Antarctic Treaty Consultative Meeting, to be held in Paris in June 1976.

The new U.S. scientific station in Antarctica was formally opened in January. The dome-covered base includes three two-story buildings with quarters for as many as 35 resident and visiting scientists and technicians.

U.S. NAVY

Scientific Programs. The completion of the Soviet program in the Prince Charles Mountains marked the end of a concentrated effort in that region. The U.S. and the U.K. continued to cooperate in an airborne ice-thickness-sounding project in both east and west Antarctica. The international Dry Valley Drilling Project involving the U.S., New Zealand, and Japan completed another successful season. The first major effort of the International Antarctic Glaciological Project (IAGP) was marred by the loss of two LC-130 aircraft belonging to the U.S. at Dome Charlie, a local high on the east Antarctic Ice Sheet, as the planes were picking up a French glaciologic team that had been working at the site. No one was injured.

Ships from the U.S. and Argentina began an oceanographic study in the Drake Passage as part of the International Southern Ocean Study. The program was principally one of physical oceanography, with the aim of understanding the formation, dynamics, and interaction of Antarctic water masses. It was scheduled to continue with increased participation by additional countries.

Argentina. The Argentine programs continued to be concentrated in the Antarctic Peninsula area and in the adjacent seas. Geologic studies on Seymour Island were conducted with U.S. geologists as part of the cooperative effort in the Drake Passage. Biologic research was carried out at most of the seven stations maintained by the Argentines.

Australia. Glaciologic studies inland from Casey concentrated on changes that may have accrued since the 1973 traverse. Small geologic parties worked in several areas inland from the stations, and one geologist worked with the Dry Valley Drilling Project. Upper atmospheric physics and meteorological studies were major elements of the Australian programs, and seal and bird studies were carried out at Mawson, Davis, and Macquarie Island stations.

Chile. A small but balanced scientific effort was carried out at three bases in the Antarctic Peninsula area. Scientists joined U.S. parties on the research vessel "Hero" to conduct geologic studies.

France. The party of glaciologists that began preliminary studies at Dome Charlie included a Soviet exchange scientist with the U.S. program and a U.S. topographic engineer. The site had been selected for drilling and coring a 1,000-m. hole as part of the IAGP. Meteorological observations and sampling of pit and shallow drill holes provided information on accumulation of snow and average annual temperatures (−53.5° C).

Japan. About 30 people wintered at Syowa Station. Activities in upper atmospheric physics were continued, a geodetic control survey was completed along the Soya Coast, and two precise traverse surveys using a laser distance-meter were completed in the vicinity of Syowa. Biologic studies of freshwater algae and of the plant communities along the Soya Coast were completed. Limnological research in the dry (ice-free) valley area was conducted as part of the Dry Valley Drilling Project.

New Zealand. A 15-man drilling team participated in the Dry Valley Drilling Project. Studies in atmospheric sciences continued at Scott Base, the focus of New Zealand activities on Ross Island. Evidence of biologic material was found in seawater discovered by a small party in cracks adjacent to an unmanned ice rise on the Ross Ice Shelf, about 400 km. SE of

Ross Island. Biologic studies were conducted on Weddell seals, penguins, and the ecology of small ponds and lakes on Ross Island and the mainland.

Norway. Four geologists were placed in the Heritage Range, Ellsworth Mountains, by U.S. aircraft. This group spent about six weeks in the area before returning to the U.S. station at McMurdo. Two glaciologists joined a U.S. drilling team at Amundsen-Scott South Pole Station and assisted in the recovery of a 101-m. ice core. In the fall it was announced that Norway would send a research vessel to Antarctica during the 1976–77 season.

South Africa. SANAE continued as the only permanent station maintained by South Africa on the continent. The ice-strengthened vessel "RSA" supplied the station and provided a platform for some oceanographic and marine mammal research. Geologic and glaciologic/geophysical traverses were conducted out of SANAE, and a new all-sky camera was installed.

United Kingdom. The British Antarctic Survey (BAS) utilized one of their Twin Otter aircraft to extend the ice-thickness measurements to the base of the Antarctic Peninsula and south to the Ellsworth Mountains. On one of these flights rock samples were collected from one of the unmanned islands on the Ronne Ice Shelf. This feature was first sighted in the early 1960s and was put on the map, but by 1970 it had been removed from the map because of verification problems. Stonington Island (Base E) was closed at the end of the 1974–75 season.

U.S.S.R. With six stations in operation, the Soviet Union again maintained the largest winter-over complement in Antarctica. Experiments with deep ice drilling at Vostok concentrated on the use of a nonfreezing fluid in the drill hole. A special 105-m. hole was drilled for sterile micrometeorologic research. The exchange program with the U.S. continued, with a Soviet glaciologist spending a year at McMurdo while a U.S. meteorologist wintered at Molodezhnaya.

United States. The Dry Valley Drilling Project was the major effort in the McMurdo area. Early ice breakout canceled plans to drill into the sediments on the floor of McMurdo Sound, but five holes were drilled in the dry valleys on the west side of the sound. A marine seismic reflection project completed over 1,600 km. of profiling in McMurdo Sound, and sedimentary basins over 1,000 m. deep were discovered.

The drilling phase of the Ross Ice Shelf Project was canceled, but the geophysical and glaciologic efforts continued. The strain nets placed during the previous year were resurveyed, and detailed radio-echo sounding profiles of the ice thickness were made at the proposed drill site. Preliminary maps of sea-floor elevations, ice thickness, and water depth for the Ross Ice Shelf area were prepared. Icebreaker support late in the season allowed geologists to work in the Terra Nova Bay area. Evidence for an expansion and grounding of the Ross Ice Shelf seemed compelling, and organic materials from deposits would allow dating of these events.

The study of the dynamics of the Weddell seal population was producing good results. A diving program to study benthic fauna of the McMurdo Sound area was carried on into the austral winter. Siple Station continued to be the focus of U.S. research in upper atmospheric physics. A new program at the Amundsen-Scott South Pole Station facility was to begin a more sophisticated study of the dynamics of the atmosphere. (ROBERT H. RUTFORD)

Anthropology

The year 1975 produced substantial progress toward the resolution of two basic and related questions in anthropology: the clarification of our fundamental human nature as a biological species, and the general evolutionary course of the social transition from nonhuman to human. These advances were due in part to the maturation of the new synthetic perspective called sociobiology, whose area of inquiry, methods, and body of relevant data were impressively assembled in a large volume of that title published by E. O. Wilson of Harvard University. There was, however, a lack of summary evaluations of the subfields of anthropology contributing most to this perspective, primatology and biocultural ecology.

During the past 15 or 20 years, intensive research on the ranges of variation in the socioecology of nonhuman primates and on human gathering and hunting societies has facilitated—but not simplified—the attempt to understand the actual paths to humanity taken by intermediate forms. Because there are no living analogues of the intermediate forms (australopithecines and habilines), this portion of the human story must remain speculative. It is the critical portion of the story, however. The fundamental humanizing events—systematic hunting; regular, patterned food sharing; speech and the articulation of thought; sexual avoidance and bonding behaviours and rules—all occurred in some unknown sequence among creatures that were no longer apes and not yet quite men during the one million to 15 million years between *Ramapithecus* and *Homo erectus.*

The recent renewed interest in extant human hunter-gatherers has provided a new perspective on many aspects of the lives of human foragers. One of the most suggestive elements has been the realization that the difficulties encountered in characterizing band-level societies in positive terms (*vide* "unstratified," "acephalous," "stateless," "pre/nonliterate," "pre/nonindustrial") derive not from prejudice or

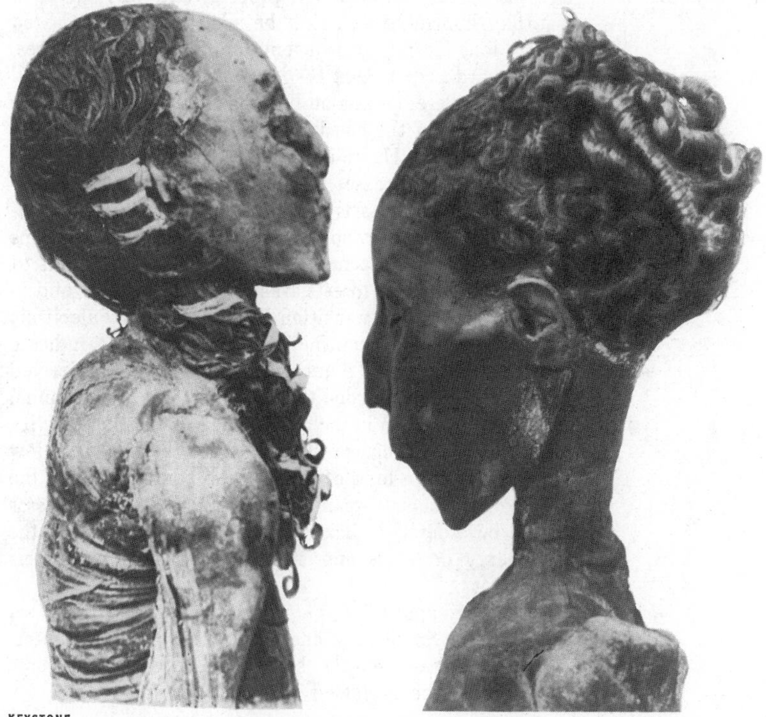

KEYSTONE

Mummies found at Luxor indicate that Egyptian noblewomen favoured wigs and coiffures 4,000 years ago that were not unlike some current styles.

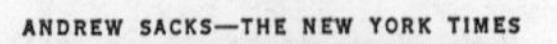

Paleopathology team at Wayne State University in Detroit conducted a complete autopsy on an Egyptian mummy in an investigation of human health and disease in ancient times.

lack of skill on the part of the observers, but from the very nature of the societies themselves. The egalitarian nature of band society is not simply an early primordial lack of sophisticated differentiation; it is an achieved condition and, in fact, a remarkable social adaptation. Thus, Paleolithic tool kits, and the gathering and hunting subsistence base they serviced, remained unchanged for so many pebble-tool-using hundreds of millennia partly because the hunting sector of the foraging economy constitutes a stable adaptive plateau. It is also an activity that exerts a strong organizing influence on social organization disproportionate to its dietary contribution.

The problem for anthropology is to understand how the emphasis on hunting became incorporated into the basically omnivore primate base, the relation of this to the hominization process, and why, given a fully human-sized brain, the adaptive plateau lasted so long despite major environmental disturbances. Richard Lee, in *Man the Hunter* (1968), first pointed to the overemphasis on hunting in general and on the harshness of the hunting life in the subsistence foraging economy. He noted that the hunting sector of such economies decreases as one moves toward the Equator. The faunal basis for this observation is just beginning to be understood as earlier, exaggerated notions of productivity in medium- to large-size mammals of the tropical rain forests are corrected. But new understandings of the transition from the Upper Paleolithic "golden age of hunting" to the Mesolithic indicate that this reduced hunting sector is itself a derived post-Pleistocene condition. Unless there is no animal protein fraction in the diet at all, it is hunting activity that carries social prestige. Despite the relatively low proportion in bulk of the hunting contribution to the diet, the social organization of band societies seems to be ordered in large measure to accommodate the energy demands and structural constraints of this sector.

There appear to be extremely narrow limits of variation in density and group size for the hunter-gatherer band society, based on a sustained adequate yield of the preferred food per person per day. By current estimates, optimum density lies below a maximum of one person per 5 sq.km. and optimum group size lies roughly between 10 and 100. If populations expand beyond these limits, in order to survive they must break up into emigrating "founder" units. Such units are characterized by as high a rate of reproduction as is consistent with the female capacity to support dependent young and the male capacity to supply them with protein. Other traits include cooperative foraging, food exchange, spatial clustering, and altruistic behaviour, all of which favour survival of the group. Surviving children are felt to belong to the band, and are freely adopted, borrowed, or exchanged. Through extension of the sharing rights of siblings to their age-mates, the band as a whole comes to lie under an altruistic umbrella of sharing. Inmarried spouses form the links in a yet wider network of inter-band hospitality and generosity.

The maximal enjoyment of abundant leisure time, a feature of hunter-gatherer societies that has been appreciated only since Lee's study of Bushman bands, is also an important aspect of the foraging adaptation. The hunter who is too efficient, too hard-working, too innovative, and too successful is likely to initiate divisive processes of dependency or competition that will lead to overexploitation. As Michael Gilpin shows in *Group Selection of Predator-Prey Communities* (1975), the more efficient the extraction process, the greater the expectation of an early population crash. In foraging societies these divisive processes are apparently held in check by the continuous operation of a complex, redundant set of social leveling mechanisms including curbs on boasting, curbs on recognition of individual property, unlimited recognition of status based on individual skills, emphasis on the need for supernatural assistance, and an ethic of generosity that is based, paradoxically, on perceived self-interest.

With the domestication of certain flora and fauna—the so-called Neolithic revolution—the economic base shifted from animal to vegetable sources of protein and carbohydrate. Now much denser populations were tolerable, although the precise causal relationship is the subject of controversy. This situation may have been foreshadowed in foraging societies situated in habitats with rich, stable food supplies, typically in border zones where the resources of land, marine, river, and air biotas lie within walking distance of one another.

In addition to raising the limits of human density, the Neolithic revolution brought a behavioural shift toward competitiveness, minimization of mutual aid, reduced fertility, delayed maturation, specialization, and self-imposed limits on resource utilization. In such a population, density is adjusted to long-range limits based on the capacity to store surplus production for later consumption, support of specialists, or trade, and this requires complex forms of regulation governing tribute and distribution. In a nomadic foraging economy controls may occur in an unsystematized form or on a daily basis, but they are not directed at stored resources except among transitional sedentary groups.

Thus we can resolve the paradox of the classical opposing theories of the basic nature of man. On the one hand, the liberal, beneficent Lockean view has been favoured by those fieldworkers who observed egalitarian band society at first hand, but it cannot account for the sudden appearance in the 4th millennium, apparently out of nowhere, of the widespread inequality, boastfulness, greed, competition, dependency, and the hoarding behaviour that apparently underlie the fact of social stratification. On the other side is the darker, Hobbesian view of man, classically expressed by Konrad Lorenz in *On Aggression,* which finds aggressiveness to be genetically based, ever present, and inescapable. This view, in turn, is embarrassed by the manifestly generous, self-disciplined, egalitarian nature of band society. An environmentally based hypothesis can account for both.

The present state of knowledge in primatology permits postulation of a direct line of continuity between a prior primate baseline model of society and the human foraging group. Based on our understanding of the socioecology of advanced higher primate omnivores, the changes in question very likely occurred within a grouping of about 40–80 male and female animals, internally structured by relations of dominance favouring males. It probably incorporated a multilevel subgrouping pattern and was open or semipermeable in that males and perhaps females changed groups. Most of the time the group was anchored by a set of ranked, female-centred genealogies attached to a particular, defensible home range.

Finally, the emerging model of the transition to humanity points up a fundamental ambivalence. The strokes of genius represented by the Promethean taming of fire, the invention and perfection of language, tools, and special breeding behaviour rules should all be the products of strong individual selection for more agile, teachable brains, a likely possibility in small breeding groups. But this classical individual selection was contained and diffused by countervailing kin selection. It seems, as Wilson suggests in the final ominous passages of *Sociobiology,* that the price of human genius has been an eternal vigilance in foragers against pride, ambition, competition, independence, and individual difference. The incorporation of the fruits of genius into the commonweal must be accomplished by means of kin ties binding the innovator to the only available means of effecting his or her genetic and social continuity, the kin band. The survival of both mandates that the exceptional individual be denied a personal claim to his own merit, just as the generous man must deny his own generosity, the altruist his own altruism, and the successful forager feast-giver any claim to the real wealth that has passed through his hands. Among nonforagers the opposite occurs. (SUZANNE RIPLEY)

See also Archaeology.
[411; 431; 432; 10/36.B]

Archaeology

Eastern Hemisphere. In spite of continued unrest in various parts of the Old World, the 1974–75 archaeological year was one of considerable activity. There was a marked increase in the reports of finds in mainland China, many of largely academic interest but some truly spectacular. The accidental discovery of a great tomb, probably that of the emperor Ch'in Shih Huang Ti (221–210 B.C.), was one such find. Some 6,000 life-size pottery effigies of men-at-arms and of horses were recovered. Thermoluminescence age determinations of clay artifacts found at Glozel in France in 1924 yielded "dates" of *c.* 300 B.C. The Glozel finds were first thought to date to around 8000 B.C., but an international commission subsequently considered them to be of modern manufacture. Hints that the matter was not yet completely resolved remained. UNESCO announced plans for a $14 million scheme to preserve Mohenjo-daro in Pakistan, the site of the two major cities of the Indus civilization of about 2000 B.C.

Vassos Karageorghis reported that excavations had resumed on Cyprus, the most interesting clearance being that at the site of Kition, a cosmopolitan town of some 3,000 years ago. Earlier reports of looting and destruction of archaeological materials in the Turkish zone proved to have been largely fabrications. The controversy persisted between East and West Germany over which country's museums should possess the bust of the Egyptian queen Nefertiti and over a thousand artifacts removed from the site of Troy by Heinrich Schliemann. (*See* GERMAN DEMOCRATIC REPUBLIC.)

As an indication of the increasing popularity of amateur public participation in archaeology in France, the section *Où ferez-vous des fouilles cet été?* ("Where will you dig this summer?") in the June issue of the journal *Archeologia* covered eight pages of classified advertisements offering opportunities.

Pleistocene Prehistory. Political unrest in Ethiopia tended to curtail work in the southwestern (Omo-Kenya frontier) region of very early Pleistocene finds, but equally early or earlier hominid fossil bones were being recovered in the northern part of the country. Mary Leakey announced that she had found bones and teeth of 11 creatures in Tanzania that indicated the presence there of true man almost 3,750,000 years ago, a million years earlier than previous estimates. Typologically early pebble tools were reported as surface finds from two regions of Iran. Several potassium-argon determinations suggested that the "Middle Stone Age" in East Africa began prior to 180,000 years ago. Interesting archaeological-paleoenvironmental investigations in the region of Cape Town, South Africa, undertaken jointly by University of Chicago and South African colleagues, proceeded, but there the "Middle Stone Age" did not appear to have begun so early.

Most excavations of the Pleistocene period reported from Europe were of the later or Upper Paleolithic time range. There was continuing concentration on open-air sites as contrasted with cave occupations. Age determinations (by the paleomagnetic method) of polychrome cave paintings of the Magdalenian V-VI type in Spain yielded "dates" of *c.* 11,500 years ago. A "castanet bracelet" of mammoth ivory, recovered from the Ukrainian site of Mezin, was interpreted by Soviet archaeologists as evidence that music dated back some 20,000 years.

The Near East. In Egypt the half-finished (and unused) 250-sq.ft. tomb of the pharaoh Horemheb was found near Saqqarah. Horemheb evidently began this tomb while still a general in Tutankhamen's army; he subsequently became pharaoh and was then buried in the Valley of the Kings at Thebes. The staff of the epigraphic survey being carried on by the Oriental Institute of the University of Chicago at Luxor began to copy and photograph the 19th-dynasty battle reliefs of the pharaoh Seti I on the temple walls at Karnak, which depict Egypt's campaigns into Palestinian and Syrian territories and also into Libya.

In Israel a joint Hebrew University-Illinois University expedition recovered important epipaleolithic material in Sinai. In the northern tip of Israel a combined Israeli-U.S. team, with over 100 volunteers, excavated at the site of Tell Dan. An important Upper Paleolithic into late Natufian sequence of living floors was being cleared at the Nachcharini cave in Lebanon

Antimony:
see Mining and Quarrying

Arabia:
see Bahrain; Kuwait; Middle Eastern Affairs; Oman; Qatar; Saudi Arabia; United Arab Emirates; Yemen, People's Democratic Republic of; Yemen Arab Republic

Arabic Literature:
see Literature

by Bruce Schroeder of the University of Toronto. At Tell Hadidi near Aleppo, Syria, a Milwaukee Museum expedition uncovered a tomb of *c.* 2200 B.C.

Not all of the various foreign field staffs who normally work in Iraq were given permission to return during the 1974–75 field year. A Soviet group was working at Tell Sotto, where a lead bracelet of *c.* 6000 B.C. was discovered. Robert McC. Adams of the Oriental Institute was allowed to continue his long-range surface surveys in the alluvial southland, so important in recovering evidence of land-use patterns and population distributions through historical ranges of time. Adams was also involved, in an advisory capacity, in developing a program for future archaeological investigations in Saudi Arabia.

In Iran P. E. L. Smith of the University of Montreal neared the end of his clearances at the important early village site of Ganj Dareh, while the Royal Ontario Museum team continued its explorations, also near Kermanshah. The large French expedition at Susa (one of the longest persisting archaeological efforts on record) divided its time between excavations on monumental buildings of the great Achaemenid Persian capital city and on nearby prehistoric villages such as Djaffarabad. The joint Chicago-Los Angeles University staff recovered a 5th-millennium house at Choga Mish.

The details of the archaeological year in Turkey, as reported in Machteld Mellink's yearly survey in the *American Journal of Archaeology,* included Tahsin Ozguc's important recovery of a number of Hittite tablets at Masat Huyuk near Zile, well east of Ankara in northeast-central Anatolia. The site has at least a Phrygian, two Hittite, and some earlier levels, and yielded some richly decorated Hittite pottery and also Mycenaean vessels, which must have been imports. Bahadir Alkim continued his excavations at Ikiztepe near the Black Sea, with yields of Hittite and Early Bronze Age materials. Both Masat and Ikiztepe promised very important new historical information.

The Greco-Roman Regions. In the eastern end of the Mediterranean, the most remarkable find of the year was probably the bronze statue of Hadrian, discovered in a field near Beit Shean in Israel by a New York stockbroker and amateur archaeologist armed with a mine detector. It was broken, but the pieces were very well preserved and could easily be reassembled. There was no word available as to the statue's context or why it happened to lie in the field. Work continued at both Sardis and Pergamon in Turkey in 1974, although excavations at Ephesus were interrupted by the tension over Cyprus.

Excavations from a burial pit near the tomb of the emperor Ch'in Shih Huang Ti revealed these magnificent life-size pottery figures of warriors and their horses. The relics are more than 2,000 years old.

UPI COMPIX

In Greece itself, the accidental discovery of an ancient military cemetery near Larissa in Thessaly was reported. Perhaps the year's most spectacular finds were the frescoes and other Minoan materials found by Spyridon Marinatos on the island of Thera before his death in 1974. The U.S. group excavating on the Agora of Athens conducted more work beneath and around the Royal Stoa. The British cleared more of the Menelaion at Sparta and undertook prehistoric work at Ayios Stephanos.

In his résumé of archaeology in central Italy and Etruria in *Archaeological Reports for 1973–74,* David Ridgway noted a general trend toward broadening and deepening interest in the nonfunerary archaeology of the Etruscans and their Italic neighbours. Few reports of work on strictly Roman finds in Italy were available, but—as usual—notes on Roman finds from all corners of the empire appeared. An Agricolan fort was identified and partially cleared at Corbridge in northern England, while a joint French-Tunisian team recorded fortifications along the Limes Tripolitanus on the Saharan frontier.

For later historic Europe, there was news of a town site near Senta, northeastern Yugoslavia, accidentally exposed as preparations were made for building a dam. The suggested inhabitants were Sarmatians and Huns, and it was speculated that the grave of Attila might be nearby.

Asia and Africa. Two U.S. expeditions worked on Harappan sites in Pakistan during the 1974–75 season, but there were no reports of work in India. The increase of archaeological activity in China could be a reflection both of increasing contact with the West and of the resumption of publication by the major Chinese archaeological journals after a six-year hiatus. Archaeological excavations were encouraged during the Cultural Revolution of the late 1960s in the belief that the finds would illustrate the oppressive nature of ancient Chinese society. More recently, the anti-Confucius campaign appeared to have given added stimulus to digging. The impressive summaries in *American Antiquity* were mainly of finds made before the 1974–75 archaeological year and concerned the historic range of time. The tomb assigned to the emperor Ch'in Shih Huang Ti, as well as a remarkably well-preserved body of a man of about 200 B.C. and a Shang dynasty city as far south as the Yangtze River, were all current finds, however.

An impressive amount of archaeological clearance was taking place in Japan, but perhaps 90% of it was of a "salvage" nature (undertaken before roads and building foundations are laid). New work on Jomon sites again resulted in age determinations of 13,000 years ago for the ribbon-appliqué pottery.

Important new early Iron Age exposures were reported from both the Transvaal in South Africa and Zambia. J. Vogel of the Livingstone (Zambia) Museum exposed the remains of 14 huts and two smelting areas at Kalondo Kumbo in southern Zambia. Little news of archaeological activity farther north was reported, presumably because of the political unrest in various parts of sub-Saharan Africa. There were, however, signs of a trend that would bring cultural-historical concern with Africa's post-Pleistocene and recent developments into better balance with the more conventional attention given to the continent's remote Pleistocene prehistory. (ROBERT J. BRAIDWOOD)

Western Hemisphere. U.S. archaeologists faced major problems during 1975 because of their accelerated involvement with projects designed to satisfy the requirements of such legislation as the National Environmental Policy Act of 1969 and the National Historic Preservation Act of 1966. Implementation of these laws as they related to archaeological resources created a demand for trained archaeologists that strained the capabilities of the profession. The National Park Service considered adopting a certification program for archaeologists involved in federally related projects, and the question of registration or licensing for archaeologists was intensely debated at the annual meeting of the Society for American Archaeology. Professionals were also attempting to develop the regional research strategies needed to integrate the great mass of data generated by service-oriented archaeology.

The innovative methodological developments of the so-called new archaeology became part of standard operating procedure, and schisms between proponents of alternative approaches were less pronounced. Studies of settlement systems and other ecologically oriented topics continued to receive attention, as did research into various aspects of exchange relationships. Sociocultural change was also emphasized through investigations of urbanization, the development of social stratification, and the emergence of complex political systems.

Analyses of stone-tool-manufacturing technologies continued, but with a growing emphasis on the contribution such studies could make toward the understanding of cultural systems. After comparing the stone-tool technologies of several groups on different levels of sociopolitical complexity, Payson D. Sheets, University of Colorado, concluded that personal innovation in tool-manufacturing methods declined as the complexity of the society increased. John R. Cole, Hartwick College (Oneonta, N.Y.), found that stone-tool traditions from a series of sites in southwest Ecuador changed much more conservatively than ceramics, probably because lithics were more closely tied to basic adaptive changes.

David S. Brose of Case Western Reserve University (Cleveland, Ohio) reported a replication study of the use of stone flakes in butchering. The results indicated that most flakes lost their effectiveness as tools after three to four minutes of use, due to the buildup of animal fats along the working edges. Since significant patterns of wear usually take longer to develop, this suggested that flakes utilized in prehistoric butchering may not always be recognized by archaeologists. Working in another research area, Michael Kliks of the University of California, Berkeley, found that coprolites (dried human fecal matter) from a series of North American sites frequently contained remains of plants that had therapeutic value in reducing the incidence of intestinal parasites.

The Aleutian Islands. W. S. Laughlin of the University of Connecticut summarized field investigations that he and A. P. Okladnikov of the U.S.S.R. had jointly directed on Anangula Island, Nikolski Bay. Among their conclusions, longevity rather than rapid population turnover contributed to the successful adaptation of the Aleuts to their environment. During the 8,700 years of documented Aleut occupation of the Nikolski Bay region, the Aleut adaptation remained comparatively stable, despite a rise in sea level and changes in coastline topography linked to tectonic uplift. A number of Siberian characteristics that were identified in the early Anangula core-and-blade industry persisted until about 4,500 years ago, when the later Aleut tradition became dominant.

Continental United States. Anne C. Sigleo of the University of Arizona utilized instrumental neutron activation analysis to determine the source of turquoise from the Gila Butte Phase (A.D. 500 to A.D. 700) at the Snaketown site in south-central Arizona. It was found that the turquoise, which occurred at Snaketown in the form of beads, derived from the Himalaya Mine in southeastern California. The result was unexpected, since a number of turquoise mines were situated closer to Snaketown.

Joseph L. Chartkoff of Michigan State University and Kerry K. Chartkoff of the University of California, Los Angeles, reported an analysis of settlement variability based upon 160 Late Period sites (A.D. 300 to A.D. 1750) along the middle Klamath River in northwestern California. It was found that rugged mountain terrain had seemed to constrain settlement, while the availability of fish coming up the rivers to spawn had promoted it.

A number of studies were designed to determine social distance between archaeological sites as measured by stylistic similarities of artifacts. Thomas G. Cook of Northwestern University (Evanston, Ill.) employed ceramics from several clusters of Basketmaker III sites in east-central Arizona to demonstrate that details of style were more closely shared within clusters of sites than between clusters, while Marvin Kay of the University of Colorado showed that stylistic details of projectile points from two central Missouri Hopewell localities were more closely shared within localities than between them.

Mesoamerica. Funding difficulties contributed to a decline in the influence of U.S. archaeologists in Mesoamerica, and local institutions and locally trained professionals, as well as archaeologists from other

WIDE WORLD

Evidence of human occupation 16,000 years ago was found at Meadowcroft Rockshelter near Pittsburgh, Pennsylvania. This is the oldest date obtained thus far for any early man site in the Western Hemisphere.

KEYSTONE

An archaeological team searches for Roman treasures in Newgate Street, London. It is thought that large buildings and an ancient road may be unearthed at this site.

countries, conducted a larger proportion of field investigations than in the past. The Instituto Nacional de Antropología e Historia de México, for example, sponsored investigations in Yucatán and Quintana Roo, focusing especially upon projects required as a result of tourist development of the Caribbean coast.

Stephen A. Kowalewski of the City University of New York reported an intensive archaeological reconnaissance near Monte Albán in the valley of Oaxaca, Mexico, conducted to assess determinants of the distribution and size of the ancient population. Also in the valley of Oaxaca, Dennis Lewarch of the University of Washington and Roger Mason, University of Texas, employed computer mapping and statistical analysis to show relationships between occupational density and a prehistoric irrigation system.

Central America. Richard W. Magnus of Yale University continued an extended ecological investigation on the Caribbean coast of Nicaragua designed to provide details of seasonal shifts between the coastal maritime communities and the dry interior. Also in Nicaragua, Jorge Espinosa Estrada, Instituto Geográfico Nacional, conducted investigations on the Monkey Bay coast. On the basis of cross dating with preceramic assemblages from Panama, it was estimated that the abundant preceramic materials that Espinosa recovered were more than 5,000 years old. Reconnaissance and test excavation in the previously unknown valleys of Pácora and Bayano in Panama, reported by Máximo Miranda, Universidad de Panamá, revealed a four-phase cultural sequence extending from *c.* A.D. 1 to A.D. 1200.

J. P. Bradbury and D. E. Puleston of the University of Minnesota reported a pollen study of prehistoric ridged agricultural fields along the Hondo River in Belize (British Honduras). The research suggested that intensive maize cultivation was an important part of Mayan riparian adaptation at least 1,500 years ago. Extensive investigations were conducted in Costa Rica by Carlos H. Aguilar, Universidad de Costa Rica, and his students. Excavations carried out at the Chaparral site in the western Central Highlands of Alajela Province showed that major occupation occurred during the Cartago Phase (A.D. 800 to A.D. 1500).

South America. A considerable amount of fieldwork was conducted throughout South America during 1975, much of it by local institutions. As in North America, numerous investigations were carried out in conjunction with modern construction. In São Paulo, Brazil, the Ilha Soltera project continued excavations in the Paraná River valley in areas that were to be flooded after completion of a hydroelectric power plant. John Erickson, University of London, completed a reconnaissance near Minas, Ecuador, in an area to be affected by dam construction, and Ruben Stehberg, Museo Nacional de Historia Natural, excavated an Inca cemetery at La Reina, Santiago, Chile, that was uncovered by construction work.

In Colombia Mary O'Neil of the California State University, Long Beach, reported on a study of central Colombian rock art in which utilization of a multidimensional scaling technique allowed the definition of core motifs for two major style areas. Gilberto Cadavid, Instituto Colombiano de Antropología, reported the discovery of 181 sites on the northern and western slopes of the Sierra Nevada de Santa Marta.

Jeffrey R. Parsons of the University of Michigan and Norbert P. Psuty, Rutgers University (New Brunswick, N.J.), presented the results of a comparative study of the sunken field agricultural sites found in several localities along the Peruvian desert coast. Such fields were excavated to form a planting surface close enough to the natural groundwater so that moisture was available for crops without irrigation. The available data indicated that the sunken field system was a relatively minor part of the subsistence pattern that appeared late in the pre-Hispanic sequence, probably after A.D. 1000, and that it never developed to the limits of its potential.

Louis Tartablia of the University of California, Los Angeles, reported on a microscopic examination of milling tools and scrapers from Guatacondo, Chile, which suggested that these tools were used for the processing of wild plant foods rather than cultivated crops. Also in Chile, Carlos Thomas and Patricio Morel, Universidad de Chile, Santiago, continued analysis of data obtained from investigations at Chiu Chiu. They determined that heads of households were buried within courtyards while others were interred outside the settlement. (DAVID A. FREDRICKSON)

See also Anthropology.

[723.G.8.c; 10/41.B.2.a.ii]

ENCYCLOPÆDIA BRITANNICA FILMS. *Sentinels of Silence (Ruins of Ancient Mexico)* (1973); *The Big Dig* (1973).

Archery:
see Target Sports

Architecture

Architecture, like many other professions, was strongly affected by the economic recession that dominated 1975. When money became tight, new building was one of the first areas to feel the pinch as existing projects were cut back or canceled and new ones delayed. Cutbacks in government spending, as in Britain, meant fewer new schools, libraries, hospitals, and public housing projects and less work for architects in the public sector. Lower profits meant that industry held back on new investment, and new offices, factories, and shops were not undertaken. Shopping developments were hit because people had less spare cash to spend. The American Institute of Architects reported gloomy prospects for 1975 as far as economic and general conditions were concerned, and private work was most severely affected. Public work increased in a few areas of the U.S., but the overall trend was downward with respect to the amount of building being undertaken. Considerable unemployment among architects and those in allied professions was reported. Hardest hit were such projects as residential developments, small commercial buildings, and speculative developments.

One region in which expansion rather than contraction was felt was the Middle East. Oil-rich nations employed Western architects on many lavish projects aimed at improving conditions and at spending some of the vast wealth being accumulated by the sale of oil to the industrialized world. Designing for the Middle East presented new sets of architectural problems. The desert climate demands structures that can be kept cool despite temperature extremes, and the character of the landscape called for a new architectural language of forms appropriate to the environment. Experiments with landscape were equally important. It was thought possible to grow certain types of imported trees in the desert soil if soil conditions could be controlled and ample water provided. One British firm was exporting trees to the Middle East in an experimental landscaping project for a new city.

The Council of Europe designated 1975 as European Architectural Heritage Year. (*See* HISTORIC PRESERVATION: *Special Report.*) Special programs of conservation, exhibitions, television programs, and other events contributed to emphasizing the importance of historic buildings and areas in European countries. It was realized that the meaning of architectural heritage must embrace not just isolated buildings but whole areas, because buildings cannot always be appreciated in isolation. Whereas in the past a typical Victorian villa might have been demolished because it was not considered to have sufficient architectural distinction in itself to merit preservation, planners would now look at the entire neighbourhood, and such a building might be restored because it formed a part of a historic area or, conversely, provided a point of reference as part of a modern development. The year's economic problems added weight to the arguments for conservation. It was often cheaper as well as more interesting to convert an old building to new use. One category of building especially suited to such conversion was that of art centres. In Britain new centres for housing the arts included such diverse structures as old warehouses, an old brewery, and even a disused church. Wherever practicable, architects were considering the option of keeping existing buildings and restoring them or incorporating them into new developments.

Another current topic of discussion was the role of women in architecture. An awareness of this subject had been increasing, especially in the United States, where organizations concerned with needs and special contributions of women in architecture were established. In Britain the August issue of *Architectural Design* was devoted to "Women in Architecture." The issue, written entirely by women, discussed the contributions being made in that country by women architects, critics, and historians and by women working in related fields.

The deaths were reported in England of two leading architects: Sir Robert Matthew (*see* OBITUARIES), perhaps best known as the architect of New Zealand House, London, and Bill Howell of Howell, Killick, Partridge and Amis, who died tragically in a car crash. One of the U.S.S.R.'s leading modern architects, Konstantin Melnikov, died late in 1974. Melnikov was the architect of the Soviet Pavilion for Decorative Arts at the 1925 Paris Exposition and was credited with helping to shape modern Soviet architecture in the 1920s.

Design Trends and Awards. Two main trends seemed to dominate new designs. These were the "neo-international style," with its emphasis on simplicity of outline and elimination of fussy detail, and the "complexity and contradiction" style, which favoured juxtaposition of materials and volumes, often in discordant ways, to create varied, complex massing and intricately detailed spaces. Raw concrete surfaces contrasted with wood interior details, and lavish use of glass skylights characterized this approach. The other approach leaned toward flat surfaces, simple high-rise structures sheathed in glass, or white-painted concrete walls. Most of the year's new designs could be placed in one category or the other. Very little of real originality was built, although students in schools of architecture continued to experiment with such ideas as tentlike canvas structures and plastic bubbles. It would be fair to say that architects still divided into two general camps, namely, followers of Le Corbusier and of Ludwig Mies van der Rohe.

Nine buildings were given Honour Awards for 1975 by the American Institute of Architects. These were Cedar Square West, Minneapolis, Minn., by Ralph Rapson and Associates; the Hanselmann residence, Fort Wayne, Ind., by Michael Graves; Columbus East High School, Columbus, Ind., by Mitchell/Giurgola

ROBERT PHILLIPS—FORTUNE MAGAZINE/© TIME, INC.

Inspired by the traditional pointed arch of Islam and the functional requirements of structures in desert regions, the new University of Petroleum and Minerals in Saudi Arabia has been termed an architectural jewel.

Associates; a high-rise office building at 88 Pine Street, New York City, by I. M. Pei and Partners; I.D.S. Center, Minneapolis, by Johnson/Burgee; The Republic, Columbus, Ind., by Skidmore, Owings and Merrill; Park Central, Denver, Colo., by Muchow Associates; the Herbert F. Johnson Museum of Art, Ithaca, N.Y., by I. M. Pei and Partners; and the Kimbell Art Museum, Fort Worth, Texas, by Louis I. Kahn.

Winners of the Royal Institute of British Architects (RIBA) awards for 1975 included Castle Park Dean Hook for the library at Leicester University; Powell and Moya for Wolfson College, Oxford; Howell, Killick, Partridge and Amis for the arts centre building of the music school at Christ's Hospital, Horsham, Sussex; Building Design Partnership for the headquarters for the Halifax Building Society, Halifax, Yorkshire; Colquhoun and Miller for Pillwood House, a vacation house in Feock, Cornwall; and Renton, Howard, Wood, Levin Partnership for the Warwick University arts centre, which incorporated a theatre, workshop, and music centre. The winner of the Royal Gold Medal for the year was Michael Scott.

According to a study carried out by the RIBA *Journal,* the best modern architecture in England was to be found at universities. Over the decade 1966–75 nearly one-third of the RIBA architecture awards went to university buildings. This implied an enlightened outlook on the part of those responsible for commissioning new university buildings, combined with the availability of sufficient funds to allow quality projects to reach fruition. Very few awards had been made for commercial buildings or private houses. Britain's standard of postwar architecture was bitterly attacked in an address given by Sir Colin Buchanan to the conference of the Royal Town Planning Institution. Sir Colin said, "We get exactly what our general standard of taste deserves. I am afraid the average taste of the community is very poor." Of the £60,000 million spent on new development between 1945 and 1970, he said, "No more than a small fraction of it is worth anything in architectural terms. No contribution to the architectural heritage is here." He singled out the tower block (high-rise) public housing developments in the 1950s and 1960s as being socially disastrous.

Solar Energy Utilization. Energy conservation continued to be a topic of great importance generally in 1975. It had particular relevance for architecture in regard to designing buildings that would maximize energy conservation. The U.S. government led the way. Congress passed several acts relating to this subject, including the Solar Heating and Cooling Demonstration Act, 1974. The American Institute of Architects Research Corp. called this a major challenge for the profession. The act provided $60 million over five years for research and would create design competitions for residential structures that used new techniques for solar heating and cooling. Other acts were passed to encourage research into energy conservation. The National Science Foundation said that it expected a substantial portion of the increase in energy demands by the mid-1980s to be met by the application of solar energy.

The winner in the governmental category of the third annual Energy Conservation Awards Program

(Top) Among the 1975 American Institute of Architects award winners is the Herbert F. Johnson Museum at Cornell University. (Bottom) Fort Worth's innovative Kimbell Art Museum by Louis I. Kahn consists of two open cycloidal vaults facing reflecting pools and a tree-filled plaza.

TOP, © NATHANIEL LIEBERMAN; BOTTOM, EZRA STOLLER © ESTO

sponsored by Owens-Corning Fiberglas Corp., announced at the end of 1974, was Smith, Hinchman and Grylls Associates, Inc., of Detroit for its Saginaw, Mich., Federal Building. This building featured an 8,000-sq.ft. flat-plate solar energy collector to take maximum advantage of the sun's heat. Another winner was Jack Miller and Associates, Inc., of Las Vegas in the institutional category for the design of the University of Nevada Systems Desert Research Institute at Boulder City, Nev. This featured a 4,000-sq.ft. solar collector, which was designed to meet 98% of the heating needs and 96% of the hot water needs generated by the building. There were no winners in the industrial and commercial categories. Some architects in Britain were also experimenting with solar energy collectors, but on the whole these were confined to private houses and had not yet been developed sufficiently to be an economic proposition in the British climate.

Domestic Architecture. The continuing trend in private house design was to leave the site apparently "undisturbed" and to use "natural" materials wherever possible. Open-planning remained popular, particularly for small vacation homes. Architects Bahr, Hanna, Vermeer and Haecker of Omaha, Neb., designed a lakefront house for Mr. and Mrs. Thomas Brandzel at Fremont, Neb. The house had a clean-cut rectangular, almost industrial look. The plan was a long rectangle with a linear interior arrangement and with windows only on the lakefront side to ensure privacy. A deep, crisscross truss made of wood dominated the lake facade to strengthen the frame and define the spaces. The structure was clad in recycled cedar shingles taken from an old barn. The house cost less than $20 per square foot to build. Architect Donald Jacobs designed a house at The Sea Ranch, Calif., for Mr. and Mrs. Richard Barrell. The design conformed to what has been termed the "new Berkeley style," with emphasis on timber cladding and clean-cut window openings. At The Sea Ranch the profile of the structure was kept low to make the house harmonize with the site. Building materials were plain board siding, redwood, and natural shingles, and a somewhat stark flavour was achieved because there were no window moldings or similar details. Inside, the house was open-plan with varied ceiling heights to define and separate spaces.

Understated elegance was the theme of a new house in the neo-international style designed by Donald Singer at Boca Raton, Fla. The sharp-edged appearance was created by exposed poured concrete walls which can be thinner than normal. The windows were of gray glass. Also neo-international in style was the Michael Tolan house at East Hampton, Long Island, N.Y., by architects Gwathmey-Siegel. The building consisted of a main house joined to separate guest quarters, the roof of the guest house forming a deck for the main house. The main house was horizontally planned with the master bedroom on the lower level and the living area occupying the second level. The juxtaposition of rounded volumes with rectangular forms showed the architect's concern with spatial geometry, and the whole complex had an air of understated elegance and simplicity. It was worlds apart from such timber-clad boxes as the houses at The Sea Ranch.

British architects Ahrends, Burton and Koralek designed an important and complex house in Jerusalem. The building was perched above the Old City walls, and a harmonizing exterior was required by planning regulations. To comply with the requirement that all external surfaces be of stone, the reinforced concrete structure had a rock-clad exterior penetrated by medieval-looking groups of small deep-set windows. The deceptively simple exterior hid three separate apartments together with a small guest flat. Maximum advantage was taken of the spectacular views of the Old City, and the client's stipulation that each apartment occupy one level only was met. Knud Holscher of Holscher and Tye built a house for himself north of Copenhagen, Den. The ingenious plan consisted of a split-level entrance with sequences of living spaces on three levels. The structure was of brick and glass simply treated. A vacation home at Albarella, Italy, by architect Federico Motterle was in direct contrast to the Holscher house. It was in the brutalist tradition—a triangular, wedge-shaped volume with the roof sloping sharply to the ground. It consisted of three triangular prisms. The rough masonry and crude detailing created a harsh effect.

LEONARDO FERRANTE

Interior of vacation home in Albarella, Italy, designed in the brutalist tradition.

Educational and Cultural Buildings. One of the largest libraries in the world was finally completed in 1974. Called "Fort Book," in reference to its monumental fortress-like quality, the John P. Robarts Research Library for the Humanities and Social Sciences at the University of Toronto was designed by architects Mathers and Haldenby of Toronto with design consultants Warner, Burns, Toan, Lunde of New York. Some criticized the library for being too massive and too concentrated. The architects explained that the form was a result of the fact that the library was originally intended to form part of a larger building complex. The larger complex was abandoned, but construction of the library went ahead because a heavy commitment had already been made to its design. The project took 14 years from start to finish. Similar factors were responsible for the sometimes outdated designs for new buildings throughout the world, particularly in the sphere of public building. Many years might elapse between the time that the design was made and completion of the building, and in that time social and economic ideas as well as aesthetic considerations might change quite radically.

KEYSTONE

A "village in the sky" was constructed on top of Sainsbury's and Woolworth's stores in Wood Green, London, as an experiment in urban housing.

The library designed by Paul Rudolph for Niagara Falls, N.Y., was more lighthearted in spirit than the one at Toronto. Known as the Earl W. Brydges Public Library, the building was of carefully detailed brick designed with a series of spiraling ramps and clerestory skylights. There was a broad plaza in front of the splayed library walls, and the whole design suggested a living, bustling, lively, man-made hill. Plans for the new music centre of North Texas State University in Denton incorporated renovated dormitories into the design and was an example of how existing buildings that had outlived their original purpose could often be given new uses rather than be torn down. Designed by Iconoplex Inc., the centre included a student commons, music practice areas, a theatre, and a performance hall. It would ultimately accommodate 1,500 music students. A complex outline of concrete and glass characterized the new Science Building at the University of La Plata, Arg., 30 mi. SE of Buenos Aires. Designed by architects Baudizzone, Diaz, Erbin, Lestard and Varas, it was intended to form part of a larger complex that would ultimately house the whole science faculty.

New educational buildings were still being constructed in many remote parts of the world. In Thailand the Asian Institute of Technology was being built under the supervision of the British firm Sir Robert Matthew, Johnson-Marshall and Partners in collaboration with Duang, Thariskdi Chaiya and Associates on a site 25 mi. N of Bangkok. The first phase included a civil engineering and hydraulics building, campus services complex, administrative offices, and dormitory. Close attention was given to the problems of climate and landscaping. All buildings were connected by covered ways. Louvred windows and cross-ventilation kept the buildings cool in the hot, wet climate. The structure was of reinforced concrete with a corrugated asbestos cement roof. All the materials used in the buildings were made locally, with the exception of the glass.

In Washington, D.C., the $15 million nine-level Temple of the Church of Jesus Christ of Latter-day Saints opened at the end of 1974. The marble-clad Mormon Temple was designed to bring to mind the famous profile of the mother church in Salt Lake City, Utah. The temple was designed by a team of four Mormon architects from Salt Lake City: Harold K. Beecher, Henry P. Fetzer, Fred L. Markham, and Keith W. Wilcox.

Commercial and Municipal Buildings. During recent years the design of federal prisons in the U.S. has changed radically to conform to new concepts of prison functions. Some of the new prisons were more like college campuses or resort complexes than old-style walled and guarded penitentiaries. The South Central Correctional Institute at Eagle River, Alaska, introduced a new approach to prison design by attempting to create a living environment as near to normal as possible. The prison buildings were small and residential in scale and were fitted out attractively with well-designed and colourful modern furnishings. The low-rise buildings were of wood and plywood with pitched roofs and large windows that recalled domestic architecture. The architects were Crittenden, Cassetta and Cannon with Hellmuth, Obata and Kassabaum. The Federal Youth Center, Pleasanton, Calif., was built by the Federal Bureau of Prisons and designed by architects Frank L. Hope and Associates. It consisted of a sort of "village" planned around a man-made lake, but the whole complex was protected by the surrounding perimeter fencing. Each of the housing subunits was designed to accommodate 30 people, and the design used wood, redwood plywood, and concrete with large areas of laminated security glass providing pleasant views.

In the field of transportation Celli-Flynn and Associates designed a prototype station for the new Pittsburgh, Pa., rapid transit system, which was expected to begin operations in 1978. The station, at a projected cost of $2.3 million, featured Vierendeel trusses spanning concrete columns, with three bays enclosed to protect passengers waiting on platforms. It was thought that as the system expanded and trains became longer it might ultimately be necessary to provide more enclosed bays.

A major retail-office-hotel complex to be called The Centrum was announced for downtown Los Angeles, following the current trend toward multi-use complexes. The design featured a 165-ft.-high atrium topped by a 15,000-sq.ft. skylight. The atrium would have interior lakes, streams, and gardens. The complex was designed by Ray Affleck and Ramesh Khosla of Arcop Associates, Montreal, who were well known for their design of Place Bonaventure, Montreal. The Los Angeles firm Gruen Associates was also involved in the project, which was expected to be completed in 1978. The first two buildings of a commercial complex, Pacific Centre in Vancouver, B.C., were completed by Cesar Pelli of Gruen Associates. The complex, which would eventually occupy two entire blocks, was expected to help revitalize the centre of Vancouver. The two completed buildings were the dark-glass Toronto Dominion Bank tower and the contrasting low, white concrete Eaton's department store.

A second office building and a hotel were currently under construction.

In Boston an 11-sided granite-faced building designed by Skidmore, Owings and Merrill, Chicago, was under construction. Sixty State Street was sited in the midst of the historic downtown area, near the new City Hall. The corners of the design were beveled to restore the line of sight between the Old State House and Faneuil Hall, previously obstructed. Nearly 60% of the site would be for pedestrian use. In Philadelphia the eight-story Federal Reserve Bank, designed by Ewing Cole Erdman Rizzio Cherry Parsky on Independence Mall, was begun. Designed to provide 800,000 sq.ft. of space, the structure featured glass-enclosed courts and was to be lavishly landscaped. The facade was of red granite and glass.

An office building in Ipswich, England, the Ipswich Centre for Willis, Faber and Dumas Insurance Brokers, exploited "the glassiness of glass." Architects Foster Associates designed the building, which incorporated two open-plan office floors enclosed by a flowing wall of tinted reflecting glass. The 1,000-ft.-long, three-story-high glass wall was said to be the longest continuous suspended glass assembly in the world. The glass was suspended like a curtain from a rail running around the perimeter of the roof. Curving glass was the dominant feature of the Lee Building on the Ginza in Tokyo. There, a witty S-shaped curve of glass rose nine stories to form a narrow commercial facade. At street level the glass was opaque. Inside, a huge chandelier descended the entire height of the building and became the dominant feature at night. Architects were KMG Architecture in collaboration with Minami Teda.

An office tower under construction for Jakarta, Indon., was said to be the tallest building in that city. Designed by Sih Timothy Seow and Partners of Singapore, the 34-story building was to be flanked by a six-story bank with a circular parking area. In Los Angeles a new 500-room hotel for the Little Tokyo section of the city was under construction. The 21-story Hotel New Otani was designed by Kajima Associates of Los Angeles with William B. Tabler Architects of New York. Completion was planned for 1976.

Two new buildings in Finland attracted critical attention. A textile factory under construction for Marimekko at Herttoniemi, near Helsinki, was criticized as lacking sufficient insulation for that climate. The structure was of light steel and aluminum and glass, and covered a volume of 110,000 cu.m. Architects were Erkki Kairamo and Reijo Lahtinen. The characteristics of the site determined the massing of a new power station by Timo Penttilä at Hanasaari, near Helsinki. It had originally been an island and some of it was infill. Thus the heavier masses were placed on the strongest part of the site. The structure of exposed steel was clad in prefabricated concrete panels or brick to create work reminiscent of the great buildings of Mies van der Rohe.

Some of the problems of building in the Middle East were overcome by British architects Trevor Dannatt and Partners, who designed a conference centre and hotel complex at Riyadh, Saudi Arabia. The complex, which included a mosque and a group of three courtyard houses, would eventually become a cultural focus for the whole city. The design had a horizontal emphasis in keeping with the desert setting. One of the problems in building in such a remote area was the availability of materials. Because the site was a long way from any existing steelworks, reinforced concrete was chosen for the building's structure. Climatic conditions were also considered in preparing the design.

A recently completed convention centre in Acapulco, Mexico, was sponsored by the Mexican government and designed to capitalize on the new influx of "package tourists" to that area by providing exhibition facilities for large groups. The centre consisted of five separate buildings joined by roofed circulation terraces and comprising more than 600,000 sq.ft. of covered floor area. The long, low, concrete buildings were designed by architect Pedro Moctezuma, and design and construction were completed in only 13 months.

Plans were in progress to restore two important historic U.S. buildings. A competition to restore the 1891 Wainwright Building in St. Louis, Mo., one of the great works of Louis Sullivan, was won by Hastings and Chivetta of St. Louis in association with Mitchell/Giurgola Associates of Philadelphia. The winning design consisted of three L-shaped low-rise units grouped around the existing building with walls of matching red sandstone. The completed project would provide a state office complex in downtown St. Louis, affording more than 200,000 sq.ft. of office space at a cost of $8.5 million. The renovation of Baltimore's Second Empire-style City Hall (completed in 1875) would increase the structure's usable area from 53,000 to 98,000 sq.ft. The work was being carried out by Architectural Heritage-Baltimore Inc./Meyers and D'Aleo Inc., whose instructions were to reinstate the historical character of the building's ceremonial spaces and at the same time increase the usable floor area. The renovation, scheduled for completion in 1976, was expected to cost approximately $6.5 million. (SANDRA MILLIKIN)

See also Engineering Projects; Historic Preservation; Industrial Review: *Building and Construction.*
[626.A.1–5; 626.C]

Arctic Regions

Throughout the year substantial progress was reported on the construction of the trans-Alaska oil pipeline, which was rapidly becoming one of the biggest and most costly man-made private projects in history. By 1975 estimated costs had risen from $4.5 billion to $6 billion, and the governor of Alaska hinted that the final figure might be as high as $10 billion. As many as 15,000 workers were engaged along the 800-mi. construction corridor stretching from the Beaufort Sea to the port of Valdez. Almost 30 new self-contained work camps had been established in areas that were previously inaccessible and uninhabited.

Although the state mounted a publicity campaign to discourage the influx of fortune seekers, they continued to arrive in unmanageable numbers, attracted by reports of weekly pay rates of $1,500 or more. The results were skyrocketing prices, a shortage of housing and other essential goods, and, strangely enough, high unemployment. The promise of billions in oil tax dollars had not yet materialized, and Alaska found itself in a cash-short position. With the $600 million fiscal 1975–76 budget producing an estimated $300 million deficit, the state was being forced to borrow on future revenues by imposing a property tax on oil and gas reserves in the ground. It was also considering the sale of additional oil and gas leases in the Beaufort Sea.

In August Canadian Arctic Gas Pipelines Ltd., one

of two companies planning to build a multibillion-dollar natural-gas pipeline down the Mackenzie River valley, announced that it hoped to adhere to the original completion date of 1981. These hopes were dimmed, however, when Canada's National Energy Board said it would probably not complete its review of the project until late 1976. Meanwhile, the Berger Commission, established by the Canadian government in 1974 to look into the social, economic, and environmental effects of northern pipeline construction, received an application for an "all Canadian" pipeline from Foothills Pipelines Ltd. The Arctic Gas proposal was for a pipeline to carry Alaskan North Slope and Canadian gas south to markets in both Canada and the U.S., while the shorter Foothills pipeline would transport only Canadian gas to customers in the Canadian provinces.

The El Paso Natural Gas Co. application for an "all Alaskan" pipeline to carry gas through Alaska for shipment in liquefied form by tanker to California was received by the U.S. Department of the Interior during the summer. In July a senior official of the department indicated there were several unfavourable aspects to the El Paso proposal, involving potential heaving in permafrost regions along the route as well as problems associated with compression-station water vapour, which could affect the local climate in certain areas. In September public hearings began in Alaska on the 9,000-page environmental impact statement prepared by the Department of the Interior for a proposed 6,280-mi. gas pipeline extending from Prudhoe Bay through Canada to terminals in California and Pennsylvania.

In March, at the opening of the hearings of his commission in Yellowknife, N.W.T., Justice T. Berger made it clear his inquiry was not merely concerned about a pipeline but was "embarked on a consideration of the future of a great river valley and its people." Adding to the commission's difficulties were native land claims to some 450,000 sq.mi. of the western Arctic, which the original peoples' groups wanted settled prior to the final decision on the pipeline. A further complication was a demand by Indian and Métis leaders in July that the natives of the Northwest Territories be recognized as the Dene ("people") nation and permitted to establish their own government. The Inuit Association, on behalf of the 12,000 Eskimos in the Northwest Territories, submitted to the government a claim proposal that could give them varying degrees of control over more than 800,000 sq.mi. of the far north, including oil, gas, and mineral deposits.

In May legislation governing exploration for oil and gas in the Canadian North was proposed by the minister of Indian affairs and northern development. He pointed out that "it was incumbent upon the Government to insure that the Canadian people, as landowners, share as fully as can be justified in the direct return from the disposal of their resources." Some initial preferences with respect to reserve frontier acreage would be given to Petro-Canada, the new government-owned energy corporation. Panarctic Oils Ltd., the partly (45%) government-owned company operating in the Canadian High Arctic Islands, reported that its exploration wells were rapidly confirming the existence of the 20 to 30 trillion cu.ft. of gas reserves necessary to justify the construction of a polar gas pipeline to eastern Canada.

The start of one of the most expensive and difficult oil exploration operations in history was signaled when Denmark's Ministry of Greenland announced its intention to offer exploration concessions to over 20 companies that had requested exploration rights. Because of the fierce climatic conditions, it was expected that the technology required to find and develop the potential petroleum resources off the Greenland coast would have to surpass that of the North Sea developments, where single test wells cost up to $6 million. Because of this and because of the short fieldwork season, no commercial recovery of oil could be expected before the late 1980s.

The Soviet newspaper *Izvestiya* reported in July that over 200 multidisciplinary field parties including geologists, topographers, and geophysicists were embarking on surveys of the vast Yakutskaya region to collect data for the creation of a mineral resources information "bank." Although emphasis was being placed on iron ore development, many other mineral resources had been identified within the region. Because of logistic and economic problems, however, only a few would be commercially exploitable.

A multimillion dollar ecological study of Alaska's outer continental shelf was under way in the northeast Gulf of Alaska. Over the next four to five years, the study would extend from the eastern Aleutians to the Beaufort Sea. The project was managed by the U.S.

A convoy of giant supply barges headed for Prudhoe Bay with materials for the Alaska pipeline was thwarted by ice floes and forced to turn back.

WIDE WORLD

National Oceanic and Atmospheric Administration. In May the U.S. government reported that four remote sensing satellites were keeping a regular watch on snow and ice movements in Canada's Northern Territories. The weekly reports pinpointed the location of snow lines, indicated ice conditions on lakes and rivers, and forecast snow and ice cover. An ice island 450 mi. N of Barrow, Alaska, became the new "farthest north" U.S. community. Manned by scientists of the Arctic Ice Dynamics Joint Experiments (Aidjex), the Beaufort Sea station was an integral part of a study designed to develop a predictive model of ice movement in the Arctic Ocean for navigation and resource development purposes.

An international agreement for the conservation of polar bears was ratified by the circum-Arctic countries early in the year. The agreement provided for better collaboration among the Arctic nations in the research and management of polar bears that cross international boundaries. In Canada native hunting rights were recognized under a quota system, provided the hunts were carried out with a native guide, using a dog team and traditional native methods. During September and October Alaska's Nunivak Island was the site of the first legal musk-ox hunt ever to be held in the U.S. Ten permits were available, and hunters had to be prepared to pay $5,000 or more for the license, transportation, and equipment. Musk-oxen returned to Siberia in 1975 after about 2,000 years. Ten of the long-haired animals, a gift from Canada, were flown to the Taymyr Peninsula.

The Carnegie Museum of Natural History reported that fossils of bony fishes, crocodilians, and primitive mammals had been found in the Northwest Territories just 800 mi. from the North Pole. The discovery indicates the existence of a near-tropical climate there about 50 million years ago.

Although they had accepted many other imported ideas and gadgets from the south, the 300 inhabitants of Igloolik, one of the most traditional-minded communities in the eastern Canadian Arctic, voted not to receive television in the community until more time had been spent studying the effects TV would have on their way of life. (KENNETH DE LA BARRE)

Arena Sports

Bullfighting. Although Spain rightly continued to be regarded as the bullfighting capital of the world, several Latin-American countries, especially Mexico, were as enthusiastic as ever in promoting corridas (bullfights), which aficionados looked upon as a national heritage. During the 1975 season in Spain, an estimated 12 million spectators (including 85% of all tourists) attended about 2,000 spectacles in some 400 arenas. Of the 12,000 bulls used in these corridas, the Miura and the Pablo Romero *ganaderías,* competing with over 600 other bull ranches, supplied 54 and 50, respectively; they thus reinforced their reputations as outstanding breeders of arena bulls. Three out of the 500 or so active matadors received special acclaim for their performances: Pedro Moya, "Niño de la Capea," who participated in 93 corridas, Paco Alcalde (87), and Antonio José Galán (75).

In Mexico, which has nearly 800 bullrings, there were 235 major corridas, featuring 1,190 bulls, during the first ten months of the year. Manolo Martínez appeared in 63 events, Mariano Ramos in 54, and Curro Rivera in 53, thus making them the most active of the

FOTOS GRUMBARTOA

Manolo Martínez, one of Mexico's premier matadors, executes a graceful pase during a contest.

63 matadors in Mexico. The Atenco *ganadería,* founded in 1552, was still functioning as one of the country's 165 active bull ranches. Colombia, which has about a dozen *ganaderías,* held annual corridas in nine top-ranked bullrings. Five of the year's most important events featured a total of 32 corridas. Among Colombia's finest matadors were Jorge Herrera, Enrique Calco, and Pepe Cáceres. Venezuela, with six large bullrings and five major *ganaderías,* held six festivals with 17 corridas in addition to a large number of other national events. Though Fermín Figueras was ranked, with Rafaél Ponzo and Jorge Jiménez, among Venezuela's best matadors, his unconventional style was severely criticized by purists. Peru, which has the third-oldest bullring in the world and about ten *ganaderías,* held numerous local corridas besides the annual festival called Señor de los Milagros. Recent outstanding performers included Rafaél Puga, Paco Chávez, and Carlos Suárez. In Ecuador many local bullrings were active, but the most important event was the festival of Jesús del Gran Poder in Quito. Matadors Armando Conde, Edgar Peñaherrera, and Fabián Mena demonstrated especially fine skills.

(RAFAEL CAMPOS DE ESPAÑA; LEE BURNETT)

[452.B.4.h.viii]

Rodeo. Following a century-old tradition that began with informal bronc riding and steer roping contests during the course of cattle drives, modern professional cowboys annually participate in 600 rodeos held in 40 U.S. states and four provinces of Canada. During 1975 more than $5 million in prize money was awarded for events sanctioned by the Professional Cowboys Association of Denver, Colo. The Calgary Exhibition and Stampede, the largest Canadian rodeo, paid out $111,653 in July, but it was the December national finals in Oklahoma City, Okla., that offered the richest purse in history, $189,300. The 1975 all-around world champion was Leo Camarillo of California, who won the team roping finals and a grand total of $50,831. Tom Ferguson of Oklahoma finished a close second with $50,719. Other world champions were Monty Henson of Texas in bronc riding, Joe

Areas:
see Populations and Areas; *see also the individual country articles*

WIDE WORLD

Canadian bronco buster Jim Clifford competes in the Canada v. U.S. Match Riding Championships held in Pueblo West, Colorado, in June.

Alexander of Wyoming in bareback riding, Don Gay of Texas in bull riding, Jeff Copenhaver of Washington State in calf roping, and Frank Shepperson of Wyoming in steer wrestling. Jimmie Gibbs of Texas won the women's barrel racing crown and a total of $22,569. (RANDALL E. WITTE)

[452.B.4.h.xxiii]

Argentina

The federal republic of Argentina occupies the southeastern section of South America and is bounded by Bolivia, Paraguay, Brazil, Uruguay, Chile, and the Atlantic Ocean. It is the second largest Latin-American country, after Brazil, with an area of 1,072,163 sq.mi. (2,776,889 sq.km.). Pop. (1975 est.): 25,384,000. Cap. and largest city: Buenos Aires (pop., 1975 est., 2,977,000). Language: Spanish. Religion: mainly Roman Catholic. President in 1975, María Estela Martínez de Perón; interim president from September 13 to October 16, Italo Luder.

Domestic Affairs. The year began with increased terrorist activity, and in February the government allowed the Army to enter the antiterrorist battle officially with ambitious operations against rural guerrillas of the People's Revolutionary Army (ERP) in Tucumán Province. Almost immediately urban terrorism spread over the provinces of Córdoba and Santa Fe, but the government took no action until the political campaign for the local elections in the northern province of Misiones was over. The elections, held on April 13, favoured the government; the Justicialist Party secured 50% of the provincial chamber's seats, although Misiones, with an agricultural system mainly based in smallholdings, was hardly typical of provincial political feeling. In fact, at the time of the Misiones campaign, a suspected conspiracy to take over control of local trade unions, as well as to paralyze the heavy industry belt along the Paraná River between Rosario and San Nicolás, was met with massive repressions of workers in the area. There were hundreds of arrests, particularly in Villa Constitución.

In June the economic shock treatment imposed by the new economy minister, Celestino Rodrigo, demanded further sacrifices from wage earners. The unions protested these measures, which included devaluation of the peso and increased prices for all basic necessities. Relations between government and workers (the highest paid and best organized in South America) reached their lowest level in July, when the Confederación General del Trabajo defied the president's ban on immediate wage increases higher than 50% and pressed for its original claims, agreed to by the employers, for up to 150%. After a two-day general strike Mrs. Perón gave in to their demands, marking the beginning of a progressive deterioration of her authority, both as head of an increasingly authoritarian government and as leader of the Justicialist Party.

A new Cabinet was appointed following the strike. Mrs. Perón was forced to give up the services of the most influential of her advisers, José López Rega (*see* BIOGRAPHY), social welfare minister and secretary of the presidency, and, soon after, of Rodrigo. A series of Cabinet changes took place during the rest of the year, adding to the growing political instability that affected all sectors, including the Army, whose third commander in chief in 1975, Gen. Jorge Videla, was committed to vigorous action against terrorists. The political crises also affected the health of Mrs. Perón, who requested a month-long leave of absence in mid-September and handed over the presidency to the provisional president of the Senate, Italo Luder. Mrs. Perón reassumed the duties of office on October 16,

ARGENTINA

Education. Primary (1973–74), pupils 3,741,456, teachers 202,256; secondary (1972–73), pupils 422,652, teachers 59,521; vocational (1972–73), pupils 703,063, teachers 88,962; higher (1972–73), students 423,824, teaching staff 38,964.

Finance. Monetary unit: peso, with (Sept. 22, 1975) a free commercial rate of 35.06 pesos to U.S. $1 (free rate of 73.86 pesos = £1 sterling) and a financial rate of 45.75 pesos to U.S. $1 (94.78 pesos = £1 sterling). Gold, SDRs, and foreign exchange, central bank: (March 1975) U.S. $899 million; (March 1974) U.S. $1,461,000,000. Budget (1974 actual): revenue 28,541,000,000 pesos; expenditure 59,544,000,000 pesos. Gross domestic product: (1972) 219.9 billion pesos; (1971) 132.7 billion pesos. Money supply: (Feb. 1975) 116,640,000,000 pesos; (Feb. 1974) 71,850,000,000 pesos. Cost of living (Buenos Aires; 1970 = 100): (April 1975) 693; (April 1974) 386.

Foreign Trade. (1973) Imports 20,917,000,000 pesos; exports 29,615,000,000 pesos. Import sources: U.S. 22%; Japan 11%; West Germany 11%; Brazil 9%; Italy 8%; U.K. 5%. Export destinations: Italy 12%; Brazil 10%; West Germany 8%; U.S. 8%; Chile 7%; Kuwait 6%; The Netherlands 6%; U.K. 6%. Main exports: meat 24%; corn 11%; wheat 8%; wool 6%; animal feedstuffs 5%.

Transport and Communications. Roads (1972) 283,775 km. Motor vehicles in use (1971): passenger 1,680,000; commercial 788,000. Railways (1973): 40,210 km.; traffic 12,334,000,000 passenger-km., freight 12,557,000,000 net ton-km. Air traffic (1973): 3,282,000,000 passenger-km.; freight 93.6 million net ton-km. Shipping (1974): merchant vessels 100 gross tons and over 366; gross tonnage 1,408,129. Shipping traffic (1973): goods loaded 14,133,000 metric tons, unloaded 9,841,000 metric tons. Telephones (Dec. 1973) 2,065,000. Radio receivers (Dec. 1970) 9 million. Television receivers (Dec. 1973) 3,950,000.

Agriculture. Production (in 000; metric tons; 1974; 1973 in parentheses): wheat 4,800 (*c.* 6,500); corn 9,900 (9,700); sorghum 6,100 (5,159); barley 386 (659); oats 316 (561); rye 310 (613); potatoes 1,798 (1,535); sugar, raw value 1,487 (1,638); linseed 370 (297); sunflower seed 970 (880); cotton, lint 118 (125); tomatoes *c.* 550 (646); oranges (1973) 805, (1972) 750; apples (1973) 233, (1972) 512; wine *c.* 2,000 (*c.* 2,000); tobacco 98 (71); beef and veal (1973) *c.* 1,990, (1972) *c.* 2,200; cheese 223 (210); wool 84 (86); quebracho extract (1973) 90, (1972) 96. Livestock (in 000; June 1974): cattle *c.* 58,000; sheep *c.* 41,500; pigs *c.* 4,333; goats (1973) *c.* 5,200; horses (1973) *c.* 3,000; chickens (1973) *c.* 29,550.

Industry. Fuel and power (in 000; metric tons; 1974): crude oil 21,135; natural gas (cu.m.) 7,242,000; coal (1973) 451; electricity (kw-hr.; 1973) 26,737,000. Production (in 000; metric tons; 1973): cement 5,220; crude steel (1974) 2,353; cotton yarn 85; nylon, etc., yarn and fibres 37; passenger cars (including assembly; units) 220; commercial vehicles (including assembly; units) 69.

but her health remained precarious. On November 17 it was announced that the presidential election, scheduled for 1977, would be held instead in 1976. The seriousness of the internal political and economic situation did not allow Mrs. Perón to continue the international policy carried out by her predecessor, and no significant developments were recorded in this area.

Meanwhile the possibility of an army coup was ever present. Such an eventuality would not have been unwelcome to many, existing anxiously between the terrorism and kidnappings of the rural and urban guerrilla organizations and the fascist Alianza Anticomunista Argentina. The "death squad" of the AAA, whose executions of leftists were estimated to number as high as 1,000 in the 12 months to May 1975, was tacitly unchecked by the government. At the same time the guerrillas had never been stronger, despite the Army's infliction of heavier casualties. In February the U.S. honorary consul in Córdoba, John P. Egan, was kidnapped by the Montoneros urban guerrillas and murdered after the government refused to negotiate for his release. After being held for over nine months, the industrialist brothers Jorge and Juan Born were released in June by the Montoneros, who received the staggering ransom of $60 million for their lives. On July 25 a group of Montoneros in combat dress made lightning attacks on points in Buenos Aires and burned hundreds of yachts at their berths between Vicente López and Tigre. In late August the Montoneros succeeded in dynamiting and extensively damaging a new destroyer being fitted out for the Argentine Navy at the shipyard at La Plata. On October 5 they mounted a major attack against the Army at the provincial capital of Formosa, seizing an airliner and attacking a military headquarters. There were 30 dead on both sides. A more serious challenge to the regime came on December 18, when right-wing air force officers seized two air bases and called on the armed forces to overthrow Mrs. Perón's government. The vast majority of the military remained loyal, however, and the rebels surrendered quietly on December 22. A few days later leftist guerrillas attacked an arsenal at Quilmes, near Buenos Aires; at least 100 were killed in the biggest clash thus far between guerrillas and the military.

The Economy. The gross domestic product expanded in real terms by 7.2% in 1974, with agriculture (8.1%), industry (6.8%), construction (12.5%), and services (6.9%) showing the greatest increases. The favourable result obtained in agriculture was mainly due to increases in the corn and sorghum crops and in the number of cattle. The high rate of consumption began to slacken in the second half of 1974.

In the external sector exports in 1974 amounted to $4,005,000,000, 22.6% over the 1973 figure, and imports rose by 59.7% to $3,570,000,000, resulting in a trade surplus of $435 million. There was a net outflow on capital movements, and the overall balance of payments result was a deficit of $51.3 million ($921 million surplus in 1973). Deterioration continued in the first months of 1975, which showed a trade deficit of $511 million as against a $355 million surplus a year earlier.

The deterioration of the international payments position, which began in mid-1974, affected the servicing of the foreign debt, which exceeded the inflow from new borrowings. The level of international reserves began to fall during the second half of 1974, reaching about $700 million at the end of June 1975. Official figures showed that the foreign debt at this time totaled $8,085,000,000 for capital only, more than half for the public sector. Repayments due in the second half of 1975 amounted to $2,520,000,000.

KEYSTONE

Strikers demanding a 100% salary increase invaded the offices of La Nación, an important Argentine newspaper, in July.

The other problem affecting the economy was the acceleration of the rate of inflation. The official cost-of-living index rose by 257.7% over the year ended September 1975, as compared with 40.1% for calendar 1974. Major causes of the rise in consumer prices were increases in overall demand, particularly for nondurables, resulting from the government's policy of income redistribution in favour of low-income groups, and the increase in the money supply brought about by rising fiscal deficits. In 1974 the treasury deficit amounted to 27,407,000,000 pesos, as compared with 19,145,000,000 pesos a year earlier; in 1975 the deficit was expected to reach 165 billion pesos as against a budget estimate of 18 billion pesos.

(JAIME R. DUHART)

[974.F.1]

Art and Art Exhibitions

Many art museums and galleries and many individuals in the art world faced financial problems in 1975 as the effects of world recession deepened. On the surface things seemed to continue as before, with important exhibitions in major museums attracting large crowds. But smaller galleries and the artists whose work was shown by their resourceful proprietors fared less well, and over the long term it is the work of young artists that determines the course of art for the future.

The whole future of the art world in Britain was in question as the government's proposed wealth tax came under discussion. Living artists feared they would suffer if their works could be taxed according to value in the same way as works by nonliving artists. If this were the case, many would be forced to sell their works to pay the tax. Similarly, private collections might cease to exist in time as owners sold works in their collections to pay the tax levied on assets. This would lead to a contraction of the art market in Britain, and many works of national importance would probably be removed from the country. In Britain as in many other countries, the export of art continued to be a major issue.

Museums in England were seriously affected by the fall in the purchasing power of the pound. At the Tate Gallery, London, for example, the government grant had remained the same for five years while prices rose

Armies:
see Defense

Art:
see Architecture; Art and Art Exhibitions; Art Sales; Dance; Literature; Museums; Theatre

steadily. Hitherto generous benefactors were also poorer, and many were being conservative in their commitments until the full effects of the wealth tax could be assessed. Special appeals had to be launched to keep individual works of national importance in the country. The economic cutbacks also meant that there would be fewer exhibitions and that installations would have to be cheaper and less lavish than in the past. The Royal Academy, London, planned to continue its policy of holding large profit-making exhibitions, such as that of J. M. W. Turner seen in 1974–75 (*see* below).

No expansion of Arts Council activities was foreseen, and less money was available to help living artists. In 1975 over 350 applications were received from practicing artists in England alone for the limited number of financial awards and bursaries available. In Wales 123 artists applied for 14 awards made by the Welsh Arts Council.

Australia continued to provide a substantial subsidy for the arts; the Australia Council, founded in 1972, had A$20 million to spend in the financial year 1974–75. A growing awareness of the arts in Australia was evident. The major show of the season was "Modern Masters: Manet to Matisse," organized by the Museum of Modern Art, New York City, and seen at the Art Gallery of New South Wales, Sydney, and at the National Gallery of Victoria, Melbourne. The exhibition of over 100 paintings was visited by more than 250,000 people in Australia. It was seen in New York City in August.

Détente between the West and the Soviet Union continued to foster exchanges of works of art. In 1975 an exhibition of masterpieces of Western European and Russian painting from collections in Soviet museums was shown in the U.S. under a Soviet-American agreement signed in Moscow in April. Forty-three canvases from the Hermitage and the Russian Museum, both in Leningrad, went on display, first at the National Gallery of Art, Washington, D.C., and later in New York City, Detroit, Los Angeles, and Houston, Texas. U.S. museums were organizing a show of works by American and Western European painters to be shown in the U.S.S.R. Agreement was reached between Britain and Moscow for the showing of the Turner exhibition at the Hermitage and at the Pushkin Museum, Moscow, in late 1975 and early 1976. An exhibition lent by the Soviet government, "Landscape Masterpieces from Soviet Museums," was held at the Royal Academy, London, October 18–November 30. Although official exchanges of art were successful, dissident "unofficial" artists working in the Soviet Union continued to suffer harassment by the authorities. Abstract art was still frowned upon by the Soviet government.

Part of Rembrandt's "The Night Watch," which was slashed by a deranged person while the famous painting was on display at the Rijksmuseum, Amsterdam, in September.

WIDE WORLD

The problem of accommodating exhibitions received attention during a two-day conference on "Housing the Arts: Why, Where, and How," held in London at the Royal Institute of British Architects. Special attention was paid to buildings originally designed for other purposes but now converted to community art centres. The British Museum introduced an arrangement whereby new acquisitions of outstanding interest could be seen in one location. These were placed on show in the main entrance hall, and the display was changed at regular intervals. At the National Gallery, London, a new extension providing additional exhibition space was opened in the spring.

The art world was saddened by the sudden death of the English sculptor Barbara Hepworth (*see* OBITUARIES), who died in a fire at her home at St. Ives, Cornwall, on May 20. Hepworth was one of the leading artists of the 20th century.

Exhibitions. *Turner and Michelangelo.* The exhibition at the Royal Academy of the work of the English painter J. M. W. Turner (1775–1851) was a major event of the winter season. The gigantic show was organized as a celebration of the bicentenary of Turner's birth. It proved extremely popular with the general public, to the extent that it was sometimes necessary to queue for admission. Once inside, the viewer had the opportunity of studying the whole range of Turner's works and his prodigious talent. The organizers tried to encourage viewers to look anew at the paintings, some of which were familiar and some from private collections not usually seen by the public. It was hoped that the literary aspect of Turner's work would not be overemphasized as it had been on occasion in the past.

An exhibition of about 300 Turner watercolours at the British Museum was assembled from that institution's own collection of over 19,000 drawings by the artist. The drawings on show spanned the whole of his career, and many aspects of his work were represented. A permanent display of Turner watercolours was planned for the Tate Gallery in 1976. There was renewed interest in making available more of the Turner works that languish unseen in the storerooms of the Tate for lack of space. One popular suggestion was that a permanent home might be found for the Turner Bequest in the restored 18th-century rooms of Somerset House, London. An exhibition of paintings and watercolours by Turner organized by the Tate Gallery and the British Council opened in Lisbon in June, one of several events marking the 600th anniversary of the first treaty of alliance between England and Portugal. Twenty-two paintings and 56 watercolours were lent to the exhibition by the Tate and the British Museum.

The 500th anniversary of the birth of Michelangelo was celebrated by an exhibition of his drawings at the British Museum, though surprisingly little attention was paid to the anniversary in Italy. (*See* Special Report.) The British Museum showed nearly 200 drawings from its own collection and those at Oxford and Windsor, as well as from private collections in Britain,

PHOTOS, FRANKENHUIS COLLECTION, COLUMBIA UNIVERSITY LIBRARIES

God bless dear Daddy
who is fighting the Hun
and send him Help

Kriegs
Anleihe
Helft den
Hütern
Eures
Glückes
W Georgi
1918

Columbia University displayed part of its large collection of World War I posters during the summer. That shown at far left is from Australia, and the German war loan poster asks support for "the guardians of your happiness."

France, and the U.S. The wide variety of drawings included pen and ink sketches, architectural plans, working drawings, and chalk compositional ideas.

American Art and Architecture. A number of exhibitions devoted to American art were held in 1975. Some were a prelude to the forthcoming American bicentennial of 1976 which promised more major shows, including one in Britain on the art of the American Indians. The British Museum held an exhibition entitled "The World of Franklin and Jefferson," which was opened in mid-September by U.S. Vice-Pres. Nelson Rockefeller. The show spanned 120 years of American history from 1706 to 1826—from colonial times to the beginning of the great westward expansion. Items on display included artifacts, paintings, manuscripts, photographs, reproductions, and reconstructions. The exhibition had been at the Grand Palais in Paris and at the Polish National Museum in Warsaw.

The American embassy in London exhibited a show entitled "Forty-eight Masterpieces of American Painting," lent by the Pennsylvania Academy of Fine Arts. An exhibition of Shaker (a religious sect) furniture at the Victoria and Albert Museum, London, was admired for its simple, straightforward designs and excellent craftsmanship. It contrasted sharply with another Victoria and Albert exhibition—on Liberty's, the great London department store, which celebrated its 100th birthday in 1975. Liberty's based its designs on motifs taken from the Orient and concentrated on beautifully designed and made luxury items. Both exhibitions were concerned with good design, but the purity and simplicity of Shaker design had a greater relevance today, perhaps, than the Oriental luxury and richness of the Liberty items. The contrast in materials was also striking: the Shaker items were of simple wood and rush; Liberty employed silver, precious stones, and luscious silks.

Interest in American painting, which had grown in recent years, was given further impetus by an exhibition devoted to American narrative painting, seen at the Los Angeles County Museum of Art, which celebrated its tenth anniversary in its present location in 1975. This was the first time that the theme of storytelling in American painting had been explored extensively in an exhibition. Among the works included were paintings in the religious, historical, and genre traditions.

American Art Deco architecture was the theme of an exhibition held at the Contemporary Wing of the Finch College Museum of Art, New York City. The exhibition was the first devoted entirely to American architecture in the Art Deco style; previous shows had included the influence of European design. The buildings, dating in the main from the 1920s and 1930s, were shown in large photomurals as well as in slides and photographs. A diverse range of building types was represented, including skyscrapers, bridges, warehouses, dams, movie palaces, and private houses. American architecture of an earlier era was the subject of an exhibition of the work of the great 19th-century architect H. H. Richardson. The show, presented by the Department of Printing and Graphic Arts, Harvard College Library, Cambridge, commemorated the architect's move from New York to Boston in 1874 as a result of winning the competition for Trinity Church, Boston. The selected drawings by Richardson and members of his office were also seen in Albany, N.Y., and Washington, D.C.

The Ringling Museum of Art, Sarasota, Fla., organized a show devoted to the work of the American designer Louis Comfort Tiffany, best known as the inventor of Tiffany glass. The exhibition emphasized the wide variety of media in which he worked. Much of the material was lent from private collections, including furnishings from his own house, Laurelton Hall at Oyster Bay, Long Island, N.Y. There were numerous drawings and sketches dating from Tiffany's first trip to Europe in 1865, as well as five "period" rooms arranged to show Tiffany's contribution to the decorative arts in America.

Art of the Orient and Ancient Civilizations. Oriental art continued to be a popular exhibition subject in

This magnificent gold comb is part of a collection of Scythian treasures from the Hermitage museum in Leningrad which was exhibited at the Metropolitan Museum of Art in New York City for two months.

COURTESY, THE METROPOLITAN MUSEUM OF ART; PHOTO, JACK MANNING—THE NEW YORK TIMES

1975, in the wake of the successful exhibition of Chinese art in London the previous winter. "Studies in Connoisseurship: Chinese Paintings from the Arthur M. Sackler Collection" was seen at Princeton, N.J., at the end of 1974 and then at the Cleveland (Ohio) Museum of Art, the Los Angeles County Museum of Art, and the Metropolitan Museum of Art, New York City. The Sackler Collection was started in the 1950s when Chinese works began to come onto the market. Most of the paintings had been purchased since 1967. The exhibition concentrated on examples of painting and calligraphy dating from the 14th to the 20th century A.D. Works were chosen not only for their inherent aesthetic values but also for research use. There were 15 magnificent examples of painting and calligraphy by Tao-chi (Shih-t'ao; 1641–*c.* 1720); a modern forgery album in the style of Tao-chi as well as two copies of his works were included for purposes of comparison.

"Chinese Jade Through the Ages" at the Victoria and Albert Museum was the largest and most comprehensive collection of jade ever shown in London. It traced the history of the ways in which this material was carved, and also chronicled its decreasing value from a material in which precious objects only were made to its modern use for cheap jewelry and souvenir ashtrays. The Los Angeles County Museum of Art mounted an exhibition of over 80 Turkish miniatures, manuscripts, and decorative objects drawn from the collection of Edwin Binney III. Binney had assembled one of the largest private collections of Turkish painting in the world, spanning the period from its beginnings to its decline in the 19th century. Turkish calligraphy was also well represented

An exhibition of works drawn from one of the finest private collections of ancient art in the U.S.—the Norbert Schimmel Collection—was seen in late 1974 at the Cleveland Museum of Art and later at the Dallas (Texas) Museum of Fine Arts. The collection, which focused on Egypt, Greece, and the ancient Near East and spanned over 600 years, had been considerably expanded since it was exhibited in 1964–65 at the Fogg Art Museum, Harvard University. The exhibition comprised 265 objects.

A traveling exhibition devoted to Egyptian art was mounted by UNESCO. Entitled "The Reign of the Sun," it was devoted to the reign of Amenhotep IV, or Akhenaton, and his wife Nefertiti. The 80 pieces lent by the Cairo Museum were displayed in Brussels, Vienna, Oslo, Stockholm, Munich, and Berlin. "A Thousand Years of Ethiopia," seen at the Petit Palais in Paris, consisted of objects accompanied by films and photographs of monuments from this little-known civilization.

Sculpture. A number of sculpture shows attracted attention. The British Council and the Museum of Modern Art, in association with the Museum of Fine Arts, Boston, organized a retrospective of the work of the British abstract sculptor Anthony Caro. The show was seen in Minneapolis, Minn., and Houston, Texas, as well as in New York City and Boston. "The Condition of Sculpture" was the title of a summer exhibition organized by the Arts Council and held at the Hayward Gallery, London. The works on display were a personal selection chosen by sculptor-writer William Tucker and were designed to illustrate how things stand today in the world of sculpture. Forty-one British and foreign artists were represented, as were a wide variety of ideas and techniques. Most exhibits were in the Constructivist tradition of Caro, but there were some examples of pop. In Tucker's view the "condition" of sculpture evolves from a basic paradox: "The world can evidently do without sculpture: sculpture cannot do without the world."

Two shows in West Germany also focused on sculptural themes. The restrained, severely cubist forms of Henri Laurens were the subject of an exhibit of sculptures and drawings at the Kunstverein, Mannheim. The delightful mobiles, stabiles, gouaches, and collages of U.S. sculptor Alexander Calder were shown at the Haus der Kunst, Munich.

France. Paris museums and galleries again presented a varied program of major exhibitions. "From David to Delacroix" at the Grand Palais dealt with painting in the period 1774 to 1830. The show pointed up the richness of style that existed in painting between the strict Neoclassicism of David and the Romanticism of Delacroix. The exhibition was also seen in Detroit and at the Metropolitan Museum of Art, New York City. The retrospective show of the work of surrealist Max Ernst, previously seen at the Guggenheim Museum, New York City, was also shown at the Grand Palais. It was the most complete retrospective of his work ever mounted, and included nearly 300 paintings and sculptures demonstrating Ernst's unique, curious mixture of humour and fantasy.

A large exhibition of works by the painter J. F. Millet was seen in Paris and then in London. Outside Paris the small town of Barbizon in the forest of Fontainebleau celebrated the centenary of Millet's death with an exhibition at the Salle des Fêtes. Barbizon was made famous by Millet, who settled there in 1849, and a group of his contemporaries who chose to paint outdoors in the area. The small exhibition included paintings by other members of what became known as the Barbizon School, as well as documents and letters lent by museums and private collectors.

England. In London the Private Rooms of the Royal Academy were opened to the public for the first time. Visitors were treated to a view of the fine rooms designed by Colin Campbell in 1716, as well as to some of the Academy's priceless collection including John Constable's "Dedham Lock" and well-known self-portraits by Thomas Gainsborough and Sir Joshua Reynolds. The Academy's greatest treasure, "The Madonna and Child with the Infant St. John," the marble tondo by Michelangelo, was also on view.

"English Influences on Vincent Van Gogh" was the subject of a show organized jointly by the Arts Council and the Fine Art Department of the University of Nottingham and seen at the Victoria and Albert Museum, as well as in a number of provincial cities. Van Gogh, who lived intermittently in England from May 1873 to December 1876, was a particular admirer of English illustrators of such popular magazines as the *Graphic* and *The Illustrated London News*. His own copies of illustrations from these magazines were included in the exhibition.

"British Sporting Painting 1650–1850" was a peculiarly English type of show, organized by the Arts Council for the Hayward Gallery. The show was also seen in Liverpool and Leicester. Many of the pictures were lent by private collectors. Such paintings had usually been appreciated more for their subject matter than for inherent artistic quality, but this exhibition proved that George Stubbs had several rivals in the field of high-quality sporting painting. Sport was widely interpreted to include not only hunting and racing subjects but also boxing, fencing, cricket, skating, and archery. "The Real Thing," a photographic show at the Hayward Gallery from March to May, featured an anthology of British photographs, 1840–1950. Organized by the Arts Council, it later toured provincial cities. There were 12 chronological sections arranged to show both a comprehensive picture of English daily life and the evolution of photographic technique. Work by both amateurs and professional photographers was included.

The Hayward Gallery was also the venue for an exhibition about the work of the Italian architect Andrea Palladio, whose designs had such a strong influence on 18th-century architecture in Britain and the U.S. Titled "Andrea Palladio 1508–1580—The Portico and the Farmyard," the exhibition included examples of furniture, pottery, and everyday objects from the period as well as drawings and photographs. Beautifully detailed large models of the important buildings formed a central attraction. An exhibition called "The Georgian Playhouse," shown concurrently with the Palladio exhibition, focused on the actors, artists, audiences, and architecture of the period 1730 to 1830.

An exhibition of works by the Swiss-born Romantic painter Henry Fuseli was mounted at the Tate Gallery in February and March. There were about 200 works on display by this artist, who was a friend of William Blake and worked mainly in England after 1764. His most famous picture, "The Nightmare" of 1781, was among those included. The show was also seen in Paris and Hamburg, West Germany. The Tate also featured a small exhibition of works by the Bloomsbury Group artist Duncan Grant, organized to celebrate his 90th birthday. The paintings were mostly small-scale and intimate still lifes, landscapes, interiors, and portraits. Several commercial galleries in London also held shows devoted to Grant. The new McAlpine Gallery at the Ashmolean Museum, Oxford, was inaugurated with an exhibition of 39 Dutch paintings from the museum's collection and from Oxford colleges. The paintings were presented in a setting of Dutch 17th-century furniture lent by the Victoria and Albert Museum, and the whole formed a sensitive and carefully displayed small exhibition.

Prints and Drawings. An exhibition devoted to the work of Charles Méryon (1821–68) was shown in April at the St. Louis (Mo.) Art Museum. Méryon was probably the greatest French etcher of all time. Although the finest collections of his works were in the U.S., the exhibition of 112 prints and drawings was the first major showing of his work in the U.S. since 1917. Méryon, who devoted himself entirely to printmaking, was acknowledged by Victor Hugo as a major source of inspiration.

KEYSTONE

This massive sculpture nearly 40 feet tall was created by Giacomo Manzu. Named "Great Creases to the Wind," the statue is on exhibit in the Piazzale del Pincio in Rome.

Drawings were also the subject of "Four Centuries of Scenic Invention," 125 stage designs from the collection of Donald Oenslager, which toured eight museums in the U.S. in 1975 under the auspices of the International Exhibitions Foundation. Oenslager, a leading stage designer, teacher, and collector, had amassed over 3,000 drawings of stage designs, providing a comprehensive survey of the subject from the mid-16th century to the present. An exhibition of 147 drawings, chiefly of architecture and design, was shown in Johnson Hall, Middlebury, Vt., in January and February. The works came from the Richard P. Wunder Collection, which concentrated on Italian and French drawings of the 17th and 18th centuries. Wunder was formerly curator of the collection at the Cooper-Hewitt Museum of Design and Decoration in New York City.

Spain. An exhibition at the Museum of Fine Arts, Madrid, entitled "The Art of Valencia and Burgos," continued the government's program of promoting the many aspects of Spanish art. Some of the pieces on display were borrowed from churches in the region and were hardly known to those from outside the area. The paintings from Valencia showed a strange mixture of Flemish, Italian, and German influences.

(SANDRA MILLIKIN)

See also Art Sales; Museums; Photography.

[612.A; 613.A–B]

ENCYCLOPÆDIA BRITANNICA FILMS. *The Louvre* (edited version, 1966); *Henry Moore—The Sculptor* (1969); *Siqueiros—"El Maestro"* (1969); *Richard Hunt—Sculptor* (1970); *Interpretations* (1970); *Paul Kane Goes West* (1972); *Textiles and Ornamental Arts of India* (1973).

QUINCENTENARY OF MICHELANGELO BUONARROTI (1475-1564)

By Alexander Perrig

Few artists have had such a lasting influence on the conceptual world of their own age and of future generations as has Michelangelo. Whatever assignment he set himself in architecture, sculpture, or painting, the solution came both to his intellect and his hands as though it were meant to fill a conceptual gap for all time. Even today, whoever thinks of David, the Creation, or the Last Judgment will find his ideas nourished by the marble colossus in Florence and by the pictures on the ceiling and altar wall in the Sistine Chapel. And anyone who encounters a domed structure or a nobleman's tomb may well unconsciously compare what he sees with the Dome of St. Peter's or the Medici Chapel. Michelangelo's figures set new standards for art and conferred a new ethos and self-awareness upon the artists who sought to master their grave solemnity, their expressive pathos, and their almost unsurpassable energy potential.

The Man and the Myth. Michelangelo became a myth and the subject of a cult even in his own lifetime—thanks primarily to the fundamental biographical work of Giorgio Vasari (1550; second expanded edition, 1568). Vasari's concept of a history of art, steadily progressing toward and culminating in Michelangelo, was never counterbalanced with a corrective of equal intellectual weight. By 1506 Michelangelo was already called *unico* (in a letter of recommendation from the Florentine head of government, Piero Soderini), and later he was called *divino*. Such adulation completely estranged an already retiring man from his milieu and caused his name to be used in justification of every possible artistic orientation and ideological viewpoint. Precisely for this reason, modern history of art is on trial whenever it treats him.

In one century of strenuous research a vast amount of source material about Michelangelo has been collected, reviewed, edited, and annotated, including letters, poems, contracts, receipts, and biographies. Biographical and artistic data have been checked and rechecked, sometimes corroborating and sometimes correcting our previous ideas, and an abundance of new facts has been revealed. Long lost works have been rediscovered and every single known piece has been studied in its formal, iconographic, genetic, and functional aspects. The artist's character, his daily habits, his working methods, his personal attitudes, and his artistic and political opinions have been traced, as well as the peculiarities of the people with whom he had contact—friends, colleagues, patrons, business partners, and assistants. Thus modern history of art has formed an image of Michelangelo that is much nearer to historical truth than those presented by his first biographers, Vasari and Ascanio Condivi (1553). And owing to an increasing number of summarizing publications this knowledge is on the verge of becoming common property.

Alexander Perrig is professor of art history at the University of Hamburg, West Germany. He is an internationally recognized authority on the works of Michelangelo, particularly with regard to problems of genesis and authenticity.

ALINARI

"La Pietà," in St. Peter's, Rome, by Michelangelo, one of the most magnificent works ever created from stone by the hand of man.

But this impressive historiographical accomplishment cannot conceal the fact that, even today, research on Michelangelo is often conducted in a manner not unlike that of a community of priests and worshipers toward the object of its cult; critical questioning is often replaced by dogmatism and ritual incantations. Symptomatic of this is the enormous discrepancy that exists between the knowledge and interest shown in Michelangelo, and that shown in his artistic surroundings.

This is demonstrated by an almost grotesque ratio of pertinent publications: whereas Michelangelo was the subject of about 2,300 articles and books between 1927 and 1975, his many coeval and in part extremely talented Florentine colleagues—such as Granacci, Bugiardini, Raffaellino del Garbo, Fra Bartolommeo, Albertinelli, Franciabigio, Torrigiani, and Rustici among others—have been afforded a total of 50–60 publications at most.

A compelling question arises, namely, whether research did not in fact try to enhance its hero's greatness by depriving his surroundings of their creative substance. In one respect it definitely did this, and with diligence. Especially in the case of drawings, which demand particularly careful treatment, scientific principles were repeatedly abandoned and blind faith in traditional judgment substituted for critical analysis. Through methods largely corresponding to those of the past, an expansion of the number of alleged Michelangelo sketches is once again taking place, the like of which was witnessed only in the heyday of Michelangelo's posthumous fame. (In response to a phenomenally rising demand during the 17th and 18th centuries, hundreds of supposedly "genuine" drawings appeared as if by magic, though Michelangelo's contemporaries, estranged by the Master's habit of periodically burning his preparatory work, had considered every surviving drawing a rarity.)

The effect of this expansion has been catastrophic: a stylistic jumble in which the verified drawings comprise only about one-tenth of all those attributed to him and which has hindered our insight into his actual modes of developing concepts, of assimilating and adapting ideas, an insight essential for an understanding of his artistic creativity. Thus critical judgment has been led into a labyrinth of blind alleys and contradictions. Instead of providing a basis for new questions and perceptions, the body of Michelangelo's alleged drawings has become a fervently worshiped but scientifically unfruitful appendant to his "actual" works.

Unfinished Works. One of the most striking peculiarities of Michelangelo's work is the great number of pieces that were left unfinished. About one-fifth of his paintings and nearly two-thirds of the sculptures were not completed; of the multipartite larger projects he worked on, such as the tomb of Pope Julius II, the Medici Chapel, the Capitoline Square, and St. Peter's, not one was finished in complete accordance with the intentions of the artist. This is all the more remarkable because, throughout his lifetime, Michelangelo subscribed to the then still current ideal of perfection, whereby the full value of a work of art was measured, independently of where it was viewed from, by the extent to which the traces of manual work had been eliminated. He found it blameworthy, for example, that some sculptures of Donatello, whom he revered highly, lost their effectiveness for lack of sufficient polish when studied from a short distance.

Not only were commissioned sculptures such as the "Bacchus" (1496–97), the "Pietà" in St. Peter's (1498–99), the marble "David" (1501–04), the Bruges "Madonna and Child" (*c.* 1504), the "Moses" for the tomb of Pope Julius II (*c.* 1513–16), the reclining figure "Night" for the Medici tombs, and the presentation sheets for Tommaso de'Cavalieri (1533) and Vittoria Colonna (*c.* 1545) completed to a non plus ultra of possible perfection; even the sculptured works undertaken later "for amusement" (as Condivi put it)—the "Pietà" in the Cathedral of Florence (1547–53) and the "Rondanini Pietà" (*c.* 1553–64)—were meant to achieve that same perfection, as is demonstrated by their most completed parts. The fact that most of his works remained unfinished, in spite of this ideal, and therefore did not meet either the demands of the patron of the time or the standards the artist set himself, irritated even his contemporaries. To them this must have seemed to contradict and undermine the enormous prestige that Michelangelo enjoyed. This provoked a chain of new questions that inadvertently led to a new understanding of art and of artists.

Reflections on Michelangelo's unfinished works first appeared in the writings of Vasari and Condivi. Both biographers were convinced that the artist would have produced fewer but more complete works if, early in his career, he had not already become enmeshed in a net of projects, each of which prevented the others from being completed. They sensed, however, that external impediments alone were not the whole explanation. They therefore thought that Michelangelo's enthusiasm for work was frustrated because in each case his imagined artistic goal proved to be of a higher level of perfection than its final material expression.

People who were interested in Michelangelo retaining an untarnished reputation would not admit to the real reasons for his unfinished works because they stemmed from a mode of artistic behaviour that went beyond the understanding of most of his contemporaries. Michelangelo felt a compelling need to execute all the manual work on his sculptured and painted productions personally, and he could only bring himself to delegate work to assistants in the most extreme emergencies, when his reputation as a contract partner was at stake. Because of this, he left himself open to the suspicion of consciously transgressing the unwritten moral law that placed every master under the obligation of passing on his artistic skill to others as best he could. ("It may please Your Highness to know that the one and only reason why he has never finished a marble work is that he has never allowed anyone to help him, in order not to produce any masters, of course . . . ," sneered Michelangelo's enemy Bandinelli in 1547 in a letter to Duke Cosimo de'Medici.) His behaviour robbed every assistant of the opportunity to become intimate with the Master's projects through active participation and to develop his artistic personality by inner assimilation. Thus the likelihood for real schooling was minimized, every potential fellow worker was burdened with the permanent status of an apprentice, and no student trained to a degree that would correspond to the educational norms of those times emerged from Michelangelo's studio. At the same time, artists educated elsewhere (Cellini, Vasari, and Condivi, among others) wished to regard themselves as "pupils" of this master out of the conviction that they had arrived at their own mastery—at true artistic power—primarily through the study of Michelangelo's works.

Method and Theory. Michelangelo's refusal to delegate actual production work was based on a personal, unorthodox working method. While the usual method was characterized by a rigorous separation of design and execution (which made possible not only the enormous production capacities but also the tremendous training potential of the art workshops of that time), Michelangelo's method represented an integration of these processes. The manual execution of his sculptures and paintings had almost nothing in common with the halfway mechanical reproduction work that could be delegated to others at any time. For Michelangelo manual execution was a vital component of the creative process and on occasion seemed part of the process of design itself.

To Michelangelo manual execution represented an act of confirmation by means of which the inner coherence and persuasive power of his concept were put to the test. Precisely because of this, the completion of a work according to his intentions became a problem of time. It depended entirely upon whether the artist could give a definite expression to his ideas in good time, before he had grown away from them in his mind (significantly—almost a miracle under the conditions of that period—such finished sculptures as the "Bacchus," the "Pietà" in St. Peter's, and the "David" were completed before the respective deadlines of their short delivery periods). If the process of execution was interrupted too often or for too long a time, the prospects of final completion became uncertain.

Despite its lightning speed—typical of Michelangelo—even the work rate in the frescoing of the Sistine Chapel ceiling did not keep pace with the inner retreat from the original concept he had had in mind. The original prophet-and-sibyl concept, based on the current idea of the "humanist in his study" and harmoniously adjusted to the illusionary architecture as well as to the motif of the medallion-holding *Ignudi* ("nudes"), already began to disintegrate after the completion of the first ceiling compartment (Zechariah, Joel, the Delphic sibyl). It became more and more displaced by the "modern" concept of the "visionary possessed with supernatural knowing," a concept that required, among other things, a successive augmentation of the format and volume of the figures and that unavoidably conflicted with the original purpose of the illusionary architecture (which could not be altered any more) and of the *Ignudo* motif (which became independent and turned the medallions, as symbols of erudition, into mere decorative additions). A similar thing occurred, for instance, after the second contract was made with Pope Julius II's heirs, when Michelangelo began to revise his first slave-concept (the Louvre "Slaves"). All at once the enlarged dimensions of the new slaves (the Boboli "Slaves") rendered the already completed lower front part of the Julius Tomb worthless in the artist's eyes.

The roots of such an unusual conception of art, which turned every artistic project into a search for truth fraught with physical exertion, extend far back into the period of his youth. Michelangelo attended the most elite of the three elementary schools existing at the time, but he never received a regular education in an art workshop except for a brief period of painting instructions (1488–89) under Ghirlandajo. His conception of himself as an artist developed outside of the norms of that time—primarily in an argument with his middle class family, which had nothing but contempt for an artist's profession. During his entire life the artist seems to have been obsessed with the thought that he had to prove to his father that the way *he* practiced art agreed quite well with the paternal concept of a calling appropriate to his class. "I was never a painter or sculptor like someone who makes a mere business out of it. I have constantly shunned that for the sake of my father's and my brothers' honour, although I did serve three popes, which I had to do." (May 2, 1548, letter to his nephew.)

Art Sales

Market Trends. When the new auction season opened in October 1974, the art market was suffering its first serious setback of the 1970s. Investment interest, which had given it two years of unprecedented boom conditions, had virtually disappeared, and rare and expensive items in almost every field failed to find buyers at prices approaching recent levels. Among the hardest hit areas were Impressionist and modern paintings, Chinese porcelain, English 19th- and 20th-century paintings, Dutch 19th-century paintings, and English clocks.

The organization of specialist sales (at Sotheby's and Christie's in London, Parke-Bernet in New York, the Palais Galliera in Paris) generally requires a lapse of three to six months between the acceptance of goods for sale and their appearance at auction. Thus many items accepted for sale at the previous season's price levels remained unsold throughout the autumn. This problem had worked itself through the system by the new year, but the new era heralded by the spring and summer sales of 1975 defied generalization. Prices in each collection field were reacting to different sets of pressures and going in different directions. The buying power of the oil-rich Middle East countries and Iran was the most important new influence.

Works of Art. In April an early 19th-century Qajar painting of the "Fifteen Sons and Grandsons of Fath Ali Shah" sold for £200,000 at Sotheby's; that the price was exceptional was demonstrated when a slightly smaller but finer portrait of the shah himself sold for £100,000 in July. In Paris in June Boisgirard had sold three small Qajar panels of Persian lady musicians at Fr. 151,000, Fr. 150,000, and Fr. 133,000. In February a colourful German painting of the Emir Bechir greeting Ibrahim Pasha in 1831 attracted Lebanese bidders to Christie's and went for £22,050; the painting, by Georg Emanuel Opiz, depicted an important event in Lebanese history. Even without historical associations, paintings of the Middle East by

SOTHEBY & CO.

This Wedgwood "Poole" copy of the famous Portland Vase was sold at Sotheby's, together with a lock of George Washington's hair, for £18,000. The original owner was Thomas Poole, a Bristol tanner, who received the vase around 1790.

19th-century European artists were much in demand. "The Carpet Merchant of Cairo" by Jean-Léon Gérôme made $19,000 in New York in October.

There were also unprecedented prices for Islamic pottery and glass. At Sotheby's in July a 13th-century Gurgan pottery ewer with a rooster-headed neck brought £11,000, while a Sassanian or early Islamic pale green glass bowl of around the 5th to 8th century A.D. made £8,500. In general, however, Middle East dealers and collectors appeared to feel more at home with the 19th century than with antiquity. A pair of 19th-century copies of pierced bronze Mamluk tables, inlaid with gold and silver, sold at Christie's for £4,410 in November 1974, a reflection of the new prices for 19th-century metalwork. Persian lacquer also soared in price. Pen boxes, or *qalamdan,* used to sell for £30 or £40; in April 1975 Christie's sold one decorated with a historic battle scene for £3,885, and in July another in 17th-century style went for £8,925. Middle East buying also contributed to the strength of oriental carpet prices.

The steady erosion of the sterling exchange rate attracted an unprecedented number of European dealers to London auctions in search of bargains. Swiss and West German dealers contributed especially to the buoyant market in continental glass and porcelain. A Venetian "calcedonio" footed glass bowl was bid to £7,500 in July, and a record price of £15,225 was paid for a Meissen snuffbox in December 1974.

German taste appeared particularly to favour the Gothic and Renaissance periods. A pair of 14th-century oak doors carved into openwork panels symbolizing the months of the year was sold to the Münster Landesmuseum for £36,000 at Sotheby's in April 1975. The same price was paid in July for a pair of north German carved oak figures of the Virgin and St. John dating from *c.* 1220.

For many years Italian buying had helped support the market for minor Old Master paintings and antique furniture. In 1975 the Italians were joined by other European dealers, particularly the Spanish. In July Francisco Ribalta's "Portrait of a Knight of Santiago and His Wife" was bid to £24,000, while two panels from a retable by Juan Rexath made £21,000 and a 17th-century Spanish walnut *vargueno,* or chest on chest, £4,800. Prices for Italian majolica had never been so high, especially for late examples hitherto unappreciated. A Gubbio plate painted with Abraham and Isaac in an Italian landscape by Giorgio Andreoli established an auction record for European pottery—£55,000 at Sotheby's in March.

The threat of international recession made it a particularly good season for small, portable items of high artistic or historic value—a private means of transferring wealth from one centre to another. This affected the markets in jewelry, coins, watches, and Japanese netsuke. A collection of English gold coins formed by Capt. K. J. Douglas-Morris sold for £569,390 in November 1974, with a 1703 five-guinea piece of the "Vigo" type fetching £26,000, an auction record for a British coin. In February 1975 a Korean War Victoria Cross brought £7,200, an auction record for a gallantry medal. At the beginning of the season an automaton watch of *c.* 1800, enameled and set with pearls, made SFr. 125,000 at the Galérie Genevoise in Geneva, and a gold and enamel verge watch by C. Bonneux made £15,000 at Christie's.

The market in Impressionist and modern paintings, the most expensive area of the entire art market, was dogged by disaster. The pattern was set at Parke-

Bernet in New York in October 1974, when well over half the major autumn auction was unsold. The only bright spot was the $340,000 for Jean Dubuffet's "Échange de Vues" of 1963. In London in December 30 out of 100 paintings were unsold at Christie's and 42 out of 109 at Sotheby's, although a Cubist Braque made £240,000 and "The Painter's Daughters" by Max Ernst, £78,000. A Jackson Pollock of 1951 was unsold at £126,000. In April an important Van Gogh portrait of "Patience Escalier" from the Chester Beatty collection was scheduled for sale at Christie's, but the owner had second thoughts and sold it to a syndicate of dealers before the auction.

Around 30 to 50% of the major spring and summer auctions were unsold, although consignors were beginning to scale down their expectations. On the whole, Impressionist paintings seemed to be holding their value better than those of the 20th century, while works of the 1950s and 1960s were the worst hit. Sotheby's July sale devoted to an unknown and unexhibited French collection was the exception that proved the rule. A Monet of Rouen Cathedral was bid to £210,000, a Braque still life of 1941 to £170,000, three Fauve Vlamincks to £130,000, £118,000, and £101,000, and two late but distinguished works by Pissarro to £120,000 and £80,000.

The speculative spiral in the Chinese porcelain market had collapsed dramatically in the summer of 1974, but the spring and summer sales of 1975 saw steadily returning confidence as a new, though lower, level of prices was established. Early Ming blue and white and the finer late polychromes suffered most. The temporary fall in prices for ceramics of the Sung and T'ang dynasties had been virtually made good by the end of the season. The most spectacular piece of porcelain to come on the market was a 14th-century Ming blue and white jar, the body superbly painted with Chinese landscapes; it was the only known example to survive with its cover. In spite of damage, it sold to a Japanese dealer at £160,000 in March. At Sotheby's in July a rare Sung Kuan-Yao bottle with a thick gray-blue glaze made £78,000.

"The Most Ancient and Most Noble Order of the Thistle," a very rare decoration given by William IV to the earl of Erroll in 1834, was sold at Sotheby's for £9,500.

KEYSTONE

This bronze horse, about one metre tall, was one of the treasures of the Barons de Rothschild and de Rédé sold at auction in March. The price was Fr. 1.5 million (about $375,000).

KEYSTONE

Uncertainty about prices deterred many owners from selling, and the season's turnover of all the major auction rooms was reduced. Nevertheless, a number of spectacular pieces came on the market and made spectacular prices. In October 1974 an album of 94 photographs by Julia Margaret Cameron, presented by her to Sir F. W. Herschel, made £52,000; it was subsequently acquired at that price by the National Portrait Gallery, London. In November a set of five Philadelphia Chippendale chairs made $227,500 in New York, and Francesco Parmigianino's painting "The Mystic Marriage of St. Catherine" was sold to the National Gallery, London, after being bought in at Christie's at £273,000.

In December an Assyrian relief of *c.* 1880 B.C. from the palace at Nimrud made £57,750, and the British Rail pension fund bought a Tiepolo sketch for £195,000. Also in December, a pair of Pierre Monlong flintlock pistols (1690–1700) made £78,000 at Sotheby's and was later sold privately to the Tower of London for £90,000. In Geneva in May Christie's sold a silver soup tureen from the Count Orloff service for SFr. 620,000 and a matching pair of table candlesticks for SFr. 140,000. In Monte Carlo, also in May, Sotheby's dispersed works of art from the collections of Barons Alexis de Rédé and Guy de Rothschild; a Renaissance bronze horse from the Bologna-Susini workshop made Fr. 1.5 million.

Several notable sales were made in June. In London a 16th-century pottery St. Porchaire ewer that had graced the collection of Sir Horace Walpole at Strawberry Hill made £44,000 and a pair of William III silver-gilt wine bottles, £62,000. Picasso's "Vollard Suite" of etchings made SFr. 480,000 at Kornfeld and Klipstein in Bern, Switz. An Utamaro print, "The Waitress China," made $70,000 in New York, and the hat worn by Napoleon during his disastrous Russian campaign made Fr. 170,000 in Paris. In July a Turner watercolour, "The Dark Rigi" from his famous series of Swiss views of 1842, made an auction record at £85,000. A William Beilby enameled goblet of the 1760s became the most expensive piece of glass ever sold at auction at £19,500, until John Northwood's cameo glass copy of the Portland vase made £30,000 a week later.

Book Sales. In contrast to the art market, the 1974–75 season saw no recession in the book trade. There had been an unusually rapid rise in prices between November 1973 and June 1974, and the opening of the new season brought a return to normality. In most fields prices marked time, although there was an increasing emphasis on illustrated books.

The 1485 edition of Aesop's *Fables* published in Naples for Francesco del Tuppo, one of the earliest and most decorative printed editions with 88 magnificent woodcuts, made £24,000 in June 1975. The same sale brought £13,000 for a richly illuminated copy of the Gospels in church Slavonic; it belonged to Boris Godunov, tsar of Russia from 1598 to 1605. A sale at Sotheby's in February highlighted the demand for topographical books. Three sets of steel-engraved views by the Batty family, including *Hanoverian and Saxon Scenery* of 1829, made £1,200. L. F. Cassas' *Voyage Pittoresque de la Syrie* of 1799–1800 and Lavalée's *Voyage Pittoresque et Historique de l'Istrie et Dalmatie* of 1802 each made £750.

The most important natural history sale of the season was that devoted to books from Arpad Plesch's *Stiftung für Botanik* at Sotheby's in June; B. Besler's *Hortus Eystettensis* of 1613 made £16,000. Parke-Bernet also had an important group of botanical books in March, with John Edwards' *Collection of Flowers Drawn after Nature* of 1793–95 and 1798 fetching $30,000. A 1640 edition of Besler made $28,000. In the travel field, Sir Robert Dudley's *Arcano del Mare* of 1661, from the Scott library, fetched £9,000 in December. Ortelius' *Theatrum Orbis Terrarum* of 1595 made £12,000, or more than £80 a map, in April.

This Paul Gauguin painting, "Hina Maruru," was sold in New York for $950,000. It was the highest price ever paid for one of Gauguin's works.

WIDE WORLD

The effect of Middle East buying was as apparent in the book field as in the arts. A 1599 manuscript of Firdausi's *Shah Nameh* or *Book of Kings,* with 44 full-page miniatures and rich illumination, made $250,000 in New York in May.

Among the major events of the year was the appearance at auction of an unpublished and unknown manuscript of Elizabethan love poems by Robert Sidney, brother of the poet Sir Philip Sidney. The manuscript failed to sell at Sotheby's November 1975 auction and was bought in at £28,000; it was subsequently purchased by the British Library for around £50,000. Also in November, a fragment of a 14th-century illuminated breviary from the Abbey of St. Andrew in Cologne made Fr. 100,000 in Paris.

In January 1975 a full score of Gilbert and Sullivan's opera *Trial by Jury,* 164 pages in the hand of Sir Arthur Sullivan, made $29,000 in New York. Sotheby's dispersed 34 manuscripts from the library of the late Major Abbey (a group formed by C. H. St. J. Hornby) for £285,900 in March. A magnificent manuscript of the Gospels made £80,000; it was written in Metz in the second quarter of the 9th century and was thought to have belonged to Queen Theutberga of Lorraine. An illuminated missal of *c.* 1240 written for the Augustinian Abbey of St. Étienne at Dijon made £42,000.

In May Christie's sold a long autograph letter from Shelley to Thomas Love Peacock, including references to Byron, at £9,800. Nearer to the present, in June the same auctioneers dispersed the library of Siegfried Sassoon (d. 1967) for £17,919.

The bursting of a literary bubble was confirmed in June when a poem by John Donne copied in the hand of Sir Nathaniel Rich, a contemporary and acquaintance, sold for £1,000. Six months before, the poem, erroneously identified as in Donne's own hand, had been claimed as the literary discovery of the century.

One of the 21 recorded copies of the first printing of the American Declaration of Independence was sold at Christie's for £40,000 in July. In the wake of the amazing $440,000 paid for another Declaration in 1969, this copy had been unsold at a Parke-Bernet auction at $120,000. (GERALDINE NORMAN)

[613.B.2.b]

Astronomy

Galaxies and Quasars. The year was an exceptionally active one for discoveries in extragalactic astronomy. The most notable finds included the largest and farthest galaxies and the brightest and nearest quasars. All of these objects are strong radio sources, three of them being listed in the third Cambridge catalogue (3C) of bright radio sources.

Under the assumption that the universe is expanding, the more distant that objects are from the Earth the faster they recede from it and the greater the shift of their spectral features toward the red (long-wavelength) end of the spectrum. In 1960, the strong radio source 3C295 was identified with a visible galaxy that had a red shift of 0.46, placing the galaxy approximately six billion light-years from the Earth. Since that time, many quasars have been found to have larger red shifts than 3C295 (up to about 3.5), but no galaxy was found to be farther away. In 1975, however, Hyron Spinrad (University of California, Berkeley) showed that the visible galaxy underlying the radio source 3C123 has a red shift of 0.637. Using the currently accepted value for the rate of expansion of the universe, this puts 3C123 at a distance of nearly eight billion light-years.

Extragalactic radio sources usually take the form of a bright pointlike object centred on the underlying galaxy or quasar, or they appear as a pair of large diffuse regions of radio emission on either side of the central object. By carefully mapping the radio galaxy 3C236 with the Westerbork synthesis radio telescope located in The Netherlands, A. G. Willis, R. G. Strom, and A. S. Wilson (Leiden Observatory) found that its radio clouds span about 18 million light-years. By comparison, the largest other objects known to date, which are clusters of 1,000 or more galaxies, are generally no larger than ten million light-years across. Though it is the largest object known, 3C236 has a mass estimated at no more than 100 billion solar masses, about one galactic mass. DA240, a second object studied by the group, is about 6.5 million light-years across and is remarkable because of the visible jetlike protuberance emanating from its parent galaxy.

Quasars are extragalactic objects that emit not starlight but rather fluxes of radio, infrared, ultraviolet, and X-radiation that are excessive in comparison with galaxies containing normal stellar populations. Their most remarkable features are their large red shifts and small sizes. Assuming their red shifts to be cosmological in origin, a question still under debate (*see* below), the luminosities of quasars are among the highest known for individual objects. For example, the highly variable quasar 3C279 has a normal optical brightness of the 15th or 16th magnitude. By searching through the past 70 years of plates from the Harvard College Observatory sky patrol, William Liller and Lola Eachus found that among several quasars showing optical flare activity, 3C279 had a truly spectacular outburst in 1937. Its brightness increased by more than a factor of 100 for about a month. At the distance corresponding to its red shift of 0.536, the luminosity of 3C279 would have been 10^{48} ergs per second, about 10,000 times as bright as the entire Milky Way galaxy. Based on the change in brightness by a factor of 5 in 13 days during 1936, one can conclude that 3C279 is no more than a few light-days across, about ten times the size of the solar system. Just how an object as luminous and probably massive as an entire galaxy can be crammed into so small a space and turned on and off in so short a time is a question to which no satisfactory answer existed as of 1975.

K. TARUSOV—TASS / SOVFOTO

The largest optical telescope in the world, with a 236-in. reflector, is housed in this Soviet Academy of Sciences Observatory in the Caucasus Mountains.

A way of avoiding this difficulty is to assume that the quasars are not at the distances indicated by their red shifts. Placing them at much smaller distances from the Earth requires them to be much less energetic and luminous. During the year astronomers focused attention on the peculiar object BL Lacertae, which exhibits highly variable radio, infrared, and optical emission reminiscent of many quasars but lacks spectral features that might indicate its red shift. Hoping that it in fact is a galaxy with a very bright nucleus, J. B. Oke and J. E. Gunn (Hale Observatories) managed to obtain a spectrum of the outer fuzzy regions of the object by occulting its bright centre with an obscuring disk. The outer regions then appeared to have a star-produced spectrum similar to that of a giant elliptical galaxy (like 3C295) and a red shift of about 0.07. Assuming this as the correct distance indicator, the astronomers showed that the central object has properties much like the more distant quasars 3C48, 3C279, and 3C345, with the exception

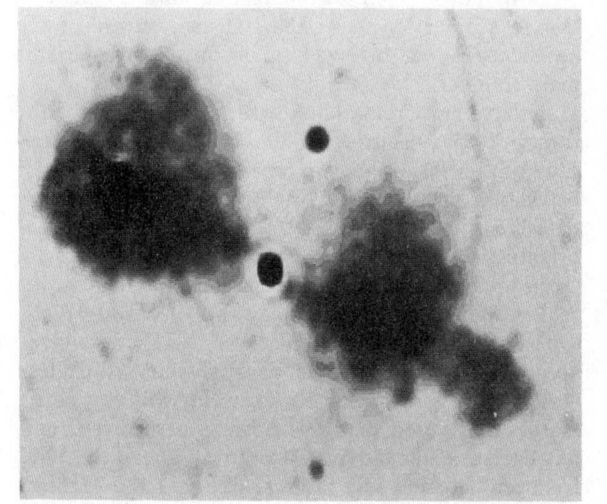

LEFT, FROM A PROJECT OF A. G. WILLIS, R. G. STROM, AND A. S. WILSON OF THE LEIDEN OBSERVATORY; RIGHT, © AEROPHOTO EELDE

Map of radio galaxy 3C236 (left), the largest object in the universe, which was detected by Dutch radio astronomers from Leiden Observatory using 12 parabolic radio telescopes arrayed on an east-west line (right). The galaxy spans a distance of 18 million light-years.

Asbestos: *see* Mining and Quarrying

Association Football: *see* Football

Astronautics: *see* Space Exploration

Earth Perihelion and Aphelion, 1976

January 4	Perihelion, 91,409,000 mi. (147,104,000 km.) from the Sun
July 3	Aphelion, 94,515,000 mi. (152,102,000 km.) from the Sun

Equinoxes and Solstices, 1976

March 20	Vernal equinox, 11:50*
June 21	Summer solstice, 06:24*
Sept. 22	Autumnal equinox, 21:48*
Dec. 21	Winter solstice, 17:36*

Eclipses, 1976

April 29	Sun, annular (begins 7:23†), visible NE of North and South America, Greenland, N. Africa, Europe, Asia
May 13	Moon, partial (begins 17:47†), visible Australia, Asia except NE part, E part of Europe, Africa except NW part, Antarctica, part of New Zealand, Indian O., E part of S. Atlantic
Oct. 23	Sun, total (begins 02:39†), visible Central and E. Africa, S. Asia, Antarctica, Australasia
Nov. 6–7	Moon, penumbral (begins 20:46†), visible W. Australia, Asia except extreme E part, Arctic regions, Africa, Greenland, extreme NE part of North America, extreme NE part of South America, most of Atlantic O., Indian O.

*Universal time.
†Ephemeris time.
Source: *The American Ephemeris and Nautical Almanac for the year 1976*, Washington, D.C. (1974).

that it has no conspicuous spectral emission lines. E. M. Burbidge and colleagues (University of California, San Diego) were unable to confirm the existence of any spectral features in BL Lac. If the proposed red shift is ultimately confirmed, BL Lac will serve as a link between quasars and galaxies, adding further weight to the argument that quasars are truly at the distance indicated by their red shifts.

Stellar Astronomy. Surely the most visible event of astronomy in 1975 was the nova that appeared in the constellation Cygnus in late August. Discovered by the Japanese amateur astronomer Minoru Honda, it quickly gained in magnitude to a peak of about 1.8 (about as bright as the pole star), the brightest nova in 33 years. Easily visible near the star Deneb in the Northern Cross, Nova Cygni 1975 was observed by hundreds of astronomers at radio, infrared, optical, ultraviolet, and X-ray wavelengths. Because it is not visible on the Palomar Observatory Sky Survey plates made in 1948, it must have brightened at least by a record 19 magnitudes, or a factor of about 100 million, before beginning to fade away. Luigi Jacchia (Smithsonian Astrophysical Observatory, Cambridge, Mass.) suggested that Nova Cygni 1975, like Nova CP Puppis 1942 which increased by 16.5 magnitudes, may be a virgin nova, ejecting radiating shells for the first time.

The binary companion of Sirius A, the brightest star in the sky, is the white dwarf Sirius B. Because of their proximity (only about 11 arc seconds separated the two stars in 1974) it is difficult to measure the spectrum of the very dim dwarf star. In 1975, however, K. D. Rakos (University Observatory of Vienna) measured the spectrum of Sirius B and found it to have the exceedingly high effective temperature of 24,000° K, making it the hottest, most luminous white dwarf known. In addition, R. Mewe and collaborators (Astronomical Institute, Utrecht, Neth.) reported detecting a flux of low-energy X-rays from Sirius B, the first X-ray flux detected from a known white dwarf. Rakos pointed out that during the time of the Roman Empire both Ptolemy and Seneca described Sirius as red in colour, in contrast to its present blue-white appearance. It seems, therefore, that 2,000 years ago Sirius B may have been a red giant whose light dominated its companion Sirius A. It perhaps later lost its outer envelope, leaving the degenerate core seen today.

Pulsars. Ever since 1967, when radio pulsars were first discovered, a curious problem about them has persisted. As is well known, more than half of all normal stars are found to be members of binary or multiple-star systems. But even though more than 140 pulsars had been detected and subjected to detailed analysis by 1974, radio astronomers had not discovered any pulsar in a binary system. Then in late 1974 two radio astronomers, R. A. Hulse and J. H. Taylor (University of Massachusetts, Amherst) discovered a radio pulsar in a binary star system, PSR 1913+16. Pulsing nearly 20 times per second, it revolves around its unseen companion star with an eccentric orbit in 7.75 hours. Based on the first few weeks of observation of the object, Kenneth Brecher (Massachusetts Institute of Technology, Cambridge), as well as A. R. Masters and D. H. Roberts (University of Illinois, Urbana), showed that the unseen companion must also be a compact star.

The brightest globular cluster known, a swarm of more than one million stars located 35,000 light-years from the Sun, is shown here as it appeared through the new 158-in. reflecting telescope at the Cerro Tololo Inter-American Observatory in Chile.

CERRO TOLOLO INTER-AMERICAN OBSERVATORY

KITT PEAK NATIONAL OBSERVATORY

The surface temperatures of Betelgeuse, a giant red star, were mapped by new imaging techniques at the Kitt Peak National Observatory, Arizona.

Galactic X-ray Sources. X-ray astronomy continued to provide surprises during the year. As a result of the launch of several new X-ray telescopes, including the British UK-5 (Ariel), U.S. SAS-3 and OSO-8, and the joint U.S.-Dutch satellite (ANS), the most unusual events seemed to be the discovery in rapid succession of more than half a dozen new transient X-ray sources. These objects suddenly appear on a time scale of a few days, and decay away in days or weeks. Two of them, A1118-61 and A0535+26, pulsated with regular periods of 405 and 104 seconds, respectively. Though pulsating much more slowly than the steadily radiating binary X-ray sources Her X-1 and Cen X-3, both of these objects were believed to be powered by accretion of matter onto a collapsed star in a binary system; the transient nature of the new sources was believed to be caused by sporadic mass transfer.

Perhaps most remarkable was the discovery of the transient X-ray source A0620-00 by the Ariel 5 satellite. Within less than two weeks of its discovery, it had flared up to be the brightest X-ray source ever detected, almost five times brighter than Sco X-1, the brightest source previously known. With the accurate position for the source having been obtained by the SAS-3 satellite, Forrest I. Boley and Richard L. Wolfson (Dartmouth College, Hanover, N.H.) discovered an optical nova there. Lola Eachus (Harvard College Observatory), searching through Harvard sky patrol plates, discovered that this nova is a recurrent one, having last exploded in 1917. In addition, the nova has been detected as a radio source at 2,380 MHz by

H. D. Craft, Jr., using the 1,000-ft. Arecibo Ionospheric Observatory radio telescope in Puerto Rico. Unlike A1118-61 and A0535+26 it neither pulsates nor emits extremely energetic X-rays, its X-rays probably arising from material ejected from the system.

Finally, the discovery of five variable X-ray sources in globular clusters came as a surprise. Because globular clusters are systems containing very old stars, one would not expect to find any currently active stars in them at all. Yet the fraction of X-ray emitting sources in globular clusters is a factor of 10 to 100 higher than for the rest of the Milky Way. Using the SAS-3 satellite, G. W. Clark (MIT) and collaborators found that several of these X-ray objects lie very close to the centres of their respective clusters. This may indicate that the high density of stars near the crowded centres of the clusters can instigate intense energetic activity in otherwise old and settled stars.

Solar System. The discovery of the 13th satellite of Jupiter was reported in September 1974 by Charles T. Kowal (Hale Observatories), Kaare Aksnes and Brian G. Marsden (Smithsonian Astrophysical Observatory), and Elizabeth Roemer (University of Arizona, Tucson). It was found first on a set of photographs of a field centred on Jupiter made by Kowal with the Palomar 122-cm. (48-in.) Schmidt telescope. Jupiter XIII has an orbital period of 239.24 days and a semi-major axis of about 11 million km. Because its photographic magnitude is about 21, 1.5 magnitudes fainter than Jupiter XII which is estimated to have a radius of about 8 km., Jupiter XIII is smaller still. Whether this tiny satellite is a captured asteroid or whether it formed at the same time as Jupiter remained a mystery. The discoverers suggested that at the faint levels they could detect, other small satellites should be found. In fact, late in 1975 Kowal reported the probable discovery of another satellite of Jupiter.

The shapes and sizes of the moons of the major planets and of the asteroids are only poorly known. Size estimates of such objects are usually made on the basis of their measured brightness and an assumed sunlight reflectivity (albedo). In 1975, however, for the first time, the size of one of the asteroids was measured directly. Brian G. Marsden and colleagues from six colleges in New England observed the occultation of the bright star Kappa Geminorum by the asteroid Eros. By combining the computed orbit and velocity of Eros with the naked-eye observations of the duration of eclipse made by amateur astronomers situated throughout the path of totality, the astronomers determined a shape and size for the asteroid. Though the results were somewhat ambiguous, Eros appears to be shaped like a squashed sphere about 20 km. long and 7 km. wide. The albedo of the object is about 0.5, considerably higher than that derived for any other planetary body.

While 1974 proved an exciting year in spacecraft studies of Jupiter, Venus, and Mercury by Pioneer 11 and Mariner 10, no comparable discoveries were made by probes in 1975. Further analysis of the Mariner 10 probe revealed, however, the surprising result that Mercury has an extended magnetic field. Whether it is internally generated or externally impressed by the solar wind remained unclear. Pioneer 11 found Jupiter to be accelerating its own cosmic rays. The launch of the Viking 1 and 2 spacecraft, scheduled to make a first soft landing on Mars on or about July 4, 1976, generated much excitement. Their main mission is to test the surface of the planet for the conditions and even direct signs of life.

Instrumentation and Techniques. Two new large telescopes for studying the southern skies were dedicated in 1975. The 4-m. (158-in.) reflector at the Cerro Tololo Inter-American Observatory in Chile and the Anglo-Australian 3.9-m. (154-in.) telescope near Siding Spring, New South Wales, Australia, both produced their first results.

The world's largest radio dish, the 1,000-ft. antenna at Arecibo Observatory in Puerto Rico, was refurbished with a new surface that consisted of nearly 40,000 aluminum panels. It replaced the original wire-mesh surface. The new surface allows observations at 4.2-cm. wavelengths, short enough to permit detection of interstellar molecules.

Perhaps the most exciting development in 1975 was the increased introduction of modern technology into optical astronomy. Unlike radio-, infrared-, and X-ray astronomy, each of which developed in the age of the computer and solid-state physics, optical astronomy was slow to adopt sophisticated new methods. By 1975, however, astronomers at the Kitt Peak National Observatory had combined traditional photography with a technique called speckle interferometry and with the data-handling capability of a large computer (Interactive Picture Processing System). This combination allows astronomers to accentuate otherwise faint details in an image by changing the contrast between different regions. By using the new system they were able to reproduce for the first time the surface features of a distant star, namely, the red supergiant Betelgeuse. (KENNETH BRECHER)

See also Earth Sciences; Space Exploration.

[131.A.3; 132.A-D; 133.A-C; 723.E.1.b and d]

ENCYCLOPÆDIA BRITANNICA FILMS. *Controversy over the Moon* (1971).

WIDE WORLD

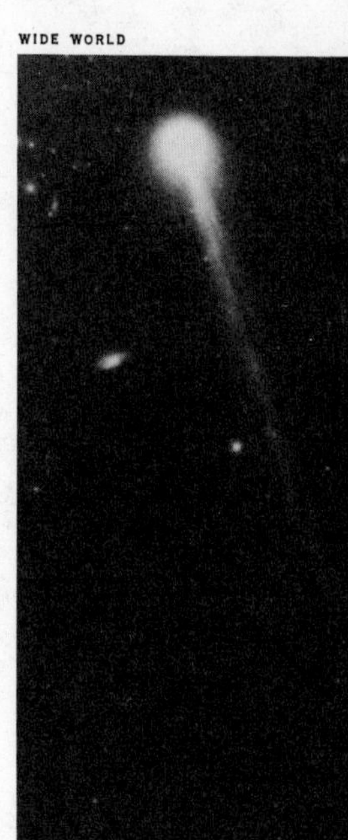

The Comet Kobayashi-Berger-Milon, discovered July 2, is shown here a month after developing a tail several million miles in length.

Australia

A federal parliamentary state and a member of the Commonwealth of Nations, Australia occupies the smallest continent and, with the island state of Tasmania, is the sixth largest country in the world. Area: 2,967,900 sq.mi. (7,686,850 sq.km.). Pop. (1975 est.): 13,542,100. Cap.: Canberra (metro. pop., 1975, 185,800). Largest city: Sydney (metro. pop., 1974, 2,898,300). Language: English. Religion (1971): Church of England 31%; Roman Catholic 27%; Methodist 8.6%; Presbyterian 8.1%. Queen, Elizabeth II; governor-general in 1975, Sir John Kerr; prime ministers, Gough Whitlam and, from November 11, Malcolm Fraser.

Domestic Affairs. On Dec. 13, 1975, Australians went to the polls for the third time in three years. The conservative Liberal-Country Party (LCP) coalition won the election with a record majority. There was a 6% swing to the LCP, and 30 Australian Labor Party (ALP) members of Parliament lost their seats in the landslide. In political terms, Australia returned to the state of equilibrium that had existed under Sir Robert Menzies in the 1950s and early 1960s, when the conservatives held majorities in both houses.

The LCP won the 1975 election on the issues of inflation and unemployment. Their leader, Malcolm Fraser (*see* BIOGRAPHY), had earlier made his mark with successful campaigns in by-elections and during the state election in Queensland. In South Australia the Labor government barely survived a general election and relied for office on the goodwill of the independent speaker.

Athletics:
see Sporting Record;
articles on the various sports

From the time that Fraser replaced Billy Snedden as leader of the opposition in March 1975, conservatives picked up ground strongly. As soon as he became leader of the LCP Fraser was asked whether he would allow the Labor Party to govern for its expected three-year term or whether he would use the opposition's numbers in the Senate to bring the government down. Fraser replied that the elected government had a right to expect that it would govern except in the most extraordinary circumstances. The extraordinary circumstances were not long in coming. Whitlam was forced to dismiss or demote senior ministers James Cairns (*see* BIOGRAPHY), Clyde Cameron, Frank Crean, and Reginald F. X. Connor, and to make matters worse the speaker of the House, James Cope, was forced to resign after a clash with Whitlam.

Most important in exposing the weakness of the Whitlam government was the series of scandals involving Deputy Prime Minister Cairns. Cairns was dismissed from the Treasury portfolio in June because of letters he had sent to a Melbourne businessman regarding huge overseas petrodollar loan negotiations. Later, in the House of Representatives, Cairns said that he had no recollection of a letter in which the businessman was offered a commission of 2.5% if loan negotiations were successful. Although a copy of the letter was subsequently produced, Cairns refused to resign from the Cabinet, saying that he had answered the question in Parliament in the sincere belief he was speaking the truth. Since Cairns did not intend to resign, Whitlam advised the governor-general to terminate his commission. Immediately Cairns protested that Whitlam had been arbitrary and unfair, and Fraser called for a judicial inquiry. Whitlam summoned a special sitting of Parliament to discuss the loan issue, but opposition members were not satisfied that all the evidence about the issue had been produced. Using his majority in the Senate, Fraser was able to summon 12 senior public servants and the solicitor general to the bar. The inquiry was unable to unearth any new evidence, as the witnesses all claimed crown privilege and declined to answer any questions. The leader of the opposition in the Senate claimed that the cloak of silence was positive proof that the government was terrified of having any inquiry into its loan-raising activities.

A constitutional crisis began on October 16 when Fraser announced his decision to defer the budget appropriation bills in the Senate in order to force Whitlam to hold a general election. The LCP had a fortuitous majority in the upper house because of the death of a Labor senator from Queensland and the decision of the Queensland prime minister to appoint a non-Labor replacement. The Labor Party had previously lost another Senate seat when Lionel Murphy was elevated to the High Court, and the New South Wales government decided to replace Murphy with a non-Labor senator.

The election was precipitated on November 11 when the governor-general, Sir John Kerr, sacked Prime Minister Whitlam, the first time the crown had dismissed an elected prime minister in 200 years. Kerr explained that he had been forced to remove Whitlam when there was a real prospect that the government would run out of money and that it was his duty as head of state to find a prime minister who could obtain "supply" (funds).

Kerr was able to get an assurance from Fraser that he could steer the budget through the Senate and thus end the crisis. Once this legislation passed, Fraser was sworn in as caretaker prime minister until the people chose a new government on December 13. The Labor Party described Fraser as "Kerr's cur" and claimed that it had been deposed by a coup d'etat. Efforts to keep the election focused on the constitutional issue failed, however, and when the public opinion polls showed strong support for the LCP many Labor men threw in the towel.

Darwin is slowly being rebuilt following the devastation wrought by Cyclone Tracy on Christmas Day 1974. Shown here are two views of the same row of stilt houses in Darwin.

PHOTOS, WIDE WORLD

AUSTRALIA

Education. (1973) Primary, secondary, and vocational, pupils 2,853,411, teachers 136,122; teacher training (third-level only), students 28,-524; higher (including 15 universities), students 116,033, teaching staff 12,026.

Finance. Monetary unit: Australian dollar, with (Sept. 22, 1975) a free rate of A$0.79 to U.S. $1 (A$1.64 = £1 sterling). Gold, SDRs, and foreign exchange: (June 1975) U.S. $4,428,-000,000; (June 1974) U.S. $4,974,000,000. Budget (1974–75 est.): revenue A$15,704,000,-000; expenditure A$16,274,000,000. Gross national product: (1973–74) A$50,140,000,000; (1972–73) A$41,160,000,000. Money supply: (March 1975) A$8,283,000,000; (March 1974) A$7,838,000,000. Cost of living (1970 = 100): (Jan.–March 1975) 155.9; (Jan.–March 1974) 132.6.

Foreign Trade. (1974) Imports A$8,640,900,-000; exports A$7,688,000,000. Import sources: U.S. 21%; Japan 18%; U.K. 14%; West Germany 7%. Export destinations: Japan 29%; U.S. 9%; New Zealand 7%; U.K. 6%. Main exports (1973–74): wool 17%; meat 12%; wheat 7%; iron ore 7%; coal 5%.

Transport and Communications. Roads (1972) 863,897 km. (including 208,198 km. paved roads). Motor vehicles in use (1973): passenger 4,596,400; commercial 1,050,200. Railways: (government; 1974) 40,349 km.; freight traffic (1973–74) 28,329,000,000 net ton-km. Air traffic (1973): 14,241,000,000 passenger-km.; freight 300.1 million net ton-km. Shipping (1974): merchant vessels 100 gross tons and over 394; gross tonnage 1,168,367. Shipping traffic (1974): goods loaded 161,241,000 metric tons, unloaded 29,787,000 metric tons. Telephones (June 1973) 4,659,000. Radio licenses (June 1974) 2,851,000. Television licenses (June 1974) 3,022,000.

Agriculture. Production (in 000; metric tons; 1974; 1973 in parentheses): wheat c. 11,500 (12,094); barley 2,500 (2,403); oats 940 (1,-111); sorghum 861 (942); corn 157 (188); rice 409 (316); potatoes 665 (693); sugar, raw value 2,850 (2,525); tomatoes c. 215 (c. 210); apples (1973) 435, (1972) 360; oranges (1973) c. 292, (1972) c. 351; wine (1973) c. 250, (1972) 286; wool, clean 400 (415); milk 7,406 (7,295); butter 175 (185); beef and veal 1,310 (1,438); mutton and lamb 457 (713). Livestock (in 000; March 1974): sheep 145,304; cattle c. 31,200; pigs 2,506; horses (1973) c. 450; chickens (1973) c. 30,000.

Industry. Fuel and power (in 000; metric tons; 1974): coal 63,608; lignite 27,270; crude oil 18,-957; natural gas (cu.m.) 4,675,000; manufactured gas (cu.m.) 8,935,000; electricity (kw-hr.) 72,771,000. Production (in 000; metric tons; 1974): iron ore (65% metal content) 96,687; bauxite 20,058; pig iron 7,250; crude steel 7,755; zinc 277; aluminum 219; copper 162; lead 192; tin 6.7; nickel concentrates (metal content; 1973) 36; sulfuric acid 2,431; cement 5,205; newsprint 195; cotton yarn 28; wool yarn 21; gold (troy oz.; 1973) 582; silver (troy oz.; 1973) 19,579; passenger cars (including assembly; units) 394; commercial vehicles (including assembly; units) 99. Dwelling units completed (1974) 150,000.

Bewildered by a result that reduced his party strength from 65 to 35, Whitlam said that he had suffered the usual fate of reforming governments in a recession. More colorfully, the federal president of the ALP, Robert J. Hawke (*see* BIOGRAPHY), said that the party had had its "guts ripped out."

Foreign Affairs. The major foreign policy problem for Australia in 1975 was caused by the revolution in Portuguese Timor. When the Portuguese government lost control of Portuguese Timor, a power struggle began between the radical Fretilin (Revolutionary Front for an Independent East Timor) and the Democratic Union of Timor. Donald R. Willesee, Australian minister for foreign affairs, indicated that Australia was in favour of self-determination by the Timorese, and Whitlam stated that Australia could not become militarily involved, except in response to a UN request to participate in a peacekeeping force. Timorese and Portuguese refugees were evacuated to Australia, and those who did not wish to proceed to Portugal were given permission to settle.

In December 1974 and January 1975 Whitlam traveled to Europe, visiting seven of the nine members of the European Economic Community (EEC). Whitlam justified his grand tour on the ground that there had been 15 years of neglect during which Australian prime ministers had avoided contact with Europe. Only a visit by a head of government, argued Whitlam, compelled the countries visited to clarify and coordinate their policies toward Australia. The EEC was Australia's second greatest trading partner, after Japan, and Whitlam hoped by his personal contact with the Community's leaders to put forward the Australian point of view fully and forcefully. Whitlam also visited Yugoslavia, a country he described as a founder and leader of the nonaligned world, and spent four days in the Soviet Union. In Leningrad and Moscow he laid wreaths at war memorial cemeteries. In a joint communiqué at the end of the visit, both Australia and the Soviet Union attached great importance to strengthening peace and stability in Asia; they also expressed their readiness to participate in seeking a solution to the problem of making the Indian Ocean an area of peace in accordance with the principles of international law.

The Whitlam government was embarrassed by the publication of secret cables and letters it had sent to Pres. Nguyen Van Thieu of South Vietnam and to the North Vietnamese foreign minister, Nguyen Duy Trinh, in an effort to spur peace negotiations. The opposition spokesman on foreign affairs, Andrew Peacock, was able to prove that there were substantial differences in the cables sent the same day to Saigon and Hanoi. The note to Thieu was curt and called upon him to adhere to the Paris peace agreements. The cable sent to Hanoi demonstrated a clear sympathy for the position of North Vietnam and the problems of the Provisional Revolutionary Government (PRG). The Australian government understood the sense of frustration that had given rise to renewed recourse to military pressure on Thieu and set out to reassure the North Vietnamese of its goodwill. Willesee subsequently announced on May 6 that Australia had decided to recognize the revolutionary government in South Vietnam. The Australian ambassador in Hanoi was authorized to inform the PRG representative in Hanoi of the decision and to discuss the question of diplomatic relations.

Relations with Papua New Guinea became strained on the eve of that country's independence. Willesee held discussions in Papua New Guinea with Papua New Guinea's ministers who were leading their country through its final stage to independence from Australia. Papua New Guinea was the largest recipient of Australian bilateral aid and was promised A$500 million for three years beginning in 1974. Willesee was determined that Australia's conduct would be

View of Canberra, Australia's capital city, as it appears today. Buildings in the foreground are a theatre centre and a government news and information complex. Black Mountain is in the distance.

CAMERA PRESS/PHOTO TRENDS

adjusted to reflect the status of Papua New Guinea and Australia as two sovereign states who were close and friendly neighbours. On the other hand, Michael Somare, Papua New Guinea's chief minister, accused Australia of economic mismanagement insofar as Whitlam refused to give a guarantee that Australia would maintain its level of aid over a five-year period following independence. Somare said that Whitlam was dumping Papua New Guinea and described Australian treasury officials as a bunch of arrogant, ignorant people. (*See* PAPUA NEW GUINEA.)

Australia's attitude toward the Palestine Liberation Organization (PLO) continued to cause concern both in domestic politics and in the United Nations. In January 1975 the government banned a visit to Australia by delegates from the PLO. When the United Nations had debated the Palestine question the Australian ambassador, Sir Laurence McIntyre, said that whatever reservations were entertained about the methods employed in asserting the right to self-determination, it was clear that there existed a new and vigorous spirit among the leaders of the displaced Arabs, a new confidence in their rights to self-determination and independence within a Palestinian state of their own. Nevertheless, Australia abstained from voting on the issues of Palestinian self-determination and PLO participation in the work of the UN General Assembly.

The Economy. Three treasurers guided the nation's finances in the fiscal year 1974–75, and to add to the confusion the prime minister made major policy initiatives in the economic field. Treasurer Frank Crean was dismissed in November 1974 after the prime minister refused to express his confidence in the way Crean had handled the portfolio. Crean's successor was James Cairns, the deputy prime minister and minister for overseas trade, who was himself removed on the eve of the scandal involving his staff and negotiations for overseas loans from Middle East oil barons. Cairns was succeeded by William Hayden.

In November 1974 the federal government had eased restrictions on foreign investment in Australian mining projects. The policy of 100% ownership was abandoned in favour of the policy of 100% control. Whitlam said that the government wanted maximum Australian ownership compatible with Australia's long-term capital requirements and its need for access to markets and advanced technology.

The Australian government also broadened the scope of foreign takeover legislation and closed existing loopholes. Under new laws the Australian government was able to examine all takeovers of Australian businesses by foreigners and to prohibit those that were against the national interest.

Unemployment continued to be a serious problem and led to reverses in the Labor Party's new economic policies. By July, 251,622 Australians were out of work. On a seasonally adjusted basis this represented 4.8% of the work force, a high percentage for a country where all major parties were committed to full employment.

In January the federal government approved a package deal to stimulate motor vehicle sales and save jobs in the industry. The sales tax on passenger vehicles was reduced, the special tax on company cars was abolished, and import quotas were imposed on light passenger vehicles. General Motors-Holden's had precipitated a crisis in December 1974 by announcing its intention to lay off 5,000 employees, and Chrysler and Ford were in comparable positions.

The export potential of beef and uranium to the EEC was of concern to the Australian government in 1975. Whitlam himself took up forcefully with European heads of government Australia's attitude to the EEC's action in imposing restrictions without warning or consultation. He pointed out that restrictions were disruptive and harmful to the Australian meat industry and tried to impress upon European leaders the need for stable long-term marketing arrangements. Whitlam was informed that the EEC would open its markets to Australian beef by mid-1976, and he was sure that the interest of the European countries in Australian uranium would make it less likely that restrictive action would be taken against Australian commodities in the future.

In May Australian workers began a three-month trial period of wage indexation (later made subject to further review), as part of a historic judgment given by the full bench of the Conciliation and Arbitration Commission. Under the judgment all wages in Australia were to be adjusted each quarter by a percentage change in the consumer price index. The intention of the commission was to preserve the real purchasing power of each worker's money wages as prices rose.

In August the treasurer, William Hayden, introduced the budget. Through a radical restructuring of the personal income tax system, the Labor Party hoped to begin a major redistribution of wealth in the community. The old method of deducting allowances to arrive at a taxable income was abolished. Instead, there was to be a new scale of seven tax steps, and deductions like education and life insurance were converted to rebates. Hayden also reduced the company tax by 2.5%, but the overall effect of the concessions was canceled out by increases in indirect taxation and levies on tobacco, beer, spirits, and gasoline. This budget was taken over by the LCP and used as the basis for government policy during the first six months of 1976. (A. R. G. GRIFFITHS)

See also Dependent States.

[977.B.2]

UPI COMPIX

The freighter "Macdili," crowded with refugees from Portuguese Timor, heads for Darwin following the outbreak of civil war on the island in August.

SPECIAL REPORT

AUSTRALIA'S DEFENSE REAPPRAISED

By Thomas B. Millar

AUSTRALIAN INFORMATION SERVICE

The Gallipoli veterans medallion.

During its 23 years in opposition (1949–72), the Australian Labor Party witnessed a series of national involvements in overseas conflicts: the Korean War, the Malayan emergency of the 1950s, the Vietnam war, and Indonesia's "confrontation" with Malaysia in the early '60s. Security treaties and arrangements relevant to these involvements had been negotiated, honoured, and matured. By December 1972, when Labor returned to power, Australia's international environment appeared more stable than it had been at any time since 1939.

It was this that enabled the Labor government, expressing its own ideological sympathies and beliefs, to wind down still further Australia's declining overseas military activities. The few advisers remaining in South Vietnam were withdrawn. Military aid to South Vietnam and Cambodia ceased. The infantry battalion stationed in Singapore as part of the ANZUK (Australia-New Zealand-U.K.) forces was brought home, although air squadrons in Malaysia—fulfilling a need that country could not meet—remained. Conscription for military service, introduced on a selective basis prior to the Vietnam war and reduced when the Australian forces returned in 1972, was abandoned.

Time for a Change. Whichever political party may have been in office, it was time for a reappraisal of Australia's defense requirements. All of Australia's involvements in Asian conflicts since 1941 had been in conjunction with one or both of its major allies, Britain and the United States. But Britain had largely withdrawn from the region, while the United States had removed its troops from Vietnam and seemed unlikely to bring such massive forces back to Southeast Asia in the foreseeable future. In an attempt to replace the assurance that ANZUK—and especially British—forces had provided, Malaysia had begun to promote the concept of a "zone of peace, freedom, and neutrality" in its region. China had become a member of the United Nations. The only discordant note was in the Indian Ocean, where Soviet naval vessels, more conspicuous than numerous, had begun to occupy strategic space previously the prerogative of Western powers.

Labor had supported the UN forces in Korea, opposed Australian operations in Malaya and Vietnam, and acquiesced in the Malaysian involvement. Traditionally it had been reluctant to send forces overseas to "other people's wars." It had never believed that China was a threat to the peace of Asia, let alone the integrity of Australia. It had welcomed the 1951 ANZUS (Australia-New Zealand-U.S.) Treaty as a guarantee of Australian security in the event of attack, but rejected the idea that Australia should therefore support U.S. policies in Asia as an insurance payment against future help. It had never accepted the concept that Australia could best be defended at a distance; *i.e.*, in Southeast Asia. It had tended to the conclusion that friendly political and economic relations with other nations were a strong deterrent to military conflict and, in some respects, a substitute for military preparedness.

Prior to his election as prime minister in 1972, Gough Whitlam had described SEATO (the Southeast Asia Treaty Organization, as distinct from the treaty) as "moribund." After taking office, his government moved with other members of the organization to shift its emphasis to less military, less ideologically oriented activities and toward eventual disbandment. In 1975 the decision was made to phase it out entirely.

Under the Liberal and Country Party government, one of the by-products of ANZUS had been the establishment in Australia of several U.S. military and scientific installations. For security reasons, the exact purpose of some of these had never been made public. In other cases, such as the communications station at North West Cape, the role of the facility was clear enough (to communicate with surface and submarine vessels including, where relevant, nuclear-powered submarines), but it was controlled entirely by the United States. The Labor government saw this as a derogation of sovereignty.

In 1974 the minister for defense, Lance Barnard, concluded negotiations to amend the 1963 agreement establishing the installation; henceforward, it was to be operated as a joint facility, with an Australian deputy commander and other Australian servicemen in various key positions. The existence and role of the North West Cape station had always carried the implication that it might draw a retaliatory attack in the event of nuclear war not of Australia's making. The amended agreement could not eliminate this risk, but Australia was assured of "full and timely information about strategic and operational developments relevant to the station and their significance for Australian national interests." It was also agreed that two U.S. monitoring facilities, at Amberley in Queensland and Alice Springs in central Australia, would be transferred to Australian management.

The withdrawal of Australian ground forces from Singapore changed the character of the five-power agreement under which they had been deployed. The rundown of the British component followed, although joint exercises were still held from time to time. The Australian government made it clear that the air units in Malaysia must also return to Australia. A small naval presence was being maintained in the area.

Looking Ahead. Shortly after taking office, Barnard asked his officials for an assessment of the strategic situation over the next 15 years. He reported to Parliament in August 1973: "We and our advisers do not at present foresee any deterioration in our strategic environment that would involve consideration of the commitment of our defence force to military operations to protect Australia's security or strategic interests." He later related this assessment to the coming decade, although he acknowledged the possibility of unforeseen changes toward the end of the period. These and other statements were widely interpreted as assuring Australians that they faced no threat for 10 to 15 years. This was an understandable if not entirely accurate interpretation, but even as given the statements contained a greater sense of optimism than of realism.

Barnard saw the favourable strategic prospect as allowing an opportunity to review, rationalize, prune, and take stock, to make savings, and to defer expenditure on new equipment wherever this could be done responsibly. He accordingly canceled (prior to the start of construction) a program that had been developed over several years to build sophisticated light destroyers in Australia; retired ahead of time the fleet transport HMAS "Sydney" and an old destroyer; and deferred construction of a fast combat-support (fleet replenishment) ship and the acquisition of new army tanks. Military and civilian manpower in the defense group of departments was reduced. Construction of the naval facility at Cockburn Sound, Western Australia, was extended by a further three years (to 1978). One of the Mirage interceptor-fighter squadrons of the Royal Australian Air Force

---

Thomas B. Millar is director of the Australian Institute of International Affairs and is a professorial fellow in international relations, the Australian National University, Canberra. His published works include Australia's Defence *(1965)*, The Commonwealth and the United Nations *(1967), and* Australia's Foreign Policy *(1968).*

was phased out. An improved retirement scheme for officers encouraged substantial numbers to leave the armed forces, whether or not that was intended by the legislation.

These reductions suited a government committed to massive new expenditures on social services, especially a national health scheme, and were compatible with the changed strategic environment—or at least with official Australian assessments of it. At the same time, the withdrawal of almost all Australian forces stationed overseas suggested to the government and the Defence Department that, for the first time since 1944, the primary purpose of the armed forces should be to defend the Australian continent *from* the Australian continent. Studies were commissioned to examine the most appropriate strategy, tactics, equipment, and distribution of defense establishments. As of 1975, many of these studies were still in progress.

Meanwhile, further changes in Australia's defense posture were signaled when Papua New Guinea—part Australian colony and part Australian-administered UN trust territory—became independent on Sept. 16, 1975. Papua New Guinea had been moving toward independence for several years, and this process was stimulated by the Labor government, which arranged for the transfer of defense and foreign relations to the Papua New Guinea government effective March 6, 1975.

Under the UN trusteeship agreement, Australia was responsible for the defense of New Guinea (the northern half of the territory, including the islands of New Britain, New Ireland, and copper-rich Bougainville). In defense, as in other government administration, however, the trust territory and the colony of Papua had long been treated as a single unit. Indigenous infantry forces had been raised during World War II and again after the war. From the early 1960s native officers and noncommissioned officers began to replace Australians, and a small naval patrol force was created.

Even after independence, Papua New Guinea remains heavily dependent on Australia, not only for economic assistance but for military expertise and logistics as well. Canberra made it clear to the Papua New Guinea government that Australian forces would not be available for internal security purposes. But the Australian government would be faced with difficult decisions if, as seemed likely, local independence movements asserted their autonomy against Port Moresby, especially in situations where national forces could only operate effectively with Australian logistic or technical help.

Reorganization. At different times the Australian defense system has been organized under one defense department and under separate service departments with a central coordinating defense department. Since 1959 the coordinating role of the Defence Department has grown in scope and authority. The Labor government took a further major step by abolishing the separate service departments with their individual ministers and splitting the Department of Supply between Defence and a new Department of Manufacturing and Industry.

A committee of inquiry report (the Tange Report) on reorganizing the whole defense system recommended, in essence, an expansion of the civilian element in the higher organization. This element would be given increased authority over all aspects of defense policy and administration; service input into the central organization would be increased; and the service chiefs, in effect, would be made commanders in chief of their respective arms, with a chief of defense force staff to command the defense force overall. Legislation introduced in mid-1975 to give effect to these proposals was adopted by both houses of Parliament after the failure of an attempt to refer it for scrutiny to the Senate Standing Committee on Foreign Affairs and Defence.

The government also decided to amalgamate the regular officer cadet colleges of the three services, at Jervis Bay, Duntroon, and Point Cook, into a single Australian Defence Force Academy. A "Development Council" was in the process of formulating appropriate proposals.

For more than a century the Australian federal and colonial armies relied on part-time volunteers for the bulk of their strength, with regulars providing the instructional and staff elements and a proportion of wartime leaders. A standing army with a regular combat force was created after World War II, but the part-time reserve, known as the Citizen Military Forces, remained to supplement the regular army in an emergency and to provide the basis for expansion during mobilization or war. The Royal Australian Navy and the Royal Australian Air Force also had small part-time reserves.

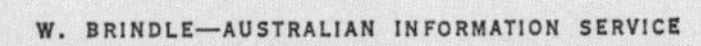
W. BRINDLE—AUSTRALIAN INFORMATION SERVICE

The 7th battalion, Royal Australian Regiment, marches through Sydney after returning from Vietnam.

In 1973 the Labor government appointed a committee of inquiry into the part-time Citizen Military Forces. Its report was issued the following year, and its recommendations were in the course of being implemented in 1975. The Forces were renamed the Australian Army Reserve, and while the Reserve retained its separate identity, it was being integrated with the regular army to a much greater degree than before. Units that were substantially understrength were being eliminated or amalgamated, while pay and some other aspects of service were brought into line with those of the regular army. The role of the Reserve was being amended to make it a reserve in fact as well as in name, available for call-up in national emergencies, including civil disasters. Its central administration was brought into a Reserve Branch at Army headquarters; formerly, it had been self-administered with regular army support.

Renewed Concern. While these changes were being carried forward, the Labor government's views on defense were affected by two dramatic events: the Middle East war of October 1973, together with the exercise of forceful oil politics by the Organization of Petroleum Exporting Countries (OPEC); and the collapse of non-Communist governments in Indochina. Within Australia, there were protests against the country's declining defense capacity, especially from retired senior officers.

In 1974 the government decided to replace some obsolete or obsolescing defense equipment, and in 1975 Barnard and his successor, William L. Morrison, announced the details. Australia would purchase two American patrol frigates (if the vessel went into production in the U.S.), eight Orion long-range maritime patrol aircraft, and 53 (later increased to 87) German Leopard tanks; a 6,000-ton logistic landing ship would be built; and the U.S. Rapier surface-to-air guided weapons system would be acquired for the Army. Other reequipment decisions were taken in principle. As an economy measure, and in the face of much public protest, the government decided to disband the 120-year-old Army cadet system.

Despite this apparent change in the mood of the government, the general defense capacity was barely being maintained. It would be several years before much of the new (and still limited) equipment became available. Meanwhile, many Australians, including some Labor supporters, were concerned that the instability of their region and/or international pressures of population on resources would pose a threat to their comfortable security in the not too distant future.

Austria

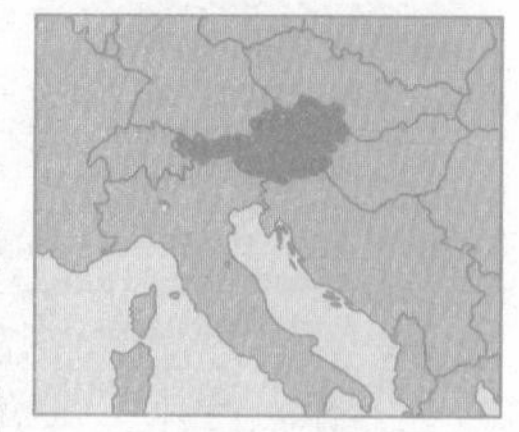

A republic of central Europe, Austria is bounded by West Germany, Czechoslovakia, Hungary, Yugoslavia, Italy, Switzerland, and Liechtenstein. Area: 32,375 sq.mi. (83,850 sq.km.). Pop. (1975 est.): 7,481,700. Cap. and largest city: Vienna (pop., 1971, 1,614,800). Language: German. Religion (1971): Roman Catholic 87%. President in 1975, Rudolf Kirchschläger; chancellor, Bruno Kreisky.

In a general election on Oct. 5, 1975, the Socialist Party of Austria (SPÖ) retained the absolute majority it had held since 1971. The distribution of seats in the National Assembly remained as before: SPÖ, 93 seats; Austrian People's Party (ÖVP), 80; and Austrian Freedom Party (FPÖ), 10. The Austrian Communist Party (KPÖ) and two splinter parties failed to gain seats. The SPÖ was thus assured of four more years in power.

The SPÖ's success was generally regarded as a personal victory for its leader, Bruno Kreisky, who remained chancellor. It also signified voter approval of the party's social reform program and economic measures to safeguard employment. The main opposition party, the ÖVP, suffered a grievous setback when its leader and chancellor-candidate, Karl Schleinzer, was killed in a car accident in July (*see* OBITUARIES). Schleinzer was succeeded by Josef Taus, a 42-year-old lawyer and bank director who, during the two months prior to the election, failed to make a sufficiently strong impression on the electorate. A bribery affair involving an ÖVP deputy also affected the party adversely. The FPÖ failed to achieve its objective of preventing either of the two main parties from obtaining an absolute majority.

During the year important legislation was introduced to complete the SPÖ's reform program. On January 1 the new penal law came into force. At the same time working hours were reduced from 42 to 40 a week, and at the end of the month Parliament approved a new law regulating the food industry. In April—in the face of considerable opposition—a complete reorganization of Austria's universities and high schools took effect. In July subsidization of the daily press was introduced as a means of ensuring democratic rights of expression for all shades of opinion. Also in July Parliament enacted the new family law according equal rights to husband and wife.

In January Otto Oberhammer was confirmed as head of the state broadcasting service (ORF), thus effectively ending controversy that had followed his appointment by ORF's governing body in October 1974. (In a special session of Parliament the opposition had attacked as politically unacceptable Oberhammer's proposals for personnel and other changes in the broadcasting services.)

Austria successfully pursued its policy of active neutrality. In November 1974 Chancellor Kreisky had submitted to the UN General Assembly proposals for a new "Marshall Plan" for concerted aid from the richer to the poorer nations of the world. In April

AUSTRIA

Education. (1973–74) Primary, pupils 984,213, teachers 50,718; secondary, pupils 165,650, teachers 11,040; vocational, pupils 168,514, teachers 3,533; teacher training, students 12,966, teachers 511; higher (including 6 universities), students 76,971, teaching staff 10,607.

Finance. Monetary unit: schilling, with (Sept. 22, 1975) a free rate of 18.75 schillings to U.S. $1 (38.85 schillings = £1 sterling). Gold, SDRs, and foreign exchange: (June 1975) U.S. $3,708,000,000; (June 1974) U.S. $2,558,000,000. Budget (1975 est.): revenue 168.1 billion schillings; expenditure 184.4 billion schillings. Gross national product: (1973) 546.3 billion schillings; (1972) 474.7 billion schillings. Money supply: (May 1975) 118,810,000,000 schillings; (May 1974) 105.4 billion schillings. Cost of living (1970 = 100): (May 1975) 141; (May 1974) 130.

Foreign Trade. (1974) Imports 168,280,000,000 schillings; exports 133,360,000,000 schillings. Import sources: EEC 62% (West Germany 40%, Italy 7%); Switzerland 7%. Export destinations: EEC 44% (West Germany 20%, Italy 10%, U.K. 6%); Switzerland 10%; Yugoslavia 5%. Main exports: machinery 19%; iron and steel 13%; textile yarns and fabrics 11%; timber 7%; chemicals 10%; paper and board 6%. Tourism (1973): visitors 10,215,000; gross receipts U.S. $2,252,000,000.

Transport and Communications. Roads (1973) *c.* 97,400 km. (including 600 km. expressways). Motor vehicles in use (1973): passenger 1,562,800; commercial 140,900. Railways: (1972) state 5,883 km., private 636 km.; traffic (1973) 6,725,000,000 passenger-km., freight 10,486,000,000 net ton-km. Air traffic (1974): 597.6 million passenger-km.; freight 8,280,000 net ton-km. Navigable inland waterways in regular use (1973) 358 km. Telephones (Dec. 1973) 1,841,000. Radio licenses (Dec. 1973) 2,157,000. Television licenses (Dec. 1973) 1,779,000.

Agriculture. Production (in 000; metric tons; 1974; 1973 in parentheses): wheat 1,102 (939); barley 1,238 (1,087); rye 415 (400); oats 290 (284); corn 857 (966); potatoes 1,997 (2,117); sugar, raw value *c.* 394 (*c.* 363); apples (1973) 287, (1972) 156; wine (1973) 240, (1972) 260; meat (1973) *c.* 485, (1972) 493; timber (cu.m.; 1973) 12,000, (1972) 12,500. Livestock (in 000; Dec. 1973): cattle 2,624; sheep 136; pigs 3,290; chickens (1972) 12,463.

Industry. Fuel and power (in 000; metric tons; 1974): lignite 3,641; crude oil 2,240; natural gas (cu.m.) 2,207,000; electricity (kw-hr.) 33,794,000 (61% hydroelectric in 1973); manufactured gas (cu.m.) 1,392,000. Production (in 000; metric tons; 1974): iron ore (30% metal content) 4,245; pig iron 3,444; crude steel 5,221; magnesite (1973) 1,414; aluminum 157; copper 27; lead 9; zinc 16; cement 6,435; paper (1973) 1,327; fertilizers (nutrient content; 1973–74) nitrogenous 231, phosphate 155; cotton yarn 20; woven cotton fabric 16; rayon, etc., filaments and fibres (1973) 100.

View of Heiligenblut, Austria, a typical alpine village nestled in a formerly glacier-filled valley.

LEPROHON—ATLAS PHOTO

1975 he was presented with the International Rescue Committee's Freedom Award in recognition of the part played by Austria in offering asylum to political refugees. Vienna was the scene of meetings between U.S. Secretary of State Henry Kissinger and Soviet Foreign Minister Andrey A. Gromyko and between U.S. Pres. Gerald Ford and Egyptian Pres. Anwar as-Sadat in May and June.

Relations with Czechoslovakia, which had been poor since the end of World War II, improved markedly with an agreement reached in December 1974 providing for compensation of Austrians for property lost in Czechoslovakia, and the way was cleared for a liberalization of trade, tourism, and other contacts between the two countries. The disagreement between Austria and Yugoslavia over the alleged discriminatory treatment by Austria of its Slovene minority continued in 1975. Austria took steps to improve contacts with the minority's representatives and announced a special census and the publication of a blue book on conditions among the Slovenes.

The Austrian economy experienced recession during 1974–75, though to a lesser degree than elsewhere in Europe. The Organization for Economic Cooperation and Development reported that for 1974 and the first half of 1975 Austria's growth rate was considerably above the group average, while its inflation and unemployment rates were considerably below the average. Tourism continued to bring in good returns. The government injected 12.5 billion schillings into the economy in a deficit spending program to combat recession and maintain employment.

(ELFRIEDE DIRNBACHER)

[972.B.2.a]

Bahamas, The

A member of the Commonwealth of Nations, The Bahamas comprise an archipelago of about 700 islands in the North Atlantic Ocean just southeast of the United States. Area: 5,382 sq.mi. (13,939 sq.km.). Pop. (1975 est.): 203,900. Cap. and largest city: Nassau (urban area pop., 1970, 101,500). Language: English (official). Religion (1970): Baptist 28.8%; Anglican 22.7%; Roman Catholic 22.5%; Methodist 7.3%; Saints of God and Church of God 6%; others and no religion 12.7%. Queen, Elizabeth II; governor-general in 1975, Sir Milo B. Butler; prime minister, Lynden O. Pindling.

With inflation at 13.5% and unemployment at 10% or more in early 1975, David Knowles, president of the Trades Union Congress, told the annual convention of the opposition Free National Movement in April that the unions would shift allegiance to the FNM from the ruling Progressive Liberal Party. The opposition denounced the recent purchase of three hotels for £8.7 million (to support flagging tourism) as intended to force socialism on The Bahamas.

In July Prime Minister Pindling announced Project Impact, a B$20 million development program to stimulate the economy and alleviate unemployment by concentrating on such labour-intensive industries as agriculture, fisheries, and low-cost housing projects. Other projects included a steel mill, extensions to oil transshipment facilities, a new oil refinery, and a petrochemical and plastics complex. Later he stated that the budget allocation for agriculture would be quadrupled. Fishing would benefit from legislation making more than 100,000 sq.mi. of international waters—including the most lucrative lobster areas—off limits to non-Bahamian fishermen from August 1. U.S. fishermen planned to take the matter to the International Court of Justice.

Tourism, which produced over 70% of the gross national product and 50% of revenue, suffered setbacks during 1974, with arrivals down 8.7%. The trend was reversed during the winter, but a small decrease was again noted by July 1975. Uncertainty in the banking sector diminished following government assurances of continuing tax haven protection.

Pindling again advocated a national program to mobilize Bahamian youth (nearly 60% of the population was under 25). He envisaged a National Cadet Corps for secondary-school boys and girls, with training in civic discipline skills. Young people in post-secondary education would continue to form the nucleus of a wider National Service welfare scheme.

(SHEILA PATTERSON)

[974.B.2.d]

BAHAMAS, THE

Education. (1971–72) Primary, pupils 34,097, teachers 751; secondary, pupils 20,648, teachers 500; vocational, pupils 427, teachers 60; teacher training, students 534, teachers 32; higher (at universities overseas; 1973–74), students 690.

Finance and Trade. Monetary unit: Bahamian dollar, with (Sept. 22, 1975) an official rate of B$1 to U.S. $1 (B$2.08 = £1 sterling). Budget (1973 est.): revenue B$109 million; expenditure B$107 million. Cost of living (1970 = 100): (Dec. 1974) 120; (Dec. 1973) 105. Foreign trade (1974): imports B$1,905,700,000; exports B$1,443,600,000. Import sources: Saudi Arabia 26%; Nigeria 17%; Iran 15%; U.S. 12%; Libya 8%; Gabon 5%; Canada 5%. Export destinations: U.S. 83%; Puerto Rico 8%. Main export petroleum products 91%. Tourism (1973): visitors 1,448,000; gross receipts U.S. $316 million.

Transport and Communications. Shipping (1974): merchant vessels 100 gross tons and over 129; gross tonnage 153,202. Telephones (Dec. 1973) 54,000. Radio receivers (Dec. 1973) 85,000. Television receivers (Dec. 1964) c. 4,500.

Bahrain

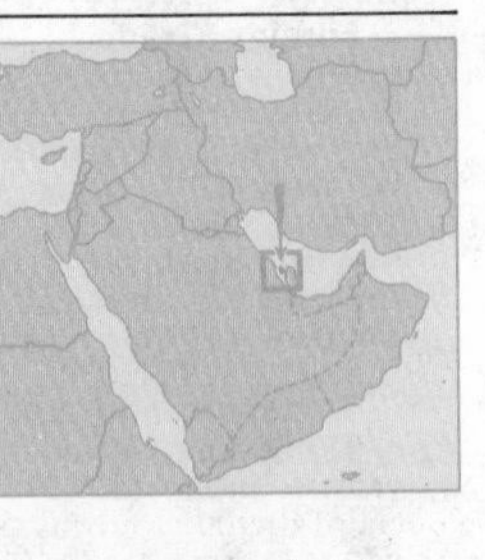

An independent monarchy (emirate), Bahrain consists of a group of islands in the Persian Gulf, lying between the Qatar Peninsula and Saudi Arabia. Total area: 256 sq.mi. (662 sq.km.). Pop. (1974 est.): 239,200. Cap.: Manama (pop., 1974 est., 98,300). Language: Arabic (official), Persian. Religion (1971): Muslim 95.7%; Christian 3%; others 1.3%. Emir in 1975, Isa ibn Sulman al-Khalifah; prime minister, Khalifah ibn Sulman al-Khalifah.

BAHRAIN

Education. (1974–75) Primary, pupils 43,409, teachers 2,126; secondary, pupils 15,949, teachers 682; vocational, pupils 1,599, teachers 70; higher, students 689, teaching staff 67.

Finance and Trade. Monetary unit: Bahrain dinar, with (Sept. 22, 1975) an official rate of 0.39 dinar to U.S. $1 (0.83 dinar = £1 sterling). Budget (1974–75 rev. est.): revenue 90 million dinars; expenditure 70 million dinars. Foreign trade (1974): imports 175,877,000 dinars; exports (excluding oil) 71,722,000 dinars. Import sources: U.S. 18%; U.K. 15%; Japan 13%; China 6%; West Germany 5%. Export destinations: Japan 35%; Saudi Arabia 31%; Dubai 5%. Main exports: crude oil and petroleum products; aluminum (44% of nonoil exports).

Industry. Production (in 000; metric tons): crude oil (1974) 3,369; petroleum products (1973) 11,841.

Automobile Industry: *see* Industrial Review; Transportation

Automobile Racing: *see* Motor Sports

Aviation: *see* Defense; Transportation

Backgammon: *see* Board Games

Badminton: *see* Court Games

MARVINE HOWE—THE NEW YORK TIMES

Harbour of Manama, Bahrain, where a large inter-Arab dry-dock complex is under construction. When completed, the facilities will provide service for the giant supertankers that pass through the Persian Gulf.

Bahrain's brief experience of a form of parliamentary democracy was temporarily halted in 1975 when the emir, on August 26, dissolved the 44-man National Assembly and suspended a constitutional provision that would have required new elections to be held within two months. The new measures were suggested to the emir by his brother, Prime Minister Khalifah ibn Sulman al-Khalifah, who resigned on August 24 saying that the National Assembly had consistently thwarted his government's legislative and development programs. Khalifah formed a new government on August 25. About half the dissolved National Assembly had formed a radical nationalist opposition bloc.

In April the emir signed a comprehensive trade and economic agreement with Saudi Arabia, and the two countries held joint military exercises in June. Trade and industry progressed during 1975 despite a small decline in oil production. Exports, which had increased by 125% in 1974 over 1973, continued their upward trend; this occurred largely because of increased aluminum sales from the ALBA complex, for which Japan replaced the U.S. as the main customer. Imports rose 37% from 1973 to 1974, with the U.S. increasing its share and replacing Britain as the nation's chief supplier. Despite some protests from the National Assembly members, the government allowed the U.S. Navy continued use of the Jufair servicing base, for which the rent was increased in 1975 by 600%. A government report in August warned against Bahrain's "explosive" birthrate, which would double the country's population by 1992.

(PETER MANSFIELD)

[978.B.4.b]

Bangladesh

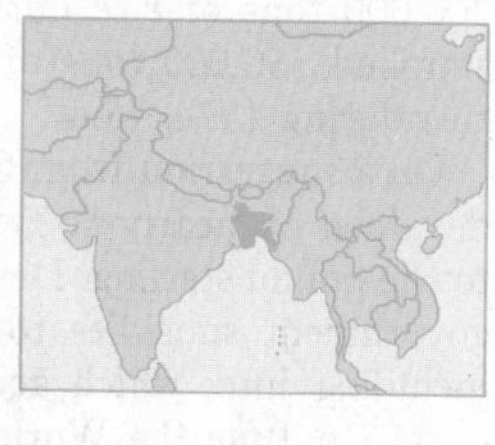

An independent republic and member of the Commonwealth of Nations, Bangladesh is bordered by India on the west, north, and east, by Burma in the southeast, and by the Bay of Bengal in the south. Area: 55,126 sq.mi. (147,776 sq.km.). Pop. (1974 est.): 74,990,800. Cap. and largest city: Dacca (pop., 1974, 1,311,000). Language: Bengali. Religion: Muslim 80%, with Hindu, Christian, and Buddhist minorities. Presidents in 1975, Mohammadullah until January 25, Sheikh Mujibur Rahman until August 15, Khandakar Mushtaque Ahmed until November 6, and, from November 6, Abu Sadat Mohammed Sayem; prime ministers, Sheikh Mujibur Rahman until January 26 and Mohammed Mansoor Ali until August 15.

The killing of Pres. Sheikh Mujibur Rahman (*see* OBITUARIES) and his close family members by army officers on Aug. 15, 1975, and his replacement by Khandakar Mushtaque Ahmed (*see* BIOGRAPHY) came as a rude shock to the long-suffering people of Bangladesh. The sheikh, "father of the nation," had rapidly been losing his charismatic hold on the Bengalis as

BANGLADESH

Education. Primary (1973–74), pupils *c.* 7,750,000, teachers 155,023; secondary (1973–74), pupils 1,955,200, teachers 80,500; vocational (1972), pupils *c.* 176,000; higher (1969), students 117,603, teaching staff 7,201.

Finance. Monetary unit: taka, with (Sept. 22, 1975) a free rate of 14.48 taka to U.S. $1 (official rate of 30 taka = £1 sterling). Foreign exchange (March 1974 est.) U.S. $95 million. Budget (1974–75 est.): revenue 5,594,000,000 taka; expenditure 4,702,000,000 taka (development budget 5,250,000,000 taka). Cost of living (Dacca; 1970 = 100): (July 1974) 314; (July 1973) 211.

Foreign Trade. (1973–74) Imports 5,013,000,000 taka; exports 2,769,000,000 taka. Import sources (1973): India *c.* 25%; U.S. *c.* 18%; Japan *c.* 10%; West Germany *c.* 10%; Canada *c.* 8%; U.K. 7%. Export destinations (1973): U.S. *c.* 29%; U.K. *c.* 15%; Italy *c.* 7%; West Germany *c.* 6%; Belgium-Luxembourg *c.* 6%; Argentina *c.* 5%; France *c.* 5%. Main exports: jute products 55%; jute 33%.

Transport and Communications. Roads (1973) *c.* 24,000 km. (excluding *c.* 150,000 km. dirt roads). Motor vehicles in use (1972): passenger 66,700; commercial (including buses) 23,300. Railways: (1973) 2,874 km.; traffic (1972–73) 2,815,000,000 passenger-km.; freight 891 million net ton-km. Navigable waterways (1973) *c.* 8,000 km. Shipping (1974): merchant vessels 100 gross tons and over 98; gross tonnage 115,612. Shipping traffic (1972): goods loaded 275,000 metric tons, unloaded 2,141,000 metric tons. Telephones (Dec. 1972) 48,000. Radio licenses (March 1969) 531,000.

Agriculture. Production (in 000; metric tons; 1974; 1973 in parentheses): rice 17,527 (19,356); potatoes 731 (759); sweet potatoes (1973) 691, (1972) 747; onions 149 (156); jute *c.* 800 (*c.* 1,080); tea 31 (28); bananas (1973) *c.* 600, (1972) 586; tobacco 42 (40); timber (cu.m.; 1973) 10,700, (1972) 10,700; fish catch (1970) 247, (1969) 277. Livestock (in 000; 1974): horses *c.* 45; cattle *c.* 26,698; buffalo *c.* 650; sheep *c.* 728; goats (1973) *c.* 11,500; chickens *c.* 29,000.

Industry. Production (in 000; metric tons; 1973–74): cement 52; petroleum products 328; salt (1968–69) 432; crude steel 73; nitrogenous fertilizers (plant nutrient content) 129; jute fabrics 508; cotton yarn 37; paper 52; electricity (kw-hr.; 1973) 1.2 million.

Balance of Payments: *see* Economy, World

Ballet: *see* Dance

Ballooning: *see* Aerial Sports

PHOTOS, WIDE WORLD

Armoured units move into central Dacca, August 15, following a military coup in which Sheikh Mujibur Rahman was killed. The new president of Bangladesh, Khandakar Mushtaque Ahmed (below), was in turn forced to resign in November after a second governmental upheaval.

the infant nation continued to reel under the blows of a disintegrating economy, famine conditions, and corruption. Bangladesh had remained a sick nation under the sheikh despite massive doses of foreign aid and generous provision with experts and goods from such friendly countries as India and Japan.

President Ahmed, trade and commerce minister under the sheikh, told a bereaved nation that the coup had been necessitated by the "rampant favouritism and corruption" of the old government. He announced a Cabinet drawn mostly from the sheikh's government. He dismissed some bureaucrats of the former regime who were known to have opposed the Army's efforts to eliminate corruption. A number of close associates of the sheikh were arrested, including former prime minister Mansoor Ali. The one-party rule imposed on the country by the sheikh in January 1975 was ended, but freedom to form political parties was withheld. Some newspapers closed by the former government were allowed to reappear but under strict censorship.

On November 6 Ahmed was forced to resign in a power struggle with the top command of the Army that apparently began with the killing, on November 3, of four imprisoned officials of Sheikh Mujibur's regime, including former prime ministers Tajuddin Ahmed and Mansoor Ali. After three days of tense maneuvering, Ahmed resigned and was succeeded by the chief justice of the Supreme Court, Abu Sadat Mohammed Sayem, who dissolved Parliament and the Council of Ministers and promised to hold elections by February 1977. Sayem was to be assisted by a three-man council composed of the Army chief, Maj. Gen. Ziaur Rahman, Navy Commodore Mosharoff Hossain, and Air Vice-Marshal G. M. Tawab. In a radio address on November 7, Ahmed promised to support the Sayem government.

Sheikh Mujibur, in the nine months before his death, had kept the country under his personal control. He had declared a state of emergency in December 1974 and made himself president under an amended constitution on January 25. Launching what he called the "second revolution," he said that he hoped to demolish the "old and rotten colonial system and usher in a new era to bring good to the exploited millions." In February he announced a one-party structure by setting up the Bangladesh Krishak Sramik Awami League (Baksal), declaring that the parliamentary system was inadequate to deal with economic offenders and terrorists. Baksal was dominated by elements of the old Awami League founded by the sheikh in 1949, causing activists of other defunct parties to become hostile to the regime. The sheikh also did away with press freedom by bringing all mass media under state control, including four permitted newspapers.

The Bangladesh economy had been a tale of woe since the establishment of the republic in December 1971. The floods of 1974 were so disastrous to food crops that the government did not expect famine conditions to be removed before early 1976 and therefore sought 600,000 tons in food aid at the World Food Council in Rome in June 1975. The U.S. announced plans to give Bangladesh 800,000 tons of wheat and 200,000 tons of rice during 1975–76; it had already supplied 550,000 tons of wheat and 300,000 tons of rice during 1974–75.

On a suggestion from the World Bank the taka was devalued by nearly 60% in May and fixed at 30 taka to the pound sterling. Devaluation was forced by huge government subsidies to producers of export items, including jute, which accounted for 80% of the exports. In June the World Bank recommended to the Bangladesh Aid Consortium a total of $1.2 billion as aid for 1975–76, 80% of it in goods and food. An estimated $800 million was needed to finance imports for 1975–76. China recognized Bangladesh in October. (GOVINDAN UNNY)

[976.A.3.b]

Banking:
see Economy, World

Baptist Churches:
see Religion

Barbados

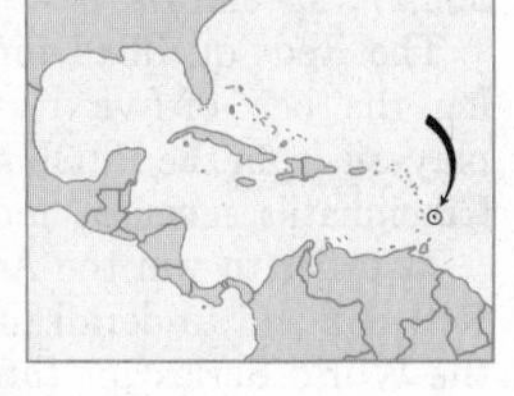

The parliamentary state of Barbados is a member of the Commonwealth of Nations and occupies the most easterly island in the southern Caribbean Sea. Area: 166 sq.mi. (430 sq.km.). Pop. (1975 est.): 251,200; 91% Negro, 4% white, 4% mixed. Cap. and largest city: Bridgetown (pop., 1970, 8,900). Language: English. Religion: Anglican 53%; Methodist 9%; Roman Catholic 4%; Moravian 2%; others 32%. Queen, Elizabeth II; governor-general in 1975, Sir Winston Scott; prime minister, Errol Walton Barrow.

In 1975 Barbados, with other independent Caribbean territories, resumed diplomatic relations with Cuba. On July 4 Caribbean Community Day was celebrated. During its two years of life, the Caribbean Community and Common Market (Caricom) had shown progress in intraregional trade, interchange of information, and fiscal and legal harmonization and in the successful conclusion of the Lomé, Togo, agreement in February with the European Economic Community. Prime Minister Barrow continued his longtime rejection of Trinidad and Tobago's claims that Trinidad-based British West Indian Airways (BWIA) should be the regional carrier for servicing the international route rights of the independent territories.

In 1975 the Barbados economy continued under pressure, with unemployment at 10%. But in May the prime minister spoke of recovery; the Barbados dollar was to have future parity fixed with the U.S. dollar rather than the pound sterling; Bar$14 million would be injected into the economy, with Bar$10 million for mortgage and housing construction and the rest for agriculture; 1974 growth of imports (29%) and exports (66%) was three times the rate of 1973, and 1975 was expected to be another year with an overall balance of payments surplus, through increased receipts from sugar exports (Bar$60 million or 100% above 1974). Barrow proposed to raise funds for his Bar$14 million injection by an additional levy on sales of sugar abroad. The Barbados Sugar Producers' Association claimed that sugar production had declined and the sugar industry itself needed a massive injection of capital. (SHEILA PATTERSON)

[974.B.2.d]

BARBADOS

Education. (1972–73) Primary, pupils 43,246, teachers 960; secondary, pupils 24,640, teachers 1,020; vocational (1971–72), pupils 1,381, teachers 80; higher (1973–74), students 942, teaching staff (1972–73) 75.

Finance and Trade. Monetary unit: Barbados dollar, with (Sept. 22, 1975) an official rate of Bar$2 to U.S. $1 (free rate of Bar$4.17 = £1 sterling). Budget (1974–75 est.): revenue Bar$146.7 million; expenditure Bar$162.5 million. Cost of living (1970 = 100): (May 1975) 228; (May 1974) 190. Foreign trade (1974): imports Bar$416,740,000; exports Bar$172,150,000. Import sources: U.K. 21%; U.S. 19%; Trinidad and Tobago 12%; Venezuela 10%; Canada 9%. Export destinations: U.K. 26%; U.S. 16%; Windward Islands 7%; Trinidad and Tobago 6%; Canada 6%. Main exports: sugar 30%; chemicals (1973) 7%; clothing (1973) 6%; rum (1973) 5%. Tourism (1973): visitors 222,000; gross receipts U.S. $70 million.

Agriculture. Production (in 000; metric tons): sweet potatoes (1973) *c.* 19, (1972) *c.* 19; sugar, raw value (1974) *c.* 112, (1973) *c.* 122.

Baseball

Baseball, America's national pastime, passed more time than usual in 1975. Not until October 22 did the World Series finish, but most observers agreed that waiting out the rain-delayed event was worthwhile. The Cincinnati Reds defeated the Boston Red Sox four games to three in a contest that many observers termed one of the most exciting in history. The 162-game regular season was more quiet, but did feature the advent of some outstanding new personalities, the passing of some familiar ones, and considerable change in the balance of power among the 24 major league franchises. All of this helped create a generally healthy situation for the sport during difficult economic times, which affected other professional athletics to a more serious degree.

World Series. The Cincinnati Reds claimed their first world championship in 35 years by downing the Red Sox 4–3 in Boston on the evening of October 22. The Red Sox leaped to a 3–0 lead, but the Reds rallied and won it in the ninth inning on a bloop single by second baseman Joe Morgan (*see* BIOGRAPHY).

The Red Sox, decided underdogs in the Series, had won the opening game at home October 11 by a 6–0 score on a six-run seventh inning. Luis Tiant (*see* BIOGRAPHY) allowed just five hits in his first World Series appearance. The Reds were in danger of losing a second straight game October 12, but they rallied for two ninth-inning runs in Boston to win 3–2. Bill Lee, a colourful left-hander whose eccentric ways earned him the nickname "Spaceman," carried a 2–1 lead into the last inning for the Red Sox, but Cincinnati catcher Johnny Bench started the rally with an opposite field double, advanced to third on a hit by Tony Pérez, and then tied the score on Dave Concepción's single. Ken Griffey's double sent Concepción home from second base with the winning run.

In Cincinnati, the Reds recorded a ten-inning 6–5 triumph October 14 to assume a 2–1 lead in games. This contest was shrouded in controversy, because after Boston rallied from a 5–1 deficit to tie matters 5–5, the Reds gained their victory on a disputed play. César Gerónimo opened the tenth inning for Cincinnati with a single. Ed Armbrister, a pinch hitter, followed with a bunt. On the play, Boston catcher Carlton Fisk collided with Armbrister in front of the plate and threw wildly to second base. Gerónimo advanced

Milt May of the Houston Astros hits a home run against the San Francisco Giants on May 4, driving in teammate Bob Watson to score the one millionth major league run.

WIDE WORLD

to third and then scored on Morgan's subsequent game-winning single.

Fisk and the Red Sox argued loudly with plate umpire Larry Barnett that Armbrister had been guilty of interference with Fisk, and that the batter should have been called out while the runner (Gerónimo) returned to first. Barnett disagreed, claiming there was no intent to interfere with the catcher on Armbrister's part, but one rule, thought by some to be relevant in this case, indicated that the question of intent was immaterial.

In the fourth game Tiant threw an exhausting 163 pitches but prevailed to beat the Reds in Cincinnati 5–4 on October 15, evening the Series again at 2–2. The Red Sox trailed 2–0 but scored five runs in the fourth inning, with the key hit a triple by Dwight Evans.

Pérez, one of Cincinnati's best clutch hitters, snapped an 0-for-15 slump in the fifth game at the Reds' Riverfront Stadium. He became the first National League player in 15 years to hit two home runs in the same World Series game, and Cincinnati whipped Boston 6–2 behind the pitching of Don Gullett, the loser in the opening game.

With the Reds leading 3–2 in games, the Series returned to Boston, where persistent rain caused three postponements of the sixth game. Finally, the inclement weather subsided on October 21, and the teams engaged in a four-hour contest replete with defensive excellence, clutch hits, and high drama. The Red Sox won 7–6 on Fisk's leadoff homer in the 12th inning to tie the series 3–3. After Cincinnati had taken a 6–3 lead, Boston tied the game 6–6 in the eighth inning on a three-run pinch homer by Bernie Carbo, a former Cincinnati player. The Red Sox then loaded the bases with none out in the ninth, and failed to score. But Fisk's blast in the 12th ignited night-long celebrations throughout Fenway Park and the city of Boston.

The Reds, however, touched off a wild celebration back in their hometown by winning the Series the next night. Manager Sparky Anderson, criticized for holding Gullett until the seventh game, got only four innings from his ace. But Cincinnati relief pitchers held the Red Sox to one hit and no runs over the next five innings. Pete Rose (*see* BIOGRAPHY), who converted from an outfielder to a third baseman early in the regular season, had 10 hits in 27 at bats during the Series for a .370 average. He was named most valuable player for the tournament, which attracted 308,272 spectators.

The Reds qualified for the World Series by sweeping the best-of-five National League championship play-off from the Pittsburgh Pirates. The pennant was Cincinnati's seventh, and third since 1970.

In order to win the American League pennant, the Red Sox had to derail the Oakland A's, who had won the World Series for three consecutive years. Boston did it decisively, upsetting the A's in three straight games for their first pennant since 1967. After the series, A's owner Charles Finley fired manager Alvin Dark, who had piloted the team to World Series titles in 1973 and 1974.

Regular Season. Races in the major leagues' four divisions were not as taut as in previous seasons. In the National League West, the Reds amassed 108 victories against just 54 losses to win by 20 games over the Los Angeles Dodgers, who had won the pennant in 1974. The National League East was closer, with the Pirates prevailing by 6½ games over the young Philadelphia Phillies, who welcomed back their recalcitrant slugger, Dick Allen.

The A's achieved their fifth straight American League West title by seven games over the Kansas City Royals, despite the absence of Jim ("Catfish") Hunter, Oakland's onetime leading pitcher who was declared a free agent in December 1974, after a salary dispute with Finley. Hunter joined the New York Yankees for approximately $3 million and enjoyed a 23-victory season, but his team finished a distant third in the American League East. Boston won the division by 4½ games over the Baltimore Orioles, who were picked to repeat as champions but never recovered from a slow start.

Mike Schmidt of the Philadelphia Phillies led the major leagues in home runs for the second straight season with 38. Oakland's Reggie Jackson and Milwaukee's George Scott tied for the American League title with 36. Minnesota's Rod Carew batted .360 to lead the major leagues for the third straight season and the American League for a fourth time. Only Ty Cobb (nine), Rogers Hornsby (six), and Honus Wagner (four) had equaled that accomplishment. Bill Madlock, third baseman for the Chicago Cubs, batted .354 for the National League crown.

Jim Palmer of the Baltimore Orioles returned from an arm injury to win 23 games and lead the American

Controversial collision at home plate (left) between Ed Armbrister of the Cincinnati Reds and Boston catcher Carlton Fisk in the 10th inning of game four of the World Series. The umpire ruled the collision unintentional and the Reds went on to win. Another dramatic moment in the Series occurred in game six (right), which was won by Fisk's deciding home run in the bottom of the 12th inning.

UPI COMPIX

WIDE WORLD

Final Major League Standings, 1975

American League

East Division

Club	W.	L.	Pct.	G.B.	Bos.	Balt.	N.Y.	Clev.	Mil.	Det.	Cal.	Chi.	K.C.	Minn.	Oak.	Tex.
Boston	95	65	.594	—	—	9	11	7	10	13	6	8	7	10	6	8
Baltimore	90	69	.566	4½	9	—	8	10	14	12	6	7	7	6	4	7
New York	83	77	.519	12	5	10	—	9	9	12	5	6	5	8	6	8
Cleveland	79	80	.497	15½	11	8	9	—	9	12	9	5	6	3	2	5
Milwaukee	68	94	.420	28	8	4	9	9	—	11	5	4	5	2	5	6
Detroit	57	102	.358	37½	5	4	6	6	7	—	5	7	6	4	6	1

West Division

Club	W.	L.	Pct.	G.B.	Oak.	K.C.	Tex.	Minn.	Chi.	Cal.	Balt.	Bos.	Clev.	Det.	Mil.	N.Y.
Oakland	98	64	.605	—	—	11	12	12	9	11	8	6	10	6	7	6
Kansas City	91	71	.562	7	7	—	14	11	9	14	5	5	6	6	7	7
Texas	79	83	.488	19	6	4	—	10	13	9	5	4	7	11	6	4
Minnesota	76	83	.478	20½	6	7	8	—	9	10	6	2	6	8	10	4
Chicago	75	86	.466	22½	9	9	5	9	—	9	4	4	7	5	8	6
California	72	89	.447	25½	7	4	9	8	9	—	6	6	3	6	7	7

National League

East Division

Club	W.	L.	Pct.	G.B.	Pitt.	Phil.	N.Y.	St.L.	Chi.	Mon.	Atl.	Cin.	Hou.	L.A.	S.D.	S.F.
Pittsburgh	92	69	.571	—	—	7	13	10	12	11	8	6	5	7	8	5
Philadelphia	86	76	.531	6½	11	—	11	10	6	11	7	5	6	5	7	7
New York	82	80	.506	10½	5	7	—	9	11	8	8	4	8	6	8	8
St. Louis	82	80	.506	10½	8	8	9	—	7	7	9	4	8	7	8	7
Chicago	75	87	.463	17½	6	12	7	11	—	9	7	1	7	5	5	5
Montreal	75	87	.463	17½	7	7	10	11	9	—	4	4	4	7	7	5

West Division

Club	W.	L.	Pct.	G.B.	Cin.	L.A.	S.F.	S.D.	Atl.	Hou.	Chi.	Mon.	N.Y.	Phil.	Pitt.	St.L.
Cincinnati	108	54	.667	—	—	8	13	11	15	13	11	8	8	7	6	8
Los Angeles	88	74	.543	20	10	—	10	11	10	12	7	5	6	7	5	5
San Francisco	80	81	.497	27½	5	8	—	10	9	13	7	7	4	5	7	5
San Diego	71	91	.438	37	7	7	8	—	11	9	7	5	4	5	4	4
Atlanta	67	94	.416	40½	3	8	8	7	—	12	5	8	4	5	4	3
Houston	64	97	.398	43½	5	6	5	9	6	—	5	8	4	6	6	4

League with a 2.09 earned run average. Other 20 game winners were Oriole Mike Torrez, Jim Kaat of the Chicago White Sox, Vida Blue of the A's, Randy Jones of the San Diego Padres, Tom Seaver (*see* BIOGRAPHY) of the New York Mets, and Hunter.

There were three no-hitters pitched during the 1975 season, one of unconventional nature. California Angel Nolan Ryan (*see* BIOGRAPHY) tossed his fourth June 1 when he beat Baltimore 1–0, and Ed Halicki of the San Francisco Giants achieved his first August 24 when he downed the New York Mets 6–0. But the most unusual no-hitter in baseball history occurred on September 28, when four Oakland pitchers combined to beat the Angels 5–0. The pitchers were Blue, Glenn Abbott, Paul Lindblad, and Rollie Fingers.

The National League won the 46th All-Star Game 6–3 at Milwaukee July 15, the Nationals' 12th win in 13 tries and 27th overall against 18 losses.

Fred Lynn, outfielder for the Boston Red Sox, became the first player in major league history to be named rookie of the year and most valuable player in the same year. The other top American League honour, the Cy Young award for the outstanding pitcher, went to Baltimore's Jim Palmer. In the National League the most valuable player was Cincinnati's Joe Morgan, and Joe Montefusco, a pitcher for the San Francisco Giants, was rookie of the year. Seaver won the Cy Young award for the third time, an achievement shared only by Sandy Koufax.

Five men were inducted into baseball's Hall of Fame at Cooperstown, N.Y. They were: Ralph Kiner, a slugger with the Pittsburgh Pirates; Billy Herman, a second baseman for the Cubs and Brooklyn Dodgers; outfielder Earl Averill of the Cleveland Indians; William (Judy) Johnson of the old Negro leagues; and Bucky Harris, a second baseman turned manager.

An arbitration panel ruled that pitchers Andy Messersmith of Los Angeles and Dave McNally of Montreal were free agents after playing a year under contracts renewed without their consent. Baseball officials planned a court appeal of the ruling, which would permit baseball players—like football players—to become free agents by playing out their option. Bill Veeck, whose showman-like tactics had startled baseball in the '40s and '50s, returned as an owner by buying the White Sox. Casey Stengel, who managed the New York Yankees to five straight world championships, died at 85 (*see* OBITUARIES).

Latin America. The winter league season of about 60 games takes place in Puerto Rico, Mexico, the Dominican Republic, and Venezuela. A player is eligible if he does not have more than four years' experience in the major leagues or if he has not batted 250 times or pitched 100 innings during the previous summer. Natives of Latin America have no limitation on their eligibility provided they play in the country where they were born.

In 1975, the Bayamón Vaqueros team from Puerto Rico captured the Caribbean championship. Bayamón won the title in the six-team Puerto Rican league, then triumphed in an elimination tournament over the other champions: the Águilas, Cibaeñas of the four-team Dominican Winter League, the Aragua Tigres of the six-team Venezuelan Winter League, and the Hermosillo Naranjeros of the seven-team Mexican Winter League.

(ROBERT WILLIAM VERDI)

Japan. The Hankyu Braves of Nishinomiya won the Japan Series, the Japanese version of the World Series, four games to two draws, over the Toyo Carp of Hiroshima. It was the first time that the Braves had captured the championship, though they had played in the Series five times since 1967. Contributing especially to the Braves' victory was rookie Takashi Yamaguchi, who pitched in the last four games. Also notable were pitcher Hisashi Yamada; catcher Shinji Nakazawa, whose batting was outstanding; and centre fielder Yutaka Fukumoto, who displayed fine fielding. For the first time in the 26 years since the team was founded, the Toyo Carp won the pennant of the Central League. In the Pacific League the Braves gained the championship by defeating the Kintetsu Buffaloes of Osaka, 4–1, in a best-of-five play-off series.

The success story of the Carp may be described as the Japanese version of the New York Mets, a case of achieving a miraculous victory after years in the cellar. Much credit was given to the 39-year-old newly appointed manager Takeshi Koba, who successfully organized the team despite a lack of star players. The prestigious Yomiuri Giants of Tokyo, who had won nine consecutive Central League titles from 1965 to 1973, fell to the bottom of the standings.

Koji Yamamoto of the Carp was chosen as the Central League's most valuable player, and Koichi Tabuchi of the Hanshin Tigers of Osaka won the home-run title for the first time in his seven-year career with a total of 43. Yamamoto was the league's leading hitter with an average of .319, while Sadaharu Oh of the Giants, winner of the league's triple crown in batting (average, home runs, and runs batted in) in 1973 and 1974 and the home-run king for 13 straight years, could only gain the runs-batted-in crown with 96.

The Pacific League's most valuable player was Hideji Kato of the Braves. Masahiro Doi of the Taiheiyo Club Lions of Fukuoka captured the home-run title with 34. Jinten Haku of the Lions was the leading hitter with .319, while Kato had the most runs batted in with 97. (RYUSAKU HASEGAWA)

[452.B.4.h.iii]

Basketball

United States. *Professional.* The Golden State Warriors delivered one surprise after another as they battled to the top of the National Basketball Association with only one proven star and a largely unknown supporting cast. Their final victims were the powerful Washington Bullets, who were expected by many observers to sweep the championship series in four straight games. Instead, the Warriors did the sweeping and wrote a fitting climax to a season that began with them expected to do little more than play out their schedule.

Golden State's linchpin was Rick Barry (*see* BIOGRAPHY), a multitalented forward who earned a reputation as a nomad in previous years by jumping from the NBA to the rival American Basketball Association, and then back to the NBA. Only rookie forward Keith Wilkes consistently complemented Barry's play during the regular season, which saw the unpredictable Warriors win the Pacific Division thanks to the collapse of the Los Angeles Lakers. But the play-offs summoned unexpected brilliance from guards Phil Smith and Charles Dudley, centres Clifford Ray and George Johnson, and forward Derrek Dickey. The Warriors overpowered Seattle and outmuscled Chicago, the NBA's most physical team, to win the Western Conference and enter the championship series.

Washington came into the finals with its well-advertised talent—Elvin Hayes, Wes Unseld, Phil Chenier —but with some problems as well. The Bullets were tired from two grueling series, that against Buffalo and against defending NBA champion Boston, which they needed to capture the Eastern Conference. More important, age and injury had cut into their already thin line of reserves.

Nevertheless, Washington was the overwhelming favourite in the finals, and Golden State altered opinion only slightly by winning the first game, 101 to 95. But when Washington missed two shots in the closing seconds of game two and lost, 92 to 91, the Warriors suddenly looked more formidable. Urged on by Coach Al Attles, a volatile former Warrior guard, Golden State never let up. Although the Warriors won the last two games by a total of just nine points, it was good enough to secure the NBA title.

Pete Trgovich (25) outmaneuvers Ross Kindel (20) in NCAA basketball championship on March 31 as UCLA defeated Kentucky 92–85.

WIDE WORLD

Major College Champions, 1975

League	Team and location
Eastern (Ivy)	Pennsylvania (Philadelphia)
Atlantic Coast	North Carolina (Chapel Hill)
Southern	Furman (Greenville, S.C.)
Southeastern	Alabama (University) Kentucky (Lexington)
Ohio Valley	Middle Tennessee (Murfreesboro)
Big Ten	Indiana (Bloomington)
Mid-American	Central Michigan (Mount Pleasant)
Big Eight	Kansas (Lawrence)
Missouri Valley	Louisville (Ky.)
Southwest	Texas A & M (College Station)
AAWU (Pacific Eight)	UCLA (Los Angeles, Calif.)
Western Athletic	Arizona State (Tempe)

Barry was voted the outstanding performer in the championship series, while Wilkes became rookie of the year. The most valuable player for the regular season was Bob McAdoo, a lithe, 6-ft. 10-in. centre from Buffalo, who won his second consecutive scoring championship with an average of 34.5 points.

Kareem Abdul-Jabbar, three times the NBA's most valuable player, demanded that Milwaukee trade him after the season, and the Bucks complied by dealing the 7-ft. 3-in. centre to Los Angeles for four young players.

Lawrence O'Brien, former U.S. postmaster general and Democratic Party national chairman, was selected as the NBA's commissioner, replacing Walter Kennedy, who retired after 13 seasons. O'Brien's first major decisions were to fine Atlanta $400,000 for tampering with another team's draft choice and to nullify New York's contract with George McGinnis because Philadelphia had first rights to him.

Despite the eye-opening debuts of 19-year-old Moses Malone of Utah and St. Louis' Marvin Barnes, who was the league's rookie of the year, Artis Gilmore of Kentucky remained the premier big man in the ABA. Dominating both ends of the court, Gilmore led the Colonels to the league title by saving his best for the championship series against Indiana.

At season's end the ABA hired 34-year-old Dave DeBusschere, a former NBA star, as commissioner, making him one of the youngest men ever to hold such a post. The Denver Nuggets signed both the ABA's first draft choice, Marvin Webster from Morgan State, and the NBA's first choice, three-time All-American David Thompson from North Carolina State, the first time an ABA team had managed such a coup. Major setbacks for the junior league followed, however. On September 25 the Nuggets and the New York Nets applied for admission to the NBA in 1976–77, a move the ABA was expected to contest. Then, before the 1975–76 season was two months old, three financially ailing teams—the Baltimore Claws, San Diego Sails, and Utah Stars—folded. DeBusschere announced that the seven remaining teams would play out the season in one division.

Collegiate. There was something old and something new about the University of California at Los Angeles capturing the National Collegiate Athletic Association (NCAA) championship. The Bruins were again on the throne, for the tenth time in the last 12 years, but this was the last season they would be coached by John Wooden. Retiring at the age of 64, Wooden, who came to UCLA 27 years and 619 victories earlier, said farewell by proving he could conquer all with a team that boasted no superstars, no overwhelming depth, and no proof of invincibility, such as the 88-game winning streak that ended in 1974. Indeed, the Bruins of 1975 lost three regular-season games, an infinitely large number for a Wooden team.

The salvation of the Bruins proved to be forward David Meyers, the team's captain and one of its two senior starters, and two rapidly improving centres, Richard Washington and Ralph Drollinger. They gave their best performances of the season in the NCAA tournament, powering UCLA past Montana, Arizona State, and Louisville to reach the finals against Kentucky.

The Wildcats traveled a tougher road to the championship game, if for no other reason than that they had to play Indiana, believed by many observers to be the best team in college basketball. Fast, physical, and intelligent, Indiana had won 34 straight games before colliding with Kentucky in the Mideastern Regionals. Kentucky did everything the Hoosiers did, got one more chance to do it, and won, 92 to 90.

UCLA and Kentucky played the championship game the way one would expect a game to be played between two teams that, together, have won more than a third of all the NCAA basketball titles. There were 15 changes of the lead and five ties in the first half, and when UCLA ran up a 12-point lead in the second half, Kentucky battled back to tie it at 76 to 76 with six minutes left. But Meyers sank two free throws, and Washington, who was named the tournament's most valuable player, scored on a tip-in to give UCLA a lead it never relinquished.

With the Bruins' 92-to-85 victory margin still glowing on the scoreboard, Wooden announced his expected retirement. He was succeeded by Gene Bartow of Illinois, who in 1973 coached the Memphis State team that lost to UCLA in the NCAA finals.

Princeton became the first Ivy League team ever to win the National Invitational Tournament as Tim van Blommesteyn scored 23 points to lead the Tigers past Providence, 80 to 69. Old Dominion University of Norfolk, Va., relied on the scoring and rebounding of 6-ft. 9-in. Wilson Washington to squeeze past the University of New Orleans, 76 to 74, and claim the NCAA's college division championship. Another deft big man, 6-ft. 10-in. Bayard Forrest, was the reason Grand Canyon College of Phoenix, Ariz., outlasted Midwestern University of Wichita Falls, Texas, 65 to 54, and became the champion of the National Association of Intercollegiate Athletics.

The player of the year in major college basketball was David Thompson, the spectacular 6-ft. 4-in. forward from North Carolina State who also won the honour in 1974. Thompson was joined on the National Association of Basketball Coaches' All-American team by Meyers of UCLA, John Lucas of Maryland, Adrian Dantley of Notre Dame, and Ron Lee of Oregon. Bob McCurdy of Richmond led major college scorers by averaging 32.9 points per game.

(JOHN SCHULIAN)

World Amateur. In the women's European championships played in Sardinia in September 1974, the U.S.S.R. gained its eighth successive title. With characteristic ease the Soviets brushed aside opposition from Czechoslovakia and Italy—which finished second and third—with triumphs of 104–58 against Czechoslovakia and 81–32 against Italy. In the seventh senior women's world championships held at Cali, Colombia, at the end of September 1975, the U.S.S.R. team took the gold medal, ahead of Japan (silver) and Czechoslovakia (bronze). In the final round the U.S.S.R. beat Colombia 92–34, Czechoslovakia 62–50, South Korea 103–78, Japan 106–75, and Italy 85–49.

WIDE WORLD

Golden State star Rick Barry scores two points for the West despite the efforts of Buffalo's Bob McAdoo in the NBA All-Star game in Phoenix, Arizona.

In the fifth African women's tournament, held in Tunisia in December 1974, the battle for the championship was between Senegal and Tunisia. The two teams had met earlier in the competition and Senegal had won easily, 58–38. The final game, therefore, seemed a formality, but this was not the case. Tunisia rose to the occasion and was narrowly beaten 47–44.

One hundred and thirty-eight teams from 28 countries took part in the 1975 edition of the European Cup for Champion Clubs. In the Men's Cup the finalists were Ignis Varese (Italy) and Real Madrid (Spain), a repeat of the 1974 final. This time, however, it was Ignis that carried off the honours in a hard-fought physical contest, 79–66. In the Women's Cup, Daugawa Riga (U.S.S.R.) won for the 12th successive time.

The 19th European Championship for Senior Men took place in Yugoslavia, June 7–15. After the qualifying rounds, which were played off in three centres, Split, Karlovac, and Rijecka, Yugos., the U.S.S.R., and Spain headed their respective sections with Italy, Czechoslovakia, and Bulgaria occupying second places. The final rounds took place in Belgrade. In the tense championship contest, between Yugoslavia and the U.S.S.R., Yugoslavia won 90–84.

The first Intercontinental Cup for National Teams took place from July 19 to August 19. Eight national teams from the Americas, Europe, and Asia competed at home and away. The matches that attracted the most interest were those between the U.S. and the U.S.S.R. In Leningrad the U.S.S.R. beat the U.S. 86–72, and in the U.S. it was again successful 71–65. The Brazilian team was particularly powerful, defeating the Yugoslavian team and narrowly losing to the U.S.S.R. in Brazil 76–72.

(K. K. MITCHELL)

[452.B.4.h.iv]

Beer:
see Industrial Review

Behavioural Sciences

During 1975 behavioural scientists had to defend their research from attacks on the grant process by Sen. William Proxmire (Dem., Wis.), who believed too much money was being spent on studies that were useless at best. Proxmire, in turn, was taken to task by members of the profession. Gardner Lindzey, director of the Center for Advanced Study in Behavioral Sciences in Stanford, Calif., felt some of the senator's criticisms were justified. He cited poor studies, cases in which good findings were overgeneralized, and some studies that raised ethical questions. But much of the criticism, Lindzey felt, was based on a naive expectation of how much social science can contribute to the solving of society's problems.

Whither Psychology? Fifty British psychologists peered into the future in an attempt to determine what tomorrow's psychology would be like. Their predictions included the following: among subdisciplines, social and occupational psychology would grow most rapidly as planners and designers in other professions called on psychological knowledge to help them communicate their ideas to the public; there would be a breakthrough in the neurophysiology of behaviour by the end of the century that would make it possible to control unwanted behaviour through drugs rather than prison.

The British scientists also foresaw that behavioural control would be a reliable, sophisticated technique by 1987. Psychology would increase its influence on education; by the year 2009, the standard educational techniques would be slide-tape packages and computer learning. Some areas would not develop as expected, however. It was unlikely that there would be any reliable applications of extrasensory perception (ESP) or convincing demonstrations of thought transference in animals.

Ethics. Continued agonizing over the effects of behavioural control and research methods resulted in new regulations governing the rights of human subjects in experiments and in the curtailing of at least one project, a Boston study on chromosomal variants. Earlier research on the XYY chromosome had showed that 2% of the inmates of prisons and mental institutions had this chromosome, compared with only one-tenth of 1% of all newborn children. This led some scientists to associate the XYY chromosome with aggressive or sexual psychopathology. Other scientists attacked the premise that the XYY is a predictor of antisocial behaviour, and they objected to programs screening children for the chromosome because of the bad effects the screening and subsequent labeling could have on the subjects. Although the Boston project had the approval of the pertinent Harvard Medical School committees and of the full faculty, the program was cut back by the project director after many groups objected to it.

Behavioural researchers in Muncie, Indiana, are testing children to determine whether perceptual or neurological problems can be detected at an early stage.

ROBERT REINHOLD—THE NEW YORK TIMES

Children. The 1970s were a difficult time for children in the United States. Urie Bronfenbrenner, a psychologist at Cornell University, Ithaca, N.Y., found statistical confirmation of this impression hidden in the mountains of figures collected by government agencies on labour, marriage, divorce, infant mortality, education, and almost every other aspect of life. For example, he found that, for the first time in the nation's history, a majority of children had mothers who worked outside the home, and most of these mothers worked full-time. This might not be a problem, but there was a serious shortage of day-care centres and other types of family support to assist working mothers in caring for their children.

Divorce rates continued to rise, with the result that more children were growing up in one-parent families. One in every six children under 18 lived in a single-parent home, double the rate of 25 years earlier. In infant mortality, the U.S. ranked 13th in the world, between East Germany and Hong Kong, and the infant mortality rate for nonwhites was twice that for whites. Adult abuse and murder of children were increasing, along with suicide rates among children, and juvenile delinquency reached new proportions.

The Children's Defense Fund, operating in Cambridge, Mass., found that two million school-age children were not in school. Most of these were not dropouts, or children physically or mentally incapable of attending school, but "pushouts"—children expelled or otherwise prevented from attending school. Another two million children were suspended at least once during the school year, usually for nonviolent, nondangerous offenses such as cutting classes, arguing with the teacher, or smoking. Suspension was used disproportionately against black children—twice as often overall and three times as often in high school.

Both the courts and government took special note of children's needs. A Philadelphia court ruled in *Bartley* v. *Kremens* that children must have legal counsel and a court hearing before being committed to a mental hospital, and that parents cannot waive these rights. The National Center for Child Abuse and Neglect, part of the U.S. Office of Child Development, began a three-year program to help agencies and professionals improve their abilities to identify, treat, and prevent child abuse and neglect.

Middle Age and the Elderly. The so-called male menopause or middle life crisis received considerable attention. At the State University of New York, Buffalo, sociologists found that the crisis is a time (which they defined as between ages 38 and 48) when men feel alienated from their jobs, their families, and their friends. Their children have started to leave home, leading them to question why they should continue with their jobs or marriages. Their careers have often reached a point where reality has spoiled earlier dreams of glory. Their own parents may die or become dependent, raising thoughts of their own advancing age and mortality. In a study of 300 men, the researchers found that lower-class workers were particularly affected. They usually had less satisfying jobs, knew less about options open to them for changing their lives, and lacked the educational and financial resources that would enable them to take advantage of opportunities that did present themselves.

The Institute of Human Development at the University of California, Berkeley, completed a study of 40 years in the lives of 143 men and women. They found that old age continued what a person's earlier years had begun. Thus, people who were preoccupied with their health and had poor health when they were young were the sickest when they became old. Similarly, those who enjoyed life and had busy social and work schedules when they were young continued that pattern in old age. The study also showed that, contrary to common belief, people do not lose their individuality with age, but often become more complex and diversified personalities.

Working Life. There was no evidence that anyone had ever been bored to death, but considerable evidence existed that many workers in industrialized countries were being bored to sickness. When researchers at the Institute for Social Research, University of Michigan, studied 2,000 male workers in 23 different occupations, they found that the traditional killers—long hours, heavy workloads, and pressing responsibilities—produced less anxiety, depression, and physical illness than less demanding jobs. For example, assembly-line workers who worked normal hours at a regular pace, with little responsibility, reported the greatest dissatisfaction with their workload, as well as high levels of depression, irritation, poor appetite, and other physical problems.

These findings matched many of those reported by the Swedish psychologist Marianne Frankenhaeuser, who found that stress could be produced both by work overloads and by the "stimulus underload" of monotonous jobs. She used an objective measure of stress, the production of adrenaline and noradrenaline by the body. These hormones increase physical and mental efficiency, but constant overproduction can lead to psychosomatic and cardiovascular illness.

Frankenhaeuser also observed that men and women reacted differently to many types of stress. In one study, excretion of adrenaline by male and female workers was compared during routine activities and while taking intelligence tests under time pressure. The women's output was about the same under both conditions, while that of the men increased significantly during the test. Frankenhaeuser found similar reactions among 12-year-old boys and girls in comparable situations. She offered two explanations: men and women may have different hormonal responses to stress or, alternatively, the difference might be a learned behaviour pattern. Type A behaviour, characterized by competitiveness, a sense of urgency and time pressure, and a need to be in control, is more common to men than to women in modern society. "One might speculate," Frankenhaeuser said, "that the ongoing change in sex-role patterns will lead to a growing proportion of Type A women," which could make them more susceptible to stress-related diseases.

Crime and Punishment. The number of murders committed in the U.S. had doubled during the past 20 years. According to recent research, the most likely murderer was still a relative of the victim, but felony murders were starting to catch up. Twenty years earlier, murders committed during the commission of another crime accounted for only 10% of the total; by 1975 they accounted for almost 30%. The homicide rate was four times as great for men as for women, and nonwhites were killed ten times as frequently as whites. About 40% of the victims and 60% of the murderers were from 15 to 29 years old. (*See* CRIME AND LAW ENFORCEMENT.)

"I'll tell you what I want. I want self-actualization as a woman in a societal modality in which a viable life-style is divorced from preconceived ideas of sexual role-conditioning, and I want it now!"

A review of 231 studies of correctional facilities by a U.S. sociologist, Paul Martinson, offered little evidence that any particular type of treatment was effective in reducing the rate of recidivism. Martinson pointed out, however, that one reason for this was that parole and probation had been so successful in the past. He hypothesized that these methods had already screened out the offenders most susceptible to rehabilitation. (*See* PRISONS AND PENOLOGY.)

(PATRICE DAILY HORN)

[432.C.7.b and 8.a; 521.B.3.c and C.3.ii; 522.A.3.d.iii and f.ii; 10/36.C and F]

ENCYCLOPÆDIA BRITANNICA FILMS. *The House of Man, Part II—Our Crowded Environment* (1969); *View from the People Wall: A Statement About Problem Solving and Abstract Methods* (1973).

Belgium

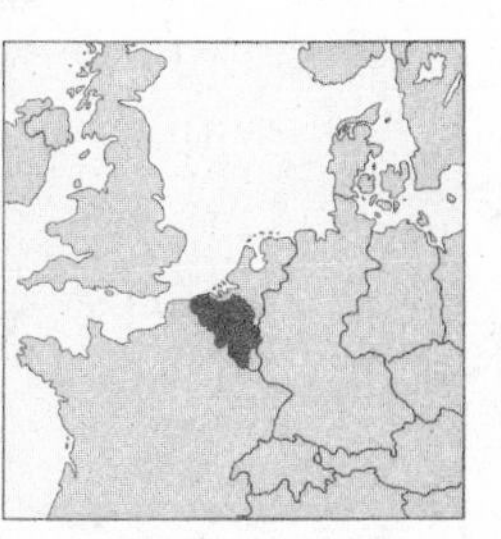

A constitutional monarchy on the North Sea coast of Europe, Belgium is bordered by The Netherlands, West Germany, Luxembourg, and France. Area: 11,782 sq.mi. (30,514 sq.km.). Pop. (1975 est.): 9,788,200. Cap. and largest urban area: Brussels (pop., 1975 est., commune 152,700, urban agglomeration 1,055,000). Language: Dutch, French, and German. Religion: predominantly Roman Catholic. King, Baudouin I; prime minister in 1975, Léo Tindemans.

As it celebrated its first anniversary in April 1975, Belgium's government was confronted with the consequences of the rapidly worsening economic situation. Caught between spiraling costs and social contributions on the one hand and lower sales figures on the other, many companies were either laying off workers or closing down operations altogether. At the end of August the unemployment figure stood at 174,413, as against 96,645 the previous year. Consumer prices, despite a 60-day price freeze from May 7 that was later extended, continued to climb at an annual rate of 11.4%. Employers and labour unions were at odds with each other over the reasons for the deteriorating situation of many companies. The Federation of Belgian Enterprises singled out automatic wage indexation, charging that it moved wages up faster

BELGIUM

Education. (1969–70) Primary, pupils 1,013,419, teachers (1967–68) 47,902; secondary, pupils 341,582, teachers (1967–68) 40,074; vocational, pupils 417,756, teachers (1966–67) 47,956; teacher training, students 23,680, teachers (1967–68) 6,089; higher (1971–72), students 145,524, teaching staff (4 universities only; 1967–68) 5,489.

Finance. Monetary unit: Belgian franc, with (Sept. 22, 1975) a free commercial rate of BFr. 40.04 to U.S. $1 (BFr. 82.95 = £1 sterling). Gold, SDRs, and foreign exchange: (June 1975) U.S. $5,338,000,000; (June 1974) U.S. $4,070,000,000. Budget (1974 est.): revenue BFr. 473,623,000,000; expenditure BFr. 548,980,000,000. Gross national product: (1974) BFr. 2,070,000,000,000; (1973) BFr. 1,783,000,000,000. Money supply: (March 1975) BFr. 617.9 billion; (March 1974) BFr. 595.9 billion. Cost of living (1970 = 100): (June 1975) 148; (June 1974) 132.

Foreign Trade. (Belgium-Luxembourg economic union; 1974) Imports BFr. 1,154,300,000,000; exports BFr. 1,097,200,000,000. Import sources: EEC 66% (West Germany 22%, France 17%, The Netherlands 16%, U.K. 6%); U.S. 6%. Export destinations: EEC 70% (West Germany 21%, France 20%, The Netherlands 17%, U.K. 5%); U.S. 6%. Main exports: iron and steel 18%; chemicals 13%; machinery 10%; textile yarns and fabrics 8%; food 8%; motor vehicles 8%; nonferrous metals 6%. Tourism (1973): visitors 7,435,000; gross receipts (Belgium-Luxembourg) U.S. $754 million.

Transport and Communications. Roads (1973) 93,679 km. (including 1,011 km. expressways). Motor vehicles in use (1973): passenger 2,362,000; commercial 224,000. Railways: (1973) 4,048 km.; traffic (1974) 8,280,000,000 passenger-km., freight 9,102,000,000 net ton-km. Air traffic (1974): 3,974,000,000 passenger-km.; freight 294,690,000 net ton-km. Navigable inland waterways in regular use (1973) 1,940 km. Shipping (1974): merchant vessels 100 gross tons and over 251; gross tonnage 1,214,707. Shipping traffic (1974): goods loaded 40,283,000 metric tons, unloaded 62,475,000 metric tons. Telephones (Dec. 1973) 2,503,000. Radio licenses (Dec. 1973) 3,662,000. Television licenses (Dec. 1973) 2,376,000.

Agriculture. Production (in 000; metric tons; 1974; 1973 in parentheses): wheat *c.* 1,000 (1,015); barley *c.* 702 (718); oats 240 (250); rye *c.* 50 (63); potatoes *c.* 1,156 (1,418); tomatoes *c.* 102 (120); apples (1973) 240, (1972) 265; sugar, raw value 607 (780); pork (1973) *c.* 600, (1972) 615; beef and veal (1973) 224, (1972) 228; milk (1973) *c.* 3,700, (1972) 3,650; fish catch (1973) 53, (1972) 59. Livestock (in 000; May 1974): cattle 2,896; pigs 4,720; sheep 74; horses *c.* 60; chickens (1973) *c.* 34,660.

Industry. Fuel and power (in 000; 1974): coal (metric tons) 8,110; manufactured gas (cu.m.) 3,499,000; electricity (kw-hr.) 42,761,000. Production (in 000; metric tons; 1974): pig iron 13,019; crude steel 16,231; copper 360; lead 110; zinc 294; tin 4.4; sulfuric acid 2,592; cement 7,468; newsprint 91; cotton yarn 70; cotton fabrics 68; wool yarn 79; woolen fabrics 31; rayon and acetate yarn and fibres 29.

than the rise in the cost of living. Socialist and Social Christian union leaders refused, however, to consider changes in the system and put the blame on prices alone. Attempts by the government to win labour union approval for a modified version of wage indexation were countered by demands for structural reforms of the economy and, in particular, the creation of a public agency that would be entitled to set up state-run companies. To cope with the crisis the Social Christian unions insisted on a limitation of dividends and of all higher incomes.

The death of André Oleffe, minister of economic affairs, who as former chairman of the Mouvement Ouvrier Chrétien (MOC) enjoyed the confidence of the Walloon Social Christian labour unions, was a serious handicap for the Tindemans government. His successor, Fernand Herman, though he shared many of Oleffe's views, wanted state-run companies to operate on the basis of the free-market system.

Once Tindemans gained approval for the second extension of his government, regional devolution was given effect with the creation of three regional ministerial councils within the Cabinet. They were to look after specific regional problems of Flanders, Wallonia, and Brussels. Regional councils had been set up on Nov. 26, 1974, in Mechelen, Namur, and Brussels. Describing these councils as unconstitutional, the Socialists refused to attend the meetings.

Regional divergences came to light over such national issues as the acquisition of new fighter aircraft and a protocol with The Netherlands on the digging of a new canal giving access to Antwerp port facilities on the left bank of the Scheldt. Finally it was agreed that 102 U.S. F-16s would be purchased, an order worth BFr. 30 billion. French-speaking Belgians (Walloons) had wanted the contract awarded to the French Mirage F-1M53. In the second case Walloon political leaders rejected the terms of the protocol because they considered it would deprive them of their precious water resources. Tension between the linguistic communities persisted in and around Brussels; in particular, a decision by the mayor of Schaerbeek, a commune of the Brussels agglomeration, to provide separate counters for Dutch- and French-speaking inhabitants stirred up strong reactions among the Flemish (Dutch-speaking) public opinion.

The government also undertook a program to increase efficiency in municipal organization. Minister of the Interior Joseph Michel launched a merger operation that would reduce the number of communes from 2,340 to 569, to the displeasure of many burgomasters, aldermen, and councillors. The Socialists for their part described the operation as gerrymandering and proclaimed an administrative boycott in communes run by party members. The federations of communes, created in 1971 around Brussels to protect the Flemish countryside against further gallicizing, were abolished.

Prime Minister Tindemans was received in Peking in April by Chairman Mao Tse-tung. He also traveled extensively in Europe on a fact-finding mission for the European Economic Community, trying to determine if progress toward a European union was possible. He and King Baudouin visited the Soviet Union in June. (JAN R. ENGELS)

[972.A.7]

Bhutan

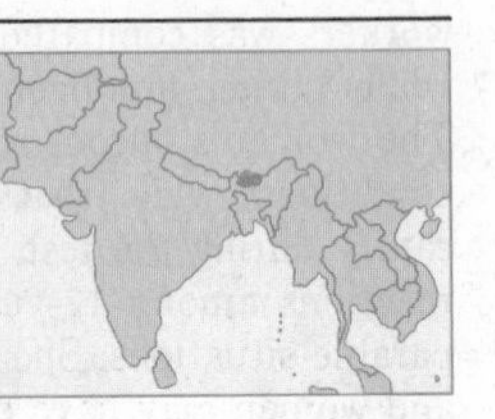

A monarchy situated in the eastern Himalayas, Bhutan is bounded by China and India. Area: 18,000 sq.mi. (47,000 sq.km.). Pop. (1974 est.): 1,146,000. Official cap.: Thimphu (pop., approximately 10,000). Administrative cap.: Paro (population unavailable). Language: Dzongkha (official). Religion: approximately 75% Buddhist, 25% Hindu. Druk gyalpo (king) in 1975, Jigme Singye Wangchuk.

King Jigme Singye Wangchuk visited India in December 1974 and September 1975, strengthening the existing close relations between the two countries. The December visit, the first since the king's coronation, closely followed the change in status of neighbouring Sikkim from an Indian protectorate to an associated state. Although Bhutan did not react to this development or to the subsequent incorporation of Sikkim into India as that nation's 22nd state, the king's visit brought reassurances from India that the 1949 Indo-

Belize:
see Dependent States

Benelux:
see Belgium; Luxembourg; Netherlands, The

Benin, People's Republic of:
see Dahomey

Bermuda:
see Dependent States

Biathlon:
see Target Sports

Bicycling:
see Cycling

BHUTAN

Education. (1971) Primary and secondary, pupils 10,176, teachers 486; vocational, pupils 275, teachers 18; teacher training, students 40, teachers 7.

Finance and Trade. Monetary unit: ngultrum, at par with the Indian rupee, with (Sept. 22, 1975) a free rate of Rs. 8.95 to U.S. $1 (official rate of Rs. 18.53 = £1 sterling). Budget: revenue (1971–72) Rs. 27.5 million; expenditure (1972–73) Rs. 71.1 million. Third five-year development plan (1971–76) total expenditure (est.) Rs. 350 million (including *c.* Rs. 330 million from India). Virtually all external trade is with India. Main exports: timber, coal, fruit and fruit products.

Bhutanese treaty would be respected and that India would continue to provide maximum help for Bhutan's economic development and modernization program. Under the treaty India looked upon the kingdom as an independent nation except in matters of foreign affairs, defense, and communications, in which India provided guidance.

During his September visit the king secured India's pledge that, as in the case of the third five-year plan, New Delhi would undertake 90% of the outlay for the fourth plan, set to begin in April 1976. The UN Development Program had also promised a total of $11 million in aid for the period of the third and fourth plans. Bhutan, admitted to the UN in 1971, was represented at several international conferences in 1975. The borders with Tibet were calm during the year. (GOVINDAN UNNY)

Billiard Games

Billiards. Three-cushion billiards, played at its highest level, is currently dominated by amateur players associated with the billiard federations of Europe, Japan, and South America. Though the U.S. is also a member of the world confederation, financial problems and differences in rules have prevented U.S. players from participating in recent competitions. In 1974 Nobuaki Koyabashi of Japan dethroned Raymond Ceulemans of Belgium, who dominated the sport for 11 years and had established a mark of 1.284 points per inning over the past 12 years.

The number of professional billiard players has dwindled considerably, partly because prize money has been too scarce to permit a player to support himself on such earnings alone. In an effort to reverse the downward trend, a group of Mexican promoters placed $25,000 in escrow for a three-cushion event, thereby hoping to attract the world's best players to a tournament scheduled for late 1975. To sustain audience interest, it was also decided to place a time limit on each shot, with the winner chosen on the basis of most points scored within a given time period. Such steps, it was believed, would also make the sport more suitable for television coverage.

Three-cushion billiards was having a modest revival in the U.S. through the efforts of the American Billiard Association. Room proprietors with three or more tables had been holding one or two ABA events a year. Perhaps the most promising of the young players frequenting these weekend events was Frank Torres of Los Angeles, who represented the U.S. in the 1974 world amateur event in Belgium and had an average of 1.142 points per inning in the six-player finals at an ABA tournament in August. Others who showed great potential were George Ashly, Bill McClelland, and James Blesse. Though private clubs also sponsored three-cushion play, participation was generally poor and the quality of play was far from spectacular. Elks Lodges on the West Coast, however, provided a notable exception. For 25 years, three-man teams from the San Francisco area had been sent to ten or more lodges a year to take part in tournaments, and the Medford-Ashland Elks in Oregon consistently drew some 25 teams to their annual competition.

U.S. Pocket Billiards Open Championships, 1975

Men	bpi*	Women	bpi*
1. D West	9.37	1. J. Balukas	4.05
2. P. Margo	10.71	2. M. Harada	2.89
3. S. Mizerak	15.26	3. G. Titcomb	2.14
4. R. Martin	6.66	4. B. Brown	1.81
5. A. Hopkins	7.26	5. P. Byrd	2.14
6. I. Crane	4.88	6. S. Bohm	1.77
7. L. Butera	10.7	7. S. Patarino	1.81
8. L. Lassiter	5.64	8. M. Girolamo	1.75
9. M. Beilfuss	9.75	9. G. Breedlove	2.55
10. D. Louie	7.77	10. M. Whitlow	2.48

*Average balls per inning.

Pocket Billiards. The tenth annual U.S. pocket billiards championships, sponsored by the Billiard Congress of America, were played in Chicago in August. Of the 32 men and 16 women who competed, two were Japanese champions and one was a German. A total of $43,000 was offered in prize money; the men's champion received $10,000 and the women's champion $3,000. All other participants were awarded a token prize of at least $150. As usual, the 32nd men's berth was allotted to a junior champion (17 years old or younger).

The defending men's champion, Joe Balsis of Pennsylvania, had to face Udo Moers, holder of the German national title, Masaru Hanatani, the Japanese champion from Osaka, Steve Mizerak of New Jersey, winner of four consecutive open titles (1971–74), Irving ("The Deacon") Crane, Luther ("Wimpy") Lassiter, Lou ("Machine Gun") Butera, and Cisero Murphy. A new champion, however, was destined to be crowned in 1975 when Dallas West of Illinois and Pete Margo of New York fought their way into the finals. West won the showdown with a 200–189 victory in 36 innings. Mizerak, who came to the tournament with high hopes after six recent victories, was upset in an early round and finished in third place.

In the women's division, Jean Balukas, a 16-year-old New York schoolgirl, continued to dominate her competition by winning her fourth consecutive national open title. In the finals she faced her old rival Mieko Harada of Japan and won 100–63 in 39 innings.

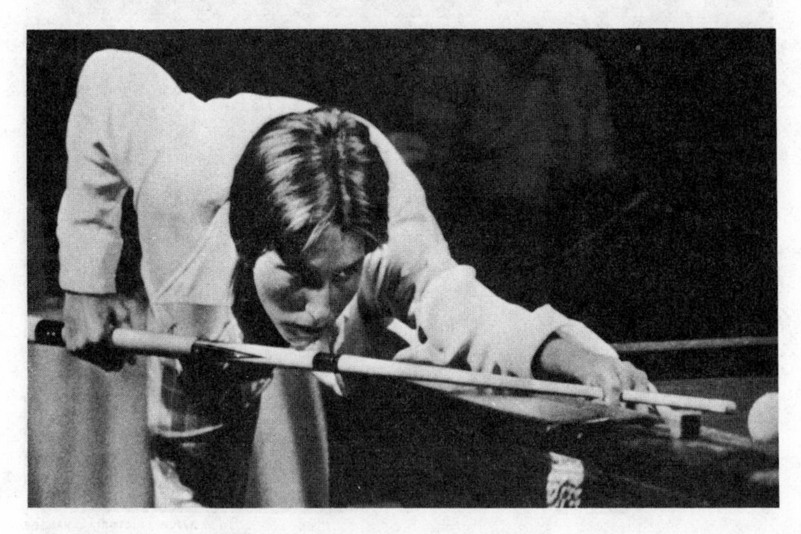

Jean Balukas of Brooklyn, New York, takes careful aim en route to the pocket billiards championship in the women's division.

In 1974 Balukas defeated Harada for the open title by a single ball, winning 100–99, after earlier losing the World Invitational championship to Harada in Los Angeles. During 1975 Balukas also won the women's invitational, New England open, National Billiard News open, and Wisconsin open.

Snooker. The world's finest snooker players gathered in Sydney, Australia, during April to vie for the hotly contested world professional championship. Ray Reardon of Wales retained his title by defeating Eddie Charlton of Australia, who was already in the record books for having made consecutive breaks of 135 and 137 on July 5, 1967. In the semifinals Reardon defeated Alex Higgins, and Charlton beat Dennis Taylor; both contenders represented Ireland. The four others who reached the quarterfinals were John Spencer and Rex Williams of England, Gary Owen of Australia, and Cliff Thorburn of Canada. Thorburn, rated tenth in world competition, won the U.S. title in 1972, held a world record with six perfect games, and earlier won top prize money of $20,000 during a televised tournament in Australia. Early in the year Spencer won the international masters tournament with a victory over Reardon.

(FREDERICK J. HERZOG)

[452.B.4.h.v]

Biochemistry: *see* Life Sciences
Biographies: *see* People of the Year *beginning on page 24*
Biological Sciences: *see* Life Sciences
Biophysics: *see* Life Sciences
Birth Statistics: *see* Demography

Board Games

Chess. It became apparent in 1974 that Bobby Fischer (U.S.) would defend his world title only on his own terms, some of which had already been rejected in June during a congress of the World Chess Federation (WCF) which convened in Nice, France. In March 1975, at an extraordinary meeting of the WCF in Bergen, Neth., the final terms of a world championship match between Fischer and Anatoly Karpov (U.S.S.R.) were decided: Fischer's demand for a limitless number of games was agreed to, but his demand that the challenger win the match (and the title) by a two-point margin was rejected. Fischer was given until April to comply with the WCF ruling. He refused, and so in late April Karpov was declared the new world champion at a ceremony in Moscow. Fischer thus became the first reigning champion never to play in competition.

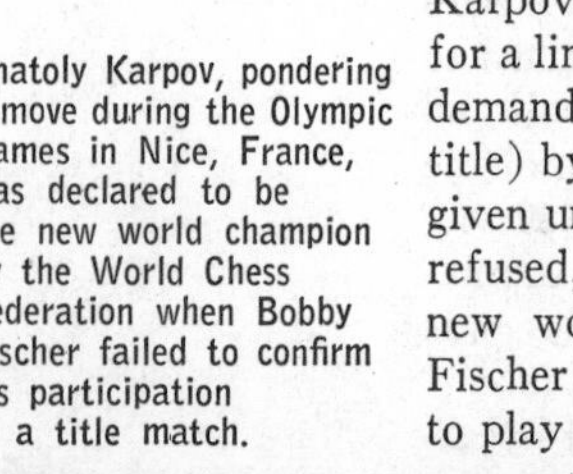

Anatoly Karpov, pondering a move during the Olympic Games in Nice, France, was declared to be the new world champion by the World Chess Federation when Bobby Fischer failed to confirm his participation in a title match.

A.F.P./PICTORIAL PARADE

Ruy Lopez, Classical Defense (played in the international tournament at Ljubljana, Yugos., 1975)

White	Black	White	Black
A. Karpov	S. Mariotti	A. Karpov	S. Mariotti
1 P—K4	P—K4	12 R—K 1 (d)	R—KKt1
2 Kt—KB3	Kt—QB3	13 Q—R5	Q—Kt2 (e)
3 B—Kt5	B—B4	14 P—Kt3	P—B3
4 O—O	Q—B3 (a)	15 B—Q3 (f)	P—Q3
5 P—B3 (b)	KKt—K2	16 Kt—B4	B—Kt5
6 P—QKt4	B—Kt3	17 Q—R4 (g)	Kt—B1
7 Kt—R3	P—Kt4 (c)	18 P—K5 (h)	P×P
8 P—Q4	P—Kt5	19 B—R6	B—Q1 (i)
9 Kt×P	Kt×Kt	20 B×Q	B×Q
10 P×Kt	Q×P	21 B×KP (j)	P—KB4
11 Q×P	Q×BP	22 Kt—R5	resigns (k)

(a) A favourite line with Mariotti which has earned him good dividends against lesser players; but against Karpov it is not effective. (b) Not with the usual idea of preparing P—Q4 since Black's set-up prevents this, but a counter-attack on the queen-side. (c) A fierce, if wild, attacking move. Quieter moves allow White to establish a positional supremacy by Kt—B4. (d) A comparison of the development of the two players shows that White's queen-side pieces are almost fully in operation whereas Black's queen-side pieces are, for the most part, on their original squares. (e) Now at least he threatens mate but he is operating with only half his pieces developed and little wonder that he soon has to pay a heavy penalty. (f) Here, rather than QB4, as he wants to reserve that square for the knight. (g) And not 17 Kt×P ch, K—Q2; when Black has succeeded in unraveling his position and has equality. (h) The decisive maneuver which allows him to break into Black's king's position. (i) If 19 . . ., Q—R1; 20 Kt×P, and Black is quite lost. (j) Threatening simply 22 B×P. (k) Black is helpless against the many threats of which 23 Kt×KtP and 23 KR—K1 are only two.

Catalan System (played in the Alexander memorial tournament at Middlesbrough, England, 1975)

White	Black	White	Black
D. Bronstein	R. Keene	D. Bronstein	R. Keene
1 P—QB4	Kt—KB3	16 P—Q5 (f)	P×P
2 P—Q4	P—K3	17 P×P	B—B1 (g)
3 P—KKt3	P—Q4	18 Kt—K4	Kt×Kt (h)
4 B—Kt2	QKt—Q2	19 Q×Kt	B×P
5 Kt—Q2	B—K2 (a)	20 Q—B5	P—Kt3 (i)
6 KKt—B3	O—O	21 Q—B4	P—B3 (j)
7 O—O	P—QKt3	22 QR—Q1	P—B5 (k)
8 P—Kt3	B—Kt2	23 Kt—Kt5	R—B4 (1)
9 B—Kt2	P—B4	24 R×B	R×R
10 P—K3	R—B1	25 P×P	P×Kt
11 R—B1	R—B2 (b)	26 Q—Kt4	R—KB4
12 Q—K2	Q—R1 (c)	27 B×Q	R×B
13 KR—K1 (d)	KR—B1	28 Q—K4	R—Q1
14 BP×P	B×P (e)	29 Q—Q4	K—B2
15 P—K4	B—Kt2	30 P—Kt4	resigns (m)

(a) The defensive system Black now employs is too passive; better was an immediate 5 . . ., P—B4. (b) This, and the succeeding maneuver, constitute an artificial system that is too complicated. Best was simply 11 . . ., BP×P; 12 P×P, P×P. (c) But now, after 12 . . ., QP×P; 13 KtP×P, White controls the centre and Black's pieces are not well placed. (d) A subtle move that shows White is looking deeply into the position and already planning the combination that starts with his 16th move. (e) The alternative of 14 . . ., KP×P; 15 Kt—K5, is not very attractive for Black. (f) An intuitive positional pawn sacrifice that gives White great attacking possibilities. (g) 17 . . ., Kt×P; 18 Kt—K4, P—KR3; 19 QR—Q1, is bad for Black but preferable seems 17 . . ., R—K1 when Bronstein had not made up his mind as to whether he was going to reply 18 Kt—K4, or 18 Kt—B4. (h) 18 . . ., R—K1; 19 B×Kt, forces Black to break up his king-side by 19 . . ., P×B; since 19 . . ., Kt×B; 20 Kt×Kt ch, wins the rook. (i) And not 20 . . ., P—KR3; 21 Kt—Kt5, P—Kt3; 22 B×B, P×Q; 23 B×P mate. (j) After 21 . . ., B—Kt2; 22 B×B, K×B; 23 R—K7, Q—B3; 24 Kt—K5, White wins easily. (k) There is a neat mate after 22 . . ., Q—B3; 23 R×B, Q×R; 24 Kt—Kt5, Q×Kt; 25 Q×Q, P×Q; 26 B—Q5. (l) This leads to the eventual loss of the queen but if 23 . . ., P×Kt; 24 Q—Q4, B×B; 25 Q—R8 ch, K—B2; 26 Q×RP ch and White mates in two moves. (m) If 30 . . ., R—B3; 31 Q—Q5 ch, or if 30 . . ., R—R4; 31 Q—R8 followed by Q×P ch.

Bobby Fischer apart, the chess world was more active than ever before. In the first programmed computer competiton, a Soviet Kaissa won the world championship. Another first, the Pan-American championship, was convincingly won by Walter Browne (U.S.) in Winnipeg, Man., during the summer. During the latter part of 1974 there were numerous other international tournaments. Of the four held in Yugoslavia, J. Timman (Neth.) won at Sombor, V. Vukic (Yugos.) at Banja Luka, and R. Vaganian (U.S.S.R.) at Kragujevac. The annual match between Yugoslavia and the Soviet Union was won by the Soviets 19½–16½ at Belgrade in November. The first of two major tournaments held in Bulgaria was won by M. Taimanov (Bulg.) at Albena, the second by V. Hort (Czech.) at Sunny Beach. In a match held in the Soviet Union, L. Polugayevsky (U.S.S.R.) easily captured the Tchigorin memorial tournament at Sochi. The 42nd Soviet championship, played in Leningrad, ended in a tie between A. Beliavsky and M. Tal. Other major international tournaments were won by E. Vasyukov (U.S.S.R.) in Manila; by M. Tal in Halle, East Germany; by V. Liberzon (Israel) in Venice, Italy; by L. Portisch (Hung.) in Wijk-ann-Zee, Neth.; and by B. Larsen (Den.) in Orense, Spain. The Asian Pacific championship was captured by R. Torre (Phil.) in Melbourne, Australia; the annual Hastings international by V. Hort; and the U.S. Chess Federation championship by R. Huebner (West Germany) in Houston, Texas. The Ladies' Chess Olympiad was played in Medellín, Colombia. Though Romania's team tied for first in regulation play, Soviet women won the play-off.

In match play, U. Andersson (Swed.) defeated B. Larsen in Stockholm in early 1975, and the late Soviet master Paul Keres (*see* OBITUARIES) won a tournament in Tallinn, U.S.S.R., and the Vancouver Open in Canada. In the finals of a women's tourney held in Moscow, Nana Alexandria defeated Irina Levitina 9–8. Between early spring and late summer, of three tournaments held in England, H. Westerinen (Fin.) was victorious in Dortmund, W. Hartston regained his British title in Morecambe, and E. Geller (U.S.S.R.) triumphed in Middlesbrough. In the U.S., V. Liberzon (Israel) won a Swiss system event in Lone Pine, Calif.; I. Csom (Hung.) won a USCF event in Cleveland, Ohio; and W. Browne retained his U.S. championship in Oberlin, Ohio.

During June Karpov became the first reigning world champion in 41 years to win a major tournament. The site of his victory was Ljubljana-Portoroz, Yugos. In other tournaments held in Yugoslavia, V. Chekhov (U.S.S.R.) won the world junior title in Tjentiste and G. Sax (Hung.) triumphed in Rovinj-Zagreb. Other tournament winners included W. Browne in Mannheim, West Germany; U. Andersson in Cienfuegos, Cuba (the Capablanca memorial tournament); Z. Ribli (Hung.) in Budapest, Hung., and in Amsterdam, Neth.; V. Hort in Brno, Czech. (the first Czechoslovak international tournament); and J. Timman in Netanya, Israel. In the four-man finals of a major tournament in Milan, Italy, Karpov defeated L. Portisch (Hung.). During August, David Goodman (Eng.) won the world cadet championship in France.

(HARRY GOLOMBEK)

Checkers. In retrospect, 1975 will be looked upon as a year of transition. Following the death of Walter Hellman, winner of four American and eight world championships in three-move checkers (the first three moves of the game are predetermined), the American Checkers Federation (ACF) named Marion Tinsley, winner of the 1974 American tourney, as Hellman's successor. Tinsley, who had been slated to meet Hellman for the world title late in 1975, quickly justified the choice by defeating a strong field of competitors at the Florida open in St. Petersburg. Later he also won the prestigious Northern States championship. Tom Wiswell, longtime holder of the world championship in freestyle checkers, announced his intention to retire in 1976 after the completion of a 40-game match between Derek Oldbury of England and Leo Levitt of the U.S. The English Draughts Association and the ACF agreed that the winner would be declared world freestyle title holder. In still another variation of checkers, two champions faced each other in a showdown 20-game match. Asa Long of Ohio, world tournament champion in 11-man ballot checkers (each player uses only 11 pieces and opening moves are predetermined), wrested the match play title from Kenneth Grover of Washington state with 4 wins, 2 losses, and 16 draws. Other current titleholders were Alfred Huggins of England (world mail play) and Dan Vestal of Texas (American mail play).

(TOM WISWELL)

Backgammon. In the early 1960s Prince Alexis Obolensky (*see* BIOGRAPHY) launched a quiet campaign to stimulate new interest in backgammon. By sponsoring tournaments and affiliating local clubs he induced tens of thousands to attempt to master a deceptively simple game. By 1975 the World Backgammon Club (WBC), which Obolensky founded in 1973, was issuing master point certificates to players indicating the quality of their play. As a consequence of such steps, interest in backgammon had spread beyond a small nucleus of the social elite to private individuals who could gain membership in the WBC and keep abreast of developments in the game through a bimonthly newspaper. Four important tournaments were held during 1975, with U.S. players emerging victorious in each event. The world championship title was won by Billy Eisenberg of Beverly Hills, Calif. The American championship was captured by Ezra Tissona of Fort Lauderdale, Fla. Bart Brooks, also of Fort Lauderdale, returned home with the European championship, and Chuck Papazian of New York City won the Grand Master tournament. Only two persons, Claude Beer and John R. Crawford, have been awarded life membership in the WBC.

(ALEXIS OBOLENSKY)

[452.C.3.c.i and ii]

Boating:
see Rowing; Sailing; Water Sports

Bobsledding:
see Winter Sports

Bolivia

A landlocked republic in central South America, Bolivia is bordered by Brazil, Paraguay, Argentina, Chile, and Peru. Area: 424,165 sq.mi. (1,098,581 sq.km.). Pop. (1974 est.): 5,470,000, of whom more than 50% were Indian. Language: Spanish (official). Religion (1971 est.): Roman Catholic 94.5%. Judicial cap.: Sucre (pop., 1972 est., 52,100). Administrative cap. and largest city: La Paz (pop., 1972 est., 574,200). President in 1975, Col. Hugo Banzer Suárez.

With President Banzer's declaration of Nov. 9, 1974, after suppression of a revolt at Santa Cruz, that political parties were officially in recess and that labour union activity was banned, the military institutionalized its grip on the Bolivian government and announced that it would retain control until 1980. Statements by military leaders suggested that Banzer would not necessarily head the government throughout this period.

The flow of oil and gas is adjusted by a worker in Bolivia's Naranjillos field.

THE NEW YORK TIMES

Bolivia's need to regain an access route to the Pacific Ocean by 1980 was stressed. It was a foreign policy aim for which the nation had sought and gained some support from the Organization of American States and from some Latin-American neighbours, including Uruguay, which President Banzer visited in July. Early in 1975 limited attempts were made to achieve this aim; in February Bolivia and Chile signed an agreement renewing diplomatic relations and providing for negotiations on the sea access issue. These moves gave rise to a greater fluidity in traditional Pacific Coast international politics and led to discussions on a nonaggression pact involving Bolivia, Chile, and Peru.

In August the republic celebrated the 150th anniversary of its founding. When Bob Dorsey, chairman of Gulf Oil Corp., disclosed in the U.S. that the corporation had made tremendous "political contributions" to Bolivian officials during 1966–71, the firm's Bolivian representative was arrested on May 20. Dorsey was summoned to appear and was asked to reveal the names of the individuals involved.

In January the government brought in a wage and price freeze policy as a measure to deal with inflation, the cost-of-living index having increased by 38.9% in 1974. Reactions to the government's economic and other policies led to two strikes by tin miners and disputes with the Roman Catholic Church, whose large proportion of foreign clerics benefited from a simultaneously privileged but vulnerable position in Bolivia.

While economic conditions for the average Bolivian citizen did not improve radically, on the national scale there were significant changes for the Bolivian economy. Although Bolivia still had an underdeveloped economy, high commodity prices rather than increased output led to record export earnings in 1974, a balance of payments surplus of $111.5 million, and an economic growth rate of 7%. Monetary reserves increased significantly, as did foreign confidence in Bolivia, resulting in loans from private and international agency sources for the nation's heavy investment program and also in the establishment of a sixth foreign bank. The boom conditions began to collapse in the last quarter of 1974, and by mid-1975 the prices of Bolivia's export commodities were 25–50% below the peak levels of 1974. Oil exports, the most dynamic sector in 1974, were greatly diminished owing to the world recession and high Bolivian prices. Tin, the most important mineral export, was subjected to export control by the International Tin Council during 1975. In spite of the setbacks, however, the boom of 1974 had given Bolivia greater strength to face future economic problems. This was reinforced in 1975 by economic agreements that Bolivia made with Chile, Paraguay, and Uruguay and by large-scale aid and cooperation agreements with Brazil and Venezuela. (JOHN HALE)

[974.D.3]

BOLIVIA

Education. (1971) Primary, pupils 694,416, teachers 28,382; secondary, pupils 84,077, teachers 5,077; vocational, pupils 10,452, teachers 549; teacher training, students 5,222, teachers (1970) 497; higher (including 8 universities; 1969), students 27,352, teaching staff 2,727.

Finance. Monetary unit: peso boliviano, with (Sept. 22, 1975) an official rate of 20 pesos to U.S. $1 (free rate of 41.43 pesos = £1 sterling). Gold, SDRs, and foreign exchange: (June 1975) U.S. $192.3 million; (June 1974) U.S. $151.2 million. Budget (1973 actual): revenue 2,478,000,000 pesos; expenditure 3,351,000,000 pesos. Gross national product: (1973) 20.9 billion pesos; (1972) 14,967,000,000 pesos. Money supply: (March 1975) 4,096,000,000 pesos; (March 1974) 3,050,000,000 pesos. Cost of living (La Paz; 1970 = 100): (Dec. 1974) 245; (Dec. 1973) 176.

Foreign Trade. Imports (1973) U.S. $255.5 million; exports (1974) U.S. $547.6 million. Import sources (1972): U.S. 26%; Japan 16%; Brazil 13%; Argentina 13%; West Germany 8%. Export destinations (1972): U.K. 22%; Argentina 15%; U.S. 15%; Japan 10%; West Germany 7%; Brazil 6%. Main exports: tin 42%; crude oil 29%; zinc 7%; antimony 5%; silver 5%.

Transport and Communications. Roads (1971) 25,637 km. Motor vehicles in use (1970): passenger c. 19,200; commercial (including buses) c. 28,800. Railways: (1973) 3,443 km.; traffic (1971) 270 million passenger-km., freight 440 million net ton-km. Air traffic (1973): 195 million passenger-km.; freight 3.1 million net ton-km. Telephones (Jan. 1974) 49,000. Radio receivers (Dec. 1968) 1,350,000. Television receivers (Dec. 1972) 11,000.

Agriculture. Production (in 000; metric tons; 1974; 1973 in parentheses): potatoes 749 (c. 729); corn (1973) 305, (1972) 268; wheat (1973) 53, (1972) 51; cassava (1973) c. 210, (1972) 242; bananas (1973) c. 235, (1972) 230; sugar, raw value 204 (139); cotton, lint c. 18 (22); rubber c. 4 (c. 4). Livestock (in 000; Oct. 1973): cattle 2,326; sheep 7,508; pigs 1,104; horses (1972) c. 310; asses c. 660; goats (1972) c. 2,400.

Industry. Production (in 000; metric tons; 1973): cement 166; crude oil (1974) 2,110; electricity (kw-hr.; 1973) 903,000 (79% hydroelectric); gold (troy oz.) 37; other metal ores and concentrates (exports; metal content) tin 29, lead 20, antimony 15, zinc 49, tungsten (oxide content) 2.8; copper 8.2; silver 0.16.

Botswana

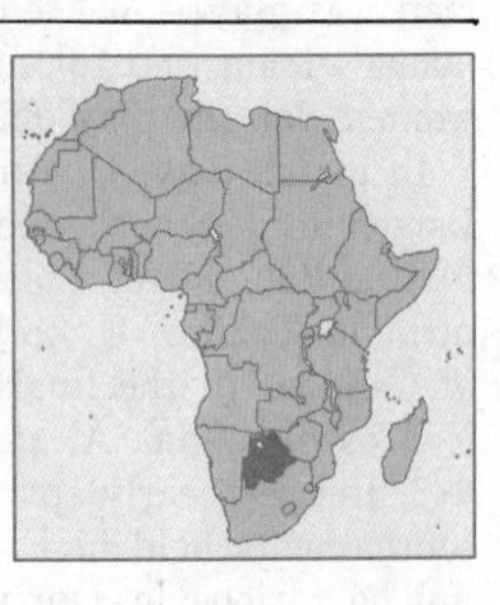

A landlocked republic of southern Africa and a member of the Commonwealth of Nations, Botswana is bounded by South Africa, South West Africa, and Rhodesia. Area: 222,000 sq.mi. (576,000 sq.km.). Pop. (1975 est.): 680,000, almost 99% African. Cap. and largest city: Gaborone (pop., 1975, 27,500). Language: English (official) and Tswana. Religion: Christian 60%; animist. President in 1975, Sir Seretse Khama.

Pres. Sir Seretse Khama and the Botswana Democratic Party, returned to power in elections at the end of 1974, had pledged to achieve racial harmony and to exert pressure for reform on South Africa, to which Botswana was linked in uneasy economic coexistence. To this end, the quadripartite monetary arrangements (with South Africa, Lesotho, and Swaziland in the South African rand monetary area) were not renewed, and Botswana threatened to take over Rhodesian railways operating within its borders. Botswana sent no delegation to the meeting of the Organization of African Unity at Kampala, Uganda, in July, in order to show its disapproval of Pres. Idi Amin's regime.

The completion of the BotZam highway linking Botswana and Zambia was postponed from 1976 to 1979. Huge coal deposits located on the border with South West Africa (Namibia) were expected to relieve fuel shortages.

The March budget revealed a depressed economy, in which inflation and adverse trade terms hindered development. Recurrent expenditure estimated at R 51.2 million represented an increase of 48% over 1973–74, while revenue, at R 73.3 million, was only

BOTSWANA

Education. (1974) Primary, pupils 103,711, teachers 3,047; secondary, pupils 10,308, teachers 492; vocational, pupils 1,123, teachers 155; teacher training, students 409, teachers 46; higher (at University of Botswana, Lesotho, and Swaziland), students 196, teaching staff 25.

Finance and Trade. Monetary unit: South African rand, with (Sept. 22, 1975) an official rate of R 0.87 to U.S. $1 (free rate of R 1.81 = £1 sterling). Budget (1974–75 est.) balanced at R. 58,086,000. Foreign trade (1973–74): imports R 102 million (65% from South Africa in 1966); exports R 58 million (18% to South Africa in 1966). Main exports (1972): mineral products 44%; meat and products 42%.

Agriculture. Production (in 000; metric tons; 1973; 1972 in parentheses): sorghum c. 50 (74); corn c. 10 (7); millet c. 6 (1); peanuts c. 6 (c. 6). Livestock (in 000; 1974): cattle c. 2,100; sheep c. 410; goats c. 1,000; chickens c. 500.

Industry. Production (in 000; 1973): diamonds (metric carats) 2,453; manganese ore (metric tons) 0.1; electricity (kw-hr.; 1972) 32,000.

Bonds:
see Stock Exchanges

Books:
see Art Sales; Literature; Publishing

Botanical Gardens:
see Zoos and Botanical Gardens

Botany:
see Life Sciences

26% above the preceding year. Development expenditure was estimated at R 40 million.

(MOLLY MORTIMER)

[978.E.8.b.ii]

Bowling

Tenpin Bowling. *World.* The annual report for 1974 of the Fédération Internationale des Quilleurs (FIQ) showed that there was increasing interest in tenpin bowling. The inauguration of the first commercial tenpin centre in the Soviet Union, in Moscow, bore witness to this, as did the granting to the FIQ of membership in the General Assembly of International Sports Federations (GAIF). GAIF was planning to conduct the first World Games of non-Olympic sports in 1977 in Manila, Phil., in which tenpin bowling would now be included.

In tenpin bowling 1974 was a year between international events. The delayed American championships were held in November 1974 in Caracas, Venezuela. Representing 16 countries of the American continents, 128 men and 66 women took part in the tournament, which was the biggest of its kind held thus far. Once again, the U.S. bowlers were dominant, capturing five of the eight championship titles. The winners in men's competition were: teams of eight, Venezuela, 12,948 (a new tournament record, which included also the team-high game of Venezuela, 1,714); teams of five, U.S., 6,200 (also a new tournament record with a team-high game of 1,146 and three-game series of 3,248); doubles, U.S., 2,606, also a new record; all-events, Ron Woolet, U.S., 6,047, another record. In the men's division as many as 12 old records were broken, and the women bettered 11 old marks. The winners of women's events were: teams of four, Venezuela, 4,459; doubles, Canada, 2,285; teams of five, 5,857; all-events (24 games), Olga Gloor, U.S., 4,679; all of these scores were new records.

Besides these FIQ championships several international bowling tournaments were conducted. The tenth Bowling World Cup national eliminations were carried out in 40 countries in 1974. The international finals took place in November, also in Caracas. During the six-day final tournament 40 men and 32 women were qualifying toward the individual grand finals. In the men's section Jairo Ocampo of Colombia defeated Belgium's Louis Wildemeersch 587 to 563 in the three-game grand finals. In the women's section grand finals Birgitte Lund of Denmark met Dale Gray of Australia and defeated her in a thrilling match by 573–565.

In 1974, 23 countries from the American continent sent teams to the annual Tournament of the Americas, sponsored by the city of Miami, Fla. The women's 15-game singles was won by Mrs. Tere Mejia of Mexico with 2,803 pins and the women's 36-game all-events by Mayorca of Venezuela with 6,548. Gary Brooks of the U.S. won the men's section, winning both the 15-game singles with 3,029 and the 36-game all-events with 7,317.

In October 1975 the eighth FIQ world championships were held at Tolworth, Surrey, England. The results were: men: teams of eight, West Germany, 12,406; teams of five, Finland, 5,769; doubles, Great Britain, 2,553; singles, all-events, Marvin Stoudt (U.S.), 5,816; women: teams of five, Japan, 5,461; teams of four, Japan, 4,551; doubles, Sweden, 2,334; individual, all-events, Annedore Haefker (West Germany), 4,615.

(YRJÖ SARAHETE)

United States. Professional bowlers endured the second year of the Earl Anthony era in 1975, and as the year neared its close there was no indication that the left-handed athlete from Tacoma, Wash., was going to lessen his dominance of the sport. In 1974 Anthony was a nearly unanimous choice of the Bowling Writers Association of America for bowler of the year after he finished first in six Professional Bowlers Association (PBA) tournaments, averaged a record 219.3, and won $99,585, the highest money total in history by a bowler. By late 1975 the 37-year-old Anthony had won six PBA events and earned more than $95,000 with a half-dozen tournaments remaining. His average for 1,005 games in 26 meets was 219.6, five pins better than his nearest challengers.

One of the professional events that Anthony did not win was the Firestone Tournament of Champions in Akron, Ohio. There, another left-hander, Dave Davis, of Cumming, Ga., captured the $25,000 first prize.

There were no professionals among the five bowlers who made up the Leisure Lanes team from Kankakee, Ill., as it rolled in the annual American Bowling Congress (ABC) tournament in Dayton, Ohio, but the group, competing in the Booster Division (for the least-proficient bowlers), shot a three-game total of 2,929, the highest score ever compiled in that division.

Other ABC tournament winners included: Classic Division—team, Munsingwear No. 2, Minneapolis, Minn., 2,980; doubles, Marty Piraino, Syracuse, N.Y., and Bill Bunetta, Fresno, Calif., 1,392; singles, Les Zikes, Chicago, 710; all-events, Bill Beach, Sharon, Pa., 1,993; Regular Division—team, Roy Black Chrysler, Cleveland, Ohio, 3,234; doubles, Bob Metz and Steve Partlow, Dayton, Ohio, 1,360; singles, Jim Setser, Dayton, Ohio, 756; all-events, Bobby Meadows, Dallas, Texas, 2,033.

In the Masters Tournament, held on the lanes used for the ABC meet, Ed Ressler, Jr., of Allentown, Pa., became the youngest champion in the 25-year history of the Masters by defeating Sam Flanagan of Parkersburg, W.Va., in two four-game matches, 944–825 and 850–814. Ressler was 20 years old.

The Women's International Bowling Congress (WIBC) tournament was held at Meadows Bowl in Indianapolis, Ind. The winners were: Open Division—team, Atlanta Bowling Center of Georgia No. 1, from Buffalo, N.Y., 2,836; doubles, Jeanette James, Oyster Bay, N.Y., and Dawn Raddatz, East Northport, N.Y., 1,234; singles, Barbara Leicht, Albany, N.Y., 689; all-events, Virginia Park, Whittier, Calif.,

Joseph da Benigno attempts to influence the ball in his challenge match with Emilio Cavazzini in a New York City bocci tournament.

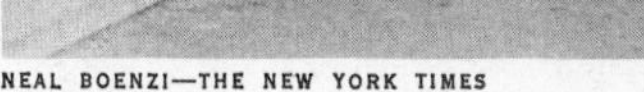
NEAL BOENZI—THE NEW YORK TIMES

1,821; Division I—team, Channel Chargers, Robinson, Ill., 2,667; doubles, Josie Freeman and Patsy Plumley, West Helena, Ark., 1,194; singles, Beatrice Orendorf, Bridgeville, Del., 664; all-events, Jeanette Pease, Richmond, Va., 1,749.

In the WIBC Queens Tournament, in Indianapolis, the champion was Cindy Powell of Navarre, Ohio, who defeated Pat Costello, Midwest City, Okla., in the final round 805–742 and 758–674.

Duckpins. The National Duckpin Bowling Congress tournament was held at Bowl America Westwood, Bethesda, Md. The winners included: men's team, Fair Lanes Westview, Baltimore, Md., 2,008; women's team, Eastwood Trophies, Baltimore, Md., 1,904; mixed team, Frank F. Favazza & Son, Baltimore, Md., 1,868; men's doubles, George Teague and Bernie Ruzin, Sr., Baltimore, Md., 867; women's doubles, Dotti Warren and Norma Gallagher, Hyattsville, Md., 804; mixed doubles, Medora Kaltenbach, Towson, Md., and Wayne Kraus, Baltimore, Md., 890; men's singles, Jeffrey Ferrand, Salisbury, Md., 469; women's singles, Delina Rock, Glastonbury, Conn., 437; men's all-events, Bob Wilson, Baltimore, Md., 1,310; women's all-events, Wilda Guerrette, Glastonbury, Conn., 1,209.

(JOHN J. ARCHIBALD)

Lawn Bowls. A year of development rather than of outstanding achievements or events, 1975 ended with bowlers thinking forward to the third World Bowling Championships, scheduled to be played at Johannesburg, South Africa, in February and March 1976. Despite concessions by South Africa, opponents of the nation's racial policies campaigned for a total boycott of the championships, but at the end of the year some 15 countries were expected to contest the series at the Zoo Lake Bowling Club. In England the official travel agents launched a tournament for bowls officials, the prize for the winner to be two free places on the trip plus spending money while in South Africa; the English Bowling Association quickly nipped the money part of the prize in the bud, but that still left a prize worth about £800 sterling, the largest ever put up in Britain and possibly in the world.

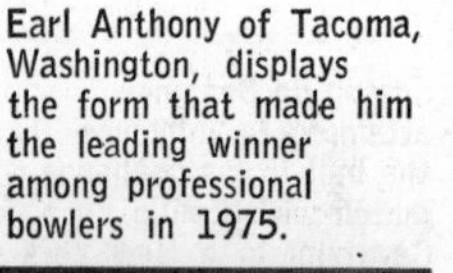

Earl Anthony of Tacoma, Washington, displays the form that made him the leading winner among professional bowlers in 1975.

WIDE WORLD

Coinciding with an escalation in sponsorship, this brought misgivings to many who, remembering the evolutionary problems of open tennis, saw lawn bowls moving toward a similarly tempestuous future. The International Bowling Board (IBB) was firmly oriented toward the amateur game, but crown green bowls, a variation of the predominant flat green game, had long been openly professional. Furthermore, it enjoyed television exposure beyond anything enjoyed by other codes of bowls, despite the fact that it was virtually confined to a handful of northern English counties. Several countries tried to define professionalism and professionals but, as in tennis and track and field, the frontiers separating professionalism and amateurism were, at times, obscure. Men who were teaching for money were classified "professional," but others who owned or ran sports shops, which enjoyed obvious benefits from the skills on the green of those owners, were not deemed to have infringed the rules. Australia and South Africa staged many open, international masters tournaments to which they invited overseas entrants, all expenses paid.

A survey showed a world average growth in numbers of players of 1.4%, Rhodesia being the top country with a 3.2% increase, as compared with 2% for Australia, 1.1% for the U.S., and 0.6% for England. Spain became the latest country to adopt the IBB game, primarily to attract those on holiday from the British Isles. A green also was established in Switzerland.

(C. M. JONES)

[452.B.4.h.vi]

Brazil

A federal republic in eastern and central South America, Brazil is bounded by the Atlantic Ocean and all the countries of South America except Ecuador and Chile. Area: 3,286,488 sq.mi. (8,511,965 sq.km.). Pop. (1975 est.): 107,145,200. Principal cities (pop., 1975): Brasília (cap.; federal district) 763,300; Rio de Janeiro 4,857,700; São Paulo 7,198,600. Language: Portuguese. Religion: Roman Catholic 93%. President in 1975, Gen. Ernesto Geisel.

Domestic Affairs. The nation was stunned by the victory of the opposition Brazilian Democratic Party (MDB) in the congressional and legislative elections of Nov. 15, 1974. Not even the opposition leaders had expected such a sweeping victory. It substantially increased the MDB membership in the federal Congress and gave it a majority in the legislatures of 5 states (out of the total 21), including São Paulo and Rio Grande do Sul, as well as in the constitutional assembly of the new Rio de Janeiro state. Some observers claimed that the elections were equivalent to a plebiscite, expressing the electorate's disapproval of the regime installed by the 1964 revolution. Others believed that the elections had strengthened the rather artificial, but operating, two-party system created by law in 1965.

The government-supporting party, National Renewal Alliance (ARENA), maintained its majority in the Chamber of Deputies, but not the two-thirds majority it had enjoyed before. In the Senate it continued to have a majority.

In an address to the nation over radio and television at the end of 1974, President Geisel congratulated the Brazilian people for their large participation in the November 15 elections (80% of a total of 36 million registered voters). As to the surprising victory of the opposition, the president pointed out that the government party still had a majority in both houses of Congress and in the legislatures of 16 states. Admitting that ARENA had suffered a serious defeat at the polls in many places, Geisel admonished the opposition to consider carefully the national problems and not to act "impulsively." The president admitted the need for radical changes in his party's organization, but he rejected the idea (advocated by some) of replacing the two existing parties with a national union party or creating two or more new parties. Although created artificially in a moment of national stress, the two-party system, said the president, had its roots in the political history of the country.

President Geisel ended his long talk by warning the opposition that he was still prepared to make use of the "emergency tools" which had been placed in his hands by Institutional Act number 5 (AI-5 of Dec. 13, 1968) and other emergency legislation. AI-5 gave the president the power to recess the federal Congress and state and local legislative bodies; to annul the mandate of any elected official; and to suspend the political rights of any citizen for ten years.

The president's warning was not an idle one. During the first year and a half of his administration he invoked AI-5 on four occasions: to annul the political rights of a judge involved in a proven corruption case in the territory of Rondônia; to settle a bitter and prolonged dispute between the governor and the legislature of the interior state of Acre over the appointment of a mayor; to annul the mandate of a federal senator (member of ARENA) and suspend his political rights as well as those of two other individuals, all implicated in a case of subornation in the northeastern state of Pernambuco; and to dismiss two diplomats who had been convicted of engaging in smuggling while on duty in a European country.

On Aug. 1, 1975, in an address to the nation, President Geisel repeated his warning that, although determined to "democratize" Brazil, he did not intend to give up his emergency powers. The president's talk was bitterly criticized by the leader of the opposition in a note issued to the press a few days later. This note was considered by many as "offensive and disrespectful" to the president. A serious political crisis ensued. There was fear that the president would invoke AI-5 to suspend the political rights of some of the opposition leaders. The crisis was aggravated by the refusal of the government to permit the minister of justice to appear before the Chamber of Deputies and answer questions regarding the recent arrest of certain persons allegedly accused of conspiring against the regime.

The Economy. The country's economy continued to suffer the restraining effects of the sudden price increase for imported oil, as well as of the economic recession in the world at large. Brazil annually imported 75–80% of the oil it consumed. Among the serious problems confronting the government, the struggle against inflation stood high. It was estimated that inflation had been running at a rate of 29% during 1974 and between 20 and 25% in the early months of 1975. Later, it was officially announced that it would be about 30% for the whole year. The crippling effects of this high rate were somewhat eased by the "monetary correction" system adopted by the government, involving the periodic readjustment of salaries and interest rates.

Another constant worry of the authorities was the deterioration of the balance of payments. This was, in the main, due to the large disparity between imports and exports. The balance of payments showed a deficit of $4.5 billion in 1974. Exports for 1975 were expected to reach at least $8 billion, but imports would probably exceed $12.5 billion. With the addition of payments for the service of the foreign debt, the total deficit was expected to be close to $7 billion. This was to be partially covered by expected incoming foreign loans and direct investments as well as by the use of some of the country's reserves, estimated at about $5.5 billion.

To discourage imports, higher import duties were imposed on foreign commodities. Also the so-called minidevaluation system of the national currency unit (cruzeiro) continued. In January the official exchange rate was set at 7.51/7.55 cruzeiros to U.S. $1. After several successive small devaluations, it became

BRAZIL

Education. (1971) Primary, pupils 13,640,967, teachers 476,663; secondary, pupils 3,464,088, teachers 228,143; vocational, pupils 797,487, teachers 68,846; teacher training, students 300.551, teachers 39,223; higher, students 569,230, teaching staff 49,507.

Finance. Monetary unit: cruzeiro, with (Sept. 22, 1975) a free rate of 8.34 cruzeiros to U.S. $1 (17.27 cruzeiros = £1 sterling). Gold, SDRs, and foreign exchange, official: (March 1975) U.S. $4,352,000,000; (March 1974) U.S. $6,396,000,000. Budget (1975 est.) balanced at 90.2 billion cruzeiros. Gross national product: (1973) 473.2 billion cruzeiros; (1972) 355.8 billion cruzeiros. Money supply: (March 1975) 123,540,000,000 cruzeiros; (March 1974) 97,470,000,000 cruzeiros. Cost of living (São Paulo; 1970 = 100): (May 1975) 249; (May 1974) 198.

Foreign Trade. (1974) Imports 94,628,000,000 cruzeiros; exports 53,226,000,000 cruzeiros. Import sources (1973): U.S. 28%; West Germany 13%; Japan 8%; Saudi Arabia 5%; Argentina 5%. Export destinations (1973): U.S. 18%; The Netherlands 10%; West Germany 9%; Japan 7%; Italy 6%; U.K. 5%. Main exports: sugar 12%; coffee 11%; iron ore 7%.

Transport and Communications. Roads (1972) 1,260,331 km. (including 59,372 km. main roads). Motor vehicles in use (1972): passenger 3,069,200; commercial (including buses) 809,300. Railways: (1973) 23,870 km.; traffic (1972) 11,489,000,000 passenger-km., freight 18,080,000,000 net ton-km. Air traffic (1974): 8,559,000,000 passenger-km.; freight 420,407,000 net ton-km. Shipping (1974): merchant vessels 100 gross tons and over 471; gross tonnage 2,428,972. Shipping traffic: goods loaded (1974) 76,296,000 metric tons, unloaded (1973) 48,190,000 metric tons. Telephones (Dec. 1973) 2,415,000. Radio receivers (Dec. 1972) 6 million. Television receivers (Dec. 1972) 6.6 million.

Agriculture. Production (in 000; metric tons; 1974; 1973 in parentheses): corn 16,065 (14,059); rice 7,329 (7,111); cassava (1973) *c.* 33,000, (1972) *c.* 31,000; potatoes 1,671 (1,557); sweet potatoes (1973) *c.* 2,350, (1972) *c.* 2,200; wheat 2,305 (2,032); coffee *c.* 1,600 (873); cocoa *c.* 196 (193); bananas (1973) *c.* 7,300, (1972) *c.* 7,000; oranges (1973) *c.* 4,005, (1972) *c.* 3,825; cotton, lint 564 (*c.* 640); sisal (1973) *c.* 260, (1972) *c.* 230; tobacco *c.* 226 (235); peanuts 479 (588); sugar, raw value *c.* 7,950 (*c.* 7,450); dry beans 2,168 (2,211); soybeans *c.* 7,900 (5,009); rubber *c.* 25 (23); timber (cu.m.; 1973) 163,800, (1972) 163,800; beef and veal (1973) *c.* 2,202, (1972) 2,096; pork (1973) *c.* 800, (1972) *c.* 772; fish catch (1972) 590, (1971) 581. Livestock (in 000; Dec. 1973): cattle *c.* 88,000; horses (1972) *c.* 9,350; pigs *c.* 34,000; sheep *c.* 26,000; goats (1972) *c.* 16,000; chickens (1972) *c.* 243,705.

Industry. Fuel and power (in 000; metric tons; 1974): crude oil 8,599; coal (1973) 2,316; natural gas (cu.m.) 1,488,000; electricity (kw-hr.; 1973) 61,381,000 (85% hydroelectric in 1971). Production (in 000; metric tons; 1974): pig iron 5,844; crude steel 7,233; iron ore (68% metal content) 59,430; bauxite (1973) *c.* 800; manganese ore (metal content; 1973) 1,035; gold (troy oz.; 1973) 161; cement 14,927; asbestos (1972) 474; wood pulp (1973) 974; paper (1973) 1,565; passenger cars (including assembly; units) 562; commercial vehicles (including assembly; units) 337.

MARVINE HOWE—THE NEW YORK TIMES

Jair Inácio, shown working on preservation of an 18th-century statue of Jesus, is chief restorer for the city of Ouro Prêto, Brazil.

Boxing:
see Combat Sports

8.62/8.67 cruzeiros per U.S. $1 at the end of October. Besides being intended to discourage imports, the system was expected to enhance the competitive position of Brazilian commodities in world markets.

At the end of 1974 the discovery of valuable offshore oil deposits at Garoupa, near the coastal city of Campos, elated the nation. It was said that these deposits would increase Brazil's daily production from 180,000 to 1 million bbl. within two years. This would enable the country eventually to become self-sufficient in oil. (RAUL D'ECA)

[974.G]

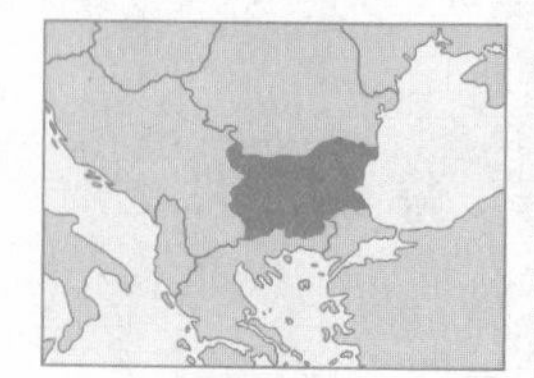

Bulgaria

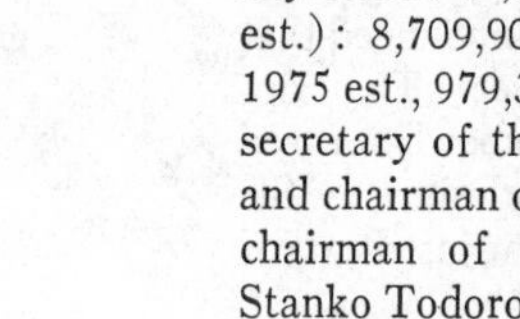

A people's republic of Europe, Bulgaria is situated on the eastern Balkan Peninsula along the Black Sea, bordered by Romania, Yugoslavia, Greece, and Turkey. Area: 42,823 sq.mi. (110,912 sq.km.). Pop. (1975 est.): 8,709,900. Cap. and largest city: Sofia (pop., 1975 est., 979,300). Language: chiefly Bulgarian. First secretary of the Bulgarian Communist Party in 1975 and chairman of the Council of State, Todor Zhivkov; chairman of the Council of Ministers (premier), Stanko Todorov.

The outstanding event of 1975 was the official visit to Sofia in July of Greece's prime minister, Konstantinos Karamanlis. It was the first visit of a Greek head of government to Bulgaria since 1878, when an independent Bulgarian principality was established by the Treaty of San Stefano.

On June 20, in Bucharest, Zhivkov and Pres. Nicolae Ceausescu of Romania signed an agreement on the joint construction of the Nikopol-Turnu Magurele dam and hydroelectric plant on the Danube. When completed, it would increase electric power for each of the two countries by 2,000,000,000 kw-hr. annually.

On June 23, Zhivkov arrived in Rome for an official visit. He was also received by Pope Paul VI, who later appointed two bishops for Bulgaria.

The question of the true nationality of the Macedonians continued to trouble relations with Yugoslavia. Speaking at Blagoevgrad, chief town of Pirin Macedonia, Ludmila Zhivkova, daughter of Todor Zhivkov and chairman of the Committee for Culture and Art, said that Macedonians were simply Bulgarians. The *Review of International Affairs* (April 20 and June 5) in Belgrade, Yugos., published strongly worded rejoinders from representatives of Yugoslav Macedonia.

Short of hard currency, Bulgaria had revalued the lev on Nov. 1, 1974. While the official commercial rate remained at 0.94 lev to U.S. $1, the tourist rate was changed from 1.65 to 1.20 lev to the dollar. Foreigners coming from the "capitalist" countries were required to change a minimum of $23 a day. Industrial production during the first six months of 1975 increased by 12% above January–June 1974.

(K. M. SMOGORZEWSKI)

[972.B.3]

Girls arrayed in their native costumes honour the rose as a symbol of beauty, youth, and love at the national Festival of the Rose held in Karlovo.

ST. MINKOV—BTA/KEYSTONE

BULGARIA

Education. (1973–74) Primary and secondary, pupils 1,107,745, teachers 54,912; vocational, pupils 152,489, teachers 9,432; teacher training, students 12,134, teachers 556; higher (including 3 universities), students 103,515, teaching staff 8,908.

Finance. Monetary unit: lev, with an official exchange rate of 0.94 lev to U.S. $1 (2.06 leva = £1 sterling) and a tourist rate of 1.20 lev to U.S. $1 (2.55 leva = £1 sterling). Budget (1974 est.): revenue 8,060,000,000 leva; expenditure 8,045,000,000 leva.

Foreign Trade. (1973) Imports 3,172,000,000 leva; exports 3,201,000,000 leva. Main import sources: U.S.S.R. 52%; East Germany 9%; Czechoslovakia 6%; Poland 5%. Main export destinations: U.S.S.R. 55%; East Germany 8%; Poland 5%. Main exports (1970): machinery 19%; tobacco and cigarettes 13%; transport equipment 7%; wines and spirits 6%; fruits and vegetables 6%; clothing 6%; iron and steel 5%. Tourism (1973): visitors 3,248,000; gross receipts U.S. $171 million.

Transport and Communications. State roads (1972) 35,706 km. (including 2,407 km. main roads). Motor vehicles in use (1970): passenger *c.* 160,000; commercial (including buses) *c.* 38,000. Railways: (1973) 4,246 km.; traffic (1974) 7,452,000,000 passenger-km., freight 17,309,000,000 net ton-km. Air traffic (1973): 360 million passenger-km.; freight 6.8 million net ton-km. Navigable inland waterways (1971) 471 km. Shipping (1974): merchant vessels 100 gross tons and over 166; gross tonnage 864,939. Telephones (Dec. 1973) 641,000. Radio licenses (Dec. 1973) 2,266,000. Television licenses (Dec. 1973) 1,383,000.

Agriculture. Production (in 000; metric tons; 1974; 1973 in parentheses): wheat *c.* 3,420 (*c.* 3,258); corn *c.* 2,500 (2,565); barley *c.* 1,400 (1,368); sunflower seed *c.* 400 (448); tomatoes 808 (801); grapes (1973) *c.* 933, (1972) 933; apples (1973) *c.* 350, (1972) 340; tobacco *c.* 150 (141); meat (1973) *c.* 464, (1972) 475. Livestock (in 000; Jan. 1974): sheep 9,765; cattle 1,454; goats 286; pigs 2,431; horses 142; asses 312; poultry 36,939.

Industry. Fuel and power (in 000; metric tons; 1974): lignite 23,994; coal 306; crude oil 144; natural gas (cu.m.; 1973) 222,000; electricity (kw-hr.) 22,801,000. Production (in 000; metric tons; 1974): iron ore (32% metal content) 2,682; manganese ore (metal content; 1973) 8.5; copper ore (metal content; 1973) 40; lead ore (metal content; 1973) 105; zinc ore (1973) 80; pig iron 1,515; crude steel 2,188; copper (1973) 48; lead (1973) 100; zinc (1973) 80; cement 4,298; sulfuric acid 761; soda ash (1973) 247; cotton yarn 80; cotton fabrics (m.) 335,000; wool yarn 30; woolen fabrics (m.) 32,000.

Burma

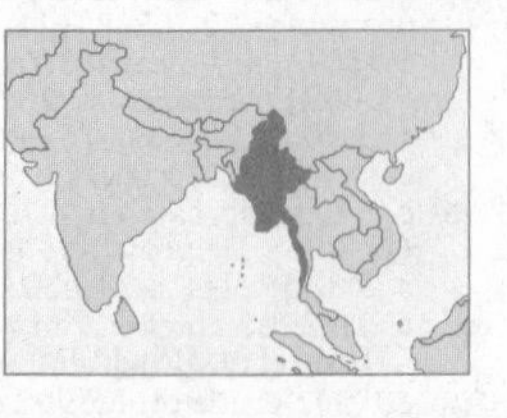

A republic of Southeast Asia, Burma is bordered by Bangladesh, India, China, Laos, and Thailand. Area: 261,789 sq.mi. (678,030 sq. km.). Pop. (1974 est.): 30,270,000. Cap. and largest city: Rangoon (metro. pop., 1971 est., 1,844,000). Language: Burmese. Religion (1970): Buddhist 85%. Chairman of the State Council in 1975, U Ne Win; prime minister, U Sein Win.

Violent student demonstrations in June 1975 gave clear proof that Chairman U Ne Win's efforts to bring about political reform by shedding the military label from his government and holding a general election in 1974 had not received widespread backing. The June riots, in which workers also took part, showed that discontent, first manifested in December 1974 when students seized the body of the late UN secretary-general U Thant, was still simmering.

Ne Win recognized the danger and ordered Central Executive Committee members of the Burma Socialist Program Party to hold countrywide crisis meetings with students and workers. The students complained about the soaring cost of living and the continued imprisonment of colleagues after the December riots; they also demanded freedom to form unions. Attempts by the government to bring in more rice to the market and lower prices of essential commodities were belated, and colleges and universities in Rangoon and Mandalay remained closed.

A government claim in March that insurgency had practically ended with the death of the Burmese Communist Party leadership during an all-out offensive in the Shan State seemed premature. In May progressive Arakan, Karen (two parties), New Mon, and Shan parties formed a Federal National Democratic Front, aimed at establishing a National Federal Union based on national self-determination, equality, and progress of all nationalities in Burma.

Foreign aid included U.S. $35 million from the UN Development Program in June and U.S. $36 million from Japan. The latter also continued to assist Burma's oil development program. Ne Win visited Peking in November. (GOVINDAN UNNY)

[976.B.1]

BURMA

Education. (1971–72) Primary, pupils 3,198,670, teachers 71,136; secondary, pupils 813,144, teachers 25,461; vocational, pupils 6,307, teachers 576; teacher training, students 2,428, teachers 180; higher, students 52,661, teaching staff 3,700.

Finance. Monetary unit: kyat, with (Sept. 22, 1975) a free rate of 6.63 kyats to U.S. $1 (13.72 kyats = £1 sterling). Gold, SDRs, and foreign exchange: (June 1975) U.S. $154.7 million; (June 1974) U.S. $191.5 million. Budget (1974–75 est.): revenue 10,652,000,000 kyats; expenditure 11,797,000,000 kyats.

Foreign Trade. (1974) Imports 614.7 million kyats; exports 953.7 million kyats. Import sources (1972): Japan 27%; China 10%; West Germany 9%; India 7%; U.K. 7%; U.S. 5%. Export destinations (1972): Sri Lanka 14%; Japan 12%; U.K. 9%; Singapore 9%; West Germany 5%; Mauritius 5%. Main exports: rice 39%; teak 22%; oilcakes 6%.

Transport and Communications. Roads (1974) 21,745 km. Motor vehicles in use (1973): passenger 31,700; commercial (including buses) 34,300. Railways: (1971) 3,100 km.; traffic (1973) 2,593,000,000 passenger-km., freight 708 million net ton-km. Air traffic (1973): 170 million passenger-km.; freight 2.4 million net ton-km. Shipping (1974): merchant vessels 100 gross tons and over 40; gross tonnage 54,877. Telephones (Dec. 1973) 29,000. Radio licenses (Dec. 1973) 627,000.

Agriculture. Production (in 000; metric tons; 1974; 1973 in parentheses): rice *c.* 8,350 (8,559); sesame seed 125 (122); peanuts *c.* 500 (459); dry beans *c.* 160 (*c.* 150); onions *c.* 130 (127); sugar, raw value *c.* 100 (*c.* 100); cotton, lint (1973) 15, (1972) 15; jute *c.* 110 (*c.* 92); tea (1973) *c.* 45, (1972) *c.* 43; tobacco *c.* 52 (*c.* 73); rubber 15 (14); timber (cu.m.; 1973) 21,200, (1972) 20,900. Livestock (in 000; March 1974): cattle *c.* 7,875; buffalo (1973) 1,768; pigs *c.* 1,961; goats (1973) *c.* 767; sheep *c.* 214; chickens (1973) 17,867.

Industry. Production (in 000; metric tons; 1974): crude oil 919; electricity (excluding most industrial production; kw-hr.) 615,000; cement (1973) 193; lead concentrates (metal content; 1972) 6.3; zinc concentrates (metal content; 1973) 3.4; tin concentrates (metal content; 1973) 0.6; tungsten concentrates (oxide content; 1973) 0.7.

A.J.C. BONE—THE NEW YORK TIMES

Ancient shrines in Pagan were reduced to rubble when an earthquake ravaged central Burma in July.

Burundi

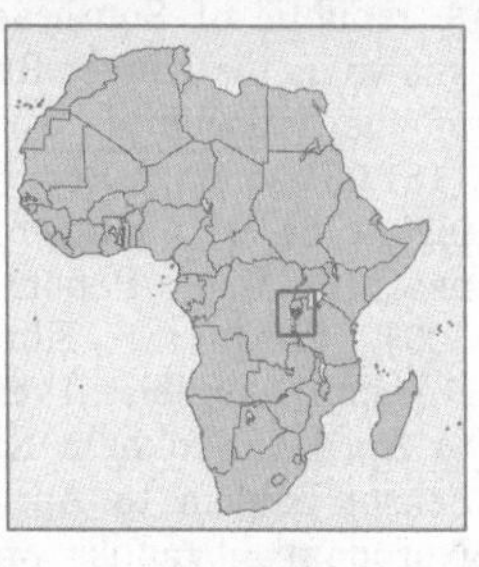

A republic of eastern Africa, Burundi is bordered by Zaire, Rwanda, and Tanzania. Area: 10,747 sq.mi. (27,834 sq.km.). Pop. (1973 est.): 3,580,000, mainly Hutu, Tutsi, and Twa. Cap. and largest city: Bujumbura (pop., 1970 est., 110,000). Language: Kirundi and French. Religion (1964): Roman Catholic 51%; animist 45%; Protestant 4%. President in 1975, Michel Micombero.

Reinstalled as president in November 1974 following October elections, Micombero on March 7–8, 1975, attended the meeting of heads of French-speaking African states at Bangui, Central African Republic. France also sent a delegate to this meeting, which was followed by a return visit to Burundi by Pierre Abelin, French minister of overseas cooperation, in May. Economic, technical, and financial cooperation were discussed, and France agreed to provide aid up to Fr. 24 million and 151 technical personnel. Burundi also supplied a vice-chairman to the UN Economic

BURUNDI

Education. (1973–74) Primary, pupils 127,176, teachers (1970–71) 4,955; secondary, pupils 4,517, teachers (1970–71) 324; vocational, pupils 1,720, teachers (1970–71) 290; teacher training, students 4,385, teachers (1970–71) 210; higher, students 774, teaching staff (1970–71) 102.

Finance. Monetary unit: Burundi franc, with (Sept. 22, 1975) an official rate of BurFr. 78.75 to U.S. $1 (free rate of BurFr. 165.45 = £1 sterling). Gold, SDRs, and foreign exchange: (June 1975) U.S. $27,740,000; (June 1974) U.S. $19,250,000. Budget (1974 est.): revenue BurFr. 2,531,000,000; expenditure BurFr. 2,820,000,000.

Foreign Trade. (1974) Imports BurFr. 3,396,000,000; exports BurFr. 2,324,000,000. Import sources (1973): Belgium-Luxembourg 24%; France 12%; West Germany 9%; Iran 6%; Kenya 5%. Export destinations (1973): U.S. 55%; Italy 11%; West Germany 10%; U.K. 9%; Spain 5%. Main export coffee 84%.

Agriculture. Production (in 000; metric tons; 1973; 1972 in parentheses): corn *c.* 500 (461); cassava *c.* 4,000 (3,558); sweet potatoes *c.* 1,200 (*c.* 900); millet *c.* 40 (35); sorghum *c.* 60 (*c.* 50); dry beans (1974) *c.* 250, (1973) 245; dry peas (1974) *c.* 30, (1973) 26; bananas *c.* 1,520 (*c.* 1,500); coffee (1974) *c.* 21, (1973) *c.* 21; cotton, lint *c.* 3 (*c.* 3). Livestock (in 000; Dec. 1973): cattle *c.* 792; sheep *c.* 315; goats (1972) *c.* 590.

Brazilian Literature: *see* Literature

Bridge: *see* Contract Bridge

Bridges: *see* Engineering Projects

British Commonwealth: *see* Commonwealth of Nations; *articles on the various member states*

British Honduras: *see* Dependent States

Brunei: *see* Dependent States

Buddhism: *see* Religion

Budgets, National: *see* Economy, World

Buildings, Historic: *see* Historic Preservation

Bullfighting: *see* Arena Sports

Commission for Africa for 1975, was represented at the ECA conference in Nairobi, Kenya, in February, and received an International Development Association loan of CFA Fr. 1.2 billion for road reconstruction from Bujumbura to Mutambara. Bad weather conditions reduced the cotton crop despite an increase in the area planted from 6,000 to 9,000 ha. between 1973 and 1975. An acute corn shortage led to acceptance of supplies from the 1,700 tons of corn sold to the UN by Uganda.

Relations with Zaire remained strained because of the border-raiding activities of the 30,000 Burundi refugees in the Kivu area. Zaire undertook to move them farther inland and promote integration.

(MOLLY MORTIMER)

Cambodia

A republic of Southeast Asia, Cambodia (officially known as the Khmer Republic) is the southwest part of the Indochinese Peninsula. Area: 69,898 sq.mi. (181,035 sq.km.). Pop. (1974 est.): 7,888,000, including (1962 est.) Khmer 93%; Vietnamese 4%; Chinese 3%. Cap.: Phnom Penh (pop., 1971 est., 479,300). Language: Khmer (official) and French. Religion: Buddhist. Presidents in 1975, Gen. Lon Nol to April 1, Saukham Khoy to April 12, Lieut. Gen. Saksut Sakhan to April 16; chief of state, Prince Norodom Sihanouk; premiers, Long Boret to April 16, and Samdech Penn Nouth.

Whether it was "liberated" or fallen depended on one's point of view, but Cambodia renewed itself in 1975. The year began with the U.S. clinging tenaciously to its goal of keeping the Lon Nol government afloat. The war was already a forgotten issue in terms of political significance and the rebel government confidently outlined the policies it would follow once in power. The New Year offensive launched by the Khmer Rouge rebels was so elaborately planned that it looked like the final putsch. By the beginning of February they had closed the Mekong River route to the sea, forcing the U.S. to organize an arms-food airlift by charter aircraft. The government troops never regained the military initiative.

Civil disorder made the going more difficult for the government. Student riots rocked the key town of Battambang, there were public protests in Phnom Penh over continuing corruption in high places, and student associations openly warned the U.S. against manipulating Cambodian affairs. In March U.S. Ambassador John Gunther Dean was still pleading for more aid for Pres. Lon Nol in order to buy time until a "controlled solution" could be reached. This was understood to entail a new leadership in Phnom Penh and then negotiations with the Khmer Rouge.

The other side was singularly uninterested. The notion of negotiations with the Lon Nol regime had been rejected with particular vehemence late in 1974 when the UN General Assembly decided to let Lon Nol retain the Cambodia seat. Prince Norodom Sihanouk, in exile in Peking, said the vote did not reflect "the genuine will of the UN" and spurned the call for a negotiated peace. Now the insurgent forces were well on their way to a military settlement. With the country's vital lifelines firmly in their hands, rebel formations laid an effective siege around the capital city. U.S. attempts to persuade Lon Nol to step down from office were dismissed by the insurgents as a "dirty and vulgar trap."

The fall of Phnom Penh signaled the Communist victory in Cambodia, April 17, 1975.

SYLVAIN JULIENNE—SYGMA

CAMBODIA

Education. (1973–74) Primary, pupils 429,110, teachers 18,794; secondary, pupils 98,888, teachers 2,226; vocational, pupils 4,856, teachers 202; teacher training, students 1,156, teachers 40; higher (including 5 universities), students 10,967, teaching staff 254.

Finance. Monetary unit: riel, with (end Feb. 1975) a free rate of 1,650 riels to U.S. $1 (4,000 riels = £1 sterling). Budget (1974 est.): revenue 22.8 billion riels; expenditure 71 billion riels.

Foreign Trade. (1973) Imports 14.2 billion riels; exports 2,732,000,000 riels. Import sources: U.S. *c.* 69%; Thailand *c.* 11%; Singapore *c.* 5%; Japan *c.* 5%. Export destinations: Hong Kong *c.* 23%; Japan *c.* 22%; Malaysia *c.* 18%; France *c.* 12%; Spain *c.* 10%. Main export rubber 93%.

Transport and Communications. Roads (1973) *c.* 11,000 km. Motor vehicles in use (1972): passenger 27,200; commercial (including buses) 11,100. Railways: (including sections not in operation; 1972) 649 km.; traffic (1973) 54,070,000 passenger-km., freight 9,780,000 net ton-km. Air traffic (1973): 51 million passenger-km.; freight 500,000 net ton-km. Inland waterway (Mekong River; 1973) *c.* 1,400 km. Telephones (Dec. 1972) 9,000. Radio receivers (Dec. 1972) 1.1 million. Television receivers (Dec. 1972) *c.* 25,000.

Agriculture. Production (in 000; metric tons; 1973; 1972 in parentheses): rice 953 (2,138); corn 73 (80); rubber *c.* 20 (15); bananas *c.* 90 (86); oranges *c.* 40 (36); dry beans *c.* 18 (18); jute *c.* 5 (5). Livestock (in 000; Dec. 1973): cattle *c.* 2,300; buffalo *c.* 850; pigs *c.* 1,150.

What had for long seemed inevitable finally happened on April 1. Lon Nol, the chief architect of Sihanouk's overthrow and Cambodia's ruler for five years, flew off to Bali with his family and close associates. From there he proceeded to Honolulu where he bought a house and settled down. He had been given $1 million to leave the country. Saukham Khoy, who succeeded Lon Nol as acting president and who later joined the refugee camps in the U.S., said the money was given to Lon Nol as a bribe. Others said it was part of an agreed settlement. Attempts made by various quarters to put a government together following Lon Nol's departure never materialized. On April 12 the U.S. pulled its entire diplomatic staff out of the capital by helicopter in what became a pattern for U.S. withdrawals from Indochina theatres. At dawn on April 17 Phnom Penh surrendered. Thousands of residents and government soldiers, who quickly shed their uniforms, turned out to welcome the conquerors as they finally rolled into the city. Five years and a month after it began, the war in Cambodia was at last over.

It was peace and friendliness as the new order began. Khmer Rouge soldiers asked people to stay calm while ministers and officials of the fallen regime were summoned to "help formulate measures to restore order." Seven days of celebration were ordered, coinciding with the Cambodian New Year on April 13. After the celebrations came what looked like a crackdown. U.S. sources, quoting themselves, reported a bloodbath and widespread revenge killings. While these remained unconfirmed by other sources, all were agreed that the new authorities in Phnom Penh were enforcing a harder discipline than their counterparts in other Indochinese states. Prominent leaders of the previous regime disappeared into obscurity. In October aides to Prince Sihanouk said that former prime minister Long Boret, the once-powerful Sirik Matak, and other former high-ranking officials had been executed and Lon Nol's brother, Gen. Lon Non, had been killed by a mob.

Leaders were not the only people whose lives were drastically disrupted. The entire population of Phnom Penh was forcibly evacuated from the city, soldiers

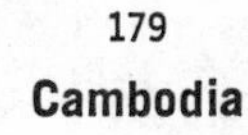

pushing the old and the sick along with the others into the countryside. It was described as a purificatory drive with the promise that the city would be repeopled in due course. The outside world inferred that the food situation in the ravaged country was so desperate that the whole populace had to be put to work in agriculture. As Phnom Penh turned into a ghost city, all foreign residents in the country were ousted. Cambodia seemed to draw the curtains round itself, leaving escapees as the only source of information on internal conditions.

A month after their triumph, however, the new rulers of Phnom Penh made headlines in an altogether unexpected manner. In what was clearly the most spectacular act of self-assertion by Indochinese nationalists, a Cambodian gunboat seized a 10,000-ton U.S. container ship, the "Mayaguez," on May 12. Calling it an act of piracy, the U.S. government ordered a naval task force to the spot. Some reports said Washington was trying to negotiate a settlement through China. But on May 14 a contingent of 250 Marines and 11 helicopters struck at Koh Tang, an island where the ship and its crew were believed to be held. The crew was not there. The ship was recaptured by U.S. forces and Cambodia subsequently released the crew. War planes from the carrier "Coral Sea" zoomed over to the Cambodian air base of Ream 200 mi. away from Koh Tang and rained bombs that destroyed 17 Cambodian planes on the ground.

There was a great deal of confusion and apparent prevarication by both sides as the incident was played out. The U.S. justified the punitive strike on Ream on the plea that it was to prevent the Cambodian Air Force from interfering with the rescue operation. Cambodia said the ship and its crew were released before the air strike, which was described as a "savage, ferocious, insane, aggressive act." Official U.S. accounts of the battle of Koh Tang tended to play it down at first, but reports from other sources soon showed that it was a major encounter in which U.S. losses were quite in excess of the objectives. The final tally announced by the Pentagon a week after the event was 15 servicemen killed, 3 missing, and 50 wounded. (Cambodia claimed that 30 U.S. Marines were killed.) Three helicopters crashed, two others were damaged.

The U.S. strike force had used Thailand as a base without consulting the Thai government. Indeed, Thailand had taken a stand against its territory being used for U.S. military operations any longer and was grievously embarrassed when Washington ignored its stated position. The State Department eventually soothed tempers by tendering an apology to Bangkok. After the "Mayaguez" incident Phnom Penh again seemed to disappear behind a curtain of its own. Reports of widespread scarcities and starvation in different areas circulated, but there was no way they could be confirmed.

Some broad outlines of the political and diplomatic reshaping of the country slowly emerged as the months passed. In the last week of April Radio Phnom Penh announced that Sihanouk would remain chief of state for life, Penn Nouth premier, and Khieu Samphan (*see* BIOGRAPHY) deputy premier. A special National Congress which met at the same time said that no foreign military bases would be tolerated in Cambodia. It also reaffirmed nonalignment as a major line of policy. By August the known leaders in the new power structure were making public appearances. Khieu Samphan, the most publicized figure after

WIDE WORLD

John Gunther Dean, U.S. ambassador to Cambodia, arrives at U Taphao air base in Thailand carrying the U.S. flag that flew over the embassy in Phnom Penh.

Sihanouk, made a fierce attack on U.S. policies and then flew to Peking along with Deputy Premier Ieng Sary. Going on to Pyongyang, North Korea, Khieu Samphan met Sihanouk, who had appeared in no particular hurry to return to his capital. There were reports that the new hierarchy in Phnom Penh was not especially anxious to see the prince in their midst either, and that Sihanouk would eventually settle in the safety and dignity of the Cambodian delegation to the UN.

In September Sihanouk returned to Phnom Penh and there was a show of public welcome. But he was quickly back in his exile home in Peking, purportedly to participate in China's 26th anniversary. Meanwhile, Ieng Sary went to Lima, Peru, in August to attend the nonaligned nations' conference and then to New York for the UN General Assembly special session on economic and social problems. He justified the mass evacuation of Phnom Penh on the twin grounds that it was impossible to ensure food supplies in the capital and that a secret political-military plan drawn up by "traitors" like Long Boret to retake power at the end of six months had been uncovered. He said that the crop situation held out the promise of Cambodia's becoming self-sufficient in food by the end of the year.

In late October Ieng Sary, at the head of an eight-man delegation, visited Bangkok, where agreement was reached on the resumption of diplomatic relations between Thailand and Cambodia. Thailand thus became the first non-Communist nation to recognize the new regime.

On the economy in general, the scanty indications available were often contradictory. At first the new leaders spurned all foreign aid saying "we want to be our own masters." By the middle of May they were admitting "great difficulties" in rebuilding the country and saying they would be prepared to accept aid without strings from any country. Khieu Samphan's visit to Peking ended with an aid agreement. There was little likelihood of significant aid forthcoming from the Soviet Union; seven Soviet diplomats were among the foreigners unceremoniously expelled from the country in the first flush of victory. Perhaps Moscow's policy of maintaining formal relations with the Lon Nol regime until it fell had damaged Soviet standing in Cambodia. (T. J. S. GEORGE)

[976.B.4.f]

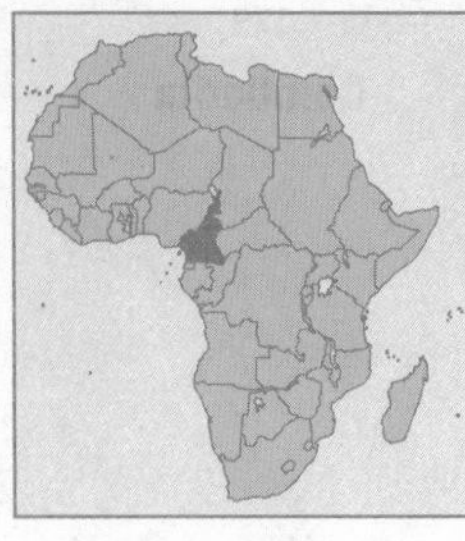

Cameroon

A republic of west Africa on the Gulf of Guinea, Cameroon borders on Nigeria, Chad, the Central African Republic, the Congo, Gabon, and Equatorial Guinea. Area: 179,558 sq.mi. (465,054 sq.km.). Pop. (1974 est.): 6,282,000. Cap.: Yaoundé (pop., 1973 est., 230,000). Largest city: Douala (pop., 1973 est., 340,000). Language: English and French (official), Bantu, Sudanic. Religion: mainly animist, with Christian and Muslim minorities. President in 1975, Ahmadou Ahidjo; prime minister from June 30, Paul Biya.

On April 5 President Ahidjo, the sole candidate, was reelected for a fourth consecutive five-year term with 99.99% of the votes cast.

Although the president retained his firm hold on power, the aftereffects of the 1970 uprising by the revolutionary Union of the Cameroon Peoples (UPC) were still much in evidence. In April there were rumours of the arbitrary arrest of Mme Marthe Moumié, widow of former UPC leader Félix Moumié who had been assassinated in Geneva in 1960. However, the following month it became known that Madame Moumié was living with her family at Ebolowa. It appeared that she had been a beneficiary of presidential clemency after a long period of detention, as had former archbishop Albert Ndongmo, who was pardoned on May 17 after having been sentenced to death (the sentence had earlier been commuted to life imprisonment). In July it became known that William Bechtel, a French national sentenced by the Swiss courts for the murder of Moumié, had been released on parole in view of his advanced age (81 years) and failing health.

In June the office of prime minister was created and taken up by Paul Biya, former secretary-general to the president. (PHILIPPE DECRAENE)

CAMEROON

Education. (1971–72) Primary, pupils 930,131, teachers 19,159; secondary, pupils 65,360, teachers 2,719; vocational, pupils 21,547, teachers 950; teacher training (1970–71), students 4,441, teachers (1969–70) 275; higher, students 3,443, teaching staff 278.

Finance. Monetary unit: CFA franc, with (Sept. 22, 1975) a parity of CFA Fr. 50 to the French franc and a free rate of CFA Fr. 227.70 to U.S. $1 (CFA Fr. 471.75 = £1 sterling). Federal budget (1974–75 est.) balanced at CFA Fr. 69.2 billion.

Foreign Trade. (1974) Imports CFA Fr. 104,830,000,000; exports CFA Fr. 114.9 billion. Import sources (1973): France 48%; West Germany 10%; U.S. 9%; Gabon 4%; Italy 4%. Export destinations (1973): France 29%; The Netherlands 24%; West Germany 10%; U.S. 7%; Japan 5%. Main exports: cocoa 27%; coffee 25%; timber 10%; aluminum 3%.

Transport and Communications. Roads (1972) 22,750 km. (including 4,838 km. main roads). Motor vehicles in use (1972): passenger 39,100; commercial (including buses) 37,300. Railways (1973): 1,173 km.; traffic 199 million passenger-km., freight 351 million net ton-km. Telephones (June 1973) 22,000. Radio receivers (Dec. 1973) 230,000.

Agriculture. Production (in 000; metric tons; 1974; 1973 in parentheses): corn *c.* 350 (*c.* 300); sweet potatoes (1973) *c.* 500, (1972) 476; cassava (1973) *c.* 1,000, (1972) *c.* 1,000; coffee *c.* 80 (*c.* 80); cocoa *c.* 126 (*c.* 125); bananas (1973) *c.* 130, (1972) *c.* 130; peanuts *c.* 230 (*c.* 166); rubber *c.* 15 (*c.* 15); cotton, lint *c.* 15 (*c.* 11); millet and sorghum *c.* 360 (*c.* 320); palm kernels *c.* 60 (*c.* 60); palm oil *c.* 60 (*c.* 60). Livestock (in 000; Dec. 1973): cattle *c.* 2,013; pigs *c.* 377; sheep *c.* 2,000; goats *c.* 2,100; chickens *c.* 8,600.

Industry. Production (in 000; 1972): aluminum (metric tons) 43; gold (troy oz.) 1.

Canadian Literature: *see* Literature

Canning Industry: *see* Food Processing

Canoeing: *see* Water Sports

Canada

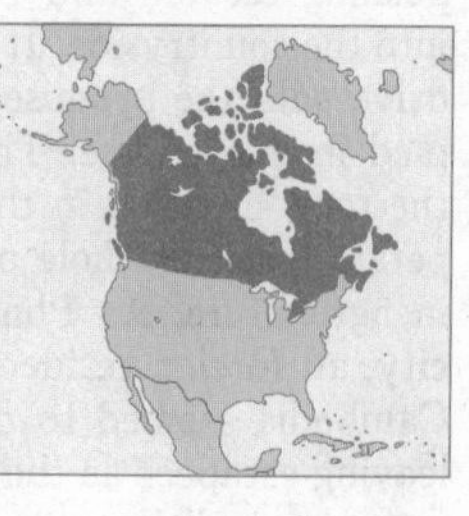

Canada is a federal parliamentary state and member of the Commonwealth of Nations covering North America north of conterminous United States and east of Alaska. Area: 3,851,809 sq.mi. (9,976,130 sq.km.). Pop. (1975 est.): 22.8 million, including (1971) British 44.6%; French 28.7%; other European 23%; Indian and Eskimo 1.4%. Cap.: Ottawa (metro. pop., 1974 est., 626,000). Largest city: Montreal (metro. pop., 1974 est., 2,798,000). Language (mother tongue; 1971): English 61%; French 27%; others 13%. Religion (1971): Roman Catholic 46%; Protestant 42%. Queen, Elizabeth II; governor-general in 1975, Jules Léger; prime minister, Pierre Elliott Trudeau.

Economic problems, especially inflation and unemployment, constituted the chief public issue throughout Canada in 1975. Although the Canadian recession was shorter and less severe than that in the U.S., it was marked by an unemployment rate running at over 7% of the labour force and price levels that climbed more than 10% during the year.

The Trudeau government found itself under attack from all sides for its failure to come forward with policies dealing with these twin problems. In the general election of July 8, 1974, it had resisted the Conservative opposition's call for wage and price controls, arguing that Canada's inflation reflected worldwide conditions. It claimed that improvements in the supply of goods would result in a general dampening of rising prices and thus bring an end to Canada's difficulties. By the early summer of 1975, however, it was apparent that these conditions, although partly achieved, were not leading to the desired results.

The Canadian people appeared to have concluded that inflation would probably continue indefinitely and that the only way to meet it was to demand incomes that would more than compensate for it. Thus 1975 was a year of widespread industrial unrest as workers attempted to improve their economic position through collective action. Throughout the country strikes and lockouts occurred in industry, transportation, construction and the public sector, including a nationwide, six-week strike by post office employees. The total of man-days lost rose at a rate double that of two years earlier.

In June Finance Minister John Turner embarked on an effort to persuade business and labour to accept voluntary restraints on prices and incomes. Limits were to be specified within which inflation would be contained, and a board would be appointed to monitor increases. After a series of meetings with the concerned parties, Turner was forced to admit that he could not obtain a consensus in favour of this approach. On September 10 the finance minister, in office since January 1972, dramatically resigned his portfolio. The only reason he gave was a desire to return to private life, although sources close to him suggested that the real reason was increasing frustration over constant disagreements with his colleagues. A financial conservative, Turner was believed to be unhappy with the high level of federal government spending and the Cabinet's reluctance to impose mandatory controls on wages and prices.

A month later, on the eve of the resumption of Parliament on October 14, Prime Minister Trudeau announced to the country that a set of guidelines would be established immediately to limit incomes and prices. The guidelines would apply with the force of law to all government employees: federal, provincial, and municipal; to 1,500 large corporations employing more than 500 persons each; to most construction workers; and to professionals who derived their income from fees. Businesses would be allowed to raise prices only to the point of recovering increased costs. Other Canadians would be expected to abide by the guidelines on a voluntary basis. An Anti-Inflation Board would be created to monitor the mandatory restraints.

The guidelines, during the first year of the plan's operation, would allow a maximum salary increase of 10%, of which 8% would be based on rises in the cost of living and 2% would reflect increased national productivity. A further 2% increase would be available for groups considered to have fallen behind in wage bargaining. In his appeal to the country Trudeau urged all Canadians to "restrain their rising demands upon the nation's wealth, so that Canada as a whole will be able to live within her means." "In this struggle," he went on, "we must accomplish nothing less than a wrenching adjustment of our expectations—an adjustment of our national lifestyle to our means." The federal government promised to do its part by arresting further growth in the public service and reducing spending in many areas.

Thus Canada moved to a measure of state intervention in the economy unknown since World War II. Success or failure in the anti-inflation drive would depend upon the public's perception of the government's sincerity and fairness in implementing the program. Organized labour immediately declared against it, while Premier David Barrett of British Columbia criticized it for imposing only weak controls on profits and prices. A stormy winter appeared to lie ahead as Canada embarked on bold measures designed, as Trudeau put it, to "knock the wind out of inflation."

Domestic Affairs. The Trudeau Cabinet was shuffled on September 26, following the Turner resignation, in an effort to put together a new team capable of taking "fast, hard action" to meet Canada's economic difficulties. Six senior ministers changed positions, while two members of the Liberal back bench were brought into the government. Donald Macdonald, formerly minister of energy, mines, and resources, took over the key finance portfolio. Otto Lang, a Saskatchewan law teacher who had been justice minister, replaced Trudeau's close associate Jean Marchand, who was suffering from poor health, as minister of transport. Another member of the Cabinet left it soon after he was appointed. Pierre Juneau, the former head of the federal regulatory agency for broadcasting, was appointed minister of communications on August 29, but when he sought election to Parliament for a Montreal riding on October 14, he was defeated and obliged to resign. On the same day the Liberals retained another seat in northern New Brunswick, leaving the standings in the House of Commons as Liberals 140; Progressive Conservatives 95; New Democratic Party 16; Social Credit 11; independent 1; vacant 1.

FINANCIAL TIMES

Prime Minister Pierre Trudeau inspects a guard of honour of the Honourable Artillery Company at Guildhall, where he received the Freedom of the City of London in March.

One of Canada's major parties gained a new leader in 1975 when the New Democratic Party (NDP) chose Edward Broadbent (*see* BIOGRAPHY), member of Parliament for the automobile-manufacturing city of Oshawa, Ont., at a convention in Winnipeg, Man., on July 7. Broadbent succeeded David Lewis, who lost his parliamentary seat in the 1974 election. Lewis

CANADA

Education. (1973–74) Primary, pupils 3,779,-900; secondary, pupils 1,885,100; preprimary, primary, and secondary, teachers 269,200; vocational (not including Quebec; 1970–71), pupils 322,000; higher (including 44 main universities), students 543,250, teaching staff 45,700.

Finance. Monetary unit: Canadian dollar, with a free rate (Sept. 22, 1975) of Can$1.02 to U.S. $1 (Can$2.12 = £1 sterling). Gold, SDRs, and foreign exchange: (June 1975) U.S. $4,662,000,-000; (June 1974) U.S. $5,780,000,000. Budget (1973–74 est.): revenue Can$19,367,000,000; expenditure Can$20,039,000,000. Gross national product: (1974) Can$139,490,000,000; (1973) Can$118.9 billion. Money supply: (April 1975) Can$27,930,000,000; (April 1974) Can$25.1 billion. Cost of living (1970 = 100): (June 1975) 142; (June 1974) 128.

Foreign Trade. (1974) Imports Can$33,805,-000,000; exports Can$33,430,000,000. Import sources: U.S. 66%; EEC 10%. Export destinations: U.S. 66%; EEC 13% (U.K. 6%); Japan 7%. Main exports: motor vehicles 17%; crude oil 11%; metal ores 8%; wheat 6%; nonferrous metals 6%; timber 6%; wood pulp 6%; newsprint 6%. Tourism (1973): visitors 38,289,000; gross receipts U.S. $1,434,000,000.

Transport and Communications. Roads (1971) 831,682 km. (including 2,765 km. expressways). Motor vehicles in use (1973): passenger 7,866,100; commercial (including buses) 2,211,800. Railways (1973): 70,131 km.; traffic 2,573,000,000 passenger-km., freight 190,906,-000,000 net ton-km. Air traffic (1973): 21,701,-000,000 passenger-km.; freight 569.9 million net ton-km. Shipping (1974): merchant vessels 100 gross tons and over 1,321; gross tonnage 2,459,-998. Shipping traffic (includes Great Lakes and St. Lawrence traffic; 1973): goods loaded 112,-535,000 metric tons, unloaded 66,554,000 metric tons. Telephones (Dec. 1973) 11,665,000. Radio receivers (Dec. 1973) 19,133,000. Television receivers (Dec. 1973) 7,705,000.

Agriculture. Production (in 000; metric tons; 1974; 1973 in parentheses): wheat 14,221 (16,-459); barley 8,585 (10,223); oats 3,929 (5,041); rye 481 (363); corn 2,589 (2,803); potatoes 2,437 (2,168); tomatoes *c.* 345 (345); rapeseed 1,200 (1,275); linseed 363 (493); soybeans 301 (397); tobacco *c.* 119 (117); beef and veal (1973) *c.* 902, (1972) 927; pork (1973) *c.* 618, (1972) 637; timber (cu.m.; 1973) *c.* 124,100, (1972) 124,100; fish catch (1973) 1,152, (1972) 1,169. Livestock (in 000; Dec. 1973): cattle *c.* 13,378; sheep *c.* 605; horses (1972) 345; pigs 7,007; chickens (1972) 94,689.

Industry. Labour force: (May 1975) 10,005,-000; (May 1974) 9,605,000. Unemployment: (May 1975) 7.1%; (May 1974) 5.4%. Index of industrial production (1970 = 100): (1974) 126; (1973) 123. Fuel and power (in 000; metric tons; 1974): coal 17,303; lignite 3,484; crude oil 84,703; natural gas (cu.m.) 96,029,000; electricity (kw-hr.) 279,199,000 (74% hydroelectric and 5% nuclear in 1973). Metal and mineral production (in 000; metric tons; 1974): iron ore (shipments; 55% metal content) 47,260; crude steel 13,622; copper ore (metal content) 826; nickel ore (metal content) 262; zinc ore (metal content) 1,207; lead ore (metal content) 301; aluminum (1973) 930; uranium ore (metal content) 4.2; asbestos 1,665; gold (troy oz.) 1,680; silver (troy oz.) 42,079. Other production (in 000; metric tons; 1974): wood pulp 19,138; newsprint 8,662; other paper and paperboard (1973) 4,109; sulfuric acid 2,627; synthetic rubber 209; passenger cars (units) 1,166; commercial vehicles (units) 362. Dwelling units completed (1974) 257,000.

was the last in a series of leaders who had been associated with the party's founding in the 1930s.

The first session of the 30th Parliament, which began on Sept. 30, 1974, sat well into the summer of 1975. Of 89 pieces of legislation brought before it, 63 bills, many of a housekeeping nature, were passed. The House spent an inordinate amount of time on three subjects: a petroleum administration bill giving the government power to set oil prices across Canada; tax changes resulting from the budget of Nov. 18, 1974; and a controversial measure to raise MPs' salaries by one-third.

The last item was originally introduced in December 1974, when a 50% raise was recommended on the ground that parliamentarians had not enjoyed a salary increase since 1971. Public reaction was so critical that the total increase, and a provision for an annual cost of living adjustment, were scaled down. When the pay increase was finally approved on April 30, former prime minister John Diefenbaker denounced it as a poor example to the people of Canada in a time of rampant inflation. Less controversial bills that were approved included the amending of a number of federal statutes to give women equal status with men, measures to stabilize farm income for a wide range of products from cereals to livestock, and a private member's bill declaring the industrious beaver an official symbol of Canada.

Four provinces held elections in 1975. The most unexpected result was in Canada's largest province, Ontario, where, after 32 years of majority government, the Conservatives were reduced to a minority position in the legislature. In the election of September 18 the Tories lost 23 seats and saw three Cabinet ministers defeated. Their share of the popular vote fell by 10%. In an enlarged legislature of 125 seats, they won 51, with the formerly second-place Liberals emerging with 36 seats and the New Democratic Party with 38. The latter party, under the leadership of David Lewis' son, Stephen, thus became the official opposition. The outcome was a severe blow to Premier William Davis, whose administration had been tarnished by scandals and criticized for its policies on land use, regional government, and education.

In Alberta another Conservative administration, this one led by Peter Lougheed, won a smashing victory on March 26. In a legislature of 75 seats, the Conservatives won 69, leaving 4 Social Credit members, one NDP member, and one independent in opposition. The Social Credit party, which had previously held 24 seats, was virtually wiped out. Lougheed's victory gave a strong vote of confidence to his government's policies emphasizing that Alberta's oil and gas resources must be developed and priced for the long-term benefit of the province.

"I must confess to feeling some trepidation over our government's meddling in percentages of Canadian content in our reading matter."

NORRIS—VANCOUVER SUN/ROTHCO

In neighbouring Saskatchewan, the NDP government of Premier Allan Blakeney also retained office in an election on June 11, although not as decisively as Lougheed had done. Blakeney's party won 38 of the 60 seats in the legislature, compared with 45 in the last election in 1971. The Conservatives showed a resurgence, electing seven members and gaining 28% of the popular vote, a spectacular improvement over the 2% they had obtained in 1971. The Liberals held the 15 seats they had won in 1971, but their share of the popular vote declined.

Finally, in Canada's easternmost province of Newfoundland, another Conservative government held onto office in an election on September 16. The Conservatives under Premier Frank Moores won 30 seats in an expanded 51-seat legislature, but the party's share of the popular vote fell from 59% in 1972 to 46%. The most exciting feature of a dull campaign was the return to public life of 74-year-old Joseph Smallwood, the first premier of the province and a long-time leader of the Liberals. Creating a splinter group of Liberals, Smallwood took votes from the official party under Edward Roberts.

Canada's oil exports to the U.S. began dropping in 1975, partly because of a ceiling designed to protect declining reserves and partly because of lower U.S. demand. Canadian government ceilings were well above the average flow over the year of 707,000 bbl. a day. Construction began on a pipeline from Sarnia to Montreal that would bring 250,000 bbl. a day of western Canadian oil to markets in Quebec and the Maritime Provinces. When completed in early 1977, this line would divert further oil from the U.S. market into eastern Canada. Imports of overseas oil into eastern Canada reached an average of almost 825,000 bbl. a day in 1975, necessitating changes in the export tax designed to bring export prices into line with import prices.

The federal government gave a substantial boost to domestic production in February when it agreed to a $300 million participation in the giant Syncrude Canada Ltd. scheme to extract oil from the Athabaska tar sands of northern Alberta. Ottawa, together with Alberta and Ontario, invested heavily in the scheme, while the three participating oil companies—Imperial Oil, Gulf Oil, and Cities Service—also put in additional funds. Oil would be separated from the sticky sand of the deposits by hot water and steam. The target for the project was an output of 125,000 bbl. a day, with production expected to start in 1978. A small plant was already producing 45,000 bbl. a day.

Strains between Canada and the U.S. over the cross-border traffic in agricultural commodities were eased in 1975 as both countries relaxed quotas on meat products. On August 7 U.S. Pres. Gerald Ford signed a proclamation lifting U.S. quotas on Canadian cattle, hogs, and pork that had been imposed in November 1974 but made retroactive to August 12. At the same time Canada removed its quota on U.S. slaughter cattle. Canadian quotas on beef and veal products remained, as well as a limit on the importation of eggs from the U.S. This had been applied on July 4 in order to protect Canadian egg producers from lower-priced imports.

Foreign Affairs. Prime Minister Trudeau made two visits to Europe in 1975 to promote the idea of a "contractual link" between Canada and the European Economic Community (EEC). This would involve, in

Trudeau's words, "an obligation to consult . . . to develop co-operatively initiatives in the economic sphere." In early March he spent 17 days visiting five European countries to explain the Canadian proposals to government leaders. In late May he returned for the NATO summit meeting in Brussels and engaged in conversations in two more countries. The Commission of the EEC lent its support on May 22 by recommending that negotiations be opened with Canada to conclude "a framework agreement for economic and commercial co-operation."

Trudeau was in Helsinki, Fin., at the end of July for the signing of the Final Act of the Conference on Security and Cooperation in Europe. During this trip he discussed Canada's dispute with the U.S.S.R. over heavy Soviet fishing catches on the Atlantic coast with Soviet Communist Party leader Leonid Brezhnev. The Soviet failure to observe internationally approved regulations on catches led Canada to close its Atlantic ports to Soviet trawlers on July 28. Following a visit by Soviet Foreign Minister A. A. Gromyko to Ottawa, an agreement was reached and the ban was lifted effective September 29.

Canada lost influence among third world countries when it declined to play host to the fifth UN Congress on the Prevention of Crime in September because of domestic controversy over the intended participation of representatives of the Palestine Liberation Organization. The Canadian Jewish community and the provincial government of Ontario had opposed the entry of members of the PLO into Canada, and the government decided that the time was not "propitious" to hold the conference. It unsuccessfully urged the United Nations to postpone the conference, which was held in Geneva on the dates originally scheduled.

Canada retreated from one of the principles underlying the contentious unification of its armed forces carried out in 1967 by setting up a separate air command to be based at Winnipeg. The new command would undertake air defense, transport, and search and rescue functions. The decision was announced by Defense Minister James Richardson on January 17. With a mobile command at St. Hubert, Que., a maritime command at Halifax, Nova Scotia, and the new air command, Canada had in effect reestablished the army, navy, and air force of preunification days. In May the minister announced that two new regions would be created within Canada for the North American Air Defense Command (NORAD) operations. Whereas most NORAD regions had straddled the U.S.-Canadian border, there would now be a western Canadian region with headquarters at Edmonton, Alta., and an eastern Canadian region using the existing headquarters of the 22nd NORAD region at North Bay, Ont.

The Economy. The Canadian economy was clearly underutilized in 1975. Canadian industrial production had begun to turn down in late 1974, following a trend that was already evident in the U.S. In the first quarter of 1975 Canada's real gross national product declined 1.4% from the last quarter of 1974, recovering only slightly in the second quarter. Over the full year it was estimated that the gross national product, on a seasonally adjusted basis, would reach $150.3 billion. This represented a gain of about 9.5% in current dollar terms, but a decline of 0.5% in real terms from the 1974 figures.

The chief brake on the economy lay in a poor export performance. The recession in the U.S. cut back that country's imports of Canadian goods, whether

CALGARY HERALD

Crossing of the Bow River by the F Troop of the North West Mounted Police in 1875 was re-created at the site of Fort Calgary as part of a centennial celebration.

automobiles, lumber, or minerals. Canada's own restraints on crude oil shipments to the U.S. reduced its exports in that sector, while U.S. quotas lowered its meat imports from Canada. Depression in other countries affected trade with them as well. Thus Canada's export trade experienced its worst decline since World War II. Yet, because consumer spending held up, imports continued to rise in 1975, resulting in a current account deficit that was expected to grow to the unusually large figure of over $5 billion by the end of the year. This deficit would be twice as large as that experienced in 1974. Only a strong inflow of capital, attracted by Canada's high interest rates, prevented a serious fall in the exchange value of the Canadian dollar.

Especially worrying to the government was the fact that Canadian wage settlements were running at a higher level than in the U.S. Productivity per worker was growing faster in the U.S., and these conditions, if they persisted, would seriously damage Canada's trading position in relation to the U.S., its major competitor as well as its chief market.

Finance Minister Turner's fifth (and last) budget, presented on June 23, was clearly directed at the persistent problem of inflation. In an effort to promote the development of new petroleum supplies, the domestic price of oil was allowed to rise to $8 a barrel from $6.50. (A number of provinces, including Ontario, applied temporary freezes on gasoline prices at this time while they assessed the new situation.) Turner announced that the federal excise tax on gasoline was to be increased immediately by ten cents a gallon, the object being to provide more revenue to meet higher compensation payments and thus hold down the price of imported oil for Canadians. The finance minister also announced that the price of natural gas would be allowed to rise 43 cents per 1,000 cu.ft. on November 1. Tax changes in the June budget were minor. The federal government showed modest restraint by cutting its proposed spending by $1 billion, but the budget still forecast a deficit of $3.6 billion for the year. Expenditures by Ottawa were expected to rise by almost $4 billion to more than $31 billion for the fiscal year 1975–76. (D. M. L. FARR)

[973.B]

ENCYCLOPÆDIA BRITANNICA FILMS. *The Legend of the Magic Knives* (1971); *The Canadians: Their Cities* (1974); *The Canadians: Their Land* (1974).

SPECIAL REPORT

THE STATE OF CANADIAN PUBLISHING

By Richard Rohmer

In the mid-1970s Canadian publishing—books, magazines, and periodicals, though not the flourishing newspapers—can be characterized as in disarray, in difficulty, and on the defensive.

The newspapers are prosperous, protected against foreign ownership or control and impervious to same-medium competition except in the communities they serve. The big ones in major cities such as Montreal, Toronto, and Vancouver are fat editorially and quite ready to stand up to the federal and provincial governments. In Ontario the jewel of Canadian journalism, the prestigious *Toronto Globe and Mail,* has taken over the mantle of opposition to the government of the province from the seemingly impotent opposition parties in the legislature. Moreover, the *Globe* has been remarkably effective in its investigative reporting, opening can after can of political worms with commendable regularity.

Canadian book publishing, however, is in a crisis situation. Whether the major Canadian-owned publishing houses can survive is a question that has troubled the industry for a decade. During the latter part of the 1960s, the decentralization of textbook selection and buying destroyed the publishers' once-firm financial base of large-scale textbook purchases by the provincial education ministries. Without the working capital provided by this assured market, many Canadian publishing houses were caught in a squeeze between high inventories and stretched-to-the-limits accounts receivable. Confronted by unsympathetic Canadian bankers who refused to enlarge their lines of credit (but were and still are happy to lend Canadian savings to wealthy U.S. publishing corporations or their Canadian subsidiaries for the purpose of buying out the sinking Canadian houses), all but a handful were compelled to sell out to U.S. firms. In 1970, after a series of American takeovers, the patriarch of educational publishing in Canada, Ryerson Press, was acquired by the U.S. publishing giant McGraw-Hill. Only two major book-publishing firms were left in Canadian ownership: McClelland & Stewart and Clarke, Irwin.

A Vanishing Canadian Voice? If there were no Canadian-owned book publishers, but only Canadian subsidiaries of foreign—predominantly American—firms, what would happen to the expression of the Canadian point of view, the Canadian novel, poetry, and nonfiction about things Canadian? The fear was, and still is, that editorial decisions to publish or not to publish Canadian manuscripts would be made, not in Canada, but in New York or Chicago where editorial knowledge of and interest in Canada are minimal or nonexistent. An examination of the track record of U.S. and British publishers and their subsidiaries in Canada demonstrates the point. Of 659 new titles of Canadian high-risk fiction, poetry, and other trade books published in the fall of 1974, 584 (88.6%) were produced by Canadian publishers, 46 by U.S. subsidiaries, and 29 by British-owned firms.

Richard Heath Rohmer, Canadian journalist and lawyer, is chairman of the Royal Commission on Publishing, Ottawa. Books he has written include The Arctic Imperative *(1973),* Ultimatum *(1973),* Exxoneration *(1974), and* Exodus/U.K. *(1975).*

Is it important to have a Canadian point of view expressed in book or magazine form? And is Canadian ownership of the publishing industry a matter for concern?

The government of Canada certainly seems to think so. In two speeches early in 1975, the secretary of state, Hugh Faulkner, who is responsible for cultural matters, said:

> The Canadian government believes strongly that the major segment of the publishing industry in Canada should be owned by Canadians. Canadian books and magazines are too important to the cultural and intellectual life of this country to be allowed to come completely under foreign control, however sympathetic or benign.
>
> We in the government are really not so much concerned with certain of the nation's industries as we are deeply committed to the nation's integrity. What happens in the area of Canadian books, magazines, and broadcasting, as in other areas of Canadian cultural expression, is not a matter of marginal interest or importance. The strength, originality, and vision we find therein is the true measure of what constitutes our national life.

For most Canadians, possessing and maintaining a separate culture and identity is an absolute necessity. This is the reason for the continuing fight against the American cultural tidal wave of television programs, book overruns, book clubs, and magazines. The acquisition of Ryerson Press by McGraw-Hill (using money borrowed from a Canadian bank) brought English-speaking Canadians face to face with the question of whether they want an indigenous book-publishing capability. The answer—delivered by public expression, by government pronouncement, by studies of commissions and other bodies—has been an emphatic yes. But the response by the governments of Canada and of Ontario, the principal province of residence of most publishers, has been almost totally monetary, ad hoc, and short term.

The Government Response. Confronted with a public outcry over the Ryerson acquisition, the government of the Province of Ontario, on Dec. 23, 1970, appointed a Royal Commission on Book Publishing. The commission's brief was to investigate the industry and to report on what steps should be taken to keep those segments of it still in Canadian ownership both Canadian and healthy. Naturally enough, since Ontario is where almost all the English-language Canadian publishers are located, the focus of the royal commission was on English-language publishing. Nevertheless, in its studies it ranged across the country, especially in its concern for the state of educational publishing. It also monitored the attempts by the Province of Quebec to assist both the French-language publishers and the retail bookstores by requiring schools to buy their books through local, accredited shops.

Within a month of the establishment of the Ontario royal commission, the president of McClelland & Stewart, the largest remaining Canadian-owned publisher, announced that he would have to sell out—probably to a U.S. firm—or go bankrupt. After assessing the crisis, the commission presented its first interim report to the government of Ontario, recommending that a loan of approximately $1 million be made to McClelland & Stewart. The government immediately accepted the recommendation, thereby rescuing the beleaguered publishing house. Later, it also accepted the commission's third interim report, which laid the groundwork for government-guaranteed loans to all Ontario-based, Canadian-owned publishers threatened by critical cash shortages. Since 1971 virtually all qualified publishers in Ontario have applied for and received this financial assistance.

But financial problems are not all that ail the Canadian book-publishing industry. In its final report, delivered in December 1972, the royal commission made 70 recommendations aimed at dealing with a variety of difficulties. Central to all of them was the proposal that the government establish a Book Publishing Board to bring cohesiveness and direction to the industry and to administer the various programs proposed by the commission. The Ontario government chose to ignore all of these recommendations—a typical fate for the considered opinions of such bodies—although it did establish a Learning Materials Development Fund in 1973 and increase the publishing grants distributed by the Ontario Arts Council.

While the Ontario government gave the Royal Commission on Book Publishing a "slick burial," the government of Canada has shown increasing concern for the health of the industry. Even so, its efforts have been far from comprehensive. Federal assistance, mainly through the Canada Council, includes support for publishers ($1,150,000 in 1975) and authors ($600,000); for the translation of Canadian books from one of the country's two official languages (English and French) to the other ($275,000); for the purchase of books for free distribution in Canada and abroad ($600,000); and for the publication of learned manuscripts. Other programs include a new, $1.5 million scheme for the promotion and distribution of Canadian publications.

Although the federal government is prepared to assist the publishing industry financially, it is not prepared to take over policy direction or control. There are no plans to establish an agency comparable to the Canadian Radio-Television Commission, which monitors (among other things) the cultural performance of Canadian broadcasting stations. Hugh Faulkner, speaking at the 1975 annual meeting of the Canadian Book Publishers' Council, confirmed the government's hands-off policy. Dealing with the need to increase the Canadian share of mass-market paperback distribution and authorship (less than 2% of the 32 million mass-market paperbacks sold annually in Canada are Canadian-authored), he said:

> The government will not act in your place. It is up to your members to decide whether it is better for each publishing house to establish its own mass paperback collection or to pool your efforts in creating one or two large national collections. It is up to you to acquire and keep the rights for books that might sell on the mass market. It is up to you to negotiate with a national distributor of proven competence the introduction of your mass paperback collections in as many sales outlets as possible across Canada.

The Development Council. In response to government urging that the various factions within Canadian publishing present a common front, a new organization emerged at the beginning of 1975. The Book and Periodical Development Council encompasses a significant cross section of the industry: the Canadian Booksellers Association, the Canadian Library Association, the Writers' Union of Canada, the Canadian Periodical Publishers Association, the Independent Publishers Association, and the Canadian Book Publishers' Council. This alliance of varied interests could well provide a new impetus for publishing in Canada. The council has moved rapidly to define its objectives and is pressing the government for action. Concerned with a market share that has declined significantly since 1972, it has proposed a series of measures which it claims would substantially increase the portion of the Canadian book market enjoyed by Canadian-owned publishers. In themselves, these proposals demonstrate the scope and scale of the difficulties facing Canadian publishers. They are:

1. The establishment of a Book and Periodical Development Agency.
2. Legislation to prevent foreign take-overs of existing Canadian businesses and the establishment of new foreign-owned firms in both publishing and distribution and to empower the agency to regulate the transfer of book-publishing agency agreements from Canadian to foreign-owned companies. The latter issue is a complex one, and exceptions to the general policy of restricting transfers of agency business to the foreign-owned firms would be necessary.
3. The development of programs of working capital loan guarantees for Canadian-owned publishers and distributors, to be administered by the agency.
4. The approval of a federally funded library purchase program to allow libraries to improve their collections of Canadian books.
5. Action to regulate book clubs doing business in Canada with respect to both ownership and the content of their offerings.
6. The establishment of a licensing system and review procedure for regulating mass paperback and periodical wholesalers in Canada.
7. Measures to provide effective access for Canadian books in the book club and mass paperback markets, including space in retail outlets.
8. A substantial strengthening and expansion of the retail bookstore system.
9. Amendment of the Copyright Act to restrict the sale in Canada of foreign editions of books for which there is a Canadian publisher.
10. A strategy for getting Canadian-owned companies actively involved again in publishing for the educational market.
11. The setting up of an Educational Materials Development Fund to provide federal support, on a cost-sharing basis with the provinces, for the development of Canadian educational material by Canadian-owned companies.
12. A commitment to implementing a public lending right program for Canadian publications whereby authors whose books are in libraries will be compensated for their use when loaned by the libraries.
13. The careful coordination of programs for improving promotion and distribution of Canadian publications with the measures listed above and with the broader objectives outlined in the text of the brief.

The Magazine Question. The Book and Periodical Development Council is concerned not only with books but also with the publishing and distribution of magazines and other periodicals. A recent study by the Canadian Periodical Publishers Association shows that newsstand sales account for only 9% of sales of Canadian magazines, compared with 55% of sales of American magazines in Canada. But the next statistic tells it all—only 3% of all the magazines sold on the newsstands in 1974 were Canadian!

It follows that probably 95% of all magazines sold by newsstands in Canada are American. Why does this pathetic situation exist? Among a multitude of causes, four main reasons stand out: (1) the free flow of magazines and other periodicals across the border with no duty restrictions, permitting high-volume, low-cost "dumping"; (2) control of the "geographic wholesalers" in Canada by ten national distributors in the United States; (3) the siphoning off of massive Canadian advertising revenues by "canadianized" versions of *Time* and *Reader's Digest;* and (4) the disinclination of the appropriate Canadian governments to enact protective legislation.

Two of these reasons deserve special comment. All the American magazines sold in Canada are in the hands of ten U.S. distributors. By some magic formula, all ten select one wholesaler in a large geographic area, whether in Canada or in the U.S., and use him exclusively. Therefore, a retailer, if he wants important magazines such as *TV Guide, Time, Newsweek,* and *Playboy,* is forced to deal with the anointed wholesaler, who has a de facto monopoly within his region. How will a Canadian magazine, with its low volume, high cost, and unattractive percentage return, fare with these wholesalers? The Canadian magazines' 3% share of newsstand sales provides the answer.

What to do? The only remedy is the imposition of protective legislation and quotas by a concerned government. As of 1975, there was no sign of any such move.

The second reason is the incongruous tax privilege given to *Time* and *Reader's Digest.* Under the 1964 amendments to the Income Tax Act, Canadian firms, in calculating income tax, are allowed to deduct the cost of advertising in Canadian magazines. The object of the legislation was to allow Canadian publications to attract enough advertising revenue to become self-sufficient. Both *Time* and *Reader's Digest* publish Canadian editions with a small Canadian segment, but their basic editorial content is prepared in the U.S. Nevertheless, through heavy lobbying and direct pressure from the U.S., both magazines were classified as "Canadian" publications under the law. The result has been that *Time* and *Reader's Digest* have carried off two lions' shares of Canadian advertising revenue—so large, it is argued, that no similar Canadian publications could ever be launched.

At the beginning of 1975 the government announced its intention to remove this special tax privilege, as of Jan. 1, 1976. Legislation to this effect was introduced in the House of Commons in May 1975. As the year drew to a close, the bill was nearing passage, although the magazines stimulated a heavy mail campaign directed at members of Parliament. But the granting of such a privilege in the first place demonstrates a fundamental Canadian weakness of purpose.

Canadians talk a great deal about protecting their economy, culture, and sovereignty, but only rarely do they do anything about it. So it is with publishing, an industry at the heart of any nation's culture. There has been much brave talk in the last five years, but precious little has been accomplished. The result? Canadian publishing in 1975 remains "in disarray, in difficulty, and on the defensive."

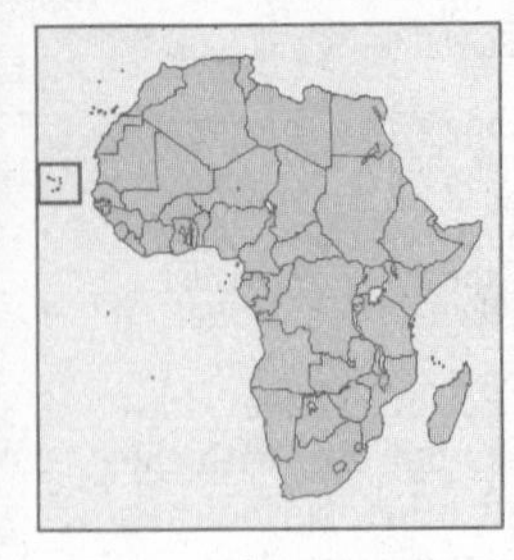

Cape Verde Islands

An independent African republic, Cape Verde is located 385 mi. (620 km.) off the west coast of Africa. Area: 1,557 sq.mi. (4,033 sq.km.). Pop. (1974 est.): 291,000. Cap.: Praia (pop., 1970, 21,500). Largest city: Mindelo (pop., 1970, 28,800). Language: Portuguese. Religion: mainly Roman Catholic. President in 1975, Aristide Pereira; premier, Maj. Pedro Pires.

Elections to the 56 seats in the National Assembly were held on June 30, 1975; the franchise embraced everyone over 17 years of age, and 84% of the 130,000 persons eligible to vote went to the polls. The only party contesting the election was the African Party for the Independence of Guinea-Bissau and Cape Verde (PAIGC). The National Assembly met on July 4 in Praia, and the country became independent on July 5, with Aristide Pereira, secretary-general of PAIGC, as president. A treaty of friendship and cooperation was signed between Portugal and Cape Verde, and on July 6 Portuguese troops withdrew from the island, taking with them a number of opponents of the PAIGC for whom Portugal had negotiated an amnesty. Major Pires became premier, and the government met for the first time on July 15.

Earlier, in April, Pres. Luis Cabral of Guinea-Bissau had proposed unification between his country and Cape Verde, and soon after independence the minister of foreign affairs in Cape Verde, Abilio Duarte, was named to head a commission that would study the proposals. The government also turned its attention to the preparation of schemes to counter the effects of the severe drought that had plagued the islands for seven years. Cape Verde was admitted to the United Nations on September 16. (KENNETH INGHAM)

CAPE VERDE ISLANDS

Education. (1973–74) Primary, pupils 63,734, teachers 1,078; secondary and vocational, pupils 3,712, teachers 186.

Finance and Trade. Monetary unit: Cape Verde escudo, at par with the Portuguese escudo and with (Sept. 22, 1975) a free rate of 27.35 escudos to U.S. $1 (56.65 escudos = £1 sterling). Budget (1973 est.): revenue 282 million escudos; expenditure 158 million escudos. Foreign trade (1973): imports 1,091,855,000 escudos; exports 306,605,000 escudos (including 258,803,000 escudos transit trade). Import sources: Portugal 53%; U.K. 13%; Angola 11%. Export destinations: Portugal 61%; U.S. 25%: ships's stores 6%. Main exports (excluding transit trade): fish 33% (shellfish 12%); fish products 20%; salt 8%; bananas 6%; metals 6%.

Transport. Ships entered (1972): vessels totaling 5,977,000 net registered tons; goods loaded 45,000 metric tons, unloaded 427,000 metric tons.

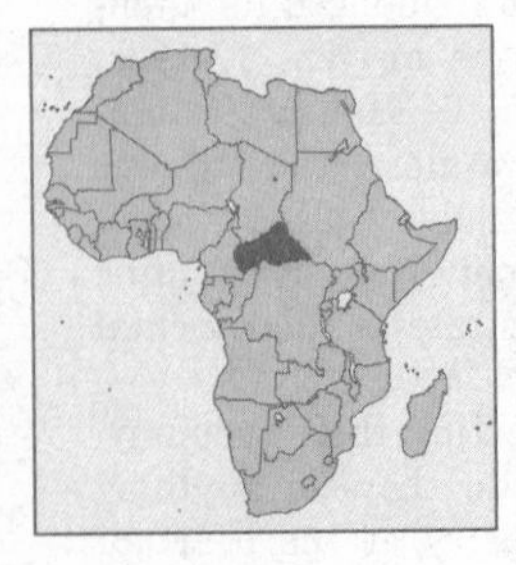

Central African Republic

The landlocked Central African Republic is bounded by Chad, the Sudan, Congo, Zaire, and Cameroon. Area: 241,305 sq.mi. (624,977 sq.km.). Pop. (1973 est.): 1,716,000 according to estimates by external analysts; recent official estimates range up to 750,000 persons higher. Cap. and largest city: Bangui (pop., 1968, 298,600). Language: French (official); local dialects. Religion: Protestant, about 40%; animist and Catholic, about 30% each. President in 1975 and premier until January 2, Jean-Bédel Bokassa; premier from January 2, Elisabeth Domitien.

WIDE WORLD

French Pres. Valéry Giscard d'Estaing is bidden farewell by African children and a presiding tribal chief upon concluding his stay in the Central African Republic.

In January, a fortnight after announcing the discovery of a plot against his regime among officers of the police force, President Bokassa appointed Elisabeth Domitien as premier—the first time a woman had held this office in an African state. Two major Cabinet reorganizations, a regular feature of Bokassa's regime, took place in January and September.

In March French Pres. Valéry Giscard d'Estaing paid an official visit to Bangui—the first by a French president in office—and took part in a Franco-African "summit." It became clear during the course of the meeting that France was openly seeking the role of spokesman for the African sector of the third world at major international conferences.

Ministerial delegations from the Central African Republic visited South Africa in February and March. It was rumoured that the rapprochement with Pretoria might ultimately lead to a visit to South Africa by Bokassa himself. (PHILIPPE DECRAENE)

[978.E.7.a.ii]

CENTRAL AFRICAN REPUBLIC

Education. (1971–72) Primary, pupils 177,924, teachers 2,599; secondary, pupils 10,475, teachers 329; vocational, pupils 1,297, teachers 121; teacher training, students 349, teachers (1970–71) 34; higher (1970–71), students 88, teaching staff 6.

Finance. Monetary unit: CFA franc, with (Sept. 22, 1975) a parity of CFA Fr. 50 to the French franc and a free rate of CFA Fr. 227.70 to U.S. $1 (CFA Fr. 471.75 = £1 sterling). Budget (1974 est.): revenue CFA Fr. 15,706,000,000; expenditure CFA Fr. 17.2 billion. Cost of living (Bangui; 1970 = 100): (Feb. 1975) 150; (Feb. 1974) 124.

Foreign Trade. (1973) Imports CFA Fr. 11,496,000,000; exports CFA Fr. 8,328,000,000. Import sources: France 57%; U.S. 9%; West Germany 7%. Export destinations: France 41%; U.S. 15%; Israel 11%; Italy 6%. Main exports: diamonds 32%; cotton 31%; coffee 30%.

Agriculture. Production (in 000; metric tons; 1973; 1972 in parentheses): cassava *c.* 1,100 (*c.* 1,100); millet and sorghum *c.* 50 (*c.* 50); corn *c.* 55 (*c.* 50); sweet potatoes *c.* 50 (*c.* 49); peanuts *c.* 90 (*c.* 85); bananas *c.* 170 (*c.* 170); coffee *c.* 11 (*c.* 11); cotton, lint *c.* 15 (*c.* 17). Livestock (in 000; 1973): cattle *c.* 455; pigs *c.* 59; sheep *c.* 70; goats *c.* 545; chickens *c.* 1,190.

Industry. Production (in 000; 1973): diamonds (metric carats) 380; cotton fabrics (m.; 1972) 11,000; electricity (kw-hr.) 51,000.

Chad

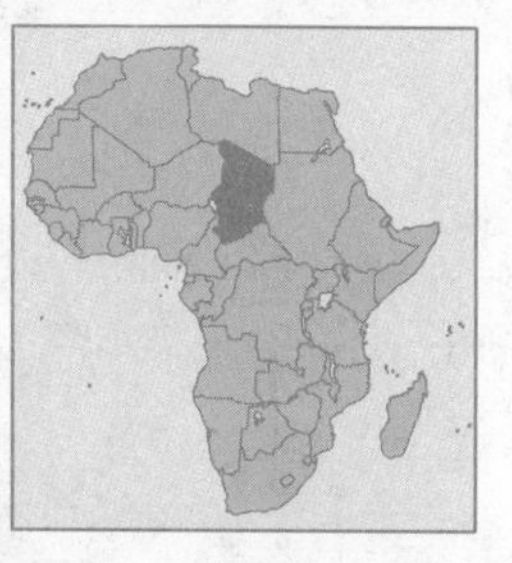

A landlocked republic of central Africa, Chad is bounded by Libya, the Sudan, the Central African Republic, Cameroon, Nigeria, and Niger. Area: 495,750 sq.mi. (1,284,000 sq.km.). Pop. (1974 est.): 3,949,000, including Saras, other Africans, and Arabs. Cap. and largest city: N'Djamena (until Nov. 28, 1973, known by its former French name, Fort-Lamy; pop., 1973 est., 193,000). Language: French (official). Religion (1964): Muslim 41%; animist 30%; Christian 29%. President and premier until April 13, 1975, N'Garta (formerly François) Tombalbaye; president of the Supreme Military Council from April 15 and head of state and premier from May 12, Brig. Gen. Félix Malloum.

After 15 years in office, President Tombalbaye (*see* OBITUARIES) was deposed and killed on April 13, 1975, in a military takeover led by Brig. Gen. Noël Odingar. The first actions of the new rulers included the release of former army chief of staff Brig. Gen. Félix Malloum (*see* BIOGRAPHY), who had been imprisoned on Tombalbaye's orders, the suspension of the constitution, and the dissolution of the National Assembly. A provisional government led by Malloum was formed on May 12, and Odingar was confirmed as head of the armed forces, a function that he had exercised since the arrest of Malloum in 1973. No firm declarations of policy were made, however, and it was difficult to forecast to what extent the new regime would differ from the old in its attitude to internal and external political issues.

CHAD

Education. (1971–72) Primary, pupils 184,020, teachers 2,788; secondary, pupils 10,079, teachers (1969–70) 313; vocational, pupils 1,104; teacher training, students 317, teachers (1969–70) 33; higher, students 46.

Finance. Monetary unit: CFA franc, with (Sept. 22, 1975) a parity of CFA Fr. 50 to the French franc and a free rate of CFA Fr. 227.70 to U.S. $1 (CFA Fr. 471.75 = £1 sterling). Budget (1974 est.) balanced at CFA Fr. 20 billion. Cost of living (N'Djamena; 1970 = 100): (April 1975) 146; (April 1974) 124.

Foreign Trade. (1973) Imports CFA Fr. 18,213,000,000; exports CFA Fr. 8,483,000,000. Import sources: France 42%; Nigeria 12%. Export destinations: not separately distinguished 62%; Nigeria 6%; Congo 5%. Main exports: cotton 63%; beef and veal 7%; cattle 5%.

One thing soon became clear, however; namely, that the new rulers were proving to be as inept as their predecessors in dealing with the guerrilla tactics of the Chad National Liberation Front (Frolinat), particularly in their attempts to secure the release of the last of the European hostages detained since April 1974 by rebel leader Hissen Habre. After a year and a half of negotiations, French ethnologist Françoise Claustre was still a prisoner; another hostage, Marc Combe, had succeeded in escaping thanks to his own initiative rather than to the efforts of the various authorities; and a French negotiator, Maj. Pierre Galopin, had been executed by the rebels. The net result of these events was a souring of relations between France and Chad, and the remaining French troops at the Shar and N'Djamena bases were ordered to leave the country. (PHILIPPE DECRAENE)

A holding pit about 290 miles south of N'Djamena stores the first oil discovered after five years of exploration in Chad.

AUTHENTICATED NEWS INTERNATIONAL

Chemistry

Physical and Inorganic Chemistry. The recent period in physical and inorganic chemistry was characterized by extensive work on the chemical aspects of nuclear processes, energy sources, and pollution. The periodic table of chemical elements was extended to element 106, discovered in late 1974. Glenn Seaborg and Albert Ghiorso of the Lawrence Berkeley Laboratory of the University of California bombarded a target of californium (element 98) with oxygen-18 ions and obtained element 106, with a mass of 263 and a half-life of 0.9 seconds. The proof of its identity was based on its decomposition chain into an alpha particle and rutherfordium (element 104 of mass 259) and the decomposition of the latter into nobelium (element 102 of mass 255) and an alpha particle. At the same time, research with different results was carried out on the production of the same element at the Joint Institute for Nuclear Research at Dubna, U.S.S.R., by Georgy N. Flerov and his associates. Preliminary results indicate that the chemistry of element 106 is similar to that of chromium, molybdenum, and tungsten.

The general economic crisis caused by the controlled production and increased price of petroleum continued to have a wide impact on chemistry. Increased emphasis on nuclear energy resulted in the development of new methods of concentrating the uranium-235 isotope more economically than could be done by the standard gaseous diffusion or centrifugation processes. Research was carried out on the use of highly monochromatic and powerful lasers to selectively decompose compounds containing specific

Catholic Church: *see* Religion
Cave Exploration: *see* Speleology
Cement: *see* Mining and Quarrying
Census Data: *see* Populations and Areas; *see also the individual country articles*
Central America: *see* Latin-American Affairs; *articles on the various countries*
Ceramics: *see* Materials Sciences
Ceylon: *see* Sri Lanka
Checkers: *see* Board Games
Chemical Industry: *see* Industrial Review

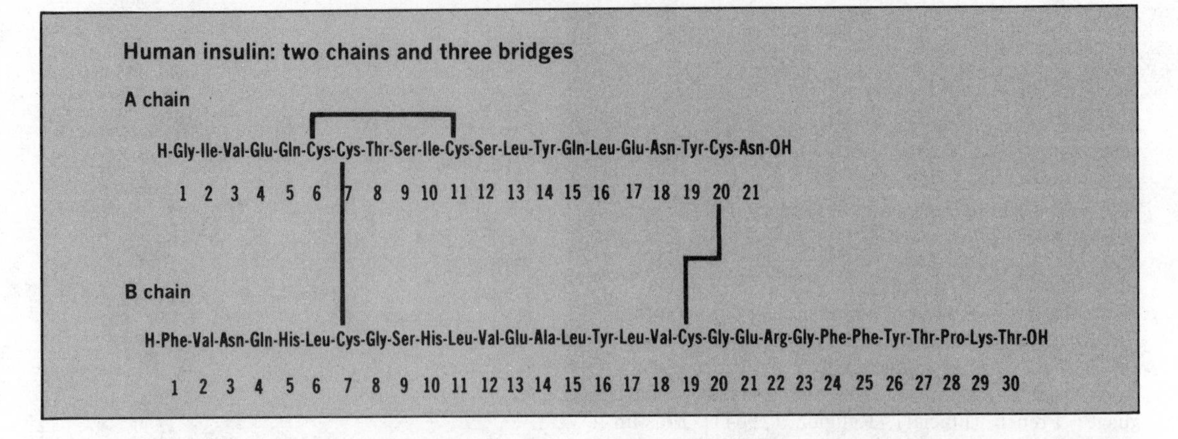

isotopes. In experimental situations success was achieved in enriching boron and sulfur isotopes by the use of a carbon dioxide laser and enriching the chlorine-37 isotope from its natural concentration of 25% to 85% by using an argon laser.

Extensive work was being carried out on the gasification and liquefaction of coal to produce fuel and on coal gasification to produce starting materials such as hydrogen and carbon monoxide for the petrochemical industry. An important development in this program was the discovery and industrial application of the catalytic production of acetic acid by low-pressure carbonylation of methanol (itself made from carbon monoxide and hydrogen), using rhodium complexes as catalysts and iodine as a promoter. This process may replace the acetic acid process based on the petrochemical ethylene.

Considerable research was under way on the role of fluorocarbon pollutants in breaking down the Earth's protective ozone layer. This apparently occurs by means of the photoreaction of the pollutants with the ozone of the upper atmosphere. This ozone layer serves as an absorbent for the extreme ultraviolet radiation of the Sun, which, if it reached the surface of the Earth, would produce serious burns in man, facilitate the occurrence of cancer, and have harmful effects on animal and plant life. Fluorocarbon-11, CCl_3F, is used extensively as a propellant in aerosols and fluorocarbon-12, CCl_2F_2, is used in refrigeration and air-conditioning units. Experiments during the year showed that the extreme ultraviolet radiation does dissociate the otherwise inert fluorocarbons and that the decomposition products react with ozone.

In another important development, R. H. Holm of the Massachusetts Institute of Technology synthesized iron-sulfur complexes of the type $[Fe_2S_2(SR)_4]^{2-}$ and $[Fe_4S_4(SR)_4]^{2-}$. These complexes are analogous to centres in certain commonly occurring iron-sulfur proteins. The analogues serve both as detailed structural models and as indicators of the oxidation levels of the protein-active sites.

(JOHN TURKEVICH)

[121.C.5; 128.B.4; 221.A.2.a; 724.C.2]

Organic Chemistry. The period under review began on a spectacular note with the publication of details on the first chemically directed total synthesis of insulin. The feat, by a Swiss team, climaxed a prodigious effort by many research groups throughout the world over the period of 20 years since the detailed structure of this important hormone became known. The synthesis, not as yet commercially feasible, involved more than 170 individual reactions. The crucial feature in the synthetic problem is the proper placement of three disulfide linkages (two sulfur atoms in tandem) that bind together the A and B polypeptide chains (*see* fig.). In the successful strategy one of the three disulfide linkages was introduced at an early stage prior to complete assembly of the polypeptide chains.

In the areas of new drugs and new insecticides synthetic activity was drastically curtailed, presumably because of greater awareness of health hazards that these substances might cause. At the same time and in response to the same pressures, interest in the organic chemistry underlying insect communication greatly increased. Following successful field trials on insect control based on synthetic sex attractants (pheromones), substantial progress was made in the identification and synthesis of the relatively simple, but species-specific, organic chemicals that appear to be vital to insect propagation. A recent synthesis was that of 3,11-dimethyl-2-nonacosanone, the contact mating pheromone of the female German cockroach.

Organic polymers are normally used as insulators; nevertheless, there was much activity in the synthesis of electrically conductive polymers. Some of these materials are conductive only under illumination and

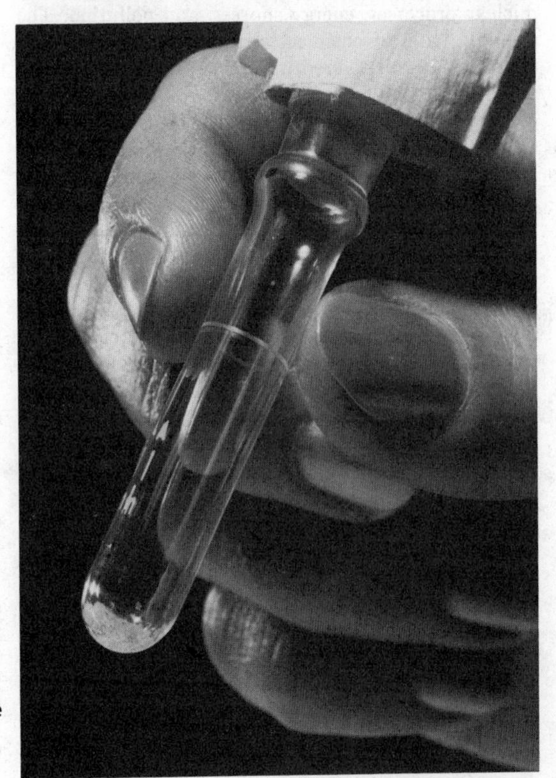

Uranium in visible quantities is being produced by laser enrichment techniques in the Lawrence Livermore Laboratory of the University of California.

COURTESY, LAWRENCE LIVERMORE LABORATORY

so find application in xerography. Others behave as semiconductors, and others based upon radical cations in stacked structures have remarkable conductivity properties but lack the desired flexibility and stability. An ultimate objective is the creation of a superconducting polymer; this was achieved experimentally during the year in a polysulfur nitride, which, strictly speaking, is inorganic rather than organic.

Progress in fundamental organic chemistry during this period was substantial in terms of new knowledge of structure and chemical mechanisms but not significant as to theoretical concepts. The introduction in 1973 of Fourier transform nuclear magnetic resonance spectroscopy, capable of revealing resonances of carbon-13 at the isotope's normal abundance level in nature (1.1%), was being applied as a new tool for the structural study of complex molecules. Another recently introduced technique, CIDNP spectroscopy (chemically induced dynamic nuclear polarization), has a unique capability of determining whether a product in a reaction arises from a diradical intermediate (hitherto a very elusive species), or, in photochemical reactions, if a product is derived from a singlet or a triplet electronic state (electrons paired or unpaired). (WELDON G. BROWN)

See also Nobel Prizes.

[122.A.6; 123.H]

Chile

A republic extending along the southern Pacific coast of South America, Chile has an area of 292,258 sq.mi. (756,945 sq.km.), not including its Antarctic claim. It is bounded by Argentina, Bolivia, and Peru. Pop. (1975 est.): 10,253,000. Cap. and largest city: Santiago (metro. pop., 1975 est., 3,263,000). Language: Spanish. Religion: predominantly Roman Catholic. President in 1975, Gen. Augusto Pinochet Ugarte.

The military government of Chile, which had seized power in a bloody coup d'etat in 1973, made it clear in 1975 that it intended to hand over power to a new generation of Chileans but not to the current political leaders. While it was impossible to conjecture when the military regime would step down, all indications were that a period of from five to ten or more years could elapse before control was returned to civilians in some form. It appeared, moreover, that whatever form of pseudo-democratic government was adopted eventually, Chile would not soon resemble the vigorous democracy that existed for more than 40 years prior to the coup that toppled the Marxist regime of the late president Salvador Allende.

On the second anniversary of the coup, Sept. 11, 1975, General Pinochet made some show of deference to constitutional processes in an effort to defuse continuing international criticism of the regime. He said the government was in transition from a state of internal defense to one of internal security. Until September 1974 the junta had said Chile was in a state of internal war. The nearest Pinochet came to any perceived shift in policy, however, was to propose establishment of a consultative Council of State that would include civilians and the three living former presidents of the country. Pinochet offered former Christian Democratic president Eduardo Frei Montalva a seat, but Frei had been a vocal critic of government economic policies in the past year.

There had been a steady deterioration of relations between the democratic leftist Christian Democrat Party and the junta, as well as an internal rift within the party itself between those who were ready to make common cause with the parties of Allende's former Marxist coalition and those who were not. The outlawed Communist Party called on the Christian Democrats to join in an antijunta alliance, and one exiled Christian Democrat leader, former senator Renan Fuentealba, urged a coalition with the Communists and Socialists in Allende's old Unidad Popular. This suggestion was flatly rejected in Chile by Christian Democrat leader Patricio Aylwin. The outlawed Socialists, headed by exiled Carlos Altamirano, asserted that the armed struggle against the junta must go on.

Aylwin contended that the Christian Democrats must work with opponents of both Allende and the military to restore democracy. The junta reacted sharply to Aylwin's words, and on September 25 said this was not why they made the revolution. The junta claimed it took power to build a new type of democracy, apart from the old-style politicians and outmoded systems and without political parties. This was

CHILE

Education. (1974) Primary, pupils 2,332,720, teachers 67,963; secondary, pupils 290,408, teachers 18,049; vocational, pupils 162,048, teachers (public only) 8,588; teacher training, students 23,939; higher (including 8 universities), students 53,040, teaching staff (1965) 8,835.

Finance. Monetary unit: peso (from Sept. 29, 1975), equal to 1,000 former escudos, with a free rate of 6.40 pesos to U.S. $1 (13.03 pesos = £1 sterling). Budget (1973 est.): revenue 167,568,000,000 escudos; expenditure 301,038,000,000 escudos. Gross national product: (1972) 228,640,000,000 escudos; (1971) 123,224,000,000 escudos. Money supply: (Dec. 1974) 836.7 billion escudos; (Dec. 1973) 224.6 billion escudos. Cost of living (Santiago; 1970 = 100): (March 1975) 16,156; (March 1974) 3,402.

Foreign Trade. Imports (1973) U.S. $1,098,000,000; exports (1974) U.S. $2.5 billion. Import sources (1972): U.S. 17%; Argentina 15%; West Germany 9%; U.K. 6%. Export destinations (1972): Japan 17%; West Germany 14%; U.K. 11%; U.S. 10%; The Netherlands 8%; Italy 7%; Argentina 6%. Main exports: copper and copper ore (1973) 86%; iron ore (1972) 7%.

Transport and Communications: Roads (1972) 63,656 km. Motor vehicles in use (1971): passenger 193,009; commercial 135,667. Railways: (1973) 8,995 km.; traffic (principal only; 1974) 2,877,000,000 passenger-km., freight 2,383,000,000 net ton-km. Air traffic (1974): 1,222,600,000 passenger-km.; freight 59,839,000 net ton-km. Shipping (1974): merchant vessels 100 gross tons and over 135; gross tonnage 364,364. Telephones (Dec. 1973) 433,000. Radio receivers (Dec. 1972) 1.5 million. Television receivers (Dec. 1972) 500,000.

Agriculture. Production (in 000; metric tons; 1974; 1973 in parentheses): wheat *c.* 1,122 (747); barley *c.* 179 (107); oats *c.* 142 (109); corn 367 (294); potatoes 957 (624); rapeseed *c.* 30 (40); dry beans *c.* 107 (65); onions *c.* 54 (*c.* 48); sugar, raw value 127 (89); apples (1973) *c.* 148, (1972) *c.* 150; wine (1973) *c.* 600, (1972) 670; beef and veal (1973) *c.* 95, (1972) 118; wool *c.* 9 (*c.* 9); timber (cu.m.; 1973) 8,500, (1972) 8,300; fish catch (1973) 664, (1972) 792. Livestock (in 000; 1974): cattle *c.* 3,170; sheep 5,094; pigs *c.* 1,177; horses (1973) *c.* 470.

Industry. Production (in 000; metric tons; 1974): coal 1,526; crude oil 1,310; natural gas (cu.m.; 1973) 4,100,000; electricity (kw-hr.) 8,766,000 (61% hydroelectric); iron ore (63% metal content) 10,270; pig iron 514; crude steel (ingots) 596; copper ore (metal content; 1973) 745; nitrate of soda (1973) 702; manganese ore (metal content; 1973) 6.4; sulfur (1973) 31; iodine (1973) 2.2; molybdenum concentrates (metal content; 1973) 4.8; gold (troy oz.; 1973) 104; silver (troy oz.) 2,926; woven cotton fabrics (m.; 1973) 72,000; fish meal 93.

Chess:
see Board Games

Child Welfare:
see Education; Social and Welfare Services

WIDE WORLD

The first detachment of women soldiers in the Chilean Army passes in review in Santiago.

the clearest indication so far that the junta meant to establish a one-party system, perhaps modeled after that of Brazil but without the minority opposition built into the Brazilian system. There seemed nowhere for the Chilean democratic leaders to go, either with the junta or with their old enemies of the Unidad Popular. Meanwhile, the junta continued the late-night curfew, although it was much less rigorous than in the days of fighting and mass arrests immediately after the coup.

While Chile seemed frozen politically into an indefinite period of military rule, the government was making stringent efforts to rebuild the economy after the disasters of the Allende years. The government's measures did succeed in slowing down the inflation rate to below 10% a month for the first time since the military uprising, but the economy also slowed. Inflation dropped from 694% in 1973 to 376% in 1974 to a projected rate of 250–300% in 1975. At the same time, a number of industries collapsed or disappeared and unemployment spiraled to unprecedented levels. It was estimated that in Santiago the unemployment rate might be as high as 50%. The result was that prices were down or holding steady but the Chileans had little money with which to buy. Many of the layoffs represented a purposeful attempt by the government to eliminate flagrant featherbedding in national enterprises, admittedly a curse of state-owned industries in Latin America.

Chile's credit abroad continued to improve as a result of budget austerity and the willingness of the U.S. and other foreign creditors to postpone payment on some of Chile's awesome international debt. Chile's foreign debts had reached more than $3.4 billion, partly as a result of the drop in copper prices and the debt service strain; 41% of this was scheduled to come due in the next four years. If Chile could maintain copper exports at the current 800,000-ton-per-year level, the nation could achieve a favourable balance of payments even if the predicted copper price of 80 cents a pound in 1976 was not realized. In September Chile introduced a new monetary unit, the peso, equal to 1,000 old escudos. The escudo would be phased out of circulation gradually.

The military coup in Peru, which removed Gen. Juan Velasco Alvarado from the presidency and replaced him with more moderate Gen. Francisco Morales Bermúdez, was expected to take some strain off the Chilean government. Despite denials in Lima, many hemispheric observers had believed the Velasco regime was intent on a military effort to recover territory lost to Chile nearly a century earlier. There was evidence that the new Lima government, which was ideologically closer to the Santiago regime, was less likely to attempt such an adventure.

As 1975 drew to a close, the Chilean government was making strong efforts to improve its international image in light of repeated condemnations abroad for its alleged tactics of repression. Many political prisoners were being sent into exile instead of being kept in prison, but Chile in 1975 remained a military-police state. Having seized and retained power for more than two years, the junta was at a loss to find a civilian process to replace barracks rule and was unlikely to relinquish control until it did.

(JEREMIAH A. O'LEARY, JR.)

[974.E]

China

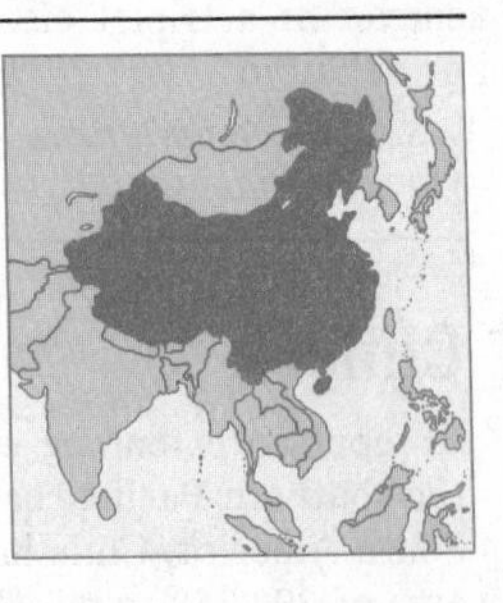

The most populous country in the world and the third largest in area, China is bounded by the U.S.S.R., Mongolia, North Korea, North Vietnam, Laos, Burma, India, Bhutan, Nepal, Pakistan, and Afghanistan. From 1949 the country has been divided into the People's Republic of China (Communist) on the mainland and on Hainan and other islands, and the Republic of China (Nationalist) on Taiwan. (*See* TAIWAN.) Area: 3,691,500 sq.mi. (9,561,000 sq.km.), including Tibet but excluding Taiwan. Pop. of the People's Republic: officially 800 million; unofficial estimates range upward to 920 million. Cap.: Peking (metro. pop., 1970 est., 7,570,000). Largest city: Shanghai (metro. pop., 1970 est., 10,820,000). Language: Chinese (varieties of the Mandarin dialect predominate). Chairman of the Communist Party in 1975, Mao Tse-tung; chairman of the Permanent Standing Committee of the National People's Congress (nominal chief of state), Marshal Chu Teh; premier, Chou En-lai.

The most significant event of 1975 was the convocation of the long-delayed fourth National People's Congress from January 13 to 17, immediately following the second plenary session of the tenth Central Committee of the Communist Party of China from January 8 to 10. The meetings of these two important bodies of the party and state were held in unusual secrecy until the issuance of the official pronouncement at the close of the People's Congress. Mao Tse-tung failed to attend either of the two meetings personally, while Premier Chou En-lai played an indispensable role despite his reported illness and hospitalization. Mao's absence without any public explanation naturally stimulated speculation. Chou's brisk and varied internal and diplomatic activities during much of the year signified that the premier was firmly in control, while Mao's prestige and authority appeared to be on the decline.

According to the official communiqué issued on

January 18, the plenum of the party discussed the preparatory work for the fourth National People's Congress; elected Teng Hsiao-p'ing, disgraced in the Cultural Revolution of the 1960s, as a member of the Standing Committee (Politburo) and a vice-chairman of the party; and approved the draft revised text of the new state constitution. These actions signaled the achievement of a compromise in the leadership struggle between radicals and moderates following the 1974 campaigns against Confucius and the late defense minister Lin Piao, and thus permitted the convening of the People's Congress announced by Chou at the tenth party congress in 1973. On the recommendation of the party plenum, the congress "unanimously" adopted the constitution, redefined the political system and state structure, appointed the leading personnel of the state, and reaffirmed Chairman Mao's revolutionary line in foreign affairs as expounded and implemented by Chou.

Less than a month after the People's Congress and upon the instruction of Chairman Mao, another nationwide ideological campaign was initiated, for the study of the theory of the dictatorship of the proletariat in order to combat revisionism and capitalism. In spite of the new unity and order hailed by the People's Congress, the continuation of ideological disputes between doctrinairism and pragmatism (or radicals and moderates), as well as the age and ill health of Mao (82) and Chou (77) and the apparently unresolved problem of succession, appeared to have left a sense of uncertainty and weariness in Mao's perpetual revolution.

New Constitution and Old Leadership. The first session of the People's Congress, attended by 2,864 out of 2,885 deputies, including a number of overseas Chinese from Taiwan, Hong Kong, and Macao, considered three main questions: revision of the 1954 constitution; the report on the work of the government; and the election and appointment of the leading personnel of the state. Keynote speeches were delivered by Chou and Chang Ch'un-ch'iao, a Politburo member and first secretary of the Shanghai Revolutionary Committee, who became prominent during the Cultural Revolution. Outlining the revision of the constitution, Chang singled out destruction of the bourgeois influence of former president Liu Shao-ch'i and Lin Piao and the consolidation and development of the socialist system under Mao's leadership as China's most significant achievements in the past two decades.

The 1975 constitution affirmed the supremacy of the party over the bureaucracy and the military. It declares the People's Republic of China to be "a socialist state of the dictatorship of the proletariat led by the working class and based on the alliance of workers and peasants" under the command of the Communist Party. Compared with the 1954 constitution of over 100 articles, the new instrument is rather short, with only 30 brief articles and about 4,500 words.

Among its more important provisions, the new constitution enshrines Mao's thought as the spiritual beacon of the Chinese revolution but deemphasizes his power position and the cult of Mao. As the first chairman or president under the 1954 constitution, Mao had been the real focus of power, serving as titular chief of state and actual commander in chief of the military forces. However, the second People's Congress in 1959 elected Liu Shao-ch'i to replace him as president, and the third congress in 1964 reelected Liu for a second term. After the purge of Liu during the Cultural Revolution, the post of president fell vacant. The issue of retaining it caused a break between Mao and Lin Piao when Mao decided to abolish it and accused Lin of scheming to obtain it.

In light of these disputes, it was decided to eliminate the central position of chairman of the People's Republic. Under the new constitution, the chairman of the Permanent Standing Committee of the Congress becomes the ceremonial or nominal chief of state, while the chairman of the party commands the country's armed forces. Instead of naming Mao personally, the constitution stipulates that the Army and militia are led by the party and commanded by its chairman.

Under the leadership of the party, the highest organ of state power is the National People's Congress, with powers to amend the constitution, make laws, and appoint and remove the premier and members of the State Council (Cabinet) on the recommendation of the party Central Committee. The State Council, consisting of a premier, 12 vice-premiers, and 29 ministers in charge of various departments, takes over the functions and dignity of government. Individual rights and duties were little changed from the 1954 document, and art. 26 of the new constitution stipulates that citizens are obliged to support the socialist system and the Communist Party of China. However, the new constitution guarantees the right of limited free enterprise to both agricultural and industrial workers.

In the elections to the various positions of state, the moderates gained an upper hand. Such important figures of the Maoist faction as Chiang Ch'ing (Mao's wife), Yao Wen-yuan, and Wang Hung-wen, who rose phenomenally to third position in the party hierarchy

KEYSTONE

An aqueduct 100 km. long will provide irrigation water in rural areas of Hopei Province.

CAMERA PRESS/PHOTO TRENDS

Chinese peasants undertake the planting of trees in order to control the shifting sands of the Maowusu Desert in Inner Mongolia.

in 1973, were excluded from key posts. At age 88, Marshal Chu Teh was elected chairman of the Standing Committee, and the majority of the 22 vice-chairmen were senior citizens with long standing in party and government.

The most notable appointments to the State Council were the confirmation of Chou as premier and the naming of Teng Hsiao-p'ing and Chang Ch'un-ch'iao as the first and second vice-premiers. Of the 29 ministerial posts, only 5 went to the Cultural Revolution faction, and the majority of the ministers were older persons and pre-Cultural Revolution bureaucrats known to be close to Chou. The election of Teng as one of five vice-chairmen of the party and a member of the Politburo at the second plenum had been a crushing blow to the radicals, and his appointment as the first deputy premier was seen as additional proof that moderates had won the day. Their victory was far from complete, however. When Teng was named chief of staff of the Army, Chang Ch'un-ch'iao was appointed its top political commissar. Only Teng and Chang held leadership posts in the three institutions of power: party, government, and Army.

The Economy. A new order of priorities in which agriculture was the foundation and industry the leading factor in economic development was especially stressed by Chou at the People's Congress and prescribed in art. 10 of the new constitution. Chou declared that the fourth five-year plan (1971–75) had been successful in meeting targets and that before the end of the 20th century the modernization of agriculture, industry, defense, and technology should build China into a powerful, modern socialist country. The successful orbiting of China's third earth satellite on July 26 was regarded as a major achievement.

The official press agency reported a big increase in crop production in 1974 over the 1973 record grain harvest of about 250 million metric tons, and an excellent spring harvest for 1975. However, drought in northern China and floods in central and southern China threatened the autumn grain harvest, which normally accounts for two-thirds of output. Despite labour unrest, official releases claimed an industrial growth rate of 9 to 11% for the first half of 1975, indicating a rebound from the economic slackness of the previous year.

China had emerged as a major oil producer and exporter, with proven reserves estimated at 11,000,000,000 metric tons of crude oil. Over 65 million tons of crude oil were produced in 1974, an increase of about 20% from 1973, and exports rose to over 4 million tons. A further 24% increase in production was reported for the first half of 1975. Exports of crude oil in 1975 were expected to exceed 8 million tons.

In July and August serious labour strife was reported in Hangchow, capital of Chekiang and famous for its silk industry, and in other industrial areas including Hsuchow in Kiangsu, Wuhan in Hupei, and Heilungkiang Province in Manchuria. The causes appeared to be factional quarrels and workers' demands for better pay and working conditions, despite the party's emphasis on ideological dedication as the chief incentive for higher production. Basic contradictions between Maoist idealistic attempts to create utopia by spiritual remolding and the pragmatists' approach of accelerating the transitional process from socialism to Communism by building up the economic infrastructure remained to be reconciled.

Foreign Affairs. In his report to the People's Congress on the work of the government, Chou reiterated China's long-term foreign policy with emphasis on

CHINA

Education. Primary (1959–60), pupils 90 million, teachers (1964) *c.* 2.6 million; secondary (1958–59), pupils 8,520,000; vocational (1958–59), pupils 850,000; teacher training (1958–59), students 620,000; higher (1962–63), students 820,000.

Finance. Monetary unit: yuan, with (Sept. 22, 1975) an official exchange rate of 1.90 yuan to U.S. $1 (free rate of 4.09 yuan = £1 sterling). Gold reserves (1973 est.) U.S. $2 billion. Budget (1960 est.; latest published) balanced at 70,020,000,000 yuan. Gross national product (1972 est.) U.S. $134 billion.

Foreign Trade. (1974) Imports *c.* U.S. $7 billion; exports *c.* U.S. $5.9 billion. Import sources: Japan *c.* 29%; U.S. *c.* 12%; Canada *c.* 6%; West Germany *c.* 6%; Australia *c.* 5%. Export destinations: Japan *c.* 22%; Hong Kong *c.* 20%. Main exports: foodstuffs (meat and products, cereals, fruits and vegetables) *c.* 40%; crude oil *c.* 20%; textiles and clothing *c.* 20%.

Transport and Communications. Roads (1974) *c.* 700,000 km. (including *c.* 400,000 km. all-weather). Motor vehicles in use (1971): passenger *c.* 1 million; commercial (including buses) *c.* 800,000. Railways: (1973) *c.* 35,000 km.; traffic (1959) 45,670,000,000 passenger-km., freight (1971) 302,000,000,000 net ton-km. Air traffic (1960): 63,882,000 passenger-km.; freight 1,967,000 net ton-km. Inland waterways (including Yangtze River; 1974) *c.* 160,000 km. Shipping (1974): merchant vessels 100 gross tons and over 360; gross tonnage 1,870,567. Telephones (1951) 255,000. Radio receivers (Dec. 1970) *c.* 12 million. Television receivers (Dec. 1969) *c.* 300,000.

Agriculture. Production (in 000; metric tons; 1974; 1973 in parentheses): rice *c.* 113,000 (*c.* 110,000); corn *c.* 31,000 (*c.* 30,300); wheat *c.* 37,000 (*c.* 36,000); barley *c.* 20,000 (*c.* 19,500); millet *c.* 23,500 (*c.* 23,000); potatoes *c.* 35,000 (*c.* 32,000); dry peas *c.* 3,550 (*c.* 3,500); soybeans *c.* 11,800 (*c.* 11,700); peanuts *c.* 2,600 (*c.* 2,600); rapeseed *c.* 1,200 (*c.* 1,150); sugar, raw value *c.* 3,500 (*c.* 3,300); pears *c.* 950 (*c.* 940); tobacco *c.* 965 (*c.* 950); tea *c.* 290 (*c.* 280); cotton, lint *c.* 2,000 (*c.* 2,000); jute *c.* 550 (*c.* 520); beef and buffalo meat (1973) *c.* 1,980, (1972) 1,970; pork (1973) *c.* 9,400, (1972) *c.* 9,200; timber (cu.m.; 1973) 178,000, (1972) 175,500; fish catch (1972) *c.* 6,920, (1971) *c.* 6,880. Livestock (in 000; 1974): horses *c.* 7,000; asses *c.* 11,600; cattle *c.* 63,300; buffalo *c.* 29,800; sheep *c.* 73,000; pigs *c.* 239,000; goats *c.* 58,000.

Industry. Fuel and power (in 000; metric tons; 1974): coal (including lignite) *c.* 400,000; coke (1973) 26,040; crude oil *c.* 65,000; electricity (kw.hr.; 1970) *c.* 75,000,000. Production (in 000; metric tons; 1973): iron ore (metal content; 1973) *c.* 39,000; pig iron (1973) *c.* 33,000; crude steel *c.* 25,000; lead *c.* 100; copper *c.* 100; zinc *c.* 100; bauxite *c.* 600; aluminum *c.* 150; antimony ore (metal content) 12; magnesite *c.* 1,000; manganese ore *c.* 300; tungsten concentrates (oxide content) *c.* 10; cement (1973) *c.* 23,000; salt (1973) *c.* 18,000; sulfuric acid (1966) *c.* 2,500; fertilizers (nutrient content; 1973–74) nitrogenous *c.* 2,730, phosphate *c.* 1,310, potash *c.* 300; cotton yarn (1969) *c.* 1,450; cotton fabrics (1971) *c.* 9,000; man-made fibres *c.* 75; paper *c.* 4,250.

the following major elements: opposition to the hegemonism of the two superpowers; solidarity with the nonaligned nations of the third world against social-imperialism and capitalist-imperalism; and friendship with countries of the second (Communist) world as a counterbalance to Soviet expansion. Specifically, Chou declared that China was ready to develop relations with all countries, including those with different social systems, on the basis of the principles of peaceful coexistence.

Resolution of internal issues at the People's Congress, China's renewed determination to build a modern economy, and the dramatic turn of events in Southeast Asia resulted in a notable shift in China's attitude in the direction of support for a U.S. military presence in Asia and the Pacific. While the end of U.S. involvement in Indochina reduced the danger of U.S.-China conflict, closer ties between North Vietnam and the Soviet Union, flanking China on two sides, created a new international situation in Asia. Viewing Soviet expansion as the main threat to its sovereignty, China assumed an active role in the major-power equilibrium, establishing formal relations with the European Economic Community (EEC) and playing down its support of liberation movements in Africa, Latin America, and Asia.

Peking continued to play host to a long list of heads of state and foreign leaders, including Asian leaders who came in the aftermath of the Communist victory in Indochina. Accompanied by his generals and ministers of foreign trade and economic affairs, Marshal Kim Il Sung of North Korea visited China from April 18 to 26. At the end of his discussions with Chinese leaders, a joint communiqué was issued in which China reaffirmed its support of the Korean people in their "just struggle for the independent and peaceful reunification of their fatherland" and for the dissolution of the U.S.-led UN command in South Korea. Evidently China had no desire to see renewed conflict on the divided peninsula, which might wreck Chinese détente with the U.S.

The visits of Pres. Ferdinand E. Marcos of the Philippines and Prime Minister Kukrit Pramoj of Thailand were diplomatic victories for Peking. On June 9 Chou and President Marcos signed an accord establishing diplomatic relations and ending 25 years of mutually hostile foreign policies. The Philippines became the 100th nation to recognize Peking as the sole legal government of China. Following weeks of discussion and maneuvering, Chou and Prime Minister Kukrit signed an agreement establishing diplomatic relations on July 1.

A delegation of senior Cambodian leaders, headed by deputy premiers Khieu Samphan and Ieng Sary, arrived in August for discussions that culminated in the signing of an aid agreement on August 18. Shortly afterward Prince Norodom Sihanouk returned to Phnom Penh after five years' exile in Peking, but by mid-October, after addressing the UN in New York, he was back in the Chinese capital. North Vietnamese Vice-Premier for Economic Development Le Thanh Nghi arrived in Peking about the same time as the Cambodians but failed to receive the same warm treatment. In late September the most senior North Vietnamese delegation to visit China since the fall of Saigon arrived in Peking under the leadership of Communist Party Secretary Le Duan for a week of discussions on foreign policy differences between the two countries and the future of Southeast Asia.

In 1975 China began to repay the dozens of unreciprocated state visits that foreign leaders had made in previous years. Delegations led by a vice-premier visited Nepal, Mexico, Pakistan, Iran, and France. In transit in Calcutta after his visit to Nepal, Vice-Premier Ch'en Hsi-lien invited India to take the initiative in talks to normalize relations, but India's incorporation of Sikkim resulted in further strain. Peking attached considerable importance to Teng's stay in France for a week in May. Paris and Peking agreed on arrangements for regular political consultation and increased commercial exchanges.

Relations between China and the Soviet Union showed no signs of improvement. The five-year talks on border issues were resumed in February, but negotiations soon became deadlocked again as Moscow refused to acknowledge, even in principle, the disputed areas acquired by the czarist regime through "unequal treaties" and rejected China's proposal for a nonaggression pact. The exchange of Sino-Soviet polemics tended to become increasingly bitter following the conclusion of the Conference on Security and Cooperation in Europe in Helsinki, Fin., on August 1.

The process of normalizing Sino-Japanese relations progressed with the signing of a fishery agreement on August 15. Negotiations for a treaty of peace and friendship were stalemated, however, because the Chinese insisted on a clause opposing hegemony by any power in Asia. Moscow lost no time in warning Tokyo that the inclusion of such a provision constituted an anti-Soviet declaration.

The relationship between China and the U.S. moved slowly on a steady course. On his return from Peking in late December 1974, Senate majority leader Mike Mansfield had reported on China's dissatisfaction with the slow progress of U.S.-China relations, but Pres. Gerald Ford's congratulatory message to Chou on his reappointment as premier was taken as a welcome sign of improvement. House Speaker Carl Albert and Republican leader John J. Rhodes visited Peking in the spring and reportedly were told that termination of

DAVE SWAN

The Ta ch'ing petrochemical plant processes crude oil from one of China's newly discovered oil fields. It symbolizes the nation's hope for future economic well-being derived from petroleum production.

WIDE WORLD

The first session of the fourth National People's Congress of China convened in January in Peking's Great Hall of the People.

U.S. diplomatic relations with the Nationalist government on Taiwan and of the U.S.-Taiwan security treaty of 1954 were prerequisites for establishing full diplomatic relations. After the Indochina collapse, President Ford reaffirmed the U.S. treaty commitment to the Nationalists. Another bipartisan congressional delegation, headed by Sen. Charles H. Percy, in China during the summer, gained the impression that Peking was not pressing Washington for immediate abandonment of Taiwan. In September, a high-ranking Chinese trade mission and a group of senior scientists arrived in Washington for an extended visit.

The year's main event in this area, the visit to Peking by President Ford in early December, passed without effecting any substantive changes in Sino-U.S. relations. U.S. Secretary of State Henry Kissinger, on a preparatory visit in October, had what was described as a "very useful" meeting with Chairman Mao, but indications were that his reception generally had been somewhat cool. The main point at issue, Chinese distrust of U.S.-Soviet détente, was brought up again during Ford's visit. In his toast at the opening banquet, Teng Hsiao-p'ing noted that "rhetoric about 'détente' cannot cover up the stark reality of the growing danger of war" resulting from appeasement of the Soviets. Ford also met with Mao, but Chou was again hospitalized, and the principal talks were held between Ford and Teng, who appeared to be carrying on the country's day-to-day business. In a briefing to the press, Kissinger suggested that Ford and the Chinese leaders had reached broad agreement on the need to counter expanding Soviet influence in Western Europe, the Pacific, and Angola.

(HUNG-TI CHU)

Chinese Literature: *see* Literature

Christianity: *see* Religion

Church Membership: *see* Religion

Cinema: *see* Motion Pictures

Cities: *see* Environment

Civil Rights: *see* Race Relations

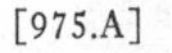

[975.A]

Colombia

A republic in northwestern South America, Colombia is bordered by Panama, Venezuela, Brazil, Peru, and Ecuador and has coasts on both the Caribbean Sea and the Pacific Ocean. Area: 439,737 sq.mi. (1,138,914 sq.km.). Pop. (1974 est.): 23,952,100. Cap. and largest city: Bogotá (pop., 1974 est., 2,975,200). Language: Spanish. Religion: Roman Catholic (91%). President in 1975, Alfonso López Michelsen.

In 1975 President López Michelsen's administration contended with mounting discontent, stemming from the government's attempts to deal with pressing economic problems and, simultaneously, to initiate long-term reforms in the country's socioeconomic structure. The prime objective of curbing inflation was pursued by containing the expansion of the money supply and reducing the fiscal deficit through expenditure cuts and higher taxes. Revised income and sales taxes were designed to shift the tax burden from the poor to the wealthier groups and from earned income to property. The measure whose effects were felt first, however, was the policy of rationalizing prices through the elimination of price subsidies, which caused a continued rise in the cost of living. At the same time, lower public expenditure and the declining demand for Colombian exports led to increased unemployment. This situation prompted demonstrations and riots, particularly by students, and strikes, some involving white-collar workers. There were also disturbances in the countryside, with peasants occupying unused land in some areas.

Against this background, guerrilla activity intensified. Clashes with the Army became more frequent, and a spate of kidnappings occurred, most of them aimed at financing the Colombian Revolutionary Armed Forces (FARC) or the National Liberation Army (ELN). Although these organizations met with some reverses—notably the capture of Segundo Ayala, a senior commander of the FARC, in June and the kill-

COLOMBIA

Education. Primary, pupils (1973) 3,551,000, teachers (1970) 85,009; secondary (public only; 1971), pupils 312,181, teachers 15,516; vocational (public only; 1971), pupils 94,265, teachers 5,431; teacher training (public only; 1971), students 43,823, teachers 2,523; higher, students 135,000, teaching staff (1970) 10,295.

Finance. Monetary unit: peso, with (Sept. 22, 1975) an official rate of 30.98 pesos to U.S. $1 (free rate of 66.11 pesos = £1 sterling). Gold, SDRs, and foreign exchange: (June 1975) U.S. $334 million; (June 1974) U.S. $490 million. Budget (1975 est.): revenue 32,282,000,000 pesos; expenditure 32,354,000,000 pesos. Gross national product: (1973) 237,330,000,000 pesos; (1972) 181,060,000,000 pesos. Money supply: (Dec. 1974) 52,866,000,000 pesos; (Dec. 1973) 41,647,000,000 pesos. Cost of living (Bogotá; 1970 = 100): (April 1975) 245; (April 1974) 188.

Foreign Trade. (1974) Imports 35,124,000,000 pesos; exports 32,910,000,000 pesos. Import sources (1973): U.S. 40%; West Germany 9%; Japan 8%; France 5%. Export destinations: U.S. 37%; West Germany 12%; Spain 5%. Main exports: coffee 47%; emeralds (1973) 7%; cotton (1973) 6%. Tourism (1973): visitors 275,000; gross receipts U.S. $98 million.

Transport and Communications. Roads (1971) 45,873 km. (including 20,017 km. main roads). Motor vehicles in use (1973): passenger 326,900; commercial (including buses) 107,000. Railways: (1973) 3,420 km.; traffic (1974) 482.4 million passenger-km., freight 1,329,200,000 net ton-km. Air traffic (1973): 2,494,000,000 passenger-km.; freight 108.4 million net ton-km. Shipping (1974): merchant vessels 100 gross tons and over 54; gross tonnage 211,083. Telephones (Dec. 1973) 1,080,000. Radio receivers (Dec. 1973) 2,793,000. Television receivers (Dec. 1972) *c.* 1.2 million.

Agriculture. Production (in 000; metric tons; 1974; 1973 in parentheses): corn 870 (824); rice *c.* 1,540 (1,124); barley *c.* 110 (94); potatoes *c.* 1,135 (*c.* 1,130); cassava (1973) *c.* 1,630, (1972) 1,600; sorghum *c.* 400 (398); soybeans *c.* 120 (*c.* 99); coffee *c.* 570 (*c.* 528); bananas (1973) *c.* 830, (1972) 828; cane sugar, raw value 897 (810); palm oil *c.* 60 (*c.* 42); cotton, lint 152 (135); tobacco *c.* 47 (*c.* 49). Livestock (in 000; Dec. 1973): cattle *c.* 22,940; sheep *c.* 2,075; pigs *c.* 1,502; goats (1972) *c.* 680; horses (1972) *c.* 860; chickens (1972) *c.* 34,000.

Industry. Production (in 000; metric tons; 1974): crude oil 8,727; natural gas (cu.m.; 1973) *c.* 1,700,000; coal (1973) *c.* 3,265; electricity (74% hydroelectric in 1969; kw-hr.) *c.* 12,000,000; crude steel 244; gold (troy oz.; 1973) 216; emeralds (carats; 1972) 1,750; salt (1973) 1,330; cement 3,360.

ing of Pedro León Arboleda, one of the founders of a third group, the Popular Liberation Army (EOL), in August—they continued to operate effectively. In September the ELN succeeded in assassinating Gen. Ramón Arturo Rincón Quiñones, the inspector general of the Army.

This groundswell of agitation provoked a reaction from the establishment. Beginning in May, army officers believed to hold progressive views were gradually removed from influential positions, and at the end of June, under pressure from the Conservatives in his government, President López Michelsen declared a national state of siege. The president also had to cope with dissension within his own Liberal Party, particularly from former president Carlos Lleras Restrepo. Lleras was even suspected of planning a realignment of the Liberal and Conservative parties to further his 1978 presidential ambitions.

Political unrest showed signs of abating in the second half of the year, partly because of improvements in the economic situation. The prospects for coffee, Colombia's major export, were much enhanced when international prices rose to record levels after frosts had destroyed much of Brazil's crop. As the cost of living began to stabilize and economic activity to regain momentum, it seemed likely that the government's targets of a 5% growth rate and inflation below 20% would be achieved. (JOAN PEARCE)

[974.C.2]

Combat Sports

Boxing. Muhammad Ali (U.S.) dominated world heavyweight boxing in 1975, successfully defending his title four times. He stopped Chuck Wepner (U.S.) in the 15th round at Richfield, Ohio, and Ron Lyle (U.S.) in 11 rounds at Las Vegas, Nev. His next title defense was in Kuala Lumpur, Malaysia, where he outpointed Joe Bugner, the European champion from England, over 15 rounds. Finally, Ali stopped Joe Frazier (U.S.) in 14 rounds at Manila. These were the first world heavyweight championship fights to take place in Malaysia and the Philippines.

Muhammad Ali (right) and Joe Frazier during their grueling heavyweight championship bout in Manila in October. Frazier's manager stopped the fight after the 14th round and Ali retained his title.

CURT GUNTHER—CAMERA 5

SYNDICATION INTERNATIONAL/PHOTO TRENDS

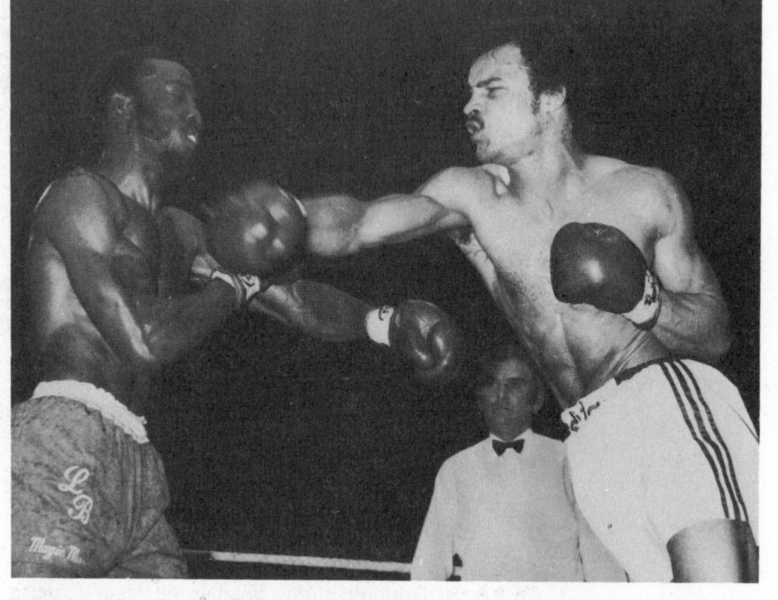

Britain's John Conteh (right) remained the World Boxing Council light-heavyweight champion after defeating challenger Lonnie Bennett of the U.S. in March.

Ali remained the only undisputed world champion in the 12 weight divisions. In the other 11 divisions the World Boxing Council (WBC) and the World Boxing Association (WBA) recognized different champions. John Conteh (England) retained the WBC light-heavyweight championship, stopping Lonnie Bennett (U.S.) in five rounds in London. Víctor Galíndez (Arg.) successfully defended the WBA version twice, outpointing Jorge Ahumada (Arg.) in New York and Pierre Fourie (South Africa) in Johannesburg. WBA middleweight champion Carlos Monzón (Arg.) retained his title by knocking out Tony Licata (U.S.) in ten rounds in New York and in December successfully defended it again by knocking out Gratien Tonna (France) in the fifth round in Paris. Tonna claimed that the knockout punch was illegal, but films of the fight upheld Monzón. Rodrigo Valdes (Colombia) defended the WBC version three times, knocking out Tonna in 11 rounds in Paris, outpointing Rudy Robles (Colombia), and stopping Ramón Méndez (Arg.) in eight rounds. The vacant WBC junior middleweight championship was won by Miguel de Oliveira (Brazil), who outpointed José Durán (Spain) in Monte Carlo but then lost his title to Elisha Obed (The Bahamas) in Paris. Yuh Jae Do (South Korea) won the WBA junior middleweight title from Koichi Wajima (Japan) with a seventh-round knockout and later retained it by stopping Masahiro Misako (Japan).

José Nápoles (Mexico) retained the WBC welterweight championship with victories against Horacio Saldano (Arg.) in three rounds in Mexico City and Armando Muñiz (U.S.) in 12 rounds and again on points. But on December 7 Nápoles surrendered his title to John Stracey (England), who stopped him in six rounds. Ángel Espada (Puerto Rico) won the vacant WBA welterweight title by outpointing Clyde Gray (Canada) in San Juan and then retained it by outpointing Johnny Grant (U.S.). Pedro (Perico) Fernández (Spain) retained the WBC junior welterweight crown, knocking out João Henrique (Brazil) in nine rounds in Barcelona; Fernández then lost the title to Saensak Muangsurin (Thailand) in eight rounds in

Coal: *see* Energy

Cobalt: *see* Mining and Quarrying

Cocoa (Cacao): *see* Agriculture and Food Supplies

Coffee: *see* Agriculture and Food Supplies

Coinage: *see* Philately and Numismatics

Colleges: *see* Education

Colonies: *see* Dependent States

Table I. Boxing Champions
As of Dec. 31, 1975

Division	World	Europe	Commonwealth	Britain
Heavyweight	Muhammad Ali, U.S.	vacant	Richard Dunn, England	Richard Dunn, England
Light heavyweight	John Conteh, England* Víctor Galíndez, Arg.†	Domenico Adinolfi, Italy	Tony Mundine, Australia	Chris Finnegan, England
Middleweight	Rodrigo Valdes, Colombia* Carlos Monzón, Arg.†	vacant	Monty Beetham, N.Z.	Alan Minter, England
Junior middleweight	Elisha Obed, Bahamas* Yuh Jae Do, South Korea†	Eckhard Dagge, West Germany	vacant	Maurice Hope, England
Welterweight	John Stracey, England* Ángel Espada, Puerto Rico†	vacant	Clyde Gray, Canada	Pat Thomas, Wales
Junior welterweight	Saensak Muangsurin, Thailand* Antonio Cervantes, Colombia†	Cemal Kamaci, Turkey	Hector Thompson, Australia	Joey Singleton, England
Lightweight	Gattu Ishimatsu, Japan* Roberto Durán, Panama†	vacant	Jonathan Dele, Nigeria	Jim Watt, Scotland
Junior lightweight	Alfredo Escalera, Puerto Rico* Ben Villaflor, Philippines†	Sven-Erik Paulsen, Norway	Billy Moeller, Australia	...
Featherweight	David Kotey, Ghana* Alexis Argüello, Nic.†	Elio Cotena, Italy	David Kotey, Ghana	Vernon Sollas, Scotland
Bantamweight	Rodolfo Martínez, Mexico* Alfonso Zamora, Mexico†	Daniel Trioulaire, France	Paul Ferreria, Australia	Paddy Maguire, Northern Ireland
Flyweight	Miguel Canto, Mexico* Erbito Salavarría, Philippines†	Franco Udella, Italy	vacant	John McCluskey, Scotland
Junior flyweight	Luis Lumumba Estaba, Venez.* Jaime Ríos, Panama†	...	...	...

*World Boxing Council champion.
†World Boxing Association champion.

Bangkok. Antonio Cervantes (Colombia) retained the WBA version, outpointing Esteban de Jesús (Puerto Rico) in Panama City.

Gattu ("Guts") Ishimatsu (Japan) retained the WBC lightweight title with wins over Rodolfo González (Mexico) in 12 rounds, Ken Buchanan (Scotland) on points, Arturo Pineda (Mexico) on points, and Alvaro Rojas (Costa Rica) in 14 rounds. Roberto Durán (Panama) retained the WBA version, stopping Masataka Takayama (Japan) in one round at San José, Costa Rica, knocking out Ray Lampkin (U.S.) in 14 rounds in Panama City, Panama, and knocking out Leoncio Ortiz (Mexico) in the 15th round in San Juan, Puerto Rico. Kuniaki Shibata (Japan) retained the WBC junior lightweight by outpointing Oult Makloufi (Alg.) but was then beaten by Alfredo Escalera (Puerto Rico) in two rounds. Escalera retained this title when he drew with Leonel Hernández (Venezuela) in Caracas and gained a technical knockout in the ninth round over European champion Sven-Erik Paulsen (Norway) in Oslo. Ben Villaflor (Phil.) retained the WBA junior lightweight crown, outpointing Kim Hyun-Chi (South Korea) in Manila.

In the WBC featherweight championship Bobby Chacon (U.S.) retained the title with a second-round knockout against Jesús Estrada (Mexico) but lost the championship when stopped in two rounds by Rubén Olivares (Mexico). Later Olivares lost the title to David Kotey (Ghana), who scored a win on points in Inglewood, Calif. Alexis Argüello (Nicaragua) took the WBA featherweight title from Rubén Olivares with a 13th-round knockout in Los Angeles and defended it with a win over Leonel Hernández on points, over Rigoberto Riasco (Panama) in two rounds, and over Royal Kobayashi (Japan) in five rounds. Rodolfo Martínez (Mexico) won the WBC bantamweight title from Rafaél Herrera (Mexico) in four rounds. Martínez retained this crown, stopping Nestor Jiménez (Colombia) in seven rounds in Bogotá. Soo Hwan Hong (South Korea) retained the WBA version with a win on points from Fernando Cabanela (Phil.), but lost the title to Alfonso Zamora (Mexico) in a fourth-round knockout. Zamora later retained the championship by stopping Thanomjit Sukhothai (Thailand) in four rounds. Miguel Canto (Mexico) took the WBC flyweight championship from Shoji Oguma (Japan) on points and retained it with victories over Betulio Gonzáles (Venezuela), Jiro Takada (Japan), and Ignacio Espinal (Dominican Republic). Susumu Hanagata (Japan) lost the WBA version to Erbito Salavarría (Phil.) on points. Salavarría repeated this victory over Hanagata. Junior flyweight was introduced as a new world championship weight class. Luis Lumumba Estaba (Venezuela) won the WBC title, knocking out Rafaél Lovera (Paraguay) in four rounds. The WBA recognized Jaime Ríos (Panama) as junior flyweight champion after he outpointed Rigoberto Marcano (Venezuela) in Panama City.

(FRANK BUTLER)

[452.B.4.h.vii]

Boris Bazaev of the Soviet Union won the 136-lb. class of the World Cup wrestling championship. He is shown in action here, placing a leg hold on Egan Beiler of Canada.

WIDE WORLD

Wrestling. The leading events in wrestling during 1975 were the World Games, held at Minsk in the Soviet Union, and the Pan-American Games, held at Mexico City. In the World Games the Soviet Union dominated both the freestyle and the Greco-Roman competition. In freestyle Bulgaria finished second, followed by Japan, Mongolia, and the United States, in that order. Poland placed second in the Greco-Roman events, followed by Romania and Hungary.

In 1975 Greco-Roman-style wrestling was added to the Pan-American games for the first time. The U.S. dominated both styles of wrestling at the tournament. Cuba finished second in the freestyle, followed by Canada, Mexico, and Argentina. In Greco-Roman the order of finish after the U.S. was Cuba, Mexico, Canada, and Argentina.

The University of Iowa moved into the elite circle of wrestling champions by sweeping to the U.S. collegiate championship. It was followed by Oklahoma University, Oklahoma State University, Iowa State University, and Lehigh University in Bethlehem, Pa.

(MARVIN G. HESS)

[452.B.4.h.xxix]

Judo. For those who expected the Japanese to repeat their 1973 sweep of world judo championships, the October 1975 world tournament in Vienna was something of a disappointment. Nonetheless, by winning four of the six world titles, Japan demonstrated its continued overall domination of the sport. In the finals of the open weight division, Haruki Uemura employed his famous seoinage (flying mare) technique to defeat former champion Kazuhiro Ninomiya, thus adding a new title to those he already possessed. In April he recaptured the All-Japan Judo Championship (AJJC), the only major world judo tournament without weight classes, and in September at Fukuoka during the Japan Weight Class Judo Championships (JWCJC) fought his way to the title as a heavyweight. Sumio Endo, who was runner-up to Uemura in the JWCJC, won the world heavyweight crown in Vienna, and Shozo Fujii emerged victorious for the third consecutive time in the middleweight division. Y. Minami, the previous lightweight champion, successfully defended his title. Though M. Ishibashi was defeated in the world finals, the month before he won the light heavyweight championship during the JWCJC.

Karate. For karate enthusiasts in Japan, 1975 offered numerous tournaments, many sponsored by specific schools of karate, by universities, by the Self-Defense Force, or by industrial organizations. The third world championships in October, however, were especially satisfying to the British who defeated the Japanese 2–1 (with 2 draws) in the team finals at Long Beach, Calif. In the individual finals, Japan's K. Murakami became the new champion with a victory over J. Hamaguchi; both were trained in the shitokai school of karate.

In March, Murakami had been forced by injuries to withdraw from the prestigious All-Japan all-styles championships. The finals in Fukuoka featured two members of the Japan Karate Association, a shotokan school of karate, which had no representative at Long Beach because of difficulties involving various organizations. In the two-minute All-Japan finals Toshiro Mori decisioned Norimasha Hayakawa with an upper punch and a straight thrust for two half-points. Tokyo Prefecture won the team title by blanking Saitama Prefecture 3–0 (with 2 draws). During the same tournament W. Yamaguchi won the women's routine exercise competition with a flawless execution of all the prescribed karate forms. Kyokushinkai, which does not belong to the million-member federation that represents virtually all Japanese karate organizations, staged the first world open karate tournament in Tokyo in November. In a rough, full-contact series of encounters, Katuaki Sato outlasted 116 karate experts from 34 countries to win the championship. Also during the year the All-Japan Federation agreed that each of the 47 Japanese prefec-

WIDE WORLD

Masakazu Takahashi (right) and Toyotaro Miyazaki demonstrate the samurai sword and karate bamboo pole during the martial arts championships held in New York City's Madison Square Garden in March.

Table II. World Games Wrestling Champions, 1975

Weight class	Competitor	Country
FREESTYLE		
105.5 lb.	H. Issaev	Bulgaria
114.5 lb.	Y. Takada	Japan
125.5 lb.	A. Massaho	Japan
136.5 lb.	Z. Oydov	Mongolia
149.5 lb.	P. Pinigin	U.S.S.R.
163 lb.	R. Ashuraliyev	U.S.S.R.
180.5 lb.	Z. Adies	West Germany
198 lb.	L. Tediashivilli	U.S.S.R.
220 lb.	K. Baynmunkh	Mongolia
Heavyweight	S. Andiev	U.S.S.R.
GRECO-ROMAN		
105.5 lb.	S. Vladimir	U.S.S.R.
114.5 lb.	K. Vitali	U.S.S.R.
125.5 lb.	M. Zargat	U.S.S.R.
136.5 lb.	O. Nelson	U.S.S.R.
149.5 lb.	Y. Chamil	U.S.S.R.
163 lb.	B. Anatolij	U.S.S.R.
180.5 lb.	N. Anatolij	U.S.S.R.
198 lb.	R. Baleri	U.S.S.R.
220 lb.	L. Kanem	Bulgaria
Heavyweight	Z. Alexandre	Bulgaria

Table III. Pan-American Games Wrestling Champions, 1975

Weight class	Competitor	Country
FREESTYLE		
105.5 lb.	G. Frías	Mexico
114.5 lb.	E. Abreu	Cuba
125.5 lb.	G. Ramos	Cuba
136.5 lb.	E. Beiler	Canada
149.5 lb.	L. Keaser	U.S.
163 lb.	F. Leberquer	Cuba
180.5 lb.	G. Hicks	U.S.
198 lb.	B. Peterson	U.S.
220 lb.	R. Hellickson	U.S.
Heavyweight	M. McCready	U.S.
GRECO-ROMAN		
105.5 lb.	S. Valdez	Cuba
114.5 lb.	B. Thompson	U.S.
125.5 lb.	D. Mello	U.S.
136.5 lb.	H. Stopp	Canada
149.5 lb.	P. Marcy	U.S.
163 lb.	I. Barbán	Cuba
180.5 lb.	D. Chandler	U.S.
198 lb.	W. Williams	U.S.
220 lb.	B. Rheingans	U.S.
Heavyweight	B. Van Worth	U.S.

Table IV. U.S. Collegiate Wrestling Champions, 1975

Weight class	Competitor	University
118 lb.	Shawn Garel	Univ. of Oklahoma
126 lb.	John Fritz	Pennsylvania State Univ.
134 lb.	Mike Frick	Lehigh Univ.
142 lb.	Jim Bennett	Yale Univ.
150 lb.	Chuck Yagla	Univ. of Iowa
158 lb.	Dan Holm	Univ. of Iowa
167 lb.	Ron Ray	Oklahoma State Univ.
177 lb.	Mike Lieberman	Lehigh Univ.
190 lb.	Al Nacin	Iowa State Univ.
Heavyweight	Larry Billenberg	Oregon State Univ.

KEYSTONE

Evasive action is taken during the world fencing championships held in Budapest, Hungary, in July. Winner of the men's individual épée title was Alexander Pusch of West Germany.

tures could henceforth award black belts up to the third degree, but the federation reserved the right to give examinations in Tokyo to all candidates seeking promotion to a higher rank.

Sumo. As always, the six annual 15-day national tournaments provided the greatest excitement of the year for sumo fans all over Japan. Kitanoumi (*see* BIOGRAPHY) finished the season with a 71–19 record, best of the year, and for the second straight time was named sumo wrestler of the year. His promotion to the rank of *yokozuna* (grand champion) in 1974 was more than justified as he captured the January *basho* (tournament) with a 12–3 record, the May *basho* in Tokyo with a 13–2 record, and was runner-up in three of the other four *basho*. Two of Kitanoumi's defeats were inflicted by Takanohana, a 6 ft. 232 lb. *sumotori*. Takanohana's triumphs, which came in March (13–2) and September (12–3), were not in themselves sufficient to secure a promotion from the second highest rank of *ozeki* to that of *yokozuna*. The July *basho* at Nagoya was won by Kongo (13–2) and the one in November by Mienoumi (13–2), who finished the season with a win-loss record of 62–28, second best of the year, and was promoted to the rank of *ozeki*. Kaiketsu was also elevated to *ozeki*, but after a mid-year attack of hepatitis and 6–9 records in September and November was demoted for not meeting required standards of performance.

Hawaiian-American Jesse Kuhaulula, who fights under the name of Takamiyama, was still the largest major league wrestler in action at 6 ft. 3½ in. and 365 lb. He had two good records during the year (10–5, 11–4) and was promoted to the fourth highest rank of *komusubi*.

The most disappointing *sumotori* of the year was Wajima, who for the first time in four years failed to win a single title. Fans had anticipated a new era in sumo with Kitanoumi facing Wajima in a replay of several dramatic finals in 1974. But after a 10–5 record in January, Wajima dropped out of the March and May *basho* after the first few days, skipped the July *basho* altogether, then made a mild comeback in September and November with 10–5 and 11–4 records. He was thus saved from forced retirement, there being no demotion from the grand champion rank of *yokozuna*. Kitanofuji and Kotozakura, two veteran *yokozuna*, and Daikirin, who held the rank of *ozeki*, all formally retired when their topknots were clipped in gala ceremonies attended by thousands of admirers.

(ANDREW M. ADAMS)

[452.B.4.h.xxix]

Fencing. The continued domination of world fencing by the Soviet Union, a burgeoning interest in the sport by China, and the jailing "on suspicion of espionage" of Lieut. Col. Jerzy Pawlowski of Poland, one of the sport's best known and most popular competitors, were among the year's key developments.

During the July world championships at the vast Neb Stadt Complex in Budapest, Hung., Soviet fencers demonstrated their superiority before more than 4,000 spectators. Vladimir Nazlimov, a 30-year-old army officer, scored four victories in the final round robin to clinch the individual sabre title. Jacek Bierkowski of Poland, whose three wins in the finals matched the record of Peter Marot of Hungary, was named runner-up on the basis of a victory over Marot in an earlier round. The failure of Viktor Sidak, the Soviet pre-tournament favourite, to qualify for the individual finals was surprising. Even so the Soviet men made a clean sweep of the sabre events by also winning the team title.

The women's foil team from the Soviet Union, led by two-time Olympic and three-time world champion Elena Belova, won a lopsided 9–3 victory over what appeared to be a dispirited and unnerved Hungarian contingent. This success marked the ninth Soviet women's team foil championship in 15 years. The individual women's foil title went to Katalin Jencsik-Stahl of Romania.

Alexander Pusch of West Germany emerged from the competition as individual épée champion, but the team title went to Sweden. France, a perennial power in the men's foil, captured the team title with a 9–4 victory over the Soviet Union and produced the individual champion in Christian Noel. The Nations Cup, decided by points amassed by the top six fencers in each event, went to the Soviet Union by a comfortable margin; Hungary was second and France third. The overall superiority and diversified strength of the Soviet athletes was undeniable, for they captured a total of three gold, three silver, and one bronze medal in eight events. Though Hungary showed its traditional prowess with two silver and four bronze medals, its overall performance was a disappointment to the vociferous gallery. Italy's poor showing was quite unusual. Mario Montano, the defending world sabre champion, was dethroned and the Italian sabre team, which had won the gold medal two years earlier, failed to live up to expectations. The frustrated Italians took only one medal, a bronze in the men's foil.

China, which appeared on the world sports scene only a few years ago, sent a full team to the competition in Budapest—a rather spectacular development considering the fact that two years earlier they were mere observers at the world fencing championships at Göteborg, Sweden. Though the Chinese fencers were clearly inexperienced, they proved to be the most intent observers at the tournament. The American coach, Hungarian-born Csaba Elthes, was somewhat startled when a Chinese coach, speaking fluent Hungarian, questioned him closely about fencing techniques. The U.S., which had never won a gold medal in world competition, made its best showing with a sixth place finish in the team sabre event.

The Pawlowski espionage incident was the chief

topic of conversation at the championships. Pawlowski, a former world sabre champion well known to most of the participants, was reportedly in a Warsaw jail and thus, for the first time in many years, failed to compete for a world title.

(MICHAEL STRAUSS)

[452.B.4.h.xii]

Kendo. Though only 200,000 women belong to the 4 million member All-Japan Kendo Federation, they held well organized national tournaments during the year, fighting with regulation length (about 47 in.) bamboo swords and standard kendo armour, including face masks, chest and waist protectors, and arm guards. In the finals of a tournament in Osaka that featured 51 female competitors, Yumiko Tanaka, a schoolteacher, won the national championship. In men's competition, one of the major events of the year was the All-Japan team championship held at Osaka on May 3. A high level of competition was assured because 85% of the participants were specially trained policemen or kendo school instructors. In the finals, the five-man team from Tokyo Prefecture defeated its Hyogo Prefecture counterpart 3–2. Tokyo Prefecture scored another victory on May 14 when Y. Ono won the individual championship in the police tournament. During the university tournament in Osaka on July 6, M. Machi of Keio University added further lustre to Tokyo's reputation by battling his way to victory over 119 other combatants. The All-Japan kendo instructors' tournament, staged in Nagoya on August 11, was won by a team from Nagasaki Prefecture. During December at the All-Japan Kendo Championships in Tokyo, kendo instructors won the top four places. In the final match, which featured former champion T. Kawazoe of Kochi Prefecture and S. Miyazawa of Miyagi Prefecture, Kawazoe won 1–0. (ANDREW M. ADAMS)

Commonwealth of Nations

The Kingston Meeting. The 20th meeting of the heads of state or government of Commonwealth countries at Kingston, Jamaica, during April 29–May 6, 1975, was attended by 28 presidents or prime ministers out of 34 (Ghana, Kenya, Malawi, Trinidad and Tobago, and Uganda were represented by other officials, and a special member, Nauru, does not take part in heads of government meetings). Eric Gairy of Grenada, which had achieved independence in February 1974, was the only representative of a new country; and there were only two changes in other heads of state since the last conference, in 1973 in Ottawa: W. E. Rowling of New Zealand and Harold Wilson of Great Britain. (Papua New Guinea, which did not celebrate its independence till September 16, was not eligible to attend; *see* DEPENDENT STATES).

Although wide-ranging discussion took place on the subjects of Cyprus, the Middle East, the Indian Ocean, South Asia, the Caribbean, and nuclear tests in the Pacific, the major preoccupations were, first, the changing situation in southern Africa and, second, a new economic order. The emphasis on Africa obscured the real and pressing needs of Malaysia and Singapore for Commonwealth support in the face of Communist expansion and externally aided insurgency. An attempt by the host government to invite the Rhodesian African National Council leader, Bishop Abel Muzorewa, to address the conference was disapproved as a precedent for unofficial pressure groups, but he was heard sympathetically at an informal session of the conference on April 30. Economic discussion resolved into a dialogue between Guyana's Prime Minister Forbes Burnham with his revolutionary proposals for reform and reconstruction of world financial bodies and Britain's Wilson, whose sober six-point reform comprised a general agreement on commodities and prices. The conference set up a group of ten experts under Alister McIntyre, secretary-general of the Caribbean Community and Common Market (Caricom), to report to the Commonwealth finance ministers' meeting at Georgetown, Guyana, on August 26–28, and to coordinate Commonwealth views for both the UN Conference on Trade and Development and the UN's seventh special session in September. The interim report commanded general support at Georgetown, but Britain, supported by Canada and Australia, did not accept indexation (automatic keying of the economy to prices), the UN's overseas development aid target of 0.7% of the donor countries' gross national product, or an increase in voting rights for less developed countries in world financial organizations. A definitive report was scheduled for 1976 when the views of both the U.S. and the European Economic Community (EEC) would be known.

The final communiqué from Jamaica routed the concept of the EEC as a divisive issue in the Commonwealth by welcoming the Lomé agreement signed in February between the EEC and the 46 countries—22 Commonwealth—of Africa, the Caribbean, and the Pacific (ACP countries). For the first time, in recognition of the International Women's Year and of the many distinguished women present, including the prime ministers of India and Sri Lanka, the final communiqué "took account" of women's need for full equality and opportunity. Queen Elizabeth II, as queen of Jamaica, continued the pattern set at Ottawa of receiving her ministers before the opening of the conference. It was agreed to synchronize the 21st meeting of Commonwealth heads of state in London in 1977 with the queen's silver jubilee of her accession as head of the Commonwealth.

The Pacific. New Zealand's contribution to the Commonwealth conference highlighted its developing role as regional leader of the South Pacific. Emphasis was placed on the South Pacific Forum centred in Wellington, N.Z., which was overtaking the international South Pacific Commission and Conference in importance. New Zealand's new membership in the Ministerial Conference for the Economic Development of Southeast Asia (MEDSEA) tied it firmly to local aid and trade. New Zealand's foreign aid (at NZ$44 million) was focused on Southeast Asia, Fiji, Tonga, Samoa, and the nation's own associates of the Cook Islands, Niue, and the Tokelau Islands. Trade, which had fallen in two decades from over 80% with Europe to under 30%, also had a corresponding local increase. New Zealand's close links with the Association of Southeast Asian Nations was epitomized by liaison with Lee Kuan Yew of Singapore, who visited the country in February and emphasized New Zealand's key role in regional development and protection in that part of the Commonwealth.

Asia. The unique election of Malaysia's *yang dipertuan agong* (supreme head of state) once every five years took place in 1975. The choice of a ruler from the state of Kelantan had strategic significance; Kelantan's border with Thailand was permanently patrolled against Chinese Communist infiltration, stepped up since the end of the Vietnamese war; in

Comecon: *see* Economy, World

Commerce: *see* Economy, World

Commercial and Trade Policies: *see* Economy, World

Commodity Trade: *see* Economy, World; Stock Exchanges

Common Market: *see* Economy, World; European Unity

particular, attacks were made on the East-West Highway under construction in northern Malaysia.

The integration of Sikkim with India in April and the coups in Bangladesh in August and November passed comparatively quietly. In Sri Lanka and the Maldive Islands a move to the right led to agreement to a temporary Royal Air Force presence in Colombo after the evacuation at the end of 1975 of the Gan staging post and until Diego Garcia should be ready. In Cyprus on February 13 the Turkish Cypriots declared a provisional republic in the Turkish-controlled 40% of the island. The position of such a breakaway state within the Commonwealth remained uncertain, but a committee was set up to cover the Commonwealth aspect of the Cyprus impasse.

Africa. Though discontent in Ghana grew (Ignatius Kutu Acheampong did not leave Africa for the Commonwealth meeting), it was Nigeria that experienced a coup in 1975. Gen. Yakubu Gowon, while at the Organization of African Unity's (OAU's) summit meeting in Kampala, Uganda, during July, had to yield to a quiet takeover by Brig. Murtala Ramat Mohammed (*see* BIOGRAPHY). Despite this upheaval, Nigeria continued to play a leading part in ACP negotiations and in particular in the establishment of the West Africa Economic Community (after June 1975 the Economic Community of West African States, or ECOWAS; French, CEDEAO), on which an agreement was reached on May 28, 1975.

Although there were initial difficulties with the French-speaking organizations, the Communauté Economique de l'Afrique de l'Ouest (CEAO) and Organisation Commune Africaine et Mauricienne or Common African and Mauritian Organization (OCAM), the Commonwealth countries of West Africa faced a more hopeful future in 1975 than did the members of the East African Community, whose rival nationalisms brought the Community to the point of collapse and even to military confrontation between Uganda and Tanzania. It was difficult to hold a balance between comparatively affluent capitalist Kenya, the vagaries of Idi Amin's Uganda, and the austere socialist experiment of Tanzania, verging on bankruptcy and heavily in debt to China.

U.K. Foreign Secretary James Callaghan's visit to Africa did little to promote Rhodesia's constitutional future, hampered by bitter divisions among local African leaders, and the meeting of Pres. Kenneth Kaunda of Zambia and South African Prime Minister B. J. Vorster on the Zambezi in August bore little more fruit. Zambia remained vulnerable politically and economically because of the declining price of its copper and lack of economical port facilities. Therefore, Zambia showed a slightly more friendly eye to permitting its copper to pass through Rhodesia again. More desperately, Zambia, like Tanzania and Malawi, was classified by the UN Economic Commission for Africa (ECA) as a food-deficit area, needing increased imports that could be obtained from Rhodesia and South Africa.

The Caribbean. Although Caricom strengthened its relations with both Canada and Cuba, the strains of economic independence increased, not least in the latest recruit, Grenada. Though Britain had agreed to provide £2,250,000 to cover 1974–77 budgetary and development difficulties, aid was held up when misuse of £250,000 was discovered, and Prime Minister Gairy threatened to take Britain to the International Court of Justice to claim compensation for economic cruelty during 191 years of colonization.

Communications: *see* Industrial Review; Television and Radio

Economic Affairs. The Secretariat of the Commonwealth expanded activities in 1975, particularly through the multidevelopment Commonwealth Fund for Technical Cooperation, which had a new budget of £5.5 million. After the resignation of Arnold Smith, the first and only secretary-general since 1965, Shridath Ramphal, foreign minister of Guyana, was chosen to succeed him. The Secretariat continued to coordinate the network of Commonwealth bodies and organized more than 100 meetings and conferences. One of the most important meetings was in March in London between Judith Hart (*see* BIOGRAPHY), Britain's minister of overseas development, and representatives from 32 Commonwealth countries. This conference proposed the setting up of a Commonwealth food production and rural development division in the Secretariat and made practical recommendations in that regard, passed on to heads of state in Jamaica and embodied in the interim report to Commonwealth finance ministers at Georgetown.

British aid to less developed countries, more than 90% of them in the Commonwealth, was estimated at more than £471 million for 1975–76, in grants and interest-free loans. As of October 1975 all official aid was "untied" and priority given to the poorest countries. The White Paper of January 1975 estimated a 14% increase in official aid over the following four years, rising from £350 million to £384 million. Britain's Ministry of Overseas Development, which in June 1975 came under Foreign Office control for the better coordination of economic relations, was concerned with providing personnel (12,000 overseas and 15,000 from overseas training in the U.K.) to operate the programs. A new scheme announced in June 1975 pledged the ministry to pound-for-pound aid to voluntary Commonwealth bodies whether in education or community development.

In the 25th year of the Colombo Plan the 25th meeting was held in Sri Lanka, to which Britain made a new grant of £3,350,000. Over 30% of British bilateral aid went to India, Bangladesh, and Sri Lanka, all badly affected by rising oil prices. The 24th meeting, held in Singapore in December 1974, had agreed that the plan should be extended to 1981.

The Commonwealth Development Corporation (CDC) commitments in 1974 rose from £243.5 million to £256.9 million. A record disbursement of £36.4 million brought total investment in 241 projects to £203.6 million. Gross income was also a record at £23.8 million, as was the operating surplus of £19.1 million. The value of exports alone produced by CDC-affiliated companies in 1974 was £135 million.

In the Lomé Convention the EEC and the ACP sugar group mutually guaranteed access and quotas to both the U.K. and the EEC. Trade among Commonwealth countries accounted for about a fifth of their total trade, still slightly in excess of EEC trade, though a number of Commonwealth African countries showed an increase in trade with the EEC.

(MOLLY MORTIMER)

See also articles on the various political units.
[972.A.1.a]

Communist Movement

The year 1975 would be remembered in the history of the Communist movement for the victory of Communist forces in South Vietnam, Cambodia, and Laos. Elsewhere, election gains by the Italian Communists brought them closer to gaining a place in the national government, and the Portuguese Communists, despite a poor showing in the national elections and subsequent difficulties with the military government, remained a major contender for power. These successes did not, however, contribute to the unity of the international Communist movement, and in fact provided new sources of friction between the Soviet and Chinese Communists and also between the Soviet and several nonruling Communist parties.

Soviet Union. The Soviet leaders placed great emphasis on the celebration in May of the Soviet victory in World War II, an event that they believed marked the height of the second major crisis in capitalism and opened the way for the first major expansion of Communism since 1917. The 35-nation summit meeting in Helsinki, Fin., in July, which brought the Conference on Security and Cooperation in Europe to its ceremonial conclusion, gave the Soviet bloc the long-sought-for international recognition of the borders established as a result of the defeat of Nazi Germany. Although the U.S.S.R. and its allies made some concessions in the area of human rights, the conclusion of the conference was hailed as a major success for Soviet party leader Leonid I. Brezhnev.

The outcome at Helsinki was, however, only one of the successes Brezhnev had apparently hoped to achieve in the months prior to the 25th party congress, scheduled for February 1976, and in several other areas he ran into difficulties. Domestically, the hopes for a successful conclusion of the ninth five-year plan were dampened by another poor harvest in 1975, while internationally Brezhnev's hopes faded for an all-European conference of Communist parties in 1975 and for a meaningful new agreement on strategic arms limitation before the end of the year. As the party congress approached and rumours spread about the possibility of Brezhnev's retirement, there was evidence of political struggle within the Soviet leadership. In April the ambitious former secret police chief Aleksandr Shelepin was dropped from his position in the Politburo and then from his job as head of the Soviet labour unions.

Italy's Communists in June scored their largest electoral gains since World War II.

KEYSTONE

Eastern and Western Europe. The Soviet hope was to have a series of regional conferences of Communist parties in various parts of the world during the first half of 1975 that would adopt joint policy statements, condemn Maoism, and open the way for a new world Communist conference in the future. The plan to hold an all-European Communist conference in East Berlin following the July summit in Helsinki was frustrated by disagreements among party representatives at several preparatory meetings concerning the joint statement. By July a major rift developed at an eight-party subcommittee session when the draft text of a common stand prepared by the East Germans and backed by the Soviet and Danish Communists proved to be completely unacceptable not only to the independent-minded Yugoslav, Italian, and Spanish Communists but even to the generally loyal pro-Soviet French Communists. At an October preparatory session the representatives of 27 European Communist parties agreed to resume work on a new draft, but in November they adjourned until January 1976.

Among the ruling parties of Eastern Europe, the pro-Chinese Albanian Communists remained adamant in their refusal to have any relations with the Soviet "social imperialists" and even refused to attend the European security conference, which they denounced as a superpower deal designed to divide up Europe. The nonaligned Yugoslav regime continued during the year to tighten political controls domestically, not only arresting Croatian and Albanian nationalists but also dismissing dissident university professors and closing down the independent philosophical journal *Praxis* in February. The Yugoslav leaders continued their efforts to improve relations with the U.S.S.R. and rejected Western concerns about a possible Soviet threat in the event of the death of aging President Tito.

The situation in Portugal particularly troubled many Western European Communists. Working closely with the revolutionary Armed Forces Movement that seized power in 1974 and particularly with the pro-Communist Premier Vasco dos Santos Gonçalves, the Portuguese Communists under the firmly pro-Moscow leadership of Alvaro Cunhal (*see* BIOGRAPHY) had gained sufficient control over the labour unions and the mass media to feel that they could dismiss their poor showing in the April elections (under 13% of the vote) as a factor of little significance. Their methods, besides evoking an increasingly violent response from the Socialists and other anti-Communist parties, embarrassed those European Communists who hoped to gain power through democratic means. Meanwhile, the pressures on the Portuguese military leadership led to the removal of Gonçalves in late August, and the Communists stood aside when left-wing junior officers attempted unsuccessfully to overthrow his moderate successor in November.

Asia. In January the opening session of the fourth National People's Congress was finally held in Peking, the first such meeting in a decade. The congress, which Mao Tse-tung did not attend, appointed a new government and ratified a new constitution for the Chinese People's Republic which eliminated the long-vacant post of president and deleted the references found in the 1954 constitution to Sino-Soviet friendship. Although the ailing Chou En-lai was reelected

Membership of the Major Communist Parties of the World*

Countries with a membership of 2,000 or more persons

Country	Membership
Albania	95,000†
Argentina	116,000
Australia	3,900
Austria	25,000
Bangladesh	2,500
Belgium	14,000
Brazil‡	7,000
Bulgaria	763,000†
Burma‡	§
Cambodia	§
Chile	§
China	28,000,000
Colombia	11,000
Cuba	170,000
Cyprus	13,000
Czechoslovakia	1,279,000
Denmark	7,750
Finland	49,000
France	410,000
Germany, East	1,950,000†
Germany, West‖	43,000
Greece	28,000
Guadeloupe	3,000
Hungary	754,000†
Iceland	2,200
India	453,000
Indonesia	§
Iraq	2,000
Israel	2,000
Italy	1,700,000
Japan	350,000
Korea, North	1,600,000†
Laos	5,000
Lebanon	2,500
Malaysia‡	2,500
Mexico	5,000
Mongolia	61,000
Nepal‡	5,000
Netherlands, The	11,500
Norway	2,500
Paraguay‡	3,500
Peru‡	3,200
Philippines‡	8,000
Poland	2,322,000†
Romania	2,480,000†
Spain‡	5,000
Sri Lanka	9,500
Sudan	7,500
Sweden	17,000
Switzerland	3,000
Syria‡	3,000
U.S.S.R.	15,000,000†
United Kingdom	30,000
United States	2,500
Uruguay‡	§
Venezuela	6,000
Vietnam, North	1,200,000
Vietnam, South	§
Yugoslavia	1,077,000

*Latest available figures.
†Official claim.
‡Communist Party illegal.
§No estimate available.
‖Including West Berlin.
Sources: U.S. Department of State, Bureau of Intelligence and Research, *World Strength of the Communist Party Organizations*, 1973; and subsequent published reports, official or otherwise.

premier and delivered a major report to the congress, during most of the year Deputy Premier Teng Hsiao-p'ing appeared to be effectively in charge of day-to-day operations.

Sino-Soviet polemics, which seemed to have moderated somewhat at the beginning of the year when Chou En-lai, in his report to the National People's Congress, called for the development of normal state relations with the U.S.S.R., soon worsened. While Soviet spokesmen denounced the new Chinese constitution as anti-Soviet and antidemocratic, the Chinese again attacked the U.S.S.R. as the more dangerous of the two superpowers. To buttress anti-Soviet forces in Europe, Chinese leaders warmly received several conservative Western politicians, established diplomatic relations with the European Economic Community, and, on the occasion of the celebration of the victory in World War II, described Brezhnev as a modern-day Hitler. It was in Asia, however, particularly following the Communist victories in Indochina, that the competition between the two Communist powers became most intense. The U.S.S.R. warned Japan in June against signing a friendship treaty with the Chinese which contained a clause opposing the dominance in Asia of a third power; accused China of plotting to extend its dominance in Asia by subversive means; and began to urge once more that an Asian security conference be called.

Caught in the crossfire of the Sino-Soviet dispute, most Asian Communist parties attempted to remain neutral and nonaligned. Exceptions included the pro-Soviet Mongolian party, but the Japanese Communists continued to be critical of both sides of the dispute and the North Vietnamese and North Koreans, both of whom were accepted into the bloc of nonaligned nations in August, tried to maintain friendly relations with both sides.

The victory of the Communist forces in South Vietnam and Cambodia in April and the subsequent steady takeover by the Communists in Laos were hailed by all Communist parties. However, as the new regimes began their efforts to reestablish order, to initiate massive reeducation programs for former enemies, and to revitalize their agricultural economies, the rivalry for influence on the part of Moscow, Peking, and Hanoi continued. The North Vietnamese overall remained the most influential power in the area. Northern troops continued to be stationed in South Vietnam, and the fourth-ranking member of the North Vietnamese Politburo, Pham Hung, seemed to be the unofficial leader in Saigon. The fiercely independent Cambodian Communists were clearly far more closely associated with the Chinese than with the Soviet Union or even with the North Vietnamese. The Laotian Communists emphasized self-reliance and nationalism but maintained close ties with the North Vietnamese and after coming to power received considerable aid, plus 1,500 technical advisers, from the Soviet Union.

Elsewhere in Southeast Asia, military activity on the part of Communist insurgents increased in Thailand, Malaysia, and Burma. This occurred in spite of the moves made by the non-Communist governments of the area to establish relations with China and the new Communist regimes in Indochina and in spite of Chinese assurances that they were not supporting the guerrillas.

As the 25th anniversary of the war in Korea approached, the renewal of North Korean propaganda attacks on the South Korean regime and the Communist victories in Indochina inspired fears that Korea might become the scene of a new military confrontation. However, when North Korean leader Kim Il Sung visited China in April, his hosts apparently urged him to be cautious, and in his subsequent trips to Africa and to Romania, Bulgaria, and Yugoslavia in May and June, Kim emphasized his desire for support in achieving a peaceful reunification and the withdrawal of UN troops from South Korea.

Other Nations. The strong Soviet influence on the Communist parties of the Middle East was reflected in the joint statement issued by the conference of eight Arab parties in April. It supported the holding of a world Communist conference, backed Soviet policy in the Middle East, and was critical of the Egyptian government both for its conservative internal policies and for its willingness to negotiate with the United States and Israel. The open Soviet opposition to the policies of Egyptian Pres. Anwar as-Sadat was also accompanied by an announcement that the Egyptian Communist Party, which had dissolved itself in 1964, was returning to action. In Africa Sino-Soviet rivalry was increasingly evident, particularly in the former Portuguese colonies. The new Marxist-Leninist-oriented government in Mozambique claimed that it was adopting the Chinese model, while in war-torn Angola the Chinese and Soviets armed and trained rival liberation movements.

Representatives of 24 Latin-American and Caribbean Communist parties assembled for a regional conference in Havana in June and agreed on a joint statement that included a condemnation of Maoism and support for Soviet efforts to convene a world Communist conference. For the Cuban Communists, 1975 was marked by a major success, the decision in July by the Organization of American States to lift its sanctions against Cuba. (DAVID L. WILLIAMS)

See also Economy, World.

[541.E.3.d.ii]

Communists rally in Lisbon following the downfall of Vasco dos Santos Gonçalves as premier. Banner in the foreground urges comrades to squeeze the capitalists.

WIDE WORLD

Comoro Islands

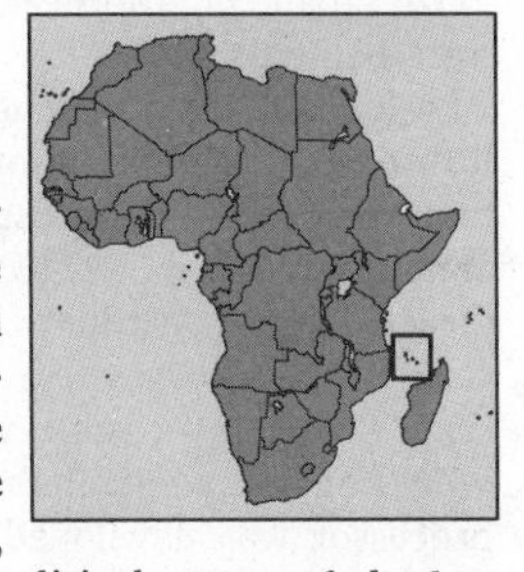

An African island state lying in the Indian Ocean off the east coast of Africa between Mozambique and Madagascar, the Comoros comprise four main islands, Grande Comore, Moheli, Anjouan, and Mayotte, although the political status of the last is not yet settled. Area: 863 sq.mi. (2,235 sq.km.). Pop. (1975 est.): 306,000. Cap. and largest city: Moroni (pop., 1973 est., 15,900), on Grande Comore. Language: French. Religion: mainly Muslim, except for the predominantly Christian population of Mayotte. President until Aug. 3, 1975, Ahmed Abdallah; head of government after August 3, Ali Soilih.

In the referendum of Dec. 22, 1974, more than 95% of the population of the Comoro Islands voted for independence. The National Assembly in France required the constitution of the future state to receive approval in each island separately before the proclamation of independence, to take account of the inhabitants of Mayotte who had voted 60% against independence. But Ahmed Abdallah, head of the islands' government, declared independence unilaterally on July 6. After a coup on August 3, however, Ali Soilih assumed power. There was a risk that Anjouan, where Abdallah had fled, might secede, but a military detachment from Moroni restored order in September. Mayotte continued to adhere to France; a new referendum would permit it to choose the status of either French *département* or overseas territory.

The UN General Assembly voted on November 12 to admit the Comoros. On November 21 the government in Moroni tried unsuccessfully to overthrow the leadership on Mayotte. The Executive Council in Moroni on November 26 ordered the takeover of French government property; French personnel were to be repatriated. (PHILIPPE DECRAENE)

TASS/SOVFOTO

Moroni, capital of the Comoro Islands, lies at the base of the active volcano Mt. Kartala on Grande Comore island.

COMORO ISLANDS

Education. (1973–74) Primary, pupils 21,557, teachers 570; secondary, pupils 2,920, teachers 121.

Finance and Trade. Monetary unit: CFA franc, with (Sept. 22, 1975) a parity of CFA Fr. 50 to the French franc and a free rate of CFA Fr. 227.70 to U.S. $1 (CFA Fr. 471.75 = £1 sterling). Budget (1972 rev. est.) balanced at CFA Fr. 2,232,000,000. Foreign trade (1973): imports CFA Fr. 3,369,000,000; exports CFA Fr. 1,106,000,000. Import source France *c.* 41%. Export destinations: France *c.* 74%; West Germany *c.* 6%. Main exports (1968): essential oils 42%; vanilla 35%; copra 17%.

Computers

Microprocessors continued to be improved substantially in 1975, causing the power of computer technology to be extended downward to levels that previously were uneconomical. New applications were developed, and new microprocessor designs went into production.

A microprocessor is a single large-scale integrated circuit with much of the capability of the central processing unit of a much larger computer. Microprocessors first became commercially available in 1972. Their development was consolidated and extended in 1973, and they burst upon the consciousness of the world the following year. Engineers began to use them in a wide variety of applications in 1975 and the man in the street was exposed to them in such devices as point-of-sale terminals in department stores, automatic cash dispensers in banks, and television-like games such as Pong®, which proliferated in hotel lobbies and barrooms.

Microprocessors represent the point at which the four classic disciplines of electronics converge and become indistinguishable. Electronics as a branch of technology has been traditionally defined as the study and utilization of electric charge moving through empty space or through a gas, as opposed to moving through metallic wires and components made of materials of varying degrees of electrical conductivity. Early investigators found themselves obliged to concentrate in one of four areas: materials, devices, circuits, and systems. Materials had to be discovered and developed that would emit electrons in desired quantities and that could control their flight; devices, notably the vacuum tube, had to be invented that capitalized on these materials and that could be incorporated into circuits which performed useful functions such as rectification, amplification, modulation, and detection. Finally, numerous functional circuits were combined into systems that were capable of achieving a desired goal.

While electronics was developing it was realized that classic rules of logic—the syllogisms of Aristotle, for example, and their derivatives—could be expressed in terms of simple mathematical relationships, which in turn could be implemented by a number of interconnected switches. These switching functions could be executed by electronic devices, which were combined to create the earliest computers.

When transistors were invented in 1948, the first signs of the fusion of materials and devices appeared. About 10–15 years later, transistor technology, by then well developed, was extended to incorporate other components, which could be manufactured by the same process at the same time; and the integrated circuit was born. Thus, for the first time the disciplines of materials, devices, and circuits became intermingled.

LONDON EVENING NEWS/PICTORIAL PARADE

Control panel of the new computer at London Bridge will be responsible for routing and charting 4,000 trains per day, including all those from Charing Cross, London Bridge, and Cannon Street.

At first, the only manufactured integrated circuits were the simplest logic functions. From the circuit design point of view, these "on-off" functions were simpler and easier to build than the older and more familiar circuits, which had to produce continuously varying outputs in response to continuously varying inputs. Later these "linear" circuits were also integrated. Then the simple logic functions were extended, first to incorporate arrays of similar circuits in one device (the device now incorporating the circuit), then to interconnect those circuits within the device to obtain more complex functions, and finally to build large numbers of dissimilar circuits within a device to achieve a true subsystem. As combined material-device-circuit-systems, microprocessors represent the ultimate in this process.

Microprocessors, and most other large-scale integrated circuits, were built with metal oxide semiconductor (MOS) technology. This is a relatively simple process, but it suffers from speed restrictions. A few attempts were made to use the intrinsically faster bipolar technology, but for the most part, until 1975, it could be applied only to smaller and less complex devices, in part because of higher power requirements that led to overheating. Then, as a result of developments over the previous two or three years in the United States, The Netherlands, and West Germany, a new circuit form was devised, called integrated injection logic (I^2L) or merged transistor logic (MTL), in which the speed of bipolar technology and the small circuits and manufacturing simplicity of MOS could be combined.

In particular, an I^2L microprocessor was introduced by Texas Instruments Inc. It could process four bits at once, the same as the earliest MOS microprocessors, most of which had since graduated to 8, 12, or 16 bits. It was, however, up to five times as fast as the fastest MOS versions and dissipated less power than the coolest previous bipolar versions, while its circuits were only half the size of the latter.

While U.S. manufacturers continued to forge ahead in microprocessor development, European companies were not far behind. For example, another I^2L microprocessor was developed by La Radiotechnique-Compelec (France), while Standard Telecommunications Laboratories in Great Britain brought out a slow but inexpensive 1-bit microprocessor for use in communications and industrial control.

In Japan, microprocessor-based industrial controls were being promoted by Tokyo Shibaura Electric Co. (Toshiba) and by Yokogawa Electric Co. For Toshiba it was a new application for the company's 12-bit microprocessor, the most powerful at the time of its announcement in 1974. One of the products was a direct digital controller that could handle up to eight stations in a loop, with more flexibility and options than would be possible with the previous eight individual analog controllers. Meanwhile, a 16-bit microprocessor was developed by Matsushita Electric Industrial Co. The circuit measured 5.58 by 5.5 mm., comparable to less complex chips made in Japan and elsewhere and to earlier 16-bit, one-chip microprocessors made in the U.S.

In the U.S., new applications for microprocessors included a computer-output printer, an automatic speech recognizer for use in warehouse sorting and baggage handling, and a portable automobile diagnostic machine for use by mechanics.

Technology. The computer industry continued to move ahead on other fronts besides microprocessors. Among the advances was the increasingly common use of 4,000-bit integrated memory circuits, edging out the previously used 1,000-bit devices and threatening seriously for the first time the dominance of the much older magnetic core memories. Their use was held back primarily by limited availability and the lack of a standardized configuration of pins for interconnection to other devices.

Late in 1974, International Business Machines Corp. (IBM) introduced a mass storage system with a capacity of 4 trillion bits; a somewhat similar system was brought out in May 1975 by Control Data Corp. Both systems consisted of a large number of small magnetic tape cartridges, each storing several

Languages prove no barrier for this desk-sized computer, jointly developed in the U.S. and England. It is programmed to understand 150 spoken words or phrases, converting them into digital signals.

TREVOR HUMPHRIES—CAMERA PRESS/PHOTO TRENDS

million characters. An access mechanism plucks a cartridge out of a honeycomb-like array (a rectangular array for Control Data) and transports it to a recording station, where the data stored on it are transferred either to a standard disk unit (both systems) or directly into the computer (Control Data only).

Other mass storage systems were developed using memories that could be addressed by electron beams. One such was a unit from Micro-Bit Corp. of Lexington, Mass., with a capacity of just over a million bits; its builders said they hoped to put together a system nearly 100 times as large. Another was a 32-million-bit system from General Electric Co.

Business. The U.S. Department of Justice, having filed its pretrial brief in its antitrust suit against IBM late in 1974, finally brought the six-year-old action to trial in May 1975. The pretrial brief was the government's first formal documentation of its charges. Evidence of an IBM monopoly, said the Justice Department, would "be largely reflected in IBM's own documents, culled from millions that have been examined," as well as its overwhelming share of the market, the inability of large companies to compete, and the existence of de facto industry standards arising from IBM's dominance of the market. Although the trial finally started in May, testimony was taken for only two months, when a recess for additional discovery was called. The trial resumed in September.

In a separate action, IBM won its appeal of a ruling against it in an antitrust suit filed by Telex Corp. Telex, a manufacturer of peripheral equipment compatible with IBM computers, had sued IBM, charging monopolistic practices, and IBM had countersued, charging Telex with theft of trade secrets. Both parties won their suits in 1973, and both parties appealed. The appeals court reversed the original finding against IBM but upheld that against Telex. As a result, Telex originally planned to appeal again to the U.S. Supreme Court, but decided against this course in October. IBM then said it would not demand payment of damages due IBM under the countersuit.

Xerox Corp. withdrew from the computer market during the summer of 1975. Xerox, known mainly for its office copiers, had purchased Scientific Data Systems in 1969, a small company that had been one of the few profitable ones in the middle 1960s. For Xerox it had been a bad investment, and showed no signs of turning around in the near future. Later, Honeywell, Inc., said it would take over servicing and marketing support of Xerox computers.

IBM's plan to enter the domestic satellite business jointly with Comsat General Corp., announced in mid-1974, was overruled by the U.S. Federal Communications Commission early in 1975. Rather than categorically deny the application, the FCC considered it a special case in view of IBM's unique position in the industry. In response, IBM, together with Comsat General Corp., made a new proposal involving themselves and a third partner, Aetna Life & Casualty, which would dilute the amount of control by IBM and thus be more likely to satisfy the FCC.

In France, Honeywell-Bull, a subsidiary of Honeywell Information Systems in the U.S., undertook a merger with Compagnie Internationale pour l'Informatique (CII). It was thought that the merger, besides improving CII's business posture, would beef up Unidata, the combine formed by CII, Philips N.V. (The Netherlands), and Siemens AG (West Germany) to protect the European computer industry against inroads from IBM. Philips and Siemens, however, opposed the merger. Philips eventually pulled out of Unidata, returning to its previous concentration on small computers as well as to its extensive involvement with other areas of electronic technology.

AUTHENTICATED NEWS INTERNATIONAL

This flat-screen video system devised by scientists at Bell Telephone Laboratories, Inc., can record handwritten signatures, reproduce pictures and charts, simulate dialing a telephone number, and serve as a desk-top calculator. Thousands of neon-gas cells that glow when energized by an electric current form the basic circuitry of the system.

Philips' departure was the final blow that sealed Unidata's doom. As a result, Siemens took over the manufacture and marketing of all four announced Unidata computers, thus becoming the European giant in the computer industry.

Late in 1974 Rockwell Microelectronics, part of Rockwell International and a leader in the development of silicon-on-sapphire (SOS) semiconductor devices, shelved its commercial effort in the SOS field to concentrate on the military market. The move forced General Automation Inc. to withdraw its LSI-12 microcomputer, announced at the end of 1973, for which Rockwell had been the prime supplier of the SOS microprocessor on which the unit was based. General Automation made a strong effort to recoup from this misadventure by introducing four new microcomputers based on more conventional MOS technology. A few months later, reverberations from Rockwell's action resulted in the bankruptcy of Inselek Corp., a small company in Princeton, N.J., that had been one of the few other organizations developing SOS and that had committed most of its resources to this technology.

Among many significant developments overseas was an agreement permitting U.S. and Japanese companies to manufacture computers in Spain. Parties to the agreement included the Spanish Instituto Nacional de Industria, Sperry Univac in the U.S., and Fujitsu in Japan.

Many new computers and related products were introduced during 1975. Among the most significant were two unusually small machines from IBM. First came the System 32, for industrial and commercial applications, using 2,000-bit MOS memory chips, a small cathode-ray tube display in the operator's console, and a small magnetic storage minidisk, known familiarly as a floppy disk, with all electronics on 24 circuit boards. Later came IBM's first truly portable computer, weighing only 50 lb., which some called a programmable calculator. It could be programmed from its keyboard in either of two machine languages, and sported in its single case a four-inch display screen and a small magnetic tape drive for cartridges. Internally it had a 48,000-bit read-only memory containing an interpretive program for the keyboard inputs. (WALLACE B. RILEY)

[735.D; 10/23.A.6–7]

ENCYCLOPÆDIA BRITANNICA FILMS. *What Is a Computer?* (1970); *A Computer Glossary* (1973).

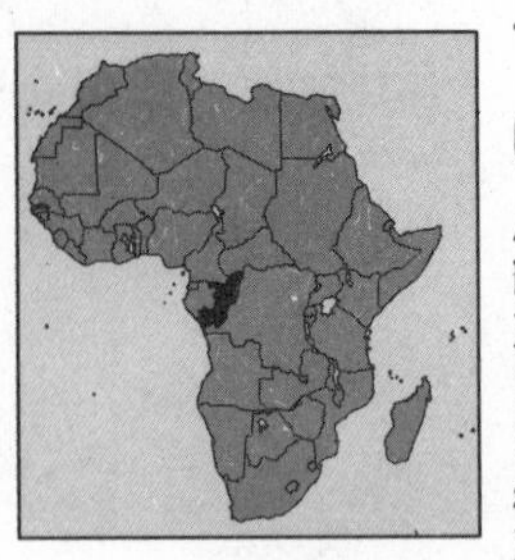

Congo

A people's republic of equatorial Africa, the Congo is bounded by Gabon, Cameroon, the Central African Republic, Zaire, Angola, and the Atlantic Ocean. Area: 132,047 sq.mi. (342,000 sq.km.). Pop. (1974 est.): 1,313,000, mainly Bantu. Cap. and largest city: Brazzaville (pop., 1974 prelim., 310,500). Language: French (official) and Bantu dialects. Religion: mainly animist, with a Christian minority. President in 1975, Maj. Marien Ngouabi; premier, Henri Lopes.

After party elections confirming the leadership of the one-party state, President Ngouabi in January 1975 decided to amalgamate the permanent secretaryship of the Congolese Labour Party with his presidency of the Central Committee and his office of head of state.

Although President Ngouabi had claimed in January that there were no more political detainees in the Congo, acute tension existed between the Brazzaville government and its left-wing opponents. In February the president accused two former officials of having created "a Communist Party of Central Africa" for the purpose of ousting his regime. In May Ngouabi denied that former president Alphonse Massamba-Débat was still under house arrest and affirmed that he was living in freedom in his native town in full enjoyment of presidential retirement. In July Ngouabi declared that all former political prisoners could thenceforward live wherever they liked without any restrictions.

Relations with France continued to be ambiguous. After sending Premier Lopes on an official visit to Paris and then warmly receiving Pierre Abelin, France's minister of cooperation, on his official visit to Brazzaville, Ngouabi announced in August that a takeover of French interests in the Congo was under consideration. In October he severely criticized the French government in the affair of Françoise Claustre in Chad (*see* CHAD).

Congolese foreign policy was firmly oriented toward the socialist nations, as evidenced by Ngouabi's visits to Moscow in March and to Havana in September, by Lopes' visit to Peking in February–March, and by the normalization of relations with Portugal in January. (PHILIPPE DECRAENE)

[978.E.7.a.iii]

CONGO

Education. (1972–73) Primary, pupils 277,386, teachers 4,373; secondary, pupils 49,984, teachers 948; vocational, pupils 4,228, teachers 331; teacher training, students 671, teachers 23; higher, students 2,098, teaching staff 194.

Finance. Monetary unit: CFA franc, with (Sept. 22, 1975) a parity of CFA Fr. 50 to the French franc and a free rate of CFA Fr. 227.70 to U.S. $1 (CFA Fr. 471.75 = £1 sterling). Budget (1974 est.) balanced at CFA Fr. 27,475,000,000.

Foreign Trade. (1973) Imports CFA Fr. 18,760,000,000; exports CFA Fr. 13,760,000,000. Import sources (1972): France 54%; West Germany 8%; U.S. 6%; China 5%. Export destinations (1972): France 16%; West Germany 14%; South Africa 8%; The Netherlands 5%. Main exports: crude oil 53%; timber (1972) 33%; potassic fertilizer (1972) 21%; veneers and plywood (1972) 14%; sugar (1972) 7%.

Transport and Communications. Roads (1973) *c.* 11,000 km. Motor vehicles in use (1971): passenger *c.* 7,500; commercial *c.* 5,500. Railways: (1973) 795 km.; traffic (1974) 206.6 million passenger-km., freight 556 million net ton-km. Air traffic (including apportionment of Air Afrique; 1973) 100 million passenger-km.; freight 9 million net ton-km. Telephones (Dec. 1973) 10,000. Radio receivers (Dec. 1973) 75,000. Television receivers (Dec. 1973) 3,800.

Agriculture. Production (in 000; metric tons; 1973; 1972 in parentheses): cassava *c.* 460 (*c.* 460); sweet potatoes *c.* 13 (*c.* 13); peanuts *c.* 20 (*c.* 20); sugar, raw value *c.* 37 (*c.* 40); bananas *c.* 10 (*c.* 10); palm kernels *c.* 3 (*c.* 3); palm oil *c.* 6 (*c.* 6). Livestock (in 000; 1973): cattle *c.* 30; sheep *c.* 33; goats *c.* 45; pigs *c.* 15; chickens *c.* 450.

Congregational Churches: *see* Religion

Conservation: *see* Environment

Construction Industry: *see* Engineering Projects; Industrial Review

Consumerism

For the second successive year the continuing rapid rise in consumer prices against a background of world economic recession made the cost of living the dominant theme of consumerism in 1975. In the industrialized countries the mounting cost of such essentials as food and household fuels, coupled with a slowdown in the growth of personal incomes, made consumers extremely price-conscious—a concern that was reflected in the increased incidence of price-control activities by many consumer organizations.

In the less developed countries higher prices brought added hardship to millions already living at or below subsistence level. This reinforced the tendency of consumer groups in these countries to apply themselves to the more basic consumer issues—food, clothing, and shelter. It also gave further encouragement to the formation of new consumer groups, so that the less developed countries were the scene of the consumer movement's most rapid growth.

The latest edition of the *Consumer Directory*, a worldwide index of consumer organizations compiled by the International Organization of Consumers Unions (IOCU), listed nine additional countries as having formed their first national consumer organizations: Hong Kong, Indonesia, Iran, Mexico, Poland, Portugal, Taiwan, Thailand, and North Vietnam. The IOCU itself was joined by 16 new members in 1975, half drawn from less developed countries. In March the organization had announced the admission of its 100th member.

In the United States the range of consumerism activities included: lobbying for new legislation on consumer issues, testing of consumer products, training of state and local advocacy groups, litigation on a widening number of consumer issues, support for the establishment of groups on college campuses to study local consumer issues, help to support local consumer groups, research on a wide range of consumer issues, reform of current marketing practice, setting up food-marketing programs in major cities, and legal action in support of nonsmokers' rights.

Recent surveys in the U.S. showed that unethical sales and marketing practices—such as pricing products to create confusion, price gouging, increasing the price to offer a rebate, misrepresentation of merchandise, designing products for servicing complexity, and marketing to achieve planned obsolescence—were on

SIDNEY HARRIS

"Clam chowder—Ingredients: clams, potatoes, water, hydrolated plant protein, sodium phosphate, calcium carbonate, butylated hydroxytoluene. For external use only."

the increase in 1975 despite new and more far-reaching legislation. Law enforcement agencies at both the federal and state levels, private organizations, and consumer groups continued to bring these practices and others to the attention of the public. Many businesses realized that unethical practices undermined their sales programs and in the long run would reduce their profits.

World Consumerism. In March nearly 200 representatives from the consumer organizations of 25 countries met in Sydney, Australia, for the eighth IOCU congress. Under the general theme of "The Cost of Living," the delegates discussed common policy and outlined plans to be followed by IOCU and its member organizations during the following triennium. The congress made it clear that inflation and rising prices were regarded as the biggest single consumer problem in 1975 and adopted a number of resolutions under this heading, including a renewal of its demand for reform of the present International Air Transport Association (IATA) cartel, which controls air fares, and an appeal to governments for freer world trade as a means of mitigating inflation and improving economic efficiency.

The congress reaffirmed the need for support and assistance for consumer groups in less developed countries and the readiness of established consumer organizations in the industrial countries to give that help. The congress also called on the United Nations to prepare a report on consumer protection in member states, to draw up a model code of consumer protection practice to be recommended to member states, and to establish a consumer protection agency to implement these proposals.

IOCU represented the views of consumers on a number of issues before the UN and other intergovernmental and international bodies, notably in the field of food standards, and before the various technical committees of the International Organization of Standardization (ISO) and the Information Exchange Center (IEC) dealing with subjects of concern to the final consumer, such as sewing machines and shoe sizing.

Consumer Organizations. Reflecting consumerism's concern at the rapid rise in the cost of living, a growing number of consumer organizations took direct action to fight prices in 1975. The Consumer Guidance Society of India, for example, organized a boycott of open-market sugar which was successful in reducing prices; consumer organizations in Switzerland collectively persuaded the public not to buy meat costing more than SFr. 15 per kilo, while the Consumers Association of Canada was the principal intervenor in hearings into airline price increases that were held in Ottawa in May. A record amount of space was also allotted to the subject of prices in the various consumer magazines.

Other subjects that predominated in consumer publications in 1975, in addition to test reports, were legislation, the environment, and "market practice" issues such as credit and advertising. There was also an increase in the number of reports on holidays and travel, and on financial matters such as choosing a bank or investing savings.

Many consumer organizations were active in the field of consumer education, and much new material for this purpose was produced, often in collaboration with government—such as the project, initiated in 1974 by two consumer organizations in The Netherlands and sponsored by the Ministry of Economic Affairs, to produce integrated film, television, and printed material for use by schoolchildren.

In January the third International Consumer Film Competition, organized by the West German Arbeitsgemeinschaft der Verbraucher, was held in Berlin and attracted 134 entries from 11 countries. First prizes were awarded to films from West Germany (four), the U.K., and The Netherlands.

Government Participation. In the United Kingdom an entirely new government body to represent consumers was launched in January, and Michael Young, president of the British Consumer Association, was nominated to serve as its chairman. In accordance with the government's pledge, made at the end of 1974, to create a body that could speak for consumers equally with industry and the trade unions, the National Consumer Council was established as a nonstatutory body, with a chairman and 19 members. Its purpose was to ensure that the consumer's voice was clearly heard when decisions were taken in gov-

Replaced by the 69-cent shop, five-and-ten-cent stores are destined for extinction in the U.S. The new shops carry such items as gum, books, and even clothes—all for 69 cents.

KEYSTONE

ernment, industry, commerce, and any other quarter where the consumer's interests were affected.

The reorganization of local government in England and Wales in 1974, with its drastic reduction in the number of authorities involved, opened the way to the creation in 1975 of large single-purpose consumer protection/trading standards authorities, offering consumer advice and education services as well as the enforcement of consumer-oriented laws and regulations. As a result Great Britain became the only member of the EEC with a locally based enforcement service to protect consumer interests. In all the other states of the Community the service continued to be provided by central government departments.

At the end of May Britain's director general of fair trading revealed that the first attempts to analyze consumers' complaints on a nationwide basis had shown that over 142,000 complaints had been made in a period of nine months to local agencies. The British government also announced in midyear that more money was to be made available for the extension of consumer advice centres operated by local authorities. The centres were expected to increase from 60 to 80 by the end of 1975.

A move to strengthen the consumer programs of local authorities also took place in Sweden, where the report of a study by the Ministry of Commerce and Industry recommended that local activities to promote consumer interests should primarily be the task of the municipalities. The report made detailed proposals for these activities and recommended that these should be implemented from the beginning of 1976. In France a working party for the study of consumer problems was set up in January within Parliament to bring together all groups represented by the members for action on behalf of the consumer interest. In Denmark a consumer ombudsman was appointed by the state on the Swedish and Norwegian models and took office in May. His main task was to oversee the implementation of the recently introduced Trade Practices Act. To deal with complaints from individual consumers, Denmark also initiated a consumer complaints office to provide consumers with more speedy redress and at less cost than the alternative of court action.

Flameproof children's nightclothes, being tested here by a textile engineer, are gaining popularity among consumers despite their higher prices.

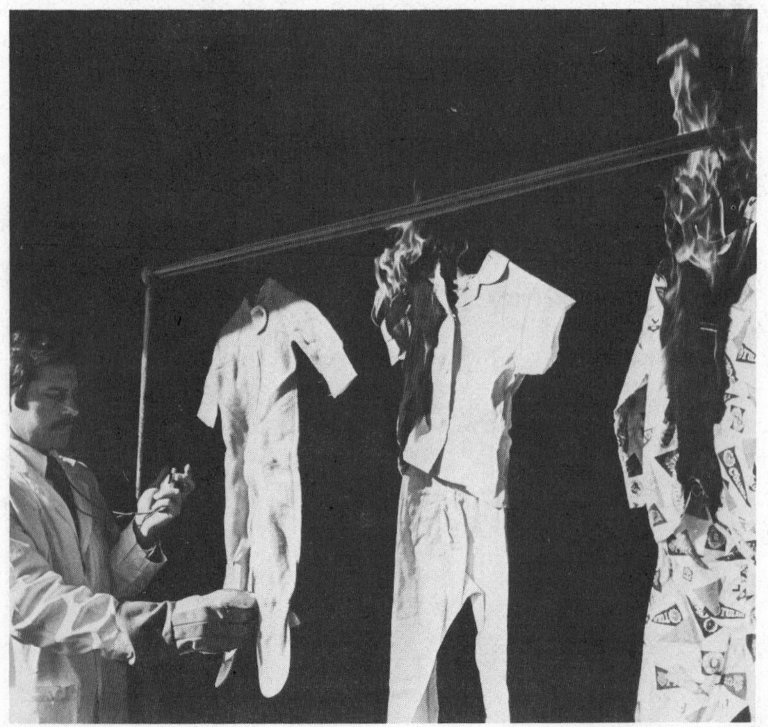

THE NEW YORK TIMES

In April the Council of Ministers of the EEC adopted a wide-ranging "Consumer Protection and Information" program that was welcomed by the Bureau Européen des Unions de Consommateurs (BEUC), the federation representing consumer organizations in the Common Market countries, as a step toward ensuring that the consumers' interests "would be represented equally with those of the other partners in the Common Market." The program specified five basic consumer rights—the right to protection of health and safety, to protection of economic interests, to redress, to information and education, and to representation.

Confronted with political pressure and an adverse court decision, the U.S. Food and Drug Administration (FDA) backed away from a rule that would have put "supervitamins" on the prescription list. Under a contested rule that the agency had issued in 1973, high-potency vitamins or mineral products were classified as drugs and could be restricted to prescription sales at FDA discretion. The new version kept them in a food classification as long as no health claims were made and the dosage was at a level "generally recognized as safe."

Because of the possibility that raw material shortages might continue to affect product ingredient formulas, the U.S. Federal Trade Commission (FTC) revised its detergent labeling requirements. An alternate method for the manufacturers of household detergents to disclose the phosphorus content of their products was authorized under a voluntary uniform labeling program. Since 1973 manufacturers had been adopting uniform labeling to disclose phosphorus content. Considerable controversy was created concerning the FTC's proposed budget for fiscal 1975–76, which earmarked less for consumer protection and more for antitrust enforcement.

Four automobile manufacturers—General Motors, Chrysler, Ford, and Volkswagen—petitioned the FTC in 1975 to issue guidelines on mileage claims in advertising. This proposal was a dramatic turnaround from the attitude taken by auto makers in 1974; at that time they were highly critical of a prior FTC proposal. The petition said "the proposed industry guides will clearly benefit the consumer. They require that the Environmental Protection Agency test results, both city and highway, be included in any fuel economy advertisements."

Voluntary industry-wide action continued in 1975 as a way of dealing with consumer problems. For example, the moving and storage industry set up an arbitration board to act as a court of last resort if a consumer failed to resolve a complaint with a particular mover. Similarly, the National Advertising Review Board prepared guidelines for advertising portraying and directed at women.

Legislation. In addition to their own direct participation in consumer programs, national and state governments in 1975 considered and enacted much new legislation within the general field of the consumer interest. Perhaps most closely related to this interest was the legislation introduced to regulate trade practices. New or amending legislation of this type was enacted or drafted in many countries, including the U.S., Canada, France, West Germany, The Netherlands, Australia, New Zealand, and Singapore. Much of this legislation reflected the influence of the landmark British Trade Descriptions Act 1968.

An equally large body of legislation and regulation directly affecting consumers introduced in 1975 was concerned with health and safety. Examples were the French requirement that medicinal drugs be labeled by a "use-by" date; the U.S. FDA ruling that cosmetics from January 1976 would have to list all ingredients on the label in order of predominance, as well as warnings about misuse; the compulsory wearing of car safety belts by front seat passengers in Belgium, Luxembourg, and The Netherlands; and, in the United Kingdom, new regulations, for which consumer organizations had long campaigned, requiring more stringent safety requirements for children's toys. In September an EEC directive laying down minimum safety requirements for appliances up to 1,000 volts (*i.e.,* any domestic electrical appliance) became mandatory in all nine Common Market countries. Other EEC directives implemented in 1975 covered sugars (standard quantities, definition, and labeling of certain types); and the licensing of manufacturers and marketers of medicines as well as new labeling requirements.

In the U.S. the Magnuson-Moss Warranty Federal Trade Commission Improvements Act was passed in January 1975. The bill sets forth requirements for the FTC in the area of consumer protection rule-making. A bill to set up an agency for consumer advocacy to represent consumer interests before federal agencies was passed by the Senate on May 15 and the House on November 6.

Sen. John V. Tunney (Dem., Calif.) introduced a bill that required print advertisements that discussed fuel or energy use for automobiles and major appliances to show average annual operating costs. Television commercials for cars and appliances would be required to show the costs visually, not verbally, and only if energy use was stressed in a visual display. Claims about energy consumption would be policed by the FTC. FTC action would be expected if the claims departed from data on energy-use labels required by the legislation for cars and household appliances such as refrigerators and air conditioners. Toasters, blenders, and other small appliances were excluded.

Trends in Consumerism. Packaging practices were a subject of public concern and criticism in 1975. The consumerism movement was bringing about important changes in materials used for packaging consumer products. A number of major manufacturers of antiperspirants and hair sprays were making immediate packaging changes. Bristol-Myers, for example, was bringing back pump hair sprays for men and women; Gillette introduced roll-on applicators for two of its antiperspirants; and Carter Products brought out a roll-on version of Arrid. Gillette stated that if research shows that aerosols are hazardous it would offer alternative packaging "quickly."

Manufacturers were responding more rapidly to sex bias in the sale of products and services. An example was in the do-it-yourself industry—traditionally male dominated. Now more products were being specifically designed for women. In addition, under the Equal Opportunity Act of 1975 sex discrimination was banned in the granting of credit.

Cents-off coupons continued to show growth and widespread consumer acceptance. The First National Bank of Chicago released a study showing that 88% of those interviewed said they redeemed coupons and 56% said that they used coupons weekly. There seemed to be some softening in the alarm over widespread misredemption that was reported in 1974. Five of six persons who had been accused of involvement in a coupon misredemption scheme subsequently pleaded guilty to mail fraud charges in U.S. district court. According to postal authorities, 33 coupon misredemption cases were investigated in 1975, compared with 39 cases in 1974 and 29 cases in 1973.

(JOHN CALASCIONE; EDWARD MARK MAZZE)

See also Economy, World; Industrial Review: *Advertising.*

[532.B.3; 534.H.5; 534.K]

Contract Bridge

The 25th Bermuda Bowl contest for the contract bridge world championship was staged in January 1975, appropriately in Bermuda. The note of celebration came to an abrupt end on the second day when an accusation of cheating installed the tournament firmly on the front pages of the world press.

Screens that prevented players from seeing their partners during the bidding were being used for the first time in a world championship. Some time before the contest a distinguished U.S. bridge journalist, Alfred Sheinwold, had written an article welcoming the advent of the screens. It was so expressed that it was considered highly inflammatory by the participating Italians and their many friends. The prospects of a harmonious tournament were thus somewhat reduced when Sheinwold was named nonplaying captain of the North American team.

The first stage of the championship was a round robin, after which the field was reduced to four teams that would play semifinals and a final. On the second day of the round robin an Italian pair, Gianfranco

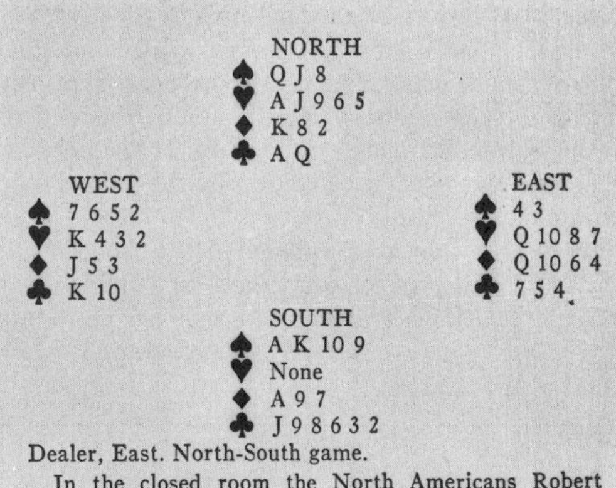
NORTH
♠ Q J 8
♥ A J 9 6 5
♦ K 8 2
♣ A Q

WEST
♠ 7 6 5 2
♥ K 4 3 2
♦ J 5 3
♣ K 10

EAST
♠ 4 3
♥ Q 10 8 7
♦ Q 10 6 4
♣ 7 5 4

SOUTH
♠ A K 10 9
♥ None
♦ A 9 7
♣ J 9 8 6 3 2

Dealer, East. North-South game.

In the closed room the North Americans Robert Hamman and Bobby Wolff had bid and made six no trumps with the North-South cards. The second auction, which was shown on a Vu-Graph screen, was:

East B. Eisenberg	South Belladonna	West E. Kantar	North Garozzo
Pass	2 ♣	Pass	2 ♦
Pass	2 ♠	Pass	3 ♥
Pass	3 no trumps	Pass	4 ♣
Pass	4 ♦	Pass	4 no trumps
Pass	5 ♦	Pass	5 ♥
Double	Redouble	Pass	5 ♠
Pass	5 no trumps	Pass	7 ♣
Pass	Pass	Pass	

Declarer ruffed the opening heart lead and led a trump. When West followed with the ten the club finesse followed by the ace of clubs gave declarer 13 tricks. Had West played the king of clubs on the first round declarer might well have lost his contract—and the championship. If declarer accepts the king as a singleton, he can make 13 tricks by way of a "trump coup" if the East hand has at least three spades and at least two cards in each red suit.

Facchini and Sergio Zucchelli, were accused of signaling under the table, the allegation being that while Zucchelli's feet were planted firmly under the table Facchini made regular contact with them with his own feet during the bidding. A meeting of officials of the World Bridge Federation (WBF), which lasted from 10 P.M. until 3 A.M., heard the evidence of several observers and ended with the resolution that Facchini and Zucchelli "be severely reprimanded for improper conduct"; the two were, however, allowed to continue playing. This resolution was adopted by 13 votes, with 2 abstentions and 1 in opposition. Fuel was added to the fire when the North American captain issued a statement on behalf of his team in which he approved the findings of the WBF but deplored the action taken as inadequate punishment.

In due course Italy and North America reached the final. Facchini and Zucchelli were in the Italian lineup for the start, and Sheinwold refused to allow his team to play until ordered to do so by officials of the American Contract Bridge League. Meanwhile, the Italians insisted that the entire incident had been engineered as part of a war of nerves.

After 32 boards of the 96-board final (a board consists of one hand dealt and played), Facchini and Zucchelli were rested from an Italian team that seemed to have little chance of retaining the title. After 51 boards the North Americans led by 77 international match points (IMP), but then the Italian quartet of Giorgio Belladonna, Benito Garozzo, Arturo Franco, and Vito Pittala found their best form and with 16 boards to play the lead had been whittled down to 24 IMP. Six hands later Italy went into the lead, but the real drama came on board 92 when Italy led by 13 IMP (*see* box).

The Italians eventually won by a margin of 26 IMP, 215–189, and were accorded such an enthusiastic reception as to suggest that much of the sympathy during the week's stormy events had been on their side. Some months later an Italian team that contained only two of the world champions retained the European title. Europe would therefore be represented in the next Bermuda Bowl contest by the second-place team, Israel.

The Italian women surrendered their European title, which they had held for four years, to a British team led by Mrs. Rixi Markus and Mrs. Fritzi Gordon.

(HAROLD FRANKLIN)

[452.C.3.a.i]

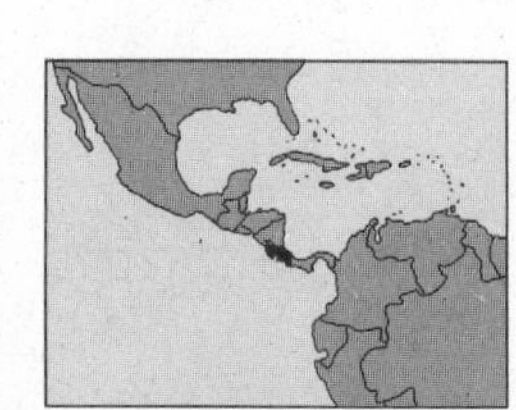

Costa Rica

A Central American republic, Costa Rica lies between Nicaragua and Panama and has coastlines on the Caribbean Sea and the Pacific Ocean. Area: 19,652 sq.mi. (50,898 sq.km.). Pop. (1974 est.): 1,921,600, including white and mestizo 98%. Cap. and largest city: San José (pop., 1974 est., 220,700). Language: Spanish. Religion: predominantly Roman Catholic. President in 1975, Daniel Oduber Quirós.

COSTA RICA

Education. (1973) Primary, pupils 384,033, teachers 12,923; secondary, pupils (1972) 68,499, teachers (1970) 3,285; vocational, pupils (1972) 9,329, teachers (1970) 406; higher, students 24,256, teaching staff (universities; 1968–69) 678.

Finance. Monetary unit: colón, with (Sept. 22, 1975) an official rate of 8.57 colones to U.S. $1 (free rate of 17.81 colones = £1 sterling). Gold, SDRs, and foreign exchange: (June 1975) U.S. $47.9 million; (June 1974) U.S. $34,460,000. Budget (1973 actual): revenue 1,387,200,000 colones; expenditure 1,725,800,000 colones. Gross national product: (1972) 7,963,000,000 colones; (1971) 7,039,000,000 colones. Money supply: (April 1975) 2,461,000,000 colones; (April 1974) 2,183,400,000 colones. Cost of living (San José; 1970 = 100): (April 1975) 183; (June 1974) 153.

Foreign Trade. (1974) Imports 5,594,200,000 colones; exports 3,384,500,000 colones. Import sources (1973): U.S. 35%; Japan 9%; Guatemala 7%; West Germany 7%; El Salvador 5%; Nicaragua 5%; Venezuela 5%. Export destinations (1973): U.S. 33%; West Germany 13%; Nicaragua 8%; Guatemala 6%; El Salvador 5%; Italy 5%. Main exports: coffee 29%; bananas 22%; meat (1973) 9%; chemicals (1973) 7%; sugar (1973) 6%. Tourism (1973): visitors 247,000; gross receipts U.S. $33 million.

Transport and Communications. Roads (1973) *c.* 17,600 km. (including *c.* 4,800 km. all-weather and 650 km. of Pan-American Highway). Motor vehicles in use (1972): passenger 47,500; commercial (including buses) 30,100. Railways: (1973) 612 km.; traffic (1972) 53 million passenger-km., freight 15 million net ton-km. Air traffic (1974): 297 million passenger-km.; freight 9,423,000 net ton-km. Telephones (Jan. 1974) 89,000. Radio receivers (Dec. 1973) 140,000. Television receivers (Dec. 1973) 122,000.

Agriculture. Production (in 000; metric tons; 1974; 1973 in parentheses): sorghum *c.* 16 (8); corn (1973) *c.* 52, (1972) *c.* 64; potatoes (1973) *c.* 35, (1972) 34; dry beans (1973) 9, (1972) 10; bananas (1973) *c.* 1,300, (1972) 1,250; oranges (1973) *c.* 65, (1972) *c.* 62; sugar, raw value 176 (174); cocoa 7 (6); coffee *c.* 86 (72); palm oil *c.* 15 (*c.* 15). Livestock (in 000; 1973): cattle *c.* 1,722; horses *c.* 114; pigs *c.* 280; chickens *c.* 4,450.

Industry. Electricity production (1973) 1,346,000,000 kw-hr. (84% hydroelectric).

The Communist Party and other left-wing organizations were granted legal status in Costa Rica in May 1975. Later President Oduber supported a constitutional change that would allow reelection of former presidents, thus permitting José Figueres Ferrer to run again. Figueres and Robert Vesco, fugitive U.S. financier, were known to be involved in business deals together, and many Costa Rican businessmen and politicians continued to demand Vesco's expulsion from the country. Rodolfo Solano, a leader of the ruling National Liberation Party, stated that "In a small country, Vesco's economic power translates into political power." Politicians also criticized special privileges, primarily tax breaks, granted U.S. citizens living in Costa Rica. Land speculation by foreigners was causing land prices to skyrocket, and the government proposed a law to control speculation and restrict foreign land ownership.

On the brighter side Costa Rica, in the first quarter of 1975, registered its first surplus, $1.4 million, with the Central American Common Market (CACM), against a deficit of $2.5 million in the first quarter of 1974. A grain self-sufficiency program was launched in early 1975, to yield 550,000 tons (1974, 330,000 tons). Export agreements were signed with China for over 700 tons of coffee, with Kuwait for 20,000 tons of sugar, and with the U.S. for 54.2 million lb. of beef. Legislation was presented to Congress in June to expropriate idle lands from United Brands, a major banana-exporting company. This was followed by invasions by land-hungry peasants. The company transferred 10,000 ac. of unused land valued at $1.5 million to the government, partly as a donation.

In July the Aluminum Company of America (Alcoa) declared its decision not to develop the Boruca bauxite deposits because of increased costs and changes in the original contract terms.

In September the government announced the nationalization of gasoline wholesaling, with $10 million compensation to the five companies concerned.

(BARBARA WIJNGAARD)

[974.B.1.e]

Copper:
see Mining and Quarrying

Corn:
see Agriculture and Food Supplies

Cosmetics:
see Fashion and Dress

Court Games

Badminton. After 11 years of persistent effort, Svend Pri of Denmark finally became the unofficial world badminton champion by dethroning Rudy Hartono of Indonesia in the finals of the All-England championships in March (15–11, 17–14). Hartono therefore returned home without capturing his eighth consecutive world title. Hiroe Yuki of Japan retained her world singles title on the Wembley court by defeating Gillian Gilks of England (11–5, 11–9). Of the two Indonesian teams that competed for the men's doubles crown, Tjun Tjun and Johan Wahjudi emerged victorious by taking two straight games (15–11, 15–5). Though Indonesians also made the finals of the women's doubles, they fell victims to the Japanese team of Machiko Aizawa and Etsuko Takenaka (12–15, 15–12, 15–9). England's only victory came in the mixed doubles when Elliott Stuart and Nora Gardner overpowered a team from West Germany (15–9, 15–3).

The Canadian Open championships, held during April in Montreal, attracted many of the top players in the world, partly because the event marked the first time that substantial prize money ($18,500) was at stake in a badminton tournament. England won both singles titles when Ray Stevens defeated Thomas Kihlstrom of Sweden (1–15, 15–5, 15–10) and Margaret Beck swept to an easy victory over Joke Van Beusekom of The Netherlands (11–4, 11–3). Stevens and Mike Tredgett won another title for England by winning the men's doubles after a nip and tuck battle with Nobutaka Ikeda and Shoichi Toganoo of Japan (17–16, 12–15, 15–12). England shared a fourth title when Margaret Beck teamed with Joke Van Beusenkom to defeat Barbara Welch and Jane Youngberg of Canada (12–15, 15–11, 15–4).

In a third major tournament of the year, the Jamaica international championships held in April in Kingston, Denmark won the men's singles (F. Delfs), the women's singles (L. Koppen), the women's doubles (L. Koppen-J. Van Beusekom), and the mixed doubles (E. Hansen-L. Koppen). Lene Koppen, who emerged as a triple-crown winner, was the star of the tournament. Denmark's only loss came in the men's doubles, won by the English team of R. Stevens and M. Tredgett.

In the triennial women's competition for the Uber Cup, a symbol of world team supremacy in badminton, Indonesia took possession of the trophy for the first time by defeating Japan (5–2), the defending champion since 1965.

(JACK H. VAN PRAAG)

Handball. The biggest handball news of the year emerged from Las Vegas, Nev., where the $50,000 Spalding eight-city professional tour held its grand finale in April. This event was immediately followed by the six annual national championships sponsored by the U.S. Handball Association (USHA). A record-breaking 909 entries necessitated marathon eliminations (best of three 15-point games) to determine the final 16 in each category.

Excitement ran high in the finals of the pro championship because the two finalists, Fred Lewis and Dennis Hofflander, had each won two previous tournaments. Lewis lost the first game 19–21, barely took the second 21–20, then won the deciding game and the championship 21–17.

In the finals of the USHA open singles, Jay Bilyeu dropped the first game 18–21 to Junior Powell, then took the next two games 21–18 and 21–5. In the open doubles, Marty Decatur, already a five-time winner, teamed with Steve Lott to beat Jim Barnett and Jerry Conine 21–14, 13–21, 21–15. The masters singles title was captured by Jack Scrivens, who defeated an exhausted Harry Hyde 21–13, 12–21, 21–2. In the masters doubles, Arnold Aguilar and Gabe Enriques became the only repeat champions with a convincing 21–7, 21–16 victory over Sol Aber and Marty Goffstein. The golden masters doubles was won by Ken Schneider and Irv Simon and the super masters doubles by Bill Keays and Jeff Capell.

In intercollegiate play, Bill Peoples of the University of Montana won the national A singles title and Lake Forest College in Illinois captured the team trophy. Future champions, however, were likely to come from the University of Illinois in Urbana, which received a $300,000 grant for handball scholarships from a famous alumnus, the late Avery Brundage.

(MORTON LEVE)

[452.B.4.h.xv]

Cotton: *see* Agriculture and Food Supplies; Industrial Review

Council for Mutual Economic Assistance: *see* Economy, World

Council of Europe: *see* European Unity

Volleyball. International competition during 1975 was especially intense because several of the tournaments determined qualifiers for the 1976 Olympic Games. The first three of the ten Olympic berths allotted to men were preempted by Canada (host country), Japan (1972 Olympic champion). and Poland (1974 world champion). Five other places were then settled through regional competitions: Asia (Korea), Europe (U.S.S.R.), South America, Africa, and North America (Cuba). Cuba's victory in Los Angeles during August highlighted the first major international volleyball tournament ever held in the U.S. and marked Cuba's first visit to the U.S. The two remaining Olympic berths would be determined in open competition to be held in Rome early in 1976.

Of the eight Olympic spots assigned to women's teams, one was automatically filled by Canada (host country), another by the U.S.S.R. (1972 Olympic champion), and a third by Japan (1974 world champion). Four other teams were chosen on the basis of victories in regional tournaments: Asia (Korea), Europe (Hungary), South America, and North America

TONY DUFFY

Svend Pri of Denmark in action during the All-England badminton championships at Wembley. He captured the men's singles title, defeating Rudy Hartono of Indonesia.

(Cuba). The eighth women's team to participate in the Olympics would be decided in Munich, West Germany, during an open competition to be held in January 1976.

In the VII Pan-American Games held in Mexico City, Cuba dominated the volleyball tournament by winning both the men's and women's titles. Second-place silver medals were awarded to Brazil (men) and Peru (women). Both Mexican teams won third-place bronze medals.

(ALBERT M. MONACO, JR.)

[452.B.4.h.xxviii]

Jai Alai. The 1974 world amateur jai alai championship got under way in Colonia, Uruguay, in late November. The round robin tournament was sponsored as usual by the Federación Internacional de Pelota Vasca, with headquarters in San Sebastián, Spain. *Pelota vasca,* "Basque ball," is a common Spanish term for *jai alai,* a Basque term meaning "merry festival." The exhausting 40-point matches were dominated by the superlative performance of Pierre Iroazoki, whose backcourt play was supported in the front court by Jean-Pierre Abeberry. This team captured the world title for France without losing a single match. Adrian Zubacheri (front court) and Alexandro Andrade (backcourt) of Mexico finished second; Spain was third and the U.S. fourth.

The eighth annual U.S. amateur championship was held on July 6, 1975, in Miami, Fla. The title, decided by cumulative scores after four 25-point games, was won by the team of Víctor Gómez (front court) and Linsey Bruce (backcourt). Second place went to Nestor García (front court) and Larry Heffer (backcourt). In late November, at a world tournament in Mexico City, the U.S. won its first international title.

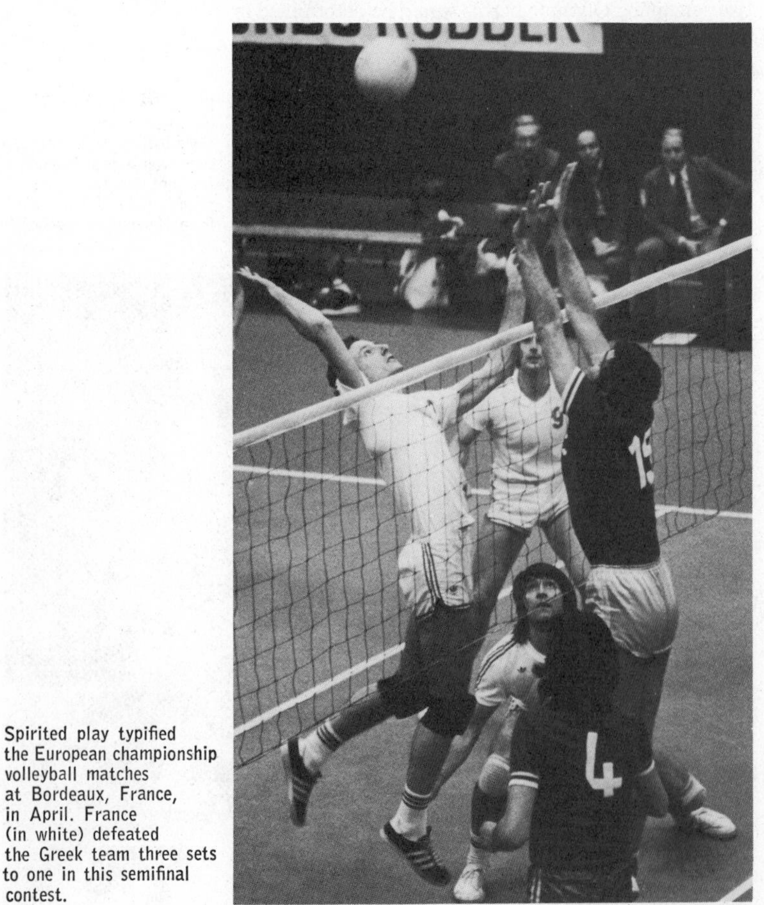

Spirited play typified the European championship volleyball matches at Bordeaux, France, in April. France (in white) defeated the Greek team three sets to one in this semifinal contest.

A.F.P./PICTORIAL PARADE

COURTESY, MIAMI-METRO DEPT. OF PUBLICITY AND TOURISM

A jai alai pelotari, armed with his wicker cesta, prepares to hurl the ball at a speed exceeding 100 mph.

Professional jai alai continued to attract such large crowds in Miami and Las Vegas that four new frontons were under construction in Connecticut and Rhode Island.

(ROBERT H. GROSSBERG)

[452.B.4.h.xix]

See also Tennis and Rackets.

Cricket

Two major cricket tours were undertaken during the Northern Hemisphere winter of 1974–75. Australia under I. M. Chappell entertained England under M. H. Denness in a six-match rubber, after which England visited New Zealand under B. E. Congdon, for two tests; and West Indies under C. H. Lloyd played five tests against India, led by M. A. K. Pataudi, and two against Pakistan under Intikhab Alam. In the northern summer of 1975 England was host to seven other countries in a tournament of one-day matches for the Prudential World Cup, after which Australia played four five-day test matches against England.

Australia v. England. Australia scored an overwhelming triumph over England, winning four tests, losing one, and drawing one. A powerful fast bowler, J. R. Thomson, who teamed up with D. K. Lillee, gave the English batsmen unaccustomed problems of pace and lift and the two shared 58 wickets.

Australia won the first test at Brisbane by 166 runs: Australia 309 (I. M. Chappell 90, G. Chappell 58, R. G. D. Willis 4 for 56) and 288 for 5 declared (G. Chappell 71, K. D. Walters 62, R. Edwards 53); England 265 (A. W. Greig 110, J. H. Edrich 48, Thomson 3 for 59, M. H. N. Walker 4 for 73) and 166 (Thomson 6 for 46). Thomson and Lillee were physically dangerous on the unprepared pitch (playing field), and only a swashbuckling century by Greig and courageous defense by Edrich kept England in the game. Australia won the second test at Perth by 9 wickets: England 208 (A. P. E. Knott 51, D. Lloyd 49) and 293 (F. J. Titmus 61, Thomson 5 for 93); Australia 481 (Edwards 115, Walters 103, G. Chappell 62) and 23 for 1. Thomson and Lillee, aided by brilliant close catching, shared 11 wickets. The third test, at Melbourne, was tied after a close match, Australia needing 8 runs to win from their last two wickets: England 242 (Knott 52, Edrich 49, Thomson 4 for 72) and 244 (D. L. Amiss 90, Greig 60, Thomson 4 for 71, A. A. Mallett 4 for 60); Australia 241 (I. R. Redpath 55, Willis 5 for 61) and 238 for 8 (G. Chappell 61, Greig 4 for 56).

Australia won the fourth test at Sydney by 171 runs and so clinched the series. Denness, out of form with the bat, dropped himself and Edrich took over the captaincy, but Australia won easily: Australia 405 (R. B. McCosker 80, G. Chappell 84, I. M. Chappell 53, G. G. Arnold 5 for 86) and 289 for 4 declared (G. Chappell 144, Redpath 105); England 295 (Edrich 50, Knott 82, Thomson 4 for 74) and 228 (Greig 54). Australia won the fifth test at Adelaide by 163 runs. Fine bowling by D. L. Underwood checked Australia, and Knott made a brilliant century: Australia 304 (T. J. Jenner 74, Walters 55, Underwood 7 for 113) and 272 for 5 declared (Walters 71 not out, R. W. Marsh 55, Redpath 52, Underwood 4 for 102); England 172 (Denness 51, Lillee 4 for 49) and 241 (Knott 106 not out, K. W. R. Fletcher 63, Lillee 4 for 69). In an extraordinary reversal of form, England won the final test at Melbourne by an innings and 4 runs. With Thomson and Lillee out with injuries, Denness and Fletcher showed their true form and fast bowler P. Lever took 9 wickets: Australia 152 (I. M. Chappell 65, Lever 6 for 38) and 373 (G. Chappell 102, Redpath 83, McCosker 76, I. M. Chappell 50, Greig 4 for 88); England 529 (Denness 188, Fletcher 146, Greig 89, Edrich 70, Walker 8 for 143).

India v. West Indies. In India, West Indies won a close-fought series 3–2. West Indies' batting strength was decisive against the all-spin attack of India, which lacked sufficient depth.

West Indies won the first test at Bangalore by 267 runs after India in the fourth innings lost Pataudi and F. M. Engineer because of injuries. West Indies won the second test at New Delhi by an innings and 17 runs, thanks to a brilliant innings by I. V. A. Richards and hard hitting by Lloyd and all-rounders B. D. Julien and K. D. Boyce. L. R. Gibbs then won the match by exploiting a drying field. India fought back at Calcutta to win the third test by 85 runs. G. R. Viswanath batted superbly in both innings; A. M. E. Roberts took 8 wickets in the match; and, when West Indies batted again, B. S. Bedi and B. S. Chandrasekhar shared 7 wickets. India then won a low-scoring fourth test at Madras by 100 runs. Viswanath made more than half the runs in India's first innings, Roberts took 12 wickets in the match, and E. A. S. Prasanna 9.

A huge innings by Lloyd virtually settled the issue in the fifth test at Bombay, which West Indies won by 201 runs. India batted bravely, but Lloyd's second innings declaration left them too many runs to make against good bowling. The scores were as follows: First test, West Indies 289 (A. I. Kallicharran 124, C. G. Greenidge 93, "Chandra" 4 for 112, S. Venkataraghavan 4 for 75) and 356 for 6 declared (Lloyd 163, Greenidge 107); India 260 (H. S. Kanıtkar 65) and 118. Second test, India 220 (P. Sharma 54) and 256 (Engineer 75, Sharma 49, Gibbs 6 for 76); West Indies 493 (Richards 192 not out, Lloyd 71, Boyce 68, Prasanna 4 for 147). Third test, India 233 (Viswanath 52, Roberts 5 for 50) and 316 (Viswanath 139, Engineer 61); West Indies 240 (R. C. Fredericks 100) and 224 (Kallicharran 57, Bedi 4 for 52). Fourth test, India 190 (Viswanath 97 not out, Roberts 7 for 64) and 256 (A. D. Gaekwad 80, Roberts 5 for 57); West Indies 192 (Richards 50, Prasanna 5 for 70) and 154 (Kallicharran 51, Prasanna 4 for 41). Fifth test, West Indies 604 for 6 declared (Lloyd 242 not out, Fredericks 104, Kallicharran 98) and 205 for 3 declared (Greenidge 54); India 406 (E. D. Solkar 102, Viswanath 95, S. M. Gavaskar 86, Gibbs 7 for 98) and 202 (B. P. Patel 73 not out, V. A. Holder 6 for 39).

Pakistan v. West Indies. West Indies drew two tests against Pakistan, at Lahore and Karachi. In the first, the main striking forces in both first innings were fast bowlers A. M. E. Roberts and Sarfraz Nawaz. Mushtaq Mohammad was the mainstay of Pakistan's second innings, and a match-saving six-hour innings by L. Baichan of the West Indies in his first test achieved a draw. There were two century

SYNDICATION INTERNATIONAL/PHOTO TRENDS

Fourth day of the second test at Lord's in the England versus Australia match. Australian skipper I. M. Chappell is batting.

Credit and Debt: *see* Economy, World

makers on each side during the first innings of the second test, in which West Indies led by 87. Four Pakistan wickets were down in that team's second innings before the deficit was wiped out, but Asif Iqbal and Sadiq Mohammad saved the game. Riots between spectators and police lost 150 minutes. The scores were: First test, Pakistan 199 (Roberts 5 for 66) and 373 for 7 (Mushtaq 123, Aftab Baloch 60 not out, Asif Iqbal 52); West Indies 214 (Kallicharran 92 not out, Sarfraz 6 for 89) and 258 for 4 (Baichan 105 not out, Lloyd 83). Second test, Pakistan 406 for 8 declared (Wasim Raja 107, Majid Khan 100, Wasim Bari 58) and 256 (Sadiq 98 not out, Asif Iqbal 77); West Indies 493 (Kallicharran 115, Julien 101, Fredericks 77, Lloyd 73) and 1 for no wicket.

New Zealand v. England. England easily won the first test against New Zealand at Auckland and drew the second at Christchurch. Denness and Fletcher continued their Melbourne form, and on a wearing pitch Greig and Underwood shared 15 wickets to give England victory by an innings and 83 runs, despite a seven-hour defensive century by J. M. Parker. The match ended in near tragedy when New Zealand's last man, Ewan Chatfield, was hit on the head by a pitch from Lever, causing his heart to stop for a few seconds. But instant action on the field saved his life, and he recovered in a hospital. England 593 for 6 declared (Fletcher 216, Denness 181, Edrich 64, Greig 51); New Zealand 326 (Parker 121, J. F. M. Morrison 58, K. J. Wadsworth 58, Greig 5 for 98) and 184 (Morrison 58, G. P. Howarth 51 not out, Greig 5 for 51). Rain made a draw in the second test match inevitable: New Zealand 342 (G. M. Turner 98, Wadsworth 58); England 272 for 2 (Amiss 164, Denness 59—both not out).

A. I. Kallicharran (West Indies) hooks for 6 in the Prudential World Cup group match between Australia and the West Indies at the Oval, London.

PATRICK EAGAR

Prudential Cup. West Indies (291) won the Prudential World Cup, beating Australia (274) in the final at Lord's, London, by 17 runs. C. H. Lloyd made a brilliant 102, and five Australian batsmen were run out. The other teams taking part were East Africa, England, India, New Zealand, Pakistan, and Sri Lanka.

England v. Australia. The four-match rubber in England brought Australia victory in the first test at Edgbaston, Birmingham, and draws in the other three, and so Australia retained "the Ashes" 1–0. Had Denness not sent Australia in to bat, the course of the series might have been different, because they had no problems with the pitch on the first day, whereas England floundered after a heavy storm that made batting difficult, and Australia won by an innings and 85 runs. Denness was replaced by Greig as captain for the remaining matches. Slow pitches that diminished the pace of the Australian fast bowlers enabled England to hold its own in high-scoring draws at Lord's and the Oval, London. The third test at Headingley, Leeds, was abandoned on the fifth day due to vandalism of the pitch during the night, though, as it happened, rain would have made a finish impossible. The scores of the matches were: First test, Australia 359 (Marsh 61, McCosker 59, Edwards 56, I. M. Chappell 52); England 101 (Lillee 5 for 15, Walker 5 for 48) and 173 (Fletcher 51, Thomson 5 for 38). Second test, England 315 (Greig 96, Knott 69, D. S. Steele 50, Lillee 4 for 84) and 436 for 7 declared (Edrich 175, B. Wood 52); Australia 268 (Edwards 99, J. A. Snow 4 for 66) and 329 for 3 (I. M. Chappell 86, McCosker 79, G. Chappell 73 not out, Edwards 52 not out). Third test, England 288 (Steele 73, Edrich 62, Greig 51, Gilmour 6 for 85) and 291 (Steele 92, Greig 49); Australia 135 (P. H. Edmonds 5 for 28) and 220 for 3 (McCosker 95 not out, I. M. Chappell 62). Fourth test, Australia 532 for 9 declared (I. M. Chappell 192, McCosker 127, Walters 65) and 40 for 2; England 191 (Thomson 4 for 50, Walker 4 for 63) and 538 (R. A. Woolmer 149, Edrich 96, Steele 66, Knott 64, Lillee 4 for 91, Walters 4 for 34).

County Cricket. Leicestershire won the title for the first time after a close struggle with Yorkshire (second) and Hampshire (third). Strong batting, varied bowling, and shrewd captaincy by R. Illingworth were responsible for the victory. Yorkshire's improved form was due to the opting out of international cricket by its captain, G. Boycott.

Winners of the one-day competitions were Lancashire, which beat Middlesex by seven wickets in the Gillette Cup final; Leicestershire, which beat Middlesex by five wickets in the Benson and Hedges Cup final; and Hampshire, which won the John Player League.

National Cricket. In Australia, Western Australia won the Sheffield Shield; in South Africa, Natal won the Currie Cup; in New Zealand, Otago won the Plunket Shield; and in West Indies, Guyana won the Shell Shield. In India, Bombay won the Ranji Trophy, South Zone the Duleep Trophy, and State Bank of India the Moin-ud-Dowlah Trophy. In Pakistan, National Bank won the Patron's Trophy, Lahore Hexangular, and A. S. Pirzada Memorial Tournament; Lahore "A" won the Punjab championship; Punjab "A" gained the Qaid-i-Azam Trophy; and Karachi Whites won the A. H. Kardar Summer Shield.

(REX ALSTON)

[452.B.4.h.ix]

Crime and Law Enforcement

Criminal violence continued to dominate international trends in crime throughout 1975. Around the world a rash of terrorist bombings, shootings, kidnappings, and hijackings left a trail of death and destruction.

Violent Crime. The victims of terrorist violence were largely the innocent and the uninvolved. Thus, in January a bomb exploding in New York City ripped apart a busy Wall Street restaurant, killing 4 patrons and injuring 53 others. A group seeking independence for Puerto Rico, the Armed Forces of the Puerto Rican National Liberation (FALN), claimed responsibility. In March a bomb blew apart a crowded bus parked in the centre of Nairobi, Kenya, killing at least 27 people and injuring 90, many of them women and children. The motive and identity of those responsible were not immediately apparent. In London, increasingly the scene of violence instigated by the Irish Republican Army (IRA), a bomb exploded in late October outside the home of Hugh Fraser, a prominent Conservative member of Parliament, killing a neighbour, a British cancer specialist. A house guest of the Frasers, Caroline Kennedy, 17-year-old daughter of the late U.S. president John F. Kennedy and Jacqueline Onassis, escaped injury. In November a gunman shot dead sportswriter and right-wing spokesman Ross McWhirter at home.

Political kidnapping was also becoming commonplace, usually to obtain money to further a cause or to secure the release of imprisoned comrades. Thus Peter Lorenz, a West German mayoral candidate, was abducted and then exchanged for five radicals being held

Homicide in Selected Countries

Country (year is latest for which figures are available)	Total homicide Number	Total homicide Rate per 000,000 pop.	Gun homicide Number	Gun homicide Rate per 000,000 pop.
United States (1973)	17,123	8.2	11,249	6.2
Australia (1970)	190	1.5	71	0.6
Canada (1973)	479	2.2	215	1.0
Denmark (1971)	48	1.0	12	0.2
England and Wales (1972)	384	0.8	41	0.1
France (1970)	373	0.7	124	0.2
Germany, West (1971)	802	1.3	203	0.3
Ireland (1972)	21	0.7	—	—
Italy (1970)	442	0.8	239	0.4
Japan (1971)	1,380	1.3	20	.0
Netherlands, The (1972)	72	0.5	13	0.1
New Zealand (1971)	25	0.9	8	0.3
Scotland (1972)	73	1.4	3	0.1
Sweden (1972)	76	0.9	19	0.2
Switzerland (1972)	57	0.9	12	0.2

in West German jails. Tough measures to suppress terrorist violence were reported from many countries, and governments of Europe and the U.S. stepped up cooperation in exchanging intelligence information about terrorist methods and movements. (See *Special Report.*)

Assassinations, successful or otherwise, were much in the news in 1975. In the U.S. it was revealed that in the early 1960s the Central Intelligence Agency (CIA) had tried to arrange for the assassination of Prime Minister Fidel Castro of Cuba, allegedly with the help of such organized-crime figures as Sam Giancana. Before Giancana could testify before a Senate investigating committee, he was found dead in his kitchen with seven bullets in the face and neck. According to police, the slaying had all the signs of a gangland execution, but CIA Director William Colby (*see* BIOGRAPHY) felt obliged to issue a statement indicating that the agency had "no involvement" in the killing.

Suggestions of possible crime syndicate involvement were also present in the disappearance of James R. Hoffa, former president of the teamsters' union, who had served time in prison for jury tampering and mail fraud and who was said to be trying to regain control of the union. Hoffa was last seen on July 30 outside a restaurant in a Detroit suburb, and as the months passed, officials inclined to the belief that he had been killed. Investigations involving teamster and organized crime figures had produced no definite answer by year's end.

U.S. Pres. Gerald Ford was the target of two unsuccessful assassination attempts in September, both by women carrying pistols. In the first incident, in Sacramento, Calif., Lynette Fromme, a member of the cult surrounding convicted murderer Charles Manson, pointed a loaded gun at the president. She was disarmed before firing a shot. In the second attempt, in San Francisco, Sara Jane Moore fired a shot at the president but missed him.

These assassination attempts raised a number of major issues, including the overall level of violence in the U.S., gun control, media coverage of the events, and the methods used to protect public figures. Homicide rates, particularly those involving guns, remained far higher in the U.S. than in other developed countries. (*See* Table.) The most recent FBI *Uniform Crime Reports* showed that about 10,000 of the 19,000 reported murders in the U.S. in 1974 were committed with handguns, and two out of three of the reported 287,000 armed robberies and about 111,000 of the 436,000 reported aggravated assaults involved firearms. The federal Gun Control Act of 1968, passed after the assassinations of Robert Kennedy and Martin Luther King, Jr., had proved ineffective. There were said to be more than 40 million handguns in the U.S., with annual average sales of 2.5 million. Over the past three decades opinion polls in the U.S. had indicated strong public support for gun-control legislation, but the opposition was highly vocal, well organized, and politically effective.

The issue was not limited to the U.S. In Australia, where gun-related crime had risen alarmingly, the most populous state, New South Wales, enacted legislation requiring licensing of all types of firearms. Federal and state legislation already banned the use of handguns to all but police, the military, licensed pistol club members, and certain private security personnel. Nevertheless, police reported quantities of handguns were being smuggled into Australia from the U.S.; one of the cheap handguns known as Saturday night specials, worth $20 in the U.S., was selling on the black market for as much as U.S. $1,000.

Media coverage of the assassination attempts against President Ford gave rise to controversy over whether the press, by prominently publicizing such events, inspired a contagion of violence. Observers, including many journalists, believed there was some cause and effect relationship; the more publicity given to bomb scares, for instance, the more bomb scares there seemed to be. Media officials, however, emphasized their responsibility to report news. The editors in chief of *Time* and *Newsweek* magazines, both of which had featured cover stories on Fromme, stressed serious policy questions raised by the attacks, including how to protect a head of state in an open society.

The attacks against Ford, the 10th and 11th against U.S. presidents or presidential candidates, led to a

WIDE WORLD

Tom Smith of the U.S. Secret Service displays almost $1 million in counterfeit 20s recovered from the trunk of a car in East Boston. Seven men and one woman were charged with the crime. One of the men was on parole, having been charged in the famous Brink's robbery 25 years earlier.

UPI COMPIX

Bomb scene at the historic Fraunces Tavern in New York City following an explosion in January killing four persons and injuring over 50. George Washington's farewell address to his officers was delivered on this site.

far-reaching review of the measures being taken to guard the president and other high officials. Of particular concern was intelligence about potential assassins. In 1969 the Secret Service had issued guidelines to major U.S. law enforcement agencies, including the FBI and CIA, on the type of threatening persons or organizations to be listed in intelligence files. For security reasons, the criteria used to select these names were not divulged, but it appeared that neither Fromme nor Moore was judged a potential threat prior to the events.

Moore was said to have been a paid informer for the San Francisco police department, the FBI, and the Bureau of Alcohol, Tobacco, and Firearms of the Treasury Department—the same department to which the Secret Service belongs. The day before her alleged attack on the president, she had been arrested by the San Francisco police because she was carrying a pistol, but since the pistol was not loaded the police, under California law, could only confiscate the weapon and issue a misdemeanour citation. Subsequently, the Secret Service interviewed Moore but concluded that she did not warrant surveillance. Failure to carry out surveillance in Moore's case may have been an error in judgment. The quandary remained of how, in a democracy, to protect free speech and privacy on one hand and the lives of leaders on the other.

The wholesale collection of dossiers on presumably law-abiding U.S. citizens was the subject of a series of congressional hearings and investigations in 1975. It was revealed that both the CIA and FBI, among other illicit activities, had monitored international mail and cable traffic and engaged in extensive wiretapping and electronic surveillance of politically suspect individuals and organizations. It was also established that the late director of the FBI, J. Edgar Hoover, had kept secret files on persons who were or might be critical of him. According to the testimony of Attorney General Edward H. Levi, these included 17 past and present members of Congress. The revelations did little to restore the shaken reputation of the FBI, already badly tarnished by disclosures of its misuse by former presidents to further their personal ambitions. Seeking to rebuild public confidence in the bureau, Attorney General Levi proposed tighter guidelines for its domestic intelligence-gathering activities.

During the year the FBI began at last to achieve some success in its long search for a number of radical fugitives. Jane L. Alpert, on the agency's ten-most-wanted persons list for four years before she surrendered to authorities in November 1974, was sentenced to 27 months in prison in January for conspiracy to bomb buildings and bail jumping. Cameron David Bishop, on the list for nearly six years in connection with the dynamiting of electric transmission towers in Colorado, was arrested in East Greenwich, R.I., in March. In September the FBI gained its most widely heralded success with the arrest, in San Francisco, of newspaper heiress Patricia Hearst and three comrades, Emily and William Harris, members of a terrorist group calling itself the Symbionese Liberation Army (SLA), and Wendy Yoshimura. The arrests came after one of the most massive manhunts in the nation's history, launched following Hearst's kidnapping by the SLA in February 1974. Pending what appeared likely to be a protracted legal battle involving determination of state and federal criminal charges against Hearst and her colleagues, there were no answers to the question of whether she was brainwashed into cooperating with her kidnappers or had been a willing convert to the SLA cause and a voluntary participant in its terrorist activities.

The number of reported kidnappings in the U.S. had risen from 1,357 in 1971 to 3,585 in 1974, although it was said that in as many as 95% of these cases the abductors were captured, the victims freed, and the ransom reclaimed. One of the year's most publicized kidnappings, that of Samuel Bronfman II, heir to the Seagram fortune, ended in this manner when the 21-year-old victim was rescued from an apartment in Brooklyn, $2.3 million in ransom money was recovered, and two suspects, a New York City fireman and a limousine service operator, were taken into custody.

Nonviolent Crime. While violent crime received the most publicity, crimes against property were causing widespread international concern. The response of governments varied widely. In Zaire a thief who was caught stealing in the marketplace would commonly be lynched on the spot. In France a corporate briber and tax evader was frequently regarded as greedy but not necessarily as criminal. In Italy tax

Peter Lorenz and his wife in West Berlin after his release by terrorist kidnappers.

WIDE WORLD

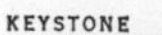

Raphael's "La Muta" ("The Mute Girl"), one of three priceless paintings stolen from the National Gallery of the ducal palace in Urbino, Italy, in February.

evasion was viewed almost as a national sport—which, according to the Italian Finance Ministry, cost an estimated $5 billion in lost revenues each year. West Germany's losses from corporate crimes, business and tax fraud were estimated to cost the government $8 billion annually. In the U.K. the total value of cash and property stolen in 1974 was said to amount to $190 million, and insurance companies reported paying out $55 million in claims because of these crimes. A growing number of insurers warned that, if the rate of property offenses did not abate, insurance would no longer be available to a significant segment of the population.

A white-collar fraud that cost the Manitoba Development Corp. as much as $30 million drew attention to this type of crime. An American promoter, Alexander Kasser, was charged with fraud by the U.S. Securities and Exchange Commission (SEC) and the Canadian government. In 1966 he obtained government loans of about $92 million to build an integrated forestry project in a depressed northern area of the province called The Pas. The companies that were to have run the project on its completion were secretly controlled by Kasser, and after they went bankrupt it appeared that much of the money paid to them had been siphoned off into Swiss bank accounts. Kasser, meanwhile, had vanished. An investigating commission concluded that the provincial government had been so eager to develop the north that it had blinded itself to obvious warning signs.

Investigators from the SEC and the Senate Foreign Relations Committee conducted extensive inquiries during the year into illegal political contributions and bribery abroad by more than a dozen large multinational corporations. It was revealed, for example, that Gulf Oil Corp. had paid over $4 million to government officials in South Korea and Bolivia. The president of Honduras was deposed in April after it was discovered that the United Brands Co. had paid $1,250,000 in illegal contributions to his government, although the new government later denied any connection.

Many difficulties were encountered by law enforcement officials attempting to prosecute white-collar criminals. As a senior French police official commented, "A murder is relatively easy. There is a crime, there is a trial, there is a penalty. But for these financial crimes the investigation may take years and then they [the offenders] march confidently into court with a battery of lawyers." To consider these and other problems of white-collar crime, the UN convened a meeting of experts in Rome in November.

The fifth UN Congress on the Prevention of Crime met in September in Geneva. It had been scheduled for Toronto, but the Canadian government withdrew its invitation after the UN decided to invite the Palestine Liberation Organization and other "liberation" groups to attend as observers. The International Association of Chiefs of Police (IACP) and some other organizations also withdrew from participation.

In the year ended June 1975 the General Secretariat of the International Criminal Police Organization (Interpol) examined 24,398 cases resulting in 630 arrests; 9,185 items of information were supplied to national central bureaus, and 426 persons were the subject of international notices.

Victims. Complaints concerning the official treatment received by crime victims were bringing about some changes. Largely as a result of pressure from feminist groups, special programs to deal with the victims of rape were being established in many U.S. cities, and police agencies stepped up the use of women, rather than men, to interview rape victims. Assisted by a Police Foundation grant, the Sacramento (Calif.) police department began a model victim advocate program. A police officer was appointed as a full-time victim advocate in cases of robbery, burglary, grand theft, auto theft, and assault. The program was designed to inform victims of the progress of the investigation, to speed return of stolen property after it was recovered, and to familiarize victims with police and court procedures.

The importance of establishing an effective federal victim-compensation program was stressed by President Ford in a message to Congress in June. The president also emphasized the need for uniform sentencing practices and mandatory prison sentences for serious

UPI COMPIX

Masked Palestinian guerrillas who seized the Egyptian embassy in Madrid on September 15 hold a news conference in Algiers after surrendering their hostages to the authorities.

crimes. More state legislatures introduced laws mandating capital punishment for murder and related crimes during the year, but the constitutionality of these measures remained to be tested in the Supreme Court. Pending such determination, no executions were carried out in the U.S. in 1975. In Canada the federal government proposed legislation outlawing capital punishment (currently available only in cases involving murder of a law-enforcement officer), but sponsors of a pro-death penalty petition obtained more than 200,000 signatures. A campaign in support of capital punishment was also said to be gathering momentum in Hong Kong. While capital punishment remained in abeyance in many nations, a number of African, Middle Eastern, and Latin-American countries exhibited little reluctance to execute criminals for a range of crimes. In Saudi Arabia the assassin of the late King Faisal was beheaded according to custom in the capital of Riyadh in June as thousands looked on.

Policing. The danger that vigilante action would proliferate in the absence of severe penalties, including capital punishment, was mentioned in a statement by the president of the Canadian chiefs of police in August. The statement reflected widespread concern among law enforcement officers over their apparent inability to stem the tide of crime by official means. As the number of police officers slain in the execution of their duties rose, traditional policies concerning the arming of police began to be questioned in such countries as England, where officers carried firearms only in emergency situations.

The use of hollow-point ammunition by police was being debated in many U.S. jurisdictions. The advocates of such ammunition claimed it had greater stopping power and caused fewer ricochets, with consequent injury to innocent bystanders, than the widely used hard-point bullets. Critics argued that it was known that hollow-point ammunition produced greater numbers of fatal or major injuries. Concerned by these issues, and the circumstances under which police fired guns, the Police Foundation began a study of police firearm use and training.

Agents of an anti-gang brigade surround a Paris bank in February, within which three gunmen held hostages to enforce their demand for $710,000 (Fr. 3 million) and safe passage from France.

POPPERFOTO

In the Soviet Union, the leadership, in an unusual display of concern over urban crime, urged citizens to provide greater assistance to local police. A front-page editorial in the Communist Party newspaper *Pravda* said that citizen auxiliary police (*druzhiniki*) were to be given a greater role in combating crime. Previously, *druzhiniki* had dealt mainly with the drunk and disorderly.

Relations between native minority populations and the police were the subject of special studies in Canada, the U.S., and Australia. The Australian government established a royal commission to examine the subject following several serious clashes between native aboriginals and police. A comparative study of the North American experience, commissioned by the Australian Department of Aboriginal Affairs, recommended vigorous efforts to recruit aboriginals into Australian law enforcement agencies and far more extensive police training in race relations.

The role of women in police work, long a matter of controversy in several countries, was the subject of a major debate in Sweden in 1975. Sweden had had policewomen since 1949. In the 1960s they were permitted to leave their traditional tasks and patrol the streets in uniform. In 1969 the National Police Board, responding to pressure groups within the force, ordered women back inside the police station, but two years later the women, alleging sex discrimination, forced a reversal of the policy. In the summer of 1975 a group of male officers petitioned to have women banned from patrol car duty. After heated exchanges between the government and the police, the Swedish attorney general stated that "We need more women police and we do not wish to exclude women from certain duties such as patrolling." Women remained a small minority of the Swedish police force, however; there were 400 women among the 15,000 officers.

Angry protests by police were not limited to Sweden. In Bangkok, Thailand, in August a mob of police in civilian clothes stormed the house of Premier Kukrit Pramoj to protest what they called the weakness of the government toward pressure from leftist students. The Thai chief of police and the Bangkok police commissioner resigned after the attack, during which the premier's house was ransacked. Earlier, in March, Italian police held unauthorized protest meetings to dramatize their demand for the right to take stronger measures against offenders, including authorization to fire before being fired on.

In the U.S. police militancy largely concerned economic issues and the right to organize and strike. A three-day strike by the San Francisco police ended when Mayor Joseph L. Alioto used his emergency powers to impose a settlement previously rejected by the city's Board of Supervisors as too expensive. Municipal officers throughout the country were apprehensive that this victory by the police of the nation's 14th largest city would encourage similar actions elsewhere. The prospect was particularly worrisome in a time of economic stringency, when most communities were seeking to hold the line on pay increases for all public employees. New York City, on the verge of bankruptcy, was forced to lay off several thousand officers. (*See* UNITED STATES: *Special Report.*) In October, police in Oklahoma City struck for three days.

(DUNCAN CHAPPELL)

See also Drug Abuse; Law; Prisons and Penology.

[522.C.6; 543.A.5; 552.C and F; 737.B; 10/36.C.5.a]

ENCYCLOPÆDIA BRITANNICA FILMS. *Our Community Services* (1969).

POLITICAL CRIME AND TERRORISM

By Brian Crozier

The great wave of transnational terrorism that first reached a climax in 1972 showed no signs of abating in 1975. Strictly speaking, the phenomenon was not new; what was new was its rapid growth in the 1970s, made possible by increasingly sophisticated technology. Some of this new technology consists of specialized equipment, such as miniaturized or remote-control detonating devices, hand-held rocket launchers, and the like, which make terrorism more lethal, more effective, and less risky for the terrorist. But even improvements in generally available technology are important. For example, self-dialing international telephone communications and jet travel facilitate conspiracies across national boundaries and the perpetration of political crimes by nationals of one country operating in another. The growth of television has contributed to the easy dissemination of terrorist techniques, such as the hijacking of aircraft and the kidnapping of diplomats or businessmen for ransom.

The Nature of the Problem. "Political crime" differs from ordinary crime only in the motivation, real or claimed, of the criminal. A holdup, a bank robbery, a burglary, drug running, kidnapping, or murder is no less a crime for being politically motivated. In this context, terrorism may be defined as "motivated violence for political ends"; this distinguishes terrorism both from vandalism and from crimes of violence in which no political motivation is discerned. Political crime is thus a wider term than terrorism, which is an extreme form of it. The relationship between the two is that between the whole and the part.

In practice, however, the crimes listed in the preceding paragraph, if politically motivated, tend to serve the ends of terrorist groups or (much more rarely) individuals. Especially in the early planning phase of terrorist action, members of the group may raid a bank to raise funds. The same is true, more often than not, of the extortion of ransom for abducted persons or hostages in an embassy or a hijacked airliner. Drug running (practiced by the Palestinian Black September group, among others) serves the same ends. Murder on contract may bring in sufficient funds to permit assassinations without financial inducement.

In recent years, terrorism (and the range of political crimes serving terrorist ends) has dramatically increased in certain countries and at certain times, creating new problems of containment and suppression with which, in many cases, the existing security services have been ill prepared to cope. The internationalization of terrorism has created still more intractable problems because of the inadequacies of existing international law and the quasi-impossibility of achieving internationally coordinated action, especially in the extradition of air pirates.

In any society, political crime poses cruel moral and political problems. These problems are particularly acute in open, pluralistic, and representative societies, which by definition are more vulnerable than others. At the other end of the political spectrum, a totalitarian regime, such as the Soviet Union, is virtually immune to terrorism, since the pervasive security apparatus of the state and its monopoly of commercial transactions makes it almost impossible for terrorist groups to acquire the necessary devices or to conspire to use them. (Even in the U.S.S.R., however, there has been at least one example of attempted aerial hijacking, the authors of which were apprehended and punished.)

Terrorism and Democracy. For the open society, the political dilemma is implicit in the need to adopt measures to suppress terrorism while preserving the traditional liberties that make a society open. It is a safe general rule that, the more open a society, the more likely it is that the authorities will be reluctant, in the first instance, to take adequate measures against political crime. Any failure to deal with the threat, however, will inevitably lead to a rapid increase of incidents, necessitating more severe measures than would have been required if action had been taken earlier.

Some examples in recent history may illustrate the problem. The most striking, perhaps, is that of Uruguay, which was exceptional in Latin America for its well-established representative democracy and social welfare programs. Between 1968 and 1971 a terrorist organization known as the Tupamaros (after Tupac Amaru, an 18th-century Inca hero of the resistance to the Spaniards) nearly paralyzed the administration, robbing banks at will, kidnapping officials or businessmen, and escaping—with obvious police complicity—if captured. The terrorists, however, failed to prevent the presidential election of November 1971, in which Juan María Bordaberry was the winner. A "state of internal war" was proclaimed, civil rights were suspended, and the Army was given a free hand to restore order. Under severe interrogation methods, the movement was broken between April and November 1972. The terrorist movement had been defeated, but at the cost of losing the country's democratic system.

In Turkey political violence fostered by the Turkish People's Liberation Army (TPLA) had caused widespread fear and suffering and brought about the closure of the Middle East Technical University. The military intervened in April 1971, forcing the creation of a government determined to restore order. A state of emergency was proclaimed, and ruthless interrogation methods enabled the security forces to break the TPLA by the end of 1972. In Brazil a similar challenge was brought under control by similar methods by late 1971. Turkey later succeeded in restoring constitutional government, but the authoritarian regimes

Ethnologist Françoise Claustre was captured by rebel forces in Chad in April 1974. The French government failed to secure her release during 1975.

FRANK SPOONER

Brian Crozier is director and co-founder of the Institute for the Study of Conflict, London, and the editor of Conflict Studies. *His books include* The Rebels *(1960)*, Neo-Colonialism *(1964)*, The Struggle for the Third World *(1966)*, Franco *(1967)*, De Gaulle *(2 vol., 1973), and* A Theory of Conflict *(1974)*.

established in Brazil and Uruguay appeared to be set for a long tenure of power.

The British response to terrorism in Ulster illustrates in still more acute form the dilemmas created by terrorism in a long-established parliamentary system. By mid-1975 the disorders had lasted seven years and showed no signs of ending. The violence of the Catholic Irish Republican Army (IRA) had provoked counterviolence from the Protestant and loyalist Ulster Defence Association (UDA). Detention without trial had been practiced by successive governments but was being phased out in 1975. Severe—although relatively mild—techniques of "interrogation in depth" (including hooding and high-pitched noise, wall-standing, and deprivation of sleep) had brought rapid results in terms of arrests, but were abandoned in 1972 after the publication of reports by two committees of inquiry, under Sir Edmund Compton and Lord Parker, respectively.

The Moral Dilemma. In their simplest formulation, the issues, then, are these: Is it better to defeat terrorism with the use of brutal methods and lose democratic freedoms in the process, or to avoid effective measures, preserve essential liberties, and leave terrorism undefeated?

Similarly invidious choices between unsatisfactory alternatives apply in the matter of hostages. The moral dilemma is inescapable, whether the decision is to be taken by a government, by an airline, or by a commercial company. In the case of a hijacked airliner, the lives of all on board are instantly at stake. In the case of a kidnapped diplomat or businessman, only one life is normally at risk, but the dilemma is not thereby reduced; on the contrary, it tends to be dramatically intensified.

For obvious reasons, there is no uniformity of response to such situations. Some governments are tougher than others, while private companies have tended to meet terrorist demands unquestioningly. Two of the most striking recent examples occurred in 1975. On April 24 six members of the West German Rote Armee Fraktion (better known as the Baader-Meinhof gang) stormed the West German embassy in Stockholm and seized 12 hostages. During the struggle, the military attaché was mortally injured. The terrorists demanded the release of 26 other members of the group about to face trial in Germany. The German government stood firm (in contrast to its actions on previous occasions), and in retaliation the terrorists blew up the building, killing one of the hostages and precipitating the suicide of one of the terrorists. In the end, the five surviving terrorists were captured; four of them were deported to West Germany by the Swedish government, and the fifth—who was seriously injured—was detained in a hospital in Stockholm.

On August 4 five members of the Japanese Rengo Sekigun (Red Army) seized a building in Kuala Lumpur, Malaysia, containing the U.S. and Swedish embassies. Using the threat to kill more than 50 hostages, they demanded the release of seven other members of the group from prison in Japan. The Japanese government agreed and released five of the seven, the other two having declined the offer of freedom. Eventually the ten terrorists (including the five released in Japan) were flown in a Japan Air Lines aircraft to Tripoli, Libya, where they were given sanctuary.

This case stands in striking contrast to events in The Netherlands on Oct. 31, 1974. Fifteen hostages held by armed criminals in Scheveningen Prison were released by a Dutch counterterrorist squad using diversionary tactics (involving excessive noise, flares, smoke bombs, and sirens), a thermal lance that sliced through a steel door in six seconds, rapid action, skilled marksmanship, and reliable background intelligence on the Arab terrorist who had organized the original incident five days earlier.

The Scheveningen "siege" introduced the beginning of a new strategy, the wearing down of trapped terrorists by patient waiting and refusal to countenance their demands. The strategy was developed fully in two London sieges—first, in September–October, of the three "Spaghetti House" robbers (not terrorists) caught in the restaurant's basement with their seven hostages (five days) and then, in December, of four IRA gunmen trapped in an apartment with its two occupant-hostages (six days). In both actions the police and their advisers skillfully applied patience and moral pressure so as gradually to phase out the risk of violence. Similar methods were used by the Dutch in December when South Moluccan gunmen seized a train and the Indonesian consulate in Amsterdam for 13 and 16 days, respectively, before surrendering, but at the cost of the lives of three train hostages.

At the end of 1975 pro-Palestinian terrorists, on the other hand, were able to speedily negotiate air transport to Algiers for themselves and their hostage oil ministers, whom they had seized at the Vienna meeting of the Organization for Petroleum Exporting Countries.

There has been a similar diversity of responses to the abduction of single hostages. A classic case was the kidnapping of the British ambassador to Uruguay, Geoffrey Jackson, in January 1971. With his informed consent, the British authorities refused to make a deal with the terrorists, who released the ambassador in September. In contrast, enormous sums have been paid by private companies in Argentina for the release of executives kidnapped, especially, by the Ejército Revolucionario del Pueblo (ERP). On March 11, 1974, for instance, the Esso Oil Co. of Argentina paid the ERP $14.2 million to obtain the release of Victor Samuelson.

In the Argentine kidnappings, and in similar cases in Italy, political crime has been shown to pay. In this context, the attitude of a private company is perhaps inevitably determined by concern for the lives of top employees rather than by considerations of general security or even the security of other employees, who are more likely to be threatened if the company pays up than if it does not.

Sanctuary for Terrorists. In any discussion of issues raised by political crime, the question of sanctuary must be given high priority. The word has at least two precise connotations: it applies to the use of contiguous sovereign territory by terrorist groups; and it also signifies the availability of a haven for escaping terrorists, particularly after a successful act of aerial piracy. In the first instance, the government of the target country is precluded from taking effective action, even in "hot pursuit," unless it receives permission from the country harbouring the terrorists or is willing to incur the odium of armed action against a neighbouring state.

The offer of sanctuary to hijackers has proved to be a particularly intractable problem. Some international legislation exists, including the Tokyo Convention on Offences and Certain Other Acts Committed on Board Aircraft (in force by the end of 1969); the Convention for the Suppression of Unlawful Seizure of Aircraft (The Hague; in force since October 1971); and the Montreal Convention for the Suppression of Unlawful Acts Against the Safety of Civil Aviation. In practice, these conventions have proved inadequate, if only because of the unwillingness of Arab states to turn away Palestinian or other Arab terrorists. Efforts to achieve a unanimous position on this problem through the United Nations (for instance, in the UN debates in June 1972) have proved abortive.

Conclusions. In a perceptive article in the July 1975 issue of the U.S. quarterly *Foreign Affairs*, David Fromkin argued strongly in favour of resisting terrorist demands, whatever the consequences. A further principle may be stated: although political crime calls for special measures because of the motivation and objectives of the criminals, on no account should a legal category of "political crimes" be created in open societies. If the criminals are apprehended, they should be dealt with under existing laws. To do otherwise would concede the claim made by terrorists and other political criminals that they are "political prisoners" and, as such, entitled to special privileges and treatment. To dignify political criminals in this way brings the law into disrepute, plays into the hands of political criminals, and may even, in extreme cases, foster the growth of private vigilantes prepared to take the law into their own hands.

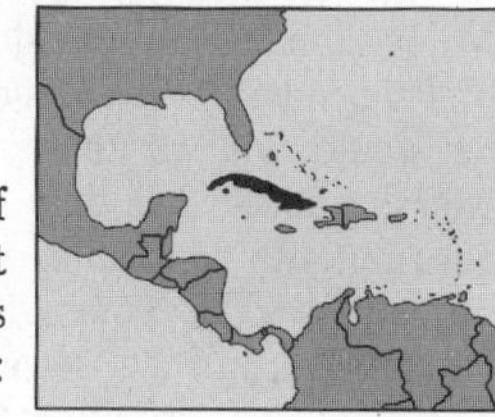

Cuba

The socialist republic of Cuba occupies the largest island in the Greater Antilles of the West Indies. Area: 42,827 sq.mi. (110,922 sq. km.), including several thousand small islands and cays. Pop. (1975 est.): 9,265,-900, including (1953) white 72.8%; mestizo 14.5%; Negro 12.4%. Cap. and largest city: Havana (pop., 1974 est., 1,838,000). Language: Spanish. Religion: predominantly Roman Catholic. President in 1975, Osvaldo Dorticós Torrado; prime minister, Fidel Castro.

A long period of ostracism for Cuba finally ended when the Organization of American States (OAS) met in San José, Costa Rica, and voted on July 29, 1975, to lift the political and economic sanctions imposed in 1964. The latter resulted from OAS confirmation of a charge by the then president of Venezuela, Rómulo Betancourt, that Cuba was furnishing arms to Venezuelan guerrillas. The U.S. joined 15 of the 21 countries of the OAS in supporting the decision.

Within Cuba the formation of permanent government institutions, to bring the administrative system more into line with those of Eastern European countries and to achieve representational local and regional government, continued in 1975. Official consultation with labour union, women's, youth, and small farmer organizations was designed to encourage greater popular participation. The committees for the defense of the revolution ceased to supervise the provision of local services. Yet policymaking was still dominated by the Communist Party, with about 80,000 members. The party's first congress was convoked in December 1975. The congress defined domestic and foreign policy aims, determined a system for management of the economy, decided on a timetable for the establishment of countrywide People's Power assemblies, and worked on the draft of a new constitution. The draft constitution provided for the establishment of a five-year elective National Assembly of Popular Power, led by a State Council that included a president, a first vice-president, five other vice-presidents, and 24 additional members.

The gross national product was estimated to have risen by 13% in 1973 and 10% in 1974; it was calculated by the World Bank at $3,970,000,000 in 1972. The official overall economic growth-rate target for 1973–83 was 6% a year. A four-year development plan (1976–80) was designed to provide for investments totaling $15 billion, of which $4.5 billion would be channeled to industry, $3.5 billion to agriculture, and $2 billion to public-works projects.

Sugar remained the mainstay of the economy. Production in 1973 and 1974 amounted to 4.7 million and 5.4 million tons, respectively, and was forecast at about 6 million tons in 1975. Observers considered that the crops between 1972 and 1975 would have been considerably lower but for the introduction of combine harvesters and the Australian method of burning off the foliage before harvesting the cane, and the modernization of the sugar mills. Agricultural production was to be increased by 10% a year: sugar by 6.5% and nonsugar agriculture by 16.4%. Incentives to private small-scale farmers were resulting in improved production; these farmers owned 32% of the land and produced 20% of the cane, 80% of tobacco, and 70% of coffee.

Output by heavy and light industry continued to rise, and consumer, fishing, and textile industries grew. Beginning in 1973 the following industries were established: glass, newsprint, chemical, copper wire, and cable. There were plans to establish between 1976 and 1980 factories to produce tires and refrigeration and merchant marine equipment; thermal and nuclear power output was also to be expanded.

Cuba was developing its extensive mineral resources. It was the world's fourth largest nickel producer, with reserves of 19 million tons; capacity was to be doubled by 1980 to 70,000 tons a year with Soviet assistance. The country was still more than 95% dependent on the U.S.S.R. for petroleum; two local wells had been established but had not yet been brought into full production in 1975. Cuba had a sizable positive balance in its international trade in 1974 and expected an even greater one in 1975.

During 1975 Cuba engaged in high-level trade missions with France, Great Britain, and Sweden. From August 1973 more than $3.3 billion in credits had been made available to the nation. Mexico and Argentina made available large credits for the industrial development plan. In 1975 Cuba established diplomatic relations with Iran, West Germany, and Colombia. The decision of the OAS to readmit Cuba permitted individual OAS member countries to formulate their own political and economic policies toward Cuba—as an increasing number of governments had already been doing in defiance of the organization's policy.

(MICHAEL WOOLLER)

[974.B.2.c]

CUBA

Education. (1972–73) Primary, pupils 1,852,714, teachers 68,699; secondary, pupils 222,481, teachers 17,724; vocational, pupils 41,940, teachers 4,652; teacher training, students 25,910, teachers 2,268; higher, students 43,261, teaching staff (1970–71) 4,129.

Finance. Monetary unit: peso, with (Sept. 22, 1975) an official rate of 0.81 peso to U.S. $1 (free rate of 1.68 peso = £1 sterling). Budget (1966; latest published) balanced at 2,718,000,000 pesos.

Foreign Trade. (1972) Imports 1,189,000,000 pesos; exports 739 million pesos. Import sources (1971): U.S.S.R. 53%; East Germany 5%. Export destinations (1971): U.S.S.R. 35%; Japan 12%; East Germany 6%; Czechoslovakia 5%. Main exports (1971): sugar 74%; nonferrous metal ores 16%.

Transport and Communications. Roads (1974) 18,900 km. (including 1,220 km. of the Central Highway). Motor vehicles in use (1971): passenger *c.* 72,000; commercial (including buses) *c.* 32,000. Railways: (1973) 14,490 km. (including *c.* 9,440 km. plantation); traffic (1971) 987 million passenger-km., freight 1,598,000,000 net ton-km. Air traffic (1973): 535 million passenger-km.; freight 14.5 million net ton-km. Shipping (1974): merchant vessels 100 gross tons and over 259; gross tonnage 409,064. Telephones (Dec. 1973) 281,000. Radio receivers (Dec. 1973) *c.* 1.8 million. Television receivers (Dec. 1973) *c.* 370,-000.

Agriculture. Production (in 000; metric tons; 1974; 1973 in parentheses): rice *c.* 400 (*c.* 375); corn (1973) *c.* 125, (1972) *c.* 120; cassava *c.* 230 (*c.* 230); sweet potatoes (1973) *c.* 245, (1972) *c.* 245; tomatoes *c.* 87 (*c.* 87); sugar, raw value *c.* 5,935 (*c.* 5,383); coffee *c.* 27 (*c.* 30); oranges (1973) *c.* 110, (1972) *c.* 100; tobacco *c.* 47 (*c.* 46); jute *c.* 7 (*c.* 7). Livestock (in 000; 1974): cattle *c.* 7,568; pigs *c.* 1,450; sheep *c.* 318; goats (1973) *c.* 86; horses (1973) 688.

Industry. Production (in 000; metric tons; 1973): crude oil 138; petroleum products (1971) 4,310; electricity (kw-hr.; 1972) *c.* 5,250,000; copper ore (metal content) 5; chrome ore (oxide content; 1972) 13; manganese ore (metal content; 1968) 28; nickel ore (metal content; 1972) 37.

Croatian Literature:
see Literature
Crops:
see Agriculture and Food Supplies

Cycling

Though Europe remained the hub of the cycling world, the radius continued to increase. The United States was producing first-class road and track riders; Australians were regularly striking gold at world and Olympic championships, in which South Americans also placed; and during 1975 for the first time a Japanese cyclist emerged in top international competition: Ryoji Abe finished third in the 1975 world professional sprint championship at Rocourt, Belgium, in August. Most sports commentators believed cycling to be a minor sport in Japan; in fact, however, the professional track scene there was busier than anywhere else in the world. At velodromes (cycle tracks) owned by the Keirin Association, spectators backed their favourites with pari-mutuel betting. Visiting European officials and riders returned with accounts of first-class Japanese sprinters, but the top men were never seen in action away from home. With Tokyo in line to stage a world championship series by 1980, Japanese stars were being encouraged to get the feel of European-style competition.

While new nations were taking part in track-racing activities, international road competition continued to be dominated by European riders—Belgians in particular. At the end of 1974 the overall record of Brussels-based Eddy Merckx included five victories in each of three of the greatest races: the one-day Milan–San Remo classic and the multistage tours of France and Italy. His entourage was confident that he would win all three in 1975. In fact, however, Merckx succeeded only in the first with a brilliant effort in the final miles into San Remo. Illness kept him out of the Tour of Italy, and in the Tour de France he finished second to French star Bernard Thévenet, who intelligently planned his season to be in peak form for his country's great stage race. This setback was expected to make Merckx more determined than ever to retain his world road title six weeks later on a hard course in the south of Belgium. His form was good, but an early crash in the 166-mi. race sapped his strength, and although fighting back strongly he had no answer to the devastating attack made by 1972 Olympic champion Hennie Kuiper (Neth.) 12 mi. from home.

Kuiper's success was the final note of triumph in a victory march to the podium by Dutch riders in the 1975 championships. Earlier in the week two compatriots had taken the women's and amateur men's championships on a neighbouring road circuit, while on the Rocourt track gold medals went to flying Dutchmen (and women) in motor-paced and pursuit championships. The series was a near disaster for host-nation Belgium, which had only one silver medal and one bronze to show at the end of 15 title races. In winning the amateur sprint, Daniel Morelon (France)

Cyclers on the 14th leg of the Tour de France in the mountains of Auvergne.

A.F.P./PICTORIAL PARADE

1975 Cycling Champions

Event	Winner	Country
WORLD AMATEUR CHAMPIONS—TRACK		
Men		
Sprint	D. Morelon	France
Tandem sprint	void	
Individual pursuit	T. Huschke	East Germany
1,000-m. time trial	K-J. Gruenke	East Germany
Team pursuit	West Germany	
50-km. motor-paced	G. Minneboo	The Netherlands
Women		
Sprint	S. Novarra	U.S.
Pursuit	C. van Oosten Hage	The Netherlands
WORLD PROFESSIONAL CHAMPIONS—TRACK		
Sprint	J. Nicholson	Australia
Individual pursuit	R. Schuiten	The Netherlands
One-hour motor-paced	D. Kemper	West Germany
WORLD AMATEUR CHAMPIONS—ROAD		
Men		
100-km. team time trial	Poland	
Individual road race	A. Gevers	The Netherlands
Women		
Individual road race	T. Fopma	The Netherlands
WORLD PROFESSIONAL CHAMPIONS—ROAD		
Individual road race	H. Kuiper	The Netherlands
WORLD CHAMPIONSHIPS—CYCLO CROSS		
Amateur	R. Vermeire	Belgium
Professional	R. de Vlaeminck	Belgium
MAJOR PROFESSIONAL ROAD-RACE WINNERS		
Het Volk	J. Bruyère	Belgium
Ghent–Wevelgem	F. Maertens	Belgium
Milan–San Remo	E. Merckx	Belgium
Paris–Roubaix	R. de Vlaeminck	Belgium
Amstel Gold Race	E. Merckx	Belgium
Flèche Wallonne	A. Dierickx	Belgium
Liège-Bastogne-Liège	E. Merckx	Belgium
Grand Prix of Frankfurt	R. Schuiten	The Netherlands
Tour of Flanders	E. Merckx	Belgium
Bordeaux–Paris	H. Van Springel	Belgium
Paris–Brussels	F. Maertens	Belgium
Tour of Lombardy	F. Moser	Italy
Grand Prix des Nations time trial	R. Schuiten	The Netherlands
Tour de France	B. Thévenet	France
Tour of Italy	F. Bertoglio	Italy
Tour of Spain	A. Tamames	Spain
Tour of Switzerland	R. de Vlaeminck	Belgium
Tour of Belgium	F. Maertens	Belgium
Tour of Luxembourg	F. Verbeeck	Belgium
Tour of Sardinia	E. Merckx	Belgium
Paris–Nice	J. Zoetemelk	The Netherlands
Dauphiné–Libéré	B. Thévenet	France
Four Days of Dunkirk	F. Maertens	Belgium
Midi–Libre	F. Moser	Italy
Semana Catalana	E. Merckx	Belgium

CENTRAL PRESS/PICTORIAL PARADE

Reg Harris (left), the 55-year-old cyclist who was five times world sprint champion, announced his intention to retire after defending his 1,000-m. sprint title in the British national track championships at Leicester Sports Centre. (Bottom) After ten years of professional cycling, Eddy Merckx celebrates his 358th professional win after his victory in the Tour of Flanders.

WIDE WORLD

equaled the record of seven world championship victories. The absence of Soviet names from the women's championship results had a simple explanation: there were no Soviet entries. Another notable name missing was that of Beryl Burton of Great Britain, a winner of several medals during an international career lasting 15 years. Although still unbeatable at home, Mrs. Burton did not take part in the Belgian races, leaving the family honour in the care of her 19-year-old daughter Denise, who finished third in the pursuit event. (J. B. WADLEY)

[452.B.4.h.x]

Cyprus

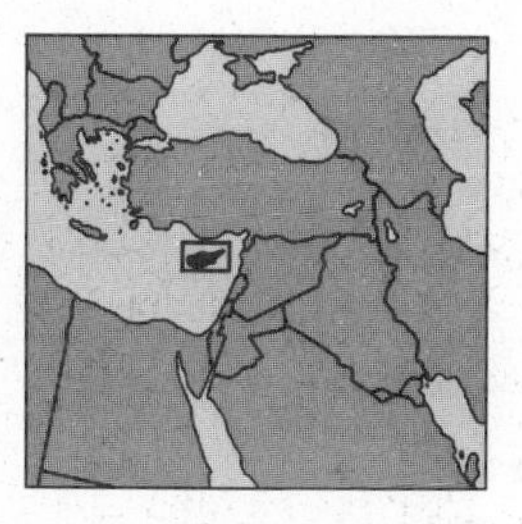

An island republic and a member of the Commonwealth of Nations, Cyprus is in the eastern Mediterranean. Area: 3,572 sq.mi. (9,251 sq.km.). Pop. (1974 est.): 639,000, including Greeks 82%; Turks 18%. Cap. and largest city: Nicosia (pop., 1974 est., 117,100). All these figures should be considered unreliable, as they do not take into account the extensive internal migration or the recent and reportedly extensive Turkish immigration and Greek emigration, for which authoritative data are not available. Language: Greek and Turkish. Religion: Greek Orthodox 77%; Muslim 18%. President in 1975, Archbishop Makarios III.

After his return to Cyprus on Dec. 7, 1974, ending his stay abroad in the aftermath of the July 1974 coup, Archbishop Makarios sought to form a government of national unity. The conservative leader Glafkos Clerides refused to be associated with such a government, which would have included left-wing elements. Therefore, on Jan. 14, 1975, the president appointed a Cabinet of nonparty men, half of whom had been in his administration at the time of the coup. Clerides continued as Greek Cypriot interlocutor in negotiations with the Turkish Cypriot leader Rauf Denktash. They met in Nicosia on January 14 for a new round

Georgios Mavros, Greek parliamentary opposition leader, addresses a mass rally in Nicosia on the first anniversary of the Turkish invasion of Cyprus. Listeners include Glafkos Clerides (left), Archbishop Makarios, and General Komninos (far right) of the Cypriot National Guard.

UPI COMPIX

of intercommunal talks. These, and four other rounds of negotiations (three in Vienna and one in New York) held between April 28 and September 9 at the insistence of the UN Security Council and under the chairmanship of UN Secretary-General Kurt Waldheim, failed to end the intercommunal crisis.

The Turkish invasion of the island following the coup had resulted in the flight of 200,000 Greek Cypriots from the north and the concentration of the majority (100,000) of the Turkish Cypriots in an area comprising 40% of the island, within which only 10,000 Greek Cypriots remained. This gave the Turkish Cypriots a strong negotiating position. It was further improved at the end of January 1975, when 10,000 Turkish Cypriots from the south were sent north from refugee camps in the British bases at Akrotiri and Episkopi, and again in August when the remaining Turkish Cypriots in the south (some 9,000) were permitted to settle in the northern third of the island, controlled by the Turkish Army.

The presence of Turkish forces helped stabilize the position of the Turkish Cypriots and compelled the Greek Cypriot community to rely on intercommunal negotiations and diplomacy to obtain redress for their losses. Makarios made numerous journeys abroad in an effort to maintain international pressures on Turkey and cause it to withdraw its troops from Cyprus. However, despite UN moves and diplomatic offensives by members of the European Economic Community and by the U.S. (which cut off military aid to Turkey in February), the Turkish Army did not pull out of the island.

In January the interlocutors began to negotiate the form of a future federated state of Cyprus and the geographic boundaries of the two communities. In April Clerides conceded that a bizonal solution might be inevitable, and Denktash agreed that the present frontier should be amended to the advantage of the Greeks. On September 8 in New York, however, Denktash failed to make the expected concrete proposals about this frontier. Lack of clarity in the talks was due to, and paralleled by, the obscure relationship between Denktash and the Turkish government. He appeared unable to stem immigration to northern Cyprus from the Turkish mainland, but he had Turkish backing in his plans to obtain half the posts in future federal establishments for Turkish Cypriots and to create a Turkish Cypriot government alongside the "government of the Greek Cypriot community" (neither Denktash nor the Turks recognized the Makarios regime as the official government of Cyprus). On February 13 a Turkish Cypriot Federated State of Cyprus (not recognized by Makarios) came into being. This, and the Turkish Cypriot referendum of June 8 which approved the constitution of this state, caused temporary breakdowns in the intercommunal talks.

In the south 18,000 Greek Cypriot refugees remained in camps. Since the Turks did not settle the new town of Famagusta or the area between the two roads from Nicosia to Famagusta, it seemed likely that about half the Greek Cypriot refugees would eventually recover their homes. It was doubtful whether more would be able to return; the Turkish Cypriots laid claim to 30% of the island, and their numbers were increasing as a result of immigration from Turkey and the return of 4,000 Turkish Cypriots from Great Britain. In the south there was 30% unemployment, and many Greek Cypriots were emigrating. On June 13 and December 13 the UN Security Council agreed to six-month extensions of its peacekeeping force on Cyprus. (L. J. D. COLLINS)

[978.A.4]

LONDON DAILY EXPRESS/PICTORIAL PARADE

The former prime minister of Turkey, Bulent Ecevit, addressed a crowd of Turkish Cypriots in July during a visit to the island.

CYPRUS

Education. (Greek schools; 1973–74) Primary, pupils 63,446, teachers 2,284; secondary, pupils 44,996, teachers 2,171; vocational, pupils 4,672, teachers 338; teacher training, students 170, teachers 14; higher, students 679, teaching staff 74. (Turkish schools; 1972–73) Primary, pupils 16,014; secondary, pupils 7,190; vocational, pupils 753; teacher training, students 13.

Finance. Monetary unit: pound, with (Sept. 22, 1975) a free rate of C£0.39 to U.S. $1 (C£0.81 = £1 sterling). Gold, SDRs, and foreign exchange: (June 1975) U.S. $255.3 million; (June 1974) U.S. $271 million. Budget (1974 est.): revenue C£60,630,000; expenditure C£51,150,000.

Foreign Trade. (1974) Imports C£148,028,000; exports C£55,177,000. Import sources: U.K. 21%; West Germany 9%; Italy 8%; Greece 7%; France 7%; U.S. 6%. Export destinations: U.K. 38%; U.S.S.R. 7%; West Germany 6%; Libya 5%. Main exports: citrus fruit 21%; copper 11%; potatoes 9%; wine 9%. Tourism (1973): visitors 264,000; gross receipts U.S. $67 million.

Transport and Communications. Roads (1971) 8,319 km. Motor vehicles in use (1973): passenger 77,682; commercial 15,470. Air traffic (1973): 371 million passenger-km.; freight 3 million net ton-km. Shipping (1974): merchant vessels 100 gross tons and over 722; gross tonnage 3,394,880. Telephones (Dec. 1973) 62,000. Radio licenses (Dec. 1972) 171,000. Television licenses (Dec. 1972) 66,000.

Agriculture. Production (in 000; metric tons; 1974; 1973 in parentheses): barley 115 (3); wheat (1973) 10, (1972) 81; grapes *c.* 140 (*c.* 168); potatoes (1973) *c.* 187, (1972) 175; oranges (1973) *c.* 170, (1972) 139; grapefruit (1973) *c.* 60, (1972) 44; olives *c.* 17 (2). Livestock (in 000; Dec. 1973): sheep 430; cattle 34; pigs (1972) 129; goats (1972) 380.

Industry. Production (in 000; metric tons; 1973): asbestos 28; iron pyrites (exports) 364; copper ore (exports; metal content) 14; chromium ore (oxide content) 15; cement (1974) 338; electricity (kw-hr.; 1974) 732,000.

Czechoslovakia

A federal socialist republic of central Europe, Czechoslovakia lies between Poland, the U.S.S.R., Hungary, Austria, and East and West Germany. Area: 49,374 sq.mi. (127,877 sq.km.). Pop. (1975 est.): 14,795,000, including (1974 est.) Czech 64%; Slovak 30%. Cap. and largest city: Prague (pop., 1974 est., 1,091,400). Language: Czech and Slovak (official). General secretary of the Communist Party of Czechoslovakia and president from May 29, 1975, Gustav Husak; president to May 29, Ludvik Svoboda; federal premier, Lubomir Strougal.

Although Czechoslovakia's slow progress toward the normalization of its international affairs continued, internal developments dominated events in 1975. Attention came to be focused on the resurgence of protest by the supporters of the 1968 reform movement, including the former party leader Alexander Dubcek.

A visit to Prague by the West German foreign minister, Hans-Dietrich Genscher, in March marked a further step in the slow improvement of relations between the two countries, although these suffered a check in August when the Czechoslovak authorities reacted angrily to a violation of the state's territory during the course of an attempt to smuggle out several East Germans by helicopter. The helicopter affair also cast a cloud over Czechoslovak-Austrian relations, much improved at the end of 1974 when the two countries signed an agreement covering compensation for Austrian properties nationalized by Czechoslovakia after World War II.

CZECHOSLOVAKIA

Education. (1973–74) Primary, pupils 1,890,081, teachers 96,781; secondary, pupils 127,451, teachers 7,829; vocational and teacher training, pupils 277,945, teachers 16,292; higher (including 10 main universities), students 135,874, teaching staff 16,628.

Finance. Monetary unit: koruna, with (Sept. 22, 1975) an official exchange rate of 5.97 koruny to U.S. $1 (12.25 koruny = £1 sterling) and a tourist rate of 11.06 koruny to U.S. $1 (21.42 koruny = £1 sterling). Budget (1973 est.): revenue 242,258,000,000 koruny; expenditure 237.2 billion koruny.

Foreign Trade. (1973) Imports 35,805,000,000 koruny; exports 35,322,000,000 koruny. Import sources: U.S.S.R. 30%; East Germany 13%; Poland 8%; Hungary 6%; West Germany 6%. Export destinations: U.S.S.R. 32%; East Germany 11%; Poland 10%; West Germany 6%; Hungary 5%. Main exports: machinery 37%; iron and steel 10%; motor vehicles 9%; chemicals 7%; metal ores 5%.

Transport and Communications. Roads (1973) 143,974 km. (including 82 km. expressways). Motor vehicles in use (1973): passenger 1,192,760; commercial 226,499. Railways (1973): 13,293 km. (including 2,659 km. electrified); traffic 19,278,000,000 passenger-km., freight (1974) 67,949,000,000 net ton-km. Air traffic (1974): 1,282,600,000 passenger-km.; freight 18,144,000 net ton-km. Navigable inland waterways (1972) 483 km. Shipping (1974): merchant vessels 100 gross tons and over 13; gross tonnage 116,148. Telephones (Dec. 1973) 2,354,000. Radio licenses (Dec. 1973) 3,793,000. Television licenses (Dec. 1973) 3,404,000.

Agriculture. Production (in 000; metric tons; 1974; 1973 in parentheses): wheat *c.* 5,000 (4,646); barley *c.* 2,950 (*c.* 2,962); oats *c.* 620 (*c.* 740); rye *c.* 660 (690); corn *c.* 750 (619); potatoes 4,522 (5,087); sugar, raw value *c.* 750 (*c.* 714); beef and veal (1973) *c.* 372, (1972) 379; pork *c.* 668 (666). Livestock (in 000; Jan. 1974): cattle 4,556; pigs 6,266; sheep 842; poultry 37,672.

Industry. Index of industrial production (1970 = 100): (1974) 140; (1973) 132. Fuel and power (in 000; metric tons; 1974): coal 27,972; brown coal 82,790; crude oil 148; manufactured gas (cu.m.) 7,689,000; electricity (kw-hr.) 55,920,000. Production (in 000; metric tons; 1974): iron ore (30% metal content) 1,689; pig iron 9,032; steel 13,868; cement 8,967; sulfuric acid 1,211; fertilizers (nutrient content; 1973–74) nitrogenous 424, phosphate 336; cotton yarn 125; cotton fabrics (m.) 620,000; woolen fabrics (m.) 57,000; rayon and acetate yarn and fibres 71; nylon, etc., yarn and fibres 48; passenger cars (units) 169; commercial vehicles (units) 64. Dwelling units completed (1974) 124,000.

CZECHOSLOVAK NEWS AGENCY/KEYSTONE

Gustav Husak signs the constitutional act which elevated him to the presidency of Czechoslovakia on May 29.

At the end of November 1974 the plenum of the party's Central Committee signaled the sensitivity of the authorities toward imported inflation, especially through higher oil prices. The increase in the price of Soviet oil, which came into effect on Jan. 1, 1975, added to this pressure, since a substantial proportion of Czechoslovakia's energy needs were met by the Soviet Union. Czechoslovakia's trade with the West was growing, and the ratio between the Council for Mutual Economic Assistance (Comecon) countries and the West was down to about 2:1. Czechoslovak imports from the West exceeded exports, however, so the country faced a growing deficit.

The resurgence of protests by the ousted leaders of the 1968 reform movement opened with the publication in the left-wing Italian weekly *Giorni-Vie Nuove* of a long interview given by Josef Smrkovsky prior to his death in January 1974. The interview, which revealed little that was new, induced the Czechoslovak authorities to launch an attack on Smrkovsky's memory. A few weeks later, the publication, in the West, of a lengthy document by Dubcek resulted in a violent personal attack on him by Gustav Husak (*see* BIOGRAPHY). Dubcek's protest—a letter to the Federal Assembly dated October 1974—dealt with the extraordinary surveillance of him by the security organs and with the failures of the present leadership.

This challenge formed the background to Husak's elevation to the presidency of the republic, which he combined with the post of secretary of the party. The ailing Ludvik Svoboda was removed from office on May 29. Husak's succession was evidently not entirely acceptable to the hard-line faction in the Czechoslovak party, however. The unusually fulsome terms used by

Andrey Kirilenko, the Soviet delegate to the 30th anniversary celebration of the country's liberation, in his praise of Husak were generally interpreted as an expression of Soviet support.

Husak made some concessions to the hard-liners, and the publication of Dubcek's letter was followed by a spate of house searches and confiscations of documents, directed against 1968 reformers. The philosopher Karel Kosik wrote of his despair to Jean-Paul Sartre, the French writer, complaining especially that the Czechoslovak authorities had illegally confiscated books, papers, and manuscripts. It appeared, however, that the Prague authorities were most concerned to prevent the emergence in the West of a lengthy analysis of the political situation in the country, with proposals for improvement, which had been prepared by Zdenek Mlynar, another 1968 reformer, for circulation at the planned conference of European Communist parties. Several parties had expressed their continued support for the ideas of 1968, and Mlynar's document could have proved embarrassing to the Czechoslovak leadership.

Despite a visit to Prague by Msgr. Agostino Casaroli, generally termed the Vatican's foreign minister, during which he negotiated over the position of the Roman Catholic Church, the campaign against religion was maintained with unabated force, especially in Slovakia. (GEORGE SCHÖPFLIN)

[972.B.2.c]

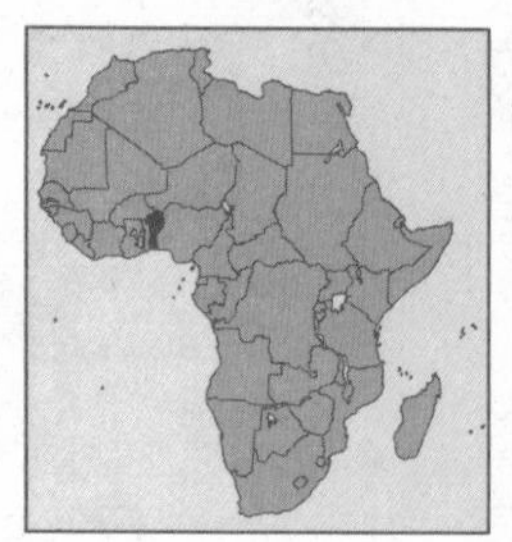

Dahomey

A republic of West Africa, Dahomey (renamed People's Republic of Benin from Nov. 30, 1975) is located north of the Gulf of Guinea and is bounded by Togo, Upper Volta, Niger, and Nigeria. Area: 43,475 sq.mi. (112,600 sq.km.). Pop. (1974 est.): 3,029,000, mainly Dahomean and allied tribes. Cap.: Porto-Novo (pop., 1972 est., 100,000). Largest city: Cotonou (pop., 1972 est., 175,000). Language: French and local dialects. Religion: mainly animist, with Christian and Muslim minorities. President in 1975, Lieut. Col. Mathieu Kerekou.

President Kerekou's regime celebrated its third anniversary in late 1975, a record in longevity under Dahomey's conditions of chronic instability. On November 30, a year after the proclamation of "Marxist-Leninist scientific socialism" as Dahomey's guiding principle and the reorganization of the government under a six-man Politburo and a 70-man National Council of the Revolution, the country's name was changed to the People's Republic of Benin.

In January 1975 the government claimed to have foiled an attempted coup instigated, it was said, by Capt. Janvier Assogba, minister of public service and of labour. Accused also of having sought to defame Kerekou, Assogba in a report made to Dahomey's inspector general of finances had questioned the integrity of the president, who he alleged had diverted to his own use a large sum earmarked for purchase of supplies. Assogba and six others were condemned to death in March.

On June 20 Capt. Michel Aikpe, minister of the interior, was killed by members of the presidential guard. The official report was that he had been discovered in the arms of the president's wife. Afterward, troops had to suppress demonstrations at Cotonou and at Abomey and to impose a curfew. A wave of strikes followed, and the curfew was not lifted for a month. Though the government was able to control the situation, opposition regrouped abroad under the Liberation Front for the Rehabilitation of Dahomey. (PHILIPPE DECRAENE)

DAHOMEY

Education. (1971–72) Primary, pupils 186,000, teachers (1970–71) 3,941; secondary, pupils 27,000, teachers (1970–71) 505; vocational, pupils 2,000, teachers (1968–69) 102; teacher training, students 2,553; higher, students 582, teaching staff 109.

Finance. Monetary unit: CFA franc, with (Sept. 22, 1975) a parity of CFA Fr. 50 to the French franc and free rate of CFA Fr. 227.70 to U.S. $1 (CFA Fr. 471.75 = £1 sterling). Budget (1974 est.): receipts CFA Fr. 12,485,000,000; expenditure CFA Fr. 13,572,000,000.

Foreign Trade. (1973) Imports CFA Fr. 26,570,000,000; exports CFA Fr. 10,020,000,000. Import sources (1972): France 40%; U.S. 7%; West Germany 6%; The Netherlands 6%; U.K. 6%. Export destinations (1972): France 37%; West Germany 16%; The Netherlands 14%. Main exports (1971): palm products 34%; cocoa 24%; cotton 19%.

Agriculture. Production (in 000; metric tons; 1974; 1973 in parentheses): sorghum 70 (64); corn (1973) *c.* 200, (1972) *c.* 170; cassava (1973) *c.* 550, (1972) *c.* 750; yams (1973) *c.* 540, (1972) *c.* 524; dry beans *c.* 25 (*c.* 17); peanuts *c.* 53 (*c.* 42); palm kernels *c.* 67 (*c.* 65); palm oil *c.* 47 (*c.* 45); coffee (1973) *c.* 2, (1972) 1.2; cotton, lint *c.* 21 (17). Livestock (in 000; 1974): sheep *c.* 690; cattle *c.* 750; goats *c.* 700; pigs *c.* 430.

Czechoslovakian Literature: *see* Literature

Dairy Products: *see* Agriculture and Food Supplies

Dams: *see* Engineering Projects

Dance

An institutional event, highlighted by a gala celebration, constituted a newsworthy occasion on the U.S. dance scene in 1975. The American Ballet Theatre celebrated its 35th birthday. In a nation that until recently had never funded the arts this internationally famous troupe had survived financial vicissitudes, even disbanding, to reach a position as one of the world's major ballet companies. Lucia Chase, its patroness from the start and its co-director (with Oliver Smith), presided over a year highlighted by birthday performances featuring the newest stars and illustrious returnees. At the first of its galas, the young prima ballerina Cynthia Gregory, who later left the company, was accompanied in the Rose Adagio from *The Sleeping Beauty* by veterans Igor Youskevitch and André Eglevsky and not-so-veteran Scott Douglas in a staging by 71-year-old Anton Dolin (all four gentlemen onetime premiers danseurs with the company). Nora Kaye, who had achieved overnight stardom in Antony Tudor's *Pillar of Fire* (1942), returned to act a scene with such members of the original cast as her partner, Hugh Laing, Miss Chase, and Tudor himself. In a scene from Jerome Robbins' *Fancy Free* (1944), danced by three boys of the current cast, a postscript was performed by the three original sailors—Robbins, John Kriza (*see* OBITUARIES), and Harold Lang. Agnes de Mille danced briefly in her own *Three Virgins and a Devil,* Sono Osato and Laing did the opening of Tudor's *Romeo and Juliet,* and there were appearances by Irina Baronova, Maria Karnilova, Karen Conrad, and others from the past. Current stars—among them Natalia Makarova, Mikhail Baryshnikov (*see* BIOGRAPHY), Ivan Nagy, and Fernando Bujones—performed. At a second gala in the summer of 1975 the major occasion was the first U.S. appearance, after a 15-year absence, of the great Cuban ballerina Alicia Alonso, who had risen from corps de ballet to prima ballerina with the American Ballet Theatre and who currently headed the Ballet Nacional de Cuba.

During the year the American Ballet Theatre presented new ballets, new productions, and revivals. The three-act *Raymonda* was staged by Rudolf Nureyev to music of Glazunov and with decor by Nicholas Georgiadis. Premieres included Tudor's *The Leaves Are Fading* to music of Antonín Dvořák, setting by Ming Cho Lee, and costumes by Patricia Zipprodt, and *Epilogue* by John Neumeier to music of Gustav Mahler, especially for Makarova and Erik Bruhn. First U.S. productions included Tudor's *Shadowplay,* with music of Charles Koechlin and decor by Michael Annals, and Glen Tetley's *Gemini,* with music by Hans Werner Henze and scenery and costumes by Nadine Baylis. Revivals presented were Robbins' *Les Noces* (Igor Stravinsky) and *Le Jeune Homme et la Mort,* with book and design by Jean Cocteau, choreography by Roland Petit, and the music of Bach.

The New York City Ballet, directed by George Balanchine, featured a Ravel festival celebrating the 100th anniversary of the birth of composer Maurice Ravel. Thirteen world premieres and Balanchine's long-popular *La Valse* were produced. Choreographers were Balanchine, Robbins, John Taras, and Jacques d'Amboise. Among the premieres were *L'Enfant et les Sortilèges, Sonatine,* and *Le Tombeau de Couperin* (Balanchine) and *Concerto in G* and *Une Barque sur l'Océan* (Robbins). During the company's summer season at Saratoga Springs, N.Y., another new Balanchine ballet, *The Steadfast Tin Soldier,* had its premiere.

The City Center Joffrey Ballet, which has an authorized (by the choreographer) production of Kurt Jooss's award-winning (1932) *The Green Table* in its repertory, added another Jooss classic, *The Big City,* to its repertory in a production supervised by Jooss. Novelties included Twyla Tharp's *Deuce Coupe II,* a new version of *Deuce Coupe* (which originally had combined the Tharp and Joffrey dancers), with an all-Joffrey cast. The live-graffiti painters were eliminated but the music of the Beach Boys was retained. Other productions included John Cranko's *Jeu de Cartes* (Stravinsky) and his *Opus I* (Webern); a new staging of Tudor's *Offenbach in the Underworld;* a new ballet, *Five Dances,* choreographed by company-principal Christian Holder (to music of Rachmaninoff); and a U.S. bicentennial production, *Drums, Dreams and Banjos,* choreographed by the troupe's principal choreographer, Gerald Arpino, to music of Stephen Foster (arranged by Peter Link).

MARTHA SWOPE

Erik Bruhn and Natalia Makarova in the sombre elegance of "Epilogue."

Among other ballet troupes producing special ballets on the eve of the U.S. bicentennial were the Pittsburgh Ballet Theatre with a revival of Ruth Page's classic *Frankie and Johnny,* Nicolas Petrov's new *Steel Concerto,* and Stuart Sebastian's new *Winterset* (based on the Maxwell Anderson play). The Houston Ballet produced three ballets comprising *Texas Trilogy—Allen's Landing* (revised from a 1974 preview), based on the founding of Houston and choreographed by James Clouser; Ruthanna Boris' *Galveston Suite* to music of Texas-born Scott Joplin; and Jan Stockman Simonds' *Moonscape,* based on radio transmissions from the Moon recorded by the National Aeronautics and Space Administration and incorporated into the score and adapted NASA designs for a Moon-landing aircraft.

Another anniversary eve celebration was that heralding the 50th anniversary of the Martha Graham Dance Company, which had its inception in 1926. The Graham gala, held at Broadway's Uris Theater in New

NORDISK PRESSEFOTO/PICTORIAL PARADE

The Royal Danish Ballet offered a lyrical ballet based on Vivaldi's "The Four Seasons." Shown is Mette Hønningen performing in "Winter."

York City, featured Miss Graham's first association with Nureyev in a work, *Lucifer,* created especially for him (title part) and Dame Margot Fonteyn, assisted by the Graham company. Seats for this performance, which benefited the company, were scaled as high as $10,000. Approximately $250,000 was taken in for the single performance. Celebrities included Mrs. Gerald Ford, a onetime Graham pupil, who appeared on stage with Miss Graham for a curtain call. The company's 1975 winter season repertory featured *Lucifer* (with Nureyev) and other Graham works with Nureyev as guest; revivals of two historic Graham solos, *Frontier* and *Lamentation;* and new Graham choreographies, *The Scarlet Letter* among them.

The first U.S. performance of Soviet emigrants Valery and Galina Panov took place at the Spectrum, a sports arena in Philadelphia, and the duo offered excerpts from *The Sleeping Beauty,* Boyarsky's *The Lady and the Hooligan,* and *Harlequinade,* supported by the Baltimore Symphony Orchestra with Robert Zeller conducting.

The San Francisco Ballet, one of the nation's oldest ballet troupes, was saved from extinction by the efforts of members of the company who performed in the streets of their city for money and pledges. The Chicago Ballet, headed by veteran dancer-choreographer Ruth Page, was established in a studio-theatre in Chicago. The Boston Ballet presented productions of Agnes de Mille's new *Summer* (music of Schubert) and *Carmina Burana* (Orff) by resident choreographer Lorenzo Monreal. The Eliot Feld Ballet featured two new ballets—*Mazurka* (Chopin) and *Excursions* (Samuel Barber). The Pennsylvania Ballet performed the first U.S. production of Dutch choreographer Hans van Manen's *Grosse Fuge* (Beethoven). The Cincinnati Ballet's new *With Timbrels and Dance Praise His Name* was choreographed by James Truitte and featured the black gospel singer Odetta. There were extensive tours by the Hartford (Conn.) Ballet and Ballet West (with headquarters in Salt Lake City, Utah). The Southeastern Regional Ballet Festival, which had launched the regional ballet movement with five companies that had increased to more than 200 by 1975, celebrated its 20th anniversary.

Modern dance events included national and international tours by the José Limón Dance Company directed by Ruth Currier; the Alvin Ailey City Center Dance Theater, continuing its choreographic tribute to the late composer Duke Ellington with *The Mooche,* choreographed by Ailey for an elaborate production designed by Rouben Ter-Arutunian and with costumes by Randy Barcelo; Pearl Lang's *The Possessed,* a dance fantasy-drama based on the play *The Dybbuk;* Pauline Koner's *Solitary Songs, Opus 3 and 4* (music of Luciano Berio), one of the features of the American Dance Festival at New London, Conn.; the Alwin Nikolais Dance Theatre in the new *Temple* and *Tribe,* with choreography, music, costumes, and lighting by Nikolais; Paul Taylor's troupe in the new *Esplanade;* and Merce Cunningham and his dancers in a series of *Events.*

The Dance Theatre of Harlem incorporated ballet and modern dance as well as Afro-American dance materials in productions of *Every Now and Then* by William Scott, Walter Raines's *After Corinth,* and a new version of Geoffrey Holder's *Dougla.* Nureyev, continuing his 1974 program of "Nureyev and Friends," added Fonteyn in 1975 to the "friends," and Dennis Wayne of the American Ballet Theatre launched a small group called Dancers as an outlet for some American Ballet Theatre performers in new roles and new ballets. There were seasons and tours by two "travesty" all-male troupes, the Trockadero Gloxinia Ballet Company and its new offshoot, Les Ballets Trockadero de Monte Carlo.

In the ethnic dance field, which saw concerts by companies and soloists representing dance traditions of many lands, the American-based EthnoAmerican Dance Theater, headed by Matteo, premiered a new work, *America Has Many Faces: A Dance Heritage,* as a bicentennial feature dedicated to the races making up the U.S.

Summertime dance festivals included the oldest, the Jacob's Pillow Dance Festival (with Norman Walker, choreographer-teacher, as the new director), the American Dance Festival, and the New York Dance Festival, free to the public, in Central Park. Awards included the Capezio Dance Award given to Robert Irving, conductor for the New York City Ballet Orchestra and the Martha Graham company; and the Dance Magazine Awards, to Cynthia Gregory, Alvin Ailey, and Arthur Mitchell. New Broadway musicals with major dance materials included *A Chorus Line* (Michael Bennett), *Chicago* (Bob Fosse), and *The Wiz* (George Faison). The ten-volume *Dictionary Catalog of the Dance Collection, Performing Arts Research Center,* published, with the help of grants, by the New York Public Library in October 1974, was a major addition to dance literature.

(WALTER TERRY)

CENTRAL PRESS/PICTORIAL PARADE

Doreen Wells emerged from retirement in January to perform the "Nutcracker" with Patrice Bart in a Royal Festival Ballet production.

Worldwide inflation and economic recession affecting life generally in 1974–75 tended to hit dance more severely than other art forms. In Britain, as elsewhere, the future of many companies seemed uncertain although there was still considerable creative activity in the smaller and more contemporary companies. Among the larger classical companies it was a year of playing safe. There were no major creations for the Royal Ballet's Covent Garden company although there were two new works from Kenneth MacMillan—*Elite Syncopations* (Scott Joplin) and *The Four Seasons* (Verdi)—and a revival, *Symphony* (Shostakovich). Hans van Manen created his first work for the company, *Four Schumann Pieces* (Schumann), and Jerome Robbins revived his *The Concert* (Chopin). The Royal Ballet's smaller company (formerly "the new group") enlarged its personnel so it could tour with some of the smaller classics—*Giselle* and *Coppélia* revived by Peter Wright. Other works taken into the repertory included Jack Carter's *Shukumei* (Stomu Yamashita), Christopher Bruce's *Unfamiliar Playground* (Hymas/Hodgson), Peter Wright's *Arpège* (Boieldieu), and *El Amor Brujo* (Manuel de Falla).

The London Festival Ballet concentrated its efforts and finance into a very spectacular production, designed by Nicholas Georgiadis, of Rudolf Nureyev's version of the Petipa/Tchaikovsky *Sleeping Beauty,* which brought enormous success to the company during its London season at The Coliseum as well as on its first trans-Australian tour with Nureyev as guest. It was with Festival Ballet at The Coliseum that the ex-Kirov dancers Galina and Valery Panov made their first London appearances. Festival Ballet appeared regularly in two other London theatres—the Royal Festival Hall and the New Victoria Theatre—as well as touring the British provinces.

Of the smaller companies, Ballet Rambert, Britain's oldest company (founded 1926), formed an almost entirely new repertory under its new director, John Chesworth, a repertory for an open-stage at the Round House as well as for a proscenium at Sadler's Wells. New creations by present and former members of the company included Chesworth's *Project 6354/9116 Mk2* (Martti Vuorenjuuri), Jonathan Taylor's *Almost an Echo* (Milhaud), Joseph Scoglio's *The Night Dances* (Downes), Judith Marcuse's *baby* (John Lambert), and Bruce's *Ancient Voices of Children* (George Crumb). New works from other British choreographers included Lindsay Kemp's *The Parades Gone By* (popular songs) and Robert North's *Running Figures* (Geoffrey Burgon). American contributions were, from Manuel Alum, *Escaras* (Krautze/Szalonek) and from Cliff Keuter, *Table* (Ravel) and *Musique di Taverni* (Couperin). Ballet Rambert also made extensive provincial and European tours.

That Britain's first modern dance company, based on the Martha Graham school, had reached maturity in only five years became apparent when the London Contemporary Dance Theatre took Graham's *Diversion of Angels* (Dello Joio) into its repertory—and triumphed. This popular company had, through a series of school and company workshops, developed a number of choreographers from within its own ranks. Artistic director Robert Cohan created several works including *Waterless Method of Swimming Instruction* (Robert Downes), *No-Man's-Land* (Barry Guy), and *Masque of Separation* (Burt Alcantara). Creations by dancers in the company were: Robert North's *Troy-Game* (Downes/Batacuda music) and *Still Life* (Downes), Siobhan Davies' *The Calm* (Geoffrey Burgon), Micha Bergese's *Hinterland* (various), and Cathy Lewis' *Extinction* (Edgar Frosse).

The economic situation curtailed any major developments in Britain's three main regional companies and the first, the Scottish Ballet, was forced to postpone an important new two-act work until 1976. However, it toured Spain in 1975 with Nureyev as guest in Bournonville's *La Sylphide.* The repertory of one-act works was enlarged with Harold King's *Intimate Pages* (Janacek), Jack Carter's *The Dancing Floor* (Subotnick), and a revival of Andrée Howard's *La Fête Étrange* (Fauré). The Scottish Ballet's splinter group, Ballet for Scotland, toured smaller Scottish towns and villages with a repertory including Anton Dolin's *Pas de Quatre* (Caesar Pugni), John Cranko's *Beauty and the Beast* (Ravel), Maurice Béjart's *Sonate à Trois* (Bartok), and Bournonville's *La Ventana* (Lumbye). The principal creations for Manchester's Northern Dance Theatre were Laverne Meyer's three-act *Aladdin* (Ernest Tomlinson) and a one-act *Three Dances from the Soldier's Tale* (Stravinsky); Jonathan Thorpe created *Stamping Ground* (Bach) and *Triptych* (Beethoven). Laverne Meyer, founder of the Northern Dance Theatre, resigned in the summer of 1975, and the artistic direction of the company was taken over by a quorum.

After a rather checkered start, Britain's youngest regional company, the Welsh Dance Theatre, settled down in Cardiff under the artistic direction of William Louther who mounted his version of *The Soldier's Tale* (Stravinsky) and *Lyric Fantasies* (various composers). The main company toured Wales and gave seasons in Cardiff's Sherman Theatre; it also broke up into smaller groups for lecture and demonstration programs for educational centres.

The New London Ballet, a group formed around Galina Samsova and André Prokovsky, toured extensively overseas and through the English provinces with occasional London seasons at Sadler's Wells. Prokovsky himself created a number of works for the repertory including *Vespri* (Verdi), *Folk Songs* (Berio), and *Simorgh* (Tjeknavorian). Other creations included Peter Darrell's *Othello* (Liszt), Jack Carter's *Pythoness Ascendant* (Berio), Ronald Hynd's *Valses Nobles et Sentimentales* (Ravel), and Ashley Killar's *Washington Square* (Bruckner).

The Irish Ballet Company, now with grant-aid guaranteed for five years, extended its work beyond its home base at the Cork Opera House with seasons in Dublin and other larger Irish towns. For its second season the repertory was enlarged with David Gordon's *First Impressions* (Mozart), Domy Reiter-Soffer's *Other Days* (Downes) and *Love Raker* (Isan Yun), Patrick Hurd's *Flights of Fancy* (Bach), and Joan Denise Moriarty's *West Cork Ballad* (Sean O'Reida). Anton Dolin revived his *Pas de Quatre.*

On the continent the Ballet of the Paris Opéra, for the first time in its history, put on the full-length *Sleeping Beauty* (Tchaikovsky) based by producer

MARTHA SWOPE

The incomparable Nureyev in the title role of "Lucifer," produced for the 50th anniversary celebration of the Martha Graham Dance Company in New York City.

THE TIMES

The Zula Dance Company performing in the African musical "Kwa Zulu" in London.

Alicia Alonso on current Soviet productions. Continuing its policy of developing a repertory mixing classics with contemporary forms, the Opéra commissioned a work from Glen Tetley, *Tristan* (Henze), for Nureyev who also revived Petipa's *La Bayadère* (Ludwig Minkus) for the company. Roland Petit returned to his former company to create *Symphonie Fantastique* (Berlioz) and revive his *Le Loup* (Dutilleux). The Opéra now had a second company, Troupe Favart, whose repertory included some Stravinsky works—Janine Charrat's *Jeux de Cartes* and Michel Fokine's *Petrushka*.

France has several regional companies. Roland Petit developed his Ballets de Marseille and created a number of new works including a full-evening work based on Proust, *Les Intermittences du Coeur* (various composers), and a Bizet program—*Jeux d'Enfants, Variations Chromatiques, L'Arlésienne,* and *Carmen;* he also mounted a modern version of *Coppélia* (Delibes). In Angers the Ballet Théâtre Contemporain increased its repertory with Brian Macdonald's *Rags* (various composers), Paul Sanasardo's *Saints and Lovers* (Mayuzumi/Penderecki), Lar Lubovitch's *Un Poco piu ma non troppo* (various composers), René Goliard's *Mobilissimo* (Ives), Oscar Araiz' *Agitor* (Groupe Arco Iris), and Édouard Saint-Denis' *Intersection II* (Thadeus Baird).

In Denmark the most important additions to the repertory of the Royal Danish Ballet were Flemming Flindt's *Dreamland* (Koppel) and John Neumeier's version of *Romeo and Juliet* (Prokofiev). In Sweden the Göteborg Ballet emerged as an important regional company for which its director, Elsa Marianne von Rosen, revived the Bournonville classics—*La Sylphide* and *Napoli*—and created *Pictures at an Exhibition* (quasi-Mussorgsky); other creations included Ulf Gadd's *Maison de Fous* (Viking Dahl) and Flemming Flindt's *Trio* (Per Nordgaard).

In The Netherlands the Dutch National Ballet continued to develop its brand of mixed repertory with revivals of *Swan Lake* and *La Bayadère,* ballets by Balanchine, and creations by its three resident choreographers, Rudi van Dantzig, Hans van Manen, and Toer van Schayk, all of whom combined in one work, *Collective Symphony* (Stravinsky); van Manen also created *Quintet* (Mozart) and van Schayk, *Eight Madrigals* (Gesualdo). The other major Dutch company, the Netherlands Dance Theatre, concentrated on American choreographers: Louis Falco's *Caterpillar* (Berio) and *Eclipse* (Alcantara), Jennifer Muller's *American Beauty Rose* (Alcantara) and full-evening *Strangers* (Alcantara), and Margot Sappington's *Juice* (Kamen).

In West Germany, where nearly every town of any size appeared to have a dance company connected with one of the many opera houses, the main interest lay in Stuttgart and Hamburg. The Stuttgart Ballet, in addition to preserving John Cranko's works, enlarged its repertory with works by its new director, Glen Tetley: *Daphnis and Chloë* (Ravel) and revivals of *Mythical Hunters* (Partos) and *Laborintus* (Berio). For the Hamburg State Opera Ballet John Neumeier made a new version of *The Nutcracker* (Tchaikovsky) and a new work, *Third Symphony* (Mahler). The principal work for the West Berlin Opera ballet was Tatyana Gzovsky and Nicholas Beriosoff's production of the full-length *Raymonda* (Glazunov). The most important event for the Frankfurt Ballet was a Schoenberg program—Alfonso Cata's *In der Zeit* and *Verklärte Nacht* and John Butler's *Epochen* and *Cult of the Night.* (PETER WILLIAMS)

See also Music; Theatre.

[625]

Danish Literature: *see* Literature

Darts: *see* Target Sports

Deaths: *see* Demography; *see also biographies of prominent persons who died in 1975, listed under People of the Year beginning on page 64.*

Debts, National: *see* Economy, World

Defense

The most dramatic strategic events of 1975 took place in Southeast Asia, where Communists came to power in South Vietnam, Cambodia, and Laos and the long

U.S. involvement in Indochina finally ended. The speed of the North Vietnamese advance in South Vietnam during March–April took most observers by surprise, since the two sides had seemed to have relatively balanced forces. But the Northern offensive, using heavy artillery, tanks, and motorized transport, was a classic example of blitzkrieg—lightning war—in which the attacker builds up a momentum that catches the defender off balance and prevents him from regrouping in new defensive positions quickly enough to stop the advance.

Although the U.S. Congress had considerably reduced the military aid appropriations for South Vietnam requested by the Ford administration, U.S. military assistance was still substantial. It had enabled South Vietnam to field an army of 450,000 men, formed into 11 infantry divisions and 1 airborne division, 2 independent infantry regiments, 3 independent armoured battalions, and 18 armoured cavalry squadrons, supported by 14 independent artillery battalions, as well as a marine division of 15,000 men. Equipment included 600 M-48 medium and M-41 light tanks, 1,000 armoured personnel carriers, 1,200 105-mm. and 300 155-mm. howitzers, TOW antitank guided weapons, and antiaircraft guns. The Air Force of 60,000 men had 509 combat aircraft, mostly geared to ground support operations, with 72 F-5A fighter/ground attack aircraft, 220 A-37B and 60 A-1H/J fighter-bombers, and 56 gunships. Helicopters included 625 Bell UH-1s and 60 CH-47s. The 40,000-man Navy was mainly tied down in antiguerrilla operations in the South, especially the Mekong Delta. Nevertheless, the South Vietnamese Army and Air Force, if properly commanded, trained, and manned, should have been able to put up a sustained resistance.

The North had an army of 685,000, composed of 24 infantry divisions of 8,000–10,000 men each, plus 3 training divisions and 10 independent infantry regiments. The artillery command comprised ten regiments. Soviet-supplied equipment included 900 T-34, T-54, and T-59 medium tanks, 800 85-mm., 122-mm., 130-mm., and 152-mm. guns and howitzers, Sagger antitank guided weapons, and antiaircraft guns. The Air Force, with 12,000 men and 268 combat aircraft, was geared to air defense; its complement included 70 MiG-21F/PF and 80 MiG-19 interceptors and 110 MiG-15/17 fighter-bombers. In addition, the North Vietnamese had invested heavily in a road and pipeline network through North Vietnam and eastern Laos that enabled them to move supplies and troops to the central highlands faster than South Vietnam could move forces from Saigon.

The initial North Vietnamese thrust came in March, with five divisions, supported by long-range artillery and tanks, advancing against 45,000 South Vietnamese troops in the highlands. They struck first at the roads into the highlands, feinted at the regional headquarters in Pleiku to draw reserves out of the provincial capital of Ban Me Thuot, then took the capital in a three-day siege, leaving the South Vietnamese without enough troops to retake the capital or open the blocked roads. The South Vietnamese Air Force, handicapped by combat losses and maintenance problems, was unable to bring in reinforcements. Pres. Nguyen Van Thieu therefore made the decision to withdraw from the highlands and concentrate his defenses in the area north of Saigon, from the Cambodian border to the coast.

South Vietnamese hopes for an orderly retreat that would allow regrouping in a more defensible position proved futile. Refugees crowded the roads to the south and to the coast, frequently coming under heavy North Vietnamese fire as they turned the retreat into a rout. Da Nang, the country's second largest city, was overwhelmed by refugees and by some 100,000 government soldiers whose units had disintegrated. (*See* REFUGEES: *Special Report*.) By mid-April the North Vietnamese had advanced to within 50 mi. of Saigon, taking, in the process, the major ports along the coast, including the former U.S. bases at Cam Ranh Bay and Phan Thiet, where the government had planned to anchor the coastal flank of its new defense line. By this time the morale of the South Vietnamese forces had collapsed completely.

Rough estimates were that in the first four weeks of fighting South Vietnam lost six divisions and vast quantities of equipment, leaving only seven divisions and a handful of combat aircraft to defend Saigon against an estimated 21 North Vietnamese divisions. A South Vietnamese attempt to make a stand at Xuan Loc failed; the defenders were encircled and destroyed by North Vietnamese units that outnumbered them by four to one and so could afford a short battle of attrition. Simultaneously, the Communists brought the major South Vietnamese air base at Bien Hoa under artillery fire and increased their pressure from the Mekong Delta. The remaining government forces crumbled rapidly, and on April 30 the North Vietnamese occupied Saigon. The value of U.S. equipment captured by North Vietnam was estimated at about $2 billion. The victory was a remarkable achievement for North Vietnam's defense minister, Gen. Vo Nguyen Giap, and his deputy chief of staff commanding forces in the South, Tran Van Tra. (*See* VIETNAM.)

The capture of Saigon followed by some two weeks the fall of neighbouring Cambodia to the forces of the Communist-dominated Khmer Rouge. These forces totaled approximately 80,000 men, organized in some four divisions and three independent regiments, equipped with Soviet, Chinese, and captured American weapons and supported by about one North Vietnamese division. The Cambodian government of Pres. Lon Nol was able to muster, on paper, a 200,000-man army of five light infantry divisions, one armoured and ten infantry brigades, and one artillery brigade with about 200 105-mm. howitzers. The 9,500-man Air Force had 64 combat aircraft equipped for ground-support operations. In practice, however, these forces lacked the organization, discipline, morale, and leadership of their opponents. After a long siege, the Khmer

"No, no, . . . it's gray and cigar-shaped with a little periscope on top . . ."

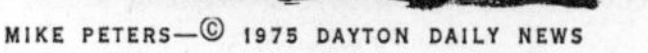
MIKE PETERS—© 1975 DAYTON DAILY NEWS

Rouge entered the capital of Phnom Penh on April 17. (*See* CAMBODIA.)

In contrast to the bloody fighting in South Vietnam and Cambodia, the Communist takeover of Laos was accomplished largely through political means, as the anti-Communists in the Cabinet yielded to the Communists to avoid a North Vietnamese reinforcement of the Communist Pathet Lao that would have left the government forces outnumbered. These comprised an army of 50,000 men, reorganized into 7 infantry brigades with 24 battalions and 5 artillery battalions, plus 50 infantry battalions under military regions, and an air force of 2,000 manning the 75 light ground-attack aircraft. Against these, the Pathet Lao could muster 35,000 men, including dissident neutralists, with some artillery, supported by North Vietnamese forces in the border areas. (*See* LAOS.) The fall of Laos seemed a partial vindication of the so-called domino theory, namely that if South Vietnam fell to the Communists the whole of Indochina would fall. It was by no means clear, however, whether the North Vietnamese victory in South Vietnam and the Communist takeovers in Cambodia and Laos meant that other countries in Southeast Asia would become Communist, or what effect this would have on U.S. interests or on the power balance at large.

In keeping with its traditional policy of bowing before whatever political force was dominant in the area, Thailand moved to placate the new rulers of Indochina by requesting the U.S. to withdraw most of the 23,000 servicemen and 350 planes still stationed there. Thai armed forces were significant numerically, though their combat value was questionable. The Army of 135,000 was divided into five infantry divisions, including four tank battalions, plus two independent regimental combat teams; equipment included 195 light tanks, 200 armoured personnel carriers, and 130 105-mm. and 12 155-mm. howitzers. The 42,000-man Air Force had 110 combat aircraft, including 10 F-5A fighters and 10 counterinsurgency squadrons, with 30 F-5Es, 20 AU-23 counterinsurgency aircraft, and 25 Bell UH-1H helicopters on order from the U.S. The 27,000 navy personnel included 9,000 Marines.

An odd footnote to the end of the 30-year war in Indochina came in May, when Cambodian forces seized the U.S. freighter "Mayaguez" in the Gulf of Thailand. After diplomatic action had failed to secure release of the ship and its crew, U.S. Pres. Gerald Ford ordered in a Marine and naval task force. Some 15 servicemen were killed, 50 wounded, and 3 missing in the subsequent action. The ship and crew were recovered, although the Cambodians later claimed that the crew would have been released in any case. Although criticized as an overreaction, this decisive intervention did go some way toward restoring U.S. diplomatic and military credibility among its allies.

FAR EAST

The strategic picture in the Far East was significantly altered by the events in Indochina. Although it seemed clear that the U.S. would never again fight a guerrilla war in Asia, and despite the decision to phase out the U.S.-founded Southeast Asia Treaty Organization (SEATO), the U.S. remained a powerful force in the Pacific. It had 16,000 men in the Philippines, 40,000 in South Korea, 51,000 in Japan and Okinawa, 11,000 in Guam, and 5,000 in Taiwan, plus the 27,000 men, 3 aircraft carriers, 2 cruisers, 20 destroyers, and support vessels of the 7th Fleet. Paradoxically, China seemed likely to regard continued U.S. involvement in the Pacific as an essential counterweight to the U.S.S.R.

Chinese defense policy continued to operate at the two extremes of nuclear deterrence against strategic attack by the U.S.S.R. and "people's war," intended to deter or repel any land invasion by mass mobilization of the country's population. China's nuclear program made little progress. An underground test of a nuclear device, the first in over a year, was held at the Lop Nor testing site in October. The stockpile of nuclear weapons, both fission and fusion, remained at about 200–300. A multistage intercontinental ballistic missile (ICBM) with a range of 3,500 mi., able to reach Moscow and most of Asia, had been ready for deployment since 1974; the longer-range (8,000-mi.) ICBM under development for some time still had not been tested. Operational forces included 20–30

The new RAF Rapier missile system on station in West Germany. It is intended principally for airfield defense.

THE TIMES

KEYSTONE

The General Dynamics YF-16 combat fighter aircraft emerged as the new U.S. choice following an intense selection process.

intermediate range ballistic missiles (IRBMs) with a range of 1,750 mi. and 50 medium range ballistic missiles (MRBMs) with a range of 700 mi. There were also about 60 Tu-16 medium bombers with a radius of action of 2,000 mi., although their chances of penetrating the U.S.S.R.'s air defense network remained doubtful. For tactical missions large numbers of nuclear-capable fighter-bombers were available.

The 2.8 million-man People's Liberation Army remained essentially a defensive force, although logistic capability was being improved and a proportion of the formations were being armed with modern weapons. Of a total of 162 divisions, 125 were infantry and only 7 were armoured. The PLA's equipment included 8,500 heavy and medium tanks; 3,600 armoured personnel carriers, and 15,000 guns, howitzers, and rocket launchers.

The shift of forces toward the Sino-Soviet border had ceased, and the major concentrations were in the northeast (Peking and Manchuria), the coastal provinces, and the Yangtze and Yellow River basins. Thus (excluding the 20 artillery divisions) in north and northeast China there were 55 divisions; in east and southeast China, 25 divisions; in south-central China, 21 divisions; in midwest China, 15 divisions; and in west and southwest China, 26 divisions. Communist Party control of the military was emphasized by the appointment of two civilians, Teng Hsiao-p'ing and Chang Ch'un-ch'iao, the first and second vice-premiers, as chief of the general staff and director of the general political department, respectively.

China's Air Force comprised 220,000 men and 3,800 combat aircraft, among them 60 Tu-16 and a few Tu-4 medium bombers; 400 light bombers; and 200 MiG-15, 1,500 MiG-17, 1,500 MiG-19, 50 MiG-21, and 400 Chinese-designed and built F-9 fighters. The Navy of 230,000, including 28,000 Marines and the Naval Air Force, had 4 Lutz-class destroyers (with more building) and 2 ex-Soviet Gordy-class destroyers, all with the Styx surface-to-surface missile (SSM), and 51 diesel fleet submarines. Air force and naval fighter planes were mostly integrated into an air-defense system providing a limited point defense of key urban and industrial areas, military installations, and advanced weapons complexes. Estimates of Chinese defense spending ranged from a low of U.S. $4 billion–$5 billion to a U.K. estimate of $10 billion–$12 billion. A decline in the level of weapons procurement had apparently occurred between 1971 and 1974, most dramatically after U.S. Pres. Richard Nixon's visit to Peking in 1972.

The forces of the other Asian powers seemed small by comparison, but they were probably adequate for self-defense and to counter internal threats. Japan's 1975–76 defense budget totaled 1,327,300,000,000 yen ($4,484,000,000), or only 0.9% of gross national product (GNP). It seemed certain to grow, however, and the possibility of a Japanese nuclear deterrent was beginning to be discussed publicly among the policy-making elite as the durability of the U.S. nuclear umbrella came into question. Existing Japanese conventional forces could offer only a limited defense. The 155,000-man Army could field 1 mechanized division and 12 infantry divisions of 7,000–9,000 men each, 1 tank, 1 airborne, 1 composite, 1 artillery, 1 helicopter, and 2 antiaircraft artillery brigades, plus 7 surface-to-air missile (SAM) groups. Armour was limited to 600 Type 61 medium tanks, 150 light tanks, and 460 armoured personnel carriers. The Air Force, with 42,000 men, had 445 combat aircraft, and the Navy, numbering 39,000 men, included a naval air arm of 2,200. The antisubmarine warfare (ASW) force was relatively small given Japan's extremely long and vulnerable sealanes.

With the death of Pres. Chiang Kai-shek, and with Taiwan's security becoming less vital to the U.S., it seemed possible that Taiwan and China might reach some form of accommodation. Taiwan's defense budget of NT$38 billion ($1 billion), representing 7.5% of GNP, provided substantial forces. Of the Army's 340,000 men, 80,000 were deployed on the offshore islands of Quemoy and Matsu. Armour included 1,620 medium and 625 light tanks. There were also two divisions of Marines, 35,000 strong, with M-47 medium tanks. The Air Force, with 82,000 men, had 216 combat aircraft.

North and South Korea preserved an armed and intensely hostile equilibrium, thanks to a U.S. guarantee that, as U.S. Secretary of Defense James Schlesinger made clear, included a U.S. intention to resort to the early use of tactical nuclear weapons if the North attacked the South. The 410,000-man Northern Army comprised 1 tank, 3 motorized, and 20 infantry divisions, plus 3 independent infantry brigades and 3 SAM brigades with 180 SA-2s. Armour included 1,000 medium and 130 light tanks. The Air Force of 40,000 had 588 combat aircraft, and naval forces included 8 submarines and 18 fast patrol boats

Approximate Strengths of Regular Armed Forces of the World

Country	Military personnel in 000s Army	Navy	Air force	Warships: Aircraft carriers/ cruisers*	Submarines†	Destroyers/ frigates	Total major surface combat vessels	Jet aircraft: Bombers‡	Fighters	Tanks§	Defense expenditure as % of GNP
I. NATO											
Belgium	62.7	4.2	20.1	—	—	—	—	90 FB	36	458	2.8
Canada	28.0	14.0	35.0	—	3	20	20	20 FB	44	330	2.0
Denmark	21.5	5.8	7.1	—	6	2	2	60 FB	40	200	2.3
France‖	331.5	69.0	102.0	2 CV, 2 CA	19, 4 SSBN	43	47	266 FB, 36 SB	135	950	3.4
Germany, West	345.0	39.0	111.0	—	13	23	23	402 FB	78	3,700	3.6
Greece	121.0	17.5	22.7	—	7	15	15	144 FB	52	860	4.3
Italy	306.5	44.5	70.0	3 CA	10	27	30	125 FB	164	1,300	2.8
Luxembourg	0.6	—	—	—	—	—	—	—	—	—	0.9
Netherlands, The	75.0	18.5	19.0	1 CA	6	17	18	108 FB	36	800	3.4
Norway	18.0	8.0	9.0	—	15	5	5	97 FB	16	116	3.2
Portugal	179.0	19.5	18.5	—	4	16	16	32 FB	25	100	6.8
Turkey	365.0	40.0	48.0	—	16	13	13	180 FB	52	1,500	3.7
United Kingdom	174.9	76.1¶	94.1	1 CV, 2 CVH, 2 CA	20, 8 N, 4 SSBN	70	75	138 FB, 95 B	135	900	5.2
United States	982.0¶	536.0	612.0	15 CV, 8 CVH, 27 CA	12, 64 N, 41 SSBN	137	187	1,400 FB, 463 SB	1,240	8,500	6.0
II. WARSAW PACT											
Bulgaria	120.0	10.0	22.0	—	4	—	—	72 FB	144	2,000	2.7
Czechoslovakia	155.0	—	45.0	—	—	—	—	168 FB	240	3,400	3.8
Germany, East	98.0	17.0	28.0	—	—	2	2	36 FB	294	2,000	5.4
Hungary	90.0	—	15.0	—	—	—	—	—	108	1,500	2.3
Poland	210.0	25.0	58.0	—	4	3	3	192 FB, 15 B	542	3,800	3.7
Romania	141.0	9.0	21.0	—	—	—	—	64 FB	180	1,800	1.6
U.S.S.R.	1,825.0	500.0	900.0	1 CV, 2 CVH, 31 CA	155, 34 N, 47 SSBN, 8 N/BMSS, 20 BMSS, 41 N/CMS, 25 CMS	97	131	100 SB, 700 B, 3,000 FB	4,000	40,000	10.5
III. OTHER EUROPEAN											
Albania	30.0	3.0	5.0	—	4	—	—	—	24	60	...
Austria	33.7	—	4.3	—	—	—	—	38 FB	—	320	1.0
Finland	30.3	3.0	3.0	—	—	3	3	—	47	...	1.4
Ireland	11.0	0.5	0.6	—	—	—	—	9 FB	—	—	1.1
Spain	220.0	46.6¶	35.7	1 CVH, 1 CA	8	23	25	18 FB	66	370	1.9
Sweden	55.7	15.0	13.0	—	22	13	13	150 FB	360	...	3.6
Switzerland	33.5	—	9.0	—	—	—	—	240 FB	36	450	1.8
Yugoslavia	190.0	20.0	20.0	—	5	1	1	120 FB	110	2,150	5.1
IV. MIDDLE EAST AND MEDITERRANEAN; SUB-SAHARAN AFRICA; LATIN AMERICA♀											
Algeria	55.0	3.5	4.5	—	—	—	—	100 FB, 25 B	35	400	4.6
Egypt	275.0	17.5	30.0	—	12	5	5	253 FB, 30 B	450	1,100	22.8
Iran	175.0	15.0	60.0	—	—	7	7	156 FB	—	1,160	9.0
Iraq	120.0	3.0	12.0	—	—	—	—	110 FB, 7 B	130	1,300	14.2
Israelδ	135.6/375.0	5.0/6.0	16.0/20.0	—	2	—	—	475 FB	—	2,700	32.0
Jordan	75.0	—	5.0	—	—	—	—	24 FB	18	440	14.2
Lebanon	14.0	—	1.0	—	—	—	—	13 FB	6	60	...
Libya	25.0	2.0	5.0	—	—	1	1	50 FB	32	345	6.8
Morocco	55.0	2.0	4.0	—	—	1	1	24 FB	20	145	3.2
Saudi Arabia	40.0	1.5	5.5	—	—	—	—	30 FB	35	175	15.0
Sudan	45.0	0.6	3.0	—	—	—	—	15 FB	18	130	4.3
Syria	150.0	2.5	25.0	—	—	—	—	140 FB	250	2,100	15.7
Ethiopia	41.0	1.5	2.3	—	—	—	—	19 FB, 4 B	—	12	3.0
Nigeria	200.0	3.0	5.0	—	—	1	1	21 FB	—	—	2.9
South Africa	38.0	4.0	8.5	—	3	8	8	160 FB, 17 B	65	161	3.2
Zaire	40.0	—	3.0	—	—	—	—	34 FB	—	—	2.0
Argentina	83.5	33.0¶	17.0	1 CVH, 3 CA	4	8	12	75 FB, 2 B	14	120	1.9
Brazil	170.0	49.5¶	35.0	1 CVH, 1 CA	8	14	16	—	16	150	1.3
Chile	40.0	21.8	12.0	3 CA	4	8	11	—	32	76	2.7
Colombia	50.0	8.0	6.3	—	2	6	6	—	18	—	0.8
Cuba	90.0	7.0	20.0	—	—	—	—	15 FB	160	600	6.2
Mexico	315.0	11.5	6.0	—	—	3	3	—	—	—	0.7
Peru	39.0	8.0	9.0	3 CL	4	7	10	24 B	42	260	2.4
V. FAR EAST AND OCEANIA♀											
Australia	31.3	16.2	21.6	1 CV	4	12	13	64 FB, 8 B	—	143	3.2
Bangladesh	30.0	0.5	5.5	—	—	—	—	—	14	—	...
Burma	153.0	7.0	7.0	—	—	2	2	—	—	—	2.9
Cambodia	80.0	—	—	—	—	—	—	—	—	—	...
China	2,800.0	230.0¶	220.0	—	51	16	16	500 FB, 520 B	3,650	8,500	...
India	826.0	30.0	100.0	1 CV, 2 CL	8	29	32	300 FB, 60 B	400	1,700	2.8
Indonesia	200.0	38.0¶	28.0	—	3	9	9	17 FB	—	—	3.2
Japan	155.0	39.0	42.0	—	15	45	45	150 FB	280	600	0.9
Korea, North	410.0	17.0	40.0	—	8	—	—	328 FB, 60 B	200	1,000	24.9
Korea, South	560.0	40.0¶	25.0	—	—	7	7	260 FB	—	1,000	4.2
Laos	50.0	—	2.0	—	—	—	—	—	—	—	11.0
Malaysia	51.0	4.8	5.3	—	—	2	2	20 FB	—	—	4.9
New Zealand	5.5	2.9	4.3	—	—	4	4	13 FB	—	—	1.7
Pakistan	365.0	10.0	17.0	—	3	8	8	260 FB, 10 B	—	950	7.6
Philippines	39.0	14.0¶	14.0	—	—	1	1	16 FB	20	—	3.6
Taiwan	375.0¶	37.0	82.0	—	2	18	18	100 FB	98	1,620	7.5
Thailand	135.0	27.0¶	42.0	—	—	7	7	10 FB	—	—	3.2
Vietnam, North□	685.0	3.0	12.0	—	—	—	—	110 FB, 8 B	150	900	21.5
Vietnam, South (1974)	465.0¶	40.0	60.0	—	—	9	9	132 FB	—	600	21.4

Note: Data exclude paramilitary, security, and irregular forces. Naval data exclude vessels of less than 100 tons standard displacement. Figures are for July 1975.
*Aircraft carriers (CV); helicopter carriers (CVH); heavy cruisers (CA); light cruisers (CL).
†Nuclear hunter-killers (N); ballistic missile submarines (SSBN); (nuclear/) ballistic missile submarines, short-range (BMSS, N/BMSS); (nuclear/) long-range cruise missile submarines, (CMS, N/CMS).
‡Medium and heavy bombers (B), fighter-bombers (FB), and strategic bombers (SB).
§Medium and heavy tanks (31 tons and over).
‖French forces were withdrawn from NATO in 1966, but France remains a member of NATO.
¶Includes Marines.
♀Sections IV and V list only those states with significant military forces.
δSecond figure is fully mobilized strength.
□Strength at cessation of hostilities, April 1975. Equipment and manpower of former South Vietnamese forces not included.
Sources: International Institute for Strategic Studies, 18 Adam Street, London, *The Military Balance 1975–1976, Strategic Survey 1974.*

with the Styx SSM. The South had a larger army of 560,000; in armour it was about equal to the North, but its artillery was inferior. Its 25,000-man Air Force had 216 combat aircraft. The Navy had 7 destroyers and 20 landing ships.

The armed forces of the other major Pacific powers were relatively small and designed for internal policing duties. Malaysia had an army of 51,000 men, a navy of 4,800 men, and an air force of 5,300 with 40 combat aircraft. About one-third of the Indonesian Army of 200,000 was engaged in civil and administrative duties. The Philippines had an army of 39,000, no armour, a coastal patrol navy, and 52 combat aircraft.

UNITED STATES

Manpower of the U.S. armed forces fell by 44,000, and defense spending dropped slightly in terms of percentage of GNP. The proposed defense budget was $92.8 billion for fiscal 1975–76. Improvements in the strategic forces continued: 550 Minuteman III ICBMs, each with three multiple independently targetable reentry vehicles (MIRVs), had been deployed, and 50 additional Minuteman IIIs were procured for flight testing. The Upgraded Silo Program was almost complete, giving U.S. ICBMs the ability to withstand overpressures of 1,000 lb. per sq.in. (psi), instead of the former 300 psi, and to resist the electromagnetic pulse of a nuclear explosion. The Command Data Buffer System enabled new target programs to be fed into the ICBMs in 36 minutes, instead of the previous 16–24 hours. Testing of the Mark 12A MIRV for the Minuteman III, with three 340-kiloton warheads as against three 170-kiloton warheads for the Mark 12, was scheduled for completion before March 1976 when the threshold test ban treaty could come into force. Further in the future, the Pave Pepper program could provide small warheads for a Minuteman IV that, married to the Advanced Inertial Reference Sphere, could reduce the circular error probable (CEP; the estimated radius of a circle within which 50% of the reentry vehicles are expected to land) to 700 ft., as against the existing CEP of 1,300 ft. With terminal guidance systems developed under the Advanced Ballistic Reentry System program, notably terrain contour matching, this could provide the U.S. with a substantial hard-target counterforce capability.

Of the 41 submarines carrying 656 submarine-launched ballistic missiles (SLBMs), 25 SSBNs (ballistic missile submarines, nuclear) each had 16 Poseidon C-3 SLBMs with MIRV. Conversion of a further six Polaris-carrying SSBNs to Poseidon was to be completed by 1977. Development of the 4,600-mi.-range Trident I SLBM continued, with deployment planned for mid-1978. The Trident I would be fitted in ten Poseidon submarines and in the new 24-tube Trident submarine, also to be operational by mid-1978. The more advanced Trident II, with a 7,000-mi. range, would not be in service until the mid-1980s and could only be carried in the Trident SSBN.

The strategic bomber force fell to 463 aircraft (66 FB-111As, 165 B-52Gs, 90 B-52Hs, 120 B-52Ds, and 22 B-52Fs in a training squadron) carrying 1,140 short-range attack missiles (SRAMs). The swing-wing supersonic B-1 bomber was flight-tested, and the decision on procurement of 241 aircraft was to be taken in the next fiscal year. A 1,750-mi.-range cruise missile, capable of being launched from aircraft, surface vessels, and submarines, was under development. The Safeguard antiballistic missile (ABM) site at Grand Forks, N.D., became operational. Air defense systems were further reduced, to a total of 374 interceptors.

SVENSKT PRESSFOTO/KEYSTONE

The new Swedish all-terrain tank S 103 is turretless and, consequently, is less vulnerable to enemy fire. It is extremely fast and the gun is directed by turning the entire vehicle to the orientation required.

The 785,000-man Army was being restructured to raise the number of divisions from 13½ to 16 by the end of 1976 and to add two brigades to the forces in Europe (without increasing manpower). This would give the U.S. four armoured, five mechanized infantry, five infantry, one airmobile, and one airborne division, each with 16,500 men, plus three armoured cavalry regiments. Equipment included 8,500 M-48, M60A1, and A2 (with the Shillelagh antitank guided weapon) medium tanks, 1,600 M-551 Sheridan light tanks with the Shillelagh, 16,000 armoured personnel carriers, 2,700 self-propelled guns and howitzers, 2,200 towed guns and howitzers, Honest John, Lance, and Pershing surface-to-surface missiles, 2,400 TOW and Dragon antitank guided weapons, 20,000 Redeye and Chaparral/Vulcan antiaircraft missile/gun systems, 900 Nike Hercules and Hawk SAMs, and 8,000 helicopters. These forces were mainly oriented toward the defense of Western Europe.

The Strategic Reserve was designed to reinforce the 7th Army in Europe, to intervene in the Middle East, or, less probably, to give limited aid to U.S. allies in the Pacific and to South Korea. It comprised 1 armoured, 2 infantry, 1 airmobile, and 1 airborne division and, to provide immediate reinforcement to the 7th Army, 1 armoured and 1 mechanized division with heavy equipment stockpiled in West Germany, 1 mechanized division with 2 dual-based brigades with heavy equipment stored in West Germany, and 1 armoured cavalry regiment. The 7th Army in Western Europe totaled 180,000 men with 2,100 medium tanks. Additional European deployments were 4,400 men in West Berlin, 800 in Greece, 3,000 in Italy, and 1,200 in Turkey. In the Pacific one oversize division with 30,000 men was stationed in South Korea and one infantry division less one brigade in Hawaii. Reserves included the Army National Guard (405,000 men) and the Army Reserves (212,000). The Marine Corps comprised 197,000 men in three large divisions of 18,000 men each, equipped with 430 M-48 medium tanks and 950 armoured personnel carriers. The three air wings had 372 combat aircraft.

The Navy, which had halted the recent decline in the number of major surface combat vessels, had 179 such vessels and 75 attack submarines (64 nuclear,

11 diesel). The carrier force, which was to be reduced from 15 to 13, included 2 nuclear-powered carriers, the "Nimitz" and the "Enterprise." The F-14 Tomcat fleet air defense interceptor began to replace the F-4 Phantom fighter. There was a reclassification of U.S. ships which placed most frigates in the cruiser class, with smaller frigates becoming destroyers and smaller escorts becoming frigates. A major gap in the Navy's armament, the lack of an antiship missile, was to be remedied by deployment of the 70-mi.-range Harpoon. The U.S. remained a substantial Pacific power, with the 3rd Fleet (Eastern Pacific) comprising 6 carriers and 51 surface combatants and the 7th Fleet (Western Pacific), 3 carriers (2 in 1975–76), 28 surface combatants, 1 marine amphibious unit, and 1 marine battalion landing team. The 6th Fleet (Mediterranean) included 2 carriers, 14 surface combatants, and 1 marine amphibious unit, and the 2nd Fleet (Atlantic), 4 carriers and 62 surface units.

The 612,000-man Air Force had about 5,000 combat aircraft, including 69 fighter/attack squadrons with F-4 Phantoms, F-105s (to be replaced by the F-15 air superiority fighter), F-111s, and A-7Ds (to be replaced by the A-10); 13 tactical reconnaissance squadrons with RF-4Cs and EB-66s; 4 electronic countermeasures squadrons; and 4 special operations squadrons. Heavy transport was provided by 17 squadrons, 4 with the C-5A Galaxy. There were 82,000 men in the 37 fighter squadrons of the Tactical Air Command and 64,500 men in the Military Airlift Command, both in the U.S., 70,000 men in U.S. Air Force, Europe, and 50,000 men in the 11 fighter squadrons of the Pacific Air Forces, including the 7th Air Force in Thailand, which was being eliminated.

KEYSTONE

The Grumman F-14 swing-wing aircraft undergoing its flight tests for the U.S. Navy over San Clemente Island, California.

In November President Ford dismissed Schlesinger as secretary of defense and nominated Donald Rumsfeld, the assistant to the president, to succeed him. There had been speculation for some time that Schlesinger and Kissinger had been at odds, particularly with regard to SALT, but Rumsfeld, testifying at his Senate confirmation hearings, announced his intention to maintain U.S. defense policy substantially without change.

U.S.S.R.

Soviet defense spending was estimated at 26.2 billion roubles (comparable to $103.8 billion at U.S. dollar prices) in 1975, representing 10.6% of GNP. The Soviet Union had again expanded its conventional forces, by 50,000 men, but the most noticeable buildup occurred in the 350,000-man Strategic Rocket Forces. Total ICBMs now numbered 1,618, the ceiling allowed under the first SALT (strategic arms limitation talks) agreement of May 1972, and a new family of more accurate, large-payload ICBMs was being introduced. The SS-18 was replacing the SS-9 as the U.S.S.R.'s "heavy" ICBM, of which it was allowed 313 under SALT I; the SS-18 had been tested in both single-warhead and MIRV modes, and 10 had been deployed. The SS-11 was being replaced by the SS-17 and SS-19, both of which had been tested with MIRV only. Tests had also been carried out with the SSX-16, which might be deployed in a land-mobile version, although the U.S. insisted this would constitute a violation of SALT I. In addition, the U.S.S.R. had about 1,000 IRBMs and MRBMs, with 100 SS-5s and 500 SS-4s deployed, most near the western border and the rest east of the Urals.

Total Soviet SLBMs had increased to 784 in 75 submarines, 724 of which counted against the SALT ceilings. The 34th Y-class submarine, carrying 16 SS-N-6 SLBMs, was launched, and two new models of the SS-N-6 were tested, one with multiple reentry vehicle (MRV) warheads and the other a longer-range, single-warhead missile. The number of D-class submarines rose to 13, each carrying 12 SS-N-8 SLBMs, with a 4,800-mi. range; construction started on a larger version that would carry 16 5,000-mi.-range SLBMs. The Long Range Air Force remained at 100 Tu-95 and 35 Mya-4 strategic bombers, plus 670 medium bombers. Twenty-five of the new Backfire-B bombers were deployed; one version was reported to be capable of in-flight refueling and thus of striking the U.S.

The Air Defense Force, with 500,000 men, was far larger than its U.S. counterpart. The ABM total remained at 64 Galosh missiles in four sites around Moscow. Some 12,000 SAM launchers were deployed at about 1,650 sites; they included 4,250 SA-2s with a slant range (launcher to target) of 25 mi., effective between 1,000 and 80,000 ft., the SA-3 low-level missile with a slant range of 15 mi., SA-4 air-transportable missiles, SA-5 high-level missiles with a slant range of 50 mi. and limited antimissile capability, and the SA-6 low-level missile, with a slant range of 17 mi. Interceptors numbered about 2,550, with the MiG-23 being introduced.

The Army of 1,825,000 men was organized in 49 tank, 110 motor rifle, and 7 airborne divisions with 40,000 tanks, 35,000 armoured fighting vehicles, 17,000 artillery pieces, and 8,000 mortars. The T-54/55 medium tank was being replaced by the T-62 and the new M-1970; new armoured fighting vehicles were deployed, as were new self-propelled field guns to replace towed artillery and new SAMs. The 1,000 nuclear-capable SSM launchers included the Frog 1–7 (10–45 mi. range), Scud A (50 mi.), Scud B (185 mi.), and Scaleboard (500 mi.), all able to carry warheads in the kiloton range. At about 10,000 men, Soviet divisions were smaller than those of the U.S., but at full strength a tank division had 325 medium tanks and a motor rifle division had 200–266 tanks. Divisions were in three degrees of combat readiness: category 1, three-quarters to full strength, with complete equipment; category 2, half to three-quarters strength, with complete fighting vehicles; and category 3, one-third strength with complete, but often obsolescent, fighting vehicles. Deployment remained relatively constant, with 31 divisions in Eastern Europe, including 20 (10 tank) in East Germany; 63 (22 tank) in the European U.S.S.R.; 43 (7 tank) on the Sino-Soviet border; 6 (1 tank) in the central U.S.S.R.; and 23 (3 tank) in the southern U.S.S.R. Deployment outside the Warsaw Treaty Organization area remained small, with 200 personnel in Afghanistan, 600 in Algeria, 1,000 in Cuba, 250 in Egypt, 600 in Iraq, 100 in Libya, 2,500 in Somalia, over 3,000 in Syria, 100 in Uganda, 100 in Yemen (Aden), and 100 in Yemen (San'a').

The Navy comprised 500,000 men, 236 major surface combat ships, and 265 attack and cruise missile submarines. The first Soviet aircraft carrier, a Kiev-class vessel of 40,000 tons with 25 short/vertical take-off and landing aircraft or 36 helicopters, was expected to enter service in 1976, and a second was under construction. Two Moskva-class ASW helicopter cruisers were already in service, but even with the new carriers the U.S.S.R. would lack the carrier-based airpower of the U.S. Instead, it relied for air cover on the Naval Air Force of 715 combat aircraft shore-based near the northwest and Black Sea coasts. Major surface forces were oriented primarily toward ASW, but they also gave the Soviet Union a powerful and flexible means of asserting its interests on a global scale.

The Air Force, excluding the Air Defense Force, had 400,000 men and 5,350 combat aircraft including the 4,500 in the Tactical Air Force, plus 1,500 aircraft in the Air Transport Force. Deployment was in 16 tactical air armies: 4 (1,500 aircraft) in Eastern Europe and one in each of the 12 military districts in the U.S.S.R. (900 aircraft in Soviet Asia). There was one Tu-22 squadron in Iraq.

DISARMAMENT

In contrast to the accelerating strategic arms race between the superpowers, progress on arms control was minimal. The 1974 Vladivostok accord had limited the U.S. and U.S.S.R. to 2,400 strategic delivery vehicles each, but attempts to translate it into a SALT II agreement ran into unexpected difficulties. The U.S.S.R. refused to accept U.S. definitions of what constituted a MIRVed missile. Furthermore, the "national-technical means of verification" allowed under SALT I could not detect whether particular missiles were MIRVed or not. The U.S.S.R. insisted that the new U.S. cruise missiles be counted against the U.S. total of strategic missiles, while the U.S. counted only air-launched ballistic missiles. The U.S.S.R. was resisting the classification of the SS-19 as a "heavy" missile, to count under the SALT I ceiling, and it insisted that any SALT III agreement, to which the parties to SALT II would be committed, should include allied (British and French) strategic nuclear forces and forward based systems for delivering tactical nuclear weapons.

The prospects for halting nuclear proliferation seemed equally gloomy. The review conference on the nuclear nonproliferation treaty, held May 5, did little to encourage those states most likely to develop nuclear weapons to adhere to the treaty. No progress was made on the crucial question of making peaceful nuclear explosives available to nonnuclear weapons states or on multinational arrangements for processing fissionable material.

NATO

No progress was made in the Vienna negotiations between NATO and the Warsaw Treaty Organization

WIDE WORLD

Two vehicles from the Royal Navy Hovercraft Trials unit during speed trials in the English Channel. The Hovercraft in the foreground is an SRN 6; that in the rear is the BH 7, a 50-ton Wellington-class craft.

on mutual and balanced force reductions. The Warsaw Pact forces continued to outnumber NATO on the Central Front (northern and central Europe) in terms of manpower (Pact 895,000; NATO 625,000) and of main battle tanks in operational service in peacetime (Pact 19,000; NATO 7,000). The Pact had 5,600 field, medium, and heavy guns, mortars, and rocket launchers against NATO's 2,700. In aircraft, the Pact had 2,000 interceptors to NATO's 350, although the two sides were roughly equal in numbers of fighter-bombers.

Improvements in the Pact forces were also eroding the qualitative lead on which NATO had relied to offset its quantitative inferiority. More than ever, NATO depended on the threat of an early resort to tactical nuclear weapons to deter a Soviet attack, and the U.S. was modernizing its theatre nuclear forces to make this threat more credible.

On the political front, NATO remained in trouble. Greece had virtually withdrawn from the alliance as a result of the 1974 Turkish invasion of Cyprus; the U.S. Congress suspended military aid to Turkey until late fall, and Turkey retaliated by closing U.S. installations. Portugal's future role in NATO, if any, remained open to question.

UNITED KINGDOM

The defense White Paper of March 19 confirmed the outlines of cuts in defense spending announced by the secretary of defense, Roy Mason, on Dec. 3, 1974. These cuts would reduce defense expenditure to about £3,690 million for 1976–77, as against the current £4,548 million ($9,974,000,000). By 1979 the Royal Navy would be cut by 5,000 men to 74,000, the Army by 15,000 to 165,000, and the RAF by 18,000 to 82,000. All forces would be withdrawn from east of Suez except the 9,300-man garrison in Hong Kong, which would be run down. Naval forces were to be withdrawn from the Mediterranean. Reinforcement capabilities for the northern and southern flanks of NATO would be largely eliminated, leaving the U.K. defense effort concentrated on the NATO Central Front.

The 55,500-man British Army of the Rhine (BAOR) remained a well-equipped, professional force. Reorganization would eliminate the brigade as a level of command, giving the BAOR four armoured divisions of five battle groups each, one infantry force of three battalions, and one artillery division comprising the two existing artillery brigades. About 15,000 troops remained committed to Northern Ireland.

The Royal Navy was still the largest in Western Europe. Its complement included 1 aircraft carrier, 2 commando carriers (each with 20 helicopters), 2 assault ships, 2 ASW cruisers, 10 destroyers, and 60 frigates. There were also 8 nuclear and 20 diesel attack submarines. The Navy provided the strategic deterrent of four SSBNs, each with 16 Polaris A-3 missiles with MRV, under independent British control. The Air Force had 500 combat aircraft, including 50 Vulcan B2 and 60 Buccaneer bombers and 138 fighter-bombers.

FRANCE

French defense spending in 1975 fell slightly in percentage of GNP to 3.4%, or Fr. 43,786,000,000 ($10,838,000,000). The development of the French independent nuclear deterrent, the *force de frappe,* continued. A fourth SSBN was to become operational in 1976, a fifth was building, and the construction of a sixth was under consideration. There were also 18 SSBS S-2 IRBMs, with a range of 1,875 mi. and a 150-kiloton warhead, in hardened silos in the Plateau d'Albion, plus 36 Mirage IV-A bombers. Sixteen Mirage IV bombers were in reserve. The major tactical nuclear weapon was the Pluton SSM, with a range of 75 mi. and a 15-kiloton warhead.

Although France had withdrawn its forces from NATO command in 1966, it remained committed to the defense of West Germany and cooperated with NATO. The cream of the 331,500-man Army (216,000 conscripts) formed the Forces de Manoeuvre with two mechanized divisions in West Germany under bilateral Franco-German arrangements and three mechanized divisions in support in France. The Territorial Defense Forces, totaling 52,000 men, could be bought up to 90 battalions on mobilization. The Force d'Intervention (strategic reserve) comprised one airborne division and one air-portable motorized brigade. Forces stationed abroad included 2,000 infantry and three frigates in the Territory of the Afars and Issas; 4,000 infantry and one destroyer in Réunion; 4,000 infantry elsewhere in Africa; two battalions in the Pacific, and one battalion in the Caribbean. French forces were withdrawn from Chad.

The Air Force, with 461 combat aircraft, provided defense for the *force de frappe* and support for the Army. The Air Defense Command had 45 Mirage III-C, 45 Mirage F-1, and 45 Super Mystère B-2 interceptors, coordinated by the Strida II automatic air defense system. The Navy remained substantial, with 69,000 men and 47 major surface combat vessels, including 2 aircraft carriers, 2 cruisers, 19 destroyers, and 24 frigates. Three new frigates entered service during the year.

WEST GERMANY

At DM. 29.9 billion ($12,669,000,000), or 3.6% of GNP, the West German defense budget was the highest in Western Europe, and West Germany provided the largest force on the NATO Central Front. The Army of 345,000 men (177,000 conscripts) comprised 16 armoured, 12 armoured infantry, 3 motorized infantry, 2 mountain, and 3 airborne brigades, organized in 3 corps and 12 divisions. Equipment included 2,300 German-built Leopard and 1,400 Patton medium tanks, over 7,000 armoured personnel carriers, and more than 1,000 tank destroyers, 350 of which were armed with the SS-11 antitank guided weapon. Missiles included 1,000 Redeye SAMs and Cobra, Milan, and TOW antitank guided weapons; the 70 Honest John and 20 Sergeant SSMs were to be replaced by the Lance.

The 111,000-man Air Force had 444 combat aircraft, including 60 F-4F Phantoms, 144 Starfighter F-104Gs, and 102 G-91 fighter-bombers. Phantoms were replacing the Starfighters and Alpha Jets were replacing the G-91s; only 18 F-104G interceptors were still in service. Missiles included 72 nuclear-capable Pershing SSMs with nuclear warheads in U.S. custody.

The Navy, with 39,000 men, had 24 coastal submarines (5 more on order), 11 destroyers (3 with the Tartar SAM), 6 fast frigates, 5 ASW frigates/patrol vessels, 10 fast combat support ships, and 38 patrol vessels (16 with the Exocet SSM). The Naval Air Arm had 96 F-104G fighter-bombers and 25 RF-104G reconnaissance aircraft.

THE MIDDLE EAST

U.S. Secretary of State Henry Kissinger persuaded the Egyptians and Israelis to agree to a second interim peace agreement in September. This involved Israel's withdrawal from the strategic Giddi and Mitla passes (although it retained positions dominating their exits into the Sinai Desert), Israeli transfer of the Abu Rudays oil fields to Egypt, and the placing of 200 U.S. technicians in the broadened buffer zone between Israeli and Egyptian forces to man electronic listening posts. In addition, the U.S. would give Egypt $500 million in grants and increased food aid while Israel would receive $2 billion–$2.5 billion in aid, including the latest U.S. air superiority fighter, the Eagle, and Lance and Pershing SSMs. This amounted to an implicit U.S. guarantee of Israel's security, so long as Israel did not initiate any new fighting.

Whether a similar disengagement could be negotiated between Israel and Syria on the Golan Heights appeared less certain. In the meantime all the protagonists in the Middle East conflict continued to build up their armed forces with outside aid. Under Pres. Hafez al-Assad, the only Arab leader still susceptible to Soviet influence, Syria had received massive Soviet assistance. The defense budget, at S£2,500 million ($668 million), represented 15.7% of GNP. Army strength had increased by 25,000 men in one year to 150,000, and equipment included 700 of the new Soviet T-62 medium tanks, 100 T-34 and 1,300 T54/55 medium tanks, 1,100 armoured personnel carriers, and Snapper, Sagger, and Swatter antitank guided weapons. The U.S.S.R. had also supplied nuclear-capable Frog-7 and Scud SSMs. The Air Force of 25,000 men had 400 combat aircraft, among them 45 MiG-23 fighter-bombers.

In contrast, Egyptian Pres. Anwar as-Sadat had received relatively limited Soviet aid since the 1973 October war, and the U.S. indicated it was considering selling arms to Egypt to lessen its dependence on the Soviets. The Egyptian defense budget of E£2,600 million ($6,103,000,000) represented 22.8% of GNP, down from 31% the previous year but still providing the largest single Arab army of 275,000 men. The U.S.S.R. had supplied 820 T-62 and 1,100 T-54/55 medium tanks, as well as armoured personnel carriers, armoured fighting vehicles, and artillery; SSMs included the Scud, Frog-7, and Samlet. The 30,000-man Air Force had 500 combat aircraft, including 48 MiG-23, 80 Su-7, and 125 MiG-17 fighter-bombers and 250 MiG-21 interceptors with the Atoll air-to-air missile. The Air Defense Command comprised 11 squadrons of MiG-21MF interceptors, 360 SA-2, 200 SA-3, and 75 SA-6 SAMs, and 2,500 antiaircraft guns, with missile, gun, and early warning radars; 44 Mirage F-1 interceptors were on order, with a further 44 Mirage F-1s and 38 Mirage IIIs being supplied via Kuwait and Saudi Arabia, respectively. The Navy included 12 submarines and 5 destroyers.

Since Jordan seemed likely to join in any future war against Israel, there was considerable U.S. opposition to the Ford administration's plan to supply it with 36 batteries of the Hawk SAM. Jordan spent 48 million dinars ($155 million; 14.2% of GNP) on defense to provide an army of 75,000 with 440 medium tanks and an air force of 5,000 with 42 combat aircraft. Iraq might also aid other Arab countries against Israel, although most of its forces were deployed against Iran. Its forces included an army of 120,000 with 1,200 T-62 and T-54/55 medium tanks and an air force of 12,000 with 30 MiG-23, 60 Su-7, and 20 Hunter fighter-bombers and 100 MiG-21 interceptors.

Israeli defense spending, at 32% of GNP (I£22,000 million; $3,503,000,000), was among the highest in the world. Its armed forces totaled 34,000 regular and 122,000 conscript troops, with mobilization to a full strength of 400,000 possible within 72 hours. Armoured forces included 2,700 medium tanks (200 Shermans converting to self-propelled artillery, 900 Centurions, 400 M-48s, 450 M-60s, 400 T-54/55s, and 150 T-62s) and 3,600 armoured fighting vehicles. The Air Force had 461 combat aircraft, among them 200 F-4E Phantoms; three fighter/ground attack squadrons were equipped with the Mirage III/Kfir that was Israeli manufactured, on the basis of Mirage-5 plans, with General Electric J-79 engines. The Navy had two submarines and three were on order. One ominous development was the deployment of the 280-mi.-range, nuclear-capable Jericho SSM. Persistent reports crediting Israel with a stockpile of ten or more nuclear weapons of at least 20 kilotons each made the U.S. intention to supply the 450-mi.-range Pershing SSM a particularly contentious issue.

This continuing military buildup in the Arab-Israeli conflict had obscured the emergence of Iran as one of the most heavily and best armed medium powers

COURTESY, U.S. NAVY

The 95,000-ton USS "Nimitz" is the largest aircraft carrier ever built as well as the most costly, at more than $1 billion. Commissioned in May, the "Nimitz" will carry approximately 100 tactical aircraft and will not need to refuel for 13 years.

in the world and the dominant military power in the Persian Gulf and the surrounding area. Its Army of 175,000 was equipped with 300 Chieftain, 400 M-47/48, and 460 M-60A1 medium tanks; 1,680 Chieftains, the heaviest main battle tank in the world, were on order. The 60,000-man Air Force had 238 modern combat aircraft, and 80 F-14 Tomcats, 190 F-4s, and 179 F-5E fighters were on order from the U.S. Naval forces included three destroyers and four frigates with the Mk 2 Seakiller SSM and Seacat SAM, plus three Tang-class submarines and six Spruance-class destroyers on order from the U.S.

INDIA AND PAKISTAN

No further tests followed India's initial detonation of a nuclear device on May 18, 1974, but India appeared to be pursuing a well-defined, long-range program to acquire a significant nuclear deterrent against China and a defensive nuclear capability. Meanwhile, India's conventional forces remained second only to China in the region, although defense spending was held to Rs. 22,740,000,000 ($2,660,000,000), or 2.8% of GNP.

The Army of 826,000 men was equipped with over 1,500 Centurion, T.54/55, and Vijayanta medium tanks, 500 armoured personnel carriers, and 3,000 artillery pieces, mostly towed. Missiles included the SS-11 and Entac antitank guided weapons and the Tigercat SAM. The 100,000-man Air Force had 725 combat aircraft, including 50 Canberra light bombers and 77 Su-7BKL, 60 Indian-designed and built HF-24 Marut 1A, and 130 Hunter F-56 fighter-bombers. The air defense system had 20 SA-2 SAM sites, and the Navy included 1 aircraft carrier, 2 cruisers, 3 destroyers, 26 frigates, and 8 ex-Soviet F-class submarines. These forces were more than sufficient to deter a Chinese or Pakistani attack and to deal with the Naga and Mizo (Lushai) border guerrillas.

Pakistan's forces just sufficed for self-defense, although the defense budget of Pak Rs. 7,020,000,000 ($722 million) represented 7.6% of GNP. This provided an army of 365,000 with 950 M-47/48, T-55, and T-59 medium tanks and 350 armoured personnel carriers, supported by 1,200 artillery pieces and the Cobra antitank guided weapon. The 17,000-man Air Force had 278 combat aircraft, including 10 B-57B Martin (Canberra) light bombers and 49 Mirage IIIEP/V, 70 F-86 Sabre, and 140 MiG-19/F-6 fighter-bombers. Naval forces included three submarines of the French Daphne class, four destroyers, and four frigates.

The sea-launched cruise missile, under development for the U.S. Navy, underwent trials during the summer. Powered by a small jet engine and directed by its own computer, the cruise missile is highly accurate within 1,500 mi. and can deliver a thermonuclear warhead.

TOP, COURTESY, U.S. NAVY; BELOW, AUTHENTICATED NEWS INTERNATIONAL

AFRICA SOUTH OF THE SAHARA

While the outcome of the power struggle in Portugal remained uncertain, the withdrawal from Portugal's African colonies continued. (*See* DEPENDENT STATES.) Merely maintaining the existing Portuguese military establishment was costing 17 billion escudos ($701 million) annually, representing 6.8% of a GNP that was falling rapidly as a result of domestic disturbances. Portuguese Guinea (Guinea-Bissau) had been granted independence in 1974, and it was followed in the summer of 1975 by the Cape Verde Islands and Mozambique. Angola was granted independence in November, but by that time civil war had broken out between the Popular Movement for the Liberation of Angola (MPLA), which held the capital of Luanda, and a coalition of the National Front for the Liberation of Angola (FNLA) and the smaller National Union for the Total Independence of Angola (UNITA). The MPLA, which was supported by the Organization of African Unity (OAU), was receiving substantial aid from Moscow, while the FNLA, supported by neighbouring Zaire, with its 40,000-man army, was strongly backed by the U.S. In late November U.S. officials reported that several thousand Cuban troops and advisers, equipped with Soviet arms, had joined the MPLA. The Soviets claimed that U.S., South African, and Western European troops were fighting with the FNLA, and both superpowers delivered strong protests concerning the other's involvement.

Talks aimed at negotiating a timetable for the phased transfer of power to the blacks in Rhodesia failed during the year, despite the encouragement of South African Prime Minister B. J. Vorster and several of the independent black African governments. The long-range prospects for Prime Minister Ian Smith's regime seemed dim. To control a black population of 5.9 million, it had only the 4,500-man Army, 10,000 in the Territorial Force, an air force of 1,200 with 40 jet fighter-bombers, and reserves of 10,000, plus the paramilitary British South African Police (8,000 actives and 35,000 reservists) and a number of African units. South African paramilitary forces which had been assisting in the anti-insurgent campaign had been withdrawn. The black opposition movements were divided, however. The Zimbabwe African National Union, which since 1972 had been operating out of Mozambique, was supported by the OAU, while the Zimbabwe African People's Union was backed by Zambia, Algeria, and, to some extent, the U.S.S.R. Rhodesian defense spending rose to R$57 million ($102 million), still only 2.6% of GNP.

By contrast, South Africa retained its ability to defend itself against most foreseeable combinations of guerrillas, including those in Namibia (South West Africa). The Army of 38,000 (31,000 conscripts) was equipped with 141 Centurion and 20 Comet medium tanks, 1,050 armoured cars, and 350 armoured personnel carriers. There was an Active Reserve of 138,000, as well as the 75,000-man commando paramilitary forces. The 8,500-man Air Force had 108 combat aircraft, sufficient to give the republic air superiority over any other African force. (ROBIN J. RANGER)

See also Space Exploration.
[535.B.5.c.ii; 544.B.5–6; 736]

SPECIAL REPORT

FOREIGN INTELLIGENCE IN A FREE SOCIETY

By John A. McCone

The collection of foreign intelligence, which is the pursuit of a special kind of information, is an indispensable service for any government having even the most elementary international associations. Vigorous nations must devise a strategy to provide for both their security and well-being. History teaches us that responsibility cannot be met without knowledge of the political, economic, and military capabilities and intentions of other nations. Indeed, advance knowledge of these matters, or its absence, could well settle the fate of a great nation, especially in an era when a single nation or consortium of nations is capable of smashing another society in a single stroke, or of cowing it under the threat of poised catastrophe. The well-being of any great nation will depend on decisions taken by others, which must be foreseen, correctly analyzed, and countered. On the military side of the balance, the maneuvering of possible hostile forces, the deployment of mass-destruction weapons and counterweapons, and, what could be the most dangerous, the hidden development of yet more advanced weaponry must all be discovered in good time, and their possible effects measured. And on the political and economic side, the traditional task of intelligence services in safeguarding the well-being of the state has lately been vastly amplified by the advent of cartels which seek economic advantage by imposing boycotts and quotas on various raw materials.

If, as Walter Lippmann wrote, foreign policy is the "shield" of the Republic, then, as Sherman Kent, a distinguished historian, said, "strategic intelligence is the thing that gets the shield to the proper place at the right time. It is also the thing that stands ready to guide the sword."

The Intelligence Process. By timeless custom, the collection and analysis of intelligence is done for governments by organizations uniquely charged with that function. The particularities of these organizations vary from country to country as do the scope of their responsibilities and the restraints imposed upon them. The observant diplomat as he moves from nation to nation is certain to find tucked away somewhere in the government at least the shadowy evidence of a foreign intelligence apparatus. Usually the authority granted and the control are both embedded at the topmost echelon of power. Invariably, the organization is clandestine. Even in open societies, practical considerations demand that the organization be kept out of public view and its work known only to the few who need to know. Intelligence findings are, therefore, usually classified and limited in circulation.

Unevaluated intelligence—raw, as it is known in the trade—comes in many ways. Through the long sweep of history, human contact, both open and covert, has been the major source. Conversations between heads of state, reports from ambassadors, and articles in newspapers and other publications all contribute to the inventory of information gathered by intelligence organizations. But the richest source is usually the secret agent. The best of these agents are highly skilled, well-trained professionals concealed under disarming cover, who usually move in the highest and most informed circles. Through this access, the secret agent has on occasion been in a position to warn his government of an imminent hostile action or, alternatively, to advise that an apparent threat is a hollow one.

The ethics of clandestine intelligence operations have long been debated. Some would do away with them. The fact is that no international covenant forbids such operations, and they go on as they have done for centuries. At least 40 nations today support clandestine services.

In the recent past, technology has enormously lengthened the reach and sharpened the penetration of intelligence. High-flying aircraft carrying sophisticated cameras, supplemented by orbital satellites equipped with even more advanced cameras, have been able to look down onto fortress societies and fix in startling detail what is actually developing. A correspondingly wide range of electronic sensing and tracking devices makes it possible to deduce quite accurately the yield of nuclear devices, as well as the performance of missiles, planes, submarines, and other military equipment being tested beyond otherwise impenetrable frontiers. Indeed, in the event of a surprise attack, these intelligence-gathering systems would probably flash the first warning of the blow being prepared.

There can be no denying the importance of mechanical intelligence-gathering systems. They supplement but can never wholly substitute for the human agent. During the present era of international strain, both the human and the technical systems must be maintained and steadily improved.

Gathering information on a possible adversary or adversaries is only the start of the intelligence process. The raw material, once in hand, must be drawn together, analyzed, correlated, and evaluated before it becomes useful knowledge. In this stage emerges an estimate of the adversary's intentions and of his ability to achieve them. From this appraisal, which points to his most likely course of action, the head of the target state, in consultation with his advisers, can chart a course of action best designed to meet the developing situation. Without both the intelligence itself and the sophisticated estimate of it, the head of a government would be, at best, groping blindly toward his decision.

Not surprisingly, the so-called superpowers, the United States and the Soviet Union, both operate elaborate though differing intelligence systems. In the confines of this space, I shall limit my analysis to the U.S. system.

Creation of the U.S. Intelligence Community. The entrance of the U.S. government into the foreign intelligence business is fairly recent. Between the two World Wars, the U.S. did not maintain a strong intelligence organization. To be sure, the Army (which then included the Air Force) and the Navy maintained separate intelligence units of their own, specifically to meet their needs in times of war. Additionally, the Department of State kept a watchful eye on world happenings, and ambassadors regularly reported their observations.

There was, however, no organization to analyze the whole flow of information from these sources, let alone to study the dangers to American security inherent in the pattern of action reported from abroad. Thus, an inquiry conducted by Congress after World War II into why the United States was surprised

---

John A. McCone is a former Director of the U.S. Central Intelligence Agency and retired Chairman of the Board of Hendy International Company.

by the Japanese attack on Pearl Harbor disclosed that the various government agencies had in hand all essential information concerning Japan's preparations for war, including the assembly and departure of the Japanese fleet, days prior to the actual attack. The intelligence essential for a correct estimate had been collected by the State, War, and Navy departments and used to meet their special departmental interests. Unfortunately for the United States, no branch of government then had the duty to put the information together and alert the president of impending danger.

After this tragic experience, the present foreign intelligence community was gradually established. The structure began with the creation of the Central Intelligence Agency under the National Security Act of 1947, the only national intelligence service except for that of West Germany to be initiated and authorized by legislative action. To ensure that it remained apart and unsullied by partisan attachments and parochial interests, the CIA was developed essentially as a civilian organization composed of men and women drawn from all the necessary disciplines and under a civilian director, who stands by law as the nation's senior intelligence officer and the statutory adviser to the president on intelligence matters.

Functions of the CIA. All raw intelligence entering the U.S. intelligence community flows on in one form or another to the CIA. The bits and pieces of information are studied at the agency by political scientists, economists, historians, linguists, engineers, physicists, and others who have devoted their lives to a study of one aspect or another of foreign societies. This scholarly body conducts a continuing analysis of the intelligence that passes before them. Their efforts produce a daily intelligence summary for the president, a succession of reports on special situations in other countries for concerned government departments, and finally the body of papers known as the National Intelligence Estimates, which present periodic comprehensive analyses of the continuing military, political, and economic situations that bear directly on the well-being of the U.S. Preparing this body of literature in its various forms is, perhaps, the most important single activity of the CIA.

Following closely in importance are the agency's intelligence-gathering responsibilities, as defined by statute or executive order. This part of the task calls for two quite different organizations. On one side is the traditional organization, manned by officers and agents both overt and covert, their true identities and missions usually being concealed under a cover. The CIA looks to them for information that can be acquired only by a man at the scene. Their reports flow to headquarters through a secure communications network.

The other organization is responsible for gathering information by sophisticated technical means, such as satellite photography, high-altitude reconnaissance, and electronic signals; these are joint activities of the CIA and the military. As an example, the signals gathered by a great number of listening and sensing devices make it possible to determine the success of a distant missile launching, the yield of an underground nuclear explosion thousands of miles distant, or the orbit and function of a space vehicle. And photographic analysis permits estimates so diverse as the characteristics of a submarine under construction and the crop yield on the steppes.

Other U.S. Intelligence Agencies. Intelligence units exist in other departments of the U.S. government. The Department of State maintains a Bureau of Intelligence and Research, a small division devoted to the assessment of information to serve the department in the conduct of foreign policy. The Department of Defense intelligence organizations are sizable and grouped under the Defense Intelligence Agency. This agency supports the secretary of defense and the joint chiefs of staff. The director of the DIA coordinates the work of the three separate service intelligence units, manages the corps of military attachés, prepares assessments of matters relating to the nation's security, and coordinates the Defense Department's contributions to the national intelligence assessments. The primary missions of the Army, Navy, and Air Force intelligence services are to serve their chiefs of service, provide current tactical intelligence information to field commanders, participate in the production of National Intelligence Estimates, and stand prepared and organized to fulfill their service's intelligence requirements in time of war.

The Department of the Treasury and the Energy Research and Development Administration maintain small intelligence units that contribute important specialized information on foreign events, within their competence. The Federal Bureau of Investigation, in the course of its extensive domestic operations, constantly unearths information that either originates in another country or has a significant foreign connection. This draws the FBI into the foreign intelligence community.

The senior body of the American intelligence community is the United States Intelligence Board. It consists of directors from the several departmental intelligence organizations. They assemble at least once a week at the headquarters of the Central Intelligence Agency to review the national estimates prepared by the Board of National Estimates and the analysts of the CIA. It is also within their purview to advise the director of the CIA on how best to supply the intelligence needs of the nation's policymakers, schedule the flights of reconnaissance satellites and photographic planes, fix the tasks of the National Security Agency, and develop precautions that may be desirable for protecting the nation's intelligence sources and methods.

Overseeing the Intelligence Community. Control over the entire intelligence apparatus in the U.S. is exercised by the president in several ways: through personal contact with the CIA director, through the Office of Budget and Management, through a subcommittee of the National Security Council that oversees certain covert activities, and through a civilian advisory board. The House of Representatives and the Senate have special committees responsible for overseeing the community's activities and for reviewing the budgets of all units of the community.

In spite of this extensive oversight recent accusations of wrongdoing by the community, particularly by the CIA—some imagined, some overstated, and some justified—have created a clamour for closer supervision of intelligence operations, especially of clandestine activities. The remedies, where needed, involve relatively simple legislative and executive actions. In applying them, however, great care must be taken not to damage the effectiveness of the intelligence organization, but, at the same time, there should be controls that will assure the public and the Congress that the intelligence services will always be confined to acceptable moral and legal standards. Also, a practical truth must be accepted: a foreign intelligence operation, to be effective at all, must by its very nature remain cloaked in privacy, but society must accept the cloak. A free society finds it difficult to accept this.

Perhaps one way to help strengthen public confidence in the intelligence function would be to make more conspicuous the CIA director's close relationship with the president and the National Security Council. Other useful reforms could include establishing a permanent staff inside the National Security Council to oversee the community's operations; giving a strongly staffed presidential civilian intelligence advisory board an effective voice; and reorganizing and strengthening the congressional oversight role by transferring that responsibility to a single joint committee on intelligence, drawn from both houses. Oversight by such a joint committee must be accepted as oversight by the Congress as a whole.

Beyond these measures, anyone who has been seriously connected with the responsibilities of national security will hope that the prolonged and painful review of the roles and missions of the CIA and the work of the intelligence community as a whole will, in the end, preserve an organization that can serve the nation's security needs and rest comfortably with American political philosophy. The nation would not be safe without one.

Demography

Birthrate trends in most of the industrialized countries, such as the U.S., Canada, Australia, New Zealand, and Western Europe, had been generally downward since 1960, with the decline more rapid in the years 1970–73. In the few other countries that had reliable annual statistics the rates fell slowly or remained within a narrow range. During the same period death rates fell slowly or rose somewhat in countries like Denmark, Sweden, and the United Kingdom with "older" populations. The most significant effect of these changes was a slowing of the rate of population growth in industrialized countries. Countries for which reliable vital statistics were not available generally tended to have higher vital rates and rapid population growth. During this period the marriage rate had risen in some industrialized countries and fallen in others, with decreases predominating in 1974. The divorce rate was rising steadily.

Birth Statistics. The rapid fall of the U.S. birthrate between 1970 and 1973 stopped in 1974. According to provisional figures, both the number of births and the birthrate (births per 1,000 population) increased about 1% from 1973 to 1974. Similar small increases occurred in the first seven months of 1975 compared with the same period in 1974. The decline of the fertility rate (births per 1,000 women aged 15–44 years) also slowed in 1974 and in the first seven months of 1975.

The birthrate and the fertility rate were 15 and 68.4, respectively, in 1974, compared with 14.9 and 69.2 in 1973. For the first seven months of 1975 the birthrate was 14.7, compared with 14.6 for the corresponding period of 1974, and the fertility rate was 66.4, compared with 66.7. The different rates of change in the birth and fertility rates could be attributed to the continuing increase in the number of women of childbearing age. Because of the slight rise in the birthrate and a decrease of the death rate, the rate of natural population increase (excess of births over deaths per 1,000 population) rose to 5.9 in 1974 from 5.5 in 1973. The rate continued to rise in the first seven months of 1975.

The latest available U.S. birth data by colour, age of mother, birth order, and other characteristics were for 1973. The rate for the white population, 13.9, continued to be much lower than for all other groups, 21.9. The fertility rate for white women in 1973, 65.3, was only 69% of the rate for women of all other races, 94.3. Of all births to white women, 6.4% were illegitimate in 1973, whereas the corresponding figure for nonwhite women was 41.7%. The number of white and nonwhite illegitimate births each rose about 1% over 1972.

Birthrates declined between 1970 and 1973 for women in all age groups except those under 15 years. The largest declines, over 30%, were in the age groups 35 years and above, and the smallest was in the 15–19-year age group. Rates for all birth-order groups fell between 1970 and 1973, the decline ranging from 12.8% for second births to more than 40% for fifth and higher-order births. The most recent survey (1975) by the U.S. Bureau of the Census indicated that this trend toward fewer births per mother was likely to continue. The number of lifetime births expected per married woman was 2.2 for women aged 18–24 years and 2.3, 2.7, and 3.1 for the next three five-year age groups of women. These expectation data, combined with the continuing rapid declines in the rates for third- and higher-order births, and for women at the higher ages, provided strong evidence that the two-child family was now regarded as the preferred size by most women. The sex ratio of births occurring in 1973 was 1,052 males per 1,000 females, a ratio that varies little from year to year.

In other countries where birth registration was considered to be 90% or more complete, UN reports indicated that the birthrate fell in 23 countries from 1973 to 1974 and rose in 10. As in the U.S., the rates of most developed countries had fallen between 1970 and 1973 but most of them did not show the increase in 1974 that occurred in the U.S. The most recent data published by the UN indicated that birthrates around the world ranged from about 10 per 1,000 population to over 50.

In recent decades the birthrate had been the most dynamic factor influencing rates of population increase in all parts of the world. The annual rate of natural increase ranged from an actual decrease, and increases of less than 10 per 1,000 population in most

Table I. Life Expectancy at Birth, in Years, for Selected Countries

Country	Period	Male	Female
Africa			
Burundi	1965	35.0	38.5
Egypt	1960	51.6	53.8
Liberia	1971	45.8	44.0
Malagasy Republic	1966	37.5	38.3
Nigeria	1965–66	37.2	36.7
Upper Volta	1960–61	32.1	31.1
Asia			
Cambodia	1958–59	44.2	43.3
Hong Kong	1971	67.4	75.0
India	1966–70	48.2	46.0
Israel	1972	70.1	70.9
Japan	1974	71.2	76.3
Korea, South	1970	63.0	67.0
Pakistan	1962	53.7	48.8
Taiwan	1971	66.1	71.7
Thailand	1964–67	53.9	58.6
Europe			
Albania	1965–66	64.9	67.0
Austria	1973	67.4	74.7
Belgium	1959–63	67.7	73.5
Bulgaria	1965–67	68.8	72.7
Czechoslovakia	1970	66.2	72.9
Denmark	1970–71	70.7	75.9
Finland	1966–70	65.9	73.6
France	1971	68.5	76.1
Germany, East	1969–70	68.9	74.2
Germany, West	1970–72	67.4	73.8
Greece	1960–62	67.5	70.7
Hungary	1972	66.9	72.6
Iceland	1966–70	70.7	76.3
Ireland	1965–67	68.6	72.9
Italy	1970–72	69.0	74.9
Netherlands, The	1972	70.8	76.8
Norway	1971–72	71.2	77.4
Poland	1970	66.8	73.8
Portugal	1970	65.3	71.0
Romania	1970–72	66.3	70.9
Spain	1970	69.7	75.0
Sweden	1972	72.0	77.4
Switzerland	1960–70	69.2	75.0
United Kingdom	1969–71	68.6	74.9
Yugoslavia	1971–72	65.6	70.4
North America			
Barbados	1959–61	62.7	67.4
Canada	1965–67	68.8	75.2
Costa Rica	1962–64	61.9	64.8
Guatemala	1963–65	48.3	49.7
Mexico	1965–70	61.0	63.7
Panama	1970	64.3	67.5
Puerto Rico	1971–73	68.9	76.1
United States	1972	67.4	75.1
Oceania			
Australia	1965–67	67.6	74.2
New Zealand	1965–67	68.7	74.8
South America			
Argentina	1965–70	64.1	70.2
Brazil	1975*	58.8	63.1
Chile	1969–70	60.5	66.0
Peru	1965–70	56.5	59.6
Surinam	1963	62.5	66.7
Uruguay	1963–64	65.5	71.6
Venezuela	1970–75*	62.9	66.7
U.S.S.R.	1968–69	65.0	74.0

*Projection.
Source: United Nations, *Demographic Yearbook* (1973); official country sources.

developed nations, to well over 30 in some countries of Africa, Latin America, and Asia. Recent rates for some of the largest countries were Egypt, 21.7; the U.S., 5.9; Nigeria, 24.7; Brazil, 28.3; China, 17.8; India, 26.1; Indonesia, 28.9; Japan, 12.8; Pakistan, 24; and the U.S.S.R., 9.

Death Statistics. The provisional crude death rate of the U.S. in 1974 was 9.1 per 1,000 population, 3% below the rate for 1973. The rate for the first seven months of 1975, at 9.3, was unchanged from that recorded for the same period in 1974. All the age-specific death rates were lower in 1974 than in 1973. Rates for the 45–54 and 55–64 age groups were the lowest ever recorded for the U.S. However, the largest percentage declines between 1973 and 1974 were in the 5–14 and 15–24 age groups, 7.3 and 6.5%, respectively.

The most recent available age-adjusted U.S. death rates were for 1973. Substantial differences by sex and by colour continued to be observed. The rate for males was 9.1 per 1,000 population and, for females, only 5.1; for white persons the rate was 6.6, and for all others, 9.5. By major causes of death, all the rates were much higher for males than for females, except for diabetes, and much lower for whites than for all other races combined except for suicide, arteriosclerosis, and bronchitis, emphysema, and asthma.

The ranking of the ten leading causes of death in the U.S. in 1974 is shown below. There was one change from the order in 1973. Suicide replaced bronchitis, emphysema, and asthma in the tenth position. However, this apparent shift was misleading. Due to changes in medical certification practices and prevailing rules of classification, a significant number of deaths were assigned to "chronic obstructive lung disease." If these deaths were combined with those assigned to bronchitis, emphysema, and asthma, the total rate would be 19.6, making this category the sixth leading cause of death.

Cause of death	Estimated rate per 100,000 population
All causes	914.4
Diseases of the heart	353.1
Malignant neoplasms (cancer)	169.5
Cerebrovascular diseases	97.2
Accidents	48.9
Influenza and pneumonia	25.7
Diabetes mellitus	17.4
Cirrhosis of the liver	16.0
Arteriosclerosis	15.2
Certain causes of mortality in early infancy	13.2
Suicide	12.5

Rates for all of the above causes were lower in 1974 than in 1973 except for cancer, suicide, and cirrhosis of the liver, which were higher. Over the longer period 1950–73, the age-adjusted death rates for 5 of the 15 leading causes of death rose—cancer, cirrhosis of the liver, suicide, homicide, and bronchitis, emphysema, and asthma.

As in the U.S., the crude death rates for European countries, Canada, Australia, New Zealand, Japan, and a few others have fluctuated within narrow limits for ten years or longer with a slowly downward trend. The few countries in other parts of the world that had reasonably complete statistics had generally reported declining rates, reflecting improvements in standards of living and health services. In 1974, among countries with at least 90% complete registration, 13 reported higher crude death rates in 1974 than in 1973, 19 showed lower rates, and 2 reported no change.

Infant and Maternal Mortality. The infant mortality rate for the U.S. continued its long downward trend, falling from 17.7 deaths under 1 year per 1,000 live births in 1973 to the provisional rate of 16.5 in 1974, the lowest annual rate ever recorded for the U.S. Rates for white and nonwhite infants were also the lowest ever recorded for those groups, 14.7 and 24.6, respectively. Both the neonatal rate (infants under 28 days) and the post-neonatal rate (28 days to 11 months) fell, the former from 13 to 12.1, the latter from 4.8 to 4.4. Improvement continued in the first seven months of 1975, when the total infant mortality rate was 16.5, compared with 16.9 for the same period in 1974.

Among countries with 90% or more complete registration, the infant mortality rate ranged from about 10 or below for Finland, Iceland, and Sweden to over 40 for Costa Rica and Chile. Rates for most countries in Africa and Asia were estimated by the UN to range from 75 to over 200, but reliable data were not available.

The provisional maternal mortality rate (deaths from complications of pregnancy per 100,000 live births) for the U.S. in 1974 was 20.8, appreciably above the record low reported final rate of 15.2 in 1973. However, because the numbers of deaths were small and the provisional figures were based on a 10% sample, it was possible that the ratio shown for 1974 would be significantly revised when the final figures became available. Because of differences in definitions and classification procedures, fetal and maternal rates are not comparable between the countries of the world.

Expectation of Life. The expectation of life at birth in the U.S. for 1974, based on final figures, was 71.9 years, the longest life expectancy ever attained for the total population. Expectation of life is the average number of years that an infant could be expected to live if the age-specific death rates observed during the year of birth were to continue unchanged throughout its lifetime. Obviously it is a hypothetical figure, but it is one that is very useful in measuring changes in the intrinsic rate of mortality.

Table II. Birthrates and Death Rates per 1,000 Population and Infant Mortality per 1,000 Live Births in Selected Countries, 1974*

Country	Birth-rate	Death rate	Infant mortality
Africa			
Egypt†	35.4	12.9	97.9
Mauritius	27.5	7.3	46.3
Tunisia	35.8†	8.0†	74.7‡
Asia			
Cyprus	18.0	9.5	28.5†
Hong Kong	19.3	5.2	17.7
Israel	28.2	7.3	23.5
Japan	18.6	6.5	11.3†
Kuwait†	45.5	5.2	44.1
Lebanon†	24.5	4.3	13.6§
Malaysia	33.2‖	6.5‖	37.4‡
Philippines	25.0	6.3	74.2†
Singapore	19.9	5.3	16.5
Thailand‖	30.8	6.9	27.0
Europe			
Austria	12.8	12.5	23.4
Belgium	12.6	11.9	17.0†
Bulgaria	17.2	9.8	25.4
Czechoslovakia	19.8	11.7	20.4
Denmark	14.2	10.2	12.2‖
Finland	13.3	9.6	10.1†
France	15.2	10.4	12.1
Germany, East	10.4	13.3	16.0†
Germany, West	10.1	11.7	23.1†
Greece	16.1	8.5	24.0
Hungary	17.8	12.0	33.9
Iceland	20.4	7.0	11.4
Ireland	22.3	11.2	17.8†
Italy	15.7	9.6	22.6
Luxembourg	11.5	12.6	13.5
Malta	16.8	8.5	20.9
Netherlands, The	13.8	8.0	11.0
Norway	14.9	9.9	11.8†
Poland	18.4	8.2	23.5
Portugal	19.3	11.1	38.4
Romania	20.3	9.1	35.0
Spain	19.3	8.4	13.7
Sweden	13.4	10.6	9.2
Switzerland	12.9	8.5	13.2†
United Kingdom†	13.9	12.0	17.2
Yugoslavia	17.9	8.5	40.4
North America			
Antigua	18.3	6.9	45.4¶
Bahamas, The†	22.4	5.7	32.2
Barbados†	20.8	9.4	37.7
Canada†	15.5	7.4	15.6
Costa Rica†	28.3	5.1	44.8
Cuba†	25.4	5.8	27.5
El Salvador†	40.3	8.3	59.1
Guatemala†	43.4	15.4	79.1
Jamaica	30.8	7.2	26.3
Mexico†	46.3	8.2	51.4
Panama	32.6	5.6	32.6
Puerto Rico†	23.3	6.5	24.2
United States	15.0	9.1	16.5
Oceania			
American Samoa	37.2	4.9	14.7
Australia†	18.9	8.4	16.5
Fiji†	28.2	5.0	21.5
Guam†	34.8	4.7	23.2
New Zealand†	20.5	8.5	16.2
Pacific Islands, Trust Terr. of	35.3	5.0	35.1
Western Samoa	26.9	3.5	15.8
U.S.S.R.	18.2	8.7	26.4†

*Registered births and deaths only.
†1973.
‡1971.
§1960.
‖1972.
¶1965.
Sources: United Nations, *Population and Vital Statistics Report;* various national demographic publications.

The life expectancy for males was 68.2 years and for females, 75.9 years. For white persons it was 72.7 years, and for all other persons, 67 years. It was significant that the expectation of life at birth in the U.S. was now 7.7 years longer for females than for males. This differential was also observed in the other technically advanced countries. In the less developed nations the female advantage was usually two or three years, and in a few countries of Africa and Asia life expectancy for females was less than for males.

Marriage and Divorce. In the U.S. both the number of marriages and the crude marriage rate per 1,000 population fell in 1974 after 15 years of annual increases. The rate for 1974 was 10.5, compared with 10.9 in 1973. The decline began in 1973 when the number increased only slightly and the rate fell slightly. The number and rate continued to go down in the first seven months of 1975, the latter figure being 9.5, compared with 10 for the corresponding months of 1974. The decline in marriages occurred even though the number of single, widowed, or divorced persons continued to increase.

Among countries where reporting was believed to be at least 90% complete, the marriage rate rose from 1973 to 1974 in 10 countries and fell in 16, with no change in 3 countries. Comparability of marriage rates between countries is limited by several factors in addition to completeness of reporting, most notably the frequency of unofficial, or common law, marriages in many countries of Africa, Asia, and Latin America.

Both the number and rate of divorces granted in the U.S. continued to increase in 1974 and 1975. Provisional data indicated that the crude rate (divorces and annulments per 1,000 married persons) in 1974 was 4.6, compared with 4.4 in 1973. The number of divorces for the first seven months of 1975 was 3% above the same period in 1974. Differences between states in divorce rates are largely due to the degree of difficulty imposed by the various state laws. In that respect, it was of interest that most states had passed laws recognizing some form of "no fault" divorce. In 13 states "irretrievable breakdown of marriage" was accepted as the sole ground for divorce.

Few or no divorces occur in Africa, Asia, and Latin America. In many countries it is forbidden or not recognized by law. Among the countries where divorce is permitted and reported with some reliability, the U.S. consistently had the highest rate. Next highest in 1973 was the U.S.S.R., with 2.8 per 1,000 population. Other countries with high rates were Czechoslovakia, Denmark, Hungary, Sweden, and the United Kingdom. The trend of the divorce rate in most reporting countries had been upward for many years.

(ROBERT D. GROVE)

See also Populations and Areas.
[338.F.5.b; 525.A; 10/36.C.5.d]

Denmark

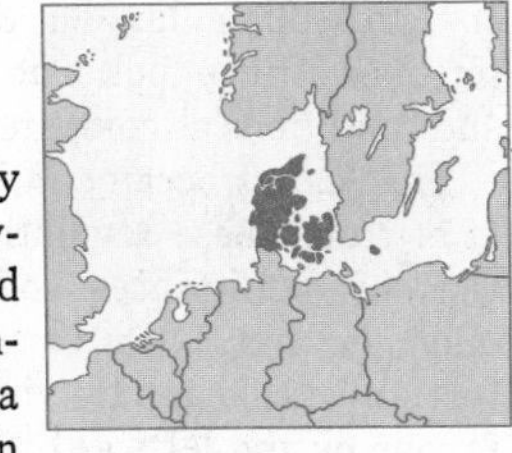

A constitutional monarchy of north central Europe lying between the North and Baltic seas, Denmark includes the Jutland Peninsula and 100 inhabited islands in the Kattegat and Skagerrak straits. Area (excluding Faeroe Islands and Greenland): 16,630 sq.mi. (43,074 sq.km.). Pop. (1975 est.): 5,054,400. Cap. and largest city: Copenhagen (pop., 1974 est., 744,500). Language: Danish. Religion: predominantly Lutheran. Queen, Margrethe II; prime ministers in 1975, Poul Hartling until January 29 and, from February 13, Anker Jørgensen.

CHRISTEN HANSEN P.P.F.—POLITIKENS PRESSE FOTO

Demonstration against unemployment in front of Christiansborg Palace in Copenhagen.

The general atmosphere of economic and political malaise that had characterized Danish affairs for some time led once again to a general election, held on Jan. 9, 1975. The most significant features of the election results were an increase in representation for outgoing prime minister Poul Hartling's Liberal Party from 22 seats to 42 and for the Social Democrats, the largest group in the 179-seat Folketing (Parliament), from 46 to 53 seats. The recently formed Progress Party led by Copenhagen tax lawyer Mogens Glistrup (*see* BIOGRAPHY) fell back slightly, although opinion polls later in the year suggested a reversal of this trend. At all events, the election did little to clarify the political situation, and the new Parliament once more included representatives of no less than ten parties.

It might have been expected that, having achieved a substantial increase in representation, Hartling's minority Liberal government would return to power. However, after a Liberal defeat in Parliament on January 28, the eventual outcome of complex negotiations was the formation of a Social Democrat minority government under Anker Jørgensen, who had been Hartling's immediate predecessor as prime minister. The problems that confronted the new Parliament, moreover, remained as grave as before. Major issues to be faced were the substantial balance of payments deficit and rapidly rising unemployment. A particular problem for Denmark had always been the country's extreme sensitivity to prevailing economic conditions overseas, due to its heavy dependence on foreign trade, and the international situation in 1975 proved unpromising.

Meanwhile, the problems of inflation, the balance of payments deficit, and rising unemployment remained serious, and the new government set about tackling them as best it could. A prices and incomes package was introduced. It involved various economies, including a cutback in public expenditure and a two-year extension of existing labour agreements. Forecasts of a brighter international economic situation in 1976 led the government to take steps to

DENMARK

Education. (1971–72) Primary, pupils 537,141; secondary and vocational, pupils 215,109; primary, secondary, and vocational, teachers 46,767; higher (including 4 main universities), students (1972–73) 97,621, teaching staff 8,708.

Finance. Monetary unit: Danish krone, with (Sept. 22, 1975) a free rate of 6.17 kroner to U.S. $1 (12.78 kroner = £1 sterling). Gold, SDRs, and foreign exchange: (June 1975) U.S. $789 million; (June 1974) U.S. $715.9 million. Budget (1973–74 rev. est.): revenue 49,956,000,000 kroner; expenditure 49,470,000,000 kroner. Gross national product: (1973) 165,370,000,000 kroner; (1972) 144,060,000,000 kroner. Money supply: (March 1975) 38,610,000,000 kroner; (March 1974) 35,380,000,000 kroner. Cost of living (1970 = 100): (May 1975) 156; (May 1974) 139.

Foreign Trade. (1974) Imports 60,138,000,000 kroner; exports 49,676,000,000 kroner. Import sources: EEC 46% (West Germany 18%, U.K. 10%, The Netherlands 6%); Sweden 13%; U.S. 6%. Export destinations: EEC 40% (U.K. 16%, West Germany 12%); Sweden 15%; Norway 6%; U.S. 5%. Main exports: machinery 16%; meat and meat products 13%; chemicals 8%; dairy products 5%.

Transport and Communications. Roads (1973) 65,112 km. (including 278 km. expressways). Motor vehicles in use (1973): passenger 1,257,300; commercial 203,900. Railways: state (1973) 1,999 km.; private (1970) 538 km.; traffic (1973–74) 3,197,000,000 passenger-km., freight 2,142,000,000 net ton-km. Air traffic (including apportionment of international operations of Scandinavian Airlines System; 1973): 2,216,000,000 passenger-km.; freight 93.1 million net ton-km. Shipping (1974): merchant vessels 100 gross tons and over 1,349; gross tonnage 4,460,219. Shipping traffic (1973): goods loaded 8,313,000 metric tons, unloaded 33,284,000 metric tons. Telephones (including Faeroe Islands and Greenland; Dec. 1973) 2,047,000. Radio receivers (Dec. 1972) 1,636,000. Television receivers (Dec. 1973) 1,412,000.

Agriculture. Production (in 000; metric tons; 1974; 1973 in parentheses): wheat 597 (540); barley 6,032 (5,432); oats 475 (444); potatoes *c.* 898 (748); sugar, raw value (1973) 368, (1972) 341; apples (1973) *c.* 120, (1972) *c.* 125; rapeseed *c.* 120 (92); butter 138 (146); cheese *c.* 145 (*c.* 127); pork (1973) *c.* 787, (1972) 783; beef and veal (1973) *c.* 186, (1972) 178; fish catch (1973) 1,465, (1972) 1,443. Livestock (in 000; July 1974): cattle *c.* 2,779; pigs 7,671; sheep *c.* 57; horses (1973) *c.* 48; chickens (1973) *c.* 18,419.

Industry. Production (in 000; metric tons; 1974): cement 2,493; pig iron (1972) 204; crude steel 535; fertilizers (nutrient content; 1973–74) nitrogenous 83, phosphate 104; manufactured gas (cu.m.) 335,000; electricity (net; kw-hr.) 17,256,000. Merchant vessels launched (100 gross tons and over; 1974) 1,125,000 gross tons.

stimulate the economy so that Danish industry would be well on the way to recovery when the hoped-for improvement materialized. These measures included an attempt to reduce unemployment, maintaining the tax reductions introduced by the Hartling government late in 1974, a reduction in the value-added tax from 15 to 10% over five months from September 29, the scrapping of a mandatory savings scheme three years before expiration and the return of funds for free consumption, grant aid for building, and subsidies to industry. After much debate the proposals received the support of 122 out of the 179 members of the Parliament.

Whether the measures would succeed in their aim and whether continuing support for the government would be forthcoming remained to be seen. Various problems had yet to be solved, and certain aspects of prices, wages, and labour relations were not included in the overall package. Moreover, the measures met with considerable opposition from the left-wing parties in Parliament, as well as from the Progress Party, which took the view that the whole package would turn out to be an expensive mistake.

(STENER AARSDAL)

See also Dependent States.

[972.A.6.a]

Dentistry:
see Health and Disease

Dependent States

Two trends developed in 1975: the claim of national minorities to be considered as potential states, and hence, as temporarily dependent territories; and the increase in importance of very small dependencies with strategic value and mineral resources.

In the first category, émigré groups from the Soviet Baltic states persevered in petitioning the UN for self-determination; similar Armenian groups also claimed the right of national secession from the U.S.S.R. and Turkey. In Iraq the long-standing rebellion of the Kurds appeared to have been put down at last. A conference on human rights and self-determination for Europe was held in April at Geneva. Bretons in France and Basques and Catalans in Spain sought autonomy at the very least, as did Scotland and Wales in Britain. (*See* UNITED KINGDOM: *Special Report.*) The Netherlands experienced terrorism by refugee groups demanding independence for the southern Moluccas, although those islands had been part of Indonesia since the Dutch withdrew in the 1940s.

Danish Greenland, with possible undiscovered mineral wealth, was promised a referendum on self-government in 1977. In the Americas land claims settlements (such as that of the Crees in northern Quebec in November 1975) no longer satisfied American Indians. The November 1974 Washington Conference of North and South American Indians was followed by a 1975 conference held in Ottawa to press for recognition and UN representation. In Africa and the Near East, apart from the Eritrean secessionists in Ethiopia and the claims of Palestinians and Omanis, the South African Bantustans were an urgent problem. Of the ten Bantustans, the Transkei was scheduled for independence in October 1976. Its leader, Chief Kaiser D. Matanzima, claimed the right to UN membership, pointing out that his three million people, 90% literate and already attracting large sums in foreign investment, were more prepared to run their own affairs than many so-called states.

The second category covered small islands that were significant in relation to strategy and offshore resources as well as other territories.

Europe and the Atlantic. On the opening of the airport in Norwegian Svalbard in September, the U.S.S.R. pressed for the right of use. The oil potential of the continental shelf brought to a head the question of conflicting Norwegian and Soviet claims in the area. Gibraltar remained a bone of contention between Britain and Spain.

In the French North Atlantic islands of Saint Pierre and Miquelon, the disgruntled inhabitants clamoured for removal of the governor and the French troops posted there. A French warship, transferred from fishery protection, lay off the capital, Saint Pierre. A series of strikes took place in protest against poor pay and conditions as compared with those of France.

The Azores became increasingly unsettled after the 1974 Portuguese revolution. Closely linked with the U.S. by remittances and emigrants and dependent upon the U.S. Lajes base for much employment and foreign exchange, the inhabitants looked with disfavour on the leftward swing in Lisbon. They forced the pro-Communist governor to resign and gave considerable support to a right-wing liberation movement. Argentina stepped up its claim to the Falkland Islands when British and Canadian companies detected potential offshore oil deposits there in 1975. Since there was no regular sea passage to the Falklands, apart from the annual wool-clip ship, access to the islands was by air from Buenos Aires and was under Argentine control. The British government's promise to improve the Falklands' airstrip was implemented during the year, but it still could not accommodate aircraft sufficiently large to bypass Argentina. The proposed British mission under Lord Shackleton to the Falklands was opposed by Argentina.

Caribbean. The associated Commonwealth Caribbean states shared problems arising from revenue shortfalls and dependence on aid; 15–20% unemployment or underemployment; the inability of tourism and local industry to provide enough jobs; and the need to develop agriculture; *e.g.,* bananas and sea island cotton. The prime ministers, except for George Walter of Antigua, favoured some integration among the islands in conjunction with eventual independence. Walter intended to press for entirely separate independence in 1976. Robert Bradshaw of St. Kitts was still faced with Anguilla's desire to secede from St. Kitts-Nevis. In October 1974 an earthquake damaged both St. Kitts and Antigua. Antigua enacted a new labour code and election legislation. Controversy continued over Walter's Newspaper Act; as a result of its provisions, including high license fees and antilibel deposits, no newspapers were being published.

In Dominica elections in March 1975 (using new electoral boundaries and enfranchising 18-year-olds) consolidated Prime Minister Patrick John's position; 16 of the 21 seats in the legislature went to his Labour government. The main issues were the economy and internal security after the Dread-induced violence of 1974. The Dreads (so-called from the braided "dread locks" in their hair), a radical black power youth movement blamed for an outbreak of antiwhite violence, had been outlawed in December 1974. They were supported, in at least such aims as the ending of foreign economic domination, by a dissident political group known as the Movement for a New Dominica. A young black militant was sentenced to death for the murder of a U.S. tourist in 1974 after a trial regarded by some as a frame-up.

Elections in St. Vincent in December 1974 had returned Milton Cato and his Labour Party, which won 10 of the 13 contested seats in the House of Assembly. Ebenezer Joshua, former deputy premier and leader of the People's Political Party (PPP), and his wife, Ivy, who had precipitated the election by breaking up their partnership with James Mitchell, retained their seats and sat on the government side. Mitchell thus became the solitary elected PPP opposition member. During his two and a half years in office, Cato had won widespread respect as a regional statesman and had led a much-needed reappraisal of the region's important but socially divisive tourist industry. By late 1975 only 21.67 in. of rain had fallen in the Kingstown area; the prolonged drought resulted in a poor crop of bananas, the main export.

In Belize Prime Minister George Price's People's United Party had been returned to power in elections in October 1974. The issue of independence for Belize was complicated by Guatemala's claim to the territory, which was supported by most Latin-American states. Price, meanwhile, repeatedly sought a defense guarantee from Britain, Canada, the U.S., and other sources. Talks between Guatemala and Britain collapsed in July 1975, when Whitehall rejected a Guatemalan compromise proposal to slice the colony in half, with Guatemala annexing the southern part. In November Britain reinforced Belize's small defense force, but at the end of the month the two governments agreed to resume negotiations.

Arson and violence on Grand Turk in the Turks and Caicos Islands in June 1975 were attributed to resentment against the presence of foreign expatriates. Earlier in the year Canada rejected the islands' request to become a Canadian province. Willard Wheatley was returned to power in the British Virgin Islands elections in September 1975. The Cayman Islands government proposed a new 15-year development plan in which all areas of the colony were earmarked for specific purposes to avoid haphazard development and sale to speculators. Vigorous local opposition to the plan was reported.

Surinam became independent on Nov. 25, 1975. The Netherlands agreed to make 3.5 billion guilders available for long-term development. It was also agreed that Surinamese able to obtain housing and employment in the Benelux countries within three months of arrival would be granted a resident's permit. Communal tensions increased the flow of mostly Asian Surinamese to The Netherlands, which over the past decade had received more than 130,000 such migrants, or one-third of the population of Surinam. Despite this efflux, unemployment in Surinam stood at 30%. (*See* SURINAM.)

In French Guiana pro-autonomy initiatives and anti-French unrest were exacerbated by the high cost of living, massive unemployment, the presence of troops, reports of a possible influx of up to 40,000 Vietnamese refugees, and the plan of the French secretary of state for overseas territories, Oliver Stirn, to open up the unexplored interior to some 30,000 French colonists from metropolitan France and elsewhere. The immediate program was concerned with

NORDISK PRESSEFOTO/PICTORIAL PARADE

This Greenland Eskimo in his kayak was observed by Queen Margrethe of Denmark during her visit to Jakobshavn in June.

LONDON DAILY EXPRESS/PICTORIAL PARADE

Queen Elizabeth II of Great Britain chats with a welcoming crowd during her Bermuda visit in February.

timber production, but there were reports that the French government planned to exploit uranium deposits found on the border.

The pattern of migration to Puerto Rico from the mainland continued, but the net in-migration in 1974, at 18,378, was considerably lower than the 34,492 recorded in 1973. There was disagreement as to whether the drop could be attributed to the economic situation on the island, which was experiencing the effects of recession imported from the U.S. In March Gov. Rafael Hernández Colón introduced a \$1.3 billion budget for fiscal 1976 that included a number of austerity measures, among them the withholding of \$100 million in pay increases for public employees. Earlier measures included imposition of a retroactive tax surcharge on 1974 incomes, a 5% excise tax on all imports other than food, and the dismissal of 1,600 government workers. Among the sectors that were particularly hard hit was tourism; the number of visitors in the 1974–75 season fell by 8.1%.

In September Tropical Storm Eloise caused 28 deaths and \$60 million in damage on the island, and Governor Hernández asked that it be declared a federal disaster area. The Armed Forces of the Puerto Rican National Liberation (FALN), a small leftist guerrilla group demanding complete independence for Puerto Rico, claimed responsibility for several bombing incidents on the mainland. After five years of protest by Puerto Rico, the U.S. Navy withdrew from the section of Culebra Island that had been used for gunnery practice since 1899.

Africa. The breakup of Portuguese Africa was completed. Mozambique was given independence on June 25, 1975, São Tomé and Príncipe on July 12, and Cape Verde Islands on July 5. Angola received a shattered and shaky independence on November 11. Cabinda, an enclave of Angola separated from it by a strip of Zaire territory, showed signs of seeking independence from Angola. It was potentially rich in offshore oil, and its situation on the northern shore of the Congo estuary made it especially attractive to neighbouring Zaire. By year's end, several other powers, including the U.S., the U.S.S.R., China, Cuba, and South Africa, were reportedly intervening to one degree or another in the struggle between warring Angolan factions. (*See* AFRICAN AFFAIRS; ANGOLA; CAPE VERDE ISLANDS; MOZAMBIQUE; SÃO TOMÉ AND PRÍNCIPE.)

In South West Africa (Namibia), the long-promised constitutional conference took place in September, under the shadow of the assassination of Ovambo Chief Elifas and a boycott by the South West African People's Organization. Before adjourning for a second meeting in November, delegations representing the various peoples laid down guidelines stating that a draft constitution for the territory should be achieved within three years, the position of Walvis Bay should be clarified, discrimination should be abolished, and relationships with South Africa should be discussed. It condemned external interference in South West African affairs.

On October 16 the International Court of Justice delivered a negative advisory opinion (recommending a referendum within the territory) on Moroccan, Mauritanian, and Algerian claims to Spanish Sahara. Morocco then stepped up its demands for the area and for Ceuta, Melilla, Peñón de Alhucemas, the Charafinas islets, and Peñón de Vélez de la Gomera. (The Canary Islands liberation movement continued with the approval of the Organization of African Unity.) King Hassan of Morocco organized a "peace march" of 350,000 civilians, which invaded the territory on November 6, despite Spanish and UN claims, backed up by Algeria, that the Sahouris must decide their own future by referendum. The march was ordered back by the king. A subsequent agreement on the territory's future reached by Spain, Morocco, and

Supporters of the Fretilin movement (Revolutionary Front for the Independence of East Timor) march through the streets of Dili, the capital city.

CAMERA PRESS

Mauritania was opposed by Algeria. (*See* MOROCCO.) At issue was control of the Spanish Sahara's huge BuCraa phosphate deposits.

In the French Territory of the Afars and Issas, increasing pressures for takeover came from Somalia and Ethiopia; rival Afar and Issas claimants fought bloodily in Djibouti during May. The French government, while promising democratic self-government under Pres. Ali Aref, also maintained and developed the port of Djibouti in the face of possible Soviet development of bases in Somalia. It also accepted over 50,000 refugees driven from Somalia by drought and famine.

Indian Ocean. Diego Garcia, part of the British Indian Ocean Territory, or BIOT, was leased as a base to the U.S. for 50 years, with a 20-year renewal option. The object of the move was to counter Soviet expansion in the Indian Ocean. The removal of the population to Mauritius caused some stir. The Seychelles, which had been promised independence in 1976 at a conference in London in March 1975, further complicated matters by demanding the return of Île Desroches, Aldabra, and the Farquhar Islands. These three territories had been detached politically from Seychelles in 1965, in return for a British-provided airport, and formed into BIOT, along with the Chagos Archipelago (including Diego Garcia), which was detached from Mauritius. BIOT, British-administered from the Seychelles, remained a flashpoint.

The French island of Réunion, with up to 50,000 unemployed, was passing through an economic crisis, though the calls for independence diminished somewhat during the year. The island's position was the more difficult because its population would shortly reach an unmanageable peak of 500,000 (after which it was expected to decline), and assisted emigration was proving inadequate to meet the crisis. The municipalities had opened workshops for the unemployed, but no unemployment benefits were provided (though social security payments were made to families). Fresh measures to alleviate the situation were announced from France.

The French Comoro Islands declared independence unilaterally on July 6 under Ahmed Abdallah, who was overthrown in a coup four weeks later. In September Abdallah attempted a further secession of Anjouan Island, where he had stayed after the coup. (*See* COMORO ISLANDS.)

Pacific. China, which took over the strategically located Paracels (Hsinan Islands) from South Vietnam in 1974 and evicted their inhabitants, also claimed the Spratlys and Senkaku and all the shallow sea from Taiwan to Korea. The status of the Australian-administered Cocos (Keeling) and Christmas islands was discussed with Indonesia and Singapore.

Hong Kong was visited by Queen Elizabeth II in May, the first such visit by a ruling British sovereign. The world's largest desalinization plant, opened in 1975, lessened Hong Kong's partial dependence on China for water supplies. Some of the colony's far-left political groups were organizing youth sections (over half Hong Kong's population was under 21). Legal and illegal immigration was estimated at 90,000 persons for 1974. Ironically, agreement was reached with China at the end of 1974 to repatriate numbers of would-be British supporters because of intense overcrowding. Though Hong Kong still provided China with over 40% of its foreign exchange earnings, China's increased trade with the West brought fears that China no longer needed an independent Hong Kong and might press for the return of Kowloon before the British lease expired in 1998.

A.F.P. / PICTORIAL PARADE

This Corsican demonstration for autonomy followed the arrest of 11 Corsicans by French police after two gendarmes were killed at Aleria in August.

Macao continued to exist as a Portuguese possession by Chinese courtesy. In Timor events overtook the promised March 1975 referendum in which the 600,000 inhabitants were to choose between a continued Portuguese link, independence, or integration with the Indonesian part of the island. Fighting broke out among rival groups, the chief of which were the left-wing Revolutionary Front for the Independence of East Timor (Fretilin) and the Democratic Union of Timor. In August Portugal admitted that it had lost control of the situation. Early in December Indonesia, claiming that it was acting at the behest of pro-integrationist groups, invaded the territory, captured the capital of Dili, and began to set up a provisional government.

Papua New Guinea became the 35th member of the Commonwealth of Nations on September 16. Copper-rich Bougainville threatened to separate from it but was pacified by regional government status and control over local revenue. (*See* PAPUA NEW GUINEA.) Internal self-government was introduced into the British Solomon Islands at the end of 1975; full independence was to come by 1977.

In the Gilbert and Ellice Islands, the Ellice Islands became a new entity, Tuvalu, in October 1975, with a new capital, Funafuti, but it remained British grant-aided. The Gilbertese opposed the desire of the Banabans from Ocean Island (who had been settled on Rabi in the Fiji Islands after World War II) for separate existence, based on control of Ocean Island's phosphate revenues and possible future association with Fiji, itself promised independence in 1977. In April this potential "state" of 2,000 people brought a suit against the British government in London for £22 million in compensation for damage done to the island by phosphate mining and underpayments of phosphate revenues. A British High Court judge visited Ocean Island to examine the alleged damage.

Following talks in London in November 1974, the Anglo-French condominium of New Hebrides was promised transfer of limited responsibility to an elected assembly. The question of citizenship re-

continued on page 254

Dependent States

ANTARCTIC

Claims on the continent of Antarctica and all islands south of 60° S remain in status quo according to the Antarctic Treaty, to which 17 nations are signatory. Formal claims within the treaty area include the following: Australian Antarctic Territory, the mainland portion of French Southern and Antarctic Lands (Terre Adélie), Ross Dependency claimed by New Zealand, Queen Maud Land and Peter I Island claimed by Norway, and British Antarctic Territory, of which some parts are claimed by Argentina and Chile. No claims have been recognized as final under international law.

AUSTRALIA

CHRISTMAS ISLAND

Christmas Island, an external territory, is situated in the Indian Ocean 875 mi. NW of Australia. Area: 52 sq.mi. (135 sq.km.). Pop. (1974 est.): 3,000. Cap.: The Settlement (pop., 1971, 1,300).

COCOS (KEELING) ISLANDS

Cocos (Keeling) Islands is an external territory located in the Indian Ocean 2,290 mi. W of Darwin, Australia. Area: 5.5 sq.mi. (14 sq.km.). Pop. (1974 est.): 640.

NORFOLK ISLAND

Norfolk Island, an external territory, is located in the Pacific Ocean 1,035 mi. NE of Sydney, Australia. Area: 14 sq.mi. (36 sq.km.). Pop. (1973 est.): 1,800. Cap. (de facto): Kingston.

DENMARK

FAEROE ISLANDS

The Faeroes, an integral part of the Danish realm, are a self-governing group of islands in the North Atlantic about 360 mi. W of Norway. Area: 540 sq.mi. (1,399 sq.km.). Pop. (1974 est.): 39,800. Cap.: Thorshavn (pop., 1974 est., 11,200).

Education. (1974–75) Primary, pupils 5,958; secondary, pupils 2,276; primary and secondary, teachers (1966–67) 299; vocational, pupils (1973–74) 1,266, teachers (1966–67) 88; teacher training, students 113, teachers (1966–67) 12; higher, students 24.

Finance and Trade. Monetary unit: Faeroese krone, at par with the Danish krone, with (Sept. 22, 1975) a free rate of 6.17 kroner to U.S. $1 (12.78 kroner = £1 sterling). Budget (1973–74 est.): revenue 168,214,000 kroner; expenditure 167,360,000 kroner. Foreign trade: imports (1972) 325.7 million kroner; exports (1973) 471,357,000 kroner. Import sources: Denmark 73%; Norway 7%; U.K. 6%. Export destinations: Denmark 22%; U.S. 13%; U.K. 13%; Spain 9%; Italy 8%; Iceland 5%; Poland 5%. Main exports: fish and products 90% (including fish meal 15%).

Transport. Shipping (1974): merchant vessels 100 gross tons and over 146; gross tonnage 44,653.

Agriculture and Industry. Fish catch (in 000; metric tons; 1973) 246, (1972) 208. Livestock (in 000; Dec. 1972): sheep 68; cattle 2.3. Electricity production (1973–74) 87 million kw-hr. (64% hydroelectric).

GREENLAND

An integral part of the Danish realm, Greenland, the largest island in the world, lies mostly within the Arctic Circle. Area: 840,000 sq.mi. (2,175,600 sq.km.), 84% of which is covered by ice cap. Pop. (1975 est.): 54,000. Cap.: Godthaab (pop., 1974 est., 8,300).

Education. (1974–75) Primary, pupils 10,834; secondary and vocational, pupils 2,411; primary, secondary, and vocational, teachers 1,044; teacher training, students 159, teachers 11.

Finance and Trade. Monetary unit: Danish krone. Budget (1972 est.) balanced at 52,118,000 kroner. Foreign trade (1972): imports 503 million kroner (92% from Denmark); exports 153 million kroner (66% to Denmark, 26% to U.S.). Main exports: fish and products 89%; cryolite 5%.

Agriculture. Fish catch (in 000; metric tons; 1973) 44, (1972) 41. Livestock (in 000; Nov. 1973): sheep 21; reindeer 0.8.

Industry. Production (in 000): cryolite (metric tons; shipments; 1972) 61; electricity (kw-hr.; 1973) 110,000.

FRANCE

AFARS AND ISSAS

The self-governing overseas territory of Afars and Issas is located on the Gulf of Aden between Ethiopia and Somalia. Area: 8,900 sq.mi. (23,000 sq.km.). Pop. (1973 est.): 180,000. Cap.: Djibouti (pop., 1973 est., 120,000).

Education. (1972–73) Primary, pupils 6,968, teachers 228; secondary, pupils 1,067, teachers 79; vocational, pupils 761, teachers 60; teacher training, students 25, teachers 12.

Finance. Monetary unit: Djibouti franc, with (Sept. 22, 1975) a free rate of DjFr. 165 to U.S. $1 (DjFr. 342 = £1 sterling). Budget (1973 est.) balanced at DjFr. 2,955,000,000.

Foreign Trade. (1973) Imports DjFr. 12,675,000,000; exports DjFr. 3,498,540,000. Import sources: France 49%; Ethiopia 12%; Japan 6%; U.K. 6%. Export destination France 84%. Main exports: ships and boats 16%; leather and shoes 7%.

Transport. Ships entered (1971) vessels totaling 5,788,000 net registered tons; goods loaded (1973) 142,000 metric tons, unloaded 728,000 metric tons.

FRENCH GUIANA

French Guiana is an overseas département situated between Brazil and Surinam on the northeast coast of South America. Area: 34,750 sq.mi. (90,000 sq.km.). Pop. (1974 est.): 58,000. Cap.: Cayenne (pop., 1967, 19,700).

Education. (1971–72) Primary, pupils 7,868, teachers 315; secondary, pupils 3,500, teachers 179; vocational, pupils 945, teachers 66.

Finance and Trade. Monetary unit: local franc, at par with the French (metropolitan) franc, with (Sept. 22, 1975) a free rate of Fr. 4.55 to U.S. $1 (Fr. 9.43 = £1 sterling). Budget (1974 est.) balanced at Fr. 117 million. Foreign trade (1973): imports Fr. 251 million (67% from France, 10% from U.S., 5% from Trinidad and Tobago); exports Fr. 23 million (81% to U.S., 9% to Surinam). Main exports (1973): shrimps 76%; ships and boats 6%.

FRENCH POLYNESIA

An overseas territory, the islands of French Polynesia are scattered over a large area of the south central Pacific Ocean. Area of inhabited islands: 1,261 sq.mi. (3,265 sq.km.). Pop. (1975 est.): 128,000. Cap.: Papeete, Tahiti (pop., 1971, 25,300).

Education. (1971–72) Primary, pupils 30,315, teachers 1,173; secondary, pupils 6,059, teachers 373; vocational, pupils 1,353, teachers 85; teacher training, students 130, teachers 11.

Finance. Monetary unit: CFP franc, with (Sept. 22, 1975) a parity of CFP Fr. 18.18 to the French franc and a free rate of CFP Fr. 82.81 to U.S. $1 (CFP Fr. 171.54 = £1 sterling). Budget (1974) balanced at CFP Fr. 8,774,000,000. Cost of living (Papeete; 1970 = 100): (March 1975) 160; (March 1974) 132.

Foreign Trade. (1973) Imports CFP Fr. 16,898,000,000 (59% from France, 15% from U.S.); exports CFP Fr. 1,497,000,000 (82% to France). Main exports: copra, vanilla, coffee, citrus fruit. Tourism (1972): visitors 111,300; gross receipts (1968) U.S. $9 million.

GUADELOUPE

The overseas département of Guadeloupe, together with its dependencies, is in the eastern Caribbean between Antigua to the north and Dominica to the south. Area: 687 sq.mi. (1,780 sq.km.). Pop. (1975 est.): 354,000. Cap.: Basse-Terre (pop., 1974 prelim., 15,500).

Education. (1974–75) Primary, pupils 75,036, teachers 2,473; secondary, pupils 35,624, teachers 840; vocational, pupils 7,516, teachers 381; teacher training (1971–72), students 382, teachers 15; higher, students 1,614, teaching staff 33.

Finance and Trade. Monetary unit: local franc, at par with the French (metropolitan) franc. Budget (1972 est.) balanced at Fr. 583 million. Cost of living (Basse-Terre; 1970 = 100): (April 1975) 164; (April 1974) 136. Foreign trade (1973): imports Fr. 895 million (75% from France); exports Fr. 210 million (82% to France, 7% to Martinique). Main exports (1973): sugar 43%; bananas 36%; rum 8%.

MARTINIQUE

The Caribbean island of Martinique, an overseas département, lies 24 mi. N of St. Lucia and about 30 mi. SE of Dominica. Area: 431 sq.mi. (1,116 sq.km.). Pop. (1975 est.): 346,000. Cap.: Fort-de-France (pop., 1971 est., 100,000).

Education. (1971–72) Primary, pupils 68,237, teachers 2,714; secondary, pupils 30,718, teachers 1,915; vocational, pupils 2,684, teachers 166; teacher training, students 564, teachers 16; higher (1969–70), students 1,673, teaching staff (1966–67) 21.

Finance and Trade. Monetary unit: local franc, at par with the French (metropolitan) franc. Budget (1972 est.) balanced at Fr. 392 million. Cost of living (Fort-de-France; 1970 = 100): (April 1975) 162; (April 1974) 141. Foreign trade (1973): imports Fr. 1,083,000,000 (72% from France); exports Fr. 244 million (80% to France, 11% to Guadeloupe).

NEW CALEDONIA

The overseas territory of New Caledonia, together with its dependencies, is in the South Pacific 750 mi. E of Australia. Area: 7,366 sq.mi. (19,079 sq.km.). Pop. (1975 est.): 135,000. Cap.: Nouméa (pop., 1974, 59,100).

Education. (1973) Primary, pupils 29,165, teachers 1,257; secondary, pupils 4,659, teachers 269; vocational, pupils 1,829, teachers 182; teacher training, students 69, teachers 22; higher, students 134, teaching staff 15.

Finance. Monetary unit: CFP franc. Budget (1974 est.) balanced at CFP Fr. 7,760,000,000 (including special French grants of CFP Fr. 1,810,000,000).

Foreign Trade. (1973) Imports CFP Fr. 17,748,000,000; exports CFP Fr. 14,907,000,000. Import sources: France 49%; Australia 12%. Export destinations: France 45%; Japan 33%; U.S. 11%. Main exports: ferronickel 45%; nickel 26%; nickel castings 24%.

Industry. Production (in 000; 1973): nickel ore (metal content; metric tons) 116; electricity (kw-hr.) 1,683,000.

RÉUNION

The overseas département of Réunion is located in the Indian Ocean about 450 mi. E of Madagascar and 110 mi. SW of Mauritius. Area: 970 sq.mi. (2,512 sq.km.). Pop. (1975 est.): 501,000. Cap.: Saint-Denis (pop., 1973 est., 98,000).

Education. (1973–74) Primary, pupils 124,120, teachers 3,942; secondary (including vocational), pupils 44,450, teachers 2,123; teacher training, students 560, teachers 47; higher, students 1,295, teaching staff 56.

Finance and Trade. Monetary unit: CFA franc, with (Sept. 22, 1975) a parity of CFA Fr. 50 to the French franc (free rate of CFA Fr. 227.70 = U.S. $1; CFA Fr. 471.75 = £1 sterling) and French (metropolitan) franc. Budget (1973 est.) balanced at CFA Fr. 88.5 billion. Cost of living (Saint-Denis; 1970 = 100): (Feb. 1975) 159; (Feb. 1974) 140. Foreign trade (1973): imports CFA Fr. 63,504,000,000 (64% from France, 6% from Malagasy); exports CFA Fr. 18,341,000,000 (75% to France, 22% to Italy). Main exports (1973): sugar 85%; essences 7%.

SAINT PIERRE AND MIQUELON

The self-governing overseas territory of Saint Pierre and Miquelon is located about 15 mi. off the south coast of Newfoundland. Area: 93 sq.mi. (242 sq.km.). Pop. (1974 est.): 5,800. Cap.: Saint Pierre, Saint Pierre.

Education. (1974–75) Primary, pupils 1,287, teachers 53; secondary, pupils 377, teachers 32; vocational, pupils 107, teachers 12.

Finance. Monetary unit: CFA franc and French (metropolitan) franc. Budget (1972 est.) balanced at CFA Fr. 736 million.

Foreign Trade. (1974) Imports Fr. 125,553,000; exports Fr. 59,352,000. Import sources: Canada 54%; France 38%. Export destinations (excluding ship's stores): Canada 70%; U.S. 25%. Main exports: petroleum products (as ship's stores) 53%; cattle 30%; fish 12%.

WALLIS AND FUTUNA

Wallis and Futuna, an overseas territory, lies in

the South Pacific west of Western Samoa. Area: 98 sq.mi. (255 sq.km.). Pop. (1975 est.): 9,000. Cap.: Mata Utu, Uvea (pop., 1969, 600).

NETHERLANDS, THE

NETHERLANDS ANTILLES

The Netherlands Antilles, a self-governing integral part of the Netherlands realm, consists of an island group near the Venezuelan coast and another group to the north near St. Kitts-Nevis-Anguilla. Area: 385 sq.mi. (996 sq.km.). Pop. (1975 est.): 242,000. Cap.: Willemstad, Curaçao (pop., 1970 est., 50,000).

Education. (1972–73) Primary, pupils 39,192, teachers 1,344; secondary, pupils 11,820, teachers 536; vocational, pupils 6,879, teachers 367; teacher training, students 321, teachers 25; higher, students 434, teachers 34.

Finance. Monetary unit: Netherlands Antilles guilder or florin, with (Sept. 22, 1975) a free rate of 1.79 Netherlands Antilles guilders to U.S. $1 (3.71 Netherlands Antilles guilders = £1 sterling). Budget (1972 rev. est.): revenue 115 million Netherlands Antilles guilders; expenditure 123 million Netherlands Antilles guilders. Cost of living (1971 = 100): (Jan. 1975) 148; (Jan. 1974) 122.

Foreign Trade. (1972) Imports 1,565,200,000 Netherlands Antilles guilders; exports 1,364,200,000 Netherlands Antilles guilders. Import sources: Venezuela 61%; U.S. 12%; Nigeria 6%; The Netherlands 6%. Export destinations: U.S. 64%; Canada 5%. Main exports petroleum products 91%. Tourism (1972) gross receipts U.S. $130 million.

Transport and Communications. Roads (1972) 1,150 km. Motor vehicles in use: passenger (1971) 36,000; commercial (including buses) 7,000. Shipping traffic (1971): goods loaded c. 36,630,000 metric tons, unloaded c. 43,690,000 metric tons. Telephones (Dec. 1973) 32,000. Radio receivers (Dec. 1973) 130,000. Television receivers (Dec. 1972) 33,000.

Industry. Production (in 000; metric tons; 1973): petroleum products c. 45,000; phosphate rock 92; electricity (kw-hr.; 1971) 1,419,000.

NEW ZEALAND

COOK ISLANDS

The self-governing territory of the Cook Islands consists of several islands in the southern Pacific Ocean scattered over an area of about 850,000 sq.mi. Area: 93 sq.mi. (241 sq.km.). Pop. (1975 est.): 25,000. Seat of government: Rarotonga Island (pop., 1971, 11,400).

Education. (1971) Primary, pupils 6,077, teachers 276; secondary, pupils 1,138, teachers 65; teacher training, students 75, teachers 10.

Finance and Trade. Monetary unit: New Zealand dollar, with (Sept. 22, 1975) a free rate of NZ$0.95 to U.S. $1 (NZ$1.96 = £1 sterling). Budget (1971 actual): revenue NZ$1,702,000 (excluding subsidy of NZ$2,943,000); expenditure NZ$4,695,000. Foreign trade (1971): imports NZ$5,766,000 (76% from New Zealand, 8% from Japan and Hong Kong in 1970); exports NZ$2,692,000 (98% to New Zealand in 1970). Main exports: citrus juices 26%; bananas 10%; pineapple juice 10%; canned pineapple 9%; copra 8%; oranges 5%.

NIUE ISLAND

The territory of Niue Island is situated in the Pacific Ocean about 1,500 mi. NE of New Zealand. Area: 100 sq.mi. (259 sq.km.). Pop. (1975 est.): 5,000. Capital: Alofi (pop., 1971, 1,000).

Education. (1975) Primary, pupils 925, teachers 69; secondary, pupils 387, teachers 23; vocational, pupils 9, teachers 2.

Finance and Trade. Monetary unit: New Zealand dollar. Budget (1971–72 actual): revenue NZ$980,000 (excluding subsidy of NZ$1,140,000); expenditure NZ$2,152,000. Foreign trade (1972): imports NZ$918,000 (79% from New Zealand in 1971); exports NZ$136,000 (90% to New Zealand in 1971). Main exports: passion fruit 29%; copra 22%; honey 5%.

TOKELAU ISLANDS

The territory of Tokelau Islands lies in the South Pacific about 700 mi. N of Niue Island and 2,100 mi. NE of New Zealand. Area: 4 sq.mi. (10 sq.km.). Pop. (1974 est.): 1,600.

NORWAY

JAN MAYEN

The island of Jan Mayen, a Norwegian dependency, lies within the Arctic Circle between Greenland and northern Norway. Area: 144 sq.mi. (373 sq.km.). Pop. (1973 est.): 37.

SVALBARD

A group of islands and a Norwegian dependency, Svalbard is located within the Arctic Circle to the north of Norway. Area: 23,957 sq.mi. (62,050 sq.km.). Pop. (1974 est.): 2,900.

PORTUGAL

MACAU

The overseas province of Macau is situated on the mainland coast of China 40 mi. W of Hong Kong. Area: 6 sq.mi. (16 sq.km.). Pop. (1975 est.): 257,000.

Education. (1973–74) Primary, pupils 20,205, teachers 676; secondary, pupils 7,786, teachers 463; vocational, pupils 2,885, teachers 120; higher (teacher training), students 7, teachers 9.

Finance and Trade. Monetary unit: patacá, with a free rate of 6.15 patacás to U.S. $1 (12.73 patacás = £1 sterling). Budget (1974 est.) balanced at 79,220,000 patacás. Foreign trade (1973): imports 804,483,000 patacás; exports 551,250,000 patacás. Import sources: Hong Kong 67%; China 26%. Export destinations: France 16%; U.S. 16%; West Germany 12%; Portugal 11%; Hong Kong 10%; Angola 6%; Belgium-Luxembourg 5%; Italy 5%. Main exports: textiles 75%; fish 5%.

Transport. Shipping traffic (1972): goods loaded 67,000 metric tons, unloaded 339,000 metric tons.

PORTUGUESE TIMOR

Portuguese Timor, an overseas province consisting of the eastern portion of the island of Timor and the exclave of Oé-Cussé in the western portion, is located about 300 mi. N of Australia. Area: 5,763 sq.mi. (14,925 sq.km.). Pop. (1975 est.): 672,000. Cap.: Dili (pop., 1970, 6,700).

Education. (1971–72) Primary, pupils 33,884, teachers 667; secondary (1970–71), pupils 411, teachers 20; vocational, pupils 930, teachers 39; teacher training, students 288, teachers 25.

Finance and Trade. Monetary unit: Timor escudo, at par with the Portuguese escudo, with (Sept. 22, 1975) a free rate of 27.35 escudos to U.S. $1 (56.65 escudos = £1 sterling). Budget (1974 est.) balanced at 211,370,000 escudos. Foreign trade (1973): imports 249,658,000 escudos; exports 169,387,000 escudos. Import sources: Portugal 25%; Singapore 15%; Australia 15%; Macao 11%; Mozambique 10%; Japan 7%. Export destinations: U.S. 27%; Italy 18%; U.K. 14%; Belgium-Luxembourg 10%; Singapore 10%; Portugal 10%. Main exports: coffee 90%; copra 6%.

Agriculture. Production (in 000; metric tons; 1973; 1972 in parentheses): corn c. 16 (c. 15); rice c. 15 (c. 13); sweet potatoes c. 15 (c. 13); cassava c. 19 (c. 20); copra c. 2.4 (c. 2.4); coffee c. 3 (c. 4). Livestock (in 000; 1973): cattle c. 78; sheep c. 47; goats c. 217; pigs c. 224; buffalo c. 136; horses c. 124.

SOUTH WEST AFRICA (NAMIBIA)

South West Africa has been a UN territory since 1966, when the General Assembly terminated South Africa's mandate over the country, renamed Namibia by the UN. South Africa considers the UN resolution illegal and has stated that it is determined to continue its jurisdiction over the area. Area: 318,261 sq.mi. (824,296 sq.km.). Pop. (1974 est.): 862,000. National cap.: Windhoek (pop., 1970, 61,300). Summer cap.: Swakopmund (pop., 1970, 5,700).

Education. Primary and secondary (1970): Bantu, pupils 95,302, teachers 2,243; Coloured, pupils 12,270, teachers 406; white (1971), pupils 22,775, teachers 1,191.

Finance and Trade. Monetary unit: South African rand, with (Sept. 22, 1975) an official rate of R 0.87 to U.S. $1 (free rate of R 1.81 = £1 sterling). Budget (1974–75): revenue R 85 million; expenditure R 91 million. Foreign trade (included in the South African customs union; 1972 est.): imports c. R 170 million (c. 80% from South Africa); exports c. R 240 million (c. 50% to South Africa). Main exports: diamonds c. 40%; fish and products 20%; livestock 15%; karakul pelts c. 14%.

Agriculture. Production (in 000; metric tons; 1973; 1972 in parentheses): corn c. 14 (c. 14); millet c. 14 (c. 14); beef and veal c. 65 (c. 64); mutton and goat meat c. 28 (c. 27); fish catch (excluding Walvis Bay; 1971) 19, (1970) 20. Livestock (in 000; 1973): cattle c. 2,650; sheep c. 4,300; goats c. 1,850; horses c. 39; asses c. 60.

Industry. Production (in 000; metric tons; 1973): lead ore (metal content) 63; zinc ore (metal content) 53; copper ore (metal content) 28; tin concentrates (metal content) 0.7; vanadium ore (metal content) 0.7; silver (troy oz.; 1972) 1,125; diamonds (metric carats) 1,600; salt (1971) 110; asbestos (1969) 90; electricity (kw-hr.; 1963) 188,000.

SPAIN

SPANISH SAHARA

Spanish Sahara is a province in northwest Africa, bordered by Morocco, Algeria, Mauritania, and the Atlantic Ocean. Area: 102,703 sq.mi. (266,000 sq.km.). Pop. (1974 est.): 108,000. Cap.: El Aaiún (pop., 1970, 24,500).

Education. (1972–73) Primary, pupils 4,680, teachers 204; secondary, pupils 590, teachers (1970–71) 54.

Finance and Trade. Monetary unit: Spanish peseta, with (Sept. 22, 1975) a free rate of 59.76 pesetas to U.S. $1 (123.80 pesetas = £1 sterling). Budget (1973 est.) balanced at 1,553,000,000 pesetas (mainly aid from Spain). Foreign trade (1973): imports 758,185,000 pesetas; exports 244,851,000 pesetas. Main export phosphate ore.

Agriculture and Industry. Livestock (in 000; 1973): camels 77; sheep 15; goats 123. Production (in 000; 1973): electricity (kw-hr.) 9,739; phosphate rock (metric tons) 696.

UNITED KINGDOM

ANTIGUA

The associated state of Antigua, with its dependencies Barbuda and Redonda, lies in the eastern Caribbean approximately 40 mi. N of Guadeloupe. Area: 171 sq.mi. (412 sq.km.). Pop. (1975 est.): 73,000. Cap.: Saint John's (pop., 1974 est., 23,500).

Education. (1973–74) Primary, pupils 12,138, teachers 440; secondary, pupils 6,300, teachers 290; vocational, pupils 153, teachers 23; teacher training, students 82, teachers 13.

Finance and Trade. Monetary unit: East Caribbean dollar, with (Sept. 22, 1975) a free rate of ECar$2.32 to U.S. $1 (official rate of ECar$4.80 = £1 sterling). Budget (1974 est.) balanced at ECar$38.9 million. Foreign trade (1972): imports ECar$90,976,000; exports ECar$34,639,000. Import sources (1968): U.K. 25%; U.S. 20%; Trinidad and Tobago 8%; Middle East 8%; Canada 7%. Export destinations (after 45% bunkering; 1968): Canada 24%; U.S. 5%; France 5%. Main exports (1968): petroleum products 79%; machinery and transport equipment 11%. Tourism (1973) 72,800 visitors.

BELIZE (formerly British Honduras)

Belize, a self-governing colony, is situated on the Caribbean coast of Central America, bounded on the north and northwest by Mexico and by Guatemala on the remainder of the west and south. Area: 8,866 sq.mi. (22,963 sq.km.). Pop. (1975 est.): 140,000. Cap.: Belmopan (pop., 1973 est., 5,000).

Education. (1970–71) Primary, pupils 32,610, teachers 1,228; secondary, pupils 3,539, teachers 238; vocational (including teacher training), pupils 312, teachers 25.

Finance and Trade. Monetary unit: Belize dollar, with (Sept. 22, 1975) a free rate of Bel$1.93 to U.S. $1 (official rate of Bel$4 = £1 sterling). Budget (1975 est.) balanced at Bel$49.5 million. Foreign trade (1973): imports Bel$80 million; exports Bel$53 million. Import sources (1970): U.S. 34%; U.K. 25%; Jamaica

7%; The Netherlands 7%. Export destinations (1970): U.S. 30%; U.K. 24%; Mexico 22%; Canada 13%. Main exports (1970): sugar 48%; orange juice 7%; grapefruit segments 5%; timber 8%; lobster 5%; clothing 5%.

BERMUDA

The colony of Bermuda lies in the western Atlantic about 570 mi. E of Cape Hatteras, North Carolina. Area: 21 sq.mi. (53 sq.km.). Pop. (1975 est.): 55,000. Cap.: Hamilton, Great Bermuda (pop., 1970, 3,000).

Education. (1973–74) Primary, pupils 7,425, teachers 346; secondary, pupils 4,536, teachers 322; vocational, pupils 456, teachers 47.

Finance and Trade. Monetary unit: Bermuda dollar, at par with the U.S. dollar (free rate, at Sept. 22, 1975, of Ber$2.07 = £1 sterling). Budget (1973–74 est.): revenue Ber$56,084,000; expenditure Ber$54,096,000. Foreign trade (1973): imports Ber$122,940,000; exports Ber$29,761,000 (including Ber$356,000 domestic). Import sources: U.S. 45%; U.K. 20%; Canada 10%. Export destinations (domestic only; 1972): U.S. 89%; Canada 6%. Main exports (domestic only): drugs and medicines 59%; liquor 5%. Tourism: visitors (1972) 340,000; gross receipts (1971) U.S. $97 million.

Transport and Communications. Roads (1973) *c.* 210 km. Motor vehicles in use (1972): passenger 11,900; commercial (including buses) 2,400. Shipping (1974): merchant vessels 100 gross tons and over 54; gross tonnage 1,153,280. Telephones (Dec. 1973) 35,000. Radio receivers (Dec. 1972) 40,000. Television receivers (Dec. 1973) 20,000.

BRITISH INDIAN OCEAN TERRITORY

Located in the western Indian Ocean, this colony consists of the Chagos Archipelago and the islands of Aldabra, Desroches, and Farquhar. Area: 85 sq.mi. (221 sq.km.). No permanent civilian population remains. Administrative headquarters: Victoria, Seychelles.

BRITISH VIRGIN ISLANDS

The colony of the British Virgin Islands is located in the Caribbean to the east of the U.S. Virgin Islands. Area: 59 sq.mi. (153 sq.km.). Pop. (1975 est.): 11,000. Cap.: Road Town, Tortola (pop., 1973 est., 3,500).

Education. (1972–73) Primary, pupils 2,138, teachers 94; secondary and vocational, pupils 745, teachers 44.

Finance and Trade. Monetary unit: U.S. dollar (free rate at Sept. 22, 1975, of U.S. $2.07 = £1 sterling). Budget (1974 est.): revenue U.S. $4,274,000; expenditure U.S. $5,436,000. Foreign trade (1973): imports U.S. $9,467,000; exports U.S. $441,400. Import sources: U.S. 24%; Puerto Rico 19%; U.K. 16%; U.S. Virgin Islands 15%; Trinidad and Tobago 8%. Export destinations: U.S. Virgin Islands 59%; Netherlands Antilles 12%; St. Martin 8%; U.K. 7%. Main exports: motor vehicles (reexports) 15%; nonelectric machines (reexports) 14%; gravel and sand 10%; fish 9%; timber (reexports) 6%; beverages (reexports) 5%.

BRUNEI

Brunei, a protected sultanate, is located on the north coast of the island of Borneo, surrounded on its landward side by the Malaysian state of Sarawak. Area: 2,226 sq.mi. (5,765 sq.km.). Pop. (1975 est.): 147,000. Cap.: Bandar Seri Begawan (urban area pop., 1972 est., 75,700).

Education. (1972) Primary, pupils 30,652, teachers 1,478; secondary, pupils 12,127, teachers 720; vocational, pupils 146, teachers 28; teacher training, students 386, teachers 32.

Finance and Trade. Monetary unit: Brunei dollar, with (Sept. 22, 1975) a free rate of Br$2.50 to U.S. $1 (Br$5.18 = £1 sterling). Budget (1974 est.): revenue Br$192 million; expenditure Br$191,065,000. Foreign trade (1973): imports Br$323,230,000; exports Br$852,056,000. Import sources (1972): Japan 20%; U.S. 19%; Singapore 15%; U.K. 14%; Malaysia 6%; The Netherlands 6%. Export destinations (1972): Japan 52%; Malaysia (Sarawak) 11%; Singapore 8%; U.S. 8%; Thailand 6%. Main export (1972) crude oil 99%.

Agriculture. Production (in 000; metric tons; 1973; 1972 in parentheses): rice *c.* 6 (*c.* 5); rubber *c.* 0.1 (*c.* 0.1). Livestock (in 000; Dec. 1973): cattle *c.* 3; buffaloes *c.* 16; pigs *c.* 14; goats *c.* 1; chickens *c.* 750.

Industry. Production (in 000): crude oil (metric tons; 1973) 11,053; natural gas (cu.m.; 1972) 453,000.

CAYMAN ISLANDS

The colony of the Cayman Islands lies in the Caribbean about 170 mi. NW of Jamaica. Area: 100 sq.mi. (259 sq.km.). Pop. (1975 est.): 11,400. Cap.: George Town, Grand Cayman (pop., 1970, 4,000).

Education. (1974–75) Primary, pupils 1,897, teachers 70; secondary, pupils 1,319, teachers 99.

Finance and Trade. Monetary unit: Cayman Islands dollar, with (Sept. 22, 1975) a free rate of CayI$0.84 to U.S. $1 (CayI$1.74 = £1 sterling). Budget (1974 est.) balanced at CayI$7,175,000. Foreign trade (1973): imports CayI$15.5 million; exports CayI$630,000. Main export turtle products. Tourism (1973) visitors 46,000.

Shipping. (1974) Merchant vessels 100 gross tons and over 48; gross tonnage 39,717.

DOMINICA

The associated state of Dominica lies in the Caribbean between Guadeloupe to the north and Martinique to the south. Area: 289 sq.mi. (750 sq.km.). Pop. (1975 est.): 75,000. Cap.: Roseau (pop., 1974 est., 10,200).

Education. (1973–74) Primary, pupils 20,993, teachers 538; secondary, pupils 2,111, teachers 111; vocational, pupils 94, teachers 13; teacher training, students 40, teachers 4.

Finance and Trade. Monetary unit: East Caribbean dollar. Budget (1973 est.) balanced at ECar$26.9 million. Foreign trade (1973): imports ECar$31,209,000; exports ECar$16,710,000. Import sources (1969): U.K. 33%; U.S. 15%; Trinidad and Tobago 11%; Canada 10%; The Netherlands and Netherlands Antilles 6%; West Germany 5%. Export destination (1969) U.K. 84%. Main exports (1970): bananas 26%; coconuts 15%; timber 5%.

FALKLAND ISLANDS

The colony of the Falkland Islands and Dependencies is situated in the South Atlantic about 500 mi. NE of Cape Horn. Area: 6,150 sq.mi. (15,930 sq.km.). Pop. (1975 est.): 2,000. Cap.: Stanley (pop., 1974 est., 1,000).

Education. (1974–75) Primary, pupils 101, teachers 9; secondary, pupils 60, teachers 12.

Finance and Trade. Monetary unit: Falkland Island pound, at par with the pound sterling, with (Sept. 22, 1975) a free rate of FI£0.48 to U.S. $1. Budget (1974–75 est.): revenue FI£862,000; expenditure FI£791,000. Foreign trade (1973): imports FI£567,000; exports FI£1,540,000. Main export wool.

GIBRALTAR

Gibraltar, a self-governing colony, is a small peninsula that juts into the Mediterranean from southwestern Spain. Area: 2.25 sq.mi. (5.80 sq.km.). Pop. (1974 est.): 29,400.

Education. (1974) Primary, pupils 3,923, teachers 185; secondary, pupils 1,549, teachers 120; vocational, pupils 52, teachers 22.

Finance and Trade. Monetary unit: Gibraltar pound, at par with the pound sterling. Budget (1973–74 rev. est.): revenue Gib£6,710,000; expenditure Gib£6,906,000. Foreign trade (1973): imports Gib£15,511,000 (57% from U.K. in 1972); reexports Gib£4,664,000 (31% to EEC, 16% to U.K. in 1971). Main reexports (1972) petroleum products 60%. Tourism (1973) 135,000 visitors.

Transport. Shipping (1974): merchant vessels 100 gross tons and over 10; gross tonnage 28,293. Ships entered (1973) vessels totaling 14,377,000 net registered tons; goods loaded 8,000 metric tons, unloaded 344,000 metric tons.

GILBERT AND ELLICE ISLANDS

The former colony of Gilbert and Ellice Islands was divided into two new colonies on Oct. 1, 1975. The Gilbert Islands retained that name, while the former Ellice Islands were constituted after October 1 as the Colony of Tuvalu. For details of area, population, and capital city, *see* entries under the respective names. Statistical data below refer to the former colony prior to its dissolution.

Education. (1973–74) Primary, pupils 14,194, teachers 471; secondary, pupils 833, teachers 54; teacher training, students 98, teachers 17.

Finance and Trade. Monetary unit: Australian dollar, with (Sept. 22, 1975) a free rate of A$0.79 to U.S. $1 (A$1.64 = £1 sterling). Budget (1973 est.): revenue A$5,497,000; expenditure A$5,509,000. Foreign trade (1973): imports A$6,670,000 (59% from Australia, 13% from U.K., 5% from New Zealand in 1972); exports A$9,732,000 (62% to New Zealand, 30% to Australia, 5% to U.K. in 1972). Main exports (1972 est.): phosphate *c.* 85%; copra *c.* 15%.

Industry. Production (in 000; 1972): phosphate rock (metric tons) 511; electricity (kw-hr.) 2,500.

GILBERT ISLANDS

The Gilbert Islands comprise 16 main islands, together with associated islets and reefs, straddling the Equator just west of the International Date Line in the western Pacific Ocean. Area: 102 sq.mi. (264 sq.km.). Pop. (1974 est.): 47,700. Seat of government: Bairiki, on Tarawa Atoll (pop., 1974 est., 17,100).

For statistics *see* GILBERT AND ELLICE ISLANDS.

GUERNSEY

Located 30 mi. W of Normandy, France, Guernsey, together with its small island dependencies, is a crown dependency. Area: 30 sq.mi. (78 sq.km.). Pop. (1971): 53,700. Cap.: St. Peter Port (pop., 1971, 16,300).

Education. (1974–75) Primary, pupils 5,563, teachers 251; secondary, pupils 4,137, teachers 279.

Finance and Trade. Monetary unit: Guernsey pound, at par with the pound sterling. Budget (1973): revenue £12,247,000; expenditure £8,868,000. Foreign trade included with the United Kingdom. Main exports: tomatoes, flowers. Tourism (1973) 289,000 visitors.

HONG KONG

The colony of Hong Kong lies on the southeastern coast of China about 40 mi. E of Macau and 80 mi. SE of Canton. Area: 403 sq.mi. (1,040 sq.km.). Pop. (1975 est.): 4,366,600. Cap.: Victoria (pop., 1971, 520,900).

Education. (1974–75) Primary, pupils 677,421, teachers 21,059; secondary, pupils 317,799; vocational, pupils 20,601; secondary and vocational, teachers 11,143; higher, students 18,200, teaching staff 1,863.

Finance. Monetary unit: Hong Kong dollar, with (Sept. 22, 1975) a free rate of HK$5.06 to U.S. $1 (HK$10.48 = £1 sterling). Budget (1974–75 est.): revenue HK$5,845,000,000; expenditure HK$5,747,000,000.

Foreign Trade. (1974) Imports HK$34,120,000,000; exports HK$30,036,000,000. Import sources: Japan 21%; China 17%; U.S. 13%; U.K. 6%; Singapore 5%; Taiwan 5%. Export destinations: U.S. 26%; U.K. 10%; West Germany 8%; Japan 7%; Singapore 5%; Australia 5%. Main exports: clothing 30%; chemicals 21%; machines 15%; textile yarns and fabrics 13%; instruments 5%. Tourism (1973): visitors 1,292,000; gross receipts U.S. $436 million.

Transport and Communications. Roads (1972) 1,010 km. Motor vehicles in use (1973): passenger 132,500; commercial 31,900. Railways: (1973) 35 km.; traffic (1974) 285.1 million passenger-km., freight 40,780,000 net ton-km. Shipping (1974): merchant vessels 100 gross tons and over 93; gross tonnage 269,945. Ships entered (1973) vessels totaling 36,094,000 net registered tons; goods loaded (1974) 4,919,000 metric tons, unloaded 13,706,000 metric tons. Telephones (Dec. 1973) 913,000. Radio licenses (Dec. 1972) 725,000. Television licenses (Dec. 1973) 748,000.

ISLE OF MAN

The Isle of Man, a crown dependency, lies in the Irish Sea approximately 35 mi. from both Northern Ireland and the coast of northwestern England. Area: 221 sq.mi. (572 sq.km.). Pop. (1975 est.): 55,600. Cap.: Douglas (pop., 1971, 20,400).

Education. (1974–75) Primary, pupils 5,641, teachers 214; secondary, pupils 4,329, teachers 251; vocational, pupils 133, teachers 32.

Finance and Trade. Monetary unit: Isle of Man pound, at par with the pound sterling. Budget (1973–74 rev. est.): revenue £14,687,000; expenditure £12,455,000. Foreign trade included with the United Kingdom. Main exports: livestock, fish products, tweeds. Tourism (1973) 529,000 visitors.

JERSEY

The island of Jersey, a crown dependency, is located about 20 mi. W of Normandy, France. Area: 45 sq.mi. (117 sq.km.). Pop. (1971): 72,600. Cap.: St. Helier (pop., 1971, 28,100).

Education. (1973–74) Primary, pupils 5,850; secondary, pupils 3,750.

Finance and Trade. Monetary unit: Jersey pound, at par with the pound sterling. Budget (1973): revenue £27,433,000; expenditure £19,508,000. Foreign trade included with the United Kingdom. Main exports: potatoes, tomatoes. Tourism (1973): visitors 1,047,000; gross expenditure (1971) £30 million.

MONTSERRAT

The colony of Montserrat is located in the Caribbean between Antigua, 27 mi. NE, and Guadeloupe, 40 mi. SE. Area: 40 sq.mi. (102 sq.km.). Pop. (1975 est.): 12,800. Cap.: Plymouth (pop., 1974 est., 3,000).

Education. (1974) Primary, pupils 2,640, teachers 108; secondary, pupils 499, teachers 108; vocational, pupils 39, teachers 8.

Finance and Trade. Monetary unit: East Caribbean dollar. Budget (1973 est.) balanced at ECar$4,987,000. Foreign trade (1973): imports ECar$12,148,000; exports ECar$130,000. Import sources (1972): U.K. 31%; West Indies 20%; U.S. 15%; Canada 12%. Export destinations (1972): West Indies 72%; U.K. 10%. Main exports (1972): hot peppers 21%; cotton 20%; tamarinds 9%; tomatoes 6%.

PITCAIRN ISLAND

The colony of Pitcairn Island is in the central South Pacific, 3,200 mi. NE of New Zealand and 1,350 mi. SE of Tahiti. Area: 1.75 sq.mi. (4.53 sq.km.). Pop. (1975): 70. Cap. (de facto): Adamstown.

ST. HELENA

The colony of St. Helena, including its dependencies of Ascension and Tristan da Cunha islands, is located in the Atlantic off the southwestern coast of Africa. Area: 119 sq.mi. (308 sq.km.). Pop. (1974 est.): 5,000. Cap.: Jamestown (pop., 1974 est., 1,600).

Education. (1971) Primary, pupils 777, teachers 39; secondary, pupils 438, teachers 30; vocational, pupils 100, teachers 1; teacher training, students 5, teachers 3.

Finance and Trade. Monetary unit: pound sterling. Budget (1973–74 est.): revenue £998,000; expenditure £964,000. Foreign trade (1973–74): imports £655,000 (61% from U.K., 28% from South Africa in 1968); exports nil.

ST. KITTS-NEVIS-ANGUILLA

This associated state consists of the islands of St. Kitts and Nevis; Anguilla was under direct British administration. Area: 135 sq.mi. (350 sq. km.). Pop. (1973 est., excluding Anguilla): 47,800 (Anguilla about 5,500). Cap.: Basseterre, St. Kitts (pop., 1970, 13,000).

Education. (1974–75) Primary, pupils 9,441, teachers 424; secondary, pupils 4,695, teachers 196; vocational, pupils 89, teachers 29; teacher training, students 95, teachers 10.

Finance and Trade. Monetary unit: East Caribbean dollar. Budget (1973 est.) balanced at ECar$34,553,000. Foreign trade (1972): imports ECar$31 million; exports ECar$11 million. Import sources (1969): U.K. 28%; Canada 14%; U.S. 14%; Trinidad and Tobago 10%; Barbados 5%. Export destinations (1969): U.K. 76%; Canada 10%. Main exports (1969) sugar and molasses 88%.

ST. LUCIA

The Caribbean island of St. Lucia, an associated state, lies 24 mi. S of Martinique and 21 mi. NE of St. Vincent. Area: 238 sq.mi. (616 sq.km.). Pop. (1974 est.): 110,800. Cap.: Castries (pop., 1970, 3,600).

Education. (1973–74) Primary, pupils 27,256, teachers 828; secondary, pupils 3,522, teachers 152; vocational, pupils 138, teachers 22; teacher training, students 178, teachers 19.

Finance and Trade. Monetary unit: East Caribbean dollar. Budget (1974 est.): revenue ECar$29,390,000; expenditure ECar$49,504,000. Foreign trade (1972): imports ECar$68,690,000; exports ECar$15,118,000. Import sources: U.K. 31%; U.S. 15%; Trinidad and Tobago 10%; The Netherlands and possessions 6%. Export destinations: U.K. 58%; Leeward and Windward islands 18%; Jamaica 7%; Trinidad and Tobago 6%. Main exports: bananas 55%; coconut oil 14%; machinery (reexports) 6%. Tourism (1973): visitors 45,800; gross receipts (1969) ECar$7.2 million.

ST. VINCENT

St. Vincent, including the northern Grenadines, is an associated state in the eastern Caribbean about 100 mi. W of Barbados. Area: 150 sq.mi. (389 sq.km.). Pop. (1975 est.): 93,000. Cap.: Kingstown (pop., 1973 est., 22,000).

Education. (1971–72) Primary, pupils 34,521, teachers 1,765; secondary, pupils 3,647, teachers (1968–69) 92; teacher training, students 362, teachers 11.

Finance and Trade. Monetary unit: East Caribbean dollar. Budget (1974 est.) balanced at ECar$31.9 million. Foreign trade (1972): imports ECar$35,240,000; exports ECar$6,590,000. Import sources (1971): U.K. 36%; Trinidad and Tobago 14%; U.S. 8%. Export destinations (1971): U.K. 59%; Barbados 19%; Trinidad and Tobago 9%; U.S. 7%. Main exports: bananas 51%; arrowroot 7%; coconut oil 6%.

SEYCHELLES

The colony of Seychelles consists of a group of about 80 islands scattered over 400,000 sq.mi. in the western Indian Ocean northeast of Madagascar. Area: 107 sq.mi. (278 sq.km.). Pop. (1975 est.): 58,000. Cap.: Victoria, Mahé (pop., 1972 est., 14,000).

Education. (1975) Primary, pupils 10,337, teachers 424; secondary, pupils 3,464, teachers 154; vocational, pupils 352, teachers 27; higher (teacher's college), students 109, teaching staff 18.

Finance and Trade. Monetary unit: Seychelles rupee, with (Sept. 22, 1975) a free rate of SRs. 6.43 to U.S. $1 (official rate of SRs. 13.33 = £1 sterling). Budget (1973 est.): revenue SRs. 49.9 million; expenditure SRs. 52.7 million. Foreign trade (1972): imports SRs. 111,671,000; exports SRs. 13,280,000. Import sources: U.K. 46%; Kenya 12%; Japan 6%; South Africa 6%; The Netherlands 5%. Export destinations: U.S. 29%; India 12%; Kenya 6%; Mauritius 6%; The Netherlands 6%. Main exports: cinnamon bark 44%; ship and aircraft bunkers 26%; copra 18%. Tourism (1973) 19,500 visitors.

SOLOMON ISLANDS

The Solomon Islands is a protectorate in the southwestern Pacific east of the island of New Guinea. Area: 10,983 sq.mi. (28,446 sq.km.). Pop. (1975 est.): 187,000. Cap.: Honiara, Guadalcanal (pop., 1973 est., 15,300).

Education. (1971) Primary, pupils 25,144, teachers 1,060; secondary, pupils 1,155, teachers 58; vocational, pupils 345, teachers 28; teacher training, students 87, teachers 13.

Finance and Trade. Monetary unit: Australian dollar. Budget (1974 est.) balanced at A$12,494,000 (including A$6,121,000 development aid). Foreign trade (1973): imports A$11,256,000; exports A$10,723,000. Import sources: Australia 45%; U.K. 13%; Japan 12%; Singapore 7%. Export destinations: Japan 53%; American Samoa 13%; West Germany 7%; Australia 7%; Norway 5%. Main exports: timber 40%; copra 29%; fish 17%.

TURKS AND CAICOS ISLANDS

The colony of the Turks and Caicos Islands is situated in the Atlantic southeast of The Bahamas. Area: 193 sq.mi. (500 sq.km.). Pop. (1975 est.): 6,000. Seat of government: Grand Turk Island (pop., 1970, 2,300).

Education. (1970–71) Primary, pupils 1,615, teachers 106; secondary, pupils 227, teachers 18.

Finance and Trade. Monetary unit: U.S. dollar. Ordinary budget (1973 actual): revenue $2,285,000; expenditure $2,241,000. Foreign trade (1973): imports $3,272,000; exports $456,000. Main exports: crayfish 90%; conchs 10%.

TUVALU

The colony of Tuvalu (formerly the Ellice Islands) comprises nine main islands, together with their associated islets and reefs, located just south of the Equator and just west of the International Date Line in the western Pacific Ocean. Area: 9½ sq.mi. (25 sq.km.). Pop. (1974 est.): 5,900. Seat of government: Funafuti (pop., 1974 est., 900).

For statistics *see* GILBERT AND ELLICE ISLANDS.

UNITED KINGDOM and FRANCE

NEW HEBRIDES

The British-French condominium of the New Hebrides is located in the southwestern Pacific about 500 mi. W of Fiji and 250 mi. NE of New Caledonia. Area: 5,700 sq.mi. (14,800 sq.km.). Pop. (1975 est.): 96,000. Cap.: Vila (pop., 1972 est., 8,500).

Education. (1971) Primary, pupils 18,878, teachers 782; secondary, pupils 580, teachers 50; vocational, pupils 213, teachers 12; teacher training, students 85, teachers 9.

Finance. Monetary units: Australian dollar and New Hebridean franc, with a free rate (Sept. 22, 1975) of NHFr. 73.61 to U.S. $1 (NHFr. 152.48 = £1 sterling). Condominium budget (1975 est.) balanced at A$11,268,000. British budget (1974–75 est.) balanced at A$7,885,000. French budget (1973 est.) balanced at A$7,524,000.

Foreign Trade. (1973) Imports NHFr. 2,498,800,000; exports NHFr. 1,498,100,000. Import sources: Australia 37%; France 17%; Japan 11%; New Zealand 8%; New Caledonia 5%. Export destinations: U.S. 55%; France 27%; Japan 10%; New Caledonia 6%. Main exports: fish 59%; copra 24%; timber 5%; beef and veal 5%.

Agriculture. Copra production (in 000; metric tons; 1974) *c.* 25, (1973) *c.* 23. Livestock (in 000; 1973): cattle *c.* 85; pigs *c.* 61.

Industry. Production (in 000): manganese ore (metal content; exports; metric tons; 1973) 10; electricity (kw-hr.; 1972) 10,000.

UNITED STATES

AMERICAN SAMOA

Located to the east of Western Samoa in the South Pacific, the unincorporated territory of American Samoa is approximately 1,600 mi. NE of the northern tip of New Zealand. Area: 76 sq.mi. (197 sq.km.). Pop. (1974): 29,200. Cap.: Pago Pago (pop., 1974, 4,700).

Education. (1974–75) Primary, pupils 7,213, teachers 333; secondary, pupils 2,367, teachers 142; vocational, pupils 800, teachers 38.

Finance and Trade. Monetary unit: U.S. dollar. Budget (1973 est.) balanced at $33,921,000 (including U.S. grants $30.4 million). Foreign trade (1973): imports $35,953,000 (91% from U.S. in 1970); exports $66,576,000 (95% to U.S. in 1970). Main exports (1970): canned tuna 90%; pet food 5%.

CANAL ZONE

The Canal Zone is administered by the U.S. under treaty with Panama and consists of a 10-mi.-wide strip on the Isthmus of Panama through which the Panama Canal runs. Area (land only): 362 sq.mi. (938 sq.km.). Pop. (1973 est.): 41,000. Administrative headquarters: Balboa Heights (pop., 1970, 200).

Education. (1973–74) Primary, pupils 6,954, teachers 329; secondary, pupils 5,324, teachers 297; higher, students 1,632, teaching staff (1971–72) 120.

Finance. Monetary unit: U.S. dollar (Panamanian balboa is also used). Budgets (1974): Canal Zone government, revenue $63.5 million, expenditure $63,171,000; Panama Canal Company, revenue $216,054,000, expenditure $227,852,000.

Traffic. (1973–74) Total number of oceangoing vessels passing through the canal 14,033; total cargo tonnage 147,907,000; tolls collected U.S. $119,420,000. Nationality and number of commercial vessels using the canal: Liberian 1,798; Japanese 1,348; Greek 1,337; U.S. 1,322; British 1,258; Panamanian 1,034; Norwegian 1,031; West German 748; Dutch 417; Swedish 344.

GUAM

Guam, an organized unincorporated territory, is located in the Pacific Ocean about 6,000 mi. SW of San Francisco and 1,500 mi. E of Manila. Area: 209 sq.mi. (541 sq.km.). Pop. (1974 est.): 110,300. Cap.: Agana (pop., 1974 est., 2,500).

Education. (1974–75) Primary, pupils 19,529, teachers 772; secondary, pupils 13,467, teachers 560; vocational, pupils 832; higher, students 2,111.

Finance and Trade. Monetary unit: U.S. dollar. Budget (1972 est.): revenue $75 million (including U.S. grants $9.6 million); expenditure $71.9 million. Foreign trade (1972): imports $167 million; exports $16.4 million. Tourism (1972) 185,000 visitors.

Agriculture and Industry. Main crops: corn, sweet potatoes, cassava, lemons, copra. Industrial production (in 000; metric tons; 1973): petroleum products 1,496; stone (1969) 593; electricity (kw-hr.) 1,010,000.

PUERTO RICO

Puerto Rico, a self-governing associated commonwealth, lies about 885 mi. SE of the Florida coast. Area: 3,421 sq.mi. (8,860 sq.km.). Pop. (1974 est.): 3,045,000. Cap.: San Juan (pop., 1972 est., 471,600).

Education. (1974) Primary (including preprimary), pupils 479,680, teachers 17,023; secondary, pupils 317,397, teachers 12,321; higher, students 74,059, teaching staff 5,185.

Finance. Monetary unit: U.S. dollar. Budget (1972–73): revenue $1,696,000,000; expenditure $1,818,000,000. Gross domestic product: (1972–73) $6,430,000,000; (1971–72) $5,793,000,000. Cost of living (1970 = 100): (April 1975) 148; (April 1974) 136.

Foreign Trade. (1973) Imports $3,580,000,000 (73% from U.S.); exports $3,093,000,000 (92% to U.S.). Main exports (1972–73): chemicals 20%; textiles 14%; fish products 9%; petroleum products 9%. Tourism: visitors (1974) 1,441,000; gross receipts (1971) U.S. $234 million.

Transport and Communications. Roads (1974) 16,827 km. Motor vehicles in use (1973): passenger 552,000; commercial 94,537. Railways (1973) 96 km. Telephones (Dec. 1973) 393,000. Radio receivers (Dec. 1973) c. 1,750,000. Television receivers (Dec. 1973) c. 600,000.

Agriculture. Production (in 000; metric tons; 1973; 1972 in parentheses): sweet potatoes 7 (7); bananas c. 113 (113); coffee (1974) c. 12, (1973) c. 14; sugar, raw value (1974) 261, (1973) 229; tobacco 2.3 (3.2); pineapples 40 (44); oranges 33 (31); grapefruit 8 (9). Livestock (in 000; Jan. 1974): cattle 541; pigs 233; chickens (1973) 4,517.

Industry. Production (in 000; metric tons; 1972): sand and gravel 6,786; stone 12,247; cement (1974) 1,793; electricity (kw-hr.) 11,256,000.

TRUST TERRITORY OF THE PACIFIC ISLANDS

The Trust Territory islands, numbering more than 2,000, are scattered over 3 million sq.mi. in the Pacific Ocean from 450 mi. E of the Philippines to just west of the International Date Line. Area: 707 sq.mi. (1,831 sq.km.). Pop. (1975 est.): 117,000. Seat of government: Saipan Island (pop., 1972 est., 10,700).

Education. (1973–74) Primary, pupils 30,746, teachers 1,433; secondary, pupils 7,358, teachers 457; vocational, pupils 268, teachers 39; teacher training, students 122, teachers 17.

Finance and Trade. Monetary unit: U.S. dollar. Budget (1972–73 est.): revenue $79,605,000 (including U.S. grant $59.4 million); expenditure $62,812,000. Foreign trade (1973): imports c. $30 million (50% from U.S., 28% from Japan in 1968); exports $1.9 million (57% to Japan in 1971). Main exports: copra 50%; fish 28%; handicraft items 10%; vegetables 5%.

Agriculture. Production (in 000; metric tons; 1973; 1972 in parentheses): sweet potatoes c. 3 (c. 3); cassava c. 5 (c. 5); copra c. 8 (c. 9); bananas c. 2 (c. 2). Livestock (in 000; June 1973): cattle c. 8; pigs c. 28; goats c. 5; chickens c. 135.

VIRGIN ISLANDS

The Virgin Islands of the United States is an organized unincorporated territory located about 40 mi. E of Puerto Rico. Area: 133 sq.mi. (344 sq.km.). Pop. (1974 est.): 65,000. Cap.: Charlotte Amalie, St. Thomas (pop., 1970, 12,200).

Education. (1973–74) Primary, pupils 14,737, teachers (1972–73) 563; secondary, pupils 7,285, teachers (1972–73) 523; higher, students 1,698, teaching staff 54.

Finance and Trade. Monetary unit: U.S. dollar. Budget (1972 est.): revenue $90.7 million; expenditure $90,280,000. Foreign trade (1973): imports $850,336,000 (41% from U.S. in 1970); exports $636,093,000 (93% to U.S. in 1970). Main exports: sugar, rum, petroleum products, watches, jewelry. Tourism (1972–73): visitors 1,312,000; gross receipts U.S. $100,020,000.

continued from page 249

mained knotty, for the division between French and English appeared to deepen during the year. The local National Party, incensed at not being consulted during the London talks, demanded total independence in 1977, but the August municipal elections showed overwhelming support for continued condominium status. In November the representative Assembly, created after an exchange of letters between France and Great Britain at the end of August, held its first meeting. The National Party, which was encouraged by the British, was the strongest group in the Assembly. In the French Pacific, the Territorial Assembly of Polynesia had a new majority of autonomists who, in June, rejected a proposed new constitution as being retrogressive.

Spanish troops search local tribesman as a security measure prior to the march on Spanish Sahara by Moroccan demonstrators in November.

UPI COMPIX

In the U.S. Trust Territory of the Pacific Islands, talks on the constitutional future were slowed by land control questions. In June a referendum in the strategically located northern Marianas resulted in a 78.5% vote in favour of U.S. commonwealth status, currently held only by Puerto Rico. Several steps remained to be taken before this became official, including approval by the U.S. Congress and UN Security Council approval for dissolution of the trusteeship, and final action was not expected until at least 1980.

Indian Protectorate (Sikkim). Sikkim's separate status as an Indian associated state ended in April 1975 when it was formally merged with India. A referendum organized by the ruling Sikkim National Congress had showed overwhelming support for integration with India and for deposing the chogyal (ruler), Palden Thondup Namgyal. The Indian move brought to a close more than 300 years of feudal rule by the Namgyal dynasty and led to the eclipse of the chogyal, whose angry protests found no echo among either the Indian leaders or his own 200,000 subjects.

Sikkim's chief minister, Kazi Lendup Dorji, whose differences with the chogyal had led to the latter's downfall, visited New Delhi several times both before and after the merger. The Indian government's Sikkim Bill making the kingdom India's 22nd state provided for representation by one member each in the two houses of the Indian Parliament. In September Sikkim nominated the two representatives who would sit in the Indian Parliament until the next Indian general election.

(PHILIPPE DECRAENE; MOLLY MORTIMER; SHEILA PATTERSON; GOVINDAN UNNY)

See also African Affairs; Commonwealth of Nations; South Africa; United Nations.

Development, Economic: *see* Economy, World

Diamonds: *see* Industrial Review; Mining and Quarrying

PROLIFERATION AND PEACE

By Lord Caradon

Of all the great changes in the history of the world none has been more revolutionary, more dramatic, or more rapid than the end of colonialism. Only 30 years ago Europe still administered its vast empires in Asia and Africa. The Germans had lost their empire in World War I; the Italians lost theirs in World War II; but the British, the French, the Dutch, and the Portuguese still ruled much more than a quarter of the population of the whole world.

Today all the great colonial empires have gone. They disappeared in less than three decades, with the Portuguese—the first colonizers—the last to go. By 1975 only a few minor scattered territories could be described as dependent or colonial in the old sense. The revolutionary transformation is virtually complete. Half a century ago such a fundamental change had not been imagined. The colonial system and the great empires seemed permanent. It was not until the end of World War II that the process of transforming colonies into independent states began, but once started it went ahead with breathtaking speed.

The Colonial Legacy. The results of these changes have been most startling at the United Nations; membership has risen from 51 states when the organization was created in 1945 to more than 140 in 1975—with probably another score to come. Writing in *Commentary* (March 1975), Daniel P. Moynihan (*see* BIOGRAPHY), the United States representative at the UN, called the end of colonialism "the British revolution" (justifying his label by the facts that the British had the largest empire and that more than half of the 87 states that had joined the UN since its founding were once part of the British empire). As he says, "a third of the nations of the world today owe their existence to the Statute of Westminster." "These new nations," Moynihan continued, "naturally varied in terms of size, population, and resources. But in one respect they hardly varied at all. To a quite astonishing degree they were ideologically uniform, having fashioned their polities in terms derived from the general corpus of British socialist opinion as it developed in the period roughly 1890–1950." Furthermore, "Before very long the arithmetical majority and the ideological coherence of those new nations brought them to dominance in the United Nations and, indeed, in any world forum characterized by universal membership."

Moynihan is a gifted phrasemaker, a provocative advocate, sometimes a mischievous commentator. He misjudges and overrates the influence of socialism in Britain and its empire in the first half of this century. But he rightly contends that British influence was dominant in the process of ending colonialism, and he was generous enough to say that "in the main it has been an immensely good thing." Certainly when Britain extended independence to its colonies this was done, in nearly every instance, with the cooperation and agreement of the people concerned. They were left with free parliaments, independent courts, and competent civil services.

Lord Caradon was minister of state for foreign and Commonwealth affairs and U.K. permanent representative at the UN from 1964 to 1970. Previously he had a distinguished career in the British colonial service and was governor of Jamaica and then of Cyprus.

British colonial administrators made no claim to be visionaries or idealists. Not until late, too late sometimes, was there recognition of where developments were leading and realization of the urgency of the preparations to be made for self-government. But they were working with the people. They were rowing on a full tide—and not against it but with it. The British have been criticized for introducing their own systems of representation and justice and administration. But they taught what they believed in for themselves, for to do otherwise would have seemed the worst form of paternalism.

The New Nations. So much for what was attempted. What of the results? How have the new nations fared since they attained the status of independence? It is perhaps too early to come to any balanced judgment on their performance, since most of them have had only a decade or two on their own. But how have they governed themselves so far? Have they advanced in prosperity? What part have they played in international affairs? Have they increased or diminished hopes of world peace?

Disappointingly, the course followed by the new nations in their internal administration has been reactionary almost everywhere. Not only have most of the free parliaments, independent courts, and uncorrupted civil services been abandoned—and it was perhaps to be expected that British institutions, in the form in which they were first established, would not survive—but nearly all the new nations are now under some form of military rule. In Africa alone there have been countless military coups since independence, and scarcely a month passes without news of another. In Bangladesh, as well as in India, democracy today is on the defensive.

To set against these reverses there have been honourable achievements. The reconciliations in Nigeria and Sudan after their fierce civil wars set an example for other divided peoples. Pres. Julius Nyerere of Tanzania and Pres. Kenneth Kaunda of Zambia are striving to make one-party systems responsive to the wishes of the people. There have been a few striking success stories—that of Singapore, for instance. Among and within the new nations, with all their confusions and conflicts, there have been outstanding examples of courage and leadership.

The flags of 16 new African member states were raised at UN headquarters in 1960 in celebration of an "African political renaissance."

UNATIONS

ALAIN NOGUES—SYGMA

Fifty thousand Moroccans assembled near the border with Spanish Sahara to await the signal for a peaceful invasion of that state in November.

But the fact must be faced that in Africa and Asia colonialism has been widely followed by a retreat to nationalism backed by military dictatorship. Economically, some progress has been made, with the help of decreasing bilateral aid but increasing multilateral aid from the World Bank and the UN Development Program. But in many third world countries the slow general progress has been overwhelmed by the rise of oil prices—which makes nonsense of their meagre development policies—and by the inexorable increase in population, which destroys their hope of escape from poverty, hunger, and squalor. Recent world conferences on the environment, population, and food marked recognition of the extent of the problems but produced no agreement on radical solutions. The special session of the UN General Assembly that met in September 1975 directed world attention to the economic needs of the new nations. There was at first little optimism that early decisions or urgent actions would be forthcoming, but in fact a wide range of agreement was reached at the session, agreement on how to proceed in tackling the main questions facing both the rich and the poor nations. An exciting new start on these vital issues is now possible.

On the World Stage. It might be argued that the internal problems of the new nations are so great that they can exercise little influence on the wider world. With all their internal troubles and failures, what part can they play in international endeavours for the preservation of peace? The dangers are greater than ever. A race war in southern Africa; another far more devastating conflict in the Middle East; a confrontation between Greece and Turkey over Cyprus; continued unrest in the Far East; growing tension throughout the world between the poor and the rich—all these are likely. It seems almost as though the world was a much safer place in the old colonial days.

Nevertheless, it is in the wider field of international affairs that the new nations intend to exercise positive and hopeful influences. It is on the new worldwide issues of poverty and population and race that they wish to take new initiatives. They applauded the words of former West German chancellor Willy Brandt when he spoke in the General Assembly on Germany's admission to the UN: "Human distress is conflict. In the long run where hunger prevails there can be no peace. Where bitter poverty prevails, there can be no justice. Where a man's very existence is threatened for want of basic daily needs, it is not possible to speak of security." It is on these issues that the new nations feel most intensely and are usually united.

It is in the open country of internationalism that the liberal and socialist influences bequeathed by "the British revolution" may eventually be felt. Against monolithic oppression and domination by armed strength, the hope is that the new nations will create a third force that is more concerned with justice than with power, more concerned with the rights of the individual than with the authority of the state, more concerned with freedom than with force.

No one can claim that the proliferation of new nations has made peace more secure. Indeed, it has greatly increased the difficulties and the dangers. But it also holds out the possibility of a growing determination not to depend for peace on the destructive power of the great nations but instead to make use of the instrument of the United Nations, where every nation can be heard and where the will of the majority of mankind for peace and justice can prevail. Many years ago, UN Secretary-General Dag Hammarskjöld said:

> It is not the Soviet Union or indeed any other big powers who need the United Nations for their protection; it is all the others. In this sense the organization is first of all their organization, and I deeply believe in the wisdom with which they will be able to use and guide it.

The Unsilent Majority. Within the UN and its related agencies, the stage is now set for a fascinating contest, or competition, in initiative. The new nations, seeing their opportunity and impatiently eager to use the instrument they believe may be their salvation, will press their voting advantage. They may continue to make grave procedural and tactical errors. They may even continue to make serious blunders, such as the attempt to oust from the UN governments that they condemn. They may thus alienate even some of the middle powers, which on most issues are on their side. But with a majority of well over 100 nations on most important international issues, they are in a strong position. We may hope that they will use their advantage more wisely in the future.

On the other hand, the United States—and other Western powers as well, though for different reasons—are turning away from international leadership in disillusion and isolation. The United States is no longer able to command a majority in the Security Council or the General Assembly and thus may seek to curtail UN influence and action. John Scali, Moynihan's predecessor at the UN, began the shrill complaint against "the tyranny of the majority," and U.S. Secretary of State Henry Kissinger, while giving lip service to the fashionable thesis of interdependence, might well continue the attempt to bypass the UN by direct big-power diplomacy. It is to be hoped that such a destructive division will not persist, and that the new procedures recently proposed unanimously by 25 experienced international leaders will show the way to more effective practical cooperation. U.S. Pres. Gerald Ford has spoken of a dialogue in the UN "of candor, directness, and respect." In such a dialogue the new nations will not fail to respond. They may well take the lead.

The emergence in the past 30 years of nearly 100 new nations, representing the majority of mankind and bringing with them the European traditions of equality and justice, may yet prove to have a salutary and, indeed, a decisive influence on endeavours to keep the peace and to make the peace tolerable.

Disasters

The loss of life and property from disasters in 1975 included the following.

AVIATION

Jan. 4 Lotru Mt., Rom. A Romanian airliner on a domestic flight crashed into a mountainous area, killing 33 persons.

Jan. 6 Near Tucumán, Arg. A two-engine military plane crashed during a storm and burst into flames; 2 of the 13 officers who died were army generals.

Jan. 8 Near Neiva, Colombia. A C-47 Satena airliner crashed and burned shortly after taking off from the Neiva airport; none of the 20 persons aboard survived.

Jan. 9 Near Whittier, Calif. A Golden West Airliner commuter plane was hit by a single-engine Cessna 150 carrying a student pilot and his instructor; all 14 persons aboard the two planes lost their lives.

Jan. 30 Near Istanbul, Turkey. A Turkish Airlines F-28 carrying 37 passengers and 4 crew members crashed into the Sea of Marmara when a citywide power failure blacked out the landing strip lights at Yesilkoy Airport; there were no survivors.

Feb. 3 Near Manila, Phil. The engine of a Philippine airliner burst into flames shortly after the pilot took off from the Manila airport; 31 of the 32 persons aboard died in a crash landing.

Feb. 9 Crete. A West German military plane heading for a NATO base crashed on the Greek island of Crete in the Mediterranean, killing all 42 persons aboard.

Feb. 27 Congonhas, Brazil. A VASP airliner scheduled to fly into the interior crashed while taking off from the Municipal Airport; 15 persons died.

Feb. 28 Near Natal, Brazil. A helicopter carrying petroleum workers to a drilling platform exploded near Natal; 12 persons lost their lives.

March 16 Near San Carlos de Bariloche, Arg. A Fokker 26, operated as a passenger plane by the Argentine Air Force, smashed into a mountain; there were at least 52 fatalities.

March 20 Near Quilcene, Wash. A U.S. military C-141 Starlifter, nearing the end of a flight from Japan, crashed inside Olympic National Park when the pilot followed landing directives intended for another plane; all 16 persons aboard perished.

April 4 Near Saigon, South Vietnam. A U.S. Air Force C-5A, the world's largest airplane, carrying 243 Vietnamese orphans and their adult escorts on the first leg of a flight to the U.S., crashed and broke apart in a soggy paddy before the pilot was able to return safely to Saigon's Tan Son Nhut Airport; improperly closed rear hatches were blamed for the disaster, which claimed the lives of more than 150 persons, most of them tiny children.

June 24 New York City. An Eastern Airlines Boeing 727 jetliner on a flight from New Orleans, La., crashed at Kennedy International Airport during a lightning storm that whipped up hazardous wind currents; 113 persons were killed when the plane disintegrated and burst into flames after striking a series of light towers.

Mid-July Near Batumi, Georgia, U.S.S.R. A Soviet Yak-40 airliner operating out of Armenia crashed near Batumi, killing at least 28 persons.

July 31 Taipei, Taiwan. A Far Eastern Air Transport turboprop on a routine domestic flight from Hualien skidded off the Taipei airport runway during a sudden rainstorm and broke into three pieces; at least 27 persons were killed and 48 injured.

Aug. 3 Near Imzizen, Morocco. A four-engine Boeing 707, carrying workers home from France for a summer vacation, crashed into a fog-shrouded mountain and burned as it approached the Agadir airport; none of the 188 persons aboard survived.

Aug. 20 Near Damascus, Syria. A four-engine Soviet-made Ilyushin 62 jetliner operated by Czechoslovakia crashed into a hill and burst into flames as it approached the Damascus airport; there were only 2 survivors among the 128 persons aboard.

Aug. 30 St. Lawrence Island, Alaska. A Wien Air Alaska F-27B turboprop crashed into a fog-veiled hillside at Gambell while on a routine flight from Nome; 10 persons died but 23 others were rescued by Eskimos living in a nearby village.

Aug. 31 Leipzig, East Germany. A Tu-134 jetliner operated by the Interflug Airline of East Germany crashed just short of the Leipzig airport runway at the completion of a flight from Stuttgart; 26 persons died in the flaming wreckage.

Sept. 24 Palembang, Sumatra, Indon. A Garuda Indonesian Airways Fokker 28 on a routine flight from Jakarta overshot the Palembang runway, then struck coconut trees and burst into flames; 29 persons were killed, including a woman farm worker who was burned to death.

Sept. 30 Mediterranean Sea. A Soviet-built Tu-154, operated by the Hungarian Malev Airlines, crashed into the sea and sank as it was preparing to land at the Beirut airport in Lebanon; none of the 60 persons aboard survived the predawn mishap.

Oct. 25 Bolivia. A Bolivian Air Force Convair 440 that was transporting military personnel and their relatives to La Paz crashed into a mountain shortly after taking off from a resort at Tomonoco; all 70 aboard were presumed dead.

Oct. 30 Prague, Czech. A twin-jet DC-9 airliner chartered by Yugoslavia crashed on the outskirts of Prague as it came in for a landing at the fog-shrouded airport; 68 of the 120 persons aboard were killed.

Nov. 25 Sinai Peninsula. An Israeli C-130E Hercules transport, on a night training flight over the Sinai desert, crashed into the summit of 2,900-ft. Jebel Halal; all 20 persons aboard were killed.

FIRES AND EXPLOSIONS

Jan. 22 Marikina, Phil. A fire that broke out in a five-story building trapped workers on the upper floors when flames engulfed the exits; in the worst Philippine fire to date, about 50 persons died, most of them women, and some 80 others were seriously injured.

Jan. 29 Taichung, Taiwan. An explosion in a firecracker factory set off a raging fire that engulfed more than a dozen buildings and claimed the lives of some 20 persons; about 50 others were severely injured.

March 27 Santa Maria Maggiore, Italy. The Excelsior Hotel, a multistory resort lodging, was consumed by an early morning fire; 16 were reported killed and about 40 others injured.

March 28 Rijeka, Yugos. Faulty electrical installation at the Dr. Zdravko Kucic Hospital was blamed for a fire that killed 25 babies whose lives were being supported by incubators.

April 18(?) Cologne, West Germany. The 270-ton Dutch excursion ship "Princess Irene" caught fire and sank while

GAMMA / LIAISON

Turkey, astride one of the major earthquake belts that girdle the globe, suffered a temblor in September that destroyed the town of Lice. The loss of life was estimated at more than 2,000 and another 30,000 persons were left homeless.

tied to its Rhine River moorings; most of the 19 persons presumed dead were elderly and infirm.

May 14 Buhut, Egypt. A fire, fanned by winds from a powerful sandstorm, destroyed a village of straw-roofed homes in the Nile delta; at least 12 persons lost their lives and more than 200 suffered injuries.

June 10 Keelathattapara, India. Explosives blew up in a southern India village killing 12 persons and injuring 65.

July 23 Near Toulon, France. An explosion and fire aboard the ferryboat "Vénus des Îles II" claimed the lives of at least 12 persons, though the number of missing was not known; scores of terrified passengers who leaped into the Mediterranean were rescued within minutes by nearby helicopters and rescue vessels.

July 23 Near Comilla, Bangladesh. A mine that was discovered on a riverbank by children exploded when it was tossed into a fire by neighbours; 10 persons were killed and 32 injured.

Dec. 13 Mina, Saudi Arabia. A fire that began with the explosion of bottled gas swept through a tent city of Muslims who were among two million religious pilgrims gathered in or near Mecca for the annual feast of Id al-Adha; 138 persons lost their lives and 151 others were injured.

Dec. 25 Sydney, Australia. An early morning fire that started in an elevator shaft swept through the Savoy Hotel located in the King's Cross area; 14 persons were killed and many others severely burned.

MARINE

Jan. 10 Hanstholm, Den. Ten seamen, trapped between their capsized Polish trawler and a pier, were crushed to death just beyond the reach of a rescue party; 17 others were saved by an air force helicopter.

Jan. 25 Off southwest English coast. The 1,093-ton British cargo ship "Lovat" was sunk by strong gales while on its way from Wales to France with a load of coal dust; only 2 of the 13 crewmen were rescued.

Jan. 25 Near Dacca, Bangladesh. A ferryboat that collided with a steamer on the Buriganga River sank about 7 mi. from Dacca; about half of the estimated 200 persons aboard were presumed drowned.

Aug. 3 Near Canton, China. Two triple-deck excursion ferries, plying the Hsi River during heavy rains in the wee hours of the morning, collided and sank; as many as 500 persons were believed to have drowned.

Aug. 25 João Pessoa, Brazil. During a festival for dependents of military personnel, a group of small army boats capsized on a lake; 29 persons died, most of them children.

Mid-September Northern Thailand. Thousands of Meo tribesmen, many of them women and children, fled their sanctuary in northern Thailand when Pathet Lao troops began firing on their village; several hundred of the refugees drowned while attempting to escape across a mountain river.

Sept. 18 Northern India. A crowded ferryboat carrying about 200 flood victims to a relief centre capsized on the Rapti River; about half the refugees perished in the swirling waters.

Oct. 24 Pyamalaw River, Burma. A two-deck ferryboat, carrying about 230 passengers, capsized and sank on a branch of the Irrawaddy River; at least 150 of those aboard were believed drowned.

Oct. 25 Near Rangoon, Burma. A ferryboat capsized and sank in the Twante Canal; 18 persons were known to have died and 49 others were missing.

Nov. 10 Near Cooper Mine Point, Ont. The 729-ft. ore carrier "Edmund Fitzgerald," battered by 20-ft.-high waves and 65-mph winds, sank in Lake Superior; though sea and air rescue parties discovered three self-inflatable lifeboats, none of the 29 crewmen survived.

Dec. 19 Gulf of Mexico. The 7,000-ton Mexican freighter "Tlaxcala" turned over when its cargo of aluminite shifted during a storm; 23 persons were missing, including the captain, his wife, and their two-year-old daughter.

MINING AND TUNNELING

Sept. 20 Near Rockhampton, Australia. An explosion and fire at the Kianga coal mine in central Queensland took the lives of 13 miners who were trapped 650 ft. underground when the accident occurred.

Nov. 3 Figols, Spain. A gas explosion in a coal mine located about 50 mi. from Barcelona killed 27 workers and seriously injured at least 2 others.

Nov. 7 Beek, Neth. An explosion caused by leaking gas at one of the State Mines Company's three naphtha cracking units ignited storage tanks containing gasoline and liquid chemicals; 12 persons were killed, 2 were missing, and 30 injured.

Nov. 27 Mikasa, Japan. A gas explosion deep inside a coal mine killed ten workers and injured seven.

Dec. 27 Near Dhanbad, Bihar State, India. Two explosions at the Chas Nala Colliery caused millions of gallons of water from old shafts to pour into underground areas where hundreds of coal miners were working; despite frantic rescue efforts, there was no hope that any of the 372 who were known to be trapped by the mine's collapse would survive.

MISCELLANEOUS

January Hobart, Australia. The "Lake Illawarra," an iron-ore carrier, crashed into a pylon of the Tasman Bridge and sank; five seamen and four motorists who were crossing the bridge lost their lives.

January Kisumu, Kenya. An epidemic of cholera, which claimed many lives in private homes before it was detected, was blamed for nearly 200 deaths.

January Florida. A virulent strain of influenza that was most severe in the St. Petersburg area was a major factor in the deaths of about 30 persons, most of whom were elderly.

March 9 Seoul, South Korea. A cement embankment supporting two buildings collapsed on several dormitories that housed young women employees of a nearby wig factory; 17 were killed and 12 injured.

Late March Dinajpur, Bangladesh. An outbreak of smallpox in a northern district of Bangladesh killed 31 persons before effective measures were undertaken to prevent further contagion.

Summer U.S. Encephalitis-bearing mosquitoes infected some 350 persons residing in 15 states, with Mississippi the most severely affected area; health authorities confirmed that the disease caused 47 deaths before the end of summer.

Late August Bihar, India. During a period of extensive flooding in the capital of Bihar State, cholera claimed the lives of at least 50 persons.

August–October Papua New Guinea. An epidemic of influenza that raged for several months took the lives of more than 400 persons.

Early November Ishiagu, Nigeria. A cholera outbreak in the village of Ishiagu claimed an estimated 30 lives.

December Nova Iguaçu, Brazil. A severe heat wave reportedly caused 56 children to die of dehydration.

NATURAL

Early January Southern Thailand. Unusually heavy rains caused widespread flooding that severely damaged rubber plantations, rice crops, and mining facilities; the disaster also claimed 131 lives.

Early January Central U.S. A blizzard with subzero temperatures and 90-mph winds was responsible for 50 deaths in the Midwest and the Central Plains.

Jan. 10 Mississippi. A tornado that leveled a shopping centre killed 12 persons and injured about 200; property damage was estimated in the millions.

Jan. 19 Himachal Pradesh State, India. A violent earthquake measuring 7 on the Richter scale destroyed numerous dwellings and buried many inhabitants alive under the rubble.

Late January Philippines. A tropical storm triggered landslides on the southern island of Mindanao and whipped up

Wreckage of an Eastern Airlines plane which crashed at Kennedy International Airport in New York on a flight from New Orleans June 24. The disaster claimed the lives of 113 passengers.

KEYSTONE

A.F.P./PICTORIAL PARADE

Fire swept the pleasure craft "Vénus des Îles II" near Toulon, France, on July 23, killing 12 and injuring about 50 persons when panic ensued.

rough seas that battered a fishing boat off the island of Panay; all told, the storm was blamed for 30 deaths on land and sea.

January–June East Africa. A severe drought that began late in 1974 and continued unbroken into June 1975 affected some 800,000 persons in the Ogaden region of Ethiopia and the neighbouring area in Somalia; an estimated 40,000 persons died, many of them while living in relief camps.

Feb. 4 Anshan, Liaoning Province, China. A violent earthquake measuring 7.3 on the Richter scale hit Anshan, a major industrial area in northeast China; though no report on casualties or damage was released, at least some of the 830,000 inhabitants were believed to have been killed or injured because of the large number of factories and homes located in the area.

Feb. 20–21 Nile River area, Egypt. In the worst Egyptian flood in 20 years, torrential rains inundated 1,000 ac. of land along the Nile River, destroyed 21 villages, and took at least 15 lives.

Mid-March Nequen Province, Arg. Rainstorms sweeping in off the Andes caused the deaths of 20 persons; about a dozen others were missing.

Late March British Columbia, Canada. A violent storm that lashed Vancouver Island and swept some 200 mi. inland to Kamloops capsized ships, destroyed aircraft, uprooted trees, downed power lines, and damaged campers, buildings, and stores; little hope was held out for 14 fishermen who were missing and presumed drowned.

Early April Alps mountain ranges. In one of the worst series of avalanches on record, huge quantities of snow buried villages, roads, and rail lines; the estimated death toll was 13 in Switzerland, 12 in Italy, and 15 in Austria.

April 21 Northern Iran. Torrential rains in the Damghan area destroyed about 150 villages and took the lives of at least 14 persons.

Mid-June Pakistan. A searing week-long heat wave that reached 119° F in some areas took at least 14 lives.

July Northwest India. Month-long monsoon rains that flooded some 400 sq.mi. of standing crops and damaged or destroyed about 14,000 dwellings took the lives of 300 persons.

August Northern Japan. Typhoon Phyllis, which killed 68 persons in mid-August when it lashed the Japanese island of Shikoku, was followed a week later by Typhoon Rita, which caused extensive damage and claimed 26 lives; 3 others were missing and 52 injured.

Late August San'a', Yemen Arab Republic. Floodwaters that swept through the capital of Yemen killed 80 persons, most of whom were women and children.

August–September Eastern India. Seasonal monsoon rains that caused hundreds of millions of dollars in damage and contributed to the spread of cholera took the lives of at least 450 persons.

Sept. 6 Lice, Turkey. An earthquake that registered 6.8 on the Richter scale leveled the town of Lice and severely affected a wide area in eastern Turkey; tremors that continued for several days collapsed additional buildings and brought the death toll to 2,312; the number of injured was placed at 3,372.

Early September Uttar Pradesh State, India. Monsoon rains flooded the town of Bulandshahr with water up to 10 ft. deep and drowned at least 30 persons.

Sept. 16 Puerto Rico. Hurricane Eloise, which packed winds up to 140 mph and dumped torrential rains on Puerto Rico, caused tens of millions of dollars in damage and killed 34 persons before striking the island of Hispaniola, where 25 more persons were killed. After severely battering Haiti and the Dominican Republic, Eloise claimed 12 more lives when it moved into mainland Florida and on to the northeastern part of the U.S., where damage was so extensive that it created a state of emergency and warranted federal aid for reconstruction.

Oct. 22–23 Gujarat State, India. A fierce two-day storm that pounded the west coast of India caused extensive damage to homes and crops and took at least 21 lives.

Oct. 24 Mazatlán, Mexico. Hurricane Olivia hit the peninsula city of Mazatlán on the Gulf of California, bringing death to 29 persons.

Dec. 24 Rhodesia. During a violent storm, 21 persons seeking temporary shelter inside a hut were killed by a bolt of lightning; 14 were children.

RAILROAD

Jan. 18 Egypt. A train, so overcrowded that some passengers were riding on the locomotive, derailed north of Cairo while traveling at great speed; 27 persons were killed and more than 50 injured.

Feb. 17 South Africa. An express train traveling from Cape Town to Johannesburg crashed into a freight train, causing the deaths of 16 persons and injuring about 30 others.

Feb. 22 Near Tretten, Norway. Two 12-car trains carrying mostly skiers to and from a winter resort crashed head-on when neither pulled onto a siding to let the other pass; 27 of the 800 passengers lost their lives, making it the worst such accident to date in Norway's history.

Feb. 28 London. In England's worst such accident to date, a six-car subway train roared into Moorgate station during the morning rush hour, plowed through a barrier of sand at full speed, then struck the dead-end wall of the tunnel with devastating impact; for more than ten hours rescue crews climbed through the wreckage with acetylene torches and hacksaws trying to remove the dead and injured; there was no sure explanation for the disaster which took 41 lives.

March 25 Argentina. A freight train heading for Paraná, 300 mi. NE of Buenos Aires, lost traction on a hill and rolled backward into a passenger train; 12 died and 30 were injured.

March 31 Linköping, Sweden. An automobile was demolished at a railroad crossing by an oncoming express train, which derailed on impact; at least 14 persons lost their lives and 39 were injured.

April 4 Lithuania. A passenger train en route from Vilna to Kaunas caused a raging fire when it slammed into a train transporting gasoline; though no accurate death toll was available, numerous persons were trapped inside the wreckage and perished.

June 8 Near Munich, West Germany. Two passenger trains traveling in opposite directions on a one-track section of the Munich–Bad Toelz line crashed with such violence that several cars telescoped on impact; at least 25 persons died and more than 50 were injured, some critically.

July 17 Near Rio de Janeiro. A speeding commuter train carrying over 1,000 passengers left the track and hurtled into a suburban dance school; local newspapers estimated the death toll at 30 and the number of injured at more than 200.

July 19 Near Belgrade, Yugos. A fast-moving express train crashed into the back of a passenger train that was standing motionless in a suburban station; 16 persons were killed and 37 injured.

Tearful Vietnamese war orphans who were aboard the ill-fated Galaxy C-5A transport jet which crashed and burned April 4 near Tan Son Nhut Airport in Saigon, South Vietnam. There were 325 children and adults on the mercy flight, more than 150 of whom perished.

UPI COMPIX

SYNDICATION INTERNATIONAL/PHOTO TRENDS

View of the remains of the first coach in the Moorgate tube disaster in London. The underground train crash on February 28 claimed 41 lives and over 70 persons were injured.

Sept. 29 Near Río Lujan, Arg. A collision involving two passenger trains about 35 mi. from Buenos Aires killed some 30 persons and injured about 16 others.

Oct. 20 Mexico City. A subway train carrying work-bound commuters into Mexico City smashed into another train that was standing motionless at a station stop; more than 20 persons died and dozens were severely injured.

Dec. 14 Fornos de Algodres, Port. A Lisbon express heading for Paris crashed headlong into a train carrying migrant workers home from France for the Christmas holidays; at least 16 persons were killed and some 60 injured.

TRAFFIC

Jan. 1 Near Nagano, Japan. A hotel bus, loaded with holiday skiers, plunged over a cliff and sank in Lake Auki; though 37 persons survived the accident, 23 others were presumed dead.

Jan. 30 Ecuador. A bus traveling from Quito to the Lago Agrio oil fields went off the road and over a precipice, killing 30 persons.

Feb. 8 Tultepec, Mexico. A passenger bus, carrying more than twice its approved capacity, was struck by a train when the driver, ignoring the screams of his riders, tried to speed over a crossing; 29 persons died and 28 were injured.

Feb. 24 Near Medellín, Colombia. While traveling through a mountainous area, a bus plunged over a precipice, killing 20 persons.

March 7 Munich, West Germany. A seven-car electric commuter train traveling 75 mph hit a public bus when it went past a protective gate that opened prematurely; of the 12 persons who died, 6 were young students.

March 10 Near Manila, Phil. An express train that smashed into a passenger bus took the lives of 10 persons and injured 28.

March 14 Near Buenos Aires, Arg. A truck and bus collided in bad weather, killing at least 11 persons and seriously injuring 5 others.

March 25 Near Rio de Janeiro, Brazil. A suburban bus that plunged into a muddy river and sank brought death to 26 of the 32 persons aboard.

March 27 Bahía Blanca, Arg. During a heavy rain, a bus was hit broadside by a freight train at an unguarded crossing; 12 persons died and 22 were injured.

April 2 Vizille, France. A crowded bus with faulty brakes missed a sharp turn, smashed through a stone barrier, then plunged off a bridge onto a river embankment about 100 ft. below; 27 of those returning from a religious pilgrimage died and 16 were injured.

April 25 Near Plovdiv, Bulg. A collision at an unguarded railroad crossing caused a freight car to derail and then strike a bus carrying workers to a mountain resort; 11 were killed and 16 seriously injured.

May 19 Near Poona, India. A truck, carrying a wedding party and guests, was hit by a train in central Maharashtra State; at least 66 persons lost their lives and 18 others suffered injuries.

May 20 Roseau, Dominican Republic. A truck fell 500 ft. into a ravine, killing 28 persons, some of whom were children.

May 27 North Yorkshire, England. In the worst such British accident to date, a chartered bus smashed through the stone siding of a bridge and dropped upside down onto a field 25 ft. below; 31 of the 45 women who had gone on the one-day outing and the driver were killed.

June 15 Villach, Austria. Brake failure caused a tour bus to plunge off a steep mountain road and hurtle 120 ft. into a rocky ravine; 21 retirees were killed and 23 others injured.

July 5(?) Near Bandar-Abbas, Iran. A head-on collision between a truck and a bus caused the deaths of 21 persons.

July 21 Near Culiacán, Mexico. A bus burst in flames after colliding with a car near the capital of Sinaloa State in western Mexico; 30 persons trapped inside the burning bus lost their lives.

Aug. 20 Near Mexico City. In a head-on collision between two buses, 15 persons were killed and 78 injured.

Sept. 20 Near Ciudad Obregón, Mexico. A crowded bus plunged into a canal and submerged; at least 18 persons lost their lives, 7 of whom were children.

Oct. 14 Eastern Hungary. A crowded bus crashed into a train at an unmanned crossing bringing death to 12 persons.

Oct. 30 Zitacuaro, Mexico. A truck that moved into the lane of oncoming traffic smashed into a school bus and killed 15 students and the bus driver.

Disciples of Christ: *see* Religion

Diseases: *see* Health and Disease

Divorce: *see* Demography

Docks: *see* Transportation

Dominican Republic

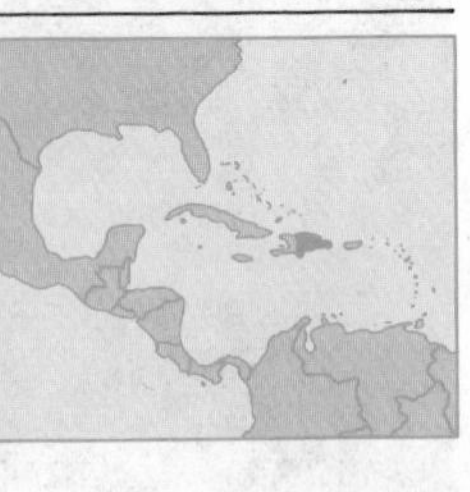

Covering the eastern two-thirds of the Caribbean island of Hispaniola, the Dominican Republic is separated from Haiti, which occupies the western third, by a rugged mountain range. Area: 18,658 sq.mi. (48,323 sq.km.). Pop. (1974 est.): 4,562,000, including (1960) mulatto 73%; white 16%; Negro 11%. Cap. and largest city: Santo Domingo (pop., 1973 est., 817,300). Language: Spanish. Religion (1971 est.): Roman Catholic 92%. President in 1975, Joaquín Balaguer.

Under the regime of President Balaguer, the Dominican Republic continued to be one of the most economically dynamic countries of Latin America during 1975. Agriculture, mining, and the tourist industry were principal areas of government investment.

DOMINICAN REPUBLIC

Education. (1971–72) Primary, pupils 823,553, teachers 15,290; secondary, pupils 126,208, teachers 5,253; vocational, pupils 3,061, teachers 218; teacher training, students 582, teachers 48; higher, students 28,873, teaching staff (1970–71) 1,038.

Finance. Monetary unit: peso, at parity with the U.S. dollar, with a free rate (Sept. 22, 1975) of 2.07 pesos to £1 sterling. Gold, SDRs, and foreign exchange: (June 1975) U.S. $164.2 million; (June 1974) U.S. $122.1 million. Budget (1974 est.) balanced at 383.4 million pesos. Gross domestic product: (1973) 2,342,000,000 pesos; (1972) 1,987,000,000 pesos. Money supply: (March 1975) 368.5 million pesos; (March 1974) 261.6 million pesos. Cost of living (Santo Domingo; 1970 = 100): (March 1975) 159; (March 1974) 137.

Foreign Trade. (1974) Imports 773.9 million pesos; exports 636.8 million pesos. Import sources (1973): U.S. *c.* 61%; Japan *c.* 9%; West Germany *c.* 7%. Export destinations (1973): U.S. 66%; The Netherlands 8%. Main exports: sugar 53%; cocoa 8%; coffee 7%; tobacco 6%.

Transport and Communications. Roads (1971) 10,467 km. Motor vehicles in use (1973): passenger 56,600; commercial (including buses) 28,200. Railways (1974) *c.* 1,700 km. (mainly for sugar estates). Telephones (Jan. 1974) 83,000. Radio receivers (Dec. 1972) 170,000. Television receivers (Dec. 1973) 155,000.

Agriculture. Production (in 000; metric tons; 1974; 1973 in parentheses): rice *c.* 215 (*c.* 205); corn (1973) *c.* 40, (1972) *c.* 50; sweet potatoes (1973) *c.* 97, (1972) *c.* 95; cassava (1973) *c.* 205, (1972) *c.* 195; dry beans *c.* 31 (*c.* 20); tomatoes *c.* 85 (*c.* 84); peanuts *c.* 75 (*c.* 81); sugar, raw value *c.* 1,214 (*c.* 1,193); oranges (1973) *c.* 63, (1972) *c.* 62; avocados (1973) *c.* 127, (1972) *c.* 126; mangoes (1973) *c.* 143, (1972) *c.* 143; bananas (1973) *c.* 310, (1972) *c.* 290; cocoa *c.* 32 (*c.* 28); coffee *c.* 49 (*c.* 46); tobacco *c.* 39 (*c.* 43). Livestock (in 000; June 1974): cattle *c.* 1,560; sheep *c.* 49; pigs (1973) *c.* 1,300; goats (1973) *c.* 750; horses *c.* 170; chickens *c.* 7,500.

Industry. Production (in 000; metric tons; 1972): cement 678; bauxite (1973) 1,411; electricity (kw-hr.) 1,201,000.

The initiation of several hydroelectric and irrigation systems was particularly significant. Among these projects was the $130 million Sabana Yegua Dam which would provide irrigation for 62,000 ac. (25,000 ha.) near Azua on the south coast. Similar, though smaller, projects were begun in the Cibao and San Juan valleys, and a multipurpose canal system was undertaken near Monte Cristi on the north coast.

Support for small farmers, including increases in credit and extension services, received major government emphasis in 1975. Agrarian reform was the item of first priority for the Balaguer government. The most severe drought in several decades drastically reduced the area sown to food crops and curtailed agricultural production. To combat economic losses caused by the drought, the government imposed emergency measures including a freeze on government wages and restrictions on luxury imports.

In May the secretary of the armed forces and the commanders of the three military branches resigned in protest over the appointment of Maj. Gen. Neit Rafael Nivar Seijas as chief of the national police. Although a coup d'etat was feared, conditions remained normal. (GUSTAVO ANTONINI)

[974.B.2.b]

Drug Abuse

Narcotics. The ambivalent attitude of society and authority toward at least some of the drugs taken for their effect upon the mind continued to prevail in 1975. In October Jack Ford, the 23-year-old son of U.S. Pres. Gerald Ford, felt able to admit in an interview with a U.S. newspaper that he had smoked marijuana occasionally, and to compare the cautious use of the drug to the moderate drinking of beer.

Ford's statement was hardly a bombshell, since he and the other three Ford children had already admitted in public to having experimented with marijuana. It might well, however, presage a change in the U.S. and, indeed, in much of the rest of the world toward this most widely used and apparently least harmful of illegal drugs. Robert DuPont, President Ford's chief adviser and spokesman on drug abuse, favoured legalizing the possession of at least small quantities of marijuana. In Alaska its personal use at home was legalized by the state supreme court in May. In 1972 a commission appointed by U.S. Pres. Richard Nixon and Congress to study the drug heavily favoured making its use legal, but the report was thereupon disowned by Nixon. At the end of 1974, however, Senators Jacob Javits (Rep., N.Y.) and Harold Hughes (Dem., Iowa) conducted hearings in their Subcommittee on Alcoholism and Narcotics aimed at putting the findings of the rejected report on record and paving the way for more liberal legislation.

At about the same time, papers appearing in two U.S. journals, *Science* and the *New England Journal of Medicine,* discounted earlier suggestions that marijuana reduces the body's ability to resist infections, or that it lowers the amount of the male sex hormone, testosterone, circulating in the blood.

In Great Britain a study group working for the Institute for the Study of Drug Dependence, chaired by Sir Kenneth Younger and including among its members prominent physicians, lawyers, and professors, was preparing a report to be published in 1976. Making the assumption that major changes in British law concerning marijuana were a real possibility, the report set out to describe a Britain in which the drug was either freely available or was sold legally but with certain restrictions.

Few of the increasing number of responsible citizens in the U.S. and elsewhere who would like to see the moderate use of marijuana made legal would claim that the drug had been proved harmless. The consensus seemed to be that young people should be discouraged from using the drug, but also that the current antimarijuana laws, by turning thousands of people into criminals, did more harm than good.

In Britain the price of marijuana rose to £30 or more per ounce, representing an increase of more than 100% in two years. The increase was believed to be due to the growing efficiency of the police in both Britain and the producing countries, and also to an increasing tendency for large drug imports to be handled by well-established and elaborately organized gangs that deliberately raised the market price. The result was that many young people turned away from marijuana to the readily obtainable, much cheaper, but at least equally dangerous barbiturates.

Despite a growing tolerance toward the smoking of marijuana, there was concern at an increasing traffic in liquid marijuana or "hashish oil." This preparation has a content of tetrahydrocannabinol (THC, the active ingredient of marijuana) over 40 times higher than that of normal marijuana. The International Narcotics Control Board of the United Nations expressed the fear during the year that the potent oil might give rise to new and more dangerous forms of consumption, and act as a bridge between the smoking of marijuana and an addiction to hard drugs. The Institute for the Study of Drug Dependence, however, expressed the view that fears concerning the oil were exaggerated and that, although those who swallow it may suffer the symptoms of an acute overdose of THC, the consequences are unlikely to be fatal. All the cases of overdosage reported by the end of 1975 involved smugglers who had swallowed balloon-like containers filled with the oil which then burst inside their stomachs. The institute's statement ended with the comforting suggestion that "with hashish oil selling at £80 (about $185) per ounce, it is doubtful that many people could afford to buy a lethal dose."

NOVOSTI

This Soviet antialcoholism poster asks the question, "Your health?," while the framed skull neatly reinforces the answer, "No!"

Drama:
see Motion Pictures; Theatre

Dress:
see Fashion and Dress; Industrial Review

The International Narcotics Control Board, which appeared to be inclined toward pessimism, expressed concern in mid-1975 about the growing use of heroin in many countries where the drug had not been a problem in the past. The organization, however, refused to name the regions involved on the grounds that this information might help drug traffickers. By contrast, a series of papers published in the *American Journal of Public Health* earlier in the year analyzed figures concerning the use of heroin in the U.S. and concluded that the peak had been reached in 1969, after which there was a dramatic decline. At the beginning of the 1960s in Washington, D.C., about 1 person in 5,000 used heroin. The number increased, at first slowly and then rapidly, to about 1 person in 240 in 1969. By 1973, however, usage was back to the 1 in 5,000 level of the early 1960s.

Poppies, the source of the raw material from which heroin is prepared, were in the news. In July Turkey harvested its first opium poppy crop in more than two years. The government had banned opium poppy cultivation in 1971 following an official complaint that much of the heroin sold illegally in the U.S. came from Turkey. The Turkish government hoped that strict controls would prevent that country from once again becoming a source of smuggled heroin.

A U.S. government study found that 90% of the heroin confiscated in 13 major U.S. cities during the first six months of 1975 came from Mexico. This contrasted with 40% from Mexico in 1972. In Europe Amsterdam was described as the centre of that continent's heroin traffic, replacing Marseilles.

Sweden announced the development of poppies with a morphine content less than one-tenth that normally found in the opium plant but which nevertheless give a good yield of thebaine, another poppy alkaloid. Thebaine is needed for the manufacture of codeine, a drug with important legitimate medical uses. Cultivation of the new poppies could end a codeine shortage, which resulted from UN efforts to persuade opium-growing countries to switch to other crops. A study of poppies low in morphine but high in thebaine was also undertaken at the School of Pharmacy at the University of London on behalf of the UN.

In the U.S. Timothy Smith, head of the department of psychiatry at the University of California, announced that a small surgical clip inserted in the lobe of each ear and placed according to the Chinese system of acupuncture provides rapid relief from the symptoms of methadone and heroin withdrawal.

Colombian police discovered a mountain valley in June which may rank as the largest marijuana plantation in the world.

UPI COMPIX

A.W. AMBLER—NATIONAL AUDUBON SOCIETY

Jimson weed, given some notoriety by mention in Carlos Castaneda's books, caused poisoning in users in Delaware and Oregon in 1975.

Figures released during the year showed that 60% of all deaths from poisoning in England and Wales during 1973 were due wholly or in part to barbiturates, women being the victims more frequently than men. Leaders of the medical profession in the U.K. launched a campaign aimed at reducing the use of barbiturates in favour of safer and newer tranquilizers and hypnotics. Physicians were being asked to accept a voluntary ban on the use of barbiturates except for the few patients, such as epileptics, who really need them. The medical use of these drugs had declined in recent years but was still high; pharmacists, therefore, carried large stocks, and as a result great quantities were stolen for sale to addicts.

In the U.S. the Drug Enforcement Administration placed several drugs, including the widely sold tranquilizers Librium and Valium, under strict government control. Manufacturers, physicians, and pharmacists were required to keep production and distribution records on the drugs, and the number of refills of prescriptions was limited.

Alcoholism. Alcoholism appeared to be increasing everywhere. A British report estimated that the disease was responsible for at least 26 million lost working days a year in the U.K. and that it cost the country an annual £210 million. In a debate in the House of Lords alcoholism was described as the country's fourth biggest killer, after heart disease, cancer, and tuberculosis, and it was said that an estimated 400,000 Britishers might have a drinking problem. Cirrhosis of the liver, regarded as one of the best indicators of the incidence of alcoholism, had increased in Britain by about 40% in ten years.

Other reports claimed that a growing number of women were becoming alcoholics, and that there was increasing drunkenness among children. In the U.K. during the mid-1960s there were eight male alcoholics to each female alcoholic, but by 1975 the ratio was three to one. In Scotland convictions for drunkenness among children doubled within recent years.

In France a campaign against excessive drinking was launched by IREB, the institute for scientific, economic, and social research on drink. This organization was backed by some of the country's leading manufacturers and importers of alcohol. They believed that a reduction of heavy drinking would improve their public image and ultimately prove good for trade. IREB issued a rough-and-ready guide, stating that whatever your drink, more than seven glasses of it a day are too much. The organization commissioned a survey, which suggested that 40% of all French men over 18 and 8% of French women of the same age drink more than the suggested seven glasses a day. Statistics published by a French government group showed that alcoholism kills 22,000 citizens a year and that the average Frenchman drinks an annual 31 gal. of wine. Social welfare officials in West Germany reported that thousands of children, some as young as ten, were becoming alcoholics.

In the U.S. a report published by NIAAA (the National Institute on Alcohol Abuse and Alcoholism) stated that nearly one out of seven 12th-grade schoolchildren admit to getting drunk at least once a week. They had no supply problem, since in some supermarkets canned beer was cheaper than soft drinks. Alcoholism was estimated to cost the U.S. at least $25 million a year, apart from the destruction brought about by traffic accidents and crimes of violence following drinking.

A leading article in the British medical journal the *Lancet* questioned the doctrine of Alcoholics Anonymous which holds that the alcoholic, even when abstinent, is always "one drink away from a drunk." The article quoted studies showing that some alcoholics are capable of reverting to a pattern of "normal," controlled drinking. It suggested that more attention should be paid to the social and other circumstances that trigger excessive drinking rather than to the mere act of drinking itself.

Tobacco. During the year considerable publicity was given to the claim by Philip Burch of the University of Leeds in England that the evidence for a causal relationship between smoking and lung cancer is inadequate, and to the equally controversial claim by Carl Seltzer of the Harvard University School of Public Health that there is no proof that smoking causes heart disease. Both men were respected experts in their fields and their arguments were closely reasoned, but physicians generally rejected their claims, even categorizing them as mischievous at a time when great efforts were being made to discourage the smoking habit.

In Britain it was announced that tobacco was to be legally designated as an addictive drug and subjected to the controls that regulated the manufacture, supply, and promotion of medicinal products. This would give the government full control over tobacco advertising. Meanwhile, the tobacco industry in Britain agreed to print tar yields on cigarette packets, and to discontinue advertisements associating smoking with a healthy, outdoor life or with sexual and social success.

The search for safer cigarettes proved discouraging. Experiments carried out by the Addiction Research Unit at Maudsley Hospital in London showed that "safe" cigarettes with a low tar and nicotine content yield as much carbon monoxide as high-tar brands, and carbon monoxide is thought to be a major cause of some of the ill effects of smoking. Also, cigarettes containing a proportion of tobacco substitutes were found to be just as irritating to the lungs and air tubes as ordinary cigarettes.

A paper published in the *Lancet* showed that the incidence of bronchitis and pneumonia in infants during the first year of life is appreciably higher when one or both parents are smokers. This is due to the inhalation of tobacco smoke in the home.

(DONALD W. GOULD)

[522.C.9]

ENCYCLOPÆDIA BRITANNICA FILMS. *Scag (Heroin)* (1970); *Ups/Downs (Amphetamines and Barbiturates)* (1971); *Weed (Marijuana)* (1971); *Acid (LSD)* (1971); *The Drug Problem: What Do You Think?* (1972); *The Tobacco Problem: What Do You Think?* (1972); *The Alcohol Problem: What Do You Think?* (1973).

Dutch Literature: *see* Literature

Earthquakes: *see* Disasters; Earth Sciences

Earth Sciences

GEOLOGY AND GEOCHEMISTRY

Perhaps the most far-reaching aspect of the reexamination in the geological sciences spurred on by the concept of plate tectonics is the conceptual revolution treating the origin of ore minerals. Many ore deposits were being shown to occur along present or past boundaries of the large crustal plates that abut and are in motion against one another. This led scientists to propose that the interaction of seawater with cooling volcanic rock may be the chief means by which many metallic elements are extracted and geochemically concentrated into ore bodies.

The accumulating data on known ore deposits coupled with evolving theoretical models provide the clues with which to look for still-undiscovered deposits. Volcanically generated oceanic crust developed at divergent plate boundaries, as in Cyprus, was demonstrated to contain concentrated deposits of copper, iron, zinc, chromium, and nickel. At the opposite end of the plate-tectonic process—converging plate boundaries—large igneous bodies form that often contain another type of copper deposit. An example is the Andes Mountains of South America.

The greenstone belts in continental interiors have historically been the source of major metal deposits.

Soviet volcanologists studied the eruption of Tolbachik, Kamchatka Peninsula, which was one of the most intensive such events in this century.

LONDON DAILY EXPRESS/PICTORIAL PARADE

COURTESY, NASA

A satellite photograph of central Asia revealed major strike-slip (horizontal) displacements along the Altyn Tagh Fault in northwestern China. Lateral movement of 25 miles has affected the dark rocks across the centre of this photograph.

These belts have been identified as relics of former oceanic island arcs caught in continental collisions.

Hot Spots. A plate tectonic process associated with volcanism and rock-melting phenomena is the formation of a hot spot in the mantle. Hot spots may mobilize metallic elements and thereby lead to such geochemical concentrations in ore deposits near the surface of the Earth as the lead-zinc deposits in northwest Africa. In addition, deposits of diamond are associated with the eruption of deep-seated mantle rock and may be indicative of hot spots.

University of Utah scientists offered further evidence that the geothermal and volcanic phenomena at Yellowstone National Park are the result of a crustal hot spot at a junction of major tectonic trends. Other geologists, from the U.S. Geological Survey, presented evidence that a large shallow body of silica-rich magma, in part still molten, underlies a wide area of Yellowstone National Park. Their findings indicate that the magma lies on top of a large body of crustal and mantle material containing pods of silicic and basaltic magma. The Yellowstone thermal phenomena may represent the present activity of a hot spot that has migrated progressively northeastward for 15 million years along the eastern Snake River Plain.

Mantle material rising along a hot spot or plume may have been the source of the natural iron-nickel alloy found along Josephine Creek in Oregon (and dubbed josephinite). The chemical and mineralogical composition of this material led to the suggestion that the material was transported outward from the hot core-mantle boundary by a deep mantle plume to a near-surface location on the Pacific Plate, which in turn deposited it on the North American Plate as the former was consumed by subduction at the plate margin. This hypothesis remains controversial.

Petroleum and Oil Shale. Giant oil fields were studied by Soviet and other geologists. These fields tend to occur on major uplifts having a long history of structural development, and most of the largest are associated with Mesozoic deposits (65 million to 225 million years of age). Most of the remainder are associated with Cenozoic beds (those formed during the last 65 million years). The relative lack of Paleozoic supergiant oil fields (formed 225 million to 570 million years ago) may be attributed to the length of time available for the processes of destruction to take their toll. The distribution of giant fields throughout the world is quite uneven, only ten being located in the Western Hemisphere.

Models were proposed for the depositional environment of the Eocene Green River Formation of Colorado, Wyoming, and Utah, host of the world's largest oil shale deposits, in the western U.S., involving deposition in a rather shallow-water lake. Wyoming geologists suggested that the lake probably underwent frequent periods of desiccation, leading to the deposition of saline minerals interbedded with the high-quality oil shale, rather than the deeper, permanently stratified lake model proposed earlier. Oil shale was deposited in the shallow water during periods of high organic productivity during more humid periods.

Climatic Change. Observers of present world climatic data have noted ominous signs that man continues to live in a geological era of great ice ages. After three quarters of a century of mild conditions the Earth's climate is cooling. Geologists have pointed out that the Earth's average temperature during continental glaciation was only about 4° C lower than during its warmest periods. On the basis of present temperature trends, the Earth may, therefore, be one-sixth of the way into the next period of glaciation. Droughts, floods, and unstable weather patterns may in the future make marked changes on the Earth's surface as well as wreak havoc with the world's food-producing system.

Geochemical evidence from oxygen and radiocarbon isotope studies accompanied by a micropaleontological analysis of deep-sea cores allowed Earth scientists to chart the major trends of global environmental change during the last 700,000 years. Samples from the ocean bottom provided evidence that at least eight major glacial cycles have occurred during this period. Related studies pushed the beginning of the Pleistocene "glacial age" back to two or three million years before the present and called into question the rigid classification of four well-defined cycles of continental glaciation.

Research reported by Florida marine geologists and geochemists confirmed the worldwide significance of the isotopic record as a paleoclimatological and a correlational tool. Their recent work on cores from the Gulf of Mexico identified what they believed to be an episode of rapid ice melting and sea-level rise about 9600 B.C.

Lunar Geology. Although the Apollo moon flight program had ended, Earth scientists from many countries continued mineralogical, geochemical, and geophysical research on the recovered samples of lunar rock to update their hypotheses concerning the development of the lunar crust and interior structure. From data that became available geologists divided the Moon's interior into five concentric layers: (1) an outer crust of plagioclase-rich rock extending to a depth of 60 km. (37 mi.); (2) an upper mantle of olivine- and pyroxene-rich rock extending from 60 to 300 km. (185 mi.); (3) a middle mantle from 300 to 800 km. (500 mi.), possibly composed of primitive lunar rock from which the outer layers formed during an earlier period of melting; (4) a lower mantle lying at a depth of 800 to 1,400 km. (865 mi.) that may be partially molten, and (5) below 1,400 km. a core, perhaps of molten iron sulfide.

Paleontology. In the Cretaceous (65 million to 136 million years ago) rocks of the Big Bend area of West Texas, paleontologists discovered three partial skeletons of a large pterosaur with a conservatively estimated wingspan of 15.5 m. These fossil remains represent the largest creature ever to fly (or soar) above the Earth; the great American condor, the largest of present-day birds, has a wing span of 3 m.

No pterodactyl remains had previously been found in this region. They were unearthed from nonmarine rocks deposited far from the nearest ancient sea. Pterodactyls are thought to have subsisted on a fish diet. The absence of any nearby body of water of any size may indicate that these giant airborne creatures were the vultures of the past, scavenging the flesh of dead dinosaurs. Their unusually long necks would aid in picking such a pile of bones.

A major area of controversy exists over the way in which these giant pterodactyls took to the air. Some scientists argue that the wings of these creatures were too large to be used for anything but gliding and that the pterodactyls had to launch themselves from some height. Geologists reported, however, that the host sediments of these bones showed no evidence of ancient hills nearby. Other scientists suggest that these reptiles could get the aerodynamic lift necessary to make them airborne by proper wing flapping in favourable wind conditions much as the smaller gooney birds and albatrosses do today. Once aloft, these giant creatures could then build up an airspeed of about ten miles per hour.

Early Earth Conditions. Interest in the complex problems of the early nature of the Earth was highlighted by a multidisciplinary conference in the U.K. Many models of processes were proposed, but agreement on many crucial issues appeared to be many years away. Most researchers agreed that the terrestrial planets completed their major accretion by 4,500,000,000 years ago. The time and genetic relationships between the Earth and the Moon remained in dispute. Data were reported on the probable form of early chemical differentiation and core formation. Earth history before 4,000,000,000 years ago can best be described as turbulent, with details forever obliterated. The oldest ages for preserved crust remained about 3,750,000,000 years. At least one participant believed that rocks as old as 4,000,000,000 years would eventually be found.

The idea of an early reducing atmosphere dominated by ammonia and hydrogen appeared to be giving way to a hypothesis allowing a slightly oxidizing atmosphere that became highly oxidizing when blue-green algae became abundant. Early ironstones, cherts, and marbles probably developed by means of inorganic precipitation.

Biogeochemistry. Biogeochemists continued to concentrate on environmental problems. They shared with inorganic geochemists the paucity of quantitative data on natural cycles, which must be understood before the superimposed effects of man and his industrial technologies can be assessed. West German researchers reported on their efforts to trace the increasing atmospheric levels of carbon dioxide back to preindustrial times. The most reliable data came from isotopic records in wood.

One group of British and U.S. scientists interested in the carbon cycle and the fate of man-made organic materials concentrated their investigations on recent sediments. A common problem for such investigators was the difficulty in differentiating natural organics from man-made pollutants. Considerable interest was being shown in using stable isotopes to "fingerprint" the source of pollutants.

(GEORGE ROBERT RAPP, JR.)

[133.E.4; 212.D.2–3; 213.A; 214.A.4; 214.C.4.b–c; 224.D.6; 242.B; 242.E]

GEOPHYSICS

Project FAMOUS (French-American Mid-Ocean Undersea Study) carried out dives in the submersibles "Alvin" (U.S.) and "Cyana" and "Archimède" (France) to depths of 8,400 ft. in the median valley of the Mid-Atlantic Ridge south of the Azores. Both the ridge and its median valley are central to plate tectonics theory as a region of upwelling of material from deep within the Earth. The submersibles used many types of probes to determine water temperature, salinity, currents, and geomagnetism just above the sea floor. Their primary work was photographing the bottom and collecting specimens for later analysis. They found areas of spectacular lava formations: pillows, cones, and tubes characteristic of recent undersea eruption. They also found little or no silt deposits and that areas not covered by lava were crisscrossed by many small fissures up to 100 m. in length and 10 m. in depth. These features, plus the patterns of paleomagnetism obtained from samples taken in the surrounding region, supported the arguments for recent and continuing upwelling.

Scientists at the Massachusetts Institute of Technology explored the conditions of collision between oceanic and continental plates as they apply to the Indian subcontinent and Asia, using Earth Resources Technology Satellite (ERTS) photographs. It was found that, though the rate of convergence has slowed, there has been approximately 1,500 km. (930 mi.) of crustal shortening since Eocene time (38 million to 54 million years ago). Combining ERTS data with recent seismic activity and fault movement, scientists mapped a broad zone of the primary and secondary effects of this collision. It indicated that the formation of the Himalayas accounts for 300 to 700 km. (185 to 435 mi.) of the shortening and that other mountain belts account for 200–300 km. (125–185 mi.); the remainder of the shortening results from strike-slip faulting more or less perpendicular to the direction of collision.

Studies at Princeton University revealed that continental plate thicknesses are much greater than the 200 km. generally postulated. Evidence of seismic wave velocities, temperature differences, and thermal gradients between oceanic and continental plates indicate depths for the latter of at least 400 km. (250 mi.) and possibly as much as 670 km. (415 mi.).

The driving forces that move the tectonic plates have not been identified but are generally accepted as some form of thermal convection. A model developed at Cornell University demonstrated that these motions could be explained by convection cells in the mantle. Convection currents, largely generated by radioactivity, form widely spaced upward and downward plume pairs, and the lithosphere, the upper 43–60 mi. of the Earth, provides a cold boundary. This creates a gravitational imbalance, causing the lithosphere to sink into the mantle at ocean trenches.

Additional forces are provided by thermal contraction of the descending plate and the elevation of the olivine-spinel transition zone, a seismic discontinuity at a depth of about 400 km. (250 mi.). The motion is opposed by the increasing viscosity of the mantle, which places an upper limit on the plate velocity.

Paleomagnetism is used as a determinant for polar wandering. Because the continental plates from which the sample data are taken are also moving, an investigator from the University of Buenos Aires was able to correlate the data from Argentina, southern Africa, and Australia and thus determine the relative positions of the plates in those areas during geologic time. He deduced that Australia began to move away from the Gondwanaland mass in Permo-Carboniferous or early Permian times (about 280 million years ago), while Africa and South America remained together until the late Paleozoic (about 225 million years ago) but not later than early Cretaceous (about 135 million years ago) when the South Atlantic was formed.

The Carnegie Institution in Washington, D.C., released a report that recommended a ten-year, $110 million program for investigating plate composition and movement and other geophysical processes by drilling deep holes in selected continental locations. The drilling was to be done in two phases; first, a series of shallow holes (30–300 m.), followed by intermediate and deep holes (300–9,000 m.) in critical areas. The first phase was to be carried out in conjunction with heat flow, thermal structure, and stress domain studies. The main thrust of the program, however, concerned the deep-hole studies. The objectives of this portion of the work were the study of the mechanism of faulting and earthquake generation; hydrothermal systems and active magma chambers; and the extent, regional structure, and evolution of the continental crust.

(RUTLAGE J. BRAZEE)

[213.A–B; 241.F–G]

HYDROLOGY

During the past year research concentrated on problems relative to the use and disposal of water in urban areas, for energy development, and for managing wastes. Much work continued to be done in applying models, system analysis, and statistical methods to water management. Advances also were made in the theories of groundwater-surface water interrelationships and of groundwater movement.

Trickle irrigation applies water sparingly and frequently to individual plants as they need it. The concept and practice were first developed extensively in Israel, but acceptance and economical use elsewhere awaited more extensive experimentation and improved controls. Work in Texas showed that the method conserves water while achieving optimum growth of food and fibre crops. Increased use of this method was expected to be of special benefit in regions where past and current demands for irrigation water have steadily diminished groundwater resources.

Studies in New York were evaluating methods to turn flood damage to the advantage of a community. Economic evaluations show that changes in the use of urban land subject to flooding can result in more viable urban environments. Even normal runoff from urban areas differs from that of nonurbanized areas. Studies in Nebraska were pinpointing these differences which included changes in concentrations of nitrogen, phosphorus, pesticides, phenols, and bacteria.

In Alaska research showed that a significant amount of water is lost by evaporation during the winter, in contrast to conditions in warmer climates. The heat lost by evaporation is critical to construction activities and the design of equipment.

The International Hydrological Decade (IHD) ended at the close of 1974. This ten-year program to upgrade education and research, and to increase technical assistance in hydrology to less developed countries, was considered so successful that nearly 90 countries joined at the end of 1974 to continue the effort. The new project, the International Hydrological Program (IHP), was planned to continue until it appeared to be no longer needed. Like the Decade, it was guided by an intergovernmental council working under the aegis of UNESCO. The IHP was to have similar objectives to those of the Decade, but with greater emphasis on education and training.

Two outstanding international scientific studies were the International Field Year for the Great Lakes (IFYGL) and the International Baltic Sea Water Balance Study. IFYGL began as a joint venture of the U.S. and Canadian national IHD committees. Final comprehensive reports on the atmospheric, terrestrial, and lake water balances; the chemical and biological

A relatively inexpensive radio-controlled sounding plane is readied for takeoff at the National Oceanic and Atmospheric Administration facilities in Boulder, Colorado. Such models are being developed to study atmospheric electricity.

AUTHENTICATED NEWS INTERNATIONAL

nutrient cycles; the physical phenomena at the lake water surface; and the patterns of internal water movement and circulation were being prepared for release by 1977. The Baltic Sea study, involving the hydrological interest of Denmark, Finland, West Germany, East Germany, Poland, Sweden, and the U.S.S.R., began in 1974, and data collection was to continue through 1976. The prime scientific focus of the study was the exchange of water between the Baltic Sea and the Atlantic Ocean through the Danish straits. The driving practical reason for making the study was the concern about the growing use of the Baltic as the sink for the metropolitan, industrial, and agricultural wastes of the countries surrounding it. The scientists hoped that a better understanding of the natural exchange mechanisms may make it possible to use them, at least in part, to "self-clean" the Baltic and so minimize the costs of effluent treatment and waste prevention.

(L. A. HEINDL)

[222.A.2; 222.D]

METEOROLOGY

Atmospheric scientists throughout the world but especially in China, the U.S., and the U.S.S.R. showed increased concern during the year about man's unplanned modification of the Earth's climate. Hundreds of research reports gave tentative conclusions and hypothesized on the many ways in which modern civilization may modify one or more of the vital constituents of the atmosphere and disturb the delicate balance involved in the climate.

This fear of unintentional man-made changes in the atmosphere was a new trend among meteorologists and their kindred scientists. Less than a decade earlier many eminent men of science were theorizing with optimism that science would soon have the means and the power to control climate and weather on a large scale to suit man's desires. While serious research on possibilities of beneficial weather control continued, its volume was exceeded during 1975 by studies of the grave consequences of unplanned and uncontrollable modification of the atmosphere. In broad categories the dangers could come from three forms of contaminants: particles sent into the atmosphere by smoke or wind-driven dust; gases set free by combustion, chemical manufacturing, and such products as aerosol spray cans; and heat and water vapour artificially introduced into the air and into the land and sea environment. There was some evidence that fluorinated hydrocarbons from spray cans and similar commercial sources have a destructive effect on the ozone layer high in the atmosphere. Scientists recognized that the evidence to date did not show significant ill effects, but voiced the warning that if the high ozone layer ever reaches a stage of serious deterioration the change would be irreversible and the final results might be fatal to many living creatures.

The approach of another period of increasing frequency and magnitude of sunspots revived the long-standing controversy about the effects of sunspots on weather and the use of such a relationship in forecasting the weather. The rather well-defined cycles in sunspot maxima and minima, chiefly the 11-year cycle, have been known for over a century, and modern science has established the extremes in solar radiant energy that are associated with sunspot changes as the cause of magnetic "storms" in the Earth's magnetic field. But the relations between sunspot changes and the Earth's climate are uncertain, if indeed they exist.

WIDE WORLD

Students fill an experimental balloon with helium in the lobby of a building at the Massachusetts Institute of Technology in Cambridge. The balloon was charged with five million volts prior to launching in March to study lightning and other electrostatic phenomena in the atmosphere.

World Meteorological Organization (WMO). One of the organizations that significantly touches the lives of humans every day is the WMO, which coordinates and promotes the collection of weather information and publishes weather forecasts throughout the world. The seventh quadrennial congress of WMO was convened in Geneva in April 1975. The aims and the vital requirements of WMO have traditionally been those of cooperation and scientific advancement, and until the seventh congress political forces in opposition to scientific goals had been kept to a minimum. But in 1975 the sweeping changes that had taken place in majority representation in the UN and its agencies caught up with the WMO. Two events were examples of the changes and their future implications. For political and sociological motives South Africa was suspended from WMO. And for the first time since the establishment of WMO Great Britain was not elected to representation on the executive committee. This committee is the powerful body that carries into operation the programs authorized by the congress. For the first time the majority of the committee comprised relatively small countries with comparatively inexperienced weather bureaus.

In view of acute shortages of food in many countries, and with the strong support of FAO (UN Food and Agriculture Organization), the WMO congress voted to increase programs and services in weather reporting and research needed for greater production of foodstuffs. The World Weather Watch (WWW) and the Global Atmospheric Research Program (GARP) were strengthened to the extent permitted by the budget. Recognizing the potential importance of weather modification by means of seeding clouds with silver iodide or "dry ice," and the uncertainty and heated controversy that continued after three decades of such experimentation, the WMO sponsored a new program of research in the hope of finding answers to the many questions relating to rainmaking.

Severe Storms Research. Year after year the universal problems caused by unfavourable weather inspire an incredible number of experiments and research projects aimed at finding causes and solutions. The year 1975 was no exception. The growing emphasis on energy conservation and search for new sources of energy induced one author to publish his proposal that under certain topographical conditions the potential and kinetic energy generated in convectively active cumulus clouds might be harnessed for power uses on the ground below. This proposal was noteworthy for its imagination rather than for any likely practical application.

Many projects during the year were designed to provide techniques for warning of severe storms. Tornadoes, the most destructive local storms, had been studied exhaustively for many years. Detection and tracking by means of radar had brought many improvements in warnings after 1950, but a major source of uncertainty remained the inability to distinguish with certainty between the severe thunderstorm with basically linear wind systems and the cumulonimbus with a tornado vortex. Many times during past years meteorologists have reported distinctive features that they hoped would prove to be the "signature" by which a tornado could be positively identified. In August 1975 the U.S. National Oceanic and Atmospheric Administration (NOAA) reported that the beginnings of a vortex which grew into a full-scale tornado had been recognized by use of Doppler radar. In this case the whirlwind was born inside the cumulonimbus at altitudes between 10,000 and 15,000 ft. By using the Doppler effect, observers could measure the net difference in wind speed on opposite sides of the vortex with respect to an outside fixed point; this difference served as an identifying signature.

In several other ways research in the U.S. on tornadoes was intensified. Local tornado detectors installed at 20 sites during 1974 in states with a high incidence of tornadoes were continued in operation and improved under leadership of the National Severe Storms Laboratory near Norman, Okla. These detectors were designed to identify destructive local storms through the unique bursts of electrical discharges within the storm.

Applied Meteorology. Cloud-seeding experiments were continued over the Everglades in Florida, where reasonably satisfactory experimental controls could be set up. Of the many thousands of rainmaking attempts taking place each year in dry parts of the world, the several projects under the direction of NOAA were among the relatively small number with scientific management adequate to satisfy research standards. Although many of the cloud-seeding operations elsewhere reported success, the impossibility of distinguishing man-made rain from that brought by natural causes left the true results unknown and added to the controversy as to the efficacy of the technique. While there was progress during 1975 in data gathering and modest refinement of techniques for weather modification and storm diminution, there was no real breakthrough.

By far the greatest advances in meteorology were in technical equipment designed for gathering data about weather over large regions and for its analysis and use in forecasting. The equipment included sophisticated computers and prognostic charters and improved satellites that gave more or less continuous views of certain atmospheric features from hundreds or thousands of miles above the Earth's surface. Another vital part of the data input was the information about hurricanes, typhoons, and other cyclonic storms, especially those far at sea. This was obtainable only by reconnaissance aircraft that could penetrate the storm centre itself. In 1975 the reporting and tracking of hurricanes in waters off the coasts of North America by reconnaissance planes added much to the accuracy and range of storm warnings.

(F. W. REICHELDERFER)

[224.A.3.e; 224.B; 224.C; 224.D.1]

OCEANOGRAPHY

As in earlier years of this decade, interest in marine resources and environment was sparked by actual and predicted shortages of raw materials and food and by the need to dispose safely of the by-products of industrial civilization. The great extent to which major scientific programs established at the beginning of the 1970s have changed man's picture of ocean circulation became evident in 1975. The political problems inherent in equitable international partitioning of marine resources were underlined by the difficulty of negotiations carried out at the UN Conference on the Law of the Sea.

The International Decade of Ocean Exploration entered its middle year in 1975. A major part of oceanographic research has been organized around the goals of IDOE. For many of the programs, 1975 marked a year of reflection upon the data obtained thus far as well as a period of pilot observations and experimental design for the remainder of the decade.

MODE and POLYMODE. The Mid-Ocean Dynamics Experiment (MODE) was typical of this pattern. In the late 1950s it was discovered that the ocean currents associated with eddying motions (mesoscale eddies) in the ocean were often more intense than permanent deep sea currents and were also unpredictably variable over distances of hundreds of miles or times of weeks to months. MODE was intended to elucidate the role played by these eddies in the overall basinwide ocean circulation of water and transportation of dissolved substances.

During the first half of the 1970s MODE prepared and carried out a four-month program of extensive current and water temperature observations in a region about 300 km. (185 mi.) across slightly southwest of Bermuda. A somewhat similar program, POLYGON, had been carried out a few years earlier by Soviet scientists in the north tropical Atlantic. The projects found that the occurrence of eddies appears to be the rule rather than the exception. Typical eddy sizes are on the order of 100 km. (60 mi.), although no firm limits exist. Water swirls about the eddy centre with speeds of 10 to 20 cm. per second (about $\frac{1}{4}$ to $\frac{1}{2}$ mph) in either a clockwise or counterclockwise direction, and the eddy centre may be either a few degrees warmer (clockwise swirling) or colder (counterclockwise swirling) than its surroundings. These flows and temperature contrasts are most pronounced at depths of several hundred to perhaps 1,000 m., although significant variations are observed to depths greater than 4,000 m.

In a number of theoretical studies of the ocean carried out on the largest of computers, ocean eddies actually generate basinwide quasi-permanent currents. Does this occur in the real ocean? To decide, oceanographers planned a program of fieldwork spanning the entire western Atlantic Ocean. One of its central goals was the determination of the distribution of eddies relative to the more persistent flow. Far too extensive for any single country to undertake, this project was, therefore, planned as a joint U.S.-Soviet experiment and was to be called POLYMODE, a combination of POLYGON and MODE. Preliminary work was under way in 1975.

Norpax and GATE. While MODE and POLYMODE studied mesoscale eddies in the Atlantic, the North Pacific Experiment (Norpax) concentrated upon understanding the larger (thousands of kilometres) and longer (months-to-years) fluctuations of heat content of the upper layer of the North Pacific. For Norpax the mesoscale eddies are "noise," and the results and methods of MODE were useful in planning experiments that "see through" them. Because North Pacific heat storage fluctuations are so large in extent and so long lasting, an entirely different approach to their study evolved in Norpax. Norpax observers regularly traverse the Pacific between the U.S. and Japan on commercial ships. Every few hours, an observer launches an expendable bathythermograph (XBT), a device having a temperature sensor that falls through the water and relays ocean temperatures as deep as 300 m. back to the ship for recording. These XBTs may be utilized at full speed and therefore do not interfere with regular ship's operations.

MODE and Norpax jointly demonstrated that the mid-latitude ocean is characterized by current and temperature variations that appear more random and only statistically predictable than they are steady or perfectly repeating and predictable in detail. The tropical ocean may be different. First results from the Global Atmospheric Research Program Atlantic Tropical Experiment (GATE) showed surprisingly regular and smooth fluctuations in the strength and position of the equatorial undercurrent, a swift (about 1 m. per second or 2 mph), narrow (few hundred km. wide), relatively shallow (about 100 m. or 300 ft.) but submerged eastward-flowing equatorial current in the Atlantic. The current appears to wander roughly 100 km. (about 60 mi.) back and forth about its equatorial centre over two to three weeks.

In contrast to mid-latitude ocean currents the equatorial flow variations are strikingly smooth and are very similar at observing stations separated by 500 km. (about 300 mi.). Similar observations were reported in the east Pacific from a Norpax-related cruise. This great difference suggests that the mid-latitude results may not be generalized to the tropics.

GEOS-C. Currents, waves, and tides cause the actual sea surface to deviate from the geoid by a few metres. To observe these deviations a specially equipped satellite, GEOS-C, was launched by the National Aeronautics and Space Administration (NASA) in 1975. It carries a radar altimeter that measures the time required for a radar pulse leaving the satellite to return after reflection from the sea below. This time indicates the altitude of the satellite with a precision of better than 1 m.

The satellite is thus the reference point from which average sea surface elevation is measured, and its location must, therefore, be accurately known. This is accomplished by a unique combination of tracking, both from ground-based stations and from another satellite.

DSDP. The Deep Sea Drilling Project (DSDP) continued in the Atlantic, Mediterranean, and Black seas, and plans for a sequel program, the International Phase of Ocean Drilling (IPOD), were being formulated. Continuing work from the specially outfitted drilling ship "Glomar Challenger," the DSDP was drilling off the west coast of Africa in the spring of 1975 studying sediments formed at a time when Africa and South America had just begun to separate. The initial region of separation appeared to have resembled the Great Rift Valley of Africa, with subsequent widening resulting in a broad, shallow sea within which great salt deposits formed.

COURTESY, WOODS HOLE OCEANOGRAPHIC INSTITUTION

The three-man research submersible "Alvin" is placed aboard its mother ship while en route to the Caribbean to explore the Cayman Trough. The latter deep is thought to mark the boundary between two major geologic plates.

Subsequent drilling in the Mediterranean Sea delineated formation times of different basins, while work in the Black Sea studied changes in that region when ice-age lowerings of sea level isolated it from the Mediterranean. The "Glomar Challenger" then returned to the northwest Atlantic to study some of the oldest (180 million years) sediments formed when the Atlantic first began to develop.

Law of the Sea. During early 1975 the "Glomar Explorer," a sister ship to the "Glomar Challenger," was reported to have raised part of a sunken Soviet submarine under the cover of engaging in development of seafloor mineral recovery techniques. Use of oceanographic research as a cover for political or military operations is of concern to scientists because it endangers traditional freedom of research on the seas.

In spite of unresolved differences in viewpoint between less developed and industrialized countries, the UN Conference on the Law of the Sea succeeded in producing an informal draft treaty that was expected to serve as the basis of further negotiations scheduled for 1976. Under the draft treaty, territorial waters would extend to 12 mi. Coastal nations could control economic exploitation (such as fishing and mining) and enforce pollution standards to a distance of 200 mi. but without restricting freedom of navigation and overflight. In the deep sea beyond, seafloor resource development and enforcement of pollution standards would be controlled by an international seabed authority. (MYRL C. HENDERSHOTT)

See also Disasters; Energy; Life Sciences; Mining and Quarrying; Physics; Space Exploration; Speleology.

[223.A; 223.C; 241.G; 552.B.c.v]

ENCYCLOPÆDIA BRITANNICA FILMS. *Erosion—Leveling the Land* (1964); *Rocks that Form on the Earth's Surface* (1964); *Evidence for the Ice Age* (1965); *What Makes the Wind Blow?* (1965); *What Makes Clouds?* (1965); *Waves on Water* (1965); *The Beach—A River of Sand* (1965); *Why Do We Still Have Mountains?* (1966); *Rocks that Originate Underground* (1966); *How Solid Is Rock?* (1968); *Reflections on Time* (1969); *Heartbeat of a Volcano* (1970); *How Level Is Sea Level?* (1970); *The Ways of Water* (1971); *A Time for Rain* (1971); *A Time for Sun* (1971); *Earthquakes—Lesson of a Disaster* (1971); *Fog* (1971); *Geyser Valley* (1972); *Glacier on the Move* (1973); *The Atmosphere in Motion* (1973); *Volcanoes: Exploring the Restless Earth* (1973); *Monuments to Erosion* (1974); *Storms: The Restless Atmosphere* (1974); *The San Andreas Fault* (1974); *Energy for the Future* (1974); *Weather Forecasting* (1975).

SPECIAL REPORT

SCIENCE AND SUPERSTITION: AN AGE OF UNREASON

By Lawrence K. Lustig

We live in a truly remarkable time. At every turn we are confronted with evidence suggesting that an age of scientific miracles has arrived. Man has walked upon the Moon and returned; he has deciphered the genetic code; organ transplants and complex surgery of every description are routinely performed; the energy of the atom has been focused and controlled; radio telescopes plumb the dark recesses of the heavens; and the nature of the Earth's interior and of distant stars is known to a degree undreamed of only a few decades ago. The magnitude of these and other scientific accomplishments is immense, but this is not to imply that no unknowns remain, or that there exist no frontiers of knowledge yet to be crossed. It is quite clear, however, that science has progressed sufficiently far to permit discrimination between the true and the untrue, the possible and the impossible, and the unknown and the patently unlikely. The ultimate origins of the universe and of the earliest matter, for example, clearly reside in the category of the unfathomable. Claims of suspension of the laws of nature by mysterious unspecified powers, on the other hand, are simply unacceptable, and must be relegated to the realm of superstition. The most remarkable aspect of our age is the parallel coexistence of sophisticated scientific knowledge and widespread beliefs of this sort. Exploration of this matter and the possible reasons for it must begin with some consideration of the methodology and general aims of the realm of science.

The Nature of Science. All scientific "miracles" are attributable to hard-won battles to acquire knowledge, wresting from the very universe a rational explanation of cause and effect and of the fundamental laws that govern natural phenomena. The procedures employed are basically invariant. Given a particular observation or question, be it the reason for the red shift in the spectra of distant astronomical bodies, or why the fabled apple struck Newton's head, all possible explanations are first set forth. These hypotheses are then subjected to rigorous experimental or theoretical tests, under specified conditions and controls, until, in the end, the erroneous postulations drop away and the correct conclusion emerges—or the fact that no conclusion is yet possible emerges. Of paramount importance is the fact that the truths revealed by this scientific method are reproducible—by any investigator, in any institution, at any time. Results or conclusions announced in Moscow, or Sydney, or Tokyo can be, and are, duplicated in Cambridge, or Zürich, or Berkeley, by following precisely the techniques and procedures used by the initial investigators. The universality of scientific knowledge is based on this replication of results upon demand, which Jacob Bronowski quite properly referred to as the very underpinning or *integrity* of all scientific knowledge.

Such integrity is indeed vital if one is concerned with truth and reason. When scientists write a chemical equation for a specific reaction, or state that the speed of light is a particular constant value, or indicate that permanent space stations can exist only at certain (Lagrangian) points of gravitational equilibrium in the Earth-Moon system, the integrity of science guarantees that these observations do not depend upon who the particular scientist is, or how he or she feels at the time, or whether the audience addressed is friendly, hostile, or skeptical. The truth in all such matters is solitary, ubiquitous, and provable whenever necessary.

And it should be emphasized that the term provable is by no means synonymous with visible. Science accepts a vast array of invisible phenomena—gravity, magnetism, the crystal lattice, chemical reactions, the transmission of disease and light, and the Coriolis effect on the winds are but a few examples in this class. In each case, acceptance is based on quantitative evidence, freely offered to all for the tests of prediction of consequences and replication of results. Religious faith aside, because it is not at issue here, science cannot accept restrictive truth, visible or otherwise, special revelation to particular individuals, suspension of the laws of nature by "mysterious and inexplicable forces beyond our ken," or advocacy of the supernatural which is based on the substitution of assertion, claim, and intuition for facts, evidence, and proof.

Science is not a closed system and the body of scientific knowledge certainly has grown with time. And because the basic goal of science is discovery of the truth, it is, as a discipline, far more open than any other to the incorporation of every new discovery, from whatever source. The question that seems to have arisen today, however, is "What is truth?" Though a philosopher might respond differently, a scientist defines truth as an elusive and abstract concept of the ideal, one which is universal and unvarying, a veritable beacon for all to see who have but the wit and desire to open their eyes. The truth holds in Toronto as in Paris, yesterday and today and tomorrow, for you and for me, and for all those who are yet to come.

So elementary a proposition seems unworthy of print. And yet it needs to be set forth, for today, in an age of scientific miracles, truth itself is clearly under attack. It has become to some a thing subjective—a mere matter of opinion, of belief, of feeling, and of the charisma of charlatans of every description whose pronouncements are given enormous distribution. Indeed, it is fair to say that a tidal wave of superstition threatens to engulf the truth today, blending the real with the imaginary, thus threatening to transform this marvelous age of scientific advance into one of delusion, mysticism, and unreason.

A Litany of Superstition. The evidence sustaining the foregoing charge seems to the writer to be great in volume and diverse in character. The listing offered here is by no means exhaustive but should suffice to indicate why many thoughtful commentators on the contemporary human condition are saddened and perplexed by the scene surveyed.

- *Witchcraft.* The ancient belief in witches, sorcery, and demonology persists today principally in parts of Africa and Oceania, and in certain Indian societies. In Western culture witchcraft was a dominant facet of life during the Middle Ages, culminating in the great European witch-hunts of the 15th to 17th centuries and the trials at Salem in the New World. From our vantage point, the cruelties of the Inquisition in the search for secular agents of Satan and the preparation of lists of enemies and scapegoats by everyman would seem to be relicts of a bygone age of darkness.

But if this is so, how then can one explain that there exist today persons in our modern cities who seriously declare themselves to be witches and warlocks? That covens of such people flourish in the West, as do numerous shops to supply them with costumes, and philtres, and various satanic paraphernalia? That formal courses are offered on witchcraft, satanism, and the occult by supposedly reputable educational institutions? That 30,000 individuals gathered in Bogotá, Colombia, in 1975 to attend the First World Congress of Sorcery? Or that hundreds of thousands of persons trooped to theatres to see the rite of exorcism per-

Lawrence K. Lustig, former university professor and research scientist, is a writer and editor who expresses here his concern with some aspects of contemporary thought.

formed on a child? Perhaps the self-styled witches of today represent a form of counterreligion, not unlike the revival of interest in pagan worship by some in Iceland, but taken as a whole witchcraft clearly is one manifestation of unreason in our time.

• *Astrology.* The roots of astrology also are ancient, and no royal court of the past was without its experts skilled in the interpretation of astral omens. Their efforts were well rewarded when favourable events transpired, but not nearly so well as the efforts of our more modern soothsayers. Syndicated newspaper columns are avidly consulted daily by millions of otherwise rational persons who wish to know "what the stars have ordained."

And in England, *Old Moore's Almanack* has been published continuously for 279 years, since its founding by the physician and astrologer to King Charles II. In recent years more than one million copies have been sold annually, a figure easily exceeding that for one-volume editions of Shakespeare in the U.K. For 1976, *Old Moore's* predicts a year "of severe austerity when conditions will impose the need for self-restraint and a simpler style of living." This is a safe forecast indeed in a country whose economic woes have produced identical predictions in a legion of public speeches, editorials, and published economic analyses during the last few years. But according to *Old Moore's'* several staff astrologers it is supposedly based on the fact that "The sign of Virgo is rising. Saturn is the main ruler and Mars the second. . . ."

Those who object to the inclusion of astrology in a litany of superstitions must offer explanation for its fundamental assumption, namely that there is a correlation between the positions of the Sun, Moon, planets, and stars in the heavens, and the affairs of man on Earth. No conceivable cause and effect relationship has ever been demonstrated and no amount of trigonometric computation for the determination of zodiacal signs and horoscopes can conceal this fact. The number of births on Earth per day now approximates 300,000. It should therefore be obvious that identical astrological predictions will pertain to the wealthy and the poor, the ignorant and the wise, the happy and the sad, and the handsome and the plain—and to a legion of others who are linked solely by their time of birth. The basis of all of astrology is simply faith or, more properly, wishful thinking. As such, its inclusion here is most appropriate—its widespread appeal signifies nothing less than general support for mysticism and an embracement of unreason.

• *Medical Magic.* If one can believe that the outcome of marriages on Earth depends upon the compatibility of the partners' "signs," it is but a short step to belief in nonmedical healing of various kinds. The Indian medicine men of the Americas and their African counterparts did their best to treat illness within the limitations of then available knowledge and drugs. Thus, dancing, prayers, chants, and fetishes played an appropriate role; the patient was at least comforted, and there is something to be said for this result.

In our time, however, despite an enormous advance in medical knowledge and methods of treatment, there exists widespread belief in the ability of numerous "healers" to effect miraculous on-the-spot cures for arthritis, kidney and liver disease, cancer—indeed, for any ill known to man. The methods involved were splendidly described by Sinclair Lewis in his satirical *Elmer Gantry* (1927), but given the advantages of television and modern advertising techniques, the number of "true believers" has been greatly increased. An investigative account by the physician William Nolen (*Healing;* 1974) clearly indicates that no true cure of any disease has ever been proved to have been achieved before professional choirs in large auditoriums.

Still farther from the pale of reason are claims of the so-called "psychic surgeons" of the Philippines and Brazil. These spiritual healers not only "cure" tennis elbow and the like, but supposedly "operate" on the critically and terminally ill without benefit of scalpel or anesthesia, removing "cancerous tissue" and other "tumours" from the credulous sufferers for substantial fees. It is perhaps understandable that those declared incurably ill will grasp at any straw of hope, however slight, but there are many in our society who are not so afflicted, who nevertheless seriously discuss or absolutely believe that the operations described actually took place. For any literate adult to believe that human skin will cleanly part at the touch of another's fingertips, that healing will be accomplished in minutes, and that no trace of any incision will remain, is to enroll in the lists of the superstitious as here defined. These "surgeons" are in every instance merely clever sleight-of-hand tricksters who have successfully perpetrated the cruelest of hoaxes on those for whom pity must certainly be felt.

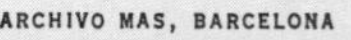
ARCHIVO MAS, BARCELONA

"The Witches' Sabbath," from an oil painting by Francisco de Goya, 1798.

• *Best Sellers of "Science Fantasy."* Historically, the public has always been willing to accept published claims of every description. In 1835, for example, the *New York Sun* included a picture of hairy creatures with wings, claiming that they were inhabitants of the Moon as seen by telescope; the "photograph" was doubted by few. Similarly, the famous radio broadcast by Orson Welles in 1938 frightened many who heard an announcement of a landing by Martians.

The sales data for certain books today are evidence of gullibility of a different stripe, however. Immanuel Velikovsky's contributions of the 1950s (*Worlds in Collision* and *Earth in Upheaval*), Erich von Däniken's efforts of the 1960s (*Chariots of the Gods?* and *Gods from Outer Space*), and such modern fare as *The Secret Life of Plants, The Bermuda Triangle,* and *The Sinking of Japan*—each a best-seller of the 1970s—have combined sales that easily exceed 35 million copies in various editions and printings. One of these best-sellers even spawned a reasoned refutation, namely, *The Bermuda Triangle Mystery—Solved* (1975). This work has had more modest success than the original "mystery," however, and it is impossible to determine how many purchasers mistakenly believed that it was the original.

Space limitations preclude a detailed analysis of the myriad flaws of fact and logic that thread the pages of these several volumes. One factor common to all, however, is the blending of a handful of scientific truths with sufficient supposition or outright fabrication to yield a new genre of literature, one that might best be termed "science fantasy." Another common factor is the aggrieved posture of each author when taken to task. Velikovsky, for example, claimed persecution by the scientific "establishment" for his views, and von Däniken takes great pains to point out that he is self-taught, and thus free from the prejudices that supposedly accompany formal training in archaeology, anthropology, and the several earth sciences in which he dabbles. The danger, of course, is that he may also be free of the knowledge that such training instills. As Stephen Gould so perceptively indicated in a review of *Worlds in Collision,* one does not attain the stature of Galileo merely because he is persecuted—it is also necessary that he be right.

Velikovsky for one is certainly not right; there is not the slightest shred of evidence to sustain his claims that Venus was torn from Jupiter, that Jupiter collided with or otherwise disturbed Mars, and that the latter planet then left its orbit to cause a variety of catastrophic upheavals on Earth—all between 1500 and 700 B.C., approximately. His thesis violates every basic tenet of historical geology and, additionally, it is disproved by the data which show that segments of the Earth's crust are in measurable motion today.

Such "science fantasy" has been equaled or exceeded by von Däniken, who offers the thesis that astronauts from a superior race sped across the cosmos in ancient time to build the pyramids of Egypt, erect the great stone megaliths on Easter Island, and construct "airfields" in Peru. A few words of refutation are perhaps in order here. The pyramids of Egypt date from the Old Kingdom (*c.* 2690–2160 B.C.) and are acknowledged by all scholars to be funerary edifices of the pharaohs. The largest is the Great Pyramid, or Pyramid of Khufu, which is constructed of nearly 2.5 million limestone blocks with an average weight of about 2.5 tons. The method of construction involved the use of sledges, rollers, and levers, combined with ample manpower and the advantage of great sloping earthen embankments, which were removed following completion of the work.

The pyramids are rightly considered one of the wonders of the ancient and modern world, but von Däniken asserts that there is great mystery in all of this, and that the Egyptians could not possibly have built the pyramids. For Easter Island as well as Egypt he raises the issue of the weight and number of stones to be moved. Apparently he did not know, or simply chose to ignore, the fact that experiments on Easter Island in 1955–56 showed that 180 persons were able to move a great stone statue over the ground using only wooden logs as rollers and levers; and that a mere 12 persons were able to lift a 25-ton statue 10 feet off the ground in order to tilt it into an upright position. In view of this physical demonstration of human capabilities on Easter Island in the 1950s, it scarcely seems necessary to invoke a visit by ancient spacemen in books written in the 1960s.

Von Däniken also asserts that these same astronauts created in the ancient Egyptians a belief in corporeal reawakening to a second life. He seems to compare the embalming of mummies with the storing of modern tissue and bodies in liquid nitrogen deep-freeze banks. Here again, one must question whether this author was aware of Egyptian embalming techniques, or simply chose to ignore them in order to sustain his fable. The Egyptian morticians always removed the vital organs and brains in order to pack the bodies with resin and myrrh and thus help to preserve them. Are we to believe that superior beings from an advanced technological civilization thought that the pharaohs would one day rise up to attest to their visit, despite being internally packed with resin?

The Peruvian "airfield" argument is much the same. Archaeologists who have studied various Andean ruins find no reason to suppose that the Incas and other terrestrial civilizations did not produce the structures of their day. Von Däniken, however, finds "landing strips" rather than walls and roadways among the lineaments to be seen on aerial photographs. The question to be asked in this instance is why beings sufficiently advanced to traverse interstellar space and land their craft in Peru should then require "airfields" in order to depart? The answer should be self-evident: There certainly would be no such requirement.

Such is the stuff of "science fantasy." If this be proof of the existence of extraterrestrial visitors, then there is little wonder that some believe in the existence of "mysterious magnetic aberrations" in the Bermuda triangle; or believe that their houseplants can hear, think, and feel; or believe that the islands of Japan will sink beneath the waves in a great cataclysm of six months duration. No notion is too fanciful to be accepted in toto, in defiance of both reason and the laws of nature.

• *Parapsychology.* This category includes a vast array of phenomena, the claims for which stem largely from the experiments of J. B. Rhine at Duke University. In 1934 he began to test the proposition that certain individuals possess extrasensory perception (ESP). A simple deck of cards bearing five basic markings—a circle, square, wave, cross, or star—was used for this purpose. The experimenter randomly drew cards from the deck in one room while the subject tried to guess the design appearing on each card from a second room. The laws of probability suggest that if large numbers of subjects are tested, and a large number of trials made, then one card out of each five drawn (or 10 out of each 50) will be guessed correctly due to chance alone. Those subjects correctly guessing a greater number of cards are said to possess ESP. The statistics are such that if a subject correctly guesses 11 cards out of each 50 trials, and continues to do so through 10,000 trials, the odds are two million to one that this result is not attributable to chance alone. And such subjects are reported to exist.

Controversy, discussion, dispute, refinement of testing, and charges of fraud have occupied the intervening 41 years. In 1974, for example, a leading investigator at Rhine's institute was forced to resign after it was discovered that he had tampered with an automated experiment. Aside from this problem, namely the emotional involvement of the investigators, who tend also to be supporters, two points should be borne in mind. First, the successes demonstrated are not nearly so spectacular as most persons seem to believe; the "ESP-sensitive" who correctly guesses 11 cards in each 50 trials is obviously failing to guess correctly 39 times in each 50 trials. And second, assuming that the results of these card-guessing experiments are acceptable, they constitute the *only* genuine evidence of so-called parapsychological phenomena that has been produced thus far. All other avenues of investigation have been permeated by carelessness, fraudulence, or emotionally based claims. This means that the principal "proof" for general telepathy, precognition, clairvoyance, and psychokinesis resides only in the fact that certain individuals can correctly guess more than 10 cards out of each 50; any assertion of such linkage would seem extravagant, to say the least.

Separate mention should be made of the host of mystics, mediums, psychics, and psychokinetic projectionists that abound in the 1970s. The Russian "sensitive" Ninel (Lenin spelled backward) Kulagina purportedly causes objects to levitate by force of will; Ted Serios, a Chicago bellboy, supposedly produces "thoughtographs" on film; Peter Hurkos, a Dutch "psychometrist," claims to be able to find missing objects and solve crimes; and the famous Israeli performer Uri Geller bends keys and cutlery by means of "special psychic powers." Geller's powers, incidentally, were attributed by Andrija Puharich, a physician who has studied psychic phenomena for 25 years, to extraterrestrial beings on the spaceship "Spectra," which is stationed 53,069 light-years from Earth. He also reported that he received permission to publish the book *Uri* (1974) from a computer on board this craft.

The most thoughtful and considered treatment of Uri Geller's performances, and those of similar psychics, is that by Milbourne Christopher (*Mediums, Mystics & The Occult;* 1975), a professional magician and head of the Occult Investigation Committee of the Society of American Magicians. It is instructive that any such individual readily recognizes Geller's act as that of a skillful conjurer and showman; indeed, James Randi, another professional magician, has duplicated many of the feats, including metal-bending, but this failed to still Geller's supporters. The latter also choose to ignore his repeated refusals to perform before professional magicians and, most surprising of all, they willingly accept his failures as "proof" of genuineness, arguing that psychics *naturally* cannot perform before skeptical or unsympathetic audiences. In this context it is worth noting that many sympathizers who witnessed Geller's televised broadcast in England called the studio to report the simultaneous bending of cutlery in their homes. Their belief remained unshaken even when they were later informed that the show had been taped—Geller was not even in the U.K. at that time.

But this line of argument is beyond the scope of this essay. More to the point is a different observation. In the writer's youth it was commonplace for magicians on stage, and in later years in televised performances, to "amaze and astound" their audiences by their proficiency at sleight of hand and illusion. When one observed a woman being "sawed in half"; or light bulbs rising and glowing "unsupported" in mid-stage; or fluids poured into one container only to disappear and rise in another distant duplicate; or rabbits and birds emerging from top hats—in all such instances one was gladdened and delighted, and one applauded to indicate awareness that a deception beyond one's ken had somehow been perpetrated. No one, however, would have claimed—or believed—that special paranormal forces produced these effects. The woman, for example, was surely not physically cut through and rematerialized; nor did the light bulb glow through inexplicable psychic powers; nor were the rabbits and birds created from nothing, by sheer force of will.

And yet today, all this and more is readily accepted by those emotionally committed to parapsychology. As Martin Gardner has indicated, the claims are immense but proofs nonexistent. The stuff of parapsychology is largely that of showmanship—and of superstition and unreason.

• *Miscellany.* This litany of superstition would be incomplete without passing mention of other phenomena of our day which suggest the prevalence of widespread superstitious belief. In this category one might include: the witnessed landing of flying saucers, whose crews kidnapped cows after interviewing their owners; enormous sales of model pyramids to customers believing that some magical "resonating energy" is to be derived from this form; tales of personal encounters with Big Foot and the Yeti, or Abominable Snowman; establishment of an "Institute of Noetic Sciences" by a former Apollo astronaut; claims that a race of intelligent beings inhabits the ocean bottoms (*Invisible Residents;* 1970); the advent of motion pictures designed to give credence to the notion that the recollection of former lives is perfectly natural (*The Reincarnation of Peter Proud*); and a search for poltergeists in Wellington, New Zealand, as recently as 1963. All this and more is taken here as evidence of the acceptance of delusionary thinking in our time.

A Summing Up. Any objective appraisal of the literature, reports, and events described above leads inexorably to one basic question, namely, why? Why do large numbers of people in our society deliberately choose mysterious, supernatural, and delusionary explanations in lieu of tried and tested rational patterns of causality? Some would answer, as did the eminent psychologist Carl Jung after an analysis of UFO sightings (*Flying Saucers;* 1958), that people do so simply because it suits them—because they *want* to believe in the mysterious. William James, psychologist of an earlier day, would doubtless have agreed. Even when defending religious faith, however, this great pragmatist said that a belief is true only if it works, and he suggested testing the effects and consequences of any given belief (*The Will to Believe;* 1897). This suggestion is obviously unacceptable to supporters of the phenomena described here and the question that remains is why people wish to believe that the unreal is real.

Elizabeth Janeway and others have said that the world of modern science and technology is too complex to be decently conveyed to the lay public by those who speak the language of science. Hence, the multitudes withdraw to the mysterious, for here, at least, they can feel as one—both with the author or performer in question, and with their own peers.

And last, one must consider the unfortunate Anglo-Saxon tendency to view intelligence with considerable resentment, suspicion, and hostility, a factor which has been noted by writers as diverse as John Erskine ("The Moral Obligation to Be Intelligent") and Richard Hofstadter (*Anti-Intellectualism in American Life;* 1963).

The truth may well comprise elements of each of these explanations. But whatever the cause it is quite clear that we may awaken tomorrow to learn that some clever promoter has discovered a new and intriguing solution to the question of how light is transmitted. The dust jacket on a first edition of two million copies may ask: "Is there evidence that light is transmitted as an infinite series of invisible aardvarks, whose tails glow when activated by a mysterious intelligence from outer space?" If we greet this absurd proposition with anything other than the ridicule it richly deserves then we will have moved one step further along a path of unreason that may well lead to one of darkness.

Those who doubt that this is so might ponder the fact that the fall of Phnom Penh, and thus all of Cambodia, was hastened by belief of the defenders in the existence of an invisible dragon beneath the city's outskirts. Obeying the portents of the stars, they severed their own supply road to relieve the pressure on this beast's tail. Obviously, their astrologers failed them in this instance.

Even the most sophisticated society ultimately must depend on the ability of its members to make rational choices between conflicting alternatives. The survival of our society would be a bit more certain if the dichotomy between scientists and their lay colleagues were bridged. This essay is offered in this spirit and with this intent.

Enigmatic stone megaliths of Easter Island, easternmost Polynesia.

ERNEST MANEWAL—SHOSTAL

Economics

Both as a profession and as a science, economics lost considerable prestige during the recession of 1974–75. The crisis that seized the Western industrialized countries, including Japan, was of a character not to be found in economics textbooks: rates of inflation exceeding 10% a year coupled with declining production and high levels of unemployment. Hitherto, peacetime inflation had been associated with high employment and an overactive economy, while high rates of unemployment went with recession or depression. The new combination was aptly called stagflation.

The press seemed to delight in printing articles about the plight of the professional economists who had, by and large, failed to predict either the magnitude of the inflation or the depth of the recession, and who seemed unable to agree on what ought to be done. The economists were no less critical of themselves. Walter Heller, who had headed the Council of Economic Advisers under Presidents Kennedy and Johnson (a period that saw economists at the very pinnacle of power and success), scolded his colleagues for losing their nerve. In his presidential address to the annual convention of the American Economic Association at the end of 1974, he said: "We have . . . readily confessed that the inflationary shocks of 1974–75 caught not just the economy but the economist by surprise. On this and other fronts, the chorus of self-criticism has risen to a new crescendo. . . . Nietzsche must have been thinking of economists when he observed that 'he who despises himself nevertheless esteems himself as a self-despiser.' "

Under the crisis of confidence lay a crisis of theory. John Maynard Keynes had rescued the profession from a similar crisis in the 1930s by supplying a theoretical rationale for government measures to combat widespread unemployment and depression. He had converted two generations of economists to his ideas, in what came to be known as the Keynesian Revolution. By 1975 the revolution seemed to have run its course. Economists were confronted with the question of whether the Keynesian revolution had really been as fundamental as it had seemed.

Keynes had argued that government spending could stimulate an economy out of a slump, and subsequent events seemed to prove him correct. But economists in increasing numbers were admitting that Keynes did not provide them with answers—or perhaps even with adequate tools—for the problems of the inflation-ridden 1970s. One of the sessions at the AEA convention was devoted to "a critical look at the Keynesian model" by four Keynesian theorists, Robert Clower and Axel Leijonhufvud of the University of California at Los Angeles, Robert Eisner of Northwestern, and James Tobin of Yale. They seemed to agree that Keynesian theory had not yet explained why large numbers of willing workers may be unable to find employment in a free-enterprise economy. Lacking agreement on the precise reasons why unemployment exists in the first place, economists could hardly be expected to agree on ways of combating it.

Clower and Leijonhufvud maintained that the followers of Keynes had misread him and oversimplified his ideas. He had attacked traditional economic theory for its assumption that the economy is self-adjusting and tends to return to equilibrium after any disturbance. Economists since Keynes have not pursued this line of inquiry, preferring to maintain that government fiscal and monetary policies can make up for any disequilibrium in the system.

To Clower and Leijonhufvud this was a serious mistake, since it turned inquiry away from reality: "We have yet to resolve the central question posed by Keynes's assault on received doctrine: Is the *existing* economic system, in any *significant* sense, self-adjusting? . . . In our judgment, the standard model is incapable of development in the directions to which the central question requires that we turn our attention." They called for a fresh approach to macroeconomic theory that would enable economists to describe how business and household units behave when the system is not in equilibrium—in short, a theory that would be more relevant to the problems of unemployment and inflation than the present "Keynesian" one.

Eisner and Tobin responded that the fault lay not in Keynesian theory but in inadequate political programs. Eisner suggested a number of things government could do to unlimber the economy and make it more responsive to changes in supply and demand. If economists would sharpen their political swords, he concluded, the Keynesian revolution might still carry the day. Tobin conceded that the analytical concepts of Keynes left something to be desired, but held that he had been right in believing that government intervention is necessary to eliminate persistent unemployment.

Along with the crisis in theory went a crisis in the art of economic forecasting. More than half of the inflation in the years 1973 and 1974 had been generated by increases in fuel costs and food prices, resulting from a quadrupling of oil prices by the Organization of Petroleum Exporting Countries and a sharp rise in world grain prices. In other words, about half of the inflation in the U.S. came from external causes. Economists could not be blamed for failing to predict what the Arabs and the Soviets would do, but they might have been better at addressing the consequences.

Arthur M. Okun, also a former chairman of the Council of Economic Advisers, pointed out in a report for the Brookings Institution that economists' forecasts throughout 1974 were overly optimistic. For example, in May the median of a sizable sample of economic forecasters were predicting that real gross national product in the U.S. for 1974 would be 0.3% less than in 1973; in the outcome, real GNP fell by 2.1%. The median forecast also predicted that the general price level would rise by 8.4%; actually, it rose by 10.3%.

Some of the forecasts had been based on elaborate computerized models of the economy. One source of error lay in the sets of equations that comprised these models. As Heller said in his presidential address, they left out certain variables that had not been very important in recent years. Thus they assumed that prices would follow the same trend as wages, allowing for slight increases in productivity. This had been a safe assumption during the previous 20 years, and one that greatly simplified the tasks of the model builders, but suddenly new variables became important. Prices were now affected by tighter commodity supplies and changes in exchange rates—variables that were not included in the equations the economists had been using. (FRANCIS S. PIERCE)

See also Industrial Relations: *Special Report;* Nobel Prizes.

[531; 10/36.D]

Eastern Orthodox Churches: *see* Religion

Ecology: *see* Environment; Life Sciences

Economy, World

General Overview. Any appraisal of the gross national product (GNP) for the world must involve some inaccuracies and estimation. This is because the nature of goods and services differs markedly for nonhomogeneous groups of countries and because national account figures in local currencies must be converted into dollars or other standard units at prevailing exchange rates. Nevertheless, it seemed probable that world product remained roughly unchanged in 1975, as recession, which affected the developed market economies, offset growth in several other areas of the world.

The National Institute of Economic and Social Research of the U.K. forecast in November 1975 that the gross product of the member countries of the Organization for Economic Cooperation and Development (OECD) would fall in real terms by 2.3% in 1975, compared with a decline of 0.2% in 1974. The recession thus was a long one and, despite the relatively gentle appearance of year-to-year changes, a severe one at its worst. For example, the annual rate of decline in the U.S. between the third quarter of 1974 and the first quarter of 1975 was 10.2%.

The severity of the recession may be attributed to two main causes, the strength of the inflationary pressures engendered by the boom throughout the developed world in 1972 and 1973 and the difficulty of bringing them under control; and the oil price increases that came into force in October 1973 and January 1974. The latter gave an important new push to costs and also had a depressive effect by reducing expenditure on everything other than petroleum.

Governments tended to be inhibited in their response to this recession by the fear that measures to stimulate economic activity, if taken too early or pushed too far, could undermine all the hard-won achievements in reducing the rate of inflation. And those achievements were considerable, as the prices of many foods and raw materials turned downward. Comparing the two periods September 1973–September 1974 and September 1974–September 1975, inflation as measured by the consumer price index declined from 11.9 to 7.9% in the U.S., from 14.7 to 10.7% in France, from 23 to 13% in Italy, from 22.6 to 10.8% in Japan, from 7.3 to 6.1% in West Germany, and from 10.9 to 10.5% in Canada. Of the seven major Western economies only the U.K. experienced a worsening of its inflation rate, from 16 to 27.7%. But even though the progress achieved in five of the other six was considerable, it was clear that inflationary forces had been scotched rather than killed, and it was understandable that governments should have been cautious about reflation.

If one considers the years 1974 and 1975 together, the OECD economies experienced a decline of about 2.5% in real GNP compared with 1973. The worst affected was the U.S., in which a 2.1% fall in 1974 was followed by one of approximately 3% in 1975. Another economy badly affected was that of West Germany, which managed a 0.6% increase in gross domestic product (GDP) in 1974 but experienced a decline in 1975 of probably 4.2%. West Germany suffered disproportionately from the decline in the volume of world trade, because exports normally provide so much of the dynamism of its economy. West Germany was also ill served by its economic forecasters, the most noted of whom were advising at the end of 1974 that there was no need for major government stimulus to the economy because the latter was likely to produce a 2.5% growth rate under its own steam in 1975.

On the other hand, the decline of GNP in Japan between 1973 and 1975 was confined to a negligible 0.3%. Affected by the recession at an early stage, it suffered a 1.8% fall in GNP in 1974 but was thought to have regained most of the lost ground in the course of 1975. The impressive thing about Japan's response to the recession was that it set out to export itself out of trouble. Between the first halves of 1974 and 1975 the volume of its exports rose by 4.6% over a period in which the volume of West Germany's exports, for instance, fell by 12.6%.

The decline in GNP in the U.K. between 1973 and 1975, with a fall of 0.4% in 1974 and one estimated at 1.9% in 1975, looks relatively modest when compared with that of the U.S. This is essentially because, in the short term at least, the government had some success in attaching a higher priority to maintaining employment than to dealing with inflation. It was not, indeed, until other governments had reached the stage of feeling it safe to reflate their economies that the U.K. authorities took any effective measures to control wage inflation. This belated anti-inflationary action meant that aggregate real demand in Britain was likely to show little if any increase in 1976, when the rest of the OECD countries would probably achieve a growth rate of about 5%.

It is perhaps instructive to look in some detail at the course of the recession in the U.S. One has a sequence, quarter by quarter, in which GNP declined at the moderate annual rates of 1.7 and 1.9% in the second and third quarters of 1974, and then at the very steep annual rates of 9 and 11.4% in the fourth quarter of 1974 and the first of 1975. Then, perhaps earlier than expected and certainly before the authorities' major reflationary stimulus had time to take effect, there was a return to growth at a 1.9% annual rate in the second quarter followed by an unsustainable 13.2% in the third quarter of 1975.

Swings in inventory accumulation or liquidation, however, had much to do with the quarterly fluctuations in the U.S. Thus, in terms of final sales, the fourth quarter of 1974 was the worst of the recession, with an 11.7% annual rate of decline, but this was disguised in the GNP figures by the fact that manufacturers and traders, taken by surprise by the strength of the recession, involuntarily had to hold an increased volume of stocks. They were busily correcting this situation in the first quarter of 1975, with the result that although the volume of final sales fell only at an annual rate of 0.7%, heavy liquidation of inventories resulted in the worst quarterly GNP figure of the recession. This liquidation continued more massively still in the second quarter, with the result that a 4.6% annual rate increase in final sales resulted only in a 1.9% annual gain in GNP. In the third quarter, final sales continued on much the same path, a 4.4% annual rate, but because inventory liquidation was much less of a drag on the economy, a 13.2% annual rate of GNP growth was possible.

The real value of housing construction had been falling before the recession proper began and continued to do so. At the low point in the first quarter of 1975, it was 34.3% less than a year earlier. The decline in business fixed investment started later in the cycle, in the third quarter of 1974. There the decline between the second quarters of 1974 and 1975, peak and trough, was 16.8%. By contrast, the slump in consumer expenditure on durable goods, in real terms, was very sharp and very short. Although it had fallen back from 1973 levels, it was rising again in the second and third quarters of 1974. Then, in the fourth quarter, sales collapsed, falling by 13.9% or an annual rate of 45.1%. Thereafter, however, it began to recover. The tax rebate and reduced tax withholding rates introduced in the spring of 1975 seemed well calculated to assist consumer spending in its recovery, but monetary policy seemed at the end of the year likely to keep the growth of GNP in 1976 relatively modest for a year of recovery from a recession, so as to prevent a resurgence of price inflation.

The full impact of the recession on primary producing countries only began to be felt well into 1975. The governments of these countries were able to keep up the value of imports, though not always their volume, by running down the reserves accumulated during the commodity price boom and by pushing their foreign borrowing close to the limits of their creditworthiness. Because this process seemed to be coming to an end in the second half of 1975, one would expect real GNP growth rates for the year as a whole to have been fairly well maintained, though on balance lower than in 1974 and with a tendency to tail off during the course of the year.

For many primary producing countries, 1976 will be a more difficult year than 1975, until demand for commodities begins to pick up in its second half. The Organization of Petroleum Exporting Countries (OPEC), of course, form a group of their own. They had no reason to feel dissatisfied with 1975, having foreseen the drop in the volume of their oil exports and compensated for it by a further price rise.

The Communist countries are relatively but not wholly immune from the effects of recession in the developed market economies. Their generally high though somewhat exaggerated rates of growth in net material product are essentially determined by their own organization of men and resources, subject to the vagaries of agricultural production. This last was a major factor in the case of the Soviet Union in 1975. Its grain harvest of 137 million tons against a target of 215 million tons caused an immediate fall in economic growth in 1975 and was expected to lead to a secondary deceleration in 1976, with food processing industries short of raw materials and imports under pressure. But trade with the West is of major importance to these countries as a means of industrial modernization, and while the Soviet Union was able to set the higher price of its petroleum exports against the higher price of the manufactured goods it imported, Eastern European countries suffered in 1975. Their terms of trade with the West worsened as a result of Western inflation, and their markets diminished as a result of Western recession.

Table I. World Shares of Population and Production

Area	Population (1973) (000,000)	Population (1973) Percent	Gross domestic product $000,000 1970	Gross domestic product $000,000 1960	Gross domestic product Percent 1970	Gross domestic product Percent 1960
World	3,860	100.0	—	—	—	—
Market economies	—	—	2,485,300	1,125,700	100.0	100.0
Developed market economies	—	—	2,098,400	—	84.4	83.8
Less developed market economies	—	—	386,900	—	15.6	16.2
Major industrial economies						
Canada	22	0.6	82,890	39,918	3.3	3.5
France	52	1.3	144,734	61,041	5.8	5.4
Germany, West	62	1.6	187,694	72,036	7.6	6.4
Italy	55	1.4	92,704	34,802	3.7	3.1
Japan	108	2.8	196,917	43,097	7.9	3.8
U.K.	56	1.5	119,811	71,244	4.8	6.3
U.S.	210	5.4	983,237	509,030	39.6	45.2
Total	565	14.6	1,807,987	831,168	72.7	73.7
Other selected industrial economies						
Australia	13	0.3	36,716	16,297	1.5	1.4
Belgium	10	0.3	25,731	11,279	1.0	1.0
Netherlands, The	13	0.3	31,650	11,011	1.3	1.0
Spain	35	0.9	32,340	10,345	1.3	0.9
Sweden	8	0.2	32,972	13,941	1.3	1.2

ECONOMIC CONDITIONS

The preceding overview examined world economic conditions in general, contrasting developments in the industrial market economies with those in the centrally planned economies and the less developed countries. In this section the examination is taken a stage further with an assessment of the impact on individuals and households of prevailing economic trends. This requires examination of those economic variables that are of most direct interest to individual citizens. These are: employment, unemployment, and hours worked; wages and prices; taxation and social benefits; housing; ownership of goods; and available credit and interest rates.

While prime interest is in developments in these variables over the last two to three years, it helps if these events can be placed in their longer-term perspective. Thus, data illustrating long-term trends are included in the tables below as well as data on recent developments. Sometimes there are, in fact, no statistics on recent developments, and all that can be discussed are trends over the past decade. And although the vast majority of the world's population lives in nations with centrally planned economies or in the less developed countries, the availability of up-to-date statistical material of good quality for both is limited compared with that available for the developed countries. The data given here concentrate, therefore, on the industrialized countries of the West. In particular, economic trends are tabulated for the seven major Western economies (U.S., West Germany, Japan, France, U.K., Italy, and Canada) as well as for some of the smaller Western countries such as Belgium, The Netherlands, Australia, Sweden, and Spain (still classified as a less developed country by some measures). Table I shows how these richer countries stand in relation to the world economy, with regard both to their share of world population and to their share of world income.

Even for Western countries, the data describe the impact of economic developments on basic social units such as the household less adequately than they describe the impact on individuals. For instance, figures on trends in the number of unemployed reveal little about the number of nonworking dependents affected, a figure that is possibly of much greater social significance.

An absorbing subject of discussion in many countries is whether the combination of slump and inflation over the last two years has led to certain sections of the population gaining a larger share of the national wealth relative to others. Unfortunately, the available data rarely permit a simple unqualified answer. In at least one major economy, the U.K., it is generally believed that high rates of price and wage inflation in recent years have led to substantial gains by manual workers relative to white-collar workers. In part this is because income-tax allowances are not "indexed" to inflation. Taxes, therefore, bite with increasing severity as money incomes increase so that, although low-paid and high-paid might get equal percentage increases in pretax terms, post-tax increases in money income favour the lower-paid.

Table II. Total Employment in Selected Countries
(1970=100)

Country	1973	1974	1975 first quarter	1975 second quarter	% change from a year earlier 1975 first quarter	% change from a year earlier 1975 second quarter
Australia	106	108	107	108	−0.9	0.0
Canada	111	116	113	119	2.7	2.6
France	101	102	101	100	0.0	−1.0
Germany, West	100	98	96	95	−3.7*	−4.0
Italy	99	101	101	100	1.0	0.0
Japan	103	102	98	103	−2.0	−1.0
Sweden	101	103	104	105	3.0	1.9
U.K.	101	101	101	100	−1.9†	−1.6
U.S.	107	109	105	107	−1.9	−1.8

*Total dependent employment.
†Employment in the production industries.
Source: OECD, *Main Economic Indicators*.

It is generally known that in times of recession the share of national income received in the form of profits, and thus the proportion going to dividend payments, diminishes relative to the share received in the form of wages and salaries. In times of inflation, a corresponding general rule is that debtors gain and creditors lose. In effect, this means that a large proportion of the moderately well-off tend to gain, particularly if they are purchasing a house or consumer durables on credit. On the other hand, the very poor and the very rich will lose: the poor because they cannot obtain much credit, the rich because they do not need it. When recession and inflation combine, as was the situation in most countries in 1975, it is more difficult to determine who is gaining and who is losing. The rich, as both creditors and receivers of dividend income (and capital gains), seem certain to be losers. The poor are also likely to lose, except to the extent that poverty and/or unemployment are cushioned by generous social benefits. One result of the recent recession has been an improvement in a number of countries in the value of the benefits available. For the rest, an individual's position depends on whether he or she has a secure job, is in debt to a substantial extent, and belongs to an occupational group with sufficient political or economic muscle to ensure that post-tax wages or salaries keep at least abreast of inflation.

Employment, Unemployment, and Hours Worked. Boom and slump affect the average individual in industrial countries most directly through their impact upon his job prospects. Will he, or she, keep his job and, if he does, will he be working less than full time or taking home extra money from overtime? If he becomes unemployed, how well do unemployment benefits cushion the blow? The following discussion examines such questions.

Employment. Employment trends in the industrial countries in recent years and in the first two quarters of 1975 can be seen in Table II. Characteristically, between one-third and one-half of the population in developed countries can be regarded as being part of the total labour force, the exact proportion depending largely on how many women work. Total employment tends to react rather sluggishly to economic recession, compared with other labour force indicators such as unemployment. Demographic factors—young people entering and old people leaving the labour market—are usually more important than economic factors.

In a prolonged and severe depression, of course, such as that which occurred in the 1930s, employment contracts sharply. But in the milder recessions since the end of World War II the downturn in employment has also been mild and may not appear until a year or more after the onset of recession. This is not entirely because of the mildness of the recessions. Another factor has been the growing proportion of the labour force that is employed in the "tertiary" sector of the economy, that is, in government or the private service industries rather than in agriculture or industry. Employment in the service industries is much less affected by recession, and the growing proportion of workers in these industries means that employment totals are likely to respond even less to future economic downturns.

Demographic factors are evident in the higher long-term rate of labour force growth in the Canadian, U.S., and Australian economies, as compared with the European countries. The percentage growth rates in the early part of 1975 reflect, however, current economic developments. Canada and Sweden can be seen to be less affected at that stage of the recession than other economies. In most cases, though, total employment had dropped by 1 to 2% when compared with a year earlier, with U.S. employment about 2% down. Second quarter developments did, however, hint at some "bottoming-out" in the downturn.

Unemployment. People who drop out of employment during a recession do not automatically join the unemployed. Married women in particular may be drawn into the labour force during a period of expansion but in a recession will not be looking for work. Others, particularly older people, may become discouraged after a prolonged period of unemployment and cease to look for work. As unemployment is gen-

Table III. Unemployment in the Developed Economies

Country	Number unemployed as of June 1975* (in 000)	Unemployment rates (Percent of civilian labour force)*: Average 1962–72	1973	1974	1975 Latest peak	1975 Latest month	Standardized annual unemployment rate (%) 1974	1975 first quarter
Major industrial economies								
Canada	725	5.1	5.6	5.4	7.2	7.2 July	5.4	7.0
France	878	1.7	2.1	3.1	5.0	5.0 second quarter	3.1	4.6
Germany, West	1,307	1.0	1.3	2.6	5.2†	4.4 September	2.1	3.0
Italy	727‡	3.4	3.5	2.9	3.4	3.4 second quarter	3.1	3.1
Japan	1,015	1.2	1.1	1.4	1.8	1.8 June	1.4	1.8
U.K.	920	2.3	2.6	2.6	4.2	4.2 July	3.0	3.5
U.S.	7,896	4.7	4.9	5.6	9.2§	8.4 July	5.6	8.3
Other industrial economies								
Australia	270	1.5	1.5	2.1	4.8	4.8 July	...	...
Belgium	180	1.9	3.6	4.1	...	...	...	...
Netherlands, The	193	1.1	2.7	3.3	...	...	...	...
Spain	241‖	—	1.4	1.4	1.9	1.9 December 1974	...	...
Sweden	80	2.0	2.5	2.0	...	...	...	...

*Seasonally adjusted.
†February 1975. ‡April 1975. §May 1975. ‖March 1975.
Sources: UN, *Monthly Bulletin*; OECD, *Main Economic Indicators*; OECD, *Economic Outlook*, July 1975 (page 29); National Institute, *Economic Review*, London, Number 73, August 1975.

Table IV. Unemployment Coverage and Benefits in Selected Countries

Country	Unemployment insurance: Coverage in 1974–75*	Size of benefits in mid-1975†	Maximum benefit period in mid-1975 (weeks)
Canada	99	67	51
France	61	40	52
Germany, West	93	60	52
Italy	51	Partly flat rate	26
Japan	45	60–80	‡
U.K.	80§	Partly flat rate (40–60 in first 26 weeks)	52
U.S.	95	51 (average)	65

Note: Unemployment systems are complex and some of the details are of necessity omitted from a general table such as this. For further information, reference should be made to A. Mittelstadt, "Unemployment Benefits and Related Payments in Seven Major Countries," OECD, *Occasional Studies*, July 1975.
*Covered employment as percent of total employment.
†As percent of gross earnings.
‡Length varies with length of insured employment and, in addition, with difficulties encountered in finding new employment.
§Estimate.

erally defined, they would then cease to be regarded as unemployed.

The number of unemployed is not, therefore, a fixed absolute, but depends in part on the statistical definitions and methods of counting used by government statisticians. Two main methods of counting are used. Labour force surveys, as conducted in the U.S., send interviewers to a selected sample of households to find the numbers out of work and seeking further work. In many countries, however, such as the U.K., a person is counted as unemployed only if he or she registers with the appropriate government department or other authorized body. Clearly a register system provides lower estimates of unemployment than a household labour force survey. A good deal of caution is needed therefore in comparing unemployment rates between countries. Most of the figures on unemployment in each country given in Table III are based on national definitions. A comparative analysis for the seven largest economies is included in the table, however, with unemployment rates for 1974 and the first quarter of 1975 adjusted to conform with the U.S. definition.

Even allowing for differences in definition, Canada and the U.S. had much higher unemployment rates than most other countries, both in the past and in recent months. West Germany and Japan tended to have low rates. For West Germany this reflects a strong rate of economic growth with the impact of cyclical swings being largely met by changes in the number of migrant workers. In Japan, the tendency is for employers to retain labour even when production is falling, while female and part-time workers move readily in or out of the labour force in accordance with cyclical fluctuations.

For most countries not only were 1975 unemployment rates well above average rates in the 1950s and 1960s, but they were also higher than the rates seen at the lowest points of other post-1950 recessions (although still in no way comparable to the worst rates in the 1930s). Even in 1973, at the crest of the last boom, unemployment tended to be higher than in earlier years. Unemployment then rose sharply in most countries, particularly in late 1974 and extending into early and mid-1975.

As can be seen from the data on latest monthly unemployment rates, most countries had not yet reached or had just receded from the peak in unemployment by mid- to late 1975. Seasonally adjusted unemployment in the seven largest economies totaled 13.5 million in June 1975, with nearly 8 million of that number being in the U.S. However, West Germany and the U.S., the two largest economies, showed a significant improvement from peak rates earlier in the year. It can be assumed that most other countries will also show declines from peak unemployment levels by mid-1976.

Certain sections of the population are more severely affected by unemployment than others. These include racial minority groups and young people just entering the labour force. In part, this reflects the standard policy of "last hired, first fired." A late 1975 report by the OECD's Directorate for Social Affairs, Manpower and Education claimed, however, that the problem of unemployment among young people is more than just a temporary cyclical effect and that a long-term deterioration is taking place, linked to structural changes in society.

A fairly common problem for young people is that they have not been in the labour force long enough to qualify for the full range of unemployment benefits. In most of the developed countries, however, most workers are now protected by unemployment insurance against immediate financial hardship should they become unemployed. A consequence of the 1974–75 recession is that a number of countries improved their unemployment insurance by such means as raising benefit rates and extending benefits for longer periods. Table IV summarizes benefit coverage, size, and duration for the seven major economies as of mid-1975. Canada and West Germany appear to have the most comprehensive systems. The U.S. system is also extensive, but it varies a good deal in application from state to state.

Hours Worked. Average weekly hours worked in manufacturing is one of the most sensitive statistical indicators of the state of a country's economy. During a boom overtime increases and so do average hours worked. In recession there is less overtime, short-time working increases, and average hours decline.

Underlying these short-term cyclical fluctuations is the downward trend in average hours worked found in almost all countries. This is clearly apparent in Table V, with Japan showing the most sizable reduction among the major industrial countries in the last decade. This reflects the tendency for most people to wish to convert a part of their share of increased national prosperity into increased leisure time.

With regard to current developments, the impact of the recession can be clearly seen from the reductions in average hours in early 1975 when compared with a year earlier. The sharpest reductions occurred in West Germany and Japan, the latter providing evidence that Japanese employers and employees prefer to spread the burden of recession by reducing hours worked rather than by laying off workers.

A comparison of second-quarter with first-quarter figures points to a coming recovery. West Germany, Japan, and the U.S. all showed smaller percentage declines in the second quarter and also experienced increases in the average number of hours worked.

Prices and Wages. The worldwide recession of 1974–75 is distinguished from other post-World War II recessions not only by its magnitude but by the extraordinarily high rates of inflation that persisted throughout 1974. Even in 1975, although declining, inflation in most countries was very high by postwar standards. (*See* Table VI.)

Of the countries listed in Table VI only West Germany was successful in keeping the annual rate of

Table V. Hours of Work in Manufacturing

Per week; seasonally adjusted

Country	1963	1973	1974	1975 first quarter	1975 second quarter	Percent change from a year earlier 1975 first quarter	Percent change from a year earlier 1975 second quarter
Major industrial countries							
Canada	40.8	39.6	38.9	38.6	38.4	−2.3	−1.5
France	46.3	43.6	42.9	42.0	41.7	−2.6	−3.2
Germany, West	44.1*	42.8	41.9	39.9	40.6	−4.5	−3.3
Italy (per day)	8.0	7.66	7.65	7.57†	...	...	...
Japan	45.5	42.0	40.0	39.4	40.0	−5.6	−4.3
U.K. (males)	46.8	44.7	44.0	—	—	...	...
U.S.	40.5	40.7	40.0	38.9	39.1	−3.7	−2.0
Other industrial countries							
Australia (males)	...	38.8	38.8	38.2	37.3	−2.8	−3.6
Belgium	42.3‡	37.6	36.6	—	—	—	—
Netherlands, The	46.6	43.0	—	—	—	—	—
Spain	44.8	44.2	43.8	44.3	—	—	—

*1965. †1974. ‡1966.
Sources: UN, *Statistical Yearbook* (1974); OECD, *Main Economic Indicators*.

inflation below 10%, and even there the rate doubled from the average of recent years. Other countries did far less well. The annual rate of inflation in the U.S. reached a peak in excess of 10% in late 1974, but in 1975 was driven back below the 10% level. In Italy and Japan inflation surged to double the U.S. level in 1974–75, but then proceeded to drop in both countries, with particular rapidity in Japan. In the U.K. inflation continued upward past the 25% per year level, stabilizing and turning down only in late 1975.

Economists still have only an imperfect understanding of the means by which inflation is generated, as can be seen by the continuing controversies over appropriate policy measures. There would be considerable agreement, however, that although the current inflation was caused in the first instance by other factors, the continuing high rate in some countries, notably the U.K., is largely a consequence of increased wages exerting strong cost pressures on industry.

In Table VI the annual rate of increase in hourly earnings in manufacturing is shown along with the rates of consumer price inflation. From these two sets of figures the annual rate of increase of manufacturing earnings in real terms—that is, the increase in the amount of goods and services that can be purchased by the increased earnings—has been obtained by deducting the price increase from the wage increase. The results appear as row C.

A number of qualifications must be made in regard to these figures. They assume implicitly that workers in manufacturing spend their earnings according to the pattern used in constructing the consumer price indexes. In fact, they could be affected by inflation to a greater or lesser extent than suggested by the consumer price indexes. For instance, food commonly makes up a higher proportion of a low-paid wage earner's budget than that of a highly paid professional worker. If food prices increase more rapidly than prices in general, then the low-paid person will in effect face a higher rate of inflation than the well-paid worker. Conversely, if food prices increase less rapidly, the effective rate of inflation for the low-paid person could be lower than that stated by the price index. Also, earnings increases in manufacturing are not necessarily representative of earnings increases going to other sections of the labour force. Finally, and a point that will be taken up again later, the earnings figures are before taxes. If measured in post-tax terms and given the progressive tax scales usually applying to normal wage and salary levels, the increases would be less.

Accepting all these qualifications, one can still find the real earnings data a useful aid to the interpretation of recent economic developments. They can be regarded as a measure of continuing upward pressure on costs, though offset at least in the long term by productivity gains. Alternatively, they show the extent to which the manufacturing worker is maintaining or improving his (pretax) income in real terms. In most countries he seems to have done reasonably well in protecting his income, the most notable exception being the U.S. In general, but with exceptions such as Canada and Italy, wage-cost pressures on prices appeared to be easing by mid-1975.

Taxation and Social Benefits. High rates of inflation had some unexpected results in the last few years. Not the least of these was that numbers of low-paid people who were formerly exempt found that their incomes were subject to taxation. Many other income earners found themselves moving into higher tax brackets, even when their pretax income had increased only in money terms and not in real terms.

Most countries did not make provision for this situation by automatic "indexation" of tax allowances and tax brackets. Eventually, adjustments were expected to be made but only after an appreciable time lag. To quite a number of economic policymakers, the "fiscal drag" caused by fixed tax rates applied to rapidly rising money increases is a welcome and politically painless means of deflating the economy and so aiding the struggle to contain inflation.

Some countries did, however, use automatic or semiautomatic methods for adjusting tax allowances and tax rates to allow for the effects of inflation. As might be expected, traditionally inflation-prone economies such as Chile, Brazil, and Iceland provide for the automatic adjustment of income taxes. But even some more stable economies have similar arrangements. For instance, The Netherlands and Canada have provisions for automatic adjustment and France has a partially automatic system. The system in The Netherlands consists of taking the basic tax table, which contains tax brackets, dependency allowances, and other deductions, and multiplying this each year by a factor representing consumer price increases. The effects of indirect taxes and subsidies on the prices of goods are excluded from the correction factor, however, and also the minister of finance has some discretion in adjusting the correction factor downward by 20% should he think it necessary. The Canadian system dates from 1974 and resembles that of The Netherlands, although no prior adjustment is made for sales tax changes. In France the personal income tax schedule must be changed whenever the annual rate of inflation exceeds 5%.

A large number of countries make provision for automatic adjustment of pensions and other welfare benefits to allow for inflation. This can be seen from Table VII, and even in those countries such as the

Table VI. Percentage Changes in Earnings, Prices, and Real Earnings

A=Hourly earnings in manufacturing
B=Consumer prices
C=Real hourly earnings in manufacturing

Country		Average 1962–72	1972–73	1973–74	1974–75 first quarter	1974–75 second quarter	Latest month 1975 from previous year
Major industrial countries							
Canada	A	6.1	8.9	13.4	17.6	18.4	18.9 June
	B	3.3	7.6	10.9	11.7	10.5	11.0 July
	C	2.7	1.2	2.3	5.3	7.1	
France	A	9.0	12.4	18.6	20.9	18.5	18.5 April
	B	4.4	7.3	13.7	14.0	12.1	11.1 July
	C	4.4	4.8	4.3	6.1	5.7	
Germany, West	A	7.5	10.7	10.6	10.8	7.9	7.9 April
	B	3.2	6.9	7.0	5.9	6.2	6.2 July
	C	4.2	3.6	3.4	4.6	1.6	
Italy	A	10.1	24.3	22.4	28.4	29.6	25.9 August
	B	4.3	10.4	19.4	23.4	20.2	15.3 August
	C	5.6	12.6	2.5	4.1	7.8	
Japan	A	13.4	22.5	26.3	32.2	7.3	0.8 June
(monthly earnings)	B	5.7	11.7	24.5	14.7	13.6	11.4 July
	C	7.3	9.7	1.4	15.3	−5.5	
U.K.	A	8.2	12.9	17.2	26.4	34.1	26.5 August
	B	4.9	8.2	16.0	20.7	24.4	26.4 September
	C	3.1	3.2	0.9	4.7	8.0	
U.S.	A	4.3	6.8	8.4	10.7	9.3	8.4 July
	B	3.3	6.2	11.0	11.0	9.6	9.7 July
	C	1.0	0.6	−2.3	−0.3	−0.3	−1.2
Other industrial countries							
Australia	A*	—	12.9	27.2	34.5	—	25.4 April
	B	3.4	9.5	15.1	17.6	16.9	16.9 May
	C	—	3.1	10.5	14.4	—	
Belgium	A	9.2	15.9	21.2	24.1	19.6	19.6 June
	B	3.8	7.0	12.7	10.6	13.5	12.0 July
	C	5.2	8.3	7.5	12.2	5.4	
Sweden	A	9.2	8.4	11.1	14.0	8.0	9.1 June
	B	4.7	6.7	13.8	10.0	9.1	9.1 May
	C	4.3	1.6	−2.2	3.6	−1.0	

*Males.
Sources: OECD, *Economic Outlook*, July 1975; OECD, *Main Economic Indicators*.

U.K. which do not apply an automatic formula, the annual increase will normally cover any cost of living increase. One result of the recent acceleration in inflation is that periodic reviews have tended to become more frequent.

Similar provisions usually exist for other welfare benefits, but total government expenditures on these, including expenditure on unemployment benefits, is usually considerably less than expenditure on old-age pensions. The number of elderly people as a proportion of the population has increased considerably in recent years, as shown in Table VII, and will continue to increase for most countries until about 1980. A slight decline will then occur for most countries between 1980 and 1985.

Table VII. Number of Persons Aged 65 and Over as a Percent of Total Population and Methods of Adjustment of Old-Age Pensions

Country	1951	1965	1975	1985	Methods of adjustment of old-age pensions (as of 1973)
Belgium	11.1	12.5	14.2	13.4	An annual increment larger than the increase in the price index.
Canada	—	7.6	8.0	—	Based on increases in the price index. From 1976, will increase with changes in national average wages.
France	11.4	12.0	13.3	11.7	Semiannual adjustment (January and July); related to increase in salaries.
Germany, West	9.3	11.9	14.2	12.6	Adjusted annually, taking account of progress in economic efficiency and productivity, and changes in the national income per employed person.
Italy	8.1	9.7	11.7	12.0	Annual adjustment (by decree), when cost of living rises 2% or more.
Japan	—	6.3	7.9	9.5	
Netherlands, The	7.8	9.5	10.6	10.8	Pensions adjusted by decree, when wage index changes by more than 3%.
Sweden	10.2	12.6	14.7	15.9	Automatic adjustment based on changes in price level.
U.K.	10.9	12.0	13.5	13.5	Special legislation, once a year.
U.S.	—	9.3	9.8	10.2	Automatic cost of living adjustment.

Sources: "Old Age Pensions' Level, Adjustment and Coverage," in *The OECD Observer*, No. 77, September–October 1975; OECD, *Demographic Trends in Western Europe and the United States;* OECD, *Demographic Trends 1970–1985 in OECD Member Countries.*

Table VIII. Trends in Housing Conditions in Selected Countries

Country		Average number of persons per household	Percent of owner-occupants	Percent of dwellings with Piped water	Flush toilet	Electric lighting	Dwellings constructed*
Australia	1966	3.5	70.8	—	—	98.3	9.7
	1971	3.3	67.3	—	89.5	98.4	11.1
Belgium	1961	3.0	49.7	76.9	47.6	99.6	4.3
	1970	—	55.9	86.6	...	...	4.8
Canada	1967	3.7	65.4	95.2	92.5	—	7.4
	1971	—	60.0	96.1	94.3	—	9.4
France	1962	3.1	42.7	78.3	37.2	97.6	7.0
	1968	3.1	43.3	90.8	51.8	98.8	8.4
Germany, West	1968	2.9	34.3	99.7	87.4	99.9	8.6
	1972	2.7	33.5	99.2	94.2	99.7	10.7
Italy	1961	3.6	45.8	62.3	—	95.9	8.2
	1971	3.3	50.9	86.1	—	99.0	6.7
Japan	1968	3.9	59.5	94.9	17.1	—	12.7
	1970	3.7	58.2	...	...	...	15.1
Spain	1960	4.0	...	45.0	—	89.3	10.0
Sweden	1965	2.7	35.5	94.3	85.3	—	12.5
	1970	2.6	35.2	97.3	90.1	—	13.6
U.K. (England and Wales)	1966	2.9	47.8	—	97.9	...	7.4
	1971	2.9	50.1	—	98.9	...	—
U.S.	1960	3.3	61.9	92.9	89.7	—	8.7
	1970	3.2	62.9	97.5	96.0	—	7.2

*Per 1,000 population.
Source: UN, *Statistical Yearbook* (1974), Table 204.

Table IX. Housing Starts in Selected Countries

(Average 1970=100)

Country	Total 1970 (000)	1972	1973	1974	1975 first quarter	1975 second quarter	Percent change from a year earlier 1975 first quarter	second quarter
Australia	138.8	105	120	94	82	96	−26.8	−8.6
Belgium	42.7	119	137	152	...	...	...	...
Canada	190.5	131	141	117	50	123	−45.1	−18.5
France	481.7	115	115	114	108	115	−1.8	−7.3
Italy	74.7	100	102	72	—	—	—	—
Japan	1,484.6	122	128	89	71	90	−17.4	+9.8
Netherlands, The	127.3	123	111	88	84	95	−6.7	−3.1
Sweden	106.7	92	75	75	31	40	−39.2	−42.0
U.K.	331.1	109	102	78	79	108	+6.8	+16.9
U.S.	1,469.0	162	140	92	53	89	−39.8	−29.6

Source: OECD, *Main Economic Indicators.*

Table X. New Consumer Credit in the U.S. and U.K.

	1971	1972	1973	1974	1975 first quarter	1975 second quarter
U.S. ($000,000,000)						
Total new credits	10.4	11.9	13.8	13.9	11.7	14.0
New credits, automobile	2.9	3.4	3.9	3.6	3.2	3.9
U.K. (£000,000)*						
New credits, retail shops	89	106	118	123	144	152
New credits, finance houses	83	102	121	86	97	100

*Seasonally adjusted.
Source: OECD, *Main Economic Indicators.*

Housing, Interest Rates and Consumer Credit, and Ownership of Assets. Tables VIII and IX examine housing in the industrial countries. The first covers improvements in housing conditions that have taken place over the long term, while the second table shows recent fluctuations in building activity.

A number of measures of housing conditions appear in Table VIII, but care is needed in their interpretation. For example, fewer persons per household may be a result of the greater freedom for persons to set up their own home, and this follows from increased national prosperity. But it may also simply reflect demographic trends toward delaying the start of a family and having smaller families. Again, a high proportion of home ownership is normally thought of as a natural consequence of national prosperity, but the given figures do not all support that hypothesis. The comparatively low proportions in such rich countries as Sweden and West Germany show how housing preferences can differ markedly from country to country. Owner-occupancy is strongly influenced also by the urban/rural distribution of a country's population, being much higher among rural populations.

Other measures of progress in housing conditions, such as the percentage of dwellings having piped water, a flush toilet, and electric lighting, are less ambiguous. Again the urban/rural composition of a country's population strongly affects these figures, but in all cases where comparable data are available there is definite evidence of progress in recent years. The final column in Table VIII gives some impression of the resources that each country devotes to constructing new houses.

Table IX reveals how seriously the recession hit housing construction. In few countries were housing starts in 1974 in excess of the number in 1970, while starts in the first half of 1975 were usually sharply down from the levels of early 1974. One of the sharpest declines occurred in the U.S. although, as with other statistical indicators, there was evidence for some recovery in the second quarter of 1975.

An important factor in housing construction is the availability of financing at reasonable rates. Interest rates rose to unprecedentedly high levels in 1973 and 1974, although by late 1975 short-term rates were declining in most countries. The high rates undoubtedly had a dampening influence on house buying and construction, as well as on the purchasing of other durables, including automobiles. Table X shows the decline in new consumer credit for automobile purchases in the U.S. and the U.K. (a substantial proportion of the new credits extended by finance houses in the U.K. is for automobile purchase). The total new credits seem, however, to have been less affected by the recession, although much of the increase was simply a result of inflation.

NATIONAL ECONOMIC POLICIES

Nations throughout the world faced the problems of inflation and recession during 1975. Their responses, in terms of monetary and fiscal policies, varied according to their particular situation and economic system, but all to a greater or lesser extent had to cope with those two overriding concerns.

Developed Market Economies. During 1974 the two major problems that had faced the industrially developed non-Communist world were an unprecedented rise in prices and a serious deterioration in the external payments position, both legacies of the quadrupling of oil prices at the end of the previous year. Most governments, therefore, were forced to adopt monetary and fiscal policies aimed at curbing inflation, and by early 1975 the external payments position had improved somewhat in most Western industrialized countries. These anti-inflationary policies, however, depressed the level of business activity.

By the end of 1974 it was clear that, in the absence of a change in policies, the recession would continue well into 1975. With the prospect of a further rise in the already high level of unemployment, recession gradually replaced inflation as the chief enemy, and most governments responded by relaxing restrictive monetary and fiscal policies. As discussed in subsequent sections, interest rates experienced a downward trend and credit restrictions were eased during the year. Several nations, including the U.S., France, and Japan, took action to provide direct stimulus to domestic demand.

In their anxiety not to endanger the modest victories against inflation, however, economic policymakers erred on the side of caution and underestimated the potential strength of the recession. In consequence, the relaxation of the restrictive fiscal and monetary policies was timid and hesitant. On the whole, governments responded to rather than anticipated the growing weakness of the economy, and it was not until the final quarter of 1975 that a full-fledged policy of reflation was adopted by the majority of the larger industrialized countries. France, for example, waited until September 1975 before announcing a really significant boost for the economy;

Table XI. Real Gross National Products of OECD Countries

(% change, seasonally adjusted annual rates)

Country	Average 1960–73	From previous year 1974*	1975*	From previous half year 1975 first half	second half*
Canada	5.2	2.8	−0.3	−2.8	5.5
France	5.8	3.9	1.0	0.0	1.5
Germany, West	4.9	0.4	−2.0	−4.5	3.0
Italy	5.5	3.4	−2.8	−1.5	−1.5
Japan	10.9	−1.8	1.5	−1.0	5.0
U.K.	3.3	−0.2	−2.0	−2.5	−1.8
U.S.	4.2	−2.1	−3.8	−8.0	5.0
Total major countries	5.5	−0.6	−1.8	−4.8	3.5
Australia	4.9	1.5	2.0	...	...
Austria	5.2	4.4	0.8	...	...
Belgium	4.9	4.3	−0.3	...	...
Denmark	4.7	1.8	0.0	...	...
Finland	5.4	3.7	0.5	...	...
Ireland	4.1	1.0	−1.5	...	...
Netherlands, The	5.1	2.0	−0.5	...	...
New Zealand	3.6	5.0	1.0	...	...
Norway	4.9	3.7	4.5	...	...
Spain	7.3	5.0	1.5	...	...
Sweden	4.1	4.1	1.0	...	...
Switzerland	4.6	−0.8	−3.3	...	...
Total OECD	5.4	−0.1	−1.5	−4.0	3.5

*Estimate.
Source: Adapted from OECD, *Economic Outlook*, July 1975.

Table XII. Economically Active Population

Latest census or estimate

Country	% of economically active population in Agriculture*	Industry†	Services‡
AFRICA			
Afars and Issas	50	—	50
Algeria	50.1	11.7	38.2
Angola	63	...	37§
Botswana	22.5	20.2	57.3
Burundi	95	1	4
Cameroon	80	10	10
Cape Verde Islands	40.1	1.2	58.7
Central African Rep.	87	...	13§
Chad	96	4	—
Comoro Islands	63.9	17.6	18.5
Congo	40	...	60§
Dahomey (Benin)	90	...	10§
Egypt	53.2	13.1	33.7
Equatorial Guinea	95	—	5
Ethiopia	85	...	15§
Gabon	84.1	7.0	8.9
Gambia, The	85	...	15§
Ghana	58.0	11.9	30.1
Guinea	83	...	17§
Guinea-Bissau	86	...	14§
Ivory Coast	86.4	1.9	11.7
Kenya	86.5	3.6	9.9
Lesotho	91	1	8
Liberia	80.9	8.5	10.6
Libya	32.5	24.3	43.2
Malagasy Republic	80	2	18
Malawi	87	...	13§
Mali	91	...	9§
Mauritania	85	...	15§
Mauritius	35.0	23.6	41.4
Morocco	50.6	15.3	34.1
Mozambique	72	...	28§
Niger	91	...	9§
Nigeria	55.9	12.1	32.0
Réunion	29.5	7.3	63.2
Rhodesia	63	...	27§
Rwanda	91	...	9§
São Tomé & Príncipe	...	...	...
Senegal	72.7	7.0	20.3
Seychelles	28.4	29.7	41.9
Sierra Leone	75.2	9.8	15.0
Somalia	82	...	18§
South Africa	28.0	21.3	50.7
South West Africa	58.5	10.2	31.3
Sudan	80	...	20§
Swaziland	19.4	6.9	73.7
Tanzania	91.0	1.7	7.3
Togo	75	...	25§
Tunisia	41.0	9.5	49.5
Uganda	86	...	14§
Upper Volta	89	...	11§
Zaire	78	...	22§
Zambia	43.7	20.0	36.3
ASIA			
Afghanistan	77.0	8.2	14.8
Bahrain	6.6	14.0	79.4
Bangladesh	70.5	...	29.5§
Brunei	11.9	22.1	66.0
Burma	68	...	32§
Cambodia	80.3	2.8	16.9
China	66.5	...	33.5§
Cyprus	33.6	25.2	57.8
Hong Kong	2.1	44.5	53.4
India	68.6	...	31.4§
Indonesia	61.8	7.5	30.7
Iran	54.6	21.4	24.0
Iraq	55.3	6.9	37.8
Israel	7.5	24.8	67.7
Japan	19.4	16.9	63.7
Jordan	35.3	10.8	53.9
Korea, North	53.2	...	46.8§
Korea, South	50.8	15.2	34.0
Kuwait	1.7	16.8	81.5
Laos	78	...	22§
Lebanon	50	10	40
Macau	0.4	0.4	99.2
Malaysia‖	47.3	12.8	39.9
Maldives	...	...	...
Mongolia	45.4	22.3	32.3
Nepal	96.8	1.1	2.1
Oman	82.7	4.0	13.3
Pakistan	56.2	13.0	30.8
Philippines	51.5	15.6	32.9
Portuguese Timor	65.6	...	34.4§
Qatar	...	...	...
Saudi Arabia	60	...	40§
Singapore	3.5	28.9	67.6
Sri Lanka	50.4	10.0	39.6
Syria	47.9	12.7	39.4
Taiwan	36.6	19.3	44.1
Thailand	82.1	4.4	13.5
Turkey	67.0	11.9	21.1
United Arab Emirates	...	...	...
Vietnam, North	77.6	...	22.4§
Vietnam, South	65	...	35§
Yemen (Aden)	62	...	38§
Yemen (San'a')	73.3	...	26.7§
EUROPE			
Albania	62	...	38§
Andorra	8.3	28.6	63.1
Austria	13.8	40.7	45.5
Belgium	4.5	34.3	61.2
Bulgaria	44.3	26.4	29.3
Czechoslovakia	16.4	48.0	35.6
Denmark	9.5	32.7	57.8
Faeroe Islands	26.2	30.7	43.1
Finland	20.3	34.3	45.4
France	6.3	15.9	77.8
Germany, East	12.6	48.8	38.6
Germany, West	7.5	48.9	56.4
Gibraltar	—	21.8	78.2
Greece	40.5	24.8	34.7
Hungary	24.5	43.2	31.4
Iceland	16.8	36.8	46.4
Ireland	24.4	27.5	48.1
Isle of Man	9.1	31.1	59.8
Italy	16.7	42.0	41.3
Liechtenstein	6.2	56.6	37.2
Luxembourg	7.5	42.7	49.8
Malta	7.5	24.3	68.2
Monaco	0.1	21.5	78.4
Netherlands, The	10.7	31.3	58.0
Norway	11.9	35.0	53.1
Poland	38.6	34.4	27.0
Portugal	31.4	31.5	37.1
Romania	56.8	19.4	23.8
San Marino	8.5	54.1	37.4
Spain	24.8	36.6	38.6
Sweden	8.1	40.3	51.6
Switzerland	7.6	48.3	44.1
United Kingdom	1.7	45.3	53.0
Yugoslavia	43.9	17.7	38.4
NORTH AMERICA			
Antigua	10.6	20.0	69.4
Bahamas, The	6.9	17.7	75.4
Barbados	21.3	13.8	64.9
Belize	33.9	12.8	53.3
Bermuda	1.6	19.4	79.0
British Virgin Islands	7.8	9.9	82.3
Canada	6.2	28.3	65.5
Cayman Islands	10.9	27.6	61.5
Costa Rica	37.5	22.5	40.0
Cuba	30.0	20.3	49.7
Dominica	39.4	7.9	52.7
Dominican Republic	44.3	10.5	45.2
El Salvador	46.6	10.4	43.0
Greenland	18.6	28.2	53.2
Grenada	71.6	17.5	10.9
Guadeloupe	32.4	25.7	41.9
Guatemala	57.0	13.9	29.1
Haiti	77	...	23§
Honduras	85.2	11.8	3.0
Jamaica	32.8	19.4	47.8
Martinique	28.1	20.4	51.5
Mexico	39.4	22.5	38.1
Montserrat	20.4	5.8	73.8
Netherlands Antilles	0.9	32.9	66.2
Nicaragua	46.4	16.3	37.3
Panama	38.4	13.8	47.8
Puerto Rico	7.3	16.9	75.8
St. Lucia	10.5	5.3	84.2
St. Pierre & Miquelon	11.3	17.5	71.2
Trinidad and Tobago	15.4	18.7	65.9
United States	3.7	32.7	63.6
Virgin Islands (U.S.)	1.2	25.5	73.3
OCEANIA			
American Samoa	2.0	32.9	65.1
Australia	7.4	32.5	60.1
Christmas Island	—	80.3	19.7
Cook Islands	21.9	24.0	54.1
Fiji	55.2	7.0	37.8
French Polynesia	37.1	22.3	40.6
Gilbert Islands¶	65.5	3.8	30.7
Guam	0.7	22.8	76.5
Nauru	0.1	31.4	68.5
New Caledonia	34.1	18.3	47.6
New Hebrides	82.5	2.5	15.0
New Zealand	11.5	34.0	54.5
Niue	11.4	—	88.6
Norfolk Island	6.1	15.9	78.0
Papua New Guinea	56.4	4.5	39.1
Solomon Islands	23.2	12.5	64.3
Tonga	34.0	1.5	64.5
Wallis and Futuna Is.	93.0	—	7.0
Western Samoa	67.3	—	32.7
SOUTH AMERICA			
Argentina	14.8	20.6	64.6
Bolivia	48	16	36
Brazil	44.3	19.2	36.5
Chile	21.4	17.8	60.8
Colombia	38.6	20.1	41.3
Ecuador	55.1	17.8	27.1
Falkland Islands	48.9	—	51.1
French Guiana	18.4	28.5	53.1
Guyana	29.6	23.1	47.3
Paraguay	49.5	18.6	31.9
Peru	45.1	16.9	38.0
Surinam	34.9	14.9	50.2
Uruguay	18.1	27.3	54.6
Venezuela	20.3	14.6	65.1
U.S.S.R.	26.3	45.1	28.6

*Includes forestry and fishing.
†Includes mining and construction.
‡Includes all other economic activities, including government employment.
§Includes all nonagricultural activities.
‖West Malaysia only.
¶Includes Tuvalu (Ellice) Islands.

Japan tinkered with reflation for about nine months before taking resolute action; and in the U.S., though fiscal policy had a strong expansionary flavour from early in 1975, the monetary strategy of the Federal Reserve Board was characterized by a high degree of caution. In sharp contrast to other countries, Great Britain entered 1975 on a note of accelerating wage and price inflation, as a result of which the authorities pursued a solidly deflationary policy throughout the year. Despite some monetary relaxation the basic character of Italian policies was also restrictive, at least until the third quarter of the year.

Because of the relaxation of fiscal policies, large budget deficits emerged during the year throughout the developed non-Communist world. By the end of 1975, it was clear that these would exceed the original estimates by a substantial margin. In the U.S., for example, the last forecast pointed to a deficit of $90 billion (accounting for some 6% of GNP) as against a plan of about $50 billion; in Japan the deficit was expected to be $33 billion, or some 8% of GNP. In the U.K. the public sector borrowing requirement was expected to reach about $25 billion in the 1975–76 fiscal year as against a plan of $19 billion. In Britain's case, this was not due to a conscious policy of reflation but to the inability of the government to control the public sector wage bill and local authority spending.

Because of the general reluctance to dismantle the restrictions on growth imposed in 1974 there was a continuing slowdown in inflation. As Chart 1 indicates, in six out of the seven principal OECD countries consumer prices rose more slowly in 1975 than in the previous year. At the same time, however, the growth of the economy fell below expectations almost everywhere, and the recovery, widely forecast for early 1975, did not get under way until the second half of the year. Thus, between the final quarter of 1974 and the first quarter of 1975, industrial production fell in virtually every OECD country. The average for the area showed a drop of more than 5% during this period, as a result of which output was about 10% below the level of the corresponding period of 1974. In the second quarter, industrial output continued to decline though at a slower rate, with the fall leveling off in the third and turning into a modest, but nevertheless potentially significant, increase in the last few months of the year.

The steep downward trend in the level of industrial output was a reflection of the weakness of aggregate demand. The weakest component of this appears to have been fixed investment. With the emergence of a very large margin of spare production capacity in most countries, there was little incentive to invest in new plant and equipment. Moreover, the liquidity of business was adversely affected by a fall in profits that resulted from a reduction of output and a rise in unit costs, a problem that was only marginally eased by the cautious monetary relaxation initiated at the start of the year.

With the benefit of the third quarter's statistics for most of the countries, it was estimated that fixed investment in the OECD area during the entire year fell by approximately 9%, compared with a decline of 5% in 1974. As the year drew to a close, there were few concrete indications of an early and decisive recovery, but in view of the modest improvement in confidence, the easier monetary conditions, and the large public works programs announced by several countries, an increase was expected in 1976.

Inventory movements also exerted a negative influence on the level of business activity. Normally, industry needs time to adjust production in response to a fall in demand, and if the fall is very sudden and deep—as it was in the second half of 1974—the result is a large, involuntary increase in stocks. The year 1975, therefore, opened with very high levels of inventories, particularly of finished products. This meant that business, already suffering from a fall in profits, found itself with very large sums of money tied up in surplus goods. The result was a determined drive to reduce inventories virtually everywhere, and it was this that played the largest role in the drastic decline in industrial output referred to earlier. As a result, the stock adjustment process was largely complete by the autumn of 1975, and it was partly for this reason that industrial output showed some signs of recovery toward the end of the year.

The largest single component of GDP, accounting for about 60% of the total, is private consumption. Although this was adversely affected by inflation, a slowdown in wage increases, and high unemployment, in comparison with other constituent parts of aggregate demand it remained relatively strong throughout 1975. During the first half of the year, for example, the volume of private consumption increased in most of the large OECD countries with the notable exceptions of the U.S. (where it fell by about 2%) and Italy. Similarly, the evidence available in December

CHART 1.

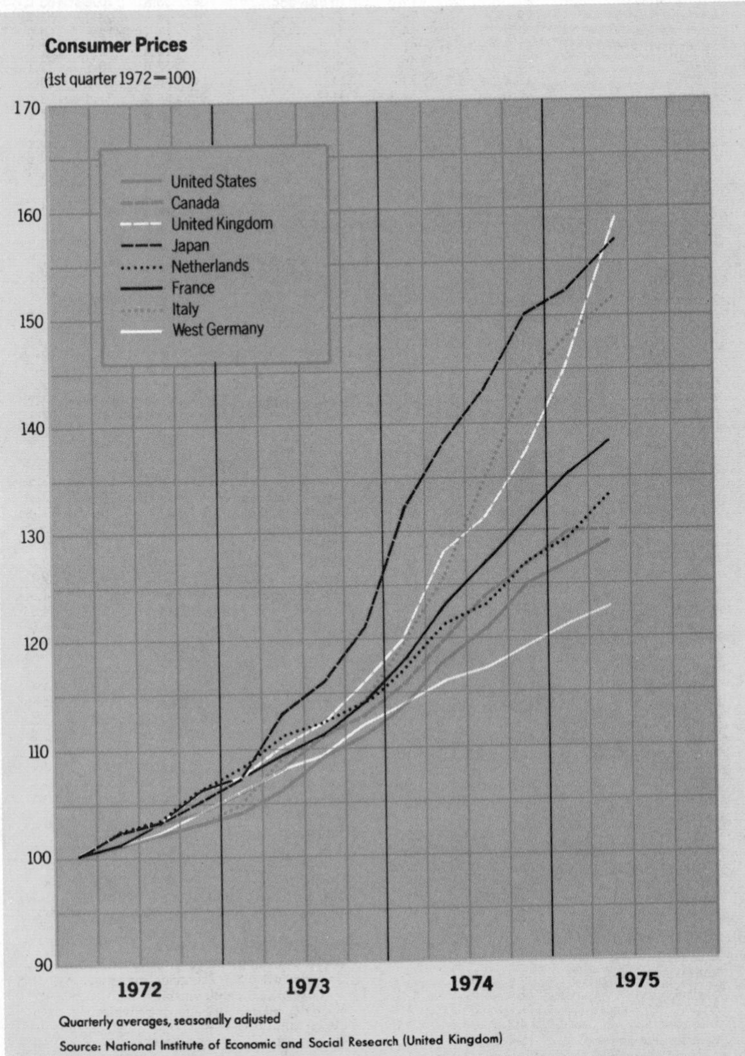

Quarterly averages, seasonally adjusted
Source: National Institute of Economic and Social Research (United Kingdom)

1975 indicated that in the second half of the year there was some increase in all of the large countries except the U.K., where the incomes policy introduced in August depressed disposable incomes in the subsequent four months.

For the year as a whole expenditure on consumer durables was weaker than on other goods and services. This was the consequence of the sluggish trend of residential construction, which had an adverse effect on the demand for furniture; the weakness of the demand for automobiles resulting from changing travel habits brought about by the rise in oil prices; and the reluctance to enter into long-term installment purchase commitments at a time of rising unemployment and general economic uncertainty.

An interesting development that had a significant effect on the level of consumers' expenditure was the increase in savings. According to previous experience, the relative importance of savings tends to decline in times of rapid inflation because consumers lose their confidence in money and turn to goods. Despite unprecedented rates of inflation, however, most countries experienced a rapid rise in the amounts saved. Although in part this may have been the result of widespread unemployment and anxiety about the future, the magnitude of the increase surprised most observers. In the U.K., for example, the savings ratio (savings as a proportion of disposable incomes) rose from 12.9% in 1974 to 14% in the first half of 1975. In other countries a large part of the additional funds pumped into the private sector did not boost consumption but instead increased savings, with the result that savings ratios reached very high levels. At the end of 1975 it was not yet clear if this was a temporary phenomenon or a basic structural change. Most forecasts at the end of 1975 were based on the expectation that the normal pattern would reassert itself during 1976; if this did not happen, the recovery might not be as strong as anticipated.

Through 1973 the volume of OECD exports had been increasing each year for more than 15 years. In 1974 and 1975, however, the quadrupling of oil prices forced member countries to cut back their imports for balance of payments reasons; but because a large part of OECD exports go to OECD countries this introduced a source of weakness in trade within the area. At first, the effect was cushioned by strong demand from other, especially oil-producing, countries, but by the first half of 1975 the volume of foreign shipments was pointing in a downward direction. During the third quarter the fall leveled off, and by late 1975 there were some indications of a modest increase. This, however, could not make up for more than a fraction of the earlier decline, and it was generally assumed that exports of goods and services, adjusted for the effects of inflation, fell by about 6% during 1975. Imports, on the other hand, probably decreased by 8–9% (the difference being accounted for by a cut in purchases from outside countries) so that the net effect of foreign trade on the level of GDP was positive in most OECD countries.

The effect of the developments discussed in this section was to delay the recovery in the world economy by about six to nine months and to create the longest recession since World War II. Although there were marked variations in the performance of the individual countries, the figures suggest that the volume of GDP for the OECD area as a whole fell for about 18 months until the middle of 1975, by which time it was about 4% below its level at the beginning of 1974. Virtually every country in this group experienced a spectacular weakening in economic activity, with the U.S. recording a decline of some 6% and West Germany 5%. The result was an unprecedented increase in the number of jobless. By September unemployment levels approached or exceeded previous peaks in virtually all developed non-Communist countries, and the total number of unemployed reached 17 million, or 5.2% of the labour force, compared with about 9 million at the beginning of 1974. Furthermore, despite some signs of a recovery, by December the overall unemployment figure was thought to be in the region of 18 million. The volume of GDP for the entire year was estimated to have fallen by about 1.5–2% for the OECD area. With most governments pursuing strongly stimulative policies by late 1975, however, the outlook for 1976 was judged to be much better; at the end of 1975, most forecasters anticipated a gain in real GDP of 4–5%.

United States. In line with Pres. Richard Nixon's "policy of fiscal responsibility," Pres. Gerald Ford began his term in 1974 with the intention of cutting back government expenditure and the budget deficit. However, the sudden weakening of the economy in the final quarter of 1974 overtook the administration's proposals. Real GNP, measured in constant 1958 prices, slumped at an annual rate of 9%, com-

CHART 2.

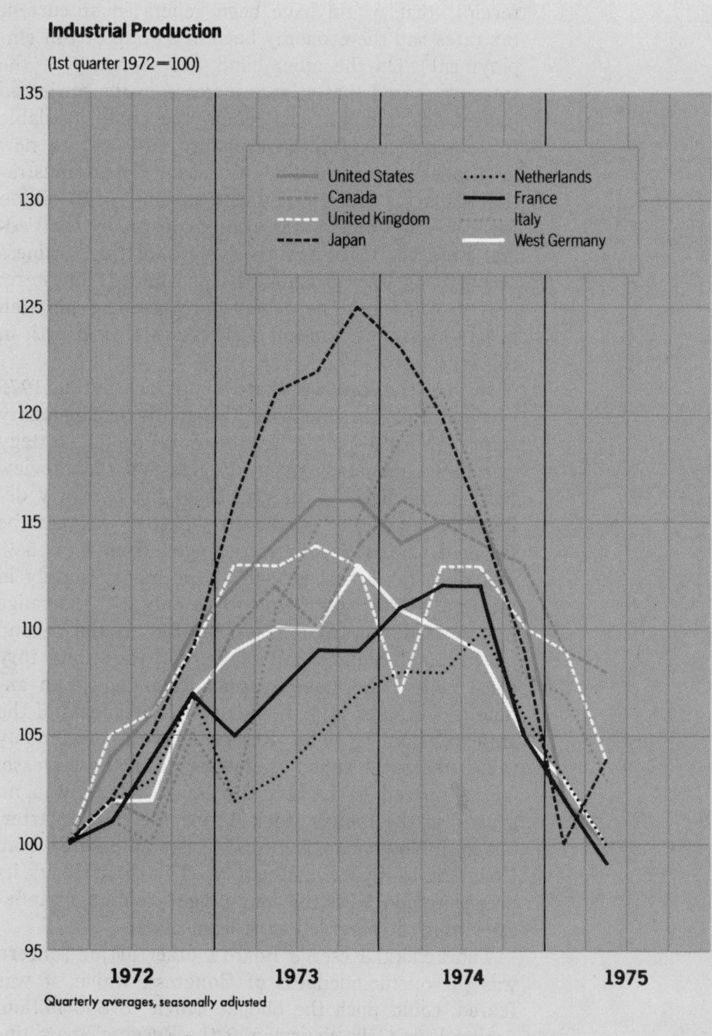

pared with 1.6 and 1.9% declines recorded in the previous two quarters. In the face of this, the administration cautiously reversed its restrictive policy. The budget proposals sent to Congress in January included tax rebates (effective from March) to prop up the sinking economy at the cost of an estimated deficit of $52 billion. Even before the new economic conditions forced a change in the direction of fiscal policy, a relaxation in monetary strategy was under way. This was evidenced by a sharp decline in short-term interest rates after September 1974, the result of the Federal Reserve Board's policy of easing the liquidity shortage.

By early 1975 there was broad agreement between the administration, the Federal Reserve Board, and Congress on the state of the economy and the kinds of policies necessary to deal with the recession. Nevertheless, the three differed on the adequacy of the measures already taken or proposed. Congress, for instance, was more concerned with the growing unemployment and favoured a level of expenditure that would bring about a quicker and stronger recovery than that officially aimed at. Some members of Congress also claimed that the 1974–75 budget had not been pulling its weight in the attempt to end the slump in the U.S. and the rest of the world. They pointed to the fact that even though it had shown an apparent deficit of $44 billion, it remained in "full employment surplus" in the amount of $6.3 billion (that is, expenditure was $6.3 billion less than the receipts that would have been generated at current tax rates had the economy been in a state of full employment). On the other hand, the secretary of the treasury feared that a large increase in the projected budget deficit might well reduce the credit available for other sectors of the economy and lead to new inflationary pressures. For this reason the administration planned a "full employment surplus" of $7 billion for 1975–76. Caution was also advocated by the Federal Reserve Board against overstimulating business activity, on the grounds that sustained long-term growth could best be achieved by keeping inflation at bay even if this meant a slower rate of growth in the short run.

In fact, the Reserve Board's approach during 1975 was not fully in line with the gently expansionary stance of fiscal policy. In broad terms its strategy was to set monetary policy targets and then review them in the light of the growth of the narrowly defined money supply. In the early part of the year the targeted annual growth rate ranged from 4 to 6%, and when the actual growth of the money supply in the first quarter was found to be only 2% the range was revised upward to 5–7.5%. But in the second quarter, mainly under the influence of the stimulatory fiscal policy, the money supply expanded at an annual rate of over 11%, reviving the worst fears of the antiexpansionists. The Reserve Board reacted by taking measures aimed at slowing down the increase. These proved to be too successful. There was no growth in the money stock during the third quarter, but until November the board resisted pressures from Congress to improve liquidity. This underlined its preoccupation with the long-range problem of inflation, which it regarded as still unsolved.

The Federal Reserve Board's other major concern was the openhandedness of Congress, which, it was feared, could push the budget deficit to $90 billion. Arthur Burns, the chairman of the Reserve Board, indicated that he was opposed to the continuation of the 1975 tax cuts into 1976 and would support the president's proposed $28 billion tax reductions only if matched by an equal cut in government spending. Late in December President Ford agreed to extend the tax cuts into 1976 after he obtained a promise from Congress to control spending during the next fiscal year.

The uneven and often unpredictable course of business during 1975 did little to help resolve the disagreements faced by U.S. economic policymakers. In spite of the promised tax rebates, the slowdown in the economy gained momentum in early 1975. Unemployment continued to climb toward the 8 million mark, and personal incomes dropped sharply. Industrial output plunged for seven consecutive months (until April), causing many investment proposals to be shelved. As a result many economists came to believe that a recovery before summer was not possible. But, as it happened, the recession bottomed out in the second quarter, and in the subsequent three months real GNP shot up by over 13% at an annual rate. Industrial production began to rise, and unemployment, which reached a peak of 8.5 million in May, fell sharply. Even though savings remained high (almost all the March tax rebates went into savings), consumers' expenditure picked up encouragingly.

Nevertheless, as 1975 drew to a close, doubts remained as to the strength of the recovery. Would it be strong enough to carry through into 1976 and in so doing set the world economy into motion, or could it run out of steam or be nipped in the bud by a restrictive monetary policy and high interest rates? These doubts arose from the fact that most of the recovery in the third quarter was due to the end of using up inventories rather than an increase in final sales. The underlying strength of consumer spending was also suspect, with sales of durable goods remaining relatively sluggish. Companies were reported to be too preoccupied with the short term and with ensuring their own survival to worry much about investment. At the same time a new bout of inflation began. In spite of the continuing slowdown in wage increases, inflationary pressures began building up after midsummer. Having slowed down to an annual rate of 5% in the second quarter of the year, the rise in prices climbed to 8.5% in the subsequent three months.

If the threat to the pace of the recovery became more severe, President Ford could be counted on to yield without too much struggle to the expansionary pressures emanating from Congress. Because 1976 was a presidential election year, and in view of the estimated 3.8% fall in real GNP during 1975, the president clearly wished to ensure that the recovery stayed on target in spite of any misgivings by the Reserve Board or the Treasury.

Japan. Partly as a result of the explosion in oil prices at the close of 1973, Japan, like most other developed countries, entered 1974 facing a runaway inflation and a deterioration in its external payments position. Unlike some other governments, however, the Tokyo authorities wasted no time in introducing corrective measures, consisting mainly of a reinforcement of the restrictive monetary policy that was instituted in the second half of 1973. In consequence, real national income fell in 1974 for the first time since World War II, but by early 1975 inflation was beginning to slow down and the large trade deficit of the first half of 1974 was turned into a respectable surplus.

By the start of 1975, therefore, Japan had successfully dealt with much of its inflation, and the way was clear for stimulating demand and economic growth. The adoption of a full-fledged expansionary policy was delayed, however, by the ultracautious attitude adopted by the government. This attitude was the result of the appointment of the economically conservative Takeo Miki as prime minister in December 1974, the desire to weaken the labour unions' hand in the nationwide spring wage negotiations, and a failure to grasp the strength of the recessionary forces in the economy. Thus, although the authorities announced increases in public expenditure and some financial help for selected enterprises in February 1975, the central bank's discount rate (which has a strong influence on the level of interest rates) was not reduced until April. Even then, the reduction was only 0.5% (to 8.5%) and was not accompanied by any meaningful relaxation in the restrictions imposed on loans extended by the major banks.

With the publication of the first quarter's national income statistics in late spring, it became clear that the recession was more stubborn than anticipated and that national income, adjusted for the effects of inflation, was still firmly on a downward trend. The government responded with a cut in the discount rate in June, followed by the announcement of further increases in public spending, an easing of restrictions on bank loans, and a relaxation of installment credit regulations for consumer durable goods. The next set of economic indicators revealed that the level of business activity remained sluggish in the second quarter, which forced the authorities to reassess their strategies. The results were another 0.5% reduction in the discount rate in August and the introduction of yet another "reflationary package" during the subsequent month. Once again, the centrepiece of this was a substantial increase in public spending (with much of the finance coming from the sale of government bonds), and there were also loans to a large number of industries. With business still not responding as fast as expected, the discount rate was reduced to 6.5% at the end of October. At the same time, the authorities let it be known that a further easing of monetary policy was under active consideration, and indeed the banks' reserve requirement ratio, which is one of the factors that govern the amount of credit extended, was reduced in November.

The government's policy succeeded in cutting inflation even further (from about 15% in the first quarter of 1975 to 10% in October) and in improvement of the foreign trade account. However, it also had a highly adverse effect on economic growth. During the first half of 1975 the volume of national income was approximately 1% lower than in the preceding six months and, even with the modest improvement that seemed to have taken place during the second half, the gain for the year was believed to have been less than 2%. Although this was a better performance than in 1974 (−1.8%), it was well below the postwar average.

The underlying weakness of the economy was reflected in most major areas of business activity. During the first nine months of the year, industrial production was approximately 11% down from 1974, with many industries facing considerable overcapacity. This in turn resulted in a rapid rise in unemployment and corporate bankruptcies. As in previous recessions, investment activities were extremely sluggish. These were affected by the reduction in corporate profits, the scarcity of money, high interest rates, and the general lack of confidence in the future. At the same time, in sharp contrast to previous experience, private consumption was also weak. In 1974 this was largely explained by inflation, but in 1975 the principal factors appear to have been the reduction in incomes arising from high unemployment, widespread short-time working and a loss of overtime, and the growing tendency to boost savings at the expense of consumption. With the weakness of domestic demand, industry had a strong incentive to promote exports; however, after some success in the early part of the year, export growth was adversely affected by the fall in world trade. At the same time, imports were running well below the previous year's levels for most of 1975, with the result that the balance of trade and external payments position improved significantly.

During the final quarter of the year, there were some signs of a cautious upturn. Although some commentators take the view that Japan is becoming a low-growth economy, it was widely anticipated that, as a result of the government's reflationary posture and the expected recovery in world trade, a comparatively rapid rise in most components of national income would take place in 1976.

Great Britain. The U.K. entered 1975 on a note of sluggish demand, declining industrial production, rising unemployment, accelerating wage and price inflation, and a substantial external payments deficit. In the final quarter of 1974, the volume of GDP declined by approximately 2% and industrial production was nearly 3% lower than in the preceding quarter. At the same time, prices were increasing at an annual rate of 23%; the pound sterling was under pressure in most major countries, and the current account of the balance of payments showed a deficit of £1,100 million. Faced with this situation, the government adopted a strategy aimed at a significant slowdown in inflation and a reduction in the external payments deficit. The methods chosen to attain these objectives included strict curbs on domestic demand, a slow increase in the money supply, the diversion of resources from private and public consumption to investment and exports, and an attempt to moderate the rise in wages (and therefore prices) with the aid of the "social contract," a vague and unenforceable agreement on the need for pay restraint between the government and the Trades Union Congress.

Accordingly, in the budget of April 1975 the chancellor of the exchequer increased income tax rates and reduced the corporation tax. He also introduced some additional investment incentives, promised a significant reduction in government expenditure, and reemphasized the government's determination to persevere with the social contract. Within a few months, it was clear that the budget strategy was not working as expected. The most conspicuous failure was the social contract. In the absence of effective sanctions and with unemployment still at a relatively low level, most pay settlements remained well above the official guidelines. The result was that the annual increase in basic wage rates accelerated from 31% during the first quarter to 35% in the following three months. This and an increase in the rates of the value-added tax (VAT) on luxury items in May had a highly adverse effect on the trend of retail prices, with the annual rate of increase during the second quarter reaching 48%, compared with 28% in the preceding three-month period.

By this time it was also becoming apparent that, in

formulating their strategy, the authorities had underestimated the extent and the influence of the underlying recessionary forces in the economy. According to the budget forecast, the level of real GDP during the first half of 1975 was to be nearly 3% higher than in the corresponding period of 1974, and the gain for the entire year was projected at about 1.5%. The result for the first half, however, showed an increase of less than 1%, and it was clear that current policies would lead to a decrease in GDP for the year. There was also mounting skepticism about the government's ability to carry out its stated policy on public expenditure. At the same time, manufacturing investment continued on a downward trend, although—thanks to the recession-induced cutback in imports—the balance of payments deficit was significantly reduced. In spite of this, the international value of sterling continued to fall, which, while helping to make British exports more competitive, created additional inflationary pressures by raising raw material costs.

By the middle of 1975 the government realized that the social contract had been a failure, and that unless prices and wages could be brought under control it would be extremely difficult and dangerous to take any antirecessionary measures. At the same time, with the rapid and continuing increase in unemployment, many union leaders came to accept the need for effective restraints on the size of pay settlements. The result was the introduction of a new incomes policy in August. The principal feature of this was a ceiling of £6 a week for most pay increases, a figure that would, if generally observed, hold the annual rise in wages to about 10%. By the end of 1975 the policy had not been backed by legal sanctions (although these can be introduced if necessary), but the initial response was encouraging. Between August and November approximately three million employees settled below the ceiling, and by the end of the year there were definite signs of a slowdown in the rates of both wage and price inflation. During the three months to October, basic wage rates rose at an annual rate of 5%, as against 37% in the previous comparable period, with the index in September and October showing hardly any advance. At the same time, the annual rate of increase in retail prices fell from 32 to 12%.

Fearing that a sizable reflation of the economy would undermine the new incomes policy and lead to a deterioration in the balance of payments situation, the authorities maintained strict curbs on demand during the second half of the year. As a result, the tempo of business activity remained subdued during this period. The volume of GDP recorded another decline in the third quarter, and the outcome for the entire year was believed to have been a decrease of approximately 2%. The level of unemployment rose steadily and reached 1.1 million in November. Industrial output continued on a downward path, although the final months of 1975 saw some evidence of an impending change in trend. Private consumption, affected adversely by the still-high rate of inflation and the limitations on the level of pay increases, also recorded a substantial decline, as did expenditure on plant and equipment investments. By contrast, however, the external payments position continued to improve, and the current account deficit for the year was reduced to a little more than half of the figure recorded in 1974. Britain, therefore, entered 1976 on a note of sluggish demand, weak industrial output, and rising unemployment. In contrast to the beginning of the previous year, however, the rate of inflation was gradually slowing and the payments deficit was being cut back to manageable proportions.

West Germany. In 1975 West Germany waited for an economic upturn that never came. In their single-minded drive against inflation, in the wake of the oil crisis, West German economic policymakers underestimated the aftereffects of their restrictive measures. They prolonged the recession by overestimating the expansionary effect of successive small doses of reflation administered in the latter half of 1974. In spite of a rapid slowdown in the tempo of economic activity in the closing months of 1974, as demonstrated by a 0.5% fall recorded in real GNP, the government entered 1975 confident that the turning point had been reached and that it would be followed by a growth of at least 2% during 1975. As the year unfolded, however, the underlying weakness of the economy became apparent; the reflationary measures had failed to have the desired effect. As a consequence, the continuing decline in economic activity pushed up the number of unemployed in February to the highest level since World War II, 1.2 million, over 5.2% of the labour force.

In the early months of 1975 consumer confidence weakened further and remained cautious for the rest of the year, making it extremely difficult for manufacturers to pass on increased costs. Moreover, fears of unemployment triggered a "savings mania" with as much as 17% of disposable incomes going into savings. Business investment, which together with increased export demand was supposed to pull West Germany out of the recession, remained basically flat except for a temporary spurt just before June. Given the chronic underutilization of productive capacity and a profit squeeze arising from the inability of manufacturers to pass on increased costs, there was little incentive to invest on a large scale. The fact that inflation was firmly under control at the beginning of 1975 contributed to a remarkable stability in wages, which, in turn, enabled West Germany to maintain the lowest rate of inflation among the major OECD countries throughout the year. In spite of the basic competitiveness of the mark and the strenuous efforts to boost exports, foreign orders remained 10% below the level of 1974. As export earnings account for well over a quarter of the GNP, low overseas demand exerted a particularly strong contracting influence that was impossible to offset by expanding domestic consumption.

After the disappointing performance of the first three quarters, firm evidence began to support the view that the worst was at last over and that the economy was definitely on a recovery course. Not only did forward indicators paint a more optimistic picture in the final quarter, but industrial output also picked up and unemployment leveled out, though at a high level (one million). But the recovery came far too late to prevent the economy from showing a real decline from the previous year. As 1975 drew to a close it was estimated that real GNP would be 3–4% below that of 1974.

The cautiously expansionary posture adopted by the government in 1974 continued largely unaltered during 1975. In addition to three separate though not very large reflationary measures launched during 1974, in August 1975 yet another initiative was unveiled to "help the economy through the winter," as the government's spokesman on economic affairs put it. Although this was aimed at easing the plight of the construction industry, when coupled with the previous measures and the incentives offered in the March 1975 budget it amounted to a comprehensive package that included tax reductions and benefits amounting to not less than DM. 14 billion. But given the projected budget deficit of more than DM. 55 billion (twice as much as the cumulative deficit between 1950 and 1974), the government steadfastly resisted demands for larger doses of reflation. Partly because of this deficit the yield on long-term government bonds rose to unacceptable levels, forcing the government to borrow from abroad.

While the government was reluctantly prepared to finance such a large budget deficit during the slump, its aim over the long term was to balance the budget. New tax measures designed to achieve this, effective from early 1977, were announced at the same time as the August reflationary package.

The Bundesbank's continued policy of easier credit and lower interest rates underpinned the government's cautious expansionary course. At the beginning of 1975, the Bundesbank's declared policy was to let the money supply rise by up to 8% during the next 12 months. But, owing to the reluctance of industry to borrow, the money supply expanded by less than the target rate, leading the Bundesbank to take action to improve liquidity and reduce interest rates. Consequently, by the autumn, the discount rate was down to 3.5%, compared with 6% at the beginning of the year. At this level, West German interest rates were significantly below those in other nations, but in order to stimulate demand for credit the central bank was prepared to risk some funds leaving the country in search of higher rates.

A reversal of this expansionary policy was expected in early 1976 because, as the demand for credit by the private sector picked up, the money markets would find it increasingly difficult to absorb the borrowing requirements of both the government and the private sector. Because the option of allowing the money supply to take the strain might unleash inflationary forces, a rise in interest rates and a reduction in liquidity seemed likely.

France. Even though France was among the countries last hit by the recession, there was a good chance that it would be one of the first to recover. The French economy began to run out of steam in the closing quarter of 1974 in response to the government's midyear anti-inflationary measures and the worsening international economic climate. Industrial output, which peaked in June 1974, fell at an annual rate of 10% in the first half of 1975. It continued to fall in the third quarter but at a slower rate before picking up cautiously from October onward. Private consumption, both final and intermediate, weakened sharply in early 1975 thanks to a rush of precautionary buying a year previously. Foreign demand was also lower than that anticipated by early forecasts, and in volume terms fell by about 5% in the first six months of 1975. In view of this weakness in demand, inventory stocks rose to unexpectedly high levels and the amount of unused productive capacity grew. Consequently, business investment suffered.

Not surprisingly, unemployment rose sharply, reaching nearly 800,000 by the end of March. In spite of a slowdown in the rate of increase in the summer, it exceeded one million in October. Short-time working also became widespread, probably more so than in any other European country, because of the generous unemployment benefits, the bill for which is shouldered by the employers.

The economic slowdown and the restrictive policies of the government combined to decelerate inflation from an annual rate of 17% in the first half of 1974 to one of just over 10% in the corresponding period of 1975. After that, however, the trend was disappointing in that the rate of inflation exceeded the government's target. Because control of retail profit margins was the selected instrument of combating inflation and no direct action was taken against wage rates, companies were unable to pass on their increased import and labour costs. This led to a profit squeeze and a sharp increase in bankruptcies.

Apart from moderating inflation, the other major short-term objective of the government was to bridge the trade gap. In spite of a fall in the volume of exports, the slowdown in domestic economic activity and lower energy consumption made significant inroads into the level of imports, virtually eliminating the trade deficit.

In the final quarter of 1975 the economic climate and businessmen's expectations improved markedly. The index of production, having touched bottom in September, recovered steadily in October and November; the improvement in the demand for consumer goods, which was already under way, also strengthened. This led to larger orders for such goods, and the long downward slide in orders for capital goods also came to an end. Yet another encouraging sign was an increase in foreign orders.

The recovery in the last few months of 1975 was the result of the increasingly expansionist policy followed during the year, reflecting the switch in priority from holding down inflation to propping up the economy. Between November 1974 and April 1975 four separate, though small, reflationary measures were announced. Collectively these measures aimed to offer moderate assistance to all the major sectors of the economy. In addition to supporting private consumption through increased pensions, unemployment benefits, and similar social transfer payments, the measures encouraged private investment through loans and additional tax relief for investment committed before the end of 1975. Liquidity shortages of companies were also eased thanks to a cancellation of the first payments due under the anti-inflation tax. Public investment was expanded by the provision of easier loans and grants for local-authority housing projects. Additional loans were given to public enterprises (notably Électricité de France and the railways). These moderate doses were, however, insufficient to counteract the powerful contractionary forces working their way through the economy.

As the recession deepened, making it impossible for companies to maintain high employment levels, the economic policymakers were criticized for having done too little too late. The government answered its critics by announcing in September an ambitious reflation plan aimed at pumping something like Fr. 30 billion into public works, consumers' pockets, and private investment. By slanting the program in favour of private investment, the government was banking on restoring business confidence. The expansionary fiscal stance inevitably resulted in a huge budget deficit of about Fr. 35 billion.

A relaxation in monetary policy at the end of 1974 first signaled the change in the attitude of the economic policymakers. The volume of permissible advances by the banks was raised, and the Bank of France's discount rate was reduced. This was followed by a further relaxation in June to stimulate the demand for commercial credit. Although the bank lending rate declined from a peak of 18% in June 1974 to 8.5% in November 1975, it remained high by historical levels and was thought to have had some dampening effect on borrowing, thus keeping the growth of money supply below the level the authorities would like. Even the special loans at subsidized rates, aimed at encouraging investment and export financing, were ineffective. As confidence returned, however, the stimulatory policies were expected to help the economy to expand by around 5% in 1976, compared with a decline of about 2% in 1975.

Less Developed Countries. In 1975, as in the previous year, the less developed countries faced enormous problems because of the world economic slowdown. Only the oil-producing countries were able to escape the cruel effects of the recession. For the one billion poorest people living in Asia and Africa, it was a year of zero growth at best and in many cases a partial reversal of the progress made in the early 1970s. The industrial slowdown and the steps taken by the industrialized nations to reduce inflation and balance of payments deficits resulted in a sharp fall in the price of major commodities (except oil), which is often the only source of export income for the less developed countries. In the meantime, the prices of manufactured goods, which accounted for more than two-thirds of the import bill of the less developed countries, continued to rise. Thus, the purchasing power of the export earnings of those countries dropped sharply, leading to large trade deficits.

The more developed primary producers, even though subject to the same nutcracker effect of falling export receipts and rising import prices, were able to cushion their economies more effectively by running down reserves and by financing the increasing trade deficits through foreign commercial sources (such as Eurodollars), though at fairly hard terms. This group of countries achieved a 4% growth rate during 1974, and in spite of the general recession in 1975, a small growth is thought to have been achieved in that year.

The major oil-producing countries managed to sustain high growth rates (about 7–8% on the average) thanks to increased efforts to develop their economies. The colossal expenditure involved was easily financed by increased oil revenues, although these had lost some of their purchasing power as a result of worldwide inflation in 1974 and 1975. Purchasing power was partially restored by the 10% upward revision in oil prices, effective from Oct. 1, 1975. This revision, coming as it did before the industrialized countries had fully recovered from the effects of the December 1973 upheaval, set a new precedent that was expected to go a long way toward protecting the earnings of the oil exporters from the ravages of inflation or from foreign currency fluctuations.

In spite of the high priority given to domestic development, oil producers were relatively generous in their aid programs. During 1974, $7 billion was offered either bilaterally or through the International Monetary Fund (IMF) and the World Bank, compared with $12 billion made available by the "rich world." More than half of the direct aid went to Egypt and Syria for obvious political reasons, but India and Pakistan also benefited enormously. The total flow of aid from the OECD nations to the less developed countries during 1975 rose very little in real terms. As a percentage of combined GNP, however, it rose slightly, although at 0.33% it remained far short of the target of 0.7%. (EIU)

Centrally Planned Economies. Piotr Jaroszewicz, the premier of Poland, speaking at a Communist Party conference in Warsaw, revealed on Feb. 6, 1975, that the Executive Committee of the Council for Mutual Economic Assistance (CMEA, or Comecon) had agreed to the Soviet demand of more than doubling the prices of fuels and raw materials exchanged between the member states. Lengthy and vigorous diplomatic negotiations among the CMEA member states preceded this fundamental change from two decades of agreed-upon practice. At the 28th plenary session held in Sofia, Bulg., in June 1974 the U.S.S.R., chief supplier of crude petroleum and raw materials to other CMEA countries, proposed that the quinquennial price fixing be abandoned and yearly changes introduced not from 1976, the first year of the next five-year plan, but from 1975, the last year of the current one. After many months of difficult discussions at the Moscow headquarters of CMEA, the Executive Committee decided on Jan. 23, 1975, that the prices for that year would be an average of world prices for the 1972–74 period, and that in the future they would be adjusted every year, always on the basis of an average of world prices based on the previous five years.

The practical result for the five European CMEA members, Romania excepted, was a 140% price increase for crude oil, namely from 15 to 36 rubles per ton. In other words, the four CMEA countries (Poland, Hungary, Czechoslovakia, and East Germany) that depended on the "Friendship" pipeline, and that had paid the U.S.S.R. about 607 million rubles for its crude, probably would pay 1,670,000,000 rubles for the 1975 deliveries. Zygmunt Szeliga, explaining in the Warsaw weekly *Polityka* (Feb. 22, 1975) why the price increases for fuels and raw materials were necessary, used the following arguments: first, in 1973 the U.S.S.R. exported to Poland 12 million tons of crude petroleum and oil products and received for these supplies the same amount of money as for 6 million tons sold to West Germany; and second, in 1974 the U.S.S.R. sold 50 million tons of crude and oil products to the CMEA countries (the four on the pipeline plus Bulgaria and Cuba, supplied by sea) for more than 1 billion rubles, but the sale of 70 million tons of the same goods to capitalist countries brought back about 4 billion rubles.

The 29th plenary session of the CMEA, held in Budapest June 24–26, was of exceptional importance for the further industrial development of member states. The session adopted the coordinated economic plans for the 1976–80 period as well as a series of multilateral integration measures aiming at the completion of the Comprehensive Program approved at the Bucharest plenary session in July 1971.

Gyula Szeker, Hungarian deputy premier and current chairman of the Executive Committee, sum-

Table XIII. Rates of Industrial Growth in Eastern Europe*

Country	1956–60	1961–65	1966–70	1971–74	1975†
Bulgaria	15.9	11.7	11.2	8.9	12.6
Czechoslovakia	10.5	5.2	6.3	6.5	7.0
Germany, East	9.2	5.9	6.4	6.5	6.8
Hungary	7.5	8.1	6.1	6.8	6.0
Poland	9.9	8.6	8.3	11.0	11.6
Romania	10.9	13.0	11.8	13.1	14.0
U.S.S.R.	10.4	8.6	8.5	7.4	7.7

*Yearly average percentages.
†First six months.
Source: National statistics.

Table XIV. Output of Basic Industrial Products in Eastern Europe, 1974
In 000 metric tons except for natural gas and electric power

Country	Hard coal	Brown coal	Natural gas (000,000 cu.m.)	Crude petroleum	Electric power (000,000 kw-hr.)	Steel	Sulfuric acid	Cement
Bulgaria	300	28,400*	—	100	22,800	2,200	761	4,300
Czechoslovakia	27,972	82,165	1,000	171	56,035	13,640	1,211	8,967
Germany, East	600	246,200*	—	—	80,300	6,200	1,005	10,100
Hungary	3,200	22,552	5,094	1,997	18,946	3,466	657	3,437
Poland	162,000	39,800	5,739	550	91,600	14,565	3,319	16,800
Romania	7,100	17,600*	29,238	14,500	49,300	8,800	1,358	11,200
U.S.S.R.	474,000	210,000	261,000	459,000	975,000	136,000	16,700	115,000
Total	675,172	...	302,071	476,318	1,293,981	184,871	25,011	169,804

*1973.
Source: National statistics.

marized the achievements of the socialist division of labour during the 1971–75 period and described the main tasks for the years 1976–80. Coordination, he declared, implied collective investments, harmonized production, and guaranteed supplies of fuels, raw materials, and machinery. During the past four years the member countries concluded more than 20 multilateral and hundreds of bilateral agreements among themselves, especially in the fields of mechanical and chemical industry.

Nikolay K. Baybakov, Soviet deputy premier and chairman of the State Planning Committee, mentioned some multilateral enterprises that should be completed during the coming five-year plan. These included the joint construction of the Kiyembayev asbestos enrichment plant in the Urals, with an estimated production of 500,000 tons yearly; the building by five Eastern European CMEA member states (Romania excepted) of a gas pipeline 2,750 km. long and 142 cm. in diameter, running from Orenburg in the U.S.S.R. to the Soviet-Czechoslovakian frontier near Uzhgorod, which by 1980 would deliver 15,500,000,000 cu.m. of gas to Czechoslovakia, Poland, East Germany, Hungary, and Bulgaria; and the enlargement of the power transmission grid Mir ("Peace"), linking five Eastern European countries (Romania excepted) with the U.S.S.R., from 65,000 Mw. capacity to more than 150,000 Mw. Ten other joint investments, costing in all about 9 billion rubles, were planned.

Opening the session, Aleksey N. Kosygin, the Soviet premier, said that during 1971–75 the economic potential of the socialist nations had increased considerably and that their system of planned economy protected them against disturbances from which the capitalist countries were suffering. He admitted, nevertheless, that the situation on the world market created some economic complications for the socialist nations because of their increasing foreign trade with capitalist developed countries.

Jaroszewicz spoke of the future foreign trade between the CMEA countries, which during the years 1976–80 was expected to rise at least by 40%. For the long-term collaboration within the CMEA area the supply of fuels and basic raw materials was of crucial importance. By 1990 the CMEA countries, excluding the U.S.S.R., were expected to consume 250% more fuel than in 1970, and 43% of their needs would have to be imported.

"For Czechoslovakia," proclaimed Premier Lubomir Strougal, "the results of the efforts at coordination constitute a decisive factor for drawing up the 1976–80 plan of economic development." Gyorgy Lazar (*see* BIOGRAPHY), the premier of Hungary, said that his country, deriving nearly half of its national income from foreign trade, had arduous problems to solve. Some resulted from the fact that Hungary had largely exhausted the sources of growth that were the easiest to tap, but the altered world economic situation contributed to the nation's difficulties.

The Budapest session of the CMEA directed its Executive Committee to prepare a long-term plan of joint supply of energy and raw materials. The committee met in Moscow October 13–15 and prepared a draft plan, which was to be discussed at the next plenary meeting in 1976. It was believed that the draft recommended the building of large nuclear power stations in Eastern European countries. By 1980 these stations would supply at least 13% of those nations' electric power consumption, and it was hoped that by 1990 this proportion would rise to 33%.

In an article in the official party periodical, the *Kommunist*, Mikhail A. Lesechko, Soviet deputy premier and permanent member of the CMEA Executive Committee, emphasized the decisive role of the U.S.S.R. in supplying its allies with fuels. "In 1975," he wrote, "the CMEA countries will receive from the U.S.S.R. about 130 million tons of fuels (expressed in hard coal equivalents). During the coming five years it is planned to increase these supplies considerably to some 800 million tons, that is 43% more than during the 1971–75 period. About half of these supplies will consist of crude petroleum and its products." As practically all this crude petroleum had to come either from Almetyevsk in Tataria or from the Tyumen area in western Siberia, both its extraction and transport to the consumer countries in central Europe would be costly. In addition, Lesechko went on, Samotlor and other oil fields in western Siberia were situated in primeval areas with a forbidding climate. Working in extremely difficult conditions, Soviet engineers completed in the summer of 1975 a new 720-km.-long single-track railroad line from Tyumen to Surgut on the Ob River that would help to open a new oil-rich area.

Following the 1964 agreement of far-reaching cooperation between the CMEA and Yugoslavia, and of a limited one concluded in 1973 with Finland, Iraq and Mexico in 1975 signed agreements with the CMEA on economic and scientific cooperation. Official contacts between the European Economic Community (EEC) and the CMEA made no progress during 1975. The February visit of four officials to Moscow, headed by Edmund Wellenstein of The Netherlands, director of the external affairs department at the Brussels headquarters of the EEC, achieved practically nothing. Under Soviet pressure the CMEA Executive Committee declined to negotiate with the Brussels Commission about trade matters and insisted that the CMEA governments preferred to negotiate bilaterally with the EEC governments.

(K. M. SMOGORZEWSKI)

INTERNATIONAL TRADE

The main features of international trade in 1975 were a sharp fall in its volume, caused principally by the recession in the industrialized countries, and a small rise in its value, due mainly to those same countries' failure to prevent a further stiff inflation of their export prices. These prices were rising more slowly, however, as the year progressed. Patterns of trade were markedly different from those that characterized 1974. In that year, the developed oil-importing countries were concerned mainly with financing the deficits that had resulted from the enormous increase in the cost of crude petroleum; in 1975 they were concerned, and able, to reduce those deficits by raising the volume of their exports to the oil-exporting countries, now that the latter were physically ready to absorb capital goods on a huge scale. The oil revenues of the petroleum-exporting countries may have been lower in the fourth quarter of 1975 than a year previously because the volume of their exports was reduced by a greater percentage than their prices rose, but by and large there were no financial constraints on their importing as much as their economies, and ports, could handle.

CHART 3.

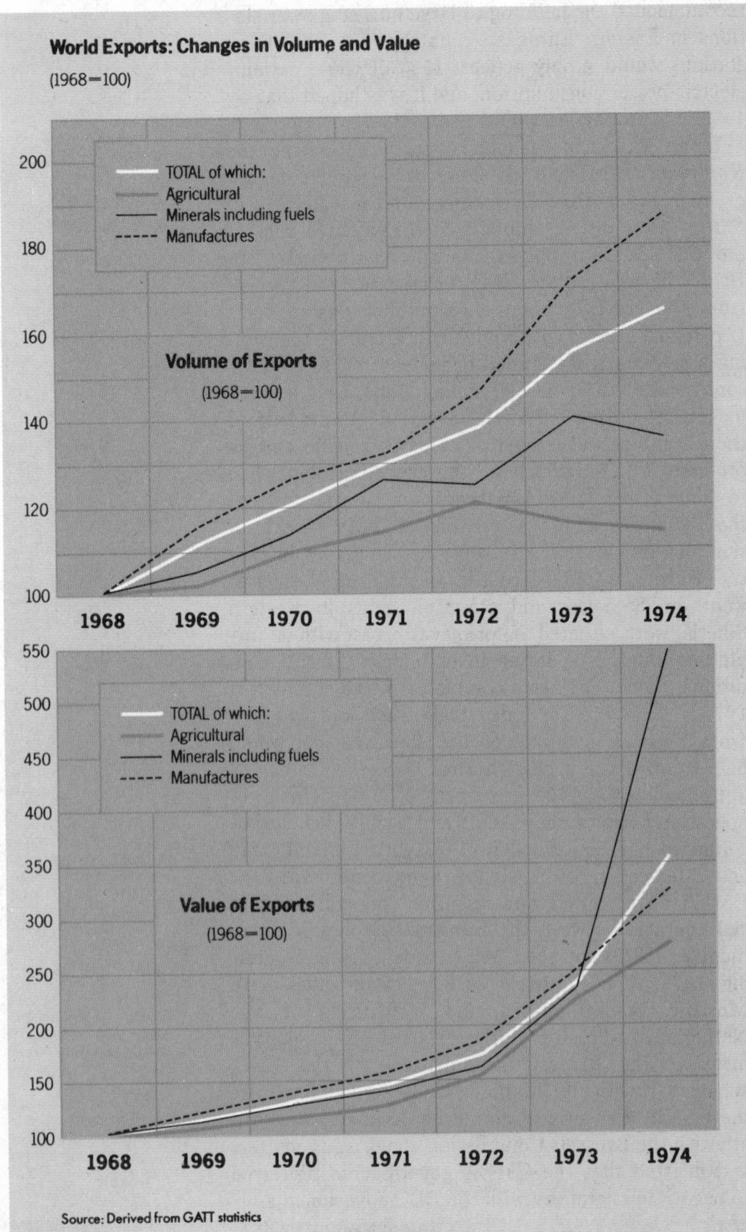

The non-oil-producing less developed countries helped contain the global contraction in the volume of world trade, at least in the early part of the year, by importing on a scale more in keeping with the prices their exports commanded in 1974 than with the commodity prices prevailing in 1975. There were clear and widespread indications in the second half of the year that the imports of these nations would either have to grow more slowly or be reduced; they had been financing current account deficits even greater than those of 1974 out of reserves or by foreign borrowing, in a way that was not sustainable.

The members of the CMEA, the Soviet Union and its allies in Eastern Europe, continued in 1975 to increase their imports from the industrial countries of the West at a pace much greater than was recorded for their imports from one another. By the end of the year, however, it was clear that the worsening of their terms of trade with the West and the consequent growth of their indebtedness to it, coupled with the harvest failure in the Soviet Union and the rising cost of Soviet oil deliveries to Eastern Europe, would soon necessitate a marked slowing down in the growth of their imports from the West.

In 1974 the value of world exports, excluding those of the centrally planned economies, was $774.6 billion. This was 49% higher than in 1973. Of this huge increase, only about 5–6% can be attributed to volume growth, compared with a gain of 11% in 1973 and 9–10% on average in the years 1963–73. Moreover, the volume increase decelerated throughout the first three quarters of the year and gave way to a decline in the final quarter. On the other hand, world export prices rose by 40.4% in terms of dollars between 1973 and 1974. Export prices in the industrial countries rose by less than this, but still by a record 24.1%, compared with 20.2% in 1973. This worsening, where in other circumstances an improvement might have been expected, was due in no small measure to the increased costs resulting from a 204.2% rise in the export prices of the oil-exporting countries, but there were also increases of over 40% in the export prices of the non-oil-exporting countries of Asia and Latin America as a result of the commodity price boom.

The picture of world trade in 1975 was very different. Its value in the first half of the year was $400.2 billion, only 7.7% greater than in the same period of 1974. This increase in value masked a fall in volume, for the unit price of exports of manufactures from the developed market economies rose by 24.2% over the same period. The National Institute of Economic and Social Research of the U.K. estimated that for 1975 as a whole, the volume of world trade fell by 9% compared with 1974.

Primary Producing Countries. The imports of the Organization of Petroleum Exporting Countries, which rose by 64% between 1973 and 1974 in dollar terms to $32 billion (representing a volume increase of perhaps 30%), continued to increase in 1975. When the figures for the full year become available, they are likely to show a considerable reduction in those countries' surplus on current account. The IMF forecast that the current account surplus of major oil-exporting countries would amount to only about $50 billion in 1975, compared with $70 billion in 1974. Figures for ten members of OPEC (not including Qatar or the United Arab Emirates) showed that exports to them by members of the OECD amounted to $21.4 billion in the first six months of 1975, compared with $16.4 billion in the second half of 1974 and $10.8 billion in the first. The increase between the two first-half periods is nearly 98%, though the increase for the year as a whole would probably prove to be less than this. The biggest absolute increase, as well as an above average relative increase, was recorded by Iran, whose imports from OECD members rose from $737 million in the first half of 1974 to $1,228,000,000 in the second half and to $1,767,000,000 in the first half of 1975.

The other factor working for a reduction in OPEC's current surplus in 1975 was the probable fall in the value of its oil exports, because even with the price increase that came into force in the last quarter of 1975 the rise in average oil prices between 1974 and 1975 was unlikely to have been sufficient to offset the drop in the volume of oil exports. The volume decline was expected to be in the region of 15%. The contrast between the rise of 7.3% in fuel export prices and that of 24.2% in those of the manufactured exports of the developed market economies, between the first halves of 1974 and 1975, shows there to have been a marked swing back in the terms of trade. Its extent, however, was expected to be somewhat smaller for 1975 as a whole than that indicated by the first half comparison.

The trading fortunes of the less developed countries that are not significant oil exporters varied considerably in 1975, the degree of their dependence on imported oil being one important variable and the commodity mix of their exports another. Mexico, which achieved oil self-sufficiency during the year, was clearly much better placed than Brazil, which began 1975 with only about 25% self-sufficiency; countries such as Zambia and Chile, which are almost wholly dependent for their export earnings on a single badly depressed commodity, in their case copper, fared worse than others with a more diversified export trade.

The less developed countries that were non-oil-producing, however, were viciously affected by the combination of recession and inflation in the developed market economies. The value of their exports was reduced and the cost of their imports increased. The value of the latter in 1974 was $123.9 billion, an increase of 60% over 1973. Of this, probably not far short of 20% represented a volume increase, while most of the rest was accounted for by the higher export prices of petroleum and manufactures. The value of exports was $97.2 billion, an increase of 43.5%, of which about nine percentage points were accounted for by a volume increase and most of the rest by higher commodity prices. Thus, some of the improvement in the terms of trade the non-oil-producing less developed countries gained in 1973 was lost again in 1974 when commodity prices fell. Also, their collective trade deficit was worsening. It rose from $9.9 billion in 1973 to $26.7 billion in 1974, and within the latter year climbed from $3.4 billion in the first quarter to $6.8 billion in the second, $7.7 billion in the third, and $8.8 billion in the fourth. It did fall back to $7.6 billion in the first quarter of 1975, but even this rate of deficit proved difficult to finance. In its 1975 *Annual Report,* the IMF forecast that this group of countries would together run a current account deficit of $35 billion in 1975, but it qualified its forecast in these terms: "The projection . . . is based on the implicit assumption that the necessary financing will be available. However, the sheer size of the aggregate deficit inevitably raises questions as to the actual ability and willingness of the countries concerned to finance it."

The IMF warning looked increasingly relevant as the year ended, in that a significant number of less developed countries came to the end of their ability to finance trade deficits out of reserves and foreign borrowing. To take a few examples, Brazil was reported to be considering a 20% cut in the value of its imports in 1976 in view of the size of the 1975 trade deficit; Kenya had had to prune its 1976 development targets severely for balance of payments reasons; and Peru had seen fit to devalue its currency by 14% against the dollar in September in order to discourage inessential imports.

OECD trade figures for the first half of 1975 show in broad outline the background of decisions of this sort. OECD imports from the non-OPEC less developed countries of Latin America, Africa, and Asia fell between the first halves of 1974 and 1975 by 3.5%, from $30.3 billion to $29.2 billion, while OECD exports to them rose by 17.7%, from $33.8 billion to $39.8 billion. The 17.7% rise in the group's imports from OECD countries probably conceals a fall in volume, because the developed market economies' prices for exported manufactures rose between the same two periods by 24.2%.

Industrial Countries. Although the collapse of the commodity boom and the growing payments difficulties of the less developed countries were among the most striking effects of the 1974–75 recession, the harshest trade effect in volume terms was that on trade between the developed market economies. Total OECD exports, which were worth $252.7 billion in the first half of 1974 and $279.9 billion in the second, continued upward in value terms in 1975. In the first

CHART 4.

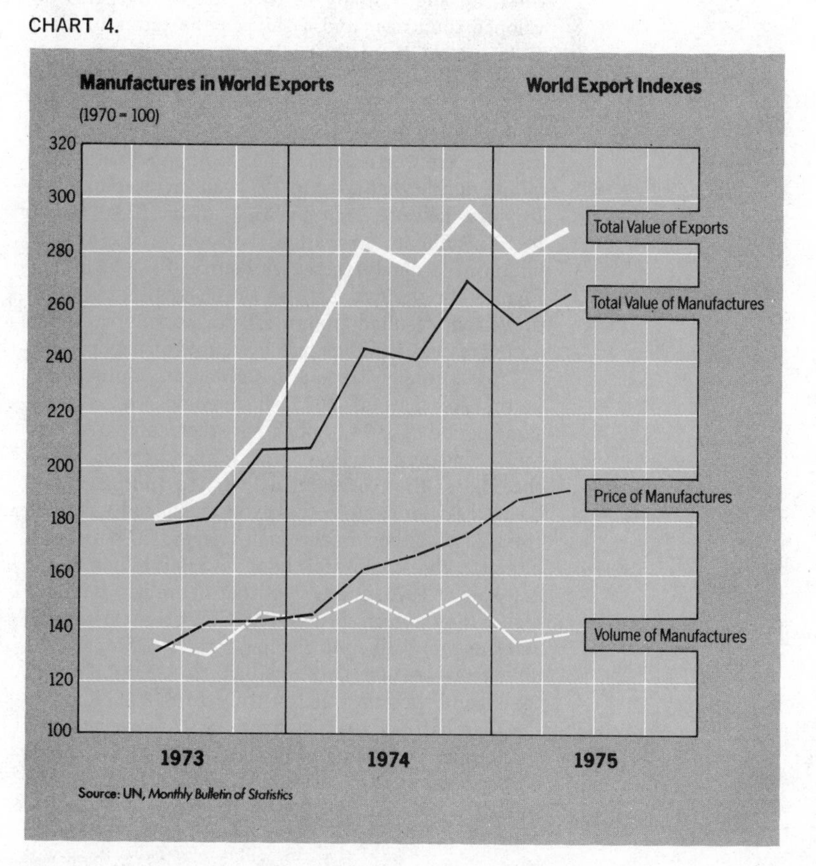

half of the year, they were valued at $287 billion, or 13.6% more than in the same period of 1974. But export prices in the industrial countries rose by 19.9%, and the price of manufactures exported by developed market economies rose by 24.2% over the same period. Therefore, the volume of OECD exports declined approximately 5–8%. Between the first halves of 1974 and 1975 the value of exports by OECD member countries to one another rose by only 5.6%, which, on the same rough reckoning, implies a volume fall of 12–15%.

Total OECD imports rose from $279.1 billion in the first half of 1974 to $302.6 billion in the second, falling back again in the first half of 1975 to $297.1 billion to give an increase between the two first half periods of 6.4%. Over the same period import prices rose by 18.1%, indicating a volume fall of about 10%. The growth in the value of imports from within the OECD helped to keep up the average; they were worth 8.5% more than in the first half of 1974, whereas, as shown above, imports from the non-OPEC less developed countries fell by 3.5% and imports from OPEC members (excluding Qatar and the United Arab Emirates) rose in value by 6.2%.

The fact that over the period between the first half of 1974 and the first half of 1975 OECD exports were growing considerably faster in value than OECD imports permitted a marked reduction in the combined trade deficit of the OECD countries. This amounted to $26.1 billion in the first half of 1974, but in the first half of 1975 it was reduced to $10.1 billion. For 1975 as a whole, the IMF's *Annual Report* projected a current account surplus of $1 billion for the industrial countries, compared with a deficit of $12 billion in 1974. This major improvement was due principally to reduced demand for petroleum, brought about by recession more than by conservation measures; strong demand from OPEC member countries and, initially at least, from other less developed countries; and a shift in the terms of trade in favour of the industrial countries vis-à-vis both oil exporters and primary commodity producers.

There was a striking turnabout in the foreign trade of the United States in 1975. In the first nine months exports were worth $79.4 billion, compared with $71.5 billion during that span in 1974, an increase of 11%. Imports, however, fell by 3.2% from $73.3 billion to $70.9 billion. Instead of a trade deficit of $1.8 billion, accordingly, there was a surplus of $8.4 billion. Figures for the first half of 1975 show that the improvement resulted from a fall in the volume of imports greater than that in the volume of exports.

Japan's foreign trade also showed an improvement in the first half of 1975 when compared with the same period of 1974, though not when compared with the second half of 1974. The FOB (free on board, that is, less the charge for delivery to and placing on board a carrier) value of its exports, which had leaped from $24.1 billion in the first half of 1974 to $31.5 billion in the second, fell back to $26.9 billion in the first half of 1975, but even at that figure it was 11.8% higher than a year earlier. The CIF (cost, insurance, and freight) value of its imports rose from $30.7 billion in the first half of 1974 to $31.4 billion in the second, but then fell sharply to $28.8 billion in the first half of 1975, a figure 6.3% lower than a year earlier. A striking characteristic of Japan's trade performance is that between the first halves of 1974 and 1975 the volume of exports increased by 4.6%, whereas in the same period every other major industrial nation recorded a volume fall. The corollary of this is that its export prices, expressed in dollars, showed a below-average increase and actually fell between the second half of 1974 and the first half of 1975. And while Japan gained a bigger share of a shrinking world market, it helped create the shrinkage by cutting back the volume of its imports by 18.6%, more than any other major economy for which figures are available.

West German foreign trade remained heavily in surplus in 1975. Its exports, worth $43 billion in the first half of 1974, rose quite strongly in the second half to $46.2 billion but then leveled off in the first half of 1975 to $46.1 billion, a figure that left them only 7.4% higher than in the previous year. Imports rose about half as fast again as exports between the first and second halves of 1974, from $33 billion to $36 billion, but they grew more slowly in the first half of 1975; at $37.5 billion they were worth 13.6% more than in the same period of 1974. Even so, there resulted a surplus of $8.7 billion, compared with surpluses of $10 billion in both the first and second halves of 1974. The volume of West German exports fell by 12.6% between the two first-half periods. This was a bigger percentage decline than was recorded by any other major Western economy. On the other hand, West German imports rose in volume, by 1.6%. It was the only major economy to record such an increase with the exception of Sweden, which was at an earlier stage of its business cycle.

Between the first halves of 1974 and 1975, the value of French exports rose much more rapidly than that of French imports. Exports were valued at $22.3 billion in the first half of 1974, rose to $23.6 billion in the second half, and then increased much more rapidly in the first half of 1975, to $27.6 billion. This left them 24% higher than a year previously. Imports, on the other hand, rose only from $26.1 billion in the first half of 1974 to $26.7 billion in the second and $28 billion in the first half of 1975, an increase over the year of 7.3%. Again it was a case, in recessionary conditions, of the volume of exports falling less severely than the volume of imports, by 6.1% as opposed to 14.8%. These figures yield a striking apparent increase in the unit value of French exports, which is probably explained by a shift in their composition; for instance, an 18.8% volume fall in exports of food, drink, and tobacco contrasted with an 11.1% gain in exports of investment goods.

While remaining heavily in deficit on its foreign trade, the U.K. also improved its position in 1975 and regained something of the market share it had been losing. Its exports rose from $18.3 billion in the first half of 1974 to $20.5 billion in the second and to $22.4 billion in the first half of 1975, an increase over the year of 22.2%. This was accounted for by price increases, but the volume fall in exports, of only 0.7%, compared favourably with the performance of all of Britain's major competitors except Japan. The value of U.K. imports rose from $26.7 billion in the first half of 1974 to $27.8 billion in the second, but fell back again to $27.5 billion in the first half of 1975. This gave an increase over the year of only 3.2%. In volume terms, there was a decline in imports over the same period of 9.5%.

Centrally Planned Economies. The figures that would permit a picture to be drawn of the foreign trade of the CMEA countries in 1975 were not available at year's end, though there was some scattered evidence on which to base a guess as to the extent that the trends it displayed in 1974 were repeated in 1975. The combined exports of the U.S.S.R., Bulgaria, Czechoslovakia, East Germany, Hungary, Poland, and Romania in 1974 amounted to $65.5 billion, according to a UN estimate. This was nearly 24% more than in 1973. The same countries' imports amounted to $70.9 billion, nearly 26% more than in 1973. As in the immediately preceding years, there was thus a trade deficit of significant proportions, when it is remembered that roughly half the trade concerned was between the countries mentioned and that the deficit was incurred only on the other half. (In 1974, of the total imports 49.3% were intraregional, 38.1% were from developed market economies, 10.8% from the less developed countries, and 1.8% from other centrally planned economies, according to the General Agreement on Tariffs and Trade or GATT, while a similar breakdown of exports yielded totals of 51.3, 32.5, 13.8, and 2.4%.) According to OECD figures, the area's exports to OECD countries amounted to $12 billion in 1973 and $17.1 billion in 1974, an increase of 42.8%, while its imports from OECD countries rose from $14 billion in 1973 to $19.6 billion in 1974, an increase of 39.3%.

CMEA trade with the West grew faster in value than its total trade, partly because the prices at which trade with the West was carried out rose much more steeply than those in intraregional trade. Thus, while CMEA imports from OECD countries had a value gain of 39% but a volume gain of perhaps only 11%, intraregional imports showed a value gain of only 15% that was mainly accounted for by a volume increase. But no matter how valuable imports from the West are in qualitative terms to the CMEA economies, Western inflation exaggerated their value in monetary terms in comparison with the still dominant trade of members with one another.

This element of exaggeration should be less important in 1975 as Western inflation was brought more nearly under control, on the one hand, and as prices in intra-CMEA trade were affected by the decision in January to revise them annually in the light of world prices over the previous three years. For 1975 this would have the effect of raising the price of Soviet exports of petroleum to Eastern Europe quite considerably and those of Eastern European supplies of raw materials to the U.S.S.R. somewhat less.

The tendency of the terms of trade of the Eastern European countries vis-à-vis the U.S.S.R. to worsen, coming on top of the fact that they had already worsened considerably with the West, meant that by the end of 1975 a number of those countries were looking hard at means of limiting imports from the West to those with economic priority. Their trade returns for 1975 may well in any case show that, while overall trade was still expanding strongly in volume and value, the value of imports from the West was no longer growing noticeably, if at all, faster than the value of those from their CMEA partners.

The most important single feature of the Soviet Union's trade with the West in 1975 was the necessity, from the summer onward, to contract for the import of grains to make good in part the huge shortage in the Soviet grain harvest. By late in the year, approximately 25 million tons had been contracted from the U.S. and elsewhere, and the operation was bound to put a strain on the Soviet Union's capacity to import industrial goods from the West.

Commodity Trade. The impact of the 1974–75 recession on world trade in commodities was most marked in the case of industrial raw materials, demand for which is more susceptible to changes in aggregate demand than is demand for many foodstuffs. Within the metals group, however, the impact on prices varied considerably with the organization of the market. In the case of copper, the North American producer price is important but responds to the dominating influence of the London Metal Exchange (LME) price. Unrestrained by any stabilization mechanism, this fell from a peak of just over £1,400 a ton in May 1974 to just under £500 a ton early in 1975, and although there was some recovery in the course of 1975 (reflecting in part the depreciation of the pound sterling), the price had drifted back to £563 by December 12. This price is below the cost of production of a significant proportion of existing capacity.

Demand for copper was so weak in 1975 that, although Western primary production was probably as much as 1 million tons less than the 6.7 million tons of 1974, stocks of refined copper rose steeply and steadily. North American mining companies cut their output, and Japanese refiners reduced purchases of concentrates. Also, CIPEC (the Intergovernmental Council of Copper Exporting Countries) decided in April that its members (then Chile, Peru, Zaire, and Zambia, later joined by Papua New Guinea and Indonesia) should extend their defensive measures from a 10% export cut adopted in late 1974 to a 15% export and production cut.

The price of tin is theoretically stabilized by the International Tin Council's buffer stock, but this is not adequately financed to do the job, and in order to keep the LME price above the floor price established under the fourth International Tin Agreement it was found necessary in April 1975 to impose export quotas on producing member countries, amounting to an 18% cutback for the period April–September. These restrictions were somewhat eased for the fourth quarter of 1975, but in December quotas for the first quarter of 1976 were cut again in response to the continuing weakness of demand and prices. The LME

Table XV. Foreign Trade of Eastern Europe
In $000,000

Country	Exports			Imports		
	1960	1970	1974	1960	1970	1974
Bulgaria	572	2,004	3,835	633	1,831	4,279
Czechoslovakia	1,929	3,792	6,898	1,816	3,695	7,360
Germany, East	2,207	4,577	8,729	2,195	4,843	9,625
Hungary	874	2,316	4,817	952	2,464	5,148
Poland	1,325	3,548	8,321	1,495	3,608	10,489
Romania	717	1,850	4,863	648	1,959	5,132
U.S.S.R.	5,564	12,799	27,769	5,628	11,731	25,219
Total	13,188	30,886	65,232	13,367	30,131	67,252

Source: National statistics.

Table XVI. Soviet Trade with Eastern European Countries
In 000,000 rubles

Country	Exports		Imports	
	1974	1973	1974	1973
Bulgaria	1,478.5	1,230.8	1,425.6	1,324.0
Cuba	926.1	679.1	716.2	430.5
Czechoslovakia	1,511.1	1,354.0	1,518.4	1,405.6
Germany, East	2,164.6	1,856.4	2,150.7	2,108.9
Hungary	1,134.5	975.6	1,147.8	1,087.9
Mongolia	285.2	250.6	119.1	87.9
Poland	1,838.2	1,445.0	1,745.4	1,555.3
Romania	578.5	519.1	612.3	611.2
Total	9,916.7	8,310.6	9,435.5	8,611.3

Note: The average official exchange rate, used only in foreign trade, was in 1973 and 1974, respectively, 0.685 and 0.78 ruble to U.S. $1.
Source: Ministry for Foreign Trade of the U.S.S.R.

spot price, which peaked at £4,195 a ton in September 1974, was not much above £3,000 for most of 1975.

Among other industrial raw materials, natural rubber and cotton were also badly affected by the recession. In the case of rubber the main cause was the depression of the tire industry, though the effect was moderated by an increase in the market share of natural rubber at the expense of synthetic rubber, as a result of the higher costs of the latter caused by increased petroleum prices. In view of the falling total demand for rubber, Malaysia had already undertaken measures to cut output in November 1974, and these were followed in May 1975 by the decision of the Association of Natural Rubber Producing Countries to establish a small buffer stock and to cut exports to the world markets to 2.8 million tons in 1975, compared with 3.2 million in 1974. These measures, and the beginnings of a recovery in demand, permitted some recovery in prices. Falling from a nominal £542 per ton for the RSS1 type in London in January 1974 to £239 in January 1975, the price stood at £350 in mid-December.

Cotton consumption in the 1974–75 season, ended in July, declined 4.2% from the previous season in non-Communist countries, and world production was about 1% up. The effect on prices in 1974 was dramatic: that of Strict Middling $1\frac{1}{16}$ in. reached a peak of 90.35 cents per pound in January 1974 and a low point of 46.35 cents per pound in January 1975. Its recovery after that (it was 57.25 cents per pound on December 12) was due partly to the prospects of some recovery in demand in 1976 but more to the likelihood that production would be sharply down in 1974–75.

To a lesser degree, the recession played its part in the decline of wheat and coarse grain prices in the first half of 1975. With the supply side of the 1974–75 equation already broadly determined, it was the lower than expected demand for animal feedstuffs that depressed prices. This factor was increasingly reinforced by the prospects of a very good North American harvest in 1975. But by the summer the prospects of a poor grain harvest in the Soviet Union led that country to make large grain purchases in North America and elsewhere, causing some recovery in prices. Even so, the Chicago wheat price on December 10, at 351.75 cents per bushel, was still well below the price of 461.50 cents a year previously.

Natural disasters combined with political disasters to transform the world coffee position in 1975. Until July, the market was dominated by problems of mild oversupply. The 1974–75 crop was estimated at 80 million bags, compared with a below-average 63 million in 1973–74, and was considered to be 2 million bags above current requirements. World imports of raw coffee, which fell from 59 million bags in 1973 to 54.8 million in 1974, were 11.4% lower in the first half of 1975 than in the same period of 1974, and prices were correspondingly weak. At that time there seemed every reason to expect another heavy crop in 1975–76. In July, however, the Brazilian crop suffered extensive frost damage. This focused attention on the 1976–77 crop by reducing the likely Brazilian output for that season by up to 16 million bags. The effect on prices was immediate and was reinforced by drought damage to the 1975–76 Brazilian crop, rain damage to the Colombian crop, and the descent of Angola into civil war, which threatened the loss of up to 75% of that country's production. The International Coffee Organization's composite average indicator price was just over 85 cents per pound in mid-December, about 43% higher than the year's lowest monthly average of 59.53 cents per pound in April. With prospects that demand would outstrip production until 1978–79, the new International Coffee Agreement coming into force in October 1976 would probably not have to operate its price-triggered export quota system for the first two years of its operation.

Despite the cartel action of OPEC, the recession had a moderating effect on the price of crude petroleum. In the first half of 1975, Japanese imports of mineral fuels were 9.1% less than in the second half of 1973; West German and U.K. imports of mineral fuels and lubricants were down, respectively, by 18.8 and 17.4%; and French imports of energy and lubricants declined 14.9%. And although U.S. imports rose in volume, this was essentially to make up for falling domestic output; total demand was about 6% below the average for 1973.

Commercial and Trade Policies. In terms of national policies on trade, 1975 was principally significant for what did not happen. In a year that experienced the low point of the longest and most severe recession since World War II, there was no major attempt to export unemployment by restricting imports, though in December, in the face of considerable international opposition, the U.K. government was still talking in terms of selective import controls. The freedom from a trade war was a notable feature of relations between the U.S. and the European Community.

The U.S. Trade Reform Act of 1974 contained a number of provisions making it easier to get a ruling on a complaint of dumping, excessive rebating of domestic taxes, and other unfair trade practices. Not surprisingly in a time of recession, use was made of these provisions. The law, however, seemed not to have been applied in a protectionist spirit, and it was significant that in 1975 the U.S. International Trade

CHART 5.

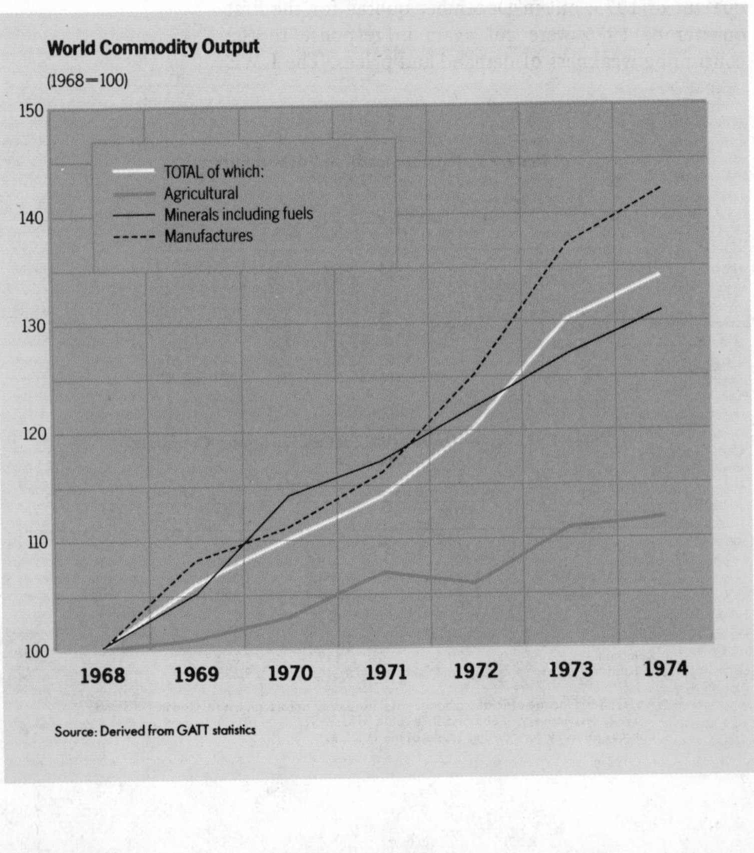

World Commodity Output
(1968=100)
150
140
130
120
110
100
TOTAL of which:
Agricultural
Minerals including fuels
Manufactures
1968 1969 1970 1971 1972 1973 1974
Source: Derived from GATT statistics

Commission ruled on three cases claiming protection against "serious injury" from imports and found in each case that the injury was not serious enough to warrant action. Certainly the application of U.S. trade legislation did not result in significant retaliatory action on the part of the EEC, despite a certain amount of grumbling. When one considers the range of issues on which the U.S. and the EEC could be at loggerheads, this must be a good augury for the Tokyo round of trade liberalization talks under GATT.

Progress in these negotiations was held up in 1975, however, by the failure of the EEC and the U.S., until December 10, to reach even procedural agreement on the way to proceed with negotiations on agricultural trade. Moreover, a general formula had not been devised for tariff reduction; little progress was made on nontariff barriers to trade; and it was clear that a major effort would have to be made early in 1976 to clear up procedural matters and make a start on substantive negotiations if the round were to be successfully completed by the end of 1977.

The Conference on International Economic Cooperation began in Paris on Dec. 16, 1975, at the ministerial level, and its work was to be continued into 1976 in four commissions dealing with energy, raw materials, development, and finance. The brainchild of the OPEC countries, it was to bring together representatives of the industrial countries, the oil-exporting countries, and the other less developed countries. The inclusion of the last-mentioned suggests that discussions on petroleum would be linked with, and doubtless confused by, a discussion of general commodity problems that would focus on the concepts of a "new economic order" and the transfer of resources to less developed countries through the regulation of commodity prices.

(EIU)

INTERNATIONAL EXCHANGE AND PAYMENTS

In 1975 the industrialized countries returned their accounts to near balance with the rest of the world, eliminating their deficit with the oil producers. The decision by some not to increase demand sufficiently to balance the deflationary effect of the rise in oil prices, and the unexpectedly rapid increase in oil producers' imports, eliminated the OECD countries' current deficit by the two routes that had seemed least promising in 1974. The low demand also raised the terms of trade of the advanced countries with both oil producers and other less developed countries, further improving the balances of the former. The shift went so far that some oil producers even became borrowers.

The apparent success was achieved at the expense of the deepest recession in international trade since the 1930s and by changes in the balances of very few countries. The reductions in imports were caused by declines in domestic output, which were aggravated by lower stocks, particularly of oil itself. For many of the smaller industrial countries and most of the less developed oil importers, the deficits remained as large as in 1974, as the reduction in demand from the major countries offset any improvement in their balances with the oil producers. The problem of reducing their deficits remained, and became more serious because of the decline in reserves and the increase in foreign borrowing that had taken place during two years of deficits. The growth in the foreign currency liabilities of these small and less developed countries would not only make them dependent on having larger increases in exports in order to finance their growing interest payments and increased imports, but also would restrict their willingness to increase exports by devaluing their currencies.

In 1974 most medium-term forecasts indicated an improvement of oil consumers' balances from 1975 to 1978–80, as the oil producers increased their imports and consumers "saved" oil. This process did not begin in 1975 because some advanced countries, in order to limit their external deficits (and inflation), cut growth and imports by unsustainable amounts. They may return to growth in 1976, but the deficits that would reappear with growing demand for oil might encourage slow growth. Also, the changes brought about by the oil price increase and in patterns of trade require time for trade to adjust before returning to former growth rates. The year 1975 thus aggravated the problems of the oil-importing less developed countries while providing no permanent solutions for the advanced industrial nations.

Interest and Other Invisibles. A major result of the 1974–75 deficits was the increased scale of borrowing and, therefore, of debt servicing. Countries with large foreign investments, such as the United States, United Kingdom, and Japan, also faced lower profits from abroad, particularly from the oil companies. The profit margins of the oil firms were squeezed by the new methods of pricing crude oil that accompanied increased government ownership and by the difficulty of raising prices in the face of weak demand. Net U.K. income from profits and interest fell in both 1974 and 1975. The increase in

CHART 6.

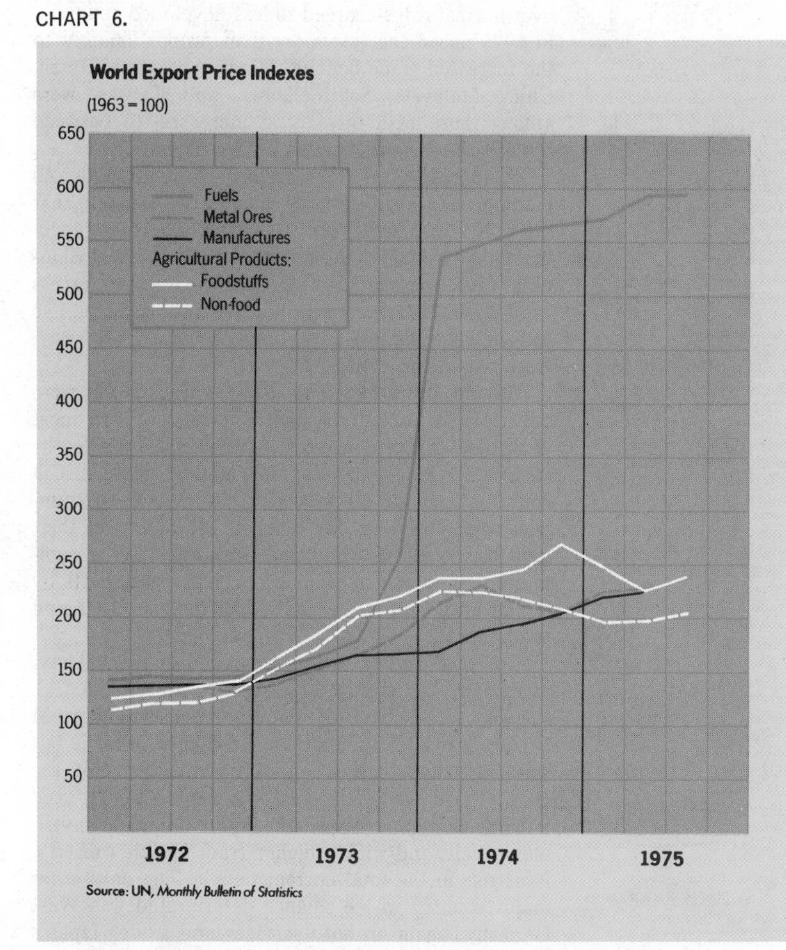

foreign investment in the U.K. in the early 1970s, the decline in British investment abroad, and continued high foreign borrowing ensured a continuing fall, although it was reduced in 1975. Low profits and devaluation reduced payments more than income. The cost of borrowing was high, as most was at short-term market rates of interest rather than through official international agencies; the expected increase in payments in 1976 was, however, reduced by an IMF loan at the end of the year. The decline in U.S. income from profits and interest between 1974 and 1975 was much sharper, but the 1974 figure had been inflated by temporary large stock profits for the oil companies.

For other advanced countries, the changes depended more closely on current borrowing and lending abroad. Belgium, The Netherlands, and Switzerland probably maintained or increased their surpluses. Other countries, notably Canada, Australia, Denmark, and South Africa, found interest a growing burden. Payments by Italy, Portugal, Greece, and New Zealand also rose, although these benefited from low-interest IMF loans. For all advanced countries such payments may have added about $4 billion to their deficit in 1975, about 40% of their total deficit although less than 1% of their exports.

For the oil-importing less developed countries, the interest payments were more damaging; the rise ($2.5 billion to $3 billion) was larger relative to their exports (perhaps 3%), and for many interest was already a significant cost. A fall in long-term foreign investment made it necessary for all less developed countries to increase their reliance on medium-term loans and short-term trade credits. The high interest rates of 1974 and 1975 and the increasing premiums over normal rates charged to less developed countries in 1975 raised the cost more than proportionately to the increased trade deficits. Israel, Argentina, Brazil, Chile, Malaysia, South Korea, and Taiwan were among those with the largest increases, to between a tenth and a quarter of export earnings.

Trade in services fell more than that in goods. As planning for such services generally assumed that demand would grow relatively rapidly, excess capacity, with falling prices, emerged more rapidly. Shipping was hardest hit, as there would have been excess capacity in 1975 even with normal trade growth. The fall in shipping earnings hurt the U.K., Norway, Greece, and the U.S.

Current Balances. The changes in invisibles were unusually large, but the principal influence on most countries' current balances (Table XVII) was the change in trade balances (*see* above). The OECD countries and the oil-importing less developed countries each suffered a fall of about $2 billion in their invisibles surpluses. The trade changes may be summarized as much lower oil imports, lower imports by the advanced countries, and higher imports by the oil producers.

Advanced Countries. In spite of reduced travel payments, the fall in interest earnings reduced the U.S. surplus on invisibles; the improvement in the current balance was slightly less than the change in trade but was only about half the total improvement for the OECD as a whole. Interest payments and reduced tourism greatly increased the usual Canadian invisibles deficit, and with a higher trade deficit caused a large rise in the total current deficit. The only other major country whose balance deteriorated was West Germany, again on both services and trade. Japan's deficit on invisibles also rose because of interest and services.

The massive improvement in the French balance was almost entirely from trade, with perhaps a small improvement in tourism. Italy, surprisingly, nearly returned to balance after a large deficit in 1974. Although it probably had a small increase in its surplus on tourism, the doubling of its net interest payments, which in 1974 were already three times their 1973 level, and stagnation of receipts from migrants gave little overall change in invisibles. The U.K. deficit was reduced by almost half, although the surplus on invisibles fell; income from tourism and air services rose but was offset by increased interest, shipping, and services payments for North Sea oil exploitation.

Net income from invisibles probably fell in the other OECD countries, approximately balancing the small improvement in trade. Most, like Canada, avoided the deep recessions of the major countries and therefore followed their trends in trade less closely than is customary. Belgium and Switzerland probably remained in surplus; the latter's reduced trade deficit and higher interest income balanced lower earnings from tourism, while the former may have improved both trade and invisibles. The other countries remained in deficit. Higher interest payments and lack of growth in tourism and transfers probably gave Ireland a deficit, but it was smaller than might have been expected given the increase in oil prices and depression in the U.K. Falls in invisibles combined with higher trade deficits increased the deficits of Norway (shipping) and New Zealand, South Africa, Denmark, and Finland (interest payments, although Denmark and Finland had higher tourism earnings). Spain's and Portugal's deficits probably rose, because of increased interest payments and reduced tourism, while the Swedish balance deteriorated because of a trade deficit.

Oil-Producing Countries. The fall of $35 billion–$40 billion in the surplus of the oil-producing countries in 1975 was almost entirely a reduction in their trade surplus; the increase in their invisibles deficit was only about $4 billion, compared with perhaps $10 billion in 1974. Although the change in services may have been similar, it was balanced by increased interest income from the 1974 surplus. Saudi Arabia had nearly a third of the group's trade and current surpluses in 1974 and in the first half of 1975 but, even though its imports rose less rapidly than those of other oil producers, may have had a greater than average decline in its surplus in the second half because it cut its oil exports to protect the poorer producers from the fall in demand. Kuwait, with a trade surplus of $9.5 billion in 1974, also increased its imports relatively slowly and kept its high surplus.

Iran had about 20% of the oil producers' surplus in 1974 and the first half of 1975, but a rapid increase in its imports of goods (by perhaps 150%) and services may have reduced its current surplus from over $10 billion to $1 billion–$2 billion. Iraq probably maintained its exports relatively well, but its doubled imports may have cut its trade surplus from $4 billion to $1.5 billion; if its services deficit rose, its current surplus may have been eliminated. The smaller Middle Eastern countries probably also increased their imports of both goods and services rapidly, thereby reducing their surpluses.

Although Algeria and Libya had slower import growth than most Middle Eastern countries, both may have moved into current deficit; they had high service imports and interest payments (on pre-1973 borrowing), and Libya's exports were particularly low in the first half of the year. Nigeria, in spite of a surplus of $4.5 billion in 1974, may also have had a deficit because its imports of goods increased by about 100% and the congestion in its ports increased its services costs. Indonesia and Venezuela had fairly slow increases in their imports and, therefore, small changes in their deficits.

Other Less Developed Countries. There was apparently little change in the overall trade balance in 1975 of the non-oil-producing less developed countries. They reduced oil imports sufficiently to balance the rise in their deficit with the developed countries. The more advanced of these nations may have had smaller deficits because they were not as dependent on basic raw materials, for which demand fell more rapidly than for manufactures; however, those such as Mexico or some North African countries that relied on tourism or transfer payments were hurt. Some Middle Eastern countries were helped by demand from oil producers, but this effect was surprisingly small. Although the total change in the deficit is small, each year's deficit is equal to about a fifth of the value of the area's merchandise imports, and the 1975 deficit required unusually low growth rates.

Table XVII. Current Balances of Payments
In $000,000

Country	1972	1973	1974	1975*
Canada	−625	+18	−1,212	−6,500
France	+284	−694	−5,849	+700
Germany, West	+776	+4,302	+9,588	+4,300
Italy	+2,266	−2,405	−7,815	—
Japan	+6,624	−136	−4,693	−1,200
United Kingdom	+320	−2,048	−8,560	−4,000
United States	−9,710	+335	−3,357	+12,000
Other OECD countries	+3,360	+3,969	−12,633	−11,300
OECD total	+3,295	+3,340	−34,531	−6,000
Other advanced countries	+200	+600	−2,500	−1,500
Centrally planned economies*	—	−800	−3,400	−5,400
Oil producers*	+1,000	+3,500	+68,000	+42,000
Less developed countries	−4,800	−7,000	−28,000	−29,500

*Estimate.
Sources: International Monetary Fund, *International Financial Statistics;* national sources.

Table XVIII. Official International Aid, 1975
In $000,000

Areas and principal borrowers and lenders	Oil facility contributions	Use of IMF credit	World Bank and IDA loans July 1974–June 1975
OECD	1,200	4,300	281
Germany, West	350	—	—
Greece	—	177	70
Italy	—	1,175	—
Netherlands, The	306	—	—
New Zealand	—	177	—
Spain	—	345	33
Turkey	—	198	158
United Kingdom	—	2,000	—
Oil producers	3,700	—	619
Indonesia	—	—	332
Iran	717	—	52
Kuwait	437	—	—
Nigeria	350	—	173
Saudi Arabia	1,674	—	—
Venezuela	463	—	—
Other countries	—	1,700	4,996
Bangladesh	—	45	150
Brazil	—	—	426
Chile	—	193	20
Egypt	—	−30	227
India	—	205	840
Israel	—	195	35
Mexico	—	—	360
Pakistan	—	117	126
Philippines	—	222	208
South Korea	—	80	298
Zaire	—	50	152
Total	4,900	6,000	5,896

*Including 2,000 committed for 1976.
Sources: International Monetary Fund, *International Financial Statistics;* World Bank, *Annual Report 1975.*

Centrally Planned Economies. The balances of the countries with centrally planned economies may not have changed much in 1975. In 1974 and 1975 these nations offered a growing market to the industrialized countries of the West. In 1975 there was an increase in their deficit with the OECD countries of about $5 billion–$7 billion, with West Germany and France benefiting the most as they had in 1974, joined by the U.S. because of grain exports at the end of the year. The earnings of the centrally planned economies from tourism probably increased, but the rising cost of interest on trade credits and medium-term loans may have balanced this.

Capital Movements. The means used to finance the 1974 deficits continued in 1975. Except for the poorest or least creditworthy countries, market borrowing remained the rule. Most of the special "oil deficit" schemes that international organizations spent much of 1974 attempting to arrange were never established; only the IMF oil facility, at about half its planned scale, survived. Short-term finance in the form of export credits, often subsidized by the governments of industrial countries, again covered an unusually high share of trade, particularly with the non-oil-producing less developed and Eastern European countries.

Official Aid. Loans from international organizations probably increased at a slower rate than in 1974. In the year to June 1975, the World Bank and the International Development Association (IDA) made loans of about $6 billion, $1.5 billion more than in the previous year. Use of IMF credit increased from $3.3 billion to $4 billion, with an additional $2 billion committed for 1976; $1.3 billion (in 1974) and $1.7 billion (in 1975) went to the less developed countries (Table XVIII). Most went to advanced countries. The World Bank did not repeat its 1974 issue of two-thirds of its bonds in oil-exporting countries, although some may still have been indirectly financed from oil surpluses. Only about $3.7 billion of the IMF oil facility was borrowed from the oil producers. The UN "special fund" was never established; the EEC plan to borrow from oil producers to lend to its members was unable to obtain adequate loans; and the OECD plan to arrange loans from surplus to deficit members was not implemented.

Bilateral aid by the industrial countries probably rose little from the $11 billion in 1974. As with aid from the World Bank (and the less developed countries' share of IMF aid), these funds were principally for the poorest countries, especially in Asia. The centrally planned countries probably did not increase their aid much above the 1974 level, about $1 billion concentrated on a few countries. OPEC aid increased in 1975; in 1974 commitments were high, but only about $3 billion was paid. In 1975 this may have risen to $5 billion. Most went to other Middle Eastern countries.

International Capital Markets. New direct investment in 1975 made a fairly small contribution to interarea flows, except for investment in oil production and refining. Eurocurrency loans in the first three quarters of 1975 were about half the total for 1974 (Table XIX). Oil producers tripled their borrowing (although it remained low relative to their probable contribution to the market), and other less developed countries had little change. The decline in lending to industrial countries was mainly in the area of government borrowing by countries whose balances improved sharply in 1975 rather than by those that still had deficits, except for the U.K. As the margins over the interbank interest rate that were charged in 1975 were about a point greater than in 1974, borrowing in 1975 increased future commitments more than did earlier loans.

Foreign bond issues increased in 1975, but except for issues by international agencies they were rarely used by less developed countries. For the advanced countries, however, they replaced some Eurodollar credits. The major countries together greatly increased their net outflow of long-term capital (Table XX), although the change may be little more than was necessary to replace the reduced OPEC support of international markets that resulted from the lower surpluses of those countries.

United States. The outflow of long-term capital flows in the first half of 1975 was at about the same rate as in 1974. The U.S. remained the principal place of issue for foreign bonds, especially by Canada and international agencies, and its interest rates were relatively low. Lower direct investment abroad offset both this and lower foreign investment. On short-term capital, however, there was a shift in the first half from the small surplus in 1974 to a large deficit, only partly reversed by an inflow in the third quarter. The decline was caused by an outflow of European funds and a lower share of the OPEC surplus, both probably related to the low interest rates. The current surplus and capital outflows left little change in net United States liabilities.

United Kingdom. In 1975 there was probably a net outflow of long-term capital, in spite of direct borrowing by the government, as disinvestment abroad was reduced and investment in North Sea oil was lower than in 1974. There was also a much smaller increase in overseas holdings of reserves in sterling, with a net outflow in the first half of the year; the reserves of non-oil producers continued to fall, and a much smaller share of the oil producers' surplus was placed in sterling. The deficit was financed by short-term movements, particularly by banks. Official reserves fell by more than $1 billion (15%), after a fall of $1 billion in December 1974, and in November it was announced that the U.K. would borrow $2 billion from the IMF in 1976, providing medium-term, low-interest financing.

France. Capital movements in France were probably fairly small in 1975, although there appeared to be some net capital inflow. International borrowing in the first three quarters was lower than in 1974, and in the fourth the government temporarily suspended such borrowing. Reserves rose by about $2 billion.

West Germany. The outflow of long-term capital exceeded the current surplus and was probably $4 billion higher than in 1974 even after a reduction in the net outflow in the fourth quarter when the government began to borrow abroad. Mark-denominated bond issues replaced dollar issues as the most common for international bonds, accounting for 40% of issues in the first half. A temporary ban on issues was imposed in August, but it was removed in November. The balance on short-term capital improved in the first half of 1975 and was probably further helped by the ending, late in the year, of the prohibition of interest payments on nonresidents' bank deposits. As West German interest rates were relatively low, ending the restrictions did not cause a massive inflow of foreign capital such as led to West German controls on capital in 1972–73. West German reserves fell by about $1 billion (4%).

Japan. Japan changed from one of the major exporters of long-term capital to a small importer in the first half of 1975, and may have returned only to balance in the second half. Controls had been imposed on foreign investment at the end of 1974. For the first time the nation became a major issuer of international bonds, after the relaxation of official controls on foreign borrowing. Its reserves fell by about $2 billion in the second half of the year because of short-term outflows.

Other Developed Countries. In spite of its return to current balance Italy borrowed additional funds from the IMF (although it repaid half its $2 billion 1974 loan from West Germany), and its reserves fell by $1 billion, indicating that it was still facing outflows of short-term capital. Of the other countries that used IMF and World Bank credit, Spain, Finland, and Greece also maintained their market borrowing, which provided substantially more than the official agencies, and had little change in their reserves. New Zealand used public and private borrowing and loss of reserves

Table XXI. Distribution of World Reserves*
End of period; U.S. $000,000 (1970)

	1970	1972	1973	1974	1975†
Developed countries	74,339	112,238	101,207	71,629	63,915
Oil producers	5,226	9,843	10,667	26,821	28,217
Other less developed countries	13,708	18,294	21,116	16,302	13,991

*Adjusted for each area's import prices.
†Estimate.
Sources: International Monetary Fund, *International Financial Statistics*; UN, *Monthly Bulletin of Statistics*; *Petroleum Economist*; estimates.

Table XIX. International Capital Markets
In $000,000

Areas and principal borrowers	Eurodollar issues 1973	1974	1975*	Foreign bond issues and issues in foreign currencies 1973	1974	1975*
OECD	11,822	19,351	4,977	5,410	5,732	10,912
Austria	30	185	—	178	476	628
Canada	51	85	71	1,210	2,403	2,492
Denmark	243	393	41	160	119	83
Finland	424	435	328	148	81	196
France	63	3,327	576	103	674	1,187
Germany, West	—	9	—	56	136	128
Greece	600	488	435	15	—	—
Ireland	—	358	485	138	134	34
Italy	4,713	3,040	15	25	50	61
Japan	150	258	237	49	249	1,077
Netherlands, The	252	540	56	160	458	559
New Zealand	—	565	113	—	33	163
Portugal	10	367	34	—	17	—
Spain	467	1,110	943	88	25	137
United Kingdom	3,070	5,986	341	1,313	271	175
United States	1,248	1,575	855	1,318	190	304
Oil producers	3,021	949	2,845	124	62	50
Algeria	1,352	22	100	71	60	—
Indonesia	478	384	992	—	—	—
Other countries	6,401	9,879	7,240	1,265	932	862
Brazil	718	1,372	1,626	61	25	—
Egypt	—	250	—	53	—	—
Israel	—	—	—	468	560	66
Mexico	1,572	1,090	1,250	177	50	221
Philippines	178	923	135	—	17	—
South Africa	498	506	243	171	50	147
South Korea	142	293	322	—	19	—
International agencies and companies	779	1,613	407	3,116	5,457	3,622
Total	22,023	31,792	15,469	9,915	12,183	15,446

*First three quarters; third quarter data incomplete.
Sources: OECD, *Financial Statistics*; International Monetary Fund, *Survey*.

Table XX. Foreign Investment by Major Countries
In $000,000

	Long-term capital flows 1972	1973	1974	1975*	Net interest, dividends, profits 1972	1973	1974	1975
Germany, West	+5,340	+5,483	−2,076	−6,600	+333	+582	−67	+200
Japan	−4,487	−9,750	−3,881	+600	+367	+490	−451	−700
United Kingdom	−1,996	−436	+5,076	−1,000	+1,451	+3,423	+3,162	+3,100
United States	−1,403	−1,312	−7,329	−8,000	+4,321	+5,179	+10,121	+6,000
Total	−2,546	−6,015	−8,210	−15,000	+6,472	+9,674	+12,765	+8,600
France	−644	−2,248	−271	—	+7	+399	+279*	+250

*Estimate.
Source: National sources.

about equally. Turkey relied mainly on IMF and World Bank borrowing, combined with a $600 million decline in its reserves. Other advanced countries financed deficits in the markets.

OPEC. Members of OPEC approaching deficits first used the high reserves accumulated in 1974 (Indonesia, Algeria, Iraq, and Libya) and then borrowed on international markets (particularly Algeria and Indonesia). Of their surpluses, $10 billion went directly and through international agencies to the less developed countries and perhaps another $3 billion in loans to advanced countries; one-third to one-half of the rest was deposited in the U.K. and the U.S., and the remainder in other European countries and banks.

Other Less Developed Countries. Brazil and Mexico were again able to cover about half their current deficits (which may have approached $3 billion) from Eurocredits. Each also received loans from the World Bank, but most of the remaining deficit was covered by direct foreign investment, export credits, and, for Brazil, a reduction of about $1 billion in its reserves. South Korea, Taiwan, and most of Latin America (except Chile) continued to use market financing but also received official aid. Argentina, in addition, used about $1 billion of its reserves. Egypt and the Philippines, which had used international loans in 1974, turned increasingly to official borrowing in 1975. Egypt was the main recipient of OPEC aid. The other Middle Eastern countries, notably Jordan and Syria, also relied mainly on OPEC. India, Pakistan, Bangladesh, and Sri Lanka used aid from OPEC, as well as international aid and bilateral aid from the OECD.

Official Reserves. Reserves were not a common method of financing deficits in 1974 or 1975, being totally inadequate compared with the increased cost of oil. Most industrial countries could attract financial deposits either directly from OPEC or from others that could. For the less developed countries, reserves remained essential for smoothing normal export and import fluctuations; in spite of the increase in their reserves in the early 1970s when commodity prices rose ($15 billion from 1970 to 1973), by the end of 1975 reserves of the less developed countries were less adequate for this purpose (Table XXI). From 1970 to 1975, the import prices of these nations more than doubled; when corrected for this change, their reserves did not rise but instead fell from 30 to 25% of their imports. The real value of the developed countries' reserves fell even faster, but these countries were less vulnerable to trade fluctuations and used their reserves mainly for marginal foreign exchange interventions. The only countries for which the decline was a problem were those where such intervention had been extensive, the U.K. and Japan.

Total reserves rose less than in 1974 and their real value continued to fall (Table XXII), but there was little change in their relation to trade. This remained lower than in 1970, but the change to floating rates by the major trading countries probably made the aggregate figure less significant than reserves of the less developed countries. There were slight declines in the shares of dollar and sterling holdings.

Interest Rates and Exchange Rates. Interest rates generally fell in the first half of 1975 (Chart 7), particularly for continental Europe. Although the U.S. rate was relatively low early in the year, by early summer it began to rise. The rate in the U.K. was among the highest, fell less, and then rose with the U.S. rate. The relative rates show the Japanese, British, and West German attempts to manage their currencies. In general, however, the spread among the levels and movements was reduced from the confusion of early 1974, reflecting the relaxation of capital controls (particularly by the U.S. in early 1974) and the adjustment to this and to the oil surpluses.

CHART 7.

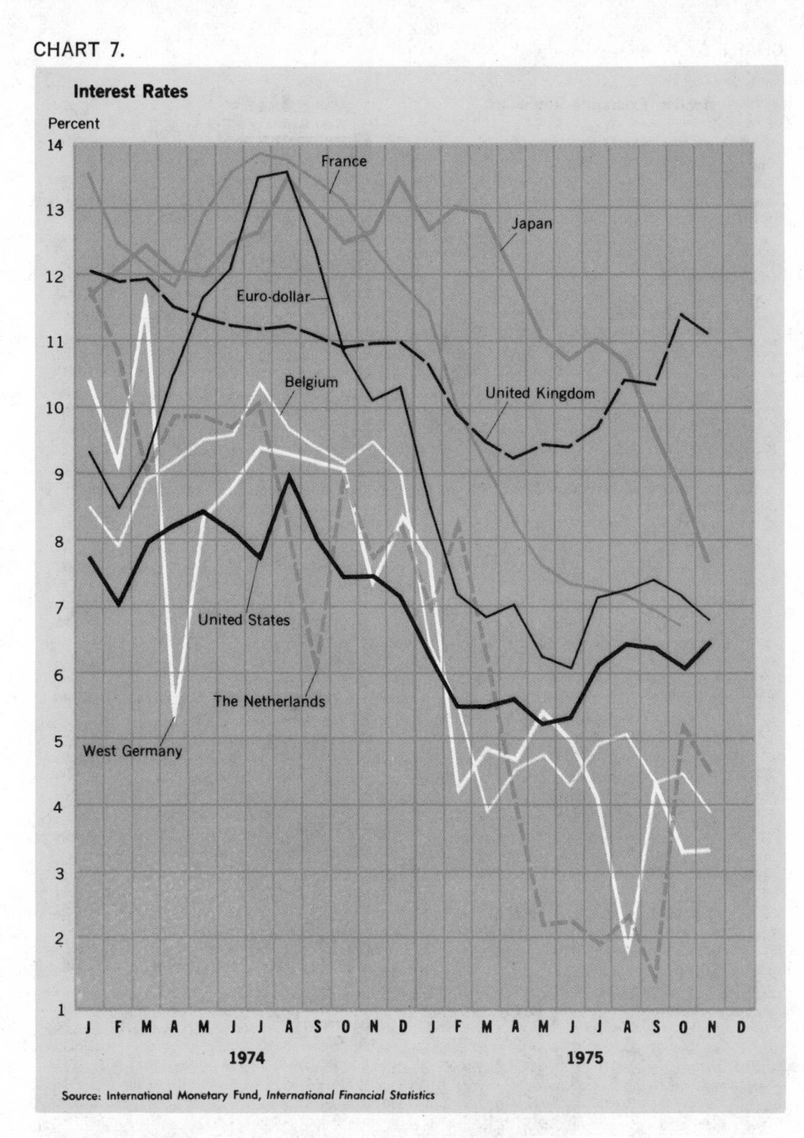

Source: International Monetary Fund, *International Financial Statistics*

The major exchange rates continued to float, with changes reflecting relative price movements. In November it was agreed that the principal central banks would cooperate to smooth temporary fluctuations, but the agreement merely formalized existing cooperation. Attempts to manage rates were not very successful except by Japan and within the EEC joint float, where all members were committed and known to be committed to using their reserves to hold the

Table XXII. World Reserves
End of period

	1970	1971	1972	1973	1974	1975*
Total reserves (U.S. $000,000)	93,631	131,715	159,428	184,104	220,948	224,680
Composition (percentages)						
Gold	39.8	29.8	24.4	23.5	19.8	18.5
Special Drawing Rights	3.3	4.8	5.9	5.8	4.9	4.5
Reserve position in IMF	8.2	5.2	4.3	4.0	4.9	6.1
United States dollars	25.4	38.4	38.6	36.3	34.7	33.6
Sterling	6.1	6.0	5.5	4.3	4.6	4.1
Other foreign exchange	17.2	15.7	21.3	26.2	31.1	33.2
Value at constant export prices (U.S. $000,000; 1970)	93,631	125,443	138,633	131,503	112,156	100,304
Value in relation to world exports (percentage)	33.2	41.6	42.3	35.1	28.4	28.3

*Estimates.
Sources: International Monetary Fund, *International Financial Statistics;* world export price index; UN, *Monthly Bulletin of Statistics.*

CHART 8.

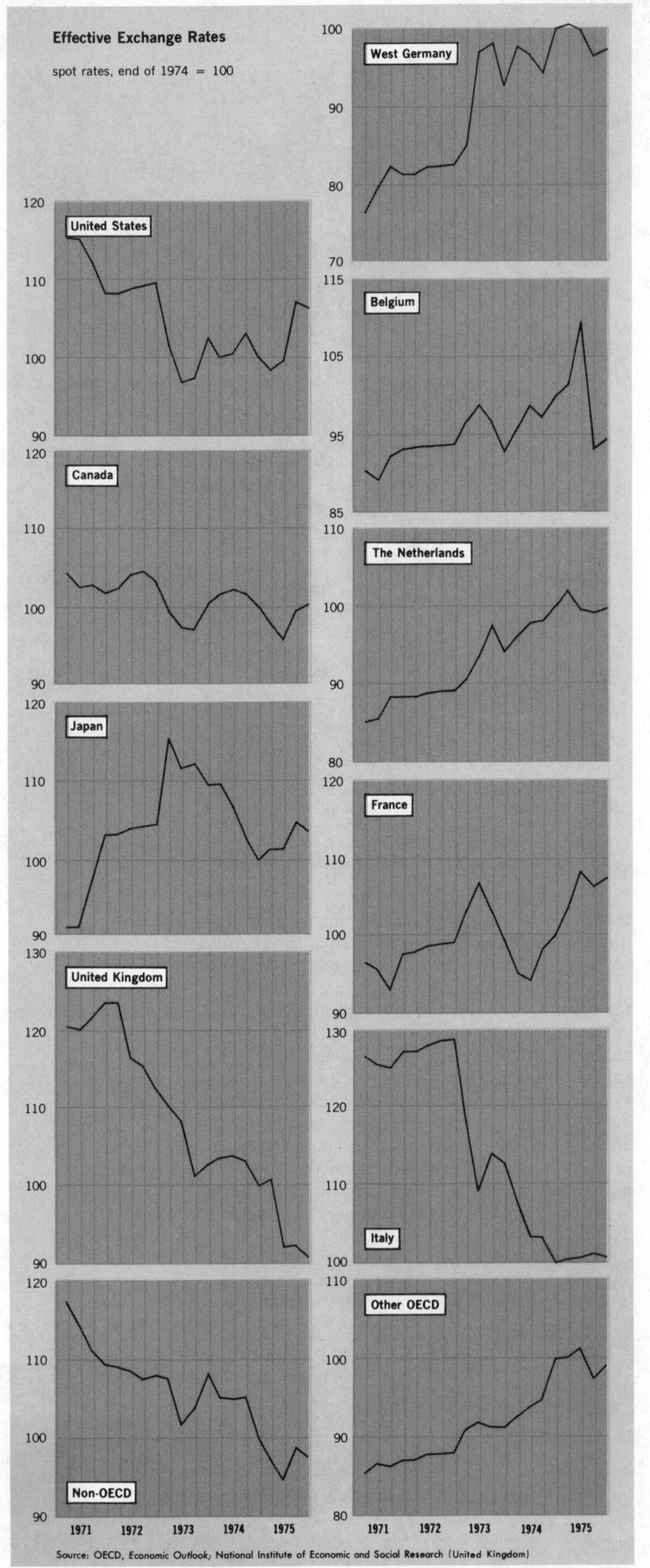

Source: OECD, *Economic Outlook;* National Institute of Economic and Social Research (United Kingdom)

relative rates. Except for a few oil producers and India, which switched to the SDR or other multicurrency units, nonindustrial countries maintained fixed rates with the dollar, pound, or franc.

The European exchange rates continued to fluctuate widely against the dollar but not among themselves, and after dollar interest rates came into line with the rest relative movements were smaller. Although floating still failed to ensure stable markets, the structure of rates at the end of 1975 was probably less distorted than at the end of 1974 and in early 1975. The dollar fell in the first quarter of 1975, but then rose by more except against the French franc. Its weighted, or effective, rate (Chart 8) fell only slightly and at the end of the year had recovered from an undervaluation that had persisted since floating began in 1973. The yen rose against the dollar in the first half of 1975, but fell after the dollar rose; the effective rate remained at average 1974 levels.

The largest major currency fall was by the pound. The effective fall, over 10%, was probably greater than can be explained by higher inflation; its decline against the dollar was more than twice as large. The French franc rose in the first half of 1975, permitting it to rejoin the EEC joint float in July, while the West German mark and the smaller countries' rates, particularly the Belgian franc, fell in the second half of the year. After two years of large declines, the Italian lira was finally stable and moved closely with the other European currencies. The Swiss franc moved with the others in the first half of 1975 but later did not fall as rapidly against the dollar.

Devaluations became increasingly common among the oil-importing less developed countries, especially among dollar-tied ones after the dollar recovered. Including some revaluing oil producers, there was little change for all non-OECD countries; oil importers may have devalued by 5%. This decline is low for countries with large deficits and high inflation. Their heavy foreign currency liabilities may have discouraged devaluation, which increases the cost of the liabilities and the interest on them.

In spite of the currency fluctuations, there was no shift to gold or bonds in multicurrency units. The price of gold fell sharply in January after the low demand when the U.S. Treasury auctioned part of its holdings; the decline continued through the year, balancing the rise during 1974. With no change in the average price between the two years, its real value fell. The agreement that the IMF should sell part of its holdings, using the difference between the official and selling prices to establish an aid fund, depressed the market as sales could equal several years' production. Multicurrency units—the SDR, European unit of account, and others—accounted for only about 5% of international bonds. There was a shift from dollars to marks (and to the Netherlands guilder when restrictions on capital were lifted in May) in the summer and then back to dollars while the West German markets were closed, but the stable level of borrowing indicated no general loss of confidence in currencies.

The IMF efforts to regulate floating or to increase the stability of exchange rates made no progress. The only reforms on which agreements were reached were the sale of gold and a revision in IMF quotas that determined voting rights as well as contributions and borrowing rights in order to give an increased share to the oil producers. Neither measure was implemented during the year. (SHEILA A. B. PAGE)

[533; 534; 535; 536; 537]

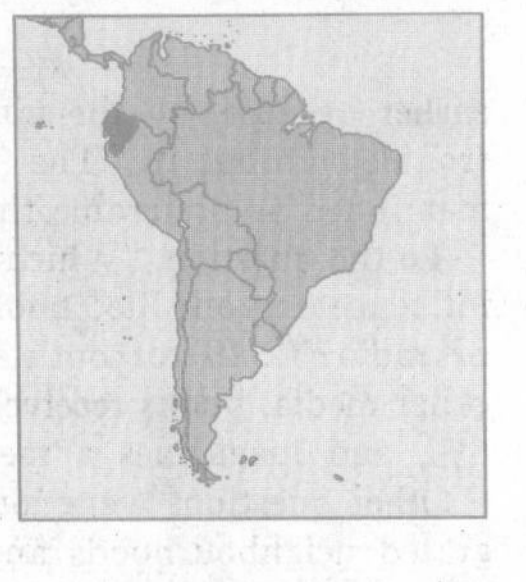

Ecuador

A republic on the west coast of South America, Ecuador is bounded by Colombia, Peru, and the Pacific Ocean. Area: 109,484 sq.mi. (283,561 sq.km.), including the Galápagos Islands (3,075 sq.mi.), which is an insular province. Pop. (1974 census): 6,552,100. Cap.: Quito (pop., 1974, 597,100). Largest city: Guayaquil (pop., 1974, 814,100). Language: Spanish, but Indians speak Quechuan and Jivaroan. Religion: mainly Roman Catholic. President in 1975, Brig. Gen. Guillermo Rodríguez Lara.

General discontent, arising from the inadequacy of the agrarian reform program and the high rate of inflation (30% in 1974, compared with 20.6% in 1973), finally erupted in an unsuccessful coup d'etat on Sept. 1, 1975. Pressure for a return to civilian rule was temporarily checked and Brig. Gen. Rodríguez remained in control as president.

The main economic feature of 1975 was the decline in petroleum revenues. High prices combined with a lack of storage facilities and damage to the trans-Andean pipeline resulted in a sharp drop in foreign exchange reserves and a weakening in the balance of payments position. In an attempt to alleviate the situation export prices of crude petroleum to the U.S. were lowered in July, and a 30% surcharge was imposed on luxury imports in September. Meanwhile, sales of petroleum were arranged with both Chile and Peru, and the government granted a contract to the Northwest Pipeline Corp. of the U.S. for oil and gas exploration in the Gulf of Guayaquil.

Top priority, however, was given to industrial expansion, with fishing (including the enforcement of the 200-mi. limit), petrochemicals, cement, pharmaceuticals, and, more recently, steel the main areas of development. To support this industrial platform the government strengthened the infrastructure, largely with the aid of international loans; $80 million was to be invested in electric power development in 1975 alone. Other projects included rural development plans, irrigation schemes in the provinces of Cotopaxi and Manabí and the Daule-Peripa Dam, and the building of a Quito–Guayaquil expressway.

(PRUDENCE JUDD)

[974.D.1]

ECUADOR

Education. (1972–73) Primary, pupils 1,117,569, teachers 28,885; secondary, vocational, and teacher training, pupils 268,388, teachers 15,099; higher, students 43,743, teaching staff (1970–71) 2,867.

Finance. Monetary unit: sucre, with (Sept. 22, 1975) an official rate of 25 sucres to U.S. $1 (free rate of 51.79 sucres = £1 sterling). Gold, SDRs, and foreign exchange, central bank: (June 1975) U.S. $242.8 million; (June 1974) U.S. $437.6 million. Budget (1974 est.) balanced at 11.2 billion sucres. Gross national product: (1973) 62,350,000,000 sucres; (1972) 45,910,000,000 sucres. Money supply: (Dec. 1974) 13,064,000,000 sucres; (Dec. 1973) 9,568,000,000 sucres. Cost of living (Quito; 1970 = 100): (April 1975) 187; (April 1974) 164.

Foreign Trade. Imports (1974): U.S. $948.2 million; exports U.S. $1,061,600,000. Import sources (1973): U.S. 34%; Japan 14%; West Germany 12%; Colombia 6%; U.K. 6%. Export destinations (1973): U.S. 32%; Trinidad and Tobago 12%; Panama 9%; Peru 6%; Netherlands Antilles 6%; West Germany 5%. Main exports: crude oil 58%; bananas 12%; cocoa 10%; coffee 6%.

Transport and Communications. Roads (1972) 18,345 km. (including 1,392 km. Pan-American Highway). Motor vehicles in use (1972): passenger 33,000; commercial (including buses) 51,500. Railways (1972): 1,071 km.; traffic 63 million passenger-km., freight 43 million net ton-km. Air traffic (1973): 220 million passenger-km.; freight 9.9 million net ton-km. Telephones (Dec. 1973) 131,000. Radio receivers (Dec. 1971) 1.7 million. Television receivers (Dec. 1971) 280,000.

Agriculture. Production (in 000; metric tons; 1974; 1973 in parentheses): barley *c.* 57 (*c.* 79); corn (1973) *c.* 230, (1972) *c.* 264; potatoes *c.* 441 (*c.* 539); rice (1973) *c.* 152, (1972) *c.* 171; cassava (1973) *c.* 370, (1972) *c.* 377; cabbages (1973) *c.* 70, (1972) *c.* 62; dry beans *c.* 38 (*c.* 30); sugar, raw value *c.* 292 (*c.* 283); bananas (1973) *c.* 3,000, (1972) *c.* 3,100; coffee *c.* 55 (*c.* 52); cocoa *c.* 60 (*c.* 54); pineapples (1973) *c.* 75, (1972) *c.* 73; oranges (1973) *c.* 170, (1972) *c.* 153. Livestock (in 000; 1974): cattle *c.* 2,690; sheep *c.* 2,060; pigs *c.* 1,440; horses *c.* 260; chickens (1973) *c.* 8,200.

Industry. Production (in 000; metric tons; 1973): petroleum products 1,405; crude oil (1974) 8,636; electricity (kw-hr.; 1972) 1,117,000; cement (1972) 482; gold (troy oz.) 10.4; silver (troy oz.; 1972) *c.* 60.

AID/AUTHENTICATED NEWS INTERNATIONAL

Modern U.S. AID-financed tractors have prepared more land for production and have led to the establishment of agricultural cooperatives in Ecuador.

Education

Education in most parts of the world was seriously affected by the world recession in 1975. In many developed countries the expansion of educational services was brought to a standstill. In the United Kingdom a moratorium was officially announced for education budgets from 1976 for at least the following three to four years, though before this took place teachers in the U.K. had received an unprecedented average raise of 30% in their salaries. The only growth areas in the U.K. were training for specific industrial skills and payments to relieve the plight of unemployed dropouts, whose number increased sharply during the summer. The British plan, following French and Canadian precedents, was for a payment of £5 a week for 26 weeks to any employer who would take on an unemployed dropout. Budgets were also restricted in Western European countries, notably West Germany, The Netherlands, and Finland.

The effects of the economic crisis caused by the escalation in oil prices were probably most severely experienced in India, which virtually abandoned its five-year plan for educational advance. Nonetheless, claims were still made by some Indian government officials that there was progress in enrollments; but most observers believed that educational provision—low as it was—was probably declining. Even in Australia, whose federal government had embarked on

Ecumenical Movement: *see* Religion

YOUTH AND EDUCATION

The opinions held by American junior high school students on a wide variety of topics were solicited in 1975 by the Encyclopædia Britannica Educational Corp. The poll covered more than a thousand students in classrooms throughout the United States. The results, in the words of Ross Sackett, president of the company, dispute "a general, if somewhat vague belief, among many of the older generation, that today's teenagers belittle marriage, that college education is now of less importance, and that parental guidance and influence have diminished."

Of the students polled, 59% said they believed in marriage as an institution and that it would be as important in the year 2000 as it is now. Notably, the percentage of affirmative replies was considerably higher among girls (66%) than among boys (52%).

Asked whether they thought a college education was important in getting a job, 84% replied that they did—although, as one said, "This, of course, depends on the job."

And an overwhelming 91% answered in the affirmative when asked if they had felt close to their parents and their home during their growing-up years and whether their parents were an important influence in their lives.

Other replies were equally revealing. Not only did the students believe in marriage, but a majority of them did not think future population should be restricted. Assuming that families were limited, two was mentioned most frequently as the optimum number of children.

In replying to the question "Is sex education taught in your junior high school?" (53% said that it was), one ninth-grade boy indicated he believed it should be taught earlier because, by the ninth grade, "you can be in big trouble without it." The sixth and seventh grades were mentioned as preferable times.

To the question, "Which do you think has had the most influence on your life: books, newspapers, magazines, TV, or radio?" 58% of both sexes named television. Of the other media, books received 19%, radio 12%, newspapers 6%, and magazines a mere 3%.

Other questions were concerned with attitudes on integrated neighbourhoods and forced busing. The vote on integrated neighbourhoods was almost evenly split, with the boys expressing a little more opposition. As to forced busing, however, both girls and boys opposed it by about 9 to 1.

A majority were in favour of the information given out on drugs, alcohol, and smoking. Many, especially the boys, thought there should be even more facts available. These same students were overwhelmingly interested in medical advice on such specific problems as cholesterol and prevention of venereal disease as well as more general facts about diet.

Less than a third answered the question "Do you have a particular hero?" and there was no agreement among those that did. No one mentioned Gerald Ford, Henry Kissinger, Robert Redford, Jackie Onassis, or John Denver. Some mentioned Winston Churchill and quite a few girls named Jennie Churchill—reflecting, in all likelihood, the influence of a current television series dramatizing her life. Some cited their junior high school teachers, past and present, and two mentioned their fathers. One concluded: "My parents are heroes to me because some day I hope I will be as happily married as they are and so deeply concerned about my children and their well being."

an ambitious educational program, cuts in real terms were made in higher education and in the schools by the federal government.

The educational system in the United States was largely in a holding pattern. The federal courts continued desegregation actions started long ago. The U.S. Department of Justice had very few suits under way to eliminate segregation. Public support for federally forced integration efforts reached its lowest level since the mid-1960s—one of several indices of a generally conservative climate among old and young alike. College students protested mildly in some places—about personal matters like finances and instructional quality. How to pay for education amid spiraling inflation boggled the minds of experts and the average citizen alike.

School enrollments dipped, but the U.S. experienced a miniboom in births and the world's population was estimated at 4,000,000,000. U.S. Commissioner of Education Terrell H. Bell estimated 1975–76 school-year enrollments would total 58.9 million persons in regular kindergarten through collegiate programs. The total included 34 million in elementary grades, 15.6 million in secondary grades, and 9.3 million in collegiate degree-granting programs. Costs of operating private and public educational institutions at all levels rose to $119 billion, an increase of $11 billion over 1974. Bell estimated that there were 3.1 million classroom teachers and another 300,000 employed as superintendents or principals and in other instructional roles. Some 650,000 people staffed the colleges. Bell's analysis at the opening of the school year noted that three of every ten Americans were directly involved in education.

The U.S. Congress passed a $7.9 billion elementary-secondary-collegiate bill—more than $1.5 billion larger than the Ford administration's request. President Ford then used his 35th veto, and Congress overrode it. Hearings were held on the renewal of the Higher Education Act. Learning that more teachers were being prepared than could secure teaching jobs, some congressional leaders talked about cutting many of the act's education personnel development provisions. Educators continued to emphasize that current staffing situations offered opportunities to decrease class sizes and to diversify needed educational offerings. The production of doctorates again outstripped demands for college professors. John E. Ryor, the National Education Association's new president, lashed out against local budget cuts for education, an issue on which the NEA and the American Federation of Teachers (AFT) agreed. He cited a study showing that 39.2% of schools surveyed were increasing class size, 42% reducing purchase of school supplies, 28% cutting some programs altogether, 25.9% decreasing special subjects, and 17% cutting some extracurricular activities.

Efforts were continued to develop alternatives to traditional approaches to education and evaluate effectiveness of experiments. The U.S. General Accounting Office reported to Congress that the advantages of Project Head Start may wane by the third grade unless special services are continued for the program's disadvantaged learners. Some $3,160,000,000 had been spent on Head Start since its inception in 1965. In another effort to offer options the National Institute of Education (NIE) awarded $597,000 for planning grants in Connecticut and New Hampshire to help set up voucher systems. The plan would enable parents to select the private or public school of their choice and presumably would stimulate schools to become more attractive to prospective consumers. The National Association of Secondary School Principals wanted students to have more choice in selecting learning programs. Addressing prominent educators, Commissioner Bell urged the American Association of School Administrators to build an effective home-school partnership to combat the nation's materialism, rootlessness, and reckless search for thrills.

A new secretary of the U.S. Department of Health, Education, and Welfare (HEW) and the director of the National Institute of Education were selected from the academic community and received ready acceptance. Appointed to the HEW post was University of Alabama president and noted historian F. David Mathews. Mathews played down what he as one person could do in the most sprawling and expensive ($120 billion) of federal agencies. Harold Hodgkinson of the University of California at Berkeley became the second regular director of the financially troubled NIE, which had been unable to convince Congress to appropriate funds approaching original legislative intent. Adding to hopes that NIE might be settling down was the appointment of John Corbally, president of the University of Illinois, to head the NIE's policy council.

Nursery and Primary Education. There was evidence in several countries of continuing concern about levels of attainment, notably in reading. In Victoria, Australia, for example, a report based on five years of research demonstrated that reading standards of children in Australian elementary schools were lower on average than those in the United States. Some blamed television for this, a survey in Sydney having shown that children viewed television for 5½ hours a day on the average.

An official report produced in England, *A Language for Life*—one of the most significant reports to appear anywhere in 1975—also arose out of a concern for reading standards. It had been suggested that reading standards had been in decline in England for ten years. The conclusions of the report (known as the Bullock Report after the chairman of the committee of inquiry, Sir Alan Bullock) were, however, that standards had gone down very little, if at all, for 15-year-olds and 11-year-olds, though the evidence was less certain for 7-year-olds. The report revealed that young children spend an average of 25 hours a week watching television in England, but it did not attach major importance to this. What had to be done was to teach reading in a more organized way. The report made a large number of specific recommendations for improving reading standards. Particular stress was put on training teachers. In the teachers' course at least 100 hours should be spent on studying the teaching of reading. One of the report's most significant assertions was the fact that there existed a respectable body of knowledge about reading and that it should form part of every teacher's education.

In Italy, following the election of new Socialist/Communist local administrations, there was evidence of changes in educational policy. In Turin, for example, it was announced that the former morning-only elementary school would be turned into full-time schooling and there would be free school lunches. It was recognized in a number of less developed countries that free school lunches were vital to the development of primary education. In Saudi Arabia progress continued to be made in the development of a novel school meal in the form of a highly nutritious biscuit. In Egypt the minister of education declared that priority should be given to the provision of a school meal for primary schools; otherwise there seemed little prospect of improving on the 40% dropout rate in Egyptian elementary schools by the age of 12. An even poorer dropout rate was reported from Brazil, but again there was evidence that where a school lunch program was operated improvements in school attendance were dramatic. Unhappily, countries with a massive defense expenditure (like Egypt) found it impossible to invest more in education (the percentage of the gross national product taken by education in Egypt was as low as 3%). In North Vietnam, on the other hand, when the war had been over for several months a change in educational policy was announced to make education almost free for the five million children at school. The parental contribution was reduced to about $1 a year per child.

In the developed countries arguments continued on the size of classes appropriate to primary schools. In the U.K. at the annual conference of the Labour Party in September 1975, the conference, quite contrary to the wishes of the Labour government, resolved that classes should be reduced to no more than 25 by 1980. Similarly, French teachers' unions demanded that classes be reduced to this figure, though this was immediately rejected by the minister of education. The average teacher-pupil ratio in French nursery schools was 1 to 40, and proposals were made by the government to bring in "education helpers" to relieve the burden. The teachers' unions, however, opposed this except where helpers might be employed outside of school hours.

The attitudes of teachers' unions no doubt had a good deal to do with the fact that the supply of teachers in 1975 was in most countries beginning to exceed the demand. There were some exceptions to this, however, notably in the Soviet Union where, for demographic reasons, there were chronic shortages of teachers in some regions.

Elementary and Secondary Education. A major document of government policy in 1975 came from The Netherlands and was compiled by Jos van Kemenade, Dutch education minister. Entitled *The Future Educational Order,* it covered the whole educational spectrum, but in its most radical aspects concerned the secondary stage. The Dutch report concerned education for the next 25 years and aimed to raise the school-leaving age from 16 to 18 by 1985, giving everyone 14 years of compulsory education.

The pattern of schooling was seen first as basic schools for the age group 4–12, middle schools for the group 12–16, and then upper schools for the group 16–19. There would be no examination at 12, and thus the middle schools would be comprehensive. In the upper schools pupils would go into a two-year theoretical stream giving access to higher education, or a three-year or two-year vocational stream.

In Italy, too, there was widespread discussion of comprehensive schooling and particularly of the form that an extended secondary education—from age 14 to 16—should take: whether it should be vocational or general. Both the Socialists and the Christian Democrats favoured the alternative of general education in the bills they presented for consideration to the Italian Chamber of Deputies.

In the French National Assembly a bill was finally passed for reforming the educational system up to university entrance. The legislation had been debated over a long period and received a hostile reception from many teachers and students on the ground that it was vague and reactionary. The main practical objective of the reform was to recast the all-important graduation examination in France, the *baccalauréat* (taken at age 18 or 19), into a more flexible form.

This reform was the latest in a line of successive changes that followed the student uprising of 1968 in France. Another consequence of the 1968 incidents was to change the form of government in schools, particularly secondary schools. This movement toward more parent and student participation also manifested itself in other countries. In February 1975 the first school council elections took place in Italy. These councils were intended to involve teaching staff, parents, and pupils in the day-to-day operation of schools. A surprisingly high proportion of parents and pupils took part in the elections. In England demands for participation in school government led to the setting up by the government of a committee of inquiry into the government and management of schools in England and Wales (the Taylor Committee). In Sweden the demand by teachers that they should be in the majority on school management committees was one of the principal areas of contention over the government proposals known as SIA (Internal Work in Schools), which were expected to become law during the spring of 1976.

As elementary-secondary schools opened in the U.S. in September, newspaper headlines were concerned with court-ordered busing in Boston and Louisville, Ky., and teacher strikes that kept some two million students from attending opening classes. After massive law enforcement assured parents that peace would be maintained, enrollments in Boston and Louisville climbed steadily. Groups in Kanawha County, W.Va., tried again to fire up interest in the "godless books" issue, but met with little success.

The number of teacher strikes in the U.S. was the largest ever. There were more than 80 teacher strikes during the opening month of the 1975–76 school year. Some 85,000 teachers were on strike in major cities such as New York and Chicago, and in a dozen states.

National Teacher of the Year for 1975, Robert G. Heyer, a science teacher in St. Paul, Minnesota, receives a crystal apple from Pres. Gerald Ford at the White House. The Teacher of the Year awards are sponsored by the Encyclopædia Britannica Companies, the Council of Chief State School Officers, and the "Ladies Home Journal," which presented a feature article on the winner in its June issue.

WIDE WORLD

Demands for better salaries and working conditions triggered the strikes.

The cliff-hanging odds that New York City would default on its financial obligations provided a dramatic proof of the power and financial position of the American Federation of Teachers. Its increasingly powerful president, Albert Shanker, as president of New York City's United Federation of Teachers, agreed to float a $150 million loan to the city. (*See* United States: *Special Report.*) The new president of the rival National Education Association set national collective bargaining legislation as his major goal. Ryor, a Michigan mathematics teacher, did not want his group to be a part of the labour movement. AFT's Shanker, on the other hand, was a major union leader in his own right, a member of the influential AFL-CIO Executive Committee.

Higher Education. Higher education budgets in most countries were trimmed in 1975, particularly in the area of research. Research projects tended to shift from major scientific matters to current problems; for example, new sources of energy and pollution control. There was also more emphasis on the improvement of teaching in higher education. At a Council of Europe symposium of 13 countries in Göteborg, Sweden, it was proposed that some form of assessment of lecturers' teaching ability should be made by students and fellow lecturers. In Western Europe the containment of higher education expenditure was made more difficult by the established tradition that all who had passed the final school-leaving examination (for example the *baccalauréat* in France and the *Abitur* in West Germany) should be allowed to enter a university. In practice it became impossible to allow unhindered entry, and various means were devised to select university students. In Sweden this was done by fixing nationally a certain level of marks, depending on the demand for places as against the supply. In both The Netherlands and West Germany a lottery plan was proposed—a complicated system in which applicants whose marks fell below a certain level would be chosen by chance. In West Germany restrictions were placed on the numbers of students accepted from outside the European Economic Community. This affected chiefly would-be students from Egypt, Iran, and Indonesia.

In France a new post of secretary of state for universities was created, first occupied by Jean-Pierre Soisson. Soisson stated that the *baccalauréat* would assure university entry, but at the same time he accepted that some restriction was inevitable. In 1975 the first products of the new diploma of general university studies (DEUG) emerged from the universities. This was after a two-year course, which would normally be followed by a one-year course leading to the *Licence* and, after a further year, to the master's degree. Similar attempts to introduce more flexibility into the university pattern had been introduced in the previous year in England with the diploma in higher education, again a two-year course though intended to be operated outside the universities.

There was evidence that standards of entry were rising in most European countries. A notable exception was Portugal, where the changes in the social order and the dominance of the revolutionary left in the universities had greatly disrupted university studies. In Brazil there was a quite different social context. The reforms in the universities in 1971 had led to a doubling of the university intake and a great lowering of standards and high dropout rates.

World Education

Most recent official data

Country	1st level (primary) Students (full-time)	1st level Teachers (full-time)	1st level Total schools	General 2nd level (secondary) Students (full-time)	General 2nd level Teachers (full-time)	General 2nd level Total schools	Vocational 2nd level Students (full-time)	Vocational 2nd level Teachers (full-time)	Vocational 2nd level Total schools	3rd level (higher) Students (full-time)	3rd level Teachers (full-time)	3rd level Total schools	Literacy % of population	Literacy Over age
Afghanistan	620,576	16,022	3,226	160,895	7,317	716	9,331	868	33	11,695	1,498	22	8.0	15
Albania	555,300	18,944	1,374	32,867	7,157	46	50,072	1,205	85	25,500	926	5	71.0	9
Algeria	2,435,365	60,179	7,794	406,565	15,340	524	23,454	1,316	46	35,887	4,041	15	26.4	15
Angola	536,599	13,230	5,585	59,209	3,060	177	15,845	1,154	99	2,942	274	1	30.0	...
Argentina	3,508,406	189,456	20,648	422,652	59,521	1,720	703,063	88,962	2,695	423,824	38,964	788	91.4	15
Australia	1,811,027	70,911	8,133	1,042,384	65,211	2,265	...	...	...	144,557	12,026*	113	...	...
Austria	540,732	61,093	5,920	607,033	†	†	267,426	14,517	995	84,349	10,607*	35	98.0	15
Bangladesh	7,750,000‡	155,023‡	36,165‡	1,955,200	80,500	8,083	7,373‡	616‡	53‡	27,940‡	1,532‡	12‡	22.7	15
Bolivia	748,506	27,046	8,887	86,365	4,116	383	8,114	1,060	80	37,692	3,026	16	39.8	15
Botswana	103,711	3,047	316	10,308	492	15	1,532	201	21	238	40	2	19.3	15
Brazil	20,135,898	837,268	186,563	688,988	142,654	5,690	788,662	...	...	772,800	77,951	...	79.8	15
Brunei	30,652	1,478	134	12,127	720	25	532	60	4	—	—	—	64.0	15
Bulgaria	996,949	49,929	3,567	116,789	7,530	328	292,779	19,009	557	124,662	10,805	49	91.4	8
Burma	3,198,670	71,136	18,299	813,144	25,461	1,748	8,735	756	35	54,502	3,827	20	68.3	8
Cambodia	429,110	18,794	1,021	98,888	2,266‡	79	5,409	220	73	11,570	276	35	36.1	...
Cameroon	754,101	14,703	3,450	65,360	2,719	191	21,547	961	134	3,559	322	11	12.0	...
Canada	3,779,900	269,200	16,000	1,885,100	†	†	...	...	...	543,250	45,700	272	95.4	14
Chile	2,332,720	67,963	8,478	290,408	18,049	587	162,048	...	288	76,979	...	32	89.1	10
China	90,000,000	...	...	8,520,000	...	...	1,470,000	...	...	820,000	...	...	40.0	...
Colombia	3,791,543	115,310	32,230	1,003,492	49,931	3,252	227,582	13,257	913	178,761	18,152	89	78.5	15
Congo	277,386	4,373	940	49,984	948	67	4,899	354	31	2,098	194	2	28.8	...
Costa Rica	356,171	12,109	2,530	78,224	...	121	7,679	462	19	17,366	1,275	5	84.7	15
Cuba	1,899,266	75,921	15,561	265,589	21,475	563	83,095	7,450	137	55,435	...	4	...	...
Czechoslovakia	1,890,081	96,781	10,247	119,563	7,829	339	560,572	26,900	1,548	108,646	16,697	44	98.5	15
Denmark	554,578	49,014	2,474	279,183	54,318	1,336	112,159	...	154	85,284	6,045	60	100.0	15
Dominican Republic	820,215	14,752	4,916	122,565	2,131	933	7,544	460	8	19,336	1,038	...	67.3	15
Ecuador	1,117,569	28,885	8,277	268,388	15,099	873	...	...	...	43,743	...	15	67.5	...
Egypt	3,873,297	99,351	8,415	1,268,060	44,197	1,705	289,812	14,300	261	241,690	5,378	106	26.3	14
El Salvador	509,985	13,919	2,787	60,870	3,531§	300	27,437	§	114	9,615	751	9	49.0	...
Fiji	133,890	4,147	759	23,780	993	95	1,895	183	26	1,031	145	1	72.7	15
Finland	393,242	21,248	4,449	405,203	17,536	1,049	111,776	11,212	748	67,881	4,940	27	100	15
France	5,662,089	255,919‖	59,967	2,028,887	173,934‡	6,282	1,212,424	69,501	4,478	773,669	38,000‡	278	100	7
Germany, East	2,608,074	151,989†	5,042	51,609	†	288	431,963	14,692	1,035	145,717	17,015	54	100	15
Germany, West	6,499,824	217,839	18,561	2,872,195	134,970	7,865	2,246,315	54,372	6,061	729,207	68,286	288	99.9	10
Greece	913,972	28,424	9,736	490,867	14,935	1,111	123,081	...	...	91,309	4,614	...	85.8	10
Guatemala	585,015	16,451	5,902	86,215	5,934	493	15,810	1,380	...	21,715	1,314	5	36.7	15
Honduras	415,851	11,354	4,245	33,392	2,516	110	7,089	2,689	13	9,204	533	4	47.3	15
Hong Kong	677,421	21,059	1,078	317,799	11,143§	309	20,601	§	39	18,200	1,863	17	80.9	...
Hungary	1,039,586	65,687	4,736	102,079	6,700	290	110,608	7,345	248	60,059	11,305	47	98.2	15
India	78,000,000	1,602,515	404,418	8,600,000§	538,684§	124,360	§	§	§	2,540,000	119,000	3,721	33.3	15
Indonesia	11,907,979	394,365	61,916	1,492,921	102,781	6,666	612,933	65,719	3,731	136,467	...	148	58.1	10
Iran	3,445,528	111,032	28,357	942,523	27,085	2,425	82,803	3,452	365	115,311	4,128	156	22.8	15
Iraq	1,523,955	57,621	6,194	457,763	16,862	1,133	29,572	1,814	82	70,247	2,440	50	36.1	15
Ireland	545,439	16,973	3,899	237,740	9,904	847	3,939	216	72	29,642	1,455	65	100	15
Israel	552,338	28,297	1,877	76,953	6,344	346	72,641	5,434	359	81,079	...	...	91.7♀	14♀
Italy	4,968,900	245,900	35,080	1,190,656	245,628	8,868	1,894,831	249,031	6,639	802,603	44,622	77	90.7	...
Ivory Coast	556,689	12,216	2,377	83,456	2,804	115	3,284δ	130δ	12δ	4,699	...	2	20.0	...
Japan	9,816,536	392,793	24,592	7,153,337	445,388	14,070	1,561,580	...	1,413	1,926,108	102,396	977	99.9	15
Jordan	371,631	10,418	1,132	137,832	6,334	906	5,494	335	10	9,302	493	18	43.8	15
Kenya	1,816,017	56,543	6,932	174,767	7,388	902	3,525*	237*	11*	8,177	...	4	43.0	15
Korea, South	5,599,074	108,126	6,367	2,674,972	67,332	2,640	451,032	15,340	479	286,142	13,885	191	88.5	13
Kuwait	94,087	5,033	162	88,922	7,283	176	3,034	488	9	3,339	152	5	61.0	10
Laos	273,357	7,320	2,125	14,633	613	37	5,977	413	27	625	106	3	58.8	...
Lebanon	497,723	32,901†	2,319	167,578	†	1,241	7,836‡	...	159	50,803	2,313	13	88.0	...
Lesotho	187,459	3,951	1,087	12,559	551	56	553	86	9	446	61	1	56.5	15
Liberia	149,687	4,111	843	26,426	1,015	275	1,511	...	6	2,214	...	3	21.5	15
Libya	538,070	24,424	2,121	107,577	8,074	523	22,429	1,779	100	12,162	596	16	52.4	15
Luxembourg	35,589	1,691	472	8,214	739	12	9,631	874	44	341	11	2	100	15
Malawi	611,678	10,524	2,091	13,900	694	59	1,812	141	14	1,146	101	3	16.5	15
Malaysia	1,834,390	57,378	6,355	790,358	28,575	1,193	22,466	1,084	85	28,002	2,081	21	60.8	10
Mali	229,879	6,614	873	3,507	290	10	4,937	424	24	731	151	4	2.2	...
Mauritius	152,417	5,568	240	60,441	1,921	125	1,212	83	10	1,341	84	2	61.6	12
Mexico	9,127,226	182,454	46,010	1,008,205	71,057	4,530	419,251	30,540	1,107	247,637	17,103	374	76.2	9
Morocco	1,337,931	37,585	1,609	361,725	23,701	...	2,567δ	120δ	...	20,055	620	...	22.2	...
Mozambique	496,381	6,607	4,095	17,831	1,150	96	2,754	292	25	1,145	213	9	7.0	...
Nepal	478,743	11,490	7,260	257,245	3,334	1,041	365δ	19δ	...	25,000	1,070	49	12.5	15
Netherlands, The	1,539,676	56,745	9,173	662,145	41,738	1,502	448,735	40,600□	2,050	83,212	7,500□	336	100	15
New Zealand	523,673	20,086	2,554	208,596	10,980	394	2,035	...	19	34,593	3,214	31	100	15
Nicaragua	314,425	8,154	2,115	54,139	1,587	185	6,945	429	44	11,618	694	6	57.6	15
Nigeria	4,662,400	136,142	14,502	452,372	17,215	1,320	64,286	3,233	229	24,999	3,604	16	25.0	15
Norway	375,004	19,109	3,395	268,197	17,799	312	57,215	5,405	598	56,664	5,491	106	100	15
Pakistan	4,441,322	111,408	48,507	1,316,428	79,024	6,829	59,958	2,969	423	246,811	12,017	423	16.3	5
Panama	312,386	10,731	2,105	79,705	3,572	80	43,355	2,208	145	21,076	843	2	81.3	15
Papua New Guinea	236,060	7,545	1,744	28,720	1,226	76	9,149	680	112	2,823	313	2	32.0	10
Paraguay	459,393	15,871	2,709	66,746	6,829	652	848	66	2	11,194	1,388◦	4	79.7	15
Peru	2,449,837	...	...	664,739	...	...	168,407	...	...	149,553	...	...	72.5	15
Philippines	7,622,424	247,551	...	1,631,363	45,594	...	159,813	...	...	634,855	29,694	...	83.4	10
Poland	4,522,466	201,006	17,802	647,992	26,166	1,249	1,866,062	74,067*	9,029	521,896	45,014	89	97.8	15
Portugal	1,191,477	48,352	17,388	211,772	10,307	464	164,393	11,897	287	59,149	4,916	147	71.0	...
Puerto Rico	479,680	17,038	3,765	317,397	11,843	272	2,749¶	177¶	63¶	74,059	5,185	10	87.1	15
Rhodesia	864,660	22,091	3,649	74,412	3,771	204	5,088	430	34	2,364	299	6	28.6	16
Romania	2,733,414	147,931†	15,175†	324,508	†	†	495,682	28,257	...	154,285	14,816	...	100	8
Rwanda	397,752	7,777	2,003	7,488	1,487§	177	3,047	‡	40	819	109	4	23.0	15
Saudi Arabia	577,734	26,384	2,711	148,520	7,831	749	16,508	1,286	78	17,253	1,454	20	5.2	...
Senegal	283,276	6,294	...	59,236	2,198	89	7,408	920	124	7,773	...	...	45.6	6
Singapore	337,816	11,913	396	174,177	7,601	123	4,947	790	13	13,823	905	4	75.6	10
South Africa	4,108,910	96,034	...	560,659	21,401	...	39,162	2,657	...	162,709	8,645	...	89.0	...
Soviet Union	39,394,000	2,417,000†	...	9,830,000	†	...	4,448,000	209,000	...	4,671,300	302,000	...	99.7	...
Spain	5,774,929	196,216	164,615	1,012,945	56,379	3,011	278,027	20,238	1,131	354,940	24,714	322	90.1	15
Sri Lanka	2,117,706	...	6,970	480,264	98,925	1,673	12,936	895	39	12,074	1,329	5	78.1	10
Sudan	1,257,339	28,926	4,440	231,311	8,651	1,075	12,077	1,073	37	22,204	750	20	20.0	9–45
Sweden	705,417	43,096	4,836	544,411	58,277	...	20,449	...	...	106,447	...	...	100	15
Syria	1,133,515	30,850	6,452	406,040	19,127	983	23,901	12,310	73	1,719	371	7	54.0	10
Taiwan	2,406,531	62,109	2,354	1,176,280	47,552	795	257,475	9,201	173	276,059	13,309	100	83.4	15
Tanzania	937,609	19,786	4,705	34,303	2,199	114	6,017	472	...	2,060	308	1	...	...
Thailand	6,228,469	192,318	30,933	666,755	28,064	1,705	178,866	12,044	278	63,940	8,348	26	82.3	10
Togo	329,443	5,627	1,199	44,306	1,111	112	4,695	393	23	1,619	243	2	10.5	...
Tunisia	934,827	18,881	...	173,433§	6,549§	...	§	§	...	10,849	628	...	32.2	10
Turkey	5,268,811	159,599	40,383	1,263,802	33,619	2,933	186,225	11,688	563	180,689	10,703	81	54.7	6
Uganda	786,899	24,032	2,937	53,887	2,341	159	6,242	501	31	4,018	470	2	31.0	15
United Kingdom	6,228,702	248,107	28,451	4,061,002	242,436	6,481	330,629	63,787	826	389,659	50,788	283	100	15
United States	31,469,000	1,293,000	...	15,347,000§	1,003,000§	...	§	§	...	8,179,000	748,000	...	99.0	14
Uruguay	366,756	13,436	2,430	138,422‡	8,154‡	233‡	44,203‡	3,251‡	97‡	18,650‡	2,201‡	1‡	90.0	15
Venezuela	1,918,655	54,387	10,591	564,167	15,665	1,018	17,429	1,199	...	99,745	9,105	35	83.4	...
Vietnam, South	3,290,387	65,984	...	908,326§	27,639§	...	§	§	...	57,574	1,348	14	80.0	...
Yugoslavia	2,869,344	126,327	13,661	203,296	10,164	450	519,957	10,540	1,475	328,536	19,197	273	83.5	10
Zaire	3,292,020	80,481	5,924	37,116	13,792	2,511	87,374	...	...	19,294	2,550	36	15.0	15
Zambia	810,234	16,916	2,654	61,354	2,880	110	7,197	...	23	2,324	...	2	47.7	...

*Excludes teacher training. †Data for primary include secondary. ‡Public schools only. §General includes teacher training and vocational. ‖Includes preprimary education. ¶Private schools only. ♀Jewish population only. δTeacher training only. □Estimate. ◦Excludes private 3rd-level teacher training.

It was in the Arab countries that higher education problems were perhaps the most acute. Saudi Arabia was investing in an enormous university expansion without having the numbers of Saudi students to fill the places. On the other hand, the Egyptians were still unable to provide jobs for their own graduates, though some 40,000 of Egypt's 250,000 university students were from other Arab countries. It was reported in 1975 that some 20,000 Egyptian-trained teachers were at work in other Arab countries. In Morocco there were as many as 6,000 French teachers known as *coopérants*. The Moroccans were planning 13 regional teacher-training colleges with the intention of replacing the French as soon as Moroccan nationals could be trained.

In the U.S. college students became more conservative. The ninth annual survey of U.S. college freshmen showed them to be more middle-of-the-road politically than in previous years and less interested in social issues such as environmental quality. Only 12.5% would use their influence to change the nation's political structure. Protests on campus were few in number and tended to deal with personal concerns such as rising costs and poor instruction.

The economic value of attending college had dropped sharply in the last five years, and job prospects continued to be gloomy, according to a study by Harvard University and Massachusetts Institute of Technology professors. The picture was brighter for black graduates, particularly males.

The Handicapped. Among the reforms proposed by The Netherlands Ministry of Education over the next two decades was the reform of special education; *i.e.,* the education of the handicapped. It was proposed that the 20 different school types for the handicapped would be reduced to 4—therapeutic, motoral, corrective, and compensatory. This was but one example of the changes taking place in thinking about teaching the handicapped. A conference held in Canterbury, England, in August 1975 brought together experts in this field from some 28 countries. It seemed that in most countries the categorizing of the handicapped was undergoing a change. The process would need to start from the listing of the needs of children. There had been progress too in dealing with the severely mentally handicapped including the autistic. It was now clear that they had to be taught, not merely placed in a stimulating environment. Judging from data gathered in England, the numbers who should be classified as handicapped had been seriously underestimated. Research carried out in one English rural county showed that one primary-school child in six had a chronic handicap, and it was estimated that in London the incidence would be double.

In the U.S. advocates of "mainstreaming" became more insistent that handicapped students could get effective education in regular classrooms. They would have handicapped students receive much of their instruction with peers, but they did point up the need for special training for regular classroom teachers, special education personnel to assist classroom teachers, and special materials. Advocates of mainstreaming recognized the necessity of having some separate special education facilities and programs.

Minorities and Discrimination. The U.S. Department of Justice was down to 20 suits to secure desegregation, largely to complete Southern desegregation actions undertaken in the mid-1950s. In another civil rights development, the Carnegie Commission on Higher Education proposed that the affirmative action concept be applied to recruiting female and minority group students to increase their numbers in college. Reverse discrimination charges were leveled by academically qualified white males who claimed that minority quotas were keeping some strong students out of professional schools.

Integration to improve learning was questioned by some very influential people. James S. Coleman, whose massive 1966 study provided the rationale for many federal desegregation efforts, concluded that forced busing speeds up resegregation as whites leave areas that reach a high black concentration. A related study by the Federal Reserve Bank of Philadelphia questioned how much integration improves post-elementary performance of minority students as measured by standardized tests.

A study by the California-based Stanford Center for Research and Development in Teaching showed that blacks and Chicanos (Mexican-Americans) have high images of their achievement and efforts. Other studies showed that minority group students are disciplined to a greater degree than are white students in many school systems, leading some civil rights groups to charge that there was harassment. In a ruling unrelated to race, the U.S. Supreme Court said that students must be given some sort of hearing and explanation before disciplinary action. The president of the NEA told a congressional committee that violence in the schools showed an alarming increase, against both students and teachers.

While the proposed Equal Rights Amendment to the U.S. Constitution, which would abolish all laws and discrimination based on sex, still had not been ratified by the requisite number of states, other efforts to promote women's rights and dignity continued. Textbook publishers created and followed guidelines on removing sex-role stereotyping in textbooks. The International Women's Year was used as a stimulus to some school studies of sexism around the world.

The Supreme Court acted on two potentially important education-related matters. It struck down Pennsylvania provisions for using tax monies for parochial school health services, crossing guards, and some kinds of remedial, visiting, diagnostic, and other special personnel. The court did let stand some student-centred services such as textbook loans and bus transportation. The justices deadlocked on a challenge to the legality of massive photocopying of copyrighted materials by the National Institutes of Health and by the National Library of Medicine. The ruling left in effect the presently vague statute (written in 1909); Congress continued its ten-year study on how to rewrite the legislation to reflect the advanced state of photocopying and computer retrieval systems.

Illiteracy. In its 1975 annual report the World Bank estimated that there were 750 million illiterates over the age of 15 in the world. It went on to add the frustrating estimate that over the next decade the number would grow by about 100 million—more or less in line with population increase. Illiteracy remained one of the major concerns of the world's educators in 1975. In a frank appraisal of 11 literacy projects sponsored by UNESCO's Experimental World Literacy Program (EWLP), it was suggested that part of the problem lay in a lack of will on the part of the countries concerned. In some cases the countries did not appear to want to have literacy extended. It was clear, however, that in those countries wholeheartedly committed to literacy programs the results could be dramatic. According to official figures the illiteracy rate in Cuba was cut from 23 to 4% in 1961 alone, but this involved radical measures, including the temporary closing of schools in order to use the pupils as literacy teachers. The two main objectives set by the EWLP, which involved about one million learners with a production of 100,000 separate sets of learning materials, were to demonstrate the economic and social returns of literacy and to pave the way for an eventual world literacy campaign. Only Tanzania was stimulated to launch a mass campaign; otherwise the latter objective was little nearer achievement than it was in 1965 when the program was initiated. National literacy, the report said, could not be drafted or transplanted from the outside. The EWLP showed, however, that the price of literacy was not unsinkably high—between $8 and $110 per head, depending on the type of project. It was found, moreover, that functional literacy—that is, literacy which formed an integral part of the learner's life as a worker—could not simply be thought of as having a vocational purpose. It carried over to political, cultural, and social aspects of development.

Efforts were made in September 1975 to bring together senior officials of the ministries of education of the 25 least developed countries; they met at UNESCO headquarters in Paris to pool information on educational development. The 25 countries were identified, using 1971 figures, on the basis of three criteria: per capita gross domestic product of $100 or less, an industrial production of 10% or less of this latter figure, and a literacy rate of 20% or less. Countries in this category were: Afghanistan, Bhutan, Botswana, Burundi, Chad, Dahomey, Ethiopia, Haiti, Laos, Lesotho, Malawi, Mali, Nepal, Niger, Rwanda, Somalia, Sudan, Tanzania, Uganda, Upper Volta, Western Samoa, Yemen (San'a'), and three not represented at the meeting—the Maldives, Guinea, and Sikkim (which was incorporated into India during the year). The conclusions reached were thought to be influential. It was first accepted that elitist systems of education inherited from the colonial past must give way to systems designed for all sectors of the population; second, that emphasis should shift away from academic learning and training for white-collar jobs; and third, that mass education had to take place in the national language, despite the difficulties of producing teaching material, and that the national printing of textbooks should therefore be given priority.

(TUDOR DAVID; JOEL L. BURDIN)

See also Libraries; Motion Pictures; Museums.
[562; 563]

ENCYCLOPÆDIA BRITANNICA FILMS. *Learning with Today's Media* (1974).

Egypt

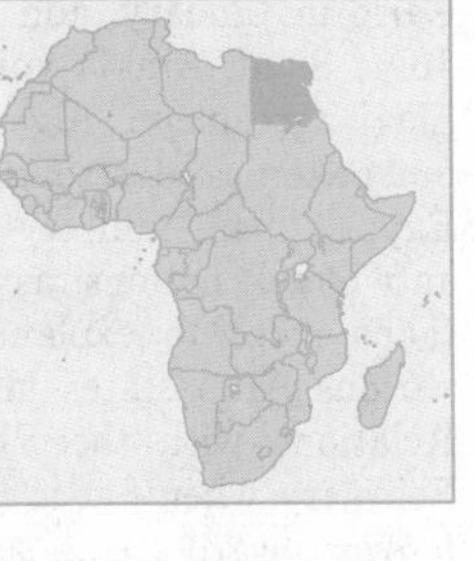

A republic of northeast Africa, Egypt is bounded by Israel, Sudan, Libya, the Mediterranean Sea, and the Red Sea. Area: 386,900 sq.mi. (1,002,000 sq.km.). Pop. (1975): 37 million. Cap. and largest city: Cairo (pop., 1975, 5,859,000). Language: Arabic. Religion: Muslim 93%; Christian 7%. President in 1975, Anwar as-Sadat; prime ministers, Abdul Aziz Hegazy to April 13 and, from April 16, Mamdouh Salem.

For Egypt 1975 was a momentous year, marked by the reopening of the Suez Canal and a new interim agreement with Israel over Sinai. This brought substantial advantages but also strong criticism from some Arab countries.

AUDREY TOPPING—THE NEW YORK TIMES

Reconstruction of the war-damaged community in Suez, Egypt, is being aided by the Kuwait Fund for Arab Economic Development, which increased its working capital in July from $600 million to $3.4 billion.

Domestic Affairs. January opened with serious rioting in central Cairo, which was touched off when a 100-man workers' delegation from Helwan was prevented by police from approaching the People's Assembly. Students joined in support of the workers, and widespread arrests were made. The government blamed leftists for provoking the violence, but there was popular discontent with inflation and shortages. Although measures were taken to provide funds to import food and other essentials, rioting broke out at the cotton textile industry centre of Mehalla el-Kubra in March. On April 13 Prime Minister Hegazy, who received much of the blame for the economic situation, resigned and was replaced on April 16 by Mamdouh Salem, minister of the interior. Salem was expected to take firm measures to restore order.

In the new Cabinet 18 former ministers were retained, and 16 new ones were appointed. A significant change was the dropping of the former planning minister, the Marxist economist Ismail Sabry Abdullah, who was regarded as an obstacle to the government's economic liberalization policies. At the same time, the president abolished the six largely honorific posts of presidential adviser held by former senior ministers, and he appointed as sole vice-president Air Marshal Husni Mubarak. Mubarak, Air Force commander since 1972, was widely regarded as being groomed by President Sadat as his successor. The other vice-president, Hussein Shafei, was asked to resign, although the constitution provided for two vice-presidents. Reports that Sadat himself would step down when his six-year term ended in 1976 were largely discounted when the Arab Socialist Union's national congress on July 23 unanimously nominated him as president for a further term (beginning in October 1976).

Foreign Relations. The most notable features of Egypt's foreign policy in 1975 were the continuing friendly relationship with the U.S. and growing coolness toward the U.S.S.R. In the spring Egyptian-U.S. ties seemed to be endangered after the failure of U.S. Secretary of State Henry Kissinger's mission aimed at a new Egyptian-Israeli settlement. It soon became clear, however, that the U.S. government blamed the breakdown of the negotiations primarily on Israel and that Egypt had not abandoned hope of

Eggs:
see Agriculture and Food Supplies

U.S. mediation. Egypt formally asked for a reconvening of the Geneva Middle East peace conference, but the U.S. suggested a postponement. President Sadat showed his determination to proceed with détente by his decision, announced on March 29, to reopen the Suez Canal. Work on clearing the canal and its banks of huge quantities of mines, bombs, shells, and other debris was carried on intensively by the Egyptian forces, with help from the U.S., British, French, and Soviet navies, and the canal was formally reopened on June 5 by Sadat, accompanied by the flagship of the U.S. 6th Fleet. Canal dues were fixed at nearly double their level before the canal's closing in 1967. Oil tanker traffic was well down from pre-1967 levels, but work on widening and deepening the canal to allow medium-sized tankers to pass through was begun almost immediately.

On June 1 and 2 President Sadat held talks with U.S. Pres. Gerald Ford at Salzburg, Austria. Diplomatic moves toward a further Egyptian-Israeli disengagement continued through July, and in the second half of August Kissinger made six visits to Egypt as part of his renewed peace mission. Difficulties centred on whether Israel would withdraw entirely from the Giddi and Mitla mountain passes in the Sinai and on the manning of early-warning systems, for which Egypt wanted U.S. technicians. The agreement reached on September 1 and initialed at Geneva on September 4 provided for an Israeli withdrawal of 12–26 mi. covering some 1,000 sq.mi. of Sinai; this left 95% of the peninsula in Israeli hands but restored to Egypt the Abu Rudays oil fields. Both sides would be allowed 8,000 men and 75 tanks in the limited forces zones bordering the demilitarized buffer zone. Egypt would allow cargoes going to and from Israel (though not Israeli ships) through the Suez Canal, and both sides agreed to settle their conflict by peaceful means rather than military force.

After the agreement U.S.-Egyptian relations improved further, and President Sadat visited the U.S. during October and November. U.S. aid of $1.5 billion to $2 billion was expected for Egypt.

The agreement with Israel did nothing to improve Egyptian-Soviet relations. A second visit (the first was in February) to Cairo by Soviet Foreign Minister Andrey A. Gromyko in November only slightly improved the atmosphere, and the long-awaited visit by Soviet Communist Party leader Leonid I. Brezhnev did not take place. Egyptian criticism of the U.S.S.R. centred on its alleged failure to supply arms to replenish the 1973 losses (as it had done for Syria), its failure to supply spare parts, and alleged reluctance to reschedule Egypt's heavy debts to the U.S.S.R. After the Sinai agreement, President Sadat was even more outspoken, accusing the U.S.S.R. of obstructing all moves toward a Middle East peace.

Egypt made clear its intention to seek alternative sources of arms. After President Sadat made a state visit to Paris in January, he said that France would supply arms, including Mirage F-1 fighter-bombers, in addition to giving technical and industrial assistance. Vice-President Mubarak also discussed arms when he visited Paris in June. The foreign minister visited London at the same time, and although a major arms deal was discussed nothing final was decided. The Egyptians made it clear that, in addition to buying British and French arms, they would like Anglo-French help in establishing a major new arms industry in Egypt, to be financed by several Arab oil-producing nations. France's willingness to assist in such an enterprise was expressed in the joint communiqué issued at the end of French Pres. Valéry Giscard d'Estaing's state visit to Cairo in December.

Relations with the Arab states and the Palestine Liberation Organization (PLO) were affected by the Sinai agreement. King Faisal of Saudi Arabia visited Cairo in January, and his successor, King Khalid, in July; Saudi Arabia voiced no public criticism of the Sinai agreement. Algeria was critical, although not outspoken, and strong opposition came from Syria, Egypt's main military ally, and from such hard-line anti-Israel nations as Iraq and Libya. Sadat had taken steps to explain Egypt's position by touring various Arab states in May but with little success. Relations with the PLO were already troubled in February when Sadat responded to PLO criticism of moves toward a U.S.-sponsored agreement with Israel by refusing to meet a PLO delegation. The breach became more serious as the year progressed, and on September 11 Egypt closed down the PLO broadcasting station in Egypt.

Relations with Libya went from bad to worse in 1975, and the two countries exchanged violent in-

EGYPT

Education. (1971–72) Primary, pupils 3,873,297, teachers 99,351; secondary, pupils 1,237,750, teachers 41,888; vocational, pupils 289,812, teachers 14,369; teacher training, students 27,247, teachers 2,172; higher (including 6 universities), students 246,558, teaching staff 13,472.

Finance. Monetary unit: Egyptian pound, with (Sept. 22, 1975) an official rate of E£0.39 to U.S. $1 (free rate of E£0.90 = £1 sterling) and a tourist rate of E£0.72 to U.S. $1 (E£1.49 = £1 sterling). Gold, SDRs, and foreign exchange: (Dec. 1974) U.S. $342 million; (Dec. 1973) U.S. $391 million. Budget (1974 est.): revenue E£2,642 million; expenditure E£2,909 million. Gross national product: (1971–72) E£3,275 million; (1970–71) E£3,086 million. Money supply: (Feb. 1975) E£1,490.7 million; (Feb. 1974) E£1,228.1 million. Cost of living (1970 = 100): (Jan. 1975) 128; (Jan. 1974) 116.

Foreign Trade. (1974) Imports E£919.2 million; exports E£593.3 million. Import sources (1973): U.S. 13%; France 8%; West Germany 8%; U.S.S.R. 7%; Australia 5%; East Germany 5%; Italy 5%; Romania 5%. Export destinations (1973): U.S.S.R. 33%; Czechoslovakia 6%; Japan 5%. Main exports: cotton 46%; cotton yarn (1973) 10%; fruit and vegetables 9%; crude oil (1973) 8%; rice 7%.

Transport and Communications. Roads (1970) *c.* 50,000 km. (including 22,100 km. with improved surface). Motor vehicles in use (1973): passenger 167,400; commercial (including buses) 48,000. Railways: (1973) 5,006 km.; traffic (1971–72) 7,306,000,000 passenger-km., freight 2,976,000,000 net ton-km. Air traffic (1974): 1,285,000,000 passenger-km; freight 17,793,000 net ton-km. Shipping (1974): merchant vessels 100 gross tons and over 134; gross tonnage 248,591. Telephones (Dec. 1973) 472,000. Radio licenses (Dec. 1973) 5.1 million. Television licenses (Dec. 1971) 584,000.

Agriculture. Production (in 000; metric tons; 1974; 1973 in parentheses): wheat *c.* 1,850 (1,838); barley *c.* 100 (97); millet *c.* 875 (853); corn *c.* 2,600 (2,508); rice *c.* 2,500 (2,274); potatoes *c.* 750 (798); sugar, raw value *c.* 605 (*c.* 590); tomatoes *c.* 1,630 (1,577); onions *c.* 520 (539); dry broad beans (1973) 273, (1972) 361; watermelons (1973) *c.* 1,000, (1972) 1,014; dates (1973) *c.* 350, (1972) *c.* 320; oranges (1973) 767, (1972) *c.* 750; tangerines and mandarin oranges (1973) 89, (1972) *c.* 90; lemons (1973) 62, (1972) *c.* 75; grapes (1973) 162, (1972) *c.* 128; cotton, lint *c.* 480 (490); cheese *c.* 189 (*c.* 187); beef and buffalo meat *c.* 233 (226). Livestock (in 000; 1973): cattle *c.* 2,138; buffalo *c.* 2,283; sheep *c.* 2,080; goats *c.* 1,300; asses *c.* 1,440; camels *c.* 120; chickens *c.* 25,450.

Industry. Production (in 000; metric tons; 1974): cement 3,160; iron ore (50% metal content) 1,302; crude oil 7,398; petroleum products (1973) 6,488; fertilizers (nutrient content; 1973–74) nitrogenous 78, phosphate 81; salt (1972) 386; sulfuric acid 198; cotton yarn 176; cotton fabrics (m.) 598,000; electricity (kw-hr.; 1973) 8,104,000.

sults. In April Sadat described Libya's Pres. Muammar al-Qaddafi as "100% sick and possessed by a devil who makes him imagine things." The Egyptian news media accused the Libyans of gross maltreatment of Egyptian citizens, of planning to seize part of Egypt's Western Desert, and, in May, of having concluded a huge arms deal with the U.S.S.R. which amounted to virtual Soviet control of Libya. In June Egypt banned its citizens from traveling to Libya. In October, however, steps were taken to repair the damage and to revive the moribund Arab federation of Egypt, Libya, and Syria.

The Economy. As in foreign policy, Egypt continued a rightward swing in domestic economic policy, although there was nothing like a concerted campaign against the left. Some de-nasserization continued to be pursued, but there was no repudiation of Nasserist policies; Sadat himself affirmed that the public sector remained the cornerstone of Egypt's development. Measures were taken to encourage foreign investment, and in May a presidential decree allowed the sale of some shares in the nationalized industries to the private sector.

Egypt's general economic position was perilous since huge arms expenditures in recent years had run down the country's economic infrastructure. The reopening of the Suez Canal and the recovery of the Sinai oil fields, which were expected to make Egypt a net oil exporter in 1976, helped to improve future prospects, and the repopulation of the canal zone cities relieved pressure on other Egyptian towns. Foreign aid, especially from other Arab oil states, was substantial, but foreign investment, often discouraged by the Egyptian bureaucracy, was more sluggish than had been hoped. The country's most immediate problem was its need to buy essential goods to keep down prices and curb mass discontent, which was difficult to accomplish because of a lack of financial liquidity. Inflation was running at an annual rate of more than 30%.

On February 3 Um Kalthoum, the most famous and popular singer in the Arab world, died in Cairo (*see* OBITUARIES). Her funeral was attended by hundreds of thousands of mourners. (PETER MANSFIELD)

[978.B.3.e]

El Salvador

A republic on the Pacific coast of Central America and the smallest country on the isthmus, El Salvador is bounded on the west by Guatemala and on the north and east by Honduras. Area: 8,124 sq.mi. (21,041 sq.km.). Pop. (1975 est.): 4,108,000. Cap. and largest city: San Salvador (pop., 1974 est., 416,900). Language: Spanish. Religion: Roman Catholic. President in 1975, Col. Arturo Armando Molina.

The Molina regime began its fourth year on July 1 with new initiatives in land reform and wage policy, but faced uncertainty caused by internal criticism and violence. The Agrarian Transformation Act, a comprehensive land-reform measure, became law in June and awaited the issuance of regulations for its implementation.

In quest of the international spotlight, El Salvador sponsored the annual Miss Universe contest. A demonstration was staged by university students on July 30

WIDE WORLD

Anne Pohtamo, representing Finland, was named Miss Universe of 1975 in the July pageant held in San Salvador.

to protest the government's large expenditure for the Miss Universe competition. This led to confrontation with government forces, resulting in perhaps as many as 12 student fatalities. The People's Revolutionary Army, a self-styled Marxist group, took credit for an armed assault on a national guard post, attacks on a radio station and a newspaper, and the kidnapping for ransom of wealthy industrialist Francisco de Sola. In action from the other side, leftist congressman and labour leader Rafael Aguiñada Carranza was shot to death by unidentified assailants.

In the midst of the violence a right-wing terrorist group came into being, with the imposing name Armed Front for the National Anti-Communist Struggle in

EL SALVADOR

Education. (1970) Primary, pupils 509,985, teachers 13,919; secondary, pupils 60,870; vocational, pupils 27,437; secondary and vocational, teachers 3,531; higher (1971), students 12,645, teaching staff 751.

Finance. Monetary unit: colón, with (Sept. 22, 1975) a par value of 2.50 colones to U.S. $1 (free rate of 5.18 colones = £1 sterling). Gold, SDRs, and foreign exchange, central bank: (June 1975) U.S. $129.7 million; (June 1974) U.S. $63,409,000. Budget (1974 actual): revenue 488.1 million colones; expenditure 542.4 million colones. Gross national product: (1973) 3,238,000,000 colones; (1972) 2,855,000,000 colones. Money supply: (Jan. 1975) 576.7 million colones; (Jan. 1974) 492.7 million colones. Cost of living (1970 = 100): (March 1975) 146; (March 1974) 119.

Foreign Trade. (1973) Imports 943.7 million colones; exports 896 million colones. Import sources: U.S. 29%; Guatemala 16%; Japan 10%; West Germany 8%; Costa Rica 5%; The Netherlands 5%. Export destinations: U.S. 33%; Guatemala 18%; West Germany 13%; Japan 10%; Nicaragua 7%; Costa Rica 6%. Main exports: coffee 45%; cotton 10%.

Transport and Communications. Roads (1971) 10,733 km. (including 625 km. of Pan-American Highway). Motor vehicles in use (1972): passenger 37,900; commercial (including buses) 21,900. Railways (1973) 623 km. Telephones (Dec. 1973) 47,000. Radio receivers (Dec. 1971) 350,000. Television receivers (Dec. 1971) 125,000.

Agriculture. Production (in 000; metric tons; 1974; 1973 in parentheses): corn *c.* 336 (391); sorghum *c.* 157 (156); rice (1973) *c.* 26, (1972) 36; dry beans *c.* 32 (37); coffee 140 (134); sugar, raw value 201 (190); cotton, lint 81 (*c.* 69); jute *c.* 5 (*c.* 5). Livestock (in 000; 1974): cattle *c.* 1,200; pigs *c.* 421; horses *c.* 65; poultry (1973) *c.* 8,400.

Industry. Production (in 000; metric tons; 1973): cement 240; petroleum products *c.* 600; cotton yarn 5.1; electricity (kw-hr.; 1972) 820,000.

Eire: *see* Ireland

Electrical Industries: *see* Energy; Industrial Review

Electronics: *see* Computers

Employment: *see* Economy, World

the War of Elimination. The initials of the title in Spanish were, significantly, FALANGE.

The nation's economy continued an uneven course. Growth of the gross national product was small (less than 1% per capita annually in the early 1970s), a high rate of inflation prevailed (23% during the year ended May 1975), and unemployment (more than 6% increase from the end of 1973 to the end of 1974) remained a serious concern. (HENRY WEBB, JR.)

[974.B.1.c]

Energy

The dominant events in the field of energy during 1975, as in 1974, were the actions of the Organization of Petroleum Exporting Countries (OPEC). In the United States the most important developments concerned national policies to cope with the OPEC actions.

The year began with the imposition of a 4% increase in the basic reference price of oil sold by the OPEC members. At the same time, the price standard was changed from the traditional "posted" price, the theoretical basis on which taxes and royalties had been computed. Adopted in its stead was the "host government take," or the revenue received by the host country from taxes and royalties and from the sale of government royalty oil. The price increase was accompanied by the announcement that the new price would be frozen until October, at which time it would be reviewed.

As the year progressed there were increasing reports of discounts and price shaving on certain kinds of crude oil. Given the combination of a general reduction in world oil use in reaction to the several hundred percent price increase in 1974 and the development of a worldwide economic recession during 1975, with consequent reduced demand, it became evident that there was a large excess of producing capacity, most of it in Saudi Arabia.

A mobile solar water heater employing a commercially available solar collector panel is used in teaching liberal arts students at the University of California at Santa Barbara about the utilization of solar energy.

SWALLING—AUTHENTICATED NEWS INTERNATIONAL

In April France called a meeting of representatives from ten developed and less developed countries to plan for an international energy conference that would consider the world economic problems created by the new oil prices. The meeting collapsed in disagreement over the demand by third world countries that the entire range of problems involving developed versus less developed nations be considered, but at another French-sponsored meeting, in October, it was agreed that a ministerial conference would be convened to consider the expanded agenda. The Conference on International Economic Cooperation, which opened in Paris on December 16, was attended by representatives of 8 industrialized countries and 19 less developed nations (including 7 OPEC members). Following initial, largely procedural sessions, the actual work of the conference was to be done by four commissions—on energy, raw materials, development, and finance—and was expected to take at least a year.

In spite of the weakness in demand for oil (OPEC production in the first half of the year was almost 17% below the 1974 level), the June meeting of OPEC debated the question of additional price increases. The members decided to continue the freeze announced in January but to change the basis of oil prices from U.S. dollars to Special Drawing Rights (an international monetary unit established by the International Monetary Fund which is the weighted average value of 16 major currencies). The effect of this decision, if the dollar lost value in relation to other currencies, would be to raise the price of oil.

At the September OPEC meeting the issue was not whether to end the price freeze but by how much the price should be raised. After the most intense dispute in OPEC history, between Saudi Arabia which argued for a rise of no more than 5% and other countries which urged as much as 40%, a compromise 10% increase was announced, effective Oct. 1, 1975. The reason given for the increase was the need to offset the declining value of the dollar and other major world currencies due to worldwide inflation. The dollar had, however, strengthened relative to other currencies since the decision in June to abandon it as the basis of account, and so the use of Special Drawing Rights as the basis would result in a small decline in the revenues of the OPEC countries. Adoption of that change was, therefore, postponed.

Efforts by the U.S. government to adopt and carry out appropriate policies in the face of the new energy situation were dominated by policy differences between Pres. Gerald Ford and Congress. In his state of the union message in January, Ford announced a goal of reducing oil imports by one million barrels a day by 1985 as the beginning of a program to achieve ultimate "energy independence." The president imposed a $1 per barrel tax on oil imports. His proposals included the removal of oil price controls and allocation, deregulation of natural gas prices, use of the Elk Hills Naval Petroleum Reserves, and an accelerated program of leasing the outer continental shelf.

A few days later the president by executive order carried out the provisions of a law enacted the previous October and abolished the Atomic Energy Com-

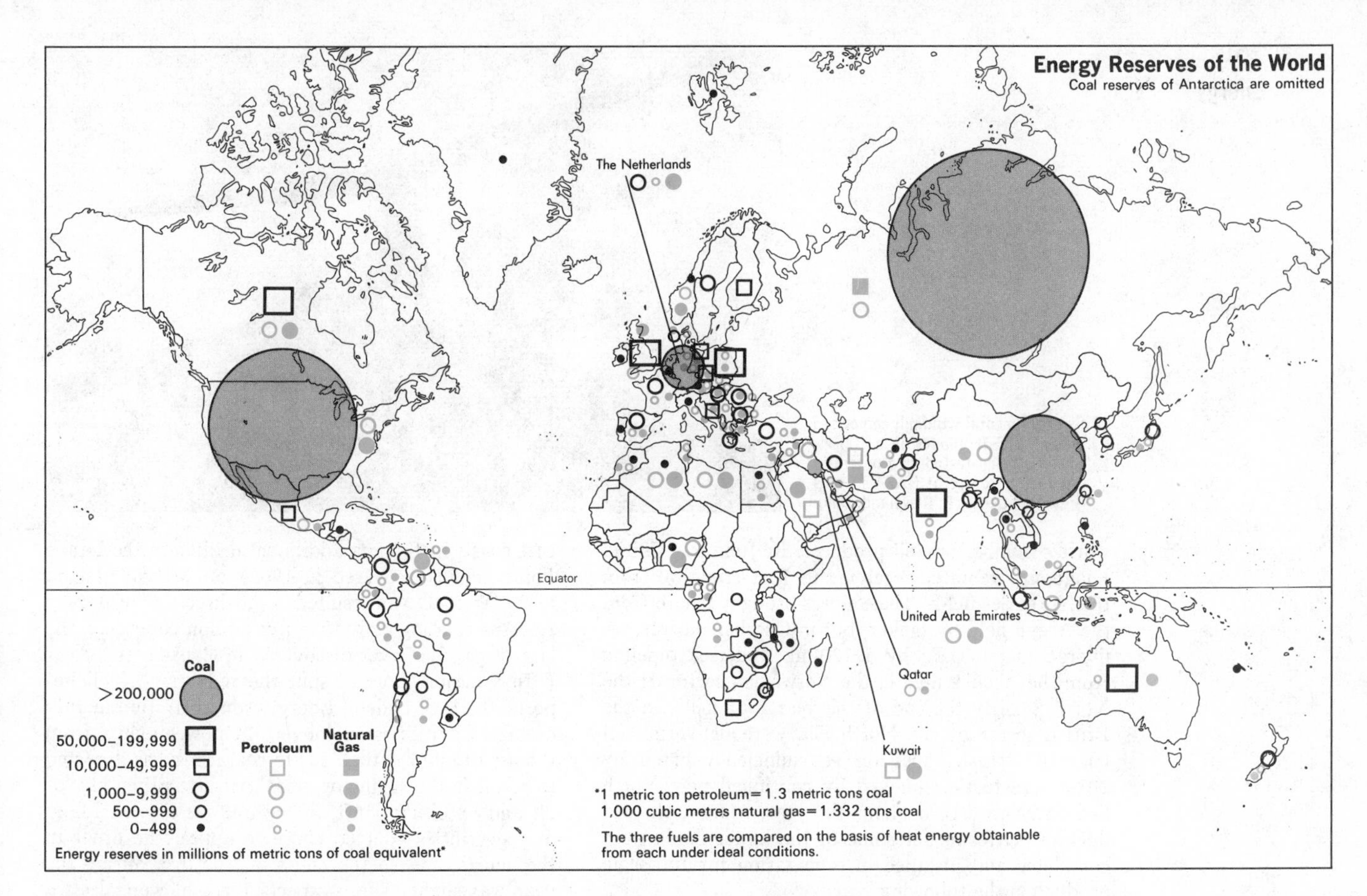

mission (AEC), creating in its place two new agencies: the Nuclear Regulatory Commission and the Energy Research and Development Administration. The former inherited the licensing and regulatory functions of the old agency; the latter combined the nuclear research and development function of the AEC with greatly expanded responsibilities for research and development in all fields of energy.

Ford's state of the union energy proposals met with a hostile reaction from Congress. Legislative leaders announced that Congress would develop its own energy legislation, and there ensued a controversy between the president and Congress that continued throughout the year. During the spring Ford twice postponed his planned additional dollar fee on imported oil, and in May he vetoed a comprehensive bill imposing environmental restrictions on the surface mining of coal, on the grounds that it would interfere with the substitution of coal for imported oil. The veto was sustained. Congress then took a recess without passing any energy legislation, whereupon the president imposed the second dollar of import fee.

The controversy intensified during the summer as Aug. 31, 1975, the date of expiration of existing authority to control oil prices, neared. President Ford proposed a phasing out of the authority over 30 months, but in July Congress passed a bill extending the Emergency Petroleum Allocation Act, which would thus retain existing control authority unchanged. Ford vetoed the bill.

The expiration of price control authority on August 31 caused both sides to compromise; ten days later Ford's veto of the extension was sustained, but the president abandoned his position of promising to veto any bill that attempted to extend controls. Congress prepared a bill temporarily extending controls until Nov. 15, 1975, with the understanding on both sides that the eventual legislation would phase out oil price controls over a period of a few years. This bill was passed as was a later one that extended the temporary controls to Dec. 15, 1975. The stalemate ended on December 22, when the president signed a compromise bill that would reduce the average price of a 42-gal. barrel of crude from the November 1 estimate of $8.75 to $7.66, after which the price would be allowed to rise gradually until controls expired in 1979. The bill also contained conservation measures designed to lessen the country's dependence on oil and presidential standby powers to deal with an energy emergency. On the same day he signed the measure, the president lifted the $2 a barrel import fee.

As in the U.S., Canada made some major energy policy changes in attempting to cope with the new circumstances in world energy markets. The allowable level of oil exports to the U.S. was cut from 900,000 to 800,000 bbl. per day on Jan. 1, 1975, and to 650,000 by July, and the government announced plans to phase out crude oil exports to the U.S. completely by 1982. In midyear the oil export tax was reduced from $5 per barrel to $4.70 per barrel in recognition of the fact that the tax was not fulfilling its purpose of subsidizing oil imports into eastern Canada. While the oil tax was being lowered, the export price of natural gas was being raised. On Jan. 1, 1975, the price of gas exports to the U.S. was increased by government edict from 60 cents to $1 per thousand cubic feet. On August 1 it was raised to $1.40 and on November 1 to $1.60. The purpose of this increase was to bring the price of Canadian gas closer to that of other energy commodities in the U.S.

In the exploration and production phase of the world oil industry it was announced during the year that, on the basis of final 1974 production statistics, the Soviet Union had replaced the United States as the

WIDE WORLD

This experimental windmill comprised of two 125-ft. blades on a 100-ft. tower is being tested as a potential energy source at NASA's Lewis Research Center in Cleveland, Ohio.

world's number one oil producer. In June the United Kingdom celebrated receiving its first crude oil from the North Sea fields. That oil was brought ashore from the Argyll field by tanker, but in October oil was delivered to the U.K. by a 220-mi. undersea pipeline from the Ekofisk field in the Norwegian sector of the North Sea. By the end of the year four fields in the British sector of the North Sea were delivering oil onshore. British hopes for self-sufficiency in oil by 1980 were further buoyed by continued new North Sea discoveries throughout the year. Mammoth production platforms for some of the larger fields were completed and installed in preparation for full-scale production the following year.

Across the Atlantic the final barrier to drilling on the outer continental shelf off the eastern U.S. was removed when the U.S. Supreme Court disposed of the last serious challenges to the legality of such action. The U.S. Department of the Interior quickly followed with the nomination of the first lease tracts for sale on the Atlantic outer continental shelf. The tracts lie in an area off New Jersey, Delaware, Maryland, and the northern coast of Virginia, known as the Baltimore Canyon Trough, which had previously been designated by the U.S. Geological Survey as the most promising area for petroleum deposits of the entire East Coast. The lease sale was scheduled for 1976.

The Interior Department also gave preliminary approval for the drilling of the first two offshore wells on the Atlantic Coast for the purpose of providing geological information for the leasing program. The two wells were to be located 80 mi. E of New Jersey in 290 ft. of water and 75 mi. E of Cape Cod, Massachusetts, in 140 ft. of water.

Europe's energy consumers, already reeling under the impact of OPEC oil prices, were dealt another blow when European gas producers raised natural gas prices to a parity with oil. At the same time, plans were announced to import large quantities of Iranian gas into western Europe. The Soviet Union increased its European gas exports, and Saudi Arabia announced ambitious plans to develop and use its own gas reserves. These plans included liquefaction for export and the domestic use of gas in a wide variety of industrial projects, from fertilizer and petrochemical manufacture to steel production.

Egypt's first gas field, on the Nile River delta about 110 mi. N of Cairo, began production. In Australia construction began on the country's largest pipeline, which was to carry gas 834 mi. from Moomba, near the centre of the continent, to Sydney on the southeast coast. In Canada additional drilling in the Drake Point field (discovered in 1968) on Melville Island in the Arctic Ocean resulted in the discovery of proved reserves totaling more than five trillion cubic feet, the largest gas field ever discovered in Canada.

In a major effort to spur the reduction of oil imports, the U.S. Federal Energy Administration in July ordered 25 utilities to convert 74 power plants from the use of oil or natural gas to coal. This was expected to result in the saving of more than 64 million bbl. of oil and 88 billion cu.ft. of natural gas a year. Many of the utilities affected chose to appeal the order in the courts, and so the effect on fuel use during the year was slight. The prospects for coal were dealt a severe blow during the year by a Court of Appeals decision in a suit by environmental organizations to prevent the development of the coal resources of the northern Great Plains, which contain half of the total U.S. coal resources. The decision sent the case back to the lower courts and was accompanied by an injunction prohibiting any new coal mining on federal lands in the region until the Department of the Interior presented a regional environmental impact statement to the court.

The debate over the safety of nuclear power intensified in the U.S. The results of a study of the safety issue, commissioned in 1973 by the U.S. Atomic Energy Commission, were published in a massive report which concluded that the possibility of a major catastrophic accident was so small as to be inconsequential. This finding was immediately challenged by opponents of nuclear power, and the scientific community was divided sharply on the issue.

The price of uranium oxide in the U.S. rose from less than $10 a pound to a range of $20–$40, depending on the future year of delivery. This prompted one of the two major suppliers of nuclear power plants in the U.S. to announce it would not honour contract commitments that called for the future delivery of a total of 81 million lb. at contract prices of less than $10. The nuclear fuel situation was further confused by the decision of the new U.S. Nuclear Regulatory Commission in May to postpone for three years a final decision on permitting the use of plutonium recovered from spent fuel as fuel in commercial reactors. In January a reactor at the Biblis nuclear power plant in West Germany achieved its full power rating of 1,200 Mw. to become the world's largest operational nuclear unit. (BRUCE C. NETSCHERT)

ENCYCLOPÆDIA BRITANNICA FILMS. *Energy: A Matter of Choices* (1973); *Energy for the Future* (1974).

COAL

In 1975 many nations looked to coal to reduce their dependence on imported oil, and those that had cut back on coal production made strenuous efforts to stabilize it at around 1974 levels. The major producing countries took steps to increase both the production of coal and its use in power generating stations.

Programs to find and evaluate reserves were expanded, and much interest was shown in the development of economically viable processes to convert coal to gaseous and liquid fuels. Interchange of technical information was common throughout the world, and even the international oil industry considered coal as an alternative energy source.

World hard coal production in 1974 was an estimated 2,278,274,000 metric tons, an increase of 33.1 million tons over 1973. Increases occurred in the U.S.S.R., China, Poland, Canada, and India. In Western Europe production again fell, registering a drop of 10% from 1973, mainly because of a strike in the U.K. Eastern European production (including the U.S.S.R.) showed an increase of just under 3%. China, with an output estimated at 430 million metric tons, an increase of 20 million tons, remained the world's third largest producer and in 1974 resumed its export trade with Japan.

U.S.S.R. A total of 684 million metric tons of raw coal and lignite was produced in 1974, about 30% of it from surface operations. Production of hard coal rose by 16 million metric tons to 524 million tons. Production of coking coal increased 1.2% to 175 million metric tons. The Donets Basin region maintained record production levels with 219.5 million tons. Lignite production increased by 3.7 million to 160 million metric tons. Production of raw coal and lignite was expected to reach 700 million metric tons in 1975.

Coal use in power stations increased in order to conserve relatively limited supplies of oil and gas. Over two million men and women were employed in the industry in 1974.

United States. In 1975 coal production was expected to exceed that of the previous two years; in the first five months of the year production was 2% ahead of the similar period for 1974. In July 1974 a Coal Task Force, set up to provide estimates for Project Independence, estimated that coal production by 1985 could be maintained economically at 1,000,000,000 metric tons a year, if world oil prices were $11 a barrel, or 900 million metric tons with oil prices at $7 a barrel, given increased production capacity and improvement of transport facilities.

Research and development of coal gasification and liquefaction continued to expand sharply, with some 40 projects under way. Several oil-fired power stations and industrial boilers were converted to coal use.

Bituminous coal production in 1974 amounted to 590 million short tons, just over half from surface operations; a strike at the year's end lost 35 million metric tons, leaving production at about the same level as in 1973. Approximately 6.3 million short tons of anthracite were produced, a decline of 6% from 1973. Coal exports totaled 61 million short tons, 45.1% going to Japan. Net exports increased by less than 3%, but their value doubled. Coal consumption decreased fractionally during 1974, though deliveries to power utilities increased slightly to 390 million short tons.

European Economic Community. Total hard coal production in 1974 amounted to 236 million metric tons, 27.4 million tons less than in 1973. Belgium's ten mines produced 8.1 million metric tons, a reduction of 8% compared with 1973. Plans were announced to increase production and to study the feasibility of underground gasification. In France, production declined by 11% to 22.9 million metric tons. Plans were revised to stabilize production at about 21 million metric tons, a 50% increase over previous targets. The Netherlands produced 758,000 metric tons from two mines that closed at the end of 1974.

Provisional figures for West Germany's hard-coal production showed a decrease of 2.5 million metric tons to 94.9 million tons, although the highest miner productivity within the EEC, 4.1 metric tons per manshift, was maintained. Lignite production increased by 10 million metric tons to a record 126 million tons.

In the U.K. the National Coal Board (NCB) finished the financial year 1974–75 with an operating profit of £34 million, compared with an operating loss of £112 million for the previous year. Output from deep mines was 115 million long tons, almost 18 million tons more than in 1973–74. Opencut operations remained at about the same level, with 9.1 million long tons, and licensed deep mines and open pits contributed an additional 1.1 million long tons. Deliveries to power stations increased 11% to 71.5 million long tons.

Under the ten-year plan for coal, the NCB aimed to stabilize the industry's output and, if possible, increase it. Planning and design of the Selby Mine were well advanced, and the NCB estimated that by the end of 1975 half the investment to provide 42 million tons replacement of annual capacity would have been initiated.

Poland. In 1974, 162 million metric tons of hard coal were produced, an increase from 1973 of 3.4%. Production of brown coal rose by 1.6% to 39.8 million tons. Coal exports in 1974 were 40.1 million metric tons, a gain of 4.2 million tons over 1973. A complex of underground coal mines was planned in a newly discovered deposit in the Lublin region, where production levels of 25 million tons annually could be expected.

India. The 1974 output of 88 million metric tons was 10 million metric tons higher than in the preceding year. Production was expected to rise to a record level of 100 million metric tons in 1975. Plans to increase production to 135 million metric tons per year and to export about 4 million tons annually required massive investment (more than $1 billion over the next four years), increases in productivity, and the modernization of coal transportation. India's estimated annual requirements by 1985 were put at 200 million metric tons.

Japan. Output of hard coal again fell during 1974, to 20.3 million metric tons, some 9.3% lower than in 1973. Imports increased to a record 64.2 million metric tons. The U.S. replaced Australia as Japan's chief supplier, with 25.4 million tons of bituminous coal, almost 8.9 million tons more than in 1973. Imports from Australia fell to 22.9 million metric tons. Canada provided nine million tons.

Although it remained cheaper to import, concern was expressed during 1975 over Japan's dependence on imported raw materials. With state subsidies and other incentives, authorities hoped to stabilize indigenous production at about 20 million metric tons and also perhaps increase it as the easiest solution to Japan's medium-term energy problems.

South America. Coal production in 1974 was 8.5 million metric tons, an increase of 469,000 metric tons over 1973. Colombia, the largest producer, had 3.6 million metric tons, while Brazil produced 2.6 million and Chile 1.4 million metric tons. The proposed exchange of Brazilian iron ore for 100 million tons of Colombian metallurgical coal was terminated in 1975, though plans to extract 5 million tons a year from the El Cerrejon deposit were continued.

Africa. Of the estimated total of 70.4 million metric tons of hard coal produced in 1974, 64.6 million tons were produced by South Africa. Rhodesia's production climbed by 16.7% to 3.5 million tons.

Australia. Production of black coal rose by some 2% in 1974 to about 62 million metric tons, compared with 60.7 million tons in 1973. The 29 million tons of lignite from Victoria represented an increase of 4 million tons.

During the year ended June 1974, exports of black coal increased by 2.6 million tons to 28.4 million metric tons, 84% of it to Japan. Queensland's exports, all coking coal, rose by only 6.7% to 15.6 million tons. The reduction in the growth rate, compared with 59.3% in 1972–73, was attributed to severe weather conditions that affected production, transport, and loading, and also to an industrial dispute. Exports from New South Wales increased 14% to 12.7 million tons, following a decline in 1972–73.

Domestic consumption during 1973–74 amounted to 27.7 million tons, an increase of only 1.1%. Domestic demand was expected to ease in 1975, due to slackening of industrial activity.

Canada. In 1974, production increased slightly to 23 million short tons, an increase of 422,871 short tons over 1973, and was expected to reach about 26 million short tons in 1975. Exports fell 1.2% from the record level achieved in 1973 to 11.9 million tons. Exports to Japan accounted for 92.6% of the total.

Lignite production in Saskatchewan fell slightly to 3.8 million short tons. Imports of coal from the U.S. declined 4 million short tons to 13.5 million short tons. During 1974, plans were announced to build a $35 million coal transfer terminal and rail system at Thunder Bay, Ont. Coal would be transported there from the western producing areas to the markets in the east.

(R. J. FOWELL)

ELECTRICITY

Consumption of electricity continued to rise in most countries during 1974 but at a rate well below the previous mean of 7.3% a year. The increase over 1973 was nil in the U.S., 6.3% in the U.S.S.R., 9.8% in Japan, and 2% in the EEC, with France's consumption up by 4.9%, Italy's by 3.9%, and West Germany's by 3%. In the U.K., however, consumption fell by 3.2%, and this decline was further accentuated during 1975.

Thermonuclear Electricity. An increase in the number of power stations using enriched uranium led to such an increase in consumption of the metal that it caused serious problems. The U.S., main supplier of enriched uranium, subjected its price to systematic review, raising it by 26% in 1975.

When their three plants for uranium enrichment by gas diffusion were working at full capacity, the European countries would be able to supply an increasing proportion of their own needs. The Eurodif group, therefore, started work in January 1975 on the construction of an enrichment plant at Tricastin in France. The cost of the plant, allowing for the need to construct a nuclear power station to provide it with electricity,

Installed Capacity and Production of Electric Power in Selected Countries, Dec. 31, 1973

Country	Hydroelectric power: Operating plants Installed capacity (000 kw.)	Hydroelectric power: Operating plants Production (000,000 kw-hr.)	Total electric power: Installed capacity (000 kw.)	Total electric power: Production (000,000 kw-hr.)
World	...	...	...	6,042,000
Afghanistan*	192	416	268	439
Algeria	286†	733†	1,107	2,371†
Angola	368	680*	499	984
Argentina	1,332	2,948	8,355	26,737
Australia	4,221*†	12,027	16,215*†	64,802
Austria	5,873	19,159	8,778	31,325
Bangladesh*	80†	300	547†	1,172
Belgium‡§	503	622	8,710	41,067
Bolivia	209	712	308	903
Brazil	10,974*	43,274‖	13,489*	61,381
Bulgaria	1,228	2,565	5,114	21,952
Burma*	101	475	263	616
Cameroon	193‖	1,080*	221‖	1,133*
Canada‡§	34,266	192,911	54,377	262,272
Chile	1,366	5,319	2,472	8,766
Colombia	1,787‖	6,058¶	3,150‖	10,300*
Costa Rica	242	1,137	361	1,346
Cuba	44†	...	1,576	4,212*†
Czechoslovakia‡§	1,591	2,403	12,122	53,473
Denmark	9	24	5,699	18,004
Ecuador*	105	445	357	1,117
Egypt	2,454†	5,157†	4,012	8,104
El Salvador	108‖	429*	207‖	820*
Ethiopia‖	95	275	184†	585
Finland	2,320	10,242	6,363	24,596
France‡§	15,618*	47,280	41,494‖	174,080
Gabon	—	4.7*	37*	165
Germany, E.‡§	697	1,260	14,300	76,908
Germany, W.‡§	4,820	15,516	62,050	298,995
Ghana*	900	3,304	976	3,344
Greece	1,041†	2,216†	3,443†	14,817
Guatemala	96†	332†	233	910
Honduras	69†	360†	130†	408
Hong Kong†	—	—	2,021	6,809
Hungary	20	99	3,230	17,641
Iceland♂□	379†	2,181†	487	2,290
India‡§	6,788*	27,718	17,990*	70,516*
Indonesia†	309*	1,257*	789*	2,932
Iran	804†	5,408	4,117	12,093
Ireland	219†‖	644†	1,678†‖	7,348
Israel	—	—	1,593	8,722
Italy‡§♂□	16,377	39,125	39,768	145,518
Jamaica	21†	141*†	658	2,134
Japan‡§♂□	21,520†	67,012	84,161†	470,082
Kenya†	71*	381*	191*	723
Korea, South	621†	1,284†	4,272†	15,234
Lebanon	246†	478	538†	1,791
Liberia*	72	266	300	846
Libya†	—	—	265*	698
Luxembourg	932*†	839	1,157†	2,165
Malagasy Republic	35‖	142*†	90‖	286*
Malaysia	...	3,986*	1,024	4,333*
Malta†	—	—	115	348
Mexico♂□	3,612	16,232	9,362	37,084
Morocco	388†	1,192†	821	2,639
Mozambique	114†‖	283*	365‖	724‖
Netherlands, The‡§	—	—	13,407	52,628
New Zealand†♂□	3,376	14,153	4,209	18,112
Nigeria	320†	1,858†	855	2,625
Norway	13,991*	72,610	14,142*	72,745
Pakistan†‡	586♀	2,524♀	1,850♀	7,449‖
Panama*	15†	83†	272	1,151
Paraguay	90*†	192*†	156*	379
Peru‖	989	4,283	1,797	5,949
Philippines*	849	2,536†	2,449	10,398
Poland	821	1,853	17,729	84,302
Portugal	1,782	7,354	2,751	9,821
Rhodesia	705*	5,591	1,192*	7,277
Romania	2,300	7,547	10,119	46,779
Singapore†	—	—	727*	3,719
South Africa	160*†	814*	12,600*	64,857
Spain‡§	11,136*	29,203	21,871*	75,765
Sri Lanka*	195	856	281	995
Sweden‡§	11,961	59,892	19,296	78,080
Switzerland‡§	9,700*	27,787	11,320*	36,538
Syria	—	—	437	1,154
Tanzania†	49*	...	131*	512
Thailand*	516†	1,728†	1,639	6,209
Tunisia	29†	71†	337	1,129
Turkey	877*	2,628	2,742*	12,289
Uganda	150*†	796*†	174*	798†
U.S.S.R.‡	35,320	122,345	195,560	914,653
U.K.‡§	2,158	4,554	78,311	282,128
U.S.‡§♂□	57,125*	275,330	457,879	1,947,079
Uruguay	252†	1,556†	546	2,430†
Venezuela	908‖	6,167	3,372	16,392
Vietnam, South†	164*	—	838*	1,625
Yugoslavia	4,624	16,394	8,545	35,062
Zaire	...	3,764	...	3,884
Zambia	425‖	3,076*	655‖	3,419

*1972. †Public sector only. ‡Includes nuclear (in 000 kw.): Belgium 11; Canada 2,666; Czechoslovakia 95; France 2,942; East Germany 75; West Germany 2,414; India 780; Italy 670; Japan 2,940; The Netherlands 524; Pakistan 125; Spain 1,073; Sweden 472; Switzerland 1,006; U.S.S.R. 3,509; U.K. 5,814; U.S. 21,070. §Includes nuclear (in 000,000 kw-hr.): Belgium ...; Canada 14,256; Czechoslovakia 232; France 13,968; East Germany 351; West Germany 11,755; India 2,204; Italy 3,142; Japan 9,480; The Netherlands 1,110; Spain 4,751; Sweden 2,111; Switzerland 3,050; U.S.S.R. ...; U.K. 27,997; U.S. 83,292. ‖1971. ¶1969. ♀1970. ♂Includes geothermal (in 000 kw.): Iceland 2; Italy 406; Japan 31; Mexico 78; New Zealand 192; U.S. 322. □Includes geothermal (in 000,000 kw-hr.): Iceland 24; Italy 2,480; Japan 248; Mexico 183; New Zealand 1,162; U.S. 1,453.
Source: United Nations, *Statistical Yearbook, 1974.*

was estimated at Fr. 12 billion. Plans were made to build a second European enrichment plant, using the same method of gas diffusion, with Iranian participation.

At the end of May 1975 there were 175 nuclear power plants operating worldwide, representing a total capacity of 71,940 Mw. Of this total 36,810 Mw. were in the U.S., 6,440 Mw. in Japan, 5,650 Mw. in the U.K., 4,373 Mw. in the Soviet Union, 3,334 Mw. in West Germany, and 2,891 Mw. in France. This capacity was distributed in the proportions of 32,795 Mw. from 58 enriched-uranium, pressurized water reactors (PWR); 23,375 Mw. from 44 boiling water reactors (BWR); 8,397 Mw. from 36 natural uranium gas-graphite reactors; and 7,373 Mw. from 37 reactors of other types. Nine of the reactors (four PWRs, four BWRs, and one enriched-uranium, graphite, boiling water reactor) had a capacity equal to or greater than 1,000 Mw. Seven reactors were in the U.S., one in the Soviet Union, and one in West Germany. The last was the most powerful, a PWR of 1,146 Mw., brought into service at Biblis in 1974.

In 1974 total production of electricity from the nuclear power stations in service, the U.S.S.R. and Eastern European countries excluded, totaled 246,000,000,000 kw-hr., an increase of about one-third over 1973. Of this, the U.S. produced 125,000,000,000 kw-hr.; the U.K., 24,000,000,000 kw-hr.; Japan, 18,000,000,000 kw-hr.; France, 15,000,000,000 kw-hr.; Canada, 15,000,000,000 kw-hr.; and West Germany, 12,000,000,000 kw-hr. The most productive nuclear power station was at Pickering, in Canada, with four heavy-water groups of 540 Mw. each; it supplied 14,000,000,000 kw-hr.

In the U.S. orders received by suppliers of reactors by the beginning of 1975 represented a total capacity of 215,780 Mw., of which 36,810 Mw. were in service, 73,840 Mw. under construction, and 105,130 Mw. projected. Westinghouse Electric had 35.1% of the orders; General Electric, 32.4%; Combustion Engineering, 15%; and Babcock and Wilcox, 14.1%.

The U.S. Atomic Energy Commission (AEC) disappeared, to be replaced by two new bodies, the Energy Research and Development Administration (ERDA) and the Nuclear Regulatory Commission (NRC). Ten days after it was set up, the NRC ordered an inspection of all U.S. boiling water reactors to discover whether a particular pipe system showed cracks similar to those found in the Dresden 2 reactor near Morris, Ill. The inspection proved negative.

In Japan 11 nuclear power plants—six BWRs, four PWRs, and one LWCHR (moderated by heavy water, cooled by ordinary water)—with a capacity of 9,040 Mw. were under construction. Total capacity in service by the end of 1979 would be 15,480 Mw. In April 1975 the Central Electricity Council inaugurated a new development program, which provided for nuclear power stations with a capacity of 24,670 Mw. to be constructed between 1975 and 1979. The U.S. General Atomic Co. set up a joint company with Mitsubishi Heavy Industries, Ltd., with the object of developing high-temperature reactors in Japan.

In West Germany there were 15 plants under construction or on order as of June 30, 1975, of which six were PWRs, seven BWRs, one THTR (high-temperature) prototype, and one rapid neutron prototype. These reactors, representing a total capacity of 15,243 Mw., were scheduled to come into service by 1980. Additional projects for 26 nuclear plants totaling more than 30,000 Mw. were announced for dates between 1980 and 1985.

In France nuclear power stations under construction or on order at the end of 1975 comprised 20 plants with a total capacity of 17,715 Mw. scheduled to come into service between 1976 and 1980. Apart from one rapid neutron reactor with a capacity of 1,200 Mw., cooled by liquid sodium, they were all PWRs. Électricité de France (EDF) had hoped to use BWRs as well as PWRs, but the government decided in August for the sake of simplicity to order only from the manufacturer holding the Westinghouse license, and options on two BWR groups were not taken up. In exchange, EDF obtained permission to increase the capacity of the two additional PWRs from 900 to 1,300 Mw.

Because of its sizable resources of con-

Cooling tower of the nuclear power plant to be constructed in Gösgen, Switzerland, which will be the third such plant in the country. Its final height will be 150 m.

KEYSTONE

Electrical Power Production of Selected Countries, 1974
By source

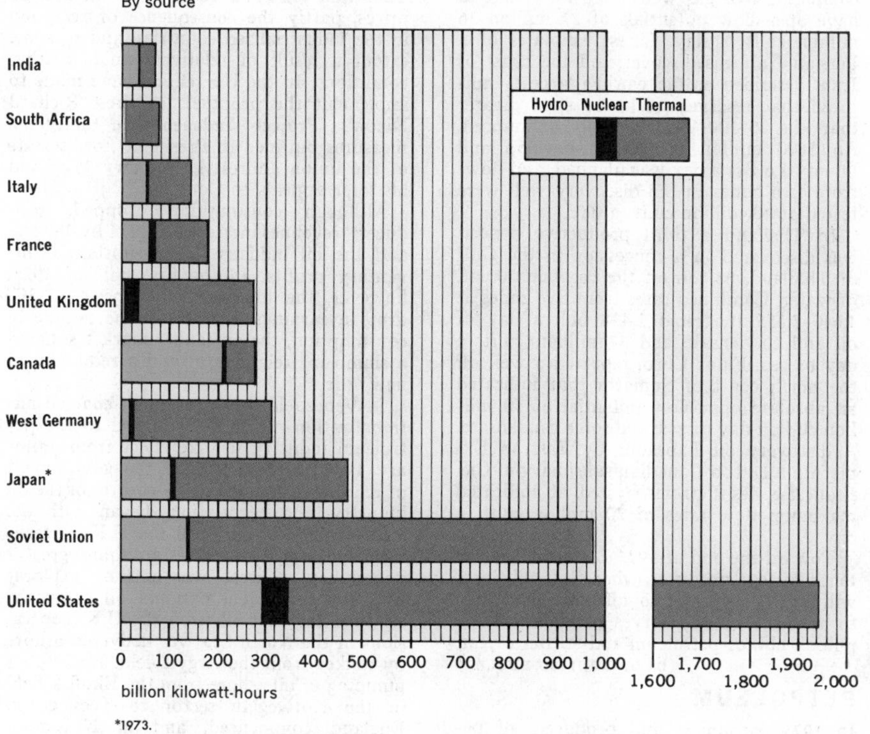

*1973.
Sources: United Nations, *Monthly Bulletin of Statistics; World Energy Supplies, 1969–1972.*

ventional power, the U.S.S.R. had been slow to develop a nuclear industry. The 17 power plants under construction, with a total capacity of 12,384 Mw., would, however, bring total capacity to 17,153 Mw. by the end of 1978. Agreements were made with seven Eastern European countries to supply 20 440-Mw. PWR plants. Three of these were in service—two in East Germany and one in Bulgaria—and 11 were under construction—four in Czechoslovakia, three in Bulgaria, two in Finland, and two in Hungary. The other six were still in the planning stage.

In June 1975 an agreement was signed in Bonn for West Germany to supply Brazil with eight nuclear power stations of 1,300 Mw. each with a factory for reprocessing irradiated fuel and a plant for uranium enrichment. The orders, worth DM. 12 billion, were to be carried out over 15 years, and the agreement gave West Germany access to Brazilian uranium deposits in return.

Hydroelectricity. The Emmasson dam in Switzerland came into service at the end of 1974, harnessing the waters from several valleys of the French and Swiss Alps and supplying two factories working in series: one at La Batiaz (160 Mw.) in Switzerland and one at Le Châtelard (189 Mw.) in France.

Japan was actively engaged in harnessing its remaining hydroelectric energy resources, particularly by means of pumped storage plants. These would allow output from a number of power stations to be regulated in the most favourable way; 11 plants of this type, with a total capacity of 7,735 Mw., were under construction.

The last of six units at the seventh of the power stations in the Snowy Mountains scheme in New South Wales, Australia, came into service during 1974. The project, first examined in 1949, had taken 25 years to complete. Total capacity of the scheme was 3,740 Mw., with an annual mean productive capacity of 5,000,000,000 kw-hr.

In Canada the ninth station of the Peace River scheme in the province of British Columbia was brought into service at the end of 1974. This brought the capacity of the installation to 2,475 Mw. and put a total capacity of 4,600 Mw. at the disposal of the British Columbia Commission.

In Brazil the Promissão power station on the Tietê River, with a capacity of 270 Mw., was inaugurated in May 1975. This raised the nation's total installed capacity to 3,944 Mw.

In Lima, Peru, a consortium of companies from five countries began work early in 1975 on a project to harness the Majes River; when completed, it would have a capacity of 600 Mw. and allow irrigation of 60,000 ha. of arid pampas in southern Peru.

In Zaire the sixth and last unit in the Inga 1 power station on the Congo came into service in December 1974, raising the mean annual productive capacity of the station to 2,400,000,000 kw-hr. Work continued on Inga 2, supplied by the same dam and consisting of eight units. It was designed to have a mean annual output of 9,600,-000,000 kw-hr.

(LUCIEN CHALMEY)

GAS

There was a good deal of soul-searching in the major energy-consuming countries in 1975 in an effort to achieve greater self-sufficiency in energy. The U.S. had particularly acute problems, which were compounded by actual cuts in available supplies of gas.

Natural gas imports to the U.S. fell by 9%, to 940 Bcf (billion cubic feet), in 1974. Consumption of natural gas declined 2.1%, to 21.78 Tcf (trillion cubic feet). Marketed gas production dropped 3.3%, to 21.9 Tcf. Gas curtailments and other restrictions on the use of gaseous fuels were reported; it was estimated that winter gas curtailments would rise 30% over the previous winter, to 1.3 Tcf.

World gas reserves at the end of 1973 totaled 2,233 Tcf, with the U.S.S.R. accounting for a 29.1% share, Iran 17%, and the U.S. 11.2%. Total production for 1973 amounted to 51.97 Tcf, of which the U.S. produced 46.2%, the U.S.S.R. 15.8%, and Canada 6.4%.

EEC countries, helped by a 15% boost in gas production in 1974, met 35% of their energy needs by means of natural gas. Production was up by 19% in The Netherlands and by 21% in the U.K., but France and Italy experienced declines of 1 and 2%, respectively. Dutch fields supplied 48% of all gas consumed in EEC countries.

The British government estimated that its sector of the North Sea held 27–45 Tcf of gas. Existing discoveries would support the production of 5–6 Bcf a day well into the 1980s. Production in 1974 averaged 3½ Bcf a day. Despite a downturn in West Germany's energy consumption in 1974, Ruhrgas, the country's largest supplier, achieved a 28% increase in total gas deliveries, and another increase was expected for 1975.

The Canadian Petroleum Association reported that proved reserves of marketable gas in Canada showed an 8.1% annual gain at the end of 1974, to 56.7 Tcf. Discoveries in the Arctic Islands were expected to produce about 12 Tcf. In the U.S.S.R. initial gas production goals for 1975 of 11.3 Tcf were expected to fall short; a revised target was set at 10 Tcf.

Methods of underground coal gasification, tested in an experiment at Hanna, Wyo., increased the 2 million cu.ft.-a-day gas production rate and 126 BTU (British thermal units)-per-cu.ft. heating value of an earlier experiment there to 2.7 million cu.ft. a day and 152 BTU per cu.ft. A 15 million cu.ft.-a-day SNG (synthetic natural gas) plant was brought into production in Hawaii by Pacific Resources Inc. After a 40-day test in April 1974 Brooklyn Union Gas Co. readied its Greenpoint (N.Y.) SNG plant for continuous 180-day operation, which began early in 1975. Half of the 250 million cu.ft.-a-day design capacity of the 166 million cu.ft.-a-day SNG plant of the Northern Illinois Gas Co. was reported operational during 1975.

An agreement between the U.S.S.R., Japan, El Paso Natural Gas Co., and Occidental Petroleum Corp., signed at the end of 1974, provided for two years of development in Siberian gas fields in the Yakutsk region. Late in 1974 deliveries of Siberian natural gas began to arrive in Moscow through a 2,000-mi., 48-in. pipeline capable of carrying 540 Bcf a year. Soviet gas exports in 1974 more than doubled the previous year's deliveries, with non-Communist European countries buying 39% of the total 520 Bcf. The Soviet Union planned to increase gas deliveries to Austria. In return the Austrian state steel company would supply the U.S.S.R. 200,000 tons of steel pipe. West Germany was also to receive gas in exchange for steel pipe. By 1980 the U.S.S.R. expected to be delivering about 1 Bcf a day to West Germany. Bolivia agreed to increase gas supplies to Argentina from 150 million cu.ft. a day to 280 million cu.ft. a day for ten years, and to deliver an additional 280 million cu.ft. a day when sufficient new reserves were developed. In return, Argentina would finance oil exploration in Bolivia.

Nigeria approved the construction of two LNG (liquefied natural gas) and LP (liquefied petroleum) gas complexes, each designed to liquefy 1 Bcf a day of natural gas. Pakistan's Sui Gas Transmission Co. chose a consultant for the construction of 265 mi. of 18-in. pipeline in Pakistan. It was to have an initial capacity of 110 million cu.ft. a day and was scheduled for completion in late 1976.

Exploration and production during the year provided some surprises. The Texas Pacific Oil Co. tested a 13,500-ft. gas well 25 mi. S of Fort Stockton, Texas, at a calculated absolute open-flow potential of 4 Bcf a day, a possible world record. The No. 2 Osborne well in Morrow County, Texas, tested 1.6 Bcf a day at 10,780–10,801 ft. In Roberts County, Texas, a well was reported as indicating 500 million cu.ft. a day. Another hydrocarbon field, in southeast Mexico, was reported by Petróleos Mexicanos to produce both oil and 10 million cu.ft. a day of gas; 24% of Mexico's gas demand was said to be satisfied by the output of two new giant oil fields, at Reforma and Samaria in southeastern Mexico, which were producing 1,650,000 cu.ft. of natural gas per 1,000 bbl. of oil, or 485 million cu.ft. a day.

During 1974 the Consolidated Gas Supply Corp. began to withdraw methane from an Eastern Associated Coal Corp. coal mine near Bula, W.Va. A year later gas still flowed from the mine at about 600,000 cu.ft. a day, only slightly down from the original rate of 700,000–720,000 cu.ft. a day. In California, Occidental Petroleum discovered a new natural-gas field in the northern Sacramento Valley. A discovery about 40 mi. SW of Oklahoma City indicated a well with a maximum daily flow rate of 11.7 million cu.ft. and 819 bbl. of condensate.

In Papua a consortium of Japanese companies began drilling in May 1975 at a place where a minimum of 1.5 Tcf of gas had been indicated. The consortium planned to drill three wells with an option to drill six more. Two well completions in the Malossa field in Italy at the end of 1974 indicated that the find was the largest in Italy's history. Reserves of 1.8 Tcf of "very pure" gas were reported. The British Gas Corp. reported a find in its first well drilled in the Irish Sea off Blackpool. Ireland's gas agency, Bord Gais Eirann Teoranta, signed a 20-year pact for the purchase of 125 million cu.ft. a day of natural gas from a field of Marathon Petroleum Ireland Ltd. off the County Cork coast. Reserves were estimated at 1 Tcf and initial production was expected to meet 10% of Ireland's energy requirements.

British Gas signed a 20-year contract with Shell U.K. Exploration and Production Ltd. and Esso Petroleum Ltd. to buy a minimum of 500 million cu.ft. a day of natural gas from the North Sea's Brent oil field. Deutsche Shell A.G. announced that it would sell gas from A/S Norske Shell from the Albuskjell field in the Norwegian sector of the North Sea to a group of European companies. Pan Ocean Oil Corp. announced tests in May that showed oil and 104 million cu.ft. a day from a well in the British sector of the North Sea. West Germany brought in its first successful wildcat operation in the North Sea, a well about 220 mi. NW of Emden which tested at 25.4 million cu.ft. a day. Tunisia reported the discovery of three natural gas fields off its Mediterranean coast estimated to contain at least 530 Bcf. Added to previous finds of 105 Bcf, these gas deposits were expected to meet all of the country's needs until 1995.

Atlantic Richfield Co. and Exxon Corp. struck oil and gas in a formation below their main discovery zone in the Prudhoe Bay field off the north coast of Alaska. In ten tests at 9,994–11,815 ft. the largest gas flow rate recorded was 7 million cu.ft. a day. Off South Padre Island, Texas, Mobil Oil Corp. completed five gas wells that were said to have open-flow potentials of 27 million–36 million cu.ft. a day. Latest estimates of a Persian Gulf gas discovery off the coast of Iran, described as the world's largest, indicated that reserves might be even greater than the 70–100 Tcf originally announced. An $800 million project to develop and liquefy 1.6 Bcf a day was planned, and flows from two zones in the discovery well were tested at 40 million cu.ft. a day.

In Thailand a third productive deposit was discovered in a concession in the Gulf of Thailand, 85 mi. off the coast in 200 ft. of water. Combined rates from five zones at 4,640–7,355 ft. tested 1,438 bbl. a day of oil and condensate and 37 million cu.ft. a day of gas. Fluor Corp. reported a well off the north coast of Sumatra that indicated an absolute open-flow potential of 50 million cu.ft. a day of gas, and some condensate. A discovery off Labrador by Eastcan Exploration Ltd., a Canadian subsidiary of Cie. Française des Pétroles, tested at indicated maximum flow rates of 20 million cu.ft. a day.

Toward the end of 1975 Zaire became the tenth African producer, when Gulf Oil Corp. withdrew oil from two offshore fields said to have combined reserves estimated at 200 million bbl. of petroleum and 50 Bcf of gas.

(DAVID RICHARD BUTLER)

PETROLEUM

In 1975 consumers and producers of petroleum products reviewed their respective positions in the light of reduced demand and falling production, industrial recession, and continuing inflationary pressures. The International Energy Agency explored the possibilities of and planned for cooperation among consumers on the security of oil supplies and alternative sources of energy. The International Monetary Fund (IMF) and World Bank tackled recycling and other financial problems caused by the sudden large oil price increases, which turned out to be less disruptive than had been feared. Divergent U.S. and French approaches to oil affairs moved closer together as a result of talks held in Martinique in December 1974. Members of OPEC held many discussions among themselves on policies, culminating in a summit conference at the beginning of March 1975. The Sinai accord between Israel and Egypt, reached in September 1975 under U.S. auspices, helped to reduce the level of political tension in the Middle East. The death by assassination of King Faisal of Saudi Arabia had no appreciable effect on oil questions.

For the average person, the overriding concern was the price of oil. After a freeze on oil prices was agreed upon by OPEC in December 1974, an OPEC meeting in Libreville, Gabon, in mid-June 1975 prolonged the standstill until October 1. There was considerable pressure by the consumers, notably the U.S., to maintain the price freeze. U.S. Pres. Gerald Ford stated that rises in oil prices would be "very disruptive and totally unacceptable." Nevertheless, OPEC argued that oil revenues had declined because of inflation, and most members wanted to offset at least part of such losses, with Iran reportedly proposing increases between 20 and 35%. At the unexpectedly long and acrimonious OPEC conference at Vienna in September, the moderate stance of Saudi Arabia prevailed and prices were raised by 10%, but other questions of crude oil differentials and output restrictions were postponed for later consideration.

In 1974 oil consumption fell by 2.9%, in contrast to the previous world five-year average annual increase of 4.9%, exclusive of the U.S.S.R., Eastern Europe, and China. This was partly a reaction to higher oil prices, partly the consequence of recession in the industrialized countries, and to some extent a result of relatively mild weather conditions. In the U.S. efforts were made to implement the proposals of Pres. Richard Nixon's Project Independence and the measures outlined in President Ford's state of the union address in January 1975 and his later appeals to Congress.

Although consumption dropped, producers' revenues increased in 1974 by 289.5% and the oil industry made substantial inventory profits. In the first half of 1975, however, the industry experienced a 33% drop in earnings. Because of the decline in consumption, the oil tanker market suffered a slump in freight rates and a reduction in new orders.

In Venezuela the government enacted nationalization measures in regard to the petroleum industry to take effect from January 1976. In March 1975 the government of Kuwait demanded 100% control of the oil industry, and negotiations began with the Kuwait Oil Co. In April the U.K. government published a bill establishing greater government control over offshore exploration and forming a national oil company. In June the first oil from the U.K. concessions in the North Sea was delivered ashore by tanker from the Argyll field. In October pumping of oil ashore from the Ekofisk field in the Norwegian sector to Teesside in England commenced, and in November Queen Elizabeth officially inaugurated the first piping of oil ashore from a U.K. concession in the North Sea, the Forties field, to Scotland. Progress on the North Slope field in Alaska was delayed by extremely severe weather conditions.

In the U.S. the year-long dispute between the president and Congress over energy policy ended in the signing of a compromise bill in December. (*See* above.) The Senate subcommittee of Sen. Frank Church (Dem., Idaho), which was investigating the role of the multinational oil companies in the oil crisis of 1973–74, came to the conclusion that the companies had not abused their position and had behaved in a responsible manner. Interest increased in the oil potential of China.

The ninth World Petroleum Congress took place in Tokyo in June 1975, with 4,800 delegates from 73 countries presenting 151 technical papers. General concern was expressed that the rate of new oil discoveries was not keeping pace with predicted growth in demand, and there was emphasis on the need to find more oil and develop alternative energy sources, irrespective of any political considerations.

Production in the first half of 1975 in the Middle East fell below that of the crisis levels of 1973, and compared with the first half of 1974 was generally down by 13.5%, with only Iraq registering a significant change, up by 14.3%. Libyan production had fallen by more than one-half since the beginning of 1973. Sharjah registered a large percentage increase, but the volume, at 39,000 bbl. a day, was small. The overall total of the non-Communist world was down by 9% from the first half of 1974, with Mexico alone recording an increase, of over 26%.

Reserves. At the beginning of 1975 total world proved and probable oil reserves were 720,400,000,000 bbl., compared with 634,700,000,000 bbl. for the previous year. The Western Hemisphere share was 90,000,000,000 bbl., 12.4% of the total. The Middle East continued to account for the largest share of the world reserves, rising to 403,400,000,000 bbl., 56.3% of the world total. U.S. reserves, at 5.4% of the total, were lower than in the preceding year, while those of the U.S.S.R., Eastern Europe, and China increased to 132,400,000,000 bbl. Canadian reserves declined for the fifth successive year. In Australia drilling activity in 1974 was the lowest for 11 years. In the Atlantic Ocean three licenses were awarded by the French authorities in April 1975. Ireland in June made its first awards of exclusive exploration and development licenses.

Production. During 1974 world crude oil production increased by 0.2%, to 57,970,000 bbl. a day, compared with an average annual increase during 1969–74 of 5.9%. The Middle East again dominated production with an increased share of 37.8%, a total of 21,720,000 bbl. a day. Saudi Arabia increased production by 11.8%, half its average of 1969–74, to 14.3% of the total, 8,210,000 bbl. a day. Iran followed with an increase of 2.7%, giving it a 10.6% share of the total with 6,060,000 bbl. a day. Iraq and Abu Dhabi, which registered large increases of 34.7 and 23.8%, respectively, in 1973, fell considerably in 1974 to a decline of 4.2% and an increase of 8.5%, respectively. Kuwait again reduced production, by 17.3%, and Libya's output fell greatly, by 29%. U.S. production at 10,485,000 bbl. a day was a lower percentage share of the total, at 17.4%, and was down 4.3% from 1973. Venezuelan production, 3,060,000 bbl., a drop of 11.6%, accounted for 5.6% of the total share. Mexico with 14.1% and Nigeria with 13.3% both recorded increases, as did West Africa, Trinidad and Tobago, Indonesia, and the U.S.S.R., whose share of the total at 15.8% was still below that of the U.S. Chinese production increased by the largest single percentage, 24.5%, to 1,050,000 bbl. a day.

Consumption. World petroleum consumption in 1974 was 55,990,000 bbl. a day, a reduction of 1.2% from 1973. Japanese demand at 5,310,000 bbl. a day, a reduction of 2.7% from the previous year, was 9.5% of total world consumption. The U.S. remained the largest single consuming nation at 16,220,000 bbl. a day, a decline from 1973 of 4% with its share of the world total at 28.6%. Western European consumption, at 14,170,000 bbl. a day, showed the largest decrease, 6.6%, with West Germany at 2,785,000 bbl., France 2,435,000 bbl., the U.K. 2,150,000 bbl., and Italy 2,010,000 bbl. a day as the chief consumers. Only Spain registered an increase (5.3%) over 1973. The Netherlands had the greatest single percentage reduction, 14.3%, a consumption of 720,000 bbl. a day, followed by Belgium and Luxembourg at 12.7%. The U.S.S.R., Canada, and Mexico went against the trend with modest rises of 7.6, 5.3, and 5%, giving the U.S.S.R. 12.5% of the total.

The pattern of imports changed little in 1974. The Middle East continued to supply most of the consumption of Japan and Western Europe and increased its supplies to the U.S. to 1,025,000 bbl. a day, compared with 820,000 bbl. a day in 1973.

Products. In the U.S. gasolines continued to dominate demand, followed by middle distillates and fuel oil. Average annual increases, 1969–74, were 3, 2.5, and 6.6%, respectively. For the same period the Benelux countries continued to show increases for gasolines but reductions in fuel oil demand as natural gas replaced it. In Japan fuel oil demand at 2,210 bbl. a day was less than that of the previous year.

Refining. World refining capacity in 1974 was 68,440,000 bbl. a day, an increase of 5.3% over 1973. The increase from 1972 to 1973 had been 7.7%. The capacity of the Western Hemisphere was 24.4 million bbl. a day, 35.6% of the total and a slight increase of 0.2% over the previous year. Western Europe, with 19,520,000 bbl. a day, had 28.5% of the total, an increase of 4.4%. Capacity in the U.S. continued its decline to 21.9% of the world total, although, at 14,970,000 bbl. a day, it was 4.2% higher than in 1973. Japan, with an increase of 4.6%, had a 7.4% share of the total at 5,095,000 bbl. a day. Southeast Asia registered an increase of 3.1%, accounting for a slightly increased share of the total at 4%.

Petrochemicals. During the first part of 1974 there was a demand for all petroleum products, caused primarily by the anticipated rise in crude oil prices and the temporary oil supply dislocations. In the second part of the year, however, there was a general decline in demand, particularly in artificial fibres, although the agricultural sector maintained its requirements. The worldwide trade recession in the first half of 1975 led to a considerable drop in sales tonnages and to some deferment of large-scale capital projects. Much attention was paid to plant efficiency, conservation, and the better utilization of energy resources.

(R. W. FERRIER)

See also Engineering Projects; Industrial Review; Mining and Quarrying; Transportation.

[214.C.4; 721; 724.B.2; 724.C.1-2; 737.A.5]

Engineering Projects

Bridges. Although many major bridges were under construction around the world in 1975, the biggest problems facing bridge engineers were those of maintenance and repair. In the U.S., where there were approximately 600,000 bridges, the annual repair bill was estimated at $200 million, and these costs were repeated throughout the world in efforts to counter erosion and corrosion, breakup of the roadway surfaces, and lack of load-carrying capacity in older bridges. Acceptable accessories, such as bearings and expansion joints, parapets, crash barriers and safety fences, surface water drainage, and a waterproofing membrane to protect the structure, had to be provided within a tight budget, but with a view to keeping down maintenance costs throughout the expected lifetime of the bridge.

Suspension Bridges. When completed, the Humber Bridge in Britain would have a main span of 1,410 m., the longest span ever built, and side spans of 280 m. and 530 m. Construction had begun in 1973, and the substructure was nearly complete by the end of 1975. The bridge would have slipformed reinforced concrete towers, the first time such towers had been used for a very-long-span suspension bridge. The north tower was finished, and the south tower was to be built during 1976. The suspended structure, consisting of a trapezoidal steel box 22 m. wide by 4.5 m. deep, had side cantilever panels for footpaths and bicycle tracks. The deck was to be carried by hanger ropes, inclined so as to assist in damping any oscillations induced by wind loading. The arrangements for the superstructure followed the success of the same designers in bridging the Severn River (England) and the Bosporus Strait (Turkey). The Humber, a toll bridge, would carry four traffic lanes. Completion was expected in 1978.

The only other major suspension bridge under construction, the Kvalsund bridge in Norway, was designed to have a main span of 525 m. It was to be completed during 1977.

Steel Box Bridges. The bridge over the Loire River at Saint-Nazaire in France was completed in 1975. With a total length of 3,356 m., it consisted of a three-span steel bridge, length 720 m., and long prestressed concrete viaduct approaches at both ends. The steel bridge had a main span of 404 m., the longest cable-stayed span ever completed, and anchor spans of 158 m. The multiple cables, of harp formation, were anchored at the top of inverted-V steel towers (68 m. high) and to the outer edges of the deck girder.

In Australia some progress was made toward the completion of the West Gate Bridge in Melbourne, which had suffered a bad setback in 1970 when one of the end spans collapsed after a number of bolts had been inexplicably cut out from the mid-span splice. The collapse of this span touched off a reassessment of the steel box concept of bridge design. The five-span bridge was to have a main span of 336 m. and would have stay cables over single central pylons above the two main piers.

The Milford Haven Bridge over the Cleddau River in Wales, the other box girder bridge to suffer a partial collapse in 1970, was completed in 1975. A seven-span bridge with a single, continuous welded-steel trapezoidal box girder running the full length of 819 m., it had a main span of 213 m. but without stays. It was built by cantilevering the box girder forward from both abutments and raising a central suspended span of 136.5 m., weighing nearly 1,000 metric tons, that had been preassembled nearby. A large number of strain gauges fixed to the steelwork provided information on its behaviour during erection and would continue to do so under service conditions.

In India work recommenced on the second Hooghly Bridge. Its cable-stayed main span of approximately 457 m. was the longest yet designed.

Steel Arch Bridges. The world's longest steel arch bridge was due to be completed in 1976. It would have a span of 518 m. over New River Canyon, near Fayetteville, W.Va., and an arch height of 266 m.

Concrete Bridges. The longest span stayed-concrete bridge yet built neared completion at Bretonne near Rouen, France. It would have a main span of 320 m. In the U.S. construction of the Pasco-Kennewick Bridge over the Columbia River in Washington state was under way, and the bridge was due for completion in 1977. With a main span of 299 m., the bridge would be 24.4 m. wide to allow four traffic lanes and side footpaths. It was to be built in 8-m.-long modules, each weighing 280 metric tons. Each module would be supported by a pair of stay cables anchored at the top of the 76-m.-high concrete towers. It would be the first major bridge of its type in North America.

Strong, straight lines of structure were one of the notable features of modern, long-span concrete bridges. The three-span Hikoshima Great Bridge over the Strait of Komon, Japan, with a main span of 236 m. and side spans of 132 m., was completed in 1975 and provided an excellent example of this kind of construction.

(DAVID FISHER)

Buildings. The worldwide economic recession and consequent reduction in demand that dominated 1975 had an unusual effect on the construction industries of the industrially developed countries—perhaps eventually to the advantage of the less developed countries. In response to the continuing energy crisis, the West began to turn away from the notion that buildings should be monuments to technological sophistication, grandiose in scale and high in energy consumption. Instead, architects and engineers began to move toward reusable, human-scaled, ecologically sensitive structures with relatively low energy requirements. With the fall in demand in the developed countries there was more interest in building in other areas, particularly in the oil-producing countries, where rapidly increasing demand could not be satisfied by internal resources. Several Middle Eastern nations hired foreign builders to construct such monuments as the new conference centres at Riyadh and Mecca, Saudi Arabia, which demonstrated the suitability of reinforced concrete construction for a desert environment. The Mecca complex, designed by Frei Otto and Rolf Gutbrod, was dominated by the roof of the 1,500-seat auditorium; it was a suspended cable system independent of the structure of the building.

The multipurpose hall and restaurant for the Mannheim Garden Exhibition in West Germany was completed. The shell construction, a doubly curved surface formed from a lattice of timber laths bolted together at uniform spacing in two directions, was the largest structure of its kind in the world, covering an area of 80,000 sq.ft.

In the U.S. an increasingly common type of permanent lightweight structure had its roof entirely supported by air. The Thomas E. Leavey Activities Center, a 70,000-sq.ft. dome of Teflon-impregnated glass fibre at Santa Clara, Calif., enclosed a 5,000-seat basketball arena, two smaller arenas, and many other courts and rooms.

The world's largest concrete dome, for the 65,000-seat King County Stadium in Seattle, Wash., had a diameter of 661 ft. The 5-in.-thick dome was cast in 40 wedge-shaped segments, each weighing 1,000 tons. The segments were cast in the air on curved plywood forms, each supported by a pair of 330-ft.-long steel trusses. Four pairs of trusses formed an X across the stadium, spanning the distance between temporary towers at the centre and rim. The towers at the rim were mounted on rails so that the form could be lowered from the segment after casting, rotated, and raised into position for casting the next segment. The world's largest indoor stadium, seating 97,000 persons, was completed in New Orleans, La. The basic shape was a squared circle, and the steel-ribbed roof had a 680-ft. clear span.

In the U.K. the new fruit and vegetable markets at Nine Elms in South London, replacing Covent Garden, provided examples of two different kinds of large-scale steel roof construction. A pair of buildings, each 1,200 ft. by 165 ft., were covered by steel sheets mounted on hollow rolled steel sections with spans varying between 100 and 130 ft. The 330-ft.-square flower market was a series of massive steel trusses supporting plastic roof units in the shape of inverted, square, truncated pyramids.

The new Saint-Nazaire Bridge across the Loire River near Nantes, France.

PHILIPPE BAUDRY

WIDE WORLD

The world's tallest reinforced concrete building, Chicago's Water Tower Place, was completed in July. It is named after the old Chicago Water Tower (landmark at lower left), which survived the great fire of 1871.

In Paris a new arts centre, the Centre Pompidou, was a major example of the innovative use of steel. The frame consisted of a perimeter of vertical hollow steel columns, from which huge warren trusses (upper and lower members connected by members in the form of a series of isosceles triangles) in welded structural steelwork were hung to provide clear spans of 147 ft. on each of the six 23-ft.-high stories. The trusses were attached to the columns by gerberettes, specially designed, pivoted, cast-steel arms. Services and communications were located on the outside of the structure, and elevators and pedestrian escalators were housed in transparent tubes.

In Toronto the CN communications and observation tower was completed. The world's tallest free-standing structure, it had a total height to the top of its antenna of 1,815 ft.; 1,464 ft. of this was constructed of slipformed, reinforced, post-tensioned concrete, for which an accelerated 48-hour concrete strength testing method was employed. The total weight of the tower was 130,000 tons. Also completed in 1975 was the tallest structural concrete building for commercial and residential use, the 76-story, 859-ft.-high Water Tower Place in Chicago.

Japan's Expo '75 contained one building that was a major "first" even in the extravagant world of international exhibitions. The main pavilion was a 328-ft.-square semisubmersible floating platform, lying 700 ft. off the shore of the Expo site in Okinawa and linked to it by a bridge. It was designed to withstand the worst typhoons by increasing its water ballast and therefore displacement.

In Montreal preparations were under way for the 1976 Olympic Games. The most spectacular structure, the velodrome, had a roof supported on three pairs of giant precast arches, spanning a maximum of 564 ft. and bearing upon only four abutments. The arches were held together by epoxy glue and posttensioning cables. A 70,000-seat stadium and 930 housing units for the athletes were planned.

The emphasis during the year seemed to be on leisure buildings, but oil exploration under the North Sea produced offshore structures of outstanding significance. These included steel structures for British Petroleum's Forties Field, where the depth of water was 200 fathoms. (PETER DUNICAN)

Dams. *Europe.* The Winscar earth-fill dam in the U.K. (height 174 ft., crest length 1,706 ft., volume 1,308,000 cu.yd., crest width 26 ft., width at base 564 ft.) neared completion in 1975. In Albania construction continued on the Fierze earth- and rock-fill dam on the Drin River, and the Ridracoli arch-gravity dam on the Bidente River was under construction in Italy.

Work continued in Greece on the Mornos earth-fill dam (height 414 ft., crest length 2,677 ft., volume 22,235,000 cu.yd., storage 632,000 ac-ft.), one of the largest earth dams in Europe. A grouting curtain was used to make the foundations watertight. The Pournari earth-fill dam, with storage to supply three 300-Mw.-capacity Francis generator units in a semioutdoor powerhouse, was scheduled for completion in 1977.

In Switzerland, at 4,311 ft. above sea level, construction continued on the 220-ft.-high Ferden double-curvature arch dam on the Lonza River, and in Norway the 230-ft.-high Eidfjord Dam, under construction in the Hardanger Mountains, was designed to supply an underground power station.

Work continued on the Sayano-Shushenskaya concrete gravity-arch dam in the U.S.S.R. When completed, it would feed a power station with 6,400 Mw. capacity.

Middle East. In Turkey the Keban earth- and rock-fill dam on the Euphrates River (height 679 ft.) was completed late in 1974, three years behind schedule. The delay had been caused by having to fill cavities in the limestone foundations. Eight 155-Mw. units were to be installed in the associated powerhouse. The Hasan Ugurlu earth- and rock-fill dam (height 574 ft., crest length 1,427 ft., volume 11,827,000 cu.yd., storage 874,000 ac-ft.) on the Yesil Irmak was in an advanced stage of construction.

The Tabka earth-fill dam (height 197 ft., crest length 14,764 ft., base width 1,640 ft., storage 11,350,000 ac-ft.) on the Euphrates was completed in 1974. The power station housed five 100-Mw. units, and three further units were to be added. Work was also completed on the Reza Shah Kabir arch dam on the Karun River in Iran, and construction started on the Lar earth- and rock-fill dam on the Lar River.

Asia. In China the Liuchia Dam (height 699 ft., storage 4,634,145 ac-ft.) on the Yellow River was completed during 1974. It was designed to supply a 1,225-Mw. power station and would regulate downstream power plants and provide for flood control, irrigation, and fish breeding.

In June 1974 the Nam Phrom Dam in northeast Thailand was formally inaugurated. During 1974 two dams had been completed in Taiwan. The Tachien arch dam (height 591 ft., crest length 951 ft., volume 598,000 cu.yd., storage 207,000 ac-ft.) on the Tachia River was built in a very steep, narrow gorge, and the vertical section of the dam overhung in a downstream direction to protect against the effects of seismic shocks. The Tehchi double-curvature arch dam (height 590.5 ft., crest length 607 ft., volume 562,440 cu.yd., storage 142,277 ac-ft.), also on the Tachia, in the mountains of central Taiwan, had taken five years to construct. Its storage supplied three 79-Mw. units installed in a powerhouse 656 ft. below ground level.

The High Island project under construction in Hong Kong was designed to include two rock-fill dams located in the Sai Kung peninsula. In India work continued on the Nagarjuna Sagar earth-fill dam on the Krishna River, and in Nepal the Kulikhani rock-fill dam on the Kulikhani River was under construction.

THE TORONTO STAR

The new CN communications tower, built in Toronto by Canadian National Railways, is the world's tallest free-standing structure at 1,815 ft. (including antenna).

WIDE WORLD

Rubber dams anchored to the riverbed near Ferrara, Italy, emerge from the water after trials were conducted in a new system to control high tides. If successful, similar dams will be placed around Venice to prevent furthur flooding of the lagoon city.

United States. Work began on the ellipse-shaped Auburn double-curvature arch dam, the world's largest of its type, on the North Fork of the American River, northeast of Sacramento, Calif. A curved powerhouse would be constructed at the dam's toe. Television cameras, lowered into boreholes under the foundations of the Gathright Dam in northwest Virginia, revealed the presence of cavities, and an 8-ft.-wide cutoff wall was built to reduce the seepage.

The Los Angeles rock-fill dam, which would replace two dams damaged by earthquake in 1971, was designed to withstand severe earthquakes and the worst of the California storms. One of the world's thinnest dams, the Crystal arch dam on the Gunnison River in Colorado, was to include a ski-jump spillway occupying one-quarter of the crest.

South America. In Colombia the Alto Anchicaya concrete-faced rock-fill dam (height 459 ft.), completed at the beginning of 1975, supplied an underground power station housing three 113.3-Mw. units. Construction continued on the Chivor rock-fill dam on the Batá River (height 777.5 ft.), the world's seventh highest such dam. In Peru construction continued on the earth-fill dam on the Colca River. The storage would be used to irrigate arid pampas near Arequipa. Work on the Gallieto Ciego zoned earth-fill dam began during 1975.

Australia. In July 1974 work started on the Dartmouth earth- and rock-fill dam (height 591 ft., crest length 2,264 ft., volume 13.7 million cu.yd. of rock-fill, 2 million cu.yd. of clay, and 1.2 million cu.yd. of filler) on the Mitta Mitta River. Scheduled for completion in 1977, it was the last of the dams on the Upper Murray River system, the largest system in Australia. The Thomson rock-fill dam on the Thomson River was designed to provide a reservoir for irrigation and water supplies to Melbourne.

Major World Dams Under Construction in 1975*

Name of dam	River	Country	Type†	Height (ft.)	Length of crest (ft.)	Volume content (000 cu.yd.)	Gross capacity of reservoir (000 ac-ft.)
Água Vermelha	Grande	Brazil	EG	295	13,090	25,689	8,900
Auburn	American (N. Fork)	U.S.	A	685	4,150	6,000	2,300
Balimela	Sileru	India	E	230	15,200	29,600	3,100
Chicoasen	Grijalva	Mexico	ER	787	1,568	15,700	1,346
Chivor	Batá	Colombia	ER	778	919	14,126	661
Dartmouth	Mitta Mitta	Australia	ER	591	2,264	16,900	5,232
Fierze	Drin	Albania	ER	518	1,312	916	2,124
Hasan Ugurlu	Yesilirmak	Turkey	ER	574	1,427	11,827	874
Inguri	Inguri	U.S.S.R.	A	892	2,513	4,967	801
Itaipu	Paraná	Brazil-Paraguay	ERG	591	25,918	35,316	23,510
Itumbiara	Paranaiba	Brazil	EG	328	21,981	47,088	13,806
Kara Kaya	Euphrates	Turkey	A	591	1,293	1,779	7,767
Kolyma	Kolyma	U.S.S.R.	ER	427	2,461	16,415	12,000
La Grande No. 2	La Grande	Canada	ER	525	9,300	30,000	50,264
La Grande No. 3	La Grande	Canada	ER	320	12,800	30,000	49,615
La Grande No. 4	La Grande	Canada	ER	385	11,400	25,000	15,322
Las Portas	Camba	Spain	A	498	1,587	977	609
Mornos	Mornos	Greece	E	414	2,677	22,235	632
Nader Shah	Maroon	Iran	E	574	722	9,418	1,313
Nurek	Vakhsh	U.S.S.R.	E	1,040	2,390	75,864	8,424
Oosterschelde	Vense Gat Oosterschelde	Netherlands, The	E	148	29,527	91,560	2,351
Patia	Patia	Colombia	ER	787	1,804	30,869	15,322
Poechos	Chira	Peru	E	164	32,808	22,890	973
Rogunsky	Vakhsh	U.S.S.R.	E	1,066	2,506	91,560	9,485
São Simão	Paranaiba	Brazil	ERG	394	11,847	35,822	10,166
Sayano-Shushenskaya	Yenisei	U.S.S.R.	A	794	3,504	11,916	25,353
Sobradinho	São Francisco	Brazil	ERG	139	12,795	17,265	27,700
Sterkfontein	Nuwejaarspruit	South Africa	E	305	10,039	22,236	2,153
Thomson	Thomson	Australia	ER	530	1,800	12,600	892
Toktogol	Naryn	U.S.S.R.	G	699	1,476	3,787	15,800
Ukai	Tapi	India	EG	226	16,165	33,375	6,900
Ust-Ilim	Angara	U.S.S.R.	EG	344	11,695	11,382	48,100
Yacyreta-Apipe	Paraná	Argentina-Paraguay	EG	125	164,000	91,560	14,079
MAJOR WORLD DAMS COMPLETED IN 1974 AND 1975*							
Beas	Beas-Indus	India	G	435	6,400	45,800	6,600
Chirkeyskaya	Sulak	U.S.S.R.	A	764	1,109	1,602	2,252
Cabora Bassa	Zambezi	Mozambique	A	561	994	667	51,900
Cochiti	Rio Grande	U.S.	E	253	26,891	64,631	513
Dworshak	Clearwater (N. Fork)	U.S.	G	717	3,287	6,500	3,453
El Chocón	Limay	Argentina	E	282	7,546	17,004	17,025
Emosson	Barberine	Switzerland	A	590	1,818	1,400	182
Idikki	Periyar	India	A	561	1,201	609	1,182
Kanev	Dnepr	U.S.S.R.	E	82	52,950	49,520	2,125
Keban	Euphrates	Turkey	ERG	679	3,881	20,900	25,110
Marimbondo	Grande	Brazil	EG	295	12,297	24,328	5,184
Mica	Columbia	Canada	ER	794	2,600	42,000	20,000
Mratinje	Piva	Yugoslavia	A	722	879	971	713
New Melones	Stanislaus	U.S.	ER	625	1,600	15,970	2,400
Reza Shah Kabir	Karun	Iran	A	656	1,247	1,570	2,351
Tabka (Thawra)	Euphrates	Syria	E	197	14,764	60,168	11,350
Tehchi (Tachien)	Tachia	Taiwan	A	591	951	598	207
Tarbela	Indus	Pakistan	ER	486	9,000	186,000	11,100
Zeyskaya	Zeya	U.S.S.R.	B	369	2,343	3,139	55,452

*Having a height exceeding 492 ft. (150 m.); or having a total volume content exceeding 20 million cu.yd. (15 million cu.m.); or forming a reservoir exceeding 12 million ac-ft. capacity (14,800 x 10^6 cu. m.).
†Type of dam: E=earth; R=rock-fill; A=arch; G=gravity; B=buttress.

(T. W. MERMEL)

Africa. The 184-ft.-high Kamburu rock-fill dam on the Tana River in Kenya was completed at the beginning of 1975. It supplied an underground power station housing three 31.4-Mw. vertical-shaft Francis turbine generator units. In South Africa the Welbedacht Dam on the Caledon River was completed, and work continued on the Sterkfontein earth-fill dam on the Nuwejaarspruit River. In Nigeria work started on the Bakolori Dam on the Niger River. The project was to include a canal, pumping stations, a hydroelectric station, and a navigation lock.

(ALDO MARCELLO)

Roads. The development of roads and road transport facilities during 1975 was influenced not only by the world economic situation, which (at least in the industrialized countries) caused a reduction of work undertaken or completed, but also by a trend toward regional rather than purely national development planning.

France offered a salient example of this trend. Over a relatively short period, approximately 3,000 km. (1,850 mi.) of expressway had been brought into service, and some 6,000 km. were planned to be open by 1980. It was possible in 1975 to travel from Dunkirk in the north or from Brussels in Belgium to Marseilles, Nice, or Narbonne without encountering a traffic signal. By 1980 this facility would extend to the Spanish frontier at Le Perthus and to the Italian frontier at Menton; or via Geneva in Switzerland and the Mont Blanc Tunnel to Turin in Italy, with access to the Italian expressway network. The international importance of the French system was expected to increase even before 1980. In 1976 the West German network would be joined with the French by completion of the link from Strasbourg or Saarbrücken via Metz to Paris, giving road traffic from central Europe direct access to the ports on the English Channel.

The Council of Europe was examining the organization of a European long-distance transportation network in relation to European regional development. Following a series of meetings it was established that future European road projects should be planned with the object of providing communications with peripheral, frontier, and isolated regions, and to provide facilities that would alleviate congestion in the densely populated industrial and urban areas. To provide the links with the peripheral regions, it was recommended that a continental coastal highway should be constructed, running from Holstein, West Germany, to Groningen, Neth., along the coasts of The Netherlands and Belgium, and to the Pyrenees via Boulogne, Le Havre, Caen, Brest, Bordeaux, and San Sebastián. Also recommended for high priority was the development of a transportation system from the centre of Europe to the southwest across the French Massif Central; to south and southeast Europe as far as Turkey over the Alpine passes; to the British Isles across the Channel; and to the Scandinavian Peninsula through Denmark.

In the nonindustrialized or less developed countries expenditure on road construction continued at an increased rate, largely through finance from international aid and development funds. The annual report of the World Bank for the fiscal year 1974-75 disclosed that of a total of $988.7 million in loans and credits for transportation projects, the largest amount was allocated for roads.

Among less developed countries the greatest activity in road construction was in Brazil, which was largely dependent on road transport for communications. Under the national development plan the government proposed to spend $4.1 billion up to 1979 and aimed to add an additional 12,400 km. (7,700 mi.) of roads to the existing 69,846-km. network. Most of the new mileage would be devoted to opening up the underpopulated Amazon region and to the construction of a road from Brasília to Manaus and from there to the Venezuelan frontier.

MARVINE HOWE—THE NEW YORK TIMES

Engineers are struggling to complete the 3,500-mi. Trans-Amazon Highway in Brazil. This aerial view is of the last section, which is badly behind schedule.

The other major project in the Americas was the Pan-American Highway, running 22,530 km. from Fairbanks, Alaska, to the southernmost tip of South America in Tierra del Fuego. In 1975 approximately 400 km. of it, in the Darien sectors of Colombia and Panama, remained to be finished. Delays were caused by the nature of the terrain and also by the special measures necessary for animal health protection in the area. Linked with the highway was a network of roads totaling some 72,000 km., to which it was planned to add a further 13,000 km.

In Africa the Trans-African Highway extending from Mombasa in Kenya to Lagos in Nigeria was well advanced. Of the total length of 6,325 km., 2,882 km. were classed as all-weather, and the majority of those sectors were bitumen-surfaced. The good progress achieved resulted in proposals for three other projects that would provide the basis for a continental highway network, namely the Trans-Sahelian, Trans-Saharan, and Coastal highways. Together, the four projects would provide a road network of 18,690 km. plus about the same length of feeder roads, and would affect 34 African countries. The Trans-Sahelian Highway would run from Dakar in Senegal through Mali, Upper Volta, Niger, and Cameroon to N'Djamena, Chad; the Coastal Highway would link the Mauritanian capital of Nouakchott to Lagos; and the north-south Trans-Saharan Highway from Algiers via Tamanrasset to Gao in Mali and Agadez in Niger would give the countries of the Sahel region south of the Sahara access to the Mediterranean.

(IRF)

Tunnels. The tunneling nonevent of 1975 was the cancellation of the second stage of the Channel Tunnel project after work had begun on the construction of a pilot bore from each side of the English Channel. It was unlikely that work would resume on the project in the near future, if at all, as the economic studies were too critically affected by external factors such as the world price of oil. In the U.K. a special exhibition commemorated the 150th anniversary of the construction of the first tunnel under the Thames River and the birth of shield tunneling pioneered by Marc Brunel. Tunneling under the Thames continued as construction work proceeded on the second Dartford Tunnel using two 10.3-m.-diameter shields. Tunneling began on the £19 million Kielder water tunnel in Northumberland, which would be the longest single drive through hard rock ever made in Britain.

In Norway tunnels were driven through the centre of Oslo to join the city's rail transit and commuter rail system on the East and West sides. Special blasting methods that employed stemming with polystyrene granules were used to reduce seismic shock, and slurry wall construction was utilized to form tunnels one above the other. In Finland the Helsinki Water Board was constructing the world's largest continuous rock tunnel, scheduled for completion in 1980. The tunnel, driven by drill and blast methods, was to be 120 km. long, with a cross-sectional area of approximately 16 sq.m. In Sweden the construction of the new main subway station in the centre of Stockholm required extensive ground treatment to control water found 30 m. above the lowest level of the construction work.

In Austria a new type of tunneling machine was used for the construction of part of Vienna's new subway system. It combined a face support system with mechanical cutters and was designed for boring in soft ground under heavy structures. At Seelisberg in Switzerland construction work continued on the largest two-way vehicular tunnel in the world. Main headings were advanced by drill and blast methods, but a special digging shield was used to enlarge a ventilation tunnel to its final size of 12 m. in diameter. Engineers in West Germany introduced a bentonite shield for the construction of a 4-m.-diameter sewer tunnel 4.6 km. long at Hamburg. Good progress was achieved, and up to 67 rings of smooth bore precast concrete lining rings were placed daily. The tunnel was driven through waterlogged gravel under a hydrostatic head of 15 m. In Munich a tunneling machine worked under compressed air in the driving of extensions to the new main subway system. On another section of the project a novel method of excavation was used involving the construction of two small-diameter tunnels and then enlarging the pair to form one single large-diameter tunnel.

Entrance to the newly built Elbe tunnel in Hamburg, West Germany. Opened for traffic in January 1975, it accommodates an estimated 65,000 cars per day and is Europe's longest tunnel (3,325 metres).

KEYSTONE

WIDE WORLD

Newly completed section of a subway system in Kharkov, U.S.S.R., connects the centre of the city with an industrial district.

In South Africa the Orange Fish tunnel was officially opened; at 82.5 km. in length it was the world's longest continuous tunnel construction to date. A second world record for South Africa was the construction of a water culvert in Durban by pipe jacking concrete units, each 8 m. wide and 4.5 m. high, over a total length of 160 m. Elsewhere on the African continent, civil engineering work was finally completed on the underground works for the North Bank power station at Kariba on the Zambezi River. Work on the project had been halted in 1973 when the civil contractor had run into financial difficulties and called in a receiver.

In Australia a wide variety of tunneling methods were used to complete the new subway in Melbourne. Heading machines and tunneling machines were employed to avoid excessive use of explosives, and it was anticipated that compressed air would be required in some sections where the four-line railway loop penetrated an old creek bed. In Sydney, after 50 years of stop-and-go policies, the first section of the new underground railway (subway) was opened.

In Japan work continued on the construction of the world's largest subaqueous tunnel, linking Honshu with Hokkaido. Despite massive water problems, Japanese engineers still expected to complete the 54-km. tunnel on time in 1979. In the city of Kobe the Japanese used posttensioned concrete slabs for the roadway on a 7-km. tunnel. Greater flexural strength and less tire noise were claimed for this method of construction, coupled with a reduction in overall cost;

the posttensioned slabs were thinner than conventional road slabs.

In the U.S. field trials of a hard-rock tunneling machine equipped with a water jet system operating at 56,000 lb. per sq.in. (psi) proved interesting. The system offered considerable promise, but several years of further development were required. Major tunneling projects included the second bore for the Eisenhower Memorial Tunnel in Colorado and the deep-level storm water system at Chicago, which would involve 200 km. of deep tunnels. In Mexico the 50-km. outfall tunnel required for Mexico City's new main drainage system neared completion during 1975.

(DAVID A. HARRIES)

See also Architecture.

[733; 734.A]

ENCYCLOPÆDIA BRITANNICA FILMS. *The Mississippi System: Waterways of Commerce* (1970).

Environment

For environmentalists, 1975 was a year of solid, if unspectacular, achievement, marked by the increasing involvement of supranational institutions in environmental issues. At one level, this may have been due to a fear that deliberate modification of environments could be used as a weapon of war. In August the U.S. told the Geneva Disarmament Conference that immediate controls should be imposed, while Soviet leaders voiced similar fears in terms that suggested they might have had specific techniques in mind.

Fears that the world was doomed to the kind of collapse predicted in the Club of Rome's *The Limits to Growth* in 1972 receded a little. Several groups in different countries, including the Systems Analysis Research Unit of the British Department of the Environment, were constructing models of their own and concluding that global catastrophe was not the inevitable consequence of the pursuit of economic growth; man had a range of options and time to choose. Attention was directed increasingly toward the economic disparities between rich and poor nations, and the Club of Rome followed this trend in several new documents.

European Architectural Heritage Year received less attention than European Conservation Year in 1970, although both were sponsored by the Council of Europe. (*See* HISTORIC PRESERVATION.) Yet the urban environment attracted increasing interest and concern as preparations proceeded for the UN Habitat conference on human settlements, to be held in Vancouver, B.C., in 1976.

In the U.K. the queen appointed Lewis Mumford, the noted U.S. writer on architecture and urban planning, an honorary knight commander of the Order of the British Empire (KBE) in recognition of his contribution to town planning in Britain. Mumford was much respected by environmentalists all over the world for his efforts to arouse public awareness of environmental issues and for his attempts to improve the quality of urban life. Earlier in the year, environmentalists had mourned the death of another champion, Sir Julian Huxley. (*See* OBITUARIES.)

INTERNATIONAL COOPERATION

UN Environment Program (UNEP). Concepts of economic growth were coming to the fore in debates at the supranational level. Most of the major institutions, including the UN, were beginning to talk of a "new economic order" that would narrow the gap between rich and poor. This theme was taken up and given a more overtly environmental twist by Maurice F. Strong, executive director of UNEP, when he spoke to the UN Association in London in July. "The 'new growth' society need not be a 'no growth' society," he said, "but rather a society of growth, which is exciting, sustainable, healthy and satisfying."

UNEP continued to carry out the tasks allotted to it. Unlike other UN agencies, it had few executive powers but existed to catalyze the other agencies and member governments into taking action to protect the environment. The U.S. $102.3 million out of which it had to finance its activities from 1975 to 1977 was being contributed by member governments, with more than half coming from the U.S., the U.S.S.R., and Japan. The Program's priority areas were human settlements and habitat; the health of people and of the environment; the management and control of terrestrial ecosystems; environment and development; the oceans; energy; and natural disasters.

In May UNEP named Richard Morse and Francesco Sella as leaders of the Earthwatch team, responsible for coordinating national monitoring systems through the proposed Global Environmental Monitoring System (GEMS) and for instituting the International Referral System (IRS). These would enable UNEP to maintain a constant and perhaps even predictive watch on variables in the global environment and, through IRS, to provide coordination of relief operations in the event of natural disasters.

UNEP's economic and political position could be inferred from Strong's own views, formed while he was president of the Canadian International Development Agency, when he gained considerable experience with the problems of less developed countries. His calls for a new approach to the implications of economic growth were criticized, however, at a meeting of the UNEP Governing Council held at UNEP headquarters in Nairobi, Kenya, in April. Christian Herter (U.S.) was supported by many other delegates when he called on UNEP to concentrate on a smaller number of strictly environmental projects because it had "enough on its plate without trying to reform the world." Delegates from socialist countries, on the other hand, argued that social and philosophical issues were at the root of environmental problems and could not be ignored.

WIDE WORLD

An estimated half million birds died from the cold after the U.S. Army sprayed a roosting area with a chemical that washed oil from their feathers at Ft. Campbell, Kentucky, in February. Large swarms of such birds pose serious problems in the region.

England: *see* United Kingdom

English Literature: *see* Literature

Entertainment: *see* Dance; Motion Pictures; Music; Television and Radio; Theatre

Entomology: *see* Life Sciences

This dispute within the Governing Council reflected a wider controversy outside. In October 1974 a symposium in Cocoyoc, Mexico, chaired by Dame Barbara Ward, English economist and president of the International Institute for Environment and Development, led to the publication of the "Cocoyoc Declaration," which began by observing that "more people are hungry, sick, shelterless and illiterate today than when the UN was first set up." The declaration rejected population growth as the cause of the present crisis. While admitting that rising levels of consumption could not be sustained indefinitely, it held that the immediate problem was political and social in nature, rather than physical.

The declaration concluded that the existing world economic system was incapable of resolving the problems confronting it and that a "new economic order" was therefore required. The debate thus initiated was continued in other forums. It echoed the growing disillusionment of the less developed countries, which saw environmental problems in terms of starvation, shantytowns, and disease, rather than polluted rivers and aesthetically displeasing landscapes.

UN Conference on the Law of the Sea. The chances of achieving a new economic order were hardly enhanced by the fate of the third Law of the Sea conference, the second working session of which was held in Geneva for eight weeks in the spring. The objective was to draft a treaty, but the conference ended without any important agreement having been reached. The aggrandizement of national claims dominated, and as the conference approached its end the president, H. Shirley Amerasinghe (Sri Lanka), took the unusual step of ordering the chairmen of the three main working committees to draw up "unified texts" reflecting the opinions expressed within their committees. These texts were accepted and formed the substance to be negotiated at the next session, to be held in New York, N.Y., in March and April 1976.

International Union for Conservation of Nature and Natural Resources (IUCN). The amalgamation of conservation and development interests took a further step in September at the 12th General Assembly of the IUCN, held in Kinshasa, Zaire. Thanks to the support of African members, the 450 organizations composing the IUCN resolved to integrate conservation programs with development, particularly in rural areas; to involve local people in conservation projects; and, wherever practicable, to assist communities whose life-styles were consistent with conservation objectives to preserve them. The Sahel drought of the late '60s and early '70s provided a warning of the dangers of failing to observe possible environmental constraints when planning for development and a reminder that the welfare of people must not be overlooked when seeking to preserve ecosystems.

Other International Developments. Ministers for science and technology from member governments of the Organization for Economic Cooperation and Development (OECD) met in June to discuss the problems of industrialized and less developed countries, particularly in the fields of energy, the environment, natural resources, and food. They stressed the responsibility of the OECD countries to help combat poverty and to make appropriate developmental technologies available to less developed nations.

The Council of Europe produced a draft European Convention on the Protection of International Watercourses Against Pollution. While the Council did not pretend that the convention afforded complete solutions, it did believe the draft represented the most that would be accepted by its member governments. It did not aim to reduce the production of polluting substances but only to regulate their discharge.

The convention was intended as part of the answer to the wider problem of managing the major European river basins. The Danube, for example, was managed by ten nations, while many other rivers marked international frontiers. Similar problems existed in the Council for Mutual Economic Assistance (Comecon) countries of Eastern Europe. In July the U.S.S.R. announced that purification installations had improved the quality of the Moskva River; the oxygen content had increased by 50%, turbidity had been reduced, and some species of fish had returned. The U.S.S.R. and Poland drew up a program for protection of the Bug River, which forms their common frontier, and the management of rivers bordering Comecon countries was being discussed by the U.S.S.R., Hungary, Romania, Czechoslovakia, and Yugoslavia.

A European satellite to monitor the quality of fresh water was proposed to the Council of Europe at a symposium in Strasbourg late in October 1974. The idea came from H. Kaminski and M. Schmidbauer of the Space Research Institute of Bochum Observatory, West Germany, who had been studying infrared photographs taken by a U.S. environmental satellite. They showed clearly that parts of the North and Baltic seas were markedly warmer than the water surrounding them and that parts of the Adriatic and Caspian were cooler, suggesting that their waters interchanged little with the adjacent seas.

The Regional Office for Europe of the World Health Organization was also concerned about the quality of European waters, in this case those adjacent to beaches used for recreation. In collaboration with the governments of The Netherlands and West Germany, it convened a working group as part of its long-term program to control environmental pollution. In a summary report issued in advance of its final report, the group called for a reduction in pollution from waste water so as to reduce or eliminate fecal contamination.

"It sort of made life exciting. I miss DDT."

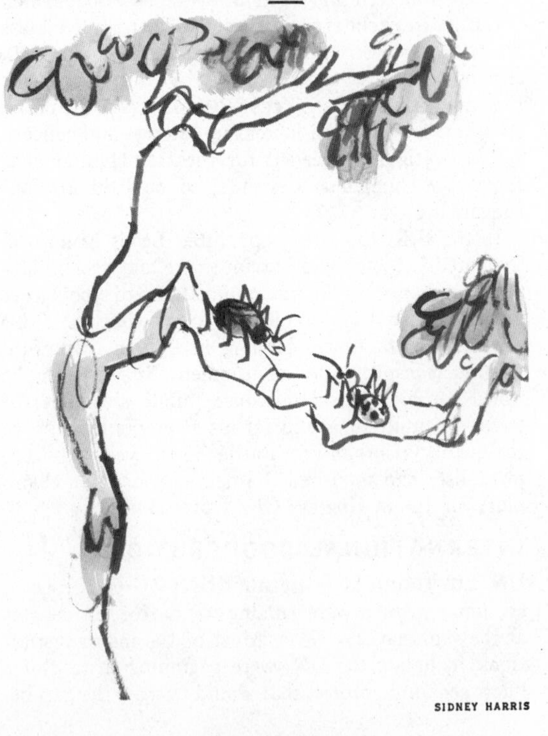

SIDNEY HARRIS

It suggested that to be considered highly satisfactory an area should have consistently less than 100 *Escherichia coli* bacteria per 100 millilitres of water and, to be considered acceptable for bathing, an upper limit of 1,000 *E. coli* per 100 ml.

European Economic Community. The Environment and Consumer Protection Service of the European Commission continued its active pursuit of environmental objectives laid down for the EEC. By the end of 1974 the Council of Ministers had adopted Commission proposals on the quality of surface water intended for drinking, on energy and the environment, on the disposal of waste oils, and on the "polluter pays" principle, which relates to the allocation of costs resulting from antipollution measures.

The Commission continued to study problems associated with organohalogen compounds, hydrocarbons, nitrogen oxides, photochemical oxidants, asbestos, vanadium, noise, and micropollutants in water. On April 25 it submitted two draft directives, one on the monitoring of populations for lead, the other on criteria for the harmfulness of lead and on air quality standards with respect to lead. A draft directive was prepared on the storage, transport, and treatment of toxic wastes.

The Commission also concerned itself with the environmental implications of farming practices, and its directive on hill and mountain farming was adopted. It made recommendations regarding the protection of migratory birds and completed a study of certain natural resources that were in limited supply, including water, mercury, platinum, fluorine, phosphorus, tin, and lead. A study of environmental problems peculiar to town centres was conducted, and the Commission began to classify urban areas according to their environmental quality. It also prepared the rules that would govern the European Foundation for the Improvement of Living and Working Conditions, which began work late in the year.

NATIONAL DEVELOPMENTS AND POLICIES

The main issues of the year were those raised by radioactive wastes and by possible chemical threats to the upper atmosphere from supersonic transport aircraft and from halocarbons, the group of chemicals used as propellants in aerosols.

Radioactive Waste. The dangers inherent in the disposal of radioactive wastes were emphasized by Maurice Strong when he announced in May that UNEP was providing the International Atomic Energy Agency with U.S. $300,000 to develop a concerted approach to the problem. In the same month, the OECD announced that an internationally supervised operation for the disposal of packaged solid radioactive wastes into the deep Atlantic was to take place during June and July. Some 4,500 metric tons of concreted and bituminized low-activity wastes from establishments in Belgium, The Netherlands, Switzerland, and the U.K., packed in metal drums, were dumped in an area 70 nautical miles across, centred at 46°15′ N and 17°25′ W. The sea there was some 4.5 km. deep, and the area had been used for this purpose before.

In October the U.K. Atomic Energy Authority announced that it was reexamining the policy of ocean dumping of wastes. The agency hoped to discover safe methods for disposing of the much larger quantities of wastes that would be produced under the expanded nuclear power program on which the U.K., like most other industrial countries, had embarked. Public fears were not allayed by news in May of the third leak in 18 months from the Windscale reprocessing plant in the U.K., where a number of elements, including cobalt-60 and cesium-137, contaminated the River Calder, probably by seepage from underground storage channels. In France there were public demonstrations against the government's nuclear power program. A report issued by the U.S. Atomic Energy Commission warned that some reactors might have to shut down because of lack of storage facilities.

The Ozone Shield and Stratospheric Flight. The controversy over the effects of man's activity on the ozone layer of the atmosphere continued. The Concorde aircraft remained a favourite target for criticism. A U.S. National Academy of Sciences report of a study on the "environmental impact of stratospheric flight," issued in April, concluded that, unless steps were taken to restrict stratospheric flights or redesign jet engines, ozone would be removed from the upper atmosphere, thus increasing the incidence of ultraviolet radiation at the earth's surface. The Federal Aviation Administration (FAA), which held hearings in April on whether to permit two landings per day by Concorde at Dulles International Airport near Washington, D.C., and four per day at John F. Kennedy International Airport, New York, encountered strong opposition led by the Sierra Club.

Later studies indicated that the number of aircraft actually operating in the stratosphere would probably be much smaller than originally suggested, that the effect of such reduced fleets on the ozone layer would be minimal, and that it might be reduced further by predictable improvements in engine design. Environmentalists returned to the attack in September, when the Environmental Defense Fund, a coalition of U.S. lawyers and environmentalists, argued that payload considerations meant Concorde would carry insufficient fuel for more than 30 minutes' circling prior to landing, necessitating special air traffic procedures. While conceding the facts, the British Aircraft Corporation pointed out that the same restriction on endurance applied to existing jumbo-type aircraft and caused no great problems. An environmental impact statement prepared by the U.S. Department of Transportation indicated that Concorde would degrade the ozone layer and also cause unacceptable noise.

Aerosols Under Attack. The National Academy of Sciences report also drew attention to the hazard from Freons. "Freon" was the trade name for a group of halocarbon compounds used in several industries but especially as propellants in aerosols. In June Oregon became the first state to ban aerosol cans containing fluorocarbon propellant, and a federal interagency task force, representing 14 agencies, recommended a ban throughout the U.S. within three years. The compounds tended to be carried up into the stratosphere, which acted as a sink, retaining them because of the permanent temperature inversion at those altitudes. Under bombardment by ultraviolet radiation in the 190- to 215-nanometre band, they would break down and release chlorine (or bromine or fluorine), which reacted with atmospheric ozone. The chemistry of the upper atmosphere was complex and still poorly understood, but the consensus of British scientists was that, while a risk existed, it should not be exaggerated.

Marine Pollution. In September J. S. Gray of the Wellcome Marine Laboratory, University of Leeds, England, announced that the Baltic Sea, believed to be dying in 1969, had recovered as a result of being

JOHN DONAT

"Autarkic," a prototype of a self-sufficient home, was developed by the Department of Architecture at Cambridge University. The building in completely free of the need for centralized services.

flushed out with clean water from the Atlantic. The U.K. proposed stringent international controls on marine pollution at the law of the sea conference in March, and in July it became one of eight countries to ratify the Oslo Convention on dumping of wastes at sea. A further five countries had signed, but not yet ratified, the convention. In October, however, the U.K. opposed an EEC proposal to define legal limits for quantities of certain highly toxic substances that could be dumped in rivers, lakes, or coastal waters; in an aide-mémoire to the European Commission it argued in favour of setting objectives for environmental quality, rather than for discharges, and then letting national governments decide what controls were appropriate to realize those objectives.

Other Pollution Issues. Environmentalist opposition continued to the increasing use of slow-releasing insecticide strips whose active ingredient was dichlorvos. A report by the U.K. Central Unit on Environmental Pollution found that such strips accounted for 70% of all insecticides used in British homes, apart from those used for the treatment of wood. The strips were banned in The Netherlands as a health hazard.

In the U.S. the automotive industry was granted a one-year extension of the date by which its vehicles must meet new, more stringent emission standards. This was the third such extension, and the industry asked for a further four-year extension. Emission standards were also relaxed for coal-fired power stations, and there were proposals to amend the Clean Air Act in order to facilitate the building of coal-fired power stations in the Great Plains and in the Southwest. The suggestion was opposed by the Environmental Protection Agency (EPA) and by the Sierra Club.

Early in the year the Japanese Environment Agency reported that a total of 14,186 persons in Japan were suffering from diseases related to pollution. This figure excluded those who had died from such diseases. The situation was improving, however, and in some respects, such as the establishment of air quality objectives, Japan was ahead of most European countries. Popular protest was intensifying; in 1970 there were known to be 292 environmental citizen groups, but by 1973 there were 1,007. Public expenditure on environmental protection rose by 62% in 1973 compared with 1972, and by a further 25% in 1974.

THE URBAN ENVIRONMENT

European Architectural Heritage Year and preparations for the 1976 UN Habitat conference were conducted amid growing doubts about the quality, and even the viability, of large cities. New York was experiencing an acute financial crisis (*see* UNITED STATES: *Special Report*), and all over the world the incidence of distress, mental illness, and violent crime, often of a spectacular nature, was rising. Urban guerrilla forces were becoming a world problem. (*See* CRIME AND LAW ENFORCEMENT: *Special Report.*) Many people began to wonder whether a causal relationship might exist between city life and antisocial behaviour. Derek Bryce-Smith of the University of Reading, England, a chemist who had specialized in the study of the toxic effects of heavy metals, was one of the scientists suggesting that behavioural abnormalities might be induced by air-borne lead.

In less developed countries the rate of growth of cities caused concern. At the biennial conference of the International Union of Local Authorities, held in Teheran, Iran, in April, delegates were told that the population of Teheran had grown from three million to more than four million in four years and that the planned population for 1990 was already in sight. On September 1 Robert McNamara, president of the World Bank, used his annual speech to the International Monetary Fund to spell out the dangers of over-rapid urbanization in conditions of great poverty.

McNamara proposed that the World Bank lend less developed countries U.S. $7 billion in the current year and about $40 billion over the next five years. He outlined a four-point program whereby the governments of less developed countries might increase economic opportunities for the self-employed, provide more employment in industry and better access to public utilities for the poorest sections of the community, and establish realistic housing policies based, for example, on upgrading existing shantytowns rather than embarking on expensive housing projects.

The aim of European Architectural Heritage Year was "to make the general public more aware and appreciative of their surroundings," according to Lord Duncan-Sandys, chairman of the EAHY organizing committee. Events held in connection with EAHY included a symposium in Krems, Austria, in April on "How to Restore a Medium-Sized Town of Historic Importance" and the Congress on European Architectural Heritage, which met in Amsterdam in October. The congress, attended by many ministers and members of royal families, adopted a European declaration on architectural heritage, a concept that had come to mean the architectural environment as a whole rather than isolated buildings and monuments.

Problems of preserving the urban physical environment were illustrated by figures showing the cost of environmental damage, published by the OECD in May. The value of property decreased the closer it was to major airports, and the deterioration of paintwork and stone caused by air pollution imposed direct costs. In April an OECD-sponsored conference in Paris on "Better Towns with Less Traffic" concluded that towns *were* better with less traffic, as long as adequate provision was made for the mobility of workers and residents and the distribution of goods. In July the British Civic Trust published figures showing the effects of traffic vibration on buildings, measured as the percentage of the life of the building that was lost. For example, at the kind of traffic densities experienced in the City of London, the life of a building might be halved. As part of its energy conservation program, the U.K. government announced new standards for the thermal insulation of new buildings. Interest in the use of solar energy for space and water heating continued to grow. (*See* ARCHITECTURE.)

(MICHAEL ALLABY)

THE NATURAL ENVIRONMENT

In a vigorous address to the first International Environmental Management Seminar, held at the Centre d'Études Industrielles, Geneva, in January, Maurice Strong reviewed the current state of the environment as a world issue affecting the future of humanity. Drastic increases in energy costs, growing scarcities of food, fertilizers, and other resources, growing population pressures, increasing signs of environmental deterioration, and galloping inflation were all, he said, warning signs of a crisis in the human experience.

Land Conservation. At the Congress of the International Union of Societies of Foresters, held at Helsinki, Fin., late in 1974, there was strong criticism of the indifference of "economic" foresters to conservation needs and values. Gerardo Budowski, a forester himself and currently director general of the IUCN, cited the situation in Peruvian Amazonia, where Japanese companies were ready to bid from U.S. $80 million to $500 million for logging concessions in the tropical rain forests. This he regarded as rampant exploitation, since practically nothing was yet known about sustained timber yield in those regions. The worst sufferers were the indigenous inhabitants, who knew how to gather a diversified and sustained crop of food and implements for their own sustenance. Not only timber but whole traditions of life appeared doomed to disappear.

Saroj Raj Choudhury, a conservator of forests in Assam, India, declared that the eucalyptus forests established to supply paper mills had decreased the amount of land available for grazing and diminished supplies of many minor products of high economic value to local tribesmen. He cited honey from wild bees, the flesh and skins of wild deer, antelopes, boars, game birds, and even song birds such as exportable singing mynahs as "forest products" that could be secured in perpetuity from indigenous forests.

Reports from North America indicated that beech bark disease, a fungal disease of beech trees spread by a scale insect, had reached epidemic proportions in parts of New England and was spreading southward. Some 50% of the beech's range was said to be affected. Plant pathologists believed the infestation was potentially as serious as the epidemics of chestnut blight, Dutch elm disease, and white pine blister rust that had almost wiped out those species on the North American continent. As in the case of the earlier blights, both the scale and the fungus had been introduced from Europe, so that North American trees had no natural resistance.

In Australia Ian Douglas, head of the Department of Geography at the University of New England, Armidale, New South Wales, took stock of the mounting pressures on Australian rain forests. He questioned the conclusions of the national Forwood Conference held in 1974; that such forests were simply a resource to be exploited for the short-term gains of timber merchants and similar entrepreneurs. He found that the relatively small areas of rain forest strung along the eastern coasts of Queensland and New South Wales were threatened by coal waste tips, sand mining, clearances for cattle ranching and real estate development, and the monoculture of the hoop pine and bunya pine (*Araucaria* species).

The forest resources of Russia and Siberia were subjected to a searching and exhaustive analysis by W. R. Sutton, a forest economist at the Rotorua Forest Research Institute, New Zealand. Traditionally, the U.S.S.R. had been thought to hold "vast areas of virgin forest that could meet the world's needs for decades, if not for centuries to come, without any need for restocking." Sutton found that the area of the Russian forests, some 900 million ha., equaled that of the forests of Canada and the U.S. combined. Growth was so slow in the northern regions, however, that the annual increment of timber, around 500 million cu.m., was no more than that maintained by the U.S. alone, and the total annual cut was already approaching this figure. Exploitation of the slow-growing Siberian forests was hampered by extreme winter cold, with temperatures down to −50° C.

At the opposite extreme of temperature, the Arabian state of Abu Dhabi established two sizable irrigated plantations, each around 200 ha. in extent. Rainfall there was so low and erratic that it could be disregarded. All the water needed to start tree growth had to be pumped up from deep wells by diesel-driven centrifugal pumps and then forced by booster pumps through polythene pipes to outlets, one for each tree. An unexpected hazard developed in the form of stem abrasion by windblown desert sand, but this was successfully checked by shelters of palm fronds. The trees selected were tough native species, namely, *Acacia nilotica, A. tortilis, Prosopis spicigera,* and *Zizyphus Spina-Christi.* If their spreading roots could tap deep soil water or surface dew, as was the case with their occasional natural neighbours, they might eventually become independent.

A remarkable project to stabilize an extreme natural environment was begun in conjunction with the trans-Alaska oil pipeline. The oil emerged from deep underground wells at 180° F, and friction with the sides of the pipe would keep it at a high temperature as it was

World's 25 Most Populous Urban Areas*

Rank	City and country	City proper: Most recent population	City proper: Year	Metropolitan area: Most recent population	Metropolitan area: Year
1	Tokyo, Japan	8,658,200	1975 estimate	22,082,000	1970 census
2	New York City, U.S.	9,809,200	1973 estimate	16,976,700	1973 estimate
3	Osaka, Japan	2,802,100	1975 estimate	14,886,000	1970 census
4	London, U.K.	7,176,600	1974 estimate	12,606,700	1974 estimate
5	Mexico City, Mexico	8,591,800	1975 estimate	11,339,800	1975 estimate
6	Shanghai, China	5,700,000	1970 estimate	10,820,000†	1970 estimate
7	São Paulo, Brazil	7,198,600	1975 estimate	10,371,300	1975 estimate
8	Ruhr, West Germany‡	—	—	10,278,000	1975 estimate
9	Los Angeles, U.S.	2,746,900	1973 estimate	10,130,400	1973 estimate
10	Paris, France	2,321,500	1975 estimate	9,594,000	1975 estimate
11	Buenos Aires, Argentina	2,977,000	1975 estimate	8,498,000	1975 estimate
12	Rio de Janeiro, Brazil	4,857,700	1975 estimate	8,328,800	1975 estimate
13	Chicago, U.S.	3,172,900	1973 estimate	7,689,300	1973 estimate
14	Peking, China	...	...	7,570,000†	1970 estimate
15	Moscow, U.S.S.R.	7,368,000	1974 estimate	7,528,000	1974 estimate
16	Calcutta, India	3,148,700	1971 census	7,031,400	1971 census
17	Cairo, Egypt	5,859,000	1975 census	6,757,000	1975 census
18	Nagoya, Japan	2,074,200	1975 estimate	6,574,900	1970 census
19	Seoul, South Korea	...	...	6,289,600†	1973 estimate
20	Bombay, India	...	...	5,970,600†	1971 census
21	Philadelphia, U.S.	1,861,700	1973 estimate	5,652,900	1973 estimate
22	Manila, Philippines	1,473,600	1974 estimate	5,369,900	1974 estimate
23	Jakarta, Indonesia	...	...	4,915,300†	1973 estimate
24	Detroit, U.S.	1,386,800	1973 estimate	4,690,700	1973 estimate
25	Tientsin, China	3,300,000	1975 estimate	4,576,000†	1975 estimate

*Ranked by population of metropolitan area.
†Municipality or other civil division within which a city proper may not be distinguished.
‡A so-called industrial conurbation within which a single central city is not distinguished.

LONDON DAILY EXPRESS/PICTORIAL PARADE

Nearly two tons of bream and roach float in Coate Water near Swindon, England, which is many miles from any known source of pollution. Scientists were unable to explain the April fish kill.

pumped. This heat was likely to thaw the frozen water in the permafrost, through which long sections of the pipe had to be laid, causing what had been an apparently solid base to become a muddy swamp. The remedy was to surround the pipe with an outside fibreglass jacket enclosing polyurethane foam. Refrigerated brine, which has a lower melting point than water, would be pumped through this to keep the surrounding permafrost permanently frozen. Fear of the environmental risks of melting the permafrost, particularly the danger to wandering caribou or reindeer, had been the basis of much of the opposition to the pipeline. (*See* ARCTIC REGIONS.)

For the second time in two years, U.S. Pres. Gerald Ford vetoed a measure that would have mandated federal regulation of strip mining, and the effort to override the veto in the House of Representatives fell three votes short of the necessary two-thirds majority. Although the bill was weaker than the one vetoed in 1974, the White House claimed it would have reduced coal output by as much as a fourth, thrown thousands of miners out of work, and raised the cost of electricity. The failure to pass federal legislation left regulation of strip mining up to the states, which exercised widely varying degrees of control.

Water Conservation. The U.S. National Environmental Policy Act of 1969 required the Council on Environmental Quality (CEQ) "to gather timely and authoritative information concerning the conditions and trends in the quality of the environment" and "to report at least once each year to the President on the state and condition of the environment." Inquiries into the actual working of this plan revealed a multiplicity of projects for assessing environmental quality. The leading federal body, the EPA, maintained 800 stations for monitoring water quality, and individual states operated a further 6,000. In addition, 24,000 stations gave simple hydrological data, *e.g.,* for streamflow predictions. Unfortunately, these stations were not all ideally sited, and there was insufficient coordination of their data-collection systems so that many valuable results could not be compiled and analyzed in reasonable time. Federal agencies spent some $8 million annually on monitoring water resources, not always to the best effect.

Congress moved in October to amend the law which permitted strip mining in national parks. Shown below is a mining site at Zabriskie Point, Death Valley.

THE NEW YORK TIMES

A study of the drinking water supplies of 79 U.S. cities, conducted by the EPA, revealed that all contained traces of organic chemicals, including some suspected carcinogens. The survey was undertaken following the discovery, in 1974, that the water supply of New Orleans, La., contained 66 chemical pollutants. At least some of the chemicals found in the EPA tests were believed to be by-products of the chlorination process, commonly used to purify drinking water from bacterial contamination. Russell Train, the EPA administrator, emphasized that the amounts discovered were minute and constituted a far smaller risk to public health than water-borne bacterial diseases. "People should not react with any sense of panic," he said, "but they should know there is a problem."

In France the Ministère de la Qualité de la Vie, the ministry responsible for environmental matters, reported substantial progress in both monitoring and preventing riverain pollution. Networks of sampling and analyzing stations, linked to purification plants, were being set up in each major catchment area. On the Marne above Paris, for example, there were five purification and testing plants and three others monitoring flow and pollution. On the Oise River live trout were being used as active monitors. If a fish that normally swam upstream in a tank facing the sample current weakened and started to drift downstream, an alarm signal was triggered.

West Germany pressed ahead with the development of highly sophisticated automatic systems for measuring and controlling the pollution of the Rhine. It was estimated that the Rhine was 20 times more polluted than in 1949, although 19 million citizens relied on it as their only source of drinking water. Some 24 million tons of contaminants and poisons were carried over the Dutch border annually, including an estimated 3 tons of arsenic and 1,000 lb. of mercury daily.

The English Water Resources Board, a new national authority, sponsored creation of the huge Kielder Reservoir in Northumberland, close to the Scottish border. Rivaling Windermere, England's largest natural lake, in extent, "Kielder Water" would be six miles long, with a surface of 2,700 ac., and would ensure an output of 200 million gal. a day. Water released below the dam would be transported 40 mi. down the River North Tyne and then diverted into a buried aqueduct. If necessary, it could then be fed into three rivers, the Tyne, the Wear, and the Tees, and taken toward the major industrial complexes of Newcastle upon Tyne, Sunderland/Durham, and Teesside.

In a convincing experiment at the flooded Ottoville Quarry in Ontario, Arlo W. Fast of Union Carbide Corp., cooperating with William J. Overholtz and Richard A. Tubb of Ohio State University, showed that it was possible to restore the fish life of a large body of still water by adding oxygen artificially. The process, known as "hypolimnetic oxygenation," involved extracting a relatively small amount of water from the lower levels of a deep lake, adding liquid oxygen to it, and then allowing it to flow back, through pipes, to its original depth. During the period April–June, the oxygen content of the untreated waters of this two-acre, 40-ft.-deep lake fell from 300 kg. to zero. The investigators then added 250 kg. of oxygen over two months, virtually all of which was retained by the lake's waters. Trout could now thrive in the rejuvenated waters, and the revenue from fishing permits would exceed the outlay on treatment.

(HERBERT L. EDLIN)

Wildlife. In January 1975 Colin Bertram, a council member of the Fauna Preservation Society (FPS), chaired a meeting in Nairobi designed to identify East African coastal areas inhabited by the dugong, *Dugong dugon.* The meeting, part of the UN Food and Agriculture Organization Advisory Committee on Marine Resources and Research, was a move in the fight to save from extermination the animals of the mammalian order Sirenia, the sea cows, of which the dugong and the three species of manatees are the only living representatives. All sirenians are harmless, all have palatable flesh, and all are easily caught in nylon fishing nets. They are scattered in small populations over an enormous range in tropical waters. To save them would be a great achievement, not only because of their scientific interest and meat but because, as the only large herbivorous mammals living in shallow waters, they might become consumers and utilizers of the uncontrollable freshwater weeds that choke waterways throughout the tropics.

On February 19, in Washington, D.C., the Pan-American Union celebrated the grant of the first J. Paul Getty Wildlife Conservation Prize to Felipe Benavides, president of Pro Defensa de la Naturaleza (Prodena—the Peruvian World Wildlife Fund national appeal). The citation referred to Benavides as "responsible for major strides in conservation in Peru, in Latin America and beyond, with respect to endangered species, notably the vicuña; moving force in creating the Manu National Park, safeguarding this fragile remnant of Amazonia's vanishing tropical rain forest; energetic pioneer providing rays of hope and inspiration for conservation, notably in Latin America, where lies a significant portion of the planet's biological heritage." Later the FPS, of which Benavides was a vice-president, announced in its journal that he was donating the whole $50,000 of his prize toward the establishment of a scientific station at Paracas in an area of splendid coastal desert.

Early in the year the government of The Netherlands amended its Delta Project, which had involved placing a permanent barrier across four of the mouths of the Rhine. One of them, the Oosterschelde, was a major marine habitat named in the international Wetlands Convention and a feeding ground for hundreds of thousands of birds. The amended—and much more expensive—scheme substituted mechanically operated gates. These would allow normal tidal flows, thus preserving the low-tide mud flats, but could be lowered when necessary to protect the land against exceptional tides or storms.

The American crocodile, formerly common in southern Florida, was among the species placed on the endangered list during the year by the U.S. Department of the Interior. Meanwhile, its relative, the alligator, was removed from the list in all but a few areas. Once hunted almost to extinction for its hide, the alligator had made such a comeback that it was becoming a public nuisance in some places. Despite this, the environmental group Friends of the Earth expressed fear that removal of a species from the list constituted a dangerous precedent.

At the 27th meeting of the International Whaling Commission, in London in June, the U.S.S.R. announced that only two, instead of the previous three, whaling expeditions would be sent to Antarctica during the 1975–76 season. At the same meeting a further mild check in the whale's voyage to extinction was made with the classification of whales into Protection Stocks, on which there would be a total moratorium, and Sustained Management and Initial Management Stocks, both under some control. Whaling nations had consistently rejected the ten-year total moratorium on whaling recommended by the 1972 UN Conference on the Human Environment.

COURTESY, GENERAL ELECTRIC RESEARCH AND DEVELOPMENT CENTER

A microbe created at the General Electric Research and Development Center, Schenectady, N.Y., can digest crude oil at a rate several times faster than any known organism. It is potentially of great importance in cleaning oil spills on waterways.

Two further developments, one threatening and the other hopeful, might radically affect the future of whales and the whaling industry. The threat was posed by experiments in direct human harvesting of the krill, the small, shrimp-like crustacean on which baleen whales are totally dependent for food. On the optimistic side, the National Research Council of the National Academy of Sciences released a report recommending cultivation of the jojoba plant for its oil. The seed of the jojoba, a hardy evergreen shrub native to the Sonoran Desert of California, Arizona, and northern Mexico, provides a colourless, odorless oil with a chemical composition virtually identical to that of sperm oil. The council reported that this oil duplicated the performance of sperm oil as a lubricant; previously, there had been no satisfactory substitute for sperm oil in this application.

On July 1 the Washington Convention on International Trade in Endangered Species of Wild Fauna and Flora came into force. At that date it had been ratified by 12 nations: Canada, Chile, Cyprus, Ecuador, Mauritius, Nigeria, Sweden, Switzerland, Tunisia, United Arab Emirates, Uruguay, and the U.S. Though the absence of the U.K., despite many assurances of intention, was deplored, the British conservation and humanitarian societies remained in the forefront of the fight against the waste and cruelty of the wildlife trade. In May the Royal Society for the Protection of Birds published *All Heaven in a Rage: A Study of Importation of Wild Birds into the United Kingdom,* which showed that, except for owls and other birds of prey, there was little restriction or detailed record of wild bird importation or of birds passing through the U.K. in transit to other countries. The study, by T. Inskipp, was based on birds placed on a voluntary basis at the facility maintained at London Airport by the Royal Society for the Prevention of Cruelty to Animals (RSPCA). It was estimated that, worldwide, at least 5.5 million birds were involved in the trade in wild-caught birds each year.

On August 1 the British Wild Creatures and Wild Plants Protection Act became law. It gave protection to certain rare British wild animals and plants and provided that others could be added. (C. L. BOYLE)

See also Agriculture and Food Supplies; Energy; Fisheries; Historic Preservation; Life Sciences; Transportation.

[355.D; 525.A.3.g and B.4.f.i; 534.C.2.a; 724.A; 737.C.1]

ENCYCLOPÆDIA BRITANNICA FILMS. *The House of Man, Part I—Our Changing Environment* (1965); *The Pond and the City* (1965); *Waterfowl: A Resource in Danger* (1966); *Problems of Conservation: Air* (1968); *The Everglades: Conserving a Balanced Community* (1968); *The House of Man, Part II—Our Crowded Environment* (1969); *Problems of Conservation: Forest and Range* (1969); *Problems of Conservation: Minerals* (1969); *Problems of Conservation: Soil* (1969); *Problems of Conservation: Water* (1969); *The South—Roots of the Urban Crisis* (1969); *The Industrial City* (1969); *The Rise of the American City* (1969); *The Garbage Explosion* (1970); *Problems of Conservation: Our Natural Resources* (1970); *Problems of Conservation: Wildlife* (1970); *A Field Becomes a Town* (1970); *What Is a Community?* (2nd ed., 1970); *The Aging of Lakes* (1971); *Turn Off Pollution* (1971); *The Ways of Water* (1971); *Noise—Polluting the Environment* (1971); *Poison Plants* (1972); *The Great Lakes: North America's Inland Seas* (2nd ed., 1972); *The Environment: Everything Around Us* (1972); *Buffalo: An Ecological Success Story* (1972); *Controversy over Industrial Pollution: A Case Study* (1972); *Our Changing Cities: Can They Be Saved?* (1972); *The Image of the City* (1973); *Energy: A Matter of Choices* (1973).

Equatorial Guinea

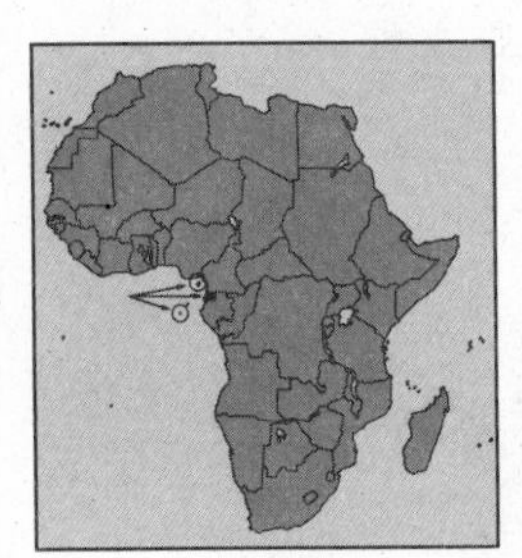

The African republic of Equatorial Guinea consists of Río Muni, which is bordered by Cameroon on the north, Gabon on the east and south, and the Atlantic Ocean on the west; and the offshore islands of Macías Nguema Biyogo (until 1973 called Fernando Po) and Pagalu (formerly Annobón). Area: 10,830 sq.mi. (28,050 sq.km.). Pop. (1974 est.): 303,000. Cap. and largest city: Malabo, on Macías Nguema Biyogo (pop., 1970 est., 19,300). Language: Spanish. President in 1975, Francisco Macías Nguema.

Rumours that an attempted coup in December 1974 had led to mass executions were officially denied, although the detention of 15 political prisoners and 10 suicides were admitted. A rumour that Vice-Pres. Miguel Eyegue had been assassinated in February 1975 was not confirmed, but former vice-president Edmundo Bosio was found dead on February 9. Bosio had been leader of the defunct Río Muni National Party, and the exiled National Association for the Restoration of Democracy claimed that he had protested against President Macías' extreme measures.

Two Roman Catholic bishops and a number of missionaries were expelled, churches were threatened with closure, and Macías had nuns and priests in Río Muni jailed for refusing to read his praises during mass. Allegations of atrocities were made by refugees in Gabon and Cameroon. Nigerian labour on the Macías Nguema Biyogo cocoa plantation was not replaced, and production fell to 13,000 tons in 1974 (40,000 tons in Spanish times).

Chinese personnel in the country increased. In January 1975 President Macías paid a state visit to the Central African Republic to sign a treaty of friendship. Contact with Gabon was maintained in connection with border and offshore disputes, of concern since the presence of oil was suspected.

(MOLLY MORTIMER)

[978.E.7.b]

EQUATORIAL GUINEA

Education. (1970–71) Primary, pupils 31,600, teachers 635; secondary, pupils 5,198; vocational, pupils 603; teacher training, students 213; secondary, vocational, and teacher training, teachers 175.

Finance and Trade. Monetary unit: Equatorial Guinea peseta (ekpwele), at par with the Spanish peseta, with (Sept. 22, 1975) a free rate of 59.76 ekpwele to U.S. $1 (123.80 ekpwele = £1 sterling). Budget (1970): revenue 709.4 million ekpwele; expenditure 589.3 million ekpwele (excludes capital expenditure of 650.7 million ekpwele). Foreign trade (1970): imports 1,472,100,000 ekpwele (80% from Spain); exports 1,740,900,000 ekpwele (91% to Spain). Main exports: cocoa 66%; coffee 24%; timber 9%. Trade with Spain (1974): imports 340 million ekpwele; exports 803.8 million ekpwele.

Agriculture. Production (in 000; metric tons; 1974; 1973 in parentheses): sweet potatoes *c.* 28 (*c.* 28); bananas *c.* 12 (*c.* 12); cocoa *c.* 12 (12); coffee *c.* 7 (*c.* 6); palm kernels *c.* 2 (*c.* 2); palm oil *c.* 4 (*c.* 4). Livestock (in 000; 1973): sheep *c.* 31; cattle *c.* 3; pigs *c.* 7; goats *c.* 7; chickens *c.* 80.

Epidemics:
see Health and Disease

Episcopal Church:
see Religion

Equestrian Sports

Thoroughbred Racing and Steeplechasing. *United States and Canada.* The tragic death of Ruffian, the continued dominance of the handicap division by Forego, and the comeback by the six-year-old mare Susan's Girl were among the leading events in U.S. Thoroughbred racing during 1975. The three-year-old filly Ruffian, undefeated in ten starts, suffered a compound comminuted fracture of both proximal sesamoid bones of the right foreleg several furlongs after the start of her match race with three-year-old colt Foolish Pleasure at Belmont Park on July 6. Efforts to save her failed.

Nonetheless, Ruffian, a Kentucky-bred daughter of Reviewer-Shenanigans, by Native Dancer, was acclaimed champion of her division in the annual poll conducted by the *Daily Racing Form,* the National Turf Writers Association, and the Thoroughbred Racing Associations. Ruffian won five races during the season for her owners-breeders, Mr. and Mrs. Stuart Janney. Her victories included the so-called Triple Crown for three-year-old fillies: the Acorn, Mother Goose, and Coaching Club American Oaks.

Mrs. Edward F. Gerry's five-year-old Forego (Forli-Lady Golconda, by Hasty Road) gained top honours by being named horse of the year for the second consecutive season. The huge Kentucky-bred gelding won the handicap division championship by scoring victories in six of nine stakes starts, the Seminole, Widener, Carter, Brooklyn, Suburban, and Woodward. Forego earned $429,521 for the year.

Susan's Girl (Quadrangle-Quaze, by Quibu), owned and bred by Fred W. Hooper, had been voted champion three-year-old filly in 1972 and best older mare the following season. Fractured sesamoids idled her during most of 1974, but she came back strongly in 1975 to win 7 of 17 starts. Her five-year career earnings of $1,251,667 set a U.S. record for a filly or mare. Her most prestigious victories came in the Matchmaker, Delaware, Beldame, and Spinster handicaps. She was retired at the season's end.

Other champions crowned were Wajima, three-year-old colt division; Dearly Precious, two-year-old filly; Honest Pleasure, two-year-old colt; Gallant Bob, sprinting; Snow Knight, turf competition; and Life's Illusion, steeplechasing.

UPI COMPIX

Ruffian joins the ranks of the "hall of fame" by winning the filly Triple Crown at the $100,000-added Coaching Club American Oaks race at Belmont Park on June 21.

Foolish Pleasure, the Florida-bred colt that annexed the two-year-old title in 1974, gained early prominence in the three-year-old division by taking the Flamingo Stakes and the Kentucky Derby. He ran second in the Preakness and Belmont Stakes but, except for his victory in the match race with Ruffian, Foolish Pleasure did not post another triumph after the Derby. As for the other winners of the Triple Crown races, Master Derby did not win again after his Preakness triumph, and Avatar won only one minor race after winning the Belmont Stakes.

East-West Stable's Wajima, who missed the Triple Crown races, projected himself into the three-year-old picture with five consecutive stakes victories starting in mid-July. The Kentucky-bred son of Bold Ruler-Iskra, by Le Haar, won the Marylander Handicap, the Monmouth Invitational, the Travers Stakes, and the Governor and Marlboro handicaps, the latter two against older competition. Wajima defeated both Foolish Pleasure and Avatar twice in his only meetings with those rivals.

Forego was among his victims in the Governor and Marlboro, but Forego defeated Wajima in the weight-for-age Woodward. Wajima finished second by a neck to Group Plan in the final start of his career, the weight-for-age Jockey Club Gold Cup. Wajima retired with earnings of $537,838 and was syndicated for a record $7.2 million to stand at stud.

Bertram Firestone's two-year-old colt Honest Pleasure (What A Pleasure-Tularia, by Tulyar), bred by Waldemar Farms in Florida as was Foolish Pleasure and also trained by LeRoy Jolley, had six firsts and two seconds in eight appearances. He won stakes races in his final four starts, the Arlington-Washington Futurity, Cowdin, Champagne, and Laurel Futurity, and accumulated $370,227.

Richard E. Bailey's Florida-bred filly Dearly Precious (Dr. Fager-Imsodear, by Chieftain) ran fifth in her racing debut and then won her other eight starts. Her last seven triumphs were in stakes races, the Polly Drummond, Fashion, Colleen, Astoria, Sorority, Spinaway, and the Arlington-Washington Lassie, to bank $250,989. Dearly Precious, like Wajima, was trained by Steve DiMauro.

A worthy rival to Dearly Precious was Mrs. Bertram Firestone's Optimistic Gal, trained by LeRoy Jolley. After Dearly Precious was retired for the season early in September, Optimistic Gal won four consecutive stakes: the Matron, Frizette, Alcibiades, and Selima.

Robert J. Horton's three-year-old gelding Gallant Bob, a Kentucky-bred son of Gallant Romeo-Wisp O'Will, by New Policy, won 13 stakes while competing mainly on the Maryland-New Jersey-Pennsylvania circuit. He scored once in New York and once in Chicago and earned $256,843.

Edward P. Taylor's English-bred Snow Knight (Firestreak-Snow Blossom, by Flush Royal), which won the 1974 Epsom Derby, triumphed in five turf stakes: the Senaca, a division of the Brighton Beach, a division of the Manhattan, the Man O'War (via disqualification of One On the Aisle) and the Canadian International. Also on the turf, the French-bred Nobiliary won the Washington, D.C., International.

L'Enjoleur, a three-year-old colt, made Canadian racing history in 1975 when he was named horse of the year for a second consecutive season. The Canadian homebred, owned by J.-L. Levesque and ridden by Sandy Hawley, dominated his division. He won two of the races in Canada's Triple Crown, the Queen's Plate and the Prince of Wales Stakes, and also triumphed in the Quebec and Manitoba Derbies. Momigi won the third leg of the Triple Crown, the Breeders' Stakes.

In other major Canadian races Pampas Host took the Canadian Derby and Auguste won the British Columbia Derby. The premier event for fillies, the Canadian Oaks, went to Reasonable Win, while the Canadian International Championship, open to older horses, was won by Snow Knight.

(JOSEPH C. AGRELLA)

Europe and Australia. Followers of National Hunt racing in Britain in 1974–75 looked to the Grand National Steeplechase at Aintree, Liverpool, in April for the climax of the season. In an attempt to become the only horse to win three Grand Nationals, and in

Grundy leads the field to finish first in the King George VI and Queen Elizabeth Diamond Stakes at Ascot in July.

KEYSTONE

successive years, Red Rum was beaten by L'Escargot, trained by D. Moore in Ireland and ridden by T. Carberry. The two horses jumped the last fence together, but L'Escargot then had the speed to draw away and win by 15 lengths. L'Escargot, owned by Raymond Guest, U.S. ambassador to Ireland, had been second and third in the race the two previous years and had won the Cheltenham Gold Cup twice.

At Cheltenham, under steady rain that on the last day required two fences to be cut out and the last three races to be abandoned, Comedy of Errors, trained by F. Rimell and ridden by K. B. White, flew away from Flash Imp and Tree Tangle to win the Champion Hurdle by eight lengths and stamp himself as one of the great hurdlers. In the Cheltenham Gold Cup, Ten Up, trained in Ireland by J. Dreaper and ridden by Carberry, had too much stamina for Soothsayer and Bula.

In November 1974 Bruslee won the Mackeson Gold Cup Steeplechase at Cheltenham and Royal Marshal II the Hennessy Cognac Gold Cup Steeplechase at Newbury; in December Garnishee won the Massey-Ferguson Gold Cup Steeplechase; Comedy of Errors beat Lanzarote in the Irish Sweeps Hurdle at Leopardstown, as he had already done in the Cheltenham Trial Hurdle; and Captain Christy won Kempton Park's King George VI Steeplechase. In April the Whitbread Gold Cup Steeplechase at Sandown Park was won by April Seventh from Captain Christy. T. Stack was National Hunt champion jockey.

In June at Auteuil, Paris, Air Landais won the Grand Steeplechase de Paris, worth more than $100,000, from Captain Christy. T. W. Dreaper, the retired Irish trainer, died on April 28; he had saddled ten winners of the Irish Grand National and five of the Cheltenham Gold Cup, among them the duchess of Westminster's steeplechaser Arkle.

An unusual feature of flat racing in England in 1975 was the preeminence of two Italian owners. C. Vittadini owned the brilliant three-year-old colt Grundy (by Great Nephew), who was trained by P. Walwyn, himself leading English trainer for 1975 with 121 winners and record stakes won of £382,527, and was ridden by P. Eddery, champion jockey in 1974 and again in 1975 with 164 winners. C. d'Alessio owned the three-year-old colt Bolkonski, who was trained by H. Cecil (second in the trainer's list with 82 winners and £206,345 won) and ridden by Sardinian-born jockey G. Dettori. Grundy won the Irish Two Thousand Guineas, the English Derby (from the French filly Nobiliary and Hunza Dancer), the Irish Derby (from King Pellinore), and the King George VI and Queen Elizabeth Diamond Stakes (from Bustino and the French mare Dahlia). Bolkonski won the Two Thousand Guineas (from Grundy), the St. James's Palace Stakes at Royal Ascot, and the Sussex Stakes at Goodwood (from Rose Bowl and Lianga). To crown their season, d'Alessio and Cecil produced the two most formidable English two-year-olds: Wollow won the Champagne Stakes at Doncaster and the Dewhurst Stakes at Newmarket, while his stable companion Take Your Place won the Observer Gold Cup from French-trained Earth Spirit. Dettori, in his brief descents on England to ride for Cecil, had 14 winners out of 29 rides.

Of the other English classics, the One Thousand Guineas was won by the Irish filly Nocturnal Spree and the Oaks by Juliette Marny, trained by J. Tree and ridden by L. Piggott; the St. Leger was won by Bruni, trained by H. Price and ridden by A. Murray. Miralla won the Irish One Thousand Guineas from Silky. Piggott rode eight winners at the Royal Ascot meeting (six for the Irish trainer V. O'Brien out of O'Brien's total of six runners), including a victory in the Ascot Gold Cup on the French horse Sagaro from another French horse, Le Bavard.

In July the King George VI and Queen Elizabeth Diamond Stakes, over 1½ mi. at Ascot, proved to be one of the great races of the English turf, the course record being broken by the staggering margin of 2.36 sec. (2 min. 26.98 sec.). Grundy won the race by half a length from Lady Beaverbrook's Bustino, winner of the 1974 St. Leger and 1975 Coronation Cup at Epsom, with Dahlia third; Dahlia ran faster than in her two previous victories in the race in 1973 and 1974. Bustino strained a leg and never ran again, while Grundy soon after failed in the Benson and Hedges Gold Cup at York against Dahlia and was retired, to stand at the National Stud, which had acquired a three-quarter share in him.

Silk Stockings won the Gold Rush in July and set a new world record for the mile for three-year-old fillies.

WIDE WORLD

May Hill won the Yorkshire Oaks at York and the Park Hill Stakes at Doncaster. Rose Bowl, trained by F. Johnson Houghton and ridden by W. Carson, took Ascot's Queen Elizabeth II Stakes and then ran another sparkling race to hold off the great Allez France and another French horse, the colt Ramirez, in the Champion Stakes at Newmarket.

Of the sprinters, the French-trained Flirting Around, perhaps the fastest sprinter in Europe, won Royal Ascot's King's Stand Stakes. French-trained Lianga took Newmarket's July Cup; Lianga rounded off the season by winning the £13,000 Vernon's Sprint Cup from Roman Warrior at Haydock Park. Roman Warrior won the Ayr Gold Cup and dead-heated with the Irish filly Swingtime in Ascot's Diadem Stakes. At York, Bay Express won the Nunthorpe Stakes and Music Boy, a two-year-old with a blinding turn of speed, took the Gimcrack Stakes.

In France the equivalents of the Two Thousand and One Thousand Guineas were won, respectively, by Green Dancer and by Ivanjica. J. Wertheimer's Val de l'Orne, trained by A. Head and ridden by F. Head, won the Prix du Jockey Club (French Derby) by a head from English-trained Patch (who, if he had won, would have given his owner Vittadini his fourth Derby in 1975, since his Orange Bay had won the Italian Derby). Val de l'Orne also won the Prix Hocquart and the Prix Noailles. The Prix du Cadran (equivalent of the Ascot Gold Cup) was won by Le Bavard, and Matahawk triumphed in the Grand Prix de Paris. Lianga won the Prix Jacques le Marois at Deauville, where the two-year-old Vitiges, who had earlier won the Prix Robert Papin, won the Prix Morny. L'Ensorceleur won the Grand Prix de Deauville from Dahlia. Allez France took the Prix Ganay, the Prix Dollar, and the Prix Foy. The Prix Royal Oak (St. Leger) went to Henri le Balafre, and the Prix de la Salamandre and the Grand Criterium to Manado, France's top two-year-old. Ivanjica won the Prix Vermeille from Nobiliary and May Hill. The Prix de l'Abbaye de Longchamp went to Lianga.

In Italy the Gran Premio di Milano was won by Star Appeal (by Appiani II), trained in West Germany by T. Grieper. Star Appeal had earlier won the Grosser Preis der Badischen Wirtschaft and, in England at Sandown Park, the Eclipse Stakes; at the end of the season, ridden by G. Starkey, he won Europe's richest race (worth about $325,000), the Prix de l'Arc de Triomphe at Longchamp, Paris, by three lengths from On My Way and Comtesse de Loir. In West Germany Athenagoras won the Grosser Preis von Nordrhein-Westfalen from Lord Udo, which won the Grosser Preis von Düsseldorf and the Aral-Pokal. Windwurf won the Preis von Europa at Cologne.

Stableboys, striking for better pay and conditions, interfered with but did not prevent the running of the Two Thousand Guineas at Newmarket, but in France they caused the Prix de Diane (French Oaks) to be abandoned. In both countries an uneasy truce followed while discussion and union organization continued. Limited graded racing based on the French system was introduced in handicaps in England, to promote better-balanced and more competitive racing by eliminating from the better races horses unworthy of the minimum weight on their past performances. A colt by Mill Reef was bought by the British Bloodstock Agency at the Newmarket Houghton Sales for £212,100, a European auction record.

In Australia the 3,200-m., A$128,000 Sydney Cup was won by the 40–1 outsider New Zealand-bred gelding Gay Master, owned by B. Hedley, trained by T. Hughes, and ridden by A. Trevena, from Participator and High Style. At Flemington, Victoria, the 3,200-m. A$153,000 Melbourne Cup went to 33–1 five-year-old Think Big, owned by R. O'Sullivan of Brisbane and Chin Nan Tan from Singapore, trained by B. Cummings, and ridden by H. White, from Holiday Waggon and Medici. Think Big's victory in the Cup was his second in a row, and the victory was Cummings' fifth in that race as a trainer.

(R. M. GOODWIN)

Harness Racing. Highlight of 1975 in Australia was the 1 min. 58.6 sec. world two-year-old record performance in the mile by Mister Karamea. Bred by N. Simpson and purchased as a yearling by J. Deane of Perth, the Meadow Al-Miss Carlisle colt was the first Australian-bred two-year-old to pace or trot a mile faster than two minutes. Turning three in August, he went on to establish a new state record over 2,000 m. (rating 1 min. 17.3 sec.). The $47,000 Hunter Cup in Melbourne was won by Royal Gaze, while Just Too Good took the 2,600-m. West Australian Pacing Cup, and Young Quinn won the Miracle Mile in Sydney. In the classics, the New South Wales Pacers

TOP, A.F.P./PICTORIAL PARADE; BOTTOM, SPORTING PICTURES

Italy's Graziana Mancinelli takes Bel Oiseau (top) to victory in the International Horse Show at Fontainebleau, France. Comedy of Errors (below) clears the last hurdle en route to the winner's circle in the Champion Hurdle at Cheltenham, England, in March.

Derby went to Wilbur Post, and New Zealand visitor Rippers Delight triumphed in the N.S.W. Pacing Oaks. In the trotting division Little William won the Victorian Derby, and the Victorian Oaks went to Radiant Destiny.

Top pacer of New Zealand was Young Quinn, which, after winning the Auckland Cup and later recording 1 min. 57 sec. in the Stars Travel Miracle Mile, went on to the U.S., where he added over $300,000 to his year's winnings. For the trotters In Or Out won the New Zealand Oaks and Rippers Delight the North Island Oaks. The remarkable pacing colt Noodlum (by Bachelor Hanover) was top three-year-old, while the smart filly Olga Korbut (by Lordship) topped the two-year-old section. The 3,200-m. New Zealand Cup provided a thrilling finish with Lunar Chance prevailing by a head over Final Decision. The 1,600-m. National Flying Pace was won by the consistent Robalan.

In the U.S. world records began to fall on the Grand Circuit when Silk Stockings paced a mile in 1 min. 55.2 sec. at Syracuse for C. and K. Mazik and went on to a string of victories. However, the 1974 champion, two-year-old Tarport Hap driven by Delvin Miller for Alan Levitt and Wilrose Farms, turned the tables on her in the New York Sires Stake and the Hanover Filly Stake. Later, at Lexington, Miller produced Meadow Bright, which he owned with H. Grant, to break the world record for trotting fillies with a 1-min. 57.4-sec. mile. She later became the greatest three-year-old trotting filly ($233,715).

The $200,000 Roosevelt International was won by the Allwood Stables' U.S. representative Savoir from Bellino II (France) and Surge Hanover (Canada). Savoir became the third trotter to win over a million dollars. The $200,000 Cane Futurity for pacers went to Nero. The $200,000 Yonkers Trot for three-year-olds was won by Surefire Hanover, while Noble Rouge took the $100,000 Kentucky Futurity for trotters. The final of the $232,193 Hambletonian trot was won by Bonefish, which had then won over $300,000 and was sold for $1 million. Young Quinn, over from New Zealand for the Yonkers International Pace, failed in that event, which was won by Handle With Care, but later proved himself with a number of victories in major stakes races.

In Europe the Norwegian Trotting Association was host to a successful World Trotting Conference at Oslo in the 100th anniversary year of trotting in Norway, and their richest race of the season ($26,500) was won by the Swedish visitor Micko Tilly. The Norwegian Derby for four-year-olds was won by Safaga Vixi from Lord Scott and Dunlop in 2 min. 13 sec. over the 2,600 m. In Sweden the $83,000 Elite Trot was won by the 1970 Hambletonian winner Timothy T., while the $23,000 three-year-old Criterium went to Top Flekt.

In the Premio Lido in Rome Bellino II nosed out Duc de Vrie and Wayne Eden in a fast 2 min. 1 sec. over 2,100 m. The Italian Derby of $124,000 over 2,100 m. was won by Maribon (by Nike Hanover), owned by Fabio-Mauro Stable, with Scellino second and Basile third in a race record of 2 min. 6.4 sec.

(NOEL SIMPSON)

PAUL HOSEFROS—THE NEW YORK TIMES

Polo now aims at the middle class enthusiast in the U.S. Shown at right is a participant in a practice clinic sponsored by the Polo Training Foundation in Old Westbury, Long Island.

Show Jumping. European show jumping was dominated in 1975 by the West German rider Alwin Schockemöhle, whose three horses Rex the Robber, Warwick, and Santa Monica swept like a scythe through the shows of Aachen, Hickstead, and the Royal International in London and went on to win him the European championship in Munich in August. His compatriot Hartwig Steenken, reigning world champion who gained his title in 1974 at Hickstead and would retain it for four years, was runner-up. Schockemöhle's most doughty rival, Britain's David Broome, was debarred, as a professional, from competing, the German federation having decreed that the 1975 championship should be for amateurs only. This produced some ill feeling, and no British riders competed in Munich.

West Germany also won the President's Cup of the International Equestrian Federation for the world team championship. Great Britain finished second.

At the Rome show in the Piazza di Siena in the spring, British rider Malcolm Pyrah won the Grand Prix, riding the volatile Australian-bred Olympic mare April Love. At Aachen the West German Grand Prix was also won by a British rider, Graham Fletcher, on the Irish horse Buttevant Boy. In Dublin, the Grand Prix was won for Italy by Raimondo d'Inzeo on the 18-year-old Irish horse Bellevue. David Broome was the most successful British rider of the year with Harris Carpets' Sportsman, Heatwave, and Philco. Harvey Smith was the leading international rider in Dublin, but the British Jumping Derby at Hickstead went to an Irish rider, Paul Darragh, riding Pele.

In the Pan-American Games at Mexico City in October the U.S. equestrian team of Buddy Brown, Dennis Murphy, Joe Fargis, and Mike Matz took the gold medal. Mexico finished second and Canada third.

(PAMELA MACGREGOR-MORRIS)

Polo. In 1975 there were nine players handicapped at ten goals, the ultimate rating in polo. Eight were Argentines and the ninth was an Australian, Sinclair Hill. In the Argentine championships held at the beginning of December, Coronel Suarez led by J. C. Harriot beat Santa Ana 13 goals to 8. Coronel Suarez totaled 40 and Santa Ana 38. In the Australasian Gold Cup at Goondiwini in July New Zealand, represented by B. Broughton (handicap 4), D. Kirkpatrick (5), J. Walker (7), and T. Wilson (4), won the final, defeating Queensland by 11 goals to 3.

In the final of the Gold Cup at Cowdray Park, Sussex, Greenhill, represented by J. R. ("Hap") Sharp (3), Tommy Wayman (8), "Red" Armour (7), and R. Ferguson (5), won the cup after the best match for many years in England, defeating Jersey Lillies 9–5. The hero of the match was a pony: Sweet William, ridden by Wayman. The Greenhill team also won the Madrid championship in April and the Soto Grande Gold Cup in August, where the best player in the world, Argentine J. C. Harriot (handicap ten), took Wayman's place. Sharp, Wayman, Joe Barry, and Bob Vilheim won the U.S. Open championship. Wayman was the most successful polo player of the year.

The Coronation Cup, played at Windsor, Berkshire, was won by South America, which defeated England 10 goals to 6. The South American team consisted of G. Pierez (3), E. Moore (9), J. J. Diaz Alberdi (7), and H. Barrantes (7). Playing for England were M. Hare (3), H. Hipwood (7), J. Hipwood (8), and P. M. Withers (7). (ANDREW HORSBRUGH-PORTER)

[452.B.4.h.xvii and xxi; 452.B.5.e]

Ethiopia

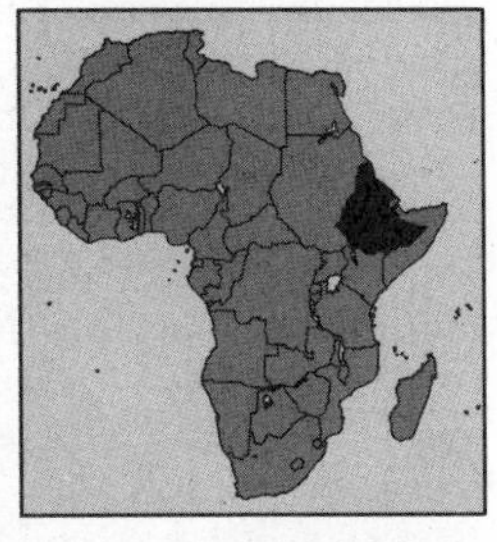

A state in northeastern Africa, which has abolished the title of kingdom but has not officially been declared a republic, Ethiopia is bordered by Somalia, the French Territory of the Afars and Issas, Kenya, the Sudan, and the Red Sea. Area: 471,800 sq.mi. (1,221,900 sq.km.). Pop. (1975 est.): 27,030,400. Cap. and largest city: Addis Ababa (pop., 1975 est., 1,174,000). Language: Amharic (official) and other tongues. Religion: Ethiopian Orthodox (Coptic) and Muslim, with various animist minorities. Head of state and chairman of the Provisional Military Administrative Council in 1975, Brig. Gen. Teferi Benti.

On September 13 of the Gregorian calendar (2 Maskarem, 1968, Ethiopian calendar), 1975, the first anniversary of the Ethiopian Revolution was celebrated in what had been Maskal Square, redesigned at a cost of Eth$2.8 million and now renamed Revolution Square. During this first year of military government, a series of proclamations announced the major contours of political and social change. On Dec. 20, 1974, a declaration of the Provisional Military Administrative Council (PMAC) defined the origins and future direction of the movement *Ethiopia Tikdem* ("Ethiopia First"). The document stated the fundamental principles of Ethiopian socialism (*Hibrettesebawinet*), summarized as equality, self-reliance, the dignity of labour, the supremacy of the common good, and the indivisibility of Ethiopian unity. Banks and insurance companies were transferred to public ownership during January, and this was followed in February by the PMAC Declaration on Economic Policy, which stated that the common good took precedence over the pursuit of private gain and brought under public ownership a further range of key industries and agro-industrial concerns.

On March 4 rural lands were nationalized by a proclamation that also announced the policy of establishing peasant farmer associations on redistributed units of 20 gashas (800 ha.). The use of land by individuals was restricted to 10 ha. By September the government announced that nearly 16,000 peasant associations had been formed.

Urban lands and properties were nationalized on July 26. All urban land became government property, and ownership was limited to one house property, excess houses reverting to the government. For future development individual home plots were defined at 500 sq.m. Community associations (300 in Addis Ababa) were established and charged with much of the responsibility of administering the proclamation with regard to registering properties, housing homeless people, and collecting government rent from small properties and other rented accommodations. On September 29 private schools were placed under the control of the urban community associations.

In December 1974 the National Work Campaign for Development through Cooperation (short name in Amharic, "Zemecha") was launched. All students above grade ten in the secondary schools and in the third-level institutions were recruited, together with their Ethiopian teachers. The 60,000 young people mobilized in the Zemecha were dispatched to rural areas throughout the country where they were engaged in development work, including a literacy campaign and the implementation of the rural lands proclamation, particularly in the formation of peasant associations. A number were also to have been involved in urban areas implementing the urban proclamation, but clashes with the authorities resulted in some 2,000 being placed in corrective detention during August and September 1975. The government declared the campaign in rural areas to be successful and extended participation by the current Zemecha for one more academic year.

Public holidays in Ethiopia were revised and limited to 13 official holidays, including 3 Muslim feasts, a newly established Revolution Day, and the official celebration of May Day. Victory Day (over the Italian forces in 1941) was moved from May 5 to April 6 because the former date marked only the day on which the former emperor Haile Selassie re-entered the capital.

The PMAC announced its intention of forming a political party in the "near future" and establishing the right "to form associations in line with the philosophy of Ethiopian Socialism." A political committee was formed under the PMAC to present proposals for "preparing the masses for active participation in running the affairs of the state on the basis of revolutionary principles." These measures would include political education campaigns.

Political and social changes were accompanied by administrative reforms. A complete restructuring of the civil service was planned, and preliminary steps included the appointment of "permanent secretaries" to the major ministries. Legal notices were published to create a number of new public enterprises to manage the nationalized industries. These included enterprises for industrial sectors, domestic distribution, and import-export. There was a redistribution of functions among the ministries with the apparent intention of establishing larger, umbrella agencies to become focal points of activity; for example, a Ministry of Culture was created with responsibility for fine arts and culture as well as youth affairs and sport. The Ministry of Public Works was the focal point of all construction activity, and among other measures established a Building Agency for Rural Developments, which included the former Elementary School Building Unit of the Ministry of Education.

On March 21 the monarchy was abolished by proclamation, annulling the appointment of Crown

UPI COMPIX

Leading a February demonstration in Addis Ababa of nearly 4,000 war veterans supporting the military junta's campaign to crush the Muslims in the northern province of Eritrea was this horseman garbed in a lion's headdress.

MOHAMED AMIN—CAMERAPIX/KEYSTONE

Somali people of Ethiopia's Ogaden region were dying at the rate of 90 per day because of the three years of drought in the region.

Prince Asfa Wossen as king-designate. Many members of the royal family and former officials remained in custody, and the investigation of their affairs continued through the Commission of Inquiry, whose chairman announced on September 23 that 74 out of the 116 cases against former government officials had been completed. Former emperor Haile Selassie (*see* OBITUARIES) died in detention on August 27, but 55 former officials were granted amnesty and released by the government on September 12, the occasion of the Ethiopian New Year.

The first year of socialism was not without its difficulties. Rebellion in Eritrea Province continued to pin down Ethiopian forces, and armed clashes were frequent and serious. A major military action occurred in the Asmara region in February when a state of emergency was declared in Eritrea, and a reported massacre of 1,000 civilians of the Afar people in June at Aisaita, near the border of the French Territory of the Afars and Issas, was later blamed on an Afar leader, Sultan Ali Mirrah.

Fighting was not restricted to Eritrea. Feudal landowners and their supporters still resisted the reform measures, and provincial disturbances and arrests of individuals resisting government forces were reported. A number of executions of captured rebels took place in Addis Ababa, and in September the chief administrator of Begemdir Province and its Semien region was ambushed and shot.

In Addis Ababa and some other larger urban centres rumblings of disagreement persisted among the more organized sectors of the population. In June the leadership of the Confederation of Ethiopian Labour Unions (CELU) was replaced. On September 24 CELU published a manifesto condemning the government's policies and threatening a general strike; at the end of September distribution of the manifesto by Ethiopian Airlines personnel at Bole (Addis Ababa) airport provoked intervention by the security forces, and seven employees were killed and a number injured. This resulted in a three-day shutdown, supported by other unions and provoking the declaration of a state of emergency in the Addis Ababa region that lasted nine weeks. Opposition to PMAC policies was growing among members of the Teachers' Association, and 18 teachers were arrested on September 24 for distributing subversive literature. There was unrest among the students, who advocated an early end to military rule.

European Economic Community:
see Economy, World; European Unity

On September 30, in the face of the increasing challenge to its authority, the PMAC declared a nationwide state of emergency and outlawed strikes.

The structure of the armed forces committee of the PMAC, the Dirgue, remained obscure, although its chairman, Brigadier General Teferi, confirmed at a press conference in September that the 120 members who had formed the military committee remained together. The first and second vice-chairmen, Maj. Mengistu Haile Mariam and Lieut. Col. Atnafu Abate, respectively, continued in office. Reference was made to Maj. Sissay Habte as chairman of the Political Committee responsible for proposing the form of political or party organization to be created, and to Lieut. Alemayehu Haile, chairman of the Administration and Organization Committee responsible for structural changes in the government and for administrative appointments.

The government had to deal with the aftermath of the drought in Wallo and Tigre provinces and with its extension into Hararge and Bale provinces and other regions in the south. Parts of 12 provinces remained affected, some seriously, particularly in the pastoral areas where livestock losses were enormous and rehabilitation measures difficult to implement. Just under three million people were in a precarious position and required continuing relief supplies. The worst conditions were now to be found in the Ogaden region of

ETHIOPIA

Education. (1972–73) Primary, pupils 767,157, teachers 16,978; secondary, pupils 162,463, teachers 5,350; vocational, pupils 5,233, teachers 500; teacher training, students 3,053, teachers 192; higher, students 9,170, teaching staff 579.

Finance and Banking. Monetary unit: Ethiopian dollar, with (Sept. 22, 1975) a par value of Eth$2.07 to U.S. $1 (free rate of Eth$4.29 = £1 sterling). Gold, SDRs, and foreign exchange: (June 1975) U.S. $282.6 million; (June 1974) U.S. $235.7 million. Budget (1974–75 est.): revenue Eth$882 million; expenditure Eth$919 million. Gross national product: (1972) Eth$4,687,000,000; (1971) Eth$4,681,000,000. Money supply: (April 1975) Eth$792.9 million; (April 1974) Eth$682 million. Cost of living (Addis Ababa; 1970 = 100): (May 1975) 118; (May 1974) 113.

Foreign Trade. (1974) Imports Eth$569.2 million; exports Eth$555.9 million. Import sources (1973): Italy 15%; Japan 12%; West Germany 12%; U.K. 9%; U.S. 9%; Iran 7%. Export destinations (1973): U.S. 30%; West Germany 9%; Italy 8%; Afars and Issas 7%; Saudi Arabia 6%; Japan 6%. Main exports: coffee 27%; pulses 19%; oilseeds 17%; hides and skins 8%.

Transport and Communications. Roads (1972) *c.* 23,400 km. (including 8,170 km. main roads). Motor vehicles in use (1972): passenger 41,000; commercial (including buses) 12,700. Railways (1973): 1,088 km.; traffic (including traffic of Afars and Issas portion of Djibouti-Addis Ababa line; excluding Eritrea) 79 million passenger-km., freight 223 million net ton-km. Air traffic (1974): 455 million passenger-km.; freight 19,460,000 net ton-km. Telephones (Dec. 1973) 61,000. Radio receivers (Dec. 1973) 175,000. Television receivers (Dec. 1973) 25,000.

Agriculture. Production (in 000; metric tons; 1974; 1973 in parentheses): barley *c.* 1,500 (*c.* 1,500); wheat *c.* 850 (*c.* 860); corn *c.* 1,000 (*c.* 1,000); millet *c.* 150 (*c.* 150); sorghum *c.* 1,100 (*c.* 1,100); sweet potatoes (1973) *c.* 262, (1972) *c.* 256; potatoes *c.* 170 (*c.* 169); linseed *c.* 75 (*c.* 72); sesame *c.* 110 (*c.* 100); sugar, raw value *c.* 131 (*c.* 139); chick-peas *c.* 198 (*c.* 196); dry peas *c.* 135 (*c.* 133); dry broad beans (1973) *c.* 149, (1972) *c.* 148; lentils (1973) *c.* 112, (1972) *c.* 110; dry beans *c.* 78 (*c.* 78); coffee *c.* 180 (*c.* 180). Livestock (in 000; 1974): cattle 24,663; sheep 22,320; goats (1973) *c.* 11,370; horses (1973) *c.* 1,442; mules (1973) *c.* 1,440; asses (1973) *c.* 3,930; camels (1973) *c.* 995; chickens *c.* 50,000.

Industry. Production (in 000; metric tons; 1970–71): cement 183; petroleum products (1973) 655; cotton yarn 9.6; cotton fabrics (sq.m.) 79,000; electricity (kw-hr.) 585,000.

Hararge Province and in El Keré subprovince of Bale.

These factors and others affected the general economy. The *Ethiopian Herald,* in an October editorial denouncing strikes and encouraging a proper attitude toward work, referred to the "abysmal" state of the Ethiopian economy. This was a particularly gloomy view, and there was no doubt that political uncertainty, nationalization, labour unrest, malfunctioning of the market apparatus, and the aftereffects of drought, as well as increased military expenditure, had had a significant short-run effect. However, shortages of imported consumer goods did not affect most of the population, and business did not seem to have been seriously inconvenienced by gasoline shortages and rationing. But there were end-of-season grain shortages in urban centres (particularly of teff, from which the unleavened pancakes known as *injera* are made). Drought and bad harvests, gasoline prices, and a disrupted communications system, combined with current measures to change the nature and direction of the economy, were not circumstances in which a buoyant economy could be expected.

The 1975–76 budget set a record of Eth$1.3 billion, Eth$432 million of which was capital expenditure. Economic services claimed 34% and social services 25% of the total. No large change was envisaged in the structure of revenue, although new tax laws were proclaimed. The main feature of this budget was that deficit financing was introduced for the first time, to be carried out through increased borrowing from the National Bank of Ethiopia to the extent of Eth$156 million.

The vigorous policy of economic reorganization emphasized the need for higher levels of productivity in both agriculture and industry. This, coupled with the likelihood of special external assistance deriving from Ethiopia's position as one of the most needy of the less developed countries and of external support from a new range of donors and the special assistance promoted by the drought situation, was a factor that would favour economic growth. The government, however, had to ensure that the 1975 coffee harvest was picked and processed under new circumstances, including redistribution of landholdings, creation of peasant associations, new regulations for the employment of agricultural labour, nationalization of coffee processing plants, and a new framework for loans to finance picking and processing. Coffee, in a somewhat reduced year, represented 27% of the value of exports in 1974.

[978.E.5.a]

European Unity

For the European Economic Community (EEC) 1975 was a disappointing year, but by no means without hope for the future. It was prepared for with cautious optimism by the Community summit conference of Dec. 9–10, 1974, which decided that unanimity should not always be necessary in the Council of Ministers; set up a working party to study the introduction of a European passport for Community citizens; instituted Community meetings (European Councils) of heads of government to be held three times a year; established the European Regional Development Fund from Jan. 1, 1975; reiterated the determination of the nine members to move toward economic and monetary union; and invited the Community to work out and implement a common energy policy. The move toward democratization of the Community through direct election of the European Parliament gathered momentum, and on Dec. 1–2, 1975, in Rome, the European Council decided that the first direct elections would be held on the same day throughout the Community, in May or June 1978 (neither Britain nor Denmark committed themselves, but did not block the vote). The Council also decided that a start would be made on introduction of a European passport in 1978. The so-called renegotiation of Britain's terms of accession and the referendum in the U.K. on the question of continued British membership delayed development in 1975. However, the British government duly declared itself satisfied with the results of the renegotiation, and in the referendum the British people voted overwhelmingly to remain in the Community.

Those who had expected the clear verdict of the British people to give a new impetus to the development of the Community were disappointed, however. Britain, with its currency chronically weak since October 1973, considered itself in no position to move forward to an economic and monetary union in which more stable exchange rates would be the first step. Further, Britain now asked for derogations from the terms of its accession treaty on transport, refused to approve the principle of control of discharge of highly toxic substances into rivers and seas, showed reserve on the formulation of a common energy policy, and alone among the nine member states insisted on a separate seat at the plenary session of the Conference on International Economic Cooperation (formerly known as the energy and raw materials conference) in Paris in December.

West Germany, intent on stemming inflation and disappointed at the lack of progress toward economic and political integration, had insisted on substantial budget cuts, not in the common agricultural policy (CAP), which absorbed some three-quarters of Community expenditure and which West Germany wished to reform, but in allocations to the Community's regional and social funds and in its aid to less developed countries. France imposed completely illegal restrictions on imports of inexpensive Italian wine.

Britain's "Renegotiation." The British government considered its renegotiation completed following the meeting of the newly baptized European Council in Dublin on March 10–11. Five of the seven points

"That's the third round he's insisted on buying—I hope he doesn't consider that's Britain's contribution to the E.E.C."

MAC—LONDON DAILY MAIL/ROTHCO

KEYSTONE

Britain, Ireland, and Denmark each claimed rights to the continental shelf around Rockall, an outcrop of rock 200 miles from land in the Atlantic. At issue are fishing rights and potential oil reserves.

on which the Labour Party had insisted in its manifesto of a year earlier had by then been resolved. Several aspects of CAP had been changed, and Britain had been able to retain deficiency payments for beef; in addition, British consumers were benefiting substantially from price stability and import and other subsidies on various foodstuffs at a time when world prices of many products had risen chaotically. The interests of most of the poor Commonwealth countries had been generously safeguarded by the Lomé Convention (*see* below) and through generalized preferences and trade agreements. Guaranteed access for Commonwealth sugar had been achieved. The question of Britain's retaining the right to determine its own regional aids and its own economic policy was glossed over. By the time the Dublin summit took place, the only outstanding matters were Britain's financial contribution to the Community's budget, the arrangements for which Britain considered unfair, and access for New Zealand butter and cheese to the Community market after 1977.

These two questions were resolved in Dublin. It was agreed that a budget refund would be given to any country whose share in the Community's gross domestic product (GDP) turned out to be less than its share in the budget, subject to a refund limit. The summit also guaranteed continued access of New Zealand butter up to 1980. The British government termed the renegotiation successfully concluded and threw its weight behind a "yes" vote for continued British membership in the Community in the referendum of June 5. The result was a surprising victory for moderate, reasoned opinion against the extremists who had made the most noise. (*See* United Kingdom.)

Energy. The general lines of the Community's strategy for reducing dependence on oil imports were set out in objectives for 1985 approved by the Council of Ministers on Dec. 17, 1974. These aimed at reducing the Community's dependence on imported energy from 63% in 1973 to below 50%, and if possible to 40%, by 1985—mainly by increasing the use of solid fuels (coal and lignite) to 17% of total consumption (from 10% forecast in 1973), that of nuclear energy to 13–16% (from 9% forecast), and that of natural gas to 18–23% (15% forecast). The share of oil in total consumption would fall to 41–49%, from 64% forecast in 1973. First, the Council limited the amounts of oil and natural gas that could be used in electricity generating stations, and it was decided to fix minimum coal stocks for power stations and raise minimum oil stocks to 90 days' supply. The Council also adopted in December 1974 a program to help bring energy consumption down to 15% below the amount previously estimated for 1985; coal production would be maintained until 1985, and Community oil and natural gas production would be increased, largely through developing North Sea resources. For nuclear power, an installed capacity of 160 gigawatts (= 160 million kw.), and if possible 200 gigawatts, was aimed at by 1985, but the member states' plans later indicated that in fact the figure would not exceed 155 gigawatts.

Economic and Monetary Union. As Western Europe passed through its worst recession since the 1930s, with GDP actually falling by 2½% in 1975, progress toward economic and monetary union was blocked by divergences between the member countries. Both Britain and Italy had deep-seated industrial problems, but Italy was able to restore its balance of payments and the stability of the lira. Britain made little headway against its rapid inflation: while average 1975 inflation rates were estimated by the European Commission at 12½% for the Community as a whole, they ranged from only 6% in West Germany to 22–23% in the U.K. and Ireland. The pound fell in value by about 10% over the year. France, West Germany, and Italy had by the spring of 1975 so restored their payments situations as to be in surplus; the U.K. still had a deficit on current account for 1975 estimated at £1,750 million.

This meant that West Germany and The Netherlands were able to combat the recession by pursuing expansionary economic policies and relaxed monetary policies early in 1975, to be followed later in the year by France, Italy, and Denmark. In Britain, however, the chancellor of the exchequer announced as late as December that no reflation was yet possible. Britain's large-scale unemployment, superficially similar in volume to that of the rest of the Community (in which five million, or 4½% of the total working population, were unemployed), was likely to persist much longer than that of other member countries.

The French franc, which was showing great strength in international currency markets, returned on July 10 to the EEC "snake" of jointly floating currencies, leaving only the pound sterling and the Italian lira still outside. The division of the Community into first-class and second-class economies seemed complete.

Industrial Policy. Proposals put to the Council by the Commission in October advocated Community financing in the aerospace industry and the coordination of member's activities in the fields of military aircraft purchase, civil aviation projects, and services and equipment specifications, and preferential purchasing arrangements in the telecommunications industry. In the computer industry, Commission hopes of forming a strong European grouping suffered a heavy blow with the breakup of the Unidata association of France's CII, The Netherlands' Philips, and Germany's Siemens when CII withdrew in May and subsequently merged with the U.S. firm Honeywell.

On May 13, 1975, the Commission sent the Council an amended draft regulation for a European Company Statute enabling companies to merge across frontiers and to form holding companies or joint subsidiaries under European rather than national legislation. The amendments would make medium-sized as well as large firms eligible for European status. European companies would have a two-tier board structure, with one-third worker representation on the upper, or supervisory, board, and compulsory works councils.

In the field of taxation, the Commission on July 30 sent the Council an action program for taxation, urging it to decide quickly on a standard basis for assessing value-added tax (VAT), harmonization of excise-duty structure, and taxes on mergers. It submitted a draft directive for harmonizing corporation tax and withholding tax on the basis of the imputation or tax-credit system.

Regional Policy. On March 18, 1975, the European Community's long-heralded Regional Development Fund was set up with the task of making an effort to reduce regional imbalances in living standards and prosperity. It disposed of 1,300,000,000 units of account ($1,568,000,000) for the three years 1975–77. Of the total, Italy was to receive 40%, Britain 28%, France 15%, West Germany 6.4%, and Ireland 6%. But there was little sign of a Community regional policy; the payments were merely handouts to governments to finance their own policies. This was largely due to the British government which, plagued by its immense public expenditure deficit, refused to accept the principle that Community regional policy measures should be additional to national measures. A Regional Policy Committee was also set up to coordinate national policies and to suggest methods for drawing up regional development programs.

Agriculture. The great "stocktaking" of CAP produced nothing like the plan for radical overhaul that the British and West Germans envisaged when it was launched in October 1974. On the contrary, the document finally agreed on by the Council in November 1975 set out from the assumption that the basic premises of CAP—market unity, with free trade and common pricing; Community preference; and financial burden-sharing—would remain untouched. It rejected as too expensive any general move to replace price support by direct income aid to farmers. The ministers did no more than list points at which CAP was not working properly and some general principles for dealing with them. But the document also set out member states' fundamental differences.

On September 29 the Commission's proposals for CAP expenditure got through the Council virtually unscathed, with 1976 spending estimated at 5,490,-000,000 units of account—20% more than the 1975 budget allocation, 9% more than the amount actually spent in 1975, and equal to nearly three-quarters of the total Community budget.

However, Commission proposals for 1976 submitted to the Council on Dec. 11, 1975, indicated its determination to stop the buildup of surpluses and to start dismantling the complex system of monetary compensatory amounts. The latter were instituted originally to compensate farmers in countries whose currencies had appreciated in value, but they were by now creating distortions in trade rather than eliminating them. The Commission proposed varying price increases averaging 7½%: for dairy products, in which the main surplus existed, a price rise of only 2% in March 1976 was to be followed by a second rise of 4.5% in September 1976, and also measures to get rid of the skim milk powder surplus—amounting to roughly a million tons by December 1975—and to prevent any further buildup of stocks; changes in the cereals policy would prevent high-yielding non-bread varieties of wheat from benefiting from the bread-wheat subsidy; sugar production quotas were to be reimposed and a reserve sugar stock of 1.5 million metric tons was to be built up. In September the Commission sent the Council proposals for a common policy for sheep meat, to come into force on Jan. 1, 1976.

Restrictive Practices and Monopolies. Two notable decisions by the European Court of Justice in Luxembourg toward the end of the year confirmed a tendency by the court to criticize explicitly or implicitly the Commission's preparation and presentation of antitrust actions against companies. On November 27 it quashed fines totaling BFr. 18 million imposed by the Commission on the Belgian Wallpaper Manufacturers Association. Its grounds were simply that the Commission had not properly made out its case, which was that the association covered every aspect of marketing and included an aggregated rebate system which effectively prevented imports. On December 16 the court took an even more powerful swipe at the Commission, reducing or annulling fines totaling 9 million units of account imposed on 16 sugar refining companies in December 1972. The court, while upholding the Commission's allegations of concerted practices to protect The Netherlands' sugar market, said the chief blame for the lack of competition must lie with the way in which the Community's sugar market had been organized.

Living and Working Conditions. The Community took modest steps forward in social policy. On June 17 the Council approved a recommendation (not binding) that the 40-hour week and four weeks' paid annual holiday be adopted throughout the Community by the end of 1978. In July the Council decided to extend assistance from the Community's Social Fund (though the fund's budget was slightly cut in September) to promote specific action to facilitate employment of young people under 25, and also to contribute to the cost of retraining workers affected by partial or total closure of firms in the iron, steel, and coal industries in Belgium, France, West Germany, and the U.K.

Free movement of people between Community countries was assisted by agreement on mutual recognition of medical qualifications (to become effective by 1977); the Commission also proposed improvements in the position of migrant workers concerning family allowances and educational facilities and submitted a draft directive on freedom to provide legal services throughout the Community. The Education Committee set up in 1974 proposed an action program, adopted on Dec. 10, 1975, for greater cooperation in the education sector.

Relations with Other Countries. The Lomé Convention, signed in the capital of Togo on February 28, was the major achievement of the Community since its enlargement in January 1973. It linked to the Community in a trade and cooperation agreement 46 African, Caribbean, and Pacific (ACP) countries with a total population of 270 million, and made available to them over a five-year period 3,390,000,000 units of account (some $4 billion), including outright grants of 2,100,000,000 units of account, and 375 million for an export stabilization scheme (Stabex), which was the most imaginative feature of the convention. The convention provided for duty-free entry into the Community of all the ACP countries' industrial products and 96% of their agricultural products (including over 1.2 million tons of sugar) without requiring any reciprocal concessions. For less developed countries as a whole, the Community's generalized scheme of preferences was again substantially improved in 1975.

The Community was still far from developing a common foreign policy. Nevertheless, the regular European Councils of heads of government, and the more effective cooperation of Community countries' ambassadors in foreign capitals, as well as the additional weight engendered by the enlargement of the Community, began to give a more political dimension to its external relations. This was reflected in the united Community attitude to Portugal, to which the Community on October 7 gave "immediate" aid of 180 million units of account, with a promise of more if the trend toward pluralistic democracy continued; toward events in Spain; toward the North-South dialogue at the seventh special session of the UN; and in a mandate for the Commission to start negotiations for a cooperation agreement with Canada.

On June 12, 1975, Greece applied for full membership in the Community and was given a favourable reply, though without a timetable; Portugal requested closer links; the Community on May 11 signed a preferential trade agreement with Israel—the first trade agreement under its new Mediterranean policy—and in December the Council agreed to the opening of negotiations with Egypt, Syria, Jordan, and Lebanon. A commercial cooperation agreement with Mexico came into force on November 1. Limited trade agreements were signed with Pakistan, Laos, Sri Lanka, and Thailand, and in December talks were held with Japan regarding nontariff barriers against European cars and allegedly unfair competition for shipbuilding orders. Talks were begun with the Arab League countries in June, and a long-term deal for the sale of food to Egypt was approved in October. China accredited an ambassador to the Community in Brussels in May. (DEREK PRAG)

See also Defense; Economy, World.
[534.F.3.b.iv; 971.D.7]

Fashion and Dress

Fullness was the watchword in the early part of 1975. Rarely had all the capitals of the fashion world offered such similarity. There was a reckless atmosphere of swirling capes worn over crushed riding boots with extra high heels. Other popular styles were simple, unlined shepherd-style coats with huge, back-dipping hoods and buttoned-up invernesses worn with long, winding wool scarves. Back-flaring chemise coats with high yokes and gathers at back and front were seen in soft, plain cashmere or velvet rather than the classical broadcloth or rough-looking baize. The capes, all descending well over the calf, covered a variety of day clothes: full-blown chemise dresses, later worn belted; wide-flaring sectioned skirts in plain woolens or printed velvet, and the inevitable shirt, pullover, and long knitted jacket. The use of heavy wools and giant-size needles gave the essential handmade look.

Early spring saw a rage for pea-soup coloured loden coats, worn by men, women, and children alike—a cheap material and a cheap-looking cut, full backed with deep inverted centre pleat and raglan sleeves. Raincoats, in extra-light water-repellent material, were worn beltless and featured the same back flare.

Eager followers of fashion rapidly abandoned this fullness, however, when the Paris couturiers replied with the "tube" line. Sheath dresses came in for the summer, and skirts rose to calf top—a hard blow for retailers who had stocked up with full chemise dresses. Having grown accustomed to the ease and comfort of the unfitted styles, women bought them all the same, adding a wide elasticized belt with triple hook fastening, which became a best-seller among summer accessories. One thing that was definitely "out" was the rippling bias cut. Skirts still offered slight ease with a few gathers at the front or were cut with a back or front side-wrap effect, the latter being most popular in plain or printed cotton, but the slimmer line was rapidly acquiring converts.

For summer the fashion colour was white with a decidedly nautical flavour. Middies and sailor collars and a multitude of navy and white stripes were to be seen at resorts such as Deauville, France. Regular, horizontal striping in cotton chenille knit appeared in loose pullovers with wide sleeves and bateau necklines to wear with or without a shirt, over skirts, pants, or bermudas. An alternative was a V-necked blouson top in bright terry velvet. Another feature of the summer season was the outfit of stark white, wide-legged shorts with matching waistcoat that left the midriff bare, while for swimming and tanning the Brazilian *tanga,* consisting mainly of string with very little fabric, was often discarded in favour of the bare-top or the all-over-bare look.

The trend in sportswear was to borrow from the worker's outfit, with clothes designed for wear and tear in reliable materials and shapes that allowed much freedom of movement. The French miller's blouse with its polo neck, full back, and wrist-length puffed sleeves was deemed ideal for relaxation. Originally in gray cotton, it was preferred in lighter, more flattering shades or striped like a man's shirt. Along much the same line was the "settler's look" from Denmark, with a striped or plain cotton farmer's blouse or dress. A favourite sailing outfit consisted of white cotton painters' overalls with legs rolled up and a knotted strap belt in khaki, the season's other fashionable colour. The popularity of overalls and jumpsuits continued into the autumn and winter.

In early spring, having decided that blue jeans had

Evangelical Churches:
see Religion

Exchange and Payments, International:
see Economy, World

Exhibitions:
see Art and Art Exhibitions; Museums; Photography

Expeditions, Scientific:
see Antarctica; Arctic Regions; Earth Sciences; Mountaineering; Speleology

Faeroe Islands:
see Dependent States

Falkland Islands:
see Dependent States

Farming:
see Agriculture and Food Supplies

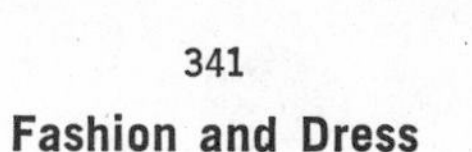

had a long enough run, fashion promoters and magazines attempted to oust the ubiquitous Levi's by launching khaki as the "in" colour, with every article from umbrella to shoes made available in this shade. In Saint-Tropez the military look borrowed from every possible source—U.S. "fatigues," British shorts as worn in the Indian Army, and even scouts' shirts. At the end of the day, however, blue jeans continued to hold their own, finding a new appeal in the original indigo blue, cigarette slim and turned up anywhere between ankle and thigh. When not turned up they were tucked into high-heeled boots or torn off in a ragged line anywhere along the thigh to make boxer shorts or briefs. The latest embroidery theme for hip pockets was a pound or dollar sign in red thread.

To accompany this outfit there were loose T-shirts —the newest with short kimono sleeves—featuring a diversity of front decorations, from portraits of film stars or even oneself to the U.S. university names popular in France and the "Snoopy" themes, adapted from the comic strip "Peanuts," popular in the U.S. The newest inspiration to be found on U.S. beaches in the summer of 1975, however, was derived from the film *Jaws,* based on the best-selling book by Peter Benchley: a gruesome pair of shark's jaws across the front of the T-shirt. Perhaps the last word in T-shirts was the U.S.-produced "scratch and smell" version. The printed front contained microscopic capsules that exhaled the appropriate smell when scratched—anything from lilac bushes, chocolate bars, pizza, or apple pie to the most sophisticated perfumes. Depending on the amount of scratching, the smell would resist up to 15 washings.

Liberty's in London had opened an Eastern Bazaar, and a new wave of Liberty prints spread through the fashion world. Pinafore dresses with wide shoulder straps were revived, and the many examples of the Early American period, inspired by the approach of the bicentennial of the Declaration of Independence, included prim, high-necked, fitted bodices and gathered skirts ending just above the ankle. Colour combinations for the Liberty prints were either romantic pink and blue pastels or bright colours on a dark background. The pinafore worn with blouses or pullovers remained popular as a winter style, further developing the layered look.

In summer dresses the romantic trend was seen in high-waisted, long-sleeved styles with frills at the neck and single or double flounces at the hem, while in Saint-Tropez romance turned to ghost-like transparency with all kinds of sheer white togas and other loose-flowing robes, some in hospital gauze to give an even more evanescent effect. A transparent effect was also provided by hem-length fringed scarves in light, silky knits with tone-on-tone embroidery, in bright colours or plain white, worn over long cotton skirts in the evening. Other prominent summer accessories were the floppy-brimmed straw hat to accompany the romantic dress, and the colonial pith hat in plaited straw with narrow leather headband, worn with jeans and T-shirt. In the footwear section, wooden or leather clogs remained popular with the teenage set, but the 20-to-30 age group turned to more elegant open-toed leather sandals, mounted on high wedge soles in string, or T-strapped sandals with thin leather soles and high heels for day and evening wear in town.

The onset of autumn brought a return of the layered or "piled on" look. The waistcoat was the newest item, worn over a loose shirt that was itself worn over a turtleneck pullover—all in varied lengths, the waistcoat shorter than the shirt, and in varied colours combined for harmonious effect: dark blue, plum, and gray for one range; rust, tomato, and faded rose for another. The usual headgear was a close-fitting bonnet in wool knit or crochet or a classic beret just skimming the eyebrows.

When pants or overalls were discarded in favour of skirts and dresses, the look was definitely slim. Many displayed high-slit side seams, frequently rounded, while slim tunics a few inches shorter than the skirts emphasized the pencil line. Slim tunics, like slim dresses, could also be worn over pants tucked into boots. To balance the slim silhouette, huge fringed

OPPOSITE PAGE: (LEFT) AGIP/PICTORIAL PARADE, (RIGHT) WIDE WORLD; BELOW: (LEFT) LONDON DAILY MAIL/PICTORIAL PARADE, (CENTRE) WIDE WORLD, (RIGHT) AGIP/PICTORIAL PARADE

Women's fashions in 1975 included the tube dress (opposite page, left) by Pierre Cardin and the "batman look" (opposite page, right) shown in London by Royal dressmaker Hardy Amies. The "khaki look," complete with berets (left), illustrates the military theme of many designers in 1975. This provides marked contrast with the elegant evening dress of silk mousse (centre) by the Paris house of Guy LaRoche, which again stands out against the layered casual air of a LaRoche design at far right.

LEFT, AGIP/PICTORIAL PARADE; RIGHT, INTERNATIONAL WOOL SECRETARIAT, LONDON

Men's evening wear assumed a tailored look, whereas a casual air was lent to daytime wear by the wide lapels, open scarf, and flaring coat and slacks at left.

scarves in very sheer wool or stoles in heavy rib knit were worn knotted at the shoulder.

From China came the vogue for quilted jackets in plain cotton or fine wool jersey, box-shaped and often displaying a lining of contrasting colour. Whether on the streets of Paris or those of Milan, all had the same dropped shoulder seam, small, stand-up collar, and braid fastening. This type of jacket was worn indifferently over slacks or dresses. In keeping with the season's Oriental look, the worker's-overall style developed a wrapover top and wide sleeves that ended below the elbow to show the wrist-length sleeve of the turtleneck pullover worn underneath.

Mandarin collars, off-centre fastenings on coats and dresses, deep armholes, braid trimming, and split side seams, all very fluid and graceful, contributed further to the Oriental look in winter fashion. Coats were either slim as a column or soft and casual as a chemise with high back and front yokes above gathers. High-slit side seams and standing mandarin collars conferred the Oriental touch on the latter style.

Capes had a look of being left over from the previous winter. The garment of the season was the poncho, often with attached hood, as supple as a cape but with a few more slits and plenty of buttoned tabs for trimming. Soft mohair was the favourite medium for long shapeless jackets with shawl collars or pullovers with high, ribbed turtlenecks. Red and fuchsia made a pretty combination, with Chinese lacquer red on its way in for the spring of 1976.

Cosmetics and Hairstyles. Transparency was the keynote for spring makeup, a "fresh air" makeup base with foundations tinted beige, honey, or sand. In tune with the times, Helena Rubinstein launched a "Persian Roses" look—cheeks reflecting a joyful rose with "Glowstick Amber" and lips a new blushing pink with "Shiraz." A new wrinkle remover, "Bye Lines Replenishing Treatment," produced by Elizabeth Arden, was claimed to have almost magical properties.

Warmer tones appeared in the autumn with pink turning to amber and red reflecting a brownish or copper tint. Nature was again the inspiration for Estée Lauder's new line, "Countrywoods," with rich red lipstick shades ranging from "Red Maple" to "Redwood" and a new bois de rose shade called "Laurel Wood." With fashions immersed in the Far Eastern mood, makeup bases followed the trend. Pale shades left all the emphasis for the eyes, with dark eyeliner along the lower lid. Lancôme named it the "Letchi" look, adding a strong "Baccara" red for lips and nail polish.

The latest hairstyles were short—cropped or bobbed—to free the neck for the huge shawls and oversize turtlenecks. For a softer effect, hair could still be fluffy as mohair, with a soft fringe over the eyes rather in the manner of a Yorkshire terrier.

(THELMA SWEETINBURGH)

Men's Fashions. During 1975 the classic two-piece suit, single-breasted and either three- or two-buttoned, continued to consolidate its position as the almost universal style for business wear. In the three major suit-wearing areas of the world—Western Europe, the U.S., and Japan—sales of suits rose 2% over the previous year to around 80 million units. The European Economic Community accounted for half of the total.

In a year of worldwide economic uncertainty, there was a certain constancy of gray as the colour choice for the businessman's suit; gray suits accounted for over 80% of sales in most countries. Blues came second in popularity, either plain or enlivened by silver-gray stripes or by pin or spot effects, usually in a contrasting colour or colours. Diagonal weaves regained some of their former popularity. Browns and greens remained consistent favourites for sports suits and jackets. There was a slight increase in the sales of green suits, notably in Europe; they were worn mainly by the younger age groups.

There was further consolidation of "put together" suits for leisure wear. Safari jacket styles in lightweight camel- and biscuit-coloured fabrics or in denim maintained their position on the holiday beaches and in the country. The layered look, consisting of one or more knitted styles worn over a knitted sports shirt, became a popular fashion.

Patterns for woven shirts were neater, with stripes of varying widths predominating. The beginning of a white shirt revival was noticed, but the white shirting was enlivened by satin stripe or cord effects.

"Safe" and "salable" were keywords often used to describe men's fashions at the major European trade exhibitions in London, Cologne, Paris, Turin, Florence, Amsterdam, and Copenhagen, no less than at those in Canada and the U.S. However, one new fashion did emerge in custom tailoring in 1975. Called the delta line, it was shown first in London and later at the International Tailoring Congress in Rome. The delta line was based on the triangular form of the Greek capital letter D. Robert Bright, president of the British Federation of Merchant Tailors, referred to it as "a natural progression of the classic cut of men's jackets over the last 50 years. It develops and extends the line of the jacket, the collar and lapels and introduces the panel theme." A fitting if somewhat unfashionable label to hang on most items of the male wardrobe in 1975 was ironically the one used for this new delta line—"economic with an absence of extraneous detail."

(STANLEY H. COSTIN)

See also Industrial Review: *Clothing; Furs.*

[451.B.2.b and d.i; 629.C.1]

ENCYCLOPÆDIA BRITANNICA FILMS. *Culture and Costumes: The Great Clothes Put-On* (1974).

Feed Grains:
see Agriculture and Food Supplies

Fencing:
see Combat Sports

Field Hockey and Lacrosse

Field Hockey. Highlights of 1975 in field hockey included the third World Cup in Malaysia in March and the women's world championship, organized by the International Federation of Women's Hockey Associations (IFWHA), at Edinburgh, Scotland, in September. Within a week of the World Cup, Poland traveled to Great Britain for international contests against England and Wales, both won by the home countries. Soon afterward the United Kingdom countries and Ireland played a four-match international competition in Dublin. In May six nations met in a tournament organized by the Royal Belgian Hockey Association in Brussels, and in July at Montreal Canada welcomed the teams of eight nations to the first international tournament ever held on artificial turf.

For the World Cup, held at Kuala Lumpur, the facilities, setting, and organization were of high standard. The only adverse factor was the weather, which compelled abandonment or postponement of a number of games and caused others to be played in hot and humid conditions. India won the coveted title of world champion, defeating Pakistan in the final 2–1. The winning goal was much disputed, but India's rating as the no. 1 team in the tournament was not. The final ranking was: (1) India; (2) Pakistan; (3) West Germany; (4) Malaysia; (5) Australia; (6) England; (7) New Zealand; (8) Spain; (9) The Netherlands; (10) Poland; (11) Argentina; (12) Ghana.

The next most significant competition was probably the meeting of eight nations (West Germany, Pakistan, The Netherlands, Argentina, Great Britain, Canada, Kenya, and Mexico, in order of finishing) at Montreal in July. It was significant because it was played on the artificial turf that was to be used for the Olympic Games in 1976. The verdict of the players on the new surface was generally favourable with one qualification: it reflected heat to a degree that caused discomfort. This could be counteracted by watering the turf, the only difficulty being the need to ensure an even distribution of water.

In the internationals between the U.K. countries and Ireland, England won the "triple crown," defeating Ireland 3–2, Scotland 2–0, and Wales 5–1. At Brussels in May, Great Britain finished first of the six nations taking part (Great Britain, Poland, France, Belgium, Czechoslovakia, and Scotland). England also won the women's U.K. internationals.

West Germany won a junior international tournament organized by the European Hockey Federation at Barcelona, Spain, as well as the European club championship which went to Sports Club 1880 of Frankfurt for the fifth year in succession. West Germany also held the European indoor championship.

In the IFWHA tournament at Edinburgh in September, England's women won the world championship from a strong field, which included The Netherlands, winners of a rival event, the Women's World Cup organized by the men's international federation, Fédération Internationale de Hockey (FIH), based in Brussels. The women's ranking at Edinburgh was: (1) England; (2) Wales; (3) New Zealand; (4) The Netherlands; (5) Australia; (6) Argentina; (7) Ireland; (8) India; (9) Scotland; (10) United States.

The IFWHA conference, held in conjunction with the world championship at Edinburgh, agreed to join with the FIH in forming a Supreme Council to deal with matters of common policy and interest. In effect, the Supreme Council was a consultative body, its resolutions requiring endorsement by the IFWHA and the FIH. The formation of the council would, it was hoped, heal the breach that opened in 1973 between IFWHA and FIH. On August 1 a common code of rules for men and women approved by the International Hockey Rules Board (IHRB) and the Women's IHRB was introduced.

(R. L. HOLLANDS)

[452.B.4.h.xvi]

TEDD CHURCH—MONTREAL GAZETTE

Flavio De Giacomi of Argentina grimaces after bout with three British players during the international field hockey action in Montreal.

Lacrosse. For the World Series, held every four years in each of the lacrosse-playing countries, Australia played host in Melbourne during June–July 1974, with the U.S., Canada, and England also participating. The U.S. was the overall winner, with three victories over the other teams, who each won once against one another. Later the U.S. visited England and lost 17–15 to England in an international game. In the U.S. teams from the eastern states continued to dominate. The University of Maryland won the 1975 National Collegiate Athletic Association tournament, defeating the U.S. Naval Academy 20–13. The

WIDE WORLD

Maryland's Terrapins (dark jerseys) upset Navy's Midshipmen 20–13 in May to become the first team ever to win two NCAA university division lacrosse championships. Their total goals and margin of victory set tournament records.

20 goals scored by the winners were a record for an NCAA tournament game.

Lacrosse has its greatest following in Canada with over 500,000 registered players. The 1975 championship of the National Lacrosse League, comprising teams from Canada and the U.S., was won by the Quebec Caribous. They defeated the Montreal Quebecois four games to two in the best-of-seven play-off series. In England in 1974 the dominant North beat the South 22–4, and Urmston defeated Lee for the English club championship, the Iroquois Cup.

(CHARLES DENNIS COPPOCK)

[452.B.4.h.xx]

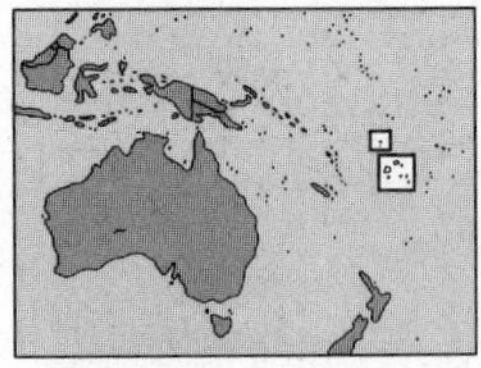

Fiji

An independent parliamentary state and member of the Commonwealth of Nations, Fiji is an island group in the South Pacific Ocean, about 2,000 mi. E of Australia and 3,200 mi. S of Hawaii. Area: 7,055 sq.mi. (18,274 sq.km.), with two major islands, Viti Levu (4,011 sq.mi.) and Vanua Levu (2,137 sq.mi.), and several hundred smaller islands. Pop. (1974 est.): 563,800. Cap. and largest city: Suva (pop., 1974 est., 71,600). Language: English, Fijian, and Hindi. Religion: Christian and Hindu. Queen, Elizabeth II; governor-general in 1975, Ratu Sir George Cakobau; prime minister, Ratu Sir Kamisese Mara.

In February 1975 Fiji signed a sugar marketing agreement with the European Economic Community under which half of the 1975 production could be sold at top prices. Unlimited access to the U.S. market was also obtained. Record prices in 1974 dropped in 1975, and production targets were not met because of unfavourable weather conditions and industrial disturbances. Fiji also took over the marketing of its sugar from the Colonial Sugar Refining Company of Australia.

There was a rise in import costs, leading to a deficit for visible trade of $94 million, and inflation reached an annual rate of 18%. Copra prices fell, together with invisible earnings from tourism. The government borrowed overseas to cushion its reserves and also imposed exchange and import controls. On April 1 the government lifted wage and price controls except for those on rent, freight charges, and certain essential household commodities.

In July, at the South Pacific Forum meeting in Tonga, Prime Minister Mara attacked the inhibiting effect of Australasian maritime unions on the development of regional shipping. Fiji continued to oppose nuclear testing and in April was host to a conference on a "nuclear-free" Pacific, attended by regional delegates. The royal commission on the electoral system, which was agreed upon at pre-independence talks, began its hearings.

(BARRIE MACDONALD)

[977.A.3]

FIJI

Education. (1973) Primary, pupils 133,890, teachers 4,147; secondary, pupils 23,780, teachers 993; vocational, pupils 1,445, teachers 141; teacher training, students 450, teachers 42; higher (University of the South Pacific; 1974), students 1,031, teaching staff 145.

Finance and Trade. Monetary unit: Fiji dollar, with (Sept. 22, 1975) an official rate of F$0.80 to U.S. $1 (free rate of F$1.77 = £1 sterling). Budget (1973 est.) revenue F$68.4 million; expenditure F$72.3 million. Foreign trade (1973): imports F$175 million; exports F$74 million. Import sources: Australia 31%; Japan 16%; U.K. 14%; New Zealand 13%; U.S. 5%. Export destinations: U.K. 29%; U.S. 17%; Australia 12%; Canada 8%; New Zealand 6%. Main exports (1973): sugar 67%; coconut products 12%; gold 12%. Tourism: visitors (1971) 152,000; gross receipts (1973) U.S. $49 million.

Transport and Communications. Roads (1973) 2,366 km. (including 2,000 km. all-weather). Motor vehicles in use (1972): passenger 16,300; commercial (including buses) 6,300. Railways (1972) *c.* 700 km. (for sugar estates). Shipping (1974): merchant vessels 100 gross tons and over 25; gross tonnage 7,048. Ships entered (1973) vessels totaling 2,789,000 net registered tons; goods loaded (1973) 457,000 metric tons, unloaded 764,000 metric tons. Telephones (Dec. 1973) 23,000. Radio licenses (Dec. 1972) 53,000.

Agriculture. Production (in 000; metric tons; 1974; 1973 in parentheses): sugar, raw value *c.* 280 (319); rice (1973) 16, (1972) 17; sweet potatoes *c.* 16 (*c.* 16); cassava (1973) *c.* 89, (1972) *c.* 88; copra *c.* 30 (*c.* 28); bananas (exports; 1973) *c.* 5, (1972) *c.* 5. Livestock (in 000; Sept. 1974): cattle *c.* 130; pigs *c.* 30; goats (1973) *c.* 31; horses (1973) *c.* 31.

Industry. Production (in 000; 1973): cement (metric tons) 92; gold (troy oz.) 80; electricity (kw-hr) 217,000.

Finance, International: *see* Economy, World

Fires: *see* Disasters

Fiscal Policy: *see* Economy, World

Finland

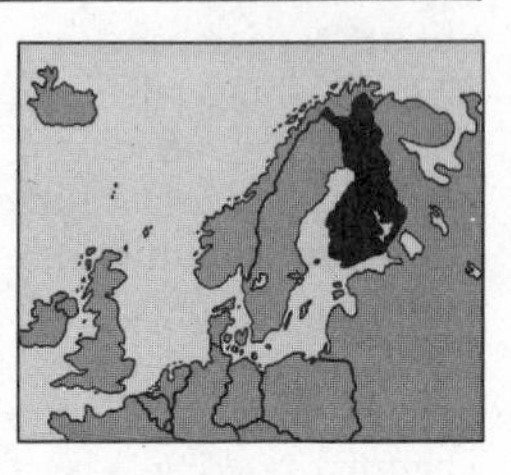

The republic of Finland is bordered on the north by Norway, on the west by Sweden and the Gulf of Bothnia, on the south by the Gulf of Finland, and on the east by the U.S.S.R. Area: 130,129 sq.mi. (337,032 sq.km.). Pop. (1975 est.): 4,697,900. Cap. and largest city: Helsinki (pop., 1975 est., 504,300). Language: Finnish, Swedish. Religion (1974): Lutheran 91.7%. President in 1975, Urho Kaleva Kekkonen; prime ministers, Kalevi Sorsa, Keijo Liinamaa from June 4, and, from November 30, Martti J. Miettunen.

The rapidly increasing foreign trade deficit (5 billion markkaa in 1974) grew even faster in 1975. The government forecast a record 8 billion markkaa deficit for the year on the basis of trade figures for the first six months of 1975. To combat this it introduced tough economic measures, including an immediate price freeze and a 15% import surcharge (later changed to a 30% import deposit, repaid after six months). In June the International Monetary Fund granted Finland a 735 million markkaa loan in Special Drawing Rights on condition that it phase out the import deposit scheme by March 1976 and maintain the current levels of the markka and the bank rate.

The Soviet Union remained Finland's largest trading partner, and the annual trade agreement between the two countries set the total value of trade for 1975 at 8 billion markkaa. Though the Soviets cut their crude oil exports to Finland, three-quarters of the imports from the Soviet Union were still in the energy sector. Continuing its normalization of trade relations with Eastern Europe, Finland on March 4 signed an agreement that removed trade barriers with East Germany. This was similar to agreements signed earlier with Bulgaria, Czechoslovakia, and Hungary and settled in principle with Poland.

Foreign policy was largely dominated by the 35-nation Conference on Security and Cooperation in Europe whose summit meeting was held at Finlandia House in Helsinki on July 30–August 1, after many months of disagreement between negotiators at Geneva on the timing of the summit. The Helsinki meeting largely put an end to speculation at home and abroad about Soviet intentions with regard to Finland, the conference being widely regarded by Finns as an

FINLAND

Education. (1973–74) Primary, pupils 393,242, teachers 21,248; secondary, pupils 405,203, teachers 17,536; vocational, pupils 110,355, teachers 10,823; teacher training, students 1,421, teachers 389; higher (including 11 universities), students 67,881, teaching staff 4,940.

Finance. Monetary unit: markka, with (Sept. 22, 1975) a free rate of 3.89 markkaa to U.S. $1 (8.05 markkaa = £1 sterling). Gold, SDRs, and foreign exchange, central bank: (June 1975) U.S. $540.9 million; (June 1974) U.S. $623.3 million. Budget (1975 est.): revenue 20,901,000,000 markkaa; expenditure 21,234,000,000 markkaa. Gross national product: (1973) 65,250,000,000 markkaa; (1972) 54,340,000,000 markkaa. Money supply: (Dec. 1974) 7,263,000,000 markkaa; (Dec. 1973) 6,111,000,000 markkaa. Cost of living (1970 = 100): (May 1975) 171; (May 1974) 147.

Foreign Trade. (1974) Imports 25,676,000,000 markkaa; exports 20,687,000,000 markkaa. Import sources: Sweden 18%; U.S.S.R. 18%; West Germany 15%; U.K. 9%; U.S. 7%. Export destinations: U.K. 19%; Sweden 16%; U.S.S.R. 14%; West Germany 9%. Main exports: paper 31%; timber 11%; machinery 10%; wood pulp 6%; ships 6%; clothing 5%.

Transport and Communications. Roads (1973) 73,210 km. (including 161 km. expressways). Motor vehicles in use (1973): passenger 894,104; commercial 119,898. Railways (1973): 5,965 km.; traffic 2,773,000,000 passenger-km., freight (1974) 7,485,000,000 net ton-km. Air traffic (1974): 1,155,800,000 passenger-km.; freight 32,605,000 net ton-km. Navigable inland waterways (1973) 6,674 km. Shipping (1974): merchant vessels 100 gross tons and over 362; gross tonnage 1,507,582. Telephones (Dec. 1973) 1,535,000. Radio licenses (Dec. 1973) 1,944,000. Television licenses (Dec. 1973) 1,224,000.

Agriculture. Production (in 000; metric tons; 1974; 1973 in parentheses): wheat 536 (462); barley 963 (992); oats 1,216 (1,169); rye 175 (124); potatoes 525 (669); sugar, raw value 82 (81); butter *c.* 78 (*c.* 80); timber (cu.m.; 1973) 43,000, (1972) 43,000; fish catch (1972) 67, (1971) 70. Livestock (in 000; June 1974): cattle *c.* 1,884; sheep *c.* 145; pigs *c.* 1,177; horses (1973) 48; chickens (1973) 10,117.

Industry. Production (in 000; metric tons; 1974): iron ore (66% metal content) 805; pig iron 1,363; crude steel 1,657; copper (1973) 43; cement 2,201; sulfuric acid 984; petroleum-based products (1973) 8,212; plywood (cu.m.; 1973) 685; cellulose (1973) 4,157; wood pulp (1973) mechanical 2,159, chemical 4,519; newsprint 1,493; other paper and board (1973) 4,060; electricity (kw-hr.) 29,058,000; manufactured gas (cu.m.) 27,700.

assurance of the country's independence and sovereignty. President Kekkonen, head of state for 19 years and a leading advocate of close ties with the Soviet Union, celebrated his 75th birthday on September 3. Kekkonen's proposal for the creation of a nuclear-free zone in Scandinavia, and similar zones in other parts of the world, became a major foreign policy goal and won strong Soviet approval. (In October 1974 Kekkonen had launched a radical reappraisal of Finland's role in World War II at the 30th anniversary celebrations in Helsinki of the Finnish-Soviet armistice agreement, attended by Soviet Pres. Nikolay V. Podgorny. Kekkonen accused his country's wartime leaders of starting hostilities against the Soviets in 1941, contradicting the generally accepted version that Finland declared war only after Soviet bombing raids on Finnish cities.)

In January 1975 Hans-Dietrich Genscher became the first West German foreign minister to visit Finland. In June Juan Carlos, king-designate of Spain, also visited Finland—the first visit to a Scandinavian country by a Spanish leader.

On June 4 the left-centre coalition government of Social Democrat Prime Minister Sorsa resigned because of internal differences after 1,004 days in office (the second-longest-lived Cabinet in Finnish history). A caretaker Cabinet, led by former state labour arbitrator Keijo Liinamaa, was appointed. General elections were held on September 21-22, four months earlier than usual, but brought only minor shifts in support for the four leading parties—the Social Democrats, Communists, Centrists, and Conservatives. The biggest gains were made by the tiny Christian Party, which won nine seats as compared with its previous four. Ten parties gained seats in the 200-seat Eduskunta (Parliament). Attempts to form a Cabinet started early in October, but nothing was achieved until November 27, when Kekkonen, in a nationally televised address, demanded formation of a "government of national emergency" within five days. The result, on November 30, was a five-party coalition headed by Martti Miettunen of the Centre Party and including four Communists, participating in a Finnish Cabinet for the second time since World War I. The remainder of the 18 places went to 5 Social Democrats, 4 Centrists (including Miettunen), 2 members of the Swedish People's Party, 1 Liberal, and 2 nonaligned ministers. In April the Social Democrats announced that they would run Kekkonen as their candidate in the 1978 presidential election, ending the inflamed debate about the succession to the presidency. (COLIN NARBOROUGH)

[972.A.6.d.i]

Fisheries

The troubles of the world's fisheries—high fuel costs, low fish prices, and the threat of a 200-mi. limit for territorial waters—worsened in 1975. Wages, materials, and operating costs all rose steadily, while prices remained low and market demand poor.

Some of the trouble stemmed from an earlier change in U.S. import policy, when a switch from Scandinavian frozen cod to Japanese pollack threw many thousands of tons of quality frozen fillets onto the European market at uncomfortably low prices. Furthermore, this came at a time when the fleets of Norway, Britain, France, and Spain were striving to meet steeply rising costs in the face of falling consumption on home markets. Fortunately for the stability of world markets, U.S. preference began to swing back to North Atlantic cod late in 1975.

"The Vulgar Boatman."

PETERSON—VANCOUVER SUN/ROTHCO

In Spain total operating costs of freezer trawlers were calculated by the fleet owners' federation as having risen by over 70% in five years, while fish prices had risen by only 2.36%. Fuel costs increased 248%. For the Spanish cod fishery, working the Newfoundland grounds, demand fell at home and prices were down by 40%. Internationally agreed quotas cut so drastically into Spanish squid catches off Boston that fishing became virtually uneconomic.

In France, Britain, and Canada, as well as in Spain, pressure grew throughout the year for government intervention to stave off impending bankruptcies. An increasing number of relatively modern vessels were tied up and idle, and many older vessels were taken out of service—sold or scrapped before their time in order to reduce fleet size and remove ships that were now too expensive to run. Among the first to be affected were a number of fish-processing factories in Norway, Canada, and Scotland which were forced to close down as a result of lack of demand. Shipyards had few new orders for fleet renewals—a situation fortunately cushioned by orders from the oil industry. Smaller shipyards were hardest hit; with little capital reserve, they faced a rush of canceled orders as vessel prices soared beyond the reach of the fishermen.

For those nations operating long-distance trawlers, the threat of an international 200-mi. limit did little to encourage investment in the future. The greater part of the world's fish were concentrated on and above the continental shelf, and under the proposed 200-mi. "exclusive economic zone" most of them would be forbidden to foreign vessels. The prospect was especially bleak for those nations having little coastline of their own or, as in the case of Spain, a continental shelf that was very narrow. The only practical solution appeared to be "joint projects" with the fish-owning nations, whereby the latter obtained financial or other benefits in return for shore bases and fishing rights. Among the Communist nations, particularly the U.S.S.R., such deals usually took the form of aid to the partner nation in developing its resources.

The third UN Conference on the Law of the Sea at Caracas, Venezuela, in 1974 had achieved little, beyond disclosing that an overwhelming majority of nations favoured the 200-mi. limit. A second meeting of the conference in Geneva in 1975 achieved little more, and those nations with the most to gain from the wider limit became impatient. Iceland and Canada hinted at early unilateral action, and British, U.S., and Norwegian fishermen petitioned their governments to do the same. In July Iceland's prime minister was the first to announce a firm date—October—for the new limit. There was considerable disappointment among Canadian fishermen when Ottawa rejected an equally precipitate course and chose to proceed, if possible, within the confines of international law. Prime Minister Pierre Trudeau indicated that this was the wisest course unless nations were prepared to risk war to enforce their revised limits.

Nevertheless, Canada began to take a tougher line with Soviet and other vessels fishing its coasts. Obvious signs of overfishing had led to agreement on quotas among the members of the International Commission for the Northwest Atlantic Fisheries (ICNAF). When Soviet vessels grossly exceeded their quotas off Newfoundland, Canada quickly imposed a ban on the use of Canadian ports by Soviet vessels for repairs and revictualing.

While capital investment dried to a trickle in Europe, the oil-rich nations of the Middle East and the South American countries of Brazil, Argentina, and Peru were building up their fleets of tuna seiners and their shrimp and fish trawlers. But the biggest order to flow from Spanish yards during 1975 was for 26 giant factory trawlers, each 286 ft. in length, for Cuba, which was rapidly emerging as a major fishing power under the tutelage—and perhaps the economic umbrella—of the Soviet Union.

The year saw the continued depression of the hitherto profitable shrimp fishery, affecting such producing areas as the Gulf of Mexico, India, and northern Australia. The downturn was attributed to the fact that shrimp, a semi-luxury item, was among the first to be eliminated by the housewife during a period of recession. When the previously insatiable shrimp markets of Japan and the U.S. cut back, the repercussions were worldwide, highlighting the inherent risk involved in building specialized fishing vessels to serve export markets that could disappear almost before the vessels were completed.

In 1974 Peru, normally the world's top fishing nation in terms of weight, was still recovering from the failure of the anchoveta harvest. The 1974 catch of 2.4 million metric tons—compared with a normal harvest of approximately 9 million metric tons—had left a large gap in international fish-meal supplies. The resulting rise in world prices had encouraged "indus-

An angry armada of fishermen protest low-priced fish imports by blockading the Channel at Newhaven, England, in April.

LONDON DAILY EXPRESS/PICTORIAL PARADE

trial fishing" by more European nations. However, the financial blow to Peru may have been the spur that prompted that nation to switch its policy—to emphasis on the catching of food fish for people rather than the processing of fish meal for export. Peru ordered two large tuna purse seiners during the year, from a British shipyard.

One of the features of 1974 had been the search for new species of fish to supplement shrinking stocks of those that had proved all too popular, such as cod, herring, and hake. In 1975, with demand for even common species falling, the need for such exploratory exercises became less important. Attention swung from the grenadier as a substitute for cod to blue whiting as an alternative to herring, especially for the fish-meal plant.

Sole and herring appeared to be disappearing rapidly from the North Sea, and scientists discovered that their estimates of herring stocks in the Irish Sea and off the northwest coast of Scotland had been over-optimistic. Drastic cuts were made in quotas by the North–East Atlantic Fisheries Commission, much to the alarm of Denmark, The Netherlands, and Scotland. By October even worse fears were being expressed over North Sea herring stocks, and the International Council for the Exploration of the Sea recommended a complete cessation of fishing for that stock, which was said to be threatened with extinction.

Warnings that ever more powerful "cutters," towing heavy twin trawls, were overfishing sole in the North Sea had been ignored by most Dutch fishing interests. Finally, the situation had to be met by the introduction of quotas by the European nations, and the size of those quotas, in conjunction with continually escalating costs, created a crisis in the Dutch fishery. Plans were made to cut the fleet by 100 vessels, with government compensation for the unlucky ones who might, at best, be diverted to other fisheries. Measures were also taken to ensure that, for example, the displaced vessels did not turn to the Dutch shrimp fishery, where stock and catching power were already in delicate balance.

In North America, where the fish trawlermen, at least, had everything to gain and nothing to lose, the prospect of territorial limits that would remove—or at least reduce—foreign competition brought a new spirit of optimism. In New England, for example, the dragger (trawler) fleet was largely obsolete, and the average age of skippers was 65. With the promise of an extended limit, investment in new vessels tentatively began again. Younger New England and Nova Scotia fishermen believed that, given the chance, they could compete with their often-subsidized European counterparts in home markets, currently dominated by imported Icelandic and Japanese fish. As the Gulf of Mexico shrimp trawler market cut back on new vessel investment, at least one large Southern shipyard was looking for orders farther north among the younger New England skippers. There was also some reason for optimism on the Canadian west coast, despite a mediocre salmon run.

"Inrybprom 75," a giant fisheries exhibition held in Leningrad under the sponsorship of the Soviet Ministry of Fisheries, followed the pattern of the previous event in 1968 and was an invitation to the West to offer its wares to the great Soviet fishing machine. A wide variety of Soviet-built equipment was also on display, indicating advancing Soviet capability in this field and perhaps the wish to penetrate the growing markets of Cuba and other aligned nations. (In November the Soviet prototype factory trawler "Gorizont," the major exhibit at "Inrybprom 75," sank

Table I. Whaling: 1973–74 Season (Antarctic); 1973 Season (Outside the Antarctic)
Number of whales caught

Area and country	Fin whale	Sei/ Bryde's whale	Hump-back whale	Minke whale	Sperm whale	Total	Percentage assigned under quota agree-ment*
Antarctic: pelagic (open sea)							
Japan	705	2,624	—	3,713	45	7,087	58.8
Norway†							1.7
U.S.S.R.	583	1,768	—	4,000	4,882	11,233‡	39.5
Total	1,288	4,392	—	7,713	4,927	18,320‡	100.0
Outside the Antarctic§							
Japan	299	1,826	—	—	4,239	6,364	
U.S.S.R.	161	759	—	—	4,329	5,427‖	
Peru	11	330	—	—	1,497	1,838	
South Africa	41	10	1	—	1,606	1,658	
Australia	—	—	—	—	971	971	
Iceland	267	139	—	—	47	453	
Others	76	497	9	—	641	1,261¶	
Total	855	3,561	10	—	13,330	17,972‖¶	

*Antarctic only.
†Norway had no expeditions in the Antarctic in the 1973–74 season.
‡Includes others (bottlenose, killer, gray, right, and blue whales).
§Excluding small whales.
‖Includes 178 gray whales.
¶Includes 38 other whales.
Source: The Committee for Whaling Statistics, *International Whaling Statistics*.

WIDE WORLD

Two assistants of Teruo Harada, the inventor of a new floating net method of fish farming, empty their catch, which includes a large yellowtail.

Table II. World Fisheries, 1973*

Country	Catch in 000 metric tons		Value in U.S. $000	
	Total	Freshwater	Total	Freshwater
Japan	10,701.9	178.6	...	...
U.S.S.R.	8,618.7	849.6	...	...
China	7,574.0	4,595.0	...	...
Norway	2,974.5	...	355,461	...
United States	2,669.9	79.0	907,400	...
Peru	2,299.3	80.0	85,940	...
India	1,958.0	747.6	443,282	...
Thailand	1,692.3	137.9	357,095	...
Korea, South	1,654.6	0.5	...	...
Spain	1,570.4	14.0	...	...
Denmark	1,464.7	14.2	238,904	78
South Africa	1,331.7	0.1	76,307	...
Indonesia	1,300.0	440.0	...	...
Philippines	1,248.5	99.2	513,254	21,112
Canada	1,151.6	41.8	300,119	11,160
United Kingdom	1,144.4	...	383,800	...
Iceland	906.2	...	...	...
Korea, North	800.0	...	...	...
France	796.8	...	505,472	...
Vietnam, South	713.5	91.3	...	...
Nigeria	664.8	337.0	...	...
Chile	664.4	...	9,157	...
Brazil	589.9	97.4	...	...
Poland	579.6	22.2	...	...
Mexico	482.1	15.0	144,969	2,195
Germany, West	475.2	15.0	180,653	15,456
Angola	470.2	...	10,821	...
Burma	463.4	125.3	93,097	...
Portugal	452.7	0.3	136,642	122
Malaysia	444.7	4.3	274,662	4,361
Morocco	397.2	0.4	...	...
Italy	389.7	17.5	308,614	18,230
Germany, East	365.8	14.2	...	...
Netherlands, The	343.8	3.0	152,903	1,043
Senegal	323.8	20.0	91,170	2,726
Argentina	302.1	7.6	68,935	3,390
Vietnam, North	300.0	85.0	...	...
Bangladesh	247.2	211.9	...	...
Faeroe Islands	246.4	...	...	...
Sweden	226.9	10.6	54,183	263
Pakistan	214.2	17.6	68,701	6,566
Ghana	195.5	41.3	57,031	9,106
Uganda	169.0	169.0	35,602	...
Tanzania	167.7	144.7	25,805	...
Turkey	166.1	14.4	...	...
Venezuela	162.4	17.9	39,288	3,126
Bermuda	161.9	...	...	...
Other†	3,598.4	999.6	...	...
World total†	65,700.0	9,760.0	...	...

*Excludes whaling.
†May include statistical discrepancy.
Source: United Nations Food and Agriculture Organization, *Yearbook of Fishery Statistics*, vol. 36.

after a collision in the English Channel.) An even larger exhibition, Japan's Expo '75, held on the island of Okinawa, had as its theme "The Sea We Would Like to See." Many nations took advantage of the opportunity to demonstrate their contribution to ocean science.

Once again the antiwhaling lobby failed to obtain a complete moratorium on the taking of whales. The U.S. had given a lead with its ban on imports of whale-based products and by legislation forbidding the taking of marine mammals such as porpoise during tuna-fishing operations. The remaining major whaling nations, the U.S.S.R. and Japan, were not so willing to relinquish an important source of oil and protein. At the meeting of the International Whaling Commission in London in June, priority protection was given to those species whose survival was most threatened —the blue, humpback, gray, and "right" whales; fin, sei, and sperm whales were protected in certain areas, and their taking was restricted in others. In 1974 there were 11 land stations and five factory ships in operation. (H. S. NOEL)

See also Food Processing.
[731.D.2.a]

Fishing:
see Hunting and Fishing

Floods:
see Disasters; Earth Sciences; Engineering Projects

Folk Music:
see Music

Food Processing

Environmental pollution and the safety of foods and food-processing procedures attracted much attention during 1975. Legislative hurdles hampered the application of food irradiation, despite considerable work including a report by an international agency on the value of the process to less developed countries. Pollution of the marine environment, with the concomitant destruction of ecosystems and contamination of edible products, was singled out at a meeting of the UN Environment Program as an area of grave concern, but proposals to control the dumping of wastes at sea remained in the talking stage.

The use of nitrates and nitrites in the curing of meat and fish products received particular attention from U.S. and British authorities, due to the possible role of these substances in the formation of carcinogenic nitrosamines. This was disputed by some experts, but the main reason no action was taken was the fear that alterations in the curing process might increase the risk of botulism. The U.S. Food and Drug Administration proposed restrictions on the use of polyvinyl chloride (PVC) in food packaging on the ground of possible carcinogenic hazard from traces of vinyl chloride monomer.

A U.S. Senate select committee held several hearings to review food-consumption patterns in relation to health and disease. A European Economic Community (EEC) directive placed limits on the use of rapeseed oil with a high erucic acid content and offered inducements to farmers to cultivate the less productive low-erucic acid varieties. The West German food regulations were completely revised, Norway issued a new list of permitted food additives, Sweden banned the use of synthetic food colours, and the EEC announced a complete review of food packaging.

Britain continued to revise its regulations on food additives in line with EEC directives. Proposals were made by the British authorities to control the composition and labeling of a number of sugar products and to restrict the use of certain food colours. It was discovered that the food colour Red 2G, which was permitted in the U.K., may break down to the nonpermitted food colour Red 10B during processing. Products containing textured vegetable protein meat analogues continued to proliferate, and two legal actions were taken by the U.K. authorities under the labeling regulations.

Technology. The energy crisis stimulated many reappraisals of food industry practices. A U.S. scientist commented on the imbalance that has arisen between food-production methods in advanced and in primitive societies as a result of high energy consumption of the former. Whereas primitive cultures obtain 50 calories for each calorie invested, highly industrialized food systems require 5–10 calories of fuel to provide one food calorie, and the amount of energy used in food production and distribution often exceeds that available in the food. As a result of mismanagement in the affluent world, one-quarter of all milk protein produced was going to waste or was being used as feed for animals.

An Australian company developed a line of sophisticated harvesters for various agricultural products, and a Nigerian research institute invented a machine for pounding yams. A spray-dried product derived from ripe mango fruits, buffalo milk, and additives was developed by an Indian dairy research institute. A plant went into operation in Finland for the manufacture, under Swiss license, of a sugar, xylose, by a process utilizing bark and other forestry wastes. Subsequently the xylose was converted to xylitol, a sweetener that, it was claimed, would not produce dental caries. It was used in chewing gum for the first time. Several companies reported the development of new enzyme preparations for use in the manufacture of high-fructose corn syrups.

Products. U.S. scientists developed a featherless breed of chickens, but the higher fuel bills for the broiler houses more than offset the money saved by eliminating defeathering. A flake-cut meat patty of consistent texture, free from gristle and bone, and with improved "bite," introduced in the U.S., was made possible by the development of a new type of meat-cutting head. Several French dairy companies introduced a new method of cheese manufacture developed by French scientists; milk was preconcentrated by ultrafiltration to the solids content of the final product, eliminating the separation of whey and increasing yield by retention of the whey protein.

An Italian company commissioned the most highly automated ice-cream plant in Europe. All the blending, product routing, and in-place cleaning were computer controlled. A process was developed in the U.S. for the manufacture of soft margarine from the tallow of cattle and sheep that had been fed polyunsaturated oil supplements. U.S. scientists found that the storage life of fruit could be extended by storage at subatmospheric pressure. A new variety of grapefruit, derived from a mutant obtained by nuclear irradiation, was introduced; it was said to be firmer, easier to section, and squirt-free. A new method for the preservation of Indian mangoes by osmotic dehydration, using a concentrated sugar solution, was developed, thereby effecting economies in fuel and packaging.

Seafoods. The UN Food and Agriculture Organization reported on methods whereby one hectare of flooded land could be made to yield some 2,000 kg. of fish annually; used for grazing, a hectare could produce only 11 kg. of beef. Chinese workers, using processed cattle and pig manure as feed, raised ducks and carp together for a yearly yield of 2,500 kg. per ha., and in Japan a new technique for the culture of algae and mollusks achieved yields of 26,000 kg. per ha. A new laboratory was established in Britain for the production of phytoplankton needed in the breeding of oysters and of clams for the French market.

A research laboratory for shrimp breeding was established in Bahrain. Artificial reefs constructed from discarded automobile tires were shown to facilitate fish culture. A Norwegian company was harvesting plankton for use in the manufacture of fish soups and sauces. A smoking and drying plant in Zambia could process 5,000–10,000 lb. of fresh fish daily.

Speakers at a conference in London alluded to the substantial resources of deepwater species, but many felt that housewives were still too traditional to accept such fish. Others considered the problem to be largely a matter of engineering; it was reported that new deboning and mincing machines were under development with a view to converting many of the unsavoury-looking deepsea fish into tasty products.

Protein-Rich Foods. While a million tons of skimmed milk powder deteriorated in EEC stores, the development of novel proteins continued unabated. The prospects of petroleum-derived protein faded with the dramatic rise in the price of oil, and attention was directed to alternative feedstocks such as carbohydrate-derived methanol and ethanol. Since cellulose in the form of vegetable fibre and timber is the most abundant polymer of glucose, the search continued for a means of breaking down these difficult materials to fermentable substrates for single-cell protein production; a U.S. Army laboratory reported some success. Many countries reported new processes for extracting edible protein from bacteria, yeasts, fungi, algae, lichens, oilseeds, cereal grains, lupin seeds, foliage, and other plant materials including sugarbeet tops, the stems and tops of pea and potato plants, water weeds, and grasses.

The technological effort was in marked contrast to the progress toward exploitation, however. Even full utilization of the more conventional oilseed proteins made relatively slow progress, largely because of consumer resistance to the flavour and texture. The U.S. Department of Agriculture (USDA) succeeded in eliminating the beany flavour of soybeans by suitable pretreatment, and improvements in the preparation of cottonseed protein were reported from Colombia. A U.S. company claimed to have produced a bland soy protein isolate by treatment with fungal amylase. Traditional methods for the fermentation of soybeans, rice, and cassava have long been known to remove off flavours, and the USDA began an extensive investigation of traditional fermented foods from India, Nepal, Pakistan, and Tibet. It reported the successful development of a commercial process for the manufacture of tempeh, an Indonesian food prepared from soybeans, and its use in snack foods.

The most progress made was in the manufacture and utilization of textured vegetable protein products as meat extenders. Japanese scientists reported a new development whereby proteins were restructured enzymatically. The products, called plasteins, have a lower molecular weight than the original protein and a bland flavour. During restructuring it was possible to introduce amino acids such as methionine to make up for deficiencies, so that a plastein derived from soy protein could be given a nutritional value equivalent to that of meat.

U.S. scientists investigating the diet of primitive man reported that, in terms of variety, man achieved the pinnacle of success 5,000 years ago, when he was a hunter and gatherer consuming many different types of grass seeds, nuts, leaves, berries, shoots, fruits, flowers, barks, roots, bulbs, tubers, saps, resins, in-

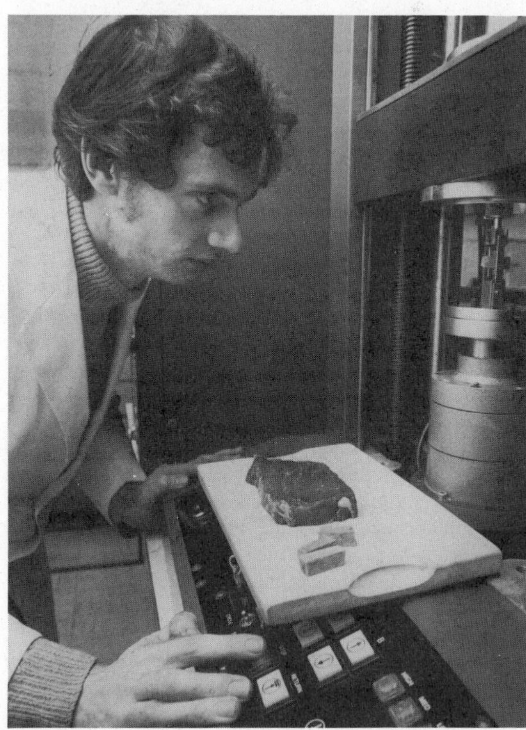
KEYSTONE

A mechanical chewing machine developed at the Meat Research Institute at Langford, England, can determine the precise toughness of a steak.

"Two breakthroughs—imitation eggs made of soybeans and imitation soybeans made of eggs."

SIDNEY HARRIS

sects, rodents, reptiles, game animals, eggs, and fish. As man became more and more dependent upon cultivation, the variety of food resources diminished.

New Foods. The USDA established a new market development service to inform foreign countries of new foods and developments in the U.S. market. In both the U.S. and Europe there was a proliferation of new and refashioned convenience foods. A line of canned Chinese meals and canned sauces was introduced in Britain, as well as a line of fresh cream fruit desserts in diaphragm-sealed containers ready for immediate use. A British-developed whole-meal pasta appeared on the Italian market. Other new products included frozen potato cakes, onion-flavoured potato-corn sticks, and a line of heat-and-eat seafood entrees.

The development of novel products with good nutritive value based on blends of indigenous raw materials was accelerated in view of the world food situation. The government of Saskatchewan reported the development of pea protein chips. U.S. scientists announced the successful development of bread fortified with defatted corn-germ (which greatly enhanced its nutritional value), a line of soy-wheat macaroni preparations, and lysine-fortified cornmeal tortillas.

In Mexico a new high-protein, low-lactose infant food derived from cheese whey was developed, and an Indian dairy research institute introduced a line of snacks based on curd and rice meal. In Japan a line of cheese-like products was developed from soy-milk curd. A research institute in South Korea introduced a range of palatable, low-cost snacks made from squid and pork. Jamaican scientists prepared a number of new products based on bananas, including a baby food made from banana meal and soy.

A novel line of vegetable paste concentrates prepared from fresh potatoes, onions, carrots, cabbage, parsley, and marrow was introduced in the U.S.S.R. A Swedish company successfully developed a new line of soft drinks with a reduced sugar content and no artificial colours, stabilizing agents, or other chemical additives; the stability of these beverages depended on the method of preparation. A new line of modified dairy products was introduced in South Africa to meet the demand for food products with enhanced polyunsaturated fatty acid content. The Canadian authorities also recognized the demand for such products and modified the labeling regulations to make their sale possible. (H. B. HAWLEY)

See also Agriculture and Food Supplies; Fisheries; Industrial Review: *Alcoholic Beverages*.

[451.B.1.c.ii; 731.E–H]

ENCYCLOPÆDIA BRITANNICA FILMS. *The Community Bakery* (1967); *Milk: From Farm to You* (3rd ed., 1972).

Food Supplies: *see* Agriculture and Food Supplies

Football

Association Football (Soccer). The story of violence surrounding soccer continued in 1975, and England seemed to be spawning the worst offenders, the followers of Leeds United (*see* below). But England had no monopoly on this modern disease. In Santiago, Chile, on June 25, after no fewer than 19 players had been sent off in the second leg of the Pinto Duran Cup between Chile and Uruguay following a brawl on the field, the players could not leave the playing area for another quarter of an hour because of a hail of stones from the spectators. The Chilean referee, Sergio Vasquez, was later fined by his national referees' association for letting things "get out of hand." Riots elsewhere in South America and in Italy were also reported.

Argentina, whose ability to stage the 1978 World Cup finals had been questioned in 1975, experienced a referees' strike. This "withdrawal of labour" was resolved, and the Argentines insisted that all would be ready for the World Cup finals.

On the field there was a slight tendency toward more goals, and the three major European club competitions produced 739 goals in 238 matches, an average of more than three a game.

European Champions' Cup. The final between the defending champions, Bayern Munich, and Leeds United in the Parc des Princes Stadium, Paris, on May 28, was ruined by the conduct of the English club's fans who ran riot after a shot by Peter Lorimer had scythed into the net but was ruled out ("offside") by the French referee, Michel Kitabdjian, in the 66th minute. The fans of Leeds United started a riot in which they fought, tore out seats and hurled them and other objects onto the playing field, and battled with riot police and stewards. Afterward the scuffling and vandalism extended into Paris itself.

Even before they left Britain the hooligan element among the "fanimals," as they were dubbed, damaged trains taking them to Dover and property in the port itself. The reaction to this from the controlling body, Union of European Football Associations (UEFA), was to slap a ban on Leeds from competing in any European competition for four years. This was later reduced on appeal by the Yorkshire club to one season upon qualification for a European competition.

Regrettably, this 20th anniversary final of the founding of the competition for national club champions did not live up to its billing. The Germans were pegged back on defense for most of the first hour by the overanxious English team, which kept pumping long passes deep into the Bayern half for the strikers Joe Jordan and Allan Clarke to head or shoot at goalkeeper Sepp Maier. Along with the Lorimer offside "goal," the referee's refusal to grant Leeds a penalty when Clarke was brought down by Franz Beckenbauer —a foul that the Bayern captain afterward admitted was such—helped stir up the fans. The vital first goal came after 70 minutes from Franz Roth, who collected a pass from Conny Torstensson and curled a left-foot shot into the far corner; a second goal by the indomitable Gerd Müller, who fastened onto a pass by Jupp Kapellmann and thumped home the ball wide of David Stewart ten minutes before the end of the contest, settled the match, 2–0.

European Cup-Winners' Cup. Dynamo Kiev became the first club from the U.S.S.R. to win one of the major European trophies by easily defeating Ferencvaros, of Hungary, in Basel, Switz., on May 14. The Soviets were in command of the game from the early phases and coasted through the final as if it were more a friendly training match than the apex of the competition. Only rarely did the Hungarians flutter into the picture, and they had little answer to the darting runs of Oleg Blochin.

The first two goals, by Vladimir Onishenko, came after 18 minutes and 40 minutes. The first was from a pass by Leonid Burjak, and the left-foot shot gave the Ferencvaros goalkeeper, Istvan Geczi, who seemed a little slow to move, no real chance. The second was a long-range effort in which the ball swung to deceive the Hungarian goalkeeper and finished in the top corner of the net. Blochin, who had troubled the shaky defense earlier, rounded off the scoring after 67 minutes when he beat a defender and thundered the ball home for the third goal.

UEFA Cup. National champions Borussia Mönchengladbach completed the first half of a West German double triumph by winning the UEFA Cup over two legs against Dutch club Twente Enschede with a 5–1 aggregate. All the goals came in the second leg.

Table I. Association Football Major Tournaments

Event	Winner	Country
European Super Cup	Dynamo Kiev	U.S.S.R.
European Champions' Cup	Bayern Munich	West Germany
European Cup-Winners' Cup	Dynamo Kiev	U.S.S.R.
UEFA cup	Borussia Mönchengladbach	West Germany
South American Champions' Cup	Independiente	Argentina
UEFA Youth Cup	England	
Inter-Continental Cup	Atletico Madrid	Spain

Table II. Association Football National Champions

Nation	League winners	Cup winners
Austria	SW Innsbruck	SW Innsbruck
Belgium	RWD Molenbeek	Anderlecht
Bulgaria	CSKA Sofia	Slavia Sofia
Czechoslovakia	Slovan Bratislava	Spartak Trnava
Denmark	KB Copenhagen	Vejle BK
England	Derby County	West Ham United
Finland	Kuopion Palloseura	Lahden Reipas
France	Saint-Étienne	Saint-Étienne
Germany, East	FC Magdeburg	Sachsenring Zwickau
Germany, West	Borussia Mönchengladbach	Eintracht Frankfurt
Greece	Olympiakos Piraeus	Olympiakos Piraeus
Hungary	Ujpest Dozsa	Ujpest Dozsa
Iceland	IA Akranes	Valur
Ireland	Bohemians	Home Farm
Italy	Juventus	Fiorentina
Luxembourg	Jeunesse d'Esch	US Ramelange
Netherlands, The	PSV Eindhoven	Den Haag
Northern Ireland	Linfield	Coleraine
Norway	Viking Stavanger	Skeid Oslo
Poland	Ruch Chorzow	Stal Rzeszow
Portugal	Benfica	Boavista
Romania	Dinamo Bucharest	Rapid Bucharest
Scotland	Rangers	Celtic
Spain	Real Madrid	Real Madrid
Sweden	Malmö	Malmö
Switzerland	FC Zürich	Basel
Turkey	Fenerbahce	Besiktas
U.S.S.R.	Dynamo Kiev	Dynamo Kiev
Wales		Wrexham
Yugoslavia	Hajduk Split	Hajduk Split

WIDE WORLD

Action at the British Isles championship at Wembley in May, as England (white jerseys) defeated Scotland 5–1.

In the opening encounter on May 7, the West Germans were without their star striker Jupp Heynckes, and this made Twente's task of containing them easier. There were few highlights as the game ground its way to a goalless draw played not on Borussia's home field but in the nearby Rhein Stadium at Düsseldorf with a capacity (70,000) double that of the home club's.

Heynckes was fit for the return a fortnight later in The Netherlands, and what a difference he made, putting, just as Dutchman Johan Cruyff did with Barcelona, a large query to the long-held belief that one man does not make a team. Heynckes proved his worth by ramming in a hat trick of goals. Twente had embarked on an attacking policy from the opening whistle, leaving gaps at the back that the West Germans exploited. Danish winger Alan Simonsen scored the first goal in the second minute and Heynckes added another in the ninth minute, virtually sealing the destination of the trophy. Although Borussia later went on to clinch the West German national title and so qualify for two European competitions, its success lost some of its gilt when the coach, Hennes Weisweiler, announced his resignation to take up a similar appointment with Barcelona.

British Isles Championship. After drawing with Northern Ireland and Wales, England emerged at Wembley Stadium on May 24 to hand out a crushing 5–1 defeat to the Scots and clinch the British Isles championship for the 30th time outright. Don Revie, England's manager, had shuffled his squad during the three games in the series and at last found a winning combination, whose task was simplified by the inadequacies of the Scottish defense. Scotland challenged briefly when Ken Dalglish (Celtic) started using the ball well in midfield, but it could not match the sharpness of England's finishing nor the tenacity of its defense. Because of fears of vandalism and injury to train and bus crews by a possible hooligan element among the Scottish fans, there was no public transport from the centre of London to Wembley Stadium—some eight miles—but it did not stop a capacity crowd from attending.

Inter-Continental Cup. Traditionally played between the winners of the South American Cup and the victors in the European Cup, the Inter-Continental Cup again experienced a deviation because Bayern Munich declined the invitation. Atletico Madrid, second place in Europe, represented the Old World and defeated Independiente of Argentina.

Although there was some rough play in the first leg of the tournament in Buenos Aires, Arg., on March 12, the playing field did not resemble a battlefield as had been the case in some other matches in this competition. The referee, Charles Corver of The Netherlands, was fairly lenient, especially when Atletico was on the defensive before Agustin Balbuena scored for Independiente from a pass by Ricardo Bertoni after 34 minutes. After that goal the Spanish team moved up players in a search for goals, but the score stood at 1–0 after the first leg. In the return leg, in Madrid on April 11, Atletico made sure of the trophy by scoring twice, the winning goal coming only four minutes before the end of the match. It was made by Argentine World Cup player Ruben Ayala. The first Atletico goal was registered by Javier Irureta after 21 minutes.

(TREVOR WILLIAMSON)

[452.B.4.h.ii]

Rugby. *Rugby Union.* The 1974–75 period was one in which the balance of power in world rugby swung away from European countries to those of the Southern Hemisphere. Late in 1974 the New Zealand All Blacks triumphed in Ireland and Wales and the South African Springboks won their two test matches in France. Then in 1975 England lost both its tests in Australia; France lost both tests in South Africa; and Scotland was beaten in its only test on its tour of New Zealand.

The All Blacks were not defeated on their eight-match tour of Ireland, Wales, and England in November 1974, a tour conceived as part of the celebrations for Ireland's centenary and including six games in that country. They won seven matches and tied the last, 13–13, against the Barbarians at Twickenham. This game was the climax of a hectic period of eight days in which the All Blacks beat Ireland 15–6 in Dublin and "a Welsh XV" 12–3 at Cardiff before traveling on to Twickenham. The All Blacks scored 127 points and had 50 scored against them.

Wales's rugby team proved the victor in a brutal match against France in Paris during the five-nation rugby tournament in January.

A.F.P./PICTORIAL PARADE

While the New Zealanders were in the British Isles, the Springboks were touring France, where they played two tests. After South Africa's defeats by the Lions (British Isles) earlier the same year, the Springboks gave renewed hope to their supporters by returning to winning ways against the French. In the first test, played at Toulouse, the Springbok forwards gained a measure of control and South Africa won 13–4. The French forward play was more effective in the second test, at the Parc des Princes Stadium in Paris, and France scored two tries to the South Africans' one. But the French failed to take their opportunities of kicking goals, whereas Gerald Bosch kicked well for the Springboks. The final score was 10–8 in favour of South Africa.

The scores in England's two test defeats against Australia's Wallabies, at Sydney and Brisbane in May 1975, were 16–9 and 30–21. This was the first time the Wallabies had won a test series at home for ten years, but the tour would also be remembered for misplaced violence. This reached a climax early in the second test when Mike Burton, the England prop forward, was sent off the field for a late and dangerous tackle. He was the first man ever sent off while playing for England and the first sent off in any test involving Australia.

France played 11 games in South Africa in May and June 1975, winning six, drawing one, and losing four. It was during this tour that a multiracial team of South Africans was fielded for the first time ever in that country. The team was known as the "South African Invitation XV," and it included two Africans and two Coloureds. The French lost this game, played on June 7 on the test ground at Newlands, Cape Town, by 18–3. The scores in the two tests were 38–25 to the Springboks at Bloemfontein and 33–18 to the Springboks at Pretoria.

Scotland played seven games in New Zealand in May and June 1975, winning four and losing three. The only test was won by the All Blacks by 24–0 at Eden Park, Auckland, in probably the wettest conditions ever known for a rugby international.

The chief feature of the home international championships was the way Wales, with a largely untried side, steadily built up confidence and technique so that, after an uncertain start to their campaign, they eventually thrashed Ireland 32–4 at Cardiff and so won the title. Ireland, Scotland, and France finished in a three-way tie for second.

Rugby League. The 1974–75 period involved the triangular tournament in the European area and the first stages of the new world championship. The first, held early in 1975 between England, Wales, and France, was won by England, which beat France 11–9 at Perpignan and Wales 12–8 at Salford. Wales finished second by beating France 21–8 at Swansea. The world championship, involving England, Wales, France, Australia, and New Zealand, was begun in Europe in March 1975 with France beating Wales 14–7 at Toulouse and England beating France 20–2 at Headingley, but the rest of the matches were played in Australia and New Zealand. Each country played four games in this stage of the championship, Australia finishing first with 7 points, New Zealand gaining 5, England 4, and Wales and France 2 each.

(DAVID FROST)

[452.B.4.h.xxiv]

U.S. Football. The Pittsburgh Steelers won the championship of U.S. professional football for the second straight year by defeating the Dallas Cowboys 21–17 in the Super Bowl on Jan. 18, 1976, in Miami. Oklahoma was voted the nation's top college team.

College. All but one of the challengers for the 1975 national championship lost a game somewhere along the way, and when the season ended the only undefeated school from a major conference was Ohio State. But the Buckeyes were then upset by UCLA 23–10 in the Rose Bowl.

Alabama was the first Goliath to fall, losing its opening game to Missouri before winning its next ten. Oklahoma, the preseason choice as the nation's best, had its 37-game unbeaten streak interrupted by a 23–3 loss against unranked Kansas, but the Sooners salvaged a tie for the Big Eight title by spoiling Nebraska's unbeaten record in the season's final game. Texas A & M also went into the last game undefeated, but lost to Arkansas. And Michigan's record was blemished by only two ties before Ohio State defeated it in the season's final game. The Wolverines then fell to Oklahoma 14–6 in the Orange Bowl. Arizona State was the only undefeated major school, beating Nebraska 17–14 in the Fiesta Bowl, but it failed to gain top ranking because it plays in the lightly regarded Western Athletic Conference. In the season's final poll, the top five teams in order were Oklahoma, Arizona State, Alabama, Ohio State, and UCLA.

Ohio State ranked first in scoring during the regular season with 34 points a game and was second to Alabama's 6-point average in defense. But Archie Griffin's unprecedented second Heisman Trophy, the annual award for the top U.S. college football player, was more spectacular than anything that the Ohio State team did. Griffin, a senior, had a record streak of 31 consecutive regular-season games with 100 yd. or more rushing before Michigan stopped it. Two of Griffin's teammates were national leaders, Pete Johnson in scoring with 13.6 points a game and Tom Skladany in punting with 46.7 yd. a kick.

Alabama's season was overshadowed somewhat by the off-field attention its coach, Paul ("Bear") Bryant, attracted. Bryant first made news by suing the National Collegiate Athletic Association over its new rule that limited visiting teams to fewer players than home teams, a move the NCAA made in the name of economy. Later, Bryant was accused of arranging major Bowl match-ups so that third-ranked Alabama would play eighth-ranked Penn State in the Sugar Bowl. Bryant won both the lawsuit and the Sugar Bowl, 13–6, Alabama's first Bowl victory in its last nine tries.

The two Orange Bowl opponents, Oklahoma and Michigan, had been among the nation's best in the previous two years, but neither had played in a Bowl game, Oklahoma because it was on NCAA probation for recruiting violations and Michigan because the Big Ten had a rule prohibiting more than one team from appearing in a Bowl game. Michigan became the second NCAA team ever to have two men run for 1,000 yd. with Gordon Bell and Rob Lytle, and Oklahoma's defensive tackle Leroy Selmon won the Outland Trophy as the nation's top lineman.

Texas A & M, loser to Southern California 20–0 in the Liberty Bowl, scored its first win over Texas since 1967 and led the nation in total defense (183.8 yd. a game) and rushing defense (80.3 yd.). California missed the Bowl season altogether despite leading the nation in total offense with 458.5 yd. a game.

WIDE WORLD

Air Force kicker Dave Lawson breaks the NCAA career scoring record of 212 points with 15 points against Army.

In the most traditional Eastern games, Harvard beat Yale 10–7 to win the Ivy League title and Navy beat Army 30–6. Army scored against Navy for the first time since 1972, while Navy's 7–4 finish gave it a winning record for the first time since 1967.

Professional. Five weeks into the National Football League season, the Baltimore Colts had a 1–4 record and appeared to be on their way to repeating their 1974 record of 2–12. Then they did not lose another game in the regular season. Their final 10–4 record was the same as Miami, but the Colts became champions of the American Conference East because their nine-game winning streak included two over Miami.

The Colts had a new coach, Ted Marchibroda, and a young team that general manager Joe Thomas began assembling when he drafted quarterback Bert Jones in 1973. Jones was one of the league's best passers, completing 59%, and his favourite receiver, halfback Lydell Mitchell, led the conference with 60 catches.

Miami missed the play-offs for the first time since 1969 in an injury-dominated season. Safety Dick Anderson and linebacker Nick Buoniconti left hard-to-fill holes in the defense with season-long injuries, and the Dolphins finished the season with third-string quarterback Don Strock after Bob Griese and Earl Morrall were hurt. Besides the injuries, the Dolphins lost offensive stars Larry Csonka, Paul Warfield, and Jim Kiick to the World Football League at the beginning of the season.

The three ex-Dolphins had nowhere to play after continuing financial troubles forced the WFL to fold in the middle of its second season. Their employer, John Bassett, honoured their contracts and hoped to enter the NFL with his Memphis team, but NFL owners did not share that desire.

The National Conference East provided the NFL's other big race, featuring three overtime games among its contenders in which Dallas beat St. Louis, Washington beat Dallas, and St. Louis beat Washington. The St. Louis victory was tied at the end of regulation time when Mel Gray caught a pass in the end zone and was immediately separated from the ball. The officials huddled before making their decision in

Table III
NFL Final Standings and Play-offs, 1975

AMERICAN CONFERENCE			
Eastern Division	W	L	T
Baltimore	10	4	0
Miami	10	4	0
Buffalo	8	6	0
New York Jets	3	11	'0
New England	3	11	0
Central Division			
Pittsburgh	12	2	0
*Cincinnati	11	3	0
Houston	10	4	0
Cleveland	3	11	0
Western Division			
Oakland	11	3	0
Denver	6	8	0
Kansas City	5	9	0
San Diego	2	12	0
NATIONAL CONFERENCE			
Eastern Division			
St. Louis	11	3	0
*Dallas	10	4	0
Washington	8	6	0
New York Giants	5	9	0
Philadelphia	4	10	0
Central Division			
Minnesota	12	2	0
Detroit	7	7	0
Chicago	4	10	0
Green Bay	4	10	0
Western Division			
Los Angeles	12	2	0
San Francisco	5	9	0
Atlanta	4	10	0
New Orleans	2	12	0

*Fourth qualifier for play-offs.

Play-offs

American semifinals
Pittsburgh 28, Baltimore 10
Oakland 31, Cincinnati 28

National semifinals
Los Angeles 35, St. Louis 23
Dallas 17, Minnesota 14

American finals
Pittsburgh 16, Oakland 10

National finals
Dallas 37, Los Angeles 7

Super Bowl
Pittsburgh 21, Dallas 17

favour of St. Louis, but that call touched off the first of many strong suggestions that NFL officials take advantage of instant-replay cameras.

Gray, along with Terry Metcalf, Jim Otis, and quarterback Jim Hart, made St. Louis the league's most explosive team as well as the National Conference East champions with an 11–3 record. Gray led the league with 11 touchdown catches and led the conference with 926 yd. on his 48 receptions. Metcalf broke a league record with 2,462 yd. on runs, receptions, and kick returns, and the offensive line tied another record by allowing only eight sacks of the quarterback. Otis led National Conference rushers with 1,076 yd., a mark far behind the league-leading total of 1,817 yd. by O. J. Simpson (*see* BIOGRAPHY).

Dallas became the National Conference's wild-card play-off team (the best second-place record) by beating Washington in the next-to-last game, and also led the conference in total offense. Cincinnati was the American Conference wild-card team, finishing 11–3 in the same conference with defending league champion Pittsburgh, which was 12–2. Quarterback Ken Anderson, the only player to pass for more than 3,000 yd., led Cincinnati's offense, while Pittsburgh relied heavily on fullback Franco Harris, whose 1,246-yd. rushing made him the first player ever to gain 4,000 yd. in his first four seasons.

Minnesota, Los Angeles, and Oakland won the championships of their respective divisions by at least five games. Oakland and Minnesota were their conference defensive leaders in yardage allowed, and Los Angeles allowed the fewest points in the league.

Minnesota quarterback Fran Tarkenton set career records for touchdown passes and completions and led the league with a completion percentage of 64.2. His favourite target, Chuck Foreman, led the league with 73 catches. Washington's Charley Taylor became the all-time reception leader, and Oakland's field-goal and extra-point kicker George Blanda scored his 2,000th point, over 600 more than anyone else.

In the play-offs Los Angeles defeated St. Louis 35–23, and Dallas beat Minnesota 17–14 on a last-minute touchdown pass. Pittsburgh defeated Baltimore 28–10, and Oakland edged Cincinnati 31–28.

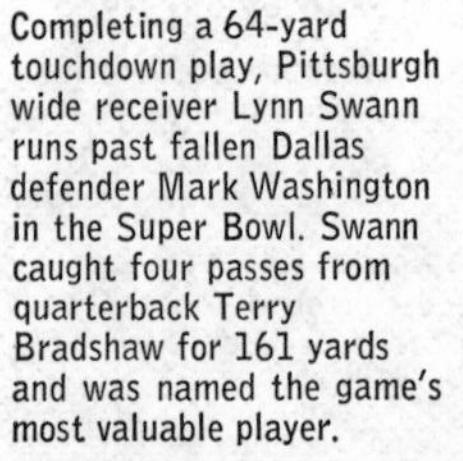
Completing a 64-yard touchdown play, Pittsburgh wide receiver Lynn Swann runs past fallen Dallas defender Mark Washington in the Super Bowl. Swann caught four passes from quarterback Terry Bradshaw for 161 yards and was named the game's most valuable player.

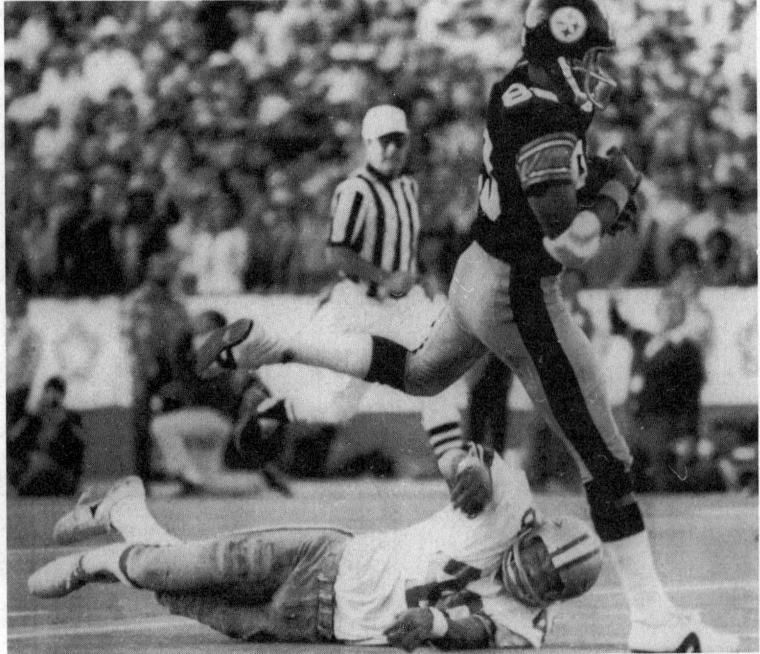
UPI COMPIX

WIDE WORLD

Michigan tailback Gordon Bell (5) is hit high and low by Oklahoma's Selmon brothers, Dewey (91) and Leroy (93), in the Orange Bowl game.

Dallas then became the first wild-card team ever to advance to the Super Bowl by routing Los Angeles 37–7 for the National Conference championship behind the outstanding passing of quarterback Roger Staubach. Pittsburgh repeated as the American Conference winner with a 16–10 triumph over Oakland under frigid conditions that caused many fumbles.

Pittsburgh won its second consecutive Super Bowl contest by defeating Dallas 21–17. Voted as the game's outstanding player was Pittsburgh receiver Lynn Swann, who made several spectacular catches of passes from quarterback Terry Bradshaw, including a 64-yd. touchdown play. Both Dallas touchdowns were scored on passes from Staubach. An unusual feature was the inclusion in the game program of the six finalists in a Slogans USA contest to choose a bicentennial slogan for the U.S.

On December 30 a U.S. district court judge ruled against the NFL and in favour of 15 players by declaring the "Rozelle rule" a violation of antitrust laws. Named for NFL commissioner Pete Rozelle, the rule states that a team signing a player who has made himself a free agent by playing out the option year in his contract must compensate that player's former team by means of players and/or draft selections; if the two teams cannot agree, Rozelle decides on the compensation. The NFL appealed the decision, claiming that it would result in a bidding war in which the richest teams would get the best players, and the judge stayed his decision pending the appeal.

Canadian Football. All of the points in the Grey Cup game for the championship of Canadian professional football were scored on kicks, with Dave Cutler providing the difference for the Edmonton Eskimos in their 9–8 victory over the Montreal Alouettes. Cutler, who set league records with 40 regular-season field goals and 169 points, kicked three field goals of 41, 25, and 52 yd. His last one broke a Grey Cup record for distance that Don Sweet of Montreal had set with a 47-yd. kick in the first quarter.

Montreal, which outgained Edmonton by 299 yd. to 193, had a 6–0 lead in the first quarter and a 7–3 lead before Cutler kicked two fields goals in the third quarter. Sweet, who set a record in the 1974 Grey Cup game with four field goals, made two against Edmonton but missed two others that went for one-point rouges (the term for a kick that is not returned out of the end zone).

Sweet had a chance to win the game for Montreal when he tried an 18-yd. field goal with 45 seconds left and the Alouettes trailing 9–7. But the holder had trouble placing the ball and Montreal had to settle for one point, and a defeat. (KEVIN M. LAMB)

[452.B.4.h.xiii]

France

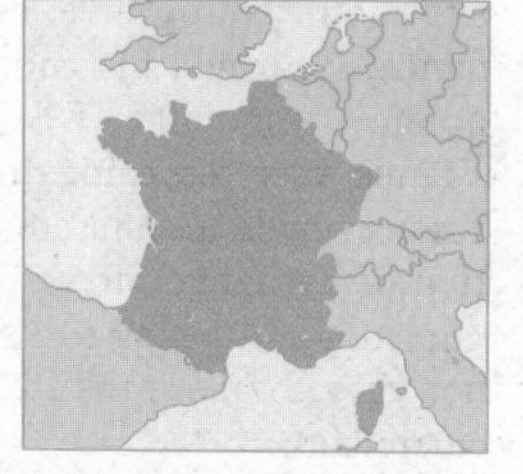

A republic of Western Europe and head of the French Community, France is bounded by the English Channel, Belgium, Luxembourg, West Germany, Switzerland, Italy, the Mediterranean Sea, Monaco, Spain, Andorra, and the Atlantic Ocean. Area: 210,039 sq.mi. (543,998 sq.km.), including Corsica. Pop. (1975 census): 52,544,000. Cap. and largest city: Paris (pop., 1975 census, 2,290,900). Language: French. Religion: predominantly Roman Catholic. President in 1975, Valéry Giscard d'Estaing; premier, Jacques Chirac.

During 1975 President Giscard determined to pursue reforms intended to change French society, to refloat the economy, and to conduct a foreign policy based on global cooperation. According to an opinion poll, in which the public was asked its views on the president's conduct of affairs, 47% considered that he had fulfilled his promises, 64% that he had made changes in certain areas, and 40% that the presidential form of government had been accentuated.

Domestic Affairs. The year opened with a minor Cabinet reshuffle. Yvon Bourges of the Union des Démocrates pour la République (UDR, or Gaullists) replaced Jacques Soufflet at defense, and Gen. Marcel Bigeard became secretary of state for the armed services, with the aim of resolving conscripts' discontent. Norbert Segard was promoted from secretary of state to minister of foreign trade. Aymar Achille Fould, vice-president of the Centre Démocratie et Progrès (CDP) and an upper-class progressive, took over from Pierre Lelong in the post office. Jean-François Deniau, former member of the European Commission, became secretary of state for agriculture. Otherwise there was no change in the team formed by Giscard on his election to the presidency in May 1974.

This did not mean, however, that the political situation was static. Premier Chirac and Michel Poniatowski, the minister of state and a member of the Independent Republicans (IR), Giscard's party, who was believed to be the influence behind Giscard, made no secret of their ambition to control the governing coalition. This explained Chirac's surprising surrender of his post of general secretary of the UDR at the annual party convention in June, a post that he had obtained six months earlier after a hard struggle. André Bord, secretary of state for war veterans, succeeded him, but Chirac remained in charge and made it clear that he meant to lead the governing coalition, and not merely his own party in it, while upholding the principles of Gaullism. Almost at the same time, the setting up of a coalition of Independents was confirmed, with Poniatowski elected as its president after a meeting of leaders of the Fédération des Indépendants and of the Centre National des Indépendants et Paysans. Poniatowski's aim was to make the IR the leading party in the coalition.

A.F.P./PICTORIAL PARADE

The French satellite Diamant prior to launching from French Guiana in September.

But this competitive loyalty to Giscard was far less strident than the controversy that arose between the two principal leaders of the Union of the Left, François Mitterrand of the Socialist Party and Georges Marchais of the Communist Party. The dispute went back to October 1974, after the midterm elections had given substantial gains to the Socialists at the expense of the Communists. At the beginning of 1975 Marchais suffered a slight heart attack and was out of action for three weeks, but this did not prevent his describing Mitterrand, shortly afterward, as "increasingly self-confident and domineering." Exchanges continued, in particular during Giscard's visit to Marseilles in February and over the situation in Portugal.

The Tarn by-election, in which the government majority candidate regained his seat in the National Assembly on the first ballot, again pointed to a drop in the popularity of the Communists as compared with that of the Socialists. Feelings were still further exacerbated in October after the by-election at Châtellerault (Vienne), where Pierre Abelin (a Reformist and the majority candidate) was returned with only 52.6% of the vote against Mme. Edith Cresson, a member of the Socialist Party national secretariat who polled 47.39%. In March 1973 the single left-wing candidate, a Communist, had received only 39.06%.

The Constitutional Council ruled on January 15 that the Abortion Bill liberalizing the previously strict abortion law did not violate the constitution. The bill, which Simone Veil (*see* BIOGRAPHY), the minister of health, had sponsored, became law on January 18. It would generally allow abortion during the first ten weeks of pregnancy.

The spring and autumn sessions saw the passage of several bills that exemplified the "principal orientation of the state's action for reform." The most important were those on reforms of the divorce laws and on education. Giscard's declared aim was still to

Foreign Aid: *see* Economy, World

Foreign Exchange: *see* Economy, World

Foreign Investments: *see* Economy, World

Forestry: *see* Environment; Industrial Review

Formosa: *see* Taiwan

raise the country's educational level. As usual, the autumn session was mainly devoted to discussion of the 1976 budget, designed on the assumption of a 4.6% growth rate and a forecast that prices would rise by around 8%. The part dealing with revenue passed quickly. Earlier, the Mazeaud bill for development of sport went through, as did the draft on property reforms; Giscard took personal responsibility for the latter since it concerned a basic structural reform. The property tax bill was set aside, however.

In June Bernard Lafay (Centrist Union, allied to the UDR) was elected president of the Council of Paris by 35 votes, against Communist (29 votes) and Paris-Avenir (20) candidates. A few days later the Council of Ministers accepted the reform in the status of Paris, to become effective from July 1, 1976. The Council of Paris, with a membership increased to 100, was made responsible for administering both the city and the *département*, the boundaries of which coincided. The prefect of Paris and the prefect of police would become the representatives of the state. The former district was replaced by a public regional administration. The Parisian region would have the same legal powers as the provincial regions.

The Parisian press was affected by a dispute between the director of the *Parisien Libéré*, Emilien Amaury, and the Communist-led Syndicat du Livre, which had called repeated strikes. *Le Monde* wrote: "Strike action should only be the last weapon in an industrial dispute." In fact, the issue was one of an attack on free expression. On *Le Figaro*, after the editorial staff had tried unsuccessfully to prevent the transfer of Jean Prouvost's shares to Robert Hersant, some 50 staff members resigned from the paper.

Early in November the Confédération Générale du Travail and the Confédération Française Démocratique du Travail ordered strikes that affected extensive sectors of the public services, and the ground staff of Air France stopped work. One of the principal demands was retirement at age 60, and in December the National Assembly passed a bill that provided for this, under certain circumstances, for persons engaged on heavy shift work or otherwise working under trying conditions. A dispute with Italy over the entry of cheap Italian wine, as permitted by EEC regulations, and the consequent undercutting of French wine prices, remained unresolved at year's end. In Corsica an autonomist movement was banned after the occupation of a vineyard and the killing of two French policemen.

The Economy. After making determined efforts to contain inflation (a satisfactory third quarter had helped to lower the annual rate to less than 10%) and strengthening the franc on the exchange market, the government decided that the time had come to return to the European joint currency float or "snake" and also to inject fresh finance into the country's economic system, even at the risk of creating a new inflationary situation. Jean-Pierre Fourcade, the minister of finance, informed his colleagues in the European Economic Community (EEC) in Brussels on July 10 that France was returning to the "snake." By so doing, France made a concrete gesture toward the stabilization of exchange rates. The exchange rate of France's currency, returning to its level of January 1974, could not vary by more than 2.25% against other European currencies.

Giscard himself told the country on television on September 4 of the plan to develop the economy which had been agreed to by the Council of Ministers. A total of about Fr. 30 billion was to be reinjected into the economy. In line with Keynesian theory, Giscard would use growth in the budgetary deficit as a motor to restart the economy. What he said, in essence, was that nations were undergoing the most serious upheaval that the world economy had felt in peacetime during the past 45 years. No EEC country had been spared its effects. In France unemployment was causing concern (it was estimated that there were already more than a million unemployed by September). The situation had to be put right through the creation of jobs, and economic activity must be stimulated.

There were four elements in the government plan. First, the measures being taken were for one time only. All the proposed credits would be granted in 1975, and from 1976 onward the budget would have to be balanced. Second, aid for social consumption (Fr. 700 for pensioners and Fr. 250 for each child for all families receiving family allowances) would amount to Fr. 5 billion. Third, state investment in-

FRANCE

Education. (1973–74) Primary, pupils 6,367,523, teachers 255,919; secondary, pupils 2,945,192, teachers 173,934; vocational, pupils 953,235, teachers 66,549; teacher training, students 27,823, teachers 2,952; higher (including 36 universities), students 763,980, teaching staff 38,000.

Finance. Monetary unit: franc, with (Sept. 22, 1975) a free rate of Fr. 4.55 to U.S. $1 (Fr. 9.43 = £1 sterling). Gold, SDRs, and foreign exchange: (June 1975) U.S. $9,909,000,000; (June 1974) U.S. $7,707,000,000. Budget (1976 est.) balanced at Fr. 294 billion. Gross national product: (1973) Fr. 1,135,800,000,000; (1972) Fr. 997.5 billion. Money supply: (Feb. 1975) Fr. 340,980,000,000; (Feb. 1974) Fr. 307,380,000,000. Cost of living (1970 = 100): (June 1975) 152: (June 1974) 136.

Foreign Trade. (1974) Imports Fr. 254.2 billion; exports Fr. 223,120,000,000. Import sources: EEC 48% (West Germany 19%, Belgium-Luxembourg 10%, Italy 7%, The Netherlands 6%); U.S. 8%; Saudi Arabia 6%. Export destinations: EEC 53% (West Germany 17%, Italy 12%, Belgium-Luxembourg 11%, U.K. 7%, The Netherlands 5%); Switzerland 6%; U.S. 5%. Main exports: machinery 18%; chemicals 12%; motor vehicles 9%; iron and steel 9%. Tourism (1973): visitors (at classified hotels) 10,158,000; gross receipts U.S. $2,478,000,000.

Transport and Communications. Roads (1973) 793,826 km. (including 2,426 km. expressways). Motor vehicles in use (1973): passenger 14,620,000; commercial 1,980,000. Railways: (1973) 34,435 km.; traffic (1974) 46,880,000,000 passenger-km., freight 76,999,000,000 net ton-km. Air traffic (1974): 21,738,000,000 passenger-km.; freight 942,419,000 net ton-km. Navigable inland waterways in regular use (1973) 7,209 km.; freight traffic 13,792,000,000 ton-km. Shipping (1974): merchant vessels 100 gross tons and over 1,341; gross tonnage 8,834,519. Telephones (Dec. 1973) 11,337,000. Radio licenses (Dec. 1972) 17,034,000. Television licenses (Dec. 1972) 12,279,000.

Agriculture. Production (in 000; metric tons; 1974; 1973 in parentheses): wheat 18,910 (17,828); rye 308 (327); barley 10,030 (10,844); oats 2,038 (2,203); corn *c.* 8,900 (10,625); potatoes 7,592 (7,459); rice (1973) 71, (1972) 52; sorghum 290 (298); rapeseed 684 (661); sunflower seed 75 (91); tomatoes (1973) *c.* 490, (1972) 490; onions 132 (136); carrots (1973) *c.* 530, (1972) 530; apples (1973) 3,428, (1972) 2,818; pears (1973) 514, (1972) 462; peaches (1973) 627, (1972) 584; flax fibres (1973) 47, (1972) 45; sugar, raw value 2,944 (3,171); wine (1973) 7,993, (1972) 5,850; tobacco 49 (50); beef and veal (1973) *c.* 1,500, (1972) 1,560; pork (1973) *c.* 1,580, (1972) 1,476; milk *c.* 29,528 (29,291); butter 540 (550); cheese 870 (840); fish catch (1973) 797, (1972) 783. Livestock (in 000; Oct. 1973): cattle 22,864; sheep 10,324; pigs 11,369; horses (1973) 480; chickens (1973) *c.* 150,000.

Industry. Index of production (1970 = 100): (1974) 123; (1973) 120. Fuel and power (in 000; 1974): coal (metric tons) 22,897; electricity (kw-hr.) 180,249,000; natural gas (cu.m.) 7,526,000; manufactured gas (cu.m.; 1973) 5,888,000. Production (in 000; metric tons; 1974): bauxite 2,910; iron ore (32% metal content) 54,265; pig iron 22,518; crude steel 27,023; aluminum 520; lead 146; zinc 283; cement 32,468; cotton yarn 268; cotton fabrics (1973) 208; wool yarn 143; wool fabrics (1973) 72; rayon, etc., filament yarn 40; rayon, etc., staple fibre 81; nylon, etc., filament yarn 91; nylon, etc., staple fibre 129; sulfuric acid 4,663; petroleum products (1973) 123,781; fertilizers (nutrient content; 1973–74) nitrogenous 1,694, phosphate 1,640; potash 2,082; passenger cars (units) 3,046; commercial vehicles (units) 418. Merchant shipping launched (100 gross tons and over; 1974) 1,342,700 gross tons.

volving major public works projects and the raising of living standards and of the social environment through improvement of such features as hospitals, resources devoted to education, and funds granted to local communities would amount to Fr. 13 billion. Fourth, aid for investment and for company funds would amount to an additional Fr. 2.8 billion, and the postponement of tax payments for private industry to April 15, 1976, would represent Fr. 9.6 billion. The opposition and the trade unions immediately rejected the plan as inadequate.

The government's plan was accepted by the National Assembly (300 votes to 182) and by the Senate (176 to 85) at an extraordinary session of Parliament called to examine the financial amendment act required to initiate it. Chirac and Giscard each saw the 22 regional prefects to urge them to carry out the plan energetically.

Unemployment, nevertheless, got worse. In the spring, the longest industrial conflict experienced by the state-owned Renault company ended on April 15 after nine weeks of cumulative strikes and a production loss of 80,000 cars. However, the Salon de l'Auto (motor show) in the autumn demonstrated that the motor industry was picking up slightly.

Foreign Policy. Giscard was active in foreign policy during the year. His style differed from that of Gen. Charles de Gaulle, but most of his policies followed the path laid down by the founder of the Fifth Republic. However, one of France's priorities was the construction of a united Europe. The British referendum in June, which produced a vote of 67.2% in favor of the EEC and only 32.8% against, was welcomed in France as removing the question mark that had hung over the continent.

France and West Germany shared similar attitudes, particularly on the subject of European political unity. This was revealed in February in a first discussion between Giscard and Chancellor Helmut Schmidt, at the meeting with West German Pres. Walter Scheel in April, and in Giscard's visit to Bonn with a large French delegation at the end of July, when a joint timetable for steps toward economic recovery was drawn up. The visit to France in April of Konstantinos Karamanlis, prime minister of Greece, and that of Giscard to Athens in September opened the way for Greece's integration into democratic Europe. At the same time, visits by Gen. Francisco da Costa Gomes, the Portuguese head of state, and Pedro Cortina y Mauri, the Spanish foreign minister, allowed Giscard to consider the role that might eventually be played in the building of Europe by new regimes in Spain and Portugal.

On April 10–12 the French president visited Pres. Houari Boumédienne in Algiers, three weeks later he held talks in Rabat with King Hassan II, and at the beginning of November he went to Tunis for a meeting with Pres. Habib Bourguiba; in all these cases, these were the first official visits by a French head of state since the North African countries had gained independence. The meetings were intended to revitalize the "grand Mediterranean design," which had a part to play in the dialogue between Europe and the Arab world. These successes in Africa were clouded by the deterioration of relations with the government of Chad during the year and by the protracted and inconclusive negotiations with rebels there for the release of a kidnapped French ethnologist, Françoise Claustre, as well as by disturbances in the Territory of the Afars and Issas and the unilateral declaration of independence of the Comoro Islands. (*See* Comoro Islands.)

AGIP/PICTORIAL PARADE

Demonstration at the Place de l'Opéra for improved benefits for workers in the publishing industry.

At the end of July, Giscard took part in the Conference on Security and Cooperation in Europe in Helsinki, Fin. He also visited Poland and was host in Paris to the Hungarian foreign minister, Frygyes Puja, and to the federal premier of Czechoslovakia, Lubomir Strougal. Chirac and Foreign Minister Jean Sauvagnargues visited Yugoslavia and Romania, respectively. During a five-day visit to the U.S.S.R. by Chirac and the minister for industry, Michel d'Ornano, in March, major economic agreements were signed covering the next five years. In October, Giscard himself went to Moscow for talks with Soviet party leader Leonid Brezhnev. In May France had given an exceptionally cordial welcome to Deputy Prime Minister Teng Hsiao-p'ing, generally recognized as the "Number Three" man in China.

Relations with the Arab countries had received considerable attention after the oil crisis. In January Pres. Anwar as-Sadat of Egypt visited Paris. France promised Egypt an unspecified number of Mirage jet fighter aircraft and other military supplies. At the end of April, Yigal Allon, the Israeli foreign minister, came to Paris for an official three-day visit immediately after King Hussein of Jordan had been welcomed at the Elysée Palace. Since the deterioration of Franco-Israeli relations after the Six-Day War, France's pro-Arab policy did not exclude recognition of the existence of both "an Israeli reality" and "a Palestinian reality." However, a second visit by Sadat to Paris at the end of October, on his way to Washington and London, acquired symbolic significance for both Paris and Cairo, as did Giscard's return visit to Cairo in December, confirming France's pro-Arab outlook and marking Egypt's return to the Western fold after a 25-year absence. Earlier, the French government was successively host to Emir Sabah as-Salim as-Sabah of Kuwait; to the president of the United Arab Emirates, Sheikh Zaid ibn Sultan an-Nahayan; to Crown Prince Fahd of Saudi Arabia and his brother; to Iraqi Vice-President Saddam Hussein (after Saudi Arabia, Iraq was France's main oil supplier); and to Sheikh Khalifah ibn Hamad ath-Thani, the emir of Qatar.

From November 15 to 17, a monetary and economic summit at Rambouillet brought together the heads of state or government of the six major Western industrial countries, the U.S., Japan, Britain, West Germany, Italy, and France. However, Giscard's outstanding success was in getting delegates from 8 industrial and 19 less developed countries to Paris on December 16 for the Conference on International Economic Cooperation. The preparatory meeting for a conference of energy producing and consuming nations had collapsed in April, but the same delegations quickly reached agreement at a French-sponsored meeting in Paris in October. A year after the idea had been put forward by Giscard, the conference was intended to demonstrate the growing willingness among nations for mutual discussion and understanding. (*See* CHRONOLOGY OF EVENTS.) (JEAN KNECHT)

See also Dependent States.
[972.A.2]

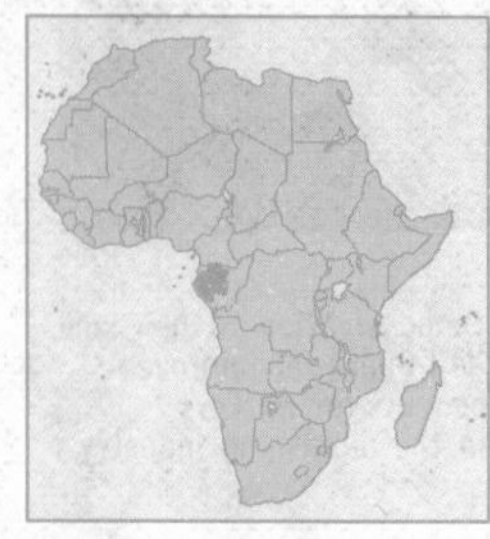

Gabon

A republic of western equatorial Africa, Gabon is bounded by Equatorial Guinea, Cameroon, the Congo, and the Atlantic Ocean. Area: 103,347 sq.mi. (267,667 sq.km.). Pop. (1975 est.): 1,155,800. Cap. and largest city: Libreville (pop., 1975 est., 169,200). Language: French and Bantu dialects. Religion: traditional tribal beliefs; Christian minority. President in 1975, Omar Bongo; premier, from April 16, Léon Mébiame.

Léon Mébiame, previously vice-president of the republic, was nominated premier on April 16, 1975, by President Bongo. In the economic field the spectacular growth of the production of petroleum resulted in Gabon's admission to full membership in the Organization of Petroleum Exporting Countries at its June conference in Libreville.

In foreign relations the leaders of Gabon appeared to have twin preoccupations: to maintain close ties with France and to develop connections with the former Portuguese African colonies. For these reasons President Bongo paid several visits to Paris and saw Pres. Valéry Giscard d'Estaing, while the latter spent his August holiday in Gabon. The leaders of Gabon attempted to mediate between France and Chad in the Claustre affair (*see* CHAD) but in the end blamed the French government for not having sent Premier Jacques Chirac to negotiate personally in Chad.

(PHILIPPE DECRAENE)

[978.E.7.a.iv]

GABON

Education. (1972–73) Primary, pupils 110,472, teachers 2,436; secondary, pupils 11,734, teachers 373; vocational, pupils 2,419, teachers 212; teacher training, students 301, teachers (1971–72) 25; higher, students (1972–73) 533.

Finance. Monetary unit: CFA franc, with (Sept. 22, 1975) a parity of CFA Fr. 50 to the French franc (free rate of CFA Fr. 227.70 = U.S. $1; CFA Fr. 471.75 = £1 sterling). Budget (1974 est.): revenue CFA Fr. 48,714,000,000; expenditure CFA Fr. 39,885,000,000.

Foreign Trade. Imports (1973) CFA Fr. 35,540,000,000; exports (1974) CFA Fr. 206,220,000,000. Import sources: France 59%; West Germany 9%; U.S. 9%. Export destinations (1973): France 37%; West Germany 10%; The Netherlands 7%; U.S. 7%; U.K. 6%. Main exports: crude oil 87%; timber *c.* 8%; manganese *c.* 5%.

Transport and Communications. Roads (1973) 6,848 km. Motor vehicles in use (1972): passenger *c.* 10,000; commercial *c.* 4,600. Railways (1973) 372 km. Construction of a Trans-Gabon railway (330 km.), to be completed in 1978, was begun in 1974. Telephones (Dec. 1973) 11,000. Radio receivers (Dec. 1971) *c.* 65,000. Television receivers (Dec. 1971) *c.* 1,300.

Agriculture. Production (in 000; metric tons; 1973; 1972 in parentheses): sweet potatoes *c.* 3 (*c.* 3); cassava *c.* 170 (*c.* 169); peanuts *c.* 2 (*c.* 2); corn *c.* 2 (*c.* 2); coffee *c.* 1 (*c.* 1); cocoa *c.* 5 (*c.* 5); bananas *c.* 10 (*c.* 10); palm oil *c.* 2.5 (*c.* 2.5); timber (cu.m.; 1973) 3,500, (1972) 3,400. Livestock (in 000; 1973): cattle *c.* 5; pigs *c.* 5; sheep *c.* 56; goats *c.* 61.

Industry. Production (in 000; metric tons; 1974): crude oil 10,202; manganese ore (metal content; 1973) 979; uranium 0.4; petroleum products (1973) 702; electricity (kw-hr.) 170,000.

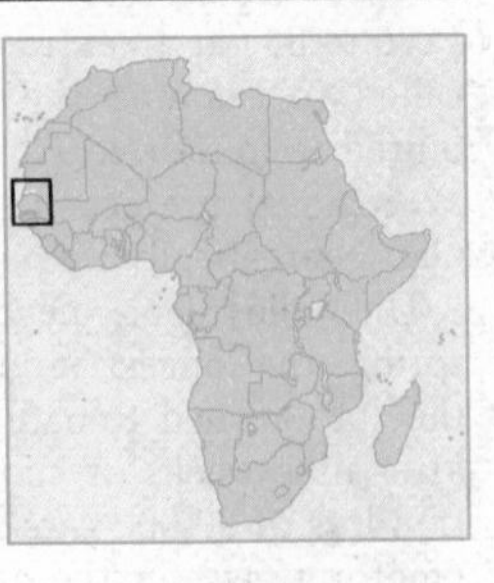

Gambia, The

A small republic and member of the Commonwealth of Nations, The Gambia extends from the Atlantic Ocean along the lower Gambia River in West Africa and is surrounded by Senegal. Area: 4,467 sq.mi. (11,569 sq.km.). Pop. (1975 est.): 524,000, including (1973) Malinke 42.3%; Fulani 18.2%; Wolof 15.7%; Dyola 9.5%; Soninke 8.7%; others 5.6%. Cap. and largest city: Banjul (pop., 1975 est., 42,400). Language: English (official). Religion: predominantly Muslim. President in 1975, Sir Dawda Jawara.

The Gambia celebrated ten years of independence in February 1975 in an atmosphere of political stability and economic confidence. Relations with Senegal improved following visits to Banjul by Premier Abdou Diouf in April and Pres. Léopold Senghor in June. Land and sea boundaries—important for fishing and potential offshore oil—were finally agreed upon. In March President Jawara visited Moscow, where he obtained a fishing aid agreement in return for granting the U.S.S.R. long-term rights in Gambian waters. China made The Gambia a five-year, interest-free loan of 28 million dalasis, largely for irrigation. Britain remained The Gambia's chief economic partner, however, providing £2.8 million for fishery development and a river communications vessel in 1975.

A record peanut (groundnut) crop of over 140,000 tons obviated President Jawara's call to "tighten belts." The president also urged Gambians to become development-oriented, since national projects were falling behind their targets. Nevertheless, the value of external trade had risen 30%, and the economic position was healthy, even though peanuts still constituted 95% of export earnings. (MOLLY MORTIMER)

[978.E.4.b.ii]

GAMBIA, THE

Education. (1974–75) Primary, pupils 22,629, teachers 854; secondary, pupils 5,791, teachers 314; teacher training, students 99, teachers 16; higher, students 272, teaching staff 29.

Finance and Trade. Monetary unit: dalasi, with (Sept. 22, 1975) a free rate of 1.93 dalasi to U.S. $1 (par value of 4 dalasis = £1 sterling). Budget (1974–75 est.): revenue 23,689,000 dalasis; expenditure 23,953,000 dalasis. Foreign trade (1974): imports 79,520,000 dalasis; exports 72,190,000 dalasis. Import sources (1973–74): U.K. 24%; China 10%; The Netherlands 6%; France 5%; Poland 5%; U.S. 5%; Senegal 5%. Export destinations: U.K. 37%; France 23%; The Netherlands 17%; Portugal 8%; West Germany 7%; Italy 6%. Main exports peanuts and products 94%.

Gambling

For the majority of proprietors of both legal and illegal gambling operations, there was no economic recession in 1975. The "handle," or wagered money, taken on U.S. pari-mutuel harness races and in Las Vegas casinos had already reached record highs in 1974 and gave strong indications that the trend would continue. As both local and national governments considered plans to move into increased competition with organized crime and the small operator, they justified the legalization of gambling less as a deterrent to illegal bookmaking and more as a major source of revenue. The Soviet Union, Italy, Israel, and 13 U.S. states, among others, offered lotteries during the year, and New York and at least six other states expressed interest in team-sport betting.

The average bettor, however, was not the only loser in 1975. A number of U.S. state lotteries experienced sagging profits and financial mismanagement; consequently, some games were dropped and others temporarily suspended. And despite the apparently paradoxical nature of U.S. gambling laws, which according to some critics were unnecessarily harsh yet unenforceable, dozens of individuals were indicted during the year for running highly lucrative, illegal bet-taking operations.

Horse Racing. A longtime money-maker for all but the wagerer, the sport of kings remained attractive as a source of revenue. In the U.S. about ten cents of each $2 bet placed legally went to taxes. North American Thoroughbred tracks handled about $5.4 billion in 1974, and 1975 estimates were running slightly ahead. According to the United States Trotting Association, harness racing's pari-mutuel handle for 1974 soared to a record $2.4 billion, with state tax revenue increasing 4.7% over 1973; total wagers in 1975 were expected to reach $2.6 billion. Canada's Department of Agriculture, which supervised the country's horse-racing operations, reported a total of $871.5 million in pari-mutuel betting during 1974, a gain of 18% over the 1973 figure.

Recent years had seen a trend toward what was called exotic betting; for example, picking the first two or three finishers in a single race or the winners of several races. Because of the enormous odds against success, payoffs often ran as high as $100,000 on a $2 bet. For some, such rewards provided an irresistible motivation to cheat. In 1975 courts took action on the two biggest scandals in racing history, both of which had involved exotic betting. In Maryland four jockeys were found guilty of fixing a "triple" race (picking the first three finishers in order) at a St. Valentine's Day program. They became the first athletes to be convicted in a U.S. federal court of conspiracy to fix a sporting event. A 1974 French steeplechase event in which the bettors also attempted to pick the first three finishers ended in suspicious fashion; the favourites trailed the rest of the field by many lengths and a score of jockeys and trainers were subsequently jailed.

In the U.K., where it had been legal for many years to make off-track bets, most of the handle was not registered with the official pari-mutuel machines but with the bookmakers, who decided the odds on each horse for themselves. On the other hand, France, which had pioneered off-track pari-mutuel betting, allowed each bet placed in thousands of cafés, tobacco

UPI COMPIX

The first ticket from the drum is drawn by a nurse in Dublin. The lucky winner of the Irish Hospitals Sweepstakes in 1975 was $840,000 richer.

shops, and other locations to be included in the pari-mutuel system and, thus, to help determine the odds. Until recently, however, the U.S. citizen who wanted the convenience of not needing to travel to the track had to deal with illegal bookmakers.

With promises of a financial windfall and the demise of the illegal bookie parlour, New York City opened the Offtrack Betting Corporation (OTB) in 1971. During its first three fiscal years, OTB lived up to expectations, increasing its handle from an annual $292 million to almost $800 million. But in the fiscal year ended June 30, 1975, despite more than 3,000 employees and an expanded network of OTB betting parlours, its handle dropped to $758 million. OTB president Paul R. Screvane predicted that for the next fiscal year the handle would slip again to $700 million. Though citing as causes the economic recession and widespread unemployment, he placed most of the blame on the New York state legislature, which had imposed a 5% surcharge effective July 1974 on all OTB winning tickets, thus making them less profitable for the bettor than those at the track. Screvane suggested OTB expansion into greyhound racing and jai alai to bolster revenues.

Casinos. In Nevada, the only U.S. state where gambling was not only legal but a major industry, casinos continued to demonstrate their imperviousness to economic crises. Nevada gambling establishments in 1974 took in a record $1 billion-plus, and figures for the first nine months of 1975 showed a gain of 17% over the corresponding period of the previous year. One Las Vegas official noted that, despite the record handles, gasoline consumption was down 3.1%, an indication that fewer people were arriving by car. On the other hand, he noted that plane travel was up 7.9%, a sign that the "high rollers" were still affluent.

Las Vegas casinos along The Strip but outside the city proper were given permission by the county liquor and gaming board to award prizes ranging from $20 to $15,000 for winning bets in lieu of cash; "downtown" casinos had already been operating for some time under such authority. Some concern was voiced, however, about the possible appearance of outlandish and cheapening advertisements for jackpot prizes outside casinos competing for patrons.

In August, after wagering $3, a 25-year-old Las Vegas resident collected the world's largest slot-machine payoff—$152,683. The pot had been building up in the machine in a Las Vegas hotel since December 1973.

Casino-type gambling became increasingly popular outside Nevada as churches, veterans' posts, and other charitable organizations pursued the monetary benefits of "Las Vegas nights." A number of states and cities lent their support by considering or approving constitutional amendments and legislation that permitted such games of chance to be operated by nonprofit groups, though not by private entrepreneurs.

Two New York state legislators took a large step toward Nevada-style gambling by calling for public hearings on a bill that would set the stage for the establishment of state-operated casinos by 1978. If passed, the legislation would let voters decide in a 1977 referendum if the state constitution should be so amended. Of the net profits from the casinos, half would belong to the state, one-fourth to the local government in which the casino was located, and the remainder to other local governments within the state. Mere passage of the bill, however, was considered a gamble in itself; the odds against its adoption ranged from 2–1 to 75–1.

Lotteries. Most lotteries owed their success to the lure of easy fortunes for only a small investment. Many countries sponsored national lotteries, which gave people a chance to become instant millionaires while financing their governments. In Australia the Sydney Opera House, whose escalating construction costs ultimately reached $140 million, finally emerged from debt in August, with great assistance from a lottery operated by the state of New South Wales. Nationally televised drawings with million-dollar first prizes highlighted Olympic Lottery Canada, a revenue-raising plan to help finance site construction for the 1976 summer Olympic Games at Montreal. Though by 1975 the original construction-cost estimates of about $220 million had more than doubled, the lottery's success already had far exceeded all predictions and was expected to provide revenues of up to $200 million.

The elegant Monte Carlo casino in Monaco.

AUTHENTICATED NEWS INTERNATIONAL

In the U.S. lottery proponents sought and gained increased legal approval for game operations. On January 2 Pres. Gerald Ford signed a bill exempting state lotteries from federal antigambling regulations to permit the transportation, mailing, and broadcasting of advertisements and information concerning the games. The legislation followed threatened legal action in 1974 by the attorney general's office, which would have sought permanent injunctions against the lotteries of 13 states. In the wake of this new law, the National Association of Broadcasters amended its television code to permit advertising of legally conducted state lotteries; the change in the NAB code also allowed the advertising of legalized betting on sports events.

For some U.S. states, the lottery proved itself a panacea for ailing budgets. Prospering well in September at the end of its first year, the Illinois lottery showed a gross income from ticket sales of more than $144 million, of which $64.9 million was paid back in prizes. Subtracting sellers' commissions, handling fees, and operating expenses, the state's take amounted to $64.6 million. Connecticut, whose three-year-old lottery was earning an annual $16 million for the general fund, instituted a second game specifically designed to raise funds for public schools in the poorer towns of the state.

Yet, what often was called the legal numbers racket also took a considerable beating in 1975, both from critics and, in some cases, from an uninterested public. In April, Delaware was forced to halt a new 50-cent lottery based on the outcome of horse races when its weekly ticket sales fell from an initial high of 172,000 to fewer than 50,000 in the fourth week. Sales originally had been expected to produce a first prize of up to $20,000 each week, but after four weeks the accumulated total of the first-prize pool amounted to less than $12,000.

All of New York's state lotteries were suspended in October when a programming error was discovered to have caused the printing of hundreds of duplicate tickets for a special $1.4 million jackpot drawing. Ironically, the special game had been devised to counteract the low popularity of the state's weekly lottery, which had been described by some critics as systematic cheating because of its practice of allowing both sold and unsold tickets the same chance of winning. The special jackpot was to have helped distribute the accumulated surplus of unwon prizes from the regular game. Further investigation by an independent management consulting firm uncovered opportunities for fraud, lax security, and other problems, and in November Gov. Hugh Carey dismissed the entire staff of the Lottery Commission and ordered a sweeping reorganization of the lottery operation.

Sports Betting. In the U.K., where bookmaking was legal, bets continued to be accepted on almost anything—sporting events, the Miss Universe contest, the space race, and even the probability of a white Christmas (in 1974, for example, the odds were 4–1 against snow falling on the Ministry of Air building in London). For the fiscal year ended in 1975, the

British government's receipts from gambling and gaming totaled $480 million, up 29% from a year earlier. By contrast, in the U.S., except for state-operated horse-race betting at the track, licensed bookmakers in Nevada, and New York's unique OTB, almost all such gambling was illegal. It was not known how much money was bet with illegal bookmakers, but estimates placed the figure at a colossal $50 billion annually for sports events alone.

In February the U.S. Commission on the Review of the National Policy Toward Gambling, created by the Organized Crime Control Act of 1970, opened hearings to consider the legalization of sports-events betting. The eight members of Congress and seven presidential appointees who comprised the panel heard testimony from the commissioners of professional football, baseball, basketball, and ice hockey, as well as from representatives of the Amateur Athletic Union and the National Collegiate Athletic Association. All argued against legalized betting, asserting that it would undermine the public's perception of integrity in team sports and raise suspicions of game fixing with every controversial play. Charles Morin, chairman of the gambling commission, called the arguments unconvincing because heavy betting, albeit in illegal form, already existed without apparent adverse effects on team sports. Later in the year, George Schwartz, president of the Philadelphia City Council, expressed his support before the panel for the legalization of sports betting, and OTB president Screvane predicted that a future New York state constitutional amendment would permit his corporation to book sports events within three years.

A new U.S. law, effective Jan. 1, 1975, reduced from 10 to 2% the federal excise tax that sports bettors were required to pay with every wager placed with Nevada's licensed bookmakers. The old 10% tax had made it virtually impossible for legal bookmaking firms to compete with illegal bet takers.

(MICHAEL KATZ)

See also Equestrian Sports.
[452.C.2]

Games and Toys

By comparison with previous years the atmosphere at 1975's international toy fairs was somewhat sober. At Brighton, England, the first of the major fairs, the mood reflected the prevailing economic gloom. The well-established product lines from the major toy manufacturers were most favoured by buyers. At Harrogate, Britain's smaller toy fair, there was an increase in attendance of nearly 8%, and business was much better than had been expected.

The fair at Nürnberg, West Germany, premier showcase of the industry, was much quieter than usual, and many West German manufacturers found levels of orders well down. The Milan, Italy, toy fair attracted 900 exhibitors from 26 countries; business there, too, was somewhat slow, with buyers showing preference for medium-priced products. The Salon International du Jouet in Paris had 560 exhibitors from 22 countries, and attendance, at 16,000, showed a 7% increase from the previous year.

At the American Toy Fair in New York City, Merlin Birk, president of Toy Manufacturers of America, predicted that U.S. wholesale toy sales in 1975 would rise about 10% above 1974's $3 billion level. This would be a return to the average level of

KEYSTONE

Child programmer Richard Scriver tries out a new miniature computer. Designed for use by a 12-year-old, it can play games and solve simple problems.

growth achieved by the U.S. industry from the mid-1960s through 1973, as against 6% in 1974.

As the year progressed it became apparent that the toy industry had been less affected than others by the world recession, and confidence returned. In June, Arthur Katz, deputy chairman of Mettoy Co. Ltd., one of the biggest British toymakers, and president of the British Toy Manufacturers Association (BTMA), forecast a minimum 5% growth rate for the year.

Two particular sectors, indoor games and craft and hobby items, were in fact growing rapidly as people tended to spend more time in their homes. Toymakers had come to realize that indoor games and crafts could be enjoyed by a very wide age range. Similarly, many craft and hobby items could be enjoyed by adults as much as by children. This was an important consideration for two reasons: the age up to which children would accept toys was falling (and was currently estimated to be as low as nine years); and birthrates were also falling.

Monopoly (boosted by the first European and world championships, held in Iceland and Washington, D.C.), Scrabble, and Risk continued to be among the most popular games, while Master Mind, a codebreaking game from the U.K., enjoyed good sales. Several action games also found sizable markets. These included Celebrity Tennis, which could be played in small lawn and driveway areas; Paddle Puff Tennis, an indoor version; and Auto-Score Basketball, featuring pushbuttons that allowed each player to shoot the ball from different angles.

A traditional toy that made one of its periodic returns to favour in 1975 was the yo-yo, now most often made of plastic rather than wood. Dolls accounted for about 11% of U.S. toy sales in 1975 with baby dolls the most popular. Innovations included a walking doll whose right and left legs move when its right and left hands are squeezed, and a "growing up" doll that increases in height and develops breasts. A popular action figure was the Six Million Dollar Man, based on the "bionic man" in the television series of the same name. Kites found considerable favour, including a hand-painted model from China made of silk paper and bamboo. One of the year's major fads in the U.S. was the "Pet Rock," an egg-shaped stone

WIDE WORLD

With a rotation of her arm, this new doll by Mattel approaches womanhood as she becomes 3/4 of an inch taller, slims at the waist, and develops a modest bust line.

handsomely packaged and offered as an "easily trainable" pet that required "little care."

Hong Kong remained the largest producer of toys, with annual export sales approaching $380 million, approximately two-thirds higher than either Japan or Great Britain. However, costs, particularly wages, were rising rapidly, and countries such as Taiwan, Brazil, South Korea, and Spain, which could still manufacture toys relatively cheaply, were expanding their business at Hong Kong's expense.

Apart from market prospects, a constant concern of toy manufacturers was product safety. In 1960 the BTMA had collaborated with the British Standards Institution in publishing a code of safety requirements for toys and playthings. Manufacturers' membership in the BTMA was made conditional upon observance of the code, which was eventually used as the basis for British government legislation covering the manufacture of toys and also as the model on which many other national standards were based. Considerable efforts were being made in 1975 to harmonize the various safety standards adopted throughout the world so as to achieve uniformity. In the European Economic Community, for example, all member countries would have to comply with a common safety code, which was being prepared in 1975. In the U.S. the Food and Drug Administration decided to discontinue its annual list of unsafe toys because manufacturers had greatly improved the safety of their products. (GORDON A. WEBB)

See also Board Games.
[452.B.6 and C-D]

Gardening

Towering 21 ft. 5½ inches, this sunflower won £1,400 for Mr. and Mrs. Frank Kellard of Exeter, England, in a national competition.

THE TIMES

There was a tremendous increase in the sales of foliage house plants in the U.S. during the year (in 1973 they totaled $111.3 million, an increase of $43 million over 1972). This was accompanied by greater concern about the quality of plants being sold. Most were grown in Florida, California, and Texas under a light intensity of 2,000 or more foot-candles. In the average home, however, away from a window facing south, the light intensity usually is less than 100 foot-candles. This is too great a change in environment, and all too often the plants lose most of their leaves or die within a few weeks. It was hoped that light acclimatization, the gradual adjustment of a plant to lower light intensity, could be improved for most plants, thus providing the consumer with a plant better adapted to indoor survival. According to Charles A. Conover, director, University of Florida Agricultural Research and Educational Center, Apopka, this is accomplished by subjecting the plant to gradually decreased light intensities over several weeks.

In Europe the trend toward growing house plants, especially those with ornamental foliage, in hydroponic systems was increasing. Garden rock wool blocks or Argex expanded clay granules were used as a growing medium. Plants grouped together in gravel beds in offices or public buildings and equipped with subirrigation and added nutrients grew well and required a minimum of maintenance. Cyclamen, a popular flowering plant, was improved by the introduction of F_1 hybrid cultivars raised in West Germany. Called Rosamund, Salmon Red, Swan Lake, and Merry Widow, they proved popular because of their uniformity, shorter growing period (five–eight months), free flowering, and long-lasting attributes.

COURTESY, BURPEE SEEDS

The new white marigold became the costliest flower in the world as David Burpee ended his 56-year search and awarded Mrs. Alice Vonk $10,000 for the treasured seed.

After a long, wet winter, the summer of 1975 in Europe was in direct contrast to 1974, being long, hot, and dry. Difficult soil conditions hampered sowing and planting, and as a result there was a great increase in the area of land sown and planted without cultivation—the weeds having been burnt off with paraquat. The upsurge in homegrown food continued, encouraged by rising unemployment and financial stringency, especially in the U.K. The season favoured the spread of Dutch elm disease, and the virulent strain in the U.K. continued to spread, killing elms of all ages.

A rare and priceless collection of 50 bonsai plants was presented to the American people by the Nippon Bonsai Association of Japan to commemorate the U.S. bicentennial. The plants were to be housed at the U.S. National Arboretum, Washington, D.C., where a viewing pavilion was being designed to permit visitors to see them to best advantage. The full collection was expected to be available for public viewing in July 1976, when formal ceremonies were planned.

In 1945 David Burpee, head of W. Atlee Burpee Co., one of the largest mail-order seed houses in the U.S., offered to pay $10,000 to the first person to come up with a white marigold. The search ended in 1975. Burpee made payment to Mrs. Alice Vonk, a gardener from Sully, Iowa, after the three judges decided her entry met all the requirements. In recent years the marigold had become a favourite of many vegetable gardeners because it was thought to repel rabbits and rid the soil of nematode worms.

Work continued on development of methods for the mechanical picking of all fruit crops. This involved the use of prototype harvesting machines and the breeding of new cultivars suited to this method of picking. The Romanian Fruit Institute established a museum-type collection of fruit of 3,500 types to facilitate the breeding of new cultivars, especially by the exchange of pollen with plant breeders working in other countries.

A new pear, named California, was developed by the department of pomology at the University of California, Davis, and would be available soon to California commercial growers. The fruit has a tantalizing aroma and delicious flavour and was expected to be used as a fresh fruit dessert and shipped throughout the country.

Scientists at Michigan State University discovered that the time needed to produce plantable trees and shrubs could be reduced considerably by growing them in large nursery houses using special lighting to supplement the daylight hours. Both conifer and deciduous species could be grown year-round until the desired size was reached. The system, called "Accel-O-Gro," also aids research, it was claimed, since the trees appear to reach sexual maturity much more rapidly.

Four new roses won 1976 All-America awards. They were America, a pink climber; Cathedral, an apricot floribunda; Seashell, a peach hybrid tea; and Yankee Doodle, a pink-yellow hybrid tea.

Three new flowers won awards in the 1975 All-America Selections: a dahlia mixture with bronze foliage called Redskin; a hybrid giant-flowered, heat resistant blue pansy called Imperial Blue; and a hybrid dwarf-flowered, fragrant red carnation called Juliet. There were three new hybrid vegetables attaining All-America winner status for 1975, namely, broccoli, Premium Crop; cauliflower, Snow Crown; and a yellow fleshed watermelon called Yellow Baby.

The U.K. Royal National Rose Society awarded the 1975 Henry Edland Memorial Medal for the most fragrant rose to Harry Edland, raised by R. Harkness & Co. Ltd. The gold medal and Uladh award at the City of Belfast International Rose Trials went to Fragrant Hour, a hybrid tea rose raised by Sam McGredy Roses International, New Zealand, and the Golden Thorn was won by Scherzo, a florabunda raised by Meilland of France. The Golden Rose of The Hague was awarded to Satchmo, raised by Sam McGredy Roses International.

Owners of Chinese chestnut trees were warned by the U.S. Department of Agriculture to check them for gall wasp, an oriental pest recently discovered for the first time in the U.S. The wasp is very small, about $\frac{1}{8}$ in. (3 mm.) long, black, with clear wings. Suspected findings should be reported to state or federal plant protection officials. The gall wasps were responsible for significant reductions in Chinese chestnut yields in Korea and Japan, and may even kill trees.

(J. G. SCOTT MARSHALL; TOM STEVENSON)

See also Agriculture and Food Supplies; Life Sciences.
[355.C.2–3; 731.B.1]

Geography

For geography, the 1960s may have been characterized as a period of rapprochement with modern science and increasing contact with other disciplines. The geographers' responses to the 1970s appeared to move from this self-conscious scientism toward humanistic and applied approaches to current educational, social, and environmental problems. In practical terms, opportunities for nonacademic employment and for multidisciplinary applied research continued to increase in 1975, while employment possibilities in institutions of higher education decreased.

Various subfields within geography, such as medical geography, transportation geography, and spatial analysis and modeling, continued to be redefined during the year according to contemporary problem areas. In addition, U.S. geographers began renewing their interests in foreign area studies, especially in non-Western and third world countries. A small but important publication, recently released by the Association of American Geographers (AAG), *The Underdevelopment and Modernization of the Third World* by Anthony R. de Souza and Philip W. Porter, examined the theories, literature, and models of underdevelopment and suggested that, despite important research efforts, much is still obscure about important aspects of underdevelopment.

The AAG completed a three-year project on comparative metropolitan analysis. A comprehensive atlas of the 20 largest standard metropolitan statistical areas in the U.S., *Comparative Atlas of America's Great Cities: Twenty Metropolitan Regions,* was scheduled to be published in 1976. Two companion volumes were also forthcoming: *Contemporary Metropolitan America: Twenty Geographical Vignettes,* and *Urban Policy Making and Metropolitan Dynamics: A Comparative Geographical Analysis.*

Seventeen U.S. geographers participated in two joint seminars with their Soviet and Hungarian counterparts to foster scientific cooperation between U.S. geographers and those of Eastern Europe. Both seminars focused on the urban environment. The Hungarian seminar, held in Budapest, considered "Geographical Characteristics of Urban Development"; the Soviet seminar, in Moscow, developed the theme of "Environment of Present and Future Cities."

A group of social and behavioural scientists, including many geographers, collaborated at the University of Colorado on a three-year assessment of research on natural hazards. Their recently released publication, *Assessment of Research on Natural Hazards* by Gilbert F. White, J. Eugene Haas, and others, provides a balanced and comprehensive basis for judging the social utility of allocating funds and personnel for various types of research on geophysical hazards. The authors hoped that the analysis would appraise the research needs systematically for policymakers.

The growth and health of the discipline of geography was exemplified by the assembly of more than 2,000 geographers in Milwaukee, Wis., in April for the largest annual meeting in the history of the AAG. In an address at the meeting, Julian Wolpert exhorted geographers to engage in social action and research on the problems of the "hidden minorities" of the population and to serve as volunteers to assist in their reintegration into community life.

In October more than 100 women attended the 50th anniversary meeting of the Society of Woman Geographers, in New York. Meanwhile, however, the 124-year-old American Geographical Society of New York (AGS), home of the major geographical research library in the U.S. and repository of one of the most comprehensive map collections in the world, was in serious financial trouble. Massive efforts were under way in an attempt to save this unique and important national resource. During 1975 the AGS produced two major publications, a new map of the Arctic region and Folio 19 of the Antarctic map folio series. The latter presents concepts of Antarctica from A.D. 43 to the 20th century and summarizes the objectives and accomplishments of Antarctic expeditions from 1772 to 1975.

The National Geographic Society, the world's largest, continued to support research on a broad range of natural and social science research projects at field sites scattered throughout the world. During 1975 more than 100 research scientists received financial support from the society. In September the society initiated a new children's magazine in geography,

Garment Industry:
see Fashion and Dress; Industrial Review
Gas Industry:
see Energy
Gemstones:
see Industrial Review
Genetics:
see Life Sciences
Geochemistry:
see Earth Sciences

DON HOGAN CHARLES—THE NEW YORK TIMES

Resurveying the 312-mile Mason-Dixon Line are members of the National Geodetic Survey who are replacing missing monuments along the boundary.

World. The November issue of *National Geographic* featured some new insights into the voyages of Columbus, and in the December issue a major definitive coverage of the Mayan civilization appeared. The journal also featured illustrated articles on exploration, environmental hazards, ice age man, oil and Iran, the impact of modernization on primitive cultures, the Mid-Atlantic Ridge, and the world's food supply.

(SALVATORE J. NATOLI)

See also Earth Sciences.

[10/33.B.1]

ENCYCLOPÆDIA BRITANNICA FILMS. *The Earth: Man's Home* (1970).

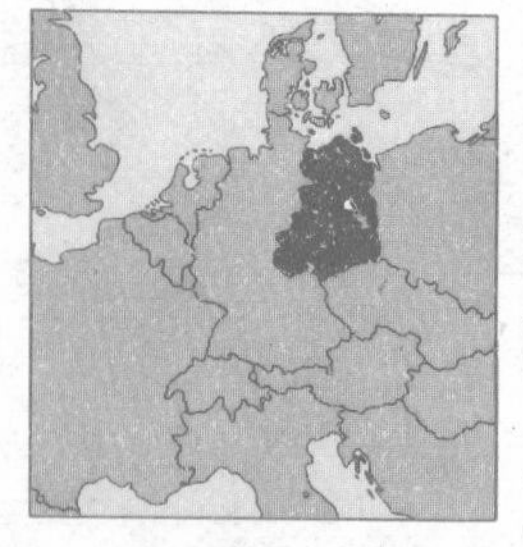

German Democratic Republic

A country of central Europe, Germany was partitioned after World War II into the Federal Republic of Germany (Bundesrepublik Deutschland; West Germany) and the German Democratic Republic (Deutsche Demokratische Republik; East Germany), with a special provisional regime for Berlin. East Germany is bordered by the Baltic Sea, Poland, Czechoslovakia, and West Germany. Area: 41,768 sq.mi. (108,178 sq.km.). Pop. (1975 est.): 16,890,800. Cap. and largest city: East Berlin (pop., 1975 est., 1,094,100). Language: German. Religion (1969 est.): Protestant 80%; Roman Catholic 10%. First secretary of the Socialist Unity (Communist) Party (SED) in 1975, Erich Honecker; chairman of the Council of State, Willi Stoph; president of the Council of Ministers (premier), Horst Sindermann.

In August the government announced that the prices of gasoline, gas, coal and electricity, cement, and several other commodities would rise substantially at the beginning of 1976, largely because of the U.S.S.R.'s decision early in the year to charge more for its raw material exports. Assurances by leaders of the Socialist Unity Party that these increases would have little effect on the nation were undercut by warnings that everybody would have to work harder if East Germany was to maintain its rising standard of living.

By any standards East Germans had prospered in the past few years. Approximately 500,000 housing units had been built after 1971. Real wages had risen by nearly 25% as had pensions and maternity benefits, while prices for most consumer goods and basic foodstuffs remained stable as a result of huge government subsidies. Erich Honecker, first secretary of the SED, thus delivered on the promise of a better, more relaxed life that he had made when he took over as East Germany's leader from Walter Ulbricht in 1971. Party leaders confirmed that the nation's capital investment program, including the ambitious plan to build or modernize three million housing units by 1990, would continue. Prices of basic foodstuffs and rents were expected to remain low, but observers believed that other prices would have to go up.

Speaking at the 14th session of the Central Committee of the SED in Berlin in June, Honecker said that, in looking back, East Germans could say they had achieved great things. Great strides had been made in building an advanced socialist society. The growing stability and authority of the workers' and farmers' state, the efficiency of its national economy, and the marked progress in raising the people's living standard reflected the success of the policies of the party and the government. The growth of production was higher than in past five-year periods.

In October East Germany signed another treaty of friendship with the Soviet Union, the third since the formation of the German Democratic Republic. In contrast to the treaties of 1955 and 1964, the new treaty contained no reference to German unity or to the possibility of German reunification. On the question of Berlin it stated that both sides, in accordance with the 1972 four-power agreement, wished to develop their relations with West Berlin on the understanding that the Western sector of the city was not

GERMAN DEMOCRATIC REPUBLIC

Education. (1972–73) Primary, pupils 2,608,074; secondary, pupils 51,609; primary and secondary, teachers 151,989; vocational, pupils 431,931, teachers 14,692; teacher training, students 25,443; higher (including 7 universities), students 308,064.

Finance. Monetary unit: Mark of Deutsche Demokratische Republik, with (Sept. 22, 1975) a nominal exchange rate of M. 2.60 to U.S. $1 (M. 6 = £1 sterling). Budget (1973 est.): revenue M. 94,926,000,000; expenditure M. 93,260,000,000. Net material product (at 1967 prices): (1973) M. 126.7 billion; (1972) M. 120.1 billion.

Foreign Trade. (1973) Imports M. 27,330,000,000; exports M. 26,171,000,000. Import sources: U.S.S.R. 32%; Czechoslovakia 9%; West Germany 8%; Poland 8%; Hungary 6%. Export destinations: U.S.S.R. 38%; Czechoslovakia 10%; Poland 9%; West Germany 7%. Main exports (1970): machinery 38%; transport equipment 11% (ships and boats 5%); chemicals; lignite; textiles; furniture.

Transport and Communications. Roads (1973) 129,900 km. (45,645 km. main roads, including 1,495 km. autobahns). Motor vehicles in use (1973): passenger 1,539,000; commercial 216,250. Railways: (1973) 14,317 km. (including 1,383 km. electrified); traffic (1974) 19,737,000,000 passenger-km., freight 49,167,000,000 net ton-km. Air traffic (1973): 1,120,000,000 passenger-km.; freight 30.8 million net ton-km. Navigable inland waterways in regular use (1973) 2,546 km.; freight traffic 1,884,000,000 ton-km. Shipping (1974): merchant vessels 100 gross tons and over 431; gross tonnage 1,223,859. Telephones (Dec. 1973) 2,326,000. Radio licenses (Dec. 1973) 6,082,000. Television licenses (Dec. 1973) 4,966,000.

Agriculture. Production (in 000; metric tons; 1974; 1973 in parentheses): wheat *c.* 3,250 (*c.* 2,861); rye *c.* 1,900 (1,699); barley *c.* 3,250 (2,848); oats *c.* 840 (805); potatoes *c.* 13,404 (11,401); sugar, raw value *c.* 577 (*c.* 584); cabbages (1973) *c.* 426, (1972) 426; rapeseed *c.* 280 (246); apples (1973) *c.* 261, (1972) 261; fish catch (1973) 366, (1972) 333. Livestock (in 000; Dec. 1973): cattle 5,482; sheep 1,742; pigs 10,849; goats 78; horses used in agriculture 82; poultry 45,667.

Industry. Index of production (1970 = 100): (1974) 129; (1973) 120. Production (in 000; metric tons; 1974): lignite 243,439; coal 592; electricity (kw-hr.) 80,286,000; iron ore (25% metal content) 53; pig iron 2,280; crude steel 6,164; cement 10,100; potash (oxide content; 1973) 2,556; sulfuric acid 1,005; synthetic rubber 139; cotton yarn (1973) 59; rayon, etc., filaments and fibres (1973) 169; passenger cars (units) 155; commercial vehicles (units) 34.

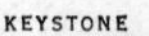
KEYSTONE

The original manuscripts of composer Johann Sebastian Bach were displayed at the International Bach Festival in Leipzig. At left is Bach's first cantata, written in 1708.

part of the Federal Republic of Germany or governed by it.

Western sources felt the new treaty made it clear that the Brezhnev Doctrine (that a Communist bloc state would not be allowed to break free) applied to East Germany. It stated "that the protection of socialist achievements was a common international duty of the socialist countries." Further, the treaty described the inviolability of state borders as "the most important prerequisite of European security." The treaty was signed in Moscow by Honecker and Leonid I. Brezhnev, and the ceremony was shown live on television in all the Eastern European countries. The official reaction in Bonn was that the treaty did not change the aim of the West German government to create conditions in which the German people would be able to attain reunification by peaceful self-determination. Nor did the treaty alter the rights and duties of the four powers and their responsibility for Germany as a whole.

In a declaration in October by the Politburo of the Central Committee of the SED and the Council of Ministers, the Conference on Security and Cooperation in Europe was described as having reinforced the turn from the cold war to détente. In his speech at the conference in Helsinki, Fin., Honecker said that, for the first time, agreement had been reached on a code for the application of the principles of peaceful coexistence between states with different social systems.

The East Germans issued a demand during the year for the return of art treasures that had been removed from museums in the eastern part of Berlin during World War II for safekeeping in the western areas of Germany. Among the notable works were the bust of Queen Nefertiti, excavated at Tell el-Amarna, Egypt, by German archaeologist Ludwig Borchardt in 1912, 21 Rembrandt paintings, among them his "Man with the Golden Helmet," 118 drawings by Rembrandt and 115 by Dürer, 558 pictures from the former Prussian national gallery, a collection of more than 3,000 Egyptian antiquities, and, as the East German Communist Party organ, *Neues Deutschland*, put it, "much more property belonging to our people."

The East Germans based their claim on The Hague convention of 1954, which stated that art treasures transferred during a war should be handed back to their owners after hostilities ceased. The West Germans countered by pointing out that the owner of this property was the state of Prussia, which ceased to exist in 1947 under a law passed by the Allied Control Council. They also argued that The Hague convention applied to countries that had been at war with each other, whereas, when the disputed art objects were moved, the nations now known as the German Democratic Republic and the Federal Republic of Germany comprised the single country of Germany. This issue continued to delay the conclusion of a cultural agreement between the two German states.

(NORMAN CROSSLAND)

[972.A.3.b.iii]

Germany, Federal Republic of

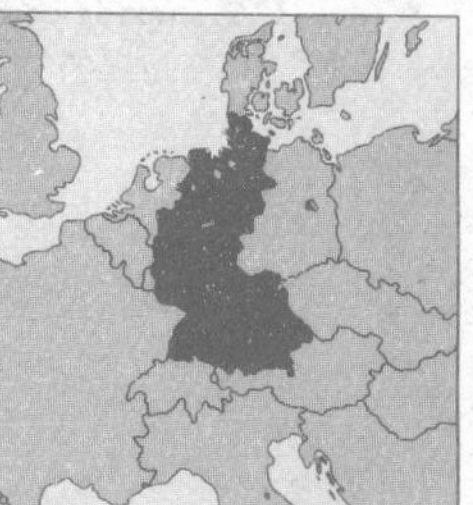

A country of central Europe, Germany was partitioned after World War II into the Federal Republic of Germany (Bundesrepublik Deutschland; West Germany) and the German Democratic Republic (Deutsche Demokratische Republik; East Germany), with a special provisional regime for Berlin. West Germany is bordered by Denmark, The Netherlands, Belgium, Luxembourg, France, Switzerland, Austria, Czechoslovakia, East Germany, and the North Sea. Area: 95,985 sq.mi. (248,601 sq.km.). Pop. (1975 est.): 61,991,000. Provisional cap.: Bonn (pop., 1974 est., 283,300). Largest city: Hamburg (pop., 1974 est., 1,751,600). (West Berlin, which is an enclave within East Germany, had a population of 2,024,000 in 1975.) Language: German. Religion (1970): Protestant 49%; Roman Catholic 44.6%; Jewish 0.05%. President in 1975, Walter Scheel; chancellor, Helmut Schmidt.

Economic affairs dominated the federal government's activities for much of 1975. Unemployment rose to well over a million; many workers were on short time; and prices continued to rise, though not as much as in most other Western countries.

Domestic Affairs. The West Germans took their recession with calm. Political extremism dwindled to insignificance; the discipline of the labour unions played a major role in keeping the rate of inflation enviably lower than in other countries (the average inflation rate was some 6%, about the same as the average rise in wages); and personal savings increased—too much for the government's liking.

The previous year's trend against the Social Democratic Party (SPD) was checked in several state elections. In March 1974 the party had lost 10.4% of its former electoral support in the election of the Hamburg Parliament. In the state election in Schleswig-Holstein in April 1975 the SPD lost only 0.9%, while the Christian Democratic Union (CDU) vote fell by 1.5%. In the election in North-Rhine Westphalia in May the SPD lost 1% and its coalition partner, the Free Democratic Party (FDP), increased its poll by 1.2%. This was the most populous and industrialized state of the republic, the home of about half the country's unemployed. The extreme right-wing National Democratic Party (NPD) was no longer represented in any state parliament. Justifiably or not, most

Geology:
see Earth Sciences
Geophysics:
see Earth Sciences
German Literature:
see Literature

GERMANY, FEDERAL REPUBLIC OF

Education. (1973–74) Primary, pupils 6,499,-824, teachers 217,839; secondary, pupils 2,872,-195, teachers 134,970; vocational, pupils 2,246,-315, teachers 54,372; higher (including 43 universities), students 729,207, teaching staff 68,-286.

Finance. Monetary unit: Deutsche Mark, with (Sept. 22, 1975) a free rate of DM. 2.66 to U.S. $1 (DM. 5.50 = £1 sterling). Gold, SDRs, and foreign exchange: (June 1975) U.S. $30,926,000,-000; (June 1974) U.S. $32,674,000,000. Budget (federal; 1974 actual): revenue DM. 128.1 billion; expenditure DM. 138.2 billion. Gross national product: (1974) DM. 995.3 billion; (1973) DM. 930.3 billion. Money supply: (March 1975) DM. 142.3 billion; (March 1974) DM. 126.7 billion. Cost of living (1970 = 100): (June 1975) 135; (June 1974) 127.

Foreign Trade. (1974) Imports DM. 177,-970,000,000; exports DM. 230,070,000,000. Import sources: EEC 48% (The Netherlands 14%, France 12%, Belgium-Luxembourg 9%, Italy 8%); U.S. 8%. Export destinations: EEC 45% (France 12%, The Netherlands 10%, Italy 8%, Belgium-Luxembourg 8%, U.K. 5%); U.S. 8%; Switzerland 6%. Main exports: machinery 28%; motor vehicles 12%; iron and steel 12%; chemicals 10%; textile yarns and fabrics 6%. Tourism (1973): visitors 7,474,000; gross receipts U.S. $2,085,000,000.

Transport and Communications. Roads (1973) 459,452 km. (including 5,481 km. autobahns). Motor vehicles in use (1973): passenger 17,036,000; commercial 1,246,000. Railways: (1973) 32,360 km. (including 9,834 km. electrified); traffic (1974) 38,616,000,000 passenger-km., freight 70,178,000,000 net ton-km. Air traffic (1974): 12,472,000,000 passenger-km.; freight 991,332,000 net ton-km. Navigable inland waterways in regular use (1973) 4,393 km.; freight traffic 48,480,000,000 ton-km. Shipping (1974): merchant vessels 100 gross tons and over 2,088; gross tonnage 7,980,453. Telephones (Dec. 1973) 17,803,000. Radio licenses (Dec. 1973) 20,586,000. Television licenses (Dec. 1973) 18,-486,000.

Agriculture. Production (in 000; metric tons; 1974; 1973 in parentheses): wheat 7,722 (7,134); rye 2,543 (2,576); barley 7,074 (6,-622); oats 3,448 (3,045); potatoes 14,547 (13,-676); apples (1973) 2,016, (1972) 1,239; sugar, raw value 2,423 (2,453); wine (1973) 979, (1972) 723; milk 21,563 (21,266); butter 510 (512); cheese 593 (570); beef and veal (1973) 1,070, (1972) 1,153; pork (1973) 2,162, (1972) 2,239; fish catch (1973) 475, (1972) 419. Livestock (in 000; Dec. 1973): cattle 14,364; pigs 20,452; sheep *c.* 908; horses used in agriculture (1973) 283; chickens (1973) 99,712.

Industry. Index of production (1970 = 100): (1974) 112; (1973) 113. Unemployment: (1974) 2.6%; (1973) 1.2%. Fuel and power (in 000; metric tons; 1974): coal 94,878; lignite 126,043; crude oil 6,192; coke (1973) 33,997; electricity (kw-hr.) 311,681,000; natural gas (cu.m.; 1973) 18,659,000; manufactured gas (cu.m.) 17,228,000. Production (in 000; metric tons; 1974): iron ore (28% metal content) 4,442; pig iron 40,505; crude steel 53,226; aluminum 1,013; copper 424; lead 321; zinc 563; cement 35,366; sulfuric acid 5,165; cotton yarn 214; woven cotton fabrics 182; wool yarn 55; rayon, etc., filament yarn 74; rayon, etc., staple fibres 99; nylon, etc., filament yarn 377; nylon, etc., fibres 390; petroleum products (1973) 115,-130; fertilizers (1973–74) nitrogenous 1,473, phosphate 962, potash 2,539; synthetic rubber 335; plastics and resins 6,255; passenger cars (units) 2,839; commercial vehicles (units) 264. Merchant vessels launched (100 gross tons and over; 1974) 2,109,000 gross tons. New dwelling units completed (1974) 604,000.

people appeared to believe that the federal government had got the economy under control and that the situation would improve.

The government had hoped that foreign workers, among whom the unemployment rate was particularly high, would go home in 1975 of their own free will. They did not do so. Indeed, the higher children's allowances, which were introduced at the beginning of the year, prompted many foreign workers to send their families to West Germany. The total number of foreigners in the country grew to some 4.1 million during the year.

In August federal Chancellor Helmut Schmidt prevailed on a rather tense Cabinet to pass measures, including hefty cuts in public spending, to reduce the government's budget deficit in 1976 by DM. 7.9 billion. Cuts were made across the board, but this was no austerity program. From the beginning of 1976 unemployment insurance contributions were to be increased by 1%, but the most painful part of the government's strategy would not come into effect until the beginning of 1977, a few months after the 1976 federal elections. If Schmidt were reelected, he would seek then to increase the value-added tax (VAT) by 2%, a proposal attacked by the unions and by the parliamentary opposition. If the opposition were to retain its slight majority in the upper house of the federal Parliament, the Bundesrat, it could block the passage of legislation raising the VAT and thereby cause a drastic revision of Schmidt's long-term plans for reducing the government's debts. This theorizing did not upset the chancellor. He expected the opposition to maintain its resistance to the VAT increase, on the grounds that it was inflationary, up to the election, but if his coalition won, to forget about it (if only because the state governments, which were represented in the Bundesrat, would not be able to resist the chance to increase their tax revenues).

Rheinstein Castle near Bingen is being offered for $120,000, in contrast to the original asking price of $1.6 million by the duke of Mecklenburg. Another 100 West German castles and country palaces are also for sale, but the maintenance cost is a major deterrent to purchasers.

WIDE WORLD

The long-awaited government program to bolster the economy, also announced in February, caused some disappointment at home and abroad. It totaled DM. 5.5 billion and was principally designed to help the enfeebled construction industry through a difficult winter.

Helmut Kohl (*see* BIOGRAPHY), chairman of the CDU and minister president of the Rhineland Palatinate, was chosen in June as the candidate to contest the chancellorship at the 1976 federal election. The Bavarian Christian Social Union (CSU), which formed a joint parliamentary party with the CDU, had insisted that the candidate should be selected only after the two parties had agreed on a common platform. The CDU jumped the gun when its general secretary and chief strategist, Kurt Biedenkopf, declared that Kohl was the party's best chancellor candidate. On May 12, while the CSU was still working out a policy program, Kohl was officially nominated by the CDU executive committee. This angered the chairman of the CSU, Franz-Josef Strauss, and his colleagues. The CDU was hoping that Kohl would be given the approval of the CSU at the first round of negotiations on June 10, but he was made to wait. The CSU had even considered making a break with the Christian Democrats and fighting the next federal election as an independent party of the right, not just in Bavaria but throughout the country. Eventually, the CSU accepted Kohl, but reluctantly.

Nearly three years after their arrest, the ringleaders of the Baader-Meinhof group of alleged terrorists went on trial in Stuttgart on May 21. Four people who had openly declared war on West German society were in the dock: Ulrike Meinhof, aged 40, former editor of the political magazine *Konkret;* Andreas Baader, 32, who was widely described as the chief of the group; Gudrun Ensslin, a clergyman's daughter and former teacher; and Jan-Carl Raspe, a sociologist. Their activities and those of their supporters outside prison placed the entire country on the alert and caused new laws to be passed, some of which restricted freedom. They were charged with involvement in 5 murders and 71 cases of attempted murder as well as in several bomb attacks and bank raids. Several defense counsel were excluded from the trial on suspicion of having a conspiratorial relationship with the accused under a law specifically enacted to suit this case. In September the court decided to carry on the trial in the absence of the accused. Under another law, drafted with the Baader-Meinhof case in mind, a prisoner who made himself unfit to stand trial might be tried in his absence. The court seized the chance to invoke the new law after psychiatrists and other physicians on September 23 pronounced the four accused to be capable of standing trial "only to a limited extent" and to be in need of treatment. One physician suggested that the proceedings of the court, which met on three days a week, should be limited to three hours a day interspersed with short breaks. The bench calculated that if this course were followed the trial would be likely to last ten years. The court decided on September 30 to exclude the accused from the trial. The defense appealed to the Federal Constitutional Court, which ruled that the prisoners could not be excluded from the trial against their will, although they could stay away if they wished.

Günter Guillaume, whose alleged spying activities had brought about former chancellor Willy Brandt's resignation in 1974, was convicted of treason in Düsseldorf on December 15 and sentenced to 13 years' imprisonment.

The chairman of the West Berlin CDU, Peter Lorenz, was kidnapped by terrorists on February 27. He was released on March 5 after the West German government agreed to the demands of the kidnappers to free five terrorists and fly them out of the country. Another condition was that they should be accompanied on their flight by a former mayor of West Berlin, Heinrich Albertz. As the kidnappers demanded, each of the released prisoners was provided with DM. 20,000. The aircraft finally landed at Aden. After its return with Albertz to Berlin, Lorenz was set free. Chancellor Schmidt said that all the political parties accepted responsibility for the decision.

The state, however, took a tougher line in April when some half-dozen terrorists seized the West German embassy in Stockholm. They shot and fatally wounded the military attaché and held the ambassador and several other members of the staff hostage while demanding the release of 26 prisoners in West Germany, including the leaders of the Baader-Meinhof group. When told that the West German government would not give in to their demands, they blew up the embassy. (*See also* CRIME AND LAW ENFORCEMENT: *Special Report*.)

Foreign Affairs. Agreements were signed in October under which West Germany was to pay Poland DM. 2.3 billion. The outlines of the deal were worked out at Helsinki, Fin., in July when both Schmidt and Edward Gierek, the Polish party leader, attended the Conference on Security and Cooperation in Europe. In a way the agreements were a "fine" on the West German government for not being careful enough over the drafting of the West German-Polish treaty signed in 1970. At that time the Germans thought that the Polish promise to allow people of "indisputably German nationality" to emigrate to West Germany meant that all the Germans still living in Poland and wishing to leave would be able to go. In fact, since the end of 1970, only about 58,000 persons had been permitted to leave. As of 1975 the West German Red Cross still had on its books an additional 284,000 applications from would-be emigrants from Poland. The new agreement provided for another 120,000–125,000 to leave over the next four years. Part of the deal was in the form of a DM. 1 billion loan to Poland at an interest rate of $2\frac{1}{2}\%$ over 25 years. The rest of the money was to cover on a once-and-for-all basis Polish citizens' pensions claims against Germany as well as to compensate Polish victims of German World War II concentration camps.

The military disengagement of the U.S. in Southeast Asia in April prompted a good deal of comment in West Germany about possible lessons to be drawn for the security of Western Europe. Open criticism of the U.S. was carefully avoided, but fears of U.S. isolationism were reawakened. Considerable coverage was given by the newspapers to an opinion poll in the U.S. which showed that only 39% of Americans would favour military action by the U.S. should the Soviet Union occupy West Berlin.

Schmidt paid a five-day visit to China at the end of October and met Chairman Mao Tse-tung. Although the chancellor and the Chinese government did not see eye to eye on the question of the West's relations with the Soviet Union and its satellites, Schmidt was a much more welcome guest in Peking than his predecessor, Willy Brandt, who had been slow to establish diplomatic relations with China, would have been. Schmidt was credited by the Chinese with having a more realistic and less nervous attitude toward the Soviet Union than had Brandt. Nonetheless, Schmidt gave several assurances to the Soviet government that Bonn would not allow its relations with China to hamper East-West détente. Consequently, the chancellor was careful in Peking not to identify himself with the Chinese view of Soviet policy. He told the Chinese that West Germany had adopted a clear policy toward Moscow at a time when the Chinese re-

KEYSTONE

The biggest fire in Germany since 1949 began in the heath area of northern Germany and, following a change in wind direction, spread over an area of 50 square miles. Damages are estimated at $12 million.

garded the Soviets as inseparable friends. There were some practical results of the visit. Two agreements were signed, one laying down regulations for shipping and the other paving the way for opening an air service between West Germany and China.

At the end of September a special Cabinet meeting was held to discuss West Germany's long-range policy toward the European Economic Community (EEC). The ministers talked about possible ways of subjecting the EEC's spending habits to stricter control. One suggestion was for the appointment of a financial commissioner in Brussels, who would have to explain the financial effects of any EEC Commission proposal to the Council of Ministers and the European Parliament, give his views on all Commission proposals that cost money, and have a delaying veto. In short, this commissioner would hold powers in the EEC similar to those held by a finance minister in West Germany.

In October Schmidt sent well-publicized private letters to the rest of the EEC's government leaders and to the EEC Commission saying, in effect, that while West Germany did not begrudge the marks it poured into the EEC, the money must go into programs that promoted European integration instead of financing member governments' private extravagances. The chancellor's sharpest rebukes were reserved for U.K. Prime Minister Harold Wilson. Schmidt asked him to think again about insisting on a separate seat for Britain beside the EEC at the Conference on International Economic Cooperation in Paris in December.

From November 15 to 17 Schmidt took part in a special "summit" meeting at the château of Rambouillet, near Paris, called by Pres. Valéry Giscard d'Estaing of France. Leaders of governments of the U.S., Japan, West Germany, France, Britain, and Italy—the six foremost non-Communist industrial countries—discussed what should be done to restore the world's economic health. Schmidt, in his statement at the conclusion of the conference, recognized that it had produced few detailed agreements, but the general consensus was that the meeting betokened a fresh cooperative approach to problems.

West Berlin. In the election of the city Parliament on March 2, the SPD lost its overall majority. Its share of the poll fell from 50.4 to 42.7%, the party's worst performance in the city since World War II. The Christian Democrats, polling 43.9%, achieved their best result and would probably have done better had it not been for the right-wing party known as Federation for a Free Germany, which managed to poll 3.4%. The Social Democrats were able to stay in power only by forming a coalition with the Free Democrats. The election was undoubtedly influenced by the kidnapping of West Berlin's CDU chairman Peter Lorenz (*see* above), who was in the hands of terrorists on polling day.

The East German authorities, in some cases supported by the Soviet government, continued to protest against any attempt to extend the links between West Berlin and West Germany. In a statement published by the East German Communist Party organ *Neues Deutschland* in January, Erich Honecker, first secretary of the party, said that West Berlin could only maintain such relations with West Germany as it maintained with other nations. The East Germans protested against the participation of the federal government in the Green Week (an agricultural show) in West Berlin and against the plan of the EEC to set up a European centre for vocational training in the city.

In May the refusal of East Berlin border guards to allow West Berlin firemen and police to rescue a boy who had fallen into the Spree River caused the head of the East German mission in Bonn to be summoned to the chancellor's office. He was told that the incident, in which a five-year-old Turkish boy was drowned, had severely strained the efforts of the West German government to improve the climate between the two German states. In October agreement was reached between the West Berlin Senate and the East German government to enable West Berlin services to assist in rescue operations in the Spree in the future, even on those stretches of the river which were completely in East German territory. (NORMAN CROSSLAND)

[972.A.3.b.ii]

Ghana

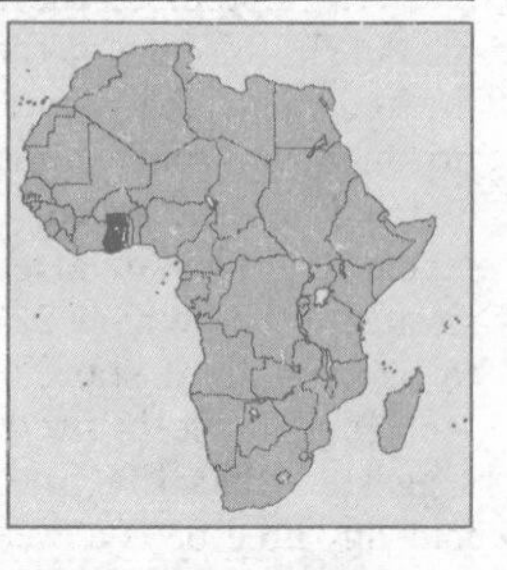

A republic of West Africa and member of the Commonwealth of Nations, Ghana is on the Gulf of Guinea and is bordered by Ivory Coast, Upper Volta, and Togo. Area: 92,100 sq.mi. (238,500 sq.km.). Pop. (1974 est.): 9,607,000. Cap. and largest city: Accra (pop., 1970, 564,200). Language: English (official); local Sudanic dialects. Religion (1960): Christian 43%; Muslim 12%; animist 38%. Chairman of the National Redemption Council and, from Oct. 10, 1975, of the Supreme Military Council, Col. Ignatius Kutu Acheampong.

The National Redemption Council government remained stable in 1975 until October, when it was downgraded in favour of a new legislative and administrative body, the Supreme Military Council. Colonel Acheampong headed both councils. Though rejecting the suggestion of life presidency, Acheampong announced that the military government would stay in office till the goals of the revolution had been achieved. Ghana was host to the February meeting of the Council of Ministers of the African, Caribbean, and Pacific countries for final discussions before the signing of the Lomé Convention in February. It also played an active part as a signatory of the Economic Community of West African States.

Discontent centred on increasing corruption, soaring prices (up 25%), and a budget featuring prestige development projects. Despite a balance of payments deficit of 30 million cedis at the end of 1974 and a gloomy forecast of reduced foreign exchange earnings, the 1975 budget allowed for a capital expenditure of more than 300 million cedis. Although medium-term debts (those not repudiated by the government) had been rescheduled, the balance of payments deficit increased and resources declined as oil prices rose and the demand for gold and timber fell. Despite the need for an increase in foreign investment, the April 30 Investment Policy Decree provided for a large-scale takeover of businesses by Ghanaian citizens; however, the Investment Policy Implementation Committee found that Ghanaians had neither the interest nor the capital to participate in the economy to the extent provided by the law. External aid remained crucial, whether the World Bank's 13 million cedis to develop oil palm in eastern Ghana to supply the soap industry or £10 million from the U.K. to finance agricultural projects. An increasing number of Chinese

GHANA

Education. (Public schools only; 1973) Primary, pupils 1,000,510, teachers 32,147; secondary, pupils 509,174, teachers 19,434; vocational, pupils 10,574, teachers 670; teacher training, students 14,299, teachers 919; higher, students 6,394, teaching staff 978.

Finance. Monetary unit: new cedi, with (Sept. 22, 1975) an official rate of 1.15 cedi to U.S. $1 (free rate of 2.39 cedis = £1 sterling). Gold, SDRs, and foreign exchange: (June 1975) U.S. $161.1 million; (June 1974) U.S. $161.2 million. Budget (1973–74 est.): revenue 561.7 million cedis; expenditure 740.3 million cedis. Gross national product: (1972) 2,787,000,000 cedis; (1971) 2,450,000,000 cedis. Money supply: (Oct. 1974) 649.6 million cedis; (Oct. 1973) 482.3 million cedis. Cost of living (Accra; 1970 = 100): (Dec. 1974) 190; (Dec. 1973) 139.

Foreign Trade. (1974) Imports 945.7 million cedis; exports 868 million cedis. Import sources (1973) U.K. 16%; U.S. 16%; West Germany 12%; Japan 7%; France 6%. Export destinations (1973): U.K. 19%; U.S. 15%; The Netherlands 9%; Japan 9%; West Germany 9%; Italy 7%; U.S.S.R. 6%. Main exports: cocoa 63%; timber 21%; aluminum 7%.

Transport and Communications. Roads (1973) *c.* 31,000 km. Motor vehicles in use (1972): passenger 40,400; commercial (including buses) 31,000. Railways: (1972) 953 km.; traffic (1971) 520 million passenger-km., freight 305 million net ton-km. Air traffic (1973): 150.5 million passenger-km.; freight 2,773,000 net ton-km. Shipping (1974): merchant vessels 100 gross tons and over 77; gross tonnage 173,018. Telephones (Dec. 1973) 52,000. Radio receivers (Dec. 1972) 775,000. Television receivers (Dec. 1973) 25,000.

Agriculture. Production (in 000; metric tons; 1974; 1973 in parentheses): corn *c.* 450 (438); cassava (1973) *c.* 2,100, (1972) 2,813; taro (1973) *c.* 1,120, (1974) *c.* 1,100; yams (1973) *c.* 750, (1972) 660; millet *c.* 120 (109); sorghum *c.* 170 (167); peanuts *c.* 125 (122); cocoa *c.* 386 (343); palm oil *c.* 65 (61); timber (cu.m.; 1973) *c.* 10,100, (1972) 10,100; fish catch (1973) 195, (1972) 281. Livestock (in 000; 1972): cattle *c.* 1,100; sheep *c.* 1,600; pigs *c.* 340; goats (1973) *c.* 1,550.

Industry. Production (in 000; metric tons; 1973): bauxite 349; petroleum products 976; gold (troy oz.) 729; diamonds (metric carats) 2,700; manganese ore (metal content) 313; electricity (kw-hr.; 1972) *c.* 3,344,000.

technicians, under a 1974 agreement, arrived to set up irrigation projects.

The most pressing problems were those of cocoa and smuggling. Cocoa prices fell and production decreased (cocoa accounted for 70% of export earnings), Ghana's proportion of world output having fallen to about 27% from nearly 40% in the 1960s. In February 1975 a special Ministry of Cocoa Affairs was set up, and on International Cocoa Day (May 31) both the ministry and Colonel Acheampong emphasized that cocoa was the lifeblood of Ghana; those who smuggled it out were "enemies of the state." Smuggling, not only of cocoa but also of gold, diamonds, and subsidized gasoline, caused an estimated revenue loss of 26 million cedis a year.

(MOLLY MORTIMER)

[978.E.4.b.ii]

Golf

Once again Jack Nicklaus was the commanding figure in world golf in 1975. Although Johnny Miller, leading money winner the previous year, began the season in explosive fashion by winning the first three U.S. tournaments with scoring of a brilliance that had rarely been approached, he could not prevent Nicklaus from winning the Masters at Augusta, Ga., for a record fifth time. Thereafter Nicklaus, with four more victories including a fourth success in the Professional Golfers' Association (PGA) championship, swept ahead. His total of major championship victories rose to 16, eight more than that of Gary Player, his nearest contemporary rival. In past years Walter Hagen won 11 and Ben Hogan 9.

KEYSTONE

Jack Nicklaus blasts out of a bunker during the British Open at Carnoustie, Scotland.

Throughout the year Nicklaus was rarely out of contention in any event, and for the seventh time in 12 years headed the money-winning list. He just failed to reach $300,000 for the third time, but his total of $298,149 was far ahead of Miller and Tom Weiskopf, his closest pursuers. In the end Nicklaus came closer to achieving the professional Grand Slam (Masters, PGA, and U.S. and British opens) than ever before. In the U.S. Open at Medinah, Ill., he finished only two strokes out of the play-off in which Lou Graham beat John Mahaffey, and he was only one out of that at the British Open, where Tom Watson beat Jack Newton of Australia.

The centrepiece of the year proved to be the Masters, which produced as fine a finish as any championship of modern times. With opening rounds of 68 and 67 Nicklaus appeared to be in complete command, but by the third evening he was one behind Weiskopf, who had a third-round score of 66 to Nicklaus' 73. Miller, who had started the day 11 behind, produced a wonderful round of 65 and gained 8 strokes, but Nicklaus appeared to be undisturbed, as if relishing the prospect of a tremendous contest to come. The final round, indeed, surpassed all expectation. Occasionally in the past two great golfers had fought shot for shot to the bitter end, but rarely, if ever, had three such men done so. Miller shot a 66, giving him an unprecedented total of 131 for the last two rounds, and on the final green he and Weiskopf had eminently makable putts to tie. When Nicklaus, playing ahead of Miller and Weiskopf, stood on the 15th fairway, he was one behind and knew that, almost for certain, he must make a birdie to remain in the running. After a long pause, while he considered the wind, Nicklaus hit a majestic no. 1 iron over the lake to the green, one of the greatest strokes under pressure of his life. The short 16th was, however, even more crucial. While Tom Watson, playing with Nicklaus, was struggling toward a horrific seven, Nicklaus was assessing

Gibraltar: *see* Dependent States
Glass Manufacture: *see* Industrial Review
Gliding: *see* Aerial Sports
Gold: *see* Economy, World; Mining and Quarrying

a putt of 40 ft. Down it went for a two on the hole, and the effect on Miller and Weiskopf, watching from the tee, can be imagined. Weiskopf changed his club, came up short of the green, and took four. Nicklaus was then one stroke ahead of Weiskopf and two ahead of Miller. He parred the last two holes, and then Miller made a birdie on the 17th. He and Weiskopf were even, both needing a birdie on the 18th to tie Nicklaus. After perfect drives and approaches Miller just missed a 20-ft. putt. Weiskopf's putt of 8 ft. seemed certain to drop, but it slipped by the hole. This was a cruel disappointment for Weiskopf, who has finished second in the Masters four times in seven years.

The severity of the course at Medinah, with its great trees overhanging the fairways, dominated the U.S. Open, and rarely have so many unfamiliar names occupied the leading places. After three rounds only Lee Trevino of the eight leaders had won a major championship. Nicklaus, as often before, had slipped behind. Frank Beard, who had not won a tournament for several years, led Tom Watson and Pat Fitzsimons by three strokes. The story of the last day was one of recession, from which the steadiness of Lou Graham and John Mahaffey just prevailed. Everyone else had vulnerable spells, notably Nicklaus, who seemed set to win with par golf but then finished with three bogeys.

Graham, a good but not conspicuously successful player for many years, played fine, composed golf to beat Mahaffey in the play-off, while his opponent, one of the strongest of the new generation, did not putt well. Britain's Peter Oosterhuis, who eventually won over $60,000 in his first season on the U.S. tour, tied for seventh with Nicklaus. Hale Irwin, defending his title, showed that his victory at Winged Foot was no accident by finishing a stroke outside the tie. He had also finished fourth in the Masters with a record-equaling 64 in the last round, and clearly established himself as one of the world's leading golfers. His consistent accuracy from tee to green probably had no equal, and he completed a fine year by retaining the Piccadilly match play championship at Wentworth, Surrey, in which he beat Oosterhuis, Newton, and, in the final, Al Geiberger.

Trevino, Jerry Heard, and Bobby Nichols suffered minor burns when they were struck by lightning during a severe thunderstorm that forced postponement of the second round of the Western Open at Oak Brook, Ill., in June. They spent the next two days in a nearby hospital, and Heard continued playing after their release. The winner of the tournament was Hale Irwin.

The 18th green at Medinah, Illinois, site of the U.S. Open in June.

WIDE WORLD

One of the features of the U.S. season was the success of Geiberger and Gene Littler, both considered veterans. Geiberger won twice and Littler three times, and both won more money than ever before. Littler's golf was remarkable in view of his serious operations three years earlier, and he completed his season by winning the Pacific Masters in Japan for the second successive year. In one of his other victories he beat Julius Boros, aged 55, after a play-off. Billy Casper also had a revival in fortunes, and in all it was a year in which the established players prevailed in America. In the PGA championship at Akron, Ohio, Nicklaus comfortably resisted the challenges of Bruce Crampton and Weiskopf and won by two strokes. This was the fourth time in major championships that Crampton had been second to him, and Weiskopf must have been heartily sick of his friend, Nicklaus, on the golf course. In the World Open at Pinehurst, N.C., Weiskopf missed from 7 ft. on the last green to join Nicklaus and Casper in the play-off, which Nicklaus went on to win.

Carnoustie, Scotland, could never have played more easily than it did for the first three rounds of the British Open. Scores in the middle 60s abounded, and on the third evening Bobby Cole of South Africa, after a 66, led Newton, whose 65 was a record, by one stroke. Miller was one further behind. Although a firm breeze from an unaccustomed direction seemed to favour the more experienced players, Tom Watson and Newton survived a tense finish. Miller, needing a four to tie, drove into a bunker on the 18th and took two to emerge; Cole dropped three strokes on the last five holes. Nicklaus could not redeem his early mistakes, but Watson finished magnificently, playing the last six holes better than anyone and finishing with a birdie to tie Newton. The following day Watson and Newton played a great match, giving precious little away until on the 18th Newton's long iron from the rough hit a bunker near the green. Watson hit a beauty, and finally Newton's putt of 15 ft. to take the Open into its first-ever sudden-death play-off just missed. Watson's performance was the greater for he had failed under the pressure of leading the last two U.S. Opens. He impressed everyone with his cool, intelligent, and pleasant manner. He hit with uncommon power for a lightly built man and clearly was the young player of the year, which he demonstrated again by winning the World Series of Golf. Oosterhuis again was the leading British player, tying for seventh with Neil Coles.

Apart from occasional performances, notably by Brian Barnes, Maurice Bembridge, and Bernard Gallacher, British golfers did not excel in the European tournaments. Dale Hayes of South Africa was the leading money winner with £17,487, and Bob Shearer of Australia finished second. Arnold Palmer's winning days in the U.S. might be over, but he delighted everyone with a spectacular victory in the Spanish Open and then gave a reminder of his greatness in the Penfold PGA championship at Sandwich, Kent. He played superbly in a gale and won the first prize of £10,000.

A strong U.S. team of amateurs, led by Ed Updegraff, several of whom turned professional soon afterward, always had control of the Walker Cup match at St. Andrews, Scotland. Although the British team, notably Mark James, the young English champion, and Richard Eyles, played well in the foursomes, U.S. supremacy in both sessions of singles was never in question. The following week at Hoylake, Cheshire, Marvin Giles swept aside Mark James in the final. In the U.S. amateur championship Fred Ridley from the University of Florida beat Keith Fergus by two holes in the final.

The Ryder Cup match was one-sided from the outset. The U.S. team, one of the most powerful of modern times, took command on the first day and by the second evening needed only four points from 16 singles matches for victory. The British and Irish played as well as could be expected but were outplayed by Palmer's men. Barnes did beat Nicklaus twice on the last day. The U.S. won 21–11.

The U.S. team of Johnny Miller and Lou Graham won the World Cup tournament, held in Bangkok in December. Miller was individual champion with a four-round total of 275. With Graham's 279 the U.S. score was 554, ten strokes ahead of second-place Taiwan. Japan finished third with 565, and Australia was fourth with 566. Trailing Miller in individual scoring were Bob Shearer of Australia, Ben Arda of the Philippines, and Hsieh Min-nan of Taiwan, all of whom tallied 277.

Sandra Palmer won the two most important women's professional events. Unshakable steadiness won her $32,000 in the Colgate-Dinah Shore Winners Circle championship in Palm Springs, Calif. Three months later she was U.S. Open champion, four strokes ahead of Joanne Carner, Sandra Post, and an amateur, Nancy Lopez. Palmer had to be content with second place in the Colgate European championship at Sunningdale, Berkshire, to Donna Caponi Young. The U.S. amateur title was won by 18-year-old Beth Daniel, while Nancy Syms combined a holiday at St. Andrews with victory in the British amateur championship. (P. A. WARD-THOMAS)

[452.B.4.h.xiv]

Greece

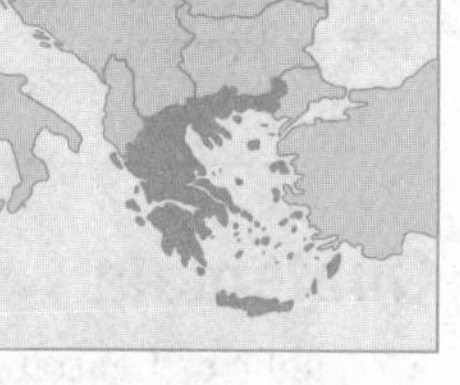

A republic of Europe, Greece occupies the southern part of the Balkan Peninsula. Area: 50,960 sq.mi. (131,986 sq.km.), of which the mainland accounts for 41,227 sq.mi. Pop. (1974 est.): 8,962,000. Cap. and largest city: Athens (pop., 1971, 867,000). Language: Greek. Religion: Orthodox. Presidents in 1975, Michael Stassinopoulos (ad interim) and, from June 20, Konstantinos Tsatsos; prime minister, Konstantinos Karamanlis.

A new constitution establishing a parliamentary republic was voted by Parliament on June 7, 1975. The new charter granted significant executive and legislative prerogatives to the president, elected by a two-thirds majority of the unicameral Parliament for five years. The opposition accused Karamanlis of using his party's large majority to have the charter approved. When, on June 19, this majority elected one of his most trusted associates, 76-year-old Konstantinos Tsatsos (*see* BIOGRAPHY), to be president, it was generally assumed that this was temporary and that Karamanlis proposed to take over as chief of state before Parliament's term expired in 1978. Leftist opposition parties scored major gains in local elections on March 30.

GREECE

Education. (1972–73) Primary, pupils 913,972, teachers 28,424; secondary, pupils 490,867, teachers 14,935; vocational, pupils 123,081; higher (including 5 universities), students 91,309, teaching staff 4,614.

Finance. Monetary unit: drachma, with (Sept. 22, 1975) a free rate of 34.18 drachmas to U.S. $1 (free rate of 70.81 drachmas = £1 sterling). Gold, SDRs, and foreign exchange: (June 1975) U.S. $890.5 million; (June 1974) U.S. $915.4 million. Budget (1975 est.) balanced at 140 billion drachmas (excluding investment of 32 million drachmas). Gross national product: (1973) 488.8 billion drachmas; (1972) 376.8 billion drachmas. Money supply: (Jan. 1975) 108,510,000,000 drachmas; (Jan. 1974) 87,070,000,000 drachmas. Cost of living (1970 = 100): (May 1975) 178; (May 1974) 157.

Foreign Trade. (1974) Imports 131,560,000,000 drachmas; exports 60,890,000,000 drachmas. Import sources: EEC 43% (West Germany 16%, Italy 9%, France 7%, U.K. 5%); U.S. 9%; Japan 6%. Export destinations: EEC 50% (West Germany 21%, Italy 9%, France 6%, U.K. 6%, The Netherlands 5%); U.S. 6%; Libya 5%. Main exports: textile yarns and fabrics 10%; petroleum products 10%; iron and steel 9%; tobacco 8%; dried fruit 5%; fresh fruit 5%; aluminum 5%; chemicals 5%. Tourism (1973): visitors 2,762,000; gross receipts U.S. $512 million.

Transport and Communications. Roads (1973) 36,415 km. (including 65 km. expressways). Motor vehicles in use (1973): passenger 346,762; commercial 150,185. Railways (1973): 2,572 km.; traffic 1,615,000,000 passenger-km., freight 798 million net ton-km. Air traffic (1974): 3,083,800,000 passenger-km.; freight 51,318,000 net ton-km. Shipping (1974): merchant vessels 100 gross tons and over 2,651; gross tonnage 21,759,449. Telephones (Dec. 1973) 1,670,000. Radio receivers (Dec. 1972) *c.* 1.3 million. Television receivers (Dec. 1972) 520,000.

Agriculture. Production (in 000; metric tons; 1974; 1973 in parentheses): wheat *c.* 2,200 (1,738); barley *c.* 980 (857); oats 114 (102); corn 600 (650); potatoes *c.* 708 (733); rice *c.* 93 (82); tomatoes *c.* 1,090 (1,188); onions *c.* 121 (*c.* 184); watermelons (1973) *c.* 630, (1972) 696; apples (1973) *c.* 240, (1972) *c.* 240; oranges (1973) *c.* 450, (1972) 482; lemons (1973) *c.* 150, (1972) 151; sugar, raw value 187 (158); peaches (1973) 250, (1972) 277; olives *c.* 1,020 (950); olive oil *c.* 250 (*c.* 285); wine *c.* 500 (*c.* 500); raisins (1973) *c.* 160, (1972) *c.* 160; figs (1973) *c.* 145, (1972) *c.* 145; tobacco 70 (77); cotton, lint *c.* 120 (108). Livestock (in 000; Dec. 1973): sheep *c.* 8,150; cattle *c.* 1,013; goats (1972) *c.* 4,120; pigs *c.* 700; horses (1972) *c.* 245; asses (1972) *c.* 335; chickens (1972) *c.* 26,900.

Industry. Production (in 000; metric tons; 1974): lignite 13,929; electricity (excluding most industrial production: kw-hr.) 13,722,000; petroleum products (1973) *c.* 10,810; bauxite 2,813; magnesite (1972) 917; cement 7,012; sulfuric acid 886; fertilizers (1973–74) nitrogenous 255, phosphate 163; cotton yarn (1973) 52. Merchant vessels launched (100 gross tons and over; 1974) 141,400 gross tons.

On January 14 the government passed special legislation proclaiming the 1967 coup d'etat a punishable crime. This signaled a series of prosecutions, beginning with that of the military regime's strong man, Gen. (ret.) Dimitrios Ioannidis. The process was speeded up by the discovery in February of a half-baked plot by pro-junta officers to seize control and force the government to grant a general amnesty to the jailed junta leaders. Twenty-one of the officers were court-martialed and 14 were sentenced to prison terms of from 4 to 12 years. The government also dismissed 225 officers who supported the defunct regime.

Georgios Papadopoulos and 19 other junta leaders went on trial for revolt and high treason on July 28. Papadopoulos and his two deputies, Stylianos Pattakos and Nikolaos Makarezos, were sentenced to death, and Ioannidis and seven others were given life imprisonment. Only two were acquitted. The government shocked the opposition by pledging that it would commute the death penalties. On September 12, 16 military police received prison terms of up to 23 years for torturing political prisoners. Some of them were also among 36 officers and privates who were court-martialed in October as torturers but for different instances. In December Papadopoulos, Ioannidis, and a number of army and police generals were convicted of complicity in the massacre after the Polytechnic revolt in November 1973, in which at least 24 civilians were killed.

During 1975 the Greek islands near the Anatolian coast were heavily fortified, in contravention of international treaties, for fear of a Turkish attack, and sophisticated weapons were ordered from abroad. On January 27 Karamanlis proposed to the Turks to refer the Aegean dispute to the International Court of Justice. Turkey agreed, but little was achieved. Tension

Government Finance: *see* Economy, World

Great Britain: *see* United Kingdom

Greek Literature: *see* Literature

Greek Orthodox Church: *see* Religion

Greenland: *see* Dependent States

eased after the Greek and Turkish prime ministers met privately in Brussels at the end of May.

In view of Greece's diplomatic isolation during the dictatorship and the need to solicit international support in the Greek-Turkish dispute, Karamanlis set out in April–May on a tour of European capitals, where he also canvassed support for the Greek application for full membership in the European Economic Community, submitted on June 12. Belgrade, Bucharest, and Sofia responded positively to his overtures for Balkan cooperation during a tour of Balkan capitals. On August 20 he proposed a Balkan meeting at the expert level to explore possible avenues of collaboration. Bulgaria, Romania, and Yugoslavia accepted, Albania declined, and Turkey's reply was delayed.

Official relations with the U.S. remained friendly, and the U.S. announced it would assent to a Greek request for economic and military aid. But anti-Americanism was rife, and on April 21 a mob tried to set fire to the U.S. embassy. The government asked the U.S. to maintain only those facilities that were also relevant to Greek defense, and two of the more conspicuous U.S. installations near Athens were closed. On December 23 Richard S. Welch, the U.S. Central Intelligence Agency station chief in Greece, was killed in front of his home in an Athens suburb by unknown gunmen. Welch, officially a special assistant to the ambassador, was one of a group of CIA officials whose identities had been revealed in an Athens English-language newspaper.

The Greek economy was burdened in 1975 with the cost of the massive rearmament program. The second half of the year showed a hopeful recovery, however, and further external borrowing to cover the balance of payments deficit was avoided. The inflation rate was held down to 15%. A flexible five-year economic plan aiming at 6–7% annual growth was outlined on October 31. (MARIO MODIANO)

[972.B.3]

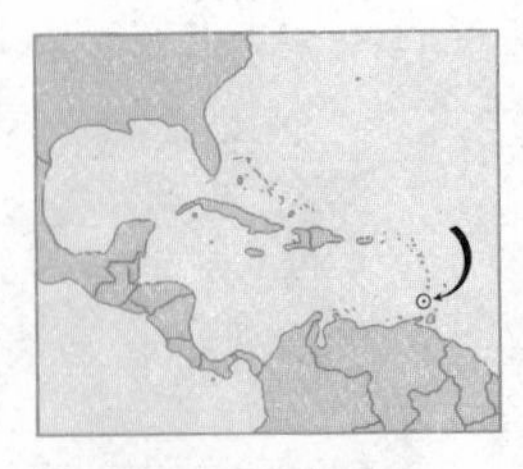

Grenada

A parliamentary state within the Commonwealth of Nations, Grenada, with its dependency, the southern Grenadines, is the southernmost of the Windward Islands of the Caribbean Sea, 100 mi. N of Trinidad. Area: 133 sq.mi. (344 sq.km.). Pop. (1973 est.): 106,200, including Negro 53%, mixed 42%, white 1%, and other 4%. Cap.: Saint George's (pop., 1970, 6,300). Language: English. Religion: Christian. Queen, Elizabeth II; governor-general in 1975, Leo de Gale; prime minister, Eric Gairy.

In March the report by the independent Duffus Commission of Enquiry into the violence of 1973–74 accused the solicitor general of "gross impropriety," charged the police with brutality, and called for the dissolution of the secret force of police aides (the Mongoose Squad). Arrests, beatings, searches, shootings, and setting fire to "subversives'" property continued. In July troops occupied the Nutmeg Growers' Association offices and its funds were frozen, and the moderately radical New Jewel Movement had its headquarters ransacked. A new law aimed at stifling the opposition press. Meanwhile, Gairy remained secure on his base of rural support.

In May 1975 Gairy threatened to file a claim against Britain at the International Court of Justice for £2,250,000 of aid funds, and at the Commonwealth conference in Jamaica Britain's foreign secretary, James Callaghan, countered with a charge of misappropriation of £250,000 by Gairy's government. Tourism declined in 1974, but signs of a gradual upturn in 1975 were reported. For the 1974–75 nutmeg year over 2 million lb. of nutmeg had been shipped, bringing in a record revenue of ECar$6.1 million. However, mace and cocoa were down in both yield and revenue. (SHEILA PATTERSON)

[974.B.2.d]

GRENADA

Education. (1970–71) Primary, pupils 30,355, teachers 800; secondary, pupils 3,039, teachers 129; vocational, pupils 985, teachers 20; teacher training, students 57, teachers 12.

Finance and Trade. Monetary unit: East Caribbean dollar, with (Sept. 22, 1975) a free rate of ECar$2.32 to U.S. $1 (official rate of ECar$4.80 = £1 sterling). Budget (1971 actual): revenue ECar$21,425,000; expenditure ECar$18,220,000. Foreign trade (1970): imports ECar$44,080,000; exports (main only; accounting for 94% of total in 1969) ECar$10,497,000. Import sources (1968): U.K. 33%; U.S. 10%; Canada 10%; The Netherlands 5%. Export destinations: U.K. 54%; Canada 22%; U.S. 10%. Main exports: cocoa *c.* 37%; nutmegs *c.* 28%; bananas *c.* 22%; mace 6%. Tourism (1972): visitors 38,000; gross expenditure U.S. $12 million.

Back in operation after a three-month strike in 1974 is the port at Saint George's.

ROBERT TRUMBULL—THE NEW YORK TIMES

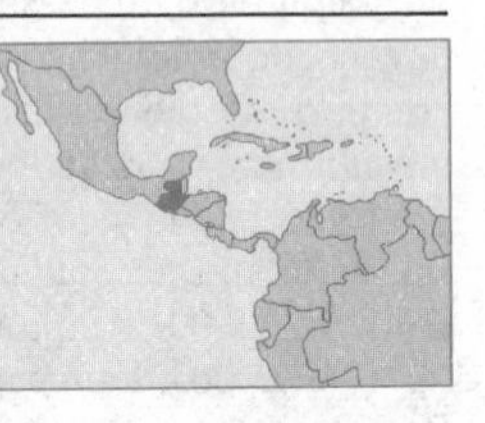

Guatemala

A republic of Central America, Guatemala is bounded by Mexico, Belize, Honduras, El Salvador, the Caribbean Sea, and the Pacific Ocean. Area: 42,042 sq.mi. (108,889 sq.km.). Pop. (1973): 5,175,400. Cap. and largest city: Guatemala City (pop., 1973, 700,500). Language: Spanish, with some Indian dialects. Religion: predominantly Roman Catholic. President in 1975, Kjell Eugenio Laugerud García.

President Laugerud's policies in 1975 were more reformist and to the centre than had been expected, losing him right-wing support and leading to accusations of Communist tendencies. The extreme right, however, lost ground in the June elections for the executive board of Congress.

The economy weathered the 1974 increase in world petroleum prices better than had been expected, and economic performance resulted in some estimates of gross domestic product growth in 1975 as high as 7%. Export growth, in both traditional agricultural prod-

GUATEMALA

Education. (1973) Primary, pupils 585,015, teachers 16,451; secondary, pupils 86,215, teachers 5,934; vocational, pupils (1970) 15,810, teachers (1969) 1,380; teacher training, students (1970) 7,980; teaching staff (1969) 1,008; higher, students 21,715, teachers (1970) 1,314.

Finance. Monetary unit: quetzal, at par with the U.S. dollar (free rate, at Sept. 22, 1975, of 2.07 quetzales to £1 sterling). Gold, SDRs, and foreign exchange: (June 1975) U.S. $287.5 million; (June 1974) U.S. $227.5 million. Budget (1975 est.) balanced at 397 million quetzales. Gross domestic product: (1973) 2,591,000,000 quetzales; (1972) 2,102,000,000 quetzales. Money supply: (March 1975) 335.4 million quetzales; (March 1974) 310.3 million quetzales. Cost of living (Guatemala City; 1970 = 100): (April 1975) 151; (April 1974) 124.

Foreign Trade. (1974) Imports 700.2 million quetzales; exports 586 million quetzales. Import sources: U.S. 32%; Venezuela 12%; El Salvador 10%; Japan 9%; West Germany 8%. Export destinations: U.S. 33%; El Salvador 11%; West Germany 11%; Nicaragua 7%; Costa Rica 6%; Japan 5%. Main exports: coffee 28%; cotton 11%; sugar 11%; bananas 6%.

Transport and Communications. Roads (1972) 13,449 km. (including 824 km. of Pan-American Highway). Motor vehicles in use (1972): passenger 54,100; commercial (including buses) 36,900. Railways: (1972) 822 km.; freight traffic (1970) 106 million net ton-km. Air traffic (1974): 100 million passenger-km.; freight 4.8 million net ton-km. Telephones (Jan. 1974) 53,000. Radio receivers (Dec. 1968) 559,000. Television receivers (Dec. 1972) 85,000.

Agriculture. Production (in 000; metric tons; 1974; 1973 in parentheses): corn *c.* 736 (*c.* 805); sugar, raw value *c.* 325 (*c.* 270); tomatoes *c.* 70 (*c.* 76); dry beans 78 (72); bananas (1973) *c.* 520, (1972) *c.* 510; coffee (1973) *c.* 132, (1972) *c.* 135; cotton, lint *c.* 116 (90). Livestock (in 000; March 1974): cattle *c.* 1,839; sheep *c.* 650; pigs *c.* 1,022; chickens (1973) *c.* 10,100.

Industry. Production (in 000; metric tons; 1973): cement 316; petroleum products 922; zinc ore (metal content; 1971) 1; electricity (kw-hr.; 1972) *c.* 910,000.

ucts and nontraditional manufactures, led to hopes of an overall balance of payments surplus for 1975.

Agreements with Mexico provided for technical assistance in the exploration and development of Guatemalan iron ore and petroleum and also for some easing of restrictions on Guatemalan trade with Mexican border areas. Tension rose over the issue of independence for the British colony of Belize (British Honduras), which Guatemala had long claimed as part of its territory, but late in the year Britain and Guatemala agreed to resume negotiations on the subject. Guatemala had general Latin-American support for its claim, but independence for Belize had gained widespread support elsewhere in the third world.

(JOHN HALE)

[974.B.1.a]

Guinea

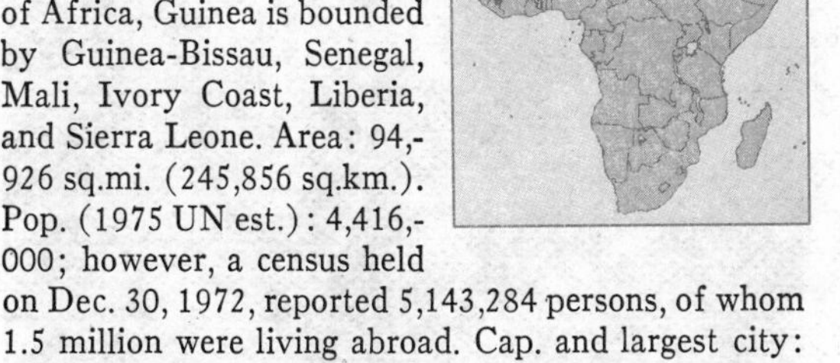
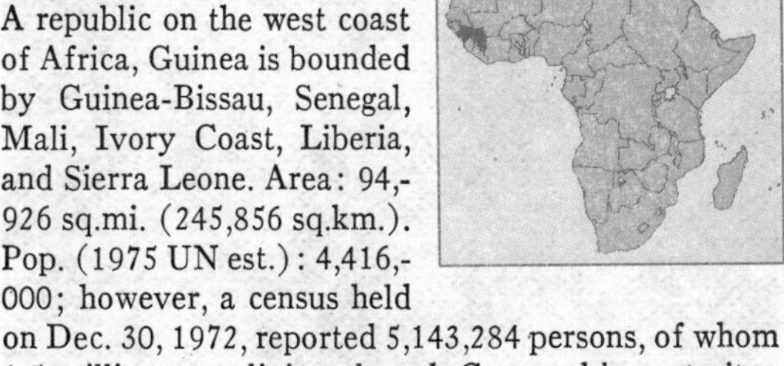

A republic on the west coast of Africa, Guinea is bounded by Guinea-Bissau, Senegal, Mali, Ivory Coast, Liberia, and Sierra Leone. Area: 94,926 sq.mi. (245,856 sq.km.). Pop. (1975 UN est.): 4,416,000; however, a census held on Dec. 30, 1972, reported 5,143,284 persons, of whom 1.5 million were living abroad. Cap. and largest city: Conakry (pop., 1974, 412,000). Language: French (official). Religion: mostly Muslim. President in 1975, Sékou Touré; premier, Louis Lansana Beavogui.

GUINEA

Education. (1970–71) Primary, pupils 191,287, teachers 5,304; secondary, pupils 59,918, teachers 2,360; vocational, pupils 2,013, teachers 150; teacher training, students 1,478, teachers 275; higher, students 1,974, teachers (1965–66) 95.

Finance. Monetary unit: syli, with an official rate (Sept. 22, 1975) of 20.46 sylis to U.S. $1 (free nominal rate of 42.40 sylis = £1 sterling). Budget (1972–73 est.) balanced at 4.5 billion sylis.

Foreign Trade. (1972) Imports *c.* 1.8 billion sylis; exports *c.* 1.6 billion sylis. Import sources: France *c.* 31%; U.S. *c.* 13%; Belgium-Luxembourg *c.* 12%; U.S.S.R. *c.* 12%; Italy *c.* 5%; West Germany *c.* 5%. Export destinations: Spain *c.* 16%; Norway *c.* 15%; West Germany *c.* 14%; Cameroon *c.* 10%; Switzerland *c.* 5%; Yugoslavia 5%. Main exports (1970): alumina and bauxite 65%; coffee 11%; pineapples 9%; palm products 6%.

The chief event of 1975 was the return to normality of Guinea's relations with France after 17 disturbed years. This was confirmed especially by the arrival of a French delegation, headed by the French minister of justice, Jean Lecanuet, in Conakry to join in the celebration of the "aggression of November 22," the repulsion five years earlier of mercenaries opposed to Sékou Touré's regime. In June Premier Lansana Beavogui visited France, and a few days later 18 Frenchmen, detained since the failed coup, were released.

But Touré's government, ever susceptible to threats of opposition and plotting, announced in March and again in August the discovery of schemes to assassinate the president. A purge of the Army was carried out, and its role was taken over increasingly by people's militias and by the civilian administration. Emigration from Guinea to neighbouring states increased.

A large-scale agricultural project progressed in 1975; with the aid of 9,000 students and 2,500 tractors the government hoped ultimately to bring 275,000 ha. of land under cultivation.

(PHILIPPE DECRAENE)

[978.E.4.b.ii]

Guinea-Bissau

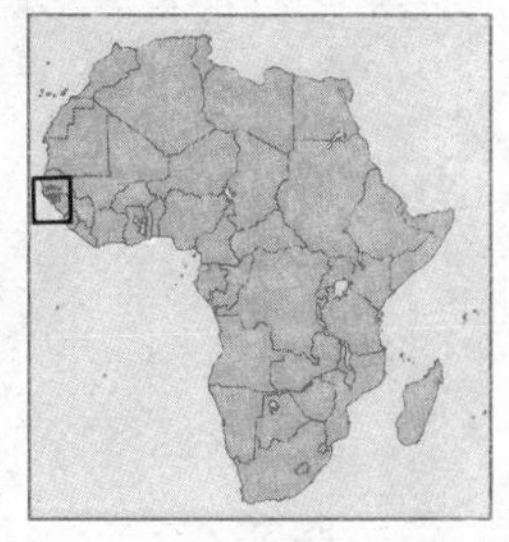

An independent African republic, Guinea-Bissau has an Atlantic coastline on the west and borders Senegal on the north and Guinea on the east and south. Area: 13,948 sq.mi. (36,125 sq.km.). Pop. (1975 est.): 525,000. Cap. and largest city: Bissau (metro. area pop., 1970, 71,200). President in 1975, Luis Cabral; premier, Francisco Mendès.

Negotiations begun in Brussels in 1973 and completed in Lomé, Togo, on Feb. 28, 1975, resulted in the establishment of a five-year trading relationship between the European Economic Community (EEC) and 46 less developed countries of which Guinea-Bissau was one. Under the Lomé Convention Guinea-Bissau was to receive development aid from the EEC and would benefit from an export stabilization scheme.

From the U.S.S.R., too, came an offer of aid when a delegation led by Premier Francisco Mendès held talks with the Soviet premier in Moscow in February. The Soviets promised assistance in the development of energy, education, and health services and agreed to set up a trade mission in Guinea-Bissau and to cooperate in economic, technical, cultural, and scientific areas. The treaty of cooperation and friendship ratified by Senegal in July 1974 was followed in January 1975 by 11 agreements between the two countries covering such topics as defense, foreign policy,

Gross National Product: *see* Economy, World

Guiana: *see* Dependent States; Guyana; Surinam

GUINEA-BISSAU

Education. (1972–73) Primary, pupils 48,007, teachers 1,148; secondary and vocational, pupils 4,133, teachers 176.

Finance and Trade. Monetary unit: Guinea escudo, with a nominal free rate (Sept. 22, 1975) of 27.35 escudos to U.S. $1 (56.65 escudos = £1 sterling). Budget (1972 est.): revenue 577 million escudos; expenditure 552 million escudos. Foreign trade (1973): imports 1,122,269,000 escudos (56% from Portugal, 7% from Spain, 5% from U.K., 5% from Japan); exports 121,698,000 escudos (90% to Portugal). Main exports: peanuts 46%; transport equipment (transit) 21%; coconuts 7%; timber 5%.

Agriculture. Production (in 000; metric tons; 1973; 1972 in parentheses): peanuts *c.* 60 (*c.* 55); rice *c.* 37 (*c.* 37); cassava *c.* 41 (*c.* 40); palm kernels *c.* 7 (*c.* 7); palm oil *c.* 5 (*c.* 5). Livestock (in 000; 1973): cattle *c.* 290; pigs *c.* 120; sheep *c.* 67; goats *c.* 177.

security, and economic and cultural affairs. A major victory was won in June by the African Party for the Independence of Guinea-Bissau and Cape Verde (PAIGC) when citizens in the nearby Cape Verde Islands voted in favour of union with Guinea-Bissau.

(KENNETH INGHAM)

[978.E.4.b.ii]

Guyana

A republic and member of the Commonwealth of Nations, Guyana is situated between Venezuela, Brazil, and Surinam on the Atlantic Ocean. Area: 83,000 sq.mi. (215,000 sq.km.). Pop. (1975 est.): 791,000, including (1970) East Indian 51%; African 30.7%; mixed 11.4%; Amerindian 4.4%. Cap. and largest city: Georgetown (pop., 1970, 63,200). Language: English (official). Religion: Protestant, Hindu, Roman Catholic. President in 1975, Arthur Chung; prime minister, Forbes Burnham.

In 1975 Guyana moved close to being a one-party socialist cooperative state. In December 1974 Burnham announced that his ruling People's National Congress was "paramount" to the government, and Deputy Prime Minister Ptolemy Reid said in September 1975 that the government was trying to achieve a dictatorship of the proletariat.

In February nationalization of the British-owned Demerara Sugar Co. was announced. A seven-week sugar workers' strike lowered estimated production for 1975 to 300,000 tons, 49,000 tons below 1974. The strike ended in late April, when Burnham recognized former prime minister Cheddi Jagan's Guyana Agricultural Workers' Union. Socialization, links with Cuba, the Communist states, and the third world, and even the institutionalization of "comrade" as the official form of address, indicated a considerable shift toward Jagan's views.

Guyana's export earnings in 1974 had almost doubled to Guy$584 million. On October 9 the Guyana dollar was pegged to the U.S. dollar at $2.55 to $1.

(SHEILA PATTERSON)

[974.B.2.d]

GUYANA

Education. (1970–71) Primary, pupils 130,484, teachers 4,485; secondary, pupils 57,093, teachers 2,262; vocational, pupils 3,060, teachers 72; teacher training, students 656, teachers 61; higher (university only; 1971–72), students 1,232, teaching staff 85.

Finance. Monetary unit: Guyanan dollar, with (Oct. 9, 1975) a par value of Guy$2.55 to U.S. $1 (free rate of Guy$5.25 = £1 sterling). Budget (1975 est.): revenue Guy$429.8 million; expenditure Guy$531.2 million.

Foreign Trade. (1973) Imports Guy$349.2 million; exports Guy$288.3 million. Import sources: U.K. 27%; U.S. 26%; Trinidad and Tobago 13%; Canada 6%. Export destinations: U.K. 30%; U.S. 17%; Trinidad and Tobago 10%; U.S.S.R. 6%; Jamaica 6%. Main exports: bauxite 48%; sugar 31%; alumina 9%; rice 9%; fish 5%.

Agriculture. Production (in 000; metric tons; 1974; 1973 in parentheses): rice 226 (164); sugar, raw value 345 (*c.* 273); cassava (1973) *c.* 14, (1972) *c.* 14; oranges (1973) *c.* 11, (1972) 10; copra *c.* 7 (*c.* 7). Livestock (in 000; 1974): cattle *c.* 265; sheep *c.* 108; goats (1973) *c.* 50; pigs (1973) *c.* 100.

Industry. Production (in 000; 1973): bauxite (metric tons) 3,497; diamonds (metric carats) 53; electricity (kw-hr.) 382,000.

Gymnastics and Weight Lifting

Gymnastics. The two major international events of the year, the tenth European and VII Pan-American championships, provided ample evidence that gymnastics in 1975 was spectacularly better than a few years earlier. The exceedingly difficult balancing bar routines introduced by Olga Korbut (U.S.S.R.) in 1972, for example, were no longer hers alone. Adopting new training techniques and taking advantage of expert coaching, top women gymnasts were able to perform similar tumbling movements in rapid sequence and strove to match Korbut's virtuosity on the uneven parallel bars. In men's competition, there were exciting new dismounts from the horizontal bars, and uncommon maneuvers requiring great strength were carried through with remarkable skill. Thus the upcoming Olympics were expected to provide a level of competition never before witnessed. A revision of the scoring system was also expected to have a positive effect on performances.

The European and Pan-American championships were generally viewed as a preview of the 1976 Summer Olympics at Montreal. Though Nikolay Andrianov clearly demonstrated his right to be ranked with such Japanese champions as Shigeru Kasamatsu and Eizo Kenmotsu, other Soviet gymnasts showed that they too would provide stiff competition for

Nadia Comaneci of Romania displays her graceful expertise on the balance beam which won her first place at the International Gymnastics competition in Montreal.

THE CANADIAN PRESS

1975 Gymnastics Champions

Event	Europe	Pan-American	U.S.
MEN			
Overall	N. Andrianov (U.S.S.R.)	J. Cuervo (Cuba)	T. Beach, B. Conner
Floor exercises	N. Andrianov (U.S.S.R.)	P. Kormann (U.S.)	P. Kormann
Still rings	D. Grecu (Rom.)	J. Cuervo (Cuba)	T. Beach
Pommel horse	Z. Magyar (Hung.)	R. Leon (Cuba)	B. Conner
Horizontal bar	E. Gienger (W. Ger.)	J. Cuervo (Cuba)	T. Beach
Parallel bars	N. Andrianov (U.S.S.R.)	R. Leon (Cuba)	B. Conner
Horse vault	N. Andrianov (U.S.S.R.)	J. Cuervo (Cuba)	T. Beach
WOMEN			
Overall	N. Comaneci (Rom.)	A. Carr (U.S.)	T. Manville
Floor exercises	N. Kim (U.S.S.R.)	A. Carr (U.S.)	K. Howard
Balance beam	N. Comaneci (Rom.)	A. Carr (U.S.)	K. Gaynor
Uneven parallel bars	N. Comaneci (Rom.)	A. Carr (U.S.) R. Pierce (U.S.)	L. Wolfsburger
Horse vault	N. Comaneci (Rom.)	C. Casey (U.S.)	C. Casey

Olympic medals. Though U.S. men gymnasts did reasonably well at the Pan-Am Games in Mexico City, the team presented no immediate threat to topflight world contenders. Peter Kormann finished first in floor exercises, but Jorge Cuervo of Cuba won four gold medals and R. Leon, also of Cuba, captured the other two. Bart Conner won the U.S. all-around national championship, Wayne Young the National Collegiate Athletic Association title, and Mike Carter the Amateur Athletic Union (AAU) crown.

Ludmila Tourischeva (U.S.S.R.), the 1972 Olympic and 1974 world champion, did not give herself fully to gymnastic competition during the year. This in part paved the way for Korean-born Nelli Kim (whose closest rival, Olga Korbut, missed part of the year's events because of injuries) to emerge as the new Soviet champion. Kim was also crowned European champion in floor exercises. But it was Nadia Comaneci, a 14-year-old Romanian girl, who created the most excitement and grabbed most of the headlines by winning four of a possible five gold medals during the European championships. Other outstanding gymnasts were Alina Goreac of Romania and Annelore Zinke and Richarda Schmeisser, both of East Germany. Though U.S. women will almost certainly do better than U.S. men at the 1976 Olympics, they were not ranked among the world's best, even though they completely dominated the Pan-Am events. Ann Carr won four gold medals, including a first-place finish shared with Roxanne Pierce, and Colleen Casey captured a Pan-Am gold medal in the horse vault. Other U.S. women gymnasts who showed promise were Diane Dunbar, Kathy Howard, Patricia Reed, and Debra Ann Willcox.

Roberto Urrutia contributed to Cuba's domination of weight lifting at the Pan-Am Games in Mexico City with this first place lift in the clean and jerk.

WIDE WORLD

CENTRAL PRESS/PICTORIAL PARADE

The Soviet Union's Nikolay Andrianov won the men's overall gold medal in a thrilling finish as he edged Japan's Hiroshi Kajiyama by 0.15 marks in the first World Cup gymnastics competition at the Empire Pool, Wembley, England.

Weight Lifting. Following a 1972 decision of the International Weightlifting Federation to eliminate the press because rule violations were too difficult to determine, only two events—the snatch and the clean and jerk—were now featured in major competitions, including the Olympics. During the past 20 years world records had been steadily pushed upward by weight lifters in all nine weight divisions despite a general decline in the number of first-class weight lifters participating in international events. While the quality of U.S. weight lifting had deteriorated in recent years (only five weight lifters, at most, would qualify for the 1976 Olympics), that of competitors in Eastern Europe had improved considerably. This development became strikingly evident during the 1975 world championships in Moscow when Soviet athletes took the team title and won four individual gold medals. Bulgaria, which followed closely with three gold medals, easily outperformed Poland and East Germany, which each won one gold medal. Hungary also ranked highly with a generous share of the silver and bronze medals. At the Pan-Am Games Cuba completely dominated the competition by winning the team title and most of the gold medals. Philip Grippaldi, perhaps the most outstanding U.S. weight lifter of the year, retained his AAU title and captured his third successive middle heavyweight Pan-Am championship. (CHARLES ROBERT PAUL, JR.)

[452.B.4.f]

1975 World Weight Lifting Champions

Flyweight	Z. Smalcerz (Pol.)
Bantamweight	A. Kirov (Bulg.)
Featherweight	G. Todorov (Bulg.)
Lightweight	P. Korol (U.S.S.R.)
Middleweight	P. Wenzel (E. Ger.)
Light heavyweight	V. Shary (U.S.S.R.)
Middle heavyweight	D. Rigert (U.S.S.R.)
Heavyweight	V. Khristov (Bulg.)
Superheavyweight	V. Alexseyev (U.S.S.R.)
Team championship	U.S.S.R.

Haiti

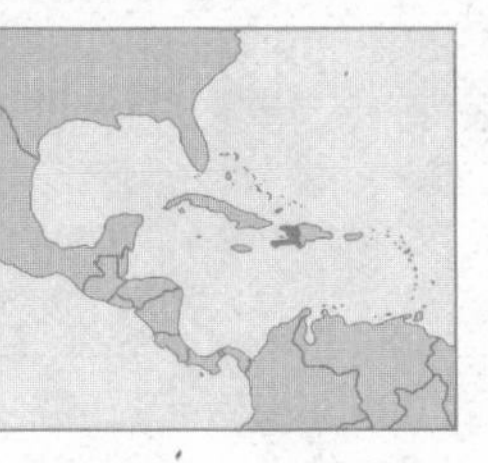

The Republic of Haiti occupies the western one-third of the Caribbean island of Hispaniola, which it shares with the Dominican Republic. Area: 10,714 sq.mi. (27,750 sq.km.). Pop. (1975 est.): 4,583,800, of whom 95% are Negro. Cap. and largest city: Port-au-Prince (pop., 1975 est., 625,000). Language: French (official) and Creole. Religion: Roman Catholic; Voodooism practiced in rural areas. President in 1975, Jean-Claude Duvalier.

Throughout 1975 President Duvalier maintained his support in the Cabinet and among the armed forces. After the resignation of the minister of finance in

HAITI

Education. (1973–74) Primary, pupils 336,511, teachers 8,470; secondary and vocational, pupils 51,-174, teachers 1,735; teacher training (1968–69), students 230, teachers 60; higher (University of Haiti), students 2,100, teaching staff 211.

Finance. Monetary unit: gourde, with (Sept. 22, 1975) a par value of 5 gourdes to U.S. $1 (free rate of 10.36 gourdes to £1 sterling). Gold, SDRs, and foreign exchange: (Jan. 1975) U.S. $21 million; (Jan. 1974) U.S. $18.1 million. Budget (1973–74 rev. est.) balanced at 195 million gourdes. Cost of living (Port-au-Prince; 1970 = 100): (March 1975) 178; (March 1974) 156.

Foreign Trade. Imports (1973) 369.7 million gourdes; exports (1974) 359.3 million gourdes. Import sources (1972–73): U.S. 41%; Japan 9%; Canada 8%; France 6%; West Germany 6%; U.K. 5%. Export destinations (1972–73): U.S. 60%; France 9%; Belgium-Luxembourg 9%; Italy 7%; The Netherlands 5%. Main exports: coffee 33%; sugar 9%; bauxite 8%.

Transport and Communications. Roads (1973) *c.* 4,000 km. Motor vehicles in use (1973): passenger 11,700; commercial (including buses) 1,300. Telephones (Jan. 1974) 9,000. Radio receivers (Dec. 1973) 90,000. Television receivers (Dec. 1973) 13,000.

Agriculture. Production (in 000; metric tons; 1974; 1973 in parentheses): coffee *c.* 33 (*c.* 33); sweet potatoes (1973) *c.* 90, (1972) *c.* 90; cassava (1973) *c.* 136, (1972) *c.* 135; sugar, raw value (1973) *c.* 138, (1972) *c.* 135; corn (1973) *c.* 260, (1972) 257; millet *c.* 219 (*c.* 216); dry beans *c.* 43 (*c.* 43); bananas (1973) *c.* 182, (1972) *c.* 180; mangoes (1973) *c.* 92, (1972) *c.* 90; sisal (1973) *c.* 17, (1972) *c.* 16. Livestock (in 000; 1974): pigs *c.* 1,682; cattle (1973) *c.* 732; goats (1973) *c.* 1,287; sheep *c.* 77.

Industry. Production (in 000; metric tons; 1973): cement 126; bauxite 779; electricity (kw-hr.) 141,000.

March over a forged order for postage stamps, the technocratic faction of the Cabinet strengthened its control of the government.

Economically 1975 was a difficult year for Haiti. World prices of coffee and sugar declined, and the recession in the U.S. and Canada reduced tourist income and remittances from Haitians resident overseas. A prolonged drought in northwest Haiti caused severe local shortages, necessitating a foreign-assisted emergency program to feed 300,000 people for five months. The cost of living rose by 13% in 1974 and 10% in the first three months of 1975. Industrial output fell by almost 14% in the first quarter.

The World Bank lent a further $20 million for the second phase of the Port-au-Prince to Cap-Haïtien highway, while the Inter-American Development Bank was negotiating a loan for the second phase of the road to the south. France lent $7 million to build a road to link Port-au-Prince and Jacmel. International currency reserves were enlarged through an International Monetary Fund standby loan from July 1; total IMF aid amounted to $6.5 million. Test drillings for a UN geologic project would determine if copper deposits in northern Haiti were as rich as estimated, and new bauxite contracts with Reynolds Metals Co. of the U.S. were expected to yield over $11 million a year to foreign reserves. (MICHAEL WOOLLER)

[974.B.2.a]

Health and Disease

General Overview. The medical scene during 1975 was marked more by problems involved in the organization and delivery of medical care than by any major epidemics, changes in the pattern of disease, or outstanding advances in medical science.

In his report to the 28th World Health Assembly, which met in Geneva in May, Halfdan Mahler, director general of the World Health Organization (WHO), stated that health services were not improving people's physical or mental welfare "as much as could be desired." A high proportion of the world's population had either poor or no access to medical aid. He also complained that such services as did exist too often operated in isolation, attempting to provide curative medicine and such strictly preventive measures as inoculations or screening for disease. The authorities concerned neglected other factors that affect human health such as food supplies, housing, education, and working conditions. Mahler proposed, and the assembly agreed, that the solution was to be found in the provision of systems of primary health care, in which the key figure would be the primary health worker, trained to deal with simple illnesses and emergencies but also serving as a link with other national and community services and facilities contributing to physical and social well-being.

In the U.S. organized political activity on the part of physicians was widespread. Angered by rising costs of malpractice insurance premiums and withdrawal of some underwriters from the field because of soaring malpractice awards, physicians in California refused to perform any but emergency surgery for a month in the late spring and were planning another, similar job action at year's end. Physicians elsewhere lobbied at state capitols for legislation placing limits on awards, outlawing contingency fees, and establishing screening panels to eliminate undeserved claims.

The first major strike of U.S. physicians occurred in New York City when 2,000 interns and residents protested long hours and other working conditions at the city's 21 metropolitan hospitals. The American Medical Association (AMA) backed the strikers' demands for shorter shifts, pointing out that exhausted physicians were more prone to mistakes in treating patients. The strike ended after four days with a new agreement. An even longer strike was carried out by 250 interns and resident physicians at Cook County Hospital in Chicago in defiance of a judge's order to return to work. On October 11 delegates representing interns and residents from 108 hospitals across the country voted at the Physicians National Housestaff Association convention in Washington, D.C., to become a labour union and applied to the U.S. Department of Labor for recognition. Unionization of senior physicians accelerated as segments of organized medicine began to adopt the weapons of organized labour. The Union of American Physicians and the American Federation of Dentists and Physicians, both founded in 1972 with a total of less than 1,000 members, claimed over 10,000 dues-paying members in 1975. The AMA created a department of negotiations to assist state and local medical societies in collective bargaining disputes with hospitals and insurance companies.

The malpractice insurance crisis appeared when the slowly increasing rates of the previous five years rose exponentially in 1975. The premium for orthopedic surgeons, for example, skyrocketed in New York from $5,000 in 1970 to $15,000 in group policies and to as much as $30,000 in the case of individual surgeons against whom a previous suit had been brought. A number of physicians announced they were giving up their practice. A few insurance companies gave up malpractice underwriting because of heavy losses through payouts that saw the average amount granted by juries in New York rise from $62,000 to nearly $350,000 in five years.

Handball: *see* Court Games

Harbours: *see* Transportation

Harness Racing: *see* Equestrian Sports

Hay: *see* Agriculture and Food Supplies

No major advances marked the continuing efforts to treat and prevent the principal causes of sickness and death. Heart disease remained the chief killer, although Jeremiah Stamler, a noted U.S. epidemiologist, claimed early in 1975 that there was a dramatic reduction in the number of deaths from heart disease among middle-aged U.S. men. Within a decade coronary deaths in the U.S. had decreased by more than 8%, a saving of 10,000 lives a year. Stamler gave principal credit for the improvement to a reduction in smoking. In 1955 60% of U.S. males were smokers; by 1970 the figure had dropped to 40%. Two further factors, Stamler believed, may have been the increasingly widespread and effective drug control of high blood pressure and a national tendency to eat a less fatty diet.

Doubt was cast upon a popular theory that people living in hard-water areas are less likely to suffer heart attacks than those who consume soft water. A study in Los Angeles involved the communities of Reseda, Burbank, and Downey. Each uses water of a different degree of hardness, but no correlation was found between water hardness and the incidence of heart disease. A second U.S. study involved the twin communities of Kansas City, Kan., and Kansas City, Mo. Both towns draw water from the same source, but the supply for Kansas City, Mo., is artificially softened. The hard-water consumers suffered a 36% higher death rate from heart diseases and associated kidney disease than their soft-water neighbours, which contradicted most previous studies. The authors of this report pointed out that the softening process reduces the cadmium content of the water and suggested that the hard-water drinkers of Kansas City, Kan., in fact suffer from cadmium poisoning, which may produce high blood pressure. These two studies did not destroy the hypothesis that the risk of contracting heart disease may be related to the nature of the water people use, but it seemed likely that it was not a matter of the degree of hardness per se but rather the presence of injurious substances in some waters.

A suggestion that coffee drinkers were at extra risk of a heart attack was contradicted by a finding in the Framingham study, in which several thousand inhabitants of this Massachusetts township had been followed for 25 years in an attempt to discover what factors may encourage heart disease. Coffee had no clear influence, but coffee addicts tended to be heavy smokers, and it was the cigarette that goes with the cup that seemed to be the dangerous element. (See *Coronary Artery Disease and Its Complications*, below.)

Several reports appeared concerning successful attempts to reduce an abnormally high heart rate or blood pressure using biofeedback techniques or yoga-like relaxation methods. When biofeedback was employed the patients were attached to an instrument that allowed them to observe their pulse rates, and they learned to "will" the instrument to show a lower reading. If the reports were valid it seemed likely that a high proportion of sufferers from cardiovascular disease could be taught to control their condition in this manner, reducing the need for drugs with dangerous or unpleasant side effects.

The American Cancer Society reported in 1975 a reduction in a 22-year period of 10% in ovarian cancer death rates, 23% in cancer of the esophagus, 26% each in cancer of the uterus, cancer of the rectum, and cancer of the bladder in women. Increases, on the other hand, were shown for cancer of the lung (125%) and cancer of the prostate, bladder, colon, and pancreas in men (about 20% each). Despite the immense amount of money and effort being devoted to the study of cancer, which, after diseases of the heart and circulation, was the second commonest cause of death in the developed nations, no major research advances were reported during the year. Toward the end of 1974, however, Denis Burkitt published what he later described as "the most important paper of my life." Burkitt, a British researcher, was internationally known for his earlier work on a cancer common among African children (known as Burkitt's lymphoma). His latest work was a major survey correlating the principal diseases characteristic of various national diets. In Africa, for example, coronary heart disease was virtually unknown, and cancer of the colon and rectum was rare (although such growths ranked second only to lung cancer among the malignancies common in the West). Burkitt believed that the high incidence of both heart disease and intestinal cancer in the West was due to the small amount of fibre in the Western diet. This lack, claimed Burkitt, slows down the passage of materials through the intestines. One consequence is a greater absorption and higher blood level of cholesterol. A second is the manufacture within the gut of chemicals capable of producing cancer.

WHO's hope of ridding the world of smallpox during 1975 was not achieved, but by the end of the year only a very few small pockets of the infection remained. By contrast WHO's director general in his annual report had this to say about malaria: ". . . the general situation has further deteriorated and malaria is now raging in some countries where, a few years ago, eradication seemed about to be attained."

Portugal suffered a minor cholera epidemic in the autumn of 1975, and the spread of this infection from the tropics northward into Europe continued. In São

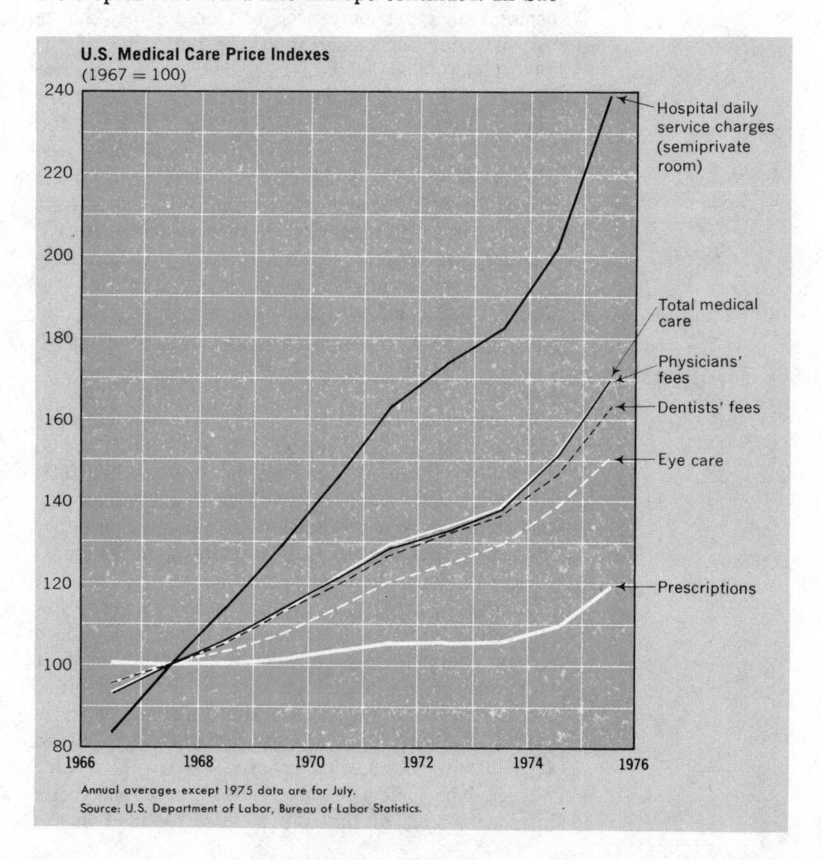

Annual averages except 1975 data are for July.
Source: U.S. Department of Labor, Bureau of Labor Statistics.

LONDON DAILY EXPRESS/PICTORIAL PARADE

A surgical and medical team in the Soviet Union works within these pressure chambers which are designed to aid in the cure of serious anaerobe diseases. These are caused by the ingestion of contaminated substances.

Paulo, Brazil, there were 2,500 deaths from meningitis during 1974, and an upsurge in this once common dangerous infection continued in Britain and Scandinavia. At the beginning of the year the death in Britain from Lassa fever of a doctor newly returned from Nigeria was a reminder that the increased amount of jet travel lays communities open to infections that they may not have encountered in the past and against which, therefore, they have no natural immunity.

In the U.S. treatment for almost all types of childhood cancers had achieved five-year survival rates of at least 50% in the best cancer centres. Patients with osteosarcoma, a bone cancer, had only a 6% chance for surviving for one year at the beginning of the 1970s. As 1975 ended half the patients were alive two to four years after beginning treatment. A new antibiotic, adriamycin, was licensed by the U.S. Food and Drug Administration (FDA) after it demonstrated effectiveness in reducing cancers resistant to other drugs. Physicians found adriamycin useful in cancers of the bone and in soft tissue cancers such as breast, bladder, and thyroid. From 5 to 8.6% of the adults who received irradiation in childhood to shrink enlarged tonsils and adenoids were developing thyroid cancer 25 years later. An estimated 70,000 children in the Chicago area alone were irradiated in what was believed to be a safe procedure at the time.

A promising candidate in the quest to identify a virus believed to cause cancer in humans was reported by Robert Gallo of the National Cancer Institute, Bethesda, Md. Gallo acknowledged the possibility that it might be a contaminant but pointed out that the same virus was isolated from the same leukemia patient on three different occasions.

Among the medical innovations in 1975 was another pioneering effort by Christiaan Barnard, the South African thoracic surgeon who transplanted the first human heart in 1967. He became the first surgeon to give a patient two hearts, working together, when he placed the heart of a 10-year-old girl killed in an accident into the chest cavity of a 58-year-old factory worker. The child's heart was grafted in piggyback fashion to 40% of the adult's heart retained in the body. The two hearts beat synchronously so that one was working while the other rested. Although the patient died five months after the operation as a result of a blood clot in his lung, Barnard was satisfied that the surgical spectacular was a success, and by year's end two more grafting operations were performed in South Africa.

Surgeons in New Orleans, La., used a novel method to repair a hole in the wall separating the chambers of the heart of a 17-year-old girl. They avoided costly and traumatic open-heart surgery by plugging the opening with two small patches that were pleated and folded, then fitted into a tiny capsule. The capsule was inserted into a large vein of the thigh and threaded through a pathway of veins into the heart by catheter. The first patch was pushed through the hole and opened like an umbrella as the catheter was pulled back through the hole. The second patch on the near side was opened and locked to the first to seal the hole.

In the past the only available treatment for an ankle that was diseased or injured beyond repair was to fuse the joint and stiffen the ankle. A two-piece prosthesis of chromium and cobalt, designed by Theodore Waugh of the University of California at Irvine, could be inserted in the body and would duplicate actions of a normal joint.

Diabetics were warned that an oral drug, phenformin, taken to reduce blood sugar, was associated with a marked increase in death rate. In 1970 tolbutamide, also a widely used antidiabetic pill, was similarly classed. In 1975 a study group known as the University Group Diabetes Program linked phenformin to high blood pressure, rapid heart rate, and heightened risk of death from heart disease. Diabetics who took tolbutamide and phenformin died at twice the rate of those who took either insulin or a placebo.

Results of another drug study showed that clofibrate and niacin, two agents widely used in an effort to lower the level of fats in the bloodstream, were not effective in preventing a second heart attack. The investigators pointed out that once hardening of the arteries has advanced sufficiently to cause a heart attack, drug therapy to lower cholesterol is not effective, but it may help to prevent the first attack.

A new warning was issued to users of the contraceptive pill, especially women over 40. The FDA notified physicians to advise their older patients to use another type of contraceptive because of an association between the pill and heart attacks. British and U.S. women aged 30 to 39 who used the pill showed a heart attack incidence of 5.6 per 100,000; for age 40 to 44, the rate was 56.9. For women not using the pill, the incidence was 2.1 and 9.9, respectively.

The first successful treatment in the womb to prevent mental retardation was published in the *New England Journal of Medicine* by Mary G. Ampola of Tufts-New England Medical Center. The fetus was discovered at midterm to have a chemical deficiency that typically impairs intellect and development and leads ultimately to early death. The mother's first child had died of the same disease 14 months earlier. The disorder often is caused by a failure to convert vitamin B_{12} to a useful form, resulting in an accumulation of acid in the fetus' body tissue. The mother was treated with massive doses of B_{12}, which entered the fetal circulation. An editorial in the journal hailed the prenatal treatment as "a new venture in medical science."

Treatment of fetuses in the womb has been a subject of controversy and led to a moratorium imposed by the U.S. Department of Health, Education, and Welfare on all fetal research. The 18-month ban was lifted in August 1975, when the National Commission for the Protection of Human Subjects of Biomedical and Behavioral Research issued guidelines governing research in the womb and on aborted fetuses. Investigators may neither kill an aborted fetus nor keep it alive artificially. (*See* Special Report.)

In an extremely controversial trial Kenneth Edelin (*see* BIOGRAPHY) of Boston City Hospital was convicted of manslaughter in 1975 for killing a "well-nourished fetus" by depriving it of oxygen while performing an abortion on a 17-year-old woman. The verdict was appealed.

A new definition declared that death has occurred irrevocably when there is no sign of brain wave activity for at least 30 minutes, even though the patient can be kept breathing with a respirator. The conclusion was reached on the basis of a collaborative study by nine institutions on more than 500 terminal patients. The criteria suggested by Harvard researchers in 1968, which require a flat brain wave for 24 hours, were found too rigid by the study sponsored by the National Institute of Neurological Diseases and Stroke.

An unprecedented petition filed in New Jersey sought court authority for a respirator to be discontinued in the case of a 21-year-old woman who had been in a coma for more than six months but whose brain waves were not flat. The adoptive parents of Karen Ann Quinlan took legal action after physicians refused their request that the plug be pulled. After an emotion-packed 11-day trial in November, Superior Court Judge Robert Muir, Jr., of Morris County, N.J., ruled that "judicial conscience and morality" led him to believe that Karen's fate was being handled properly by "the treating physician." This meant that because her doctor refused to discontinue use of the respirator, for the time being Karen would live. Her parents were expected to appeal the decision.

(DONALD W. GOULD; ARTHUR J. SNIDER)

[423; 424; 10/35]

MEDICAL-SOCIAL POLICY

Problems of inflation, inefficient organization of medical care, maldistribution of physicians, shortages of primary care practitioners, and uneven access to medical care continued in 1975. In the U.S. medicine felt acutely the results of the recession and federal restrictions on health programs, problems of malpractice insurance, and increased government regulation of medical practice and research. With health expenditures exceeding $100 billion a year, it was clear that there must be a limit on medical care costs, and an important objective of government health policy in the U.S. and elsewhere was to ensure that resource allocations were made more carefully.

Medicine also faced a crisis of confidence. Physicians were being criticized both from within the profession and by the public at large. In the previous few years there had been an enormous proliferation of legislation affecting almost every aspect of medical care organization. Federally mandated professional standards review organizations (PSROs) were in operation in some places and gearing up elsewhere. During the year Congress passed the National Health Planning and Development Act which would further develop regional authorities and health care planning in anticipation of national health insurance. Although there were issues of organization and financing to be settled, it was increasingly clear to most physicians that the practice of medicine as they had come to know it was undergoing fundamental changes.

The Malpractice Crisis. The escalation of malpractice rates and the reaction of physicians threatening to withhold services, and actually doing so, signaled the growing crisis of medical practice. The malpractice crisis was deeply rooted in the organization of medical practice and larger social forces. After World War II medicine experienced an enormous growth in knowledge and an expansion of technology. It had greater capability than ever before, but its technology also engendered greater risks. Heightened public expectations accompanied such achievements as hemodialysis and transplantation, and patients expected medicine to compensate for problems of health resulting from the risks of modern living and poor health habits. The growth of malpractice litigation apparently resulted from the disappointment of such heightened expectations, a growing acceptance of the use of litigation to express grievances and seek compensation, the inevitable injuries and adverse results concomitant with the use of risky technology, growing accessibility of legal assistance, and dissension within medicine itself as to the appropriate standards for medical practice. But the malpractice dilemma, like many other problems in medical care, probably also reflected alterations in medical organization with the growth of science and technology and changing social forces.

Medicine had become highly specialized and excessively dependent on hospital care, and there were too few generalists who concerned themselves with the total patient. The result was fragmented care in which patients were treated by a wide variety of specialists but had no personal doctor who looked after their overall welfare. Although this pattern of care may be technically excellent, discontinuities occurred and breakdowns in communication and rapport between patients and doctors were common. The erosion of such personal relationships, in conjunction with other factors, contributed to the patient's sense of grievance and his willingness to make a legal claim against the physician.

Health Care Delivery. From a public policy standpoint the main challenge was to develop a framework for providing the public with equitably distributed accessible services that were of reasonable quality and tolerable cost. Because there was no clear standard for how much care was necessary or cost-effective, the extent of expenditure was governed by the availability of resources. Throughout the world governments were struggling with the problem of how to meet needs and expectations within the allowable resources. Methods of financing medical services in the U.S. were open-ended, and further regulation was inevitable if the nation and the government were to control their costs successfully.

Manpower problems remained an intractable difficulty, particularly the distribution of physicians. A variety of efforts were made in the U.S. to encourage a more equitable distribution, but with very limited success. In other parts of the world efforts to ameliorate the effects of the shortage of fully trained medical workers by using the services of paraprofessionals for certain limited tasks continued. A report from rural Bangladesh told how women who had been given

This portable tester is used to detect lead poisoning quickly and inexpensively by examination of a drop of blood.

AUTHENTICATED NEWS INTERNATIONAL

only two months of part-time training were sterilizing their fellow countrywomen by dividing their Fallopian tubes—the operation of tubectomy. The results were as good as those obtained by qualified physicians and, indeed, their patients suffered a 15% lower infection rate. In the face of a shortage of hospital beds in Nigeria outpatient surgery was attempted at a number of hospitals and clinics. All operations were performed under general anesthesia, and hernia was the commonest condition treated. The patients did just as well as those in comparable experiments in the U.K. and other technically advanced communities.

In Britain the medical scene was marked by expressions of discontent from the workers in the National Health Service (NHS). At the start of the year the consultants—the senior and most highly paid doctors in the NHS—went on a "work to rule" in protest against a proposed new contract that would favour those who worked full time for the service at the expense of the majority who worked part-time and accepted, on average, an 18% reduction in salary in order to retain the right to private practice.

Barbara Castle, the secretary of state for health and social security, announced in addition the government's determination to remove all "private" beds from NHS hospitals. She also announced her intention to control private practice outside the NHS by placing a limit on the growth of private hospitals and other facilities available for the treatment of private patients in order to ensure that the state service would not be deprived of resources.

In the autumn the so-called junior hospital doctors who manned Britain's state hospitals under the direction of the consultants, and who ranged from newly qualified interns to fully qualified specialists, staged a series of strikes, during which they dealt only with emergencies, in protest against what they considered to be inadequate and unfair government proposals for overtime pay (many worked or were on call for 100 hours a week or more).

UPI COMPIX

Entertaining passers-by in Union Square, San Francisco, is anesthesiologist Louis Lewis, playing his flute as he awaits the California Legislature's solution to soaring malpractice insurance rates.

Some commentators felt that the action taken first by the consultants and then by their juniors was not so much a response to the particular irritations that triggered the protests as it was a symptom of a growing and more general frustration felt by all grades of staff within an NHS faced with the task of meeting an unlimited demand on an increasingly inadequate budget.

Notwithstanding their discontent, the great majority of NHS staff retained a firm belief in the principles and ideals behind the service, and there was a general welcome for the announcement by Prime Minister Harold Wilson in October that a royal commission was to be appointed "to consider in the interests both of the patients and of those who work in the national health service the best use and management of the financial and manpower resources of the national health service."

Migrant doctors became an issue in a number of countries. In Britain the NHS was able to continue only because of the admission of at least 2,500 overseas-born doctors each year. But after June 1975 most overseas doctors seeking a temporary license to practice in Britain were required to undergo a test of their knowledge of English and of their clinical ability. There was a 60% failure rate among the first few batches of the foreign graduates to take this test. In June Jean Lupien, Canada's deputy health minister, said that his country was no longer dependent upon immigrant doctors. Those admitted (apart from a few specialists) would have to go to remote areas such as the Prairie Provinces of Alberta, Manitoba, and Saskatchewan, which native Canadians tended to find unattractive. However, in February Caspar Weinberger, the U.S. secretary of health, education, and welfare, told a House of Representatives committee that he was strongly against restricting the entry of foreign physicians to the U.S., despite complaints from U.S. doctors and state medical associations (notably New York's) that the country was experiencing a glut of immigrant doctors, many of whom had language problems and inadequate medical skills.

In February the European Economic Community (EEC) approved directives, to come into force during 1976, allowing the free movement of doctors between member nations, subject to the requirement that they acquire the linguistic knowledge necessary for the exercise of their profession in the country to which they wished to move.

An official government document published in Canada at the end of 1974, with a preface by the minister of national health and welfare, described the health field as being traditionally concerned almost exclusively with the treatment of existing illness but emphasized that future improvements must "lie mainly in improving the environment, moderating self-imposed risks, and adding to our knowledge of human biology." It seemed possible that Canada might pioneer a new and more fruitful approach to community health care.

There was awareness at all levels of policymaking that medical care, no matter how proficient, cannot substitute for healthful ways of living. Medical care has only a limited effect on patterns of health and illness, and improved functioning and longevity depend as much on how people choose to live as on the remedies of medical science. There was realization that growing efforts were necessary in the area of preventive and environmental medicine and in health

continued on page 383

SPECIAL REPORT

ABORTION AND FETAL RESEARCH: A RECONSIDERATION

By Marc Lappé

By 1970 public policy on abortion had become enveloped in intense political controversy and public debate, incited in part by the exponential rise in the number of women seeking legal and illegal abortions. In January 1973 the U.S. Supreme Court issued its ruling in the cases of *Roe* v. *Wade* and *Doe* v. *Bolton*, in which it barred states from interfering with a woman's right to an abortion before a fetus becomes viable (in the first two trimesters of pregnancy). This decision permitted a further increment in the number of women seeking abortions and raised the stakes in resolving the potential long-range moral, political, and public health implications of mass use of abortion facilities. Whereas some 1,575,000 women sought abortion services in the U.S. between 1967 and 1973, a like number were expected to obtain abortions in 1974–75 alone. Increasing numbers of people have become concerned that abortion practiced on this scale might have deleterious consequences.

This concern spilled over into the legislative arena with the introduction of state and federal legislation (most notably in Massachusetts) intended to restrict the availability of abortion services to women in the second or third trimester of pregnancy. In a parallel development, bills and amendments intended to restrict the practice of fetal research were introduced in at least 15 states, two municipalities, and the U.S. House of Representatives in 1974 and 1975. In November 1973 and again in August 1974 the Department of Health, Education, and Welfare issued its own regulations for fetal research. It was in part to resolve these often conflicting regulations that the National Commission for the Protection of Human Subjects of Biomedical and Behavioral Research was appointed on Dec. 3, 1974. The secretary of health, education, and welfare directed the commission to assess the extent and nature of fetal research and offer recommendations for its regulation. A moratorium was called on federally funded fetal research until the commission's recommendations were received.

Fetal Research. To many ethicists the commingling of abortion and fetal research mixes two discrete moral issues. An abortion involves the right of a woman to assert her privilege to determine reproductive decisions privately, and this is counterbalanced against the growing prospects for independent existence of the fetus. But in fetal research it is society that claims to have a right (*e.g.*, for medical knowledge) that overrides that of the fetus. Because experiments conducted on the fetus only rarely aid that fetus directly, the social good of fetal research must be obtained at the cost of risk of some harm to the fetus. For some ethicists this trade-off violates the maxim that a person not be used for nonbeneficial research to which he or she has not consented. For others no violation occurs because the fetus is not a person.

Research on the fetus embraces a gamut of medical and physiological studies intended to increase medical knowledge generally or to offer specific therapeutic options to the practitioner. Among the types of research performed are prenatal diagnosis, intrauterine therapies (as for Rh hemolytic disease), and studies of fetal behaviour, placental transfer, nutrition, fetal physiology, abortion techniques, and techniques for facilitating delivery. A primary issue that the commission took up was whether or not such research is desirable in and of itself. A second question was whether some studies should be performed on a fetus that is about to be aborted rather than on one that is intended to go to term. Another question concerned whether or not different standards for fetal research should be applied when death and abortion are imminent. In what ways, if any, is the fetus in a moral category distinct from adults or from children—or from animals? In resolving these difficult issues the commission recommended, in part, that only minimal or no-risk nontherapeutic research was permissible on all fetuses, independent of whether or not they were to be taken to term. These recommendations were accepted by the secretary of health, education, and welfare in June 1975. The commission thus took a middle ground in protecting fetuses from harm, while allowing medical science to advance society's interests.

In supporting society's right to regulate medical practices and experimentation that may be beneficial and proscribe those that may be harmful, the commission strengthened social controls over scientific research. It insisted that where society subordinates the claims of human beings, even fetuses, at the very least it is necessary to give good reasons. By analogy, we might ask: if abortion were found to have deleterious effects on social institutions or public health, would a continued policy of social sanction be justified?

The Abortion Debate. In legalizing abortion, it was not initially clear even to the most ardent supporter whether the long-term benefits of abortion would outweigh its costs. Many Eastern European countries that have a long history of liberal abortion policies have seriously reassessed the overall consequences of these policies. Concern was expressed for deleterious effects on birthrates, maternal health, and subsequent pregnancies. At least four critical issues were introduced by the practice of widespread abortion.

Abortion as a Substitute for Contraception. Because abortion carries a greater risk of maternal death and morbidity than does average contraceptive use, any population-wide trend that leads to a greater reliance on abortion than on contraception will also result in an increase in maternal morbidity and mortality. Fortunately, available evidence indicates that widespread abortion has been accompanied by a general increase rather than a decrease in the utilization of family planning services and thus, by inference, a rise in contraceptive use.

Although statistically unremarkable, data on abortion "repeaters" indicate that replacement of contraception by abortion definitely does occur in individual cases. This substitution becomes a moral problem if the fetus is regarded as a developing organism with increasing human and biological potential. In this view, developed most thoroughly by Daniel Callahan in *Abortion: Law, Choice, and Morality* (1970), the fetus incrementally acquires properties that enhance its status as a person. As it moves through stages of development that bring its human potential closer to fruition, Callahan and other moral philosophers assert, its claims on us for protection and support mount. Thus procedures that prevent conception or an intrauterine device that "aborts" a newly implanted embryo interrupts the reproductive process at a stage when personhood and human potential are less well developed than they would be later. According to this view, as pregnancy progresses, abortion—and, by inference, fetal research—becomes an increasingly weighty moral decision. In contrast, many Roman Catholic theologians regard the conceptus itself as a person and find both contraception and abortion at any stage in pregnancy morally repugnant.

Reproductive Impairment Following Abortion. The World Health Organization (WHO) is currently studying the long-term

Marc Lappé is associate for the biological sciences at the Institute of Society, Ethics, and the Life Sciences, Hastings-on-Hudson, New York.

effects of abortion procedures on subsequent pregnancies. Among the postulated deleterious effects of these procedures are increased rates of infecundity, spontaneous abortions, extrauterine pregnancies, and premature births. While some early studies performed in Japan suggested a statistical association between one or more of these factors and abortion technique, an extensive review performed in Skopje, Yugos., demonstrated that such associations can be spurious because of sampling errors. In contrast, studies conducted in Prague, Czechoslovakia, and Opole, Poland, appear to indicate that abortions performed in the 6th to the 12th week of pregnancy by dilatation and curettage have a deleterious influence. In the Opole study previous abortions were thought to injure the cervix and its musculature in a way that increased the incidence of prematurity and prolonged labour in abortion users as compared with control subjects who had not had prior abortions.

Health-Related Effects of Abortion. If single or repeated abortions introduce appreciable medical complications for the woman patient or her subsequent pregnancies, such an eventuality would seriously undermine one of the justifications given by U.S. Supreme Court Justice Harry A. Blackmun for affording women the option to interrupt a pregnancy. In its decision on abortion the Supreme Court placed great weight on the proportionate safety of abortions performed under adequate medical conditions as compared with the risk of childbearing or illegal abortions. Legal abortion carries a risk of roughly 5 maternal deaths per 100,000 procedures, compared with 14 deaths per 100,000 live vaginal deliveries and at least 40 deaths per 100,000 illegal abortions.

The experience during the first two years following the Supreme Court's decision and the period immediately after New York State liberalized its abortion statutes in 1970 strongly vindicated the view that legal abortion reduces mortality among women in their childbearing years. Statistics showed that between 1958 and 1973 there was a marked decline in abortion-related deaths, a factor that can be attributed largely to the increased availability of legal abortion procedures and the resultant decline in illegal operations.

Psychological Effects of Abortion. Abortion, especially late in the second trimester, can carry with it the knowledge that something very near to being a child has been killed. Historically, social policy in the U.S. has operated on the understanding that not wanting a child per se does not provide a moral or legal warrant for killing. Roman Catholic teachings generally hold that human life has sanctity wherever and whenever it is present. Hence, some persons may be deeply confused over the moral weight to attach to an abortion decision. This will probably continue as long as the legal distinction between killing a pre-viable fetus (now condoned by the court) and a viable one (here the court encouraged the states to limit abortion) is in conflict with church or secular teachings.

Conventional wisdom indicates that many women would face potentially serious emotional conflicts and psychological sequelae following abortion. But, surprisingly, there is little reliable data substantiating any lasting psychopathological effects of first-trimester or early second-trimester abortion. Virtually no reliable information is available regarding the effect of abortion on marital relationships, family cohesiveness, or child abuse. All that can be said is that abortions performed on teenagers appear to be associated with higher psychological hazards and that late (*i.e.*, mid-trimester) abortions are more often accompanied by grief and a loss reaction than are earlier procedures.

Medical Personnel and Abortion. A more subtle psychological problem concerns the effect of abortions on the medical personnel who perform them. Some physicians and nurses who were politically active in the drive to liberalize abortion laws expressed misgivings in the year following the Supreme Court's decision. Their concern centred on the possible erosion of the health worker's traditional life-supporting role. The sole stipulation the court made regarding a woman's right to abortion was that such a right could only be exercised in conjunction with (and with the acquiescence of) an attending physician. Some have interpreted this to mean that the physician's duty to his patient's well-being is preeminent over the claims of a fetus for continued existence. The traditional source for defining medical duties, the Hippocratic oath, expressly forbids the physician from performing an abortion. (Some medical historians, notably Henry Sigerist, believe that this injunction is a historical artifact.) But if the physician's duty to his patient overrides his duty not to harm, he must violate this oath.

An alternative to abortion performed by an attending physician would be utilization of the paraprofessional. However, many nurses, who often bear the brunt of abortion services, are increasingly disturbed by their primary role in terminating pregnancy. Further, paraprofessionals might not be able to afford a woman the degree of medical care that a physician can provide.

Physicians are left with another dilemma: If they perform abortions according to traditional guidelines for protecting maternal welfare, they will occasionally choose abortifacient methods, *e.g.*, saline abortion, which inevitably compromise the prospect for post-abortion survival of the fetus. If techniques are employed that mimic labour closely, *e.g.*, polypeptide substances called prostaglandins that are likely to produce live but perhaps only marginally viable fetuses, what are the physician's obligations to this new "patient"? If the physician were truly identified with the fetus' needs he would have insisted on leaving it in the womb, since, short of toxemia of pregnancy, that is the safest place for a fetus to complete its gestation.

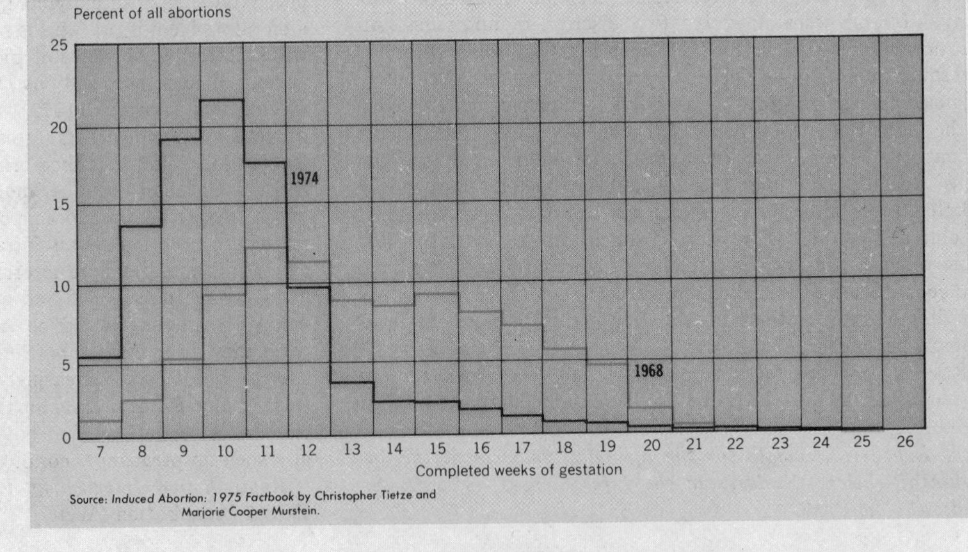

Chart showing shift of timing of abortions in Sweden between 1968 and 1974. The dramatic concentration of abortions in weeks 8 through 12 in 1974 accounts in part for a drop in maternal morbidity and mortality seen in that year. Abortions performed in the first trimester are safer for the mother than those performed later. This trend has moral significance as well, since early abortion reduces the chance of delivering a viable fetus.

continued from page 380

education. The crisis of confidence in medicine was also an important opportunity for significant redirection of priorities and commitments. The problems would remain for many years; important structural changes do not occur overnight. Policymakers must decide how to cope with such problems as catastrophic costs, the enhancement of the health of children, elevation of dignified care of the aged, and the humanization of nursing homes and facilities for the handicapped and disabled. They must also come to terms with how to balance the needs of society in allocating limited resources and in fulfilling social goals against the needs of the individual for assistance, for privacy, and for control over his own fate.

(DONALD W. GOULD; DAVID MECHANIC)

[425.D.1-2; 425.J]

CANCER AND CANCER RESEARCH

Cancer refers to a group of over 100 different diseases. The impact of cancer is significant—it was the second leading cause of death in the U.S., second only to heart disease. In 1975 cancer would account for 665,000 new patients, in addition to more than one million patients under treatment, and 365,000 deaths. About 53 million persons in the U.S. (about one in four) eventually would have cancer. Cancer would strike approximately two out of every three families. Its financial burden, often catastrophic for a family, was estimated at $15 billion–$25 billion annually, or nearly one-fifth of the national costs for all health care. Almost half of the persons who died of cancer were under 65. Cancer, particularly leukemia, was the largest disease killer of children between the ages of 1 and 15 years. It was the leading cause of death among women between the ages of 30 and 54. Most of the major site cancers—cancer of the lung, breast, colon and rectum, pancreas, and bladder—were increasing in incidence, while the incidence of cancer of the stomach was decreasing steadily in the U.S., for reasons not completely understood but which may have been related to diet.

All cancer starts in living cells, but scientists did not know exactly the cause that allows cells to deviate from normal orderly mitotic division to a disordered growth that is generally lethal if left untreated. Research advances in fields such as cell and tumour biology, molecular biology, virology, and immunology offered the promise of increased capability for the production of much-needed basic knowledge about the nature of cancer. In addition to research on the basic cancer process, scientists were working on methods to determine the causes of cancer, to prevent cancer, to detect and diagnose cancer, and to treat, cure, and rehabilitate cancer patients so that they could return to a nearly normal life-style.

Progress had been made in the effort against cancer: in the 1900s cancer was nearly always fatal; by the 1930s one out of five cancer patients was saved; by 1975 treatment was successful in one out of every three cancer patients. Scientists believed that half of all cancer patients could be saved if present knowledge were applied promptly in every case. Even with the new emphasis, the solution to the cancer problem would not be immediate. From the time a preliminary study shows that a new treatment will be effective until its final acceptance in national health delivery, approximately 15 years are required.

Cause and Prevention. Scientists estimated that 60–80% of cancers were due to environmental causes: such factors may include (1) industrial or occupational exposures, (2) certain consummative behaviours on the part of individuals such as smoking or alcohol ingestion, and (3) drugs, hormones (diethylstilbestrol exposure *in utero* may predispose young girls to vaginal cancer), and X-ray given for diagnostic or therapeutic medical indications. The time from exposure to the carcinogen until the onset of the cancer takes many years. For example, in women who were exposed to high doses of radiation at Hiroshima and in women with tuberculosis who were treated by artificial pneumothorax monitored by repeated treatment, there was an increased risk of developing breast cancer. This increased incidence occurred more than 15–20 years after irradiation but appeared to be less if women were over the age of 35 at the time of radiation exposure.

With regard to industrial exposures, industry and unions estimated that several million individuals had been exposed to asbestos, many minimally but several hundred thousand significantly. Asbestos workers were at risk of developing lung cancer, mesothelioma (an unusual tumour of the tissue surfaces which surround the lungs and the abdominal cavity), and gastrointestinal tract cancer. New evidence suggested that the high risk for lung cancer occurred in asbestos workers who smoked. Research also pointed out that vinyl chloride, a common plastic feedstock, was the cause of angiosarcoma of the liver in workers in certain chemical plants.

The laboratory testing of potential cancer-causing chemicals that enter the environment each year by the thousands was a time-consuming and expensive operation. In 1975 alone 450 chemicals were being tested. It required about $100,000, nearly four years, and several hundred mice and rats to evaluate each chemical. Much effort was going into the development of short-term test systems such as the use of the mutagenic activity of a chemical in cultured cells as a warning of possible carcinogenic activity.

The determination of the characteristics of cancer patients was an important facet of cancer prevention research. The preliminary results from the third National Cancer Survey, which collected demographic

WIDE WORLD

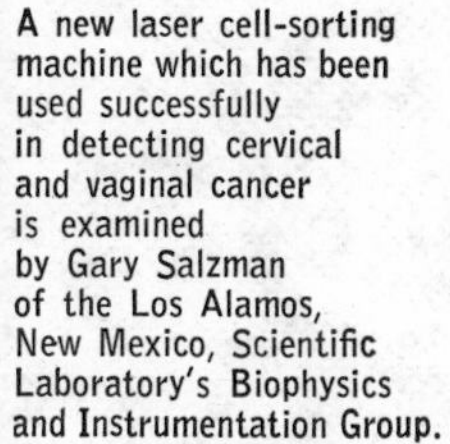

A new laser cell-sorting machine which has been used successfully in detecting cervical and vaginal cancer is examined by Gary Salzman of the Los Alamos, New Mexico, Scientific Laboratory's Biophysics and Instrumentation Group.

THE NEW YORK TIMES

Technicians leave the new $6 million Naylor Dana Institute for Disease Prevention in Valhalla, New York, which will be linked with the Westchester County Medical Center at Grasslands. The institute will deal solely with the prevention of cancer.

and medical information on all cancers newly diagnosed during the three-year period 1969–71 in seven metropolitan areas and two entire states, indicated an increase in cancer among U.S. black men, particularly cancer of the prostate and esophagus, and a trend toward a more uniform national incidence of cancer. Knowledge of risk factor was important in determining the individuals who should be subjected to close evaluation. The risk of dying from lung cancer among heavy smokers was 20 times greater than for nonsmokers. Women at high risk of developing breast cancer were obese, aged 40–60 years, childless, or had had a child after 30 years of age, or had a family history of breast cancer among blood relatives.

Detection and Diagnosis. Early diagnosis of cancer may be the key to successful treatment. The means for early detection of cancer of the cervix were available in the Pap test, which could eliminate cervical cancer. Yet many thousands of women still died of the disease each year. Breast cancer can be detected in its earliest stages. It had been shown that early detection methods of clinical history, physical examination, and X-ray examination (mammography) could result in a reduction of mortality from breast cancer, especially in women older than 50 years. Research was under way to develop detection methods for large-scale screening for lung cancer (sputum cytology and fiberoptic bronchoscopy) and bowel cancer (colonoscopy, purified carcinoembryonic antigens, and tests specific for human hemoglobin in body excreta).

Treatment. Advances in cancer treatment were based on several concepts. There was growing evidence that combinations of therapeutic methods tailored to have a maximum effect on individual cancers produced significantly increased survival rates. Treatment planning also must recognize that cancer is seldom a localized phenomenon and that drugs (chemotherapy) should be introduced early in the treatment before cancer is far advanced with a large tumour burden. The first treatment decision is crucial. The wrong type of initial decision can limit the effectiveness of advanced therapies later. Most cancer patients have the best chance for extended survival if evaluated first by a team of physicians such as surgeons, radiation therapists, and medical oncologists so that all effective therapies are used initially. This approach of several types of treatment given early in the course of cancer was termed the combined modality approach. Treatment of acute lymphocytic leukemia of childhood and Hodgkin's disease with a combination of anticancer drugs or irradiation or both dramatically improved the survival of patients with these diseases. A new study that investigated postoperative chemotherapy in breast cancer patients who had positive axillary lymph nodes indicated that the rate of cancer recurrence was significantly reduced for women who received the anticancer drug immediately after surgery. In osteogenic sarcoma the use of surgery and anticancer drugs (methotrexate and adriamycin) resulted in long disease-free intervals. There were indications that immunotherapy (stimulation of the body's immune system) combined with other treatments might be of value. For example, chemoimmunotherapy with anticancer drugs and BCG (attenuated tubercle bacillus) might induce definite increases in the remission rate in malignant melanoma.

In certain hormonally dependent cancers, such as breast cancer, it was hoped that the new estrogen receptor tests (estrogen-binding proteins) would help to predict response to hormone therapy. These laboratory tests would determine if cancer cells removed at surgery had these hormone receptors on their surface. Their presence indicates significant possibility for hormone responsiveness. Those patients without receptors could be given other therapies without delay.

Treatments were most effective when the tumour burden was low. Research was under way to determine the presence of biological markers in the blood or urine of cancer patients. Early results suggested that these markers might serve as guideposts for treatment continuation once obvious clinical evidence of cancer disappeared but while small numbers of cancer cells persisted.

Rehabilitation. Rehabilitation of the cancer patient had become an important new activity. Cancer detection, diagnosis, and treatment lead to definite numbers of cancer patients who, if not cured, can at least expect long periods of cancer-free life. Cancer rehabilitation involves physical problems such as amputations, stomata, and maxillofacial reconstruction. It also includes activities to help life adaptation such as psychosocial adjustments of the patient, his family, and his social contacts, and vocational considerations. The aim of cancer rehabilitation is to produce as normal a life as possible in the patient.

(DIANE J. FINK)

[424.B]

CORONARY ARTERY DISEASE AND ITS COMPLICATIONS

The major emphasis of investigative studies in the field of cardiovascular disease continued in the area of coronary artery disease—that is, disorders of the small blood vessels (arteries) feeding the heart muscle. Whereas structural changes due to degeneration (atherosclerosis) and leading to narrowing and even total obstruction of the blood vessels had long been recognized as the basic problem in coronary artery disease, there was increasing recognition that a minority of patients having a type of chest discomfort (angina) typical of coronary artery degeneration or even having a full-blown heart attack had no such process present.

Some of these individuals were shown to have a reversible spasm of the arteries without organic change in these arteries. Some were suspected of having small aggregates, or clumps, of blood platelets that briefly blocked the channel of an artery. (This was especially considered in the case of young women on the pill who developed heart attacks.) In certain others the reasons for the appearance of angina or a heart attack remained mysterious. While such cases were decidedly unusual, it was clear that more and more of them were being identified.

Questions were also being asked regarding the role of clotting in the genesis of the typical heart attack. The concept that a heart attack was due to the formation of an occluding clot (thrombus) in an area of local disease or atherosclerosis of a coronary artery accounted for the frequent use in the past of the terms coronary thrombosis and coronary occlusion. A recent report of international experts in the field could not resolve the issue of whether a thrombus actually initiated a heart attack or was a secondary consequence or complication of it. Attempts also were being energetically pursued to limit the amount of damage done to the heart muscle should a heart attack occur. It appeared possible that certain drugs tending to diminish the work of the heart (called blockers) might be useful in this regard. Some salvage of heart muscle also seemed to be achieved in certain patients with heart attacks through the use of drugs that lowered the blood pressure and decreased the work load on the heart, and also in those with very severe heart attacks where resort was made to pumping devices that lessened the mechanical load on the heart as well as providing it with a better circulation through its own arteries.

The mid-1970s continued to be the era of coronary artery surgery. The voices of those skeptical of the current operations, which provided a detour or bypass around a narrowed diseased area in a coronary artery, were heard less often. The operations were not too difficult technically, and many surgeons were hard at work performing them. The operative risk in major medical centres was reasonably low (certainly less than 10% and often less than 5%), and the benefits in terms of relief of discomfort (angina) were well demonstrated. It was, however, generally accepted that these procedures did not usually help a heart in which the muscle was severely damaged and that their role in prolonging life or averting future attacks had not been well demonstrated. It was also evident that in hospitals in which the operation was only occasionally performed, the risk to the patient rose as compared with the risk in centres in which such surgery was a daily occurrence.

There was also increasing preoccupation with the electrical record of the heart (electrocardiogram) taken under circumstances other than the routine of the doctor's office, the hospital heart station, or the hospital bed. One group of investigators reported on the information in a single electrocardiographic record obtained over a period of many hours using a portable recording device. This technique permitted a correlation of the electrocardiogram with the events in the day (eating, walking, arguments, and the like). It was especially useful in exposing the frequency of irregularities of heart rhythm but might also reveal signs of latent coronary heart difficulty. Other investigators extended earlier observations on the utility of electrocardiograms recorded during the stress of exercise—usually on a treadmill. Many physicians believed that the findings of such electrocardiograms were predictive of future disability or death from coronary artery disease. Some physicians, pointing to the lack of a 100% correlation of the findings with

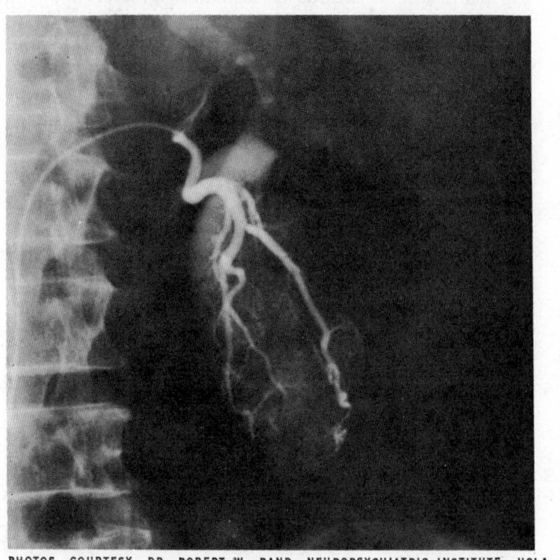

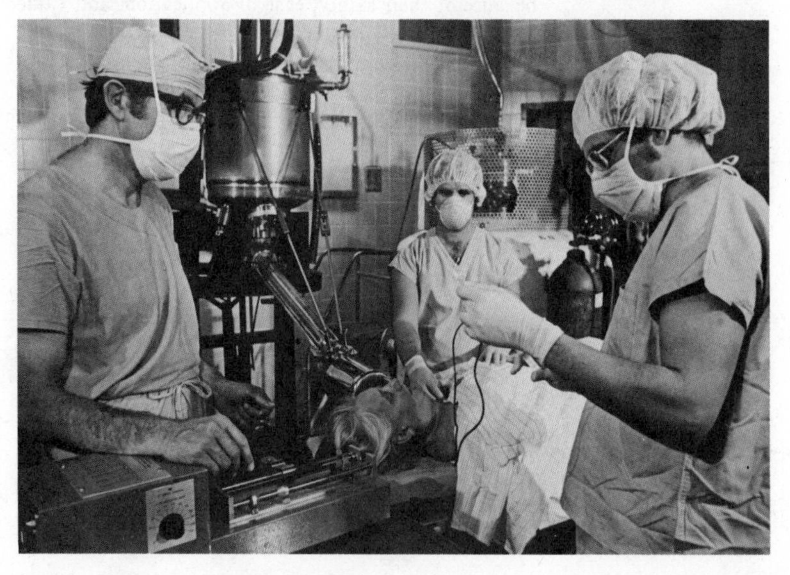

Selective destruction of brain tumours prior to surgery is accomplished by a new technique. At left, a ferrosilicone material is injected by catheter into a tumour and viewed by X-ray photography. A superconducting magnet placed against the patient's head (right) causes occlusion of the blood supply to the tumour and, hence, its destruction.

PHOTOS, COURTESY, DR. ROBERT W. RAND, NEUROPSYCHIATRIC INSTITUTE, UCLA

PHOTOS, KEYSTONE

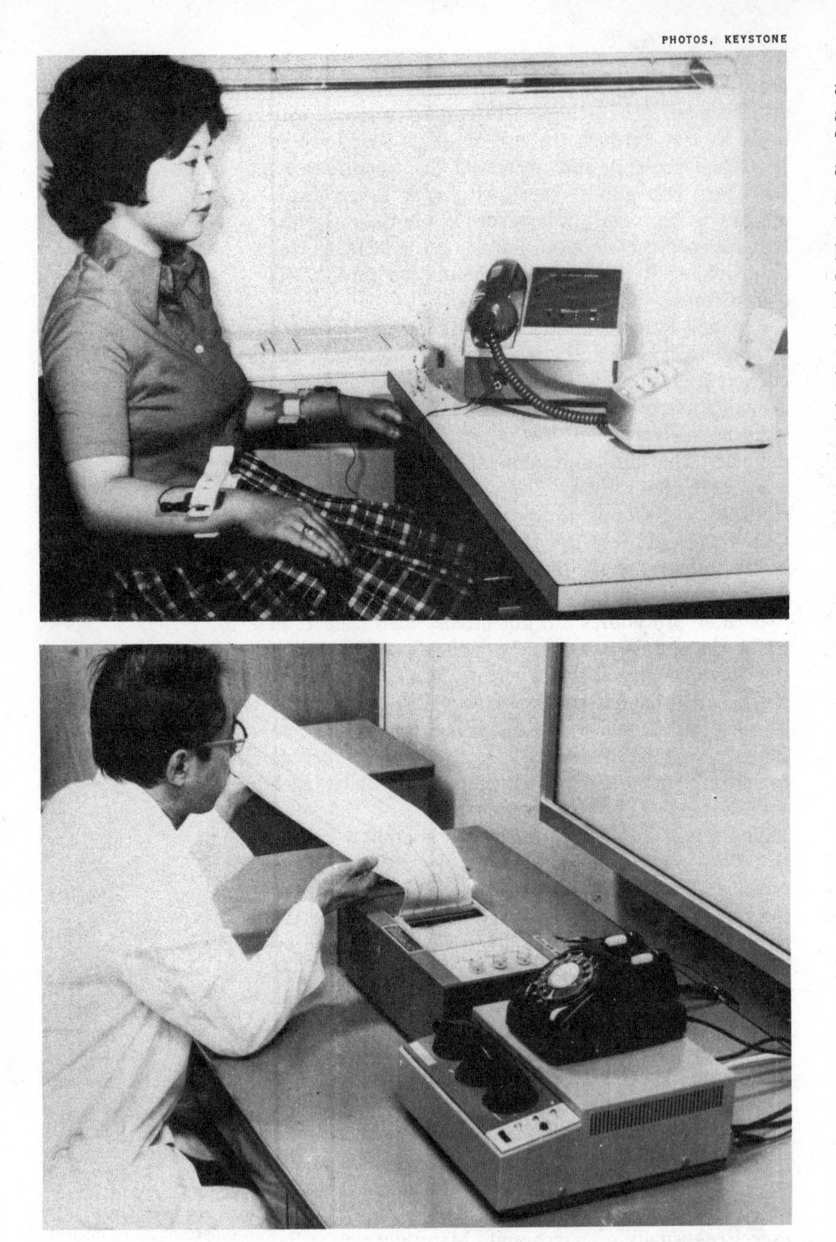

A doctor in Tokyo analyzes this woman's heartbeat with the aid of a new type of machine utilizing telephone transmission.

other accepted sources of information (such as special X-rays, or arteriograms, outlining the coronary arteries), were more cautious. However, both of these noninvasive approaches were seeing increasing use because of their safety, ease of application, and value as an additional source of information about heart response.

Hypertension. High blood pressure, or hypertension, was receiving almost as much attention as coronary heart disease. The need to identify the cause or causes of the commonest type of high blood pressure —usually called essential hypertension—continued. It was suggested that the production by the kidney of a substance called renin was closely related to certain types of high blood pressure; *i.e.*, patients whose kidneys produced a low level of renin might have high blood pressure with a better outlook than those patients in whom the output of renin was high. It would clearly be valuable if such a measurement could provide an index for a given patient of the risk of complications (including death) from high blood pressure. Unfortunately the use of the level of renin as a risk factor was receiving much criticism, and the majority of workers questioned its utility as a predictor of future disability or death.

A great deal of attention was directed internationally to the better detection of high blood pressure and to improved methods of treatment and follow-up. There was increasing use of nurses and various other allied health personnel in high blood pressure programs, partly because of the vast extent of the hypertension problem, partly in order to save expense, and partly because they had been shown to be exceedingly effective if properly supervised by physicians. Just how often mild high blood pressure should be treated remained unclear. That the medical profession must take a greater interest in the earliest phases of high blood pressure in children was widely accepted. The possible disadvantages or hazards of certain of the drugs used (rauwolfia and breast cancer, for example) received considerable publicity, but fortunately the record of safety and efficacy of the drugs most commonly employed was extraordinarily good.

Effect of Cigarettes. The unfavourable effects of cigarette smoking on the heart had been described in the past, but the exact basis for these deleterious effects was not clarified. Some investigators believed nicotine to be the culprit, and there was some experimental work in animals indicating that large doses of nicotine in conjunction with cholesterol feeding and vitamin D could produce a disease of arteries resembling that seen in humans. An alternative explanation was offered by other scientists who pointed to the possible role of carbon monoxide inhaled with the cigarette smoke. Whatever the exact mechanism or mechanisms, there were ever increasing data demonstrating how the nonsmoker or ex-cigarette smoker experienced fewer heart attacks than the habitual cigarette smoker. The long-term population study in Framingham, Mass., showed that among men who were followed for 18 years, those who were cigarette smokers when first seen and who subsequently stopped had attack rates for coronary heart disease one-half those experienced by men who continued to smoke. A study in Göteborg, Sweden, investigated a group of men who had already experienced a heart attack and observed that after two years those who continued to smoke cigarettes had twice as many new heart attacks and twice the death rate from heart attacks as those who had given up smoking.

Formation of Blood Clots. Prevention of clotting within the heart or arteries leading from the heart and within the veins carrying blood back to the lungs continued to be actively pursued. Clots formed within the heart under various circumstances: after a heart attack, in some patients in whom the upper chambers, or atria, were beating chronically with a rapid and often irregular rhythm (atrial fibrillation), and in persons with artificial valves. Clots might also form in diseased arteries. The clot formation in the veins seemed especially liable to be found after injuries to the veins, after surgery, with slowing of the flow of blood in these veins from any cause, such as pressure on veins behind the knees from prolonged sitting, and at times in women taking oral contraceptive pills. Clots in both the arteries and veins and in the heart interfered with blood flow. More critical, however, was their tendency to break off from the sites of formation and migrate as free clots, or emboli, to produce an obstruction to blood flow elsewhere in the body. Strokes, gangrene of the legs, acute circulatory deficiency to the intestinal tract, and blockage of the vessels in the lungs were potentially lethal consequences. Most of the efforts at prevention of clot formation and clot dislodgement were concentrated

WIDE WORLD

This horseshoe-shaped blood bypass device implanted into a human heart can correct the effects of a certain congenital disease. The apparatus is explained here by Christopher G. LaFarge of the Children's Hospital Medical Center in Boston.

on the use of the drug heparin and drugs in the coumarin family. Both of these were somewhat difficult to use—the effect on blood clotting had to be carefully monitored and they had definite hazards. Recent work suggested that clots might be prevented from forming in the heart and in arteries more simply by taking moderate and regular doses of aspirin or a substance called dipyrimadole. Other studies also suggested that doses of heparin much smaller and safer than those employed in the past might be given by injection twice a day to patients after surgery to prevent clots from forming in veins. These quests for better means of averting undesirable coagulation of blood were being watched with special interest. Improved techniques for detecting the presence of clots in the legs and elsewhere in the circulatory system were becoming increasingly available. The rate of incorporation of radioactive fibrinogen, one of the substances in a clot, was measured over the legs; this was one of several means of registering interference with or alteration of blood flow (Doppler technique).

(OGLESBY PAUL)

[421.B.3; 422.A]

RHEUMATIC DISEASES

Rheumatic diseases is a term that connotes pain and disability of the musculoskeletal system. Medically the term encompasses a large and diverse group of over 100 diseases, which include arthritis (inflammation of a joint) and rheumatism (aches and pains in either the joints or soft tissues of the musculoskeletal system). Over 20 million Americans, or at least 10% of the population, were afflicted with rheumatic diseases and required medical care. The incidence of rheumatic diseases increased with age, and females had a higher overall prevalence than males. These diseases were the leading cause of crippling in the U.S. with a cost to the nation in medical expenses and lost wages of over $9 billion and immeasurable pain, suffering, and disability.

A major milestone was achieved when the National Arthritis Act was enacted on Jan. 4, 1975. The act created a National Commission on Arthritis and Related Musculoskeletal Disorders to formulate a long-range plan with specific recommendations for the use and organization of national resources to combat arthritis.

The etiology of most rheumatic diseases is unproven, a fact that hampers both accurate classification and optimal therapy. Other systems of the body besides the musculoskeletal may be affected and many rheumatic diseases have manifestations that mimic those of other diseases, especially in the early course. A discussion of some of the major disabling or life-threatening rheumatic diseases and concepts of causation follows.

Rheumatoid Arthritis. This chronic disease may be mild or relentlessly progressive with painful, often deforming, arthritis that may lead to partial or complete disability. The hallmarks are chronic inflammation and overgrowth of joint linings, erosion of adjacent bone cortex, and a destruction of the cartilage that normally provides a smooth cushion over articulating bones. The patient with rheumatoid arthritis tends to have constitutional manifestations, for example, tiring more easily, decreased appetite, prolonged stiffness of joints after arising, weakness, and a tendency to emotional depression, which reflect the systemic nature of this disease. Progressive disease may affect internal organ function in both children and adults.

The etiology or underlying predisposition is unknown. Once the abnormal conditions are established or set into motion, inflammatory processes contribute to the progression of joint damage and to the manifestations of pain, heat, swelling, tenderness, and limitation of joint motion. Intensive search for a possible viral agent as the underlying cause was under way throughout the world, but no specific organism or indicator of infection had been found in man. Immunologic abnormalities were discovered in the blood and joints of rheumatoid arthritis patients, which may be contributing to inflammation. The immunologic

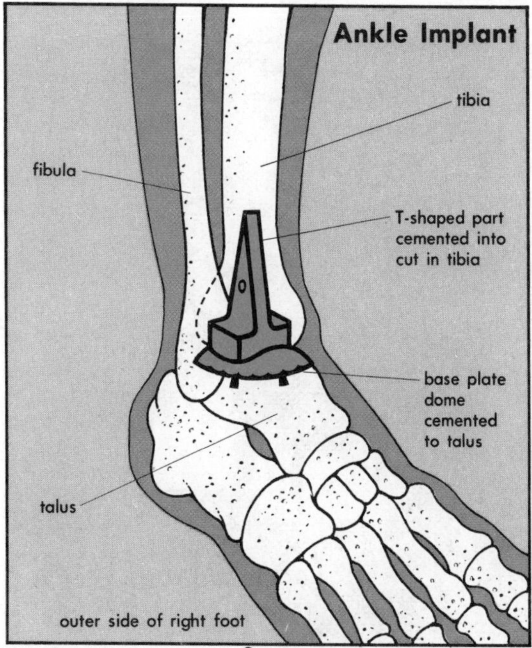

FROM V. PUGLISI—TIME MAGAZINE, © TIME INC. 1975

A new ankle implant operation may bring relief to thousands of crippled persons. A T-shaped metal wedge is inserted at the base of the tibia and aligned to rotate on a domelike base plate as shown. The new ankle prosthesis was devised by Theodore Waugh of the University of California at Irvine.

changes are more prominent in advanced disease, and it was not known if they were a cause or result of the disease.

Persons of all ages were susceptible to rheumatoid arthritis with 5 to 10% of cases having onset in juvenile ages and about half by age 45 years. The clinical pattern and the ratio of females to males varied with age of onset. The female incidence was only slightly greater than that of the male in juvenile onset, but in early adulthood it considerably exceeded the male, until about age 60 when it again approached equality. Childhood or juvenile onset arthritis was more likely to remit spontaneously than rheumatoid arthritis beginning in adult ages. The juvenile disease affected fewer joints at the onset but tended to be associated with more systemic manifestations; *e.g.*, fever, rash, and internal organ involvement. In the U.S. and Europe the proportion of the population with rheumatoid arthritis increased with age, in both males and females. Certain Oriental populations were believed to have less rheumatoid arthritis than was found in the U.S. or northern Europe, and population studies suggested a familial predisposition to progressive or erosive disease. Such clinical and epidemiologic findings suggested that host factors were important in the pathogenesis of rheumatoid arthritis whether or not microbiologic factors were involved in the onset or perpetuation of disease.

Connective Tissue Disorders (Acquired). These disorders were originally associated on the basis of common histologic changes found in the collagen and blood vessels of persons with these diseases and led to the older term collagen-vascular diseases. Collagen, the major structural protein of the body, was, however, believed in the 1970s to be normal in these diseases, the microscopic changes being attributed to leakage of plasma proteins altering the appearance. Abnormalities of blood vessels, especially those of smaller size, were still considered to play an important role in these diseases, but the pathogenesis of the vessel changes was not proven. As with rheumatoid arthritis, the possibility of circulating antigen-antibody complexes inciting vascular damage due to inflammatory mechanisms was suspected.

Also in this group of diseases, as in rheumatoid arthritis, an increased concentration of lymphocytes around blood vessels and in certain tissues exists, suggesting lymphocyte-related pathogenetic mechanisms. Whether lymphocyte changes observed during clinical disease activity precede or follow the initial manifestations was a crucial question, undergoing intensive research.

The major diseases in this group, namely, systemic lupus erythematosus, scleroderma, polymyositis and dermatomyositis, and various forms of vasculitis, affect various internal organs and may seriously compromise function, as well as survival. Differential diagnosis among these diseases was complex and was the subject of active research, since proper treatment (and evaluation of treatment) requires accurate diagnosis.

Degenerative Joint Disease. Osteoarthritis, or degenerative joint disease, is a slowly progressive, usually noninflammatory, type of arthritis found increasingly with age. It is characterized pathologically by deterioration of articular cartilage and by alterations of bone, including formation of spurs, cysts, and increased densities. The disorder is ubiquitous and not unique to man, modern or ancient, but is evident in most vertebrate species, with such bony changes even found in fossil dinosaur skeletons. The disorder is considered primary when it occurs as a concomitant of aging alone. However, when local or systemic factors are recognized that accelerate the pace of degeneration, such as certain occupational stresses affecting particular joints (*e.g.*, baseball pitchers' elbow), trauma, congenital deformity, or other factors, the osteoarthritis is considered secondary, and such patients tend to have more advanced lesions and onset at a younger age. In practice, it is difficult in many instances to distinguish between the two processes, clinically or anatomically.

Osteoarthritis was probably the most common form of arthritis, although its true frequency and distribution in the population were difficult to estimate because pain and other clinical manifestations do not always correlate with the extent or severity of the process. It was estimated that in the U.S. over 40 million people had osteoarthritic changes, but only a minority of these needed specialized care. Although the etiology and pathogenesis of osteoarthritis were unestablished, it was generally believed to result from an interaction of multiple factors, with perhaps physical stresses and impacts on joints being most important, but with other contributions to pathogenesis including heredity, joint lubrication and cartilage elasticity factors, articular cartilage cell and matrix function, as well as aging per se.

Gout. Gout is the most painful type of arthritis. It predominantly affects males and was well known clinically by the early Greeks and Romans. However, its relationship to blood uric acid was not discovered until the late 18th century. Uric acid is the final excretory product of the metabolism of purines (nucleic acid base molecules) in man, who is almost alone among mammals in lacking the enzyme uricase, which further degrades uric acid to a more soluble excretory product. The role of sodium urate microcrystals in causing joint inflammation was recognized in the late 1890s, but the observations were not generally accepted, and it was rediscovered in the early 1960s when active research in these mechanisms of inflammation was being carried out. The role of microcrystals in gout stimulated the recognition of other crystals causing acute joint inflammation and led to a more general concept of crystal-induced arthritis.

Surgeons minimize the chance of infection during an operation by wearing these futuristic "space suits" at the Nuffield Orthopaedic Centre in Oxford, England.

SYNDICATION INTERNATIONAL/PHOTO TRENDS

Gout is an excellent example of metabolic imbalance that leads to an inflammatory joint disease and can be treated specifically with drugs that lower the blood uric acid level by either decreasing the overproduction of uric acid or increasing its excretion in the urine. Such treatment decreases the likelihood of joint attacks and prevents complications due to accumulation of sodium urate crystals in joint and other tissues.

Like osteoarthritis, gout may be classified into primary and secondary categories, with the term primary gout applied to the majority of cases in which the elevated blood uric acid results from an apparently inherited overproduction or retention of uric acid. Secondary gout refers to those cases in which the elevated uric acid levels are due to another, usually acquired, disorder. Although the complex metabolic pathways of uric acid production had been defined, the imbalances causing uric acid overproduction in most gouty patients had not as yet been discovered.

(ALFONSE T. MASI)

[422.I.3-5; 424.L.1-4]

NEUROLOGICAL DISEASES

The most striking advance in the management of patients with neurological disorders during 1975 was the widespread introduction of computerized tomography (CT) of the skull and brain. Initially developed at the Central Research Laboratories of EMI Ltd. in England by G. N. Hounsfield, the technique permits one to delineate brain structures without administering foreign materials, such as gases or radiopaque media, to the patient. CT scanning was one of the single most important tests in the diagnosis and management of patients with neurological disease.

In CT scanning, the patient's head is held in an elastic hemispherical cap filled with water. X-ray signals are detected by a sodium iodide crystal that gives off photons of visible light when struck by a narrow beam of X-rays. The quantity of light emitted by the crystal is measured by a photomultiplier tube that is, in turn, connected to a high-speed computer. Projections are obtained by rotating the X-ray source and detector in a 180° arc around the patient's head. During a single scan, which averages four minutes, it is possible to determine the X-ray absorption coefficients of approximately 20,000 individual areas of the brain. The information is then processed by the computer to form a reconstruction of a cross section of the patient's head, which is displayed on a cathode-ray tube and photographed. The total dose of X-rays is equivalent to or less than that received in conventional radiography.

Very small variations in X-ray absorption coefficients, which normally exist in the different parts of the brain, are defined, rendering the subarachnoid space, cerebral cortex, white matter, and ventricular system visible (fig. 1). Calcification, which may elude detection by conventional X-ray methods, is readily identified. Dilatation and displacement of the cerebral ventricles are also easily defined (fig. 2 and 5). CT scans can detect intraorbital and intracerebral tumours (fig. 3 and 5), blood clots (fig. 4), or swelling. Intravenous administration of iodine-containing compounds to supplement the CT scan can be used to enhance differences in absorption coefficients and permits outlining of brain tumours (fig. 6). CT scans obviate the use of potentially hazardous substances and can be performed readily in 35 to 40 minutes.

The year 1975 also brought notable advances in the understanding of myasthenia gravis, a perplexing neuromuscular disorder manifested by weakness and fatigability of muscle. In 1973 Jim Patrick and Jon Lindstrom produced an experimental myastheniclike syndrome in rabbits by repeatedly injecting them with acetylcholine receptor substance purified from the electric eel (*Electrophorus electricus*). This experimental disease was then produced in other animals and could be reversed by treatment with anticholinesterase drugs similar to those used in treatment of myasthenia gravis. In normal neuromuscular transmission acetylcholine is delivered from the presynaptic tip of the nerve, crosses the neuromuscular junction, and interacts with an acetylcholine receptor on the post-synaptic membrane of the muscle. This provokes an action potential that is propagated along the muscle and results in contraction. Investigators in a number of laboratories demonstrated serum factors in patients with myasthenia gravis that were capable of tying up or blocking acetylcholine receptors at the human neuromuscular junction. In addition an apparent reduction in the number of available acetylcholine receptors was demonstrated in muscle biopsies obtained from myasthenia gravis patients. Development of a new experimental animal model and demonstration that serums of certain patients with myasthenia gravis contain factors that bind to acetylcholine receptors would permit closer examination of the cause of the disease and suggest novel and more rational methods of treatment.

(DONALD H. HARTER)

[422.K.1-2; 424.M.1-6]

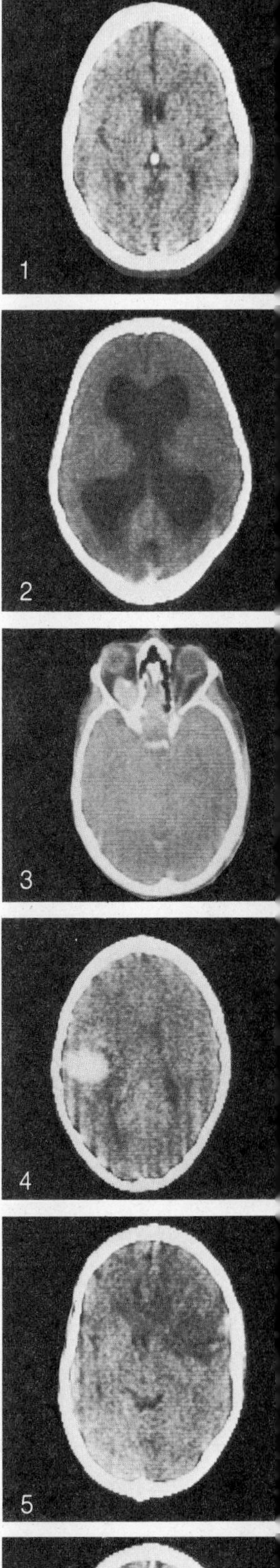

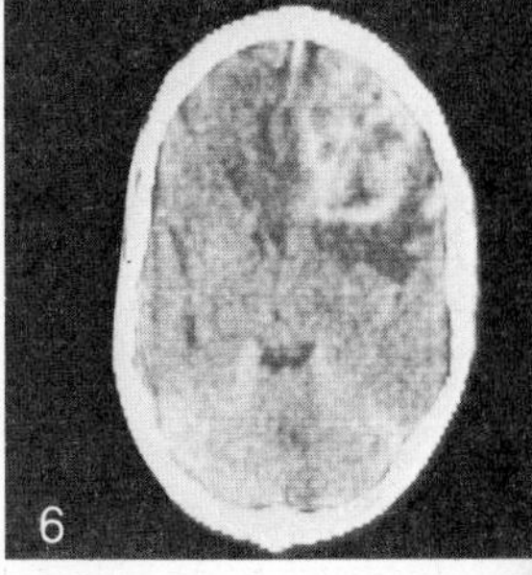

(Left) Patient lies under a new X-ray scanner which takes well-defined pictures of the soft internal parts of the body. The CT scans (fig. 1–6; top to bottom, at right) are discussed in text.

RIGHT: PHOTOS, COURTESY, DR. SADEK K. HILAL, NEW YORK NEUROLOGICAL INSTITUTE, THE PRESBYTERIAN HOSPITAL; ABOVE: WIDE WORLD

MENTAL HEALTH

The field of mental health in 1975 struggled to meet the challenges of change, and the task of keeping pace with societal change drained energy from verifying existing knowledge and making new inroads. Research lagged as enormous service demands usurped the time of the professional. Yet it became more and more apparent that as the wheels of psychological research ground relentlessly on, the more that was known, the more needed to be known.

Much progress had been made in meeting new challenges in mental health. But in the previous few years, and especially in the economic downturn of 1974–75, there was a widespread pulling back of the support systems of research in the behavioural sciences. In the U.S. federal funding was decreased by economy-minded, but shortsighted, legislators. Departments of psychiatry struggled to maintain a respectable identity in many medical schools, where the hard sciences of chemistry and physics, with their inherent structure and better defined boundaries, had overruled the soft sciences, especially those dealing with human behaviour. Psychiatric chairmanships in respected medical schools remained unfilled for months at a time. Training programs in clinical psychology and social service disappeared or were severely reduced, due primarily to diminished state and federal support.

In the face of increasing societal problems, the community mental health movement of the 1960s, aimed at bridging the disparities in mental health care between the poor and the more affluent, was not able to meet initial expectations in its delivery of services. No theoretical framework of community mental health had evolved and been accepted to provide the cognitive context for such a movement to succeed with meaning. Long-term financing for delivery of services was becoming increasingly rare as inflation gouged budgets, making them obsolete before they could be implemented.

There was continued effort to reduce the number of patients in state mental hospitals and shift the burden to the communities, which had neither the trained personnel, the physical facilities, nor sufficient finances to carry this enormous burden of care and treatment, especially for schizophrenia, a psychotic condition that accounted for more hospital beds than any other diagnostic category. Pharmaceutical agents were being used increasingly for treatment, but since they only covered the symptom and did not uncover the cause, their effects were often short-term.

Kenneth Donaldson was released from Florida State Hospital after 15 years of confinement and was awarded $38,500 in damages. The U.S. Supreme Court ruled that every mental patient must be treated or released, and Donaldson had not been treated while confined.

UPI COMPIX

The incidence of alcoholism continued to increase, and hard drugs maintained a substantial grip on youth despite fluctuating availability and cost. Among 14- and 15-year-olds, marijuana use more than doubled from 1973 to 1975, rising from 10 to 22%, according to the National Institute of Drug Abuse in Washington, D.C. At least one-half of the nation's three million high school seniors had tried marijuana, and 6% used it daily.

Suicide continued to be a major mental health problem in the U.S., with 25,000 recorded annual deaths attributed to self-destruction, placing suicide fourth as a cause of death in younger age groups, even though most suicides were never recorded as suicides. There were an estimated 800,000 suicide attempts annually, many resulting in serious physical injury and deep psychological scars. In Britain there were about 2,000 fewer suicides a year than ten years earlier, and the suicide rate was about 12 per 100,000 of the population as compared with, for example, 18 per 100,000 in California and 30 per 100,000 in Hungary. The remarkably low British figure was due, it was claimed, to an organization called the Samaritans, a countrywide network of voluntary workers who were available by telephone, day and night, for anybody who was in despair and sought help.

With clinical research in mental health currently being curtailed, the quality of services tended to stagnate. One consequence was the overstimulation of mental health services covered by insurance, as a national health insurance act moved closer to reality. There was a serious concern that overutilization of mental health insurance coverage would lead to abuse, although many hoped it would lead to prevention. Here again relevant research was needed to help answer such questions as whom should therapists see, how often, under what circumstances, and how should one pay? Discrimination among mental health disciplines remained a problem, with many MDs trying to maintain the stance that only they should have the right to insurance reimbursement for mental health services rendered, while other professional groups—psychologists, social workers, and clergy—strove for inclusion in the national health insurance acts being formulated.

The diminution of clinical training, mainly due to cutbacks in federal and state support systems, led to serious concerns about rationing existing services. As a result, a new phenomenon emerged—the neglect of the middle-class wage earner. Lower socioeconomic classes could seek help from clinics and governmental agencies, although the quality of service was often uneven. Increasingly only the upper classes were able to seek the expensive private practitioner, whereas the middle class struggled within the confines of insurance to diagnose and treat both mental and medical problems.

The American Psychiatric Association dropped the classification of homosexuality as a mental disorder but added that those "who are either bothered by, in conflict with, or wish to change their orientation, still can be diagnosed as ill under a new category, 'sexual orientation disturbance.' "

Esoteric new therapeutic treatment modalities emerge, run their cycle, and generally meet the fate of indifference or eventual rejection once their novelty has been tested. With the need for closeness and involvement and for immediate "cures," marathon encounter groups continued, although their popularity waned in the face of increasing concern that the casual selection of group participants and the inadequate training of group leaders had resulted in many psychological casualties. Behaviour modification gained more widespread circulation, although its lasting effects were yet to be tested, and the question remained as to whether it could have the same results in increasing effective personality change as the more traditional forms of individual psychotherapy, which bring about a much more gradual and voluntary change.

Advances in other fields also made imprints in the field of mental health. Kirlian photography, which substitutes electricity for light as the photographic medium, produces photographs that capture an aura of pulsating light rays emanating from the edges of an object. Such a tool was used for measuring that indefinable something that presumably links (or repels) individuals during an interpersonal interaction. Thus, for example, physical attractiveness allegedly was measured, in ways never before utilized, by the electrical aura created in Kirlian photographs. This might be a first step toward solving the dilemma of quantification, which had plagued the behavioural sciences.

The trend toward treating sexual offenders by surgery or with drugs that are designed to reduce or abolish sexual drive was strongly condemned in a WHO expert report prepared for the UN Congress on the Prevention of Crime. "It is not," said the report, "a generally accepted medical opinion that castration or hormonal demasculinisation are effective treatments for sexual offenders." A pharmaceutical company had introduced an antimale sex hormone preparation (cyproterone acetate) which, it was claimed, proved of value in the treatment of male patients who had committed repeated sexual offenses, but the value of chemical or surgical treatments for people inclined toward unorthodox sexual behaviour remained in dispute.

Concern continued over the high incidence of mental invalidism apparently caused not so much by any chemical or anatomical defect in the mechanism of the brain as by the fact that the pattern of contemporary life—at least, urban life—imposed strains too difficult to be borne. The escalating use of tranquilizers supported the idea that a majority of citizens of industrialized communities were subjected to a degree of mental and emotional stress from which they sought some kind of release. In the U.S. an estimated 25 million prescriptions a year were written for Valium alone. In March the U.S. Justice Department's Drug Enforcement Administration placed Valium and Librium under federal control. Prescriptions for these drugs remained valid for six months only, and pharmacists could not refill the same prescription more than five times in six months.

Why are some people born with a far lower intelligence than others? The popular explanation had always been that it was a question of who you happened to choose for your parents, but there was increasing evidence that environmental factors might play a major role. In particular, exposure to lead poisoning gained attention. A team of Scottish researchers found a positive correlation between the levels of lead in drinking water and the incidence of mental retardation among local infants. Similarly, a reduced performance in intelligence tests and certain other tests of brain function was reported by doctors examining children living near a lead-emitting smelter in El Paso, Texas. Other studies supported the idea that contamination of the atmosphere or of the water supply by lead might be a significant cause of mental illness and deficiency.

Psychosurgery had attracted vociferous criticism on the grounds that it altered personality, that its effects were irreversible, and that its efficacy was, at best, not proven. There was therefore a cautious welcome for the plans of Britain's Royal College of Psychiatrists to organize a prospective controlled trial in which the fate of patients subjected to psychosurgery would be compared with that of another group of closely similar patients. A sound assessment of psychosurgery was urgently needed, but the ethical and practical difficulties facing the organizers of the trial were formidable.

(DONALD W. GOULD; ROBERT I. YUFIT)

[438.D]

DENTISTRY

As congressional activity toward the adoption of some form of national health insurance regained some impetus in the U.S. during 1975, organized dentistry reiterated its insistence that a dental care component must be included. The ultimate goal for dentistry's involvement in a national health scheme would be to establish some type of priority scale, starting with children, to bring dental care to more Americans. One important step in this direction was the phenomenal expansion of dental insurance provided on a group basis. Most of this growth stemmed from union-management negotiations. Dental care had grown in popularity as a fringe benefit in local contract negotiations for 20 years. The number of Americans covered by dental insurance grew from 4.7 million in 1967 to 25 million in 1975 and was expected to reach 60 million, or over 25% of the population, by 1980.

Tooth Decay. Dental researchers were possibly moving closer to developing a type of immunization process to protect against tooth decay in humans. This was reported in April at the annual meeting of the International Association for Dental Research in London by a British scientist who said that such immunization had been accomplished in animal studies. Thomas Lehner of Guy's Hospital, London, said that experiments with rhesus monkeys had shown a significant decrease in the incidence of tooth decay through a cell-mediate immune response against *Streptococcus mutans*, the organism chiefly implicated in decay.

That the texture of foods as well as the composition might be a factor in the development of tooth decay was suggested by an investigator from the University of Alabama. Hady Lopez of Birmingham told the annual session of the American Association for Dental Research in New York City in April that this idea came from her animal study evaluating the effect on decay caused by changing the texture parameter of a test snack food. Earlier investigations by the same research team had revealed that modifications in the composition or the consistency of foods could affect their decay-promoting qualities. From her latest findings she concluded that food texture might affect

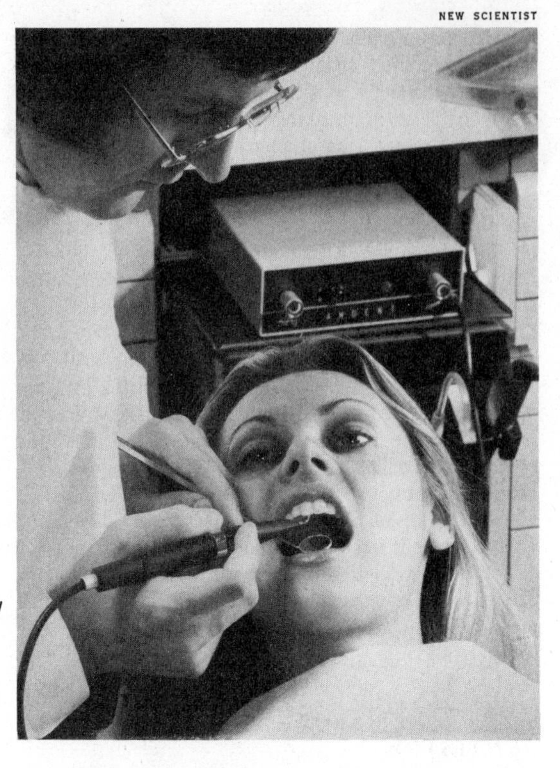

An ultrasonic dental instrument designed by the West German Siemens firm may one day replace the grinding, chiseling, and chopping associated with the standard methods used for removing tartar from teeth.

decay and therefore should not be overlooked in the design of low-decay-causing snacks.

Gum Disease. National Institute of Dental Research (NIDR) scientists studying the origin of periodontal or gum disease—the major cause of tooth loss in adults—turned up another possible clue. They found that corn nut extracts induced immunological reactions on the part of human white blood cells, thus adding substance to a long-held concept that foods probably contribute at times to gum disease. In their experiments, leukocytes (white blood cells), when separated from the rest of the blood and maintained for about a week in culture fluid containing corn extract, demonstrated a very rapid proliferation as compared with those lymphocytes (a type of white blood cell) not exposed to corn products. The researchers felt that corn hulls, nut particles, and possibly other foods might cause local destruction of gum tissue, especially when they lodge in crevices around teeth.

Other Developments. Researchers from the State University of New York at Buffalo discovered that by studying the frequency of certain dental trait anomalies commonly associated with cleft lip, with or without cleft palate, a greater degree of accuracy in determining the risk of the cleft condition in the unborn might be possible. Affecting one in every 800 births, in severe forms, cleft palate prevents the individual from eating normally and can also cause serious speech impediment unless surgically corrected. Data collected on 16 twin sets and 25 of their siblings showed that, despite heredity factors, there was a surprising drop in the number of dental defects in an identical twin without a cleft whose co-twin had the condition.

A Medical College of Georgia researcher suggested that there was an association between smoking, abnormal coloration in the soft part of the roof of the mouth, and lung cancer. Hubert W. Merchant of Augusta said his study of 19 patients with unusual soft palate pigmentation revealed that virtually all were long-term smokers, all had some kind of lung disorder, and five had lung cancer. He concluded that the "occurrence of smoking, abnormal pigmentation and lung disorders is not a coincidence and more studies need to be done to see if we can use this to predict lung disorders." (LOU JOSEPH)

See also Demography; Drug Abuse; Life Sciences; Nobel Prizes; Social and Welfare Services.

[422.E.1.a; 10/35.C.1]

ENCYCLOPÆDIA BRITANNICA FILMS. *Work of the Heart* (1968); *The Ears and Hearing* (2nd ed., 1969); *Muscle: Chemistry of Contraction* (1969); *Muscle: Dynamics of Contraction* (1969); *Radioisotopes: Tools of Discovery* (1969); *Respiration in Man* (1969); *The Nerve Impulse* (1971); *Health: Eye-Care Fantasy* (1972); *Health: Toothache of the Clown* (1972); *The Drug Problem: What Do You Think?* (1972); *Work of the Kidneys* (2nd ed., 1972); *Regulating Body Temperature* (2nd ed., 1972); *The Tobacco Problem: What Do You Think?* (1972); *Intern: A Long Year* (1972); *Venereal Disease: The Hidden Epidemic* (1973); *The Alcohol Problem: What Do You Think?* (1973); *Exercise and Physical Fitness* (1973); *The Heart and Circulatory System* (1974); *The Living Cell: An Introduction* (1974); *The Lungs and Respiratory System* (1975).

Historic Preservation

Despite the economic recession experienced in many countries, preservation projects continued to attract public interest and support in 1975. This was reflected in news coverage and in growing public resistance to development for its own sake.

Among international campaigns sponsored by UNESCO, the operation in Egypt to salvage the temples on the island of Philae and transfer them to the neighbouring island of Agilkia continued steadily. Drainage was completed, and deposits of silt were removed to allow completion of the photogrammetric record of the buildings before dismantling began. Preparation of the Agilkia site also continued rapidly. The first draft of an annotated bibliography of all published material resulting from the Nubian campaign, aimed at salvaging monuments endangered by the Aswan High Dam, comprised more than 600 titles covering many different aspects of conservation. The definitive bibliography was to appear in 1976.

In Indonesia the international campaign to restore the Buddhist monument at Borobudur was subject to some delays, although heavy equipment was already on site and trucks and forklifts were in operation. Additional tests on the fill underlying the terraces led the Consultative Committee to recommend that the four lower terraces should all be dismantled and waterproof layers inserted to avoid the danger of damage due to differential absorption of rainwater if some terraces only were dismantled. The new scheme was approved by the Indonesian government, which stated that it was "prepared to pay the price and bear the burden of the restoration of Borobudur." Meanwhile, UNESCO's international fund-raising campaign continued, with new pledges or contributions from the governments of Iran, Luxembourg, Nigeria, and The Netherlands, as well as private contributions from Japan and the U.S.

In Italy there were delays in the government's application of the special law for Venice adopted in 1974, but regulations put into effect in March allowed the provisions of the law to be carried out. These dealt with the problem of the hydrogeologic balance and ecology of the lagoon and the protection and enhancement of the natural environment, limiting the expansion of industry and of the port, and establishing pollution limits. The equivalent of U.S. $8.5 million was made available, permitting work to begin on restoration and on the improvement of sanitation. Taking

Hebrew Literature: *see* Literature

Highways: *see* Engineering Projects; Transportation

Hinduism: *see* Religion

into account the delays experienced, the regulations also extended the period covered by the special law.

A report prepared by a team of city planners under Leonardo Benevelo, set up by the Italian government to prepare a plan for the development of Venice, was reviewed in June by a committee of UNESCO experts which included the Italian team as well as international experts. The committee unanimously rejected an earlier plan to divide the city into two zones—one encompassing the historic centre and principal monuments, to be rigorously protected, the other allowing for expansion and redevelopment—and stressed the need to consider the whole city as a unit. It also recommended the carrying out of two pilot studies, one in Venice itself and another on one of the islands in the lagoon, to establish guidelines on which plans could be based. In August the head of the Venice Geographical Research Laboratory said that the sinking of Venice, caused by the draining of underground water from wells, had halted.

Studies with a view to safeguarding the Bronze Age site at Mohenjo-daro in Pakistan were well under way. At the suggestion of UNESCO experts, a series of observation wells were to be drilled around the two experimental tube wells already installed in order to determine the effective area that would be drained and the subsidence that might take place. Of the operations planned, first priority was now being given to the construction of a diversion dam on the Indus River; the current meander pattern of the river was rapidly bringing it closer to the site.

Following the report of a UNESCO mission sent to Cyprus after the upheavals of 1974, an adviser on the cultural heritage was appointed, with the agreement of the Cypriot authorities; most of the principal areas of cultural importance were inspected and, in the spring of 1975, recommendations were made for their preservation. While some looting and damage had occurred during the fighting, it was clear that press accounts had been exaggerated.

The Council of Europe's European Architectural Heritage Year 1975 was marked by considerable publicity and a number of exhibitions in member countries, with parallel programs in several nonmember states including Czechoslovakia, Finland, Ghana, Hungary, Poland, Romania, the U.S.S.R., and the Vatican. Many governments adopted special budgets for conservation purposes; for example, grants amounting to £1 million a year were awarded to the British Building Council for conservation zones of exceptional interest. Among the exhibitions was one in Paris entitled "Artistic and Historic Cities and Traditional Villages"; the most outstanding of these were transferred to Amsterdam, where the year reached its climax in October with an international congress coinciding with the celebration of the 700th anniversary of the founding of that city. (See *Special Report.*)

In June the International Council of Monuments and Sites (ICOMOS) celebrated its tenth anniversary at its general assembly in Rothenburg, West Germany. The number of national committees had grown to 53, and the council had its permanent headquarters in the "coach house" of the Hotel Saint Aignan in the historic Marais quarter of Paris. During 1975 specialized committee meetings were held on various subjects, the most important being one on "The Preservation of Historic Quarters and Communities" held in Bruges, Belgium. Raymond Lemaire (Belgium) was elected president and Ernest A. Connally (U.S.) secretary-general of the organization.

New legislation in the U.K. provided for government control of demolition of historic buildings and protection of the countryside, especially trees, and

continued on page 396

Repair plans (right) submitted by members of a British consortium to save the Leaning Tower of Pisa from collapse were discussed at a press conference at Kenilworth House, London, in September.

PHOTOS, KEYSTONE

EUROPEAN ARCHITECTURAL HERITAGE YEAR

By Barbara Hilborne

Restoration of the rural village of Conques, France, has been undertaken with public and private funding. Visible here are the towers of Saint-Foy rising above the slate-roofed buildings of this charming town.

ETIENNE REVAULT

Historic buildings, including the Frauenkirche, form part of a pedestrian precinct created in central Munich, West Germany, from which all traffic, including former streetcars, is now banned.

EUROPA NOSTRA

CIVIC TRUST

The Engelberg ironworks was built around 1820. Its restoration and preservation are part of a Swedish project to create a museum on the site.

A view of Cologne, West Germany, with the ancient cathedral towering above its modern surroundings.

PICTOR LTD.

Part of the Rows at Chester, England, showing its distinctive double-tier shops which date from the 16th and 17th centuries.

VERNON D. SHAW

The medieval church of St. Giles, Cripplegate, in London is the only remaining ancient structure in an area destroyed by World War II bombing. It is preserved within a modern steel-and-concrete housing development.

A. F. KERSTING

NORWEGIAN SECRETARIAT

All houses in the fishing village of Nusfjord have been registered with the Norwegian office of historic monuments. Some of these buildings date from the 18th century.

The Council of Europe proclaimed 1975 as European Architectural Heritage Year and launched an extensive campaign under the slogan "A Future for Our Past." The campaign covered the whole of Europe and was conducted at international, national, and local levels. Its central aims were to awaken the interest and pride of European peoples in their common architectural heritage; to draw attention to the dangers which threaten that heritage; and to secure the action needed for its conservation. The world is squandering its resources at a frightening rate and some of these, like the great works of art inherited from the past, are irreplaceable; once lost, they can never be recovered. European Architectural Heritage Year should create greater awareness of this peril. The pictorial review on these pages illustrates but a few examples of historic structures that will serve to remind future generations of their architectural heritage.

Barbara Hilborne is Senior Picture Editor in the London office of the Britannica Book of the Year.

continued from page 393

government circulars stressed the need for continuous renovation of housing rather than demolition. In designated conservation areas even unlisted buildings could not be demolished without authorization, and a duty was placed upon local authorities to formulate and publish proposals for preservation and enhancement of conservation areas. Where appropriate, it would be possible for authorities to purchase listed buildings at current use value.

Much of the historic preservation program in the U.S. was linked with the bicentennial of the founding of the republic, inaugurated at a ceremony attended by Pres. Gerald Ford at North Bridge, Concord, Mass., on April 19. The National Park Service, which had undertaken one of the largest programs in its history, designated 23 areas as having special historical significance, many of them closely connected with events in the War of Independence. In October 1974 matching grants had been announced amounting to $20.3 million for preservation purposes, as well as $2.7 million for the National Trust for Historic Preservation. These grants supported ongoing projects in addition to those connected with the bicentennial.

In Canada the restoration of the old city of Quebec progressed rapidly. Artillery Park had been designated as a national historical park, and a number of buildings within it were being restored. Others, such as the Quebec Gas Co. building, which did not fit the character of the park, had been demolished, and a parking lot was relocated outside the walls. The open spaces were being laid out as green spaces and gardens.

In the spirit of the U.S. bicentennial, the National Trust of Great Britain has bestowed Washington Old Hall, in Washington, England, upon the American people for a token rent of about five cents per year. George Washington's ancestors settled there in 1183.

WIDE WORLD

A large number of experts from UNESCO and the UN Development Program were taking part in the project to preserve and develop sites and monuments in the Cuzco/Machu Picchu area of Peru, financed in part by a loan from the Inter-American Development Bank. A regional training program had been established in Cuzco financed under the UNDP's regional program, with fellowships available to suitable candidates from the Andean countries, where other programs for conservation and development were also being undertaken. In Ecuador, for example, a grant from UNESCO had enabled a group of students and professors of architecture to carry out the first inventory of historic buildings in the city of Cuenca.

The UNESCO general conference of November 1974 had passed a resolution calling for "an integrated solution" for the preservation of the cultural and natural heritage of the Kathmandu valley in Nepal. The country had been closed to visitors until the 1950s, and its natural sites and communities had persisted with little change over the previous century. The opening up of the country had led to rapid changes, however, some of them beneficial but others more questionable. The latter included the disappearance of many historic buildings and the effect on the environment of even the relatively small-scale industrial development.

Under the UNESCO/UNDP program, aided by a grant from the Japanese government, the restoration of the Hanuman Dhoka royal palace was undertaken, and work on the buildings surrounding the courtyard, scene of the coronation of King Birendra in February, was completed on schedule. As restoration proceeded, old skills such as wood carving and the manufacture of traditional forms of brick and roofing tiles were revived. The restoration and modernization of the ancient city of Bhaktapur had been undertaken by the West German government, which had also contributed toward the next phase of the reconstruction of Hanuman Dhoka. In the early summer a team of UNESCO/UNDP experts, together with a World Health Organization expert on water supplies and sewage disposal, carried out a survey of the entire valley, and a master plan was drafted for the preservation and development of the cultural and natural heritage.

An earthquake in Burma in July caused considerable damage to many of the ancient pagodas of the 11th-century Pagan site. Reports stated that many of the spires had fallen, and that the most ancient of the pagodas, Buphya, which had been a landmark on the banks of the Irrawaddy, had fallen into the river. This was regarded as an event of ill omen by many Burmese. A UNESCO expert was sent to the area to assess the extent of the damage and to determine the work required for restoration.

In Australia legislation was passed to establish an Australian Heritage Commission on the lines of the U.S. Advisory Council on Historic Preservation.

From all these developments, it was clear that citizens and their governments, in both the developed and the less developed countries, were becoming ever more aware of the importance of conservation. This was also evident in the growing trend in city planning away from wholesale demolition and toward a policy of gradual renewal through a continuous program of renovation and rehabilitation.

(HIROSHI DAIFUKU)

See also Architecture; Environment; Museums.
[612.C.2.d]

Honduras

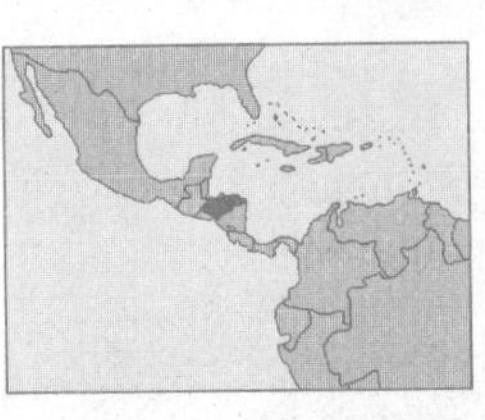

A republic of Central America, Honduras is bounded by Nicaragua, El Salvador, Guatemala, the Caribbean Sea, and the Pacific Ocean. Area: 43,277 sq.mi. (112,088 sq.km.). Pop. (1975 est.): 3,037,000, including 90% mestizo. Cap. and largest city: Tegucigalpa (pop., 1974, 303,900). Language: Spanish; some Indian dialects. Religion: Roman Catholic. Presidents in 1975, Gen. Oswaldo López Arellano and, from April 22, Col. Juan Alberto Melgar Castro.

Military rule of Honduras continued in 1975, with a movement inside the military establishment toward leadership by younger officers. President López Arellano was replaced as commander of the armed forces on March 31 by Col. Juan Alberto Melgar Castro. In April, when United Brands, a U.S. firm, revealed it had paid a $1,250,000 bribe to unnamed Honduran officials for concessions in the application of a banana export tax, López Arellano was removed as chief of state in a bloodless coup by the Army on April 22 and, again, replaced by Melgar. Although no evidence on which to incriminate López was revealed, Melgar remained at the nation's helm throughout the year. The government in August canceled contracts and concessions granted United Brands and the U.S.-owned Standard Fruit and Steamship Co. early in the century, but continued to work with the companies in a mutual desire for a harmonious operation.

Agitation led by the Christian Democrat-controlled National Peasants' Union for accelerated implementation of the land reform law resulted in the murder of 14 individuals, including peasants, students, and two priests, one from the U.S. and one from Colombia, in June. Two landowners and the military commander of Olancho, where the tragedy occurred, were held for trial by the military government, which repeatedly stated its determination to proceed with land reform. At least 15 peasants were killed in a similar incident in November.

Catastrophic conditions resulting from 1974's Hurricane Fifi were aggravated by a severe drought in 1975. Low prices for exports and high ones for imported products, especially petroleum, produced another bleak year for the nation's economy.

(HENRY WEBB, JR.)

[974.B.1.b]

HONDURAS

Education. (1973) Primary, pupils 420,714, teachers 11,712; secondary and vocational, pupils 56,692, teachers 3,038; teacher training, students 1,134, teachers 67; higher (university only), students 8,070, teaching staff 466.

Finance. Monetary unit: lempira, with (Sept. 22, 1975) a par value of 2 lempiras to U.S. $1 (free rate of 4.16 lempiras = £1 sterling). Gold, SDRs, and foreign exchange: (June 1975) U.S. $38,930,000; (June 1974) U.S. $34,030,000. Budget (1974 actual): revenue 256.8 million lempiras; expenditure 244 million lempiras. Gross domestic product: (1973) 1,798,000,000 lempiras; (1972) 1,634,000,000 lempiras. Money supply: (Dec. 1974) 250.8 million lempiras; (Dec. 1973) 246.2 million lempiras. Cost of living (Tegucigalpa; 1970 = 100): (April 1975) 133; (April 1974) 126.

Foreign Trade. (1974) Imports 764.5 million lempiras; exports 516.6 million lempiras. Import sources (1973): U.S. 41%; Japan 10%; Venezuela 8%; Guatemala 6%. Export destinations (1973): U.S. 57%; West Germany 12%; Canada 7%. Main exports: bananas 27%; coffee 16%; timber 16%; meat (1973) 9%.

Transport and Communications. Roads (1973) 5,943 km. (including *c.* 150 km. of Pan-American Highway). Motor vehicles in use (1972): passenger 16,700; commercial (including buses) 17,400. Railways (1973) *c.* 1,080 km. (mainly for banana plantations). Air traffic (1973): 205 million passenger-km.; freight 3.5 million net ton-km. Shipping (1974): merchant vessels 100 gross tons and over 56; gross tonnage 69,561. Telephones (Jan. 1974) 15,000. Radio receivers (Dec. 1973) 155,000. Television receivers (Dec. 1973) *c.* 60,000.

Agriculture. Production (in 000; metric tons; 1974; 1973 in parentheses): corn *c.* 255 (*c.* 295); cassava (1973) *c.* 42, (1972) *c.* 40; coffee *c.* 48 (*c.* 42); sorghum *c.* 35 (*c.* 42); sugar, raw value (1973) *c.* 90, (1972) *c.* 96; sugar, noncentrifugal (1973) *c.* 29, (1972) *c.* 31; dry beans 32 (*c.* 36); bananas (1973) *c.* 1,600, (1972) *c.* 1,366; oranges (1973) *c.* 54, (1972) *c.* 52; cotton, lint (1973) *c.* 6, (1972) *c.* 4; beef and veal (1973) *c.* 43, (1972) *c.* 41; timber (cu.m.; 1973) 4,500, (1972) 4,400. Livestock (in 000; 1973): cattle *c.* 1,638; pigs *c.* 837; horses *c.* 278; chickens *c.* 7,600.

Industry. Production (in 000; metric tons; 1973): petroleum products 628; silver (1972) 0.11; gold (troy oz.; 1971) 3.5; lead ore (metal content) 18; zinc ore (metal content) 20; electricity (kw-hr.) 408,000.

Hungary

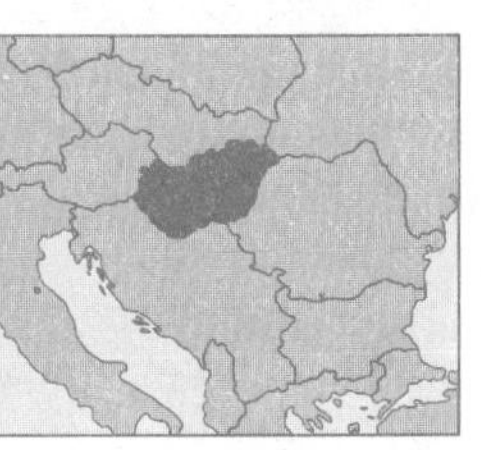

A people's republic of central Europe, Hungary is bordered by Czechoslovakia, the U.S.S.R., Romania, Yugoslavia, and Austria. Area: 35,920 sq.mi. (93,032 sq.km.). Pop. (1975 est.): 10,510,000, including (1970) Hungarian 95.8%; German 2.1%. Cap. and largest city: Budapest (pop., 1975 est., 2,058,000). Language (1970): Magyar 95.8%. Religion (1970): Roman Catholic about 60%, most of remainder Protestant or atheist. First secretary of the Hungarian Socialist Workers' (Communist) Party in 1975, Janos Kadar; chairman of the Presidential Council (chief of state), Pal Losonczi; presidents of the Council of Ministers (premiers), Jeno Fock and, from May 15, Gyorgy Lazar.

Mayors from the capital cities of neighbouring socialist countries met in Budapest on Feb. 13, 1975, to celebrate the 30th anniversary of the city's liberation from Nazi occupation. Much larger celebrations took place in the Hungarian capital on National Day, April 4.

The 11th congress of the Hungarian Socialist Workers' Party (HSWP) met in Budapest from March 17 to 22 to assess the work done since the tenth congress in November 1970 and to map future plans. Addressing the 848 delegates representing 754,353 party members (an increase of 93,000 since 1970), Janos Kadar said that all the conditions existed for the successful fulfillment of the 1971–75 five-year plan. In 1974 the national income was 29% above the 1970 level, industrial output was 30% higher, and agricultural production was on the average 17% higher than during the 1966–70 period. Plans for 1976–80 were designed to maintain this pace of development. The experiences since 1970, Kadar went on, had proved that it was correct to "develop the Hungarian system of economic management," but he insisted that "the decentralization of a significant part of the spheres of authority demanded still greater and more effective central guidance and supervision."

Rezso Nyers, Lajos Feher, and Gyorgy Aczel, the chief architects of the 1968 New Economic Mechanism, were sitting on the congress platform during Kadar's speech, but the new Central Committee of 125 members reelected only the last-named to the

Hockey:
see Field Hockey and Lacrosse; Ice Hockey

Hogs:
see Agriculture and Food Supplies

Holland:
see Netherlands, The

Honduras, British (Belize):
see Dependent States

Hong Kong:
see Dependent States

Horse Racing:
see Equestrian Sports; Gambling

Horticulture:
see Gardening

Hospitals:
see Health and Disease

Housing:
see Architecture; Industrial Review

Hungarian Literature:
see Literature

RUDOLF JARAI—CAMERA PRESS/PHOTO TRENDS

Dividing Budapest into Buda on the left and Pest on the right is the Danube River. Connecting the city are the Liberty Bridge, the Elizabeth Bridge, the Szechenyi Chain Bridge, and the Margaret Bridge.

new 13-member Politburo. New members of this key body were: Gyorgy Lazar (*see* BIOGRAPHY); Laszlo Marothy, 33-year-old first secretary of the Young Communist League; Miklos Ovari, 51, a member of the party secretariat from 1974; and Istvan Sarlos, 56, secretary-general of the Patriotic People's Front. Later, on May 15, Lazar succeeded Jeno Fock, retiring at his own request, as premier. A general election was held on June 15, and the new National Assembly reelected Antal Apro as speaker and Pal Losonczi as chairman of the Presidential Council. The latter body, jointly with the Politburo of the HSWP, went into session to consider proposals for a new Council of Ministers. Among the five deputy premiers two were new: Ferenc Havasi, 46, a member of the Central Committee who had spent three years studying in the U.S.S.R., and Gyula Szeker, former minister of heavy industry. There were also three new ministers: Tivadar Nemeslaki, 52, who held various labour union and party posts, now received the portfolio of metallurgy and machine engineering; Pal Simon, 46, former deputy minister of heavy industry, became the head of that ministry; and Pal Romany, 46, former head of the party's regional economic development department, became minister of agriculture and food industry.

In three constituencies no candidate received an absolute majority at the 1975 elections, and by-elections were held on June 29. Six clergymen were elected as nonparty members. Among the three Roman Catholics elected, the most prominent was Father Imre Varkonyi, director of *Actio Catholica*. As Kadar reported to the party congress, "We can state with satisfaction that in Hungary state and church relations have been settled." (K. M. SMOGORZEWSKI)

[972.B.2.b]

HUNGARY

Education. (1974–75) Primary, pupils 1,039,586, teachers 65,687; secondary, pupils 102,079, teachers 6,700; vocational, pupils 107,567, teachers 7,049; higher (including 18 universities), students 60,059, teaching staff 11,305.

Finance. Monetary unit: forint, with (Sept. 22, 1975) an official exchange rate of 9.39 forints to U.S. $1 (nominal rate of 19.50 forints = £1 sterling), a tourist rate of 22.20 forints to U.S. $1 (46 forints = £1 sterling), and a commercial rate of 47.25 forints to U.S. $1 (97.87 forints = £1 sterling). Budget (1974 est.): revenue 261,406,000,000 forints; expenditure 263,676,000,000 forints. National income: (1974) 370.6 billion forints; (1973) 354 billion forints.

Foreign Trade. (1974) Imports 51,010,000,000 forints; exports 46,927,000,000 forints. Import sources: U.S.S.R. 28%; West Germany 10%; East Germany 9%; Czechoslovakia 8%; Austria 5%; Poland 5%. Export destinations: U.S.S.R. 32%; East Germany 10%; Czechoslovakia 9%; West Germany 6%; Poland 6%. Main exports (1973): machinery 22%; transport equipment 11%; chemicals 7%; fruit and vegetables 6%; iron and steel 5%; cereals 5%; clothing 5%; livestock 5%.

Transport and Communications. Roads (1973) 109,649 km. (including 158 km. expressways). Motor vehicles in use (1973): passenger 407,551; commercial 98,304. Railways: (1973) 8,527 km.; traffic (1974) 13,879,000,000 passenger-km., freight 22,472,000,000 net ton-km. Air traffic (1973): 420 million passenger-km.; freight 5.8 million net ton-km. Inland waterways in regular use (1973) 1,277 km. Telephones (Dec. 1973) 968,000. Radio licenses (Dec. 1973) 2,533,000. Television licenses (Dec. 1973) 2,199,000.

Agriculture. Production (in 000; metric tons; 1974; 1973 in parentheses): corn (1973) 5,963, (1972) 5,554; wheat 4,860 (4,502); rye *c.* 175 (178); barley *c.* 840 (874); oats *c.* 65 (72); rice *c.* 74 (69); potatoes 1,364 (1,355); sugar, raw value *c.* 303 (320); cabbages (1973) *c.* 207, (1972) 207; tomatoes *c.* 450 (478); onions *c.* 154 (144); rapeseed *c.* 70 (68); sunflower seed *c.* 150 (153); dry peas *c.* 73 (*c.* 72); peaches (1973) *c.* 132, (1972) 132; plums (1973) *c.* 251, (1972) 251; apples (1973) *c.* 709, (1972) 709; wine (1973) *c.* 608, (1972) 503; tobacco *c.* 19 (20); beef and veal (1973) *c.* 185, (1972) 170; pork (1973) *c.* 455, (1972) *c.* 480. Livestock (in 000; March 1974): cattle *c.* 1,998; pigs 6,980; sheep 1,813; horses (1973) 189; chickens (1973) 55,219.

Industry. Index of production (1970 = 100): (1974) 129; (1973) 120. Production (in 000; metric tons; 1974): coal 3,209; lignite 22,552; crude oil 1,996; natural gas (cu.m.) 5,095,000; electricity (kw-hr.) 18,946,000; iron ore (25% metal content) 545; pig iron 2,299; crude steel 3,468; bauxite 2,751; aluminum 69; cement 3,437; petroleum products (1973) 7,995; sulfuric acid 657; fertilizers (1973–74) nitrogenous 424, phosphate 195; cotton yarn 58; wool yarn 12; commercial vehicles (units) 12.

Hunting and Fishing

Despite recession and soaring prices, an estimated 20 million persons purchased hunting licenses in the U.S. in 1975. In 1974 the number was 16.4 million and those hunters poured $143 million into state coffers in license fees. Pennsylvania led the states in hunting license sales, followed by New York, California, Michigan, Texas, and Virginia.

Several strides were made in the hunting field in 1975. National Hunting and Fishing Day, begun several years earlier as a brainchild of Warren Page, president of the National Shooting Sports Foundation, had become an institution. It had been proclaimed an official celebration by the governors of every state and was celebrated each September by more and more sportsmen's groups across the nation.

The fifth annual convention of Game Conservation International met in San Antonio, Texas, in May, and delegates from every organization connected with hunting attended the huge gathering sponsored by the nonprofit, tax-exempt Game Coin. It was at that convention that the first legal defense fund in the U.S. was established to protect the civil rights of the hunting public from harassment and abuse by preservation groups using the media to attack hunting as a sport and game management tool.

The large volunteer organizations, such as Ducks Unlimited, which had their beginnings in the 1930s, were growing rapidly in membership—a healthy sign for the hunting community. The membership of Ducks Unlimited in 1975 was approximately 150,000, and this did not include the approximately 500,000 persons who contributed varying amounts of money through game and fish departments across the country.

Rising costs and dwindling numbers of animals plagued big-game hunters in many parts of the world during 1975. The average expense per person of a three-week safari from the U.S. to Africa was estimated at $12,000; this included the pay of a professional hunter, fees, transportation, and taxidermy. At the same time, the rapid increase in population in many countries depleted the supply of animals by eliminating much of their natural habitat. Among those nations in which big-game hunting continued to be good to excellent in 1975 were Botswana, the Central African Republic, Zambia, and the Sudan.

According to state game and fish departments and the U.S. Fish and Wildlife Service, over 29 million persons purchased fishing licenses in 1975. However, the figures do not indicate the total number of persons who fished in the U.S. Youngsters below the age of 14 and in some states senior citizens were not required to purchase a license to fish. The largest bloc of people not included in the figures were those who engaged in saltwater fishing, which did not require a license in most states.

The National Marine Fisheries Service estimated that participation in marine recreational fishing in the northeastern states from Maine to Virginia alone totaled almost 11 million anglers. If the trend toward saltwater fishing continued, fishing could become one of the largest participation sports in the U.S. It was thought that the total number of people fishing each year was in the neighbourhood of 60 million.

The trend toward saltwater recreational fishing could be attributed to several factors. Developers and other commercial interests had made deep inroads into areas where there were once virgin lakes and streams. Much of the freshwater fishing was a crowded situation and those seeking solitude were forced to backpack into wilderness areas to find fishing the way it once was. Also, the recession and the rise in food costs led many to fish the shores, jetties, docks, and from boats in salt water for food fish. Another reason for the increase in marine angling was the development of better equipped, faster, and safer small boats within the price range of the average family and of such improvements as fibreglass hulls, built-in flotation, smaller and more efficient engines, and more sophisticated fishing tackle.

A number of encouraging successes marked the effort to introduce exotic fish species into certain areas and to reintroduce fish into old haunts. The most notable was the restocking of Atlantic salmon in a number of northeastern rivers—particularly in the area of Maine and Connecticut. Efforts by the U.S. and Canadian governments to stop commercial netting at the mouths of salmon rivers resulted in a highly satisfying return of the Atlantic salmon for sport fishing. In rivers such as the Connecticut, fisheries biologists had to begin the migration and spawning cycle all over again by raising eggs in hatcheries and stocking small salmon fry in the river headwaters in order to induce salmon to return for spawning. Results were highly favourable. The striped bass, which was at one time strictly an Atlantic Ocean saltwater game and food fish, was successfully stocked into many inland freshwater lakes and rivers—from the Carolinas to the arid southwestern deserts of Arizona and Nevada—and even into the Pacific Ocean at San Francisco Bay.

Biologists at the Florida Game and Fresh Water Fish Commission developed a new hybrid game fish, which they referred to as a "reciprocal bass." The unnamed hybrid was a cross between a female white bass and a male striped bass. A similar hybrid had been developed in South Carolina in 1965, but was a cross between a striped female and a white male. The new reversed hybrid was reported to be an extremely hardy fish capable of putting up a harder fight than the South Carolina original.

A tragic situation was confronting the giant bluefin tuna. Its population was declining steadily because of heavy commercial fishing for the past several decades and its numbers alarmed marine biologists to the point where they asked for a moratorium on both sport and commercial fishing of these great fish. Overfishing by foreign fleets in northern Atlantic territorial waters of the U.S. led to introduction of several

Hunters near Aspen, Colorado, in the Rocky Mountains pursue what they call the "highest hunt in the world" as they gallop after coyotes and rabbits.

GARY GUISINGER—THE NEW YORK TIMES

NOVA SCOTIA INFORMATION SERVICES

An 845-lb. bluefin tuna won for members of the U.S. team the 26th International Tuna Cup Match off Yarmouth, Nova Scotia, in September.

bills in the U.S. Congress to establish a 200-mi. commercial fishing limit along the lines being suggested at the UN Conference on the Law of the Sea. It was not just commercial fishing in waters off the U.S. that had decimated the population of the giant bluefin tuna. The tuna's numbers had also dropped all along its migration routes from across the North Atlantic Ocean, down the coast of Europe, and into the Mediterranean. Over-harvesting of the very young fish was thought to be the main cause.

Saltwater big-game fish—particularly the marlin, swordfish, and the sailfish—were taking a beating from commercial Japanese long-line fishermen in the Pacific and South Atlantic oceans and attempts were being made to enter into international treaties to establish some sort of control over the harvest of these species. (JACK SAMSON)

[452.B.5.b–c; 731.D]

Ice Hockey

North American. Economic disaster hit the National Hockey League in 1975. The Pittsburgh Penguins declared bankruptcy at the close of the 1974–75 season; plans for 1976 expansion into Denver and Seattle were scrapped, and, because of poor ratings, the NHL lost its national television contract with NBC-TV, a prime source of revenue.

Despite the league's financial troubles, player salaries were higher than ever. For the first time in NHL history players were allowed to become free agents when their contracts expired. Thus, because he could entertain offers from a number of teams in the league, Marcel Dionne of the Detroit Red Wings was able to obtain a five-year, $1.5 million contract with the Los Angeles Kings. Responding to the money crunch, some NHL teams tightened their belts by sharing minor league affiliates. As a result the American Hockey League shrank from nine teams to eight while the Central Hockey League went from eight to six.

The NHL's Stanley Cup was won for the second consecutive year by the boisterous Philadelphia Flyers. They defeated the Buffalo Sabres in the finals, four games to two. The expansion teams triumphed over the older, established clubs by placing three of their number in the semifinals. The New York Islanders, just three seasons old, defeated Pittsburgh in the quarterfinals, winning the last four games of a best-of-seven-game series. Only one other team in Stanley Cup history, the 1942 Toronto Maple Leafs, had ever rallied from a three-game deficit to win. With a surge of local interest in hockey generated by their involvement in the play-offs, the Penguins were able to find new owners over the summer.

The Islanders were defeated in the semifinals by the defending champion Flyers. Buffalo made it to the finals by defeating the Montreal Canadiens. The lengthy, 80-game regular season schedule served to push the Stanley Cup play-offs far into May, with a bizarre result. The heat in the last week of post-season play was such that a fog rose on the ice in Buffalo's Memorial Auditorium, which was not air-conditioned.

For the second time in three seasons, Bobby Clarke (*see* BIOGRAPHY) of the Flyers won the Hart Trophy as the league's most valuable player. Bobby Orr of Boston became the first player in NHL history to win eight consecutive awards as the league's outstanding defenseman. Eric Vail of Atlanta won rookie-of-the-year honours, and Detroit's Dionne won the Lady

Hurricanes: *see* Disasters; Earth Sciences
Hydroelectric Power: *see* Energy; Engineering Projects
Hydrology: *see* Earth Sciences
Ice Boating *see* Winter Sports

Table I. NHL Final Standings, 1974–75

	Won	Lost	Tied	Goals	Goals against	Pts.
JAMES NORRIS DIVISION						
Montreal Canadiens	47	14	19	374	225	113
Los Angeles Kings	42	17	21	269	185	105
Pittsburgh Penguins	37	28	15	326	289	89
Detroit Red Wings	23	45	12	259	335	58
Washington Capitals	8	67	5	181	446	21
CHARLES F. ADAMS DIVISION						
Buffalo Sabres	49	16	15	354	240	113
Boston Bruins	40	26	14	345	245	94
Toronto Maple Leafs	31	33	16	280	309	78
California Golden Seals	19	48	13	212	316	51
LESTER PATRICK DIVISION						
Philadelphia Flyers	51	18	11	293	181	113
New York Rangers	37	29	14	319	276	88
New York Islanders	33	25	22	264	221	88
Atlanta Flames	34	31	15	243	233	83
CONN SMYTHE DIVISION						
Vancouver Canucks	38	32	10	271	254	86
St. Louis Blues	35	31	14	269	267	84
Chicago Black Hawks	37	35	8	268	241	82
Minnesota North Stars	23	50	7	221	341	53
Kansas City Scouts	15	54	11	184	328	41

Table II. WHA Final Standings, 1974–75

	Won	Lost	Tied	Goals	Goals against	Pts.
EAST DIVISION						
New England Whalers	43	30	5	274	279	91
Cleveland Crusaders	35	40	3	236	258	73
Chicago Cougars	30	47	1	261	312	61
Indianapolis Racers	18	57	3	216	338	39
WEST DIVISION						
Houston Aeros	53	25	0	369	247	106
San Diego Mariners	43	31	4	326	268	90
Minnesota Fighting Saints	42	33	3	308	279	87
Phoenix Roadrunners	39	31	8	300	265	86
Baltimore Blades	21	53	4	205	341	46
CANADIAN DIVISION						
Quebec Nordiques	46	32	0	331	299	92
Toronto Toros	43	33	2	349	304	88
Winnipeg Jets	38	35	5	322	293	81
Vancouver Blazers	37	39	2	256	270	76
Edmonton Oilers	36	38	4	279	279	76

Table III. World Ice Hockey Championships, 1975

GROUP A	Won	Lost	Tied	Goals	Goals against	Pts.
U.S.S.R.	10	0	0	90	23	20
Czechoslovakia	8	2	0	55	19	16
Sweden	5	5	0	51	34	10
Finland	5	5	0	36	34	10
Poland	2	8	0	18	78	4
United States	0	10	0	22	84	0

Byng Memorial Trophy for sportsmanship and gentlemanly conduct. Bernie Parent of the Flyers won the Vezina Trophy as the league's outstanding goalkeeper for the second year in a row.

In the World Hockey Association play-offs for the Avco World Trophy, the defending champion Houston Aeros defeated the Quebec Nordiques in four straight games. Gordie Howe, 47 years old, announced he would return to retirement after the first game of the 1975–76 season. He had come out of retirement in 1973 to help start the new league. Bobby Hull of the Winnipeg Jets was voted the league's most valuable player. Although WHA attendance was up, some teams experienced financial problems, and several franchises were moved.

In the American Hockey League the Springfield (Mass.) Indians came from a fourth-place finish during the regular season to win the play-off championship for the Calder Cup. They defeated the New Haven Nighthawks four games to one in the finals. In the Central Hockey League the Salt Lake City Golden Eagles defeated the Dallas Black Hawks, four games to three, for the championship.

During a stick-swinging brawl in a game between the Boston Bruins and the Minnesota North Stars on January 4, Henry Boucha of the North Stars suffered a fracture of an eye cavity that left him with residual double vision. NHL Pres. Clarence Campbell suspended Boston left-winger David Forbes for ten games without pay for his part in the incident. On January 14 Forbes was indicted by a Hennepin County (Minn.) grand jury on a charge of aggravated assault with a deadly weapon—his hockey stick. The case was heard in July and was believed to be the first criminal assault trial in the U.S. involving a professional athlete's actions during a sports contest. Forbes denied that his stick had struck Boucha's eye. The jury could not reach a verdict, and a mistrial was declared.

(ROBIN CATHY HERMAN)

European and International. Ice hockey was held back in Europe during 1975 by a failure to merge amateur and professional interests enough to encourage major rink operators to progress with ambitious plans. Leading existing clubs and projected new ones thus could not develop the hoped-for international competitions calculated to draw big box-office receipts, which in turn could inspire an improved standard of play at all levels. A previous trickle of top talent from North America to Europe tended to be reversed, and Sweden in particular lost several star national players.

A new and much-heralded European League for club teams did not begin in October, as had been planned. Protracted efforts to reach agreement broke down because of friction between some national amateur associations and rink managements. Without a guarantee of participation by the strong Scandinavian clubs from the outset, other nations considered it imprudent to go ahead. This meant delaying the return to Wembley, England, of the London Lions team, composed mainly of North American professionals, but officials were optimistic that the difficulties could be resolved.

Sweden's startling withdrawal from the 1976 Winter Olympic tournament meant that two nations with medal-winning potential would be nonstarters, Canada also having refused to compete. Neither was happy about the Olympic eligibility rules, which bar Western European and North American professionals but allow state-subsidized players from Eastern Europe.

The 42nd world championships were contested by 21 nations during March and April 1975. The six major entrants competed in Group A at Munich and Düsseldorf, West Germany, each team playing the other twice. The U.S.S.R. comfortably retained the

WIDE WORLD

Philadelphia Flyer Bob Kelly (9) shoots the puck past Buffalo Sabre goalie Roger Crozier to put the Flyers ahead 1–0 during the third period of the sixth game of the Stanley Cup series. (Below) Buffalo's Rick Martin (7) smashes puck past Philadelphia goalie Bernie Parent in the first period of the third game of the series.

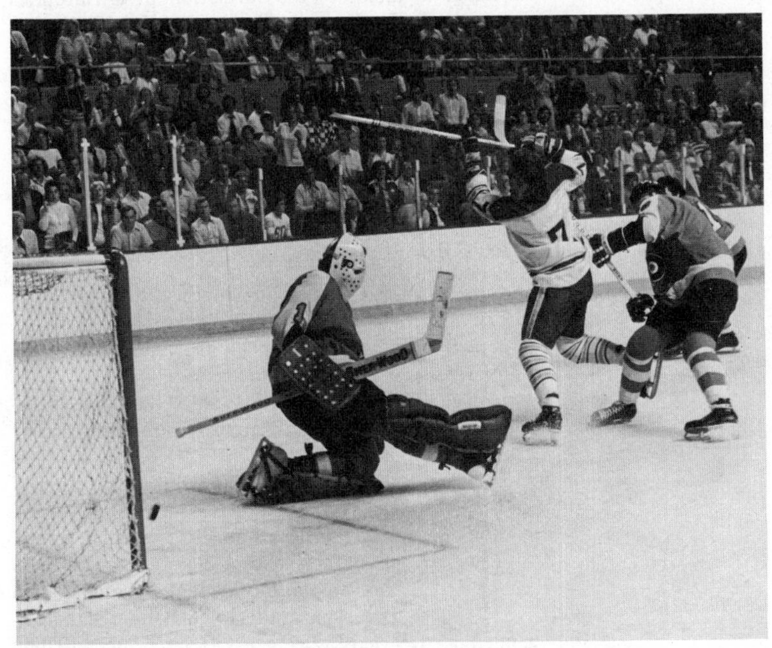

UPI COMPIX

title, its 14th victory and the 12th in 13 years, winning all 10 matches and scoring 90 goals in the process. Its only serious rival was Czechoslovakia, runner-up by six points over the third- and fourth-place teams, Sweden and Finland. Poland finished fifth, above a surprisingly weak U.S. team, which did not score a point and was relegated to Group B.

As had become customary in recent years, the two games between the Czechoslovak and Soviet teams were the vital ones. The champions won the first 5–2 and the second 4–1. Victor Shalimov, the Soviet right-winger, was top point scorer with 19, from 11 goals and 8 assists. His compatriot, left-winger Aleksandr Jakushev, and the Swedish left-winger, Tord Lundstrom, also scored 11 goals apiece. The most successful goalkeeper was Jiri Holecek of Czechoslovakia, who allowed four goals fewer than his Soviet counterpart. Canada, winner of the title the most times, declined to enter for a sixth successive year in protest against the regulations defining amateur and professional status.

East Germany, leader of the eight teams in Group B, at Sapporo, Japan, gained promotion back to Group A after only one season out of it. East Germany and West Germany each won six of their seven games to finish even on points, the East Germans gaining promotion because of their superior goal average. Italy and The Netherlands, at the bottom of the Group B standings, moved down to Group C. Norway and Bulgaria gained promotion to Group B from Group C, played at Sofia, Bulg.

Dynamo Moscow, of the U.S.S.R., won the international club competition for the Ahearne Cup, at Stockholm in January. Sparta Prague of Czechoslovakia was runner-up. The historic Allan Cup, first contested in 1908 and emblematic of world amateur club supremacy, was won for the first time by a U.S. Hockey League team, the Thunder Bay Twins, which beat the Barrie Flyers, of the Ontario Senior Hockey League, 4–2 in a best-of-seven play-off series.

The International Ice Hockey Federation, meeting in July at Gstaad, Switz., decided to throw the world championships open to professionals as well as to amateurs, beginning in 1976. An agreement to admit clubs to the federation as associate members was expected to facilitate the formation of a European League. John F. Ahearne, 75, of the U.K. retired after 22 years as the federation's president. He was succeeded by Günther Sabetzki from West Germany and was then made honorary president for life.

(HOWARD BASS)

[452.B.4.h.xviii]

Iceland

Iceland is an island republic in the North Atlantic Ocean, near the Arctic Circle. Area: 39,769 sq.mi. (103,000 sq.km.). Pop. (1974 est.): 216,600. Cap. and largest city: Reykjavik (pop., 1974 est., 84,800). Language: Icelandic. Religion: 98% Lutheran. President in 1975, Kristjan Eldjarn; prime minister, Geir Hallgrimsson.

In order to conserve its fishing resources, Iceland had extended its fishing limit from 12 mi. to 50 mi. as of Sept. 1, 1972. The 50-mi. limit was, in effect, observed by all nations except West Germany and Great Britain, the two nations principally affected. On Nov. 13, 1973, Iceland and Great Britain had concluded a two-year agreement under which British trawlers were permitted to fish within designated areas inside the 50-mi. limit. The dispute with West Germany remained unsettled but appeared to be approaching settlement near the end of the year.

On Oct. 15, 1975, Iceland further extended its fishing limit to 200 mi. The area within the new limit covered 758,000 sq.km., more than seven times the area of Iceland itself. Both Great Britain and West Germany disputed the validity of this extension as well as that of the 50-mi. limit. Other nations, *e.g.*, the Soviet Union, asked for fishing rights within the 200-mi. zone. The agreement on fishing rights with Great Britain expired on Nov. 13, 1975, and no new agreement was concluded. Great Britain contended that the expiry of the agreement entitled it to fish anywhere outside the 12-mi. zone, whereas Iceland did everything within its power to prevent British vessels from catching within the new fishing limit, with special emphasis placed on protecting the 50-mi. zone.

National income in real terms had increased by 9.5% in 1973. The rapid expansion was led by an export boom, which subsided in early 1974 as export prices for fish products began to decline. At the same time, prices of imports rose sharply, helping to bring the rate of inflation to over 50% in 1974; national income in real terms remained unchanged at the 1973 level. The business downturn continued in 1975. Export prices declined still further, although less than in 1974, and import prices continued to rise, but more moderately. The domestic economy had been kept operating at a high level in 1974 by running a balance of payments deficit equivalent to 12% of the gross national product (GNP). In 1975 it was beginning to contract, as the government adopted a restrictive economic policy. The krona was devalued by 20% in February 1975, following a 17% devaluation

ICELAND

Education. (1971–72) Primary, pupils 27,336, teachers (including preprimary) 1,431; secondary, pupils 18,823, teachers 1,513; vocational, pupils 4,647, teachers 724; teacher training, students 635, teachers 81; higher, students 1,970, teaching staff 260.

Finance. Monetary unit: króna, with (Sept. 22, 1975) a free rate of 162.56 krónur to U.S. $1 (336.75 krónur = £1 sterling). Gold, SDRs, and foreign exchange: (June 1975) U.S. $42.6 million; (June 1974) U.S. $64.7 million. Budget (1974 est.): revenue 29,180,000,000 krónur; expenditure 29,402,000,000 krónur. Gross national product: (1973) 92,403,000,000 krónur; (1972) 66,270,000,000 krónur. Money supply: (May 1975) 14,694,000,000 krónur; (May 1974) 12,278,000,000 krónur. Cost of living (Reykjavik; 1970 = 100): (1975) 293; (1974) 199.

Foreign Trade. (1974) Imports 52,558,000,000 krónur; exports 32,949,000,000 krónur. Import sources: West Germany 12%; U.K. 11%; U.S.S.R. 10%; Denmark 9%; Norway 8%; U.S. 8%; Sweden 7%; The Netherlands 7%; Australia 5%. Export destinations: U.S. 22%; Portugal 10%; West Germany 9%; U.K. 9%; U.S.S.R. 8%; Denmark 6%; Switzerland 6%; Spain 5%. Main exports: fish 65%; aluminum 15%; fish meal 10%. Tourism: visitors (1972) 68,000; gross receipts (1973) U.S. $13 million.

Transport and Communications. Roads (1973) 11,137 km. Motor vehicles in use (1973): passenger 56,274; commercial 6,070. There are no railways. Air traffic (1974): 1,930,700,000 passenger-km.; freight 31,155,000 net ton-km. Shipping (1974): merchant vessels 100 gross tons and over 350; gross tonnage 148,695. Telephones (Dec. 1973) 81,000. Radio licenses (Dec. 1973) 66,000. Television licenses (Dec. 1972) 46,000.

Agriculture. Production (in 000; metric tons; 1973; 1972 in parentheses): potatoes 6 (9); hay *c.* 320 (*c.* 330); milk 128 (126); mutton and lamb 14 (13); fish catch 906 (726). Livestock (in 000; Dec. 1973): cattle 37; sheep 829; horses 39; chickens *c.* 210.

Industry. Production (in 000): electricity (public supply only; kw-hr.; 1974) 2,341,000; aluminum (metric tons; 1973) 71.

PHOTOS, GYLFI GUNN & BERTEL THOMSEN—NORDISK PRESSEFOTO/PICTORIAL PARADE

Although 4,000 have returned to their homes, 1,000 persons are still homeless on the Icelandic island of Heimaey, where their houses were covered in a shower of ashes during a volcanic eruption in January 1973. Some of the windows were covered with tin to prevent ashes from invading the homes. Pictured is a view of the island immediately after the disaster (left) and two years later.

in September 1974. Real national income was expected to decline by about 8–9% between 1974 and 1975. The current account deficit for 1975 was estimated at approximately 10% of GNP. By the end of 1975 inflation was at an annual rate of about 25%.

Construction of the 150-Mw. Sigalda hydropower plant continued during the year, and a 95-Mw. geothermal-generated power plant at Krafla was begun. Both were to be completed in 1976.

(BJÖRN MATTHÍASSON)

[972.A.6.d.ii]

India

A federal republic of southern Asia and a member of the Commonwealth of Nations, India is situated on a peninsula extending into the Indian Ocean with the Arabian Sea to the west and the Bay of Bengal to the east. It is bounded (east to west) by Burma, Bangladesh, China, Bhutan, Nepal, and Pakistan; Sri Lanka lies just off its southern tip in the Indian Ocean. Area: 1,269,420 sq.mi. (3,287,782 sq.km.), including the Pakistani-controlled section of Jammu and Kashmir and Sikkim (annexed in 1975). Pop. (1975 est.): 600 million; Indo-Aryans and Dravidians are dominant, with Mongoloid, Negroid, and Australoid admixtures. Cap.: New Delhi (pop., 1971, 301,800). Largest cities: Calcutta (metro. pop., 1971, 7,031,400) and Greater Bombay (metro. pop., 1971, 5,970,600). Language: Hindi and English (official). Religion (1971): Hindu 83%; Muslim 11%; Christian 3%; Sikh 2%; Buddhist 0.7%. President in 1975, Fakhruddin Ali Ahmed; prime minister, Indira Gandhi.

In 1975 India experienced the most serious political crisis in its 25 years as a republic. The government arrested a large number of opposition leaders and introduced press censorship under a proclamation of emergency. Repudiating suggestions that these amounted to the imposition of authoritarianism, Prime Minister Gandhi maintained that the action was within the framework of the constitution and had to be taken to save the country from anarchy and to restore democracy.

Domestic Affairs. The year began with a political assassination. L. N. Mishra, the controversial minister of railways, was fatally injured in Samastipur, Bihar, in a bomb blast on January 2. On March 20 there was an unsuccessful attempt on the life of the chief justice, A. N. Ray. The police traced both incidents to the Anand Marg, a politico-religious organization. Meanwhile, prominent opposition parties (with the exception of the Communist Party of India) formed an alliance and intensified their challenge to the government. Their efforts received some encouragement from the activities of a junior minister of the union, Mohan Dharia, and some congressmen known as Young Turks. Mrs. Gandhi asked for Dharia's resignation in March. In the following month Morarji Desai, leader of the Opposition Congress party, undertook a political fast to dramatize his demand for immediate elections in Gujarat. After initially refusing, the prime minister conceded the demand. Polling took place in the state on June 8 and 11.

The opposition's chance came with the judgment of the Allahabad High Court on June 12 setting aside Indira Gandhi's election to the Lok Sabha (lower house) in the 1971 general election. Her defeated rival, Raj Narain, had filed an election petition, and the case had dragged on for four years. The judge, J. M. L. Sinha, rejected charges that there had been bribing of voters or exploitation of their religious sentiments, but he held that the construction of rostrums for the prime minister's meetings by state officials and electioneering by an official aide while in service amounted to corrupt practices.

The verdict threw the nation into confusion. Although the judge allowed Mrs. Gandhi to appeal to the Supreme Court and stayed the enforcement of his order, the opposition front called for her resignation and set up an action committee to mobilize the people. Their morale was reinforced by the results of the Gujarat election, announced the same day, which showed that the prime minister's Congress party, with 75 seats, had trailed behind the opposition front, which obtained 86 (12 seats went to the Kisan Mazdoor Lok Paksha or KMLP and 8 to independents). With the KMLP's promise of support, the opposition front formed a ministry in the state under Babubhai J. Patel. Meanwhile, in Delhi, the Congress parliamentary party unanimously resolved on June 18 that Mrs. Gandhi should continue to be its leader. On June 20 a massive rally of support was held in the capital.

Ice Skating
see Winter Sports

Income, National:
see Economy, World

ED VALTMAN—ROTHCO

"You, too!!"

The prime minister's appeal was admitted by the Supreme Court on June 24, and Justice V. R. Krishna Iyer ruled that she could continue to hold office but without the right to vote in the Lok Sabha. This led to a renewed call for her resignation. At a public meeting in Delhi on June 25, the opposition front announced its resolve to start a countrywide civil disobedience from June 29. Jayaprakash Narayan (*see* BIOGRAPHY), guide and philosopher of the opposition, asked the police and armed forces to disobey orders if they were immoral.

Mrs. Gandhi struck back with speed and ferocity. On her recommendation, Pres. Fakhruddin Ali Ahmed signed a proclamation around midnight under art. 352(i) of the constitution declaring "that a grave emergency exists whereby the security of India is threatened by internal disturbances." A large number of opposition leaders (including Narayan, who was, however, released in November) were rounded up all over the country the same night. In a succession of orders the arrested persons were denied the right to appeal in courts and newspapers were forbidden to publish the names or the number of those arrested or anything calculated to defeat the emergency order.

On July 1 Mrs. Gandhi announced a wide-ranging package of economic measures which came to be described as the Twenty-Point Program. Because of its appeal to various segments of the population, the Twenty-Point Program was widely welcomed. In fact, there was very little opposition to the emergency as a whole, and virtually no major demonstrations or clashes took place, even in the two states with governments opposed to the Congress—Tamil Nadu and Gujarat. Underground activity was confined to the production of leaflets opposing "governmental tyranny." On July 4 an ordinance was issued outlawing various groups of extremists, but no parliamentary party was banned. On grounds of violation of censorship rules, six foreign journalists were expelled.

The two houses of Parliament were summoned to meet on July 21 to transact government business. The emergency proclamation was ratified in the Lok Sabha by 336 votes to 59 and in the Rajya Sabha (upper house) by 136 votes to 33. The opposition front parties withdrew from the session, although they continued to participate in parliamentary committees. Parliament also gave approval to some emergency ordinances and amendments to the constitution designed to strengthen the government's position.

Between August 25 and October 9 the Supreme Court heard the prime minister's appeal and a counterappeal by Narain, whose counsel challenged Parliament's right to amend the constitution to cover specific cases. On November 7 the court unanimously quashed the lower court's debarment of the prime minister from elective office for six years and declared her 1971 election valid, but it rejected the constitutional amendment invalidating the earlier High Court decision. In December Mrs. Gandhi won the approval of the party leaders to continue the emergency and to postpone parliamentary elections, due in March 1976, for a year—the first such postponement since independence.

Among the ordinances issued after the adjournment of Parliament were those fixing the level of the bonus to industrial workers at 4% and linking it to profits; decreeing equal remuneration to men and women workers and preventing discrimination in employment on grounds of sex; enabling the opening of regional rural banks; and abolishing bonded labour throughout the country.

There were two other major political developments during the year. During February a political settlement was reached with Sheikh Muhammad Abdullah whereby the accession of the state of Jammu and Kashmir to India was treated as final and irrevocable. Sheikh Abdullah assumed office as the state's chief minister and formed a government on February 25. The other development concerned Sikkim. On April

INDIA

Education. (1971–72) Primary, pupils 78 million, teachers (1970–71) 1,602,515; secondary and vocational, pupils 8.4 million, teachers (1970–71) 523,341; teacher training (1967–68), students 190,075, teachers (1965–66) 13,460; higher (including 86 universities), students 2,540,000, teaching staff (1970–71) 119,000.

Finance. Monetary unit: rupee, with (Sept. 29, 1975) a free rate of Rs. 9 to U.S. $1 (Rs. 18.32 = £1 sterling). Gold, SDRs, and foreign exchange: (April 1975) U.S. $1,405,000,000; (April 1974) U.S. $1,439,000,000. Budget (central government; 1974–75 est.): revenue Rs. 67,267,000,000; expenditure Rs. 88,490,000,000. Gross national product: (1971–72) Rs. 429.7 billion; (1970–71) Rs. 402.5 billion. Money supply: (March 1975) Rs. 115,070,000,000; (March 1974) Rs. 107,880,000,000. Cost of living (1970 = 100): (March 1975) 173; (March 1974) 149.

Foreign Trade. (1974) Imports Rs. 40,754,000,000; exports Rs. 31,375,000,000. Import sources (1973–74): U.S. 17%; Iran 9%; U.S.S.R. 9%; West Germany 7%. Export destinations (1974–75): U.S. 11%; U.S.S.R. 13%; U.K. 9%; Japan 9%; Iran 6%. Main exports (1974–75): sugar 10%; jute fabrics 9%; tea 7%; cotton fabrics 7%; iron ore 5%.

Transport and Communications. Roads (1972) 1,021,819 km. (including 28,819 km. main highways). Motor vehicles in use (1972): passenger 646,463; commercial 346,020. Railways: (1972) 60,149 km.; traffic (1973–74) 131,452,000,000 passenger-km., freight (1974) 126,351,000,000 net ton-km. Air traffic (1973): 5,454,000,000 passenger-km.; freight 204.9 million net ton-km. Shipping (1974): merchant vessels 100 gross tons and over 451; gross tonnage 3,484,751. Telephones (Dec. 1973) 1.6 million. Radio licenses (Dec. 1972) 12,772,000. Television licenses (Dec. 1972) 62,000.

Agriculture. Production (in 000; metric tons; 1974; 1973 in parentheses): wheat 22,073 (*c.* 24,735); rice *c.* 60,000 (65,613); barley 2,327 (2,379); corn *c.* 5,000 (5,643); millet *c.* 9,500 (11,082); sorghum *c.* 7,500 (8,992); potatoes 4,626 (4,451); cassava (1973) 6,312, (1972) 6,026; chick-peas 4,006 (4,537); mangoes (1973) *c.* 8,550, (1972) *c.* 8,400; bananas (1973) *c.* 2,900, (1972) *c.* 2,700; sugar, raw value 4,336 (4,170); sugar, noncentrifugal (1973) 6,760, (1972) 6,750; tea *c.* 480 (470); tobacco 441 (364); rapeseed 1,692 (1,808); linseed 471 (428); peanuts *c.* 5,200 (5,798); cotton, lint 1,214 (1,193); jute *c.* 1,080 (1,373). Livestock (in 000; 1974): cattle *c.* 177,010; sheep *c.* 40,000; pigs *c.* 4,780; buffalo (1973) *c.* 55,149; goats *c.* 69,229; poultry *c.* 117,705.

Industry. Production (in 000; metric tons; 1974): coal 83,262; lignite 3,016; iron ore (61% metal content) 34,230; pig iron 7,425; crude steel 6,684; electricity (excluding most industrial production; kw-hr.) 68,158,000; aluminum 129; cement 14,263; cotton yarn 1,009; woven cotton fabrics (m.; 1973) 7,833,000; petroleum products (1973) *c.* 18,700; sulfuric acid 1,294; caustic soda 430; gold (troy oz.; 1973) 95; manganese ore (metal content; 1973) 542.

10 the Sikkim Assembly adopted a resolution favouring merger in India, and this was confirmed by referendum on April 14. Parliament made Sikkim the 22nd state of the union through the Constitution (36th Amendment) Act, passed on April 26 and ratified on May 16. By another amendment of the constitution (37th), the union territory of Arunachal Pradesh was enabled to have its own elected legislative assembly and Cabinet from August 15.

A technological development of importance was the placing in orbit on April 19 of a wholly Indian-built scientific satellite. It was launched from the Soviet Union. Yet another milestone was the eradication of smallpox as the result of a coordinated effort by the medical administration and the World Health Organization.

The Economy. There was cause for some satisfaction on the economic front. The inflation rate of 30%, registered in the early part of 1974, had been reversed as early as July 1975. The emergency further helped the downward trend. An official document in October stated that on September 27 the price index was 7.8% lower than a year earlier.

The union government's budget (February) placed the overall deficit for 1974–75 at Rs. 6,250,000,000. Revenue for 1975–76 was estimated at Rs. 71,140,000,000 (including new levies of Rs. 2,390,000,000) and expenditure at Rs. 64,910,000,000. With capital receipts of Rs. 34,290,000,000 and capital expenditure of Rs. 42,770,000,000, a net deficit of Rs. 2,250,000,000 was left uncovered. External assistance was anticipated at Rs. 6,130,000,000.

The monsoon proved to be uniformly good. Although there was extensive damage to crops from floods in Bihar and Orissa, agricultural output for 1975–76 was expected to set a record. The improvement of power supply and the marked absence of strikes after the emergency presaged a rise in industrial production as well. The offshore oil wells near Bombay began production and were expected to yield an annual output of ten million metric tons by 1980.

Defending her policies, Prime Minister Indira Gandhi addresses a mass rally in New Delhi in June while awaiting the result of the appeal of her conviction for corrupt campaign practices.

WIDE WORLD

Foreign Affairs. The coup in Bangladesh on August 15 caused considerable disquiet in India. While expressing strong condemnation of the politics of assassination, India declared, however, that the governmental changes were an internal affair, and it dealt in the normal course with the Khandakar Mushtaque Ahmed government. The government brought to power in the further coup of November 6 appeared to be somewhat friendlier toward India. Earlier an agreement had been signed with Bangladesh on the Ganges-Brahmaputra waters, as a result of which the Farakka Barrage went into operation in May.

The announcement of the resumption of U.S. arms supplies to Pakistan ruffled tempers, as did U.S. Pres. Gerald Ford's observation after the emergency that 600 million Indians had lost the liberty they once had. The prime minister participated in the conference of Commonwealth heads of government in Kingston, Jamaica, in April. The Palestine Liberation Organization was permitted to open an office in New Delhi.

(H. Y. SHARADA PRASAD)

[976.A.2]

Indonesia

A republic of Southeast Asia, Indonesia consists of the major islands of Sumatra, Java, Kalimantan (Indonesian Borneo), Celebes, and Irian Jaya (West New Guinea) and approximately 3,000 smaller islands and islets. Area: 782,663 sq.mi. (2,027,087 sq.km.). Pop. (1975 est.): 129,082,600. Cap. and largest city: Jakarta (pop., 1975 est., 5,490,000). Language: Bahasa Indonesian (official); Javanese; Sundanese; Madurese. Religion: mainly Muslim; some Christian, Buddhist, and Hindu. President and prime minister in 1975, General Suharto.

For the first time in a decade under the Suharto administration, the Indonesian economy in 1975 suffered a balance of payments deficit, arising largely from the financial plight of the state-owned oil enterprise, Pertamina. This setback took place at the same time that Indonesia was experiencing alarm over the swift Communist takeovers in South Vietnam, Cambodia, and Laos and the emergence of areas of instability in the eastern end of the archipelago, notably in Portuguese Timor and Papua New Guinea.

Despite an oil income of about $5 billion in 1974, the government was embarrassed by Pertamina's inability to repay short-term commercial loans early in the year. In March the Suharto government stunned the world's business and diplomatic communities with the disclosure that "the government has taken over Pertamina's financial problems."

Although no Pertamina loan was formally declared in default, President Suharto found himself in a politically awkward position because he had given a free hand to the director of the state enterprise, a flamboyant army general, Ibnu Sutowo. Sutowo raised oil production spectacularly and, in the process, borrowed more than $2 billion from abroad to finance operations. Pertamina overextended itself, building hotels and golf courses, operating large fleets of aircraft and merchant ships, partly financing a $1 billion steel complex on Java, and involving itself in several other ambitious projects. As a result of the 1975 world economic recession, set in motion by the 1973–74 oil embargo, Pertamina was unable to cover outstanding debts with new short-term loans. By the end of 1975, however, following the introduction of

INDONESIA

Education. (1971) Primary, pupils 13,474,730, teachers 414,799; secondary, pupils 1,394,593, teachers 97,936; vocational, pupils 589,541, teachers 56,118; teacher training, students 120,600, teachers 10,143; higher, students 251,870, teaching staff (1967) 21,309.

Finance. Monetary unit: rupiah, with (Sept. 22, 1975) an official rate of 415 rupiah to U.S. $1 (free rate of 860 rupiah = £1 sterling). Gold, SDRs, and foreign exchange: (Feb. 1975) U.S. $1,308,000,000; (Feb. 1974) U.S. $850 million. Budget (1974–75 est.): revenue 1,363,000,000,000 rupiah; expenditure 1,577,000,000,000 rupiah. Gross national product: (1973) 6,378,000,000,000 rupiah; (1972) 4,404,000,000,000 rupiah. Money supply: (Dec. 1974) 942.4 billion rupiah; (Dec. 1973) 671 billion rupiah. Cost of living (Jakarta; 1970 = 100): (April 1975) 237; (April 1974) 202.

Foreign Trade. (1974) Imports U.S. $3,754,100,000; exports U.S. $7,090,300,000. Import sources: Japan 30%; U.S. 16%; West Germany 8%; Singapore 7%. Export destinations: Japan 53%; U.S. 20%; Singapore 7%. Main exports: crude oil 68%; rubber 7%.

Transport and Communications. Roads (1972) 84,891 km. Motor vehicles in use (1973): passenger 306,700; commercial (including buses) 173,300. Railways (1973): 7,801 km.; traffic 2,726,000,000 passenger-km., freight 1,068,000,000 net ton-km. Air traffic (1974): 2,204,500,000 passenger-km.; freight 44,893,000 net ton-km. Shipping (1974) merchant vessels 100 gross tons and over 616. Telephones (Dec. 1973) 269,000. Radio receivers (Dec. 1970) 13,796,000. Television receivers (Dec. 1973) 237,000.

Agriculture. Production (in 000; metric tons; 1974; 1973 in parentheses): rice *c.* 22,800 (*c.* 21,500); corn 2,760 (2,912); cassava (1973) *c.* 10,099, (1972) 10,099; sweet potatoes (1973) *c.* 2,150, (1972) 1,944; sugar, raw value 1,600 (937); sugar, noncentrifugal (1973) *c.* 250, (1972) 243; tea *c.* 67 (*c.* 67); copra *c.* 720 (660); soybeans *c.* 550 (529); palm oil (1973) *c.* 300, (1972) 269; peanuts *c.* 530 (505); coffee *c.* 168 (164); tobacco *c.* 81 (*c.* 79); rubber *c.* 985 (886); fish catch (1973) 1,300, (1972) 1,268. Livestock (in 000; Dec. 1973): cattle *c.* 6,292; pigs *c.* 3,300; sheep *c.* 3,000; horses *c.* 670; buffalo (1972) *c.* 2,850; goats *c.* 7,000; chickens *c.* 90,000.

Industry. Production (in 000; metric tons; 1974): crude oil 67,979; petroleum products (1972) 14,389; coal 153; tin concentrates (metal content) 25; bauxite 1,289; electricity (excluding most industrial production; kw-hr.; 1973) 2,932,000.

sweeping reforms in Pertamina's financial operations, the Suharto government had restored confidence in the economy at home and abroad.

The sudden collapse of South Vietnam in the spring generated concern in Indonesia about further Communist encroachment in Southeast Asia and misgivings about the reliability of the United States as an ally. "If I were a Vietnamese," said Adam Malik, Indonesia's outspoken foreign minister, "I would feel that America failed to maintain its commitment." The official armed forces journal in Indonesia, *Angkatan Bersendjata,* also voiced fears of a possible chain reaction in Indonesia following a midsummer increase in armed Communist incidents in Malaysia and Thailand, two countries sandwiched between Indonesia and Indochina. The journal expressed concern that the morale of the underground Indonesian Communist Party, which was smashed following an abortive coup in 1965, had been bolstered by South Vietnam's collapse and recent developments in Malaysia and Thailand. Indonesia's principal fear was increased infiltration along the country's long coastline. This concern was heightened by the Communists' capture of South Vietnam's stockpile of military hardware.

In July President Suharto flew to the United States to confer with U.S. Pres. Gerald Ford. The visit was returned in December, when Ford stopped in Jakarta following his trip to China.

Downtown Jakarta today is a bustling modern city whose appearance differs markedly from that of impoverished villages elsewhere in Indonesia.

IAN STEWART—THE NEW YORK TIMES

Indonesian concern about regional developments was deepened by the eruption of civil war in Portuguese Timor, on an island that Indonesia shared with Portugal. In the late summer, the radical Revolutionary Front for the Independence of East Timor (Fretilin), which sought an independent Timor and had Communist support abroad, gained control of large segments of the island, including the capital, Dili. In early December, following incidents between Indonesian and Fretilin forces on the border between the Portuguese and Indonesian parts of the island, Indonesian troops, with naval and air support, seized control of Dili, and the Fretilin forces retreated to the hills. Foreign Minister Malik claimed that Indonesia had taken action at the request of two pro-Indonesian parties, the Popular Democratic Association and the Timorese Democratic Union. Portugal broke relations with Indonesia and took the matter to the UN, which called on Indonesia to withdraw its forces. The enclave of Ocussi Ambeno in Indonesian Timor was formally incorporated into Indonesia on December 13.

In another development, Papua New Guinea, which shares the island of New Guinea with Indonesia, achieved its independence from Australia. Among the least developed of the newly emergent nations, the young state was immediately threatened by secessionist movements. In a joint statement, Indonesia and Papua New Guinea declared their opposition to separatism. (ARNOLD C. BRACKMAN)

[976.C.1]

Industrial Relations

During recent years many long-established industrial relations systems have come under stress, particularly in advanced industrial countries. The stress may be diagnosed as resulting largely from two groups of forces. On the one hand, a number of factors have been affecting workers' attitudes to work and the workplace. Among these are the generally higher standards of education now prevalent; full employment (in many countries); and the higher threshold of expectations resulting from long-continued economic growth. On the other hand, there are the technological and organizational changes in industry itself, resulting in larger-scale units, closer integration and greater capital-intensiveness, and more remote decision-making, which have added to the difficulty of achieving good human relations and, at the same time, made industry more vulnerable to disruptive action.

The interplay of these forces would seem certain to

make for tension and change in industrial relations systems—as, indeed, has been apparent in recent years. In 1975, however, new factors entered the scene. First, the substantial increase in oil and other raw material costs worked its way through countries' economies, producing higher prices. And second, the downward turn of the economy in many countries produced unemployment levels greater than any experienced since World War II. In these circumstances, it was not surprising that much of the activity in the industrial relations field during the year was concerned with wage negotiation in an inflationary environment and with employment and job security.

Wages, Inflation, and Job Security. Faced with rapidly rising prices, wage and salary earners in industrialized market economies naturally expected collective bargaining to preserve, and if possible improve, their living standards. Economically, few countries achieved much in the way of economic growth, and for many growth was negative. There was not much scope, therefore, for real wage increases, and there was a danger that unemployment might increase if high wage settlements were made. Accordingly, many trade unions chose a policy of moderation.

Relatively few of the important U.S. wage contracts were up for renewal during the year, but the general level of the settlements that were made was modest, despite the fact that, for many people, real earnings had fallen for two consecutive years. In the Japanese "spring wage round" the unions settled for less than half the level of their increases in 1974. West German wage increases were even more modest. In Britain the "social contract" of 1974 began to look increasingly unrealistic when measured against the settlements actually being concluded, and in the summer the Trades Union Congress (TUC) agreed to support a new program of restraint, broadly on the lines of a government White Paper proposing a level of increase not to exceed £6 a week.

There were often difficulties. In Denmark the likelihood of large-scale strikes was averted only when the government imposed a national wage settlement. In June the Irish government, on the basis of economic measures designed to bring down the cost of living, felt it necessary to ask the unions and employers to renegotiate the national wage agreement that had been concluded in April. But the year passed without any major upheaval on wage issues. In Australia the central wage-fixing body, the Commonwealth Conciliation and Arbitration Commission, adopted, for a trial period, a policy of reviewing wage increases on the basis of movements in the cost of living. In October the Canadian government opted for a statutory prices and incomes policy, limiting wage increases in its first year of operation to a maximum of 10% for most workers.

Many countries legislated measures to maintain or create employment, and sometimes both legislative and collectively bargained measures were taken. Thus, in France the government-initiated central national agreement of October 1974, on unemployment payments, was followed by a law of January 1975 concerning procedures for dealing with layoffs. A particularly interesting collective agreement was that concluded by Fiat with the Italian engineering union in November 1974, for its automobile section, in which the union accepted a share of responsibility for production levels in return for the ending of short-time work and for certain guarantees concerning manning levels and layoffs.

Participation and Quality of Working Life. Interest in workers' participation and in the quality of working life continued in many countries, though the economic recession tended to overshadow such developments.

In April the Commission of the European Communities adopted a revised proposed statute for a European company (the first draft having appeared in 1970). The new proposal envisaged a two-tier supervisory and management board structure with one-third of the supervisory board representing shareholders, one-third representing workers, and the remaining one-third being independent members, coopted by the shareholder and worker representatives. There would also be a works council, elected by the workers. A second relevant proposal by the Commission, concerned with the harmonization of company law, was revised during the year. While more flexible than the original proposal put forward in 1972, this too argued strongly for a two-tier board structure with workers' interests reflected in the supervisory board.

Underlying the discussion about workers' representation on company boards was the question of the role of the enterprise in modern industrial society, and whether the traditional form of the company, as basically established over a century ago, should continue. A broad and searching review of this question was made by the French Committee on the Reform of the Enterprise, headed by Pierre Sudreau. The committee's report, issued in February, proposed a whole series of reforms, including the idea of "co-surveillance" (co-supervision) by up to one-third representation of worker members, sitting with shareholder representatives on supervisory boards or boards of directors exercising supervisory functions.

In West Germany the political compromise reached in 1974, providing for equal employee and shareholder representation on the boards of large concerns but including elected managerial representation among the employee representatives, came under strain. Dispute arose as to the managerial representation and the importance of a clear separation of the two sides of industry in collective bargaining. There were also

West German truckers protest traffic problems by hoisting a truck in Bocholt, West Germany, with a banner on the side reading "Long distance traffic business is in a stranglehold by the government." They claimed that better conditions prevailed elsewhere in the Common Market countries.

WIDE WORLD

legal arguments that the proposal infringed the provision of the West German constitution concerning ownership of property. However, near the end of the year a new compromise solution was found, although it did not entirely satisfy trade-union aspirations.

Another—wide-ranging—approach to participation was that found in Sweden, where an extensive union-backed legislative program, much of it bearing on participation, had been enacted in recent years. In January 1975 the report of the Committee on Labour Relations Legislation set forth radical proposals to strengthen the influence of workers in what happens at the enterprise. Proposals included extension of the subject matter of collective bargaining to include virtually any question concerning employer-employee relations; giving employees the right of interpretation concerning certain issues instead of the employer; placing a duty on employers to negotiate before any substantial change could be introduced at the workplace; extension of the requirement that employers make information available; and a liberalization of the legal position of strikers.

In Europe, particularly, discussion on participation related to gain and ownership as well as to participation in management. The most advanced proposal to date, embodied in the Danish government's "economic democracy" bill of 1973, did not succeed, though the issue was by no means dead. In The Netherlands, however, a government White Paper in May 1975 proposed that an element of companies' profits should be contributed to a central fund, which would be used (1) for supplementary pensions, (2) for shares to be made available to employees, and (3) for cash payments to employees on retirement. A new formula put forward in the summer by a Swedish trade-union group proposed that a proportion of companies' annual profits, in the form of new stock issues, should be paid annually into a workers' shareholding fund.

The improvement of life at the workplace was a major item of discussion at the International Labour Organization (ILO) conference. It was decided to launch a European Community Foundation for the Improvement of Living and Working Conditions in Ireland, and the Commission itself promulgated guidelines concerning humanization of work and safety, hygiene, and health protection at the workplace. The West German government published guidelines for research into working conditions and organization. A central "framework" collective agreement, concluded in France in March, set out principles concerning work standards and work loads; encouraged flexible organization of working time; deprecated large variations in earnings under systems that paid according to results; stressed the need for more safety measures; and proposed increased emphasis on the role of supervisory staff.

National Developments. In Britain the close partnership between the government and the TUC continued. In addition to trying to reverse certain clauses which it had been forced to accept in its industrial relations legislation of 1974, the government legislated an Employment Protection Act, extending the rights of workers in a variety of ways. Against a background of economic difficulties, the industrial relations scene remained troubled, though the volume of disputes subsided to some extent.

The industrial relations scene in Italy continued to be turbulent, though less so than in some recent years. In a generally depressed economy, there were signs that both unions and employers were seeking new and constructive forms of dialogue that would take them beyond the attitudes of confrontation that had persisted since the "hot autumn" of 1969. In the long-drawn-out effort at unification of the three national trade-union organizations, the three executive committees agreed in August that unification should be achieved by 1977. Doubts were expressed, however, that this target would be attained.

Japan appeared to have adjusted well to the shock of recession following years of extremely high growth rates. Attention was now turning toward what could be accomplished with lower growth rates than hitherto. More attention was being paid to social security and to social policy generally. Other trends in Japan were toward raising the normal retirement age to 60 and toward the full operation of a five-day week. In May the Spanish government approved new legislation on the right to strike, but this right remained more restricted than in most industrial countries. The Spanish labour scene continued to be disturbed, with numbers of strikes backed by the unofficial trade unions. In Portugal the uneasy political situation was reflected in industrial relations, with much working time lost and considerable militant action against employers. Legislative decrees created a new framework for trade unions, including establishment of a national trade-union organization.

In recent years government, state, and municipal employees had become increasingly restless in a number of countries. The trend toward fuller recognition of trade unions and procedures for collective bargaining for such workers continued in 1975. There were some quite serious disputes in this sector, notably in the U.S. and Canada.

The World Scene. Like so many subjects, industrial relations was tending to become more internationalized. Partly this was a result of growing international cooperation at the government level, as in the European Economic Community. Much of it, however, stemmed from the growth of multinational enterprises and the efforts of trade unions to protect workers' interests vis-à-vis those enterprises.

For some time trade unions had followed a dual policy to this end. First, they stepped up coordination through the international trade-union organizations, particularly the industry-based international trade secretariats. Second, they sought to persuade international agencies to establish procedures for monitoring, and in some respects regulating, the activities of these enterprises.

The UN Economic and Social Council (Ecosoc), the Organization for Economic Cooperation and Development (OECD), and the ILO were all concerned with this matter, and the OECD was considering the possibility of guidelines with respect to multinational enterprises. Union strategy was reviewed at the World Congress of the International Confederation of Free Trade Unions in Mexico City in October, when it was decided to press for further international action on the subject. (R. O. CLARKE)

R. O. Clarke is a principal administrator in the Social Affairs and Industrial Relations Division of the Organization for Economic Cooperation and Development, Paris. The views expressed in this article are his own and should not be attributed to the OECD.

See also Economics; Economy, World; Industrial Review.

[521.B.3; 534.C.1.g; 552.D.3 and F.3]

ENCYCLOPÆDIA BRITANNICA FILMS. *The Rise of Labor* (1968); *The Industrial Worker* (1969); *The Rise of Big Business* (1969); *The Progressive Era* (1971).

UNEMPLOYMENT AND INFLATION

By Harford Thomas

The study of economics has engaged some of the most powerful minds of this century. Despite this fact, none of them foresaw that persistent inflation would coexist with persistent unemployment, or that growth would stagnate as government spending was poured into the economy, or that, with world prices moving up, world trade would move down. This has been a worldwide experience, in one form or another, in the mid-1970s.

The primary objectives of government have been to maintain full employment, to stabilize prices, to sustain economic growth, and to maintain a balance of export earnings that will cover the cost of imports in foreign trade. It has not been uncommon for a government to fail on all counts at once—and not for want of employing and following the most expert economic advice. No finance ministry is complete without its team of top-flight economists and its backup of computer forecasts.

Nor is it unprecedented for theories and forecasts to fail. Between World Wars I and II the classical economics of a laissez-faire free market still prevailed. Left to itself, it was argued, equilibrium with full employment would be achieved, with each man selling his labour at the price it would bring and with the producer pricing his goods at the level they would bring. It was not so. In Britain for 20 years unemployment never fell below 10%. In the United States the 1920s boom blew up in the 1929 crash and collapsed into the depression of the 1930s, with unemployment reaching 25%. In Germany there were 6 million unemployed when Hitler came to power in 1933.

Harford Thomas was formerly deputy editor and also financial and city editor of The Guardian, *London, and has written widely on economic and social topics.*

The Keynesian Theory. In 1936 John Maynard Keynes published his *General Theory of Employment, Interest and Money.* Writing in the 1930s, his focus was on unemployment. Why did it persist? His answer (to reduce it to the briefest terms) was that employment was determined by the level of output, and this was determined by demand (comprising individual spending, business investment in plant and equipment, and public expenditure). Therefore the level of employment could be regulated by managing the aggregate level of demand. This the government could and should do by adjusting its taxation and expenditure.

Rearmament and war eliminated the unemployment of the 1930s before Keynes's theory had made much impact on government, but by the end of World War II it had been embodied in Britain's full employment policy for the postwar period. Later it was taken up by most other Western governments (in the U.S. first under Pres. John F. Kennedy). Since 1945 demand management to secure the twin objectives of economic growth and full employment has become the common practice of developed countries throughout the world.

Keynes had been not much concerned with inflation (prices in Britain had been remarkably stable, at a depressed level, between the wars), nor was his theory a prescription for economic growth. Rather, it was designed to foster stabilization of the economy with full employment. He died in 1946, too soon to apply his formidable intellect to an aspect of full employment policies that became apparent only with the experience of practice. Price inflation appeared to be inseparably linked with a high level of employment.

In 1958 the economist A. W. H. Phillips (*see* OBITUARIES) was able to show from U.K. statistics that there was a consistent relationship between the rate of price inflation and the level of employment: the higher the level of employment the higher the rate of price inflation. So a government had to choose: it could have stable prices at the cost of more unemployment, or full employment at the cost of some inflation. The Phillips curve, as it is called, has become famous in economic argument. But it did not allow for accelerating inflation which has virtually driven it off the chart. Around 1960, when it was first being discussed, it seemed that prices would stabilize (in the U.K.) with around $2\frac{1}{2}$% unemployment. By the mid-1970s many countries were experiencing 5% unemployment or more with two-digit inflation.

The Monetarists. Meanwhile a rival school of economists, the monetarists, headed by the American Milton Friedman, had

DONALD MC CULLIN—MAGNUM

Seeking work on a cold winter morning in the north of England.

mounted a set of fundamental objections to the Keynesian theories of demand management. Keynes had assumed that varying the level of demand, provided it did not exceed the capacity of the economy when fully employed, would influence output rather than prices. Therefore it need not be inflationary to pump extra spending power into the economy by reducing taxation, increasing public expenditure, and running a budget deficit. The monetarists approach the argument from the other way round.

Their primary concern is with inflation. They say that if the amount of money in circulation rises much faster than the increase in productive capacity, then the effect is seen not in more jobs and more output but in higher prices, coming into effect a year or so later. Correspondingly, by restricting the amount of money in circulation prices can be forced down because there will not be sufficient money around to pay high prices and high wages. This, they admit, will cause considerable unemployment while the economy readjusts itself.

How much unemployment and of what duration is the question their critics ask of them. Monetarists hold that there is what they call a "natural" level of employment which depends not on fiscal or monetary techniques but on the freedom and flexibility of the market to create enough viable jobs for the available work force. From the monetarist point of view it is self-defeating and inflationary for a government to try to spend its way into a higher level of employment than the economy can sustain naturally. This, they say, sets up accelerating inflation, and the higher it goes, the more unemployment there will be when excess demand ultimately has to be removed by deflation.

Theory and Reality. Both sides of the argument, it may seem to observers, suffer a mismatch between the untidiness of the facts and the neatness of the theory. Consider unemployment itself. There is much dispute over the statistics. In August 1975 the number of unemployed in the U.K. was officially given as 1,250,000, but this figure includes students on vacation, men retired early on company pensions, recent school leavers, workers changing jobs, and hard-core unemployables. The figure for true involuntary unemployed seeking jobs could be as little as half the official total. Alternatively, the total could understate the real situation because it does not include short-time working. Nor do we know how much labour hoarding there is by employers maintaining their work force in the hope of an upturn in activity, or being prevented by union pressure from dismissing underemployed workers. There is the further complication that unemployment varies from region to region. In the favoured areas of London and the south there could still be labour shortages in particular places and particular skills.

Such discrepancies complicate the political judgment of what is an acceptable level of unemployment at a time when the primary objective of most governments has come to be the containment of inflation. Furthermore, generous terms for severance pay and unemployment compensation have made unemployment less painful, for a short time at least, than it was on the starvation-level doles of the 1920s and 1930s. In 1975 some of West Germany's unemployed, drawing 68% of their last net income, were reported to have gone away on extended foreign holidays, and in some other countries payments are even more generous. Hence the fear of civil strife provoked by high unemployment is less in some countries than in others, and some governments will therefore be more inclined than others to choke off inflation as promptly and decisively as possible, even at the cost of heavy unemployment.

So there are significant variations in the performance of different countries. This is important because both inflation and recession are worldwide phenomena moving like an infection along linkages of foreign trade. No country can shut itself off from the rest, and each will depend to a large extent on creating more employment from its exports to others. Therefore a government will want to see other governments reflating their economies, though it may hesitate to do so itself for fear that further inflation will undermine its own export competitiveness. The policy pulls are in opposite directions. If wide divergences develop between different countries in their success in containing inflation, this will create new instability in foreign exchange rates.

National Experience. In mid-1974 some unemployment and inflation rates were estimated as follows: U.S., unemployment 8.4%, inflation 9.5%; Japan, 1.9% and 13.5%; West Germany, 3.5% and 6.5%; France, 4.9% and 12%; U.K., 5.6% and 25%. These figures also illustrate the fact that inflation and unemployment in different countries will depend greatly on their history and on particular and local circumstances. Japan has a disciplined, conservative, and traditional labour force, which has enabled it to cut its inflation rate by half in one year and at the same time mount an intensive export drive. The U.S. has become used to a higher unemployment rate than most other Western countries. Germany's history makes West Germany more fearful of inflation than unemployment, and with a modernized postwar union and management structure it has had little industrial unrest. Britain's history makes it more fearful of unemployment than inflation, and with out-of-date union and management structures it suffers from chronic industrial strife.

It follows that a country's history, national characteristics, and politics can falsify some of the generalizations of economic theory. The textbook free market no longer exists. Unions exercise industry-wide monopoly power in wage fixing. Public industries, and big corporations in the private sector, exercise monopoly power in fixing prices. Unions and producers are highly resistant to reducing wages and prices. These are the political facts of economics. In addition, the psychology of rising expectations has institutionalized wage claims that take account of future inflation and price increases that assume the consumer's continuing ability to pay. For two decades countries of the developed world have enjoyed continuously rising standards of living, mostly with full employment, on these assumptions.

Can Full Employment Return? The orderly expansion of the 25 years after World War II, albeit with some continuing and slowly accelerating inflation, was wrecked by the world price explosion in foodstuffs, industrial commodities, and oil in 1972 and 1973. For the first time since the war, products were priced out of their markets, people were priced out of their jobs, and firms were priced out of existence. The speed and violence of the breakdown of sustained growth and full employment has been traumatic. There were indeed new factors at work. Initially the hyperinflation of world prices of foodstuffs and industrial raw materials was set off by world demand exceeding supply. In many sectors we had run into the buffers of capacity limits. If this is a correct analysis it may not be possible to return to the 5% growth rates (which imply a doubling of output in 15 years) on which full employment had been based.

Few political leaders and few of their economic advisers have thought out the implications of this possibility. It could mean a "natural" level of very high unemployment, because the present level of industrial capacity cannot provide enough jobs for everybody. It could necessitate the redirection of much industrial output to the export markets of the less developed countries —which need their own kind of growth breakthrough but currently do not have the money to pay for it.

In any event, there will have to be some slowing down of the growth rates of recent years in developed countries, not least for environmental reasons. This will exacerbate the problems of what is known as structural unemployment—the loss of jobs arising from the decline of old industries, the obstinate difficulties of regional unemployment, and the low demand for labour in new automated plants. This kind of unemployment may call for nothing less than the restructuring of society, with radical changes in habits, attitudes, and expectations. There will have to be much retraining for new skills. There may even have to be planned sharing of what work there is to do and a quite new emphasis on leisure and its desirability. If unemployment proves persistent it is unlikely to be resolved by economic policy alone, whatever the theory in current fashion.

Industrial Review

During 1972 and 1973 the rise of world manufacturing production was the fastest since the end of World War II, amounting to 18%. This was followed by a stagnation in the first half of 1974 and then by a recession, which in 1975 developed into the deepest since the war. Toward the middle of 1975 manufacturing activity in the developed countries returned to the level that had preceded the start of the boom.

The year 1974 ended as it had begun, in an atmosphere of crisis for the world economy. But while the initial obstacle, the oil shortage, was quickly overcome and it appeared that the feared international monetary crisis could be avoided, rapid inflation became increasingly serious. The effects of inflation on purchasing power seriously depressed demand, which was weakening anyway. Apart from the growing but still relatively small market provided by the oil-exporting countries, the stagnation of demand was general in the Western world. The income of the less developed countries was adversely affected by falling commodity prices and by the significantly higher cost of their oil supplies. The latter influenced the developed countries as well, but in the case of the less developed countries there were other more prominent factors.

By early 1974 inflation had reduced purchasing power and business confidence started to fall. In the course of 1974, restrictive monetary and fiscal measures of varying severity were introduced in most industrial countries, intended to check the rise in domestic prices and the deterioration of the balance of payments; the higher oil prices had contributed to both. By the end of the year these measures had achieved some success; demand stopped rising and later actually fell, and the rate of inflation had been braked as well. The other consequences included declining industrial activity and rapidly rising unemployment; in mid-1975 both of these indicators pointed to the worst situation in many countries since the recovery from World War II. In the early autumn of 1975 any marked revival was still a promise of the future; although various measures aimed at stimulating demand were taken in some countries, these were unlikely to have much effect before 1976.

In mid-1975 manufacturing output in the industrial countries was more than 10% below the level of the same period a year earlier. Most industries began their recessive course in the second half of 1974. Industrial production in the less industrialized world turned down considerably later, while in the centrally planned economies its rate of advance, although slowing somewhat, was well maintained.

The magnitude of the recession became clear in the first quarter of 1975. The worst hit were the basic metals and textile-clothing groups; in the developed economies, their output was about 15% lower in early 1975 than in early 1974. The production of chemicals fell by about 12% in the same period and that of

Table I. Index Numbers of Production, Employment, and Productivity in Manufacturing Industries
1970 = 100

Area	Relative importance 1963	1970	1974	Production 1973	1974	Employment 1973	1974	Productivity* 1973	1974
World†	1,000	1,000	1,000	120	122	...	...	...	...
Industrial countries	876	896	883	119	120	...	...	...	...
Less industrialized countries	124	104	117	126	137	...	...	...	...
North America‡	480	409	402	120	120	...	...	...	...
Canada	28	27	29	122	126	106	109	115	116
United States	452	381	372	119	118	103	103	116	115
Latin America§	49	59	68	129	140	...	...	...	...
Mexico	8	13	13	122	122	...	...	...	...
Asia‖	88	137	144	127	128	...	...	...	...
India	16	11	9	108	109	...	...	...	...
Japan	55	99	103	130	127	104	104	125	122
Pakistan	3	3	3	110	117	...	...	...	...
Europe¶	350	365	353	116	118	...	...	...	...
Austria	7	6	6	122	127	108	107	113	119
Belgium	11	11	11	118	124	...	...	...	...
Denmark	6	5	5	115	...	101	99	114	...
Finland	4	4	4	121	123	104	111	116	111
France	51	67	69	122	126	103	103	118	122
Germany, West	89	104	94	113	110	98	...	115	...
Greece	2	3	4	145	142	117	118	124	120
Ireland	1	1	1	121	124	103	103	118	120
Italy	36	37	36	114	119	103	107	111	111
Netherlands, The	12	13	12	113	115	93	92	122	125
Norway♀	4	4	4	113	119	99	101	107	110
Portugal	2	3	3	110	...	...	...	...	...
Spain	12	12	15	141	155	111	115	127	135
Sweden	14	13	13	110	117	98	108	112	108
Switzerland	10	12	11	110	111	95	95	116	117
United Kingdom	73	54	48	110	108	94	94	117	115
Yugoslavia	13	13	15	127	140	115	121	111	116
Rest of the world♂	33	30	30	115	117	...	...	...	...
Australia	14	14	13	117	116	101	103	116	113
South Africa	5	6	6	115	122	109	113	106	108
Centrally planned economies□	...	...	...	130	142	...	...	...	...

*This is 100 times the production index divided by the employment index, giving a rough indication of changes in output per person employed.
†Excluding Albania, Bulgaria, China, Czechoslovakia, East Germany, Hungary, Mongolia, North Korea, North Vietnam, Poland, Romania, and the U.S.S.R.
‡Canada and the United States.
§South and Central America (including Mexico) and the Caribbean islands.
‖Asian Middle East and East and Southeast Asia, including Japan.
¶Excluding Albania, Bulgaria, Czechoslovakia, East Germany, Hungary, Poland, Romania, and the U.S.S.R.
♀Employment and productivity based on 1972=100.
♂Africa and Oceania.
□These are not included in the above world total and consist of Albania, Bulgaria, Czechoslovakia, East Germany, Hungary, Poland, Romania, and the U.S.S.R.
Sources: UN *Monthly Bulletin of Statistics;* U.K. National Institute of Economic and Social Research, *Economic Review.*

KEYSTONE

This experimental impulse water gun is capable of penetrating two metres of granite in 2.5 hours. It is being tested for use in the U.S.S.R.

COURTESY OF LOCKHEED ELECTRONICS CO.

A new Lockheed Electronics Co. air traffic control system can automatically handle up to 256 aircraft simultaneously. Prototypes have been installed in the Wilkes-Barre–Scranton airport in Pennsylvania and in Atlantic City, New Jersey.

metal manufactures by 10%. Within the latter group there were large variations; electrical machinery was down only 4%, but motor vehicles suffered a much greater decline (production of automobiles fell by one-third in Italy, one-fifth in the U.S. and the U.K., and one-ninth in France and West Germany).

The stagnation of consumer demand was aggravated by the generally rather low industrial investment activity, which was the outcome of excess capacity and the depressed business climate; by the decline in world trade, which in 1975 might be as much as 8–10% lower than in 1974; by the huge fall in residential investment, which in some countries had started in 1973; and by the high level of inventories accumulated in 1974, which in some cases (such as steel and automobiles) might have accounted for the bulk of the production decline.

The status of manufacturing industries in the various countries is shown in Table I, but the annual figures do not reflect the downturn in activity which started from a high level at various times, mostly during 1974. (The "relative importance" figures for 1963 and 1970 are the weights officially assessed by the UN Statistical Office and indicate the changes in this period; the 1974 figures are estimates.)

The importance of U.S. industry in relation to the rest of the world declined from 45 to under 40% between 1963 and 1974, but the U.S. still accounted for well over one-third of the manufacturing output of the world, excluding the U.S.S.R. and Eastern Europe. Including these, but not China, the share of the U.S. was 27% in 1970, as compared with a 21% share for the U.S.S.R. After a year of virtual stagnation U.S. manufacturing activity started to fall toward the end of 1974, and by the second quarter of 1975 its level was 12% lower than a year earlier, raising industrial unemployment alarmingly. The downswing was led by the automobile industry; producers of investment goods felt the decline of business fixed investment; and demand for residential investment, on a downtrend since early in 1973, fell further.

The recession was somewhat less severe in Canada. The annual decline in industrial output was about 7% in the year to mid-1975, but it was nevertheless the steepest since 1961. Local consumption and industrial investment were maintained, and demand from those quarters alleviated the unavoidable effects of the U.S. recession.

Capacity utilization in Japanese industry fell to under 80% in 1975, with output running some 15% below the level of the first half of 1974. The decline in world trade and weak home demand, caused by high unemployment, inflation, and stagnating investment, were the main reasons why output in 1974 lagged behind that of the previous year. In mid-1975 industrial production started to improve marginally from its trough in the spring.

Table II. Manufacturing Production in the U.S.S.R. and Eastern Europe*
1970 = 100

Country	1972	1973	1974
Bulgaria†	119	131	142
Czechoslovakia	124	133	142
Germany, East†	112	120	129
Hungary	113	120	130
Poland	121	135	151
U.S.S.R.	115	124	134

*Romania not available.
†All industries.
Source: UN *Monthly Bulletin of Statistics*.

Output in the U.K. was reduced in the first three months of 1974 by a coal miners' strike and the temporary imposition of a three-day workweek. Subsequently, production recovered but could not reach the prestrike level. Rapid inflation and high unemployment depressed home consumption, and generally low business confidence hampered investment. The declining exchange rate of the pound partly balanced rapidly rising wage costs and helped to preserve a measure of export competitiveness in 1974, but in 1975 the fall in world trade depressed exports too.

The downturn in West Germany started in the early months of 1974 but was gradual until the autumn, when industrial output started to fall sharply; by mid-1975 it was 10% below the level of a year earlier. The slow rise in consumers' expenditures was outweighed by falls in exports and investment in plant and machinery, as well as by weak building and construction activity. At mid-1975 the inflow of new orders was still well below the previous year's level, though in some sectors—notably the motor industry—there were indications that further decline might be avoided.

Manufacturing activity in the less developed countries rose fairly rapidly in 1974, their output totaling about 8% more than in 1973 (in contrast to the 1% rise in the industrial countries). But already there was industrial stagnation in some regions (such as the Indian subcontinent), and this became more general during 1975.

In the centrally planned economies manufacturing output continued to rise during 1974. The growth rate was 8%, about the same as previously, in the U.S.S.R. and ranged from 7% (Czechoslovakia) to 12% (Poland) in Eastern Europe. Preliminary estimates indicated a slowing down of growth in 1975 (Table II).

Productivity in manufacturing rose much more slowly in 1974 than in the two preceding boom years. Output per man-hour in the six largest Western industrial countries (weighted by their importance) rose by more than 5% in 1972 and by almost 7% in 1973. In 1974 this aggregate growth was reduced to $2\frac{1}{2}$%; in the United Kingdom productivity did not rise at all, in Japan relatively little, and in the other major countries the earlier rate of growth was halved. The 1975 recession caused productivity to fall in many countries and halted its rise elsewhere.

(G. F. RAY)

ADVERTISING

International advertising expenditures increased in 1975 over 1974. More than $14 billion was spent on international advertising in 1975, double the total of 1961. During those years the industry witnessed such developments as the formation of multinational agencies and increased governmental control over local advertising. Statutes regulating the advertising and labeling of foods, drugs, cosmetics, and a host of other products were enacted in many nations, especially those most advanced economically. In 1975, for example, Norway passed a law that forbids giveaways, free offers, and premiums if they are not available to everybody and if the consumers have to buy a product to get the premium.

Despite the recession, inflation, energy problems, shortages, and consumer reluctance to spend money for major products, the U.S. advertising industry enjoyed an increased level of activity in 1975. Advertising spending during the year was expected to total about $28,670,000,000, up 6.9% from 1974. If such a growth rate were to continue, total advertising volume in the United States would reach $40 billion in 1980 and $60 billion in 1985. One aspect of the year 1975 that favoured advertisers was unprecedented decline in personal selling expenditures, with manufacturers turning more of their marketing budgets over to advertising.

In the U.S. the top 100 national advertisers spent $6 billion in eight media in 1974, up from $5,680,000,000 in 1973 according to *Advertising Age.* The largest national advertiser was Procter & Gamble Co., followed by General Motors Corp., Sears, Roebuck and Co., General Foods Corp., and Warner-Lambert Co. Procter & Gamble spent $325 million for national advertising. The U.S. government was the tenth-largest national advertiser, spending $110.8 million, with recruiting advertising for the military obtaining most of the expenditure. Local advertising spending by retailers increased 7% in 1975 over 1974. Classified newspaper linage, however, dropped significantly for real estate and help-wanted advertisements.

In 1975 the advertising rates for media in the U.S. continued to rise. A 30-second prime time television slot increased to $40,900 in 1975, up 18% from 1974 and 66% from 1970. A consumer magazine black-and-white page was priced at about $15,500 in 1975, 8% over 1974 and 19% over 1970.

The advertising business employed about 1.3 million persons in 1975 and there were approximately 5,500 advertising agencies, ranging in size from one person to 7,000. The largest agency in world billings continued to be J. Walter Thompson, with $867.5 million in 1974.

The U.S. Federal Trade Commission on Nov. 7, 1974, announced rules to cover nutrition claims made in food advertising. Simultaneously, the FTC published a staff recommendation that all advertisements be required to disclose certain brand-specific nutritional information. According to the director of the Bureau of Consumer Protection, J. Thomas Rosch, the food advertising rule was the most complex and comprehensive rule-making effort ever undertaken by the agency.

In April 1975 the FTC proposed new guidelines for endorsements in advertising. Under these guidelines, every endorsement would reflect the endorser's honest views, avoid distortion of meanings, and apply only as long as the advertiser had good reason to believe the endorser was using the products or subscribed to the advertised viewpoint.

The Children Review Unit of the National Advertising Division of the Council of Better Business Bureaus in 1975 called for reduced emphasis on the use of premiums in advertising. The unit also advised against directing advertising for medication, drugs, and supplemental vitamins to children.

A National Advertising Review Board panel in the U.S. concluded that although there was no conscious, concerted effort among advertisers to offend women, a problem existed because advertising is a part of a changing society in which old ways of thinking sometimes outlive new conditions. The most frequent complaints were that advertising portrays women too often as only housewives and mothers (shoppers, cleaners, family cooks), minimizing their roles in the business and professional world and in community activities, and that advertisements feature women's sexuality to the neglect of their individualities. The panel developed a checklist of questions for advertisers and agencies to consider when creating and approving an advertisement. The panel also suggested extreme caution in using humour, particularly in making fun of efforts to improve the status of women and the opportunities available to them.

A threat to establish more controls over advertising in the United Kingdom continued in 1975. To avoid additional gov-

Advertisements aimed at world problems included Bell Helicopter Co.'s effort to promote the sale of combat helicopters in Asia and the CARE campaign against hunger.

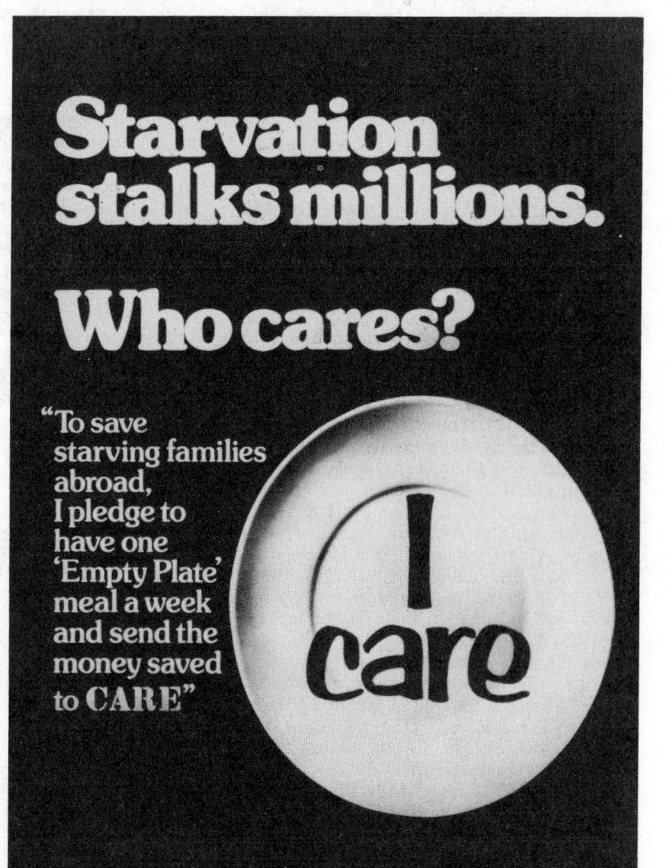

PHOTOS, WIDE WORLD

ernment control, the Advertising Standards Authority in May launched an advertising campaign to make the public aware of the British Code of Advertising Practice and the steps being taken to protect the consumer. Large advertisements were placed in newspapers and periodicals, and a film was shown in theatres. The advertisement explained the control system and asked the public to help bring poor practices to the attention of the authority.

An international advertisers' conference held under the auspices of the International Advertising Association took place in Rio de Janeiro, Brazil, from May 22 to May 23, 1975. It had as its theme "the contribution of advertising to developing countries and emerging consumers." The internationality of the world's consumers was stressed.

(EDWARD MARK MAZZE)

[534.I; 629.C.4.c]

AEROSPACE

The U.S. aerospace companies continued to record a healthy growth in 1975. Estimates made at the beginning of the year put total sales of all U.S. equipment, military and civil, at $29 billion, very close to the peak figure reached during the critical years of the Vietnam war. Great Britain's industry also expanded, despite industrial unrest and uncertainty caused by the Labour government's plans to nationalize the largest companies. Exports for 1974 were up by 20% to $1.4 billion, and 1975 seemed likely to show similar growth. Britain's best customer for aircraft and engines was the U.S., followed by France, West Germany, and China, the last-named mainly through the purchase of Tridents. In France, Aérospatiale, a nationalized company and the country's biggest aerospace producer, was reorganized following a succession of difficult years.

Despite economic uncertainties, some airlines continued to plan for reequipment. One significant sign was the emergence of the Airbus A-300B on the world market; in 1975 this consortium-built European airliner, dismissed only a year earlier by a Boeing official as a "government airplane," outsold all the U.S. wide-body transports (Boeing 747, McDonnell Douglas DC-10, and Lockheed L-1011 TriStar) together. The A-300B faced no competition until McDonnell Douglas proposed the DC-X-200, an airliner with a similar configuration although smaller and intended as a replacement for the DC-9.

At the Paris Air Show at Le Bourget in May, Boeing dusted off plans for its 7X7 three-engined 727 replacement, first unveiled two years earlier. Perhaps its most significant feature was the use of engines having a thrust of about 22,000 lb. each, or 10 metric tons, under development by Pratt & Whitney, General Electric, and their European partners. A new version of the Boeing 727, the world's best-selling airliner, known as the 727-300, was also offered, but this project was shelved later in the year for lack of support. After a two-year absence, the Soviet Tu-144 supersonic transport reappeared at the Le Bourget show, apparently little changed. Late in December it went into regular service, carrying mail and cargo between Moscow and Alma-Ata; passenger flights were to begin in 1976.

Preparations to put the Anglo-French Concorde into service continued, following extensive British and French route-proving flights throughout the world. In October the French government approved its version for commercial operation, in advance of a similar British action. The major "new" commercial aircraft, the Boeing 747SP, a special version of the Jumbo Jet for low-density, long-haul routes, made its maiden flight in July.

In the military field the first flight of the Rockwell International B-1 in December 1974 showed that the U.S. would not renounce the concept of the manned strategic bomber. The huge swing-wing bomber, as large as the Concorde, was designed to travel to its target at the speed of sound but at an altitude of only about 200 ft.

The major news of the year was the adoption of two experimental aircraft to play a central part in Western defense systems. In May the U.S. Navy announced that it had selected a lightweight fighter known as the Northrop F-17 as the model on which to base a new carrier-borne fighter-bomber, the F-18; this would be built jointly by Northrop and McDonnell Douglas and masterminded by the latter company, which had long experience in building combat aircraft for the U.S. Navy. Even more controversial was the selection by The Netherlands, Belgium, Denmark, and Norway of General Dynamics' F-16 as the European replacement of the squadrons of F-104 Starfighters. The competitor, the Mirage F-1 from Dassault-Breguet of France, had a new engine, the Snecma M53. European companies were assured that they would be responsible for much of the industrial effort in producing the F-16.

Another reverse for Dassault was the decision by the French government in October to shelve the projected Super Mirage interceptor planned for service in the 1980s. Continuing affirmation of the versatility of Britain's Harrier vertical takeoff fighter came from two directions. In August the Royal Navy announced its decision to buy 25 Sea Harriers to equip its new "through-deck" cruisers, and in September the U.S. Navy approved the purchase of a more advanced version of the AV-8A Harrier already in service with the Marines. Some 340 of the new AV-8Bs would also be operated by the Marine Corps.

The long-held dream of a European space organization came true in May when the European Space Agency came into existence. More spectacular was the much-publicized Apollo-Soyuz flight, perhaps less of a scientific mission than a public-relations exercise to strengthen the Soviet-U.S. détente. For the U.S., this was the last of the Apollo flights, with their historic Moon landings, and the last manned flight before the reusable space shuttle took over the job of putting satellites and probes into space. The U.S.S.R. stepped up its space activities, and there were rumours of a new space station design and of a new launch vehicle even larger than the U.S. Saturn V. (*See* SPACE EXPLORATION.)

(MICHAEL WILSON)

[732.B.1]

ALCOHOLIC BEVERAGES

Beer. During 1974 there was an overall increase in world beer production of 20 million hectolitres (hl.), the estimated total reaching 750 million hl. (1 hl. = about 26.5 U.S. gal.). Of this, the U.S. produced 183,344,000 hl., West Germany 92,783,000 hl., and the U.K. 63,039,000 hl. In the countries in which excise duty was a sizable proportion of the retail price, there was evidence that sales declined, particularly in Britain, where the duty was increased by twopence a pint (1 pint = approx. 0.57 litre) in April. The long, hot, dry summer in Western Europe in 1975 bolstered sales, but as inflation continued to bite, consumer retrenchment during the fall and winter was expected.

The strain on profits led South African Breweries Ltd. to note that future expenditures would have to be watched, and several British breweries reported declines in profits despite increased production. Belgium, top of the beer-drinking league in 1973 with a per capita consumption of 150 l., slumped to 140 l. in 1974 and slipped to fourth place—the first time in many years it had not been among the top three. Czechoslovakia took the lead at 152.7 l., followed by West Germany at 147 l. Third place went to Australia at 141.3 l., a sharp advance from 1973. The United States increased per capita consumption from 76.5 l. in 1973 to 79.8 l. in 1974. (*See* Table III.)

In Europe and in North America there was some concern about the barley crop. Farmers reported that high temperatures and low rainfall had kept pests at bay but that the corns were small and the crop would be light. In some countries nitrogen levels were high, which could reduce yield in the mashing process and could also cause trouble at retail outlets if the high-nitrogen barley produced beer that would foam on pouring.

The crop of European hops was light in several countries. In the U.K. total tonnage was expected to be 10% below optimum requirements, but with stockpiles good this shortage was unlikely to cause problems. Some varieties of hops did well in the dry weather, and irrigation helped minimize drought damage. Hop growers looked for a small crop of high quality. In northwest Europe, in 1975, hop harvesting started earlier than usual.

More brewing countries accepted modern methods of dispensing draft beer. Many customers liked to see beer served from a bulk container, and the habit gained support. In Japan, where the idea was new, British-style "pubs" were erected that included modern draft-beer service equipment. This move was fortunate for the brewers, since the environmentalists were still preaching against the use of one-trip containers and sometimes even against returnable bottles.

(ARTHUR T. E. BINSTED)

Spirits. The spirits market showed remarkable resilience in the first half of 1975 despite prevailing economic conditions. In the U.K. the April budget brought an increase in the duty on spirits (and wines), thus widening the gap between the taxes imposed by the U.K. and those in the rest of the EEC. British liquor dealers predictably took a gloomy view of prospects for the year, but by September business was by no means discouraging.

Sales of vodka, with a 9.6% share of the total U.K. spirits market, rose by no less than 26%, to 1,387,000 proof gal. in the January–July period, as a result of considerable promotion. Imported vodkas accounted for 27,000 proof gal. In several European markets vodka enjoyed a 15% share of spirits sales, and industry observers expected U.K. sales eventually to overtake those of gin, which at 2,421,000 proof gal. showed a modest increase of 4.1%.

For Scotch whisky the picture was mixed. In the 12 months to July 1975 releases from bond in the U.K. totaled 27.6 million proof gal., a rise of 10%. But whisky profitability in the home market was restricted by rising costs and price controls. Consequently some distillers, notably the industry leader, the Distillers Company Ltd., decided to cut back production. During the year a large number of countries increased their taxes or duties on Scotch.

In the U.S., according to figures published in *Advertising Age,* per capita consumption of spirits increased from 1.5 gal.

Table III. Estimated Consumption of Beer in Selected Countries
In litres* per capita of total population

Country	1972	1973	1974
Czechoslovakia	147.7	145.5	152.7
Germany, West	145.3	146.7	147
Australia†	127.3	130.5	141.3
Belgium‡	140	150	140
Luxembourg	133.5	144.2	135
New Zealand	121.1	125.2	126.1
Germany, East	107.3	112	114.9
United Kingdom	105.6	112	114.3
Denmark	108.05	113.52	111.96
Austria	103.7	110.1	106.2
Canada§	83.5	86	89.1
Ireland	76.92	80.19	86.74
United States	73.4	76.5	79.8
Netherlands, The	65.7	73.46	75.72
Switzerland	73.6	75.6	75.7
Hungary	57.3	61.6	66
Sweden	57.4	56.6	58.6
Finland	53.8	54.3	56.2
France	40.3	44.47	44.19
Norway	41.22	42.02	43.85
Bulgaria	39.51	43.62	...
Spain	36	42.5	42
Venezuela	41.1	40.7	...
Yugoslavia	35.2	37.2	...
Poland	35.5	37.8	36.1

*One litre=1.0567 U.S. quarts=0.8799 imperial quart.
†Years ending June 30.
‡Including so-called "household beer."
§Years ending March 31.

Table IV. Estimated Consumption of Potable Distilled Spirits in Selected Countries
In litres* of 100% pure spirit per capita of population

Country	1972	1973	1974
Poland	3.9	4.2	4
Japan	...	...	3.74
Germany, East	2.9	3.2	3.4
Canada†	2.86	2.96	3.38
Hungary	3.05	2.91	3.25
Luxembourg	2.8	3.3	3.1
United States	2.97	3.03	3.09
Spain	2.9	3.1	3
Yugoslavia	3	3	...
Sweden	2.63	2.66	2.94
Finland	2.19	2.45	2.9
Czechoslovakia	2.4	2.64	2.82
Netherlands, The	2.28	2.55	2.75
Germany, West	2.93	3.02	2.65
Iceland	2.49	2.53	2.65
Surinam	2.5	...	...
France‡	2.3	2.4	2.4
Romania	2.4§	...	...
Switzerland	2.08	2.12	2.15
Italy	1.9	2.2	2
Bulgaria	2	2	...
Austria	2.36	2.3	1.96
Ireland	1.69	1.82	1.92
Belgium	1.59	1.75	1.9
Norway	1.66	1.66	1.82

†Years ending March 31.
‡Including aperitifs.
§1970.

Table V. Estimated Consumption of Wine in Selected Countries
In litres* per capita of total population

Country	1972	1973	1974
Italy	110.9	109.3	110.5
France†	106.88	105.49	103.04
Portugal	82.4	80.4	80
Argentina	79.7	72.5	77.2
Spain	67	92	75
Switzerland‡	44.4	46.4	45
Luxembourg	41.5	40.9	40.3
Chile	44	38.2	40
Hungary	38.4	38.5	38
Austria	34	35.5	36.8
Greece	40	37	36.5
Yugoslavia	28.9	29.2	...
Uruguay	25	25	...
Romania	21.8	35.6	22.8
Germany, West	21.8	21.5	20.2
Bulgaria	20	20	...
Belgium	15.6	15.3	15.8
Czechoslovakia	14.6	14.5	12.5
U.S.S.R.	11.8	12	...
Australia	9	9.9	11.1
Netherlands, The	7.81	8.89	10.38
South Africa	9.97	10.72	10.17
Denmark	7.48	10.74	9.66
Finland	4.79	6.42	9.2
New Zealand	7.55	8.7	9.2

†Excluding cider (c. 20 litres per capita annually).
‡Excluding cider (c. 6.85 litres per capita 1972–73).

Source: Produktschap voor Gedistilleerde Dranken, *Hoeveel alcoholhoudende dranken worden er in de wereld gedronken?*

The Henriot wine cellar in Reims, France, occupies a former chalk mine. More than five million bottles of champagne are being aged there.

A.F.P./PICTORIAL PARADE

in 1965 to 2 gal. in 1974. Total whiskey imports during January–August 1975 fell 3%, to 56.3 million tax gal., compared with a year earlier, while Scotch whisky imports fell 7% to 30.9 million tax gal. Brandy imports rose 6% to 1.8 million tax gal., with French brandies rising 11% to 1.3 million tax gal. Cordial and liqueur imports fell 2% and gin imports 4%, but rum imports soared 71% to 486,000 tax gal. In 1974 rum ranked fifth in popularity among the various types of spirits in the U.S.

(COLIN PARNELL)

Wine. In 1975 world production of wine was expected to exceed 300 million hl. for the fourth time in six years, being estimated at 318 million hl., compared with an actual 340 million hl. in 1974, 350 million hl. in 1973, and 306 million hl. in 1970. The decrease in production during 1975 was mainly due to a decline in Europe, which accounted for some 80% of world production. Output was also down, by about 10%, in North Africa (Algeria, Morocco, and Tunisia). In South America, Argentina produced 30 million hl., compared with 27 million hl. in 1974. U.S. production was estimated at 14 million hl., compared with 11 million hl. in 1974.

The French harvest of 65 million hl. was 13% below that of 1974 but of better quality. In the Bordeaux region quantity was down by 25%, but quality was excellent and the year promised to be among the finest for these wines. The same applied to Burgundy, with an appreciably smaller harvest of excellent quality. Alcoholic content was high, and the colour of the red wines was very good. Beaujolais was harder hit than other regions by rain and frost, but some individual vintages were spared and reached high quality. Côtes du Rhône, also among the regions with the greatest decrease, showed a 40% fall in production, but the wines were in general of better quality. The harvest fell by 10% in Champagne, but the wines were considered harmonious and of very high quality.

Italy's production, estimated at 60 million hl., was down by 25% compared with 1974, and below the average of the ten preceding years. In Piedmont the decrease was less, but quality was only average. Harvests in Lombardy and Venezia also fell by between 15 and 30%, with no marked improvement in quality. The same applied, with some higher percentage decreases, to other Italian regions, in particular Apulia, Tuscany, Sicily, and Sardinia. Under pressure from its own growers, France imposed a 12% import tax on Italian wines, which the European Commission held to be illegal.

In the United States the unprecedented expansion of vineyards that took place during 1970–74, combined with a leveling off of wine consumption, caused grape prices in 1975 to be about 45% below their 1973 highs. One industry source estimated that the supply of traditional table wine might be twice the consumer demand by 1978, leading to a price-cutting situation that could drive many small wineries out of business.

In Spain the 1975 harvest was 28 million hl., 26% lower than that of 1974 (which had been well above average in quantity). In the region of Jerez the harvest was quantitatively larger than during the previous year, but all other centres of production suffered a decrease. Fine weather during the year produced wines of superior quality almost everywhere in the country. In the Mancha, Untiel-Requena, and other regions alcoholic content reached 12° or more. (*See* DRUG ABUSE.)

(PAUL MAURON)

[731.E.8.a–c]

AUTOMOBILES

Automakers looking for an end to the troubles that had built up for them since the Arab oil embargo of 1974 found solace in 1975. Car sales, which started showing some recovery in the final weeks of 1974, gained real momentum in the fall of 1975. However, U.S. car production in 1975, at 6,725,682, was 8% below 1974 and the lowest since 1970, when General Motors was hit by a two-month strike.

Auto sales in the U.S. reached their low point in November 1974, when the industry was selling at an annual rate of 6.9 million units. In January 1975 the situation began to improve, with sales at an annual rate of 8 million. By October and November, after the U.S. manufacturers had introduced their new models, the annual selling rate swelled to 9.2 million. At that time import sales slumped to an annual rate of 1.2 million, the lowest rate for the foreign cars in a year.

Table VI. Production and Exports of Motor Vehicles by the Principal Producing Countries, 1974

Country	Passenger cars	Commercial vehicles
Production		
United States	7,324,504	2,746,538
Japan	3,931,842	2,619,998
France	3,045,283	417,564
Germany, West	2,839,596	260,181
Italy	1,630,686	141,829
United Kingdom	1,534,119	402,566
Canada	1,165,635	359,239
U.S.S.R.	1,119,000	727,000
Australia	400,287	89,052
Sweden	326,743	41,616
Other countries	2,628,860	980,688
World total	25,946,555	8,786,271
Exports		
France	1,765,297	183,265
Japan	1,727,396	890,691
Germany, West	1,540,808	340,745
Canada	840,803	222,494
Italy	686,244	47,524
United States	600,902	214,605
United Kingdom	564,722	170,722
Sweden	163,970	32,685

Source: Motor Vehicle Manufacturers Association of the United States, Inc.

AUTHENTICATED NEWS INTERNATIONAL

The 1975 Volkswagen Rabbit typified the trend toward smaller, more efficient cars, achieving a gas consumption rating of 38 miles per gallon in highway driving.

Imports, which had been strong at the outset of the year and zoomed to a record of more than 22% of total new car sales, settled down when their manufacturers started having supply problems. In the fall when the U.S. manufacturers brought out their new cars and the foreign car makers had not yet unveiled their next season's models, the sales fortunes of the former took a decided edge. At that time General Motors Corp. introduced the Chevrolet Chevette, with a 94-in. wheelbase, the smallest car ever built by a U.S. manufacturer.

Designed specifically to compete with small imported cars, the Chevette did surprisingly well against the Volkswagen Beetle and Rabbit, Datsun B-210, and Toyota Corolla. Its $3,098 price tag also was less than those of most of its competitors. Sales averaged 15,000 a month.

When the U.S. manufacturers brought out their new cars in the fall, they announced price increases averaging more than $200 per vehicle and boosted optional equipment prices 5 to 6% as well. But consumers did not resist the price hikes as they had a year earlier, when increases averaging more than $400 kept people away from showrooms. Ample gas supplies, consumer demand from those who had held back from a new car purchase in 1974 because of the controversy over fuel shortages, and an upswing in consumer confidence were seen as positive factors in the auto sales recovery.

The luxury car market was a benchmark of how adequate gasoline supplies affected sales. The more expensive models moved well in 1975. Cadillac, for example, sold everything it built. Recreational vehicles, hard hit by gasoline shortages because owners typically travel great distances to out-of-the-way places, showed recovery.

But there was also in 1975 a strong switch in buyer preferences, which first started appearing in 1974. While consumers found gas supplies ample, the higher prices made them more fuel-conscious. As a result small cars —the compacts, subcompacts, minis, and economy imports—did well, capturing about 50% of total new car sales.

Leading the charge of the auto industry out of its 1974 doldrums were the mid-size cars, those normally associated with about a 116-in. wheelbase. In this group the Oldsmobile Cutlass surprised even General Motors Corp. Not only was it the industry's leading intermediate but it also became the industry's second largest selling U.S.-made model, behind the full-size Chevrolet.

The cars that suffered most from fuel consciousness were the standard-size Ford, Chevrolet, Dodge, and Plymouth models. One reason that these big cars declined was the emphasis that automakers put on the fuel economy achieved by their small models in 1975. Though such an accomplishment had been considered an idle boast or simply a pipe dream by consumers in 1974, automakers actually produced several cars that achieved 40 mi. per gal. (mpg) in the fall of 1975, such as the Honda Civic (43 mpg on the highway), the Mazda 808 piston Mizer (42 mpg), the Datsun B-210 (41 mpg), and the Chevette (40 mpg).

The industry as a whole showed a 12.8% increase in fuel economy over 1974, when the industrywide fuel economy average was 13.9 mpg. In 1975 it rose to 15.6 mpg. The 1976 models averaged 17.6 mpg.

The most significant factor in boosting economy was the fact that there were no new emissions laws dictated to the automakers by the U.S. government, thereby allowing the manufacturers to design engines for optimum performance and economy. The emissions standards were to toughen up again in 1977, however, to 2 grams per mile of nitrogen oxide, 1.5 grams per mile of hydrocarbons, and 15 grams per mile of carbon monoxide.

Because of such factors as anticipated federal legislation on fuel economy levels and because of anxieties over another oil embargo or at least ever increasing gasoline prices, the automakers announced in 1975 that they would spend more than $7 billion by the end of the decade to resize their cars in order to cut weight and improve fuel economy. Actually, the automakers had been laying the groundwork for increasing fuel economy for some time through the ploy of dropping those cars with the poorest mileage so that the weighted average of the remaining models showed an improvement. Chrysler, for example, discontinued the Imperial luxury model in the fall of 1975.

In the fall of 1974 the domestic automakers offered consumers 325 models to choose from. In the fall of 1975 these were trimmed down to 295, the lowest number of offerings out of Detroit since 1962. This reduction not only was intended to help overall fuel economy ratings but also was aimed at easing the economic burden automakers experienced because of the recession and continued inflation during the year. By reducing the number of models and continuing to make them smaller, the industry hoped to save on the cost of materials.

Because so many changes were in store for the fall of 1976, when the resized 1977

WIDE WORLD

The American Motors Pacer was well received by U.S. buyers who appreciated the freshness of its styling.

models would appear, there were few changes introduced in 1975. The most dramatic new entry was the Chevette.

At Ford there were no new models in 1975. Instead, the company decided to put catalytic converters on its Pinto, Bobcat, and Mustang models to increase fuel economy. A year earlier Ford's fuel economy ratings were the worst in the industry, mainly because the company had decided to combat emissions without the converter. In the spring it adopted the converter and obtained 30 mpg readings from its small cars. Ford's competitor for the Chevette, announced late in 1975, was to be an import from West Germany.

Chrysler brought out the Plymouth Volaré and Dodge Aspen compacts, which originally were supposed to replace the Dodge Dart and Plymouth Valiant but instead were additions to the corporation's small car line. With small cars becoming more popular, the automakers wanted more rather than fewer small car offerings.

While U.S. manufacturers did not make much news with new offerings during 1975, automakers in other countries did. In France Renault started exporting the Renault 5 to the U.S., a mini in the 40 mpg category that already had been on sale in the home market. Renault also announced that it was taking aim at the U.S. market in earnest. In 1955 Renault had been the import sales leader in the U.S., but then lost out to Volkswagen. The French firm planned to expand its dealer network in the U.S., set up parts warehouses, and aim for sales of 100,000 units within five years, versus 5,000 units in 1975.

Mazda, the Japanese firm that used the rotary engine, introduced the Cosmo sport coupe in 1975. It was a dual rotor model rated at 18 mpg in the city and 29 mpg on the highway. The car listed for $5,900, highest priced offering ever from Mazda. Mazda also made news with the Mizer, a piston engine car that achieved 42 mpg in the Environmental Protection Agency's highway tests. Mazda, especially hard hit by the Arab oil embargo and one of the first cars labeled a gas guzzler for its 10 mpg rating on earlier models, worked diligently on economy in 1975 and began giving new emphasis to its piston engine models as well as the rotaries.

Datsun announced that the car known as the Cherry in Japan would soon be marketed in the U.S. as the F-10. It would be a front-wheel-drive model using a four-cylinder engine. At the Tokyo Auto Show, Nissan unveiled an experimental two-seater model with the engine mounted crossways amidships. The sporty model was 152 in. long on a 92-in. wheelbase and tipped the scales at a meagre 1,630 lb.

Toyota showed two hatchback versions of the Corolla. At Subaru the featured attraction was the four-wheel-drive Leone 1600 sedan with a sun roof, but no production date was set for it.

In Great Britain Jensen showed off a new coupe based on the Jensen Interceptor. It was powered by a 7.2-l. Chrysler V-8 engine. Ford unveiled its new subcompact Escort in West Germany. Volkswagen let it be known that its Polo, which is smaller than the Golf (called the Rabbit in the U.S.), would probably never make it into the U.S. since the addition of U.S. emission and safety equipment would rob it of fuel economy and cause its U.S. price to equal or exceed that of the Rabbit.

Auto production in many countries was affected adversely by the recession. In West Germany, for example, there were several layoffs that cut production dramatically. As a result, in October Volkswagen lost its title as the leading import in the U.S. to the Japanese Toyota. Volkswagen was also hurt by the time-consuming shutdown of assembly lines for conversion to the new Dasher, Scirocco, and Rabbit models. As a result, West Germany, which had been the world's leading exporter of vehicles, looked as though it might fall to third place behind Japan and France in 1975.

In the U.K. serious labour problems and capital shortages plagued the auto industry. Car prices rose about 60% over the year. British Leyland and Vauxhall joined Chrysler in losing money, and the former was taken over by the government in April. Chrysler's British subsidiary, after unsuccessfully seeking a £35 million loan and at the same time offering worker profit-sharing and participation, threatened a complete shutdown of its plants. Faced with the politically disastrous prospect of a loss of more than 25,000 jobs, the British government in December announced a £162 million deal to bail Chrysler out. Inflation affected the market so much that many motorists not only looked for cheaper transportation but also questioned ownership of a car at all.

As for new cars in Britain, Chrysler introduced the Simca 1307/1308 and called it the Alpine. Vauxhall brought out the Cavalier, a version of the Opel Manta made in Belgium from West German components.

Enthusiasm for the rotary engine continued to decline except, of course, at Mazda. Meanwhile, the diesel engine enjoyed new popularity. Mercedes-Benz said that 40% of its total sales in 1975 were diesel cars, up from 15% in 1973. Noting the popularity of the high-economy diesel engine and the low cost of diesel fuel, Volkswagen began working on a four-cylinder diesel engine for possible inclusion in the Rabbit within two years. General Motors also was working on a V-8 diesel for Oldsmobile. Both Volkswagen and General Motors admitted that development was hindered by nitrogen oxide emissions.

(JAMES L. MATEJA)

[732.B.2]

BUILDING AND CONSTRUCTION

At midyear 1975 the total expenditures for new construction in the United States were at an annual rate of $122 billion; expectations were that total outlays for the year would be close to the midyear rate. This meant that the dollar outlays would be above the construction expenditures in 1971 and approximately equal to 1972 but below those in 1973 and 1974, when they had exceeded $135 billion annually.

The downturn in construction activity that had started in 1974 continued into 1975. As in 1974, however, public construction continued at a high level. These expenditures, at the seasonally adjusted annual rate, were $38.7 billion during the first seven months of 1975, compared with $38.4 billion for the year 1974. Expenditures for private construction in 1975 were at a much lower level than in 1974, and it did not appear that recovery in the industry would get under way during the last half of 1975. On the basis of the seasonally adjusted annual rate, private construction expenditures were $85.7 billion in the first seven months of 1975, compared with $97.1 billion in 1974. Thus it appeared that private construction expenditures would be the lowest since 1971.

The doldrums in residential construction in the U.S., which started in 1973, continued into 1975. In constant (1967) dollars the value of new housing units had been $32.9 billion in 1973, $23.2 billion in 1974, and $16.2 billion (seasonally adjusted annual rate) during the first seven months of 1975. In the third quarter of 1975 housing starts had slowed and were at an annual adjusted rate of 1,260,000 units.

In 1975 builders continued to be confronted with uncertain costs due to the inflationary movements in prices. The composite cost index of the U.S. Department of Commerce reached 189.2 (1967 = 100) in May 1975. The price index for new single-family houses continued to move up also and in the first quarter of 1975 was 170.1 (1967 = 100), compared with 152 in the first quarter of 1974. The indexes reflected increases in the prices of both materials, especially steel products, and labour.

In Canada demand for housing remained weak in 1975. During the first quarter of the year investment in dwellings fell by 10%. With a slight easing in financial conditions, however, there were expectations of some recovery. Substantial change was not expected because the government was following a somewhat neutral budget policy for fear of stimulating inflation.

In Western Europe the conditions of inflation and depression had a continuing adverse effect on building and construction. In Great Britain at midyear there were some signs of recovery in the housing sector. During the first half of 1975 housing starts had been up to 50% higher than in 1974 in both the public and private sectors. The outlook in the nonhousing sector was bleak, however, and it was anticipated that unemployment in the industry would increase.

In West Germany in 1975 the situation in

the building industry was described as desperate. There was little to indicate improvement within the year because of the anticipated slow recovery of the overall economy. The severe recession in Italy continued, with a reduction in the volume of fixed gross investments below the 1974 level. It was expected that the depressed conditions would continue into 1976. In Switzerland the situation was similar. The volume of building, which had been falling since 1973, was expected to experience even greater declines, with a drop in 1975 of 51% in dwelling construction. In Belgium the economic conditions were a bit more encouraging, but a decline in residential building in 1975 appeared certain. In The Netherlands the situation was much the same.

There was little recovery in business confidence during the year in Australia. Overall production and building starts were declining. Similar conditions prevailed in New Zealand.

In Japan the government's strong anti-inflation measures and the general economic conditions gave the country its first decline in output since its involvement in World War II. At midyear the government took action to increase public financing for private housing.

(CARTER C. OSTERBIND)

[733.A]

CHEMICALS

Chemical industries in the industrialized countries of the world established new highs in production and sales during 1974. But a sluggishness that made its first appearance early in the fourth quarter of the year turned out to be an indicator of a relatively sharp drop in chemical activity that continued well into 1975. By the second quarter of 1975, however, the U.S. chemical industry showed signs of reviving, and by the end of the third quarter it appeared to be back on its growth track. Chemical industries in other countries, which in the past had followed the lead of the U.S., were also expected to recover.

In the U.S., the Federal Reserve Board's index of chemical production climbed from 150.2 (1967 = 100) in 1973 to 154.3 in 1974. It reached its high point in September 1974, when it hit 158.3 (seasonally adjusted), and then dropped each month to 132.8 in April 1975. But in May it began to move up and by July reached 138.5.

Chemical prices, which had been depressed for an extended period because of overcapacity, soared in 1974 due to a combination of general inflation and a shortage during most of the year of a wide variety of chemical products. The U.S. Department of Labor's index of wholesale prices for chemicals and allied products rose 33.5%, from 110 (1967 = 100) in 1973 to 146.8 in 1974. Despite depressed demand for chemicals, the price index continued to inch up each month during the first four months of 1975, reaching a high point of 182.4 in April. In May it started to decline somewhat and by July was down to 181.4.

The modest production increase and significant boost in prices resulted in a chemical sales increase of 21.4% in 1974. The U.S. Department of Commerce reported that shipments of chemicals and allied products rose from $67,034,000,000 in 1973 to $81,377,000,000 in 1974. The increase was registered in spite of fourth-quarter shipments that were 5% lower than those of the third quarter. But shipments in the first half of 1975, at $41,861,00,000, were 4.4% higher than in the same period of 1974.

Chemicals again made an important contribution to U.S. trade. In 1974 net chemical exports were worth $4,801,500,000. This was 46.1% higher than the 1973 net export figure of $3,286,400,000. For the first half of 1975 the favourable chemical trade balance amounted to $2,465,300,000, which was 4.1% lower than the $2,569,900,000 recorded for the first half of 1974.

West Germany's chemical industry posted sales of $33.1 billion in 1974, according to the German Chemical Industry Association (GCIA). Though that represented a 29.1% increase over 1973's sales figures, inflation was responsible for most of the growth. Physical volume increased approximately 3%, making 1974 the slowest growth year from that standpoint since 1952. The GCIA reported that chemical sales in the first quarter of 1975 were off 9.4% in value and 15.2% in volume. For the first six months, it reported, sales were $14.8 billion, 12.6% lower in value than they had been in the first half of 1974; exports were $5.8 billion, off 23%; and profits were down 60%.

Japanese chemical companies rang up record sales in 1974, increasing sales figures 22.5% to an estimated $29.1 billion. Higher prices accounted for almost all of the rise, however; real growth was close to zero. As 1974 ended, the Japanese chemical industry was facing 1975 with considerable optimism. It was looking for a 10% increase in sales, at least a portion of which would be generated by real growth. In Japan as elsewhere, however, the slump in demand for chemicals was causing companies to reexam-

This 240-ton chemical reactor of Soviet-East German design was built at the Germania Chemical plant, Karl-Marx-Stadt, East Germany.

CAMERA PRESS/PHOTO TRENDS

ine their expansion projects. The fibre industry was especially hard hit, but fertilizer makers seemed to be weathering the recession in good shape. One reason was a continued strong demand for fertilizer in Asia, with China alone expected to import one billion tons of urea from Japan in 1975.

The economic storms that buffeted the U.K. had a sharp impact on chemical activity during the last two months of 1974. Nevertheless, chemical companies managed to show a 43% increase in sales for the full year to $18.4 billion, and exports increased 68% to $4.9 billion. The bright spot for chemical makers in the U.K. was the petroleum supply from the North Sea. During the first half of 1975, approximately 35,000 bbl. of oil per day started flowing in from the Argyll field, 200 mi. E of Edinburgh.

By late 1975 the chemical industries of the world seemed to have left their major economic ills behind them. They did, however, face a number of other problems. The industry as a whole had enormous requirements for energy, in the form of electricity and steam to run the factories, and hydrocarbon raw materials for petrochemical production. Companies were working on methods to conserve energy and to utilize different raw materials. Oil-rich nations were making ambitious plans to manufacture petrochemicals. Because these countries lacked managerial and technical skills, domestic markets, and the infrastructure required to support complex industrial processing, however, they seemed likely to require considerable time before those plans could be brought to fruition.

Problems on the toxicity of certain chemicals or their effect on the environment continued worrisome. The link between inhalation of vinyl chloride monomer (VCM) and angiosarcoma, a rare liver cancer, led to stringent new procedures in factories making VCM and polyvinyl chloride (PVC), its most important product. In addition, there was concern that direct ingestion of VCM could cause cancer. The Cancer Research Institute (Bologna, Italy) was studying the problem. The U.S. Food and Drug Administration, worried about the danger of VCM migrating into food, proposed a ban on rigid and semirigid PVC packaging that would come into contact with food. Industry agreed with the goals of the proposal but contended that it was developing new PVC products that contained so little VCM that there could be no "reasonable expectation" of VCM migration.

(DONALD P. BURKE)

[732.D.1]

CLOTHING

Buying practices of the apparel industry took an important new direction during 1975 as trade show attendance began to rival visits to individual showrooms as a way of shopping the fabric market. The second edition of the American Fashion Textiles Exposition, Texpo '75 for short, staged in New York City, gave apparel manufacturers from the U.S. and other countries an opportunity to view and select from the widest range of U.S. fashion fabrics ever assembled at one time under one roof.

The U.S. Department of Commerce, on the basis of a detailed survey of exhibitors, credited Texpo '75 with the sale of nearly $10.7 million in U.S. fabrics to foreign apparel firms alone. And foreign buyers accounted for only about 14% of total attendance, approximating 12,000, at the three-day event.

The year 1975 would also be remembered as that in which clothing manufacturers began shifting into high gear in producing and promoting flame-resistant (FR) garments,

COURTESY, GENERAL ELECTRIC RESEARCH & DEVELOPMENT CENTER

A water-cooled gas turbine under development by General Electric Co. generates twice the power of those currently in use. It operates at a temperature of 2,800° F.

particularly for children. A U.S. federal regulation covering infants' and other small-size sleepwear, in effect since 1973, was joined by a slightly less stringent standard applicable to children's sleepwear sizes 7 to 14. Several major manufacturers announced plans to produce a variety of FR children's clothing, including boys' shirts and pants and girls' dresses, even though the government had yet to issue standards for such items. Also, several leading mail-order houses said that an assortment of FR apparel for adults would be included in their fall catalogs, again prior to any federal standards.

On the economic front, the U.S. apparel industry was hard hit by the unfavourable business climate that existed during the first six months of 1975. And because the U.S. is a major importer of apparel, the nation's recession was also felt by most European and Far Eastern countries that supply the American market.

In most apparel categories, output during the first half of 1975 in the U.S. was down an estimated 10 to 12% from year-earlier levels, while total industry employment slumped about 15%. The situation was aggravated by unusually conservative new-order policies on the part of apparel retailers. But as tax rebates found their way into the spending stream and other economic indicators turned upward, the U.S. apparel industry began experiencing a sharp recovery early in the second half of 1975. Retailers, with only a limited supply of goods on hand, sought frantically to replenish their depleted inventories, and many manufacturers in both the U.S. and other nations found it difficult to meet the sudden upsurge in demand. (*See* FASHION AND DRESS.)

(JOHN DAVID DRUCKENBROD)

[732.B.3]

ELECTRICAL

The economic recession had less effect on the electrical industry in 1975 than had been expected. Activity in building plants to generate electricity remained high, largely on orders received two or three years earlier. A less marked but similar time lag in the production of industrial equipment, plus rising sales in the less developed countries, helped maintain the industry's performance. Profits, however, were down, because of severe inflation and unpredictable changes in monetary exchange and interest rates. Typical of the performances of many large companies was the Swedish Allmänna Svenska Elektriska Aktiebolaget (ASEA), which showed a 30% increase in turnover but a rise in profits of only 18%.

The electrical industry could withstand temporary changes in the economic climate because of the long construction times of the capital projects in which it was involved. Cancellations of many new power station projects in 1974, with little prospect of short-term reinstatement, would not begin to affect the industry until 1976. Management policies in most companies began to shift the emphasis from growth to profitability. Reductions in manufacturing capacity and manpower were consolidated in 1975 as managements became determined never again to expand their plant capacities in order to meet peak sales demands. This would mean some loss of business in peak years, but industry leaders believed that it was better to have a small overhead structure that would maintain profits in lean years and to subcontract excess work in good years.

In the U.S., Westinghouse Electric Corp. decided to give high priority to shortening the cycle from raw material to finished product. This required a major effort to standardize production components and, thereby, reduce the product range. The luxury of tailor-made production equipment could no longer be afforded and, although some orders would be lost as a result, Westinghouse was confident that others would be gained by selling the advantages of interchangeability.

With near-zero, and in some cases negative, growth in the consumption of electricity in the industrialized countries, the EEC issued a Working Paper in September 1975 which advised coordination of investment in facilities to generate electricity and in manufacturing capacity. In the U.K., the

Central Electricity Generating Board (CEGB) announced the closing of 47 power stations and received approval for a very small new construction program. In the U.S., General Atomic Co. (GA) negotiated a revision of its one remaining commercial order for a high-temperature-reactor nuclear power station and sought financial aid from the government. With other companies, GA faced difficulties posed by environmental regulations in the U.S., order cancellations, and delays to existing contracts.

In August 1975 the Swiss Brown Boveri Group publicly sought links with British consulting engineers. Following the oil crisis, consulting engineers had become much more active in Middle East markets and were even finding it difficult to recruit sufficient experienced installation staff. At the same time, "oil" money was finding its way back into the industry. In April, Babcock & Wilcox Ltd. sold its 25% share in Deutsche Babcock & Wilcox AG to the government of Iran for about DM. 178.5 million.

The economic changes caused by the energy crisis led to a move to audit resources in terms of "potential energy." Much potential energy, it was argued, was released recklessly at temperatures well above the utilization requirements, and the development of heat pumps to recover such waste heat simply, easily, and cheaply should be encouraged. The heat pump is a reversed refrigerator, with the cold coil placed in an exhaust air or water stream and the hot coil placed in the inlet duct of a warm air heating system. No excess heating would be necessary, and the output of a heat pump, in terms of useful heat, was found to be equivalent to two or three times that produced by an electric resistance heater consuming the same quantity of electricity.

(T. C. J. COGLE)

[732.C.6; 10/37.B.5.d]

FURNITURE

The energy shortage, coupled with the business recession, had a marked effect on the world's furniture industry in 1975. Man-made materials, most of them derived from petrochemicals, increased sharply in price while their availability diminished. This caused severe problems, particularly in Europe where plastic materials are widely used in furniture.

In the U.S. the precipitous drop in the rate of housing starts depressed furniture sales. The decline in residential building cut back the demand for hardwoods for flooring and paneling, and this caused manufacturers of bedroom and dining room furniture to switch from solid plastic components to natural hardwoods. Mediterranean, which required heavy use of plastic moldings in moderately priced suites, faded in popularity after five years as a leading bedroom and dining room style. The leading wood furniture style in 1975 was the "Country Look," which featured natural wood tones and simple lines. Man-made upholstery materials continued to be used in ever increasing volume, however.

Retail furniture sales in the U.S. totaled slightly under $11 billion in 1975, virtually unchanged from 1974. Retailer inventories of furniture were at a record high at the beginning of the year, and there was a sharp reduction in orders placed with furniture manufacturers. As a result, manufacturers' sales of bedroom and dining room furniture were down 13% and upholstered furniture sales fell 10%. Summer and casual furniture, the healthiest segment, equaled the 1974 sales record. At the low point of the year manufacturers' shipments of household furniture were off as much as 20% compared with 1974, but business improved in the second half and shipments rose to within 10% of the previous year's level. The European furniture industry also suffered a severe economic recession, and Great Britain, Canada, Italy, Romania, and the Scandinavian countries stepped up their efforts to export furniture, particularly to the U.S. market.

The fastest growing trend in the U.S. was the increase in sales of modular wooden wall units, constructed to serve as bookcases, desks, hi-fi cabinets, and for general storage. Another growing trend was the increased popularity of K-D (knockdown) furniture, shipped unassembled and set up in the home. Summer and casual furniture, once used exclusively outdoors, had become popular for interior furnishing.

The U.S. industry was increasingly occupied with government regulations. The Consumer Product Safety Commission prepared a draft standard for cigarette burn-proof upholstered furniture. A study by the Battelle Memorial Institute estimated that the cost of implementing the draft standard might raise the price of upholstered furniture as much as 30%.

(ROBERT A. SPELMAN)

[732.B.4]

FURS

The international fur industry prospered in 1975, despite adverse economic pressures. Fashion was probably the most significant factor. Not only did leading designers endorse furs or include them in their collections but the increased importance of dresses—as opposed to pants—and the return to an elegant classic look added impetus to the demand. Another positive factor was economic. The traditional customer for furs was less affected by the recession than the general population.

Vertically banded furs were an important design element of the 1975 fashions.

ROBERT COHEN—AGIP/PICTORIAL PARADE

The U.S. fur industry experienced an unprecedented fourth consecutive successful year. The outlook was even better than in the previous three because, to some extent, the manufacturing segment was better prepared. However, a shortage of skilled labour prevented manufacturers from taking full advantage of the retail demand. Too many poor seasons in the 1960s had discouraged the entry of new labour, and itinerant workers from such countries as Greece were attracted by greater wage potentials in West Germany, Switzerland, and Italy.

Figures for 1975 were incomplete at the end of the year, but estimates were that retail fur sales in the U.S. exceeded $500 million, 15 to 20% above 1974 and the largest volume in more than 30 years. Significantly, this not only represented an increase in unit sales but it did not include the inexpensive, so-called fun furs from foreign sources, which accounted for at least $50 million more at retail.

Prices were higher in the primary skin markets, reflecting increased costs of feed, labour, and overhead on ranches as well as for trappers and collectors. Since the demand was there, however, there was little resistance. Generally, prices for pelts rose 10 to 20% internationally. Long-haired furs like fox and lynx were especially strong, and mink, sable, karakul, and fur seal also did well. Demand for seal had been declining, largely because of the efforts of wildlife protectionist groups, but the downtrend appeared to have been reversed in 1975.

Mink production increased about 3% in the 1974 crop year (sold in 1975), to about 18.3 million pelts. This total was exclusive of the U.S.S.R., which did not supply production figures. (*See* FASHION AND DRESS.)

(SANDY PARKER)

[724.C.8.e; 732.C.4]

GEMSTONES

The gemstone and jewelry industry had an excellent year in 1975. Diamonds again were dominant, with imports to the United States estimated at three to four times the value of all other gemstones. The estimated 1.5 million engagement rings sold during the year in the U.S., the increased use of lasers to remove impurities from the stones, the introduction of new cuts such as the star cut, uneasiness about inflation, and aggressive sales practices all helped.

It was reported that the third largest diamond ever found, the 968.9-carat Star of Sierra Leone, discovered Feb. 14, 1972, was cut into 11 fine stones, the largest weighing 143.2 carats. A large 223.6-carat yellow diamond octahedron, found at the Kimberley Mine in South Africa in October 1973, was also cut. It yielded, among others, the largest modern cut round brilliant known, at 86 carats. The 601-carat diamond found in 1967 in Lesotho and later cut stimulated prospecting in that area. Another famous gem, the notorious Hope Diamond, was the subject of a television program in March that explored the history of the legend-encrusted gem. Later in the year the Hope Diamond was removed from its setting and reweighed. The gem was found to weigh 45.5 carats instead of 44.5 carats, as had been previously believed.

The year brought the first general distribution of gadolinium gallium garnet (GGG), a new synthetic substitute for diamond. Its specific gravity is about twice that of diamond so that a two-carat GGG is the size of a one-carat diamond.

The most important trend for the year in gemstones was the explosive expansion of public interest in coloured and orna-

LEE BOLTIN

The Hope Diamond, object of study by authorities at the Smithsonian Institution during the year, was removed from its setting and reweighed. Its correct weight is 45.5 carats.

mental stones. This happened in spite of rising prices caused by inflation, shortage of supply, and disruption of customary sources due to political unrest and economic uneasiness. Thailand, for example, normally supplies more than half the new rubies and sapphires, but unrest and inflation there pushed prices up dramatically at the source. To compensate for decreased supplies, new sources were being developed. These included a major discovery of quality green jadeite-type jade from the Soviet Union, small quantities of natural pearls from China, fine new rubies from Afghanistan, increased supplies of bright blue topaz from Brazil, a large supply of excellent tourmaline from Maine, and a source of fine purplish amethyst in Colombia.

New kinds of gems also appeared during the year. The best of these was a vanadium-bearing grossular garnet (Tsavorite) from near the Tsavo National Park in Kenya. Having several of the best gem characteristics of emerald, it gained instant popularity. Tanzanite, a sapphire-like variety of zoisite from Tanzania, continued in high demand. A quantity of intense lavender and purple jade reached the market. Much of it was probably colour-treated but, if so, this was undetectable. "Gold coral," really an alga from Hawaii; an alexandrite-like garnet from Japan; a transparent blue sodalite from Burma; irradiated but permanently blue topaz from Brazil; and a jumble of commoner gemstones such as aventurine, rhodonite, rose quartz, rutilated quartz, lapis lazuli, malachite, coral, onyx, tigereye, chrysoprase, and jasper all helped stimulate the boom in coloured-gem materials. The pearl industry, plagued by water pollution and declining sales, had applied strict quality controls in 1971. Results were visible in 1975 with fewer but better quality pearls reaching the market.

(PAUL ERNEST DESAUTELS)

[724.C.4]

GLASS

Economic recession caused problems in 1975. Drastic reductions in the demand for glass products were reported, with concomitant closing down of plant, laying off of workers, and cutting back in investment. The flat-glass sector was the first to feel the pinch as demand for buildings and automobiles declined. The container industry was next and, later, as the purchasing power of the consumer began to fall, domestic products such as television tubes and table glass were affected.

In common with other industries in which energy is an important factor in the manufacturing process, the glass industry had been facing massive increases in production costs. Natural gas, although an acceptable alternative to oil, was not always obtainable, and when contracts came up for renewal, users were subject to substantially higher charges. Electricity, except where hydroelectric power was available, was too expensive an alternative.

Technical development continued despite the recession. In the U.K. Pilkington Brothers Ltd. developed an alkali-resistant glass fibre as a reinforcement for portland cement. Considerable interest was shown in the new process, both for existing uses of concrete and as a substitute for such materials as timber, cast iron, and sheet steel. In its annual report, Pilkington stated that its float-glass process was continuing to make significant progress toward universal acceptance as the preferred method of manufacturing flat glass. Fifty-five float-glass plants were currently in operation and nine more were under construction.

The French company Saint-Gobain-Pont-à-Mousson, with a view to strengthening its position in the Japanese markets, planned to build a factory for the manufacture of glass fibre for insulation purposes together with the Nippon Cement Co. Looking to the west, Saint-Gobain formed a U.K. marketing company, Vetrotex, to promote and distribute a full line of glass-fibre reinforcements and yarns. The leading sheet-glass company, Asahi of Japan, concentrated on expansion in Europe and the Middle East. Glaverbel-Mécaniver SA of Belgium, part of the French industrial group Boussois-Souchon-Neuvesel, agreed to sell its Canadian glass-distribution operations to Pilkington Brothers Canada.

Within the EEC, directive legislation relating to the capacities of containers for liquids was approved for intra-EEC trade. Several major glass-container manufacturers in West Germany, Belgium, France, Italy, and The Netherlands were ordered to nullify agreements on prices, discounts, and trading conditions. The trend toward use of the metric system continued. The U.K. glass industry was almost completely in line with its EEC colleagues, and in the U.S. customers of the container industry were advised of the advantages of the change.

Finally, concertgoers who knew the frustration of having a portion of the orchestra, or even the conductor, cut off from view by the open top of a grand piano were delighted to learn that the U.S. company Libby-Owens-Ford had developed a clear glass lid that, it was claimed, did not affect the tone.

(CYRIL WEEDEN)

[724.C.5.a; 733.A.4.a.vii]

INSURANCE

Private insurance sales in 1975, measured by annual world premium volume, exceeded $200 billion for the first time. These expenditures included almost 7% of gross national product in the U.S.; between 4–6% in such nations as the U.K., Australia, New Zealand, Canada, Switzerland, West Germany, and Japan; and generally under 2% in the less developed countries.

Life Insurance. A landmark of $2 trillion of life insurance in force was reached by midyear 1975 in the U.S. Amounts purchased for the first six months increased more than 7%, to $133 billion, from the previous year. Assets grew by $20 billion, to $278 billion. Recession and inflationary pressures, however, increased policy loans to $24 billion, or 8.5% of assets.

Major sales efforts were directed toward the pension area, as thousands of private pension plans were undergoing review and revision to meet new actuarial and fiduciary requirements of the Employee Retirement Income Security Act. This pension reform act, which required an employee's benefits to be fully vested within 15 years, also created new and increased opportunities for life insurance and annuity sales to self-employed persons and to workers without other pension plans, in individual retirement accounts (IRAs).

In the U.K. annual income for life insurers had risen 16% by early 1975. Declines in stock and bond values, however, lowered total assets by approximately 3%, to £19,600 million.

Property and Liability Insurance. Serious underwriting losses in the property and liability field caused rising concern in the U.S. During the first six months of 1975 losses (premiums earned, less claims paid and reserves) were in excess of $2 billion; this exceeded the losses for the whole previous year, which had been the worst in history. Gains on investments were expected to remain high, but not high enough to offset underwriting losses.

In spite of rate increases by most major insurers of 5–15% in both automobile and homeowners' insurance, steeper rises appeared likely. Although traffic deaths in the U.S. had been reduced by the 55 mph speed limit, this gain was small compared with the generally escalating costs of medical treatment and car repairs. Automobile no-fault insurance legislation appeared deadlocked at the federal level, and only one state, North Dakota, had added a new no-fault plan by late 1975.

Disasters in 1975 were highlighted by Hurricane Eloise in the U.S., which caused $100 million of insured damages including one-half of that written in the new national flood insurance program. In Australia a Dec. 25, 1974, hurricane caused $400 million in damages in Darwin.

Medical malpractice insurance problems were the most severe of the generally rising liability claims in all areas. Some insurers withdrew from the medical liability market. Many states attempted to solve the problem by such means as special "joint underwriting associations" of insurers, pre-trial panels, restricted fees for lawyers, and medical peer review of malpractice claims.

Guaranty funds for insurance companies were feeling the strain in 1975, as U.S. funds in various states coped with 26 insurer failures in the first nine months. In the U.K. a guaranty fund was established to protect both life and nonlife policyholders against insurance company insolvencies.

(DAVID L. BICKELHAUPT)

[534.J]

IRON AND STEEL

Even in the context of an industry accustomed over decades to extreme fluctuations of fortune, 1975 could be characterized as a catastrophic year for steel. No other post-World War II year approached it in severity. Over the preceding 20 years world steel output had fallen only in 1958 and in 1971 and those experiences in no way could be compared with the likely drop in 1975 to some 660 million metric tons, a decline of 7% from 1974.

By late 1974 it was already clear that the 1973–74 steel boom was over. During the last weeks of 1974 through 1975 demand fell with such severity that any tension remaining in the market gave place to slackness and then to burgeoning surplus. Prices on the world market collapsed; the markets of the major producing nations came under severe pressure from imports; and company finances suffered, in some cases to an acute degree.

THE NEW YORK TIMES

Junked automobiles are converted to scrap metal. The steel industry consumes 70% of all recycled metal in the U.S.

The misfortunes of the steel industry were one inevitable aspect of the worldwide depression. Real steel consumption fell during 1975 by amounts ranging up to 15% in the worst affected areas. Heavy de-stocking by consumers and merchants, characterizing the low points of the regular steel cycle, resulted in declines of up to 25% in apparent steel consumption. The exceptionally sharp decline in demand resulted in reductions in crude steel output that, in certain countries, approached 30% as compared with the production registered in 1974, and virtually no established Western producer of steel escaped the debacle unscathed.

Underutilization of production capacity on such a scale had serious financial implications for the heavily capital-intensive iron and steel industry. For steel the problem was greatly exacerbated by sharp falls in prices, provoked by intense competition on an international basis. The price realized by certain finished products on the international market was down by 40% from the peak 1974 levels, and in some cases major price declines spread extensively into the

Table VII. World Production of Crude Steel
In 000 metric tons

Country	1970	1971	1972	1973	1974	1975 Year to date	1975 No. of months	Percent change 1975/74
World	595,600	582,600	630,200	697,200	710,100	...	...	...
U.S.	119,140	109,055	120,750	136,460	132,020	81,660	9	−18.4
U.S.S.R.	115,890	120,640	125,590	131,480	136,300	46,300	4	+ 3.8
Japan	93,320	88,560	96,900	119,320	117,140	78,190	9	−11.6
Germany, West	45,040	40,310	43,700	49,520	53,230	31,200	9	−22.0
U.K.	27,850	24,240	25,390	26,720	22,500	15,010	9	−10.1
France	23,770	22,840	24,050	25,270	27,000	16,220	9	−18.6
China*	18,000	21,000	23,000	25,000	27,000	...	...	...
Italy	17,280	17,450	19,810	21,000	23,860	16,550	9	− 6.7
Belgium	12,610	12,440	14,530	15,520	16,230	8,810	9	−29.1
Poland	11,750	12,690	13,420	14,060	14,800	7,360	6	+ 2.0
Czechoslovakia	11,480	12,070	12,730	13,160	13,650	7,220	6	+ 5.7
Canada	11,200	11,040	11,860	13,390	13,590	9,840	9	− 2.2
Spain	7,390	8,020	9,530	10,800	11,500	8,280	9	− 2.1
Australia	6,840	6,750	6,750	7,700	7,810	5,950	9	+ 6.7
Romania	6,520	6,800	7,400	8,160	8,900	2,310	3	+ 7.8
India	6,280	6,100	6,860	6,890	6,970	5,910	9	+15.1
Sweden	5,500	5,270	5,260	5,660	5,990	4,220	9	− 3.9
Luxembourg	5,460	5,240	5,460	5,920	6,450	3,510	9	−27.6
Germany, East	5,420	5,740	6,060	5,850	6,170	3,210	6	+ 6.3
Brazil	5,390	6,000	6,520	7,150	7,570	6,190	9	+ 9.1
Netherlands, The	5,040	5,080	5,580	5,620	5,830	3,670	9	−14.8
South Africa	4,760	4,880	5,340	5,720	5,840	5,160	9	+19.6
Austria	4,080	3,960	4,070	4,240	4,700	3,090	9	−12.4
Mexico	3,880	3,820	4,430	4,760	5,130	3,920	9	+ 4.0
Hungary	3,110	3,110	3,270	3,330	3,450	1,820	6	+ 6.5
Yugoslavia	2,230	2,450	2,590	2,680	2,800	1,430	6	+ 1.1
Argentina	1,820	1,910	2,150	2,200	2,370	1,640	9	− 5.6
Bulgaria	1,800	1,950	2,120	2,250	2,300	920	5	− 2.4

*Estimated.
Source: International Iron and Steel Institute; British Steel Corporation.

Table VIII. World Production of Pig Iron and Blast Furnace Ferroalloys
In 000 metric tons

Country	1970	1971	1972	1973	1974
World	425,930	422,550	446,940	495,430	508,593
U.S.S.R.	85,930	89,250	92,300	94,900	99,600
U.S.	83,300	74,110	81,110	91,610	87,010
Japan*	68,050	72,740	74,060	90,000	90,440
Germany, West	33,630	29,990	32,000	36,830	40,220
France	19,220	18,340	19,000	20,290	22,520
United Kingdom	17,670	15,420	15,320	16,850	13,900
China†	16,500	19,000	21,000	23,000	26,000
Belgium	10,960	10,530	11,900	12,660	13,020
Italy	8,350	8,550	9,440	10,030	11,690
Canada*	8,220	7,830	8,490	9,540	9,420
Czechoslovakia	7,550	7,960	8,360	8,530	9,030
India	6,990	6,940	7,020	7,340	7,260
Poland	6,980	7,190	7,420	8,140	8,210
Australia*	5,960	6,240	6,000	7,660	7.250
Luxembourg	4,810	4,580	4,670	5,130	5,470
South Africa	3,950	4,040	4,430	4,330	4,620
Romania	4,210	4,380	4,890	5,710	6,050
Brazil*	4,200	4,690	5,290	5,470	5,980
Spain*	4,160	4,850	5,930	6,290	6,890
Netherlands, The	3,590	3,760	4,290	4,710	4,800
Austria*	2,960	2,850	2,850	3,000	3,440
Sweden	2,610	2,580	2,360	2,570	2,980
Germany, East	1,990	2,030	2,150	2,200	2,280
Hungary	1,830	1,980	2,060	2,110	2,300
Mexico*	1,650	1,680	1,890	2,800	3,210
Yugoslavia*	1,280	1,510	1,820	1,960	2,130
Bulgaria	1,200	1,340	1,510	1,610	1,490

*Pig iron only.
†Estimated.
Source: British Steel Corporation.

markets of the major producers themselves. Against this, the cost of raw materials, except scrap, remained firm or rose, and wage levels generally continued to rise with living costs. This cost/price squeeze rendered the financial position of some major companies critical.

The steel recession was general throughout the Western world, but its timing and extent varied. In the U.S., crude steel production seemed unlikely to exceed 105 million tons in 1975, against 130 million in 1974. Producers pursued their traditional policy of resistance to price cutting in recession, but imports took a larger share of the reduced demand. The consumer goods sector had led the decline in the U.S. economy in 1974, and a steep fall occurred in the first half of 1975 as demand weakness spread to the construction and investment sectors. By midyear, however, there were clear signs of recovery in the U.S. economy, spurred by some revival in consumer spending. Observers hoped that this might be reflected in an improvement in the steel industry's fortunes in 1976, probably ahead of the experience of most other producing regions. Although the steel companies' ability to invest was affected by reduced earnings in 1975, it proved possible to continue with expansion plans. Investment expenditure was likely to show gains of up to 50% in 1975.

The effects of the energy crisis and of government counterinflation policies made 1974 a difficult year for the Japanese steel industry, and in 1975 there was another much larger fall in crude steel output, from 117 million tons to about 103 million tons. Steel consumption in Japan was expected to be down by about 11%, and the industry's exports fell. But investment schemes launched before the full effect of the recession had been felt were continued, and the industry's spending was likely to rise by some 40% in 1975.

The steel industries of the EEC suffered severely from the recession in terms of output, realized prices, and profitability. The timing and extent of the impact varied somewhat as between the member countries, but steel consumption in the Community as a whole was likely to be down by 17% in 1975 and production by about 18%. Most severely affected were the export-oriented industries of Belgium and Luxembourg.

In contrast with the situation in the West, the steel industries of the Eastern European countries continued to develop broadly in accordance with current national plans during 1975. The iron and steel industry of the U.S.S.R. appeared certain to produce more than 140 million tons during the year, and further expansion was projected in the context of the 1976–80 five-year plan.

Iron and steel production in the less developed countries was growing, especially in Brazil, Mexico, and India. Many less developed countries, as well as the smaller traditional producers, had ambitious expansion plans.

(TREVOR J. MACDONALD)

[724.C.3.g; 732.C.2]

MACHINERY AND MACHINE TOOLS

Prospects at the end of 1974 had given machine tool builders hope that 1975 would be a good year, but the upward trend did not develop. Orders for cutting and forming tools in the U.S. in the first three months were less than one-third of those in the comparable period of 1974. Part of the sluggish market was due to waiting on the part of buyers for the increase in the investment tax credit from 7 to 10%, which was signed into law on March 29 by U.S. Pres. Gerald Ford. Also, because consumer demand remained low in the automobile and appliance markets, these large users of machine tools were not making any sizable orders for new equipment. By the fourth quarter of 1975 shipments had exceeded orders in every month since August 1974. This reduction in backlogs caused some companies to cut production and lay off workers.

Two significant problems faced the U.S. machine tool industry. The falling off of sales resulted in a decline in research and development funding. Observers feared that unless this trend was reversed, the industry would lack new technologies needed to maintain the U.S. position in the world marketplace. Another serious problem was the maintenance of a skilled work force given the uncertain pattern of employment in the industry. The average age of the skilled worker was rising, and because of the fluctuation of the employment pattern fewer young people were attracted to the industry.

West German machine tool builders were experiencing similar problems in sales of their equipment, with the world recession accelerating the export trade decline. They were also faced with an uncertain domestic market.

West Germany was host to a tool exhibit by China June 13–25 in Cologne. The show indicated that China's 30-year-old machine tool industry had made significant gains. Of the 16 machines on display, 6 of the units featured numerical control. Most of the machines were lathes.

A large international machine tool show was staged at Exhibition Park at Porte de Versailles, on the southern edge of Paris, June 17–26. Approximately 4,000 machine tools were on display, representing 26 countries. Technological advances in cutting tool developments were the most impressive features of the machines on display. Ceramic cutters were used by many of the exhibitors. The show was viewed by 76,000 French and 37,000 foreign visitors, but international economic conditions limited buying.

During 1975 demand softened for farm machinery, even though the dollar sales remained very high. Increases in their costs indicated that companies needed to have about 30% more in revenue to show true dollar gains. Inventories were building up in some lines, but the demand for large tractors and combines remained strong.

Companies manufacturing machinery for the oil and gas industry had a very good year in 1975. Drilling activity continued to rise throughout the world in 1975, and the prospects for 1976 indicated that there would be an increase of 5.2% in the number of drilling rigs. Manufacturers of machinery for mining of coal also were not affected by the recession. The recession was not good for the construction machinery industry, however. The cutback in most phases of the construction industry caused demand for this type of equipment to be weak.

(ORLAND B. KILLIN)

[722.B–C; 732.C.7]

This comparator scope permits detailed analysis of special threads. The latter deflect to prevent loosening in "True-flex," a new bolt design of Standard Pressed Steel in Pennsylvania.

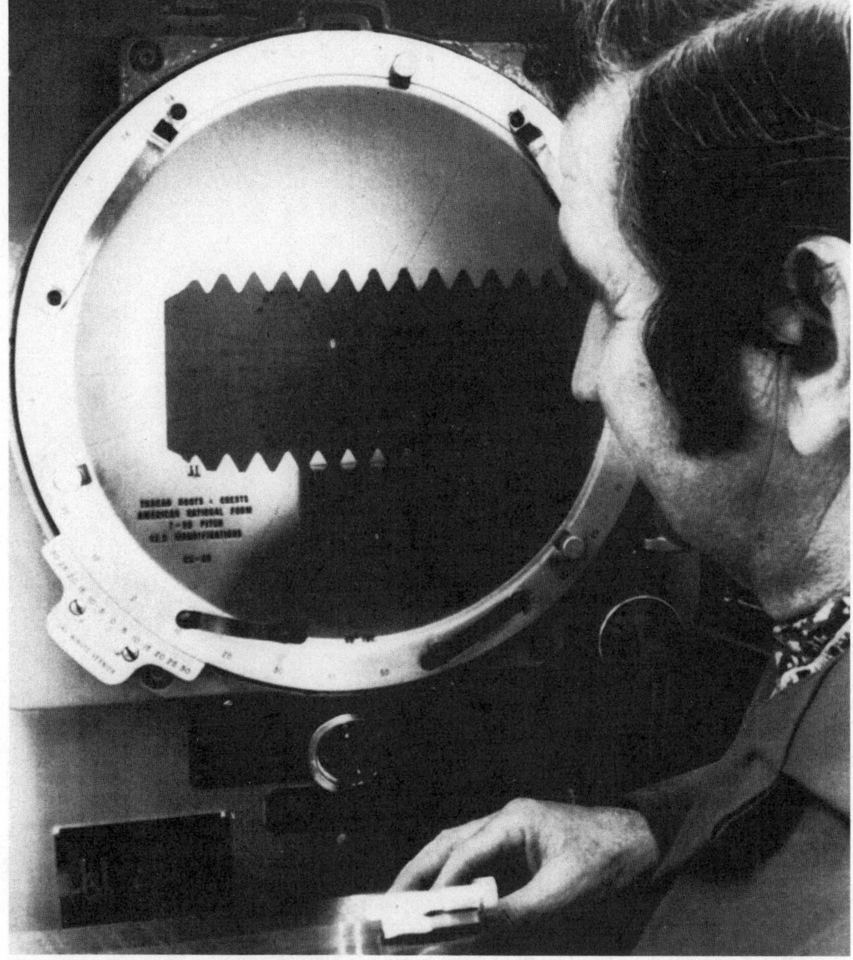

UPI COMPIX

NUCLEAR INDUSTRY

The political position of nuclear power became of critical importance during 1975. Public opinion polls in the U.S. (Harris) and in France (Sofres) indicated that more than half the population were in favour of continuing the construction of nuclear power plants, while only 20 and 30%, respectively, were against it. The situation in some other countries was considerably different, however. In Switzerland, for example, after a sit-in had been held at a construction site, the government agreed to consider demands that the local population be allowed to vote on whether construction should proceed.

In the U.S. the scientific community that supported nuclear power began to speak out in favour of it. Hans Bethe, the "father" of nuclear physics, organized a petition of scientists, and a group called "Americans for Energy Independence" began to counter the antinuclear lobbying of some of the environmental groups.

The operation of nuclear power stations in 1975 confirmed the economic benefits of nuclear over fossil fuels, according to nuclear proponents. They claimed that in the U.S. total costs, including capital charges, were 40 to 50% cheaper than for fossil fuel plants. Similar results were recorded for commercial nuclear plants throughout the world.

At the Browns Ferry plant of the Tennessee Valley Authority in the U.S., two operating stations had to be closed for several months when a workman started a fire in the cable trays underneath the reactor control room. The fire destroyed several of the control and safety systems of the reactors, which had to be shut down by manual controls. The incident shook public confidence in the foolproofness of current nuclear safety systems.

In the U.S., because growth in the demand for electricity continued sluggish, several nuclear power projects were slowed down or canceled, and few new orders were placed. Outside the U.S., however, there was continuing expansion. Iran ordered two units from the French Framatome firm and two from the West German Kraftwerk Union. Luxembourg, South Korea, and Brazil also furthered their commitments. Spain ordered additional units from the Westinghouse Electric Corp. (U.S.), as well as plants from General Electric Co. (U.S.) and from Kraftwerk Union.

The regulatory role of the former U.S. Atomic Energy Commission was vested in the Nuclear Regulatory Commission (NRC), and the research activities in the Energy Research and Development Administration (ERDA). The NRC, careful to ensure that its rulings could withstand appeals to the courts, quickly showed its independence of both the industry and the public lobbying groups and solved a number of previously unresolved problems such as the establishment of safe radiation levels and important emergency criteria. ERDA had more difficulty in establishing a cohesive policy on energy matters, supporting nuclear power as the only near-term solution to the nation's energy problems but refusing to consider the fast breeder reactor as anything but a long-term possibility.

The world's first steel net cooling tower is being installed for a West German nuclear power station. It is suspended from a 180-metre concrete pylon.

KEYSTONE

A Brazilian contract with West Germany included nuclear power reactors, two ordered and six planned, and facilities for enriching uranium and reprocessing spent fuel produced in reactors. The plutonium removed from the reactors could also be used in weapons, and the contract emphasized the difficulty of maintaining adequate safeguards against this possibility.

France decided on a single builder for nuclear equipment, Framatome. Framatome had been established by the French Creusot-Loire and U.S. Westinghouse firms to build Westinghouse-designed plants. The French government, through the Commissariat of Atomic Energy (CEA), took a 30% interest in Framatome at the expense of Westinghouse, and the CEA was reorganized.

Reprocessing plants, particularly in the U.S., were beset by technical problems. Storage facilities for used fuel were expensive and not available in sufficient quantities. A two-year-long study by the NRC was designed to determine whether plutonium produced by reprocessing plants could safely be used as a reactor fuel.

Work on the tripartite British-Dutch-West German centrifuge project and the Eurodif plant being built under French leadership proceeded. South Africa developed a new and unspecified type of enrichment plant, and the government commissioned a pilot project.

The U.S. government's attempts to involve private enterprise in building enrichment facilities were not successful. Many politicians believed that such plants were best built and operated by the government, and commercial interests were unwilling to commit resources without strong government guarantees.

Of the two advanced reactor systems under development, the fast breeder reactor and the high-temperature reactor (HTR), the HTR was in most trouble. In Europe the Dragon project, run by the Nuclear Energy Agency of the Organization for Economic Cooperation and Development, was to be shut down. In the U.S. the General Atomic Co., which offered commercial HTRs, lost all previous orders except one and asked ERDA for financial assistance, which ERDA seemed unwilling to give. But ERDA had to step in and assume total management of the demonstration fast breeder reactor project.

Other uses of nuclear energy continued to be developed. The West German chemical giant BASF wanted a reactor built to produce power and process steam (that used for heat and moisture but not for power) at their chemical plant, and sought government aid. The French developed small reactors to generate process steam or for merchant ship propulsion. A second nuclear icebreaker was launched in the U.S.S.R.

The use of radioisotopes in the medical industry continued to grow at something over 20% a year. The radiopharmaceutical market for diagnosis and therapy grew as fast as new isotopes could be produced. Development continued on the technology of treating sewage and sludge by radiation.

(RICHARD W. KOVAN)

[721.B.9]

PAINTS AND VARNISHES

Waste disposal and the soaring costs of raw materials and energy were major problems for paint manufacturers in the industrialized countries in 1975. In the EEC, several directives issued by the Commission caused further worry. A directive on dangerous substances, issued in 1967, had been only partially implemented in most countries and had already been amended five times. A new solvents directive, effective in 1976, would control the labeling of some paint solvents, including white spirit. The most far-reaching directive, which was nearing approval, would affect the labeling of many paints, with the death's-head or St. Andrew's cross appearing on products classified as toxic or noxious. The reaction of users to these symbols was awaited with trepidation. The EEC's concern about pollution arising from the manufacture of titanium dioxide, the paint industry's major white pigment, seemed likely to result in stricter controls and higher prices.

The paint industry had had to work hard to hold its ground in 1974. The U.S. achieved a modest 3.9% growth in real terms and approached the 1,000,000,000 gal.-a-year mark. The U.K. experienced a fall of some 3%, while the French industry suffered a 5.4% decline in volume. Optimists preferred to look at the value of sales, which showed large gains due to inflation. Total U.S. sales were worth 17.2% more than in 1973, while the corresponding U.K. figure was 24%. Sales to industrial users were depressed by the general slackening of manufacturing activity during the recession—by some 3% in the U.S. and about 20% in the U.K.—but demand for decorative and building paints generally held up well. In countries where the trend was to "do-it-yourself," shorter working hours and increased unemployment often boosted paint sales.

Trade continued to expand among member countries of the EEC, which produced about half the world's total paints. The U.K. recorded a 15% increase by volume in paint exports and a 7% growth in imports in 1974. The world's largest exporter was again West Germany, with the U.S. second and The Netherlands, which emphasized marine paints, third. The fourth largest producer, France, was also the largest importer, followed by West Germany, Belgium, and The Netherlands.

The Japanese paint industry, third largest in the world, experienced growth of some 7% in 1974. The Japanese automotive industry used about 20% of the country's total paint production. Large companies specializing in paints continued to dominate the Japanese industry; this contrasted with the situation in Europe and the U.S., where the largest manufacturers tended to be part of the big chemical groups, such as du Pont and Imperial Chemical Industries.

The trend toward amalgamation continued in the U.S. and European paint industries. In 1974 there were only some 260 manufacturers in France, compared with more than 400 ten years earlier. The number of U.K. manufacturers had nearly halved in 30 years. Switzerland was an exception, with a population of some five million and about 100 paint factories. In Italy there were estimated to be about 730 paint factories, three-quarters of them employing fewer than 20 workers.

(LIONEL BILEFIELD)

[732.D.7]

PHARMACEUTICALS

Despite persistent materials shortages and higher prices for packaging and for some key ingredients in 1975, the drug industry continued in a good—if not exuberant—state of health. In the U.S., the major contributing factors continued to be Medicare and state health payment plans, plus a recent upsurge in "third party payment" for prescriptions through labour unions, management insurance schemes, and other, similar programs.

Materials shortages remained spotty. A persistent shortage of heparin, derived from hog intestines, showed signs of easing when drug companies decided to invest in new extraction equipment at hog-butchering facilities to encourage the butchers to do the processing. Toward year's end, hopes that renewed Turkish production of opium poppies might alleviate shortages of codeine faded when Turkey said it would deliver only 30% of the poppy straw it had originally promised to U.S. drug manufacturers. This prompted industry pressure on the government to allow experimental cultivation of a nonopium poppy in at least one Western state. The supply of plastic, paperboard, and other packaging materials, critically short in mid-1974, was improving.

The effect of inflation on drug company profits was reflected in the nine-month financial reports. Some major drug firms cited higher labour and transportation costs, which could not be reflected in retail price increases. At the same time, there was evidence of an increase in productivity. The U.S. Bureau of Labor Statistics reported that in 1974 output per employee man-hour in the industry rose 5.7%.

Preliminary figures supplied by the Pharmaceutical Manufacturers Association showed that U.S. domestic sales of ethical or prescription drugs amounted to $5,260,000,000 in 1974, compared with $4,770,000,000 the previous year. Leading in sales were products for the central nervous system ($1.4 billion), followed by anti-infectives ($834 million), drugs to combat neoplasms and endocrine disorders ($531 million), digestive and genitourinary ($519.9 million), cardiovascular ($479 million), vitamins and nutrients ($457 million), respiratory ($335.9 million), dermatologicals ($178 million), biologicals ($141 million), diagnostic agents ($113 million), and "other pharmaceutical preparations" ($273 million).

There were signs of stronger competitive pressures on drug prices, and these were expected to continue into 1976 and 1977. Several key patents had expired, or would very shortly, opening the way for competition from generic (non-brand-name) manufacturers. The U.S. Department of Health, Education, and Welfare's policy of reimbursing prescription costs on the basis of the lowest-priced drug on the market could encourage the prescribing of generic drugs even in non-Medicare situations. A series of congressional hearings also stressed differences between the prices of brand name and generic drugs, thus contributing to consumerist pressures.

Pressures on prices were even more pronounced outside the U.S. This was especially true in countries with nationalized health schemes, since under such systems the government, as a major purchaser, exercises a very strong influence on pharmaceutical prices. Britain and West Germany utilized "jawboning" to drive down the prices of the two most prescribed tranquilizers. Sweden was studying a plan to nationalize its drug industry.

(DONALD A. DAVIS)

[732.D.4]

PLASTICS

The plastics industry proved particularly vulnerable to recession in 1975, because of its dependence on oil as a raw material and for energy and also because its major customer industries were themselves hard hit.

During the 1973–74 shortages, inventories had been kept as large as possible, and when recession came, stocks were run down. As a result most polymer plants had to operate at a fraction of capacity; in the U.S. and Japan, 20% of capacity was not untypical in late 1974 and early 1975. The trough for Europe came later in the spring and output fell less precipitously, although the situation was serious enough. One or two countries, such as Norway and Sweden, showed relative immunity.

At midyear the U.S. showed signs of recovery, and the plastics industry benefited as confidence returned and restocking began. Japan followed the U.S. pattern and, at the end of 1975, the improvement, although still rather fragile, appeared sustained. The European situation was less clear. At the quadrennial Kunststoffe exhibition (K'75), held in Düsseldorf, West Germany, in October, a strongly optimistic atmosphere was evident. Most observers predicted a real upturn in the first half of 1976.

Verband Kunststofferzeugende Industrie (Association of Plastics Producers) expected plastics output in West Germany—the world's second largest producer—to fall in 1975 by some 15%, from the 1974 figure of 6,380,000 metric tons to around 5,470,000 metric tons, about the same level as in 1972. A similar or even greater fall was predicted for total world plastics production (41 million metric tons in 1974). Another source estimated U.S. plastics production in 1975 at 14,150,000 metric tons, which was scarcely more than in 1974 (14,130,000) or 1973 (13,740,000).

Price cutting, the traditional response to easy supply, was not a strong feature of early 1975, and in the second half of the year an upward price trend became evident. The big chemical manufacturers maintained that, if they were unable to get an adequate return on their operations, new investment would be prevented. Reinforcing this argument was the prediction that, given the underlying capacity position, acute shortages would return when a more normal level of activity was resumed.

Development work was overwhelmingly concentrated on new grades, combinations or copolymers of existing plastics, and improved additives, often with the object of tailoring a material for a given end-use requirement. Improved flame retardance continued to be important. Structural foams, made from "engineering" plastics, remained a major development area, largely because of the material and processing economies they made possible. Such factors, and possibilities for recycling plastics and conserving scrap, were of prime value in helping to offset rising costs. Work on processing machinery was concerned with greater efficiency in materials utilization.

In the wake of the oil crisis there had been considerable research into the possibilities of alternative feedstocks for polymer production, either through new chemistry or by reassessing older sources such as coal tars, celluloses, and other natural or agricultural products. However, petroleum would remain the industry's basic raw material for the foreseeable future.

Techniques to minimize hazards of pollution during manufacture and toxicity during use remained areas of anxious concentration. The alleged cancer risk presented by vinyl chloride monomer continued to

KEYSTONE

This plastic elephant was displayed at an international fair in Düsseldorf, West Germany, to illustrate the versatility of synthetic materials.

have repercussions on the enormous polyvinyl chloride (PVC) industry. In the U.S. proposed legislation limiting the permitted amount of vinyl chloride in PVC manufacturing locations or as a residue in food-packaging applications was so severe as to be thought unrealistic, although dramatic reductions in exposure levels—to less than two parts per million for an eight-hour shift—were reported by KemaNord of Sweden.

In the face of its commercial and other problems, the plastics industry did not doubt that its long-term prospects were excellent. A *Modern Plastics* editorial symposium predicted that, over the remaining years of the century, the industry would become production—rather than market—oriented and more integrated with the feedstock suppliers, and that there would be long-term stability in prices. Other forecasts included development of a more efficient scrap technology; more sophisticated fillers to extend resin usage; design to get the same product from less material; a decline in the number of resin grades available; growing importance of the single product manufacturing line; greatly increased markets; and even more internationalism in the industry.

(ROBIN C. PENFOLD)

[732.D.5]

PRINTING

Economic recession touched the printing industry in 1975. Several large printers closed down in West Germany, and in France the government stepped in to save the country's largest printing group. Most European printing-machine manufacturers went on short-time working. Order books were well below 1972–73 levels, although Scandinavia, Spain, South America, and North Africa continued to buy machines.

Ultra-fast phototypesetting speeds were claimed on both sides of the Atlantic with the introduction of the Harris Fototronic 7400 systems and the Linotron 606 systems. Both machines offered the prospect of fully automatic page makeup. The manufacturers of the APS CRT phototypesetters announced a new APS-5 system in competition with Harris and Linotron. Visual display terminals, permitting electronic editing and makeup of newspaper pages, became the accepted standard, and very large orders were placed by the international news agencies' wire services and by U.S. newspapers. In Italy the *Corriere della Sera* became the first large European newspaper to go electronic.

Electronic composition had barely affected book production, however. Britain's Monotype Corp., with its 400 Series of phototypesetters and the related ACE electronic systems—some exported to Eastern Europe—led in the book field. Crosfield Electronics' new Magnascan 550 electronic colour scanner used laser light sources, a method pioneered by Dr.-Ing. Rudolf Hell of Kiel, West Germany. Automatic page imposition camera systems were introduced by Pictorial Machinery Ltd. in Britain, with cooperation from Kodak and U.S. manufacturers. Laser platemaking systems, such as the U.S.-made Eocom, were ordered by U.S. newspapers, and European orders were expected.

In the U.S. the *National Geographic* magazine announced that it was switching to gravure. The two-metre-wide rotogravure press ordered by West Germany's Burda Druck & Verlag from Cerutti in Italy was said to be the fastest in the world, and Italian rotogravure press makers made important advances in packaging. Andreotti-Graphicart obtained substantial orders in Spain and Britain. The West German Walter company became the market leader in gravure cylinder-making equipment.

Heat-transfer printing became a boom market. Strachan & Henshaw and Cobden Chadwick of the U.K., Windmöller & Hölscher of West Germany, and makers of reel-fed screen-process machines reported a growing demand from Europe and Asia. In Britain, Lyndan Press found an economical method of producing short-run heat transfers by sheet-fed offset on Roland machines. Several U.S. newspapers offered readers two-colour cartoons to be ironed off onto T-shirts.

Harris Corp. announced that it would discontinue building sheet-fed offset presses in Italy, France, and the U.S. On the other hand, at the Print 74 exhibition in Chicago the West German Heidelberg company had announced a new "72" line of multicolour unit presses, and the company later introduced a line of "102" perfecting presses in the medium format. The market for large-format presses suffered as the change to web offset became more economical. In West Germany the Springer newspaper group opened Europe's largest newspaper web offset plant using MAN presses.

(W. PINCUS JASPERT)

[735.E.3–4]

RUBBER

The rubber industry was being markedly affected in 1975 by factors resulting from the increased price of oil. Reduced automobile sales decreased original equipment tire sales, while the high cost of fuel curtailed the use of automobiles (and hence tire wear) to some extent. Lower speed limits in the U.S. designed to conserve gasoline also increased mileage per tire. The longer-lasting radial tire was in wide use, and the trend to smaller cars with smaller tires also contributed to reduced rubber usage. It appeared that, after 30 years of steady growth, the rubber industry might have to adjust for a time to an essentially zero-growth market. Less developed countries might be the exception.

Natural rubber was one of the few raw materials used in rubber manufacture that did not reflect a marked price change during the year. On Oct. 1, 1974, it was 32 cents per pound and on Oct. 1, 1975, it was 30 cents per pound, although it had fluctuated between 24 and 34 cents in the intervening period. The government of Malaysia began stockpiling rubber in order to reduce price fluctuations and, it was hoped, make the price of rubber reflect inflationary trends to some degree. Consumption of natural rubber had essentially equaled production for many years.

The Management Committee of the International Rubber Study Group (IRSG) estimated world production of natural rubber in 1974 at 3,475,000 metric tons, a decrease of 37,000 tons from 1973; production for 1975 was estimated at 3.4 million tons. World natural rubber supplies were estimated at 3.4 million tons in 1975; synthetic rubber supplies at 7.1 million tons; and consumption at 3,480,000 tons of natural rubber and 7.1 million tons of synthetic rubber.

The U.S. remained the largest single buyer of natural rubber, using 719,079 tons in 1974. World consumption of natural rubber latex (dry basis) was estimated at 268,750 tons. Statistics on world consumption of synthetic latices were incomplete, but U.S. consumption was 86,854 tons (dry basis) of the SBR type. Total consumption of both natural and synthetic rubbers worldwide was estimated at 10,792,500 tons for 1974.

Production of reclaimed rubber declined somewhat, from 289,021 tons in 1973 to 239,904 tons in 1974. This was a long-term trend resulting from changes in rubber compounding, but it might be reversed for economic reasons in the changing raw materials situation. Pollution problems in the manufacture of reclaimed rubber could be over-

Goodyear Tire and Rubber Co. in Toronto produced these cube-treaded low-pressure tires for highway and off-the-road driving conditions.

Table IX. Natural Rubber Production
In 000 metric tons

Country	1972	1973	1974
Malaysia	1,304	1,567	1,549
Indonesia	774	886	895*
Thailand	337	382	379
Sri Lanka	140	155	132
India	109	123	128
Liberia	83	84*	88
Nigeria	41	49	60†
Zaire	40	40	27
Brazil	26†	23†	19
Others	271	203	198
Total	3,125	3,512	3,475

*Preliminary.
†Estimate, or includes estimate.

Table X. Synthetic Rubber Production
In 000 metric tons

Country	1972	1973	1974
United States	2,455	2,607	2,517
Japan	819	967	858
France	368	458	463
United Kingdom	307	353	327
Germany, West	300	350	317
Italy*	186	230	250
Netherlands, The	186	263	245
Canada	195	230	209
Brazil	95	125	155
Germany, East	133	134	139
Poland	78	94	101
Romania	73	83	96*
Spain	50	65*	80*
Mexico	53	54	66
Belgium*	60	65	65
Czechoslovakia	52	50*	50*
Argentina	44	47	50
Australia	42	43	45
South Africa	30	28	32
Others*†	1,104	1,257	1,393
Total	6,630	7,503	7,458

*Estimate, or includes estimate.
†Includes estimated production for the U.S.S.R (about 1,308,000 tons in 1974) and China (about 50,000 tons in 1974).
Source: The Secretariat of the International Rubber Study Group, *Rubber Statistical Bulletin*.

come, and the price of scrap tires was low.

A new family of rubber-like materials called TPR (for thermoplastic rubber) was introduced. They are mechanical mixtures of ethylene-propylene-diene rubber (EPDM) with varying amounts of an olefinic polymer such as polyethylene or polypropylene. Projected uses were for automotive parts such as bumper guards where the good weather resistance, low cost, and easy processing of this material would offer particular advantages. Several U.S. manufacturers followed the lead of their European counterparts in developing special snow-tread tires. The tires are compounded to give essentially the same traction as a studded tire but without damaging the pavement. A number of states had outlawed studs because of the damage to roads. The Chevette subcompact announced by the Chevrolet Division of General Motors was the first all-metric car manufactured in the U.S. The tires were in metric dimensions except for the rim size, which was still in English units.

Sri Lanka was in the process of nationalizing its rubber plantations, which were largely British owned, and it was feared that this could have an adverse effect on production. Mexico planned to increase production of guayule from 30,000 to 50,000 tons per year by 1980. Extraction of the woody part of this shrub yields about a 50:50 mixture of natural rubber (polyisoprene) and resin, and the mixture can be used as a natural rubber substitute.

(J. R. BEATTY)

[732.D.6]

SHIPBUILDING

The state of world shipbuilding became a source of great anxiety during 1975 as orders for new vessels fell dramatically. By midyear, orders stood at 4,798 vessels totaling 102,137,238 gross registered tons (grt), considerably below the mid-1974 figure. Tonnage reductions were greatest for tankers. On order were 804 tankers with a carrying capacity of 123,110,000 tons; this was 233 ships and 41,342,900 tons less than were on order at the beginning of the year.

Deliveries of new ships by world shipyards during 1974 kept close to the 1973 figures, with 2,949 vessels totaling 33,541,289 grt, compared with 2,999 ships totaling 30,408,930 grt in 1973. Deliveries in 1975 were expected to compare favourably with 1974, but a sharp decline in completions was anticipated for 1976.

Japan continued to head the list of leading shipbuilding countries in 1975 with a total order book of 42,537,674 grt. Sweden, with an order book of 7,180,452 grt, was a distant second, followed by West Germany with 6,099,466 grt, the U.K. with 5,390,870 grt, and Spain with 5,306,680 grt. With the slump in new orders, shipbuilding capacity exceeded demand in many sectors and Japanese yards in particular had to find alternative orders. Because new orders for tankers were nonexistent, interest turned to bulk carriers ranging from 30,000 to 100,000 tons deadweight (dw.). Most orders for new carriers went to Japan, but at non-profitmaking prices.

There was a considerable amount of new shipbuilding and repairing activity in the Middle and Far East. A new 477,000-ton drydock opened at Sembawang in Singapore, and the new yards at Bahrain and Dubai in the Persian Gulf made progress. Two new South Korean yards were under construction; the first was due for completion early in 1976 and the second about a year after that. In Scandinavia and Japan, docks originally intended for new building were used for repair work or for the construction of smaller vessels, oil rigs, and offshore supply ships. Only a few yards were able to convert canceled tanker contracts into orders for dry-cargo vessels, and cancellation fees ranged from $400,000 to $10 million or more. Some builders were reluctant to accept cancellations, while others were only too glad to cut their losses.

Yards in Sweden, Portugal, and the U.K. faced nationalization. Financial aid was essential for survival, and nations had to decide if they needed and could afford a shipbuilding industry. Attention was paid to market surveys that identified trade growth over a period of five to ten years. The correct analysis of a market would allow a shipbuilder to estimate the most efficient size and type of vessel and to adjust his yard facilities accordingly.

Productivity in itself was not the key to shipbuilding success. A 65,000-strong labour force in the U.K. completed 1.5 million grt of shipping, while in Sweden during the same period a labour force of 25,000 accounted for 2,250,000 grt, most of it tankers. Yet despite better productivity, the Swedish shipbuilding industry also experienced unprofitable orders.

Other types of ships that generated interest among builders during the year were products carriers and both liquefied natural gas (LNG) and liquefied petroleum gas (LPG) vessels, but a survey warned that the last two types of vessels would not be required in large quantities. Orders for containerships increased during the year, and shipowners were clearly adding such vessels to their fleets. Most of the orders went to West German yards for 27-knot containerships capable of carrying 2,500 containers of the 20-ft. type. Nearly all the new vessels were diesel-powered.

UPI COMPIX

The oil tanker "Massachusetts" has a capacity of 86.3 million gallons. It is the largest ship ever built in the U.S.

Competition for the few new orders for dry-cargo ships was fierce, and in the summer Bremer Vulkan of West Germany outbid a Japanese yard for three fast 16,450-ton-dw. cargo liners with heavy-lifting cargo gear. Better loan terms helped secure the contract. Stratton Shipyards in Singapore succeeded in securing an order for ten mini-bulk carriers of 3,000 tons dw. each. During the year the Brazilian government announced a program to build 150 ships with nearly all the vessels to be built in Brazilian yards. This vast order, including all types of vessels and totaling approximately 5 million tons dw., would not stop Brazilian yards from accepting orders from foreign customers.

(W. D. EWART)

[734.E.7]

TELECOMMUNICATIONS

Major developments in telecommunications during 1975 included the launching of the first in a new series of international communications satellites, the first demonstration of a private branch telephone exchange that contained a miniaturized computer with its own memory, and completion of the final section of a cable between Australia and New Zealand.

Satellites. The first Intelsat 4A was launched by the U.S. National Aeronautics and Space Administration (NASA) on Sept. 25, 1975, into synchronous orbit (always above the same point on the Earth's surface) over the Atlantic Ocean. The 23-ft., 3,280-lb. satellite was the first of six which would replace the seven smaller Intelsat 4s that had been placed in synchronous orbit over the Atlantic, Pacific, and Indian oceans since 1971. Each Intelsat 4A was designed to provide 6,250 two-way transoceanic telephone circuits and two colour television channels that would serve 52 nations in North America, South America, and Europe.

Plans to expand the U.S. domestic satellite network were made during the year. RCA Global Communications Inc. launched the Satcom I into synchronous orbit over the Equator late in December. It was equipped with transponders, each of which could handle one television channel or 600 two-way voice signals at one time. In a joint venture the American Telephone and Telegraph Co. (AT & T) and Comsat General Corp. planned to launch three satellites in February 1976. Comsat was to build all three of the satellites and then lease two of them to AT & T, which would use them as part of its Comstar domestic network. The U.S. Federal Communications Commission (FCC) had previously restricted AT & T to using satellites only for its existing customers for at least three years.

Other nations also continued to build and launch satellites. The Soviet Union added to its already numerous fleet of Molniyas, which were not synchronous but were instead so situated as to give a long transmission period over the U.S.S.R. Late in December the Soviets launched a satellite in the Molniya 3 series that was to be used primarily for domestic telephone, television, and telegraph links; it was placed in a high, elliptical orbit.

Indonesia planned to launch its first satellite, to be built in the U.S., in 1976, and NASA launched the French-West German experimental satellite Symphonie in January. Japan expected to put into orbit in 1977–78 two satellites built jointly by U.S. and domestic firms; one was to broadcast tele-

Table XI. Countries Having More Than 100,000 Telephones

Telephones in service, 1974

Country	Number of telephones	Percentage increase over 1964	Telephones per 100 population	Country	Number of telephones	Percentage increase over 1964	Telephones per 100 population
Algeria	220,814	58.3	1.37	Luxembourg	134,560	81.8	38.12
Argentina	2,065,273	44.9	8.30	Malaysia	234,137	93.4	2.05
Australia*	4,659,182	74.5	35.36	Mexico	2,222,654	236.9	4.20
Austria	1,841,234	112.5	24.55	Morocco	181,000	27.3	1.11
Belgium	2,503,036	82.6	25.72	Netherlands, The	4,317,006	113.4	32.00
Brazil	2,415,000	98.4	2.34	New Zealand	1,410,532	56.4	46.35
Bulgaria	640,842	184.3	7.37	Nigeria	106,326	76.0	0.15
Canada	11,668,292	75.3	52.31	Norway	1,308,420	56.1	32.93
Chile	433,682	73.8	4.20	Pakistan	195,325	62.1	0.29
China*	596,663	...	3.90	Panama	120,500	190.8	7.98
Colombia	1,079,645	190.1	4.65	Peru	301,679	135.5	2.02
Cuba†	274,949	20.2	3.16	Philippines	410,290	170.7	1.04
Czechoslovakia	2,354,313	81.3	16.09	Poland	2,237,603	105.5	6.68
Denmark	2,047,497	64.1	39.99	Portugal	948,003	95.4	10.02
Ecuador*	117,961	171.2	1.79	Puerto Rico	425,876	127.8	14.43
Egypt	471,791	56.5	1.33	Rhodesia	160,322	69.0	2.67
Finland	1,535,406	110.7	32.91	Romania	886,166	135.0	4.25
France	11,337,000	112.4	21.66	Singapore	250,159	215.9	11.36
Germany, East	2,326,143	53.5	13.67	South Africa	1,816,291	69.8	7.54
Germany, West	17,802,646	134.3	28.73	Spain‡	6,331,474	177.3	18.13
Greece	1,670,132	368.6	18.67	Sweden	4,984,370	54.7	61.20
Hong Kong	913,411	412.3	21.65	Switzerland	3,604,034	80.4	55.44
Hungary	968,459	91.7	9.27	Syria	143,320	98.1	2.08
India	1,590,000	132.4	0.27	Taiwan	742,304	460.1	4.77
Indonesia	268,963	31.6	0.21	Thailand	264,548	305.8	0.65
Iran	552,500	243.5	1.74	Turkey	807,294	181.8	2.09
Iraq	129,418	108.7	1.22	U.S.S.R.	14,260,700	119.3	5.68
Ireland	366,265	77.7	12.00	United Kingdom	19,095,317	104.3	34.06
Israel	685,382	269.8	20.73	United States	138,285,699	63.7	65.47
Italy	12,611,653	149.4	22.86	Uruguay	245,884	29.8	8.22
Japan	38,697,901	262.3	35.40	Venezuela	504,000	108.0	4.38
Korea, South	1,014,016	493.8	3.09	Yugoslavia	1,003,550	211.4	4.77
Lebanon*	227,000	129.8	7.67				

*1973. †1972. ‡Including Spanish North Africa.

Source: American Telephone & Telegraph Company, *The World's Telephones, 1974;* Statistical Office of the United Nations, *Statistical Yearbook 1967.*

vision programs to community antennas and the other was for telephone communications.

Telephones. AT & T in January demonstrated Dimension PBX, a private branch exchange that featured a miniaturized computer with its own memory. The exchange could provide automatic intraoffice calling when two lines were free, automatic route selection to achieve placement of calls at the most economic rate, and a three-way conference transfer that would permit privacy between two parties of a conference call.

Scientists at the Bell System during the year tested a 2.5-in.-diameter hollow steel pipe lined with copper and polyethylene and filled with nitrogen, to be used in an underground transmission system. They believed that it would be capable of carrying up to 230,000 telephone conversations at one time, more than twice the capacity of the largest buried coaxial cable being used by Bell in 1975.

In April the General Telephone and Electronics Corp. obtained a $500 million contract to update and expand the telephone system of Iran. The project included installation of high-speed, computer-controlled switching systems in more than 500 telephone exchanges throughout the nation; these systems were expected to provide Iran with an additional 950,000 telephone lines.

The FCC in February approved a $365 million rate increase for interstate service by AT & T, and in April the rates for U.S.–Canada phone calls were raised by an average of 7%. Nevertheless, both AT & T and International Telephone and Telegraph Corp. reported declines in net income.

Cables. The last section of an undersea cable stretching 12,000 nautical miles from Sydney, Australia, to Auckland, N.Z., was completed in September. The cable was designed to provide 640 telephone links between the two countries.

Nine firms from various parts of the world announced in August that they planned to cooperate in building two undersea cables connecting the U.S. with the Caribbean and South America. One was to provide 640 telephone links between Venezuela and the Virgin Islands, and the other, 3,000 links between the Virgin Islands and the U.S. Both were scheduled to be completed in 1977.

(DAVID R. CALHOUN)

[732.I.2–3 and 6]

TEXTILES

Reduced demand for yarns and fabrics in 1975 was rapidly reflected in lower production of natural and man-made fibres and overstocking in many lines of finished goods. In the U.K., repeated appeals to the government by both management and labour unions for measures to reduce the unprecedented high levels of textile imports met with little response, and more mills were permanently closed. Labour shortages created production problems.

The seventh International Textile Machinery Exhibition in Milan, Italy, in October attracted more than 1,100 exhibitors. The vast show displayed the world's best machinery, dyeing and finishing plants, and a wide variety of accessories for every section of the industry.

Throughout the year there was no lack of research developments and inventive ingenuity aimed at higher production rates and improved quality. In Britain a Yorkshire firm reduced its daily usage of water from mains by 20,000 gal. by recycling the final rinse water in piece-scouring machines. The latest British "tunnel-type" vacuum steamer, of 420-kg. capacity, could handle any type of fibre and operated over a wide range of temperatures. One-pack polymers for coating foams, fabrics, leathers, and plastics were introduced. A new nonwoven cloth was claimed to be flame-resistant with excellent solvent-, water-, and oil-absorbing properties.

(ALFRED DAWBER)

Natural Fibres. *Cotton.* World stocks at the beginning of the 1974–75 season increased for the fourth consecutive year to 25 million bales. Production improved by approximately 300,000 bales to 63 million bales with an increase in the harvested acreage compensating for lower yields.

In the U.S. extreme weather conditions early in the season caused a decline of about 1.5 million bales, a cut in average yields of 16%. Output also decreased in Central America, Brazil, Egypt, and Uganda. The U.S.S.R., however, reported a record crop of more than 13 million bales, 1 million more than in the previous season. Significant increases were also reported from Mexico, Turkey, and Iran.

Carry-over stocks at the beginning of the 1975–76 season were at their highest level in a decade, 29.5 million bales. Most of the increases occurred in the net exporting regions, North America, the Middle East, and the U.S.S.R.

The Liverpool index of average values began the 1974–75 season at about 62 cents a pound after touching an unprecedented peak of 91.5 cents in mid-January 1974. Values weakened during the subsequent six months to less than 46.5 cents but then steadily recovered, reaching nearly 56 cents by early October 1975.

The downward slide in fibre consumption was particularly severe in the U.S. and the Far East, with Japan experiencing a drop of nearly 20%. In Eastern European countries and many less developed nations, cotton use continued to grow in response to sustained textile demand.

(ARTHUR TATTERSALL)

Wool. Recession in the wool textile industry continued in 1975. Wool prices had declined throughout 1974, falling spasmodically from the peaks of March 1973. Floor prices fixed by the Australian Wool Corporation (AWC) at the start of the 1974–75 wool-selling season were reaffirmed with only fractional changes for the 1975–76 season. The 250 cents (Australian) per kilogram for 21 micron wool, clean basis, applied until April 1975, when demand raised the price to 275 cents by mid-May. After the May 1975 peak, prices moved back toward the floor-price support level.

Wool textile activity in leading consuming countries remained on a low level, and the minor recovery did not follow through. With demand poor and the outlook uncertain, AWC floor-price purchases were again a major supporting factor. The crossbred wool market showed greater strength, and New Zealand wool sold well in August. Wool markets strengthened in October. Crossbred prices rose in New Zealand and the U.K. Demand for South American wool led to price increases, and wool was sold in Australia at slightly above floor price.

World production of wool in the 1974–75 season was estimated by the Commonwealth Secretariat to have totaled 2,599 metric tons (greasy basis), compared with 2,474 metric tons in 1973–74. Recovery in 1974–75 followed a slightly declining trend. Large stocks had accumulated in Australia to support the floor price, but in other wool-producing countries the accumulation had been relatively small or negligible. A reasonable balance between demand and supply now seemed possible.

(H. M. F. MALLETT)

Silk. In February 1975 the price of Chinese raw silk stood at 37.40 yuan per kilogram, nearly 60% lower than the peak of April 1973 and cheaper than at any time since the 1960s. At each successive fall, manufacturers and merchants had had to write down the value of their stocks, and by now they lacked the courage to enter into new commitments. In September 1975 a 3% price rise, an attempt by the Chinese corporation to reverse the trend to which the market had grown so accustomed, was greeted with a cautious welcome.

The Japanese silk market was still insulated from the outside world by the ban on raw silk imports (except through the semi-official Raw Silk Corporation) imposed in 1974, which had been extended until May 1976. This was particularly hard on countries such as Korea and Brazil, which had greatly increased production in the expectation of catering to an expanding Japanese

Viewdata is a new telecommunication system proposed by the London Post Office.

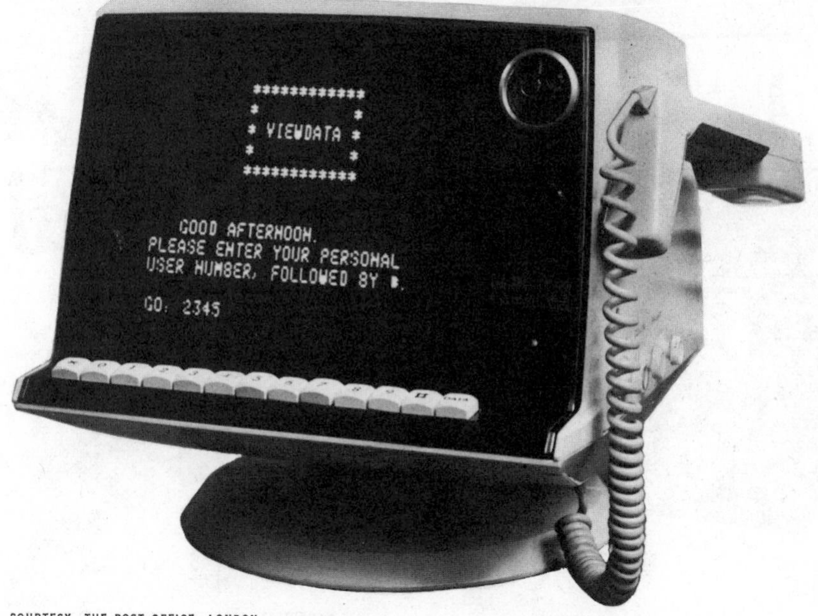

COURTESY, THE POST OFFICE, LONDON

POPPERFOTO

One woman supervises 16,500 automatic spindles in this textile plant in the U.S.S.R.

market. The restriction was confined to raw silk, however, and Japanese importers were not slow to build up a trade in cocoon, thrown silk, fabric, and wild silks, thus offering some alleviation to the producing countries.

Thus the two-tier silk market—dating to the mid-1960s when China had first replaced Japan as Europe's supplier—continued. If the inevitable European resales to Japan at an easy profit could have been prevented, all might have been well, but China's efforts in this direction had prompted the drastic price increases of 1973 that led to the market's current hard times.

(PETER W. GADDUM)

Man-Made Fibres. The depression that had affected the industry in 1974 continued into 1975, but fibre producers were forced to raise prices by amounts calculated on the basis of what the market could afford. Contraction in production was reflected in plant closures and underutilization. Even so, producers made strenuous efforts to develop new products.

Fibre producers pressed ahead with the production of producer textured yarns (PTY) to be sold to the trade ready for weaving or knitting. At the same time, the partially oriented yarns (POY), which were textured by commission processors, continued to sell. Where POY yarns were available, the trade was able to produce a wide variety of different products in comparatively small quantities, whereas PTY yarns were for a bulk market based on a standard product.

Nylon 4 was the subject of a pilot run in the U.S., and an Italian company took out a license for the process. The new nylon was said to be more "comfortable" since it absorbed more moisture than the volume nylons types 6 and 66, but this was by no means proven. Aromatic polyamides (aramids), such as Nomex, Kevlar, and Arenka, were developed for high-temperature-resistant industrial applications.

(PETER LENNOX-KERR)

[732.C.1; 732.D.9]

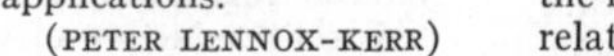

TOBACCO

The 1974 world tobacco crop was a record 11,300,000,000 lb., 6% larger than in 1973. The harvest considerably alleviated the tight supply situation for light, flue-cured, Burley or oriental tobaccos. Higher production was recorded in China, the U.S., India, Brazil, Turkey, Argentina, Mexico, Pakistan, and Thailand, although some countries showed declines, notably Greece, Japan, South Korea, and Malawi. The 1975 crop was also expected to increase but not on the same scale. Acreage was expanded by 3% but, because of adverse weather, only 2% growth in production was anticipated.

Processors and manufacturers utilized 4% more tobacco in 1974 than in 1973, but the rate of increase was below that of the previous year. Despite stock replenishment, the ratio of primary stocks to utilization was relatively low in 1975 as compared with the previous ten years.

Leaf prices in 1974 continued to rise, reflecting firm demand and the growers' increased costs. Prices at U.S. flue-cured auctions rose by 20% to a record average, and a similar increase was recorded for American-grown Burley. Prices for oriental leaf also rose sharply—by about 50% in Greece and about 40% in Turkey. A slight weakening in demand and consequent easing of average price increases was expected in 1975.

Trade in leaf tobacco was exceptionally buoyant in 1974. Exports rose by a recorded 14% to 2,870,000,000 lb., with Italy, Brazil, Greece, South Korea, and the U.S. all showing significant increases. Imports of leaf appeared to stagnate because of changes in the method of data compilation. A reversal of the pattern was expected for 1975, with reduced exports and much heavier imports.

The growth rate of tobacco usage—most accurately assessed by the output of tobacco producers—appeared to slow even more in 1975 as the effects of world recession on per-

High-speed shuttleless looms are slowing the inroads made by knitted fabrics.

COURTESY, CROMPTON & KNOWLES CORPORATION

sonal income, together with increased manufacturing costs and higher taxes in some countries, began to be felt. At year's end an increase in usage of barely 2% was forecast, with half of that accounted for by the industrialized countries.

The overall output of tobacco products in the U.S. was practically static—0.7% higher in the first half of 1975 than in 1974—and was expected to fall slightly by the end of the year. Growth also slowed in the EEC. The continental member countries recorded a 1% rise, compared with 4% in 1974, and U.K. output did not increase at all. In the U.S. the filter cigarette market was the only sector to expand in 1974; sales of cigars and smoking tobacco both diminished, as did per capita consumption of cigarettes, although only slightly. A similar situation pertained in the original six members of the EEC, where filter-cigarette output rose 2% in 1975 and cigars and smoking tobacco declined 2% and 7%, respectively.

The harmonization of excise duties in the EEC was still causing dissent, and no firm picture of future structures had yet emerged. Meanwhile, the less developed countries began to benefit more fully from preferential tariff rates on both manufactured and unmanufactured tobacco goods.

Synthetic tobacco substitutes continued to make steady, if rather slow, progress. Toward the end of 1974 several brands containing a proportion of substitutes were marketed in Europe, but they had little effect on sales. The first report of the U.K.'s Independent Scientific Committee on Smoking and Health—set up to investigate substitutes and additives—was published in mid-1975; it recommended a fairly lengthy and costly three-stage testing process. No significant cost saving resulted from the use of substitutes, but constant supplies could be more easily ensured.

There was continued pressure from anti-smoking lobbies during 1975. Renewed calls for more controls were made by, among others, the delegates at a World Health Organization meeting. (*See* DRUG ABUSE.)

(MARINA THAINE)

[731.B.4.e]

TOURISM

International tourism made a marked recovery in 1975, and a number of European countries recorded substantial increases in arrivals. Italy, Portugal, Spain, and Switzerland, however, had more moderate gains. The recovery of the U.S. dollar in the late summer came too late for the vacation plans of most Americans, and U.S. departures to Europe in 1975 were about 10% below the 1974 figure.

Prospects for travelers in 1975 had never looked so varied, with vacation possibilities matching every budget and taste. On the crest of the rising value of the French franc, French people found attractions in crossing the English Channel for "le shopping anglais." Heads of states led the crowd to visit the once forbidden Chinese capital of Peking. Student explorers continued to trek across the Sahara. The Trans-Siberian Express held no secrets for intrepid European or American globe-trotters, while postmarks of Ulan Bator or Kathmandu became almost commonplace. Resort tourism remained the predominant summer preference of Europeans, but walking or cycling holidays found new favour as they saved gasoline, respected the environment, and helped office-bound executives shed unwanted weight. Cruising retained its popularity.

In 1974, for the first time since World War II, tourist arrivals throughout the world declined from the previous year, by 3% to 209 million, while receipts grew by barely 5% to $29 billion. Higher oil prices, uncertainty about the timing of economic recovery, and rising unemployment caused postponement of vacation plans, cuts in family travel budgets, shorter trips abroad, and tours to fewer countries. Domestic tourism gained, with nights spent by people in hotels of their own nation rising by 4% in 1974, and travel to neighbouring countries increased. U.S. travelers to Europe and the Mediterranean area were 15% fewer than in 1973 (at an average trip cost of $1,035); travel spending by U.S. nationals in Latin America and the Caribbean rose by 20%.

Restrictive monetary and credit policies affected the tourist trade, and operators and agents acted to pare costs and to put their activities on a firm financial basis. Programs were pruned, charges raised, and retail outlets closed. Currency surcharges were imposed to offset the risk of floating exchange rates. The U.K. government set up a bonding scheme to guard against the consequences to holidaymakers of operator failures. Because the travel market had contracted in 1974, demand was substantially underestimated in 1975 and by late spring many operators reported tours fully booked. Tourism appeared to have become a staple for the many rather than a luxury for the few—a theme promotional campaigns were to exploit throughout 1975.

World international air passenger traffic grew by only 4% in 1974, and charter traffic dropped even more dramatically, by 17%, to barely three million passengers. Steep air fare increases in March and November of 1975 produced an even steeper decline in passengers carried on both scheduled and nonscheduled services, as both business and pleasure travelers sought less expensive alternatives such as railroads and automobiles. Passenger traffic on European railways registered increases in 1974 of between 5 and 12% in passengers carried or passenger-kilometres; in many cases this was the first upturn since the late 1950s.

Rising personnel costs and other overhead expenses caused hotel room rates to rise, particularly in city centres; consequently, occupancy rates eased. Switzerland dropped 3%, to 41% occupancy, and West Germany and Austria lost about 1% each. Some managements sold night lodgings to tour operators at up to 50% off published rates, but lack of medium-priced accommodations remained a problem. France's secretary for tourism, recalling the effort made and needed to build budget-priced hotels, appealed for "something to be done" about the 10% of French people who never took a vacation because they could not afford one.

With travel expenditures in 1974 worth $5,973,000,000, U.S. tourists took second place to West Germans ($7,041,000,000). Of the 6,467,000 U.S. travelers who made overseas trips in 1974, 47,000 went by sea and the rest by air; 3,325,000 visited Europe and the Mediterranean. U.S. visitors averaged 24 days in Europe, 18 days in South Africa, and between 6 and 10 days in Central America and the Caribbean. The U.K. earned most from U.S. overseas travel, $368 million; France earned $198 million; Italy $188 million; West Germany $153 million; Spain $138 million; and Switzerland $117 million. By comparison, neighbouring Mexico earned $1,475,000,000 from U.S. visitors, of which $904 million was spent in the Mexican border zone, and Canada earned $1,352,000,000. The Caribbean and Central America earned $685 million from U.S. travel; South America $209 million; and Japan $102 million.

In the U.S. the Japanese spent $402 million in 1974, the British $142 million, and the West Germans $126 million. Spending by Canada and Mexico exceeded that by overseas countries, with Canadians spending $1,225,000,000 and Mexicans $1,142,000,000.

With growing emphasis worldwide on the need for consumer protection, a number of countries made moves to safeguard the traveler. French legislation in 1974 gave, for the first time, a recognized professional status to the travel agent and provided for

Owners of seven stately homes have joined forces with the British Tourist Authority to encourage visitors from abroad by opening the homes to the public. Previously rivals, they now designate themselves "The Magnificent Seven."

CENTRAL PRESS/PICTORIAL PARADE

a strict licensing system under which solid financial guarantees became essential. In Spain a registration scheme for travel agents was established, while in the U.K. codes of practice reflecting the interest of consumers were adopted by operators and agents under the supervision of the director general of fair trading. In Austria new legislation came into force governing the relationship of hotelkeepers and their guests.

The new intergovernmental World Tourism Organization came into existence in November 1974 following ratification of the statutes by 51 nations. Delegates from 89 countries attended the first General Assembly in Madrid in May 1975. The organization marked a growing desire on the part of governments to play an active role in welcoming and protecting visitors from abroad and ensuring the orderly growth of the tourism and leisure industries. It also provided international recognition of the new status of tourism: a billion dollar business, a valuable invisible export sector, and a fruitful area of contact between nations, cutting through political barriers and social and economic differences.

(PETER SHACKLEFORD)

[732.F.1]

KEYSTONE

A new Swedish tree-felling machine pulls out trees and cuts off their roots in one operation.

WOOD PRODUCTS

The forest products industry, which produces lumber, plywood, pulp, paper, and thousands of related products, struggled back in 1975 from its worst slump in more than a generation. The worldwide recession that began in 1974 sharply cut demand for and production of forest products. In the United States the decline in housing starts to 1.3 million in 1974 from 2.1 million in 1973 severely affected U.S. and Canadian lumber mills; in 1975 the still sluggish housing industry was expected to start construction of less than 1.2 million new homes. Building also fell off sharply in Japan, the world's largest importer of logs and chips.

By the fall of 1975, wood consumption and production in the U.S. were still down. Lumber production was projected by the National Forest Products Association at only about 31,000,000,000 bd-ft. for the year, compared with 34,900,000,000 bd-ft. in 1974. The industry expected production in 1975 to be the lowest in any year since World War II.

In the less developed countries more than 1,000,000,000 people who relied on wood for heating and cooking faced increasing shortages. As fuel derived from oil became more costly, many Asian and African landscapes were denuded to meet firewood needs. Though in developed countries wood is used mainly for construction and papermaking, about half of all timber cut throughout the world in 1975 was still used as fuel.

Both the U.S. and Canada were also hit by an unusual decline in the pulp and paper segments of the industry. Historically, when markets for wood products have been down, the market for pulp and paper has been up.

Paced by strong demand for paper and paperboard, pulpwood production grew until the latter months of 1974. Recession hit the paperboard segments first. Then, just before the end of the year, paper production plunged. The industry had rarely experienced such a drastic and sudden swing from scarcity to oversupply.

After a sharp drop in paper and paperboard production early in 1975, production rose so that by late summer it had climbed 18% to an annual rate of about 54 million tons, the American Paper Institute reported. Production in 1974 was 61 million tons.

Particle board, an engineered product of wood chips or flakes bonded together into a panel, was off 25% in 1974, the first production drop since the industry began after World War II. Softwood plywood, a structural product made mainly in the western and southern states of the U.S., declined 10% in 1974, and decorative hardwood plywood dropped 27%.

As demand shrank and production fell, hundreds of sawmill and plywood operations shut down in 1974 and 1975. Companies with integrated operations in wood products and pulp and paper kept plants going in order to make wood chips for pulp production until early in 1975, when that market also fell off. The softwood plywood industry turned to such markets as packaging, crating, and remodeling to keep production going.

Important technological developments occurred during the depressed period. They included Plystran, a sheathing with a core of mechanically oriented fibres, and Com-Ply studs, which sandwich particle board between wood veneer and which could greatly increase the amount of structural material normally available from a tree. Industry increased its investment in genetics nurseries for faster growing of so-called supertrees.

By the end of 1975 the U.S. Forest Service was scheduled to complete an assessment of timber and related resources in the national forests, which contain nearly half of the nation's softwood sawtimber used for construction, as well as in other forests. This was mandated by a law enacted in 1974 called the Forest and Rangeland Renewable Resources Planning Act. Under the law, the Forest Service also was to draft a 50-year management plan to be updated every five years.

One of the most significant recent developments in world trade was the formation of the Southeast Asia Lumber Producers Association. It represented the major producers of tropical hardwoods, the Philippines, Malaysia, and Indonesia, and its purpose was to control supply and prices.

(TAIT TRUSSELL)

[732.D.3]

See also Agriculture and Food Supplies; Computers; Consumerism; Economy, World; Energy; Food Processing; Games and Toys; Industrial Relations; Materials Sciences; Mining and Quarrying; Photography; Television and Radio; Transportation.

Information Science and Technology: *see* Computers

Insurance: *see* Industrial Review

International Law: *see* Law

International Monetary Fund: *see* Economy, World

International Organizations

The following table on pages 433 and 434 shows the membership of the world's sovereign states in various international organizations in 1975. The growing realization that political and economic problems transcended national boundaries led to a proliferation of international organizations after World War II. The International Bank for Reconstruction and Development (World Bank), originally established to provide help to war-devastated nations, turned more and more in succeeding years toward concentration on the problems of economic development. Organizations with more restricted membership included regional political groupings (OAS, OAU), military alliances (NATO, the Warsaw Treaty Organization), and organizations with a primarily economic orientation (EEC, Comecon). Such groupings as the Colombo Plan were chiefly vehicles for channeling aid from the developed to the less developed countries.

[544.A]

Membership in International Organizations, December 1, 1975

Country	UN 1	FAO 2	IMCO 3	IAEA 4	ICAO 5	ILO 6	IBRD 7	IDA 8	IFC 9	IMF 10	ITU 11	UNESCO 12	UPU 13	WHO 14	WMO* 15	GATT 16	CE 17	LAS 18	OAS 19	OPEC 20	OCAS 21	C-Plan 22	Comecon 23	Euratom 24	ECSC 25	EEC 26	EFTA 27	IDB 28	LAFTA 29	OECD 30	CN 31	WIPO 32	NATO 33	OCAM 34	WTO 35	CFA 36	OAU 37	SPC 38
Afghanistan	●	●		●	●	●	●	●	●	●	●	●	●	●	●							●																
Albania	●	●		●							●	●	●	●	●																							
Algeria	●	●	●	●	●	●	●	●		●	●	●	●	●	●			●		●												●					●	
Argentina	●	●	●	●	●	●	●	●	●	●	●	●	●	●	●	●			●									●	●			●						
Australia	●	●	●	●	●	●	●	●	●	●	●	●	●	●	●	●						●								●	●	●						●
Austria	●	●	●	●	●	●	●	●	●	●	●	●	●	●	●	●	●										●			●		●						
Bahamas, The	●				●		●			●	●		●	●	●																●							
Bahrain	●	●			●		●			●	●	●	●	●				●																				
Bangladesh	●	●		●	●	●	●	●		●	●	●	●	●	●	●						●									●							
Barbados	●	●	●		●	●	●			●	●	●	●	●	●	●			●									●			●							
Belgium	●	●	●	●	●	●	●	●	●	●	●	●	●	●	●	●	●							●	●	●				●		●	●					
Belorussia	●			●		●	●				●	●	●	●	●																	●						
Bhutan	●												●									●																
Bolivia	●	●		●	●	●	●	●	●	●	●	●	●	●	●				●									●	●									
Botswana	●	●					●	●		●	●		●	●	●																●						●	
Brazil	●	●	●	●	●	●	●	●	●	●	●	●	●	●	●	●			●									●	●			●						
Bulgaria	●	●	●	●	●	●					●	●	●	●	●								●									●			●			
Burma	●	●	●	●	●	●	●	●	●	●	●	●	●	●	●	●						●																
Burundi	●	●			●	●	●	●		●	●	●	●	●	●	●																					●	
Cambodia	●	●	●	●	●	●	●	●		●	●	●	●	●	●							●																
Cameroon	●	●	●	●	●	●	●	●	●	●	●	●	●	●	●	●																●				●	●	
Canada	●	●	●	●	●	●	●	●	●	●	●	●	●	●	●	●						●						●		●	●	●	●					
Cape Verde Islands	●																																				●	
Central African Rep.	●	●			●	●	●	●		●	●	●	●	●	●	●																●		●		●	●	
Chad	●	●			●	●	●	●		●	●	●	●	●	●	●																●				●	●	
Chile	●	●	●	●	●	●	●	●	●	●	●	●	●	●	●	●			●									●	●			●						
China	●	●	●	●	●	●	●	●	●	●	●	●	●	●	●																							
Colombia	●	●	●	●	●	●	●	●	●	●	●	●	●	●	●				●									●	●									
Comoro Islands	●														●																						●	
Congo (Brazzaville)	●	●	●		●	●	●	●		●	●	●	●	●	●	●																●				●	●	
Costa Rica	●	●		●	●	●	●	●	●	●	●	●	●	●	●				●		●							●										
Cuba	●	●	●	●	●	●					●	●	●	●	●	●			●				●									●						
Cyprus	●	●	●	●	●	●	●	●	●	●	●	●	●	●	●	●	●														●	●						
Czechoslovakia	●	●	●	●	●	●					●	●	●	●	●	●							●									●			●			
Dahomey	●	●			●	●	●	●		●	●	●	●	●	●	●																●		●		●	●	
Denmark	●	●	●	●	●	●	●	●	●	●	●	●	●	●	●	●	●							●	●	●				●		●	●					
Dominican Rep.	●	●	●	●	●	●	●	●	●	●	●	●	●	●	●	●			●									●				●						
Ecuador	●	●	●	●	●	●	●	●	●	●	●	●	●	●	●				●	●								●	●									
Egypt	●	●	●	●	●	●	●	●	●	●	●	●	●	●	●	●		●														●					●	
El Salvador	●	●		●	●	●	●	●	●	●	●	●	●	●	●				●		●							●										
Equatorial Guinea	●		●		●		●	●		●	●		●																								●	
Ethiopia	●	●	●	●	●	●	●	●	●	●	●	●	●	●	●																						●	
Fiji	●	●			●	●	●	●		●	●		●	●								●									●	●						●
Finland	●	●	●	●	●	●	●	●	●	●	●	●	●	●	●	●														●		●						
France	●	●	●	●	●	●	●	●	●	●	●	●	●	●	●	●	●							●	●	●				●		●	●					●
Gabon	●	●		●	●	●	●	●	●	●	●	●	●	●	●	●				●												●		●		●	●	
Gambia, The	●	●					●	●		●	●	●	●	●		●															●						●	
Germany, East	●		●	●							●	●	●	●	●								●									●			●			
Germany, West	●	●	●	●	●	●	●	●	●	●	●	●	●	●	●	●	●							●	●	●				●		●	●					
Ghana	●	●	●	●	●	●	●	●	●	●	●	●	●	●	●	●															●						●	
Greece	●	●	●	●	●	●	●	●	●	●	●	●	●	●	●	●	●													●		●	●					
Grenada	●						●	●	●	●		●		●					●												●							
Guatemala	●	●		●	●	●	●	●	●	●	●	●	●	●	●				●		●							●										
Guinea	●	●			●	●	●	●		●	●	●	●	●	●																						●	
Guinea–Bissau	●	●										●	●	●	●																						●	
Guyana	●	●			●	●	●	●	●	●	●	●	●	●	●	●															●							
Haiti	●	●	●	●	●	●	●	●	●	●	●	●	●	●	●	●			●									●				●						
Honduras	●	●	●		●	●	●	●	●	●	●	●	●	●	●				●		●							●										
Hungary	●	●	●	●	●	●					●	●	●	●	●	●							●									●			●			
Iceland	●	●	●	●	●	●	●	●	●	●	●	●	●	●	●	●	●										●			●		●	●					
India	●	●	●	●	●	●	●	●	●	●	●	●	●	●	●	●						●									●	●						
Indonesia	●	●	●	●	●	●	●	●	●	●	●	●	●	●	●	●				●		●										●						
Iran	●	●	●	●	●	●	●	●	●	●	●	●	●	●	●					●		●										●						
Iraq	●	●	●	●	●	●	●	●	●	●	●	●	●	●	●			●		●																		
Ireland	●	●	●	●	●	●	●	●	●	●	●	●	●	●	●	●	●							●	●	●				●		●						
Israel	●	●	●	●	●	●	●	●	●	●	●	●	●	●	●	●																●						
Italy	●	●	●	●	●	●	●	●	●	●	●	●	●	●	●	●	●							●	●	●				●		●	●					
Ivory Coast	●	●	●	●	●	●	●	●	●	●	●	●	●	●	●	●																●		●		●	●	
Jamaica	●	●		●	●	●	●		●	●	●	●	●	●	●	●			●									●			●							
Japan	●	●	●	●	●	●	●	●	●	●	●	●	●	●	●	●						●								●		●						
Jordan	●	●	●	●	●	●	●	●	●	●	●	●	●	●	●			●														●						
Kenya	●	●	●	●	●	●	●	●	●	●	●	●	●	●	●	●															●	●					●	
Korea, North				●							●	●	●	●	●																	●						
Korea, South		●	●	●	●		●	●	●	●	●	●	●	●	●	●						●																
Kuwait	●	●	●	●	●	●	●	●	●	●	●	●	●	●	●	●		●		●																		
Laos	●	●			●	●	●	●		●	●	●	●	●	●							●																
Lebanon	●	●	●	●	●	●	●	●	●	●	●	●	●	●	●			●														●						
Lesotho	●	●			●		●	●	●	●	●	●	●	●																	●						●	
Liberia	●	●	●	●	●	●	●	●	●	●	●	●	●	●	●																						●	
Libya	●	●	●	●	●	●	●	●	●	●	●	●	●	●	●			●		●																	●	
Liechtenstein				●							●		●																			●						
Luxembourg	●	●		●	●	●	●	●	●	●	●	●	●	●	●	●	●							●	●	●				●		●	●					
Malagasy Rep.	●	●	●	●	●	●	●	●	●	●	●	●	●	●	●	●																●				●	●	
Malawi	●	●			●	●	●	●	●	●	●	●	●	●	●	●															●	●					●	

Membership in International Organizations, December 1, 1975 (*Continued*)

Country	UN 1	FAO 2	IMCO 3	IAEA 4	ICAO 5	ILO 6	IBRD 7	IDA 8	IFC 9	IMF 10	ITU 11	UNESCO 12	UPU 13	WHO 14	WMO* 15	GATT 16	CE 17	LAS 18	OAS 19	OPEC 20	OCAS 21	C-Plan 22	Comecon 23	Euratom 24	ECSC 25	EEC 26	EFTA 27	IDB 28	LAFTA 29	OECD 30	CN 31	WIPO 32	NATO 33	OCAM 34	WTO 35	CFA 36	OAU 37	SPC 38
Malaysia	●	●	●	●	●	●	●	●	●	●	●	●	●	●	●	●						●									●							
Maldives	●	●	●								●		●	●								●																
Mali	●	●		●	●	●	●	●		●	●	●	●	●	●																	●				●	●	
Malta	●	●	●		●	●				●	●	●	●	●		●	●														●	●						
Mauritania	●	●	●		●	●	●	●	●	●	●	●	●	●	●	●		●														●				●	●	
Mauritius	●	●		●	●	●	●	●	●	●	●	●	●	●	●	●															●			●			●	
Mexico	●	●	●	●	●	●	●	●	●	●	●	●	●	●	●				●									●	●			●						
Monaco				●							●	●	●	●																		●						
Mongolia	●	●		●		●					●	●	●	●	●								●															
Morocco	●	●	●	●	●	●	●	●	●	●	●	●	●	●	●			●														●					●	
Mozambique	●													●	●																●						●	
Nauru					●						●		●																									●
Nepal	●	●			●	●	●	●	●	●	●	●	●	●	●							●																
Netherlands, The	●	●	●	●	●	●	●	●	●	●	●	●	●	●	●	●	●							●	●	●				●		●	●					
New Zealand	●	●	●	●	●	●	●	●	●	●	●	●	●	●	●	●						●								●	●	●						●
Nicaragua	●	●			●	●	●	●	●	●	●	●	●	●	●	●			●		●							●										
Niger	●	●		●	●	●	●	●		●	●	●	●	●	●	●																●		●		●	●	
Nigeria	●	●	●	●	●	●	●	●	●	●	●	●	●	●	●	●				●											●	●					●	
Norway	●	●	●	●	●	●	●	●	●	●	●	●	●	●	●	●	●										●			●		●	●					
Oman	●	●	●		●		●	●	●	●	●	●	●	●	●			●																				
Pakistan	●	●	●	●	●	●	●	●	●	●	●	●	●	●	●	●						●										●						
Panama	●	●	●	●	●	●	●	●	●	●	●	●	●	●	●				●									●										
Papua New Guinea	●						●	●	●	●												●									●							
Paraguay	●	●		●	●	●	●	●	●	●	●	●	●	●	●				●									●	●									
Peru	●	●	●	●	●	●	●	●	●	●	●	●	●	●	●	●			●									●	●									
Philippines	●	●	●	●	●	●	●	●	●	●	●	●	●	●	●	●						●										●						
Poland	●	●	●	●	●	●					●	●	●	●	●	●							●									●			●			
Portugal	●	●		●	●	●	●		●	●	●	●	●	●	●	●											●			●		●	●					
Qatar	●	●			●	●	●			●	●	●	●	●	●			●		●																		
Rhodesia											●				●	●																						
Romania	●	●	●	●	●	●	●			●	●	●	●	●	●	●							●									●			●			
Rwanda	●	●			●	●	●	●		●	●	●	●	●	●	●																		●			●	
San Marino												●	●																			●						
São Tomé and Príncipe	●																																				●	
Saudi Arabia	●	●	●	●	●		●	●	●	●	●	●	●	●	●			●		●																		
Senegal	●	●	●	●	●	●	●	●	●	●	●	●	●	●	●	●																●		●		●	●	
Sierra Leone	●	●	●	●	●	●	●	●	●	●	●	●	●	●	●	●															●						●	
Singapore	●		●	●	●	●	●		●	●	●	●	●	●	●	●						●									●							
Somalia	●	●			●	●	●	●	●	●	●	●	●	●	●			●																			●	
South Africa	●			●	●		●	●	●	●	●		●	●	●	●																●						
Spain	●	●	●	●	●	●	●	●	●	●	●	●	●	●	●	●														●		●						
Sri Lanka (Ceylon)	●	●	●	●	●	●	●	●	●	●	●	●	●	●	●	●						●									●	●						
Sudan, The	●	●	●	●	●	●	●	●	●	●	●	●	●	●	●			●														●					●	
Swaziland	●	●			●	●	●	●	●	●	●		●	●																	●						●	
Sweden	●	●	●	●	●	●	●	●	●	●	●	●	●	●	●	●	●										●			●		●						
Switzerland		●	●	●	●	●					●	●	●	●	●	●	●										●			●		●						
Syria	●	●	●	●	●	●	●	●	●	●	●	●	●	●	●			●														●						
Taiwan							●	●	●	●																												
Tanzania	●	●	●		●	●	●	●	●	●	●	●	●	●	●	●															●	●					●	
Thailand	●	●	●	●	●	●	●	●	●	●	●	●	●	●	●							●										●						
Togo	●	●			●	●	●	●	●	●	●	●	●	●	●	●																●		●		●	●	
Tonga											●		●	●																	●							
Trinidad and Tobago	●	●	●		●	●	●	●	●	●	●	●	●	●	●	●			●									●			●	●						
Tunisia	●	●	●	●	●	●	●	●	●	●	●	●	●	●	●	●		●														●					●	
Turkey	●	●	●	●	●	●	●	●	●	●	●	●	●	●	●	●	●													●		●	●					
Uganda	●	●	●	●	●	●	●	●	●	●	●	●	●	●	●	●															●	●					●	
Ukraine	●			●		●					●	●	●	●	●																	●						
United Arab Emirates	●	●			●	●	●			●	●	●	●	●				●		●												●						
United Kingdom	●	●	●	●	●	●	●	●	●	●	●	●	●	●	●	●	●					●		●	●	●				●	●	●	●					●
United States	●	●	●	●	●	●	●	●	●	●	●	●	●	●	●	●			●			●						●		●		●	●					●
Upper Volta	●	●			●	●	●	●	●	●	●	●	●	●	●	●																●		●		●	●	
Uruguay	●	●	●	●	●	●	●		●	●	●	●	●	●	●	●			●									●	●			●						
U.S.S.R.	●		●	●	●	●					●	●	●	●	●								●									●			●			
Vatican City				●							●		●																			●						
Venezuela	●	●		●	●	●	●		●	●	●	●	●	●	●				●	●								●	●									
Vietnam, South		●		●	●	●	●	●	●	●	●	●	●	●	●							●										●						
Western Samoa							●	●	●	●				●																	●							●
Yemen (Aden)	●	●			●	●	●	●		●	●	●	●	●	●			●																				
Yemen (San'a')	●	●			●	●	●	●	●	●	●	●	●	●	●			●																				
Yugoslavia	●	●	●	●	●	●	●	●	●	●	●	●	●	●	●	●																●						
Zaire	●	●	●	●	●	●	●	●	●	●	●	●	●	●	●	●																●					●	
Zambia	●	●		●	●		●	●	●	●	●	●	●	●	●																●	●					●	

*Includes members not shown: Afars and Issas, Angola, British Caribbean Dependencies, Hong Kong, New Caledonia, French Polynesia, Netherlands Antilles, Saint Pierre and Miquelon, and Surinam.

1 United Nations.
2 Food and Agriculture Organization of the United Nations.
3 Intergovernmental Maritime Consultative Organization.
4 International Atomic Energy Agency.
5 International Civil Aviation Organization.
6 International Labour Organization.
7 International Bank for Reconstruction and Development.
8 International Development Association.
9 International Finance Corporation.
10 International Monetary Fund.
11 International Telecommunication Union.
12 United Nations Educational, Scientific, and Cultural Organization.
13 Universal Postal Union.
14 World Health Organization.
15 World Meteorological Organization.
16 General Agreement on Tariffs and Trade.
17 Council of Europe.
18 League of Arab States (Arab League).
19 Organization of American States.
20 Organization of Petroleum Exporting Countries.
21 Organization of Central American States.
22 Colombo Plan for Co-operative Economic Development in South and South-East Asia.
23 Council for Mutual Economic Assistance.
24 European Atomic Energy Community.
25 European Coal and Steel Community.
26 European Economic Community.
27 European Free Trade Association.
28 Inter-American Development Bank.
29 Latin American Free Trade Association.
30 Organization for Economic Cooperation and Development.
31 Commonwealth of Nations.
32 World Intellectual Property Organization.
33 North Atlantic Treaty Organization.
34 Common African and Mauritian Organization.
35 Warsaw Treaty Organization.
36 African Financial Community.
37 Organization of African Unity.
38 South Pacific Commission.

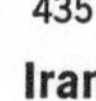

Iran

A constitutional monarchy of western Asia, Iran is bounded by the U.S.S.R., Afghanistan, Pakistan, Iraq, and Turkey and the Caspian Sea, the Arabian Sea, and the Persian Gulf. Area: 636,000 sq.mi. (1,648,000 sq.km.). Pop. (1975 est.): 32,923,000. Cap. and largest city: Teheran (pop., 1974 est., 3,931,000). Language: Farsi Persian. Religion (1972 est.): Muslim 98%; Christian, Jewish, and Zoroastrian minorities. Shah-in-shah, Mohammad Reza Pahlavi Aryamehr; prime minister in 1975, Emir Abbas Hoveida.

The remarkable economic and social progress of Iran, resulting from the systematic employment of oil revenues in the promotion of national development, continued throughout 1975. The shah, with the avowed purpose of enlisting the masses in support of his far-reaching plans, announced in a decree of March 2 that the two-party system would be abolished and that all men of good will in Iran should join a new national party, the Rastakhiz ("National Resurrection"). Among the purposes of the new party, of which the prime minister, Emir Abbas Hoveida, was secretary-general, would be a great extension of worker participation in both public and private industrial enterprises, the only exceptions being certain entirely state-owned key industries.

WIDE WORLD

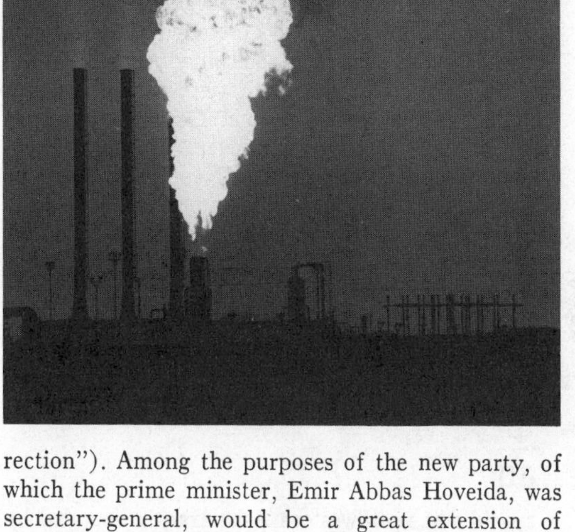

A gas burnoff at the Abvaz oil field symbolizes the petroleum-derived wealth that is transforming Iran.

IRAN

Education. (1972–73) Primary, pupils 3,445,528, teachers 111,032; secondary, pupils 942,523, teachers 27,085; vocational, pupils 56,745, teachers 2,817; teacher training, students 26,058, teachers 635; higher (including 8 universities), students 115,311, teaching staff 4,128.

Finance. Monetary unit: rial, with (Sept. 22, 1975) a free rate of 67.92 rials to U.S. $1 (140.70 rials = £1 sterling). Gold, SDRs, and foreign exchange: (June 1975) U.S. $9,015,000,000; (June 1974) U.S. $5,439,000,000. Budget (1973–74 actual): revenue 774,333,000,000 rials; expenditure 731,752,000,000 rials. Gross domestic product: (1973–74) 2,033,200,000,000 rials; (1972–73) 1,298,600,000,000 rials. Money supply: (Feb. 1975) 386,850,000,000 rials; (Feb. 1974) 289,060,000,000 rials. Cost of living (1970 = 100): (April 1975) 163; (April 1974) 136.

Foreign Trade. (1974) Imports 383.6 billion rials; exports 1,623,000,000,000 rials. Import sources (1973): West Germany 19%; Japan 14%; U.S. 14%; U.K. 10%; U.S.S.R. 5%; France 5%. Export destinations (1973): Japan *c.* 28%; West Germany *c.* 9%; U.K. *c.* 9%; The Netherlands *c.* 8%; Italy *c.* 7%; U.S. *c.* 6%; France *c.* 5%. Main export crude oil 96%. Tourism (1973): visitors 403,000; gross receipts U.S. $91 million.

Transport and Communications. Roads (1972) 43,442 km. Motor vehicles in use (1972): passenger 393,900; commercial (including buses) 87,600. Railways: (1972) 4,560 km.; traffic (1973) 2,144,000,000 passenger-km., freight 4,432,000,000 net ton-km. Air traffic (1973): 1,125,000,000 passenger-km.; freight 15.6 million net ton-km. Shipping (1974): merchant vessels 100 gross tons and over 115; gross tonnage 291,928. Telephones (Jan. 1974) 552,000. Radio receivers (Dec. 1973) *c.* 8 million. Television receivers (Dec. 1973) *c.* 1.7 million.

Agriculture. Production (in 000; metric tons; 1974; 1973 in parentheses): wheat 4,100 (4,600); barley 826 (923); rice 1,357 (1,333); sugar, raw value *c.* 710 (*c.* 700); onions *c.* 310 (306); tomatoes *c.* 220 (*c.* 200); watermelons (1973) *c.* 820, (1972) *c.* 800; melons (1973) *c.* 370, (1972) *c.* 350; dates (1973) *c.* 300, (1972) *c.* 320; grapes (1973) *c.* 671, (1972) 655; sunflower seed *c.* 44 (*c.* 47); tea *c.* 24 (23); tobacco *c.* 19 (16); cotton, lint *c.* 220 (*c.* 201). Livestock (in 000; Oct. 1973): cattle *c.* 5,760; sheep *c.* 38,000; goats (1972) *c.* 14,700; horses *c.* 380; asses (1972) *c.* 2,070; chickens (1972) *c.* 31,556.

Industry. Production (in 000; metric tons; 1974): crude oil 300,863; petroleum products (1973) 27,588; natural gas (cu.m.) 22,297,000; cement (1973) 3,489; coal (1973) 1,050; lead concentrates (metal content; 1973) *c.* 30; chrome ore (oxide content; 1973–74) 86; electricity (excluding most industrial production; kw-hr.; 1973–74) 12,093,000.

The constitution and aims of the new party were approved in May by a conference attended by more than 4,000 delegates, and elections for the Chamber of Deputies (268 seats) and for the 30 elected seats in the Senate were held on June 20. The electorate was invited to choose between three candidates selected by the Rastakhiz for each seat. It was estimated that some 52% of the electorate duly cast their votes, with Teheran showing the highest turnout at 70%. The success of the shah's plan to enlist "new blood" in the parliamentary machine was demonstrated by the fact that some 80% of the deputies entered the Chamber for the first time.

As in 1974, Iran repudiated the use of oil supplies as a political weapon. Rather, it preferred to employ its new resources to secure, on advantageous terms, the industrial and technical know-how that it needed to obtain from the West and to acquire a stake in a number of leading industrial enterprises in Europe and elsewhere. In an effort to ensure that this dual process was not unduly slowed by the alarming rate of inflation in Western countries, Iran pressed for and obtained a further increase in the price of oil at the meeting of the Organization of Petroleum Exporting Countries in Vienna in September.

Cooperation with France, the U.S., Great Britain, and West Germany along the lines laid down in 1974 proceeded smoothly. Perhaps the clearest indication of Iran's new economic strength and political influence in western Asia was a far-reaching agreement with the Soviet Union in February, under which,

Investment:
see Economy, World; Stock Exchanges

among other projects, Iran provided the financing for a new paper mill in the U.S.S.R. and the Soviet Union undertook to pay an increase of 85% in the price of natural gas supplied by Iran from the enormous new field at Kangan on the Persian Gulf. Both the aims and scope of Iran's current five-year plan were greatly extended, and in spite of heavy investment expenditure at home and abroad, current reserves rose from the rial equivalent of U.S. $1,237,000,000 to $8,383,000,000. The previous link between the rial and the U.S. dollar was superseded in February 1975 by links between the rial and the International Monetary Fund's Special Drawing Rights.

Iran was liberal in using its economic and political strength to assist less fortunate nations, including Pakistan and Turkey, its partners in the long-standing Regional Cooperation for Development scheme. A number of new projects were begun in both countries, and credits also were granted to a number of Muslim states, among them the United Arab Emirates. One of the most significant developments in Iran's foreign relations was a formal reconciliation with Iraq, concluded in June after several months of careful negotiations in which the UN played a part. In order to gain Iran's goodwill—important to Iraq in the final stages of the suppression of the Kurdish insurrection—the Baghdad government made a number of concessions, territorial and otherwise, on Iranian claims that until then had been stoutly resisted. (*See* IRAQ.) (L. F. RUSHBROOK WILLIAMS)

[978.C.1]

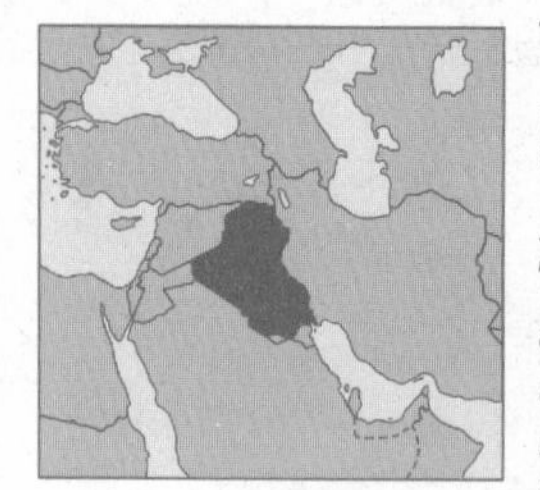

Iraq

A republic of southwestern Asia, Iraq is bounded by Turkey, Iran, Kuwait, Saudi Arabia, Jordan, Syria, and the Persian Gulf. Area: 168,928 sq.mi. (437,522 sq.km.). Pop. (1975 est.): 11,124,300, including Arabs, Kurds, Turks, Assyrians, Iranians, and others. Cap. and largest city: Baghdad (pop., 1974 est., 2,800,000). Language: Arabic. Religion: mainly Muslim, some Christian. President in 1975, Gen. Ahmad Hassan al-Bakr.

Iraq's national and international position underwent important changes in 1975 as a result of the agreement with Iran in March, formalized in June, which settled border differences and led to the collapse of the year-old Kurdish rebellion. However, Iraq remained fairly isolated in the Arab world.

In the early part of the year relations with Iran were bad; several border clashes were reported, and Iraq moved troops to the frontier. The Iraqi foreign minister's talks in Istanbul, Turkey, in January were inconclusive. The war against the Kurdish rebels led by Mulla Mustafa al-Barzani intensified in February; both sides claimed successes, but the Kurds were heavily dependent on Iranian support for supplies and for artillery protection of their mountain refuges from across the border.

The situation was transformed as a result of the agreement reached between the shah of Iran and the Iraqi strong man, Vice-Pres. Saddam Takriti, at the summit meeting of the Organization of Petroleum Exporting Countries in Algiers in March. Through Algerian mediation, both sides decided to settle all their border disputes, notably in the Shatt al-Arab waterway. The new boundary was fixed on the thalweg, or median line of maximum depth; under the 1937 agreement, which Iran had previously denounced, it had been on the Iranian bank. In return for this major Iraqi concession, Iran withdrew support for Barzani's rebellion.

Without Iran's assistance, the Kurdish rebels' position became hopeless. The Iraqi Army launched a major offensive on March 7, and on March 13, after Barzani's military commanders had told him the struggle could not be continued, a cease-fire was announced. The Iraqi government offered the Kurdish fighters a choice between refuge in Iran and surrender. An amnesty for the rebels, to last until April 1, was later extended. There were conflicting reports of subsequent Iraqi treatment of the Kurds. Foreign observers generally agreed that there were no mass reprisals and that substantial sums were being devoted to the revival of war-ravaged areas, but some executions and forced resettlement of Kurds outside Kurdish majority areas were also reported. It was alleged that Egyptian peasants invited into Iraq under an agreement with Egypt would be settled in Kurdish areas. The Iraqi Army's casualty figures for the year of Kurdish war were 1,640 killed and 7,903 wounded, but the Kurds claimed the real figures were several times higher.

Throughout the year Iraq remained a firm member of the Arab "rejection front" in its attitude toward a settlement with Israel. Iraq denounced the Sinai troop disengagement agreement between Israel and Egypt in September, but its strongest criticisms were re-

IRAQ

Education. (1974–75) Primary, pupils 1,523,955, teachers 57,621; secondary, pupils 457,763, teachers 16,862; vocational, pupils 21,033, teachers 1,508; teacher training, students 8,539, teachers 306; higher, students 70,247, teaching staff 2,440.

Finance. Monetary unit: Iraqi dinar, with (Sept. 22, 1975) an official rate of 0.296 dinar to U.S. $1 (free rate of 0.612 dinar to £1 sterling). Gold, SDRs, and foreign exchange: (June 1975) U.S. $2,560,200,000; (June 1974) U.S. $2,845,300,000. Budget (1973–74 est.): revenue 592.6 million dinars; expenditure 820,190,000 dinars (including development expenditure of 310 million dinars). Gross national product: (1971) 1,268,700,000 dinars; (1970) 1,121,600,000 dinars. Money supply: (Feb. 1975) 495.2 million dinars; (Feb. 1974) 329.7 million dinars. Cost of living (Baghdad; 1970 = 100): (June 1975) 135; (June 1974) 121.

Foreign Trade. Imports (1973) 270.3 million dinars; exports (1974) 2,382,600,000 dinars. Import sources: U.S.S.R. 9%; U.K. 9%; France 8%; Japan 7%; Brazil 6%; U.S. 6%; Czechoslovakia 6%. Export destinations (1973): Italy *c.* 25%; France *c.* 23%; Brazil *c.* 10%; U.S.S.R. *c.* 6%. Main export crude oil 96%. Tourism (1973): visitors 488,000; gross receipts U.S. $77 million.

Transport and Communications. Roads (1973) 10,824 km. Motor vehicles in use (1973): passenger 77,317; commercial 34,336. Railways: (1971) 2,528 km.; traffic (1972–73) 604 million passenger-km., freight (1971–72) 1,514,000,000 net ton-km. Air traffic (1974): 387.9 million passenger-km.; freight 5,765,000 net ton-km. Shipping (1974): merchant vessels 100 gross tons and over 49; gross tonnage 229,603. Telephones (Jan. 1974) 129,000. Radio receivers (Dec. 1971) 1,072,000. Television receivers (Dec. 1972) 520,000.

Agriculture. Production (in 000; metric tons; 1974; 1973 in parentheses): wheat 1,339 (*c.* 957); barley 533 (462); rice *c.* 200 (157); aubergines (1973) *c.* 130, (1972) 132; watermelons (1973) *c.* 550, (1972) 519; melons (1973) *c.* 160, (1972) 145; tomatoes *c.* 167 (165); dates (1973) *c.* 400, (1972) *c.* 350; sesame *c.* 14 (*c.* 6); tobacco *c.* 10 (*c.* 9); cotton, lint (1973) *c.* 15, (1972) 16. Livestock (in 000; 1974): sheep *c.* 15,500; goats (1973) *c.* 2,561; cattle 2,059; buffalo *c.* 300; camels (1973) *c.* 311; horses (1973) *c.* 128; asses *c.* 600.

Industry. Production (in 000; metric tons): cement (1971) 1,856; crude oil (1974) 91,216; petroleum products (1973) 4,313; electricity (excluding most industrial production; kw-hr.; 1972) 2,358,000.

served for the rival Baathist regime in Syria, which it accused of deviousness as compared with Egypt's frankness about its decision to reach a new interim agreement with Israel. Iraq offered to revive the northern front against Israel, but only on condition that Syria repudiate UN Security Council resolutions 242 and 338, which implied recognition of Israel. Iraqi-Syrian relations were exacerbated by the dispute over the Euphrates waters, which flared up in March and continued throughout the summer despite attempts at mediation by the Arab League and Saudi Arabia. Iraq accused Syria of taking nearly twice the share of Euphrates water proposed for it in a World Bank report and claimed that 70% of the winter crop in the Euphrates basin had been lost as a result.

Iraq's oil output was reduced by about one-third in the early part of the year as a result of world oversupply, and the government announced that future production would be geared to the country's needs. Revenues continued to rise steadily, however, and the budget announced for the last nine months of 1975 was 700 million dinars above that for the whole of 1974. The sum of 1,076,000,000 dinars was devoted to development. Allocations for agriculture under the third five-year plan totaled 3 billion dinars, or ten times as much as in the previous five-year plan. An agreement signed with the U.S.S.R. in May provided for Soviet engineers to build a 1.5 million-ton-capacity iron and steel complex at Basrah. In December the government completed nationalization of the oil industry by taking over the remaining shares of the Basrah Petroleum Company. (PETER MANSFIELD)

[978.B.3.c]

Ireland

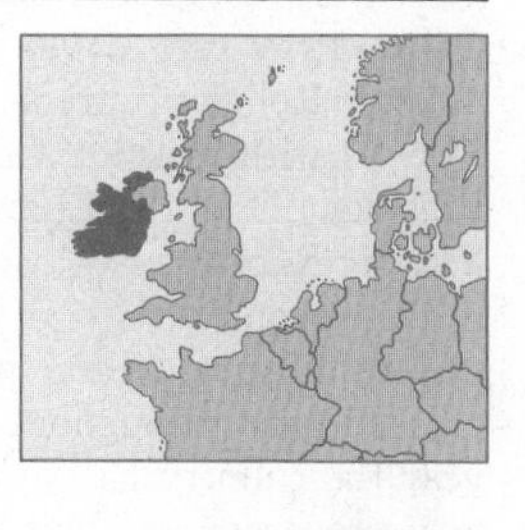

Separated from Great Britain by the North Channel, the Irish Sea, and St. George's Channel, the Republic of Ireland shares its island with Northern Ireland to the northeast. Area: 27,136 sq.mi. (70,283 sq.km.), or 83% of the island. Pop. (1974 est.): 3,086,000. Cap. and largest city: Dublin (pop., 1971, 567,900). Language (1971): non-Irish, mostly English (72%), and Irish (28%). Religion: predominantly Roman Catholic (95%). President in 1975, Carroll O'Daly; prime minister, Liam Cosgrave.

In the face of a 30% increase in gasoline and oil prices at the end of 1974 and a steep rise in unemployment from 80,000 to more than 100,000 over the Christmas period, the main concern of the government during early 1975 was the economy. This was emphasized by the fact that the budget date was shifted, for the first time, from the traditional one in the spring to January, and there was an early start to Parliament with the introduction of the coalition's third budget since it assumed power in March 1973.

The budget was judged to be a set of moderate proposals, including further social welfare increases, some incentives to industry, the blocking of taxation loopholes, and an increase in the duty on certain luxury items. It was not by any means the sort of hairshirt collection of measures that speeches by the prime minister and the minister for finance, Richie Ryan, had led the country to expect. But it was not the only budget of the year. A second was introduced on June 26 in response to the continuing effect of the international economic crisis, the high inflation rate of approximately 24% in the republic, and the seeming intransigence of labour. The unions were demanding the strict observance by government and employers of what was regarded as an overgenerous national wages agreement giving workers across-the-board increases in excess of 30% during a one-year period.

The combination of high inflation, falling international markets for increasingly expensive Irish goods, and unbending demands for wages to keep pace with prices dominated almost all government action between the two budgets and continued on into the late summer. At that point a modest renegotiation of the national wages agreement, combined with the beneficial effects of measures in the second budget aimed at bringing down the consumer price index, produced a slight easing of the crisis. In one month, September, the consumer price index actually went down by 0.8%, the first such decline in a decade. Unfortunately, it was widely expected that the measures taken during midsummer to relieve the crisis would be neutralized in the autumn when further price increases and wage demands would become inevitable. Unemployment, after the steep rise early in the year, remained level at around 103,000. Any worsening of this after June was partly offset by the introduction, in the budget of that month, of special employment premiums paid for the reemployment of laid-off workers in manufacturing industries and part-time labour.

It was fortunate for the coalition government, under continual pressure from an economic crisis that the prime minister described as the "gravest in the country's history," that it was not as hard-pressed as it had been in the previous year by the situation in Northern Ireland. It became strict government policy during 1975 to make no gestures of help or interference in the direction of the Northern Ireland politicians or the constitutional convention.

At the same time, a security drive, undertaken at

Eamon de Valera, former president of the Republic of Ireland, was laid to rest in the family plot in Glasnevin Cemetery on September 2.

LENSMEN PRESS PHOTO AGENCY/KEYSTONE

the beginning of the year, resulted in several notable successes. The first was the arrest of a leading Provisional Irish Republican Army (IRA) escapee, Kevin Mallon, who was recaptured on January 8 in a suburb of Dublin and was sentenced in April to ten years' penal servitude. In the same month a hunger strike began in the main prison in the republic, at Portlaoise, where Provisional IRA prisoners sought segregation from nonpolitical prisoners. On February 5 the justice minister revealed that the lives of two members of the Cabinet had been threatened, and on February 7 explosives were discovered in the same prison. The combination of these events reduced sympathy for the prisoners' case, and after considerable negotiation the hunger strike came to an end. The following month saw a major breakout attempt from Portlaoise. It was foiled by the military guards, although one prisoner was killed by a ricocheting bullet. In July David O'Connell, the most wanted of all Provisional leaders, was arrested in Dublin and sentenced to one year in prison for membership in the IRA.

In October the most serious threat to security in the state emerged with the kidnapping of a Dutch industrialist, Tiede Herrema, and the threat that he would be killed unless Bridget Rose Dugdale and two other IRA prisoners were released. The government's reaction was an absolute and unbending refusal, and this was supported by the Fianna Fail opposition party. On October 18 the police captured two men in a car associated with the kidnapping, and this led to the location of the Dutch industrialist with two of his captors, Eddie Gallagher and Marion Coyle, in a council house in the midland town of Monasterevin. A siege of the house, aimed at wearing down the resistance of the two kidnappers, was carried out by the police and terminated in surrender and the release of Herrema on November 7. A further security success was also recorded in October, when three people were arrested in connection with the murder of a policeman in Dublin a month before.

On August 29 Eamon de Valera (*see* OBITUARIES), former prime minister and president of Ireland, died at the age of 92. His wife, Sinead, had died less than eight months before him, in January, at the age of 96. One of the leaders of the 1916 Easter Rising, and the last to survive, Eamon de Valera had played a major part in founding and shaping the Irish state. He was prime minister in 1932–48, 1951–54, and 1957–59 and president for the 14 years that followed.

(BRUCE ARNOLD)

See also United Kingdom.
[972.A.1.b.i]

IRELAND

Education. (1973–74) Primary, pupils 545,439, teachers 16,973; secondary, pupils 237,740, teachers 9,904; vocational, pupils 3,939, teachers 216; higher, students 29,641, teaching staff 1,455.

Finance. Monetary unit: Irish pound, at par with the pound sterling, with a free rate (Sept. 22, 1975) of U.S. $2.07 = £1. Gold, SDRs, and foreign exchange: (June 1975) U.S. $1,284,000,000; (June 1974) U.S. $916 million. Budget (1973–74 rev. est.): revenue £793 million; expenditure £803 million. Gross national product: (1974) £2,881 million; (1973) £2,675 million. Money supply: (May 1975) £629.6 million; (May 1974) £541.6 million. Cost of living (1970 = 100): (May 1975) 188; (May 1974) 151.

Foreign Trade. (1974) Imports £1,620.9 million; exports £1,123 million. Import sources: U.K. 46%; West Germany 8%; U.S. 6%; France 5%. Export destinations: U.K. 56%; U.S. 9%; West Germany 6%. Main exports: meat 16%; chemicals 9%; machinery 9%; textiles 8%; dairy products 8%; livestock 6%. Tourism: visitors (1973) 1,619,000; gross receipts (1972) U.S. $176 million.

Transport and Communications. Roads (1972) 88,180 km. Motor vehicles in use (1973): passenger 476,721; commercial 49,040. Railways (1973): 2,189 km.; traffic 868 million passenger-km., freight (1974) 572.8 million net ton-km. Air traffic (1974): 1,648,200,000 passenger-km.; freight 89,625,000 net ton-km. Shipping (1974): merchant vessels 100 gross tons and over 88; gross tonnage 208,700. Telephones (Dec. 1973) 366,000. Radio licenses (Dec. 1971) 615,000. Television licenses (Dec. 1973) 532,000.

Agriculture. Production (in 000; metric tons; 1974; 1973 in parentheses): potatoes *c.* 1,160 (1,332); wheat 208 (229); oats 125 (162); barley (1973) *c.* 843, (1972) 981; sugar, raw value *c.* 147 (*c.* 193); milk *c.* 4,180 (*c.* 4,129); butter *c.* 72 (*c.* 87); cheese *c.* 58 (42); beef and veal (1973) *c.* 300, (1972) *c.* 318; pork (1973) *c.* 143, (1972) *c.* 159; fish catch (1974) 85, (1973) 86. Livestock (in 000; June 1974): cattle 7,270; sheep 3,999; pigs 935; horses 94; chickens 10,232.

Industry. Index of production (1970 = 100): (1974) 124; (1973) 120. Production (in 000; metric tons; 1973): coal 62; cement 1,680; petroleum products *c.* 2,610; electricity (kw-hr.; 1973–74) 7,348,000; manufactured gas (cu.m.) 270,000; beer (hl.; 1970–71) 4,155; wool fabrics (sq.m.; 1972) 5,000; rayon, etc., fabrics (sq.m.; 1972) 7,300.

Ireland, Northern: *see* United Kingdom

Iron and Steel: *see* Industrial Review; Mining and Quarrying

Islam: *see* Religion

Israel

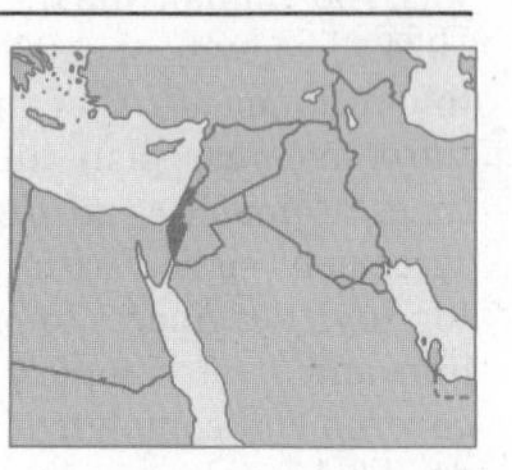

A republic of the Middle East, Israel is bounded by Lebanon, Syria, Jordan, Egypt, and the Mediterranean Sea. Area (not including territory occupied in the June 1967 war): 7,992 sq.mi. (20,700 sq.km.). Pop. (1975 est.): 3,450,000. Cap.: Jerusalem (pop., 1974 est., 344,200). Largest city: Tel Aviv-Yafo (pop., 1974 est., 357,600). Language: Hebrew and Arabic. Religion: predominantly Jewish (1975 est., 84.6%) with Muslim, Christian, and other minorities. President in 1975, Ephraim Katzir; prime minister, Yitzhak Rabin.

The reconstruction of Israel's military equilibrium and confidence, begun in 1974, continued at an increased pace throughout 1975, and by the end of the year the country had achieved a high degree of military preparedness. This applied as much to doctrine, which had been radically reassessed, as to armament, which had been improved and increased. The standing army and the total of potential reserves available for immediate call-up had also been enlarged.

Essentially, however, 1975 was the year for reassessing Israel's special relationship with the U.S. This issue dominated all else—even the critical state of the economy. It went much further than the parallel reassessment of U.S. policy in the Middle East, which remained unformulated at the end of the year, nine months after it had been set in motion. The year was also marked by Israel's critical confrontation with the UN, as represented by its third world majority in the General Assembly and in the specialized agencies. This reached a climax in the three hostile votes of November 10, which lent the support of the UN General Assembly to the unspecified demands of the Palestinians and to the claim of the Palestine Liberation Organization (PLO) to be represented in all negotiations with Israel, including the Geneva conference on peace in the Middle East, and which branded Zionism and, by implication, Israel as "racist." (*See* RACE RELATIONS). However, Israel's relationship with the U.S., particularly the areas of defense, diplomacy, and economy, remained central to this issue as to all others.

Israel had satisfied the Americans that a strong, self-reliant Israel Defense Force (IDF) was a factor for peace and stability in the Middle East. The supply of U.S. equipment and arms, suspended in April and May during the initial period of the reassessment of Middle East policy in Washington, was resumed and proceeded on schedule. On October 30 Pres. Gerald Ford indicated that the U.S. administration's purpose was "to provide Israel with the assistance needed to maintain security and to persevere in the negotiating process." To this end, the president proposed that Congress approve $740 million in security-supporting assistance and $1.5 billion in military credits.

The defense relationship was accompanied by a parallel forward movement in the diplomacy of peacemaking. U.S. Secretary of State Henry Kissinger's negotiations in Cairo and Jerusalem during February and March came to an abrupt halt on March 22, when Kissinger decided to return to Washington with the mission unfinished. There was some recrimination between the U.S. administration and the Israel government about the causes of the breakdown, followed by the suspension of U.S. arms deliveries to Israel and by some weeks of diplomatic tension. The differences were resolved by the late summer, however, and Kissinger completed his negotiations for a second Egyptian-Israeli disengagement agreement, which was reached on September 1. The agreement stipulated that the conflict between Egypt and Israel "shall not be resolved by military force but by peaceful means" (art. 1); that they would "not resort to the threat or use of force or military blockade against each other" (art. 2); and that "they are determined to reach a just and final peace settlement by means of negotiations" (art. 1). It set out the details of the new military position in the Sinai Peninsula and the extent of the Israeli withdrawal to the eastern entrances of the Giddi and Mitla passes and from the Abu Rudays oil fields. (*See* Middle Eastern Affairs.)

Thus, an acceptable new version of the special relationship with the U.S. had been established in the areas of defense and diplomacy, but the question of Israel's economic viability remained unsettled. The foreign debt had risen to $7.5 billion and was still increasing. The balance of payments deficit for 1975 was estimated at $3.5 billion and was expected to increase to $4.1 billion in 1976. The cost of "defense consumption" in 1975 was put at I£23,500 million, and this was scheduled to increase by 54% in 1976 to I£36,000 million. But it was not the actual finance that caused concern so much as the entire conduct of Israel's economic and financial affairs. A number of major scandals involving public and semipublic corporations had shaken public confidence. The reports of the state controller concerning the high-spending government departments and such bodies as the Israel Aircraft Industries were far from reassuring.

In a sense, these three areas of sensitive relations with the U.S. were reflected in Israel's domestic affairs. Almost every step taken at home had to be considered in terms of its repercussions abroad—especially in Washington. This was particularly evident in the standing of the prime minister, Yitzhak Rabin. He made an uncertain start at the beginning of the year when his old friend and colleague Aharon Yariv, the former chief of military intelligence whom he had appointed as minister of information, resigned from the government. Yariv cited shortcomings in the conduct of affairs by the Cabinet and its attitude toward the Palestinian question as reasons for his withdrawal.

CAMERA PRESS/PHOTO TRENDS

Golda Meir, former prime minister of Israel, received the Israel Prize in April for her services to the state.

In the Knesset (Parliament), the government had a dubious majority estimated variously at one or three votes over the combined opposition.

All this changed dramatically when Rabin refused to accept Egyptian conditions for the disengagement that Kissinger had been negotiating throughout February and March. Rabin's majority in Parliament, his popularity in the country, and his political standing generally were greatly enhanced by his firmness. And though there was criticism when Rabin concluded the agreement on September 1, there was no doubt that he had obtained a better agreement, militarily and politically, in September than he would have in March. His personal position was thus greatly strengthened, despite the brittle nature of the government coalition. The Cabinet was noticeably dominated by the prime minister and by the defense minister, Shimon Peres. The two men did not always agree, but they had succeeded in working together—especially on the major issues of reconstructing the defense forces and doctrine and of relations with the U.S.

The uncertain state of the economy remained a negative factor. The government had succeeded in slowing the high rate of inflation—some 56% during 1974—to rather less than half that during the first six months of 1975, but unemployment was increasing and had reached the possibly underestimated official level of 3½% by late summer. There was also a measurable slowdown of the economy, and the target of a 3% increase in gross national product for 1975, stipulated in the budget, had not been reached halfway through the year. The economic difficulties, to a large extent a reflection of world conditions, had severe domestic repercussions. The combination of inflation and unemployment caused serious labour problems. The government's attempts to eliminate featherbedding by privileged segments of organized labour met with opposition from some quarters and led to a number of crippling wildcat strikes.

More serious in some respects was the effect of the faltering economy in the administered areas of the West Bank, where the change from the previous boom

ISRAEL

Education. (1974–75) Primary, pupils 552,338, teachers 28,297; secondary, pupils 76,953, teachers 6,344; vocational, pupils 72,641, teachers 5,434; teacher training, students 11,079, teachers 1,147; higher, students *c.* 70,000, teaching staff (universities only; 1972–73) 7,681.

Finance. Monetary unit: Israeli pound, with (following the devaluation of Sept. 28, 1975) a par value of I£7 to U.S. $1 (free rate of I£14.26 = £1 sterling). Gold, SDRs, and foreign exchange: (June 1975) U.S. $1,483,200,000; (June 1974) U.S. $1,392,000,000. Budget (1974–75 est.) balanced at I£27,630 million. Gross national product: (1973) I£37,585 million; (1972) I£28,958 million. Money supply: (May 1975) I£9,840 million; (May 1974) I£7,449 million. Cost of living (1970 = 100): (May 1975) 290; (May 1974) 206.

Foreign Trade. (1974) Imports I£24,249 million (including I£5,183 million military goods); exports I£8,214 million. Import sources: U.S. 18%; West Germany 16%; U.K. 13%; Italy 5%; The Netherlands 5%. Export destinations: U.S. 17%; U.K. 9%; Belgium-Luxembourg 5%; France 5%. Main exports: diamonds 35%; chemicals 15%; citrus fruit and products 10%; machinery 7%; clothing 5%; textiles 5%. Tourism (1973): visitors 604,000; gross receipts U.S. $233 million.

Transport and Communications. Roads (1972) *c.* 9,000 km. (including 3,336 main roads). Motor vehicles in use (1973): passenger 238,000; commercial (including buses) 113,400. Railways (1973): 809 km.; traffic 355 million passenger-km., freight 445 million net ton-km. Air traffic (1974): 3,659,000,000 passenger-km.; freight 141,033,000 net ton-km. Shipping (1974): merchant vessels 100 gross tons and over 76; gross tonnage 611,300. Telephones (Dec. 1973) 685,000. Radio receivers (Dec. 1972) 680,000. Television licenses (Dec. 1972) 370,000.

Agriculture. Production (in 000; metric tons; 1974; 1973 in parentheses): wheat 270 (242); sorghum *c.* 47 (30); potatoes *c.* 165 (*c.* 165); watermelons (1973) *c.* 107, (1972) 126; tomatoes *c.* 190 (193); oranges (1973) *c.* 1,150, (1972) 1,179; grapefruit (1973) *c.* 412, (1972) 334; lemons (1973) *c.* 40, (1972) 40; grapes *c.* 82 (78); sugar (1973) *c.* 24, (1972) 28; olives *c.* 30 (*c.* 20); bananas *c.* 55 (38); cotton, lint 45 (37); fish catch (1973) 27, (1972) 29. Livestock (in 000; Dec. 1973): cattle 280; sheep *c.* 185; goats (1972) *c.* 136; chickens (1972) *c.* 12,200.

Industry. Index of production (1970 = 100): (1974) 135; (1973) 129. Production (in 000; metric tons; 1974): cement 1,428; petroleum products (1973) 6,687; sulfuric acid 187; electricity (kw-hr.) 9,152,000; salt (1973) 61; potash (oxide content; 1973–74) 515. New dwelling units completed (1974) 50,500.

conditions for labour and business was particularly evident. This added to the government's difficulty in evolving a viable policy on the question of the Palestinians, and it was a problem that would not go away. The government remained determined not to treat with the PLO, despite the formal backing it had received from the UN, until the PLO recognized the Israeli state. Contacts were established with all levels of Palestinian thinking, however. The result was a serious reassessment of earlier assumptions—as much by moderates as by hard-liners.

The votes taken by the UN General Assembly confirmed the government—and the public generally—in the view that the time was not ripe for a settlement, except in such limited areas as the disengagement agreement with Egypt. The paradox of the UN vote was that, while it was designed to formalize the Palestinian claim, in Israel it had the opposite effect. In a way, it broke the diplomatic isolation of Israel in relation to the Western world. Politically it left the Rabin government in a strong position, leading a people united by the hostility of the UN majority and not inclined to make concessions. It was in this context that the Cabinet decided not to participate, in early 1976, in the full-scale Security Council discussion on the Middle East, to be attended by the Palestinians, which Syria had obtained as its price for renewing the UN peacekeeping force in the Golan Heights. (JON KIMCHE)

[978.B.3.d.i]

ENCYCLOPÆDIA BRITANNICA FILMS. *Israeli Boy: Life on a Kibbutz* (1973); *Kibbutz Kfar Menachem: Crossroads* (1974).

Italy

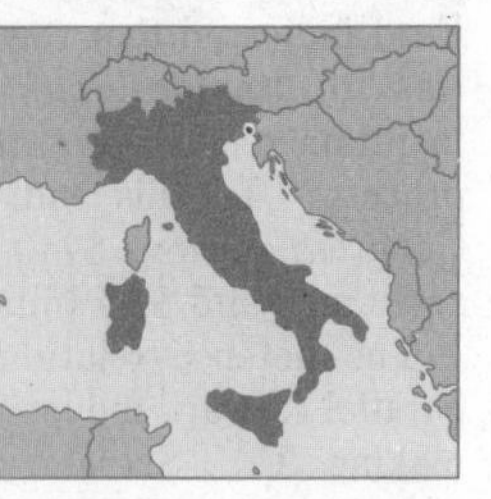

A republic of southern Europe, Italy occupies the Apennine Peninsula, Sicily, Sardinia, and a number of smaller islands. On the north it borders France, Switzerland, Austria, and Yugoslavia. Area: 116,313 sq.mi. (301,245 sq.km.). Pop. (1975 est.): 55,613,000. Cap. and largest city: Rome (pop., 1974 est., 2,833,100). Language: Italian. Religion: predominantly Roman Catholic. President in 1975, Giovanni Leone; premier, Aldo Moro.

Politically motivated violence, kidnappings, and a dangerous worsening of the economic situation were dominant in Italy in 1975, a year that saw the Communist Party, led by Enrico Berlinguer (*see* BIOGRAPHY), gain beyond expectations at the local elections on June 15.

Domestic Affairs. The Christian Democrats' uninterrupted enjoyment of power from 1947 onward received a setback on June 15, when over 30 million voters (including almost 3 million who had just reached the new age of majority of 18) expressed a vote of no confidence in the party. In the municipal elections the Christian Democrats collected 34.7% of the votes, as compared with 37.3% in 1970—not, apparently, a great loss. Much more significant, however, was the Communists' gain, from 25.2% in 1970 to 32.2%. The other principal parties of latter-day centre-left coalition governments fared as follows: Socialists 13.3% (11.5% in 1970), Social Democrats 5.8% (7%), Republicans (who were partners in a coalition government with the Christian Democrats from 1964) 3.6% (3%). The Liberals suffered a loss, 2.3% from 4.3%, while the neofascist Social Movement-National Right (MSI-DN) made a slight gain, 5.7% from 4.8%.

At the same time, elections were held for provincial and regional administrations in most parts of Italy. The trend was duly repeated: provincial elections, Christian Democrats 34.8% (37.3% in 1970), Communists 32.7% (26.7%), Socialists 12.7% (11%), Social Democrats 5.8% (7.3%), MSI-DN 6.8% (6%); regional elections, Christian Democrats 35.3% (37.9%), Communists 33.4% (27.9%), Socialists 12% (10.4%), Social Democrats 5.6% (7%), MSI-DN 6.4% (5.9%).

One of the immediate effects was a crisis among the Christian Democrats, who secured the resignation of their secretary, former premier Amintore Fanfani, on July 22; on July 26 Benigno Zaccagnini (*see* BIOGRAPHY) succeeded him. The effects of the elections on the country as a whole were marked. A series of towns previously held by the Christian Democrats and their allies acquired Communist administrations. With the support of the Socialists, Communist Diego Novelli became mayor of Turin, and Genoa, Naples, and Milan followed suit (the latter with a Socialist mayor). Many of Italy's regions were given "popular front" governments.

Italian Literature: *see* Literature

ITALY

Education. (1973–74) Primary, pupils 4,968,900, teachers (1972–73) 245,628; secondary, pupils 3,053,863, teachers (1972–73) 264,860; vocational, pupils 1,111,589, teachers (1972–73) 95,639; teacher training, students 195,184, teachers (1972–73) 18,606; higher (including 37 universities), students 802,603, teaching staff 44,622.

Finance. Monetary unit: lira, with (Sept. 22, 1975) a free rate of 687 lire to U.S. $1 (1,422 lire = £1 sterling). Gold, SDRs, and foreign exchange: (June 1975) U.S. $6,694,000,000; (June 1974) U.S. $4,987,000,000. Budget (1974 actual): revenue 18,785,000,000,000 lire; expenditure 25,532,000,000,000 lire. Gross national product: (1973) 80,574,000,000,000 lire; (1972) 68,880,000,000,000 lire. Money supply: (Sept. 1974) 54,712,000,000,000 lire; (Sept. 1973) 47,899,000,000,000 lire. Cost of living (1970 = 100): (June 1975) 171; (June 1974) 143.

Foreign Trade. (1974) Imports 26,608,000,000,000 lire; exports 19,677,000,000,000 lire. Import sources: EEC 42% (West Germany 18%, France 13%); U.S. 8%; Saudi Arabia 7%; Libya 6%. Export destinations: EEC 45% (West Germany 18%, France 13%, U.K. 5%); U.S. 8%. Main exports: machinery 18%; chemicals 10%; motor vehicles 10%; textile yarns and fabrics 9%; petroleum products 8%; food 7%; clothing and footwear 7%. Tourism (1972): visitors 10,608,000; gross receipts U.S. $2,733,000,000.

Transport and Communications. Roads (1973) 288,400 km. (including 5,090 km. expressways). Motor vehicles in use (1973): passenger 13.6 million; commercial 1,025,000. Railways: (1972) 20,193 km.; traffic (1973) 36,359,000,000 passenger-km., freight 17,574,000,000 net ton-km. Air traffic (1974): 11,379,000,000 passenger-km.; freight 464,958,000 net ton-km. Shipping (1974): merchant vessels 100 gross tons and over 1,710; gross tonnage 9,322,015. Telephones (Jan. 1974) 12,612,000. Radio licenses (Dec. 1973) 12,448,000. Television licenses (Dec. 1973) 11,426,000.

Agriculture. Production (in 000; metric tons; 1974; 1973 in parentheses): wheat 9,590 (8,899); corn 5,193 (4,923); barley 552 (458); oats 460 (419); rice 988 (1,043); potatoes 2,896 (2,947); dry broad beans (1973) 265, (1972) 334; onions 496 (444); sugar, raw value *c.* 968 (*c.* 1,149); tomatoes 3,592 (3,295); grapes 11,823 (11,842); wine (1973) 7,700, (1972) 5,989; olives 2,400 (2,836); oranges (1973) 1,573, (1972) 1,554; tangerines and mandarin oranges (1973) 334, (1972) 265; lemons (1973) 800, (1972) 726; apples 1,886 (2,050); pears 1,507 (1,570); peaches (1973) 1,200, (1972) 1,273; figs (1973) 157, (1972) 147; tobacco 96 (96); cheese *c.* 505 (501); beef and veal (1973) *c.* 700, (1972) 663; pork (1973) *c.* 640, (1972) 653. Livestock (in 000; Jan. 1974): cattle *c.* 8,948; sheep *c.* 7,890; pigs 8,341; goats 948; poultry *c.* 110,000.

Industry. Index of production (1970 = 100): (1974) 120; (1973) 114. Unemployment: (1974) 2.9%; (1973) 3.5%. Fuel and power (in 000; metric tons; 1974): lignite 1,180; crude oil 1,026; natural gas (cu.m.) 15,272,000; manufactured gas (cu.m.) 3,493,000; electricity (kw-hr.) *c.* 146,500,000. Production (in 000; metric tons; 1974): iron ore (50% metal content) 658; pig iron 11,939; crude steel 23,806; aluminum 223; zinc 193; lead 41; cement 36,256; cotton yarn 150; rayon, etc., filament yarn 54; rayon, etc., fibres 88; nylon, etc., filament yarn 133; nylon, etc., fibres 207; fertilizers (nutrient content; 1973–74) nitrogenous 1,123, phosphate 450; sulfuric acid 3,151; petroleum products (1973) 121,612; passenger cars (units) 1,631; commercial vehicles (units) 142. Merchant vessels launched (100 gross tons and over; 1974) 868,100 gross tons. New dwelling units completed (1974) 166,000.

The political balance that resulted from this expression of popular choice was faced, during the year, with incidents of violence from extremist groups, pledging their faith to a Communist-oriented revolution (but with the declared disapproval of the Communist Party) or to extreme-right fascist ideals. On the "black" front, after a series of bomb attacks on railway lines, right-wing extremist Mario Tuti shot and killed two policemen who were trying to arrest him at Empoli on January 24. Tuti was finally caught after a shoot-out on the French Riviera on July 27. On April 16 a 17-year-old student, Claudio Varalli, was shot in a Milan square by 21-year-old Antonio Braggion; in the demonstrations that followed, another young Communist was killed when a police armoured car collided with him. On October 1 a group of wealthy young Roman neofascists were arrested for the murder of a young woman and the attempted murder of her companion after the women had rejected their demands at a "political" orgy.

On the "red" front, February 18 saw the escape from Casale prison of Renato Curcio, regarded as the leader of the Red Brigades (BR). On March 11, in Naples, a student belonging to the Armed Proletarian Units (NAP) was killed by the explosion of a bomb he was manufacturing. On the same day, in Milan, Sergio Ramelli, 19, a student connected with the MSI, was attacked by left-wing extremists with iron bars; he died on April 29. On May 6 in Rome an NAP group kidnapped Judge Giuseppe Di Gennaro and offered his return in exchange for companions in jail. The magistrate was freed after three prisoners were transferred from a Viterbo jail to one in northern Italy. On June 4 a commando of the Red Brigades in Turin kidnapped Vittorio Gancia of the well-known wine company. On the following day he was freed after a gunfight near Acqui between his kidnappers and carabinieri, one of whom was killed. A BR woman who also died turned out to be Curcio's wife, Margherita Cagol.

In January a Catanzaro tribunal was called upon to try Pietro Valpreda, at his third trial for the Milan bomb massacre (16 dead) of Dec. 12, 1969, and another group including Franco Freda and Giovanni Ventura, accused of acts of terrorism in 1969. The trial was postponed on February 1 and Valpreda was released, since the term of preventive imprisonment had long since expired. In March self-declared anarchist Gianfranco Bertoli, accused of the Milan police headquarters bombing of May 17, 1973, which killed 4 people and injured 46, received life imprisonment. On February 24, in Rome, a trial began related to the burning in 1973 of the house of a local MSI official, whose two sons had died in the fire; during the trial a series of fights between left-wing and right-wing extremists resulted in a student's death. A few days earlier steps had been taken to obtain Parliament's permission to prosecute 40 MSI-DN deputies and senators accused of reconstituting the fascist party. On November 5, 78 members of the alleged "1970 coup" led by the late Prince Valerio Borghese were formally charged, among them Vito Miceli, former head of the Italian secret service. A new law against "improper weapons," such as spanners and chains, was introduced on May 6 and another on public order on May 7.

Kidnappings for ransom also increased. The most

A campaign has been launched to save and preserve the unique cone-shaped architectural form termed "trulli" in southeastern Italy. This building style is thought to be more than 1,000 years old.

ROBERT CRANDALL—THE NEW YORK TIMES

notable included those of five-year-old Pietro Garis, nine-year-old Luciano Privitera, Verona football club chairman Saverio Garonzi, and shipowner Giuseppe d'Amico. The body of Cristina Mazzotti, 18, who disappeared near Milan on July 1, was found on September 1 in a rubbish dump after ransom had been paid. A special squad formed in February to fight kidnappings met with limited success.

Italian culture lived through triumph and despair at the end of the year: the Nobel Prize for Literature awarded to poet Eugenio Montale (*see* NOBEL PRIZES) had just been announced when, on November 2, writer, poet, and film director Pier Paolo Pasolini (*see* OBITUARIES) was savagely murdered by a 17-year-old boy.

Foreign Affairs. The price of oil largely governed Italy's foreign activity. At the beginning of March President Leone and Foreign Minister Mariano Rumor paid an official visit to King Faisal of Saudi Arabia and Sultan Qabus ibn Sa'id of Oman to obtain economic cooperation. A "package" of commercial agreements with Libya was signed in May.

A long-standing emotional issue was settled in October, when agreement was reached with Yugoslavia about the final partition of the Trieste territory. The new official borders reflected reality, with the old "A" zone remaining in Italy's hands and the "B" zone in Yugoslavia's. A small "wine war" was staged between Italy and France when Paris imposed an import surcharge to protect its southern region's wines from Italian competition.

On the diplomatic front the main events were Canadian Prime Minister Pierre Trudeau's talks with Premier Moro (Rome, March 5); U.S. Pres. Gerald Ford's visit to Rome on June 3 and his talks with Leone, Moro, and Rumor; and Soviet Foreign Minister Andrey Gromyko's Rome trip in June, followed a few days later by that of British Foreign Minister James Callaghan. Portugal's Pres. F. da Costa Gomes also visited Rome in October, and on November 17 Leone embarked on a visit to Moscow. In October a delegation of the Italian Industrial Federation, led by Giovanni Agnelli, its president and the chairman of Fiat, visited Peking.

The Economy. The economic crisis centred on the automobile industry, but it was apparent in all sectors of the economy. By September 265 million hours had been lost through short-time working, and the forecast for the whole year was approximately 350 million hours. Unemployment remained well above one million, and by October it was feared the two million mark might be reached by spring. In the automobile industry Fiat lost over 40 days' production, but no mass reduction of the work force was attempted. British Leyland announced in November that its Italian subsidiary, Innocenti, would be put into liquidation. Maserati went into liquidation, and the Pirelli tire manufacturing company asked for the dismissal of 1,450 workers in November.

In the first nine months of 1975, industrial production was 12.4% below the corresponding period of 1974. Inflation rose 12.7% in the year ended September 1975. An economic plan was announced by the government on August 8: up to 4 trillion lire were to be spent in two years to assist small and medium industries, agriculture, exports, and housing and to build hospitals and improve public transport.

The only positive news came from a sharp improvement of the balance of payments deficit, which was limited to 382.4 billion lire for the first eight months. The trade balance showed a deficit of 966 billion lire, compared with 5,048 billion lire in the first eight months of 1974. (FABIO GALVANO)

[972.A.4]

Workers destroy illegal housing in Torre Angela, a village of 4,000 inhabitants on the outskirts of Rome. Officials believe as many as 800,000 Romans may be living in such dwellings.

KEYSTONE

SPECIAL REPORT

ITALY'S POLITICAL CRISIS: TRANSITION OR DISRUPTION?

By P. A. Allum

The Italian crisis continued in 1975. The economy remained in the throes of a recession, bombings and kidnappings were a daily occurrence, and the government lingered in office because people feared the consequences of its fall. But 1975 also witnessed a turning point in postwar Italian political life. It was certain that the Italian political system could not continue to operate in the same way that it had done for the last 28 years.

The Politics of Immobility. Since the expulsion of the Communist Party from the government in May 1947, the Roman Catholic-based Christian Democrat Party has totally controlled state and parastate institutions. The Christian Democrats have always received the largest share of the vote (around 40%), and this has been linked to the fact that the Communists (with votes rising from 19% in 1946 to 27% in 1972) have constituted the largest opposition party, regarded by the Christian Democrats as a totalitarian Trojan horse and shunned as a prospective coalition partner. Government coalitions were formed of an alliance between the Christian Democrats and some combination of the smaller lay parties, Socialists, Republicans, Social Democrats, and Liberals, with occasional support from the monarchist and neofascist extreme right.

The chief consequence of the Christian Democrats' impregnability has been a stagnant parliamentary situation characterized by intrigue and factionalism. The Christian Democrats have had powerful incentives to resist dynamic policies; since their party had a religious base, action provoking social mobility was likely to undermine its strength. Ironically, spontaneous social change set in motion by the "economic miracle" (which, culminating in 1958–62, transformed Italy into one of the ten leading industrial nations) did just that. First, the result of the divorce referendum of May 12–13, 1974 (59% in favour of retaining the 1970 law permitting divorce), showed that the church could no longer mobilize a majority of the Italian people. Second, the regional elections of June 15, 1975, in which the Communists polled over 33% to the Christian Democrats' 35%, indicated that the Christian Democrats could lose their dominating position as the largest single party in Parliament at the next general election, due to be held in the spring of 1977.

The cold war enabled the Christian Democrat Party and its centrist allies, the Social Democrats, Republicans, and Liberals, to mobilize the support of all sections of society, except the hard core of the working class organized by the Communist Party and its trade union confederation. Thus forged into a provincial power bloc, the middle classes were strong enough to offset the electoral power of organized labour. The government dispensed subsidies and patronage to cement anti-Communist fervour and tie whole populations to state institutions.

P. A. Allum is reader in politics at the University of Reading, England, and is associated with the University's Centre for the Advanced Study of Italian Society. He is also maître de conférence associé in the University of Paris VIII. He is the author of Politics and Society in Post-war Naples *and* Italy: Republic Without Government? *(both 1973).*

This system created the economic miracle, but its contradictions became apparent in 1963. Despite the persistence of unemployment in the south, industrial expansion in the north had created full employment for skilled labour. This gave the unions a bargaining power that they had not known for a decade. A wage explosion followed, setting off a consumer demand that provoked a balance of payments deficit of $1.2 billion.

It was to avoid this kind of economic situation that the "opening to the left" (*apertura a sinistra,* an alliance between the Christian Democrats and the Socialists) had been initiated in 1962. Its object was to carry through a program of democratic reforms that, by correcting the imbalance between north and south, improving the social services and state administration, and controlling economic development through planning, would both satisfy industry and benefit the workers.

The apparently all-powerful reformist alliance was in reality dangerously weak. The support of the advanced sectors of industry was only halfhearted; in addition, the Communists, an essential element of any successful reformist alliance, were kept on the sidelines. At the same time, the opponents of the centre-left alliance were more powerful than its promoters realized. These representatives of the Christian Democrat-created provincial power groups dominated the parliamentary standing committees, the ministries, and, above all, the many state-level agencies that control so many areas of Italian life. Their interests were directly threatened by the proposed reforms. Had it carried the reforms through, the Christian Democrat Party would have lost its powerful support altogether—as the party was to discover in the riots in Reggio di Calabria in 1970–71. Finally, fear of political crisis kept the Socialists in the coalition.

End of a Miracle. The deflationary measures of 1964 rapidly reduced inflation and the trade deficit, but they changed the pattern of Italian economic growth in the later 1960s. Higher wages resulted in a profits squeeze in industry and dried up private investment. Demands for improved working conditions were a major component in the new explosion of militant union activity and acute social unrest, known as the "hot autumn" of 1969, which brought the expansion of the 1960s to an abrupt halt.

The period since 1969 has been one of what Antonio Gramsci (1891–1937), a founder of the Italian Communist Party, called "organic crisis," resulting from problems that could not be solved under the existing political system and foreshadowing major transformations in its functioning. Certainly the factors that permitted the Italian political system to function adequately have disappeared one by one. First, political indifference: the years 1969–75 witnessed a political mobilization without precedent. The unions, split into three major confederations (Communist, Catholic, and Social Democrat) since 1948, made rapid strides toward unity of action and began also to turn their attention to social reform. They organized a series of one-day national strikes in the winter of 1970–71 and subsequently pressed for those reforms not yet introduced.

Second, low wages: trade-union action after 1969 won the Italian workers exceptional wage rises that brought unit labour costs in Italy even with those of its European partners. Italian products were thus priced out of international markets, and the immediate consequence was the country's worst and longest recession (1969–72) since World War II. On top of this, the international monetary crisis made it necessary to float the lira and accelerate inflation. Moreover, when the economy had been brought under control, an incipient boom was cut short by the energy crisis, and the economy was thrown into an even worse recession.

Finally, civic order: terrorism became endemic after 1969. It was initiated by neofascist extremists as a "strategy of tensions," designed to mobilize the "silent majority" in support of an authoritarian response to leftward trends. It developed throughout 1969 and culminated in December, when 16 persons were killed in the bombing of a Milan bank. Since then acts of terrorism by neofascist extremists and some leftists have become common. The major massacres (*e.g.*, the bombing of an antifascist rally in Brescia, May 1974; the bombing of the "Italicus" express train, August 1974) and three mysterious but failed coups were the work of neofascist extremists.

Searching for a Cure. Two strategies for solving the crisis have been promoted on and off since 1969. The first is authoritarian: to rally conservative support and subordinate the labour movement, introducing, if necessary, constitutional changes, such as a presidential system on the model of the French Fifth Republic. The latest proponent of this tendency has been a former premier, Amintore Fanfani; hence it has been dubbed *Fanfangollismo*. The progressive strategy is centred on a package of reforms negotiated between government, employers, and unions with support in Parliament. The Communists see it as a first step toward their "historical compromise" between the major forces in Italian society—Catholic, Communist, and Socialist—in the national interest. Both strategies have been explored hesitantly. Both have provoked opposition, much of it violent.

Major gains were registered by the neofascists in the 1971 local elections, particularly in the south, which had suffered most from the post-1969 recession. The Christian Democrats quickly moved toward a more authoritarian stance and liquidated the centre-left alliance. A southern Christian Democrat notable, Giovanni Leone, was elected president of the republic with the help of neofascist votes in December 1971. In February 1972 he dissolved Parliament a year before its term, after appointing one of the party's leading conservative figures, Giulio Andreotti, as premier. The centre-right government that was formed in the wake of the May 1972 elections made little headway against the economic crisis, despite floating the lira, and within a year it had lost the confidence of Parliament, provoking Andreotti's resignation in June 1973.

With inflation accelerating under the impetus of the floating lira and with the economy expanding again at last, the government needed union support if another wage explosion was to be avoided. In June 1973 Fanfani was recalled to the secretaryship of the Christian Democrat Party, and the centre-left coalition was relaunched under the premiership of Mariano Rumor. The Communist Party demonstrated its goodwill by throwing its votes behind the government's progressive measures in Parliament and urging moderation on the unions. It was in September 1973, in reaction to the overthrow of the Marxist Salvador Allende in Chile, that the Communist Party secretary, Enrico Berlinguer (*see* BIOGRAPHY), spelled out his proposal for a "historical compromise" between Communists and Catholics.

Workers in Rome march past the Colosseum en route to a national general strike rally in January.

WIDE WORLD

Meanwhile, Fanfani threw all his energy into attempting to reorganize, on the Christian Democrats' behalf, the ruling power bloc of business, bureaucracy, and provincial middle classes. He sought both to reduce factionalism inside the party and to increase its power over outside decision-making centres such as state agencies, radio, and the press. Single-mindedly, he pursued the divorce referendum to the vote. Against the wishes of all parties except the neofascists, and of many Christian Democrat supporters, he was determined to demonstrate that, when faced with a choice between the Christian Democrats and the other parties, the majority of the Italian people will always rally to the Christian Democrats.

Fanfani's plans received a sharp rebuff. For the first time since 1948, large numbers of Catholics ignored the appeals of their party and the church, and the political consequences were enormous. The most immediate was a Cabinet crisis, but it was patched up because of the need to take harsh measures to combat inflation and an $8 billion-plus balance of payments deficit caused by the rise in oil prices. The squeeze had the desired effect, cutting inflation and the trade deficit, but only at the expense of industrial activity and by raising unemployment.

The inevitable was only delayed a few months. The centre-left coalition collapsed in October 1974, provoking one of the longest postwar Cabinet crises. It was late November before Aldo Moro, father of the "opening to the left" and former premier (December 1963–68), formed a two-party (Christian Democrat and Republican) minority government, with the parliamentary support of the Socialists and Social Democrats.

Pandora's Box. Despite the gravity of the economic situation and the discreet support that the Communists offered the government, Fanfani was set on revenge, convinced that, if he could turn the next elections into a simple confrontation with the Communists, he could reverse the verdict of the referendum. He found an issue in law and order and converted the campaign for the regional elections of June 1975 into an anti-Communist crusade. The results were a disaster. If his tactics limited Christian Democrat losses to about 3%, they also contributed to the largest Communist advance since the war (5.5%).

The regional elections not only confirmed the verdict of the divorce referendum, interpreted unanimously as a vote for change, but emphasized dramatically the crisis of the Christian Democrats. The coalition that had given them unlimited power in Italy for nearly 30 years had begun to fall apart. They had lost votes to the extreme right before when they embarked on modest progressive policies, but they had always recovered those votes when the policies were dropped. Now, for the first time, they had lost large numbers of votes to the left (while recouping others from the right). The Christian Democrat leaders knew that these votes were lost forever because, if the party attempted to recover them by revamping itself in a progressive mold, desertion on the right wing would take place on an even larger scale, probably provoking a split. In July Fanfani was forced to resign the party secretaryship.

The regional elections have opened a sort of political Pandora's box in Italy. They have left open the question of how the political system will operate in the future. The regional and local administrations formed after the elections did not reflect the formation of alliances on the lines of the "historical compromise"; as of 1975, five regions and many large cities possessed left-wing (Communist-Socialist) majorities, with the Christian Democrats preferring to go into opposition rather than share local power with the Communists.

All the signs were that the Communist Party had taken another step nearer power. What would happen if it were to find its way into a government coalition, either with the Christian Democrats in the immediate future or as the leading member of a left-wing alternative government in the next Parliament? In such an event, it might well be that Italian democracy would have more to fear from the right and from the Army's efforts to restore "normality" than from the Communists' misuse of power.

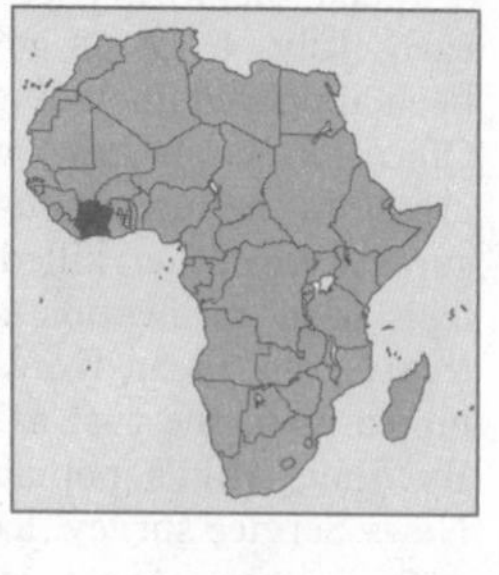

Ivory Coast

A republic on the Gulf of Guinea, the Ivory Coast is bounded by Liberia, Guinea, Mali, Upper Volta, and Ghana. Area: 123,484 sq.mi. (319,822 sq.km.). Pop. (1975): 6,673,000. Cap. and largest city: Abidjan (pop., early 1970s est., 650,000). Language: French and local dialects. Religion: animist 65%; Muslim 23%; Christian 12%. President and premier in 1975, Félix Houphouët-Boigny.

Houphouët-Boigny, the sole candidate, now in his 70th year, was reelected to the presidency on Nov. 18, 1975, with 99.9% of the votes cast by 99.8% of the electorate, and 120 deputies were elected to the National Assembly from a single-party list. The constitution was amended to allow the premier to succeed automatically to the presidency if the incumbent should die.

In foreign affairs, the "dialogue" with South Africa preoccupied the Ivory Coast's leaders. In May, South Africa's prime minister, B. J. Vorster, confirmed that he had met President Houphouët-Boigny secretly at Yamoussoukro in 1974. In April, Houphouët-Boigny reaffirmed his views in favour of a dialogue, and in September the minister of information, Laurent Dona-Fologo, with his white wife, paid a ten-day official visit to South Africa during which he pressed for relaxation of discrimination against black Africa. In October, Houphouët-Boigny said he hoped that all black African states would one day establish diplomatic relations with South Africa.

The country's economy continued to be one of Africa's most successful. Goods handled by the port of Abidjan stood at 6.6 million metric tons in 1974 (1.2 million metric tons in 1960), and a ten-year port enlargement plan was announced. Coffee and cocoa production rose. (PHILIPPE DECRAENE)

IVORY COAST

Education. (1972–73) Primary, pupils 556,689, teachers 12,216; secondary, pupils 83,456, teachers (public only) 2,804; vocational, pupils (1971–72) 5,242, teachers (1970–71) 613; teacher training, students 3,284, teachers 130; higher, students 4,699, teaching staff (1971–72) 465.

Finance. Monetary unit: CFA franc, with (Sept. 22, 1975) a parity of CFA Fr. 50 to the French franc (free rate of CFA Fr. 227.70 = U.S. $1; CFA Fr. 471.75 = £1 sterling). Gold, SDRs, and foreign exchange: (April 1975) U.S. $82.6 million; (April 1974) U.S. $79.3 million. Budget (1974 est.) balanced at CFA Fr. 97.7 billion. Money supply: (April 1975) CFA Fr. 166,220,000,000; (April 1974) CFA Fr. 135,820,000,000.

Foreign Trade. (1974) Imports CFA Fr. 232,286,000,000; exports CFA Fr. 291,771,000,000. Import sources: France 39%; U.S. 7%; West Germany 6%; Iraq 6%; Nigeria 5%. Export destinations: France 26%; The Netherlands 15%; Italy 9%; West Germany 9%; Dahomey 8%; U.S. 7%; Taiwan 6%. Main exports: coffee 22%; cocoa 21%; timber 18%.

Agriculture. Production (in 000; metric tons; 1974; 1973 in parentheses): corn *c.* 108 (*c.* 108); yams (1973) *c.* 1,550, (1972) *c.* 1,550; cassava (1973) *c.* 575, (1972) 570; rice (1973) *c.* 400, (1972) 360; millet *c.* 35 (*c.* 30); peanuts *c.* 42 (*c.* 42); coffee *c.* 300 (290); cocoa *c.* 220 (*c.* 210); bananas *c.* 230 (227); palm kernels *c.* 55 (30); palm oil *c.* 135 (118); cotton, lint *c.* 23 (*c.* 20); rubber *c.* 16 (16); timber (cu.m.; 1973) *c.* 9,800, (1972) 9,800. Livestock (in 000; 1974): cattle *c.* 480; pigs *c.* 195; sheep *c.* 950; goats *c.* 950; poultry *c.* 6,200.

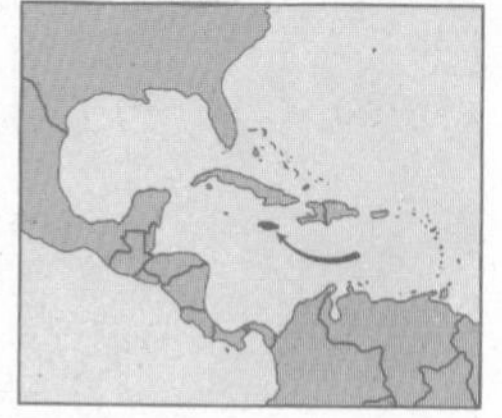

Jamaica

A parliamentary state within the Commonwealth of Nations, Jamaica is an island in the Caribbean Sea about 90 mi. S of Cuba. Area: 4,244 sq.mi. (10,991 sq.km.). Pop. (1975 est.): 2,025,000, predominantly Negro, but including Europeans, Chinese, Indians, and persons of mixed race. Cap. and largest city: Kingston (pop., 1974 est., 169,800). Language: English. Religion: Christian, with Anglicans and Baptists in the majority. Queen, Elizabeth II; governor-general in 1975, Florizel Glasspole; prime minister, Michael Manley.

The Jamaican economy benefited during 1975 from an increase in the revenues from bauxite and sugar. Imports were expected to rise to about Jam$1 billion and, despite increased port earnings, a substantial trade deficit was likely. Foreign borrowing was expected to finance the bulk of a budget deficit of Jam$146.9 million. Inflation continued during the year, and the government introduced an anti-inflation package in September that included tougher import controls and currency regulations and a wage-and-price freeze pending introduction of a workable prices and incomes policy. Industrial unrest continued, with demands for wage increases ranging up to 90%.

The Jamaica Labour Party (JLP) conference elected Edward Seaga leader to succeed Hugh Shearer. Sir Alexander Bustamante, former JLP leader, was elevated to the exclusive position of "the Chief." Political gang warfare and violent crime erupted in antiopposition mob violence at the House of Representatives, a direct threat to constitutional order.

A survey of educational changes in the 13 years since independence in August 1962 showed great increases in enrollment at all grades—81% in the 12- to 14-plus age group and an expected 35% in the 15- to 16-plus age group. Teacher-training colleges produced 1,057 teachers in 1974–75, as against 250 in 1962–63. More than 17.7% of the 1975–76 budget was allocated for education, plus Jam$3 million to combat adult illiteracy. (SHEILA PATTERSON)

[974.B.2.d]

JAMAICA

Education. (1972–73) Primary, pupils 410,942, teachers 9,888; secondary and vocational, pupils 80,673, teachers 3,549; teacher training, students 2,146, teachers 142; higher (university only), students 3,516, teaching staff 330.

Finance. Monetary unit: Jamaican dollar, with (Sept. 22, 1975) a par value of Jam$0.91 to U.S. $1 (free rate of Jam$1.89 = £1 sterling). Gold, SDRs, and foreign exchange: (June 1975) U.S. $179.3 million; (June 1974) U.S. $174.3 million. Budget (1974–75 est.): revenue Jam$447,777,000; expenditure Jam$584,338,000.

Foreign Trade. (1974) Imports Jam$850,781,000; exports Jam$664,446,000. Import sources: U.S. 35%; Venezuela 15%; Canada 5%; Trinidad and Tobago 5%. Export destinations: U.S. 46%; U.K. 15%; Norway 12%; Canada 5%. Main exports: alumina 52%; bauxite 20%; sugar 12%. Tourism (1973): visitors 418,300; gross receipts U.S. $127 million.

Agriculture. Production (in 000; metric tons; 1974; 1973 in parentheses): sweet potatoes *c.* 20 (*c.* 20); yams (1973) *c.* 130, (1972) 127; cassava *c.* 22 (*c.* 22); sugar, raw value *c.* 387 (331); bananas *c.* 190 (*c.* 190); oranges (1973) *c.* 80, (1972) 83; grapefruit (1973) *c.* 37, (1972) 36; copra *c.* 13 (13). Livestock (in 000; 1973): cattle *c.* 272; goats *c.* 360; pigs *c.* 210.

Industry. Production (in 000; metric tons; 1974): bauxite 15,220; cement 399; petroleum products (1973) *c.* 1,830; electricity (kw-hr.; 1973) 2,134,000.

Jai Alai:
see Court Games

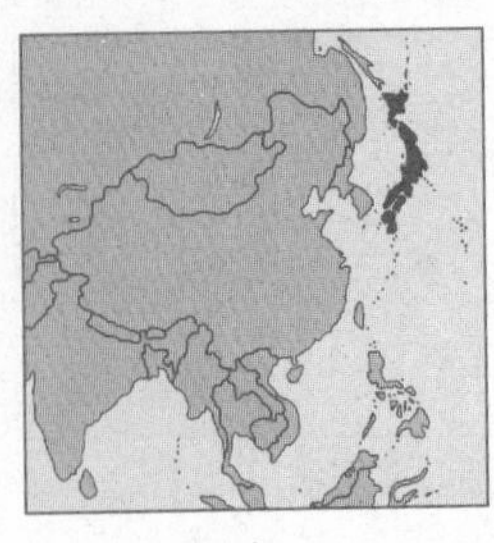

Japan

A constitutional monarchy in the northwestern Pacific Ocean, Japan is an archipelago composed of four major islands (Hokkaido, Honshu, Kyushu, and Shikoku), the Ryukyus (including Okinawa), and minor adjacent islands. Area: 145,747 sq.mi. (377,484 sq.km.). Pop. (Oct. 1975 census): 104,665,200. Cap. and largest city: Tokyo (pop., 1975 est., 8,658,200). Language: Japanese. Religion: primarily Shinto and Buddhist; Christian 0.5%. Emperor, Hirohito; prime minister in 1975, Takeo Miki.

Domestic Affairs. On Dec. 9, 1974, Prime Minister Takeo Miki (*see* BIOGRAPHY) formed his first Cabinet with Kiichi Miyazawa as foreign minister, Takeo Fukuda as deputy prime minister, Masayoshi Ohira as finance minister, Michio Nagai as education minister, and Yasuhiro Nakasone as secretary-general of the majority Liberal-Democratic Party. Five days later he made his maiden policy speech before an extraordinary session of the Diet, stressing the importance of international cooperation in combating recession, inflation, monetary uncertainties, and shortages of energy and food. An opinion poll in January rated the prime minister's popularity at 48.8% and that of his Cabinet at 59.4%.

When the 75th ordinary Diet opened in late January, party representation was as follows: (lower) House of Representatives: Liberal-Democrats (LDP) 277, Japan Socialists (JSP) 114, Japan Communists (JCP) 39, Komeito (KMT) 30, Democratic Socialists (DSP) 20, independents 1, vacancies 10 (total 491); (upper) House of Councillors: LDP 128, JSP 61, KMT 24, JCP 20, DSP 10, Niin Club 4, independents 3, vacancies 2 (total 252).

In elections held on April 13, both conservative and progressive camps claimed "comforting victories," the LDP winning overwhelming majorities in 12 gubernatorial races while leftist parties maintained strongholds in Tokyo and Osaka and brought in the first progressive governor of Kanagawa Prefecture. On April 27 conservative candidates scored victories in 121 of the 165 mayoral elections.

When the 75th Diet ended its 190-day session in early July, 43 of 68 government-sponsored bills had been approved, including the important revised Public Offices Election Law, which provided a 20-seat increase in the lower house of the Diet. Four key measures were either killed or held over: antimonopoly legislation, ratification of the nuclear nonproliferation treaty, the Japan-Korea continental shelf pact, and increases in the cost of liquor, tobacco, and postage. By June Miki's popularity, according to a Kyodo News Service survey, had plunged to 36.2%.

Preliminary reports indicated that Japan's inflation-adjusted gross national product (GNP) fell by 1.8% during 1974, marking the first net annual decline since World War II. The Economic Planning Agency (EPA) placed the 1974 GNP at 89,190,000,000,000 yen (U.S. $297.3 billion) in 1970 prices. The economy turned slightly upward during the second quarter (April–June) of 1975, but EPA officials predicted that the annual growth rate for the fiscal year ending in March 1976 would be below the government's target of 4.3%. Unemployment in June stood at 920,000 (1.7% of the labour force).

In January the government had announced a general account budget for fiscal year 1975 totaling 21,288,000,000,000 yen (coupled with a 9,310,000,000,000 yen loan and investment program). The 24.5% increase over the 1974 budget was largely attributable to social security payments. On September 16 the government announced a fourth antirecession package of 2,090,000,000,000 yen to promote public works, housing, antipollution projects, and trade.

A government survey in July discovered that although 90% of those interviewed still considered themselves "in the middle class," 48.3% felt they were worse off than they had been a year earlier. In January the rate of increase in Tokyo's consumer prices fell, for the first time in a year, below 20% (compared with the year before). The Tokyo index in June showed the first monthly decline in 20 months (0.1%), but the retail price level was still 13.7% higher than that of the previous year. The index stood at 171.4 (1970 = 100) in August, the first time since April 1973 that the annual increase was held to a 10% level, but in September it climbed to 174.5.

Among the exhibitions seen by visitors to Japan's Expo '75 (below, left) was the world's largest glass-walled aquarium containing more than 12,000 fish.

(LEFT) ORION PRESS/KATHERINE YOUNG; (RIGHT) WIDE WORLD

The Finance Ministry announced a substantial deficit of $6,843,000,000 in the overall balance of payments for 1974. For the first six months of 1975, however, the deficit of $1,860,000,000 was a dramatic improvement over the $6,692,000,000 deficit during the comparable period in 1974.

On July 17 Crown Prince Akihito and Princess Michiko narrowly escaped injury from a Molotov cocktail hurled at them while they paid homage to war dead in Naha, Okinawa. The crown prince later officially opened the world's first International Ocean Exposition, called Expo '75, which occupied a 250-ac. site on the tip of Motobu Peninsula.

On November 26 more than 800,000 government employees, in an effort to win the right to strike, began an illegal strike that tied up the nation's transportation and communications systems. The government refused to yield to their demands, and the strike was called off after eight days.

On June 3, 1975, former prime minister Eisaku Sato (*see* OBITUARIES), recipient of the Nobel Peace Prize in 1974, died in a Tokyo hospital at the age of 74.

Foreign Affairs. In September U.S. ambassador to Japan James D. Hodgson urged Japan-U.S. cooperation to keep respective policies "compatible through constant consultations" and to maintain the current "no-problem era" in bilateral relations. Foreign Minister Miyazawa and U.S. Secretary of State Henry Kissinger met on April 10 in Washington to discuss the U.S.-Japan Security Treaty.

Early in July Miki prepared for the first Japan-U.S. summit meeting since he and U.S. Pres. Gerald Ford came to power. Miki and Ford wound up their two-day summit in Washington on August 6 after agreeing that "the security of the Republic of Korea is essential to the maintenance of peace on the Korean peninsula, which in turn is necessary for peace and security in East Asia, including Japan." They also agreed that the U.S. should continue to maintain military forces in South Korea and that the U.S.-Japan Security Treaty was an "indispensable element" in the basic international structure of Asia, the continuation of which would serve "the long-term interests of both countries."

On September 30 a more symbolic, but perhaps more important, event got under way when Emperor Hirohito and Empress Nagako left Tokyo for a historic 15-day visit to the U.S. After resting two days in Williamsburg, Va., the imperial couple visited the U.S. capital on October 2–4, then toured New York City and the headquarters of the UN. The emperor, a marine biologist, also inspected the Woods Hole Oceanographic Institute on Cape Cod, Massachusetts. The couple then moved on to Chicago, Los Angeles, San Diego, San Francisco, and Honolulu. After a rest in Hawaii, they returned to Tokyo on October 14. The visit marked the end of the Pacific war era for Hirohito who, on several occasions, expressed regret that the conflict had marred Japan-U.S. relations.

HIROTAKA YOSHIZAKI—THE NEW YORK TIMES

The harbour at Kobe will be the site of the world's largest man-made island. Fill for the project, intended to increase port facilities, is obtained from Mount Yoko, west of the city, and transported to shore by conveyors.

Memories of the war, however, continued to intrude on Japan-U.S.S.R. relations. Foreign Minister Miyazawa admitted that talks in Moscow (Jan. 15–17) had not produced progress toward the solution of the "northern territories" issue (the Soviet occupation of the Kurils). In February Oleg Troyanovsky, the Soviet ambassador in Tokyo, delivered a letter to Prime Minister Miki from Soviet Communist Party chief Leonid Brezhnev. It proposed that both nations conclude a treaty of "good neighbourliness and co-operation." Miki in effect rejected the proposal by

JAPAN

Education. (1972–73) Primary, pupils 9,816,536, teachers 392,793; secondary, pupils 7,153,337, teachers 445,388; vocational, pupils 1,561,580; higher (including 41 state universities), students 1,926,108, teaching staff 102,396.

Finance. Monetary unit: yen, with (Sept. 22, 1975) a free rate of 303 yen to U.S. $1 (627 yen = £1 sterling). Gold, SDRs, and foreign exchange: (June 1975) U.S. $13,782,000,000; (June 1974) U.S. $12,781,000,000. Budget (1974–75 est): revenue 20,389,000,000,000 yen; expenditure 21,815,000,000,000 yen. Gross national product: (1974) 131,682,000,000,000 yen; (1973) 111,034,000,000,000 yen. Money supply: (May 1975) 44,415,000,000,000 yen; (May 1974) 40,994,000,000,000 yen. Cost of living (1970 = 100): (June 1975) 171; (June 1974) 152.

Foreign Trade. (1974) Imports 18,067,000,000,000 yen; exports 16,220,000,000,000 yen. Import sources: U.S. 20%; Saudi Arabia 8%; Iran 8%; Indonesia 7%; Australia 6%. Export destinations: U.S. 23%; South Korea 5%. Main exports: machinery 21% (telecommunications apparatus 6%); iron and steel 19%; motor vehicles 13%; ships 10%; chemicals 7%; textile yarns and fabrics 6%.

Transport and Communications. Roads (1973) 1,049,710 km. (including 1,403 km. expressways). Motor vehicles in use (1973): passenger 14,473,600; commercial 10,422,400. Railways: (1973) 27,517 km.; traffic (1974) 324,661,000,000 passenger-km., freight 54,693,000,000 net ton-km. Air traffic (1974): 16,273,000,000 passenger-km.; freight 733,557,000 net ton-km. Shipping (1974): merchant vessels 100 gross tons and over 9,974; gross tonnage 38,707,659. Telephones (April 1973) 38,698,000. Radio receivers (Dec. 1972) 70,794,000. Television licenses (Dec. 1973) 24,797,000.

Agriculture. Production (in 000; metric tons; 1974; 1973 in parentheses): rice 15,826 (15,717); wheat 232 (202); barley 233 (216); sweet potatoes (1973) *c.* 2,000, (1972) 2,107; potatoes 2,824 (3,302); sugar, raw value 492 (656); tea *c.* 97 (95); onions 1,000 (994); tomatoes 865 (*c.* 900); cabbages (1973) *c.* 3,000, (1972) 2,385; watermelons (1973) *c.* 1,200, (1972) 1,131; apples *c.* 924 (963); pears *c.* 495 (495); oranges (1973) *c.* 290, (1972) 290; tangerines and mandarin oranges (1973) *c.* 3,329, (1972) 3,568; grapes 165 (271); tobacco *c.* 139 (157); pork (1973) *c.* 940, (1972) 885; eggs *c.* 1,655 (*c.* 1,805); timber (cu.m.; 1973) 44,500, (1972) 44,500; fish catch (1973) 10,702, (1972) 10,273; whale and sperm oil (1973–74) 16, (1972–73) 50. Livestock (in 000; Feb. 1974): cattle 3,714; sheep 19; pigs 7,985; goats (1973) 137; chickens (1973) *c.* 243,689.

Industry. Index of production (1970 = 100): (1974) 126; (1973) 129. Fuel and power (in 000; metric tons; 1974): coal 20,333; crude oil 675; natural gas (cu.m.) 2,847,000; manufactured gas (cu.m.; 1973) 3,488,000; electricity (kw-hr.) 460,705,000. Production (in 000; metric tons; 1974): iron ore (55% metal content) 779; pig iron 92,705; crude steel 117,131; petroleum products (1973) 224,306; cement 73,108; cotton yarn 511; woven cotton fabrics (sq.m.) 2,163,000; rayon, etc., filament yarn 116; rayon, etc., fibres 358; nylon, etc., filament yarn 523; nylon, etc., fibres 652; sulfuric acid 7,128; fertilizers (nutrient content; 1973–74) nitrogenous 2,204, phosphate 736; cameras (units) 6,644; radio receivers (units) 18,026; television receivers (units) 13,406; passenger cars (units) 3,933; commercial vehicles (units) 2,629; motorcycles (units) 4,510. Merchant vessels launched (100 gross tons and over; 1974) 17,584,000 gross tons. New dwelling units started (1974) 1,470,000.

insisting that Japan hoped to conclude a treaty based on a settlement of the territorial issue.

Prime Minister Miki declared in the Diet on June 24 that Soviet protests against negotiations between Japan and China concerning a treaty of peace and friendship were based on a misunderstanding. "We have no particular country, such as the Soviet Union, in mind when we negotiate with Peking," Miki stated. "The so-called antihegemony clause [opposing hegemony by any power in Asia] is nothing more than a principle of peace which will be universally accepted."

Moscow's nervousness had arisen from the negotiations that began on January 20 when Shigeru Hori, a senior LDP member, carried a personal letter from Miki to China's Premier Chou En-lai. Further talks led to the first meeting of foreign ministers held on September 24 at the residence of the Japanese ambassador to the UN in New York. The talks, however, failed to narrow the gap on the controversial antihegemony clause in the proposed treaty. Meanwhile, two-way trade between Japan and China in the first half of the year totaled $1.8 billion, up 30% from the corresponding 1974 period.

Japan also took steps to improve its relationship with Taiwan. Air service between the two countries had been severed in April 1974 when Tokyo signed a civil aviation agreement with Peking. An agreement was signed in Taipei on July 9 whereby civil aviation service was resumed on a strictly private basis. On September 15 Japan Asia Airways (a thinly disguised subsidiary of Japan Air Lines) reopened service between Tokyo and Taipei.

Relations with another neighbour, South Korea, took a turn for the better in late July when Miyazawa held talks in Seoul with his counterpart, Kim Dong Jo. In a verbal note, the South Korean government deliberately skirted the question of the involvement of Kim Dong Woon (a former staff member in its Tokyo embassy) in the 1973 abduction from Tokyo of Kim Dae Jung, an opposition leader. Apparently Seoul had stripped Kim Dong Woon of official status. Another verbal note concerned Mun Se Kwang, a South Korean resident in Japan, who tried to assassinate Pres. Park Chung Hee in Seoul in 1974. Tokyo promised to make every effort to prevent the recurrence of such incidents. These developments opened the way for the long-delayed eighth ministerial conference, which convened in Seoul's Chosun Hotel on September 15. The ten-point communiqué reconfirmed cooperation at the UN and elsewhere.

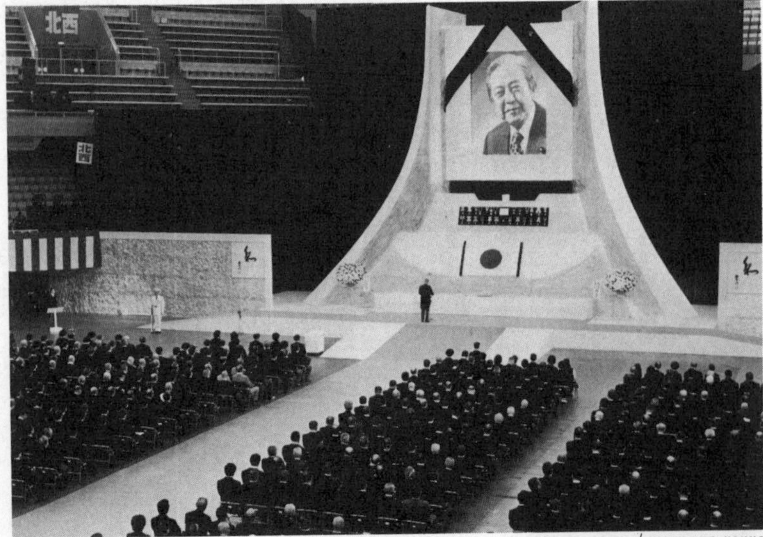

ORION PRESS/KATHERINE YOUNG

Funeral ceremony for former prime minister Eisaku Sato at the Budokan Hall in Tokyo in June.

ORION PRESS/KATHERINE YOUNG

Tree-planting ceremony at Akasaka Palace during a visit by Queen Elizabeth II in May.

In August, Tokuma Utsunomiya, an LDP member of the Diet, notified Miki that North Korean Pres. Kim Il Sung wished to negotiate a Korean peace settlement with Washington. Kim told Utsunomiya on July 15 that he did not intend to resort to military means to achieve unification. Tokyo's doubts about this were revived on September 2 when a North Korean patrol boat fired on and captured the Japanese fishing boat "Shosei-maru" in the Yellow Sea. Because Tokyo had no diplomatic ties with Pyongyang, a message was sent through the Red Cross stating that the fishing boat had been mistaken for a U.S. or South Korean spy ship and that two persons were dead and two wounded.

Concern over Korea had been heightened by what Japan (and the rest of Asia) regarded as the U.S. defeat in Indochina. In early May, following the surrender of the Saigon government to Communist-led forces, Miyazawa stated that Japan would have to conduct a thorough review of its Asian policies, which had been formulated on the basis of the U.S.-Japan Security Treaty. Tokyo and Hanoi announced in July that Japan would give 5 billion yen to North Vietnam for relief and reconstruction. Negotiations revolved around Japan's plans to open an embassy in Hanoi.

Indonesia's President Suharto, at a meeting in July, asked Miki for further Japanese economic cooperation so that Indonesia could continue its "national resilience to the Communist offensive." Japan promised to maintain closer ties with the Association of Southeast Asian Nations (ASEAN).

Japan's fishery agency and its whaling industry were shocked in midyear by a decision of the International Whaling Commission, which voted to restrict quotas, particularly catches of finback whales. The Japanese delegation vainly protested the unreasonableness of claims made by countries, specifically the U.S. and Norway, that strongly opposed whaling.

During the year Japan played host to Queen Elizabeth II and Prince Philip, who departed for England on May 12 after a successful six-day visit. It was the first visit by the British royal family and reciprocated the imperial family's tour of England in 1971.

(ARDATH W. BURKS)

[975.B]

Jordan

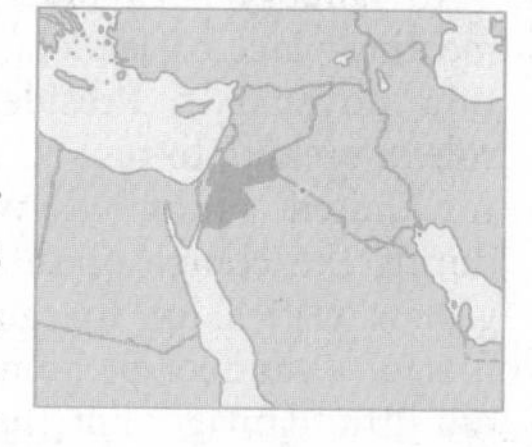

A constitutional monarchy in southwest Asia, Jordan is bounded by Syria, Iraq, Saudi Arabia, and Israel. Area (including territory occupied by Israel in the June 1967 war): 36,832 sq.mi. (95,394 sq.km.). Pop. (1975 est.): 2,674,000. Cap. and largest city: Amman (pop., 1975 est., 615,000). Language: Arabic. Religion (1961): Muslim 94%; Christian 6%. King, Hussein I; prime minister in 1975, Zaid ar-Rifai.

In 1975 Jordan's long-standing position as a pro-Western state was affected by the refusal of the U.S. Congress to endorse a major arms deal. Jordan threatened to turn to the Soviet Union and moved closer to Syria. Egyptian and Syrian efforts to mediate between Jordan and the Palestine Liberation Organization (PLO) achieved only modest results. Talks were held in Cairo on January 3–4 between Egyptian, Syrian, Jordanian, and PLO representatives, but mutual suspicion remained deep and Jordan maintained its flat refusal to allow PLO forces on the east bank of the Jordan, while the PLO accused Jordan of continued persecution of its supporters. Jordan's attitude was that, in view of the Arab states' October 1974 decision to recognize the PLO as the sole legitimate representative of the Palestinian people, it was no longer Jordan's role to represent the Palestinians in international negotiations.

The U.S. approved the transfer of 24 F-5 jet fighters from Iran to Jordan in January, but the direct supply of 35 F-5E interceptors, which had been promised in February 1973, was repeatedly delayed, reportedly because of production problems. King Hussein visited the United States April 28–May 11, and while he was there it was announced that the U.S. government was ready to sell Jordan 200 Hawk antiaircraft missiles. However, when U.S. Pres. Gerald Ford informed Congress on July 11 that the U.S. planned to sell Jordan a comprehensive air defense system costing about $350 million and including Vulcan antiaircraft guns and Redeye antiaircraft missiles as well as the Hawks, strong opposition was raised, and on July 28 Ford temporarily withdrew notice of the sale. The possibility that Saudi Arabia, which was due to finance the arms deal, would provide funds for Jordan to buy Soviet arms was seriously considered. Jordan announced that it had received 46 million dinars in Arab aid in 1974 and the amount was expected to increase in 1975. In September, however, after some hesitation over the conditions set by President Ford under congressional pressure, Jordan told the U.S. it would purchase the Hawk missiles, with the stipulation that they be used strictly for defense purposes.

Dismayed by the U.S. reluctance to supply arms and also alarmed by the moves toward a new Egyptian-Israeli interim agreement in Sinai which could mean Egypt's neutralization in a future Arab-Israeli war, King Hussein and his government moved closer to Syria. The king visited Damascus in April, and on June 10–12 Pres. Hafez al-Assad became the first Syrian head of state to visit Jordan since 1957. On June 12 a Jordanian-Syrian joint high commission to coordinate the two countries' foreign policies and armed forces was formed. But Jordan did not go as far as forming a joint military command, and it was clear that Jordan was not prepared to make a full alliance with Syria. Its chief concern was that, in the event of a Syrian-Israeli war, Syria's strong defenses might cause Israel to launch a "right hook" offensive through Jordanian territory. After a visit to Jordan in July by Syrian Prime Minister Mahmoud Ayoubi, a major economic and trade agreement and the creation of joint ventures was announced, Hussein paid a

WIDE WORLD

Jordan's King Hussein (left) escorted King Faisal to the Amman airport in January following a three-day visit by the Saudi Arabian monarch.

JORDAN

Education. (East Bank only; 1974–75) Primary, pupils 371,631, teachers 10,418; secondary, pupils 137,832, teachers 6,334; vocational, pupils 5,494, teachers 335; higher, students 9,302, teaching staff 493.

Finance. Monetary unit: Jordanian dinar, with (Sept. 22, 1975) a free rate of 0.325 dinar to U.S. $1 (0.67 dinar = £1 sterling). Gold, SDRs, and foreign exchange: (June 1975) U.S. $482.5 million; (June 1974) U.S. $320.4 million. Budget (1975 est.): revenue 206 million dinars; expenditure 218 million dinars. Gross national product: (1973) 287 million dinars; (1972) 263.2 million dinars. Money supply: (May 1975) 183,950,000 dinars; (May 1974) 153,190,000 dinars. Cost of living (Amman; 1970 = 100): (May 1975) 169; (May 1974) 153.

Foreign Trade. (1974) Imports 156,430,000 dinars; exports 49,770,000 dinars. Import sources: U.S. 11%; West Germany 9%; U.K. 8%; Lebanon 5%; Japan 5%; Egypt 5%. Export destinations: India 13%; Saudi Arabia 11%; Lebanon 8%; Japan 8%; Syria 6%; Kuwait 6%; Iran 5%. Main domestic exports: phosphates 21%; vegetables 13%; aircraft (reexports) 12%; cement 7%; oranges 7%; tobacco 5%. Tourism (1973): visitors 307,700; gross receipts U.S. $31 million.

Transport and Communications. Roads (1973) 5,909 km. (including 28 km. expressways). Motor vehicles in use (1973): passenger 19,011; commercial 6,933. Railways (1973) 480 km. Air traffic (1974): 373.8 million passenger-km.; freight 7,417,000 net ton-km. Telephones (Dec. 1973) 40,000. Radio receivers (Dec. 1972) 500,000. Television receivers (Dec. 1973) 80,000.

Agriculture. Production (in 000; metric tons; 1974; 1973 in parentheses): wheat *c.* 225 (50); barley (1973) 6, (1972) 34; lentils (1973) *c.* 10, (1972) 22; tomatoes c. 130 (83); watermelons (1973) *c.* 15, (1972) 40; olives *c.* 30 (5); oranges (1973) *c.* 19, (1972) 10; grapes (1973) 12, (1972) 18; bananas (1973) *c.* 7, (1972) 7; tobacco *c.* 1 (*c.* 1). Livestock (in 000; 1973): cattle *c.* 39; goats *c.* 350; sheep *c.* 650; camels *c.* 9; asses *c.* 44; chickens *c.* 2,676.

Industry. Production (in 000; metric tons; 1973): phosphate rock 1,081; petroleum products 633; cement (1974) 596; electricity (kw-hr.) 281,000.

Japanese Literature: *see* Literature

Jazz: *see* Music

Jehovah's Witnesses: *see* Religion

Jewish Literature: *see* Literature

further visit to Damascus in August, with his prime minister.

Internally Jordan remained fairly stable, despite the continued opposition of some Palestinian guerrilla elements who claimed widespread disaffection within the Army. The decision to send more military aid, including troops and 31 Hawker Hunter planes, to Oman to help fight against the Dhofar rebels was not popular with all Jordanians. On March 17 King Hussein announced that elections for a new Parliament to replace the one that was dissolved in November 1974 had been postponed indefinitely.

(PETER MANSFIELD)

See also Middle Eastern Affairs.
[978.B.3.d.ii]

Kenya

An African republic and a member of the Commonwealth of Nations, Kenya is bordered on the north by Sudan and Ethiopia, east by Somalia, south by Tanzania, and west by Uganda. Area: 224,961 sq.mi. (582,646 sq.km.), including 5,172 sq.mi. of inland water. Pop. (1975 est.): 13,413,000, including (1969) African 98.1%; Asian 1.5%. Cap. and largest city: Nairobi (pop., 1975 est., 700,000). Language: Swahili (official) and English. Religion: Protestant 36%; Roman Catholic 22%; Muslim 6%; others, mostly indigenous 36%. President in 1975, Jomo Kenyatta.

KENYA

Education. (1973) Primary, pupils 1,816,017, teachers 56,543; secondary, pupils 174,767, teachers 7,388; vocational, pupils 3,525, teachers 237; teacher training, students 8,905, teachers 578; higher, students 8,177.

Finance. Monetary unit: Kenyan shilling, with (Sept. 22, 1975) an official rate of KShs. 7.14 to U.S. $1 (free rate of KShs. 14.88 = £1 sterling). Gold, SDRs, and foreign exchange: (June 1975) U.S. $191.7 million; (June 1974) U.S. $203.6 million. Budget (1974–75 est.): revenue KShs. 4,240,000,000; expenditure KShs. 3,720,000,000. Gross national product: (1973) KShs. 15,790,000,000; (1972) KShs. 14,066,000,000. Cost of living (Nairobi; 1970 = 100): (April 1975) 149; (April 1974) 122.

Foreign Trade. (1974) Imports KShs. 7,327,000,000; exports KShs. 4,306,000,000. Import sources: U.K. 17%; Japan 11%; Iran 10%; West Germany 10%; Saudi Arabia 7%; U.S. 6%. Export destinations: Uganda 13%; Tanzania 9%; U.K. 9%; West Germany 8%; The Netherlands 5%. Main exports: petroleum products 19%; coffee 18%; tea 9%; sisal 8%; chemicals 7%. Tourism (1973): visitors 398,000; gross receipts U.S. $64 million.

Transport and Communications. Roads (1973) 48,206 km. Motor vehicles in use (1973): passenger 116,984; commercial 18,487. Railways: (1973) 2,070 km. (operated under East African Railways Corp., serving Kenya, mainland Tanzania, and Uganda with a total of 5,860 km.); traffic (total East African; 1966) 4,529,000,000 passenger-km., freight (1973) 4,442,000,000 net ton-km. Air traffic (apportionment of traffic of East African Airways Corp.; 1973): 549 million passenger-km.; freight 19.1 million ton-km. Telephones (Dec. 1973) 105,000. Radio receivers (Dec. 1973) 508,000. Television receivers (Dec. 1972) 37,000.

Agriculture. Production (in 000; metric tons; 1974; 1973 in parentheses): corn *c.* 1,400 (*c.* 1,300); wheat (1973) *c.* 172, (1972) *c.* 185; millet and sorghum *c.* 360 (*c.* 365); sweet potatoes (1973) *c.* 530, (1972) *c.* 530; cassava (1973) *c.* 640, (1972) *c.* 640; coffee *c.* 75 (71); tea (1973) *c.* 57, (1972) 53; sugar, raw value *c.* 133 (149); sisal (1973) *c.* 58, (1972) *c.* 41; cotton, lint *c.* 5 (*c.* 5); fish catch (1973) 29, (1972) 30. Livestock (in 000; May 1974): cattle *c.* 7,400; sheep *c.* 3,200; pigs *c.* 78; goats (1973) *c.* 3,600; camels (1973) *c.* 325; chickens (1973) *c.* 14,300.

Industry. Production (in 000; metric tons; 1973): salt 35; soda ash 206; cement (1974) 856; petroleum products 2,637; electricity (kw-hr.; 1974) 806,000.

In January 1975 and again in June, Kenya was the meeting place of leaders of the three Angolan liberation movements. President Kenyatta took an active role in seeking to resolve their rivalries and to provide for united action. Kenya itself, however, suffered during the course of the year from the activities of groups critical of the government. In February the first of a number of bomb explosions occurred. Most did little damage, but the worst, on March 1 in Nairobi, destroyed a bus, killing 27 people and injuring some 90 more. Telephone messages suggested that the outrages were the work of a poor people's movement but the government was unable to track down the offenders.

More disturbing still was the disappearance at the beginning of March of Josiah Kariuki, a member of Parliament who was critical of the government for its failure to distribute the country's wealth fairly. Shortly afterward he was found murdered and the implication of police or security officers was suspected. Demonstrations by students in Nairobi and violent criticisms from members of Parliament induced President Kenyatta to appoint a select committee of Parliament, which submitted its report on Kariuki's death at the beginning of June. The committee accused senior police officers of trying to cover up evidence and of failing to investigate the crime thoroughly. Ben Gehti, commander of the parliamentary police general service unit, was accused of having either taken an active part in the murder or of having been an accomplice.

A government attempt to postpone a debate on the report by the National Assembly was defeated, and after vigorous discussion the report was accepted by 62 votes to 59. Simultaneously, a minister and two assistant ministers who had criticized the government and given approval to the report were dismissed from office by the president. In the early hours of June 13 two further bombs exploded in Nairobi, and Kenyatta announced later in the day that anyone who thought of overthrowing the lawful government would find his plans doomed to failure. In October two leaders of Parliament were arrested and placed in detention, allegedly for being disloyal to the government, and Kenyatta warned that dissidents would no longer be tolerated.

There was rioting at Nairobi University on May 26 when police broke up a meeting called to protest the arrest of students during a demonstration that had taken place a few days earlier. The university was closed indefinitely, but charges against 103 students were withdrawn on the order of Kenyatta.

Kenya's neighbours created further problems for the government. In December 1974 Tanzania decided to expel all Kenyan nationals from Dar es Salaam and many parts of northern Tanzania and also banned heavy trucks from using the highways in the north. This latter decision delayed the transit of goods from Mombasa to Lusaka, Zambia, with heavy financial loss to Kenya. Uganda's growing military strength was also a source of worry. In June 1975 a convoy transporting Soviet military vehicles to Uganda was held up in Kenya but later completed its journey after reassurances from Pres. Idi Amin. In August the Kenyan government concluded a $5 million arms deal with the U.S. and also purchased arms from West Germany and France.

The increasing cost of imports, particularly oil, fostered inflation, and in spite of the continued investment in Kenya by foreign countries the economy was

Journalism:
see Publishing
Judaism:
see Israel; Religion
Judo:
see Combat Sports
Karate:
see Combat Sports
Kashmir:
see India; Pakistan
Kendo:
see Combat Sports
Khmer Republic:
see Cambodia

under pressure. In mid-April the government ordered 463 businesses, mainly owned by Asians, to be closed as a further installment in the campaign to transfer trade to Kenyan citizens. Two weeks later the president announced an increase in the legal minimum pay of Kenyans, particularly of low-paid agricultural workers, but reminded the public that strikes were still banned. In June the government signed an agreement with the Federal Home Loan Bank of New York by which the latter body would lend $38.4 million, repayable over 30 years, to build 4,300 low-priced houses in Kenya. (KENNETH INGHAM)

[978.E.6.b.v]

Korea

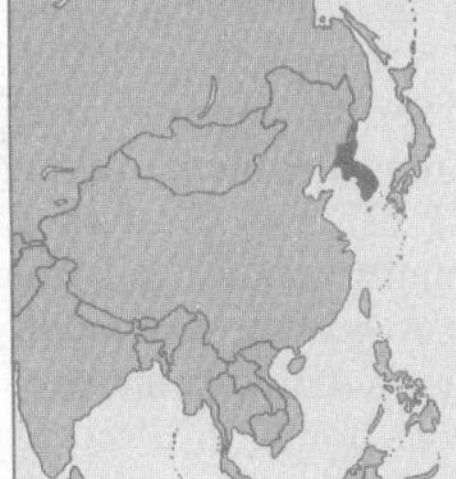

A country of eastern Asia, Korea is bounded by China, the Sea of Japan, the Korea Strait, and the Yellow Sea. It is divided into two parts at the 38th parallel.

The collapse of the U.S. commitment in Vietnam, Cambodia, and Laos turned worldwide attention to Korea in the second quarter of 1975. Two aspects of the question formed the subject of speculation: would the victory of Communist forces in Indochina inspire Korean Communists to go on the offensive? And, would the Americans honour their military commitments in Korea even if it meant another war?

The U.S. government seemed anxious to eliminate all speculation on the second point. It lost no time in announcing its intention to honour all its pledges to South Korea. In May Defense Secretary James Schlesinger, who personally visited Seoul in August, emphasized Washington's continuing solidarity with Seoul. He said the U.S. might "go for the heart of the opponent's power" if North Korea were to invade the South. Senate majority leader Mike Mansfield frankly acknowledged that the prospects of a new Asian war worried him, because if North Korea attacked the South, the U.S. would have no choice but to intervene. Reports in June indicated that the U.S. had quietly increased its military presence in South Korea by an additional 4,000 troops during the previous 12 months, thus reaching the authorized maximum of 42,000. In October South Korean Defense Minister Suh Jyong Chul said plans were afoot to establish a combined U.S.-South Korean military command in preparation for the expected dissolution of the UN command in January 1976.

In the circumstances, the diplomatic dialogue started between the two Koreas three years previously remained moribund. The South proposed a resumption of contacts, but the North refused to consider any such move until Seoul abandoned its anti-Communist policies.

Republic of Korea (South Korea). Area: 38,130 sq.mi. (98,758 sq.km.). Pop. (1974 est.): 33,459,000. Cap. and largest city: Seoul (pop., 1973 est., 6,289,600). Language: Korean. Religion: Buddhist; Confucian; Tonghak (Chondokyo). President in 1975, Gen. Park Chung Hee; prime ministers, Kim Chong Pil to December 19 and Choi Kyu Hah.

The post-Vietnam atmosphere prompted President Park to stress repeatedly the danger from the North and to ask his people to concentrate on preparing for an all-out fight for survival. Many in the nation responded to this call, believing the threat to be of utmost seriousness; but others protested, and there was widespread disappointment when a ranking party official said there would be no elections in 1975. However, a referendum was held in February, and Park received a strong mandate to continue his policies. A number of political prisoners were released following the referendum.

Reports of massive arrests, persecution, and other repressive actions continued to circulate widely. Political opponents, journalists, church leaders, lawyers, and students staged rallies, sit-ins, and strikes. In April, Yonsei University was closed after a violent student demonstration, and eight leftists accused of instigating a student plot were executed on April 10. Prime Minister Kim Chong Pil said at one point that the government, in the circumstances, could not indefinitely tolerate attempts to "create social confusion" by raising demands for the restoration of democratic practices. At the same time, it was reported that many

KOREA: Republic

Education. (1974–75) Primary, pupils 5,599,074, teachers 108,126; secondary, pupils 2,674,972, teachers 67,332; vocational, students 451,032, teachers 15,340; higher, students 286,342, teaching staff 13,885.

Finance. Monetary unit: won, with (Sept. 22, 1975) an official rate of 485 won to U.S. $1 (free rate of 1,005 won = £1 sterling). Gold, SDRs, and foreign exchange: (June 1975) U.S. $1,097,400,000; (June 1974) U.S. $1,020,600,000. Budget (1974 est.): revenue 780,730,000,000 won; expenditure 967,440,000,000 won. Gross national product: (1974) 6,942,900,000,000 won; (1973) 4,928,700,000,000 won. Money supply: (Dec. 1974) 945.7 billion won; (Dec. 1973) 730.3 billion won. Cost of living (1970 = 100): (July 1975) 208.3; (May 1974) 161.

Foreign Trade. (1974) Imports 2,771,000,000,000 won; exports 1,805,900,000,000 won. Import sources: Japan 38%; U.S. 25%; Saudi Arabia 10%. Export destinations: U.S. 33%; Japan 31%; West Germany 5%. Main exports: clothing 21%; textile yarns and fabrics 11%; electrical machinery and equipment 11%; iron and steel 10%; food 7%. Tourism (1973): visitors 67,800; gross receipts U.S. $264 million.

Transport and Communications. Roads (1973) 43,580 km. (including 1,013 km. expressways). Motor vehicles in use (1973): passenger 78,300; commercial (including buses) 83,500. Railways: (1973) 5,521 km.; traffic (1974) 10,908,000,000 passenger-km., freight 8,797,000,000 net ton-km. Air traffic (1973): 2,496,000,000 passenger-km.; freight 128.3 million net ton-km. Shipping (1974): merchant vessels 100 gross tons and over 650; gross tonnage 1,225,679. Telephones (Dec. 1973) 846,000. Radio receivers (Dec. 1972) 4,115,000. Television receivers (Dec. 1972) 955,000.

Agriculture. Production (in 000; metric tons; 1974; 1973 in parentheses): rice 6,067 (5,854); wheat *c.* 280 (162); barley 1,881 (1,778); potatoes *c.* 470 (470); sweet potatoes (1973) 1,669, (1972) 1,887; soybeans *c.* 323 (246); cabbages (1973) *c.* 1,000, (1972) *c.* 1,000; tomatoes *c.* 57 (*c.* 57); onions *c.* 100 (*c.* 100); apples *c.* 300 (291); grapes *c.* 57 (57); tobacco *c.* 112 (*c.* 112); fish catch (1973) 1,655, (1972) 1,339. Livestock (in 000; Dec. 1973): cattle *c.* 1,260; pigs *c.* 1,450; goats (1972) *c.* 135; chickens (1972) *c.* 29,000.

Industry. Production (in 000; metric tons; 1974): coal 15,289; iron ore (50% metal content) 493; steel 1,935; cement 8,843; tungsten concentrates (oxide content; 1973) 2.8; zinc (1973) 13; kaolin (1972) 184; fluorite (1972) 29; limestone (1971) 11,213; gold (troy oz.; 1973) 14; silver (troy oz.; 1973) 1,479; sulfuric acid 474; petroleum products (1973) 14,302; electricity (excluding most industrial production; kw-hr.) 16,833,000.

KOREA: Democratic People's Republic

Education. (1973–74 est.) Primary, pupils *c.* 1.5 million; secondary and vocational, pupils *c.* 1.2 million; primary, secondary, and vocational, teachers *c.* 100,000; higher, students *c.* 300,000.

Finance and Trade. Monetary unit: won, with (Sept. 22, 1975) a nominal official exchange rate of 1 won to U.S. $1 (2.07 won = £1 sterling). Budget (1973 est.) balanced at 8,544,000,000 won. Foreign trade (1973): approximate imports *c.* 1 billion won (50% from China, 30% from U.S.S.R., 10% from Japan, 6% from France); exports *c.* 1 billion won (65% to China, 18% to U.S.S.R., 7% to Japan). Main exports (1964): metals 50%; minerals 12%; farm products 11%.

Agriculture. Production (in 000; metric tons; 1973; 1972 in parentheses): rice *c.* 1,450 (*c.* 1,350); corn *c.* 900 (*c.* 800); barley *c.* 330 (*c.* 320): millet *c.* 400 (*c.* 380); potatoes *c.* 1,050 (*c.* 1,000); sweet potatoes *c.* 300 (*c.* 290); soybeans *c.* 250 (*c.* 235); apples *c.* 125 (*c.* 120); tobacco *c.* 40 (*c.* 40); fish catch (1967) 1,200, (1964) 770. Livestock (in 000; Dec. 1973): cattle *c.* 767; pigs *c.* 1,491; sheep *c.* 200; goats *c.* 180; chickens *c.* 20,000.

Industry. Production (in 000; metric tons; 1973): coal 30,000; iron ore (metal content) *c.* 4,420; pig iron *c.* 2,700; steel *c.* 2,630; lead *c.* 80; zinc *c.* 130; magnesite *c.* 1,700; silver (troy oz.) *c.* 700; cement *c.* 5,800; tungsten concentrates (oxide content) *c.* 2.7; electricity (kw-hr.; 1965) 13,300,000.

WIDE WORLD

Entrance to a tunnel which was dug by North Koreans beneath the demilitarized zone 65 miles northeast of Seoul. The UN Command protested this activity in March.

South Koreans felt that the circumstances warranted even stricter controls on criticism of government policies than were actually imposed.

The worldwide business recession adversely affected production and prices in 1975. The 1974 gross national product was officially estimated to be $17 billion, representing an annual growth rate of 8.2%, whereas the projected growth rate for 1975 was 7%. Exports in the first five months of 1975 aggregated $1.7 billion, only 29% of the year's $6 billion target. Officials predicted that it would take until the end of 1976 for the economy to absorb completely the impact of the fourfold rise in the price of crude oil.

Democratic People's Republic of Korea (North Korea). Area: 46,800 sq.mi. (121,200 sq.km.). Pop. (1974 est.): 15,439,000. Cap.: Pyongyang (metro. pop., 1974 est., 1.5 million). Language: Korean. Religion: Buddhist; Confucian; Tonghak (Chondokyo). General secretary of the Central Committee of the Workers' Party of Korea, president, and chairman of the Council of Ministers (premier) in 1975, Marshal Kim Il Sung.

Pres. Kim Il Sung raised many eyebrows around the world when he paid a rare visit to Peking in April 1975 in the aftermath of the Vietnam war. Western speculation was that he was trying to enlist Chinese backing for a putsch against the South. But China's moderate line of recent years and its anxiety to stay on the right side of the U.S. for its own reasons made any such collusion unlikely. Kim subscribed to the U.S. view that another Asian war was quite possible. In June he charged that the U.S. had placed large quantities of nuclear weapons in South Korea and that war could break out at any moment. Visiting Eastern Europe and Algeria in May, he proclaimed that the U.S. would face a disaster worse than Indochina if it did not withdraw its forces from South Korea. July was observed as "the month of the anti-U.S. joint struggle," with rallies throughout the country. However, Kim told a visiting Japanese mission in July that he would not use military force against South Korea. A secret meeting he later held with a close confidante of Japanese Prime Minister Takeo Miki gave rise to reports that he was trying to establish contacts with the U.S. Japanese and Chinese leaders meanwhile maintained the position that there was no danger of another Korean war breaking out in the immediate future.

Whatever the speculation about war, North Korea did gain diplomatically during the year. The nonaligned nations' conference in Lima, Peru, approved its application for membership while rejecting that of South Korea. In the UN the question of Korean membership was dominated by Pyongyang's stand that separate membership was unnecessary; strong backing by the U.S. for Seoul's membership application was of no avail. In his UN speech in September, U.S. Secretary of State Henry Kissinger proposed a conference between North and South Korea and China and the U.S. Reacting coldly to the proposal, the North Korean spokesman, Li Yun Gyon, said it did not touch on what his government thought to be the crucial issue; namely, the withdrawal of U.S. troops from South Korea.

Serious payment arrears cast shadows across North Korea's economy during the year. Estimates of trading debts to Western Europe, Japan, and the Communist bloc ranged from $700 million to $1.7 billion in August. It was reported that North Korea was the first socialist country to fail to pay its trade obligations promptly. Sweden and West Germany suspended the issuing of export insurance on deals with Pyongyang and other countries lodged complaints. The government reaffirmed its intention to settle all outstanding bills and, with a $200 million loan from Iran, began making some arrears payments to Japan.

(T. J. S. GEORGE)

[975.C.]

Kuwait

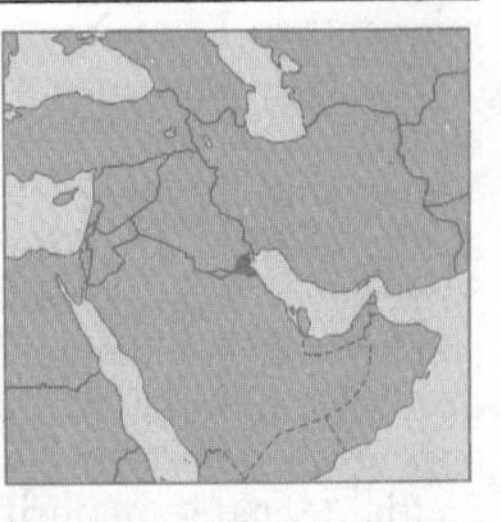

An independent emirate, Kuwait is on the northwestern coast of the Persian Gulf between Iraq and Saudi Arabia. Area: 6,880 sq.mi. (17,818 sq.km.). Pop. (1975 prelim.): 991,400. Cap.: Kuwait (pop., 1975 prelim., 78,000). Largest city: Hawalli (pop., 1975 prelim., 130,300). Language: Arabic. Religion (1970): Muslim 94.7%; Christian 4.6%. Emir in 1975, Sheikh Sabah as-Salim as-Sabah; prime minister, Crown Prince Sheikh Jabir al-Ahmad al-Jabir as-Sabah.

Kuwait's revenues and financial reserves increased in 1975, as did foreign aid and investment. From an average oil output of 2,250,000 bbl. a day in 1974 (17% below 1973), production fell to 2 million bbl. a day in early 1975. Revenues for fiscal 1975–76, estimated by the Central Bank of Kuwait at 2 billion dinars, represented a 23% drop from the previous year—owing to a decline in the world demand for oil. In March the Kuwaiti dinar was temporarily tied to the International Monetary Fund's Special Drawing Rights, to the exclusion of the U.S. dollar. A Swiss bank estimated that in 1974 Kuwaitis had the highest per capita gross national product in the world—$11,500. In April the government announced aid of $415 million for the three Arab states confronting Israel, the Palestine Liberation Organization, and four poorer Arab states—Mauritania, Somalia, and the two Yemens. Relations with Saudi Arabia were close, and in March an economic and cultural agreement was signed. Pres. Anwar as-Sadat of Egypt visited Kuwait in May and secured Kuwait's participation in an arms project. In May the emir of Kuwait visited Paris, and Kuwaiti purchases of French armaments

KUWAIT

Education. (1973–74) Primary, pupils 94,087, teachers 5,033; secondary, pupils 88,922, teachers 7,283; vocational, pupils 2,187, teachers 390; teacher training, students 847, teachers 98; higher, students (1972–73) 3,339, teaching staff (1971–72) 250.

Finance. Monetary unit: Kuwaiti dinar, with (Sept. 22, 1975) a free rate of 0.294 dinar to U.S. $1 (0.610 dinar = £1 sterling). Gold and foreign exchange: (June 1975) U.S. $1,194,600,000; (June 1974) U.S. $959.2 million. Budget (1974–75 est.): revenue 960 million dinars; expenditure 574 million dinars.

Foreign Trade. (1974) Imports 455,090,000 dinars; exports 3,214,759,000 dinars. Import sources: Japan 17%; U.S. 14%; West Germany 11%; U.K. 8%. Export destinations: Japan 26%; U.K. 16%; France 10%; Singapore 5%; Italy 5%. Main exports: crude oil 81%; petroleum products 15%.

Transport. Air traffic (1973): 795 million passenger-km.; freight 18.3 million net ton-km. Shipping (1974): merchant vessels 100 gross tons and over 161; gross tonnage 681,692. Shipping traffic (1972): goods loaded 174.6 million metric tons, unloaded 1,439,000 metric tons.

Industry. Production (in 000; metric tons; 1973): petroleum products 18,974; crude oil (1974) 114,627; natural gas (cu.m.) 5,267,000.

were announced. A census estimate in May showed that Kuwaitis constituted only 47.4% of the population; the remainder were principally temporary inhabitants. In elections in January 258 candidates contested 50 seats in the National Assembly and 60–65% of the 40,000 eligible voters cast ballots.

In March the government formally took over British Petroleum's and Gulf Oil's 40% share of the Kuwait Oil Co. Talks with the companies were broken off in April, but in December the government agreed to pay at least $50.5 million in compensation.

(PETER MANSFIELD)

[978.B.4.b]

Laos

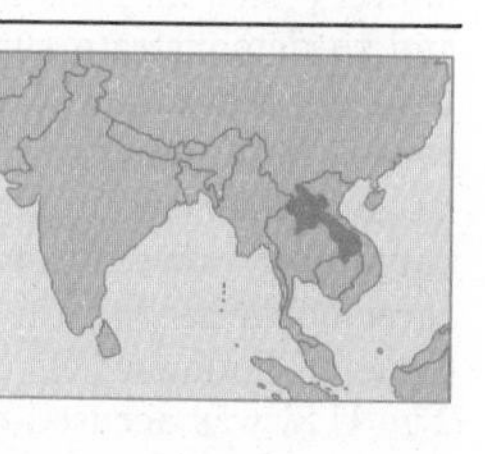

Nominally a constitutional monarchy until Dec. 3, 1975; on that date the People's Democratic Republic of Laos was proclaimed. A landlocked country of Southeast Asia, Laos is bounded by China, North and South Vietnam, Cambodia, Thailand, and Burma. Area: 91,400 sq.mi. (236,800 sq.km.). Pop. (1975 est.): 3,303,000. Cap. and largest city: Vientiane (pop., 1973, 176,600). Language: Lao (official); French and English. Religion: Buddhist; tribal. King until December 3, Savang Vatthana; president from December 3, Prince Souphanouvong; premiers, Prince Souvanna Phouma and, from December 3, Kaysone Phomvihan.

Laos in 1975 achieved a revolutionary transformation as historic as that of Cambodia and South Vietnam, but the style was vastly different. As the year opened it was clear that Communist successes across the border would be influencing events in Laos. The collapse of the Phnom Penh and Saigon regimes in April and May not only gave massive encouragement to pro-Communist forces in Laos; it dampened the rightists' last-ditch hope that the U.S. would intervene in case of a showdown. The Pathet Lao began what appeared to be a concerted program to force the rightists out of the government. On the one hand, it began actively wooing the moderates in the government and, on the other, it organized military and social pressure. A series of localized battles invariably went in favour of the Pathet Lao.

LAOS

Education. (1972–73) Primary, pupils 273,357, teachers 7,320; secondary, pupils 14,633, teachers 613; vocational, pupils 1,946, teachers 186; teacher training, students 4,031, teachers 227; higher, students 625, teaching staff 106.

Finance. Monetary unit: kip, with (Sept. 22, 1975) a nominal official exchange rate of 750 kip to U.S. $1 (nominal free rate of 1,550 kip = £1 sterling). Budget (1973–74 rev. est.): revenue (excluding foreign aid) 13,785,000,000 kip; expenditure 28,785,000,000 kip (including defense expenditure of 14 billion kip).

Foreign Trade. (1973) Imports 34,304,000,000 kip; exports 3,045,000,000 kip. Import sources: Thailand 47%; Japan 13%; France 10%; U.S. 7%; Switzerland 5%; Singapore 5%. Export destinations: Thailand 65%; Malaysia 29%. Main exports: tin 57%; timber 36%.

Transport and Communications. Roads (1972) c. 7,300 km. (including c. 3,300 km. all-weather). Motor vehicles in use (1973): passenger 13,600; commercial (including buses) 2,400. Air traffic (1973): 22 million passenger-km.; freight 500,000 net ton-km. Inland waterways (Mekong River) 715 km. Telephones (Dec. 1973) 5,000. Radio licenses (Dec. 1973) c. 150,000.

Agriculture. Production (in 000; metric tons; 1973; 1972 in parentheses): rice 883 (817); corn c. 29 (27); melons c. 20 (c. 20); oranges c. 17 (c. 17); pineapples c. 26 (c. 26); coffee c. 2 (c. 3); tobacco c. 4 (c. 4). Livestock (in 000; 1973): cattle c. 450; buffalo c. 960; pigs c. 1,250; chickens c. 13,000.

Industry. Production (1973): tin concentrates (metal content; metric tons) 748; electricity (excluding most industrial production; kw-hr.) c. 245 million.

Workers' strikes, demonstrations by civil servants and war veterans, and continual rioting by students spread an atmosphere of social unrest throughout the country. The southern town of Pakse was "occupied" by students and the governor and other officials held hostage. In the royal capital of Luang Prabang, students took over the radio station and demanded the dismissal of the city's right-wing governor. Rallies in key centres singled out rightist leaders for criticism.

By the second week of May, the rightists began to yield. Those who had been publicly condemned by rioters told the prime minister they were prepared to "make sacrifices for national concord." On May 9, as elements of Pathet Lao troops marched ostentatiously toward Vientiane along Highway 13, their leaders accused Defense Minister Sisouk Na Champassak of planning a coup with Thailand's support. That night Champassak and four other ministers resigned, along with several rightist generals. On May 11, as the country held ceremonies to mark the 28th anniversary of its Constitution Day, the rightist leaders were reported to have escaped quietly to unknown destinations. A Pathet Lao leader became the new defense minister, and King Savang Vatthana asked all troops to take orders only from the Defense Ministry. The leftists had taken over Laos although, formally, the coalition continued.

Attention now turned to forcing the Americans out of the country. Riots broke out around U.S. establishments. A dozen or more U.S. officials of the Agency for International Development (AID) in Savannakhet were detained for about nine days by student demonstrators, who demanded the expulsion of Americans and the abolition of all U.S. AID agreements. Pressure on the U.S. seemed to mount in proportion to fears in Vientiane that the rightist leaders who fled were planning to set up a government in exile. The Pathet Lao news agency gave details of the invasion the rightists were said to have planned, but no invasion took place. Throughout the turmoil, the U.S. remained inactive. It agreed to wind down the AID program and withdrew the last AID personnel on June 26.

Labour Unions: *see* Industrial Relations

Lacrosse: *see* Field Hockey and Lacrosse

WIDE WORLD

Buddhist monks sat among the guests at an August rally in Vientiane designed to introduce the new revolutionary administration in Laos.

Although Laos was virtually Communist by the end of May, the Pathet Lao leadership insisted that it wished to abide by the 1973 peace formula, which had put the coalition government in power. It found four moderate right-wingers to join the Cabinet. By June something of a cultural revolution was under way, with a reshuffling of civil servants, a radical poster campaign, and a program to reeducate the officers of the former loyalist Army.

The general impression in the following months was that moderates in positions of power were being replaced by Hanoi-leaning hard-liners. In a sudden turn of events three leading members of the hierarchy—Deputy Premier Phoumi Vongvichit, Information Minister Souk Bongsak, and Economics Minister Soth Petrasy—were reported to be going abroad on leave. Their positions were quickly filled by new men from the inner circle of the Pathet Lao headquarters in Sam Neua. Finally, on December 3, it was announced that both the coalition government and the 600-year-old monarchy had been abolished. Interest focused on the new leadership, but this remained a matter for speculation. The new president, Prince Souphanouvong, was the most publicized Pathet Lao leader, but it was widely believed he was no more than that. Kaysone Phomvihan, the premier and secretary-general of the Laos People's Party, had reportedly been directing Pathet Lao operations from the North Vietnam border area. Neither he nor the new first deputy premier, Neuhak Phoumsavan, had been seen in public for many years.

With U.S. subsidies gone and exports negligible, the country was expected to enter a period of economic austerity. In March the kip was devalued by 25% against the U.S. dollar. The system of bolstering the currency with international contributions continued; although the U.S. declined to make any more contributions, France, Japan, Britain, and Australia announced continuation of their quotas. In September Laos announced a new red, white, and blue national flag. (T. J. S. GEORGE)

See also Southeast Asian Affairs: *Special Report.*

[976.B.4.e]

Latin-American Affairs

The new U.S. Trade Act, signed by Pres. Gerald Ford on Jan. 3, 1975, led to a period of strained relations between the U.S. and the Latin-American countries early in the year. The sanctions established in the act, particularly that preferential access to the U.S. market should not be extended to any member of the Organization of Petroleum Exporting Countries (OPEC) or any other group that withheld supplies of vital commodity resources from international trade or regulated its prices, could affect most Latin-American countries.

On Jan. 27, 1975, the Argentine minister of foreign affairs, Alberto Vignes, announced that, after consulting with his Latin-American colleagues, he had received their consent to postpone the third meeting of "new dialogue" between Latin America and the U.S., scheduled for March in Buenos Aires. The Latin-American representatives on the Permanent Council of the Organization of American States (OAS) had already unanimously determined that the act contravened basic doctrines of the OAS Charter and violated the principles of the Charter of Economic Rights and Duties of States, approved by the UN General Assembly on Dec. 12, 1974. Another reason for the cancellation was the OAS's decision in November 1974 to maintain sanctions against Cuba, which was not supported by some countries. As a result, U.S. Secretary of State Henry Kissinger suspended his February tour of the region.

The Trade Act had the effect of moving U.S.-Latin-American relations in a new direction. Mexico and Venezuela proposed an exclusively Latin-American system of consultation and economic cooperation to organize multinational concerns and to establish joint programs and projects to develop the region's natural resources. The idea was well received, and Mexico and Venezuela agreed to coordinate the project.

At the end of March, presidents Alfonso López Michelsen of Colombia, Daniel Oduber Quirós of Costa Rica, Carlos Andrés Pérez of Venezuela, and Gen. Omar Torrijos Herrera of Panama (*see* BIOGRAPHY) met in Panama to study regional problems and to demonstrate support for Panama in its effort to negotiate a new canal treaty with the U.S. The four-nation meeting reflected the attempt by reformist Latin-American governments to reinforce their bargaining power vis-à-vis the U.S. by coordinating agreements among themselves. Meanwhile, the U.S. Congress indicated its opposition to Panama's claims. The U.S. was accused of delaying the treaty negotiations to avoid possible embarrassment to President Ford during a presidential campaign year.

The annual General Assembly of the OAS, held in Washington, D.C., May 8 to 19, reversed the trend toward confrontation with the U.S., and a constructive dialogue was initiated. The U.S. announced that it did not intend to apply the restrictive measures specified in the Trade Act to OPEC countries in Latin America (Venezuela and Ecuador). The Special Commission for Consultation and Negotiation was to meet to seek the best courses the act offered for promoting trade between the U.S. and the other OAS countries. Also lessening tension was the joint report of the U.S. and Panamanian delegations on the state of bilateral Canal Zone negotiations. The report affirmed that the U.S. would transfer sovereign power over the Canal Zone to Panama and that the operation of the waterway would be so arranged that the U.S. would continue to act through the Panama Canal Company and to provide military protection.

The key problem in inter-American relations continued to be U.S. predominance in Latin America. In turn, the OAS had been constrained by the limitations placed on it as a political mechanism. A reform of its charter and of the 1947 Inter-American Treaty of Reciprocal Assistance (Rio Treaty) was called for, and the General Assembly scheduled a special meeting in July at San José, Costa Rica, to discuss the matter. During the San José meeting it was agreed to change the voting procedure established by the Rio Treaty, thus opening the way to the lifting of sanctions against Cuba. The OAS action put pressure on the U.S. to develop a more open policy toward Cuba, since the U.S. had insisted that it could not proceed with Cuban détente until the multilateral OAS sanctions were ended. It also removed one of the major irritants in inter-American relations. In concrete terms, however, the OAS move would have little immediate effect; those Latin-American countries wishing to trade with Cuba had already gone ahead despite the OAS ban and, although Cuba and the U.S. appeared headed toward reconciliation, the process promised to be long, painful, and complicated.

On May 17 Alejandro Orfila (*see* BIOGRAPHY), the Argentine ambassador to the U.S., was elected to a five-year term as secretary-general of the OAS. He succeeded Galo Plaza Lasso of Ecuador.

The system of consultation put forward by Mexico and Venezuela gained momentum on August 2, when representatives of 25 Latin-American countries, meeting in Panama, voted to establish the Sistema Económico Latino Americano (SELA), 23 signing then and 2 signing later. Conceived as an alternative to the U.S.-dominated OAS, SELA was designed to promote regional development on a variety of fronts, including creation of Latin-American multinational companies to develop regional resources; establishment of mechanisms to maintain prices and guarantee joint marketing; adoption of a regional policy to ensure that decisions of international companies or industrialized countries operating in the region conformed to the region's development objectives; improvement of regional production of basic goods, especially food; regional interchange of technology; and intraregional communications and transport systems. The formal establishment of SELA took place on October 18, when 23 Latin-American and Caribbean countries signed its charter in Panama. Two Latin-American multinationals founded in 1975, the Cafés Suaves Centrales coffee-marketing company and Namucar, a Caribbean shipping company, were not directly part of SELA but exemplified its spirit.

RENAULT—SACRAMENTO BEE/ROTHCO

Uncle Quixote

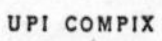
UPI COMPIX

Mexican Pres. Luis Echeverría (centre) was greeted by Cuban Prime Minister Fidel Castro (left) and Cuban Pres. Osvaldo Dorticós on his arrival in Havana for a visit in August.

Regional and Subregional Integration. Collective negotiations under the Latin American Free Trade Association (LAFTA) continued during 1975, but no agreement on changes in the organization and the tariff-cutting mechanism was reached. LAFTA was operating under the broad mandate of the 1969 Caracas Protocol calling for free trade within the region by 1980. This had become an excuse for delay once it became apparent that the group's original 1973 deadline could not be met, but LAFTA failed to devise a new plan. It was recommended that the Annual Conference and Permanent Executive Committee be replaced by a commission similar to that of the Andean Group, but Argentina, Brazil, Mexico, and the smaller nations were divided on the issue.

The six-nation Andean Group advanced its tariff-reduction program. Tariffs in force between Chile, Colombia, Peru, and Venezuela were again reduced by 10% from January 1, bringing to 40% the total reduction since annual reductions began on Jan. 1, 1972. The program envisaged the abolition of tariff barriers among these four countries on Dec. 31, 1980. Imports from Bolivia and Ecuador were already allowed to enter the other member countries duty-free. Bolivian and Ecuadorean tariffs on products from Chile, Colombia, Peru, and Venezuela were to be lowered in a series of automatic reductions starting in 1976, with free entry postponed until the beginning of 1986. The group was also working to establish a common external tariff, with similar timing.

The difficulties encountered by the Andean Group in reaching agreement on the final allocations for the petrochemical and motor vehicle programs reflected both the importance of the programs and the problems of integration. The integration program had survived political changes in some of the member countries, but its development was being hindered by differences in levels of economic development, even though special provisions had been made for preferential treatment of less developed Bolivia and Ecuador.

The Central American Common Market (CACM) continued its progress toward integration. At the end of 1974 the Secretariat submitted, for discussion by the High Level Committee, a draft treaty on the creation of a Central American Economic and Social Community. Among other things, the draft called for common treatment of foreign investment and technology; rules on repatriation of profits and reinvestment; foreign acquisition of existing domestic firms; and the creation of multinational Central-American companies. Adoption of the treaty would probably await normalization of relations between Honduras and El Salvador and the return of Honduras to the CACM. In the meantime, a short-term action plan based on a program of the UN Economic Commission for Latin America was adopted.

Inter-American Development Bank. The IDB annual survey on economic and social progress in Latin America showed that the combined gross domestic product of the Latin-American and Caribbean countries had increased impressively in 1973 and 1974, by an average annual rate of 7.4%. The economic expansion in Latin America was suggested by the increase in gross domestic investment. Investment outlays in 1972 and 1973 (at constant prices) grew at rates of 10.5 and 10.1%, respectively (5.1% during 1961–65 and 7.8% in 1966–70). Exports, which helped to accelerate economic growths, rose (in real terms) 14.6% in 1973 and about 10% in 1974 (4.6% in 1961–70). The share of national savings in the region's total investment increased from 85% in 1971 to 94% in 1973.

The 16th meeting of the Board of Governors of the IDB was held in Santo Domingo, Dominican Republic, on May 19–21, 1975. The IDB's president, Antonio Ortiz Mena, reported that the bank had granted 53 loans totaling $1,111,000,000 to Latin-American countries in 1974. This amount, the highest in the bank's history, represented a rise of more than $200 million over the amount approved in 1973.

(JAIME R. DUHART)

See also articles on the various political units.

[971.D.8; 974]

ENCYCLOPÆDIA BRITANNICA FILMS. *Venezuela: Oil Builds a Nation* (1972); *Central America: Finding New Ways* (2nd ed., 1974); *Costa Rica: My Country* (2nd ed., 1974).

Law

Court Decisions. Many similar problems were resolved, sometimes differently, by the courts of the world in 1975. These problems involved such matters as abortion laws, freedom of speech, family law, educational rights, election laws, and distinctions between private and public activities for purposes of determining whether those activities are permissible.

Abortion. Abortion laws came under judicial scrutiny in four countries, paralleling litigation in the U.S. in 1973. The Italian Constitutional Court surprised some observers by ruling that abortions were permissible where the continued pregnancy would endanger the physical or mental health of the mother. It held that a 1930 law prohibiting abortions was unconstitutional in that it recognized no exceptions. French and Austrian courts similarly upheld laws allowing abortions, but the West German Federal Constitutional Court took a different stance. It held by a 6 to 2 vote that no law could allow abortion in violation of the rights of the unborn. Art. 2 of the West German constitution provides that "Everyone has a right to life and to inviolability of his person." This provision had been assumed to protect individuals against the "liquidations" carried out by the National Socialist regime as government policy, but it had been uncertain whether it applied to "life developing in the mother's womb."

Latin-American Literature: *see* Literature

Latter-day Saints: *see* Religion

Freedom of Press. The English courts had been trying for several years to strike a balance between freedom of press and the right to a fair trial. This balance is admittedly difficult to achieve; the criminally accused frequently have contended that they do not have a fair trial if the crime in question is unduly publicized, and the press is determined that the public shall be informed. In two cases in 1975 the English courts seemed to tip the balance in favour of the press, but in a third they appeared to go the other way.

In one case the Court of Appeal held that members of the press had a right to view allegedly obscene publications shown by the prosecution in a criminal trial, even though members of the public could be barred from such showings. The court reasoned that the press should have this right in order to be able to provide the public with information needed to form opinions on sexual and moral standards and the correct legal posture on these matters. In a second case a high court held that the press had the right to publish detailed accounts of past Cabinet meetings supplied by a member of the Cabinet, even though some of the participants in those meetings still occupied important government positions. In a third case, however, the court held members of the press in contempt for releasing the names of witnesses, even though the order of the court not to release the names was not specifically directed to the press but to another party.

Family Law. A West German court and the U.S. Supreme Court appeared to take different views on the right of a widower to receive a pension after the death of his wife. The West German Constitutional Court upheld a law providing that a man is only entitled to a widower's pension if the wife had worked and contributed to the support of her family. The Supreme Court, on the other hand, held portions of the U.S. Social Security law unconstitutional because they made distinctions between widows and widowers respecting survivor's benefits (*Weinberger* v. *Wiesenfeld*, 95 S.Ct. 1225). The law provided that survivor's

William O. Douglas, who served as justice of the U.S. Supreme Court for over 36 years, longer than any other justice in history, tendered his resignation to President Ford in November. Douglas indicated that the effects of a stroke suffered in December 1974 prevented satisfactory performance of his duties on the bench.

UPI COMPIX

benefits would be paid to a widow and the minor children of a man covered by the act, but only to the minor children, and not to the widower, of a woman covered by the act. The court said this provision violated the right to equal protection secured by the Fifth Amendment to the U.S. Constitution; women wage earners were required by the law to pay Social Security taxes but were afforded less protection for their survivors than was provided for men wage earners.

Education. In a significant opinion, the European Court of Justice overturned a decision of the French government to restrict educational financial aid to French students. The court found that this restriction violated rulings based on the Treaty of Rome guaranteeing equal protection to migrant workers within the European Economic Community (EEC) with respect to all rights arising from admission to educational courses. In Switzerland the Basel-Stadt Administrative Court held that students may not be forced to join a student union since such a requirement would violate their right of free access to education.

In *Goss* v. *Lopez* (95 S.Ct. 729), the U.S. Supreme Court held that students facing temporary suspension from public schools were entitled to be given notice of the charges on which the suspension was based and the right to present their version of the facts to the appropriate authorities, in most cases prior to removal from school. Though the majority opinion in this 5 to 4 decision stopped short of finding that there is a constitutionally guaranteed right to an education, it did find that a student's interest in statutorily defined education was a property right protected by the due process clause of the U.S. Constitution.

Election Laws. Perhaps the most important judicial decision handed down during the year took place in India, where Prime Minister Indira Gandhi was convicted by a provincial court of election law violations. This conviction was upheld by an intermediate appellate court and was appealed to the Supreme Court of India. If the high court had sustained her conviction, Mrs. Gandhi would not have been eligible under Indian law to continue as prime minister. Before the Supreme Court could act, however, Mrs. Gandhi induced the Indian Parliament to approve a declared state of emergency and suspension of civil rights, repeal retroactively the laws under which she had been convicted, and change the Indian Constitution so as to deny the courts power to hear cases involving the election of prime ministers. Many of her political opponents were imprisoned under the terms of the declared emergency. The Supreme Court finally acquitted Mrs. Gandhi, but the state of emergency continued in force. (*See* INDIA.)

Permissible Private and Public Action. Some systems of law, particularly the Anglo-American legal systems, draw sharp distinctions between permissible private and public activities. Under this distinction, discriminatory private action is usually permitted whereas such public action is prohibited. There are difficulties, however, in identifying activities that are private as opposed to those that are public. In 1975 two important cases on these matters reached the U.S. Supreme Court, and one reached the House of Lords, the highest court in England.

In *Jackson* v. *Metropolitan Edison Co.* (95 S.Ct. 449), a customer brought suit against a privately owned and operated utility corporation that had a monopoly by virtue of a certificate of public convenience issued to it by the state of Pennsylvania, seeking damages on account of a termination of her electric service. The utility company responded by alleging that the customer had not paid her electric bill. She replied that the utility had no right to suspend service without giving her an opportunity to be heard on possible legitimate reasons for nonpayment. In this connection she argued that the utility company's activities involved "state action" and its refusal to give her an opportunity to be heard denied her due process of law.

Under the U.S. Constitution a state or governmental unit cannot deprive any person of due process, but private activities are beyond the reach of this proscription. Thus the U.S. Supreme Court had held that a private club could arbitrarily exclude a person from membership on account of race, whereas public facilities could not make such an exclusion. The customer in the Jackson case admitted this, but contended that a utility holding a monopoly by virtue of governmental action was not a private entity for purposes of this rule. The Supreme Court did not agree; it held that the state of Pennsylvania was not sufficiently connected with the challenged termination of electrical service to make the utility company's conduct "state action" for purposes of making it conform to the due process clause.

The Jackson decision was considered to be one of the most important handed down by the Supreme Court during the year because of its potential effect on the commercial community and on consumers' rights. Specifically, most legal observers thought it portended a decision that sec. 9-503 of the Uniform Commercial Code would be held constitutional. That provision permits secured creditors to use "self-help" in recovering property sold to consumers and others on the installment plan where a default in payments has occurred, even though no opportunity to be heard is provided to the consumer prior to the seizure.

The House of Lords, in *Dockers' Labour Club* v. *Race Relations Board,* made the same kind of distinction between private and public action that was made in the Jackson case. The House of Lords held that a private club is not guilty of wrongful discrimination by refusing to serve an individual because of his race. The decision would have been otherwise if the club in question had been a public facility.

The mere fact that "state action" is present, however, does not necessarily mean that its employment violates one's right to due process, because deprivation of due process does not occur unless arbitrary or capricious action has been taken. Normally, the U.S. Supreme Court had held that action not affording the affected party an opportunity to be heard is arbitrary and capricious within the meaning of this doctrine, but it had appeared to waver on this matter over the last several years where prejudgment remedies are employed to seize property prior to a trial on the merits.

Important prejudgment remedies include replevin, attachment, and garnishment. All involve the state providing the means for a claimant to seize property in the possession of another upon the mere allegation of the claimant that the property belongs to him or is about to be put beyond the reach of any judgment that he might subsequently acquire. In 1972 the Supreme Court invalidated the replevin statutes of Florida and Pennsylvania because they directed a sheriff, operating under a writ issued by a clerk of court, to seize goods prior to any hearing on whether or not the claimant was entitled to the goods (*Fuentes* v. *Shevin,* 92 S.Ct. 1983). But in 1974 the Supreme Court sustained a

PHOTOS, WIDE WORLD

Former Nixon administration officials appeared before the courts for sentencing during the year. Former attorney general John N. Mitchell (top) and presidential advisers John D. Ehrlichman (second from top) and H. R. Haldeman (bottom) appealed their convictions as Watergate cover-up conspirators, whereas former commerce secretary Maurice H. Stans pleaded guilty to five counts of violating federal campaign finance laws.

UPI COMPIX

WIDE WORLD

Two controversial legal decisions involving ethical questions were handed down during the year. The parents of Karen Ann Quinlan (above) petitioned to remove her life-sustaining mechanical respirator because she had been in a coma since April 15 and physicians believed that there was no chance for her recovery. The petition was denied. Kenneth Edelin (below), a Massachusetts physician, was convicted of manslaughter by a Boston jury for the death of an aborted fetus. He was sentenced to one year on probation, but the celebrated case was appealed.

Louisiana sequestration statute that was remarkably similar (*Mitchell* v. *W. T. Grant Co.*, 94 S.Ct. 1895).

This led some observers to conclude that the Supreme Court now regarded the prejudgment remedies as valid, and they attributed the difference between *Fuentes* and *Mitchell* to differences in the makeup of the court. In 1975 these observers were astounded when the Supreme Court declared the Georgia garnishment statute unconstitutional (*North Georgia Finishing, Inc.* v. *Di-Chem*, 95 S.Ct. 719). Legal scholars were now trying to reconcile the three decisions. The most plausible reconciliation seemed to be that there were differences between the statutes involved in the three cases, and that such differences must be taken into account in any prediction as to the constitutionality of any particular prejudgment remedy.

Other Significant Cases. In *Faretta* v. *California* (95 S.Ct. 2525), the U.S. Supreme Court held that one accused of crime has a constitutional right to proceed at the trial without counsel if he voluntarily and intelligently elects to do so, and that the state cannot force a lawyer upon him. The decision did not impair the doctrine of earlier cases which held that the criminally accused are guaranteed the right to assistance of counsel, including the furnishing of counsel to indigents at no cost. The European Court of Human Rights held that England must allow a prisoner the right to see counsel and to have access to the courts for the purpose of bringing a civil action of defamation against a prison guard.

In the U.K. the House of Lords held that it would be incorrect to convict a man of rape if he honestly believed that the woman had consented to sexual intercourse, even if his belief was improbable and unreasonable.

The efforts of the U.S. government to prevent or reduce illegal immigration from Mexico appeared to suffer a setback by the Supreme Court's decision in *United States* v. *Brignoni-Ponce* (95 S.Ct. 2574). At a checkpoint 62 air miles and 66 road miles north of the Mexican border, a patrol stopped a car for the sole reason that the three occupants appeared to be of Mexican descent. In fact the occupants were Mexicans who had entered the U.S. illegally. They were arrested, and the driver was charged with knowingly transporting illegal immigrants. He was convicted, but the Court of Appeals reversed the conviction. The Supreme Court affirmed the Court of Appeals, holding that the Fourth Amendment to the Constitution permits searches to be made at border points but prohibits searches at points distant from the border unless the patrolling officer is aware of specific articulable facts, together with rational inferences therefrom, reasonably warranting suspicion that the vehicle contains illegal aliens.

(WILLIAM D. HAWKLAND)

International Law. *Maritime Affairs.* The UN law of the sea conference at Caracas, Venezuela, in 1974, which had failed to achieve any substantive results, was followed in 1975 by a further meeting at Geneva. This also proved inconclusive, and it was hoped that the 1976 session would be more successful. Meanwhile, all the topics discussed at the conference were the subject of piecemeal actions.

Maritime boundary discussions took place between France and the U.K. (continental shelf in the Western approaches; submitted to arbitration with the award expected at the end of 1976), India and Bangladesh, The Gambia and Senegal (agreement signed), Libya and Tunisia (agreement reached), Greece and Turkey (agreement in principle to refer the dispute over the continental shelf in the Aegean to the International Court of Justice), and Cameroon and Niger (agreement on territorial waters). Fishery limits had been extended to 200 mi. by Iceland, Ecuador, and Mexico. Norway introduced a number of trawl-free zones within a 50-mi. line and was discussing their extension with interested states. Denmark formally reserved its position on the U.K. claim to the continental shelf around the uninhabited North Atlantic island of Rockall. (*See* FISHERIES.)

A number of bilateral fishery treaties were concluded during the year. In May Canada, the U.S., West Germany, and Japan signed an equal-sharing agreement for the mining of deep-sea manganese nodules. Japan agreed to finance exploration of the Soviet continental shelf off Sakhalin in return for a 50% share of any profits. Saudi Arabia and Sudan signed an agreement on the basic principles to be applied to the exploitation of the resources of the Red Sea, and Iran and Oman concluded an agreement on patrolling the Persian Gulf, particularly in the Strait of Hormuz and around oil terminals.

Concern for pollution was centred primarily on the Mediterranean. A 16-state meeting in Barcelona, Spain, agreed on the framework of a UN convention to protect the Mediterranean, and a working party of legal experts was drafting the legal instruments for consideration by a plenipotentiary conference in February 1976 under the auspices of the UN Environment Program. A conference of all the littoral states of the North and Irish seas was held in London in October to consider a draft convention on liability for oil pollution resulting from seabed-drilling activities. The private Offshore Pollution Liability Act, signed by 26 oil companies in September 1974, came into force in May, as did the 1969 international conventions on Civil Liability for Oil Pollution Damage and Intervention on the High Seas in Cases of Oil Pollution Casualties.

The Inter-Governmental Maritime Consultative Organization was concentrating on marine safety. Its 1971 convention relating to civil liability in the field of maritime carriage of nuclear material came into force in July, and in October its Maritime Safety Committee agreed on improved procedures, mainly through accelerated exchange of information, to enable the authorities of port states to exercise more efficiently the functions laid down by the various conventions on the safety of life at sea. In December 1974 it opened for signature a convention on carrier liability relating to the carriage of passengers and their luggage by sea.

Also in the field of maritime transport, the 1974 UN Conference on Trade and Development (UNCTAD) Convention on a Code of Conduct for Liner Conferences had led to serious constitutional issues within the EEC. The European Commission recommended that no member state sign the convention on the ground that it conflicted with the aims of the Treaty of Rome, and it threatened legal proceedings before the European Court of Justice against three member states that did sign.

Territory. In December 1974 the UN General Assembly had asked the International Court of Justice for an advisory opinion on the legal status of Spanish Sahara. The king of Morocco sent his subjects on a "peace march" into the territory in the autumn of 1975 in order to take it over, but he withdrew them without incident after a symbolic crossing of the frontier. Subsequently, Spain agreed to withdraw its forces by Feb. 28, 1976, after which the territory would be divided between Morocco and Mauritania. The arrangement was denounced by Algeria, which favoured self-determination. (*See* DEPENDENT STATES.)

Boundary disputes arose or were settled between Iran and Iraq (agreement to set up three joint working committees to settle all outstanding boundary disputes and demarcate the disputed sectors of the frontier); Iraq, Turkey, and Syria (agreement to settle problems concerning use of the Euphrates River); Ghana and Togo (border demarcation commission set up); Italy and Yugoslavia (settlement of the sovereignty of Trieste and the surrounding territory); and Mali and Upper Volta (mediation commission to settle the border dispute). Portugal and India signed a treaty recognizing Indian sovereignty over the Portuguese territories annexed by India in 1961.

International Organizations. The European Space Agency was created to replace the European Space Research Organization (ESRO) and the European Launcher Development Organization (ELDO). The treaty establishing the 15-member Economic Community of West African States (ECOWAS) was signed and by July was in force between Upper Volta, Dahomey, Ivory Coast, Ghana, The Gambia, Guinea, Liberia, Nigeria, Togo, and Niger. Members of the Southeast Asia Treaty Organization (SEATO) agreed to dissolve the alliance. Australia, in a trade agreement with the Philippines, recognized the Association of South East Asian Nations as a trading bloc. The 1971 agreement to set up an International Institute for Managerial Tasks in the Technological Field came into force in October 1974 for Austria, The Netherlands, West Germany, Italy, and the U.K.

The World Intellectual Property Organization became a new specialized agency of the UN. The 25-man expert panel on restructuring of the UN issued a report proposing new negotiating procedures in the UN on controversial economic questions, the appointment of a director general for development and international economic cooperation, changes in the weighted voting system in the International Monetary Fund and the World Bank, and the consolidation of UN funds dealing with special issues such as population and environment into a single development authority. The U.S. gave notice of its withdrawal from the International Labour Organization in two years.

Other "Traditional" International Law Matters. After more than 40 years of unsuccessful attempts to define "aggression," a definition was finally adopted by the UN General Assembly in December 1974. It stated that aggression is "the use of armed force by a State against the sovereignty, territorial integrity or political independence of another State, or in any other manner inconsistent with the Charter of the United Nations, as set out in this definition." The Final Act of the Conference on Security and Cooperation in Europe, signed by 35 nations at Helsinki, Fin., in August, covered the inviolability of frontiers, economic cooperation, and freer movement of people and ideas. The Biological Weapons Convention entered into force for the U.K., the U.S., and the U.S.S.R.

Other significant events included the adoption of the Convention on the Representation of States in Their Relations with International Organizations of a Universal Character and of a draft convention on diplomatic immunity. In December 1974 the General Assembly had adopted the Charter of Economic Rights and Duties of States, and throughout the year discussions continued on the UNCTAD proposals for a code of conduct for the transfer of technology.

International Private Law. In January 1975 the Inter-American Conference on Private International Law, meeting in Panama under the aegis of the Organization of American States, concluded no less than six conventions: on bills of exchange, promissory notes, and invoices; checks of international circulation; power of attorney for use abroad; letters rogatory; obtaining evidence abroad on civil and commercial matters; and international commercial arbitration. In the field of industrial property, the Strasbourg Agreement on the International Patent Classification 1971 entered into force for ten Western European countries, while the EEC countries agreed in December on a convention that would create a

WIDE WORLD

A Soviet fishing trawler approaches the 12-mile limit at the entrance to New York Harbor as it draws up a net full of herring, whiting, and ling.

UNITED NATIONS/ICJ

Members of the World Court pondered the legalities of Morocco's claim to Spanish Sahara at The Hague in July.

single Community-wide patent. The 1974 Executive Regulations of the Madrid Trademarks Convention entered into force, as did the 1974 additional protocol to the European Convention on the Protection of Television Programs.

There was a notable increase of interest in product liability, stimulated by the legal proceedings against the McDonnell Douglas Corp. following the crash of a Douglas DC-10 in France in March 1974 and by a series of cases in Scandinavia involving women who suffered death or disability after taking contraceptive pills. The possible introduction of strict liability for manufacturers was being studied in a number of countries. The European Commission was preparing the preliminary draft of a directive, and the Council of Europe had completed a very thorough draft convention on the subject.

(NEVILLE MARCH HUNNINGS)

See also Crime and Law Enforcement; Prisons and Penology; United Nations.

[552; 553]

Lebanon

A republic of the Middle East, Lebanon is bounded by Syria, Israel, and the Mediterranean Sea. Area: 3,950 sq.mi. (10,230 sq.km.). Pop. (1975 est.): 2,550,000. Cap. and largest city: Beirut (metro. pop., 1975 est., 1,172,000). Language: Arabic. Religion: Christian and Muslim. President in 1975, Suleiman Franjieh; prime ministers, Rashid as-Solh until May 15 and, from May 29, Rashid Karami.

In 1975 Lebanon faced the most serious challenge in its 32-year history to its existence as an independent state. Israeli raids on south Lebanon were overshadowed by the civil strife that developed along Muslim-Christian lines, causing in a nine-month period nearly 6,500 deaths, 13,000 wounded, and immense damage and virtually bringing the country's services-based economy to a halt. By year's end nearly 20 cease-fire declarations had been made as fighting continued between the right-wing Christian Phalangist Party and left-wing Muslim groups—a feud that began over the distribution of power in Lebanon. Under the contested political system, based on a census taken in 1932 when Christians held a slight majority, the president and the commander of the armed forces must be from the Maronite Christian sect, the prime minister must be a Muslim, and the legislative assembly must consist of a 6–5 Christian to Muslim ratio. In 1975, however, the population was estimated to be 60% Muslim.

Heavy Israeli raids on south Lebanon in January in retaliation for Palestinian guerrilla attacks caused scores of casualties and the evacuation of several hundreds of individuals from border villages. Lebanon twice protested to the UN Security Council. The Arab League's Joint Defense Council meeting in Cairo in February approved Lebanon's request for military aid reportedly worth $27 million.

The first signs of sectarian trouble began appearing in principally Muslim Tripoli, Lebanon's second largest city, and in late March and in mid-April the clashes spread to the capital city of Beirut. Some Palestinian guerrilla elements joined with the Muslims in fighting but their leaders declared their intention to keep out of internal Lebanese affairs. On May 15 Prime Minister Rashid as-Solh resigned after placing full responsibility on the Phalangists. Additional fierce fighting broke out in the second half of May and on May 23 President Franjieh announced the formation of a Cabinet of seven army officers and one civilian but, lacking any support from the main political groups, the Cabinet resigned on May 26. Franjieh then called on seven-time prime minister Rashid Karami (*see* BIOGRAPHY), but he faced difficulties in forming a government because of the refusal of the Progressive Socialist Party (PSP) to serve with the Phalangists. This led to more fighting on June 2. Finally, Karami formed on June 30 a six-man Cabinet without Phalangists or the PSP,

Violent fighting between the Muslim and Christian communities of Beirut left much of the once-splendid city in ruins.

CLAUDE SALHANI—SYGMA

LEBANON

Education. (1972–73) Primary, pupils 497,723; secondary, pupils 167,578; primary and secondary, teachers 32,901; vocational, pupils 4,603, teachers (1970–71) 508; teacher training, students 3,233, teachers 218; higher, students 50,803, teaching staff 7,999.

Finance. Monetary unit: Lebanese pound, with (Sept. 22, 1975) a free rate of L£2.23 to U.S. $1 (L£4.62 = £1 sterling). Gold and foreign exchange: (June 1975) U.S. $1,659,800,000; (June 1974) U.S. $1,059,000,000. Budget (1975 est.) balanced at L£1,607 million. Gross national product: (1972) L£6,358 million; (1971) L£5,646 million. Money supply: (May 1975) L£3,111 million; (May 1974) L£2,648 million. Cost of living (Beirut; 1970 = 100): (March 1975) 132; (March 1974) 124.

Foreign Trade. (1973) Imports L£3,636 million; exports L£1,837 million; transit trade L£1,345 million. Import sources: U.S. 12%; West Germany 11%; France 10%; Italy 10%; U.K. 8%. Export destinations: Saudi Arabia 15%; France 9%; U.K. 8%; Libya 7%; Kuwait 6%; Syria 5%. Main exports: machinery 14%; fruit and vegetables 12%; chemicals 8%; aircraft 6%; clothing 6%; textile yarns and fabrics 6%; motor vehicles 5%. Tourism (1973): visitors 1,504,000; gross receipts U.S. $216 million.

Transport and Communications. Roads (1971) 7,400 km. Motor vehicles in use (1973): passenger 185,900; commercial 19,200. Railways: (1973) 417 km.; traffic (1974) 1,890,000 passenger-km., freight 42 million net ton-km. Air traffic (1974): 1,773,800,000 passenger-km.; freight 423,608,000 net ton-km. Shipping (1974): vessels 100 gross tons and over 88; gross tonnage 120,130. Telephones (Jan. 1973) 227,000. Radio receivers (Dec. 1971) 605,000. Television receivers (Dec. 1972) 320,000.

Agriculture. Production (in 000; metric tons; 1974; 1973 in parentheses): potatoes *c.* 120 (117); wheat (1973) *c.* 30, (1972) 64; sugar, raw value (1973) *c.* 11, (1972) 27; tomatoes *c.* 70 (59); grapes *c.* 115 (107); olives *c.* 50 (30); figs (1973) *c.* 10, (1972) 11; bananas (1973) 38, (1972) 39; oranges (1973) *c.* 180, (1972) 184; lemons (1973) *c.* 85, (1972) 86; apples *c.* 200 (166); tobacco (1973) *c.* 8.5, (1972) 8.3. Livestock (in 000; 1973): cattle *c.* 91; goats *c.* 355; sheep *c.* 226; chickens *c.* 6,378.

Industry. Production (in 000; metric tons; 1974): cement 1,744; petroleum products (1972) 2,041; electricity (excluding most industrial production; kw-hr.) 1,975,000.

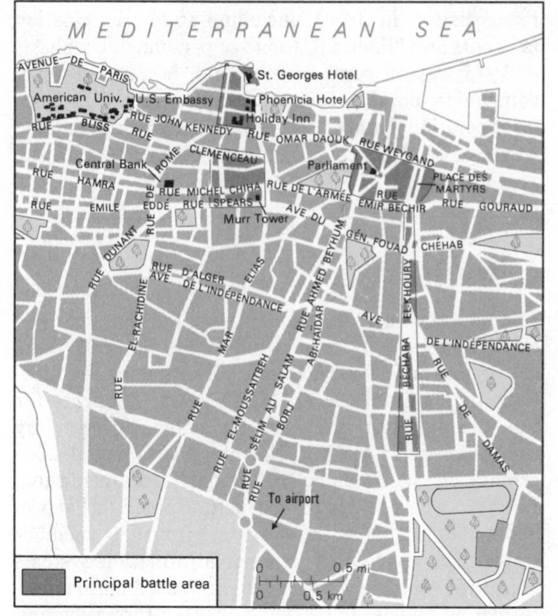

Contested areas in Beirut.

but including former president Camille Chamoun as minister of the interior to represent right-wing Christian interests. The situation improved temporarily in Beirut and a cease-fire took effect on July 2. But sectarian trouble revived in Zahle in the last week of August and on September 7 spread to Tripoli after an incident involving Christian villagers from neighbouring Zgharta. Fighting raged in Tripoli and on September 10 the Cabinet decided to send the Army to establish a buffer zone separating the combatants.

The situation in north Lebanon improved for a time, despite sporadic clashes, but on September 15 trouble again broke out in Beirut and spread from the western suburbs to the central commercial area. The ordinary security forces were too weak to cope with the warring armed gangs. Scores of buildings were bombed or burned and numerous kidnappings occurred. Hopes that the formation of a committee for national reconciliation representing all elements would restore calm were belied. Karami appealed to the Syrian foreign minister and to the Palestine Liberation Organization (PLO) leader, Yasir Arafat, to help restore confidence and the Arab League convened in Cairo to try to end the crisis. Lebanese Muslims were demanding a total restructuring of Lebanon's political system to give them more power. Many also demanded the resignation of President Franjieh and were joined in this by some moderate Christians who saw the president as an ally of the Phalangists.

Fighting intensified in October and left- and right-wing militiamen began fighting to capture territory for the first time since factional fighting began in April. Elements of the PLO, which until then had played a peacekeeping role, also entered the battle for control of part of Beirut. Machine-gun fire and explosions were commonplace in the embattled city and its suburbs, where property damage was high. The once flourishing economy was at a standstill as foreign businesses and banks abandoned Beirut for Athens, Rome, and London.

The final days of December witnessed more truce violations but the Lebanese radio reported that Muslim and Christian factions were ready to adopt a Syrian formula which would make the 17th truce in three months a reality. The main points of the Syrian proposal provided for a 50:50 parliamentary representation of Muslims and Christians, election of the prime minister by Parliament instead of by consultation with the president, and abolition of hiring based on religion for public jobs at all levels.

(PETER MANSFIELD)

[978.B.3.a]

Lesotho

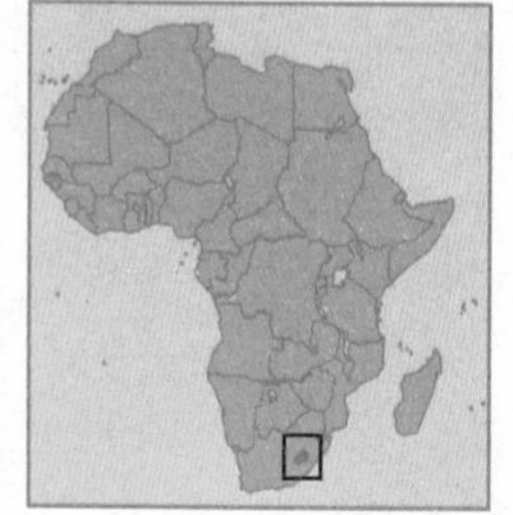

A constitutional monarchy of southern Africa and a member of the Commonwealth of Nations, Lesotho is entirely within South Africa. Area: 11,720 sq.mi. (30,355 sq.km.). Pop. (1975 est.): 1,142,600. Cap. and largest city: Maseru (pop., 1972 est., 18,800). Language: English and Sesotho (official). Religion: Roman Catholic 38.7%; Lesotho Evangelical Church 24.3%; Anglican 10.4%; other Christian 8.4%; non-Christian 18.2%. Chief of state in 1975, King Moshoeshoe II; prime minister, Chief Leabua Jonathan.

At a treason trial of opposition members of the Basutoland Congress Party (BCP), held in March 1975, following failure of their attempted coup in January 1974, 15 of the defendants were convicted of high treason and sentenced to prison terms. At another trial in July, 18 supporters of the BCP were found guilty of high treason and sentenced similarly. The government issued proposals in December 1974 to scrap the 1966 independence constitution, make King Moshoeshoe a constitutional monarch, make local government elective, banish criminal fugitives and traitors permanently, and pass a vote of confidence in the government to carry on. Chief Jonathan continued an aggressive policy against South Africa, claiming large tracts of Cape and Orange Free State lands as having once been part of Basutoland. Nevertheless, close links remained with South Africa and, in accordance with a monetary agreement of December 1974, deferred payments to miners working in the republic were to be paid into the Lesotho Bank.

The 1975–76 budget showed hope for the second five-year plan: revenue from agriculture and tourism had increased, though estimated expenditure at R 42.6 million was an increase of 54% over the previous year. Optimism was generated by new industrial projects and a new policy of transferring retail trade into Basuto hands, and also by increased international investment. In March 1975 the De Beers company signed an agreement with the Lesotho government to develop diamonds in the Maluti Mountains.

(MOLLY MORTIMER)

[978.E.8.b.ii]

LESOTHO

Education. (1973) Primary, pupils 187,459, teachers 3,951; secondary, pupils 12,559, teachers 551; vocational (1972), pupils 623, teachers 170; teacher training, students 383, teachers 59; higher, students 724, teaching staff 127.

Finance and Trade. Monetary unit: South African rand, with (Sept. 22, 1975) an official rate of R 0.87 to U.S. $1 (free rate of R 1.81 = £1 sterling). Budget (1974–75 est.): revenue R 17,251,000; expenditure R 16,008,000. Foreign trade (1973): imports R 60.5 million; exports R 8.8 million. Main exports: wool 36%; cattle 18%; mohair 17%; sheep 5%. Most trade is with South Africa.

Agriculture. Production (in 000; metric tons; 1973; 1972 in parentheses): corn *c.* 70 (59); wheat *c.* 40 (21); sorghum *c.* 40 (14); wool *c.* 2.4 (*c.* 2.3). Livestock (in 000; 1973): cattle *c.* 570; goats *c.* 920; sheep 1,557.

Law Enforcement: *see* Crime and Law Enforcement

Lawn Bowls: *see* Bowling

Lawn Tennis: *see* Tennis and Rackets

Lead: *see* Mining and Quarrying

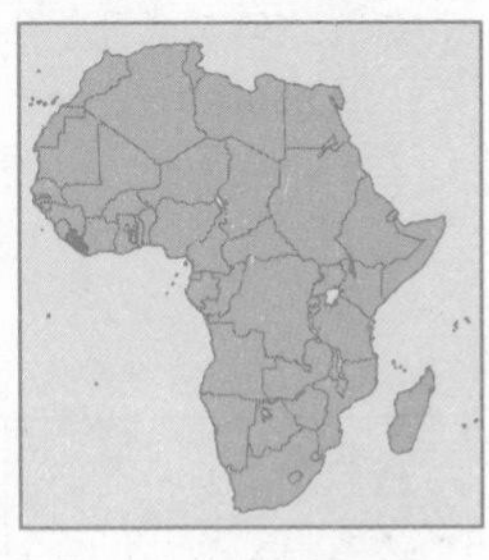

Liberia

A republic on the west coast of Africa, Liberia is bordered by Sierra Leone, Guinea, and Ivory Coast. Area: 43,000 sq.mi. (111,400 sq.km.). Pop. (1974): 1,496,000. Cap. and largest city: Monrovia (pop., 1974, 180,000). Language: English (official) and tribal dialects. Religion: mainly animist. President in 1975, William R. Tolbert, Jr.

In his March 1975 message to the legislature, President Tolbert indicated grounds for political and economic optimism. A setback occurred, however, when the president's brother Stephen Tolbert (*see* OBITUARIES), an outstandingly capable minister of finance, died in an airplane crash in April. William Tolbert's stature as an African statesman was epitomized by visits from leaders in southern Africa, especially that of B. J. Vorster, prime minister of South Africa, in February. Vorster outlined his terms for racial détente in southern Africa: that the peoples of South West Africa must decide their own future and that there must be no interference in the domestic affairs of other states. Although left-wing African states attacked Tolbert for his dialogue, his legislature on March 11 supported him, as did the Ivory Coast, which he visited during March 13–22.

The March budget showed annual growth (62%) in gross domestic product greater than much of the rest of Africa, and there had been a favourable balance of trade in 1974. In May a decree banning aliens from many areas of trade came into effect, and in July two commissions were set up for the summary trial of persons accused of currency forgery, bank fraud, and dealing in narcotics.

Tolbert redefined Liberia's relations with the U.S. by imposing more stringent conditions for foreign-owned companies (particularly the U.S. Firestone Tire and Rubber Co. whose agreement came up for renegotiation in July), including state participation in profits and "liberianization" of personnel. Emphasis in 1975 was on rural development, in which foreign companies, notably Firestone and the Swedish iron-ore operation Lamco, had shown the government the way.

(MOLLY MORTIMER)

[978.E.4.a]

LIBERIA

Education. (1974) Primary, pupils 149,687, teachers 4,111; secondary, pupils 26,426, teachers 1,015; vocational, pupils 1,087, teachers (1970–71) 66; teacher training, pupils 424, teachers 41; higher, students 2,214, teaching staff (1970–71) 164.

Finance. Monetary unit: Liberian dollar, at par with the U.S. dollar, with (Sept. 22, 1975) a free rate of L$2.07 to £1 sterling. Budget (1973 actual): revenue L$89.8 million; expenditure L$70 million.

Foreign Trade. (1974) Imports L$288,440,000; exports L$400,270,000. Import sources (1973): U.S. 28%; West Germany 12%; U.K. 10%; Japan 6%; Sweden 5%. Export destinations (1973): U.S. 20%; Belgium-Luxembourg 18%; West Germany 17%; The Netherlands 13%; Italy 12%; France 6%; Japan 5%. Main exports: iron ore 65%; rubber 16%; diamonds 7%.

Transport and Communications. Roads (main state roads only; 1972) *c.* 4,800 km. Motor vehicles in use (1972): passenger 12,200; commercial (including buses) 10,000. Railways (1973) 493 km. Shipping (1974): merchant vessels 100 gross tons and over 2,332 (mostly owned by U.S. and other foreign interests); gross tonnage 55,321,641. Telephones (Jan. 1974) 3,000. Radio receivers (Dec. 1971) 155,000. Television receivers (Dec. 1973) 8,500.

Agriculture. Production (in 000; metric tons; 1973; 1972 in parentheses): rice 155 (152); cassava *c.* 250 (*c.* 267); bananas *c.* 62 (*c.* 62); rubber (1974) *c.* 91, (1973) 91; palm kernels *c.* 15 (*c.* 15); palm oil *c.* 7 (*c.* 7); cocoa *c.* 2.5 (3.2); coffee *c.* 4.8 (*c.* 5.6). Livestock (in 000; 1973): cattle *c.* 32; pigs *c.* 86; sheep *c.* 165; goats *c.* 160.

Industry. Production (in 000; metric tons; 1973): iron ore (metal content) 23,542; petroleum products 555; diamonds (exports; metric carats; 1972) 890; electricity (kw-hr.; 1972) 846,000.

Libraries

The importance of libraries through the centuries was marked in 1975 by celebration of the first 500 years of the Vatican Library, Rome, with its famous collections dating from the 3rd century A.D. Thoughts for the future of libraries were dominated, however, by the responses to UNESCO's Intergovernmental Conference on the Planning of National Documentation, Library and Archives Infrastructures, held in Paris in September 1974, with delegates from 86 member states. The concept of national information systems (NATIS) which was formulated required national information policies to be coupled with information and manpower resources and with users' needs.

Other international activities during the year included the foundation of the Islamic Library Information Centre in Karachi, Pak.; the installation of the International Federation of Library Associations (IFLA) Office for International Lending at the British Library Lending Division, Boston Spa, Yorkshire; the first issue of the *ISDS Bulletin* under the International Serials Data System, as part of the UN network of cooperative scientific information systems (UNISIST); and a recommendation that an International Centre for Paper Study, concerned with rare and historic documents, be established. In Western Europe the nine countries of the European Community had decided in 1971 to create a European network for scientific, technical, social, economic, and legal information, to cost nearly two million units of account (about $2 million). It would embrace existing "sectoral groups" on metallurgy, agriculture, patents, biomedicine, energy, and environmental information. Work on this was accelerated in 1975 when 550,000 units of account were allocated for these sectors and an additional 660,000 for the creation of a coordinated computer network. In May the British Library Association held a seminar at Banbury, England, on the interchange of bibliographic information in machine-readable form, attended by more than 30 delegates from Western Europe.

Some national responses to the NATIS proposals of UNESCO were: a plan to create the new Pahlavi Cultural, Scientific and Resource Centre at the National Library of Iran; a resolution in Tunisia to coordinate national information systems in the Maghreb countries of North Africa; a Hungarian seminar under the auspices of UNESCO in August on the selective dissemination of information; a conference of Southeast Asian libraries in December on the integrated planning of library and documentation services within the framework of NATIS; and a decree passed by the Romanian government ordaining the organization of a national information and documentation system on NATIS principles. Other national developments included the third draft of a "National Program" in the U.S. by the National Commission on Libraries and Information Science. In France the governmental library structure was transformed by the abolition of the Direction des Bibliothèques et de la Lecture Publique and by the separation of the public libraries (now to be under the State Secretariat for Cultural Affairs) from the research and university libraries, which were to remain under the Ministry of National Education; the Bibliothèque Nationale was to be an autonomous institution. In East Germany the Deutsche Bücherei, Leipzig, assumed the functions of a registration centre for periodicals for the International Serials Data System, Paris, and for the International Centre for Scientific and Technical Information, Moscow. Work began on building the National Library in Jakarta, Indonesia, while in Tanzania an act was passed establishing the Tanzania Library Services Board with functions in accordance with the NATIS concept. A long-awaited new law on public libraries went into effect in The Netherlands in July; in the U.S.S.R. the State V. I. Lenin Library and its important Centre for Recommendatory Bibliography celebrated their 50th anniversary.

The U.S. Senate in September confirmed Daniel J. Boorstin as librarian of Congress. Boorstin had previously served as senior historian of the Smithsonian Institution, and there was some debate in the Senate about possible conflicts between his roles as a historian and as administrator of the Library of Congress. His lack of previous professional library experience also aroused some opposition.

The trend in library techniques continued toward greater use of microforms and mechanization, including the application of computers in library administration and in information work. For example, in France after January 1 the first part of the weekly *Bibliographie de la France* (works received by legal deposit at the Bibliothèque Nationale) was computerized and photocomposed, and index cards were expected to be available soon to all libraries. In Belgium a data bank was set up by the Société pour la Diffusion de la Presse in February 1974 to give information on periodicals published throughout the world. The National Library in Canberra, Australia, undertook a program of cataloging-in-publication (catalog cards produced at the publication of each book). In the United Kingdom an index on microfiche was produced by University Microfilms Ltd., while the British Standards Institution published a standard for magnetic tape for data-interchange. Audiovisual materials were increasingly used, and an international meeting at UNESCO in July tried to coordinate methods of cataloging such "nonbook" materials.

Some countries encountered difficulty in training librarians, notably Brazil and Denmark, because of a shortage of qualified staff; and in France, with a view to development of training, the École Nationale Supérieure des Bibliothèques was transferred from Paris to Lyons in 1974 and held its first academic year in 1974–75. In Calcutta, India, a new Institute of Librarians organized on a voluntary basis ran courses to train more workers for employment in libraries. In Canada's Quebec Province, however, too many had been trained at the library technician level for the market to absorb. Toward the end of 1974 the new regional school of librarianship for the West Indies, as a department of the University of the West Indies in Jamaica, produced its first graduates, the school having been founded with initial support from UNESCO, the British Council, the Canadian International Development Agency, and the Organization of American States, with an international staff.

Library associations increased their activity, and 135 associations from 98 countries were members of the IFLA in 1975. In Indonesia the profession was integrated into a single association.

THE GUARDIAN

Toys designed for handicapped children were displayed at the Toy Libraries Association exhibit which opened in June at Toynbee Hall, London.

Finally, an important section of the terminology of libraries and documentation was completed by a subcommittee of the International Organization for Standardization (ISO). It was chapter one of a *Vocabulary of Information and Documentation* compiled in English and French, comprising basic terms, terms on copyright and patents, and on organizations in the field. (ANTHONY THOMPSON)

[441.C.2.d; 613.D.1.a; 735.H]

ENCYCLOPÆDIA BRITANNICA FILMS. *Library Story* (1952); *The Library—A Place for Discovery* (1966); *Library of Congress* (1969); *Look in the Answer Book* (1972).

Libya

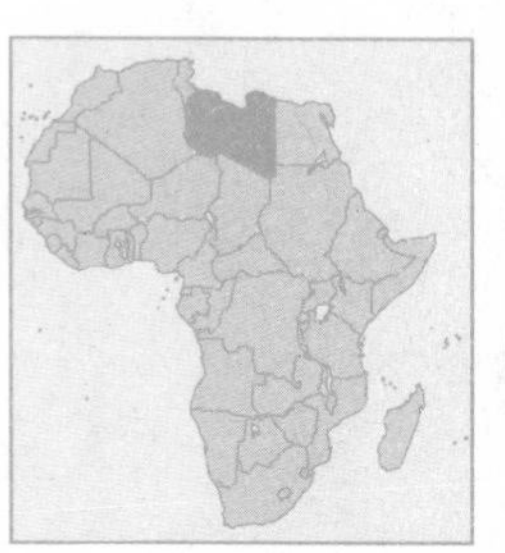

A socialist republic on the north coast of Africa, Libya is bounded by Egypt, the Sudan, Tunisia, Algeria, Niger, and Chad. Area: 675,000 sq.mi. (1,749,000 sq.km.). Pop. (1973 census): 2,257,000. Cap. and largest city: Tripoli (pop., 1973 census, municipality, 551,000). Language: Arabic. Religion: predominantly Muslim. Leader of the Revolutionary Command Council in 1975, Col. Muammar al-Qaddafi; prime minister, Maj. Abdul Salam Jalloud.

Libyan oil revenues fell in 1975 for the first time. The threefold increase in revenues experienced in 1974 had resulted from the price rises of late 1973, and had occurred despite a fall in output. Production of crude oil declined further in 1975; in the early months of the year it was running at less than one million barrels a day, one-third of the 1969 level. At the same time, local and foreign contractors engaged in development of the nation's infrastructure, agriculture and industry, were pressing the government for massive interim payments to cover contract costs that had risen as a result of inflation. This pressure came at a time when other assets were frozen in medium- and long-term investments overseas.

Libya was understandably unwilling to concede that oil price increases alone were to blame for world inflation, and it was among the loudest of the group of oil producers that pressed for a compensating rise in oil prices at the Organization of Petroleum Exporting Countries meeting in September. Oil production

LIBYA

Education. (1974–75) Primary, pupils 538,070, teachers 24,424; secondary, pupils 107,577, teachers 8,074; vocational, pupils 2,883, teachers 265; teacher training, students 19,546, teachers 1,514; higher, students 12,162, teaching staff 596.

Finance. Monetary unit: Libyan dinar, with (Sept. 22, 1975) a par value of 0.296 dinar to U.S. $1 (free rate of 0.613 dinar = £1 sterling). Gold and foreign exchange: (June 1975) U.S. $2,348,000,000; (June 1974) U.S. $2,989,000,000. Budget (1972 actual): revenue 858,122,000 dinars (including petroleum revenue of 624,575,000 dinars); expenditure 882,962,000 dinars. Gross national product: (1973) 2,193,000,000 dinars; (1972) 1,798,000,000 dinars. Money supply: (March 1975) 729.6 million dinars; (March 1974) 641.7 million dinars. Cost of living (Tripoli; 1970 = 100): (March 1974) 121; (March 1973) 111.

Foreign Trade. (1974) Imports 993 million dinars; exports 2,318,300,000 dinars. Import sources (1973): Italy 26%; West Germany 10%; France 8%; U.K. 7%; Japan 6%; U.S. 5%. Export destinations: Italy 28%; West Germany 21%; U.K. 12%; U.S. 8%; France 5%. Main export crude oil 99.6%.

Transport and Communications. Roads (with improved surface; 1972) *c.* 5,000 km. (including 1,822 km. coast road). Motor vehicles in use (1973): passenger 197,900; commercial (including buses) 89,800. About 500 km. of railways are planned. Air traffic (1973): 356 million passenger-km.; freight 4 million net ton-km. Shipping (1974): vessels 100 gross tons and over 25; gross tonnage 160,180. Ships entered (1973): vessels totaling 5,127,000 net registered tons; goods loaded (1973) 102,405,000 metric tons, unloaded 5,051,000 metric tons. Telephones (Dec. 1971) 42,000. Radio licenses (Dec. 1972) 100,000. Television licenses (Dec. 1973) *c.* 15,000.

Agriculture. Production (in 000; metric tons; 1974; 1973 in parentheses): barley *c.* 200 (205); wheat (1973) *c.* 30, (1972) 42; potatoes (1973) *c.* 25, (1972) 21; watermelons (1973) *c.* 85, (1972) 85; tomatoes (1973) *c.* 140, (1972) 170; olives *c.* 95 (149); dates (1973) *c.* 60, (1972) 60. Livestock (in 000; 1973): goats *c.* 1,105; sheep *c.* 2,400; cattle *c.* 110; camels *c.* 123; asses *c.* 77.

Industry. Production (in 000; metric tons; 1973): petroleum products 442; crude oil (1974) 75,221; electricity (Tripolitania; excluding most industrial production; kw-hr.) 698,000.

and revenues picked up later in the year, partly because of concessions on the premium normally charged for Libyan oil but mainly because of higher offtake by the oil companies.

Relations with Egypt were as bad as at any time in the past, and Egyptian citizens employed in Libya had to endure government hostility. Their numbers did not change significantly, however, and there was evidence that many farms in both western and eastern Libya were becoming dependent on an Egyptian work force. Soviet Premier Aleksey N. Kosygin visited Libya in May and signed cooperation agreements.

Libya's position as a source of finance for other Middle Eastern and African countries was weaker than in the past, and it played a less dramatic role in Middle Eastern and world affairs. Nevertheless, the share of its national income allocated to overseas aid was greater than that of the Western industrial nations. The high level of investment envisaged in the national development plans was achieved. The northern coast enjoyed another favourable season of winter rains, and the Ministry of Agriculture was able to announce self-sufficiency in barley.

Two coups were attempted, one on July 25 and the second on August 17. The second was the more significant in that it involved a member of the Revolutionary Command Council, Maj. Omar Meheishi. Both were unsuccessful, but they were taken as signs that some elements were uneasy about the direction of economic and social development.

(J. A. ALLAN)

[978.D.2.a]

Life Insurance:
see Industrial Review

Liechtenstein

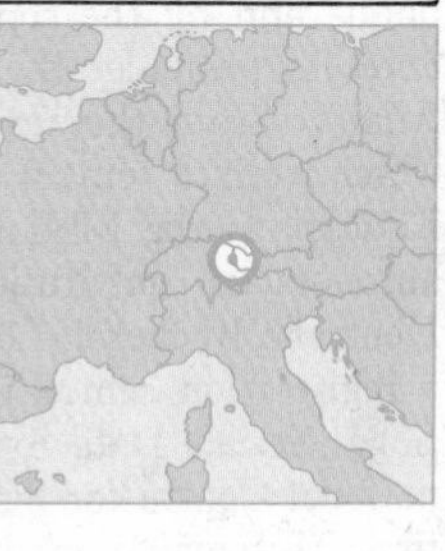

A constitutional monarchy between Switzerland and Austria, Liechtenstein is united with Switzerland by a customs and monetary union. Area: 62 sq.mi. (160 sq.km.). Pop. (1974 est.): 23,700. Cap. and largest city: Vaduz (pop., 1974 est., 4,400). Language: German. Religion (1970): Roman Catholic 90%. Sovereign prince, Francis Joseph II; chief of government in 1975, Walter Kieber.

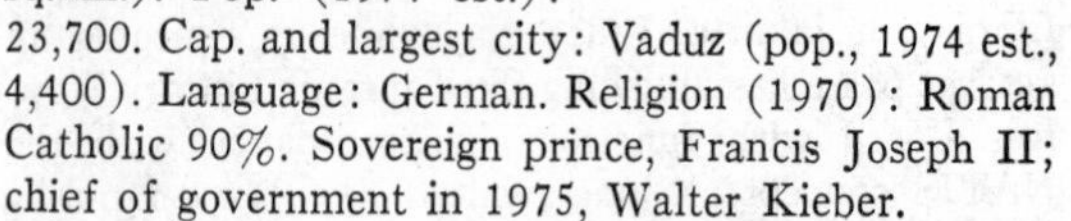

In 1975 only 5% of Liechtenstein's labour force worked on the land; some 60 small industrial enterprises manufactured a wide assortment of goods, from artificial teeth (the principality was a major world producer) to precision instruments. Until 1945 Liechtenstein had been predominantly agricultural.

Exports in 1974 earned more than SFr. 500 million (about $166 million), 95% of which represented the value of manufactured goods. According to Hugo Meier, head of the government Philatelic Department, sales of postage stamps covered 18% of the principality's yearly income. The banking and financial facilities attracted hundreds of "letter box" foreign companies every year, and by 1974 about 20,000 of them were registered in Liechtenstein. A company paid 2% of its declared capital on registering and only 1% a year afterward. As a result the principality had a high standard of living. An unskilled labourer earned the equivalent of about $5,700 annually, while a dentist earned $38,000.

Walter Kieber, the chief of government, signed the Final Act of the Conference on Security and Cooperation in Europe in Helsinki, Fin., on August 1, along with the representatives of 34 other countries.

(K. M. SMOGORZEWSKI)

LIECHTENSTEIN

Education. Primary (1974), pupils 2,053, teachers 82; secondary, pupils 1,525, teachers 106; vocational, pupils 70, teachers 26.

Finance and Trade. Monetary unit: Swiss franc, with (Sept. 22, 1975) a free rate of SFr. 2.73 to U.S. $1 (SFr. 5.66 = £1 sterling). Budget (1974 est.): revenue SFr. 93.9 million; expenditure SFr. 93,984,000. Exports (1972) SFr. 421 million. Export destinations: Switzerland 44%; EEC 26%. Main exports: metal manufactures, furniture, pottery. Tourism: visitors (1972) 82,000; gross receipts (1971) *c.* SFr. 18 million.

Life Sciences

The quarter century that ended in 1975 was one of the great revolutionary periods in the history of biology. Electronic instrumentation widened the range and precision of observations both in the laboratory and in the field as much as the microscope had done three centuries earlier. With the discovery of the double helix less than 25 years old, molecular biology, by interpreting in principle all biological processes in molecular terms, finally closed the gap between the physical and biological sciences. Though the relation between mind and matter remained mysterious, expanded knowledge of the behaviour of organisms, especially in communication and migration, revealed an unbroken continuity from single cells and simple multicells, to which the attribution of mind in any definable sense seemed impossible, to primates and other mammals, to which its denial seemed equally impossible. The end of the period coincided with the end of the historic ten-year International Biological Programme and the inauguration of the various new enterprises derived from it.

Research in 1975 concentrated on the exploitation of these developments, the addition of details, and application to practical problems. Work in the earlier years of the period had unveiled the basic processes of gene activity in the naked DNA threads of bacteria and viruses; it was now, however, concerned with the regulation of these processes in eukaryotic cells, where DNA is packed into chromosomes in intimate association with histones and other proteins. Apart from applications to special medical problems, this research included studies on the activation and deactivation of particular genes in the cells of embryos at appropriate times in relation to their positions in the embryo, the action of molting hormones in insect pupation, and the role of cytoplasmic protein in promoting DNA replication. The determination of the neural connections in the developing brain, *e.g.,* in the optic tract of vertebrates and in the neurons of cats' whiskers, continued as a major multidisciplinary study. Gene regulation was also found to be important in evolution. Earlier work had shown that, broadly speaking, gene mutation continues relentlessly at much the same rate in such slowly evolving groups as frogs and in such rapidly evolving ones as mammals. It now appeared, however, that the adaptive changes which lead to speciation result mainly from differential changes in the regulatory mechanisms. The differences between chimpanzees and men appeared to be an example.

The year 1975 saw a growing concern for the fate of tropical forests, whose flora is by far the richest in quantity and in variety of all terrestrial habitats, but whose destruction was going on rapidly in almost complete ignorance of the consequences. An international conference on this issue was planned by the UN Food and Agriculture Organization (FAO) in October, and both the International Union for Conservation of Nature and Natural Resources and the World Wildlife Fund inaugurated campaigns for conservation of representative areas. The problems were also discussed at the 12th International Congress of Botany, held in Leningrad during the summer, where it was pointed out how much progress was held up by lack of suitably trained botanists, especially taxonomists. One of the losses that accompany progress came from the excitements of the "new biology," which attracted students from the important but less exciting traditional disciplines.

The losses accompanying progress were also dramatically demonstrated in the disastrous failure of the Indonesian rice crop. The Green Revolution of latter years had led to the abandonment of traditional varieties in favour of the new "miracle rice." This, however, proved unable to resist the insect-borne grassy stunt virus, resulting in the almost complete loss of the year's crop. Such loss of valuable genetic resources through disappearance of local varieties with special adaptive characteristics emphasized the need for such worldwide efforts as the FAO's International Bank of Plant Genetic Resources at Izmir, Turkey, for Middle East food plants. For animals the difficulties of conservation were greater, but the establishment in the U.K. of the Rare Breeds Survival Trust was a useful step.

Rapid growth of the influence of science outside its ivory towers inevitably involved biologists more and more in public affairs. Conservationists were continually in conflict with commercial and political interests, from village concerns to such international affairs as the UN Conference on the Law of the Sea and the International Whaling Commission. Some scientifically essential international activities, *e.g.,* the imaginative UN Environment Program with headquarters at Nairobi, Kenya, were supported lukewarmly or even opposed by some countries, which argued that such efforts were wasted until the urgent problem of human hunger had been solved. The Research Unit on Genetic Control of Mosquitoes at New Delhi, India, was abandoned in the face of local controversy (see *Entomology,* below). Much emotion surrounded the ethics of fetal research (*see* HEALTH AND DISEASE: *Special Report*). Recent fears about the dangers of work on genetic engineering in bacteria were partly allayed by the establishment of guidelines for future research by an international conference of scientists (see *Genetics,* below). However, the entry of at least one commercial firm into this field caused new concern.

(HAROLD SANDON)

ZOOLOGY

Some surprising findings involving a variety of animals were reported during 1975. A South American peccary, previously thought to be extinct, was found alive and well and living in western Paraguay. Peccaries belong to the family Tayassuidae and are New World relatives of the Suidae (pigs). Until this discovery, only two species were thought to have survived to the present, the collared peccary or javelina (*Dicotyles tajacu*) and the white-lipped peccary (*Tayassu pecari*). R. M. Wetzel and his co-workers studied 29 specimens of the new peccary from the Gran Chaco region of Paraguay and classified it as *Catagonus wagneri,* previously known only from fossils. Its discovery was probably delayed because the thorn forests of the Gran Chaco, which extend from southeastern Bolivia through western Paraguay to northern Argentina, are relatively unstudied. There are important differences between *C. wagneri* and the two other existing species, including many in the skulls and dentition. Evidently this peccary has survived in a scrub-thorn and grass habitat. It is one of the major mammals hunted for food in western Paraguay and thus may be in danger of extinction.

Another discovery involved the distribution of the primitive, unsegmented mollusk *Neopilina,* the only living genus of the class Monoplacophora. *Neopilina* was first reported in 1957 by H. Lemche as a living specimen from the ocean floor in the Pacific near Costa Rica. Five or six segmentally arranged pairs of gills, nephridia (excretory structures), and gill hearts bear witness to the internally segmented body. Specimens have since been reported in other regions of the Pacific, the northern Indian Ocean, and the Antarctic part of the Atlantic. The specimen from the Antarctic was immature, but a second, mature specimen was reported from the Atlantic at 56°29′ S, 50°51′ W by Soviet oceanographers as a result of a cruise during 1971–72. It measured 19 mm. long and was found among mud, sand, and pebbles at a depth of about 5,000 m. It is possible that the immature specimen, which was only 2.3 mm. long, was a member of the same species. The bottom fauna was very rich where the specimen was found, with more than 20 inverte-

LOS ANGELES ZOO PHOTO

Coyotes have displayed a remarkable ability to adapt to environmental change and they occur today within a number of metropolitan areas of the western U.S. Those shown above were captured in Los Angeles during the summer.

brate groups represented. It was felt that floating ice would act to disperse the hard substrata (stones, manganese nodules, or pebbles) to which *Neopilina* adheres.

A number of interesting observations concerning reproduction were also reported. A unique form of parental care, completely without parallel among the vertebrates, was described by C. J. Corben and co-workers in an Australian leptodactylid frog, *Rheobatrachus silus*. This is an aquatic, stream-dwelling frog, first described in 1973 near Brisbane. It is unlike any other Australian genus but resembles the African pipid frog *Xenopus*. The discovery was made in 1973, when an adult of unusually large girth was about to be transferred from one aquarium to another. After some rocks and other material had been removed, the frog swam around, seeking refuge. It then rose to the surface, compressed its lateral body muscles, and propulsively ejected six living tadpoles from its mouth. Three of these were preserved and found to be unusual, exhibiting both large amounts of abdominal yolk and large tails; such tails would not be needed, as the yolk appeared sufficient to support the whole of development. With respect to the size of the tail the tadpoles resembled those of *Rhinoderma darwini* of Chile, which are carried in the enlarged vocal sac of the male. The ejected frogs survived only two days in water. Eighteen days after the initial observation, a juvenile frog was discovered with the adult. Some days later the adult was grasped by its hind legs, whereupon it flexed dorsally, elevated its head, opened its mouth, and ejected eight more juvenile frogs. Postmortem examination of the adult frog confirmed its sex as female. Its stomach was found to be exceptionally large and thin-walled, occupying the midline, rather than the usual left position. The muscles surrounding the lateral and ventral borders of the abdominal cavity were exceptionally thin, due to their recent, prolonged distension. In many fish species, the eggs are transported by mouth but not swallowed. In some, the eggs are retained in the oral cavity during incubation. Corben and his colleagues assumed that there must be total inhibition of gastric secretion and digestive processes in the case of *R. silus*, presumably involving the action of reproductive hormones. Although frogs are noted for bizarre examples of embryo transport and inhibition, this instance of gastric brooding is the strangest yet encountered.

A reproductive finding of evolutionary importance involves the true position of the free-living flatworms of the class Turbellaria in the phylum Platyhelminthes, always considered as representative of the most primitive Bilateria (bilaterally symmetrical metazoans with a digestive cavity). However, recent findings of biflagellate spermatozoa in turbellarians have been a serious obstacle to complete acceptance of their primitiveness. Such complex sperm would not be expected in primitive organisms. Thus, the recent observation by S. Tyler and R. M. Rieger of uniflagellate sperm in the primitive marine turbellarian *Nemertoderma* sp. is of importance because such sperm are similar to those of sponges, cnidarians, and ctenophores, which are lower on the evolutionary tree. Consequently, it is still possible to regard the Turbellaria as primitive Bilateria, with the biflagellate sperm of most members of the group explained as a specialization.

Evidence was obtained that synchronous breeding may have adaptive value. S. T. Emlen and N. J. Demong studied colonies of bank swallows (*Riparia riparia)* and found that two-thirds of the nests fledged their young within a period of only six days. They also found that reproductive fitness increased as a function of synchronization of the colony. They concluded that late-fledging birds would be at a disadvantage in obtaining food, because they would emerge from the nest to encounter large flights of birds departing to unknown destinations and would be less able to learn where food could be found. They analyzed the growth and mortality of nestlings with respect to the peak date of synchronization in each colony. The loss of retarded birds (runts) to starvation occurred much more frequently among late nesters than among any other category, in agreement with their hypothesis regarding synchronized breeding.

Predation is another area in which interesting results were obtained. H. C. Mueller studied the colour of mice preyed upon experimentally by American kestrels (*Falco sparverius*) and found that these hawks tend to select odd-coloured prey. Six tamed kestrels were allowed to prey on laboratory white mice, some of which had been dyed gray with food colouring. Illumination and background conditions were held constant. There were two parts to the experiment. In part A each hawk was first given ten opportunities to capture a single white mouse. On the 11th trial, a choice between a white and a gray mouse was offered. Once a gray mouse was taken, the experiment involving choice was repeated daily for 15 more days. Under these conditions the hawks selected gray mice much more frequently. In part B the conditions were reversed: ten opportunities to capture a gray mouse were followed by a choice. During this part hawks selected white mice to a much greater degree. Statistical calculations clearly showed a deviation from random selection and indicated a strong preference for odd or novel mice. In contrast to the other five hawks, one bird, Walda, never chose a gray mouse in part A, even after 16 days of experiments. Mueller concluded that Walda exhibited a strong "specific searching image" or SSI, a term used by L. Tinbergen to describe a strong tendency for birds to select prey of the colour to which they have become accustomed. SSI did not account for the results obtained with the other five hawks. When Walda's results in part B also disclosed a strong SSI, it was decided not to include them in the calculations. The American kestrel normally encounters only one prey at a time; thus the present experiments were quite natural. Because odd animals are almost invariably unfit animals, Mueller felt that such selection of odd prey would benefit both predator and prey by driving the predator-prey system to optimal yield. He called the present situation sequential oddity, as opposed to simultaneous oddity, where a predator is exposed to a single odd animal in an aggregate. Previous work has provided only slight evidence for simultaneous oddity, but the experimental conditions may make it difficult to reveal such behaviour.

The Convention on International Trade in Endangered Species of Wild Fauna and Flora, initialed by 80 nations when first drafted in 1973, went into effect on July 1. Relying on a system of permits from countries of origin and destination, it constituted the first all-encompassing attempt at international trade regulation of endangered species and, it was hoped, would slow the increasing rate of species extinction.

(RONALD R. NOVALES)

[10/34.B.5.1]

Entomology. An international controversy developed during the period 1972–75 over the work of the Research Unit on Genetic Control of Mosquitoes, which had been established at New Delhi, India, in 1970 by the UN World Health Organization (WHO) and the Indian Council of Medical Research with the use of funds subscribed by the U.S. Public Health Service. Indian journalists accused the unit of carrying out experiments with chemical sterilizing agents that would not have been allowed in the U.S. and that served principally to provide the U.S. with information on biological warfare. A committee of the Indian government investigated the project and in its report of April 1975 repeated the allegations, stating that the unit had concentrated its research on *Aëdes aegypti*, a vector of yellow fever, despite the fact that the disease did not occur in India. As a result of the report, WHO officially withdrew from the project. Reviewing these incidents, the influential British science journal *Nature* (July 31, 1975) found the accusations inaccurate or misleading and scientifically irrational, but it placed part of the blame on WHO officials who had remained unreasonably uncommunicative when asked to release information on the work of the unit.

If the Indian genetic research had run into difficulties, a kindred project on sheep blowfly in Australia showed considerable promise. Max Whitten and Geoff Foster of the Commonwealth Scientific and Industrial Research Organization had bred a strain of *Lucilia cuprina* that had a pair of "compound" chromosomes; *i.e.*, chromosomes that had been broken under irradiation and had rejoined in the wrong way, with the same ends of the sister chromosomes linked. When sex cells are formed in this strain, some receive both compound chromosomes, or a double set of genetic information; some receive one chromosome, or only half of the genetic information doubled up; and some receive neither. As a result, crosses between compound and wild strains were always infertile, and when the compound strain interbred, only about one-quarter of the zygotes or fertilized eggs (those in which a full and balanced set of genetic information had by chance been added back together) were viable. Whitten and Foster showed that, by releasing their compound

COURTESY, WAITE AGRICULTURAL RESEARCH INSTITUTE

Oechalia consocialis, a shield bug, preys on caterpillars of the vine moth in Australian vineyards rather than on the plants themselves.

strain among wild blowflies, they could effectively sterilize the wild strain and replace it with the compound one. Tests were in progress in 1975 to see whether the fertility of the compound strain would be low enough to reduce blowfly strike to acceptable levels.

In the U.S., the Environmental Protection Agency (EPA), which had banned agricultural use of aldrin and dieldrin in 1974, released the news that it would permit continued use of these insecticides against termites, on nonfood plants, and against clothes moths in some circumstances.

Earl Butz, U.S. secretary of agriculture, announced the U.S. Department of Agriculture was pulling out of the effort to eradicate the imported fire ant *Solenopsis* from the Southern states. The insects, although not strictly agricultural or household pests, attacked agricultural workers, and their stings could lead to secondary infections and allergic reactions. Despite annual expenditures rising to $7 million in 1974, plus grants from the affected states, the fire ants had continued to hold their own over some 126 million ac. The failure of the eradication program, which had depended on the pesticide Mirex, was due, according to Butz, to the restrictions placed on use of the chemical by the EPA.

Many workers continued to explore the use of aggregating and sex pheromones to trap insects or disrupt their mating behaviour. L. B. Hendry and coworkers at Pennsylvania State University also speculated on the evolutionary origin of these secretions. They had noted that not only were phytophagous insects attracted to the scents of the plants on which they fed but also that some then secreted or excreted such chemicals in a concentrated or modified form which, to other individuals of the species, was even more attractive than the original source. Hendry's team suggested that sex pheromones may have originated in the same way, from attractants in natural diets. They reported that females of the oak leaf roller moth, *Archips semiferanus*, produce sex pheromones that contain 21 isomeric tetradecenyl acetates, of which 17 attracted males to field-emplaced lures. Fresh oak leaves also contained tetradecenyl acetates, and males became sexually excited in the presence of the leaves, attempting to copulate with them.

WIDE WORLD

The first successful photo of the green lacewing (Chrysopa) insect in free flight was taken by Stephen Dalton.

Tsetse flies, the vectors of sleeping sicknesses in both man and his domestic animals in Africa, were the latest targets of hormonal insecticides. The female tsetse produces only one offspring at a time and carries the larva in her uterus, nourished by a special "milk gland" until it is fully grown. The flies have a very low reproductive potential, therefore, but more than compensate for this by maternal care. David Denlinger of the International Centre of Insect Physiology and Ecology, Nairobi, showed that the administration of small doses of either molting hormone or juvenile hormone caused abortions and could be used as a potent weapon to reverse the value of the insect's reproductive strategy.

James Lloyd of the University of Florida and Steve Nelson of the State University of New York at Stony Brook and co-workers observed that females of *Photuris versicolor* were the femmes fatales of the firefly world. The male lampyrid beetles fly at night, emitting flashes with a timing that is characteristic for each species; the females remain stationary on perches, responding with their own characteristic signals, and the males home in on them. *P. versicolor* virgin females responded typically to their own males until they had mated. Two days later, however, they began to mimic the responses of a number of other lampyrid species and, when they arrived, ate them.

(PETER W. MILES)

[321.B.9.c.i; 321.E.2.a]

The first whooping crane born to parents hatched and raised in captivity was born at the Patuxent Wildlife Research Center, Laurel, Maryland, in May. The chick was named Dawn.

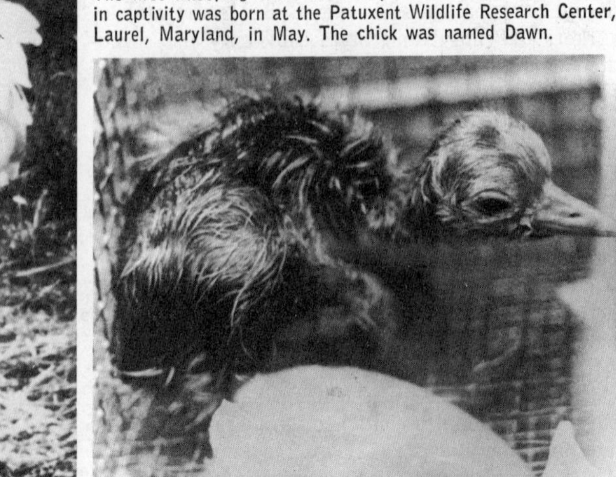

LEFT, DR C. KEPPEL—U.S. FISH AND WILDLIFE SERVICE; RIGHT, THE NEW YORK TIMES

Ornithology. Ornithological history was made when a tree surgeon working in the Santa Cruz Mountains in the western United States discovered the nest of a marbled murrelet, the only bird believed to nest in North America whose nest had never been found. The murrelet, a type of auk, is a seabird, but it has been known to nest inland in trees. The first nest to be seen by man was merely a depression atop a horizontal moss-covered branch 45 m. (148 ft.) above the ground. From such sites, the young birds were believed to fly directly to the sea.

Ross's gull, a rosy-chested, gray-winged seabird that has been observed only rarely even in its own Arctic habitat, made an unprecedented appearance in March on the eastern coast of North America. After a number of early unconfirmed sightings, the bird was identified and photographed by a small army of birders who had gathered at the mouth of the Merrimack River near Salisbury, Mass. Ross's gull normally breeds in northeastern Siberia and occasionally has been observed off Point Barrow, Alaska.

The years 1968–69 saw a dramatic 77% decrease in the British breeding population of the common whitethroat, a small insectivorous warbler. Corresponding with a population fall in other parts of Western Europe, the decline was attributed to reduced rainfall in the arid steppe region of the southern fringe of the Sahara, where the bird spends the winter. West German ornithologists, however, attributed the same decline to pesticide contamination in winter quarters or during migrations.

Ornithologist Stanley Cramp described increases in the variety and numbers of insectivorous birds breeding in central London, with special reference to the 17-year periods before and after the U.K.'s Clean Air Act of 1956. Possible reasons for the improvement included reduced smoke pollution, leading in turn to greater supplies of insect food.

The biology and behaviour of phalaropes, small wading and swimming birds of the Arctic, were of particular interest because of the reversed role of the sexes in events linked with reproduction. The studies of the Soviet ornithologist A. A. Kistchinsky on the gray phalarope in eastern Siberia showed that the birds did not engage in territorial defense, that all courtship displays were initiated by females (the more brightly coloured of the two sexes), and that no permanent pairs were formed. After egg laying, the females were driven away; the males incubated the eggs and cared for the young themselves.

A West German ornithologist, S. Langner, found that the hill star hummingbird (*Oreotrochilus estella*) lived the entire year at an altitude of nearly 4,000 m. (13,000 ft.) in the Bolivian Andes. During the cold, barren winter, the birds made a daily trip of 120 km. (74 mi.) in each direction to the nearest flowers and slept clinging to vertical rock crevices, which at night were on average about 20° C warmer than the surrounding open country.

In the U.S., the number of blackbirds and starlings in a roosting congregation was estimated from calculations involving the weight of droppings deposited per unit area below the roost. The single dormitory was reckoned to contain 2,294,700 birds! Studies by Janet Kear of Salvadori's duck, one of the least observed of the world's waterfowl, revealed that the New Guinean bird was adapted to living in mountain torrents and was highly territorial. The species might be related to the blue duck of New Zealand and the torrent ducks of South America, which also inhabit waterfalls.

A royal albatross ringed with a numbered identity bracelet as a breeding adult in 1937 was still alive at its nesting colony in December 1974, making the bird the longest-lived individual wild bird revealed by ringing. Because the great albatrosses do not begin breeding until the age of nine, this particular individual must have been at least 46 years old.

In *Birds of Prey in Europe* (1974), Dutch ornithologist Maarten Bijleveld presented a masterly synthesis tracing for over 200 years the history of the relationship between man and the diurnal raptors of Britain and continental Europe. It documented the decline and near fall of these noble birds, including the rarest of them all, the imperial eagle, of which no more than 80 pairs were left. Looking to the future, the author discussed various means of preservation: monetary rewards for successful broods; the acquisition of areas of land for roosting places such as that purchased in Austria for griffon vultures; the protection of nests; the establishment of feeding places like the vulture "hard table" in northern Spain; and the reintroduction of birds bred in captivity to areas where they had formerly lived but from which they had disappeared.

The Biology of Penguins (1975), edited by Bernard Stonehouse, presented 21 papers on various aspects of one of the most primitive of avian families. One paper concerned the Magellanic penguin, the least studied of the world's 18 species, a bird that lives in temperate and subantarctic South America. Various aspects of its breeding biology were described for the first time. A 1951 work by Erwin Stresemann, published in an English translation during 1975 under the title *Ornithology: From Aristotle to the Present,* seemed well on its way to becoming the standard text on the history of the subject.

(JEFFERY BOSWELL)

[313.J.6]

MARINE BIOLOGY

A solar eclipse affords a rare opportunity to study the effects of sudden and unprecedented withdrawal of light from the natural daytime environment of marine animals. A report of such a study on deepwater organisms during the eclipse of June 30, 1973, was published in 1975. Observations were made on a plankton community depicted as a sonic scattering layer 40 mi. N of Cape Verde Islands at a depth of 200 m. The layer, which had migrated downward at dawn, rose again by 50 m. at eclipse totality, some three hours after sunrise, lagging slightly because the rate of swimming was too slow to permit the animals to maintain themselves exactly in the optimal photoenvironment.

The anglerfish *Cryptopsaras couesi,* a resident of the darkness and great pressures of the ocean depths below 500 m., is a well-known example of the reproductive strategy of sexual parasitism. In an environment where food is difficult to procure and a chance meeting between sexual partners is rare, the males of the species have evolved into dwarfed parasites that permanently attach themselves with pincerlike denticles to the female. The males then degenerate into little more than sperm factories, the epidermal tissues of the partners fuse, and their circulatory systems forever unite. It had always been assumed that, before receiving parasitic males, female anglerfish mature sexually to a large adult stage. However, the recent discovery of two sexually immature parasitized female specimens led T. W. Pietsch of the Harvard University Museum of Comparative Zoology to speculate that parasitic attachment may necessarily precede sexual maturity in the female. Because neither free-living pregnant females nor free-living males with developed testes have ever been found, Pietsch suggested that gonadal development in both sexes may be dependent on the attachment.

Plans to increase ship traffic through the Panama Canal by pumping seawater into Gatun Lake were criticized by marine biologists. Currently the lake was of low salinity and acted as a major barrier to the interchange of Atlantic and Pacific marine faunas. If it were made more saline there could be dangerous consequences for the faunal assemblages at each side of the canal. The Japanese seaweed *Sargassum muticum,* which colonized along the Pacific coastline of North America in 30 years, was recently introduced to Britain. Intensive efforts to eradicate the alga there failed, and it seemed likely to spread from The Solent, to some extent at the expense of other brown algae such as indigenous *Laminaria* and *Cystoseira.* Organisms that live on the surface of the indigenous species seemed unlikely to be affected since they were also present on *Sargassum.*

South African work on fish physiology showed that the elasmobranch gill is more important in salt regulation than had hitherto been considered, and work on Antarctic teleost fish considered the problem of how bladder urine with a capillary tube freezing point of $-1°$ C resists freezing at $-1.8°$ C. It was suggested that glycoprotein "antifreeze" is present in coelomic fluid surrounding the bladder, thus preventing freezing of the supercooled urine.

The repellent saponins produced by starfish, previously thought to be used to induce shell opening in bivalve mollusks, were now being studied as possible defense mechanisms. Solutions of the saponins of *Marthasterias glacialis* caused considerable damage to the gill epithelium in the plaice or flounder *Pleuronectes platessa.* Avoidance of starfish by mollusks was well known after contact with the starfish, but relatively few data were available on remote sensing. The limpet *Acmaea* was clearly able to detect the predatory starfish *Pisaster* at a distance in response to the saponins in solution.

Growth of corals still presented problems after 100 years of study; for example, whether calcification

THEO BROWN—AUSTRALIAN INFORMATION SERVICE

Experiments testing the reactions of marine animals to various sound frequencies has resulted in an electronic device which Theo Brown, an Australian marine investigator, claims will repel five species of man-eating sharks.

takes place within or outside of the cell. New studies by electron microscopy and X-ray microprobe analysis of certain calcium-secreting tissues of newly settled larvae and adult corals suggested that skeletal formation is extracellular to the epidermis.

Pollution studies identified barnacles as possible indicators of zinc pollution; *Balanus balanoides, Elminius modestus,* and *Lepas anatifera* all accumulate the metal as insoluble zinc salt granules in the gut tissues. In the polychaete *Phyllodoce,* death by copper poisoning was considered to relate to the rate of uptake rather than to the amount of copper accumulated. Ten years' work by the Marine Laboratory, Aberdeen, Scotland, on the sand ecosystem of O-group plaice (*Pleuronectes platessa*) provided background data for the study of the long-term effects of sublethal concentrations of metal pollutants. Copper sulfate added to the food chain showed dose-dependent accumulations of copper in the sand, in flesh and shell of the mollusk *Tellina tenuis,* and in plaice viscera; no plateau concentration was reached with doses up to 100 micrograms of copper per litre. Phytoplankton standing crop was reduced, filter-feeding *Tellina* showed adversely affected condition, and *Pleuronectes* flatfish, feeding on *Tellina* siphons, showed reduced growth.

(ERNEST NAYLOR)

[354.B]

BOTANY

Much of the new information acquired in 1975 in the field of plant physiology related to some very old problems. One of these was the mechanism of transport of indolylacetic acid (IAA), a member of a class of plant hormones called auxins that promote lengthwise growth. IAA moves in a polar manner, from the apex of the stem toward the base, and its movement across cell membranes from one cell to the next had been believed to be an important step in such polar transport. It was shown that in crown-gall cells there are two separate mechanisms of auxin transport across cell membranes. IAA in the undissociated state enters cells by diffusion across the membrane, while dissociated IAA anions leave via a carrier-mediated mechanism. An inhibitor of polar IAA movement, called TIBA, was shown to inhibit the efflux of IAA anions but not the influx of the undissociated IAA. It was suggested, therefore, that once IAA diffuses into cells it dissociates; the dissociated anions then reach a higher concentration inside the cell than outside, and are secreted preferentially through the basal ends of the cell via the carrier system, resulting in a net polar transport.

The control exerted by changes in light quality, independent of photosynthesis, on the physiological and developmental responses of plants and plant cells is known as photomorphogenesis. Those responses mediated by the pigment phytochrome continued to receive much attention. One major issue for debate concerned the mechanism governing phytochrome-mediated increases in enzyme activities. While de novo synthesis of molecules of several enzymes (as opposed to the utilization of activated preexisting molecules) was again demonstrated using techniques that separate "new" molecules from "old" molecules by centrifugation, some results suggested the possibility that the induction of activity of the enzyme phenylalanine ammonia-lyase (PAL) in mustard seedling cotyledons was a consequence of phytochrome-mediated activation of preexisting molecules. Differently designed experiments carried out on the same material, however, clearly supported the idea of de novo synthesis as the mechanism responsible for the increase in PAL activity, as is the case for other enzymes.

Another interesting observation concerning phytochrome was that illumination of mustard seedling cotyledons with far-red light (the wavelengths that reversibly convert phytochrome to its active form) resulted in a decrease in the levels of cyclic AMP. This decrease was fully reversible by illumination with red light, indicating that indeed phytochrome was responsible for the effect. The investigators were careful to point out, however, that the relationship of the changed levels of cyclic AMP, an important compound in developmental processes in animal cells, to photomorphogenesis in the mustard seedling was not established, and that it may be an insignificant one.

Resistance to low temperatures can be acquired by plants following gradual exposure to low temperatures through a kind of physiological adaptation known as hardening. In an attempt to describe some of the changes that occur during this process, biochemical analyses of leaves of hardened species were carried out. It was shown that during the hardening process the proportion of unsaturated fatty acids in membrane phospholipids increased; such a change would lower the temperature at which phase changes in membranes, leading to cellular damage, would occur. Changes in the fatty acids were detected only in cold-sensitive species which harden readily, and not in chill-resistant species or in chill-sensitive species which do not harden. It had also been shown, however, that by midwinter some Arctic plants can acquire a tolerance of temperatures of $-80°$ C; membrane changes alone were considered insufficient for such tremendous tolerance.

The present-day cultivated bread wheat, *Triticum vulgare* (or *aestivum*), is known to have evolved from three separate ancestors. Three separate sets of chromosomes, each from a different diploid ancestor, constitute the genome or genetic complement of the hexaploid *T. vulgare.* These ancestors had been identified as the diploid species *Triticum monococcum, Aegilops squarrosa,* and *Triticum speltoides.* However, the application of chromosome banding techniques, which permit the identification of individual chromosomes, to the chromosomes of wheat and its putative an-

C. E. MOHR—NATIONAL AUDUBON SOCIETY

LOUISE K. BROMAN—NATIONAL AUDUBON SOCIETY

Franklinia (left) and French's shooting star, two of perhaps 2,000 species of plants native to the U.S. that are in danger of extinction according to a Smithsonian Institution study.

cestors cast doubt on the identification of *T. speltoides* as a donor of one of the chromosome sets. Clear banding similarities between the chromosomes of both *T. monococcum* and *A. squarrosa* and those of *T. vulgare* were recognized, but the banding patterns of *T. speltoides* were so different from the remaining *T. vulgare* chromosomes that it was suggested *T. speltoides* be eliminated as a possible donor to the wheat genome. No substitute donor, however, was offered. (*See also* GARDENING.)

(PETER L. WEBSTER)

[321.B.9.d; 323.A; 338.B.1.c]

MOLECULAR BIOLOGY

Biochemistry. The actions of hormones have long elicited in man a sense of awe and curiosity. One could not fail to be impressed by such devastating consequences of hormonal deficiencies as cretinism, infantile diabetes, or dwarfism. As early as 1902 the British physiologists Sir William Bayliss and Ernest Starling established that hormones are diffusible substances, produced by one part of the body and acting upon another. They selected the word "hormone" because its Greek root means to stimulate or arouse; the hormone they were studying stimulated the pancreas to secrete its digestive juice.

The general properties of a hormone permit certain presumptions: (1) Because the level of a hormone can be modulated in response to the needs of the moment, it must be both released by the source tissue and removed by the target tissue. Consider, for example, a momentary fright. The brain signals the adrenal glands, which release stored epinephrine (adrenaline), causing the liver to raise the level of blood sugar, the heart to beat faster, the bronchioles leading to the lungs to dilate, and the arterioles of the gut to contract. As fright passes these changes must subside and will do so only if the hormone that caused them is removed. (2) Because the effects are selective, the target cells must contain receptors for the given hormone that are absent from other cells. (3) Because miniscule amounts of a hormone may have a profound effect, the specific receptor sites must exhibit great affinity for the hormone. In addition, the action of the hormone must be mediated by devices that greatly amplify the original signal. Within living things such amplification is achieved by enzymes that catalyze metabolic interconversions; a substance that modifies the activity of an enzyme or a cascade of enzymes can therefore achieve a great effect. (4) Because many hormones are rather large molecules, which are not likely to penetrate the outer membrane of cells, the essential action of such hormones must be exerted at these outer membranes.

Much of the recent work aimed at understanding the mechanism of action of hormones is a direct outgrowth of the pioneering labours of Earl W. Sutherland, Jr., who died in 1974. During his studies of the hormonal control of glycogen breakdown, he discovered the mediating action of cyclic adenosine monophosphate (cyclic AMP) and thereby opened a trail that others have broadened and extended. Cyclic AMP is now seen to be a common factor in the action of numerous hormones. Indeed, if the hormones are messengers which operate between tissues, then cyclic AMP is a messenger operating within the cell. It has in fact been called the second messenger.

A specific example of a complex enzyme cascade will serve to illustrate the mediating activity of cyclic AMP and can be used as a model for the action of many hormones. Adenylyl cyclase is a membrane-bound enzyme that catalyzes the conversion of adenosine triphosphate (ATP) into cyclic AMP. Epinephrine activates the adenylyl cyclase of liver cells, producing a rise in the rate of production of cyclic AMP and an increase in the concentration of this compound inside the liver cells. Cyclic AMP in turn activates another enzyme, a protein kinase, that catalyzes the transfer of a phosphate group from ATP onto various proteins. In this particular case, the protein kinase catalyzes the phosphorylation and consequent activation of glycogen phosphorylase kinase. This latter enzyme then catalyzes the transfer of a phosphate group from ATP onto glycogen phosphorylase, which is thereby made more active in catalyzing the breakdown of glycogen into a glucose phosphate. This is the desired effect since glycogen, the polymeric storage form of glucose, must be broken down to make the sugar available to the muscles needed in the emergency that caused the release of epinephrine.

Many tissues contain membrane-bound adenylyl cyclases, which are activated only by specific hormones. Kidney tubules contain one which responds to antidiuretic hormone; heart muscle contains one which is activated by glucagon; and thyroid tissue contains one which is activated by the thyroid-stimulating hormone. Just as hormones must be both made and destroyed, so must the cyclic AMP be removed to allow modulation of its effects. Phosphodiesterases catalyze the hydrolytic destruction of cyclic AMP; their action is also under the control of hormones. In addition, there is another second messenger, cyclic guanosine monophosphate (cyclic GMP), which mediates the regulation of cellular events that are distinct from the effects of cyclic AMP. In the rat uterus the hormones oxytocin, serotonin, and prostaglandin $F_{2\alpha}$ raise the level of cyclic GMP but have no effect on the level of cyclic AMP. There is, of course, a phosphodiesterase that acts upon cyclic GMP. The stacked membranous discs found in retinal rod cells contain such a membrane-bound phosphodiesterase; it is activated by light and thus serves as one stage in the amplifying cascade that allows the absorption of one photon of light to initiate a nerve signal.

(IRWIN FRIDOVICH)

[321.B.7 and 9; 333.C.2.a; 422.F.1]

Biophysics. Perhaps the single most exciting and certainly the most promising advance in 1975 was the report of a new method for mapping genes in human chromosomes. Developed by S. J. Goss and H. Harris of the University of Oxford, the technique will complement and expand present more qualitative approaches such as dye staining and fluorescent microscopy and provides for the first time a systematic and quantitative approach to the mapping problem.

Goss and Harris demonstrated its efficacy by measuring the distances between four human genes on the X chromosome. Their approach began with exposure of human cells to large doses of ionizing radiation. These cells were then fused to nonirradiated cells of a different mammal, usually rodent, by the addition of inactivated Sendai virus to the mixed cell suspension. The fused cells became mononucleate hybrids capable of indefinite growth and multiplication, though most human chromosomes were eliminated from rodent-human cell hybrids during subsequent generations of growth. Nevertheless, different human chromosomes survived in different hybrid clones and thereby provided different functioning human chromosomes for analysis. At this point Goss and Harris applied some well-established techniques in radiation and molecular genetics to determine the relative distances between genes linked on single chromosomes. X-rays are known to break chromosomes, separating normally linked genes; the probability that any two genes will remain together, or be cotransferred, on the same chromosome fragment is inversely proportional to the distance between them. Goss and Harris studied the cotransfer of three other genes known to be linked to the gene that directs the production of the enzyme hypoxanthine guanine phosphoribosyl transferase (HGRT); namely, the genes for phosphoglycerate kinase (PGK), glucose-6-phosphate dehydrogenase (G6PD), and α-galactosidase (α-gal). Each of these three enzymes can be identified using electrophoretic techniques. The approach measured the reduction in frequency of occurrence of each of these enzymes with HGRT as radiation exposure was increased. Their results showed that the gene for G6PD remained with that for HGRT more frequently than did the other two genes and therefore was the closest to the HGRT gene of the three. The data indicated the gene order PGK—α-gal—HGRT—G6PD and provided provisional map distances between these genes, accurate to about 30%.

In another application of the somatic-cell hybrid technique it was found that a human tumour-inducing virus must be carried in a particular human chromosome for establishment of the tumour. C. M. Croce and H. Koprowski of the Wistar Institute of Anatomy and Biology, Philadelphia, found that human chromosome 7 carries the genome, or genetic complement, of the simian tumour-inducing virus SV40. They examined a large number of independently selected clones of human-mouse hybrids formed by the fusion of either of two mouse strains with certain human fibroblasts (connective-tissue cells) that had been genetically altered, or transformed, by infection with the genome of the SV40 virus. All of the transformed hybrid cells showed the visible characteristics of the typical SV40 tumour cell. The chromosomal content of 80 of these transformed hybrid clones was analyzed, and all were found to contain human chromosome 7. Furthermore, in 15 of these clones chromosome 7 was the only human chromosome present. Because the same investigators had shown earlier that normal chromosome 7, without the integrated SV40 genome, could not produce tumour-cell characteristics in these hybrids, the results clearly demonstrated that the infected chromosome 7 is the locus of this cancerous virus.

Patients with the rare recessive disease xeroderma pigmentosum (XP) are hypersensitive to sunlight. Exposure of the skin leads to multiple recurring neoplasms. Several years earlier, J. E. Cleaver of the University of California, San Francisco, had discovered that cells from XP patients were deficient in excision repair, a process by which ultraviolet light-induced lesions in one strand of the DNA duplex are excised and replaced with new DNA replicated from the undamaged strand. It was thought that, in the absence of this repair system, the unrepaired damage caused light-induced cancer. More recently, however, XP patients have been found who do have the normal excision-repair systems; thus the mechanism of light-induced cancer in these persons was obscure. Recently A. R. Lehmann (University of Sussex, England), D. Bootsma (Erasmus University, The Netherlands), and their collaborators showed that these patients were defective in an alternate repair process called recombination repair, which replaces damaged strands with material replicated from a second, undamaged duplex of the same cell. These studies clearly demonstrate the importance of DNA repair to light-induced cancer and suggest that many other kinds of cancer may be due to DNA lesions induced either chemically or by viral agents.

(H. E. KUBITSCHEK)

[339.C and E; 424.B.1.a.v]

Genetics. *Escherichia coli,* a common intestinal inhabitant and one of the most intensively studied organisms in the laboratory, became the centre of a scientific controversy in 1974 when a group of prominent scientists proposed a voluntary moratorium on certain experiments that could render the bacterium dangerous to human life. Recently developed techniques of genetic manipulation had enabled research scientists to introduce completely functional genes from plant and animal origins into the bacterial cell, thereby providing it with capabilities it would not normally possess. Such manipulations conceivably could also increase the resistance of *E. coli* to known antibiotics, making it highly infectious and potentially deadly. In February 1975, responding to the warning, an international conference of scientists convened at the Asilomar Conference Center in Pacific Grove, Calif. The group voted to lift the moratorium, but they established strict guidelines to be followed in any future research.

In drawing up safety precautions the conference evolved a guiding principle—match risk with containment. Experiments in which risk appears minimal would require only the standard laboratory practice used in working with pathogenic microorganisms. In this situation eating, smoking, and drinking would not be allowed in the laboratory. Protective coats would be worn, and liquid transfer would be handled with cotton-plugged pipettes or with mechanical pipettors. An example of such an experiment might be the combining of bacterial genes between nonpathogenic strains that could also exchange these genes by natural means.

By contrast, a high-risk experiment would require a very special environment. The laboratory would be maintained under negative air pressure to prevent contaminated dust from escaping. The air leaving the laboratory would be specially filtered or incinerated. Work with recombinant DNA molecules or organisms

Electron photomicrograph of a plasmid or separately existing DNA molecule, which was introduced to the bacterium Escherichia coli. It was then spliced with a different DNA molecule and replicated, thus becoming the first example of genetic manipulation. The experiment was conducted by A. C. Y. Chang, H. W. Boyer, and R. B. Helling.

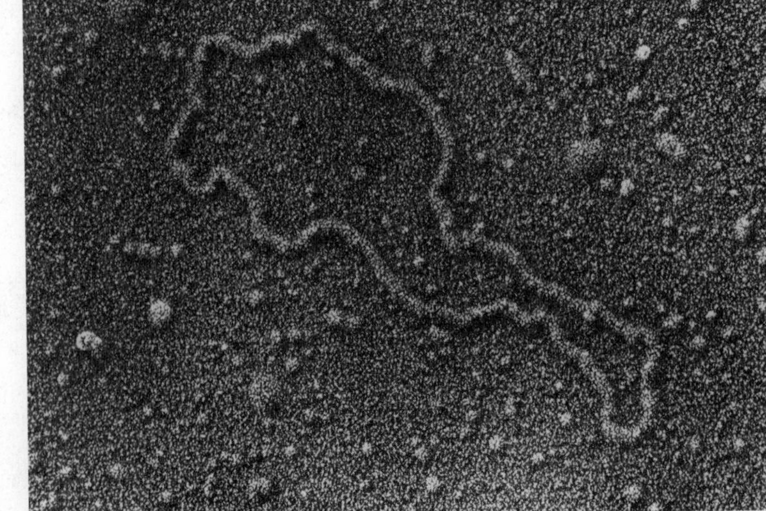

COURTESY, DR. STANLEY N. COHEN, FROM "PROCEEDINGS OF THE NATIONAL ACADEMY OF SCIENCES, U.S.A.," 1973

containing them would be carried out in a hood that restricts movement of particles to or from the work area. Only mechanical pipetting would be allowed, and all materials would be decontaminated or destroyed before leaving the laboratory. Researchers would wear protective clothing that would be discarded, and they would disinfect themselves in a shower before leaving the containment area. Experiments using recombinant DNA molecules that would confer upon a pathogenic microorganism increased resistance to therapeutically useful antibiotics would fall into the high-risk category. Experiments with intermediate levels of risk would require a matched level of containment. Work in which the hazards are not clearly defined would be performed under conditions of high-level containment. Only when proven safe could the work be transferred to low-level containment conditions. It was also suggested that some potentially dangerous experiments be deferred; *e.g.*, the cloning of DNA molecules from highly pathogenic organisms or of DNA containing toxin genes.

To provide further precautions for work with recombinant DNA molecules, the Asilomar conference recommended that safe vectors and hosts be developed. A vector is the vehicle—plasmid or phage—from which the recombinant DNA molecule can be formed; it has the property of self-reproducibility. To be made safe, particular genetic traits must be introduced to limit the vector to infection and reproduction in only one particular host. Furthermore, the host, which harbours the vector and is usually a microorganism, must be made safe by combining genetic traits that make its growth and survival impossible outside of a contrived laboratory environment.

In a study on DNA replication in *Bacillus subtilis*, A. T. Ganesan (Stanford University) found that nascent DNA, that is, DNA synthesized in small fragments as precursors to the longer strands, will not pair up in complementary fashion to form short double strands. This observation showed that only one strand of the double-stranded DNA molecule is being synthesized in fragments.

An interesting characteristic of *B. subtilis* is that all strains studied have been found to contain a defective phage, a virus that is normally infectious in bacteria. Upon induction the cells lysed or disintegrated and phage particles were produced. The particles were noninfectious and, hence, defective, because they contained host DNA rather than phage DNA and because they lacked the ability to eject the DNA. Anthony Garro of the Mount Sinai School of Medicine, New York City, had obtained mutants of this defective phage and found that all defective phage functions were located in one close segment on the host chromosome. This finding disproved an earlier hypothesis that genes for the defective phage would be located at more than one site on the host chromosome, a factor that could have contributed to the defective nature of the phage. He postulated that the ubiquitous occurrence of defective phage among *B. subtilis* strains could indicate that the defective phage was a protophage, a product of incomplete evolution. Another possibility was that the genome of a phage-infected bacterium lost some vital phage functions, thus rendering it defective. This alteration would have had to occur early in the evolution of *B. subtilis* to impart the defective phage to all subsequent strains.

(JAMES C. COPELAND)

See also Earth Sciences; Environment.
[313.B; 339.C.2.b.ii]

ENCYCLOPÆDIA BRITANNICA FILMS. *The Ears and Hearing* (2nd ed., 1969); *Muscle: Dynamics of Contraction* (1969); *The Origin of Life: Chemical Evolution* (1969); *Radioisotopes: Tools of Discovery* (1969); *Theories on the Origin of Life* (1969); *The Nerve Impulse* (1971); *Seed Dispersal* (3rd ed., 1971); *The World of Up Close* (1971); *How Do They Move?* (1971); *Some Friendly Insects* (1971); *Investigating Hibernation* (1972); *A Bird of Prey—The Red-Tailed Hawk* (1972); *The Cactus: Profile of a Plant* (1973); *Nematode* (1973); *The Mayfly: Ecology of an Aquatic Insect* (1973); *Insect Life Cycle* (*The Periodical Cicada*) (2nd ed., 1975).

Literature

The 1975 Nobel Prize for Literature was awarded to the 79-year-old Italian poet and prose writer Eugenio Montale—a compromise choice of the Swedish Academy, it was rumoured. Montale, the translator of T. S. Eliot, with whose temperament and technique he had some affinity, was known as a difficult, visionary, and intensely private poet—"an hermetic if ever there was one," according to the prize citation, which went on to describe his work as "an expression of deep pessimism." (*See* NOBEL PRIZES.)

That struck a note appropriate to a year in which the writer's room between unrelenting political and economic pressures seemed to shrink detectably. In the West inflation continued to push up the costs of paper and printing, increasing the price of books generally and reducing the amount of money available for the publication of new and experimental work. There was a growing sense, in the world of literature no less than in other spheres of production, that this crisis must involve changes that would be neither simple nor temporary. The point was well put in an article in the *Daily Telegraph* (London) by Frank Kermode: "The shapes and forms of books are not part of the nature of things. A book of poems hasn't always been a 'slim volume,' and the fact that volumes of modern poetry are usually slim is a fact bearing on the kind of poetry they contain as well as on the economics of their production."

In Britain one or two attempts were being made, though on a much smaller scale than in West Germany, to respond to the situation by forming small

KEYSTONE

Eugenio Montale, Italian poet, was the recipient of the Nobel Prize for Literature in 1975.

Liquors, Alcoholic: *see* Drug Abuse; Industrial Review

publishing cooperatives of writers, but where *samizdat,* or "do-it-yourself" publishing, flourished, it was as a response to political rather than economic difficulties. In the Soviet Union the state's efforts to control dissidence among writers and intellectuals might have grown a shade more circumspect out of deference to the much-invoked "spirit of Helsinki," but there were few signs of a thaw in Czechoslovakia, where several manuscripts were seized in police raids in May, among them that of a new novel, *The Hoof,* by Ludvik Vaculik (*see* CZECHOSLOVAKIA).

Not all the pressures felt by writers were of the overt thought-policing sort, however. Saul Bellow, in "An Interview with Myself" published in the September issue of *The New Review,* complained of a kind of "malign" neglect. "Our intelligentsia, completely politicized and analytical in temper," he wrote, "does not take much interest in literature. The members of this elite ('professors, commentators, editors') *had* literature in their student days and are now well beyond it . . . sometimes I sense they feel they have replaced writers." Bellow was describing primarily the condition of writers in the United States, but noted an even more drastic collapse of creative confidence in Europe. "At this moment in evolution, so miraculous, atrocious, glorious and hellish, the firmly established literary cultures of France and England, Italy and Germany can originate nothing. They look to us, to the 'disadvantaged' Americans, and to the Russians."

On August 12, when the time limit stipulated by the author of 20 years after his death had expired, sealed packets containing 32 of Thomas Mann's notebooks were opened in the Mann archives in Zürich, Switz. The most important part of this belated *Nachlass* seemed likely to be the four books dealing with 1918–21, critical years for the author and for Germany.

The centenary of Mann's birth was one of the year's more resonant anniversaries: Saul Bellow might have called in aid his affirmation of the act of artistic creation as the essential testimony of our full humanity. Carl Jung's centenary, too, came as a timely reminder of teaching which might be unfashionable among professional psychologists but seemed full of insights of value to artists in an age that was beginning to mourn the death of God once more. Doris Lessing in her latest novel, *The Memoirs of a Survivor,* was clearly one of those writers who had found inspiration in Jung's insistence that men must understand their fantasies and create their own myths to live by, and in his insights into the therapeutic effects of creativity, whereby recurring and fundamentally insoluble human contradictions might be reconciled at the symbolic level of art.

ENGLISH

United Kingdom. The strains of the crisis which seemed to have become the usual, if hardly settled, condition of English life showed both in the books that appeared in 1975 and in the creaking arrangements by which they were published.

It seemed uncomfortably symbolic that the fictional event of such a year should have been an ending—the publication of *Hearing Secret Harmonies,* the final volume of Anthony Powell's *A Dance to the Music of Time,* bringing up to date at last his emblematic history of the English ruling class in its 20th-century decline. Other accomplished novelists—Doris Lessing, Maureen Duffy, Constantine FitzGibbon—produced visions of an England where civilization was on or over the brink of collapse. And a crisis in historiography was confronted in the remarkable concluding chapter of *Whigs and Hunters,* a study of repressive legislation in Walpole's England by the distinguished social historian E. P. Thompson. ("As the last imperial illusions of the twentieth century fade, so preoccupation with the history and culture of a small island off the coast of Europe becomes open to a charge of narcissism. . . . . Alternative perspectives must diminish the complacency of national historical preoccupation.") And yet it was a "good year": these uneasy cultural symptoms were to be found, after all, in novels and historical work of high quality. If the "Titanic" was going down—a wan, recurring joke that grew paler still as the year went on—at least there would be something to read in the lifeboats.

Fiction. "*The Music of Time,* with its loving aggregation and recapitulation of detail, hoarded like bedtime tales or sagas in families": John Bayley's review, in the *Times Literary Supplement* (*TLS*), of Anthony Powell's 12th and final installment, caught the mood of the occasion well. The social focus of the whole work, as Bayley acknowledged, might remind some readers of Orwell's characterization of England—a family with the wrong members in control—but *Hearing Secret Harmonies* was received like news of a death in the family, with emotional gratitude for what had been vouchsafed, and a numb awareness that there really wasn't going to be any more. With its perspectives completed, most reviewers were content to be gratefully amazed that so grand a structure could have been achieved in such hard times.

The most impressive single work in fiction was probably *Guerrillas,* by V. S. Naipaul, a novelist with a reputation as an almost too fluently accomplished prizewinner who won more thoughtful praise with this bleak and painful vision of moral and political disintegration set in a Caribbean island that bore some resemblance to his native Trinidad. Its central figure resembled very closely indeed the former black power leader Michael X: a "charismatic" militant taken up flatteringly by trendy liberals in England, then dropped and sent back home powerless and full of curdled illusions. There seemed something disturbingly and precisely representative about the characters' threatened life and moral paralysis, an all-too-recognizable climate of despair redeemed by its author's fine attentiveness to his people, the close subtleties of their interaction, and landscapes as tangible and important to the book's moral atmosphere as Joseph Conrad's.

Doris Lessing called *The Memoirs of a Survivor* "an attempt at autobiography," which turned out to mean partly a narrative of dreams and spiritual development, partly fictional projection of an elderly but recognizable version of herself into the dire future of a decaying civilization toward which her experience of life seemed inexorably to point. It was definitely a Jungian experiment and evidently influenced by her recent involvement with Sufi teaching. Some of her projections articulated with unnerving clarity fantasies and intuitions that one would guess were widely shared. It was a disturbing book in more ways than one, however. Many problems of tone and structure were not resolved, and worried admirers felt that it was difficult to see where so autobiographical a writer could go from there. Maureen Duffy's *Capital* was less radically experimental, though ambitious and anxious enough in its commuting between the past, present, and future of a beloved and threatened Lon-

FAY GODWIN—HEINEMANN

Anthony Powell's 12th and final installment of "The Music of Time" was well received during the year.

don. Most of the traffic took place in the wounded head of an elderly autodidact trying to prove, as a talisman for the future, that the city had actually survived through the Dark Ages after the Roman withdrawal. *The Golden Age* by Constantine FitzGibbon, in more traditional future-fic territory beyond the holocaust, attempted a Revelation, juggled dangerously with the myths of Orpheus and Faust, and struck some sparks of the authentic visionary gleam through the sheer energy of his wild and willful imagining. To these might be added Kingsley Amis' son Martin's *Dead Babies,* whose holocaust was the Old Permissiveness that left in its druggy wake a generation very lost indeed in what seemed to be the naughty 1990s. Very fin de siècle, anyway, Amis' relishy disgust at the elegantly vicious goings on these young are heir to.

Ruth Prawer Jhabvala's Booker Prize-winning *Heat and Dust* interwove the Indian experience of two Englishwomen separated by 50 years. Other novels about India were *A Division of the Spoils,* in which Paul Scott concluded his quartet of novels on British India, bringing the Raj to a sticky end on the eve of the transfer of power; and *Flashman in the Great Game,* an episode in the annals of "our poltroon Ulysses," as *The Guardian*'s reviewer called George MacDonald Fraser's resurrected antihero, indicating the affectionate respect that these hilarious Victorian entertainments rightly commanded. In *Sweet William,* Beryl Bainbridge had another of her ingenious ingenues getting her men wrong and somehow surviving the heartaches. Iris Murdoch's *A Word Child* was equally characteristic, plotted like opera buffa, as readable as a novelette and otherwise about as easy to describe as an extended proposition in symbolic logic. *Docherty* by William McIlvanney was a tender, careful recovery of the life of a Scottish mining town in the first two decades of the century, and there were two decent first novels—Dominic Cooper's *The Dead of Winter* (a dark-toned story of a Hebridean feud) and, at the other end of the British sensibility spectrum, M. T. Wadey's nervous trio of human needs and insecurities, *Sleight of Heart.*

Short stories seemed to be published now chiefly as reluctant occasional rewards for successful novelists who would persist in this sweet and uneconomic form. Two good collections that did appear were Paul Theroux's far-flung *Sinning with Annie* and William Trevor's *Angels at the Ritz,* which confirmed him as one of the most finely skilled and dedicated of surviving practitioners. A collectible item was *Out of the War,* remarkably assured stories written 30 years ago by Francis Wyndham who had since been a marvelous midwife and sponsor to new and unjustly neglected writing in London.

History, Biography, Letters. It was a vintage year for historical writing: nearly all the more interesting and readable scholars seemed to have a book on the lists. E. P. Thompson's *Whigs and Hunters* answered the questions he had raised about parochialism and relevance, first by the quality of his research and historical insight into the meaning of the Black Act, that savage leap forward in what E. J. Hobsbawm called the "progressive conquest of England by the gallows," but also by his tough and scrupulous defense, against the new schematists of the intellectual left, of the "autonomy" of the rule of law. The "hard Whigs" may have "played the game of power according to rules which suited them, but they could not break those rules or the whole game would be thrown away." Hence, "the notion of the regulation and reconciliation of conflicts through the rule of law" as it developed in 18th-century England, whatever the motives of its promulgators, might be seen as "a cultural achievement of universal significance."

Thompson was one of those on whose work one might build a case that the best prose in England was now being written by historians; Richard Cobb was another. His *Paris and Its Provinces 1792–1802,* evoking from the archives a vivid account of the tensions between the capital and its hinterland, was the fourth in a sequence of works which, as Gwyn Williams wrote, "is creating a veritable popular theatre of revolutionary France." Christopher Hill, Cobb's Balliol College master, widened and deepened the argument about whether the English Revolution was the first social revolution in the essays collected in *Change and Continuity in Seventeenth-Century England;* Norman Cohn's *Europe's Inner Demons* was a penetrating study of the origins of the witch hunts that tortured Europe in the two preceding centuries; and in *Astraea,* Florence Yates produced a richly suggestive set of essays on the handling of the myth of empire in the 16th-century culture.

The Use and Abuse of History was a wide-ranging collection of studies grounded in problems of the classical world by another forceful and lucid writer, M. I. Finley—that "historian's historian who yet remains doggedly accessible," as John Rosselli remarked. But for sheer adventurousness and intellectual reach the most remarkable work of the year was to be found in two volumes by a young historian writing outside the protecting walls of academe. Perry Anderson's *Passages from Antiquity to Feudalism* and *Lineages of the Absolutist State* were really one work examining with formidable erudition the radical question of why East and West, especially Eastern and Western Europe, developed so differently. Professor Finley himself, no light dispenser of praise, found it brilliantly enlightening.

With one exception, it was not a particularly good year for historical biography. Robert Skidelsky's *Oswald Mosley* contained valuable information about

William Trevor, one of the most skillful practitioners of the art of the short story, contributed "Angels at the Ritz" in 1975.

FAY GODWIN—BODLEY HEAD

his subject's earlier career, but came uncomfortably close to apologia in its treatment of the fascist years; *Life with Lloyd George,* the diaries of his secretary, A. J. Sylvester, edited by Colin Cross, was a moderately interesting account of the last 15 years, and *My Darling Pussy* a moderately embarrassing book made by A. J. P. Taylor out of Lloyd George's letters to his mistress. The exception was Karl Miller's *Cockburn's Millennium,* a study of the Edinburgh lawyer and Whig reformer that was both a valuable contribution to the understanding of Scottish cultural history and a moving personal meditation on the peculiarly difficult nature of the father-son relationship in Scotland.

Two large literary projects got under way: there was the first of Leon Edel's four volumes of the *Letters of Henry James,* full of travels and ponderings of "the complex fate," and—a good deal less exhilarating—*The Flight of the Mind,* the first of six volumes of Virginia Woolf's letters, these mostly domestic, whimsical, only negatively revealing. Christopher Sykes's thick but flatly written biography of *Evelyn Waugh* was nevertheless full of good stories about his extraordinary, self-caricaturing subject; *Young Thomas Hardy* by Robert Gittings satisfactorily cleared up some myths and mysteries (there was no son by his cousin Tryphena); and Susan Chitty, in *The Beast and The Monk,* made hay on the occasion of the Charles Kingsley centenary with Kingsley's hectic sexuality and abundant contradictoriness.

There was much poets' prose: autobiographical books by Edward Lucie-Smith (*The Burnt Child*—a little premature, it was thought), Norman Nicholson (*Wednesday Early Closing*), Laurie Lee (mostly travel pieces called *I Can't Stay Long*), and best of all Kathleen Raine, whose *The Land Unknown* P. J. Kavanagh thought a brave and "ruthless narrative" and "an account, on as important a level as Yeats's *Autobiographies,* of what it is to be a poet, which is to say under orders not always easy to understand and fatal to disobey." The travel book of the year was *The Great Railway Bazaar,* Paul Theroux's narrative of a vast train journey, out from Calais to Japan and back from Vladivostok to the Hook, which earned a chorus of enviously admiring reviews.

Finally, a scholarly ending and a beginning. Geoffrey Bullough completed his invaluable *Narrative and Dramatic Sources of Shakespeare* with an eighth volume devoted to *Cymbeline, The Winter's Tale,* and *The Tempest;* and there appeared the first four of 50 volumes of a mighty English translation of Karl Marx, "the product of the most serious and painstaking scholarship," David McLellan assured us in the *TLS*—bigger than the German *Werke,* more than half of it never in English before, and the bargain of the year at £3 each for volumes of around 800 pages each.

(W. L. WEBB)

Seamus Heaney, lyrical poet of Irish history, treated the tragic conflict in Northern Ireland in "North."

FABER & FABER

Poetry. Despite the restrictive influence of the grave economic situation and government efforts to combat inflation, a large number of books, booklets, and collected editions were published by poets both old and young, established and unestablished, not to mention collections by children still at school.

Once again it was the small "shoestring" presses that contributed most toward the publication of works by new poets, although Faber & Faber continued their *Poetry Introduction* anthologies with a third volume and Chatto & Windus brought out a new series entitled *Treble Poets.* The list of volumes by established poets was also longer than might have been expected in the prevailing economic conditions. An interesting new development was the publication of the first collection of poems to result from the Arvon Foundation's creative writing courses held at Totleigh Barton Manor in Devon. Entitled *Lamb and Thundercloud,* the collection was edited by Peter Redgrove.

Among the best of the numerous first collections was Roger Garfitt's *West of Elm,* in which the author gave clear evidence of his ability to call upon a wide variety of form and subject. The collection was remarkable for its quality of verbal surprise and aptness of phraseology (the heron who "shakes out his pac-a-mac of wings," the hitchhiker's "shy elocution of the thumb"). Other features of Garfitt's work were his skillful use of extended metaphor and imaginative identification with his material.

From the established poets came a large number of new volumes, including collections by Edwin Brock, Robert Graves, John Fuller, Christopher Middleton, Peter Porter, Alan Ross, Vernon Scannell, Alan Sillitoe, John Wain, and others. In *End of Drought* Ruth Pitter exhibited her usual concern for craftsmanship and her affirmative view of things, but George MacBeth's *In the Hours Waiting for the Blood to Come* seemed calculated to disturb rather than to delight its readers. In the 63 poems (one for each year of the author's life) of *From the Joke Shop,* Roy Fuller addressed his shrewd intelligence and keen sense of irony to a series of entertaining reflections on the inconveniences and embarrassments of growing old and expressed feelings of inadequacy in coping with the crudity and violence of the present era. Elizabeth Jennings, on the other hand, seemed to have taken on a new lease of life with *Growing-Points,* which showed new depth, fresh purpose, and greater warmth than her earlier books.

Perhaps the most striking development of all was to be observed in the work of Ulster poet Seamus Heaney. Always a lyrical poet, drawing on Irish history and his own childhood experiences for his inspiration, Heaney had tended previously to avoid any direct confrontation with the current conflict in Northern Ireland. With the publication of *North,* however, readers encountered a far more vigorous and outspoken Heaney, prepared to tackle head-on some of the tragic consequences of a situation in which, as an Ulster Catholic, he could not avoid being personally involved. Yet in this notable volume, which placed Heaney as perhaps the most significant Irish poet since Yeats, the author never allowed his personal sympathies or the political implications of the situation to betray him into partisan attitudes or oversimplification of the issues involved.

An equally surprising number of collected editions were also published in the course of the year, among them the *Collected Poems* of Charles Causley, Stevie Smith, James Reeves, Arthur J. Ball, and Edgell Rickword, as well as the *Selected Poems* of Thomas Blackburn and Henry Shore. The collections from Smith and Causley were perhaps among the most important volumes to be published during the year. Other collections worthy of attention were *Born Early* by Michael Ivens, *A Song of Good Life* by Alan Brownjohn, *Laboratories of the Spirit* by R. S. Thomas, *The Penguin Book of English Pastoral Verse* edited by John Barrell and John Bull, *Poems of Black Africa* edited by the Nigerian Wole Soyinka, and *A Choice of Comic and Curious Verse* edited by J. M. Cohen.

(HOWARD SERGEANT)

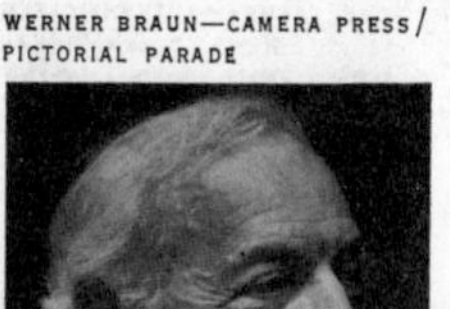

WERNER BRAUN—CAMERA PRESS/ PICTORIAL PARADE

Saul Bellow, American novelist, was widely acclaimed for "Humboldt's Gift," which appeared in August.

United States. *Fiction.* The American novel showed increasing tolerance for fantasy and incongruity in 1975. If the fallout from the 1960s of eroticism, comic surrealism, and the absurdist manner affected contemporary fiction by their antic and anarchic spirit, so did the post-Watergate depressions of the day. A post-existential vision—sometimes playful, sometimes violent, always nostalgic—vaulting over the various genres and subcultures, at once parodic and desperate, erudite and trivial, challenged the assumptions of art, of history, of being. The novel, in short, was still engaged in an epistemological quest of its own origins, though at times it seemed to anticipate a sudden lexical death. But out of its own exhaustion fiction discovered some striking new insights from the country's past.

The genre continued to respond to a more jagged, roguish, or grotesque sense of reality, veering toward more picaresque modes. Typically, its hero, or heroine, was still a rebel-victim, a lone emissary of the self in the repressive land of culture, an ironic self-confessed redeemer of reality. But the lines that formerly separated comedy from tragedy, satire from sentimentality, rigid from improvisational forms, the future from the past, blurred. To this antiformalist or antiacademic tendency, almost every U.S. writer of fiction gave his spontaneous energy. What the novel's imagination would ultimately reveal of itself in the 1970s was still uncertain. But the quest for the future undertaken amid the detritus of the past remained the nation's largest novel, daily revised.

The symbolic state and presence of U.S. fiction was gauged once again by one of its major authors, Saul Bellow. Bellow has written in the main, intelligent tradition of the novel: in his work the European realism of Balzac and Dickens was modified by the greater liberty of native fable and romance. His concerns were freedom and love: freedom as the interplay between what is given and what is made in the life of man, and love as the interplay between man's identity and his completion in others. Insistently he asked what it meant to be human in the contemporary world; insistently he sought "the axial lines of existence." His urban Jewish characters recalled their heritage at the same time that they embodied the complexities of the Jew in America; their comic, painful quests adduced dignity to all men.

In 1975 at the age of 60 Bellow produced *Humboldt's Gift,* a novel of energized chaos and retrenchment that sprawls in picaresque fashion, but without the humour of *Herzog* or the humanity of *Mr. Sammler's Planet,* a novel whose art is querulous and whose imagination awaits the fulfillment of death. The story of Humboldt, he of the gift, poet, trickster, genius with a gift of gab, is told by his protégé and heir, Charlie Citrine, who has won a Pulitzer Prize and knows the "glory and gold" that attend success. Citrine is left the "gift"—an outline for a movie script that will net a good deal of that gold. Some of Bellow's central concerns throughout: the sense of destiny that is never far from the abyss; that for "self-realization it's necessary to embrace the deformity and absurdity of the inmost being"; that death becomes an almost daily pressure. Still if one is left with a "kind of light-in-the-being" that can overcome the terminal terror, it will represent underachiever Humboldt's (*scio* Bellow's) great achievement.

"Divided between power and the dream" is the way F. Scott Fitzgerald saw it in his luminous projection of lost innocence, *The Great Gatsby.* In *Ragtime,* E. L. Doctorow plays a dazzling variation on that theme in a slightly earlier era: the final days of America's privileged childhood. *Ragtime* is a great billiard game of events, social epiphanies, and personages at the turn of the century, where the real protagonist is the U.S. itself captured in the last gasps of complacency and social Darwinism—waging territorial wars abroad for God, Mammon, and country, breaking strikes and throwing charity balls at home while World War I hovers in the wings. Doctorow's *The Book of Daniel* (1971) mythified the Rosenbergs and their children, but *Ragtime* galvanizes the headlines and heroes of an entire formative era in an antinostalgic political work of even greater magnitude—all watched over by the spirit of Scott Joplin.

At the heart of the story is a stultifying Victorian model family of a respectable manufacturer of flags, fireworks, and patriotic odds and ends whose somewhat Moses-like recovery of an abandoned illegitimate black infant leads to an exemplary tale of racism, insurrection, and injustice. This is fleshed out by a succession of wildly imaginative run-ins with (and among) Henry Ford, Houdini, J. P. Morgan, Zapata, and of course—the Archduke Ferdinand. At that time "There were no Negroes. . . . There were no immigrants"—and that's the bluntly hammered-out theme that pulls it all together: the vulgarity of the wealthy and their oppression of the lower classes. Nevertheless, *Ragtime* is a high achievement in comedy and irony that hinges on distancing; and if not history's revenge (the last laugh belongs to a deranged parasitic scion), then the revenge of art.

The jolt of discovering a past can be especially distressing in the U.S., where history itself tends to be regarded not so much as bunk but as a variety of quaint, slightly boring, comic fiction. Confronting the general U.S. conviction that history is unreal, Larry Woiwode in *Beyond the Bedroom Wall* set out to explore his Midwestern past, producing as first-rate fiction the collective memory of one family, small towners from North Dakota and Illinois named the Neumillers. Woiwode has seized in rapt fascination the flotsam and minutiae of childhood memory, the scrap heap of family stories, jokes, anecdotes, to make his fictional family album something like a saga. There is much here about the life and death of the Midwestern generations, much about the changing landscape, much about the love between parents and children. Consistently tinged with the sound of autobiography, this is a novel in search of roots, self-consciously seasoned throughout with the salt of the earth, an excellent novel whose silhouettes and rags not only make fiction out of history but also reveal the fictions out of which history is made.

Continuing one of the major trends taken by fiction in the 1960s, many authors were drawn to the novel of fantasy. Satire, burlesque, and nightmare were elements of this form that claimed for itself the widest imaginative freedom. Donald Barthelme went still further in his experiments with nonlinear narratives and absurdist techniques in *The Dead Father,* a collage including fragments, captions, fictions of detritus, trivia—to say nothing of "Blague" and "Dreck," Barthelme's special touchstones. The dead father is a giant 3,200-cubit construct lugged across the countryside, issuing ukases in his golden robes, strung up on cables, with one mechanical leg and a seven-metre-high foot—a "great endifarce teeterteeterteetertotter-ing." *The Underground Woman* by Kay Boyle was a

ALAN CARUBA—AUTHENTICATED NEWS INTERNATIONAL

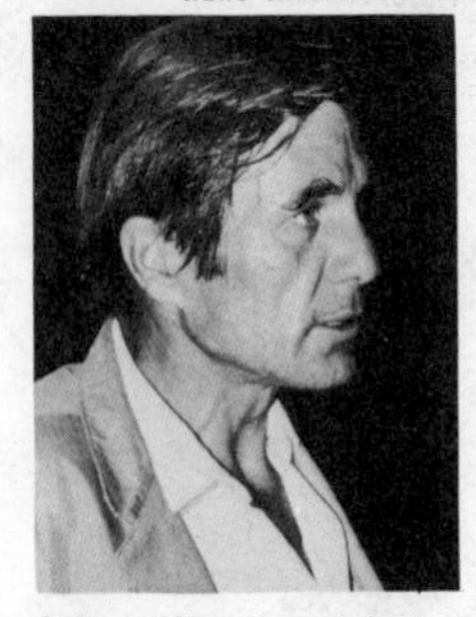

Galway Kinnell, recipient of the 1975 American Academy of Arts and Letters Award of Merit for poetry.

metamythic fugue of modern times set in a prison in California where a number of women war protesters are penned up together, and where Athena—mother of three, one-note Greek chorus—defends the validity of myth as the timeless and universal history of all men and all morals.

Another entrepreneur of the next-to-impossible was Richard Condon in *Money Is Love*. The story involves a league of Judeo-Christian seraphs about to hold a convention in Liederkranz Hall, the entire pantheon of Greek gods (particularly Joe V. Zeuss), a clairvoyant bookmaker, and a whole new economy based on the New York Plate Exchange with its vast consignments of Wedgwood and Spode. *The Last Words of Dutch Schultz* was William S. Burroughs' most accessible hallucination, a gruesome exposition of the dying words of Prohibition mobster Dutch Schultz, a demented aria filled with unconscious gutter poetry laid out as a stripped-down movie script.

If *Steps* (1968) was an enigma, Jerzy Kosinski's *Cockpit*, as Jonathan Baumbach said in the *New York Times Book Review*, was "a return to [its] seemingly random, picaresque mode, and in many ways a more audacious and elaborate version of it." It was a vicious peepshow-parable about a world we reluctantly recognize through the eyes of a distant god-like narrator named Tarden. With his assumed names and disguises his missions take him everywhere, but they are not as explicit as his self-appointed tasks: injecting toxic substances in supermarket food containers, stealing rare *objets*, or photographing his blatant sexual encounters until he is overcome by the pointlessness of it all.

In *Moise and the World of Reason*, Tennessee Williams offered an extended if prolapsed memoir in neofictional form of some of his favourite recurring themes: the assorted memories of a Southern writer—failed at 30, a homosexual who had been a "little library queen" back in Alabama and at 15 had his one real love with a light-skinned Negro (the link with Moise, a painter who has left the world of reason).

Still standing apart from the flock after nearly two decades of distinguished service was John Updike in *A Month of Sundays*. The striving hero is the Rev. Thomas Marshfield, a lacerated Calvinist as divided as sin and salvation particularly when it comes to adultery. When his trysts with the church organist and other assorted supplicants are exposed, Marshfield is shipped off for a month's rest to a desert spa for troubled clergymen. Mornings are spent at an obligatory typewriter, where orgies of therapeutic confession are the order of the day. Concerned in some dry way with death and dread, the counterfeits of love, the slow atrophies of spirit, Updike seems to have reported everything he knows about the sexually tormented middle class in a vision adroitly cerebral in a culture of drugged feelings.

In the burgeoning canon of women's writing, Judith Rossner's *Looking for Mr. Goodbar* scored a popular success. Rossner's strongest book to date is based on one of those nocturnal New York horror stories about the schoolteacher who seemed to live an irreproachable life except that she sought out her sexual partners in a singles bar. The last of them bashed in her skull on New Year's Day 1973. A tour de force of writing and timing create this complex and chilling portrait of a woman's descent into hell: overlooked and undiscovered until a professor at CCNY taught her a little about sex, less about love, and just enough to leave her looking for Mister Goodbar on nights when she was restless—also enough to leave her still fuller of guilt and contrition after encounters with abusive men, much too religious, too devoted, too nice, and too late.

A number of short-story collections were notable in their substance and resonance: Isaac Bashevis Singer's *Passions*, his seventh collection, centred on the lives of Yiddish-speaking Polish Jews in Europe and the Americas before and after the Holocaust—and here as with so much of Singer, "the whims and passions" that destroy, illuminate, and possess a life often slip into the supernatural dimension. Mark Helprin's *A Dove of the East and Other Stories* concerned essences which lead from the heart. In the title story an "ill-fitting refugee" serves as a patrol in Israel where he is spooked into shooting a dove—a dove that dies alone and unattended, perhaps like the wife he has lost. Johanna Kaplan's *Other People's Lives* are caught in transit from the old world (Poland) to the new (Bronx), but they have an animation all their own since Kaplan hustles experience with great mobility. One miniaturist masterpiece: "Loss of Memory Is Only Temporary"—in which a young psychiatrist resists the attachments of her past while dismissing the effects of electroshock therapy on memory. Finally, ubiquitous Joyce Carol Oates produced two more collections: *The Seduction & Other Stories*, containing some of her best revelations of complexity in lives ordinarily thought to be without depth or value; and *The Poisoned Kiss*, co-authored by a being named Fernandes, who does not exist, and "discovering" stories that "come out of nowhere" and seem best categorized by the author's own phrase, "cerebral/Gothic."

History, Biography, and Belles Lettres. The national scandals and constitutional crises following the disclosures of Watergate, having brought the presidency to a nadir of confidence, also pushed the theme of the eclipse of liberty to centre stage. The future of the U.S. became open to virtually any utopian or dystopian scenario; henceforth, for better or worse, the U.S. would never appear the same to others or to itself. But the very burden of self-awareness in a time of national anxiety drove Americans to seek more compelling formulations of their situation than mere politics could provide. These formulations, which drew on sociology and law, psychology and science, amounted to a comprehensive view of man's relation to himself and society.

Four important prescriptions for normalcy and for crisis-avoidance appeared, each seeking to answer the question: how to preserve liberty in a nation where the vast majority of people have no appreciation of it, except when it is taken away. In *Thinking About Crime*, James Q. Wilson rejects the idea—promulgated since the Enlightenment—that malefactors are affected by their social climate and not simply born bad: "Wicked people exist. Nothing avails but to set them apart from innocent people." Wilson is led of necessity to repression as the sole remedy. An untidy accommodation of a similar kind was offered by the late Alexander Bickel's *The Morality of Consent*, which argues that the press and government exist in an adversary relationship whose rules are set down in the First Amendment. In a sound society, however, the "reliance is upon self-discipline and self-restraint, and on public opinion, not on law." "Law," for Bickel, "can never make us as secure as we are when we do not need it."

Edgar Friedenberg's disquieting *The Disposal of*

Liberty and Other Industrial Wastes identifies spite or *ressentiment* as the prime moving force in U.S. society. Iconoclastic and unabashedly elitist, Friedenberg argues that liberty and equality are antagonistic impulses and, moreover, that the lower middle classes are the sworn enemies of liberty that is defended, if it is defended at all, by a privileged minority. Reversing conventional wisdom, Friedenberg concludes that "democracy is not an alternative to fascism, but a stage in its development." In *Twilight of Authority,* Robert Nisbet asserted that the U.S. had allowed the raw power of politics to eclipse the traditional moderating authority of the family, the church, and the community. The result: an immense concentration of might, a "democratic royalism" with profoundly dangerous implications for the future health of American society.

Complementing these sociological and juridical views, psychoanalysis also widened its claims on the American intellect and imagination. Erik H. Erikson's *Life History and the Historical Moment* represented the consolidation of the psychohistorical approach Erikson first proposed in his studies of Luther and Gandhi; but here, pushing forward beyond individuals, even beyond the charismatic influence of the chosen on the masses, Erikson considers mass psychology and the widening concentric circles of history. Also noteworthy was *The Mind's Fate: Ways of Seeing Psychiatry and Psychoanalysis* by Robert Coles, very largely an indictment of America's inadequate social consciousness.

In *Synergetics: Explanations in the Geometry of Thinking,* visionary-scientist Buckminster Fuller went even further in applying the principles of his "comprehensive anticipatory design science" to the human situation. Its central fact: synergetics (viewing the part in relation to the whole) comprehends the universe as an infinitely various repetition of simple forms related to the tetrahedron (and not the cube). Now 80, Fuller continued to assert the scientist's faith in man's capacity to conquer scarcity and conflict through technology, and to reverse physical entropy through metaphysical organization of thought.

The existential drive to meaning was perhaps most secular in character in important but disparate works on education: Fred and Grace Hechinger's *Growing Up in America* surveyed the 200-year period of U.S. educational history, viewed as a cyclical struggle between elitists and egalitarians; and Jonathan Kozol's eloquent *The Night Is Dark and I Am Far from Home,* an anguished document of grief, pain, and hunger in the slums, dealing finally with the systematic desensitizing of the children of the privileged so they will not question the existing balance of oppression.

Against Our Will: Men, Women and Rape by Susan Brownmiller was the feminist book of the year par excellence by one of the movement's leading theoreticians. In this declaration of war on the war of the sexes Brownmiller demonstrates: how rape has its genesis in power (and the need to preserve the appearance of power) rather than eroticism; that women do not "precipitate" rape by provocative behaviour; that resistance does not increase the chance of physical harm; that rapists are usually hardened criminals. The most impressive entry in the mode of "new journalism" was *A Time to Die* by Tom Wicker, detailing the "one essential contradiction" of the Attica prison riot story—that in the end, it was the respectable, law-and-order prison authorities who behaved in a dehumanized, bestial manner.

PATT MEARA—FARRAR, STRAUS & GIROUX, INC.

Isaac Bashevis Singer continued to enthrall his many fans with "Passions," which appeared in October.

A brief word must also be accorded the continuing post-mortem: the unmaking of a president. Four professional president watchers and one street-wise verbal brawler have dared to look back in anger and regret—*U.S. v. Richard M. Nixon* by Frank Mankiewicz, *The Last Nixon Watch* by John Osborne, *Watchmen in the Night* by Theodore Sorensen, *Breach of Faith* by Theodore H. White, and *How the Good Guys Finally Won* by Jimmy Breslin—and most notably, these books (albeit rushed, flawed, repetitive, sometimes contradictory) provide small, sharp, almost novelistic, insights into the personal struggles of individuals caught up in the scandal.

Finally, there was more than a little comfort, to say nothing of fortuity, in the appearance of three candidly patriotic histories of America's genesis: *1776: Year of Illusions* by Thomas Fleming was a solid and trenchantly written bicentennial volume that rejoiced in its own virtuosity at upsetting clichés, while it convincingly upheld the biggest one of all—Washington as brave, solitary commander. Bernhard Knollenberg's *The Growth of the American Revolution, 1766–1775* offered contagious scholarly excitement, unabashed pro-Revolutionary sentiments, and a passionate insistence upon the world-historical importance of the conflict. *The Spirit of '76: The Growth of American Patriotism Before Independence, 1607–1776* by Carl Bridenbaugh charted the country's sense of national identity beginning with the first settlement at Jamestown.

Several major biographies of U.S. literati appeared in 1975. Reed Whittemore's *William Carlos Williams* was an accomplished study of the late poetic bloomer who is now justly acclaimed as the central figure of the 20th-century American pantheon. It is Whittemore's achievement as a biographer to have captured, as if in a cubist painting, the double exposure where the modest, self-effacing physician merges with a lonely, gifted writer.

In *Thurber* by Burton Bernstein the imaginative genius is observed progressing from the bookish, daydreamy, nervous child (who lost that eye early on)

NANCY CRAMPTON—AUTHENTICATED NEWS INTERNATIONAL

John Gardner was recipient of $3,000 in awards for literary merit from the American Academy of Arts and Letters and the National Institute of Arts and Letters in 1975.

CHRISTOPHER LITTLE—CAMERA 5

Judith Rossner, author of "Looking for Mr. Goodbar," a 1975 best-seller about a woman seeking fulfillment.

to the tentative late-starter as both man and writer. Most memorable is the report of his first marriage to the demanding Althea, the prototype of all emasculating Thurber women ("it was like sleeping with the Statue of Liberty"), who would only promote his innate sense of menace and misery as later epitomized by all those droopy dogs and woebegotten little men.

A long, full-fashioned and eminently just biography was Virginia Spencer Carr's *The Lonely Hunter: A Biography of Carson McCullers,* accomplished primarily through those who knew her. Always unhappy, McCullers is remembered best as Frankie Addams, "a member of nothing in the world." In addition, *Edith Wharton* by R. W. B. Lewis was a scrupulous and commodious life, extending Wharton's portrait to the margins of her life, however neurasthenic and insulated she remained behind the conventions of social breeding, wealth, and her own immaculate taste.

In the domain of the perilous self was Frederick Exley's soggy *Pages from a Cold Island,* an improvident part II of an autobiographical trilogy from and about the bottle and "life's hard fact of famelessness"; Judy Chicago's *Through the Flower: My Struggle as a Woman Artist*—a work that wrests from the contradictions of existence a finer fate for woman in a man's profession; and the frankly querulous *Tennessee Williams: Memoirs.*

The myth of the self as stage-personality scored on the popular front as well. Speedily assembled biographies included: Charles Higham's *Kate: The Life of Katharine Hepburn* and a double entry for Judy Garland—Christopher Finch's *Rainbow: The Stormy Life of Judy Garland* and *Judy* by Gerold Frank.

Especially noteworthy belletristic studies included: *The Poetry Wreck,* a collection of vitriolic essays by prizewinning poet Karl Shapiro, hurling myth, symbolism, the poetry of ideas, classicism, and high culture out the window; Edmund Wilson's posthumously gathered, long-awaited notebooks, entitled *The Twenties,* wherein we meet for the first time the distinctly personal Wilson, including revelatory glimpses into his boudoir; and *Vision and Resonance: Two Senses of Poetic Form* by formalist poet-critic John Hollander, offering essays sensitive to the calibrations of style, curling comfortably around the roots of classical English prosody.

Poetry. The old dichotomies in attitude to subject as well as to form reemerged with increasing clarity in 1975's poetry output. On the one hand, there were the various movements based on the conception of *le poésie pur*—aleatoric poetry, the New York School, and concretism—and on the other, the poetry based on commitment to social action. Chief among practitioners of the former was John Ashbery; in his seventh collection, *Self-Portrait in a Convex Mirror,* the words are not "composed" so much as they quirkily "occur." His poems' absurd arbitrariness, their tangle of indecisions and open questions, their rush of fragmentary imagery and endless linguistic ambiguities are so much more fun than the clipped formal gardens of poets like Pound and Stevens. If nothing is finally knowable, then this whirlwind of "ideas about thoughts" becomes as viable an approach as any to the abstract.

The total undermining of received structure, where texture is all, was also apparent in A. R. Ammons' *Diversifications: Poems,* where as often as not the purity and the swill come in separate stages, beginning in a mood that is cool, clean, Japanese, lovely, and working up to a verbal debauch of silly word games and unpoliced typewriter reeling. The running theme is a meditation on form, which, for Ammons, summarizes everything. Another minimalist offering was Charles Wright's volume *Bloodlines,* where one has to do some conjuring over discontinuous images and assonant Joycean compounds to focus on his locale. It turns out to be the fertile back country of the South; but instead of rustic poems, one gets sound riddles ("snow-rotted, ooze-rooted, cold blossom") occasionally juxtaposed to a much freer colloquialism. Also eluding definition was the posthumous third volume of *The Maximus Poems* by projectivist-guru Charles Olson. Olson, who died in 1970, had great underground *réclame* during the 1950s for his "open" structure, or "high-energy construct," a technique that looked both back to Pound and ahead to the beat generation.

The problem of making good poetry from arguments with others remained what it has always been. Unsurpassed in her effort to forge the consciousness of her gender was Erica Jong (*see* BIOGRAPHY) in *Loveroot,* a sensational collection of poems with that cover-girl glow, returning to her still-unfinished task of taking female sexuality out of the closet: "The flesh is flesh./The word is on its own." Joyce Carol Oates, the most prolific writer to win the National Book Award, struck out once again in *The Fabulous Beasts.* Written in Oates' usual monotone of numbed anger, the poems blur together in what finally and ironically becomes a celebration of death—death of the body, of the spirit, of a relative; nothing else is apparently as real to her.

Finally, and most notable, was *Poems: Selected and New, 1950–1974* by Adrienne Rich, a selection edited from seven previous volumes of poetry plus eight uncollected and eleven new poems—which marks the first plateau of great achievement for feminist Rich, who shared the National Book Award for poetry with Allen Ginsberg in 1974. Her newest poems are lucid visions, bold bloodlettings, knife-clean products of experience and courage and a terrific will to rethink the world in order to change it—all in a fashion unmatched for intellect, brilliance, and originality.

(FREDERICK S. PLOTKIN)

Canada. Canadian fiction enjoyed a prosperous year with several significant works and concrete promises for the future. Hugh Hood's *A Swing in the Garden* began the projected 12-volume Proustian remembrance of life in 20th-century Canada with a social portrait of Toronto in the 1930s. Ending his trilogy with *World of Wonders,* Robertson Davies unraveled the haunting mystery surrounding Paul Dempster, the small-town minister's son turned Magnus Eisengrim, the world's greatest magician. The plight of the artist in his social environment was the subject of Morley Callaghan's *A Fine and Private Place,* featuring a neglected Toronto writer and a student with an impossible quest—total knowledge of the artist's work. Brian Moore symbolized the relationship between the artist and his own creation in *The Great Victorian Collection,* a fantasy involving a McGill University history professor whose dream materializes in a motel parking lot. Fantasy and conflict in male-female relationships were treated in both Kent Thompson's *Across from the Floral Park,* in which a wealthy eccentric, inspired by the view in his telescope, fancies buying a house complete with a decrepit landlady and an elegant mistress; and Sylvia Fraser's *The Candy Factory,* a satiric and grotesquely violent attempt to shatter the illusions surrounding the sexual relationships of factory employees.

Ernest Buckler's *The Rebellion of Young David and Other Stories* realistically portrayed the psychological relationships of a pastoral Nova Scotian lifestyle. From the west came W. D. Valgardson's *God Is Not a Fish Inspector*—encounters with Manitoba farmers, hunters, and fishermen. In *The Snow Walker* the Canadian north was the setting for Farley Mowat's stories about the clashing civilizations of Eskimos, Indians, and whites.

The Island Means Minago, poems from Prince Edward Island by Milton Acorn, reflected the history and struggles of the local people with richly textured images. In *Borderlands* Don Gutteridge presented finely crafted verse dealing with the exploration of Canada's northwest coast. David McFadden's *A Knight in Dried Plums* had a humour that often was black and satirical. George Woodcock in *Notes on Visitations: 1936–1975* gave a significant collection of his poetry. Clara Thomas in *The Manawaka World of Margaret Laurence* provided a study of the evolution of the much-loved and respected Canadian writer Margaret Laurence (*see* BIOGRAPHY).

Charm, wit, and concerned interest in his country pervaded *One Canada: Memoirs of the Right Honourable John Diefenbaker, The Crusading Years 1895–1956,* which recounts his homestead years and his years as a student and young lawyer, concluding with his attainment of the leadership of the Progressive Conservative Party in 1956. The final volume in Lester Pearson's autobiography *Mike: The Memoirs of the Right Honourable Lester B. Pearson, Volume 3, 1957–1968,* edited by John Munro and Alex Inglis, concerned his years as leader of the opposition and his period as prime minister and ended as Pierre Elliott Trudeau took over as leader of the Liberal Party. From his viewpoint as a civil servant and later as a member of Parliament, J. W. Pickersgill explored his relationship with another one of Canada's notable prime ministers in *My Years with Louis St. Laurent: A Political Memoir. Edward Blake: The Man of the Other Way (1833–1881)* by Joseph Schull recorded the career of the man who, as an earlier head of the Liberal Party, was John A. Macdonald's major rival.

CAMERA PRESS/PHOTO TRENDS

Canadian Morley Callaghan, a chronicler of urban life, published "A Fine and Private Place" in 1975.

Robert Laird Borden, Volume 1 by Robert Craig Brown revealed the most notable period of Borden's political career—first as a backbencher, then opposition leader, and finally as prime minister. Interviews with expressive Canadian women were provided for *Her Own Woman: Profiles of Ten Canadian Women* by Myrna Kostash.

Books on Canadian history covered a broad range of periods and topics. Events in the exploration and development of the west coast were narrated by George and Helen Akrigg in *British Columbia Chronicle, 1778–1846.* Two studies documented the treatment of native Indians: J. E. Chamberlin's *The Harrowing of Eden* was a fresh, finely written comparative study of Canadian and U.S. attitudes and policies, whereas Howard Adams presented a more disturbing account from the Métis point of view in *Prison of Grass.* James Gray continued his popular social history of the Prairie Provinces, covering an exciting decade in *The Roar of the Twenties.* Several books examined aspects of Canada's role during World War II: *The Forgotten Heroes: The Canadians at Dieppe* by John Mellor; *Broadcast from the Front: Canadian Radio Overseas in the Second World War* by A. E. Powley; and *Canada's War: The Politics of the Mackenzie King Government, 1939–1945* by J. L. Granatstein.

Willy Amtmann in *Music in Canada* provided a scholarly study of early Canadian music and the struggles and achievements of its pioneers. Keith MacMillan and John Beckwith edited *Contemporary Canadian Composers,* an authoritative reference work, which included critical studies of the works of 144 composers that have appeared since 1920. John Hofsess' *Inner Views: Ten Canadian Filmmakers* was a valuable assessment of the fast-growing Canadian film industry. Marion MacRae and Anthony Adamson in *Hallowed Walls: Church Architecture in Upper Canada* provided an impressive study of buildings, customs, and social history of churches in Canada contributed by the many countries from which Canadian settlers came.

Walter L. Gordon in *Storm Signals: New Economic Policies for Canada* recommended the gradual removal of foreign, especially U.S., control of Canadian corporations and natural resources and stressed the need for wage and price controls. Evelyn Dumas in *The Bitter Thirties in Quebec* examined 12 examples from among the hundreds of strikes that occurred in Quebec during the 1930s and early 1940s and showed that labour militancy in Quebec was not exclusively a postwar development. Frank H. Epp's *Mennonites in Canada, 1786–1920: The History of a Separate People* provides a record of their escape from persecution in Europe, subsequent wanderings, and ultimate arrival in Canada.

(H. C. CAMPBELL)

FRENCH

France. *Fiction.* The year 1975 saw the brilliant conclusion to some vast cycles of historical novels: Henri Troyat's *Le Moscovite* with *Les Feux du matin;* Jules Roy's moving series on Algeria with *Le Tonnerre et les anges,* which won the Grand Prix de la Ville de Paris; Luc Estang's *Il était un p'tit homme,* the story of a Chouan, one of the royalist insurgents in western France at the time of the Revolution, with *À la chasse aux perdrix* and *Boislevent;* and *Nous l'appelions Bismarck,* in which Marc Blancpain achieved a delightful marriage of tragedy and humour, set in France under the German occupation in 1914. René Barjavel's *Les Dames à la licorne* went back to the 11th century for its retelling of an Irish legend.

Michel Tournier's *Les Météores,* a work of characteristic depravity and brilliance, had as its theme two twins united by strange ties and by a homosexual. Hervé Bazin turned his sharp pen to the story of a divorce, *Madame Ex,* which took a pitiless view of woman. *Le Jeune Homme vert* by Michel Déon, the story of a foundling who spends his adolescence wandering through Normandy, England, and Italy, was in the tradition of the great 19th-century novels. Jean Fougère's *Les Passagers* admirably captured the atmosphere of a cruise. *Les Moyens du bord,* one of Michel Mohrt's best works, described a troubled relationship between father and son during one summer in Brittany. Michel del Castillo's *Le Silence des pierres,* about a family in decline, recalled François Mauriac and won the new Prix Chateaubriand. The Prix Interallié for the best novel by a journalist went to Voldemar Lestienne, deputy editor of *France Dimanche,* for his *L'Amant de poche,* the story of a liaison between a 15-year-old boy and a woman of 25. *Le Trouble Source,* perhaps Jacques Perry's best-written novel to date, concerned a man who has the task of depolluting a small river.

FAYARD

The publication of Henri Troyat's "Les Feux du matin" concluded a three-volume cycle entitled "Le Moscovite."

Among books inspired by current events, Michel Bataille's *Cendres sur la mer* was a passionate attack on abortion methods, Michel de Saint-Pierre's *Je reviendrai sur les ailes de l'aigle* an essay-novel in praise of Israel, and Marie Cardinal's *Les Mots pour le dire* a daring confession on psychoanalytical treatment that gained an outstanding success.

Comedy was predominant in Jean Duché's *L'Enlèvement de M. Rémi-Potel,* about a man taken hostage, studded with erotic episodes, and in Albert Cossery's *Un Complot de saltimbanques,* about a gang of unscrupulous layabouts in a small Egyptian town. Absurd and burlesque, *Achète-moi les Amériques* by Claude Klotz imagined the collapse of civilization and New York City overrun by weeds.

The French Academy announced that it would not award its Grand Prix du roman in 1975 because of the mediocrity of recent novels. The jury for the Prix Goncourt enjoyed some dangerous publicity from protesters with pen and bomb: the prize was awarded to *La Vie devant soi* by Émile Ajar, a pseudonymous writer who told of the childhood of an Arab boy in Belleville, brought up by an old Jewish woman, in a book reminiscent of Céline. The same slang, the same, sometimes cruder, obscenities were to be found in *Les Rois et les voleurs* by the young writer Muriel Cerf. Jean Joubert's *L'Homme de sable,* awarded the Prix Renaudot, described an architect's passionate conception of a town which could never be completed. In the same mysterious tone, *Villa triste* by Patrick Modiano developed nostalgically among suspicious adventurers and aristocrats. Didier Decoin, still in search of spiritual enlightenment, moved his characters from London to Scotland in a symbolic fable, *Un policeman.* The Prix Femina went to Claude Faraggi for *Le Maître d'heure,* an avant-garde work about an engineer in charge of building a railway line who comes up against unsurmountable occult forces. Rachid Boudjedra in *Topographie idéale pour une agression caractérisée* used interminable sentences to encompass the Kafkaesque perambulations of an Algerian in the Paris métro. Jeanne Champion's *Dans les jardins d'Esther,* a dreamlike story in which the statues and pictures at Versailles come to life, confirmed an unusual and personal talent.

The literary season began with novels inspired by politics or by personal experiences: *L'Indésirable,* in which Régis Debray evoked the life of a guerrilla fighter in dialogue and soliloquy, and Olivier Todd's *Les Canards de Ca Mao* on the trials and tribulations of three journalists in Vietnam. Jean Lartéguy's *Les Rois mendiants,* showing the author as a true virtuoso, also had as its theme the disillusionment of journalists, this time in the Sahara in 1957. *Ne pleure pas, la guerre est bonne* by Guy Croussy was a fictional documentary, firmly antimilitaristic, inspired by the Algerian war. Jacques Almira won the Prix Médicis for *Voyage à Naucratis,* a difficult work, confused and plotless, but including some superb passages.

Poetry. The popular novelist Robert Sabatier, himself a refined poet, began a monumental, authoritative, and exemplary undertaking in *Histoire de la poésie française,* bringing his talents as biographer, critic, and scholar to bear on each of the poets selected to represent the Middle Ages and the 16th century; volumes on the 17th and 18th centuries were added late in the year. In *La Foire à la ferraille,* Jean l'Anselme adopted an unusual and delightful burlesque style. Philippe Dumaine's *Aux Passeurs de la nuit* was made up of "aphoristic" and prose poems showing perfection of form in a register that was sometimes crude and had tragic overtones: intelligence shone from these works of epigrammatic brevity. The Prix Apollinaire was awarded to Charles Le Quintrec, a Breton who celebrated his country and his religious faith in *Jeunesse de Dieu.* Close-knit, condensed *Racine de tout* spanned a vast horizon and won for its author Gabriel Audisio the French Academy's Grand Prix de poésie. The material of Pierre Loubière's *Poèmes à la craie* was dense, substantial, and vibrant. *L'Enfant-soleil et la croix* by Charles Bory was a collection of finely wrought but mysterious poems. Nature inspired the nostalgic poems in Jean Pourtal de Ladevèze's collection *De La Source azurine,* while Jean-Louis Vallas turned to the historic sites of the City of Paris in *Resonances de Paris.*

Nonfiction. A number of politicians felt the need to put pen to paper and the year was marked by the quality of these literary productions as well as by their critical and popular success. Jacques Chaban-Delmas in *L'Ardeur* asserted his desire for public service, though not without bitterness at losing power; the same applied to Michel Jobert, whose *Mémoires d'avenir* also evoked the past and his childhood in Meknès (Morocco); sensitivity to nature enriched François Mitterrand's *La paille et le grain,* while Michel Poniatowski's *Conduire le changement* was distinguished by its calm lucidity and Olivier Guichard's *Un chemin tranquille* by common sense.

Works of outstanding interest also came from political commentators. In *Charles de Gaulle ou la France en général,* André Frossard outlined the life of his country during the de Gaulle period. *Journal secret. Une année pas comme les autres* by Jean-Raymond Tournoux revealed unsuspected political secrets and was compared to the work of Saint-Simon. *Maurice Thorez, vie secrète et vie publique* by Philippe Robrieux provided some surprising firsthand accounts of the life of the great Communist leader, while in *Roger Wybot et la bataille pour la D. S. T.* Philippe Bernert detailed 15 years of political intrigue under the Fourth Republic. Gilles Perrault devoted *La Longue Traque* to Roland Farjon, a resistance leader accused of treason in 1947. *L'Adieu à Saigon* by Jean Lartéguy described the corruption of the Vietnamese by the U.S. dollar and how they in turn perverted the U.S. forces with drugs. An enthusiastic biography of King Faisal, *Fayçal, Roi d'Arabie,* was not without interest, but its author, Jacques Benoist-Méchin, excelled in *L'homme et ses jardins*—the gardens including those of China, Japan, and Arabia. The Bourse Goncourt for historical writing was justly awarded to René Vigo for *Tragédie à Clairvaux,* the story of a double murder and the biography of the criminals who were eventually sentenced to death, and to Henri Vincenot for *Dans les chemins de fer au XIXe siècle.*

Some writers chose precisely defined subjects as pivots around which to recount the history of France at given periods: for example, Bernard Morice in *Paris en son Hôtel de Ville* evoked earlier monuments and the people of the time; René Héron de Villefosse took his *L'histoire des grandes routes de France* back to animal tracks and the Roman roads, ending with the contemporary expressway, while in *L'Anti-Versailles ou le Palais-Royal de Philippe Égalité* the same writer described not only the history of an architectural masterpiece but also that of the royal house of Orléans. Claude Pasteur's *L'Elysée hier et aujourd'hui,* delightfully written, was a careful study of the construction of the Elysée Palace and the various alterations it had undergone since the 18th century. Ghislain de Diesbach's *Histoire de l'émigration. 1789–1814* gave a remarkable insight into the life of French émigrés in several countries, among which England seemed to have proved the most hospitable. José Cabanis with *Saint-Simon l'admirable* (Prix de la critique littéraire) provided what was indeed an admirable critique of the work of this celebrated writer of memoirs, acid commentator on the French court, and avid collector of scandals, before reaching stature as a politician and a man of undoubted spirituality. Pierre Daix, in *Aragon: une vie à changer,* traced the political, literary, and emotional career of the poet, including his youthful liaisons with distinguished women and his great love for Elsa Triolet—a massive work of undoubted value, despite the criticism it aroused from some quarters. Henry de Montherlant's last notebooks, *Tous feux éteints,* characteristically imperious in tone, left off shortly before his suicide; a biography by Pierre Sipriot (his second), rich and concise, gained the Prix Ève Delacroix. Charles Moeller's *Amours humaines,* the fifth volume of his *Littérature du XXe siècle et Christianisme,* oddly linked the names of Françoise Sagan, Bertolt Brecht, and Saint-John Perse: the last-named, with Paul Valéry, provided the most interesting portions of the book. Jacques Robichon's *Le Défi des Goncourt* was an admirable history of the private academy that had had a predominant influence on the success of the French novel. François Nourissier, an outstanding drama critic, confided in *Lettre à mon chien* that he preferred dogs to human beings and engaged in autobiographical reflections that were valuable chiefly for the quality of the writing. In a highly flavoured, colourful, inspirational style, Lucien Bodard's *Le Fils du consul* told of his childhood in China at the time

KEYSTONE

Prolific author René Barjavel came out with yet another fine work in 1975—"Les Dames à la licorne."

of the warlords. Georges Walter, the writer responsible for Chow Ching Lie's *Le Palanquin des larmes,* provided a firsthand account of the life of a Chinese woman before Mao and under Mao, which proved very popular.

During the past few years well-known writers had described their personal philosophy in the series *Ce que je crois,* but none of these books had attracted as much comment or as many readers as that by Maurice Clavel, an active left-winger. In strident tones, with attacks and contradictions, he examined two centuries of philosophy and described how religious faith "struck him like lightning." Similar in tone, as well as in its success, Roger Garaudy's *Parole d'homme* described a conversion from Christianity to Communism and a painless return to Christianity. Benoîte Groult's pamphlet *Ainsi soit-elle* left an unpleasant taste, though the savage humour of this fanatical feminist won popular success for the work.

The French Academy's Grand Prix de littérature was awarded to Henri Queffélec, while the prize for the *nouvelle* form went to Roger Grenier's *Le Miroir des eaux.* Father Ambroise-Marie Carré and Félicien Marceau were elected to the Academy. Losses to French literature were Robert Aron, Saint-John Perse, one of its greatest poets and winner of the 1960 Nobel Prize for Literature, and the poet Patrice de la Tour du Pin. (*See also* OBITUARIES.)

(ANNIE BRIERRE)

Canada. Primed for several years, the French-Canadian literary movement showed no sign of slowing down in 1975. On the contrary, it gained momentum and the list of literary notables grew constantly with the addition of newcomers.

The need to probe and examine every aspect of man's ordinary daily life, present or past, became more and more pressing and vital. This theme was found in the novels of Pierre Châtillon, *La Mort rousse;* Pierre DesRuisseaux, *Le Noyau;* Marie-France Dubois, *Le Passage secret;* Francine Dufresne, *Dieu le clown;* Jocelyne Felx, *Les Vierges folles;* Roland Lepage, *La Pétaudière;* Marie LeTellier, *On n'est pas des trous-de-cul;* Andrée Maillet, *À la Mémoire d'un héros;* Eric Martel, *Conrad l'imaginaire;* and Josette Marchessault, *Comme une enfant de la terre I.*

Similar concerns were found in the works of more established authors. Written at the beginning of the "quiet revolution" of 1960 but published only in 1975, *La Commensale* by Gérard Bessette recounted in the same simple, precise style of *L'Incubation* the loneliness of a woman who, through her own personal intrigues, comes to view all men as scoundrels. To describe the isolation of the heroine in *New Media,* Monique Bosco used a compositional technique borrowed from the theatre: a prologue and five acts.

With *La Partie pour le tout,* Nicole Brossard continued to search for a style of writing that unveiled both reality and fantasy and permitted a brutally accurate but nonetheless caring exploration of each of these realms. The author's popularity as well as the quality of *Les Enfants du sabbat* would surely contribute to making a best-seller of Anne Hébert's novel, set in 1944 in a religious institution.

Novelist Yves Thériault continued an earlier saga with *Agaok,* about the grandson of the title character in his first novel, *Agaguk.* The tale of Agaok's long voyage and of the desperate sadness of the young Eskimo woman awaiting his return, however, lacked the inspiration of his first novel, perhaps because of the degeneration of the protagonists, contaminated by civilization.

In theatre, three plays were worthy of mention. Jean Barbeau's *Citrouille* told the tale of the kidnapping of a playboy by three women who want to shatter the myth of the woman as object and make their prisoner submit to the fate reserved by man for the woman. In Marcel Dubé's *L'Été s'appelle Julie* all of Dubé's themes come back into play, with the author's vision of the world synthesized in the character of Ludovic. In *Une Soirée en octobre* André Major dealt with the events of an October evening via five characters shut in a hotel room.

Two noteworthy literary essays were *Des Choses à dire* by Adrien Thério, a literary chronicle written for the author's pleasure with his habitual verve and candid language; and Philippe Haeck's *L'Action restreinte de la littérature,* a study inspired by Marxist thought on the function, teaching, and reading of literature.

(ROBERT SAINT-AMOUR)

DUTCH

In general Dutch literature continued to move away from experimental writing and was going through a phase of consolidating traditional techniques and themes. True, there were exceptions, such as the novel *Erwin, 5 October 1972* by a young writer who called himself Joyce & Co. and who described in his novel what the novel he describes could have been. It was "the dream of a masterpiece," as the poet and critic Gerrit Komrij aptly said. Other experiments were being made with the form and the thematic range of the novel, but on the whole the writers who published in 1975 did not depart very far from the conventions. It might seem that Gerard Kornelis van het Reve—who had now reduced his name to Gerard Reve—broke new ground with *Ik had hem lief* ("I Loved Him"), an epistolary novel about a homosexual love affair, but in the light of former books in a similar style and on similar subjects it appeared that Reve was really reaffirming the new genre that he created some years earlier. In The Netherlands, therefore, his new novel did not have the impact of the earlier books, but Reve's work was so outstanding that had it been published in a language more widely known than Dutch it would have been hailed as a literary event of the first order. Reve had certainly lost none of his extraordinary verbal powers nor his ability to write a novel that was deeply melancholy and at the same time very funny.

Willem Frederik Hermans, always a more traditional writer than Reve, published *Onder Professoren* ("Among Professors"), in which he attacked the new democracy in Dutch universities. Hermans was The Netherlands' most eloquent pessimist, an intelligent and dogged analyst of the foibles and faults of modern civilization, and not surprisingly his view of progress in university life was one of utter derision. A writer who had been in the background for some years, Albert Alberts suddenly rose to prominence with *De Vergaderzaal* ("The Meeting Room"), an evocative description of a businessman's mental breakdown under the stress of a surfeit of meetings and negotiations. Alberts' contemporary Anton Koolhaas, famous for his animal stories, gave in *De Geluiden van de eerste Dag* ("The Sounds of the First Day") an excellent account of a chain of uncontrollable events that result when the delicate balance of a small community is disturbed by a seemingly meaningless accident.

Following the success of his collection of short stories *Bang Weer* ("Thundery Weather"), Henk Romijn Meijer reprinted a number of earlier stories in *Tweede Druk* ("Second Edition") and seemed on the way to receiving the recognition that had long since been his due. The most talked-about literary event of the year was the publication of Tymen Trolsky's *Aliesje,* an account of the relationship between a young man and a seven-year-old girl. Trolsky's real identity remained a well-guarded secret but he was clearly a young writer with a great deal of pent-up energy who in a very short time had published two novels and two volumes of poetry. His style combined passionate romanticism, parody, and pastiche inextricably woven together, resulting in a not entirely satisfying mixture but on the other hand obviously showing the hand of a born writer.

(REINDER PIETER MEIJER)

GERMAN

The centenary of the birth of Thomas Mann provided opportunity for stocktaking on the state of German letters and for writers to mark out their positions with regard to the great master. At the same time it provoked the question: who was the Mann of 1975? Where Mann succeeded in relating great issues of political and social import to fictitious individuals with interesting private personalities, contemporary novelists seemed to concentrate either on the social or on the private. Thus Heinrich Böll, on whom the mantle of *praeceptor Germaniae* had devolved, appeared to be exclusively preoccupied with the "order of the day." His latest work, *Berichte zur Gesinnungslage der Nation,* a satire on West Germany's current brand of McCarthyism, was amusing but as ephemeral as anything he had written.

There were a number of fine evocations of recent history. Horst Bienek scored a notable success with *Die erste Polka.* Set in Upper Silesia on Aug. 31, 1939, it skillfully juxtaposed wedding celebrations with the preparations for and outbreak of war. The uneasy relationship between Germans, Poles, and Jews in this focal geographic area was well captured. Hermann Lenz's *Die neue Zeit* followed the fortunes of a student of art history in the war itself. And Walter Kempowski reached volume 3 of the Kempowski saga; *Ein Kapitel für sich* covered the years 1948–56 in a now familiar mosaic of surface impressions. If it was gloomier than the earlier volumes, this could be attributed to the situation of the three narrators, all in East German prisons.

CAMERA PRESS/PICTORIAL PARADE

Nobel Prize winner Heinrich Böll continued to narrate contemporary German life. His 1975 contribution was the satirical "Berichte zur Gesinnungslage der Nation."

East German novelist Rolf Schneider achieved success with his "Die Reise nach Jaroslaw," the story of a troubled teenage girl.

PIPER & CO. VERLAG

Other writers besides Böll were concerned about current problems in West Germany. Jürgen Lodemann's *Anita Drögemöller* imputed scandalous connections between business, politics, prostitution, and the media in the Ruhr. Gerhard Zwerenz turned the Guillaume espionage affair into a novel, *Die Quadriga des Mischa Wolf.* Perhaps the most controversial novel of the year, however, was Karin Struck's *Die Mutter,* which, punctually for International Women's Year, analyzed the position of woman in society. If Ibsen's Nora broke out of the role of motherhood imposed on her by society, Frau Struck's Nora Hanfland had to fight against the contemporary attitude that "mere motherhood" was something inferior.

At the opposite pole were a number of works that discounted social and political "relevance" and explored the private world of the individual. In *Die Stunde der wahren Empfindung* Peter Handke continued his search for the exact reproduction of emotional states. Gregor Keuschnig dreams that he is a murderer, whereupon his life is transformed, he experiences the strangeness of everything, objects take on an independent existence, he can no longer relate either to his own individuality or to what he has in common with others. Handke excelled in the precision of his language, this time in a work redolent of his Austrian predecessors, Hofmannsthal, Rilke, and Kafka. Hans Jürgen Fröhlich's *Im Garten der Gefühle* was a novel about marriage, loosely patterned on Goethe's *Elective Affinities.* Gabriele Wohmann's *Schönes Gehege* studied the tension between individual existence and the persona forced on a prominent writer by the media. Robert Plath is forced by preparations for a television feature on his life to analyze himself and finds he has been more concerned with his image than with being himself.

This same concentration on the intimate realm of the self characterized Max Frisch's *Montauk.* Subtitled "a tale" and therefore ostensibly his first major narrative work since 1964, it in fact continued his more recent series of autobiographical works in an extraordinary public baring of his private life, in particular a recent affair with an American girl half his age. Indeed, autobiographies continued to be popular: besides that of Kempowski, there were Geno Hartlaub's volume of reminiscences *Wer die Erde küsst* and Thomas Bernhard's *Die Ursache,* which told of his early years in Salzburg and launched a remarkably vehement attack on that town. In widely divergent areas there were the highly successful *Spandauer Tagebücher* of Albert Speer and Hildegard Knef's best-selling account of her operation for breast cancer, *Das Urteil,* while the publication of Bertolt Brecht's diaries and autobiographical notes of the years 1920–54 was a further landmark in Brecht scholarship.

Lyric poetry was represented by Frank Geerk's *Notwehr,* which included the notorious poems which brought about his prosecution in Basel for blasphemy; Klaus Konjetzky's autobiographical *Poem vom Grünen Eck;* and Rolf Dieter Brinkmann's important posthumous collection *Westwärts 1 und 2.* But in many ways the most impressive volume came from Herbert Asmodi, whose *Jokers Gala* succeeded as others did not in expressing personal feelings about life in the 1970s in language and rhythms public and memorable enough for others to identify with.

In East Germany the success of the year was Rolf Schneider's *Die Reise nach Jaroslaw,* an account of a teenager's revolt against parental and social authority. Gittie breaks away, seduces a Polish student, but is eventually brought back to conformity. The jargon in which it is told owed much to Ulrich Plenzdorf, but ultimately the novel remained irritatingly superficial. Max Walter Schulz's *Triptychon mit sieben Brücken* also included a rebellious teenager, who distributes anti-Soviet leaflets on the occasion of the invasion of Czechoslovakia in 1968. Schulz grasped the nettle that Schneider invariably avoided, but his novel was pedestrian and the conflicts never appeared more than academic. Stefan Heym treated a similar episode in East Germany's past, the June 1953 uprising, in his novel *5 Tage im Juni.* While leaving the reader in no doubt about the correctness of the official party line, Heym did introduce elements of genuine conflict and wrote, for all its shortcomings in characterization, an exciting narrative.

Other novels went further back in East German history. Erik Neutsch brought out the first volume of an ambitious work, *Der Friede im Osten.* Covering the years 1945–50, it took the traditional form of a novel of education, in this case concentrating to such an extent on the development of a fanatical Hitler Youth boy into a member of the Communist youth movement that at times historical events were obscured. Eberhard Panitz' *Die unheilige Sophia* treated the same period in rather more novelesque form. However, one of the most attractive works to appear in the East was a collection of stories by Manfred Jendryschik, *Jo, mitten im Paradies,* in which the child's-eye perspective was used to good effect.

As more and more East German writers were invited and received permission to lecture in the West, signs of the times were Günter Kunert's *Der andere Planet* and Rolf Schneider's *Von Paris nach Frankreich,* travel impressions of the United States and France, respectively.

(J. H. REID)

SCANDINAVIAN

Danish. During 1974–75 there was a noticeable shift from the esoteric and the politically engaged in Danish literature. The novel moved toward social realism, as in Åge Hansen-Folehaven's *Vi venter på fællesskab* (1974). Related in their approach were Henning Mortensen's *Yvonnes verden,* Jens Smærup Sørensen's *Byggeri,* Arne Harløv Petersen's *Imod fremtids fjerne mål,* and Christian Kampmann's *Rene linjer,* the third volume in a family saga. It was perhaps the same trend that produced an anthology of poems of ordinary life, *Splinter fra hverdagen nr. 2.* Even Sven Holm, awarded the Danish Academy's prize for 1974, turned to the portrayal of middle-class life in *Det private liv* (1974). With his *Protestanten* Willy-August Linnemann completed his cycle of novels concerned with the Sunesen Schleswiger family. A young writer, Martha Christensen, dealt with the good and bad qualities in a number of boys in an approved school in *Som de vil ha' dig* (1974). Further from social realism was Aage Dons's *Et behageligt opholdssted,* telling of a woman's return to Copenhagen after 20 years in London, and of the way in which she comes to terms both with the new conditions she finds and with her own relatives. Based partly on family recollections, but unsentimental and with general relevance, was Hans Lyngby Jepsen's *Et bedre forår,* while on the borderline between realism and fantasy was Poul-Henrik Trampe's *Gidselsaffæren,* a novel about a bank robber and the holding of hostages. Leif Panduro, whose television plays enjoyed a high reputation, published a further two: *Bertram og Lisa* and *Anne og Paul.*

Noteworthy autobiographies and memoirs were H. V. Brøndsted's *Et liv—tre tidsperioder* (1974) and Johannes Wulff's *Tyk og glad som sædvanlig* (1974). Soya made his contribution with *Ærlighed koster mest,* and in *Vink fra fjern virkelighed* Jacob Paludan, who died in September 1975, gave brief glimpses from

Sven Holm, winner of the 1974 Danish Academy literary award, recounted middle-class existence in Denmark in "Det private liv."

LUTFI ÖZKÖK

his youth. Memoirs of more recent years were Thorkild Hansen's diaries from 1943–47, *De søde piger.* Two other collections of essays came into the memoir category: Steen Eiler Rasmussen's *Også et sovemiddel* and Carl Bergstrøm-Nielsen's *Analfabeternes forlægger og den glade magister.*

A novel with autobiographical overtones was Klaus Rifbjerg's *En hugorm i solen,* recounting a boy's experience of the summer of 1939. Rifbjerg published a volume of poems in 1974, *25 desperate digte,* and followed this with a humorous novel, *Tak for turen,* a portrayal of a young man just after World War II. From the less prolific but highly regarded Peter Seeberg came a volume of short stories, *Dinosaurusens sene eftermiddag* (1974), varied in character, but all looking to the future with anxiety.

Poetry made its contribution in Vagn Steen's *Fuglens flugt i halvkrystal* (1974), Poul Borum's *Sang til dagens glæde* (1974), and Jørgen Gustava Brandt's *Her omkring* (1974).

(W. GLYN JONES)

Norwegian. The fundamental problem of attitudes about death was at the centre of Sigbjørn Hølmebakk's intense novel *Karjolsteinen,* focusing on a left-wing novelist and his meeting with a parson whose brother, executed as a Nazi, was most likely the father of the parson's presumed daughter who died as a drug addict, followed by the death of the parson's wife from cancer.

An outstanding thriller was Michael Grundt Spang's *Aksjon Ullersmo,* with breathtaking action set in motion by a gang of international terrorists organizing an airlift escape from a Norwegian prison. Apocalyptic visions inspired Finn Carling's *Fiendene* and Knut Faldbakken's *Uår. Aftenlandet.* Carling presented a dehumanized world where television had turned people into unfeeling robots no longer able to distinguish between the unreality of the screen and the actual world around them. An element of hope inspired Faldbakken's presentation of a small colony seeking refuge from a run-down technological metropolis in its enormous dumping site. Edvard Hoem's *Kjærleikens ferjereiser,* composed in a fascinating Chinese box narrative technique, was a collective novel dealing with the problems of a small outlying district in a centralized world. Pessimistic in tone also was Dag Solstad's *25. september-plassen,* centred on a small industrial town in southern Norway and expressing deep frustration at the state of affairs after more than three decades of social democratic rule in Norway. Rich in perspectives was a multifaceted collection of short stories by Johan Borgen, *Lykke til!,* combining psychology, philosophy, and humour. More serious was the same author's *I dette rom,* a collection of four short stories and a play for radio, "Stemmen." Mikkjel Fønhus' *Hallingsvarten,* published posthumously, was a moving account of the relationship between a man and his horse.

Feminist ideas were discussed in Ebba Haslund's fine portrait of upper middle-class family life, *Bare et lite sammenbrudd.* The same theme was dealt with from a number of angles in Bjørg Vik's collection of short stories, *Fortellinger om frihet,* and from a lesbian angle in Tove Nilsen's *Helle og Vera.* Several historical novels appeared. Kåre Holt's *Sjøhelten* was little more than a pale rendering of an episode in the life of the 18th-century naval hero Peder Wessel Tordenskjold. Vera Henriksen's *Staupet* added a fourth volume to her series of novels with action laid in the 16th century.

LUTFI ÖZKÖK

Sweden's Tore Zetterholm, a master of the psychological novel, added "Turisterna" to his list of published works.

The fourth of Einar Gerhardsen's books of memoirs, *Unge år,* contained a fascinating account of the former Labour prime minister's proletarian childhood in Oslo at the beginning of the century. Tim Greve's *Fridtjof Nansen 1905–1930* concluded a well-documented two-volume biography. Outstanding scholarly contributions were Johannes Lunde's *Liv og kunst i konflikt,* dealing in great detail with the novelist Alexander L. Kielland's life and works during 1883–1906; Finn Thorn's *Sigrid Undset: kristentro og kirkesyn,* tracing the influence of Roman Catholic ideas in her novels; and Audun Tvinnereim's *Risens hjerte,* a detailed analysis of six central works by Sigurd Hoel. The publication of a new comprehensive history of Norwegian literature was brought to a conclusion with the appearance of volumes 3 to 6. Nearly three volumes were devoted to the 20th century.

(TORBJØRN STØVERUD)

Swedish. Many books by or about women reflected International Women's Year. Kerstin Ekman's *Häxringarna* was a moving study of an unmarried mother's world 80 years ago; Eva Runefelt's *I svackan* concerned the search for meaning in life of a girl of 19; Ulla Isaksson, who for 35 years had been writing about women, published short stories on this theme in *Kvinnorna;* and Margareta Sarri wrote the lively, provocative *Ta dej en slav,* about a woman who rebels against marital and parental authority. A prostitute exploited by men in a man's world in 1875, yet who manages to retain her human dignity, was the heroine of Hans Granlid's *Flickan Kraft.*

Barbro Lindgren's remarkable gift for presenting mentally handicapped or abnormal people from within was seen in *Molnens bröder,* a moving little book suggesting that these people are reassuringly like the rest of us. Per Gunnar Evander, a leading novelist in the near-documentary style, wrote about a teacher's nervous breakdown and struggle to regain his balance in *Härlig är jorden,* a convincing psychological study realistically set in a residential adult education college. Biting psychological analysis, the hallmark of Tore Zetterholm, was evident in *Turisterna,* in which a Swedish woman archaeologist has an affair in Greece with a Greek student, who then blackmails her trendy, media-lionized husband into taking him back to Sweden as a supposed victim of the colonels' regime (when in fact he is a collaborator). Zetterholm's couple act from a mixture of naiveté and a desire to salve their liberal consciences. Another form of naïveté, which leads to even more disastrous results, was found in the husband-wife relationship in film director Vilgot Sjöman's novel *Garaget.* A Greek village at war during 1944–47 provided the epic centre of Theodor Kallifatides' *Plogen och svärdet.* In *Oredans natt* Håkan Boström examined the events that took place in the provincial town of Eskilstuna in 1937, where a brawl turned into a riot; the subsequent trial punished those least able to defend themselves.

In poetry, scholar and university teacher Kjell Espmark published *Det obevekliga paradiset,* the last part of a poetic trilogy. Espmark's constant concern is how life can be made more human in an advanced welfare state (the relentless Paradise of his title). The same concern for human beings and values was voiced by poet and doctor Claes Andersson in *Rums kamrater,* with versatile changes of mood and style. The gifted Ylva Eggehorn, young best-selling Christian poet, published *Han Kommer,* in which she, too, voices the dilemma of helpless individuals—and sees Christ as saviour.

The death of Per Wahlöö (*see* OBITUARIES), who collaborated with his wife, Maj Sjövall, in a series of best-selling detective stories, occurred in June.

(KARIN PETHERICK)

ITALIAN

The award of the 1975 Nobel Prize for Literature to the 79-year-old poet Eugenio Montale—the fifth Italian recipient of the prize since its inception—met with general approval in literary circles. (*See* NOBEL PRIZES.)

Horcynus Orca by Stefano D'Arrigo, one of the most publicized and best-selling books of 1975, was a 1,300-page novel describing the experiences, dreams, evocations, and feelings of a Sicilian soldier during his short journey home from Calabria after the September 1943 armistice. Although providing the background of the story, the war was not the main theme of the novel, which dealt with a ferocious species of dolphins and with the *Orca* herself, a death symbol and a fetid sea monster. The novel contained a number of powerful episodes which, however, failed to justify its publisher's exaggerated claim that the book deserved "an absolute position of first class in the literature of our century."

Another best-seller, *Berlinguer e il professore,* an anonymous satire of Italian politics and in particular of the secretary-general of the Italian Communist Party, Enrico Berlinguer (*see* BIOGRAPHY), was more manageable both in size and in content, occasionally pleasant and refreshing for its humour, but on the whole rather facile and superficial.

The most prestigious literary prize, the Premio Strega, was awarded to Tommaso Landolfi, ostensibly for his latest book, *A caso,* a collection of short stories, but perhaps more appropriately in recognition of his four decades of successful activity as a writer. Landolfi, a Florentine by adoption, of the same generation as the better-known Vasco Pratolini, had always been an isolated writer, difficult to fit into any 20th-century literary school or movement. This was perhaps why, despite his qualities, he had never been quite so popular as Pratolini. The Strega award seemed likely to redress the balance, as it coincided with the republication of his earlier works.

An inspiration of remarkable artistic and moral value was shown by Paolo Volponi, whose *Il sipario ducale* (Premio Viareggio), set in Urbino in December 1969 at the time of the Milan bomb outrages, was structured as two series of alternating chapters, developing two parallel stories that interreacted upon each other as the narrative proceeded. On one side was the heir of the count Oddi-Semproni of Urbino, mad and cunning, completely obsessed by his passion for TV advertisements and by the dream of his family's past glories. On the other were an old couple of anarchists, Subissoni and Vives, antinationalist, antiunitarian, also slightly mad, who had lived together since meeting during the Spanish Civil War. Volponi mixed history and chronicle and closely followed the reactions of his characters to the bomb outrages. At the end of the novel Subissoni, left alone by the death of Vives, is made aware of present history and of the necessity to live its challenge by breaking through the *sipario ducale.*

Memory novels were still very popular in Italy, all pervaded by that kind of lucid and deceptively critical nostalgia that Italian writers seem to be so well versed in. In this field Susanna Agnelli excelled with her *Vestivamo alla marinara,* which was awarded the Premio Bancarella. This was the story of a girl and her family (which incidentally owns Fiat) between the rise and fall of Fascism. Primo Levi published *Il sistema periodico,* the autobiography of a chemist in 21 chapters, each one of them drawing inspiration from a mineral element. The book, however, also was the story in 21 moments of a generation of Italians, through Fascism, war, resistance, deportation, concentration camps, and, finally—for some—the return home. *Pomo pero* by Luigi Meneghello was ostensibly an appendix to his *Libera nos a malo* of 1963, but in fact was a more deeply personal recollection, halfway between prose and poetry, in which the author made full use of his personal experience of the languages and the cultures of Italy and England.

The Premio Campiello was awarded to *Il prato in fondo al mare* by Stanislao Nievo, great-grandson of Ippolito Nievo, one of the great Italian writers of the 19th century, who was shipwrecked in 1861 at the age of 30, in circumstances never fully explained. The book gave a gripping account of the author's varied attempts at unraveling that mystery.

Among the experimental novels, the most curious one was *a a.: Il libro dell'utopia ceramica* by Sebastiano Vassalli, a "repertory of tiles," as the author called it, juxtaposed by chance and containing all sorts of material, from classic quotations to slogans, names, numbers, pictures, and all kinds of words by which the middle-brow Italian is daily persecuted through the media. A different kind of pastiche was *Specchio delle mie brame* by Alberto Arbasino, a thoroughly amusing little book described as "kitsch Italian style in narrative form."

Comparatively smaller was the number of new books of poetry. Arnoldo Mondadori's *Almanacco dello Specchio* for 1975 (edited by Marco Forti) printed isolated works by Montale (in much the same vein as his *Diario del '71 e del '72*), Mario Luzi, Albino Pierro, Pratolini, Pier Paolo Pasolini (*see* OBITUARIES), Giovanni Testori, Giovanni Guiducci, Rossana Ombres, and others. Pasolini confirmed his

THOMAS VICTOR

Italian author Stefano D'Arrigo gained literary and monetary success with his lengthy novel "Horcynus Orca."

reputation as a poet with *La nuova gioventú,* but Giovanni Raboni with *Cadenza d'inganno* was the only Italian poet to produce an entirely new volume of poetry in 1975.

In the field of essay writing, Guido Piovene, before dying in London in 1974, had collected a number of his articles, previously published in an Italian newspaper between 1953 and 1973. These were printed under the general title *Idoli e ragione* and with a preface in which the author explained the meaning of "enlightened conservative," the epithet he had chosen for himself. A different kind of approach to similar problems was offered in Pasolini's *Scritti corsari,* a collection of articles, reviews, interviews, and unpublished fragments, dated 1973–75, in which the author dealt with some of the most urgent questions of Italian society in his characteristically vigorous and provoking manner.

(LINO PERTILE)

SPANISH

Spain. Most of the good novels and memoirs published in 1975 were by politically committed writers. Those who were not Spanish-American by birth were, in the main, allies in every sense of those who were making Latin-American literature well known around the world. At the same time, two outstanding South Americans, Mario Vargas Llosa (*see* BIOGRAPHY) of Peru and Gabriel García Márquez of Colombia, were becoming—by ever longer residence—Spanish by adoption, or at least expatriates in Europe, and creating "Spanish-American literature from Spain." There seemed to be no special purpose in their staying away from their former homelands and they gave no public reason. The political balance was somewhat righted by the presence in Spain of refugees from Cuba and Argentina.

A book that had aroused considerable expectation in Spain was García Márquez' *El otoño del patriarca,* written in Barcelona, the portrait of a magical and almost indestructible dictator who summarized in himself all the world's dictators. Some critics did not find the book up to their expectations, considering the generally acknowledged masterpiece the same author had produced in *Cien años de soledad* (1967).

While key Spanish-American novels were issued first in Spain, a novel by a self-designated "ex-Spaniard" was first issued in Mexico for censorship reasons: this was *Juan sin tierra,* the latest in a series, by Juan Goytisolo, which inevitably reflected Spain and its history. Despite the prohibition, Goytisolo's novel circulated in Spain, along with its predecessors in the series.

Notable memoirs were those of two close friends centred in Barcelona: Jaime Gil de Biedma's *Diario del artista seriamente enfermo* and Carlos Barral's *Años de penitencia.* Both books were evocative of the 1920s and '30s in Catalonia and of the artistic life there in subsequent years.

Among the year's prizes, the Premios de la Nueva Crítica went to Mariano Antolín-Rato for the 1974 novel *Cuando 900 mil Mach aprox;* to Eugenio Trías in the essay category for *Drama e identidad;* and to Juan E. Cirlot, cited posthumously for the totality of his work. These prizes, issued from Madrid, were given for works designed to mark new directions in literary forms; remarkably little attention was paid to political stances among the prizewinners. Antolín-Rato, winner in the novel class, produced a second work in 1975 in the same line of abstraction, *De vulgari Zyklón B manifestante.*

Works of specialized interest were *Diez siglos de poesía castellaña,* a selection by Vicente Gaos intended as a companion volume to the recent *Poesía catalana.* Luis Cernuda's *Antología poética* appeared, with an introduction and selection by Philip Silver. Also notable in this field was *Historia de la hispania romana* by A. Tovar and J. M. Blázquez; subtitled *La península ibérica desde 218 a.C. hasta el siglo v,* it included an excellent account of all 300 pagan gods of Iberia. Juan Bonet issued *El entrevistario, entrevistas imaginarias,* imaginary interviews with such people as Gertrude Stein during her 1916 stay in Mallorca.

(ANTHONY KERRIGAN)

Latin America. The tragic death in 1975 of the talented Salvadorian poet Roque Dalton occurred under circumstances that remained unclear. His most recent collection of writings, *Las historias prohibidas del pulgarcito,* which appeared in 1974, was a collage of the cultural history of San Salvador including his own compositions and poems by other poets and documents, which together formed an underground history of his country.

The French Cino de Duca Prize was awarded to Alejo Carpentier. The 1975 Casa de las Américas prizes were more numerous than in previous years and included two poetry prizes, one to Omar Lara of Chile for his collection *¡Oh buenas maneras!* and the other to Manuel Orestes Nieto of Panama for the collection *Dar la cara.* The prizes for new plays went to Alejandro Sieveking of Chile for *Pequeños animales abatidos,* to Jorge Goldenburg of Argentina for *Relevo 1923,* and to Guillermo Maldonado Pérez of Colombia for *Por estos santos latifundios.* The prizes for the novel were awarded to Haroldo Conti of Argentina for *Mascaro, el cazador Americano* and to Eduardo Galeano of Uruguay for *La canción de nosotros;* the two prizes for short story collections

THOMAS VICTOR

The publication of "Blue Spaces" in 1975 brought the first translation of Mexican poet Homero Aridjis' poems to the English-speaking world.

went to Colombia's Carlos Bastides Padilla Barrios for *Definición de la ira* and to the Chilean Juan Gabriel Leonardo Carvajal Barrios for *Definición del olvido.*

On the darker side, recession and political uncertainty seemed to have had their effects on publishing, especially in Buenos Aires, which had been superseded by Mexico City as the major publishing centre of Latin America. In Peru there were restrictions early in 1975 when some magazines were forced to close, though the situation changed for the better when the government was reorganized. A new magazine, the excellent *Revista de crítica literaria,* began publication in September 1975.

Fiction. Historical and documentary fiction dominated Latin-American writing in 1975. Gabriel García Márquez' long-awaited novel *El otoño del patriarca* proved to be a tour de force of black humour. The patriarch of the title is a 150-year-old dictator of an imaginary Caribbean country with a savage sense of fun and an almost infinite capacity for survival. The veteran Cuban novelist Alejo Carpentier, who has a predilection for historical themes, brought out *Concierto barroco,* a fantasy inspired by Vivaldi's opera *Motezuma.* Also published in 1975 was *Terra Nova,* a historical novel by Carlos Fuentes.

The historical period that most attracted Bolivian writers has been the period of the Chaco War in the 1930s. Néstor Taboada Terán's new novel, *El signo escalonado,* was a critical account of the events leading up to the hostilities. The Chilean novelist Fernando Alegría, on the other hand, was concerned with more recent history. His *El paso de los gansos* incorporated documents, newspaper reports, and photographs as well as fantasy and personal experience to reconstruct the death of Salvador Allende in September 1973 and its tragic aftermath.

Having reached a venerable age, the Argentine writer Jorge Luis Borges allowed a premature *Obras completas* to be published in 1974. In 1975 he came out with a new collection of 13 narratives, *El libro de arena.*

If any other trend could be detected, it was perhaps in the direction of satirical fantasy. One of the most amusing examples was the Mexican novelist Gustavo Saínz's *La princesa del palacio de hierro,* in which a middle-class girl, one of the habitués of Mexico City's Zona Rosa, pours out in implacable detail her private fantasies and adventures among the *jeunesse dorée.* The Argentine writer Hector Libertella, who in 1971 won the Monte Ávila Prize, also satirized the young jet set in *Personas en pose de combate.*

Several Argentine writers of the older generation brought out new works; among these were Eduardo Mallea's *Los Papeles privados,* Manuel Mujica Lainez' *Laberinto,* Roger Pla's *Intemperie,* and Arturo Cerratani's collection of three novellas, *Matar a título.* Rodolfo Walsh, an Argentine writer whose work had been unjustifiably neglected abroad, issued *Cuentos completos.* In Mexico Juan García Ponce's new novel. *Unión,* proved to be a love story much in the mood of his earlier writing. Among recent Peruvian novels the most interesting were Marcos Yauri Montero's *El otoño después de mil años,* which won the Casa de las Américas Prize in 1974, and Fernando Ampuero's *Mamotreto.*

Poetry. Some interesting critical works with a bearing on poetry appeared in 1975, notably Octavio Paz's *Children of the Mire: Modern Poetry from Romanticism to the Avant-Garde,* the text of his Charles Eliot Norton lectures at Harvard for 1971–72. This is an essay of major theoretical importance and a brilliant analysis of modern movements in poetry. The Nicaraguan writer José Coronel Urteche, who for decades had been instrumental in introducing modern North American poetry to Latin America, also brought out a book of critical essays, *Rápido tránsito.* In other respects the year was an arid one for poetry except for the publication of retrospective collections

Jorge Luis Borges, pride of Argentina and author of "El libro de arena."

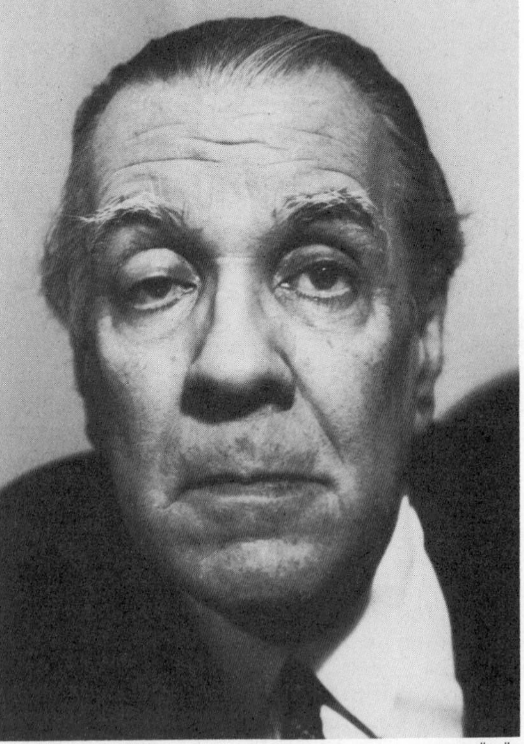

LUTFI ÖZKÖK

LUTFI ÖZKÖK

The year 1975 brought Cuban novelist Alejo Carpentier the Cino de Duca Prize and also saw the publication of his "Concierto barroco."

by several established poets. In Peru Juan Gonzalo Rose brought out an *Obra poética* and Javier Sologuren published a collection of translations from Swiss, Italian, and French, *Las uvas del racimo.* In Argentina an *Antología poética* of the poetry of the recently deceased Raúl González Tuñón provided interesting insights into one of the members of the Boedo group of writers; and one of Argentina's most important poets, Juan Gelman, brought out an *Obra poética,* which included all his poetry up to and including *Relaciones* (1973). There were several new collections by established poets: *Tierra que habla* by the Nicaraguan poet Pablo Antonio Cuadra, *Cuaderno paralelo* by the Cuban Roberto Fernández Retamar, *Informe personal sobre la situación* by Jorge Enrique Adoum of Ecuador, *Museo salvage* by the Argentine poet Olga Orozco, and *El que a hierro mata* by Hernán Lavín of Chile. Of great interest to all poetry lovers this year was the long-awaited first volume of popular poetry collected by Margit Frenk in the *Cancionero folklórico.*

(JEAN FRANCO)

PORTUGUESE

Portugal. With publishers' lists and booksellers' displays virtually restricted to political titles, readers, deprived of alternatives, appeared to confirm the belief that there was no market for anything else. In fact, the constant political tension made it difficult for readers and writers alike to bring their minds to bear on literature. Among the few volumes of new verse were A. Ramos Rosa's *Animal Olhar,* Fiama Brandão's *Novas Visões do Passado,* and *Sem Palavras nem Coisas* by A.-F. Alexandre.

In his semiautobiographical *Cão Velho entre Flores* (1974)—a *Bildungsroman* with mingled echoes of Joyce, the archetypal Quest, and *Huckleberry Finn* —Baptista Bastos superimposed the map of modern Lisbon on that of Vasco da Gama's voyage in *The Lusiads,* restating Camões' epic in terms of a working-class child's progress to manhood in the 1940s: a temporal journey epitomized in a long summer day's return on foot from the far East to the far West of the capital in the company of a mysterious "Magician" (Camões himself?). Vergílio Ferreira's *Rápida, a Sombra,* while breaking no new ground, maintained his usual high standard, and was perhaps the best full-length novel of the year.

The greater adaptability of the theatre to changed conditions was reflected almost exclusively in the conversion of the traditional Lisbon revue into a vehicle of political satire, rather than in drama. In criticism as well, political concerns were conspicuous in the two most significant large-scale works to appear during the period under review: Alexandre Pinheiro Torres' study of a modern social poet, *Vida e Obra de José Gomes Ferreira,* and *Nós: uma Leitura de Cesário Verde,* a brilliant revaluation by Helder Macedo that firmly established Verde as the greatest 19th-century poet in the language.

(STEPHEN RECKERT)

Brazil. The most striking publications in 1975 were the *Novo Dicionário da Língua Portuguesa,* edited by Aurélio Buarque de Holanda, and the *Enciclopédia Mirador Internacional,* edited by Antônio Houaiss. The dictionary, with 140,000 to 150,000 entries, and the encyclopaedia, in 20 volumes and 11,000 pages, far surpassed any similar projects previously undertaken in Brazil and represented a level of scholarship comparable to that of other such projects produced in countries with long scholarly traditions. There were interesting works of fiction, long and short, and several noteworthy books of nonfiction. In many ways the most fascinating of all was Gilberto Freyre's *Tempo Morto e Outros Tempos,* excerpts from diaries kept between his 14th and 30th year. They furnished a picture of a brilliant youth who, as he grew up in Brazil and studied in the U.S. and Europe, developed the culture and the broad interests that were to give depth to his mature writings. Four veterans published novels; Rachel de Queiroz's first novel since 1939, *Dôra, Doralina,* has as its protagonist a familiar figure, a young woman who leaves her farm home in Ceará to seek other experiences. Dinah Silveira de Queiroz novelized the life of Christ in *Eu Venho, Memorial do Cristo.* The playwright Guilherme de Figueiredo wrote his second novel, *14 Tilsitt, Paris,* and José Geraldo Vieira continued his career of 55 years with *A Mais Que Branca,* which portrays Rio life in the middle of the 20th century. Another good book by a woman was Elisa Lispector's existentialist *A Última Porta.*

There was a spate of collections of short stories and novellas representing different literary trends. Several of the established short story writers brought out excellent books: Rubem Fonseca wrote *Feliz ano Nova;* Dalton Trevisan *A Faca na Mão;* and Clarice Lispector *Visão do Esplendor.* The poet Renata Pallotini brought together her first collection of short stories, *Maté É a Cor da Viuvez.* Rachel Jardim's "estórias," *Cheiros e Ruidos,* was based on recollections of childhood and youth in a provincial town.

The field of nonfiction was well represented by worthwhile books. Joaquim Mattoso Câmara's posthumous *História e Estrutura da Língua-Portuguesa* was a notable contribution to the study of Portuguese linguistics. *O Governo Castelo Branco* was a solidly documented study by Luís Viana Filho, chief of Castelo Branco's civil Cabinet and first minister of justice of his government. Two other books dealing with the period were Hélio Silva's *Golpe ou Contra-Golpe* and Carlos Castelo Branco's *A Revolução de 1964*. Fernando Pedreira's *Brasil Político* consisted of essays on the political development of the country. *Formas Criativas no Desenvolvimento do Brasil* by Mário Simonsen and Roberto Campos was an analysis of the country's fiscal, economic, and monetary policies, and the anthropologist Thales de Azevedo questioned the genuineness of Brazilian racial tolerance in *Democracia Racial*.

(RAYMOND S. SAYERS)

NOVOSTI

Historical novelist, poet, and playwright Konstantin Simonov published "Days of the War" to add to his long list of works dealing with World War II.

RUSSIAN

Soviet Literature. The 1974–75 period saw the publication of many outstanding works of fiction and nonfiction. The Soviet people's experiences in World War II (the "Great Patriotic War") were portrayed in different genres and styles, and especially in epic fiction and fictionalized documentary works. Konstantin Simonov's *Days of the War*, written in diary form, covered the events of the war in accurate detail; Aleksandr Chakovsky's *The Blockade*, describing the heroic defense of Leningrad, was largely based on documentary material; in Yury Bondarev's *The Shore* and Vasil Bykov's psychological narrative *The Pack of Wolves* (translated from Belorussian) the story of the tragic days of the war was closely interwoven with latter-day events.

A number of works were devoted to Allied cooperation in the war years. K. Kudiyevsky's novel *The Bitter Fog of the Atlantic* celebrated the courage of Soviet, British, and U.S. sailors fighting together against the common enemy, while Savva Dangulov's *Kuznetsky Most Street* was concerned with the activities of Soviet and foreign diplomats and Allied leaders, and with the strategic plans of the two sides locked in combat.

Historical events that had left a deep imprint on the lives of different nationalities of the Soviet Union were described in Arseny Semyonov's short novel *The Edge of the World*, about the first Russian explorers of Siberia and the Soviet Far East; in I. Yesenberlin's novel *The Charmed Sword* (translated from Kazakh), about the emergence of the Kazakh state after the fall of the Golden Horde; in Vasily Lebedev's novel *The Doomed Will*, about the peasant revolt led by Kondrati Bulavin; and in I. Kalashnikov's novel *The Cruel Age*, about the first years of Genghis Khan's rule.

Soviet poet Rasul Gamzatov.

NOVOSTI

Dramatic works included M. Shatrov's *Weather Forecast*, G. Nikitin's *My Friend Mozart*, S. Dneprov's screenplay *A Front Without Flanks*, and E. Pashnev and G. Drozdov's reportage *The Chronicle of One Day*, about the coup against Chile's President Allende.

Much poetry was published during the year, and again the 30th anniversary of victory in the Great Patriotic War provided the theme for many collections. Among these were N. Dorizo's *The Sword of Victory. Verses, Poems and Songs*, Yu. Drunina's *The Star of the Trenches. New Poems*, and K. Vanshenkin's *Campfire Reminiscences. Wartime Lyrics*. Historical themes predominated in Ya. Smelyakov's *Verses of Many Years*, B. Kunyayev's *Devotion. Poems*, I. Molchanov's *Half a Century. Verses*, and G. Korshak's *The Stellar Hour*. The unity of the Soviet peoples was the underlying theme of *Winds of Different Colours* (collected verse by various authors), I. Ulyanova's *Birch Tree Rain*, A. Roshka's *Steel and Flint* (translated from Moldavian), and S. Eraliyev's *Herald's Word* (from Kirgiz).

State prizes for literature went to, among others, F. Abramov for his trilogy *Priasliny;* V. Bykov for *Obelisk* and *Live to See the Dawn;* B. Vasilyev for his short novel and screenplay *It's Quiet Here in the Morning;* K. Kuliyev for his verse collection *The Book of the Earth;* L. Martynov for his verses *Hyperboles;* and A. Nurpinsov for his trilogy *Sweat and Blood*.

(NOVOSTI)

Expatriate Russian Literature. Inevitably the copious works and formidably accusing personality of Aleksandr I. Solzhenitsyn continued to dominate the Russian expatriate scene in 1975. There were few signs, especially in fiction, from the writers who had left the Soviet Union since 1973 that a new course of the stream of experimental writing that flowed so vigorously in the U.S.S.R. in the 1920s might somehow emerge from underground. The wild symbolist novella published in London with the title of *Nobody* was a sole modest freshet, a *samizdat* work dated 1966.

Solzhenitsyn, with his almost archaic style, was not to be overlooked, however, like the atavistic history he insisted on bearing witness to, however inconvenient it might be in the year of the Helsinki agreement. His lengthening time in exile left his energies and sense of mission undimmed, and with more of him and his work and contradictions plainly in view he began to emerge as a less idealized but no less extraordinary figure than the doyen of "dissident Moscow writers" established when Nikita Khrushchev put Solzhenitsyn's fame into orbit with the publication of *One Day in the Life of Ivan Denisovitch* in 1962. His unrelenting reluctance to allow Khrushchev some moral credit as a uniquely reformed and reforming character among the post-Stalin leadership troubled many Western liberals and socialists. More widely antagonizing was his claim to be above the political battle. "I insist that not only am I no politician but that I have no political ideas," he affirmed in an interview given in the spring in which he also described Henry Kissinger's Vietnam cease-fire agreement as different "in no way from the Munich agreement signed with Hitler."

Solzhenitsyn produced two works in the course of the year. *Bodalsya Telenoks Dubom* ("The Calf Butting the Oak"), published in Russian in Paris, was an absorbing book of "literary memoirs" setting out his attempts to get his works published in Moscow, his fights with the Writers' Union, and his friendship with Aleksandr Tvardovsky of *Novy Mir,* together with a commentary on his own writings and some extraordinary descriptions of how eventually he smuggled them out of the country. *From Under the Rubble,* the other volume, consisted of essays by him and six writers still living in the Soviet Union, consciously echoing the Orthodox Christian, quietist position adopted in *Landmarks,* a famous conservative manifesto of 1909.

A possible focus for a new aesthetic, the ex-*Novy Mir* critic Andrey Sinyavsky appeared in an interview published in Paris in April to launch his large and very personal study of Gogol. ("My speciality is creating images by a process of transformation, and that is all. . . . I have no programme except art.") But Vladimir Maximov's *Seven Days of Creation,* published in London in May, an account of the lives of the Soviet industrial proletariat painted in strong primary colours, was squarely in the realist tradition.

(W. L. WEBB)

GREEK

The fall of the dictatorship in July 1974 produced various changes in intellectual life in Greece, creating a democratic climate absent in that country, except briefly, since 1936. The new climate permitted the repatriation of intellectuals who had fled after the coup of 1967, and also of figures like Dimitris Hatzis —the most significant prose writer of the generation of 1940—who had been in exile since the Civil War. The end of censorship stimulated the immediate appearance of numerous political, sociological, and historical books about the dictatorship, the German occupation, the Resistance (1941–44), and the Civil War (1946–49).

The calamity of the dictatorship inspired one of the most significant publications of 1975, Kostas Varnalis' posthumous *Orgi laou,* a collection of bitter, enraged, sarcastic, and satirical poems by an outstanding poet of the Greek left. Other poetry inspired by the dictatorship and expressing the people's rage, despair, or resistance included Nikiforos Vrettakos' *Diamartiria,* Kostas Stergiopoulos' *Eklipsi,* Yiorgos Yeralis' *Elliniki nikhta,* and Yannis Ritsos' *Kodonostasio.* The prolific Ritsos published four additional works in 1975. *O tikhos mesa ston kathrefti* and *Hartina* consisted of epigrammatic, sometimes cryptic poems in which the real and the imaginary alternate within a context of nightmare. *Petrinos khronos* made available the poems written by Ritsos in the Makronisos concentration camp in 1949, none of which could have been published previously in Greece. *Imnos kai thrinos yia tin Kipro* expressed the people's sentiments after the Turkish invasion of Cyprus. Another important publication of 1975 was *Ta eterothali,* a volume which brought together all of Odysseas Elytis' previously uncollected poems.

The most significant novel of 1975 was Aris Alexandrou's *To kivotio,* about the Civil War. Menis Koumandareas' *Viotekhnia Ialikon* traced the defeat of individuals by their society. Spiros Plaskovitis' *To sirmatoplegma,* a collection of short stories composed in prison, brought personal experience to its treatment of the dictatorship. Vasilis Vasilikos' *Glafkos Thrasakis* was drawn from the author's vicissitudes while he was exiled in Western Europe. Also noteworthy were Maro Douka's *I pigada* and Hatzis' *Diigimata.* The new climate permitted Hatzis to reissue an earlier work that had been banned: *Fotia,* the first prose narrative to treat the Resistance. The year also saw the posthumous publication of George Seferis' only novel, *Exi kai mia nikhtes stin Akropoli.*

Elytis' *Anikhta hartia,* Ritsos' *Meletes,* and the expanded edition of Seferis' *Dokimes* were among the most important essay collections published in 1975. In these, the three leading poets of the generation of 1930 illuminated not only their own poetry but also the aesthetic and ideological tendencies of their generation. The same might be said of Seferis' two posthumous volumes of memoirs: *Meres A, 16 Fevrouariou 1925–17 Avgoustou 1931* and *Meres tou 1945–51.*

(CHRISTOS ALEXIOU)

The relaxation of censorship in Greece resulted in a number of significant publications in 1975, including poet Yannis Ritsos' "Petrinos khronos," which included poems written when Ritsos was incarcerated at the Makronisos concentration camp.

NICHOLAS TSIKOURIAS—GREEK PHOTO AGENCY/KEYSTONE

EASTERN EUROPEAN LITERATURE

Polish. In Polish publishing circles the date of publication is often anachronistic. For various reasons books regularly appear bearing the previous year's date, and 1975 was no exception. Drama is worst affected: plays submitted for publication to *Dialog* (the literary organ for theatre and drama) often appear two or three years late. For example, *White Marriage* by Tadeusz Rozewicz was written in 1973, published in 1974, and produced in 1975. The play, undoubtedly Rozewicz' finest work and the best example of postwar Polish drama, was scheduled for production in dozens of theatres throughout the world. In this tragicomedy Rozewicz dealt honestly with the subject of sex and the effect of traditional role-playing by both men and women. With his new collection of plays, *Dialogues,* Stanislaw Grochowiak demonstrated conclusively that he belongs among the best of modern dramatists. Several notable works about the theatre also appeared: *The History of*

THOMAS VICTOR

Polish poet Zbigniew Herbert, author of the acclaimed "Mr. Cogito."

Puppet Theaters, volume 2, including the period from 1800 to the present, richly illustrated, by Henryk Jurkowski; and *Apocalypsis Cum Figuris* by Malgorzata Dzieduszycka, a description of Grotowski's final theatrical production.

Several interesting novels made up for previous uneventful years: *Microclimate* by Zofia Posmysz, a psychological study of a divorcee who involuntarily gets caught up in the lives of people with real and imagined problems; *A Bet on an Unlucky Horse* by Zdzislaw Uminski, a sometimes controversial depiction of people who return to ruined Warsaw and about their failure to understand and accept postwar sociopolitical changes; *Death Knell* by Stanislaw Grochowiak, the eminent poet-dramatist who was fast becoming an eminent novelist; and *The Anatomical Atlas of Love* by Michal Choromanski, a posthumously published unfinished novel.

A number of collections by distinguished poets were published and works of deceased poets were reissued. *Poems and Notes* by Julian Przybos, who died in 1970, included some of his finest lyrics and notes regarding the circumstances under which the poems were written. Zbigniew Herbert astounded critics with *Mr. Cogito,* translated into 15 languages and dramatized.

An important publishing project was the monumental *History of Polish Literature Series,* under the editorship of the recently deceased Kazimierz Wyka. Three excellent volumes had appeared (with subsequent augmented editions to follow): *The Enlightenment* by Miecyzslaw Klimowicz, *The Baroque* by Czeslaw Hernas, and *The Renaissance* by Jerzy Ziomek. These studies marked the first attempt in Poland at a definitive approach to literary periods. Two Polish writers were nominated for the prestigious *Books Abroad* Neustadt Prize: Tadeusz Rozewicz and Czeslaw Milosz.

(EDWARD J. CZERWINSKI)

Czechoslovakian. Since the mid-1960s the literature of Czechoslovakia has experienced a significant rebirth. It was gradually able to free itself from the propagandistic norms of socialist realism and address itself to significant moral, social, and political issues. The works that prepared the ground for a critical reexamination of the effects of Stalinism on the nation's moral fibre were Vladimir Minac's *Notes* and Ladislav Mnacko's *Belated Reports.*

Czechoslovakian novelist Ludvik Vaculik, author of "The Axe."

LUTFI ÖZKÖK

Other works, more subtle in their design but even more profound in their exploration of Czechoslovakian society, began to appear in the late 1960s. Foremost among these was Ludvik Vaculik's *The Axe,* one of the outstanding prose masterpieces of recent literature. The novel was a fictionalized reminiscence of an intense emotional confrontation between the narrator (a questioning critic) and his father (a dedicated Communist).

Milan Kundera's novel *The Joke* examined how dogmatic ideologies poison human behaviour, forcing men into situations where all personal attempts to forge a more meaningful existence are futile. Bohumil Hrabal's collections of short stories and his novel *Closely Watched Trains* used the comic and the grotesque in opposing the thoughts and concerns of the eccentric individual to the demands of governments and ideologies. The novellas of Ivan Klima, *The Jury* and *A Ship Named Hope,* employed compelling and haunting settings in an allegorical exploration of ever tightening constrictions on individual freedom. Echoes of Kafka were also to be found in Klima's highly influential absurdist drama *The Castle.*

Poetry since the mid-1960s has been distinguished by its experimentation with free verse forms and by its willingness to confront themes of personal and social morality. The poems of Miroslav Holub created precise and sober images for the moral paradoxes that confront this age. Jan Skacel's lyrics spoke of basic human values and truths, searching with great pathos for a moral order that would be in harmony with the laws of nature.

In about 1970 stringent censorship was reinstituted in Czechoslovakia, accompanied by an outright ban on authors who supported the Dubcek government of 1968 and refused to recant their beliefs. Reprisals such as confiscation of personal manuscripts steadily increased. Significant novels by Kundera and Vaculik were published abroad, but not in Czechoslovakia. Even the work of talented writers who were allowed to continue to publish, most notably the stylistically rich prose of Vladimir Paral and Ladislav Fuks, declined in quality under the reimposed constraints. The most significant works of recent years, produced under extremely difficult personal circumstances, were the new novels of Vaculik and Klima. These, however, might remain in manuscript form until the government allowed its prominent writers to publish.

(HERBERT J. EAGLE)

Hungarian. The most talked-about Hungarian literary work of 1975—George Konrad's *A varosalapito* —remained in manuscript, the delay in publication apparently prompted by political considerations. More experimental in form and more brilliant in content than *The Case Worker,* his highly acclaimed first novel, *A varosalapito* ("The City-Founder") was a stunning fusion of abstract and concrete—of political and personal history. Ironically, Konrad's social criticism was quite oblique, for while his focus was a medium-sized Eastern European city, a living memorial to centuries of turbulent history, he dealt ultimately with larger, supraregional realities. Another writer, Miklos Meszoly, whose intensely intellectual, innovative prose bears a resemblance to Konrad's, was more fortunate; after years of mild official disapproval and indifference, his collected stories were published under the title *Alakulasok* ("Transfigurations"). The latest work of yet another experimentalist—Gyula Hernadi's *Voros rekviem* ("Red

LUTFI ÖZKÖK

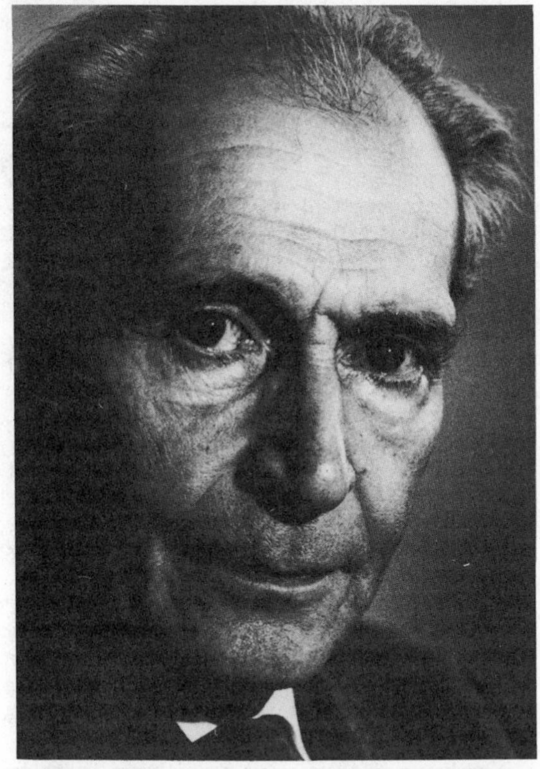

Tibor Dery, doyen of Hungarian literature, contributed two works in 1975.

Requiem")—was openly political; in a series of narrative fragments Hernadi depicted the final hours of a condemned Communist revolutionary.

Some of the more conventionally realist novels of the year were written by Gyorgy Moldova, Gyula Fekete, and Erzhebet Galgoczi. Moldova's *A Szent Imre-indulo* ("Saint Emeric-March") concerned itself with the tragedy of Hungarian Jewry in 1944. Fekete's *Mezeshetek* ("Honeymoon") also had a historical background; it was a new bride's diary, begun in 1945, immediately after the war. In her new novel *Kozos bun* ("Collective Guilt"), Erzhebet Galgoczi explored moral dilemmas faced by people in a small village in the wake of the 1956 uprising.

Octogenarian Tibor Dery, the grand old man of Hungarian literature, published two works in 1975: *A felfulu* ("The One-Eared Young Man"), a satiric thriller, and *Kyvagioken,* a mock-autobiography. Dery's ironic ruminations on human foibles and societal ills were still captivating, although in recent years they had become somewhat self-conscious and predictable. The problems of old age seem to be perennial themes in contemporary Hungarian literature—perhaps because there are so many aging Hungarian writers. Fear of death and nostalgia for the past preoccupied Zoltan Zelk in his new collection of poems, *Ahogy a koteltan-cosok* ("As the Tightrope-Walkers"). A somewhat younger writer, Ivan Mandy also tried to capture the ambience of a fast-vanishing world in his dreamlike narratives; *Zsamboky mozija* ("Zsamboky's Movie") was the title of Mandy's latest collection of stories, in which the well-known hero is visited by the glamorous Hollywood stars of the 1920s and '30s.

Laszlo Nemeth, one of the most influential figures in modern Hungarian literature, as well as Jozsef Lengyel (*see* OBITUARIES), the noted novelist, died in 1975.

(IVAN SANDERS)

Romanian. The first volume of Marin Preda's *Delirul* was popular not only because it came from the man considered by many as Romania's leading novelist, but also because it treated in a rather personal manner situations and characters linked to the years 1940 and 1941 (the Fascist revolt in Romania leading to the establishment of a military dictatorship and intervention in World War II). While much of the straight historical comment seemed less than sophisticated, the aesthetically valid episodes of the book remained those dealing with the effect of the events on the village community and on the Moromete family. Ion Lancranjan's huge two-volume *Caloianul* was a partly successful attempt to describe Romania's recent past through the eyes of a talented writer who, owing to cynicism, self-deceit, and cowardice, gradually abandons during the 1950s his ideals and his willingness to speak up for his own peasant background as well as for the dignity of his fellow writers. Al. Ivasiuc gave in *Iluminatii* another of his novelistic disquisitions on the relationship between the intellectuals and the socialist system. Radu Petrescu's *O singura virsta,* M. H. Simionescu's whimsical travelogues, and particularly Tudor Topa's *Incerearea scriitorului* confirmed again that a psychological-intellectual vein in Romanian fiction was still strong, if less apparent. Among the younger writers, George Balaita's applauded *Lumea in doua zile* was valuable perhaps more for its accurate portrayal of provincial life in contemporary Romania than for a rather improbable detective-story plot.

In poetry the most important publishing events were the massive retrospective selections of the works of Nichita Stanescu and Ion Alexandru, both leading poets of the generation that in the mid-1960s brought about a genuine revival of modern Romanian poetry.

That 1975 was somehow a retrospective year, a year devoted to accounting and analyzing, was seen also in the spate of interesting books of literary history and criticism published. Foremost among these were the studies of Dumitru Micu (*Gindirea si gindirismul*) and Ileana Vrancea (*Confruntari in critica deceniilor IV–VII*). The first discussed a leading literary journal

LUTFI ÖZKÖK

Ion Alexandru, leading Romanian poet who had a retrospective selection of his work published in 1975.

Mahmoud Darwish, Palestinian poet.

of the 1920s and '30s, the intention of which was to impose a traditionalist and irrationalist directive on Romanian intellectual life, and investigated the varying involvement of prominent writers with the journal, a subject that had not yet been approached by critics. The second analyzed a parallel literary current (the Lovinescu group) which, the author claimed, had been mistakenly labeled "aestheticist"; in fact, it was functioning as a vigorous opposition to the racist and nationalist distortions of literature in the 1930s. Among other scholarly and balanced reinterpretations of the Romanian literary heritage were the studies of 19th-century literature by Z. Ornea, M. Gafita, and P. Cornea. *Engrame* by I. Negoitescu confirmed again the position of its author as a leading practitioner of aesthetic criticism.

(VIRGIL PETRE NEMOIANU)

Serbian. Serbian literature, like other Yugoslav literatures, was dominated in 1975 by two events: the death of Ivo Andric (*see* OBITUARIES) and the eighth congress of the Union of Yugoslav Writers, held in Belgrade, October 2–4. The death of Andric, the only Yugoslav Nobel Prize winner (1961), marked the end of an illustrious career dating back to 1918. The key themes of the congress were the role of the writer in a self-managing society, the development of Yugoslav literatures since 1945, theoretical problems of contemporary literature, and the role and state of book publishing.

In fiction Dobrica Cosic added a third volume of *Vreme smrti* ("The Time of Death") to his semihistorical epic of World War I. Branko Copic, another veteran writer, pursued in *Delije na Bihacu* ("The Heroes of Bihac") his favourite theme of the War of Liberation in Bosnia. In poetry, Ivan V. Lalic's *Smetnje na vezama* ("Interference in Connections"), Adam Puslojic's *Religija psa* ("The Religion of a Dog"), and Vitomir Markovic's *Nasmejana zrtva* ("A Smiling Victim") were outstanding. The most remarkable book of the season, however, was Milan Kasanin's sweeping *Srpska knjizevnost u srednjem veku* ("Serbian Literature in the Middle Ages").

Croatian. Croatian literature in 1975 was also preoccupied with the eighth congress of the Union of Yugoslav Writers. A venerable Croatian writer, Gustav Krklec, was reelected the president of the union, while Predrag Matvejevic delivered the keynote address. Matvejevic's theoretical work *Prema novom kulturnom stvaralastvu* ("Toward a New Cultural Creativity"), dealing with the basic concepts of cultural activity in the society, further established him as the driving force in renewed attempts to alert writers to the social nature of their work. Otherwise 1975 had again revealed a puzzling stagnation in Croatian publishing. In fiction Vojin Jelic returned in *Pobozni djavo* ("A Pious Devil") to the tragic events in his home region in World War II. The novel *Zagrepcanka* ("A Zagreb Woman") by Branislav Glumac enjoyed great success despite the absence of punctuation. In poetry the recipient of the NIN Prize, Jure Franicevic-Plocar, published a new collection, *Zedna sidra* ("Thirsty Sails"). A new magazine for poetry, *Pjesnici* ("Poets"), was launched by the noted poet Milivoj Slavicek. In criticism the leading Croatian writer Miroslav Krleza continued to receive the most attention. The first of five volumes of his quotations and *Struktura Krlezinih "Zastava"* ("The Structure of Krleza's *Banners*") by Stanko Lasic were published.

(VASA D. MIHAILOVICH)

ARABIC

Jack Burk's book *Langage arab du présent* expressed the efforts Arabs were making to absorb current cultural trends and to transfer themselves from the past into the horizons of tomorrow. Like other peoples in the third world, Arabs seemed unable to affirm their civilization except by raising two pillars: liberation from imperialism and an industrial and social revolution. The modern Arab literary movement was thus in a state of evolution. Dramatists, particularly, were confronting a new art that was not rooted in the classical Arab tradition and were exploring new dimensions in social realism and experimental and revolutionary theatre.

In 1975 dramatists Samih al-Qasem of Palestine, Sa'dallah Wannous of Syria, Sa'd Iddin Wahbeh of Egypt, and Yousef al-Ani' and Abdel Amir Mu'alaa of Iraq seemed most representative. The group Al-Ballaline ("The Balloons"), founded by François Abu Salem, struggled to produce plays, the last of which was *Sarkhat Al Sa'alik* ("The Cry of the Strays"). Samih al-Qasem of Palestine constantly produced plays for this group, starting with *Quarakash* and most recently *Al-Ibn* ("The Son"). Yousef el-Sayegh of Iraq, influenced by Tawfiq el-Hakim of Egypt, further developed the "drama novel" in his latest, *Almassafa* ("The Distance").

Novelists and short story writers were trying to solve an equation between tradition and modernization. Al-Tayyeb Saleh of the Sudan, Yousef Iddriss of Egypt, and Katib Yassin of Algeria started this attempt. They were followed by Jamal Alghitani of Egypt with *Awraq Sh'ab A'sh Munthu Alfi A'm* ("The Notes or Papers of a Young Man Who Lived 1,000 Years Ago") and Salah Hafez, also of Egypt, with *Alkitar* ("The Train").

Egyptian Najib Mahfouz excelled in his recent works *Hikayat Ha'ratuna* ("The Stories of Our Quarter") and *Al Karnak* ("The Karnak"). *Al Ya'ter* ("The Anchor") and *Bakaya Sowar* ("The Remainder

Syrian novelist Hanna Minah gained kudos for two new works.

RAHEB

of Pictures") by the Syrian Hanna Minah and *Al Wakai Al-Ghariba* ("The Strange Incidents") by Palestinian Emil Habibi also received critical acclaim. UNESCO chose Lebanese Tawfiq Yousef Awwad's *Tawaheen Beirut* ("The Windmills of Beirut") for the 1975 series "Les Écrivains les plus représentatifs de leur temps."

Modern poetry was constantly developing and the poet Adonis gave the movement a very strong innovative impetus, freeing it from the bonds of its traditional structure. His *Al-Aghani al-Thania Li Mehyar al-Dimashki* ("The Second Songs of Mihyar al-Dimashki") was representative. Other successful poets included Mahmoud Darwish (Palestine), Abdel Wahhab al-Bayyati (Iraq), and Amal Dankal (Egypt).

The centre of the more progressive literary activity had transferred from Cairo to other Arab capitals, mainly Beirut, Baghdad, and Damascus, due to the reversion of the Egyptian regime to the classical literary currents.

(ABDUL RAHMAN YAGHI)

JEWISH

Hebrew. The year or two following the 1973 Arab-Israeli war and the ensuing economic hardships had not noticeably discouraged the publication in Israel of volumes in every genre of fiction and nonfiction. A posthumous novel by the Nobel Prize recipient Shmuel Agnon, *Be-hanuto shel Mar Lublin,* appeared, as did a volume of stories, *Paamon ve-Rimmon,* by the late eminent novelist H. Hazaz. The young Abraham Yehoshua struck a more contemporary note in *Ad Horef 1974,* while A. Appelfeld in *Ke-Maia Eidim* again proved faithful to the theme of the Holocaust and its aftermath. Y. Kaniuk's saga *Hasippur Al Doda Shlomtzion Hagedola* was provocative, while B. Tammuz' *Mishlai Bakbukim* described the alienation of the Jew from the West. Of interest were Y. Orpaz' *Baiyit he-Adam Ehad,* Rachel Eytan's *Shidah ve-Shidoth,* S. Golan's *Bericha Lamerchakim Ketsarim,* and Mordecai Tabib's *Ka-Kisev ha-sadeh.*

A comprehensive exposition of the diverse aspects of the Diaspora was J. Tsur's *Deyuknah shel h-Tefutsah,* while Chaim Herzog, Israeli ambassador to the UN, keenly analyzed some of the effects of the 1973 war in *Milhemet Yom Hakippurim.*

A critical study of modern literature was J. Dan's *ha-Mandarin ve-Hanachri;* and H. Barzell in *Sippurai ha-Ahavah shel Sh. Y. Agnon* discussed the love element in this author's writings. *Exzistenzialism* by R. Sigurd was both trenchant and lucid. Y. Bronovsky's slim volume *Massah al ha-Lashon* dealt with the nature of language. Somehow related to this was R. Gurfein's *Milim U-Maiver Lahen.*

To be noted in poetry were three slim volumes by Y. Ratosh, which appeared simultaneously. *Olam Kazeh Olam Kaba* was Y. Tan-Pai's contribution, and I. Pinkas' distinctive *Al Kav Hamashveh* also appeared. Other books published included A. Trainin's *Ha-Shaar Hasotum,* D. Rokeah's *Ir Shezemana Kayitz,* M. Dor's *Mappot Hazeman,* and an elegiac *Shirim* by Nathan Yonathan.

In the U.S. Hebrew literary life was rather subdued. However, there appeared in Israel, posthumously, another volume of the works of A. Zeitlin. One of the writers who emigrated to Israel was Sh. Grodzensky, whose reflections on literature were collected, also posthumously, in *Al Kol Panim.*

(GABRIEL PREIL)

COURTESY, THE NOBEL FOUNDATION, STOCKHOLM

In Shmuel Agnon's posthumous novel "Be-hanuto shel Mar Lublin" a young Agnon relates the problems encountered by Polish Jews in Germany during World War I.

Yiddish. Thematically, Yiddish prose in 1975 was concerned with Jewish life in the interwar period, the tension and struggle between the generations, and the Holocaust and the struggle of its survivors to adjust to new circumstances, as well as with considerably earlier periods. Four novels gave evidence of this trend: Isaac Bashevis Singer's *The Lost Tribe;* Chaim Grade's *The Rabbi's House;* part three of Elya Schechtman's *Erev;* and Nathan Zabare's *In the Middle of the Day,* about Jewish life in medieval France, Italy, and Spain.

Haskel Tabachnikov's *Borshever Motifs* dealt with the reconstruction of the *shtetl* in Russia during the 1930s. Rivka Rubin, in *A Thread Is Being Woven,* told about World War II and Nazi atrocities. Wolf Tambor's *Marmorosh Stories* and D. Zakalik's *The Return* dealt with World War II and its aftermath.

In poetry, Hirsh Osherovitch's *The World of Sacrifices* had an intellectual tone; Arie Shamri's *Rings in Stem* was rich in imagery and symbolism; Hillel Shargel's *A Tree in the Window* was visionary and melancholy. In *In Imagination Sealed* M. Shklar lamented those who perished in the Holocaust. Moshe Nadir nostalgically recaptured his youth in *A Day in a Garden,* as did Alef Katz in *Morning Star.* The late Hasidic scion Yakov Friedman's three-volume *Poems and Songs* constituted a major contribution to contemporary Yiddish poetry, combining with moving expressiveness both traditional and modern Jewishness.

In the final volume of his trilogy "World Jewry," *Old-New Problems,* Vladimir Grossman analyzed current issues with remarkable vigour. Zev Baumgold collected a number of his essays concerning Zionist and Israeli problems in *Footprints of a Generation.* Itzkhak Janosowicz discussed a number of literary and topical issues in *Without Exclamation Points,* while Yaakov J. Maitlis' *Wake of Generations* contained erudite essays on biblical themes and evaluations of some leading writers. The poet M. Szulsztein reminisced about life in France during the occupation in *A Link in a Link,* concerning several Yiddish writers who perished in that period. In *From Josephus to Ringelblum* Tevia Groll discussed Jewish historians and Jewish historiography.

(ELIAS SCHULMAN)

CHINESE

The short story dominated the literary scene in Taiwan in 1975. The major theme—explored with a vivid sense of time and place in such collections as Shu Ch'ang's *Prose Selection,* Wang Chen-ho's *Dowry in a Bullock Cart, Selected Stories of 1974* edited by Cheng Chieh-kuang and T'an Yun-sheng, and Kao Shang-ch'in's *Collected Contemporary Chinese Stories*—revolved around the fate of small men from small places and their search for personal authenticity. Huang Ch'un-ming's works represented this genre at its best. His *Young Widows* dealt with the life of villagers, workers, the petty bourgeois class, and those existing beyond the fringe of respectability.

Two longer works deserve attention. *The Diary of Hsia Tsi-an,* brought out by C. T. Hsia, charted the daily naivetés, insights, searing self-analysis, and inconsequential meanderings of an intelligent, engaging Prufrockian personality in love at a distance. In Chang Hsi-kuo's novel *The Chess Prodigy,* the lower-middle-class world continued to provide the mundane setting for a witty yet compassionate dramatization of the meaning of genius to society and the experiences of an artist of modest talents who finally reaches an accommodation with that sense of blankness that is in the heart of things.

In the literature of mainland China, there was considerably more interest in society than sensibility. Perhaps the aim of Chinese writers to create a literature for the broad masses was best exemplified in such poetry collections as Mo Shaoyün's *With Ardour We March, Shanghai New Folksongs,* published by the People's Publication Press, and *I Make Iron Horses for My Country,* written by factory hands and published by the People's Literature Press. Some of these poems were topical, criticizing Lin Piao and Confucius in ringing tones. Yet they displayed a directness and simplicity of language that justified their role as folk literature.

The problems of collectivization and migration to remote regions were explored in such novels as Chou Chia-chun's *Mountain Wind,* Wang Shih-mei's *Iron Whirlwind,* and K'e Fei's *Spring Tide Hurrying,* dramatizing through a series of confrontations the communications gap between the politically committed and the lukewarm.

(JOHN KWAN-TERRY)

JAPANESE

The predominant mood of the Japanese literary scene in 1975 seemed to be introspective, reflective, and even nostalgic. One factor was, of course, economic, and the sales of literary books decreased remarkably. Some publishers seemed to be more engrossed with paperback editions of previously issued books than with new ones.

It was a full 30 years since the end of the war in the Pacific, and this proved to be long enough for the Japanese to reflect upon the war years with detachment and objectivity. Hiroyuki Akawa's *Kuroi ushio* ("Dark Tide") was a monumental war novel, specifically concerned with the reactions and experiences of university graduates in the Japanese Navy. The important characters were killed in action, and the whole mood of the novel was, of course, dark. However, it was a panoramic novel, broad and far-reaching in scope and perspective, and Akawa's style remained effectively cool, objective, and in some situations even humorous. It was an impressive achievement, quite different from the vociferous "protest" novels that proliferated during the postwar years, and symptomatic of the mood of the 1970s.

There were two remarkable autobiographies, or literary memoirs: *Kono hi ano hi* ("Those Days") by Kazuo Ozaki and *Shonen* ("A Boy") by Shohei Ooka. Ozaki's memoir consisted of two big volumes, starting with a vivid evocation of the big earthquake of 1923 and covering the turbulent 20 years until the end of the Pacific war. Ozaki was one of the so-called *watakushi-shosetsuka* ("I" novelists or personal chroniclers), and his recollections were mainly concerned with the private aspect of life. However, his attitude was remarkably frank and straightforward, and he was successful in conveying the uncensored reactions of the average Japanese during those cataclysmic years. The whole memoir, however trivial and personal in detail, read like a vivid and evocative chronicle novel. Ooka's *Shonen* was as factual and detailed in description as *Kono hi ano hi,* probably more so, and the author's preoccupation with the "exact" accuracy of the locations and dates related to his boyhood was sometimes distracting. However, his description of the cultural milieu of the 1910s and '20s was broad in perspective and was effective.

There were several impressive achievements in the short story genre, in which modern Japanese literature has been so remarkable. Tetsuo Miura's *No* ("The Fields") and subsequent stories serialized in *Gunzo* magazine were mainly concerned with rural life in northern Japan. The contrast between the rural and urban ways of life in present-day Japan was portrayed with brilliant skill. Tsuneko Nakasato's *Hanagatami* ("Flower-basket") and Hiroko Takenishi's *Tsuru* ("Cranes") were both impressive collections of short stories by women. They shared something of the technique and atmosphere, both classical and personal, of literature concerned with the traditional aspect of life. Rather nostalgic in tone, they were reminiscent of the hidden continuity found in classical Japanese literature. This was also true of the tour de force novel *Usuzumi no sakura* ("The Old Cherry-tree") by Chiyo Uno, who seemed to owe some of her literary effects to classical dramas, especially the narrative technique in *bunraku* ("puppet theatre").

Tsutomu Minakami's *Ikkyu,* a biographical analysis of the famous Buddhist priest-eccentric of the 16th century, Takeshi Muramatsu's *Themes of Death in Japanese Literature,* Satoshi Wakasugi's *Literary Sketches of Takashi Nagatsuka,* Fujio Noguchi's *My Kafu,* and Kenkichi Yamamoto's *Hakucho Masamune* were important in the areas of biography and literary criticism.

(SHOICHI SAEKI)

See also **Art Sales; Libraries; Nobel Prizes; Philosophy; Publishing; Theatre.**

[621]

ENCYCLOPÆDIA BRITANNICA FILMS. *Bartleby by Herman Melville* (1969); *Dr. Heidegger's Experiment by Nathaniel Hawthorne* (1969); *The Lady, or the Tiger? by Frank Stockton* (1969); *The Lottery by Shirley Jackson* (1969); *Magic Prison* (1969); *My Old Man by Ernest Hemingway* (1969); *James Dickey: Poet* (1970); *Shaw vs. Shakespeare—Part I: The Character of Caesar, Part II: The Tragedy of Julius Caesar, Part III: Caesar and Cleopatra* (1970); *The Deserted Village* (1971); *The Lady of Shalott* (1971); *The Prisoner of Chillon* (1971); *Greek Myths—Part I: Myth as Fiction, History, and Ritual* (1971); *Greek Myths—Part II: Myth as Science, Religion, and Drama* (1971); *Walt Whitman: Poet for a New Age* (1972); *The Crocodile by Fyodor Dostoyevsky* (1973); *The Secret Sharer by Joseph Conrad* (1973); *John Keats: His Life and Death* (1973); *John Keats: Poet* (1973); *The Bible as Literature—Part I: Saga and Story in the Old Testament* (1973); *The Bible as Literature—Part II: History, Poetry and Drama in the Old Testament* (1973); *Talking with Thoreau* (1975); *The Hunt* (1975).

Luxembourg

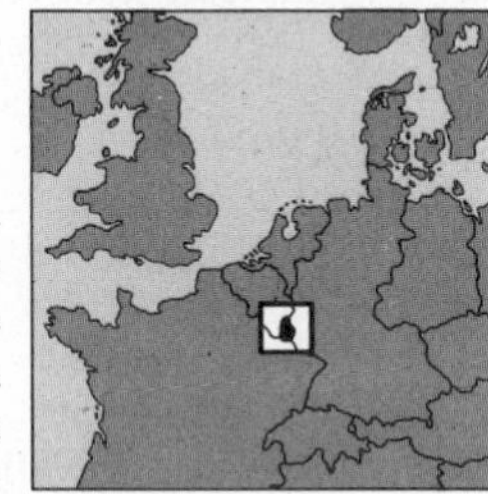

A constitutional monarchy, the Benelux country of Luxembourg is bounded on the east by West Germany, on the south by France, and on the west and north by Belgium. Area: 999 sq.mi, (2,586 sq.km.). Pop. (1975 est.): 357,400. Cap. and largest city: Luxembourg (pop., 1975 est., 78,300). Language: French, German, Luxembourgian. Religion: Roman Catholic 97%. Grand duke, Jean; prime minister in 1975, Gaston Thorn.

Grand Duke Jean, accompanied by Grand Duchess Joséphine-Charlotte and Prime Minister Thorn, arrived in Moscow on June 5, 1975, on an official visit. Speaking at a dinner in honour of his guests, Nikolay Podgorny, chairman of the Presidium of the Supreme Soviet, said that Soviet-Luxembourg relations offered an example of the implementation of the principle of peaceful coexistence of states with different social systems. Replying, the grand duke expressed his satisfaction at the signing of agreements testifying to the common desire to deepen mutually beneficial cooperation. The following day Thorn and Premier Aleksey Kosygin signed agreements on air service, cultural cooperation in 1975-76, and scientific and technical cooperation.

On August 1, in Helsinki, Fin., Thorn signed the Final Act of the Conference on Security and Cooperation in Europe on behalf of Luxembourg. On September 16 he was elected president of the 30th General Assembly of the United Nations in New York City.

During 1975 Mme Colette Flesch, a Liberal, was the mayor of the city of Luxembourg, and Arthur Useldinger, a Communist, was elected mayor of the second-largest town, Esch-sur-Alzette.

(K. M. SMOGORZEWSKI)

[972.A.7]

LUXEMBOURG

Education. (1973–74) Primary, pupils 35,589, teachers 1,691; secondary, pupils 8,214, teachers 739; vocational, pupils 9,631, teachers 874; higher, students 341, teaching staff (1971–72) 125.

Finance. Monetary unit: Luxembourg franc, at par with the Belgian franc, with (Sept. 22, 1975) a free commercial rate of LFr. 40.04 to U.S. $1 (LFr. 82.95 = £1 sterling). Budget (1975 est.): revenue LFr. 24,825,000,000; expenditure LFr. 24,858,000,000. Gross domestic product: (1973) LFr. 70.9 billion; (1972) LFr. 59.2 billion. Cost of living (1970 = 100): (June 1975) 141; (June 1974) 127.

Foreign Trade. *See* BELGIUM.

Transport and Communications. Roads (1973) 4,465 km. (including 25 km. expressways). Motor vehicles in use (1973): passenger 119,700; commercial 10,010. Railways: (1973) 271 km.; traffic (1974) 278 million passenger-km., freight 866 million net ton-km. Air traffic (1973): 125 million passenger-km.; freight 200,000 net ton-km. Telephones (Dec. 1973) 135,000. Radio licenses (Dec. 1972) *c.* 176,000. Television licenses (Dec. 1972) 85,300.

Agriculture. Production (in 000; metric tons; 1974; 1973 in parentheses): wheat *c.* 36 (*c.* 36); oats *c.* 34 (*c.* 34); barley (1973) 56, (1972) 54; potatoes (1973) *c.* 61, (1972) 61; apples (1973) *c.* 11, (1972) 110; grapes *c.* 20 (26); wine (1973) *c.* 12, (1972) 14. Livestock (in 000; May 1974): cattle 216; sheep 3; pigs 91; poultry 269.

Industry. Production (in 000; metric tons; 1974): iron ore (30% metal content) 2,617; pig iron 5,469; crude steel 6,447; electricity (kw-hr.) 2,079,000; manufactured gas (cu.m.; 1972) 19,000.

Malagasy Republic

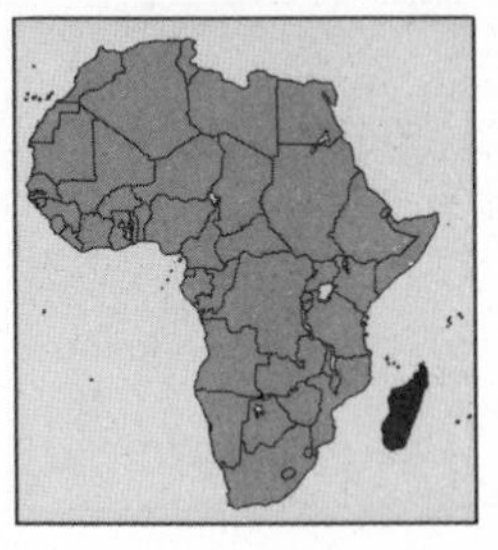

The Malagasy Republic occupies the island of Madagascar and minor adjacent islands in the Indian Ocean off the southeast coast of Africa. Area: 226,444 sq.mi. (586,486 sq.km.). Pop. (1975 est.): 8,020,000. Cap. and largest city: Tananarive (pop., 1972 est., 336,500). Language: French and Malagasy. Religion: Christian (approximately 50%) and traditional tribal beliefs. Heads of government in 1975, Gen. Gabriel Ramanantsoa until January 25, Col. Richard Ratsimandrava February 5–11, Gen. Gilles Andriamahazo from February 11 to June 15, and, from June 15, Comdr. Didier Ratsiraka.

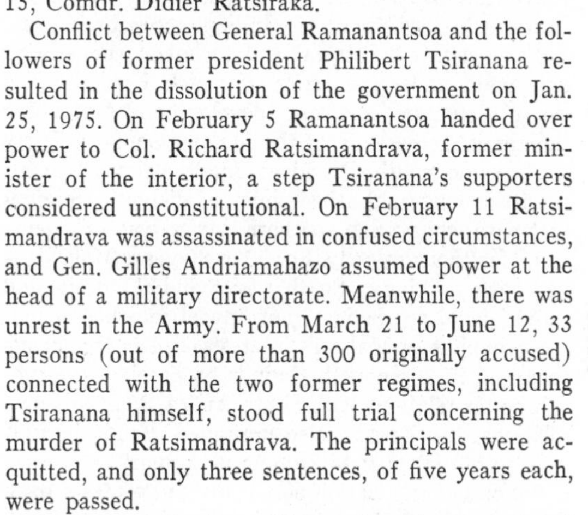

Conflict between General Ramanantsoa and the followers of former president Philibert Tsiranana resulted in the dissolution of the government on Jan. 25, 1975. On February 5 Ramanantsoa handed over power to Col. Richard Ratsimandrava, former minister of the interior, a step Tsiranana's supporters considered unconstitutional. On February 11 Ratsimandrava was assassinated in confused circumstances, and Gen. Gilles Andriamahazo assumed power at the head of a military directorate. Meanwhile, there was unrest in the Army. From March 21 to June 12, 33 persons (out of more than 300 originally accused) connected with the two former regimes, including Tsiranana himself, stood full trial concerning the murder of Ratsimandrava. The principals were acquitted, and only three sentences, of five years each, were passed.

On June 15 the military directorate invested Comdr. Didier Ratsiraka (*see* BIOGRAPHY) as head of state and dissolved itself. Ratsiraka proceeded to nationalize banks and insurance companies and, in September, the country's mineral resources. In a referendum on December 21, Ratsiraka's presidency and a new constitution were approved by 95% of the voters in a 90% turnout. (PHILIPPE DECRAENE)

[978.E.6.c]

MALAGASY REPUBLIC

Education. (1972) Primary, pupils 1,004,000, teachers 15,600; secondary, pupils *c.* 175,000, teachers (1970) 6,858; vocational, pupils 10,200, teachers 684; teacher training, students (1971) 2,019, teachers 215; higher (1971), students 6,683, teaching staff 260.

Finance. Monetary unit: Malagasy franc, at par with the CFA franc, with (Sept. 22, 1975) a parity of MalFr. 50 to the French franc (free rates of MalFr. 227.70 = U.S. $1 and MalFr. 471.75 = £1 sterling). Gold, SDRs, and foreign exchange: (June 1975) U.S. $32.1 million; (June 1974) U.S. $56.2 million. Budget (1974 est.): revenue MalFr. 71 billion, expenditure MalFr. 93.4 billion.

Foreign Trade. (1973) Imports MalFr. 45,160,000,000; exports MalFr. 44,750,000,000. Import sources: France 49%; West Germany 8%; U.S. 7%; Japan 5%. Export destinations: France 37%; U.S. 17%; Réunion 9%; Japan 6%; Malaysia 6%. Main exports: coffee 30%; cloves 9%; vanilla 5%.

Agriculture. Production (in 000; metric tons; 1974; 1973 in parentheses): rice 1,918 (1,848); corn (1973) *c.* 120, (1972) 108; cassava (1973) *c.* 1,300, (1972) 1,233; sweet potatoes (1973) *c.* 350, (1972) 345; potatoes (1973) *c.* 125, (1972) 124; dry beans *c.* 61 (*c.* 61); bananas *c.* 280 (260); oranges (1973) *c.* 65, (1972) *c.* 60; pineapples (1973) *c.* 50, (1972) *c.* 49; peanuts *c.* 50 (*c.* 50); sugar, raw value *c.* 114 (*c.* 104); coffee *c.* 65 (*c.* 65); cotton (1973) *c.* 9, (1972) 9.1; tobacco (1973) *c.* 6, (1972) 5.4; sisal (1973) *c.* 28, (1972) 27; fish catch (1972) 49, (1971) 48. Livestock (in 000; Dec. 1973): cattle *c.* 9,710; sheep *c.* 500; pigs *c.* 610; goats *c.* 900; chickens (1972) *c.* 11,500.

Livestock and Animal Products:
see Agriculture and Food Supplies

Lumber:
see Industrial Review

Lutheran Churches:
see Religion

Macau:
see Dependent States

Machinery and Machine Tools:
see Industrial Review

Madagascar:
see Malagasy Republic

Magazines:
see Publishing

Magnesium:
see Mining and Quarrying

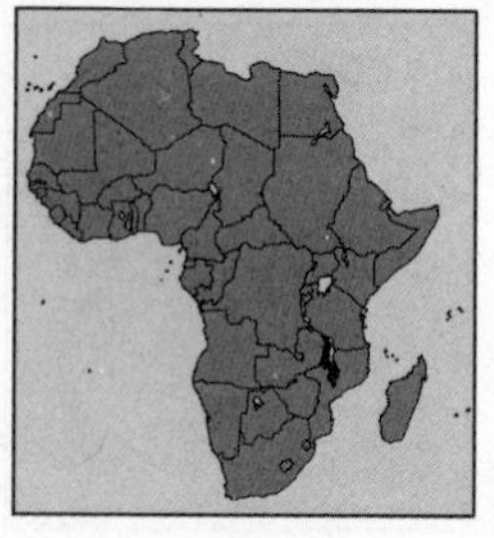

Malawi

A republic and member of the Commonwealth of Nations in east central Africa, Malawi is bounded by Tanzania, Mozambique, and Zambia. Area: 45,747 sq.mi. (118,484 sq.km.). Pop. (1974 est.): 4,916,000. Cap.: Lilongwe (pop., 1974 est., 86,900). Largest city: Blantyre (pop., 1972, 160,100). Language: English (official) and Nyanja (Chichewa). Religion: predominantly traditional beliefs. President in 1975, Hastings Kamuzu Banda.

Although the high cost of oil burdened the country's balance of payments, agricultural production improved in 1975 and foreign investors retained confidence in Malawi's progress. In September France and Malawi signed a cultural and technical cooperation agreement under the terms of which France would assist in economic and social development. Addressing the annual convention of the Malawi Congress Party in the same month, President Banda claimed that his country's long-established policy of dialogue and contact with white-ruled southern Africa was producing results, although slowly. For 70 or 80 years Malawians had been working in South Africa and Rhodesia, and Banda could not believe that boycotting those countries could be in Malawi's interests. Following the attempt of Pres. Kenneth Kaunda of Zambia to establish better relations with South Africa, Malawi's own relations with Zambia also improved. Banda himself paid an official visit to Zambia in January.

Banda's africanization policy aroused protests from the country's 12,000 Asians, mostly subsistence farmers, who feared they would be driven from the land and be unable to find a livelihood in the three already overcrowded towns to which they were to be restricted. Meanwhile, thousands of Jehovah's Witnesses, who had fled six years earlier when their sect was banned, were being forced to leave their refuge in Mozambique and return to Malawi, where reportedly they were being systematically persecuted.

(KENNETH INGHAM)

[978.E.8.b.iii]

MALAWI

Education. (1974–75) Primary, pupils 611,678, teachers 10,524; secondary, pupils 13,900, teachers 694; vocational, pupils 529, teachers 46; teacher training, students 1,283, teachers 95; higher (University of Malawi), students 1,146, teaching staff 101.

Finance. Monetary unit: kwacha, with (Sept. 22, 1975) a free rate of 0.90 kwacha to U.S. $1 (1.86 kwacha = £1 sterling). Gold, SDRs, and foreign exchange: (June 1975) U.S. $75,220,000; (June 1974) U.S. $72,720,000. Budget (1974–75 est.): revenue 52,690,000 kwachas; expenditure 67.6 million kwachas.

Foreign Trade. (1974) Imports 156,270,000 kwachas; exports 100,140,000 kwachas. Import sources: South Africa 23%; U.K. 23%; Rhodesia 13%; Japan 5%; West Germany 5%. Export destinations: U.K. 31%; U.S. 9%; Rhodesia 7%; The Netherlands 7%. Main exports: tobacco 39%; tea 17%; peanuts 5%.

Transport and Communications. Roads (1973) 11,814 km. Motor vehicles in use (1973): passenger 10,540; commercial 8,700. Railways (1973): 566 km.; traffic 69.8 million passenger-km., freight (1974) 251 million net ton-km. Air traffic (1974): 79.9 million passenger-km.; freight 1,170,000 net ton-km. Telephones (Dec. 1973) 17,000. Radio receivers (Dec. 1973) 112,000.

Agriculture. Production (in 000; metric tons; 1974; 1973 in parentheses): corn *c.* 1,100 (*c.* 1,200); cassava (1973) *c.* 150, (1972) *c.* 150; sweet potatoes (1973) *c.* 49, (1972) *c.* 49; sorghum *c.* 35 (*c.* 35); sugar, raw value *c.* 53 (*c.* 53); peanuts (1973) *c.* 190, (1972) *c.* 190; tea *c.* 23 (24); tobacco *c.* 31 (30); cotton, lint *c.* 7 (*c.* 7). Livestock (in 000; 1974): cattle *c.* 596; sheep *c.* 120; goats (1973) *c.* 650; pigs *c.* 180; poultry *c.* 8,500.

Industry. Production (in 000; 1974): electricity (public supply; kw-hr.) 211,000; cement (metric tons) 81.

Malaysia

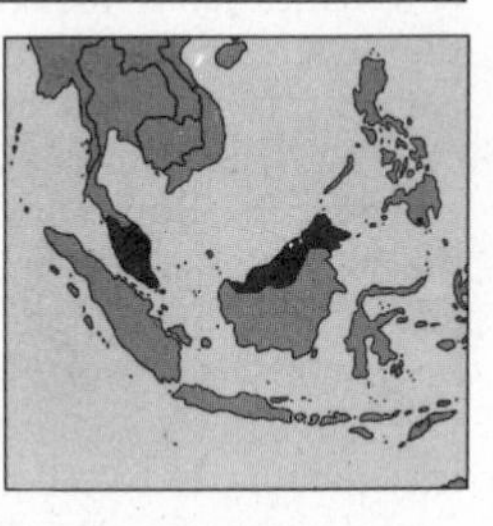

A federation within the Commonwealth of Nations comprising the 11 states of the former Federation of Malaya, Sabah, Sarawak, and the federal territory of Kuala Lumpur, Malaysia is a federal constitutional monarchy situated in Southeast Asia at the southern end of the Malay Peninsula (excluding Singapore) and on the northern part of the island of Borneo. Area: 127,316 sq.mi. (329,747 sq.km.). Pop. (1975 est.): 12,093,000. Cap. and largest city: Kuala Lumpur (pop., 1970, 451,800). Official language: Malay. Religion: Malays are Mus-

MALAYSIA

Education. *West Malaysia.* (1974) Primary, pupils 1,554,611, teachers 48,176; secondary, pupils 705,825, teachers 25,361; vocational, pupils 20,649, teachers 901; higher, students 28,002, teaching staff 2,081. *East Malaysia:* Sabah. (1973) Primary, pupils 121,912, teachers 4,553; secondary, pupils 42,435, teachers 1,593; vocational, pupils 264, teachers 27; teacher training, students 642, teachers 73. *East Malaysia:* Sarawak. (1973) Primary, pupils 157,867, teachers 4,649; secondary, pupils 42,098, teachers 1,621; vocational, pupils 323, teachers 26; teacher training, students 588, teachers 57.

Finance. Monetary unit: Malaysian dollar, with (Sept. 22, 1975) a free rate of M$2.58 to U.S. $1 (M$5.34 = £1 sterling). Gold, SDRs, and foreign exchange: (June 1975) U.S. $1,384,000,000; (June 1974) U.S. $1,452,000,000. Budget (1974 est.): revenue M$3,534,000,000; expenditure M$5,364,000,000. Gross national product: (1973) M$16,434,000,000; (1972) M$13,475,000,000. Money supply: (March 1975) M$4,103,000,000; (March 1974) M$3,781,000,000. Cost of living (West Malaysia; 1970 = 100): (May 1975) 141; (May 1974) 135.

Foreign Trade. (1974) Imports M$9,988,000,000; exports M$10,185,000,000. Import sources: Japan 22%; U.S. 10%; U.K. 9%; Singapore 8%; Australia 7%; West Germany 6%; China 5%. Export destinations: Singapore 22%; Japan 17%; U.S. 14%; U.K. 7%; The Netherlands 5%. Main exports: rubber 28%; timber 15%; tin 15%; palm oil 11%; crude oil 7%.

Transport and Communications. Roads (1972) 24,389 km. (including 17,867 km. in West Malaysia). Motor vehicles in use (1973): passenger 382,600; commercial (including buses) 123,800. Railways: (1974) 1,814 km.; traffic (including Singapore; 1973) 824 million passenger-km., freight 1,157,000,000 net ton-km. Air traffic (1974): 1,297,700,000 passenger-km.; freight 22,212,000 net ton-km. Shipping (1974): merchant vessels 100 gross tons and over 122; gross tonnage 337,511. Shipping traffic (1973): goods loaded 18,543,000 metric tons, unloaded 11,381,000 metric tons. Telephones (Jan. 1974) 234,000. Radio licenses (Dec. 1973) 462,000. Television licenses (Dec. 1973) 359,000.

Agriculture. Production (in 000; metric tons; 1974; 1973 in parentheses): rice *c.* 1,790 (1,728); rubber *c.* 1,568 (*c.* 1,566); copra *c.* 155 (*c.* 163); palm oil *c.* 1,022 (816); tea *c.* 3 (*c.* 3); bananas *c.* 460 (430); pineapples (1973) *c.* 290, (1972) 315; pepper (Sarawak only; 1973) 23, (1972) 26; timber (cu.m.; 1973) 32,000, (1972) 26,500; fish catch (1973) 445, (1972) 359. Livestock (in 000; Dec. 1973): cattle *c.* 359; pigs *c.* 1,095; goats *c.* 390; sheep (West Malaysia only) *c.* 41; buffalo *c.* 310; chickens (1972) *c.* 30,838.

Industry. Production (in 000; metric tons; 1974): tin concentrates (metal content) 68; bauxite 948; cement (West Malaysia only) 1,362; iron ore (West Malaysia only; 56% metal content) 468; crude oil (Sarawak only) 3,845; petroleum products (Sarawak only; 1973) *c.* 2,100; gold (troy oz.; 1973) 4.1; electricity (kw-hr.) 5,144,000.

DAVID K. ANDELMAN—THE NEW YORK TIMES

Ginger root sold in Kuala Lumpur has increased in price from 20 to 80 cents in five years.

lim; Indians mainly Hindu; Chinese mainly Buddhist, Confucian, and Taoist. Supreme heads of state in 1975, with the title of *yang di-pertuan agong,* Tuanku Abdul Halim Mu'azzam Shah ibni al-Marhum Sultan Badlishah and, from September 21, Tuanku Yahya Putra ibni al-Marhum Sultan Ibrahim; prime minister, Tun Abdul Razak.

Student disturbances erupted in Kuala Lumpur and other education centres in December 1974. They marked a climax of protest over the alleged impoverished condition of rural small landholders. In April 1975 a bill amending the Universities and University Colleges Act 1971 was passed forbidding student membership in or support for any party or union and bringing Malaysia's institutions of higher learning directly under the minister of education.

At the United Malays National Organization's General Assembly in June, Prime Minister Tun Abdul Razak and Deputy Prime Minister Hussein bin Dato Onn were returned unopposed as president and deputy president. In the contested elections for the three posts of vice-president, the successful candidates were Ghafar Baba, minister of agriculture; Tengku Razaleigh Hamzah, head of the state-controlled oil company; and Mahathir Muhammad, minister of education. Dato Harun, chief minister of Selangor, was unsuccessful in these elections despite his role in sponsoring the world heavyweight boxing championship fight between Muhammad Ali and Joe Bugner in Kuala Lumpur in July. On September 21 Sultan Yahya Putra of Kelantan became sixth elected head of state of Malaysia for a five-year term.

Terrorism by members of the fractured Malaysian Communist Party increased significantly and in a spectacular manner. In April a rocket attack was launched on the Malaysian Air Force base outside Kuala Lumpur with some damage to aircraft. In August the National Monument in the capital was blown up, and in September grenades were thrown with devastating effect at the barracks of the paramilitary police force in Kuala Lumpur.

On August 4 five gunmen from the Japanese Red Army entered the U.S. embassy in Kuala Lumpur and held some 50 people hostage. They demanded the release of fellow terrorists from prison in Japan and Sweden. After negotiations, the Japanese government agreed to release the detainees and, of these, five were flown to Kuala Lumpur. The siege at the embassy ended on August 7 when a Japan Air Lines DC-8 took off for Libya carrying both sets of terrorists together with Japanese and Malaysian hostages who volunteered to travel with them in return for the release of the hostages held at the U.S. embassy.

In July a major political revolt occurred in the state of Sabah against the rule of Chief Minister Tun Mustapha. An indication of federal government support for his opponents was manifest at the opponents' press conference to announce a new party, the Sabah People's Union (Berjaya). Conspicuous protection at the conference was provided by the police, who had previously enjoyed a reputation for arresting opponents of the chief minister. The new party was led initially by Datuk Haris Salleh, but he was succeeded by Tun Muhammad Fuad, who resigned from the office of head of state of Sabah to challenge Tun Mustapha. Although Tun Mustapha secured a vote of confidence in the State Assembly, he resigned on October 31. (MICHAEL LEIFER)

[976.B.2]

Maldives

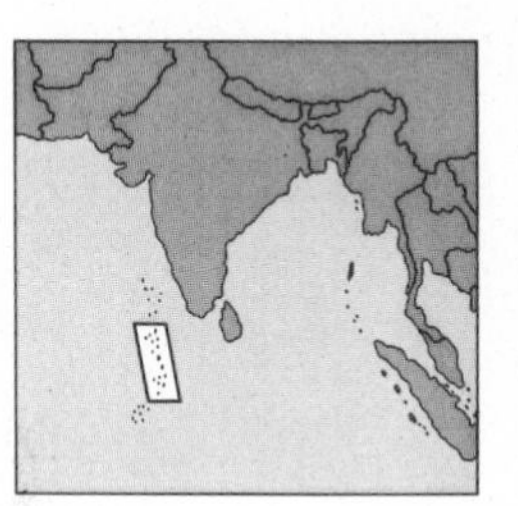

Maldives, a republic in the Indian Ocean consisting of about two thousand small islands, lies southwest of the southern tip of India. Area: 115 sq.mi. (298 sq.km.). Pop. (1974): 128,700. Cap.: Male (pop., 1974, 16,250). Language: Divehi. Religion: Muslim. Sultan, Emir Muhammad Farid Didi; president in 1975, Ibrahim Nasir; prime minister to March 6, Ahmed Zaki.

Presidential rule was instituted following a bloodless coup on March 6, 1975, when President Nasir forestalled an alleged left-wing coup by Prime Minister Zaki and banished him to a remote atoll. Zaki had been reelected when his supporters obtained 36 of the 54 seats in the Majlis (Parliament) in elections on February 22. Foreign pressure on the islands had increased after Zaki's visit to Britain in 1974, when it became known that Britain would dismantle its RAF base on Gan before the lease expired in 1986. Zaki had supported Sri Lanka's aim of neutrality in the Indian Ocean and condemned U.S. use of Diego Garcia (*see* DEPENDENT STATES); his talks with Indian Prime Minister Indira Gandhi and the Soviet ambassador to India, who visited the Maldives in January, precipitated right-wing pressure from Ahmed

MALDIVES

Education. (1972–73) Primary, pupils 8,668, teachers 351; secondary, pupils 1,431, teachers 61.

Finance and Trade. Monetary unit: Maldivian rupee, with (Sept. 22, 1975) a nominal free rate of MRs. 7.50 to U.S. $1 (MRs. 15.60 = £1 sterling). Budget (1973) expenditure MRs. 20,670,000. Foreign trade (1973): imports U.S. $4,378,000; exports U.S. $3,426,000. Trade mainly with Sri Lanka and Japan. Main exports (metric tons): fish 7,760; shells 65; copra 20.

Manikku, economic adviser to the president, who wished to see a U.S. occupation of Gan. British withdrawal (completed by December 31) would seriously affect the Maldives economically.

Mrs. Gandhi pledged Indian aid to the Maldives for a Rs. 40 million fishery plant and the provision of 19 atoll schools. New Zealand set up a teacher-training scheme under the Colombo Plan, while Britain, India, Sri Lanka, the U.S., and Japan launched a general modernization plan, including tourism and communications. (MOLLY MORTIMER)

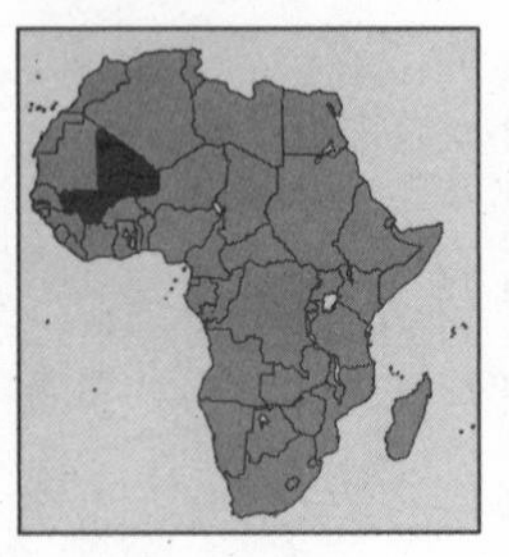

Mali

A republic of West Africa, Mali is bordered by Algeria, Niger, Upper Volta, Ivory Coast, Guinea, Senegal, and Mauritania. Area: 478,822 sq.mi. (1,240,142 sq.km.). Pop. (1975 est.): 5,697,000. Cap. and largest city: Bamako (pop., 1970 est., 196,800). Language: French (official); Hamito-Semitic and various tribal dialects. Religion: Muslim 65%; animist 30%. Head of military government in 1975, Col. Moussa Traoré.

The little frontier war between Mali and Upper Volta provoked a number of efforts at mediation in 1975, on the part of France, the Organization of African Unity (OAU), Senegal, Togo, and Guinea, which, upon the fresh outbreak of hostilities in June, urged both sides to call an immediate halt to all fighting. A conference at Lomé, Togo, on June 18 brought together Pres. Gnassingbe Eyadema of Togo, Pres. Léopold Senghor of Senegal, Pres. Seyni Kountche of Niger, and others in an attempt to resolve the quarrel. The communiqué issued at the end of the conference spoke of Upper Volta and Mali as undertaking to resolve their differences according to the recommendations of the OAU Mediation Commission. Nevertheless the problem remained basically unchanged.

In accordance with his announcement in January, Colonel Traoré in June set free 15 political figures of the old regime who had remained in custody since the coup of November 1968; 6 more were set at liberty in November. A five-year plan to wipe out the effects of the drought and to achieve economic independence was published in April. Already international loans were financing livestock rehabilitation programs, and several schemes for large dams were approved.

(PHILIPPE DECRAENE)

[978.E.4.b.ii]

MALI

Education. Primary (1971–72), pupils 243,886, teachers 6,984; secondary (1970–71), pupils 3,507, teachers 290; vocational (1970–71), pupils 3,386, teachers 332; teacher training (1970–71), students 1,551, teachers 92; higher (1970–71), students 731, teaching staff 151.

Finance. Monetary unit: Mali franc, with (Sept. 22, 1975) a parity of MFr. 100 to the French franc and a free rate of MFr. 455 to U.S. $1 (MFr. 943 = £1 sterling). Gold, SDRs, and foreign exchange: (May 1975) U.S. $7.3 million; (May 1974) U.S. $7.6 million. Budget (1974 est.) balanced at MFr. 29 billion.

Foreign Trade. (1973–74) Imports MFr. 48,050,000,000; exports MFr. 16,990,000,000. Import sources (1973): France *c.* 57%; Ivory Coast *c.* 15%; U.S. *c.* 7%; West Germany *c.* 6%; Belgium-Luxembourg *c.* 5%. Export destinations (1973): France *c.* 34%; Ivory Coast *c.* 28%; Upper Volta *c.* 8%; Japan *c.* 6%; West Germany *c.* 5%; U.K. *c.* 5%. Main exports: cotton 36%; peanuts 10%.

Agriculture. Production (in 000; metric tons; 1974; 1973 in parentheses): millet and sorghum *c.* 750 (*c.* 600); rice (1973) *c.* 100, (1972) *c.* 130; corn (1973) *c.* 60, (1972) *c.* 60; peanuts *c.* 180 (*c.* 100); sweet potatoes (1973) *c.* 60, (1972) *c.* 60; cassava (1973) *c.* 120, (1972) *c.* 120; cotton, lint *c.* 22 (*c.* 18); beef and veal (1973) *c.* 33, (1972) *c.* 37; mutton and lamb (1973) *c.* 20, (1972) *c.* 22. Livestock (in 000; 1973): cattle *c.* 3,700; sheep *c.* 3,900; goats *c.* 3,800; camels *c.* 150; horses *c.* 120; asses *c.* 320.

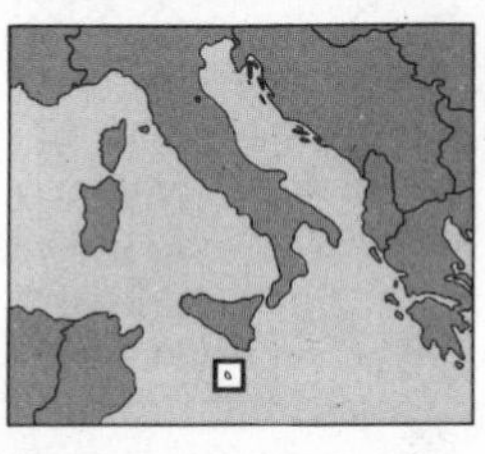

Malta

An island in the Mediterranean Sea, between Sicily and Tunisia, Malta is a republic and a member of the Commonwealth of Nations. Area: 122 sq.mi. (316 sq. km.), including Malta, Gozo, and Comino. Pop. (1975 est.): 297,600. Cap.: Valletta (pop., 1974 est., 14,000). Largest city: Sliema (pop., 1974 est., 20,000).

Saharan fringe near Timbuktu where drought has persisted for over six years.

WIDE WORLD

MALTA

Education. (1973–74) Primary, pupils 32,569, teachers 1,611; secondary, pupils 25,509, teachers 1,829; vocational, pupils 4,161, teachers 331; higher, students 1,420, teaching staff 173.

Finance. Monetary unit: Maltese pound, with (Sept. 22, 1975) a free rate of M£0.40 to U.S. $1 (M£0.84 = £1 sterling). Gold, SDRs, and foreign exchange: (June 1975) U.S. $438.5 million; (June 1974) U.S. $351.7 million. Budget (1973–74 actual): revenue M£56,020,000; expenditure M£52,410,000.

Foreign Trade. (1974) Imports M£138,850,000; exports M£51,580,000. Import sources: U.K. 25%; Italy 17%; West Germany 8%; The Netherlands 6%; U.S. 6%; France 5%. Export destinations: U.K. 28%; West Germany 10%; Belgium-Luxembourg 9%; Italy 7%; Sweden 6%; Libya 5%. Main exports: clothing 38%; petroleum products 11%; textile yarns and fabrics 10%; machinery 7%; rubber products 6%; food 6%. Tourism (1973): visitors 211,200; gross receipts U.S. $44 million.

Transport and Communications. Roads (1973) 1,224 km. Motor vehicles in use (1973): passenger 47,300; commercial 11,000. There are no railways. Air traffic (1974): 219.2 million passenger-km.; freight 2,874,000 net ton-km. Shipping (1974): merchant vessels 100 gross tons and over 22; gross tonnage 38,011. Ships entered (1973) vessels totaling 1,472,000 net registered tons; goods loaded (1974) 89,000 metric tons, unloaded 913,000 metric tons. Telephones (Dec. 1973) 46,000. Radio licenses (Dec. 1973) 129,000. Television licenses (Dec. 1973) 61,000.

Language: Maltese and English. Religion: mainly Roman Catholic. President in 1975, Sir Anthony Mamo; prime minister, Dom Mintoff.

Toward the end of 1974 the government published a development plan for 1973–80. Its purpose was to increase productive activity to such an extent that Malta would be independent of foreign military bases after 1979, thus disengaging the island from power-bloc affiliations.

After negotiations with the European Economic Community for a new agreement had been deadlocked for several months, agreement was eventually reached in December 1975. The EEC foreign ministers had raised the offer of financial assistance to Malta from 21 million units of account to 26 million (about £13 million sterling). France had at first opposed the increase.

The government budgeted for an estimated expenditure of M£80.3 million in 1975–76. Allowances for not more than three children under 16 were introduced. During 1975 the government took over the cable and wireless service by agreement with the owners. The Rediffusion Group agreed to transfer its entire radio and television business to the government. A new bank was set up to take over all the assets and liabilities of Barclays branches in Malta.

(ALBERT GANADO)

Materials Sciences

The most significant problems faced in the materials sciences during 1975 were those associated with protection of the environment and the energy shortage. These were aggravated by the continued cost squeeze and difficulty in raising capital. Adding to the problems were the decreasing grade of available ore and political factors adversely affecting mineral supplies. Metal shortages were common during the year in spite of reduced demand.

Ceramics. Reflecting energy concerns, many of the year's outstanding developments in ceramics were directly associated with producing new materials for the more efficient generation and storage of energy.

High-Temperature Turbine Applications. High turbine temperatures offer increased thermodynamic efficiency and less atmospheric pollution. Unfortunately, metallic components are severely limited in their use in turbines by their loss of strength and oxidation resistance at high temperatures; air cooling schemes developed to protect such components significantly reduce turbine efficiency. Ceramic components that could operate at much higher temperatures without the need for cooling air could lead to tremendous fuel savings.

Despite this potential, until recently the future for ceramics in these applications seemed bleak. Traditional ceramics, based on metal oxides, tend to fracture when they are exposed to sudden changes in temperature. In recent years, however, new fabrication processes have produced silicon nitride and silicon carbide that offer dense, strong ceramics that are resistant to thermal shock and may well survive the hostile environment of a turbine.

Recent studies in a number of laboratories, including the U.S. Army Materials and Mechanics Research Center, the U.S. Naval Research Laboratory, and the U.S. Air Force Materials Laboratory, concentrated on the use of yttrium oxide, zirconium dioxide, and rare-earth oxides as densification aids in hot-pressed silicon nitride to improve its high-temperature mechanical properties. Perhaps the most important recent advance in ceramic technology was the development at General Electric Co. of a means of sintering silicon carbide by the controlled addition of boron and carbon. Previously, silicon carbide could be densified only under intense pressures and temperatures. Studies were under way to determine similar approaches to the densification of silicon nitride.

Scientists at General Electric, United Technologies Corp., and Avco Corp. recently made significant progress in determining and improving the impact resistance of silicon carbide and silicon nitride for

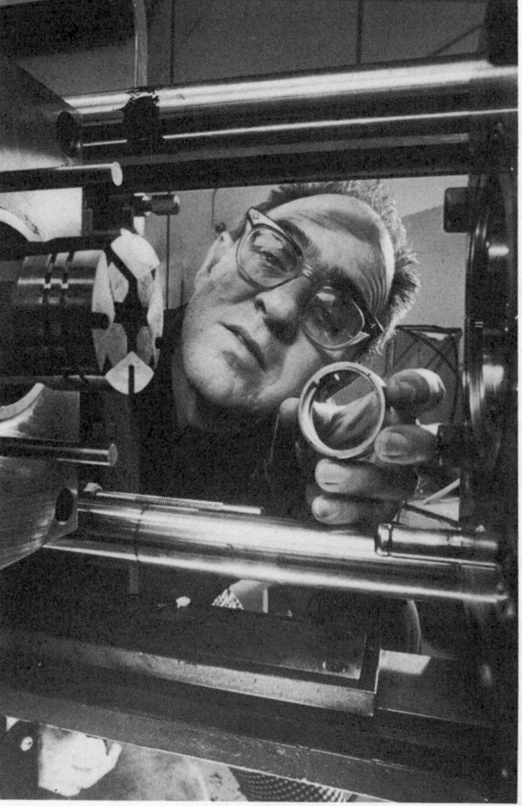
LEONARD NADEL

Metalworkers have adopted the Wiech process in which metal and ceramic powders are forced by injection molding into complicated shapes.

Manganese: *see* Mining and Quarrying

Manufacturing: *see* Economy, World; Industrial Review

Marine Biology: *see* Life Sciences

Marketing: *see* Consumerism; Economy, World

turbine applications, particularly by the use of energy-absorbing surface layers and fibre reinforcements. One of the most promising advances in high-temperature composites was the development at General Electric of silicon reinforced with silicon carbide. In this process low-cost graphite yarn can be wound into complex shapes to take maximum advantage of its directional strength and stiffness capabilities. The component is then infiltrated with silicon, and the fibres are converted to silicon carbide. The resulting composite has excellent properties to about 1,400° C, and work on the production of practical demonstration components was under way.

Energy Generation and Storage Applications. Virtually every process proposed for the harnessing of new energy sources, for the more efficient conversion of available resources to usable energy, and for its effective storage has underlying materials problems that will at least in part require new ceramic solutions. Ceramic turbine components can certainly play an important role, allowing much more efficient gas/steam turbine combined-cycle electric power plants.

Another high-efficiency process under active development is magnetohydrodynamic (MHD) power generation, in which an ionized gas produced by fuel combustion is passed through a magnetic field to generate power without the need for moving parts. Though long a dream of engineers, this process imposes especially harsh requirements on materials, particularly in the generating duct itself. Electrodes that can conduct electricity better than the ionized gas itself and at the same time resist the extremely corrosive high-temperature environment are needed. With the efforts and support of such U.S. agencies as the National Bureau of Standards and the Energy Research and Development Administration, progress was made in the use of modified zirconium dioxide, strontium-doped lanthanum chromite, and other highly conductive ceramics for this application.

Macor, a new glass-ceramic material produced by Corning Glass Works, can be machined to any desired shape and may replace aluminum- and beryllium-bearing materials, as well as Teflon plastic, for many purposes.

COURTESY, CORNING GLASS WORKS

One of the most active and important ceramic areas during 1975 was the development of new battery materials. There are a variety of energy storage applications, ranging from load leveling at the generating station itself to battery-powered cars, that impose strong demands for compact, lightweight cells that can store large amounts of energy and can be charged and discharged rapidly. Sodium/sulfur and lithium/sulfur cells emerged as leading candidates, but a solid electrolyte is required to separate the electrodes physically and yet permit rapid motion of the sodium or lithium ions at moderate temperatures. A new class of ceramic materials, the beta aluminas, were receiving a great deal of study in this connection. Amazingly, these and a number of other ceramic compounds were found to contain paths in their crystal structures along which charged atoms move almost as rapidly as they do in a liquid.

(NORMAN M. TALLAN)

Metallurgy. There were no outstanding developments in pollution control. Only the minimum required action seemed to be taken in gaseous emission reduction; apparently further action was awaiting evaluation of the control measures and contaminant-removal pilot plants previously started. Most companies seemed to be seeking pollution-control devices instead of attempting major changes in metallurgical operations. Hydrometallurgy for treating sulfide ores, which could eliminate the sulfur dioxide problem, had the drawbacks of greater energy consumption and greatly increased water pollution.

Metal processing moved into space during the Apollo-Soyuz manned mission with the casting of rare earth-cobalt magnets under weightless conditions. On the Earth the high-density magnetic particles freeze before the bulk of the metal; therefore, they tend to settle out, causing the magnet to be weaker.

Extractive Metallurgy. Extractive metallurgy remained in the forefront of the field as many nations sought ways of economically utilizing their own low-grade mineral deposits instead of depending on imports. Cartels and the growing trend of governments of ore-producing countries to strictly control and heavily tax mining were threatening to cause large price increases and ore shortages. A small pilot plant using a promising method of extracting nickel from laterite deposits in the United States began operation and the first commercial production of nickel directly from laterite ore began in the Philippines. Bauxite, currently the only ore of aluminum, was largely under the control of a cartel. This led to intensified efforts to use aluminum silicate minerals, especially clay, for production of the metal. The U.S. Bureau of Mines and several large aluminum producers were jointly carrying out pilot plant studies to determine which of several processes was economically and technically the most favourable for full-scale aluminum production.

The rising costs and increasing shortages of ores also encouraged the recovery and recycling of metal wastes. A possible improvement in the recovery of nonmagnetic metals from urban waste was offered by the "aluminum magnet," basically a high-frequency, current-carrying coil that repelled electrically conducting material. The aluminum and other metals could then be further separated by conventional means. In Japan one of the world's largest prereduced iron pellet plants, built to reclaim normally wasted fine ore and particulate material from plant gases, started operation. Coal was used as the reducing agent, and the pellets were charged into the blast furnace to decrease the amount of scarce metallurgical coke required.

The severe shortage of coking coal with low sulfur content led to iron-smelting experiments in which high-sulfur coke was used. The iron produced was then desulfurized with magnesium before conversion into steel. Calcium carbide was being used in the U.S. to achieve greater than usual reduction in the sulfur content of steel, in part to reduce the amount of manganese necessary to overcome the tendency of sulfur to make steel brittle. The U.S. produces very little manganese.

Alloys. Much of the activity during the year centred on the development of alloys that could resist stress-corrosion, which causes metals to crack unexpectedly if used under load in even mildly corrosive conditions. A stainless steel with a high chromium content and containing 4% molybdenum was developed in Europe and found wide acceptance in the U.S. In comparison with nickel-containing stainless steel, it better resisted corrosion environments containing chloride, was less expensive, and was not threatened by the worldwide nickel shortage. The U.S., with a large reserve of molybdenum, viewed this substitution as a particularly valuable one.

More stainless steel than in previous years was refined by the argon-oxygen process for removing carbon; by this means the alloy could be made with regular rather than special low-carbon ferrochromium and with the more readily available and less expensive ferronickel instead of electrolytic nickel. A new titanium alloy containing molybdenum and nickel retained high strength and resisted corrosion in boiling chloride solutions, a harsh environment frequently encountered in industry. Parts made of an aluminum-magnesium alloy experienced temperatures up to 120° C in a desalination plant that operated for three years. Aluminum alloys would be cheaper than alternate materials for desalination plants, but most cannot withstand high-temperature saltwater.

Metal Forming. Much of the development in metal forming took place in the processing of metal powder into semifinished or finished parts. The greatest change from usual practice was the loose-pack process. Relatively inexpensive atomized metal powder mixed with a binder was poured into a paper pulp mold and compacted by vibration. It was then put into a sintering furnace, where the mold was burned away but not before the binder had carbonized. The carbon did not burn out until sintering had begun so that the part being formed was supported or had fair strength at all times. Strong molds and large presses were not needed, and so large parts could be economically formed.

The commercial availability of the high-power carbon dioxide laser allowed it to be used for metal cutting, where it was giving clean narrow cuts even on complex shapes, and for welding, where it had most of the advantages of electron-beam welding without the need of working in a vacuum. In both applications the zone affected by heat was very thin.

(DONALD F. CLIFTON)

See also Industrial Review: *Glass; Iron and Steel; Machinery and Machine Tools;* Mining and Quarrying.
[725.B]

Mathematics

Mathematics in the mid-1970s was experiencing an upsurge of interest in new applications made possible by theoretical advances of recent years. Whereas traditional applications of mathematics depend largely on the classical tools of calculus, algebra, and probability, the new ones employ methods from fields like combinatorics (the study of patterns in which things can be arranged) and mathematical logic (the study of the reasoning processes of mathematics itself).

During the past quarter century the core of mathematics—algebra, analysis, geometry—has transcended its traditional role of modeling physical science and soared to unprecedented heights of abstraction. But the demand of the computer scientist for methods that will actually produce (correct) numbers within a reasonable time has refocused mathematical attention on the concrete world of numbers, arrangements, and events. A similar refocusing has been accomplished by the cautious skepticism of the logician, who examined and strengthened the tether that ties mathematics to the language in which it is expressed.

Combinatorics. Many practical problems concerning scheduling (of school classes, assembly line processes, and airline flights, for instance) involve so many combinations of events that even the fastest computers cannot cope with them. Many problems grow exponentially with the number of variables, and so adding one more variable is likely to double the amount of work involved in achieving a solution; adding ten variables to the problem can increase the work by a thousandfold.

Typically, mathematicians and computer scientists use various algorithms, step-by-step solution procedures, to attack combinatorial problems. Ideally, a proposed algorithm for a particular problem is analyzed theoretically to determine if it will actually yield a solution, and then it is programmed on a computer to carry out the solution. But for most complex scheduling problems, mathematicians have been confronted by a frustrating "Catch-*22*" barrier: those algorithms known to work in theory were too inefficient to use on a computer, while those that could be used were not guaranteed to succeed.

Stephen Cook of the University of Toronto and Richard Karp of the University of California at Berkeley found a way to penetrate this barrier: they were able to classify many combinatorial problems as being essentially equivalent in the sense that an algorithm that would solve one of them could be adapted to solve them all. This class of problems, termed NP complete, was during the year the subject of investigations to determine how extensive it is and whether

Nonstandard numbering involves expansion of the real number sequence as shown here. New number series are generated by consideration of infinitesimal and infinite quantities.

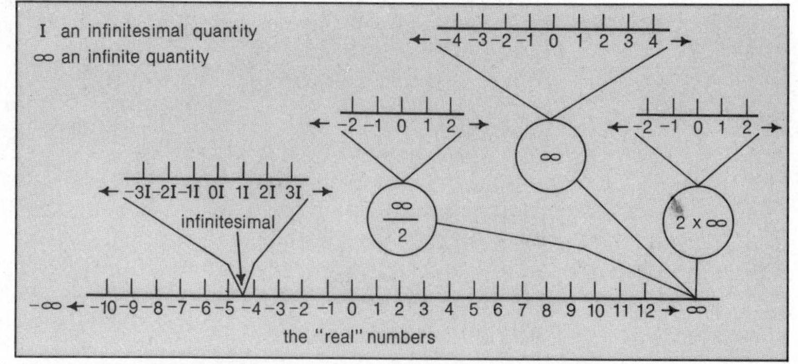

FROM THE NEW YORK TIMES, FEB. 15, 1975

it is possible to solve any (and, therefore, all) NP complete problems by any efficient algorithm.

The major conjecture—as yet unproved—is that no efficient algorithms can exist that provide exact solutions to NP complete problems. Accordingly, many mathematicians began seeking good approximate algorithms, having abandoned hope for theoretically perfect ones. Others struggled to resolve the general conjecture itself: to determine whether these problems really cannot have efficient algorithms or whether perhaps this question, like many others in mathematics, might itself be undecidable on the basis of the present axiomatic structure of the discipline.

Nonstandard Analysis. Tough combinatorial problems arise because of the difficulty of dealing with large but still finite numbers of events. Other mathematical models require the analysis of infinite numbers, and recent applications of mathematical logic have provided surprising new insight into this esoteric and nearly unimaginable realm. Over a decade earlier, the late Abraham Robinson of Yale University had discovered that there exist, in addition to the standard system of so-called real numbers (which include positive and negative whole numbers, fractions, and irrational numbers), certain larger systems that contain both infinitely large and infinitesimally small numbers. At a conference at Yale in May—on the first anniversary of Robinson's death—logicians, mathematicians, physicists, and economists gathered to explore ways in which this "nonstandard analysis" of infinitely large and infinitesimally small numbers could provide new approaches to outstanding problems in pure and applied mathematics.

Just as the solution to a combinatorial problem requires a precisely stated algorithm, so the description of an infinitely larger or infinitesimally small number requires a precise definition setting forth its properties. Robinson explored the relationship between the language in which mathematics is expressed and the objects described by that language to produce a totally new model of numbers that contains whole "galaxies" of infinitely large numbers and "monads" of infinitesimally small numbers.

Scientists often need to analyze infinite models because they are good approximations to excessively complex situations involving a large finite number of events. Formerly, when approaching an infinite model, scientists had to develop many kinds of ad hoc devices that had little scientific reality simply in order to avoid contradictions in the mathematical model. Nonstandard methods permit scientists a direct transition from the well-known finite models to the little-known infinite ones. (LYNN ARTHUR STEEN)

[10/22.E.2]

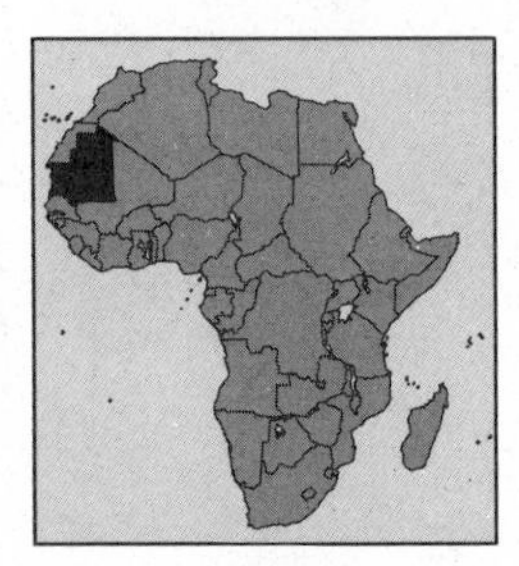

Mauritania

The Islamic Republic of Mauritania is on the Atlantic coast of West Africa, adjoining Spanish Sahara, Algeria, Mali, and Senegal. Area: 398,000 sq.mi. (1,030,700 sq.km.). Pop. (1974 est.): 1,290,000. Cap.: Nouakchott (pop., 1975 est., 103,500). Language: Arabic, French. Religion: Muslim. President in 1975, Moktar Ould Daddah.

Ould Daddah, as sole candidate, was reelected president, with 99.99% of the votes from 94% of the electorate on Oct. 26, 1975. At the same time, 70 deputies (20 more than previously) as single-list candidates were elected to a new National Assembly.

The Spanish Sahara question governed Mauritania's foreign policy in 1975. At midyear Mauritania and Morocco appeared to have agreed on a division of the territory and on the exploitation of its phosphate beds. Later the Mauritanian leaders moved away from the Moroccans, partly because King Hassan of Morocco and his advisers seemed determined to "go it alone" and also because Ould Daddah was unwilling to risk a possible rupture with Algeria. In the event, the agreement reached with Spain following the Moroccan "peace march" into Spanish Sahara in November provided for a joint administration by Spain, Morocco, and Mauritania until Spain's withdrawal, scheduled for Feb. 28, 1976, when the territory was to be divided between Mauritania and Morocco.

Prospects in the economic sphere appeared to be good, particularly since the nationalization of the iron

A fragile oasis village in Arat stands amid the advancing sands of the Sahara.

WIDE WORLD

MAURITANIA

Education. (1972–73) Primary, pupils 38,900, teachers (1971–72) 1,585; secondary, pupils 4,073, teachers (1971–72) 156; vocational, pupils 247; teacher training (1971–72), students 145.

Finance. Monetary unit: ouguiya, with (Oct. 31, 1975) a free rate of 41.37 ouguiya = U.S. $1 (market rate of 94.35 ouguiya = £1 sterling). Gold, SDRs, and foreign exchange: (June 1975) U.S. $94.4 million; (June 1974) U.S. $68.3 million. Budget (1974 est.) balanced at 3,125,000,000 ouguiya.

Foreign Trade. (1974) Imports 7,676,000,000 ouguiya; exports 7,999,000,000 ouguiya. Import sources (1972): France 41%; U.S. 11%; U.K. 7%; Senegal 7%; West Germany 5%; China 5%. Export destinations (1972): France 20%; U.K. 18%; Italy 14%; Belgium-Luxembourg 12%; Spain 11%; Japan 9%; West Germany 8%. Main exports: iron ore 73%; fish (1972) 11%; copper concentrates (1972) 10%.

ore mines of the Société des mines de fer de Mauritanie (Miferma), effective from November 1974. The monetary reserves of Mauritania were eight times higher in 1975 than in 1973, not only because of developing mineral exportation but also on account of loans and deposits coming chiefly from the Arab countries. (PHILIPPE DECRAENE)

Mauritius

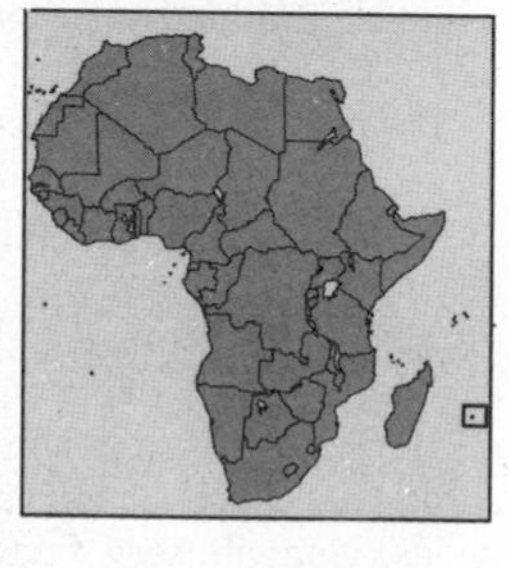

The parliamentary state of Mauritius, a member of the Commonwealth of Nations, lies about 500 mi. E of the Malagasy Republic in the Indian Ocean; it includes the island dependencies of Rodrigues, Agalega, and Cargados Carajos. Area: 787.5 sq.mi. (2,040 sq.km.). Pop. (1974 est.): 872,000, including (1972) Indian 50%; Pakistani 16%; Creole (mixed French and African) 31%; others 3%. Cap. and largest city: Port Louis (pop., 1973 est., 136,600). Language: English (official). Religion (1974 est.): Hindu 51%; Christian 30%; Muslim 16%; Buddhist 3%. Queen, Elizabeth II; governor-general in 1975, Sir Abdul Rahman Muhammad Osman; prime minister, Sir Seewoosagur Ramgoolam.

Mauritius during 1975 became involved in the Diego Garcia dispute (*see* DEPENDENT STATES). From the end of the 1960s more than a thousand settlers had been removed from the Indian Ocean island of Diego Garcia to Mauritius, and for their resettlement the British government allowed £650,000 in 1972 to Mauritius (as distinct from the £3 million paid for loss of sovereignty over the Chagos Archipelago, in which Diego Garcia is situated). Sir Seewoosagur Ramgoolam claimed the payment was insufficient. The matter remained under discussion.

Cyclone Gervaise, which left about 90,000 people homeless and caused more than £50 million in damage, also destroyed over 30% of the sugar harvest and made it doubtful that Mauritius could meet its 1975 production quota. Aid came from Great Britain (£5 million, bringing the 1976–80 development total to £13 million), the UN Development Program (a 40% increase, to $1.4 million a year, mainly for agricultural and industrial schemes), and France (Fr. 180 million). In view of the expiration of the defense agreement with Britain in 1976 and the closing down of the British naval communications base, French use of naval facilities was discussed tentatively during Prime Minister Ramgoolam's May visit to Paris. The 1975–76 budget outlined a largely foreign-financed five-year plan to achieve full employment. Texaco began oil-drilling operations in June.

(MOLLY MORTIMER)

MAURITIUS

Education. (1973) Primary, pupils 154,830, teachers 5,270; secondary, pupils 55,893, teachers 1,870; vocational, pupils 1,210, teachers 93; higher (university and teacher training at this level), students 1,263, teaching staff 65.

Finance and Trade. Monetary unit: Mauritian rupee, with (Sept. 22, 1975) a free rate of MauRs. 6.44 to U.S. $1 (par value of MauRs. 13.33 = £1 sterling). Gold, SDRs, and foreign exchange: (June 1975) U.S. $92.9 million; (June 1974) U.S. $27.4 million. Budget (1973–74 est): revenue MauRs. 606 million; expenditure MauRs. 519 million. Foreign trade (1974): imports MauRs. 1,756,400,000; exports MauRs. 1,771,800,000. Import sources: U.K. 14%; South Africa 9%; Taiwan 8%; Iran 8%; France 8%; West Germany 6%; Japan 6%; U.S. 5%; Australia 5%. Export destinations: Canada 36%; U.K. 35%; U.S. 8%. Main export sugar 89%. Tourism (1973): visitors 68,000; gross receipts U.S. $15 million.

Agriculture. Production (in 000; metric tons; 1974; 1973 in parentheses): sugar *c.* 676 (723); bananas (1973) *c.* 11, (1972) 10; tea *c.* 5 (*c.* 5); tobacco *c.* 0.6 (0.6); milk (1973) *c.* 23, (1972) 22. Livestock (in 000; April 1973): cattle *c.* 50; pigs *c.* 4; sheep *c.* 3; goats *c.* 66; chickens *c.* 420.

Mexico

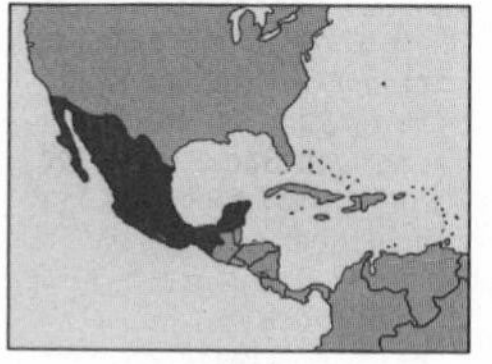

A federal republic of Middle America, Mexico is bounded by the U.S., Belize, and Guatemala. Area: 761,604 sq.mi. (1,972,546 sq.km.). Pop. (1975 est.): 60,145,300, including about 55% mestizo and 29% Indian. Cap. and largest city: Mexico City (pop., 1975 est., federal district 8,591,800, metro. area 11,339,800). Language: Spanish. Religion: predominantly Roman Catholic. President in 1975, Luis Echeverría Álvarez.

Foreign Relations. President Echeverría in 1975 again emphasized the need for closer relations with countries other than the U.S. In May Mexico, together with Colombia, Costa Rica, Cuba, Jamaica, Nicaragua, Panama, and Venezuela, established the new shipping line Empresa Naviera Multinacional del Caribe, which aimed to reduce those countries' dependence on foreign shipping concerns. New or increased trade contacts were established with Jamaica, the Council for Mutual Economic Assistance (Comecon) countries, China, Finland, and Switzerland. A five-year economic cooperation and trade agreement was reached with the European Economic Community in June.

During July and August the president traveled officially to Guyana, Cuba, Senegal, Algeria, Iran, India, Sri Lanka, Tanzania, Kuwait, Saudi Arabia, Egypt, Israel, Jordan, and Trinidad and Tobago. The outcome of these visits was the signing of 27 agreements covering economic, cultural, and scientific matters. The president also received Queen Elizabeth II of the U.K. and her husband, Prince Philip, on a state visit in February. On June 19 the UN Conference on International Women's Year opened in Mexico City. (*See* UNITED NATIONS: *Special Report.*)

Domestic Affairs. A number of major disturbances occurred, including bomb explosions in Guadalajara, Oaxaca, and Mexico City in November 1974 and again in the last two cities and in San Luis Potosí in January 1975. At the beginning of December 1974 Lucío Cabañas, a well-known guerrilla leader, and 27

Medicine: *see* Health and Disease
Mental Health: *see* Health and Disease
Merchandising: *see* Consumerism; Economy, World
Merchant Marine: *see* Transportation
Mercury: *see* Mining and Quarrying
Metallurgy: *see* Materials Sciences
Metals: *see* Industrial Review; Materials Sciences; Mining and Quarrying
Meteorology: *see* Earth Sciences
Methodist Churches: *see* Religion

UPI COMPIX

The traditional symbolic torch is lighted to signal the opening of the Pan-American Games at Aztec Stadium, Mexico City, in October.

of his followers were killed by government forces in an isolated mountain area in the state of Guerrero. In August 1975 five policemen and three government inspectors were killed by guerrillas in Mexico City.

Following prolonged negotiations, the Confederación de Trabajadores Mexicanos (CTM), the official trade union organization, had accepted an across-the-board 22% wage increase in September 1974. Wage rises averaging about 16% for state employees and 15% for other sectors were granted in August 1975.

Political activity in 1975 concentrated mainly on the 1976 presidential elections and the choice of a candidate by the official party, the Partido Revolucionario Institucional (PRI). On September 22 José López Portillo, the current secretary of finance, emerged as the PRI candidate. This came as a surprise; it had been widely expected that Mario Moya Palencia, the secretary of the interior, would be chosen, since the post he occupied was traditionally the stepping-stone to the presidency. López Portillo's career in government began in 1959. He had worked in the Secretariat of National Resources and the office of the Presidency. After a short term as director general of the Federal Electricity Commission (CFE), he became secretary of finance in 1973.

On December 29 Alfonso García Robles, Mexico's permanent representative at the UN, replaced Emilio Rabasa as foreign minister. Rabasa's resignation reportedly was influenced by Mexico's support of the UN resolution condemning Zionism as a form of racism. The Mexican tourist industry was feeling the effects of a boycott by Jewish groups in the U.S. and Canada. The boycott continued at year's end despite President Echeverría's assurances to representatives of major U.S. Jewish organizations that, even though it had voted for the resolution, Mexico "in no way identified Zionism with racism."

The Economy. The growth of the Mexican economy in 1974 was estimated at 6% in real terms, as against 7.3% in 1973; major growth was recorded in petroleum and petroleum products, mining, and electrical energy. The 1974 performance compared favourably with that of other less developed countries in the context of the world economic situation. Inflation and the external sector continued to be the main problem areas. The rate of growth of the gross domestic product was expected to slow to about 4–5% in 1975.

The national retail price index rose by an estimated 16.2% in the first six months of 1975, as against 10.4% in 1974. The high rate of inflation persisted despite the government's attempts to curb inflationary pressures through tighter supervision over public expenditure and the money supply, strengthening of official price controls and price freezes, and tax measures to reduce consumption of energy and luxury goods. Contributory factors included the high prices of imported essential commodities, insufficient domestic agricultural and industrial output, and increased production costs resulting from the recent wage increases for unionized workers. The government's decision in April to increase the money supply sharply and to raise public service charges and guarantee prices to farmers caused a further rise. This departure from original policy was justified by Echeverría in his annual address to the nation on September 1 as an essential measure to ensure adequate domestic supplies and to further the promotion of crucial industrial projects for Mexico's future development.

There was a weakening in the country's external trade position in the first half of 1975. The trade

MEXICO

Education. (1972–73) Primary, pupils 9,860,933, teachers 219,565; secondary (1971–72), pupils 1,008,205, teachers 71,057; vocational, pupils 359,927, teachers 25,091; teacher training (1970–71), students 52,852, teachers 5,131; higher (including 40 universities; 1970–71), students 247,637, teaching staff 17,103.

Finance. Monetary unit: peso, with (Dec. 16, 1975) a par value of 12.50 pesos to U.S. $1 (free rate of 25.25 pesos = £1 sterling). Gold, SDRs, and foreign exchange, central bank: (June 1975) U.S. $1,278,000,000; (June 1974) U.S. $1,429,000,000. Budget (1975 estimate) balanced at 298,420,000,000 pesos. Gross domestic product: (1975 est.) 994.2 billion pesos; (1974) 812.9 billion pesos. Money supply: (Aug. 1975) 96,381,800,000 pesos; (Aug. 1974) 77,861,300,000 pesos. Cost of living (Mexico City; 1970 = 100): (May 1975) 189; (May 1974) 165.

Foreign Trade. (1974) Imports 81,297,000,000 pesos; exports 44,245,000,000 pesos. Import sources (1974): U.S. 62%; West Germany 8%; Japan 4%. Export destinations (1974): U.S. 53%; Japan 4%. Main exports (1974): nonferrous metals 13%; textile yarns and fabrics 9%; chemicals 9%; sugar 7%; cotton 6%; machinery 6%; coffee 5%; fish 4%; petroleum and petroleum products 4%. Tourism (1974): visitors 3,362,000; gross receipts U.S. $2,192,000,000.

Transport and Communications. Roads (1974) 172,100 km. (including 58,616 km. paved). Motor vehicles in use (1974): passenger 1,947,000; commercial 745,000. Railways (1974): 24,700 km.; traffic 4,534,000,000 passenger-km., freight 30,819,000,000 net ton-km. Air traffic (1974): 5,894,000,000 passenger-km.; freight 70,798,000 net ton-km. Shipping (1975): merchant vessels 100 gross tons and over 274; gross tonnage 574,857. Telephones (1974) 2,549,600. Radio receivers (Dec. 1973) 16,870,000. Television receivers (Dec. 1973) 4,339,000.

Agriculture. Production (in 000; metric tons; 1974; 1973 in parentheses): corn 8,000 (9,900); wheat 2,764 (2,000); barley 310 (305); sorghum 2,950 (2,900); rice *c.* 400 (392); dry beans 896 (1,009); soybeans *c.* 380 (375); tomatoes *c.* 930 (900); bananas *c.* 1,155 (1,115); oranges 2,013 (1,900); lemons 236 (233); coffee *c.* 210 (195); sugar, raw value 2,837 (2,821); tobacco *c.* 67 (65); agaves (1973) 142, (1972) 141; cotton, lint 412 (326); fish catch (1973) 482, (1972) 459. Livestock (in 000; Dec. 1973): cattle *c.* 27,500; sheep *c.* 5,844; pigs *c.* 13,024; horses (1972) 4,334; mules (1972) 2,707; asses (1972) 2,887; chickens (1972) 147,200.

Industry. Production (in 000; metric tons; 1974): cement 10,498; crude oil 29,702; coal (1973) 4,230; natural gas (cu.m.) 21,087; electricity (kw-hr.) 40,326,000; iron ore (metal content) 3,338; pig iron 3,197; steel 5,011; sulfur 2,278; petroleum products (1973) *c.* 25,500; sulfuric acid 2,025; fertilizers: sulfate of ammonia 551, ammonium anhydrite 523, calcium superphosphate 508, urea 335; lead 186; zinc 102; copper, smelter 82; aluminum 41; manganese ore (metal content) 145; antimony ore (metal content) 2.4; gold (troy oz.) 134; silver (troy oz.) 37,545; cotton yarn (1973) 163; woven cotton fabrics (1973) 138; wool yarn (1971) 26; rayon, etc., filaments and fibres 35; nylon, etc., filaments and fibres (1973) 112.

deficit for the first half of 1975 was officially estimated at $1.7 billion, compared with $1.4 billion in January–June 1974. Imports amounted to $3.1 billion ($2.8 billion in 1974) and exports, $1.4 billion ($1.3 billion in 1974), indicating rises of 11.8% and 3.8%, respectively. The trade deficit for 1975 as a whole was unofficially estimated at $4 billion, compared with $3.2 billion in 1974. The deterioration was attributed to the recessionary trends in the U.S. and other industrially developed countries, which were responsible for a reduction in the growth of Mexican exports and a marked decline in tourism. At the same time, import costs soared. Previously, direct foreign investment and loans had compensated for this in the overall balance of payments. In the meantime, the government issued a series of measures designed to avoid a further widening of the trade gap.

As of Dec. 31, 1974, Mexico's total public foreign debt was $9,692,000,000, compared with $7,070,000,000 at the end of 1973. The deterioration of the external position, high debt repayments for 1975, and the increased disparity between the Mexican and U.S. inflation rates, as well as the political uncertainty that was traditional before a presidential election, caused rumours that the Mexican peso (which had been maintained at 12.50 pesos per U.S. dollar since 1954) might be devalued. On September 1 President Echeverría stated that, with gross foreign reserves at $1,475,000,000 on August 29, standby credits and loans of $1,285,000,000, and $400 million obtainable from the revaluation of the country's gold reserves, the current parity of the peso was assured.

During 1974 and 1975 new discoveries of oil were made in Chiapas-Tabasco, Veracruz, and Campeche, and total production rose to more than 830,000 bbl. a day. Gas was found in Nuevo Laredo and Soto la Marina. The deposits of phosphoric rock found in Baja California Sur were estimated at up to 3,000,000,000 tons. (BARBARA WIJNGAARD)

[974.A]

Middle Eastern Affairs

An important new step away from Israeli-Egyptian confrontation was taken in an agreement reached in September 1975 for an Israeli withdrawal in Sinai, the freedom of passage for nonmilitary Israeli cargoes through the Suez Canal, and a declaration by both parties that they would use peaceful means to settle their conflict. However, the agreement aroused strong criticism in several Arab quarters, and some observers believed it had increased rather than diminished the dangers of a new Middle East war.

The Arab-Israeli Dispute. The year opened with talks held in Cairo between Egyptian, Syrian, Jordanian, and Palestine Liberation Organization (PLO) representatives aimed at achieving cooperation between Jordan and the PLO in the light of resolutions taken at the Arab summit meeting in October 1974. The talks had little success; Jordan and the PLO remained hostile and mutually suspicious. Both Syria and the PLO also made clear their opposition to any new interim agreement between Egypt and Israel without a simultaneous Israeli withdrawal from Syrian territory and Jordan's West Bank.

A press declaration by U.S. Secretary of State Henry Kissinger, published on January 2, in which he said the U.S. might use force against Arab oil producers in certain circumstances, though it would

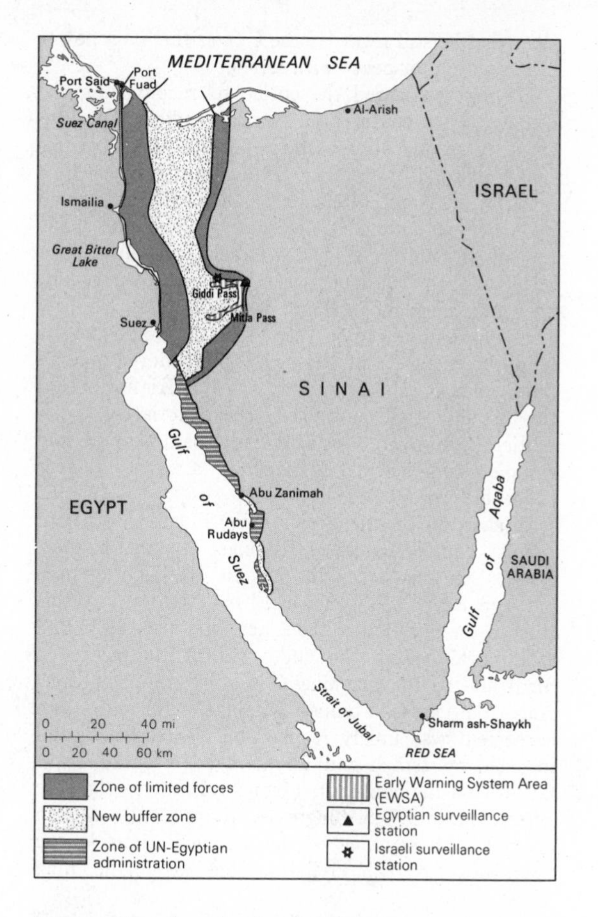

be considered only in "the gravest emergency," aroused strongly critical reactions in several Arab states. However, Kissinger felt the chances of a new stage in Arab-Israeli disengagement were sufficient for him to make an exploratory visit to Israel, Egypt, Syria, Jordan, and Saudi Arabia in February and to begin a new round of shuttle diplomacy in March. His efforts concentrated on securing agreement on a further partial Israeli withdrawal in Sinai rather than in the Syrian Golan Heights. But despite several visits to Egypt and Israel and many hours of talks, it was clear that he had failed when the suspension of his mission was announced on March 22. Declaring that shuttle diplomacy had come to an end, Egypt formally asked the U.S. and the Soviet Union to reconvene the Geneva Middle East peace conference. However, in announcing (March 29) his decision to reopen the Suez Canal in June, Egyptian Pres. Anwar as-Sadat gave a clear indication that he wished to avoid a renewal of tension in the area.

The U.S. government did not conceal the fact that it placed the main blame for the breakdown of talks on Israel's hard-line attitude, and it suspended its decision on Israel's request for military and economic aid totaling $2.5 billion as a means of pressuring the Israeli government to relax its stance. The U.S. dialogue with both Israel and Egypt continued when the Israeli foreign minister visited Washington in April. U.S. Pres. Gerald Ford and Kissinger met President Sadat in Salzburg, Austria, on June 1 and 2, and Israeli Prime Minister Yitzhak Rabin visited Washington on June 11 and 12. Kissinger said the talks with President Sadat "provided a proper basis for constructive talks with Israel," and President Ford declared bluntly that the U.S. would not allow a stalemate to develop in this all-essential progress toward peace. In return, President Sadat made it

Microbiology: *see* Life Sciences

clear that he still regarded the U.S. as the main power in the search for peace with Israel.

Having considered the option of reconvening the Geneva peace conference, the U.S. indicated its decision to resume its own peace efforts instead. U.S.-Israel relations were still strained because of U.S. pressure on Israel, although this was publicly denied by leaders of both sides, but some progress was made toward an interim Egyptian-Israeli agreement as a result of further talks between the Israeli prime minister and Kissinger in Bonn, West Germany, on July 12. Egypt announced on July 15 that it would not extend the mandate of the UN Emergency Force in Sinai when it expired on July 24, and Kissinger said this "complicated enormously the negotiating possibilities." However, President Sadat said that he had complete confidence in Kissinger as "a man who never broke his word to me."

Intense diplomatic activity continued throughout August, and on August 21 Kissinger resumed his personal peace mission in the Middle East. Differences between Egypt and Israel had been narrowed by this time to the question of the exact extent of the Israeli withdrawal behind the Giddi and Mitla passes in Sinai and to the manning of early-warning stations above the passes. Through Kissinger's mediation, an agreement was finally reached on September 1 and initialed by Israeli and Egyptian representatives at Geneva on September 4. (Israel refused to sign the agreement until U.S. congressional approval had been given to the manning of the watch stations in the Sinai passes by U.S. civilians. This was forthcoming in October.)

The agreement provided for an Israeli withdrawal of between 12 and 26 mi., from a total of about 1,000 sq.mi., of Sinai. Although the strategic Mitla and Giddi passes were to be effectively demilitarized, Israel would retain a surveillance station at Umm Khashiba near the western end of the Giddi Pass and would continue to control the Wadi Jundi, leading to Ras Sudr on the Gulf of Suez. Egypt also would man a surveillance station, to the east of the Israeli post. In addition, three manned and three unmanned electronic early warning posts to verify the operations of the Egyptian and Israeli stations would be controlled by 200 U.S. civilian personnel, who would also oversee the Israeli and Egyptian stations. In the areas of limited forces bordering the buffer zone, Egypt and Israel would be permitted to station a maximum of 8,000 men and 75 tanks.

The Abu Rudays oil fields were to be returned to Egypt, but there would be joint Israeli-Egyptian use of the road down the eastern coast of the Gulf of Suez, which passes near the oil fields. Egypt agreed to allow ships carrying nonmilitary cargoes for Israel to pass through the Suez Canal provided they did not fly the Israeli flag. The two parties undertook not to resort to the threat or use of force or military blockade against each other, but to resolve any conflict between them or in the Middle East by peaceful means.

The Israeli Knesset approved the agreement by 70 votes to 43. In the debate that preceded this action, the Israeli prime minister said he agreed with President Sadat that the agreement was "a turning point in the Arab-Israeli conflict." But there was strong opposition from the Israeli right wing, which said Israel should have insisted on a formal Egyptian declaration of nonbelligerency. The former defense minister, Moshe Dayan, voted with the opposition. There was also opposition in the Arab world from those who believed that Egypt had made too many concessions for too little return. The only Arab states to praise the agreement were Saudi Arabia and Sudan. Jordan and Kuwait refrained from criticizing it directly, but open opposition came from Iraq, Libya, Algeria, and Syria. Demonstrations against the agreement took place in Lebanon and Syria. The Central Council and Executive Committee of the PLO condemned it as a political agreement rather than a military disengagement.

President Sadat responded vigorously to his critics. He claimed that Egypt had been offered the return of the whole of Sinai as the price for ending the state of war with Israel, but had refused because it was negotiating for the Syrian and Palestinian cause as well as its own. He said the Arabs had emerged from the agreement militarily and politically stronger than before, and that Egypt would continue to strive for the return of occupied Arab territory and the recognition of the Palestinians' national rights. President Sadat's most bitter attacks were reserved for the Soviet Union, which he accused of "flagrant incitement and attempts to divide the Arab nation."

On September 11 the Egyptian government closed down the Voice of Palestine radio station in Cairo after it had broadcast the PLO denunciation of the agreement. Controversy in the Arab world over the agreement thereafter centred on whether the U.S. had given any understanding to Egypt that it would press for a further Israeli disengagement on Syria's Golan Heights and for some restitution of Palestinian rights. Egypt maintained that the U.S. had made such a commitment, but both the Syrians and the PLO denied it and the U.S. government made no public statement on the matter. Israeli spokesmen said that Israel would not withdraw in the Golan Heights except as part of a general Arab-Israeli settlement, and Syria's Pres. Hafez al-Assad said that Syria would negotiate over Golan only if there were simultaneous negotiations between Israel and the Palestinians. On October 17, following criticism of Egyptian policy by the Syrian Air Force commander, Egypt announced that it was withdrawing its aircraft stationed in Syria.

Differences among the Arabs over the Arab-Israeli conflict were also reflected in their attitudes toward Israel's possible expulsion from the UN. The sixth conference of Islamic foreign ministers, held in Jidda, Saudi Arabia, unanimously adopted a resolution proposed by Syria and the PLO calling on Islamic states to sever all relations with Israel and to press for its expulsion from the UN. A similar proposal was put to the Organization of African Unity (OAU) summit meeting at Kampala, Uganda, on July 28–August 1 by Yasir Arafat, chairman of the PLO, who attended the meeting, but it was rejected in favour of a compromise resolution calling on OAU members to take measures to reinforce pressure on Israel at the UN and its specialized agencies "including the possibility of eventually depriving it of its membership in these institutions." Egypt supported this resolution against the PLO and Libya, which demanded Israel's immediate expulsion. President Sadat later explained his view that "Israel would love to be expelled from the UN because it would rally the whole of American public opinion behind her." Egypt's opposition was crucial in preventing the demands for Israel's expulsion from being pressed successfully at the UN.

For the PLO and the Palestine guerrilla organizations in general, 1975 was a somewhat disappointing year after the diplomatic triumphs of the previous year when the Arab states recognized the PLO as the sole legitimate representative of the Palestinians and Arafat was invited to address the UN General Assembly. The General Assembly passed resolutions inviting the PLO to participate in all UN deliberations on the Middle East, creating a committee to work out a program for Palestinian self-determination, and condemning Zionism as "a form of racism." However, no satisfactory relationship was established between the Palestinians and Jordan, which continued to refuse to allow PLO guerrilla forces on its territory. Syria remained a staunch supporter and agreed to the principle of forming joint Syrian-PLO political and military committees, but the PLO was concerned by Syria's rapprochement with Jordan.

Palestinian guerrilla activity against Israel was largely confined to the Lebanese border area where it provoked the usual heavy Israeli reprisals from air, land, and sea against Palestinian refugee camps that the Israelis alleged were used as guerrilla bases. Guerrilla operations outside the Middle East, such as the two attempts on Israeli airliners at Orly airport, near Paris, during January, were disowned by the PLO. It likewise denounced the spectacular exploit at year's end by gunmen of the "Arm of the Arab Revolution" who took over OPEC headquarters in Vienna, holding hostage 11 oil ministers, among them Sheikh Ahmed Zaki Yamani of Saudi Arabia, Iran's interior minister, Jamshid Amouzegar, and numerous officials. (The Austrian government, ceding to the terrorists' demands, flew them and some of their hostages to Tripoli in Libya, where eight hostages were released, and on to Algiers where the remaining hostages, including Yamani and Amouzegar, were freed and their captors granted asylum.) On the other hand, the PLO claimed responsibility for the night attack by eight al-Fatah guerrillas on Tel Aviv, Israel, on March 5. This was seen as a move to upset Kissinger's mission to achieve a further Egyptian-Israeli disengagement agreement.

The rift between the PLO and Egypt served to conceal the division that existed among the Palestinian organizations over relations with Jordan and the possibility of negotiations with Israel. After the talks between Egypt, Syria, Jordan, and the PLO in Cairo in January, the Palestinian "rejection front" of four small groups led by George Habash's Popular Front for the Liberation of Palestine strongly criticized attempts to reconcile Jordan and the Palestinians; these efforts, it said, "had uncovered the truth about the defeatist party in the PLO leadership." After the suspension of Kissinger's Middle East mission, when it seemed that the Geneva peace conference might be reconvened, the Palestinian leadership was again faced with a decision as to whether it should take part in negotiations. But Arafat rightly predicted that Kissinger would resume his shuttle diplomacy, and when the new Israeli-Egyptian agreement was reached, the Palestinian organizations were united in their condemnation. The difficult questions raised by a resumption of the Geneva conference receded.

The balance of advantage emerging from the developments of 1975 remained a subject of hot dispute among all parties to the conflict. Foreign military experts were generally agreed that the military advantage still lay with Israel. After the Sinai settlement it was due to receive large quantities of additional U.S. weapons, as well as compensation for the loss of the Sinai oil fields and some $2.5 billion in economic aid. The Arabs were also more divided than at any time since the 1973 war. But Israel was more dependent than ever on U.S. help and ultimately had to give in to U.S. pressure. Furthermore, even U.S. aid could not entirely restore Israel's parlous economic condition or—most serious of all—prevent the clear trend toward an excess of Jewish emigrants from Israel over immigrants in 1975.

Through Kissinger's achievement, the U.S. consolidated its new relationship with the Arab world at the expense of the Soviet Union. If this was to be more than a short-term advantage, further progress would have to be made toward a general Middle East peace settlement of the kind that Ford and Kissinger repeatedly insisted they were determined to achieve. But the Syrian reaction to the Sinai agreement and Israel's rejection of further disengagement on the Golan Heights (where it continued to establish new settlements in 1975) made the prospects of further progress extremely doubtful.

Inter-Arab Relations. The rift over Egypt's decision to make a bilateral agreement with Israel affected all aspects of inter-Arab relations. In February the Arab League Defense Council met at Lebanon's request to discuss the repeated Israeli raids on Lebanese territory and reportedly agreed to all Lebanon's demands. As the year progressed, however, the Lebanon-Israel situation was overshadowed by the threat of civil war in Lebanon as fighting in Beirut between right-wing Christian and leftist Muslim groups in that country escalated markedly. All Lebanon's Arab neighbours felt deeply concerned, and the Arab League secretary-general and the Syrian foreign minister attempted to mediate between the warring factions. Egypt, which felt that Palestinian extremists, with support from Libya, Iraq, and other members of the Arab "rejection front," were exacerbating the trouble in Lebanon, showed some sympathy for Lebanese Pres. Suleiman Franjieh and the right-wing Lebanese nationalists. Syria and the PLO did not accept this view, although as far as possible they tried to maintain their mediating role.

When the Arab League foreign ministers met urgently in Cairo on October 15 and 16 at Kuwait's request to discuss the Lebanese crisis, both Syria and the PLO boycotted the meeting on the ground that it was an attempt to divert attention from the Egyptian-Israeli interim peace agreement. The Arab ministers attending the meeting could only appeal to the warring factions to exercise restraint and promise financial aid to help reconstruct what was destroyed

U.S. Secretary of State Henry Kissinger (centre left) conferred with Egyptian Pres. Anwar as-Sadat (second from right) in August at the Naqmura Palace, Alexandria.

CLAUDE SALHANI—SYGMA

WIDE WORLD

As part of the Middle East accords, Israeli tanks leave a limited armaments zone near the Suez Canal.

during the fighting. They warned Israel against exploiting the troubled situation in Lebanon. However, when the Egyptian foreign minister said that Egypt would regard any intervention in Lebanon as an aggression against itself, it was widely understood that the warning was directed to Damascus as well as Jerusalem.

Another consequence of Egypt's move toward a bilateral agreement with Israel was the rapprochement between Jordan and Syria, which was sealed with the formation of a joint high commission, first announced in June, to coordinate policies. Because of the differences in political outlook of the two regimes, this stopped short of a full-scale military alliance. Clearly, however, Jordan and Syria felt the need to close ranks now that Egypt was effectively withdrawing from the confrontation with Israel.

No similar rapprochement took place between Syria and Iraq, which offered to revive the "northern front" with Israel, as it had existed in the October 1973 war, provided Syria renounced UN Security Council resolutions 242 and 338 which implied Arab recognition of Israel. Relations between the rival Baathist regimes in Iraq and Syria deteriorated further during the year. This was partly due to the dispute over the use of the Euphrates waters, but each party accused the other of plotting against it and maltreating its citizens. Iraq also accused Syria of trying to promote the cause of the Kurdish nationalists even after the collapse of their rebellion in March following Iranian withdrawal of support.

Iraq's position in the Arab world was strongly affected by its agreement in March to settle its differences with Iran, which was achieved through Algerian mediation. While Iraq's military and economic positions were both enhanced by the end of the Kurdish rebellion and the relaxation of tension on the Iraq-Iran frontier, its prestige as the leading member of the Arab "rejection front" and the champion of Arabism in the Persian Gulf inevitably suffered. Iraq's hitherto outspoken support for the Dhofari rebels in Oman, opposed by the sultan with the aid of some 4,000 Iranian troops, was no longer very convincing. (The rebels were finally routed in December.)

While Egypt's ties with Syria, the PLO, and Algeria all suffered during 1975 because of the Sinai agreement, its relations with Saudi Arabia, Sudan, and the Persian Gulf states were unaffected. Its ties with Libya, which went from bad to worse in the first half of the year until a complete break in relations was seriously expected, took a surprising turn for the better in mid-October. Senior officials of the Syrian-Egyptian-Libyan Federation of Arab Republics helped to mediate between the two sides, and Libyan Pres. Muammar al-Qaddafi was reportedly grateful for a warning from pro-Egyptian elements in Libya of an attempted coup against him.

Oil and Economics. Because of the worldwide economic recession and the oversupply of oil, all the major Arab oil-producing states reduced their oil output in 1975 below 1974 levels. Their oil revenues increased because of the rise in oil prices, but they claimed that this was more than outweighed by imported inflation. At the opening of the UN's seventh special session on development and international economic cooperation on September 1, the Algerian foreign minister said there had been progress in the attitude of the developed countries since the failure of the consumer-producer conference in Paris in April; they now "formally recognized the need to give equal attention to the problems of energy, raw materials and development." The speech by Kissinger which followed strongly attacked any further oil price increases, since "the enormous and arbitrary increases in the price of oil in 1973 and 1974 have already exacerbated both inflation and recession worldwide."

This question was the centre of interest at the Organization of Petroleum Exporting Countries (OPEC) meeting in Vienna on September 24. Before the meeting a clear division had appeared. Saudi Arabia, concerned over the effect on the world economy and the oil market, favoured no price increases while most of the other producers, with Iran as their leading spokesman, advocated an increase of 15–20%. Questions of national prestige and rivalry for OPEC leadership were also involved, and the meeting was often stormy. Saudi Arabia was nearly isolated, although it had some support from Algeria, but it was able to use the threat that it would act alone by freezing its own oil prices to enforce a compromise 11% increase. The Saudi attitude was later strongly criticized by Iran.

By reopening the Suez Canal and opening up the Egyptian economy to foreign investment, Egypt made a clear bid to recover some of its former status as an international financial and commercial centre. The troubles in Lebanon, its main rival for this position in the Arab Middle East, improved its chances, but there was little indication that many of the international companies would move their regional offices to Cairo; as the situation in Lebanon worsened, the companies that fled Beirut appeared to prefer Athens. In general, however, increasing oil revenues, which benefited not only the oil producers, made the whole Middle East the scene of strong commercial competition between the industrialized countries.

(PETER MANSFIELD)

See also Energy; articles on the various political units.
[978.B]

Migration, International

Western and Northern European countries, which for over a decade had relied on increasing supplies of foreign labour from labour-exporting countries, strove in 1975 to limit or even halt the influx of migrant workers, including illegal immigrants, because of recession and unemployment conditions.

The movement of migrant workers, overwhelmingly Italians, within the European Economic Community (EEC) could not be stopped, but their numbers fell from about three-quarters of the total of foreign workers in the EEC in 1960 to one-quarter in 1975. West Germany and France, which between them accommodated two-thirds of the EEC's migrants, had turned to Turks, Yugoslavs, Spaniards, Portuguese, and North Africans. By 1974 it was estimated that there were more than three million Muslim workers and their families in Europe, from North Africa, Yugoslavia, Asia, and Turkey. In West Germany a recruitment ban of November 1973 was followed in April 1975 by restrictions on migrant workers' movements within Germany, aiming to limit them to 12% of the labour force in any one area. Legal migrant labour was estimated at over two million, with 7.4% unemployed in 1975. France, with nearly two million legal migrants, had barred immigration to non-EEC workers in July 1974 and introduced a rule preventing illegal immigrants from "regularizing" their position to avoid deportation. From March 1, 1975, the squeeze was extended to African migrant workers other than Algerians. Belgium, with 265,000 legal migrants, stopped non-EEC immigration in August 1974. The Netherlands (*c.* 160,000 foreign migrants) also introduced local restrictions; an additional 130,000-odd Surinamese with unrestricted entry from the Netherlands Antilles caused ethnic tensions, and their numbers were augmented in 1975 by tens of thousands of Asians fleeing Surinam before independence on November 25 under a black government and the possible ending of The Netherlands' "open door" colonial policy. Luxembourg had nearly 28% foreign workers (mostly EEC) in its labour force.

Switzerland (nearly 600,000 settled or annual workers, 152,000 seasonal workers, and 98,000 daily border commuters), Sweden (197,000, including over 100,000 Finns), and Austria (229,000, including 166,000 Yugoslavs) were major non-EEC labour-importing countries in Europe. In August 1975 the Swiss government began to stabilize its foreign population, and a ruling banned new quotas for permits for annual workers and cut the maximum number of seasonal workers. Denmark and Norway reintroduced stricter curbs on immigrants from outside the Nordic community. In Britain, because of prior curbs, dependents constituted 99.8% of New Commonwealth immigrants (20,424 in 1973). Another 13,433 U.K. passport holders (mainly Asians from East Africa) were accepted in 1974. Foreign nationals (including EEC countries) accepted for settlement totaled 26,800.

Restrictionist moves in Europe reflected not only economic weakness but concern over such social problems as native unrest and immigrant militancy. Most governments were unable to make major reductions in foreign manpower, essential particularly in the public services. Curbs on immigration were accompanied by policies designed to integrate foreign workers already in the country and their families.

Immigration and Naturalization in the United States

Year ended June 30, 1975

Country or region	Total immigrants admitted	Quota immigrants	Nonquota immigrants: Total	Nonquota immigrants: Family—U.S. citizens	Aliens naturalized
Africa	6,729	5,163	1,566	1,411	2,757
Asia*	132,469	94,032	38,437	33,539	44,915
China†	18,536	14,881	3,655	3,318	9,683
Hong Kong	4,891	4,179	712	632	...
India	15,773	14,827	946	746	2,720
Iran	2,337	1,534	803	791	601
Iraq	2,796	2,594	202	190	526
Israel	2,125	1,510	615	506	1,844
Japan	4,274	2,017	2,257	1,930	1,548
Jordan	2,578	2,124	454	422	1,364
Korea, South	28,362	19,782	8,580	6,391	6,007
Lebanon	2,075	1,701	374	350	796
Philippines	31,751	18,984	12,767	11,936	15,330
Thailand	4,217	1,348	2,869	2,603	411
Vietnam, South	3,039	411	2,628	2,267	1,369
Europe‡	73,996	54,499	19,497	17,445	50,268
Germany, West	5,154	1,556	3,598	3,209	5,187
Greece	9,984	8,023	1,961	1,822	6,647
Italy	11,552	9,213	2,339	2,143	8,798
Poland	3,941	3,042	899	830	3,069
Portugal	11,845	10,732	1,113	1,037	3,728
Spain	2,549	1,628	921	801	922
U.S.S.R.	5,118	4,908	210	167	550
United Kingdom	10,807	6,336	4,471	3,944	8,532
Yugoslavia	3,524	3,020	504	452	3,273
North America	146,668	109,714	36,954	31,564	34,794
Canada	7,308	3,342	3,966	3,300	3,548
Cuba	25,955	24,794	1,161	309	15,546
Dominican Republic	14,066	11,550	2,516	2,261	1,518
El Salvador	2,416	1,676	740	706	342
Haiti	5,145	4,498	647	594	1,966
Jamaica	11,076	9,357	1,719	1,600	2,152
Mexico	62,205	41,977	20,228	17,146	5,781
Trinidad and Tobago	5,982	5,060	922	889	987
Oceania	3,347	2,208	1,139	1,037	595
South America	22,984	15,944	7,040	6,508	6,722
Argentina	2,227	1,675	552	485	1,378
Colombia	6,434	4,032	2,402	2,241	1,699
Ecuador	4,727	3,758	969	915	807
Guyana	3,169	2,692	477	436	524
Peru	2,256	1,276	980	955	710
Total, including others	386,194	281,561	104,633	91,504	141,537

Note: Immigrants listed by country of birth; aliens naturalized by country of former allegiance.
*Includes Turkey. †Taiwan and People's Republic. ‡Includes U.S.S.R.
Source: U.S. Department of Justice, Immigration and Naturalization Service, *1975 Annual Report*.

Illegal immigration posed a worldwide problem. At its 60th conference in June 1975 the International Labour Organization adopted a convention dealing with "migration in abusive conditions" and "equality of opportunity and treatment," though 81 delegates abstained. Illegal immigrants were a source of concern in the U.S., and a Committee on Illegal Aliens chaired by the attorney general was established. In the year ended June 30, 1975, 386,194 immigrants were admitted and 141,537 naturalized, as compared with 394,861 and 131,655, respectively, in the previous year. Statistics for 1974 showed 35,483 professional and technical workers, including 6,422 from Europe, 21,644 from Asia, 1,376 from Africa, 4,228 from North America, and 1,365 from South America.

In 1974 Canada admitted 218,465 immigrants, 18.6% over the previous year. The U.K. continued to be the major sending country, with almost 40,000, while the U.S. came second, with 27,000. Portugal, Greece, and Italy were the main European sending states, but India (13,000), Hong Kong (13,000), Jamaica (11,000), and the Philippines (10,000) provided larger contingents than did Greece or Italy.

Analyses made in connection with International Women's Year (*see* UNITED NATIONS: *Special Report*) of world migration of women threw light on migration trends in Europe and three major overseas countries of traditional migration. In Western Europe women were more than one-third of the 12 million migrant population. In the U.S. women had exceeded men every year in the decade 1964–73, with an average of 54.8% of immigration over that period (3,615,536); in 1973, the percentage of women migrants to the U.S. was highest for Germany (70.9% of all migrants), Sweden (66.7%), Vietnam (81%), and Japan (71.3%). In Canada immigration figures for 1964–73 showed a much closer balance between male and female immigrants. The Australian statistics showed a percentage of women to all immigrants ranging from 46 to 49%. (SHEILA PATTERSON)

See also Refugees.
[525.A.1.c]

Military Affairs: *see* Defense

Mining and Quarrying

With a few notable exceptions 1975 was a recession year in mining. Demand for metals was well below supply; prices were sharply reduced; and inflation eroded profits. Coal, uranium, and precious metals were among the exceptions. Copper was the hardest hit, with production at U.S. mines estimated to be 25 to 30% below 1974. Iron ore was in demand at the beginning of the year, but by June inventories were accumulating.

Nations that exported copper, iron ore, and bauxite, with the example of the Organization of Petroleum Exporting Countries before them, renewed efforts to control commodity prices through associations formed among producing countries. The copper-exporting countries announced cutbacks, but these appeared to have amounted to only 10% from 1974. Such nations as Chile, Zambia, and Zaire, which are heavily dependent for foreign exchange on copper, were subject to a marked economic downturn and a consequent slowing of development plans.

Compounding the woes of mining companies in the adverse economic situation were the high costs of meeting environmental standards and the delays in obtaining necessary permits. A case in point was found in the concentrated copper mining industry of Arizona, which collectively spent $84.1 million in 1974 on environmental control facilities. This expenditure raised to $313.4 million the total spent by the industry since the enactment of clean air statutes. Also, whereas capital expenditures had always been under the control of corporate management, this was not the case with the many millions of dollars that had to be spent for environmental protection according to timetables established by governmental bodies.

Industry Developments. The financial structure of mining companies continued the change that had begun in the mid-1960s. Historically, U.S. mining companies provided capital investment out of cash flow derived from earnings, and also from provisions for depreciation and depletion. By 1975, however, approximately 30% of the capital investment came from external sources such as long-term debt, bonds, and production payments. Industry leaders projected that in the future from 33 to 50% of capital required by mining companies would be derived from external sources. One reason that internal sources were no longer sufficient was that capital requirements escalated dramatically with inflation; the rate for the next five years was projected by one of the largest engineering and construction firms at 10% per year.

MIKE PETERS—©1975 DAYTON DAILY NEWS

WIDE WORLD

Open-pit mining of nickel by Société Imetal in New Caledonia. The French firm, controlled by the Rothschilds, began attempts to acquire Copperweld Corp. in September.

The high cost of new mines and processing facilities was expected to be reflected in higher mineral commodity prices in the years ahead. For example, the recent depressed U.S. producer copper price of 60 to 63 cents per pound yielded a profit at only a few operations. It was generally believed in industry circles that a price of $1 per pound would be required to stimulate development of new ore bodies.

Phelps Dodge Corp. completed late in the year in Hidalgo County, N.M., the first new copper smelter built for many years in the U.S. It was designed to operate in an environmentally acceptable manner by the flash smelting process. Of the $200 million cost, $70 million was for antipollution facilities. Capacity was to be 100,000 tons per year of fire-refined copper. Universal Oil Products Co. Inc. announced plans to build a pilot plant at Tucson, Ariz., to test a new process that would recover nickel from refractory laterite ore in an environmentally acceptable manner.

In the mid-1960s the New Jersey Zinc Co. discovered a new zinc area in middle Tennessee in limestone formations under deep cover. But it was not until the end of 1974 that the first mine was brought in by that company, a small one at Elmwood. Many companies were exploring in the area, which was proven to extend into Kentucky.

Uganda nationalized the mines of Kilembe Copper Cobalt Ltd., owned principally by Falconbridge Nickel Mines Ltd. of Canada. Civil disorders in Angola interrupted rail service of the Benguela railroad, which reduced the copper shipments from Zaire and Zambia that are normally delivered to the port at Lobito.

The surge to unprecedented heights of the price of

copper, among other commodities, in 1974 caused the poor exporting nations to consider that the private mining companies were enjoying windfall profits. In 1975 numerous unilateral moves were made by governments, such as Papua New Guinea, Australia, Canada, and others, to take a greater share of income, particularly among the Caribbean bauxite countries.

The Peruvian government nationalized and expropriated the properties of Marcona Mining Co. in Peru. The only iron-mining company in Peru, Marcona mined approximately 10 million tons per year. Compensation had not been settled at the end of 1975. Also in Peru a new copper refinery was built at Ilo, and plans were under way to expand it. Southern Peru Copper Corp., which operated the Toquepala mine and processing facilities, planned to double its capacity by completing the Cuajone project in 1976. This company was owned by Asarco, Cerro Corp., Phelps Dodge, and Newmont Mining Corp. Another partner in the new project was the Dutch firm Billiton International Metals BV. In addition, Peru planned to develop several new mines, such as the Torro Mocho and Cerro Verde copper deposits, with the help of foreign capital. These plans moved more slowly in 1975 because of economic conditions.

South Africa supplanted Canada and Australia as a favourable place to which foreign investors looked for mineral development. In northwestern Cape Province, Newmont and Phelps Dodge had promising zinc deposits under study.

The first major new gold mine in the Western Hemisphere in many years began production in 1975 in the Dominican Republic. Owned by Rosario Resources Corp. and J. R. Simplot Co. of the U.S. with the government of the Dominican Republic, it was expected to produce 350,000 oz. of gold and 1.5 million oz. of silver per year.

Uranium exploration was undergoing a boom because the price for U_3O_8 contained in yellow cake jumped from $10 per ton to $20. This reflected the shortage envisioned in meeting delivery schedules for reactors in operation or under construction. To achieve the U.S. government's goals for energy self-sufficiency by 1985 would require increasing the production of nuclear energy from about 1% of the national total energy output to 30%. The annual uranium requirement in the U.S. in 1975 was 11,000 tons; to meet the goal this would have to increase to 25,000 tons per year in 1980 and 45,000 tons in 1985. Canada was also undergoing a uranium exploration and development boom.

Technological Developments. Increasingly efficient mechanized equipment was the prime factor in the rising productivity at underground mines. Innovations and improvements included all-hydraulic drills in which better environmental effects were coupled with greater penetration and lower maintenance costs. In-the-hole drills produced large-diameter long holes, which reduced development costs and introduced large open-pit techniques to underground mining. Development and stoping drills that can perform various functions interchangeably were designed. They have compact configurations and hydraulic functioning to increase productivity. Mechanized loaders for blasting gels were being introduced. The use of high explosives was being reduced. Despite their higher maintenance costs LHD (load-haul-dump) machines were in the ascendancy in mines that produce in excess of 500 tons per day because of their high productivity per man employed. Increasing the size of the scoop bucket was part of the trend to even greater productivity.

Raise boring had been a major development over the past decade. Most recent improvements included improved cutter heads, variable thrust and torque control, hydraulic drive, and more compact machine profiles. Holes up to 15 ft. in diameter and up to several thousand feet in depth could be bored. Metallic piping in mines for compressed air and water was all but obsolete, having been displaced by polyvinyl chloride and fibreglass-reinforced plastic pipe.

In situ leaching of uranium, which had been in the experimental stage, was being developed on a production scale by at least one company with more to follow. In this process, leach solutions are injected through holes drilled into the deposits, and the uranium is recovered from the extracted solution. The process can be used for deposits too small for economic mining and for those in structurally poor ground that would be too expensive to mine.

(JOHN V. BEALL)

Production. The years 1974 and 1975 were for most mineral commodities periods of stagnation or decline in production levels. Only those commodities made more attractive by rising petroleum costs—coal (*see* ENERGY) in energy production; rock phosphate, potash, and sulfur among fertilizer bases; and gemstones purchased as hedges against inflation—showed production increases as a group during 1974. Available production figures for the first six to nine months of 1975 indicated little overall strength in the mining sector of the developed countries except among the centrally planned countries of Eastern Europe. Of the major metals, only aluminum managed to swim against the current of the worldwide recession, in both price levels and production levels. It was anticipated, moreover, that despite a 25% decline in consumption in the first quarter of 1975, aluminum would continue to show strength, mostly because of an anticipated worldwide shortage during 1976–77.

The strongest overall growth in production levels during the early and mid-1970s was among the less developed countries, in which investment and new capacity had been heavily favoured by development planners, and among the socialist countries of Eastern Europe, which had to a degree been insulated from the

Special containers and handling procedures are used for enriched uranium shipments from Oak Ridge, Tennessee. A shortage of this nuclear fuel by 1978 was foreseen by users.

COURTESY, UNION CARBIDE CORPORATION

worst effects of the recent inflation. For the developed countries, the continuing prospects of rising labour and fuel costs, reduced industrial demand, and continuing transportation problems reduced expectations for 1975 and, overall (especially in North America and the countries of the European Economic Community), combined to drive production back to levels of 1971 and earlier. Value of production for all minerals in 1974 was up an apparent 49%, but after elimination of inflation was in fact down about 1%.

Aluminum. Production of bauxite, the primary ore of aluminum, rose by an estimated 12% to about 78.3 million metric tons in 1974. Australia continued to lead all producers, with 20.1 million tons, followed by Jamaica (15.3 million tons), Surinam (7.1 million tons), and Guinea (an estimated 6.6 million tons). Production of aluminum metal rose by 8.4% to a total of about 13.2 million tons. The major producer was the U.S., which refined some 4,450,000 tons, about one-third of which was produced from imported alumina; the U.S. domestic production of alumina was based almost 90% on imported bauxite. Other important producers of aluminum metal were the U.S.S.R. (estimated at 1.1 million tons) and Japan (1.1 million tons). Despite the rise in worldwide output and the reduction in demand resulting from the economic slowdown, transportation problems caused supplies to remain tight in virtually every consuming country.

Antimony. World production (in terms of metal content of ores) rose slightly in 1974 by about 1.3%, an increase of only about 940 tons, to a total of 70,790 tons. South Africa continued to lead producers with 15,300 metric tons, followed by Bolivia, which showed a substantial decline but continued as the second-leading producer. The U.S. Bureau of Mines estimated that China and the Soviet Union were the third- and fourth-ranked producers, with 12,000 and 7,300 tons, respectively. Other producers remained at levels corresponding to those of previous years, except Morocco, which nearly doubled its output to some 2,140 tons. Because of many recent mine and transportation regulations involving flame-proofing materials, it was anticipated that overall demand for antimony would rise by 3.5% annually during 1974–80.

Asbestos. Production of asbestos in 1974 increased only 0.3% from 1973, reaching a total of 4,068,000 tons. Canada and the Soviet Union were responsible for 74% of world production, having extracted 1,650,000 and 1,350,000 metric tons, respectively. The only other countries producing in excess of 100,000 tons were South Africa, China, Italy, and the U.S. In the U.S., the world's leading consumer (18% of the world's production), imports fell, which, combined with a decline in mine production, led to an overall drop in consumption of about 7%.

Cement. The worldwide fuel crisis imposed limits on cement production, and as a result 1974 showed only a 0.4% increase over 1973; the total production for all countries was estimated to be 704 million metric tons, of which the major producers were the U.S.S.R. (115 million tons), the U.S. (75.2 million), Japan (73.1 million), West Germany (47.6 million), Italy (36.3 million), France (32.5 million), and China (an estimated 27 million). Consumption in the U.S. in 1974 was approximately 66% for ready-mixed concrete; 14% for products such as building blocks, drainage pipe, and pre-stressed units; and 20% for all other uses.

Chromium. World mine output of chromite ore rose by about 7% in 1974 to a total of 7.2 million metric tons, approximately 53% of which was accounted for by the two major producers, the U.S.S.R. with 1,950,000 tons and South Africa with an estimated 1,875,000 tons; other major producers (more than 500,000 tons) were Albania, Rhodesia, the Philippines, and Turkey. Consumption of chromite ores in the U.S. during 1974 rose by only about 2%, but demand for chrome in alloys and in carbon and silicon compounds continued strong.

Cobalt. World mine output of cobalt ores (in terms of metal content) rose nearly 15% in 1974 to an estimated total of approximately 30,400 metric tons. About 60% of this total originated in Zaire. Other major producers (over 1,000 tons) were Zambia (3,200 tons), Canada (1,900), Morocco and the U.S.S.R. (about 1,750 tons each), Cuba (1,600), and Finland (1,300). Consumption in the U.S., which absorbs about one-third of world production, also rose in 1974. Because it is not possible to substitute other metals for cobalt in a number of its applications, demand was expected to rise by 6% or so annually during the remainder of the 1970s, although a modest oversupply was expected in 1975.

Copper. World mine production of copper ores in 1974 increased about 3.9% over 1973, rising to a total in excess of 7,350,000 metric tons; North American production, predominantly in the U.S. and Canada, amounted to nearly a third of the world total, the U.S. (the world leader) having produced some 1,445,000 metric tons (a 7% decline from 1973) and Canada 840,000. Chile, the second-leading producer, recovered its position in the world market (although prices did not bring the expected benefits in trade balances) by increasing its production (906,000 tons) nearly a quarter over the production levels of 1972 and 1973. Following these, the major producers were the U.S.S.R. (740,000 tons), Zambia (698,000), and Zaire (499,000). Smelter production of copper in 1974 rose less than copper ores (only about 2.3%), and U.S. domestic production declined 10% to approximately 1,450,000 tons. All other major smelting countries showed substantial increases, with the exceptions of East Germany and South Africa, which experienced slight declines.

Diamonds. World production of diamonds rose slightly in 1974 to 44,085,000 carats, an increase of about 2.2% over 1973. The major producers were unchanged, with the three leading producers being Zaire with an estimated 13 million carats, the U.S.S.R. with an estimated 9.8 million carats, and South Africa with 7.5 million carats. All other major producers were in Africa; Angola, Botswana, Ghana, Sierra Leone, and South West Africa each produced in excess of 1.5 million carats. U.S. Bureau of Mines estimates suggested that approximately 72% of world output was industrial.

Gold. World production of gold in 1974 was estimated to have fallen off slightly from 1973 levels, to about 41.7 million troy ounces, an overall decline of about 4.4%. The leading producer continued to be South Africa, with about 60% of world production, or about 25 million troy ounces, followed, according to external estimates, by the Soviet Union, with about 7.5 million. Expectations that had been raised by high gold prices in recent years were dashed by their decline in 1975. In South Africa, particularly, estimated revenues of the central government were substantially lower than originally expected because preliminary budget estimates had been based on a higher world market price. Nevertheless, prices remained high enough to stimulate examination of some marginal South African properties and led to the active study of gold recovery from mine tailing and waste heaps.

Iron and Steel. During 1974 world output of iron ore rose by about 1.9%, from 834.9 million metric tons to 851.1 million; production of pig iron rose comparably, by about 1.4%, from 496.3 million metric tons to about 503.2 million; and raw steel production showed a 1.7% increase from 694.5 million metric tons to an estimated 706.3 million. The U.S.S.R. was the major producer of all three commodities—iron ore 225 million tons, pig iron 98 million tons, and raw steel 136 million tons—followed by the U.S. in only one category, raw steel 135 million tons. Australia attained the position of second-leading producer of iron ore, with some 96.7 million tons, displacing the U.S., now third. Production in Japan's import-based iron and steel industry gained some ground against the U.S., displacing it as the second-leading producer of pig iron; Japanese output rose slightly to some 90.4 million tons while the U.S.'s declined to 87 million tons. On Oct. 12, 1975, the Association of Iron-Ore Exporting Countries came into being, 30 days after ratification by Peru (the requisite seventh country) of the April 1975 agreement creating the association. Charter members (with Peru) were Mauritania, Algeria, Venezuela, Chile, India, and Australia.

Lead. Preliminary data indicated that the total production of lead from mines declined slightly in 1974 (0.8%) to a total of about 3,488,000 metric tons. Leading producers continued to be the United States, with 602,000 metric tons, and the U.S.S.R., with an estimated 475,000 tons. Other countries producing in excess of 200,000 tons were Australia (377,000 tons), Canada (331,000 tons), Mexico (218,000 tons), and Peru (204,000 tons). Smelter production of lead showed a slight increase, probably indicating utilization of stocks and inventory, with a 1974 production level of approximately 3,460,000 tons, up about 20,000 tons from 1973.

Magnesium. World production of magnesite ore rose during 1974 and attained a total of approximately 9,248,000 metric tons, an increase of about 2% over 1973. The leading producer was thought to be North Korea with an estimated 1.7 million metric tons, followed by the U.S.S.R. with an estimated 1,570,000 tons and Austria with 1,455,000 tons. China and Greece were the only other countries believed to have produced more than 1 million tons during 1974. Among lesser producers the strongest increases were shown by Yugoslavia and India, which increased production by 42 and 35% over 1973, respectively. In the U.S., the major consumer, about 44% of consumption occurred in aluminum-based alloy metals.

Manganese. According to preliminary figures, world mine production of manganese ore rose about 2.9% during 1974 to a total of 24,568,000 metric tons (metal content), as against the 1973 total of about 24,175,000 tons. Major producers remained unchanged, with the U.S.S.R. ranked first with about 8 million metric tons of ore, followed by South Africa with 4.5 million tons, Brazil (2.2 million tons), Gabon (1.9 million tons), Australia (1,750,000 tons), and India (about 1,350,000 tons). Manganese demand remained steady because its primary uses in industrial countries, especially in steel and other metallurgical applications, were lightly affected by the general economic climate.

Mercury. Production of mercury in 1974 declined by about 2.2% from 1973 to a total of about 9,040 metric tons. Spain and the U.S.S.R. were the leading producers, with about 2,075 and 1,860 tons, respectively. Other major producers were relatively unchanged, although Algeria lost ground to Canada. The second rank of producers included China (900 tons), Italy (860), Mexico (730), Yugoslavia (546), Canada (483), and Algeria (458). Mercury production in the U.S. in 1974 fell to a new low, although new production capacity was planned for 1975. Environmental legislation in the principal developed countries was expected to cut into a number of applications of mercury, especially in paints, pharmaceutical products, and agriculture.

Missiles: *see* Defense

Molecular Biology: *see* Life Sciences

Molybdenum: *see* Mining and Quarrying

Molybdenum. Production of molybdenum in terms of contained metal rose during 1974 to a total of 85,400 metric tons, an increase of about 0.5% over levels of 1973. The U.S. with almost 60% of world production was by far the leading producer. Canada maintained its second rank with about 16% of world production, followed by Chile at about 11.5% and the U.S.S.R. with an estimated 10%. Among other producers only China was believed to exceed 1,000 tons. As with many other metals, the price stability of the 1960s and early 1970s ended in 1974, with substantial increases instituted.

Nickel. Mine and smelter production increased strongly during 1974, showing among the largest increases of any of the metals. Mine production increased to some 752,000 metric tons, up 9%, or some 63,000 tons over 1973, while smelter production rose by nearly 11%, approximately 71,000 tons more than 1973 to a total of about 724,000 tons. The leading producing countries in mining were unchanged, with Canada supplying more than a third of the world total, about 272,000 tons, followed by New Caledonia and the U.S.S.R., with about 125,000 tons each. Other major producers included Australia (40,000), Cuba (an estimated 32,000), the Dominican Republic (30,000), Greece (25,000), and South Africa and Indonesia (about 21,000 each). Smelter production was led by Canada (about 177,000 tons), the U.S.S.R. (about 145,000), and Japan (104,600, entirely from imports and scrap).

Phosphate Rock. World production of rock phosphate in 1974 was 110.3 million metric tons, up about 11.6% from 1973. Much of the increased demand could be attributed to the increased cost of other fertilizers and of petrochemicals for similar applications. About 80% of all world production of phosphate is consumed as fertilizer; Morocco, which was the largest net exporter of phosphate during 1974, was only the third-leading producer (19.7 million tons), after the United States (41,445,000 tons) and the U.S.S.R. (estimated 22.5 million tons). Although enormous amounts of phosphates were expected to be needed for world agriculture during the next five years, a softening of prices by major producers during 1974 and 1975 was interpreted by some observers as an indication that substantial overcapacity may already have developed and might become fully apparent during 1977–78. The political status of Spanish Sahara, which was under numerous strains during 1975, was expected to cause substantial realignments of market positions when it was finally determined whether Mauritania and Morocco would obtain the territory's Bu Craa phosphate deposits by annexation.

Platinum-Group Metals. World production of platinum-group metals during 1974 increased substantially over 1973, reaching a level of some 5,760,000 troy ounces, an increase of about 10% over 1973. South Africa and the U.S.S.R. accounted for about 92% of the world's production, some 2,832,000 troy ounces having been produced in South Africa and an estimated 2.5 million in the U.S.S.R. Canada was the only other significant producer, with about 360,000 troy ounces. Consumption in 1974 increased significantly in the U.S., the leading market, but fell in Japan, the second-leading consumer during the second half of 1974. Prices of osmium and ruthenium rose during 1974, but the other four platinum-group metals, platinum, palladium, rhodium, and iridium, all fell.

Potash. Production of potash rose slightly in 1974 to a total of about 23,865,000 metric tons, an increase of 8.3% over 1973. The two leading producers, the U.S.S.R. and Canada, both increased their output, with Canada showing a 24% increase over 1973. After these two the other major producers were East Germany (2,865,000), West Germany (2,620,000), the U.S. (2,513,000), and France (2,276,000).

Silver. World mine production of silver was estimated to have declined slightly during 1974 from 1973's all-time high of 305.9 million troy ounces to about 299,999,000 ounces. Preliminary figures were available for the leading producing countries in the Americas, although the U.S.S.R. had not published any official figures. Canada led all producing countries with some 43,765,000 troy ounces, followed closely by Peru (43.5 million), Mexico (39.8 million), and the U.S. (33.8 million). Only the U.S.S.R. had production of an order approaching these countries, estimated to be about 42 million troy ounces. Handy & Harman characterized the year 1974 as "perhaps the most chaotic period in the history of world silver markets." Prices not only doubled the previous record to a high of 670 cents per troy ounce in February, but also fluctuated within much wider limits than in the past.

Sulfur. World production of elemental sulfur was estimated to have risen by about 2.5 million metric tons to a total of about 34 million tons in 1974. The U.S. was the leading producer with some 11,490,000 tons, followed by Canada (about 7.8 million tons), the U.S.S.R., Poland, Mexico, and France. In the U.S., despite production increases of 5% in both native and recovered sulfur, imports also rose, nearly doubling over 1973. The U.S. continued to be a net exporter, however, as exports also rose (by about 46%). It was anticipated that the relatively strong position shown by sulfur against the general economic situation might be expected to continue during 1975 and 1976 as additional fertilizer plants under construction, or contracted for, went into production.

Tin. World mine production of tin declined by approximately 2% during 1974 according to U.S. Bureau of Mines estimates, with total production at 231,507 metric tons. Major producers were virtually unchanged, with most of the decline having occurred in Malaysia, the largest producer, off some 4,000 tons, and in Zaire, off about 1,000 tons. After Malaysia, with 68,125 tons, the leading producers were the U.S.S.R. (about 30,000 tons), Bolivia (29,500), Indonesia (25,000, up some 2,700 tons, the largest gain of any producing country), China (estimated at 20,500), and Thailand (20,300). Smelter production of tin also declined during 1974, but by only about 1%, down from 232,200 tons in 1973 to an estimated 229,300 in 1974. Malaysian smelter production rose to about 84,400 tons; it was the world leader. After Malaysia, leading countries were, or were estimated to be, the U.S.S.R. (30,000 tons), China (20,500), Thailand (19,800), Indonesia (15,100), and the United Kingdom (12,100).

Titanium. Mine production of titanium in 1974 declined by about 1% from levels of 1973 to a total of about 849,000 metric tons. Norway was the leading producer of ilmenite concentrates, with about 848,000 metric tons, continuing to show remarkable growth (12.6% in 1974 and 11.7% in 1973); Australia, the second-leading producer of ilmenite concentrates, showed even more remarkable growth, a nearly 15% increase over levels of 1973. After these two the leading producers were Malaysia (190,000 tons) and Finland (152,000 tons). Australia was also the overall leader among titanium producers as it shipped some 322,000 tons of rutile concentrates; there were no other major producers of rutile.

Tungsten. Worldwide, production of tungsten ore (in terms of contained metal) was virtually unchanged from 1973 (38,414 metric tons in 1974, as compared with 38,401 in 1973, according to estimates by the U.S. Bureau of Mines). The two leading producers were thought to be China and the U.S.S.R., with estimated production of 8,500 and 7,600 tons, respectively. The U.S. was probably the third-ranking producer, with 3,348 tons in 1974, down about 2.6% from the preceding year, followed by South Korea (3,078 tons), Thailand (2,204 tons), North Korea (an estimated 2,150 tons), and Bolivia (2,028 tons). Imports of tungsten for consumption into the U.S. amounted to about 5,260 tons, the highest level since 1957. Consumption in the U.S. rose by about 10%, primary uses being tungsten carbide materials 65%, tungsten metal mill products 15%, and tool steels 10%.

Uranium. Despite increased interest in alternatives to petroleum or natural gas energy sources, production of uranium (in terms of U_3O_8) showed a nearly 6% decline in 1974, as world production fell from 23,253 metric tons in 1973 to 21,933 tons in 1974. This was an estimated total prepared by the U.S. Bureau of Mines, which noted that there were some dozen producing countries for which available information was so meagre that the bureau was unable even to estimate levels of production; these countries included not only the U.S.S.R. and China, but also Australia, Brazil, and several other nonsocialist countries. Among the countries for which information was available, the U.S. was the leading producer with 10,458 tons, followed by Canada (4,265), South Africa (3,074), and France (about 2,000). At a meeting in London in 1975 the Uranium Institute was established by 16 producing companies and governmental agencies from five countries to promote research, development, and information exchange. Because U.S. production declined by some 13% in 1974, concurrent with a strong rise in domestic demand, prices rose sharply, nearly doubling during the year.

Zinc. Both mine and smelter production of zinc rose modestly in 1974. Mine production rose by about 1.5% in 1974, reaching a total of some 5,795,000 metric tons (metal content of ore). Canada was the leading producer, with fully one-fifth of world production, amounting to some 1,160,000 tons. The U.S.S.R. was estimated to be the second-leading producer at about 680,000 tons; it was followed by the U.S. and Australia, both with preliminary totals for the year of 453,500 tons. Smelter production increased by about 2.1% in 1974. Japan's import-based smelting industry was the world leader with output of almost 850,000 tons; it was followed by the U.S.S.R. (with an estimated 680,000 tons), the U.S. (504,000 tons), and Canada (426,000 tons).

(WILLIAM A. CLEVELAND)

See also Earth Sciences; Energy; Industrial Review: *Gemstones; Iron and Steel;* Materials Sciences.

[724.B.1 and C.3]

ENCYCLOPÆDIA BRITANNICA FILMS. *Problems of Conservation: Minerals* (1969).

Monaco

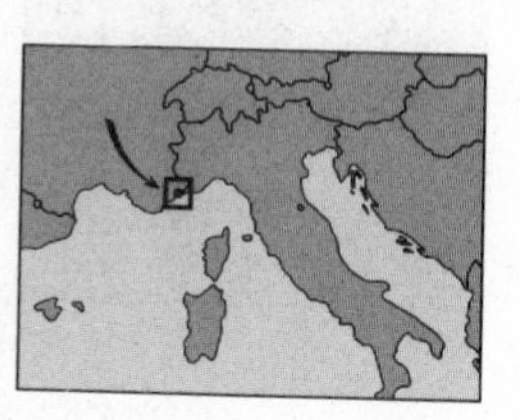

A sovereign principality on the northern Mediterranean coast, Monaco is bounded on land by the French département of Alpes-Maritimes. Area: 0.73 sq.mi. (1.89 sq.km.). Pop. (1974 est.): 25,000. Language: French. Religion: predominantly Roman Catholic. Prince, Rainier III; minister of state in 1975, André Saint-Mleux.

During the summer of 1975 old-timers in the ornate Casino de Monte Carlo were looking askance at the scene just down the road. There, in the principality's

WIDE WORLD

Prince Rainier and Princess Grace attended the annual Red Cross ball in Monaco in August with their lovely daughter Princess Caroline.

newly completed $65 million Loews Corp. hotel complex, U.S. millionaire Robert Tisch was challenging the whole concept of Monaco's character with a garish new casino reminiscent of Las Vegas. Not only did Tisch introduce three U.S.-style crap games and a device called the money wheel but he also brought in John Licini, former director of Caesar's Palace in Las Vegas. The gala opening of the new gaming rooms in November 1974 was part of Prince Rainier's plan to enlarge the clientele to boost Monaco's finances.

In May Prince Rainier and Princess Grace bought an elegant three-story house in Paris in the Square de l'Avenue Foch, not far from their former apartment residence, for about $1.7 million. The move to larger quarters was made to enable the family to live together during the education of the children in Paris.

André Saint-Mleux, the minister of state, signed the Final Act of the Conference on Security and Cooperation in Europe in Helsinki, Fin., on August 1.

(K. M. SMOGORZEWSKI)

MONACO

Education. (1971–72) Primary, pupils 1,486, teachers 71; secondary, pupils 2,089, teachers 165; vocational, pupils 458, teachers 61.

Finance. Monetary unit: French franc, with (Sept. 22, 1975) a free rate of Fr. 4.55 to U.S. $1 (Fr. 9.43 = £1 sterling). Budget (1974 est.): revenue Fr. 289 million; expenditure Fr. 354 million.

Foreign Trade. Included with France. Tourism (1973) 137,100 visitors.

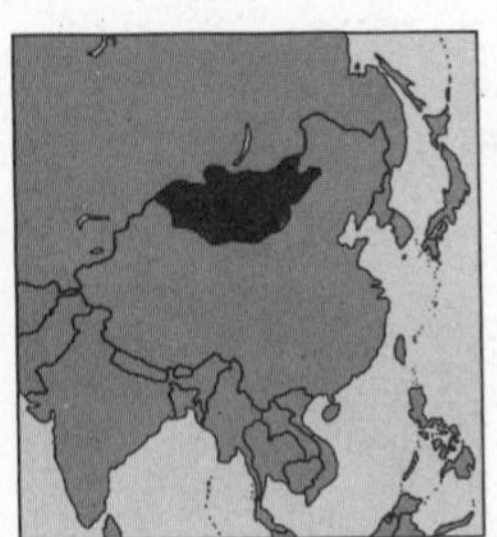

Mongolia

A people's republic of Asia lying between the U.S.S.R. and China, Mongolia occupies the geographic area known as Outer Mongolia. Area: 604,000 sq.mi. (1,565,000 sq.km.). Pop. (1975 est.): 1,446,000. Cap. and largest city: Ulan Bator (pop., 1974 est., 312,000). Language: Khalkha Mongolian. Religion: Lamaistic Buddhism. First secretary of the Mongolian People's Revolutionary (Communist) Party in 1975 and chairman of the Presidium of the Great People's Hural, Yumzhagiyen Tsedenbal; chairman of the Council of Ministers (premier), Zhambyn Batmunkh.

At the celebration in Ulan Bator in August 1975 of the 30th anniversary of Japan's unconditional surrender, speeches and press articles emphasized the "decisive" part played by the Soviet-Mongolian operations against the Japanese forces in Inner Mongolia and Manchuria—operations that started only five days before Japan capitulated. In a message to Tsedenbal, the Soviet leader Leonid I. Brezhnev said that the Soviet people would never forget the assistance given by the people of Mongolia in the common struggle against Japanese militarists. Later in August Tsedenbal visited Moscow to discuss the question of increased Soviet-Mongolian collaboration with Brezhnev and other Soviet leaders.

On June 15 more than 14,000 candidates were elected to the local councils of *aymags* (regions), *somons* (districts), and towns of the republic; 96.3% of the electorate took part in these elections.

Mongolia's goods exchange with the Council for Mutual Economic Assistance (Comecon) countries, accounting for 95% of its total trade, increased in 1974 by 7.2% as compared with 1973. The first British trade mission ever to visit Mongolia, organized by the East European Trade Council, returned to London in June 1975. In 1974 Anglo-Mongolian trade reached the modest sum of £127,000, but it was expected that the turnover would approach £1 million by 1976.

(K. M. SMOGORZEWSKI)

MONGOLIA

Education. (1971–72) Primary, pupils 153,604, teachers 4,921; secondary, pupils 91,401, teachers 4,276; vocational, pupils 9,260, teachers 545; teacher training, students 1,864, teachers 136; higher (including University of Ulan Bator), students 8,525, teaching staff 710.

Finance. Monetary unit: tugrik, with (Sept. 22, 1975) a nominal exchange rate of 3.40 tugriks to U.S. $1 (6.98 tugriks = £1 sterling). Budget (1974 est.): revenue 2,620,000,000 tugriks; expenditure 2,610,000,000 tugriks.

Foreign Trade. (1970) Imports *c.* 460 million tugriks; exports *c.* 330 million tugriks. Import sources: U.S.S.R. *c.* 80%; Czechoslovakia *c.* 5%. Export destinations: U.S.S.R. *c.* 70%; Czechoslovakia 9%. Main exports: agricultural raw materials 58%; raw materials for food 20%; foodstuffs 10%.

Transport and Communications. Roads (1970) *c.* 75,000 km. (including *c.* 9,000 km. main roads). Railways (1973) 1,425 km. Telephones (Jan. 1974) 27,000. Radio receivers (Dec. 1970) 166,000. Television receivers (Dec. 1973) 34,000.

Agriculture. Production (in 000; metric tons; 1973; 1972 in parentheses): wheat *c.* 400 (*c.* 170); oats *c.* 40 (*c.* 17); barley *c.* 27 (*c.* 17); potatoes *c.* 37 (*c.* 10); milk *c.* 155 (*c.* 155); beef and veal *c.* 71 (*c.* 70); mutton and goat meat *c.* 116 (*c.* 114). Livestock (in 000; Dec. 1973): cattle *c.* 2,206; sheep *c.* 14,077; goats (1972) *c.* 4,338; horses (1972) *c.* 2,239; camels (1972) *c.* 670.

Industry. Production (in 000; metric tons; 1973): coal 118; lignite 2,206; salt 11; cement 146; electricity (kw-hr.) 669,000.

Morocco

A constitutional monarchy of northwestern Africa, on the Atlantic Ocean and the Mediterranean Sea, Morocco is bordered by Algeria and Spanish Sahara. Area: 177,117 sq.mi. (458,730 sq.km.). Pop. (1974 est.): 16,880,000. Cap.: Rabat (pop., 1971, 367,600). Largest city: Casablanca (pop., 1971, 1,506,400). Language: Arabic; Berber. Religion: Muslim. King, Hassan II; prime minister in 1975, Ahmed Osman.

Trying to keep his promise to "liberate" the phosphate-rich Spanish Sahara in 1975, King Hassan announced on October 16 that he would send 350,000 unarmed Moroccans across the southern frontier to achieve this by peaceful means. His announcement came after months of minor clashes in the territory and wrangling among the countries mainly concerned, which included Spain, Mauritania, Algeria, and Morocco itself. The announcement also came the same day that the International Court of Justice, requested by the UN General Assembly to give a ruling, advised that neither Morocco nor Mauritania had any historic claim to sovereignty over the territory. Despite appeals from the UN Security Council and the strengthening of Spanish defenses, some 200,000 Moroccans, armed only with the Koran, started the "Green March" across the border on November 6 and encamped a few miles inside Spanish Saharan territory. Spanish forces had withdrawn from the area but laid down a minefield along their front. The Moroccans withdrew on King Hassan's orders three days later, and both sides were thus able to avoid a seeming defeat. On November 14 Spain undertook to hand over the territory to joint Moroccan-Mauritanian control by the end of February 1976.

Relations with Spain had already been strained. Spanish fishing vessels were detained, and the Spanish enclaves of Ceuta and Melilla on the Mediterranean coast were harassed. After the march relations deteriorated with Algeria, which had stood for self-determination in the Sahara.

The king's policy on the Sahara issue rallied the Moroccan people behind the throne. There were no serious discussions during the year toward widening the political base of royal rule, the government continuing under the leadership of the king's brother-in-law, Ahmed Osman, as prime minister. The need to ensure Saharan liberation was given by King Hassan in March as the reason for once more postponing the holding of elections. In July he promised that elections would be held within 18 months.

French Pres. Valéry Giscard d'Estaing visited Morocco in May, the first French president to do so since the end of the protectorate in 1956. His visit was used by the Moroccan government to press for better terms of association with the European Economic Community. Amicable arrangements were reached on the vexed question of compensation for French-owned property taken over by the state.

The steep rise in the export price of Moroccan phosphates introduced in 1974 led to a sharp curtailment of demand in 1975, and original production estimates of 22.5 million tons had to be revised to 16.5 million tons, well below the previous year's level. Another severe deficit in the balance of trade was expected for 1975. (PETER KILNER)

[978.D.2.c]

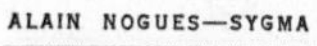
ALAIN NOGUES—SYGMA

A column of trucks snaked its way through western Morocco in October carrying volunteers for the march into Spanish Sahara.

MOROCCO

Education. (1973–74) Primary, pupils 1,337,931, teachers (including preprimary; 1970–71) 34,277; secondary and vocational, pupils 361,725, teachers (1971–72) 15,590; teacher training (1971–72), students 1,877, teachers 171; higher, students (1971–72) 16,971, teaching staff 692.

Finance. Monetary unit: dirham, with (Sept. 22, 1975) a free rate of 4.11 dirhams to U.S. $1 (8.51 dirhams = £1 sterling). Gold, SDRs, and foreign exchange: (June 1975) U.S. $431 million; (June 1974) U.S. $237 million. Budget (1973): revenue (actual) 7,678,000,000 dirhams; expenditure (est.) 5,760,000,000 dirhams. Gross domestic product: (1973) 21.3 billion dirhams; (1972) 20.2 billion dirhams. Money supply: (May 1975) 11,073,000,000 dirhams; (May 1974) 9,280,000,000 dirhams. Cost of living (Casablanca; 1970 = 100): (Jan. 1974) 126; (Jan. 1973) 110.

Foreign Trade. (1974) Imports 8,292,000,000 dirhams; exports 7,397,000,000 dirhams. Import sources (1973): France 32%; U.S. 11%; West Germany 8%; Spain 5%; Italy 5%. Export destinations (1973): France 34%; West Germany 10%; Italy 7%; Spain 5%; U.K. 5%. Main exports: phosphates 55%; citrus fruit 5%. Tourism (1973): visitors 1,340,600; gross receipts U.S. $245 million.

Transport and Communications. Roads (1973) 25,414 (including 14 km. expressways). Motor vehicles in use (1972): passenger 260,411; commercial 84,710. Railways: (1973) 1,756 km.; traffic (1974) 713.7 million passenger-km., freight 3,591,000,000 net ton-km. Air traffic (1973): 673 million passenger-km.; freight 7.7 million net ton-km. Shipping (1974): merchant vessels 100 gross tons and over 43; gross tonnage 52,564. Telephones (Dec. 1973) 208,000. Radio licenses (Dec. 1973) 1.2 million. Television licenses (Dec. 1973) 331,000.

Agriculture. Production (in 000; metric tons; 1974; 1973 in parentheses): wheat 3,048 (1,774); barley 2,062 (1,257); corn 323 (217); potatoes *c.* 240 (226); sugar, raw value *c.* 289 (239); dry broad beans (1973) *c.* 270, (1972) 267; tomatoes *c.* 460 (*c.* 460); grapes 290 (282); oranges (1973) 733, (1972) *c.* 688; tangerines and mandarin oranges (1973) 145, (1972) 150; olives *c.* 241 (*c.* 229); figs *c.* 67 (*c.* 67); dates (1973) *c.* 92, (1972) *c.* 92; fish catch (1973) 397, (1972) 246. Livestock (in 000; 1974): cattle *c.* 3,820; sheep *c.* 19,000; goats (1973) *c.* 8,900; horses *c.* 420; mules *c.* 420; asses *c.* 950; camels *c.* 230; poultry *c.* 16,000.

Industry. Production (in 000; metric tons; 1974): coal 575; crude oil 25; cement 1,914; iron ore (55–60% metal content) 534; phosphate rock (1973) 17,077; manganese ore (metal content; 1973) 122; lead concentrates (metal content) 83; zinc concentrates (metal content) 14; petroleum products (1973) 2,038; electricity (kw-hr.; 1973) 2,639,000.

Monetary Policy: *see* Economy, World

Money and Banking: *see* Economy, World

Mormons: *see* Religion

Motion Pictures

Worldwide economic uncertainty in 1975 inevitably affected cinema production in most film-making countries; but against rising costs and (comparatively) ever dwindling returns, there was the dubious comfort that in the past economically hard times always seemed to have driven audiences into the movie theatres. Optimists in the film industries of the Western world took heart from apparent signs that the decline in attendance had stopped; in the U.S. and Great Britain there were even signs of an upswing in audience figures.

The cinema's obituary list during the year included veteran Hollywood directors George Marshall and George Stevens, respectively 84 and 70; Italian directors Pietro Germi, 60, and Pier Paolo Pasolini, 53; Fredric March, 77; Evelyn Brent, a star of silent films, 74; Pierre Blaise (Louis Malle's *Lacombe, Lucien*), 20; Richard Conte, 59; Minta Durfee, star of old-time slapstick, 78; Larry Fine and Moe Howard, respectively 73 and 78, the survivors of The Three Stooges; Mark Frechette, star of Michelangelo Antonioni's *Zabriskie Point,* 27; Therese Ghiese, 77, the great German stage star who played in *Lacombe, Lucien;* John Gregson, 55; James Robertson-Justice, 69, irascible star of British comedy; John McGiver, 62, lugubrious character actor in Hollywood films; Ljuba Orlova, 73, the U.S.S.R.'s first musical star; Larry Parks, 60; and—symbols of the French cinema of the 1930s—Michel Simon, 80, and Pierre Fresnay, 77. (*See* also OBITUARIES.)

The cinema's most famous pioneer, Charles Chaplin (86 on April 16), played in a role far removed from the experience of Charlie the tramp when on March 4 he was knighted by Queen Elizabeth II.

English-Speaking Cinema. *United States.* Once again the U.S. cinema reflected the strange economic pattern of an intense focus of public interest on a small handful of films, whose enormous profits alone appeared to have ensured the survival of the industry as a whole. In 1975 the happy conquerors at the box office included most notably *The Godfather, Part II,* directed like its predecessor by Francis Ford Coppola, and *Jaws.* The success of *Jaws,* the saga of a killer shark that terrorizes the inhabitants of a New England town, directed by Steven Spielberg, seemed symptomatic of a distinctive trend in contemporary American cinema. Public reaction to the grave economic and political insecurity of the era appeared to be to look for a synthetically contrived experience of fear. Similarly, the great age of German silent horror films in the 1920s and the flowering of spine-chillers in early 1930s Hollywood both coincided with periods of grave economic difficulty.

The great white shark in "Jaws" became a motion-picture celebrity in 1975.

COURTESY OF UNIVERSAL PICTURES

In this connection, *The Exorcist* bred its followers and imitators, reflecting a curiosity about satanism and the supernatural. Among the most unpleasant was the chiller *Race with the Devil.* Quite the most spectacularly repellent film of the year, Tobe Hooper's *The Texas Chainsaw Massacre,* was no more nor less than its title indicated, an all too literal description of the fate of a group of young people who fall into the hands of a crazed homicidal family.

Other films predicted fearsome futures. Norman Jewison's *Rollerball,* a film of great technical expertise but small originality of thought, predicted a world in which an international totalitarian government solves national disputes by means of a stadium sport of murderous violence. A film of much more modest scope, Paul Bartel's *Death Race 2000,* treated a similar story with greater humour and less pretension.

A number of films found varied metaphors for U.S. society. Robert Altman's (*see* BIOGRAPHY) great frieze of American life and character, *Nashville,* sought a symbol in the hopes and failures and betrayals of the country music industry. Michael Ritchie's *Smile* probed small-town folkways and the tensions brought to the surface by the preparation of a beauty contest. Even the Western was brought to bear as allegory: Kirk Douglas directed *Posse,* which showed how a too efficient political machine can get out of the hands of its creator and turn into a monster. Hal Ashby's *Shampoo,* set on the eve of the 1968 presidential election, reflected corruption and social inadequacy through the central figure of a woman's hairdresser and amateur gigolo (Warren Beatty). Bob Fosse's *Lenny* was a sincere if muted biography of comedian Lenny Bruce, portrayed as a precocious and prophetic social critic of the nation. Through its central character, a private detective, Arthur Penn's *Night Moves* explored the difficulties of knowing one another and resolving conflicts between people. In *Dog Day Afternoon,* a story of a bank robbery in Brooklyn, Sidney Lumet showed how public reporting of an event can affect the actions of those involved in it.

Films continued to visit the past in a nostalgic search for former times of carefree security. There was a revival of interest in idols of the 1950s (20 years after his death, James Dean was the subject of a feature-length film portrait by an English director, Ray Connolly), a period to which John C. Avildsen's *W. W. and the Dixie Dancekings* also turned. Musicals of the year—Herbert Ross's biography of Fanny Brice, *Funny Lady,* and Peter Bogdanovich's disappointing *At Long Last Love*—were set in the 1920s and 1930s. Menachem Golam's *Lepke* looked back to the early gangster era. *The Great Waldo Pepper,* a much undervalued study by George Roy Hill of a man at odds with his time, looked at the life of stunt flyers in the years immediately after World War I. Michael Anderson's *Doc Savage* was a lightly satirical treatment of 1940s comic strip characters. John

Lee Strasberg (left) and Al Pacino confer in "The Godfather, Part II," a successful continuation of the original story of a Mafia family in the U.S.

Schlesinger's *Day of the Locust* was a disappointing attempt to re-create Nathanael West's 1930s Hollywood, foundering under the weight of its own overelaboration.

One of the happiest of these flights of nostalgia was John Milius' *The Wind and the Lion,* a lusty desert melodrama about the taming of a North African bandit by a formidable American lady and her two small children; it recalled the Teddy Roosevelt spirit of romantic opportunism. Roosevelt and his swashbuckling America seemed due for a revival of interest: his name was often invoked in Richard Brook's Western *Bite the Bullet,* the saga of a marathon cross-country horse race promoted by a newspaper—an image of heroic pioneer America exploited by Eastern commercialism.

Even comedy tended to look back to Hollywood's former joys and glories. Thus Brian De Palma's *Phantom of the Paradise* was a whipped-up 1970s reading of *The Phantom of the Opera;* while Mel Brooks's zany *Young Frankenstein* coincided with Paul Morissey's Italian-made *Flesh for Frankenstein.* Woody Allen's *Love and Death* parodied every Napoleon-in-Russia epic back to *War and Peace.*

Hollywood was inclined also to revert to old favourite genres. The 1940s-style private eye was again in vogue, with Dick Richards remaking *Farewell My Lovely,* starring Robert Mitchum as Raymond Chandler's Philip Marlowe, and Paul Newman re-creating his own private-eye character from *Harper* in Stuart Rosenberg's *The Drowning Pool.*

Ely Landau's American Film Theatre continued its systematic program of filming—most often in Britain—stage successes. Among the more notable productions of 1975 were Joseph Losey's interpretation of Bertolt Brecht's *Galileo,* with Topol uncomfortably cast in the central role, and Lindsay Anderson's record of his own stage production of David Storey's *In Celebration.*

In the annual awards of the U.S. Academy of Motion Picture Arts and Sciences, *The Godfather, Part II* almost swept the board, as its predecessor *The Godfather* had done in 1973. It received "Oscars" for best film of the year, best direction (Francis Ford Coppola), best adapted screenplay (Coppola and Mario Puzo), best art direction (Dean Tavoularis, Angela Graham), best set decoration (George R. Nelson), best original dramatic score (Nino Rota and Carmine Coppola, the director's father), and best supporting actor (Robert De Niro). The awards for best actor and actress went to Art Carney for *Harry and Tonto,* the story of an old man's revolt against relegation, and to Ellen Burstyn for Martin Scorsese's *Alice Doesn't Live Here Anymore.* The best supporting actress was Ingrid Bergman in *Murder on the Orient Express.* The best original screenplay was adjudged *Chinatown,* written by Robert Towne.

The best documentary short subject was adjudged Robin Lehman's *Don't;* the best documentary feature, Peter Davis and Bert Schneider's *Hearts and Minds.* Schneider provided the year's obligatory awards ceremony *scandale* by reading a message from a Viet Cong leader. Further discomfiture was produced by Dustin Hoffman's statement that the ceremony was "obscene, garish, and embarrassing." The award for the best foreign language film went to Federico Fellini's *Amarcord.* The veteran French director Jean Renoir (81) and the great Hollywood old-timer Howard Hawks (78) both received special honorary awards.

Britain. It was a dispiriting year for the British cinema. New native production shrank almost to nonexistence. Meanwhile, outside attack from puritan quarters continued. An attempt to abolish film censorship in the Greater London area was defeated by a vote in the Greater London Council. Subsequently, a private person brought a successful action against the distributors and exhibitors of the Swedish sex instruction film, *More About the Language of Love,* and followed up that success with an attempt to prosecute the president and secretary of the British Board of Film Censors. This was unsuccessful, but the litigator persisted with an action against an earlier film, *The Language of Love.*

In August the government set up a working party to consider "the requirements of a viable and prosperous British film industry over the next decade," whose report was eagerly awaited at year's end. Amid the general depression, there was a comforting touch of nostalgia in the celebration of the 50th anniversary of the foundation in London of the original Film Society, which exerted a profound influence upon the changing attitudes to motion pictures of intellectuals in the 1920s and 1930s.

Annual Cinema Attendance*

Country	Total in 000	Per capita
Afghanistan	19,200	1.1
Albania	8,400	4
Algeria	89,300	6
Angola	3,500	0.6
Argentina	51,400	2.1
Australia	32,000	3
Austria	26,700	3.6
Bahrain	1,400	6
Barbados	1,800	7.5
Belgium	29,800	3.1
Bolivia	3,200	0.9
Brazil	234,700	3
Brunei	2,900	20.4
Bulgaria	112,400	13.1
Burma	222,500	8.1
Cambodia	20,000	3
Cameroon	6,200	1
Canada	92,300	4.3
Chad	1,300	0.4
Chile	44,600	5
Colombia	92,800	5
Cuba	124,300	14.2
Cyprus	6,100	9.5
Czechoslovakia	98,400	6.8
Dahomey	1,200	0.4
Denmark	20,700	4.1
Dominican Republic	5,200	1.2
Ecuador	16,000	2.5
Egypt	65,400	2
El Salvador	10,400	3
Finland	10,000	2.2
France	184,700	3.6
Germany, East	81,500	4.8
Germany, West	149,800	2.4
Ghana	18,7C0	2
Guatemala	8,300	1.5
Guyana	10,300	13.7
Haiti	1,500	0.3
Hong Kong	71,300	17.5
Hungary	74,400	7.1
Iceland	1,600	7.6
India	3,490,000	6.2
Iran	28,200	0.9
Iraq	8,300	1.3
Ireland	38,000	13
Israel	32,100	10.1
Italy	555,400	10.1
Ivory Coast	11,500	2.5
Japan	187,000	1.7
Jordan	3,200	1.8
Korea, South	125,200	3.9
Kuwait	3,700	4
Laos	1,000	0.3
Lebanon	49,700	18
Liberia	1,000	0.6
Luxembourg	1,100	3.2
Macau	3,896	15.7
Malaysia	90,000	8.2
Mali	2,500	0.5
Martinique	2,100	6
Mauritius	8,300	9.7
Mexico	235,500	4.5
Morocco	18,200	1.3
Mozambique	3,200	0.4
Netherlands, The	25,000	1.9
New Zealand	14,300	5
Nicaragua	7,500	5
Norway	18,9C0	4.8
Pakistan	194,800	3
Panama	7,100	4.8
Poland	136,100	4.1
Portugal	25,800	3
Puerto Rico	8,700	3
Réunion	1,200	3
Romania	179,700	8.7
Senegal	5,200	1.5
Singapore	37,400	17.1
Somalia	4,700	1.7
Spain	293,100	8.5
Sri Lanka	98,100	7.7
Sudan	16,000	1
Surinam	1,700	5
Sweden	22,900	2.8
Switzerland	29,000	4.5
Trinidad and Tobago	8,400	8
Tunisia	8,000	1.6
Turkey	246,700	6.7
U.S.S.R.	4,569,000	18.5
United Kingdom	156,600	2.8
United States	920,600	5
Upper Volta	1,000	0.2
Venezuela	37,000	3.4
Vietnam, South	62,100	3.3
Yemen (San'a')	3,500	2.4
Yugoslavia	83,500	4
Zaire	1,100	0.1

*Countries having over 1 million annual attendance.
Source: United Nations, *Statistical Yearbook 1974.*

A scene from Robert Altman's "Nashville," a box-office success treating the world of country music.

The major British success of the year was Sidney Lumet's elegant all-star period piece *Murder on the Orient Express,* from Dame Agatha Christie's novel and with Albert Finney as her well-loved detective hero, Hercule Poirot. Ken Russell made a flamboyant version of the 1960s rock musical *Tommy* and the equally flamboyant *Lisztomania,* a film in which Franz Liszt and the cult that grew around him were compared with modern rock music stars and their adoring fans. Terry Gilliam and Terry Jones translated to the screen the distinctive comedy style of the Monty Python television series team in *Monty Python and the Holy Grail.* A film about rural life, *All Creatures Great and Small,* based on a series of fictionalized autobiographical books by a country veterinarian, achieved considerable popular success. Joseph Losey's *The Romantic Englishwoman* abounded in an elegant mannerism that failed to obscure the deficiencies of the theme, the entangling of the life and art of a writer caught in a dramatic emotional triangle.

Reprises were numerous. After *Alfie* came *Alfie Darling* (Ken Hughes); after *Confessions of a Window Cleaner, Confessions of a Pop Performer;* after *The Three Musketeers,* the anticlimactic *The Four Musketeers* (officially designated Panamanian); after *That'll Be the Day, Stardust.* A new James Bond adventure, *The Man with the Golden Gun,* had a new James Bond, Roger Moore.

There was lively activity in independent production, with the British Film Institute Production Board financing a notable group of films. David Gladwell's *Requiem for a Village* drew from Lindsay Anderson the compliment that it "is one of that handful of works which prove that the English poetic genius is fully capable—given the right, rare circumstances—of expressing itself in cinema, as it always has in literature and painting." Nicholas Broomfield and Joan Churchill's *Juvenile Liaison* compared, as *cinéma vérité,* with the films of the U.S. documentarist Fred Wiseman. *Fly a Flag for Poplar,* made by a collective of directors, explored the changing spirit of a London borough through the juxtaposition of 50-year-old archive photographs and film and contemporary material. *Pressure,* directed by West Indian Horace Ove, recorded the problems of a West Indian boy growing up and trying to find a job appropriate to his talents in a white London.

Australia. Sequels were also prominent in Australia: *Alvin Purple* was succeeded by *Alvin Purple Rides Again;* and *The Adventures of Barry McKenzie* by *Barry McKenzie Keeps It Up;* but neither recaptured the crude jollity of the originals. The outstanding Australian film of the year was Ken Hannam's *Sunday Too Far Away,* a study of itinerant sheepshearers that had something of the scale and humanity of a John Ford Western.

Canada. With official encouragement and an effective organization for overseas exploitation and publicity, Film Canada, Canadian feature film production continued to expand and export. Two horror films made their mark at international festivals: Robert Clark's *Black Christmas* and David Cronenberg's *The Parasite Murders,* about an organism that infects the population of an entire apartment complex with a combination of aphrodisiac and acute venereal disease. More portentously, a good political film by the Quebec director Michel Brault, *Les Ordres,* recalled events of 1970 when the Canadian government, alarmed at a series of kidnappings, invoked the War Measures Act and arrested several hundred inoffensive Canadian citizens for no very good reason.

Western Europe. *France.* Pres. Valéry Giscard d'Estaing made clear his intention of a reform of censorship. The government's first move in this direction was to overrule some of the more restrictive decisions of the Censorship Board, and later in the year a bill of censorship reform was approved by the French Cabinet. At the same time, restrictions on publicity and economic sanctions to curb pornographic material were strengthened. Parisians reacted by flocking to the cinemas which promised *le porno;* and two of the year's biggest box-office successes—Just Jaeckin's adaptation of *L'Histoire d'O* and Bertrand Blier's *Les Valseuses* adapted from his own novel—undoubtedly triumphed from the promise, at least, of sexual titillation. Other major commercial successes, of a less specialized appeal, were Jacques Deray's sequel to *Borsalino, Borsalino et Cie,* and Edouard Molinaro's likable zany comedy *L'Emmerdeur.*

The best of the year's production came from those established directors who had shaped the cinema for at least the past decade. Claude Chabrol added to his growing repertory of murder thrillers *Les Innocents aux mains sales,* an adaptation of a U.S. novel of multiple story twists, and *Une Partie de plaisir,* an extraordinary undertaking in which the scenarist, Paul Gegauff, and his wife virtually re-created on screen the trauma of their own broken marriage, with an effect that was perhaps more horrific than Chabrol's purely fictional thrillers. After looking to France's past in *Lacombe, Lucien,* Louis Malle made *Black Moon,* a futurist fantasy about a French town torn by a merciless intersexual war.

In *Daguerreotypes* Agnes Varda returned to her documentary origins, recording a touching self-portrait of the ordinary people of the rue Daguerre and the fast-vanishing modes of life of their little Parisian backwater. Another French woman director, Marguérite Duras, made *India Song* from a play she had originally written for Britain's National Theatre. Nominally set in the India of 1937, it was in fact an exploration, in terms of extreme artifice, of an "India of the soul." Of the younger French directors,

Bertrand Tavernier's *Que la fête commence* was a lively study of the France of Philippe d'Orléans, interpreted in the light of the impending revolutionary events of his times. Jean Eustache, after the heavyweight study of a series of intense relationships in *La Maman et la putain,* made an altogether lighter work in *Mes Petites Amoureuses,* a surprisingly gentle study of a boy's sexual awakening.

Italy. Perhaps the oddest cinema event of the year was the "kidnapping" of the negatives of a number of Italian films, including the latest works of Federico Fellini and Pier Paolo Pasolini (*see* OBITUARIES). Otherwise memorable were Michelangelo Antonioni's return to activity and renewed virtuosity with *The Passenger,* a philosophical thriller in which a man assumes the identity of another in order to escape the responsibilities of his own life and identity; and the return to full power of Roberto Rossellini, with *Italy Year One,* an intelligent and forceful re-creation of the rise and death of Alcide De Gasperi in the post-World War II era, and *The Messiah,* which examined the philosophical implications of the Hebrew proclamation of "The Kingdom of the Poor" and expectation of the Messiah.

West Germany. The West German film industry, perhaps because of its good relations with television, appeared the most productive in Western Europe. Apart from the prolific Rainer Werner Fassbinder (*see* BIOGRAPHY), all the other new directors who had emerged in the last ten years or so were in full activity. Werner Herzog's *Jeder für sich und Gott gegen Alle* was a retelling of the tale of Kaspar Hauser, the mysterious "wild boy" who was found in the streets of Nürnberg in 1828. Herzog's impeccably paced film showed the disturbing effect of this boy from another, mysterious existence upon the settled life of the town. The central performance, by Bruno S., a Berlin street musician, isolated and molded by his own background in institutions, was particularly remarkable.

Following his stylized re-creation of the life of Ludwig of Bavaria, Hans-Jürgen Syberberg examined the life of the writer Hans May, a formative influence upon the psychology of the Third Reich. The cast was mainly formed of actors from the German cinema of the 1930s. Jean-Marie Straub made a dry and uncompromising film rendering of Arnold Schoenberg's *Moses und Aron,* shot in a Roman arena in the Abruzzi Mountains, and with a personal—antinationalist—interpretation. In *Falsche Bewegung* Wim Wenders also interpreted the contemporary situation through a work of the past: his hero was a 1970s Wilhelm Meister. Bernhard Sinkel made a notable debut with *Lina Braake,* a touching and funny film about two old people resentful of relegation to an old people's home and rejuvenated by committing a bank deception. Sinkel's experience as a lawyer in Munich gave authority to the detail of the film.

West German cinema and television sought co-producers in order to employ outstanding young artists from other countries. The Iranian director Sohrab Saless made *In der Fremde,* a quiet—even Chekhovian—study of the isolation of foreign workers in West Germany; while U.S. director James Ivory continued his explorations of India with *Autobiography of a Princess,* which used old newsreel footage of court life in imperial India and an encounter between an exiled princess and an elderly Englishman (played by James Mason) to explore the nature of British colonial rule.

Sweden. Ingmar Bergman followed his six-part television film *Scenes from a Marriage* with a splendid filmed opera, *The Magic Flute.* Otherwise it seemed an uneventful and unproductive year for Sweden's normally lively cinema. A director of the Stockholm Marionette Theatre, Michael Meshke, made his feature debut with *Purgatorio,* which depicted the hallucinations reflecting the inner breakdown of a fashionable writer. Stig Bjorkmann, a film critic turned director, adopted a more objective approach to a case history in *The White Wall,* in which a newly divorced woman (a dazzling interpretation by Harriett Andersson) tries to come to grips with her altered situation.

Candice Bergen and Sean Connery in "The Wind and the Lion," an entertaining account of a U.S. citizen held hostage by the Riff of Morocco.

Denmark. Three women directors—Mette Knudsen, Elisabeth Rygaard, and Li Vilstrup—collaborated to demonstrate that sociopolitical tracts could be made to speak widely and cheerfully to a large audience. *Take It Like a Man, Ma'am* was a jolly, absurdist comedy with a central dream sequence in which the heroine speculates what life would be like if the roles of men and women were reversed.

Belgium. Jeanne Dielman, 23 Quai du Commerce, 1080 Bruxelles, directed by Chantal Anne Akerman, was another approach to the woman's situation. Delphine Seyrig sustained the role of a widow observed in the day-to-day routine of her living, as it, and she, adapt to crisis and the growing awareness of the prison created around her. A Belgian-French-Tunisian co-production, *Le Fils d'Amr est Mort,* won the Grand Prix at the Locarno Film Festival in October; this virtuoso feature debut of Jean-Jacques Andrion was a journey of self-discovery, with the hero seeking reasons for the suicide of a Tunisian he had befriended.

Spain. Besides producing conventional comedies and melodramas, the younger and more progressive Spanish directors continued to reflect something of the political realities of Spain's situation and recent history. José Luis Borau, after producing a number of films by young directors, himself directed *Furtivos (Poachers),* a baroque tale that contrasted the corruption and hypocrisies of established society with the attempts of the young hero and heroine to find romantic escape from society's snares.

Greece. Repressive censorship and competition from television had left the Greek film industry as a whole in a state of artistic impoverishment, but even before the overthrow of the dictatorship there was a movement toward a new cinema that managed to convey some sort of commentary on the contemporary

EMI

Ingrid Bergman was one of more than a dozen stars appearing in the fine production of "Murder on the Orient Express," a classic mystery tale by Agatha Christie.

situation. The outstanding Greek film of 1975, and indeed for many years, was Theodor Angelopoulos' *O Thiassos* (*The Traveling Players*), which recounted the political history of Greece between 1939 and 1952 as reflected in the experiences of a small theatrical troupe. An older director of the Greek cinema, Michael Caccoyannis, made a moving documentary about the history and plight of his native Cyprus, *Attila 74*.

Eastern Europe. *U.S.S.R.* The major Soviet productions of 1975 included a Moscow-Tokyo co-production directed by Akira Kurosawa (*see* BIOGRAPHY), *Dersu Uzala,* a quiet period epic about the friendship of a scientist and a hunter that won the Grand Prix of the 1975 Moscow Film Festival; Andrey Tarkovsky's massive and complex exploration of a man's memories and personality, *The Mirror;* and Sergey Yutkevitch's *Mayakovsky Laughs.* Yutkevitch was the only active survivor of the first generation of Soviet cinema, and his film captured something of the creative enthusiasm of those years. Using live action, animation, and puppets in combination, he

Jack Nicholson and Maria Schneider in "The Passenger," a Michelangelo Antonioni film about a man who assumes another's identity in order to escape from reality.

CINEMA INTERNATIONAL

extended an adaptation of Vladimir Mayakovsky's classic play *The Bedbug* with commentary and an updating to show Mayakovsky's worker hero as a 1970s pop star. Otherwise the main focus of creative activity seemed to have been away from the large studios of Moscow and Leningrad, in other republics. Georgia, with a 50-year-old cinema tradition, had an outstanding school of young directors. In 1974 Eldar Shengelaya, brother of Georgy Shengelaya, who made *Piorsmani,* directed *The Eccentrics,* a wonderland adventure of a 19th-century peasant youth who discovers the big city, love, villainy, and a flying machine. Moscow's 119th movie theatre opened during the year, bringing the total number of seats in the capital's cinemas to more than 95,000.

Poland. Historical themes were in vogue. Andrjez Wajda's *The Promised Land* was a huge operatic epic about the rise and fall of late 19th-century capitalist opportunists in industry. Jerzy Hoffman adapted Henryk Sienkiewicz's *The Deluge,* about the Swedish invasion of Poland in 1655. Walerian Borowczyk, returning home after several productions in France, adapted a novel about misguided love in 19th-century Poland, *The Story of Sin.* Among the few important directors who essayed films on contemporary subjects was Krzysztof Zanussi, who made *The Balance,* a study of a good-natured woman's breakout from her marriage.

Hungary. A notable run of major international prizes continued with the award of the Berlin Golden Bear to Marta Meszaros' *Adoption,* a realistic study of a middle-aged woman whose craving for motherhood finds expression first in friendship with an orphan and then in the adoption of a child. Peter Bacso's comedy *Don't Pull My Beard* and Gyula Gazdag's bizarre fantasy *74 Bastion Promenade* both satirized inefficient bureaucracy. An extraordinary feat of *cinéma vérité,* Judit Elek's *Hungarian Village,* exposed vividly in its two parts the spiritual vacuum and the unbridgeable generation gap in a peasant community where the young people learn their aspirations from television while their parents doggedly pursue the life-styles and prejudices of their ancestors.

East Germany. The DEFA studios continued to maintain an annual output of a score or so of films, including a high proportion of children's features. The year's productions included a reworking of the story of *Til Eulenspiegel,* seen now as a socialist hero, and a pedestrian *Orpheus in the Underworld.* Two films achieved international notice: Egon Günther's *Lotte in Weimar,* with Lili Palmer as the romantic heroine who meets her romantic poet too many years afterward, when Goethe is ossified into a pompous celebrity; and *Jakob der Lügner* (directed by Frank Beyer), a comedy set, improbably, in the Warsaw ghetto, with its hero an incurable teller of optimistic untruths.

Asia. *Japan.* Production continued to be fairly clearly departmentalized, with the Nikkatsu Company, for instance, mainly concerned with the production of soft-core pornographic films, while Toei specialized in Yakuza pictures. The latter was a species of gangster film that had so successfully supplanted the old samurai stories in the popular audience's imagination that production of them now stood at about 100 a year; Warner Brothers tried to introduce the style to the U.S. with Sydney Pollack's *The Yakuza.* Shochiku continued to specialize in popular comedy, while the "big" pictures were mostly left to Toho. The immense popular success of *The Towering In-*

ferno overshadowed the Japanese-made "disaster" film, Junya Sato's *The Bullet Train.* A story of sabotage on a super-express, the film was done with brilliant special effects work and with political and symbolic overtones.

Amid the predominantly commercially oriented productions, two films stood out. The veteran Tadashi Imai's painstaking reconstruction of the life and death (by torture in a Tokyo police cell in 1933) of the socialist writer *Takiji Kobayashi* was highly praised. The avant-garde dramatist, poet, novelist, and sports columnist Shuji Terayama added to his rapidly growing works a surrealist revisiting of childhood, *Pastoral Hide and Seek,* and a series of short films in which he spectacularly explored new relationships between screen and audience, frequently with active participation by the public in events on the screen.

Japan's greatest living director, Akira Kurosawa, worked away from home during the year; his first film in five years, since *Dodeska Den,* was made in the U.S.S.R. (*see* above). Meanwhile, new and younger directors were making their mark. At Toei, Kinji Fukasaku brought a new dimension of reality to the conventions of the Yakuza genre with *Battle Without Obligation;* in the same way Kumashiro Tatsumi endeavoured to give psychological depth to the standard soft-core pornographic product with *Joy Street,* and went on to make an interesting and more ambitious *Love Stories* for Toho. Regarded as a natural successor to the great Yasujiro Ozu, who had also begun his career as a director of domestic comedy, Yuji Yamada made *Companion,* which was highly regarded by Japanese critics.

India. The unchanging staples of Indian film production had been the production in large numbers of authentically popular films—musicals, romance, adventure—by the Bombay studios. A growing movement of independent producers and directors, calling themselves "The Parallel Cinema" and receiving a degree of support from India's National Film Corporation, demonstrated, however, a new impulsion toward concerted action when they formed a union organization during the 1975 Delhi Film Festival. Most of these directors were under 40, and their films showed a determination to deal with present-day Indian life and problems. They included M. S. Sathyu (*Hot Winds*), Basu Chatterji (*Rajhiganda*), Mani Kaul (*Duvidha*), Girish Karnad (*Kaadu,* a remarkable study of rural life), and Chidamanda Das Gupta (*Blood,* a black comedy of remarkable brutality and irony).

Satyajit Ray, master of the Bengal cinema, meanwhile completed two new films in 1975. *The Golden Fortress,* adapted from his own story, was a comic fantasy about a little boy who recalls a treasure glimpsed in a previous existence. *The Middle Man* was a contemporary story about social malaise and corruption with a hero who fails to find a job and so ends up in the business of supplying call girls.

Hong Kong. The Hong Kong martial arts film continued to sustain its fascination to a large world market and to inspire co-production, with kung-fu films being made in Europe and even in Australia (*The Man from Hong Kong*). A new style appeared in the films of King Hu, characterized by historical veracity and by a dazzling mise-en-scène that elevated kung-fu combats to the level of ballet. King Hu's *A Touch of Zen* received its first showing in its integral form at the Cannes Film Festival, after years of problems with producers and distributors. Another King Hu epic, *The Valiant Ones,* was seen at the Edinburgh, London, and Chicago festivals.

Iran. If the new Iranian cinema seemed to have lost something of its first momentum, the two films from the 1974 Teheran Film Festival made a striking entry on the European festival scene in 1975. Bahman Farmanara's *Prince Ehtejab* was a sardonic comedy about a crumbling aristocrat and despot who recalls regretted days of the corruption and tyranny of his heritage. Bahram Beiza'i's *The Stranger and the Fog* was an ambiguous, meditative, poetic spectacle, about a man who drifts, wounded, in an open boat to be beached among a strange, primitive, and altogether alien community.

Africa. *Algeria.* An Algerian film, Mohammed Lakhdur-Hamma's *Chronicle of the Years of Heat,* won the Grand Prix of the Cannes Film Festival. A massive, three-hour nationalist epic, it told the story of the rise of revolutionary nationalism in Algeria between 1939 and 1945 through the experiences of a single, poor family. Its scale, scope, and historical oversimplification led to its being styled "a third-world *Gone with the Wind.*"

Senegal. Ousmane Sembene, father of the black African cinema, made in *Xala* a ferocious and funny satire upon the new business elites. The bawdy tale concerned an elderly businessman who marries a young wife and neglects his business to worry about his lost virility.

(DAVID ROBINSON)

Nontheatrical Motion Pictures. U.S. nontheatrical films were finding new audiences in other nations as the export of educational and related subjects climbed steadily in recent years. Export sales jumped 50% between 1973 and 1975. In 1974 approximately 4% of the total sales of educational films came from exports, compared with about 3% for the previous year. One factor behind the increase was the Beirut Agreement, which allows films of a scientific, cultural, or educational nature to enter a country duty-free. In 1975 U.S. certificates issued in accordance with the treaty increased 7%.

AGIP/PICTORIAL PARADE

Christine Lambert in "Cold Soup," the story of two Parisian girls who provoke intrigue and jealousies in a small-minded village.

IN—BILD/AUTHENTICATED NEWS INTERNATIONAL

"Lina Braake," the story of an elderly woman who is forced to live in a home for the aged, was awarded the Federal Film Prize for 1975 as the year's best West German film.

Although there were no particularly outstanding nontheatrical films in 1975, the overall quality was good. The American Film Festival singled out *Antonia: A Portrait of the Woman* for its top "Emily" award. Made by newcomers Judy Collins and Jill Godmilow, it is the story of an orchestra conductor, Antonia Brico, a woman in a field dominated by men. The 1975 Grierson Award went to three young filmmakers, Howard Blatt, Joel Sucher, and Steven Fischler, for their social documentary *Frame-Up! The Imprisonment of Martin Sostre.*

Among the year's television documentaries, a David Wolper production sponsored by the National Geographic Society was outstanding. "The Incredible Machine" described the workings of the human body "through microscopic photography of human organs in action." The Council on International Nontheatrical Events found that Robin Lehman was a talent to watch. Two of his films emerged as prizewinners: *See,* an ecology motion picture; and *Don't,* using both underwater cinematography and butterfly sequences. Both films won foreign honours, and *Don't* received an Academy Award in 1975.

Three sponsored motion pictures were honoured in at least four film events. *Freedom 2000,* produced by Hanna-Barbera Productions for the U.S. Chamber of Commerce; *Highfire! Plan for Survival,* made by William Brose Productions for Syska & Hennessy, Inc.; and *Portrait of a Railroad,* produced by Francis Thompson for Burlington Northern, Inc.

Approximately 19,000 nontheatrical motion pictures were produced in the United States in 1974, up 11% from 1973. While some subjects were being made on videotape (usually subjects for which film is not the best medium), film production was increasing. During the past 65 years more nontheatrical films had been turned out worldwide than any other kind, an estimated 460,000 titles. This compares with approximately 435,000 theatrical feature and short subject films (including newsreels) produced during the same period. In 30 years about 390,000 television programs and documentaries had been made on film. The world total of all films ever produced exceeds two million titles. (THOMAS W. HOPE)

See also Photography; Television and Radio.

[623; 735.G.2]

ENCYCLOPÆDIA BRITANNICA FILMS. *Growing* (1969)—a computer-animated film; *Practical Film Making* (1972).

Vittorio Gassman in "Woman's Perfume," an offering at the Cannes International Film Festival.

A.F.P./PICTORIAL PARADE

Motor Sports

Grand Prix Racing. Formula One Grand Prix motor racing continued under unchanged general rules in 1975. Apart from BRM and Ferrari, most competitors raced F1 cars that consisted of a rear-mounted, 3-litre, gasoline-burning Cosworth-Ford V8 engine driving through a Hewland gearbox, with very wide slick rear tires; road grip was enhanced by the use of airfoils. At the end of the season Ken Tyrrell introduced his controversial car with two pairs of front wheels.

The Argentine Grand Prix at Buenos Aires in January gave promise of a good year for the sport, being competitive and intense. Emerson Fittipaldi of Brazil drove a tactical race to win from Britain's James Hunt. The victorious McLaren M23 averaged 190.861 kph (100 kph equals 62 mph) for the 53-lap, 316.314 km. race, held in hot, dry weather. Hunt's Hesketh 308 was just under six seconds behind, third place going to the Brabham BT44B of an Argentine, Carlos Reutemann.

The drivers then went to São Paulo for the Brazilian Grand Prix. Again, Jean-Pierre Jarier of France in the Shadow was the sensation of the practice rounds, and he led the race for 32 of the 40 laps, when he retired with fuel-feed problems. Carlos Pace of Brazil had been pressing hard in the Brabham BT44B, and he went on to win at 182.488 kph. Fittipaldi's McLaren was second, with third place going to West German Jochen Mass's McLaren, both M23s.

In the South African Grand Prix at Kyalami Jody Scheckter became the host country's hero by winning at 185.897 kph over the 320.1-km. course in a Tyrrell 007. Reutemann finished second for Brabham.

The Spanish Grand Prix took place at Barcelona. The Montjuich Park circuit had been criticized by the drivers as unsafe, and on the 26th lap West German Rolf Stommelen's Embassy-Hill went out of control and crashed into the spectator area, killing four and injuring nine. Stommelen suffered a broken leg. This unhappy race went to Mass in a McLaren, from the Lotus of Belgian Jackie Ickx, at an average of 153.764 kph. The Monaco Grand Prix was a happier affair and provided a foretaste of Austrian Niki Lauda's successful season, for he was never challenged, the flat-12-cylinder Ferrari covering the 245.85 km. at 121.552 kph. Fittipaldi was second for McLaren, ahead of Pace's Brabham.

In the Belgian Grand Prix at Zolder the Italian Ferrari gave a demonstration of its 1975 superiority, with Lauda fastest in practice and winner of the 298.34-km. race at 172.285 kph. That racing was still open and strongly contested was demonstrated when Scheckter's 007 Tyrrell took second place and Reutemann's Brabham BT44B third. Next Sweden had its world championship race, at Anderstorp, where Ferrari was again to the fore with Lauda first and Gianclaudio Regazzoni of Switzerland third. Second place went to Reutemann in the Brabham. The winning speed was 161.6 kph. On the Zandvoort 4.2-km. circuit the Dutch Grand Prix in June went to Hunt, who averaged 177.81 kph in his Hesketh 308 to gain his first championship success. He vanquished both Ferraris, and these three were the only ones to complete the full 75 laps. It was Ferrari in front again at Le Castellet, where the 1975 French Grand Prix was held. Lauda pulled out a surprise last-moment best practice lap after fine efforts by Shadow and Hesketh cars and then enjoyed a runaway victory in the 313.74-km. race, averaging 187.654 kph and being followed home by Hunt and Mass.

The British Grand Prix in July at Silverstone was a fiasco. Rain caused almost the entire field to crash, and the race was stopped after 56 of the 67 laps had been completed, during which time the lead had changed repeatedly. The officials took the placings after 55 laps, and this caused much comment and discontent. They gave the race to Fittipaldi's McLaren M23, at a speed of 193.15 kph, which represented 82 min. 5.0 sec. of racing. Pace's Brabham was declared second and Scheckter's Tyrrell 007 third.

Proper racing conditions returned when drivers traveled to Nürburgring in West Germany for the German Grand Prix in August. Over this punishing 319.609-km. course of 14 laps in hot weather, only 9 cars finished out of 24 starters. Reutemann in the BT44B Brabham received the checkered flag of victory, having averaged 189.473 kph to defeat comfortably Jacques Lafitte of France in a Williams-Cosworth FW. Lauda was third.

There remained the Austrian and Italian Grand Prix before the performers went off to North America to finish the season. At Monza over a race-distance of 300.56 km. the Italians got what they came to see, a Ferrari victory, achieved by Regazzoni at 218.034 kph. Second was Fittipaldi in the McLaren, and third place was secured by the other Ferrari, driven by Lauda, who thereby gained the world drivers' championship. It was a great day for Ferrari, with the winning car setting a new lap record of 223.501 kph. It was well that this race had been so satisfactory, because the preceding Austrian Grand Prix at the Österreichring was a shambles. Rain caused the contest to be stopped after 29 of the intended 54 laps. Italian Vittorio Brambilla drove a very good race under the circumstances and was declared to have won, at 173.30 kph, from Hunt and Tom Pryce of Great Britain driving a Shadow DN5. In the Swiss Grand Prix, held at Dijon-Prenois in France, the 197.34-km. event was won by Regazzoni's Ferrari at 194.091 kph, with Patrick Depailler of France second.

WIDE WORLD

Niki Lauda of Austria takes his fourth Grand Prix victory of the year, this one at Le Castellet, France.

The start of the 59th Indianapolis 500, a race marred by heavy rains at the finish.

WIDE WORLD

An exciting and eventful Formula One season closed with the U.S. Grand Prix at Watkins Glen, N.Y. With the championship safely under his belt, Lauda won again, without serious opposition, at 116.1 mph (186.9 kph) from Fittipaldi's Texaco-Marlborough-McLaren Ford and Mass's McLaren. As the Canadian Grand Prix had been canceled, the championship points were: Lauda 64½, Fittipaldi 45, Reutemann 37, and Hunt 33. The Formula One manufacturers' championship was won by Ferrari. Graham Hill, who announced his long-pending retirement as a driver during the year, was killed in an airplane crash in November (*see* OBITUARIES).

In Britain the *Daily Express* International Trophy Race was won by Lauda's Ferrari. In long-distance sports car racing Alfa Romeo gained the world championship of makes. The 3-litre Gulf DFV GR8 of Derek Bell of Britain and Ickx won the Le Mans 24-hour race at 191.48 kph for 4,595.6 km. from a Ligier DFV and another Gulf. The Tourist Trophy race, held at Silverstone, was a victory for British Stuart Graham's Fabergé Camaro Chevrolet coupe.

(WILLIAM C. BODDY)

U.S. Racing. Two veterans dominated major U.S. driving championships and two other veterans lost their lives during a 1975 auto racing season marked by an extraordinary number of keenly competitive finishes. A. J. Foyt won his sixth United States Auto Club (USAC) crown, clinching it by July 20. Richard Petty (*see* BIOGRAPHY) won his sixth National Association for Stock Car Auto Racing (NASCAR) championship and the Winston Cup. But former Indianapolis and Sports Car Club of America champion Mark Donohue returned from retirement for a try at the Grand Prix circuit and found death instead while practicing for the Austrian Grand Prix in August. And DeWayne ("Tiny") Lund was the lone fatality in a six-car crash at Talladega, Ala.

At the Indianapolis 500, shortened by rain to 435 mi., the race cars spun and slid into a series of collisions. The red flag stopping the contest actually dropped during the 175th circuit of the 2½-mi. oval, but scoring reverted to lap 174, the last full go-around. Bobby Unser won the race for the second time by staying just off the pace set by Foyt, Wally Dallenbach, and Johnny Rutherford and then taking the lead

Motorboating: *see* Water Sports

Motor Industry: *see* Industrial Review

on the 165th lap. At the end he was picking his way through the spins in the rain at 20 mph but was credited with an average speed of 149.21 mph.

Rutherford and Foyt finished second and third, completing the same number of laps as Unser, with fourth-place Pancho Carter five laps back and Roger McCluskey another two laps behind that. Unser collected $265,921 for just under three hours of racing. He damaged a knee in a subsequent accident and missed several of the USAC races.

In the Ontario, Calif., and Pocono, Pa., 500s which carry equal points if not equal purses with the Indianapolis event, Foyt and his Ford-engined car won. Averaging 154.34 mph, Foyt won a race-long duel with Unser at Ontario. At Pocono, he managed to be in front when rain ended that contest at 425 mi. Only Dallenbach was in the same lap. The huge lead from these three Triple Crown races propelled Foyt to the USAC championship, and the $342,000 in winnings from these three races alone sent him well past the $2 million mark in career race winnings. Rutherford and Unser finished second and third in points.

Jimmy Caruthers won the national dirt track championship, and Ramo Stott ended Butch Hartman's four-year monopoly on the USAC stock car crown. Larry Dickson won the sprint car title. Brian Redman of the U.K. won the successful Formula 5000 road racing championship sponsored jointly by USAC and the Sports Car Club of America.

Richard Petty won his sixth NASCAR season championship and joined Foyt in career earnings of more than $2 million as his STP Dodge dominated the Winston Cup superspeedway circuit. He scored 10 victories in 30 races including his first in the World 600 at Charlotte, N.C. Former Detroit taxi driver Benny Parsons won the Daytona 500, and David Pearson took the Purolator 500 in Pocono and the Michigan International's 400. Bobby Allison beat Petty by about 25 seconds to win the Southern 500 at Darlington, S.C., and Buddy Baker won one of the two Talladega, Ala., 500s. Except for a couple of victories won by Cale Yarborough, it was all Petty the rest of the way.

Veteran Don Garlits was the main story in drag racing in 1975, sweeping through to the World Finals and besting Shirley ("Cha Cha") Muldowney in the Summernational finals at Indianapolis Raceway Park. Garlits then retired from driving. In the Sports Car Club of America National Road Racing Classic at Road Atlanta, Jerry Hansen of Minneapolis, Minn., won his fifth straight Formula A crown in a Lola-Chevrolet.

(ROBERT J. FENDELL)

Barry Sheene sweeps to victory in the John Player British Grand Prix at Silverstone in August.

KEYSTONE

Motorcycles. In road racing, reigning 500-cc champion Phil Read of Britain had to yield the title to the man from whom he had wrested it two years previously, Italian Giacomo Agostini (*see* BIOGRAPHY). Read was riding the Italian four-stroke MV Agusta, which through the season proved to be distinctly inferior in performance as compared with the best of the Japanese two-stroke vehicles, such as the Yamaha ridden by Agostini. Other champions were Johnny Cecotto of Venezuela in the 350-cc class, Walter Villa of Italy (250 cc), Angel Nieto of Spain (50 cc), and Rolf Steinhausen of West Germany (sidecar).

Barry Sheene of the U.K., riding a Japanese Suzuki, beat Read with ease in the Hutchinson 100 at Brands Hatch, England, and beat Agostini at the Pesaro circuit on the Adriatic coast. Sheene had made a startlingly quick recovery from a horrendous 170-mph crash at the beginning of the season at the U.S. Daytona Classic. That race was won by Gene Romero of the U.S. in an augury of the success that the Americans were to achieve in the annual Anglo-U.S. match races series held in Britain.

In the Isle of Man Tourist Trophy (TT) competition Mick Grant on a Kawasaki broke the absolute lap record with a circuit at 109.82 mph in the Open Classic. The race winner, at 105.33 mph, was British John Williams (350-cc Yamaha). Other event winners were: Steinhausen (König), 500-cc sidecar; Grant (Kawasaki), 500-cc; C. Mortimer of Britain (Yamaha), 250-cc.

In motocross Roger de Coster of Belgium (Suzuki) took the 500-cc championship. The Moto Cross des Nations, held at Sedlcany near Prague, was headed by Czechoslovakia.

In the International Six Days' Trial, held on the Isle of Man, West Germany won the trophy. The Scottish Six Days' Trial was won by Mick Andrews (Yamaha). In Britain the league riders champion (speedway) was Laurie Etheridge, and the *Motor Cycle News* drag racing champion was Brian Chapman. O. Olsen of Denmark was speedway world champion.

Don Vesco of the U.S. became the first man to beat 300 mph on two wheels, with a two-way average of 302.928 mph. He achieved the record on a double-engined (1,500-cc) Yamaha at the Bonneville Salt Flats, Utah. (CYRIL J. AYTON)

[452.B.4.c]

See also Water Sports.

Mountaineering

The year 1975 was decidedly a Himalayan one, and in particular a Mt. Everest year: no fewer than three expeditions, of three nationalities, climbed the mountain successfully, and by three separate routes. Pride of place must go to the first ascent of the southwest face (after five unsuccessful attempts by expeditions of various nationalities) in September, by the post-monsoon British expedition led by Chris Bonington. Masterly organization and a very strong and experienced team enabled two parties to reach the summit only 33 and 35 days after the expedition had reached its base camp. A third party ran into disaster; after one member had retired with equipment trouble the other man, who continued solo, died during a violent storm on the mountain.

The Japanese women's expedition in May climbed the mountain by the original route via the South Col—the first ascent by a woman, Junko Tabei (*see* BIOGRAPHY). The third successful expedition was a Chinese-Tibetan one in May which climbed the route attempted by successive pre-World War II British expeditions via the North Col; nine members reached the top, one Chinese and eight Tibetans, including Mme Phantog—the second woman's ascent in two weeks. There had always been some doubt about a previous Chinese claim to have climbed Everest, but there could be no such doubt about this one because a surveying tripod left on the summit by the Chinese expedition was found there by the British expedition.

A big increase occurred in expeditions obtaining permission to climb in the Karakoram, with the result that porters and other resources were considerably overstrained, and many expeditions were completely or partly frustrated. Many first-rate climbs were carried out, however, by far the most notable being the first ascent of the northwest face of Gasherbrum I (Hidden Peak) by Reinhold Messner (West Germany) and Peter Habeler (Austria). They applied Alpine tactics to their climb, with the result that they completed it in the astonishing time of four days for the complete climb from base and back to base. The British ascent of Everest could be regarded as representing a landmark in Himalayan climbing; but even more so must Messner and Habeler's climb be considered as the start of a new epoch in that endeavour.

Pre-monsoon expeditions in the Himalayas in 1975 included successful attempts by the French on the southwest ridge of Pumori, by an Austro-German expedition on Yalung Kang, by a Japanese team on Dhaulagiri IV and V, and by the Spanish on Manaslu. A British team failed on Nuptse, Italians on Lhotse, Austrians on Annapurna, Indians and British on the Nanda Devi traverse, and Japanese on Dhaulagiri II, Baudha, Peak 29, and Himalchuli. In the Karakoram the Japanese climbed Kampa Dior, the Austrians Sia Kangri Central Peak, the French Gasherbrum II, and the Poles Gasherbrum II and III.

In the winter of 1974–75 in the Alps the making of first winter ascents of high-standard climbs continued. Some of the more notable were routes on the Grand Pilier d'Angle of Mont Blanc de Courmayeur (the Cecchinel-Nominé and the Bonatti-Zapelli routes), on the north face of the Grandes Jorasses, on the northwest face of the Ailefroide, on Mont Blanc du Tacul and the Punta Gugliermina, and on the northeast face of the Zermatt Breithorn. In the summer of 1975 the notable new climbs included ones on the Grand Pilier d'Angle, the east face of Mont Blanc du Tacul, the north face of the Grandes Jorasses, the west face of the Petit Dru, and the north face of the Aiguille de la Grande Rocheuse.

In Norway a development was winter ascents of major routes, in the winter of 1974–75 on the west ridge of Store Vengetind in Romsdal and on the Lakselvtinder ridge in northern Norway. In New Zealand in the summer of 1974–75 important new climbs were made on Vancouver, Hicks, and Tasman, and in the Southern Alps, Darrans, Wilkinson, Aspiring, and Dart Glacier areas. New routes in Africa included Batian on Mt. Kenya in late summer 1974 and some first winter ascents of routes on Mt. Kenya in the winter of 1974–75.

In North America, too, ice climbs became a feature in Yosemite in the winter of 1974–75. In 1975 in Alaska and Yukon a first winter ascent of Foraker was made, and in summer new routes on Foraker, Mt. Deborah, and the Moose's Tooth. In South America in 1974 new climbs were made on Huascarán Norte, Huantsan, Huandoy Norte, the Nevado Colqueroz, Illimani, Huayna Potosí, Condoriri, Aconcagua, and Bifida in the Cerro Torre group. (JOHN NEILL)

[452.B.5.d]

THE SUNDAY TIMES

Dougal Haston en route to conquest of Mt. Everest's southwest face in September. He and his compatriot Doug Scott were the first climbers to complete this ascent.

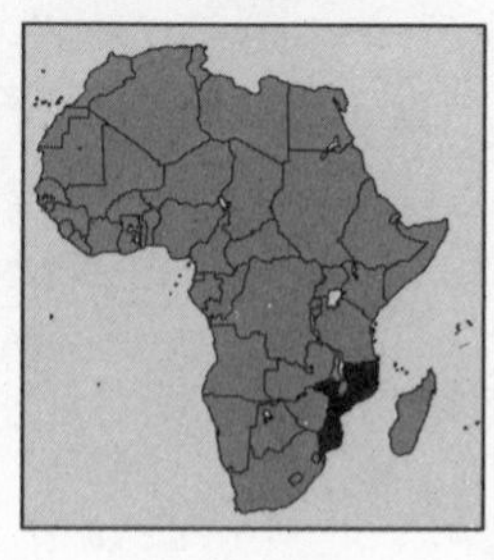

Mozambique

An independent African state, the People's Republic of Mozambique is located on the southeast coast of Africa, bounded by Tanzania, Malawi, Zambia, Rhodesia, South Africa, and Swaziland. Area: 308,642 sq.mi. (799,380 sq.km.). Pop. (1975 est.): 9,239,000. Cap. and largest city: Lourenço Marques (Can Phoumo; pop., 1970, 354,700). Language: Bantu languages predominate; Portuguese is also spoken. Religion: traditional beliefs 70%, Christian about 15%, Muslim 13%, with Hindu, Buddhist, and Jewish minorities. President in 1975, Samora Machel; premier, Joaquin Chissano.

During negotiations that took place in March 1975 between Portugal and the leaders of the Mozambique Liberation Front (Frelimo) in Dar es Salaam, Tanzania, to discuss economic arrangements for Mozambique after independence, the Portuguese foreign minister pledged his country's fullest assistance. Further discussions took place in May when an agreement was reached on a plan for administering the Cabora Bassa hydroelectric project; the plan envisaged the setting up of a corporation, led by the Portuguese government and including all who had invested in the project, to control the operations of the dam until all investors had recovered their capital. After an estimated period of another ten years, the dam would become a government asset. These arrangements saved the new government from becoming involved in the sale of electricity to South Africa, the only customer in the immediate vicinity.

On June 23 the Frelimo leader Samora Machel returned to Lourenço Marques to become president of the republic on independence day, June 25. Delegates from 60 nations (not including the governments of the U.S., France, West Germany, South Africa, Rhodesia, Japan, and Italy, which received no invitations) assembled for the independence celebrations, which took place two days later. South Africa, Mozambique's second most important trading partner and main supplier of the country's imports, closed its consulate, which was replaced by a trade mission.

The new constitution, which upheld the political supremacy of Frelimo over all other branches of government, provided for a one-party People's Assembly of 210 members. Although the republic was to be socialist in ideology, President Machel made it clear that he did not seek a confrontation with South Africa, and although the struggle with Rhodesia would continue, it was hoped that the regime of Ian Smith would reach a negotiated settlement with its opponents. In the following months Machel was consulted on a number of occasions by Rhodesian African leaders, and he played his part in trying to encourage a settlement of Rhodesia's constitutional problems. As a step toward reducing the country's economic dependence on South Africa, agreements were signed in July with China and India providing for loans and technical assistance. Britain also discussed the possibility of offering substantial financial aid.

In March Father Alexandre José Maria dos Santos became the first black archbishop of Lourenço Marques. It was not an easy position for the new incumbent, for although President Machel declared that Frelimo would permit freedom of religion, he had previously spoken of the Roman Catholic Church as an instrument of colonial repression. Church leaders feared the effect upon the Christian community of a state governed on Marxist principles. These fears were to some extent substantiated when, in the course of a statement on socialist policy in July, the president announced that all schools and colleges would be taken over by the state, along with hospitals and private medical practices. The churches, he said, were dominated by the capitalist system; some were using religion to slow down development, and some of the black priests were imperial agents.

Early in August the Defense Department announced compulsory military training for every young member of the state, regardless of sex, together with compulsory politico-military instruction for all citizens. It also declared the country's support for the independence of South West Africa (Namibia) and denounced South Africa's government as fascist and inhuman. Later in the same month new citizenship regulations denied residence to any foreigner who

WIDE WORLD

A medal commemorating Mozambique's independence on June 25 shows a relief map of the former Portuguese colony and Samora Machel, the new president, on its faces.

MOZAMBIQUE

Education. (1970) Primary, pupils 526,962, teachers 6,855; secondary (1968), pupils 18,431, teachers 1,188; vocational, pupils 11,458, teachers 744; teacher training, students 1,164, teachers 117; higher (university only), students 1,071, teaching staff 220.

Finance and Trade. Monetary unit: Mozambique escudo, at par with the Portuguese escudo, with (Sept. 22, 1975) a free rate of 27.35 escudos to U.S. $1 (56.65 escudos = £1 sterling). Budget (1973 actual): revenue 11,789,000,000 escudos; expenditure 11,682,000,000 escudos. Foreign trade (1973): imports 11,415,000,000 escudos; exports 5,541,000,000 escudos. Import sources: South Africa 20%; Portugal 19%; West Germany 13%; France 8%; U.K. 8%; Japan 5%; U.S. 5%. Export destinations: Portugal 36%; U.S. 14%; South Africa 9%; U.K. 6%. Main exports: cashew nuts 22%; cotton 20%; sugar 10%; minerals 6%; vegetable oils 5%.

Transport and Communications. Roads (1973) 39,173 km. Motor vehicles in use (1972): passenger 83,600; commercial (including buses) 20,000. Railways: (1973) 3,733 km.; traffic (1972) 346 million passenger-km., freight 3,455,000,000 net ton-km. Ships entered (1972) vessels totaling 15,927,000 net registered tons; goods loaded (1973) 12,146,000 metric tons, unloaded 4,793,000 metric tons. Telephones (Dec. 1973) 53,000. Radio licenses (Dec. 1972) 110,000. Television licenses (Dec. 1972) 1,000.

Agriculture. Production (in 000; metric tons; 1974; 1973 in parentheses): corn *c.* 550 (*c.* 500); sorghum *c.* 215 (*c.* 213); cassava (1973) *c.* 2,150, (1972) *c.* 2,140; peanuts (1973) *c.* 150, (1972) *c.* 140; sugar, raw value *c.* 300 (*c.* 370); copra *c.* 63 (*c.* 63); bananas (1973) *c.* 67, (1972) 66; tea *c.* 20 (*c.* 20); cashew nuts (1973) *c.* 202, (1972) 200; cotton, lint *c.* 35 (*c.* 48); sisal (1973) *c.* 27, (1972) 24. Livestock (in 000; Dec. 1973): cattle *c.* 2,250; sheep *c.* 250; goats *c.* 900; pigs *c.* 280.

Industry. Production (in 000; metric tons; 1973): petroleum products *c.* 729; cement 611; bauxite 6; electricity (excluding most industrial production; kw-hr.; 1974) 587,000.

stayed outside the country for more than 90 days without a valid reason, while any resident wishing to retain Portuguese nationality would have to obtain permission by explaining his reasons for wanting to do so.

In December an attempted rebellion by some 400 soldiers and policemen, apparently touched off by a crackdown on "corruption" in the armed forces, was put down after two days of fighting in the capital.

(KENNETH INGHAM)

[978.E.8.b.iv]

Museums

Fiscal problems were prominent in the concerns of the U.S. museum world. Perhaps emblematic of the situation was the reopening of the Pasadena (Calif.) Art Museum, which had been rescued from severe financial difficulties only by permitting the prominent West Coast financier and art collector Norton Simon to restructure the administration and policy of the museum. The economic recession made these difficulties especially burdensome, and museum endowments were severely affected. The Museum of Modern Art in New York City announced a deficit of $1.5 million for the years 1973–74 and predicted $1,250,000 as the 1975 deficit. Trustees felt that immediate action should be taken so that the museum's endowment would not be severely depleted and, like other museums across the U.S., the Museum of Modern Art announced that it would reduce the length of its week by closing on Wednesdays. Likewise, the Metropolitan Museum of Art in New York City announced that, in addition to its Monday closing, it would also be closed on Tuesdays. The Detroit Institute of Arts was closed for a month after a 29% budget cut and reopened in late summer with a five-day week with only a quarter of its 101 galleries open at any one time. The Cincinnati (Ohio) Art Museum began to charge admission, and the Boston Museum of Fine Arts raised its admission to $2.50 and reduced its week to six days. If there was a bright side to these events, it might be found in the intensified search for new avenues of income and a larger audience. New York City's Museum of Modern Art, for instance, offered a new "membership-for-a-day," a trial introduction to the advantages of membership, while a corporate grant from the Mobil Oil Corp. permitted the Whitney Museum of American Art in New York City to remain open on one evening during the week.

Worldwide, the financing of museums and museum associations was a perennial problem, but it was worsening in 1975. A science museum in Milan, Italy, existed on its cinema, which was originally intended for scientific purposes but now showed commercial films. Museum directors who could defend their museums turned into businessmen. International organizations concerned with museums were critically affected, owing to devaluations of currencies to which part of their income was linked and to the forced restrictions on expenditure of governmental or intergovernmental bodies on which they relied for subsidies. In 1975 the atmosphere in international nongovernmental organizations was one of foreboding.

In the U.S., on the other hand, at a conference of the New York State museums it was reported that approximately 35% of museum funding was governmental; of this amount 67% came from cities and counties, 24% from the state, and 9% from the federal government. Since the amount contributed by government would in all probability increase throughout the country, members of the museum profession began to consider the problems for policymaking implicit in such large-scale public funding. Another aspect of the concern for public responsibility was felt when the New York attorney general's office accused the director and board of trustees of the Museum of the American Indian in New York City of financial fraud and mismanagement and sought their removal from office because they "allowed the assets of the museum to be wasted." Several members of the board and the director resigned, and the museum was closed while an inventory of the collections was taken.

The year 1975 witnessed a number of international and regional meetings on themes relating to museums. A seminar on the problems and plans of museums in the Arab countries was organized by UNESCO in Cairo in December 1974, as part of a series of regional meetings devoted to the adaptation of museums to the needs of the modern world. One such meeting for museums in English-speaking Africa had already been held, and UNESCO planned seminars in 1976 for Asian countries and for French-speaking Africa. Viewing museums in the context of actual modern needs was part of the work of the intergovernmental conference on cultural policies in Africa held in Accra, Ghana, in October–November 1975. In the United Kingdom the Group for Educational Services in Museums organized a meeting on the theme of "museums as an influence in the quality of life" at the Victoria and Albert Museum in April. In June UNESCO held a conference in Paris on "the exchange of original objects and specimens among institutions in different countries." This has been a delicate matter for a number of reasons, one of them being that institutions are not always in agreement about the relative value of the objects they exchange, and cases occur where each of the partners feels defrauded. Also in June the second International Congress of Friends of Museums was held in Brussels. The first congress, held in Barce-

PETER L. GOULD—KEYSTONE

The new wing of the Metropolitan Museum of Art in New York City, which will house the Robert Lehman Collection, is itself a work of art, blending a graceful geometry with utilitarian needs.

CENTRAL PRESS/PICTORIAL PARADE

The new National Railway Museum at York, England, opened in September on the 150th anniversary of the first public passage by steam railway, from Stockton to Darlington. The museum contains 2 turntables, 24 locomotives, and 20 carriages, including a number of royal saloons of yesteryear.

lona, Spain, in 1972, recommended that the over 500 local clubs of "friends of the museum" in various countries and the national federations some of them had formed should be brought together in one international body. A special committee presented the proposed statutes for that body to the second congress, and on their adoption a new international nongovernmental organization was born: the World Federation of Friends of Museums, comprising units throughout the world—but mostly in Western countries. Some were devoted to one museum only, others to museums in general, and they participated actively in the life and work and solution of problems of museums, the improvement of their collections, acquisitions and exchanges, financing, the promotion of museums, and their better integration with the life of the community.

UNESCO's quarterly review *Museum* continued to explore new paths for the advance of museums. After a monumental double issue, practically a textbook, on "Museum Architecture," it published during the year a number of special issues including one on museums of exact and natural sciences, another partly devoted to the recent conversion of historic buildings into museums as a means of preserving them, and a third on traditional methods of conserving museum material in countries of South and Southeast Asia.

International organizations continued to struggle in 1975 with the problem of theft in museums, churches, and other places, as well as vandalism and international traffic in stolen objects. The results were not satisfying. The theft situation in Italy, to take only one example, was appalling. Despite all its efforts, Interpol was handicapped by the fact that only a small percentage of thefts were reported. And the heavy demand for works of art and archaeology made it more and more difficult to repress illegal excavations of sites and international illicit traffic.

While U.S. museums suffered only one major theft in 1975—the Boston Museum of Fine Arts had a Rembrandt portrait stolen—the vast and proliferating problem in Europe made U.S. museums all the more security conscious. The publication of a new international monthly, *Stolen Paintings and Objets d'Art,* was vivid testimony to the urgency of the situation. Several other publications of interest to the museum world also appeared. *Understanding Art Museums* was the book form of the deliberations of the 46th American Assembly, a yearly public affairs forum sponsored by Columbia University. Among the many recommendations: art museums should be more aware of public needs; more attention should be paid to the training of guards because they constitute the largest ongoing contact between museums and their visitors; more effective educational alternatives to group tours and electronic talks should be explored; artists should be encouraged to become part of the museum policy body; and there should be more intermuseum cooperation and interaction. The three-year study by the National Endowment for the Arts, *Museums USA,* was published. Among the interesting statistics garnered by the study: museums account for more than $500 million in yearly revenue; 308.2 million admissions were counted by the 1,821 participating museums in the year 1971–72. Disheartening perhaps was the information that the museum world, which employed 113,300 people, depended too heavily upon volunteer and unpaid labour: while 30,400, or 27%, of museum employees were full-time and 18,700, or 16%, were part-time, more than 64,000 volunteers completed this labour force.

New Facilities. A more optimistic aspect of the museum world was found in continuing building activity. The American Museum of Natural History in New York City added the multimillion-dollar, ten-story Childs Frick Wing to its facilities; the structure would house Frick's vast collection of mammalian bones and fossils. The St. Louis Art Museum began a major renovation that would close its facilities for some time; in Philadelphia both the Pennsylvania Academy of the Fine Arts and the Philadelphia Museum of Art closed for a full year. It was hoped that the drastic measure would expedite construction and ready these museums for the bicentennial year.

The Smithsonian Institution in Washington, D.C., which normally can display less than 1% of its total collections, planned a vast 1,280,000-sq.ft. structure on 70 ac. in suburban Maryland, eight miles from Washington. Approximately 30 million objects would be housed and available for study in the computerized centre. Miami (Fla.) planned a downtown facility for its Metropolitan Museum and Art Center. The Charleston (S.C.) Museum had a multimillion-dollar bond issue approved by the voters of the county; the inadequate 1907 facility was to be replaced by a new building that would be a permanent bicentennial monument. The Palm Springs (Calif.) Desert Museum, a combined art and natural history facility, opened during the year. With a gift from the Spencer Foundation, the Museum of Art at the University of Kansas planned to quadruple its quarters. The Milwaukee Art Center opened its new wing on Lake Michigan, vastly expanding its exhibition areas and allowing the museum to install a multimedia centre. In New York the Metropolitan Museum of Art opened the huge $7 million Robert Lehman wing, housing the "last of the great American collections," valued at $100 million and especially rich in drawings. The Metropolitan Museum also opened its new Islamic galleries featuring jewelry, carpets, metalwork, and glass. A gift from the museum's president emeritus, Arthur Houghton, Jr., aided the construction.

Belgium was engaged in a complete review of its museum policy. In the United Kingdom the Group for Educational Services in Museums and the Museum Assistants' Group organized a meeting on "museums and the handicapped." In Iran the new Museum of 18th and 19th Century Iranian Art, containing the vast collections of the Empress Farah, was opened in

April. Japan inaugurated its National Aquarium at Okinawa-Motobu in May. In the same month the Galleria d'Arte Moderna in Bologna, Italy, opened its new building.

The northern extension of the National Gallery in London was opened on June 10. In Paris the Musée des Arts et Traditions Populaires moved into a spacious new building in the Bois de Boulogne. The national museum of Qatar in the capital (Doha) was inaugurated on June 23. The building represented an experiment in designing a museum for the needs of an Arab public interested in renewing its traditions. The building complex endeavours neither to bring in an imported style nor to give a mere pastiche of traditional architecture. On July 5 the Deutsches Schiffahrt Museum, a maritime museum, made its appearance at Bremerhaven, West Germany. At the Ciudad Universitaria of Madrid the Museo Español de Arte Contemporáneo opened its new building on July 11. The Joan Miró Foundation for the study of contemporary art was established in July in Barcelona.

Perhaps as a reflection of bicentennial concern in the U.S., the establishment of an American Folklife Center in the Library of Congress received strong backing in both houses of Congress. Folklife was defined as the traditions, customs, beliefs, dances, and arts and crafts common to a group of people within the U.S. Some $2.6 million was to be budgeted over three years to support the centre, to produce materials, and to award grants to those working on and studying American folklore and crafts. Other governmental actions of interest to the museum world included the Treasury Department's offer to reverse its former stance on the treatment of charitable deductions. In view of the dire financial position in which inflation had left so many private charities, the House Ways and Means Committee voted to allow deductions for gifts of appreciated value to all charitable institutions, including museums. Under the original proposals for minimum taxable income of several years earlier, charitable deductions were to be treated like any other personal deduction and could not be used in combination with other personal deductions and exclusions to eliminate more than 50% of a taxpayer's income.

Acquisitions. In the U.S. the Cleveland Museum of Art obtained a major Cubist painting by Pablo Picasso—the 1918 "Harlequin with Violin (Si Tu Veux)." The work had been in a private family collection since 1920. A rare work by the 17th-century French Caravaggist Georges de La Tour, "St. Philippe," was acquired for the Walter Chrysler Museum of Art in Norfolk, Va. Clyfford Still, a mysterious and influential U.S. abstract artist, donated 28 paintings to the San Francisco Museum of Art, which planned a major exhibition of his work in early 1976. The Metropolitan Museum of Art, New York City, purchased 412 rare Japanese art objects comprising the Packard Collection, at a cost of $5.1 million. The transaction was a controversial one, as it was reputed to have exhausted the Metropolitan's purchase funds for five years. The Kimbell Art Museum in Fort Worth, Texas, acquired a "Raising of Lazarus" by the great Sienese master Duccio from David Rockefeller. The small wooden panel is one of a group of long-dispersed paintings from the still-intact altarpiece in Siena, the "Maestà."

Two Fragonards were among the many acquisitions of important works of art. "Les Verroux" went to the Louvre and "La Parmesane" was acquired by the National Gallery in London.

KEYSTONE

Taxidermy workshop near Nairobi, Kenya, where full-body preservation of Ahmed, Kenya's world-famous giant elephant, is under way. The animal will be placed in Nairobi's National Museum.

The new museum of African art and culture that was being planned in Dakar, Senegal, was doing its best to accumulate whatever had escaped the hands of foreign collectors. The national museum of Papua New Guinea was showing pathetic zeal in attempting to acquire the art and artifacts that had been disappearing from New Guinea. And there were great private collections throughout the world that faced acquisition problems. One of them, the Hooper Collection, now in England but in danger of immediate dispersion, comprised a priceless series of artifacts of Oceania, Indian North America, and Africa. The problem of its disposal was almost insoluble if the scattering effect of the auction block was to be avoided. The establishment of a museum in Britain would require funds for both the settlement of the late owner's estate and the museum itself, and sending the items back to their innumerable countries of origin also raised vast difficulties.

(JOSHUA B. KIND; CONRAD WISE)

See also Art and Art Exhibitions; Art Sales; German Democratic Republic.

[613.D.1.b]

Music

Johann Strauss would have been 150 years old in 1975, and the fact was noted throughout the musical world. Vienna naturally led the way with new productions of several of his operettas, a special exhibition featuring many rare photographs, scores, and documents, and concerts during the May–June festival, each of which included a work by the waltz king. The centenary of Georges Bizet's premature death in 1875 brought many reassessments of his work. The British Broadcasting Corporation (BBC) on Radio 3 surveyed all of his operas and included a performance of the rarely heard *Ivan IV* and *Carmen,* first performed in the year of Bizet's death. Few composers had been dealt with so harshly by posterity, in the sense that true editions of his operas were hard to come by because of the cavalier treatment of the autograph scores after his death by those who wished him well—and those who did not. At least some of the misdemeanours were now corrected.

Besides marking Bizet's death, 1975 also marked the 100th anniversary of the birth of Maurice Ravel, and that occasion too was noted in the world's concert halls. In Ravel's case, the problems were interpretative rather than textual. Even so, the English Bach Festival managed to unearth two cantatas that Ravel wrote as his Prix de Rome entry, which had never before been performed publicly. Among minor celebrations, the centenary of Samuel Coleridge-Taylor, best known for *Hiawatha's Wedding Feast,* was noted in England, where Luciano Berio's 50th birthday was marked by a London Sinfonietta concert devoted to his music in October. The centenary of Reynaldo Hahn's birth also was remembered. This minor French composer, conductor, and singer added much to the sum of human pleasure through his witty pen and thin but expressive voice, immortalized on a few, much-prized old 78-rpm records.

Since the end of World War II musical competitions have proliferated. Among the many such events that took place during 1975 were the 27th Busoni Piano Competition held at Bolzano, Italy; the 26th Viotti Violin Competition at Vercelli, Italy; the 25th International Competition for conductors at Besançon, France; the 24th International Music Competition of West German Radio (piano, violin, and organ in 1975); the 22nd International Singing Competition at 's Hertogenbosch, Neth.; the 28th Singing Competition at Toulouse, France; the 4th Montevideo (Uruguay) Piano Competition; the 4th Leeds (England) Piano Competition; the Marguerite Long-Thibaud Violin and Piano Competition at Paris; the 31st International Performers' Competition at Geneva; the Queen Elizabeth Violin Competition at Brussels; the Chopin Piano Competition at Warsaw; and the Moscow Piano Competition.

The value of such competitions was perhaps open to doubt, for it is not always the most talented performer who shines under competitive conditions. Furthermore, with the age of entrants generally ranging from 20 to 30, a younger player obviously could not have the same experience of a particular work as a player perhaps ten years older. And one player's performance of, say, a Bach concerto could not be gauged against another's rendition of a Prokofiev work. Nevertheless, such contests had become a fact of musical life and had undoubtedly helped further the careers of the winners. One "discovery" in 1975 was the hugely talented Soviet pianist Dmitry Alekseyev, who won at Leeds. In this important competition, performers were judged on what they had achieved over four appearances and not on the final concerto performance alone.

Sarah Caldwell directing the Opera Company of Boston.

MARTHA SWOPE

Among prizes offered to established artists in recognition of their achievements, the prestigious Shakespeare Prize, presented by the FVS Foundation in Hamburg, West Germany, was awarded in 1975 to the British conductor John Pritchard. Malcolm Williamson (*see* BIOGRAPHY), an Australian composer, was appointed master of the queen's music in succession to Sir Arthur Bliss, who died in March.

Death robbed the musical scene of many famous figures during 1975. Of composers, the most serious loss was Dmitry Shostakovich. To the end, he remained a conservative figure, one true to his own methods even when under political pressure. It was unlikely that the century would see a more significant symphonist; he surpassed even Jean Sibelius in the breadth and scope of his 15 works in that genre. His contribution to the realm of chamber music was no less important, and in his quartets the private man was perhaps more to the fore than in the symphonies. His single major opera, *Katerina Ismailova,* would probably soon take its deserved place in the repertory. His piano music and songs also added to the stature of this individual and often profound composer.

Luigi Dallapiccola, one of the leading Italian composers of the past 50 years, a writer who managed to bridge the gulf between the world of Italian lyricism and serial technique, would also be sorely missed. Boris Blacher, Sir Arthur Bliss, and André Jolivet were probably of more local interest, but each was revered in his own country. Robert Stolz, an Austrian composer, gave much pleasure in a lighter vein and was also noted as a conductor. Vittorio Gui, the doyen of Italian conductors, died at the age of 90; he had continued to work within weeks of his death. Basil Cameron, a British conductor, was the same age but had been inactive for some years prior to his death.

Among a long list of singers who died were Max Lorenz (the Austrian Wagnerian tenor), Toti Dal Monte, Ludwig Weber, Frida Leider, Richard Tucker, Aksel Schiøtz, Martyn Green, and, among a younger generation, Amy Shuard and Norman Treigle. Other losses were Lionel Tertis, the veteran viola player, who was 98; Sir Jack Westrup, an eminent British musicologist; and Sir Neville Cardus, a critic. (*See also* OBITUARIES.)

At Ottawa in September a World Music Week was held, including a symposium entitled "Music as a Dimension of Life." Musicians from all parts of the world attended the proceedings, and several concerts featuring new works by Canadian composers were given.

Symphonic Music. The New York Philharmonic faced problems in 1975. Pierre Boulez announced that he was to retire as music director after the 1976–77 season (being currently solely concerned with his new Institut de Recherche et de Coordination Acoustique-Musique, a centre in Paris for the development of new music). Leonard Bernstein made it known that he would be willing to appear more often with the orchestra in his position as conductor laureate, but if he were to conduct more often the post of music director might be thought to be downgraded and, therefore, might be harder to fill. In any case, any likely contender of comparable rank to Boulez would be unlikely to provide the orchestra with the regular relationship so needed to give an orchestra a true profile of its own. Such conductor-orchestra relationships existed in Philadelphia (Eugene Ormandy), Cleveland (Lorin Maazel), Boston (Seiji Ozawa), and Chicago (Sir Georg Solti), although even in those cases the conductors, with the exception of Ormandy, seldom conducted the orchestras for more than half the year. Just as opera singers were no longer willing to remain in one house season after season, so leading conductors also wished to be peripatetic. The star system—and jet aircraft—were to blame.

Boulez also retired from the London scene insofar as he gave up his regular post as principal conductor of the BBC Symphony Orchestra in June, to be succeeded by Rudolf Kempe, who himself held a similar post with the Munich Philharmonic. Kempe, in turn, was succeeded as principal conductor of the Royal Philharmonic by Antal Dorati. Riccardo Muti, who took up his post as principal conductor of the New Philharmonia in 1974, began to make his mark on the orchestra, whose performances improved in shape and purpose. All the London orchestras were striving to have three or four conductors at their service and so eliminate the need for too many guests. This led the London Symphony into a dispute that threatened at one point to tear it apart. The eminent German Eugen Jochum was made conductor laureate by the self-governing board, apparently without consulting the orchestra's chief conductor, André Previn. Previn was not unnaturally surprised at the development, particularly because it seemed that some members of the board were anxious to end his contract. In the end, members of the orchestra indicated their continuing support for Previn, and Howard Snell, chairman of the board, resigned in October. The only orchestra in London not to undergo any change was the London Philharmonic; Solti, Daniel Barenboim, and Carlo Maria Giulini were confirmed as the orchestra's regular guests. There continued to be rumours that the Arts Council might withdraw its support from one or more of these organizations, London being one of the few cities in the world to sport more than two main orchestras. Nonetheless, standards remained high in all four when the right man was conducting. Those standards were in fact remarkable considering that London players were not under permanent contract and often worked three three-hour sessions daily for several days in a week, a necessity if they were to make a reasonable living.

Broadcast Music. In the U.K., Humphrey Burton left Independent Television to return to the BBC to take control of all arts programs, and was replaced on ITV's "Aquarius" by Peter Hall of the National Theatre. A great deal of opera was shown by both channels, with the question undecided as to whether direct transmissions from a theatre or productions made purposely for television were to be preferred. What was not in dispute was that dubbing the voices on after the visual side had been produced was unsuccessful. The BBC followed both courses during 1975, transmitting *Un ballo in maschera* direct from Covent Garden (and thereby justifying to some extent the huge grant that theatre received from the Arts Council), and staging its own *Flying Dutchman,* the first time a Wagner opera had been produced in the studio. Southern Television (ITV) continued its arrangement with Glyndebourne. It screened on the whole network, after a long struggle, *Il ritorno d'Ulisse in patria,* recorded as much earlier as 1973, and filmed *Cosi fan tutte* for later transmission.

In the concert field the BBC screened Promenade concerts from the Albert Hall but also continued its studio series with Previn and the London Symphony. In both Britain and West Germany programs associated with personalities were popular. West German television made a feature to celebrate Dietrich Fischer-Dieskau's 50th birthday (the record company Deutsche Grammophon also gave him a party at the Nymphenburg Palace outside Munich), while the BBC presented profiles and documentaries about various aspects of music.

In the U.S. the New York Philharmonic resumed its radio broadcasts in October, after an eight-year absence. The Boston Symphony was in its second season of weekly concerts selected and edited for television from the year's live concerts.

Recorded Music. In spite of the general recession, the record industry seemed able to issue almost as many discs as in former years, although there was in all countries a steep increase in prices, causing even a so-called cheap reissue to become hardly that. The greatest interest continued to be shown in issues containing a composer's whole output in a particular field. For example, Decca (London) completed its massive project of issuing all the Haydn symphonies under Dorati, who went over to Philips to begin recording all the Haydn operas. Solti, Kempe, and Kurt Masur each in turn recorded all the Beethoven symphonies, adding to other similar sets already on the market.

While the demand for such popular classics seemed to be insatiable, there was definitely a desire for the unusual and, in some cases, the esoteric. Among important additions to the recorded repertory were the first-ever issue of Carl Maria von Weber's *Euryanthe* (HMV/Angel), a work that revealed itself as a neglected masterpiece, extraordinarily advanced for its year of composition, 1823, in both its harmonic daring and flexible structure. It seemed overdue for a major revival on the stage. Philips continued its much-valued renaissance of Verdi's early operas with *I Masnadieri.* From HMV/Angel came the premier recording of Ralph Vaughan Williams' *Sir John in Love,*

LONDON DAILY EXPRESS/PICTORIAL PARADE

Dmitry Alekseyev, Soviet pianist who won the prestigious Leeds Piano Competition by unanimous vote, prepares for his debut with the Royal Philharmonic Orchestra in London as Marion Thorpe, a founder of the competition, looks on.

THE TIMES

Artur Rubinstein rehearses for a concert with the London Philharmonic Orchestra at Albert Hall in March.

his opera based on *The Merry Wives of Windsor*, covering much the same territory as Verdi's *Falstaff*. Philips continued its series of "live" recordings from Bayreuth with *Die Meistersinger*.

All of Shostakovich's symphonies were issued by HMV/Melodiya, an issue that sadly became a memorial one. Fischer-Dieskau, in his continuing quest for the unknown in song, resurrected some of Meyerbeer's lieder (Deutsche Grammophon), while Gérard Souzay revived some of Gounod's melodies, delightful pieces of exceptional charm.

Chamber music continued to flourish on records, if not always in the concert hall. The Aeolian Quartet continued its series of the Haydn quartets for Argo, while in a related field John McCabe, himself a composer of no small talent, began his integral recording of the Haydn piano sonatas for Decca. Pinchas Zukerman and Daniel Barenboim recorded Brahms's sonatas for violin and for viola and piano. Zukerman and Barenboim were artists who had been brought up to consider the recording studio as part of their professional existence, thereby largely banishing nervous tension from their activities there. Previn was another in the same category. Other young artists such as the Romanian pianist, resident in London, Radu Lupu and the Korean violinist Kyung-Wha Chung still found the studio an ordeal.

Barenboim completed his recording of the Mozart piano concertos (Friedrich Gulda began his) and of the Mozart opera *Don Giovanni* in the Edinburgh Festival production, as conductor. Outside the studio he continued his Herculean program of recitals and concerts, conducting a new production of Mozart's *Le nozze di Figaro* at Edinburgh and concerts with the London Philharmonic, the Orchestre de Paris, and many others.

Opera. New appointments in the operatic field included that of Anthony Bliss as executive director (a new post) of the Metropolitan Opera in New York, while James Levine was appointed musical director of the Metropolitan as of the 1976–77 season. Richard Bonynge was to succeed Edward Downes as musical director of Australian Opera. August Everding was appointed general manager of Bavarian Opera, to take effect in 1977, and was succeeded in Hamburg by Christoph von Dohnanyi in a similar capacity. Lofti Mansouri succeeded Herman Geiger-Torel (*see* BIOGRAPHY) as general director of Canadian Opera. These appointments were indicative of the difficulty of maintaining continuity, and thereby creating a consistent artistic policy, in the running of major opera houses, with administrators and musicians often unwilling to remain for more than a few years in a particular post. The Metropolitan was perhaps in this respect a peculiar case. With the untimely death of Göran Gentele in a car accident in 1972, the company fell back on Schuyler Chapin, who was to have been Gentele's assistant. For whatever reason, the board of the company decided on a further reorganization during 1975. No true successor to Gentele was appointed, and a triumvirate took charge of the house, comprising Bliss, Levine, and John Dexter, who was named director of productions. Chapin declined an offer to head a new fund-raising activity. It was hoped that this reorganization would give the Met stability.

Soprano Beverly Sills, in her debut at the Metropolitan Opera in New York City, performing in Rossini's "The Siege of Corinth."

WIDE WORLD

At the Royal Opera and Ballet, Covent Garden, Christopher Hunt was made opera administrator and John Hart ballet administrator. It was hoped that these appointments would rationalize the organization of the two companies and also help pare costs. As with artistic enterprises everywhere during 1975, Covent Garden was plagued by the inflationary spiral, which caused the house to postpone the completion of its ambitious, expensive *Ring* production for a season. Both the opera and ballet were much aided, however, by help from industrial and banking firms, support that was not always forthcoming for smaller enterprises. The English Music Drama Company, with Colin Graham and Steuart Bedford as artistic directors, arose from the ashes of the English Opera Group, but providing the money needed to support this new touring company meant that the Arts Council had to withdraw its support for the equally worthwhile Phoenix Opera.

Götz Friedrich's *Ring* at Covent Garden was an arrestingly new view of Wagner's tetralogy, in line with, but not as extravagant as, several other productions begun or continued during the year. Luca Ronconi produced a modernistic *Siegfried* to follow his *Die Walküre* at La Scala, Milan, with Alberich in a top hat and frock coat seen as a 19th-century Jewish banker and the giant Fafner in a motorcycle jacket. At Marseilles, Jean-Pierre Ponnelle set *Das Rheingold* in Victorian times as a melodrama with kidnapped virgin (Freia), perfidious lord (Wotan), armour, hidden treasure, and dwarfs, all like something out of Edgar Allan Poe. At Frankfurt there was even a court case, this time over *Götterdämmerung*, which was to have inaugurated a new *Ring* produced by a gifted young Munich man, Peter Mussbach. It was withdrawn after a single performance at the end of March. Apparently Dohnanyi, Frankfurt's departing music director, demanded changes in the staging which the authors were not prepared to make. An impasse was reached, although at the single performance changes must have been made as Mussbach brought a court case against the opera company on the grounds of infringement of copyright and won, at least in the lower court.

The Paris Opéra continued to be the most lavishly run opera house in the world. Its governmental subsidy ran to some $20 million in 1975, with artists' fees at a correspondingly high level. To justify this huge expenditure, the house's administrator, Rolf Liebermann, at the instigation of the minister for cultural affairs, Michel Guy, saw to it that at least the new *Don Giovanni* was televised, so that more than a metropolitan audience might benefit from the state's financing of the Opéra.

The high cost of opera was the concern of all in the business of maintaining large houses. At festivals the consequence was a sharp increase in seat prices; $40 was considered a cheap seat at the Salzburg Festival, $30 or more was quite normal at Bayreuth, and even Glyndebourne topped out at near £12 ($24). In the first two cases, at least, the public was not deterred, and most performances were completely sold out. At Salzburg, Herbert von Karajan offered a new and sumptuous *Don Carlos* on the Cinerama-like stage of the Grosses Festspielhaus with himself as producer and conductor and Mirella Freni, Placido Domingo, and Nicolai Ghiaurov in the cast. At Munich, Otto Schenk produced the same opera in its longer, five-act version. At Bayreuth, Wolfgang Wagner produced *Parsifal.* Thus ended an era, as this staging replaced that by Wieland Wagner, which had survived in the repertory since 1951 and was a classic of its time. The new staging returned, partially, to realism, with a real flower garden and recognizable trees in the forest. The BBC created history at Bayreuth by being allowed to film a whole scene of an opera (the last of *Die Meistersinger*), the first time this had been permitted by the Wagners. Meanwhile, in London, Friedelind Wagner helped bring about a revival of her father Siegfried's opera *Der Friedensengel,* a totally neglected score presented in concert form.

Glyndebourne was responsible for two arresting productions: Jonathan Miller's of Leos Janacek's *The Cunning Little Vixen,* where the animals were given human characteristics, and John Cox's of Stravinsky's *The Rake's Progress,* with adventurous sets designed by David Hockney. Other festival events of importance included the English National Opera's successful visit to Vienna with *Patience* and Benjamin Britten's *Gloriana* (the local press commenting on the fine ensemble work), the revival in Vienna of Franz Schmidt's rarely performed *Notre Dame,* the premiere of Robin Orr's *Hermiston* at Edinburgh, the premiere of Aulis Sallinen's *The Horseman* at Savonlinna (Finland), the visit of the Dresden State Opera and Moscow's Stanislavsky Opera Company to Wiesbaden (both examples of excellent ensemble work), and Götz Friedrich's controversial staging of Offenbach's *Orphée aux Enfers* at the Holland Festival. Giselher Klebe's eighth opera, *Ein wahrer Held,* based on Synge's *Playboy of the Western World,* had its premiere at the Zürich Festival.

(ALAN BLYTH)

Jazz. The fact that nothing particularly dramatic happened in the jazz world in 1975 was, in a way, the most damaging thing that could be said about it, for more urgently than ever before, jazz music was an art in desperate need of a distinctive identity. For some years there had been a steady erosion of that identity, particularly its borders with modern-classical and contemporary-pop music. While the attempts of such aging enfants terribles as John Lewis and William Russo to incorporate jazz techniques in some larger musical context faded to an almost inaudible tinkle, onslaughts by the armies of commerce continued to take effect, and it could be said that by the end of the year bogus categorizations like "hard-rock" had so confused the lines of stylistic demarcation that it was no longer possible to judge some jazz artists by strictly jazz criteria.

The saddest case of all was surely that of trumpeter-composer Miles Davis, who in the 1950s and early 1960s had been the rallying point for so many hopes for the jazz future. By 1975 he appeared to have succumbed entirely to the blandishments of a pop culture whose virtuosity, remarkable as it undoubtedly was in the areas of publicity and advertising, remained rare almost to the point of nonexistence in the musical sense. Although musicians like Davis could now command fees more extravagant than they could ever have dreamed of in the world of specialist jazz, their music showed an alarming decline in subtlety, control, and richness of ideas. Even saxophonist Stan Getz, whose efficacy had always depended on sweetness of sound, surrendered, in his "Captain Marvel" album, to those forces of electronic gadgetry best calculated to disturb the serenity of his music.

The very fact that men of the generation of Davis (b. 1926) and Getz (b. 1927) should continue to be regarded as "modernists" was some indication of the degree to which jazz stood in danger of stultification. For the first time in the history of the music there existed no sizable group of undisputed masters under the age of 30. The most prolific recording artist of the year was the pianist Oscar Peterson, who continued to widen his audience without diluting the intensity of his music and who, in his 50th year, might well be at the apex of his powers, both as a solo performer and as a small-group player.

That the demand for jazz remained large was hinted at in the fall, when the impressario Norman Granz revived for a few weeks the old concept of a touring jazz concert party, "Jazz at the Philharmonic." His troupe played most of the major cities of Europe, attracting large audiences and grossing over $1 million. Bearing in mind that the musicians who did the barnstorming included veterans like Roy Eldridge, Eddie "Lockjaw" Davis, Dizzy Gillespie, and Peterson, it could be realized that a substantial jazz public continued to exist and would make its presence known when it sensed the proximity of good music. All the "Jazz at the Philharmonic" artists recorded copiously for the Pablo label, which celebrated in 1975 the undeniable emergence as a major jazz attraction of the guitar virtuoso Joe Pass.

One figure sadly missing from the ranks of "Jazz at the Philharmonic" was that of saxophonist Julian "Cannonball" Adderley (*see* OBITUARIES), who died after a stroke during the summer, on the eve of his recruitment to Granz's tour. Adderley shared with Sonny Stitt the distinction of being the most brilliant of all the disciples of the alto saxophonist Charlie Parker (1920–55) and was also a more original player that Stitt. Through the 1960s Adderley, like so many of his contemporaries, had flirted with experimental improvisation and, at least on the surface, damaged his fluent and melodious style. Musicians who knew his full capabilities were always sure, however, that the contours of that style remained intact; his premature death was tragically timed at just the point where Adderley was about to work again in a musical environment sympathetic to his original aims as an improviser.

An even younger man, Oliver Nelson died within a few months of Adderley, and although his past was not quite so glorious as Adderley's, Nelson too was a talent that jazz could ill afford to lose. Born in 1932, he had developed into an excellent saxophonist and an orchestrator whose best work showed a rare ability to integrate progressive harmonic ideas with a more traditional orchestral style. Another death was that of Chicago trumpeter Marty Marsala, whose best years were those of the 1930s and 1940s, working in the band of his clarinetist brother, Joe.

UPI COMPIX

Pearl Bailey announced her intention to retire from the commercial world of show business in November and turn her talents toward helping people in any way possible.

Perhaps the most symbolic death of 1975 was that of the singer-saxophonist Louis Jordan (*see* OBITUARIES), because of what his music had represented. Born in 1908, he played with the Chick Webb Orchestra before launching out as the leader of a small group called The Tympany Five. It was with this group that Jordan, in the early 1940s, became a best-selling recording artist by combining a lusty jazz saxophone style with a brand of slapstick vocal comedy whose Uncle Tom overtones were virtually obliterated by the candid ridiculousness of most of the musical material. His "Is You Is or Is You Ain't My Baby?" and "Ain't Nobody Here but Us Chickens" made him known to millions of people who thought they disliked jazz, but his significance in 1975 was that his music, technically defined as "rhythm-and-blues," was the forerunner of rock 'n' roll.

(BENNY GREEN)

Popular. Scottish artists dominated many aspects of popular music during 1974–75. "Teeny-bopper" favourites were the Bay City Rollers, five youngsters from Edinburgh, who, backed by skillful management, drew mass fan worship reminiscent of Beatlemania. Their clean-cut image was complemented by undemanding songs. Several of the year's rock stars came from Glasgow, most notably The Sensational Alex Harvey Band. In the fall of 1972 Alex, a musician since the 1950s, had taken over the Scottish band Tear Gas, and the vivid, violent stage act they developed conquered audiences everywhere. Scots influenced even soul music; in March 1975 the Average White Band, six instrumentalists from Dundee, topped the U.S. charts with their tightly disciplined playing of basic music that could be danced to. Dancing was one of the liveliest aspects of the scene, and discotheques flourished. A specific "disco" style of music, soul with a beat, emerged, and the market became quite specialized.

There was a general shortage of concert arenas. London's Rainbow closed at the end of March, and the Wolman Rink in Central Park, New York City, was acquired for conversion. However, New York's NSE Theatre (formerly Fillmore East) opened in December 1974, and some London theatres admitted rock shows. Sports stadiums held large audiences, but some were at the mercy of the weather.

Despite the lack of sites and rising costs, many major events took place. Warner Brothers presented a six-group "Music Show" in the U.K.; the Rolling Stones toured the U.S., and in April Bill Graham presented a student benefit concert in San Francisco's Golden Gate Park with a bill including Santana, Joan Baez, and Bob Dylan. Baez also appeared at Phil Ochs's celebration of the end of the Vietnam war in Central Park. One enterprising British tour, "Naughty Rhythms," showcased three emergent bands, of which Dr. Feelgood showed the most promise.

Price increases affected the entire music business. Record sales were generally down, but cassettes increased in popularity. Record companies were unwilling to sign up new artists, preferring to concentrate on established best-sellers. There was still an unhealthy appetite for "oldies"; alongside rereleases (Gary Puckett's "Young Girl," for example) appeared new recordings of old hits such as "Sherry" and "Lollipop." Nostalgia boosted the success of the Manhattan Transfer's slick cabaret act and the Pasadena Roof Orchestra's recreations of 1920s dance band music.

New bands that gained acclaim included Ace, with an international hit "How Long," and The Tubes, latest of the "outrageous" groups. September saw the "arrival," after years of minority acclaim, of singer-writer Bruce Springsteen. Comebacks included those of The Bee Gees, with a hit single "Jive Talkin," and former teenage star Lesley Gore. Of the ex-Beatles, Paul McCartney was the most active in performing. All four continued recording, and in December 1974 each had a single in the U.S. Top Forty. The Beatles' heyday was recalled in Willy Russell's play *John, Paul, George, Ringo . . . and Bert.*

Leaders in rock theatre were Genesis, who presented a new show *The Lamb Lies Down on Broadway,* regarded by many as their crowning achievement. In August, however, leader Peter Gabriel left the group, and a change of style appeared inevitable. Pop films included *Stardust* (sequel to *That'll Be the Day*), *Flame,* which gave Slade their U.S. breakthrough, and The Who's *Tommy,* directed by Ken Russell.

West German groups led European rock; Tangerine Dream impressed audiences with their skillful handling of electronic keyboards, and Kraftwerk became the first synthesizer-based group to have a U.S. hit, with "Autobahn."

Black music was enormously varied, ranging from lush (Barry White) to percussive (Hamilton Bohannon). An outstanding female trio was Labelle, combining strong vocals with stunning presentation. Also excitingly presented was a new band, Earth, Wind and Fire. In reggae the authentic music of Bob Marley and The Wailers earned great respect and acclaim; the more commercial recordings by Ken Boothe and Johnny Nash were discotheque favourites.

It was an exciting year for country music. In February radio history was made when Bill Anderson's broadcast on the BBC's "Country Club" was heard throughout the U.S. via a Nashville linkup. Loretta Lynn's record "The Pill" caused some controversy; a more serious disturbance occurred when several stars broke away from the Country Music Association due to a disagreement over awards.

Personnel shifts occurred throughout the business. Mick Taylor left the Rolling Stones, who "borrowed" the Faces' guitarist Ron Wood for their tour. Having fragmented Mott the Hoople, Ian Hunter teamed up with guitarist Mick Ronson, but the partnership proved erratic.

Outstanding records of the year included 10cc's

international hit "I'm Not in Love" and Elton John's (*see* BIOGRAPHY) "Captain Fantastic" album, which totaled 12 weeks at the top of the U.S. charts. Bob Dylan's "Basement Tapes" was issued, after years of bootleg availability. British band Camel impressed listeners with "The Snow Goose," an instrumental work based on Paul Gallico's novel. Novelties included The Goodies' "Funky Gibbon" and a spoken version by Telly Savalas of David Gates's "If."

The singer and songwriter Tim Buckley was found dead in his Santa Monica, Calif., apartment on June 29. In July three members of Ireland's Miami Showband were killed by terrorists.

Despite some aimlessness, the pop scene contained a number of good things. Notably, rock and "serious" music were being drawn closer by such works as Stomu Yamash'ta's ballet score *Shukumei* and the compositions of David Bedford.

(HAZEL MORGAN)

Folk. In the 1975 calendar issued by the National Folk Festival Association 465 folk festivals were listed to take place in the U.S. and Canada. Included were many different sorts of festivals and shows, indicating that great numbers of North Americans were interested and involved, actively or passively, in folk music. An example of growing activity among minority groups was the second annual convention of the Asociación Nacional de Grupos Folkloricos, held in August at California State University in San José. With the object of making Mexican and Chicano traditional dances, music, and related folklore better known and understood, musicians were invited from six states of Mexico, as well as from the U.S.

In Latin America, work continued at the Instituto Interamericano de Etnomusicologia y Folklore in Caracas, Venezuela, directed by Isabel Aretz de Ramón y Rivera. Established as a multinational centre in 1973 by agreement between the Venezuelan government and the Organization of American States (OAS), it was training specialists in ethnomusicology and folklore from OAS member nations. It also undertook recording expeditions in the Americas.

"The Daughters of Heaven," a popular Japanese guitar group, performed in London in May.

THE TIMES

The collection of traditional music took place throughout the world but was often undertaken by outsiders who stayed only briefly in the area studied. Among the outstanding exceptions was the long-term study by Laszlo Vikar of the Hungarian Academy of Sciences and Gabor Bereczki, professor of Finno-Ugric languages at the University of Budapest, in the central Volga region of the U.S.S.R., the region from which the Hungarians came to Europe. Beginning in 1957, with the latest (sixth) expedition in the summer of 1975, they had recorded music and texts in the area near Kazan from the Cheremis (Maris), Chuvash, Tatars, Votyaks, and Mordvinians.

Meanwhile, specialists working in their own countries were making more field recordings available on records. Outstanding were an Italian series led by Roberto Leydi on the Albatros label and a series presenting traditional Greek church chant and folk music produced by the Society for Dissemination of National Music in Athens, aided by a Ford Foundation grant.

Computers were increasingly used for folk music research. In October the sixth Slovak Ethnomusicological Seminar concerned folk music classification and computers, with participants from ten European countries. Active computer research was under way in Budapest, Vienna, East Berlin, and Estonia.

In a separate development at the Canadian Centre for Folk Culture Studies in the Museum of Man, the Ethnomusicology Section sponsored a computerized analysis of Canadian folk music in 1973–74, directed by Victor Grauer. It was based on samples from nearly 24,000 folk songs from 33 Canadian subgroups. In 1974 a new computer project, to index the opening bars of Canadian folk tunes, began under Benjamin Suchoff.

The prestige of research in traditional music was enhanced by the appointment of Anna Czekanowska, noted ethnomusicologist, to the highest post in musicology in Poland, that of director of the Musicological Institute at Warsaw University. At the same time, Jan Streszewski, also an ethnomusicologist, became director of the Musicological Institute at the University of Poznan.

Moscow's first scholarly meeting on folk-music instruments, sponsored by the Union of Composers of the R.S.F.S.R., was held in December 1974. New data were presented on non-Slavic Soviet peoples and on two-part instrumental music and solo singing in two parts among the Bashkirs. Also treated were Russian instruments.

The International Folk Music Council (IFMC) held its 23rd international conference in Regensburg, West Germany, in August 1975, with sessions on recent trends in folk music research, on the study of orally transmitted music, and on dance research. Special emphasis was given to musical instruments and to improvisation. Maud Karpeles, IFMC's founder and honorary president, celebrated her 90th birthday in London.

(BARBARA KRADER)

See also Dance; Motion Pictures; Television and Radio; Theatre.

[624.D–J]

UPI COMPIX

Charley Pride, first black man to achieve fame in the country and western music field, made a concert appearance in New York's Madison Square Garden in November.

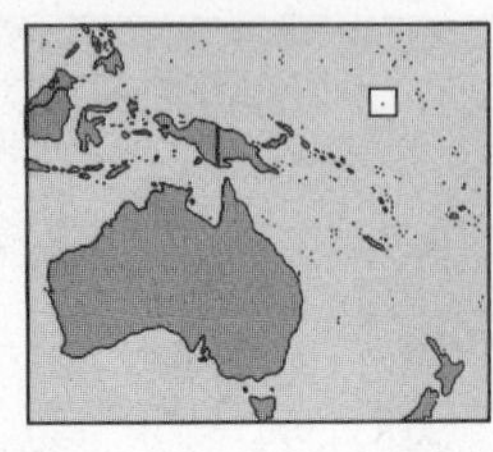

Nauru

An island republic in the Pacific Ocean, Nauru lies about 1,200 mi. E of New Guinea. Area: 8 sq.mi. (21 sq.km.). Pop. (1975 est.): 7,000. Capital: Yaren. Language: English and Nauruan. Religion: Christian. President in 1975, Hammer DeRoburt.

President DeRoburt took a major part in the sixth South Pacific Forum, held at Nukualofa, Tonga, in July. Speaking during the opening ceremony on behalf of all the delegates, DeRoburt suggested that an annual meeting was not sufficient to meet the new problems confronting South Pacific leaders. DeRoburt also spoke strongly on the regional aviation question. He argued that the Forum should not set up its own single line but that those governments which already operated airline services should concentrate on improving them.

Nauru made an investment of A$40 million in a building project in Melbourne, Australia, as a hedge against the time when the island's phosphate deposits run out. Nauru House dominated the city skyline and was designed to house more Melbourne office workers than there were native Nauruans.

Nauru continued to be generous in dispensing overseas aid. The republic gave A$250,000 to the South Pacific Bureau for Economic Cooperation for investment, with interest to be applied to financing natural disaster insurance in the islands. Three Melbourne hospitals were given A$210,000, and cyclone-shattered Darwin was helped with a gift of A$100,000.

(A. R. G. GRIFFITHS)

[977.A.3]

NAURU

Education. (1973) Primary, pupils 1,506, teachers 87; secondary, pupils 463, teachers 34; vocational, pupils 51, teachers 3.

Finance and Trade. Monetary unit: Australian dollar, with (Sept. 22, 1975) a free rate of A$0.79 to U.S. $1 (A$1.64 = £1 sterling). Budget (1972–73): revenue A$11,035,000; expenditure A$10,355,000. Foreign trade (1973 est.): imports A$14 million (*c.* 54% from Japan, *c.* 46% from Australia); exports A$24 million (*c.* 67% to Australia, *c.* 22% to New Zealand, *c.* 11% to Japan). Main export phosphate.

Industry. Production (in 000): phosphate rock (metric tons; 1971–72) 1,906; electricity (kw-hr.; 1972) 21,000.

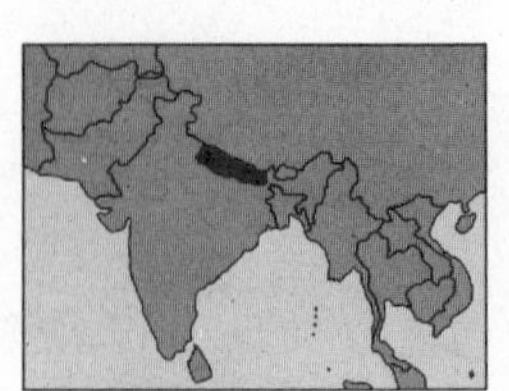

Nepal

A constitutional monarchy of Asia, Nepal is in the Himalayas between India and Tibet. Area: 54,362 sq.mi. (140,797 sq.km.). Pop. (1975 est.): 12,572,000. Cap. and largest city: Kathmandu (pop., 1971, 150,400). Language: Nepali (official); also Newari and Bhutia. Religion (1971): Hindu 89.4%; Buddhist 7.5%. King, Birendra Bir Bikram Shah Deva; prime minister in 1975, Nagendra Prasad Rijal.

More than three years after he had ascended the throne, 29-year-old King Birendra was formally crowned monarch of the world's only Hindu kingdom on Feb. 24, 1975. The week-long ceremonies were witnessed by royalty, heads of state, and ambassadors from nearly 60 countries. In a proclamation the king vowed to utilize all available resources for the development of the Nepalese people and directed that primary education be made universal and free. A Constitutional Reforms Commission was appointed in February, and in December the king announced changes in the constitution designed to further the partyless panchayat system.

In April, in a major Cabinet reshuffle, the foreign affairs portfolio was given to the former education minister, Krishna Raj Aryal. Differences over the Indian decision to merge neighbouring Sikkim with India had cooled relations between India and Nepal, but they improved after the prime minister visited New Delhi in December 1974. The king stated that Nepal would maintain an evenhanded policy toward its two big neighbours, China and India.

The economy continued to suffer from worldwide inflation and high oil prices, but food prices dropped as the result of a bumper rice crop. In July the fifth five-year plan was launched with an outlay of U.S. $1,140,000,000, 55% of which would be met through internal resources.

(GOVINDAN UNNY)

[976.A.6]

NEPAL

Education. (1973–74) Primary, pupils 392,229, teachers 18,074; secondary and vocational, pupils 216,309, teachers 7,749; teacher training, students (1969–70) 365, teachers (1966–67) 19; higher, students 19,198, teaching staff 1,499.

Finance. Monetary unit: Nepalese rupee, with (Sept. 22, 1975) an official rate of NRs. 10.56 to U.S. $1 (nominal free rate of NRs. 21.90 = £1 sterling). Gold, SDRs, and foreign exchange: (March 1975) U.S. $112.4 million; (March 1974) U.S. $126.8 million. Budget (1974–75): revenue NRs. 960 million; expenditure NRs. 1,741,000,000.

Foreign Trade. Imports *c.* NRs. 885 million (*c.* 75% from India, *c.* 10% from Japan); exports NRs. 489.2 million (*c.* 60% to India, *c.* 10% to Belgium-Luxembourg, *c.* 5% to Japan). Main exports: rice 36%; jute 9%; jute products 6%; butter 5%.

Agriculture. Production (in 000; metric tons; 1974; 1973 in parentheses): rice *c.* 2,200 (*c.* 2,402); corn *c.* 680 (*c.* 800); wheat (1973) 311, (1972) 223; potatoes (1973) *c.* 293, (1972) 293; millet and sorghum *c.* 105 (*c.* 130); mustard seed (1973) *c.* 60, (1972) 57; jute (1973) *c.* 63, (1972) *c.* 55; buffalo milk (1973) *c.* 430, (1972) *c.* 420; cow's milk (1973) *c.* 208, (1972) *c.* 193. Livestock (in 000; 1973): cattle 6,450; buffalo 3,762; pigs 300; sheep 2,250; goats 2,300.

The coronation of King Birendra in Kathmandu on February 24.

J.P. LAFFONT—SYGMA

Namibia:
see Dependent States; South Africa

Narcotics:
see Drug Abuse

NATO:
see Defense

Navies:
see Defense

KEYSTONE

Princess Maria Christina of The Netherlands was married to Jorge Guillermo, Cuban-born New York teacher of deprived children, in the 13th-century cathedral at Utrecht in June.

Netherlands, The

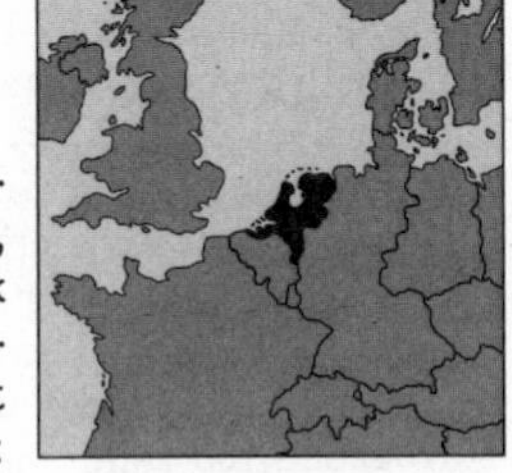

A kingdom of northwest Europe on the North Sea, The Netherlands, a Benelux country, is bounded by Belgium on the south and West Germany on the east. Area: 15,892 sq.mi. (41,160 sq.km.). Pop. (1974 est.): 13,491,000. Cap. and largest city: Amsterdam (pop., 1975 est., 13,621,000). Seat of government: The Hague (pop., 1974 est., 494,700). Language: Dutch. Religion (1971): Roman Catholic 39.6%; Dutch Reformed 23%; no religion 22.4%; Reformed Churches 7%. Queen, Juliana; prime minister in 1975, Joop den Uyl.

With Dutch exports showing a downturn for the first time since World War II and unemployment at a level of more than 200,000, the government in 1975 urged the need to check the rise in labour costs and sought to reduce government expenditure, notably in social security, and limit increases in taxation. Finance Minister Willem F. Duisenberg's budget forecast a deficit of 15 billion guilders. The economic recession seriously affected some social groups, such as canal bargemen, as cargoes dropped steadily. During August 25–28 barge masters, led by 21-year-old Leo van Laak, blockaded the Dutch inner harbours in a successful effort to prevent passage of a bill which would abolish the system of proportional distribution of cargo by way of shipping exchanges.

In May 1974 the governments of Belgium, Denmark, Norway, and The Netherlands had decided to form a consortium to purchase some 350 jet fighters to replace their obsolete F-104 Starfighters. Despite intensive diplomacy by the Belgian government on behalf of the French Mirage, the Dutch, in May, followed the lead of Denmark and Norway by choosing the U.S.-made F-16. In June Belgium also decided to accept the F-16, and the deal was completed.

On September 17, four Neptune aircraft of the Royal Netherlands Naval Aviation Service flew low over the Parliament building to demonstrate against the government's measures for economy in the Navy. A protest by NATO's secretary-general, Joseph Luns, and pressure from a majority in the upper house caused the government to modify its plans.

On August 23 the Congress of the Christian Democratic Appeal (CDA), consisting of representatives of the Antirevolutionary Party (ARP), Christian Historical Union (CHU), and the Catholic People's Party (KVP), met for the first time in The Hague. The majority of the congress voted for a resolution of the CDA's board declaring that the Bible should be the party's guide in its political activities. The resolution divided the CDA, because most of the representatives of the ARP minority supported the opinion of Willem Aantjes, leader of the faction of ARP in the upper house, that the Bible ought to guide not only the party but its representatives also. Thus what was intended to be a presentation of a new spirit in a strong new party turned out to reveal established parties divided among themselves.

NETHERLANDS, THE

Education. (1972–73) Primary, pupils 1,539,676, teachers 56,745; secondary, pupils 662,145, teachers 41,738; vocational, pupils 438,050; teacher training, students 10,685, teachers 1,000; higher (including 10 universities), students 83,212, teaching staff c. 7,500.

Finance. Monetary unit: guilder, with (Sept. 22, 1975) a free rate of 2.73 guilders to U.S. $1 (5.65 guilders = £1 sterling). Gold, SDRs, and foreign exchange: (June 1975) U.S. $6,119,000,000; (June 1974) U.S. $5,221,000,000. Budget (1975 est.): revenue 58,120,000,000 guilders; expenditure 66,198,000,000 guilders. Gross national product: (1973) 166,790,000,000 guilders; (1972) 147,480,000,000 guilders. Money supply: (April 1975) 42,470,000,000 guilders; (April 1974) 37,090,000,000 guilders. Cost of living (1970 = 100): (June 1975) 150; (June 1974) 136.

Foreign Trade. (1974) Imports 91.7 billion guilders; exports 88,513,000,000 guilders. Import sources: EEC 57% (West Germany 26%, Belgium-Luxembourg 14%, France 7%, U.K. 5%); Iran 9%; U.S. 9%. Export destinations: EEC 70% (West Germany 30%, Belgium-Luxembourg 13%, France 10%, U.K. 9%, Italy 5%). Main exports: chemicals 17%; food 17%; petroleum products 12%; electrical machinery and equipment 7%; nonelectrical machinery 6%; textile yarns and fabrics 5%; iron and steel 5%. Tourism (1973): visitors 2,558,000; gross receipts U.S. $967 million.

Transport and Communications. Roads (1973) 82,488 km. (including 1,367 km. expressways). Motor vehicles in use (1973): passenger 3,230,000; commercial 320,000. Railways: (1973) 2,833 km. (including 1,645 km. electrified); traffic (1974) 8,532,000,000 passenger-km., freight 3,369,000,000 net ton-km. Air traffic (1974): 9,361,000,000 passenger-km.; freight 635,854,000 net ton-km. Navigable inland waterways (1973): 4,802 km. (including 1,679 km. for craft of 1,500 tons and over); freight traffic 31,997,000,000 ton-km. Shipping (1974): merchant vessels 100 gross tons and over 1,358; gross tonnage 5,500,932. Ships entered (1972) vessels totaling 142.8 million net registered tons; goods loaded (1974) 85,119,000 metric tons, unloaded 250,915,000 metric tons. Telephones (Dec. 1973) 4,317,000. Radio licenses (Dec. 1973) 3,811,000. Television licenses (Dec. 1973) 3,462,000.

Agriculture. Production (in 000; metric tons; 1974; 1973 in parentheses): wheat 746 (725); barley 315 (383); rye 78 (105); oats 163 (134); potatoes 5,595 (5,771); tomatoes 350 (366); onions 394 (380); apples 370 (450); pears 105 (55); sugar, raw value c. 772 (831); cabbages (1973) 218, (1972) 230; cucumbers (1973) 343, (1972) 339; carrots (1973) 140, (1972) 136; rapeseed 45 (41); linseed 10 (6); fresh milk c. 10,150 (9,530); condensed milk (1973) 475, (1972) 458; butter 170 (169); cheese 371 (333); eggs c. 276 (285); beef and veal (1973) 308, (1972) 278; pork (1973) 882, (1972) 862; fish catch (1973) 343, (1972) 348. Livestock (in 000; May 1974): cattle 4,978; pigs 6,713; sheep 674; chickens 62,388.

Industry. Index of production (1970 = 100): (1974) 121; (1973) 118. Production (in 000; metric tons; 1974): coal 759; crude oil 1,460; natural gas (cu.m.) 83,724,000; manufactured gas (cu.m.) 1,078,000; electricity (kw-hr.) 55,350,000; pig iron 4,803; crude steel 5,840; cement 4,091; petroleum products (1973) 67,729; sulfuric acid 1,674; fertilizers (nutrient content; 1973–74) nitrogenous 1,262, phosphate 455; cotton yarn 40; wool yarn 10; rayon, etc., filament yarn and fibres 43; nylon, etc., filament yarn and fibres (1972) 113. Merchant vessels launched (100 gross tons and over; 1974) 721,000 gross tons. New dwelling units completed (1974) 146,000.

During the year the integration of mainly Asian Surinamese into the Dutch population caused trouble, especially in the big cities. Almost every week thousands of "state partners" disembarked at Schiphol Airport. The Dutch government's endeavours to secure the cooperation of the government of Surinam over this problem did not succeed, though some partial restriction on emigration to The Netherlands was agreed upon in talks in July between Dutch Prime Minister Joop den Uyl and Surinamese Prime Minister Henk Arron. Asians were leaving Surinam because they feared that independence would result in black dominance. In October both houses of Parliament, enlarged with a deputation from Surinam, passed the bill granting Surinam independence.

Another legacy of the former Dutch colonial empire, the South Moluccan community in The Netherlands, figured in a tragic and disturbing incident late in the year. Thousands of South Moluccans had fled to The Netherlands in 1950, when their home islands were incorporated into Indonesia. On December 2 a train with some 50 persons aboard was seized near the town of Beilen by terrorists demanding Dutch help in gaining an independent South Moluccan state, and two days later another group invaded the Indonesian consulate in Amsterdam, where they held some 25 persons hostage. The government said there could be no question of meeting the demands. Dutch forces surrounded the train and the consulate, and after a prolonged siege the terrorists on the train surrendered on December 14 and those in the consulate on December 19. The engineer and two passengers on the train had been shot, and an Indonesian official died after leaping from a consulate window. The remaining hostages were reported to be in good condition.

(DICK BOONSTRA)

See also Dependent States; Surinam.
[972.A.7]

New Zealand

New Zealand, a parliamentary state and member of the Commonwealth of Nations, is in the South Pacific Ocean, separated from southeastern Australia by the Tasman Sea. The country consists of North and South islands and Stewart, Chatham, and other minor islands. Area: 103,747 sq.mi. (268,704 sq.km.). Pop. (1975 est.): 3,095,000. Cap.: Wellington (pop., 1975 est., 143,400). Largest city: Christchurch (pop., 1975 est., 172,500). Largest urban area: Auckland (pop., 1975 est., 796,700). Language: English (official), Maori. Religion (1971): Church of England 31%; Presbyterian 20%; Roman Catholic 16%. Queen, Elizabeth II; governor-general in 1975, Sir Denis Blundell; prime ministers, Wallace Edward Rowling and, from December 12, Robert David Muldoon.

The general election of Nov. 29, 1975, which dominated events in New Zealand during the year, resulted in an upset victory for the National Party led by Robert Muldoon. The National Party won 53 seats in the 87-seat House of Representatives, as against 34 for Labour. Three Labour ministers, Thomas McGuigan (health), Norman J. King (social welfare), and Philip A. Amos (education), failed to retain their parliamentary seats.

The size of the three-year-old Labour government's majority, 25 seats, should have indicated only the prospect of a routine erosion in voting strength, but so controversial did the government's economic policies become that both the Labour and National parties were on the hustings virtually all year. The mildly conservative National Party, in office for 12 years before Norman Kirk brought Labour back to power, charged that a fanatical determination to avert any unemployment had caused Prime Minister Rowling to borrow like a gambler. The National attack was the more ferocious because the pugnacious Muldoon, the party's former finance minister, had replaced the gentlemanly Sir John Marshall as leader, and he was happy to turn the election campaign into a meeting of shareholders examining a failing company.

In February Rowling visited London, Brussels,

Overview of Wairakei Bore Field in Auckland Province, North Island. New Zealand continues to be a world leader in the development of geothermal resources.

AUTHENTICATED NEWS INTERNATIONAL

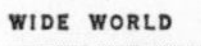
WIDE WORLD

Lynne Cox, 18-year-old distance swimmer, became the first woman to successfully traverse the 14-mile Cook Strait between North and South islands in February. Her time was 12 hours 3 minutes.

Bonn, and Paris to obtain continued New Zealand access to the European Economic Community market and favourable terms within it. New Zealand's vital agricultural exports were bringing lower prices on overseas markets while, at the same time, production and transport costs were rising and the nation was paying more for its raw material and manufactured imports.

Labour had exacerbated its troubles by abolishing the wages authority, introducing an overly expansionary first budget, and approving inflationary wage increases. The 1975–76 budget, while raising basic wage rates, held Post Office, railway, and electricity charges level and offered some tax relief to companies. More stringent criteria of age and skills for Britons wishing to emigrate to New Zealand went into effect. In August the New Zealand dollar was devalued by 15%.

A major election issue was the government's ban on white South African sports teams, an approach to dealing with apartheid that did not appear to have a consensus behind it. The restructuring of broadcasting into separate corporations (without responsibility through a minister to Parliament) for two television networks and a radio complex worked reasonably well, though the cost of the scheme threatened to endanger the scale of competition between the TV networks.

Social issues predominated in Parliament. Attempts to legislate reforms in the laws governing abortion and homosexuality failed, the first because of a technical defect and the second on a free vote in the House on a private member's bill. Children's courts were replaced by less formal boards. An act that proved highly controversial, even in its first months of operation, suppressed the names of defendants and accused persons before the courts until such time as they might be convicted. The Official Secrets Act seemed destined for reform after it was invoked (unsuccessfully) against a retired secretary of the Department of Industries and Commerce, W. B. Sutch, who was found not guilty of passing secrets to a Soviet agent. Sutch, a prominent economic consultant and historian, died seven months later.

Visitors included Singapore Prime Minister Lee Kuan Yew and Malaysian Prime Minister Tun Abdul Razak. Sir Keith Park (*see* OBITUARIES), a veteran of the Battle of Britain, died in February at the age of 82. Sixteen persons died when the 3,600-ton freighter "Capitaine Bougainville" caught fire off North Auckland during a voyage from Auckland to Sydney. (JOHN A. KELLEHER)

See also Dependent States.

[977.C]

NEW ZEALAND

Education. (1974) Primary, pupils 523,673, teachers 20,086; secondary and vocational, pupils 210,631, teachers 10,983; teacher training (third-level), students 8,004, teachers 535; higher (including 7 universities), students 25,589, teaching staff 2,679.

Finance. Monetary unit: New Zealand dollar, with (Sept. 22, 1975) a free rate of NZ$0.95 to U.S. $1 (NZ$1.96 = £1 sterling). Gold, SDRs, and foreign exchange: (June 1975) U.S. $611 million; (June 1974) U.S. $580 million. Budget (1973–74 actual): revenue NZ$2,617,000,000; expenditure NZ$2,626,000,000. Gross national product: (1973–74) NZ$8,593,000,000; (1972–73) NZ$7,297,000,000. Cost of living (1970 = 100): (1st quarter 1975) 153; (1st quarter 1974) 136.

Foreign Trade. (1974) Imports NZ$2,615,100,000; exports NZ$1,733,900,000. Import sources: Australia 20%; U.K. 18%; Japan 15%; U.S. 13%. Export destinations: U.K. 20%; U.S. 14%; Japan 13%; Australia 11%. Main exports (1973): meat and meat products 30%; wool 23%; lamb and mutton 15%; beef and veal 14%; butter 7%; milk 6%; hides and skins 5%. Tourism: visitors (1972) 242,500; gross receipts (1973) U.S. $99 million.

Transport and Communications. Roads (1973) 92,005 km. (including 116 km. expressways). Motor vehicles in use (1974): passenger 1,122,100; commercial 200,900. Railways: (1974) 4,797 km.; traffic (1972–73) 491 million passenger-km., freight (1974) 3,757,000,000 net ton-km. Air traffic (1974): 3,877,700,000 passenger-km.; freight 107,846,000 net ton-km. Shipping (1974): merchant vessels 100 gross tons and over 113; gross tonnage 163,399. Telephones (Dec. 1973) 1,444,000. Radio receivers (Dec. 1973) 2.7 million. Television licenses (Dec. 1973) 900,000.

Agriculture. Production (in 000; metric tons; 1974; 1973 in parentheses): wheat 248 (378); barley 290 (251); oats 59 (47); corn (1973) 119, (1972) 116; potatoes (1973) 325, (1972) 220; dry peas *c.* 64 (59); tomatoes *c.* 55 (49); apples *c.* 170 (143); milk *c.* 6,100 (6,080); butter 219 (242); cheese 88 (101); mutton and lamb (1973) 555, (1972) 558; beef and veal (1973) 449, (1972) 397; wool 203 (220); sheepskins (1973) *c.* 114, (1972) *c.* 114; timber (cu.m.; 1973–74) 8,800, (1972–73) 8,800; fish catch (1973) 66, (1972) 58. Livestock (in 000; Jan. 1973): cattle 9,415; sheep 55,883; pigs 507; chickens (1973) *c.* 5,600.

Industry. Fuel and power (in 000; metric tons; 1974): coal 396; lignite 2,212; crude oil (1973) 156; natural gas (cu.m.) 302,000; manufactured gas (cu.m.) 79,000; electricity (excluding most industrial production; kw-hr.) 18,264,000. Production (in 000; metric tons; 1974): cement 1,111; petroleum products (1973) 3,458; phosphate fertilizers (1973–74) 420; wood pulp (1973–74) 669; newsprint (1973–74) 214; other paper (1973–74) 240.

Nicaragua

The largest country of Central America, Nicaragua is a republic bounded by Honduras, Costa Rica, the Caribbean Sea, and the Pacific Ocean. Area: 50,000 sq.mi. (130,000 sq.km.). Pop. (1974 est.): 2,084,000.

NICARAGUA

Education. (1972–73) Primary, pupils 314,425, teachers 8,154; secondary, pupils 54,139, teachers 1,578; vocational, pupils 5,613, teachers 336; teacher training, students 1,332, teachers 93; higher, students 11,618, teaching staff 694.

Finance. Monetary unit: córdoba, with (Sept. 22, 1975) a par value of 7 córdobas to U.S. $1 (free rate of 14.55 córdobas = £1 sterling). Gold, SDRs, and foreign exchange: (June 1975) U.S. $145,550,000; (June 1974) U.S. $186,740,000. Budget (1974 est.): revenue 1,267,000,000 córdobas; expenditure 1,627,000,000 córdobas. Gross national product: (1973) 7,464,000,000 córdobas; (1972) 6,538,000,000 córdobas. Money supply: (June 1975) 1,198,200,000 córdobas; (June 1974) 1,471,600,000 córdobas.

Foreign Trade. (1974) Imports 3,939,100,000 córdobas; exports 2,671,400,000 córdobas. Import sources (1973): U.S. 34%; Guatemala 9%; Costa Rica 8%; El Salvador 8%; West Germany 7%; Japan 7%; Venezuela 5%. Export destinations (1973): U.S. 33%; Japan 12%; West Germany 9%; Costa Rica 8%; El Salvador 5%. Main exports: cotton 36%; coffee 12%; meat 6%.

Transport and Communications. Roads (1971) 13,147 km. (including 485 km. of Pan-American Highway). Motor vehicles in use (1972): passenger *c.* 32,000; commercial (including buses) *c.* 13,000. Railways (1972): 348 km.; traffic 28 million passenger-km., freight 14 million net ton-km. Air traffic (1973): 76 million passenger-km.; freight 2 million net ton-km. Telephones (Dec. 1973) 17,000. Radio receivers (Dec. 1973) 125,000. Television receivers (Dec. 1973) 62,000.

Agriculture. Production (in 000; metric tons; 1974; 1973 in parentheses): corn *c.* 193 (220); rice (1973) *c.* 81, (1972) 74; sorghum *c.* 59 (*c.* 44); dry beans *c.* 52 (47); sugar, raw value *c.* 160 (144); bananas *c.* 250 (*c.* 240); oranges (1973) *c.* 52, (1972) *c.* 50; coffee 42 (36); cotton, lint *c.* 147 (128). Livestock (in 000; 1973): cattle *c.* 3,750; pigs *c.* 660; horses *c.* 175; chickens *c.* 3,300.

Industry. Production (in 000; metric tons; 1973): petroleum products 564; cement (1971) 99; gold (exports; troy oz.) 76; electricity (kw-hr.; 1971) 649,000.

Netherlands Overseas Territories: *see* Dependent States

New Guinea: *see* Indonesia; Papua New Guinea

Newspapers: *see* Publishing

WIDE WORLD

Veiled women nomads of Niger cross an arid plain by traditional camel transport.

Cap. and largest city: Managua (pop., 1974 est., 313,400). Language: Spanish. Religion: Roman Catholic. President in 1975, Anastasio Somoza Debayle.

Open and clandestine opposition to President Somoza continued during 1975. Pedro Joaquín Chamorro, leader of the coalition Democratic Liberation Union, whose components ranged from ultraconservative to Communist, remained the human symbol of antigovernment sentiment. The minority opposition within the national Congress became increasingly vocal on various issues, especially the continuation of press censorship imposed following the December 1974 kidnapping of officials and other prominent citizens and the murder of four individuals.

Clandestine action by the Sandinist National Liberation Front, which had carried out the kidnapping-murder, continued in the form of sporadic encounters with military detachments sent to flush the guerrillas from their mountain hideouts. These clashes resulted in an undetermined number of fatalities on both sides.

President Somoza, although reportedly shaken by the December event and humiliated by the necessity to pay a large ransom and free political prisoners for the release of hostages, remained publicly defiant. He accused the Sandinistas of being influenced strongly by foreign elements and announced that the state of siege, including press censorship, would remain in effect indefinitely. (HENRY WEBB, JR.)

[974.B.1.d]

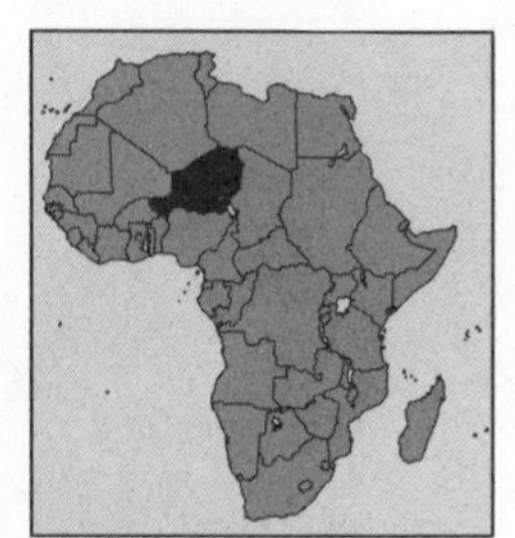

Niger

A republic of north central Africa, Niger is bounded by Algeria, Libya, Chad, Nigeria, Dahomey (Benin), Upper Volta, and Mali. Area: 489,000 sq.mi. (1,267,000 sq.km.). Pop. (1974 est.): 4,476,000, including (1970 est.) Hausa 53.7%; Zerma and Songhai 23.6%; Fulani 10.6%; Beriberi-Manga 9.1%. Cap. and largest city: Niamey (pop., 1973 est., 121,900). Language: French and Sudanic dialects. Religion: Muslim, animist, Christian. President in 1975, Lieut. Col. Seyni Kountche.

The country's military regime reacted with a mixture of repression and clemency in 1975. In February Capt. Gabriel Cyrille, minister of public works, transport, and town planning, was relieved of his post for endangering state security. In August Maj. Sani Souna Sido, until then the regime's second in command after President Kountche, was accused of plotting with two others, including Djibo Bakary, former leader of a proscribed political party, to seize power; all three men were arrested. In October a dozen associates of Bakary were also arrested. But five former ministers of former president Hamani Diori who had been imprisoned since the 1974 coup were released.

The renegotiation of cooperation agreements with France announced by President Kountche after his visit in June with Pres. Valéry Giscard d'Estaing in Paris began in Niamey in December.

For the first time in five years adequate rain fell in 1974 and the harvest was good. The military coup of that year had brought more efficient food distribution, and the refugee camps began to empty. France was to participate in further prospecting for uranium (20% of Niger's export value). Industrialization and Niger River dam projects awaited foreign capital. Meanwhile, aid loans came from various sources. (PHILIPPE DECRAENE)

NIGER

Education. (1973–74) Primary, pupils 110,437, teachers 2,736; secondary, pupils 10,494, teachers 474; vocational, pupils 237, teachers 25; higher, students 280, teachers 47.

Finance. Monetary unit: CFA franc, with (Sept. 22, 1975) a parity of CFA Fr. 50 to the French franc (free rate of CFA Fr. 227.70 = U.S. $1; CFA Fr. 471.75 = £1 sterling). Gold, SDRs, and foreign exchange: (April 1975) U.S. $41.8 million; (April 1974) U.S. $45.5 million. Budget (1973–74 est.) balanced at CFA Fr. 15,268,000,000.

Foreign Trade. (1973) Imports CFA Fr. 19,098,000,000; exports CFA Fr. 13,817,000,000. Import sources: France 43%; West Germany 8%; U.S. 7%; Nigeria 6%. Export destinations: France 51%; Nigeria 26%; Italy 6%; West Germany 5%. Main exports: uranium 39%; peanuts 14%.

Transport and Communications. Roads (1972) 6,998 km. Motor vehicles in use (1973): passenger 7,800; commercial (including buses) 9,300. There are no railways. Inland waterway (Niger River) *c.* 300 km. Telephones (Dec. 1971) 4,000. Radio receivers (Dec. 1971) 150,000.

Agriculture. Production (in 000; metric tons; 1974; 1973 in parentheses): millet *c.* 550 (*c.* 400); sorghum *c.* 250 (*c.* 125); cassava (1973) *c.* 70, (1972) *c.* 100; rice (1973) *c.* 12, (1972) *c.* 15; dry beans *c.* 25 (*c.* 25); peanuts *c.* 180 (*c.* 80); dates (1973) *c.* 5, (1972) *c.* 5. Livestock (in 000; 1973): cattle *c.* 3,000; sheep *c.* 2,000; goats *c.* 5,000; camels *c.* 350.

Nickel: *see* Mining and Quarrying

Nigeria

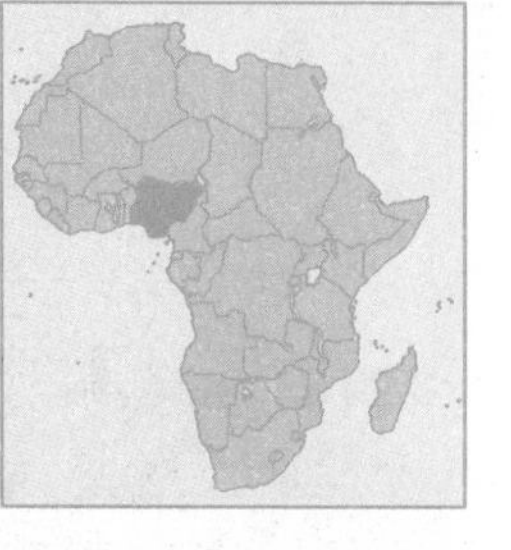

A republic and a member of the Commonwealth of Nations, Nigeria is located in Africa on the north coast of the Gulf of Guinea, bounded by Dahomey, Niger, Chad, and Cameroon. Area: 356,669 sq.mi. (923,768 sq.km.). Pop. (1974 est.): 72,833,000, including: Hausa 21%; Ibo 18%; Yoruba 18%; Fulani 10%. Cap. and largest city: Lagos (pop., 1973 est., 970,300). Language: English (official). Religion (1963): Muslim 47%; Christian 34%. Heads of provisional military government in 1975, Gen. Yakubu Gowon and, from July 29, Brig. Murtala Ramat Mohammed.

On July 29, 1975, General Gowon was deposed while attending the summit meeting of the Organization of African Unity in Kampala, Uganda. His dignified acceptance and exile to England permitted a bloodless coup. Discontent had been building since October 1974, when the indefinite postponement of a return to civilian rule and a continuance of the ban on political activities had been announced. Adding to the unrest were economic hardship resulting from price inflation and the unchecked open corruption within state governors' administrations.

Gowon's successor, Brigadier Mohammed (*see* BIOGRAPHY), at once abrogated the census (which had aroused misgivings by showing a new preponderance of Northerners—from 52% of the population to 64% in ten years), canceled the extravagant African Festival of Arts and Culture, and stated that foreign obligations would be honoured. Nearly half of his first Cabinet were civilians, though he relied on the support of the largest army in Africa (250,000 men), which took half the national budget. The 1966 state of emergency remained in force. The old administration was purged, with civil servants, police chiefs, and even state governors forced into retirement.

Wigs proved to be one of the best-selling items in the new Western-style market stalls in Onitsha, Nigeria.

THOMAS A. JOHNSON—THE NEW YORK TIMES

NIGERIA

Education. (1973) Primary, pupils 4,662,400, teachers 136,142; secondary, pupils 452,372, teachers 17,215; vocational, pupils 21,515, teachers 1,111; teacher training, students 42,771, teachers 2,122; higher, students 24,999, teaching staff 3,604.

Finance. Monetary unit: naira, with (Sept. 22, 1975) a free rate of 0.67 naira to U.S. $1 (1.39 naira = £1 sterling). Gold, SDRs, and foreign exchange: (June 1975) U.S. $6,036,000,000; (June 1974) U.S. $2,113,000,000. Federal budget (1974–75): revenue 2,496,000,000 naira; expenditure 2,634,000,000 naira (includes 1,639,000,000 naira capital expenditure). Gross domestic product: (1973) 17,801,000,000 naira; (1972) 15,364,000,000 naira. Money supply: (Jan. 1975) 1,748,400,000 naira; (Jan. 1974) 931.6 million naira. Cost of living (Lagos; 1970 = 100): (March 1975) 168; (March 1974) 136.

Foreign Trade. (1974) Imports 1,715,400,000 naira; exports 6,030,900,000 naira. Import sources (1973): U.K. 27%; West Germany 15%; U.S. 10%; Japan 9%; France 7%. Export destinations (1973): U.S. 24%; U.K. 19%; The Netherlands 13%; France 13%; Japan 5%. Main export crude oil 91%.

Transport and Communications. Roads (1971) 89,000 km. Motor vehicles in use (1972): passenger *c.* 120,000; commercial (including buses) *c.* 69,000. Railways: (1973) 3,505 km.; traffic (1972–73) 1,033,000,000 passenger-km., freight 1,372,000,000 net ton-km. Air traffic (1973): 334 million passenger-km.; freight 8.2 million net ton-km. Shipping (1974): merchant vessels 100 gross tons and over 78; gross tonnage 121,301. Telephones (Dec. 1973) 106,000. Radio receivers (Dec. 1972) 1,550,000. Television receivers (Dec. 1973) 85,000.

Agriculture. Production (in 000; metric tons; 1974; 1973 in parentheses): millet *c.* 2,800 (*c.* 2,150); sorghum *c.* 3,300 (*c.* 3,000); corn *c.* 1,000 (608); rice (1973) *c.* 550, (1972) *c.* 500; sweet potatoes (1973) *c.* 205, (1972) *c.* 204; yams (1973) *c.* 14,300, (1972) *c.* 14,300; taro (1973) *c.* 1,780, (1972) *c.* 1,770; cassava (1973) *c.* 9,600, (1972) *c.* 9,570; cowpeas (1973) *c.* 750, (1972) *c.* 800; tomatoes *c.* 220 (*c.* 190); peanuts *c.* 600 (*c.* 350); palm oil *c.* 450 (*c.* 430); cocoa *c.* 230 (*c.* 214); cotton, lint *c.* 99 (*c.* 92); rubber *c.* 100 (91). Livestock (in 000; 1973): cattle *c.* 10,920; sheep *c.* 7,550; goats *c.* 22,400; pigs *c.* 872; poultry *c.* 81,000.

Industry. Production (in 000; metric tons; 1974): crude oil 112,591; natural gas (cu.m.; 1973) 303,000; cement (1973) 1,222; tin 5.6; petroleum products (1973) 2,033; electricity (kw-hr.; 1973) 2,625,000.

A Federal Council of States was to be set up to examine the creation of new states and the suitability of Lagos as the federal capital. Mohammed promised a return to an elected civil government by Oct. 1, 1979; this goal was to be reached through five stages, beginning with the creation of new states.

Mismanagement of public funds and general incompetence and corruption were epitomized by the convergence of hundreds of vessels on Lagos in September, with huge quantities of cement which no one would admit ordering. The wage settlement of the Udoji Public Services Commission review of January, backdated to April 1974, gave raises of up to 130% to some civil servants and was followed by an avalanche of other pay settlements. The result was to worsen the inflation and draw agricultural workers from the country into the towns.

Thanks to its oil exports, Nigeria showed a record trade surplus in 1974 of 4 billion naira, a 284% increase over 1973 (oil exports, representing 92% of the total value, increased by 153%). Nigeria was foremost in the new Economic Community of West African States, established by a treaty signed in Lagos on May 28. The cost of the third national plan (1975–80) was estimated at 30 billion naira.

(MOLLY MORTIMER)

[978.E.4.b.ii]

Norway

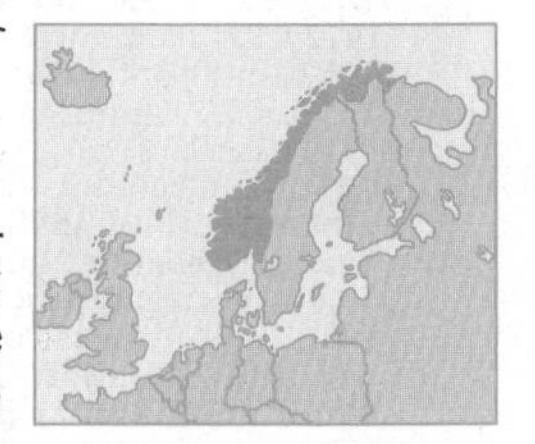

A constitutional monarchy of northern Europe, Norway is bordered by Sweden, Finland, and the U.S.S.R.; its coastlines are on the Skagerrak, the North Sea, the Norwegian Sea, and the Arctic Ocean. Area: 125,053 sq.mi. (323,886 sq.km.), excluding the Svalbard Archipelago, 23,957 sq.mi., and Jan Mayen Island, 144 sq.mi. Pop. (1975): 4,002,700. Cap. and largest city: Oslo (pop., 1974, 465,300). Language: Norwegian.

Nobel Prizes: *see* People of the Year *beginning on page 61*

Religion: Lutheran (96.5%). King, Olav V; prime minister in 1975, Trygve Bratteli.

Norway began to feel the effects of the international recession in 1975, though the repercussions on the economy were milder than in most industrial nations. There was a sharp fall in demand for key exports such as metals, paper and pulp, and fish, and, with the steep decline in tanker freight rates, earnings of the merchant fleet dropped. By the second half of 1975 more than one-quarter of the merchant fleet was laid up.

The minority Labour government gave priority to antirecession policies, relying mainly on measures to stimulate domestic consumption, including tax concessions, subsidies to hold prices down, and increased social security and unemployment benefits. In addition, to help export industries hit by the slump, it introduced various selective support measures, including credit facilities to allow companies to produce for stock. One result of the new economic situation was a big rise in Norway's external deficit; domestic demand was strong, leading to increased imports, while foreign earnings were falling. Several times during the year the government had to revise its estimate of the likely 1975 payments deficit. Toward the end of the year, it looked as if the deficit would reach 14.3 billion kroner, as compared with the forecast of 7.3 billion kroner made a year earlier.

This unexpected increase in the payments gap did not appear to worry the government. It was official policy to borrow against future revenues from offshore oil and gas in order to finance the deficit and keep the economy going. The government had little difficulty in raising several large loans abroad—foreign lenders regarded Norway as a good credit risk because of its offshore resources.

CENTRAL PRESS/PICTORIAL PARADE

This 220,000-ton drilling platform located off Stavanger, Norway, rests on the seabed under its own weight. It is the first of a new generation of concrete structures that will be used for oil exploration in the North Sea.

Despite this pump-priming, unemployment rose steadily. By mid-August it had reached 1.1% of the labour force—a low figure by international standards but double the level of a year earlier and much higher than Norwegians were accustomed to. In September the government announced a new package of measures to curb unemployment, including direct financing of public works at the national and local level, an increase in lending limits for the state-financed credit institutions, and an increase in special liquidity loans to industry. Some industrialists began urging more rapid development of offshore oil and gas.

There was considerable activity on the Norwegian continental shelf in 1975. This followed the allocation, late in 1974, of five new petroleum exploration and production licenses in Norway's sector of the North Sea. The licenses covered eight blocks or parts of blocks, six of them adjoining the British sector. Statoil, the Norwegian state oil company, was given a 50% interest in four of the five and a 55% stake in the fifth. The foreign companies involved included Exxon, Conoco, Amoco/Mobil, and the French-Norwegian consortium Petronord. One U.S. company, Chevron, declined to accept the 35% stake it was offered in one of the licenses because it disliked an impending new oil tax law, which considerably raised the state tax "take" from oil companies' North Sea production. Chevron's stake in the license was awarded to British Petroleum.

The world shipping crisis affected Norwegian shipowners—particularly those with large tanker fleets—financially. Shipyards that had specialized in building large tankers were hit by a wave of order cancellations. One tanker magnate, Hilmar Reksten, was forced to sell his shareholdings in a number of Norwegian shipping and industrial companies to the government in

NORWAY

Education. (1972–73) Primary, pupils 375,004, teachers 19,109; secondary, pupils 268,197, teachers 17,799; vocational (1971–72), pupils 66,772, teachers 10,616; higher (including 4 universities), students 56,664, teaching staff (1971–72) 5,291.

Finance. Monetary unit: Norwegian krone, with (Sept. 22, 1975) a free rate of 5.70 kroner to U.S. $1 (11.80 kroner = £1 sterling). Gold, SDRs, and foreign exchange: (June 1975) U.S. $1,980,300,000; (June 1974) U.S. $1,546,700,000. Budget (1975 est.): revenue 34,724,000,000 kroner; expenditure 39,127,000,000 kroner. Gross domestic product: (1974) 128,210,000,000 kroner; (1973) 111,170,000,000 kroner. Money supply: (Dec. 1974) 28,810,000,000 kroner; (Dec. 1973) 25,750,000,000 kroner. Cost of living (1970 = 100): (June 1975) 149; (June 1974) 132.

Foreign Trade. (1974) Imports 46,457,000,000 kroner; exports 34,434,000,000 kroner. Import sources: Sweden 19%; West Germany 14%; U.K. 10%; U.S. 8%; Japan 6%; Denmark 6%. Export destinations: Sweden 18%; U.K. 17%; West Germany 10%; Denmark 8%; U.S. 5%. Main exports: ships 18%; machinery 10%; chemicals 8%; iron and steel 7%; aluminum 7%; paper 7%; fish 6%; petroleum and products 5%.

Transport and Communications. Roads (1973) 74,796 km. (including 138 km. expressways). Motor vehicles in use (1973): passenger 913,400; commercial 163,000. Railways: (1973) 4,241 km. (including 2,440 km. electrified); traffic (state only; 1974) 1,870,000,000 passenger-km., freight 2,950,000,000 net ton-km. Air traffic (including Norwegian apportionment of international operations of Scandinavian Airlines System; 1974): 2,737,000,000 passenger-km.; freight 107,930,000 net ton-km. Shipping (1974): merchant vessels 100 gross tons and over 2,689; gross tonnage 24,852,917. Ships entered (1972) vessels totaling 18,088,000 net registered tons; goods loaded (1972) 37,457,000 metric tons, unloaded 20,399,000 metric tons. Telephones (Dec. 1973) 1,308,000. Radio licenses (Dec. 1973) 1,255,000. Television licenses (Dec. 1973) 986,000.

Agriculture. Production (in 000; metric tons; 1974; 1973 in parentheses): barley 632 (535); oats 370 (351); potatoes 847 (672); apples (1973) *c.* 50, (1972) 50; milk *c.* 1,776 (1,749); cheese *c.* 58 (*c.* 51); beef and veal (1973) 60, (1972) 54; pork (1973) 76, (1972) 76; timber (cu.m.; 1972–73) 8,600, (1971–72) 8,300; fish catch (1973) 2,974, (1972) 3,163. Livestock (in 000; June 1974): cattle *c.* 963; sheep *c.* 1,632; pigs *c.* 785; goats (1973) 72; chickens (1973) *c.* 6,200.

Industry. Fuel and power (in 000; metric tons; 1974): crude oil 1,707; coal (Svalbard mines; Norwegian operated only) 436; manufactured gas (cu.m.) 25,000; electricity (kw-hr.) 76,618,000. Production (in 000; metric tons; 1974): iron ore (65% metal content) 3,916; pig iron 1,522; crude steel 970; aluminum 652; zinc 72; copper 25; cement 2,659; petroleum products (1973) *c.* 6,010; sulfuric acid 384; fertilizers (nutrient content; 1973–74) nitrogenous 445, phosphate 128; fish meal (1973) 354; wood pulp (1973) mechanical 1,140, chemical 1,145; newsprint (1973) 531; other paper (1973) 855. Merchant vessels launched (100 gross tons and over; 1974) 997,500 gross tons. New dwelling units completed (1974) 41,400.

order to meet commitments to foreign and Norwegian creditors.

The year saw a handover of power to a new generation in the ruling Labour Party. At the party's national conference in April, Labour Prime Minister Trygve Bratteli resigned as chairman and Reiulf Steen, the party's leftist, 41-year-old deputy chairman, was elected his successor. The party's more conservative wing managed to prevent Steen's nomination as the candidate for the premiership. This went to Odvar Nordli, who was the leader of Labour's parliamentary group. In September, after a little prodding from the party hierarchy, Prime Minister Bratteli announced that he would retire early in January 1976.

(FAY GJESTER)

[972.A.6.c]

Oman

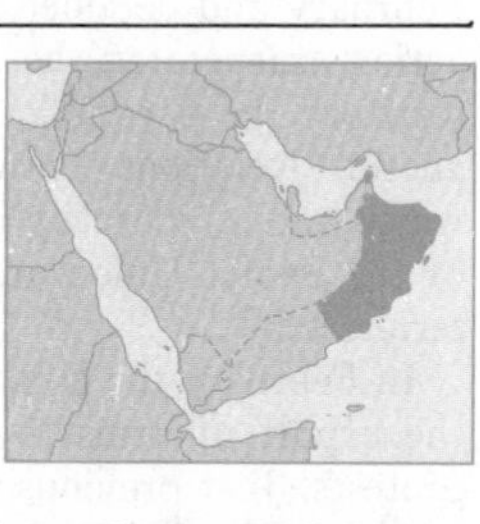

An independent sultanate, Oman occupies the southeastern part of the Arabian Peninsula and is bounded by the United Arab Emirates, Saudi Arabia, the Gulf of Oman, and the Arabian Sea. A small part of the country lies to the north and is separated from the rest of Oman by the United Arab Emirates. Area: 82,000 sq.mi. (212,400 sq.km.). Pop. (1974 est.): 700,000 to 750,000. Cap.: Muscat (pop., 1973 est., 15,000). Largest city: Matrah (pop., 1973 est., 18,000). Language: Arabic. Religion: Muslim. Sultan in 1975, Qabus ibn Sa'id.

In December 1975 the ten-year-old Dhofar rebellion led by the Popular Front for the Liberation of Oman (PFLO) was finally defeated by the sultan's British-led forces, which included Iranian and Jordanian troops. In March the Arab League's secretary-general had visited Oman and Yemen (Aden), a country that supported the Dhofar rebels, but a general meeting of the league's mediation committee in Cairo in May produced no results. The PFLO rejected mediation efforts because the league committee had not visited Dhofar, where the committee said its members' safety could not be guaranteed. The PFLO received strong verbal support from Iraq and Libya, but there had been signs that support from Iraq was falling off as a result of the Iraqi-Iranian rapprochement.

In January Sultan Qabus visited Washington, D.C., and there were widespread reports that the U.S. had asked for base facilities on Masira Island; this was vigorously denied by the Oman government. With nearly half of Oman's revenues (estimated at $1 billion in 1974) being spent on defense, the country suffered a severe cash flow problem. In spite of some aid from Kuwait and a $100 million loan from Saudi Arabia, substantial cuts were expected in all nonmilitary expenditures.

(PETER MANSFIELD)

[978.B.4.b]

OMAN

Education. (1973–74) Primary, pupils 34,572; secondary, pupils 341; primary and secondary, teachers 1,230; vocational, pupils 79, teachers 12.

Finance and Trade. Monetary unit: rial Omani, with (Sept. 22, 1975) an official rate of 0.345 rial to U.S. $1 (free rate of 0.719 rial = £1 sterling). Budget (1973 est.): revenue 68.5 million rials; expenditure 63 million rials (excludes development expenditure of 30 million rials). Foreign trade (1973): imports 85.8 million rials; exports 61.9 million rials. Import sources: United Arab Emirates 23%; U.K. 19%; Japan 9%; The Netherlands 9%; West Germany 5%; Australia 5%; India 5%. Export destinations: Japan *c.* 35%; Spain *c.* 18%; France *c.* 12%; U.K. *c.* 9%; Norway *c.* 7%. Main export crude oil 99%.

Industry. Production (in 000): crude oil (metric tons; 1974) 14,500; electricity (kw-hr.; 1973) 171,000.

WIDE WORLD

A ten-year campaign neared its end as Oman's British-led Army confined the Communist-led rebellion to isolated guerrilla warfare near the Yemen (Aden) border.

Pakistan

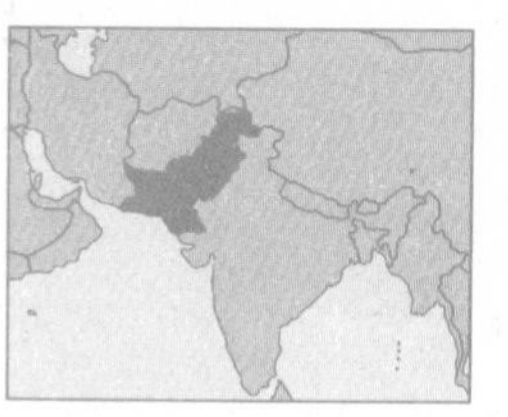

A federal republic, Pakistan is bordered on the south by the Arabian Sea, on the west by Afghanistan and Iran, on the north by China, and on the east by India. Area: 307,374 sq.mi. (796,095 sq.km.), excluding the Pakistani-controlled section of Jammu and Kashmir. Pop. (1974 est.): 68,214,000. Cap.: Islamabad (pop., 1972, 77,000). Largest city: Karachi (metro. area pop., 1972, 3,469,000). Language: Urdu and English. Religion: Muslim 90%, Hindu and Christian minorities. President in 1975, Chaudhri Fazal Elahi; prime minister, Zulfikar Ali Bhutto.

The year began badly for Pakistan. An earthquake disaster struck parts of Swat in the last days of December 1974, and an area some 70 mi. long on one side of the Indus Valley, including a stretch of the Karakoram Highway (opened in 1971), was devastated. More than 5,000 lives were lost, and three times that number were injured. Relief work was hampered by the inaccessible nature of the region and the danger to airplanes because of violent air currents, but Army engineers cleared the highway in 13 days. An appeal to governments and international relief agencies produced aid to the value of $60 million.

In July a great wave of floodwater inundated much of the country around Lahore and submerged over 1,500 villages; then a second wave affected more than 10 million ac., 4.5 million of which were under crop. Sind suffered as well as the Punjab, although the loss of life was small in comparison with the damage to property and crops. Rehabilitation on a large scale was begun, but instead of the self-sufficiency in food grains that had been hoped for, heavy purchases of wheat from Australia and other sources had to be arranged. Fortunately, the Tarbela Dam, now repaired and tested with international help, came into operation in October in time for the seasonal sowings.

Throughout the year, the Pakistan People's Party government was preoccupied by serious unrest in the North-West Frontier Province (NWFP) and in

Norwegian Literature: *see* Literature

Numismatics: *see* Philately and Numismatics

Obituaries: *see* People of the Year *beginning on page 64*

Oceanography: *see* Earth Sciences

Oil: *see* Energy

Opera: *see* Music

Organization of African Unity: *see* African Affairs

Organization of American States: *see* Latin-American Affairs

Ornithology: *see* Life Sciences

Orthodox Churches: *see* Religion

Painting: *see* Art and Art Exhibitions; Art Sales; Museums

PAKISTAN

Education. (1972–73) Primary, pupils 4,441,322, teachers 111,408; secondary, pupils 1,316,428, teachers 79,024; vocational, pupils 23,450, teachers 1,580; teacher training, students 36,508, teachers 1,389; higher, students 246,811, teaching staff 12,017.

Finance. Monetary unit: Pakistan rupee, with (Sept. 22, 1975) a par value of PakRs. 9.90 to U.S. $1 (free rate of PakRs. 20.50 = £1 sterling). Gold, SDRs, and foreign exchange, state bank: (June 1975) U.S. $470 million; (June 1974) U.S. $376 million. Budget (1974–75 est.): revenue PakRs. 14,591,000,000; expenditure PakRs. 20,952,000,000. Gross national product: (1972–73) PakRs. 62,750,000,000; (1971–72) PakRs. 53,370,000,000.

Foreign Trade. (1974) Imports PakRs. 17,202,000,000; exports PakRs. 11,052,000,000. Import sources: U.S. 23%; Japan 10%; West Germany 8%; U.K. 7%; Saudi Arabia 6%; Kuwait 6%. Export destinations: Indonesia 6%; Iran 6%; U.K. 6%; Hong Kong 6%; Japan 6%; Saudi Arabia 6%; Sri Lanka 5%; U.S. 5%. Main exports: rice 21%; cotton fabrics 20%; cotton yarn 18%; leather 7%.

Transport and Communications. Roads (1972) 62,800 km. Motor vehicles in use (1973): passenger 177,300; commercial (including buses) 79,100. Railways: (1973) 8,663 km.; traffic (1974 est.) *c.* 12,400,000,000 passenger-km., freight *c.* 7,700,000,000 net ton-km. Air traffic (1974): 1,845,000,000 passenger-km.; freight 95 million net ton-km. Shipping (1974): merchant vessels 100 gross tons and over 88; gross tonnage 494,065. Telephones (Dec. 1973) 195,000. Radio receivers (Dec. 1971) 1,630,000. Television licenses (Dec. 1972) 129,000.

Agriculture. Production (in 000; metric tons; 1974; 1973 in parentheses): wheat 7,631 (7,442); barley 140 (109); corn *c.* 675 (767); rice 3,225 (3,578); millet *c.* 320 (351); sorghum *c.* 315 (378); sugar, raw value 609 (464); sugar, noncentrifugal (1973) 1,228, (1972) 1,473; chick-peas 575 (554); onions *c.* 196 (*c.* 187); peanuts *c.* 50 (*c.* 54); rapeseed 293 (*c.* 287); oranges (1973) *c.* 330, (1972) *c.* 325; mangoes (1973) *c.* 670, (1972) 535; tobacco 66 (*c.* 63); cotton, lint 640 (659). Livestock (in 000; 1973–74): cattle *c.* 13,120; buffalo (1972–73) *c.* 9,600; sheep *c.* 18,070; goats (1972–73) c. 9,250; camels (1972–73) *c.* 800.

Industry. Production (in 000; metric tons; 1974): cement 3,519; crude oil 428; coal and lignite (1972–73) 1,161; natural gas (cu.m.; 1973) 4,400,000; electricity (excluding most industrial production; kw-hr.; 1971) 7,449,000; sulfuric acid 34; soda ash (1972–73) 74; nitrogenous fertilizers (nutrient content; 1973–74) 301; cotton yarn 377; woven cotton fabrics (m.; 1973–74) 648,000.

Baluchistan, encouraged in particular by Afghanistan. The government's policy in both these areas was to improve communications, encourage education, and provide liberal grants for development to raise living standards until they approached those prevailing in the more advanced regions. In the NWFP this policy was making headway despite the opposition of the Pakhtunistan movement, but in Baluchistan, where communications were poor and where the word of the tribal chiefs was law in many areas, the difficulties were greater. Conservative elements bitterly resented restrictions on their arbitrary authority, and they were encouraged in this attitude by elements desiring to foment movements for an independent Baluchistan and Pakhtunistan.

An earthquake devastated many villages in the Rawalpindi District of Pakistan in July 1975.

A.F.P./PICTORIAL PARADE

In Baluchistan overt resistance crumbled when the regular troops restored order, but there followed a spate of bombings and assassinations which spread to the NWFP. The government, satisfied that there was a close connection between these subversive activities and the National Awami Party, banned that party in February and detained a number of its leaders. This action exasperated the Afghan government, in whose territory the party's leaders had often been welcome guests. Relations between Kabul and Islamabad, which had temporarily improved thanks to the efforts of the Soviet Union and the shah of Iran, again deteriorated.

In February the U.S. lifted its ten-year embargo on the export of arms to Pakistan, in spite of India's protests. Just previously, Sheikh Muhammad Abdullah, the Muslim leader in Indian-held Jammu and Kashmir who had formerly supported Pakistan, reached agreement with India, to Pakistan's indignation. In general, good relations continued between Pakistan and the outside world, however, and relations with India, though delicate, improved steadily. The overthrow in August of Sheikh Mujibur Rahman and his replacement by a regime anxious to improve Bangladesh's connections with the Islamic world received cautious diplomatic handling in deference to India's natural sensbilities.

National finances continued to be managed with skill and prudence. The budget for fiscal 1975–76 provided for a second development outlay for less advanced areas and envisaged the end of deficit financing. A third gas field was found in Sind; major industrial complexes financed by the Soviet Union and China took shape. Cooperation with Iran and Turkey in regional development projects was further extended, and close connections with Saudi Arabia, Iran, and other oil-producing countries somewhat eased the burden on foreign exchange.

(L. F. RUSHBROOK WILLIAMS)

[976.A.3]

Panama

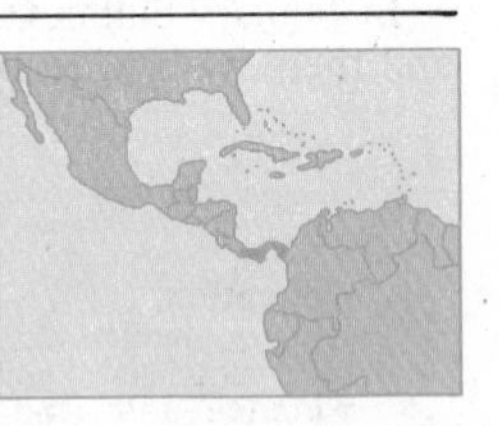

A republic of Central America, bisected by the Canal Zone, Panama is bounded by the Caribbean Sea, Colombia, the Pacific Ocean, and Costa Rica. Area: 29,209 sq.mi. (75,650 sq.km.). Pop. (1975 est.): 1,667,100. Cap. and largest city: Panama City (pop., 1975 est., 404,200). Language: Spanish. Religion (1971 est.): Roman Catholic 90%. President in 1975, Demetrio Lakas Bahas.

With his control over Panama unimpaired, Gen. Omar Torrijos (*see* BIOGRAPHY) faced a variety of economic problems in 1975. Confronted by the unnatural marriage of inflation and recession, he accomplished a 4% reduction of prevailing interest rates on loans to the agricultural and livestock enterprises

PANAMA

Education. (1974) Primary, pupils 312,386, teachers 10,731; secondary, pupils 79,705, teachers 3,572; vocational, pupils 36,169, teachers 1,937; teacher training, students 7,186, teachers 271; higher, students 21,076, teaching staff 843.

Finance. Monetary unit: balboa, at par with the U.S. dollar, with a free rate (Sept. 22, 1975) of 2.07 balboas to £1 sterling. Gold, SDRs, and foreign exchange: (Dec. 1974) U.S. $39.4 million; (Dec. 1973) U.S. $33.1 million. Budget (1974 est.) balanced at 261 million balboas. Gross domestic product: (1974) 1,332,000,000 balboas; (1973) 1,287,000,000 balboas. Money supply (deposits only): (Dec. 1974) 222.9 million balboas; (Dec. 1973) 184.1 million balboas. Cost of living (Panama City; 1970 = 100): (June 1975) 142; (June 1974) 133.

Foreign Trade. (1974) Imports 800,310,000 balboas; exports 205,190,000 balboas. Net service receipts, etc., from Canal Zone (1973) 247 million balboas. Main import sources: U.S. 27%; Ecuador 17%; Venezuela 11%; Saudi Arabia 8%; Japan 6%. Main export destinations: U.S. 52%; Canal Zone 17%; West Germany 6%; Italy 6%; The Netherlands 5%. Main exports: petroleum products 42%; bananas 25%; shrimps 7%.

Transport and Communications. Roads (1973) *c.* 7,100 km. Motor vehicles in use: passenger (1972) 53,600; commercial (including buses; 1973) 21,600. Railways (1973) 720 km. Shipping (1974): merchant vessels 100 gross tons and over 1,962 (mostly owned by U.S. and other foreign interests); gross tonnage 11,003,227. Telephones (Dec. 1972) 100,000. Radio receivers (Dec. 1973) 255,000. Television receivers (Dec. 1972) 200,000.

Agriculture. Production (in 000; metric tons; 1974; 1973 in parentheses): rice 171 (*c.* 162); sugar, raw value 104 (81); bananas *c.* 970 (*c.* 960); oranges *c.* 59 (58); coffee *c.* 4 (5); cocoa *c.* 0.5 (*c.* 0.5). Livestock (in 000; 1973–74): cattle *c.* 1,361; pigs *c.* 188; horses *c.* 164; chickens 3,706.

Industry. Production (in 000; metric tons; 1973): petroleum products 4,060; cement (1971) 192; manufactured gas (cu.m.) 15,000; electricity (kw-hr.; 1972) 1,151,000.

and a 3% decline on those to industry. He urged industry and agriculture to plow earnings back into production and to increase exports. His 1975 budget reflected a further effort to stimulate the economy by allocating an amount for public works projects greater than that for all of the other functions of government combined.

The great financial drain of these expenditures required an increase in revenues. Expanded domestic taxes offered little promise. For example, a 5% tax on lottery earnings was given up because of public clamour. The Union of Banana Exporting Countries, organized in 1974 to regulate the market so as to produce more profit, was disappointing because the increase of the tax to $1 a case was resisted by the producer, United Brands Co., and was resulting in a loss of trade to the lower-priced Ecuador bananas. At the end of 1974 Panama returned to the tax of 35 cents per case.

If the immediate outlook for increased revenues was bleak, the long-range prospect appeared bright. Torrijos could point to the government takeover of approximately 30,000 ac. of idle lands from a subsidiary of United Brands, a first step toward nationalization of the banana industry. A new fishing port at Punta Vacamonte, for which the World Bank approved a loan of $24 million, augured well for the important tuna and shrimp fishing industry. Most exciting of economic developments was the discovery of the Cerro Colorado copper deposits in the northwest. When discussions with Canadian Javelin Ltd. over the exploitation of these broke down, the government decided to take over the development.

These rosy dreams of future prosperity scarcely helped in the day-to-day problem of oil supply. From 1972 to 1974 oil import costs rose from $48 million to $260 million. These costs represented about 11% of all the import expenses in 1972 and 42% in 1974. Because of the Panamanians' taste for North American cars, the nation's consumption of gasoline was about four times that of neighbouring Costa Rica. Although Venezuela, the chief supplier of oil, offered several easy payment plans, the problem of paying now or later remained.

For Panama one other avenue of partial relief remained. This was the canal. If Panama could wrest from the United States control over the tolls charged for its transit, it would not only benefit from a substantial income but could also apply a powerful weapon against the trade of other nations. The heads of government of Panama, Venezuela, Costa Rica, and Colombia signed an agreement on March 24, 1975, and issued a declaration that upheld Panama's claims over the Canal Zone; promised Colombia and Costa Rica toll- and tax-free transit of the canal when the new treaty with the U.S. took effect; and indicated that Panama, Colombia, and Costa Rica would give priority to development of their border areas.

When U.S. negotiator Ellsworth Bunker and Panama's foreign minister, Juan Tack, resumed their conversations in mid-September, it seemed clear that the former had conceded the ultimate control of the canal to Panama. Among the immediate questions yet to be solved were the duration of the new treaty, the land and water spaces within the Zone still needed by the U.S., the number of military bases required for defense, the amount of annuity due to Panama, and the question of building a new canal. Any agreement that might be made, however, faced obstacles. On September 24 several hundred youths, demanding withdrawal of U.S. troops from the Zone and accusing Torrijos of complicity, damaged the U.S. embassy by their rock throwing. U.S. Ambassador William J. Jorden protested and President Lakas apologized. In the U.S. Senate more senators than were needed to defeat a treaty already had indicated a preference for the retention of "undiluted United States sovereignty." The U.S. House of Representatives overwhelmingly voted to deny funds for the negotiation of concessions to Panama but later receded from that position. (ALMON R. WRIGHT)

[974.B.1.f]

Papua New Guinea

Papua New Guinea is an independent parliamentary state and a member of the Commonwealth of Nations. It is situated in the southwest Pacific and comprises the eastern part of the island of New Guinea, the islands of the Bismarck, Trobriand, Woodlark, Louisiade, and D'Entrecasteaux groups, and parts of the Solomon Islands, including Bougainville. It is separated from Australia by the Torres Strait. Area: 178,260 sq.mi. (461,690 sq.km.). Pop. (1975 est.): 2,756,500. Cap. and largest city: Port Moresby (pop., 1975 est., 104,500). Language: English (official), Papuan and Melanesian languages, and Pidgin English, the lingua franca. Religion (1966): Roman Catholic 31.2%; Lutheran 27.3%; indigenous 7%. Queen, Elizabeth II; governor-general in 1975, Sir John Guise; prime minister, Michael T. Somare.

The Australian flag was lowered in Port Moresby on Sept. 16, 1975, and the governor-general of Papua

Palestine: *see* Israel; Jordan

Panama Canal Zone: *see* Dependent States; Panama

Paper and Pulp: *see* Industrial Review

A New Guinea MP abandons his usual collar, tie, and suit while visiting his constituents in the new state.

New Guinea, Sir John Guise (*see* BIOGRAPHY), declared the nation independent. Prince Charles represented Queen Elizabeth II at the celebrations. The other guests included Gough Whitlam, prime minister of Australia, with whom the leaders of Papua New Guinea had fallen out on the eve of independence. Whitlam had refused to meet a request for help in addition to the A$500 million promised for the three financial years beginning 1974–75.

Foreign policy priorities of the new nation included the establishment of close contact with China and the maintenance of a cordial relationship with Australia. Sir Maori Kiki, Papua New Guinea's minister for defense, foreign relations, and trade, visited Peking in February 1975. Kiki said that China had been "apologetic" that the balance of trade between the two countries was all in China's favour.

(A. R. G. GRIFFITHS)

[977.A.3]

PAPUA NEW GUINEA

Education. (1974) Primary, pupils 236,060, teachers 7,545; secondary, pupils 28,720, teachers 1,226; vocational, pupils 6,918, teachers 480; teacher training, students 2,231, teachers 200; higher, students 2,823, teaching staff 313.

Finance. Monetary unit: kina (introduced on April 19, 1975), at par with the Australian dollar, with (Sept. 22, 1975) a free rate of 0.79 kina to U.S. $1 (1.64 kina = £1 sterling). Budget (1973–74): revenue 313 million kinas (including 133 million kinas grant by Australian government); expenditure 305 million kinas.

Foreign Trade. (1972–73) Imports A$233,870,000; exports A$229,450,000. Import sources: Australia 54%; Japan 16%; U.S. 9%. Export destinations: Japan 35%; West Germany 23%; Australia 20%; U.S. 5%. Main exports: copper ores 55%; coffee 10%; cocoa 5%.

Transport. Shipping (1974): merchant vessels 100 gross tons and over 53; gross tonnage 17,598.

Agriculture. Production (in 000; metric tons; 1974; 1973 in parentheses): cocoa *c.* 30 (*c.* 24); coffee *c.* 41 (*c.* 39); copra *c.* 140 (*c.* 140); cassava (1973) *c.* 405, (1972) *c.* 400; taro (1973) *c.* 78, (1972) *c.* 76; yams (1973) *c.* 68, (1972) *c.* 78; rubber *c.* 6 (*c.* 6); timber (cu.m.; 1972–73) 5,300, (1971–72) 5,500. Livestock (in 000; March 1973): cattle *c.* 110; pigs *c.* 8; chickens *c.* 180.

Industry. Production (in 000; troy oz.; 1972–73): gold 601; silver (1971–72) 997; copper (metric tons; 1972–73) 495.

Paraguay

A landlocked republic of South America, Paraguay is bounded by Brazil, Argentina, and Bolivia. Area: 157,048 sq.mi. (406,752 sq.km.). Pop. (1974 est.): 2,584,000. Cap. and largest city: Asunción (pop., 1972, 387,700). Language: Spanish (official), though Guaraní is the language of the majority of the people. Religion: Roman Catholic. President in 1975, Gen. Alfredo Stroessner.

Though effective opposition was silenced, there were signs in 1975 of growing friction between the government and its critics, including the political opposition and the church. Rumours of plans to manipulate the constitution so as to make Stroessner president for life were unconfirmed, but his oldest son, Gustavo, was being brought into the limelight.

Self-sufficient in electric power, Paraguay could become the world's leading exporter of that commodity if all proposed hydroelectric projects were completed. Loans for further expansion were made and, in addition, construction of the world's largest hydroelectric complex, at Itaipú on the Paraná River, with a capacity of 12,000 Mw., was due to begin. Costs ($4.2 billion) and output of the complex were to be shared between Brazil and Paraguay, with Paraguay's share of output to be sold to Brazil. Similar projects were planned. The prime minister of South Africa, B. J. Vorster, visited Paraguay in August to complete a $9 million loan for housing and agricultural projects.

The 1974 value of exports ($169.8 million) represented a 33% increase over 1973. Though meat exports fell, Paraguay benefited from high world prices for timber, oilseeds, tobacco, edible oils, oil cake, and sugar. Imports in 1974 cost $151.4 million, as compared with $104.8 million in 1973. The cost of living increased 25.2% in 1974, but only 2.6% during the first half of 1975 as government measures slowed down the increase in prices.

(MICHAEL WOOLLER)

[974.F.3]

PARAGUAY

Education. (1973) Primary, pupils 459,393, teachers 15,871; secondary and vocational, pupils 67,594, teachers 6,895; higher, students 11,700, teaching staff 1,820.

Finance. Monetary unit: guaraní, with an official rate (Sept. 22, 1975) of 126 guaranies to U.S. $1 (free rate of 259 guaranies = £1 sterling). Gold, SDRs, and foreign exchange: (June 1975) U.S. $97.1 million; (June 1974) U.S. $71,260,000. Budget (1975 est.) balanced at 18,329,000,000 guaranies. Gross national product: (1973) 123,320,000,000 guaranies; (1972) 94,950,000,000 guaranies. Money supply: (Dec. 1974) 15,120,000,000 guaranies; (Dec. 1973) 12,494,000,000 guaranies. Cost of living (Asunción; 1970 = 100): (May 1975) 170; (May 1974) 163.

Foreign Trade. (1974) Imports 21,810,000,000 guaranies; exports 20,978,000,000 guaranies. Import sources: Argentina 28%; Brazil 18%; U.S. 10%; West Germany 9%; U.K. 7%. Export destinations: Argentina 23%; West Germany 13%; U.S. 11%; The Netherlands 9%; Switzerland 9%; U.K. 9%. Main exports: meat 21%; timber 15%; cotton 10%; oilseeds 8%; tobacco 7%.

Transport and Communications. Roads (1970) 11,225 km. Motor vehicles in use (1971): passenger *c.* 16,000; commercial (including buses) *c.* 14,000. Railways (1973): 498 km.; traffic 26 million passenger-km., freight 30 million net ton-km. Navigable inland waterways (including Paraguay-Paraná River system; 1973) *c.* 3,000 km. Telephones (Dec. 1973) 24,000. Radio receivers (Dec. 1972) 175,000. Television receivers (Dec. 1972) 52,000.

Agriculture. Production (in 000; metric tons; 1974; 1973 in parentheses): corn 276 (236); cassava (1973) 1,208, (1972) 1,197; sweet potatoes (1973) 87, (1972) 72; soybeans (1973) 120, (1972) 128; peanuts *c.* 16 (14); dry beans *c.* 33 (32); sugar, raw value (1973) 69, (1972) 57; tomatoes *c.* 50 (*c.* 48); oranges *c.* 119 (113); tangerines and mandarin oranges *c.* 31 (30); bananas *c.* 264 (*c.* 255); tobacco 26 (24); palm kernels *c.* 22 (*c.* 21); cotton, lint (1973) 25, (1972) 15; beef and veal 123 (121). Livestock (in 000; 1973–74): cattle *c.* 6,016; sheep *c.* 347; pigs *c.* 659; horses (1972–73) *c.* 720; chickens (1972–73) *c.* 6,600.

Industry. Production (in 000; metric tons; 1973): petroleum products *c.* 330; cement (1972) 75; cotton yarn (1972) 13; electricity (kw-hr.) 379,000.

Peru

A republic on the west coast of South America, Peru is bounded by Ecuador, Colombia, Brazil, Bolivia, Chile, and the Pacific Ocean. Area: 496,224 sq.mi. (1,285,215 sq.km.). Pop. (1974 est.): 14,370,000, including approximately 52% whites and mestizos and 46% Indians. Cap. and largest city: Lima (metro. area pop.,

PERU

Education. Primary, pupils (1972) 2,449,837, teachers (1970) 71,000; secondary, pupils (1972) 664,739, teachers (1970) 28,400; vocational, pupils (1972) 159,922, teachers (1970) 8,900; teacher training, students (1972) 8,485, teachers (1970) 1,075; higher, students (1972) 149,553, teaching staff (1971) 12,127.

Finance. Monetary unit: sol, with (after devaluation of Sept. 29, 1975) an official exchange rate of 45 soles to U.S. $1 (free rate of 91.70 soles = £1 sterling). Gold, SDRs, and foreign exchange: (Jan. 1974) U.S. $477.9 million; (Jan. 1973) U.S. $442.2 million. Budget (1973 actual): revenue 53,556,000,000 soles; expenditure 61,949,000,000 soles. Gross domestic product: (1972) 292.3 billion soles; (1971) 262.5 billion soles. Money supply: (March 1975) 106,140,000,000 soles; (March 1974) 73,650,000,000 soles. Cost of living (Lima and Callao; 1970 = 100): (March 1975) 169; (March 1974) 139.

Foreign Trade. Imports (1974) 59,241,000,000 soles; exports 58,465,000,000 soles. Import sources: U.S. 31%; Japan 12%; West Germany 10%; Ecuador 5%. Export destinations: U.S. 36%; Japan 13%; West Germany 8%; China 5%. Main exports: copper 23%; fish meal 13%; silver 11%; zinc 11%; sugar 10%; cotton 6%.

Transport and Communications. Roads (1973) 52,102 km. (including 180 km. expressways). Motor vehicles in use (1972): passenger 256,400; commercial 136,100. Railways: (1973) 2,105 km.; traffic (1970) 248 million passenger-km., freight 610 million net ton-km. Air traffic (1973): 404 million passenger-km.; freight 12.5 million net ton-km. Shipping (1974): merchant vessels 100 gross tons and over 675; gross tonnage 513,875. Telephones (Dec. 1973) 309,000. Radio receivers (Dec. 1972) 2 million. Television receivers (Dec. 1973) 411,000.

Agriculture. Production (in 000; metric tons; 1974; 1973 in parentheses): rice 361 (451); corn 473 (616); wheat 117 (115); barley *c.* 170 (159); potatoes 1,155 (1,277); sweet potatoes (1973) 179, (1972) 173; onions *c.* 170 (177); cassava (1973) 482, (1972) 479; dry beans *c.* 50 (*c.* 59); sugar, raw value 1,019 (914); apples 73 (77); grapes *c.* 63 (*c.* 63); oranges 214 (186); lemons (1973) *c.* 90, (1972) *c.* 80; coffee 43 (57); cotton, lint *c.* 87 (*c.* 81); fish catch (1973) 2,299, (1972) 4,768. Livestock (in 000; 1973–74): cattle *c.* 4,377; sheep *c.* 17,600; pigs *c.* 2,200; goats (1972–73) *c.* 1,970; horses (1972–73) *c.* 720; poultry (1972–73) 29,300.

Industry. Production (in 000; metric tons; 1973): crude oil (1974) 3,758; coal *c.* 80; natural gas (cu.m.) *c.* 510,000; cement (1972) 1,428; iron ore (metal content) 5,648; pig iron 258; steel 360; lead 83; zinc 67; copper 39; tungsten concentrates (oxide content) 1; gold (troy oz.; 1972) 90; silver (troy oz.; 1972) *c.* 40,000; fish meal 423; petroleum products 4,960; electricity (kw-hr.; 1971) 5,949,000.

1972, 3,317,600). Language: Spanish and Quechua are official; Indians also speak Aymara. Religion: Roman Catholic. Presidents of the military government in 1975, Juan Velasco Alvarado to August 29 and, from August 30, Francisco Morales Bermúdez.

An outbreak of rioting in Lima in February 1975, after a police pay strike, resulted in 100 deaths and injuries to 600, and a nationwide state of emergency was imposed until May. Political uncertainty continued until August 29, when a peaceful coup removed ailing President Velasco Alvarado from office. The new president, Gen. Francisco Morales Bermúdez (*see* BIOGRAPHY), previously commander in chief of the Army and premier from February 1, at once consolidated his position by reaffirming the economic and social policies of the revolution begun by the military in 1968. On September 2 a free pardon was granted to political deportees of all parties.

At least seven companies categorized as basic industries were taken over by the state in 1975, the most important being the West Coast Cable Co., Gulf Oil, and Marcona Mining. Compensation was by no means guaranteed, especially for Gulf Oil and Marcona Mining, both of which were charged with immoral conduct. The national newspapers dispute was concluded; at the end of July, one year after they had been expropriated, their control was transferred from editorial committees to representative popular organizations appointed by the government. It was the foundation of the social-property companies (EPS), however, that was considered top priority. The government set up a National Social Property Fund to provide such companies with initial working capital. Nevertheless, progress was slow, and careful planning would be required to avoid potential conflict; already Moto Andina, an EPS, and a "reformed" private company, Honda, were both building motorcycle assembly plants in Trujillo.

A second plan (1975–78) was to begin the task of modernizing the economy, since the ownership reforms undertaken during the 1969–74 plan were complete. The state was to channel investment into the basic industrial sectors and to bring the massive oil and copper projects into operation in 1977 and 1978. The rate of economic growth slowed in 1975, the result of inflation estimated at about 40%, a foreign debt that caused concern, tight money conditions, and a trade deficit. Only the manufacturing and fishing sectors registered a sharp upturn in production. Anchoveta fishing had recovered fully from its 1973 collapse. Manufacturing benefited from embargoes on imports of consumer durables and from expansion in public investment.

Oil exploration continued, but with uneven results, and there was doubt that eventual production would support the $600 million trans-Andean pipeline. The mining sector was unable to expand during the year because of oversupply, and both the production and export of copper were voluntarily reduced by 15%. Agriculture remained constrained by an inadequate marketing structure, declining world commodity prices, and the need for new arable land, which would not be available until the Olmos and Majes irrigation projects were completed. At the end of June the government abandoned its anti-inflationary policy and ended the subsidies on basic foodstuffs, consumer goods, and fuels. Wages in both the public and private sectors were raised.

Notwithstanding the restrictive Andean Pact investment regulations and the expropriation policies, foreign confidence in some basic sectors remained buoyant. At the beginning of the year, the Southern Peru Copper Corp. announced completion of the financing for the Cuajone copper project in the department of Moquegua. More important still was the approval in April by the World Bank consultative group for Peru of the ambitious program to invest $3.5 billion in development projects in 1975–77, essential to tide the economy over until revenues from the oil and copper projects were forthcoming.

In August Lima was the site of a meeting of foreign ministers and other officials from over 80 nonaligned countries, held in preparation for the special UN General Assembly session on economic development and cooperation in September. In June Quechua was made Peru's official second language. (PRUDENCE JUDD)

[974.D.2]

Philately and Numismatics

Stamps. Despite the continuing general economic stringency during 1975 there was no evidence of a slump in the philatelic market. Values of most of the accepted rarities among stamps and postal history

Parachuting: *see* Aerial Sports

Payments and Reserves, International: *see* Economy, World

Penology: *see* Prisons and Penology

Pentecostal Churches: *see* Religion

Petroleum: *see* Energy

Pharmaceutical Industry: *see* Industrial Review

material advanced faster than inflation, producing increased capital value in real terms.

The British-based Stanley Gibbons International Ltd. held its first major auction in Frankfurt am Main, West Germany, since acquiring the Briefmarkenhaus Merkur business. Profits from the auction totaled £600,000, and the gross turnover was £1,505,000. The total for H. R. Harmer's (session ended July 1975) was £3,237,000, to which the London office contributed £1,105,000, New York $4,084,000 (almost £2 million), and Sydney, Australia, just over £210,000. Robson Lowe International reported an auction turnover of £2,106,000, which included its first sale held in Geneva (in conjunction with Christie's), at which the profits were £724,000.

Two International Philatelic Federation-class international exhibitions were held in Europe. The sites and major awards were: Madrid—J. Gálvez-Naranjo, Spain (Grand Prix d'Honneur for specialized Chile), P. Provera, Italy (Grand Prix International for Austria and Lombardy-Venetia cancellations), A. P. Serbia, Brazil (Grand Prix National for 19th-century Spanish stamps); Paris—Samad Khorchid, Iran (Grand Prix d'Honneur for classic stamps of Persia 1868–80), Hiroyuki Kanai, Japan (Grand Prix International for Mauritius 1847–62), Plastiras Foster, France (Grand Prix National for France 1849–76).

R. A. G. Lee succeeded Lieut. Col. S. E. Hands as president of the Royal Philatelic Society, London, and Stuart Rossiter succeeded Arnold M. Strange as editor of the society's journal, *The London Philatelist.* The year's signatories to the Roll of Distinguished Philatelists (RDP) were A. Ronald Butler (U.K.), Ernest A. Kehr (U.S.), Jules L. Placquaert (Belgium), and Bengt E. Zimmermann (Finland). The Philatelic Congress Medal (U.K.) was awarded to Miroslaw A. Bojanowics of the U.K., who became the third holder of both the RDP award and the medal. The Lichtenstein Medal, awarded by the Collectors Club of New York for international philatelic services, went to Joseph Schatzkés of France.

Eleven arrests by the FBI in Boston, Los Angeles, and San Francisco led to the recovery in November 1974 of much of the material stolen from a Boston stamp dealer in 1971 and the Cardinal Spellman Philatelic Museum at Weston, Mass., in 1973. In England, two arrests resulted in the recovery of a £75,000 general collection stolen from Col. E. P. Dickson in September 1974. A sensational trial in London ended suddenly in December 1974 with the acquittal of Julian Clive and his son Michael, on charges of conspiring with George Yussuf Korot (who did not surrender to his bail) and Bruce Condé (who never appeared in court) to defraud by falsely representing that certain "labels" issued by the Kingdom of Yemen (Yemen [San'a']) were genuine postage stamps usable in an operative postal service. The prosecution case lasted six weeks, but the judge accepted the opening defense plea that there was no case to answer, conspiracy in the legal sense not having been proved, and dismissed the defendants. The judge ordered all the costs (estimated at over £100,000) to be met out of public funds.

Sales of Britain's experimental $4\frac{1}{2}$ pence + $1\frac{1}{2}$ pence (surcharge for charity) stamp were just over 5.5 million and provided a net revenue of £57,000 for distribution among the ten participating charities. The Post Office announced that it had no plans for any further charity stamps. The U.S. Postal Service announced that the bicentennial year (1976) would be marked by sheets of 50 stamps in which each stamp would bear one of the flags of the 50 states of the Union. The Postal Service also announced that the two 1975 Christmas stamps would be the first in U.S. history to bear no denomination; they would be valid for postage at ten cents.

(KENNETH F. CHAPMAN)

Commemorative issues for 1975 include the U.S. Christmas stamps without indication of price, American Revolutionary War heroes in honour of the U.S. bicentennial, Sweden's acknowledgment of archaeological discoveries on the island of Öland and of the International Women's Year, and the Soviet depiction of the successful docking of their Soyuz with the U.S. Apollo spacecraft.

TOP LEFT, WIDE WORLD; TOP RIGHT, BOTTOM LEFT, AUTHENTICATED NEWS INTERNATIONAL

Coins. With fitting ceremonies the three U.S. coins bearing bicentennial designs were put into circulation during 1975, the half dollar in Minneapolis, Minn., on July 7, the quarter in Chicago on August 18, and the dollar in Atlanta, Ga., on October 13. All three bore the double date 1776–1976 and would continue to be issued with those dates through 1976. The Bureau of the Mint expected to produce at least 300 million of the dollars, 550 million half dollars, and 1,600,000,000 quarters.

The Mint continued its series of pewter reproductions of ten of the earliest medals of the U.S., the originals having been issued in recognition of Revolutionary War military men and battles. Of the numerous medals produced in observance of the nation's bicentennial, only one had the official status of being authorized by Congress and struck in a U.S. mint. In a ceremony on Jan. 20, 1975, the Denver Mint began striking a medal observing the state of Colorado centennial, the only state in the Union observing its centennial in the year (1976) of the United States bicentennial. This was the first congressional medal ever struck in the 70-year-old Denver Mint.

The 175th issue of the United Nations Food and Agriculture Organization's (FAO) "Grow More Food —Food For All" coin series took place during the

TOP, KEVIN DOWLING—CAMERA PRESS/PHOTO TRENDS; BOTTOM, LONDON DAILY EXPRESS/PICTORIAL PARADE

Despite the minting of eight million beautiful 50-franc silver coins (above), it is impossible to find one circulating in France. The 20-billion Mark bank note shown below was printed in 1924 by the German Reichsbank at the height of postwar inflation. It was sold for £135 in London.

year. More than 80 nations had taken part in the program since its introduction in 1968, and all of the FAO coins had become part of the circulating legal tender of the issuing countries.

The price of gold and silver bullion rose to new heights during late 1974, and this was reflected in coin prices. Both metals, however, dropped appreciably on the market early in 1975. The U.S. public did not react as expected to removal of the ban on owning gold after Dec. 31, 1974. This weakness in the demand for the precious metals, and possibly economic conditions in general, depressed numismatic activities somewhat. The American Numismatic Association, with headquarters in Colorado Springs, Colo., had accepted a record 6,100 new members in its previous fiscal year but reported that enrollment was running about one-fourth lower in the current year.

Coin collectors continued to have many new issues of countries throughout the world available to them. Among the new coins of 1975 were: Austria, 100 schillings, noting 50 years of schilling currency, and another (dated 1976) for the XII Winter Olympics at Innsbruck; Canada, 1 dollar, centennial of Calgary, established in 1875 as a North West Mounted Police post; Czechoslovakia, 50 koruny, poet S. K. Neumann birth centennial; Dominican Republic, 10 pesos, depicting a 16th-century coin of Hispaniola; Finland, 10 markkaa, commemorating Pres. Urho Kekkonen's 75th birthday; West Germany, the first West German nonsilver 5-mark coin, and another in silver honouring Friedrich Ebert, its first president; Haiti, four denominations of FAO coins; Jamaica, 10 dollars (sterling), picturing discoverer Christopher Columbus (May 1494); Norway, two 5-kroner coins commemorating 150 years of emigration to the U.S. and the centennial of its present monetary system; Peru, 200 soles, honouring aviation heroes Jorge Chávez and José Quiñones; Poland, two 10-zloty coins honouring novelist Boleslaw Prus and poet Adam Mickiewicz; Singapore, 10 dollars, commemorating ten years of independence; Turks and Caicos Islands, seven coins relating to the "Age of Exploration"; and Vatican City, eight denominations (1 to 500 lire) of Holy Year coins. A set of eight coins (1 cent to $10) dated 1974 and issued by Belize depicts a different native bird on each denomination.

Among the significant medals, aside from those relating to the bicentennial, was one by noted sculptress Elizabeth Jones observing the Jubilee or Holy Year of the Roman Catholic Church (*see* RELIGION) and inscribed "1300 / JUBILÆUM / 1975." Others included those observing the 1975 international figure-skating championships and the Apollo/Soyuz linkup in space, and one honouring Nathaniel Hawthorne, one of 16 authors enshrined in the Hall of Fame for Great Americans. (GLENN B. SMEDLEY)

[452.D.2.b; 725.B.4.g]

Philippines

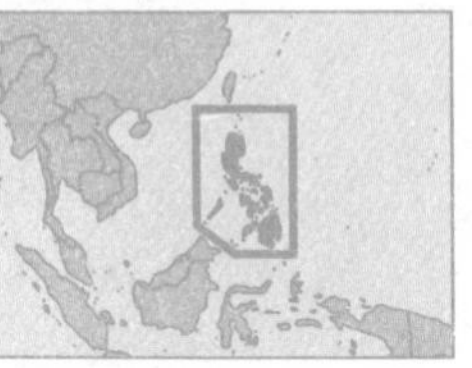

Situated in the western Pacific Ocean off the southeast coast of Asia, the Republic of the Philippines consists of an archipelago of about 7,100 islands. Area: 115,800 sq.mi. (300,000 sq.km.). Pop. (1975 est.): 42,108,000. Capital: Quezon City (pop., 1974 est., 946,400). Largest city: Manila (pop., 1974 est., 1,473,600). Language: Pilipino (based on Tagalog), English, Spanish, and many dialects. Religion (1960): Roman Catholic 84%; Aglipayan 5%; Muslim 5%; Protestant 3%. President in 1975, Ferdinand E. Marcos.

The defeat of U.S.-supported regimes in Indochina in 1975 led the Philippines to reassess its foreign relations. The government opened discussions with the U.S. on the status of the two largest U.S. military bases in the western Pacific, Clark Air Force Base and Subic Bay naval base on Luzon Island. President Marcos said that, while his government wanted to assume control of the bases, it also wished to allow the U.S. to "maintain an effective presence over air and sea lanes of the Western Pacific" from them. The U.S. "shall remain our good friend and ally," Marcos declared on June 12.

Earlier, he had said that "the only way to insure our security and survival" was to establish closer ties with Communist countries and called for an adjustment of Philippines' policy to "the emerging realities in Asia." As part of this readjustment, he visited China June 7 to 11 and signed an agreement with Premier Chou En-lai establishing diplomatic relations. Formal relations were broken with the Chinese Nationalists on Taiwan. The president also announced intentions to visit the Soviet Union.

In July Marcos sought the support of the World Conference of Islamic Nations in settling the Muslim rebellion in the southern islands. He told the conference that Muslim areas would be given greater autonomy, and the conference promised development aid if a settlement was reached. A government claim on August 14 that the Moro National Liberation Front had accepted a cease-fire proposal was quickly denied, however. Despite government success in winning over some rebels, guerrilla warfare continued. A separate guerrilla movement, the New People's Army of Maoist Communists, also flared sporadically. The government claimed limited success in eliminating some of its bases. Marcos, who believed that Peking was aiding the Maoists, hoped this would end with the establishment of diplomatic relations with China.

The September 1972 declaration of martial law, by which Marcos increased his power and extended his time in office indefinitely, was declared legal by the

Supreme Court in a 10–1 decision February 1. A national referendum was held February 27 by show of hands in village meetings, despite complaints by some Roman Catholic Church leaders and others that the system was rigged. The announced result gave 90% approval for Marcos' assumption of emergency powers and 80% support for his appointing local officials who had formerly been elected. One appointment was that of his wife, Mrs. Imelda Romualdez Marcos, as manager of a new Metropolitan Manila Commission.

Former senator Benigno S. Aquino, Jr., who had been Marcos' leading political opponent before martial law, staged a 40-day hunger strike in prison during April and May to protest efforts to put him on trial. Under arrest since September 1972, he had repeatedly denied the government's authority to try him on charges of murder and conspiracy to overthrow the government.

During celebrations of the third anniversary of martial law, Marcos said that corruption and inefficient administration had not yet been wiped out and that the authoritarian controls had even made new forms of corruption possible. He announced a "sweeping, complete and exhaustive reorganization of the government."

Officials claimed that a 1972 land reform program was proceeding effectively, although some independent studies suggested that its effect had been limited. Finance Secretary Cesar Virata said October 23 that the Philippines was weathering the worldwide recession quite well, with an economic growth rate for 1975 of 4 or 5%. High prices for imported oil and low prices for primary exports raised the balance of payments deficit to $350 million for the year.

(HENRY S. BRADSHER)

[976.C.2]

PHILIPPINES

Education. (1972–73) Primary, pupils 7,622,424, teachers 247,551; secondary, pupils 1,631,363, teachers 45,594; vocational, pupils 159,813, teachers 12,378; higher (including 40 universities), students 634,835, teaching staff 29,694.

Finance. Monetary unit: peso, with (Sept. 22, 1975) a free rate of 7.57 pesos to U.S. $1 (15.67 pesos = £1 sterling). Gold, SDRs, and foreign exchange: (June 1975) U.S. $1,593,000,000; (June 1974) U.S. $1,-539,000,000. Budget (1974–75 est.): revenue 14,768,-000,000 pesos; expenditure 17,842,000,000 pesos. Gross national product: (1974) 94.8 billion pesos; (1973) 69,560,000,000 pesos. Money supply: (March 1975) 10,125,000,000 pesos; (March 1974) 8,298,-000,000 pesos. Cost of living (Manila; 1970 = 100): (Feb. 1975) 233; (Feb. 1974) 188.

Foreign Trade. (1974) Imports 23,486,000,000 pesos; exports 18,020,000,000 pesos. Import sources: Japan 27%; U.S. 24%; Saudi Arabia 11%; Kuwait 5%. Export destinations: U.S. 42%; Japan 35%; The Netherlands 6%. Main exports: sugar 27%; coconut products 22%; copper 15%; timber 9%.

Transport and Communications. Roads (1974) 92,775 km. Motor vehicles in use (1973): passenger 362,500; commercial (including buses) 252,500. Railways: (1972) 1,169 km.; traffic (1973) 796 million passenger-km., freight 58 million net ton-km. Air traffic (1973): 1,750,000,000 passenger-km.; freight 48.4 million net ton-km. Shipping (1974): merchant vessels 100 gross tons and over 379; gross tonnage 766,478. Telephones (Jan. 1974) 410,000. Radio receivers (Dec. 1972) 1.8 million. Television receivers (Dec. 1971) 421,000.

Agriculture. Production (in 000; metric tons; 1974; 1973 in parentheses): rice 5,720 (5,594); corn *c.* 2,350 (2,342); sweet potatoes (1973) *c.* 650, (1972) 640; cassava (1973) *c.* 480, (1972) 450; copra *c.* 1,504 (1,739); sugar, raw value 2,450 (2,245); coffee *c.* 54 (51); bananas *c.* 1,100 (1,013); tobacco *c.* 65 (65); rubber *c.* 22 (23); manila hemp (1973) *c.* 56, (1972) 73; pork (1973) *c.* 353, (1972) 318; timber (cu.m.; 1973) 35,700, (1972) 33,400; fish catch (1973) 1,248, (1972) 1,132. Livestock (in 000; March 1974): cattle *c.* 2,125; buffalo (1973) 4,937; pigs *c.* 9,000; goats (1973) 1,248; horses (1973) *c.* 310; chickens (1973) 49,965.

Industry. Production (in 000; metric tons; 1974): coal *c.* 50; iron ore (55–60% metal content) 1,616; chrome ore (oxide content; 1973) 232; manganese ore (metal content; 1973) 2; copper ore (metal content; 1973) 221; gold (troy oz.; 1973) 572; silver (troy oz.; 1973) 1,900; cement (1973) 4,059; petroleum products (1973) *c.* 8,600; sulfuric acid 321; electricity (excluding most industrial production; kw-hr.) 8,885,000.

Philosophy

Professional philosophers shared with other academicians in the hardships of the economic decline and inflation of 1975. It was a particularly frustrating year for those trying to enter the profession because new teaching and research positions were generally unavailable. Still philosophy itself remained a vigorous enterprise: its teachers and students were as numerous as ever; government and foundation support for its projects hovered at a historically high level; and the volume of publications devoted to its various branches grew. An estimated 270 periodicals presented philosophical studies throughout the world, and plans for a new journal, *Philosophy in Literature,* were announced.

The areas of most pronounced philosophical interest during 1975 reflected the concerns of society at large. Analyses of sexual roles, of the morality of abortion and euthanasia, of the ethical implications of new biological and psychological techniques for controlling behaviour and redesigning human nature, of the justice of war, and of the proper role of the state were copious and, numerically, of paramount importance. Discussion of these and related topics was increasingly influenced by Robert Nozick's *Anarchy, State, and Utopia,* a work that challenges central tenets of socialist and liberal political ideologies, together with their bases in variants of utilitarian moral theory. Nozick's book promised to become the focal point of debate in social and political philosophy for the next several years. (*See* Feature article: "Free Enterprise in America.")

Although less prominently represented, other areas of philosophy were not neglected. P. F. Strawson's *Subject and Predicate in Logic and Grammar* was an important contribution to the philosophy of language. *The Actor and the Spectator* by Lewis White Beck challenged current theories of psychological determinism, while *Kant and the Problem of History* by William A. Galston, *Aspects of Aristotle's Logic* by Richard Bosley, and volume two of *Studies in Pre-Socratic Philosophy,* edited by R. E. Allen and David J. Furley, were all expressions of the abiding interest of philosophers in the history of their subject.

The three schools of thought that have dominated philosophy in the middle decades of the 20th century —existentialism, phenomenology, and Anglo-American analytic philosophy—continued to show strong signs of vitality. Although diverse in their histories and often opposed in their approaches to basic philosophical issues, these three schools would appear to be moving toward a cautious but sympathetic examination of each other's position. The exploratory essays by U.S., English, and continental writers compiled by Edo Pivcevic in *Phenomenology and Philosophical Understanding* are especially noteworthy as evidence of a growing desire among philosophers to understand more fully, not merely the differences that divide, but also the similarities that unite them.

Apart from its scholarly activities, philosophy has always had an important popular function to counsel and to console. Often of a nonacademic origin and, in recent years, with heavy debts to Oriental systems of thought, this side of philosophy enjoyed a wide appeal in 1975. New popularizations of Japanese, Indian, and Persian spiritual teachings all appeared. Of the works belonging to this group, Robert M. Pirsig's *Zen and the Art of Motorcycle Maintenance: An Inquiry into Values* achieved the most notoriety and was, because of its novel analyses of Oriental and classical Greek points of view, of particular interest.

(JERRY S. CLEGG)

[10/51; 10/52; 10/53]

ENCYCLOPÆDIA BRITANNICA FILMS. *The Medieval Mind* (1969); *The Spirit of the Renaissance* (1971); *An Essay on War* (1971); *The Reformation: Age of Revolt* (1973).

Photography

Despite a worldwide climate of recession and inflation, photography in 1975 continued to experience growth as a technological and cultural force. Although there was little in the way of major innovations or technical breakthroughs in cameras, lenses, lighting equipment, or sensitized materials, the trend in photographic equipment continued toward miniaturization and electronic automation. As a hobby and a method of personal documentation, photography's popularity remained high; in the U.S. alone, more than 5,000,000,000 pictures were taken. As a tool of scientific research, photography assisted in providing the first look at the surface of Venus and may have yielded the first direct evidence for the existence of the magnetic monopole. In its acceptance as an art form, photography made dramatic strides in many countries, with museums, galleries, collectors, historians, and critics giving it the serious attention they once reserved exclusively for more traditional forms of graphic art.

Shown with 40 of Prince Philip's photographs at the Asahi Pentax Gallery, London, on behalf of the World Wildlife Fund, was this view of marine inhabitants of the Galápagos Islands.

H.R.H. PRINCE PHILIP

KEYSTONE

"Motocross Sculptures," taken by Soviet photographer E. Metchnik, won a gold medal at the World Photo Exhibition, "Interpress-Photo 75," in East Berlin.

Cameras. The 35-mm. single-lens reflex (SLR) continued to dominate advanced camera design with a number of new models offering fully automatic exposure control. Of particular interest was the Contax RTS, named after a famous but long-discontinued 35-mm. rangefinder camera formerly manufactured by Zeiss. The result of a joint venture between Zeiss (West Germany) and Yashica (Japan) with exterior design advice by Porsche, the new Contax featured an aperture-preferred, fully automatic exposure system, a 50-mm. Planar *f*/1.4 prime lens, and an electronically controlled focal-plane shutter having a top speed of 1/2000 sec. Among its unusual features were an electromagnetic shutter release, a vertical array of 16 light-emitting diodes visible in the viewfinder to indicate the automatically selected shutter speed, and a battery-powered film-winder accessory for rapid sequential exposures.

In recent years, 35-mm. SLR cameras have grown larger and heavier as manufacturers added more features, especially automatic exposure systems. The Olympus OM-1, a remarkably compact design, represented an opposite trend, and in 1975 a number of camera makers introduced, or were developing, their own versions. Miranda, for example, brought forth its dx-3, a semiautomatic-exposure model with a top shutter speed of 1/1000 sec. and a 50-mm. *f*/1.8 or optional *f*/1.4 prime lens, measuring a relatively trim 135 x 89 x 86 mm. ($5\frac{1}{4}$ x $3\frac{1}{2}$ x $3\frac{3}{8}$ in.) and weighing 825 g. (29 oz.). The Asahi Pentax K2 was a fully automatic-exposure SLR using a new Asahi-Seiko electronically controlled metal focal-plane shutter that permitted relatively compact camera dimensions. The Olympus OM-2, still under development with a late-1976 availability date, offered full exposure automation in the same compact size as the OM-1.

Although 1974 sales of 110-size pocket cameras in the U.S. fell somewhat from a peak of eight million in 1973, interest remained high. Selling well in Europe and projected to reach a record 1975 annual sales level of one million units in Japan, the 110 had firmly established itself as the "box brownie" of the 1970s. Eastman Kodak introduced a new line of Trimlite Instamatic 110s that utilized an ingenous FlipFlash flash pack from General Electric. At the top of the new line, the model 48 provided a coupled rangefinder, an *f*/2.7 lens, and fully automatic exposure

WIDE WORLD

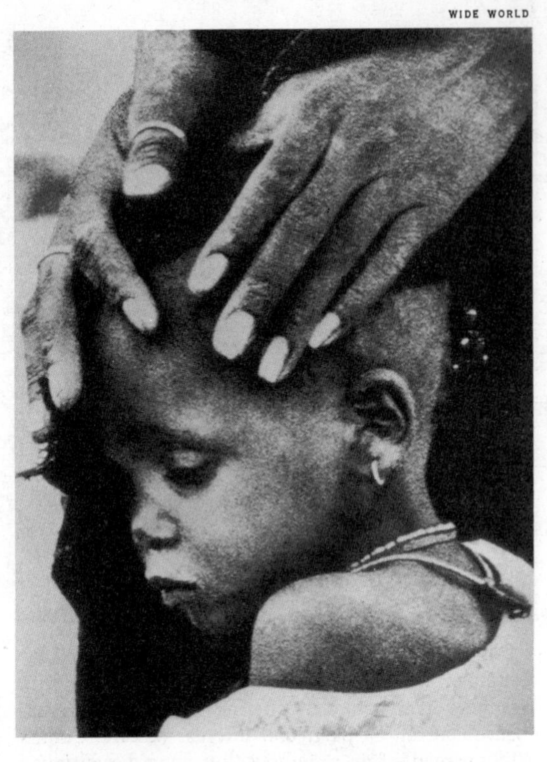

"Suffer Little Children" won the World Press Photo Prize for Ovie Carter of the "Chicago Tribune" in the annual competition in Amsterdam.

control. An interesting fifth new Kodak 110 was the Tele-Instamatic 608 with two built-in *f*/11 single-element lenses, a 25-mm. normal, and a 43-mm. moderate telephoto. By dialing his choice, the user could slide the desired lens and viewfinder mask simultaneously into position. No 110 SLRs for general use or any models with fully interchangeable or zoom lenses actually reached the market in 1975, although a number of prototypes were built. Canon offered a high-quality pocket model, the 110 ED, with a 26-mm. *f*/2 lens, coupled rangefinder, and aperture-preferred exposure automation, and Rollei introduced its tiny (6½ oz.) A110, with a 23-mm. Tessar *f*/2.8 lens, full exposure automation, and an unusual push-pull design for film advance and shutter cocking.

Of particular interest in large-format cameras was the Mamiya M645, a relatively compact roll-film SLR with interchangeable lenses and a 6 x 4.5 cm. (2¼ x 1⅝-in.) "ideal" format that provided 15 or 30 exposures per load of 120 or 220 film. Among instant photography cameras, Polaroid introduced its SX-70 Model 3, a less expensive version of the original, with similar features except for a nonreflex viewfinding and focusing system.

Lenses. Lenses proliferated in 1975, although many were duplications or modifications of existing design concepts. By far the greatest number were designed for 35-mm. SLRs. Lens manufacturers strove to produce lightweight, compact lenses of high optical quality and performance at commercially feasible prices. One example was the long-awaited introduction of the Vivitar Series 1 600-mm. *f*/8 solid cat telephoto lens. An extremely compact solid catadioptric (mirror) design, it measured only about 3¼ in. long by 4¼ in. in diameter and weighed about three pounds. Many new zoom lenses were introduced in the telephoto range and the normal-to-moderate-telephoto range, and some even bridged the difficult gap from moderate wide-angle to moderate telephoto. In the last category, the already well-established 43–86-mm. *f*/3.5 Zoom Nikkor and 35–70-mm. *f*/2.8–3.5 Canon S.S.C. were joined by the 35–105-mm. *f*/3.5 Soligor C/D, the 38–100-mm. *f*/3.5 Tamron, and numerous others. Many of the zoom lenses that appeared in 1975 included a macro focusing provision that enabled the user to switch to a mode permitting a considerably closer minimum focusing distance than was possible in the usual zoom mode. The popularity of this feature indicated it would become standard for many zoom lenses in the future. Considerable interest was generated by such nonfisheye, ultrawide-angle lenses as Nikon's 15-mm. Nikkor *f*/5.6, which corrected for the curvature of horizontal or vertical lines traditionally associated with such short focal lengths.

Lighting. Electronic flash units for every use continued to follow a trend toward miniaturization, automation, and energy-saving "quench" circuitry that utilized a thyristor and capacitor. Amateur units for hot-shoe camera mounting were available at relatively low cost and in sizes comparable to a pack of cigarettes. One ingenious application of electronic flash was found in the Konica C35-EF zone-focus camera, which featured a built-in electronic flash unit that popped up when needed. The Sunpak Auto 511 and 311 allowed manually adjustable, continuously variable light output from 1/64 to full power while still maintaining an energy-saving feature.

For use with the new Kodak line of Trimlite Instamatic 110 cameras, General Electric introduced its FlipFlash, a bar containing an array of eight flash elements and a piezoelectric firing device that eliminates the need for batteries. When one end of the bar is plugged into the camera, the four flash elements at the top can be fired in sequence; inverting the bar allows the remainder to be used. The FlipFlash itself acts as a flash extender to minimize the danger of red eye, the red or pink reflections from the retina of a subject's eyes that sometimes result when a flash source is too close to the axis of the camera lens.

Films and Papers. Polaroid introduced Polacolor 2, a self-processing, one-minute colour film packaged for use in a wide range of Polaroid Land cameras. Like the old Polacolor, the new film involves a disposable negative, but it incorporates some of the chemistry developed for SX-70 colour film and is designed to provide brighter, more stable colours at a speed of ASA 75. For photographers in much of the world it was a time of transition among Kodak colour films, as the recently introduced Kodachrome 25 and 64 (numerical designations referring to their film speeds) replaced Kodachrome II. Kodak's widely rumoured ASA 400 colour-negative film was not introduced, but the company indicated it was working on a number of new colour print and transparency films, some of which might reach consumers in 1976. At Kodak's annual stockholders' meeting, a colour slide was shown of a print from Kodak's forthcoming self-processing, instant colour system, which was expected to be announced in 1976. For super 8 movie users, Kodak introduced a Type G Ektachrome 160 film with a colour-temperature balance somewhere between daylight and tungsten illumination so that the film can be used either with or without colour-correction filters.

Increased interest in colour darkroom activity during 1975 was supported by Ilford's introduction of a Cibachrome in modified form for amateur use. A positive-to-positive colour-printing process utilizing azo dyes, Cibachrome had been available as a professional dye-bleach process for a number of years and claims colour permanence on the order of that provided by the more expensive and complicated dye-transfer process.

In 1975 many darkroom workers abandoned conventional black-and-white printing papers for such resin-coated papers as Kodak's Kodabrome RC and Ilford's Ilfospeed. These water-resistant papers, impregnated with plastic, require less processing, washing, and drying time than do conventional papers but, in the opinion of many critical users, at some loss in tonality and the richness of blacks.

Cultural Trends. A significant aspect of photography in 1975 was its increasingly enthusiastic acceptance as a major cultural force, a visual art form on a par with the much older arts of painting and printmaking. An extraordinary phenomenon, one which some objective observers questioned as over-exploitation, was the escalating price placed on photographic prints, especially signed originals from 19th- and early 20th-century photographers. Collectors, major galleries, and entrepreneurs of the art world created an environment in which unprecedented prices were paid for certain photographs, although on the average these still were less than the prices commonly being paid for signed, limited-edition prints from graphic artists. The highest price known to have been paid for a photograph was the reported $38,000 from collector Arnold Crane for a daguerreotype of Edgar Allan Poe. Gravure reproductions from Alfred Stieglitz' magazine *Camera Work* sold for $250 each and up, depending upon the photograph and the photographer. Christie's auction house in London sold an album of 39 signed and dated photographs by the Victorian photographer Henry Peach Robinson for nearly $7,000.

Museums and art galleries increased the number of photographic exhibitions and the importance they attached to them. Perhaps the most highly publicized exhibition in the world during 1975 was Richard Avedon's controversial one-man show in New York City, which featured large-scale portraits, rarely flattering and often disturbing, of celebrities and intimates. The Museum of Modern Art provided a broad retrospective view of the work of Edward Weston, including a number of previously unexhibited Weston prints, and a small but electrifying exhibit of photographs by Czechoslovak photographer Josef Koudelka, a highly original talent in the tradition of Henri Cartier-Bresson. The Minamata photographs of W. Eugene and Aileen E. Smith, documenting the horrors of mercury poisoning in a fishing village in Japan, reached their apogee of public display and recognition in 1975, and Irving Penn exhibited a series of platinum-print photographs of decayed cigarette and cigar butts, much to the dismay of many of his *Vogue* magazine aficionados.

Rollei intensified the marketing of its first 35-mm. range-finder camera in 1975. The miniature 35 S model has a retractable f/2.8 lens and weighs only 13 oz.

COURTESY, ROLLEI OF AMERICA, INC.

The publication of photographic books continued unabated during the year. Among the more interesting was the $150 limited-edition (2,000 copies), gravure-reproduced book on the U.S. by the Japanese photographer Ikko. Also on the U.S. theme was a stunning collection of landscapes in both colour and black-and-white, titled *Eternal America,* by the Japanese photographer Yoshikazu Shirakawa; a romantic evocation of the land and its people, *In America,* by Ernst Haas; and *These United States,* a sentimental journey across the land by Fred Maroon. A more critical view was provided by Robert D'Alessandro in *Glory* (1974), a visual documentation of the uses and abuses of the American flag. (ARTHUR GOLDSMITH)

See also Motion Pictures.
[628.D; 735.G.1]

Physics

The year 1975 was notable for some exciting claims by physicists from all parts of the world, in all branches of the subject. Some have been supported by further experiments and by weight of opinion in the scientific community, whereas others are already under attack.

Nuclear Physics. The nuclear physicists have recently unveiled a series of experimental discoveries which, at the present time, seem to support some of the most novel ideas of the theoreticians. The new developments began with the announcement in 1974 by two separate groups in the U.S. of the discovery of a new uncharged elementary particle with a mass, when converted entirely to energy, of 3.1 GeV (billion electron volts). The existence of this particle was immediately confirmed by workers in Frascati, Italy. A second particle with a mass of 3.7 GeV was found two weeks later by the U.S. group at the Stanford (Calif.) Linear Accelerator Center. The lifetime of the particles, known as the psis, is unusually long for particles that are three to four times heavier than the proton.

The psis were hailed as the first of a series of particles that are composed of quarks and antiquarks. (A quark is the proposed basic constituent or building block of all the elementary particles.) Initially, it had been postulated that there were three different quarks, but theoreticians working in the area of weak interactions required a fourth quark, which was differentiated from the other three by the possession of "charm." Charm has been described as a property of a particle, such as electric charge, that must survive a reaction. For example, the net electric charge of particles emerging from a reaction must be identical with that of the particles entering it.

Much of the excitement during the year was caused by the possibility that the new particles may be constructed of quarks possessing charm. The psi particles were, in fact, believed to be formed from one charmed quark and its antiparticle, the charmed antiquark. The strong nuclear interaction causes the two particles to be attracted to and, therefore, to circle around one another. It was quickly found that the heavier 3.7 GeV particle decays into the lighter 3.1 GeV one, and the first test of the charm theory was in the nature of this decay. The initial decay mode was the emission of two pions (pi mesons), but the charm theory required a decay process involving the release of gamma rays. This second decay mode was later reported by

COURTESY (TOP LEFT, RIGHT) DR. EDWARD K. SHIRK, UNIV. OF CALIF., BERKELEY; PHOTO (BOTTOM) UPI COMPIX

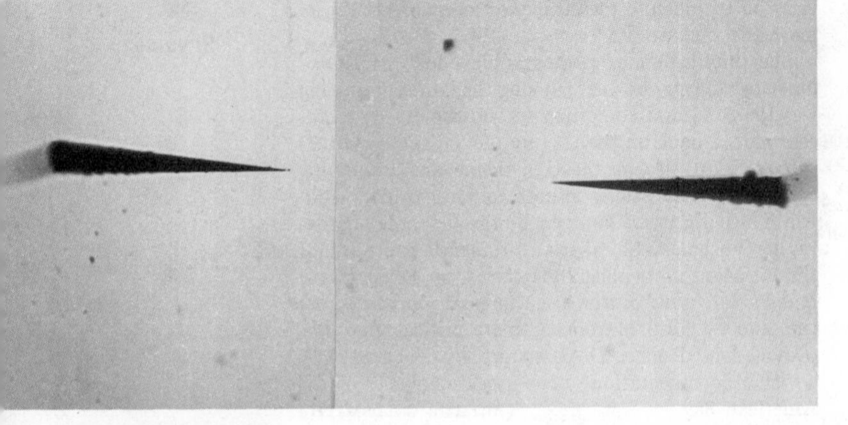

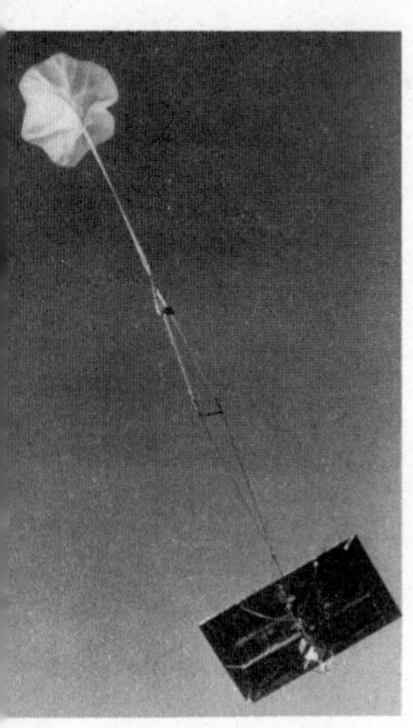

(Above) Apparatus used in the cosmic ray experiment which may have detected a magnetic monopole. (Top left and right) Photographs of two of the conical holes found in the plastic sheeting of the apparatus.

physicists at the DESY atomic centre in Hamburg, West Germany, and separately by the Stanford accelerator team. The U.S. group reported that the 3.7 GeV particle first emits a 200 MeV (million electron volts) gamma ray and therefore has an intermediate mass of 3.5 GeV (known as the chi) before it decays by emitting a 400 MeV gamma ray or four charged particles. The intermediate energy is in line with the predictions of charm theory.

In 1975 experimentalists intensified their search for the remaining members of the family, all of which basically are excited states of the 3.1 GeV particle. It has been predicted that there should be three chi particles having masses about 3.5 GeV, and there were rumours late in the year that the Stanford group had found all three of them and that the West Germans had observed at least two.

The majority of these experiments were carried out with electron accelerators in which high-energy electrons and antielectrons (or positrons) collide. It appeared that this technique would continue to lead the field in the production of the new particles, although one of the U.S. groups was bombarding beryllium targets with protons.

The Stanford accelerator project also provided a spin-off result in the production of a new charged particle, known as the U particle. Also produced in electron-positron collisions, this particle has a mass between 1.6 and 2.0 GeV and can take both positive and negative charges. In fact, the U particles are always produced simultaneously in pairs with opposite charge. These particles are thought by some theoreticians to be composed of one charmed quark and one uncharmed quark, and as such would have half the mass of the lightest psi and would be closely associated with the psis and chis.

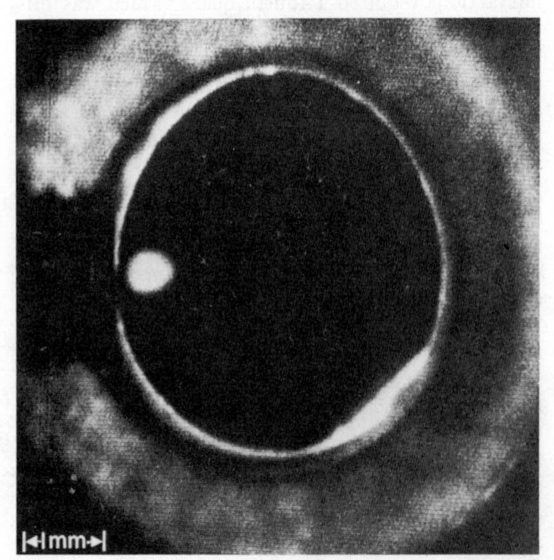

Electricity in liquid form was photographed for the first time by physicists at the University of California at Berkeley in May. The laser-produced electron-hole drop shown here is 1/30 in. in diameter and contains an estimated ten thousand billion electrical charges.

WIDE WORLD

The structure of the new particles is reminiscent of that of positronium, which consists of one electron and one positron circling one another, held together by the weak electromagnetic interaction. Thus, the new particles could form a bridge between the weak and strong interactions as well as allowing a detailed study of the concept of charm and the quarks. It should perhaps be emphasized that a single independent quark has still not been observed.

Positronium itself was first produced in the laboratory more than 20 years ago by bombarding a gas with a positron source. In 1975, after many unsuccessful experiments, the first excited (higher energy) state of positronium was produced by workers in the U.S. Production of more highly excited particles should allow a detailed study of the predictions of quantum electrodynamics.

High Pressures. Physicists have predicted for many years that liquid hydrogen can be solidified at 4.2° K (−269° C) by the pressure of several megabars. In the solid state, hydrogen should behave like a metal because its electronic structure is analogous, for example, to that of copper. It has only one electron in its outer, and only, shell. Late in 1975 the solidification of hydrogen was reported by three Soviet physicists working at the U.S.S.R. Academy of Sciences. Their surprising finding, which caused some concern among high-pressure physicists, is that the solidification took place at a pressure of only one megabar at 4.2° K. There must, however, be large error limits placed on the measurement of such a high pressure because of the difficulty of calibration at that level.

The change of phase from liquid to solid was monitored by measuring the electrical conductivity of the hydrogen layer in the high-pressure apparatus. The scientists reported a drop in the resistance of six orders of magnitude at the phase change. If this work can be confirmed, it could have major implications in the world of astrophysics because those pressures and temperatures are expected to be present in major planets and many other astronomical bodies.

Magnetic Monopoles. It has been common knowledge for many years that the positive and negatively charged elementary particles can be separated and exist independently. For example, the negative charge is carried by the electron, while the positive charge is carried by the positron or the proton. Similarly, it is well known that a moving electric charge sets up a magnetic field. Many years ago Paul A. M. Dirac predicted that there should exist independent magnetic particles, which are equivalent to one pole of the conventional magnetic dipole. These independent particles are termed magnetic monopoles, and a moving magnetic monopole should produce an electric field. A pair of monopoles should be produced from a high-energy photon in a manner analogous to the production of an electron and a positron from a gamma-ray photon of energy greater than 1 MeV.

Ever since Dirac's prediction there have been extensive searches for the elusive monopoles. They have been sought in the products of high-energy particle collision experiments, in cosmic ray showers, in meteorites, and in regions of the very deep ocean floor, all without success. In 1975, however, a team from the University of California at Berkeley and the University of Houston reported the discovery of a magnetic monopole in a cosmic ray shower. The monopole was recorded by using three separate detectors in a balloon-borne experiment high in the atmosphere.

Two of these detectors limit the particle either to a heavy nucleus or a monopole; the final detector, a stack of 33 polycarbonate sheets, should decide between these alternatives. The Berkeley-Houston scientists interpreted their results on the polycarbonate stack as evidence in favour of the monopole, but they later received severe criticism from other experts in the field who indicated that the particle tracks in the detector can be interpreted just as convincingly in terms of a heavy platinum nucleus that undergoes two collisions.

This latter interpretation was supported by the calculation of magnetic monopole flux from the one experimental observation. The flux is in direct conflict with findings in other monopole searches. It is also noteworthy that Dirac himself was quoted as saying that he no longer believes in the monopole.

(S. B. PALMER)

See also Nobel Prizes.
[111.H; 124.G.3; 127.C]

ENCYCLOPÆDIA BRITANNICA FILMS. *Introduction to Holography* (1972); *Introduction to Lasers* (1973); *Time: Measurement and Meaning* (1974); *Learning About Electric Current* (2nd ed., 1974); *Learning About Heat* (2nd ed., 1974); *Learning About Magnetism* (2nd ed., 1975); *Learning About Nuclear Energy* (2nd ed., 1975); *Learning About Sound* (2nd ed., 1975).

Poland

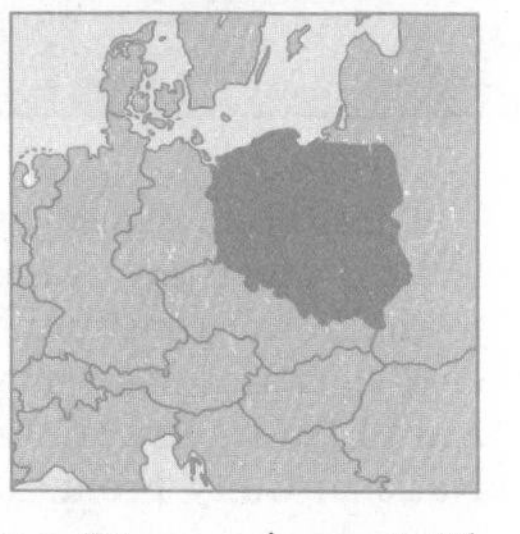

A people's republic of Eastern Europe, Poland is bordered by the Baltic Sea, the U.S.S.R., Czechoslovakia, and East Germany. Area: 120,725 sq.mi. (312,677 sq.km.). Pop. (1975 est.): 33,959,000. Cap. and largest city: Warsaw (pop., 1975 est., 1,427,400). Language: Polish. Religion: predominantly Roman Catholic. First secretary of the Polish United Workers' (Communist) Party in 1975, Edward Gierek; chairman of the Council of State, Henryk Jablonski; chairman of the Council of Ministers (premier), Piotr Jaroszewicz.

The administrative reform that began in 1973 when the 4,671 smallest units, *gromady*, or villages, were reduced to 2,365 *gminy*, or communes, was completed on June 1, 1975, when the 22 *wojewodztwa*, or provinces, including five self-governing cities, as well as 392 *powiaty*, or districts, including 78 urban districts, were replaced by 46 smaller provinces and three self-governing cities (Warsaw, Krakow, and Lodz). The reform did away with the three-tier local government system. Except for the metropolitan cities, the new provinces ranged from 3,700 to 12,300 sq.km. in area, from 283,000 to 1,221,000 inhabitants, and from 28 to 96 primary units. The dismantling of the 22 provinces weakened the resistance of local party bosses to directives from Warsaw.

In May Tadeusz Bejm, first secretary of the Gdansk provincial party organization, was appointed minister of administration with the task of implementing the reform, which simplified the procedure of decision making. Instead of many departments there was only the provincial council, whose chairman was solely responsible for all decisions. His status was further reinforced through the adoption of the principle that the first secretary of the Polish United Workers' Party (PUWP) was ex officio chairman of the provincial council.

U.S. Pres. Gerald Ford visited Poland on July 28-29. The first meeting of the Polish-American Economic Council took place in Warsaw on September 8. Between 1971 and 1974 Poland's trade turnover with the U.S. grew from $180 million to $661.5 million.

The British foreign secretary, James Callaghan, visited Poland July 13–15. On September 4 a British-Polish ten-year program of industrial cooperation was signed. Between 1971 and 1974 Polish-British trade both ways rose from 124 million zlotys to 248.9 million zlotys.

The president of the French Republic, Valéry Giscard d'Estaing, paid a state visit to Poland June 17–20. On that occasion a long-term agreement on industrial cooperation was signed, and France granted Poland a credit of Fr. 7 billion. The turnover of Franco-Polish trade rose between 1971 and 1974 from $158.5 million to $637.9 million.

On August 1, in Helsinki, Fin., Edward Gierek, first secretary of the PUWP, and West German Chancellor Helmut Schmidt approved the text of three documents further normalizing relations between their two countries. The agreements were finally signed in

Pipelines: *see* Energy; Transportation

Plastics Industry: *see* Industrial Review

Platinum Group: *see* Mining and Quarrying

Poetry: *see* Literature

POLAND

Education. (1974–75) Primary, pupils 4,522,466, teachers 201,006; secondary, pupils 647,992, teachers 26,166; vocational, pupils 1,846,553, teachers 74,067; teacher training, students 19,509, teachers (1971–72) 2,251; higher (including 10 main universities), students 521,896, teaching staff 45,014.

Finance. Monetary unit: zloty, with (Sept. 22, 1975) a basic rate of 20 zlotys to U.S. $1 (42 zlotys = £1 sterling) and a tourist rate of 33.20 zlotys to U.S. $1 (70 zlotys = £1 sterling). Budget (1974 est.): revenue 539 billion zlotys; expenditure 537 billion zlotys. National income (net material product): (1974) 1,209,300,000,000 zlotys; (1973) 1,064,800,000,000 zlotys.

Foreign Trade. (1974) Imports 34,823,000,000 zlotys; exports 27,625,000,000 zlotys. Import sources: U.S.S.R. 22%; West Germany 12%; East Germany 7%; Czechoslovakia 6%; U.K. 5%; U.S. 5%. Export destinations: U.S.S.R. 29%; East Germany 9%; Czechoslovakia 7%; West Germany 6%. Main exports: machinery 29%; coal 13%; chemicals 11%; food 10%; textiles and clothing 9%; metals 8%; ships and boats 5%.

Transport and Communications. Roads (1973) 299,876 km. (including 139 km. expressways). Motor vehicles in use (1973): passenger 780,874; commercial 324,268. Railways: (1973) 23,577 km. (including 4,700 km. electrified); traffic (1974) 41,668,000,000 passenger-km., freight 125,155,000,000 net ton-km. Air traffic (1974): 1,075,000,000 passenger-km.; freight 13,644,000 net ton-km. Shipping (1974): merchant vessels 100 gross tons and over 648; gross tonnage 2,292,318. Telephones (Dec. 1973) 2,238,000. Radio licenses (Dec. 1973) 5,872,000. Television licenses (Dec. 1973) 5,687,000.

Agriculture. Production (in 000; metric tons; 1974; 1973 in parentheses): wheat *c.* 6,150 (5,807); rye *c.* 7,620 (8,268); barley *c.* 3,740 (3,158); oats *c.* 3,100 (3,220); potatoes 48,580 (51,928); sugar, raw value *c.* 1,589 (1,817); rapeseed *c.* 524 (512); linseed *c.* 60 (51); cabbages (1973) *c.* 1,298, (1972) 1,298; onions *c.* 330 (*c.* 326); tomatoes *c.* 390 (382); carrots (1973) *c.* 458, (1972) 458; cucumbers (1973) *c.* 472, (1972) 457; apples *c.* 690 (683); tobacco *c.* 78 (*c.* 78); flax fibre (1973) *c.* 60, (1972) 57; butter 277 (245); cheese *c.* 329 (*c.* 306); eggs *c.* 440 (416); beef and veal (1973) *c.* 550, (1972) 536; pork (1973) *c.* 1,705, (1972) *c.* 1,350; timber (cu.m.; 1973) 21,800, (1972) 20,600; fish catch (1973) 580, (1972) 544. Livestock (in 000; June 1974): cattle 13,023; horses (1973) 2,373; pigs 21,496; sheep 3,023; chickens (1973) 149,700.

Industry. Index of industrial production (1970 = 100): (1974) 149; (1973) 133. Fuel and power (in 000; metric tons; 1974): coal 162,002; brown coal 39,826; coke (1973) 16,505; crude oil (1973) 392; natural gas (cu.m.) 5,739,000; manufactured gas (cu.m.; 1973) 7,145,000; electricity (kw-hr.) 91,597,000. Production (in 000; metric tons; 1974): cement 16,765; iron ore (metal content; 1973) 432; pig iron 8,212; crude steel 14,564; aluminum (1973) 102; zinc (1973) 235; copper (1973) 156; lead (1973) 68; petroleum products (1973) 10,482; sulfuric acid 3,319; fertilizers (nutrient content; 1973) nitrogenous 1,366, phosphate 814; cotton yarn 214; wool yarn 97; rayon, etc., filament yarn and fibres 97; nylon, etc., filament yarn and fibres 95; cotton fabrics (m.) 885,000; woolen fabrics (m.) 117,000; rayon and synthetic fabrics (m.; 1973) 113,000; passenger cars (units) 133; commercial vehicles (units) 74. Merchant vessels launched (100 gross tons and over; 1974) 589,000 gross tons. New dwelling units completed (1974) 190,000.

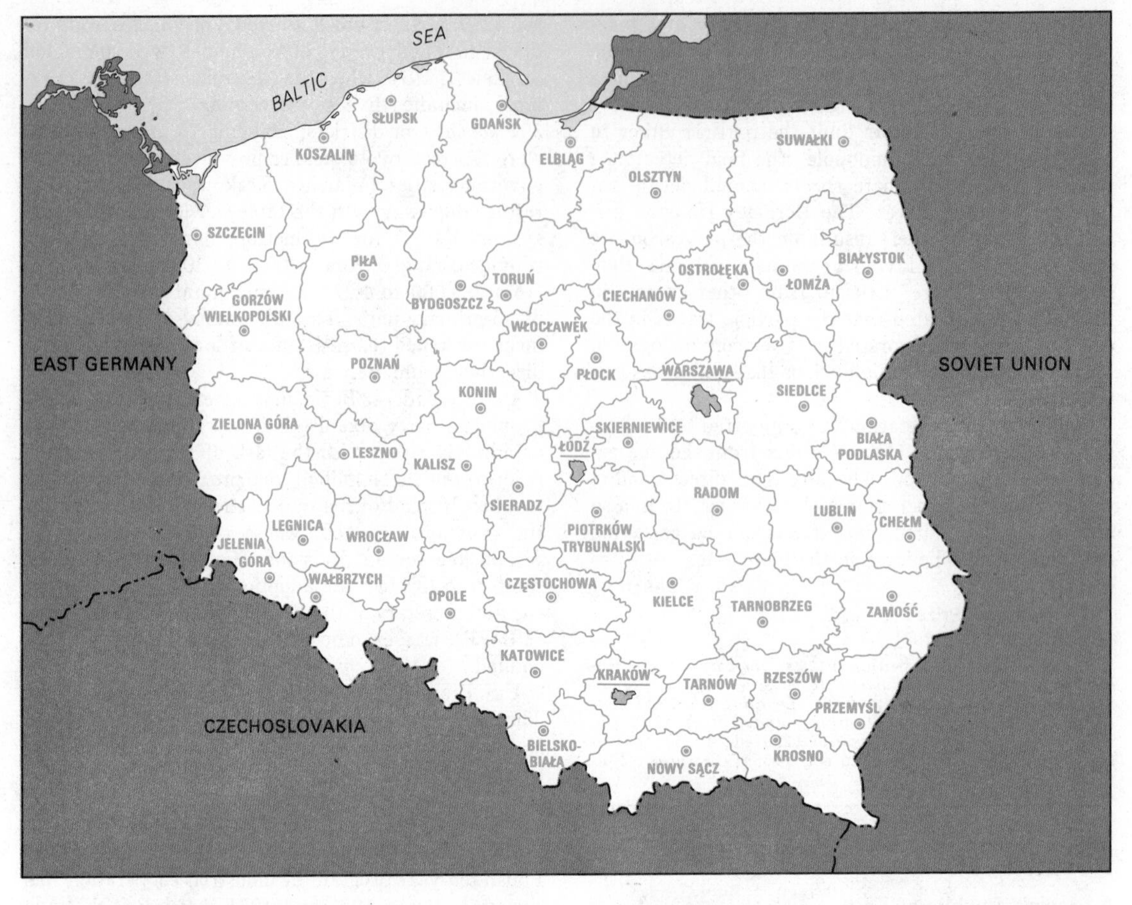

The provinces of Poland. The name of the province and its capital city are the same; Warszawa, Łódź, and Kraków are also province-level cities, independent of the provinces in which they are located.

Warsaw on October 9 by the West German and Polish foreign ministers, Hans-Dietrich Genscher and Stefan Olszowski. Poland agreed to grant emigration permits to another 120,000–125,000 Polish citizens of German extraction and members of mixed families. The Federal Republic agreed to pay Poland DM. 1.3 billion to cover the pensions that the Polish state had been paying since 1945 to former German citizens. The Federal Republic also granted Poland a loan of DM. 1 billion. Polish-West German trade turnover in 1974 amounted to DM. 4,041,400,000.

In October Deputy Premier Mieczyslaw Jagielski ceased to be chairman of the State Planning Commission. Tadeusz Wrzaszczyk, former minister of engineering industry, took over the chairmanship of this key body and was also appointed deputy premier. Tadeusz Pyka, first deputy chairman of the commission, joined the Cabinet as the eighth deputy premier.

The seventh congress of the PUWP met in Warsaw on Dec. 8, 1974, to approve the guidelines of the 1976–80 development plan and to elect the new Central Committee. Under the plan national income was expected to rise by 42% and wages by 18%. Industrial production in 1980 would be 50% greater than in 1975; hard-coal extraction would reach 200 million tons, generation of electric power 132,000,000,000 kw-hr., and production of steel 22 million tons. Agricultural production would rise by 16%, and Poland's livestock in 1980 would include 23 million pigs and 15 million head of cattle.

On December 12 the congress elected a new Central Committee, increasing its membership from 115 to 140 (including 67 old members reelected, 10 former deputy members, and 63 new). This body reelected Gierek as first secretary and elected a Politburo that was enlarged from 11 to 14 members.

A manifesto signed by 59 writers and other intellectuals protesting against the proposed amendments to the Polish constitution, which would further limit civil liberties, was sent to the speaker of the Sejm and to the leaders of the four political parties of the National Unity Front. (K. M. SMOGORZEWSKI)

[972.B.2.d]

Political Parties

The following table is a general world guide to political parties. All countries that were independent on Dec. 31, 1975, are included; there are a number for which no analysis of political activities can be given. Parties are included in most instances only if represented in parliaments (in the lower house in bicameral legislatures); the figures in the last column indicate the number of seats obtained in the last general election. The date of the most recent election follows the name of the country.

The code letters in the affiliation column show the relative political position of the parties within each country; there is, therefore, no entry in this column for single-party states. There are obvious difficulties involved in labeling parties within the political spectrum of a given country. The key chosen is as follows: F—fascist; ER—extreme right; R—right; CR—centre right; C—centre; L—non-Marxist left; SD—social-democratic; S—socialist; K—Communist; and EL—extreme left.

The percentages in the column "Voting strength" indicate proportions of the valid votes cast for the respective parties, or the number of registered voters who went to the polls in single-party states.

[541.D.2]

Police:
see Crime and Law Enforcement

Polish Literature:
see Literature

COUNTRY AND NAME OF PARTY	Affiliation	Voting strength (%)	Parliamentary representation
Afghanistan			
Presidential rule since July 17, 1973	—	—	—
Albania (October 1974)			
Albanian Labour (Communist)	—	99.9	270
Algeria			
Presidential regime since June 19, 1965	—	—	—
Angola			
After independence on November 11, rival governments were set up by warring factions in Luanda and Nova Lisboa (Huambo)			
Argentina (March 1973)			
Frente Justicialista de Liberación (Frejuli)	CR	49.6	145
Unión Cívica Radical	C	21.3	51
Alianza Popular Federalista	C	14.6	20
Alianza Popular Revolucionaria	L	7.1	12
Others	—	6.7	15
Australia (November 1975)			
Liberal-Country	CR	52.2	92
Democratic Labor	C	...	0
Australian Labor	L	43.5	35
Austria (October 1975)			
Freiheitliche Partei Österreichs	R	5.4	10
Osterreichische Volkspartei	C	42.9	80
Sozialistische Partei Österreichs	SD	50.4	93
Kommunistische Partei Österreichs	K	1.2	0
Bahamas, The (September 1972)			
Progressive Liberal Party	C	60.0	30
Free National Movement	L	...	8
Bahrain			
Emirate, no parties	—	—	—
Bangladesh			
Revolutionary government since August 1975	—	—	—
Barbados (September 1971)			
Democratic Labour	C	...	18
Barbados Labour	L	...	6
Belgium (March 1974)			
Front Démocratique Francophone } Rassemblement Wallon	R	11.0	25
Volksunie (Flemish)	R	0.2	22
Parti pour la Liberté et le Progrès	CR	15.2	30
Parti Social Chrétien	C	32.3	72
Parti Socialiste Belge	SD	26.7	58
Parti Communiste Belge	K	3.2	4
Bhutan			
No parties	—	—	130
Bolivia			
Military government since Nov. 9, 1974	—	—	—
Botswana (October 1974)			
Botswana Democratic Party	C	...	27
Botswana People's Party	L	...	2
Botswana National Front	EL	...	2
Brazil (November 1974)			
Aliança Renovadora Nacional	CR	...	...
Movimento Democrático Brasileiro	L	...	...
Bulgaria (June 1971)			
Bulgarian Communist 266 } People's Agrarian Union 100 } Nonparty 34 } Fatherland Front	—	99.9	400
Burma (February 1974)			
Burma Socialist Program Party	—	99.0	—
Burundi			
Tutsi ethnic minority government since Nov. 28, 1966	—	—	—
Cambodia			
Khmer Rouge in power from April 1975	—	—	—
Cameroon (May 1973)			
Cameroonian National Union	—	—	120
Canada (July 1974)			
Social Credit	R		11
Progressive Conservative	CR		95
Liberal	C		141
New Democratic	L		16
Independents	—		1
Cape Verde Islands (June 1975)			
African Party for the Independence of Guinea-Bissau and Cape Verde (PAIGC)	—	—	56
Central African Republic			
Military government since Jan. 1, 1966	—	—	—
Chad			
Military government since April 13, 1975	—	—	—
Chile			
Military government since Sept. 11, 1973	—	—	—
China, People's Republic of			
Communist (Kungchantang)	—	—	—
Colombia (April 1974)			
Partido Conservador	R	...	66
Partido Liberal	C	...	113
Others	—	...	20
Congo			
Military government since September 1968	—	—	—
Costa Rica (February 1974)			
Partido de Liberación Nacional	R	...	27
Partido de Unificación Nacional	C	...	16
Others (six parties)	—	...	14
Cuba			
Partido Comunista de Cuba	—	—	—
Cyprus			
Military government since July 15, 1974	—	—	—
Czechoslovakia (November 1971)			
Communist Party of Czechoslovakia } Czechoslovak People's Party } Czechoslovak Socialist Party } Communist Party of Slovakia } Slovak Freedom Party } Party of Slovak Revival } National Front	—	99.8	350
Dahomey (Benin)			
Military government since Oct. 26, 1972	—	—	—
Denmark (January 1975)			
Conservative	R	5.5	10
Liberal Democratic (Venstre)	CR	23.3	42
Christian People's	CR	5.3	9
Progress (M. Glistrup)	C	13.6	24
Radical Liberal (Radikale Venstre)	C	7.1	13
Single-Tax (Retsforbund)	C	1.8	0
Centre Democrats (E. Jakobsen)	L	2.2	4
Social Democrats	SD	30.0	53
Socialist People's	EL	4.9	9
Left Socialists	EL	2.1	4
Communists	K	4.2	7
Dominican Republic (May 1974)			
Partido Quisqueyano Demócrata	ER	...	...
Partido Reformista	R	...	...
Partido Reformista Dominicano	C	...	...
Partido Revolucionario Social-Cristiano	L	...	...
Partido Demócrata Popular	L	...	...
Ecuador			
Military government since Feb. 15, 1972	—	—	—
Egypt (September 1971)			
Arab Socialist Union	—	...	338
El Salvador (March 1974)			
Partido de Conciliación Nacional	R	...	32
Union Nacional de Oposición	C	...	14
Partido Popular Salvadoreño	L	...	4
Others	—	...	2
Equatorial Guinea			
Partido Único Nacional de los Trabajadores	—	—	—
Ethiopia			
Military government since Sept. 12, 1974	—	—	—
Fiji (April 1972)			
Alliance Party (mainly Fijian)	—	...	33
National Federation Party (mainly Indian)	—	...	19
Finland (September 1975)			
Conservative Party	R	18.4	34
Swedish People's Party	R	4.7	10
Centre Party (ex-Agrarian)	C	17.7	39
Liberal Party	C	4.4	9
Christian League	C	3.3	9
Rural Party	L	3.6	2
Social Democratic Party	SD	25.0	54
People's Democratic League	K	19.0	41
Others	—	4.0	2
France (March 1973)			
Union des Démocrates pour la République	CR	31.3	185
Independent Republicans	CR	7.7	54
Centre Démocratie et Progrès	C	3.9	21
Other majority coalition	C	3.2	15
Radicals	L	3.8	12
Socialists	SD	21.9	89
Parti Socialiste Unifié	EL	0.3	3
Communists	K	20.6	73
Others	—	...	38
Gabon (February 1973)			
Parti Démocratique Gabonais	—	—	70
Gambia, The (March 1972)			
People's Progressive Party	C	...	28
United Party	L	...	3
German Democratic Republic (November 1971)			
Sozialistische Einheitspartei } Christlich-Demokratische Union } National-Demokratische Partei } Liberal-Demokratische Partei } Demokratische Bauernpartei } National Front	—	99.8	434
Germany, Federal Republic of (November 1972)			
Nationaldemokratische Partei Deutschlands	F	0.6	0
Christlich-Demokratische Union	R }	44.8	177
Christlich-Soziale Union	R }		48
Freie Demokratische Partei	C	8.4	41
Sozialdemokratische Partei Deutschlands	SD	45.9	230
Deutsche Kommunistische Partei	K	0.3	0
Ghana			
Military government since Jan. 13, 1972	—	—	—
Greece (November 1974)			
New Democracy Party	CR	54.4	220
Centre Union—New Forces	C	20.4	60
Pan-Hellenic Socialist Movement	S	13.6	12
United Left	K	9.5	8
Grenada (February 1972)			
United Labour Party	L	59.0	13
Others	—	...	2
Guatemala (March 1974)			
Partido Institucional Democrático } Movimiento de Liberación Nacional	CR	41.2	...
Frente Nacional de Oposición } Partido Demócrata Cristiano	C	35.7	...
Partido Revolucionario } Frente Democrático Guatemalteco	L	23.1	...

COUNTRY AND NAME OF PARTY	Affiliation	Voting strength (%)	Parliamentary representation
Guinea (December 1974)			
Parti Démocratique de Guinée	—	100.0	150
Guinea-Bissau (1975)			
African Party for the Independence of Guinea-Bissau and Cape Verde (PAIGC)	—	...	92
Guyana (July 1973)			
People's National Congress	C	...	37
People's Progressive Party	EL	...	14
Others	—	...	2
Haiti			
Presidential dictatorship since 1957	—	—	—
Honduras			
Military government since Dec. 4, 1972	—	—	—
Hungary (June 1975)			
Communist-controlled Patriotic People's Front	—	97.6	352
Iceland (June 1974)			
Independence (Conservative)	R	42.7	25
Progressive (Farmers' Party)	C	24.9	17
Union of Liberals and Leftists	L	4.6	2
Social Democratic	SD	9.1	5
People's Alliance	K	18.3	11
India (March 1971)			
Jan Sangh (Hindu Nationalist)	ER	...	22
Dravida Munnetra Kazhagam	R	...	23
Telengana Praja Samiti	R	...	10
Swatantra (Freedom)	R	...	7
Ruling Congress Party	C	...	349
Opposition Congress Party	L	...	16
Praja Socialist	SD	...	2
Samyukta Socialist	S	...	3
Communist-Marxist (pro-Chinese)	K	...	25
Communist (pro-Soviet)	K	...	24
Independents and others	—	...	33
Indonesia (July 1971)			
Sekber Golkar (Functional Groups)	—	65.5	261
Nahdatul Ulama (Muslim Teachers)	R	...	58
Partai Nasional	R	...	20
Parmusi (Liberal Muslims)	C	...	24
Sarikat Islam (United Muslims)	C	...	10
Partai Keristen Indonesia (Protestants)	C	...	7
Partai Katholik Indonesia	C	...	3
Perti (Islamic Party)	C	...	2
Partai Murba (Party of the Masses)	EL	...	0
West Irian	—	...	9
Iran (June 1975)			
Rastakhiz (National Resurgence) Party	—	52.0	268
Iraq			
Military and Baath Party governments since 1958	—	...	...
Ireland (February 1973)			
Fianna Fail (Sons of Destiny)	C	46.2	69
Fine Gael (United Ireland)	C	35.1	54
Irish Labour	L	13.7	19
Sinn Fein (We Ourselves)	...	1.1	0
Others	—	3.9	2
Israel (December 1973)			
Likud (Herut, Liberal Alignment, Free Centre, and State List)	R	...	39
Tora Front (Agudat Israel and Poalei Agudat Israel)	CR	...	5
National Religious	C	...	10
Independent Liberal	C	...	4
Civil Rights List (Mrs. S. Aloni)	L	...	3
Maarakh (Mapam, Mapai, Rafi, and Abdut Avoda)	SD	...	51
Moked (pro-Israel Communists)	K	...	1
Rakah (pro-Soviet Communists)	K	...	4
Pro-government Arabs	—	...	3
Italy (May 1972)			
Movimento Sociale Italiano Partito di Unitá Monarchica	F R	8.7	56
Partito Liberale Italiano	CR	3.9	20
Democrazia Cristiana	C	38.8	267
Partito Repubblicano Italiano	C	2.9	15
Partito Social-Democratico Italiano	L	5.1	29
Partito Socialista Italiano	SD	9.6	61
Partito Socialista Italiano di Unitá Proletaria	EL	—	—
Partito Comunista Italiano	K	27.2	179
Südtiroler Volkspartei	—	0.5	3
Ivory Coast (November 1970)			
Parti Démocratique de la Côte d'Ivoire	—	...	100
Jamaica (February 1972)			
People's National Party	L	...	35
Jamaica Labour Party	S	...	18
Japan (December 1972)			
Liberal-Democratic	CR	46.9	271
Komeito	CR	8.5	29
Democratic Socialist	SD	7.0	19
Socialist	S	21.9	118
Communist	K	10.5	38
Independents	—	...	14
Jordan			
Royal government, no parties	—	—	60
Kenya (October 1974)			
Kenya African National Union	—	...	158
Korea, North			
Korean Workers' (Communist) Party	—	...	...
Korea, South (February 1973)			
Democratic Republican	CR	38.7	73
New Democratic	L	32.6	52
Democratic Unification	...	10.1	2
Independents	—	18.6	19
Kuwait			
Princely government, no parties	—	—	30
Laos			
Since Dec. 3, 1975, republican government dominated by Pathet Lao (Communists)			
Lebanon (April 1972)			
Maronites (Roman Catholics)	—	...	30
Sunni Muslims	—	...	20
Shia Muslims	—	...	19
Greek Orthodox	—	...	11
Druzes (Muslim sect)	—	...	6
Melchites (Greek Catholics)	—	...	6
Armenian Orthodox	—	...	4
Other Christian	—	...	2
Armenian Catholics	—	...	1
Lesotho			
Constitution suspended Jan. 30, 1970	—	—	—
Liberia			
True Whig Party	—	...	41
Libya			
Military government since Sept. 1, 1969	—	—	—
Liechtenstein (February 1974)			
Vaterländische Union	CR	...	7
Fortschrittliche Bürgerpartei	C	...	8
Christlich-Soziale Partei	C	...	0
Luxembourg (May 1974)			
Parti Chrétien Social	CR	28.0	18
Parti Libéral	C	22.1	14
Parti Ouvrier Socialiste	SD	29.0	17
Parti Social Démocratique	S	9.1	5
Parti Communiste	K	10.4	5
Malagasy Republic			
Military government since Oct. 13, 1972	—	—	—
Malawi			
Malawi Congress Party	—	...	58
Malaysia (August 1974)			
Barisan Nasional (National Front, 12 parties)	—	61.6	135
Democratic Action Party (mainly Chinese)	—	...	9
Pekemas (Social Justice Party)	—	...	1
Maldives			
Government by the Didi family	—	—	—
Mali			
Military government since Nov. 19, 1968	—	—	—
Malta (June 1971)			
Nationalist Party	R	48.1	27
Labour Party	SD	50.8	28
Mauritania (August 1971)			
Parti du Peuple Mauritanien	—	95.1	50
Mauritius (1967)			
Independence Party (Indian-dominated)	—	...	39
Parti Mauricien Social-Démocrate	L	...	23
Mexico (July 1973)			
Partido Revolucionario Institucional	CR	...	189
Partido Acción Nacional	C	...	4
Partido Auténtico de la Revolución	L	...	1
Partido Popular Socialista	S	...	0
Monaco			
Union Nationale et Démocratique	—	...	18
Mongolia (1973)			
Mongolian People's Revolutionary Party	K	99.0	295
Morocco (August 1970)			
Independents (pro-government)	CR	...	159
Popular Movement (rural)	CR	...	60
Istiqlal (Independence)	C	...	8
National Union of Popular Forces	L	...	1
Others	—	...	12
Mozambique, People's Republic of (1975)			
Frente da Libertação do Moçambique (Frelimo)	—	—	—
Nauru (January 1972)			
No political parties	—	—	—
Nepal			
Royal government since December 1960	—	—	—
Netherlands, The (November 1972)			
Boerenpartij (Farmers' Party)	R	1.9	3
Anti-Revolutionaire Partij (Calvinist)	CR	8.8	14
Christelijk Historische Unie (Protestant)	CR	4.8	7
Katholieke Volkspartij	C	17.7	27
Volkspartij voor Vreiheid en Democratie	C	14.4	22
Democraten '66	C	.4.2	6
Democraten-Socialisten '70	L	4.1	6
Partij van de Arbeid	SD	27.4	43
Communistische Partij	K	4.5	7
Five other parties	—	12.2	15
New Zealand (November 1975)			
National (Conservative)	CR	...	53
Labour Party	L	...	34
Nicaragua (September 1974)			
Partido Liberal Nacionalista (A. Somoza)	R	60.0	42
Partido Conservador Tradicionalista	R	...	...
Partido Demócrata Cristiano	C	...	...
Niger			
Military government since April 17, 1974	—	—	—

COUNTRY AND NAME OF PARTY	Affiliation	Voting strength (%)	Parliamentary representation
Nigeria			
Military government since Jan. 15, 1966	—	—	—
Norway (September 1973)			
Høyre (Conservative)	R	17.3	29
Kristelig Folkeparti	CR	11.8	20
Senterpartiet (Agrarian)	C	6.8	21
Venstre (Liberal)	C	3.4	1
Anti-EEC Venstre	C	2.3	2
Arbeiderpartiet (Labour)	SD	35.5	62
Socialistisk Folkeparti	S	11.2	16
Kommunistiske Parti	K		
Oman			
Sultanate	—	—	—
Pakistan			
Presidential government since Dec. 20, 1971	—	—	—
Panama (August 1972)			
No-party assembly of "corregidores"	—	—	500
Papua-New Guinea (1972)			
United Party	...	...	40
Pangu Party (M. T. Somare) National coalition	...	...	24
People's Progress Party	...	...	12
National Party	...	...	12
Paraguay (February 1973)			
Partido Colorado (A. Stroessner)	R	84.0	40
Partido Liberal Radical	C	12.0	16
Partido Liberal	C	3.0	4
Peru			
Military government since Oct. 3, 1968	—	—	—
Philippines			
Martial law since Sept. 23, 1972	—	—	—
Poland (March 1972)			
Polish United Workers' Party	Front of National Unity	99.9	255
United Peasants' Party	—		117
Democratic Party			39
Nonparty			49
Portugal (April 1975)			
Centre Democratic Social Party	CR	8.0	16
Popular Democratic Party	C	26.0	80
Socialist Party	SD	38.0	116
Portuguese Democratic Movement	EL	4.0	5
Communist Party	K	12.5	30
Qatar			
Emirate	—	—	—
Rhodesia (July 1974)			
Rhodesian Front (European)	R	72.0	50
Centre Party (mainly African)	C	...	6
Independents	—	...	2
African National Council (boycotted the elections)			
Romania (March 1975)			
Communist-controlled Socialist Unity Front	—	99.9	349
Rwanda			
Military government since July 5, 1973	—	—	—
San Marino (September 1974)			
Partito Democratico-Cristiano	CR	...	25
Partito Social-Democratico	SD	...	9
Partito Socialista	S	...	8
Partito Comunista	K	...	15
Others	—	...	3
São Tomé and Príncipe (1975)			
Movimento de Libertação de São Tomé e Príncipe	—	—	...
Saudi Arabia			
Royal government	—	—	—
Senegal (January 1973)			
Union Progressiste Sénégalaise	—	99.9	100
Sierra Leone (May 1973)			
All People's Congress	—	...	84
Others	—	...	13
Singapore (September 1972)			
People's Action Party (Lee Kuan Yew)	C	70.0	65
Four opposition parties	—	30.0	0
Somalia			
Military government since Oct. 21, 1969	—	—	—
South Africa (April 1974)			
National Party	R	57.1	123
United Party	C	32.7	41
Progressive Party	L	5.3	7
Others	—	4.9	1
Spain (1971)			
Movimiento Nacional	—	...	558
Sri Lanka (May 1970)			
United National (D. Senanayake)	R	...	17
Sri Lanka Freedom (S. Bandaranaike)	C	...	91
Federal (Tamil)	C	...	13
Lanka Sama Samaja (pro-Chinese)	K	...	19
Communist (pro-Soviet)	K	...	6
Others	—	...	5
Sudan			
Military government since May 25, 1969	—	—	—
Surinam (1975)			
National Unity coalition (H. Arron)	—	...	22
Vatan Hitkarie Party (J. Lachmon)	...	...	17
Swaziland			
Royal government	—	—	—
Sweden (September 1973)			
Moderata Samlingspartiet (ex-Höger)	R	14.3	51
Centerpartiet (ex-Agrarian)	CR	25.1	90
Folkpartiet (Liberal)	C	9.4	34
Socialdemokratiska Arbetarepartiet	SD	43.5	156
Vänsterpartiet Kommunisterna	K	5.3	19
Switzerland (October 1975)			
Christian Democrats	R	...	46
National Action (V. Oehen)	R	...	2
Republican Movement	R	...	4
Evangelical People's	R	...	3
Swiss People's (ex-Middle Class)	CR	...	21
Radical-Democrats (Freisinnig)	C	...	47
League of Independents	C	...	11
Liberal Democrats	L	...	6
Social Democrats	SD	...	55
Socialist Autonomous	EL	...	1
Communist (Partei der Arbeit)	K	...	4
Syria			
Baath and military government	—	—	—
Taiwan (Republic of China)			
Nationalist (Kuomintang)	—	...	773
Tanzania (October 1975)			
Tanganyika African National Union	C	—	...
Zanzibar Afro-Shirazi (nominated)	L	—	...
Thailand (January 1975)			
Social Nationalist Party	R	...	16
Democratic Party	CR	...	72
United Thai People's Party	CR	...	28
Social Agrarian Party	C	...	19
Social Justice Party	L	...	45
Social Action Party	L	...	18
Socialist Party	SD	...	15
United Socialist Front	EL	...	10
New Forces Party	K	...	12
Others (13 parties)	—	...	34
Togo			
Military government since Jan. 13, 1967	—	—	—
Tonga (June 1972)			
Legislative Assembly (partially elected)	—	—	21
Trinidad and Tobago (May 1971)			
People's National Movement (E. Williams)	C	...	36
Action Committee for Dedicated Citizens	L	...	0
Tunisia (November 1974)			
Parti Socialist Destourien	—	99.0	112
Turkey (October 1973)			
Nationalist Action	ER	3.4	3
National Salvation (N. Erbakan)	R	11.8	49
Turkish Justice (S. Demirel)	CR	29.8	149
Democratic	C	11.9	44
Republican Reliance (T. Feyzioglu)	C	5.3	13
Republican People's (B. Ecevit)	L	33.3	185
Turkish Unity	EL	1.1	1
Others	—	...	6
Uganda			
Uganda People's Congress	—	—	—
Union of Soviet Socialist Republics (1974)			
Communist Party of the Soviet Union	—	99.8	767
United Arab Emirates			
Federal government of seven emirates	—	—	—
United Kingdom (October 1974)			
Conservative	R	35.8	276
Liberal	C	18.3	13
Labour	L	39.3	319
Scottish National Party	...	...	11
United Ulster Unionists	...	...	10
Plaid Cymru (Welsh Nationalists)	—	...	3
Others	—	...	3
United States (November 1974)			
Republican	CR	...	144
Democratic	C	...	291
Upper Volta			
Military government since Feb. 8, 1974	—	—	—
Uruguay			
Rule by Council of State as of June 1973	—	—	—
Venezuela (December 1973)			
Cruzada Cívica Nacional	ER	4.3	7
Unión Republicana Democrática	R	3.2	5
COPEI (Social Christians)	C	30.2	64
Acción Democrática	L	44.3	102
Movimiento al Socialismo	SD	5.3	9
Fuerza Democrática Popular	S	1.2	2
Movimiento Electoral del Pueblo	EL	5.0	8
Partido Comunista Venezuelano	K	1.2	2
Others (four parties)	—	...	4
Vietnam, North			
Lao Dong (Communist Party)	—	...	420
Vietnam, South			
People's Republican government	—	—	—
Western Samoa			
No political parties	—	—	—
Yemen, People's Democratic Republic			
National Liberation Front	—	—	—
Yemen Arab Republic			
Military government since June 13, 1974	—	—	—
Yugoslavia (May 1974)			
Communist-controlled Federal Chamber	—	—	220
Zaire (1975)			
Mouvement Populaire de la Révolution	—	98	420
Zambia (1973)			
United National Independence Party	—	80	125

(K. M. SMOGORZEWSKI)

Populations and Areas

In its 200 years of existence, the United States has experienced explosive changes in the size and character of its population. In 1776 there were some 2.5 million to 3 million Americans, living for the most part on farms or in very small towns. The largest cities of the day, New York and Philadelphia, had approximately 25,000 residents each. The largest state, Virginia, had a reputed population of 692,000 people in 1790.

The American population increased rapidly during the 1800s, spreading westward to the Pacific and settling in an ever increasing number of towns. As industry grew, the towns became cities. By the start of the Civil War, in 1860, the population of the country numbered more than 31 million. New York, the first stop for many immigrants, had become the largest state with 3.9 million people, followed by Pennsylvania with 2.9 million. Largely rural Virginia had slipped to ninth place. New York City was the largest city with 814,000 people.

By 1900 Americans numbered in excess of 75 million, a population swelled by heavy immigration from Europe as well as some from Africa and Asia. More than 46 million people have immigrated to the U.S. since 1820, almost 9 million of them between 1900 and 1909. In the last decennial census, in 1970, the U.S. reported over 203 million people, and by 1975 there were an estimated 213 million. Almost three out of every four lived in cities or suburbs, which occupied only 1.5% of the land. California, which had only sparse Spanish and Indian settlements in 1776, had become the most populous state by 1970, with 20 million people. New York remained first among cities with 7.9 million in the city and 17 million in its three-state metropolitan area.

Though the U.S. experienced high growth in its first two centuries—the number of infants born each year in the 1970s was greater than the total population in 1776—there had been a definite slowdown in recent years. The birthrate dropped to an all-time low of 14.9 per 1,000 population in 1974. At the same time, the death rate decreased to 9.1 per 1,000, so the nation was currently growing at less than 1% a year. During colonial times the birthrate was estimated at 55 per 1,000, but the high incidence of disease took a heavy toll. Life expectancy was only 35, whereas in 1970 the average person could expect to live to 72. In the last few years the Census Bureau noted another trend. The older—and largest—metropolitan areas were beginning to lose population while retirement centres such as Phoenix, Ariz., and Miami-Fort Lauderdale and Tampa-St. Petersburg in Florida were receiving a great influx of newcomers.

The remarkable growth of the U.S. was the result of both high birthrates and heavy immigration.

continued on page 567

Polo:
see Equestrian Sports; Water Sports

World Populations and Areas*

Country	AREA AND POPULATION: MIDYEAR 1974			POPULATION AT MOST RECENT CENSUS					AGE DISTRIBUTION (%)†					
	Area in sq.mi.	Total population	Persons per sq.mi.	Date of census	Total population	% Male	% Female	% Urban	0 to 14	15 to 29	30 to 44	45 to 59	60 to 75	75 and over
AFRICA														
Afars and Issas	8,900	220,000	24.7	1960–61	81,200	...	...	57.4	...	...	...	...	...	...
Algeria	896,593	16,275,000	18.2	1966	11,833,126	50.2	49.8	38.8	47.1	22.4	14.9	8.7	5.0	1.8
Angola	481,350	6,204,000	12.9	1970	5,673,872	...	...	14.9	...	...	...	...	...	...
Botswana	222,000	661,000	3.0	1971	574,094	45.7	54.3	8.4	46.1	21.7	12.8	9.0	5.0	5.4
British Indian Ocean Territory	85	—	—	1971	110	...	...	...	...	...	...	...	...	...
Burundi	10,747	3,678,000	342.2	1970–71	3,350,000	...	...	3.5	...	...	...	...	...	...
Cameroon	179,558	6,282,000	35.0	1960–65	5,017,000	...	...	...	...	...	...	...	...	...
Cape Verde Islands	1,557	291,000	186.9	1970	272,071	...	...	19.7	...	...	...	...	...	...
Central African Rep.	241,305	1,752,000	7.3	1959–60	1,177,000	47.8	52.2	6.8	40.0	21.9	25.7	10.4	—2.0—	
Chad	495,750	3,949,000	8.0	1964	3,254,000	48.2	51.8	7.8	45.6	22.2	19.3	9.3	—3.6—	
Comoro Islands	863	298,000	345.3	1966	244,905	49.2	50.8	13.5	44.1	23.6	15.7	8.7	4.2	3.8
Congo	132,047	1,313,000	9.9	1974	1,300,120	48.7	51.3	39.8	...	...	...	...	...	...
Dahomey (Benin)	43,475	3,029,000	69.7	1961	2,082,511	49.0	51.0	9.3	46.0	22.7	16.4	9.3	—5.6—	
Egypt	386,900	36,417,000	94.1	1966	30,075,858	50.5	49.5	41.2	...	...	...	...	...	...
Equatorial Guinea	10,830	303,000	28.0	1965	277,240	52.8	47.2	...	35.1	—48.5—		—16.4—		
Ethiopia	471,800	27,239,000	57.7	1970	24,068,800	50.7	49.3	9.7	43.5	27.0	16.3	8.8	3.7	0.7
French Southern and Antarctic Lands	2,844	—	—	—	—	—	—	—	—	—	—	—	—	—
Gabon	103,347	1,106,000	10.7	1970	950,009	47.9	52.1	26.9	35.4	19.2	22.2	16.3	6.3	0.6
Gambia, The	4,467	510,000	114.2	1973	494,279	50.9	49.1	13.1	41.3	26.5	17.6	8.3	4.3	1.7
Ghana	92,100	9,607,000	104.3	1970	8,559,313	49.6	50.4	28.9	46.9	24.4	15.8	7.5	3.8	1.6
Guinea	94,926	4,309,000	45.4	1972	5,143,284	...	...	...	...	...	...	...	...	...
Guinea-Bissau	13,948	517,000	37.1	1970	487,448	48.7	51.3	11.5	...	...	...	...	...	...
Ivory Coast	123,484	6,673,000	54.0	—	—	—	—	—	—	—	—	—	—	—
Kenya	224,961	12,912,000	57.4	1969	10,942,705	50.1	49.9	9.9	48.4	25.1	13.6	7.5	3.9	1.5
Lesotho	11,720	1,016,000	86.7	1966	852,631	43.2	56.8	4.4	43.5	22.1	13.9	11.5	6.8	2.0
Liberia	43,000	1,667,000	38.8	1974	1,496,000	...	...	...	...	...	...	...	...	...
Libya	675,000	2,352,000	3.5	1973	2,257,037	53.2	46.8	...	...	...	...	...	...	...
Malagasy Rep.	226,444	7,785,000	34.4	1966	6,200,000	49.2	50.8	...	46.5	22.3	15.2	10.1	—5.8—	
Malawi	45,747	4,900,000	107.1	1966	4,039,583	47.4	52.6	5.0	43.9	25.2	15.5	9.7	—5.7—	
Mali	478,822	5,557,000	11.6	1960–61	3,484,500	...	...	...	...	...	...	...	...	...
Mauritania	398,000	1,290,000	3.2	1964–65	1,030,000	50.1	49.9	...	43.9	24.5	16.3	10.0	—5.3—	
Mauritius	787	872,000	1,108.0	1972	851,334	50.0	50.0	42.9	40.3	28.6	14.5	11.0	4.9	0.7
Morocco	177,117	16,880,000	95.3	1971	15,379,259	50.1	49.9	35.4	46.2	22.4	16.0	8.3	5.3	1.8
Mozambique	308,642	9,029,000	29.3	1970	8,233,834	...	...	...	...	...	...	...	...	...
Niger	489,000	4,476,000	9.2	1959–60	2,611,473	49.7	50.3	...	...	...	...	...	...	...
Nigeria	356,669	61,219,000	171.6	1973	79,760,000	...	...	...	...	...	...	...	...	...
Réunion	970	490,000	505.2	1967	416,525	48.8	51.2	42.8	45.7	23.5	15.8	9.7	4.2	1.1
Rhodesia	150,873	6,100,000	40.4	1969	5,099,340	50.3	49.7	16.8	47.2	25.4	15.7	8.4	—3.3—	
Rwanda	10,169	4,123,000	405.4	1970	3,735,585	47.8	52.2	3.2	43.8	24.2	15.2	11.6	—5.2—	
St. Helena	119	5,000	42.0	1966	4,649	48.0	52.0	0	39.0	21.2	13.9	13.2	10.0	2.7
São Tomé and Príncipe	372	79,000	212.4	1970	73,811	50.8	49.2	...	...	...	...	...	...	...
Senegal	78,685	4,231,000	53.8	1960–61	3,109,840	...	...	...	...	...	...	...	...	...
Seychelles	107	58,000	542.1	1971	52,650	49.8	50.2	26.1	43.4	21.0	15.1	11.2	7.0	2.3
Sierra Leone	27,925	2,707,000	96.9	1974	2,730,000	...	...	...	...	...	...	...	...	...

World Populations and Areas* *(Continued)*

Country	AREA AND POPULATION: MIDYEAR 1974 Area in sq.mi.	Total population	Persons per sq.mi.	POPULATION AT MOST RECENT CENSUS Date of census	Total population	% Male	% Female	% Urban	AGE DISTRIBUTION (%)† 0 to 14	15 to 29	30 to 44	45 to 59	60 to 75	75 and over
AFRICA (cont.)														
Somalia	246,300	3,086,000	12.5	—	—	—	—	—	—	—	—	—	—	—
South Africa	471,445	24,920,000	52.9	1970	21,448,169	49.2	50.8	47.9	40.8	26.1	16.7	10.0	5.0	1.3
South West Africa (Namibia)	318,261	852,000	2.7	1970	746,328	50.8	49.2	24.9	...	...	...	...	...	...
Spanish Sahara	103,000	108,000	1.0	1970	76,425	57.5	42.5	45.3	42.9	27.2	16.3	7.4	4.4	1.8
Sudan	967,500	17,324,000	17.9	1973	14,171,732‡	...	...	...	...	...	...	...	...	...
Swaziland	6,704	478,000	71.3	1966	374,571	47.7	52.3	7.1	46.7	24.6	14.4	8.5	4.5	1.3
Tanzania	364,943	14,763,000	40.5	1967	12,313,469	48.8	51.2	5.5	43.9	24.7	15.4	8.6	4.1	3.3
Togo	21,925	2,171,000	99.0	1970	1,953,778	48.1	51.9	...	...	...	...	...	...	...
Tunisia	63,379	5,641,000	89.0	1966	4,533,351	51.1	48.9	40.1	46.3	21.4	16.6	10.1	4.4	1.2
Uganda	91,452	11,172,000	122.2	1969	9,548,847	50.5	49.5	7.7	46.2	24.0	15.7	8.3	4.2	1.6
Upper Volta	105,869	5,895,000	55.7	—	—	—	—	—	—	—	—	—	—	—
Zaire	905,365	24,222,000	26.8	—	—	—	—	—	—	—	—	—	—	—
Zambia	290,586	4,751,000	16.3	1969	4,056,995	49.0	51.0	29.6	46.3	24.0	16.6	9.4	3.0	0.7
Total AFRICA	11,680,700	393,764,000												
ANTARCTICA total	5,500,000	§	—											
ASIA														
Afghanistan	252,000	18,796,000	74.6	—	—	—	—	—	—	—	—	—	—	—
Bahrain	256	239,000	933.6	1971	216,078	53.8	46.2	78.1	44.3	25.3	16.9	9.0	3.7	0.8
Bangladesh	55,126	74,991,000	1,360.4	1974	71,316,517	...	...	...	...	...	...	...	...	...
Bhutan	18,000	1,146,000	63.7	1969	1,034,774	...	...	...	...	...	...	...	...	...
Brunei	2,226	144,000	64.7	1971	136,256	53.4	46.6	63.6	43.4	28.0	15.7	8.1	3.9	0.9
Burma	261,789	30,310,000	115.8	1973	28,885,867	...	...	...	...	...	...	...	...	...
Cambodia	69,898	7,888,000	112.9	1962	5,728,771	50.0	50.0	10.3	43.8	24.9	16.8	9.8	4.1	0.6
China	3,691,500	824,961,000	223.5	1953	574,205,940	51.8	48.2	13.3	35.9	25.1	18.8	12.9	6.3	1.0
Cyprus	3,572	641,000	179.5	1973	631,778	49.5	50.5	42.2	...	...	...	...	...	...
Hong Kong	403	4,249,000	10,543.4	1971	3,948,179	50.7	49.3	...	35.8	24.3	18.1	14.3	6.2	1.3
India	1,266,602	586,266,000	462.9	1971	547,949,809	51.8	48.2	19.9	41.9	24.1	17.8	10.2	4.9	1.1
Indonesia	782,663	127,586,000	163.0	1971	118,459,845	49.2	50.8	17.5	44.1	24.0	18.6	9.0	3.7	0.6
Iran	636,000	31,955,000	50.2	1966	25,788,722	51.8	48.2	38.0	46.1	21.7	17.6	8.0	5.4	1.2
Iraq	168,928	10,765,000	63.7	1965	8,047,415	51.0	49.0	44.1	47.9	21.0	15.3	8.7	4.9	2.2
Israel	7,992	3,299,000	412.8	1972	3,147,683	50.3	49.7	85.3	32.6	26.9	15.6	13.6	9.2	2.0
Japan	145,747	109,671,000	752.5	1970	104,665,171	48.6	51.4	72.1	23.7	27.5	22.9	14.4	8.4	3.1
Jordan	36,832	2,618,000	71.1	1961	1,706,226	50.9	49.1	43.9	45.4	26.1	13.7	7.5	5.1	1.8
Korea, North	46,800	15,439,000	329.9	—	—	—	—	—	—	—	—	—	—	—
Korea, South	38,130	33,459,000	877.5	1970	31,435,252	48.4	51.6	40.4	42.1	24.9	17.5	10.1	4.5	0.9
Kuwait	6,880	929,000	135.0	1975	990,389	...	...	...	...	...	...	...	...	...
Laos	91,400	3,257,000	35.6	—	—	—	—	—	—	—	—	—	—	—
Lebanon	3,950	2,782,000	704.3	1970	2,126,325	50.8	49.2	60.1	42.6	23.8	16.7	9.1	—7.7—	
Macau	6	266,000	44,333.3	1970	248,636	51.4	48.6	100.0	37.6	28.9	15.0	11.3	5.9	1.1
Malaysia	127,316	11,700,000	91.9	1970	10,434,034‖	50.4	49.6	26.7	...	...	...	...	...	...
Maldives	115	129,000	1,121.7	1974	128,697	53.1	46.9	—	44.9	22.8	19.0	9.4	3.4	0.4
Mongolia	604,000	1,403,000	2.3	1969	1,197,600	49.9	50.1	44.0	...	...	...	...	...	...
Nepal	54,362	12,321,000	226.6	1971	11,555,983	49.7	50.3	13.8	40.5	25.5	18.7	9.7	—5.6—	
Oman	82,000	743,000	9.1	—	—	—	—	—	—	—	—	—	—	—
Pakistan	307,374	68,214,000	221.9	1972	64,892,000	53.0	47.0	...	...	...	...	...	...	...
Philippines	115,800	41,457,000	358.0	1970	36,684,486	49.8	50.2	31.8	43.1	27.1	15.4	9.0	4.3	1.1
Portuguese Timor	5,763	658,000	114.2	1970	609,477	51.9	48.1	...	35.5	25.5	19.9	12.3	5.8	1.0
Qatar	4,400	170,000	38.6	—	—	—	—	—	—	—	—	—	—	—
Saudi Arabia	872,000¶	8,702,000	10.0	—	—	—	—	—	—	—	—	—	—	—
Singapore	227	2,219,000	9,775.3	1970	2,074,507	51.2	48.8	100.0	38.8	28.1	16.9	10.5	4.9	0.8
Sri Lanka	25,332	13,679,000	540.0	1971	12,771,143	51.3	48.7	22.4	39.3	27.8	15.9	10.5	5.2	1.3
Syria	71,498	7,121,000	99.6	1970	6,304,685	51.3	48.7	43.5	49.3	22.4	14.3	7.5	4.8	1.7
Taiwan	13,893	15,701,000	1,130.1	1970	14,693,036	52.3	47.7	...	40.5	26.4	17.5	10.9	4.0	0.7
Thailand	198,500	41,023,000	206.7	1970	34,397,374	49.6	50.4	13.4	45.5	24.9	16.1	8.6	—4.9—	
Turkey	300,948	38,270,000	127.2	1970	35,605,176	50.6	49.4	61.5	41.9	25.0	17.3	8.9	—6.9—	
United Arab Emirates	37,000	430,000	11.6	1968	179,126	62.1	37.9	...	33.6	34.4	25.3	4.0	2.0	0.6
Vietnam, North	63,360	23,767,000	375.1	1974	23,767,300	...	...	...	...	...	...	...	...	...
Vietnam, South	67,293	19,582,000	291.0	—	—	—	—	—	—	—	—	—	—	—
Yemen (Aden)	111,074	1,633,000	14.7	1973	1,590,275	49.5	50.5	33.3	47.3	20.8	15.8	8.6	—6.6—	
Yemen (San'a')	77,200	5,238,000	67.8	1975	5,237,893	47.6	52.4	8.2	...	...	...	...	...	...
Total ASIA♀	17,224,700	2,269,072,000												
EUROPE														
Albania	11,100	2,378,000	214.2	1960	1,626,315	51.4	48.6	30.9	42.7	—57.3—				
Andorra	179	25,000	139.7	1975										
Austria	32,375	7,528,000	232.5	1971	7,456,403	47.0	53.0	51.9	24.4	20.5	18.3	16.5	15.5	4.8
Belgium	11,782	9,772,000	829.4	1970	9,650,944	48.9	51.1	...	23.5	21.0	19.4	17.1	14.4	4.6
Bulgaria	42,823	8,679,000	202.7	1965	8,227,866	50.0	50.0	46.5	17.8	22.6	23.8	16.5	10.3	9.0
Channel Islands	75	126,000	1,680.0	1971	126,363	48.5	51.5	...	21.8	21.4	18.4	18.1	14.9	5.3
Czechoslovakia	49,374	14,686,000	297.4	1970	14,344,787	48.7	51.3	55.5	23.1	24.8	18.4	16.7	13.6	3.4
Denmark	16,630	5,045,000	303.4	1970	4,937,784	49.6	50.4	79.9	23.2	23.8	17.7	17.8	13.4	4.1
Faeroe Islands	540	40,000	74.1	1970	38,612	52.2	47.8	...	31.8	23.0	16.5	16.0	9.4	3.3
Finland	130,129	4,682,000	36.0	1970	4,598,336	48.3	51.7	50.9	24.3	26.0	18.6	16.6	11.6	2.9
France	210,039	52,507,000	250.0	1968	49,654,556	48.7	51.3	70.0	23.7	21.9	19.7	15.9	13.7	5.1
Germany, East	41,768	17,166,000	411.0	1971	17,068,318	46.1	53.9	73.8	23.3	19.9	20.1	14.7	16.9	5.1
Germany, West	95,985	62,041,000	646.4	1970	60,650,599	47.6	52.4	...	23.2	21.3	19.7	16.6	15.0	4.2
Gibraltar	2.25	29,000	12,888.9	1970	26,833	48.1	51.9	91.9	22.9	22.7	21.1	18.7	11.2	3.4
Greece	50,960	8,962,000	175.9	1971	8,768,640	49.8	50.2	53.2	24.9	20.4	21.9	16.5	12.5	3.8
Hungary	35,920	10,458,000	291.1	1970	10,322,099	48.5	51.5	45.2	21.1	23.6	20.5	17.7	13.6	3.5
Iceland	39,769	215,000	5.4	1970	204,930	50.6	49.4	...	32.3	25.1	16.4	13.7	9.0	3.5
Ireland	27,136	3,086,000	113.7	1971	2,978,248	50.2	49.8	52.2	31.3	22.0	15.2	15.9	11.6	4.0
Isle of Man	221	56,000	253.4	1971	56,289	47.0	53.0	55.7	19.9	18.3	14.9	19.0	20.9	7.0
Italy	116,313	55,361,000	476.0	1971	54,136,547	48.9	51.1	...	24.4	21.2	20.7	17.0	12.8	3.9
Liechtenstein	62	24,000	387.1	1970	21,350	49.7	50.3	...	27.9	27.1	18.6	14.5	9.3	2.6
Luxembourg	999	342,000	342.3	1970	339,812	49.0	51.0	68.4	22.1	20.5	21.4	17.5	14.6	3.9
Malta	122	298,000	2,442.6	1967	314,216	47.9	52.1	94.3	29.8	25.9	17.6	13.8	10.2	2.7
Monaco	0.73	24,000	32,876.7	1968	23,035	45.2	54.8	100.0	12.9	17.5	18.4	20.9	21.2	9.1
Netherlands, The	15,892	13,541,000	852.1	1971	13,045,785	50.0	50.0	...	...	...	...	...	...	...
Norway	125,053	3,987,000	31.9	1970	3,888,305	49.7	50.3	42.6	24.4	22.5	16.0	18.8	13.5	4.8
Poland	120,725	33,691,000	279.1	1970	32,642,270	48.6	51.4	52.3	26.4	25.5	20.4	14.6	10.6	2.5
Portugal	35,383	8,735,000	246.9	1970	8,545,120	47.4	52.6	...	28.4	21.9	19.0	16.2	11.2	3.3
Romania	91,700	21,029,000	229.3	1966	19,103,163	48.9	51.1	38.2	26.3	23.1	23.3	15.3	9.9	2.1
San Marino	24	19,000	791.7	1947	12,100	49.3	50.7	...	...	...	...	...	...	...
Spain	194,885	35,225,000	180.7	1970	33,956,047	48.9	51.1	54.7	27.8	22.0	19.9	16.1	10.8	3.4
Svalbard and Jan Mayen	24,101	—	—	1960	3,431	...	...	...	...	...	...	...	...	...
Sweden	173,732	8,161,000	47.0	1970	8,076,903	49.9	50.1	81.4	20.6	22.8	17.4	19.3	14.8	5.1

World Populations and Areas* *(Continued)*

Country	AREA AND POPULATION: MIDYEAR 1974 Area in sq.mi.	Total population	Persons per sq.mi.	POPULATION AT MOST RECENT CENSUS Date of census	Total population	% Male	% Female	% Urban	AGE DISTRIBUTION (%)† 0 to 14	15 to 29	30 to 44	45 to 59	60 to 75	75 and over
EUROPE (cont.)														
Switzerland	15,943	6,481,000	406.5	1970	6,269,783	49.3	50.7	52.0	23.4	23.7	20.2	16.3	12.5	3.9
United Kingdom	94,217	56,056,000	595.0	1971	55,515,602	48.5	51.5	...	24.1	21.0	17.6	18.3	14.3	4.7
Vatican City	0.17	1,000	5,882.4	—	—	—	—	—	—	—	—	—	—	—
Yugoslavia	98,766	21,153,000	214.2	1971	20,522,972	49.1	50.9	38.6	27.2	24.6	22.7	13.5	9.8	2.2
Total EUROPE♀	4,055,700	660,418,000												
NORTH AMERICA														
Antigua	171	70,000	409.4	1970	64,794	47.2	52.8	33.7	44.0	24.2	12.0	11.7	——8.0——	
Bahamas, The	5,382	197,000	36.6	1970	168,812	50.0	50.0	71.4	43.6	24.3	16.8	9.8	4.4	1.1
Barbados	166	244,000	1,469.9	1970	235,229	48.0	52.0	3.7	35.9	27.2	12.9	12.8	8.7	2.5
Belize (British Honduras)	8,866	136,000	15.3	1970	119,934	50.6	49.4	54.4	49.3	22.5	13.0	8.7	5.0	1.5
Bermuda	21	55,000	2,619.0	1970	52,976	50.2	49.8	6.9	30.0	25.8	20.5	14.4	7.7	2.0
British Virgin Islands	59	11,000	186.4	1970	10,298	53.0	47.0	21.9	39.2	29.1	14.7	10.0	5.1	1.9
Canada	3,851,809	22,479,000	5.8	1971	21,568,211	50.0	50.0	76.1	29.6	18.6	25.1	10.6	10.9	5.2
Canal Zone	362	46,000	127.1	1970	44,198	53.9	46.1	5.8	31.8	31.3	19.8	14.1	2.2	0.8
Cayman Islands	100	11,000	110.0	1970	10,249	46.8	53.2	61.1	...	...	...	...	...	...
Costa Rica	19,652	1,921,000	97.7	1973	1,871,780	50.1	49.9	40.6	43.3	27.0	14.2	8.4	4.4	2.7
Cuba	42,827	9,090,000	212.2	1970	8,569,121	51.3	48.7	60.3	27.0	25.0	16.9	12.1	6.8	2.2
Dominica	298	74,000	248.3	1970	70,302	47.4	52.6	46.2	49.1	21.2	11.2	10.0	6.3	2.2
Dominican Republic	18,658	4,562,000	244.5	1970	4,006,405	50.4	49.6	40.0	47.2	24.8	15.2	7.8	3.8	1.2
El Salvador	8,124	3,980,000	489.9	1971	3,541,010	49.6	50.4	39.4	46.2	25.1	15.2	8.2	4.3	1.0
Greenland	840,000	49,000	0.06	1970	46,531	52.5	47.5	...	43.4	24.8	18.8	8.5	3.9	0.6
Grenada	133	107,000	804.5	1970	96,542	46.2	53.8		47.1	23.0	11.6	9.4	6.6	2.2
Guadeloupe	687	335,000	487.6	1974	324,500	...	...	41.9	41.2	22.8	14.3	10.4	5.3	1.7
Guatemala	42,042	5,175,000	123.1	1973	5,211,929	50.0	50.0	33.6	45.1	26.7	15.1	8.3	——4.8——	
Haiti	10,714	4,514,000	421.3	1971	4,314,628	48.2	51.8	20.4	41.5	25.8	16.5	9.5	5.0	1.7
Honduras	43,277	2,654,000	61.3	1974	2,653,857	49.5	50.5	37.5	...	...	...	...	...	...
Jamaica	4,244	1,998,000	470.8	1970	1,813,594	49.8	50.2	41.4	37.5	25.1	15.2	12.4	7.5	2.3
Martinique	431	358,000	830.6	1967	320,030	48.5	51.5	45.8	43.5	22.5	15.2	11.1	5.8	1.9
Mexico	761,604	58,118,000	76.3	1970	48,225,238	49.9	50.1	58.7	46.2	25.6	14.6	8.0	4.4	1.2
Montserrat	40	13,000	325.0	1970	11,458	46.9	53.1	88.9	37.9	20.6	9.8	12.1	10.7	8.9
Netherlands Antilles	385	238,000	618.2	1972	223,196	48.8	51.2	...	38.0	26.7	16.7	10.3	6.4	1.9
Nicaragua	50,000	2,084,000	61.7	1971	1,877,972	48.3	51.7	48.0	48.1			——51.9——		
Panama	29,209	1,631,000	55.8	1970	1,428,082	50.7	49.3	47.6	43.4	26.1	15.2	9.6	4.3	1.4
Puerto Rico	3,421	3,031,000	886.0	1970	2,712,033	49.0	51.0	58.1	36.5	26.1	15.9	11.9	7.1	2.5
St. Christopher-Nevis-Anguilla	135	65,000	481.5	1970	44,884	46.9	53.1	31.7	48.4	18.9	9.5	12.1	8.7	2.4
St. Lucia	238	111,000	466.4	1970	101,064	47.5	52.5	54.2	49.6	21.3	11.6	9.8	5.5	2.2
St. Pierre and Miquelon	93	6,000	64.5	1974	5,762	...	...	...	...	...	...	...	...	...
St. Vincent	150	94,000	626.7	1970	89,129	47.4	52.6	...	...	...	...	...	...	...
Trinidad and Tobago	1,980	1,062,000	536.4	1970	931,071	49.4	50.6	...	42.1	——40.4——			——17.5——	
Turks and Caicos Islands	193	6,000	31.1	1970	5,588	47.4	52.6	—	47.1	20.4	12.0	11.1	7.0	2.5
United States	3,615,122	211,909,000	58.6	1970	203,211,926	48.7	51.3	73.5	28.6	24.0	17.0	16.3	10.4	3.7
Virgin Islands of the U.S.	133	65,000	488.7	1970	62,468	49.9	50.1	24.4	35.7	28.3	19.4	10.8	4.4	1.4
Total NORTH AMERICA	9,360,700	336,499,000												
OCEANIA														
American Samoa	76	29,000	381.6	1974	29,200	...	...	...	...	...	...	...	...	...
Australia	2,967,900	13,339,000	4.5	1971	12,755,638	50.3	49.7	...	28.8	24.6	19.9	15.4	8.6	2.2
Canton and Enderbury Islands	27	—	—	1970	0	—	—	—	—	—	—	—	—	—
Christmas Island	52	3,000	57.7	1971	2,691	64.4	35.6	0	30.8	34.6	22.0	10.8	1.4	0.4
Cocos (Keeling) Islands	6	1,000	166.7	1971	618	50.5	49.5	0	...	...	...	...	...	...
Cook Islands	93	19,000	204.3	1971	21,317	51.2	48.8	0	51.6	22.5	12.5	——14.4——		
Fiji	7,055	560,000	79.4	1966	476,727	50.9	49.1	33.4	46.7	26.6	14.6	8.2	2.9	1.0
French Polynesia	1,261	124,000	98.3	1971	117,664	53.1	46.9	19.0	45.5	23.7	16.6	9.0	3.7	1.5
Gilbert Islands	102	48,000	470.6	1968	44,206	49.5	50.5	...	45.0	23.8	14.3	9.9	5.2	1.3
Guam	212	110,000	518.9	1970	84,996	55.7	44.3	25.5	39.7	29.1	19.3	8.9	2.5	0.5
Johnston Island	1	1,000	1,000.0	1970	1,007	...	...	0	...	...	...	...	...	...
Midway Islands	2	2,000	1,000.0	1970	2,220	...	...	0	...	...	...	...	...	...
Nauru	8	7,000	875.0	1966	6,055	53.3	46.7	0	40.0	24.7	23.9	9.2	2.1	0.1
New Caledonia	7,366	126,000	17.1	1969	100,579	52.3	47.7	41.6	34.8	26.6	19.2	12.4	5.4	1.6
New Hebrides	5,700	93,000	16.3	1967	77,988	52.1	47.9	12.0	45.6	26.0	15.5	8.5	——4.4——	
New Zealand	103,736	3,027,000	29.2	1971	2,862,631	50.0	50.0	81.4	31.8	23.9	16.8	15.1	9.4	3.0
Niue	100	4,000	40.0	1971	4,990	50.2	49.8	0	50.7	21.0	13.3	7.8	5.2	2.0
Norfolk Island	14	2,000	142.9	1971	1,683	49.0	51.0	0	25.2	20.7	19.7	18.9	12.5	2.9
Pacific Islands, Trust Territory of the	707	115,000	162.7	1973	114,782	51.5	48.5	...	...	...	...	...	...	...
Papua New Guinea	178,260	2,652,000	14.9	1971	2,489,937	52.0	48.0	11.1	45.2	24.5	17.4	9.9	1.4	1.6
Pitcairn Island	2	70	35.0	1975	70	...	...	0	...	...	...	...	...	...
Solomon Islands	10,983	185,000	16.8	1970	160,998	52.9	47.1	7.0	44.6	25.3	15.9	8.9	4.0	1.3
Tokelau Islands	4	2,000	500.0	1972	1,599	46.1	53.9	0	48.2	18.3	14.3	9.4	6.9	2.7
Tonga	225	98,000	435.6	1966	77,429	51.5	48.5	...	46.3	25.2	15.6	8.1	3.8	1.0
Tuvalu (Ellice) Islands	10	6,000	600.0	1968	5,782	44.8	55.2	...	44.8	20.9	14.8	11.5	6.0	1.7
Wake Island	3	2,000	666.7	1970	1,647	...	...	0	...	...	...	...	...	...
Wallis and Futuna Islands	98	9,000	91.8	1969	8,546	48.9	51.1	0	——95.7——				——4.2——	
Western Samoa	1,133	155,000	136.8	1971	146,627	51.8	48.2	20.6	50.6	24.3	13.1	7.9	3.3	0.8
Total OCEANIA	3,285,100	20,719,000												
SOUTH AMERICA														
Argentina	1,072,163	25,050,000	23.4	1970	23,364,431	49.7	50.3	80.4	29.3	24.6	19.9	15.4	8.6	2.2
Bolivia	424,165	5,470,000	12.9	1950	2,704,165	49.0	51.0	34.9	39.6	27.2	16.6	9.4	5.5	1.7
Brazil	3,286,488	104,243,000	31.7	1970	93,139,037	49.7	50.3	55.9	41.7	27.0				
Chile	292,258	10,405,000	35.6	1970	8,884,768	48.8	51.2	75.1	39.0	25.5	16.6	10.4	5.6	2.9
Colombia	439,737	23,952,000	54.5	1973	12,962,204	...	...	...	...	...	...	...	...	...
Ecuador	109,484	6,552,000	59.8	1974	6,552,095	50.1	49.9	41.3	44.6	26.5	14.7	8.4	4.6	1.3
Falkland Islands	6,150	2,000	0.3	1972	1,957	55.2	44.8	44.7	26.7	22.4		——51.9——		
French Guiana	34,750	58,000	1.7	1967	44,392	54.2	45.8	52.2	35.6	27.4	18.1	12.1	5.5	1.3
Guyana	83,000	774,000	9.3	1970	699,848	49.7	50.3	33.3	47.1	25.1	13.4	9.0	4.4	1.0
Paraguay	157,048	2,572,000	16.4	1972	2,354,071	49.7	50.3	37.4	44.9	25.4	14.5	9.2	4.5	1.5
Peru	496,224	14,531,000	29.3	1972	13,567,939	50.0	50.0	59.6	43.9	25.8	15.6	8.7	——5.9——	
Surinam	70,060	385,000	5.5	1971	384,903	50.0	50.0	...	48.0			——52.0——		
Uruguay	68,536	2,764,000	40.3	1975	2,763,964	49.1	50.9	...	...	...	...	...	...	...
Venezuela	352,144	11,557,000	32.8	1971	10,721,522	50.0	50.0	75.0	35.1	31.7	17.5	10.0	4.4	1.3
Total SOUTH AMERICA	6,892,200	208,315,000												
U.S.S.R.♀	8,649,500	252,064,000	29.1	1970	241,720,134	46.0	54.0	56.3	30.9	19.9	23.5	13.8	——11.8——	
in Asia♀	6,498,500	63,255,000	18.1											
in Europe♀	2,151,000	188,809,000	87.8											
WORLD totalδ	57,999,100	3,888,787,000	74.0											

*Any presentation of population data must include data of varying reliability. This table provides published and unpublished data about the latest census (or comparable demographic survey) and the most recent or reliable midyear 1974 population estimates for the countries of the world. Census figures are only a body of estimates and samples of varying reliability whose quality depends on the completeness of the enumeration. Some countries tabulate only persons actually present, while others include those legally resident, but actually outside the country, on census day. Population estimates are subject to continual correction and revision; their reliability depends on: number of years elapsed since a census control was established, completeness of birth and death registration, international migration data, etc.

†Data for persons of unknown age excluded, so percentages may not add to 100.0.

‡Sudan census excludes three southern autonomous provinces.

§May reach a total of 2,000 persons of all nationalities during the summer.

||West Malaysia only.

¶Includes 7,000 sq.mi. of Iraq-Saudi Arabia neutral zone.

♀Asia and Europe continent totals include corresponding portions of U.S.S.R.

δArea of Antarctica excluded in calculating world density.

continued from page 564
Growth in the rest of the world proceeded more slowly until recently. Some 20 years before the American Revolution the world boasted 730 million people; one hundred years later the population had passed the billion mark, and by 1930 it had reached two billion. As in colonial America, birthrates were exceedingly high, but high death rates held growth to under 1% a year. By the end of World War II medical advances in the less developed countries had drastically curbed the death rate. As a result, it took only 30 years to reach three billion, in late 1960, and 15 years later, in 1975, the world's peoples numbered four billion. At the current rate of growth, 2% annually, a doubling of population could be expected by the year 2010.

In 1975 the world's fastest-growing nations were in Latin America and Africa. The former region, growing by 2.7% annually, could double its 324 million people in only 26 years. Africa was growing at a similar rate, and that continent could double its 401 million people by the year 2000 if its 2.8% growth rate continued. Asia, with 2.3 billion people, was growing by 2.1% annually; it would take 33 years to double its population. The United States and Canada, growing by 0.9%, would require 77 years to double their 237 million, while Europe (excluding the Soviet Union), slowest growing of all, would add another 473 million people in 116 years at its current growth rate of 0.6%.

(WARREN W. EISENBERG)

See also Demography.
[525.A]

Portugal

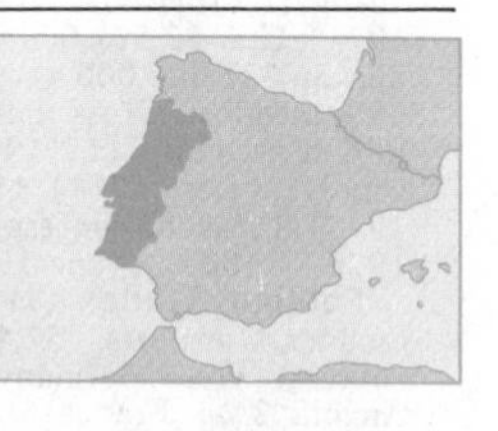

A democratic republic of southwestern Europe, Portugal shares the Iberian Peninsula with Spain. Area: 35,383 sq.mi. (91,641 sq. km.), including the Azores (905 sq.mi.) and Madeira (308 sq.mi.). Pop. (1974 est.): 8,735,000. Cap. and largest city: Lisbon (pop., 1973 est., 757,700). Language: Portuguese. Religion: Roman Catholic. President in 1975, Gen. Francisco da Costa Gomes; premiers, Brig. Gen. Vasco dos Santos Gonçalves and, from August 29, Adm. José Pinheiro de Azevedo.

Domestic Affairs. After an attempted coup, which was led by Gen. António de Spínola on March 11, 1975, and involved a paratroop regiment and two small aircraft, a 28-member Supreme Revolutionary Council, replacing the Junta of National Salvation, was set up by the Armed Forces Movement (AFM) with power to enact legislation without Cabinet approval. At the beginning of April the council drew up a draft constitution which made it clear that the representatives of the AFM intended to retain control of Portugal for three to five years. The political parties agreed reluctantly to accept this even though they were at the time conducting an election campaign for a constituent assembly whose task it was to draft a new constitution for Portugal within 90 days.

The elections were held on April 25, the anniversary of the overthrow of the Caetano regime in 1974. The Socialists led by Mário Soares (*see* BIOGRAPHY) gained about 38% of the votes and the Popular Democrats some 26%, while the Communist Party under Alvaro Cunhal (*see* BIOGRAPHY) received 12.5% of the votes. Despite the success of the Socialist and Popular Democrat parties in the elections, Premier Gonçalves declared that there would be no changes in his 21-member Cabinet, which had only two Socialist and two Popular Democrat representatives.

MINGAM—SIPA PRESS/LIAISON

Communist headquarters north of Oporto were ransacked and the contents burned in April as 5,000 demonstrators, joined by troops sent to protect the headquarters, protested the imposition of Communist influence in Portugal.

On July 8–9 the AFM adopted a plan for a people's democracy in Portugal. The document proposed a pyramidal system, rising from neighbourhood and works councils to local, district, and regional people's assemblies, with a People's National Assembly as the central legislative body. The assemblies were to be elected by a show of hands and would be composed of representatives of the AFM, labour unions, and local authorities. The plan was condemned by the Socialists and Popular Democrats, and they resigned from the government. After the resignations, the fourth provisional government was dissolved by the AFM on July 17.

On July 25 the AFM created the Revolutionary Directorate, a triumvirate composed of President Costa Gomes, Premier Gonçalves, and the commander of the internal security forces (Copcon), Gen. Otelo Saraiva de Carvalho (*see* BIOGRAPHY). The directorate replaced the Supreme Council as the state policymaking body. With widespread anti-Communist riots in the north, a political crisis then developed around the premier and nine politically moderate armed-forces officers on the Supreme Council. After three weeks of endeavours the fifth provisional government was installed on August 8, composed of left-wing officers and civilians. The new government was immediately denounced by "the nine," led by Maj. Melo Antunes, the former foreign minister, as an attempt to install a "bureaucratic dictatorship," and splits already evident in the AFM became very marked. The nine were dismissed from their posts on the Supreme Council on August 9. In order to begin to heal the splits, President Gomes on August 29 appointed Adm. José Pinheiro de Azevedo (*see* BIOGRAPHY), a moderate, as premier and the former premier as chief of staff of the armed forces. The immediate indications were that

The last monument to António de Oliveira Salazar, in the village of his birth, was found decapitated following the riots in late April.

AEI / KEYSTONE

the various units of the armed forces rejected the authority of their new commander in chief, and on September 5 Gonçalves resigned. He and three other supporting members in the Supreme Revolutionary Council were removed and "the nine" reappointed.

On September 19 the sixth provisional government was sworn in. The membership of the government reflected the relative strength of the three main political parties and the moderates of the AFM. It had strong hopes of appealing to a majority of the Portuguese as a government of national unity, capable of carrying the country forward on a socialist path, while guaranteeing liberty, freedom of the press and media, and elections. The government then set about creating authority. The AFM had been split in its support of Gonçalves between the moderates who supported the ideas of the new government and those who wanted to turn Portugal into a people's democracy. The government found it could not rely on many units and Copcon to impose security and thereafter created a new internal security force of units with loyal commands. Lack of discipline in the military remained evident, marked by refusals to embark for foreign duties and participation in antigovernment demonstrations. At the end of September the government fulfilled a pledge to the political parties by taking over all Portuguese radio and television stations; at the same time the Supreme Revolutionary Council banned the dissemination of news on military matters or communiqués unless they came from the president, the chiefs of staff, or the commander of Copcon.

Communist-led labour unions on November 16 organized an antigovernment demonstration in Lisbon that drew a crowd of more than 100,000. On subsequent days mass demonstrations were staged in the capital by both pro- and antigovernment forces, and Azevedo and his Cabinet suspended their activities on the ground that they lacked the military authority to govern. On November 25 the Supreme Council announced that Carvalho was being replaced as military commander of the Lisbon region by the politically moderate Capt. Vasco Lourenço. Subsequently, several other left-wing military commanders were replaced, including the army chief of staff, Gen. Carlos Fabião, and Adm. Antonio Rosa Coutinho.

At the news of Carvalho's dismissal left-wing troops staged an armed revolt and captured four Air Force bases in the northern and central parts of the country. By the next day, however, the revolt had collapsed as the Communist Party criticized the action and government forces recaptured the bases. The premier on November 28 announced that the government would resume operations. He also dismissed the management and editors of eight daily newspapers following accusations by some military leaders that the newspapers had fomented the revolt. Many of the military officers who took part in the revolt were arrested.

Colonial Affairs. At a conference in Macau at the end of June preparations were made for the eventual decolonization of Portuguese Timor (*see* DEPENDENT STATES), in which a struggle for power was taking place. Hopes of a peaceful transition to independence were dashed there, as they also were in Angola where white settlers lined up for plane flights to Lisbon. (*See* ANGOLA.) On December 8 Portugal broke off diplomatic relations with Indonesia, accusing it of military aggression against Portuguese Timor.

The Economy. Much of the economic program published in February was overtaken by political events. In that program no mention was made of the nationalization of banks, but these (with the exception of foreign interests) and insurance companies were afterward nationalized. A wide range of nationalizations took place in the shipbuilding, petrochemical, fertilizer, paper and pulp, cement, tobacco, brewing, mining, oil refining, and steel industries; the Portuguese airline TAP was also nationalized, as were the railways, urban and rural road passenger transport, and electrical generation and distribution networks. Through these nationalizations, as well as by other means of government intervention, the state gained control of over 70% of the national means of production. Stagnation of production, lack of investment, and rising unemployment were compounded by a rising deficit in the balance of payments, an estimated 30 billion escudos in 1975, compared with 15.6 billion escudos in 1974. The main contributory factors were a substantial trade deficit of 22.5 billion escudos in January–June 1975, as compared with 16.9 billion escudos in the corresponding period in 1974. Net receipts from tourism were estimated to be down 30% from 1974, while net private transfers fell in

PORTUGAL

Education. (1973–74) Primary, pupils 1,191,477, teachers 48,352; secondary, pupils 211,772, teachers 10,307; vocational, pupils 157,261, teachers 11,568; teacher training, students 7,132, teachers 329; higher (including 7 universities), students 59,149, teaching staff 4,916.

Finance. Monetary unit: escudo, with (Sept. 22, 1975) a free rate of 27.35 escudos to U.S. $1 (56.65 escudos = £1 sterling). Gold, SDRs, and foreign exchange: (June 1975) U.S. $2,077,000,000; (June 1974) U.S. $2,527,000,000. Budget (1975 est.): revenue 56,282,000,000 escudos; expenditure 45,185,000,000 escudos. Gross national product: (1973) 276.6 billion escudos; (1972) 233.9 billion escudos. Money supply: (Dec. 1974) 182,510,000,000 escudos; (Dec. 1973) 165.6 billion escudos. Cost of living: (Lisbon; 1970 = 100): (June 1975) 202; (June 1974) 173.

Foreign Trade. (1974) Imports 113,310,000,000 escudos; exports 57,470,000,000 escudos. Import sources: West Germany 14%; U.K. 9%; U.S. 9%; Angola 8%; France 8%; Italy 5%; Spain 5%. Export destinations: U.K. 23%; U.S. 10%; West Germany 8%; Sweden 6%; Angola 6%; France 6%. Main exports: textile yarns and fabrics 17%; machinery 11%; clothing 11%; chemicals 8%; wine 7%; electrical equipment 7%; cork and manufactures 6%; fruit and vegetables 5%. Tourism (1973): visitors 4,079,700; gross receipts U.S. $521 million.

Transport and Communications. Roads (1972) 43,197 km. (including 75 km. expressways). Motor vehicles in use (1973): passenger 769,500; commercial 70,397. Railways: (1973) 3,563 km.; traffic (1974) 3,440,000,000 passenger-km., freight 1,004,000,000 net ton-km. Air traffic (1974): 4,159,800,000 passenger-km.; freight 115,571,000 net ton-km. Shipping (1974): merchant vessels 100 gross tons and over 431; gross tonnage 1,243,128. Telephones (Dec. 1973) 948,000. Radio licenses (Dec. 1973) 1,505,000. Television licenses (Dec. 1973) 569,000.

Agriculture. Production (in 000; metric tons; 1974; 1973 in parentheses): wheat 505 (506); oats 94 (79); rye 156 (134); corn *c.* 500 (*c.* 574); rice *c.* 143 (168); potatoes *c.* 1,116 (*c.* 1,086); onions *c.* 65 (*c.* 63); tomatoes *c.* 1,000 (*c.* 1,001); figs (1973) *c.* 195, (1972) *c.* 195; oranges *c.* 149 (149); apples *c.* 100 (143); wine (1973) 1,075, (1972) 859; olives *c.* 240 (*c.* 285); olive oil 32 (42); milk *c.* 479 (*c.* 466); meat (1973) 312, (1972) 288; timber (cu.m.; 1973) 7,400, (1972) 7,000; fish catch (1973) 453, (1972) 437. Livestock (in 000; 1973–74): sheep *c.* 3,925; cattle (1972–73) *c.* 1,335; pigs *c.* 1,994; chickens (1972–73) 15,204.

Industry. Fuel and power (in 000; 1974): coal (metric tons) 230; manufactured gas (Lisbon; cu.m.) 132,000; electricity (kw-hr.) 10,635,000. Production (in 000; metric tons; 1974): iron ore (50% metal content) 24; steel 376; sulfuric acid 285; fertilizers (nutrient content; 1973–74) nitrogenous 164, phosphate 90; cement 3,147; tin 0.6; tungsten concentrates (oxide content; 1973) 2; gold (troy oz.; 1972) 14; cotton yarn 82; woven cotton fabrics 53; preserved sardines (1973) 27; wood pulp (1973) 528; cork products (1973) 365.

real terms. By September reserves of foreign exchange were exhausted, and Portugal resorted to funding through its gold reserves, which at the time were estimated to be equivalent to a year's imports.

Industry was depressed, with small and medium-sized firms reporting an average 50% decrease in sales from 1974. The Lisbon stock exchange resumed operations in October but served primarily as a base for floating state and municipal loans. The construction industry was seriously affected by a rent freeze, while the wine, textile, and consumer durable industries suffered from a depressed market. Plans in preparation for the steel industry (40 billion escudos), the Sines petrochemicals and harbour project, and roads and irrigation were expected to have "pump-priming" effects on employment and liquidity. In mid-November thousands of construction workers went on strike for higher wages, besieging the premier's residence as they demonstrated in Lisbon. The government capitulated on November 14 and granted the workers a 40% wage increase. Applications for aid from the European Economic Community ($700 million) and the U.S. received favourable consideration with the change in government. (MICHAEL WOOLLER)

See also Dependent States.
[972.A.5.b]

Prisons and Penology

The year 1975 opened with the coming into force of a new penal code in West Germany on January 1. This limited the prison population at the upper and lower ends of the range of sentences. The maximum fixed sentence that any court might pass became 15 years and sentences below one month were abolished. At the same time, the penal code introduced day fines—a system that related the amount of the fine to the daily income of the person being fined. These ranged from a minimum of five days' pay and a bottom rate of DM. 2 a day to a maximum of 360 days' pay and a top rate of DM. 10,000 a day.

This attempt to limit prison confinements was also reflected in the sentiments expressed by crime policy officials from the 18 member states of the Council of Europe which met in Strasbourg, France, in March. They reiterated that prison sentences should be used mainly as security measures for dangerous criminals and that consideration should be given to alternative methods of dealing with the less dangerous offenders and to crime prevention. Ideas of this kind were current in most countries and backed by practical measures such as the countrywide introduction of community service orders in the U.K. Such orders, instead of confining offenders to a penal institution, required them to perform some service useful to the community—such as the preparation of a playground for disadvantaged children, or teaching physically handicapped children to swim. The offenders, though deprived of leisure periods (the element of deterrence), could also see themselves in helpful roles, which might be a new and rewarding experience (the element of rehabilitation) and one from which the community benefited (the element of restitution).

Penal Reform and Public Opinion. The debate about the extent to which imprisonment should be replaced by other methods was by no means over, however. On the side of sweeping reductions in prison populations were criminologists such as Gordon Hawkins of Australia and John Conrad of the U.S. Academy for Contemporary Problems. Both had served as correctional administrators and knew practice as well as theory. Their main case, restated in the symposium on "Progress in Penal Reform" (1975), rested on the premise that penal institutions, while expensive, did not effectively rehabilitate or deter a considerable number of those currently held captive in them. An even more extreme stand in the debate, exemplified by such sociologists as the Norwegian T. Mathiesen, saw the eventual abolition of imprisonment as a political aim. Prison represented to them the ultimate means of control by the established order. Mere reform, in such a view, became suspect because it might "relegitimize" this control.

VANCOUVER SUN

A guard at the British Columbia Penitentiary in Vancouver stands at alert as three prisoners serving life sentences held 15 penitentiary workers hostage in June.

The opinion of the man in the street was different, however. With crime on the increase, he saw a simple relationship between crime and punishment: the more crime there was committed, the heavier should be the punishment. Research demonstrating that matters were less simple did not convince him. After the June referendum on whether the U.K. should remain in the European Economic Community or not, the British weekly *New Society* published a survey of other subjects on which people might like referenda. Capital punishment came first. There could be little doubt that a majority favoured its return. Law enforcement agents usually took a similar view. In the three years since the 1972 U.S. Supreme Court decision ruling the death penalty unconstitutional, 33 states had enacted new death penalty laws designed to satisfy court objections. In April the court heard oral arguments on the constitutionality of capital punishment, but in June, without explanation, postponed the reexamination until the 1975–76 court session. In Canada, which had abolished capital punishment in 1967 except in the murder of policemen and prison guards on duty, police officials, members of Parliament, and a number of citizens' groups joined in a nationwide movement urging restoration of the death penalty for murder; the effort followed an outbreak of killings in the country.

After years of trying, a number of penal experts in the United States admitted they had not really been able to reform criminals in prison. In February it was announced that the U.S. federal penal system

Portuguese Literature:
see Literature

Portuguese Overseas Provinces:
see Dependent States

Potash:
see Mining and Quarrying

Poultry:
see Agriculture and Food Supplies

Power:
see Energy; Engineering Projects; Industrial Review

Presbyterian Churches:
see Religion

Prices:
see Economy, World

Printing:
see Industrial Review

WIDE WORLD

Women relatives of 16 imprisoned Irish Republican Army men began a hunger strike in January outside the gates of a Dublin prison, in support of a strike within. A 17th man received last rites after 27 days of fasting.

would no longer stress rehabilitation in its prisons. In explaining this change, Norman Carlson, director of the federal Bureau of Prisons, said, "The unfortunate truth of the matter is that we don't know very much about the causes or cures for crime. For a long time we said we did—or kidded ourselves that we did. But I think a new sense of reality is now sweeping over the entire criminal justice system of this country." Correctional institutions would begin to put more importance on confinement of criminals. Even if it did not deter crime, it might lower the incidence of crime by getting the criminals off the streets. In England Lord Justice Lawton, while not denying that bad social conditions played a part in crime, felt that in the correctional system the carrot had been used too much and the stick too little in the last 70 years.

Radicalism v. Moderation. Arguments on penal policies had raged for long, but one dramatic episode put them into sharp focus. This was the kidnapping in May of Giuseppe Di Gennaro, an Italian judge in the Ministry of Justice, connected with the UN Social Defense Institute in Rome. The background to this incident was that overdue reforms of the Italian penal system still had not been carried out. Only in July did Parliament approve sweeping new reform legislation which, by the end of August, had not yet been put into effect. Meanwhile, unconvicted individuals were still waiting many months in jail before their trial; there was terrible overcrowding, insufficient communication with the outside world, and a sense of neglect. Many riots occurred in Italian jails, including one in late August at the modern Rebibbia prison in Rome.

The kidnappers belonged to the extreme left-wing Armed Proletarian Units (NAP), and it was no accident that they selected Di Gennaro, who was known as a reforming judge. When released he said that they saw him as the person most responsible for dividing the views of prisoners and confusing the proletariat. This echoed the opinion of those sociologists who saw moderate reform as the enemy of radical change. For many years politically conscious prisoners had been using bad conditions in correctional institutions as a means of fomenting unrest and as useful propaganda for their cause.

Those responsible for administering penal policies were faced with difficult decisions. Sandwiched between the advocates of a drastic reduction in sanctions on the one hand and of stiffer penalties on the other, they had to weigh what course might retain public confidence. While research findings indicated that some decrease in the prison population could be undertaken safely and while experiments such as crisis intervention centres in The Netherlands showed that treatment in the community could be as effective as prison, the increasing level of social conflict in some countries aroused public anxiety. The more uncertain and depressed people were, the more punitive they were likely to become. It was doubtful whether any society was mature enough to abandon its sanctions wholesale, least of all when it was increasingly divided.

Financial Problems. Correctional administrators also had to face financial problems. Penal systems had always been among the first to be affected by inflation or recession. Reductions in public expenditure impinged on everything, including prisoners' earnings. Fewer manufacturing activities and rises in unemployment were reflected in loss of contracts for work in prisons. For prisoners it meant more enforced idleness, a growing black market in scarce supplies, and a heightening of tensions inside. For ex-prisoners there were fewer chances of lawful employment. A study of work in prison, prepared by British expert Ken Neale, which examined its role and organization as well as prisoners' motivation and their earnings, was acclaimed by top administrators both at the Council of Europe meeting in the spring and at the UN Congress on the Prevention of Crime in Geneva in September.

Financial stringency lent urgency to efforts to divert more offenders away from expensive prisons. In The Netherlands, on the decision of public prosecutors with wide discretionary powers, 40% of those charged did not go on to be tried. Countries with parole systems resorted to them more frequently and for longer periods. Denmark increased the use of conditional prison sentences. California, which had been closing penal institutions for some time, had one probation officer for roughly each 2,000 inhabitants.

Prisoners' Rights. A number of countries had strengthened the legal rights of prisoners, including their right to have more contacts with the outside world. In Sweden prisoners were allowed to use telephones; other countries, including Italy, followed suit. In the U.K., as a result of a ruling by the European Court of Human Rights, prisoners were given access to legal advice and to the courts in order, for example, to sue a member of the prison service. The censorship of letters was also being eased. In the U.S. Joanne Little (*see* BIOGRAPHY), a black woman prisoner, was acquitted of second-degree murder in the death of her white male guard; she claimed she had acted in self-defense when he made forcible sexual demands on her.

An individual's real punishment sometimes began when his official punishment ended. This was particularly true when jobs were scarce. When two candidates had equal qualifications, employers were likely to pick the one without previous conviction. In order to give small-time offenders who had remained crime-free for a certain period a chance, the Rehabilitation of Offenders Act came into force in the U.K. in July. The principle was that convictions of less than 2½ years' imprisonment became inadmissible in evidence in most judicial proceedings if the individual concerned had managed to stay clear of crime for a period of up to ten years. For lesser convictions the period was shorter. This made it possible for many to declare that they had no previous convictions and to compete on equal terms for jobs or promotion.

The penal philosophy of 1975 was foreshadowed by Norval Morris of the University of Chicago, a lawyer and criminologist with wide experience of the legal and penal systems of many countries. In *The Future of Imprisonment* (1974), he pleaded that criminal justice systems should be more selective in their sanctions and suggested that no punishment should be greater than that which was deserved by the last crime or series of crimes. And he insisted that respect for the rights of the individual—whoever he might be—required drawing precise, justiciable restraints on the powers that government should be able to assume over him. This principle, if it were applied universally, would affect most correctional systems. It would impinge on the use of indeterminate sentences, of parole, and of minor but arbitrary decisions in correctional administration, however benevolent their intent might be. Gerhard Muller, executive secretary of the UN Congress on the Prevention of Crime, even claimed that "no UN member country is entirely free from acts of degrading treatment of prisoners."

"Abuse of governmental power is a central problem of the human condition," wrote Morris, "and the treatment of the criminal is closely bound up with that." Many lawyers and penologists in liberal democracies felt that this was indeed the vital issue. The lessons of Auschwitz and of the "Gulag Archipelago" must never be forgotten. (HUGH J. KLARE)

See also Crime and Law Enforcement.
[521.C.3.a; 543.A.5.a; 10/36.C.5.b]

Publishing

The economic difficulties that beset the publishing world almost everywhere in 1975 were compounded by new attacks from many different quarters on the freedom of the press. In India the state of emergency declared in June was accompanied by strict censorship; in Greece, a year after the restoration of democracy (July 1974), the freedom of journalists to write as they wished was still in question; at the meeting of the Inter-American Press Association in São Paulo, Brazil, in October, the president of its Freedom of the Press committee, G. Ornes, said that censorship, self-censorship, and government decrees prevented or inhibited the right to expression throughout Latin America, with few exceptions; and according to the International Press Institute, reporting in December, more than half the world had no free press.

In Britain a Writers and Scholars Educational Trust was set up to alert public opinion to the growth of censorship throughout the world, including Britain and Europe.

European Newspapers. By midsummer it was clear that 1975 would prove a critical year for Britain's national newspaper industry. In parallel with the country as a whole, its politics were stormy and its economy depressed, but there was, at last, a recognition on all sides that if the national newspapers were not to crumble they had only one option: change.

TIME MAGAZINE © 1975 TIME INC.

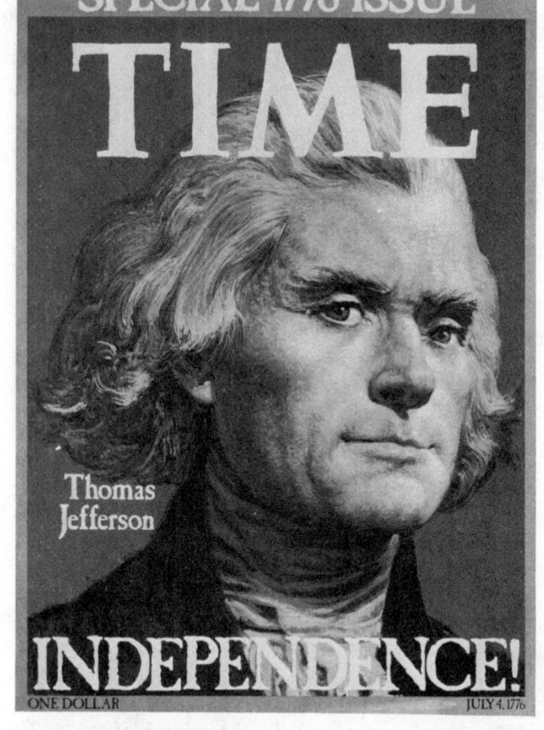

Cover of the special bicentennial issue of "Time."

At the end of November the six main printers' and journalists' unions met to discuss a common approach to the modernization of the industry. In a statement issued later the unions accepted "that the more effective use of manpower at all levels and the introduction of new technology requiring a smaller labour force could be a contributing factor to reducing the production costs of national newspapers." If agreement could be reached on ways of protecting those who would lose their jobs, "the unions on their part would be prepared to examine the effects of technological changes on existing lines of demarcation, recognizing that by the very nature of new technology rigid lines of demarcation are bound to be blurred." At a subsequent (December 5) meeting of four of the unions, representing four-fifths of the national newspapers' labour force, with the Newspaper Publishers Association (NPA) and Mirror Group Newspapers Ltd., the unions agreed to cooperate with managements with regard to the introduction of new technology in return for a pledge that there would be no compulsory layoffs.

The *Financial Times* was one of several national newspapers that announced plans for change to more modern, labour-saving technologies during the course of the year. First, and biggest, in the field was the International Publishing Corporation Ltd. (IPC). In the spring, IPC, owners of the Mirror group (*Daily Mirror, Sunday Mirror, The Sunday People*), announced a £2.8 million computerization plan. It included computerized typesetting and composition of pages; the transmission of entire pages electronically to printing plants in Glasgow and in Plymouth, where a new satellite plant would be built; the closing of one London printing works; and the use of mechanical publishing. The *Daily Telegraph* announced its own plans later in the year. And *The Guardian* proposed to introduce facsimile printing in 1976; this would involve substantial cuts in its Manchester work force.

These decisions were not made overnight. Some managements, including those of *The Guardian* and the Mirror group, had been considering them for 15

Profits:
see Economy, World
Protestant Churches:
see Religion
Psychiatry:
see Health and Disease
Psychology:
see Behavioural Sciences; Health and Disease
Public Utilities:
see Energy; Industrial Review; Transportation

WIDE WORLD

Donald L. Barlett (left) and James B. Steele of the "Philadelphia Inquirer" received the 1975 Pulitzer Prize for National Reporting for a seven-part series on the Internal Revenue Service.

years. The relative costs of installing composing equipment for a small (100,000 circulation) newspaper were £292,000 for traditional "hot-metal" methods, as against £448,000 for the most advanced computerized technology; but the relative labour costs, it was said, would be £209,000 a year for the old system and only £85,000 for the new.

For two years or more, British newspapers had pushed up their prices under the pressure of rising costs. The latest round, in the winter of 1974–75, brought them to levels that would not have been conceivable two years before, *The Sunday Times* leading at 15 pence with the *Observer* at 12 pence and *The Times* and *The Guardian* at 10 pence. But whereas previously sales had proved more resilient than had been feared, in 1975 the consumer resisted. Only one national paper did not lose circulation, and that was the *Sun,* which apart from being the brashest of tabloids was the only publication not to raise its price during the period. All the others slipped back, some of them substantially, and the slide continued.

One single event catalyzed the change. In August, a week after IPC had announced its big investment plans, David Astor, editor and owner of the *Observer,* told his staff that the paper was suffering an annual loss approaching £500,000, that circulation was dropping, and that the wage bill would have to be cut by a massive 30% if the paper was to survive. Further, in the long run, simple staff cuts would not be enough; the new technology must be employed. The *Observer* survived the summer, though not without a struggle with the unions that lost it one week's edition and threatened a quick death.

In November the gloom lightened when Beaverbrook Newspapers Ltd. reported a substantial turnaround from loss in 1973–74 to a useful profit in 1974–75. The closing of the Glasgow plant and other economies such as ending the unprofitable Saturday edition of the London *Evening Standard* contributed to this. Consequent to the Glasgow closure, the year saw the birth and death of the *Scottish Daily News,* a cooperative venture by several hundred of the men laid off. With government aid their paper was launched on May 5, but it failed after 162 issues.

In France too 1975 was a critical year for the press. Most of the large Paris newspapers (*Le Monde* being a notable exception) were reported in the red, with the most popular evening paper, *France-Soir,* down to a circulation of 727,000, from 1.2 million ten years previously. This was in spite of tax concessions, a newsprint subsidy, and no great competition from television. There were many strikes against newspapers, the main target being the largest circulation (786,000) daily, *Le Parisien Libéré,* whose editor, Emilien Amaury, alleged a Communist conspiracy to ruin the French newspaper industry. France's oldest daily, the conservative *Le Figaro* (circulation 408,000), facing a deficit of Fr. 5 million on operating costs in 1975, changed hands in July when proprietor Jean Prouvost sold his majority shareholding to Robert Hersant, owner of a chain of provincial papers. The change was protested by *Le Figaro*'s journalists, who feared loss of editorial freedom.

The situation in Italy was much the same, with *La Stampa* reporting a $4 million deficit in 1974. State subsidies to newspapers and magazines amounting to more than $50 million annually were under consideration.

West German newspapers were in not quite such bad shape, but even there losses were growing. A publishers' survey said that 88.6% of their sampled 176 newspapers had been profitable in 1973 but that only 52.2% were 18 months later. In May the Hamburg daily *Die Welt* moved to Bonn.

(PETER FIDDICK)

U.S. Newspapers. In the U.S., 1975 was a year of retrenchment, lowered expectations, and even diminished physical dimensions for newspapers. As the price of newsprint leveled off at a record high of $275 to $285 a ton, up from a low of $175 a ton two years earlier, more and more newspapers sought to cut costs by trimming the width of their pages. In most such cases, pages were narrowed by about three-quarters of an inch, and the standard news format went from eight columns to six slightly wider ones. The *Los Angeles Times,* which made the switch just before the year began, estimated that it would save $4.2 million in newsprint costs in 1975.

Newspapers were not only smaller, they were also less numerous. According to the *1975 Editor & Publisher International Year Book,* 24 newspapers were closed and only 19 new ones were started during 1974, bringing the total number of dailies down to 1,768. There were 1,449 evening newspapers, a net decline of two from the year before, and 340 morning newspapers, a net decline of three. The number of so-called "all day newspapers," which publish editions continually throughout the day, rose to 21. (The figures add up to more than 1,768 because some papers fall in more than one category.) Sunday newspapers increased by seven to a new high of 641. Total evening circulation declined by 2.45% to 35,732,231; total morning circulation dropped by 1.43% to 26,144,966; total Sunday circulation was down 0.07% to 51,678,726.

The circulation losses had a number of causes. An increasing number of newspapers raised their newsstand prices and subscription rates in 1975 to help cover rising production costs. Some papers deliberately limited the number of copies circulated to outlying areas to hold down newsprint consumption and costly distribution by truck. The recession led many readers to stop buying more than one newspaper a day.

Economic conditions were reflected in the newsroom as well. Approximately 13,000 students graduated from colleges and universities with degrees in journalism in 1975, but there were fewer than 3,000 editorial openings for them. The *Boston Globe, New York Times, Wall Street Journal, Washington Post,* and dozens of other prominent newspapers imposed hiring freezes. The *Christian Science Monitor* eliminated 100 positions through attrition and layoffs. At the *Washington* (D.C.) *Star-News,* an afternoon paper that had been losing money for years, employees agreed to work a four-day week, at a 20% cut in pay, in order to avoid layoffs.

The *Star-News*'s struggle for survival was one of the year's most dramatic episodes. Texas banker Joe L. Allbritton bought the paper in 1974 from the families that helped found it more than a century before and began pouring in millions of dollars in an effort to reverse its losses. Allbritton also attempted to buy the paper's six money-making broadcast stations, comprising Washington Star Communications, Inc., which he said he needed to help offset the publishing deficits. The Federal Communications Commission, however, bans any transfer of broadcast properties that would perpetuate a local media monopoly, as would be the case with the *Star-News.* Allbritton asked the FCC for a waiver of its rule, and offered to exchange Star Communications stations for comparable broadcast outlets in other cities. While FCC officials decided to hold hearings on the case, the *Star-News* continued to lose money. Allbritton completed purchase of the stations in September, agreeing to sell them within two to three years. At the *Washington Post,* meanwhile, the pressmen went on strike in October after damaging all the paper's presses. Other labour union employees of the *Post* denounced the action, and the paper continued to publish.

Opinion surveys showed that public respect for reporters was still higher than in the years before newspapers helped uncover the Watergate scandals, but that that esteem was being replaced by a renewed skepticism about journalistic responsibility. After Sara Jane Moore made the second attempt in 17 days on U.S. Pres. Gerald Ford's life, readers and officials began to question the extent to which news coverage of such attempts encouraged other would-be assassins. (*See* CRIME AND LAW ENFORCEMENT.)

In at least two other instances in 1975, newspapers did attempt to restrain their coverage, but that self-censorship produced controversial results. Early in the year William Colby, director of the Central Intelligence Agency, persuaded a number of major newspapers and broadcasters not to disclose the fact that the CIA had recovered part of a sunken Soviet submarine from the floor of the Pacific, on the grounds that disclosure would be harmful to the national security. After columnist Jack Anderson finally broke the story, many journalists contended that disclosure did not affect national security and that the Soviets may have known of the recovery all along. A few months later, newspapers in Louisville, Ky., adopted a set of guidelines limiting their coverage of the start of school busing. Though the guidelines were not unduly restrictive, there were complaints that serious incidents of police brutality went unreported.

Pulitzer Prizes in 1975 also seemed to reflect a retreat from the aggressive investigative reporting that had characterized the Watergate years. One of the year's most publicized investigative feats, a series on CIA involvement in domestic spying by *New York Times* reporter Seymour Hersh (*see* BIOGRAPHY), did not receive a Pulitzer. Instead, prizes went to generally less controversial efforts: an exposé on inequities in application of federal tax laws by Donald L. Barlett and James B. Steele of the *Philadelphia Inquirer,* a series on famine in Africa and India by William Mullen and Ovie Carter of the *Chicago Tribune,* editorials on a local school textbook controversy by John Daniell Maurice of the *Charleston* (W.Va.) *Daily Mail,* coverage of a local tornado disaster by the *Xenia* (Ohio) *Daily Gazette,* investigation of local police corruption by the *Indianapolis Star,* and the "massive and balanced" coverage of the start of school busing in Boston by the *Boston Globe.*

(DONALD M. MORRISON)

Magazines. In comparison with newspapers, British magazines were having an easier time. At least one prominent title went under, however. This was *Nova,* the women's monthly founded by IPC in 1965 to lead the way in appealing to the intelligent and independent —in short, "liberated"—young woman. Its circulation peak of about 170,000 was reached as far back as 1967; under pressure from such newcomers as *Cosmopolitan,* it had fallen to little above 100,000, and in midsummer, after a desultory attempt at a change of format, the IPC announced that it would cease publication. A more obvious indicator of the economic slump in the consumer industries came when *Adweek,* one of the weeklies catering to the advertising business, was merged into its rival, *Campaign.*

The *Spectator,* the 147-year-old right-wing weekly journal of political and literary comment, changed hands. Its new proprietor was Henry Keswick, a young businessman who was said to have made himself a millionaire in business in the Far East but was now returning to Britain with an eye on politics. The *Spectator,* for all its long history, had withdrawn from the Audit Bureau of Circulations' (ABC) lists several years previously. It was reputed to be selling only about 20,000 copies per week.

In the Far East, a newcomer was *Asiaweek,* a news weekly published in Hong Kong under the editorship of T. J. S. George.

(PETER FIDDICK)

Both recession and inflation plagued U.S. periodicals in 1975. Newsstand prices of almost all magazines were raised an average of 30%, and *Publishers Weekly* estimated that the average cost of a periodical to college and university libraries was $87. The projected cost in 1978–79 was $121. At the same time, the 200

NATIONAL GEOGRAPHIC
world
A totally new magazine!

"National Geographic World," a new monthly magazine designed specifically for children 8 through 12 years old, carries brain-teasers, craft ideas, and lavish photographs among its regular features.

World Daily Newspapers and Circulations, 1974–75*

Location	Daily newspapers	Circulation per 1,000 population
AFRICA		
Algeria	4	16
Angola	4	15
Botswana	2	21
Cameroon	2	3
Central African Republic	1	0.3
Chad	1	0.2
Congo	3	...
Dahomey (Benin)	2	0.7
Egypt	14	22
Equatorial Guinea	1	4
Ethiopia	9	2
Gabon	1	1
Ghana	7	46
Guinea	1	1
Guinea-Bissau	1	1
Ivory Coast	3	10
Kenya	4	14
Lesotho	1	...
Liberia	1	4
Libya	7	17
Malagasy Republic	13	15
Malawi	1	...
Mali	3	0.6
Mauritius	12	17
Morocco	11	15
Mozambique	6	8
Niger	1	0.5
Nigeria	17	3
Réunion	2	60
Rhodesia	4	15
Senegal	1	6
Seychelles	2	55
Sierra Leone	5	17
Somalia	2	1
South Africa	21	47
Sudan	22	8
Tanzania	7	4
Togo	3	6
Tunisia	4	28
Uganda	7	9
Upper Volta	1	0.3
Zaire	13	9
Zambia	2	17
Total	229	
NORTH AMERICA		
Bahamas, The	3	162
Barbados	1	113
Belize	1	24
Bermuda	1	252
Canada	121	234
Costa Rica	8	93
Cuba	16	107
Dominican Republic	5	35
El Salvador	12	76
Guadeloupe	2	144
Guatemala	8	27
Haiti	7	16
Honduras	12	42
Jamaica	3	100
Martinique	2	137
Mexico	216	...
Netherlands Antilles	5	187
Nicaragua	4	38
Panama	7	86
Puerto Rico	3	89
Trinidad and Tobago	3	139
United States	1,768	293
Virgin Islands (U.S.)	3	343
Total	2,211	
SOUTH AMERICA		
Argentina	180	180
Bolivia	17	37
Brazil	261	35
Chile	128	...
Colombia	36	105
Ecuador	22	47
French Guiana	1	39
Guyana	4	104
Paraguay	11	...
Peru	56	...
Surinam	6	...
Uruguay	54	...
Venezuela	42	91
Total	818	
ASIA		
Afghanistan	18	6
Bangladesh	4	...
Burma	8	8
Cambodia	16	10
China	392	...
Cyprus	12	123
Hong Kong	81	367
India	793	16
Indonesia	120	10
Iran	39	25
Iraq	5	...
Israel	24	183
Japan	172	529
Jordan	4	23
Korea, North	6	...
Korea, South	42	138
Kuwait	6	44
Laos	6	2
Lebanon	52	...
Macau	6	...
Malaysia	40	77
Mongolia	2	103
Nepal	30	3
Pakistan	71	...
Philippines	19	17
Saudi Arabia	5	7
Singapore	10	193
Sri Lanka	17	48
Syria	5	9
Taiwan	32	...
Thailand	35	24
Turkey	432	...
Vietnam, North	7	...
Vietnam, South	56	67
Total	2,567	
EUROPE		
Albania	2	58
Austria	31	328
Belgium	55	...
Bulgaria	13	206
Czechoslovakia	27	280
Denmark	53	361
Finland	60	425
France	106	233
Germany, East	40	425
Germany, West	1,093	330
Gibraltar	2	226
Greece	104	...
Hungary	27	216
Iceland	5	439
Ireland	7	233
Italy	78	142
Liechtenstein	1	263
Luxembourg	6	451
Malta	6	...
Netherlands, The	95	307
Norway	79	391
Poland	44	231
Portugal	33	245
Romania	57	173
Spain	115	99
Sweden	108	515
Switzerland	98	390
U.S.S.R.	647	347
United Kingdom	109	437
Vatican City	1	...
Yugoslavia	25	89
Total	3,127	
OCEANIA		
American Samoa	1	103
Australia	58	321
Cook Islands	1	30
Fiji	1	30
French Polynesia	3	87
Guam	2	170
New Caledonia	1	65
New Zealand	40	367
Niue	1	60
Papua New Guinea	1	6
Tonga	2	16
Total	111	
Grand total	9,063	

*Only newspapers issued four or more times weekly are included.
Sources: UN, *Statistical Yearbook 1974* (1975); *Editor & Publisher International Year Book 1975; World Communications* (UNESCO Press, 1975); *Europa Year Book 1975, A World Survey.*

leading U.S. consumer magazines reported that advertising revenues slipped by 2% in the first six months of 1975 and the number of advertising pages dropped almost 10%.

Rising subscription prices and lower advertising revenues supported the argument of the past decade that the general magazine was an anachronism and the specialized magazine the survivor. Only titles that were putting out a quality editorial product targeted at a well-defined audience flourished or were able to withstand the general economic downward trend of 1975. For example, significant gainers in total paid circulation were specialized magazines such as *Smithsonian, Money,* and *People;* and the interest in the U.S. bicentennial increased the circulation of *Early American Life* by 30%. Losers included *TV Guide, Reader's Digest,* and *Playboy.*

Circulation figures, however, were no longer an accurate measure of success. The question was not how large was the number of readers but who was reading the magazine. Publishers voluntarily cut circulations to guarantee advertisers a specific type of reader and, equally important, to reduce rising production and mail costs. In an effort to avoid the errors of *Life, Look, The Saturday Evening Post,* and other mass circulation titles that overextended their readership, the consumer magazines cut back giant circulations. In 1975 *Ladies' Home Journal, McCall's, Redbook,* and *Good Housekeeping* lowered circulations 7 to 14%, at the same time reducing cost per advertiser by 12 to 25%. A parallel trend was that of more dependence on revenue from subscribers and less from advertisers. In mid-1975 *Ladies' Home Journal* announced that it had a true profit on its circulation. Reader revenues exceeded all manufacturing, editorial, circulation, and distribution costs.

A major success story of 1975 was *High Times.* Devoted to stories and articles on drugs and other "highs," the magazine won instant success, jumping its circulation from a beginning 25,000 to over 300,000 in less than eight months.

More conventional new titles of 1975 included: *National Geographic World,* a children's magazine by the publishers of *National Geographic; Book Digest,* the self-explanatory title by John Veronis and Nicolas Charney, who founded *Psychology Today* and then floundered with *Intellectual Digest* and *Saturday Review; African Book Publishing Record,* a type of *Publishers Weekly* for African titles; *Harper's Weekly,* a rerun of the popular 1857–1916 illustrated magazine but this time with contributions primarily written by readers; and *Maclean's,* one of Canada's oldest magazines but transformed by a new format and publishing schedule in an effort to replace *Time* as a news magazine for Canadian readers. Some new magazines employed the newspaper tabloid format of *Rolling Stone.* These included *Alive Magazine,* a Marxist literary review; and *Madness Network News,* for those involved in psychology.

There were hundreds of other new titles, ranging from technical and trade journals to literary "little" magazines—so many in fact that at least one more effort was launched to stop the flood. A two-year, $400,000 study by the American Council of Learned Societies hoped to find a means of checking the ever growing number of new journals. The rising cost of publishing coupled with slashed library budgets underlined the question of whether many of the 10,000 or so scholarly U.S. journals were necessary. The study would investigate such factors as duplication among journals, bibliographic methods, and technological innovations in publishing.

The problem of copyright and photocopying of periodical articles might be solved by a simple solution: magazines printed on paper resistant to duplication by Xerox, IBM, or anyone else. The new paper, developed by a subsidiary of Cornell Aeronautical Laboratories, was being tested in late 1975. Its drawbacks included cost, approximately $1.50 per pound, and colouring, a brown that sometimes dims the typeface.

(WILLIAM A. KATZ)

Books. *International Developments.* The announcement that an antitrust suit had been filed against 21 U.S. publishing companies and the British publishers who were members of the British Publishers Association was the bombshell of the year in the book publishing world. The defendant firms were Addison-Wesley Publishing Co.; Bantam Books, Inc.; Columbia Broadcasting System, Inc.; Dell Publishing Co., Inc.; Doubleday & Co., Inc.; Grosset & Dunlap, Inc.; Harcourt Brace Jovanovich, Inc.; Harper & Row, Publishers, Inc.; Houghton Mifflin Co.; Intext, Inc.; Litton Educational Publishing, Inc.; Macmillan, Inc.; McGraw-Hill, Inc.; Oxford University Press, Inc.; Penguin Books, Inc.; Prentice-Hall, Inc.; Random House, Inc.; Simon & Schuster, Inc.; the Times Mirror Co.; The Viking Press, Inc.; and John Wiley & Sons, Inc. The British publishing houses were named as co-conspirators but not as defendants. The plaintiff was the United States.

The suit, filed on Nov. 25, 1974, charged the U.S. firms and the British co-conspirators with dividing the world book market into exclusive territories allocated among themselves; it asserted that they "participated in agreements entered into by members of the Publishers Association pursuant to which such members refrain from negotiating any copyright license or sublicense agreement with a U.S. or other foreign publishing house or author, unless the British publishing house is granted the exclusive rights for all countries within the British traditional market." "The British traditional market" included virtually all present and former members of the Commonwealth of Nations, some 70 English-speaking countries. The plaintiff complained among other things that competition in the sale of English-language copyrighted books among U.S. and U.K. publishing houses had been suppressed and the exportation and importation of books from and to the U.S. had been restrained.

After ten months of lengthy discussions the Publishers Association announced its withdrawal of the British Traditional Market Agreement, and the U.S. Department of Justice advised the association that it had obtained the agreement of the great majority of the 21 defendants to entry of a consent decree. The decree enjoined each defendant from preventing any person lawfully acquiring a book from importing or exporting the book to or from the U.S. The consequences of the suit for the worldwide distribution of English-language books had yet to be fully estimated at year's end, but fiercer competition among publishers could certainly be foreseen.

Contrary to forecasts, in most countries the number of new titles published was higher in 1975 than in past years, even in countries with high rates of inflation and unemployment such as Great Britain and Italy. On the other hand there seemed to be fewer copies sold per title and fewer reprints in most of the developed countries. Book clubs, encyclopaedia publishing companies, and mail order book companies were hard hit by postage increases, higher manufacturing costs, and recession.

WIDE WORLD

Pressroom of the "Washington Post" following destruction by striking employees in October.

A number of takeover agreements or mergers took place during 1975. Gulf & Western Industries, Inc., the conglomerate with interests in paper, building, and Paramount Pictures, acquired Simon & Schuster at an estimated cost of $11 million. The Hamlyn Group (U.K.) acquired the A & W Promotional Book Corp. in the U.S. The Elsevier Publishing Co. (The Netherlands) acquired E. P. Dutton & Co. (U.S.). In January the library wholesaler Richard Abel & Co. of Portland, Ore., was taken over by the Blackwell Group of Oxford, England. The acquisition in November by Penguin, the British paperback publisher, of the Viking Press, to form Viking-Penguin, was seen as a partial consequence of the antitrust suit.

(JOSEPH A. KOUTCHOUMOW)

United Kingdom. The mood in the British book publishing industry during 1975 was one of caution and anxiety. With the continuing high cost of credit and other factors creating a cash squeeze, publishers were acutely aware of the heavy sums they had tied up in stock and the long periods of waiting for payment, particularly from overseas customers. By midyear, however, although there were signs of customer resistance against the prices of new books and reductions in institutional spending were beginning to take effect, publishers' turnover appeared to be holding up remarkably well.

The size of the British industry continued to depend heavily on its export performance, which was threatened by three factors. The first of these was inflation. In 1975, for the first time ever, it became cheaper to print many categories of books in the U.S. than in Britain. This naturally made it more difficult to negotiate sheet and co-edition deals with U.S. publishers and also eroded the price advantage of British books in world markets, although this was balanced by the decline of the value of the pound. Second, inflation of production costs was compounded by a disproportionate increase in overseas postal rates. The full brunt of these raises would not be borne until 1976, and meanwhile the Book Development Council was working to establish alternative distribution methods. The third threat was the U.S. antitrust suit (*see* above), the outcome of which was expected to be increased pressure by U.S. publishers on the British publishers' "traditional market."

In the meantime British publishers continued to produce even more titles than before. In the first

ISRAEL SHENKER—THE NEW YORK TIMES

A Middle English dictionary was begun at the University of Michigan at Ann Arbor 50 years ago and published in parts. A final editorial deadline of 1982 was established during the year.

seven months of 1975 there were 20,747 produced, against 17,866 for the same period of 1974.

(MARTIN BALLARD)

West Germany. Despite the prevalent recession and unemployment, publishing and bookselling continued to expand. With 49,761 titles published in 1974 the West German (including West Berlin) industry ranked third after the U.S. and the U.S.S.R. in book production. Nearly 10% of the 1974 production was in paperback, and more than 12% consisted of translations from 50 foreign languages, with English originals comprising 62.5%. Book prices, especially of paperbacks, rose, but the reading and book buying habits of West Germans were not noticeably affected.

(SIGFRED TAUBERT)

U.S.S.R. More than 200 central and local publishing houses in the Soviet Union published 86,000 titles in 1974, totaling over 1,694,000,000 copies. Prominence in 1975 was again given to Marxist-Leninist classical literature. Nearly 450 works of Marx, Engels, and Lenin were issued, and the works of Communist Party leader Leonid I. Brezhnev were printed in large editions in all languages of the Soviet nationalities.

The Prosveshcheniye (Enlightenment) publishing house, the biggest producer of school textbooks, issued 190 million copies. A similar number was produced for secondary specialized schools and higher educational institutions. Fiction and children's literature made up more than 21% of the total number of titles.

The International Book Fair in Moscow was attended by more than 500 publishing firms from 42 countries and drew 750,000 visitors. Its theme was "Books in the Service of Peace and Progress."

(NOVOSTI)

Australia. During the year ended June 30, 1975, a total of A$1,570,000 in Public Lending Right (PLR) fees was disbursed to writers and their Australian publishers. In the same period, the Literature Board of the newly formed Australia Council paid out approximately $6.5 million in scholarships to both established and young authors and in subsidies to publishers to bring out commercially risky books. The intention was to keep the prices of sponsored books at a lower level than would otherwise be possible, ensure a reasonably high margin to booksellers, and, in some cases, contribute to the cost of promotion.

(ANDREW FABINYI)

U.S. Inflation, recession, and widespread unemployment in the U.S. caused book publishers to fear that 1975 would be a crisis year for them. The events of the year did not, however, bear out the bleak outlook. Publishers began the year cautiously, many announcing sharp cutbacks in their 1975 publishing lists. Despite the retrenchments, book title output increased for the first six months of the year. Paper supplies, which were seriously short during 1974, were adequate in 1975, and prices were also slightly down. Sales in the education markets continued to rise despite declining enrollments.

Viking Press pulled off the publishing coup of the year when it announced in the fall that it had retained Jacqueline Kennedy Onassis as a consulting editor. Part of her role would be to scout for possible Viking manuscripts, drawing upon her wide circle of social, political, and international contacts.

Despite publishers' complaints about the economy and the issuance of "too many books," more new books were published in the first six months of 1975 than in the comparable period of 1974. A total of 14,998 new titles were issued from January through June, compared with 14,775 in 1974. (These figures do not include government publications or university theses.) New editions in the first six months of 1975 decreased slightly from 4,637 in 1974 to 4,575 in 1975. New fiction was up markedly, to 1,382 titles in 1975 against 1,044 in 1974. Total sales by U.S. book publishers passed the $3.5 billion mark in 1974, an increase of 10.5% over 1973 receipts.

Based on sales alone, elementary and high-school textbooks were the industry's best sellers. In 1974 these books were sold by publishers for a total of $598.8 million, an increase of 9.3% over 1973. Sales of adult trade hardbound books showed an increase of 16.4%; trade books showed an overall increase of 13.6%. Professional books showed an overall increase of 15%, the most significant in several years. College textbook sales rose by 15.6%, compared with a 4.5% increase the prior year. Preliminary sales figures for 1975 indicated that sales for elementary and high-school textbooks, college textbooks, and professional (technical, scientific, and medical) books were showing a steady increase over 1974.

The U.S. Central Intelligence Agency made headlines in the publishing industry. The U.S. Supreme Court refused to review a federal court decision which maintained that former CIA agent Victor L. Marchetti, co-author of *The CIA and the Cult of Intelligence* (Knopf, Dell), had waived his right to invoke the First Amendment guarantee of press freedom when he signed an oath of secrecy with the CIA. The case went back to 1972, when the U.S. government sought and obtained an injunction against the publication of classified materials by Marchetti. Philip Agee avoided the problems encountered by fellow agent Marchetti by publishing his *Inside the Company: CIA Diary* abroad. Released by Penguin Books in Great Britain, the book became an instant best-seller.

One of the largest prepublication rights deals in publishing took place after a hectic open auction March 6, when Pocket Books, a mass-market paperback subsidiary of Simon & Schuster, secured the paperback rights to Agatha Christie's *Curtain* for $925,000. Written by Christie in the mid-1940s, the book marks the final appearance of Hercule Poirot, her famous Belgian detective.

Ragtime by E. L. Doctorow was sold by Random House, on the eve of its 50th anniversary, to Bantam Books for $1,850,000, the highest price ever paid for paperback rights. The previous largest known payment was the New American Library's $1.5 million for the *Joy of Cooking* in 1973.

Some mergers, some staff cutbacks, and the recession accounted for there being more well-qualified and professional job seekers than there were jobs in publishing during the year. David McKay cut back on the acquisition of trade books. Praeger Publishers, a subsidiary of Encyclopædia Britannica, Inc., announced in September plans to phase out the company's trade publishing program by 1976. Praeger's other publishing divisions, special studies and college, did well. Another publisher sought a different approach for its ailing hardcover trade department. Harcourt Brace Jovanovich planned to merge its trade department with its wholly owned mass market subsidiary, Pyramid Communications, by December 1975.

(DAISY G. MARYLES)

See also Literature.

[441.D; 543.A.4.e]

ENCYCLOPÆDIA BRITANNICA FILMS. *Newspaper Story* (2nd ed., 1973).

Puerto Rico: *see* Dependent States

Qatar

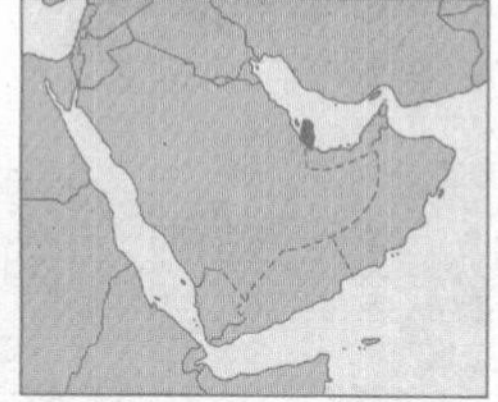

An independent emirate on the west coast of the Persian Gulf, Qatar occupies a desert peninsula east of Bahrain, with Saudi Arabia and the United Arab Emirates bordering it on the south. Area: 4,400 sq.mi. (11,400 sq.km.). Pop. (1972 est.): 170,000. Capital: Doha (pop., 1972 est., 130,000). Language: Arabic. Religion: Muslim. Emir in 1975, Sheikh Khalifah ibn Hamad ath-Thani.

During 1975 Qatar pursued its generally nonpolitical role as a small and prosperous Arab Gulf state with a substantial surplus of revenues. The 1975 budget of 1.8 billion riyals (about $450 million) marked a 60% increase over 1974; about one-third went to public works, one-sixth to industrial development, and one-seventh to education. Imports continued to increase, with Japan becoming the leading supplier. Aid and loans to various Arab states and international agencies were announced, and Qatar doubled its share in the Arab Fund for Loans to African Countries from $10 million to $20 million.

Oil output was deliberately reduced because of unabsorbable resources, and production, at 480,000 bbl. a day in February, was about 7% below that of 1974. In April the government announced its intention to buy the remaining shares retained by Royal Dutch/Shell in the Shell Company of Qatar (40%) and the Qatar Petroleum Co. (less than 10%); between $25 million and $35 million reportedly was offered. On March 17 Qatar announced that it was severing its currency's ties with the U.S. dollar and linking the riyal to the International Monetary Fund's Special Drawing Rights. At the same time the riyal was revalued by 5%. In April Sheikh Khalifah extended the life of his Advisory Council for a further three years.

(PETER MANSFIELD)

[978.B.4.b]

QATAR

Education. (1972–73) Primary, pupils 19,182, teachers 1,002; secondary, pupils 5,279, teachers 347, vocational, pupils 178, teachers 45; teacher training, students 306, teachers 48.

Finance and Trade. Monetary unit: Qatar riyal, with (Sept. 22, 1975) a free rate of 4.10 riyals to U.S. $1 (8.49 riyals = £1 sterling). Budget (1975 est.) balanced at 1.8 billion riyals. Foreign trade (1974): imports 1,069,000,000 riyals; exports 9,094,000,000 riyals. Import sources: Japan 18%; U.K. 14%; U.S. 10%; Lebanon 6%; West Germany 6%. Export destinations (1973): U.K. *c.* 24%; The Netherlands *c.* 22%; France *c.* 20%; Italy *c.* 12%; West Germany *c.* 5%. Main exports crude oil and products 98%.

Industry. Crude oil production (1974) 25,025,000 metric tons.

Sheikh Khalifah ibn Hamad ath-Thani, emir of Qatar.

JULIEN QUIDEAU—CAMERA PRESS/PHOTO TRENDS

Race Relations

World Review. The escalation of Communist and third world "antiracist," "anti-imperialist" rhetoric reached a peak at the UN in October 1975, when the UN Social, Humanitarian, and Cultural Committee passed (70 to 29, with 27 abstentions and 16 absent) an Arab resolution condemning Israel as "the racist regime in occupied Palestine," declaring that Zionism was "a form of racism and racial discrimination," and calling upon all nations to oppose Zionism as "a threat to world peace and security" and a "racist and imperialist ideology." Supporting the resolution were all Soviet bloc countries (where anti-Zionism had become an acceptable euphemism for anti-Semitism) except Romania; all Arab and most Muslim countries; India, Sri Lanka, Uganda, Tanzania, Senegal, and Chad; Cambodia, China, Cuba, Spain, Chile, Malta, and Mexico. Those who voted against the resolution included Ivory Coast, Barbados, The Bahamas, Costa Rica, Ecuador, Nicaragua, and Uruguay; Australia, New Zealand, Canada, and the U.S.; Iceland and Finland; and all Western Europe except Portugal. The anti-Israel campaign at the UN was carried further by Pres. Idi Amin of Uganda, chairman of the Organization of African Unity (OAU), who charged that the U.S. had been "colonized by Zionists" and called for "the extinction of Israel as a state." Daniel Patrick Moynihan (*see* BIOGRAPHY), the U.S. representative to the UN, expressed the growing U.S. impatience by referring to Amin as a "racist murderer" and an enemy of democracy, and calling on the OAU to disavow him. In November the anti-Zionism resolution was adopted by the General Assembly.

Portugal evacuated its large African colonies of Mozambique and Angola in great haste in 1975. About 300,000 white and mixed-blood settlers went from Angola to Portugal, where they seemed likely to create a new centre of antiradical unrest. Meanwhile, whites electing to remain in the former Portuguese African territories faced the possibility of some racial discrimination. Elsewhere in Africa, the black liberation struggle aimed at Rhodesia and South Africa continued. Internal differences appeared in the Rhodesian black independence movement and, to a lesser extent, in South West Africa.

After gaining power in a bloodless coup in late July, the new head of state of Nigeria, a Muslim northerner,

Quakers: *see* Religion

Quarrying: *see* Mining and Quarrying

ALEX WEBB—MAGNUM

Students outside Hyde Park High School in Boston waited to board buses after a new busing program was initiated.

Brig. Murtala Mohammed, did not immediately attempt to further his region's interests. One of his first acts was to cancel the 1973 census, which found that Muslim northerners made up 65% of the population—an explosive issue for the federal-ethnic balance of Nigeria's aggregation of 200 tribes. Tribal and ethnic dissensions, partly the result of European colonial boundary drawing, still bedeviled most newly independent African states. The Eritrean attempt to secede from Ethiopia continued without support from the OAU; other Ethiopian separatist minorities in revolt were the Galla and Tigre peoples. Farther west in Chad, the ten-year-old rebellion of the nomadic Muslim Toubous against the non-Muslim black government came into the news after they kidnapped a French ethnologist, Françoise Claustre. The coup of Didier Ratsiraka in the Malagasy Republic derived from the traditional schism between the African coastal people and the former highland elite of Indonesian stock.

In Lebanon the delicate Christian-Muslim equilibrium was threatened by economic class and right-left political divisions and a demographic shift toward a Muslim majority. The situation there deteriorated through most of the year following the outbreak of fighting in April. Meanwhile, the dispossessed Palestinians received international backing at the UN and elsewhere from the oil-rich Arab countries. By contrast, the Kurds, one of the Middle East's most ancient peoples (Muslim but not Arab), dispersed over Turkey, Iran, Iraq, Syria, and the Soviet Union, lost the only active supporter of their rebellion in Iraq and had to surrender after Iran and Iraq reached an agreement. The Turkish occupation of 40% of Cyprus in the name of the Turkish ethnic minority of 18% of the population was followed by the flight of Greeks from the northern part of the island. In late 1975 there were reports that Turks from the mainland were colonizing the Turkish-held areas.

In Europe manifestations of regional nationalism became more evident in 1975. Apart from the continuing violence in Northern Ireland, Scots and Welsh made demands for greater autonomy. (*See* below; *see* UNITED KINGDOM: *Special Report*.) Similar movements also were growing stronger in France, notably in regions possessing a language other than French. This was true not only in Brittany, which had a right-wing movement (the Breton Revolutionary Army) and a left-wing movement (the Movement of National Liberation by Socialism), but also in Occitania (centred on Languedoc), Alsace, Savoy, and Corsica, where violence flared in the summer of 1975. Even the authoritarian administration in Spain faced regionalist pressure for ethnic and cultural rights.

In Asia the resident Chinese community in Malaysia was nervous about accelerated "malayanization," *e.g.*, in the use of the Malay language for education and the civil service. Northern Burma had dissident Shan, Kachin, and other minorities, and remnant Kuomintang and Chinese Communist groups operating in the Golden Triangle were not controlled by the government. Thailand received minority refugees from Burma as well as an influx of Meo highlanders from Laos. Other Meos were on the move from Vietnam after their hills were overrun by the North Vietnamese. In India the war against the Nagas was intensified in September. Continuing caste discrimination and violence against the 110 million or more Harijans or untouchables were reported, particularly in rural areas. Since independence many Harijans had become Christians or Buddhists to escape the stigma, while others, like the Dalit Panthers in Bombay, chose militant action.

South Africa. Détente between white South Africa and black Africa was in the air in 1975, but it took one form internally and quite another in the republic's external relations. The latter were exemplified by South Africa's relationship with Pres. Kenneth Kaunda of Zambia, who was also committed to détente over Rhodesia. South Africa withdrew its paramilitary forces from Rhodesia in 1975 and exerted consistent pressure on it to come to a constitutional settlement with its black majority. But détente inside the republic showed a different face.

The "six months' chance" requested by Prime Minister B. J. Vorster in November 1974 (and widely understood to mean internal policy changes acceptable to all) expired on May 6. While welcoming all that Vorster had done toward external détente, the director of the South African Institute of Race Relations, F.

J. van Wyk, pointed out that lasting détente could not be reached without easing certain areas of tension on the home front, notably influx control and the pass laws. Cautious moves toward internal détente included the opening of some hotels and restaurants to nonwhites, the phasing out of petty apartheid in municipal amenities, a slight easing of the sports policy, the opening of the Nico Malan Theatre in Cape Town to nonwhites, the inclusion of a few nonwhites in the diplomatic service, some relaxation of job reservation, the recruitment of nonwhites for the defense force, and a plan to build a medical school for blacks near Pretoria.

The main factor for change had been the inability of the white labour force to supply enough skilled workers to meet demands from industry and commerce. Many jobs reserved for whites were being given openly to blacks (*e.g.*, 15,000 jobs on the railways), and many employers had covertly taken on nonwhites in reserved skilled jobs. In October 1975 the government announced draft legislation to allow black African workers to set up industrial committees and negotiate binding wage agreements on a regional basis, an arrangement halfway toward full trade unionism. South Africa's first black bank, the African Bank of South Africa Ltd., was established during the year.

Influx control and pass laws continued to work hardships on most urban blacks (though the 515,608 tried under the pass laws in 1972–73 represented a sizable decrease from the 615,825 of 1971–72). Nearly 140,000 Africans arrested under pass law regulations were referred to government aid centres, which sent 92,886 of them to various "homelands." New regulations contained in Proclamation R133, for Rehabilitation Institutions in the Bantu Homelands (published on June 6, 1975), evoked widespread comment and criticism. They provided for the establishment of institutions in the homelands where, potentially, any African found guilty of a pass offense would be received, trained in habits of industry, and reoriented into the customs and culture of the national homeland unit over a period of three years under prison-like conditions.

Wrapped in an American flag, this Indian protester dances in front of a police roadblock surrounding the Alexian Brothers novitiate, near Gresham, Wisconsin, which was seized by a group of Menominee Indians in January.

UPI COMPIX

In 1973 the Bantu Affairs Administration (BAA) took over control of all Africans in white areas, including farm workers—3,310,565 Africans were living on white-owned farms according to the 1970 census. The BAA boards were interpreting regulations dealing with the job placement of African farm workers very strictly; in theory such workers could move only to work on another farm, but in practice many went to seek work in the towns. Farm wages continued low, and the minister of agriculture opposed minimum wage regulations. Real wages for blacks, although still unsatisfactory, had risen since 1960; there were improvements in some indicators of wealth, such as education, and output per worker had increased markedly. Since World War II, however, the white share of total income had remained constant at nearly 75% and the African share at under 20%. In 1973 a total of 475,387 foreign African workers were recruited from nearby African countries.

The right of partial home ownership by Africans in black townships, taken away in 1967, was restored in May 1975, in terms of 30-year leases that could be sold or left to one's family, but little was done for Africans in the public low-cost housing field. In Cape Town there was a housing backlog of 50,000 for the Coloured population, and a major "squatters" crisis was reported. The local authorities and the BAA board virtually declared war on an estimated 100,000–200,000 Coloured squatters and large numbers of Africans.

Reflecting the national government's more pragmatic and flexible stance, the minister of justice, J. T. Kruger, stated in April that the creation of too many petty offenses bred contempt for the administration of justice. In 1973 a recorded 364,000 sentenced and 268,487 unsentenced prisoners had been admitted to prison. An average of 95,015 people, most of them nonwhites, were in prison every day, the equivalent of 413 for every 100,000 of population, as compared with 25 per 100,000 in The Netherlands, 70 in France, and 72 in Britain. In 1948 treason, murder, and rape were the three capital crimes in South Africa; since then terrorism, sabotage, armed robbery, kidnapping, and housebreaking with aggravating circumstances had been added. A peak of judicial killings was reached in 1968 with 118 executions, but a decline followed. In 1972, 1973, and 1974, South African courts sentenced 241 people to death. Of these 129 were executed (91 Africans, 32 Coloured, 4 whites, and 2 Asians).

The lawlessness in the nonwhite community was a product of the segregated, overcrowded townships in which so many lived. In Soweto, the one million-strong black labour reservoir for Johannesburg, as many as 80 murders a month were reported. Repressive moves by the authorities included declaring the Christian Institute of Southern Africa to be an "affected organization" and therefore forbidden to receive funds from abroad. The trial of 13 persons being held in connection with a September 1974 rally in

WIDE WORLD

Marching to New York's City Hall, an estimated 5,000 Chinese-Americans protested police brutality and demanded equal opportunity for Asians and other minority groups.

support of the Frelimo liberation movement in Mozambique was begun in March and subsequently postponed. These prisoners, and later others, were held in indefinite detention under the Suppression of Terrorism Act. (*See* SOUTH AFRICA.)

It was difficult to gauge political attitudes and trends among black Africans. There appeared to be a split in the banned African National Congress. Leaders in South Africa believed that the organization should turn from armed struggle to a peaceful, evolutionary policy, while exiles in London were divided between a Communist group and a wing favouring closer relations with other African nationalists.

White attitudes toward the Coloured people seemed more flexible. In an opinion poll, white voters were asked whether they would like to see Coloured people represented in Parliament by their own Coloured members. Among Afrikaans-speaking respondents, 47% replied affirmatively and only 35% negatively, with 18% undecided; among the white community as a whole, 57% were in favour of Coloured MPs. Sectors of the Afrikaans press also talked of "reintegrating" the Coloured people into the white community, but simultaneously many Coloured people were choosing to call themselves black and identifying with Africans and Indians. Relations between the (Coloured) Labour Party, led by Sonny Leon, and the government moved nearer to a collision course after the antiapartheid Labour Party won an overall victory in the Coloured Persons' Representative Council. The Labour Party's aim was full citizenship, and in September 1975 it adjourned the council until March 1976, giving Vorster six months to add substance to his "equal neighbours" policy for the Coloureds.

United Kingdom. In April 1975 the 20-year period of New Commonwealth immigration into Britain was drawing to a close. Current immigration was mainly restricted to East African holders of U.K. passports who had no other citizenship and to dependents of Commonwealth citizens already in Britain. The government was reviewing the law of citizenship. Before the current Parliament ended, it hoped to define a U.K. citizen for the first time in history. Immigration law would then be recast on the basis of U.K. requirements, without racial or ethnic discrimination.

In September the government published a White Paper, "Racial Discrimination," foreshadowing a new statute to replace the existing Race Relations Act. Among other things, this would create a single new agency, the Race Relations Commission, to replace the Race Relations Board and the Community Relations Commission; extend the definition of unlawful discrimination to cover nationality and citizenship (not just nationality), education, discrimination in private clubs, and such current exceptions as the preservation of a "racial balance" in some jobs; do away with the conciliation committees and allow alleged victims of racial discrimination to have direct access to legal remedies in the courts and tribunals; and make the law governing incitement to racial hatred more effective. The White Paper's proposals were strongest and most definite on the legal side; nothing definite was said about the future of such existing programs as the Urban Program, or of the 85 local community relations councils working with the Community Relations Commission.

By 1975 a substantial proportion of coloured immigrants were U.K. citizens, and two-fifths had been born and bred there. In 1974 the total of Commonwealth citizens admitted for settlement (mostly dependents) was 24,605 (20,424 in 1973), plus 13,433 U.K. passport holders, also mostly dependents (10,440 in 1973). As of April 30 a total of 1,539 Commonwealth citizens and citizens of Pakistan who had entered the country illegally before Jan. 1, 1973, had applied to have their positions regularized, and 785 of these had been given indefinite leave to remain; 45,910 Commonwealth citizens acquired U.K. citizenship in 1974, most of them Pakistani citizens who had become aliens on Sept. 1, 1973, after Pakistan left the Commonwealth.

The 1974 report of the Race Relations Board stated that 1,007 complaints had been registered, the highest total since 1970 and 27% more than in 1973. The board disposed of 1,050 cases; in 224 of these opinions of discrimination were formed. The Community Relations Commission in its 1974 report described its strategy of establishing contacts with minority groups, pressing government to meet their needs, and developing techniques for monitoring the progress of community relations.

Between November 1973 and May 1975 unemployment of coloured people rose by 156%, compared with a rise of 65% for the whole work force. Countrywide, there were 27,573 jobless coloured workers, or 3.4% of the unemployed, but in certain areas the situation was much worse. In some long-term depressed areas, like Brixton in South London and Liverpool, the position was especially bad for school dropouts, with coloured youth, particularly West Indians equipped only for unskilled jobs, bearing the brunt.

The 13,000 or so overseas-trained physicians, most of them Asians, had found less difficulty in getting positions; they accounted for around half the medical staff of some departments of the British hospital service and a sixth of the National Health Service's general practitioners. Concern about language ability and clinical competence led the General Medical Council to announce that, from May 22, 1975, no medical qualifications obtained in India would be recognized for full registration in Britain. Doctors qualifying in India would be eligible for temporary registration only, provided that they passed a test of linguistic and professional competence. An Overseas Doctors Association was formed to ensure that the viewpoint and concerns of these doctors should be represented.

A high incidence of homelessness as well as unemployment was reported for young West Indians, and in January £2 million was injected into the youth service in an effort to alleviate these problems. A majority of the nearly 1,000 cases of robbery (less than 500 categorizable as "muggings") reported in Lambeth in 1974 were carried out by blacks on white victims. Increasing aggressiveness on the streets was accompanied by a growing hostility to the police. In October a major drive was launched to recruit more coloured policemen to join the 41 officers already serving in London.

A study of Bradford, Leicester, Manchester, and Wolverhampton, published by the Runnymede Trust in November 1975, showed that 57% of the coloured population lived in bad housing conditions. In September 1975 a government White Paper, "Race Relations and Housing," was published in tardy response to recommendations made by the parliamentary Select Committee on Race Relations four years earlier. Among other things, it noted that "the most important question was not that of concentration versus dispersal" but of improving the housing, environment, and employment opportunities for inner urban areas where large numbers of coloured families would continue to live for some time to come. A new Political and Economic Planning report, *Racial Minorities and Public Housing,* recommended making dispersal an explicit aim of housing policy, with immigrants grouped to form small communities.

(SHEILA PATTERSON)

United States. Race relations in the U.S. in 1975, unlike those of the 1960s, were far more the product than the shaper of events. The nation's economic and political retrenchment fell hardest on racial minorities, and progress in civil rights was limited.

In 1974 recorded black unemployment averaged 13.7%, compared with 7.6% for whites. These figures rose with each month of 1975 until May, when they reached 14.7 and 8.7%, respectively, and then began to recede slowly. However, the National Urban League calculated that, if those who had despaired of finding a job and those forced to work part-time were included, "actual black unemployment" in the first quarter of 1975 was 25.7%.

Not surprisingly, black family income and purchasing power lost ground to inflation in both 1974 and 1975. The U.S. Census Bureau classified 31.4% of blacks and 8.9% of whites as "poor" in 1974. Pres. Gerald Ford, addressing the National Association for the Advancement of Colored People meeting in July in Washington, D.C., conceded that the recession hit hardest at minorities, but he blamed the recession on "the federal government's spending spree" on social programs. In May the congressional Black Caucus, noting the Ford request for aid to Vietnam refugees, had called for expanded social aid to "domestic refugees"—minorities, the poor, and the unemployed.

Throughout the year considerable attention was given to minority employment by government. In May the General Accounting Office reported to Congress that there was a pattern of "almost nonexistence of enforcement actions" under a 1965 executive order prohibiting job discrimination by federal contractors. Rep. John Moss (Dem., Calif.) released Civil Service Commission studies demonstrating how many federal agencies violated both civil service and equal employment regulations designed to protect minorities and women. At the local level, Mayor Richard J. Daley of Chicago agreed in April to hire 200 more police officers, mostly blacks and women, in order to recover $76 million in withheld revenue-sharing funds, but the funds remained tied up pending settlement of a dispute over compliance. Also in April, the U.S. Justice Department obtained a consent decree from Tallahassee, Fla., requiring the hiring of qualified blacks to all types of city jobs.

Federal courts were active in private hiring cases. The 5th Circuit Court of Appeals in New Orleans, La., banned "separate-but-equal" racial locals of the longshoremen's union. The court also ruled that last-hired, first-fired seniority principles were constitutional, even though past discrimination placed most blacks at the bottom of the seniority ladder. If upheld, this ruling would be a blow to minority employment. However, the Supreme Court let stand a ruling that ordered Massachusetts cities to give preference to black and Spanish-surnamed applicants for jobs as fire fighters.

Another blow was a 5–4 Supreme Court ruling in a case challenging zoning restrictions in Penfield, N.Y., a suburb of Rochester, that made housing too expensive for poor and most minority families to afford. The court dismissed the case for want of legal standing. However, the court did let stand a lower-court ruling that a Black Jack, Mo., ordinance banning construction of multiple-family dwellings had the effect of excluding blacks.

The most important political development for minorities in 1975 was the extension and expansion of the Voting Rights Act. The original 1965 act had been the most effective of all recent civil rights laws. Applied to seven Southern states and parts of several others, it required federal approval of any voting law

This group of New Yorkers demonstrated their support of Jews abroad.

PETER L. GOULD—KEYSTONE

changes. Moreover, federal registrars could be sent in to oversee elections, and a temporary ban was placed on literacy qualifications for voting. The 1975 version extended the act for seven years, made the literacy test ban permanent, applied the act to all of Texas and Alaska and parts of 12 other states, and extended its coverage to include native Americans, Asian-Americans, Alaskan natives, and Spanish-speaking Americans as well as black Americans. From 1965 to 1975, this act had helped to increase the number of black elected officials in the South from 100 to 1,500. Meanwhile, in the North, Albert Wheeler was elected in April as the first black mayor of Ann Arbor, Mich., and Richard Hatcher was reelected to a third four-year term as the first black mayor of Gary, Ind.

Detroit's black mayor, Coleman Young, personally calmed serious racial disturbances in his city in July. The trouble was touched off by the shooting of a black youth by a white tavern owner. Violence also marked the actions of a terrorist group called the Armed Forces of the Puerto Rican National Liberation (FALN). In January the FALN set off a bomb in a New York City tavern that killed 4 and injured 53, and in October it claimed responsibility for nearly simultaneous early morning bombings in New York City, Washington, and Chicago.

Indian militancy continued. Two FBI agents were shot and killed in June at Oglala, S.D., on the Pine Ridge Reservation, and an Indian from Idaho was killed in a later shoot-out. Other Indians seized buildings in three states. In January Menominees in Wisconsin occupied an unused novitiate belonging to the Alexian Brothers, a Roman Catholic monastic order. In March and May, Yankton Sioux in Wagner, S.D., occupied a pork-processing plant in which the tribe owned a 51% interest; they demanded better pay and working conditions. In April Kickapoos and Pottawatomis occupied the Bureau of Indian Affairs office at Horton, Kan., and won a demand for replacement of the reservation superintendent.

White violence also flared during 1975. In Louisville, Ky., the federal district court ordered busing, for desegregation purposes, of 22,600 pupils in the city and adjoining Jefferson County. Protests against the order escalated into violence during September. In Boston six visiting blacks were attacked by whites on a public beach in July, but the city began its second year of school desegregation without the violence that had marred 1974. President Ford continued to attack "forced busing," and James Coleman, the University of Chicago sociologist whose 1966 report had indicated that the scholastic achievement of black students improved when they were placed in integrated classes, stated that court-ordered school desegregation in large cities accelerated the flight of whites to the suburbs. Other social scientists, using similar data, found no such relationship, however.

Nonetheless, some progress in school desegregation was achieved. In March a federal judge ordered the administration to enforce desegregation guidelines in 164 Southern and border school districts. In May the Internal Revenue Service announced that church-affiliated schools refusing, except on solely religious grounds, to accept pupils of all racial and ethnic backgrounds would lose their tax-exempt status. In August a federal judge ordered Indianapolis, Ind., to transfer 6,500 black students into eight school systems in the surrounding metropolitan area.

Wide publicity was given to the trial of Joanne Little (*see* BIOGRAPHY) in Raleigh, N.C. She was acquitted in August by an interracial jury of killing a white jailer in the Beaufort County Jail.

Three prominent black Americans died during 1975. Josephine Baker, the famous entertainer of the 1920s, died in Paris in April, just four days after the opening of a revue celebrating her 50 years in show business. Percy Julian, the renowned chemist, died in April in Waukegan, Ill., at the age of 76. He had isolated soya protein and was an early synthesizer of cortisone. Elijah Muhammad died in February in Chicago after heading the Black Muslims for over 40 years. His fourth son, Wallace Muhammad, was immediately proclaimed as the Black Muslims' new leader. (*See* OBITUARIES.)

Gen. Daniel James, Jr., of the U.S. Air Force became the first black four-star general when he assumed command of the North American Air Defense Command in August. Joan Winn became the first black female judge in Texas, and Joseph Hatchett of Florida became the South's first black state supreme court justice since Reconstruction. William T. Coleman, Jr., named U.S. secretary of transportation in March, was the second black Cabinet member in U.S. history. (THOMAS FRASER PETTIGREW)

[522.B]

ENCYCLOPÆDIA BRITANNICA FILMS. *Heritage in Black* (1969); *The Mexican-American Speaks: Heritage in Bronze* (1972); *The American Indian Speaks* (1973).

Refugees

The Office of the United Nations High Commissioner for Refugees (UNHCR) in 1975 again devoted a substantial proportion of its resources to special tasks as distinct from its annual program of material as-

Cambodian heads of families assemble to receive rations to feed their starving families after the fall of Phnom Penh.

UPI COMPIX

Rackets: *see* Tennis and Rackets
Radio: *see* Television and Radio
Railroads: *see* Transportation
Real Tennis: *see* Tennis and Rackets
Recordings: *see* Music
Reformed Churches: *see* Religion

sistance. In fact, of the $74 million contributed to UNHCR up to mid-November, $61 million was for this purpose.

The absence of a political agreement in Cyprus obliged UNHCR to continue its role as coordinator of humanitarian assistance there throughout the year. The UN secretary-general had asked the high commissioner, Sadruddin Aga Khan, to extend for four months his original action, which was to have finished at the end of 1974, and UNHCR appealed for $9 million to cover needs for that period. Following the secretary-general's request, no new appeal was made but funds continued to be received, notably from the United States ($9.9 million), the United Kingdom, and West Germany. With relief needs met for the most part, the trend was toward measures that promoted basic self-sufficiency, and UNHCR participated in the financing of a variety of such projects.

The expected repatriation of refugees to former Portuguese territories that had achieved their independence got under-way. Approximately 25,000 persons were returned by UNHCR from Senegal to Guinea-Bissau between March and June, when the rainy season forced a suspension of the operation. Between mid-October and mid-November 20,000 refugees who had been living in Tanzania were repatriated to Mozambique with UNHCR assistance, and in November the agency helped 1,500 refugees return from Zambia to Mozambique. There was also substantial individual repatriation from both countries. The high commissioner appealed for $4 million and $7.1 million, respectively, for its Guinea-Bissau and Mozambique operations. The warlike conditions prevailing in Angola prevented a similar program there.

By far the largest special operations that UNHCR was called upon to undertake during the year were in Indochina. In the early part of 1975 the agency continued to implement projects begun in 1974 to further the return of displaced persons to their home villages within Laos and Vietnam. The end of the Vietnam war in April led to an emergency relief operation carried out in conjunction with UNICEF (the United Nations Children's Fund). More than $16 million was contributed to UNHCR for the purchase and delivery of 22,500 tons of food, medicine, clothing, and shelter material. This operation subsequently phased into an expanded program of assistance for displaced persons within Laos, North Vietnam, and South Vietnam. Following a three-week fact-finding mission to the Indochinese Peninsula, the high commissioner appealed for $20 million to finance these measures until the end of 1976.

UNHCR was also active in facilitating resettlement of Indochinese. In May the high commissioner appealed twice to governments to open their doors to displaced Indochinese. The bulk of the 237,000 persons who left their country of origin went to the U.S. Substantial numbers also found new homes in France, Canada, Malaysia, and Australia.

Within the annual program, the most acute problem was in Latin America, where refugees, mostly from Chile, formed a backlog in Argentina and Peru. Though some governments opened their doors in response to the high commissioner's appeals, the overall shortage of resettlement opportunities caused mounting bitterness and frustration among those awaiting a chance to begin life in a new country. The gravity of this situation was underlined dramatically on October 8 when ten refugees, some of them armed, entered the UNHCR regional office in Buenos Aires and took the staff hostage. Algeria agreed to accept the refugees, including family members, and the hostages were released unharmed after two days.

WIDE WORLD

Unaccustomed to the cool temperatures in the U.S., these young Vietnamese refugees were pleased to have oversized GI-issue coats at Camp Pendleton, California.

As in the past several years, the largest allocation within the annual program was for refugees in Africa. Emphasis was on completing projects begun in earlier years. Nearly $2 million went for the consolidation of two settlements in Tanzania. Each accommodated 50,000 refugees from Burundi, the largest settlements ever established with UNHCR aid.

In the field of international protection, UNHCR's prime function, the high commissioner publicly criticized growing violations of basic rights in the treatment of refugees. Before both the 31-country UNHCR Executive Committee and the Third Committee (the Social, Humanitarian, and Cultural Committee) of the General Assembly, he noted that governments were to an increasing extent guilty of abuses such as the forcible return of refugees to their country of origin, illegal detention, and abduction. The Executive Committee endorsed a proposal that the high commissioner make a new appeal to governments to respect humanitarian principles in dealing with refugees.

(UNHCR)

See also Migration, International.

[525.A.1.c.iii]

SPECIAL REPORT

FLIGHT IN VIETNAM

By Richard West

The flight of refugees in South Vietnam in March and April 1975 was both a result and a cause of the Saigon government's military setbacks. Yet some observers think that the Saigon government and its United States advisers may have encouraged the panic exodus south to Saigon and then out of Saigon to exile abroad. The flight of refugees puzzled foreign reporters, Vietnamese officials, and even the refugees themselves, many of whom had no clear reason for running.

Flight from the Central Highlands. The flight began from the town of Ban Me Thuot in the central highlands of South Vietnam, whose political problems were different from those of the rest of the country. The aboriginal inhabitants of the highlands are not Vietnamese but tribespeople, known to the French as Montagnards, who are thought to be possibly Polynesian by race. Under French rule the Vietnamese were not allowed to settle in the highlands, but in post-colonial times they have bought or seized Montagnard land and established large towns like Ban Me Thuot which are largely Vietnamese. The Vietnamese are much resented by many Montagnards, especially the Rhade people who live in the Ban Me Thuot area.

According to Vietnamese and French witnesses in Ban Me Thuot in early March, the fighting began as a revolt of the Montagnards, some of them led by Communist Vietnamese officers. The rebels killed several officials whom they regarded as their oppressors; the rest of the Vietnamese fled in fear of a racial massacre. Soon troops and civilians started to flee east to the coast from other highland towns such as Kontum, Pleiku, and Da Lat. Most of the refugees left before they had seen any signs of a major Communist presence, lending weight to the theory that the Communists too were taken by surprise. Many Vietnamese fled from the highlands because they had heard about a collapse of that area on the British Broadcasting Corporation's radio broadcasts, which Pres. Nguyen Van Thieu blamed publicly for creating panic. On the other hand, it was widely believed in diplomatic circles that Thieu himself had planned to evacuate the highlands because he thought his army was no longer strong enough to hold such a large, underpopulated region.

Panic at Hue and Da Nang. By the middle of March the panic had spread from the highlands to the narrow east coast lowlands, which are very densely populated. The people at Quang Tri, on the then border with the Communists, went south to Hue where it was thought the South Vietnamese would stand and fight. Its military commander had pledged his honour to hold the historic city or die in the attempt, and he commanded some of South Vietnam's best troops, including the crack Marines who had fought off the last major offensive in 1972. But in the last week of March, the regional government ordered that Hue be evacuated. At the time it was said that two-thirds of the citizens left for the south, but that estimate may be too large. They went by road, plane, or boat, mostly to Da Nang, the country's second largest city and a former U.S. base. Some soldier refugees got off the boats at Da Nang missing the trousers and boots they had shed to swim out to safety. Most of them carried personal weapons, but they had left behind 200 field guns and the 60 tanks of an armoured brigade.

At first the Da Nang police kept control of the refugee traffic and found shelter for people in private homes. Then, on March 27, Da Nang fell into panic as it was learned that Communist troops were drawing nearer. Thousands went to the airport to try to get on a scheduled flight to Saigon or on one of the charter planes brought into service by enterprising U.S. businessmen. There was much fighting at ticket counters to buy black market tickets. One Caravelle plane, with seating space for 125 people, took off with 197. Yet a chartered Boeing 727 left almost empty because the pilot feared so many people would board that he would not be able to take off.

The combined air services could not fulfill their plan of evacuating more than 5,000 people a day. There were menacing scenes at the airport as armed soldiers forced civilians off the planes in order to take their places. The representatives of a British charity organization went to the airport armed with revolvers and submachine guns in order to keep off the Vietnamese who might try to force them away. Because foreigners seemed to be getting away more easily, many Vietnamese turned on them. Government troops fired many random shots into the French Cultural Centre where most of the French had gathered. The U.S. crew of one of the refugee ships had to lock themselves into a cabin for fear of being attacked by soldiers. Other troops on the refugee ships raped women and robbed and beat up men. When one refugee ship arrived at Phu Quoc Island, off the coast of Cambodia, the soldiers identified as offenders were promptly shot on the beach after a drumhead court-martial.

Trail and Boat to Saigon and Vung Tau. In the first ten days of April, refugees started to leave Quang Ngai, Qui Nhon, Nha Trang, Cam Ranh, Phan Rang, and Phan Thiet, the chain of towns running down the coast. Most seem to have headed for Saigon, although the government had tried to prevent this. After the years of bombing and fighting, there were so many refugees in the capital that almost everyone in the country had a relative there and could find shelter.

Those who went south by boat came first to Vung Tau, a seaside resort and fishing port about 40 mi. SE of Saigon. The officers commandeered the luxury holiday hotels, equipped with fountains and tennis courts. The cafés and restaurants enjoyed a boom. Many prostitutes who had left Vung Tau with the Americans reappeared from Saigon to ply their trade with Vietnamese troops, at much reduced rates. The organization for coping with refugees worked better at Vung Tau than it had at Da Nang. Military police ensured that the troops handed over their weapons; the civilian police drove about in jeeps with loudspeakers, trying to regroup families. As Stewart Dalby wrote in the *Financial Times* of London: "It is very like English fun-fair or football crowd stuff—'Will Mr. Jones come to the Red Cross tent where his three-year-old son George is asking for him.'" When the present writer went to Vung Tau about three days before the Communists came, almost all the refugees had been dispersed.

The Question of Numbers. In the confusion and anxiety, it was impossible to estimate how many refugees there were. In early April, the estimates given by South Vietnamese and U.S. officials ran up to two million; others put the figure as low as 250,000. Certainly the number was less than the actual population of the refugee camps that had been set up around Saigon. It is probable that the Saigon government exaggerated the number of refugees in order to suggest to the world—above all to the United States from whom it wanted more military aid—that the mass of people feared the Communists. It was reported but never verified that an army commander on leaving Hue had threatened to shell the city to force people to leave.

It had long been a policy of the United States to create refugees in order to depopulate country areas and drive the inhabitants into towns or "new" villages where they would not be

Richard West was in Vietnam from 1966 until 1975 as correspondent for the London Daily Mail, *the* New Statesman, *the* Irish Times, *and the British Broadcasting Corp. He has written* Sketches from Vietnam *(1968) and* Victory in Vietnam *(1974).*

open to Communist influence. "Refugees Make Solid Citizens," one U.S. aid manifesto explained. Gen. William Westmoreland, formerly U.S. commander in South Vietnam, once justified his "search and destroy" operations: "I expect a tremendous increase in the number of refugees." His colleague in antiterrorist work, Ambassador Robert Komer, once said: "If we can attrite the population base of the Viet Cong it'll accelerate the progress of degrading the VC." To encourage the flow of refugees in March and April, the Saigon government and the U.S. embassy in Saigon put out stories of Communist atrocities that were, to say the least, hard to verify. For example, it was said that in coastal towns like Nha Trang, the Communists had cut off the heads of all children fathered by Americans. On the other hand, the flight of refugees may even have helped the Communists, who used the exodus as a way of infiltrating a fifth column. The panic involved in the refugee flight created a feeling of pessimism that made it almost impossible for the government to stage a military rally in front of Saigon.

There is also disagreement about why the refugees fled. Some, such as senior army officers, policemen, and intelligence agents, undoubtedly feared for their lives. But the *New York Times,* whose reporters had interviewed hundreds of refugees, stated on March 26 that most of them had answered: "Because everyone else is going." Not one of them had told their interviewers that he or she feared or hated Communism as such. They all feared bombing and shelling and, as one woman refugee said, "It's better to go to the Saigon side because the Communists have no airplanes."

Evacuation of Saigon. On April 2 the U.S. government announced that some 2,000 South Vietnamese war orphans would be flown from Saigon to the United States for adoption there. The Australian government followed with an offer to take in over 200 orphans, and some flights were made to Britain and other European countries. After a U.S. Air Force transport plane carrying more than 240 children had crashed shortly after takeoff from Saigon on April 4, killing over 140 children and more than 60 adults, there was widespread protest in South Vietnam and in other countries, and the concept of the operation came under criticism. On April 7 the South Vietnamese government announced that orphan children would be allowed to leave only if they had prospective adoptive parents waiting for them.

In Saigon itself, which had been surrounded and then besieged by the middle of April, great fear was evident among middle-class people. Saigon people, unlike the villagers, had never had any contact with the Communists and were apt to believe the most alarming stories. They also felt, perhaps with justification, that the Communists regarded Saigon as the hub of corruption, vice, and U.S. influence, and therefore would punish it. There was also much fear of street fighting such as had twice taken place in 1968. Of those who managed to leave Saigon, most were top men in the Army, government, and police, many of whom had sent money abroad and could afford a comfortable exile. There were also many businessmen, especially from the Chinese community, who could afford to bribe officials for exit visas, and many employees of U.S. commercial firms, news agencies, banks, and the embassy itself, who feared reprisals. Finally, there were the wives and children of Americans; many Americans married their mistresses in last-minute embassy weddings.

The final evacuation took place on April 29 under the cover of a 24-hour curfew throughout Saigon. The sky was filled with clatter as small Huey helicopters landed on rooftops in downtown Saigon and big CH 53 "Jolly Green Giants" landed in the U.S. embassy compound. Two U.S. Marines were killed when the Communists shelled Tan Son Nhut Airport. The helicopters flew to a 40-vessel U.S. naval armada off the coast. The aircraft, having unloaded their passengers, were thrown into the sea to make room for more. Most of the refugees were taken to the U.S. island base of Guam, where about one-third decided later they wanted to return to Vietnam. Some turned out not to be refugees at all but fishermen seen off the coast who were whisked away on the assumption that they wanted to flee. Some, on reading reports that the Communists were behaving correctly, decided to chance a return. Others apparently had escaped only because they feared the fighting.

Later reports from Saigon indicated that most of the refugees from the north who fled there had gone home. Whatever their political views, they could feel fairly confident, for the first time in 30 years, that they would not have to flee again.

View of friends and relatives left behind from the last boat to evacuate Da Nang, South Vietnam, on April 1.

SYGMA

Religion

Halfway through the 1970s, the most marked trend and most publicized events in religion were new tensions and conflicts within the churches. The emerging pattern differed vastly from that of the mid-'60s.

In the 1960s many churches were polarized and almost torn apart because, within most of them, two factions were attracted to opposite sides of divisive public issues. Those issues, in contrast to the ones upsetting denominations a decade later, resulted from the pressure or appeal of causes that were basically external to the life of the churches.

By far the most publicized of these causes was the civil rights movement. Black church leaders and members debated whether to take militant or revolutionary attitudes or to go quieter and more moderate ways. Some white churches were almost sundered when their leaders moved ahead of more conservative clienteles in support of integration and, later, militancy in the black cause. The Vietnam war similarly divided the churches almost exactly as it divided the society: into hawks and doves.

Almost every other social movement of the day had both defenders and detractors in the churches. Most members regarded the extremes with distaste, arguing that religious organizations need not or should not take stands on social questions. But the minorities on the left who worked for change and on the right who supported the status quo drew most attention.

Church bodies, in the end, did not split as a result of these controversies, though race was at least an underground problem in the largely Southern Presbyterian Church in the United States, from which the new Presbyterian Church in America parted. But splits or schisms were being threatened on other grounds in 1975. Because of battles over property and pensions, as well as the fact that traditions and family ties help hold churches together, it is difficult for denominations to break up. But observers foresaw that a number of troubled churches would face wars of attrition or joyless infighting because of doctrinal or policy differences for some years to come.

Few had foreseen such a situation. Many analysts had thought that the power of denominations themselves had largely disappeared in the age of ecumenism. The separate churches did not seem worth fighting about. Others considered the spirit of the age to be one in which belief and doctrine were themselves too unimportant to inspire debate. Whatever the reasons, however, people did engage in verbal civil wars over beliefs and behaviour patterns alike.

Examples were plentiful, beginning with the largest churches. Roman Catholicism is held together by a formal creed and a hierarchical organization. But it celebrated the tenth anniversary of the closing of the Second Vatican Council by recognizing ten years of internal stress over theological interpretation. At the moment the most visible quarrels were generated by the presence of several hundred thousand "charismatics." People in these movements believe in faith healings, their own styles of prayer meetings, emotional rallies, and the practice of glossolalia or "speaking in tongues." They had brought both new vitality and new dissension. In 1975 they were received by Pope Paul VI when they held a meeting in Rome, but in the same year criticism of their separateness became acute in America. (See *Roman Catholic Church,* below.)

The charismatic or Pentecostal issue also caused controversy in most of the large mainline Protestant churches, but each of them had other, distinctive problems. The largest Protestant body in the U.S., the Southern Baptist Convention, was partly protected from schism by the fact that its 12.3 million members insisted on the complete autonomy of each

Estimated Membership of the Principal Religions of the World*

Religions	North America†	South America	Europe‡	Asia	Africa	Oceania§	World
Total Christian	229,006,000	164,884,000	354,894,600	87,683,000	101,144,100	17,155,000	954,766,700
Roman Catholic	131,596,500	154,067,000	174,141,000	45,285,000	32,314,500	3,200,000	540,704,000
Eastern Orthodox	4,120,000	55,000	63,900,600	1,781,000	16,442,000‖	355,000	86,653,600
Protestant¶	93,289,500	10,762,000	116,833,000	40,617,000	52,367,600♀	13,600,000	327,509,100
Jewish	6,653,725	686,700	3,489,750	3,089,150	359,465	75,000	14,353,790
Muslim♂	242,100	195,300	8,370,000	430,267,000	99,073,500	66,000	538,213,900
Zoroastrian□	250	—	—	229,650	480	—	230,380
Shinto°	60,000	92,000	—	60,004,000	—	—	60,156,000
Taoist△	16,000	12,000	—	30,375,700	—	—	30,403,700
Confucian△	96,000	85,000	30,000	185,850,700	500	42,000	186,104,300
Buddhist+	150,500	190,300	222,000	249,296,500	2,000	16,000	249,877,300
Hindu⊕	75,000	533,000	350,000	522,184,500	490,550	640,000	524,273,050
Totals	236,299,675	166,678,300	367,356,350	1,568,980,200	201,070,595	17,994,000	2,558,379,120
Population**	342,609,000	218,325,000	728,166,000	2,255,458,000	401,138,000	21,308,000	3,967,004,000

*Religious statistics are directly affected by war and persecution; for example, recent events in Uganda, Bangladesh, and Cyprus alter the estimates of religious affiliation substantially. There are about 18 million refugees throughout the world who are not as yet integrated into the population statistics and religious estimates of their land of temporary (?) residence.

†Includes Central America and the West Indies.

‡Includes the U.S.S.R., in which the effect of a half century of official Marxist ideology upon religious adherence is evident, although the extent of religious disaffiliation and disaffection is disputed. The same difficulty in estimating religious adherence obtains in other nations with officially Marxist governments, although the degree of persecution varies from country to country and from time to time.

§Includes Australia and New Zealand as well as the islands of the South Pacific.

‖Includes Coptic Christians, numerous in Egypt and Ethiopia.

¶Protestant statistics outside Europe usually include "full members" only, rather than all baptized persons, and are not comparable to the statistics of ethnic religions or of churches counting all adherents.

♀Including many sects and cults of recent appearance and rapid growth.

♂The chief base of Islam is still ethnic, although missionary work has lately been undertaken in Europe and America. In countries where Islam is the official state religion, minority religions are frequently persecuted and reliable statistics are scarce. In some, such as Saudi Arabia, no general census has been taken.

□Zoroastrians (Parsees) are found chiefly in Iran and India.

°A Japanese ethnic religion, Shinto has declined markedly since the Japanese emperor gave up the claim to divinity (1947); neither does it transplant readily with Japanese moving out from the homeland, in contrast to Buddhism. Japanese religious statistics are problematical because adherents are frequently related to several different religions simultaneously.

△General population figures for China are highly speculative, although minimal population growth has apparently been achieved. Religious statistics are problematical, with the effect of the Maoist-Marxist revolution not yet measured definitively.

+Buddhism has produced several modern renewal movements, with energetic missions outside the traditional ethnic-Buddhist areas.

⊕Hinduism's strength in India has been enhanced by nationalism but eroded by modern industrialization and contemporary secular ideologies. Modern Hinduism has also developed several renewal movements with vigorous missions in Europe and America.

**Source: United Nations, Department of Economic and Social Affairs; data refer to midyear 1975.

(FRANKLIN H. LITTELL)

local congregation. Yet for some years their "ambassadors," meeting in national convention, had served notice that they did not welcome the growing moderate group's experiments in theology. The interpretation of the Bible was usually the controverted point.

The United Methodist Church, next in size in the U.S. with some 10 million adherents, was threatened from within by a "conservative evangelical" movement popularly called The Good News. "Has Good News become Bad News?" asked a headline in a Methodist newsletter, *The Interpreter*. The September issue commented on the militant conservative spokesmen's recent challenge to the denomination's Global Ministries Board and its Program-Curriculum Committee. In June The Good News people began to seek ways to bypass the official missionary program. In July, at their sixth annual convocation, a speaker lashed out at Methodism's "sick denomination" and "sick seminaries." This theological right wing wanted its own seminaries and possibly a separate jurisdiction within Methodism. Statistically small, it was still unsettling.

One of the most publicized disputes concerned Lutheranism. For several years the Lutheran Church —Missouri Synod had provided either the first or the second most important religious news story of the year, according to the vote of the Religion Newswriters Association. The conservative faction that came to power within the denomination in 1969 could summon 55–60% majorities at biennial conventions, where they insisted that a belief in biblical inerrancy had to be held by all members. The more moderate minority claimed that the freedom of the gospel and of local congregations was at stake. (See *Lutheran Churches*, below.)

The United Presbyterian Church in the U.S.A. had been in the avant garde of controversy with debates over its new confession in 1967, but some internal tension carried into the 1970s. A combination of theological and social issues led the Presbyterian Church in America to take away up to 100,000 members from the Presbyterian Church in the U.S. The larger church reported a lessening of troubles since their departure.

KEYSTONE

This hand with nails was designed for St. Gallen's section of Amnesty International in Switzerland, where a congress met in September to discuss torture throughout the world. The sign states "He who tortures man, tortures God."

Sharing headlines with the Missouri Synod Lutherans was the Episcopal Church, the U.S. branch of Anglicanism, where the dispute centred on the ordination of women to the priesthood. In 1974 and 1975 a number of women were ordained, despite opposition from most active bishops. (See *Anglican Communion*, below.) Discontent over a proposed revision of the Book of Common Prayer and over trial liturgies was less noticed but almost equally heated. Dissident movements were formed calling themselves the Anglican Episcopal Church in North America and the Anglican Church in America.

The Reverends Carter Heyward (left) and Alison Cheek celebrate communion in the church of the Rev. L. Peter Beebe, who risked suspension from the priesthood for allowing women to participate in this rite.

WIDE WORLD

The list could be extended almost indefinitely. Support of Israel and fear for survival had helped prevent overt disruptions in the three major branches of Judaism, but reform Judaism had been torn by arguments over whether rabbis should take part in religiously mixed marriages. The public watched for but did not yet see open breaks within the Black Muslim movement following the death of prophet Elijah Muhammad (*see* OBITUARIES). Here the line between factions would probably be drawn on the issue of "theological" change in attitudes toward whites. Just before his death the prophet had announced that he no longer wanted whites to be thought of as "devils," and his son and successor, Wallace Muhammad, enlarged on this policy. Even the so-called New Religions or Eastern cults experienced troubles. The Foundation Church replaced all but a remnant of its parent The Process Church, and the Divine Light Mission experienced trauma when the mother of the Maharaj Ji, regarded by his followers as divine, chided and repudiated him.

The outsider had good reason to be puzzled by this sudden turn. Denominations were designed to gather people of like mind. Conflict should be between groups, or against "the world." Besieged groups do tend to think and act together, but when the pressure is off, as in America in the '70s, they often act like people in families, who can have the liveliest fights with their own relatives. Some lauded the conflicts as a sign of vitality in the churches: there must be something there worth fighting for. But, taken as a whole, the quarrels revealed to other observers a disease of the spirit. Religious people who claim to be agents of human reconciliation and concord are embarrassed when they cannot recognize these qualities in their own circles.

Nonmembers found less at stake for themselves in these internal doctrinal wars than when churchly disputes touched on the shape of the larger society. Until and unless churches succeeded in demonstrating that the hopes of other people are bound up with the outcomes of their conflicts, it was likely that the churches would be distracted from their purposes and that nonmembers would become progressively dismayed or bored. At the very least, the conflicts drew attention away from the many creative activities most members claimed still existed within their denominations.

More than 700 delegates representing nearly 300 non-Roman Catholic Christian denominations gathered in Nairobi, Kenya, in late November for the fifth General Assembly of the World Council of Churches. Beset with crises and internal pressures since its last assembly in 1968, the ecumenical body grappled with such concerns as shrinking financial contributions, claims of religious persecution and racism, diminished fervour for interfaith activity, and calls by black African churches for greater independence from parent denominations.

Philip A. Potter, WCC general secretary, touched upon an issue sensitive to Arab delegates of Mideast Eastern Orthodox churches when he asked for a repudiation by the assembly of the recent UN condemnation of Zionism. After a long debate over new claims of religious persecution in the U.S.S.R., the council adopted a resolution calling upon the Soviet Union to safeguard religious freedom. Another controversial topic was the mandate of the 1968 assembly that had established a fund to aid liberation forces, primarily African blacks fighting white supremacist regimes; the 1975 assembly approved a policy document supporting both liberation efforts and struggles against racism and sex discrimination. Turning inwardly on the issue of sexism, the council elected two women—a Ghanaian jurist and a U.S. psychologist—to its six-member presidium.

(MARTIN E. MARTY)

The Most Rev. Stuart Blanch beats upon the door three times and awaits the threefold "welcome" shouted by the congregation at the beginning of the traditional ceremony enthroning him as the 94th archbishop of York.

ANDREW DAVIDSON—CAMERA PRESS/PHOTO TRENDS

PROTESTANT CHURCHES

Anglican Communion. The cohesion of the Anglican Communion depends to a great extent on the way the archbishop of Canterbury, officially "the principal focus of unity" for the whole institution, discharges the functions of his office. Donald Coggan, duly enthroned at Canterbury on Jan. 24, 1975, in succession to Michael Ramsey, lost no time in impressing his personal style of strong evangelical conviction on the church at home and overseas. His enthronement sermon, preached before an unprecedentedly wide representation of both Anglicans and other Christians, consisted of a powerful appeal to Anglicans everywhere to be both realistic and confident in facing the radical moral and spiritual sickness of the times.

The Anglican Consultative Council, an advisory liaison body for inter-Anglican relationships at the highest level, had intended to hold its biennial meeting in the late summer in Australia, in close connection with the World Council of Churches General Assembly in Indonesia. The change in venue and date of the WCC conference caused the Anglican council to postpone its own meeting until 1976, a nonevent that disappointed those who set store by the communion's effectual cohesion.

The traditional bond of unity formed by the common use of a virtually identical prayer book throughout the communion was further eroded by the continued invention and use of new, modern-language services. This growing diversity was not merely a matter of outward forms. Widespread argument continued among Anglicans over the basic Christian doctrines which such forms of service are used to express. Particularly controversial was the question of whether Anglicans should relax their general prohibition on the church marriage of the divorced.

Still more divisive was the vexed question of whether women should be ordained to the priesthood. In England on July 3, 1975, following a precedent set by Wales in April, the church's General Synod voted, by a two-to-one majority, that there was no objection in principle to the ordination of women but that any such ordinations would be inexpedient as long as a numerous minority within the church remained bitterly opposed. Canadian Anglicans grasped the nettle; in June the General Synod authorized the ordination of women to the priesthood, and the decision was ratified by the bishops in November. In the Episcopal Church (U.S.), the House of Bishops, which had previously voted in favour of ordination of women, censured three retired or resigned bishops for ordaining women as priests in violation of canon law. At the urging of the presiding bishop, John Allin (*see* BIOGRAPHY), the House did not order a trial. Some of the women who had been ordained in disputed ceremonies continued to exercise priestly functions in local churches friendly to their cause. No binding decision on the question could be taken until the next General Convention, due to be held in 1976.

In June Canadian Anglicans announced their formal withdrawal from union negotiations with two Protestant churches. A joint Anglican-Roman Catholic commission, meeting in Venice, Italy, in June, recorded unanimous agreement on the theological implications of "mixed marriages." To be effective, however, this

WIDE WORLD

"Heaven's Angels," a group of Anglican clergymen, demonstrate agility on their newly acquired vehicles as they receive a travelers' blessing from the bishop of Norwich and go forth to spread the word of God.

agreement, like its predecessors on the Eucharist and the ministry, required the official approval of the Vatican authorities, and this appeared problematical.

An unprecedented reorganization of the Anglican Church in the Middle East was announced in July. The Anglican archbishopric in Jerusalem was to be replaced by a synod consisting of four bishops (Jerusalem, Iran, Egypt, and Cyprus), together with clerical and lay members, to which (from January 1976) the archbishop of Canterbury was to delegate his powers over the 20,000 Anglicans in the area. Some fears were expressed that the standing of the Anglican presence in Jerusalem vis-à-vis that of other Christian churches might be adversely affected by the abolition of the archbishopric and that the choice of an Arab to be the first bishop in Jerusalem might be viewed with some displeasure by Israel.

(R. L. ROBERTS)

Baptist Churches. The 13th quinquennial congress of the Baptist World Alliance met in Stockholm during July 1975, with 9,600 delegates from 84 nations in attendance. The theme of the congress was "New People for a New World Through Jesus Christ." The significant use of the word "people" instead of the scriptural "men" (II Corinthians 5:7) demonstrated a sensitivity to such contemporary problems as sexism. A balanced program of speakers, both racially and nationally, indicated an awareness of the needs of less developed nations and sensitivity to the multinational, worldwide constituency of over 33 million Baptists.

More than 130 delegates from Communist nations were present. There were also 21 émigrés from the so-called underground churches in the U.S.S.R., who had fled since 1972 to West Germany, but they were not registered as official delegates. The congress voted to make the first constitutional changes in the structure of the BWA since its inception in 1905. David Y. K. Wong, a Hong Kong architect and chairman of the Asia Baptist Fellowship, was elected president of the BWA to succeed V. Carney Hargroves of the U.S. He was the first Asian and the first layman to hold the office. The delegates contributed $12,500 in 22 currencies toward the BWA's worldwide goal of a $1 million relief offering in 1975–76.

In the U.S. the Southern Baptist Convention, the largest non-Catholic denomination in the nation, met in Miami, Fla., in July. Southern Baptist membership continued to grow, reaching 12.3 million in 1974. A budget of $51 million was adopted at Miami, an increase of 25% over 1975; half would go to "foreign" missions. Roiling of the waters continued on such issues as the inerrancy of the Scriptures, but there was no floor debate on the matter.

The second biennial meeting of the American Baptist Churches in the U.S.A. was held in Atlantic City, N.J., in June. Charles Z. Smith, an attorney and professor of law at the University of Washington, became the second black president of the largely white denomination in recent years. The general secretary, Robert C. Campbell, reported that the Fund of Renewal, a joint effort with the predominantly black

UPI COMPIX

Martin Luther King, Sr., at the age of 75, ended his 44-year ministry with a sermon directed to the spirits of his wife and son at the Ebenezer Baptist Church, Atlanta, Georgia, in July.

Progressive National Baptists to raise $7.5 million for minority education, had reached $2 million.

Upholding the Baptist tradition of separation of church and state, James E. Wood, executive director of the Baptist Joint Committee on Public Affairs in Washington, D.C., representing various Baptist groups, wrote a letter to the American Revolution Bicentennial Administration protesting its proposal to provide matching grants of up to 50% of the cost of bicentennial projects undertaken by religious and other private groups.

(NORMAN R. DE PUY)

Christian Church (Disciples of Christ). In what was termed the most significant church union decision in the Christian Church (Disciples of Christ) since "Christians" and "Disciples" merged in 1832, the church's General Assembly, held in San Antonio, Texas, Aug. 15–20, 1975, overwhelmingly approved steps toward full recognition of members of other denominations. Although Disciples had always been leaders in the ecumenical movement, they baptize only by immersion, and many congregations accept transfers from other denominations only if they are immersed. The action to work toward "removing any impediments" to recognition of members of other churches clearly supported continued involvement of Disciples in the Consultation on Church Union. Many observers had felt that COCU, a proposal to unite nine U.S. denominations, had been losing momentum in recent years.

In their 1975 assembly the Disciples also took a liberal position on abortion, reiterated opposition to capital punishment, declared higher education to be a major priority, and called on members to support agricultural aid programs and to have a symbolic sacrificial meal each week. James A. Moak, the church's regional executive in Kentucky, was elected moderator of the church in the U.S. and Canada for a two-year term, succeeding Jean Woolfolk of Little Rock, Ark.

Heads of church bodies in Japan, Thailand, India, and Indonesia met with Disciples leaders in Indianapolis, Ind., in a session aimed at determining the church's role in Asia. Among the findings: Christians have an allegiance to each other that rises above politics and national boundaries.

(ROBERT L. FRIEDLY)

Churches of Christ. Emphasis on evangelism, relief work, and printed communications marked the work of the estimated two million members of the Churches of Christ in 1975. Over 150 periodicals of a teaching, news, or devotional nature were published during the year according to a study by Star Publications, Inc. Since Churches of Christ have no central organization, these efforts were by local congregations or private publishing companies.

Three thousand persons attended the 39th annual Yosemite Family Encampment in California, and the Blue Ridge Family Encampment in North Carolina had record attendance. The busing ministry was proving to be a primary evangelistic tool of local churches. About 200,000 persons were bused each Sunday, and many churches ran 10 to 20 buses at a single service. "Heartbeat," a one-minute daily Herald of Truth program, signed a 13-week contract to broadcast during evening newscasts on the NBC Radio Network. The Mid-America Mobilization Seminar held in April by the South National Church in Springfield, Mo., drew students from 55 colleges and universities in 32 states.

Food and medicine were distributed to Honduran hurricane victims under the supervision of the Garden Oaks Church in Houston, Texas. Vietnamese refugees at Camp Pendleton, California, were served by such Churches of Christ as the Village Church in Oklahoma City, which resettled about 100 Vietnamese Christians in that area.

(M. NORVEL YOUNG)

Church of Christ, Scientist. During 1975 the Church of Christ, Scientist marked the 100th anniversary of the publication of the Christian Science textbook, *Science and Health with Key to the Scriptures* by Mary Baker Eddy. Mrs. Eddy discovered Christian Science in 1866 and founded the church in 1879. As of 1975, there were more than 3,000 branches in 57 countries.

At the annual meeting of the First Church of Christ, Scientist, in Boston in June, some 13,000 members from around the world were told that "Renewed devotion and dedication in works of Christian healing are the needs of this hour." Otto Bertschi of Zürich, Switz., was named as the first chairman of the board of directors to come from outside the U.S. Jules Cern of New York City became president of the Mother Church for 1975–76, succeeding Mrs. Georgina Tennant of London.

Twenty meetings for youth interested in Christian Science were held throughout the world during the year. New translations of *Science and Health* into Japanese and Indonesian were announced.

(J. BUROUGHS STOKES)

Church of Jesus Christ of Latter-day Saints. In mid-1975 Latter-day Saint leaders began an extensive restructuring of administrative jurisdiction over the church's major geographic divisions. Church missions in the U.S. and Canada were divided into 12 supervisory areas. One member of the Council of Twelve Apostles would serve as adviser in each area, with another General Authority to supervise all missions within the area. Six assistants to the Twelve Apostles would supervise all ecclesiastical and proselytizing work in six other areas of the world. At the same time, programs that tended primarily to benefit members in the western U.S. were modified to serve the needs of church members worldwide.

Two area general conferences were held in South America and five in Asia as part of an effort to bring the full program of the church to regions outside the U.S. Church leaders announced plans for the construction of temples in São Paulo, Brazil, and Tokyo. Church membership grew to approximately 3.6 million in 1975. By the end of the year there were more than 700 stakes (dioceses), including the first stake organized in Sweden.

Each Mormon within the U.S. was asked to give the equivalent of one 24-hour day in service to his community or state as part of the U.S. bicentennial commemoration. Church president Spencer W. Kimball and his two counselors urged every family to adopt a seven-point program to promote health and prevent shortages of food and fuel.

(LEONARD JAMES ARRINGTON)

Jehovah's Witnesses. During 1975 the work of the society of Christian evangelizers and teachers known as Jehovah's Witnesses was organized by 38,250 congregations and carried on in 210 countries and territories. Some 295,000 new Christian evangelizers were baptized, raising the total worldwide to well over two million.

A successful series of "Divine Sovereignty" assemblies was held in the Northern Hemisphere during the summer. Over 1.2 million persons in the U.S., Canada, and the British Isles and thousands in other areas heard the lecture "One World, One Government, Under God's Sovereignty." A new Bible study aid, *Man's Salvation Out of World Distress at Hand!*, was released in English, Spanish, and German. A record 4,925,000 persons attended the annual celebration of the Lord's Evening Meal.

The Watch Tower Bible and Tract Society, Inc., the legal corporation and publishing agency of Jehovah's Witnesses, installed new presses in its plants in New York, Argentina, West Germany, Italy, Japan, and the Philippines. Circulation of *The Watchtower* reached 9.9 million in 78 languages, and its companion magazine, *Awake!*, 9.5 million in 31 languages.

Freedom to carry on Christian worship and to enjoy peaceable assembly was granted to Jehovah's Witnesses in Greece after years of legal struggle. However, intense opposition was still being encountered in Eastern Europe, the Arab countries, Cuba, and Malawi and some other African nations.

(N. H. KNORR)

Lutheran Churches. At the close of 1975, the Lutheran Church—Missouri Synod hovered on the brink of schism. In July the Synod's 51st General Convention, at Anaheim, Calif., paved the way for the ouster of moderates who disavow the theological stance of the dominant conservatives demanding literal interpretation of the Bible. In August the Synod's dissidents met in Chicago for the third assembly of Evangelical Lutherans in Mission (ELIM) and endorsed a series of actions predicated on withdrawal from the oldest (128 years) and second largest (2.8 million members) Lutheran body in the U.S. At the same time, ELIM said it would "support, encourage and assist" those who continue within the strife-torn denomination.

Jacob A. O. Preus, LCMS president, laid the central issue before delegates at Anaheim when he noted that "for the past two decades at least we have had two opposing theologies," and, he stressed, "no church body can long support two theologies which are in conflict." By a vote of nearly 3–2, conservatives declared ELIM to be "schismatic" and told those active in its functions "to cease such roles, . . . or terminate their membership in the Synod." Eight and possibly more of the Synod's 35 district presidents were warned of possible removal from office for ordaining graduates of Concordia Seminary in Exile (Seminex), the breakaway school formed by faculty and students of the Official Concordia Seminary in St. Louis, Mo. All the censured leaders spoke in defiance of the edict. Meanwhile, John H. Tietjen, former president of Concordia and president of Seminex, was absolved on all counts of heresy.

Later Preus issued several conciliatory statements that drew sharp attacks from both sides of the doctrinal dispute. In a letter to overseas churches, he expressed hope that ELIM could find its "proper place" within the Synod, and in a pastoral letter, he said he was "moving more into the middle" of the controversy in the church because of "words and deeds by both extremes that I simply do not like." In response, Samuel Roth, president of ELIM, wrote the LCMS leader that "First you employ every bit of power that you possess as president of the Synod . . . to crush your opposition. Then, having accomplished your objective, you call for patience on the part of all."

The Lutheran World Federation (LWF) set its

WIDE WORLD

An artist's conception of the Mormon temple which will be constructed in Tokyo.

sixth Assembly for June 13–25, 1977, on the campus of the University of Dar es Salaam in Tanzania. The theme was to be "In Christ—A New Community." The federation received three new members: the 67,000-member Moravian Church in South Africa, the 3,000-member Bolivian Evangelical Lutheran Church, and the 140,000-member Christian Protestant Church in Indonesia.

In South West Africa (Namibia), five prominent members of two black Lutheran churches were detained and placed in solitary confinement by South African security police during a wave of arrests following the assassination of the Ovamboland chief minister, Filemon Elifas, in August. Urgent appeals for help in obtaining their release were made by church leaders to the UN and to other governments. The German Evangelical Lutheran Church in South West Africa, which once resisted attempts to bring about closer relations with blacks, voted to begin unity negotiations with the Evangelical Lutheran Church and the Evangelical Lutheran Ovambokavango Church, both predominantly black and in the process of forming the United Lutheran Church of Namibia.

In early October, Bishop Helmut Frenz of the Evangelical Lutheran Church in Chile (ELCC) was declared persona non grata by the Chilean government and refused permission to return to Chile from Europe, where he had been attending an international consultation sponsored by the LWF. The LWF, the WCC, and many other church groups formally protested the ban. The government's action was supported by the schismatic Lutheran Church in Chile, organized in June by former members of the ELCC who objected to Bishop Frenz's refusal to endorse the military regime of Gen. Augusto Pinochet. Bishop Frenz had come under sharp criticism from a large portion of his 25,000-member church for his activities following the coup of September 1973. For his "inspiring example" in helping refugees, he had been awarded the 1974 Nansen Medal of the UN.

With terrorism growing in Argentina, several Lutheran leaders slipped quietly out of the country to seek asylum in the U.S. Among them was Juan Cobrda, 45-year-old president of the Argentine United Evangelical Lutheran Church and third vice-president of the LWF. During a year's "leave of absence," he was serving as pastor of St. John Lutheran Church in Trenton, N.J.

U.S. Lutheran and Roman Catholic theologians, marking the 21st meeting since their talks were launched in mid-1965, hoped to arrive at a consensus on papal infallibility early in 1976. A series of dialogues with the Reformed Churches was completed without definite recommendations. Dialogue resumed with the Episcopal Church, and conversations were scheduled with Pentecostals and jointly with Reformed and Orthodox churches.

For the sixth successive year, membership in the Lutheran church bodies of North America declined; in 1974 it was 8,964,383, a loss of 40,830 from the previous year. The six-year decrease of 274,891 represented nearly 3% of the all-time high of 9,239,274 members recorded in 1968.

(ERIK W. MODEAN)

Methodist Churches. The dominant theme for Methodists in 1975 was worldwide evangelism. Preparations by the Methodist conferences culminated in a World Consultation and Convocation in Jerusalem in November 1974, with a commissioning service and communications, including a message from Methodists to the world. The United Methodist Church in the U.S. embarked on an innovative New World Mission program, which brought international leaders from as far away as Australia and Africa to 370 communities across the U.S. to engage in local one-week missions. In a similar program in Australia later in the year, missioners from the U.S. visited churches in that country.

With church membership in the U.S. and Britain declining, the need for a more vigorous and comprehensive proclamation of the faith was recognized. There was, nevertheless, an increase in financial support, and United Methodists made a massive response to world hunger. By midyear, statistics showed an 11.5% increase in church giving and an increase of 216% for overseas relief.

The place of women in the church received attention during International Women's Year. The structures of church councils and committees were adjusted, and women were elected to positions of leadership. United Methodists in 73 annual conferences elected delegates to the 1976 quadrennial General Conference, and at least 12 delegations were to be headed by women. The number of women candidates for the ministry increased in Britain, and the Caribbean Methodist Church accepted its first women for training as ministers.

The British Conference, meeting in Liverpool, agreed to send the Methodist Church bill to Parliament. The bill would change the legal position of trustees, who were holding church property at the local level. In the future, the Property Division would act centrally as custodian trustee for all Methodist properties, and the local church councils (introduced in 1974) would act as managing trustees. The bill would also give the Methodist Church in Britain freedom to amend its statement of doctrine.

In Australia preparations continued for the Act of Union which would unite the Methodist Church of Australia and the majority of the congregations of the Presbyterian Assembly of Australia. The conferences of Fiji, Samoa, and Tonga, previously members of the General Conference of the Methodist Church of Australasia, would not be part of the uniting church.

Conversations with the Roman Catholic Church continued, and at a meeting in Bristol, England, in August a report was drawn up to be submitted to the World Methodist Council in 1976 and to the Roman Catholic Synod of Bishops. Remarkable understanding was reached in areas relating to the ministry and the Eucharist.

The executive committee of the World Methodist Council met in Accra, Ghana, in August and approved plans for the 13th World Methodist Council and Conference, to be held in Dublin, Aug. 25–31, 1976, with "The Day of the Lord" as its theme. The Rev. Joe Hale of the Board of Discipleship of the United Methodist Church was nominated to succeed Lee F. Tuttle as the general secretary, and the Rev. Kenneth Greet, secretary of the British Conference, was nominated to follow Bishop Prince Taylor as chairman of the executive committee.

(PETER H. BOLT)

Pentecostal Churches. In 1975 Pentecostal churches around the world mourned the death of Lewi Pethrus, founder of the Swedish Pentecostal movement. Pethrus had built the Philadelphia Pentecostal Church in Stockholm, the largest free congregation in Europe.

Growth and development characterized the Pentecostal denominations in the U.S. The general council of the Assemblies of God reported 5% growth in Sunday schools and 1,000 new churches organized in five years. The Church of God (Cleveland, Tenn.) also reported growth, with 884 new congregations formed in only two years. This church announced the opening of a new graduate school of theology in Cleveland, Tenn. The Pentecostal Church of God dedicated a new headquarters building in Joplin, Mo., and announced plans for establishing 1,000 new churches during the next decade. The Pentecostal Holiness Church dedicated its new $6 million headquarters complex in Oklahoma City.

The Pentecostal movement continued to gain momentum in the traditional denominations as charismatic members became more open. Methodist charismatics published a new quarterly entitled *Crossfire.* Daniel Joyce, past president of the world organization of the Christian Church, estimated that 5 to 10% of all Disciples were now neo-Pentecostal, and there were reports that the charismatic renewal was beginning to move into the Greek Orthodox Church. Roman Catholic charismatics gathered 10,000 strong in May for a conference in Rome. (See *Roman Catholic Church,* below.)

(VINSON SYNAN)

Presbyterian and Reformed Churches. With only one vote against, the executive committee of the World Alliance of Reformed Churches (Presbyterian and Congregational), at its 1975 meeting at Geneva on February 23–28, took the unprecedented step of calling off the next WARC General Council (world assembly) scheduled for St. Andrews, Scotland, in 1977. Although financial difficulties were among the reasons for the cancellation, there were others that were more basic and significant. The committee stressed the need for responsible Christian stewardship in the face of the worsening division between affluence and poverty in the world and, in an official statement, saw the cancellation of the assembly as "an opportunity to underline the seriousness with which Reformed Christians must be intent on developing new and simplified life-styles, thus giving a clear Christian witness in society today." In place of the assembly, an "augmented executive committee" was being planned. Worldwide study on the theme originally chosen for St. Andrews ("The Glory of God and the Future of Man") would still be pursued by the member churches.

Two new churches were admitted into membership: the Protestant Church of Senegal (160 families) and the National Church of Lippe, West Germany (287,000 members). In January 1975 the formal dissolution of the Presbyterian Church in Singapore and Malaysia took place, and two autonomous churches were constituted for the separate nations. Following the withdrawal of the Associate Reformed Presbyterian Church of Mexico because of "dissent on doctrinal issues," the number of churches belonging to the WARC stood at 142.

At the meeting of the North American Area Council (NAAC), held in Montreal, January 7–9, the possibility of forming a transnational Reformed Church in North America was debated and referred for further consideration. The South Korean government's harsh suppression of dissent was again sharply criticized by the NAAC. William P. Thompson, WARC president and stated clerk of the United Presbyterian Church in the U.S.A. (UPCUSA), urged Congress to make U.S. aid to the South Korean government conditional upon its concern for human rights. In October Thompson was elected to a three-year term as president of the National Council of Churches of Christ in the U.S.A.

A vote on the reunion of UPCUSA and the Presbyterian Church in the U.S.—the largest Presbyterian denominations—could come as early as 1977 according to the Joint Committee on Union, which was "prepared to have documents ready for final study or for voting at the General Assemblies that year." Negotiations had been going on since 1969.

The forcible takeover of the Federal Theological Seminary in Alice, Cape Province, by the South African government early in 1975, despite earlier assurances by the minister for Bantu affairs that it would not be expropriated, caused indignation. Five of the seven denominations using the seminary for ministerial training belonged to the WARC. The Alliance executive committee cabled a protest to South Africa's prime minister, but in mid-March expropriation was effected and the seminary staff and students were moved to temporary accommodations in Transkei.

The 100th anniversary of the founding of the WARC was marked by a thanksgiving service in London, Sept. 28, 1975, and by the publication of *A Century of Service,* a history of the WARC written by former general secretary Marcel Pradervand.

(FREDERIK H. KAAN)

Religious Society of Friends. The American Friends Service Committee was increasingly concerned during 1975 over the exploitation of farm workers and for the rights of native Americans—a concern echoed among Australian Friends, who for some years had supported the cause of the aborigines. American Quakers continued to be preoccupied with Southeast Asia, and a number of yearly meetings pressed for unconditional amnesty for men who had refused to fight in the Vietnam conflict.

In Britain the vigorous campaign against the increasing use of torture as an instrument of government in many parts of the world, started by a Friend and taken up by Amnesty International, was supported by the Society of Friends. The Friends World Committee for Consultation, which coordinates worldwide Quaker activities, was represented at the UN conference held in Mexico City in connection with International Women's Year. The same body sponsored the fourth Conference of European and Near East Friends, at Driebergen in The Netherlands. This was the first time that one of the scattered groups of European Friends had played host to this gathering.

On a lighter note, British Quaker railway enthusiasts enjoyed reflected glory during the 150th anniversary celebrations of the first public steam railway, from Stockton to Darlington, an enterprise in which their ancestors had played a leading role.

(DAVID FIRTH)

Salvation Army. Gen. Clarence Wiseman, the Canadian-born tenth general of the Salvation Army, traveled some 60,000 mi. in his first year of office. Large public meetings were held in every country he visited. While in New York, he conducted the retirement meetings of the national commander, Commissioner Paul Carlson. The chief of staff, Commissioner

KEYSTONE

Present at the press conference at Salvation Army headquarters in London to launch the book "No Discharge in This War" are (left to right) Gen. Frederick L. Coutts, author, the Most Rev. Donald Coggan, archbishop of Canterbury, and Gen. Clarence Wiseman, the current international leader of the Army.

Arthur Carr, installed Commissioner William E. Chamberlain as the new national commander for the U.S. General Wiseman was present at Donald Coggan's enthronement as archbishop of Canterbury in January 1975, the first Salvation Army general to be invited to such an occasion. In turn, Coggan became the first archbishop of Canterbury to visit the international headquarters of the movement in London.

Salvationists from the Caribbean had been among the first on the scene when Hurricane Fifi devastated Honduras in September 1974. With reinforcements from the U.S. and Canada, they established four relief camps and a 200-bed field hospital, presented by Gov. George Wallace of Alabama and 80 U.S. Salvationists. Seven months later, the retiring relief teams left the hospital behind to serve the continuing needs of the area. Salvationists also launched a massive relief operation when Cyclone Tracy struck the city of Darwin, Australia, on Christmas Day 1974. The relief work of Maj. Eva den Hartog of The Netherlands in Bangladesh was aided by Dutch shipyard workers who built and donated a boat that became a floating clinic.

(HARRY READ)

Seventh-day Adventist Church. Approximately 1,730 church leaders and delegates, representing the 193 countries in which the church operates, met in Vienna, Austria, July 10–19, 1975, for the 52nd General Conference of the world church. This was the first time in the 112-year history of the organization that a General Conference, currently held every five years, had been convened outside the U.S., although four-fifths of the church's 2.5 million members live outside North America. For the first time since 1918 delegates from the Soviet Union were present. Robert H. Pierson, president of the General Conference since 1966, was reelected for another five years. A special offering for missions, received during the conference, totaled more than $3 million, the largest offering ever received on one day in the church's history.

When the South Vietnamese government collapsed, the church closed its hospital in Saigon and assisted in evacuating refugees. Approximately 600 Adventists were among the refugees who arrived at Camp Pendleton, California. The church made housing facilities available and helped place the refugees in jobs, schools, and homes.

Attempts by labour unions to organize personnel at church health-care institutions in Addis Ababa, Eth., and Hackettstown, N.J., were countered successfully. The church position on the subject is that no organization—labour, industrial, government, church, or any other—may impinge on the freedom of the individual to make all his decisions in harmony with his religious convictions.

(KENNETH H. WOOD)

Unitarian Churches. Throughout North America and in Great Britain, 1975 was observed as the sesquicentennial of the founding of the Unitarian institutional movements in both areas—coincidentally on the same day, May 25, 1825.

The annual business meetings of the General Assembly of Unitarian and Free Christian Churches of Great Britain were held April 7–11 in Liverpool. The Rev. Evan David Davies became the third successive president of the movement to come from Wales.

The annual General Assembly of the Unitarian Universalist Association, embracing all North America, met in Minneapolis, Minn., June 24–29, with 820 delegates and many visitors in attendance. Concern was expressed that, while the yearly income of local congregations had been increasing steadily, giving to the denomination had been falling by 5–6% annually.

Parallel concerns arose independently on both sides of the Atlantic. In both cases, attention was focused on the world food situation, civil rights for homosexuals, social responsibility in church institutional investments, abortion, law reform, and peace. The question of changing from annual to biennial sessions remained unresolved. Curiously, an acute shortage of clergy leadership in Great Britain was reversed in North America, where there was a growing surplus. Roughly one-sixth of all pastoral settlements in the U.S. during the year were women.

The International Association for Religious Freedom held its triennial congress, August 15–22, in Montreal. Morning devotions each day were conducted in French, Czech, Hindi, and English. Four commissions dealt with the effect of world change on Christianity, relations among the world's major faiths, liberal religion in today's world, and peace, justice, and human rights.

The first continental colloquium of Unitarian Universalist religious leaders, held March 31–April 5 in Buck Hill Falls, Pa., was attended by 130 clergy and 17 religious education directors. Consensus statements

KEYSTONE

Roman Catholic prelates, including five cardinals, met near Rome to discuss the role of the church in Africa.

The 1975 Holy Year medal, of beautiful design, measures 2½ in. in diameter.

emerged on the questions: What is humanness? What is church? What is ministry? The group concluded that the obvious diversity in liberal ranks rests in attitudes and beliefs but not in core values.

The 100th anniversary of Albert Schweitzer's birth was honoured in Unitarian churches around the world on January 12.

(JOHN NICHOLLS BOOTH)

United Church of Canada. In 1975 the church celebrated the 50th anniversary of the union of Congregationalists, Methodists, and Presbyterians in Canada. Part of the celebration was a consultation of 15 united churches and church union committees in 11 countries. The consultation recommended that each united church be recognized as a true church with one church as the ultimate goal.

In recent years a group of younger ministers within the United Church had brought about a resurgence of evangelical principles in the spirit of Methodism. Church membership in 1975 totaled more than 2 million Canadians. In 1973 churchmen and women gave a record $78 million to the church, more than $15 million of which went to meet human needs in Canada and throughout the world.

The United Church of Canada has always regarded itself as "a united and uniting church," but its only significant union had been that with the Canada Conference of the Evangelical United Brethren Church in 1968. For various reasons, the proposal of union with the Anglican Church of Canada appeared to be in abeyance for the foreseeable future. On the other hand, those Presbyterians who opted out of the union in 1925 proposed closer relations through discussions with the United Church on matters of doctrine and practice.

There had been an assumption on the part of many that the church's services of baptism, marriage, and burial are freely available, regardless of whether the persons involved have an active relationship to the church or show any sign of spiritual concern. In the future, the United Church and other Canadian churches intended to require a serious commitment to the life of the church as a prerequisite.

The missionary motive has been deeply entrenched in the United Church, but the All African Conference of Churches in 1974 made it clear that there must be a moratorium on the giving of money and personnel. All too often, well-meaning Westerners virtually exploit converts to impress the home church and to raise money. The African churches indicated a desire to "go it alone" with the gospel and their own culture.

(ARTHUR GUY REYNOLDS)

United Church of Christ. In June 1975 the tenth General Synod, the church's representative body composed of some 750 delegates, met in Minneapolis to evaluate the programs of the denomination, to speak on certain social issues that have moral implications, and to determine priorities for the next two years.

Three pronouncements were adopted. One, on "Civil Liberties Without Discrimination Related to Affectional or Sexual Preference," called for federal, state, and local legislation that would guarantee the civil liberties of homosexual persons as well as others. The General Synod also called for a major study of the biblical and theological foundations of the church's teachings about human sexuality. A second pronouncement, on the world food crisis, called on members and agencies of the denomination to become aware of the critical nature of the crisis, to make changes in their life-style in order to release resources for the meeting of human hunger, and to engage in citizen action that would contribute to the resolution of the hunger problem at home and abroad. A third pronouncement, on "The Role of Transnational Business in Mass Economic Development," affirmed that the church is called by its faith to ask those engaged in transnational business to accept, as an integral part of their responsibility, a concern to improve the welfare and enlarge the dignity of the people in those countries where they operate.

The General Synod also directed that national programs be developed relating to priorities it approved, including the role and status of women in church and society, revitalizing the local church, evangelism, Christian education, stewardship, the search for faith, racial and economic justice, and criminal justice and penal reform.

At the beginning of 1975 membership of the United Church of Christ stood at 1.8 million. Total giving by church members rose from $196,845,805 in 1973 to $214,328,960 in 1974, despite a decline of 26,000 in membership and negative economic trends. In 1975 the denomination reached $13 million in its campaign to raise $17 million for six predominantly black colleges and several overseas educational institutions by 1976. The number of regional judicatories (conferences) comprising the United Church was reduced from 39 to 38 through the union of two western conferences to form the Rocky Mountain Conference.

(ROBERT V. MOSS)

[827.D; 827.G.3; 827.H; 827.J.3]

ROMAN CATHOLIC CHURCH

Pope Paul VI had declared 1975 a Holy Year and prayed that it would be dedicated to renewal and reconciliation. Millions of pilgrims flocked to Rome, and there was less emphasis on "indulgences" than in previous Holy Years. One of the most significant Roman events was the gathering of 10,000 members of the charismatic movement on the day after Pentecost in St. Peter's Basilica. Forbidden to dance in the presence of the pope, they had broken into spontaneous song during Sunday mass. The charismatics had found a powerful patron in Léon Cardinal Suenens of Belgium. His book *A New Pentecost?* was a plea for official recognition of the movement.

Many political situations, however, failed to prove amenable to the spirit of reconciliation. In February the Portuguese bishops denounced "the campaign of defamation, violence and calumny" directed against the church. Though soldiers of the Armed Forces Movement went on pilgrimage to Fátima and publicly declared the compatibility of Christianity and the revolution, the church was deprived of its radio station, Renascença, and in August fiery episcopal speeches prompted Catholic crowds to burn Communist headquarters in northern Portugal. (*See* PORTUGAL.) These events were followed with anxiety in Spain, where the bishops adopted a resolution proposing an amnesty for political prisoners, though they prudently used the less-loaded term "an indulgence of grace." Relations with the government, already tense, were not helped by the wave of violence in the Basque region.

In Latin America the developing "theology of liberation," more accurately described as a theology *for* liberation, led to the charge that the church was supporting Communism. In Uruguay the Christian review *Vespera* was suppressed by the government; the Bolivian Justice and Peace Commission was suspended; and there were reports of arrests and tortures in Paraguay. Refugees were still being sheltered in the papal nunciature of Santiago, Chile.

Throughout the world, the existence of justice and peace commissions, set up to advise bishops, made for greater sensitivity to injustice and oppression. In May the Rhodesian commission published a report called "The Man in the Middle," which said that there were no victors and no vanquished in the Rhodesian conflict; all Rhodesians were trapped "in the middle."

Despite Communist gains in the Italian regional elections in June, the Holy See continued its policy of détente toward Eastern Europe. Msgr. Agostino Casaroli represented the Vatican in Helsinki, Fin., at the concluding meeting of the Conference on Security and Cooperation in Europe. He read a letter from Pope Paul, who made himself the spokesman of the "peoples" of Europe as distinct from the "nations." They wanted, he wrote, not only security and stable frontiers, but equally "human rights and fundamental freedoms." Meanwhile, a form of diplomatic relations had been established with Poland, the five vacant sees of Hungary were at last filled, and Monsignor Casaroli spent a week in East Germany in June. The main points for negotiation were the rearrangement of diocesan boundaries to make them independent of West Germany, and the appointment of a Vatican diplomat to Berlin.

There was opposition in West Germany to Monsignor Casaroli's visit, however. Julius Cardinal

UPI COMPIX

WIDE WORLD

This portrait (left) of Mother Elizabeth Seton was brought to Rome in September for the ceremony in St. Peter's Square in which Pope Paul VI proclaimed her the first native-born United States Roman Catholic saint. (Right) A tapestry depicting Irish Saint Oliver Plunkett was hung from the balcony of St. Peter's Basilica for another canonization ceremony in October.

Döpfner of Munich protested to Pope Paul two days before it was due, and Bishop Heinrich Mario Jannsen of Hildesheim denounced it on television. But the most serious challenge to the Vatican's *Ostpolitik* was to be found in the *Memoirs* of József Cardinal Mindszenty (*see* OBITUARIES), published in English in late 1974. Based on his experiences in Hungarian prisons, it was a searing attack on the dangers of compromise. Mindszenty died in Vienna on May 6.

Holy Year was also International Women's Year. On September 14, the Sunday set aside as the church's woman's day in support of IWY, the pope canonized the United States' first native-born saint, Elizabeth Ann Bayley Seton (1774–1821), who founded the first religious order in the U.S. At least 15,000 Americans were among the 100,000 who attended the open-air ceremony in St. Peter's Square in Rome. Mother Teresa (*see* BIOGRAPHY) of Calcutta was a member of the Holy See's delegation to the UN IWY conference in Mexico.

Although Pope Paul welcomed the presence of women in Vatican offices, he held out little hope of the eventual ordination of women to the Catholic priesthood. Several U.S. women's organizations declared that they found his argument that Christ did not call women to the priesthood unsatisfactory, and thought that the pope had not meant to say the last word on the subject. Meanwhile, there were demonstrations outside various churches in San Diego, Calif., after a pastoral letter forbade the sacraments to those who publicly favoured the cause of abortion. An unobtrusive portent for the future was the emergence of the first two women doctors of canon law from the Catholic University of America.

On February 15 the Sacred Congregation for the Doctrine of the Faith (formerly the Holy Office) published a long document in which the Tübingen, West Germany, theologian Hans Küng was "admonished" for his alleged errors, particularly on papal infallibility. Although there were complaints about "judgment without trial," Küng himself pointed out that the rebuke was of the mildest kind and was not accompanied by any disciplinary sanctions. Provided he avoided the disputed doctrines, he could continue to teach.

Similar clemency was not extended to the seminary at Ecône in Switzerland. Ecône, headed by Archbishop Marcel Lefebvre, formerly of Dakar, Senegal, had become a centre of traditionalist thinking. In November 1974 Archbishop Lefebvre had declared his refusal to go along with "that neo-modernist, neo-Protestant tendency in Rome which came into the open during Vatican II, and afterward in all the reforms instigated by the Council." This was too much, and "canonical status" was withdrawn from Ecône on June 2. An appeal to Rome was refused. François Cardinal Marty of Paris commented that "one doesn't train priests for the year 2000 with the methods of the 18th century."

The Jesuit attempt to adapt to the 20th century in their 32nd General Congregation did not meet with complete approval, however. Two-thirds of the Jesuit delegates voted in favour of eliminating grades of membership, but they received a strongly worded letter from Pope Paul forbidding such a departure from tradition.

Apart from a document mildly reasserting censorship (the imprimatur system) and a semiofficial text on "Christian Faith and Demonology," the most significant Vatican documents were concerned with ecumenism. In December 1974 came "Guidelines on Jewish-Christian Relations," which were intended to "cleanse all Christian teaching and preaching of any kind of anti-Judaism." But the arrest and trial of Msgr. Hilarion Capucci, found guilty of smuggling arms into Israel for the use of Palestinian guerrillas, combined with the Vatican's reluctance to condemn him, provided a persistent obstacle to good relations with the Jewish state.

On July 7 the Secretariat for the Promotion of Christian Unity published a long document on "Ecumenical Collaboration at the Regional, National and Local Levels." Although it was unenthusiastic about the sharing of churches, guarded on intercommunion, and suspicious about the place of "spontaneous groups" in ecumenism, it nevertheless was a record of much progress in the ecumenical field. The decision about whether Catholics should belong to local councils of churches was left to the bishops of the area. The document seemed like a negative answer to a number of questions that had been raised. In January, for example, the Catholic and Lutheran clergy of Wyandanch, Long Island, N.Y., petitioned the bishop for intercommunion, but without success. In France a joint Catholic Protestant Commission proposed that baptism be celebrated ecumenically, provided this was not regarded as a "right" or done purely for social reasons, but was the expression of "a dynamic movement toward unity of the married couple."

U.S. theologian Avery Dulles had suggested in January that a good way to mark the Holy Year would be to withdraw the anathemas against those Christians who could not accept the doctrines of the Immaculate Conception and the Assumption. This suggestion met with no response. On the other hand, Catholic theologians helped in the preparation of the fifth General Assembly of the World Council of Churches in Nairobi. Its theme, "Jesus Christ Frees and Unites," echoed some aspects of the Holy Year celebrations.

(PETER HEBBLETHWAITE)

See also Vatican City State.
[827.C; 827.G.2; 827.J.2]

EASTERN CHURCHES

The Orthodox Church. Several significant meetings, gathering together representatives of all Orthodox churches, took place in connection with the preparation of the fifth General Assembly of the World Council of Churches. Following the meeting of Orthodox theologians in Cernica, Rom. (June 4–8, 1974), pan-Orthodox theological meetings were held in Crete (April 1975) and Echmiadzin, U.S.S.R. (September 1975). The consultations produced papers that prefigured the attitude of Orthodox delegates in Nairobi: a very cautious if not entirely negative attitude toward the "secular" theology that tends to identify Christianity with social and political ideologies. In the U.S. the Orthodox continued to hold ecumenical dialogues with, respectively, the Roman Catholics, the Episcopalians, and a combined Presbyterian-Lutheran theological group. Both in the U.S. and Europe, Orthodox spokesmen voiced opposition to the principle of ordaining women to the priesthood.

The installation of a democratic regime in Greece had, as a side effect, the stabilization of the ecclesiastical situation in Cyprus, where Archbishop Makarios resumed his duties as both archbishop and president in those areas not under Turkish occupation. In Greece itself Archbishop Seraphim of Athens retained his position, but other bishops installed during

KEYSTONE

Mrs. Jacqueline Tabick was ordained as England's first woman rabbi at a thanksgiving service at the Liberal Jewish Synagogue in St. John's Wood.

the dictatorship were under indictment. Although some voices began to defend the idea of a separation between church and state, the new constitution, voted by Parliament in April, confirmed Orthodoxy as the state religion. In July the Greek church broke relations with the Vatican in protest against the decision to appoint a new bishop for the Uniate Church of Greece, a small Eastern rite body in communion with Rome.

In the U.S.S.R. the government's hostility toward religious practices was expressed in the fact that the Orthodox Easter—Sunday, May 4 in 1975—was a working day. Significantly, however, Russian Orthodox prelates who visited the U.S. in February as guests of the National Council of Churches broke their long tradition of silence and were generally candid about both the official antireligious policy and the increased religious fervour of the young.

In April the Orthodox Church in America announced that the process of canonizing John–Innocent Veniaminov, an Orthodox missionary among the Aleuts and Indians of Alaska (1822–79), had been initiated.

Eastern Non-Chalcedonian Churches. This group of churches, which includes the "Monophysite" churches of Egypt (Copts), Ethiopia, Syria, Armenia, and India, as well as the "Nestorians" of Iraq, participated in the consultations of Orthodox theologians at Cernica, Crete, and Echmiadzin, thus expressing their desire for common witness with the Orthodox on the ecumenical scene. The new regime in Ethiopia appeared to have been very careful not to antagonize the influential church of Ethiopia. However, the future of the church would obviously depend on its capacity to adapt to forthcoming social reforms. In April Armenian Christians throughout the world mournfully commemorated the 60th anniversary of the massacres during World War I that decimated the Armenian communities in Turkey.

(JOHN MEYENDORFF)

[827.B; 827.G.1; 827.J.1]

JUDAISM

Judaism viewed as a religion, not reduced to the cultural and political facts affecting the Jews as a group, is subject to two polar concerns, Torah and Messiah. "Torah" stands for the totality of revelation, both that contained in Scriptures and that handed on through oral tradition and finally written down in the Talmud and related literature. "Torah" addresses a world above history. "Messiah," by contrast, conveys an intense interest in historical events, in the meaning of what happens and the direction and ultimate end of time. In contemporary Judaism, discussions on the nature and meaning of law, on the one side, and on the destiny of Jewry in relation to the state of Israel, on the other, express those two concerns.

In 1975 three important statements constituted major religious events of Judaism: one on the matter of law, two on the condition of Israel, meaning both the state and the people. These issues, which perennially set the limits of Judaic discourse, defined the distinctive issues of the year.

At the Rabbinical Assembly (Conservative) meeting in April, Rabbi Arthur Hertzberg, president of the American Jewish Congress and professor at Columbia University, as well as rabbi in Englewood, N.J., faced head-on the issue of the role of law (Halakha) in contemporary Judaism. He argued that modern Jews have lived for two centuries in an essentially post-halakhic situation. While they remain responsive to the requirements of the law, they do so eclectically. Conservative Judaism in particular, the largest sector of American Judaism, claims to carry forward classical law but in fact, he said, picks and chooses within it. But those things which are chosen bear "central and transcendent importance." The choices are "the importance of the Jewish enterprise, Hebrew, Israel, and a decent traditionalism." Hertzberg strikes at the roots of the apologetic of change-within-tradition constructed by Conservative Judaism, while at the same time laying the foundations of a fresh, perhaps more responsible, apologetic. Within his address are contained principles for a new approach to the nature of "Torah" in modern Judaism.

The second major turning was signaled by Rabbi Emanuel Rackman, professor of Judaic studies at the City University of New York and a leading Orthodox rabbi. In the name of Torah, Rackman, addressing the Rabbinical Council of America in June, criticized Israeli Orthodoxy. He said: "Many of us—Orthodox rabbis in Israel and elsewhere—are giving Jewish law a bad image. We make it appear that Jewish law is concerned only with rituals . . . we become exercised over violations of the sanctity of Sabbaths and remain silent with regard to unconscionable rates of interest prevailing in the Jewish state, despite biblical and Talmudic prohibitions against them." Similarly, he held that the status of women is unacceptable.

At the same time, Rabbi Walter Wurzburger, an officer of the council, held that religious leadership in the state of Israel has failed to provide "an example of ethical sensitivity in confronting courageously the grave social and moral issues besetting society." Rackman, Wurzburger, and others thus raised age-old issues inherent in Judaism, issues of the relationship between ethics and ritual, between religious institutions and moral professions.

"Towards a Great Debate" was the title of the third striking example of the discussion, within contemporary Judaism, of the classical issues of Judaic theology. In October 1974 Dean Herbert Chanan Brichto, Hebrew Union College-Jewish Institute of Religion, Cincinnati, Ohio, proposed a debate, first, on the centrality of Israel, meaning the state of Israel, in the life of the Jewish people; second, on Reform Judaism and its relation to tradition, or Torah; and third, on unity within the Reform movement itself. The first two themes, it is clear, are none other than the perennial issues of Judaic theology. The Reform approach, Brichto said, is "an ever-continuing reexamination both of tradition and of change," an approach characteristic of all sectors of Judaism in modern times, producing, to be sure, varied results. The role of the state of Israel in Judaism similarly requires reconsideration. "The universalism of a prophetic faith should keep us from the pendulum-swings from triumphalism to despair."

What was striking in these several intellectual events was the attention of Conservative, Orthodox, and Reform theologians to the classical issues of rabbinic Judaism, issues phrased in historically authentic language. The meaning of Torah, the commands of revelation, and the imperative of tradition were reconsidered. The place of Israel, the Jewish people, in the life of the nations, and the meaning of the state of Israel, the Jewish nation, in the life of Israel were reexamined. In 1975, as in the preceding two centuries in the history of Judaism, discussion centred upon law and its continuing demands, autonomous of events and divorced from history, on the one side, and nationhood and its messianic, deeply historical aspirations, on the other. The newsworthy events of the year fell into the rubrics of Judaic theology and were debated by theologically significant minds—evidence that Judaism, as a religion, continued to play a significant part in the formation of the imagination and world view of Jews.

Rabbi W. Gunther Plaut of Holy Blossom Temple in Toronto examines volume I of the commentary on the Torah which he prepared in consultation with a theological advisory board.

WIDE WORLD

In October the Central Conference of American Rabbis (Reform) announced publication of *Gates of Prayer: The New Union Prayer Book,* its first completely new prayer book in 80 years.

(JACOB NEUSNER)

[826]

BUDDHISM

The most important event of 1975 was the 11th General Conference of the World Fellowship of Buddhists, held in Bangkok, Thailand, in mid-November in conjunction with the jubilee for the 25th anniversary of the WFB's founding. It was followed by a Conference on Buddhist Culture, sponsored jointly by the WFB and UNESCO.

The fate of the Tibetan refugees continued to present serious problems. Fifteen years after the abortive rebellion in Tibet, 80,000 were living in India, Nepal, Sikkim, and Bhutan, and 1,000 or more were scattered elsewhere. The Dalai Lama was evidently willing to return to Tibet as a purely religious leader, but Peking's response so far had been cool.

In 1974 a new association of Himalayan Buddhists, the Simant Pradeshiya Boudha Maha Sabha, was formed and passed a resolution urging the Indian government to safeguard and promote Buddhist education and culture, including the use of the Bodhi script. In Lumbini, Nepal, the Buddha's birthplace, a World Brotherhood Centre was established by a committee of Buddhist leaders from ten Asian nations. The Japan Buddha Sangha and the Buddhist Congress of Sri Lanka strongly protested the destruction of the World Peace Pagoda (Shanti Stupa) by the Nepalese government on the ground that its construction had not received prior approval. Sri Lanka reported the establishment of an International Buddhist Library at the historic Aluvihare Rock Temple in Matela and an International Buddhist Centre in Colombo.

In a colourful ceremony at Buddh Gaya, India, on Nov. 16, 1974, U Nu, the former prime minister of Burma, was ordained in the Buddhist holy order; thereafter he was known as the Venerable Buddhanukura. The Japan Communist Party (JCP) and the powerful lay Buddhist organization Soka-gakkai signed a surprising ten-year agreement whereby the JCP pledged to defend freedom of religion and Soka-gakkai vowed not to view scientific socialism and Communism with hostility.

Bidya Dandaron, a Buddhist leader and orientalist, died in a labour camp at Vydrino in Soviet Asia. Hungarian Buddhists celebrated the 190th anniversary of the birth of Csosma de Koros, a pioneer in Buddhist activities in Hungary. During 1974 the Akademie der Wissenschaften in Göttingen, West Germany, sponsored an international symposium on "Buddhism in Ceylon." In the U.S. a Society for Buddhist Studies was formed at Columbia University, and Anagarika Sujata, who founded the Sasana Yeiktha Meditation Center in Denver, Colo., established the Stillpoint Institute for the promotion of Buddhist meditation practices at Capitola, Calif.

(JOSEPH M. KITAGAWA)

[824]

HINDUISM

The death of Sarvepalli Radhakrishnan in April 1975 at the age of 86 brought to an end the brilliant career of Hinduism's leading intellectual interpreter to the West in the 20th century (*see* OBITUARIES). A scholar, teacher, and statesman, Radhakrishnan had held academic posts in India and England and served as president of India from 1962 to 1967. The revitalization of traditional Indian philosophy among educated Hindus was in large measure the product of his pioneer work and sponsorship.

Because of the absence of specific organizational structures within Hinduism, it is impossible to document precisely the numbers and groups that go to make up its variety of traditions, movements, and expressions. During the year Bhakti ("adoration and love of the Adorable Lord") continued to be the most noticeably active expression of Hinduism. Usually under the leadership of a "holy" man or woman, the Indian Bhakti groups, while distinct from most of the "Hindu" cultic movements that had spread to Europe and America in the preceding decade, were similar in their fervour and dedication. Meanwhile, the traditional Hinduism associated with the great regional temples and local village shrines continued to be practiced by the majority of the Indian people. Modernizing forces appeared to have little or no effect upon Hindu religious beliefs or practices. On the contrary, modern educational and communications techniques were being used increasingly to popularize and strengthen traditional Hinduism.

It remained to be seen what effect Prime Minister Indira Gandhi's imposition of a state of national emergency in late June would have on the role of Hinduism in the political life of India. Among the groups banned in July was the Rashtriya Swayamsevak Sangh (National Volunteer Organization), a "nonpolitical" activist religious association dedicated to the training of youth and the mobilization of Hindus in a crusade to establish Hindu religious principles and practices as the basis for the modern Indian state. Subsequently, Mrs. Gandhi accused the organization's political ally, the Bharatiya Jan Sangh (Indian People's Party), of being the chief source of disunity in the country and of conspiring to seize power by nondemocratic methods. The Jan Sangh was the country's largest opposition political party. (*See* INDIA.)

(PHILIP H. ASHBY)

Buddhist leader Shoko Masunaga was appointed in July as chaplain for the California State Senate, a position usually held by a minister of Christian or Jewish faith.

WIDE WORLD

[823]

ISLAM

In recent years political events in the Muslim world have shaped and sometimes engulfed religious developments. During 1975 the most noteworthy occurrences were legacies of the immediate past. There was sporadic fighting in the Middle East and southern Philippines, though U.S. Secretary of State Henry Kissinger's efforts to negotiate a new interim agreement between Israel and Egypt appeared to bear some fruit. The presence of Palestinian guerrillas in Lebanon provoked raids and counterraids and exacerbated the already unstable political and confessional situation there. Fighting broke out between Lebanese Muslim and Christian groups, becoming extremely serious in Beirut and the north coastal city of Tripoli in September and escalating into virtual civil war. (*See* LEBANON; MIDDLE EASTERN AFFAIRS.)

In the Philippines the situation of the Muslim minority in Mindanao remained unresolved, despite Pres. Ferdinand Marcos' attempt to use the offices of the Conference of Islamic States in January and the appointment in July of government administrators who were Muslims or sympathizers with Muslims. (*See* PHILIPPINES.) In two areas fighting came to an end, however. In January India announced that Sheikh Muhammad Abdullah would head the Indian-controlled state of Kashmir and that it would be given more autonomy than any other Indian state. In March the Kurdish rebellion in northern Iraq was substantially crushed after Iran apparently withdrew its support. The Kurdish leader, Mustafa al-Barzani, reportedly fled to Iraq.

Another violent occurrence was the assassination of King Faisal of Saudi Arabia in March (*see* OBITUARIES); his assailant was subsequently tried and beheaded in accordance with that nation's religious law. King Faisal had been a generous benefactor, particularly of Muslim religious efforts outside the Middle East. In December 1974 it was announced that he had contributed toward a fund to build a mosque in Rome, the first Islamic place of worship to be constructed there, and in February 1975 he was quoted as promising aid for building a $3.5 million mosque in Los Angeles.

The birth-control issue reappeared with the announcement by Saudi Arabia in April that contraceptives would henceforth be banned; the basis for the decision was announced as a ruling by the World Muslim League. Muslim concern over Israeli archaeological work and social relocation continued to be expressed. These complaints were underscored in a statement issued by the UN Committee on Human Rights in February; pro-Israeli groups condemned the statement as false and the committee as biased.

Representatives of Islam participated in the first Interreligious Peace Colloquium in Bellagio, Italy, in June. The colloquium had been proposed by the Syna-

CLAUDE SALHANI—SYGMA

One of the last photographs taken of King Faisal (centre) prior to his assassination in Riyadh, Saudi Arabia, this view shows him at prayer with Syrian Pres. Hafez al-Assad (second from right) during Faisal's visit to that country in March.

gogue Council of America. Also in June, the Islamic Development Bank and the Dubai Islamic Bank were formed to lend out money accrued from oil revenues. They were to operate under Islamic law, which allows charging a handling fee on loans but forbids interest.

The sixth conference of Islamic foreign ministers was held in Jidda, Saudi Arabia, in July with 40 countries represented; the subject matter was essentially political. Shortly after Prime Minister Gandhi's assumption of extraordinary authority in India, it was reported that a number of Indian Muslims supported her action, which they saw as weakening the ultraconservative Hindu political groups.

In May the ruler of Abu Dhabi was reported to have paid $1.2 million for a letter—either the original or a contemporary copy—purportedly dictated by the Prophet Muhammad to be sent to the Byzantine Emperor Heraclius in about A.D. 628, inviting him to accept Islam. Muslim and Western scholars had subjected the document to rigorous scrutiny and believed it was not a forgery. It had belonged to the widow of the late King Abdullah of Jordan, grandfather of King Hussein.

(R. W. SMITH)

[828]

WORLD CHURCH MEMBERSHIP

The study of religious statistics is still in its infancy. Some churches keep very exact information on their members but will not release the data to outsiders. Others, and this is particularly true of the ethnic religions and some branches of Christianity with centuries-old ethnic foundations, base their own reports on percentages of population figures. Finally, no census of any kind has as yet been taken in some nations.

Some religions have "adherents," others designate "constituents," and others count "communicants"; only on the mission fields of Christianity, Buddhism, Islam, and Hinduism are precise figures available. A typical instance is Sri Lanka. A reliable government report indicates there are about 6,200 Buddhist temples in the island with about 18,000 priests, and 1,784 Hindu kovils (temples) with about 2,000 officiating kurukkals (priests). The number of adherents in both cases can only be estimated.

A second major problem for the statistician is the uncertainty of religious reports from areas of persecution. Many millions of the world's refugees are religious as well as cultural, political, and/or economic victims. Their exact religious composition can only be estimated, along with the numbers still left in their lands of origin. The effect of an enforced Marxist ideology in the U.S.S.R. and China, and in allied (Eastern Europe) or occupied (Tibet) areas, can only be estimated. Some official Eastern Orthodox tables still show 100 million Russian Orthodox; a recent government study conceded that there were 30 million "hard core" Christians. Presumably, some place in between is a figure that might be comparable to the statistics of active Christians in Spain or Sweden.

The data for countries with free churches, where membership is based upon a clear and uninhibited choice, are generally far more reliable than those for areas in which governments have intervened to sponsor or to persecute. That is to say, the statistics of membership of a Zen Buddhist Society in Boston or a Baptist congregation in Burma are "hard" figures; the Buddhist figures for Thailand and the Lutheran figures for Lower Saxony are considerably less dependable, if membership rather than very loose adherence is the issue. Accordingly, though the table on page 586 is revised regularly to reflect the latest surveys and informed estimates, the reader is advised to use it with the awareness that mixed styles of reckoning are necessarily involved.

(FRANKLIN H. LITTELL)

Rhodesia

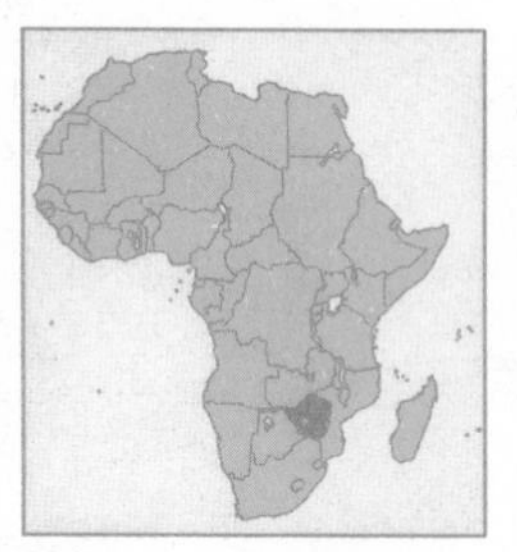

Though Rhodesia declared itself a republic on March 2, 1970, it remained a British colony in the eyes of many other nations. It is bounded by Zambia, Mozambique, South Africa, and Botswana. Area: 150,873 sq.mi. (390,759 sq.km.). Pop. (1975 est.): 6.2 million, of whom 95% are African and 5% white. Cap. and largest city: Salisbury (urban area pop., 1975 est., 555,000). Language: English (official) and Bantu. Religion: predominantly traditional tribal beliefs; Christian minority. President in 1975, Clifford W. Dupont; prime minister, Ian D. Smith.

An agreement between representatives of the Rhodesian government and leaders of the African National Council (ANC), concluded in Lusaka, Zambia, in December 1974, was to have led to constitutional discussions, and the British foreign secretary, James Callaghan, visited southern Africa to enlist the support of heads of state for Britain's efforts to achieve a

Resources, Natural: *see* Environment
Retail Sales: *see* Economy, World

CAMERAPIX/KEYSTONE

Bishop Abel Muzorewa (left), the Rev. Ndabaningi Sithole, and Joshua Nkomo arrive in Dar es Salaam after release of the latter two from prison by the Rhodesian government.

settlement. Although the ANC continued to argue that any constitutional conference must take place with Britain rather than with Ian Smith's Rhodesian government, it became clear during 1975 that it was the heads of Rhodesia's neighbouring states rather than the government of Britain who would exert the most effective pressure.

Throughout 1975 the ANC leaders were in communication with presidents Kenneth Kaunda (Zambia), Julius Nyerere (Tanzania), and Sir Seretse Khama (Botswana), and later with Pres. Samora Machel of Mozambique, while the South African prime minister, B. J. Vorster, played his part in trying to convince Smith of the need to negotiate. For some time, Smith maintained that he could not start negotiations as long as the ANC failed to fulfill its part of the Lusaka agreement by calling off guerrilla activities. The ANC counterclaimed that Smith's government was defaulting on the agreement by failing to release political detainees. The main stumbling block, however, was the ANC's insistence that majority rule must form the basis of any constitutional agreement while Smith continued to affirm that he did not contemplate handing over power to Africans during his lifetime.

The ANC cause was weakened by disagreements among its leaders, and in March Herbert Chitepo (*see* OBITUARIES), a prominent figure in the Zimbabwe African National Union (ZANU), was killed when a bomb exploded beneath his car in Lusaka. The government of Zambia reacted by arresting a number of Rhodesian Africans, mainly members of ZANU, and by closing the offices of both ZANU and the Zimbabwe African People's Union (ZAPU) in Lusaka. In an attempt to put an end to the feuding, President Kaunda said that he would recognize only the ANC as representing the Rhodesian African nationalists. He also closed the guerrilla camps in Zambia, rounding up the guerrillas into one camp with the dual aim of encouraging unity and of having available a stronger military force for possible eventual use against the Smith government. For, in spite of his annoyance at the divisions among the black Rhodesian nationalists, Kaunda still insisted that unless Smith accepted majority rule he must be prepared to face more intensive guerrilla action.

Another consequence of Chitepo's death and other acts of violence in Zambia was the arrest in Rhodesia of the ZANU leader, the Rev. Ndabaningi Sithole, on charges of plotting to assassinate other black leaders. A special court ordered that he be kept in detention because he was an advocate of violence and had failed to fulfill his promise to order the guerrillas to cease operations. He was released shortly afterward, however, to attend a conference of the Organization of African Unity in Dar es Salaam, Tanzania, and did not return to Rhodesia.

Preliminary talks between the Rhodesian government and the ANC did take place at intervals throughout the early part of 1975, but the ANC insisted that there could be no full-scale negotiations before political detainees were released. Smith replied that the ANC was simply procrastinating and threatened to begin negotiations with other sections of the African population (presumably the chiefs, who in council at the end of May claimed that they were the only true representatives of the African people). There was a greater setback on June 1 when police fired on rioting groups at an ANC meeting in the Highfield African township of Salisbury, killing about a dozen Africans and wounding several more. Joshua Nkomo (*see* BIOGRAPHY), leader of ZAPU, was accused by his rivals of having planned a deal with Smith.

At the end of June Britain again attempted to intervene by sending the Foreign Office minister of state, David Ennals, to Rhodesia, but although both Smith and the ANC agreed to take part in a constitutional conference, the idea foundered over the question of venue. Smith insisted that it should take place in Rhodesia, but the ANC, anxious that those members liable to arrest if they returned to Salisbury be free to attend, refused.

RHODESIA

Education. (1975) Primary, pupils 864,660, teachers 22,091; secondary, pupils 74,412, teachers 3,771; vocational, pupils 3,004, teachers 299; teacher training, students 2,084, teachers 131; higher, students 2,364, teaching staff 299.

Finance. Monetary unit: Rhodesian dollar, with (Sept. 22, 1975) a free rate of R$0.63 to U.S. $1 (R$1.28 = £1 sterling). Budget (1974–75 est.): revenue R$399 million; expenditure R$427 million. Gross domestic product: (1973) R$1,535,000,000; (1972) R$1,391,000,000.

Foreign Trade. (1973) Imports *c.* R$325 million; exports R$390 million. Import sources (1965): U.K. 30%; South Africa 23%; U.S. 7%; Japan 6%. Export destinations (1965): Zambia 29%; U.K. 20%; South Africa 11%; West Germany 8%; Malawi 6%; Japan 5%. Main exports (1965): tobacco 51%; asbestos 12%; machinery 9%; meat 7%; copper 7%; clothing 6%; chemicals 5%.

Transport and Communications. Roads (1973) 78,900 km. Motor vehicles in use (1971): passenger 127,000; commercial (including buses) 56,000. Railways: (1973) 3,257 km.; freight traffic (including Botswana; 1972–73) 6,623,000,000 net ton-km. Telephones (Jan. 1974) 160,000. Radio receivers (Dec. 1973) 225,000. Television receivers (Dec. 1972) 57,000.

Agriculture. Production (in 000; metric tons; 1973; 1972 in parentheses): corn *c.* 635 (*c.* 1,540); millet *c.* 220 (*c.* 220); wheat *c.* 88 (*c.* 78); sugar, raw value (1974) *c.* 259, (1973) *c.* 243; peanuts *c.* 130 (*c.* 130); tobacco *c.* 56 (*c.* 73); cotton, lint *c.* 35 (*c.* 43); beef and veal *c.* 95 (*c.* 94); milk *c.* 253 (*c.* 250). Livestock (in 000; 1972–73): cattle *c.* 4,150; sheep *c.* 480; goats *c.* 720; pigs *c.* 149.

Industry. Production (in 000; metric tons; 1973): coal 3,060; asbestos *c.* 80; chrome ore (oxide content) *c.* 272; iron ore (metal content) *c.* 320; gold (troy oz.) *c.* 500; electricity (kw-hr.) 7,277,000.

At the end of July a curfew was imposed on the eastern border to prevent Africans from crossing to Mozambique to train as guerrillas, and early in August similar restrictions were brought into force on the southwest border with Botswana. Later in the month Smith flew to South Africa for talks with Vorster and, with Kaunda, Nyerere, and other African heads of state bringing pressure to bear on the ANC, it was agreed that a meeting would take place in a railway coach on a bridge over the Zambezi River just below the Victoria Falls between Rhodesia and Zambia at the end of August.

The meeting was held but the discussions broke down, despite the presence of both Vorster and Kaunda, because Smith refused to offer an indemnity to those believed to have been guilty of acts of violence to enable them to take part in further talks in Salisbury. Shortly afterward the ANC suffered further setbacks when Nkomo accused the leaders who refused to return to Salisbury of running away. When he insisted that a congress of the ANC be held in Salisbury in September, Bishop Abel Muzorewa, president of the ANC, expelled him from the party. The congress met, however, and in the absence of Muzorewa, Sithole, and other leaders, Nkomo was elected president by a convincing majority. On December 1 Smith and Nkomo signed a pact providing for joint talks, for which an agenda was approved on December 11.

Rhodesia also had problems on the economic front. Prices were affected by continuing inflation, while defense expenditure led to the reimposition of the 10% war tax on individual and commercial incomes. In 1974 the value of imports had risen 42% while exports had risen only 26%, leading to a reduction in foreign exchange allocations that had serious effects on a number of businesses; 1974 was also the worst year for immigration since 1966.

(KENNETH INGHAM)

[978.E.8.b.iii]

Romania

A socialist republic on the Balkan Peninsula in southeastern Europe, Romania is bordered by the U.S.S.R., the Black Sea, Bulgaria, Yugoslavia, and Hungary. Area: 91,700 sq.mi. (237,500 sq.km.). Pop. (1974 est.): 21,029,000, including (1966) Romanian 87.7%; Hungarian 8.5%. Cap. and largest city: Bucharest (pop., 1973 est., 1,528,600). Religion: Romanian Orthodox 70%; Greek Orthodox 10%. General secretary of the Romanian Communist Party, president of the republic, and president of the State Council in 1975, Nicolae Ceausescu; chairman of the Council of Ministers (premier), Manea Manescu.

On May 9, 1975, on the occasion of the 30th anniversary of the capitulation of Germany, President Ceausescu spoke at a meeting in Bucharest summarizing Romania's role in World War II. Although he exaggerated the part of the then very small Romanian Communist Party in the "antifascist" resistance, he recognized that the "historic act" of Aug. 23, 1944, which overthrew Gen. Ion Antonescu's dictatorship and brought Romania into the war against the Nazi Third Reich, was made possible by the collaboration of the Communist leaders with "other democratic forces, the Army's higher command, and the king."

In conformity with the mandate of the 11th congress of the Romanian Communist Party, held in November 1974, two important documents were published by the Central Committee at the beginning of 1975: the party's new program (a book of 220 pages) and the directives concerning the 1976–80 five-year economic and social development plan (a booklet of 77 pages). The basic targets of the plan were that by 1980 national income and industrial production would rise at least by 54% as compared with 1975. The generation of electric power would reach 75,000,000,000 kw-hr., the extraction of crude petroleum 15.5 million tons, the production of steel 17 million tons, and production of cement 19 million tons. By 1980 Romania would produce yearly at least 60,000 tractors, 50,000 trucks, 150,000 automobiles, 330 electric and diesel locomotives for main lines, 900,000 deadweight tonnage of seagoing shipping, and 50 large river-going ships.

The success of the current five-year plan, to be completed in 1975, was jeopardized by the effects of catastrophic floods at the end of June that damaged

ROMANIA

Education. (1973–74) Primary and secondary, pupils 3,057,922, teachers 147,931; vocational, pupils 474,245, teachers 26,880; teacher training, students 21,437, teachers 1,377; higher (including 12 universities), students 154,285, teaching staff 14,816.

Finance. Monetary unit: leu, with (Sept. 22, 1975) a commercial rate of 4.97 lei to U.S. $1 (10.46 lei = £1 sterling) and a tourist rate of 12.40 lei = U.S. $1 (25.68 lei = £1 sterling). Budget (1973 actual): revenue 175,972,000,000 lei; expenditure 168,091,000,000 lei.

Foreign Trade. (1974) Imports 25,563,000,000 lei; exports 24,226,000,000 lei. Import sources: West Germany 15%; U.S.S.R. 15%; U.K. 6%; East Germany 5%; U.S. 5%. Export destinations: U.S.S.R. 17%; West Germany 10%; East Germany 6%; Italy 5%; U.K. 5%; Czechoslovakia 5%. Main exports: machinery and transport equipment 21%; food 20%; chemicals 11%; petroleum products 11%; industrial raw materials 7%.

Transport and Communications. Roads (1973) 76,806 km. (including 96 km. expressways). Motor vehicles in use: passenger (1972) *c.* 125,000; commercial *c.* 50,000. Railways (1973): 11,019 km.; traffic 21,228,000,000 passenger-km., freight 57,103,000,000 net ton-km. Air traffic (1974): 584 million passenger-km.; freight 6,710,000 net ton-km. Inland waterways in regular use (1973) 1,588 km. Shipping (1974): merchant vessels 100 gross tons and over 106; gross tonnage 610,982. Telephones (Dec. 1973) 886,000. Radio licenses (Dec. 1973) 3,077,000. Television licenses (Dec. 1973) 2,145,000.

Agriculture. Production (in 000; metric tons; 1974; 1973 in parentheses): wheat 4,970 (5,490); barley *c.* 911 (*c.* 740); corn *c.* 7,500 (7,397); potatoes *c.* 3,500 (2,644); cabbages (1973) *c.* 630, (1972) 610; onions 279 (264); tomatoes *c.* 1,200 (1,207); sugar, raw value *c.* 607 (*c.* 567); sunflower seed *c.* 670 (756); dry beans *c.* 90 (83); soybeans *c.* 320 (244); plums (1973) *c.* 800, (1972) 761; apples *c.* 300 (288); grapes 1,700 (1,576); tobacco *c.* 50 (38); linseed *c.* 50 (45). Livestock (in 000; Jan. 1974): cattle 5,705; sheep 14,302; pigs 8,987; horses (1973) 631; poultry 66,511.

Industry. Fuel and power (in 000; metric tons; 1973): coal 7,172; lignite 17,711; coke 1,589; crude oil 14,287; natural gas (cu.m.) 27,630; manufactured gas (cu.m.) 522,000; electricity (kw-hr.) 46,779,000. Production (in 000; metric tons; 1973): cement 9,848; iron ore (metal content) 873; pig iron 5,713; crude steel 8,161; petroleum products *c.* 17,200; sulfuric acid 1,311; fertilizers (nutrient content) nitrogenous 854, phosphate 361; cotton yarn (1972) 130; cotton fabrics (sq.m.) 571,000; wool yarn (1972) 42; woolen fabrics (sq.m.) 83,000; rayon, etc., filament yarns and fibres (1972) 62; nylon, etc., filament yarns and fibres (1972) 38; newsprint 53; other paper 531. New dwelling units completed (1973) 155,000.

Rice:
see Agriculture and Food Supplies

Roads:
see Engineering Projects; Transportation

Rockets:
see Defense; Space Exploration

Rodeo:
see Arena Sports

Roman Catholic Church:
see Religion

the wheat harvest and disrupted transport. On the brighter side, the U.S. Congress on July 28 passed a resolution granting most-favoured-nation trade status to Romania. In keeping with the provisions of the Trade Act of 1974, Pres. Gerald Ford had previously assured Congress that he was satisfied Romania would permit free emigration. In the weeks before the matter was to come before Congress for consideration, it was reported that Romania had accelerated emigration to Israel and the U.S.

On March 9, 1975, about 99% of Romania's 14.9 million registered voters elected 349 deputies from among 488 candidates. More than 88% of the members of the new Grand National Assembly were ethnic Romanians, 8.2% were Magyars, 2.2% were Germans, and the rest belonged to other nationalities. On March 17 the assembly reelected Ceausescu as president of the republic; elected the new State Council of 17 (president, four vice-presidents, and 12 members), and the Council of Ministers of 42 (premier, eight deputy premiers, 29 departmental ministers, and four heads of mass organizations).

There were two new deputy premiers: Mihai Marinescu, who was also chairman of the State Planning Committee, and Angelo Miculescu, who was also minister of agriculture, food industry, and water administration. Teodor Coman was appointed minister of the interior to succeed Emil Bobu, who was made a party secretary and replaced Vasile Vilcu as a vice-president of the State Council. Constantin Ionescu was nominated minister of machine tools, building, and electrical engineering in place of Virgil Actarian, who was dismissed for "deviation from the principles of socialist ethics."

During 1975 Ceausescu paid official visits to 12 countries including the United States, Great Britain, and Japan. Foreign heads of state or of government who visited Romania included: Queen Juliana of The Netherlands, President Ford of the U.S., Pres. Kim Il Sung of North Korea, prime ministers Harold Wilson of Great Britain, Jacques Chirac of France, Konstantinos Karamanlis of Greece, Suleyman Demirel of Turkey, Emir Abbas Hoveida of Iran, and Chancellor Bruno Kreisky of Austria. In March Col. Gen. Ion Coman visited the United States, and in September Gen. Fred C. Weyand, chief of staff of the U.S. Army, led a military delegation to Romania.

(K. M. SMOGORZEWSKI)

[972.B.3]

Romanian Literature:
see Literature

Rubber:
see Industrial Review

Rugby Football:
see Football

Russia:
see Union of Soviet Socialist Republics

Russian Literature:
see Literature

Rowing

East Germany won most of the major honours in world rowing in 1975. For the second year in succession it won 15 titles out of a possible 23 in the men's, women's, and junior world championships; there were no contestants from East Germany for the lightweight events, which were accorded world championship status for the first time. The U.S.S.R., which also excluded the lightweight events from its racing program, and West Germany were the other principal title winners. The junior championships, held in Canada, gave the Montreal course a useful tryout in preparation for the 1976 Olympic Games, and Great Britain was for the first time the host for all the other world championship events, at the National Water Sports Centre in Nottingham.

In the men's heavyweight events East Germany regained the eights title, beating the U.S.S.R. by 2.33 sec. with New Zealand finishing 2.27 sec. behind the Soviet crew in third place. East Germany lost the coxed fours title to the U.S.S.R., which led all the way to avenge its defeat of the previous year by more than 5 sec. East Germany also lost the double sculls title to the brothers Frank and Alf J. Hansen of Norway, who had been on the brink of success in this event for some years. Although East Germany led by more than 3 sec. at the halfway mark, the Norwegians hung on with great tenacity until the last 100 m., where they finally proved too strong for the defending champions by 0.21 sec. Great Britain took the bronze medal for the third year.

No one could stop the twins Bernd and Jorg Landvoigt from East Germany from retaining the coxless pairs title, but behind them Bulgaria raced up from fifth place at the halfway mark to squeeze The Netherlands out of the silver medal. Hopes for a gold medal in single sculls for Irishman Sean Drea, who had been forced to withdraw through illness during the 1974 championships, were foiled narrowly by Peter Michael Kolbe (West Germany), who crossed the line just clear of Drea. Martin Winter (East Germany) finished third behind Drea by one-third of a length, after holding the lead himself until halfway through the race.

East Germany won the three remaining titles, coxed pairs, coxless fours, and quadruple sculls, and was the

Harvard's varsity rowing crew glides across the finish line after defeating the University of Washington crew by three lengths in a four-mile race on the Thames River, Connecticut. This marked Harvard's second consecutive undefeated season.

WIDE WORLD

KEYSTONE

Cambridge sweeps past Oxford at Hammersmith Bridge, winning the race from Putney to Mortlake by 3¾ lengths.

only country to win medals in all eight events. Twenty-eight countries competed, and the remaining medals were shared by 11 of them. The U.S.S.R. with four medals and West Germany with three were next best, but unlike East Germany neither of them managed to qualify for every final.

The lightweight events attracted 19 countries, of which 7 won medals. West Germany narrowly defeated the United States by 1.79 sec. after a close tussle all the way in the eights. France gained a similar verdict over Great Britain in coxless fours after Australia had set the pace for 1,500 m. before dropping to third place. In single sculls William Belden (U.S.) set the early pace until Reto Wyss (Switz.) passed him at 1,500 m. At the finish Raimond Haberl (Austria) squeezed Belden out of the silver medal.

In the women's events East Germany won five events and finished second in the sixth, which was won by the U.S.S.R. The Soviets also collected three other medals. Bulgaria and Romania were prominent with five minor medals between them, and the only Western success was a well-earned silver medal for the United States in eights. After qualifying for the final via the repêchage, they finished 1.38 sec. behind East Germany and a similar distance ahead of Romania.

In Canada the Olympic course at Montreal was ready just in time for the world junior championships. East Germany reached every final and scored five wins; the U.S.S.R. took two titles; and one went to West Germany, which was the only nation to win a medal in every event. Soviet crews collected three minor medals, and the most successful Western nation was Great Britain with two silver medals. The only others of the 28 competing countries to finish in the medal table were Canada, France, and Yugoslavia.

At the Henley Royal Regatta in England there were five winners from overseas. Potomac Boat Club became the first U.S. crew to win the Stewards' Cup for coxless fours. The Netherlands' first victory in the Silver Goblets for coxless pairs was recorded by H. A. Droog and R. J. Luynenburg, while Garda Siochana—the Irish police eight—took the Thames Cup to Ireland for the first time. There was a second Irish triumph when Sean Drea retained the Diamond Sculls. The fifth trophy to go abroad was the Princess Elizabeth Cup to Ridley College, Canada. Hart Perry, president of the National Association of American Oarsmen, became the first Henley steward from outside the U.K. Cambridge scored its 68th victory over Oxford in the 121st university boat race.

(KEITH OSBORNE)

[452.B.4.a.ii]

Rwanda

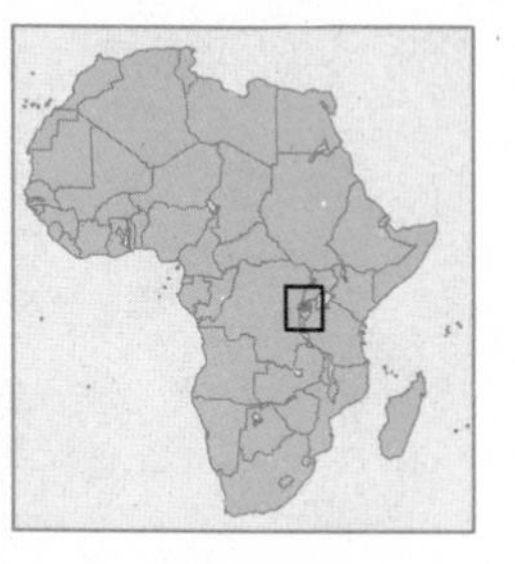

A republic in eastern Africa, and former traditional kingdom whose origins may be traced back to the 15th century, Rwanda is bordered by Zaire, Uganda, Tanzania, and Burundi. Area: 10,169 sq.mi. (26,338 sq.km.). Pop. (1975 est.): 4,160,400, including (1970) Hutu 90%; Tutsi 9%; and Twa 1%. Cap. and largest city: Kigali (pop., 1971 est., 60,000). Language (official): French and Kinyarwanda. Religion (1970): animist 43%; Roman Catholic 46%; Protestant 7%; Muslim 1%. President in 1975, Gen. Juvénal Habyalimana.

President Habyalimana announced in July 1975 the formation of the National Revolutionary Movement

CAMERAPIX

A tranquilized elephant is transported to a new home in Rwanda's Kagera National Park.

RWANDA

Education. (1973–74) Primary, pupils 397,752, teachers 7,777; secondary, pupils 7,488; vocational, pupils 1,487; teacher training, students 1,500; secondary, vocational, and teacher training (1969–70), teachers 736; higher, students 819, teaching staff 109.

Finance. Monetary unit: Rwanda franc, with (Sept. 22, 1975) a par value of RwFr. 92.84 to U.S. $1 (free rate of RwFr. 195 = £1 sterling). Gold, SDRs, and foreign exchange: (June 1975) U.S. $16,320,000; (June 1974) U.S. $15,020,000. Budget (1972 actual): revenue RwFr. 1,880,000,000; expenditure RwFr. 2,696,000,000.

Foreign Trade. (1974) Imports RwFr. 5,394,000,000; exports RwFr. 3,450,000,000. Import sources: Belgium-Luxembourg 16%; Kenya 10%; Japan 9%; West Germany 9%; France 7%; Italy 7%; Iran 7%; U.S. 5%. Export destinations (1973): U.S. *c.* 36%; Kenya *c.* 19%; Belgium-Luxembourg *c.* 18%. Main exports: coffee 64%; tin 12%; tea 6%; pyrethrum extract 5%.

Agriculture. Production (in 000; metric tons; 1974; 1973 in parentheses): sorghum *c.* 140 (*c.* 142); corn (1973) *c.* 50, (1972) 50; potatoes *c.* 120 (*c.* 140); sweet potatoes (1973) *c.* 430, (1972) 414; cassava (1973) *c.* 360, (1972) 350; dry beans *c.* 90 (*c.* 133); dry peas *c.* 30 (*c.* 56); pumpkins (1973) *c.* 55, (1972) *c.* 53; bananas (1972) 1,681, (1971) 1,679; coffee *c.* 20 (*c.* 19); tea *c.* 3 (*c.* 3). Livestock (in 000; July 1974): cattle *c.* 812; sheep *c.* 258; goats (1973) *c.* 600; pigs *c.* 65.

for Development (MRND). It was to form a mass political base for the militarily controlled Committee for Peace and National Unity, of which he was leader, and its aim was to eradicate tribal differences and combat "bandits and parasites." Pierre Abelin, French minister for overseas cooperation, visited Rwanda during May and agreed to provide Rwanda with up to Fr. 25 million and 83 technical personnel. A Japanese loan of 1,107,000,000 yen over a period of 30 years was also negotiated during the year.

Rwanda suffered crop failures and, after devastating storms that aggravated food shortages in March, the British Ministry of Overseas Development, with Red Cross support, arranged for a food airlift to Kigali to feed 50,000 children. The pressure of rapid population growth led to the extinction of the nation's 200-strong herd of wild elephants. Under the auspices of wildlife organizations based in Nairobi, Kenya, the majority of the elephants were shot, although the youngest were tranquilized and airlifted to safety.

(MOLLY MORTIMER)

Sabah:
see Malaysia

Salvador, El:
see El Salvador

Salvation Army:
see Religion

Samoa:
see Dependent States; Western Samoa

Sailing

The main interests in international yacht racing during 1975 centred on the Admiral's Cup series and on several pre-Olympic regatta series, which gave some indication of the probable winning entry in the 1976 Olympic Games.

In the closing hours of 1974 Hobart, Tasmania, was receiving the finishers of the Sydney-to-Hobart ocean race. Huey Long, who at one time held the elapsed time record for a record 11-year period, returned again in his new "Ondine III," a mammoth 79-ft. centreboard ketch designed by Britton Chance, in the hope of creating a new record. But light winds at the start and finish finally beat him and his 3 days, 13 hours was some 12 hours outside the record. Peter Kurt's "Love and War" took the corrected time honours, approximately two hours ahead of John Kahlbetzer's "Bumblebee 3."

Early in the year the Southern Ocean Racing Conference series, held annually in the Caribbean, attracted many new U.S. designs and, with Admiral's Cup selection in mind, crews worked hard. "Stinger," owned and sailed by Dennis Conner of San Diego, Calif., and designed by Doug Peterson, was the overall winner with "Inflation," owned by Dick Nordstrom of Honolulu, second.

The Admiral's Cup series, sailed off the south coast of Great Britain, attracted 19 nations, each with three yachts. The racing included the Channel Race and two inshore races during Cowes Week, and ended with the Fastnet. Great Britain fielded a strong team consisting of "Yeoman XX," "Noryema," and "Battlecry," but defending champion West Germany with "Rubin," "Duva," and "Pinta," the U.S. with "Robin," "Tenacious," and "Charisma," and Australia with "Bumblebee 3," "Mercedes IV," and "Love and War" were all capable of winning. As it turned out, in a generally light wind series that favoured smaller yachts, Ron Amey in his Frers-designed "Noryema" unexpectedly improved and ended up with the top points in the fleet, followed by the consistent Robin Aisher in "Yeoman XX," a Peterson two-tonner. These two gave the British a commanding final total

The German yacht "Pinta" edges the French "Corilan" on the run back for the first mark at the Admiral's Cup Inshore Race at Cowes.

KEYSTONE

A.F.P./PICTORIAL PARADE

Graham Woodruffe of New Zealand sailed to victory in the second race in the quarter-ton series off Deauville.

of 980 pt., over 100 pt. more than runner-up West Germany, with the U.S. third. Very light winds and strong tides for the inshore races during Cowes Week followed by calms during the Fastnet race affected the chances of a number of good boats and teams.

In various parts of the world, the one-ton series produced some very close contests. The one-ton series sailed from Newport, R.I., gave Lowell North (U.S.), an Olympic gold medalist in the Star class, a well-earned victory in "Pied Piper," followed by Berend Beilken (West Germany) sailing 1974's winner, "Gumboots." Once more, Peterson designed both boats. In the quarter-ton series, Murray Crockett (N.Z.) sailed his Bruce Farr-designed "45° South" remarkably quickly, particularly on the two sail reaches, to win the series easily. This small quarter-tonner was an eye-opener to many European yachtsmen. The series, sailed from Deauville, France, under difficult conditions and with less than adequate organization, was brought up short by a French fishermen's blockade of the marina in a protest over pollution in the Seine estuary. The half-ton series sailed in Lake Michigan at Chicago was won by Tom Stephenson of Australia sailing "Foxy Lady" from the U.S. boats, "Checkered Demon" (L. Charbonnet, U.S.) and "Accolade" (P. O'Neill, U.S.). The third race had to be resailed after misplaced marker buoys brought a string of protests against the committee. The three-quarter-ton series, from Hankø in Norway, was won by John McCarthy (U.K.) sailing "Solent Saracen," a Peterson design, from Ron Holland of New Zealand sailing "Golden Delicious" and Lars Anderson of Sweden sailing "Amoress II."

The rush for Olympic honours in 1976 began with a vengeance in 1975. A special pre-Olympic regatta in Canada and two major regattas at Kiel, West Germany, when added to the European and world championships of the Olympic classes, kept top crews busy all summer. In the Finn class Serge Maury (France) won the European championship. The class remained open, however, with U.K.'s D. Howlett, Belgium's J. Rogge, and Australia's John Bertram near the top. The 470 class had a mass of new talent and M. Laurent (France), J. and C. Fountaine (France), J.-C. Vuithier (Switz.), and F. Hübner (West Germany) looked good. In the Flying Dutchman class in 1975, the brothers Y. and J. Pajot from France won most honours in their boat constructed using Kevlar, but in 1976 they could be pressed by Rodney Pattisson (U.K.), who won the European championship, or by J. Dreisch and his brother from West Germany. In the Tempest class four names were consistently at the top: Uwe Mares (West Germany), Jan Albrechtson (Sweden), Allan Warren (U.K.), and Giuseppe Milone (Italy). In the Soling class Australian Star gold medalist David Forbes looked good, with reigning Olympic gold medalist Bud Melges, fellow U.S. world champion Bill Buchan, and Willi Kuhweide and E Hirt of West Germany in hot pursuit. In the Tornado class two men, Jorg Spengler (West Germany) and Reg White (U.K.), appeared to be the most consistent. (ADRIAN JARDINE)

[452.B.4.a.ii]

World Class Boat Champions

Class	Winner	Country
Tornado	J. Spengler	West Germany
Soling	W. Buchan	U.S.
505	J. Loveday	U.K.
470	M. Laurent	France
Flying Dutchman	Y. Pajot	France
G.P. 14	W. Whisker	Ireland
420	B. Whitehurst	U.S.
International 14	D. Owen	U.K.
Enterprise	M. Holmes	U.K.
O.K.	P. Kirketerp	Denmark
Tempest	G. Milone	Italy
Albacore	B. Shore	U.S.
Cadet	I. Videlo	U.K.
Youth 420	B. Whitehurst	U.S.
Youth Laser	C. Buchan	U.S.
Canoe	L. Lundgren	Sweden

San Marino

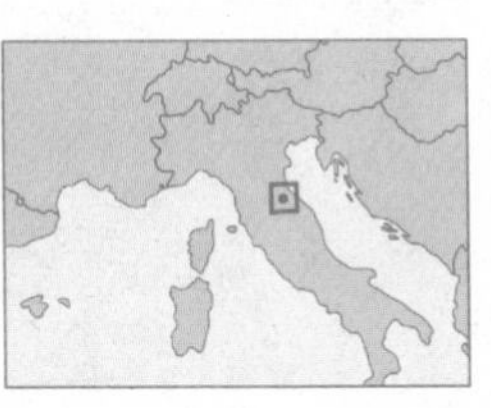

A small republic, San Marino is an enclave in northeastern Italy, 14 mi. SW of Rimini. Area: 24 sq.mi. (61 sq.km.). Pop. (1975 est.): 19,700. Cap. and largest city: San Marino (metro. pop., 1974 est.,

AUTHENTICATED NEWS INTERNATIONAL

This view of San Marino reflects the flavour of life in the small hilltop republic in northeastern Italy.

4,400). Language: Italian. Religion: Roman Catholic. The country is governed by two *capitani reggenti,* or co-regents, appointed every six months by a Grand and General Council. Executive power rests with two secretaries of state: foreign and political affairs and internal affairs. In 1975 the positions were filled, respectively, by Gian Luigi Berti and Giuseppe Lonfernini.

Gian Luigi Berti, secretary of state for foreign and political affairs, represented San Marino in Helsinki, Fin., at the last stage of the Conference on Security and Cooperation in Europe and signed its Final Act on Aug. 1, 1975.

On November 10 the Socialist Party (three members) withdrew from the two-party coalition formed with the Christian Democrats (CD, seven members) in the ten-member executive Council of State elected from the Grand and General Council. Ten days later, on November 20, the Grand and General Council dismissed the government, and the co-regents, Giovannito Marcucci and Giuseppe Della Balda, took over the administration of the republic pending negotiations between the Socialists and the Christian Democrats that would lead to the formation of a new coalition. The Socialists had resigned from the government in protest against the CD's inactivity concerning essential reforms and development plans. The Communist Party secretary, Umberto Barulli, also complained of the CD government's tolerance toward the overtaking of traditional craft skills by the easier sale of mass-produced souvenir junk to the two million visitors visiting the republic each year.

(K. M. SMOGORZEWSKI)

SAN MARINO

Education. (1972–73) Primary, pupils 1,683, teachers 99; secondary, pupils 1,115, teachers 83.

Finance. Monetary unit: Italian lira, with (Sept. 22, 1975) a free rate of 687 lire to U.S. $1 (1,422 lire = £1 sterling); local coins are issued. Budget (1974 est.) balanced at 14,083,000,000 lire. Tourism (1973) 2,584,000 visitors.

São Tomé and Príncipe

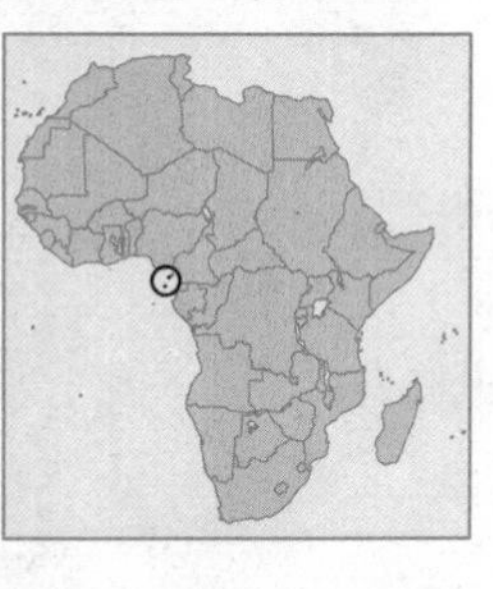

An independent African state, the Democratic Republic of São Tomé and Príncipe comprises two main islands and several smaller islets that straddle the Equator in the Gulf of Guinea, off the west coast of Africa. Area: 372 sq.mi. (964 sq.km.), of which São Tomé, the larger island, comprises 330 sq.mi. (854 sq.km.). Pop. (1974 est.): 79,000. Cap. and largest city: São Tomé (pop., 1970, 17,400). Language: Portuguese. Religion: mainly Roman Catholic. President in 1975, Manuel Pinto da Costa; premier, Miguel Trovoada.

After nearly 500 years of Portuguese rule the independent republic of São Tomé and Príncipe came into being on July 12, 1975, and Manuel Pinto da Costa, an economist and secretary-general of the Movement for the Liberation of São Tomé and Príncipe (MLSTP), was inaugurated as first president. Particular thanks were expressed by the president to Gabon, where the MLSTP had been based prior to independence. He also announced a policy of nonalignment and peaceful cooperation with all countries, a stand that was reflected in the attendance at the independence ceremonies of representatives of the U.S.S.R., East Germany, China, and Cuba on the one hand and of West Germany, Italy, France, and the U.S. on the other.

A provisional government was appointed on July 15 with Miguel Trovoada holding the offices of premier, foreign minister, and minister of defense. The MLSTP then called upon the constituent assembly to approve a new constitution, after which presidential elections would be held and a government appointed. The armed forces of the country consisted of 150 local commandos equipped with matériel the Portuguese troops left behind when they withdrew on July 11. The archipelago was admitted to the Organization of African Unity on July 18 and to the UN on September 16.

The country's economy was at a virtual standstill as the world price for cocoa, São Tomé's main crop, fell to about half of what it was in mid-1974. This, and the exodus of most of the white plantation managers, were factors that contributed to a bleak outlook for the fledgling nation.

(KENNETH INGHAM)

SÃO TOMÉ AND PRÍNCIPE

Education. (1972–73) Primary, pupils 10,015, teachers 303; secondary, pupils 2,114, teachers 86; vocational, pupils 256, teachers 30.

Finance and Trade. Monetary unit: Guinea-Bissau escudo, at par with the Portuguese escudo and with a free rate (Sept. 22, 1975) of 27.35 escudos to U.S. $1 (56.65 escudos = £1 sterling). Budget (1972 est.): revenue 171.1 million escudos; expenditure 170.8 million escudos. Foreign trade (1973): imports 247,259,000 escudos; exports 322,591,000 escudos. Import sources: Portugal 47%; Angola 23%; The Netherlands 6%; France 5%. Export destinations: Portugal 36%; The Netherlands 32%; West Germany 12%; U.S. 8%. Main exports: cocoa 87%; copra 8%.

Agriculture. Production (in 000; metric tons; 1974; 1973 in parentheses): cocoa *c.* 11 (*c.* 11); copra (1973) *c.* 6.5, (1972) *c.* 6.5; bananas *c.* 2 (*c.* 2); palm kernels *c.* 2 (*c.* 2); palm oil *c.* 1 (*c.* 1). Livestock (in 000; 1973): cattle *c.* 3; pigs *c.* 3; sheep *c.* 2; goats *c.* 1.

Saudi Arabia

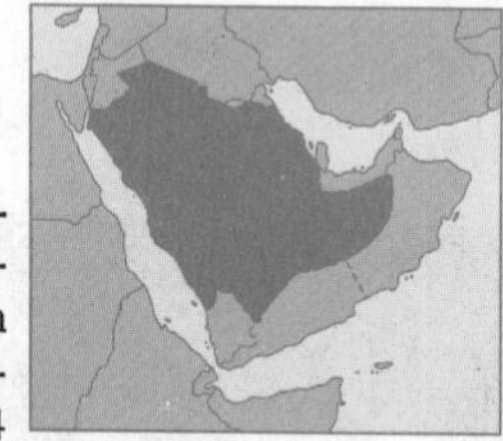

A monarchy occupying four-fifths of the Arabian Peninsula, Saudi Arabia has an area of 865,000 sq.mi. (2,-240,000 sq.km.). Pop. (1974 est.): 8,706,000. Cap. and largest city: Riyadh (pop., 1965 est., 225,000). Language: Arabic. Religion: Muslim. Kings and prime ministers, Faisal to March 25, 1975, and, from that date, Khalid.

Saudi Arabia and the whole Arab world were shaken by the assassination of King Faisal (*see* OBITUARIES) on March 25, 1975. However, the smooth and instant succession of his 62-year-old half brother, Crown Prince Khalid (*see* BIOGRAPHY), maintained stability, and Saudi Arabia's influence, based on its increasing financial power, continued to grow.

In January a $750 million arms deal with the U.S. included the supply of F-5E Tiger jet fighters. The U.S. was reported to have insisted that the agreement require U.S. approval of any transfer of the weapons to other Arab states. Also in January, King Faisal toured those Arab states in confrontation with Israel, and substantial increases in military and nonmilitary aid from Saudi Arabia to Jordan, Syria, and Egypt were announced.

On February 9 it was announced that a $77 million U.S. Defense Department contract had been awarded to the Vinnell Corp. of Los Angeles to recruit 1,000 U.S. Special Forces soldiers (the Green Berets) and Vietnam war veterans to train Saudi Arabia's National Guard. Under strong pressure from Sen. Henry Jackson (Dem., Wash.), the U.S. Senate Armed Services Committee announced that it would investigate the agreement, part of the $335 million U.S.-Saudi defense deal negotiated in April 1974. In March a subcommittee of the House Armed Services Committee, following a tour of the Middle East, reported that it saw nothing wrong with the arrangement.

The assassin who fired the fatal shots at King Faisal during a private majlis (audience) in Riyadh on March 25 was the king's 27-year-old nephew, Prince Faisal ibn Musad. Though said by some to be mentally unbalanced, he was pronounced sane by investigating doctors and was publicly beheaded on June 18. King Faisal died shortly after the shooting, and within an hour Crown Prince Khalid was proclaimed king of Saudi Arabia. The late king's funeral on March 26 was attended by 13 kings and heads of state and a crowd estimated at 100,000. The new king at once nominated the second deputy prime minister and minister of the interior, his half brother Prince Fahd (*see* BIOGRAPHY), as crown prince and first deputy prime minister; Prince Abdullah, the commander of the National Guard, was named second deputy prime minister. The deputy minister of oil and minerals, Prince Saud al-Faisal, was appointed minister of state for foreign affairs, a key post that had remained vacant since the death of Omar Saqqaf in 1974.

The new king was popular among the desert tribes but had little experience in or taste for international diplomacy, and his health was poor. The 52-year-old Crown Prince Fahd was expected to carry a large share of responsibility for domestic and foreign affairs. The rest of the Cabinet remained largely unchanged.

King Khalid announced that the country's policies would be guided by Islamic law and would aim toward social advancement and construction, as well as solidarity and unity both inside and outside the country. He stressed all the traditional Saudi goals of Islamic and Arab solidarity but said the intended policy of the government would be "to reorganize the relationship between the authority and the subjects." On April 6 an amnesty was declared for all political prisoners. The departure from the scene of King Faisal, with his high personal prestige, inevitably meant some relaxation of the authoritarian character of the government. Decisions on matters of importance were henceforth more of a collective nature, with all the ruling princes participating. However, this did not mean that parliamentary democracy was in the offing. In August Crown Prince Fahd told an Egyptian journalist that plans were being made for the formation of a consultative council to take part in running Saudi affairs. He said the council's members would be selected, not elected, "because we all know the results of elections in the world at large. . . . I do not think such elections reflect true public opinion."

Because of falling demand, oil output by Aramco declined sharply from 1974 levels (when total output was some 12% above that of 1973). In January production averaged 7.6 million bbl. a day, as compared with 8.5 million bbl. a day authorized by the government. In April it fell to 6.5 million bbl. a day, 23.5% below the 1974 average, and in June to 5.7 million bbl. a day, the lowest since 1972. In February the flow of oil in Tapline's pipeline, which takes Saudi oil to the Mediterranean via Jordan and Lebanon, was cut off because the fall in tanker rates was making

SAUDI ARABIA

Education. (1973–74) Primary, pupils 577,734, teachers 26,384; secondary, pupils 148,520, teachers 7,831; vocational, pupils 2,576, teachers 333; teacher training, students 13,932, teachers 953; higher (including 3 universities), students 17,253, teaching staff 1,454.

Finance. Monetary unit: riyal, with (Sept. 22, 1975) a free rate of 3.55 riyals to U.S. $1 (7.35 riyals = £1 sterling). Gold, SDRs, and foreign exchange: (Aug. 1975) U.S. $21,300,000,000; (June 1974) U.S. $7,047,000,000. Budget (1974–75 est.): revenue 98,-247,000,000 riyals; expenditure 45,743,000,000 riyals (excluding amounts allocated under the second development plan, 1975–80). Gross national product: (1973–74) 87,773,000,000 riyals; (1972–73) 30,094,-000,000 riyals. Money supply: (Dec. 1974) 7,481,-000,000 riyals; (Dec. 1973) 5,285,000,000 riyals.

Foreign Trade. (1974) Imports 12,330,000,000 riyals; exports 131.8 billion riyals. Import sources (1972): U.S. 19%; Japan 14%; Lebanon 12%; U.K. 7%; West Germany 6%. Export destinations (1972): Japan 15%; The Netherlands 12%; Italy 11%; France 9%; U.K. 8%; U.S. 5%. Main exports: crude oil 94%; petroleum products 6%.

Transport and Communications. Roads (1973) 15,680 km. Motor vehicles in use (1973): passenger 54,100; commercial 39,300. Railways (1973): 610 km.; traffic 61 million passenger-km., freight 62 million net ton-km. Air traffic (1973): 939 million passenger-km.; freight 27.9 million net ton-km. Shipping (1974): merchant vessels 100 gross tons and over 43; gross tonnage 61,275. Telephones (Jan. 1974) 85,000. Radio receivers (Dec. 1971) 87,000. Television receivers (Dec. 1970) 18,000.

Agriculture. Production (in 000; metric tons; 1973; 1972 in parentheses): wheat *c.* 150 (*c.* 150); barley *c.* 18 (*c.* 20); millet *c.* 130 (*c.* 135); sorghum *c.* 175 (*c.* 190); tomatoes *c.* 100 (*c.* 90); onions *c.* 35 (*c.* 34); grapes *c.* 25 (*c.* 25); dates *c.* 250 (*c.* 250). Livestock (in 000; 1972–73): cattle *c.* 300; sheep *c.* 3,000; goats *c.* 1,700; camels *c.* 580; asses *c.* 143.

Industry. Production (in 000; metric tons; 1973): petroleum products 31,516; crude oil (1974) 407,557; natural gas (cu.m.) 3,150,000; electricity (excluding most industrial production; kw-hr.; 1972) 1,000,000; cement (1972) 964.

CLAUDE SALHANI—SYGMA

Thirteen monarchs and heads of state attended the funeral of King Faisal of Saudi Arabia in March. The assassinated ruler was buried in an unmarked grave near El Eid mosque in Riyadh, in accord with Muslim custom.

the pipeline unprofitable as compared with sea routes. Strong pressure was exerted by the Lebanese government to persuade the Saudis to reopen the pipeline. At the meeting of the Organization of Petroleum Exporting Countries (OPEC) in Vienna in September, Saudi Arabia was alone among major producers in favouring an oil price freeze or a maximum increase of 5%. (*See* ENERGY.)

Despite the fall in oil output, Saudi Arabia's reserves of gold, SDRs, and foreign currencies continued to rise during 1975 to reach $21.3 billion by the end of August. By February they had surpassed those of the U.S. for the first time and had become second only to those of West Germany. In March the Saudi riyal was revalued by 2.3% against the U.S. dollar. In April it was revealed that the country's currency in circulation had increased by 85% in two years. The fiscal 1975–76 budget of 110,935,000,000 riyals, announced on July 9, was a record as compared with expenditure of 45,743,000,000 riyals budgeted in the previous year. However, 1975–76 revenues (90% derived from oil) were estimated at 95,850,000,000 riyals, and the budget was therefore expected to show the first deficit since 1969–70.

On July 10 King Khalid approved Saudi Arabia's second five-year plan, 1975–80, which provided for expenditure of 498 billion riyals, compared with 41 billion riyals for the 1970–75 plan. The announced aims of the new plan were the reduction of dependence on oil, diversification, industrialization, and the rapid development of education and social services. The bulk of industrial development funds were allocated to the state organization Petromin for oil refineries and a petrochemical complex with components in various parts of the country. Education was allocated 73 billion riyals, water resources 34 billion riyals, and agriculture 4 billion riyals. Plans to increase the capacity of the port of Dammam from 1.7 million tons to 7 million tons were announced in May.

During 1975 there were several cases of Saudi private financiers seeking control of major U.S. enterprises and meeting strong resistance from U.S. interests. In January Adnan Khashougji failed in an attempt to buy a one-third share in the First National Bank of San Jose, Calif., but another Saudi, Ghaith Pharaon, finally succeeded in buying a controlling share in the Bank of the Commonwealth, sixth largest in the state of Michigan. Later the First Boston Corp. formed a joint investment body with the National Commercial Bank of Saudi Arabia. A Saudi Arabian merchant bank based in London was established, with the Saudi Arabian Monetary Agency holding 50% and various foreign interests holding the rest.

In May a subcommittee of the U.S. Senate Foreign Relations Committee began investigating allegations that Khashougji had been paid a very substantial commission on a Saudi contract to the Northrop Corp. of Los Angeles for the maintenance of the 110 F-5 jet fighters purchased by Saudi Arabia. Northrop admitted paying a $450,000 bribe to the former and present heads of the Saudi Air Force, but in September Khashougji admitted that he had taken the bribe himself to avoid the Saudi generals' taking it.

Saudi Arabia continued to be active in Arab politics after the death of King Faisal. In an interview published in the *Washington Post* on May 25, King Khalid said that Saudi Arabia would concede Israel's right to exist within its pre-1967 borders in return for a total Israeli withdrawal from the territories it had occupied in the 1967 Arab-Israeli war. Close relations with Egypt were maintained, and King Khalid visited Egypt July 16–20. Saudi Arabia notably did not join in the widespread Arab criticism of Egypt's interim agreement with Israel in September. Crown Prince Fahd played an important diplomatic role. Heading a senior delegation to Iran July 1–3, he declared a complete identity of Saudi and Iranian interests. Later he visited London and Paris, where he announced a wide-ranging Franco-Saudi trade and technical agreement. During the summer Saudi Arabia made persistent efforts to mediate between Syria and Iraq in their dispute over the Euphrates waters and between Egypt and Syria in their disagreement over Egypt's moves toward a bilateral agreement with Israel in Sinai. (*See* SYRIA.)

The Saudi oil minister, Sheikh Ahmad Zaki Yamani, was among the 11 oil ministers taken captive at an OPEC meeting in Vienna December 21 and held hostage by terrorists believed to be extremist Palestinians. He was freed in Algiers on December 23.

(PETER MANSFIELD)

[978.B.4.a]

Savings and Investment: *see* Economy, World

Scandinavian Literature: *see* Literature

Schools: *see* Education

Scotland: *see* United Kingdom

Scuba Diving: *see* Water Sports

Sculpture: *see* Art and Art Exhibitions; Art Sales; Museums

Securities: *see* Stock Exchanges

Seismology: *see* Earth Sciences

Senegal

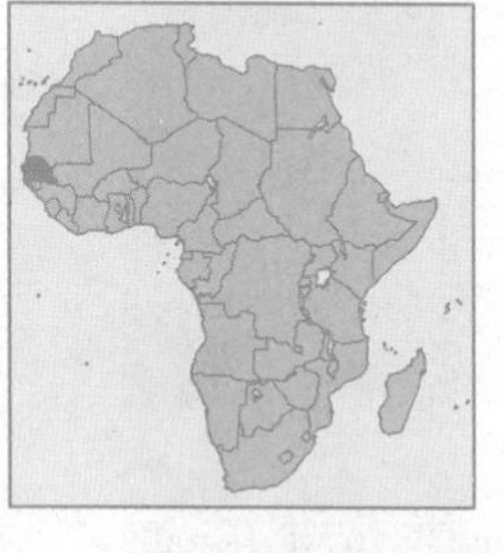

A republic of northwestern Africa, Senegal is bounded by Mauritania, Mali, Guinea, and Guinea-Bissau, and by the Atlantic Ocean. The independent nation of The Gambia forms an enclave within the country. Area: 78,685 sq.mi. (203,793 sq.km.). Pop. (1974 est.): 4,230,700. Cap. and largest city: Dakar (pop., 1974 est., 714,100). Language: French (official); Wolof; Serer; other tribal dialects. Religion: Muslim 90%; Christian 6%. President in 1975, Léopold Sédar Senghor; premier, Abdou Diouf.

Senegal continued to offer a relatively bright image of democratic politics in 1975, notwithstanding the imprisonment of members of two extreme left-wing groups in April and July. The 100,000-strong Senegalese Democratic Party (PDS), led by Abdoulaye Wade, was allowed to function as an opposition party. A year after being freed from imprisonment for plotting against the government, former premier Mahmadou Dia reentered public life in April as organizer of an association concerned with scientific project studies.

President Senghor was active diplomatically throughout the year, visiting Lisbon, Mexico, Paris, several African countries—he played a key role in resolving the frontier dispute between Mali and Upper Volta—Belgrade, Yugos., and Algiers. In retaliation for French treatment of the 70,000 Senegalese immigrants living in France, he required the 17,500 French residents in Senegal to carry identity cards from March 1.

Economic and security cooperation agreements with Guinea-Bissau were signed in January. In September the government began to arrest former African colonial soldiers who had fought for the Portuguese in Guinea-Bissau. (PHILIPPE DECRAENE)

[978.E.4.b.ii]

SENEGAL

Education. (1973–74) Primary, pupils 283,276, teachers 6,294; secondary, pupils 59,236, teachers 2,198; vocational, pupils 5,482, teachers 465; teacher training, students 1,926, teachers 455; higher, students 7,773, teaching staff (university only; 1970–71) 237.

Finance and Trade. Monetary unit: CFA franc, with (Sept. 22, 1975) a parity of CFA Fr. 50 to the French franc (free rate of CFA Fr. 227.70 = U.S. $1; CFA Fr. 471.75 = £1 sterling). Budget (1975 est.) balanced at CFA Fr. 55 billion. Foreign trade (1974): imports CFA Fr. 107,890,000,000; exports CFA Fr. 86,690,000,000. Import sources (1973): France 46%; U.S. 7%; China 5%; West Germany 5%. Export destinations (1973): France 49%; Ivory Coast 8%; Mauritania 7%. Main exports (1973): peanut oil 19%; peanut oil cake 15%; phosphates 11%; fish and products 9%.

Sierra Leone

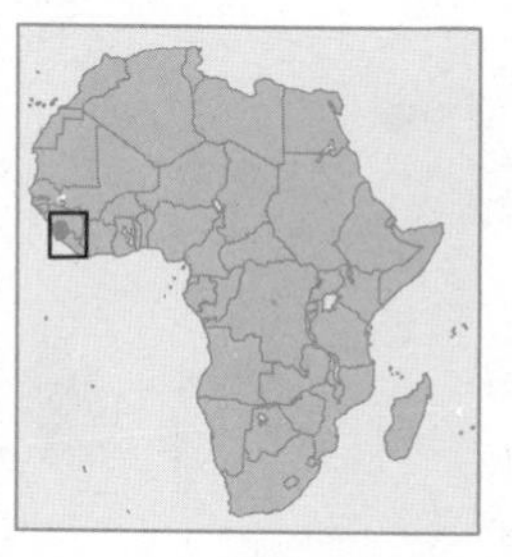

A republic within the Commonwealth of Nations, Sierra Leone is a West African nation located between Guinea and Liberia. Area: 27,925 sq.mi. (72,325 sq. km.). Pop. (1974): 3,002,400, including (1963) Mende and Temne tribes 60.7%; other tribes 38.9%; non-African 0.4%. Cap. and largest city: Freetown (pop., 1974, 274,000). Language: English (official); tribal dialects. Religion: animist 66%; Muslim 28%; Christian 6%. President in 1975, Siaka Stevens; prime ministers, Sorie Ibrahim Koroma and, from July 8, Christian A. Kamara-Taylor.

The treason trials and courts-martial following the alleged July 1974 coup attempts ended in January 1975 with 7 military men and 15 civilians receiving the death sentence. Eight of them were executed on July 19, including former ministers of finance and

View of the Dakar waterfront with phosphate silos in the background.

COMET, ZÜRICH

Serbian Literature: *see* Literature

Seventh-day Adventist Church: *see* Religion

Seychelles: *see* Dependent States

Sheep: *see* Agriculture and Food Supplies

Ships and Shipping: *see* Industrial Review; Transportation

Shipwrecks: *see* Disasters

Shoes: *see* Fashion and Dress

PICTORIAL PARADE

The tin roofs of Freetown serve to deflect the deluge of each rainy season.

information and the former commander of the country's military forces. President Stevens appeared to be in firm control. In a Cabinet reshuffle in July Vice-Pres. Sorie I. Koroma relinquished his post as prime minister to Christian A. Kamara-Taylor and became minister of finance.

Sierra Leone drew closer to Liberia during the year, the Mano River Union of 1973 between the two countries being extended to include a customs union and to help stem diamond smuggling. The diamond industry remained in the doldrums, but expansion in other mineral exports—iron ore, rutile, and bauxite—was the industrial basis of the £310 million 1974–79 plan, together with diversification in agriculture and intensified fish production. The 1974 rice deficit of 63,000 tons cost 24 million leones in foreign exchange. In presenting his 1975 July budget, the finance minister castigated the inefficiency of the government-subsidized corporations and announced that a team of British accountants was auditing the accounts.

(MOLLY MORTIMER)

[978.E.4.b.ii]

SIERRA LEONE

Education. (1970–71) Primary, pupils 166,107, teachers 5,265; secondary, pupils 33,318, teachers (1969–70) 1,364; vocational, pupils 930, teachers (1969–70) 60; teacher training, students 1,053, teachers (1969–70) 129; higher, students (1971–72) 1,266, teaching staff (1969–70) 202.

Finance and Trade. Monetary unit: leone, with (Sept. 22, 1975) a free value of 0.97 leone to U.S. $1 (par value of 2 leones = £1 sterling). Budget (1974–75 est.): revenue 86.7 million leones; expenditure 84.7 million leones. Foreign trade (1974): imports 190,450,000 leones; exports 122,310,000 leones. Import sources: U.K. 21%; Japan 10%; Nigeria 8%; West Germany 7%; Pakistan 5%; France 5%; China 5%. Export destinations: U.K. 61%; The Netherlands 15%; U.S. 6%; Japan 5%. Main exports: diamonds 60%; iron ore 10%; palm kernels 6%.

Agriculture. Production (in 000; metric tons; 1974; 1973 in parentheses): rice 530 (479); cassava (1973) *c.* 83, (1972) *c.* 83; palm kernels *c.* 52 (*c.* 41): palm oil *c.* 55 (*c.* 51); coffee (1973) *c.* 6.9, (1972) *c.* 7.5; cocoa *c.* 8 (*c.* 7). Livestock (in 000; 1972–73): cattle *c.* 270; sheep *c.* 62; goats *c.* 165; chickens *c.* 3,100.

Industry. Production (in 000; metric tons; 1973): iron ore (metal content) 1,443; bauxite 663; petroleum products 303; diamonds (metric carats) 1,670; electricity (kw-hr.; 1972) 212,000.

Sikkim: *see* Dependent States

Silk: *see* Industrial Review

Silver *see* Mining and Quarrying

Singapore

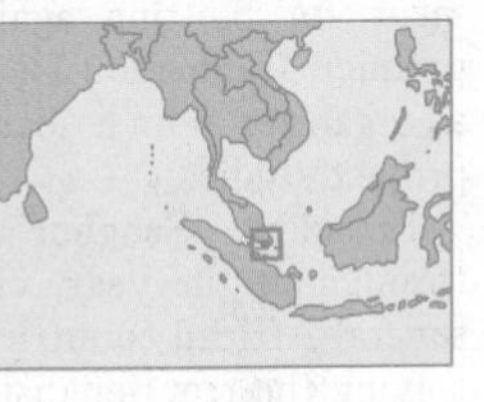

Singapore, a republic within the Commonwealth of Nations, occupies a group of islands, the largest of which is Singapore, at the southern extremity of the Malay Peninsula. Area: 227 sq.mi. (588 sq.km.). Pop. (1975 est.): 2,249,900, including 76% Chinese, 15% Malays, and 7% Indians. Language: official languages are English, Malay, Mandarin Chinese, and Tamil. Religion: Malays are Muslim; Chinese, mainly Buddhist; Indians, mainly Hindu. President in 1975, Benjamin Henry Sheares; prime minister, Lee Kuan Yew.

In February 1975 Tan Wan-piow, president of the University of Singapore students' union, was sentenced to a year's imprisonment for rioting and criminal trespass at the office of the Pioneer Industries Employees Union in Jurong the previous October. The Singapore government in August announced the arrest of five leading Communists, including Cheong Siew-teng, a long-time district committee member of the Malayan Communist Party. In September, Wee Toon Boon, minister of state for the environment and a founding member of the ruling People's Action Party, was sentenced to 4½ years of imprisonment after having been found guilty on five charges of corruption.

A Japanese supertanker, "Showa Maru," ran aground three miles off the most southerly of Singapore's minor islands in January and lost more than one million gallons of oil through leakage. On February 17 and 18, the foreign ministers of Indonesia, Malaysia, and Singapore conferred in Singapore and agreed that a traffic separation scheme be established for the Strait of Malacca and Singapore and that a limit be set on the size of supertankers allowed to pass through them.

In March Foreign Minister S. Rajaratnam led Singapore's first official goodwill mission to China. He met Premier Chou En-lai, who stated that he understood Singapore's foreign policy and was pre-

SINGAPORE

Education. (1974) Primary, pupils 337,816, teachers 11,913; secondary, pupils 174,177, teachers 7,601; vocational, pupils 4,496, teachers 689; teacher training, students 451, teachers 101; higher, students 13,823, teaching staff 905.

Finance. Monetary unit: Singapore dollar, with (Sept. 22, 1975) a free rate of Sing$2.50 to U.S. $1 (Sing$5.18 = £1 sterling). Gold, SDRs, and foreign exchange: (Dec. 1974) U.S. $1,751,500,000; (Dec. 1973) U.S. $1,225,300,000. Budget (1974–75 est.): revenue Sing$2,323,000,000; expenditure Sing$2,299,000,000. Cost of living (1970 = 100): (June 1975) 125; (June 1974) 121.

Foreign Trade. (1974) Imports Sing$20,406,000,000; exports Sing$14,157,000,000. Import sources: Japan 18%; U.S. 14%; Malaysia 13%; Kuwait 6%; Saudi Arabia 6%; Iran 6%; U.K. 5%. Export destinations: Malaysia 17%; U.S. 15%; Japan 11%; Hong Kong 6%; Australia 5%. Main exports: petroleum products 26%; machinery 17%; rubber 14%; chemicals 6%; food 6%. Tourism (1973): visitors 1,134,000; gross receipts U.S. $218 million.

Transport and Communications. Roads (1972) 2,070 km. Motor vehicles in use (1973): passenger 194,300; commercial (including buses) 50,300. Railways (1973) 26 km. (for traffic *see* MALAYSIA). Air traffic (1974): 4,021,000,000 passenger-km.; freight 117,030,000 net ton-km. Shipping (1974): merchant vessels 100 gross tons and over 511; gross tonnage 2,878,327. Shipping traffic (1974): goods loaded 23,105,000 metric tons, unloaded 38,288,000 metric tons. Telephones (Dec. 1973) 250,000. Radio licenses (Dec. 1973) 303,000. Television licenses (Dec. 1973) 231,000.

pared to wait for Singapore's convenience to establish full diplomatic relations. In September Prime Minister Lee Kuan Yew traveled to Bali, where, for the first time, he engaged in a series of informal discussions with President Suharto of Indonesia.

(MICHAEL LEIFER)

[976.B.2]

Social and Welfare Services

Social Security. Social welfare programs, including social security systems, were the object of sharply increased public attention and controversy during 1975 in the face of continuing economic recession. The international economic crisis was reflected in several countries as a growing crisis in social policy. Simply stated, the debate centred around the problem of whether governments could continue to spend more each year, as in the past, on social security and other social expenditures while national budgets remained under the heavy constraints imposed by inflation combined with slow or stagnant economic growth.

The critical attention given to social security programs was often positive and constructive. There was renewed interest in several countries in the role of social security as a measure to prevent poverty and as a stabilizer of public demand during periods of economic slowdown, and proponents of these views argued that benefits should be increased significantly. Nevertheless, a survey of recent legislative and administrative changes indicated that while there were appreciable increases in social security benefits—often up to 15% during 1975—these increases represented more nearly an effort to catch up with wage and price movements than any real improvement in the level of benefits. Moreover, 1975 was not a year of major program changes and innovations in countries with developed social security systems. There were, as would be expected, important adjustments in unemployment insurance in response to increasing numbers of beneficiaries and longer periods of unemployment. But with a few notable exceptions (*e.g.*, the new Pensions Act in the United Kingdom), most industrialized nations were forced to postpone or withdraw ambitious social welfare legislation—such as establishment of a national health insurance system in the U.S.

Unemployment Insurance. The number of unemployed in 18 European countries, the U.S., Canada, Japan, Australia, and New Zealand jumped to an estimated total of 17.1 million in September 1975, according to statistics compiled by the International Labour Organization (ILO). Revealing an increase of 6 million from a year earlier, the figure represented both the largest total and the largest 12-month increase recorded by the ILO in the past 40 years. Expecting continued high levels of unemployment, many social security institutions began to revitalize and improve their unemployment insurance programs. In the case of Switzerland, which in past years had experienced steady economic expansion characterized by persistent manpower shortages, unemployment simply had not become a public issue, and only about 20% of the population was insured against unemployment. Under a proposed constitutional amendment that was scheduled to be put to popular vote in 1976, the present cantonal systems would be replaced by a compulsory federal system covering all wage and salary earners. In countries where compulsory nationwide systems had been in operation for many years improvements were made in the extension of coverage, liberalization of qualifying conditions, extension of the maximum eligibility period, and increases in the levels of unemployment insurance benefits.

In Belgium a national collective bargaining agreement was reached, under which employees of at least 60 years of age who were dismissed and became eligible for unemployment benefits were to be entitled to a "pre-pension" supplementary allowance. Payable until normal retirement age, the amount of the supplementary allowance would be equal to half the difference between the unemployment insurance benefit and the previous wage, up to a maximum of BFr. 37,925. It would be tied to the cost-of-living index in the same manner as unemployment benefits.

The French equivalent of the pre-pension, which guarantees 70% of previous earnings for unemployed workers between the ages of 60 and 65, was implemented in 1972; three years later there were more than 70,000 beneficiaries. In 1975 an additional benefit, known as the supplementary waiting allowance, was added to the system. Aimed at workers of less than 60 years of age who were discharged as a result of economic circumstances and offered for a maximum eligibility period of one year, the waiting allowance would bring total unemployment benefits to 90% of a worker's previous earnings, up to a maximum of Fr. 11,000 a month.

The Federal Republic of Germany instituted a series of emergency measures to combat an unemployment rate that hovered around 5% throughout 1975. The National Employment Institute was authorized to pay a subsidy to firms for taking on unemployed persons from regions that had higher than average unemployment rates. This subsidy could amount to 60% of salary for workers engaged for a maximum period of six months. To pay for the subsidy and other special benefits, as well as for increased regular unemployment benefits, the combined employer-employee contribution was increased from 2 to 3%.

Skating:
see Ice Hockey; Winter Sports

Skeet Shooting:
see Target Sports

Skiing:
see Water Sports; Winter Sports

Skin Diving:
see Water Sports

Soccer:
see Football

An employment insurance law that replaced Japan's unemployment insurance program in April 1975 increased significantly the normal maximum 12-month eligibility period for the insured who was having particular difficulty in finding reemployment or was undergoing a vocational training course—or if nationwide unemployment exceeded a prescribed level. The law also introduced a special provision that permitted unemployment benefits up to a maximum of four years for female workers who wished to remain home to care for children. In order to improve the employment structure, the law offered financial assistance to employers who (1) raised their mandatory retirement age or employed more older workers; (2) employed workers from declining industries; (3) transferred their establishments to regions with high unemployment rates; or (4) were economically compelled to lay off their employees.

In the U.K. a temporary employment subsidy plan was introduced in August which paid £10 per week for the continued employment of workers by companies that had long-term viability but a temporary need to cut their labour force. Britain's Manpower Services Commission also received an additional £30 million to create 15,000 new jobs in regions of high unemployment by providing such labour-intensive projects as the construction of playgrounds and the maintenance of public buildings. Companies recruiting unemployed youths who had recently left school were to be subsidized, under another new measure, at the rate of £5 per week per worker during the first 26 weeks of employment.

Old-Age Pension Programs. A number of factors operated simultaneously to make pensions, and old-age pensions in particular, a major social security issue. The immediate cause for concern was the detrimental influence of rapid inflation on the incomes of the retired. By undermining the monetary value of private savings as well as occupational pension benefits, which were often readjusted inadequately if at all, inflation was pressuring public pension programs to guarantee a decent standard of living for the elderly. Hence, in many countries the concept of public pensions was evolving from relatively low-cost supplements to private incomes to a high-cost system that was expected to support retired persons adequately in their own homes.

A second factor of appreciable effect on the total expenditures of public pension systems was of a demographic nature. Recent statistics indicated that most of the advanced industrialized countries were experiencing marked rises in the number of persons of age 65 and over in proportion to the actively employed population, a trend that increased the burden of pension costs on those in the active work force.

Britain's Social Security Pensions Act was finally adopted, the effective date of operation being April 1978. The act would phase out the flat-rate retirement pension and introduce an earnings-related pension based on earnings-related contributions. The new pension would, in fact, consist of two parts—a base benefit of £1 for every £1 of average weekly earnings up to a basic level, and an additional pension of a quarter of earnings between that level and an upper limit. Members of occupational pension plans that satisfied the standards laid down by the act could contract out of the additional pension part of the plan by paying a reduced contribution on earnings above the basic level and receiving less benefit. Unlike the old pension plan, women would receive the same benefit as men and pay the same rate of contributions; they would also have their pension rights protected if they left work to care for children or other family members. Also, a woman widowed after the age of 50

Stephen Wiesenfeld and his son Jason were the first beneficiaries of a U.S. Supreme Court decision granting widowers with dependent children the same Social Security benefits as women presently receive in those circumstances.

WIDE WORLD

would receive the entire pension that her husband had earned.

Designed to supplement basic pensions, occupational pension plans were considered in many countries to be integral parts of old-age pension structures and consequently were being subjected to increasingly detailed governmental regulations. Noteworthy moves in this direction were taken in late 1974 by West Germany and the U.S., which hitherto had refrained from any close regulation of occupational pension plans. The main effect of the German legislation was to guarantee pension rights under plans operated at the employer level. Even if a worker left the firm before the age of retirement, his claim to a pension would be protected under the law, provided that ten years had passed since the commitment to pay such a pension was made by the employer. In case of bankruptcy of the firm, claims for old-age pensions would be guaranteed by a mutual-aid association set up by the employers' organizations. Employers were required to make cost-of-living adjustments and would not be able to reduce pensions already being paid on the grounds of increased public pension benefits.

Pension systems in many countries felt steady pressure, particularly from trade unions, to lower the age at which old-age pensions could be granted or to adopt flexible or phased retirement provisions. Sweden took an interesting step toward this end when it adopted a national partial pension plan. Financed by a special employee contribution, the partial pension could be obtained between the ages of 60 and 65 provided that the insured transferred to part-time work and was covered by the plan at least ten years after age 45. The pension would be about 65% of the income lost when the insured changed to part-time employment. Total income, therefore, would amount to between 85 and 90% of previous full-time earnings. In France legislation was introduced providing for retirement at age 60 with full pension rights for certain classes of industrial workers.

Financing of Future Benefits. As mentioned above, one of the dominant themes of 1975 was the financial difficulty of many national social security systems. In theory, social security administrators faced two alternatives: reduced benefits or additional financing through increased contributions or tax revenues. Although the first alternative obviously was undesirable, the second immediately raised serious questions. For example, what are the limits that social security financing can place on the national economy without adversely affecting its economic potential?

In France the controversy over financing was sparked by a growing deficit in the social security system, which was expected to exceed Fr. 8 billion in 1976. The deficit in the health insurance branch was not a new phenomenon, but in 1976, for the first time, it would also affect pensions and family allowances, which previously had been balanced or even in surplus. Employers, who were paying the highest social security contributions in Europe (28% of wages and salaries), were expected to resist any further contribution increases, and employees were certain to protest what they felt to be an imbalance in cost and benefit sharing, since much of the deficit was attributable to special plans for farmers, self-employed persons, and other occupational groups. In the background of this debate was a 1974 law that envisaged the establishment in stages by 1978 of an automatic system of financial compensation to ensure minimum protection among the three main branches of social insurance—health insurance, old-age pension insurance, and family allowances. Among the proposals considered by the French government to cover the current deficit and to implement the 1974 law were the partial or total abolition of the earnings ceilings used for contribution purposes; increases in the contribution rates for employees; increased subsidies from the national budget; and the creation of a special social security tax.

(DALMER HOSKINS)

U.S. Developments. Social welfare spending reached all-time highs in the U.S. in 1975, as recession and unemployment increased the need for all types of aid. At the same time, the philosophy and general approach of social services came under strong criticism, and some specific programs were rocked by charges of fraud, error, and mismanagement.

The general attack on social assistance was led by the administration of U.S. Pres. Gerald Ford. In his last major speech as secretary of health, education, and welfare (HEW), Caspar W. Weinberger warned in July that federal programs to solve social ills were leading the U.S. toward "egalitarian tyranny." President Ford stated in October that "if we go on providing more benefits and more services than we can pay for, then a day of reckoning will come."

The administration began a broad review of the country's entire lineup of social programs, which by 1975 accounted for $134 billion a year or more than one-third of the total federal budget. A special task force headed by Vice-Pres. Nelson Rockefeller conducted hearings around the nation, seeking proposals for sweeping reform.

The viability of the Social Security system was questioned during the year in the face of inflation, an increase in the number of beneficiaries, and a decline

WIDE WORLD

A supplemental food program in Detroit focused upon mothers and young children who qualified as "medically indigent" because of recessionary conditions in that city.

in the birthrate. A panel of experts commissioned by the Senate Finance Committee warned that the Social Security trust fund would soon be seriously eroded if the financing and benefit structure was not overhauled. Although acknowledging that financing problems do exist, five former HEW secretaries and three former Social Security commissioners responded in a joint statement that the system faced no financial crisis in the next 25 years.

Social Security benefits and taxes both rose in 1975. An automatic cost-of-living increase in July lifted the average benefits for a retired worker from $184 to $200 a month and for a married couple from $314 to $341. The tax rose to a maximum of $824.85 for employees and to $1,113.90 for the self-employed.

The maximum tax was scheduled to rise again in 1976. Starting January 1, earnings up to $15,300 were to be taxed, compared with a $14,100 base in 1975. Since the tax rate of 5.85% would remain the same, the maximum tax on an employee would be $895.05, an increase of $70.20. Self-employed workers, whose tax rate would continue at 7.9%, would pay up to $1,208.70, an increase of $94.80 over the 1975 maximum. HEW estimated that 18 million workers, about one out of every five covered by Social Security, would be affected by the increase, which would bring $2.1 billion in additional revenue.

Social Security benefits also were scheduled to increase in 1976. Effective January 1, beneficiaries could earn $2,760 a year and still qualify for full Social Security payments. In 1975 they were allowed to earn only $2,520 before starting to lose benefits. An automatic cost-of-living increase in benefits was expected in July 1976.

Two other major programs—food stamps and Supplemental Security Income (SSI)—were jarred by charges of mismanagement and error. Critics charged that the food stamp program was beset by fraud, abuse, and poor administration and that families earning as much as $16,000 a year were sneaking onto the rolls. Although some cheating and a large number of unintentional errors were acknowledged, most of the charges were denied or called exaggerated by supporters of the program. Part of the problem arose from the rapid expansion of the plan since the early 1970s to combat the effects of the recession. By mid-1975 it was helping to feed 19.2 million persons at a cost of about $6 billion a year, compared with 10.5 million recipients and a $1.6-billion price tag in 1971.

Two major proposals aimed at reform of the food stamp program were introduced in Congress. The Ford administration plan would reduce total spending $1.2 billion a year by eliminating or sharply cutting benefits for 8.7 million persons while increasing assistance for the most destitute. Eligibility would be strictly limited to families whose income was below the poverty level. A more moderate reform, proposed by Senators George McGovern (Dem., S.D.) and Robert Dole (Rep., Kan.), would set income eligibility at higher levels and provide for a gradual reduction of benefits as income increased.

President Ford vetoed a bill to extend school lunch and other child nutrition plans, saying that they exceeded his budget and gave subsidies to non-needy children. The veto was overridden, however, by votes of 397–18 in the House of Representatives and 79–13 in the Senate. Estimated to cost $2.7 billion for fiscal 1976, the measure would extend all nonschool food programs, including supplemental feeding for mothers and young children, and would make the school breakfast plan permanent.

Newspaper reports of errors and overspending prompted an investigation of the new federal Supplemental Security Income plan, which in January 1974 had replaced federal-state welfare for the needy aged, blind, and disabled. Authorities admitted that overpayments of $461 million were made during the first 18 months of the program. Despite its problems, however, SSI did accomplish the goal of providing more money to more needy people. HEW reported that in its first full year of operation in 1974 the program served one million more aged, blind, and disabled recipients than were aided in 1973.

In his January state of the union address, President Ford dampened hopes for enactment of some kind of comprehensive national health insurance plan when he imposed a spending moratorium and said it would apply to national health insurance. Four health insurance plans that had been introduced in previous sessions of Congress were reintroduced in 1975, but a jurisdictional dispute blocked prospects for any early action.

The nation's first government-sponsored health insurance programs, Medicare and Medicaid, celebrated their tenth anniversary in 1975. They received mixed reviews for their efficiency, but no one denied the magnitude of their effect. Together, the two programs spent about $9.3 billion in 1975. Medicare covered

U.S. Social Security Financing Schedule for Calendar Years 1937–76

Calendar years	Contribution and benefit base	Tax rate in %, employer and employee, each: OASDI*	HI†	Total	Maximum employee tax	Tax rate in %, self-employed: OASDI*	HI†	Total	Maximum self-employment tax
1937–49	$3,000	1.0	—	1.0	$30	—	—	—	—
1950	3,000	1.5	—	1.5	45	—	—	—	—
1951–53	3,600	1.5	—	1.5	54	2.25	—	2.25	$81
1954	3,600	2.0	—	2.0	72	3.0	—	3.0	108
1955–56	4,200	2.0	—	2.0	84	3.0	—	3.0	126
1957–58	4,200	2.25	—	2.25	94.50	3.375	—	3.375	141.75
1959	4,800	2.5	—	2.5	120	3.75	—	3.75	180
1960–61	4,800	3.0	—	3.0	144	4.5	—	4.5	216
1962	4,800	3.125	—	3.125	150	4.7	—	4.7	225.60
1963–65	4,800	3.625	—	3.625	174	5.4	—	5.4	259.20
1966	6,600	3.85	0.35	4.2	277.20	5.8	0.35	6.15	405.90
1967	6,600	3.9	0.5	4.4	290.40	5.9	0.5	6.4	422.40
1968	7,800	3.8	0.6	4.4	343.20	5.8	0.6	6.4	499.20
1969–70	7,800	4.2	0.6	4.8	374.40	6.3	0.6	6.9	538.20
1971	7,800	4.6	0.6	5.2	405.60	6.9	0.6	7.5	585
1972	9,000	4.6	0.6	5.2	468	6.9	0.6	7.5	675
1973	10,800	4.85	1.0	5.85	631.80	7.0	1.0	8.0	864
1974	13,200	4.95	0.9	5.85	772.20	7.0	0.9	7.9	1,042.80
1975	14,100	4.95	0.9	5.85	824.85	7.0	0.9	7.9	1,113.90
1976	15,300	4.95	0.9	5.85	895.05	7.0	0.9	7.9	1,208.70

*Old-Age, Survivors, and Disability Insurance.
†Hospital Insurance.
Source: Social Security Administration.

about 40% of the health costs for 21.9 million elderly and 3 million disabled persons. Medicaid, a joint federal-state program that subsidized health care for the poor, had been used since its inception by about one out of every five Americans.

Economic conditions placed increased pressure on all U.S. social assistance programs. During the fiscal year ended June 30, 1975, spending on all welfare programs—Aid to Families with Dependent Children (AFDC) and medical and social services—totaled $22,591,000,000, up $3,750,000,000 or 20% over 1974. The number of AFDC recipients increased 2.1% over the previous year to a record average monthly caseload of 11,078,000, and expenditures rose 14.7%.

To ease the effect of prolonged high unemployment, jobless benefits were liberalized. A measure passed by Congress in June and signed by President Ford made the eligibility period for emergency benefits dependent on the severity of unemployment in a particular state. After Jan. 1, 1976, if the state's jobless rate rose over 6%, unemployed workers would be eligible for benefits up to 65 weeks.

Other highlights of the year included the formation of an independent Legal Services Corporation to provide legal assistance to the poor; it replaced the program of legal help that had been pioneered by the Office of Economic Opportunity. F. David Mathews, president of the University of Alabama since 1969, was appointed in July to succeed Caspar Weinberger as secretary of health, education, and welfare.

The U.S. Supreme Court ruled in June that an unemployed parent was not required to accept unemployment benefits if doing so would make his or her family ineligible for higher welfare payments. In May the court also ruled that U.S. states could not reduce the shelter allowance for welfare recipients simply because a nonpaying lodger lived in the same household.

(DAVID M. MAZIE)

See also Education; Health and Disease; Industrial Review: *Insurance.*

[522.D; 535.B.3.c; 552.D.1]

Somalia

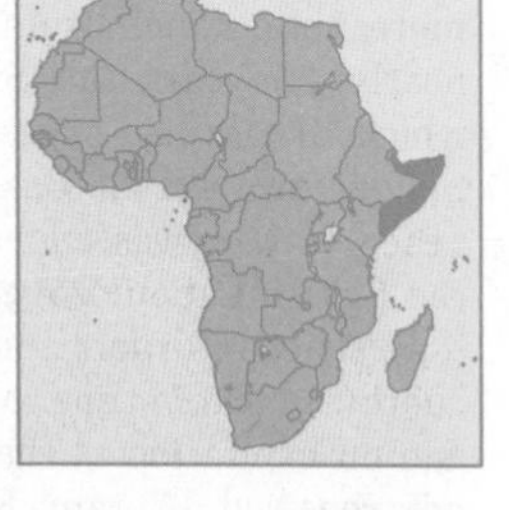

A republic of northeast Africa, the Somali Democratic Republic, or Somalia, is bounded by the Gulf of Aden, the Indian Ocean, Kenya, Ethiopia, and Afars and Issas. Area: 246,300 sq.mi. (638,000 sq.km.). Pop. (1975 est.): 3,170,000, predominantly Hamitic, with Arabic and other admixtures. Cap. and largest city: Muqdisho (pop., 1972 est., 230,000). Language: Somali. Religion: predominantly Muslim. President of the Supreme Revolutionary Council in 1975, Maj. Gen. Muhammad Siyad Barrah.

By the end of 1974, after four years of poor rainfall, drought conditions became so severe that on December 1 the government declared a state of emergency. Between one-quarter and one-third of the republic's population was thought to have been affected, mainly in the riverless north and centre of the country, where the people are nomadic sheep and camel herders. An estimated 800,000 were facing starvation. With aid from abroad, principally from the U.S.S.R. and the European Economic Community, the Somali government distributed relief to about one million nomads and set up 20 camps for the totally destitute early in 1975.

UPI COMPIX

Somalian refugees from the drought-stricken parts of the country were airlifted by Soviet planes to resettlement camps. The refugees shown here are enjoying their first meal following such transfer.

Abundant rains that fell in May–June ended the drought, but by then deaths were estimated at 18,000. There had also been enormous loss of livestock, which constituted the nomads' only resource. Many of the survivors had lost everything. The government planned, with Soviet aid, to introduce most of them to a less precarious way of life as farmers in the more fertile southern part of the country or as fishermen on the coast. By August about 120,000 people had been resettled, though the process was hampered by flooding after the rains which left a further 8,000 people homeless.

SOMALIA

Education. (1971–72) Primary, pupils 40,222, teachers 1,133; secondary, pupils 26,696, teachers 1,162; vocational, pupils 1,297, teachers 129; teacher training, students 351, teachers 17; higher (1970–71), students 964, teaching staff 58.

Finance. Monetary unit: Somali shilling, with (Sept. 22, 1975) an official rate of 6.23 Somali shillings to U.S. $1 (nominal free rate of 13 Somali shillings = £1 sterling). Gold, SDRs, and foreign exchange, central bank: (June 1975) U.S. $65.2 million; (June 1974) U.S. $33.8 million. Budget (1975 est.): revenue 667 million Somali shillings; expenditure 583 million Somali shillings. Cost of living (Muqdisho; 1970 = 100): (Jan. 1975) 139; (Jan. 1974) 111.

Foreign Trade. (1973) Imports 687.8 million Somali shillings; exports 340.5 million Somali shillings. Import sources (1972): Italy 29%; U.S.S.R. 10%; U.S. 6%; U.K. 6%; China 6%; Japan 6%; Kenya 5%; West Germany 5%. Export destinations (1972): Saudi Arabia 53%; Italy 18%; U.S.S.R. 6%; Kuwait 6%; Yemen (Aden) 5%. Main exports (1972): livestock 54%; bananas 26%; meat and products 8%; hides and skins 6%.

Transport and Communications. Roads (1971) 17,223 km. Motor vehicles in use (1972): passenger 8,000; commercial (including buses) 8,000. There are no railways. Shipping (1974): merchant vessels 100 gross tons and over 276; gross tonnage 1,916,273. Telephones (Jan. 1971) *c.* 5,000. Radio receivers (Dec. 1973) 65,000.

Agriculture. Production (in 000; metric tons; 1973; 1972 in parentheses): corn *c.* 50 (105); millet *c.* 15 (25); cassava *c.* 26 (*c.* 26); sesame *c.* 6 (*c.* 6); sugar, raw value *c.* 50 (51); bananas *c.* 135 (152). Livestock (in 000; 1972–73): cattle *c.* 2,900; sheep *c.* 3,900; goats *c.* 5,000; camels *c.* 3,000.

Sociology: *see* Behavioural Sciences

Soil Conservation: *see* Environment

In January new laws were announced giving equal rights to men and women, particularly in the inheritance of property. Ten religious men who preached against the inheritance clauses as contravening Islamic religious law were executed by firing squad on charges of subverting state authority.

On March 23 the French ambassador to Somalia, Jean Gueury, was kidnapped in Muqdisho by members of the Front for the Liberation of the Somali Coast, an organization seeking the removal of the French presence from the French Territory of the Afars and Issas. They demanded the release of two of their own men who were being held prisoner in France and $100,000 in gold. On March 26 the French government agreed to the demands, and as a further concession the Somali ambassador to Paris, Muhammad Said Samantar, accompanied the kidnappers as a second hostage to Aden, where both he and the French ambassador were released.

In June reports that the Soviet Union had established a military base at the port of Berbera were contradicted by the Somali foreign minister and by the Soviet press. Allegations to the same effect had been discussed in the world press and had led the U.S. Senate Armed Services Committee to approve the expansion of military facilities on the British island of Diego Garcia.

On October 21 former prime minister Muhammad Haji Ibrahim Egal, in detention since the coup of 1969, was set free, along with other political prisoners.

(VIRGINIA R. LULING)

[978.E.6.b.i]

South Africa

A republic occupying the southern tip of Africa, South Africa is bounded by South West Africa, Botswana, Rhodesia, Mozambique, and Swaziland. Lesotho forms an enclave within South African territory. Area: 471,445 sq.mi. (1,221,037 sq.km.), excluding Walvis Bay, 372 sq.mi. Pop. (1974 est.): 24,920,000, including Bantu 71.2%; white 16.7%; Coloured 9.3%; Asian 2.8%. Executive cap.: Pretoria (pop., 1974 est., 604,700); judicial cap.: Bloemfontein (pop., 1974 est., 216,000); legislative cap.: Cape Town (pop., 1974 est., 790,900). Largest city: Johannesburg (pop., 1974 est., 1,319,900). Language: Afrikaans and English. Religion: mainly Christian. State presidents in 1975, Jacobus J. Fouché and, from April 19, Nicolaas J. Diederichs; prime minister, B. J. Vorster.

Domestic Affairs. At the end of his seven-year term of office as state president of South Africa, Jacobus J. Fouché was succeeded in April 1975 by Nicolaas J. Diederichs, former minister of finance. On January 31 Sen. Owen P. F. Horwood had been appointed minister of finance and was succeeded as minister of economic affairs by J. Chris Heunis, while S. J. Marais Steyn was appointed minister of Indian affairs and of tourism. Early in the parliamentary session four United Party members of the House of Assembly, headed by the Transvaal leader, Harry Schwarz, and one senator broke away from the party and ultimately formed a new Reform Party, with a program to the left of the official opposition. In the Transvaal the majority of the United Party provincial councillors joined the Reform Party, which thus became the official opposition in the council. The Reformists in July formed a coalition with the Progressive Party under the name of the Progressive Reform Party (PRP), with Colin Eglin as leader. The PRP, with a parliamentary strength of 11 members, supported nonracialism and nondiscrimination and a federal constitution. Cooperation with African homeland leaders and other population groups was a keynote of its program.

The publication of the final report of the Schlebusch-Le Grange Commission inquiring into the activities of certain organizations was followed by the declaration of the Christian Institute as an "affected organization" in terms of legislation adopted in 1974. This meant that the institute was barred from receiving or using funds from foreign sources, which accounted for more than 91% of its income. Like the National Union of South African Students, named an affected organization in 1974, the institute had to curtail activities. Its chairman, C. F. Beyers Naudé, faced charges of refusing to testify before the commission. Members of the South African Students Organization (an all-black body) and of the Black Peoples' Convention, arrested in September 1974 for holding an unauthorized meeting in Durban favouring independence for Mozambique, were tried under the Terrorism Act. The trial continued until the latter part of 1975, some of the accused being released during the proceedings.

Defense expenditure for 1975–76 was estimated at R 948 million, an increase of R 256 million over the previous year's estimate. Giving details of the defense program, the minister of defense, P. W. Botha, said that the arms boycott against South Africa had in effect been largely neutralized, as the country now had the technical knowledge required to manufacture electronic equipment. More than R 500 million of the total defense bill was for armaments. The Army was reorganized into two main forces, a conventional fighting force and a counteremergency force. A new Air Force unit was equipped with missiles and antiaircraft guns. Additional aircraft were equipped for ground support and reconnaissance purposes, and three citizen-force squadrons were equipped with modern aircraft. For maritime defense the Navy acquired two missile-carrying corvettes, and the purchase of two more submarines from France was planned. After nearly 20 years the Simonstown agreement, under which Britain had access to the naval facilities at the Simonstown Naval Base under certain conditions in peace or war, was ended in June on the initiative of the British Labour government.

Restrictive orders and bans under the security laws continued. From time to time existing bans were lifted, and on expiration at the end of the period some were not renewed. Abram Fischer, South African Communist Party leader sentenced in the 1964 Rivonia sabotage trial, died shortly after release on parole (*see* OBITUARIES). On November 25 Breyten Breytenbach, a leading Afrikaans poet, was convicted of conspiring to overthrow the government.

In the field of race relations there were some moves away from discrimination on grounds of colour: certain theatres were opened to all races. Public parks, libraries, and museums were also opened in some cities. Racial signboards in public places were removed in a number of cases. "Mixed" sports to a limited extent were permitted. The basic principles of the policy of separate development (apartheid) were maintained.

Final proposals for the territorial consolidation of the African homelands (Bantustans) in terms of the Bantu land legislation of 1936 were adopted by Parliament, in the face of criticism that the homeland lead-

Sorghum Grains:
see Agriculture and Food Supplies

ers themselves had not been adequately consulted and their objections heard. The effects were to grant more land to the homelands, almost up to the target levels set in J. B. M. Hertzog's 1936 act, and to reduce the number of fragmented areas in the different territories. Only in Transkei, the oldest of the partially self-governing homelands, was the consolidation complete. The homelands reserved the right to claim more land later. Following consultations between Prime Minister Vorster and the homeland leaders, the homelands were granted more administrative powers, both political and economic. Constitutional machinery was established with a view to the proposed independence of the Transkei under Chief Minister Kaiser Matanzima, and Oct. 26, 1976, was set as its tentative date.

In May, after talks between Vorster and the homeland leaders, the right to home ownership by Africans in their own urban areas (withdrawn in 1967) was restored on a limited leasehold basis. Trading restrictions for Africans in their townships were relaxed. An investigation was made into the influx control system and the pass laws regulating the movements and employment conditions of urban Africans. Migrant labourers from the homelands and neighbouring territories working in the white areas were to be protected under a charter granting them the right to visit their families periodically while under contract. Rehabilitation centres were set up in the homelands for Africans found guilty under various laws.

In accords reached in discussions with representatives of the main opposition parties, homeland leaders identified themselves with the principles of federalism, power-sharing, equality of opportunity, and nondiscrimination. They advocated the acceptance of the urban Africans as permanent, stable communities in contrast with the official view. In Johannesburg and several other industrial areas, in agreement with labour unions, training centres were opened to equip Africans for work previously reserved for whites. In both the public and private sectors there was some tendency for the gap between the wages of white and black workers to be narrowed.

General elections for the Coloured Persons' Representative Council in March resulted in a majority for the Labour Party (31 seats) over the Federal Party (8 seats). The Labour Party was further strengthened by the addition of a proportion of the government-nominated seats. The Labour leader, S. L. (Sonny) Leon, was appointed chairman of the council's executive committee. Before the election, faced with the Labour Party's threat, if it won, to make the council unworkable, the minister of Coloured affairs, S. W. van der Merwe, was given statutory powers to take over the functions of the council if necessary. On assuming office, the Labour Party did not carry out its threat but did reiterate its demand for full citizenship, equal rights, and representation in Parliament for Coloured persons. At its first session in September the council refused to pass the budget and adjourned until March 1976 to await the government's reaction to the Labour Party's demands. The government's answer was to remove the chairman of the council's executive committee and appoint an independent in his place; the whole executive resigned in protest and the independent formally adopted and gave effect to the budget. In order to improve white-Coloured relations, committees representing both groups were set up under official sponsorship to establish communication between them.

In response to representations by the South African Indian Council, restrictions on the movement and settlement of Indians across provincial boundaries were lifted, except in the Orange Free State and northern Natal. Additional powers and status for the Indian Council were envisaged on the same basis as for the Coloured people but were regarded as inadequate by some Indians.

TOM BLAU—CAMERA PRESS/PHOTO TRENDS

The capital city of Pretoria, viewed from the University of South Africa.

Development projects during the year included a second oil-from-coal plant to be constructed in the Evander-Trichardt area in the eastern Transvaal, supplementing the existing one at Sasolburg, Orange Free State. It was due to begin operating in 1981. The search for oil by the Soekor organization, which had cost R 95 million by the end of 1974, was intensified under a program costing an additional R 18 million. Part of a plant for the development of a uranium enrichment process devised by South African atomic scientists was put into operation at Valindaba, and plans were made for the future marketing of enriched uranium for peaceful purposes. It was estimated that when the enrichment project was in full production, uranium valued at current prices at R 225 million a year would be sold abroad. The installation itself was estimated to cost R 910 million. Another iron and steel undertaking by the Iron and Steel Industrial Corp. (Iscor) was sited at Newcastle in Natal. Preliminary work was begun on the laying out of three new gold mines, in the western Transvaal and the Orange Free State.

A detailed national development plan, drawn up by the Department of Physical Planning and the Environment, was published. It projected potential development for the next 25 years. Three major new metropolitan areas were singled out, Richard's Bay, Saldanha Bay, and East London-King William's Town.

Foreign Affairs. In pursuit of the policy of détente and peaceful cooperation with black African states, Vorster visited the Ivory Coast in September 1974 and Liberia in February 1975. The minister of information of the Ivory Coast, Laurent Dona-Fologo, paid a formal visit to South Africa and associated his country with the détente efforts. For the first time, Vorster met Zambia's president, Kenneth Kaunda, at the Victoria Falls conference in an attempt to effect a settlement of the constitutional dispute in Rhodesia. With the presidents of Botswana, Tanzania, and Mozambique, Kaunda joined Vorster in the moves to promote peace in southern Africa. South African

SOUTH AFRICA

Education. (1971–72) Primary, pupils 4,108,-910, teachers 96,034; secondary, pupils 560,659, teachers 21,401; vocational, pupils 39,162, teachers 2,657; teacher training (third-level), students 25,720, teaching staff 1,298; higher, students 136,989, teaching staff 7,347.

Finance. Monetary unit: rand, with (Sept. 22, 1975) an official rate of R 0.87 to U.S. $1 (R 1.81 = £1 sterling). Gold, SDRs, and foreign exchange, official: (June 1975) U.S. $1,046,000,-000; (June 1974) U.S. $1,110,000,000. Budget (1974–75 est.): revenue R 4,869,000,000; expenditure R 5,502,000,000. Gross national product: (1974) R 21,657,000,000; (1973) R 18,-183,000,000. Money supply: (March 1975) R 3,907,000,000; (March 1974) R 3,502,000,000. Cost of living (1970 = 100): (June 1975) 156; (June 1974) 137.

Foreign Trade. (1974) Imports R 5,355,700,-000; exports (excluding gold bullion) R 3,386,-900,000. Import sources: West Germany 19%; U.K. 17%; U.S. 16%; Japan 12%. Export destinations: U.K. 29%; Japan 11%; West Germany 9%; U.S. 7%. Main exports: diamonds 10%; gold coins 10%; cereals 8%; sugar 7%; iron and steel 7%; copper 6%; metal ores 5%; textiles 5%.

Transport and Communications. Roads (1973) *c.* 320,000 km. (including 185,846 km. main roads). Motor vehicles in use (1973): passenger 1,737,000; commercial 620,800. Railways: (1973) 22,200 km.; freight traffic (including Namibia; 1974) 60,910,000,000 net ton-km. Air traffic (1974): 5,342,000,000 passenger-km.; freight 154,813,000 net ton-km. Shipping (1974): merchant vessels 100 gross tons and over 270; gross tonnage 535,322. Telephones (Dec. 1973) 1,816,000. Radio receivers (Dec. 1972) 2,350,-000.

Agriculture. Production (in 000; metric tons; 1974; 1973 in parentheses): corn 11,035 (4,-160); wheat 1,547 (1,865); oats 107 (91); sorghum 620 (*c.* 222); potatoes *c.* 600 (635); tomatoes *c.* 270 (269); sugar, raw value *c.* 2,111 (1,732); peanuts 561 (207); sunflower seed 276 (233); oranges *c.* 600 (*c.* 575); grapefruit (1973) *c.* 146, (1972) *c.* 138; apples 260 (243); grapes 1,085 (1,062); tobacco 29 (*c.* 31); cotton, lint *c.* 37 (17); wool *c.* 47 (*c.* 47); meat (1973) *c.* 788, (1972) *c.* 785; milk *c.* 2,850 (2,834); fish catch (1973) 1,332, (1972) 1,123. Livestock (in 000; June 1974): cattle *c.* 10,600; sheep *c.* 31,000; pigs *c.* 1,050; goats (1973) *c.* 5,700; horses (1973) *c.* 430; chickens *c.* 12,600.

Industry. Index of manufacturing production (1970 = 100): (1974) 122; (1973) 115. Fuel and power (in 000; 1974): coal (metric tons) 65,018; manufactured gas (cu.m.; 1973) 1,928,-000; electricity (kw-hr.) 70,782,000. Production (in 000; metric tons; 1974): cement 7,301; iron ore (60–65% metal content) 11,555; pig iron 5,256; crude steel 5,838; copper ore (metal content; 1973) 153; asbestos (1973) 334; chrome (oxide content; 1973) 724; antimony concentrates (metal content; 1973) 15; manganese ore (metal content; 1973) 1,375; uranium (1973) 2.7; gold (troy oz.) 24,400; diamonds (metric carats; 1973) 7,565; petroleum products (1972) 11,088; fish meal (including Namibia; 1973) 278.

police forces stationed in Rhodesia on the Zambezi River border with Zambia were withdrawn in March on the ground that in the changed circumstances their presence there was no longer needed to check guerrilla infiltration. In August Vorster paid a state visit to Paraguay, signing agreements for loan and development aid, and a less formal one to Uruguay.

South Africa maintained economic relations with newly independent Mozambique but did not establish diplomatic ties. Thousands of fugitives from Mozambique and Angola found refuge in South Africa, where a number were permitted to settle permanently, the rest being repatriated to Portugal. Responding to reports that South African troops were fighting on the side of the anti-Soviet faction in the Angolan civil war, the defense minister said in late November that a small South African force from South West Africa (Namibia) had been stationed across the Angolan border to protect water installations there. In mid-December it was announced that three South Africans and 61 South West African guerrillas had been killed in a battle inside Angola. At about the same time, two captured South Africans were publicly exhibited in Lagos, Nigeria.

A constitutional conference representing all population groups in South West Africa held its preliminary session in September in Windhoek (*see* DEPENDENT STATES). At the UN a triple veto by the U.S., Britain, and France defeated an African-sponsored resolution in the Security Council calling for a mandatory ban on the export of arms to South Africa. South Africa abstained from attending the regular session of the UN General Assembly in September.

The Economy. A sustained drop in the free market price of gold, occasioned mainly by the International Monetary Fund's decision to sell part of its gold holdings, coupled with a balance of payments deficit nearing R 1 billion, led to the devaluation of the rand by 17.9% in terms of the U.S. dollar. It came into effect on September 22 and was followed by various financial measures, including an increase in interest rates and in liquidity restrictions on the commercial banks by the Reserve Bank. Effects of the high devaluation rate, according to the minister of finance, Owen Horwood, were expected to be an improved balance of payments, an inflow of investment capital, the expansion of exports and gold mining, incentives to local industrial production, and possible tax adjustments.

In his first budget, providing for expenditure totaling R 6,562,000,000 on loan and revenue account for 1975–76, Horwood defined his priorities as defense and the provision of an adequate infrastructure for future growth. The budget was largely based on a continuing high price for gold, and in changed circumstances the government was committed to a reduction in spending and other adjustments.

(LOUIS HOTZ)

See also Dependent States.

[978.E.8.b.i]

Southeast Asian Affairs

Shock waves from Indochina made 1975 a year of reckoning for Southeast Asia. As the U.S. position collapsed and the Cambodian and South Vietnamese presidents went into ignoble exile, Southeast Asian countries hurriedly plunged into self-examination and readjustments. Disillusionment about the U.S. and its treaty obligations ran parallel to a general awakening to the possibilities of new options and policy attitudes. On the whole, governments in the region seemed to conclude that anti-Communism was not a worthwhile national objective in itself, and the U.S. was not a guarantor of safety for non-Communist regimes. The emerging consensus was that only through internal political-economic strength built on a basis of wise policies and genuine popular support could Southeast Asian governments exercise control over their own fates.

Articulating the region's new mood, Philippine Pres. Ferdinand E. Marcos said in April that events in Indochina had "set in motion serious and agonizing appraisals of our respective national interests and how, in the changed circumstances, we might best promote them." He said the "one indelible lesson" from Indochina was that no amount of foreign aid or arms could ensure a nation's stability. Prime Minister Lee Kuan Yew of Singapore, who had journeyed to Thailand in January 1973 to get it to act as a buffer against continental Communism from the north, now called on Thailand to align itself with China as the salvation not only of Thailand but of all Southeast Asia. He wanted the Thai government to make a "U-turn" from its alliance with the U.S.

Indeed, something like a one-way traffic developed in the region during the year. Appalled by the failure of the U.S.'s massive military might in Indochina, all Southeast Asian governments seemed anxious to put some distance between themselves and the U.S. The movement was in the direction of the Communist bloc. Nonalignment became a glamorous word. The process of recasting foreign policies, which had begun with former U.S. president Richard M. Nixon's visit to Peking in early 1972, accelerated and expanded in scope. Countries such as the Philippines and Thailand had a special problem because they had come to be known as staunchly pro-American and had been partisans with the U.S. in the Indochina wars. They were not only embarrassed by the turn of events in Indochina; it became a clear necessity for them to shed their pro-American image. They moved publicly for the closing or restricting of operations of U.S. military bases in their territories. Philippine Foreign Secretary Carlos P. Romulo, known for decades as a particular friend of the U.S., argued that the presence of U.S. bases on its soil could make the Philippines suspect as an "American Trojan horse" in the region.

Ironically, China seemed to favour a continuation of the U.S. presence in Southeast Asia. It often expressed concern that a U.S. withdrawal would create a power vacuum that the Soviet Union would seek to fill. China was reported to have been especially "understanding" about U.S. bases in discussions with visiting Philippine and Thai heads of government. Despite the Chinese position, however, Southeast Asian leaders continued to back away from the U.S. In so doing, they also evinced interest in the Soviet Union so as to balance their enthusiasm for China. Lee Kuan Yew, himself Chinese and strongly anti-Communist, singled out China as "the more benign" of the Communist powers and said that China was the key to regional equilibrium in Southeast Asia. But other leaders appeared anxious to distribute their favours more evenly. Immediately after his visit to Peking in June, Marcos began planning a trip to Moscow. The return of Thai Premier Kukrit Pramoj (*see* BIOGRAPHY) from his official visit to Peking was followed by a Thai invitation to Soviet Foreign Minister Andrey Gromyko to visit Bangkok and sign a special cultural agreement. The five members of the Association of Southeast Asian Nations (ASEAN) as a group recognized the victorious insurgents of Cambodia on April 18, the day after the fall of Phnom Penh. They left no doubt about their interest in establishing diplomatic relations with Hanoi.

Admittedly there was an element of apprehension in all Southeast Asian countries as they sought new ties and established new norms of policy. Almost all were worried about what the Communist victories in Indochina would do to the insurgencies in their own countries. A marked increase in guerrilla activities in Thailand tended to confirm their fears. Also, Peking's avowed policy of supporting governments in power did not prevent the Chinese Communist Party from sending fraternal greetings publicly to the Malaysian Communist Party (MCP). Coincidentally or otherwise, the MCP went on to score spectacular strikes against the Malaysian government in Kuala Lumpur as well as in the border jungles.

In August U.S. intelligence analysts said that Thailand and Malaysia had about 18 months to prepare for major Communist insurgencies. They predicted that massive infiltration into Thailand would begin in 1977 and that the consolidation of Communist power in Vietnam and Laos at about the same time would lead to a concerted Communist offensive in the region. The U.S. tried to back up its prediction with assurances of continuing interest in Southeast Asian defense arrangements. Secretary of State Henry Kissinger said in May that the U.S. would formulate a new Asian policy after close consultations with the leaders of Thailand, the Philippines, and Singapore, among others. The following month Assistant Secretary of State Philip Habib toured the region and declared that the U.S. was not withdrawing militarily from Asia. In September the U.S. ambassador in Singapore said that the U.S. 7th Fleet might be able to fill the psychological void created by the phased withdrawal of British, Australian, and New Zealand forces from Singapore and Malaysia.

ASEAN. A notable result of the devaluation of the U.S. in post-Vietnam Southeast Asia was the ascendancy of ASEAN and the final demise of the Southeast Asia Treaty Organization (SEATO). ASEAN, always projected as a mainly economic and occasionally cultural grouping, finally came to grips with its political destiny. Meeting in Bali, Indon., in September, Indonesian President Suharto and Singapore Prime Minister Lee said that an ASEAN summit conference, the first in the group's eight-year history, would be held soon to boost its political development. Indications that an extraordinary summit meeting was in the offing had appeared in the very month of the U.S. debacle in Indochina.

Thereafter various ASEAN leaders kept airing their views on how best the organization could cope with the new realities. Marcos wanted Communist states in the region included in the group, for only through relations with them could regional security be achieved. Kukrit Pramoj saw ASEAN emerging as the main security vehicle for the region "widened and intensified to cover fields which in the past we have not considered." Malaysian Prime Minister Tun Abdul Razak asked that ASEAN be raised to the institutional status of the Organization of African Unity and other such bodies.

When the foreign ministers of the five ASEAN countries (Indonesia, Malaysia, the Philippines, Singapore, and Thailand) met in Kuala Lumpur in May for their annual meeting, no major decision was taken, perhaps because of the impending meeting of the five heads of state. The foreign ministers called for a

Women and children sought shelter in shallow bunkers in Phnom Penh as Communist forces launched their final assault on the city.

WIDE WORLD

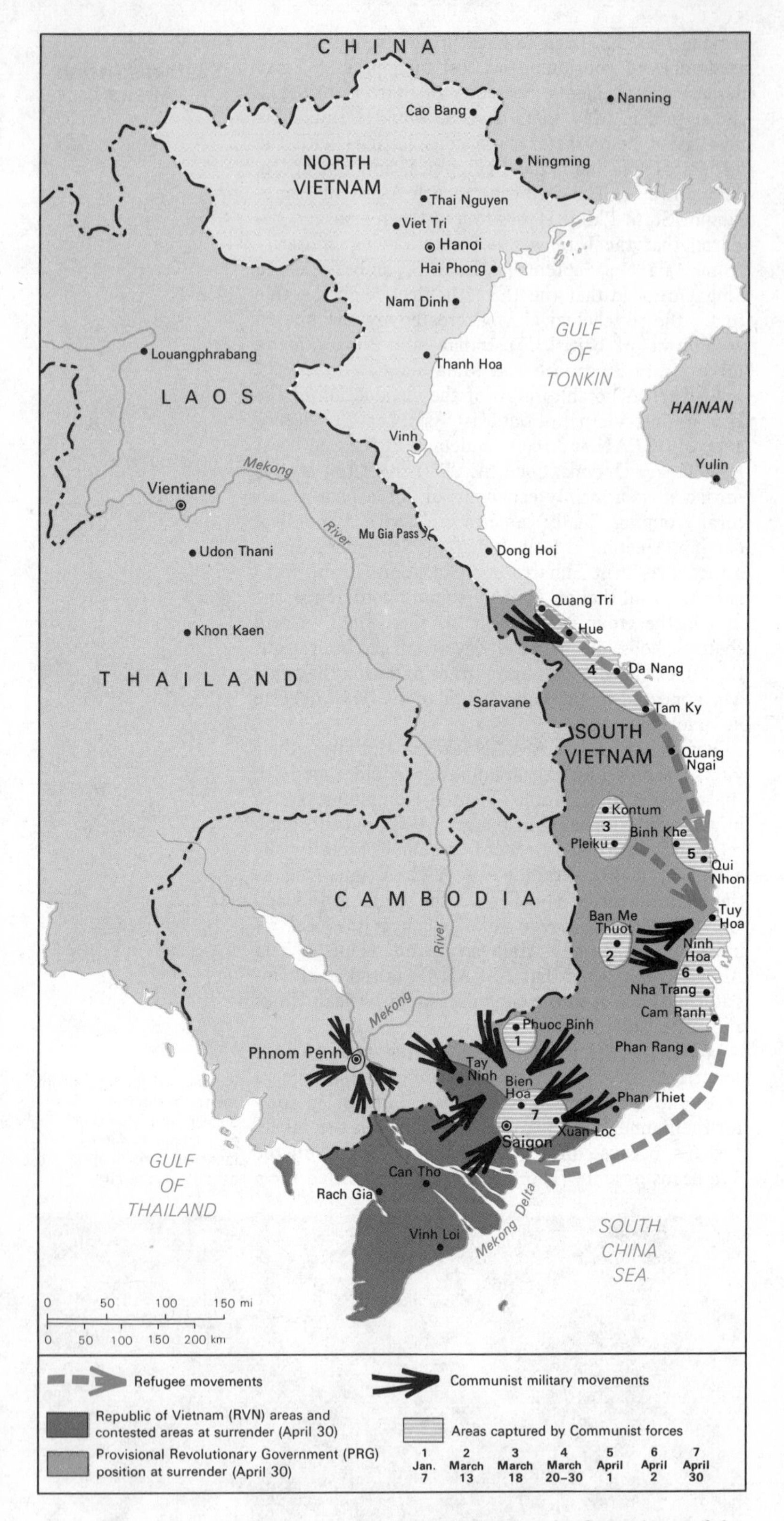

reassessment of ASEAN's place in the region and for coexistence with the new governments of Indochina. They also prepared a draft treaty on peaceful settlement of regional disputes for ratification at the summit. As if in recognition of the new significance of ASEAN, China paid a rare compliment to it in August. Noting that the organization had "achieved positive results in recent years," it held up ASEAN as an example for African states. Australia and Japan identified themselves with ASEAN's economic goals and pledged support to its expanding activities.

SEATO. If SEATO met with an entirely different fate in 1975, it was hardly surprising. Its establishment in 1955 was directly linked to the Indochina war; the then U.S. Secretary of State John Foster Dulles had admitted at the time that he was looking for a legal device that would make it possible for the U.S. to intervene in Indochina, which the French were rapidly abandoning. "This area is demonstrably important to the U.S.," Dulles had said in Bangkok, "and the treaty assures our interest in it and assures that we have allies here." With the allies in jitters and the interest admittedly somewhat muted, it was natural that the treaty had to die. It had already reached a state of living death with the withdrawal of France and Pakistan and the loss of interest of other members. In July the U.S. finally saw the handwriting on the wall and said that it would dissolve the organization if Thailand and the Philippines wished to do so. It turned out that they wished it dearly. Thai Foreign Minister Chatichai Choonhavan made it a recurring theme in his frequent travels. In Australia he called for the phaseout of SEATO and added that Thailand was not seeking another defense pact to replace it. "The war is over. We do not need collective defense any more," he said. The joint communiqué at the end of Kukrit Pramoj's state visit to the Philippines in July called for the phasing out of the organization. The Malaysian government, a persistent advocate of a neutral zone in Southeast Asia, was quick to welcome the communiqué as a "good thing." Australia and New Zealand, both SEATO members, also welcomed the idea. On September 24 the SEATO ministerial council, meeting at the U.S. mission to the UN, formally decided to wind down SEATO's remaining civil activities, though the treaty would nominally stay in being.

ESCAP. The economic picture in Southeast Asia was rather blurred in 1975 by what was called aid weariness among developed countries and uncertainty over raw materials. While several countries in the region were significant producers of some raw materials, they were in a bargaining position with respect to only a few commodities. The boom in commodity prices over the previous two years had, however, generally benefited Indonesia, Malaysia, the Philippines, Singapore, and Thailand.

The UN Economic and Social Commission for Asia and the Pacific (ESCAP) met in annual session in India from February 26 to March 7 and issued a "New Delhi declaration" calling for a new international economic order and a development strategy based on equality and social justice. It stressed the importance of food production, land reforms, and regional cooperation. However, the ESCAP report for 1974, released in February 1975, painted a grim picture of the future and forecast "death for millions of people" unless Asian governments changed their development priorities. It said Asian countries were particularly vulnerable to the effects of global economic phenomena such as food shortages and energy crises. This had already contributed to "immediate problems of famine," and Asian governments would witness a desperate situation getting worse if they did not plan, in the long term, "for the masses." Economically as well as politically, events seemed to support the Malaysian prime minister's thesis that the people of Southeast Asia were now entering a new era "fraught with unprecedented perils as well as exciting opportunities." (T. J. S. GEORGE)

See also articles on the various countries.
[976.B]

THE END OF A WAR

By Robert Shaplen

The long war in Vietnam came to a swift and sudden end on April 30, 1975, when the South Vietnamese government, in a state of military and political collapse, surrendered in Saigon to its North Vietnamese conquerors. A fortnight earlier Cambodia had fallen to the Khmer Communists, and within another month it was apparent that the Communists in Laos had made a fiction of the coalition government and had taken over that country. Thirty years after the end of World War II, all of what was once French Indochina was thus in Communist hands, and North Vietnam emerged as the dominant military power in Southeast Asia—in fact, after China, in all of Asia.

For the major powers, the United States, the Soviet Union, and China, and for the other countries of Asia, the North Vietnamese victory was an event of momentous significance. As the residue of Americans fled from Vietnam under conditions of near panic and humiliation, the U.S. came to the end of its adventure in Indochina. Whatever new relationship it might develop would take time and patience, and a totally new outlook. It seemed certain that the Soviets and Chinese, locked in their deep ideological conflict, would not only extend their competition for influence to the former Indochina nations but would intensify it throughout Southeast Asia. And the North Vietnamese, though closer to Moscow than to Peking, seemed bound to play an important new role of their own throughout the region.

The Roots of Involvement. To most Western observers, the Communist victory in Vietnam was a painful inevitability, given the degeneration of South Vietnamese morale and the vast disillusionment in the U.S. about the war. For the Communists, the victory was equally inevitable, but for different reasons. Though never fully unified, the Vietnamese have historically considered themselves as one people and one nation. For nine centuries they withstood sporadic attempts by Chinese dynasties to conquer them. Then, in the middle of the 19th century, began the French colonial conquest of Indochina.

Nearly a century of French domination, during which the colonial rulers did virtually nothing to prepare the Vietnamese for self-government, began to unravel when World War II started, but the French did not give up. They established an adjunct of their wartime Vichy government in their former Asian empire, working out compromises with the occupying Japanese that lasted almost until the end of the war. The Vietnamese nationalists, in turn, created an underground revolutionary movement to fight both the Japanese and the French. Under the guiding genius of the late Ho Chi Minh, who had formed the Indochinese Communist Party in 1930, the Viet Minh, an amalgam of nationalist parties and groups guided by Ho's Communists, continued its rebellion. In August 1945, after Japan's surrender to the Allies, Ho and his partisans marched into Hanoi, the capital of the former French protectorate of Tonkin in the north, and set up an independent government.

Robert Shaplen is the Far Eastern correspondent for The New Yorker *magazine and has written numerous articles, documentaries, and books on Southeast Asia, including* The Lost Revolution: The U.S. in Vietnam *(rev. ed. 1966) and* The Road from War *(rev. ed. 1971).*

The Vietnamese part of Indochina had been peremptorily divided by the Allied powers for purposes of occupation at the 16th parallel. This hasty partition, based purely on military expediency, made the ensuing conflict unavoidable. In the south, in the colony of Cochinchina, the Viet Minh succeeded briefly in establishing a government in Saigon, but they were driven out by British occupation troops and the returning French, who attempted to reestablish a colonial government. Though the French recognized Ho's new government in Hanoi as part of their murky French Union, they had no intention of surrendering any part of Vietnam.

In December 1946, after vain efforts by Ho to foster further agreements with the French, the French Indochina War broke out. This bitter war, during which the French suffered 74,000 dead and 200,000 wounded, lasted until 1954. The Americans gave military and economic help to the French, though, ironically, the Office of Strategic Services, a forerunner of the Central Intelligence Agency, had given some assistance to Ho during World War II. Despite wartime pronouncements in behalf of postwar freedom for Allied colonies, the Americans believed they had to support the French to obtain France's cooperation in the European Defense Community. At the end of the French Indochina War, during the siege of the French bastion of Dien Bien Phu, the Americans almost came into the conflict themselves, and there was even some talk of nuclear weapons.

With France's departure from Indochina—formalized at the Geneva Conference in the summer of 1954—the Americans entered the vacuum, a decision chiefly engendered by Secretary of State John Foster Dulles. When Ngo Dinh Diem, a mandarin nationalist and a Catholic, returned to Vietnam as the head of a new, anti-Communist South Vietnamese government, the U.S. helped prop him up in the face of chaotic resistance from minority religious sects and gangster elements in Saigon. Then, starting in the administration of Pres. Dwight D. Eisenhower and increasingly during that of Pres. John F. Kennedy, it gave Diem's regime economic and military assistance and advice. This marked the beginning of direct U.S. involvement.

The Unwinnable War. As the Diem government became more corrupt and inefficient, the Communist guerrillas, who came to be called the Viet Cong, stepped up their attacks in the south. Following serious Buddhist demonstrations, in November 1963—with the secret but effective support of the U.S.—Diem was overthrown in a military coup, and he and his nefarious brother, Ngo Dinh Nhu, were brutally murdered. The coup failed to solidify the ranks of the South Vietnamese, however. As coups and countercoups followed one another in a series of revolving-door governments, the military situation grew worse, and in March 1965 the Americans sent their first contingent of Marines to guard the northern air base of Da Nang. The U.S. involvement was ultimately to reach 550,000.

Had it not been for the Americans, the Communists would probably have cut Vietnam in half, from the central highlands to the coast of the South China Sea, in mid-1965, with repercussions that would have reached throughout Southeast Asia and, among other things, might have led to the success rather than the failure of the Communist coup in Indonesia in September of that year. In response to North Vietnamese attacks on U.S. warships in the Gulf of Tonkin—attacks that may have been encouraged by prior U.S. shelling of North Vietnamese radar stations—the first U.S. air raids on the north began in the summer of 1964. By the following year such raids on North Vietnamese highways, bridges, and rail lines had become almost a daily occurrence. As much as anything else, the bombings of the north created a deep opposition to the war in the U.S.

The Viet Cong, increasingly supported by North Vietnamese regular forces, demonstrated their capacity to attack in battalion and even regimental strength. Despite their greater firepower, the Americans and the South Vietnamese were unable to cope with the clever and ever shifting strategy and tactics of the Communists. The Americans won the major fixed battles, but the

Communists always reconsolidated and struck at the weakest points of the South Vietnamese defenses. Schemes originated by the Americans to "pacify" the South Vietnamese countryside never worked well, chiefly because of poor South Vietnamese organization, lack of leadership and zeal, and corruption.

Politically—and the war, despite its military ferocity, was always essentially a political one—the Communists proved themselves far more adept than the disputatious South Vietnamese. In 1960 they created the National Liberation Front, and five years later established the covert People's Revolutionary Party as an adjunct of the Lao Dong, Hanoi's Workers'—or Communist—Party, whose cadres ran the war under direct orders from Hanoi. As the Chinese and then the Soviets increased their supply of military equipment to their Vietnamese "brothers," it became apparent that the war could not be won by the Americans and the South Vietnamese and that, at best, it could only be settled by negotiations. Efforts to get negotiations started were made from time to time, but they never materialized, mainly because there was no clear rationale as to what to negotiate about. The Communists were adamant about ending the war on their terms, through direct talks with the Communist-dominated National Liberation Front, which was to be recognized as an independent entity, and only after the Americans had withdrawn their forces. Washington and Saigon rejected these conditions as opening the way to Communist domination of the south.

In January 1968, during the lunar new year holiday known as Tet, the Communists mounted wide-scale attacks on southern cities, including Saigon, where they even tried to capture the U.S. embassy. The Tet attacks, and subsequent ones that spring and summer, cost the Viet Cong and the North Vietnamese extremely heavy casualties, but they served finally to disillusion the U.S. government, by now beset by rising public resentment of the war. Pres. Lyndon Johnson, to whom the war had become a near obsession, decided not to run for reelection. In March 1968 he halted the bombing of North Vietnam, thus setting in motion serious peace talks in Paris.

The talks were to prove protracted and difficult. It was not until January 1973, after Johnson's successor, Pres. Richard Nixon, had resumed the bombing, that an agreement was signed establishing the mechanism for a cease-fire and a political solution in Vietnam. But while the Americans withdrew, and obtained the release of their prisoners of war in North Vietnam, the North Vietnamese were permitted to keep their troops in the south, much to the dismay of the South Vietnamese.

Both sides violated the cease-fire from the outset, and the war was soon resumed on a major scale. The Americans had poured a vast amount of military supplies into South Vietnam just after the cease-fire, but gradually, as Congress refused to grant sufficient funds, they stopped replacing weapons and equipment lost by the South Vietnamese on the one-for-one basis stipulated at Paris. Meanwhile, the Communist powers, especially the Soviets, increased their support to the North Vietnamese, who by now were completely dominating the war in the south.

Late in December 1974 the North Vietnamese began their final, all-out offensive in the southern province of Phuoc Long, which they quickly captured. In mid-March 1975 they attacked in the highlands. The South Vietnamese withdrawal toward the coast began in orderly fashion, but degenerated into panic. The northern cities of Hue and Da Nang fell at the end of March, and the whole string of coastal provinces promptly collapsed. By the end of March, Hanoi had secretly made its decision to go for broke instead of negotiating, and though Pres. Nguyen Van Thieu of South Vietnam finally resigned under pressure on April 21, neither of his successors, Vice-Pres. Tran Van Huong and retired Gen. Duong Van Minh, could set up a functioning government. It would have done no good anyway. By April 28 Saigon was under heavy rocket and artillery attack. The next day the remaining Americans escaped in their helicopters while more than 100,000 South Vietnamese fled by air or by sea. The long, tragic war was finally over.

More than one million Vietnamese, both southerners and northerners, had been killed, along with over 56,000 Americans. The war in Indochina had cost the U.S. nearly $150 billion. Both halves of Vietnam had been devastated, and the Americans had suffered their gravest defeat in history. The lessons of Vietnam had proved the inefficacy of trying to fight a massive land war on the Asian continent and had demonstrated that it was impossible to take over a war when the will to resist on the part of the native people being defended was not great enough. It had also demonstrated that a determined enemy, imbued with revolutionary fervour and strongly supported by its powerful Communist friends, would sooner or later prevail.

Aftermath. After the surrender the North Vietnamese consolidated their hold on South Vietnam, diminishing the role of the Provisional Revolutionary Government established in the south in 1969. The situation in neighbouring Cambodia and Laos remained in flux. Cambodia, invaded by U.S. and South Vietnamese forces in May 1970, following the overthrow of the government of Prince Norodom Sihanouk in a right-wing coup, had fallen to the Khmer Communists in mid-April. Chaos ensued, in contrast to the relatively quiet takeover in South Vietnam, and it was estimated that scores of thousands of Cambodians ordered out of the cities and told to resettle in the countryside by the new rulers were dead or dying of starvation. There was no love lost between the Khmer Communists and the North Vietnamese, and some skirmishes between the two took place. Among outside powers, the Chinese appeared to have the greatest influence in Cambodia, though the new Khmer rulers, determined to preserve what was left of their once-great empire, would not readily countenance any interference in prosecuting their own revolution, however bloody it might prove. Nor was Hanoi likely to accept easily any permanent dominance by Peking.

In Laos the unique coalition government of the suave, dignified Prince Souvanna Phouma had been replaced by a new Cabinet dominated by Pathet Lao military men and hard-line members of the Lao Communist Party. The influence of Hanoi seemed to be predominant there, especially since most of the important new Communist figures had had close ties with North Vietnam all along. Peking, anxious to avoid having either Hanoi or Moscow or both become the prevailing outside influence, continued to maintain its presence in the northwestern part of the country, where Chinese engineers had been building roads and fortifications for some years.

The repercussions of the Communist victories in Indochina were felt from Indonesia to Korea. In Southeast Asia a jittery and politically shaky Thailand quickly moved to accommodate both Hanoi and Peking—as, in the case of Peking, Malaysia and the Philippines had already done. The fragile Association of Southeast Asian Nations sought to solidify its ranks and proclaim neutrality for the region, but it seemed likely that Communist insurgency movements, especially in Thailand, Burma, and Malaysia, would continue to grow and that, despite their disclaimers, the Chinese would continue to support them clandestinely, as would the North Vietnamese. All in all, the chances for stability in Southeast Asia, where all governments, with the momentary exception of Thailand, had grown more authoritarian during the period of the Vietnam war, did not seem good.

In North Asia the shock effect of the war's end was felt particularly in South Korea, where the government of Park Chung Hee had also grown more authoritarian and repressive. The South Koreans feared that the North Korean dictator, Kim Il Sung, would be encouraged by the Communist victory in Vietnam to attack the South once more, as he had done in June 1950. More than ever, throughout Asia, it appeared that only the major powers, the Soviet Union, China, and the United States, could preserve peace—if they wanted to. Much would depend on how the respective policies of détente, between the United States and the Soviet Union and the United States and China, materialized. On this score, there was certainly as much room for skepticism as for hope.

Space Exploration

During 1975, for the first time in the 14 years since man first entered space, seven men were orbiting the Earth at the same time. Four were Soviet cosmonauts and three were U.S. astronauts. Two of the cosmonauts were aboard the Salyut 4 space station, while two more were linked together with the three astronauts in the joint U.S.-Soviet Apollo/Soyuz Test Project (ASTP).

For the U.S., ASTP was a grand finale to a decade that had seen Americans go from a brief 15-minute flight through the lower reaches of near-Earth space to the landing of 14 men on the Moon. With the end of the ASTP flight, the U.S. withdrew from manned space flight for at least five years, if not longer. Several well-known figures in the U.S. space program announced their retirement, including Thomas P. Stafford, who returned to the U.S. Air Force, Harrison H. ("Jack") Schmitt, who resigned to enter politics in New Mexico, and William R. Pogue and Alfred M. Worden, who left to join former astronaut James B. Irwin in his evangelistic organization known as High Flight.

On April 15 a special meeting of the European Space Conference settled the final problems of converting the old European Space Research Organization into the new European Space Agency. The new organization became a reality in May. Appointed to head the agency as director general was Roy Gibson of the U.K. The first priority of ESA was the development of a European launch vehicle.

Manned Flight. On January 10 the U.S.S.R. launched Soyuz 17 manned by Lieut. Col. Aleksey A. Gubarev and civilian Georgy M. Grechko. They were headed for a rendezvous with the Salyut 4 space station, which had been launched on Dec. 26, 1974, and placed in a circular orbit at an altitude of about 214 mi. Soyuz 17 docked with the Salyut 4 space station on January 12.

The mission of Gubarev and Grechko was to carry out a program of scientific studies in the fields of meteorology, solar astronomy, atmospheric physics, astrophysics, Earth resources, geography and geology, and biomedical studies. In addition, they tested new instruments for guiding and controlling the Salyut. After 30 days in space, Grechko and Gubarev returned to Earth.

On May 24 Soyuz 18 lifted off from Tyuratam. Aboard were veteran cosmonauts Lieut. Col. Pyotr I. Klimuk and civilian engineer Vitaly I. Sevastyanov. On May 26 the two docked with Salyut 4 and went aboard to continue the experiments of their predecessors in the space station. After two months in space they returned to Earth on July 26.

The astronauts selected for the Apollo/Soyuz Test Project consisted of a seasoned veteran and two rookies. Commander of the mission was Brig. Gen. Thomas P. Stafford, who had flown in both the Gemini and Apollo missions. He was accompanied by Vance D. Brand, who had not been in space, and by a veteran of the manned space-flight program, who also had not flown. He was 51-year-old Donald K. ("Deke") Slayton, who had been one of the first seven astronauts in the U.S. program. Grounded by a minor heart irregularity in 1962, Slayton worked his way back onto flight status in time for his last chance to reach space.

WIDE WORLD

An artist's conception of the successful docking of the U.S. Apollo and Soviet Soyuz spacecraft on July 17.

The primary Soviet crew was experienced. Commander of Soyuz 19 was Col. Aleksey A. Leonov, who had been the first man to leave a spacecraft and walk in space, during his Voskhod 2 mission in 1965. Valery N. Kubasov, a civilian engineer, was aboard Soyuz 6 in 1969.

On July 15 the two Soviet cosmonauts were launched. Stafford and his crew lifted off about 7½ hours later on the same day. On the morning of July 17, Brand sighted the Soyuz at a distance of 242 mi. and reported to Mission Control, at Houston, Texas, "OK, we got Soyuz in the sextant."

As the two spacecraft narrowed the distance between them, communications between them were relayed to the ground and on to mission control centres by the ATS-6 and Intelsat satellites. Actual docking of the two occurred at about noon on July 17 as the two craft were above a point 620 mi. W of Portugal.

The ASTP mission consisted of five joint experiments. One of these was the use of the Apollo, while it was not docked with the Soyuz, to act as an "artificial Moon" to eclipse the Sun while photographs of the solar corona were made from the Soyuz. Another was also performed while the two craft were not joined. A light beam from Apollo was aimed at reflectors on Soyuz and bounced back to a spectrometer on the Apollo, an experiment that helped determine the amount of atomic oxygen and nitrogen in the upper atmosphere. In the area of the life sciences, each crew took into orbit cultures of a fungus, the growth of which was visible like the rings of a tree. Photographs of the growth were taken by the crews, and several cultures were exchanged in orbit. Thus, not only could the effect of weightlessness upon such life forms be determined but also the change in the fundamental circadian or biological rhythms. One experiment was of an applied science nature. It consisted of melting various metals and semiconductor materials by Slayton and Kubasov in the zero-gravity of space inside a furnace in the docking adapter.

Perhaps the most significant experiment from the viewpoint of future manned spaceflight was one that investigated the exchange of microorganisms among crewmen and their spacecraft. Cultures were taken of both Soviet and U.S. spacemen before, during, and after the mission.

Southern Rhodesia: *see* Rhodesia

South West Africa: *see* Dependent States; South Africa

Soviet Bloc Economies: *see* Economy, World

Soviet Literature: *see* Literature

Soviet Union: *see* Union of Soviet Socialist Republics

Soybeans: *see* Agriculture and Food Supplies

Major Satellites and Space Probes Launched Oct. 1, 1974–Sept. 30, 1975

Name/country/ launch vehicle/ scientific designation	Launch date, lifetime*	Physical characteristics: Weight in kg.†	Shape	Diameter in m.†	Length or height in m.†	Experiments	Orbital elements: Perigee in km.†	Apogee in km.†	Period (min.)	Inclination to Equator (degrees)
Meteor 19/U.S.S.R./A II/1974–083A	10/28/74	‡	Cylinder with two panels	1.5 (4.92)	5 (16.4)	Meteorological satellite	840 (522)	908 (564)	102.4	81.1
Luna 23/U.S.S.R./D Ie/1974–084A	10/28/74 11/9/74	‡	‡	‡	‡	Lunar probe damaged in landing on Moon	Trajectory to the Moon			
Intercosmos 12/U.S.S.R./B I/ 1974–086A	10/31/74	1,100 (2,425)	Octagon and octagonal pyramid with eight panels	1.1 (3.61)	2.5 (8.2)	Scientific satellite to study atmosphere, ionosphere, and micrometeorites; joint project of U.S.S.R., Hungary, East Germany, Czechoslovakia, and Romania	243 (151)	707 (439)	94.1	74
NOAA 4/U.S./Delta/1974–089A	11/15/74	409 (902)	Cube with three rectangular solar panels	1 (3.28)	1.2 (3.94)	Meteorological satellite	1,447 (899)	1,461 (907.8)	114.9	101.7
ITOS 4/U.S./Delta/1974–089B	11/15/74	900 (1,984)	Cube with three solar panels	1 (3.28)	1.2 (3.94)	Meteorological satellite	1,441 (895)	1,462 (908)	114.8	101.7
Intasat/Spain/Delta/1974–089C	11/15/74	20 (44)	Twelve-sided polygon	0.43 (1.42)	0.46 (1.5)	Measure electron content of ionosphere (launched piggyback with ITOS 4)	1,444 (897)	1,461 (907.8)	114.9	101.7
Oscar 7/U.S./Delta/1974–089D	11/15/74	29 (64)	Octahedron	0.41 (1.33)	0.43 (1.42)	Amateur radio operators' satellite (launched piggyback with ITOS 4)	1,441 (895)	1,462 (908)	114.8	101.7
Molniya 3/U.S.S.R./A IIe/1974–092A	11/21/74	‡	‡	‡	‡	Communications satellite	650 (404)	40,690 (25,284)	717.6	62.9
Intelsat 4 (F-8)/U.S./Atlas Centaur/1974–093A	11/21/74	706 (1,556)	Cylinder	2.4 (7.87)	2.8 (9.19)	Communications satellite	35,776 (22,230)	35,800 (22,245)	1,436.2	1.8
Skynet 2B/U.K./Delta/1974–094A	11/23/74	435 (959)	Cylinder	1.37 (4.49)	0.8 (2.62)	Defense communications satellite	‡	‡	‡	‡
Soyuz 16/U.S.S.R./A II/1974–096A	12/2/74 12/8/74	6,000 (13,228)	Sphere and cylinder	3.1 (10.17)	10.7 (35.1)	Practice mission for Apollo/Soyuz flight	194 (121)	280 (174)	89.3	51.8
Helios 1/West Germany-U.S./ Titan IIIE Centaur/1974–097A	12/10/74	349 (770)	Sixteen-sided polygon	2.74 (9)	2.13 (7)	Solar probe to investigate magnetic fields, solar wind, cosmic particles, and micrometeorites	Orbit around Sun			
Symphonie 1/France-West Germany/Delta/1974–101A	12/19/74	‡	Octagon with three panels	1.83 (6)	0.46 (1.5)	Communications satellite	35,017 (21,759)	35,852 (22,277)	418.1	0.5
Salyut 4/U.S.S.R./D I/1974–104A	12/26/74	19,000 (41,888)	Cylinder	4 (13.12)	10 (32.81)	Manned space station	337 (209)	350 (217)	88.5	51.6
Soyuz 17/U.S.S.R./A II/1975–001A	1/10/75 2/9/75	6,500 (14,330)	Sphere and cylinder	3.1 (10.17)	10.7 (35.1)	Docked with Salyut 4; crew spent 30 days in orbit, a Soviet record	186 (116)	249 (155)	88.9	51.6
Landsat 2(ERTS-B)/U.S./Delta/ 1975–004A	1/22/75	900 (1,984)	Annular body with two panels	1.52 (4.99)	3.32 (10.89)	Earth resources satellite	903 (561)	914 (568)	103.2	99.09
Starlette/France/Diamant BP 4/ 1975–010A	2/6/75	48.3 (106.5)	Sphere	0.24 (0.79)		Geodesic satellite covered with 60 laser reflectors	806 (501)	1,139 (708)	104.1	49.8
SMS 2/U.S./Delta/1975–011A	2/6/75	628 (1,385)	Cylinder	1.905 (6.25)	2.3 (7.55)	Meteorological satellite	35,780 (22,233)	35,800 (22,245)	1,436.3	1
Taiyo (SRATS)/Japan/Mu 3c/ 1975–014A	2/24/75	86 (190)	Octagonal cylinder	2.75 (9.02)	0.65 (2.13)	Measure solar radiation and examine thermosphere	249 (155)	3,048 (1,894)	120.2	31.5
Intercosmos 13/U.S.S.R./B I/ 1975–022A	3/27/75	1,100 (2,425)	Octagon and octagonal pyramid with eight panels	1.1 (3.61)	2.5 (8.2)	Joint Soviet-Czechoslovakian experiment to study Earth's magnetosphere and polar ionosphere	286 (178)	1,680 (1,044)	104.7	82.9
Molniya 3 (2)/U.S.S.R./A IIe/ 1975–029A	4/14/75	‡	‡	‡	‡	Communications satellite	593 (368)	39,750 (24,700)	717.5	62.8
Aryabhata/India/B I/1975–033A	4/19/75	360 (794)	Polyhedron with 26 flat surfaces	1.47 (4.82)	1.1 (3.61)	Studies in X-ray astronomy, Sun's radiation, and radiation flows in ionosphere	563 (350)	619 (385)	96.4	50.4
Explorer 53/U.S./Scout/1975–037A	5/7/75	195 (430)	Cylinder with four panels	0.66 (2.17)	0.61 (2)	Study X-rays from Milky Way and other galaxies	508 (316)	516 (321)	94.9	3
Anik 3/Canada/Delta/ 1975–038A	5/7/75	544 (1,199)	Cylinder	1.71 (5.61)	1.52 (4.99)	Communications satellite	35,786 (22,236)	35,789 (22,238)	1,436.2	0
Castor (D5-B)/France/ Diamant B/1975–041A	5/17/75	76 (167)	Twenty-four-sided polygon	0.8 (2.62)	0.8 (2.62)	Study variations in atmospheric density and gravitational fields	277 (172)	1,279 (795)	100	29.95
Pollux (D5-A)/France/ Diamant B/1975–041B	5/17/75 8/5/75	36 (79)	Sixteen-sided polygon	0.6 (1.97)	0.6 (1.97)	Test small rocket motor for future satellites	277 (172)	1,279 (795)	100	29.95
Intelsat 4 (F-1)/U.S./Atlas Centaur/1975–042A	5/22/75	706 (1,556)	Cylinder	2.4 (7.87)	2.8 (9.19)	Communications satellite	35,787 (22,237)	36,182 (22,482)	1,446.3	0.4
Soyuz 18/U.S.S.R./A II/ 1975–044A	5/24/75 7/26/75	6,000 (13,228)	Sphere and cylinder	3.1 (10.17)	10.7 (35.1)	Manned satellite to rendezvous with and board Salyut 4 space station	198 (123)	229 (142)	88.6	51.69
Venera 9/U.S.S.R./Proton/ 1975–050A	6/8/75	4,536 (10,000)	‡	‡	‡	Investigate planet Venus with orbiter and lander	Trajectory to Venus			
Nimbus 6/U.S./Delta/ 1975–052A	6/12/75	715 (1,576)	Annular base with two panels	3.35 (10.99)	3.05 (10)	Meteorological satellite	1,097 (682)	1,104 (686)	107.2	99.9
Venera 10/U.S.S.R./Proton/ 1975–054A	6/14/75	4,536 (10,000)	‡	‡	‡	Investigate planet Venus with orbiter and lander	Trajectory to Venus			
OSO 8/U.S./Delta/ 1975–057A	6/21/75	1,064 (2,346)	Decahedron with solar panel	2.19 (7.2)	3.2 (10.5)	Study effects of Sun on weather and communications	539 (335)	557 (346)	95.6	32.9
Soyuz 19/U.S.S.R./A II/ 1975–065A	7/15/75 7/21/75	6,800 (14,991)	Sphere and cylinder	2.72 (8.92)	7.48 (24.54)	Soviet part of Apollo/Soyuz Test Project	191 (119)	218 (135)	91	62.9
Apollo/U.S./Saturn 1B/ 1975–066A	7/15/75 7/24/75	14,737 (32,490)	Cone and cylinder	3.57 (11.7)	11.89 (39)	U.S. part of Apollo/Soyuz Test Project	152 (94)	166 (103)	87.7	51.8
China 3/China/CSS-X3/ 1975–070B	7/26/75 9/14/75	‡	‡	‡	‡	Earth resources experiments or military reconnaissance	183 (114)	455 (283)	90.9	69
COS-B/European Space Agency/Delta/1975–072A	8/9/75	278 (613)	Cylinder	1.52 (5)	1.52 (5)	Study extraterrestrial gamma radiation	442 (275)	99,002 (61,517)	2,203.9	90.3
Viking 1/U.S./Titan IIIE Centaur/1975–075A	8/20/75	3,527 (7,775)	Hexagonal base with three legs (lander); octagon with four panels (orbiter)	3.66 (12)	5.24 (17.2)	Search for life on Mars, make atmospheric measurements, take pictures of surface	On trajectory to Mars			
Symphonie 2/France-West Germany/Delta/1975–077A	8/27/75	‡	Octagon with three panels	1.83 (6)	0.46 (1.5)	Communications satellite	35,364 (21,974)	35,870 (22,289)	1,427.4	0
Viking 2/U.S./Titan IIIE Centaur/1975–083A	9/9/75	3,527 (7,775)	Hexagonal base with three legs (lander); octagon with four panels (orbiter)	3.66 (12)	5.24 (17.2)	Search for life on Mars, make atmospheric measurements, take pictures of surface	On trajectory to Mars			
Intelsat 4A (1)/U.S./Atlas Centaur/1975–091A	9/25/75	1,387 (3,058)	Cylinder	2.38 (7.81)	5.28 (17.33)	Communications satellite	35,294 (21,931)	35,821 (22,258)	1,424.4	0.1
Aura (D2B)/France/ Diamant BP 4/1975–092A	9/27/75	110 (243)	Octahedron	0.9 (2.95)	1 (3.28)	Study ultraviolet radiation of Sun and other stars	715 (444)	503 (313)	98	37.16

*All dates are in universal time (UT).
†English units in parentheses: weight in pounds, dimensions in feet, apogee and perigee in statute miles.
‡Not available.

(MITCHELL R. SHARPE)

On July 19 the two craft separated and docked again to prove out both the techniques of docking and the common docking mechanism. The final separation of Apollo and Soyuz occurred later in the day. Soyuz 19 landed safely on July 21 some 85 mi. NW of Arkalyk. The U.S. astronauts continued in orbit for another five days, splashing down in the Pacific Ocean on July 24 in a landing that was marred by a serious mishap. At an altitude of 24,000 ft. the spacecraft began filling with toxic gases from its attitude control propulsion system. The crew put on oxygen masks but not before Brand had passed out briefly. Later physical examinations showed no permanent damage to the astronauts' lungs.

The continuing economic inflation had its effect on the space shuttle during the year. As a means of offsetting rising costs, NASA decided that construction of a second launch pad at Kennedy Space Center in Florida would be deferred. Also to be deferred was the development of improved space suits, life-support backpacks, and astronaut maneuvering units for use with the shuttle.

The budget also forced NASA to reschedule a significant amount of work on the shuttle main engine to stay within projected costs. It involved moving the appropriation of funds for testing from fiscal year 1976 to fiscal year 1977.

Space Probes. On March 15, Helios 1, the West German-U.S. solar probe launched on Dec. 10, 1974, passed by the Sun at a distance of 28,699,800 mi. and a velocity of 147,312 mph, setting a record for closest distance to the Sun. More interesting to the scientists monitoring its instruments was the fact that the solar wind leaves the Sun at a rate of 1,897,200 mph, a figure much higher than previously thought.

On September 21 Helios 1 passed within 28,580,000 mi. of the Sun. Slightly higher temperatures were noted on the probe; its solar cells were 270° F, compared with 262° F on the first perihelion. The difference was thought to be caused by degradation of the probe's insulating material.

On June 8 and June 14 the Soviet Union launched Venera 9 and Venera 10 toward Venus. Venera 9 landed on the planet on October 22 and began transmitting pictures of rugged rock-strewn terrain near its landing site. Venera 10 touched down on the planet on October 25. Pictures of its landing site, about 1,375 mi. from that of Venera 9, revealed a landscape that featured smooth rounded rocks that resembled huge pancakes; between the rocks were areas of cooled lava or debris of weathered rock.

On March 16 Mercury was revisited by Mariner 10 for the third time since its launch in November 1973. The quality of the pictures of the planet's surface was not as good as desired, but features as small as 150 to 300 ft. were photographed. On its final visit to Mercury, the probe also proved that the planet has a magnetic field but no entrapped radiation belt. It also detected the presence of a very tenuous atmosphere of helium and provided data that permitted a much more accurate determination of the planet's orbit and its mass to be made.

Originally scheduled for launch to Mars on August 11, Viking 1 was postponed because of a balky valve in one of the solid-propellant boosters of the Titan IIIE Centaur rocket. The probe was launched successfully, however, on August 20. While as many as four mid-course correction burns had been planned for the probe on the way to a landing on Mars, the one made on August 27 proved to be so accurate that subsequent ones would not be required. The probe was scheduled to enter an orbit 3,450 mi. above Mars on June 19, 1976.

Viking 2 was launched on September 9. Launch on that day meant that the probe would enter an orbit around Mars on Aug. 7, 1976. A highly accurate mid-course correction burn of its engine also ensured that no additional firings would be needed during the remainder of the trip.

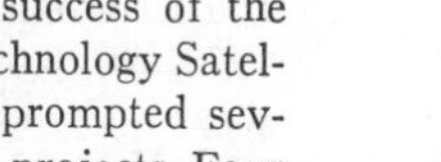

Unmanned Satellites. The great success of the U.S. in the field of Earth Resources Technology Satellites (the Landsats, formerly ERTS) prompted several countries to express interest in such projects. Four nations showed definite interest in establishing ground receiving stations for information that was being transmitted from the Landsats. They were Iran, Italy, Brazil, and Zaire.

The U.S. and Japan, in mid-July, signed an agreement for the launching by the U.S. of Japanese satellites by Delta vehicles in 1977 and 1978. The U.S.S.R. and France also signed a protocol laying out a joint ten-year program of space research, though it called for no manned flights. On June 5 a small French satellite, MAS-2, was launched "piggyback" with a Molniya 1 communications satellite by the Soviets under an earlier cooperative plan.

The Soviet Union also signed an agreement with the U.S. for a joint series of experiments in space biology. An invitation to do so had been extended by Soviet scientists to visiting U.S. scientists at the fifth meeting of the U.S./U.S.S.R. Working Group on Space Biology and Medicine in late 1974.

Spain, on Nov. 15, 1974, became a member of the growing list of countries with a scientific satellite in orbit. It was launched for that nation by the U.S. from Vandenberg Air Force Base, California, aboard a Delta rocket. The jointly developed French-West German communications satellite Symphonie was orbited by a U.S. Delta rocket from Kennedy Space Center on Dec. 19, 1974. India also joined the group of nations with domestic scientific satellites. Its Aryabhata, designed to measure radiation from the Sun, was orbited by a Soviet launch vehicle on April 19.

(MITCHELL R. SHARPE)

See also Astronomy; Defense; Earth Sciences; Industrial Review: *Aerospace, Telecommunications;* Television and Radio.

[738.C]

ENCYCLOPÆDIA BRITANNICA FILMS. *Man Looks at the Moon* (1971); *Controversy over the Moon* (1971); *Space Exploration: A Team Effort* (1972).

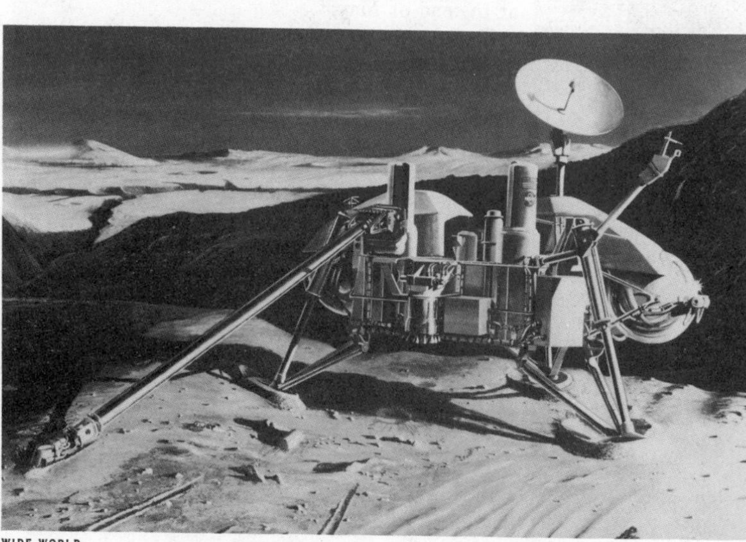

WIDE WORLD

An artist's conception of the unmanned Viking spacecraft which is scheduled to land on the surface of Mars in 1976.

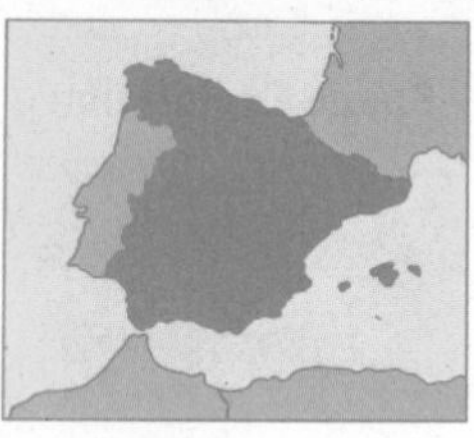

Spain

A monarchy of southwest Europe, Spain is bounded by Portugal, with which it shares the Iberian Peninsula, and by France. Area: 194,885 sq.mi. (504,750 sq.km.), including the Balearic and Canary islands. Pop. (1975 est.): 35,471,900, including the Balearics and Canaries. Cap. and largest city: Madrid (pop., 1975 est., 3,634,000). Language: Spanish. Religion: Roman Catholic. Prince of Spain and king-designate until Nov. 22, 1975, and interim chief of state from October 30 to November 20, Don Juan Carlos de Borbón y Borbón, who on November 22 became King Juan Carlos I; chief of state to October 30, Gen. Francisco Franco Bahamonde; premier, Carlos Arias Navarro.

The year 1975 was dominated by speculation as to how much longer Generalissimo Franco (*see* OBITUARIES) would remain in power and by uncertainty about the subsequent course that Spain would take. The expectation of change prompted an upsurge of political activity; extremists of both left and right adopted terrorist tactics, whereas groups nearer the centre presented themselves as democratic alternatives to the existing ruling party. The government professed a policy of gradual liberalization, but as the year progressed it resorted increasingly to force to counter extremist groups, as well as to placate its right-wing supporters.

The liberalization policy was marked by several developments in the early part of the year. The law permitting the establishment of political associations came into force, and by the autumn eight associations had been approved, though the Christian Democrats and Socialists declared that they were unable to comply with the law's requirements and the Communists were specifically excluded from its provisions. Five new government ministers were appointed, more progressive than their predecessors. New legislation introduced an element of popular election into the appointment of mayors, and certain narrowly defined forms of strike action were legalized. While some of the regime's supporters claimed that these steps indicated a weakening of the government's resolve, many Spaniards considered them not radical enough. It was also suggested that they were window dressing, in preparation for pressing the case for Spain's admission to NATO during U.S. Pres. Gerald Ford's visit at the end of May.

Prince Juan Carlos (right) and Generalissimo Francisco Franco in one of the latter's last public appearances in Madrid. Following Franco's death in November, Juan Carlos acceded to the throne, becoming king of Spain.

UPI COMPIX

During the summer the government was challenged by a widening range of political groups. Several prominent politicians, including former ministers Manuel Fraga Iribarne and Pío Cabanillas, founded Fedisa, which, though nominally a limited company set up to conduct research, clearly had a political objective. The Military Democratic Union was formed by a few junior officers, but evidently enjoyed wider tacit support. A growing number of priests came into conflict with the authorities, particularly in the Basque region. The non-Communist left launched the Platform of Democratic Convergence, and in the elections for workers' representatives, organized by the official labour unions, many left-wing candidates, including some members of the illegal workers' commissions, were voted into office.

In the Basque region strike action and disturbances earlier in the year led first to press censorship and then on April 25 to the imposition of a three-month state of emergency in the provinces of Guipúzcoa and Vizcaya. Unrest continued, and there was terrorist activity by Euzkadi ta Azkatasuna (ETA) and other separatist groups, and by a right-wing organization called the Guerrillas of Christ the King, in which some members of the security forces were thought to participate when off duty. On August 22 the Cabinet approved an antiterrorist law applying to the whole of Spain. It provided for terrorists to be summarily tried by a military court, and made the death penalty mandatory for those found guilty of killing members of the security forces. In the following ten days new measures extended and reinforced police powers and imposed further press censorship.

As a result of the antiterrorist law, between August 29 and September 20 three Basques and eight members of a Marxist organization, the Revolutionary Anti-Fascist and Patriotic Front, were sentenced to death for killing policemen in four separate incidents. Despite public demonstrations throughout Europe and elsewhere and appeals for clemency from heads of state, the pope, and international bodies, on September 26 Franco approved 5 of the 11 sentences. The executions took place the next day by firing squad. In response more than a dozen European countries withdrew their ambassadors from Madrid. East Germany broke off diplomatic relations with Spain; Mexico proposed Spain's expulsion from the UN; and the European Economic Community suspended negotiations on a new trade agreement. The outcry subsided when it was announced that no further summary trials would be held in the near future, and by mid-October most of the ambassadors had returned to Madrid. By that time, however, Spain was under pressure from another source. King Hassan of Morocco declared that he would lead a march to El Aaiún, capital of Spanish Sahara, to claim the territory. At the beginning of November, Prince Juan Carlos, who had been appointed acting head of state on October 30 after Franco had become seriously ill, flew to El Aaiún to boost the morale of the forces stationed there. Using the clever stratagem of mining the frontier, the Spanish troops withdrew from the area. The Moroccan marchers ultimately retreated without bloodshed, and an agreement was reached. (*See* MOROCCO.)

After General Franco's death on November 20, the prince was proclaimed King Juan Carlos I. Despite some conciliatory statements, he made no immediate departure from Franco's policies. A limited pardon was granted, but it excluded most political prisoners; one of the few who was released, Marcelino Camacho, a leader of the workers' commissions, was rearrested early in December. It was also announced that Carlos Arias Navarro, who had served under Franco, was to remain as premier. On December 10 Arias made some Cabinet changes.

The pessimism in business circles stemming from political uncertainty accentuated the decline in economic activity. Growth slowed to less than 2% while unemployment rose to an effective level of more than 4%, and the rate of inflation was only slightly lower than the 17% recorded in 1974. The overall performance of the external sector of the economy was poor; despite slower growth of imports and an improvement in tourism over 1974, the balance of payments was expected to show a deficit at least as large as in 1974. Both the public and the private sector had recourse to large-scale foreign borrowing. (JOAN PEARCE)

See also **Dependent States.**

[972.A.5.a]

SPAIN

Education. (1973–74) Primary, pupils 5,774,-929, teachers 196,216; secondary, pupils 1,012,-945, teachers 56,379; vocational, pupils 233,467, teachers 18,072; teacher training, students 44,-560, teachers 2,166; higher (including 27 universities), students 354,940, teaching staff 24,714.

Finance. Monetary unit: peseta, with (Sept. 22, 1975) a free rate of 59.76 pesetas to U.S. $1 (123.80 pesetas = £1 sterling). Gold, SDRs, and convertible currencies: (June 1975) U.S. $6,248,-000,000; (June 1974) U.S. $5,976,000,000. Budget (1974 actual): revenue 588.4 billion pesetas; expenditure 619 billion pesetas. Gross national product: (1973) 3,543,000,000,000 pesetas; (1972) 2,992,000,000,000 pesetas. Money supply: (March 1975) 1,465,000,000,000 pesetas; (March 1974) 1,303,000,000,000 pesetas. Cost of living (1970 = 100): (May 1975) 174; (May 1974) 149.

Foreign Trade. (1974) Imports 885.8 billion pesetas; exports 408.8 billion pesetas. Import sources: EEC 36% (West Germany 11%, France 8%, Italy 5%, U.K. 5%); U.S. 15%; Saudi Arabia 12%. Export destinations: EEC 47% (France 12%, West Germany 11%, U.K. 9%, Italy 5%, The Netherlands 5%); U.S. 11%. Main exports: food 17%; machinery 12%; chemicals 8%; petroleum products 7%; ships and boats 6%; footwear 5%; motor vehicles 5%. Tourism: visitors (1972) 32,506,600; receipts (1973) U.S. $3,225,000,000.

Transport and Communications. Roads (1973) 142,136 km. (including 807 km. expressways). Motor vehicles in use (1973): passenger 3,803,700; commercial 887,980. Railways: (1973) 15,975 km. (including 4,119 km. electrified); traffic (1974) 16,080,000,000 passenger-km., freight 12,669,000,000 net ton-km. Air traffic (1974): 10,105,000,000 passenger-km.; freight 222,140,000 net ton-km. Shipping (1974): merchant vessels 100 gross tons and over 2,520; gross tonnage 4,949,146. Telephones (Dec. 1973) 6,331,000. Radio receivers (Dec. 1971) 7,174,-000. Television receivers (Dec. 1973) 5,719,000.

Agriculture. Production (in 000; metric tons; 1974; 1973 in parentheses): wheat 4,443 (3,-966); barley 5,404 (4,402); oats 559 (425); rye 254 (252); corn 1,961 (2,037); rice 384 (386); sorghum 148 (164); potatoes 5,504 (5,-579); dry broad beans (1973) 104, (1972) 117; other dry beans 113 (123); chick-peas 80 (88); tomatoes 2,383 (1,933); onions 917 (944); cabbages (1973) *c.* 630, (1972) 666; melons (1973) 769, (1972) 754; apples 992 (1,015); pears (1973) 452, (1972) 471; peaches (1973) 328, (1972) 331; oranges 1,830 (2,061); tangerines and mandarin oranges 579 (598); lemons (1973) 221, (1972) 197; sugar, raw value *c.* 546 (816); sunflower seed 316 (294); bananas 380 (452); olives 1,650 (2,257); olive oil 350 (481); wine (1973) 3,994, (1972) 2,656; tobacco 22 (25); cotton, lint *c.* 65 (46); milk 5,134 (4,940); eggs 453 (420); meat (1973) 1,493, (1972) 1,274; fish catch (1973) 1,570, (1972) 1,617. Livestock (in 000; 1973–74): cattle *c.* 4,450; pigs 8,750; sheep 16,306; goats 2,403; horses 266; mules 377; asses 310; chickens (1972–73) *c.* 50,903.

Industry. Index of industrial production (1970 = 100): (1974) 153; (1973) 140. Fuel and power (in 000; metric tons; 1974): coal 10,241; lignite 2,920; crude oil 1,676; manufactured gas (cu.m.) 2,445,000; electricity (kw-hr.) 80,998,-000. Production (in 000; metric tons; 1974): cement 23,660; iron ore (50% metal content) 8,583; pig iron 7,154; crude steel 11,258; aluminum 189; copper 146; lead 79; zinc 129; petroleum products (1973) 41,500; sulfuric acid 2,-506; fertilizers (nutrient content; 1973) nitrogenous 753, phosphate 683, potash 490; cotton yarn 83; cotton fabrics 78; wool yarn 36; rayon, etc., yarn and fibres 63; nylon, etc., yarn and fibres 127; passenger cars (units) 714; commercial vehicles (units) 132. Merchant vessels launched (100 gross tons and over; 1974) 1,426,-000 gross tons.

Speleology

The two longest caves in the world were extended still farther by new discoveries. The Mammoth Cave-Flint Ridge system in Kentucky became 166 mi. long, and the Hölloch cave in Switzerland reached a length of $76\frac{1}{2}$ mi. with a total vertical extent of 2,887 ft. An international group broke the world depth record by descending to 4,363 ft. in a cave near Pau in the French Pyrenees.

Also in the Pyrenees, the Gouffre André-Touya was explored to a depth of 3,064 ft. late in 1974, and the nearby Gouffre Krakoukass was found to end in a sump at 2,073 ft. Explorers from Lyons, France, also reached a depth of 3,064 ft. in the Gouffre Jean Bernard on Jan. 1, 1975. Late in 1974 the Monte Cucco Cave became the deepest known in Italy, at 3,025 ft., when a passage was found leading to a new high-level entrance. The Gouffre Cappa, close to the French border of Italy, ended in a sump 2,234 ft. down, and the nearby Gouffre des Perdus was blocked similarly at 1,772 ft.

More deep caves were descended in Mexico, including the Sotano del Buque (1,647 ft.), Sotano Itamo (1,470 ft.), and Sotano de Otates (800 ft.). The Sotano de Sendero (732 ft.) had a vertical entrance shaft of 712 ft., while that of the Sotano de Socavon (656 ft.) was 590 ft. In January the Alberta Speleological Society of Canada explored the 689-ft.-deep cave of Sumidero Yochip in Mexico.

A French expedition in Guatemala finished exploring the Río Candelaria Cave and mapped a total passage length of $15\frac{1}{2}$ mi. there. In Brazil the Ouro Grosso River Cave was linked with a pothole above it and thus became the deepest in Brazil at 623 ft. The longest cave there was that of São Mateus (8 mi.).

A 24-man British expedition spent six months studying the karst regions of New Guinea and was reported to have found many large new caves there. In Jamaica another British expedition carried out water-tracing tests and also made first descents of four shafts. One of these, Morgan's Pond Hole, was established as the deepest cave in Jamaica, at 610 ft.

The polypropylene rope broke when David Huxtable, in December 1974, attempted to descend the 340-ft. main shaft of Gaping Ghyll (Yorkshire), and he fell some 300 ft. to his death. In May 1975, T. G. Yeadon passed the 2,600-ft.-long terminal sump in Boreham Cave (Yorkshire) and found approximately 500 ft. of open passage beyond, ending in a 20-ft. pitch that he did not descend. To reach this point involved a total underwater journey, in and out, of more than $1\frac{1}{4}$ mi. In September two French potholers, trapped by rising waters after exceptional rains, died in the Gouffre Berger, southeastern France, and four British explorers were rescued after six days at a depth of 1,600 ft. An international conference on cave diving took place in Barcelona, Spain, in September. Besides the formal proceedings, dives were arranged to explore caves and freshwater karst springs beneath the Mediterranean.

Dating of stalactites and similar formations was carried out by R. S. Harmon and others in several North American caves, using the thorium-230/uranium-234 disequilibrium method. The ages obtained, which ranged from 8,000 to 204,000 years, were mostly beyond the reliable capability of the better-known carbon-14 method. Thus they extended previous knowledge of the absolute dates of various Pleistocene phenomena such as river canyons and terraces, low sea levels, and glacial deposits, as well as rates of erosion and sedimentation and also the growth rates of the speleothems (cave deposits) themselves. Pierre Strinati carried out extensive biological collecting in the caves of West Malaysia and also in little-known caves in Thailand and the Philippines.

(T. R. SHAW)

[232.C.10.c]

WIDE WORLD

A member of a Chinese research team explores an ice cave of Mt. Everest on the China-Nepal border.

Sporting Record

In former years, SPORTING RECORD supplied readers with performance tables on a wide variety of sports that were not covered by text articles. Beginning with this issue, however, such sports as rodeo, handball, karate, table tennis, and gymnastics will receive more extensive treatment in the form of annual text articles.

These reports will follow the usual *Book of the Year* format in focusing on principal athletic competitions and on all major developments within each sport.

Another departure from the past is the grouping of certain related sports under a single heading. The new article entitled AERIAL SPORTS, for example, will have separate sections on *Gliding, Parachuting,* and *Ballooning*. COMBAT SPORTS will absorb the formerly independent entry on *Boxing* and be amplified to include *Wrestling, Judo and Karate, Sumo, Fencing,* and *Kendo*. Another new category, called TARGET SPORTS, will review *Archery, Shooting* of various types, and *Darts*.

To locate articles on specific sports, the simplest approach is through the Index at the back of the book. There are, however, numerous marginal references that serve much the same purpose. Thus readers who might turn to the middle of the book expecting to find *Motorboating* under MOTOR SPORTS, will quickly discover a boldface reference in the margin indicating that *Motorboating* is now relocated under WATER SPORTS along with *Canoeing, Surfing, Scuba and Skin Diving, Water Skiing,* and *Water Polo*.

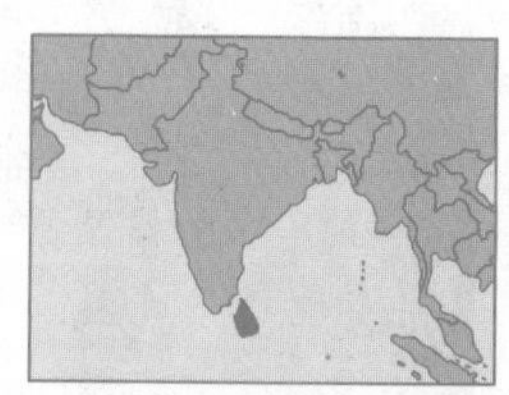

Sri Lanka

An Asian republic and member of the Commonwealth of Nations, Sri Lanka (Ceylon) occupies an island off the southeast coast of peninsular India. Area: 25,332 sq.mi. (65,610 sq.km.). Pop. (1974 est.): 13,393,000, including Sinhalese about 72%; Tamil 21%; Moors 7%. Cap. and largest city: Colombo (pop., 1972 est., 607,000). Language: Sinhalese (official), Tamil, English. Religion (1971): Buddhist 67%; Hindu 18%; Christian 7%; Muslim 7%. President in 1975, William Gopallawa; prime minister, Mrs. Sirimavo Bandaranaike.

A political crisis in July 1975 over the government takeover of three British-owned prime tea estate groups wrecked the five-year-old United Front coalition of the Sri Lanka Freedom Party (SLFP), the Trotskyist Lanka Sama Samaja Party (LSSP), and the pro-Moscow Communists. Angered by the persistent attacks on the government's policies by LSSP leaders, Mrs. Bandaranaike sacked the three LSSP ministers—N. M. Perera (finance), C. de Silva (plantation industry), and Leslie Gunewardene (transport)—in early September and reached a new agreement with the Communists who remained in the Cabinet. The LSSP opposed her decision to entrust the tea estates to the SLFP agriculture minister. The Trotskyists quit the coalition and became the second largest opposition group in the National Assembly, after the United National Party headed by J. R. Jayawardene. Jayawardene and leaders of the Tamil United Front were demanding full regional autonomy for the north and east where they dominated.

The economy worsened during the year, but the government rejected a proposal by the International Monetary Fund (IMF) in June to do away with the free rice ration or make another indirect devaluation of the rupee as a precondition for further standby credit facilities. The IMF agreed to provide a "soft loan" of over $50 million in June to meet the country's oil bill. (GOVINDAN UNNY)

[976.A.4]

One of the many British-owned tea plantations in Sri Lanka which were nationalized during the year.

THE NEW YORK TIMES

SRI LANKA

Education. (1973) Primary and secondary, pupils 2,597,970, teachers 98,925; vocational, pupils 3,648, teachers 302; teacher training, students 9,288, teachers 593; higher, students 12,074, teaching staff 1,329.

Finance. Monetary unit: Sri Lanka rupee, with (Sept. 22, 1975) a free rate of SLRs. 7.53 to U.S. $1 (official rate of SLRs. 15.60 = £1 sterling) and an effective tourist rate of SLRs. 12.41 to U.S. $1 (SLRs. 25.70 = £1 sterling). Gold, SDRs, and foreign exchange: (June 1975) U.S. $67 million; (June 1974) U.S. $76 million. Budget (1974 actual): revenue SLRs. 4,679,000,000; expenditure SLRs. 5,830,000,000. Gross domestic product: (1973) SLRs. 17,128,000,000; (1972) SLRs. 14,375,000,000. Money supply: (March 1975) SLRs. 3,019,000,000; (March 1974) SLRs. 3,009,000,000. Cost of living (Colombo; 1970 = 100): (May 1975) 143; (May 1974) 132.

Foreign Trade. (1974) Imports SLRs. 4,570,000,000; exports SLRs. 3,456,000,000. Import sources (1973): U.S. 9%; Japan 9%; France 8%; China 8%; U.K. 7%. Export destinations (1973): U.K. 11%; China 9%; Pakistan 8%; U.S. 7%; Japan 5%. Main exports: tea 39%; rubber 21%; coconut products 11%.

Transport and Communications. Roads (1973) 22,339 km. Motor vehicles in use (1973): passenger 89,900; commercial 34,400. Railways: (1973) 1,536 km.; traffic (1972–73) 3,220,000,000 passenger-km., freight 325 million net ton-km. Air traffic (1974): 258.6 million passenger-km.; freight 3,020,000 net ton-km. Telephones (Dec. 1973) 68,000. Radio licenses (Dec. 1972) 505,000.

Agriculture. Production (in 000; metric tons; 1974; 1973 in parentheses): rice *c.* 1,640 (1,319); cassava (1973) 332, (1972) 318; sweet potatoes (1973) *c.* 60, (1972) 56; onions (1973) 68, (1972) 62; pineapples (1973) 88, (1972) 45; tea *c.* 201 (211); coffee *c.* 11 (*c.* 11); copra *c.* 150 (*c.* 105); rubber *c.* 145 (155). Livestock (in 000; June 1974): cattle *c.* 1,650; buffalo *c.* 700; sheep *c.* 27; goats *c.* 570; pigs *c.* 112; chickens (1973) *c.* 10,500.

Industry. Production (in 000; metric tons; 1972): salt 156; cement (1974) 474; graphite (1971) 7.6; petroleum products (1973) 1,620; cotton yarn 4.9; electricity (kw-hr.) 995,000.

Stock Exchanges

Major world stock and commodity price indexes followed divergent patterns in 1975. Reflecting expectations of economic recovery from the worst business recession since the 1930s, 14 of 16 major stock market indexes in Europe, Asia, and Africa were higher at the end of 1975 than at the end of 1974. Stock markets in the United States registered their best gains in more than two decades. In contrast, commodity prices, as measured by selected indicators in London and Tokyo, fell from the end of 1974 to the end of 1975. The year-long commodity price weakness, particularly in industrial materials, could be traced to liquidation of excessive inventories and reduced demand in consuming industries.

The 1975 rise in stock prices was well above average in the U.S., Great Britain, Hong Kong, Singapore, Australia, West Germany, and Switzerland. Significant advances were recorded in France, Denmark, and Sweden, while moderate gains were recorded in Canada, Belgium, Japan, and South Africa. Also on the plus side, but with relatively smaller increases, were Spain and Austria. Lower stock market prices prevailed in The Netherlands and Italy (Table I).

During 1975 the industrialized world attempted to recover from the worst economic decline in 40 years. While business recovery was evident in some countries, seemingly structural deterioration existed in others. In general, real gross national product, industrial production, and the rate of unemployment had not improved as sharply as after previous business downturns. Whipsawed by inflation on one hand and deep recession on the other, business and consumer spending was sluggish and demand uncertain.

Consequently, the rapid rises in equity values in most countries in 1975 were often in the opposite direction from changes in economic conditions in those countries. This is explainable, in part, by the tendency of stock prices to rise during recessions, well before an economic recovery is actually under way. Moreover, at major turning points in business cycles, stock prices tend to be among the leading, rather than lagging, economic indicators. In short, the strength of stock markets throughout the world in 1975 did not match the tempo of business activity. But only the future could tell if the 1975 bull market was actually a prelude to new highs in worldwide economic activity.

(ROBERT H. TRIGG)

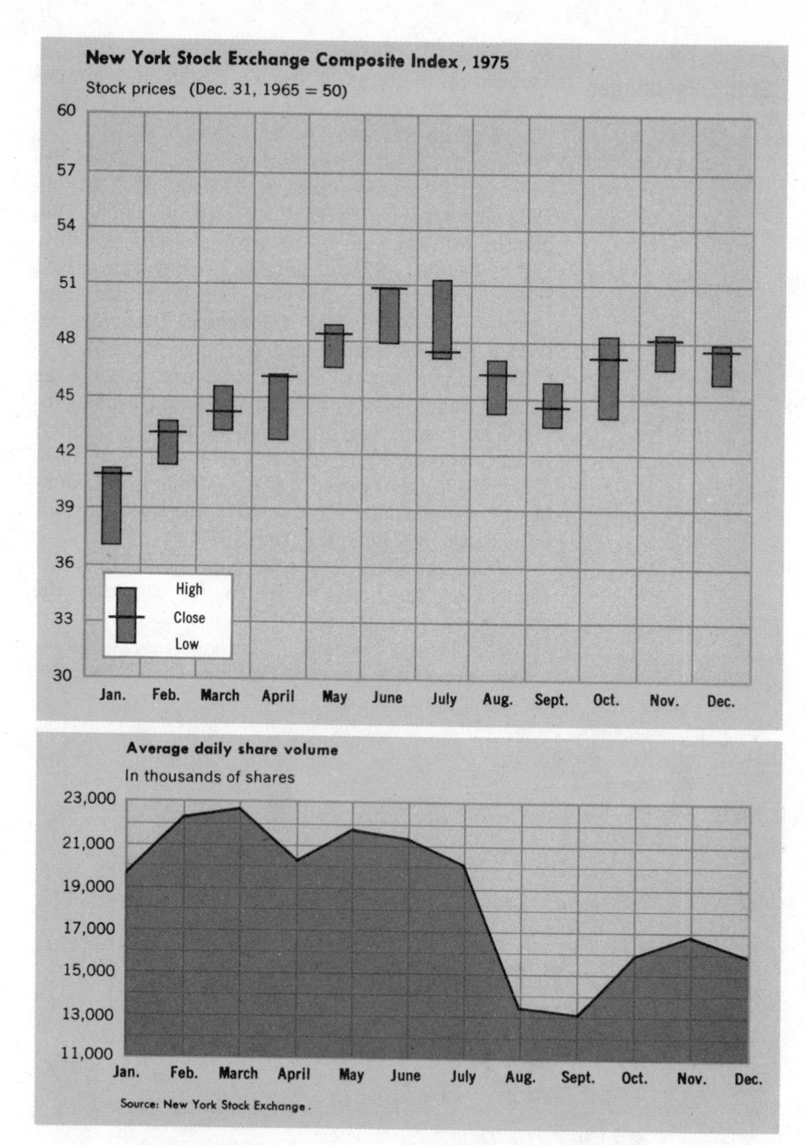

United States. Stock markets in the U.S. enjoyed their best gains in more than 20 years as the Dow Jones industrial average rose by 38.3% in 1975. This was the best percentage gain since 1954, when it rose 44%, and the third largest advance on record. (In 1933 the average rose 67%.) The major gains occurred during the first half of 1975 when the market's deeply oversold condition of December 1974 gave way to a 53% advance that extended into July. Most analysts regarded the first half of 1975 as the primary phase of a new bull market. Trading volume swelled to record levels on the New York Stock Exchange, a gain of 34.3% over the 1974 levels. In February a one-day trading record was set with turnover of 35,160,000 shares. The price-earnings ratio on the stocks in the Dow Jones industrial average for the 12 months ended Sept. 30, 1975, was 11.4, contrasted with the year-earlier level of 6.4.

Average prices on the New York Stock Exchange rose briskly in the first half of 1975 (Table II). The 500 stocks in Standard and Poor's composite index rose from a December 1974 level of 67.07 to a high of 92.49 in July, a gain of 37.9%. The daily high for the year was 95.61 and the low 70.04. The index closed the year at 90.19. The 425 stocks in the industrial average moved from 74.80 in December 1974 to a high of 103.84 in July 1975, a climb of 38.6%. This average then traced a ragged pattern during the last half of the year.

Public utility stocks staged a recovery from the December 1974 low of 32.85 to a high of 40.37 in February and then to a peak of 43.67 in June and July. Even at the year-end close of 44.45, the utilities were well below the early 1974 price levels, however.

The railroad index reflected a less vigorous recovery, moving within a narrow range throughout the year. The high for the year was 40.18 and the low 34.02. Between December 1974 and June 1975 the rise was only 11.8%.

The yields on common stocks declined to a low of 4.18 in June 1975 after an irregular decline from the 6.31 level achieved in September of the previous year. The so-called reverse spread between stocks and bonds expanded sharply during 1975, with dividend yields on the 30 stocks in the Dow Jones industrial average during November averaging 4.53%, compared with an 8.87% average yield on Barron's best-grade corporate bonds.

Long-term government bond prices continued to drift downward during 1975 despite the substantial strengthening of prices in those with short maturities. From a high of 60.27 in February, the average price dropped slightly to 57.05 in April, rose to 58.33 in June, and then settled back to 55.23 in the fall (Table III). Bond yields, which had been declining since the average of 7.33% in August 1974, fluctuated within a narrow range during most of the year and rose to the 7.29% figure in September and October 1975. A record $29.2 billion of new state and city bonds was sold to the public in 1975, an increase of 28% from the $22.8 billion sold in 1974. It far exceeded the previous record of $24.4 billion set in 1971. This was regarded as particularly significant in the light of the

Squash Rackets: *see* Tennis and Rackets

Stamp Collecting: *see* Philately and Numismatics

Steeplechasing: *see* Equestrian Sports

New York City financial crisis, which aggravated the financial rating status of New York State and resulted in a severe depression in the municipal bond markets. (*See* UNITED STATES: *Special Report.*)

Corporate bond prices during 1975 fluctuated between a very narrow range of 55.6 and 56.7 (Table IV). The spread between the prices for comparable months in 1974 and 1975 narrowed fairly steadily, and by October 1975 the average price had surpassed the level of the previous year. Yields on long-term securities remained high throughout the year, although they were more moderate than in 1974.

The market was an institutional one in 1975, as pension funds, insurance companies, and banks provided an ever larger proportion of trading activity. A stockholder census conducted by the New York Stock Exchange revealed a sharp decline in the number of shareholders. By mid-1975 they totaled 25.2 million, an 18% decrease from 1970.

Volume for the year on the New York Stock Exchange was 4,693,386,258 shares, far exceeding the 3,517,742,638 shares traded in 1974 and well above the previous record of 4,138,188,000 shares posted in 1972. Bond sales rose from the 1974 level of $4,052,123,400 to $5,178,337,500, a gain of 27.5%. On the American Stock Exchange (Amex), the volume of shares traded in 1975 was 541,141,421, a 12.3% increase from the 482,194,424 shares traded in 1974 but still well below the record 1,117,989,153 achieved in 1972. Bond trading on the Amex was up slightly at $259,625,000 in 1975, a 1.1% increase over 1974. The Pacific Stock Exchange recorded a rise in volume of 25.6% in 1975 to 215,509,642 shares.

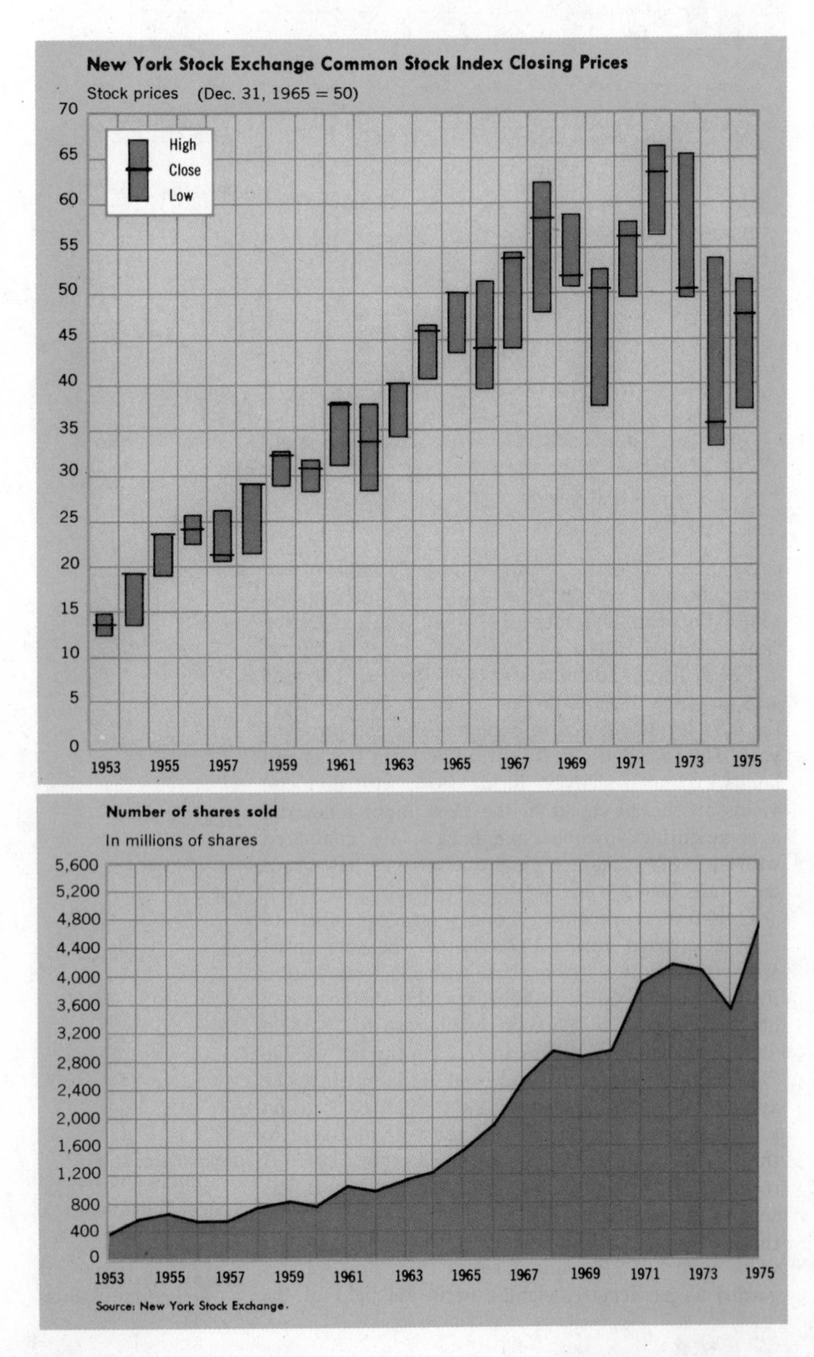

Perhaps the most striking development in the stock markets was the continuing upsurge of trading in options. This activity, which had been strictly over-the-counter until 1973, was launched by the Chicago Board Options Exchange. Its success led to listings of options on the American Stock Exchange, the Philadelphia-Baltimore-Washington Exchange, and Canadian exchanges. While only "calls" were traded in 1975, permitting an investor to buy a stock at a predetermined price at some point in the future, it was anticipated that "puts" (permissions to sell) would be traded in 1976. The turnover in options was estimated at nearly one billion in 1975.

The Securities and Exchange Commission undertook a number of major policy changes, which had a material effect on the securities markets in 1975. Rule 394 of the New York Stock Exchange, which prohibited member brokers from doing business with nonmembers, was sharply liberalized to permit off-board trading; brokerage activities of banks were given recognition; fixed commissions for brokers were abandoned; a Municipal Securities Rulemaking Board was established to draw up rules to regulate banks and investment firms that sell municipal bonds, providing for fuller financial disclosure; a National Market Advisory Board was set up to develop a blueprint for a national stock market; the New York Stock Exchange was required to open its membership to foreign-controlled brokerage firms; and the SEC encouraged establishment of markets in odd lots.

Canada. Canadian stock prices followed the U.S. pattern, rising briskly during the first half of 1975 and settling back during the last six months. The Canadian index of stock prices, which achieved a level of 146 in March 1974, had declined to 93 in December and rose to a peak of 118 in July 1975 before falling back to the 107 range in October and November. Industrials on the Toronto Stock Exchange rose from a level of 150 in January 1975 to a peak of 180 in March, and then drifted to a climax of 195 in July before easing off to close the year at about 170. A similar pattern was observed on the Montreal Stock Exchange. Gold stocks on the Toronto Stock Exchange moved from 340 to 440 by March, but by the end of the year had fallen 45.4% to the 240 level.

Interest rates were high in 1975, and yields rose irregularly throughout the year. Long-term Canada bonds started the year about 7% and ended above 8.5%. The prime rate in December 1975 was $9\frac{3}{4}$%. Canada $5\frac{1}{4}$% bonds due 1990 yielded 9.67%. Long-term corporate bonds, such as the Bell 10% of 1996, yielded 10.72% at the year's end. Ninety-day Treasury bills dropped sharply in the first half to 6.3% but rose to 8.5% by the end of 1975. In October a sharp rise in short-term interest rates, spurred in part by the increase in the bank rate from $8\frac{1}{4}$ to 9%, spilled over to all areas of the bond market, pushing current yields to levels at or near their highs for recent years.

The 1975 trading volume on Canada's three major stock exchanges dropped 19% to 1,090,000,000 shares from 1,350,000,000 in 1974. Dollar volume of transactions fell 12% to $5,780,000,000, from $6,570,000,000 in 1974.

(IRVING PFEFFER)

Western Europe. The largest gain among the major world stock market indexes in 1975 was enjoyed by Great Britain (+134%). The *Financial Times* index of 30 British industrials reached a 20-year low of 146 on January 6, which was 73% below its peak in May 1972. Over the next eight weeks, however, the London Stock Exchange experienced one of the sharpest rallies in its history. The surge in prices from the January 6 low to March 7 added an average of 115% to equity values. This was achieved despite Britain's serious economic problems.

Although stock prices on the average were down for March as a whole; the market resisted efforts at further profit-taking and buyers gained the upper hand. From March 21 to June 6, the average rise in equity values was 32%. This rally was touched off by the U.K. government's expressed intention to bring down interest rates even though inflation was accelerating. As a result, investors continued to switch from short-term, fixed-income securities to common stocks and other similar investments that might act as a hedge against a rapidly depreciating pound.

The summer witnessed a period of profit-taking that cut equity values by an average of 23%. Stock prices jumped sharply in August (+16%), however, and added to those gains in September (+17%) despite new reductions imposed on corporate dividend payments. Equity values rose almost 7% in October.

The continuing upward movement in stock prices received added momentum in early November, when the government promised priority to industrial development over consumption and social objectives. The subsequent rally carried stock prices into new high territory for the year. Occasional profit-taking trimmed some gains, but average prices at the end of 1975 were only fractionally below the peak reached on November 19.

The equity markets in West Germany sustained the impressive momentum evidenced since the fourth quarter of 1974. After reaching its lowest point in October 1974 at 520 and finishing that year up 1%, the index of West German stock prices rose 40% in six months to a peak of 726 in mid-April. Investor optimism was largely based on the hope that the government's December 1974 tax and investment-incentive proposals would stimulate economic growth by increasing domestic demand, thereby offsetting an expected lag in export demand. When it became apparent that this goal would not be achieved by mid-1975 and that the expected business revival would not arrive until sometime in 1976, a mild correction in stock prices ensued. This dropped equity values about 10% in nine weeks.

The rebound in stock prices, from June 13 until August 1, restored all but 1% of the previous correction. Prices drifted lower over the next ten weeks, but beginning in late October embarked on a strong upward move that caused them to surpass the April peak in early November and close the year 38% above the 1974 year-end level.

Beginning with the first trading session of 1975, the stock market in Switzerland entered an upward phase of considerable proportions. From year-end 1974 to year-end 1975, prices on the Zürich Stock Exchange rose 37%. Like other investors the Swiss seemed to ignore the surrounding economic gloom, preferring to concentrate on the economic upturn that was expected to take shape as 1976 progressed.

In France the Paris Bourse staged a vigorous advance in 1975 as the first signs of an improving economic environment began to appear. After falling 33% in 1974, the stock market reversed its bearish trend and rose 33% for 1975 as a whole. Factors contributing to the market's rise were a declining inflation rate, lower interest rates, and government actions designed to stimulate economic growth and combat un-

Table I. Selected Major World Stock Price Indexes*

Country	1975 range High	1975 range Low	Year-end close 1974	Year-end close 1975	Percent change
Australia	443	290	297	443	+ 49%
Austria	2,654	2,532	2,569	2,630†	+ 2
Belgium	112	89	89	105	+ 18
Denmark	101	73	76	100	+ 32
France	73	52	52	69	+ 33
Germany, West	780	574	564	776	+ 38
Hong Kong	353	160	171	350	+105
Italy	109	75	88	83	− 6
Japan	4,565	3,527	3,837	4,359	+ 14
Netherlands, The	108	83	107	97	− 9
Singapore	269	153	151	237	+ 57
South Africa	239	183	189	212	+ 12
Spain	111	92	100	104	+ 4
Sweden	410	311	308	396	+ 29
Switzerland	295	206	206	282	+ 37
United Kingdom	378	146	161	376	+134

*Index numbers are rounded, and limited to countries for which at least 12 months' data were available on a weekly basis.
†As of Dec. 19, 1975.
Sources: *Barron's*, *The Economist*, *Financial Times*, and *The New York Times*.

Table II. U.S. Stock Market Prices and Yields

Month	Railroads (15 stocks) 1975	Railroads (15 stocks) 1974	Industrials (425 stocks) 1975	Industrials (425 stocks) 1974	Public utilities (55 stocks) 1975	Public utilities (55 stocks) 1974	Composite (500 stocks) 1975	Composite (500 stocks) 1974	Yield (200 stocks; %) 1975	Yield (200 stocks; %) 1974
January	37.31	44.37	80.50	107.18	38.19	48.60	72.56	96.11	5.19	3.98
February	37.80	41.85	89.29	104.13	40.37	48.13	80.10	93.45	4.78	3.99
March	38.35	42.80	93.90	108.98	39.55	47.90	83.78	97.44	4.69	4.11
April	38.55	40.26	95.27	103.66	38.19	44.03	84.72	92.46	4.47	4.29
May	38.90	37.04	101.56	101.17	39.69	39.35	90.10	89.67	4.26	4.42
June	38.94	37.31	103.68	101.62	43.67	37.46	92.40	89.79	4.18	4.51
July	38.04	35.63	103.84	93.54	43.67	35.37	92.49	82.82	4.47	4.99
August	35.13	35.06	96.21	85.51	40.61	34.00	85.71	76.03	4.47	5.55
September	34.93	31.55	94.96	76.54	40.53	30.93	84.67	68.12	...	6.31
October	36.92	33.70	99.29	77.57	42.59	33.80	88.57	69.44	...	5.49
November	....	35.95	.....	80.17	....	34.45	....	71.74	...	5.69
December	....	34.81	.....	74.80	....	32.85	....	67.07	...	5.78

Source: U.S. Department of Commerce, *Survey of Current Business*. Prices are Standard and Poor's monthly averages of daily closing prices, with 1941–43=10. Yield figures are Moody's composite index.

Table III. U.S. Government Long-Term Bond Prices and Yields

Average price in dollars per $100 bond

Month	Average 1975	Average 1974	Yield (%) 1975	Yield (%) 1974	Month	Average 1975	Average 1974	Yield (%) 1975	Yield (%) 1974
January	59.70	60.66	6.68	6.56	July	58.09	55.97	6.89	7.18
February	60.27	60.83	6.61	6.54	August	56.84	54.95	7.06	7.33
March	59.33	58.70	6.73	6.81	September	55.23	55.13	7.29	7.30
April	57.05	57.01	7.03	7.04	October	55.23	55.69	7.29	7.22
May	57.40	56.81	6.99	7.07	November	....	57.80	...	6.93
June	58.33	57.11	6.86	7.03	December	....	58.96	...	6.78

Source: U.S. Department of Commerce, *Survey of Current Business*. Average prices are derived from average yields on the basis of an assumed 3% 20-year taxable U.S. Treasury bond. Yields are for U.S. Treasury bonds that are taxable and due or callable in ten years or more.

Table IV. U.S. Corporate Bond Prices and Yields

Average price in dollars per $100 bond

Month	Average 1975	Average 1974	Yield (%) 1975	Yield (%) 1974	Month	Average 1975	Average 1974	Yield (%) 1975	Yield (%) 1974
January	56.4	62.3	8.83	7.83	July	56.6	58.5	8.84	8.72
February	56.6	62.0	8.62	7.85	August	55.6	57.6	8.95	9.00
March	56.2	61.3	8.67	8.01	September	55.8	56.2	8.95	9.24
April	55.8	60.0	8.95	8.25	October	56.0	55.8	8.86	9.27
May	56.6	59.7	8.90	8.37	November	...	56.3	...	8.89
June	56.7	59.5	8.77	8.47	December	...	56.1	...	8.89

Source: U.S. Department of Commerce, *Survey of Current Business*. Average prices are based on Standard and Poor's composite index of A1+ issues. Yields are based on Moody's Aaa domestic corporate bond index.

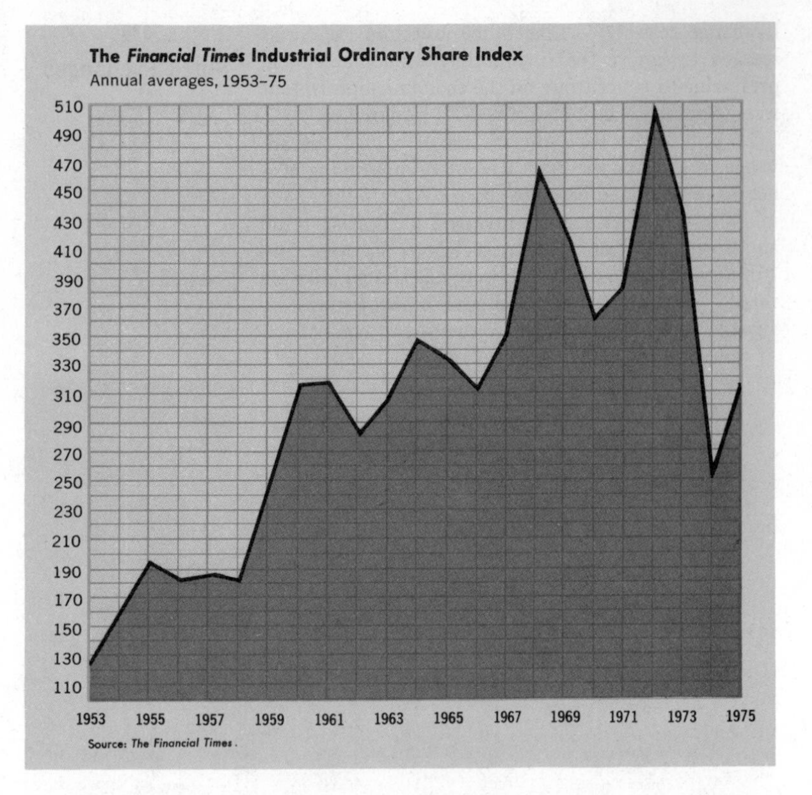

employment. These favourable influences were offset, however, by investor fears that the slow recovery of the economy would cause the government to apply fiscal and monetary stimuli at the wrong time.

Stock markets in Denmark and Sweden followed a similar bullish pattern. The Stockholm Stock Exchange recorded its 1975 low on January 9, while in Denmark the year's low was reached on January 13. Stock prices ended the first half of 1975 with a gain of 23% in Sweden, compared with 17% on the Copenhagen Exchange. Denmark, however, outperformed Sweden during the final six months. After falling 29% in 1974, the stock market in Belgium reversed its bearish trend in 1975. For the year as a whole, the average rise in stock prices was 18%.

The stock market in Spain was plagued by political problems. For 1975 as a whole, equities rose an average of 4%. Prices peaked in April and then steadily moved lower until mid-September. As the year drew to a close, stock prices were rising strongly though they did not exceed the April 22 high.

The Austrian stock market also followed a bullish pattern. For the fourth consecutive year stock prices on the Vienna Stock Exchange ended on the plus side. The stock market price index rose steadily throughout 1975 except for periods of profit-taking in June and September, finishing approximately 2% higher than the year before.

In The Netherlands the price index of shares traded on the Amsterdam Stock Exchange finished 1975 with the largest loss (−9%) among the major world stock price indexes, after losing 16% the year before. Equity prices reached their high on May 6, and then dropped steadily until November before turning upward. In Italy the price index of shares traded on the Milan Stock Exchange fell for the second year in a row. From the end of 1974 to the end of 1975 the average decline in stock prices was 6%.

Strikes:
see Industrial Relations

Sugar:
see Agriculture and Food Supplies

Sulfur:
see Mining and Quarrying

Sumo:
see Combat Sports

Surfing:
see Water Sports

Other Countries. The broad trend of prices in Japan in 1975 was upward (+14%). After a sustained increase from early October 1974, stock prices began rising sharply on January 27 and by mid-May were up nearly 21%. This appeared to coincide with the first signs that the Japanese government's strong measures to suppress aggregate demand and control inflation were beginning to bear fruit. The Japanese inflation rate, as measured by consumer prices, dropped from an annual rate of 25.5% in October 1974 to below 14% in April. Moreover, investors reasoned that the existing large production gaps in the domestic economy would permit a further moderation of inflation and lower interest rates.

The index of 225 issues traded on the Tokyo Stock Exchange drifted lower during the summer months, but the downtrend began to accelerate in September following a series of bankruptcy filings that numbed the investment community. The decline was halted by the expressed intention of the Japanese government to end the recession. It predicted that its massive spending program of more than $5 billion would increase Japan's annual growth rate to 6% by March 31, 1976. The ensuing rally in stock prices was vigorous, with a gain in October of nearly 12%. After a brief pause in November, the uptrend resumed until labour unrest in December halted the rally.

The Australian market in Sydney rose 49%, after declining 32% in 1974. After rising strongly during the first two months of the year, the market withstood mild profit-taking in March and April. Prices rose an average of 6% in May, but the gain was cut by two-thirds over the next three months. The fall of Prime Minister Gough Whitlam's antibusiness government in mid-November created a bullish atmosphere, and on the final trading day of 1975 the index was at its highest level since mid-1974.

After falling more than 60% in 1974, stock prices in Hong Kong experienced a remarkable and almost unbroken rise from January through June (+88%). Equity values fell during July and August, but the Hang Seng index resumed its uptrend in September. During the final four months of 1975, equity values gained an average of 17%. Average share prices in Singapore also experienced a bull market in 1975 (+57%), following a 43% decline in 1974.

In South Africa prices on the Johannesburg Exchange advanced sharply during the first half of 1975, with the industrial average rising more than 168 points (+109%) from its October 1974 low of 154. Following its 1975 high of 239 on July 16, however, the average entered a steep downtrend. Although industrial shares ended the year with a 12% gain, prices were off 11% from the July peak.

Commodity Markets. World commodity markets experienced generally lower prices in 1975. Reuter's United Kingdom commodity index is a geometric average that measures spot or futures quotations in sterling terms for 17 primary commodities weighted by their relative importance in international trade. After reaching an all-time peak on Feb. 26, 1974, this index dropped steadily until late June 1975 before the downside momentum was arrested. That decline, which amounted to 26%, was led by sharply falling base metal prices, particularly copper and lead, and significantly lower quotations for wheat and sugar. The index, however, jumped 13% from June 26 to August 18. Heavy Soviet purchases of U.S. wheat were largely responsible. Nevertheless, when economic recovery failed to take hold in Europe commodity markets weakened. The Reuter's index ended 1975 virtually unchanged from the end of 1974.

The Economist's world commodity price indicator,

which measures spot prices in U.S. dollar terms for 29 price-sensitive commodities traded in Great Britain, is a chain-linked index weighted periodically according to changes in the value of imports into Organization for Economic Cooperation and Development countries. It dropped from 233 at the end of 1974 to 205 near the end of 1975.

In the U.S. the Dow Jones commodity index also registered a decline in 1975, in both the spot and futures markets. On Dec. 31, 1975, the futures index stood at 287.88, compared with 357.27 a year earlier, while the corresponding figures for the spot market were 296.33 and 384.53.

The Nikkei Index of Commodity Prices, covering 17 major commodities traded in Tokyo, fell nearly 5% from the end of 1974 to mid-December 1975. Reflecting the building of commodity inventories in anticipation of a business cycle upturn, the Nikkei commodity index in mid-May was nearly 2% higher than at the end of 1974. When the economic upturn failed to materialize and weakness in demand became evident, commodity prices dropped sharply.

(ROBERT H. TRIGG)

See also Economy, World.
[534.D.2.g.i]

Sudan

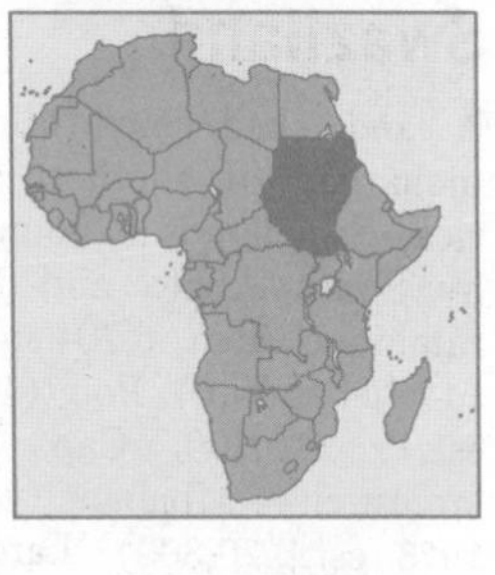

A republic of northeast Africa, the Sudan is bounded by Egypt, the Red Sea, Ethiopia, Kenya, Uganda, Zaire, the Central African Republic, Chad, and Libya. Area: 967,500 sq.mi. (2,505,813 sq.km.). Pop. (1974 est.): 17,324,000, including Arabs in the north and Negroes in the south. Cap. and largest city: Khartoum (pop., 1972 est., 300,000). Language: Arabic; various tribal languages in the south. Religion: Muslim in the north; predominantly animist in the south. President and prime minister in 1975, Maj. Gen. Gaafar Nimeiry.

In January 1975 President Nimeiry dismissed Finance Minister Ibrahim Mansour, who had been under fire over the granting of commercial concessions, and downgraded three other ministers who had been close advisers. In April he warned of plots by the banned Sudan Communist Party (SCP), and in May it was reported that left-wing army officers had planned a coup. On September 5 an attempt by a small group of officers to overthrow the regime was quickly suppressed, with the loss of about ten lives. Subsequently, the constitution was amended to provide the president with additional emergency powers and to extend police powers to arrest and detain.

In the Southern Region there was uncertainty centring on the promised integration of northern and southern military units. After a southern unit at Akobo, in Upper Nile Province, mutinied in March, members of the southern Executive Council with a hard-line attitude toward the north were dismissed.

Loan capital for agricultural development projects flowed from the oil-rich Arab states, in the belief that the Sudan would become a major supplier of foodstuffs in the 1980s. The Kenana project, to produce a million tons of sugar a year using irrigation waters from the White Nile, was finally approved, and agreement was reached with the Arab Fund for Economic and Social Development on an agricultural development plan envisioning expenditure of $5 billion over a ten-year period.

A severe drop in the export value of long-staple cotton and gum arabic necessitated further borrowings from the International Monetary Fund and budget support from friendly Arab states. The acreage under wheat and peanuts was expanded at the expense of cotton, two million bales of which remained unsold. Economic difficulties were aggravated in the summer by floods in the north and east, which rendered 100,000 people homeless and washed out the main railway line to the Red Sea coast.

President Nimeiry visited Saudi Arabia, Iraq, and the Persian Gulf states and received the emir of Kuwait in Khartoum. He used his good offices to overcome strained relations between Libya and Egypt and between Uganda and Britain. Nimeiry was one of the few Arab leaders quickly to endorse Egyptian Pres. Anwar as-Sadat's action in concluding the Sinai agreement with Israel.

(PETER KILNER)

[978.E.5.b]

SUDAN

Education. (1974–75) Primary, pupils 1,257,339, teachers 28,926; secondary, pupils 231,311, teachers 8,651; vocational, pupils 6,397, teachers 445; teacher training, students 5,680, teachers 628; higher, students 22,204, teaching staff 750.

Finance. Monetary unit: Sudanese pound, with (Sept. 22, 1975) an official rate of Sud£0.35 to U.S. $1 (free rate of Sud£0.72 = £1 sterling). Gold, SDRs, and foreign exchange: (June 1975) U.S. $43.3 million; (June 1974) U.S. $48 million. Budget (1974–75 est.): revenue Sud£277 million; expenditure Sud£268 million. Money supply: (June 1975) Sud£230,020,000; (June 1974) Sud£192,860,000. Cost of living (1970 = 100): (June 1975) 212; (June 1974) 172.

Foreign Trade. (1974) Imports Sud£223,580,000; exports Sud£122,010,000. Import sources (1973): U.K. 17%; China 8%; U.S. 7%; India 7%; Brazil 7%; West Germany 6%; U.S.S.R. 5%; Japan 5%. Export destinations (1973): China 14%; Italy 11%; Japan 11%; West Germany 9%; France 6%; India 6%; The Netherlands 5%. Main exports: cotton 35%; peanuts 15%; gum arabic 12%.

Transport and Communications. Roads (1972) *c.* 50,000 km. (mainly tracks, including 335 km. asphalted). Motor vehicles in use (1972): passenger 29,200; commercial (including buses) 21,200. Railways: (1972) 4,756 km.; freight traffic (1971) 2,636,000,000 net ton-km. Air traffic (1973): 168 million passenger-km.; freight 2 million net ton-km. Inland navigable waterways (1972) 4,068 km. Telephones (Jan. 1974) 51,000. Radio receivers (Dec. 1972) 1,310,000. Television receivers (Dec. 1972) 70,000.

Agriculture. Production (in 000; metric tons; 1974; 1973 in parentheses): millet *c.* 300 (268); sorghum *c.* 1,600 (1,498); wheat (1973) 149, (1972) 140; sweet potatoes (1973) *c.* 470, (1972) *c.* 450; sesame *c.* 271 (235); peanuts 991 (543); sugar, raw value *c.* 118 (*c.* 98); watermelons (1973) *c.* 305, (1972) *c.* 295; dates (1973) *c.* 74, (1972) *c.* 72; cotton, lint (1973) 195, (1972) 239; milk (1973) *c.* 1,420, (1972) *c.* 1,400; beef and veal (1973) *c.* 201, (1972) *c.* 194; mutton and goat meat (1973) *c.* 112, (1972) *c.* 108. Livestock (in 000; 1973–74): cattle *c.* 14,000; sheep *c.* 11,900; goats (1972–73) *c.* 10,200; camels (1972–73) *c.* 3,400; asses (1972–73) *c.* 660.

Industry. Production (in 000; metric tons; 1971): salt 55; cement 189; petroleum products (1973) 1,195; electricity (kw-hr.) 259,000.

Surinam

An independent republic (from Nov. 25, 1975) of northern South America, Surinam is bounded by Guyana, Brazil, French Guiana, and the Atlantic Ocean. Area: 70,060 sq.mi. (181,455 sq.km.). Pop. (1975 est.): 350,000, including (1971) Hindustanis 37%, Creoles 30.8%, Indonesians 15.3%, Bush Negroes 10.3%, Amerindians 2.6%. Cap. and largest

MARVINE HOWE—THE NEW YORK TIMES

Henk Arron (centre), new premier of Surinam, visited the interior by motorized canoe to explain independence to the inhabitants.

city: Paramaribo (pop., 1971, 102,300). Language: Dutch. Religion: predominantly Hindu, Christian, and Muslim. Prime minister in 1975, Henk Arron.

On Nov. 25, 1975, Surinam became an independent state, not as the result of armed struggle but at the urging of the Dutch government. Independence had been pursued by the National Party Alliance (NPK), a coalition of Creole parties, headed by Prime Minister Henk Arron. The Progressive Reform Party (PRP), mainly supported by Hindu Indians and led by Jaggernath Lachmon, opposed speedy independence for fear the Creoles, once in power, would oppress them. When the resignation of three National Party members of Parliament jeopardized the pro-independence majority, the PRP tried to prevent formation of a delegation to attend Parliament in The Netherlands to dissolve the statute governing the Netherlands-Surinam relationship. It succeeded only in that a delegation of the National Party alone went to The Hague, though in the end the PRP also sent representatives. On October 24 the 20-year-old statute was dissolved.

Independence coincided with a deterioration in Surinam's economy. More than half the food and almost all industrial products had to be imported, and 90% of exports, mainly alumina, were in the hands of foreign concerns. With an unemployment rate of some 25%, ethnic diversity became a serious threat to peaceful national development. In the spring the Dutch government promised 3.5 billion guilders in aid over 15 years, but the question was whether this would be enough. The government also faced a major exodus to The Netherlands, which had been mounting in recent years; the number of emigrants was estimated at between 130,000 and 140,000 people, most of them skilled Indians.

On December 5 the UN General Assembly admitted Surinam as the 144th member country of the world body. (DICK BOONSTRA)

[974.B.2.e]

SURINAM

Education. (1974–75) Primary, pupils 136,363, teachers 5,271; secondary, pupils 2,158, teachers 327; vocational, pupils 2,522, teachers 148; higher, students 2,138.

Finance. Monetary unit: Surinam guilder or florin, with (Sept. 22, 1975) a free rate of 1.79 Surinam guilder to U.S. $1 (3.71 Surinam guilders = £1 sterling). Budget (1975 est.): revenue 184 million Surinam guilders; expenditure 238 million Surinam guilders.

Foreign Trade. (1973) Imports 281 million Surinam guilders; exports 320 million Surinam guilders. Import sources: U.S. 34%; The Netherlands 24%; Trinidad and Tobago 11%; U.K. 5%. Export destinations: U.S. 35%; West Germany 14%; The Netherlands 12%; Norway and Sweden 10%. Main exports: alumina 45%; bauxite 27%; aluminum 14%.

Transport and Communications. Roads (main; 1973) *c.* 2,000 km. Motor vehicles in use (1973): passenger 21,460; commercial (including buses) 6,500. Railways (1972) 86 km. Shipping traffic (1970): goods loaded *c.* 4.8 million metric tons, unloaded *c.* 1,080,000 metric tons. Telephones (Jan. 1974) 12,430. Radio receivers (Dec. 1973) 108,000. Television receivers (Dec. 1972) 32,000.

Agriculture. Production (in 000; metric tons; 1973; 1972 in parentheses): rice 164 (123); oranges 10 (*c.* 10); eggs (number) 32,600 (42,000); bananas *c.* 42 (44); sugar, raw value 9 (12); milk (litres) 6,570 (7,500). Livestock (in 000; Jan. 1974): cattle *c.* 47; goats *c.* 6; sheep *c.* 3; pigs *c.* 13.

Industry. Production (in 000; metric tons; 1974): aluminum 57; bauxite 6,863; gold (troy oz.; 1972) 0.5; electricity (kw-hr.) 1,492,000 (*c.* 75% hydroelectric).

Swaziland

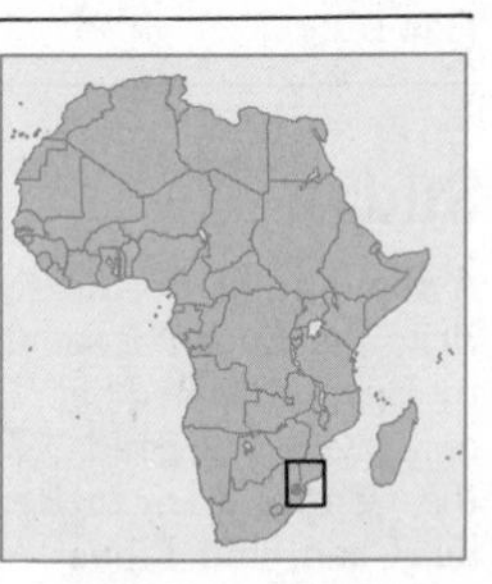

A landlocked constitutional monarchy of southern Africa, Swaziland is bounded by South Africa and Mozambique. Area: 6,704 sq.mi. (17,364 sq.km.). Pop. (1975 est.): 510,200. Cap. and largest city: Mbabane (pop., 1973 est., 20,800). Language: English and siSwati (official). Religion: Christian 60%; animist 40%. King, Sobhuza II; prime minister in 1975, Prince Makhosini Dlamini.

In January 1975 the Royal Commission on Constitutional Affairs proposed a new constitution embodying an independent judiciary, a bicameral House (a lower chamber of 26 elected by secret ballot and an upper chamber of 16, 8 nominated by the Lower House and 8 by the king), and powers of veto left to

SWAZILAND

Education. (1973) Primary, pupils 81,694, teachers 2,112; secondary, pupils 12,459, teachers 550; vocational, pupils 483, teachers (1969) 10; teacher training, students 339, teachers (1969) 31; higher, students 395, teaching staff (1969) 15.

Finance and Trade. Monetary unit: lilangeni (plural emalangeni), at par with the South African rand, with (Sept. 22, 1975) an official rate of 0.87 lilangeni to U.S. $1 (free rate of 1.81 lilangeni = £1 sterling). Budget (1973–74 est.): revenue R 28.1 million; expenditure R 23.9 million. Foreign trade (1973): imports 68.2 million emalangeni; exports 75.4 million emalangeni. Export destinations (1970): U.K. 25%; Japan 24%; South Africa 21%. Main exports: wood pulp 20%; sugar 18%; iron ore 11%; asbestos 9%; timber 8%; citrus fruit 5%; meat and products 5%.

Agriculture. Production (in 000; metric tons; 1973; 1972 in parentheses): corn *c.* 95 (120); rice *c.* 6 (6); sugar, raw value (1974) *c.* 195, (1973) *c.* 173; oranges *c.* 70 (73); pineapples *c.* 13 (13); cotton, lint *c.* 5 (4); beef and veal *c.* 33 (32). Livestock (in 000; 1973–74): cattle *c.* 610; sheep *c.* 40; pigs *c.* 16; goats *c.* 290; asses (1972–73) *c.* 660.

Industry. Production (in 000; metric tons; 1973): coal 140; iron ore (metal content) 1,374; asbestos 37; electricity (kw-hr.) 121,000.

the king, who would provide for a constitutional committee to ratify bills of a constitutional nature and would maintain his traditional *Liqoqo*, or council. Though the king at 76 retained good health, the question of succession was urgent.

Swaziland was affected by the accession to independence of neighbouring Mozambique. Political refugees sought refuge in Swaziland, and there were also economic repercussions, since Lourenço Marques was the lifeline for Swazi exports of iron ore, sugar, timber, citrus fruit, and asbestos. As a safety measure an agreement was reached with South Africa to complete a new railway line to Richard's Bay by 1977. A monetary agreement was negotiated with South Africa and Lesotho, within the rand area. The 1975–76 budget forecast revenue estimated at 57.6 million emalangeni, compared with 40.3 million emalangeni in 1974–75. Over half of total capital expenditure was to be locally financed, with the rest from foreign loans.

(MOLLY MORTIMER)

[978.E.8.b.ii]

Sweden

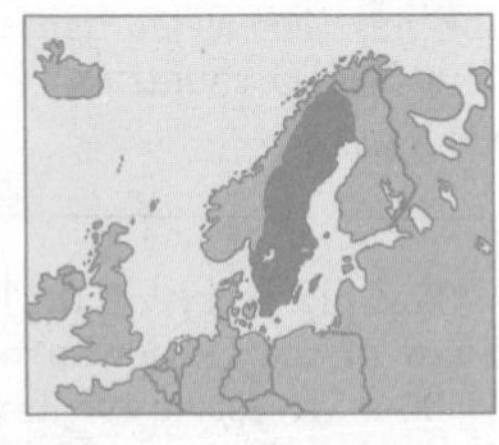

A constitutional monarchy of northern Europe lying on the eastern side of the Scandinavian Peninsula, Sweden has common borders with Finland and Norway. Area: 173,732 sq.mi. (449,964 sq.km.). Pop. (1975 est.): 8,195,900. Cap. and largest city: Stockholm (pop., 1975 est., 681,300). Language: Swedish, with some Finnish and Lapp in the north. Religion: predominantly Lutheran. King, Carl XVI Gustaf; prime minister in 1975, Olof Palme.

A royal Swedish prerogative faded into history with the opening of the Riksdag (Parliament) on Jan. 10, 1975. Carl XVI Gustaf, reduced to a figurehead under a new constitution which came into effect on January 1 and dressed in a civilian suit, was invited by the speaker to declare the session open. In previous years Parliament would have been bidden to assemble at Stockholm Palace for its formal opening amid pomp and pageantry.

Sweden's heavy consumption of imported oil and slackening export orders produced an estimated shortfall of 5 billion kronor in the 1975 budget and required borrowing abroad to compensate for a growing balance of payments deficit. By the year's end Sweden showed no economic growth, and its balance of payments deficit was estimated at nearly 9 billion kronor.

LEIF JANSSON—SVENSKT PRESSFOTO/PHOTO TRENDS

Opening of the Swedish Parliament on January 10 was conducted in accord with new rules. The ceremony began with a concert performance by the Stockholm Philharmonic orchestra.

During the spring, as the export picture darkened, the ruling Social Democrats entered into understandings with opposition parties, the private sector, and the unions. It was decided to ride out the recession by maintaining high employment and by priming industry for an upswing in 1976—also an election year. A midyear budget released about 8 billion kronor to assist industry. In October proposals costing up to 2 billion kronor were introduced, again to assist industrial investment through guarantees for loans and tax relief. The tax measures were criticized as overgenerous by some left-wing critics within the Social Democratic Party and the unions.

The Social Democrats announced plans to send a bill to Parliament putting trade unions on a par with

Swedish Literature: *see* Literature

SWEDEN

Education. (1974–75) Primary, pupils 705,417, teachers 43,096; secondary, pupils 544,411, teachers 58,277; vocational, pupils 7,445; teacher training, students 13,004, teachers 831; higher (including 8 universities), students 106,447, teaching staff (1973–74) 6,000.

Finance. Monetary unit: krona, with (Sept. 22, 1975) a free rate of 4.51 kronor to U.S. $1 (9.35 kronor = £1 sterling). Gold, SDRs, and foreign exchange: (June 1975) U.S. $2,270,000,000; (June 1974) U.S. $1,674,000,000. Budget (1974–75 rev. est.): revenue 71,942,000,000 kronor; expenditure 80,319,000,000 kronor. Gross domestic product: (1974) 247,340,000,000 kronor; (1973) 219,080,000,000 kronor. Money supply: (April 1975) 27.3 billion kronor; (April 1974) 23,010,000,000 kronor. Cost of living (1970 = 100): (June 1975) 146; (June 1974) 132.

Foreign Trade. (1974) Imports 69,993,000,000 kronor; exports 70,390,000,000 kronor. Import sources: West Germany 19%; U.K. 11%; Denmark 7%; Norway 7%; U.S. 7%; Finland 6%; The Netherlands 5%. Export destinations: U.K. 13%; Norway 10%; West Germany 10%; Denmark 8%; Finland 7%; U.S. 5%; France 5%. Main exports: machinery 24%; paper 10%; motor vehicles 9%; iron and steel 8%; wood pulp 8%; timber 6%; chemicals 5%; ships and boats 5%.

Transport and Communications. Roads (1973) 112,925 km. (including 804 km. expressways). Motor vehicles in use (1973): passenger 2,502,900; commercial 144,045. Railways (1973): 12,114 km. (including 7,520 km. electrified); traffic 4,899,000,000 passenger-km., freight 18,260,000,000 net ton-km. Air traffic (including Swedish apportionment of international operations of Scandinavian Airlines System; 1974): 3,479,000,000 passenger-km.; freight 160.3 million net ton-km. Shipping (1974): merchant vessels 100 gross tons and over 785; gross tonnage 6,226,659. Telephones (June 1973) 4,829,000. Radio receivers (Dec. 1973) 3,020,000. Television licenses (Dec. 1973) 2,758,000.

Agriculture. Production (in 000; metric tons; 1974; 1973 in parentheses): wheat 1,443 (1,335); barley 2,040 (1,768); oats 1,446 (1,209); rye 361 (323); potatoes 1,164 (947); sugar, raw value 304 (263); rapeseed 340 (338); apples 135 (132); milk *c.* 2,994 (2,994); butter 45 (44); cheese *c.* 75 (71); beef and veal (1973) *c.* 132, (1972) 131; pork (1973) *c.* 260, (1972) 272; timber (cu.m.; 1973) 57,900, (1972) 55,500; fish catch (1973) 227, (1972) 227. Livestock (in 000; June 1974): cattle 1,841; sheep *c.* 364; pigs *c.* 2,320; horses (1973) *c.* 52; chickens (1973) 13,100.

Industry. Index of industrial production (1970 = 100): (1974) 118; (1973) 111. Production (in 000; metric tons; 1974): cement 3,309; electricity (kw-hr.) 78,080,000 (77% hydroelectric); iron ore (60–65% metal content) 36,956; pig iron 2,965; crude steel 5,969; silver (troy oz.; 1973) 4,690; petroleum products (1972) 11,764; sulfuric acid (1972) 945; rayon, etc., yarn and fibres (1972) 37; wood pulp (1973) mechanical 1,800, chemical 8,003; newsprint 1,210; other paper (1973) 4,128. Merchant vessels launched (100 gross tons and over; 1974) 2,214,000 gross tons. New dwelling units completed (1974) 85,000.

managements in running companies, with the right of access to all information, including company secrets, and full negotiating rights in agreements and related matters as well as matters of production methods.

Sweden's political stability was underlined in May, when the minority Social Democratic government once again averted a potential parliamentary deadlock. Since the 1974 session the Socialist and opposition blocs had each had 175 seats, but for the second successive year Prime Minister Palme weaned the small Liberal Party away from the non-Socialist bloc by agreeing to the maintenance of high domestic consumption. On May 28 Parliament approved the government's controversial energy development program, which would eventually make Swedes the biggest per capita consumers of nuclear power in the world. In 1973 it was expected that 24 reactors might rim Sweden's long coastlines, providing two-thirds of the country's energy needs by 1990. The program was opposed by environmental organizations, a number of scientists, and the Centre Party, which suggested that technical and safety problems remained to be solved.

Sweden continued to adhere to an outspoken foreign policy stance geared toward the less developed world; the foreign aid program amounted to 1% of the nation's gross national product. Throughout the 1970s diplomatic relations between Stockholm and Washington had been strained by outspoken Swedish criticism of U.S. policy in Vietnam. In February the U.S. embassy in Stockholm confirmed reports that Pres. Gerald Ford had declined to meet a top-level Swedish trade delegation scheduled to visit Washington later that month. The presidential rebuff was viewed as a response to a January criticism of the U.S. role in Vietnam by the Swedish foreign minister.

Sweden, a refuge for Chilean exiles, maintained a hostile posture toward the military government in Santiago. In October some 7,000 screaming demonstrators in southern Sweden unsuccessfully tried to distract players at a Davis Cup tennis tournament between Chile and Sweden. In the same month Sweden recalled its ambassador to Madrid for consultations following the execution of five Basques in Spain. Nonetheless, the Palme government reaffirmed its policy of neutrality following the disclosure that the defense minister, in a secret undertaking, had promised that Sweden could guarantee delivery of parts for its Viggen jet fighter, even during wartime, to four NATO countries. (ROGER N. CHOATE)

[972.A.6.b]

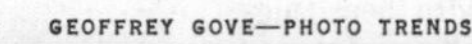
GEOFFREY GOVE—PHOTO TRENDS

Diana Nyad successfully swam 28 miles around Manhattan Island in the record time of 7 hours 57 minutes in October.

Swimming

The World Aquatics Championships, conducted by the Fédération Internationale de Natation Amateur, the governing organization, provided a preview of what would almost certainly be exciting competition in the 1976 Olympic Games. Swimmers from 39 nations competing at Cali, Colombia, July 19–27, saw little to raise their hopes that the United States male swimmers and the East German girls would not dominate the Montreal Olympics.

The exciting ten-day world tournament, the second in swimming history, was viewed by approximately 130,000 spectators, something of a record in itself. The U.S. swimmers won 11 gold, 11 silver, and 9 bronze medals for a total of 31, to lead all countries. Eight of the 11 gold medals were won by the men's team. East Germany, the runner-up with 11 gold, 7 silver, and 5 bronze for a total of 23 medals, was led by its young teenage girls, who won 10 of their country's 11 gold medals. East Germany's Roland Matthes won the 100-m. backstroke but suffered his first defeat in international games competition since 1967 when he lost the 200-m. backstroke to Hungary's Zoltan Verraszto. The tournament produced a total of five world records.

The big story of the tournament concerned Tim Shaw of the U.S., who won the 200-m., 400-m., and 1,500-m. freestyle events and also swam on the 800-m. freestyle relay team that erased the world mark. His team was disqualified, however, because one of its members had prematurely entered the water on his relay leg.

A month later, the 17-year-old Shaw, a 6-ft., 175-lb., Long Beach, Calif., high-school graduate, lowered his own world record in the 400-m. freestyle at the Amateur Athletic Union (AAU) championships in Kansas City, Kan., from 3 min. 53.95 sec., set in June at the U.S. World Championships team trials, to 3 min. 53.31 sec. At the team trials, in Long Beach, Calif., Shaw also lowered the 1,500-m. freestyle world standard of 15 min. 27.79 sec. set by Australia's 17-year-old Steve Holland in January to a sensational 15 min. 20.91 sec., almost 11 sec. faster than the 1973 World Championship time for the event.

East Germany's Kornelia Ender, who turned 16 in October, was the outstanding woman swimmer at the World Championships. Despite a poor start in the 100-m. freestyle, she won the event in 56.50 sec. after setting the first of her two world records at the tournament by clocking 56.22 on her freestyle leadoff of the East German 400-m. freestyle relay team that raced on to lower the world mark from 3 min. 51.99

Greg Jagenburg, winner of the men's 100-m. butterfly at Cali, Colombia, in July.

TONY DUFFY

sec., held by the U.S., to 3 min. 49.37 sec. Miss Ender lowered her world mark for the 100-m. butterfly to 1 min. 1.24 sec. Leading for 190 m., Miss Ender lost to Shirley Babashoff of the U.S. in the 200-m. freestyle but retained her world record in that event of 2 min. 2.27 sec., set at the East German Championships in June. Because of her two world records, Miss Ender was named outstanding athlete of the World Championships. Birgit Treiber, 15, emerged as a bright new face for East Germany, setting a world mark in the 200-m. backstroke of 2 min. 15.46 sec.

Four weeks after the World Championships at Cali, the AAU Championships at Kansas City saw the U.S. men continue where they left off. Five world and 11 U.S. marks were set in the four-day meet, August 20–23.

At the VII Pan American Games held in Mexico City in October, the U.S. men won 14 of 15 swimming events, losing only the 200-m. freestyle to Ecuador's Jorge Delgado. This feat was duplicated by the U.S. girls as they accounted for 13 gold medals out of 14 races, losing only the 100-m. backstroke to Canada's Lyne Chenard. Pan American records were set in all but three events.

Diving. After the World Championships at Cali, it became clear that the Soviet Union loomed as the greatest threat to the U.S. in diving in the forthcoming Olympic Games. Irina Kalinina, only 5 ft. 2 in., surprised the Americans as she and her teammate Tatiana Volynkina placed first and second in the women's 3-m. springboard diving. Christine Loock, of the U.S., was third. In the 10-m. platform, Janet Ely of the U.S. finished first. Miss Kalinina came in second after trailing midway through the competition, and Ulrike Knape of Sweden was third.

Phil Boggs, a U.S. Air Force lieutenant, successfully defended his 3-m. springboard crown. Klaus Dibiasi of Italy placed second, and Viatcheslav Strakhov of the Soviet Union was third. In the 10-m. platform, Dibiasi joined Boggs as a repeat winner from the 1973 World Championships. The U.S. failed to win a medal in this event, as Nikolay Mikhailin of the Soviet Union finished second and Mexico's Carlos Giron was third.

(ALBERT SCHOENFIELD)

[452.B.4.a.i]

World Records Set in 1975

Event	Name	Country	Time
MEN			
100-m. freestyle	Jim Montgomery	U.S.	51.12 sec.
100-m. freestyle	Andy Coan	U.S.	51.11 sec.
100-m. freestyle	Jim Montgomery	U.S.	50.59 sec.
200-m. freestyle	Bruce Furniss	U.S.	1 min. 51.41 sec.
200-m. freestyle	Bruce Furniss	U.S.	1 min. 50.89 sec.
200-m. freestyle	Bruce Furniss	U.S.	1 min. 50.32 sec.
400-m. freestyle	Tim Shaw	U.S.	3 min. 53.95 sec.
400-m. freestyle	Tim Shaw	U.S.	3 min. 53.31 sec.
800-m. freestyle	Steve Holland	Australia	8 min. 15.20 sec.
800-m. freestyle	Steve Holland	Australia	8 min. 15.02 sec.
800-m. freestyle	Tim Shaw	U.S.	8 min. 13.68 sec.
800-m. freestyle	Mike Bruner	U.S.	8 min. 10.20 sec.
800-m. freestyle	Tim Shaw	U.S.	8 min. 09.60 sec.
1,500-m. freestyle	Steve Holland	Australia	15 min. 27.79 sec.
1,500-m. freestyle	Tim Shaw	U.S.	15 min. 20.91 sec.
200-m. individual medley	Bruce Furniss	U.S.	2 min. 06.08 sec.
400-m. freestyle relay	U.S. national team (Bruce Furniss, Jim Montgomery, Andy Coan, John Murphy)	U.S.	3 min. 24.85 sec.
800-m. freestyle relay	Long Beach Swim Club (Rex Favero, Tim Shaw, Steve Furniss, Bruce Furniss)	U.S.	7 min. 30.54 sec.
WOMEN			
100-m. freestyle	Kornelia Ender	E.Ger.	56.38 sec.
100-m. freestyle	Kornelia Ender	E.Ger.	56.22 sec.
200-m. freestyle	Kornelia Ender	E.Ger.	2 min. 02.27 sec.
400-m. freestyle	Shirley Babashoff	U.S.	4 min. 14.76 sec.
800-m. freestyle	Jenny Turrall	Australia	8 min. 43.48 sec.
200-m. backstroke	Nancy Garapick	Canada	2 min. 16.33 sec.
200-m. backstroke	Birgit Treiber	E.Ger.	2 min. 16.10 sec.
200-m. backstroke	Birgit Treiber	E.Ger.	2 min. 15.46 sec.
100-m. butterfly	Kornelia Ender	E.Ger.	1 min. 01.33 sec.
100-m. butterfly	Kornelia Ender	E.Ger.	1 min. 01.24 sec.
200-m. individual medley	Ulrike Tauber	E.Ger.	2 min. 18.83 sec.
400-m. individual medley	Ulrike Tauber	E.Ger.	4 min. 52.20 sec.
400-m. freestyle relay	East German national team (Kornelia Ender, Barbara Krause, Claudia Hempel, Ute Bruckner)	E.Ger.	3 min. 49.37 sec.

Switzerland

A federal republic in west central Europe consisting of a confederation of 25 cantons, Switzerland is bounded by West Germany, Austria, Liechtenstein, Italy, and France. Area: 15,943 sq.mi. (41,293 sq.km.). Pop. (1974 est.): 6,481,000. Cap.: Bern (pop., 1974 est., 157,700). Largest city: Zürich (pop., 1974 est., 410,100). Language (1970): German 65%; French 18%; Italian 12%; Romansh 1%. Religion (1970): Roman

SWITZERLAND

Education. (1971–72) Primary, pupils 516,311, teachers (excluding craft teachers; 1961–62) 23,761; secondary, pupils 321,385, teachers (full-time; 1961–62) 6,583; vocational, pupils 157,444; teacher training, students 12,820; higher (including 10 universities), students 44,624, teaching staff 4,318.

Finance. Monetary unit: Swiss franc, with (Sept. 22, 1975) a free rate of SFr. 2.73 to U.S. $1 (SFr. 5.66 = £1 sterling). Gold and foreign exchange; (June 1975) U.S. $8,712,000,000; (June 1974) U.S. $8,413,000,000. Budget (1975 est.): revenue SFr. 14,133,000,000; expenditure SFr. 14,727,000,000. Gross national product: (1974) SFr. 139.5 billion; (1973) SFr. 129.4 billion. Money supply: (May 1975) SFr. 54,930,000,000; (May 1974) SFr. 53,540,000,000. Cost of living (1970 = 100): (June 1975) 145; (June 1974) 134.

Foreign Trade. (1974) Imports SFr. 42,890,000,000; exports SFr. 35,163,000,000. Import sources: EEC 67% (West Germany 29%, France 14%, Italy 9%, U.K. 6%); U.S. 7%; Austria 5%. Export destinations: EEC 44% (West Germany 14%, France 9%, Italy 8%, U.K. 7%); U.S. 7%; Austria 7%. Main exports: machinery 29%; chemicals 23%; watches and clocks 10%; textile yarns and fabrics 5%; precious metals 5%; instruments 5%. Tourism: visitors (1973) 6,818,000; gross receipts U.S. $1,389,000,000.

Transport and Communications. Roads (1973) 61,212 km. (including 555 km. expressways). Motor vehicles in use (1973): passenger 1,656,400; commercial 159,700. Railways: (1972) 4,984 km. (including 4,956 km. electrified); traffic (1974) 8,300,000,000 passenger-km., freight 6,985,000,000 net ton-km. Air traffic (1974): 7,091,000,000 passenger-km.; freight 295,020,000 net ton-km. Shipping (1974): merchant vessels 100 gross tons and over 28; gross tonnage 199,732. Telephones (Dec. 1973) 3,604,000. Radio licenses (Dec. 1973) 2,003,000. Television licenses (Dec. 1973) 1,627,000.

Agriculture. Production (in 000; metric tons; 1974; 1973 in parentheses): wheat 355 (355); barley 198 (174); oats 42 (*c.* 40); rye 40 (44); corn (1973) 130, (1972) 100; potatoes 1,085 (910); rapeseed *c.* 22 (20); apples *c.* 320 (380); pears *c.* 120 (167); sugar, raw value (1973) *c.* 78, (1972) 67; wine (1973) 107, (1972) 93; milk *c.* 3,380 (3,335); butter *c.* 33 (31); cheese *c.* 99 (96); beef and veal (1973) *c.* 126, (1972) 124; pork (1973) *c.* 238, (1972) 224. Livestock (in 000; April 1974): cattle 1,972; sheep *c.* 334; pigs *c.* 2,209; chickens (1973) *c.* 6,610.

Industry. Index of industrial production (1970 = 100): (1974) 111; (1973) 110. Production (in 000; metric tons; 1974): cement 5,250; aluminum 88; petroleum products (1973) 5,989; rayon, etc., yarn and fibre (1973) 6.5; nylon, etc., yarn and fibre (1973) 74; cigarettes (units; 1973) 31,076,000; watches (units; 1973) 59,674; manufactured gas (gasworks only; cu.m.; 1973) 421,000; electricity (kw-hr.; 1973) 36,538,000.

KEYSTONE

The Geneva grenadiers commemorated the 175th anniversary of Napoleon's passage of the Alps to Marengo, Italy, in 1800.

Catholic 49.4%; Protestant 47.7%. President in 1975, Pierre Graber.

At national parliamentary elections, held on Oct. 26, 1975, for the two chambers of the Federal Assembly—the popularly elected National Council and the canton-elected Council of States—the Social Democrats with a total of 55 seats (46 previously) emerged as the strongest party in the lower house; the Christian Democrats obtained 46 (44 previously) and the Radical Democrats 47 (49). The Social Democrats also won a seat in the traditionally conservative Council of States, bringing their share to 5 (out of a total of 44 seats), a figure wholly out of proportion to their actual strength in the country, due to institutional and political reasons. The high percentage of abstention (only 52.4% voted) was a matter of concern to many observers.

In the process of settling the Jura region dispute (involving creation of a new, 23rd canton), the three southern districts decided in a plebiscite in March to remain with the "old" canton of Bern; the allegiance of a number of border communes was decided by two additional plebiscites in September. A project undertaken by the Federal Council in 1975 indicated that the excessive number of initiatives and referendums submitted to the Swiss people was the reason for the high percentage of abstention in popular plebiscites; accordingly, the number of signatures required to make initiative and referendum proposals was to be doubled (to 100,000 and 60,000, respectively).

The construction of nuclear power plants was opposed by large sections of the public. The Kaiseraugst project, in the canton of Aargau, was delayed as a result of large-scale demonstrations and occupation of the site by thousands of opponents demanding reconsideration of the project.

The lower house of the Federal Assembly passed a measure legalizing abortion under certain circumscribed socio-medical conditions, and the upper house gave its approval at its December session.

In October the index of consumer prices stood at 163.9, compared with 153.6 a year earlier. Industrial output was 17% below that of 1974. The rate of unemployment reached 0.3% of the gainfully employed population, and about 100,000 foreign workers left the country. Exports declined to SFr. 2,167,900,000 in August 1975, as compared with SFr. 2,423,000,000 in 1974, and imports fell to SFr. 2,310,900,000 from SFr. 3,178,400,000; the largest percentage of trade was with the EEC. Thus Switzerland did not escape the recession affecting other industrialized countries. A proposed constitutional amendment that would have authorized the federal government to conceive and execute a comprehensive economic policy was defeated in the plebiscite of March 3, and the authorities were obliged to adapt existing emergency powers to the new situation. They accordingly proposed (and Parliament approved) the investment of about SFr. 1.1 billion in building roads, an increase of the export risk guarantee, and a rapid improvement of the rudimentary unemployment insurance.

The strength of the Swiss franc with its negative effects on the export and tourist industries became a matter of considerable concern. According to a study published in September, the rise of the Swiss franc exchange rate, inflationary components taken into account, amounted to about 37%. The deficit of the national budget for 1974 was announced as a record SFr. 1,040,000,000 and it was expected to exceed the SFr. 1 billion mark again in 1975, despite various measures adopted to increase some (indirect) taxes and drastic economies that were effected in the federal administration.

Early in the year the Federal Assembly approved Swiss membership in the International Energy Agency as a realistic step that would not compromise the country's traditional neutrality. According to the chief of staff of the Swiss armed forces, international relations had not improved sufficiently to justify any relaxation of defense efforts. Early in the year the federal government submitted an arms program and budget calling for the expenditure of SFr. 508 million.

(MELANIE STAERK)

[972.A.8]

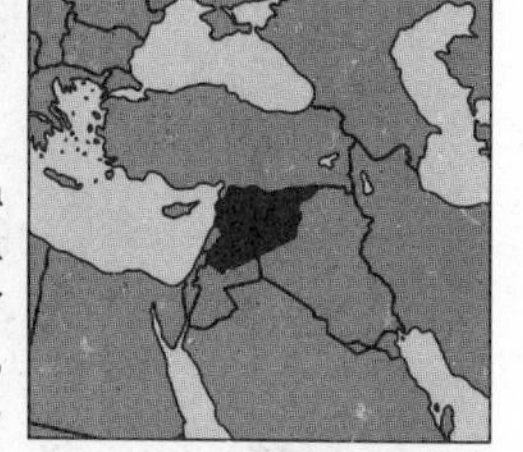

Syria

A republic in southwestern Asia on the Mediterranean Sea, Syria is bordered by Turkey, Iraq, Jordan, Israel, and Lebanon. Area: 71,498 sq.mi. (185,180 sq.km.). Pop. (1975 est.): 7,346,100. Cap. and largest city: Damascus (pop., 1975 est., 974,900). Language: Arabic (official); also Kurdish, Armenian, Turkish, and Circassian. Religion: predominantly Muslim. President in 1975, Gen. Hafez al-Assad; premier, Mahmoud Ayoubi.

For Syria, the key event in 1975 was the conclusion on September 1 of a bilateral interim settlement between Egypt and Israel. Feeling isolated in its confrontation with Israel, Syria moved closer to Jordan. Throughout the year Syria was also closely concerned with the civil-war situation developing in Lebanon.

Syrian diplomacy remained fairly flexible despite the strains it was undergoing. Syria maintained good relations with Saudi Arabia and the Persian Gulf states and avoided a complete break with Egypt, despite its differences with Cairo. The foreign minister participated with Egypt in the talks between Jordan and the Palestine Liberation Organization (PLO) in Cairo, January 3–4, and continued to work for a Jordanian-PLO reconciliation. On January 7 President Assad became the first Syrian president to visit Lebanon in 25 years, and later in the year the foreign minister repeatedly tried to mediate between the warring factions in Lebanon. In January King Faisal of Saudi Arabia visited Damascus, and it was announced that Saudi Arabia was providing Syria with $350 million in aid for development and military needs. The Soviet foreign minister, Andrey A. Gromyko, visited Damascus on February 1–3 and Syrian-Soviet relations remained close. In June new Soviet arms supplies were reported. U.S. Secretary of State Henry Kissinger also visited Damascus in February and again in March, but President Assad was reportedly cool toward U.S. diplomatic initiatives and was quoted as saying that if there were an Egyptian-Israeli agreement Syria would not attend a Geneva Middle East peace conference.

In March Syria declared its readiness to form joint political and military committees with the PLO. This was approved by the PLO joint command, but there was some delay in establishing the committees. The Jordanian prime minister visited Damascus in March and agreed to economic cooperation and the lifting of trade restrictions. In April, and again in August, King Hussein of Jordan visited Damascus, and in June President Assad visited Amman, where on June 12 the formation of a Syrian-Jordanian joint high commission was announced. The commission was empowered to coordinate the two countries' foreign policies and armed forces, but it did not extend to joint military command.

Despite Syria's disappointment with the lack of any moves toward a further Israeli withdrawal from Syrian territory, it agreed to a six-month extension of the mandate of the UN Emergency Force on the Golan Heights after May 30. In April President Assad went to Riyadh for a Saudi-sponsored meeting with Pres. Anwar as-Sadat of Egypt, and it was announced that a Syrian-Egyptian permanent coordinating committee would be set up. President Sadat visited Damascus May 17–18, and the Syrian prime minister visited Alexandria on June 21 for a meeting of the coordinating committee. But as Egypt's determination to conclude a bilateral agreement with Israel became

CAMERA PRESS/PHOTO TRENDS

Syrian troops reoccupy part of the Golan Heights following the Israeli withdrawal negotiated by U.S. Secretary of State Henry Kissinger in 1974.

SYRIA

Education. (1973–74) Primary, pupils 1,133,515, teachers 30,850; secondary, pupils 406,040, teachers 19,127; vocational, pupils 18,533, teachers 11,932; teacher training, students 5,368, teachers 378; higher (including 3 universities), students 1,719, teaching staff 371.

Finance. Monetary unit: Syrian pound, with (Sept. 22, 1975) an official exchange rate of S£3.675 to U.S. $1 (free rate of S£7.60 = £1 sterling). Gold, SDRs, and foreign exchange: (May 1975) U.S. $1,147,000,000; (May 1974) U.S. $739 million. Budget (1975 est.) balanced at S£4,500 million. Gross domestic product: (1973) S£9,404 million; (1972) S£8,891 million. Money supply: (Dec. 1974) S£5,514 million; (Dec. 1973) S£3,797 million. Cost of living: (Damascus; 1970 = 100): (May 1975) 172; (May 1974) 139.

Foreign Trade. (1974) Imports S£4,571 million; exports S£2,914 million. Import sources: West Germany 12%; Italy 9%; France 9%; Lebanon 8%. Export destinations: Greece 18%; West Germany 15%; U.S.S.R. 14%; U.K. 10%; Lebanon 7%; China 5%. Main exports: crude oil 55%; cotton 26%.

Transport and Communications. Roads (1971) 16,710 km. (including 63 km. expressways). Motor vehicles in use (1973): passenger 34,700; commercial (including buses) 23,100. Railways (1973): 902 km.; traffic 69 million passenger-km., freight 132 million net ton-km. Air traffic (1973): 305 million passenger-km.; freight 2.5 million net ton-km. Ships entered (1973): vessels totaling 17,430,000 net registered tons; goods loaded (1973) 34,751,000 metric tons, unloaded 2,211,000 metric tons. Telephones (Dec. 1973) 143,000. Radio receivers (Dec. 1972) 2.5 million. Television receivers (Dec. 1973) 179,000.

Agriculture. Production (in 000; metric tons; 1974; 1973 in parentheses): wheat 1,381 (593); barley 714 (102); lentils (1973) 101, (1972) 96; tomatoes 384 (269); onions 102 (99); watermelons (1973) *c.* 350, (1972) 460; melons (1973) *c.* 100, (1972) 130; grapes 215 (147); olives 194 (73); cotton, lint *c.* 141 (*c.* 154). Livestock (in 000; 1973–74): cattle *c.* 510; sheep 5,738; goats (1972–73) 997; horses (1972–73) *c.* 60; asses (1972–73) *c.* 240; chickens (1972–73) *c.* 4,000.

Industry. Production (in 000; metric tons; 1974): crude oil 6,535; petroleum products (1973) 1,842; cement 946; cotton yarn (1973) 29; electricity (kw-hr.; 1973) 1,154,000.

clear, Syria was increasingly critical of Egypt. On October 6 President Assad openly attacked the September 1 agreement as breaking Arab solidarity and said that Syria would only negotiate a further Israeli withdrawal in Golan if similar talks were held between Israel and the PLO for a withdrawal from the West Bank (of the Jordan River). In November Syria agreed to an extension of the mandate of the UN peacekeeping force in Golan, but only after obtaining agreement that the PLO could participate in Middle East talks at the UN in January 1976.

Relations with the rival Baathist regime in Iraq were strained throughout the year. In April several members of an alleged pro-Iraqi faction were arrested in Damascus, and in July the Iraqi military attaché was expelled. The dispute over sharing of the Euphrates River waters flared up and was not resolved. Economic development was pursued intensively, and despite a fall in cotton output in 1974 both exports and imports were double the 1973 levels. State socialist policies were maintained in general, but one striking departure was the granting by the government of an offshore oil exploration concession to the U.S. firm Tripco Petroleum—the first to a foreign company in 20 years. (PETER MANSFIELD)

[978.B.3.b]

Table Tennis

The 33rd biennial world table tennis championships were played during February 1975 in Calcutta, India, at the newly constructed 12,500-seat Netaji Stadium. Weeks before the teams were due to arrive, an uproar was created when the Indian government refused to grant visas to athletes from Israel and South Africa. Because such discrimination directly contravened the code of the International Table Tennis Federation, various groups made vigorous protestations, but to no avail. There were also attempts to withdraw recognition from the Table Tennis Federation of India for condoning a violation of its charter. Finally, however, the matches got under way, with 64 national groups participating. When the action was over, new champions were crowned in every category.

In the men's singles, which featured two European finalists for the first time since 1953, Istvan Jonyer of Hungary defeated Anton Stipancic of Yugoslavia 3–1. In the women's singles Pak Yung Sun, making her first appearance in international competition, upset the Chinese veteran Chang Li 3–1. The men's doubles was won by the Hungarian team of Istvan Jonyer and Gabor Gergely and the women's doubles by Maria Alexandru of Romania and Shoko Takahashi of Japan. The mixed doubles title was captured by the Soviet team of Stanislav Gomozkov and Tatjana Ferdman. In team competition, China's men players repossessed the Swaythling Cup, which they had lost to Sweden in 1973, by defeating Yugoslavia 3–1. China's women athletes duplicated the victory with a 3–2 win over their South Korean counterparts, thereby regaining the Corbillon Cup for the first time since 1965.

China's Hsi En-ting (right) practices with his partner prior to the international competition in Calcutta.

LONDON DAILY EXPRESS/PICTORIAL PARADE

CENTRAL PRESS/PICTORIAL PARADE

Hu Yu-lan of China defended her 1974 women's title in the 33rd world table tennis championship in Calcutta.

During the Calcutta tournament, the congress of the International Table Tennis Federation gave formal recognition to the Asian Table Tennis Union, making that group, with its 30 affiliated associations, the largest one-sport organization in Asia. Standards were also established to qualify umpires for international competitions, and action was taken to ensure that tables and nets would consistently meet specified norms. During the year the federation admitted 17 new members, bringing the total to 121.

The second Asian, African, Latin-American International Tournament was held in Lagos, Nigeria, dur-

1975 World Table Tennis Championships

MEN'S SINGLES	WOMEN'S SINGLES
1. Istvan Jonyer (Hung.)	1. Pak Yung Sun (North Korea)
2. Anton Stipancic (Yugos.)	2. Chang Li (China)
3. Dragutin Surbec (Yugos.)	3. Ke Hsin-ai (China)
4. Mitsuru Kohno (Japan)	4. Chung Hyan Sook (South Korea)
5. {Kjell Johansson (Sweden)	5. Tatjana Ferdman (U.S.S.R.)
5. {Norio Takashima (Japan)	6. Maria Alexandru (Rom.)
7. Hsü Shao-fa (China)	7. Chu Hsiang-yün (China)
8. Liang Ko-liang (China)	8. Yukie Ohzeki (Japan)

MEN'S DOUBLES: Istvan Jonyer and Gabor Gergely (Hung.)
WOMEN'S DOUBLES: Maria Alexandru (Rom.) and Shoko Takahashi (Japan)
MIXED DOUBLES: Stanislav Gomozkov and Tatjana Ferdman (U.S.S.R.)

WORLD TEAM STANDINGS

Men		Women	
1. China	6. Japan	1. China	6. U.S.S.R.
2. Yugoslavia	7. U.S.S.R.	2. South Korea	7. Yugoslavia
3. Sweden	8. West Germany	3. Japan	8. Czechoslovakia
4. Czechoslovakia	9. France	4. Hungary	9. Romania
5. Hungary	10. South Korea	5. England	10. West Germany

ing July. The Chinese men and women not only repeated their victories at Calcutta by winning both team titles, but captured both singles titles as well when Liang Ko-liang took the men's finals and Chang Li the women's. Mitsuru Kohno joined with Katsuyaki Abe to win the men's doubles title, then paired with Yukie Ohzeki in the mixed doubles to give both titles to Japan. Pak Yong Ok and Cha Kyung Mi of North Korea won the women's doubles championship.

Great Britain continued to dominate the Commonwealth championships by sweeping all team and individual titles during a late January tournament held in Melbourne, Australia. In the European League, Sweden captured the 1974–75 Premier Division title and Poland the Second Division championship. The 42 member countries in the African Federation were reorganized into seven zones to facilitate competition and diminish the need for extensive travel.

(ARTHUR KINGSLEY VINT)

[425.B.4.h.xxvi]

Taiwan

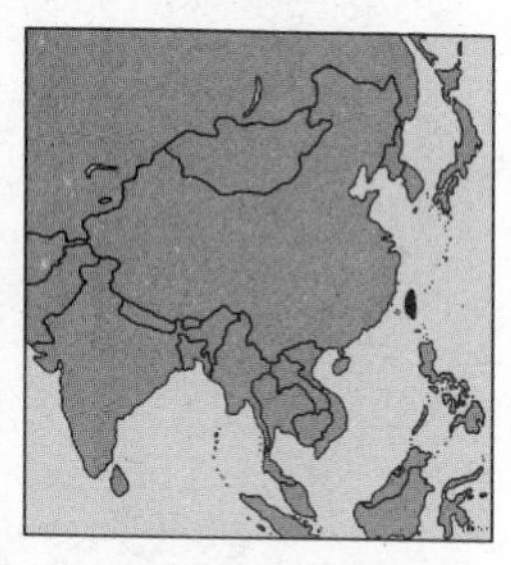

Taiwan, which consists of the islands of Formosa and Quemoy and other surrounding islands, is the seat of the Republic of China (Nationalist China). It is situated north of the Philippines, southwest of Japan, and east of Hong Kong. The island of Formosa has an area of 13,815 sq.mi.; including its 77 outlying islands (14 in the Taiwan group and 63 in the Pescadores group), the area of Taiwan totals 13,893 sq.mi. (35,981 sq.km.). Pop. (1975 est.): 16,049,100. Cap. and largest city: Taipei (pop., 1975 est., 2,022,500). Presidents in 1975, Chiang Kai-shek and, from April 5, Yen Chia-kan; president of the Executive Yuan (premier), Chiang Ching-kuo.

On April 5, 1975, Chiang Kai-shek, the last of the "Big Four" Allied leaders of World War II, died of a heart attack in the middle of his fifth six-year term as the first president of the Republic of China under the 1947 constitution (*see* OBITUARIES). Chiang's death created neither a problem of succession nor a change in policy. On April 6 Vice-Pres. Yen Chia-kan was sworn in as president. However, the real power continued to be held by Premier Chiang Ching-kuo, who had been the effective head of the administration since 1972; on April 28 the Central Committee of the ruling Kuomintang unanimously elected him to succeed his father as chairman of the party.

At a simple Chinese and Christian memorial service on April 16, U.S. Vice-Pres. Nelson A. Rockefeller, envoys from other countries that continued to recognize the Republic of China, and a multitude of Chinese paid their last respects to Chiang. In his memory the Nationalist government passed a commutation act giving freedom to some 8,000 convicts in Taiwan.

Strong economic growth in Taiwan continued; for the first half of 1975 the gross national product totaled U.S. $6,882,000,000 and per capita income was $694. Externally, however, the Nationalist claim to be the legitimate government of all China could no longer be sustained. Over 100 countries now recognized the People's Republic of China. The Chinese Nationalist diplomats were withdrawn from Saigon and Phnom Penh following the Communist victories in Cambodia and South Vietnam, and the Philippines and Thailand recognized the Peking regime as the sole legal government of China on June 9 and July 1, respectively. Because of Taipei's long-standing and close economic, commercial, and cultural ties with Manila and Bangkok, it was mutually agreed that "nongovernment relations" for the promotion of trade and cultural exchange would remain intact. Nevertheless, this reduced the number of countries officially recognizing Nationalist China to only 25.

The U.S. was the only major power that continued to maintain a fully staffed, functioning embassy in Taipei and continued to deal with the governments in Taipei and Peking as competent authorities over the territory each controlled. Following the U.S. withdrawal from Indochina, U.S. military personnel in Taiwan were reduced to a minimum. On May 6 Pres. Gerald Ford said it was his aim to "reaffirm our commitments to Taiwan." In April the U.S. State Department canceled a visit by a Peking performing arts troupe because its program included a song entitled "We Shall Certainly Liberate Taiwan."

During the year, trade missions visited several European and Asian countries that no longer maintained diplomatic relations with Nationalist China and the Nationalist government decided to establish trade offices in Latin America, Europe, the Middle East, and Africa. New air service agreements with Saudi Arabia and Jordan, new trade pacts with South Africa and

TAIWAN

Education. (1974–75) Primary, pupils 2,406,531, teachers 62,109; secondary, pupils 1,176,280, teachers 47,552; vocational, pupils 255,965, teachers 9,201; teacher training, students 1,510, teachers (1969–70) 14; higher (including 11 universities), students 276,059, teaching staff 13,309.

Finance. Monetary unit: new Taiwan dollar, with (Sept. 22, 1975) a par value of NT$38 to U.S. $1 (free rate of NT$78.72 = £1 sterling). Gold and foreign exchange: (June 1975) U.S. $1,161,000,000; (June 1974) U.S. $1,080,000,000. Budget (1973–74 est.): revenue NT$86,021,000,000; expenditure NT$76,257,000,000. Gross national product: (1974) NT$536,610,000,000; (1973) NT$388,580,000,000. Money supply: (May 1975) NT$92,830,000,000; (May 1974) NT$74,889,000,000. Cost of living (1970 = 100): (2nd quarter 1975) 176; (2nd quarter 1974) 167.

Foreign Trade. (1974) Imports NT$265,340,000,000; exports NT$209,720,000,000. Import sources: Japan 32%; U.S. 24%; West Germany 7%; Kuwait 6%; Saudi Arabia 5%. Export destinations: U.S. 37%; Japan 15%; Hong Kong 6%; West Germany 6%. Main exports: electrical machinery and equipment 17%; clothing 16%; textile yarns and fabrics 11%; sugar 6%; wood manufactures 5%; fruit and vegetables 5%; footwear 5%.

Transport and Communications. Roads (1973) 16,400 km. Motor vehicles in use (1974): passenger 95,113; commercial (including buses) 78,518. Railways: (1972) 4,400 km.; traffic (1973) 8,020,000,000 passenger-km., freight 2,960,000,000 net ton-km. Air traffic (1970): 954 million passenger-km.; freight 25,175,000 net ton-km. Shipping (1974): merchant vessels 100 gross tons and over 407; gross tonnage 1,416,833. Telephones (Sept. 1974) 570,000. Radio licenses (Sept. 1974) 1,480,000. Television licenses (Sept. 1974) 910,000.

Agriculture. Production (in 000; metric tons; 1973; 1972 in parentheses): rice 2,255 (2,440); sweet potatoes 3,204 (2,928); corn 84 (70); cassava 328 (325); peanuts 98 (94); sugar, raw value *c.* 900 (*c.* 850); citrus fruit 332 (291); bananas 422 (366); pineapples 328 (334); tea 29 (26); pork 523 (428). Livestock (in 000; Dec. 1973): cattle 234; pigs 3,638; goats 181; chickens (1970) 14,269.

Industry. Production (in 000; metric tons; 1973): coal 3,327; crude oil 150; natural gas (cu.m.) 1,454,000; electricity (kw-hr.) 19,805,000; cement 6,096; crude steel (ingots only) 507; salt 381; sulfuric acid 609; petroleum products *c.* 7,000; cotton yarn 96; man-made fibres 131; paper 465.

Paraguay, and economic cooperation agreements with Swaziland and Costa Rica were concluded.

In 1974 Taipei had terminated the lucrative air services of Japan Air Lines and China Air Lines between Tokyo and Taipei after the then Japanese foreign minister, Masayoshi Ohiro, declared that his country did not recognize China Air Lines' flag insignia as the flag of a nation. Following Foreign Minister Kiichi Miyazawa's statement to the Diet on July 1 that the flag of the Republic of China is a national flag, the East Asia Relations Association of Taiwan and the Exchange Association of Japan (in reality consulates of the respective nations) signed a new agreement that provided for resumption of air services between the two countries in late summer.

(HUNG-TI CHU)

See also China.
[975.A.6]

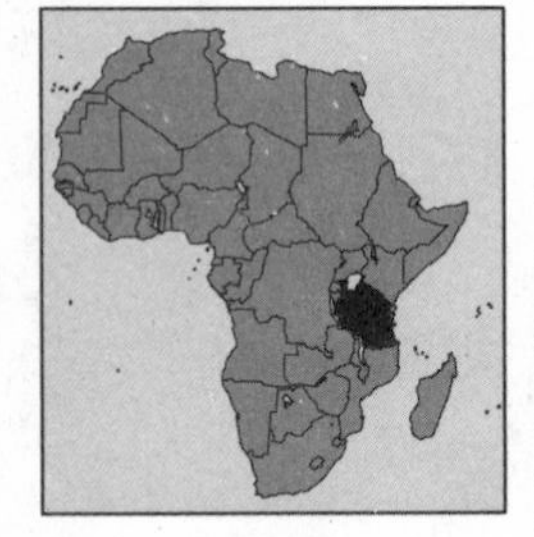

Tanzania

This republic, an East African member of the Commonwealth of Nations, consists of two parts: Tanganyika, on the Indian Ocean, bordered by Kenya, Uganda, Rwanda, Burundi, Zaire, Zambia, Malawi, and Mozambique; and Zanzibar, just off the coast, including Zanzibar Island, Pemba Island, and small islets. Total area of the united republic: 364,943 sq.mi. (945,198 sq.km.). Total pop. (1974 est.): 14,763,000, including (1966 est.) 98.9% Africans and 0.7% Indo-Pakistani. Cap. and largest city: Dar es Salaam (pop., 1972 est., 396,700) in Tanganyika. Language: English and Swahili. Religion (1967): traditional beliefs 34.6%; Christian 30.6%; Muslim 30.5%. President in 1975, Julius Nyerere.

The prolonged drought in 1974 and the need to import vital foodstuffs deflated Tanzania's foreign exchange reserves, while the rural upheaval caused by the move to would-be self-reliant *ujamaa* (community) villages—intended to be complete by 1976—continued to affect production in 1975. In June, however, it was learned that Tanzania would receive a grant of £10 million from Britain for development projects and an additional £2.5 million to buy British goods.

At a meeting of the Organization of African Unity (OAU) in Dar es Salaam in April, President Nyerere urged support for the liberation of southern Africa and, with Presidents Kenneth Kaunda of Zambia and Sir Seretse Khama of Botswana, advised the members of the African National Council in their attempts to negotiate a settlement of the Rhodesian constitutional question. Tense relations with Uganda were further strained when Tanzania criticized the OAU for planning to hold its summit meeting in Kampala in July in view of the murders and massacres said to have been perpetrated by the Uganda government. The summit meeting took place, but Nyerere, along with Kaunda and Seretse Khama, boycotted it.

In May some 40 armed men abducted four students, including three Americans, from a zoological research camp on the shore of Lake Tanganyika but later released them on payment of a ransom to the "People's Revolutionary Party of Zaire."

(KENNETH INGHAM)

[978.E.6.b.iii]

TANZANIA

Education. (1971) Primary, pupils 922,083, teachers 20,168; secondary and vocational, pupils 43,352, teachers 2,199; teacher training, students 4,218, teachers 327; higher, students 2,220, teaching staff 308.

Finance. Monetary unit: Tanzanian shilling, with (Sept. 22, 1975) a par value of TShs. 7.14 to U.S. $1 (free rate of TShs. 14.87 = £1 sterling). Gold, SDRs, and foreign exchange: (June 1975) U.S. $50.5 million; (June 1974) U.S. $73.3 million. Budget (1973–74 actual): revenue TShs. 2,934,000,000; expenditure TShs. 4,103,000,000. Gross national product: (1973) TShs. 12,418,000,000; (1972) TShs. 11,088,000,000. Money supply: (Dec. 1974) TShs. 3,575,000,000; (Dec. 1973) TShs. 2,775,000,000. Cost of living (Dar es Salaam; 1970 = 100): (June 1975) 226; (June 1974) 156.

Foreign Trade. (1974) Imports TShs. 5,791,000,000; exports TShs. 3,001,000,000. Import sources: China 11%; U.K. 10%; Japan 9%; West Germany 8%; Saudi Arabia 7%; Iran 7%; U.S. 7%; Kenya 7%. Export destinations: U.K. 13%; U.S. 7%; Kenya 6%; Hong Kong 6%; India 5%; West Germany 5%; Belgium-Luxembourg 5%. Main exports: cotton 17%; sisal 15%; coffee 13%; petroleum products 10%; cashew nuts 7%; sisal fabrics 5%.

Transport and Communications. Roads (1972) *c.* 17,500 km. Motor vehicles in use (1973): passenger 36,400; commercial (including buses) 39,600. Railways (1973) 2,560 km. (excluding the new 1,860-km. Tanzam railway linking Dar es Salaam with Kapir Mposhi in Zambia; for traffic *see* KENYA). Air traffic (apportionment of traffic of East African Airways Corporation; 1973): 127 million passenger-km.; freight 3.1 million net ton-km. Shipping traffic (mainland only; 1973): goods loaded 971,000 metric tons, unloaded 2,622,000 metric tons. Telephones (Dec. 1973) 51,000. Radio receivers (Dec. 1973) 230,000. Television receivers (Dec. 1969) 4,000.

Agriculture. Production (in 000; metric tons; 1974; 1973 in parentheses): corn *c.* 550 (888); sweet potatoes (1973) *c.* 310, (1972) *c.* 320; millet *c.* 100 (136); sorghum *c.* 130 (146); rice *c.* 130 (314); cassava (1973) *c.* 3,350, (1972) *c.* 3,250; sugar, raw value *c.* 124 (*c.* 115); dry beans *c.* 130 (160); citrus fruit (1973) *c.* 150, (1972) *c.* 150; mangoes (1973) *c.* 150, (1972) *c.* 150; bananas *c.* 720 (*c.* 700); cashew nuts (1973) *c.* 130, (1972) *c.* 130; coffee *c.* 58 (*c.* 58); cotton, lint *c.* 83 (88); sisal (1973) *c.* 155, (1972) 157; timber (cu.m.; 1973) 32,700, (1972) 32,700. Livestock (in 000; 1973–74): cattle *c.* 12,098; sheep *c.* 2,850; pigs *c.* 23; goats (1972–73) *c.* 4,400; asses *c.* 160; chickens (1972–73) *c.* 19,300.

Industry. Production (in 000; metric tons; 1973): cement 314; salt (1972) 44; magnesite *c.* 0.8; diamonds (metric carats) 580; petroleum products 786; electricity (excluding most industrial production; kw-hr.) 512,000.

Barbara Smuts (centre), one of four students kidnapped from Jane Goodall's primate research centre in Tanzania by terrorists, is supported by fellow students following her negotiated release in June.

CAMERA PRESS/PHOTO TRENDS

Target Sports

Archery. The number of nations belonging to the International Archery Federation (FITA) increased during 1975 to 57, a clear indication that interest in archery was growing at a remarkable pace. But even more remarkable were the results of two major tournaments, the first of which was held in June at Interlaken, Switz. During the 28th world archery championships all 12 world records in the double FITA round were broken, six by men and six by women. Then in August, during the 92nd U.S. national championships, nine world records for the single FITA round were also shattered. Beyond question, the bowman of the year was Darrell Pace, a high school student from Cincinnati, Ohio, who personally broke nine world records and led the U.S. men's team to two

Table I. World Archery Champions

Event	Winner	Year	Record	Old record	Maximum possible
	Double FITA Round				
MEN					
FITA	D. Pace (U.S.)	1975	2,548	2,445	2,880
90 m.	D. Pace (U.S.)	1975	569	550	720
70 m.	W. Szymanczyk (Pol.)	1975	626	620	720
50 m.	D. Pace (U.S.)	1975	656	626	720
30 m.	D. Pace (U.S.)	1975	698	675	720
Team	United States	1975	7,444	7,194	8,640
WOMEN					
FITA	Z. Rustamova (U.S.S.R.)	1975	2,465	2,380	2,880
70 m.	Z. Rustamova (U.S.S.R.)	1975	590	574	720
60 m.	Z. Rustamova (U.S.S.R.)	1975	618	610	720
50 m.	L. Myers (U.S.)	1975	608	587	720
30 m.	Z. Rustamova (U.S.S.R.)	1975	661	649	720
Team	U.S.S.R.	1975	7,252	6,907	8,640
	Single FITA Round				
MEN					
FITA	D. Pace (U.S.)	1975	1,316	1,291	1,440
90 m.	D. Pace (U.S.)	1975	309	303	360
70 m.	D. Pace (U.S.)	1975	333	325	360
50 m.	D. Pace (U.S.)	1975	331	328	360
30 m.	D. Pace (U.S.)	1975	354	350	360
Team	United States	1975	3,757	3,643	4,320
WOMEN					
FITA	I. Lorensen (U.S.)	1975	1,256	1,249	1,440
70 m.	L. Myers (U.S.)	1974	310	307	360
60 m.	J. Szoszler-Wilejto (Pol.)	1971	324	324	360
50 m.	L. Sjoholm (Swed.)	1975	319	311	360
30 m.	I. Lorensen (U.S.)	1975	344	342	360
Team	U.S.S.R.	1972	3,670	3,626	4,320
	World Distance Record				
	Bruce Odle (U.S.)	1975	2,767⅓ ft.		

world records. The only other archer to attract considerable attention was Zebiniso Rustamova of the Soviet Union who set four individual world records in the women's division of the double FITA round and helped the Soviet women set a new team record. During the U.S. national flight championship in August, Bruce Odle set a world distance record when he shot an arrow 922 yd. 1 ft. 4 in.

(CLAYTON B. SHENK)

[452.B.4.h.i]

Shooting. Target shooting with firearms, both in tournaments and for purely personal enjoyment, continued to engage a large number of sportsmen during 1975. For the finest marksmen, however, the 1976 Olympics in Montreal provided an added incentive to intensify their training.

Trap and Skeet. Though international trap and skeet competitions have obvious similarities—shot loads are limited to 32 grams, 12-gauge shotguns are generally featured, and 200 targets are released in individual events and 400 (100 × 4) in four-man team events—the differences between trap and skeet are so significant that they constitute two distinct sports.

Table II. World Rifle Records

Event	Individual	Score	Team	Score
WORLD CHAMPIONS				
Free rifle (300 m.)				
3 x 40 shots	G. Anderson (U.S.)	1,157	United States	4,602
40 shots prone	R. Pojer (Czech.)	400	U.S.S.R.	1,583
40 shots standing	L. Wigger (U.S.)	379	United States	1,478
40 shots kneeling	V. Kornev (U.S.S.R.)	392	U.S.S.R.	1,554
Standard rifle				
3 x 20 shots (300 m.)	D. Kimes (U.S.)	575	United States	2,280
	D. Wigger (U.S.)			
3 x 20 shots (50 m.)	J. Writer (U.S.)	579	U.S.S.R.	2,297
Small-bore rifle (50 m.)				
3 x 40 shots	L. Wigger (U.S.)	1,167	United States	4,656
40 shots prone	J. Kurka (Czech.)	400	United States	1,595
	J. Waibel (Austria)			
	W. Parchimovich (U.S.S.R.)			
	J. Writer (U.S.)			
40 shots standing	M. Murdock (U.S.)	385	United States	1,508
40 shots kneeling	B. Klingner (W. Ger.)	396	United States	1,563
60 shots prone	Ho Jun Li (N. Kor.)	599	Romania	2,380
Normal runs	H. Bellingrodt (Col.)	577	U.S.S.R.	1,527
	V. Postoianov (U.S.S.R.)			
Mixed runs	V. Postoianov (U.S.S.R.)	385	U.S.S.R.	1,533
Air rifle (10 m.) 40 shots	O. Vasquez	393	Poland	1,529
WOMEN'S COMPETITION				
Standard rifle (50 m.)				
60 shots prone	E. Rolinska (Pol.)	598	Poland	1,780
	M. Murdock (U.S.)			
3 x 20 shots	A. Pelova (Bulg.)	580	U.S.S.R.	1,717
Air rifle (10 m.) 40 shots	B. Zarina (U.S.S.R.)	391	U.S.S.R.	1,150

The flight angles of the targets in trap are more varied and always directed away from the marksman, who fires from five designated positions well back of the traps. In skeet, the shooter fires from seven equidistant positions along the perimeter of a large semicircle and from an eighth position midway along the diameter; the clay targets, which are released from a high and a low trap located, respectively, at the left and right extremities of the semicircle, are flung across the area of what would be the other half of the circle. The gun butt, moreover, must touch the waistline until each target appears.

During 1975 a four-man U.S. team set a new world record in trap shooting by downing 391 birds during a tournament in Mexico City. The individual record of 199 hits, held jointly by A. Scalzone of Italy (1972) and M. Carrega of France (1974), was neither broken nor equaled. In skeet, H. Rasmussen of Denmark and W. Gawlikowski of Poland both had perfect 200 scores during a competition in Vienna, thereby earning a share of the world title previously held by the three Soviet marksmen E. Petrov (1970), J. Tsuranov (1971), and T. Zhgenti (1973). During the same

Darrell Pace of the U.S. breaks the existing world record by 103 points and simultaneously wins the Archery World Championship at Interlaken, Switzerland.

KEYSTONE

WIDE WORLD

René Arpin of France took first place in the international biathlon contest at Urnerboden, Switzerland.

Vienna tournament the Swedish team established a new world record by shattering 391 of the birds.

In women's competitions, four world records were erased during the year. At Vienna, two team records were established when Soviet women scored 267 hits (100 × 3 shots) in trap shooting and the West German women's team shattered 280 birds on the skeet range. In individual events at Munich, West Germany, S. Nattrass of Canada set a new trap record by hitting 188 of 200 targets and L. Gurwich of the Soviet Union became the new woman skeet champion with a score of 191.

Rifle. Even though many top-rated marksmen participated in international tournaments during 1975, only one world record for big-bore rifles was established in the men's competition. In a standard-rifle event at 50 m. (3 × 20 shots), a Soviet team established a new mark by scoring 2,297 points at Bucharest, Rom. In small-bore competition, a 50-m. record was also established at Bucharest when M. Teca of Romania scored 599 points in the running target event. A second small-bore record fell when Margaret Murdock of the U.S. scored 385 points in Mexico City when she fired 40 shots at 50 m. from a standing position. O. Vasquez of Mexico also entered the record books by amassing 393 points while firing 40 shots with an air rifle at 10 m. The Union Internationale de Tir, which controls all international firearms tournaments, requires that all air rifle precision shooting be confined to slow fire and that .177-cal. guns be used at 10 m. from a standing position. A new world record for women was set during the year by A. Pelova of Bulgaria, who scored 580 points firing 60 shots from a standard rifle at 50 m.

Herschel Anderson of Columbus, Georgia, won the gold medal in the pistol shooting competition in Mexico City, scoring 559 points.

UPI COMPIX

Handguns. Under rules established by the Union Internationale de Tir, all international handgun competitions at 50 m. feature slow-fire (precision) shooting with 5.6-mm. rim-fire cartridges. A 25-m. range is used for rapid-fire events and for competitions in which centre-fire cartridges are used. In U.S. tournaments .22 rim-fire, centre-fire, and .45 cal. are all employed. Each type of handgun is fired in slow fire, timed fire, and rapid fire; the usual distances are 25 and 50 yd. During 1975 Harold Vollman of East Germany tied the world record with 572 points while firing 60 shots from a free pistol at 50 m. Another record was established by a four-man team from Romania which scored 2,380 points in rapid fire at 25 m. (60 × 4). Though no women's record was broken, N. Stoljarova of the Soviet Union equaled her 1974 score of 587 for 60 shots with a small-bore pistol fired at 25 m.

Table III. World Pistol Records

Event	Individual	Score	Team	Score
MEN				
Free pistol				
60 shots (50 m.)	G. Kossych (U.S.S.R.) H. Vollman (E.Ger.)	572	U.S.S.R.	2,244
Rapid-fire pistol				
60 shots (25 m.)	G. Liverzani (Italy)	598	Romania	2,380
Centre-fire pistol				
60 shots (25 m.)	T. D. Smith III (U.S.)	597	United States	2,353
Standard pistol				
60 shots (25 m.)	L. Falta (Czech.)	582	U.S.S.R.	2,303
Air pistol				
40 shots (10 m.)	G. Kossych (U.S.S.R.)	392	U.S.S.R.	1,552
WOMEN				
Small-bore pistol				
Centre-fire				
60 shots (25 m.)	N. Stoljarova (U.S.S.R.)	587	U.S.S.R.	1,752
Air pistol				
40 shots (10 m.)	N. Stoljarova (U.S.S.R.)	387	U.S.S.R.	1,147

Biathlon. A unique and challenging sport, the biathlon has shown a steady growth in popularity as expert cross-country skiers and outstanding marksmen have each tried to master the other's major skill. Two quite distinct talents are needed for the biathlon because participants must not only traverse the snow-covered course in the shortest time possible, but along the way are required to fire five rifle shots at each of four targets from both a standing and prone position. Regulation rifles must have a trigger pull of at least one kilogram and bores may not exceed 8 mm.

In February, at the 18th world biathlon championships in Anterselva, Italy, Aleksandr Elisarov of the Soviet Union won the 10-km. event and a Finnish skiing marksman, Heikki Ikola, captured the 20-km. title. The four-man relay, introduced in recent years, was won by Finland, with the Soviet Union a very close second.

(ROBERT N. SEARS; ASHLEY HALSEY, JR.)

[452.B.4.e]

Darts. Though no estimate is possible of the number of dart players who train systematically and seriously to become genuine experts, untold thousands, especially in Britain and the U.S., play the game for pure enjoyment whenever an opportunity arises. Among those who demonstrated high proficiency in English darts during the year, Conrad Daniels of New Jersey performed with the greatest consistency and skill. He not only won the North American open darts tournament in California and the U.S. championship in New York, but also captured the Champion of Champions competition in London. In American darts, the championship was won for the fifth consecutive time by Edmund Carl Hady of Pennsylvania who in 1969 scored the highest single-game score on record: 62 points with four perfect frames.

(EDMUND CARL HADY)

Television and Radio

Television and radio sets in use throughout the world numbered approximately 1,092,500,000 in 1975. All major nations had some form of radio service, and with the introduction of tests in South Africa early in the year none lacked some form of television service. An estimated 757.5 million radio sets were in use, with 401.6 million, or slightly more than half, in the United States. Approximately 335 million television receivers were in use throughout the world, with 121 million of those in the U.S.

The Soviet Union, with about 45 million, ranked next to the U.S. in the number of TV sets, according to estimates published in the 1975 *Broadcasting Yearbook*. Japan was third with 25 million and the United Kingdom fourth with 20 million. Other *Broadcasting* estimates of television sets included West Germany, 17.4 million; France, 14.3 million; Italy, 11 million; Brazil, 8.8 million; Canada, 8 million; Spain, 6.8 million; Poland, 5.2 million; East Germany, 5 million; and Argentina, Australia, Mexico, and The Netherlands, 4 million each.

Television stations on the air throughout the world numbered about 6,660. They were distributed approximately as follows: 2,200 in the Far East, 2,100 in Western Europe, 1,020 in the U.S., 920 in Eastern Europe, 180 in South America, 104 in Mexico, 96 in Canada, and 40 in Africa. About 14,550 radio stations were in operation, most of them of the amplitude modulation (AM) type but with an increasing number of frequency modulation (FM) stations. The U.S. had 8,214, or 56%, of the world's radio stations; of these, 3,716 were FM.

Organization. Efforts to reach an agreement on the future international distribution of television programs via satellite relays remained deadlocked in the United Nations in 1975. The impasse centred on the question of control of the airwaves when broadcasting from one country directly into home television sets in other countries becomes feasible, probably by 1985. The U.S. held to its position that there should be a free flow of information among countries, while the U.S.S.R. and its supporters held that broadcasters should not be permitted to send programs into any country without the prior consent of that country's government. Nor was there progress in attempts by private broadcasting organizations to agree on voluntary controls. Partial agreement on one such plan foundered when the European Broadcasting Union (EBU) withdrew the endorsement it had given subject to other support that, in the end, did not materialize.

Although they were unable to agree on future broadcasting directly to foreign homes, broadcasters continued to be successful in organizing satellite distribution of current news programs to foreign broadcasters. International broadcasting by satellite had in fact become routine for major news events. An outstanding example in July was the cooperative U.S. and U.S.S.R. Apollo-Soyuz manned space flight. With that venture the Soviet Union made its entry into space flight coverage, sharing its broadcasts of the launching and, ultimately, the recovery of the Soyuz spacecraft with the U.S. and also carrying U.S. coverage of the Apollo launch and recovery and of the historic docking of the two craft. Coverage of the joint mission was transmitted around the world by satellites and landlines. In an international venture of another kind, the government of India in August used a U.S. satellite to transmit health, agricultural, and educational material and news to 2,400 remote villages by television.

The EBU celebrated the 25th anniversary of its founding in February. From an original membership of 25, the union had grown to a worldwide membership of 102 organizations in 72 countries. The anniversary was marked by celebrations at EBU headquarters in Switzerland. Régis de Kalbermatten of Switzerland was elected as secretary-general.

During the year the EBU was involved in long, complex, and, at times, apparently futile negotiations with the Canadian Olympic Games Organizing Committee (COJO) in an attempt to secure at a realistic price the television rights for the 1976 Olympic Games in Montreal. During the EBU general assembly at St. Moritz in June, representatives of the Asian Broadcasting Union (ABU), Asociación Interamericana de Radiodifusión (AIR), Arab States Broadcasting Union (ASBU), Organización de la Televisión Iberoamericana (OTI), and the Union of National Radio and Television Organizations of Africa (URTNA), as well as the EBU and the International Radio and Television Organization (OIRT) expressed their determination not to accede to COJO's financial demands. Canadian rejection of an offer of Can$9.3 million threatened the Olympics with a blackout of television outside North America until the International Olympic Committee protested to the Canadians and made it clear the problem had to be resolved in favour of the broadcasting unions. In September COJO agreed to accept U.S. $9,450,000, and the way was cleared for worldwide coverage of the Olympic Games.

The EBU and CBS entered into a news agreement in July by which a half-hour-long CBS news tape would be flown each day to London for insertion into the Eurovision network. The agreement also covered satellite transmissions, and talks were held between U.S. and European telecommunications organizations to settle new regulations governing the amount of satellite traffic and the required tariffs in the forthcoming year.

On the EBU's behalf the British Broadcasting Corporation (BBC) was host to the first interunion workshop aimed at improving standards in television sports coverage. A similar workshop, on sound origination, was held in Cologne, West Germany, and at a conference in London EBU members also exchanged views on techniques for the presentation of modern music. During the year the first recording was made, by Antal Dorati, in a collaborative venture between the EBU and the Philips recording company to record all the operas of Haydn.

Tariffs:
see Economy, World
Taxation:
see Economy, World
Tea:
see Agriculture and Food Supplies
Telecommunications:
see Industrial Review

The second session of the International Telecommunications Union's Longwave/Medium Wave Broadcasting Conference, held in the fall at Geneva, was less successful. Almost all the 112 countries attending submitted requests for excessive frequency requirements, involving a threefold increase in power and a dramatic increase in the number of transmitters. In the end, many of these transmitters were restricted to day- or nighttime operation only, and the need for additional directional aerials, even for relatively weak transmitters, was anticipated because of growing interference on overcrowded frequencies. For many European networks the proposals, due to become effective from 1978, meant a considerable capital expenditure at a time when broadcasting finances in general were in a weak state.

United States. Approximately 51 million U.S. homes, 74% of all TV households in the U.S., had colour television sets in mid-1975, reflecting a 12-month gain of 2.4 million, or 5%, according to estimates compiled by *Broadcasting* magazine. Virtually the only programs not broadcast in colour were old movies filmed originally in black-and-white. Almost 90% of all television homes were also equipped to receive programs from ultrahigh-frequency (UHF) stations; 43% had more than one TV set; and 15% were connected to cable television (CATV). A small but rapidly growing number of the CATV subscribers, approximately 160,000 homes in April, were paying additional fees to receive special programming on pay television, popularly called pay cable.

Cable television gained relief from some restrictions in 1975, but not as much as CATV operators thought they should have. In July the Federal Communications Commission (FCC) yielded to the pleas of CATV owners and canceled the March 31, 1977, deadline for reconstruction of older systems to comply with enlarged channel-capacity and access requirements that went into effect in 1972. The commission said its own analysis supported the argument of system operators that the "rebuild rule," which would have applied to all systems constructed before March 31, 1972, was unrealistic because the industry could not raise the $275 million to $375 million required for it. The FCC also adopted in July a blackout rule prohibiting a cable system from importing a sports event into a 35-mi. zone around the local TV station in a city that is blacked out for that particular contest.

Being consumed in soapsuds are spacemen from "Space: 1999." The series about life on the Moon, renowned for its special effects, was sold directly to local stations.

COURTESY, INDEPENDENT TELEVISION CORPORATION

The commission adopted new rules in March governing pay-TV operations via cable, or pay cable, and was promptly taken to court by a group of pay-cable operators and subsequently by broadcasters as well. The rules would, among other things, relax somewhat the restrictions on pay cable as a competitor with broadcasting for rights to motion pictures, and set up elaborate guidelines for determining what sports events might be available to a pay system. Specific events such as the Rose Bowl and the World Series, for example, would be denied pay cable (and over-the-air pay TV as well, if over-the-air pay TV is developed) unless they had been off free television for five years, while regular-season events would be available in varying degrees determined by complex formulas. CATV owners claimed that the rules would inhibit their competition with broadcasters; the latter claimed that they would lead to a loss of some of free broadcasting's best programs to pay cable, with the public being the real loser.

For all the disputes in the courts and at the FCC, however, pay cable began to make significant strides in 1975. Home Box Office Inc., a pay-cable program service owned by the Time Inc. publishing organization, launched the distribution of pay programs by satellite in September 1975. The first such service was from the firm's headquarters in New York City to systems at Fort Pierce and Vero Beach, Fla., and at Jackson, Miss. A canvass conducted by *Broadcasting* produced estimates that pay cable would expand from about 275,000 homes in the latter part of 1975 to as many as 3.5 million by 1980. The envisioned total of 17.5 million cable-equipped homes would represent a 75% increase from the 10 million total that *Broadcasting* found in 1975.

Public broadcasting's financial problems remained troublesome in 1975, but its hope for long-term rather than year-to-year financing appeared to be nearing reality. Leaders in both houses of Congress were moving toward adoption of a plan for three-year funding for the Corporation for Public Broadcasting, after a House appropriations subcommittee scaled down a measure that called for five-year funding. The House bill and a pending Senate measure would both authorize expenditures for CPB on a matching-funds basis within ceilings that increased in annual steps from $88 million in 1976 to $160 million in 1980. They differed somewhat in their matching-funds formulas, but for the first three years were identical in calling for $1 in federal funds for every $2.50 raised by CPB from other sources.

In fiscal 1974, according to a CPB report in May 1975, income from all sources for public television was $259,209,574 and for public radio, $31,350,280. The combined total, $290,559,854, represented a 14.1% increase over the preceding year. Approximately $223 million were said to have come from nonfederal sources. Thus, CPB officials noted, the federal share for the ensuing fiscal year should be $89.2 million under the $1-to-$2.50 ratio, or somewhat more than the $88 million maximum established in the pending legislation.

After five years of deliberation over ways to promote diversification of media control, the FCC banned future acquisitions that would result in common own-

WIDE WORLD

Susan Seaforth Hayes and Bill Hayes are the long-suffering Julie and Doug in "Days of Our Lives," one of two daytime soap operas lengthened to an hour by NBC.

ership of a newspaper and a radio or television station within the same community. In addition, it ordered the breakup within five years of 16 small-market newspaper-television and newspaper-radio combinations that it said were media monopolies.

Europe. In Britain television license fees were increased in April (for black and white, from £7 to £8; for colour, from £12 to £18), but despite this increased revenue the BBC was still forced to make program cuts. Sales of programs overseas continued to improve, however, with the value of these exports reaching about $40 million a year.

In reports to the Annan Committee considering the future shape of broadcasting in the U.K., producers and directors argued that the proposed fourth channel should be used by independent program makers, while the BBC called for it to be devoted to educational and specialist use. The committee's report was expected by 1977.

In France the state broadcasting organization, Office de Radiodiffusion et Télévision Française (ORTF), was dissolved, and was succeeded by four national program companies, one for radio and three for television. The new channels broadcast 171 hours of television a week, as against 97 hours previously, but by April (less than four months after the demise of ORTF) artists and technicians were already complaining of a decline in program standards.

The long-awaited reform of the state-owned RAI-ITV network in Italy finally took effect in April. A new law set up a 40-member parliamentary committee to supervise broadcasting services and to elect 10 of the 16 members of the board of governors.

Italy's reformed broadcasting structure took account of financial difficulties by stressing accountability and also the right of viewers and listeners to protest against programs they considered offensive. This was also the case in Austria, where new legislation was effective throughout 1975. Broadcasts were to be objective, and were to reflect varying shades of public opinion, with regional interests in particular being considered.

Australasia and Africa. The New Zealand Broadcasting Corporation (NZBC) ceased to exist from April 1975, when a new radio and two competitive but complementary television corporations began operating. A national broadcasting council provided joint services for the three corporations.

South Africa began experimental television transmissions in May, with programs in English and Afrikaans. Initial broadcasts were in colour, using the West German PAL system. Sales of sets were rather slow due to their high cost, and by the end of 1975 approximately 250,000 had been distributed. Regular service was scheduled to start from January 1976.

Programming. Coverage of news having international significance continued to receive international distribution by satellite in 1975. There were no events to match the protracted drama of the 1974 Watergate hearings or the sudden impact of a presidential resignation in the U.S., but the closing weeks of the Vietnam war; the launchings, linkup, and landings of the U.S. Apollo and Soviet Soyuz spacecraft; and filmed or taped reports on the assassination attempts against U.S. Pres. Gerald Ford and coverage of his journeys abroad were seen in many countries via satellite relays.

In entertainment programming, Westerns, mysteries, and comedies produced in the U.S. ranked among the biggest television attractions in many countries. "Bonanza," "Gunsmoke," "Bewitched," and "Perry Mason" were some of the most widely sold series, each in scores of countries. Foreign sales by U.S. TV film distributors were estimated by *Broadcasting* to be about $130 million in 1975, up from its revised estimate of $128 million in 1974. A single motion picture, *The Godfather,* was reported to have been sold to Japanese television for an estimated $2.2 million for one showing.

United States. The initial months of the 1975–76 network television season, which opened in September, were distinguished by two features in particular: the introduction of the so-called "family viewing hour" by the networks at 8–9 P.M. Eastern and Pacific time (7–8 P.M. Central and Mountain time), and by far the closest race, in terms of audience ratings, that the three networks had experienced for years. Whether the second factor stemmed from the first was a matter of unresolved debate.

Wedding bells ended "Upstairs, Downstairs," television saga of the Bellamy family, as Georgina Worsley (Lesley-Anne Down) married the marquis of Stockbridge (Anthony Andrews).

SYNDICATION INTERNATIONAL/PHOTO TRENDS

WIDE WORLD

Howard Cosell's own variety show, "Saturday Night Live," appeared during the fall season, but was subsequently canceled by ABC-TV. Cosell remained a dominant figure on the sports scene, however, with a large following for "Monday Night Football."

A scene from the highly successful "Carol Burnett Show," with (left to right) Vicki Lawrence, Harvey Korman, Tim Conway, and Carol Burnett.

The networks created the "family hour" as a period during which programs generally would contain no "sex and violence." If an occasional program did so, viewers were to be alerted in advance. ABC's "The Rookies" and "Movie of the Week," CBS's "All in the Family" and "Kojak" (and subsequently "M*A*S*H"), and NBC's "Sunday Mystery Movie" (and later "Chico and the Man") all moved to 9 P.M. and were replaced by other shows such as "That's My Mama" and "Welcome Back, Kotter" on ABC, "The Jeffersons" and "Cher" on CBS, and "The Family Holvak" on NBC. The result, in the view of many critics, was excessively bland programming in the family hour. A. C. Nielsen Co. ratings showed, however, that in the season's first two weeks, at least, more teenagers and children, though somewhat fewer adults, were watching during that time period.

The family hour was part—but only an incidental part—of the most extensive new-season overhaul that network programming had ever experienced. In all, 27 new series were introduced in September, 9 each by ABC, CBS, and NBC. In addition, 20 holdover shows were moved into new time periods. Situation comedies and nonviolent melodrama were the dominant formats among the new shows, with nine entries in each category. To make room for the new series, the networks necessarily canceled a record number, including some long-time favourites. CBS dropped "Gunsmoke," whose 20-year run had set an endurance record, and also "Mannix," an eight-year veteran. ABC and NBC canceled their made-for-TV movies, which had declined in popularity during the 1974–75 season.

By mid-November, the shakedown was well under way and seemed likely to prove once more that, as Nielsen statistics for the past season had demonstrated, six out of ten network television programs do not last beyond their first year. Eleven new entries had already been canceled: "Barbary Coast" by ABC, whose main changes were yet to come; "Big Eddie," "Kate McShane," "Three for the Road," and "Beacon Hill" by CBS; and "The Montefuscos," "The Family Holvak," "Fay," "The Invisible Man," "Doctors Hospital," and "Medical Story" by NBC. In their places came, effective in December or January, programs that were again predominantly situation comedies, police shows, or comedy-variety offerings.

One of 1975's most spectacular failures was that of CBS's "Beacon Hill," a "quality" drama set in Boston

COURTESY, CBS TELEVISION NETWORK

but patterned after the British "Upstairs, Downstairs," which had been highly successful on public television. The series of one-hour episodes was widely publicized in advance, and its initial presentation, a two-hour special production, achieved a 42% share of the TV audience. Its ratings after that, however, went downhill week by week until, at the announcement of its cancellation in late October, its audience share was less than 15%.

In the overall prime-time ratings, which CBS had dominated for 20 years and in which ABC had been an especially poor third in 1974–75, less than one percentage point separated the three networks at mid-November. In averages covering the season from September through November 16, NBC was first with an 18.8 Nielsen rating and CBS and ABC were tied at 18.2. (Each network rating point in the 1975–76 season was equal to approximately 696,000 homes.)

The highest-rated series in mid-November were "All in the Family" (CBS), "Sanford and Son" (NBC), and "Chico and the Man" (NBC), in that order. They were followed by "The Six Million Dollar Man" (ABC), "The Waltons" (CBS), "Maude" (CBS), "Starsky and Hutch" (ABC), "M*A*S*H" (CBS), "Good Times" (CBS), and "Happy Days" (ABC). "Starsky and Hutch" and "Phyllis" (CBS) were among the new shows that placed most consistently in the top 15 or 20. At the other extreme, NBC's "Ellery Queen" and ABC's "Saturday Night Live with Howard Cosell" and "When Things Were Rotten," in addition to the shows already canceled by all three networks, were usually in the bottom third of the ratings. Several former ratings leaders were also doing less well than usual in the fall of 1975, including "Cher" and the long-running "Hawaii Five-O" on CBS and "Marcus Welby, M.D." on ABC.

The family-viewing principle adopted by the National Association of Broadcasters (NAB) applied to local programming at 7–8 P.M. (6–7 P.M. Central and Mountain) as well as to network programming an hour later. Actually, however, it had relatively little effect on programming by most stations. Network-affiliated stations already tended to schedule game shows, contests, nature programs, public affairs, or other nonviolent, nonsexual material at the early hour, and independent stations in effect were exempt from the family-viewing concept until Sept. 1, 1977. The independent stations often did schedule strong action shows in early-evening hours as counterprogramming to the fare being carried by network affiliates, but the NAB allowed them a two-year grace period in which to play off series that might not meet the "family viewing" test but which they had acquired prior to the NAB's adoption of the rule in April 1975.

Several former and current network series were being offered on a station-by-station basis in 1975 for the first time. These included past episodes of "Marcus Welby, M.D.," which were being sold to stations as "Robert Young, Family Doctor" while new episodes of "Welby" continued to appear on ABC; "Adam-12," a half-hour police series that ended a seven-year run on NBC in 1975; and "Emergency," a series of paramedical stories that was continuing on NBC.

Children's programming commanded the attention of both networks and stations in 1975. A midyear canvass by *Broadcasting* found several new trends. Increasingly, groups of stations were combining forces to produce programs more elaborate or more specialized than any one station could afford, on subjects ranging from books and travel to rodeos, magic, and opera. News for children was getting increased attention; on a number of stations children were interpreting the news for other children, while others were producing and scheduling children's versions of regular newscasts in weekend periods. Beyond the news, *Broadcasting* found both specials and regular local series oriented toward children's interests in music, literature, games, comedy, sports, and, especially with the nation's bicentennial approaching, history.

The networks in 1975 changed much of their children's programming. They replaced many of their Saturday-morning cartoons with live-action series and new stories in animation, reduced the volume of action/adventure in response to complaints of too much violence, and continued to curtail advertising in children's shows (commercial time, which had been cut from 16 minutes per hour to 10 minutes on Jan. 1, 1975, was due to go to 9½ minutes on Jan. 1, 1976). ABC's program additions included "The Great Grape Ape," "Speed Buggy," and "The New Tom and Jerry Show"; CBS added two live-action half hours, "Far Out Space Nuts" and "Ghost Busters," among others; and NBC scheduled a new live-action travel series called "Westwind" and three new animation series.

Television received a new early-morning network program in 1975 with ABC's introduction on January 6 of its two-hour information/entertainment series "AM America," in competition with NBC's highly successful "Today" show. The new show made no headway in the ratings, however, and was replaced in November by "Good Morning, America," also on at 7–9 A.M. Eastern time but putting primary emphasis on entertainment.

The big departure in daytime programming by the television networks in 1975 was the 60-minute soap opera, an expansion from the conventional 30-minute length. NBC started the trend in January by lengthening "Another World" to a full hour and then expanded "Days of Our Lives" in April. Both were almost immediate audience successes, and their gains boosted NBC's entire daytime standings in the ratings. By August NBC was in first place in six of the nine daytime periods in which all three networks competed. With NBC's successes, CBS announced it would expand "As the World Turns" to an hour, effective December 1, and ABC officials said that they probably would expand "General Hospital." The 60-minute trend also rubbed off on daytime game shows.

In its 27th annual Emmy Awards, the National Academy of Television Arts and Sciences voted "The Mary Tyler Moore Show" the outstanding comedy series of the 1974–75 season and again chose "Upstairs, Downstairs" as the outstanding dramatic series. A "mini-series" dramatizing periods in the life of Benjamin Franklin won five awards, including that for outstanding limited series. Other program winners included "The Carol Burnett Show" as the outstanding comedy-variety or music series, "The Law" as the outstanding dramatic or comedic special, "An Evening with John Denver" as the outstanding comedy-variety or music special, and "Profile in Music: Beverly Sills" as the outstanding classical music program.

Sports remained one of broadcasting's biggest attractions and also one of its highest priced. *Broadcasting* estimated that television and radio networks and stations in 1975 paid $80.7 million for broadcast rights to professional and college football games, and $44.5 million for rights to major-league baseball. The spiraling price increases evident in earlier years appeared to have tapered off, however. The football rights, whose cost had jumped by $10 million in 1974, increased by less than $500,000 in 1975, while baseball rights costs were about $1,250,000 higher than in 1974. Part of the leveling off in costs might be attributable to the economic recession, but many authorities thought it also could be traced to the abundance of sports events of all kinds that were available on TV.

WIDE WORLD

The theme of a mechanical man's fight against evil monsters is portrayed by Kikaider, a mechanical man who wards off androids in a popular Japanese-language series broadcast in Honolulu.

There were some indications that viewers were losing interest in televised sports. The ratings of professional football on CBS and ABC had been declining (but appeared to stabilize at least in the early weeks of the 1975 fall season), college football ratings had been dropping (but increased in 1975 thanks in considerable part to the scheduling of more games in prime time, when bigger audiences were available), and regular-season baseball had been barely holding its own. NBC dropped ice hockey from its prime-time schedule for lack of viewers. CBS had tried soccer, but it never caught on. Tennis, despite the success of events tailored for television and featuring such stars as Jimmy Connors, Billie Jean King, and Chris Evert, rarely achieved ratings higher than 5.

If sports audiences were growing at a slower rate generally and in some cases declining, the year produced a spectacular exception in baseball's World Series. NBC's coverage of the seventh game between Cincinnati and Boston, played in prime time, scored a 39.6 rating, highest in Series history, with an estimated average of 27,560,000 homes tuned in per minute. The sixth game, also played at night, ranked second with an average of 23,180,000 homes. The closest approach in previous World Series was 22,240,000 homes per minute for the third game of the 1973 series between Oakland and the New York Mets. In 1976 there would be far more sports than ever before, as ABC planned to televise 43½ hours of the winter Olympics from Innsbruck, Austria, and 76½ hours of the summer Olympics from Montreal.

News remained a staple of television broadcast schedules, not only in coverage of spectacular events like the Apollo-Soyuz space flights, the end of the Vietnam war, and the apparent attempts on the life of President Ford but also in reporting on day-to-day events in government and business. The public signified once more, in a survey conducted by the independent Roper Organization, that television was the source of most of its news.

In both radio and TV, a major 1975 news trend was the increasing attention being paid to inflation-fighting tips and other shopping and marketing news of special concern to consumers, along with increasing use of trained economists and other specialists in preparing news coverage. The trend was sufficiently far advanced that some leading newsmen suggested a new era had begun, in which "reality" reporting—that is, news about energy, the environment, the economy, and other subjects that affect the lives of most people—would supersede traditional "crisis-type" reporting.

Among news reports that claimed special attention in 1975 was a two-part interview by CBS News with H. R. Haldeman, White House chief of staff during the administration of former president Richard Nixon. The interview made headlines less for Haldeman's revelations, however, than for the fact that CBS News had paid him for it, which gave rise to widespread criticism of "checkbook journalism." CBS News at first defended the payment on grounds that the interview was more like "memoirs," which are conventionally paid for, than like hard news. Later, however, CBS News officials acknowledged that payment to Haldeman probably was a mistake.

Television lost a nationwide news service in 1975, and radio gained one. Television News Inc. (TVN), which for two years had been supplying daily "feeds" of national and international news coverage to subscribing stations, discontinued the service on October 31, citing financial losses. The Adolph Coors Co., a brewing company and principal owner of TVN, said that the losses totaled more than $5 million. The new radio news organization was News and Information Service (NIS), set up by NBC to provide national, international, and regional news and features to all-news radio stations. Started in June with 33 station subscribers, NIS had more than 60 by the end of 1975.

Late in 1975 the U.S. House of Representatives Rules Committee was preparing for hearings on a proposal by its special subcommittee that would permit a one-year experiment in live television and radio coverage of proceedings on the House floor. All floor proceedings would be covered; networks and stations could carry them wholly or in part but with commercial sponsorship. Tests during August, while the House was in recess, had shown that acceptable TV pictures could be produced without additional lights, up to then a principal concern.

KEYSTONE

Robert Powell, famous for his part in the "Doomwatch" television series, portrays Jesus in a joint British-Italian production entitled "The Life of Jesus."

The Public Broadcasting Service schedule for 1975–76 included a number of new series, among them two educational programs on weekday mornings: "Ourstory," a series of monthly dramas designed to coincide with the monthly calendar of the American Issues Forum of the National Endowment for the Humanities' bicentennial effort, and "Classic Theater—The Humanities in Drama." Other new series included "Gettin' Over," for high-school-age members of minority groups; "Erica," featuring lessons in various arts and crafts; "The First Poetry Quartet," a weekly literature program; "Realidades," a bilingual program with a magazine format; *National Geographic* documentaries; "Decades of Decision," consisting of five one-hour dramas with bicentennial themes; and a musical program, "Austin City Limits," billed as "the new sound of country rock." Among the holdover programs on the new PBS schedule were "Nova," "Best of Evening at the Pops," "Evening at the Symphony," and "Masterpiece Theatre."

In radio, music and news remained the dominant formats. The "nostalgia" boom that started earlier in the 1970s, featuring replays of classic dramas and comedies from earlier years or new dramas specially produced for contemporary listening, continued to accelerate. "The Green Hornet," "The Shadow," and the "Fibber McGee and Molly" comedy series were among the old-time programs being heard again on hundreds of radio stations.

Enjoying considerable growth during the year were sales of citizens' band radios, two-way sets in which the user could transmit or receive in 23 channels in the high-frequency band. They had first become popular in 1973 when truck drivers installed them in their vehicles to warn one another of traffic police enforcing the new 55-mph speed limit. Police forces, in turn, acquired them, and by the end of the year many people had installed sets in their cars as a means of exchanging information while traveling.

Europe. In Britain the BBC eroded the independent channel's domination of the audience ratings, chiefly by scheduling comedy shows and drama series, including U.S. imports, at peak hours on BBC 1. A BBC comedy series, "The Goodies," won the Silver Rose award at Montreux. Another BBC comedy series that won critical acclaim was "Fawlty Towers," written by John Cleese (*see* BIOGRAPHY) and with himself as the central character, the disaster-prone hotel proprietor Basil Fawlty.

Drama, in one form or another, was the mainstay of programming. Thames Television's "Shades of Greene" was based on stories by novelist Graham Greene, while Granada's "The Stars Look Down" dramatized A. J. Cronin's book about life in the industrial area of Tyneside in the early years of the century. The past, recent and not-so-recent, was a rich source of material for series creators. ATV's "Edward the Seventh" featured fine performances by its principals, including Timothy West as Edward, Helen Ryan as Queen Alexandra, and Annette Crosbie as Queen Victoria. BBC 2's expertise with the classic serial produced "Madame Bovary," "Moll Flanders," and "Prometheus," a life of Balzac written by David Turner; to be followed by "How Green Was My Valley" and a co-production with the U.S.S.R. of "Anna Karenina." For its home-produced series, BBC 1 relied on espionage in "Quiller," North Sea oil in "Oil Strike North," nursing in "Angels," and 18th-century Cornish romance in "Poldark."

More controversial were four highly praised films by Ken Loach and Tony Garnett, entitled "Days of Hope" and comprising a study of the British labour movement from 1916 to 1926. The documentary series "The Explorers," filmed with actors on location, was a major BBC venture in the expensive area of international co-production. "The Tribal Eye" examined exotic cultures through their art forms, while BBC 1's "Tomorrow's World" won a British Association award for the most effective presentation of a scientific or technical subject to a nonspecialist audience with "The Seed of an Idea," a film about plant breeding. Thames Television's "The Final Solution" was a harrowing study of Nazi extermination camps. The same source produced "Warrior," a film about soldiers and death.

Financial cuts affected the production of original plays for television. The independent channel abandoned its long-running Sunday night play, but screened a successful series, "The Nearly Man," about a contemporary Labour Party politician. BBC's "Play of the Month" showed versions of established theatrical successes, while BBC 2 featured Harold Pinter's *Old Times,* Peter Nichols' *Forget-Me-Not Lane,* and Christopher Hampton's *Savages.* There were small helpings of opera, *The Flying Dutchman* on BBC 2 and *La Bohème* on the independent network, and movies from young filmmakers in "The First Picture Show" on BBC 2.

One of the most successful British exports, London Weekend's "Upstairs, Downstairs," ended its British run, with the close of the final chapter on the Bellamy fortunes. In the U.S. it had won its second Emmy award as best dramatic series, with co-creator Jean Marsh winning a best actress award.

For the first time in Britain, live radio transmissions of parliamentary proceedings were broadcast from the House of Commons by the BBC and Independent Radio News. The experimental broadcasts were used to provide material for newscasts and edited daily reviews of parliamentary proceedings.

At the Florence festival the BBC won the Prix Italia for drama with "Just Another Saturday" by Peter McDougall, first shown in the "Play for Today" series. The BBC also won the documentary award for "Joey," a sensitive film about a spastic's struggle to communicate.

In general European festival offerings were earnest and didactic. Florence produced a Swiss film about Bangladesh, a West German drama about a family living under the Nazis, a Norwegian view of industrial unrest, and an East German account of the possibilities inherent in the successful implantation of electrodes in the brain. The Italian play "Living Pictures" re-created an old woman's memories of her youth. By contrast, Denmark showed a film about a sect of snake handlers in Virginia.

In Eastern Europe many of the program titles had a familiar ring: "Civil Courage," "The Road to Victory," "Encounters Preceding the Party Congress." Music played an important role in Hungarian broadcasting; other programs reflected the social position of women in International Women's Year. East Germany, however, did offer audiences a medley of topical humour, music, and geographic information in "Old Love Does Not Rust." In Poland a popular program was "Duel," in which each of two participants from different professions had to perform tasks requiring his opponent's particular skill.

Television in The Netherlands was controlled by seven major broadcasting organizations, which used up to 60% of air time, and a central news, sports, outside broadcast, and education service (NOS) with which all groups were affiliated. While allowing more opportunity for minority groups to gain access to the screen, the system did not guarantee exciting or worthwhile television. Neither did the West German system, with all three channels financed by a mixture of license money and advertising revenue. West German television continued to set high standards of technical expertise, but programs were often dull and derivative.

Australia. Although the proportion of home-produced material was on the increase in Australia (accounting for about 70% of the program budgets of the 49 commercial television stations), local programs were often derivatives of the shows imported from the U.K. and U.S. Colour television using the West German PAL system began in March; within six months 12% of the nation's homes had a colour receiver.

New radio stations began transmitting in Sydney, Melbourne, Canberra, and Adelaide. Two were "ethnic community" stations and two were FM stations financed by the Music Broadcasting Society. The Australian Broadcasting Commission (ABC) opened a nonstop rock music station in Sydney and a community access station in Melbourne.

Japan. March 1975 marked the 50th anniversary of the start of broadcasting in Japan. The first television transmissions were made in 1953, and by 1975 television reached an audience of 26 million (92% of all households). Nippon Hoso Kyokai (NHK) was the world's largest and richest broadcasting organization, transmitting on two television channels and three radio frequencies. There were also five commercial television and six commercial radio stations broadcasting from Tokyo.

Although it gave prominence to topics such as pollution, commodity prices, energy resources, social welfare, and cultural history, NHK's output of drama and melodrama earned it highest ratings. Its strong educational interest showed in its sponsorship of the tenth annual Japan Prize for international educational programs, with Hungary and the U.K. (BBC) winning prizes for radio and television, respectively.

(RUFUS W. CRATER; TERENCE HUGHES; BARRIE H. PARSONS; SOL J. TAISHOFF; ICHIRO TSUJIMOTO; MICHAEL TYPE; BRIAN WILLIAMS)

See also Industrial Review: *Advertising; Telecommunications;* Motion Pictures; Music.

[613.D.4.b; 735.I.4-5]

ENCYCLOPÆDIA BRITANNICA FILMS. *TV News; Behind the Scenes* (1973).

Tennis and Rackets

Lawn Tennis. A survey of lawn tennis in the United States, where growth of the sport was greatest, estimated that there were nearly 34 million players, about 23.4 million playing more than three times a month. During 1975 record numbers attended the Italian championships in Rome, the French championships in

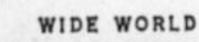
WIDE WORLD

Jimmy Connors returns a Rod Laver serve in the $100,000 winner-take-all match in Las Vegas, which Connors won 6–4, 6–2, 3–6, and 7–5.

Paris, the Wimbledon championships in London, and the U.S. championships at Forest Hills, N.Y. The total attendance at Wimbledon was 338,591, and at Forest Hills 216,683, each tournament lasting 12 days.

Large amounts of prize money continued to be offered. Arthur Ashe of the U.S. (*see* BIOGRAPHY) received $50,000 for winning the World Championship Tennis (WCT) final tournament in Dallas, Texas, and £10,000 for winning at Wimbledon. Björn Borg of Sweden, who became 19 during the tournament, received Fr. 120,000 for winning the French championship. Manuel Orantes of Spain won $25,000 as U.S. Open champion. Chris Evert of the U.S. earned the same amount for winning the U.S. women's singles title, and she also won $40,000 in the final event of the Virginia Slims circuit of tournaments. By the end of the year Miss Evert's earnings in prize money were estimated at about $350,000. Jimmy Connors of the U.S., Wimbledon and U.S. singles champion in 1974, earned $350,000 for challenge matches against the Australians Rod Laver and John Newcombe early in 1975 at Las Vegas, Nev.

Commercial sponsorship was mainly responsible for the big prize money. The Wimbledon championships relaxed traditional dignity and freedom from commercial interests to the extent of allowing a betting shop within the grounds. In the U.S. Open championships at Forest Hills there was a striking change of surface. Grass courts, used since the first U.S. national championship in 1881, were replaced by the slower "Har-Tru," a hard-surface court similar in playing qualities to courts in Europe. Prior to the change the American governing body altered its name, formally, from the U.S. Lawn Tennis Association to the U.S. Tennis Association.

The purely commercial World Team Tennis, which brought problems in international control of the game when it began in 1974, continued to operate but on a diminished scale. The number of U.S. cities taking part in this league competition was reduced from 16 to 10.

The administration of the game was maintained without major dispute. A Women's International Professional Tennis Council was formed, the International Lawn Tennis Federation (ILTF) sharing membership on it with the Women's Tennis Association, the leading organization of professional women players. This matched the men's council formed the year before. The difficulties met in promoting tournaments elsewhere than in the U.S. brought about an attempt to strengthen the organization in Europe. European members of the ILTF formed a European Tennis Association with a secretariat of its own. Its first task was to reorganize the King of Sweden's Cup, the indoor team championship, into a league basis between nations, starting in 1976.

In December the International Professional Tennis Council issued a "code of conduct." Fines for violating it ranged from $50 for throwing a ball out of the court in anger or appearing on court in unprofessional dress to $10,000 for "conduct detrimental" to the game. The council imposed the guidelines after Ilie Nastase was disqualified for unprofessional conduct in a match against Arthur Ashe in Stockholm.

Men's Competition. The Grand Prix, administered by the ILTF, sponsored by Commercial Union Assurance Co. Ltd., and based on performance at participating tournaments throughout the year, finished toward the end of 1974 with a surprise winner, Guillermo Vilas of Argentina. He did not distinguish himself in the major events but had consistent success in the later tournaments of the series. He excelled in the subsequent Masters' tournament, staged in Melbourne, Australia. In the semifinals Vilas beat Raúl Ramírez (Mexico) 4–6, 6–3, 6–2, 7–5, while Ilie Nastase (Romania) beat John Newcombe (Australia) 6–3, 7–6, 6–2. In the final Vilas beat Nastase 7–6, 6–2, 3–6, 3–6, 6–4 to equal Nastase's 1973 record as winner of both the Grand Prix series and the Grand Prix Masters' tournament. Vilas earned $100,000 for this joint success.

The Australian championship, also played in Melbourne and ending on the first day of 1975, was won for the second time by Newcombe. The field was not very strong, and he won the final from the 1974 champion, Jimmy Connors, 7–5, 3–6, 6–4, 7–6.

Manuel Orantes won the British Hard Court title at Bournemouth. The meeting was notable for the disqualification of Nastase in the quarterfinal round for refusing to continue playing after disputing a line decision. Later in the year Nastase was ordered to relinquish his prize of $8,000 for his conduct in the final of the Canadian Open championship in Toronto.

Orantes also won the German championship in Hamburg. He lost a week later in the final of the Italian championships in Rome, bowing to Ramírez 7–6, 7–5, 7–5. In the semifinals, during which Orantes beat Vilas, Ramírez was given a default by Nastase. Ramírez led 6–2, 5–2 when the Romanian declared he was too distraught to play properly, having been kept waiting for his match.

The WCT finals in Dallas brought notable success for Ashe. In successive rounds the American beat Mark Cox of the U.K., John Alexander of Australia, and Borg in the final by 3–6, 6–4, 6–4, 6–0. One of the finest contests of the year was the semifinal in which Borg beat Laver 7–6, 3–6, 5–7, 7–6, 6–2.

Borg easily retained his French championship. He lost a set only in the semifinal round, to Adriano Panatta of Italy, and in the final he defeated Vilas 6–2, 6–3, 6–4.

Ashe was an unexpected victor in the Wimbledon championships, taking the title for the first time at nearly 32. The defending champion, Connors, played with increasingly impressive form, culminating in a semifinal win against Roscoe Tanner (U.S.) in which he hit so hard and with such control that he passed into the final as the strongest favourite for many years. Ashe, however, played the match with an astuteness that robbed Connors of his confidence and won 6–1, 6–1, 5–7, 6–4.

The U.S. tournament, apart from the change of surface, was different also in that only during the last four rounds was a match decided by the best of five sets; in the early rounds the best of three sets determined the victor. Orantes was the unexpected champion. In the semifinal he beat Vilas 4–6, 1–6, 6–2, 7–5, 6–4. He trailed love–5 in the fourth set, and saved five match points in the course of the sixth and seventh games. At the same stage Connors, defending his title, beat Borg 7–5, 7–5, 7–5. In the final Orantes easily beat Connors 6–4, 6–3, 6–3.

Connors thus lost both his Wimbledon and U.S. singles titles in the final round. Early in the year he won two widely publicized challenge matches in Las Vegas. On February 2 he beat Laver 6–4, 6–2, 3–6, 7–5, and on April 26 he defeated Newcombe 6–3, 4–6, 6–2, 6–4.

Doubles. The Australian title was taken by Alexander and Phil Dent (Australia), but otherwise the first half of the year was dominated by the joint skill of Ramírez and his U.S. partner, Brian Gottfried. They won the WCT final event, staged in Mexico City, and also the Italian and French titles. Wimbledon had unseeded victors, Vitas Gerulaitis and Alex Mayer of the U.S. Connors and Nastase won the U.S. title.

Davis Cup. Sweden, led by Borg, and Czechoslovakia, led by Jan Kodes, were the two European Zone winners. Sweden won the final of section A 3–2 against Spain, the key rubber a victory by Borg against Orantes. Spain beat Romania in the semifinals despite a win by Nastase against Orantes. Czechoslovakia beat Hungary 4–1 in the semifinal of section B, and then defeated France 3–2 in the final, the latter having won its semifinal 3–2 against Italy.

Australia won the Eastern Zone with a 4–1 win against Japan and a 4–0 win against New Zealand. Chile won the American Zone. This followed an unexpected setback for the United States when at Palm Springs, Calif., Mexico won 3–2. There was disruption in the zone because of the presence of South Africa, winners of the 1974 competition by default in the final from India. Mexico refused to play South Africa and forfeited in the third round, and Colombia did the same in the semifinal. Chile played South Africa at Santiago in the final in July and won 5–0.

Women's Competition. As in 1974 the outstanding player was Chris Evert, impeccably steady, consistent, and with a style of play less dependent on volleying skill than that of most leading players of recent years. A striking newcomer to the top ranks of the women's game was Martina Navratilova (born in Prague, Czech., Oct. 18, 1956). In September she asked the U.S. authorities for political asylum.

The Australian championship was won by Evonne Goolagong (Australia), who later became Mrs. Roger Cawley and qualified for British nationality. In the final, Miss Goolagong beat Miss Navratilova 6–3, 6–2. The latter had defeated Margaret Court of Australia 6–4, 6–3 in the quarterfinal.

The Virginia Slims indoor circuit in the U.S. was dominated by Miss Evert. She won 4 of the 11 tournaments it comprised, including the last in Los Angeles 6–4, 6–2 over Miss Navratilova.

Miss Evert retained her Italian championship in Rome, defeating Miss Navratilova in the final 6–1, 6–0. Miss Evert also won the French title in Paris for the second year in a row. Once again she beat Miss Navratilova in the final, this time by 2–6, 6–2, 6–1.

Wimbledon brought a change of pattern. Billie Jean King of the U.S., having announced the event to be her last in singles, beat Miss Evert in the semifinal round 2–6, 6–2, 6–3. In a quarterfinal match Mrs. Court beat Miss Navratilova 6–3, 6–4, but Mrs. Cawley beat her in the semifinal 6–4, 6–4. In the final Mrs. King overwhelmed Mrs. Cawley 6–0, 6–1.

It was Mrs. King's sixth Wimbledon singles championship and her 19th Wimbledon championship in all. This equaled the record set in 1934 by another Californian, Elizabeth Ryan (born Feb. 5, 1892), who won 12 women's doubles and 7 mixed doubles but never the singles.

The U.S. championship was won for the first time by Miss Evert, who in four previous attempts neither fell below nor passed beyond the semifinal. She was extended only in the final, where she beat Mrs. Cawley, a losing finalist for the third straight year, 5–7, 6–4, 6–2.

Doubles. Miss Evert and Miss Navratilova won the Italian and French championships, respectively. Wimbledon brought unexpected success to Ann Kiyomura, an American of Japanese descent, and Kazuko Sawamatsu, a Japanese citizen. The U.S. title went to Mrs. Court in partnership with Virginia Wade of Great Britain.

Federation Cup. Played in Aix-en-Provence, France, this cup was won for the first time by Czechoslovakia, with Miss Navratilova playing the leading part. Supported by Renata Tomanova, she was personally invincible as Czechoslovakia in turn beat Ireland, The Netherlands, West Germany, France, and Australia. France beat Great Britain in the quarterfinals, and Australia defeated the U.S. in the semifinals.

Wightman Cup. Great Britain won 5–2 against the United States at Cleveland, Ohio. The British team included Miss Wade, Glynis Coles, Sue Barker, and Mrs. Ann Jones. The U.S. team included Miss Evert, Mona Schallan, Julie Anthony, and Janet Newberry.

(LANCE TINGAY)

WIDE WORLD

Spain's Manuel Orantes moments after winning the men's singles U.S. Open tennis championship at Forest Hills, New York, over the heavily favoured Jimmy Connors.

Squash Rackets. World control of squash rackets was tightened as a result of a three-day meeting of the International Squash Rackets Federation (ISRF) in London in June 1975 at which a new and much tougher definition of what an amateur may or may not do was adopted as an ISRF rule. Although it was unanimously agreed that the rule should come into force immediately, there was some doubt as to whether all member countries would implement it. Another attempt, this time by Sweden, to abolish amateur status was again heavily defeated. The International Squash Professional Players Association, formed in 1974, negotiated increased prize money in several tournaments.

Only Geoff Hunt of Australia was able, with ever increasing difficulty, to withstand the advance of the young Pakistanis, whose most successful amateurs, Mohibullah Khan and Qamar Zaman, reached the final of the British Amateur championship. Khan won the title, and both turned professional. Zaman won the British Open. Thirteen teams competed in the third European championships, held in April in Dublin. England won for the third straight year.

In the U.S. the most successful competitor was Victor Niederhoffer, who won both the U.S. amateur and the North American Open championships before turning professional in November. In the Open he beat the leading professional and six-time titleholder, Sharif Khan.

In women's squash the domination of Australia continued. Heather McKay of that nation won the British Women's Open championship for the 14th successive year, and the Australian women's team beat Great Britain 3–0 in a test series in England.

(JOHN H. HORRY)

Rackets. William Surtees, a 27-year-old Englishman living in Chicago, regained the world championship from Howard Angus, the British open champion, winning the challenge match by five games to one in Chicago and at Queen's Club, London, in March 1975. Surtees, having gained a commanding 4–0 (15–8, 15–12, 15–10, 15–11) lead in Chicago, needed only one more game to win the title. Angus, knowing that he must win 5–0 and concede fewer aces than he had gained in Chicago, went flat out in the opening game. Gaining the serve at 11–12, Angus ran out for the game at 15–12. When Angus gained a lead of 11–1 in the second game it looked as if a struggle would develop, but suddenly Surtees had an inspired spell. Although Angus held three game points at 14–11 he was beaten by brilliant returns, and during his next serve Surtees ran out for victory at 17–14.

Real Tennis. Howard Angus was again outstanding in British real tennis during the 1974–75 season. He won the amateur singles championship for the tenth successive year, beating Alan Lovell 6–1, 6–2, 6–5 in the final at Queen's Club, and he also retained the open challenge championship, beating the Manchester professional Frank Willis in a best of 13 sets match, 7 sets to 6. Angus also defeated the Queen's Club professional Norwood Cripps in the Cutty Sark British open singles championship. Charles Swallow and Cripps retained the Cutty Sark British open doubles championship, beating Angus and David Warburg in the final. Great Britain regained the Bathurst Cup in the international team championship, beating Australia 5–0 in Melbourne and the U.S. 5–0 in Hobart, Tasmania.

(CHRISTINA MARGARET WOOD)

[452.B.4.h.xxii and xxvii]

Textiles:
see Industrial Review

Thailand

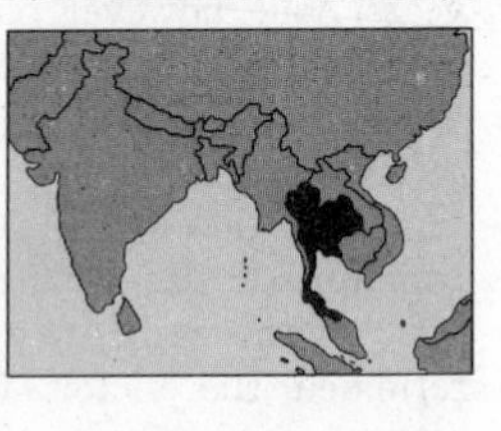

A constitutional monarchy of Southeast Asia, Thailand is bordered by Burma, Laos, Cambodia, and Malaysia. Area: 198,500 sq.mi. (514,000 sq.km.). Pop. (1975 est.): 41,334,200. Cap. and largest city: Bangkok (pop., 1975 est., 4,129,600). Language: Thai. Religion (1970): Buddhist 95.3%; Muslim 3.8%. King, Bhumibol Adulyadej; prime ministers in 1975, Sanya Dharmasakti, Seni Pramoj from February 21 to March 6, and, from March 17, Kukrit Pramoj.

Two preoccupations filled Thailand's calendar for 1975: finding a government and reorganizing its tattered foreign relations. When the country went to the polls on January 26 under the constitution passed in October 1974, there were as many as 2,193 candidates from 42 parties competing for 269 seats. None of the 22 parties that finally won seats in the Assembly was in any position to form a government. On Febru-

THAILAND

Education. (1972–73) Primary, pupils 6,228,469, teachers 192,318; secondary, pupils 666,755, teachers 28,064; vocational, pupils 129,025, teachers 8,277; teacher training, students 49,841, teachers 3,767; higher, students 63,940, teaching staff 8,448.

Finance. Monetary unit: baht, with (Sept. 22, 1975) a par value of 20 baht to U.S. $1 (free rate of 42.24 baht = £1 sterling). Gold, SDRs, and foreign exchange: (June 1975) U.S. $2,084,000,000; (June 1974) U.S. $1,790,000,000. Budget (1974–75 est.): revenue 37,881,000,000 baht; expenditure 45,672,000,000 baht. Gross national product: (1973) 187,280,000,000 baht; (1972) 159,840,000,000 baht. Money supply: (March 1975) 34,010,000,000 baht; (March 1974) 32,180,000,000 baht. Cost of living (Bangkok; 1970 = 100): (May 1975) 152; (May 1974) 149.

Foreign Trade. (1974) Imports 62,957,000,000 baht; exports 50,318,000,000 baht. Import sources: Japan 31%; U.S. 13%; West Germany 7%; Qatar 6%; Kuwait 5%; Saudi Arabia 5%; U.K. 5%. Export destinations: Japan 26%; The Netherlands 9%; Singapore 8%; U.S. 8%; Hong Kong 7%; Taiwan 7%; Malaysia 5%. Main exports: rice 19%; corn 12%; rubber 10%; sugar 7%; tapioca 7%; tin 6%. Tourism (1973): visitors 1,038,000; gross receipts U.S. $167 million.

Transport and Communications. Roads (main; 1972) 17,686 km. Motor vehicles in use (1972): passenger 282,600; commercial 158,900. Railways (1973): 3,765 km.; traffic 4,694,000,000 passenger-km., freight 2,070,000,000 net ton-km. Air traffic (1974): 2,845,000,000 passenger-km.; freight 63,248,000 net ton-km. Shipping (1974): merchant vessels 100 gross tons and over 80; gross tonnage 176,315. Telephones (Dec. 1973) 255,000. Radio receivers (Dec. 1973) 3,009,000. Television receivers (Dec. 1971) 241,000.

Agriculture. Production (in 000; metric tons; 1974; 1973 in parentheses): rice 13,274 (14,650); corn *c.* 2,300 (2,343); peanuts *c.* 233 (*c.* 221); sweet potatoes (1973) *c.* 285, (1972) *c.* 270; sorghum *c.* 200 (*c.* 130); dry beans *c.* 250 (*c.* 210); soybeans *c.* 132 (*c.* 106); cassava (1973) 6,398, (1972) 3,687; sugar, raw value (1973) 761, (1972) 709; pineapples (1973) *c.* 225, (1972) *c.* 215; bananas *c.* 1,300 (*c.* 1,250); tobacco *c.* 47 (*c.* 45); rubber (1973) 382, (1972) 337; cotton, lint *c.* 21 (*c.* 20); jute *c.* 15 (24); kenaf *c.* 350 (645); timber (cu.m.; 1973) 19,500, (1972) 19,500; fish catch (1973) 1,692, (1972) 1,679. Livestock (in 000; 1973–74): cattle *c.* 4,751; buffalo *c.* 5,630; pigs *c.* 4,573; chickens (1972–73) *c.* 53,000; ducks (1972–73) *c.* 7,300.

Industry. Production (in 000; metric tons; 1973): tin concentrates (metal content) 21; tungsten concentrates (oxide content) 2.7; lead concentrates (metal content) 3.5; manganese ore (metal content) 12; cement (1974) 3,923; petroleum products 7,848; electricity (kw-hr.; 1972) 6,209,000.

ary 13, after 18 days of maneuvering, Seni Pramoj of the Democratic Party was elected prime minister and began to put together Thailand's first elected government in more than 25 years. Formed on February 21, it fell on March 6, under right-wing pressure. After another round of hectic maneuvering, a new Cabinet led by Kukrit Pramoj (*see* BIOGRAPHY) and the Social Action Party was sworn in on March 17.

No sooner had the government settled in than troubles began. Strikes for more pay by tire factory workers and a baton charge by police on women strikers in a garment factory generated tensions in June. In August growing hostility between opposing political forces erupted into street battles. Students incited riots demanding the release of eight farmers and a student who had been arrested during disturbances in northern Thailand. When a public prosecutor yielded to the demands, resentment grew among policemen. A crowd of 1,000 off-duty policemen stormed the prime minister's house, and some of them broke in and ransacked it. Although the police attack was the most sensational episode, the most virulent was the looting and burning of some buildings of Thammasat University by bomb-throwing vocational students from other institutions.

In foreign affairs there was some confusion about the evolving role of the U.S. Outwardly at any rate, Thailand seemed anxious to show that it was disengaging itself from the U.S. American troop strength in the country was reduced from 25,000 in May to 16,000 in November as part of a reported agreement to withdraw U.S. forces altogether by March 1976. Following the U.S. use of a Thai base to strike at Cambodia after the seizure of the U.S. merchant ship "Mayaguez," Bangkok announced it would review all its agreements with the U.S.

Prime Minister Kukrit visited other member countries of the Association of Southeast Asian Nations—Malaysia, Indonesia, the Philippines, and Singapore. On June 30 he received an enthusiastic welcome in Peking, and an agreement establishing diplomatic relations with China was signed July 1. Relations with Thailand's immediate neighbours in Indochina were more troublesome. Delegations from North and South Vietnam came visiting, and Thailand was plainly eager to win their goodwill, but Hanoi's postwar political strength and plans for the future remained a source of some apprehension. The new regime in Cambodia was hostile to begin with. As streams of Cambodian refugees poured into Thailand, Bangkok was accused of espionage and sabotage activities in Cambodia. There were incidents of violence, including the capture by Cambodians of a 900-year-old temple on the border. By year's end, however, Cambodian Deputy Premier Ieng Sary had visited Bangkok and the two countries had agreed to establish formal relations. Tensions with Laos mounted steadily after the rightist Laotian leaders fled to Thailand. The Laotian border was closed November 18 after a two-day gunfight in which a Thai naval officer was killed, but on December 30 Thailand announced that Laos had promised not to shoot at Thai patrol boats in the Mekong and that the border would be reopened on New Year's Day.

Kukrit Pramoj presented a $3 billion national budget in October. It provided $900 million for defense and internal security, $350 million for health and education, and $300 million for ameliorative measures such as rural development and transport.

(T. J. S. GEORGE)

[976.B.3]

Theatre

Worldwide inflation continued to make inroads into theatre budgets. Despite this, however, several Eastern European countries continued policies that equated the public's need for theatre with its need to receive proper education and other social amenities at public expense. Thus, drama did not suffer unduly. In Western countries, on the other hand, particularly in those with a very young tradition of public subsidy, the reverse was true.

A typical example in Britain involved the Royal Shakespeare Company (RSC), which celebrated the centenary of the Stratford-upon-Avon Festival with a worldwide appeal for funds to prevent its premature demise. This was combined with a warning that its London home, the Aldwych Theatre, might have to close before the end of the year. Though the appeal spurred the government into action, the reprieve thus gained was only of a few months' duration, and the expected deficit of £200,000 for 1975–76 remained uncovered. A similar deficit was incurred at the Royal Opera House; it could have been made good by removal of the hampering value-added tax, but the state continued this levy.

Impediments to completing the new National Theatre complex in Britain were finally cleared away with a special government grant of £300,000. This would permit partial opening in March 1976, when the Old Vic Theatre, currently in use by the company, would be vacated. But a second request for £3 million by the Arts Council to meet unforeseen inflationary costs for all its clients was answered by a parliamentary vote for only £2 million. This seemed to ensure an early demise for some clients. It also appeared that the famous Old Vic Theatre would be "dark" for the foreseeable future for want of funding. Renée Short, chairman of the Theatres Advisory Council, indicated that the £50 million spent by Britain on all the arts was at least £150 million short of the realistic needs.

This bleak outlook was partly reflected in the U.S.,

CORINNE MC CARTHY—FINANCIAL TIMES

Hermione Gingold made her farewell performance in "A Little Night Music" at London's Adelphi Theatre in September.

KEYSTONE

Opening night of "The Rat-Catcher" by Carl Zuckmayer. Helmut Lohner appeared with Christine Hörbiger in the Zürich production.

where operating costs had virtually put an end to off-Broadway production, and a similar threat to all productions seemed likely to be averted only if union rules could be relaxed to that end. Two significant moves occurred in France and in Switzerland, each typifying by contrast the attitude toward the arts in these countries. The French government guaranteed an increase in overall subsidies of 25% per annum for the next three years, and in Switzerland 40% of the voters of Zürich favoured spending the equivalent of $6 a head on refurbishing their city theatre in 1976.

Great Britain and Ireland. The campaign for saving historic theatres threatened by property developers took the form of a concerted move by representatives of the theatrical professions. Led by numbers of leading players, the state was called upon to set up a Theatres' Trust, on the lines of the National Trust (for the protection of historic houses). Despite mounting costs, several new theatres opened both in the regions and in London, including the Greenwood, near London Bridge, one of the country's most hospitable and well-designed playhouses.

A direct outcome of financial problems was the change in repertorial policy at the RSC's Aldwych Theatre, where it was found advisable to put on plays for short runs of one month, thus robbing both public and actors of the artistic benefits of alternating repertory. This also affected the box office because the less popular plays had to play to half-empty houses, whereas smash hits such as Trevor Nunn's new production of *Hedda Gabler*, starring Glenda Jackson, could not satisfy the public demand for seats. Into the former category fell *Jingo*, Charles Wood's nostalgic new drama about the decline of British colonial attitudes, the first revival for half a century of Granville Barker's social comedy *The Marrying of Ann Leete*, and John Barton's well-judged *King John*. In the latter, smash-hit category were Shaw's *Too True to Be Good*, which earned a transfer to a West End commercial theatre, the witty version of *Love's Labour's Lost*, starring Ian Richardson (after its New York tryout), Peter Gill's first RSC production, *Twelfth Night*, with Nicol Williamson as Malvolio, Trevor Nunn's intermissionless 110-minute-long *Macbeth*, with Williamson and Helen Mirren, and Graham Greene's first play in 12 years, the cynical pastiche-Edwardian comedy, *The Return of A. J. Raffles*, based on the gentleman-burglar of the famous E. W. Hornung novels.

At the Old Vic the National, too, had its ups and downs. Among the latter were *Engaged* by W. S. Gilbert, of Gilbert and Sullivan fame, nicely staged and played but of little import, and an imposing Peter Hall production of Ibsen's *John Gabriel Borkman*, which Peggy Ashcroft's distinctive performance failed to save. On the credit side were an unusual number of well-knit performances, including those by Anna Massey in John Schlesinger's compelling production of Shaw's *Heartbreak House*, Diana Rigg in Tony Harrison's updated version of *Phèdre*, transposed to 19th-century British India and retitled *Phaedra Britannica*, Stephen Rea in Bill Bryden's realistic production of Synge's *Playboy of the Western World*, Jonathan Pryce in Trevor Griffiths' drama of the dying music-hall tradition, *Comedians* (transferred in toto from the Nottingham Playhouse), Albert Finney in Hall's four-hour-long uncut version of *Hamlet*, set in John Bury's single austere set, and, in the same couple's claustrophobic staging of Harold Pinter's most recent comedy of equivocation, *No Man's Land*, two unparalleled comic performances by Ralph Richardson and John Gielgud. The last-named play subsequently packed a West End theatre nightly for months on end.

A new production of *Othello*, which had toured South America before being seen in London, was among the attractions at the Young Vic, whose revival of Stoppard's *Rosencrantz and Guildenstern Are Dead* also achieved a long West End run. The Royal Court Theatre, compelled to shut down its studio stage (the Theatre Upstairs) as an economy measure, enjoyed an unusually successful season on the large stage that began with David Williamson's outspoken drama of an Australian election, *Don's Party*, directed by Michael Blakemore (of the National), included a season of three Joe Orton comedies (two of which had a West End transfer), Caryl Churchill's feminist *Objections to Sex and Violence*, starring Rosemary McHale, and, after Peter Gill had taken over the theatre's management, ended with Howard Barker's antiestablishment drama *Stripwell*, David Hare's story of a pop group's collapse called *Teeth 'n' Smiles*, with Helen Mirren, and Edward Bond's tragic parable of the artist spurned by society, entitled *The Fool*, with Tom Courtenay as the mad 19th-century poet John Clare.

Outstanding successes at the remaining subsidized theatres were few and far between. At the Greenwich Theatre, only the second of two John Osborne plays, *The Picture of Dorian Gray*, based on the Wilde novel, had real merit; audiences compared this with the first of two Noel Coward revivals, *The Vortex*, which had anticipated Osborne's early manner by 30 years. Jonathan Miller's revival of Wilde's *The Importance of Being Earnest* featured a Lady Bracknell with a strong German accent. Of two interesting novelties at the Hampstead Theatre, Brecht's *The Good Woman of Setzuan* was an import from Wales, and Michael Frayn's popular comedy of life in a provincial newspaper office, *Alphabetical Order*, was later transferred to the West End. Two plays by Shaw, *The Doctor's Dilemma*, starring Kenneth Cranham, and *On the Rocks*, with Stephen Murray as the Liberal prime minister who discovers Karl Marx, enlivened the fare at the Mermaid. Joan Littlewood's Theatre Workshop company suffered the death of her partner and fellow manager, Gerry Raffles, but recovered enough, under his successor (Maxwell Shaw), to inaugurate a new and popular season, with Miss Littlewood pulling strings behind the scenes, that included a Dickensian musical called *Nickleby and Me.* Of several go-ahead productions at Charles Marowitz' Open Space the most challenging was his own *Artaud at Rodez,* which was premiered in Rome on a prior-to-London tour.

The Actors Company returned to London with a season of four plays in alternating repertory at the Wimbledon Theatre, an example followed by Prospect Theatre Company with *A Month in the Country* (the Chichester Festival production) and their own adaptation of E. M. Forster's *A Room with a View,* both featuring Jane Lapotaire. Another commercial repertory season, launched by the firm of H. M. Tennant at the Lyric Theatre, was headed by Helen Mirren and Joan Plowright, each actress, alongside a distinguished crew, winning fresh laurels in *The Seagull* and the world premiere of *The Bed Before Yesterday,* the 89-year-old Ben Travers' sex comedy, set in the 1930s but written with all the freedom of the 1970s.

Highlights in the purely commercial sector, unusually fertile despite the managerial cries of "woe," ranged from the macabre thriller *Murderer* by Anthony Shaffer, starring Robert Stephens, to Ronald Millar's deft stage version of C. P. Snow's novel *The Case in Question,* with John Clements, and also included memorable performances by Alec Guinness in Julian Mitchell's stage version of Ivy Compton-Burnett's *A Family and a Fortune,* Richard Briers in Alan Ayckbourn's sour comedy of family hatreds, *Absent Friends,* Alan Bates as a cynical loner in Simon Gray's *Otherwise Engaged* (skillfully directed by Harold Pinter), Paul Scofield in the Leeds Playhouse production of *The Tempest,* Barbara Mullen in a revival of the stage version of Agatha Christie's *Murder at the Vicarage,* Edward Woodward in Frederick Lonsdale's *On Approval,* and Hermione Gingold in *A Little Night Music,* this being one of the few musicals, either American or British, to make the grade. The others to stay the course were two black South African musical shows, *Ipi Tombi* and *Kwa Zulu,* an all-black (bar Michael Denison as Pooh-Bah) *The Black Mikado,* in which Sullivan's music got the Caribbean treatment, and two nostalgic reminders of wartime bravado, *Happy as a Sandbag* and *Dad's Army.*

American contributions to the London stage included *The Sunshine Boys, Kennedy's Children* by Robert Patrick, the first "fringe" production to make the West End, *Harvey* with James Stewart, *Clarence Darrow* with Henry Fonda, *Lenny* with Marty Brill, and *The Charles Pierce Show,* in which the drag comedian came close to outshining the native transvestite of the species, Danny La Rue in his latest extravaganza called *Queen Daniella.* There were a number of Brecht productions of varying merit. Other impressive foreign imports included several plays by Franz Xaver Kroetz, two by Arrabal, a bowdlerized Strindberg, a comedy called *Roger's Last Stand,* starring Roy Kinnear, which hailed from The Netherlands (under another title), and, equally hard to identify, C. P. Taylor's *The Plumber's Progress,* starring Harry Secombe, which began life as Carl Sternheim's *Burger Schippel* and found its way to the West End via the Edinburgh Traverse and the London "fringe." Probably the hardest hit in London were the little fringe theatres operating on a shoestring or as lunchtime venues. Nevertheless, they doggedly continued staging all sorts of drama, from two plays about modern dropouts at the Bush by Stephen Poliakoff (who later became resident National Theatre dramatist) to two plays of strong socialist propaganda content by John McGrath at the Half Moon and at the Shaw, several by Richard Crane (sometime resident National Theatre dramatist) in various fringe theatres, as well as a children's musical by him which transferred from the Arts, home of the Unicorn Children's Company, to the Round House, and, at the Terrace Theatre, David Hare's semidocumentary of the Chinese Revolution, *Fanshen,* and the Pip Simmons anti-Nazi *An die Musik,* which premiered in The Netherlands.

The last World Theatre Season, the 11th, followed soon after by the untimely death of Sir Peter Daubeny (*see* OBITUARIES), its creator and artistic director, included productions from four countries: the Göteborg Stadsteater presented Strindberg's *Gustav III;* the Krakow Stary Theatre rendered Andrzej Wajda's production of Stanislaw Wyspianski's *November Night* and, performed in Southwark Cathedral, the ritualistic *Forefathers' Eve* by Adam Mickiewicz, staged by Konrad Swinarski; Edmo Fenoglio's Italian productions of Italo Svevo's *Regeneration* and Ibsen's *An Enemy of the People* constituted the third; and the Ugandan Abafumi Company, from Kampala, presented *Renga Moi,* written and staged by Robert Serumaga.

In Eire the Dublin Theatre Festival offered the largest selection ever, although its director, Brendan Smith, feared that it might well be the last. The Abbey Theatre, which had earlier staged the Irish premiere of O'Casey's *Purple Dust* and Brian Friel's symbolic drama about a group of political prisoners, *Volunteers,* put on two world premieres: *The Sanctuary Lamp,* a controversial religious drama by Tom Murphy that sent some spectators out midway, about the church's failure to provide for the more wayward of its flock; and *Innish,* a musical version by Fergus Linehan of Lennox Robinson's *Drama at Innish.* Elsewhere, two interesting novelties were the European premiere of Hugh Leonard's one-act trilogy *Irishmen,* and *Spokesong,* a musical play by the Ulsterman Stewart Parker, about the "troubles" as seen through the eyes of a couple who run a bicycle shop.

AGIP/PICTORIAL PARADE

Marcel Marceau, world-famous mime, portrayed a samurai at the Champs Elysées Theatre in Paris.

France. The year began excitingly with a carry-over from the 1974 Paris Autumn Festival, Peter Brook's production of *The Ik,* adapted by Jean-Claude Carrière, Colin Higgins, and Denis Cannan from Colin Turnbull's study of the decline of an African tribe (*The Mountain People*) set in arena form in the Bouffes du Nord. The 1975 festival offerings included a new play by Kateb Yacine about the Algerian independence struggle (*The 2,000 Years' War*), in Arabic, three co-productions with the 1975 Brussels Europalia Festival (devoted this year to France), and several international events such as the appearance of New York's La Mama Company in Andrei Serban's adaptation of three classic Greek plays, Luca Ronconi's Aristophanes collation *Utopia,* and the Milan Piccolo's *Il Campiello,* staged by Georgio Strehler.

In December the Comédie Française's incomparable actor and director, Jacques Charon, died in harness, just as his model, Molière, had done three centuries before him. His production of a Labiche comedy was a fitting memorial to his passing. Two new directors making guest appearances there were Antoine Vitez, with the lovely Ludmila Mikael breaking all hearts as Ysé in his revival of Claudel's *Break of Noon,* and Henri Ronsse, with a spectacular version of Strindberg's *Ghost Sonata* at the Odéon, where Jean-Claude Grumberg's satire on 19th-century mores, *At the Exhibition,* was also much admired. Both Jean Mercure at the Théâtre de la Ville and Jean-Louis Berrault at his Théâtre d'Orsay relied strongly on revivals, though the latter also ventured into original adaptations of Nietzsche's *Thus Spake Zarathustra* and Restif de la Bretonne's *Paris Nights.* Guy Retoré staged O'Casey's *Cock-a-Doodle-Dandy* and Georges Wilson transferred *Othello* from the Avignon Festival, both at the Théâtre de l'Est Parisien. Ariane Mnouchkine's Théâtre du Soleil's latest collective effort was a searingly poetic, circuslike indictment of the acquisitive society entitled *The Golden Age,* which later went to the Warsaw Festival.

New works included *The Scales,* a first play by Claude Reichmann, about a Box and Cox situation, René de Obaldia's *M. Krebs and Rosalie,* about a latter-day Pygmalion, Françoise Dorin's new comedy of manners, *The Other Waltz,* the latest commercial hit by Barillet and Grédy, called *Peau de Vache,* about a thick-skinned bully of a wife, a first play by François-Marie Bernier, *Hotel du Lac,* about an aging actress and her young lover, and one each from Anouilh, Ionesco, and Arrabal. Three interesting imports were *Ah Q,* based on Lou Sin's novel about the poverty-stricken Chinese countryside of 1911, Kuan Han Chin's musical play *The Riverside Pavilion* (from the Avignon Festival), and Pierre Daninos' adaptation of *The Black Mikado.*

MARTHA SWOPE

"The Wiz," an all-black version of "The Wizard of Oz," was well received on Broadway.

Switzerland, Germany, Austria, The Netherlands. The new Basel Stadttheater was inaugurated with a mammoth three-day-long program, staged by its manager, Hans Hollmann, with something for all tastes. One novelty was the world premiere of Brecht's early one-act play *He's Driving Out the Devil.* The Zürich Schauspielhaus, due for a face-lift, housed Carl Zuckmayer's new epic drama, *The Rat-Catcher,* based on the Pied Piper legend, with music by Gottfried von Einem, and revealing the author's belated conversion to the Brechtian epic manner and to the world outlook of the rebellious young. At the Neumarkt, the retiring manager Horst Zankl's swan song was a vivid realization of the Russian anti-imperialist agitprop drama of the 1920s, *Roar China!* by Sergey Tretyakov, staged with a French-speaking Genevan troupe.

In West Berlin two productions above all fired the public imagination: Tankred Dorst's parabolic *On Mount Chimborazo,* in which a group of West Germans vainly try to lighten the hearts of their Eastern counterparts by lighting a symbolic beacon on a border mountaintop; and Samuel Beckett's own austere production of *Waiting for Godot.* At the Berliner Ensemble across the frontier the talking point was Strindberg's *Miss Julie,* translated by Peter Weiss and staged by B. K. Tragelehn and Einar Schleef as a modern commedia dell'arte tragicomedy with strong sexual overtones and a happy ending. It displeased the authorities and was quickly closed. Among several classical revivals at the Volksbühne was Benno Besson's colourful one of *As You Like It,* newly translated by Heiner Müller.

In West Germany the season was marked by an unprecedentedly large number of new works by native and other writers, pride of place among them going to Peter Weiss's politically slanted stage version of Kafka's *The Trial,* world-premiered simultaneously in Bremen and Krefeld. Georg Tabori's psychodrama *Sigmunds Freude,* or "Sigmund's Joy," in Bremen was a collective effort to dramatize Fritz Perls' Gestalt-therapy theories. Martin Walser had a new play, *Das Sauspiel* ("Sow's Play"), about the suppression of the 16th-century Nürnberg peasant uprising, in Hamburg, with Mikis Theodorakis' music, while his translation of Mark Medoff's *When You Comin' Back, Red Ryder?* was premiered in Frankfurt. Here, too, Luc Bondy fulfilled earlier directorial promise with a sumptuous production of Marivaux's *La double inconstance,* about the fickleness of aristocratic passions. Also in Hamburg, Rudolf Noelte scored twice with Molière's *Le Misanthrope* and O'Neill's *Long Day's Journey into Night,* each starring Will Quadflieg, and Peter Zadek, on loan from Bochum, once with Ibsen's *The Wild Duck.* The Molière and the Ibsen proved to be the highlights of the 1975 Berlin Theatre Festival. Other notable new plays were *Familiar Faces, Mixed Feelings,* by Botho Strauss, a black comedy in a hotel setting, in Stuttgart, and *The Battle,* an anti-Nazi wartime drama by the East German Heiner Müller, in Essen, where *Carnival Monday,* about the drudgery of work, by Karl Otto Mühl had its world premiere. Ernst Wendt, who gave up the Berlin Schiller Theatre's literary department for directing, staged Thomas

ÉVA KELETI—KEYSTONE

"Return of Odysseus," a Monteverdi opera presented by the Hungarian State Opera Company, starred Maria Sudlik as Penelope.

Bernhard's *The President*, about the nature of tyranny, at the Vienna Burgtheater, where no less stimulating were Gerhard Klingenberg's production of *Richard II*, starring Michael Heltau, and Georgio Strehler's of *Henry VI*, retitled *The Game of the Mighty*, with Andrea Jonasson as the Queen.

The Belgian National Theatre celebrated its 30th anniversary with a splendid revival of *Le Malade Imaginaire* with André Debaar directing and playing the lead. The highlights of the Europalia Festival were Michel Legrand's musical of *Monte Cristo*, Philippe Adrien's *De Sade and the 18th Century*, and the latest offering of the Paris-based TSE company, all Franco-Belgian co-productions and later restaged in Paris.

Italy. Giorgio De Lullo, co-founder of the defunct Compagnia dei Giovani, teamed up with Romolo Valli once more to stage Pirandello's *All for the Best* in Pier Luigi Pizzi's decor, in Rome, where Franco Zeffirelli revived d'Annunzio's *Dead City*, with Sarah Ferrati. In Turin Aldo Trionfo staged Carl Dreyer's unrealized film of *Jesus* as a play, and in Genoa Luigi Squarzina put on Tullio Kezich's adaptation of a Pirandello novel (*The Late Matthew Pascal*) with Giorgio Albertazzi in the lead. An interesting feature of a revival of *Our Town* in Milan by a new actors' cooperative was the interpolation of songs from *Spoon River Anthology*. Georgio Strehler's latest Pirandello, *Il Campiello* (*The Little Town Square*), delighted audiences in Warsaw, Berlin, and Paris as much as in Milan's Piccolo Theatre.

Eastern Europe. Two plays by Rustam Ibrahimbekov, the antibureaucratic *Unpublished Report* at the Mayakovsky and *With the Looks of a Lion*, a farcical family melodrama, at the Moscow Art, ushered in a new wave of non-Russian dramatists. Also at the Moscow Art, Mikhail Roshchin's *Special Train*, staged by guest director Anatoli Efros, was one of several devoted to wartime themes in commemoration of the 30th anniversary of the victory over Fascism. A parallel production of the same play was put on by Galina Volchyok at the Contemporary. Two other novel events occurred during the season: Peter James directed *Twelfth Night* at the Contemporary, in the first English guest appearance since Gordon Craig staged *Hamlet* in 1911; and the first Brecht play was performed at the Moscow Art when Vladimir Bogomolov directed *Galileo Galilei*, starring guest artist Andrey Popov. Yury Liubimov's *Fasten Your Seat-Belts* at the Taganka was yet another wartime drama. At Efros' own theatre, Leonid Zorin's elegiac comedy *The Pokrovsky Gate* and Gogol's *The Marriage* were the main draws.

In Warsaw, at the rebuilt Popular Theatre on the right bank, reopened on the 30th anniversary of the city's liberation, Andrzej Wajda staged in the round Stanislawa Przybyszewska's prewar *The Danton Affair*. Warsaw's latest playhouse, owned by Polish TV, the Kwadrat, opened with Thurber's *The Male Animal*, staged by Edward Dziewonski. At the National Adam Hanuszkewicz put on (for the third time in his career) Wyspianski's *The Wedding* with some amusing anachronisms, and at its Small Theatre, the scandalizing theme of Rozewicz' *White Marriage*, how fin de siècle adolescent girls learn what rogues the opposite sex can be, was equally provocative in its frank use of language. Provocative in quite a different way was Slawomir Mrozek's *The Slaughterhouse*, about the debasement of culture in present-day society, an original radio-play spectacularly adapted and mounted by Jerzy Jarocki at the Dramatic. The first season of the reorganized peripatetic Theatre of the Nations brought countless visitors to the capital for four weeks to see performances of more than 20 plays by companies from 17 countries.

Roger Planchon's *Tartuffe*, Peter Stein's *The Summer Guests*, and Andrei Serban's La Mama Company shared the top honours at the annual "bitef" festival in Belgrade, with Philip Prowse's production of Webster's *The Duchess of Malfi*, with the Glasgow Citizens' Theatre, the runner-up. At the Bucharest National the outstanding new play was Mihnea Gheorghiu's *The Zodiac Bull*, and at the Small Theatre Marin Sorescu's poetic drama of *The River Bed*, inspired by the catastrophic flooding of the Danube, impressed enough to earn a trip to the Warsaw Festival. Lucian Pintilie returned from the West to stage *The Seagull* at the Bulandra City Theatre, where Liviu Ciulei was once again much in evidence as director and designer with Gorky's *The Lower Depths*, Paul Foster's *Elizabeth I*, and a play about Dracula.

Ellen Burstyn and Charles Grodin starred in Bernard Slade's widely acclaimed comedy about love and adultery, "Same Time, Next Year."

MARTHA SWOPE

Scandinavia. Ingmar Bergman's *Twelfth Night* at Stockholm's Dramatic Theatre was acted as a play within a play in an Elizabethan setting designed by Gunilla Palmstjerna-Wéiss. It, too, like the previous year's Göteborg production of *Gustav III*, visited Warsaw, among other festivals. Of special interest at the Dramatic were Alf Sjöberg's productions of *Antony and Cleopatra* and *The Playboy of the Western World*, Lars Göran Carlsson's of Strindberg's historical *The Folkung Saga*, and a first play by Per Olov Enquist, the pseudo-biographical *A Sapphic Night*, showing Strindberg being torn apart by two rival lesbians. Norwegian star Liv Ullmann made her Swedish stage debut in *Pygmalion*. Lennart Hjulström followed up his Strindberg historical series with a telling performance of *Gustav Vasa* in Göteborg, where Sven Wollter made his directing debut with Yasar Kemal's *The Drums*, set in Anatolia, and Kent Andersson played in his own partly autobiographical *The Hole*. The National Theatre in Oslo put on a new *Peer Gynt*, with three actors dividing the title role between them as the young, middle-aged, and old Gynt. Rozewicz' *White Marriage* in Danish astonishingly succeeded in shocking the usually unshockable Danes at the Copenhagen Royal Theatre. In Finland interest was divided between Helsinki and Turku: in the former the main events included Eugen Terttula's striking production of Dürrenmatt's *King John* at the National and Paavo Liski's of Lauri Leskinen's biographical drama *Minna*, about the Finnish 19th-century feminist writer Minna Canth, at the City Theatre; in the latter they were Ritva Holmberg's stage version of the Topelius classic *Tales of an Army Surgeon* and the world premiere of *Juan Palmieri*, a drama of the Tupamaro struggle by the dissident Uruguayan Antonio Larreta. A curious feature of Vili Auvinen's adaptation in Tampere of David Storey's football drama, *The Changing Room*, to local conditions was the presence of three real-life footballers in the cast.

(OSSIA TRILLING)

U.S. and Canada. The most surprising development in U.S. theatre during 1975 was that the Broadway season of 1974–75, in spite of the nation's economic difficulties, was by general agreement the best in recent years. It may not have been overwhelmingly distinguished artistically, but there were more hits than usual, more sold-out performances, greater attendance, and a general air of liveliness.

The year's most outstanding success, winner of the New York Drama Critics' Circle Award as best musical, was *A Chorus Line*, which dealt poignantly and powerfully with the lives and hopes and disappointments of a group of dancers auditioning for a Broadway show. *A Chorus Line* was based on a book by James Kirkwood and Nicholas Dante, with music by Marvin Hamlisch and lyrics by Edward Kleban. The true creator of the play, however, was director-choreographer Michael Bennett, who began by bringing a group of Broadway dancers together and encouraging them to talk about themselves; the show evolved from these sessions. *A Chorus Line* opened off-Broadway at Joseph Papp's Public Theatre and soon transferred to Broadway.

"A Chorus Line" portrayed the hopes and dreams of dancers who back up the stars and must train like Olympic athletes for the few jobs available.

MARTHA SWOPE

Other 1975 musicals were *The Wiz*—a very popular all-black soul-music version of *The Wizard of Oz*—which won the American Theatre Wing's Tony Award for best musical; *Shenandoah*, a sentimental, Rodgers-and-Hammersteinish affair about a pacifist Virginia farmer during the Civil War; and *Chicago*, a hard-edged, razzle-dazzle show, staged by Bob Fosse and starring Gwen Verdon and Chita Rivera as a couple of 1920s murderesses.

Musicals aside, Broadway was largely dominated, as usual, by British imports. The 1975 Tony and Drama Critics' Circle awards for best play went to *Equus* by Peter Shaffer, which came to Broadway late in 1974 in a production from the National Theatre of Great Britain. There were also glamorous British revivals on Broadway of *Private Lives* by Noel Coward, with Maggie Smith, and *The Misanthrope* by Molière, in an updated version by the British poet Tony Harrison, with Alec McCowen and Diana Rigg. And in the fall of 1975 there was an invasion of British comedies: *Travesties* by Tom Stoppard (with a virtuoso performance by the British actor John Wood; *see* BIOGRAPHY), *Habeas Corpus* by Alan Bennett, and *The Norman Conquests*, a trilogy of interrelated farces by Alan Ayckbourn.

Several American light comedies had substantial Broadway runs. The most successful was *Same Time, Next Year* by Bernard Slade; it dealt with a man and a woman who steal away from their respective spouses for a weekend together once a year, and Ellen Burstyn (*see* BIOGRAPHY) and Charles Grodin constituted its entire cast. *All over Town* by Murray Schisgal was directed by Dustin Hoffman and starred Cleavon Little; *The Ritz* by Terrence McNally, set in a homosexual bathhouse, featured a much admired performance by Rita Moreno.

The Circle in the Square presented two distinguished revivals of American plays on Broadway during 1975. George C. Scott scored a personal triumph as Willy Loman in Arthur Miller's *Death of a Salesman*, and an attractive production of *Ah, Wilderness!* Eugene O'Neill's only comedy, was brought in from the Long Wharf Theatre in New Haven. *Seascape* by Edward Albee, produced on Broadway with Deborah Kerr, Barry Nelson, and Frank Langella in the cast, about a pair of humans and a pair of talking lizards, received the 1975 Pulitzer Prize for drama. *The Red Devil Battery Sign* by Tennessee Williams, starring Anthony Quinn and Claire Bloom, closed in Boston on its way to Broadway. Among the younger dramatists produced in noncommercial theatres, there was a new play by Michael Weller entitled *Fishing*, which marked no advance over his previous work, and an opaque double bill by Sam Shepard, *Killer's Head* and *Action*. The Critics' Circle Award for best American play went to Ed Bullins for *The Taking of Miss Janie*, a chronicle of interracial sexual relationships during the 1960s; it was produced originally at the New Federal Theatre off-Broadway and then moved to Joseph Papp's small Newhouse Theatre in Lincoln Center. Another play about the blasted hopes of the '60s was *Kennedy's Children*, which finally came to Broadway in the fall after having been seen off-off-Broadway, in London, on the continent, and in Canada. Clearly, Broadway lost its primacy as a source of serious American drama during 1975.

It was not a good year for Joseph Papp, the dynamic entrepreneur of the New York Shakespeare Festival, in spite of the success of *A Chorus Line*, which he produced. At the Vivian Beaumont Theater in Lincoln Center, which he controls, there were sold-out houses to see Liv Ullmann in Ibsen's *A Doll's House,* but the new American plays he presented at the Beaumont were generally denounced in the press and avoided by the public. With the end of the 1974–75 season, therefore, Papp dropped his cherished policy of new American plays at the Beaumont and began a season of classical revivals there in the fall of 1975 with an indifferent revival of *Trelawney of the "Wells"* by Arthur Wing Pinero. Meanwhile, he had announced an ambitious season of five new American plays at the Booth Theatre on Broadway for 1975–76, but when the first of them, *The Leaf People* by Dennis Reardon, proved an expensive disaster, the rest of the Booth season was canceled.

Among the avant-garde, the long, slow, strange, indescribable works of Robert Wilson won a great deal of attention—notably *A Letter for Queen Victoria,* which had a brief Broadway engagement. A program of short works by Samuel Beckett, presented by a group called Mabou Mines, was favourably received. But *A Fable,* written by Jean-Claude van Itallie, directed by Joseph Chaikin, with music by Richard Peaslee—all stalwarts of the now-defunct Open Theatre—was considered a disappointment.

There were two significant labour disputes in the New York theatre during 1975. In August, Actors Equity, the stage performers' union, instituted a new "Showcase Code" ("showcase" being Equity's term for off-off-Broadway), outlining conditions under which Equity members would be allowed to appear for no pay in "showcase" productions. The new code demanded payment of carfare to actors and demanded also that if a play went on from a showcase production to commercial success, a share of the profits in perpetuity be assigned to the original showcase actors. The off-off-Broadway producers insisted that these provisions would force them either to operate without Equity actors or to go out of business, and the new code was repealed by a vote of Equity's members—indicating that even in a season of relative prosperity professional actors felt that the right to work unpaid was too precious to jeopardize.

Then, on September 18, all Broadway musicals were closed when their orchestras went on strike. The main issues between the musicians' union and the producers were wages, reduction of the workweek, and the question of "walkers," musicians who were paid for doing no work. The producers demanded the abolition of "walkers"; the union refused. Public opinion was against the strikers, but when the strike was settled on October 12, the new contract included retention of "walkers"—with, however, a reduction in the minimum number of required musicians—for the next six years.

Outside New York there were births and deaths of theatres, with the former gratifyingly outnumbering the latter. The Rochester Shakespeare Theatre (Rochester, N.Y.) went out of business at the end of 1974. But in 1975 the Cohoes Music Hall (Cohoes, N.Y.), Pittsburgh Public Theatre, and the Hartman Theatre Company (Stamford, Conn.) began operations. Center Stage in Baltimore resumed operations in a new theatre after a year's hiatus, the Seattle Repertory Theatre inaugurated a new second theatre for experimental work, and the Tyrone Guthrie Theatre in Minneapolis, Minn., announced that its second house would open in January 1976.

The bicentennial stimulated a tendency to revive American plays, bringing new popularity to *Seven Keys to Baldpate* by George M. Cohan and *Once in a Lifetime* by George S. Kaufman and Moss Hart. The American Bicentennial Theater, a project of the Kennedy Center for the Performing Arts, financed by the Xerox Corp., presented a series of eight star-cast revivals in Washington, D.C., and sent them on tour; they included *The Skin of Our Teeth* by Thornton Wilder (*see* OBITUARIES), *The Scarecrow* by Percy MacKaye, *Bus Stop* by William Inge, *Sweet Bird of Youth* by Tennessee Williams, *The Royal Family* by George S. Kaufman and Edna Ferber, and *Long Day's Journey into Night* by Eugene O'Neill.

But it is now standard practice, as it was not a few years ago, for regional theatres to include one or more new American or foreign plays in their regular subscription seasons. Among the American plays that had world premieres in regional theatres during 1975 were *You're Too Tall, But Come Back in Two Weeks* by Richard Venture (Long Wharf Theatre, New Haven, Conn.), *Continental Divide* by Oliver Hailey (Berkeley Repertory Theatre, Berkeley, Calif.), *Afternoon Tea* by Harvey Perr (Hartford Stage Company, Hartford, Conn.), *The Shaft of Love* by Charles Dizenzo (Yale Repertory Theatre, New Haven, Conn.), and *Cathedral of Ice* by James Schevill (Trinity Square Repertory Company, Providence, R.I.). *The Robber Bridegroom,* a musical with book and lyrics by Alfred Uhry and music by Robert Waldman, based on a novella by Eudora Welty, was produced by the Acting Company, which toured the U.S. with the play.

Among the British plays introduced to America in regional theatres during 1975 were *Afore Night Come,* David Rudkin's grim play of ritual murder, at the Long Wharf Theatre in New Haven, and *Bingo,* Edward Bond's play about the last days of William Shakespeare, at the Cleveland Play House. The Arena Stage in Washington, D.C., gave the American premiere of a new Soviet play about the legacy of Stalinist terror, *The Ascent of Mount Fuji* by Chingiz Aitmatov and Kaltay Mukhamedzhanov.

In Canada it was British director Robin Phillips' first season as artistic director of the Stratford Festival. The success of several Festival productions —notably *Measure for Measure,* directed by Phillips, with Brian Bedford, Martha Henry, and William Hutt in the cast—went far toward defusing the controversy that had surrounded his appointment.

The network of small "alternative theatres" continued to grow. During the 1974–75 season, theatres closed in Halifax, Nova Scotia, and Victoria, B.C., but others opened in Newfoundland, Montreal, Toronto, Saskatoon, and Victoria. Among these were three new feminist theatres, two in Toronto and one in Montreal, and two new black theatres, both in Toronto.

On the other hand, there were no new Canadian plays of any particular significance. One event that some observers saw as symbolic was the closing for a year of the Tarragon Theatre in Toronto, known for its productions of plays by leading contemporary Canadian playwrights. It was suggested that the closing of the Tarragon represented the end or slowing of the burst of energy that had produced a new, native Canadian dramatic movement. (JULIUS NOVICK)

See also Dance; Literature; Music.

[622]

ENCYCLOPÆDIA BRITANNICA FILMS. *Shaw vs. Shakespeare —Part I: The Character of Caesar, Part II: The Tragedy of Julius Caesar, Part III: Caesar and Cleopatra* (1970); *Medieval Theater: The Play of Abraham and Isaac* (1974).

Theology:
see Religion

Timber:
see Industrial Review

Tin:
see Mining and Quarrying

Titanium:
see Mining and Quarrying

Tobacco:
see Drug Abuse; Industrial Review

Tobogganing:
see Winter Sports

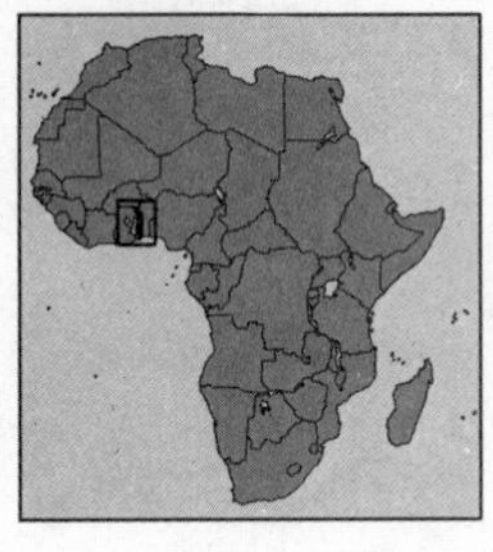

Togo

A West African republic, Togo is bordered by Ghana, Upper Volta, and Dahomey (Benin). Area: 21,925 sq.mi. (56,785 sq.km.). Pop. (1975 est.): 2,197,900. Cap. and largest city: Lomé (pop., 1975 est., 214,200). Language: French (official). Religion: animist; Muslim and Christian minorities. President in 1975, Gen. Gnassingbe Eyadema.

In January 1975 President Eyadema announced a general increase of salaries. Despite a sharp drop in phosphate exports (1.5 million metric tons estimated for 1975, as against 2.5 million metric tons in 1974), Togo's budget receipts were satisfactory because the price of phosphates had risen steeply.

Cooperation between Togo and France became closer, particularly in the military sphere. Pierre Abelin, French minister of cooperation, was an official guest of Togo in February, and Eyadema visited France privately in September. The French government undertook to provide Togo with the pilots and technical staff needed to maintain the squadron of five Fouga Magister aircraft ordered in France, as well as for two coastal patrol vessels under construction in French naval shipyards.

Relations with Ghana deteriorated as a result of the activities of militants of the National Liberation Movement of Western Togoland, who demanded the cession of former British Togoland from Ghana and its reunification with Togo.

Although 80% of the population was engaged in agriculture, they produced only enough food for local needs. Development plans included extension of palm plantations, cotton planting (20,000 tons forecast for 1975, as compared with 12,000 tons in 1974), fruit growing, stock breeding (most meat was still imported), fishing, and plans for tourist centres.

(PHILIPPE DECRAENE)

[978.E.4.b.ii]

TOGO

Education. (1974–75) Primary, pupils 329,443, teachers 5,627; secondary, pupils 44,306, teachers 1,111; vocational, pupils 4,497, teachers 336; teacher training, students 198, teachers 57; higher, students 1,619, teaching staff 243.

Finance. Monetary unit: CFA franc, with (Sept. 22, 1975) a parity of CFA Fr. 50 to the French franc (free rate of CFA Fr. 227.70 to U.S. $1; CFA Fr. 471.75 = £1 sterling). Budget (1974 est.) balanced at CFA Fr. 16,245,000,000.

Foreign Trade. (1974) Imports CFA Fr. 28,612,000,000; exports CFA Fr. 45,174,000,000. Import sources (1973): France 38%; West Germany 10%; U.K. 7%; The Netherlands 7%. Export destinations (1973): The Netherlands 36%; France 31%; West Germany 12%; Belgium-Luxembourg 5%. Main exports (1973): phosphates 46%; cocoa 26%; coffee 14%.

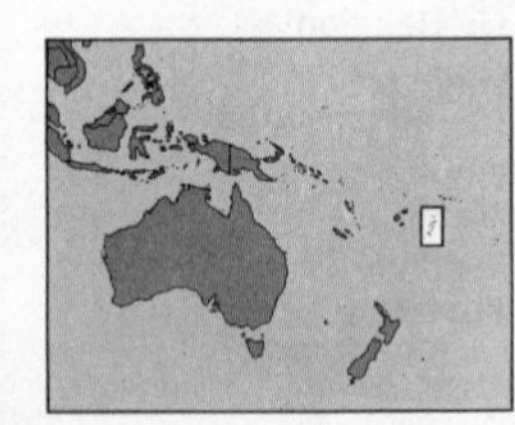

Tonga

An independent monarchy and member of the Commonwealth of Nations, Tonga is an island group in the Pacific Ocean east of Fiji. Area: 225 sq.mi. (583 sq.km.). Pop. (1975 est.): 101,000. Cap.: Nukualofa (pop., 1974 est., 25,000). Language: English and Tongan. Religion: Christian. King, Taufa'ahau Tupou IV; prime minister in 1975, Prince Tu'ipelehake.

Prices for coconut products, Tonga's major source of overseas earnings, fell in 1975, while the cost of imports, particularly foodstuffs and oil products, continued to rise. Many Tongans sought a cash income through short-term migration to New Zealand. The difficulties associated with this migration were reviewed by both governments, and henceforth the Tongan government would act as the sole recruiting agent for prearranged employment for periods of up to six months. The Bank of Tonga, jointly owned by the Tongan government and three banks with established interests in the Pacific, attracted 5 million pa'angas in 20,000 deposits (representing one-fifth of the population) in its first six months of operation. It would invest its funds in local development projects.

In July Tonga was host to the South Pacific Forum, where the idea of a nuclear-free Pacific was endorsed. Further steps were taken to establish a regional shipping line, and Tonga, despite substantial losses on its existing fleet, was attempting to purchase a bulk carrier for charter work. Tonga planned to engage in a search of the seabed of the Tonga Platform to establish whether manganese nodules or phosphoric deposits existed in commercial quantities. The search for oil continued.

(BARRIE MACDONALD)

[977.A.3]

TONGA

Education. (1971) Primary, pupils 16,416, teachers 648; secondary, pupils 10,164, teachers 503; vocational, pupils 199; teacher training, students 92, teachers 12.

Finance and Trade. Monetary unit: pa'anga (dollar), with a free rate (Sept. 22, 1975) of 0.76 pa'anga to U.S. $1 (1.58 pa'anga = £1 sterling). Budget (1974–75 est.): revenue 4,197,000 pa'angas; expenditure 4,602,000 pa'angas. Foreign trade (1974): imports 11,819,000 pa'angas; exports 4,561,000 pa'angas. Import sources: New Zealand 39%; Fiji 24%; Australia 22%. Export destinations: The Netherlands 40%; Australia 29%; New Zealand 22%; Fiji 6%. Main exports: copra 70%; desiccated coconut 9%; bananas 8%.

Track and Field Sports

It took mankind 21 years to improve by 10 seconds at running one mile. John Walker (*see* BIOGRAPHY), a rugged, blond, 23-year-old New Zealander, became the first man to run the distance in less than 3 min. 50.0 sec. when he sped around four laps of a track in Göteborg, Sweden, on Aug. 12, 1975, in 3 min. 49.4 sec., a time exactly 10 seconds faster than Roger Bannister's historic 3 min. 59.4 sec. mark of May 1954. Walker covered the first lap in 55.8 sec. and reached the halfway mark in 1 min. 55.1 sec. His third lap was 57.9 sec. (2 min. 53.0 sec. at 1,320 yd.), and he rushed past the 1,500-m. point in 3 min. 32.4 sec. Earlier in the year, Tanzania's Filbert Bayi in Kingston, Jamaica, had clipped a tenth of a second off the eight-year-old world mile mark of 3 min. 51.1 sec. set by Jim Ryun of the U.S.

International Competition: Men. *Sprints.* The dual lists of sprint marks (hand and electronic timing) continued to confuse all concerned. In the U.S. the Amateur Athletic Union (AAU) recognized electronic timing over hand times in a given race, provided that it had given approval of the type of electronic device being used. Three men—Silvio Leonard (Cuba), Steve Williams (U.S.), and Reggie Jones (U.S.)—ran 100-m. races hand-timed at 9.9 sec., while the top electronic timing was 10.05 sec. by

Steve Riddick (U.S.), who downed Williams (10.08 sec.) with that effort. A high-school sensation named Houston McTear (U.S.) sped 100 yd. in 9.0 sec., but this was not accepted as a world-record-equaling performance because the electronic apparatus in use at that meeting in Florida registered 9.32 sec.

When Don Quarrie (Jamaica) and Steve Williams locked horns over 220 yd. at Eugene, Ore., in June, they ran stride for stride before Quarrie just edged out his taller opponent at the wire. Both were timed at 19.9 sec., a world record. The 200-m. watches read 19.8 sec., and so they received a share of that record also; though the electronic-timed record remained at 19.81 sec.

Over 400 m., Britain's David Jenkins lost only once (to Alfons Brijdenbach of Belgium) and won the U.S. AAU title in 44.93 sec. before capturing the European Cup race in 45.52 sec. in Nice. Ken Randle and Benny Brown of the U.S. ran the 440-yd. dash in 45.1 sec. and 45.08 sec., respectively, and professional John Smith was credited with 44.5 sec. in London in June, although there was doubt over this time, hailed as a world professional record.

Middle Distance. The "big three" of two-lap running, Rick Wohlhuter (U.S.), Mike Boit (Kenya), and Luciano Susanj (Yugos.), were joined by an unknown from Utah named Mark Enyeart. This 21-year-old led all the way to beat Wohlhuter in the AAU championships. The ablest competitor over 800 m./880 yd. during the year was Boit. He missed the world record by 0.1 sec. in clocking 1 min. 43.8 sec. in Zürich, Switz., in August, and defeated Wohlhuter (6 times to 2) and Susanj (4–2) throughout the summer. In all, he had six marks at 1 min. 45.0 sec. and faster, and a personal best mile of 3 min. 54.9 sec. John Walker clocked the fastest 1,500-m. time of 1975 with 3 min. 32.4 sec. in Oslo. He won 17 races in a remarkable summer campaign, ending with times of 3 min. 53.6 sec. (mile) and 4 min. 56.8 sec. (2,000 m.) on successive days in London and Göteborg, besides his record mile. A U.S. team consisting of Ronnie Ray, Robert Taylor, Maurice Peoples, and Stan Vinson set a world mile-relay record of 3 min. 2.4 sec. at Durham, N.C., on July 19.

Distance. Britain's Brendan Foster (*see* BIOGRAPHY) won the European Cup race over 5,000 m. in August and shortly afterward made the greatest debut ever over 10,000 m., winning narrowly from Frank Shorter (U.S.) in 27 min. 45.4 sec. for the world's fastest performance at that distance of 1975 and seventh-fastest of all time. Emiel Puttemans of Belgium returned marks of 13 min. 18.6 sec. and 13 min. 20.8 sec. in 5,000-m. races.

A couple of weeks after finishing third to Foster and Shorter over 10,000 m. in London, Jos Hermens of The Netherlands broke the world 10-mi. record with 45 min. 57.6 sec. on his way to a remarkable 20-km. clocking of 57 min. 48.4 sec.

Hurdles and Steeplechase. Guy Drut (France) and Charles Foster (U.S.) traded early season wins in the 110-m. hurdles, but later in the year there was no holding Drut, who won everything open to him in August, clocking 13.0 sec. (hand) for a world record and 13.28 sec. (electronic). In Nice, he won the European Cup race with contemptuous ease in 13.57 sec. Rod Milburn, a U.S. professional, sped over the 120-yd. hurdles in a blistering 13.0 sec. (hand) in winning from Lance Babb (13.1 sec.). In the 400-m. hurdles, Alan Pascoe (U.K.) enjoyed another fine season, losing just once to Olympic champion John Akii-Bua

WIDE WORLD

João Oliveira of Brazil traveled 58 ft. 8½ in. for a new world record and gold medal win in the triple jump in the Mexico City Pan Am games.

(Uganda) in July when recovering from an ankle injury. Though Jim Bolding (U.S.) clocked the year's fastest of 48.55 sec. (48.4 sec. hand), Pascoe defeated him every time out in stacking up five marks at 48.9 sec. or better (best at 48.59 sec.).

One of the most convincing world records of the year was the steeplechase mark (8 min. 9.8 sec.) set by Anders Garderud of Sweden. A week earlier he had cut the record by 3.6 sec. to 8 min. 10.4 sec., and then in a torrid duel with European champion Bronislav Malinowski (Poland) he took another six-tenths off that mark in covering the last 200 m. in 27.5 sec. Malinowski was surprisingly outkicked in the European Cup race by Michael Karst and Frank Baumgartl of West Germany, but in London on August 30 the front-running Malinowski burned off both Karst and Garderud in 8 min. 18.2 sec.

Jumping. Dwight Stones (U.S.) had ten efforts of 2.26 m. (7 ft. 5 in.) or better in the high jump, with a best of 2.28 m. (7 ft. 5¾ in.) indoors. New men Tom Woods (U.S.) and Paul Poaniewa (France) jumped 2.27 m. (7 ft. 5½ in.) and 2.26 m. (7 ft. 5 in.), respectively, while Aleksandr Grigoryev of the U.S.S.R. won a tense European Cup competition with 2.24 m. (7 ft. 4¼ in.). Using one of the new "pre-bent" poles, Dave Roberts (U.S.) achieved a world record pole vault of 5.65 m. (18 ft. 6½ in.) in March; but injury curtailed the rest of his season. Professional Steve Smith vaulted consistently over 5.50 m. (18 ft. ½ in.) with a best of 5.61 m. (18 ft. 5 in.), and the best amateur competitor was Wladyslaw Kozakiewicz of Poland, who set a European record of 5.60 m. (18 ft. 4½ in.) in June and won the European Cup event with 5.45 m. (17 ft. 10½ in.).

Tornadoes: *see* Disasters; Earth Sciences

Tourism: *see* Industrial Review

Toys: *see* Games and Toys

Long jump action was rather subdued with just 4 men leaping over 27 ft. (8.23 m.) and 17 over 8 m. (26 ft. 3 in.). The year's most surprising result in this event occurred when Nenad Stekic of Yugoslavia sailed out to 8.45 m. (27 ft. 8¾ in.), second best mark of all time, at the Montreal pre-Olympic meet in July, assisted by a wind of 1.9 m. per sec. At the Pan American Games in October João Carlos Oliveira of Brazil set a remarkable triple jump world record of 17.89 m. (58 ft. 8½ in.).

Throwing. The mighty professional Brian Oldfield (U.S.) had things all his own way in the shot put, using his rotational technique to toss a stunning world best of 22.86 m. (75 ft. 0 in.) in Texas in May. Best amateur throw was the 21.33 m. (70 ft. 0 in.) effort by Hans Hoglund of Sweden.

Amateur discus and hammer throws more than made up for poor shot put marks with four world records set by four men. South Africa's John Van Reenen threw the discus 68.48 m. (224 ft. 8 in.) in Stellenbosch in March, only to lose the mark five weeks later to John Powell (U.S.) who unwound a toss of 69.08 m. (226 ft. 8 in.) at Long Beach, Calif. East Germany's Wolfgang Schmidt bested Powell in several meetings and won the European Cup final in Nice. Karl-Hans Riehm (West Germany) bettered the previous listed world record on every one of his six hammer throws, ending up with 78.50 m. (257 ft. 6½ in.). His countryman Walter Schmidt unloaded a huge throw of 79.30 m. (260 ft. 2 in.) at Frankfurt in August. In a remarkable year for hammer throwing, 15 men—all Europeans—threw 73.20 m. (240 ft. 2 in.) or better. Nikolay Grebneyev (U.S.S.R.), rated no better than seventh in the world lists, won the European Cup javelin with 84.30 m. (276 ft. 7 in.), and Hungarian Miklos Nemeth sprang back to prominence with a world-leading effort of 91.39 m. (299 ft. 10 in.).

Decathlon. Bruce Jenner (U.S.) rolled up a world record of 8,524 points at Eugene in August, turning back Olympic champion and previous record holder Nikolay Avilov of the U.S.S.R. in the process. During the year Avilov twice scored over 8,200 points, and Fred Dixon of the U.S. had a best of 8,277.

International Competition: Women. *Sprints.* Renate Stecher (East Germany) gained revenge over Irena Szewinska (Poland) for her defeats in the 1974 European championships by trouncing her in both the European Cup sprints, winning the 100 m. in 11.29 sec. from Andrea Lynch (U.K.) and Szewinska, and the 200 m. in a decisive 22.63 sec. from Szewinska. Top electronic timings were Stecher's 11.13 sec. and Lynch's 11.16 sec. in scoring over Szewinska in London in July. Stecher's 22.44 sec. paced the 200-m. listings, in which both she and Szewinska shared a 22.4 sec. hand timing. Christina Brehmer (East Germany) set a world junior best of 50.84 sec. in the 400-m. run.

Table I. World 1975 Outdoor Records—Men

Event	Competitor, country, date	Performances
100 m.	Silvio Leonard, Cuba, June 5	9.9 sec.*†
	Steve Williams, U.S., July 16	9.9 sec.*†
	Reggie Jones, U.S., July 26	9.9 sec.*†
	Steve Williams, U.S., August 22	9.9 sec.*†
220 yd.	Don Quarrie, Jamaica, June 7	19.9 sec.†
	Steve Williams, U.S., June 7	19.9 sec.†
	(both timed at 19.8 for 200 m. to equal world record on hand timing)	
1 mi.	Filbert Bayi, Tanzania, May 17	3 min. 51.0 sec.
	John Walker, New Zealand, August 12	3 min. 49.4 sec.
3,000-m. steeplechase	Anders Garderud, Sweden, June 25	8 min. 10.4 sec.
	Anders Garderud, Sweden, July 1	8 min. 09.8 sec.
110-m. hurdles	Guy Drut, France, August 22	13.0 sec.†
Pole vault	David Roberts, U.S., March 28	5.65 m. (18ft. 6½ in.)
Triple jump	João Carlos Oliveira, Brazil, October 15	17.89 m. (58 ft. 8½ in.)
Discus	John Van Reenen, South Africa, March 14	68.48 m. (224 ft. 8 in.)
	John Powell, U.S., May 4	69.08 m. (226 ft. 8 in.)
Hammer throw	Karl-Hans Riehm, West Germany, May 19	78.50 m. (257 ft. 6½ in.)
	Walter Schmidt, West Germany, August 14	79.30 m. (260 ft. 2 in.)
Decathlon	Bruce Jenner, U.S., August 9–10	8,524 pt.
10-mi. (track)	Jos Hermens, The Netherlands, September 14	45 min. 57.6 sec.
20-km./1-hr. run (track)	Jos Hermens, The Netherlands, September 24	57 min. 31.8 sec./20,907 m.
Mile relay	U.S. national team, July 19	3 min 02.4 sec.
Professional Marks		
110-m. hurdles	Rod Milburn, U.S., May 10	13.0 sec.
Shot put	Brian Oldfield, U.S., May 10	22.86 m. (75 ft. 0 in.)

*Ties record.
†Hand timing.

Table II. World 1975 Outdoor Records—Women

Event	Competitor, country, date	Performance
3,000 m.	Grete Andersen, Norway, June 24	8 min. 46.6 sec.
10,000 m.	Christa Vahlensieck, West Germany, August 20	34 min. 01.4 sec.
Shot put	Marianne Adam, East Germany, August 6	21.60 m. (70 ft. 10½ in.)
Discus	Faina Melnik, U.S.S.R., August 20	70.20 m. (230 ft. 4 in.)

Middle Distance and Distance. Nina Morgunova (U.S.S.R.) ran the year's best 800 m. with a time of 1 min. 59.4 sec. Tatyana Kazankina (U.S.S.R.) paced the women in the 1,500 m. with 4 min. 5.5 sec. but could finish only third in the European Cup when Waltraud Strotzer (East Germany) sprinted to victory in 4 min. 8.0 sec. Norway's Grete Andersen churned out a world record 3,000 m. of 8 min. 46.6 sec. at Oslo in June, and her 4 min. 6.6 sec. in the 1,500 m. ranked second in the world lists.

Hurdling and Jumping. Annelie Ehrhardt (East Germany) won the European Cup 100-m. hurdles as expected (12.83 sec.) and clocked a hand-timed 12.8 sec. Arch-rival Grazyna Rabsztyn (Poland) ran a hand-timed 12.6 sec. (12.82 sec. electric) and at the European Cup finished just inches behind Ehrhardt (12.85 sec.). Rosemarie Ackermann (East Germany) dominated the high jump again with 1.94 m. (6 ft. 4½ in.) to win the European Cup and turn back Olympic champion Ulrike Meyfarth (West Germany). Lidiya Alfeyeva (U.S.S.R.) picked the best occasion to produce her leading long-jump effort of the year in the European Cup final, a leap of 6.76 m. (22 ft. 2¼ in.).

Faina Melnik of the Soviet Union hurled the discus 70.2 m., thus breaking the women's world record in Zürich during the international athletics meet.

KEYSTONE

Throwing. Shot putter Marianne Adam (East Germany) blasted beyond 70 ft. again to raise her world mark to 21.60 m. (70 ft. 10½ in.) at East Berlin in August, and won the European Cup title as she pleased, putting 21.32 m. (69 ft. 11½ in.) there to turn back the U.S.S.R.'s Esfir Krachevskaya. Faina Melnik (U.S.S.R.) kept the women's world discus record with an astonishing 70.20 m. (230 ft. 4 in.) throw on August 20 in Zürich. Ruth Fuchs (East Germany) threw the javelin 66.44 m. (218 ft. 0 in.) during an unbeaten season. East Germany's relay teams, as usual, could not be stopped and ran world leading times of 42.7 sec. (4 x 100 m.) and 3 min. 24.0 sec. (4 x 400 m.).

(DAVID COCKSEDGE)

United States Competition. Three U.S. records fell in regularly contested events, and another five were broken in events with less frequent competition. Tommy Haynes triple jumped 56 ft. 5½ in. in the Pan American Games in Mexico City; Marty Liquori ran two miles in 8 min. 17.2 sec. at Stockholm on July 17; and Will Rodgers won the Boston Marathon in 2 hr. 9 min. 55 sec. on April 21. Four U.S. records in one race were collected by Gary Tuttle. At Goleta, Calif., on July 26 he set new figures of 44 min. 53.4 sec. for 15,000 m.; 48 min. 10.4 sec. for 10 mi.; 59 min. 52.4 sec. for 20,000 m.; and 12 mi., 811 yd. for one hour.

The final national mark was achieved by Steve Prefontaine, who ran 2,000 m. in 5 min. 1.4 sec. at Coos Bay, Ore., on May 10. It was his sixth U.S. outdoor record, covering all distances from 2,000 to 10,000 m. It was also his last, for Prefontaine was killed May 30 in a single-car accident shortly after he had won another race in his hometown of Eugene, Ore.

Indoors, where there are no officially approved world records, all-time bests were achieved in five events. Dwight Stones increased the high-jump standard four times and tied it a fifth. He jumped 7 ft. 5 in. at Pocatello, Idaho, January 17; 7 ft. 5¼ in. and 7 ft. 5⅜ in. at Los Angeles January 18 and 19, respectively; 7 ft. 5½ in. at Oklahoma City, Okla., February 15; and 7 ft. 5¾ in. at New York City, February 21.

Professional pole vaulter Steve Smith highlights the International Track Association meet as he sets a world indoor record of 18 ft. 4 in.

UPI COMPIX

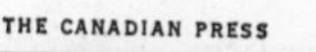

THE CANADIAN PRESS

Annelie Ehrhardt of East Germany takes the 50-yd. hurdles in a world record 6.2 sec. at the 13th annual Toronto Star-Maple Leaf indoor games at Toronto.

Dan Ripley raised the amateur pole vault indoor best to 18 ft. 1 in. at Los Angeles, January 18. But the indoor vaulting action was dominated by professional Steve Smith. He cleared a world best 18 ft. 2½ in. at Montreal on January 17 and 18 ft. 4 in. at Portland, Ore., on April 12.

Oldfield put the shot an indoor record 72 ft. 6½ in. at San Francisco on April 4, and Stan Vinson got the indoor season off to a fast start on Dec. 19, 1974, at Ypsilanti, Mich., with 1 min. 2.4 sec. for 500 m.

Team action was highlighted by increased international competition. The United States defeated the Soviet Union, 98 to 62, indoors at Richmond, Va., March 3. But the Soviets won the outdoor match, 129 to 89, at Kiev, July 5. The international decathlon contest at Eugene, Aug. 9–10, was won by the U.S. with 48,899 points to 46,328 for the U.S.S.R. and 46,091 for Poland.

Following the Kiev meet, the U.S. had a double dual meet at Prague on July 8, defeating Czechoslovakia 127 to 88 and Poland 113 to 102. Then, at Durham, N.C., in July, the U.S. scored 164½ points to 134 for West Germany and 111½ for a Pan African squad. In junior (under 20 years of age) competition, the U.S. outscored the Soviets 217 to 163 at Lincoln, Neb., on July 5. Final event on the international schedule was the Pan American Games in Mexico City in October, with the U.S. leading the way after stiff competition from Cuba. No point totals were kept.

Collegiate track champion was the University of Texas at El Paso, winner of the indoor meet at Detroit on April 6 and the outdoor tournament at Provo, Utah, on June 7. The Beverly Hills Striders won the outdoor AAU meet at Eugene, Ore., June 21. Indoors, the New York Athletic Club captured the AAU title at New York on February 28.

U.S. women bettered national records 15 times in 13 events. Francie Larrieu, Kathy Schmidt, and Madeline Jackson were double record breakers. Larrieu ran the mile in 4 min. 31.6 sec. at Wichita, Kan., May 31 and the 1,500 m. in 4 min. 8.5 sec. at Saint-Maur, France, July 9. Schmidt threw the javelin 209 ft. 3

in. at Los Angeles on May 31, and 209 ft. 7 in. at White Plains, N.Y., on June 28. Jackson ran 800 m. in 2 min. 0.5 sec. at White Plains on June 28 and 2 min. 0.3 sec. at Kiev on July 5.

Other U.S. record breakers were Rosalyn Bryant, 220 yd. in 23.2 sec., Chicago, June 7; Jane Frederick, 4,676 points in the pentathlon, Los Alamos, N.M., June 21; and at White Plains, N.Y., June 21, Debra Sapenter, 400 m. in 51.6 sec.; Lisa Metheny, 1,500-m. walk in 6 min. 46.6 sec.; Debbie Esser, 400-m. hurdles in 57.3 sec.; and Blue Ribbon Track Club, two-mile relay in 8 min. 46.4 sec. The U.S. national team ran the 440-yd. relay in 44.2 sec. and the mile relay in 3 min. 30.9 sec., both at Durham on July 18. And in the Pan American Games Chandra Cheesborough ran 200 m. in 22.7 sec.

Indoors, Larrieu scored six world all-time bests. She lowered the 1,500-m. mark three times, to a best of 4 min. 9.8 sec. at Richmond, Va., on March 3, and the best of her two records at one mile was 4 min. 28.5 sec. in the same Richmond race. She also covered 1,000 m. in 2 min. 40.2 sec. at Los Angeles on January 18. Angel Doyle equaled the 60-yd. mark with 6.5 sec. at Philadelphia on February 7, while Bryant ran 220 yd. in 23.6 sec. at New York on February 28.

The U.S. women had mixed success in international team contests. They defeated the U.S.S.R. indoors, 73 to 44, but lost outdoors, 96 to 49. Also outdoors, they beat Poland, 76 to 70, and Czechoslovakia, 82 to 64, while placing second to West Germany, 131 to 99, ahead of Pan Africa, 40. The junior meet with the Soviet Union was won 88 to 58, but the Soviets captured a three-way pentathlon match as Canada placed second. (BERT D. NELSON)

[452.B.4.b]

Transportation

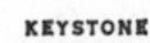

A new electric taxi developed by Lucas Industries is noise and pollution free and can travel at a top speed of 55 mph with a 100-mi. range.

The economic recession combined with inflation dampened demand for all forms of transport in 1975. Consequently, dreams of a major switch from private cars to public transport as a result of rising gasoline prices came to nothing. True, car sales remained in the doldrums, but there were signs of road traffic reviving in some countries during the year. True also, U.S. mass transit ridership rose 5.7% in 1974, but because public transport accounted for only about 7% of total travel it still had a long way to go. In general, governments were looking more critically at subsidies for public transportation, and inflation hit the labour-intensive buses and trains as hard as the motorist. How much the decline in ridership that followed fare increases was caused by inflation and how much by general economic depression was a matter for debate.

Views about the long-term trends in transport differed. The British Transport and Road Research Laboratory (TRRL) published controversial estimates of the growth in the number of road vehicles. The highly respected TRRL predicted a minimum in Britain of 23.8 million vehicles by 1990, very little less than it had estimated before the oil crisis. Others regarded the assumptions as optimistic, and *The Times* published an estimate of 19.5 million vehicles. (The actual figure for 1974 was 17.2 million vehicles.) London Transport asked motorists what they would do if their driving was severely restricted; to its chagrin, it found that rather than use public transport they would tend to stay at home.

Trade, International: *see* Economy, World

Trade Unions: *see* Industrial Relations

Traffic Accidents: *see* Disasters

Authorities began to realize that transport policy was not as simple as had been thought. But some sucesses were reported. In Besançon, France, a policy of banning through traffic, combined with more frequent buses, minibuses, and taxis, led to a 35% increase in public transport ridership. In Bologna, Italy, 50 km. of bus lanes, severe traffic restraint, and zero fares in peak hours led to a 20% drop in automobile traffic in the historic centre, a 15–20% increase in public transport ridership, and a 27% decline in road accidents. In Nagoya, Japan, a study showed that staggered working hours could cut rush-hour congestion on streets, buses, and trains by more than 30%. Singapore introduced, with dramatic success, a system of charging a daily fee to motorists wanting to drive in the city centre (but London rejected a similar proposal).

In the U.S. Pres. Gerald Ford, formerly a defender of the Highway Trust Fund, proposed that most of the $6 billion a year income that it derived from gasoline taxes should be turned over directly to the Treasury or to the states, rather than being kept entirely for road construction. In The Netherlands the government announced almost a tripling of the road tax on the largest cars, to approximately $670 a year. But France was pushing ahead with plans to double its 3,000-km. auto-route system by 1978.

(RICHARD CASEMENT)

AVIATION

Financially, 1975 was a difficult year for the airline industry, with only meagre increases in traffic. In the U.S. the situation was particularly bad, with the Air Transport Association (ATA) predicting that U.S. carriers would have lost more than $250 million by the year's end, the worst annual result on record. Cost inflation and the continuing rise in fuel prices were blamed. The 11 U.S. trunk carriers, which together carried approximately 40% of the world's scheduled traffic, covered 166,000,000,000 revenue passenger-km. in the first eight months of 1975, 2% less than in the equivalent period of 1974 (1 km. = 0.62 mi.). The nine local service carriers covered 78,000,000,000 revenue passenger-km. in the first half of 1975, a decline of 8% from 1974.

In Europe traffic continued to increase but at a slower rate than in recent years. Member airlines of the Association of European Airlines (AEA) covered 333,000,000,000 passenger-km. on intra-European scheduled services and 85,000,000,000 on inter-

The world's first flying saucer, measuring 30 ft. in diameter, makes its first flight in the great airship hangar at Cardington, England. The odd-shaped skyship was designed for military transport purposes.

CENTRAL PRESS/PICTORIAL PARADE

continental scheduled services in the 12 months to August 1975, increases of 5 and 4%, respectively. Scheduled freight traffic declined 2% on intra-European services, to 575 million metric ton-km., and 1% on intercontinental services, to 42,000,000,000 ton-km.

Traffic growth was lower than at any time in the preceding ten years, although continuing to increase in certain relatively minor and underdeveloped markets, such as within Central America and Africa. Figures from the International Civil Aviation Organization (ICAO) for 1974 showed that the increase of total scheduled traffic, excluding China, was only 5.5% over 1973. With the U.S.S.R. excluded, the overall increase in 1974 was 5.3%, the lowest recorded in any of the preceding ten years and well below the annual average for the period.

Up to the beginning of 1975 freight had been the fastest-growing sector of scheduled services. International freight was up by 13.7% in 1974, and had grown an average of 18.1% annually from 1965 to 1974 (U.S.S.R. excluded). There was an 11% decline in nonscheduled passenger traffic in 1974. Of the 897,000,000,000 passenger-km., 36% was carried by scheduled airlines and the remainder by charter airlines. European airlines carried 62% of the total.

The utilization of available aircraft capacity (load factor) continued to improve, although a sharp deterioration was noted among U.S. trunk carriers during 1975. Passenger load factor for these airlines in the first eight months was 53.8%, compared with 57.6% during the equivalent period of 1974. The European airlines in AEA achieved passenger load factors of 54.2% on intra-European services and 56.1% on intercontinental services in the 12 months to August 1975, a slight deterioration from the previous period. The International Air Transport Association (IATA) noted that although trends in load factor and in operating results had tended to follow parallel paths in the past, with higher load factors being accompanied by higher profits, by 1974 such was no longer the case because of the rapid rise in fuel prices. The 1975 decline in load factors could only add to the economic gloom, in spite of moves to increase fares.

The world's airlines (U.S.S.R. and China excluded) faced cost increases of about 17% in 1974. Revenue increased only 16%. The operating profit for the year was put tentatively at $1 billion, or 3.2% of operating revenue, compared with $1,159,000,000 in 1973. For most of the world's major scheduled airlines the 1974–75 financial year was the second worst in IATA's history, with an operating loss of 0.3% of revenue, compared with a profit of 4.2% in 1973–74. A slight improvement in 1975–76, to perhaps a profit of 2.5%, was forecast, but such a result was far from sufficient to allow a reasonable rate of return and a net profit.

The most significant cost factor was the price of aviation fuel. Fuel and oil costs accounted for one-fifth of total operating costs in 1974, compared with little more than one-tenth prior to the 1973 oil crisis. In 1975 the airlines also faced considerable cost increases in maintenance and passenger services, and in landing fees and navigational charges levied by governmental and airport authorities as governments increasingly tried to recover the full cost of navigational services from users.

U.S. trunk carriers reported an aggregate operating loss of $59.8 million in the first half of 1975, on revenue of $68 billion; their net loss was $107.2 million. In the first half of 1974 they had returned an operating surplus of $325 million and a net profit of $137

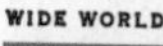

WIDE WORLD

The new short-takeoff-and-landing transport at the McDonnell Douglas plant in Long Beach, California, is equipped with supercritical wings designed to cut fuel costs. It also offers a high-lift system channeling jet exhaust through wing flaps to facilitate short takeoffs.

million. Chief losers were TWA ($86.8 million net loss) and Pan Am ($55 million net loss), followed by American Airlines and United Airlines, with Eastern Airlines only marginally in the black for the half year. Most profitable was Northwest Airlines ($21 million net profit).

In October President Ford released details of his 1975 aviation bill, which proposed major changes and aimed at increasing consumer protection and removing the protectionist features of the old system, but Congress took no action on it during the year. Major features were emphasis on competition, with freer access to new routes and fewer grounds on which the Civil Aeronautics Board could deny applications for route authority; airlines' ability to transfer, sell, or lease route authority; freedom for airlines to abandon routes; and access for the supplemental carriers to scheduled routes, previously denied them. A number of leading airline presidents attacked the administration's proposals, and ATA said that the bill, if passed, would tear the national air transportation system apart and lead to reduced service and increased cost to consumers.

The U.S. administration, invoking the 1975 Fair Competitive Practices Act, threatened to cause international difficulties toward the end of 1975. The Department of Transportation accused Australia and the U.K. of discrimination against U.S. airlines in the assessment of airport and air navigation charges. The act empowered the department to impose a penalty in retaliation against airlines of countries with whom the U.S. was in dispute should negotiations with those countries break down. Neither the British nor the Australian governments were prepared to back down. Both claimed that the charges levied were the same for all airlines and therefore not discriminatory.

In Canada, Montreal's new international airport, Mirabel, was dedicated in October. It would eventually occupy 17,000 ac., with a further 71,000 ac. zoned for environmental and noise-protection purposes.

The U.S. Federal Aviation Administration published a consultative document on aircraft noise and also organized a series of hearings. IATA expressed concern at the failure of research programs to produce effective modifications for older aircraft types which would reduce noise, and claimed that modifications so far devised would increase fuel consumption without improving noise generated at takeoff.

(DAVID WOOLLEY)

SHIPPING AND PORTS

The dry cargo and tanker markets continued to decline in 1975. Tankers became totally uneconomic,

World Transportation

Country	Railways: Route length in 000 km.	Railways Traffic: Passenger in 000,000 pass.-km.	Railways Traffic: Freight in 000,000 net ton-km.	Motor transport: Road length in 000 km.	Motor transport: Vehicles in use: Passenger in 000	Motor transport: Vehicles in use: Commercial in 000	Merchant shipping (Ships of 100 tons and over): Number of vessels	Merchant shipping: Gross reg. tons in 000	Air traffic: Total km. flown in 000,000	Air traffic: Passenger in 000,000 pass.-km.	Air traffic: Freight in 000,000 net ton-km.
EUROPE											
Austria	6.5*	6,725	10,486	c.97.4	1,562.8	140.9	60	97	12.7	598	8.3
Belgium	4.0	8,280	9,102	93.7	2,362.0	224.0	251	1,215	46.0	3,974	294.7
Bulgaria	4.2	7,452	17,309	35.7*	c.160.0*	c.38.0*	166	865	9.0	360	6.8
Cyprus	—	—	—	8.3*	77.7	15.5	722	3,395	5.7	371	3.0
Czechoslovakia	13.3	19,278	67,949	144.0	1,192.8	226.5	13	116	24.0	1,283	18.1
Denmark	2.0†	3,197†	2,142†	65.1	1,257.3	203.9	1,349	4,460	31.3‡	2,216‡	93.1‡
Finland	6.0	2,773	7,485	73.2	894.1	119.9	362	1,508	26.9	1,156	32.6
France	34.4	46,880	76,999	793.8	14,620.0	1,980.0	1,341	8,835	229.1	21,738	942.4
Germany, East	14.3	19,737	49,167	129.9	1,539.0	216.2	431	1,224	...	1,120	30.8
Germany, West	32.4	38,616	70,178	459.5	17,036.0	1,246.0	2,088	7,980	158.5	12,472	991.3
Greece	2.6	1,615	798	36.4	346.8	150.2	2,651	21,759	43.1	3,084	51.3
Hungary	8.5	13,879	22,472	109.6	407.6	98.3	17	49	10.2	420	5.8
Ireland	2.2	868	528	88.2*	476.7	49.0	88	209	20.1	1,648	89.6
Italy	20.2*	36,359	17,574	288.4	13,600.0	1,025.0	1,710	9,322	150.6	11,379	465.0
Netherlands, The	2.8	8,532	3,369	82.5	3,230.0	320.0	1,358	5,501	96.3	9,361	635.9
Norway	4.2	1,870†	2,950†	74.8	913.4	163.0	2,689	24,853	49.1‡	2,737‡	107.9‡
Poland	23.6	41,668	125,155	299.9	780.9	324.3	648	2,292	21.1	1,075	13.6
Portugal	3.6	3,440	1,004	43.2*	769.5	70.4	431	1,243	53.2	4,160	115.6
Romania	11.0	21,228	57,103	76.8	c.125.0*	c.50.0*	106	611	12.6	584	6.7
Spain	16.0	16,080	12,669	142.1	3,803.7	888.0	2,520	4,949	121.9	10,105	222.1
Sweden	12.1	4,899	18,260	112.9	2,502.9	144.0	785	6,227	59.1‡	3,479‡	160.3‡
Switzerland	5.0*	8,300	6,985	61.2	1,656.4	159.7	28	200	81.6	7,091	295.0
U.S.S.R.	259.9*†	296,619	3,100,000	1,398.0	c.3,000.0	c.4,000.0	7,342	18,176	...	98,418	2,350.9
United Kingdom	18.2§	35,204§	25,514§	362.5*	13,106.0*	1,686.2*	3,603	31,566	367.6	c.27,700	c.1,050.0
Yugoslavia	10.4	10,591	22,979	107.2	1,140.5	125.9	398	1,778	23.6	1,419	10.6
ASIA											
Bangladesh	2.9†	2,815	891	c.24.0	66.7*	23.3*	98	116	...	...	...
Burma	3.1*	2,593	708	21.7	31.7	34.3	40	55	6.6	170	2.4
Cambodia	0.6*	54	10	c.11.0	27.2*	11.1*	3	2	1.1	51	0.5
China	c.35.0	45,670*	301,000*	c.700.0	c.1,000.0*	c.800.0*	360	1,871	...	64*	2.0*
India	60.1*	131,452	126,351	1,021.8*	646.5*	346.0*	451	3,485	73.2	5,454	204.9
Indonesia	7.8	2,726	1,068	84.9*	306.7	173.3	616	762	38.8	2,204	44.9
Iran	4.5*	2,144	4,432	43.4*	393.9*	87.6*	115	292	15.9	1,125	15.6
Iraq	2.5*	604*	1,514*	10.8	77.3	34.3	49	230	5.6	388	5.8
Israel	0.8	355	445	c.9.0*	238.0	113.4	76	611	30.4	3,659	141.0
Japan	27.5	324,661	54,693	1,049.7	14,473.6	10,422.4	9,974	38,708	253.0	16,273	733.6
Korea, South	5.5	10,908	8,797	43.6	78.3	83.5	650	1,226	31.9	2,496	128.3
Malaysia	1.8	824‖	1,157‖	24.4*	382.6	123.8	122	338	20.2	1,298	22.2
Pakistan	8.7	c.12,400	c.7,700	62.8*	177.3	79.1	88	494	22.9	1,845	95.0
Philippines	1.2*	796	58	92.8	362.5	252.5	379	766	39.1	1,750	48.4
Saudi Arabia	0.6	61	62	15.7	54.1	39.3	43	61	17.5	939	27.9
Syria	0.9	69	132	16.7*	34.7	23.1	9	3	6.8	305	2.5
Taiwan	4.4*	8,020	2,960	16.4	95.1	78.5	407	1,417	18.0*	954*	25.2*
Thailand	3.8	4,694	2,070	17.7*	282.6*	158.9*	80	176	23.1	2,845	63.2
Turkey	8.1*	5,219	6,799	59.3	234.6	159.3	369	972	20.3	1,444	11.8
AFRICA											
Algeria	4.0†	943	1,577	78.4	176.9	96.7	75	240	14.8	760	5.3
Central African Republic	—	—	—	c.19.3	6.5*	3.2*	...	...	1.8¶	95¶	8.8¶
Chad	—	—	—	30.7*	5.8	6.3	...	...	2.5¶	108¶	9.8¶
Congo	0.8	207	556	c.11.0	c.7.5*	c.5.5*	6	2	2.2¶	100¶	9.0¶
Dahomey (Benin)	0.6	93	115	8.1	14.0*	7.9*	4	—	1.4¶	91¶	8.8¶
Egypt	5.0	7,306*	2,976*	c.50.0	167.4	48.0	134	249	18.4	1,285	17.8
Gabon	0.4	...	...	6.8	c.10.0*	c.4.6*	13	32	3.0¶	117¶	8.9¶
Ghana	1.0*	520*	305*	c.31.0	40.4*	31.0*	77	173	3.7	150	2.8
Ivory Coast	0.6	848	548	c.39.0	c.90.5*	c.57.4*	46	121	1.8¶	98¶	9.0¶
Kenya	2.1	4,529*♀	4,442♀	48.2	117.0	18.5	21	22	10.0δ	549δ	19.1δ
Malawi	0.6	70	251	11.8	10.5	8.7	...	...	2.3	80	1.2
Mali	0.6	95	152	c.13.0	4.5*	5.7*	...	...	1.7	73	1.8
Morocco	1.8†	714	3,591	25.4	260.4*	84.7*	43	53	11.2	673	7.7
Nigeria	3.5	1,033	1,372	89.0*	c.120.0*	c.69.0*	78	121	9.1	334	8.2
Rhodesia	3.3	...	6,623□	78.9	127.0*	56.0*	...	...	5.9	241	1.9
Senegal	1.0	279*	218	15.4*	44.2	24.0	48	20	2.0¶	101¶	8.8¶
South Africa	22.2	...	60,910◇	c.320.0	1,737.0	620.8	270	535	47.9	5,342	154.8
Tanzania	2.6	4,529*♀	4,442♀	c.17.5	36.4	39.6	14	28	3.7δ	127δ	3.1δ
Tunisia	2.1	534	1,522	18.8	90.2	50.2	25	29	8.1	699	5.8
Uganda	1.2	4,529*♀	4,442♀	25.7*	25.7*	13.6*	1	6	2.8δ	122δ	7.9δ
Zaire	5.2*	437*	2,387*	c.140.0	81.4*	54.3*	9	39	13.9	623	34.5
Zambia	1.3	...	...	35.0*	74.7*	40.0*	1	6	6.8	339	16.4
NORTH AND CENTRAL AMERICA											
Canada	70.1	2,573	190,906	831.7*	7,866.1	2,211.8	1,231	2,460	268.1	21,701	569.9
Costa Rica	0.6	53*	15*	c.17.6	47.5*	30.1*	13	6	6.0	297	9.4
Cuba	14.5	987*	1,598*	18.9	c.72.0*	c.32.0*	259	409	8.0	535	14.5
El Salvador	0.6	...	...	10.7*	37.9*	21.9*	2	—	...	...	...
Guatemala	0.8*	...	106*	13.4*	54.1*	36.9*	6	8	1.4	100	4.8
Honduras	c.1.1	174*	3*	5.9	16.7*	17.4*	56	70	6.7	205	3.5
Mexico	19.2	4,057	26,244	154.7	1,672.1	652.0	261	515	78.6	5,894	70.8
Nicaragua	0.3*	28*	14*	13.1*	c.32.0*	c.13.0*	14	33	2.2	76	2.0
Panama	0.7	...	...	c.7.1	53.6*	21.6	1,962	11,003	...	...	...
United States	332.8	16,630	1,253,180	6,094.1*	101,237.0	23,201.0	4,086	14,429	3,939.4	262,194	8,952.1
SOUTH AMERICA											
Argentina	40.2	12,334	12,557	283.8*	1,680.0*	788.0*	366	1,408	51.8	3,282	93.6
Bolivia	3.4	270*	440*	25.6*	c.19.2*	c.28.8*	...	...	4.6	195	3.1
Brazil	23.9	11,489*	18,080*	1,260.3*	3,069.2*	809.3*	471	2,429	139.5	8,559	420.4
Chile	9.0	2,877	2,383	63.7*	193.0*	135.7*	135	364	19.7	1,223	59.8
Colombia	3.4	482	1,329	45.9*	326.9	107.0	54	211	53.8	2,494	108.4
Ecuador	1.1*	63*	43*	18.3*	33.0*	51.5*	38	128	10.4	220	9.9
Paraguay	0.5	26	30*	11.2*	c.16.0*	c.14.0*	26	22	...	...	...
Peru	2.1	248*	610*	52.1	256.4*	136.1*	675	514	7.7	404	12.5
Uruguay	3.0	351	196	49.6	220.0	80.0	37	130	1.2	30	0.2
Venezuela	0.2	36*	13*	44.3	778.6*	256.1*	143	480	36.1	1,935	87.6
OCEANIA											
Australia	40.3†	...	28,329†	863.9*	4,596.4	1,050.2	394	1,168	203.2	14,241	300.1
New Zealand	4.8	491	3,757	92.0	1,122.1	200.9	113	163	43.8	3,878	107.8

Note: Data are for 1973 or 1974 unless otherwise indicated.
(—) Indicates nil or negligible; (. . .) indicates not known; (c) indicates provisional or estimated.
*Data given are the most recent available.
†State system only.
‡Including apportionment of traffic of Scandinavian Airlines System.
§Excluding Northern Ireland.
‖Including Singapore.
¶Including apportionment of traffic of Air Afrique.
♀Total for Kenya, Tanzania, and Uganda (East African Railways Corp.).
δIncluding apportionment of traffic of East African Airways Corp. and Caspair Ltd.
□Including traffic for Botswana.
◇Including Namibia (South West Africa).

Sources: UN, *Statistical Yearbook 1974*, *Monthly Bulletin of Statistics*, *Annual Bulletin of Transport Statistics for Europe 1973*; Lloyd's Register of Shipping, *Statistical Tables 1974*; International Road Federation, *World Road Statistics 1974*; *Jahrbuch des Eisenbahnwesens 1973*.

(M. C. MacDONALD)

operating at rates that covered only running costs with nothing left to cover interest, depreciation, and capital charges. The dry cargo market was helped somewhat by the movement of grain from the U.S. to the U.S.S.R.

In July 1975 the world tanker fleet (vessels over 1,000 tons gross) totaled 267 million tons deadweight (dw.); combined carriers 42 million tons; bulk carriers 98.5 million tons; and other dry cargo vessels 106.5 million tons, making a total of nearly 514 million tons dw. Millions of tons of completed ships remained undelivered to customers, particularly in the tanker section, where cancellations were expected to reach 80 million tons dw. by the end of 1975. The reopening of the Suez Canal in June 1975 had little effect, the overall freight rate for tankers, irrespective of size, being so low that nothing could be gained by using the canal.

Liberia headed the list of merchant fleets (65,820,000 tons gross), followed by Japan (39,740,000 tons gross) and the U.K. (33,157,000 tons gross). Norway (26,154,000 tons gross) and Greece (22,527,000 tons gross) were both in trouble because of the predominance of their tanker tonnage. North Sea oil operations prevented a collapse of Norwegian shipping.

World shipping continued to be troubled by the widespread adoption of protectionist policies. The Code of Conduct for Liner Conferences proposed by the Shipping Committee of the UN Conference on Trade and Development would affect many of the maritime nations. Third world countries, such as Brazil, Argentina, and Chile, were determined to increase their own merchant fleets regardless of the provisions of the code.

Competition from the low freight rates of the Soviet Trans-Siberian Railway threatened some of the ships operated by the Far Eastern Freight Conference Lines services. The journey time from Hamburg, West Germany, to Vladivostok by the rail route was about 30 days, compared with 29 by the traditional sea route via the Cape of Good Hope, and eventually the only way to combat the competition from the Soviet service might be the use of the Suez Canal.

There was little port development during 1975, except in South Africa, where preparations to provide facilities to cope with the introduction of containerized cargo continued. Most of the ports involved were owned by South African Harbours and Railways. Excessive congestion was reported at West African and Persian Gulf ports, where delays of from 100 to 300 days were caused by totally inadequate facilities. Far Eastern ports were further developed, with new container facilities at Singapore and Hong Kong. In China the twin ports of Dairen and Lushon, which provided facilities for handling export oil, were enlarged to be able to berth 100,000-ton tankers.

In Europe the new two-berth Cap d'Antifer terminal at Le Havre, France, commissioned in late 1975, was designed to handle 350,000-tonners initially and later 500,000-ton vessels. In The Netherlands work was well advanced for a vast man-made island off the Hook of Holland to provide four basins for tankers of up to 500,000 tons.

(W. D. EWART)

FREIGHT MOVEMENTS

The biggest move in the freight business was the proposed merger of seven bankrupt railroads, including Penn Central, in the northeastern U.S. In a form of nationalization, a new company, ConRail, was set up to absorb and reorganize these lines. Federal financing amounting to $2.1 billion was approved by Congress in late December. It was hoped to turn the railroads into a viable enterprise by eliminating duplication of services, closing some lines outright, improving operating methods, and reducing restrictive practices by labour. But many experts were severely critical. One bank suggested that $20 billion would be required to repair the tracks, and the Interstate Commerce Commission forecast losses of up to $10 billion. Furthermore, ConRail intended to pay Penn Central only $470 million for its assets, but Penn's trustees said that they were worth $7.4 billion.

In most countries, both rail and truck freight suffered from the economic recession. Switzerland, the main junction for rail journeys across Europe, experienced declines in traffic of up to 30%. One exception was the boom in traffic to the Middle East, with long-distance trucks flourishing, but there were congestion problems at Arab terminals. The U.S.S.R. reported that it had achieved its 1975 rail freight target of 3 trillion ton-km. in 1974. The Tanzania to Zambia (Tanzam) railway, built by the Chinese, was opened.

The Commission of the European Communities proposed a free market in truck transport for Europe.

PICTORIAL PARADE

"Conoco Europe," the third very large crude carrier (VLCC) to enter service for Continental Oil Co., is equipped to carry more than two million barrels of crude oil as it operates between the Middle East and northwestern Europe. The 1,108-ft. tanker was christened at Oppama, Japan.

SYNDICATION INTERNATIONAL

"Titan," the world's largest truck, was developed by General Motors. The huge vehicle is powered by a 3,300-hp engine and can carry 350 tons in a single load.

International truck movements had been severely restricted by both rigid quotas and strict controls on the rates charged by shippers. The West German transport industry remained opposed, but both its customers and the West German Economics Ministry began to see that there might be advantages. The Commission put forward a compromise, including freer quotas in 1976 and almost complete liberalization in the 1980s.

British Rail completed computerization of its wagon (rail car) movements (similar measures were being taken on other European railways), and the National Freight Corp. developed a mini-container service, called Scids, for road-rail use. But there was only one successful application for the subsidy offered by the British government to firms wishing to build private rail sidings. The Greater London Council became interested in copying the Paris transshipment depots, which enabled heavy trucks to be banned from the city centre.

PIPELINES

Construction of the trans-Alaska pipeline was finally allowed to begin, after a delay of five years and an escalation in cost from $900 million to $6 billion. The 798-mi. pipeline was designed to carry 2 million bbl. of oil a day. The U.S.S.R. was building large pipelines for oil and gas; one was a 1,000-mi. link to the Pacific, and another 1,500-mi. pipeline was to join the Urals to the western frontiers. Panama was planning a pipeline across the isthmus, while a $210 million pipeline was completed by Iraq.

The Tapline from Saudi Arabia to the Mediterranean was closed for much of the year because of the decline in demand for oil, and a pipeline from the North Sea to Scotland suffered two bomb attacks by militant Scottish nationalists, but without serious damage. In the U.S. public utilities planned a 1,000-mi. pipeline to carry coal slurry between Wyoming and Arkansas. Railroads feared that this might cost them $150 million a year in revenue.

INTERCITY RAILWAYS

In 1975, the 150th anniversary of public passenger transport by rail, several railways suffered acute financial crisis, especially those in the U.S., West Germany, and Britain. Methods of accounting made railways particularly vulnerable to the combination of economic recession and inflation. Whereas the road user could drive less, paying less road tax but still getting the same road spending out of governments, the railway manager had to continue maintaining his track and running the same trains though he was earning less revenue for doing so. Also, because two-thirds of railway costs were labour, expenses increased rapidly.

"Shaoshan," an electric locomotive designed and made in China, operates in the mountainous regions traversed by the electrified Poaki-Chengtu railway.

A.F.P./PICTORIAL PARADE

In the U.S. the main crisis was on the freight railroads (*see* above), but Amtrak, the nationalized passenger network, was also in trouble. Amtrak asked Congress to wipe out $900 million in federal loans, and predicted an operating deficit of $870 million for the 27 months up to September 1977. Rival firms claimed that for that price a free bus ticket could be given to every rail traveler and money still be saved. The federal government intimated that the $3.5 billion needed to introduce 150-mph trains on the poorly maintained New York to Washington, D.C., line was a bad investment. But Amtrak planned to introduce 125-mph trains, bought from France, on the New York–Buffalo service in 1976.

In Britain the Railways Act 1974 came into effect in January 1975, but it was clear that the £300 million a year passenger subsidy provided for by the act would not be enough. The first sign that the government might balk at the increasing cost of rail subsidies came early in the year with publication of a transport report by an influential group of Labour Party experts, under the chairmanship of Leslie Huckfield. The experts pointed to overstaffing on the railroads, the low return on rail investment, and the high incomes of most rail travelers. Eventually, the government fixed the passenger subsidy at £330 million for 1975, and made it clear that it would continue to set tough targets. British Rail enforced a series of steep fare increases and announced cuts in services. But the railway workers won a 30% pay increase, the second consecutive year in which they were near the top of the wage settlement league. Rail investment was cut and other long-term economies were discussed. Nonetheless, because railway accounts almost invariably disguised the true extent of subsidies, it was not immediately apparent that in 1975 British Rail was beginning to contain the growth of its deficit. On the best comparable basis, the total loss rose from £185 million in 1973 to £394 million in 1974, with £404 million forecast for 1975.

The West German government was also alarmed by the soaring cost of rail subsidies. The Bundesbahn expected a loss of DM. 3.7 billion in 1975, after federal subsidies of DM. 11 billion. The government asked the Bundesbahn what sort of network it could operate without loss. In September *Der Spiegel* magazine reported that the results were that only 6,000 mi. of the 18,000-mi. network could be operated profitably, though possibly another 6,000 mi. could be kept open, with federal subsidy, as a social service. Nevertheless, the West Germans said that they intended to go ahead with building four new railway lines, although the scheduled date for starting these was delayed because of problems in establishing their exact routes.

Britain dropped a bombshell on other European railways in January when it pulled out of the Channel Tunnel project. The main reason was that the estimated cost of the new rail link from London to the coast, to be paid for entirely by the British, had risen threefold in two years, to £373 million. Later in the year, plans were reported for reducing the London–Paris rail journey to 4½ hours by using Hovercraft for the sea crossing.

Japan, which was building three undersea rail tunnels, extended its express trains from Okayama to Kyushu Island. In Italy the Rome–Florence Direttissima line was due to open in 1976, and the French were going ahead with the new Paris–Lyon link. The Dutch announced support for several new rail lines, including a railway to Schiphol airport.

A major study of intercity railways was being prepared by the Organization for Economic Cooperation and Development. It was expected that the report would prove skeptical of the justification for new railway lines. Three reasons seemed to be behind this: first, earlier forecasts of travel by all modes, including air, had set the number of travelers too high; second, a very-high-speed line had to exclude freight, and fast passenger trains alone could seldom recoup the cost of the track; and, third, cheaper alternatives, such as short stretches of relief line, were generally available where existing lines were overloaded.

URBAN MASS TRANSIT

The U.S. Department of Transportation set the tone for a more cost-conscious approach to mass transit investment by announcing that, if a city wanted to build a rapid transit line when a reserved bus lane could do the job more cheaply, the federal subsidy would be based on the cost of the bus lane. The Bay Area Rapid Transit (BART) in San Francisco, which was supposed to be the showpiece of the new rapid transit era, continued to display teething troubles. It needed a $40 million subsidy toward its $65 million annual operating cost; intervals between trains had to be six minutes, instead of the 90 seconds planned; and at any time 40% of the rail cars were liable to be in the repair shops. Travelers liked BART, but it had not made a big dent in auto traffic. The 98-mi. subway in Washington, D.C., due to open in January 1976, seemed to have technical difficulties similar to those of BART. The cost was put at $4.6 billion, against the $2.5 billion projected in 1969. Some cities turned toward trolleys as a cheaper alternative, including San Francisco itself and Boston.

One city that did give the go-ahead for a subway in 1975 was Hong Kong, but only for a much-truncated 10-mi. line. The cost was estimated at $120 million a mile. In London a study of commuter rail needs concluded that an investment of £1,400 million would be needed just to maintain existing services. A report submitted to the government claimed that for the cost of equipping one line with new coaches, the whole line could be paved with concrete and turned into a profitable bus service.

A more futuristic alternative to the automobile remained personal rapid transit (PRT), but this too experienced difficulties. PRT prototypes generally consisted of computerized, driverless minibuses, on a fixed guideway. The case for them was, in theory, that the guideway was cheaper than a subway and that, with very short intervals between the coaches, a flexible service akin to a private car could be provided. Also, they were supposed to save labour. After many difficulties, one PRT was opened in 1975, at Morgantown, W.Va., on a smaller scale than originally hoped for. At a cost of $119 million, the 2.2-km. (1.4-mi.) route joined two university campuses with the downtown area. The 12-seat coaches achieved intervals of only 15 seconds, and speeds were up to 30 mph. The French continued work on PRTs. But the Dallas-Fort Worth airport shut down its new Airtrans rail system and sued its suppliers for $200 million, while the British government rejected a proposed Minitram system for Sheffield. The province of Ontario in Canada continued to study PRTs.

KEYSTONE

Replacing the noisy diesel engine is this new natural gas-driven bus passing the Place de la Concorde in Paris.

Transport officials, and their paymasters, increasingly talked about developing services that were not only cheaper to construct than rapid transit or PRT but that also could be installed more quickly. Thus, the British engineering consultants Freeman Fox & Partners proposed using disused railway tracks in Nottingham, England, for reserved bus lanes. Bus companies, however, experienced mounting deficits during the year. The total deficit for mass transit in the U.S. was $1.3 billion in 1974, and in September 1975 New York City introduced the 50-cent fare. The British government announced that bus operating subsidies would be reduced.

Para-transit was the rather sinister name given to another range of cheap solutions aimed at bridging the gap between private cars and conventional public transport. Para-transit covered a multitude of services, including shared taxis, jitney buses, dial-a-ride, and car pools. It was inspired partly by the success of jitneys in less developed countries, but a U.S. report published in 1974 found a number of places where they were operating in the U.S., often outside the law. (A jitney is a taxicab or small bus that operates over a regular route on a flexible schedule.) Existing transport monopolies were generally skeptical of para-transit, but in Spain Madrid's bus company introduced highly successful microbuses in the city centre. These traveled at two-minute intervals at times of peak traffic along former streetcar lines. The luxury coaches charged a 50% premium over normal fares. Their key advantage was in getting motorists out of their cars; whereas only one-fifth of passengers on normal buses had cars, the figure was 80% on microbuses. (RICHARD CASEMENT)

See also Energy; Engineering Projects; Environment; Industrial Review: *Aerospace; Automobiles.*

[725.C.3; 734; 737.A.3]

ENCYCLOPÆDIA BRITANNICA FILMS. *The Mississippi System: Waterways of Commerce* (1970); *Rotterdam-Europort: Gateway to Europe* (1971); *The Great Lakes: North America's Inland Seas* (2nd ed., 1972); *Airplane Trip* (4th ed., 1973); *All the Wonderful Things that Fly* (1974).

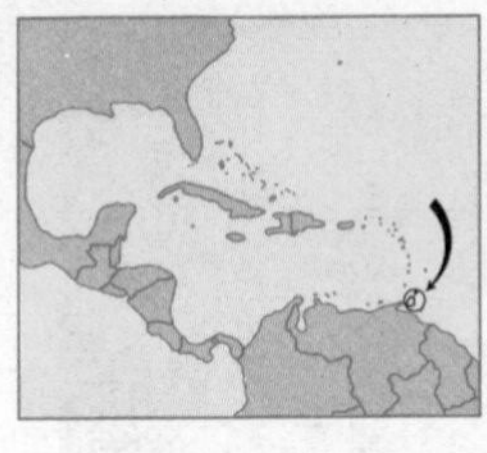

Trinidad and Tobago

A parliamentary state and a member of the Commonwealth of Nations, Trinidad and Tobago consists of two islands off the coast of Venezuela, north of the Orinoco River delta. Area: 1,980 sq.mi. (5,128 sq.km.). Pop. (1973 est.): 1,061,900, including (1970) Negro 43%; East Indian 40%; mixed 14%. Cap. and largest city: Port-of-Spain (pop., 1973 est., 60,400). Language: English (official); Hindi, French, Spanish. Religion (1960): Christian 66%; Hindu 23%; Muslim 6%. Queen, Elizabeth II; governor-general in 1975, Sir Ellis Clarke; prime minister, Eric Williams.

Growing political self-confidence and economic euphoria, deriving from the oil boom, were apparent in the late summer of 1975. Earlier, in February–April, a United Labour Front of oil and sugar workers, in an unprecedented racial alliance, had brought the country's two major industries to a standstill for six weeks, and on April 10 Prime Minister Williams called in troops to deliver gasoline and sugar. The strikers returned to work with a 40% wage rise for oil workers and a 100% rise for sugar workers, but no formal recognition for Raffique Shah's new Island-wide Indian Cane Farmers' Trade Union.

Williams reshuffled his Cabinet in September 1975, giving added responsibilities and the important Petroleum and Mines Ministry to Errol Mahabir. The prime minister bitterly opposed Venezuela's growing influence in the Caribbean. He accused Venezuela of trying to "sabotage" the proposed aluminum smelter plant announced in 1974 as a joint project by Trinidad, Jamaica, and Guyana.

Trade with other Caribbean Community countries contracted during the first half of 1975, but Trinidad was developing trade with the Soviet Union, Eastern Europe, and China. Unemployment had risen to 17–18% by the end of 1974.

Black Power advocate Michael Abdul Malik ("Michael X"), convicted of murder in 1971, was executed on May 16. (SHEILA PATTERSON)

[974.B.2.d]

TRINIDAD AND TOBAGO

Education. (1970–71) Primary, pupils 225,689, teachers (1971–72) 6,408; secondary, pupils 45,112, teachers 1,894; vocational (1969–70), pupils 2,729; teacher training (1969–70), students 707, teachers 83; higher, students 2,496, teaching staff (1970–71) 412.

Finance and Trade. Monetary unit: Trinidad and Tobago dollar, with (Sept. 22, 1975) a free rate of TT$2.32 to U.S. $1 (par value of TT$4.80 = £1 sterling). Budget (1974 est.): revenue TT$975 million; expenditure TT$974 million. Foreign trade (1974): imports TT$3,777,600,000; exports TT$4,165,900,000. Import sources: Saudi Arabia 36%; Indonesia 18%; U.S. 11%; Iran 9%; Ecuador 7%; U.K. 5%. Export destinations: U.S. 61%; Puerto Rico and U.S. Virgin Islands 7%; ship and aircraft bunker stores 6%. Main exports: petroleum products 61%; crude oil 29%.

Transport and Communications. Roads (1971) 7,050 km. (including 2,823 km. main roads). Motor vehicles in use (1973): passenger 82,700; commercial (including buses) 24,500. There are no railways in operation. Air traffic (1973): 620 million passenger-km.; freight 13.3 million net ton-km. Ships entered (1972) vessels totaling 24,244,000 net registered tons; goods loaded 20,624,000 metric tons, unloaded 14,808,000 metric tons. Telephones (Dec. 1973) 66,000. Radio receivers (Dec. 1971) 296,000. Television licenses (Dec. 1972) 82,000.

Agriculture. Production (in 000; metric tons; 1974; 1973 in parentheses): sugar, raw value *c.* 192 (184); rice *c.* 12 (*c.* 12); oranges *c.* 13 (*c.* 8); grapefruit (1973) *c.* 12, (1972) *c.* 10; copra *c.* 6 (12). Livestock (in 000; 1972–73): cattle *c.* 70; pigs *c.* 57; goats *c.* 39; poultry *c.* 5,750.

Industry. Production (in 000; metric tons; 1974): crude oil 9,460; natural gas (cu.m.; 1973) 1,549,000; petroleum products (1973) 19,216; cement 251; nitrogenous fertilizers (nutrient content; 1972–73) 67; electricity (kw-hr.) 1,200,000.

Trapshooting:
see Target Sports

Tunisia

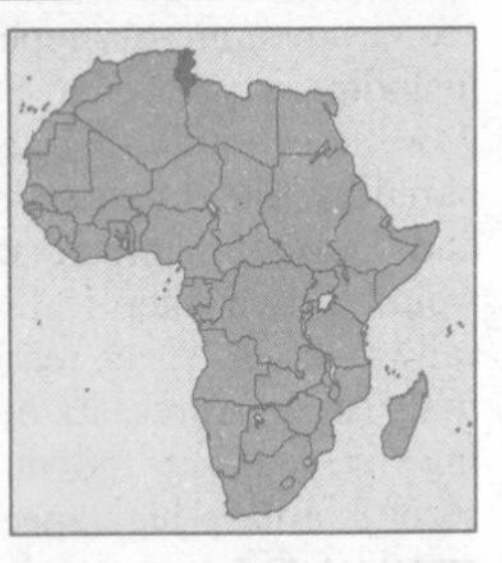

A republic of North Africa lying on the Mediterranean Sea, Tunisia is bounded by Algeria and Libya. Area: 63,379 sq.mi. (164,150 sq. km.). Pop. (1975 est.): 5,572,200. Cap. and largest city: Tunis (pop., 1966, 469,000). Language: Arabic (official). Religion: Muslim; Jewish and Christian minorities. President in 1975, Habib Bourguiba; prime minister, Hedi Nouira.

On March 18, 1975, Tunisia's National Assembly unanimously bestowed the presidency of his country on President Bourguiba for life. The commemoration in June of the 20th anniversary of his return from exile was celebrated with exceptional brilliancy.

Nevertheless, the opposition remained vigilant. On January 28 a university students' strike led to the suspension or dismissal of several dozen students. On March 19 in the Assembly the president reminded the legislators of the dangers of social conflict and de-

TUNISIA

Education. (1971–72) Primary, pupils 934,827, teachers 18,881; secondary, vocational, and teacher training, pupils 173,433, teachers 6,549; higher, students 10,849, teaching staff 628.

Finance. Monetary unit: Tunisian dinar, with (Sept. 22, 1975) a free rate of 0.42 dinar to U.S. $1 (0.86 dinar = £1 sterling). Gold, SDRs, and foreign exchange: (June 1975) U.S. $384.4 million; (June 1974) U.S. $366.8 million. Budget (1974 est.) balanced at 247 million dinars. Gross domestic product: (1974) 1,386,100,000 dinars; (1973) 1,117,300,000 dinars. Money supply: (March 1975) 415,940,000 dinars; (March 1974) 336,080,000 dinars. Cost of living (Tunis; 1970 = 100): (June 1975) 129; (June 1974) 116.

Foreign Trade. (1974) Imports 488,660,000 dinars; exports 397.7 million dinars. Import sources: France 31%; Italy 11%; U.S. 8%; West Germany 8%. Export destinations: Italy 25%; France 22%; Greece 10%; Brazil 6%; U.S. 5%; West Germany 5%. Main exports: crude oil 34%; olive oil 18%; phosphates 12%; fertilizers 9%. Tourism (1973): visitors 722,000; gross receipts U.S. $186 million.

Transport and Communications. Roads (1973) 18,774 km. Motor vehicles in use (1973): passenger 90,200; commercial 50,200. Railways: (1973) 2,089 km.; traffic (1974) 534 million passenger-km., freight 1,522,000,000 net ton-km. Air traffic (1974): 699 million passenger-km.; freight 5,790,000 net ton-km. Telephones (Dec. 1972) 96,000. Radio receivers (Dec. 1972) 400,000. Television receivers (Dec. 1972) 80,000.

Agriculture. Production (in 000; metric tons; 1974; 1973 in parentheses): wheat 760 (885); barley 200 (210); potatoes (1973) *c.* 108, (1972) 105; tomatoes *c.* 180 (180); watermelons (1973) *c.* 141, (1972) *c.* 140; wine (1973) *c.* 92, (1972) *c.* 90; dates (1973) *c.* 50, (1972) *c.* 50; figs (1973) *c.* 21, (1972) *c.* 20; olives *c.* 525 (706); oranges *c.* 72 (41). Livestock (in 000; 1973–74): sheep *c.* 3,300; cattle *c.* 690; goats (1972–73) *c.* 460; camels (1972–73) *c.* 180; poultry (1972–73) *c.* 11,100.

Industry. Production (in 000; metric tons; 1974): crude oil 4,139; natural gas (cu.m.) 202,000; cement 520; iron ore (55% metal content) 818; phosphate rock (1973) 3,474; lead (1973) 26; petroleum products (1973) 999; sulfuric acid (1973) 730; electricity (excluding most industrial production; kw-hr.) 1,099,000.

CAMERA PRESS/PHOTO TRENDS

The city of Tunis is a bustling port and modern commercial centre.

nounced striking as "equivalent to a dagger thrust in the back for this regime fashioned by the people." In July, 30 persons and then, in October, 67 more were sentenced to close imprisonment for subversive activities. Abroad, various groups of opponents kept up their active opposition to Bourguiba's regime.

In foreign policy, the Tunisian government was above all concerned with increasing cooperation with France. In June Norbert Ségard, France's secretary of state for external trade, arrived in Tunis, five months ahead of Pres. Valéry Giscard d'Estaing. Prime Minister Hedi Nouira was France's official guest in July. Nouira had also visited China and the United States, both in April. Premier Aleksey N. Kosygin of the U.S.S.R. was received officially in Tunis in May.

Relations with other Arab nations were strengthened by visits to Tunis of the vice-president of Iraq and the president of Libya, Col. Muammar al-Qaddafi, in March; by Nouira's visits to five Persian Gulf states in October; and by the public expressions of regret of Bourguiba at criticisms formulated by Algeria against Tunisia. But because of Tunisia's support of the Eritrean Liberation Front, Ethiopia broke off diplomatic relations in July.

Introducing the 1975 budget, Nouira claimed that Tunisia had succeeded in doubling investment expenditure in 1974, achieving an annual growth in production of 6.6%, in exports of 7.8%, and in per capita income of 3.5%. Agriculture, phosphate mining, and petroleum exports all recorded some growth in 1974. Deficit financing (70 million dinars in 1975, as against 30 million dinars in 1974) was to be met by investment from abroad and an easier balance of payments position. Large sugar-beet development in growing and processing, eventually expected to satisfy 50% of the country's sugar requirements, was planned. Exports of olive oil were seriously affected with the cessation of sales to countries of the European Economic Community (EEC) after the levy imposed on Tunisian exports by the EEC during the summer. On September 8–12 an international conference in Tunis on Maghreb and Euro-African cooperation, attended by representatives of EEC and Arab countries, concerned itself with the "equal" development, particularly through industrialization, of the Maghreb region (Tunisia, Algeria, and Morocco).

(PHILIPPE DECRAENE)

[978.D.2.b]

Turkey

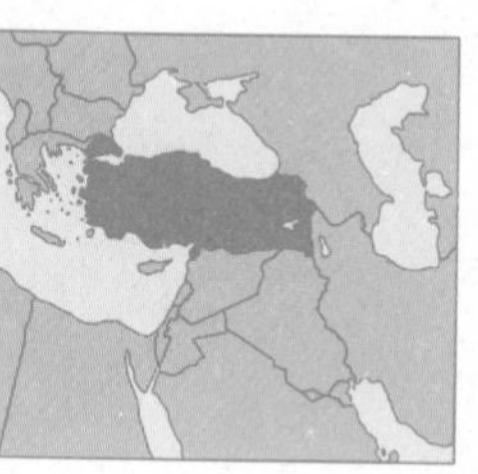

A republic of southeastern Europe and Asia Minor, Turkey is bounded by the Aegean Sea, the Black Sea, the U.S.S.R., Iran, Iraq, Syria, the Mediterranean Sea, Greece, and Bulgaria. Area: 300,948 sq.mi. (779,452 sq.km.), including 9,150 sq.mi. in Europe. Pop. (1974 est.): 38,270,000. Cap.: Ankara (pop., 1970, 1,467,300). Largest city: Istanbul (pop., 1970, 2,203,300). Language: Turkish, Kurdish, Arabic. Religion: predominantly Muslim. President in 1975, Fahri Koruturk; prime ministers, Sadi Irmak and, from March 31, Suleyman Demirel.

The year 1975 was one of slow maneuvers and deferred decisions in Turkey. On January 3, the Justice Party (JP), led by Suleyman Demirel (*see* BIOGRAPHY), set up a Nationalist Front with three smaller right-wing parties: the National Salvation Party (NSP), the Republican Reliance Party (RRP), and the Nationalist Action Party (NAP). The rightist Democratic Party (DP) stayed out, but lost a few supporters to the Nationalist Front. As political tension erupted in clashes between left- and right-wing radicals, President Koruturk appealed to the parties on March 1 to support the caretaker prime minister, Sadi Irmak. Both this appeal and the efforts of Bulent

A Turkish farmer of Akyurt displays the fine wheat crop he grew using methods developed in the U.S. Pacific Northwest.

JUAN DE ONIS—THE NEW YORK TIMES

Trucking Industry: *see* Transportation

Trust Territories: *see* Dependent States

Tungsten: *see* Mining and Quarrying

Tunnels: *see* Engineering Projects

Ecevit, leader of the left-of-centre Republican People's Party (RPP), to organize fresh elections failed. As a result, the Nationalist Front assumed office on March 31. Demirel resumed the premiership, from which he had been ousted by the armed forces in March 1971. On April 12 the Grand National Assembly endorsed the new government's program by 222 votes to 218.

In midterm Senate elections and by-elections to the Grand National Assembly held on October 12, the JP regained some of the ground it had lost to right-wing rivals in October 1973. The RPP returned 25 senators and one deputy (winning 44% of the vote, as against 35% in the same provinces in 1973); the JP 27 senators and 5 deputies (with 41%, as against 31% in 1973); and the NSP 2 senators (with its share of the poll down from 11 to 8%). Demirel declared that the Nationalist Front (in which his position was now strengthened) would remain in office.

TURKEY

Education. (1972–73) Primary, pupils 5,268,811, teachers 159,599; secondary, pupils 1,263,802, teachers 33,619; vocational, pupils 139,862, teachers 9,003; teacher training, students 46,363, teachers 1,685; higher (including 9 universities), students 180,689, teaching staff 10,703.

Finance. Monetary unit: Turkish lira, with (Sept. 22, 1975) a free rate of 15 liras to U.S. $1 (31.05 liras = £1 sterling). Gold, SDRs, and foreign exchange: (June 1975) U.S. $1,169,000,000; (June 1974) U.S. $2,124,000,000. Budget (1973–74 est.): revenue 75,658,000,000 liras; expenditure 82,411,000,000 liras. Gross national product: (1973) 294,890,000,000 liras; (1972) 237.6 billion liras. Money supply: (Nov. 1974) 85,350,000,000 liras; (Nov. 1973) 37,090,000,000 liras. Cost of living (Istanbul; 1970 = 100): (June 1975) 234; (June 1974) 193.

Foreign Trade. (1974) Imports 53,362,000,000 liras; exports 21,273,000,000 liras. Import sources: West Germany 18%; U.S. 9%; Iraq 9%; Italy 7%; U.K. 7%; Saudi Arabia 7%; France 6%; Switzerland 6%; Japan 5%. Export destinations: West Germany 22%; U.S. 9%; Lebanon 7%; Switzerland 6%; Italy 6%; U.K. 5%; U.S.S.R. 5%. Main exports: cotton 16%; tobacco 13%; hazelnuts 11%. Tourism (1973): visitors 1,341,000; gross receipts U.S. $172 million.

Transport and Communications. Roads (1973) 59,279 km. Motor vehicles in use (1973): passenger 234,600; commercial 159,300. Railways: (1972) 8,132 km.; traffic (1973) 5,219,000,000 passenger-km., freight 6,799,000,000 net ton-km. Air traffic (1974): 1,444,000,000 passenger-km.; freight 11,840,000 net ton-km. Shipping (1974): merchant vessels 100 gross tons and over 369; gross tonnage 971,682. Telephones (Dec. 1973) 807,000. Radio licenses (Dec. 1973) 4,033,000. Television receivers (Dec. 1973) 257,000.

Agriculture. Production (in 000; metric tons; 1974; 1973 in parentheses): wheat 11,082 (10,080); barley 3,330 (2,900); corn 1,100 (1,100); rye 560 (690); oats 380 (380); potatoes 2,200 (2,200); tomatoes 2,160 (2,050); onions 635 (610); sugar, raw value *c.* 815 (*c.* 736); sunflower seed 520 (560); chick-peas 190 (185); dry beans 150 (150); string beans (1973) *c.* 350, (1972) 300; cabbages (1973) 420, (1972) 598; pumpkins (1973) *c.* 400, (1972) 334; cucumbers (1973) 420, (1972) 434; oranges 578 (562); lemons (1973) 140, (1972) 149; apples 860 (850); pears 200 (195); peaches (1973) 120, (1972) 140; plums (1973) *c.* 120, (1972) 131; grapes 3,120 (3,344); raisins (1973) *c.* 320, (1972) *c.* 315; figs (1973) *c.* 220, (1972) 216; olives 814 (333); tea (1973) 22, (1972) 47; tobacco 190 (130); cotton, lint 550 (513). Livestock (in 000; Dec. 1973): cattle 12,408; sheep 36,608; horses (1972) 962; asses (1972) 1,701; buffalo (1972) 1,039; goats (1972) 18,463; chickens 38,300.

Industry. Fuel and power (in 000; metric tons; 1974): crude oil 3,429; coal 5,100; lignite 5,662; electricity (kw-hr.; 1973) 12,289,000. Production (in 000; metric tons; 1974): cement 8,938; iron ore (metal content; 1973) 1,455; pig iron (1973) 896; crude steel 1,470; sulfur (1973) 17; petroleum products (1973) 12,253; sulfuric acid (1973) 24; fertilizers (nutrient content; 1973) nitrogenous 153, phosphate 142; manganese ore (metal content; 1973) 2.5; chrome ore (oxide content; 1973) 215; cotton yarn (factory only; 1970) 185; wool yarn (1971) 26; man-made fibres (1973) 37.

In Cyprus, Turkish governments promoted the consolidation of the Turkish-held area. On January 14, as a result of Turkish pressure, Britain agreed to the transfer to Turkey of the 10,000 Turkish Cypriots who had taken refuge in the British sovereign base areas in the island. The Turkish authorities immediately shipped them back to northern Cyprus. The imposition on February 5 of the U.S. congressional embargo on all arms shipments to Turkey did not affect Turkish policy in Cyprus.

On February 13 the Turkish prime minister welcomed the proclamation by Turkish Cypriots of the Turkish Cypriot Federated State of Cyprus. Turkey then supported the inconclusive Cypriot intercommunal talks which took place in three stages in Vienna, resulting in September in the transfer to northern Cyprus of the 9,000 Turkish Cypriots who had remained in the Greek part of the island.

Relations with the U.S. were strained when on July 25, after the failure of the U.S. Congress to lift the arms embargo, the Turkish government denounced the joint defense cooperation agreement (of July 3, 1969) and took over all U.S. bases, with the exception of the major air base at Incirlik (Adana), designated as a NATO base. On October 21, however, after Congress had partially lifted the embargo, the Turkish government invited the U.S. to negotiate a new defense agreement, and also promised to support a resumption of intercommunal negotiations on Cyprus in "all its aspects"—a phrase interpreted as covering also a redrawing of the line between the Greek and Turkish zones in the island.

The dispute with Greece over continental shelf rights in the Aegean dragged on. On February 6 Turkey accepted in principle the Greek proposal that the matter be referred to the International Court of Justice at The Hague. Turkey, however, did not agree to a joint submission of the matter. The problem was discussed between the prime ministers of the two countries on May 31 following the NATO conference in Brussels.

The Turkish ambassador in Vienna was assassinated on October 22, and the ambassador in Paris two days later. The men were believed to have been killed either by Greek Cypriots or by Armenians.

On July 9 the U.S.S.R. granted Turkey a credit of $700 million for the extension of industrial installations built under the agreement of March 25, 1967, and for additional projects. On October 17 Iran agreed to lend Turkey $1.2 billion, to be used largely on improving facilities for the transit trade to Iran.

(ANDREW MANGO)

See also Cyprus.
[978.A.1–3]

Uganda

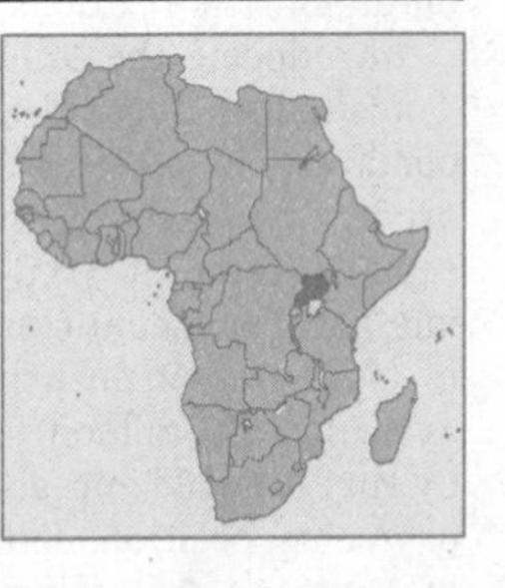

A republic and a member of the Commonwealth of Nations, Uganda is bounded by Sudan, Zaire, Rwanda, Tanzania, and Kenya. Area: 93,104 sq.mi. (241,138 sq.km.), including 15,235 sq.mi. of inland water. Pop. (1975 est.): 11,549,400, virtually all of whom are African. Cap. and largest city: Kampala (pop., 1969, 330,700). Language: English (official), Bantu, Nilotic, Nilo-Hamitic, and Sudanic. Religion: Christian, Muslim,

UGANDA

Education. (1972–73) Primary, pupils 786,899, teachers 24,032; secondary, pupils 53,887, teachers 2,341; vocational, pupils 1,521, teachers 159; teacher training, students 4,721, teachers 342; higher, students 4,018, teaching staff 470.

Finance and Trade. Monetary unit: Uganda shilling, with (Sept. 22, 1975) a par value of UShs. 7.14 to U.S. $1 (free rate of UShs. 14.87 = £1 sterling). Budget (1974–75 est.): revenue UShs. 1,880,000,000; expenditure UShs. 2,035,000,000. Foreign trade (1974): imports UShs. 1,522,000,000; exports UShs. 2,336,000,000. Import sources: Kenya 36%; U.K. 17%; West Germany 9%; Japan 5%; Italy 5%. Export destinations: U.S. 23%; U.K. 18%; Japan 9%; West Germany 5%. Main exports: coffee 71%; cotton 12%; copper 5%; tea 5%.

Transport and Communications. Roads (1972) 25,714 km. Motor vehicles in use (1972): passenger 25,700; commercial 13,600. Railways (1973) 1,230 km. (for traffic *see* KENYA). Air traffic (apportionment of traffic of East African Airways Corp.; 1973): 122 million passenger-km.; freight 7.9 million net ton-km. Telephones (Dec. 1972) 34,000. Radio receivers (Dec. 1972) 275,000. Television receivers (Dec. 1972) 15,000.

Agriculture. Production (in 000; metric tons; 1974; 1973 in parentheses): millet *c.* 600 (*c.* 600); sorghum *c.* 300 (*c.* 300); corn (1973) *c.* 350, (1972) *c.* 375; sweet potatoes (1973) *c.* 720, (1972) *c.* 713; cassava (1973) *c.* 1,000, (1972) *c.* 1,040; peanuts (1973) *c.* 170, (1972) *c.* 180; dry beans *c.* 160 (*c.* 160); coffee *c.* 200 (*c.* 252); tea 22 (21); sugar, raw value *c.* 62 (*c.* 94); cotton, lint *c.* 65 (*c.* 78); timber (cu.m.; 1973) 14,700, (1972) 14,700; fish catch (1973) 169, (1972) 166. Livestock (in 000; Dec. 1973): cattle *c.* 4,100; sheep *c.* 750; goats (1972) *c.* 1,700; pigs *c.* 75; chickens (1972) *c.* 10,700.

Industry. Production (in 000; metric tons; 1974): cement 153; copper, smelter 9; tungsten concentrates (oxide content) 0.11; phosphate rock (1972) 23; electricity (excluding most industrial production; kw-hr.) 784,000.

traditional beliefs. President in 1975, Gen. Idi Amin.

In January 1975 Finance Minister Emmanuel Wakhweya fled to Great Britain and resigned his post, claiming that Uganda was facing economic catastrophe. Foreign exchange was indeed difficult to obtain, and imported goods were in short supply. There were serious declines in the production of some of the country's main crops, including cotton and sugar. The nation also experienced a sharp rise in the cost of living, which particularly affected the poorer section of the population.

Relations with Great Britain became tense in the middle of the year when President Amin (*see* BIOGRAPHY) attempted to use a British lecturer as a hostage to extract concessions from the U.K., including the supply of military equipment, the return of Ugandan exiles from Britain, and a ban upon radio and press criticism of his policy. Denis Hills, sentenced to death for alleged spying and sedition, was eventually released after mediation by Pres. Mobutu Sese Seko of Zaire.

The Organization of African Unity (OAU) summit meeting took place in Kampala in July, but the presidents of Tanzania, Zambia, and Botswana did not attend because they disapproved of Amin's policies. In June Amin was elected OAU chairman for a year but failed to get general support for vigorous and militant action against the white regimes of southern Africa. In October he violently criticized the U.S., Britain, and Israel before the UN and called for the expulsion of Israel from membership. The U.S. ambassador to the UN, Daniel Moynihan (*see* BIOGRAPHY), in turn referred to Amin as a "racist murderer," a charge that provoked much criticism from African states. (KENNETH INGHAM)

[978.E.6.b.iv]

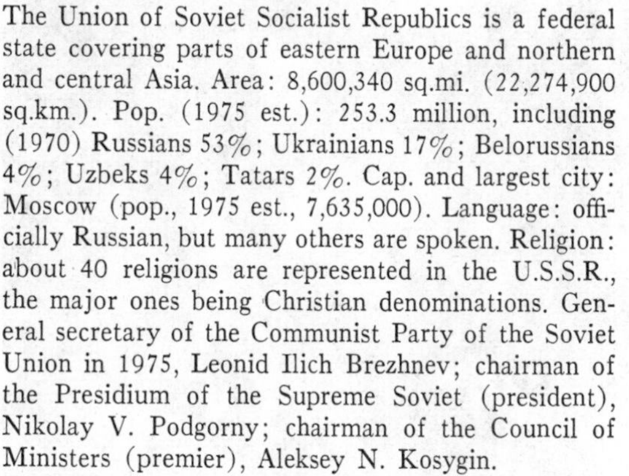

Union of Soviet Socialist Republics

The Union of Soviet Socialist Republics is a federal state covering parts of eastern Europe and northern and central Asia. Area: 8,600,340 sq.mi. (22,274,900 sq.km.). Pop. (1975 est.): 253.3 million, including (1970) Russians 53%; Ukrainians 17%; Belorussians 4%; Uzbeks 4%; Tatars 2%. Cap. and largest city: Moscow (pop., 1975 est., 7,635,000). Language: officially Russian, but many others are spoken. Religion: about 40 religions are represented in the U.S.S.R., the major ones being Christian denominations. General secretary of the Communist Party of the Soviet Union in 1975, Leonid Ilich Brezhnev; chairman of the Presidium of the Supreme Soviet (president), Nikolay V. Podgorny; chairman of the Council of Ministers (premier), Aleksey N. Kosygin.

For the Soviet Union the year 1975 was marked by relative success in foreign policy and absolute failure in agriculture, a difficult combination of circumstances that was bound to complicate East-West relations in 1976. The culmination of the Conference on Security and Cooperation in Europe in a ceremonial summit meeting at Helsinki, Fin., in the summer represented the achievement of at least two of the Soviet Union's major middle-term foreign policy goals. The frontiers drawn at the end of World War II were now solemnly ratified, and the world at large finally accepted the existence of two German states, a view that had been pressed with determination by the Soviet government for at least 20 years. Prospects for extending economic relations between East and West were also improved. The Western powers, which originally had embarked upon the European security conference with the intention of linking it to substantive progress in the concurrent talks on mutual force reductions, had to accept a separation of the two sets of negotiations. On the other hand, in the final accord at Helsinki, the Soviet Union put its signature to an undertaking to facilitate the free movement of ideas and people across the East-West divide, although by the end of 1975 there was little to indicate that the Soviet regime intended to fulfill the substance of this part of the agreement.

WIDE WORLD

Visitors view 100 masterpieces of the Metropolitan Museum of Art which were brought to the Hermitage from the U.S. for an exhibition in May.

Unemployment: *see* Economy, World; Social and Welfare Services

CAMERA PRESS/PHOTO TRENDS

Лосиный
ЗАКАЗНИК.
ВСЯКАЯ ОХОТА
ЗАПРЕЩАЕТСЯ !

This large shaggy elk becomes accustomed to its new home on an experimental farm in Sumarokova. The intended purpose is to domesticate the elk to perform the tasks of a horse and to replace the less-sturdy reindeer now being used.

Dissent in the U.S.S.R. was not silenced by the promise of better things to come. This was underscored by the award of the 1975 Nobel Peace Prize to the most prominent of the dissenters, Soviet physicist Andrey D. Sakharov (*see* NOBEL PRIZES), who was refused permission to travel to Oslo for the presentation ceremony. Indeed, the Soviet government officially denied that its decision ran counter to its undertaking at Helsinki, because "the participating states undertook to respect each other's right to make their own laws and administrative regulations."

The worst news came toward the end of the year with reports of a disastrous grain harvest. Exceptionally adverse weather reduced the harvest to 137 million tons, from a target of 215 million tons. This inability to cope with unpredictable weather conditions had characterized Russian agriculture for centuries, and the massive investments in the farming sector made in recent years failed to overcome the effects of poor management. The 1975 results were particularly disappointing after the record harvests of 1973 and 1974. In the short term the Soviet Union would need to buy grain on the world market, having already purchased some 25 million tons in 1975. This not only would affect its relations with the United States and other major grain exporters, but also would push up world prices. The Eastern European countries, which relied on imports of Soviet grain, also would have to shop on the world market. At the end of 1975 livestock had already been slaughtered in large numbers throughout the Soviet Union. Due to the grain shortage, the rate of livestock production would have to be reduced, transforming the glut of meat into later shortages.

Domestic Affairs. Though the voices of Soviet dissenters continued to be heard throughout 1975, their political significance was difficult to assess. For years there had been reports of courageous individuals calling for the protection of human rights in the Soviet Union, of repressive and restraining reaction by the regime, of Jewish intellectuals clamouring to be allowed to emigrate to Israel, and of complaints about the maltreatment of some of the non-Russian inhabitants of the U.S.S.R. The regime's reaction had moved a long way from the brutalities of the Stalin era, not only because of the gradually increasing network of East-West relations which made the Soviet Union more responsive to world opinion, but also because the nature of Soviet society and of its leaders had changed. Nevertheless, in the final analysis the regime still relied on the use of repressive power. As a scientist of great prestige, Andrey Sakharov enjoyed a relatively privileged position in a country that highly emphasized the achievements of science and technology. His Nobel Prize, which his wife accepted on his behalf, might have helped other Soviet dissenters by calling world attention to their efforts. Yet, it also might have weakened them by giving the regime the opportunity to brand them as traitors who had to rely on the acclaim of foreigners and the capitalist press.

Western reactions, however, were significant. The French Communist Party asked some awkward questions about Soviet prison camps, and the decision to release Leonid Plyush, a dissident Ukrainian mathematician, from a psychiatric prison hospital in November owed something to the intervention of French

U.S.S.R.

Education. (1973–74) Primary, pupils 39,394,000; secondary, pupils 9,830,000; primary and secondary, teachers 2,417,000; vocational and teacher training, pupils 4,448,000, teachers 209,000; higher (including 116 universities), students 4,671,000, teaching staff 302,000.

Finance. Monetary unit: ruble, with (Sept. 22, 1975) a free rate of 0.75 ruble to U.S. $1 (1.56 ruble = £1 sterling). Budget (1975 est.): revenue 208.5 billion rubles; expenditure 208.3 billion rubles.

Foreign Trade. (1974) Imports 18,834,000,000 rubles; exports 20,738,000,000 rubles. Import sources: Sino-Soviet area 59% (East Germany 11%, Poland 9%, Czechoslovakia 8%, Bulgaria 8%, Hungary 6%); West Germany 7%. Export destinations: Sino-Soviet area 58% (East Germany 10%, Poland 9%, Czechoslovakia 7%, Bulgaria 7%, Hungary 5%); Finland 5%. Main exports: machinery and transport equipment 19%; crude oil 11%; petroleum products 10%; timber 7%; iron and steel 7%; nonferrous metals 5%.

Transport and Communications. Roads (1973) 1,398,000 km. (including 598,400 km. surfaced). Motor vehicles in use: passenger (1974) *c.* 3 million; commercial *c.* 4 million. Railways: (1972) 259,900 km. (including 136,300 km. public and 123,600 km. industrial); traffic (1973) 296,619,000,000 passenger-km., freight (1974) 3,100,000,000,000 net ton-km. Air traffic (1973): 98,418,000,000 passenger-km.; freight 2,350,900,000 net ton-km. Navigable inland waterways (1973) 145,600 km.; traffic 189,500,000,000 ton-km. Shipping (1974): merchant vessels 100 gross tons and over 7,342; gross tonnage 18,175,918. Telephones (Dec. 1973) 14,261,000. Radio licenses (Dec. 1973) 110.3 million. Television licenses (Dec. 1973) 49.2 million.

Agriculture. Production (in 000; metric tons; 1974; 1973 in parentheses): wheat 83,800 (109,784); barley *c.* 54,800 (55,044); oats *c.* 18,000 (17,516); rye *c.* 12,000 (10,759); corn 12,100 (13,216); rice 1,900 (1,765); millet *c.* 3,200 (4,416); potatoes 80,700 (108,201); sugar, raw value *c.* 8,315 (*c.* 9,470); tomatoes *c.* 3,550 (*c.* 3,500); watermelons (1973) *c.* 3,500, (1972) *c.* 3,000; sunflower seed 6,760 (7,385); linseed *c.* 495 (407); dry peas *c.* 6,300 (6,066); soybeans *c.* 500 (*c.* 424); wine (1973) *c.* 3,143, (1972) 2,930; tea *c.* 75 (75); tobacco *c.* 300 (305); cotton, lint *c.* 2,700 (2,473); flax fibres (1973) 443, (1972) 458; wool 277 (258); eggs *c.* 3,024 (2,828); milk *c.* 90,600 (86,500); butter 1,360 (1,350); cheese 1,292 (1,211); meat (1973) *c.* 13,476, (1972) 13,609; timber (cu.m.; 1973) *c.* 383,000, (1972) 383,000; fish catch (1973) 8,619, (1972) 7,757. Livestock (in 000; Jan. 1974): cattle 106,266; pigs 70,032; sheep 142,634; goats (1973) 5,604; horses (1973) 7,075; chickens (1973) 671,090.

Industry. Index of production (1970 = 100): (1974) 134; (1973) 123. Fuel and power (in 000; metric tons; 1974): coal and lignite 680,800; crude oil 454,100; natural gas (cu.m.) 260,100,000; manufactured gas (cu.m.; 1973) 35,269,000; electricity (kw-hr.) 952,000,000. Production (in 000; metric tons; 1974): cement 115,100; iron ore (60% metal content) 225,000; pig iron 99,600; steel 136,600; aluminum (1973) *c.* 1,360; copper (1973) *c.* 1,300; lead (1973) *c.* 470; zinc (1973) *c.* 670; manganese ore (metal content; 1973) 2,839; tungsten concentrates (oxide content; 1973) 9.3; magnesite (1973) *c.* 1,550; gold (troy oz.) *c.* 7,400; silver (troy oz.) *c.* 41,000; sulfuric acid 16,644; caustic soda 2,200; plastics and resins (1973) 2,320; fertilizers (nutrient content; 1973) nitrogenous 7,241, phosphate 3,240, potash 5,918; newsprint (1973) *c.* 1,212; other paper (1973) *c.* 6,213; cotton fabrics (sq.m.; 1973) 7,137,000; woolen fabrics (sq.m.; 1973) 919,000; rayon and acetate fabrics (sq.m.; 1973) 960,000; passenger cars (units) 935; commercial vehicles (units) 608. New dwelling units completed (1973) 2.3 million.

Communist leader Georges Marchais. Yet, Andrey Amalrik, the well-known dissident author who was released in May after five years in prison, was rearrested and expelled from Moscow in September.

Published by Amnesty International in November, a comprehensive report on the barbarities of the Soviet prison system and on the inadequacy of the Soviet legal system in protecting basic human rights described the U.S.S.R. as "a very black spot on the human rights map." It did not, however, draw any comparisons with the Stalin years. Twenty-five years ago it would have been impossible for almost 80 prisoners to appeal for recognition of their political status and to have this information relayed to foreign journalists at a privately organized press conference in Moscow, as happened in October.

About 1,000 Jews left the Soviet Union every month in 1975, compared with a monthly average of 2,900 in 1973. There was some attempt to explain this sharp decline by claiming that most of those who wanted to go had now left and that Israel's economic difficulties made emigration to that country less attractive. But bureaucratic pressure and the official campaign to discourage emigration also must have played a part.

The customary speculations about changes in the Soviet leadership proliferated through the year. In particular, the health of Leonid Brezhnev, general secretary of the Central Committee of the Soviet Communist Party, gave much cause for concern to Western kremlinologists. Brezhnev was 68, and indisposition was given as the reason for his absence from public engagements on several occasions, notably during French Pres. Valéry Giscard d'Estaing's visit to the Soviet Union in October. Yet there was no evidence to show that his position within the Soviet leadership had been weakened in any way, although the secretive nature of decision-making processes in the Soviet Union made it impossible to estimate the political prospects reliably. There was only one major change in the leadership: the removal from the Politburo in April of Aleksandr N. Shelepin, a former chief of the KGB, or state security police. This followed immediately on Shelepin's visit to Britain where he had been invited as head of the Soviet labour unions and where he had been the target of hostile demonstrations protesting against violations of human rights in the U.S.S.R. Shelepin might have resigned at his own request, feeling perhaps that the Soviet government should have reacted more strongly to the demonstrations. His departure at age 56 displaced one of the youngest among the potential successors to Brezhnev and was interpreted by some as a preparatory maneuver for a possible restructuring of the venerable Politburo at the 25th congress of the Soviet Communist Party, due in February 1976.

Détente posed a problem for the Soviet regime by opening up a range of ideological issues that could not be ignored. Peaceful coexistence would not be allowed to impinge upon the basic ideological contest between capitalism and the Soviet brand of socialism, for the regime could not admit that there were viable alternatives to the social and economic order it was trying to maintain in the Soviet Union and Eastern Europe. On his visit to the Soviet Union, Giscard d'Estaing was publicly snubbed for advocating some degree of ideological coexistence in a speech made at an official dinner at the Kremlin. Similar remarks made later and on a similar occasion by Walter Scheel, the West German president, were simply left out of the version of his speech published in the Soviet press. The Soviet media gave no indication at all that the Helsinki accords on the free movement of ideas and people would be implemented. On the contrary, they emphasized that the conflict of ideologies continued unabated and seized upon the economic recession in the West as proof of the inherent self-destructive shortcomings of the capitalist system. The Soviet press also attacked Western commentators for allegedly distorting the significance of the Helsinki accords by concentrating on the human rights aspects of the agreement.

The Soviets also feared that détente might weaken the resolve of revolutionaries of Communist leanings in the West and the third world. A significant article published in *Pravda,* the official Communist Party newspaper, by Konstantin I. Zarodov, a leading Communist theoretician, criticized the more moderate policies espoused by some Communist parties in the West, advising them to adopt a "clear perspective of ultimately achieving socialism." Zarodov stressed that revolution "consists in the fact that it suppresses reaction's resistance by force" and warned his comrades in the West against regarding a democratic majority as an arithmetical rather than a political concept. Zarodov's article was not in itself unique, but the fact that shortly after its publication he was received by Brezhnev and that Tass, the Soviet news agency, bothered to report the meeting shed some light on Soviet regard for the meaning of détente.

Soviet intervention in the strife in Angola showed quite clearly that the U.S.S.R. had no worries about the weakening of détente whenever there was an opportunity to exploit a revolutionary situation without undue risk of a confrontation between superpowers. In addition, Brezhnev was careful to emphasize the Soviet Union's determination to maintain the unity of the Communist bloc in Eastern Europe. In a speech to the Polish United Workers' Party congress in December, he made it quite clear that this solidarity must not be undermined by détente or, as he put it, by "ideological infiltration."

The Economy. The disastrous grain harvest overshadowed most other economic news because the shortfall of nearly 80 million tons would impede the development of the economy as a whole. In early De-

WIDE WORLD

Lake Baikal, the world's deepest and largest reservoir of fresh water, 381 miles in length, became the focus of a Western-type controversy between those favouring industrialization of the area and those with environmental concerns.

cember the Supreme Soviet met to consider the plan for 1976; the deputies were informed by Nikolay K. Baibakov, chairman of the State Planning Committee, that the projected increase in industrial output would be held at 4.3%, the lowest in more than 20 years. The production of consumer goods in 1976 would be allowed to rise by only 2.7%, one of the lowest peacetime increases since the 1930s, thus further reducing the expectations of Soviet consumers who had been encouraged by the consumer boom of 1971–72. Baibakov indicated that the poor harvest also had caused some reassessment of planning priorities.

The Soviet minister of finance, Vasily F. Garbuzov, presented the 1976 draft budget to the same session of the Supreme Soviet. With respect to the ruble, he at least spoke from a position of strength. Since 1970 its purchasing power had remained stable. As Tass pointed out in February, one ruble in 1975 bought as much milk or beef as it had ten years earlier. Garbuzov stressed that defense spending would be kept at the 1975 level of 17.4 billion rubles (7.8% of total expenditure), thus officially indicating a certain measure of restraint in this sensitive category. He foresaw a 4.2% increase in expenditure for social and cultural purposes and announced special provision for increased investments in the engineering, oil, chemical, and gas industries.

By making necessary further grain purchases abroad, the farm crisis was expected to exert an adverse effect on the Soviet balance of payments with the West, which was already in deficit. Sales of raw materials abroad were reduced by the recession in the West, while inflation increased the cost of Western imports. Throughout 1975, the U.S.S.R. sold large quantities of gold and borrowed extensively in Western Europe.

In a speech to the Central Committee of the Soviet Communist Party in December, Brezhnev claimed that the 1971–75 five-year plan "was the best in our country's history as regards the scale of absolute growth in social production," but that the impact of the grain crisis would have a bearing upon long-term planning. The targets determined by the 1976–80 five-year plan, published on December 14, were rather modest, not only because of the immediate effects of the poor harvest but also because many of the goals set for the 1971–75 plan had to be reduced in 1973. The 1976–80 plan called for a 24–28% rise in national income, compared with 28% in 1971–75. Total growth of agricultural production was expected to rise by 14–17% over the previous plan, with the average annual grain harvest set at 215 million to 220 million tons. Industrial output would grow by 35–39%, heavy industry being given priority with a projected rise of 38–42%, compared with 30–32% for consumer goods. The plan also called for special efforts to reduce atmospheric pollution in some of the major cities, including Leningrad, Moscow, and Kiev.

In its search for oil, the Soviet Union launched a fourth oil-drilling rig anchored in the Caspian Sea off Baku, in January.

WIDE WORLD

In the short term the U.S. was the obvious source of grain supplies for the Soviet Union. According to the U.S. Bureau of Mines, the U.S.S.R. had now overtaken the U.S. as the world's leading petroleum producer, and negotiations centred on the possibility of trading Soviet oil for American grain. The Soviets, however, continued to insist on a formal separation of the two issues.

In the long term the future of the Soviet economy depended on the development of the vast resources of its Far Eastern territories. It appeared that the construction of the Baikal-Amur Mainline railway was proceeding according to plan. Exploratory work on the new line yielded important geologic discoveries. Vast copper deposits, estimated at about 1,200,000,000 tons of ore, were found at Udokan in eastern Siberia. Reserves of coking coal, amounting to some 500,000,000,000 tons, were opened up in Yakutiya, where there were also important iron-ore deposits. Japanese cooperation was sought in the construction of a deep-water port near Nakhodka and in prospecting and drilling for oil and natural gas in Yakutiya and in the sea around Sakhalin Island. In September a new railway bridge across the Amur River at Komsomolsk was completed, cutting more than 600 mi. off the Trans-Siberian railway to Vladivostok. In November a new 1.2 million-kw. hydroelectric power station went into operation on the Zeya River.

Foreign Policy. The Central Committee of the Soviet Communist Party held a special plenary session in April to discuss problems of foreign policy, at which time it reaffirmed its devotion to the principles of peaceful coexistence. The Central Committee recorded its view that political détente must be supplemented by military détente, but it also described the "Leninist foreign policy" of the U.S.S.R. as "helping to spread the realization in the minds of very broad masses of the people of the advantages of the new social system, which are seen with particular clarity against the background of the present economic crisis and other upheavals in capitalist countries." Finally, "the Party of Lenin" proclaimed its intention "to do all in its power to ensure the close unity of the world Communist movement."

With respect to détente, Brezhnev achieved his apotheosis at the Helsinki summit that concluded the Conference on Security and Cooperation in Europe. Ritual visits by Western leaders to Moscow were described as an important part of the process. The prime minister of Australia, Gough Whitlam, paid his respects in January. In February it was Harold Wilson, the British prime minister, who returned with an agreement on raising the level and improving the structure of Anglo-Soviet trade over the next five years. He was followed in March by Jacques Chirac, the French premier; the foreign minister of Iceland in April; the queen of Denmark in May; the grand duke of Luxembourg in June; and the king of the Belgians in June-July. A delegation of U.S. senators led by Hubert H. Humphrey (Dem., Minn.) and Hugh Scott (Rep., Pa.) visited in June, and a group of U.S. congressmen headed by Carl Albert, speaker of the House of Representatives, was received in August. Pres. Giovanni Leone of Italy, who came in November, avoided the disputations over the meaning of détente that characterized earlier visits by the presidents of France and the Federal Republic of Germany. Soviet Premier Kosygin traveled to Turkey in December.

Soviet actions, however, showed less dedication to the principles of peaceful coexistence than the rhetoric of the Central Committee's April session seemed to indicate. An important article by Georgy A. Arbatov, director of the influential Institute of U.S. and Canada Studies of the Soviet Academy of Sciences, published in the government newspaper *Izvestia* in early September, pointed out that the socialist countries "did not and could not commit themselves to guaranteeing the social status quo in the world or to stop the processes of class and national liberation struggle." The U.S.S.R. definitely acted with determination to assist the Marxist Popular Movement for the Liberation of Angola (MPLA), despite repeated warnings by the United States that the massive introduction of Soviet military equipment and advisers, together with large numbers of Cuban troops, represented a serious threat to détente. On December 25, *Izvestia* made it clear that aid for the MPLA would continue and rejected U.S. attempts "to put pressure on the Soviet Union."

Soviet support for the Communist Party in Portugal, however, did not prevent the marked diminution of left-wing influence there by the end of the year, and this setback added another contentious issue to the ongoing debate over ideology and tactics among the Communist parties of Europe. In addition, the unity of the world Communist movement, so strongly endorsed by the Soviet Central Committee in April, remained plagued with problems. Some of the Western European parties, notably the French and the Italian, were less than reticent in expressing doubts about the condition of human rights in the Soviet Union. Disagreements over a summit conference of European Communist parties remained unresolved after 12 months of trying to reconcile the demands of unity with the attractions of ideological diversity.

Relations between Moscow and Peking did not improve, although in December the Chinese released the crew of a Soviet helicopter that had come down in northern China two years previously. After the U.S. withdrawal from Indochina, the Soviet Union had become somewhat alarmed by the prospect of increased Chinese influence in Southeast Asia, but an October visit to Moscow by Le Duan, the first secretary of the Vietnamese Communist Party, was a diplomatic success and resulted in Soviet promises of economic aid to North Vietnam. The Sino-Soviet controversy followed familiar lines, and the September issue of the Soviet Communist Party's monthly *Kommunist* surprised no one when it called on all comrades to "smash Maoism." China barred a Soviet delegation from celebrations of the 30th anniversary of the victory over Japan, and on December 27 the *Peking People's Daily* denounced the "social imperialists" in Moscow for pushing the world closer to war by the policies they pursued in 1975, a somewhat extreme expression of the Chinese view that Soviet ambitions for expansion were encouraged by Western weakness.

In the Middle East, the Soviet role seemed to have been reduced, and the U.S.S.R. did not succeed in diminishing the ascendancy of U.S. influence in Egypt. Even Syria, the Soviet Union's closest Middle Eastern ally, which agreed on new deliveries of Soviet arms after Pres. Hafez al-Assad's visit to Moscow in October, seemed anxious to reduce Communist influence in its affairs. And in October Kosygin told visiting U.S. political figure Sargent Shriver that the U.S.S.R. was prepared to guarantee the integrity of Israel, provided the Israelis withdrew to their 1967 frontiers and conformed to UN resolutions. Yet, a communiqué issued after Moscow talks between Yasir Arafat, leader of the Palestine Liberation Organization, and Soviet Foreign Minister Gromyko in November referred to "the Palestinians' right to create a national state of their own on the territory of Palestine." (OTTO PICK)

[972.B.1]

ENCYCLOPÆDIA BRITANNICA FILMS. *The Soviet Union: Epic Land* (1972); *The Soviet Union: A Student's Life* (1972); *The Soviet Union: Faces of Today* (1972).

United Arab Emirates

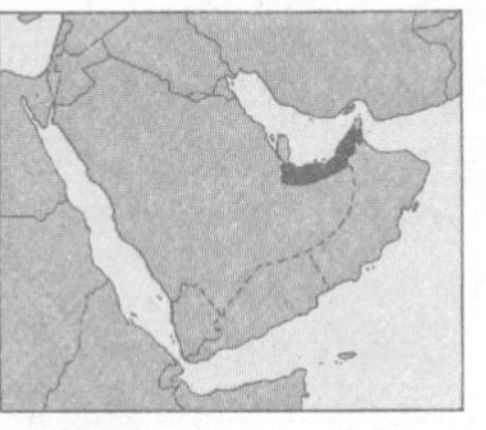

Consisting of seven emirates, the United Arab Emirates is located on the eastern Arabian Peninsula. Area: 37,000 sq.mi. (96,000 sq.km.). Pop. (1974 est.): 430,000, of whom (1968) 68% were Arab, 15% Iranian, and 15% Indian and Pakistani. Cap.: Abu Dhabi town (pop., 1973 est., 60,000). Language: Arabic. Religion: Muslim. President in 1975, Sheikh Zaid ibn Sultan an-Nahayan; prime minister, Sheikh Maktum ibn Rashid al-Maktum.

During 1975 the United Arab Emirates (UAE), especially Abu Dhabi, continued to develop its role as a major financial centre and source of investment aid. Sheikh Zaid, the UAE president and ruler of Abu Dhabi, claimed that Abu Dhabi was spending 35% of its gross national product on aid and that reserves had fallen to $1 billion despite 1974 oil revenues of $4 billion. Abu Dhabi criticized the oil companies when output was reduced in January by some 40%, but after price reductions of 55 cents a barrel, production rose again to 1.2 million bbl.

Sheikh Zaid led attempts to give the UAE greater unity in the face of complaints that individual rulers were pursuing independent policies in oil, defense, and other matters. A meeting of rulers, or their representatives, of the seven emirates broke up in disagreement on May 2, but after a further meeting it was

UNITED ARAB EMIRATES

Education. (1972–73) Primary, pupils 26,203, teachers 1,023; secondary, pupils 12,217, teachers 757; vocational, pupils 333, teachers 53; teacher training, students 117, teachers 12.

Finance. Monetary unit: dirham, with (Sept. 22, 1975) a par value of 3.95 dirhams to U.S. $1 (free rate of 8.23 dirhams = £1 sterling). Budget (1974 est.) balanced at 1,692,000,000 dirhams.

Foreign Trade. (1974 est.) Imports *c.* 7 billion dirhams; exports *c.* 29,080,000,000 dirhams. Import sources: Japan *c.* 18%; U.K. 16%; U.S. *c.* 13%; West Germany 5%. Export destinations (1973): Japan *c.* 33%; France *c.* 21%; West Germany *c.* 15%; U.K. *c.* 10%; The Netherlands *c.* 5%. Main export crude oil *c.* 98%.

Industry. Crude oil production (1974) 81,480,000 metric tons.

Unions:
see Industrial Relations

Unitarian Universalist Association:
see Religion

United Church of Canada:
see Religion

United Church of Christ:
see Religion

MARC RIBOUD—MAGNUM

Tradition merges with modern technology on the edge of this oil field in Abu Dhabi.

announced on May 12 that the seven would unite their military forces and coordinate oil policies. In July Dubai announced that it was taking over full ownership of the oil companies operating in its territory. Compensation was fixed at about $110 million. Abu Dhabi announced in April that it had abandoned plans to take over the remaining 40% of the oil companies not in its hands because it still lacked the technical and managerial expertise. (PETER MANSFIELD)

[978.B.4.b]

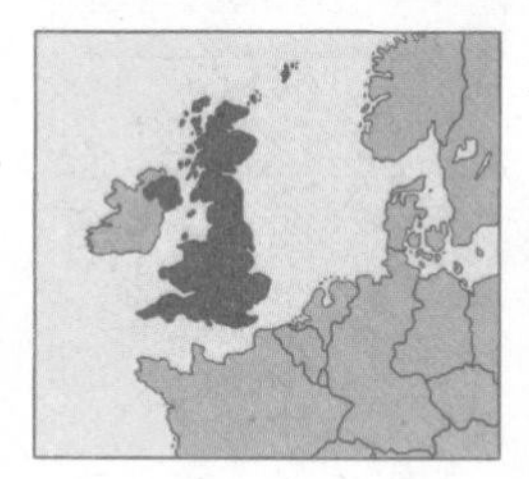

United Kingdom

A constitutional monarchy in northwestern Europe and member of the Commonwealth of Nations, the United Kingdom comprises the island of Great Britain (England, Scotland, and Wales) and Northern Ireland, together with many small islands. Area: 94,217 sq.mi. (244,021 sq.km.), including 1,191 sq.mi. of inland water but excluding the crown dependencies of the Channel Islands and Isle of Man. Pop. (1974 est.): 56,056,000. Cap. and largest city: London (Greater London pop., 1974 est., 7,281,100). Language: English; some Welsh and Gaelic also are used. Religion: mainly Protestant with Catholic, Muslim, and Jewish minorities, in that order. Queen, Elizabeth II; prime minister in 1975, Harold Wilson.

Britain in Europe. The United Kingdom confirmed its membership in the European Economic Community (EEC) by referendum on June 5. A two-to-one majority voted "yes" to the question "Do you think that the United Kingdom should stay in the European Community?" With 65% of the voters going to the polls, 17,378,581 voted "yes" (67.2%) and 8,470,073 "no" (32.8%). Only two areas returned a "no" majority—the outer fringe Scottish islands of Shetland and the Western Isles. There were "yes" votes in Scotland, Wales, and Northern Ireland, where the nationalist parties were opposed to membership, and in Greater London, the southeast, the southwest, East Anglia, and the East Midlands "yes" votes averaged over 70%.

The referendum was without precedent in British history. The device had been adopted in Labour's 1974 election program, since the party itself was divided. Prime Minister Harold Wilson (*see* BIOGRAPHY) had promised a referendum after the terms on which the U.K. had joined the EEC in 1973 had been renegotiated. Almost a year of renegotiation was concluded at an EEC summit meeting in Dublin in March, when new terms were arranged for the U.K. contribution to the EEC budget and for access to the British market for New Zealand dairy products. With the renegotiation objectives substantially achieved, the government recommended that the country vote "yes." In Parliament on April 9 a majority of 396 to 170 in the House of Commons backed the government on a free (nonparty) vote, but the Labour Party was split, 145 MPs voting "no" against 138, with 32 not voting. The Cabinet was divided, with seven ministers (Michael Foot, Anthony Wedgwood Benn, Peter Shore, Barbara Castle, William Ross, John Silkin, and Eric Varley) taking up a "license to differ" accorded to them on this issue. More than 90% of Conservative MPs and all the Liberals were in favour of continuing British membership.

The size of the "yes" majority was accepted as conclusive. The Labour Party ended its boycott of the European Parliament and took up its 18 places. The Trades Union Congress also lifted its boycott and sent trade-union representatives to the various Brussels committees.

UNITED KINGDOM

Education. (1973–74) Primary, pupils 6,228,702, teachers 248,107; secondary and vocational, pupils 4,391,631, teachers 306,223; higher, students 389,659, teaching staff 50,788.

Finance. Monetary unit: pound sterling, with (Sept. 22, 1975) a free rate of £0.48 to U.S. $1 (U.S. $2.07 = £1 sterling). Gold, SDRs, and foreign exchange: (March 1975) U.S. $7,042,000,000; (March 1974) U.S. $6,303,000,000. Budget (1975–76 est.): revenue £28,110 million; expenditure £30,858 million. Gross national product: (1974) £82,384 million; (1973) £72,879 million. Money supply: (March 1975) £14,735 million; (March 1974) £12,774 million. Cost of living (1970 = 100): (June 1975) 188; (June 1974) 149.

Foreign Trade. (1974) Imports £23,116.7 million; exports £16,494.3 million. Import sources: EEC 33% (West Germany 8%, The Netherlands 7%, France 6%); U.S. 10%; Saudi Arabia 5%. Export destinations: EEC 33% (West Germany 6%, The Netherlands 6%, France 6%, Belgium-Luxembourg 5%, Ireland 5%); U.S. 11%. Main exports: nonelectric machinery 19%; chemicals 13%; motor vehicles 8%; electrical machinery and equipment 7%; diamonds 5%; textile yarns and fabrics 5%. Tourism (1973): visitors 7,609,000; gross receipts U.S. $1,665,000,000.

Transport and Communications. Roads (1972) 362,539 km. (including 1,761 km. expressways); Great Britain only (1973) 340,956 km. Motor vehicles in use (1972): passenger 13,106,000; commercial 1,686,200. Railways (excluding Northern Ireland; 1973): 18,224 km.; traffic 35,204,000,000 passenger-km., freight 25,514,000,000 net ton-km. Air traffic (1974): *c.* 27,700,000,000 passenger-km.; freight *c.* 1,050,000,000 net ton-km. Shipping (1974): merchant vessels 100 gross tons and over 3,603; gross tonnage 31,566,298. Ships entered (1970) vessels totaling 137,888,000 net registered tons; goods loaded (1972) 50,714,000 metric tons, unloaded 206,092,000 metric tons. Telephones (Dec. 1973) 19,095,000. Radio receivers (Dec. 1972) *c.* 37.5 million. Television licenses (Dec. 1974) 17,435,000.

Agriculture. Production (in 000; metric tons; 1974; 1973 in parentheses): wheat 6,017 (5,003); barley 9,017 (9,006); oats 976 (1,080); potatoes 6,791 (6,711); sugar, raw value 616 (1,047); cabbages (1973) *c.* 850, (1972) 838; cauliflowers (1973) *c.* 340, (1972) 337; green peas (1973) 554, (1972) 554; carrots (1973) 464, (1972) 502; apples 365 (490); pears 51 (46); dry peas 97 (70); dry broad beans (1973) 187, (1972) 166; tomatoes *c.* 125 (120); onions 244 (223); eggs 828 (823); milk 14,834 (14,619); butter 53 (97); cheese *c.* 218 (181); beef and veal 930 (920); mutton and lamb 245 (226); pork 951 (926); wool 33 (32); fish catch 913 (928). Livestock (in 000; June 1974): cattle 15,241; sheep 28,639; pigs 8,651; poultry 139,927.

Industry. Index of production (1970 = 100): (1974) 106; (1973) 110. Fuel and power (in 000; metric tons; 1974): coal 110,576; crude oil 400; natural gas (cu.m.) 32,862,000; manufactured gas (cu.m.; 1973) 10,788,000; electricity (kw-hr.) 273,332,000. Production (in 000; metric tons; 1974): cement 17,781; iron ore (28% metal content) 3,320; pig iron 13,901; crude steel 22,428; petroleum products 103,059; sulfuric acid 3,903; fertilizers (nutrient content; 1973–74) nitrogenous 984, phosphate 533; cotton fabrics (m.) 409,000; woolen fabrics (sq.m.) 175,000; rayon and acetate fabrics (m.) 506,000; passenger cars (units) 1,533; commercial vehicles (units) 403. Merchant vessels launched (100 gross tons and over; 1974) 1,262,000 gross tons. New dwelling units completed (1974) 276,000.

Constitution. Having ceded some measure of sovereignty to the EEC, the Westminster Parliament came under growing pressure to grant effective political power to Scotland and Wales. Since the *Report of the Royal Commission on the Constitution 1969–73* (Kilbrandon Commission) in 1973, all parties had been committed to the idea of devolution in principle. In practice it began to appear particularly tricky. A White Paper of Sept. 17, 1974, promised elected assemblies for Scotland and Wales and legislation "as soon as possible," but there was increasing unease among ministers and MPs as the implications of the separatist inclinations came to be considered. Could devolution imply the breakup of the United Kingdom (formed by the Act of Union of 1707)? The government decided to give more time for public debate and to defer legislation until the 1976–77 session. A White Paper published on November 27 set out the terms for another "great debate."

More than 12 months of dispute over the terms of a bill legitimizing the trade-union closed shop led to a conflict between the House of Commons and the House of Lords. Because the Lords refused to give way on points that might infringe the freedom of the press by undermining the independence of editors, the government invoked the 1949 Parliament Act to overrule the Lords—the first time these powers had been exercised.

Politics. The Conservative MPs elected Mrs. Margaret Thatcher (*see* BIOGRAPHY) as their new leader in place of Edward Heath, who had led the party since 1965 and had lost two general elections in 1974. She was the first woman in British history to lead one of the main political parties. In a reorganized Conservative "shadow" cabinet, Heath withdrew to the back benches, as did former Cabinet ministers Peter Walker, Geoffrey Rippon, and Robert Carr. Former chancellor of the exchequer Anthony Barber left the Commons (later to take his seat in the Lords as Lord Barber). William Whitelaw remained deputy leader. Other key members of Mrs. Thatcher's team were Sir Keith Joseph (in a new post with responsibility for policy and research), Reginald Maudling (foreign affairs), Sir Geoffrey Howe (economic affairs), and Ian Gilmour (home affairs).

In a small reshuffle of Cabinet posts after the referendum, Benn and Varley switched jobs; Benn became secretary of state for energy to concentrate on the speedy landing of North Sea oil, and Varley, secretary of state for industry to work closely with Chancellor of the Exchequer Denis Healey on the revival of industry. Fred Mulley became minister for education, displacing Reginald Prentice (*see* BIOGRAPHY), who replaced Judith Hart (*see* BIOGRAPHY) at the Ministry of Overseas Development. The Labour Party in the country and in Parliament was troubled by a potentially divisive dispute between militants and moderates. Prentice, an outspoken moderate, was turned down by the militant majority in his constituency organization as their candidate for the next general election, and a number of other moderate Labour MPs were similarly threatened. In the elections for the national executive committee at the October party conference, a leading left-winger, Eric Heffer, displaced Healey. In Parliament, the constituencies, and the trade unions, the moderates began to organize themselves. In the Amalgamated Engineering Workers Union, Britain's second largest union, two leading left-wingers were defeated by moderates who gained control of the executive.

The incidence of violent crime continued to rise disturbingly, and Sir Robert Mark (*see* BIOGRAPHY), commissioner of police of the metropolis, called more than once for a legislative amendment on crime, as well as a less lax social attitude to the prosecution and sentencing of criminals and greater support and freedom of action for the police. In July the runaway MP John Stonehouse (*see* BIOGRAPHY), who had vanished in Miami, Fla., and turned up in Australia under an assumed name, was returned to England to face charges of fraud, theft, and forgery.

The Economy. The turn of the year found the economy floundering. During December 1974 Britain's worst-ever trade deficit, £534 million in November, was reported. Share prices had dropped to their lowest level since 1954, with the *Financial Times* (FT) industrial shares index touching 150—lower in terms of real value than at any time since the 1920s. Wage increases were about eight percentage points ahead of inflation, which (in November figures) was 18.3% year-on-year. In three years the sterling exchange rate had fallen by 22% on average against other leading trading currencies. On New Year's Eve the Bank of England had to come to the rescue of Burmah Oil, Britain's 25th-largest company, with a guarantee to meet its $650 million of foreign debts.

KEYSTONE

The Liberian tanker "Theogennitor" arrived at the British Petroleum refinery on the Isle of Grain in June with the first delivery of North Sea oil.

The FT index fell to 146 on January 6, but this proved to be the bottom. The Bank of England began to bring down interest rates, the pound was rising against the dollar, the December trade deficit was the lowest for more than a year. The FT index rose an extraordinary 70% by the end of the month—the steepest gain on record—and reached 300 by the end of February. With some ups and downs, it moved to 375 by mid-November—still far short of the 1972 peak of around 540.

The City of London, which had reechoed with the sound of crashing banks and exploding big names in 1974, had two more stunning events still to come. Early in October the First National Finance Corp. had to be bailed out by the Bank of England and the clearing banks with £360 million in loans after losing £73 million in six months—thought to be a record in London's financial history. Later that month the prototype financial whiz-kid of the 1960s, Jim Slater, resigned the chairmanship of Slater Walker at a time when Slater Walker associate companies in Singapore and Hong Kong were under investigation. The price of Slater Walker shares, which had reached around 1,150 pence in 1972, fell to 20 pence.

The stock exchange recovery reflected the long-term view of institutional investors. Meanwhile, inflation went from bad to worse. Wage increases were now the main component of inflation. With the year-on-year inflation rate running at 19 to 20% in the early months of 1975, wage increases of 30% and more were being conceded by both public and private industries. It was plain that the "social contract," the agreement between the government and the trade unions for voluntary restraint of wage claims, had broken down. Healey noted in his budget speech on April 15 that wages were running 8 to 9% ahead of prices. In April wages increased 33%, prices 21%, and industrial production less than 2%.

The April budget was severe. Income tax was raised by two percentage points at all levels except the top slice (already at 83%), bringing the lowest rate to 35%. The value-added tax (VAT) was raised from 8 to 25% on luxury goods and a wide range of domestic electric equipment. Increases in the taxes on alcoholic drinks raised the price of a bottle of whisky or gin by about 25% and a bottle of cheap wine by about 30%.

LES WILSON—CAMERA PRESS/PHOTO TRENDS

Volunteers at London's Earl's Court count ballots from the Common Market referendum in June. The ayes had it.

The control of public expenditure became a matter of increasing concern during the year, as the deficits of government, local authorities, nationalized industries, and public services seemed likely to reach £12,000 million, or about 12% of the gross national product (GNP). Local authorities were instructed to hold their programs to the existing level, and nationalized industries were required to reduce or even eliminate their deficits. The immediate result was to pass on huge increases in charges to the consumer. By October postal charges had doubled and telephone charges trebled in two years, and some services had been withdrawn. Local authority taxes in some areas increased by more than 50% in 1975. There were similarly large increases in charges for gas and electricity and in fares on railways and buses.

The search for a new policy of incomes restraint began soon after the budget. Jack Jones (*see* BIOGRAPHY), leader of the largest trade union, the Transport and General Workers, suggested a flat maximum rate of increase across the board for all workers for the next 12 months, and this became the basis of a new policy set out in a White Paper, "The Attack on Inflation," published on July 11. From August 1 there was to be a £6 a week limit on all pay increases, and no increases were to be granted on salaries of more than £8,500 a year. The objective was to get the inflation rate down to 10% by the third quarter of 1976 and possibly to single figures by the end of that year.

Labour thinking remained adamantly opposed to a statutory incomes policy, but reserve powers of enforcement were called into play by way of price control on private employers and by withholding grants and subsidies to public industry and services. Cash limits on public expenditure were to be set for the financial year beginning in April 1976. The £6 a week limit was accepted by the trade unions. After inflation peaked at 26.9% in August, the year-on-year rate began to subside slowly, and by November it was calculated that over the previous six months the annual rate had fallen to 21.9%.

The government became embroiled with consultants (senior specialists and surgeons) in the National Health Service over its decision to phase out pay beds in NHS hospitals. It was then faced with a revolt by junior hospital doctors who rejected the government compromise offer (itself looking beyond the £6 limit) to meet their demands for increased overtime pay. By a narrow majority they voted on November 17 to take industrial action, treating emergency cases only. A week later the ancillary hospital workers' and nurses' union demanded talks with the government to prevent cuts in hospital staff. A further serious blow was the recommendation by the leaders of the consultants that they too should treat emergencies only, as a protest against plans to separate private practice from the NHS, and should consider resignation from the NHS. Meanwhile, the prime minister on October 20 announced the setting up of a royal commission on the NHS. (*See* HEALTH AND DISEASE.)

Another inflationary element was the decline in the exchange rate of sterling. In January the average depreciation of the pound against major trading currencies was 21.6%. Britain's failure to curb inflation brought about a sharp fall in the value of the pound in June, when the level of depreciation reached 29%, and it stayed around that figure for some months. The effect was to raise the cost of imports considerably. However, the trade figures in the latter part of the year were encouraging, mainly as the result of a decline in imports. October yielded a record value (largely due to inflation) for exports of £1,740 million and a current account deficit of £96 million, a vast improvement over a year earlier. To maintain the exchange rate of the pound, the Bank of England brought the minimum lending rate to 12% in September. Deposits of oil producers' funds in London had been slowing, and in November the U.K. sought a $2 billion International Monetary Fund loan.

Industry and Employment. Industry was severely hit by the deep recession in demand, both at home and abroad. In August and September industrial production had fallen below the level of 1970. The automobile industry was the most severely affected. For Europe as a whole automobile production capacity was as much as double the market demand in 1975. In Britain one-third of the reduced demand was taken up by imported foreign automobiles. The U.S.-based Chrysler group threatened to close down its operations in Britain, putting more than 25,000 jobs at risk, and in December the government was forced to come to its rescue with a £162.5 million deal. In April the government had been obliged to take over British Leyland, the United Kingdom's largest motor-vehicle manufacturer, when it was, in effect, bankrupt. It was estimated that £900 million would have to be injected into the company in the next three years to make it viable. Another company that had to be taken over by the government was Alfred Herbert, one of the most important machine-tool makers. The combination of reduced business and inflated costs threatened the existence of many other companies and led to widespread short-time working and reduction of labour forces. Unemployment rose from 742,000 in January to 1,250,000 in August (a figure inflated by school-leavers) but fell back to 1,165,000 (5% of the labour force) in October. There were predictions that it would rise to 1.5 million during the winter, though the Confederation of British Industries in November was saying that the recession had bottomed out. (*See* INDUSTRIAL RELATIONS: *Special Report*.)

In "An Approach to an Industrial Strategy," published on November 5, the government set a new order of priorities. Greater weight would be given to the regeneration of industry. "For the immediate future this will mean giving priority to industrial development over consumption or even our social objectives." Resources would be concentrated on sectors with the best prospects. It acknowledged the need for industry to earn adequate profits to finance investment: "the government accepts the importance of sustaining a vigorous, alert, responsible and profitable private sector of industry."

The main instruments of the strategy were to be the National Economic Development Council ("Neddy"), which would serve as a forum for research and discussion between industry, the unions, and the government; and the National Enterprise Board (NEB), set up by the Industry Act with powers to inject cash into private industry in exchange for a share in the equity (and thus a say in the management) and to negotiate planning agreements on development projects with private industry. The first chairman of the NEB was Lord Ryder (*see* BIOGRAPHY), a notably successful industrialist.

SYNDICATION INTERNATIONAL/PHOTO TRENDS

Pierre Trudeau, Canadian prime minister, received the Freedom of the City of London at a Guildhall ceremony on his four-day official visit to Britain in March.

There remained the promise of North Sea oil. On November 3 Queen Elizabeth II inaugurated the opening of the pipeline to British Petroleum's Forties Field, the biggest field in the U.K. sector. Though many North Sea projects were a year or more behind schedule, and some were troubled by escalating costs, it still seemed probable that the U.K. would be self-sufficient in oil by 1980. During the year the Petroleum and Submarine Pipeline Act, providing for government control of North Sea oil development and a major share in the ownership, was passed by Parliament. The British National Oil Corporation was set up as the instrument of this policy, with Lord Kearton, formerly head of Courtaulds, as chairman.

The Anglo-French Concorde supersonic airliner project continued. There were plans to establish commercial services to the Middle East, Southeast Asia, Australia, and South America. British Airways had hoped to open a route to New York in January 1976, but unfavourable reports on Concorde's noise levels and pollution effects aroused strong opposition both in and outside of Congress. At year's end the U.S. government had not yet decided whether to permit the aircraft to land on its territory. During the year the cost of the Concorde development program topped £1,000 million. The Anglo-French Channel Tunnel project was suspended in January after the British government decided it could not afford the estimated cost of the rail link from London to Folkestone, which had trebled in less than two years to £373 million.

Defense and Foreign Policy. The rundown in the scale of Britain's armed forces continued. The policy statement of the minister of defense, Roy Mason, in December 1974 was amplified in a defense White Paper on March 19. A progressive reduction over the ten years to 1983–84 was expected to reduce defense expenditure from 5.5% of GNP to 4.5%. British land and air forces would be concentrated in the central region of Europe, and sea and naval air forces in the eastern Atlantic and the Channel areas. In June the agreement with South Africa on the Royal Navy's use of the Simonstown base was formally terminated.

Prime Minister Wilson and Foreign Secretary James Callaghan were both active in pursuit of détente between the Communist and non-Communist worlds. Agreements on economic, industrial, scientific, and

TERRY FINCHER—PHOTOGRAPHERS INTERNATIONAL/PICTORIAL PARADE

This young British soldier in the market square of Crossmaglen, County Armagh, typified the continuing tragedy unfolding in Northern Ireland.

technological cooperation were made with the U.S.S.R., Poland, and Romania.

The "cod war" with Iceland over fishing limits broke out again in mid-November when Iceland unilaterally claimed rights to the fishing within 200 mi. of its coast. Iceland proposed to cut the quota of fish British trawlers would be permitted to take from these waters by half. The U.K. sent naval vessels to the area after Iceland's ships cut away the nets from some British trawlers.

There was irritation in the EEC when Wilson tried to insist that Britain (as a major oil producer-to-be) should be given separate representation from the rest of its EEC partners at the Conference on International Economic Cooperation, which opened December 16 in Paris. The demand was refused, but a compromise was reached whereby Britain was to be permitted to speak with a separate voice on occasion. (*See* CHRONOLOGY OF EVENTS.)

Northern Ireland. For most of 1975 the Provisional wing of the Irish Republican Army (IRA) had declared a cease-fire. This, however, did not stop continuing sectarian and factional killings and occasional attacks on the Army. In November the number of civilians killed in the Northern Ireland troubles since 1969 reached 1,000. Murder and deliberate maiming marked feuds between the Provisional IRA, the Official IRA, the Republican clubs (Official IRA), and the Irish Republican Socialist Party. The Protestant Ulster Volunteer Force (UVF) was proscribed for a second time in October for its responsibility for many sectarian murders of Roman Catholics.

The Northern Ireland secretary of state, Merlyn Rees (*see* BIOGRAPHY), was pursuing two main objectives: to restore the processes of law and order, and to devise a new constitution for Northern Ireland acceptable to both the Protestant and Catholic communities. Rees had considerable success in substituting trial in the courts for detention without trial under emergency powers. Detention was ended in December, despite protests against the release of known terrorists. Meanwhile, the police had greater success in bringing terrorists to court and securing convictions. More than 1,000 were charged with serious crimes in the first ten months of 1975 (118 for murder, 77 for attempted murder, and 283 for carrying guns). "I am determined that criminals should be brought to justice through the courts," Rees said.

The search for common ground on a new constitution proved abortive. Elections for a constitutional convention on May 1 produced a massive United Ulster Unionist Council (UUUC) majority, with 46 seats against 17 for the Social Democrat and Labour (SDLP) parties representing the Catholic community and only 8 for the middle-of-the-road Alliance Party. The UUUC majority was not prepared to concede either power-sharing with the SDLP in government or arrangements for some formal association with the Republic of Ireland, and on October 24 it expelled William Craig, leader of the Vanguard Party and former hard-liner, for calling for an emergency coalition government. The UUUC proposals submitted in November would return virtual total control of Northern Ireland, including internal security, to an Ulster Unionist and Protestant government—terms that had no chance of acceptance by the Westminster Parliament.

In August the IRA switched its bombing attacks to England. There were attacks on London suburban pubs, fashionable West End restaurants and hotels, and the cars of some MPs. In a new phase—for England—of terrorist attack, the sports and political writer Ross McWhirter (*see* OBITUARIES), who had launched an appeal to raise £50,000 to establish a reward fund for information leading to the arrest of terrorist bombers, was fatally shot on his own doorstep at the end of November, supposedly by IRA terrorists. The police located a cache of 400 lb. of gelignite at a working-class block of flats in Southampton. In August six terrorists responsible for the Birmingham pub bombing in November 1974 which killed 21 and injured 120 were sentenced to life imprisonment, and in September another four were sentenced for two pub bombings in the London suburbs in 1974. (HARFORD THOMAS)

See also Commonwealth of Nations; Dependent States; Ireland.

[972.A.1.a]

SPECIAL REPORT

NEW NATIONALISMS IN BRITAIN

By Martin Walker

The British Parliament that adjourned in the summer of 1975 was the last that could claim to embody the full sovereignty of the United Kingdom. In June a national referendum finally and formally ratified British entry into the European Economic Community. A small but increasing proportion of economic legislation was thus placed in the hands of the EEC Council of Ministers in Brussels. But of more profound significance for British parliamentary sovereignty was the acceptance in principle by the Parliament of 1975 of the government's plan to establish national assemblies in Scotland and Wales. In that Parliament sat 14 members who had been elected on a platform of eventual independence for what had traditionally been two integral provinces of the British nation.

Growth of Nationalist Parties. Eleven of the 14 MPs were members of the Scottish National Party (SNP). With a program of full independence for Scotland, the SNP won 30% of the Scottish vote in the October 1974 general election. They had replaced the Conservatives as the main rival for the Labour Party in its long dominance of Scotland, and in a regional council by-election in September 1975 they startled political experts by wresting from Labour the old stronghold of Lothian, with 48% of the vote. The rise in votes had been rapid. Until 1964, the SNP was something of a national joke, concerned with the retention of the Gaelic language and the use of the kilt on all possible occasions. In 1964 the party won 2.4% of the Scottish vote; in 1966 it won 5%; in 1970 it doubled to 11.4%, then doubled again to 21.9% in the first election of 1974 and rose to 30.4% in the second. The most obvious cause of that growth was the new wealth of oil that had been discovered beneath the North Sea, which the SNP was quick to claim as "Scotland's Oil." By so doing the SNP's politicians were able, for the first time, to make a convincing economic case for independence. In 1975 the proved oil reserves of the North Sea fields were valued at £150,000 million, with an almost guaranteed annual return of £3,000 million by 1981.

But oil alone cannot explain the growth of Scottish nationalism, for nationalism was not simply a Scottish phenomenon. In Wales, where the prospects of offshore oil discoveries are slender, the independence party Plaid Cymru had won three seats in the House of Commons in 1974 and 10% of the Welsh vote. And in scarred and war-weary Northern Ireland, the objective of the Roman Catholic militants also was independence from Britain. There, even the Ulster Unionist Party, whose name and ethic is based upon a determination to maintain the union with Britain, became so disenchanted with the British government's unsuccessful attempts to find an equable and negotiable solution that it publicly mused about the example of Rhodesia—a unilateral declaration of independence. In England itself, the extreme right-wing National Front, led by a self-avowed admirer of Adolf Hitler with a prison record for organizing paramilitary groups, rose from the undistinguished fringe of ultrapatriot politics to 113,000 votes in the October 1974 election.

Martin Walker is a journalist on the London staff of The Guardian. *His studies of the growth of nationalistic feeling within the U.K. are summarized in* The National Front *(in preparation).*

CHARLES FERGUSON—CAMERA PRESS/PHOTO TRENDS

Robert the Bruce, king of Scots (1306–29), at the ancient victory site of Bannockburn.

The explanations for this loosening of the old ties and political loyalties within the United Kingdom, whether serious academic studies or glib journalistic accounts, have agreed that the causes are both psychological and economic. The end of global empire and Britain's reduction in rank to a middling power and a middling economy have caused a crisis of loyalty among those who enjoyed belonging to the British state while it guaranteed prosperity at home and prestige abroad. Since 1964 the Scottish and Welsh economies have been annually subsidized by the British Exchequer to the extent of £300 million and £110 million, respectively. But by 1974 Scottish and Welsh nationalists felt that they no longer needed the British connection—a brighter economic future lay in store with independence. For Scotland, the magic new guarantor of prosperity was oil. For Wales, it was water, which the industrial centres of the English Midlands and North West withdraw at the rate of 300 million gal. daily. Ironically, Welsh communities living in the shadow of the reservoirs pay up to eight times more for water than do the English consumers, because the thrifty city fathers of Birmingham and Liverpool bought the land, water, and pipelines 60 years ago.

Economic Decline. In spite of the economic subsidies from London, Welsh and Scottish nationalists claimed with some justice that their nations had long borne the brunt of the British economic decline. The average Welsh industrial wage was 15% lower than the British norm in 1974. A government report on housing in Britain, published in 1975, found that 95% of the very worst category of slums in Britain were to be found in the single Scottish area of Clydeside. Scots also complained that they did not control their own economy; a study by the University of Glasgow's Department of Social and Economic Research found that of Scottish manufacturing employment, 39.8% was controlled by English firms and 15% by U.S. companies. Moreover, "In the five fastest growing sectors, Scottish-owned companies only account for some 13.5% of total employment."

There was nothing new in this. The logic of the unified British state had long and logically meant that economic as well as political control should be vested in London. But by 1970 it had become apparent that London was no longer able to deliver the economic goods. The British gross national product had been overtaken by those of West Germany, Japan, and France and was being challenged by that of Italy. It is wrong to say that Britain went into economic decline; it simply grew more slowly, at an average rate of about 3% annually during the early 1960s compared with the 5% or even higher rate of West Germany. But there was a very real decline in the old heavy industries upon which the Industrial Revolution had been based—mining, iron and steel, shipbuilding, and the railways. During

1950–70 approximately 1.4 million jobs were lost in these industries, the bulk of them in Scotland and Wales, and more automation was yet to come. "The Welsh and the Scots are being made to pay the price for England's economic problems," Plaid Cymru's leader told the approving audience at the SNP conference in Perth, Scotland, in 1975. And as British unemployment rose above the dangerous one million level that year, the highest proportions of joblessness were to be found in Scotland, Wales, and Northern Ireland.

Militancy and Responsive Measures. Some of the nationalists, although denounced by the SNP and Plaid Cymru, have taken up arms to secure independence. The Irish Republican Army with its bombs in Belfast and London may have won the most headlines, but in Glasgow in 1975 five Scots describing themselves as belonging to the "Army of the Provisional Government" were sent to prison for organizing bank raids and blowing up electricity pylons and oil pipelines. In Wales the threat of the "Free Wales Army" was met by brisk arrests and prison terms for possession of arms in the 1960s. But the militancy survived until 1969, when two Welshmen blew themselves up with their own bomb days before the investiture of Prince Charles as prince of Wales.

So far, these incidents can be dismissed as atypical adventures, but the dreadful escalations of violence in Ulster have finally killed off the comforting British myth of "it can't happen here." More ominously, no public figure has yet dared to confront the very real danger that lies in the future. Should the rise of the SNP continue to the point at which it clearly commands the support of the majority of Scottish voters, London may consent to grant independence, but it is difficult to imagine that it would ever consent to give up North Sea oil, much of it already pledged for foreign loans to cover the £5,000 million trade deficit sustained in 1974.

In response to this rising tide of nationalism, the British government has agreed to grant a measure of autonomy to both Wales and Scotland. The degree of power that the proposed regional assemblies will wield has yet to be determined by Parliament, but both Welsh and Scottish independence parties have made it clear that although they will work with and through the new assemblies, their policy remains full independence. The decision to create these assemblies was taken in 1975, as a result of the findings of a royal commission that had been appointed in 1968–69 after a wave of by-election successes by the nationalists in Scotland and Wales. At the time, the royal commission was widely dismissed as a political maneuver to appease nationalist sentiment and buy time for the government, which hoped that the nationalist tide would recede as quickly as it had risen.

The name of this Welsh railway station appeared again after a seven-year struggle with unsympathetic authorities.

KEYSTONE

The commission, chaired by Lord Kilbrandon, announced its findings in 1974, when the elections of that year were showing that the nationalist vote was growing quickly. The 13 members of the commission could not agree on their recommendations. Indeed, two of them refused to endorse the report and submitted a resolution of their own. Six favoured granting both Scotland and Wales assemblies with wide legislative powers; two wanted the assemblies to have executive but not legislative powers; and three believed that the Scots had a better case than the Welsh, who should be granted a council with deliberative and advisory functions only. In the meantime, a number of measures have been taken to meet nationalist grievances. In 1975 the British Broadcasting Corporation created a Radio Cymru to broadcast in the Welsh language; this was dismissed by Plaid Cymru as "the most cynical act since Queen Elizabeth I ordered the Bible to be translated into Welsh to ensure that the Welsh were Protestants." In another move, the headquarters for the new national oil corporation would be located in Scotland.

Possible Consequences. The major parties in Britain all argue that a nationalist voter is not necessarily a separatist, and doubtless many electoral supporters are simply registering a protest vote. And so far, the bulk of voters in Wales and Scotland are not voting for the nationalists, although most of them now agree that a degree of devolution of power from London is desirable. A Scottish poll on the government's proposals found that 44% believed the proposals did not go far enough; 35% said they went too far.

There are influential institutions that bitterly oppose the nationalists, including the Scottish Trades Union Congress and the Scottish Labour Party. Indeed, at its first conference in 1975, the SLP voted heavily against the government's plans for devolution; it was then persuaded to hold a second conference, which belatedly endorsed the Labour government's policy. The main fear of the Labour Party is that devolution of power to Welsh and Scottish assemblies will mean that the number of MPs from Wales and Scotland will be reduced. If the House of Commons were composed only of English MPs, then the government would always be Conservative; Labour victories in the United Kingdom depend on the party's dominance of the Welsh and Scottish votes.

It is a traumatic experience for a nation and a government to accept that its sovereignty, and even perhaps its frontiers, may soon be diminished. So far, successive British governments have reacted with calm and with timely promises of reform to the nationalist revival. The Breton and Corsican separatists of France and the Basque nationalists of Spain have in contrast faced bitter official opposition. In spite of the friendly links and statements of mutual esteem that the European and Welsh and Scottish nationalist movements exchange, they appear to have little in common except the international economic crisis, which has tended to hit the remoter provinces, with their older and obsolescent economies, particularly hard. There may also be another, more tenuous, link. The recent stagnation in the international growth economy of the 1960s has given many people in the West pause for thought. Perhaps economic growth and bigger and more powerful corporations and governments with ever more sweeping economic powers do not guarantee human happiness. Perhaps old crafts, local traditions, and regional cultures and languages are valuable in providing a sense of continuity, of human roots, and of identity in a world that seems dedicated to technological and social change. In the linguistic revival in Wales, and the return of Scottish theatre groups and singers to their Gaelic traditions, there is something that goes far beyond politics. The British government has gone some way to satisfy Welsh and Scottish political demands and is trying to cope with their economic grievances. But whether governments can ever find a way to satisfy those deeper human yearnings, and to understand those ancient cultural loyalties, is another and very different matter. They may yet prove to be more crucial than Scottish oil, Welsh water, or Irish religion.

United Nations

Marking the 30th anniversary of the signing of the UN Charter on June 26, Secretary-General Kurt Waldheim spoke of the UN as a "unique human experiment" that had survived and expanded beyond recognition, in both membership and scope of activity, and that had made remarkable strides in closing the gap between the lofty aspirations of nations and their actual practices. He warned, however, that "the world cannot be safe, secure, or economically sound when global military expenditures are nearing $300 billion a year." He referred also to the increasing dangers of proliferating nuclear weapons; stressed the importance of taking a global approach to massive problems of economic and social development; and urged renewed efforts to achieve peaceful solutions in the Middle East, Cyprus, and southern Africa.

Economic and Social Development. The seventh special session of the General Assembly (September 1–16) addressed itself solely to the world's economic and social problems. At the start of the session, U.S. representative Daniel Moynihan (*see* BIOGRAPHY) presented several proposals to foster the economic growth and security of less developed countries (LDCs). These included: establishing a $10 billion International Monetary Fund (IMF) "facility" that would stabilize the export earnings of LDCs, expanding the International Finance Corporation of the World Bank, creating an International Energy Institute, arranging for more rapid sharing of technology, establishing a world reserve of 30 million tons of wheat and rice, and improving commodity trade agreements. The delegates adopted resolutions intended to improve the lot of LDCs by expanding and diversifying their trade and by opening to their exports, under favourable terms, the markets of wealthier nations. The assembly stressed the need for nations to curb excessive swings in commodity markets, to ensure stable export earnings through compensatory financing, and to study schemes for linking the prices of commodity exports to industrial imports. Delegates from developed nations set 0.7% of their nations' gross national products by 1980 as a target for aid to LDCs (the rate in 1975 was about 0.32%).

A panel of 25 experts from as many countries reported to the secretary-general on May 20 that the UN economic system should be recast to foster cooperation between rich and poor countries and to deal more effectively with the world's massive economic problems. They recommended that the UN establish negotiating procedures to help nations agree on controversial economic questions rather than continue the practice of merely casting "yes" or "no" votes. They also proposed a new post of director-general for development and international economic cooperation to guide the entire UN economic system.

Middle East. On September 2 Waldheim transmitted to the Security Council the text of the interim Sinai accord, which U.S. Secretary of State Henry Kissinger had helped Israel and Egypt negotiate. The relevant documents were initialled in Geneva on September 4, and in late September and periodically thereafter Egyptian and Israeli military representatives met under the chairmanship of Lieut. Gen. Ensio P. H. Siilasvuo, chief coordinator of UN peacekeeping operations in the Middle East, to complete detailed arrangements. Israel gradually withdrew from some of its positions in the Sinai, giving up the Ras Sudr and Abu Rudays oil fields, and both parties agreed to establish a new UN buffer zone. Beginning in 1976 U.S. civilians were to monitor electronic surveillance devices for detecting unauthorized troop movements in the area.

Ill feeling between Arabs and Israelis resulted on November 10 in the adoption by the General Assembly (72–35, with 32 abstentions) of a resolution determining that "Zionism is a form of racism and racial discrimination." (*See* RACE RELATIONS.) The president of the assembly, Prime Minister Gaston Thorn of Luxembourg, speaking as a delegate and not as an assembly officer, took the unusual step of saying that the vote had "destroyed" the climate of conciliation cultivated at the UN earlier in the year.

On November 10 the assembly also decided (93–18–27) to establish a committee to guarantee the "inalienable rights" of the Palestinian people to deal with their "right to return to their homes and property from which they have been displaced and uprooted" and approved (101–8–25) still another resolution calling for the Palestine Liberation Organization (PLO) to participate in all efforts to secure peace in the Middle East. On November 30, after negotiating intensively with Syria, the secretary-general cleared the way for the Security Council to extend the life of the UN Disengagement Observer Force on the Syrian-Israeli frontier for six months. On Syrian insistence, however, the council linked the extension to a full-scale debate on the Middle East, scheduled for Jan. 12, 1976, in which the council would allow the PLO to participate.

Israel had already condemned the assembly's anti-Zionist resolution as anti-Semitic and announced that it would not participate in any Middle East conferences where the PLO was represented. After the council vote, Israel repeated its refusal to negotiate with the PLO. On December 2, however, Israel told the assembly that it was prepared to negotiate on the Middle East "at any moment without any preconditions whatsoever."

After the assembly's anti-Zionist vote Kissinger said that the U.S. would ignore the resolution, but the vote led to calls in Congress for the U.S. to reconsider its role in the UN. On November 6 the U.S. had given the required two-year notice that it would withdraw from the International Labour Organization (ILO) largely because of what it regarded as unjustified ILO involvement in political questions, as, for instance, the ILO vote in June to give the PLO observer status.

Violence continued to flare up in the Middle East, particularly on the Israel-Lebanon border. In early March a Palestinian guerrilla assault on a beach hotel in Tel Aviv ended with the death of six Israelis and seven of the eight assailants, and the secretary-general condemned the attack as violence tending only to heighten tension. Also, in Jerusalem on November 13, a guerrilla bomb killed 6 people and wounded 46; and on November 20, guerrillas attacked a settlement in the occupied Golan Heights, killing three Israelis and wounding two. In retaliation, on December 2 Israeli jets attacked Palestinian camps in northern and southern Lebanon, reportedly killing 75 and wounding 120. Israeli spokesmen said that the raids were designed to protect Israel from attacks organized on Lebanese territory by the PLO and other terrorist organizations. The ferocity of the attack, however, aroused misgivings even in Israel, and, at the request of Egypt and Lebanon, the Security Council met in December to consider the situation. Over U.S. objections, the council agreed to allow the PLO to participate in the debate, a decision that caused Israel to boycott the meetings. On December 5 the assembly adopted (84–17–27) a resolution condemning Israeli occupation of Arab territories and asking the council to set a timetable for a general Middle East settlement based on all relevant UN decisions. The assembly also requested states to withhold economic and military aid from Israel. On December 8 the U.S. vetoed a draft resolution—the vote was 13–1–1, Costa Rica abstaining—that would have condemned the Israeli air strikes and warned of "appropriate steps" if such attacks recurred. The U.S. argued that the council should have condemned Arab terrorist attacks against Israel as well as the Israeli raids, since the two were linked—violence producing counterviolence.

Cyprus. Talks between Greek and Turkish Cypriots, begun in January, were broken off after Turkey on February 13 unilaterally proclaimed a Turkish Federated State of Cyprus in the northern part of the island. The UN Security Council, after eight meetings between February 20 and March 12 in addition to private consultations, adopted a resolution by consensus. It expressed regret at the Turkish move as tending to compromise negotiations aimed at a freely agreed settlement; reaffirmed UN support for the sovereignty, independence, territorial integrity, and nonalignment of Cyprus; asked all nations to respect those conditions; and specified that no nation should attempt to partition the island or to annex it.

The council authorized Waldheim to try to get the Greek and Turkish sides talking to each other again, and the secretary-general succeeded in arranging a series of meetings in Vienna and New York. The talks, however, proved inconclusive. On December 13 the council extended Waldheim's mission as mediator for another six months.

Decolonization. In August the Special Committee of 24 on decolonization marked the 15th anniversary of the UN Declaration on the Granting of Independence to Colonial Countries and Peoples by unanimously reaffirming the need to bring a swift and unconditional end to all forms of colonialism. Actually, significant steps toward that goal were taken in 1975, largely, though not entirely, because of the change in government in Portugal in April 1974. The committee held a week-long meeting in Lisbon in mid-June as a tribute to the Portuguese government's policy of granting independence to its now-former colonies: Guinea-Bissau (Portuguese Guinea) on Sept. 10, 1974; Mozambique on June 25, 1975; the Cape Verde Islands on July 5, 1975; São Tomé and Príncipe on July 12, 1975; and Angola on Nov. 11, 1975. On December 22 the Security Council unanimously called on Indonesia to remove without delay its military forces from Portuguese Timor (where it had sent them December 7) so as to allow the people self-determination.

The Committee of 24 and other UN organs continued throughout the year to register their distress over South Africa's apartheid (racial separation) policies and the absence of status for blacks in Rhodesia. The nonaligned countries presented a draft resolution to the Security Council on May 30 designed to get South Africa to withdraw from Namibia (South West Africa) and to see the territory constituted as an independent state. The resolution would have imposed a mandatory arms embargo against South Africa on the grounds that its continued occupation of Namibia was a threat to peace. The resolution failed, though it received ten votes, because the U.S., the U.K., and France vetoed it (Japan and Italy abstained). The minority conceded that much could be charged against South Africa's role in Namibia, denied that the problem constituted a threat to the peace, and confirmed that they were maintaining arms embargoes against South Africa.

In late August the Trusteeship Council examined for the last time the situation in Papua New Guinea, which became independent of Australian administration on September 16 and became the 142nd member of the UN on October 10. The only territory under UN trusteeship at the end of 1975 was the Pacific Islands (Micronesia), which the U.S. administered. UN membership rose to 143 on November 12 with the admission of the Comoro Islands, which declared its independence of France in July, and to 144 on December 5, when the assembly admitted the former Dutch colony of Surinam.

On May 23, while the International Court of Justice was considering the status of the Spanish (Western) Sahara, Spain announced that it intended to end its rule, and, fearing violence, suggested that UN observers go there. On October 14 a UN visiting mission recommended that the UN arrange for consultations among Algeria, Mauritania, Morocco, Spain, and the Saharans in an effort to organize some expression of self-determination. Two days later, the court stated unanimously that the Spanish Sahara had some legal ties with both Morocco and Mauritania when Spain colonized it, even though the ties did not constitute territorial sovereignty. The court said, however, that those ties were no impediment to applying to the area the principle of self-determination.

Rejecting the court's suggestion, King Hassan II of Morocco organized a "peaceful" march of Moroccans into the territory to dramatize his claims. The Security Council, meeting on November 6, adopted a resolution deploring the march and asking that all the parties concerned undertake to cooperate with the secretary-general in continued talks in an effort to avoid a danger to the peace. The marchers withdrew from Spanish Sahara on November 9 while talks proceeded in Madrid, and on November 14 Spain agreed, much to the dismay of Algeria (which argued for self-determination), to allow Morocco and Mauritania to assume control of the area in February 1976.

Asia. On November 18 the General Assembly adopted two conflicting resolutions on Korea. Although both called for an end to the UN command there, one resolution (adopted 59–51–29 and supported by the U.S. and other Western countries) called for negotiations among all concerned to find other ways of preserving the Korean armistice. Because North Korea refused to negotiate with South Korea, the North Koreans preferred a second resolution (adopted 54–43–42), supported by China, the Soviet bloc, and third world countries, that called for only the U.S. and North Korea to negotiate and asked that all foreign (that is, U.S.) troops withdraw.

In the aftermath of the war in Vietnam, the Commissioner for Refugees posted representatives at three camps in the U.S. to help any Vietnamese or Cambodians who wished to return to their countries. Both parts of Vietnam were denied admission to the UN on September 30; the U.S. vetoed their applications because the council declined to consider membership for South Korea. (RICHARD N. SWIFT)

[552.B.2]

INTERNATIONAL WOMEN'S YEAR

By Abigail McCarthy

COURTESY, UNITED NATIONS

The celebration of International Women's Year in 1975 had one unqualified result. Despite every effort to bend the new consciousness of women to political purposes, despite every effort to drive a wedge between the women of the developed world and those of the less developed countries, women everywhere—and the men who had heeded the observance—were reinforced in their knowledge of the need, recognized 30 years earlier in the UN Charter, to call for "equal rights for men and women."

In 1975, for the first time in the history of the world, women *representing their countries* met in international conferences in which they outnumbered men, and gave consideration to their own destinies. The women of the Cameroon might express concern with the removal of bride price; the American woman might express concern with unequal property division in divorce law; a Ghanaian woman might cite her denial of access to television; the English or Australian women might complain of media "stereotypes": all were giving evidence of discrimination. The Iranian, African, or Latin-American rural woman, who is a primary agricultural worker, may not be accepted in an agricultural school and does not receive development aid to improve her efficiency and reduce her work load. Women struggle against illiteracy in the less developed world; they are just beginning to break through the barriers in law school, medical school, and engineering school in the developed nations. Worldwide, the effort is to achieve full personhood and citizenship.

At the end of International Women's Year, it was apparent that the response to its call had not been all that was hoped for. Compared with International Human Rights Year and World Population Year, IWY was underfunded (UN countries pledged less than half the allotment for World Population Year, and many failed to live up to their pledges). Not all nations cooperated enthusiastically with the plans for IWY. The U.S., although its National Commission was created by the president on January 9, did not actually have a commission until April, when 35 private citizens and 4 congressional members were finally named. And Bogotá, Colombia, eventually withdrew its offer to serve as host for the international conference.

In comparison with World Population Year, IWY also received very little attention from the media. What attention was given centred largely around the so-called sharp conflict between the women delegates from the developed nations and those from the less developed countries—a very simplified description of the multitude of conflicting concerns that surfaced during meetings. And yet there seems to be a growing agreement among thoughtful commentators that much was accomplished by IWY's concentration on the inequality of women. An international network was established. Leaders were identified. Thousands of women experienced the mechanics of international organization through participation. Perhaps the greatest single achievement was the adoption of the World Plan of Action and the Declaration (with accompanying resolutions) at the international conference held in Mexico City in June.

Abigail Quigley McCarthy is a columnist for Commonweal *and the* New York Times *("One Woman's Voice") and a free-lance writer. Her works include the widely acclaimed* Private Faces/Public Places *(1972).*

World Plan of Action. The World Plan of Action is a landmark ten-year plan. The 48-page document produced by the delegates is not legally binding, but it is hoped that the member nations of the UN will take it into account in their own planning. It emphasizes the need to increase the role of women in decision-making within their countries and in the UN itself, where women represent only 8% of the employees—few at the decision-making level. It provides for a drastic yet realistic improvement in the condition of women over a wide range of areas. The document discusses ways of improving women's education, training, health facilities, and their participation in decision-making processes. It condemns the "stereotypes about women" created by education and calls on the mass media to make a critical review of their role in projecting the image of women. In separate chapters devoted to politics, education and training, health and nutrition, the family, housing, and mass communications, the document recognizes all these as fields in which women have been disadvantaged.

The following are significant excerpts:

> The achievement of equality between men and women implies that they should have equal rights, opportunities and responsibilities to enable them to develop their talents and capabilities for their own personal fulfillment and the benefit of society. To that end a reassessment of the functions and roles traditionally allotted to each sex within the family and the community at large is essential.
>
> . . . Governments should ensure for both women and men equality before the law, the provision of facilities for equality of educational opportunities and training, equality in conditions of employment, including remuneration and adequate social security. . . . The State has also the responsibility to create conditions that promote the implementation of legal norms providing for equality of men and women and in particular the opportunity for all individuals to receive free general and primary education, and eventually compulsory general secondary education, equality of conditions of employment, and maternity protection.
>
> Governments should strive to ameliorate the hard working conditions and unreasonably heavy work load, especially that fall upon large groups of women in many countries and particularly among underprivileged social groups.
>
> A major objective of this Plan is to ensure that women shall have, in law and in fact, equal rights and opportunities with men to vote and to participate in public and political life at the national, local and community levels. . . .
>
> Individuals and couples have the right freely and responsibly to determine the number and spacing of their children and to have the information and means to do so. The exercise of this right is basic to the attainment of any real equality between the sexes. . . .
>
> Improved access to health, nutrition and other social services is essential to the full participation of women in development activities. . . . To be fully effective these services should be integrated into over-all development programmes with priority being given to rural areas.
>
> In the total development process the role of women, along with men, needs to be considered in terms of their contribution to the family as well as to society and the national economy. Higher status for this role in the home—as a parent, spouse and homemaker—can only enhance the personal dignity of a man and a woman.

Although the Plan is projected for a decade, a number of minimum targets were set for 1980. These include: an increase in literacy for women; recognition of the value of women's work in the home, in domestic food production, and in voluntary activities that are not traditionally remunerated; and the promotion of women's organizations as an interim measure within workers' organizations and within educational, economic, and professional institutions.

Controversy over the Plan. At every recent international conference, an alliance of less developed and Communist bloc nations has attempted to make the "new international economic order" the first priority. It is held that there can be no liberation for individuals without a massive redistribution of economic and natural resources; that the first liberation must be from "capitalistic imperialism" and the great discrepancy in wealth between the developed and less developed countries. Only then can human rights be established. The conflict between this view and the effort to concentrate on the position and needs of women had surfaced in the preparatory consultations for IWY. It emerged full-blown at the international conference when Pres. Luis Echeverría Álvarez of Mexico, in his opening address, voiced a blistering attack on capitalism and asked for a "radical transformation of the world economic order to make possible the true liberation of women."

Confusion and bitterness over this issue were apparent throughout the conference, but it can safely be said that the politicization of IWY was firmly rejected by the majority of women delegates. Helvi Sipila of Finland, UN assistant secretary-general for social development and humanitarian affairs, chief UN conference officer, and the first woman speaker, declared firmly: "I do not see a conflict between the prevailing conditions in developing and industrialized countries as regards the real aspirations of women for social justice and a better life." Elizabeth Reid, leader of the Australian delegation, was unequivocal in rejecting diversion from women's issues, as was Françoise Giroud, the French minister for women's affairs.

Other controversies over the Plan were more subtle and philosophical. Even before the draft Plan of Action was prepared by the UN Secretariat and revised by a committee of 23 nations in March, criticisms were varied. Some argued that the Plan failed to state unequivocally that woman *as person* is the only acceptable definition (the Plan, it was thought, tended to view woman in terms of her childbearing and child-rearing functions). Others felt that primary importance was placed not on justice to women but on that justice in relation to other world problems, thus dealing with women in a relational framework. And it was also said that the Plan overemphasized economic development, and that by failing to call for total disarmament, it overlooked the most harmful of all things for women—war as a solution to world conflict.

An underlying and seldom well-articulated conflict was inherent in the fact that the vast majority of the world's women clearly thought of themselves in relation to family and children and were more strongly motivated by these concerns than by any others. Avant-garde feminists saw this as a weakness, as did some women theologians; others saw it as a strength auguring new relationships and better rapport between men and women.

The Tribune. As in the two previous UN conferences on population and food, the official conference was twinned with a Tribune, meeting concurrently, planned by a committee designated by the nongovernmental organizations in consultative status with the UN Economic and Social Council, and thought of primarily as an international forum.

Over 5,000 representatives attended the Tribune, as individuals and as representatives of organizations ranging from the World YWCA, international Girl Scouts, and church organizations through newer groups like the World Population Society to such feminist groups as the National Organization for Women, the Women's Equity Action League, and the International Lesbian Caucus. Because of a bad geographical situation—the meeting places were far apart—rather sketchy planning, and a lack of means of communication with the official conference, the Tribune was a centre of discontent.

By UN custom the presiding officer of such a conference is the head of the delegation of the host country—in the case of Mexico, a man, Attorney General Raúl Ojeda Paullada—but misunderstanding of this and other mechanics of the official meeting led to consistent attacks on the conference by feminists who felt it was unrepresentative of women. There were also more or less vociferous confrontations between different groups, but eventually a group called The Voice of the United Women of the Tribune, organized by such seasoned activists as Betty Friedan of the U.S., Dookja Hong of South Korea, and Victoria Mojekwo of Nigeria, managed to mobilize 2,000 persons who agreed to suggested changes in the Plan of Action. These changes, which were largely designed to put teeth into enforcement of the Plan, included the establishment of a permanent office at the secretary level at the UN and of a monitoring agency. They could not be presented to the conference in accordance with UN rules, but the fact that they were received by Ms. Sipila was considered to be precedent-setting.

Structure and Observance of IWY. International Women's Year 1975 was proclaimed by the UN General Assembly on Dec. 18, 1972, as a year to be devoted to intensified action to promote equality between men and women; to ensure the full integration of women in the total development effort, particularly during the Second Development Decade; and to increase the contribution of women to the strengthening of world peace.

The UN Commission on the Status of Women, established in 1946, took formal initiative in promoting IWY. At its meeting in Geneva early in 1972, it urged that the General Assembly proclaim 1975 as International Women's Year and that Secretary-General Kurt Waldheim be asked to prepare a draft program of IWY, to be submitted to the commission at its 25th session in 1974. The fact that the UN had already designated International Human Rights Year and World Population Year—both of which had a great deal to do with the lives of women but had lacked much participation by women—served as an incentive. So did the rise of the women's movement and realization of the role women have in solving world problems, especially those relating to population and food.

A program of activities for IWY, including an international conference, was adopted by the Commission on the Status of Women in January 1974 and approved by its parent organization, the Economic and Social Council, in May. The main themes for the year were to be equality, development, and peace. In resolution 1851 (LVI), Ecosoc requested the secretary-general to convene an international conference to launch an international action program including short- and long-term goals, and in resolution 1950 (LVI), it established a fund for voluntary contributions for IWY.

In addition to the Mexico City conference, official UN meetings during IWY included a journalistic encounter preceding the conference in which 50 journalistic fellows met at the invitation of the Center for Economic and Social Concerns at the UN; the New York Seminar on Peace and Disarmament, May 7–9; the Caracas, Venezuela, regional seminar for Latin America on integration in development with specific reference to population factors, April 28–May 2; and the Bangkok, Thailand, Regional Conference of Non-Governmental Organizations on the Integration of Women in Development in the context of the UN Development Decade, May 27–29. Meetings preparatory to the Mexico City conference were held in Eastern Europe, and an international meeting of young women's organizations was held in Moscow. In the U.S. the official National Commission was set up under the leadership of Jill Ruckelshaus. A congressional symposium on International Women's Year, sponsored by Senators Hubert Humphrey and Charles Percy, Rep. Elizabeth Holtzman, and Rep. Millicent Fenwick, was held on May 14.

No UN-designated year has received such enthusiastic response from national and international nongovernmental organizations. This is understandable: women's strength lies in such groups, since they are largely excluded from the policy-making levels of government. Examples of this response on the international level were the 69th International Labor Organization meeting in Geneva, which was devoted to the discussion of the woman worker; the follow-up to the Mexico City conference planned by the Women in Development section of the Society for International Development; and the inclusion of a day devoted to the subject of women at the World Council of Churches meeting in Nairobi, Kenya.

As the symbol of IWY, the UN adopted a design by Valerie Pettis. It consists of a stylized dove, representing peace, combined with the biological symbol for the female sex and the mathematical sign for equality. It was fervently desired by all that this design would one day become a reflection of reality, and future IWYs thus become unnecessary.

United States

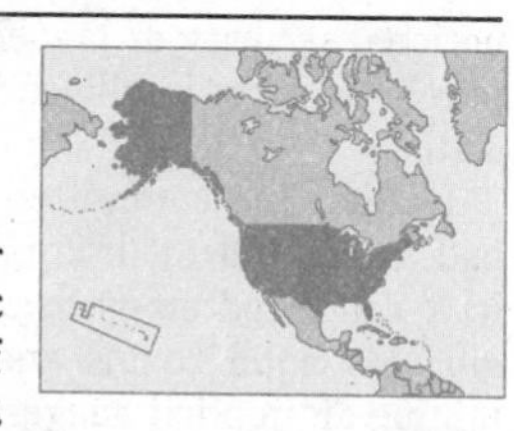

The United States of America is a federal republic composed of 50 states, 49 of which are in North America and one of which consists of the Hawaiian Islands. Area: 3,615,122 sq.mi. (9,363,123 sq.km.), including 78,267 sq.mi. of inland water but excluding the 60,-306 sq.mi. of the Great Lakes that lie within U.S. boundaries. Pop. (1975 est.): 213,631,000, including 87% white and 11.5% Negro. Language: English. Religion (early 1970s est.): Protestant 72 million; Roman Catholic 48 million; Jewish 6 million; Orthodox 3.7 million. Cap.: Washington, D.C. (pop., 1973 est., 745,800). Largest city: New York (pop., 1973 est., 7,716,600). President in 1975, Gerald Rudolph Ford.

After a decade of foreign wars and domestic discord, the United States found itself at peace both at home and abroad in 1975. But peace did not bring contentment. Continued high unemployment and a sluggish recovery from the economic recession inflicted hardship on millions of Americans and raised doubts about the government's ability to manage the economy. Disillusionment with the government was further heightened by disclosures of improper and illegal activities of the Central Intelligence Agency and the Federal Bureau of Investigation, formerly two of the most respected federal agencies.

Ordinarily, dissatisfaction with an incumbent administration might be expected to generate support for the party out of power, in this case the Democrats. But this did not happen in 1975. Although public opinion surveys indicated that President Ford's popularity was slipping, none of the ten announced Democratic candidates for their party's presidential nomination in 1976 aroused widespread enthusiasm among the electorate. For most Americans in 1975, politics at the national level apparently was perceived as irrelevant to their concerns.

Activities of Federal Agencies. Although the long ordeal of Watergate ended with Richard Nixon's resignation as president in August 1974, its aftereffects carried over into 1975 as congressional committees investigated the activities of the CIA and FBI, both of which had been involved in the Watergate cover-up. In a report made public on November 20, the Senate Select Committee on Intelligence said that U.S. government officials, operating through the CIA, had ordered the assassination of two foreign leaders and had been involved in assassination plots against three other foreign officials. Although four of the five were assassinated, none of them died as the direct result of plans initiated by U.S. officials, the report concluded.

According to the committee's report, which was released over the strong opposition of the Ford administration, Fidel Castro of Cuba and Patrice Lumumba of the Congo (now Zaire) were the targets of death plots originated in Washington. The others—Rafael Leónidas Trujillo of the Dominican Republic, Ngo Dinh Diem of South Vietnam, and Gen. René Schneider of Chile—died as the result of coup plots, which U.S. officials had encouraged or were at least privy to.

The committee said it was unable to determine if any president had explicitly ordered the death of a foreign leader, but stated that "the system of executive command and control was so inherently ambiguous that it is difficult to be certain at what level assassination activity was known and authorized. This creates the disturbing prospect that assassination activity might have been undertaken by officials of the United States government without its having been incontrovertibly clear that there was explicit authorization from the president."

PHOTO TRENDS

Emperor Hirohito of Japan and his wife, Empress Nagako, are shown San Francisco Bay and the Golden Gate Bridge by Mayor and Mrs. Joseph Alioto during the imperial couple's visit to the U.S. in October.

PICTORIAL PARADE

Pres. Gerald Ford called upon the Marines to rescue the U.S. freighter "Mayaguez" and its 30-man crew from the Cambodians after he and Secretary of State Henry Kissinger (foreground) listened to a briefing from Defense Secretary James Schlesinger.

The committee recommended that Congress pass a law making it a federal offense to assassinate or plot to assassinate foreign leaders. Directives, issued by CIA directors in 1972 and 1974, that prohibited assassination as an intelligence tool were not enough, the report said. (*See* DEFENSE: *Special Report.*)

The Senate intelligence committee also conducted hearings on FBI political abuses over the past 35 years and concluded that Presidents Roosevelt, Truman, Eisenhower, Kennedy, Johnson, and Nixon all had received reports from the bureau on journalists, political opponents, and critics of administration policies. "The FBI intelligence system developed to a point where no one inside or outside the bureau was willing or able to tell the difference between legitimate national security or law enforcement information and purely political intelligence," a committee staff report stated.

Earlier, the committee had revealed that the FBI had attempted to discredit Martin Luther King, Jr., in a concerted six-year campaign that included bugging his hotel rooms and mailing him a letter containing an implicit suggestion that he commit suicide. According to the committee, King received an anonymously sent tape recording and an accompanying note in November 1964, only 34 days before he was to accept the Nobel Peace Prize. The recording supposedly revealed instances of unsavoury behaviour King was alleged to have engaged in.

F. A. O. Schwarz III, chief counsel to the committee, said that the panel's staff had determined that the tape was made with the aid of an electronic surveillance device placed by the FBI and that FBI officials had written the note. Moreover, in December 1964, the FBI mailed anonymously a second tape, possibly of the same incident, to King's wife, Schwarz said.

These and other disclosures of improprieties by the CIA and FBI contributed to the growing demand for new investigations of the assassinations of King and John and Robert Kennedy, as well as the near-fatal shooting of Gov. George C. Wallace of Alabama. Critics of the original investigations charged, without offering any supporting evidence, that the two intelligence agencies may have been involved in the assassinations or may have withheld vital information from investigatory bodies.

Ford Assassination Attempts. Two attempts on the life of President Ford further fueled the assassination controversy. In the first incident, a young woman pointed a pistol at Ford from a distance of two feet while he was shaking hands with the public in Sacramento, Calif., on September 5. A Secret Service agent spotted the gun and leaped to grasp it and the arm of the woman holding it. The woman was quickly subdued and the president was escorted hurriedly to the California capitol, where he was scheduled to address the legislature on violent crime.

UNITED STATES

Education. (1973–74) Primary, pupils 31,469,000, teachers (1971–72) 1,293,000; secondary and vocational, pupils 15,347,000, teachers (1971–72) *c.* 1,003,000; higher (including teacher-training colleges), students 8,179,000, teaching staff (1971–72) *c.* 748,000.

Finance. Monetary unit: U.S. dollar, with (Sept. 22, 1975) a free rate of U.S. $2.07 to £1 sterling. Gold, SDRs, and foreign exchange: (June 1975) $14,350,000,000; (June 1974) $13,940,000,000. Federal budget (1975–76 est.): revenue $299 billion; expenditure $358.9 billion. Gross national product: (1974) $1,397,400,000,000; (1973) $1,294,900,000,000. Money supply: (June 1975) $285.5 billion; (June 1974) $270.5 billion. Cost of living (1970 = 100): (June 1975) 130; (June 1974) 126.

Foreign Trade. (1974) Imports $107,996,000,000; exports (excluding military aid exports of $599 million) $97,907,000,000. Import sources: Canada 22%; Japan 12%; West Germany 6%; Venezuela 5%. Export destinations: Canada 20%; Japan 11%; West Germany 5%; Mexico 5%; U.K. 5%. Main exports: machinery 24%; cereals 11% (wheat 5%); chemicals 9%; motor vehicles 8%; aircraft 6%. Tourism: visitors (1972) 12,884,800; gross receipts (1973) U.S. $3,277,000,000.

Transport and Communications. Roads (1972) 6,094,124 km. (including 56,346 km. expressways). Motor vehicles in use (1973): passenger 101,237,000; commercial (including buses) 23,201,000. Railways: (1973) 332,832 km.; traffic (class I only; 1974) 16,630,000,000 passenger-km., freight 1,253,180,000,000 net ton-km. Air traffic (1974): 262,194,000,000 passenger-km. (including domestic services 216,944,000,000 passenger-km.); freight 8,952,150,000 net ton-km. (including domestic services 5,876,620,000 net ton-km.). Inland waterways freight traffic (1972) 494,500,000,000 ton-km. (including 159,000,000,000 ton-km. on Great Lakes system and 231,000,000,000 ton-km. on Mississippi River system). Shipping (1974): merchant vessels 100 gross tons and over 4,086; gross tonnage 14,429,076. Ships entered (including Great Lakes international traffic; 1973) vessels totaling 253,931,000 net registered tons; goods loaded (1974) 245,517,000 metric tons, unloaded 424,877,000 metric tons. Telephones (Jan. 1974) 138,286,000. Radio receivers (Dec. 1973) 368.6 million. Television receivers (Dec. 1973) 110 million.

Agriculture. Production (in 000; metric tons; 1974; 1973 in parentheses): corn 118,145 (143,435); wheat 48,807 (46,408); oats 9,007 (9,680); barley 6,708 (9,180); rye 490 (667); rice 5,175 (4,208); sorghum 15,954 (23,623); soybeans 33,569 (42,108); dry beans 944 (743); dry peas 193 (117); peanuts 1,664 (1,576); potatoes 15,431 (13,588); sweet potatoes (1973) 561, (1972) 565; onions 1,517 (1,347); tomatoes *c.* 7,500 (6,263); sugar, raw value 5,034 (5,215); apples 2,900 (2,830); pears (1973) 650, (1972) 552; oranges 8,740 (9,042); grapefruit (1973) 2,428, (1972) 2,380; lemons (1973) 806, (1972) 615; peaches (1973) 1,265, (1972) 1,174; grapes 3,805 (3,804); sunflower seed 291 (353); linseed 339 (409); tobacco 890 (790); cotton, lint 2,624 (2,821); butter 431 (418); cheese 1,687 (1,564); eggs 3,861 (3,927); beef and veal (1973) 9,751, (1972) 10,280; pork (1973) 5,729, (1972) 6,166; softwood timber (cu.m.; 1973) *c.* 272,300, (1972) 272,300; hardwood timber (cu.m.; 1973) *c.* 83,400, (1972) 83,400; fish catch (1973) 2,670, (1972) 2,650. Livestock (in 000; Jan. 1974): cattle 127,540; sheep 16,394; pigs 61,100; horses (1973) *c.* 8,500; chickens (1973) 406,241.

Industry. Index of production (1970 = 100): (1974) 117, (1973) 118; mining (1974) 100, (1973) 101; manufacturing (1974) 118, (1973) 119; electricity, gas, and water (1974) 117, (1973) 119; construction (1974) 99, (1973) 114. Unemployment: (1974) 5.6%; (1973) 4.9%. Fuel and power (in metric tons; 1974): coal 541,051; lignite (1973) 12,848; crude oil 432,357; natural gas (cu.m.) 617,161,000; manufactured gas (cu.m.) 26,171,000; electricity (kw-hr.) 1,941,095,000. Production (in 000; metric tons; 1974): iron ore (55–60% metal content) 85,917; pig iron (1973) 93,522; crude steel 131,991; cement (shipments) 68,062; newsprint 2,923; petroleum products (1973) 608,190; sulfuric acid 29,458; caustic soda 9,851; fertilizers (including Puerto Rico; nutrient content; 1973–74) nitrogenous 9,152, phosphate 6,013, potash 2,346; plastics and resins (1972) 11,755; synthetic rubber 2,519; passenger cars (units) 7,332; commercial vehicles (units) 2,728. Merchant vessels launched (100 gross tons and over; 1974) 810,000 gross tons. New dwelling units started (1974) 1,351,000.

Ford's assailant was identified as Lynette Alice Fromme, 26, a follower of Charles Manson, leader of a cult convicted of the brutal killing of actress Sharon Tate and six others in 1969. Fromme was taken that afternoon before a U.S. magistrate in the federal courthouse and charged with attempted assassination of the president under provisions of a 1965 law. It was the first time anyone had been so charged. Bond was set at $1 million.

Ford again escaped harm when a shot fired at him from a crowd in San Francisco on September 22 apparently was deflected. The president was leaving the St. Francis Hotel, waving to a crowd of about 3,000 persons who had gathered to see him. About 40 ft. away, on the other side of the street, a woman raised a .38-calibre handgun and pointed it toward him. But Oliver Sipple, a former Marine, noticed the weapon and grabbed the woman's arm. The gun went off but the bullet's path was not determined. It apparently hit an object before ricocheting some distance away from Ford and striking a cabdriver, who suffered a minor injury.

The woman assailant, seized immediately by police, was identified later as Sara Jane Moore, 45. She had been questioned the night before by the Secret Service as a potential threat to the president and released. It was learned that Moore had operated as a police and FBI informer. In fact, she had phoned her city police contact two days before the incident and, citing plans for an anti-Ford protest at one of his appearances in California, said she might "test the system." Moore was ordered to undergo psychiatric examination to determine if she was competent to stand trial on charges of having attempted to assassinate President Ford. She was held under $500,000 bond.

Fromme was convicted of the charge of attempted assassination on November 26. She refused to testify in her own defense and also declined to be present in the courtroom for much of the trial. In December she was sentenced to life in prison. Moore pleaded guilty to the charge of attempted assassination and awaited sentencing at the year's end.

The Hearst Case. A 19-month search for newspaper heiress Patricia Hearst ended September 18 with her arrest by FBI agents in a San Francisco apartment. Hearst, 21, had been forcibly abducted from her Berkeley, Calif., apartment on Feb. 4, 1974, by members of the Symbionese Liberation Army (SLA), a radical terrorist group. Less than three months after her abduction, Hearst renounced her parents and affirmed her commitment to the SLA. A short time before apprehending Hearst, FBI agents captured two SLA members, William and Emily Harris, on a nearby street corner. Neither Hearst nor the Harrises offered resistance to arresting officers.

Hearst, who faced more than 30 separate state and federal charges, was taken before the local U.S. magistrate and charged with bank robbery. The Harrises, who faced numerous criminal charges, were charged with possession of illegal firearms. After a team of doctors examined Hearst, U.S. District Court Judge Oliver J. Carter declared her mentally competent and ordered her to stand trial starting Jan. 26, 1976, on federal charges of armed bank robbery and use of a firearm to commit a felony. Meanwhile, the Harrises were ordered to stand trial in Los Angeles on Feb. 2, 1976, on 11 felony counts of robbery, kidnapping, and assault.

Domestic Politics. The Ford administration underwent a major shake-up in early November as the president dismissed Secretary of Defense James Schlesinger and CIA Director William E. Colby (*see* BIOGRAPHY) and nominated Elliot Richardson, the U.S. ambassador to Great Britain, to replace Secretary of Commerce Rogers Morton, who was resigning to return to private life. In addition, Vice-Pres. Nelson Rockefeller announced that he was removing himself from consideration as Ford's running mate in 1976. Ford nominated White House Chief of Staff Donald Rumsfeld to replace Schlesinger and George Bush, head of the U.S. liaison office in China, to replace Colby.

There was speculation that the shake-up stemmed from friction between Schlesinger and Secretary of State Henry Kissinger. Schlesinger had publicly criticized Kissinger's policy of détente with the Soviet Union, especially as it applied to military matters. However, most observers attributed the moves primarily to Ford's desire to assert more positive leadership and counter an apparently growing threat from former California governor Ronald Reagan against Ford's nomination as the Republican presidential candidate in 1976. The removal of Rockefeller from the

WIDE WORLD

White House Chief of Staff Donald Rumsfeld (left) replaced James R. Schlesinger as secretary of defense after the latter was dismissed by President Ford in November.

Estimates of Total Cost of U.S. Wars

In $000,000

War	Estimated ultimate costs	Original war costs*	Veterans' benefits: Total costs under present laws†	Veterans' benefits: Percent of original war costs	Veterans' benefits: Total costs to 1974‡	Estimated interest payments on war loans: Total	Estimated interest payments on war loans: Percent of original war costs
World War II	664,000	288,000	290,000	100	101,621	86,000	50
Vietnam conflict§	352,000	128,000‖	220,000¶	200¶	10,847	22,000♀	20♀
Korean conflict	164,000	54,000	99,000	184	17,949	11,000	20
World War I	112,000	26,000	75,000	290	55,233	11,000	42
Civil War (Union only)	12,952	3,200	8,580	260	8,573	1,172	37
Spanish-American War	6,460	400	6,000	1,505	5,566	60	15
American Revolution	190	100	70	70	70	20	20
War of 1812	158	93	49	53	49	16	17
Mexican War	147	73	64	83	66	16	14

*Based on expenditures of departments of the Army and Navy to World War I and major national security expenditures thereafter. Usually the figures begin with the year the war began, but in all cases they extend one year beyond the end of the actual conflict.

†To World War I, estimates are based on Veterans Administration data. For World War I, World War II, and Korean conflict, estimates are those of the 1956 report of the President's Commission on Veterans' Pensions plus 25% (the increase in the average value of benefits since the commission made its report).

‡Source: U.S. Veterans Administration, *Annual Report of Administrator of Veterans Affairs*.

§Estimates based on assumption that war would end by June 30, 1970 (except for original war costs and for veterans benefit costs to 1974).

‖Estimated Department of Defense expenditure in support of Southeast Asia for fiscal year 1965 to 1972.

¶Medium-level estimate of 200% based on figures expressing relationship of veterans' benefits payments to original costs of other major U.S. wars.

♀Medium-level estimate of 20% based on figures showing interest payments on war loans as percentage of original costs of other major U.S. wars.

Source: Except as noted, U.S. Congress, Joint Economic Committee, *The Military Budget and National Economic Priorities*, Part 1, 91st Congress, 1st session. (Statement of James L. Clayton, University of Utah.)

ticket was seen as an effort to appease the party's conservatives, who had never been happy with his selection as vice-president. Rumsfeld was confirmed by the Senate in November and Richardson in December. Bush was expected to be confirmed early in 1976.

The so-called Halloween massacre was only the most spectacular of Ford's personnel changes. Of the Cabinet members in office a year earlier, only Kissinger, Treasury Secretary William E. Simon, and Agriculture Secretary Earl L. Butz remained at year's end. Edward H. Levi (*see* BIOGRAPHY), president of the University of Chicago, took over the embattled Department of Justice from William Saxbe, who became ambassador to India. Another college president, F. David Mathews of the University of Alabama, became secretary of health, education, and welfare, succeeding Caspar W. Weinberger (resigned). William T. Coleman, a specialist in transportation law, and Carla A. Hills, head of the Justice Department's civil division, became the second black and the third woman, respectively, to serve in a U.S. Cabinet. Coleman succeeded Claude S. Brinegar (resigned) at the Department of Transportation. Hills's predecessor at Housing and Urban Development was James T. Lynn, who became director of the Office of Management and Budget.

John T. Dunlop, who had been director of the Cost of Living Council under Nixon, replaced Peter J. Brennan as secretary of labour and, at year's end, was himself threatening to resign if Ford vetoed the common situs picketing bill (*see* below). Following Morton's transfer from Interior to Commerce, where he succeeded Frederick Dent (named the president's special representative for trade negotiations), Ford nominated Stanley K. Hathaway, former governor of Wyoming, as secretary of the interior; Hathaway resigned after six weeks because of ill health and was replaced by Thomas S. Kleppe, head of the Small Business Administration.

Ford's first opportunity to name a justice of the U.S. Supreme Court came with the retirement in November of William O. Douglas, who had served on the court longer than any other man. The president selected John Paul Stevens, 55, a judge on the U.S. Court of Appeals for the 7th Circuit in Chicago. Stevens was regarded as a centrist, neither extremely conservative nor extremely liberal. His nomination was quickly approved by the Senate.

Congress in 1975 extended the Voting Rights Act of 1965 for seven years and expanded its coverage to language minorities. The expansion applied to Texas, Alaska, and parts of 12 other states. As signed by the president, the act would continue to cover for seven years six Southern states, most of a seventh, and various counties in Northern states that were covered in the expiring legislation. Those states and political subdivisions were required to submit any election law changes to the attorney general for prior clearance. If the attorney general found that a proposed change had the intent or effect of discrimination, he could veto it.

Congress also ended one chapter of U.S. involvement in Southeast Asia when it authorized $455 million for assistance programs for Vietnamese and Cambodian refugees who fled their countries before the Communists took them over and were resettling in the United States. (*See* REFUGEES: *Special Report.*) The costs to the U.S. of the principal wars in which it has been involved are listed in the accompanying table.

In an effort to help the ailing home building industry, Congress passed an emergency housing bill. Major provisions of the bill permitted, but did not require, the Department of Housing and Urban Development to buy up another $10 billion in mortgages carrying 7.5% interest rates under a 1974 mortgage assistance program. The purchases were designed to encourage lenders to make mortgage money available at below-market interest rates. Another section of the bill allowed HUD to make loans of up to $250 a month for two years to jobless homeowners unable to meet their mortgage payments. Alternatively, HUD could insure lenders against losses if they made the same kind of assistance available directly to unemployed homeowners facing foreclosure.

Congress and President Ford remained at odds throughout 1975 on national energy policy. Both the House and the Senate passed legislation authorizing the president to propose a gasoline rationing plan,

(Left) Fifty-nine members of the Old Believers are sworn in as U.S. citizens in the Alaskan village of Nikolaevsk. Originally from Russia, the sect had traveled to China, South America, and finally Alaska, where they found a permanent home to practice their religion. (Right) Confederate Gen. Robert E. Lee regained his citizenship, lost after the Civil War, by an act of Congress in 1975.

PHOTOS, WIDE WORLD

establish oil price controls, and encourage conservation of energy. Federal energy administrator Frank Zarb worked out a compromise on the bill with Congress that would roll back the price of domestic crude oil by about 12% and then gradually phase out controls over 40 months. The president signed the bill in December, although he favoured higher fuel prices as a method of limiting energy use.

The threat of presidential vetoes also hovered over legislation to extend income tax reductions enacted in the spring as a recession-fighting measure and to allow a labour union in a dispute with one construction contractor to picket all other contractors at the same construction site (common situs picketing). Ford stated that he favoured continuation of the tax reductions but only if they were coupled with a ceiling on federal spending. Congress refused to set such a ceiling. Ford then vetoed the tax bill, but on December 19 he and Congress reached an agreement in which the reductions were extended and a nonbinding commitment to control government spending was made. On December 22 Ford announced that he would veto the construction site bill.

Although unemployment remained above 8%, other economic indicators suggested that the country was emerging from recession at the end of 1975. The consumer price index for October was 7.6% higher than a year earlier, a substantial drop from the double-digit inflation that plagued the nation in 1974. Industrial production rose by 0.4% in October, the sixth monthly advance in a row. New housing starts and auto sales also increased in October, and the Department of Commerce announced that the nation's balance of payments had improved in the third quarter of 1975.

Foreign Affairs. The most momentous event in foreign affairs in 1975 for the United States was the fall of much of Indochina to the Communists, ending more than a decade of U.S. military involvement in Southeast Asia. (*See* SOUTHEAST ASIAN AFFAIRS: *Special Report*.) The war in South Vietnam ended on April 30, when the government surrendered to the Communists and Viet Cong and North Vietnamese troops entered Saigon. Hours before the fall of the capital, the U.S. completed a limited emergency airlift from the city ordered by President Ford, bringing out virtually all Americans remaining in Vietnam as well as thousands of refugees who feared that their lives would be endangered by a Communist takeover.

Three weeks earlier, on April 10, Ford had appealed to Congress and the nation for $972 million in military and "humanitarian" aid for South Vietnam. He asked for $722 million to give the country a chance to "save itself" from Communist domination and $250 million for economic and humanitarian purposes. But Congress refused to accede to his request.

On May 12 a U.S. merchant ship, the "Mayaguez," was fired on, boarded, and seized by the crewmen of a Cambodian gunboat 60 mi. off the Cambodian coast and about 8 mi. from the Wai Islands, a small group of rocky islets claimed by both Cambodia and South Vietnam. Ford called the ship's seizure an "act of piracy," demanded its immediate release, and warned that "failure to do so would have the most serious consequences." Two days later the U.S. regained the ship and freed the crew by force but suffered substantial casualties. (*See* CAMBODIA.)

Resorting once again to "shuttle diplomacy" in the Middle East, Secretary of State Kissinger mediated an interim agreement between Israel and Egypt that provided for a further Israeli withdrawal in the Sinai Peninsula and the stationing of U.S. civilians in the region to monitor the accord. Israel was to receive a number of concessions from Egypt and a pledge of increased U.S. economic, military, and political assistance. Egypt was also promised U.S. economic aid. The establishment of the U.S. presence in the Sinai was subject to U.S. congressional approval, which was later given. Israel had said it would not implement the agreement without such an endorsement.

WIDE WORLD

Perched at the foot of encircling mountains, accessible only by ferry or air, is Alaska's capital city of Juneau. For these reasons the capital may be moved to a site closer to oil-related growth areas.

Although the U.S. and the Soviet Union continued to adhere to the policy of détente, relations between the two countries were somewhat strained in 1975. Nevertheless, the two negotiated a five-year agreement under which the Soviet Union was to buy six million to eight million tons of U.S. grain annually, starting Oct. 1, 1976. The U.S.-Soviet accord, it was hoped, would prevent a repetition of "the great grain robbery" of 1972 or "the grain drain" of 1975. Both were caused by large and unexpected Soviet purchases of foreign grain, most of it U.S. The resulting sharp rise in consumer prices, particularly in 1972, had led many Americans to wonder aloud whether détente was in their country's best interests. President Ford hailed the five-year agreement as promoting "American economic stability" and said that the Soviet commitment for a minimum annual purchase of six million tons would represent $1 billion a year in export earnings for the U.S.

The U.S.-Soviet strategic arms limitation talks (SALT) bogged down amid charges that the Soviet Union had violated earlier SALT agreements. Kissinger had planned to go to Moscow to see what could be done about breaking the deadlock, but his trip was

WIDE WORLD

American minutemen battle British soldiers on Lexington Green, Massachusetts, a reenactment for the U.S. bicentennial celebration.

postponed. "There is no sense going to Moscow until we have our positions prepared in great detail," he told a news conference, "and until we are confident that on the Soviet side there is sufficient understanding of what is needed." Kissinger also acknowledged that the United States was indirectly channeling aid to two non-Communist groups in newly independent Angola. He said that the U.S. "tried to give some assistance to some neighboring countries" but "not South Africa" to be used in Angola. Kissinger added that "whatever we have done was started long after massive Soviet involvement became evident" and said the U.S. believed "that outside powers should stay out of Angola." (*See* ANGOLA.)

President Ford traveled overseas four times in 1975, three times to Europe and once to China. On his first trip to Europe, May 28–June 3, the president sought to reassure the nation's allies of continued U.S. strength, support, and commitment in the wake of U.S. defeats in Indochina. The highlight of the trip was a summit meeting of North Atlantic Treaty Organization heads of state in Brussels. Ford later held talks with Egyptian Pres. Anwar as-Sadat in Austria and with Spanish and Italian leaders in their respective capitals.

The president returned to Europe in July, primarily to attend a 35-nation summit meeting in Helsinki convened for the purpose of signing the Final Act of the Conference on Security and Cooperation in Europe. The meeting marked the final stage of the conference, which had held preparatory talks in Helsinki in 1972 and had begun negotiations in Geneva in 1973. The document expressed principles for assuring a permanent peace in Europe, for cooperation between nations, and for establishment of inviolable boundaries within the continent; it was nonbinding and had no legal status as a treaty.

Ford traveled to France in November to attend an economic summit conference of six major industrial nations. Besides Ford, the participants included the leaders of France, Great Britain, Italy, Japan, and West Germany. At the close of the three-day meeting, the six leaders issued a declaration that their "most urgent task" was to assure economic recovery and reduce unemployment.

The talks were marked by a spirit of compromise that extended even to the problem of how to achieve currency stability, a matter of long-standing dispute between the U.S. and France. The U.S. had favoured continuation of floating exchange rates, while France urged a return to a system of fixed parities, which had been in effect from 1945 to 1973. It was reported on the final day of the conference that French Finance Minister Jean-Pierre Fourcade and U.S. Secretary of the Treasury Simon signed an agreement that apparently resolved the "fixed versus floating" debate. Although the text was not published, the agreement reportedly set forth conditions under which central banks could intervene in currency trading to prevent "erratic" fluctuations in exchange rates, particularly between the generally free-floating U.S. dollar and the controlled float of the currencies of France, West Germany, Belgium, The Netherlands, Luxembourg, Norway, Sweden, and Denmark.

Ford's trip to China in December was largely ceremonial, although he did confer with Communist Party Chairman Mao Tse-tung for almost two hours. At a stopover in Honolulu on his return trip to Washington, Ford delivered a speech in which he proclaimed a "new Pacific Doctrine" based on the premise of "peace with all—and hostility toward none." The Pacific Doctrine consisted of six main points: "American strength is basic to any stable balance of power in the Pacific"; "partnership with Japan is a pillar of our strategy"; "normalization of relations with the People's Republic of China"; "our continuing stake in the stability and security of Southeast Asia"; "peace in Asia depends upon a resolution of outstanding political conflicts"; and "peace in Asia requires a structure of economic cooperation reflecting the aspirations of all the people in the region."

(RICHARD L. WORSNOP)

See also Dependent States.

[973.A]

ENCYCLOPÆDIA BRITANNICA FILMS. *The Rise of Labor* (1968); *Heritage in Black* (1969); *The Pacific West* (1969); *The South—Roots of the Urban Crisis* (1969); *The Industrial Worker* (1969); *The Presidency: Search for a Candidate* (1969); *The Rise of Big Business* (1969); *The Rise of the American City* (1969); *Chicano from the Southwest* (1970); *Linda and Billy Ray from Appalachia* (1970); *The Mississippi System: Waterways of Commerce* (1970); *Jesse from Mississippi* (1971); *Johnny from Fort Apache* (1971); *The Progressive Era* (1971); *An Essay on War* (1971); *The Great Lakes: North America's Inland Seas* (2nd ed., 1972); *Valley Forge* (1972); *The Shot Heard Round the World* (1972); *The Boston Tea Party* (1972); *The United States Congress: Of, By and For the People* (2nd ed., 1972); *President of the United States: Too Much Power?* (1972); *The United States Supreme Court: Guardian of the Constitution* (2nd ed., 1973).

The Spanish training ship "Juan Sebastian de Elcano" is welcomed to New York Harbor to publicize the bicentennial "Operation Sail '76." The twin towers of the World Trade Center dominate the skyline.

WIDE WORLD

NEW YORK CITY'S FISCAL CRISIS

By Richard L. Worsnop

New York City's fiscal crisis, which had been building for at least a decade, reached the point of near catastrophe in 1975. Time and again, as the year wore on, the nation's largest city appeared on the brink of defaulting on its maturing debt obligations. In desperation, Mayor Abraham Beame (*see* BIOGRAPHY) and other city officials appealed to the New York state government in Albany and to the federal government for financial assistance. Gov. Hugh Carey and Pres. Gerald Ford both were reluctant to come to the city's aid. State and federal assistance finally was forthcoming, but only under terms by which the city surrendered control over its fiscal affairs. As 1975 drew to a close, there was widespread doubt that the emergency aid would achieve the goal of steering the city toward fiscal solvency.

The city's basic problem was that its expenses had increased by about 12% a year over the past decade, while its tax revenues rose only 4 to 5% a year. To make up the difference, the city resorted to massive, short-term borrowing. At the same time, it employed a number of questionable accounting devices to convince potential lenders that the municipal budget was balanced.

"To accomplish this," Ken Auletta wrote in *New York* magazine (Dec. 1, 1975), "officials have systematically overestimated revenues and underestimated expenses. Year after year they smuggled [current] expense charges into the [long-term] capital budget, and accrued future state aid and tax revenues in current budgets. They postdated one year's teachers' salaries to the next, and labeled expenses as 'advances.' All of this artistic energy—much of it sanctioned by the state—inevitably resulted in bigger and bigger budget deficits year after year. To close that ever-widening gap, the city had to borrow more and then still more money. Soon the city was borrowing to repay its previous borrowing."

A decade of borrowing produced a staggering burden of debt. The total city debt in 1975 was $12.3 billion, compared with $5.2 billion in 1965. The city's budget was $12.2 billion in 1975, compared with $3.8 billion in 1965. About $1.8 billion, or 14%, of the 1975 municipal budget was earmarked for debt service.

The first intimations of possible fiscal collapse came in July 1974, when New York City Controller Harrison Goldin announced that the city would have to pay the highest interest rate ever for short-term notes, 8.586%. Goldin began issuing muted warnings that borrowing would have to be curtailed, and Mayor Beame issued low-key warnings of a huge budget deficit. In November and December 1974 Beame announced the dismissal of more than 5,000 city employees.

The crisis atmosphere thickened in the early months of 1975. A default in February by New York State's Urban Development Corporation sent shock waves through the municipal bond market and made it more difficult for the city to borrow on the basis of anticipated tax revenues. The following month Beame began to talk of help from the state or federal government and announced a plan to borrow only $1 billion of the $3 billion the city needed.

Beame was rebuffed in his initial attempts to pry money out of Albany or Washington. But in June, with the city facing immediate default of $792 million in notes, the New York state legislature approved the creation of a new state agency, the Municipal Assistance Corporation (MAC), designed to alleviate the city's immediate cash-flow problem and oversee its long-range borrowing policies. MAC was authorized to raise $3 billion through bond sales to bail out the city from July to September but, despite a high-pressure selling campaign, it was able to sell only $1 billion of its first $1.5 billion bond offering. Beame responded by imposing wage freezes, raising the transit fare, and taking a tough stand with the leaders of public-employee labour unions.

At Governor Carey's urging, the legislature approved a second rescue plan for New York City in September. MAC was authorized to issue bonds "guaranteed" by city revenues from sales taxes. The legislation also provided for the creation of an emergency financial control board to oversee all city spending and directed that all city income be placed in MAC bank accounts to be doled out to Beame as needed.

Beame, Carey, and MAC officials then stepped up their pressure for federal assistance in the form of U.S. guarantees of MAC notes. President Ford and Secretary of the Treasury William Simon turned these entreaties aside, arguing that New York's fiscal problems were an internal matter and that federal help would set a dangerous precedent. Default thus seemed inevitable on October 17, a day when the city was scheduled to pay off $453 million in short-term notes. The city was saved at the last minute by the United Federation of Teachers, which agreed to purchase $150 million worth of MAC bonds from its pension funds.

Even this close call failed to sway the federal government. In a speech at the National Press Club on October 29, Ford ruled out any kind of pre-default federal aid, proposing instead post-default legislation to assure the maintenance of essential city services once New York went into bankruptcy. The president asserted that "the primary beneficiaries" of a federal loan-guarantee program "would be the New York officials who would thus escape responsibility for their past follies."

But Ford changed his mind after the New York state legislature approved still another package of aid for the city. More than $200 million in new taxes were imposed, payments to the city's noteholders were postponed, and interest payments were reduced. These and other actions by the state and the city convinced Ford that "New York has finally taken the tough decisions it had to take to help itself." Accordingly, he said he would ask Congress "to provide a temporary line of credit to the State of New York to enable it to supply seasonal financing of essential services for the people of New York City."

Legislation to that end moved swiftly through Congress. The bill authorized the treasury secretary to lend money to New York City to tide it over temporary cash shortfalls over a three-year period. All loans made in any one fiscal year must be repaid by the end of that year, and the total of loans outstanding at any given time could not exceed $2.3 billion. If the secretary finds that New York is unable to repay these loans, on which interest is to be 1% higher than the prevailing Treasury borrowing rate, Congress may withhold other federal funds from the city.

Passage of the federal aid bill was hailed by New York's creditors and also by mayors of other large cities, which might have found it difficult to raise money in the commercial bond market if New York had been allowed to default on its obligations. At the same time, there was concern that the economies and cutbacks in municipal services in New York, combined with higher taxes, would further weaken the city's economic base and thus impede recovery.

Meanwhile, legislation to revise municipal bankruptcy laws moved toward final passage in Congress. As passed by the House, the bill would permit a city to petition for bankruptcy without the consent of its creditors, allow a city to continue limited borrowing while it worked out a plan to adjust payment of its debts, and make it easier for this plan to win the creditors' final approval.

Richard L. Worsnop is a free-lance writer and associate editor of Editorial Research Reports *in Washington, D.C.*

United States Statistical Supplement

Developments in the states in 1975

Ethics and energy were at centre stage among events in the 50 states during 1975, along with offshoots from the states' always-delicate relationship with the federal government. An unusual number of indictments and prosecutions of public officials for corruption were reported. In the energy field, states chafed against each other and vied to influence federal policies as their local and regional interests were affected.

A national recession, plus a continuing high rate of inflation and high energy prices, forced legislatures to increase state taxes significantly for the first time in three years. A financial crunch emanating from New York City threatened to affect public bond offerings nationwide. And steadily growing opposition appeared to kill the proposed Equal Rights Amendment to the U.S. Constitution as it was just a few state votes away from ratification. Forty-nine states (all except Kentucky) held regular legislative sessions, and four staged special sessions during the year.

Party Strengths. Democrats continued to benefit from traditional Southern support and easily held onto their decisive advantage in governorships during 1975. Democratic gubernatorial nominees were victorious in elections in Kentucky, Louisiana, and Mississippi, leaving the prospective 1976 statehouse lineup identical to that of 1975: 36 Democrats, 13 Republicans, and one independent.

Although Republicans were able to score marked gains in November state legislative balloting, the partisan breakdown for 1976 remained the same as in 1975, when Republicans controlled both houses of only four state legislatures. Democrats had a majority in both houses of 37 legislatures, dominating the lawmaking process in every state except Idaho, Kansas, North Dakota, and Vermont (where Republicans controlled both houses); Arizona, Indiana, Colorado, Maine, New York, and South Dakota (where each party controlled one chamber); Wyoming and New Hampshire (where the upper chamber was tied); and Nebraska (which had a nonpartisan, unicameral legislature).

Women continued to make inroads in top state offices. During 1975, Connecticut's Ella Grasso (*see* BIOGRAPHY) served as the nation's first female governor who had not been preceded by her husband. During the year Kentucky and Mississippi elected female lieutenant governors, bringing to three (with New York) the states boasting women as second-ranking executive officers.

Federal-State Relations. Although a logjam over distribution of federal water pollution and road-building funds was broken by the national administration and court action, the revenue-sharing partnership between state and federal governments continued to be an uneasy one during 1975. States increasingly turned to federal courts to enforce their rights.

On February 12, a federal judge in Washington, D.C., ordered the release of up to $11.1 billion in highway construction funds impounded by the administrations of U.S. Pres. Gerald Ford and former president Richard Nixon over five years as an inflation-fighting move. A survey at midyear indicated, however, that budget problems in at least six states were causing part of the released funds to go unused. The states were unable to come up with the 10–30% matching share needed to obtain the federal money.

In the first impoundment case to reach the nation's highest court, former president Nixon was judged to have exceeded his authority in withholding half of the $18 billion appropriated by Congress to states for sewage treatment plant construction under the Federal Water Pollution Control Act Amendments of 1972. The U.S. Supreme Court ruled that the act made no provision for presidential delay or withholding of the authorized funds.

The governors of eight northeastern states won a federal court ruling that invalidated a $2 per barrel surcharge on imported oil imposed by President Ford. Although the administration was permitted to continue collecting the surcharge pending appeal, Ford removed it in late December after signing a new energy bill.

A Supreme Court decision on March 17 dismissed the contention of 13 Atlantic Coast states that they, not the federal government, owned title to gas and oil resources lying more than three miles off their coasts. Similar claims to offshore reserves by Louisiana and Texas were simultaneously rejected. The high court had overturned similar demands by other states in 1947, but the Atlantic Coast states claimed that their original royal charters gave them title to seabed resources out to 100 mi. Following the decision, the U.S. Department of the Interior took initial steps toward leasing oil concessions off the coast of Delaware, to be the first major East Coast offshore exploration area.

A squabble among a half-dozen eastern states over taxation of nonresidents was decided on March 19 when the U.S. Supreme Court ruled that an earnings tax levied by New Hampshire exclusively on out-of-staters working in the state was unconstitutional. Six months later, after New Hampshire refused to refund $14 million collected under the levy in recent years, Massachusetts, Maine, and Vermont sued in the Supreme Court for recovery. In July, Pennsylvania announced that it would sue New Jersey for proceeds from a similar commuter tax imposed on Pennsylvania residents.

Finances, Taxes. A two-year trend toward reducing state taxes was reversed in 1975, with 22 states moving to establish new levies or raise existing ones during the year. Although the recession and energy shortage put pressure on state treasuries, a few states were able to hold the line or enact modest tax reductions. A survey by the Tax Foundation revealed that while proposals for upward of $4 billion in new taxes were placed before state legislatures during the year, increases amounting to little more than $1 billion were approved.

For the third consecutive year, no state imposed new corporate, income, or sales taxes, though Michigan replaced its corporate income tax with a single business (value-added) tax and New Jersey enacted a limited personal levy on unearned income. North Dakota reduced its income tax rates, while Arkansas, Illinois, Iowa, Minnesota, New Mexico, and Oklahoma granted tax relief to low-income or elderly persons.

General personal income tax rate increases were enacted in Massachusetts, Michigan, Nebraska, Rhode Island, and Utah, and legislatures in six other states (Connecticut, Alaska, Maryland, Oregon, Vermont, and Wisconsin) tightened previous taxing provisions, generally enlarging the personal income tax base. Corporate taxes were raised in Connecticut, Massachusetts, Nebraska, New Jersey, New York, and Oregon, while Alaska, Maryland, Minnesota, and Wisconsin boosted expected corporate levies by tightening tax table provisions. Montana and North Dakota provided for slight reductions in effective corporate taxes.

Connecticut hiked its sales tax rate from 6 to 7%, making it again the highest state sales tax in the nation. Massachusetts also raised its sales tax rate, from 3 to 5%. The sales tax base was broadened in Connecticut and Wisconsin and narrowed in Michigan.

The most popular form of added taxation continued to be excise levies, with motor-fuel tax increases jumping alongside gasoline prices. Hawaii, Massachusetts, Minnesota, Montana, Oregon, Rhode Island, South Dakota, and Wyoming boosted motor fuel excises. Cigarette taxes were hiked in Maryland, Massachusetts, New Hampshire, New York, Oregon, and Rhode Island, and alcoholic beverage levies were raised in Massachusetts, New Hampshire, and Oregon.

State tax collections in the 1974 fiscal year totaled $74.2 billion, up 9% from 1973. Of the new total, $22.6 billion was from general sales and gross receipts taxes; $17.9 billion from selective sales taxes; $17.1 billion from individual income taxes; $6 billion from corporate income taxes; and $6.1 billion from motor vehicle and miscellaneous licenses.

Figures accumulated in 1975 showed that state revenue from all sources totaled $140.8 billion in fiscal 1974, an increase of 8.4% from the preceding year. General revenue (excluding state liquor and state insurance trust revenue) was $122.3 billion, up 8.1%. Total state expenditures rose 11.2% to $132.1 billion, creating a surplus for the year of $8.6 billion. General expenditures, not including outlays of the liquor stores and insurance trust systems, amounted to $119.9 billion, up 10.9% for the year. Of general revenue, 60.7% came from state taxes and licenses; 12.2% from charges and miscellaneous revenue, including educational tuition; and 27.1% from intergovernmental revenue (most from the federal government).

The largest state outlay was $46.9 billion for education, of which $15.4 billion went to state colleges and universities and $27.6 billion to other schools, including local public institutions. Other major outlays were $22.5 billion for public welfare, $15.8 billion for highways, and $8.4 billion for health and hospitals.

Structures, Powers. Maine and Alabama authorized their legislatures to meet in annual sessions, continuing a post–World War II trend. Even with Montana voters, in a rare move, revoking the annual authorization granted two years previously, 36 states were providing for every-year legislative meetings by the close of 1975.

Attempts to update aged state constitutions met with mixed results. Washington legislators optimistically scheduled a constitutional convention for 1976. Texas voters turned down all major constitutional revision proposals. And a constitutional convention in Arkansas, limited by the legislature to considering specific revisions only, was canceled by the state supreme court as interfering with the grant of final power "inherent in the people."

Connecticut, Indiana, New Hampshire, Maine, and Montana approved new collective bargaining laws for public employees, bringing to 18 the states with comprehensive laws mandating such labour dealings. By the year's end 36 states had specific laws prohibiting strikes by public employees.

Reform of state governmental organization continued at a slow pace. Oklahoma voters approved consolidation of state agencies, and the reform of judicial departments was endorsed by law in Kentucky, Mississippi, and New York.

Looking toward the 1976 presidential elections, state legislatures set up partial or complete regional primaries in the South, the Northeast, and the Northwest. Competition by states determined to conduct an individual primary, such as New Hampshire, threatened to derail the regional primary trend, however. Voter registration laws were liberalized in a number of states. Louisiana, New York, Tennessee, and Utah approved registration by letter, while Wisconsin enacted a postcard registration system and New Jersey set up registration by telephone.

Ethics. Spurred by public opinion polls showing widespread citizen distrust of public officials, prosecutors and investigators launched inquiries into governmental conduct at all levels. An unusually high number of indictments were reported. During the year, for example, one sitting governor was indicted, two former governors were convicted on corruption charges, and four other present or former governors were reportedly undergoing grand jury scrutiny.

Gov. Marvin Mandel, who succeeded former U.S. vice-president Spiro Agnew as Maryland's chief executive in 1969, was indicted along with five associates on 24 counts of mail fraud and racketeering in November. The central charge was that Mandel had used his influence to enrich friends who owned a small racetrack.

Former Oklahoma governor David Hall was convicted of four counts of bribery and extortion on March 14 by a federal jury and sentenced to three years in prison. Hall had been indicted on January 16, three days after his term expired, for attempting to guide investment of state pension funds into an associate's company. Former Michigan governor John B. Swainson, an associate justice of the Michigan Supreme Court, was convicted on November 2 on charges of perjury growing out of allegations that he accepted a bribe to have a burglary conviction reviewed in 1972.

Federal grand juries were reliably reported to be investigating current or former governors of Louisiana, West Virginia, Pennsylvania, and Missouri on a variety of corruption charges. All of the target governors were Democrats, and the U.S. attorneys directing the grand juries in each instance were Republicans, leading some of those being investigated to charge that they were victims of a political conspiracy.

August Mardesich, Washington state Senate majority leader, was indicted January 8 on charges of extorting $10,000 from disposal company officials in return for supporting trash-hauling legislation. The former state treasurer of West Virginia, John Kelly, pleaded no contest on July 7 to charges of eliciting bribes from the state's largest bank.

Alleged misconduct among public officials in Oklahoma and Florida resulted in extensive legal action. After being impeached by the state House of Representatives for soliciting illegal funds, Oklahoma Secretary of State John Rogers resigned on June 27. The Oklahoma state treasurer, Leo Winters, was acquitted on May 19 on four counts of mail fraud.

States responded to the crisis in confidence by continuing to approve laws mandating disclosure of campaign finances, setting codes of ethical conduct, and ordering open meetings, continuing a trend that began in 1973. Mississippi adopted a "sunshine" law, leaving Rhode Island and West Virginia as the only states without a law requiring most meetings to be open to the public. Connecticut, California, and Ohio tightened existing sunshine laws, and financial disclosure was mandated for public officials in New Jersey, North Carolina, Wisconsin, and South Carolina. Ethics commissions were established in South Carolina and South Dakota.

Education and Health. School finance reform continued on a limited basis during 1975, though much of the impetus for action faded with the U.S. Supreme Court's acceptance in 1973 of local property taxes as the basis for school finance. Texas, New Jersey, and Kentucky changed their school aid formulas, providing increased assistance to poorer districts. New Hampshire approved a law allowing voluntary school prayer, and Connecticut authorized silent meditation in public schools.

Buffeted by skyrocketing medical malpractice claims, nearly half of the states prescribed remedies to relieve resulting pressures on the cost of medical malpractice insurance. When some insurers abandoned the field, most states set up insurance pools to assure all physicians of malpractice coverage. The moves were hastened by widespread, drastic boosts in insurance premiums; physician and hospital strikes; and occasional refusal by insurance companies to write malpractice insurance. New laws authorizing medical malpractice pools were passed in 17 states. In addition, panels to review malpractice claims were provided in Arkansas, Indiana, Nevada, New York, and Florida. The New York and Florida laws established committees to discipline errant physicians. In other moves designed to ease the crisis, Oregon limited lawyer's fees in malpractice awards, Michigan required 50 hours of continuing education annually for physicians, and Texas mandated disclosure by insurers of liability insurance figures.

A U.S. Supreme Court decision on June 26 promised major changes in state mental institutions by prohibiting the involuntary commitment of harmless mentally disturbed individuals. According to figures accumulated by the National Institute of Mental Health, about 1.6 million inpatients are treated at mental hospitals nationwide in a typical year, with a substantial minority receiving care partially or fully against their will. With the high court establishing a "right to liberty" for those involuntarily committed who are dangerous neither to themselves nor to others, officials estimated that a sizable fraction of inpatients at state and county mental institutions might be eligible for outright release.

Law and Justice. For the eighth consecutive year, no death sentences were carried out in the U.S. as the Supreme Court continued to delay a new interpretation of state capital punishment laws. In the meantime, five more states (for a total of 35) enacted new death penalty statutes designed to meet objections to capital punishment enumerated by the high court in its 5 to 4 decision in 1972. To overcome objections that death was "arbitrarily and capriciously" invoked, thus making it cruel and unusual punishment, the new laws in Alabama, Maryland, Missouri, Virginia, and Washington mandated death for certain types of crimes. A sixth state, Massachusetts, also enacted a capital punishment law, but it was vetoed by the governor. After hearing oral arguments in a North Carolina case that was to test the new laws, the Supreme Court in June failed to arrive at a verdict and held the matter over for later consideration.

Two attempts on the life of President

Ford in California spurred efforts for more stringent gun control laws. Hawaii, New Jersey, Connecticut, and Illinois restricted firearms sales during the year, typically banning the sale of small handguns known as Saturday night specials. Rape laws were liberalized in Washington, Hawaii, Alaska, Tennessee, Louisiana, New York, Michigan, Connecticut, and Delaware, narrowing the amount of corroboration needed to convict and restricting inquiry into the victim's past sex life during the defendant's trial.

Drugs. A dramatic change in traditionally tough strictures against marijuana possession occurred in 1975 as five additional states followed Oregon's 1973 initiative in decriminalizing possession of small amounts of the weed. Alaska, California, Colorado, Maine, and Ohio legislatures decreed that such offenses should not result in criminal arrests or records but should be subject to traffic-ticket-type citations, usually carrying a $100 maximum fine for the first offense. In addition, the Alaska Supreme Court ruled that possession of larger quantities (more than the one-ounce limit specified in the six state laws) by an individual in his home was constitutionally protected by the right to privacy that was specified in the state constitution.

Similar decriminalization legislation was rejected in 21 states, but proponents of the measures promised increased pressure for such laws in 1976. Results of Oregon public opinion polls, showing citizen satisfaction with the state's two-year decriminalization experiment and no marked increase in marijuana usage, contributed to the national trend. One survey, conducted by the Drug Abuse Council, revealed that in two years of decriminalization, the percentage of adults regularly using marijuana actually dropped slightly, from 9 to 8%, while 58% of the voters favoured the new law's general approach.

Environment. Concern over the energy crisis and a series of adverse court decisions made the year a disappointing one for state environmental protectionists. The number of new state laws protecting air and water standards declined drastically in comparison with past legislative sessions, although several new initiatives were successful. California, Minnesota, and Vermont prohibited flip-top beverage cans; Oregon banned aerosol spray containers; Texas began regulation of strip mining; California adopted the nation's first smog control regulations for motorcycles; and Kentucky courts upheld the state's wild-river protection law.

Environmentalists suffered a major setback on May 12 when the U.S. Supreme Court ruled, in an Alaska pipeline case, that environmentalists bringing class action lawsuits could not recover attorney's fees as "private attorneys general" unless specifically authorized by law. The ruling was viewed as making many environmental court tests economically unfeasible. In another adverse decision, a federal appeals court upheld the sufficiency of an environmental impact statement for a Washington state interstate highway bypass; the March 20 ruling was a significant boost to highway planners delayed by environmentalists.

Energy. Uneasy relations between the federal government and various states over oil and energy policies continued during the year. The debate over energy also tended to pit state against state as various regions competed to promote and protect their own interests.

Typifying energy regionalism, Texas stopped shipments out of state of natural gas that might be needed at home, and New Mexico imposed a tax on electricity generated instate but used outside state lines. Governors of western, southwestern, and northeastern states formed separate energy groups to advance regional interests.

One aspect of the battle pitted the energy-poor Northeast, lobbying for elimination of taxes on imported oil, against oil-producing states, which were advocating an end to federal controls on oil-gas prices and production. Promised exploitation of the West's ample supply of low-sulfur coal, made increasingly valuable by the rise in oil prices, caused numerous moves to protect the region's environment and guard against the effects of strip mining. Warned New Mexico Gov. Jerry Apodaca: "Let there be no mistake. The West will not become an energy colony for the rest of the nation."

The situation was clouded by growing controversy over nuclear power, once thought to be the unchallenged energy source of the future. Numerous small accidents and the rising costs of production slowed plans for nuclear plant development. New laws prohibited construction of new atomic energy plants in Rhode Island and Vermont without the express approval of their state legislatures. At the urging of Illinois, a federal appeals court permanently halted establishment of a nuclear plant that was to have been built in the Lake Michigan dunes area of Indiana.

Equal Rights. The drive for a proposed 27th Amendment to the U.S. Constitution, a bill of women's rights known as the Equal Rights Amendment, sputtered and apparently died during 1975. The legislature in one additional state, North Dakota, ratified the ERA during the year, bringing the total to 34 of 38 needed for final passage. But ratification moves were defeated in Illinois, Missouri, Florida, North Carolina, and South Carolina, and prospects for final approval by the March 1979 deadline appeared remote.

After Congress passed the amendment in 1972 as a guarantee that "Equality of rights under the law shall not be denied or abridged . . . on account of sex," the ERA appeared to be heading toward immediate acceptance. Twenty-two states ratified it later that year, and eight more followed suit in 1973. But a diverse collection of opponents, raising the spectre of combat duty for women, unisex bathrooms, homosexual marriage, and abolition of maternity benefits, successfully limited the ratifications to four states in 1974 and one in 1975.

A congressional report on the amendment's impact revealed that actual changes would not be nearly as drastic as anti-ERA lobbyists feared, but noted that state laws in a wide variety of areas would be affected. Fathers would no longer be automatically responsible for child support after divorce; women would be liable for any reinstated military draft (but not necessarily for combat duty); labour laws designed to protect women would be unlawful; women would gain equal rights to credit; and rape laws would have to provide equal protection to both men and women.

As the controversy swirled, voters in New Jersey and New York handily defeated proposed equal rights amendments to their state constitutions in November balloting. Fourteen states had previously approved equal rights amendments to their state constitutions. Several court decisions during the year indicated that present laws and constitutional protections might be sufficient to outlaw egregious forms of sex discrimination. Although a national poll showed that the public favoured the Equal Rights Amendment by a three to one margin, anti-ERA forces predicted that the amendment was virtually dead in the state legislatures.

The drive for sexual equality produced a number of interesting court decisions. Following a 1974 New Jersey decision that gave girls the right to play Little League baseball, the Washington state supreme court ruled that girls must be allowed to try out for all high-school athletic teams, including football. A Massachusetts law holding the male, but not the female, guilty of a misdemeanour with the birth of an illegitimate child was ruled unconstitutional sex discrimination. And a Utah law setting the age for marriage without consent at 21 for men and 18 for women was judged unconstitutionally discriminatory toward males.

Consumer Protection. State fair trade laws, allowing manufacturers to set retail prices for their products, were repealed by 15 legislatures during 1975. At the year's end, the federal government removed anti-trust exemptions from the books for such state laws, a move that effectively killed fair trade in 21 states where such laws were still in effect.

The fair trade concept, first enacted into law during the depression of the 1930s, was designed to protect small retailers from price-cutting by big competitors and was at one time endorsed by 43 states. An accelerating attack on the laws was based on anti-inflationary principles; the U.S. Department of Justice estimated that freeing retail prices from manufacturers' controls would save consumers $2.1 billion per year.

North Dakota enacted a no-fault bodily injury auto insurance law, bringing to 24 the number of states with at least partial no-fault automobile coverage. A drive to mandate no-fault insurance in all states, including consumer protection standards that had not yet been met by any state, was mounted in Congress at the year's end. In the meantime, a crisis developed in Massachusetts, the only state to have adopted a no-fault provision for property damage auto claims. Under the law one-third of all drivers submitted claims in a year's period, twice the national average. Although the legislature attempted to mollify insurers by ordering a $200 deductible clause on such claims, the outbreak of small claims caused several insurance companies to schedule withdrawal from Massachusetts in early 1976.

The practice of refusing mortgage applications in marginal neighbourhoods, known as "redlining," was attacked by new regulations in California and Illinois. The Colorado state treasurer promised to withhold state funds from banks failing to meet their "social responsibilities" in such matters.

(DAVID C. BECKWITH)

Area and Population

Area and population of the states

State	AREA in sq.mi. Total	Inland water*	POPULATION (000) July 1, 1970	July 1, 1975†	Percent change 1970–75
Alabama	51,609	549	3,451	3,614	4.9
Alaska	586,400	15,335	305	352	16.3
Arizona	113,909	334	1,792	2,224	25.3
Arkansas	53,104	605	1,926	2,116	10.0
California	158,693	2,120	19,994	21,185	6.1
Colorado	104,247	363	2,225	2,534	14.7
Connecticut	5,009	110	3,039	3,095	2.1
Delaware	2,057	79	550	579	5.7
Dist. of Columbia	69	8	753	716	−5.4
Florida	58,560	4,308	6,845	8,357	23.0
Georgia	58,876	602	4,602	4,926	7.4
Hawaii	6,424	9	774	865	12.3
Idaho	83,557	849	717	820	14.9
Illinois	56,400	470	11,137	11,145	0.3
Indiana	36,291	106	5,208	5,311	2.2
Iowa	56,290	258	2,830	2,870	1.6
Kansas	82,264	216	2,248	2,267	0.8
Kentucky	40,395	532	3,224	3,396	5.4
Louisiana	48,523	3,417	3,644	3,791	4.1
Maine	33,215	2,203	995	1,059	6.6
Maryland	10,577	703	3,937	4,098	4.4
Massachusetts	8,257	390	5,699	5,828	2.4
Michigan	58,216	1,197	8,901	9,157	3.1
Minnesota	84,068	4,059	3,822	3,926	3.1
Mississippi	47,716	493	2,216	2,346	5.8
Missouri	69,686	548	4,693	4,763	1.8
Montana	147,138	1,402	697	748	7.7
Nebraska	77,227	615	1,490	1,546	4.1
Nevada	110,540	752	493	592	21.1
New Hampshire	9,304	290	742	818	10.9
New Jersey	7,836	315	7,195	7,316	2.0
New Mexico	121,666	156	1,018	1,147	12.7
New York	49,576	1,637	18,260	18,120	−0.7
North Carolina	52,712	3,645	5,091	5,451	7.2
North Dakota	70,665	1,208	618	635	2.7
Ohio	41,222	250	10,688	10,759	1.0
Oklahoma	69,919	1,032	2,572	2,712	6.0
Oregon	96,981	733	2,102	2,288	9.4
Pennsylvania	45,333	326	11,817	11,827	0.2
Rhode Island	1,214	156	951	927	−2.4
South Carolina	31,055	783	2,596	2,818	8.8
South Dakota	77,047	669	666	683	2.6
Tennessee	42,244	482	3,932	4,188	6.7
Texas	267,338	4,499	11,254	12,237	9.3
Utah	84,916	2,577	1,069	1,206	13.8
Vermont	9,609	333	447	471	5.9
Virginia	40,815	977	4,653	4,967	6.8
Washington	68,192	1,483	3,414	3,544	3.8
West Virginia	24,181	102	1,746	1,803	3.4
Wisconsin	56,154	1,449	4,433	4,607	4.3
Wyoming	97,914	503	334	374	12.5
TOTAL U.S.	3,615,210	66,237	203,805	213,121‡	4.8

*Excludes the Great Lakes and coastal waters.
†Preliminary.
‡State figures do not add to total given because of rounding.
Source: U.S. Department of Commerce, Bureau of the Census, *Current Population Reports.*

Largest metropolitan areas*

Name	Population 1970 census	1973 estimate	Percent change 1970–73	Land area in sq.mi.	Density per sq.mi. 1973
New York-Newark-Jersey City SCSA	17,033,367	16,976,700	−3.0	5,072	3,347
New York City	9,973,716	9,809,200	−1.6	1,384	7,088
Nassau-Suffolk	2,555,868	2,609,600	2.1	1,218	2,142
Newark	2,057,468	2,077,700	1.0	1,008	2,061
Norwalk-Stamford	792,814	787,800	−0.6	627	1,256
Jersey City	607,839	617,700	1.6	47	13,143
New Brunswick-Perth Amboy	583,813	597,100	2.3	312	1,914
Long Branch-Asbury Park	461,849	477,600	3.4	476	1,003
Los Angeles-Long Beach-Anaheim SCSA	9,983,017	10,130,400	0.7	34,007	298
Los Angeles-Long Beach	7,041,980	6,944,800	−1.4	4,069	1,707
Anaheim-Santa Ana-Garden Grove	1,421,233	1,580,300	11.2	782	2,021
Riverside-San Bernardino-Ontario	1,141,307	1,192,000	4.4	27,293	44
Oxnard-Simi Valley-Ventura	378,497	413,300	9.2	1,863	222
Chicago-Gary SCSA	7,610,978	7,689,300	1.0	4,657	1,651
Chicago	6,977,611	7,048,500	1.0	3,719	1,895
Gary-Hammond-East Chicago	633,367	640,800	1.2	938	683
Philadelphia-Wilmington-Trenton SCSA	5,627,719	5,652,900	2.2	4,946	1,143
Philadelphia	4,824,110	4,819,200	−0.1	3,553	1,356
Wilmington	499,493	517,600	3.6	1,165	444
Trenton	304,116	316,100	3.9	228	1,386
Detroit-Ann Arbor SCSA	4,669,154	4,690,700	2.2	4,627	1,014
Detroit	4,435,051	4,446,800	0.3	3,916	1,136
Ann Arbor	234,103	243,900	4.2	711	343
San Francisco-Oakland-San Jose SCSA	4,425,224	4,544,400	0.4	5,390	843
San Francisco-Oakland	3,108,782	3,125,100	0.5	2,480	1,260
San Jose	1,065,313	1,156,200	8.5	1,300	889
Vallejo-Fairfield-Napa	251,129	263,100	4.8	1,610	163
Boston-Lawrence-Lowell SCSA	3,376,328	3,418,200	1.2	1,769	1,932
Washington, D.C.	2,909,355	3,041,800	4.6	2,812	1,082
Cleveland-Akron-Lorain SCSA	2,999,811	2,933,700	−0.4	2,917	1,006
Cleveland	2,063,729	1,996,900	−3.2	1,519	1,315
Akron	679,239	674,800	−0.7	903	747
Lorain-Elyria	256,843	262,000	2.0	495	529
Dallas-Fort Worth	2,378,353	2,441,800	2.7	8,360	292
St. Louis	2,410,492	2,387,600	−0.9	4,935	484
Pittsburgh	2,401,362	2,366,800	−1.4	3,049	776
Houston-Galveston SCSA	2,169,128	2,316,000	0.1	7,193	322
Houston	1,999,316	2,138,400	7.0	6,794	315
Galveston-Texas City	169,812	177,600	4.6	399	445
Baltimore	2,071,016	2,116,500	2.2	2,259	937
Miami-Fort Lauderdale SCSA	1,887,892	2,105,700	0.1	3,261	646
Miami	1,267,792	1,367,100	7.8	2,042	669
Fort Lauderdale-Hollywood	620,100	738,600	19.1	1,219	606
Minneapolis-St. Paul	1,965,391	1,993,900	1.4	4,647	429
Seattle-Tacoma SCSA	1,836,949	1,786,100	−0.4	5,902	303
Seattle-Everett	1,424,605	1,384,900	−2.8	4,226	328
Tacoma	412,344	401,200	−2.7	1,676	239
Atlanta	1,595,517	1,728,400	8.3	4,326	399
Cincinnati-Hamilton SCSA	1,611,310	1,620,800	1.7	2,620	619
Cincinnati	1,385,103	1,383,200	−0.1	2,149	644
Hamilton-Middletown	226,207	237,600	5.0	471	504
Milwaukee-Racine SCSA	1,574,722	1,604,200	0.5	1,793	895
Milwaukee	1,403,884	1,432,000	2.0	1,456	984
Racine	170,838	172,200	0.8	337	511
San Diego	1,357,854	1,469,500	8.2	4,261	345
Denver-Boulder	1,239,477	1,366,100	10.2	4,651	294
Buffalo	1,349,211	1,353,500	0.3	1,590	851
Kansas City	1,273,926	1,294,900	1.6	3,341	388
Tampa-St. Petersburg	1,088,549	1,270,700	16.7	2,045	621
Indianapolis	1,111,352	1,138,900	2.5	3,072	371

*Standard Metropolitan Statistical Area, unless otherwise indicated. SCSA is a Standard Consolidated Statistical Area, which may be comprised of SMSAs, or of Metropolitan State Economic Areas (Boston only).
Source: U.S. Dept. of Commerce, Bureau of the Census, *Current Population Reports.*

Population change

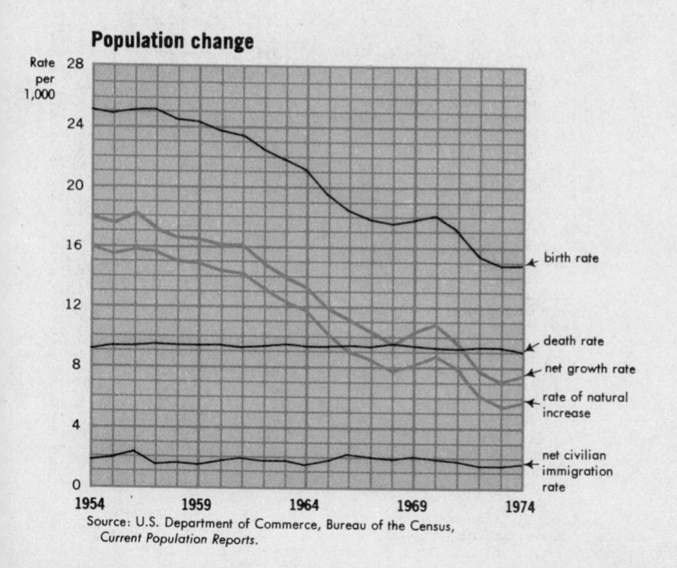

Source: U.S. Department of Commerce, Bureau of the Census, *Current Population Reports.*

Marriage and divorce rates

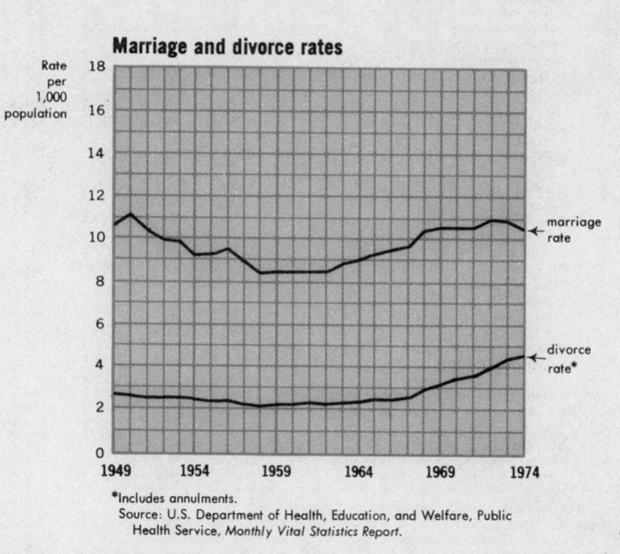

*Includes annulments.
Source: U.S. Department of Health, Education, and Welfare, Public Health Service, *Monthly Vital Statistics Report.*

Church membership

Religious body	Total clergy	Inclusive membership
Adventist, Seventh-day	3,606	479,799
Baptist bodies		
American Baptist Association	4,070	1,071,000
American Baptist Churches in the U.S.A.	8,564	1,579,029
Baptist General Conference	1,055	111,093
Baptist Missionary Association of America	2,650	211,000
Conservative Baptist Association of America	...	300,000
Free Will Baptists	3,700	215,000
General Baptists (General Association of)	1,125	70,000
National Baptist Convention of America	28,754	2,668,799
National Baptist Convention, U.S.A., Inc.	27,500	5,500,000
Natl. Bap. Evang. Life and Soul Saving Assembly	137	57,674
National Primitive Baptist Convention	601	1,645,000
Primitive Baptists	...	72,000
Progressive National Baptist Convention, Inc.	863	521,692
Regular Baptist Churches, General Assn. of	...	250,000
Southern Baptist Convention	54,150	12,513,378
United Free Will Baptist Church	784	100,000
Brethren (German Baptists): Church of the Brethren	1,948	179,387
Buddhist Churches of America	101	100,000
Christian and Missionary Alliance	1,196	144,245
Christian Church (Disciples of Christ)	6,567	1,312,326
Christian Churches and Churches of Christ	6,272	1,034,047
Christian Congregation	506	59,600
Church of God (Anderson, Ind.)	2,905	161,401
Church of the Nazarene	7,130	430,128
Churches of Christ	6,200	2,400,000
Congregational Christian Churches, Natl. Assn. of	475	90,000
Eastern churches		
American Carpatho-Russian Orth. Greek Catholic Ch.	68	100,000
Antiochian Orthodox Christian Archdiocese of N. Am.	124	130,000
Armenian Apostolic Church of America	34	125,000
Armenian Church of America, Diocese of the (Including Diocese of California)	67	372,000
Bulgarian Eastern Orthodox Church	11	86,000
Greek Orthodox Archdiocese of N. and S. America	675	1,950,000
Orthodox Church in America	558	1,000,000
Romanian Orthodox Episcopate of America	52	40,000
Russian Orth. Ch. in the U.S.A., Patriarchal Parishes of	60	51,500
Russian Orthodox Church Outside Russia	168	55,000
Serbian Eastern Orth. Ch. for the U.S.A. and Canada	64	65,000
Syrian Orthodox Church of Antioch	14	50,000
Ukrainian Orthodox Church in the U.S.A.	131	87,745
Episcopal Church	11,573	2,907,293
Evangelical Covenant Church of America	683	69,960
Evangelical Free Church of America	...	70,490
Friends United Meeting	611	67,431
Independent Fundamental Churches of America	1,252	87,582
Jehovah's Witnesses	None	539,262
Jewish congregations	6,400	6,115,000
Latter Day Saints		
Church of Jesus Christ of Latter-day Saints	18,096	2,683,573
Reorganized Church of Jesus Christ of L.D.S.	15,179	156.687
Lutherans		
American Lutheran Church	6,483	2,437,862
Lutheran Church in America	7,579	2,986,970
Lutheran Church—Missouri Synod	7,331	2,769,594
Wisconsin Evangelical Lutheran Synod	1,041	388,865
Mennonite Church	2,370	92,390
Methodists		
African Methodist Episcopal Church	7,089	1,166,301
African Methodist Episcopal Zion Church	6,873	1,024,974
Christian Methodist Episcopal Church	2,259	466,718
Free Methodist Church of North America	1,760	65,210
United Methodist Church	35,106	10,063,046
Moravian Church in America	203	54,892
North American Old Roman Catholic Church	109	60,098
Pentecostals		
Apostolic Overcoming Holy Church of God	350	75,000
Assemblies of God	12,810	1,239,197
Church of God	2,737	75,890
Church of God (Cleveland, Tenn.)	8,650	328,892
Church of God in Christ	6,000	425,000
Church of God in Christ, International	1,502	501,000
Church of God of Prophecy	5,475	62,743
International Church of the Foursquare Gospel	2,690	89,215
Pentecostal Church of God of America, Inc.	1,900	135,000
Pentecostal Holiness Church, Inc.	1,878	74,108
United Pentecostal Church, International	5,555	270,000
Polish National Catholic Church of America	144	282,411
Presbyterians		
Cumberland Presbyterian Church	713	93,948
Presbyterian Church in the U.S.	5,092	896,203
United Presbyterian Church in the U.S.A.	13,736	2,723,565
Reformed bodies		
Christian Reformed Church	1,065	206,000
Reformed Church in America	2,742	354,004
Roman Catholic Church	59,287	48,701,835
Salvation Army	5,178	366,471
Spiritualists, International General Assembly of	...	164,072
Triumph the Church and Kingdom of God in Christ	1,375	54,307
Unitarian Universalist Association	864	192,510
United Church of Christ	9,526	1,841,312
Wesleyan Church	2,489	94,215

Table includes churches reporting a membership of 50,000 or more and represents the latest information available.
Source: National Council of Churches, *Yearbook of American and Canadian Churches*, 1976.

(CONSTANT H. JACQUET)

The Economy

Gross national product and national income

in billions of dollars

Item	1965	1970	1974	1975*
GROSS NATIONAL PRODUCT	684.9	977.1	1,397.4	1,440.9
By type of expenditure				
Personal consumption expenditures	432.8	617.6	876.7	938.6
Durable goods	66.3	91.3	127.5	130.6
Nondurable goods	191.1	263.8	380.2	410.1
Services	175.5	262.6	369.0	397.9
Gross private domestic investment	108.1	136.3	209.4	148.1
Fixed investment	98.5	131.7	195.2	179.1
Changes in business inventories	9.6	4.5	14.2	−31.0
Net exports of goods and services	6.9	3.6	2.1	16.2
Exports	39.2	62.9	140.2	136.0
Imports	32.3	59.3	138.1	119.8
Government purchases of goods and services	137.0	219.5	309.2	338.1
Federal	66.9	96.2	116.9	128.4
State and local	70.1	123.3	192.3	209.7
By major type of product				
Goods output	347.2	471.2	670.3	680.5
Durable goods	139.7	183.7	256.9	247.0
Nondurable goods	207.7	287.4	413.4	433.5
Services	262.9	410.3	590.3	635.3
Structures	74.8	95.6	136.8	125.2
NATIONAL INCOME	564.3	800.5	1,142.5	1,175.4
By type of income				
Compensation of employees	393.8	603.9	855.8	885.4
Proprietors' income	57.3	66.9	93.0	86.1
Rental income of persons	19.0	23.9	26.5	27.1
Corporate profits and inventory valuation adjustment	76.1	69.2	105.6	104.9
Net interest	18.2	36.5	61.6	71.9
By industry division				
Agriculture, forestry, and fisheries	21.0	25.6	45.6	38.8
Mining and construction	35.2	50.5	72.0	69.0
Manufacturing	172.6	217.5	306.1	303.1
Nondurable goods	66.3	88.9	124.0	125.4
Durable goods	106.3	128.6	182.1	177.8
Transportation	23.2	29.8	43.4	42.5
Communications and public utilities	22.6	31.5	42.0	46.2
Wholesale and retail trade	84.3	121.3	166.2	176.9
Finance, insurance, and real estate	61.9	89.9	127.3	135.5
Services	64.1	102.9	150.1	162.6
Government and government enterprises	75.2	126.9	177.9	192.5
Other	4.2	4.6	11.9	8.3

*Second quarter, seasonally adjusted at annual rates.
Source: U.S. Department of Commerce, Bureau of Economic Analysis, *Survey of Current Business*.

Personal income per capita

State	1950	1960*	1970*	1974*
Alabama	$ 880	$1,522	$2,948	$4,215
Alaska	2,384	2,806	4,644	7,062
Arizona	1,330	2,021	3,665	5,127
Arkansas	825	1,389	2,878	4,200
California	1,852	2,709	4,493	6,032
Colorado	1,487	2,286	3,855	5,515
Connecticut	1,875	2,828	4,917	6,455
Delaware	2,132	2,788	4,524	6,306
District of Columbia	2,221	2,963	5,079	7,044
Florida	1,281	1,948	3,738	5,416
Georgia	1,034	1,649	3,354	4,751
Hawaii	1,386	2,365	4,623	6,042
Idaho	1,295	1,857	3,290	4,918
Illinois	1,825	2,649	4,507	6,234
Indiana	1,512	2,174	3,772	5,184
Iowa	1,485	1,986	3,751	5,279
Kansas	1,443	2,165	3,853	5,500
Kentucky	981	1,578	3,112	4,442
Louisiana	1,120	1,668	3,090	4,391
Maine	1,186	1,881	3,302	4,590
Maryland	1,602	2,342	4,309	5,943
Massachusetts	1,633	2,463	4,340	5,757
Michigan	1,701	2,351	4,180	5,883
Minnesota	1,410	2,074	3,859	5,422
Mississippi	755	1,222	2,626	3,803
Missouri	1,431	2,116	3,781	5,036
Montana	1,622	2,035	3,500	4,956
Nebraska	1,490	2,113	3,789	5,278
Nevada	2,018	2,803	4,563	6,016
New Hampshire	1,323	2,037	3,737	4,944
New Jersey	1,834	2,728	4,701	6,247
New Mexico	1,177	1,860	3,077	4,137
New York	1,873	2,742	4,712	6,159
North Carolina	1,037	1,585	3,252	4,665
North Dakota	1,263	1,751	3,086	5,583
Ohio	1,620	2,345	4,020	5,518
Oklahoma	1,143	1,879	3,387	4,581
Oregon	1,620	2,216	3,719	5,284
Pennsylvania	1,541	2,267	3,971	5,447
Rhode Island	1,605	2,210	3,959	5,343
South Carolina	893	1,390	2,990	4,311
South Dakota	1,242	1,792	3,123	4,685
Tennessee	994	1,571	3,119	4,551
Texas	1,349	1,935	3,606	4,952
Utah	1,309	1,982	3,227	4,473
Vermont	1,121	1,868	3,468	4,534
Virginia	1,228	1,863	3,712	5,339
Washington	1,674	2,358	4,053	5,710
West Virginia	1,065	1,621	3,061	4,372
Wisconsin	1,477	2,187	3,812	5,247
Wyoming	1,668	2,274	3,815	5,404
United States	1,496	2,222	3,966	5,448

*Revised.
Source: U.S. Department of Commerce, Bureau of Economic Analysis, *Survey of Current Business*.

Income by industrial source, 1974

State and region	SOURCES OF PERSONAL INCOME					SOURCES OF CIVILIAN INCOME % OF TOTAL										
	Total personal income	Farm income	Govt. income disbursements: Federal	Govt. income disbursements: State, local	Private nonfarm income	Total	Farms	Mining	Construction	Mfg.	Wholesale, retail trade	Finance, insurance, real estate	Transportation, communications, public util.	Service	Govt.	Other
United States	$1,151,622	$33,037	$58,134	$99,449	$705,701	$896,321	%3.7	%1.1	%6.3	%26.8	%16.5	%5.2	%7.2	%15.3	%17.6	%0.3
New England	69,263	514	2,227	5,539	42,809	51,089	1.0	0.1	6.0	31.5	16.1	6.1	5.9	17.7	15.2	0.4
Maine	4,806	256	288	388	2,626	3,558	7.2	0.1	6.5	26.4	15.8	4.0	6.3	14.0	19.0	0.6
New Hampshire	3,995	22	151	297	2,329	2,798	0.8	0.2	7.1	32.7	16.6	5.0	5.6	15.7	16.0	0.3
Vermont	2,131	57	66	207	1,253	1,581	3.6	0.6	6.4	28.3	15.4	4.4	6.7	17.1	17.2	0.2
Massachusetts	33,391	75	1,037	2,828	21,041	24,981	0.3	0.1	5.9	28.6	16.8	6.3	6.4	19.7	15.5	0.4
Rhode Island	5,006	10	232	407	2,940	3,589	0.3	‡	5.3	33.3	16.3	5.3	5.2	16.1	17.8	0.4
Connecticut	19,934	94	454	1,412	12,621	14,582	0.6	0.1	5.9	37.2	14.8	7.0	5.1	16.0	12.8	0.3
Mideast	254,838	1,441	12,578	23,693	159,614	197,327	0.7	0.4	5.6	†	16.1	6.4	7.6	17.7	18.4	†
New York	111,541	488	2,840	12,217	71,039	86,584	0.6	0.2	4.7	23.4	16.7	8.8	8.2	19.8	17.4	0.2
New Jersey	45,790	134	1,371	3,707	27,619	32,831	0.4	0.1	5.9	31.8	17.0	4.8	8.0	16.2	15.5	0.3
Pennsylvania	64,471	531	2,081	4,747	42,548	49,908	1.1	1.3	6.2	35.2	15.4	4.5	7.4	15.0	13.7	0.2
Delaware	3,614	104	136	282	2,409	2,931	3.5	0.1	6.9	38.6	13.5	4.2	5.0	13.5	14.3	0.3
Maryland	24,329	183	2,487	2,081	12,329	17,080	1.1	0.1	8.2	18.2	17.1	4.9	6.2	17.1	26.7	0.3
District of Columbia	5,093	*	3,664	660	3,670	7,993	*	‡	4.2	†	7.8	4.3	5.8	20.1	54.1	†
Great Lakes	233,749	4,815	5,724	18,757	156,904	186,200	2.6	0.6	5.5	38.2	15.7	4.3	6.6	13.2	13.1	0.2
Michigan	53,520	766	990	4,978	36,198	42,932	1.8	0.4	5.0	42.7	14.6	3.5	5.2	12.8	13.9	0.2
Ohio	59,245	791	1,662	4,275	41,014	47,743	1.7	0.7	5.5	40.0	15.4	3.9	6.8	13.3	12.4	0.2
Indiana	27,631	758	768	1,928	19,137	22,591	3.3	0.4	5.9	42.5	14.6	4.0	6.4	10.8	11.9	0.2
Illinois	69,396	1,725	1,887	5,414	45,547	54,574	3.2	0.7	5.8	31.8	17.2	5.4	7.8	14.6	13.4	0.2
Wisconsin	23,957	775	417	2,161	15,008	18,361	4.2	0.2	5.7	36.7	15.8	4.2	5.9	12.9	14.0	0.2
Plains	87,747	8,322	3,480	7,108	49,843	68,753	12.1	0.8	5.8	22.5	17.6	4.6	7.9	13.0	15.4	0.3
Minnesota	21,238	1,852	472	1,960	12,616	16,899	11.0	1.1	5.8	23.9	17.8	4.7	7.5	13.6	14.4	0.2
Iowa	15,072	1,731	296	1,199	8,280	11,506	15.0	0.3	5.9	26.3	16.8	4.4	6.4	11.5	13.0	0.4
Missouri	24,056	759	1,221	1,811	15,768	19,558	3.9	0.6	5.6	26.7	18.5	5.0	9.3	14.6	15.5	0.2
North Dakota	3,556	1,129	256	247	1,285	2,918	38.7	0.8	5.7	4.7	15.2	2.7	5.6	9.2	17.2	0.2
South Dakota	3,195	680	207	267	1,294	2,448	27.8	1.2	5.5	8.2	16.9	3.5	6.0	11.2	19.4	0.4
Nebraska	8,144	981	376	697	4,243	6,297	15.6	0.3	6.5	15.6	18.1	5.5	8.5	12.7	17.0	0.4
Kansas	12,485	1,190	652	928	6,357	9,127	13.0	1.2	5.9	20.2	16.9	4.3	8.1	12.6	17.3	0.4
Southeast	220,870	7,845	14,959	17,770	.130,130	170,704	4.6	1.7	7.5	23.9	16.6	4.8	7.2	14.1	19.2	0.4
Virginia	26,205	398	3,704	2,071	13,488	19,661	2.0	1.3	7.2	19.7	14.8	4.4	6.9	14.0	29.4	0.3
West Virginia	7,829	31	219	633	5,106	5,990	0.5	13.1	7.1	26.5	14.3	2.9	8.8	12.3	14.2	0.1
Kentucky	14,912	775	940	1,060	8,854	11,629	6.7	5.1	6.2	27.4	14.6	3.5	6.9	12.1	17.2	0.2
Tennessee	18,789	348	914	1,516	12,419	15,196	2.3	0.6	6.4	32.0	17.5	4.7	6.2	14.1	16.0	0.2
North Carolina	25,017	1,291	1,566	2,001	15,911	20,769	6.2	0.2	5.9	32.9	15.3	4.2	6.1	11.7	17.2	0.3
South Carolina	12,003	324	1,086	975	7,350	9,735	3.3	0.2	7.5	32.9	13.8	3.9	5.1	11.9	21.2	0.3
Georgia	23,196	803	1,566	1,954	14,569	18,892	4.2	0.4	6.4	23.2	19.2	5.7	8.4	13.5	18.6	0.4
Florida	43,816	1,133	2,080	3,583	23,862	30,658	3.7	0.4	10.6	12.6	19.6	7.0	7.9	19.1	18.5	0.6
Alabama	15,076	369	1,210	1,222	8,978	11,779	3.1	1.1	7.0	28.4	15.6	4.1	6.6	13.1	20.6	0.3
Mississippi	8,839	613	568	754	4,914	6,849	9.0	1.0	6.5	26.6	14.8	3.9	6.0	12.4	19.3	0.4
Louisiana	16,528	808	735	1,417	9,963	12,923	6.2	5.6	8.8	17.1	17.1	4.5	9.5	14.1	16.6	0.4
Arkansas	8,660	951	372	585	4,715	6,622	14.4	0.7	5.8	26.0	15.5	4.0	7.0	11.7	14.4	0.5
Southwest	87,759	2,602	6,206	7,212	52,361	68,381	3.8	4.1	7.6	18.4	18.2	5.3	7.7	14.8	19.6	0.4
Oklahoma	12,409	554	1,002	958	6,873	9,387	5.9	5.5	6.3	17.8	16.9	4.8	8.0	13.4	20.9	0.4
Texas	59,699	1,518	3,925	4,594	36,892	46,929	3.2	3.6	7.5	20.1	18.9	5.4	7.9	14.9	18.2	0.4
New Mexico	4,642	140	543	557	2,341	3,581	3.9	6.3	7.9	7.1	15.8	4.2	7.8	15.9	30.7	0.3
Arizona	11,039	390	736	1,104	6,255	8,484	4.6	4.2	9.9	15.1	16.4	5.6	6.3	15.8	21.7	0.4
Rocky Mountain	28,524	1,974	2,279	2,565	15,834	22,652	8.7	3.3	8.3	14.7	17.0	4.7	7.9	13.6	21.4	0.3
Montana	3,643	514	238	348	1,719	2,819	18.2	3.4	6.7	9.4	16.2	3.5	8.8	12.5	20.8	0.4
Idaho	3,929	675	207	311	1,970	3,163	21.3	1.3	7.4	15.6	15.6	3.4	6.4	12.1	16.4	0.5
Wyoming	1,940	101	129	195	1,104	1,530	6.6	13.6	14.0	6.2	14.0	2.9	10.3	10.6	21.2	0.5
Colorado	13,765	583	1,158	1,227	7,971	10,939	5.3	2.1	8.5	16.0	17.7	5.7	7.6	14.9	21.8	0.3
Utah	5,247	101	546	484	3,071	4,202	2.4	4.2	7.5	17.2	17.8	4.4	8.4	13.4	24.5	0.2
Far West	161,387	5,415	9,199	16,008	94,140	124,761	4.3	0.5	5.6	†	16.9	5.3	7.2	17.4	20.2	†
Washington	19,849	1,064	1,354	1,909	10,801	15,128	7.0	0.2	5.7	22.4	16.8	4.6	7.0	14.1	21.6	0.6
Oregon	11,973	515	433	1,163	7,285	9,395	5.5	0.3	6.5	25.4	18.5	4.5	7.8	14.0	17.0	0.5
Nevada	3,447	45	217	329	2,275	2,866	1.6	1.9	8.2	†	14.8	4.2	7.8	37.4	19.0	†
California	126,118	3,792	7,195	12,607	73,780	97,372	3.9	0.5	5.4	22.2	16.9	5.5	7.2	17.7	20.3	0.4
Alaska	2,380	1	506	352	1,459	2,319	‡	3.0	17.8	6.2	10.8	3.0	10.1	10.6	37.0	1.5
Hawaii	5,105	107	977	444	2,605	4,134	2.6	‡	10.2	6.0	15.2	6.0	8.3	17.0	34.4	0.4

Dollar figures in millions. *Less than $500,000. †Figures not shown to avoid disclosure of confidential information. Data are included in totals. ‡Less than 0.05%.
§Percentages may not add to 100.0 because of rounding.
Source: U.S. Department of Commerce, Bureau of Economic Analysis, *Survey of Current Business*.

Farms and farm income

State	Number of farms 1974*	Land in farms 1974 in 000 acres*	CASH RECEIPTS, 1974, IN $000*: Farm marketings		
			Total	Crops	Livestock and products
Alabama	77,000	14,500	1,383,968	605,892	778,076
Alaska	310	1,710†	5,003	1,749	3,254
Arizona	5,900	38,400	1,232,366	603,523	628,843
Arkansas	68,000	17,300	2,547,129	1,661,830	885,299
California	63,000	36,100	8,212,334	5,478,777	2,733,557
Colorado	29,000	39,900	2,050,656	612,190	1,438,466
Connecticut	4,300	535	200,418	68,840	131,578
Delaware	3,600	698	257,362	102,124	155,238
Florida	34,000	14,500	2,028,932	1,460,002	568,930
Georgia	75,000	17,000	2,224,940	1,138,371	1,086,569
Hawaii	4,300	2,300	266,026	205,760	60,266
Idaho	27,200	15,500	1,424,489	1,004,767	419,722
Illinois	126,000	29,200	6,256,263	4,405,567	1,850,696
Indiana	106,000	17,500	3,249,702	2,027,173	1,222,529
Iowa	137,000	34,300	7,698,327	3,895,478	3,802,849
Kansas	84,000	49,900	4,361,814	2,308,900	2,052,914
Kentucky	126,000	16,200	1,587,236	917,623	669,613
Louisiana	47,000	11,800	1,258,453	897,656	360,797
Maine	7,600	1,710	465,959	241,514	224,445
Maryland	17,800	2,955	620,389	252,311	368,078
Massachusetts	5,700	700	194,889	85,727	109,162
Michigan	79,000	12,200	1,690,793	977,335	713,458
Minnesota	118,000	30,600	4,754,041	2,773,125	1,980,916
Mississippi	84,000	17,100	1,614,328	979,984	634,344
Missouri	139,000	32,800	2,849,437	1,414,958	1,434,479
Montana	24,900	62,500	1,153,542	714,886	438,656
Nebraska	69,000	48,100	4,027,993	1,936,610	2,091,383
Nevada	2,000	9,000	140,469	38,260	102,209
New Hampshire	2,500	540	74,032	18,144	55,888
New Jersey	8,100	1,035	341,470	225,482	115,988
New Mexico	11,600	47,100	732,598	175,250	557,348
New York	55,000	10,800	1,524,561	490,716	1,033,845
North Carolina	135,000	14,000	2,575,071	1,674,940	900,131
North Dakota	41,500	41,700	2,417,262	2,021,621	395,641
Ohio	117,000	17,400	2,668,379	1,614,833	1,053,546
Oklahoma	86,000	36,900	1,944,309	823,501	1,120,808
Oregon	32,500	19,600	1,118,594	746,985	371,609
Pennsylvania	71,000	9,900	1,499,565	466,799	1,032,766
Rhode Island	660	64	24,658	13,213	11,445
South Carolina	47,000	7,800	907,272	632,798	274,474
South Dakota	43,500	45,500	1,937,427	797,176	1,140,251
Tennessee	124,000	15,400	1,134,093	545,939	588,154
Texas	209,000	141,800	5,967,495	2,915,692	3,051,803
Utah	12,400	13,000	330,301	93,068	237,233
Vermont	6,500	1,840	217,972	16,078	201,894
Virginia	73,000	11,100	1,030,607	552,294	478,313
Washington	40,000	16,500	1,765,853	1,318,382	447,471
West Virginia	26,500	4,850	152,589	46,058	106,531
Wisconsin	105,000	19,600	2,522,378	560,999	1,961,379
Wyoming	8,200	35,500	360,000	115,531	244,469
TOTAL U.S.	2,820,570	1,086,937	95,003,744	52,676,431	42,327,313

*Preliminary. †Exclusive of grazing land leased from the U.S. Government, Alaska farmland totals about 70,000 acres.
Source: U.S. Department of Agriculture, Economics Research Service.

Principal minerals produced

State	Principal minerals, in order of value, 1973	Value in $000		% of U.S. total	
		1972	1973	1972	1973
Alabama	Coal, cement, petroleum, stone	$371,241	$413,056	1.15	1.12
Alaska	Petroleum, sand and gravel, natural gas, stone	286,138	328,789	0.89	0.89
Arizona	Copper, molybdenum, sand and gravel, cement	1,091,004	1,304,988	3.39	3.55
Arkansas	Petroleum, bromine, natural gas, cement	241,179	273,705	0.75	0.75
California	Petroleum, cement, sand and gravel, natural gas	1,851,365	2,041,686	5.75	5.55
Colorado	Petroleum, molybdenum, coal, sand and gravel	425,841	532,776	1.32	1.45
Connecticut	Stone, sand and gravel, feldspar, lime	33,123	36,804	0.10	0.10
Delaware	Sand and gravel, magnesium compounds, clays	2,871	3,889	0.01	0.01
Florida	Phosphate rock, petroleum, stone, cement	424,287	601,100	1.32	1.63
Georgia	Clays, stone, cement, sand and gravel	258,041	305,479	0.80	0.83
Hawaii	Stone, cement, sand and gravel, pumice	28,074	35,147	0.09	0.10
Idaho	Silver, phosphate rock, lead, zinc	106,206	136,081	0.33	0.37
Illinois	Coal, petroleum, stone, sand and gravel	769,737	825,608	2.39	2.24
Indiana	Coal, cement, stone, sand and gravel	322,608	351,405	1.00	0.96
Iowa	Cement, stone, sand and gravel, gypsum	134,496	158,800	0.42	0.43
Kansas	Petroleum, natural gas, natural gas liquids, cement	584,537	646,299	1.81	1.76
Kentucky	Coal, stone, petroleum, natural gas	976,910	1,164,762	3.03	3.17
Louisiana	Petroleum, natural gas, natural gas liquids, sulfur	5,411,543	5,819,610	16.80	15.82
Maine	Sand and gravel, cement, zinc, stone	22,922	33,493	0.07	0.09
Maryland	Stone, cement, sand and gravel, coal	115,501	131,907	0.36	0.36
Massachusetts	Stone, sand and gravel, lime, clays	52,428	59,682	0.16	0.16
Michigan	Iron ore, cement, copper, sand and gravel	694,767	789,022	2.16	2.14
Minnesota	Iron ore, sand and gravel, stone, cement	659,669	852,785	2.05	2.32
Mississippi	Petroleum, natural gas, sand and gravel, cement	260,681	281,738	0.81	0.77
Missouri	Lead, cement, stone, iron ore	451,817	512,634	1.40	1.39
Montana	Copper, petroleum, coal, sand and gravel	307,676	385,285	0.96	1.05
Nebraska	Petroleum, cement, sand and gravel, stone	73,675	80,821	0.23	0.22
Nevada	Copper, gold, sand and gravel, diatomite	181,702	201,813	0.56	0.55
New Hampshire	Sand and gravel, stone, clays, gem stones	10,111	14,119	0.03	0.04
New Jersey	Stone, sand and gravel, zinc, titanium concentrate	113,760	114,016	0.35	0.31
New Mexico	Petroleum, natural gas, copper, natural gas liquids	1,097,292	1,305,644	3.41	3.55
New York	Cement, stone, salt, sand and gravel	320,453	375,866	0.99	1.02
North Carolina	Stone, sand and gravel, cement, feldspar	116,323	146,930	0.36	0.40
North Dakota	Petroleum, coal, sand and gravel, natural gas	98,086	111,853	0.30	0.30
Ohio	Coal, stone, cement, lime	724,748	806,979	2.25	2.19
Oklahoma	Petroleum, natural gas, natural gas liquids, stone	1,210,728	1,323,626	3.76	3.60
Oregon	Sand and gravel, stone, cement, nickel	76,516	81,466	0.24	0.22
Pennsylvania	Coal, cement, stone, sand and gravel	1,231,485	1,401,900	3.82	3.81
Rhode Island	Sand and gravel, stone, gem stones	4,291	4,340	0.01	0.01
South Carolina	Cement, stone, clays, sand and gravel	82,313	88,361	0.26	0.24
South Dakota	Gold, sand and gravel, cement, stone	65,200	81,139	0.20	0.22
Tennessee	Stone, coal, cement, zinc	269,814	275,690	0.84	0.75
Texas	Petroleum, natural gas, natural gas liquids, cement	7,211,551	8,442,494	22.38	22.95
Utah	Copper, petroleum, coal, gold	542,809	674,210	1.68	1.83
Vermont	Stone, asbestos, sand and gravel, talc	34,868	29,366	0.11	0.08
Virginia	Coal, stone, sand and gravel, cement	489,791	540,595	1.52	1.47
Washington	Sand and gravel, cement, coal, stone	109,806	114,329	0.34	0.31
West Virginia	Coal, natural gas, stone, cement	1,430,632	1,503,045	4.44	4.09
Wisconsin	Sand and gravel, stone, iron ore, cement	89,353	114,339	0.28	0.31
Wyoming	Petroleum, sodium compounds, uranium, natural gas	746,743	928,105	2.32	2.52
TOTAL U.S.		$32,217,000	$36,788,000	100.00	100.00

Source: U.S. Department of the Interior, Bureau of Mines, *Minerals Yearbook.*

Principal crops, 1974, production and value*

State	Corn, grain (bu.)		Hay (tons)		Soybeans (bu.)		Wheat (bu.)		Tobacco (lbs.)		Cotton† lint (bales)		Sorghum (bu.)		Potatoes (cwt.)	
	Production	Value	Production	Value	Production	Value	Production	Value	Production	Value	Production	Value	Production	Value	Production	Value
Ala.	29,900	$106,145	1,044	$42,804	24,480	$186,048	2,990	$11,063	1,134	$1,134	530	$116,261	1,056	$3,189	3,336	$27,957
Alaska	...	...	...	...	...	...	...	...	...	...	...	...	...	...	...	...
Ariz.	340	1,258	1,511	86,127	...	...	15,510	48,857	...	...	965	234,379	11,907	42,984	2,236	11,739
Ark.	1,012	3,643	1,170	48,555	86,000	657,900	10,400	37,960	...	...	920	233,165	6,720	19,757	...	...
Calif.	25,787	103,148	7,695	488,633	...	...	38,994	152,497	...	...	2,550	614,448	14,760	55,350	24,623	151,010
Colo.	46,000	156,400	2,728	141,856	...	...	67,809	271,273	...	...	...	...	7,685	23,670	10,622	36,286
Conn.	...	...	173	8,996	...	...	...	...	8,065	34,434	...	...	...	...	598	2,093
Del.	12,416	43,456	51	2,091	4,810	36,556	1,120	4,144	...	...	...	...	...	...	1,530	7,574
Fla.	19,104	64,954	414	23,598	7,533	58,381	600	2,280	27,764	35,249	12	2,246	...	...	5,533	42,733
Ga.	105,280	363,216	1,069	39,019	25,755	190,587	3,680	12,144	161,420	167,598	410	93,086	1,260	3,604	...	...
Hawaii	...	...	...	...	...	...	...	...	...	...	...	...	...	...	...	...
Idaho	2,408	8,548	4,427	190,361	...	...	61,860	263,789	...	...	...	...	...	...	80,045	336,189
Ill.	830,830	2,990,988	3,154	123,006	207,515	1,608,241	53,700	209,430	...	...	0.3	66	3,384	9,475	248	1,054
Ind.	387,660	1,356,810	2,017	95,808	97,750	762,450	50,040	202,662	16,800	19,320	...	...	990	2,911	1,481	7,793
Iowa	948,000	3,318,000	6,321	271,803	199,080	1,542,870	1,230	5,228	...	...	...	...	874	2,570	660	2,706
Kan.	131,480	453,606	4,229	202,992	20,600	157,590	319,000	1,291,950	...	...	...	...	132,800	409,024	...	...
Ky.	95,200	333,200	2,996	113,848	29,250	226,688	12,285	46,683	424,596	485,428	2	371	1,716	4,221	...	...
La.	3,672	12,118	752	30,456	44,880	343,332	600	2,370	125	156	570	126,677	1,200	3,696	252	1,764
Maine	...	...	371	16,324	...	...	...	...	...	...	...	...	...	...	36,400	120,120
Md.	44,940	157,290	621	26,082	7,838	58,785	5,328	19,714	28,800	26,064	...	...	...	...	310	1,581
Mass.	...	...	241	12,773	...	...	...	...	2,408	11,719	...	...	...	...	800	2,800
Mich.	110,410	380,915	2,906	101,710	13,230	100,548	37,600	150,400	...	...	...	...	...	...	9,926	42,841
Minn.	359,900	1,241,655	7,496	322,328	84,840	657,510	80,862	394,816	...	...	...	...	...	...	17,425	59,628
Miss.	5,904	21,550	1,128	43,992	46,713	359,690	3,888	13,802	...	...	1,640	388,090	1,312	3,936	190	1,767
Mo.	149,050	521,675	5,491	230,622	95,700	736,890	37,990	144,362	5,060	5,870	230	57,960	22,440	68,442	...	...
Mont.	910	3,458	4,261	196,006	...	...	120,108	550,570	...	...	...	...	...	...	1,750	10,500
Neb.	380,800	1,313,760	6,462	281,097	28,560	217,056	98,600	404,260	...	...	...	...	64,350	202,059	1,542	5,470
Nev.	...	...	913	54,780	...	...	946	3,737	...	...	2	384	...	...	3,188	...
N.H.	...	...	168	8,400	...	...	...	...	...	...	...	...	...	...	144	547
N.J.	7,743	26,713	271	14,905	2,088	14,929	2,214	8,413	...	...	...	...	...	...	2,430	10,206
N.M.	2,695	9,028	915	53,985	...	...	2,835	11,907	...	...	140	37,094	8,800	29,040	840	2,478
N.Y.	35,200	126,720	5,333	213,320	253	1,822	8,400	31,080	...	...	...	...	...	...	13,986	60,480
N.C.	116,180	395,012	530	25,970	31,950	238,028	10,150	33,495	789,395	834,580	133	27,643	3,710	10,685	1,790	13,818
N.D.	7,301	25,188	4,580	180,910	2,864	21,623	205,062	1,113,515	...	...	...	...	...	...	22,950	78,030
Ohio	266,450	945,898	3,151	133,918	79,750	618,063	64,680	268,422	21,750	22,901	...	...	...	...	2,546	13,537
Okla.	8,008	28,829	3,087	151,263	5,037	36,770	134,400	530,880	...	...	300	49,968	22,800	72,048	...	...
Ore.	828	3,229	2,491	146,969	...	...	52,770	242,742	...	...	...	...	...	...	17,482	76,522
Pa.	89,100	311,850	4,292	193,140	1,144	8,408	12,600	47,250	22,750	11,830	...	...	...	...	7,360	33,120
R.I.	...	...	17	918	...	...	...	...	...	...	...	...	...	...	1,034	4,136
S.C.	31,262	106,291	440	20,020	23,750	174,563	3,950	13,628	172,000	178,708	280	70,963	570	1,516	...	...
S.D.	76,890	265,271	5,016	240,768	7,860	59,736	57,770	276,156	...	...	...	...	5,400	16,794	371	1,447
Tenn.	34,770	128,649	1,818	69,993	31,920	239,400	9,425	32,988	114,305	124,102	310	68,002	1,829	4,920	540	4,185
Texas	73,600	250,240	5,106	245,088	7,830	57,942	52,800	205,920	...	...	2,620	440,160	312,000	926,640	3,206	29,160
Utah	1,680	6,132	1,695	79,665	...	...	8,814	37,019	...	...	...	...	...	...	1,481	5,628
Vt.	...	...	844	40,512	...	...	...	...	...	...	...	...	...	...	220	836
Va.	43,320	149,454	1,737	76,428	10,105	75,282	10,175	33,578	141,328	151,007	2	252	518	1,274	4,030	20,755
Wash.	4,128	15,274	2,577	154,620	...	...	122,220	550,648	...	...	...	...	...	...	41,160	168,756
W.Va.	5,016	18,308	1,007	41,492	...	...	561	2,160	2,888	3,206	...	...	...	...	323	2,503
Wis.	154,360	555,696	10,600	349,800	4,340	32,550	2,853	11,492	17,626	10,681	...	...	...	...	14,000	56,000
Wyo.	1,633	5,960	1,644	85,488	...	...	6,503	28,020	...	...	...	...	...	...	1,528	4,890
TOTAL	4,651,167	$16,329,535	126,960	$5,723,239	1,233,425	$9,480,238	1,793,322	$7,723,304	1,958,214	$2,123,987	11,616	$2,561,215	628,081	$1,917,805	340,116	$1,460,639

*In thousands. †Excludes pima cotton (86,300 bales). Source: U.S. Department of Agriculture, Statistical Reporting Service, Crop Reporting Board, *Crop Production* and *Crop Values.*

Livestock and products, with fisheries, 1974

State	Cattle and calves (lbs.)		Hogs and pigs (lbs.)		Sheep and lambs (lbs.)		Milk (lbs.)		Eggs (no.)		Chicken (lbs.)		Fisheries (lbs.)	
	Amount produced in 000	Value in $000	Amount produced in 000	Value in $000	Amount produced in 000	Value in $000	Amount produced in 000,000	Farm value of milk produced in $000	Amount produced in 000,000	Gross income in $000	Amount sold plus farm con-sumption	Gross income in $000	Commer-cial landings in 000	Value in $000
Alabama	617,750	169,443	284,170	97,186	156	47	710	72,704	2,945	131,789	57,250	4,981	36,962†	17,087†
Alaska	1,486	533	184	78	*	*	18	2,577	6	507	90	17	456,864	141,120
Arizona	696,535	271,706	30,008	11,103	21,025	6,631	810	74,196	149	5,823	1,897	129	...	...
Arkansas	876,965	281,799	86,030	30,455	313	75	709	61,967	3,601	189,053	122,825	11,669	13,067‡	2,872‡
California	1,909,440	750,735	41,158	13,994	64,263	23,418	10,601	903,205	8,485	338,693	81,444	5,619	745,047	130,381
Colorado	1,681,375	677,613	104,112	34,773	60,888	23,077	866	78,979	385	17,358	5,946	357	...	...
Connecticut	23,170	6,317	2,351	776	314	94	613	60,013	864	53,712	19,234	2,001	6,530	1,897
Delaware	9,650	3,259	20,505	7,423	115	34	132	11,840	134	7,537	3,277	328	8,576	1,618
Florida	727,530	225,110	70,328	23,982	177	30	1,902	216,638	2,852	108,376	45,049	2,748	171,394	66,367
Georgia	520,850	152,883	516,589	175,640	113	32	1,194	119,281	5,827	286,008	118,210	11,585	18,157	7,094
Hawaii	56,000	20,227	11,195	6,146	...	...	139	19,613	207	11,385	1,256	183	10,463	5,458
Idaho	645,845	238,105	31,937	10,859	55,300	19,786	1,555	116,625	186	8,262	2,718	217	1,310	47
Illinois	1,057,600	411,654	2,641,605	908,712	13,840	4,330	2,596	206,901	1,543	63,006	21,413	1,885	5,317†	955†
Indiana	622,845	236,504	1,568,308	537,930	11,099	3,709	2,275	192,920	2,639	110,398	39,337	2,754	334†	121†
Iowa	2,891,905	1,102,377	4,473,269	1,525,385	27,804	10,798	3,947	290,894	2,046	71,098	35,647	1,961	5,774	856
Kansas	2,740,010	941,051	743,475	255,755	15,158	5,645	1,403	114,906	601	20,534	15,058	1,129	49	14
Kentucky	930,800	307,744	439,655	154,759	3,719	1,445	2,370	193,866	527	22,793	11,980	1,306	2,728‡	659‡
Louisiana	485,640	155,066	46,314	16,117	504	98	1,059	105,900	664	30,931	16,001	1,488	1,228,906†	86,694†
Maine	26,680	7,364	2,413	772	870	254	615	60,147	1,656	82,800	32,913	3,390	147,822	41,410
Maryland	102,875	36,506	58,199	21,068	1,047	306	1,490	133,206	335	18,900	6,111	612	63,004	20,439
Massachusetts	30,475	8,390	18,295	6,037	302	90	594	57,974	510	27,413	10,067	1,037	268,659	61,784
Michigan	456,965	166,855	255,473	91,459	10,660	3,862	4,588	376,675	1,375	55,458	22,105	1,835	15,454	3,926
Minnesota	1,400,825	481,338	1,406,447	479,598	24,524	8,576	9,382	682,071	2,385	89,040	41,436	1,740	10,399†	1,065†
Mississippi	718,650	212,473	146,357	50,932	246	52	907	83,353	1,908	97,785	54,358	5,817	304,794†	16,355†
Missouri	1,951,705	680,909	1,454,354	498,843	12,517	4,584	3,008	237,030	1,149	49,886	32,768	3,506	929	152
Montana	1,010,580	309,962	85,115	27,918	35,183	9,646	294	24,255	201	9,799	4,560	319	793	117
Nebraska	3,006,430	1,120,547	1,224,630	412,700	16,030	5,966	1,477	104,128	722	23,766	8,676	460	158	16
Nevada	196,065	66,338	2,914	1,020	8,890	3,209	167	14,479	5	199	57	4	...	...
New Hampshire	14,465	3,947	3,761	1,204	297	94	333	31,135	275	14,598	8,004	824	2,488	1,057
New Jersey	29,830	9,853	24,476	8,004	535	151	551	50,416	736	36,678	8,725	1,125	166,962	16,607
New Mexico	592,380	214,289	24,390	8,658	18,636	5,952	338	33,327	197	9,604	2,032	122	...	...
New York	404,390	121,763	28,099	9,666	3,535	1,299	9,822	826,030	2,030	89,659	38,270	2,334	35,189	25,379
North Carolina	254,220	80,102	619,818	216,936	530	165	1,534	158,002	3,037	161,974	96,200	14,430	206,683	17,544
North Dakota	993,260	338,744	110,659	37,071	19,951	6,080	1,055	71,529	151	4,694	3,525	254	212	23
Ohio	597,830	228,674	681,989	238,014	29,081	11,017	4,195	363,706	2,057	81,252	30,009	2,251	8,573	1,746
Oklahoma	2,252,140	761,513	125,236	43,332	5,355	1,822	1,137	104,263	428	18,654	9,805	1,000	740‡	169‡
Oregon	452,810	155,905	36,088	12,270	26,378	8,198	1,004	87,750	543	23,530	6,900	552	95,542	34,450
Pennsylvania	437,975	157,185	173,710	60,972	6,731	2,533	6,971	635,058	3,492	157,140	78,714	13,381	442	155
Rhode Island	2,259	620	2,398	791	99	24	63	5,897	66	4,070	1,073	111	96,066	15,695
South Carolina	173,570	49,881	190,285	65,839	44	12	503	52,916	1,301	57,786	21,690	1,887	18,402	6,861
South Dakota	1,981,280	738,607	822,287	276,288	66,601	21,835	1,518	105,805	770	23,677	12,737	892	3,151	276
Tennessee	766,210	233,830	282,450	96,598	964	331	1,892	165,739	1,026	49,761	14,082	1,775	6,054‡	1,187‡
Texas	5,515,375	1,874,835	350,811	116,820	111,205	32,839	3,378	312,803	2,276	106,593	47,250	5,670	97,203†	72,455†
Utah	239,080	75,813	14,715	4,885	41,520	14,341	922	76,618	311	12,000	3,547	212	...	...
Vermont	69,960	18,940	1,541	493	378	110	1,950	173,940	131	6,507	2,388	246	...	...
Virginia	438,650	134,594	182,554	62,799	12,803	4,953	1,699	156,478	760	39,900	24,700	2,371	507,293	33,836
Washington	445,340	159,529	27,005	9,614	5,452	2,233	2,312	200,450	1,089	42,743	17,407	1,218	115,973	59,031
West Virginia	135,705	41,265	22,322	7,723	8,853	2,766	333	29,737	248	12,152	4,151	411	2	1
Wisconsin	1,024,040	301,074	552,665	180,721	6,935	2,284	18,362	1,411,961	1,183	47,813	18,940	2,443	55,135†	3,524†
Wyoming	518,235	163,422	9,652	3,195	52,545	15,096	123	10,307	30	1,448	472	32	—	—
TOTAL U.S.	42,735,650	14,907,193	20,052,301	6,863,313	803,485	269,929	115,416	9,680,210	66,045	2,934,542	1,262,304	122,618	4,939,600	898,500

*Decrease in inventory and large death loss of sheep resulted in a deficit in number of pounds produced. †Catch in interior waters estimated. ‡Estimate.
Sources: U.S. Department of Agriculture, Statistical Reporting Service, Crop Reporting Board, *Chickens and Eggs, Meat Animals, Milk, Milk Production;* U.S. Department of Commerce, National Oceanic and Atmospheric Administration, National Marine Fisheries Service, *Fisheries of the United States.*

Value of construction contracts

in millions of dollars

State	1971	1972	1973			
			Total	Non-resi-dential	Resi-dential	Non-build-ing
Alabama	1,187	1,351	1,637	477	676	484
Alaska	259	373	421	176	94	151
Arizona	1,220	1,671	1,725	488	823	414
Arkansas	607	829	837	206	451	180
California	8,317	8,943	9,379	3,053	4,777	1,549
Colorado	1,151	1,708	1,991	575	867	549
Connecticut	969	1,217	1,020	376	478	166
Delaware	259	280	240	60	147	33
Dist. of Columbia	726	640	571	290	40	241
Florida	4,212	6,482	7,924	1,580	5,480	864
Georgia	2,124	2,533	2,708	941	1,390	377
Hawaii	502	655	796	192	440	164
Idaho	163	299	355	109	120	126
Illinois	3,956	4,772	5,065	1,620	2,191	1,254
Indiana	1,766	2,154	2,499	829	1,188	482
Iowa	752	829	1,100	386	414	300
Kansas	705	779	811	289	355	167
Kentucky	1,668	1,508	1,477	378	672	427
Louisiana	1,702	2,026	1,856	582	822	452
Maine	256	306	355	101	160	94
Maryland	1,655	1,752	2,096	661	1,014	421
Massachusetts	2,268	2,178	2,185	888	936	361
Michigan	3,034	3,388	4,362	1,207	1,856	1,299
Minnesota	1,332	1,339	1,791	642	787	362
Mississippi	929	885	1,005	220	444	341
Missouri	1,652	1,437	2,078	632	789	657
Montana	226	273	515	99	132	284
Nebraska	426	611	684	227	253	204
Nevada	432	627	613	151	348	114
New Hampshire	295	301	324	90	161	73
New Jersey	2,410	2,949	2,528	970	1,086	472
New Mexico	396	478	683	256	291	136
New York	5,786	6,016	5,814	2,024	2,276	1,514
North Carolina	2,041	2,646	2,465	678	1,425	362
North Dakota	189	331	298	96	128	74
Ohio	4,037	3,898	4,166	1,548	1,930	688
Oklahoma	941	1,328	1,391	438	589	364
Oregon	979	968	1,022	333	441	248
Pennsylvania	4,383	3,360	4,310	1,403	1,222	1,685
Rhode Island	231	207	257	98	107	52
South Carolina	989	1,307	1,788	386	814	588
South Dakota	255	210	249	70	103	76
Tennessee	1,528	1,843	2,252	727	1,177	348
Texas	4,969	5,819	6,247	2,495	2,734	1,018
Utah	417	509	596	218	280	98
Vermont	131	170	165	44	85	36
Virginia	2,547	2,735	3,087	923	1,599	565
Washington	1,155	1,557	1,653	542	630	481
West Virginia	609	586	605	202	125	278
Wisconsin	1,342	1,552	1,801	631	849	321
Wyoming	104	361	270	154	52	64
TOTAL U.S.	80,188	90,977	100,067	31,761	46,248	22,058

Source: U.S. Department of Commerce, Social and Economic Statistics Administration, Bureau of the Census, *Statistical Abstract of the United States 1974;* data compiled by F. W. Dodge Division, McGraw-Hill Information Systems Company.

Principal manufactures, 1973

monetary figures in millions of dollars

Industry	Employees (000)	Cost of labour*	Cost of materials	Value of shipments	Value added by manufacture
Food and kindred products	1,551	$13,670	$97,434	$135,583	$39,693
Meat products	301	2,595	32,391	37,942	6,341
Dairy products	186	1,665	13,675	18,016	4,414
Preserved fruits and vegetables	234	1,658	8,074	13,071	5,043
Grain mill products	110	1,102	12,050	16,096	4,175
Beverages	205	2,092	8,098	14,663	6,690
Tobacco manufactures	69	557	3,447	6,341	2,900
Textile mill products	980	6,605	18,011	31,073	13,017
Apparel and other textile products	1,400	7,707	15,722	30,084	14,648
Lumber and wood products	722	5,471	15,844	27,981	12,357
Furniture and fixtures	479	3,532	5,981	12,610	6,736
Paper and allied products	645	6,482	17,654	32,752	15,166
Printing and publishing	1,084	10,523	11,072	32,855	21,871
Chemicals and allied products	852	9,440	28,596	65,008	36,239
Industrial chemicals	237	2,896	9,546	20,221	10,634
Plastics materials and resins	164	1,769	5,311	11,720	6,068
Drugs	140	1,599	2,335	8,750	6,628
Soap, cleaners, and toilet goods	114	1,140	4,082	10,578	6,484
Paints, allied products	69	718	2,330	4,268	1,960
Agricultural chemicals	47	460	2,526	4,649	2,097
Petroleum and coal products	136	1,716	27,421	34,899	7,740
Leather and leather products	268	1,595	3,076	6,022	2,962
Stone, clay, and glass products	644	6,079	10,180	23,862	13,801
Primary metal industries	1,222	14,148	44,027	72,727	28,614
Blast furnace, basic steel products	392	7,467	21,060	36,240	14,935
Iron, steel foundries	236	2,551	2,784	6,858	4,066
Primary nonferrous metals	61	705	5,363	7,439	2,143
Nonferrous drawing and rolling	201	2,152	11,173	15,996	4,870
Nonferrous foundries	88	819	1,246	2,691	1,478
Fabricated metal products	1,567	15,374	28,521	58,556	30,573
Machinery, except electrical	1,994	21,598	35,566	78,093	44,559
Engines, turbines	124	1,512	3,169	6,312	3,267
Farm machinery	145	$1,486	$3,837	$6,868	$3,198
Construction and related mach.	302	3,369	6,473	13,144	6,997
Metalworking machinery	296	3,428	3,167	9,099	6,281
Special industry machinery	205	2,154	3,095	7,298	4,372
General industrial machinery	285	3,018	4,260	9,981	6,037
Service industry machines	213	2,098	5,145	9,818	4,846
Office, computing machines	223	2,573	4,700	10,320	5,959
Electrical equipment and supplies	1,797	17,151	27,166	60,865	34,984
Electric test, distributing equip.	125	1,170	1,799	4,125	2,404
Electrical industrial apparatus	210	1,964	2,859	6,554	3,797
Household appliances	174	1,546	3,974	7,749	3,886
Electric lighting, wiring equip.	186	1,567	2,800	6,315	3,600
Radio, TV receiving equipment	112	887	3,300	5,712	2,569
Communication equipment	464	5,246	5,787	14,751	9,363
Electronic components, access.	395	3,474	4,437	10,783	6,596
Transportation equipment	1,836	22,572	65,556	110,711	45,685
Motor vehicles and equipment	888	11,265	49,733	74,799	25,518
Aircraft, parts	459	5,785	7,914	18,532	10,659
Ship, boat building, repair	196	1,872	2,371	5,104	2,780
Railroad equipment	53	596	1,563	2,771	1,246
Travel trailers, trailer coaches	38	264	841	1,304	461
Instruments and related products	485	4,801	5,977	17,794	12,224
Mechanical measuring, control devices	168	1,631	1,561	4,678	3,246
Medical instruments and supplies	96	840	1,204	3,162	2,033
Photographic equipment and supplies	101	1,235	1,821	6,435	4,736
Miscellaneous manufacturing industries	447	3,351	5,969	13,046	7,166
Ordnance and accessories	112	1,081	1,433	3,093	1,716
Ammunition, except small arms†	56	523	932	1,666	778
All establishments, including administrative and auxiliary	19,898	193,325	478,277	875,244	404,376

*Payroll only. †Includes guided missiles. Source: U.S. Department of Commerce, *1973 Annual Survey of Manufactures.*

Manufacturing activity by sector, 1972

selected industrial groups, percent of total value added

State	Total value added by mfg. ($000,000)	Food	To-bac-co	Tex-tiles	Ap-parel	Lum-ber & wood	Fur-ni-ture	Paper prods.	Print-ing & publ.	Chem-icals	Petro-leum & coal	Rubber & plas-tics	Leather	Stone, clay, glass	Prim. metal ind.	Fabr. metal ind.	Machin-ery, except elec.	Elec-tric equip.	Trans-port equip.	In-stru-ments	Misc. mfg.
Ala.	5,065	7.3	—	9.0	7.3	6.8	1.5	9.3	2.5	7.7	—	7.3	0.2	3.1	15.9	6.7	2.7	4.9	5.3	0.5	0.9
Alaska	170	34.0	—	—	—	17.3	—	—	5.6	—	—	—	—	3.6	—	—	—	—	—	—	—
Ariz.	1,880	7.2	—	—	2.4	3.6	0.9	1.1	6.2	3.2	—	1.3	—	5.6	16.5	3.6	16.4	17.7	9.1	3.7	1.1
Ark.	2,800	13.1	—	2.3	4.6	9.7	4.7	8.7	4.2	4.7	1.2	4.4	2.9	3.0	4.0	6.2	4.8	12.3	3.3	—	—
Calif.	31,195	12.9	—	0.7	2.9	3.6	2.0	2.3	5.5	5.5	2.3	3.0	—	3.6	2.7	7.2	8.6	10.6	21.5	3.0	1.8
Colo.	2,504	20.4	—	—	1.1	2.2	1.1	1.2	7.3	3.4	1.0	5.8	—	5.6	5.2	8.2	12.1	3.4	10.3	7.9	1.6
Conn.	6,828	3.7	—	2.9	2.0	0.3	1.1	2.4	5.2	6.4	—	3.4	0.3	2.1	6.7	13.5	13.6	10.5	17.0	5.4	3.4
Del.	1,292	16.2	—	1.1	1.2	0.4	0.3	—	2.0	—	—	9.2	—	—	2.8	1.8	3.3	0.9	—	—	—
D.C.	376	12.9	—	—	0.5	—	—	—	74.5	—	—	—	—	—	—	2.1	0.8	2.4	—	—	0.9
Fla.	5,787	16.7	0.9	1.0	4.0	4.6	2.1	6.1	8.1	8.9	0.5	2.1	0.5	6.5	1.3	7.4	5.0	10.0	12.1	1.2	1.2
Ga.	7,386	11.3	—	21.2	8.7	5.0	1.7	8.1	3.4	7.0	0.6	2.8	0.5	4.1	1.8	4.0	2.9	3.1	12.2	—	1.4
Hawaii	410	50.1	—	—	7.2	3.2	1.9	—	11.3	—	—	—	—	7.7	—	—	1.2	—	0.7	—	1.7
Idaho	821	31.3	—	—	0.6	32.8	—	—	2.8	12.9	—	1.3	—	2.5	—	2.8	1.3	—	—	—	—
Ill.	25,849	12.1	—	0.3	1.3	0.7	1.4	2.8	8.6	8.1	1.6	2.6	—	3.0	7.4	11.0	16.3	12.0	4.8	3.3	2.1
Ind.	14,112	6.9	—	0.1	0.8	2.5	2.0	1.6	3.2	8.8	1.5	3.5	—	3.3	15.5	7.9	9.2	16.5	13.8	1.4	1.2
Iowa	4,758	23.4	—	0.1	0.7	1.5	1.4	1.9	4.8	8.2	0.2	5.3	0.2	2.8	2.9	6.3	25.3	8.5	3.3	1.0	2.3
Kan.	2,915	15.0	—	—	2.6	2.0	1.1	—	5.3	10.8	5.7	5.8	—	5.5	—	5.0	11.3	2.4	23.5	—	—
Ky.	5,682	12.4	—	1.8	3.9	2.0	1.0	2.1	3.1	8.6	—	2.4	1.0	3.3	7.1	5.3	12.1	14.5	7.3	1.4	1.2
La.	4,273	13.6	—	0.3	1.6	4.9	0.4	9.2	2.8	31.6	10.4	0.3	—	3.0	3.4	4.9	2.9	3.4	6.7	0.2	0.4
Maine	1,383	11.9	—	6.5	3.0	10.8	0.7	24.9	3.0	1.1	—	3.4	13.2	1.6	—	2.7	3.3	—	—	0.3	0.6
Md.	4,707	14.6	—	0.4	4.6	1.6	0.9	3.4	7.3	8.8	0.7	3.0	0.5	5.9	13.3	5.4	8.4	10.8	9.4	1.0	1.0
Mass.	10,678	6.0	—	3.9	4.6	0.8	1.1	4.6	7.0	5.6	—	5.2	2.8	2.4	2.2	7.9	16.2	12.5	4.5	8.2	4.2
Mich.	23,376	5.6	—	0.3	1.8	1.0	1.6	2.1	3.0	5.2	0.7	2.1	—	2.4	8.3	11.9	12.7	3.3	36.6	0.7	0.7
Minn.	5,524	16.7	—	0.6	1.2	2.6	1.0	9.3	7.3	4.8	1.3	2.3	—	2.4	2.3	10.5	20.6	6.4	4.0	4.1	—
Miss.	2,825	7.9	—	2.9	9.8	10.4	6.2	6.0	1.5	7.9	3.0	3.4	0.9	4.1	1.7	6.8	5.4	8.7	9.5	1.0	2.9
Mo.	8,169	12.4	—	—	3.5	1.4	1.4	2.4	7.9	8.9	—	1.9	—	3.3	4.2	7.4	6.9	7.0	24.7	—	1.2
Mont.	463	14.2	—	—	—	32.3	—	—	5.4	2.1	—	—	—	5.4	—	1.1	—	—	0.7	—	0.6
Neb.	1,733	33.5	—	0.2	1.0	1.8	1.8	1.0	5.4	5.3	0.4	3.8	—	3.1	5.1	6.6	11.1	9.9	4.0	4.8	1.1
Nev.	208	1.7	—	—	—	0.3	0.1	—	1.6	2.0	—	—	—	2.1	—	0.7	0.5	0.7	—	—	0.4
N.H.	1,279	6.7	—	7.3	1.4	3.9	1.9	9.3	5.4	1.0	—	6.2	9.6	3.2	3.2	3.8	13.8	13.2	2.0	6.5	1.5
N.J.	16,409	9.2	—	2.8	4.2	0.5	0.9	3.4	4.6	24.4	—	3.8	0.6	4.3	3.5	6.9	7.9	9.7	5.6	3.1	2.6
N.M.	358	19.1	—	—	4.5	8.8	—	—	8.8	3.0	3.0	0.9	—	8.9	—	3.0	8.0	—	5.3	2.0	2.8
N.Y.	30,404	7.7	—	2.6	10.4	0.8	1.3	2.8	13.9	6.6	—	1.9	1.2	2.4	3.4	5.3	9.8	9.6	4.5	11.6	3.9
N.C.	11,015	5.8	11.5	27.4	5.8	3.3	7.5	2.9	1.9	8.1	0.1	2.5	0.3	2.3	1.2	2.7	6.6	6.2	1.7	1.4	0.9
N.D.	201	33.3	—	—	—	2.6	—	—	10.0	—	—	—	—	10.2	—	3.1	19.7	—	—	—	1.4
Ohio	27,171	6.4	—	0.5	1.1	0.7	1.0	2.5	4.4	7.3	1.1	7.3	—	4.6	11.9	11.6	14.5	8.4	14.0	1.1	1.1
Okla.	2,270	10.6	—	1.0	3.4	3.1	1.0	2.0	5.8	1.9	4.7	6.1	—	7.9	3.5	9.9	21.0	8.9	6.6	—	—
Ore.	3,490	12.0	—	—	—	42.7	1.0	8.5	3.4	2.1	—	0.6	—	2.1	—	4.4	5.3	1.6	—	5.2	0.8
Pa.	23,519	8.8	0.5	3.0	5.5	1.4	1.3	3.3	5.0	7.6	1.5	2.8	1.0	4.7	15.7	7.8	10.1	9.4	5.8	2.6	2.3
R.I.	1,764	5.9	—	10.7	2.0	0.3	0.6	1.9	5.8	2.8	0.2	6.9	1.6	2.5	10.0	6.5	7.8	6.9	1.4	4.0	22.3
S.C.	4,966	3.5	0.1	34.7	8.0	3.4	1.1	5.9	1.6	16.4	—	—	—	3.6	1.2	2.3	8.2	3.7	0.9	1.6	1.6
S.D.	285	44.6	—	—	—	8.4	—	—	8.0	—	—	2.0	—	4.3	—	4.6	14.0	—	—	—	0.6
Tenn.	7,662	9.0	0.4	4.4	7.7	2.6	3.7	4.7	3.6	18.2	0.2	5.4	2.8	4.7	3.5	5.8	6.8	9.0	5.0	0.6	1.8
Texas	15,259	11.2	—	0.4	3.7	2.4	1.3	2.2	4.3	20.9	8.8	2.3	—	4.0	5.1	7.1	9.5	6.2	8.3	1.2	0.9
Utah	1,069	13.4	—	—	3.1	2.4	1.1	—	4.5	2.8	4.3	—	—	5.5	—	6.5	10.8	—	14.1	0.4	1.7
Vt.	576	7.0	—	1.0	1.4	5.0	4.4	9.7	10.1	1.2	—	3.8	0.6	6.5	—	7.4	16.4	—	—	3.3	1.9
Va.	6,178	9.9	9.4	8.5	4.5	4.5	5.5	4.9	3.7	13.7	—	4.1	0.5	3.1	2.2	3.8	3.1	9.0	8.0	—	0.6
Wash.	4,721	12.5	—	0.2	1.4	19.9	0.7	10.0	3.7	3.9	2.6	0.6	0.1	2.4	7.7	3.1	3.6	1.3	24.1	1.2	0.9
W.Va.	2,647	3.6	—	0.3	1.3	2.3	0.4	1.0	2.7	35.9	1.0	—	—	12.8	20.1	4.8	3.0	4.2	2.2	1.9	1.0
Wis.	9,443	14.0	—	1.1	0.8	2.6	1.3	8.9	4.5	3.9	0.1	2.4	—	1.8	4.4	10.4	21.1	8.8	8.3	1.3	2.2
Wyo.	144	13.5	—	—	—	10.1	—	—	7.5	—	36.8	—	—	15.1	—	—	—	—	—	—	—
Total U.S.	353,994	10.1	0.7	3.3	3.8	2.9	1.7	3.7	5.7	9.2	1.6	3.3	0.8	3.6	6.6	7.6	10.6	8.6	11.2	3.0	1.9

State and U.S. totals include all component industry groups, regardless of whether separate data are shown by state for industry groups.
— Figure not shown because (1) no industry in this category; (2) industry too small (based on number of employees); or (3) to avoid disclosure of data for individual companies.
Detail may not add to 100.0 because of omissions or rounding.
Source: U.S. Department of Commerce, Social and Economic Statistics Administration, Bureau of the Census, *1972 Census of Manufactures.*

Retail sales

in millions of dollars

Kind of business	1960	1965	1970	1974
Durable goods stores*	70,733	93,718	114,288	167,313
Automotive group	39,509	56,266	64,966	93,089
Passenger car, other automotive dealers	36,981	53,217	59,388	84,733
Tire, battery, accessory dealers	2,528	3,049	5,578	8,316
Furniture and appliance group	10,598	13,737	17,778	25,544
Furniture, home furnishings stores	6,770	8,538	10,483	15,364
Household appliance, TV, radio stores	3,828	4,223	6,073	8,006
Lumber, building, hardware, farm equipment group	14,819	16,274	20,494	32,547
Lumberyards, building materials dealers	8,618	9,302	11,995	18,328
Hardware stores	2,693	2,813	3,351	5,163
Nondurable goods stores*	148,796	190,232	261,239	370,469
Apparel group	13,708	15,752	19,810	24,864
Men's, boys' wear stores	2,619	3,258	4,630	5,668
Women's apparel, accessory stores	5,329	6,243	7,582	9,551
Family clothing stores	2,728	2,981	3,360	4,448
Shoe stores	2,450	2,571	3,501	3,979
Drug and proprietary stores	7,530	9,335	13,352	16,785
Eating and drinking places	16,096	21,423	29,689	41,840
Food group	53,837	66,920	86,114	119,763
Grocery stores	48,339	61,068	79,756	111,347
Meat and fish markets	1,560	1,552	2,244	2,948
Bakeries	1,034	1,142	1,303	1,445
Gasoline service stations	17,594	21,765	27,994	39,910
General merchandise group	24,007	35,840	61,320	89,286
Department stores and dry goods general merchandise stores	16,994	27,939	55,812	67,982
Variety stores	3,899	5,320	6,959	8,714
Mail-order houses (department store merchandise)	1,857	2,581	3,853	5,839
Liquor stores	4,880	6,305	7,980	10,285
TOTAL	219,529	283,950	375,527	537,782

*Includes some kinds of business not shown separately.
Source: U.S. Department of Commerce, Bureau of the Census, *Monthly Retail Trade*.

Services

Kind of service	NUMBER OF SERVICES 1972	NUMBER OF SERVICES 1973	NUMBER OF EMPLOYEES* 1972	NUMBER OF EMPLOYEES* 1973
Hotels and other lodging places	51,302	52,327	828,532	898,638
Hotels, tourist courts, and motels	34,156	34,225	675,358	732,591
Rooming and boarding houses	6,905	6,963	106,984	113,241
Personal services	166,095	163,479	917,065	909,415
Laundries and dry-cleaning plants	42,224	39,758	416,706	388,180
Photographic studios	6,608	6,598	36,626	39,136
Beauty shops	70,309	70,475	278,061	281,634
Barber shops	18,203	15,476	38,283	33,500
Funeral service and crematories	12,922	13,009	67,876	69,558
Miscellaneous business services	97,255	105,426	1,670,653	1,856,903
Advertising	8,120	8,308	107,083	109,958
Credit reporting and collection	5,509	5,375	66,338	66,094
Duplicating, mailing, stenographic	5,284	5,482	60,206	62,990
Building services	16,735	17,716	317,650	351,520
Private employment agencies	5,300	5,613	51,380	63,970
Research and development laboratories	1,966	1,982	74,133	77,650
Business consulting services	21,179	22,781	301,982	326,111
Detective and protective services	3,822	4,182	182,665	202,561
Equipment rental and leasing	7,801	8,140	73,452	81,281
Photofinishing laboratories	1,609	1,663	40,878	45,799
Temporary help supply services	2,149	2,304	167,455	203,706
Auto repair, services, and garages	73,275	76,841	405,871	435,549
Automobile rentals, without drivers	5,405	5,611	66,538	73,600
Automobile parking	3,428	3,293	37,136	35,976
Automobile repair shops	56,852	58,638	235,901	251,247
Automobile laundries	5,038	5,060	50,693	52,561
Miscellaneous repair services	38,586	40,798	212,509	222,642
Radio and television repair	8,281	8,315	38,248	38,361
Motion pictures	11,076	11,506	186,501	190,137
Motion picture filming and distribution	2,973	3,195	53,726	58,045
Motion picture theatres	7,627	7,495	120,658	118,948
Other amusement and recreation services	37,143	38,492	467,716	494,019
Producers, orchestras, entertainers	5,695	5,646	57,041	58,927
Bowling and billiard establishments	8,424	8,163	95,461	97,512
Golf clubs and country clubs	4,763	4,890	93,586	98,909
Race tracks and stables	1,420	1,489	37,018	40,338
Medical and other health services	223,732	231,495	3,240,295	3,425,013
Physicians' and surgeons' offices	108,484	110,872	438,478	470,349
Dentists' and dental surgeons' offices	66,406	67,973	190,945	208,818
Hospitals	5,135	5,098	1,868,469	1,922,794
Medical and dental laboratories	7,389	7,654	60,330	65,298
Sanatoria, convalescent and rest homes	11,097	11,081	517,271	563,645
Legal services	70,456	73,885	269,904	298,218
Educational services	37,074	39,577	959,860	1,012,312
Elementary and secondary schools	26,496	28,244	364,964	401,225
Colleges and universities	1,930	1,947	462,286	470,934
Correspondence and vocational schools	3,474	3,589	53,006	53,305
Museums, botanical, zoological gardens	869	912	20,447	21,266
Nonprofit membership organizations	128,515	132,719	1,248,140	1,312,704
Business associations	11,999	12,101	75,129	76,356
Labour organizations	20,829	20,690	147,234	148,679
Civic and social associations	28,872	29,230	260,255	267,806
Religious organizations	46,096	47,169	326,427	358,423
Charitable organizations	6,768	6,887	160,074	170,057
Miscellaneous services	63,066	68,918	620,896	698,946
Engineering and architectural services	23,343	25,019	268,478	303,647
Nonprofit research agencies	3,640	3,709	110,818	116,712
Accounting, auditing, bookkeeping	30,958	31,799	213,826	234,298
TOTAL†	1,000,729	1,038,505	11,102,077	11,830,536

*Mid-March pay period.
†Includes administrative and auxiliary businesses not shown separately.
Source: U.S. Department of Commerce, Bureau of the Census, *County Business Patterns 1972* and *1973*.

Sales of merchant wholesalers

in millions of dollars

Kind of business	1960	1965	1970	1974
Durable goods*	56,803	82,861	111,970	202,341
Motor vehicles, automotive equipment	7,883	12,140	19,482	32,928
Electrical goods	8,660	12,681	16,667	26,347
Furniture, home furnishings	2,910	3,777	5,199	7,012
Hardware, plumbing, heating equipment	6,422	8,364	10,598	17,997
Lumber, construction supplies	6,680	9,765	10,863	17,821
Machinery, equipment, supplies	14,287	20,561	27,638	50,666
Metals, metalwork (except scrap)	5,708	9,162	13,647	32,027
Scrap, waste materials	3,296	4,789	6,040	14,421
Nondurable goods*	80,477	104,470	135,029	245,786
Groceries and related products	27,661	37,730	51,492	80,513
Beer, wine, distilled alcoholic beverages	7,424	9,464	13,332	18,296
Drugs, chemicals, allied products	5,370	7,223	9,375	15,343
Tobacco, tobacco products	4,164	4,960	5,955	7,882
Dry goods, apparel	6,675	8,804	10,577	15,107
Paper, paper products	4,153	5,612	7,679	12,622
Farm products	11,683	13,711	13,987	46,015
Other nondurable goods	13,346	16,966	22,632	50,007
TOTAL	137,281	187,331	246,999	448,127

*Includes some kinds of business not shown separately.
Source: U.S. Department of Commerce, Bureau of the Census, *Monthly Wholesale Trade*.

Business activity

Category of activity	WHOLESALING 1960	WHOLESALING 1965	WHOLESALING 1970	WHOLESALING 1971	RETAILING 1960	RETAILING 1965	RETAILING 1970	RETAILING 1971	SERVICES 1960	SERVICES 1965	SERVICES 1970	SERVICES 1971
Number of businesses (in 000)												
Sole proprietorships	306	265	274	319	1,548	1,554	1,689	1,765	1,966	2,208	2,507	2,593
Active partnerships	41	32	30	28	238	202	170	166	159	169	176	172
Active corporations	117	147	166	168	217	288	351	367	121	188	281	288
Business receipts (in $000,000)												
Sole proprietorships	17,061	17,934	21,556	23,880	65,439	77,760	89,315	94,286	23,256	29,789	40,869	42,423
Active partnerships	12,712	10,879	11,325	11,028	24,787	23,244	23,546	24,270	9,281	12,442	18,791	19,571
Active corporations	130,637	171,414	234,885	254,599	125,787	183,925	274,808	306,048	22,106	36,547	66,460	70,266
Net profit (less loss; in $000,000)												
Sole proprietorships	1,305	1,483	1,806	1,957	3,869	5,019	5,767	5,923	8,060	11,008	15,063	15,244
Active partnerships	587	548	557	536	1,612	1,654	1,603	1,648	3,056	4,402	6,189	6,404
Active corporations	2,130	3,288	4,441	4,816	2,225	4,052	5,217	6,487	849	1,505	1,199	1,471

Data refer to accounting periods ending between July 1 of year shown and June 30 of following year.
Source: U.S. Department of the Treasury, Internal Revenue Service, *Statistics of Income, U.S. Business Tax Returns*, and *Corporation Tax Returns*.

Commercial banks*

December 31, 1974

State	Number of banks	Total assets or liabilities $000,000	SELECTED ASSETS ($000,000) Loans†	Investments	Reserves, cash, and bank balances	SELECTED LIABILITIES ($000,000) Deposits Total	Demand	Time	Capital account
Ala.	293	9,850	8,290	2,522	1,207	8,367	3,669	4,698	761
Alaska	10	1,173	909	288	211	1,004	494	510	75
Ariz.	17	7,084	5,957	1,319	785	5,710	2,147	3,563	421
Ark.	258	6,287	5,169	1,673	935	5,428	2,477	2,951	470
Calif.	186	96,897	77,011	15,599	12,956	79,184	27,916	51,268	5,244
Colo.	263	8,336	6,618	1,677	1,380	6,988	3,360	3,629	603
Conn.	70	8,257	6,591	1,488	1,321	6,983	3,584	3,399	609
Del.	17	2,352	2,021	716	231	1,840	816	1,025	175
D.C.	16	4,304	3,506	858	664	3,586	2,069	1,517	349
Fla.	712	28,138	23,175	7,825	3,953	24,094	10,694	13,400	2,192
Ga.	443	15,409	12,464	2,436	2,012	12,157	5,905	6,251	1,193
Hawaii	8	2,840	2,386	641	297	2,444	964	1,480	196
Idaho	24	2,769	2,318	583	361	2,433	999	1,434	171
Ill.	1,183	71,631	60,419	16,287	8,295	58,610	21,729	36,881	4,606
Ind.	408	19,909	16,778	5,291	2,336	16,513	6,271	10,242	1,338
Iowa	657	12,110	10,335	3,511	1,505	10,589	4,127	6,462	885
Kan.	612	9,284	7,834	2,680	1,172	7,964	3,662	4,302	763
Ky.	341	10,792	9,009	2,675	1,435	9,090	4,412	4,678	748
La.	249	13,353	11,066	3,339	1,835	11,017	4,898	6,120	916
Maine	45	2,136	1,847	472	213	1,825	730	1,095	162
Md.	114	9,578	8,124	2,039	1,077	8,012	3,557	4,455	720
Mass.	147	18,451	14,964	3,605	2,450	14,788	7,407	7,381	1,354
Mich.	346	33,147	27,862	7,549	4,080	28,102	9,263	18,838	2,365
Minn.	742	16,994	14,411	4,013	2,061	13,887	5,263	8,624	1,157
Miss.	181	5,902	4,901	1,527	805	5,144	2,336	2,809	453
Mo.	694	20,056	16,553	5,164	2,921	16,159	7,781	8,378	1,499
Mont.	152	2,994	2,573	782	337	2,617	977	1,640	205
Neb.	448	6,791	5,671	1,625	935	5,767	2,681	3,086	500
Nev.	8	1,997	1,649	482	258	1,752	710	1,042	145
N.H.	80	1,724	1,470	302	201	1,485	546	939	150
N.J.	218	24,235	20,543	6,467	2,720	20,882	8,252	12,631	1,827
N.M.	76	3,058	2,514	694	433	2,651	1,115	1,536	223
N.Y.	271	171,241	125,922	21,007	31,405	132,714	65,941	66,773	11,731
N.C.	91	14,351	11,674	3,278	1,919	11,895	5,177	6,717	1,084
N.D.	168	2,550	2,260	854	236	2,235	907	1,327	187
Ohio	496	36,531	30,956	9,182	4,094	29,636	11,194	18,442	2,878
Okla.	455	10,804	8,783	2,891	1,660	9,210	4,111	5,098	823
Ore.	47	6,949	5,501	1,464	996	5,577	2,281	3,296	501
Pa.	399	54,029	46,113	11,053	5,369	42,661	15,480	27,180	4,012
R.I.	14	3,688	3,202	540	313	3,099	905	2,194	248
S.C.	89	4,624	3,836	1,050	618	3,867	2,194	1,674	369
S.D.	158	2,921	2,534	844	318	2,614	911	1,703	206
Tenn.	334	14,666	12,032	3,244	2,000	12,287	4,849	7,438	1,060
Texas	1,306	50,715	40,244	11,931	8,504	42,516	20,692	21,824	3,661
Utah	54	3,410	2,760	660	525	2,959	1,269	1,689	236
Vt.	33	1,388	1,227	252	125	1,237	349	889	103
Va.	288	15,544	13,095	3,165	1,785	13,084	4,914	8,170	1,116
Wash.	87	11,051	8,887	1,766	1,513	8,699	3,549	5,150	613
W.Va.	214	6,064	5,309	1,851	574	4,980	1,855	3,124	473
Wis.	620	16,390	13,917	3,825	1,840	13,951	4,898	9,052	1,146
Wyo.	74	1,632	1,373	462	209	1,422	572	849	122
TOTAL	14,216	906,385	734,561	185,446	125,388	741,713	312,858	428,855	63,043

*Detail may not add to total given due to rounding; excludes noninsured banks. †Includes investment securities, federal funds sold, and securities purchased under agreements to resell.
Source: Federal Deposit Insurance Corporation, *Assets and Liabilities—Commercial and Mutual Savings Banks—December 31, 1974, 1974 Report of Income.*

Life insurance, 1974

Number of policies in 000s; value in $000,000

State	Total: Number of policies	Total: Value	Ordinary: Number of policies	Ordinary: Value	Group: Number of certificates	Group: Value	Industrial: Number of policies	Industrial: Value	Credit*: Number of policies	Credit*: Value
Ala.	11,538	$31,596	1,597	$14,788	1,470	$12,024	6,608	$2,362	1,863	$2,422
Alaska	445	3,868	97	1,326	235	2,391	12	3	101	148
Ariz.	3,875	20,925	1,340	12,056	982	6,908	190	106	1,363	1,855
Ark.	2,565	12,158	774	6,585	531	4,184	543	276	717	1,113
Calif.	29,476	194,708	9,859	96,111	10,492	88,689	2,349	1,479	6,776	8,429
Colo.	4,096	26,228	1,558	14,070	1,232	10,540	258	142	1,048	1,476
Conn.	5,590	35,288	2,344	17,915	1,667	15,742	382	250	1,197	1,381
Del.	1,384	8,148	433	3,214	360	4,314	251	154	340	466
D.C.	3,800	15,730	427	3,298	1,228	11,054	610	325	1,535	1,053
Fla.	15,270	67,934	4,482	38,406	2,889	22,187	4,132	2,560	3,767	4,781
Ga.	12,171	47,789	2,697	23,740	1,965	17,841	4,714	2,811	2,795	3,397
Hawaii	1,498	12,526	514	5,998	634	6,008	7	3	343	517
Idaho	1,110	5,931	463	3,400	342	2,092	30	14	275	425
Ill.	22,096	120,758	8,784	62,565	5,824	51,018	3,500	2,026	3,988	5,149
Ind.	10,192	48,984	3,778	25,881	2,202	18,923	1,942	1,118	2,270	3,062
Iowa	4,489	24,608	2,361	15,688	977	7,287	285	139	866	1,494
Kan.	3,955	21,466	1,745	12,867	1,000	7,108	390	202	820	1,289
Ky.	5,994	24,963	1,813	12,266	1,081	10,062	1,747	890	1,353	1,745
La.	8,806	31,085	1,611	15,315	1,394	11,416	4,050	2,136	1,751	2,218
Maine	1,595	7,846	662	4,328	398	2,921	106	61	429	536
Md.	7,842	39,761	2,565	20,084	1,625	16,657	1,980	1,056	1,672	1,964
Mass.	9,392	53,166	3,959	27,672	2,378	22,786	1,040	600	2,015	2,108
Mich.	16,360	94,090	5,355	38,188	5,214	49,309	2,221	1,287	3,570	5,306
Minn.	5,759	34,699	2,304	18,215	1,952	14,535	300	152	1,203	1,797
Miss.	3,374	14,468	766	7,321	721	5,340	832	459	1,055	1,348
Mo.	8,584	44,669	3,391	22,798	2,103	18,801	1,464	804	1,626	2,266
Mont.	960	5,510	391	3,264	289	1,787	28	11	252	448
Neb.	2,550	15,273	1,299	9,432	598	4,939	147	75	506	827
Nev.	1,118	6,025	217	2,325	340	2,903	17	8	544	789
N.H.	1,296	6,792	597	4,165	269	2,186	108	63	322	378
N.J.	11,908	81,295	5,401	42,029	2,919	35,623	1,548	1,086	2,040	2,557
N.M.	1,589	8,717	494	4,194	466	3,776	121	72	508	675
N.Y.	27,898	182,448	11,605	88,302	7,384	84,199	2,450	1,511	6,459	8,436
N.C.	11,750	46,815	3,134	22,413	2,295	19,177	3,788	2,069	2,533	3,156
N.D.	908	5,304	398	3,016	256	1,820	5	3	249	465
Ohio	20,021	104,512	7,692	55,612	4,579	40,731	3,752	2,252	3,998	5,917
Okla.	3,974	22,570	1,485	12,039	935	8,692	470	270	1,084	1,569
Ore.	2,869	17,438	1,100	9,338	1,007	7,109	106	49	656	942
Pa.	24,417	110,538	9,584	58,989	4,869	42,343	5,333	2,915	4,631	6,291
R.I.	1,872	9,000	765	4,936	532	3,491	218	123	357	450
S.C.	7,043	23,574	1,987	11,324	1,161	9,296	2,578	1,447	1,317	1,507
S.D.	868	5,185	476	3,380	193	1,444	6	3	193	358
Tenn.	9,086	35,128	2,104	16,936	1,945	13,808	2,873	1,626	2,164	2,758
Texas	20,919	111,534	6,845	58,297	5,259	44,488	3,493	2,048	5,322	6,701
Utah	1,833	9,556	647	5,107	670	3,691	111	47	455	711
Vt.	800	3,655	319	2,244	163	1,101	45	27	273	283
Va.	10,165	49,521	2,925	22,845	2,107	22,493	2,850	1,565	2,283	2,618
Wash.	4,423	27,769	1,738	15,118	1,562	11,428	206	92	917	1,131
W.Va.	2,980	11,999	890	5,631	629	4,956	628	368	833	1,044
Wis.	6,959	38,881	3,214	22,361	2,126	14,553	531	290	1,088	1,677
Wyo.	502	3,221	209	1,646	145	1,379	10	6	138	190
TOTAL U.S.	380,014	$1,985,652	131,195	$1,009,038	93,594	$827,550	71,365	$39,441	83,860	$109,623

*Life insurance on loans of ten years' or less duration.
Source: Institute of Life Insurance, *Life Insurance Fact Book 1975.*

Savings and loan associations

Dec. 31, 1974*

State	Number of assns.	Total assets ($000,000)	Per capita assets
Alabama	62	$2,333	$652
Alaska	4	164	487
Arizona	15	3,102	1,441
Arkansas	68	1,970	955
California	175	50,785	2,429
Colorado	47	4,228	1,694
Connecticut	36	2,637	854
Delaware	15	173	302
District of Columbia	16	3,343	4,623
Florida	133	21,263	2,628
Georgia	100	5,730	1,174
Guam	2	15	148
Hawaii	11	1,493	1,763
Idaho	11	502	628
Illinois	469	22,263	2,000
Indiana	178	5,724	1,074
Iowa	83	3,503	1,227
Kansas	88	3,720	1,639
Kentucky	115	2,954	880
Louisiana	107	3,802	1,010
Maine	24	369	353
Maryland	239	5,280	1,290
Massachusetts	176	5,636	972
Michigan	66	8,479	932
Minnesota	68	5,589	1,427
Mississippi	84	1,593	686
Missouri	116	7,943	1,663
Montana	16	487	662
Nebraska	45	2,519	1,632
Nevada	7	810	1,414
New Hampshire	18	581	719
New Jersey	262	11,778	1,607
New Mexico	37	973	867
New York	158	17,106	944
North Carolina	179	5,847	1,090
North Dakota	11	1,011	1,588
Ohio	437	21,098	1,965
Oklahoma	55	2,693	994
Oregon	28	3,119	1,376
Pennsylvania	479	13,129	1,109
Puerto Rico	11	872	291
Rhode Island	6	554	591
South Carolina	74	3,061	1,099
South Dakota	19	475	696
Tennessee	90	3,481	843
Texas	298	14,041	1,165
Utah	12	1,559	1,329
Vermont	7	142	303
Virginia	76	3,871	789
Washington	50	4,388	1,262
West Virginia	36	713	398
Wisconsin	123	6,422	1,407
Wyoming	13	336	937
TOTAL U.S.	5,102	$295,616	$1,378

*Preliminary. Components do not add to totals because of differences in reporting dates and accounting systems.
Source: U.S. League of Savings Associations, *1975 Savings and Loan Fact Book.*

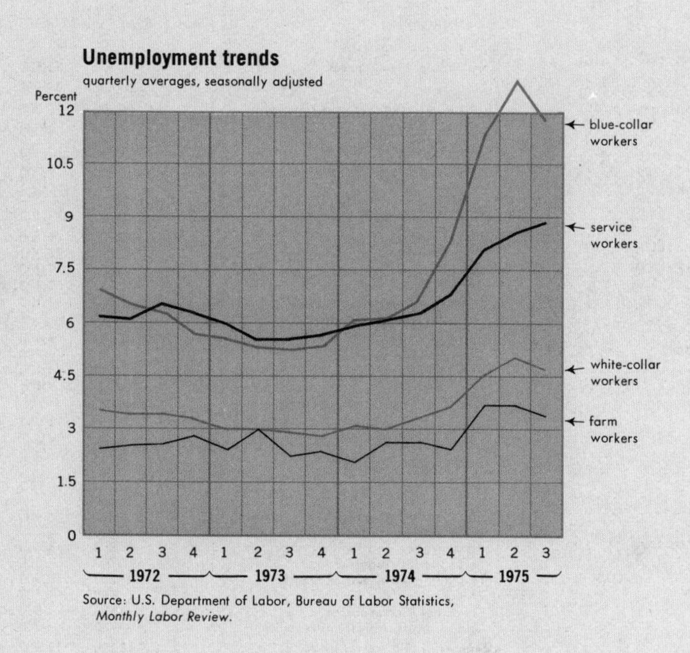

Source: U.S. Department of Labor, Bureau of Labor Statistics, *Monthly Labor Review.*

Average employee earnings

September figures

Industry	AVERAGE HOURLY EARNINGS 1974	1975*	AVERAGE WEEKLY EARNINGS 1974	1975*
MANUFACTURING				
Durable goods	$4.83	$5.24	$198.03	$212.22
Ordnance and accessories	4.82	5.43	200.03	227.52
Lumber and wood products	4.05	4.41	159.98	175.96
Furniture and fixtures	3.59	3.80	140.73	149.34
Stone, clay, and glass products	4.65	5.00	193.91	206.50
Primary metal industries	5.81	6.39	246.34	258.16
Fabricated metal products	4.74	5.16	196.24	209.50
Nonelectrical machinery	5.05	5.46	215.64	223.31
Electrical equipment and supplies	4.27	4.67	171.23	186.33
Transportation equipment	5.64	6.15	228.42	252.77
Instruments and related products	4.29	4.61	173.32	184.86
Nondurable goods	4.09	4.41	160.74	175.52
Food and kindred products	4.22	4.61	173.02	191.32
Tobacco manufactures	4.05	4.27	157.95	166.10
Textile mill products	3.28	3.48	128.90	143.03
Apparel and related products	3.09	3.22	109.08	116.24
Paper and allied products	4.64	5.10	195.81	216.75
Printing and publishing	5.08	5.49	192.53	205.33
Chemicals and allied products	4.98	5.48	206.67	226.32
Petroleum and coal products	5.78	6.59	247.96	277.44
Rubber and plastics products	4.12	4.42	168.10	179.89
Leather and leather products	3.07	3.26	111.75	124.53
NONMANUFACTURING				
Metal mining	5.66	6.33	239.98	260.16
Coal mining	6.26	7.30	256.03	289.81
Oil and gas extraction	5.03	5.46	223.84	241.33
Contract construction	7.01	7.39	263.58	277.13
Local and suburban transportation	4.49	5.00	180.05	199.00
Electric, gas, and sanitary services	5.61	6.12	230.57	251.53
Wholesale trade	4.63	4.95	180.11	191.07
Retail trade	3.16	3.39	103.02	109.16
Hotels, tourist courts, and motels†	2.67	2.83	86.51	88.58

*Preliminary. †Excludes tips. Source: U.S. Dept. of Labor, Bureau of Labor Statistics, *Employment and Earnings.*

Government and Politics

The national executive

December 1, 1975

Department, bureau, or office	Executive official and official title
PRESIDENT OF THE UNITED STATES	Gerald R. Ford
Vice President	Nelson A. Rockefeller
EXECUTIVE OFFICE OF THE PRESIDENT	
Assistant to the President	Brent Scowcroft
	Richard B. Cheney
Press Secretary to the President	Ronald H. Nessen
Counsel to the President	Philip W. Buchen
Special Assistant to the President for Labor-Management Negotiations	W. J. Usery, Jr.
Special Consultant to the President	Robert A. Goldwin
Office of Management and Budget	James T. Lynn, director
Council of Economic Advisers	Alan Greenspan, chairman
National Security Council	*
Central Intelligence Agency	William E. Colby, director (George Bush, nominated)
Domestic Council	James M. Cannon, director
Office of the Special Representative for Trade Negotiations	Frederick B. Dent, special representative
Council on Environmental Quality	Russell W. Peterson, chairman
Office of Telecommunications Policy	John M. Eger, (acting) director
Council on International Economic Policy	J. M. Dunn, (acting) executive director
Federal Property Council	vacancy (chairman)
Council on Wage and Price Stability	Michael H. Moskow, director
Energy Resources Council	Frank G. Zarb, executive director
DEPARTMENT OF STATE	Henry A. Kissinger, secretary
	Robert S. Ingersoll, deputy secretary
Political Affairs	Joseph J. Sisco, undersecretary
Economic Affairs	Charles W. Robinson, undersecretary
Security Assistance	Carlyle E. Maw, undersecretary
Management	Lawrence S. Eagleburger, deputy undersecretary
Ambassador at Large	U. Alexis Johnson
Counselor of the Department	Helmut Sonnenfeldt
Agency for International Development	Daniel Parker, administrator
Permanent Mission to the Organization of American States	William S. Mailliard, permanent representative
Mission to the United Nations	Daniel P. Moynihan, permanent representative
African Affairs	William E. Schaufele, Jr., asst. secretary
European Affairs	Arthur A. Hartman, asst. secretary
DEPARTMENT OF STATE (continued)	
East Asian and Pacific Affairs	Philip C. Habib, asst. secretary
Inter-American Affairs	William D. Rogers, asst. secretary
Near Eastern and South Asian Affairs	Alfred L. Atherton, Jr., asst. secretary
DEPARTMENT OF THE TREASURY	William E. Simon, secretary
	Stephen S. Gardner, deputy secretary
Monetary Affairs	Edwin H. Yeo III, undersecretary
Comptroller of the Currency	James E. Smith, comptroller
Bur. of Government Financial Operations	Dario A. Pagliai, commissioner
U.S. Customs Service	Vernon D. Acree, commissioner
Bureau of Engraving and Printing	James A. Conlon, director
Bureau of the Mint	Mary T. Brooks, director
Bureau of the Public Debt	H. J. Hintgen, commissioner
Internal Revenue Service	Donald C. Alexander, commissioner
Office of the Treasurer	Francine I. Neff, treasurer
Savings Bond Division	Francine I. Neff, national director
U.S. Secret Service	H. Stuart Knight, director
Bureau of Alcohol, Tobacco, and Firearms	Rex. D. Davis, director
Consolidated Federal Law Enforcement Training Center	William B. Butler, director
DEPARTMENT OF DEFENSE	Donald H. Rumsfeld, secretary
	William P. Clements, Jr., deputy secretary
Joint Chiefs of Staff	Gen. George S. Brown, USAF, chairman
Chief of Staff, Army	Gen. Frederick C. Weyand, USA
Chief of Naval Operations	Adm. James L. Holloway III, USN
Chief of Staff, Air Force	Gen. David C. Jones, USAF
Commandant of the Marine Corps	Gen. Robert E. Cushman, Jr., USMC
Department of the Army	Martin R. Hoffmann, secretary
Department of the Navy	J. Wm. Middendorf II, secretary
Department of the Air Force	John L. McLucas, secretary
DEPARTMENT OF JUSTICE	
Attorney General	Edward H. Levi
Solicitor General	Robert H. Bork
Community Relations Service	Benjamin F. Holman, director
Law Enforcement Assistance Administration	Donald Santarelli, director
Antitrust Division	Thomas E. Kauper, asst. attorney general
Civil Division	Rex E. Lee, asst. attorney general
Civil Rights Division	J. Stanley Pottinger, asst. attorney general

(continued on page 712)

The national executive (continued)

Department, bureau, or office	Executive official and official title
DEPARTMENT OF JUSTICE (continued)	
Criminal Division	Richard L. Thornburgh, asst. attorney general
Land and Natural Resources Division	Wallace H. Johnson, Jr., asst. attorney general
Tax Division	Scott P. Crampton, asst. attorney general
Administrative Division	Glen E. Pommerening, asst. attorney general
Federal Bureau of Investigation	Clarence M. Kelley, director
Bureau of Prisons	Norman A. Carlson, director
Immigration and Naturalization Service	Leonard F. Chapman, Jr., commissioner
Drug Enforcement Administration	Henry F. Dogin, (acting) administrator
U.S. Marshals Service	Wayne B. Colburn, director
DEPARTMENT OF THE INTERIOR	Thomas S. Kleppe, secretary
	Dale K. Frizzell, undersecretary
Fish and Wildlife and Parks	Nathaniel P. Reed, asst. secretary
National Park Service	Ronald H. Walker, director
Fish and Wildlife Service	Lynn A. Greenwalt, director
Bureau of Outdoor Recreation	James G. Watt, director
Energy and Minerals	Jack W. Carlson, asst. secretary
Office of Research and Development	Harry R. Johnson, (acting) director
Office of Minerals Policy Development	vacancy
Geological Survey	Vincent E. McKelvey, director
Bureau of Mines	Thomas V. Falkie, director
Land and Water Resources	Jack O. Horton, asst. secretary
Bureau of Land Management	Curtis J. Berklund, director
Bureau of Reclamation	Gilbert G. Stamm, commissioner
Commissioner of Indian Affairs	Morris Thompson, commissioner
DEPARTMENT OF AGRICULTURE	Earl L. Butz, secretary
	J. Phil Campbell, undersecretary
Rural Development	William H. Walker III, asst. secretary
Rural Electrification Administration	David A. Hamil, administrator
Farmers Home Administration	Frank B. Elliott, administrator
Marketing and Consumer Services	Richard L. Feltner, asst. secretary
Agricultural Marketing Service	Erwin L. Peterson, administrator
Commodity Exchange Authority	Alex C. Caldwell, administrator
International Affairs and Commodity Programs	Clayton K. Yeutter, asst. secretary
Commodity Credit Corporation	Clayton K. Yeutter, president
Conservation, Research, and Education	Robert W. Long, asst. secretary
Forest Service	John R. McGuire, chief
Soil Conservation Service	Kenneth E. Grant, administrator
Agricultural Economics	Don A. Paarlberg, director
Statistical Reporting Service	Harry C. Trelogan, administrator
DEPARTMENT OF COMMERCE	Rogers C. B. Morton, secretary (Elliot L. Richardson, nominated)
	James A. Baker III, undersecretary
Domestic and International Business	Travis E. Reed, asst. secretary
Economic Affairs	James L. Pate, asst. secretary
Social and Economic Statistics Admin.	Edward D. Failor, administrator
Bureau of the Census	Vincent P. Barabba, director
Bureau of Economic Analysis	George Jaszi, director
Science and Technology	Betsy Ancker-Johnson, asst. secretary
Office of Environmental Quality	Sidney R. Galler, director
National Bureau of Standards	Richard W. Roberts, director
Patent and Trademark Office	C. Marshall Dann, commissioner
Maritime Affairs	Robert J. Blackwell, asst. secretary
Tourism	Creighton Holden, asst. secretary
National Oceanic and Atmospheric Administration	Robert M. White, administrator
DEPARTMENT OF LABOR	John T. Dunlop, secretary
	Robert O. Aders, undersecretary
Administration and Management	Fred G. Clark, asst. secretary
Manpower	William H. Kolberg, asst. secretary
Labor-Management Relations	Paul J. Fasser, Jr., asst. secretary
Employment Standards	Bernard E. DeLury, asst. secretary
Occupational Safety and Health	Morton Corn, asst. secretary
Labor Statistics	Julius Shiskin, commissioner
DEPARTMENT OF HEALTH, EDUCATION, AND WELFARE	F. David Mathews, secretary
	Marjorie Ward Lynch, undersecretary
Education Division	Virginia Y. Trotter, asst. secretary
Office of Education	Terrel H. Bell, commissioner
National Institute of Education	Harold L. Hodgkinson, director
Public Health Service	Theodore Cooper, M.D., asst. secretary
Food and Drug Administration	Alexander M. Schmidt, M.D., commissioner
National Institutes of Health	Robert S. Stone, director
Health Resources Administration	Kenneth M. Endicott, administrator
Health Services Administration	Harold O. Buzzell, administrator
Center for Disease Control	David J. Sencer, M.D., director
Social and Rehabilitation Service	James S. Dwight, Jr., administrator
Social Security Administration	James B. Cardwell, commissioner
DEPARTMENT OF HOUSING AND URBAN DEVELOPMENT	Carla A. Hills, secretary
	John B. Rhinelander, undersecretary
Community Planning and Development	David O. Meeker, Jr., asst. secretary
Housing Production and Mortgage Credit	David S. Cook, asst. secretary
Housing Management	H. R. Crawford, asst. secretary
Equal Opportunity	James H. Blair, asst. secretary
Policy Development and Research	Charles J. Orlebeke, asst. secretary
DEPARTMENT OF TRANSPORTATION	William T. Coleman, Jr., secretary
	John W. Barnum, deputy secretary
United States Coast Guard	Adm. Owen W. Siler, USCG, commandant
Federal Aviation Administration	John L. McLucas, administrator
Federal Highway Administration	Norbert T. Tiemann, administrator
National Highway Traffic Safety Administration	James B. Gregory, administrator
Federal Railroad Administration	Asaph H. Hall, administrator
Urban Mass Transportation	Robert E. Patricelli, administrator
St. Lawrence Seaway Development Corp.	David W. Oberlin, administrator

*Council comprised of the President of the United States and certain other members.

The federal administrative budget

in millions of dollars; fiscal year ending June 30

Source and function	1974	1975 estimate	1976 estimate
BUDGET RECEIPTS	$264,900	$278,800	$297,500
Individual income taxes	119,000	117,700	106,300
Corporation income taxes	38,600	38,500	47,700
Excise taxes	16,800	19,900	32,100
Social insurance taxes and contributions	76,800	86,200	91,600
Estate and gift taxes	5,000	4,800	4,600
Customs duties	3,300	3,900	4,300
Miscellaneous receipts	5,400	7,700	10,900
BUDGET EXPENDITURES	268,400	313,400	349,400
National defense	78,600	85,300	94,000
Department of Defense military functions	77,600	83,000	89,800
Military assistance	800	1,800	3,000
Atomic energy defense activities	1,500	1,600	1,800
Defense-related activities	−1,300	−1,100	−500
Deductions for offsetting receipts	—*	—*	—*
International affairs	3,600	4,900	6,300
Conduct of foreign affairs	600	700	800
Foreign economic and financial assistance	2,800	4,100	5,500
Foreign information and exchange activities	300	400	400
Deductions for offsetting receipts	−200	−200	−400
General science, space, and technology	4,200	4,200	4,600
Agriculture	2,200	1,800	1,800
Farm income stabilization	1,500	900	900
Agricultural research and services	800	900	900
Deductions for offsetting receipts	—*	—*	—*
Natural resources, environment, and energy	6,400	9,400	10,000
Water resources and power	2,500	3,300	3,300
Conservation and land management	800	1,300	900
Recreational resources	700	800	900
Pollution control and abatement	2,000	2,900	3,000
Energy	600	1,500	2,200
Other natural resources	500	500	600
Deductions for offsetting receipts	−700	−900	−900
Commerce and transportation	13,100	11,800	13,700
Mortgage credit and thrift insurance	1,500	−1,000	200
Payment to the Postal Service	1,700	1,800	1,500
Other advancement and regulation	700	700	700
Air transportation	2,200	2,500	2,700
Water transportation	1,400	1,500	1,700
Ground transportation	5,600	6,400	6,900
Other transportation	100	100	100
Deductions for offsetting receipts	−100	−100	−100
Community and regional development	4,900	4,900	5,900
Community development	3,000	3,300	4,100
Area and regional development	1,100	1,100	1,400
Disaster relief and insurance	800	500	500
Deductions for offsetting receipts	—*	—*	—*
Education, manpower, and social services	11,600	14,700	14,600
Elementary, secondary, and vocational education	3,800	4,200	4,200
Higher education	1,300	2,100	2,300
Research and general education aids	900	900	800
Manpower training	2,900	4,100	4,200
Other manpower services	200	300	300
Social services	2,500	3,100	2,700
Deductions for offsetting receipts	—*	—*	—*
Health	22,100	26,500	28,000
Health care services	18,500	22,300	24,100
Health research and education	2,300	2,700	2,500
Prevention and control of health problems	800	900	900
Health planning and construction	500	600	600
Deductions for offsetting receipts	—*	—*	—*
Income security	84,400	106,700	118,700
General retirement and disability insurance	58,600	67,500	74,400
Federal employee retirement and disability	5,600	7,100	7,900
Unemployment insurance	6,100	14,700	18,200
Public assistance and other income supplements	14,100	17,400	18,400
Deductions for offsetting receipts	—*	—*	—*
Veterans benefits and services	13,400	15,500	15,600
Income security for veterans	6,800	7,700	7,700
Veterans education, training, and rehabilitation	3,200	4,000	3,600
Hospital and medical care for veterans	3,000	3,600	3,900
Veterans housing	—*	−300	−100
Other veterans benefits and services	400	500	500
Deductions for offsetting receipts	—*	—*	—*
Law enforcement and justice	2,500	3,000	3,300
Federal law enforcement and prosecution	1,300	1,600	1,700
Federal judicial activities	200	300	400
Federal correctional and rehabilitative activities	200	200	300
Law enforcement assistance	800	900	1,000
Deductions for offsetting receipts	—*	—*	—*
General government	3,300	2,600	3,200
Legislative functions	500	600	700
Executive direction and management	100	100	100
Central fiscal operations	1,300	1,700	1,800
Central property and records management	1,000	200	200
Central personnel management	100	100	100
Other general government	400	500	500
Deductions for offsetting receipts	−200	−500	−200
Revenue sharing and general purpose fiscal assistance	6,700	7,000	7,200
Interest	28,100	31,300	34,400
Allowances for contingencies, civilian agency pay raises	—	700	8,000
Undistributed offsetting receipts	−16,700	−16,800	−20,200
Employer share, employee retirement	−3,300	−4,100	−3,900
Interest received by trust funds	−6,600	−7,800	−8,300
Rents and royalties on the Outer Continental Shelf	−6,700	−5,000	−8,000

*Less than $500,000. Source: Executive Office of the President, Office of Management and Budget, *The United States Budget in Brief: Fiscal Year 1976.*

Senate January 1976

State, name, and party	Term expires
Ala.—Allen, James B. (D)	1981
Sparkman, John J. (D)	1979
Alaska—Stevens, Ted (R)	1979
Gravel, Mike (D)	1981
Ariz.—Fannin, Paul J. (R)	1977
Goldwater, Barry M. (R)	1981
Ark.—Bumpers, Dale (D)	1981
McClellan, John L. (D)	1979
Calif.—Cranston, Alan (D)	1981
Tunney, John V. (D)	1977
Colo.—Hart, Gary W. (D)	1981
Haskell, Floyd K. (D)	1979
Conn.—Ribicoff, Abraham (D)	1981
Weicker, Lowell P., Jr. (R)	1977
Del.—Biden, Joseph R., Jr. (D)	1979
Roth, William V., Jr. (R)	1977
Fla.—Stone, Richard (D)	1981
Chiles, Lawton M. (D)	1977
Ga.—Nunn, Sam (D)	1979
Talmadge, Herman E. (D)	1981
Hawaii—Fong, Hiram L. (R)	1977
Inouye, Daniel K. (D)	1981
Idaho—Church, Frank (D)	1981
McClure, James A. (R)	1979
Ill.—Percy, Charles H. (R)	1979
Stevenson, Adlai E., III (D)	1981
Ind.—Bayh, Birch (D)	1981
Hartke, Vance (D)	1977
Iowa—Clark, Richard (D)	1979
Culver, John C. (D)	1981
Kan.—Dole, Robert J. (R)	1981
Pearson, James B. (R)	1979
Ky.—Ford, Wendell H. (D)	1981
Huddleston, Walter (D)	1979
La.—Long, Russell B. (D)	1981
Johnston, J. Bennett, Jr. (D)	1979
Maine—Muskie, Edmund S. (D)	1977
Hathaway, William D. (D)	1979
Md.—Beall, J. Glenn, Jr. (R)	1977
Mathias, Charles McC., Jr. (R)	1981
Mass.—Brooke, Edward W. (R)	1979
Kennedy, Edward M. (D)	1977
Mich.—Hart, Philip A. (D)	1977
Griffin, Robert P. (R)	1979
Minn.—Mondale, Walter F. (D)	1979
Humphrey, Hubert H. (D)	1977
Miss.—Stennis, John C. (D)	1977
Eastland, James O. (D)	1979
Mo.—Symington, Stuart (D)	1977
Eagleton, Thomas F. (D)	1981
Mont.—Metcalf, Lee (D)	1979
Mansfield, Mike (D)	1977
Neb.—Curtis, Carl T. (R)	1979
Hruska, Roman L. (R)	1977
Nev.—Laxalt, Paul (R)	1981
Cannon, Howard W. (D)	1977
N.H.—Durkin, John A. (D)	1981
McIntyre, Thomas J. (D)	1979
N.J.—Case, Clifford P. (R)	1979
Williams, Harrison A., Jr. (D)	1977
N.M.—Domenici, Pete V. (R)	1979
Montoya, Joseph M. (D)	1977
N.Y.—Javits, Jacob K. (R)	1981
Buckley, James L. (C-R)	1977
N.C.—Helms, Jesse (R)	1979
Morgan, Robert B. (D)	1981
N.D.—Young, Milton R. (R)	1981
Burdick, Quentin N. (D)	1977
Ohio—Taft, Robert, Jr. (R)	1977
Glenn, John H., Jr. (D)	1981
Okla.—Bellmon, Henry L. (R)	1981
Bartlett, Dewey F. (R)	1979
Ore.—Hatfield, Mark O. (R)	1979
Packwood, Robert W. (R)	1981
Pa.—Scott, Hugh (R)	1977
Schweiker, Richard S. (R)	1981
R.I.—Pell, Claiborne (D)	1979
Pastore, John O. (D)	1977
S.C.—Thurmond, Strom (R)	1979
Hollings, Ernest F. (D)	1981
S.D.—McGovern, George (D)	1981
Abourezk, James G. (D)	1979
Tenn.—Brock, William E., III (R)	1977
Baker, Howard H., Jr. (R)	1979
Texas—Tower, John G. (R)	1979
Bentsen, Lloyd M. (D)	1977
Utah—Garn, Jake (R)	1981
Moss, Frank E. (D)	1977
Vt.—Leahy, Patrick J. (D)	1981
Stafford, Robert T. (R)	1977
Va.—Scott, William L. (R)	1979
Byrd, Harry F., Jr. (I)	1977
Wash.—Jackson, Henry M. (D)	1977
Magnuson, Warren G. (D)	1981
W.Va.—Byrd, Robert C. (D)	1977
Randolph, Jennings (D)	1979
Wis.—Nelson, Gaylord (D)	1981
Proxmire, William (D)	1977
Wyo.—McGee, Gale W. (D)	1977
Hansen, Clifford P. (R)	1979

Supreme Court

Chief Justice Warren Earl Burger (appointed 1969)

Associate Justices (year appointed)

William J. Brennan, Jr.	(1956)	Harry A. Blackmun	(1970)
Potter Stewart	(1958)	Lewis F. Powell, Jr.	(1972)
Byron R. White	(1962)	William H. Rehnquist	(1972)
Thurgood Marshall	(1967)	John Paul Stevens	(1975)

House of Representatives membership at the opening of the second session of the 94th Congress in January 1976

State, district, name, party

Ala.—1. Edwards, Jack (R)
2. Dickinson, W. L. (R)
3. Nichols, William (D)
4. Bevill, Tom (D)
5. Jones, Robert E., Jr. (D)
6. Buchanan, John H., Jr. (R)
7. Flowers, W. W. (D)
Alaska—Young, Don (R)
Ariz.—1. Rhodes, John J. (R)
2. Udall, Morris K. (D)
3. Steiger, Sam (R)
4. Conlan, J. B. (R)
Ark.—1. Alexander, Bill (D)
2. Mills, Wilbur D. (D)
3. Hammerschmidt, J. P. (R)
4. Thornton, Ray (D)
Calif.—1. Johnson, Harold T. (D)
2. Clausen, Don H. (R)
3. Moss, John E. (D)
4. Leggett, Robert L. (D)
5. Burton, John L. (D)
6. Burton, Phillip (D)
7. Miller, George, III (D)
8. Dellums, Ronald V. (D)
9. Stark, Fortney H. (D)
10. Edwards, Don (D)
11. Ryan, Leo J. (D)
12. McCloskey, Paul N., Jr. (R)
13. Mineta, Norman Y. (D)
14. McFall, John J. (D)
15. Sisk, B. F. (D)
16. Talcott, Burt L. (R)
17. Krebs, John (D)
18. Ketchum, William M. (R)
19. Lagomarsino, Robert J. (R)
20. Goldwater, Barry M., Jr. (R)
21. Corman, James C. (D)
22. Moorhead, Carlos J. (R)
23. Rees, Thomas M. (D)
24. Waxman, Henry A. (D)
25. Roybal, Edward R. (D)
26. Rousselot, John H. (R)
27. Bell, Alphonzo (R)
28. Burke, Yvonne B. (D)
29. Hawkins, Augustus F. (D)
30. Danielson, George E. (D)
31. Wilson, Charles H. (D)
32. Anderson, Glenn M. (D)
33. Clawson, Del (R)
34. Hannaford, Mark W. (D)
35. Lloyd, Jim (D)
36. Brown, George E., Jr. (D)
37. Pettis, Shirley N. (R)
38. Patterson, Jerry M. (D)
39. Wiggins, Charles E. (R)
40. Hinshaw, Andrew J. (R)
41. Wilson, Bob (R)
42. Van Deerlin, Lionel (D)
43. Burgener, Clair W. (R)
Colo.—1. Schroeder, Patricia (D)
2. Wirth, Timothy E. (D)
3. Evans, Frank (D)
4. Johnson, J. P. (R)
5. Armstrong, W. L. (R)
Conn.—1. Cotter, William R. (D)
2. Dodd, Christopher J. (D)
3. Giaimo, Robert N. (D)
4. McKinney, Stewart B. (R)
5. Sarasin, Ronald A. (R)
6. Moffett, Anthony J. (D)
Del.—duPont, Pierre S., IV (R)
Fla.—1. Sikes, Robert L. F. (D)
2. Fuqua, Don (D)
3. Bennett, Charles E. (D)
4. Chappell, William, Jr. (D)
5. Kelly, Richard (R)
6. Young, C. William (R)
7. Gibbons, Sam (D)
8. Haley, James A. (D)
9. Frey, Louis, Jr. (R)
10. Bafalis, L. A. (R)
11. Rogers, Paul G. (D)
12. Burke, J. Herbert (R)
13. Lehman, William (D)
14. Pepper, Claude (D)
15. Fascell, Dante B. (D)
Ga.—1. Ginn, R. B. (D)
2. Mathis, Dawson (D)
3. Brinkley, Jack (D)
4. Levitas, Elliott H. (D)
5. Young, Andrew (D)
6. Flynt, J. J., Jr. (D)
7. McDonald, Lawrence P. (D)
8. Stuckey, W. S., Jr. (D)
9. Landrum, Phil M. (D)
10. Stephens, Robert G., Jr. (D)
Hawaii—1. Matsunaga, S. M. (D)
2. Mink, Patsy (D)
Idaho—1. Symms, S. D. (R)
2. Hansen, George V. (R)

State, district, name, party

Ill.—1. Metcalfe, Ralph (D)
2. Murphy, Morgan (D)
3. Russo, Martin A. (D)
4. Derwinski, Edward J. (R)
5. Fary, John G. (D)
6. Hyde, Henry J. (R)
7. Collins, Cardiss (D)
8. Rostenkowski, Dan (D)
9. Yates, Sidney R. (D)
10. Mikva, Abner J. (D)
11. Annunzio, Frank (D)
12. Crane, Philip M. (R)
13. McClory, Robert (R)
14. Erlenborn, J. N. (R)
15. Hall, Tim L. (D)
16. Anderson, John B. (R)
17. O'Brien, G. M. (R)
18. Michel, Robert H. (R)
19. Railsback, Thomas F. (R)
20. Findley, Paul (R)
21. Madigan, E. R. (R)
22. Shipley, George E. (D)
23. Price, Melvin (D)
24. Simon, Paul (D)
Ind.—1. Madden, Ray J. (D)
2. Fithian, Floyd J. (D)
3. Brademas, John (D)
4. Roush, J. Edward (D)
5. Hillis, Elwood H. (R)
6. Evans, David W. (D)
7. Myers, John (R)
8. Hayes, Philip H. (D)
9. Hamilton, L. H. (D)
10. Sharp, Philip R. (D)
11. Jacobs, Andrew, Jr. (D)
Iowa—1. Mezvinsky, E. (D)
2. Blouin, Michael T. (D)
3. Grassley, Charles E. (R)
4. Smith, Neal (D)
5. Harkin, Tom (D)
6. Bedell, Berkley (D)
Kan.—1. Sebelius, Keith G. (R)
2. Keys, Martha E. (D)
3. Winn, Larry, Jr. (R)
4. Shriver, Garner E. (R)
5. Skubitz, Joseph (R)
Ky.—1. Hubbard, Carroll, Jr. (D)
2. Natcher, William H. (D)
3. Mazzoli, Romano L. (D)
4. Snyder, Gene (R)
5. Carter, Tim L. (R)
6. Breckinridge, J. B. (D)
7. Perkins, Carl D. (D)
La.—1. Hébert, F. Edward (D)
2. Boggs, Lindy (D)
3. Treen, David C. (R)
4. Waggonner, Joe D., Jr. (D)
5. Passman, Otto E. (D)
6. Moore, W. Henson, III (R)
7. Breaux, John B. (D)
8. Long, Gillis W. (D)
Maine—1. Emery, David F. (R)
2. Cohen, W. S. (R)
Md.—1. Bauman, Robert E. (R)
2. Long, Clarence D. (D)
3. Sarbanes, Paul S. (D)
4. Holt, Marjorie S. (R)
5. Spellman, Gladys N. (D)
6. Byron, Goodloe E. (D)
7. Mitchell, Parren J. (D)
8. Gude, Gilbert (R)
Mass.—1. Conte, Silvio O. (R)
2. Boland, Edward P. (D)
3. Early, Joseph D. (D)
4. Drinan, Robert F. (D)
5. Tsongas, Paul E. (D)
6. Harrington, M. J. (D)
7. Macdonald, Torbert H. (D)
8. O'Neill, Thomas P., Jr. (D)
9. Moakley, John J. (D)
10. Heckler, Margaret (R)
11. Burke, James A. (D)
12. Studds, Gerry E. (D)
Mich.—1. Conyers, John, Jr. (D)
2. Esch, Marvin (R)
3. Brown, Garry E. (R)
4. Hutchinson, Edward (R)
5. Vander Veen, R. F. (D)
6. Carr, Bob (D)
7. Riegle, D. W., Jr. (D)
8. Traxler, Bob (D)
9. Vander Jagt, Guy (R)
10. Cederberg, Elford A. (R)
11. Ruppe, Philip (R)
12. O'Hara, James G. (D)
13. Diggs, Charles C., Jr. (D)
14. Nedzi, Lucien N. (D)
15. Ford, W. D. (D)
16. Dingell, John D. (D)
17. Brodhead, William M. (D)
18. Blanchard, James J. (D)
19. Broomfield, Williams S. (R)
Minn.—1. Quie, Albert H. (R)
2. Hagedorn, Tom (R)
3. Frenzel, William (R)
4. Karth, Joseph E. (D)
5. Fraser, Donald M. (D)
6. Nolan, Richard (D)
7. Bergland, Bob S. (D)
8. Oberstar, James L. (D)
Miss.—1. Whitten, Jamie L. (D)
2. Bowen, D. R. (D)
3. Montgomery, G. V. (D)

State, district, name, party

4. Cochran, Thad (R)
5. Lott, Trent (R)
Mo.—1. Clay, William (D)
2. Symington, James W. (D)
3. Sullivan, Leonor K. (D)
4. Randall, William J. (D)
5. Bolling, Richard (D)
6. Litton, Jerry (D)
7. Taylor, Gene (R)
8. Ichord, Richard H. (D)
9. Hungate, W. L. (D)
10. Burlison, Bill D. (D)
Mont.—1. Baucus, Max S. (D)
2. Melcher, John (D)
Neb.—1. Thone, Charles (R)
2. McCollister, John Y. (R)
3. Smith, Virginia (R)
Nev.—Santini, James (D)
N.H.—1. D'Amours, Norman (D)
2. Cleveland, James C. (R)
N.J.—1. Florio, James J. (D)
2. Hughes, William J. (D)
3. Howard, J. J. (D)
4. Thompson, Frank, Jr. (D)
5. Fenwick, Millicent (R)
6. Forsythe, Edwin B. (R)
7. Maguire, Andrew (D)
8. Roe, Robert A. (D)
9. Helstoski, Henry (D)
10. Rodino, Peter W., Jr. (D)
11. Minish, Joseph G. (D)
12. Rinaldo, M. J. (R)
13. Meyner, Helen S. (D)
14. Daniels, Dominick V. (D)
15. Patten, Edward J. (D)
N.M.—1. Lujan, Manuel, Jr. (R)
2. Runnels, Harold L. (D)
N.Y.—1. Pike, Otis G. (D)
2. Downey, Thomas J. (D)
3. Ambro, Jerome A., Jr. (D)
4. Lent, Norman F. (R)
5. Wydler, John W. (R)
6. Wolff, L. L. (D)
7. Addabbo, Joseph P. (D)
8. Rosenthal, Benjamin S. (D)
9. Delaney, James J. (D)
10. Biaggi, Mario (D)
11. Scheuer, James H. (D)
12. Chisholm, Shirley (D)
13. Solarz, Stephen J. (D)
14. Richmond, Frederick W. (D)
15. Zeferetti, Leo C. (D)
16. Holtzman, Elizabeth (D)
17. Murphy, John M. (D)
18. Koch, Edward I. (D)
19. Rangel, Charles B. (D)
20. Abzug, Bella (D)
21. Badillo, Herman (D)
22. Bingham, J. B. (D)
23. Peyser, Peter A. (R)
24. Ottinger, Richard L. (D)
25. Fish, Hamilton, Jr. (R)
26. Gilman, B. A. (R)
27. McHugh, Matthew F. (D)
28. Stratton, Samuel S. (D)
29. Pattison, Edward W. (D)
30. McEwen, Robert (R)
31. Mitchell, D. J. (R)
32. Hanley, James M. (D)
33. Walsh, W. F. (R)
34. Horton, Frank J. (R)
35. Conable, B., Jr. (R)
36. LaFalce, John J. (D)
37. Nowak, Henry J. (D)
38. Kemp, Jack F. (R)
39. Hastings, James F. (R)
N.C.—1. Jones, Walter B. (D)
2. Fountain, L. H. (D)
3. Henderson, David N. (D)
4. Andrews, Ike F. (D)
5. Neal, Stephen L. (D)
6. Preyer, L. R. (D)
7. Rose, C. G., III (D)
8. Hefner, Bill (D)
9. Martin, J. G. (R)
10. Broyhill, James T. (R)
11. Taylor, Roy A. (D)
N.D.—Andrews, Mark (R)
Ohio—1. Gradison, Willis D. (R)
2. Clancy, Donald D. (R)
3. Whalen, Charles W., Jr. (R)
4. Guyer, Tennyson (R)
5. Latta, Delbert L. (R)
6. Harsha, William H., Jr. (R)
7. Brown, Clarence J., Jr. (R)
8. Kindness, Thomas N. (R)
9. Ashley, Thomas L. (D)
10. Miller, Clarence E. (R)
11. Stanton, John W. (R)
12. Devine, Samuel L. (R)
13. Mosher, Charles A. (R)
14. Seiberling, John F., Jr. (D)
15. Wylie, Chalmers P. (R)
16. Regula, R. S. (R)
17. Ashbrook, John M. (R)
18. Hays, Wayne L. (D)
19. Carney, Charles J. (D)
20. Stanton, James V. (D)
21. Stokes, Louis (D)
22. Vanik, Charles A. (D)
23. Mottl, Ronald M. (D)
Okla.—1. Jones, James R. (D)
2. Risenhoover, Ted (D)

State, district, name, party

3. Albert, Carl (D)
4. Steed, Tom (D)
5. Jarman, John (D)
6. English, Glenn (D)
Ore.—1. AuCoin, Les (D)
2. Ullman, Al (D)
3. Duncan, Robert (D)
4. Weaver, James (D)
Pa.—1. Barrett, William A. (D)
2. Nix, Robert N. C. (D)
3. Green, William J., III (D)
4. Eilberg, Joshua (D)
5. Schulze, Richard T. (R)
6. Yatron, Gus (D)
7. Edgar, Robert W. (D)
8. Biester, E. G., Jr. (R)
9. Shuster, E. G. (R)
10. McDade, Joseph M. (R)
11. Flood, Daniel J. (D)
12. Murtha, John P. (D)
13. Coughlin, R. L. (R)
14. Moorhead, William S. (D)
15. Rooney, Fred B. (D)
16. Eshleman, Edwin D. (R)
17. Schneebeli, Herman T. (R)
18. Heinz, H. John, III (R)
19. Goodling, William F. (R)
20. Gaydos, Joseph (D)
21. Dent, John H. (D)
22. Morgan, Thomas E. (D)
23. Johnson, Albert W. (R)
24. Vigorito, J. P. (D)
25. Myers, Gary A. (R)
R.I.—1. St. Germain, Fernand (D)
2. Beard, Edward P. (D)
S.C.—1. Davis, Mendel (D)
2. Spence, Floyd D. (R)
3. Derrick, Butler C., Jr. (D)
4. Mann, James R. (D)
5. Holland, Kenneth L. (D)
6. Jenrette, John W., Jr. (D)
S.D.—1. Pressler, Larry L. (R)
2. Abdnor, James (R)
Tenn.—1. Quillen, James H. (R)
2. Duncan, John J. (R)
3. Lloyd, Marilyn (D)
4. Evins, Joseph L. (D)
5. Allen, Clifford (D)
6. Beard, R. L., Jr. (R)
7. Jones, Edward (D)
8. Ford, Harold E. (D)
Texas—1. Patman, Wright (D)
2. Wilson, Charles (D)
3. Collins, James M. (R)
4. Roberts, Ray (D)
5. Steelman, Alan (R)
6. Teague, Olin E. (D)
7. Archer, William R. (R)
8. Eckhardt, Robert C. (D)
9. Brooks, Jack (D)
10. Pickle, J. J. (D)
11. Poage, W. R. (D)
12. Wright, James C., Jr. (D)
13. Hightower, Jack (D)
14. Young, John (D)
15. de la Garza, E. (D)
16. White, Richard C. (D)
17. Burleson, Omar (D)
18. Jordan, Barbara C. (D)
19. Mahon, George (D)
20. Gonzalez, Henry B. (D)
21. Krueger, Robert (D)
22. Casey, Robert R. (D)
23. Kazen, Abraham, Jr. (D)
24. Milford, Dale (D)
Utah—1. McKay, Koln G. (D)
2. Howe, Allan Turner (D)
Vt.—Jeffords, James M. (R)
Va.—1. Downing, Thomas N. (D)
2. Whitehurst, G. W. (R)
3. Satterfield, D. E., III (D)
4. Daniel, R. W. (R)
5. Daniel, W. C. (D)
6. Butler, M. C. (R)
7. Robinson, James K. (R)
8. Harris, Herbert E. (D)
9. Wampler, William C. (R)
10. Fisher, Joseph L. (D)
Wash.—1. Pritchard, Joel (R)
2. Meeds, Lloyd (D)
3. Bonker, Don (D)
4. McCormack, Mike (D)
5. Foley, Thomas S. (D)
6. Hicks, Floyd V. (D)
7. Adams, B. (D)
W.Va.—1. Mollohan, R. H. (D)
2. Staggers, Harley O. (D)
3. Slack, John M., Jr. (D)
4. Hechler, Ken (D)
Wis.—1. Aspin, Leslie (D)
2. Kastenmeier, Robert W. (D)
3. Baldus, Alvin J. (D)
4. Zablocki, Clement J. (D)
5. Reuss, Henry S. (D)
6. Steiger, William A. (R)
7. Obey, David R. (D)
8. Cornell, Robert J. (D)
9. Kasten, Robert W. (R)
Wyo.—Roncalio, Teno (D)

State government revenue, expenditure, and debt

1974 in thousands of dollars

State	GENERAL REVENUE: Total	State taxes: Total	State taxes: General sales	State taxes: Individual income	Intergov-ernmental	Charges & misc.	GENERAL EXPENDITURE: Total	Education	Highways	Public welfare	Hospi-tals	DEBT: Total	Issued 1974*	Retired 1974*
Alabama	1,847,606	1,017,367	321,199	169,801	578,502	251,737	1,808,667	879,473	285,311	245,802	106,618	873,184	68,047	42,709
Alaska	477,069	124,162	...	49,219	191,111	161,796	665,521	227,730	102,556	40,010	6,511	560,820	114,136	17,484
Arizona	1,158,198	743,201	308,058	137,698	262,799	152,198	1,160,845	510,661	171,825	78,666	41,605	84,079	—	3,224
Arkansas	996,776	605,419	191,948	117,022	308,658	82,699	946,459	377,912	182,698	161,850	47,027	113,352	7,767	8,531
California	13,610,502	7,971,715	2,670,811	1,803,080	4,355,503	1,283,284	13,702,881	5,109,847	1,177,021	3,556,028	349,552	6,246,943	326,260	269,706
Colorado	1,449,742	797,599	243,470	250,527	409,229	242,914	1,328,270	651,508	162,166	235,769	70,571	126,663	12,580	6,844
Connecticut	1,756,291	1,092,900	451,191	18,796	434,960	228,431	1,697,745	529,163	220,510	293,950	129,984	2,595,028	367,400	149,873
Delaware	475,687	308,133	...	108,488	90,740	76,814	465,736	233,410	55,464	47,524	21,179	555,640	65,400	34,952
Florida	3,954,925	2,786,602	1,196,571	...	796,748	371,575	3,904,324	1,659,184	665,177	376,633	155,561	1,487,955	260,905	33,221
Georgia	2,521,011	1,514,922	537,311	340,040	771,718	234,371	2,500,496	1,060,673	343,244	416,611	146,482	1,073,792	59,635	44,366
Hawaii	867,994	494,870	244,353	151,733	226,608	146,516	921,144	331,348	76,886	115,656	51,024	1,063,947	110,000	32,897
Idaho	458,520	256,237	69,840	72,183	150,397	51,886	457,680	165,281	95,963	54,663	5,794	37,405	2,550	3,564
Illinois	6,532,526	4,082,987	1,382,780	1,046,675	1,985,759	463,780	6,079,399	2,394,461	798,367	1,563,879	298,726	2,327,347	284,515	88,481
Indiana	2,543,718	1,674,183	831,654	328,071	484,055	385,480	2,124,371	1,029,077	397,954	246,916	109,954	607,338	37,150	25,773
Iowa	1,567,062	1,005,059	285,240	320,594	353,742	208,261	1,494,560	620,543	319,423	158,942	72,419	129,242	10,000	4,390
Kansas	1,139,672	702,709	234,730	147,143	281,560	155,403	1,048,623	439,047	182,529	160,696	82,678	194,785	1,265	11,148
Kentucky	1,889,937	1,106,130	334,192	212,324	551,196	232,611	1,698,250	713,887	341,464	247,743	61,982	1,858,515	75,637	39,720
Louisiana	2,376,006	1,319,521	337,457	99,956	619,333	437,152	2,237,167	837,917	369,271	316,078	155,298	1,214,796	71,138	45,001
Maine	622,848	336,347	132,673	39,033	205,275	81,226	563,183	160,058	96,067	123,845	30,600	378,025	42,705	17,588
Maryland	2,496,841	1,578,155	364,705	573,728	568,183	350,503	2,628,506	913,710	398,114	411,460	152,542	1,759,367	259,342	87,360
Massachusetts	3,583,916	2,204,744	258,214	971,030	1,007,832	371,340	3,823,694	1,195,057	322,278	1,102,589	252,042	3,176,881	213,075	147,893
Michigan	5,903,074	3,681,154	1,187,246	965,704	1,485,924	735,996	5,702,035	2,310,612	635,524	1,373,277	265,109	1,437,367	111,274	79,028
Minnesota	2,799,207	1,843,129	348,141	701,389	629,209	326,869	2,630,426	1,163,801	338,545	350,954	122,704	779,496	185,270	48,513
Mississippi	1,301,142	746,480	360,880	82,533	412,768	141,894	1,290,078	541,013	224,382	195,063	58,118	623,647	63,926	23,875
Missouri	2,025,085	1,300,435	450,617	315,481	547,686	176,964	1,918,604	806,650	375,316	329,692	116,190	212,955	34,500	7,550
Montana	444,761	219,984	...	79,029	149,085	75,692	408,376	165,162	82,608	47,808	14,988	88,962	15	4,688
Nebraska	721,036	405,615	127,984	79,334	201,368	114,053	674,117	250,777	144,172	100,465	42,049	73,235	—	5,722
Nevada	390,398	251,415	82,626	...	95,175	43,808	359,489	144,952	65,089	32,402	6,422	55,200	6,570	3,230
New Hampshire	330,416	165,164	...	8,344	105,390	59,862	356,435	99,599	80,693	57,142	17,309	195,575	35,920	11,592
New Jersey	3,711,389	2,056,302	735,066	44,035	1,016,481	638,606	3,741,324	1,184,971	493,359	817,706	196,685	3,611,221	746,910	99,542
New Mexico	831,506	437,674	182,203	57,946	236,176	157,656	756,133	379,802	112,094	86,933	16,507	157,819	13,300	16,749
New York	13,823,928	8,516,363	1,863,241	3,431,993	3,722,993	1,584,572	14,115,653	4,585,798	827,979	3,311,427	1,031,148	13,375,207	1,782,954	352,261
North Carolina	2,809,404	1,806,433	410,422	504,319	688,697	314,274	2,606,344	1,351,214	354,318	263,480	151,109	498,602	2,221	35,329
North Dakota	474,432	218,693	81,146	45,435	121,141	134,598	411,729	164,620	72,729	33,175	14,951	65,495	8,050	1,798
Ohio	4,573,747	2,788,875	878,123	419,174	1,184,316	600,556	4,608,500	1,767,598	731,200	801,987	248,205	2,447,509	260,145	117,504
Oklahoma	1,482,711	777,522	144,293	120,773	443,558	261,631	1,408,570	551,423	242,071	284,755	82,799	833,499	88,685	21,444
Oregon	1,325,674	701,616	...	352,396	404,982	219,076	1,297,995	450,509	200,607	193,149	53,769	1,268,261	222,545	40,856
Pennsylvania	6,919,734	4,609,141	1,190,553	1,115,612	1,665,465	645,128	6,949,309	2,619,566	951,898	1,480,625	416,352	5,096,503	658,375	157,383
Rhode Island	593,240	333,653	100,496	73,898	171,879	87,708	570,519	197,998	37,565	151,402	46,851	408,847	57,115	22,512
South Carolina	1,492,255	901,540	314,726	192,712	392,406	198,309	1,547,114	666,551	210,020	136,557	76,380	859,843	288,100	31,365
South Dakota	369,862	165,626	75,517	...	130,961	73,275	356,482	122,975	88,177	46,458	11,572	40,843	—	1,090
Tennessee	1,863,566	1,092,405	451,072	16,464	547,621	223,540	1,810,114	742,553	344,925	255,036	102,228	690,585	60,017	27,261
Texas	5,517,809	3,287,923	1,130,649	...	1,415,809	814,077	4,788,737	2,407,663	670,681	792,750	277,106	1,815,507	245,162	67,060
Utah	705,004	363,095	149,455	90,032	229,592	112,317	680,716	357,004	101,805	74,831	26,044	87,613	2,937	6,424
Vermont	371,638	179,641	26,504	52,662	125,716	66,281	368,451	123,881	61,068	59,908	13,334	413,094	21,990	22,599
Virginia	2,543,427	1,507,852	337,175	468,967	643,425	392,150	2,618,183	1,088,414	565,927	327,819	176,563	585,387	194,095	35,947
Washington	2,249,078	1,359,740	784,028	...	593,358	295,980	2,230,443	967,526	307,721	388,610	65,110	1,160,275	117,965	52,589
West Virginia	1,139,511	610,107	270,722	99,563	430,147	99,257	1,116,214	379,628	378,318	112,722	42,580	927,596	107,100	31,334
Wisconsin	3,020,413	2,032,164	477,590	802,995	647,616	340,633	3,065,899	1,137,926	316,008	460,505	157,205	945,765	59,600	37,146
Wyoming	267,098	124,235	54,879	...	97,381	45,482	245,848	90,015	68,105	15,714	10,416	75,215	37,135	970
TOTAL	122,327,392	74,206,938	22,611,751	17,077,931	33,170,233	14,950,221	119,891,358	46,860,148	15,847,192	22,537,662	6,207,952	65,296,227	7,801,383	2,478,086

Fiscal year ending June 30, 1974, except Alabama, September 30; New York, March 31; and Texas, August 31. *Long term only.
Source: U.S. Department of Commerce, Bureau of the Census, *State Government Finances in 1974.*

Education

Public elementary and secondary schools

Fall 1974 estimates

State	ENROLLMENT: Elementary	ENROLLMENT: Secondary	INSTRUCTIONAL STAFF: Total*	Principals and super-visors	Teachers, ele-mentary	Teachers, second-ary	TEACHERS' AVERAGE ANNUAL SALARIES: Ele-mentary	Second-ary	STUDENT-TEACHER RATIO: Ele-mentary	Second-ary	Expendi-ture per pupil
Alabama	390,830	373,656	37,482	2,102	17,240	18,140	$9,230	$9,414	22.7	20.6	$827
Alaska	47,431	39,145	4,649	216	2,011	2,079	16,550	16,218	23.6	18.8	1,527
Arizona	384,311	163,633	24,389	1,579	15,287	6,432	10,499	11,555	25.1	25.4	1,152
Arkansas	243,758	210,648	23,361	1,418	10,406	10,272	8,573	8,922	23.4	20.5	869
California	2,646,000	1,750,000	206,200	9,800	113,500	74,000	14,098	15,171	23.3	23.6	1,156
Colorado	305,570	267,930	30,500	1,400	12,865	13,335	10,575	10,990	23.8	20.1	1,120
Connecticut	467,405	192,785	40,889	1,985	19,793	15,681	11,031	11,783	23.6	12.3	1,387
Delaware	67,214	63,402	7,263	379	2,677	3,672	11,380	11,690	25.1	17.3	1,362
District of Columbia	74,432	57,259	8,008	474	3,982	2,960	...	...	18.7	19.3	1,522
Florida	834,121	736,729	82,369	3,900	36,908	35,082	10,123	10,457	22.6	21.0	1,007
Georgia	673,197	408,252	52,880	2,169	30,584	20,127	9,982	10,365	22.0	20.3	922
Hawaii	93,290	83,710	10,841	604	4,900	3,624	14,186	13,011	19.0	23.1	1,009
Idaho	92,014	95,538	9,619	571	3,998	4,566	9,151	9,321	23.0	20.9	...
Illinois	1,388,000	893,000	127,818	8,190	63,423	47,845	12,623	13,820	21.9	18.7	1,273
Indiana	613,523	577,921	58,584	3,300	25,700	26,584	10,600	11,200	23.9	21.7	985
Iowa	330,044	290,919	37,789	1,414	16,150	16,353	9,770	10,609	20.4	17.8	1,150
Kansas	243,296	206,268	28,547	1,400	12,892	12,681	9,104	9,475	18.9	16.3	1,208
Kentucky	440,000	265,000	35,025	1,850	19,400	11,850	8,700	9,210	22.7	22.4	805
Louisiana	508,400	333,841	43,180	2,225	22,600	18,355	9,320	9,650	22.5	18.2	912
Maine	172,503	71,778	13,034	1,095	7,141	4,673	9,469	10,321	24.2	15.4	878
Maryland	483,091	413,181	49,667	3,046	22,039	22,034	12,358	12,894	21.9	18.8	1,380
Massachusetts	669,702	547,938	72,760	4,755	29,200	31,750	11,300	11,500	22.9	17.3	1,160
Michigan	1,099,000	1,032,000	103,497	5,947	48,500	43,000	12,545	13,194	22.7	24.0	...
Minnesota	445,000	449,000	51,110	2,540	21,060	25,150	11,835	12,996	20.6	17.9	1,285
Mississippi	289,164	224,312	26,417	1,608	13,100	10,480	7,893	8,261	22.1	21.4	787
Missouri	680,224	321,481	54,281	3,121	24,623	23,860	9,880	10,176	27.6	13.5	...
Montana	115,143	57,015	9,749	404	4,945	3,700	10,024	11,080	23.3	15.4	981
Nebraska	162,630	159,038	19,975	1,225	9,400	8,800	8,955	10,156	17.3	18.1	1,331

Public elementary and secondary schools (continued)

Fall 1974 estimates

State	ENROLLMENT Elementary	ENROLLMENT Secondary	INSTRUCTIONAL STAFF Total*	INSTRUCTIONAL STAFF Principals and super-visors	INSTRUCTIONAL STAFF Teachers, ele-mentary	INSTRUCTIONAL STAFF Teachers, second-ary	TEACHERS' AVERAGE ANNUAL SALARIES Ele-mentary	TEACHERS' AVERAGE ANNUAL SALARIES Second-ary	STUDENT-TEACHER RATIO Ele-mentary	STUDENT-TEACHER RATIO Second-ary	Expendi-ture per pupil
Nevada	72,800	63,950	6,567	382	2,978	2,752	$12,030	$12,293	24.4	23.2	$1,024
New Hampshire	102,660	71,340	9,725	677	4,565	3,870	9,818	10,210	22.5	18.4	892
New Jersey	941,000	529,000	95,000	6,800	48,000	31,300	12,567	13,031	19.6	16.9	1,469
New Mexico	131,959	141,937	14,448	1,095	6,582	6,191	10,050	10,250	20.0	22.9	1,036
New York	1,782,200	1,643,300	215,100	12,300	88,900	100,800	14,100	14,600	20.0	16.3	1,810
North Carolina	818,594	359,266	56,574	2,561	33,973	17,500	10,788	11,300	24.1	20.5	1,003
North Dakota	85,746	47,495	8,400	370	4,785	2,925	8,579	9,214	17.9	16.2	998
Ohio	1,375,300	947,700	120,186	6,680	54,745	50,790	10,400	10,950	25.1	18.7	1,058
Oklahoma	317,000	274,000	32,160	1,900	15,360	13,800	8,800	9,200	20.6	19.9	961
Oregon	276,874	197,226	27,204	1,580	11,671	10,433	10,310	10,783	23.7	18.9	1,355
Pennsylvania	1,162,500	1,137,100	126,800	5,300	52,900	60,400	11,400	11,900	22.0	18.8	1,349
Rhode Island	105,000	73,662	10,691	541	5,277	4,052	12,132	12,626	19.9	18.2	1,386
South Carolina	374,228	231,322	32,143	2,363	16,291	10,889	9,102	9,431	23.0	21.2	921
South Dakota	102,559	51,033	9,166	439	5,375	3,013	8,285	8,915	19.1	16.9	929
Tennessee	528,856	349,174	43,537	2,150	24,004	15,274	9,400	10,130	22.0	22.9	852
Texas	1,526,324	1,253,866	150,279	7,510	71,996	63,973	9,574	9,842	21.2	19.6	926
Utah	160,785	145,603	14,005	780	6,350	6,165	9,820	10,130	25.3	23.6	886
Vermont	63,217	41,707	7,292	454	3,100	3,259	8,993	9,771	20.4	12.8	1,188
Virginia	680,543	412,766	60,650	4,100	32,400	24,150	10,066	10,836	21.0	17.1	1,050
Washington	400,548	384,909	40,245	3,165	18,740	14,770	11,540	12,245	21.4	26.1	...
West Virginia	228,658	175,785	21,292	1,420	10,563	8,644	8,516	9,273	21.6	20.3	854
Wisconsin	550,893	423,440	52,690	2,430	26,720	23,540	10,960	11,690	20.6	18.0	1,396
Wyoming	43,323	43,261	5,220	410	2,200	2,360	9,800	10,200	19.7	18.3	1,228
TOTAL U.S.	25,790,920	19,284,221	2,429,257	134,124	1,161,799	997,935	$11,234	$11,826	22.2	19.3	$1,163

Kindergartens included in elementary schools; junior high schools, in secondary schools.
*Includes librarians, guidance and psychological personnel, and related educational workers.
Source: National Education Association, Research Division, *Estimates of School Statistics, 1974-75* (Copyright 1975. All rights reserved. Used by permission).

Level of school completed

25 years old and over, by race

Level of school completed	April 1950	April 1960	March 1970	March 1972	March 1974
Less than 5 years elementary school, percent:					
White	8.7	6.7	4.2	3.7	3.5
Nonwhite	31.4	23.5	14.7	12.8	12.2
4 years of high school or more, percent:					
White	35.5	43.2	57.4	60.4	63.3
Nonwhite	13.4	21.7	36.1	39.1	44.3
4 years of college or more, percent:					
White	6.4	8.1	11.6	12.6	14.0
Nonwhite	2.2	3.5	6.1	6.9	8.0
Median school years completed:					
White	9.7	10.8	12.2	12.3	12.4
Nonwhite	6.9	8.2	10.1	10.5	11.1

Source: U.S. Department of Health, Education, and Welfare, Office of Education, *Digest of Educational Statistics*. Data compiled by U.S. Department of Commerce, Bureau of the Census.

Cost of attending college

in current dollars

Expenditure	1964–65 Public	1964–65 Private	1969–70 Public	1969–70 Private	1974–75 Public	1974–75 Private
Tuition and required fees						
Universities	298	1,297	427	1,809	691	2,781
Other 4-year institutions	224	1,023	307	1,469	458	2,266
2-year institutions	99	702	178	1,034	263	1,551
Board rates						
Universities	462	515	540	608	717	814
Other 4-year institutions	402	479	483	542	624	699
2-year institutions	361	464	465	546	648	699
Charges for dormitory rooms						
Universities	291	390	396	503	707	733
Other 4-year institutions	241	308	347	409	522	582
2-year institutions	178	289	308	414	497	596

Data are estimated for the entire academic year and are average charges per full-time resident degree-credit student.
Source: U.S. Department of Health, Education, and Welfare, Office of Education, *Digest of Educational Statistics*.

Universities and colleges

state statistics

State	NUMBER OF INSTITUTIONS 1974–1975 Total	NUMBER OF INSTITUTIONS 1974–1975 Public	Enroll-ment* fall, 1974	EARNED DEGREES CONFERRED† 1971–1972 Bachelor's and first professional	Master's except first professional	Doctor's
Alabama	52	31	131,433	14,278	3,261	276
Alaska	3	1	13,176	520	258	3
Arizona	21	15	127,628	8,161	3,550	386
Arkansas	21	9	54,223	7,325	1,282	147
California	228	118	1,269,586	83,342	22,260	3,490
Colorado	33	21	125,348	14,041	3,593	714
Connecticut	45	21	145,082	13,158	4,863	578
Delaware	7	3	28,133	2,103	511	85
District of Columbia	17	3	81,278	8,310	4,683	554
Florida	68	37	268,236	23,733	5,799	761
Georgia	63	32	146,975	16,702	4,911	489
Hawaii	12	9	35,945	3,472	1,554	80
Idaho	9	6	32,536	2,996	507	58
Illinois	135	50	452,907	47,947	14,906	2,142
Indiana	46	6	192,040	24,760	9,263	1,316
Iowa	57	18	100,656	15,755	2,606	625
Kansas	51	28	107,070	13,263	3,027	382
Kentucky	36	8	104,268	13,239	3,424	198
Louisiana	23	12	136,478	15,103	3,699	449
Maine	19	4	32,964	4,450	710	28
Maryland	47	26	161,888	14,497	3,678	617
Massachusetts	119	33	331,545	35,496	12,166	1,818
Michigan	89	42	370,173	39,502	13,649	1,710
Minnesota	58	26	159,991	20,327	2,904	599
Mississippi	42	24	75,838	9,272	1,873	253
Missouri	73	22	186,196	22,002	6,101	751
Montana	12	9	26,617	4,159	662	72
Nebraska	29	15	62,294	10,081	1,548	210
Nevada	6	5	19,066	1,346	303	21
New Hampshire	25	10	30,921	4,701	623	63
New Jersey	58	28	254,506	23,054	6,835	621
New Mexico	11	8	48,803	4,831	1,490	188
New York	268	80	930,224	83,357	33,301	3,607
North Carolina	100	57	176,529	21,646	3,909	763
North Dakota	13	9	25,265	4,009	709	83
Ohio	104	34	357,617	48,874	10,660	1,475
Oklahoma	41	27	124,013	13,584	3,228	509
Oregon	40	20	106,147	10,895	3,223	573
Pennsylvania	145	32	409,070	55,514	14,096	1,817
Rhode Island	13	3	56,650	5,605	1,494	208
South Carolina	45	22	106,306	8,992	1,398	130
South Dakota	16	6	25,753	4,881	897	51
Tennessee	62	19	159,039	18,212	3,829	524
Texas	138	83	490,358	48,237	10,583	1,457
Utah	13	9	72,525	9,774	2,165	491
Vermont	21	6	27,368	3,411	853	35
Virginia	70	36	198,784	16,623	3,600	331
Washington	44	31	158,708	17,671	3,402	541
West Virginia	26	15	64,836	8,276	1,493	134
Wisconsin	57	29	174,012	24,593	4,880	861
Wyoming	8	8	17,207	1,429	376	78
TOTAL U.S.	2,739	1,206	8,994,211	927,509	250,595	33,352

Excludes service academies. *Excludes non-degree-credit students. †Estimated.
Source: U.S. Department of Health, Education, and Welfare, Office of Education, *Digest of Educational Statistics, Education Directory, 1974-1975, Higher Education.*

Universities and colleges, 1974–75*

Selected four-year schools

Institution	Location	Year founded	Total students†	Total faculty‡	Bound library volumes
ALABAMA					
Alabama A. & M. U.	Normal	1875	4,046	234	157,500
Alabama State U.	Montgomery	1874	3,158	179	113,000
Auburn U.	Auburn	1856	15,705	862	691,000
Birmingham-Southern	Birmingham	1856	872	76	103,000
Jacksonville State U.	Jacksonville	1883	5,606	240	241,200
Troy State U.	Troy	1887	3,483	143	250,000
Tuskegee Institute	Tuskegee Institute	1881	3,284	322	217,000
U. of Alabama	University	1831	13,819	756	783,400
U. of South Alabama	Mobile	1963	6,146	366	202,000
ALASKA					
U. of Alaska	Fairbanks	1917	4,762	204§	345,000
ARIZONA					
Arizona State U.	Tempe	1885	31,021	1,239	4,211,300
Northern Arizona U.	Flagstaff	1899	10,165	487	530,000
U. of Arizona	Tucson	1885	29,123	1,768	693,400‖
ARKANSAS					
Arkansas State U.	State University	1909	6,687	297	430,300
State Col. of Arkansas	Conway	1907	4,685	265	200,000
U. of Arkansas	Fayetteville	1871	11,448	676	685,000
U. of A. at Little Rock	Little Rock	1927	6,155	265	157,900
U. of A. at Monticello	Monticello	1909	1,563	112	70,000
CALIFORNIA					
California Inst. of Tech.	Pasadena	1891	1,544	458	285,000
Cal. State, Bakersfield	Bakersfield	1965	2,900	176	130,000
Cal. State, Dominguez Hills	Dominguez Hills	1960	5,100	275	146,500
Cal. State, San Bernardino	San Bernardino	1962	3,500	205	200,000
Cal. State, Sonoma	Rohnert Park	1960	5,845	304§	210,000
Cal. State, Stanislaus	Turlock	1957	2,903	189	150,000
Cal. State Polytech. U.	Pomona	1938	11,000	600	240,000
Cal. Polytech. State U.	San Luis Obispo	1901	13,000	740	375,000
Cal. State U., Chico	Chico	1887	12,683	898	420,400
Cal. State U., Fresno	Fresno	1911	15,100	1,059	447,200
Cal. State U., Fullerton	Fullerton	1957	19,628	840	354,600
Cal. State U., Hayward	Hayward	1957	11,743	769	440,000
Cal. State U., Humboldt	Arcata	1913	7,500	506	150,000
Cal. State U., Long Beach	Long Beach	1949	31,228	1,400	600,000
Cal. State U., Los Angeles	Los Angeles	1947	24,865	1,278	600,000
Cal. State U., Northridge	Northridge	1958	25,377	1,359	520,000
Cal. State U., Sacramento	Sacramento	1947	18,751	1,020	460,000
Cal. State U., San Francisco	San Francisco	1899	22,983	1,300	488,100
Cal. State U., San Jose	San Jose	1857	26,500	1,600	700,000
Golden Gate U.	San Francisco	1901	8,350	588	150,000
Loma Linda U.	Riverside	1905	3,873	1,285	264,000
Loyola Marymount U.	Los Angeles	1911	5,250	311	316,000
Occidental	Los Angeles	1887	1,750	120	270,000
Pepperdine U.	Los Angeles	1937	3,830§	311	95,400
Stanford U.	Stanford	1885	12,469	1,327	3,982,000
U. of C., Berkeley	Berkeley	1868	29,909	1,430	4,310,000
U. of C., Davis	Davis	1905	15,622	791	1,070,000
U. of C., Irvine	Irvine	1964	8,384	397	575,000
U. of C., Los Angeles	Los Angeles	1919	31,086	1,753	3,280,000
U. of C., Riverside	Riverside	1868	5,376	286	736,000
U. of C., San Diego	La Jolla	1912	7,950	533	997,000
U. of C., Santa Barbara	Santa Barbara	1944	12,526	500	1,600,000
U. of C., Santa Cruz	Santa Cruz	1965	5,080	237	420,000
U. of the Pacific	Stockton	1851	4,200	272§	257,200
U. of Redlands	Redlands	1907	2,498	111	193,500
U. of San Francisco	San Francisco	1855	5,942	409	342,000
U. of Santa Clara	Santa Clara	1851	6,794	299	270,000
U. of Southern California	Los Angeles	1880	20,289	1,500	1,600,000
Whittier	Whittier	1901	1,394	108	120,000
COLORADO					
Colorado	Colorado Springs	1874	1,925	160	300,000
Colorado School of Mines	Golden	1874	1,687	174	158,000
Colorado State U.	Fort Collins	1870	16,798	858§	922,400
Metropolitan State	Denver	1963	10,256	331	150,000
Southern Colorado State	Pueblo	1933	5,458	607	165,000
¶U.S. Air Force Academy	USAF Academy	1954	4,400	600	400,000
U. of Colorado	Boulder	1876	22,420	1,102§	1,525,800
U. of Denver	Denver	1864	8,500	552	1,000,000
U. of Northern Colorado	Greeley	1889	11,110	670	323,300
CONNECTICUT					
Central Connecticut State	New Britain	1849	12,277	654	255,900
Fairfield U.	Fairfield	1942	4,865	273	245,000
Southern Connecticut State	New Haven	1893	12,601	500	300,000
Trinity	Hartford	1823	2,002	154	536,000
¶U.S. Coast Guard Acad.	New London	1876	1,088	130	90,000
U. of Bridgeport	Bridgeport	1927	8,194	494	278,400
U. of Connecticut	Storrs	1881	20,946	1,915§	1,325,000
U. of Hartford	West Hartford	1877	7,934	560	230,000
U. of New Haven	West Haven	1920	5,835	400	100,000
Wesleyan U.	Middletown	1831	2,289	255	714,100
Western Connecticut State	Danbury	1903	5,123	180	104,500
Yale U.	New Haven	1701	9,427	2,507	6,300,000
DELAWARE					
Delaware State	Dover	1891	2,219	114	61,000
U. of Delaware	Newark	1833	18,511	1,166	945,400
DISTRICT OF COLUMBIA					
American U.	Washington	1893	14,207	764	410,200
Catholic U. of America	Washington	1887	6,800	560	881,000
George Washington U.	Washington	1821	21,529	2,384	632,200
Georgetown U.	Washington	1789	10,717	2,246	722,000
Howard U.	Washington	1867	9,506	876	809,000

Institution	Location	Year founded	Total students†	Total faculty‡	Bound library volumes
FLORIDA					
Florida A. & M. U.	Tallahassee	1887	5,130	250	243,000
Florida Atlantic U.	Boca Raton	1961	6,647	292	223,700
Florida State U.	Tallahassee	1857	20,589	1,233	1,017,100
Florida Tech. U.	Orlando	1963	8,500	453	200,000
Rollins	Winter Park	1885	3,535	170	172,000
U. of Florida	Gainesville	1853	28,332	2,667	1,725,200
U. of Miami	Coral Gables	1925	12,142	725	803,100
U. of South Florida	Tampa	1960	19,300	900	300,000
U. of Tampa	Tampa	1931	2,001	141	140,600
U. of West Florida	Pensacola	1963	4,906	258	229,900
GEORGIA					
Atlanta U.	Atlanta	1865	1,118	156	280,000
Augusta	Augusta	1925	3,904	126	149,000
Emory U.	Atlanta	1836	6,746	1,024	1,051,700
Georgia	Milledgeville	1889	3,490	173	117,000
Georgia Inst. of Tech.	Atlanta	1885	8,300	700	800,000
Georgia Southern	Statesboro	1906	6,125	346	168,900
Georgia State U.	Atlanta	1913	17,443	975	440,500
Mercer U.	Macon	1833	2,205	130	180,000
¶Morehouse	Atlanta	1867	1,275	100	275,000
Oglethorpe U.	Atlanta	1835	980	41	57,000
♀Spelman	Atlanta	1881	1,155	100	38,600
U. of Georgia	Athens	1785	21,233	1,933	1,435,500
West Georgia	Carrollton	1933	5,201	281	176,000
HAWAII					
Brigham Young U.-Hawaii	Laie	1955	1,104	77	60,000
U. of Hawaii	Honolulu	1907	21,526	1,347	1,400,000
IDAHO					
Boise State U.	Boise	1932	9,927	448	176,500
Idaho State U.	Pocatello	1901	8,516	448	242,000
U. of Idaho	Moscow	1889	7,138	528	815,100
ILLINOIS					
Augustana	Rock Island	1860	2,288	149	172,300
Bradley U.	Peoria	1897	5,025	320	325,000
Chicago State U.	Chicago	1869	6,520	325	200,000
Concordia Teachers	River Forest	1864	1,272	101	111,000
De Paul U.	Chicago	1898	10,010	552	290,200
Eastern Illinois U.	Charleston	1895	8,035	643	325,000
Illinois Inst. of Tech.	Chicago	1892	6,325	291	1,200,000
Illinois State U.	Normal	1857	17,980	993	626,000
Knox	Galesburg	1837	1,220	95	158,800
Lake Forest	Lake Forest	1857	1,050	90	152,000
Loyola U.	Chicago	1870	14,000	610	654,000
Northeastern Ill. State U.	Chicago	1869	9,945	420	259,900
Northern Illinois U.	DeKalb	1895	19,971	1,355	648,000
Northwestern U.	Evanston	1851	10,108	1,039	2,349,400
Southern Illinois U.	Carbondale	1869	19,342	2,600	1,700,000
at Edwardsville	Edwardsville	1957	12,608	699	588,900
U. of Chicago	Chicago	1892	7,792	1,099	3,485,100
U. of Illinois	Urbana	1868	35,045	1,844	5,073,000
Chicago Circle Campus	Chicago	1965	19,393	1,098	518,500
Western Illinois U.	Macomb	1899	14,218	729	321,000
Wheaton	Wheaton	1860	2,234	163	156,000
INDIANA					
Ball State U.	Muncie	1918	17,215	900	700,000
Butler U.	Indianapolis	1855	4,138	300	200,000
De Pauw U.	Greencastle	1837	2,412	183	314,000
Indiana State U.	Terre Haute	1865	10,729	643	614,500
Indiana U.	Bloomington	1820	30,623	1,682	2,722,000
Purdue U.	West Lafayette	1869	27,466	1,847	1,150,000
U. of Evansville	Evansville	1854	4,760	251	200,000
U. of Notre Dame	Notre Dame	1842	8,808	651	1,115,000
Valparaiso U.	Valparaiso	1859	4,550	298	250,000
IOWA					
Coe	Cedar Rapids	1851	1,162	125	140,000
Drake U.	Des Moines	1881	7,244	...	350,000
Grinnell	Grinnell	1846	1,278	130	192,000
Iowa State U.	Ames	1858	19,914	1,637§	1,076,400
U. of Dubuque	Dubuque	1852	915	66	183,200
U. of Iowa	Iowa City	1847	21,271	1,481	1,812,900
U. of Northern Iowa	Cedar Falls	1876	9,314	575	400,000
KANSAS					
Kan. State C. of Pittsburg	Pittsburg	1903	5,017	274	360,000
Emporia Kansas State	Emporia	1863	6,243	231§	36,300
Kansas State U.	Manhattan	1863	16,422	1,330	700,000
U. of Kansas	Lawrence	1866	20,395	1,147§	1,637,400
Wichita State U.	Wichita	1895	14,768	1,012	468,000
KENTUCKY					
Berea	Berea	1855	1,411	133	200,000
Eastern Kentucky U.	Richmond	1906	11,088	500	440,700
Kentucky State U.	Frankfort	1886	2,000	150	100,000
Morehead State U.	Morehead	1922	6,765	350	300,000
Murray State U.	Murray	1922	7,349	349	295,000
U. of Kentucky	Lexington	1865	20,000	1,500	1,200,000
U. of Louisville	Louisville	1798	12,230	1,567	843,100
Western Kentucky U.	Bowling Green	1906	12,266	640	340,000
LOUISIANA					
Grambling	Grambling	1901	3,627	252	110,000
Louisiana State U.	Baton Rouge	1860	22,915	1,293	1,359,000
Louisiana Tech. U.	Ruston	1894	7,967	416	195,600
Northeast Louisiana U.	Monroe	1931	9,216	378	150,000

Institution	Location	Year founded	Total students†	Total faculty‡	Bound library volumes
Northwestern State U.	Natchitoches	1884	6,290	320	190,000
Southeastern Louisiana U.	Hammond	1925	6,410	303	155,600
Southern U.	Baton Rouge	1880	8,685	397	260,000
Tulane U.	New Orleans	1834	9,048	787	1,192,100
U. of Southwestern La.	Lafayette	1898	11,799	539	350,000
MAINE					
Bates	Lewiston	1864	1,250	100	200,000
Bowdoin	Brunswick	1794	1,296	107	486,400
Colby	Waterville	1813	1,577	122	314,100
U. of Maine, Farmington	Farmington	1864	1,777	98	63,000
U. of Maine, Orono	Orono	1865	8,978	600	500,000
U. of Maine, Portland-Gorham	Portland	1957	8,080	289	185,000
MARYLAND					
♀Goucher	Towson	1885	1,038	119	181,600
Johns Hopkins U.	Baltimore	1876	8,260	578	1,655,000
Morgan State	Baltimore	1867	5,599	348	171,000
Towson State	Baltimore	1866	13,041	573	255,600
¶U.S. Naval Academy	Annapolis	1845	4,000	545	324,000
U. of Maryland	College Park	1807	34,667	2,368	1,400,000
MASSACHUSETTS					
Amherst	Amherst	1821	1,329	161	470,800
Babson	Wellesley	1919	2,217	...	56,000
Boston	Chestnut Hill	1863	12,749	1,051	900,000
Boston U.	Boston	1869	24,622	1,582	1,820,300
Brandeis U.	Waltham	1948	3,507	371	561,200
Clark U.	Worcester	1887	3,237	256	330,000
Harvard U.	Cambridge	1636	20,602	5,170	8,859,500
♀Radcliffe	Cambridge	1879	1,673	δ	□
Holy Cross	Worcester	1843	2,694	183	310,000
Lowell Tech. Institute	Lowell	1895	10,000	300	145,000
Mass. Inst. of Tech.	Cambridge	1861	8,584	1,650	1,500,000
♀Mt. Holyoke	South Hadley	1837	1,850	236	370,000
Northeastern U.	Boston	1898	42,709	1,800	375,000
Salem State	Salem	1854	4,373	292	100,000
♀Simmons	Boston	1899	2,804	150	170,000
Smith	Northampton	1871	2,404	240	803,000
Tufts U.	Medford	1852	5,126	486	415,300
U. of Massachusetts	Amherst	1863	24,128	1,000	850,000
♀Wellesley	Wellesley	1870	2,026	245	500,000
♀Wheaton	Norton	1834	1,191	118	172,000
Williams	Williamstown	1793	1,901	180	400,000
MICHIGAN					
Albion	Albion	1835	1,757	122	190,000
Central Michigan U.	Mt. Pleasant	1892	14,270	695	375,000
Eastern Michigan U.	Ypsilanti	1849	18,568	746	456,700
Ferris State	Big Rapids	1884	8,584	433	226,600
Grand Valley State	Allendale	1960	6,677	350	200,000
Hope	Holland	1866	2,198	150	150,000
Michigan State U.	East Lansing	1855	40,624	2,311	2,000,000
Michigan Tech. U.	Houghton	1885	5,366	402	184,000
Northern Michigan U.	Marquette	1899	8,187	312	281,200
Oakland U.	Rochester	1957	9,704	400	250,000
U. of Detroit	Detroit	1877	8,879	592	450,000
U. of Michigan	Ann Arbor	1817	36,895	4,974	4,548,500
Wayne State U.	Detroit	1868	13,064	1,856	1,550,000
Western Michigan U.	Kalamazoo	1903	20,922	1,195§	605,000
MINNESOTA					
Carleton	Northfield	1866	1,636	150	242,900
Concordia	Moorhead	1891	2,402	168	198,000
Gustavus Adolphus	St. Peter	1862	1,959	132	130,400
Hamline U.	St. Paul	1854	1,327	100	125,000
Macalester	St. Paul	1874	1,748	166	255,000
Mankato State	Mankato	1867	13,130	629	400,000
Moorhead State	Moorhead	1885	6,103	320	210,000
♀St. Catherine	St. Paul	1905	1,688	105	195,000
St. Cloud State	St. Cloud	1869	10,093	405	426,500
¶St. John's U.	Collegeville	1857	1,888	101	250,000
St. Olaf	Northfield	1874	2,760	251	268,700
¶St. Thomas	St. Paul	1885	2,707	149	169,000
U. of Minnesota	Minneapolis	1851	42,970	5,055	3,000,000
Winona State	Winona	1858	4,533	231	172,000
MISSISSIPPI					
Alcorn State U.	Lorman	1871	2,568	106	65,000
Jackson State U.	Jackson	1877	5,205	350	200,900
Mississippi	Clinton	1826	2,490	107	145,000
Mississippi U. for Women	Columbus	1884	2,700	164	350,000
Mississippi State U.	Mississippi State	1878	10,008	768	435,000
U. of Mississippi	University	1848	7,777	510	800,000
U. of Southern Mississippi	Hattiesburg	1910	9,200	600	525,500
MISSOURI					
Central Missouri State U.	Warrensburg	1871	7,346	425	300,000
Northeast Missouri State U.	Kirksville	1867	5,231	295	238,000
Northwest Missouri State U.	Maryville	1905	4,633	262	110,300
St. Louis U.	St. Louis	1818	10,329	1,759	853,000
Southeast Missouri State U.	Cape Girardeau	1873	7,632	376	225,000
Southwest Missouri State U.	Springfield	1906	9,673	601	273,100
U. of Missouri-Columbia	Columbia	1839	22,961	3,552	1,700,000
U. of Missouri-Kansas City	Kansas City	1929	11,004	1,486	544,000
U. of Missouri-Rolla	Rolla	1870	4,064	671	220,000
U. of Missouri-St. Louis	St. Louis	1963	11,394	683	420,400
Washington U.	St. Louis	1853	10,917	2,085	1,500,000
MONTANA					
Eastern Montana	Billings	1927	2,757	140	102,000
Montana State U.	Bozeman	1893	8,503	548	639,200
U. of Montana	Missoula	1893	8,566	466	500,000

Institution	Location	Year founded	Total students†	Total faculty‡	Bound library volumes
NEBRASKA					
Creighton U.	Omaha	1878	4,551	707	369,300
Kearney State	Kearney	1905	5,119	200	228,600
U. of Nebraska	Lincoln	1869	20,892	990	1,160,300
U. of Nebraska at Omaha	Omaha	1908	13,575	542	368,000
Wayne State	Wayne	1910	2,032	94	138,100
NEVADA					
U. of Nevada-Las Vegas	Las Vegas	1951	7,088	321	272,300
U. of Nevada-Reno	Reno	1874	7,536	445	489,000
NEW HAMPSHIRE					
Dartmouth	Hanover	1769	3,849	383	1,000,000
U. of New Hampshire	Durham	1866	9,877	670	680,700
NEW JERSEY					
Fairleigh Dickinson U.	Rutherford	1941	4,921	345	137,400
Glassboro State	Glassboro	1923	12,213	720	350,000
Jersey City State	Jersey City	1927	10,965	440	160,400
Kean Col. of N.J.	Union	1855	12,462	681	190,000
Monmouth	West Long Branch	1933	4,185	196	180,000
Montclair State	Upper Montclair	1908	14,790	585§	209,400
Princeton U.	Princeton	1746	5,735	725	3,000,000
Rider	Trenton	1865	5,905	261	260,000
Rutgers U.	New Brunswick	1766	40,740	1,700	1,400,000
Seton Hall U.	South Orange	1856	9,719	568	283,600
Stevens Inst. of Tech.	Hoboken	1870	2,075	189	93,000
Trenton State	Trenton	1855	12,231	528	250,000
Upsala	East Orange	1893	1,703	97	132,300
William Patterson	Wayne	1855	12,981	443	235,000
NEW MEXICO					
New Mexico State U.	Las Cruces	1889	9,591	426	350,000
U. of New Mexico	Albuquerque	1889	19,488	889	735,000
NEW YORK					
Adelphi U.	Garden City	1896	9,740	632	270,000
Alfred U.	Alfred	1836	2,339	188	210,000
Canisius	Buffalo	1870	3,827	249	195,000
City U. of New York					
Bernard M. Baruch	New York	1919	17,746	1,250	200,000
Brooklyn	Brooklyn	1930	33,882	2,505	541,000
City	New York	1847	19,000	1,600	867,000
Herbert H. Lehman	Bronx	1931	13,693	1,250	286,000
Hunter	New York	1870	24,000	2,500	400,000
Queens	Flushing	1937	30,077	2,007	439,500
Richmond	Staten Island	1965	4,011	280	165,000
York	Jamaica	1966	3,435	265	120,000
Colgate U.	Hamilton	1819	2,502§	200	280,000
Columbia U.	New York	1754	15,432	3,500	4,474,000
♀Barnard	New York	1889	2,005	141	135,000
Teachers	New York	1887	5,922	351	425,000
Cooper Union	New York	1859	893	156	100,000
Cornell U.	Ithaca	1865	16,208§	1,460	4,000,000
Elmira	Elmira	1855	3,337	153	120,000
Fordham U.	Bronx	1841	6,081	359	1,075,300
Hofstra U.	Hempstead	1935	11,761	649	600,000
Iona	New Rochelle	1940	4,698	195	150,000
Ithaca	Ithaca	1892	4,000	350	220,000
Juilliard School	New York	1905	1,233	186	42,000
Long Island U.	Greenvale	1926	18,788	1,000	400,000
¶Manhattan	Bronx	1853	4,229	282	200,000
¶Marymount	Tarrytown	1907	1,038	102	96,000
New School for Soc. Res.	New York	1919	3,639	500	70,000
New York U.	New York	1831	39,676	1,322	2,390,400
Niagara U.	Niagara University	1856	3,750	199	175,000
Pace U.	New York	1906	8,513	455	189,600
Polytechnic Inst. of N.Y.	Brooklyn	1854	4,500	235	203,900
Pratt Inst.	Brooklyn	1887	4,517	493	215,000
Rensselaer Polytech. Inst.	Troy	1824	4,815	332	236,600
Rochester Inst. of Tech.	Rochester	1829	11,971	942	138,900
Russell Sage	Troy	1916	1,219	140	150,000
St. Bonaventure U.	St. Bonaventure	1859	2,347	160	210,000
St. John's U.	Jamaica	1870	12,872	644	705,300
St. Lawrence U.	Canton	1856	2,330	146	241,000
Skidmore	Saratoga Springs	1911	1,973	154	180,000
State U. of N.Y. at Albany	Albany	1844	14,521	913	800,000
SUNY at Binghamton	Binghamton	1946	9,107	538	546,100
SUNY at Buffalo	Buffalo	1846	24,983	1,840	1,500,000
SUNY at Stony Brook	Stony Brook	1957	14,193	1,251	905,500
State U. Colleges					
Brockport	Brockport	1867	10,668	587	275,900
Buffalo	Buffalo	1867	12,383	560	280,000
Cortland	Cortland	1868	6,117	346	218,200
Fredonia	Fredonia	1867	5,232	279	206,500
Geneseo	Geneseo	1867	6,335	350	259,300
New Paltz	New Paltz	1828	8,497	450	300,000
Oneonta	Oneonta	1889	6,806	396	256,000
Oswego	Oswego	1861	9,143	468	305,400
Plattsburgh	Plattsburgh	1889	5,708	420	250,000
Potsdam	Potsdam	1816	5,045	301	232,900
Syracuse U.	Syracuse	1870	19,356	1,303	1,637,400
¶U.S. Merchant Marine Acad.	Kings Point	1938	1,000	92	74,900
¶U.S. Military Academy	West Point	1802	4,000	500	400,000
U. of Rochester	Rochester	1850	7,200	632	1,000,000
Vassar	Poughkeepsie	1861	2,190	221	444,000
Wagner	Staten Island	1883	2,500	195	250,000
Yeshiva U.	New York	1886	3,428	2,425	605,100
NORTH CAROLINA					
Appalachian State U.	Boone	1899	8,014	429	261,400
Catawba	Salisbury	1851	1,147	82	100,000
¶Davidson	Davidson	1837	1,217	96	200,000
Duke U.	Durham	1838	8,766	815	2,530,100

Institution	Location	Year founded	Total students†	Total faculty‡	Bound library volumes
East Carolina U.	Greenville	1907	11,788	650	600,000
Lenoir Rhyne	Hickory	1891	1,333	101	93,100
N. Carolina A. & T. St. U.	Greensboro	1891	4,937	288	262,500
N. Carolina Central U.	Durham	1910	4,062	262	272,200
N. Carolina State U.	Raleigh	1887	15,751	1,120	693,600
U. of N.C. at Chapel Hill	Chapel Hill	1789	20,031	1,725	2,000,000
U. of N.C. at Charlotte	Charlotte	1946	6,656	438	189,300
U. of N.C. at Greensboro	Greensboro	1891	7,549	475	750,000
U. of N.C. at Wilmington	Wilmington	1947	2,787	168	110,800
Wake Forest U.	Winston-Salem	1834	4,195	502	510,800
Western Carolina U.	Cullowhee	1889	5,934	300	215,000
NORTH DAKOTA					
North Dakota State U.	Fargo	1890	6,639	342§	271,000
U. of North Dakota	Grand Forks	1883	8,763	460	320,000
OHIO					
Antioch	Yellow Springs	1852	1,330	98	214,000
Bowling Green State U.	Bowling Green	1910	16,049	702	486,400
Case Western Reserve U.	Cleveland	1826	8,843	1,400	1,556,400
Cleveland State U.	Cleveland	1964	16,261	674	427,500
Denison U.	Granville	1831	2,162	157	207,200
John Carroll U.	Cleveland	1886	3,770	219	225,500
Kent State U.	Kent	1910	31,168◊	1,740	1,100,000
Kenyon	Gambier	1824	1,404	110	223,000
Marietta	Marietta	1835	1,795	119	200,000
Miami U.	Oxford	1809	14,293	655	940,100
Oberlin	Oberlin	1833	2,757	187§	860,000
Ohio State U.	Columbus	1870	49,275	3,428◊	2,911,800◊
Ohio U.	Athens	1804	13,572	733	616,800
U. of Akron	Akron	1870	20,504	1,075	600,000
U. of Cincinnati	Cincinnati	1819	33,302	2,782	1,502,000
U. of Dayton	Dayton	1850	7,843	370	385,000
U. of Toledo	Toledo	1872	15,742	670	306,400
Wooster	Wooster	1866	1,850	150	200,000
Wright State U.	Dayton	1967	12,373	590	271,400
Xavier U.	Cincinnati	1831	6,022	285	160,900
Youngstown State U.	Youngstown	1908	13,917	689	339,800
OKLAHOMA					
Central State U.	Edmond	1890	11,953	341	322,400
Oklahoma State U.	Stillwater	1890	19,281	1,475	1,132,000
Oral Roberts U.	Tulsa	1963	2,534	171	128,800
U. of Oklahoma	Norman	1890	22,496	1,075	1,145,800
U. of Tulsa	Tulsa	1894	6,092	345	520,000
OREGON					
Lewis and Clark	Portland	1867	2,333	145	118,200
Oregon State U.	Corvallis	1868	15,915	2,000	875,000
Portland State U.	Portland	1955	13,163	650	402,000
Reed	Portland	1909	1,183	105	238,000
U. of Oregon	Eugene	1872	53,654	826§	1,200,000
PENNSYLVANIA					
Allegheny	Meadville	1815	1,738	144	218,600
♀Bryn Mawr	Bryn Mawr	1885	1,526	177	400,000
Bucknell U.	Lewisburg	1846	3,148	239	360,000
Carnegie-Mellon U.	Pittsburgh	1900	4,510	514	489,500
Dickinson	Carlisle	1773	1,683	110	240,000
Drexel U.	Philadelphia	1891	9,405	598	390,000
Duquesne U.	Pittsburgh	1878	8,002	484	360,000
Edinboro State	Edinboro	1857	7,039	415	298,000
Franklin and Marshall	Lancaster	1787	2,132	140	228,000
Gettysburg	Gettysburg	1832	1,915	169	220,000
Indiana U.	Indiana	1875	10,859	652	450,000
Juniata	Huntingdon	1876	1,173	100	165,000
Lafayette	Easton	1826	2,262	163	300,000
La Salle	Philadelphia	1863	5,522	348	187,400
Lehigh U.	Bethlehem	1865	6,213	417	620,000
Moravian	Bethlehem	1742	1,672	80	119,200
Muhlenberg	Allentown	1848	1,605	123	155,000
Pennsylvania State U.	University Park	1855	39,077	1,739	1,332,500
St. Joseph's	Philadelphia	1851	5,834	155	152,000
Slippery Rock State	Slippery Rock	1889	6,299	374	327,600
Susquehanna U.	Selinsgrove	1858	1,433	126	105,000
Swarthmore	Swarthmore	1864	1,254	146	347,800‖
Temple U.	Philadelphia	1884	31,049	3,000	1,000,000
U. of Pennsylvania	Philadelphia	1740	19,435	4,635	2,500,000
U. of Pittsburgh	Pittsburgh	1787	32,540	2,141§	1,456,600‖
Ursinus	Collegeville	1869	1,799	135	110,000
Villanova U.	Villanova	1842	9,910	474	530,000
West Chester State	West Chester	1812	8,547	511	310,000
PUERTO RICO					
Catholic U.	Ponce	1948	8,101	438	124,000
Inter American U.	San Germán	1912	16,952	774	78,000
U. of Puerto Rico	Río Piedras	1903	26,357	...	879,000
RHODE ISLAND					
Brown U.	Providence	1764	6,758	494	1,484,600
Rhode Island	Providence	1854	8,385	362	170,000
U. of Rhode Island	Kingston	1892	10,585	900	527,800
SOUTH CAROLINA					
¶The Citadel	Charleston	1842	2,964	154	100,000
Clemson U.	Clemson	1889	10,112	689	507,000
Furman U.	Greenville	1826	2,563	139	214,400
U. of South Carolina	Columbia	1801	20,278	712	1,140,000
SOUTH DAKOTA					
South Dakota State U.	Brookings	1881	6,181	504	255,000
U. of South Dakota	Vermillion	1882	5,190	391	361,600
TENNESSEE					
Austin Peay State U.	Clarksville	1929	4,124	175	150,000
East Tennessee State U.	Johnson City	1911	9,285	641	370,000
Fisk U.	Nashville	1867	1,559	110	167,000
Memphis State U.	Memphis	1909	21,445	1,662	700,000
Middle Tennessee State U.	Murfreesboro	1911	9,706	432	264,200
Tennessee State U.	Nashville	1909	4,670	319	221,400
Tennessee Tech. U.	Cookeville	1911	7,062	300	361,000
U. of Tennessee	Knoxville	1794	28,011	1,447	1,191,300
Vanderbilt U.	Nashville	1873	6,923	1,540	1,259,400
TEXAS					
Austin	Sherman	1849	1,164	95	15,800
Baylor U.	Waco	1845	10,938	441	700,000
East Texas State U.	Commerce	1889	8,441	399	430,000
Hardin-Simmons U.	Abilene	1891	1,630	110	139,500
Lamar U.	Beaumont	1923	11,236	403	270,000
North Texas State U.	Denton	1890	15,875	1,084	1,034,700
Pan American U.	Edinburg	1927	7,031	144	75,000
Prairie View A. & M.	Prairie View	1876	4,573	292	90,000
Rice U.	Houston	1891	3,475	408	800,000
Sam Houston State U.	Huntsville	1879	10,144	363	429,200
Southern Methodist U.	Dallas	1911	10,079	861	1,202,500
Southwest Texas State U.	San Marcos	1899	12,894	532	365,000
Stephen F. Austin State U.	Nacogdoches	1923	19,142	450	307,000
Sul Ross State U.	Alpine	1917	2,871	130	173,000
Texas A. & I. U.	Kingsville	1925	6,896	297	325,000
Texas A. & M. U.	College Station	1876	21,245	1,276	858,800
Texas Christian U.	Fort Worth	1873	6,132	468	809,800
Texas Southern U.	Houston	1947	7,367	348	228,600
Texas Tech. U.	Lubbock	1923	21,927	1,339	1,501,000
U. of Houston	Houston	1927	29,389	1,769	794,900
U. of Texas at Arlington	Arlington	1895	14,866	556	533,000
U. of Texas at Austin	Austin	1881	41,841	1,618§	3,518,700
U. of Texas at El Paso	El Paso	1913	11,418	514	400,000
West Texas State U.	Canyon	1910	6,645	264	203,100
UTAH					
Brigham Young U.	Provo	1875	27,567	1,279	1,000,000
U. of Utah	Salt Lake City	1850	21,751	1,222	1,400,000
Utah State U.	Logan	1888	8,049§	403§	400,000
Weber State	Ogden	1889	9,875	432	158,800
VERMONT					
Bennington	Bennington	1925	600	75	63,000
Middlebury	Middlebury	1800	1,941	149	265,000
U. of Vermont	Burlington	1791	10,475	989	498,500
VIRGINIA					
Madison	Harrisonburg	1908	6,841	403	209,400
Old Dominion U.	Norfolk	1930	11,768	527§	253,700
U. of Richmond	Richmond	1830	5,951	213	286,700
U. of Virginia	Charlottesville	1819	14,382	1,393	1,951,000
Virginia Commonwealth U.	Richmond	1838	17,571	2,151	348,900
¶Virginia Military Inst.	Lexington	1839	1,158	135	240,000
Va. Polytech. Inst. & State U.	Blacksburg	1872	18,816	1,000	627,000
¶Washington & Lee U.	Lexington	1749	1,602	157	257,400
William & Mary	Williamsburg	1693	6,727	464	500,000
WASHINGTON					
Central Washington State	Ellensburg	1890	8,677	352	180,000
Eastern Washington State	Cheney	1882	6,200	366	250,000
Gonzaga U.	Spokane	1887	3,185	196	467,000
U. of Washington	Seattle	1861	34,500	2,009	2,012,000
Washington State U.	Pullman	1890	15,613	1,500	1,000,000
Western Washington State	Bellingham	1893	8,601	442	343,000
Whitman	Walla Walla	1859	1,126	81§	173,000
WEST VIRGINIA					
Bethany	Bethany	1840	1,190	85	126,000
Marshall U.	Huntington	1837	9,774	369	240,000
West Virginia U.	Morgantown	1867	19,258	868	721,100
WISCONSIN					
Beloit	Beloit	1846	1,663	135	220,000
Lawrence U.	Appleton	1847	1,420	145	200,000
Marquette U.	Milwaukee	1881	10,987	672	600,000
St. Norbert	De Pere	1898	1,384	108	87,000
U. of W.-Eau Claire	Eau Claire	1916	9,434	427§	254,000
U. of W.-Green Bay	Green Bay	1965	3,943	211	200,000
U. of W.-La Crosse	La Crosse	1908	7,600	402	390,000
U. of W.-Madison	Madison	1849	35,931	5,727	2,600,000
U. of W.-Milwaukee	Milwaukee	1956	25,421	2,350	800,000
U. of W.-Oshkosh	Oshkosh	1871	10,624	448§	443,000
U. of W.-Parkside	Kenosha	1965	5,478	357	260,000
U. of W.-Platteville	Platteville	1866	3,821	290	208,000
U. of W.-River Falls	River Falls	1874	4,213	224	160,000
U. of W.-Stevens Point	Stevens Point	1894	8,042	517	242,000
U. of W.-Stout	Menomonie	1893	5,461	350§	143,000
U. of W.-Superior	Superior	1893	2,579	221	185,000
U. of W.-Whitewater	Whitewater	1868	8,355	437§	260,000
WYOMING					
U. of Wyoming	Laramie	1886	7,949	740	458,000

*Latest data available; coeducational unless otherwise indicated. †Total includes part-time students. ‡Total includes part-time or full-time equivalent faculty. §Total includes full-time equivalent only. ‖1971 federal survey figure; latest information did not permit separation of microforms and maps. ¶Men's school. ♀Women's school. δStudents taught by faculty of Harvard University. ☐Included with Harvard University. ◊Includes main campus and other regional campuses.

Living Conditions

Public assistance

June 1975

State	NUMBER OF RECIPIENTS: Old-age assistance*	Aid to the disabled*	Aid to dependent children†	AVERAGE MONEY PAYMENTS: Old-age assistance*	Aid to the disabled*	Aid to dependent children†
Ala.	102,180	39,683	166,553	...	...	$29.56
Alaska	1,505	1,455	11,494	...	...	94.12
Ariz.	14,219	12,638	71,364	...	...	37.07
Ark.	60,375	25,951	106,329	$ 74.45	$100.03	39.02
Calif.	326,822	293,958	1,399,068	123.52	187.51	76.02
Colo.	20,859	14,434	98,405	...	...	61.58
Conn.	9,328	12,630	128,497	...	...	84.57
Del.	3,498	2,962	32,504	72.04	114.15	52.33
D.C.	5,489	10,194	104,049	86.03	130.65	74.61
Fla.	92,217	54,610	261,597	88.30	114.69	37.33
Ga.	95,553	61,838	363,460	77.57	104.65	32.61
Hawaii	5,345	3,638	49,143	111.16	165.62	93.64
Idaho	4,238	4,510	19,666	...	...	67.95
Ill.	47,906	85,172	809,589	...	...	79.90
Ind.	23,619	18,948	166,425	60.84	94.46	48.99
Iowa	17,580	9,516	90,022	67.58	106.11	87.29
Kan.	12,885	10,252	69,834	65.58	92.09	68.26
Ky.	60,029	35,769	167,583	...	...	55.55
La.	97,569	48,971	236,461	84.07	111.59	33.69
Maine	13,687	10,151	83,561	67.95	118.95	50.70
Md.	18,688	27,609	219,343	75.97	126.22	51.53
Mcss.	82,080	44,045	362,842	131.32	192.08	77.57
Mich.	52,285	61,983	651,420	94.14	143.60	81.37
Minn.	20,108	18,804	126,165	65.01	98.47	85.84
Miss.	83,208	38,542	188,854	75.74	111.17	14.37
Mo.	67,192	31,813	264,723	...	...	38.72
Mont.	3,935	4,108	21,790	62.11	110.35	49.02
Neb.	8,924	7,073	38,675	...	...	56.25
Nev.	3,696	1,705	14,310	91.56	114.80	47.15
N.H.	3,131	2,056	26,948	...	...	75.00
N.J.	40,072	37,725	448,634	88.71	134.48	79.96
N.M.	12,520	12,553	62,071	...	...	42.10
N.Y.	179,102	210,734	1,218,044	104.66	172.95	100.95
N.C.	80,471	60,173	184,516	...	...	53.96
N.D.	5,078	2,960	13,925	...	...	80.62
Ohio	54,994	70,460	570,067	71.46	117.80	54.71
Okla.	53,171	30,089	99,014	...	...	60.35
Ore.	11,124	13,699	105,593	...	...	68.56
Pa.	66,525	72,210	629,100	89.11	136.13	76.39
R.I.	7,323	8,517	53,216	73.69	127.48	73.35
S.C.	46,271	29,157	141,247	71.27	107.30	27.30
S.D.	5,764	2,958	25,086	65.90	98.47	64.28
Tenn.	80,187	53,034	203,759	71.20	108.34	35.00
Texas	192,709	73,556	392,705	...	...	31.75
Utah	3,712	5,347	35,746	71.67	104.65	77.36
Vt.	4,828	4,094	22,368	88.20	141.89	75.53
Va.	42,413	28,322	180,685	...	...	61.96
Wash.	21,371	30,330	145,867	82.11	140.53	75.63
W.Va.	20,735	20,429	73,358	...	...	50.85
Wis.	38,250	25,696	171,078	97.39	143.68	89.73
Wyo.	1,384	1,107	6,912	65.62	104.51	52.39
TOTAL U.S.	2,326,330‡	1,788,323‡	11,133,665	...	...	$65.52§

*Supplemental security income program. †Data for April 1975. ‡Totals include some persons not distributed by state. §Incl. Guam, Puerto Rico, Virgin Is.
Source: U.S. Dept. of Health, Education, and Welfare, *Social Security Bulletin*.

Social insurance beneficiaries and benefits

State	OLD AGE, SURVIVORS, DISABILITY, AND HEALTH INSURANCE — Retired workers: Beneficiaries, monthly, at end of Dec. 1974	Retired workers: Benefits, monthly, at end of Dec. 1974 (in $000)	Disabled workers: Beneficiaries, monthly, at end of Dec. 1974	Disabled workers: Benefits, monthly, at end of Dec. 1974 (in $000)	Medicare enrollment,* July 1, 1973	UNEMPLOYMENT INSURANCE FEDERAL PROGRAMS — Beneficiaries, weekly, May 1975	Benefits, May 1975 (in $000)
Ala.	238,198	$39,252	48,923	$9,441	357,613	62,051	$14,578
Alaska	6,607	1,211	1,168	252	7,531	6,664	2,237
Ariz.	160,866	31,007	22,094	4,726	194,090	43,837	10,832
Ark.	179,782	28,578	35,409	6,627	258,621	45,956	8,946
Calif.	1,476,338	283,286	230,140	49,697	1,933,935	460,065	127,746
Colo.	144,236	26,368	17,458	3,617	202,404	25,331	6,569
Conn.	237,789	49,923	25,053	5,426	306,559	87,940	28,500
Del.	37,487	7,345	5,278	1,107	48,518	12,019	4,152
D.C.	45,747	7,719	7,217	1,298	69,202	13,974	5,163
Fla.	919,022	174,879	99,295	20,485	1,134,378	134,121	28,142
Ga.	285,382	46,753	65,176	12,156	402,389	90,046	22,259
Hawaii	44,410	8,372	5,140	1,071	51,837	13,343	4,008
Idaho	59,230	10,798	7,710	1,581	75,395	10,167	2,382
Ill.	807,610	160,677	90,394	19,443	1,131,180	232,373	62,697
Ind.	387,156	76,016	48,523	10,528	516,129	104,079	25,533
Iowa	251,762	46,936	24,073	4,943	362,432	30,010	7,921
Kan.	193,488	35,831	16,612	3,407	279,873	21,470	5,800
Ky.	240,884	40,133	44,433	8,804	359,822	56,055	13,733
La.	202,927	33,867	47,448	9,319	329,473	61,771	9,998
Maine	96,444	17,140	11,942	2,348	126,391	23,292	5,451
Md.	232,574	44,103	30,186	6,301	319,045	68,056	17,761
Mass.	482,710	94,823	48,909	10,189	653,992	166,960	45,077
Mich.	603,339	123,185	94,627	21,199	800,103	247,502	73,070
Minn.	310,895	56,791	26,891	5,545	431,339	60,792	17,329
Miss.	162,711	24,193	34,704	6,212	243,901	35,058	6,503
Mo.	419,649	76,358	53,390	10,744	585,479	95,258	26,164
Mont.	54,204	10,016	7,312	1,501	72,992	10,135	2,308
Neb.	132,214	24,052	10,595	2,090	190,289	15,165	3,868
Nev.	33,489	6,282	5,454	1,171	38,687	14,223	4,244
N.H.	71,623	13,781	6,685	1,385	87,745	18,590	4,484
N.J.	556,165	114,874	70,018	15,164	732,925	199,712	63,489
N.M.	61,932	10,850	11,196	2,267	84,511	15,596	3,127
N.Y.	1,487,993	305,104	175,720	37,580	2,000,636	411,786	120,263
N.C.	353,345	58,778	67,049	12,434	460,388	122,855	30,796
N.D.	50,702	8,782	4,528	842	71,929	4,861	1,489
Ohio	723,500	141,656	105,600	22,936	1,040,066	211,082	71,332
Okla.	217,995	37,961	32,777	6,477	319,542	31,298	6,111
Ore.	200,253	38,500	26,480	5,625	244,843	53,894	13,092
Pa.	958,215	190,736	126,993	27,240	1,332,840	305,488	92,594
R.I.	87,276	16,904	10,899	2,205	109,649	29,660	10,010
S.C.	161,559	26,741	38,215	7,114	214,650	70,686	18,024
S.D.	58,866	10,167	5,353	1,012	84,174	4,761	1,115
Tenn.	294,522	48,418	56,510	10,701	419,645	92,935	18,435
Texas	745,165	128,251	106,523	21,168	1,086,548	87,613	17,418
Utah	64,751	12,393	7,258	1,556	85,131	16,950	3,955
Vt.	38,677	7,151	4,621	924	52,137	11,015	2,761
Va.	288,683	50,069	49,509	9,681	398,976	69,857	17,155
Wash.	275,953	53,875	34,686	7,464	347,335	81,622	18,010
W.Va.	135,295	24,770	35,185	7,626	208,508	26,426	5,622
Wis.	378,575	73,352	38,907	8,294	500,509	94,635	27,966
Wyo.	24,303	4,479	2,477	500	32,727	2,426	578
TOTAL†	15,958,450	$3,003,589	2,236,882	$460,084	21,814,825	4,280,685	$1,148,090

*Includes persons aged 65 and over, and hospital and/or medical insurance. †Includes data for American Samoa, Guam, Puerto Rico, Virgin Islands and for beneficiaries or enrollees living abroad for all categories except unemployment insurance federal programs, which includes Puerto Rico only. Source: U.S. Department of Health, Education, and Welfare, Social Security Administration, Office of Research and Statistics.

Health personnel and facilities

State	Physicians Dec. 31, 1973	Dentists Dec. 31, 1972	Registered Nurses 1972*	Hospital facilities Sept. 30, 1974: Hospitals	Beds	Nursing homes 1973: Facilities	Beds
Alabama	3,384	1,173	10,235	150	26,534	197	14,844
Alaska	293	125	2,030	26	1,601	8	606
Arizona	3,500	951	12,383	80	10,901	88	6,430
Arkansas	1,950	679	5,033	96	11,577	211	17,952
California	42,438	14,077	103,385	650	123,951	4,145	150,956
Colorado	4,342	1,405	15,515	98	14,812	214	16,670
Connecticut	6,447	2,060	23,612	68	20,263	365	23,294
Delaware	822	255	4,389	14	4,710	36	2,213
District of Columbia	3,210	646	5,545	20	11,512	72	3,147
Florida	13,293	4,189	38,398	228	53,504	360	34,956
Georgia	5,655	1,690	17,423	183	33,385	306	25,936
Hawaii	1,338	534	4,117	30	4,989	142	2,726
Idaho	771	387	3,755	52	3,746	64	4,190
Illinois	16,819	6,259	60,806	293	81,162	1,039	80,151
Indiana	5,774	2,341	21,481	139	36,195	495	34,247
Iowa	3,055	1,477	17,812	147	21,689	678	35,152
Kansas	2,813	1,093	12,655	164	19,028	468	22,889
Kentucky	3,704	1,279	11,734	127	19,942	312	18,177
Louisiana	4,683	1,451	11,524	157	26,820	212	17,004
Maine	1,291	469	7,440	56	7,826	341	9,227
Maryland	8,208	2,039	22,462	81	29,666	204	17,755
Massachusetts	12,905	4,005	56,567	198	52,223	945	53,858
Michigan	12,203	4,741	46,681	255	55,317	577	48,567
Minnesota	6,314	2,686	23,638	192	33,179	589	44,661
Mississippi	1,996	647	6,288	113	17,194	143	7,886
Missouri	6,631	2,389	18,823	168	36,737	502	33,644
Montana	779	393	4,429	66	4,406	105	4,759
Nebraska	1,915	967	9,798	105	11,209	251	17,396
Nevada	643	271	2,564	24	3,118	41	1,482
New Hampshire	1,180	384	7,044	35	6,275	130	5,873
New Jersey	11,629	4,488	51,061	145	49,908	549	34,430
New Mexico	1,342	383	4,077	55	6,428	66	3,345
New York	44,555	14,735	125,794	415	168,471	1,083	92,888
North Carolina	6,370	1,791	21,366	160	34,375	838	22,145
North Dakota	614	281	3,653	61	5,908	107	6,631
Ohio	14,958	5,210	57,052	244	74,359	1,163	65,134
Oklahoma	2,814	1,063	8,698	147	17,436	417	29,512
Oregon	3,550	1,524	11,382	88	11,959	312	18,306
Pennsylvania	18,951	6,656	96,414	321	101,614	768	65,963
Rhode Island	1,680	484	6,638	21	7,830	159	6,493
South Carolina	2,774	808	10,187	89	19,412	123	8,131
South Dakota	550	293	3,852	63	6,054	160	7,795
Tennessee	5,257	1,813	12,051	157	32,376	244	14,827
Texas	14,717	4,864	40,372	577	79,282	967	80,510
Utah	1,726	701	4,531	40	4,844	120	4,556
Vermont	922	231	4,521	21	4,050	101	3,902
Virginia	6,520	2,057	23,935	128	35,724	348	16,732
Washington	5,527	2,361	21,953	127	16,750	382	31,147
West Virginia	2,019	675	7,314	87	16,214	137	4,753
Wisconsin	5,879	2,602	23,318	182	33,486	516	51,960
Wyoming	360	169	1,922	31	2,733	34	1,896
TOTAL U.S.	357,839†	123,349‡	1,127,657	7,174	1,512,684	21,834	1,327,704

*Preliminary. †Including 26,769 federally employed physicians who are not distributed by state. ‡Including 9,098 federally employed dentists who are not distributed by state.
Sources: American Medical Association, *Distribution of Physicians in the U.S., 1973;* American Hospital Association, *Hospital Statistics,* 1975 Edition; American Dental Association; American Nurses' Association; U.S. Department of Health, Education, and Welfare, Public Health Service.

Crime rates per 100,000 population

State or metropolitan area	VIOLENT CRIME Total 1970	Total 1974	Murder 1970	Murder 1974	Rape 1970	Rape 1974	Robbery 1970	Robbery 1974	Assault 1970	Assault 1974	PROPERTY CRIME Total 1970	Total 1974	Burglary 1970	Burglary 1974	Larceny 1970	Larceny 1974	Auto theft 1970	Auto theft 1974
Alabama*	295.7	372.9	11.7	15.0	18.5	22.7	50.3	99.6	215.2	235.6	1,569.7	2,627.2	763.1	1,057.9	583.2	1,308.7	223.5	260.6
Alaska	278.0	453.1	12.2	13.6	26.1	**49.3**	71.8	88.4	167.8	301.8	2,412.5	4,786.6	789.9	1,166.8	1,071.2	2,972.1	551.3	647.8
Arizona	370.3	566.7	9.5	9.6	27.0	37.5	120.2	204.2	213.7	315.5	3,074.9	**7,654.9**	1,493.0	**2,534.0**	1,080.7	**4,518.6**	501.2	602.3
Arkansas*	222.3	316.2	10.1	11.2	17.1	23.9	45.6	80.7	149.5	200.5	1,381.4	2,984.4	685.1	1,075.2	587.4	1,745.3	109.0	163.9
California	474.8	610.6	6.9	9.5	35.1	40.6	206.9	252.7	225.9	307.8	**3,832.1**	6,236.2	**1,753.0**	2,072.0	**1,389.9**	3,525.5	689.2	638.8
Colorado	356.7	429.8	6.2	6.0	**36.0**	36.5	129.1	165.7	185.4	221.6	3,305.5	5,736.0	1,380.9	1,843.1	1,336.1	3,354.2	588.4	538.6
Connecticut	170.4	228.1	3.5	3.3	9.1	11.2	70.4	92.3	87.4	121.4	2,404.5	4,178.8	1,084.2	1,353.9	836.1	2,275.0	484.2	549.9
Delaware	256.0	443.1	6.9	10.3	16.8	17.3	102.0	127.9	130.3	287.6	2,460.1	5,506.5	979.0	1,517.8	936.5	3,459.9	544.6	528.8
Florida	498.2	677.6	12.7	14.7	22.2	36.0	186.1	275.2	277.2	351.8	3,101.5	6,709.7	1,561.8	2,287.3	1,143.1	3,939.5	396.6	482.9
Georgia	304.5	442.2	**15.3**	**17.8**	16.1	27.1	95.8	176.5	177.3	220.8	1,902.2	3,470.2	899.9	1,462.4	693.7	1,660.8	308.6	347.1
Hawaii	121.8	208.0	3.6	8.3	11.8	26.1	63.3	121.6	43.1	52.1	3,274.4	5,863.6	1,456.1	1,784.8	1,237.2	3,492.8	581.1	586.1
Idaho	123.3	183.4	4.6	5.6	12.3	16.0	20.5	37.9	85.8	123.8	1,661.8	3,899.2	673.6	1,001.8	844.0	2,683.5	144.2	214.0
Illinois	467.9	627.1	9.6	11.8	20.4	27.7	251.1	313.4	186.8	274.2	1,879.2	4,557.1	765.4	1,264.2	596.0	2,761.5	517.8	531.4
Indiana*	225.5	293.3	4.8	8.0	17.9	23.5	107.5	134.4	95.3	127.3	2,045.0	4,043.6	860.0	1,254.6	756.1	2,396.0	428.9	393.0
Iowa	79.3	121.0	1.9	1.9	6.2	10.1	28.5	48.7	42.8	60.4	1,356.0	3,292.6	507.3	791.5	673.7	2,282.1	175.0	219.1
Kansas	202.8	276.3	4.8	6.9	14.5	19.7	75.1	107.8	108.5	141.9	1,941.0	4,024.1	881.7	1,268.6	802.7	2,516.9	256.6	238.6
Kentucky	222.3	234.0	11.1	10.3	13.7	17.6	72.8	92.3	124.7	113.7	1,702.2	2,525.7	703.9	830.1	651.9	1,466.8	346.3	228.8
Louisiana	413.5	472.7	11.7	16.0	23.1	25.2	140.8	156.3	237.8	275.1	1,991.2	3,343.7	890.0	1,045.7	716.4	1,956.2	384.7	341.7
Maine*	82.8	137.5	1.5	2.9	7.0	8.7	12.6	27.9	61.7	98.1	1,058.8	3,462.7	562.4	1,318.9	350.3	1,946.0	146.1	197.7
Maryland	624.9	719.1	9.2	11.7	23.9	29.8	338.6	360.6	253.3	316.9	2,722.1	4,931.0	1,051.2	1,402.9	1,123.3	2,944.8	547.6	583.3
Massachusetts	202.9	338.7	3.5	4.4	12.0	15.6	99.5	212.4	87.9	156.3	2,801.1	4,994.2	1,134.1	1,549.8	788.9	2,078.8	**878.1**	**1,365.6**
Michigan	562.8	659.4	8.9	13.0	22.9	37.1	348.4	337.2	182.6	272.0	3,096.3	5,860.2	1,493.5	1,903.9	1,143.8	3,331.6	459.0	624.7
Minnesota	152.0	207.3	2.0	3.0	9.7	17.7	89.1	104.1	51.2	82.5	1,951.4	3,723.7	801.7	1,121.8	804.0	2,228.2	345.7	373.7
Mississippi	179.3	334.9	11.5	12.9	8.9	17.4	19.0	48.0	139.8	256.5	684.1	1,914.3	351.2	755.7	254.6	1,034.5	78.4	124.1
Missouri	405.9	452.4	10.7	9.8	27.4	26.9	200.8	216.7	167.0	199.0	2,359.1	4,335.6	1,137.0	1,471.3	684.2	2,437.3	537.8	427.1
Montana	111.5	162.4	3.2	4.2	10.5	12.2	22.3	35.6	75.5	110.3	1,525.3	3,921.4	593.7	887.9	709.8	2,750.5	221.8	283.0
Nebraska	184.1	239.6	3.0	3.6	9.3	18.9	57.3	91.0	114.5	126.2	1,333.1	3,104.7	504.5	773.8	536.7	2,053.5	291.9	277.5
Nevada	398.6	682.4	8.8	14.8	19.6	45.2	188.4	277.8	181.7	344.5	3,597.6	7,144.7	1,660.6	2,452.5	1,276.3	4,086.0	660.7	606.1
New Hampshire	56.0	91.5	2.0	3.5	6.0	8.4	12.1	25.9	35.9	53.7	1,136.7	3,052.5	565.6	820.4	399.1	1,973.0	172.0	259.0
New Jersey	287.1	403.4	5.7	6.8	12.9	19.7	169.4	216.6	99.0	160.3	2,457.1	4,368.3	1,041.4	1,429.4	858.2	2,392.2	557.4	546.7
New Mexico*	292.8	450.4	9.4	11.3	21.7	34.8	66.1	124.6	195.7	279.6	2,572.6	4,762.6	1,141.5	1,583.1	1,039.1	2,873.4	392.0	306.1
New York	**676.0**	**791.6**	7.9	10.6	15.5	28.4	**443.3**	**476.3**	209.3	276.3	3,246.0	4,065.5	1,414.2	1,443.6	1,149.6	2,054.4	682.2	567.5
North Carolina	362.5	488.9	11.1	11.7	12.6	15.5	49.2	92.3	**289.6**	**369.4**	1,498.9	3,022.3	708.6	1,186.9	639.7	1,647.1	150.6	188.3
North Dakota	34.2	50.1	0.5	1.4	6.2	7.8	6.5	12.9	21.0	27.9	812.0	2,110.0	286.4	433.0	434.6	1,544.7	91.0	132.3
Ohio	284.3	364.1	6.6	8.9	16.0	23.9	145.9	191.2	115.9	140.2	2,092.4	3,859.3	853.9	1,171.8	745.8	2,285.1	492.8	402.4
Oklahoma	197.8	280.1	5.9	8.1	15.6	25.0	53.8	83.5	122.4	163.5	1,753.2	3,815.9	793.3	1,455.2	684.4	1,999.0	275.4	361.7
Oregon	256.9	367.4	4.6	5.6	18.0	32.3	102.5	130.8	131.7	198.7	2,730.4	5,977.3	1,273.4	1,843.2	1,124.1	3,665.5	332.8	468.7
Pennsylvania*	212.2	315.0	5.3	6.7	11.3	17.8	106.0	159.5	89.6	131.0	1,329.1	2,738.5	594.3	927.8	394.7	1,435.0	340.1	375.7
Rhode Island	204.7	282.9	3.2	3.8	3.6	7.4	78.3	91.0	119.6	180.7	2,721.1	4,831.1	1,018.9	1,296.1	843.2	2,612.0	859.0	923.1
South Carolina	285.2	455.7	14.6	16.2	17.1	26.2	60.0	127.4	193.4	285.9	1,781.6	3,709.5	905.8	1,562.4	629.3	1,864.7	246.5	282.4
South Dakota	92.5	180.9	3.8	2.1	11.1	10.7	17.1	20.4	60.5	147.8	1,059.7	2,489.9	471.3	597.1	494.7	1,735.3	93.7	157.5
Tennessee	274.9	386.8	8.8	13.4	15.5	25.7	82.0	157.2	168.6	190.4	1,613.4	3,272.4	806.7	1,350.1	517.4	1,575.6	289.3	346.7
Texas	361.5	386.0	11.6	13.7	21.0	29.2	134.1	161.2	194.8	182.0	2,344.3	4,309.1	1,151.3	1,531.6	798.7	2,405.8	394.3	371.7
Utah	137.7	214.6	3.4	3.2	10.9	22.3	53.1	75.8	70.3	113.4	2,235.0	4,735.6	915.0	1,132.9	1,003.8	3,272.9	316.3	329.8
Vermont	74.0	75.1	1.3	3.4	10.3	12.3	7.6	13.8	54.6	45.5	1,195.1	2,799.6	730.6	1,019.4	340.7	1,606.6	123.9	173.6
Virginia	259.0	309.0	8.4	8.6	15.4	23.3	92.0	122.8	143.2	154.3	1,890.2	3,505.7	805.6	1,005.0	787.2	2,234.7	297.4	266.0
Washington	221.3	346.3	3.5	5.1	18.0	29.0	93.5	115.5	106.3	196.6	2,935.2	5,662.8	1,444.5	1,772.5	1,129.0	3,484.8	361.8	405.5
West Virginia	123.7	137.4	6.2	6.0	6.7	10.0	27.3	35.2	83.5	86.1	835.0	1,632.0	388.5	551.8	354.0	953.3	92.4	126.9
Wisconsin	85.8	140.4	2.0	3.0	6.7	11.3	33.1	66.3	44.0	59.9	1,428.6	3,500.7	538.5	836.9	672.5	2,417.8	217.6	246.1
Wyoming	113.1	144.6	5.7	5.0	12.3	15.3	22.0	42.6	73.1	81.6	1,632.0	3,505.8	645.9	827.3	821.6	2,464.1	164.6	214.5
Baltimore	**1,008.3**	1,026.1	13.2	16.8	34.9	35.7	564.4	543.0	**395.9**	430.5	3,361.5	5,555.1	1,351.4	1,653.8	1,309.1	3,194.6	701.0	706.7
Boston	250.3	475.5	4.4	5.6	14.8	18.5	136.2	282.5	95.0	168.9	2,847.7	5,088.2	1,053.9	1,470.8	809.9	1,978.4	983.9	**1,639.0**
Chicago	633.6	793.9	12.9	15.9	25.4	34.8	362.5	431.2	232.7	312.1	2,155.1	5,171.9	829.6	1,352.7	617.2	3,117.7	708.4	701.5
Cleveland	453.2	606.7	14.5	17.2	18.7	27.8	287.9	361.8	132.1	199.9	2,629.5	4,080.2	826.1	1,108.0	595.2	2,053.9	**1,208.1**	918.3
Detroit	916.8	949.0	14.7	**20.2**	31.1	45.7	648.5	576.4	222.5	306.6	4,232.1	6,434.0	1,986.3	2,010.2	1,488.2	3,396.0	757.6	1,027.8
Houston	562.4	517.3	**16.9**	18.7	27.1	31.6	335.3	352.0	183.2	115.0	3,030.3	4,745.0	1,532.1	1,917.7	757.6	2,165.4	740.6	661.9
Los Angeles	737.5	890.4	9.4	12.9	**50.0**	**54.5**	307.3	376.3	370.8	**446.6**	4,326.4	6,101.8	1,980.5	**2,249.8**	1,401.3	2,953.6	944.6	898.4
Minneapolis	286.5	348.7	2.6	4.2	16.8	28.4	178.6	184.3	88.6	131.9	2,959.2	4,970.0	1,198.4	1,511.7	1,146.1	2,872.8	614.7	585.5
Newark	545.1	585.3	9.5	9.6	20.5	24.2	333.1	341.5	182.1	210.1	2,934.8	4,560.3	1,315.4	1,495.8	952.6	2,403.0	666.8	661.5
New York	980.7	**1,307.5**	10.5	16.3	19.9	42.8	**664.8**	**811.8**	285.6	436.6	4,239.3	4,764.6	1,821.0	1,820.7	1,471.2	2,121.5	947.1	822.4
Philadelphia	321.1	517.8	9.3	11.9	15.2	28.1	173.3	281.7	123.4	196.2	1,758.1	3,661.2	754.0	1,211.1	470.0	1,829.9	534.1	620.2
Pittsburgh	271.6	313.3	4.4	5.3	14.0	17.8	145.1	162.8	108.1	127.3	1,758.5	2,621.6	695.5	891.1	526.1	1,258.8	537.0	471.6
St. Louis	531.4	673.3	14.8	13.9	34.4	35.0	279.5	337.3	202.7	290.1	3,034.6	5,746.3	1,458.2	1,952.5	736.2	3,113.3	840.2	680.5
San Francisco	625.1	688.1	8.3	11.6	42.9	42.2	347.7	337.1	226.1	297.2	**4,704.2**	**6,789.3**	**2,163.7**	2,145.9	**1,583.4**	**3,946.3**	957.0	697.2
Washington, D.C.	769.9	687.2	11.4	13.4	23.0	41.0	503.5	409.1	232.0	223.7	3,340.7	5,253.0	1,432.5	1,403.2	1,141.4	3,303.0	766.8	546.8

Boldface: highest rate among states or listed metropolitan areas. *1974 figures may not be comparable to 1970. Source: U.S. Dept. of Justice, FBI, *Uniform Crime Reports*.

Transport, Communication, and Trade

Transportation

State	Road and street mi.* 1974	Motor vehicles† in 000s, 1974 Total	Auto-mobiles	Trucks and buses	Railroad mileage 1975	Airports 1975	Pipeline mileage 1974
Ala.	85,845	2,410	1,854	556	4,543	126	1,532
Alaska	9,043	188	125	63	20	766	79
Ariz.	51,415	1,474	1,082	392	2,034	196	1,334
Ark.	78,088	1,246	848	398	3,559	161	1,432
Calif.	169,564	13,684	11,162	2,522	7,317	769	1,723
Colo.	83,586	1,862	1,395	468	3,457	228	2,008
Conn.	18,734	1,991	1,829	163	656	91	93
Del.	5,150	344	285	59	291	32	3
D.C.	1,099	263	246	16	30	14	1
Fla.	98,129	5,616	4,705	911	4,107	341	41
Ga.	100,335	3,244	2,534	709	5,408	236	1,874
Hawaii	3,666	485	421	65	—	47	—
Idaho	55,910	633	405	229	2,633	174	633
Ill.	130,494	6,195	5,277	918	10,572	829	9,219
Ind.	91,111	3,269	2,542	726	6,374	232	2,850
Iowa	112,944	2,034	1,506	528	7,587	248	3,872
Kan.	134,770	1,785	1,252	533	7,616	314	12,815
Ky.	69,791	2,164	1,626	538	3,516	81	419
La.	54,124	2,135	1,616	519	3,683	286	8,067
Maine	21,499	637	498	139	1,665	158	354
Md.	26,859	2,346	2,000	346	1,091	123	219
Mass.	29,811	3,042	2,726	316	1,405	131	128
Mich.	118,310	5,401	4,536	865	5,963	403	3,165
Minn.	128,235	2,532	1,942	590	7,366	295	2,741
Miss.	66,686	1,341	965	376	3,644	141	3,296
Mo.	114,966	2,825	2,142	683	6,062	346	6,282
Mont.	77,932	585	363	222	4,898	168	2,614
Neb.	98,017	1,145	807	337	5,415	297	2,901
Nev.	49,659	456	338	118	1,573	111	86
N.H.	15,024	490	404	86	752	56	108
N.J.	32,422	4,168	3,753	416	1,687	222	519
N.M.	70,307	763	532	231	2,057	134	5,932
N.Y.	107,776	7,481	6,663	818	5,310	478	1,301
N.C.	87,922	3,570	2,773	797	4,115	236	900
N.D.	106,247	527	321	206	5,070	196	1,352
Ohio	109,965	6,965	6,098	868	7,727	543	5,047
Okla.	108,509	2,041	1,395	645	4,944	273	13,031
Ore.	101,397	1,580	1,282	298	3,043	273	772
Pa.	114,497	7,117	6,167	950	8,020	579	4,950
R.I.	5,540	579	510	69	139	17	17
S.C.	60,295	1,671	1,334	337	3,034	117	669
S.D.	82,720	507	331	176	3,351	124	563
Tenn.	80,656	2,568	1,988	580	3,184	128	707
Texas	251,489	8,053	6,007	2,046	13,306	1,192	52,193
Utah	47,653	810	589	221	1,726	93	1,009
Vt.	13,924	285	230	55	716	59	177
Va.	62,351	3,172	2,656	516	3,875	227	824
Wash.	81,202	2,444	1,826	618	4,767	296	392
W.Va.	36,323	935	692	243	3,494	54	2,916
Wis.	104,290	2,578	2,132	446	5,808	292	939
Wyo.	40,602	307	188	119	1,779	86	6,592
TOTAL	3,806,883	129,943	104,898	25,045	200,389	13,019	170,691

*Includes federally controlled rural roads. †Registrations, excluding military. Detail may not add to totals because of rounding.
Sources: Interstate Commerce Commission; Department of Transportation, Federal Aviation Administration; Federal Highway Administration.

Communications facilities

State	Post Offices July 1, 1975	TELEPHONES January 1, 1975: Total	TELEPHONES: Residential	COMMERCIAL BROADCAST STATIONS, 1973: Radio AM	Radio FM	TV	Public TV stations 1971	NEWSPAPERS Daily: Number Feb. 1, 1975	Daily: Circulation Sept. 30, 1974	Weekly April 1, 1975*: Number	Weekly: Circulation	Sunday: Number Feb. 1, 1975	Sunday: Circulation Sept. 30, 1974
Alabama	635	1,965,000	1,494,600	136	56	16	8	24	736,950	111	469,826	17	662,360
Alaska	193	167,000	95,200	17	3	7	—	7	82,807	11	19,312	2	29,900
Arizona	212	1,372,400	978,000	59	18	11	2	15	523,271	58	397,029	4	425,168
Arkansas	645	1,139,800	855,800	85	44	8	1	33	443,814	126	337,781	14	437,807
California	1,126	15,755,300	11,237,300	231	161	50	9	121	5,754,889	446	5,917,905	40	4,913,607
Colorado	409	1,746,700	1,221,800	66	30	11	1	21	772,534	125	365,294	9	805,542
Connecticut	249	2,332,600	1,719,400	38	21	5	3	28	932,831	54	404,334	8	667,013
Delaware	56	447,600	326,800	10	5	—	—	3	160,326	13	124,492	1	28,336
District of Columbia	1	984,600	488,000	6	7	6	1	2	900,713	...	...	2	1,050,492
Florida	464	6,017,000	4,385,300	195	97	26	9	51	2,237,616	137	710,795	34	2,178,221
Georgia	646	3,225,300	2,378,900	172	71	16	10	39	1,065,792	165	579,899	13	976,310
Hawaii	76	545,000	343,300	24	4	10	2	5	238,065	3	101,611	2	200,691
Idaho	265	488,600	356,700	43	7	6	1	15	189,471	58	129,185	5	146,578
Illinois	1,273	8,294,200	6,063,600	122	110	23	5	91	3,512,993	581	2,886,189	20	2,632,630
Indiana	758	3,476,800	2,658,500	86	79	17	4	72	1,679,116	201	666,745	18	1,159,801
Iowa	954	1,912,700	1,462,800	73	43	13	1	42	950,031	347	732,143	9	803,661
Kansas	694	1,554,000	1,167,200	58	31	12	2	51	671,041	242	495,578	14	456,901
Kentucky	1,267	1,832,100	1,382,000	108	67	12	13	26	782,077	138	571,244	12	599,057
Louisiana	535	2,170,300	1,633,800	92	48	16	1	26	831,618	95	419,950	13	718,669
Maine	497	619,100	473,600	36	15	7	4	9	269,992	40	159,873	1	110,323
Maryland	427	2,937,400	2,160,500	53	35	7	1	12	751,129	69	650,574	4	699,083
Massachusetts	435	3,969,900	2,785,500	64	40	11	2	46	2,120,033	144	1,123,069	8	1,509,609
Michigan	863	6,064,800	4,577,200	126	87	21	4	55	2,526,919	265	1,477,969	14	2,269,359
Minnesota	858	2,708,900	2,024,100	87	45	12	4	34	1,126,791	325	887,104	11	1,033,511
Mississippi	470	1,166,600	895,400	101	42	10	1	23	376,499	96	159,074	10	279,677
Missouri	968	3,207,500	2,381,000	109	50	24	2	56	1,727,110	259	855,884	18	1,438,038
Montana	377	450,200	326,100	41	10	11	—	11	192,873	72	138,243	7	186,825
Nebraska	553	1,082,800	813,300	48	17	14	9	19	497,592	204	457,914	4	364,569
Nevada	92	477,900	308,700	21	11	7	1	8	167,717	16	39,543	4	153,135
New Hampshire	243	537,600	408,100	27	14	3	5	9	168,652	31	187,750	2	64,960
New Jersey	520	5,542,000	4,100,500	36	27	4	—	31	1,747,557	204	1,584,419	11	1,320,271
New Mexico	330	637,400	436,600	58	19	7	1	20	239,134	25	138,914	12	207,212
New York	1,634	12,902,300	8,971,300	160	100	28	9	77	7,179,356	407	2,419,519	24	6,703,825
North Carolina	780	3,144,700	2,384,000	202	75	18	6	53	1,340,144	134	534,884	22	1,028,229
North Dakota	453	409,500	305,400	27	10	12	1	11	177,281	89	197,533	4	100,611
Ohio	1,083	7,125,700	5,364,900	119	113	26	8	97	3,582,714	267	1,747,123	23	2,473,789
Oklahoma	635	1,820,300	1,331,700	66	37	10	3	53	863,715	202	362,245	42	844,378
Oregon	352	1,494,300	1,084,300	77	21	13	2	22	677,334	95	520,889	5	544,674
Pennsylvania	1,794	8,508,900	6,433,800	170	119	24	9	105	3,906,765	228	1,473,657	12	2,925,144
Rhode Island	56	611,800	454,000	15	7	2	1	7	313,366	14	91,255	2	216,065
South Carolina	392	1,593,800	1,191,100	102	43	11	5	18	575,746	75	271,294	7	458,450
South Dakota	413	416,800	323,300	30	10	10	4	13	182,675	151	220,535	4	127,614
Tennessee	576	2,530,900	1,907,600	150	68	17	5	35	1,147,110	119	467,658	15	990,660
Texas	1,520	8,000,600	5,774,100	287	134	55	5	114	3,329,745	516	1,313,542	86	3,405,841
Utah	220	786,700	573,200	32	10	3	3	5	247,911	54	179,818	4	246,141
Vermont	288	288,600	206,300	18	6	2	4	10	123,830	15	38,543	1	6,523
Virginia	908	3,120,100	2,277,600	127	62	12	5	34	1,047,859	104	558,341	14	775,108
Washington	473	2,384,100	1,739,500	97	42	15	6	23	1,066,718	136	1,122,692	14	1,020,166
West Virginia	1,030	893,400	679,400	60	27	9	2	30	478,815	80	252,944	10	379,377
Wisconsin	781	2,857,900	2,103,400	99	79	18	3	36	1,233,854	236	754,575	6	846,114
Wyoming	169	252,000	178,400	29	1	3	—	9	83,092	29	75,720	3	56,701
TOTAL U.S.	30,649	143,971,500	105,222,900	4,295	2,278	691	189	1,768	61,877,197	7,612	35,892,409	641	51,678,726

*Excluding District of Columbia. Sources: U.S. Postal Service; Federal Communications Commission; American Telephone and Telegraph Co.; The Editor & Publisher Co., Inc., *International Year Book, 1975* (Copyright 1975. All rights reserved. Used by permission); American Newspaper Representatives, Inc.; U.S. Department of Health, Education, and Welfare, National Center for Educational Statistics, *Broadcast and Production Statistics of Public Television Licensees: Fiscal Year 1971.*

Major trading partners, by value

in millions of dollars

Country	EXPORTS 1970	EXPORTS 1974	IMPORTS 1970	IMPORTS 1974
North America	12,367	27,886	13,970	31,728
Canada	9,079	19,932*	11,092	22,282
Mexico	1,704	4,855	1,218	3,386
South America	3,244	7,858	2,958	8,974
Argentina	441	597	172	381
Brazil	840	3,089	670	1,705
Chile	300	452	157	310
Colombia	395	659	269	517
Peru	214	647	340	609
Venezuela	759	1,768	1,082	4,679
Europe	14,817	30,071	11,395	24,636
Belgium and Luxembourg	1,195	2,285	696	1,681
France	1,483	2,942	942	2,305
Germany, West	2,741	4,986	3,127	6,428
Italy	1,353	2,752	1,316	2,593
Netherlands, The	1,651	3,979	528	1,453
Spain	712	1,899	353	899
Sweden	543	542	399	876
Switzerland	700	1,150	459	900
United Kingdom	2,536	4,574	2,194	4,021
U.S.S.R.	119	609	72	350
Asia	10,105	26,239	9,644	27,570
Hong Kong	406	882	944	1,637
India	574	760	298	561
Indonesia	266	531	182	1,688
Iran	326	1,734	67	2,132
Israel	592	1,206	150	282
Japan	4,652	10,679	5,875	12,455
Korea, South	643	1,546	370	1,460
Malaysia	67	377	270	773
Philippines	373	747	472	1,091
Saudi Arabia	141	835	20	1,671
Singapore	240	988	81	553
Taiwan	527	1,427	549	2,108
Oceania	1,189	2,697	871	1,503
Australia	986	2,157	611	1,042
Africa	1,502	3,204	1,090	6,547
Algeria	62	315	10	1,091
Nigeria	129	286	71	3,286
South Africa†	563	1,160	290	609
Total	43,224	98,506	39,952	100,972

*Excludes grains and oilseeds transshipped through Canada to unidentified overseas countries. †Includes South West Africa. Source: U.S. Dept. of Commerce, Domestic and International Business Administration, *Overseas Business Reports.*

Major commodities traded, 1974

in millions of dollars

Item	Total*	Canada	American Republics	Western Europe	Far East†
TOTAL EXPORTS	98,506	19,932‡	14,504	28,639	19,875
Agricultural commodities					
Grains and preparations	10,331	164	1,362	2,393	3,482
Soybeans	3,537	100	111	2,064	866
Cotton, including linters, wastes	1,364	63	9	202	810
Nonagricultural commodities					
Ores and scrap metals	1,475	156	158	527	602
Coal, coke, and briquettes	2,487	379	121	644	1,334
Chemicals	8,822	1,213	2,245	2,665	1,702
Machinery	24,252	5,420	3,899	7,275	3,920
Agricultural machines, tractors, parts	2,028	747	384	387	186
Electrical apparatus	7,019	1,333	1,208	2,135	1,511
Transport equipment§	12,718	5,520	1,737	2,322	1,278
Civilian aircraft and parts	4,665	387	587	1,723	982
Paper manufactures	1,522	299	324	466	151
Metal manufactures	1,665	575	272	354	165
Iron and steel mill products‖	2,500	713	745	315	264
Yarn, fabrics, and clothing	1,604	293	340	502	200
Other exports	26,229	5,037	3,181	8,910	5,101
TOTAL IMPORTS	100,972	22,282	13,678	23,745	22,719
Agricultural commodities					
Meat and preparations	1,344	67	309	317	11
Fish, including shellfish	1,499	262	348	229	407
Coffee	1,504	—	962	4	67
Sugar	2,256	¶	1,316	¶	574
Nonagricultural commodities					
Ores and scrap metal	1,838	716	570	96	82
Petroleum, crude	16,482	3,370	2,333	105	1,225
Petroleum products	7,728	419	2,353	971	190
Chemicals	3,991	760	220	2,007	567
Machinery	12,083	2,214	972	4,266	4,512
Transport equipment	12,630	5,444	142	3,596	3,419
Automobiles, new	7,544	3,090	8	2,758	1,687
Iron and steel mill products	5,013	385	112	2,253	2,168
Nonferrous metals	3,042	1,032	563	592	525
Textiles other than clothing	1,629	43	180	518	793
Other Imports	29,933	7,570	3,298	8,791	8,179

*Includes areas not shown separately. †Includes Japan, East and South Asia. ‡Excludes grains and oilseeds valued at $552 million transshipped through Canada to unidentified overseas countries. §Excludes parts for tractors. ‖Excludes pig iron. ¶Less than $500,000. Source: U.S. Dept. of Commerce, Domestic and International Business Administration, *Overseas Business Reports.*

Upper Volta

A republic of West Africa, Upper Volta is bordered by Mali, Niger, Dahomey (Benin), Togo, Ghana, and Ivory Coast. Area: 105,869 sq.mi. (274,200 sq.km.). Pop. (1975 est.): 6,032,000. Cap. and largest city: Ouagadougou (pop., 1970 est., 110,000). Language: French (official). Religion: animist; Muslim and Christian minorities. President and premier in 1975, Gen. Sangoulé Lamizana.

Political life was overshadowed by the frontier conflict that broke out late in 1974 between Upper Volta and Mali. After 13 years of informal discussions, Mali's leaders openly talked of annexing a disputed zone 100 mi. along the frontier and situated in Volta territory. The zone appeared to be no more than seasonal grazing land for the nomadic Tuareg, but it was believed to contain mineral resources.

Sporadic fighting between patrols broke out on several occasions, notably in January and again in June. From July onward the conflict, which was never settled, lost its edge. This development was welcome to the Volta government, which was struggling with a series of difficulties resulting from the Sahel region's persistent drought. (*See* MALI.) In November the president announced formation of a new political party, the Movement for National Renewal. Parties had been banned since early 1974.

The country's largest sugar-beet factory came into use early in 1975. President Lamizana inaugurated the first railroad car to be built in the country, by the African Industrial Manufacturing Co. Cotton sales reached 30,562 metric tons in 1974–75, compared with 20,668 in 1973–74. (PHILIPPE DECRAENE)

[978.E.4.a.i]

UPPER VOLTA

Education. (1971–72) Primary, pupils 112,047, teachers 2,376; secondary, pupils 9,238, teachers 469; vocational, pupils 2,056, teachers (1970–71) 139; teacher training, students 819, teachers 44; higher, students 213, teaching staff 45.

Finance. Monetary unit: CFA franc, with (Sept. 22, 1975) a parity of CFA Fr. 50 to the French franc (free rate of CFA Fr. 227.70 = U.S. $1; CFA Fr. 471.75 = £1 sterling). Budget (1973 est.) balanced at CFA Fr. 11,726,000,000.

Uruguay

A republic of South America, Uruguay is on the Atlantic Ocean and is bounded by Brazil and Argentina. Area: 68,536 sq.mi. (177,508 sq.km.). Pop. (1975 census): 2,764,000, including (1961) white 89%; mestizo 10%. Cap. and largest city: Montevideo (pop., 1975 est., 1,229,700). Language: Spanish. Religion: mainly Roman Catholic. President in 1975, Juan María Bordaberry.

In 1975 the government continued to keep a tight grip on the country. Public opposition was not tolerated; censorship was strict; and there were arrests of workers and students. But the Army was not all-powerful or united, as was illustrated by disputes within President Bordaberry's coalition government.

In foreign affairs the government pursued a policy of strengthening overseas relations, in particular through trade and economic cooperation agreements signed with neighbours that helped Uruguay to diversify its export markets, provide development finance, and attempt to establish a role as a transshipment point for landlocked Paraguay and Bolivia. Other areas of growing contact included South Africa, the Arab countries, and Eastern Europe.

Internally, the government sought to liberalize the economy, reduce the role of government, contain inflation, and restructure the economy to allow export-based growth. In the long term Uruguay's resource base suggested a bright economic future, especially if oil exploration was successful, but unless there was a considerable upturn in world meat prices in 1976, tougher measures would be required to meet current economic problems. (JOHN HALE)

[974.F.2]

URUGUAY

Education. (1973) Primary, pupils 366,756, teachers 13,436; secondary (public only), pupils 137,406, teachers 8,154; vocational (public only), pupils 35,856, teachers 2,910; teacher training (public only), students 8,347, teachers 341; higher, students 6,462, teaching staff 2,201.

Finance. Monetary unit: new peso (introduced November 1975; equal to 1,000 old pesos), with (Nov. 3, 1975) an official rate of 2.52 new pesos to U.S. $1 (2.04 new pesos = £1 sterling). Gold, SDRs, and foreign exchange: (May 1975) U.S. $180 million; (May 1974) U.S. $208 million. Budget (1974 actual): revenue 587.9 billion pesos; expenditure 786.9 billion pesos. Gross domestic product: (1973) 2,495,400,000,000 pesos; (1972) 1,235,000,000,000 pesos. Cost of living (Montevideo; 1970 = 100): (March 1975) 1,221; (March 1974) 634.

Foreign Trade. (1974) Imports U.S. $486.7 million; exports U.S. $382.2 million. Import sources (1973): Argentina 21%; Brazil 16%; U.S. 9%; Nigeria 7%; West Germany 7%; Kuwait 6%; U.K. 5%. Export destinations (1973): West Germany 14%; Spain 12%; Italy 8%; The Netherlands 7%; France 7%; U.K. 6%; Brazil 5%. Main exports: meat 38%; wool 23%; hides and skins 6%.

Agriculture. Production (in 000; metric tons; 1974; 1973 in parentheses): wheat *c.* 500 (297); oats *c.* 72 (55); corn 225 (229); rice (1973) 137, (1972) 128; potatoes (1973) 133, (1972) 106; sweet potatoes (1973) *c.* 73, (1972) 66; sorghum 193 (225); linseed 26 (29); sunflower seed 48 (71); sugar, raw value (1973) 74, (1972) 72; oranges *c.* 56 (*c.* 63); wine (1973) *c.* 92, (1972) *c.* 90; wool 31 (33); beef and veal (1973) *c.* 320, (1972) *c.* 291. Livestock (in 000; May 1974): sheep 15,373; pigs *c.* 430; cattle 10,790; horses *c.* 410; chickens (1973) *c.* 7,000.

Industry. Production (in 000; metric tons; 1973): cement 526; crude steel 12; petroleum products 1,756; electricity (excluding most industrial production; kw-hr.) 2,430,000.

Uranium:
see Mining and Quarrying

Urban Mass Transit:
see Transportation

U.S.S.R.:
see Union of Soviet Socialist Republics

Utilities, Public:
see Energy; Industrial Review; Transportation

Vatican City State

This independent sovereignty is surrounded by but is not part of Rome. As a state with territorial limits, it is properly distinguished from the Holy See, which constitutes the worldwide administrative and legislative body for the Roman Catholic Church. The area of Vatican City is 108.7 ac. (44 ha.). Pop. (1975 est.): 1,000. As sovereign pontiff, Paul VI is the chief of state. Vatican City is administered by a pontifical commission of five cardinals, of which the secretary of state, Jean Cardinal Villot, is president.

Although Holy Year was at the centre of Pope Paul's activities in 1975, there was no slackening of endeavour by the Holy See in the field of international relations. In February a protocol was added to the 1940 concordat with Portugal; it recognized the

KEYSTONE

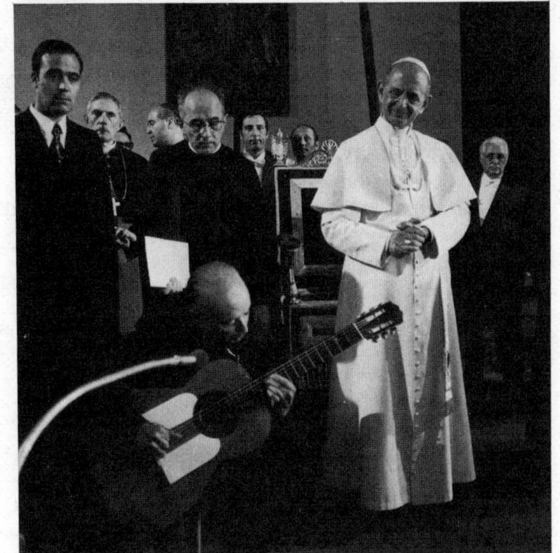

Pope Paul VI being entertained by Gypsies who traveled to Rome for the Holy Year.

civil authority's power to grant divorces to couples previously married in church. Later, in October, Portuguese Pres. Francisco da Costa Gomes visited the pope and expressed Portugal's desire to maintain good relations with the Holy See.

Some displeasure was occasioned in West Germany during the year by the Vatican's nomination of its new nuncio there as representing the Holy See "in the German Federal Republic" and not, as formerly, "in Germany"; this change in nomenclature was considered an acceptance of the division of Germany. In September the pope appealed unavailingly to Gen. Francisco Franco not to proceed with the executions in Spain of Basque terrorists; Spain's ambassador to the Holy See was recalled to Madrid, but the papal nuncio, on vacation in Italy at the time, returned to Madrid and the tension subsided.

The pope received the prime minister of Libya in April. U.S. Pres. Gerald Ford came in June and discussed Vatican support for détente in a dangerous world, particularly in the Middle East, and the securing of the future of the Holy Places in Jerusalem. A notable visitor in September was Pres. Idi Amin of Uganda, whose hostility toward Catholic missionaries in his country seemed to be ended after his talk with the pope. A high point of Holy Year in Rome was the canonization on September 14 of Elizabeth Ann Bayley Seton, the first saint born in the United States. (MAX BERGERRE)

See also Religion.

Venezuela

A republic of northern South America, Venezuela is bounded by Colombia, Brazil, Guyana, and the Caribbean Sea. Area: 352,144 sq.mi. (912,050 sq.km.). Pop. (1975 est.): 11,993,000, including mestizo 69%; white 20%; Negro 9%; Indian 2%. Cap. and largest city: Caracas (metro. area pop., 1975 est., 2,487,000). Language: Spanish. Religion: predominantly Roman Catholic. President in 1975, Carlos Andrés Pérez.

The major political preoccupations of 1975 were the nationalization of the iron industry, which took place on January 1, and passage of the Oil Nationalization Law, signed by President Pérez on August 29, to take effect on Jan. 1, 1976. A new holding company, Petróleos de Venezuela (Petrovén), would supervise and control the operations of petroleum companies, which would retain their structures, management, and personnel until changes were considered advisable. The 15 oil companies were offered $1,160,000,000 in compensation, and 22 companies conducting exploration service contracts for the government were to receive $1 billion. It was expected that the government would shortly sign two-year oil-supply contracts, renewable for two years, with the international oil companies, as well as agreements for the supply of technology for petroleum development. After nationalization, investments of more than $5.8 billion would be made over five years. Plans included bringing into production the world's largest known oil reserve, the Orinoco tar belt, with reserves of 3,000,000,000 bbl. ($1.2 billion), as well as conservation and refinery developments.

Conservationist policies and falling world demand for petroleum seem likely to produce a substantial drop in oil revenues in 1976. Based on oil production of 2.2 million bbl. a day, a 20% cut in the 1976 budget took place, and the Venezuelan Investment Fund was warned that it would not receive any additional funds under these estimates unless oil revenues or taxes rose. Government expenditure and revenue during the first half of the year totaled 23 billion bolivares and 22.4 billion bolivares, respectively; 17.6 billion bolivares of revenue came from petroleum.

The major increases in budget allocations for 1976 went to education, health, and agriculture. The government's list of priority projects included steel, aluminum, railroads, electricity, and shipbuilding, in

VENEZUELA

Education. (1971–72) Primary, pupils 1,918,655, teachers 54,387; secondary and vocational, pupils 564,167, teachers 15,665; teacher training (1970–71), students 17,429, teachers 1,199; higher, students 99,745, teaching staff 9,105.

Finance. Monetary unit: bolívar, with (Sept. 22, 1975) an official rate of 4.28 bolivares to U.S. $1 (free rate of 9.27 bolivares = £1 sterling). Gold, SDRs, and foreign exchange: (June 1975) U.S. $7,731,000,000; (June 1974) U.S. $4,474,000,000. Budget (1974 est.): revenue 41,902,000,000 bolivares; expenditure 41,272,000,000 bolivares. Gross national product: (1973) 69,640,000,000 bolivares; (1972) 58,860,000,000 bolivares. Money supply: (March 1975) 17,217,000,000 bolivares; (March 1974) 12,465,000,000 bolivares. Cost of living (Caracas; 1970 = 100): (June 1975) 132; (June 1974) 116.

Foreign Trade. (1974) Imports 17,996,000,000 bolivares; exports 46,144,000,000 bolivares. Import sources (1973): U.S. 42%; West Germany 13%; Japan 8%. Export destinations (1973): U.S. *c.* 57%; Canada *c.* 17%. Main exports: crude oil 64%; petroleum products 32%.

Agriculture. Production (in 000; metric tons; 1974; 1973 in parentheses): corn *c.* 450 (402); rice *c.* 300 (272); potatoes (1973) 108, (1972) 109; cassava (1973) 315, (1972) 318; sesame (1973) 74, (1972) 59; sugar, raw value *c.* 554 (510); cocoa *c.* 21 (19); bananas *c.* 1,000 (902); oranges *c.* 220 (217); coffee *c.* 60 (66); tobacco *c.* 15 (13); cotton, lint *c.* 28 (*c.* 21); beef and veal (1973) *c.* 210, (1972) *c.* 200. Livestock (in 000; 1973–74): cattle *c.* 8,962; pigs *c.* 1,767; sheep 100; goats (1972–73) 1,413; horses (1972–73) 445; asses *c.* 520; poultry (1972–73) 22,795.

Industry. Production (in 000; metric tons; 1974): crude oil 155,615; natural gas (cu.m.) 11,630,000; petroleum products (1972) 57,991; iron ore (64% metal content) 25,995; cement (1972) 2,765; gold (troy oz.; 1973) 19; diamonds (metric carats; 1973) 778; electricity (kw-hr.; 1973) 16,392,000.

which it would invest over $10 billion by 1979. The balance of payments remained strong, despite a further surge of 35% in imports in the first half of the year, and international reserves rose to $8,686,000,000 by September from $6,529,000,000 at the end of 1974. Exports increased 27% in value in 1974 (as compared with 47% in 1973), while imports grew by 44% in value. To bolster the government's policy of trying to make the economy more self-sustaining and less dependent on oil, the agricultural sector received over $600 million for development programs in 1975. This was to be doubled in 1976, and support of bank loans, staple prices, and purchases of agricultural equipment intensified. Despite an expected 10% agricultural growth in 1975, the food deficit remained a problem.

In October Venezuela sponsored, with Mexico, the establishment of a Latin-American economic system to integrate Latin-American diplomatic and economic relations with the rest of the world. Loans and oil aid were made available to the Central American countries, as well as to Peru and Bolivia. Agreements for bauxite supplies were signed with Jamaica and Guyana and for tourist developments with some of the smaller islands of the Caribbean. Agreement on the allocation of petrochemicals and motor vehicle production was announced by the Andean Group. The number of local automobile assemblers in Venezuela was to be drastically reduced from 14 to 4 producers, and the vehicles would have to include at least locally produced engines and transmissions. The decision on petrochemicals appeared to allow a free-for-all among the group in the production of basic products (reserved to state companies in Venezuela). The only exclusive assignments to Venezuela were for TDI and methanol.

Inflation had become serious both in terms of consumer prices and for the government's huge development plans. The rate of inflation had risen from an average of 2.5% in 1968–72 to 11% in 1973 and then to 17.2% from August 1974 to July 1975. During the last period the price of imports rose 23% and that of domestic goods and services by 15.9%, but in July the price of domestic goods began to rise faster than that of imports. (MICHAEL WOOLLER)

[974.C.1]

Veterinary Science

Concern over the supply and allocation of veterinary medical manpower had prompted studies in several countries, including a 1972 study by the National Academy of Sciences (NAS) in the U.S. and the Swann Report in Great Britain in 1975. In North America the current shortage was expected to continue for many years. Explorations concerning the feasibility of building new veterinary colleges were under way in several states, and active development of facilities and faculties was in progress in others, including Florida, Mississippi, Tennessee, and Virginia. Even so, the American Veterinary Medical Association (AVMA) estimated that the shortage of professional veterinarians in the U.S. might be as high as 8,000 by 1980. Veterinary medical manpower also was in short supply in the less developed countries. Africa, for example, had 10% of the world's total animal units and less than 2% of the veterinarians.

It was hoped that the shortage could be alleviated by the establishment of more schools to train paraprofessionals, commonly referred to as lay assistants and animal technicians.

Veterinarians removed a neck muscle from this horse with chronic gastritis to relieve its pain.

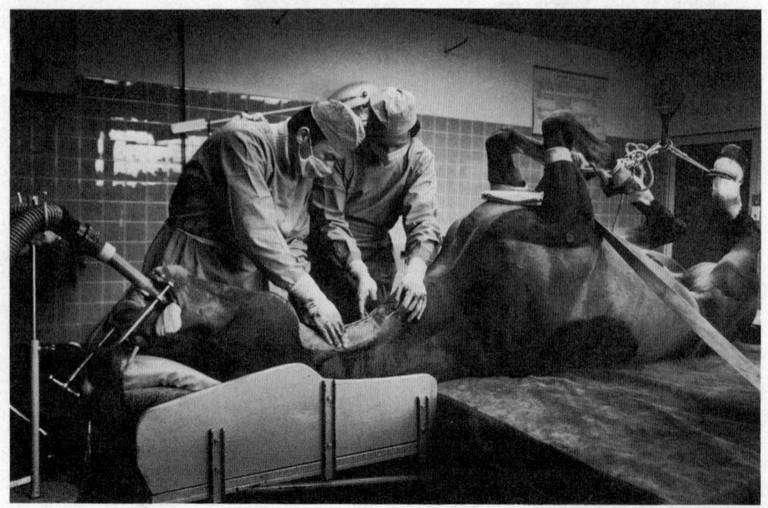

DIAMANT FOTO

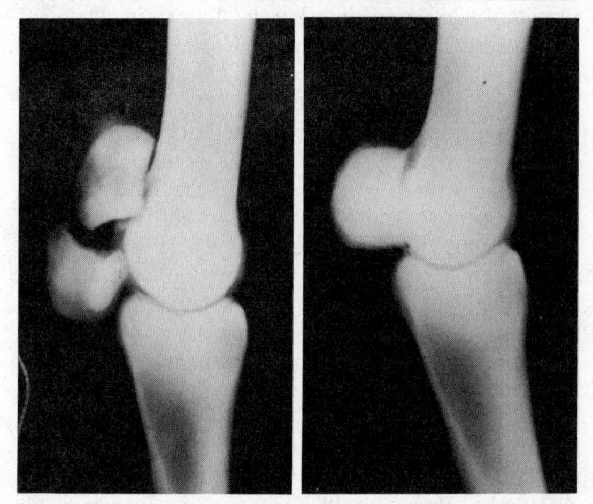

The damage to Ruffian's sesamoid bone (left), compared with a normal limb (right), was too extensive for repair. The filly was destroyed one day after the match race against Foolish Pleasure at Belmont.

WIDE WORLD

Leukemia of cats, a viral disease that is usually fatal, is considered one of the most serious diseases affecting small domestic animals. A test for identifying infected cats was developed, but there was some doubt about the consistency of results obtained in different diagnostic laboratories. Consequently, recommendations that infected cats be destroyed even though there were no overt signs of disease had not been widely accepted. Highly promising vaccines were under development in Scotland and in the U.S., but were not yet available commercially.

Brucellosis, a bacterial infection that causes abortions and whelping failures in dogs, had been reported in several countries, and the organism had been known to cause illness in humans. Until 1975 a dependable diagnosis could be obtained in relatively few specialized laboratories. During the year kits for a reliable and accurate rapid plate agglutination test, developed by the Cornell Research Laboratory for Diseases of Dogs, became available commercially.

Attempts to eradicate brucellosis from cattle were meeting with limited success. In England and Wales there was some progress, with two-thirds of the dairy herds accredited as free from the disease. Progress in the U.S. lagged, and a number of counties in several parts of the country lost their brucellosis-free certification. The slowdown was attributed to deemphasis and reduced funding.

Signs of equine infectious anemia (EIA) are not readily apparent in all affected horses, and as a result the disease can be spread unwittingly. Spread of the disease is further facilitated by rapid air transport of horses for breeding and racing. Some countries had begun to test horses, usually by the agar gel immunodiffusion (Coggins) test, to determine freedom from EIA before importation was permitted. In 1975 EIA was diagnosed for the first time in the U.K., at a stud in Newmarket in August.

Rabies continued to threaten even those countries that had made strenuous efforts to free themselves from the disease through strict quarantine measures (the U.K.) or widespread use of vaccination (the U.S. and Canada). Continental Europe was plagued during the year by epizootics among wild foxes.

Acupuncture, an ancient Chinese treatment for a wide variety of disorders in man, came under study as a treatment for animals. Some encouraging results were obtained with dogs and horses in selected cases, but the value of the method in veterinary medicine generally remained unclear. (ARTHUR FREEMAN)

[353.C]

Vietnam

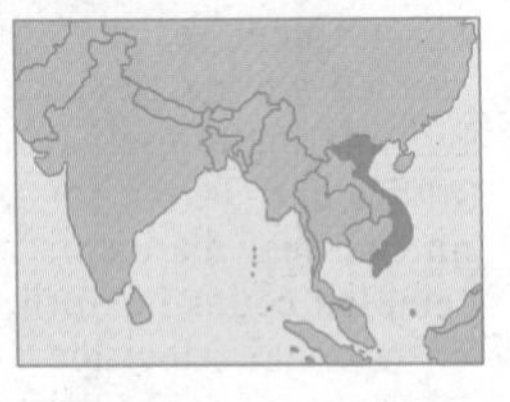

A country comprising the easternmost part of the Indochinese Peninsula, Vietnam was divided de facto into two republics in 1954.

Republic of Vietnam (South Vietnam). This is bordered by North Vietnam (along the 17th parallel), the South China Sea, Cambodia, and Laos. Area: 67,293 sq.mi. (174,289 sq.km.). Pop. (1974 est.): 19,582,100. Cap. and largest city: Saigon (metro. area pop., 1973 est., 3,805,900). Language: Vietnamese. Religion: Buddhist; pagan; Confucian; Christian. Presidents in 1975, Nguyen Van Thieu to April 21, Tran Van Huong to April 28, Duong Van Minh to April 30; premiers, Tran Thien Khiem to April 4, Nguyen Ba Can to April 23, Vu Van Mau from April 28 to April 30. Prior to April 30 the Provisional Revolutionary Government claimed legitimacy as one of two administrations. After April 30 the country was administered by an interim government including North Vietnamese and PRG elements.

On April 30, 1975, Pres. Duong Van Minh surrendered Saigon to the Communist forces surrounding it, thus ending almost 30 years of warfare. About two hours after Minh's announcement, the flag of the Provisional Revolutionary Government was raised over the U.S.-built presidential palace in Saigon. It was a surprising finale to one of the most controversial wars in modern history. In just four months the numerically superior South Vietnamese Army, well supplied with American arms, and the U.S.-backed government of South Vietnam had collapsed.

South Vietnam began the year in crisis. The economy continued to be weak, with inflation growing at an annual rate of 60 to 75% and with roughly one worker in five unemployed. An anticorruption campaign, aimed at the government in general and at President Thieu in particular, continued despite increasingly harsh attempts by the authorities to suppress it. Military morale was depressingly low. Desertions numbered over 20,000 men a month or nearly a quarter of the entire army each year.

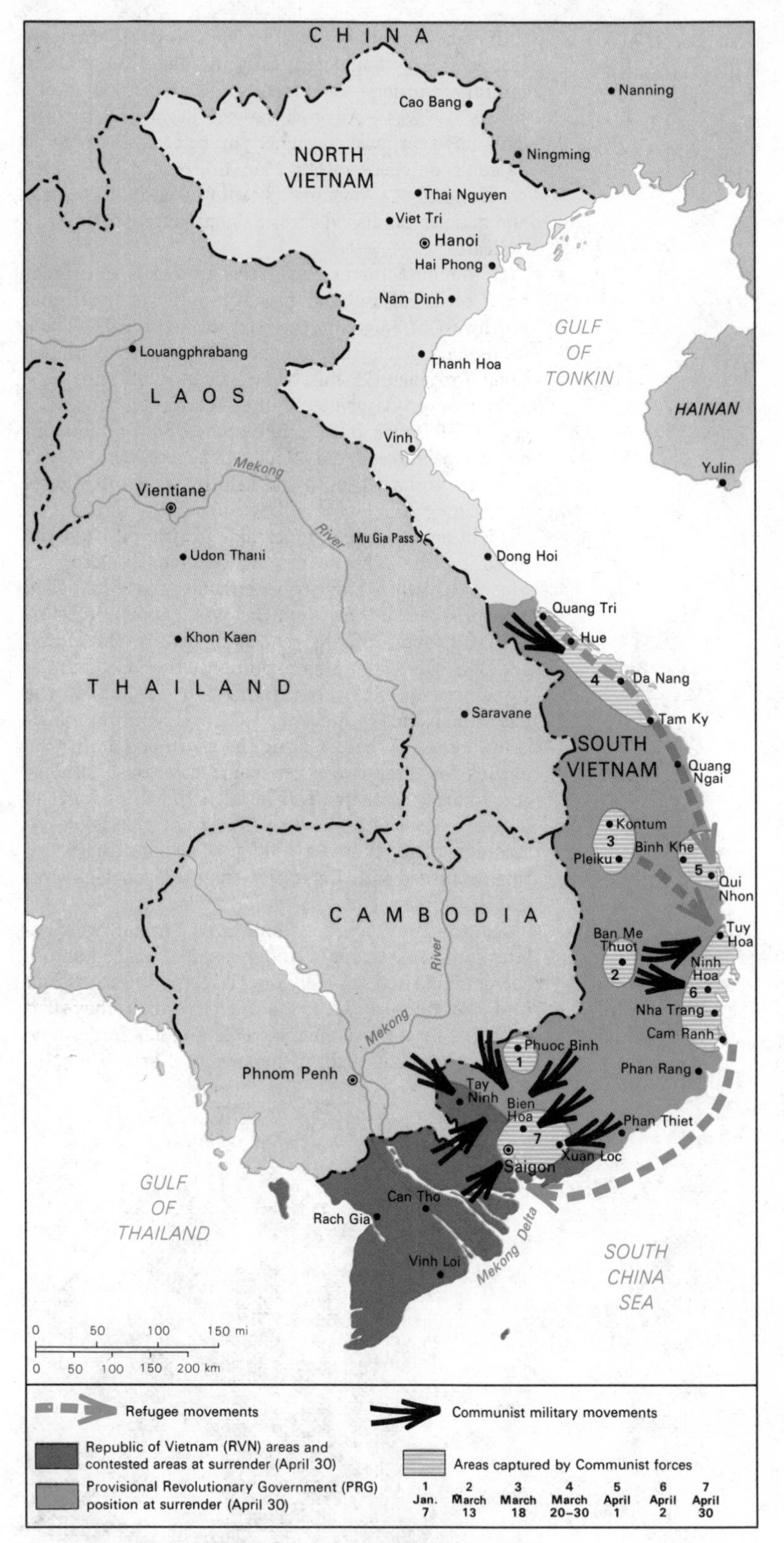

Meanwhile, U.S. economic and military aid was trimmed, and the Saigon government was hard put to provide the health and social programs once financed by the U.S. and to maintain its giant army at the same time. As the year began, the U.S. Congress indicated it was opposed to any supplemental aid for South Vietnam in fiscal 1975, and it eventually turned down a presidential request for an additional $300 million.

Increased military pressure from North Vietnamese troops—who shouldered most of the Communists' military burden—and from indigenous Viet Cong forces also was evident as the year began. Their strategy, however, was designed to test weak spots in Saigon's defenses rather than to force a "decisive" confrontation, as documents captured early in the year and articles published after Saigon's surrender clearly indicated.

Communist forces began this testing with attacks on a series of isolated military outposts north and northwest of Saigon in the final weeks of 1974. Then, in January 1975, they mounted an assault on Phuoc Long Province, 75 mi. N of Saigon. On January 7, after a seven-day siege of the picturesque provincial capital of Phuoc Binh, outnumbered South Vietnamese troops surrendered. Phuoc Long became the first province to be captured and held by the Communists in the long war.

Fighting continued to escalate, with perhaps the most important battle coming two months later, on March 10, when a major Communist force launched a surprise 3 A.M. attack on Ban Me Thuot, capital of Darlac Province in the central highlands. On March 13, Ban Me Thuot was captured. Other Communist forces, meanwhile, were preparing for assaults on the major highlands capitals of Pleiku and Kontum. President Thieu—perhaps fearing the enormous drain that battles for these two cities would have on his thinly spread army, perhaps realizing that the cities were no longer defensible—made a unilateral decision to abandon them. It was a sudden order, and the hasty retreat turned into a panicky stampede on highways leading to the secure coastal lowlands.

Kontum and Pleiku fell on March 18, and two days later North Vietnamese troops in force pushed across the demilitarized zone dividing the two Vietnams and into the ruins of Quang Tri city, which they had captured for a short time in 1972. Saigon's forces now began a headlong flight in advance of North Vietnamese troops and tanks rolling toward the old imperial capital of Hue, which fell on March 25. Perhaps as many as half a million persons began to flee southward by road, on ships, and in overloaded planes and helicopters, many of which crashed. The South Vietnamese Army in the north had degenerated into undisciplined bands of desperate men who used their weapons and uniforms to challenge the civilian population for passage to sanctuary. (*See* REFUGEES: *Special Report*.)

Demonstrators topple a monument to the South Vietnamese fighting man in May, after the fall of Saigon.

JACQUES PAVLOVSKY—SYGMA

With the fall of Hue, North Vietnam's military leaders quickly concluded that victory was within their grasp. In an article published after the surrender, two of Hanoi's top generals, Vo Nguyen Giap and Van Tien Dung, said it was at this point that they decided "to launch a historic campaign of decisive significance." Committing 21 of their 24 divisions to the conflict, they continued their push in the north while stepping up fighting around Saigon. On March 30, in a mass of confusion and lawlessness, Da Nang, the country's second largest city, was captured. By April 18 the Communists controlled three-fourths of the land area in South Vietnam and were engaged in an assault on Xuan Loc, a provincial capital northeast of Saigon that was considered the key to the defense of the capital.

With the military situation now critical, there were mounting calls for the resignation of President Thieu. His Cabinet resigned after the fall of Hue, and few seemed willing to serve in a new one. Thieu reacted by isolating himself from most of his aides, taking no advice and asking for none. He ordered a crackdown on political dissidents and thwarted at least two attempted coups in April. Finally, on April 21, he went on national television and radio to deliver an embittered attack against the U.S., which he said had failed to live up to its promises to defend South Vietnam. At the end of the speech, he announced he was resigning. Five days later he went into exile on Taiwan.

Vice-Pres. Tran Van Huong, a feeble, aging politician, was unable to form a government that could negotiate with the advancing Communists, and after seven days he resigned in favour of a neutralist, retired Gen. Duong Van ("Big") Minh. In a last-ditch effort at appeasement, Minh ordered all Americans out of the country. Even as he did so, the Communists had captured almost all military bases within 15 mi. of Saigon and were shelling and bombing the city's Tan Son Nhut Airport.

As Minh prepared to surrender Saigon, Americans were fleeing in an 11th-hour helicopter evacuation from the roof of the U.S. embassy. Meanwhile, U.S. and Vietnamese ships off the coast became havens for over 100,000 refugees who fled in the final days and hours of the U.S.-backed regime. In all, the U.S. became a new home for about 140,000 South Vietnamese. Most of them fled in fear of a Communist bloodbath. However, no signs of retribution were seen in the months following the takeover.

North Vietnamese troops occupied Saigon on April 30; the capital was given the honorific name Ho Chi Minh City. Top billing in the new administration was given to Pham Hung, identified in North Vietnamese publications as "chief of the southern branch of the Lao Dong [Vietnamese Workers] Party." While appearing to run things in Saigon, Hung, a southerner by birth, remained the fourth-ranking member of North Vietnam's governing council. Ranking second in the new Saigon government was a North Vietnamese Army general, Tran Van Tra, identified as head of the Saigon Military Management Committee, which made most of the decisions during the postwar period. Huynh Tan Phat, head of the PRG since 1969, emerged as the number three man and the individual most in the public eye. The fourth-ranking leader was Nguyen Huu Tho, who headed the National Liberation Front and was chairman of the PRG's advisory council.

The end of the war brought massive problems to South Vietnam's new leadership. The faltering economy they inherited was now under additional pressure from those newly unemployed, including the million-man army of the former regime. There were critical shortages of foreign exchange and gold, much of which had been stolen in the final days of the war. There were also at least two million new refugees, fully 10% of the population. The cities were jammed, food was in demand, severe shortages of petroleum developed, and the price of a gallon of gasoline rose to $8.

Virtually all industry was nationalized by the new government. Banks were initially closed and then nationalized, a move designed to restrict the supply of money in circulation, to control inflation, and to give the Communists full control over all future economic activity. When the banks did reopen, depositors were allowed to withdraw only about $12 a month. Because of the radically different economies of South and North Vietnam, there was no immediate move to standardize the currency, although mail and telephone services between the two countries were resumed for the first time in 21 years. Travel, with prior government approval, was also allowed for the first time since the division of Vietnam in 1954.

The Communist government signaled it was interested in resuming oil exploration off the South China Sea coast. It indicated it might be willing to negotiate with Western companies that, shortly before Thieu's resignation, had found undersea reserves of both oil and natural gas. A South Vietnamese representative to the International Monetary Fund's annual meeting in Washington in September also said his country was "open to having relations with the United States," but the U.S. showed no interest. The U.S. used its Security Council veto to block South Vietnam's admission to the UN.

One unexpected problem facing the new government was continuing military activity. For months after the capture of Saigon, scattered battles were reported almost daily, mostly in the Mekong Delta and the central highlands. Analysts said the fighting was coming from remnants of the defeated army cut off after the collapse of Saigon. "There is no long term political significance to the resistance," said one analyst. "The combat will peter out in time."

One solution to the urban problems facing South Vietnam was to get people to return to the countryside. The Thieu government had failed miserably at this task but, with the end of hostilities, the Communists were relatively successful. In their first months in power they succeeded in persuading hundreds of thousands of people to move back to farms. Some early estimates put the figure at about 535,000, and others ran as high as one million. Those who did move were given title to their land, seeds, and tools, and had their transportation paid. No specific plans to collectivize farming were announced immediately, though some experts believed such a move would come in the next few years.

While leaders in both Vietnams continually referred to the reunification of the two countries, most experts had thought such a move was years away. Late in December, however, it was announced that the reunification process was well under way and probably would be completed by April 30, 1976, the first anniversary of the fall of Saigon. Resolutions on reunification were approved by a three-day People's Representative Assembly held in Saigon and by the North Vietnamese National Assembly. There would be one constitution, and elections for a joint assembly were scheduled for early April.

Democratic Republic of Vietnam (North Vietnam). North Vietnam is bordered by China, the Gulf of Tonkin, the South China Sea, South Vietnam, and Laos. Area: 63,360 sq.mi. (164,103 sq.km.). Pop. (1974 census): 23,767,300. Cap. and largest city: Hanoi (pop., 1974, 1,378,300). Language: Vietnamese. Religion: Buddhist; pagan; Confucian; Christian. Secretary of the Vietnam Workers (Communist) Party in 1975, Le Duan; president, Ton Duc Thang, premier, Pham Van Dong.

In September, on the 30th anniversary of North Vietnam's declaration of independence, Premier Pham Van Dong hailed "the glorious spring victory." The end of the war in South Vietnam dominated not only the independence celebration but life in North Vietnam for most of the year.

Ironically, the unexpected conclusion to what Hanoi viewed as a 30-year revolution and war of independence resulted in a setback to North Vietnam's economic development plans. While some progress was made, the diversion of resources to the final military offensive and to the reconstruction of South Vietnam had a definite effect on the North Vietnamese economy.

Industrial output rose an estimated 15% but fell short of the year's target, largely because of the manpower drain necessitated by the hurried military buildup and the shifting to the South of some resources—primarily petroleum products and capital—

ANNE DOCKERY—CAMERA PRESS/PHOTO TRENDS

A woman views the flooded rice fields near Nam Dinh, North Vietnam, which must be planted, tended, and harvested if the population is to survive.

for the war and for the postwar period. North Vietnam was also forced to send large numbers of technicians, economists, and industrial managers to the South to help with the recovery. Nevertheless, Hanoi met its goal in the area of electrical power production, a particular target of U.S. bombers. Output was restored to the prebombing (but still low) level of about 35 kw-hr. per capita.

An above-average spring rice harvest (accounting for about a third of the country's yearly rice crop) was quickly offset by both civilian and military needs in South Vietnam. The spring crop was reported to be about 1.7 million metric tons of paddy rice, and it was hoped that the end-of-the-year harvest would provide another 4 million to 4.5 million tons.

By autumn there was no sign of any major military demobilization by North Vietnam, although most analysts believed that demobilization would permit more rapid economic and industrial recovery in the North. The conclusion of the war apparently would not end years of hard living for the largely rural peasant population. A July editorial in the official Communist newspaper in Hanoi cautioned: "We should not entertain the ideas that a plentiful, happy life immediately will come to us when peace is restored." The same editorial criticized rigid bureaucracy and inefficiency. It indicated that a new five-year development plan was being prepared.

Perhaps to help bolster its foreign exchange reserves, Hanoi invited arms dealers from around the world to bid on what may have been over $1 billion worth of U.S. military equipment and ammunition captured in South Vietnam. The sale, held in North Vietnam, was seen by diplomatic observers as another indication that Hanoi was running things in the South despite South Vietnam's separate diplomatic status.

With the Communist victory in the South and Communist takeovers in neighboring Cambodia and Laos, North Vietnam emerged as an important Southeast Asian power. Its position in the Southeast Asian power balance remained unclear, however. Its admission as a full member of the UN was blocked when the U.S. vetoed such a move in the Security Council. However, North Vietnam was recognized by the world's nonaligned nations. (LARRY GREEN)

See also Defense; Southeast Asian Affairs: *Special Report.*

[976.B.4.a–d]

Virgin Islands:
see Dependent States

Vital Statistics:
see Demography

Volleyball:
see Court Games

Wages and Hours:
see Economy, World; Industrial Relations

Wales:
see United Kingdom

Warsaw Treaty Organization:
see Defense

Water Resources:
see Earth Sciences; Environment

Water Sports

Motorboating. Unlimited hydroplanes enjoyed a highly successful season in the U.S., with an estimated 1.3 million spectators watching drivers and owners compete for $350,000 in prize money. Dave Heerensperger's "Pay N' Pak" won its third consecutive world championship when George Henley, who replaced starting skipper Jim McCormick, roared to victory in five of the last six races on the thunderboat circuit. The boat, with its Ron Jones hull and Rolls-Royce engines, thereby became the all-time champion with wins in 16 races (not heats) in three years; it also equaled a record by taking its third straight national crown. Billy Schumacher, who skippered the "Weisfield's" to second place, won the drivers' championship with 8,213 points. Milner Irvin, pilot of third-place finisher "Lincoln Thrift," was runner-up driver with 8,103 points, a remarkable total for a man in only his second year of thunderboat competition. Henley finished third with 7,550 points.

In international outboard racing, Dutch veteran Cees Van der Velden won the Class ON championships at Cardiff, Wales, despite a near-sinking in one of the four heats. He used a Johnson V-6, one of the new breed of 200-hp commercial outboards. Johnson outboards also thundered to victory in the world OF and OE championships. An Evinrude outboard won the OI title and a Mercury the OZ.

In world offshore powerboat racing, Wally Franz of Brazil won the international title on the Union of International Motorboating circuit. Franz began the season with wins at Mar del Plata, Arg., Punta del Este, Uruguay, and Rio de Janeiro. Though Franz did not win the Bacardi-Griffith Race in Miami, Bob Nordskog, the actual winner, was not racing for world championship points. Franz and Carlo Bonomi of Italy (who started late in the season but won four races in Europe) thus faced each other for the title in the crucial Miami–Nassau race in October. The victory, however, went to Rocky Aoki, who won the event on his very first attempt and thereby became a likely contender for the world crown in 1976. Franz missed a checkpoint, circled back to avoid disqualification, and finished fourth in a 38-ft. Bertram powered with Kiekhaefer Aeromarine engines. Bonomi finished last after blowing an engine. The U.S. offshore championship was won by Sandy Satullo using a 40-ft. Corsa and a 36-ft. Cigarette, both MerCruiser-powered.

(JAMES E. MARTENHOFF)

Canoeing. Popular interest in river running has increased dramatically in recent years. Though no exact figures are available, the number of canoeists in the U.S. alone probably exceeds five million. Attracted by the lure of solitude found only in the wilderness and by the sheer beauty of pristine nature, they have become enthusiasts after experiencing the exhilaration that attends a canoe ride on open water far from "civilization." Additional thousands have taken their first raft ride and look forward to other trips. Fortunately, rivers and streams are gradually

World Canoeing Championships, 1975

	Gold	Silver	Bronze
WILDWATER RACING			
Germany, West	4	3	2
France	3	4	2
Belgium	1	2	0
Great Britain	1	1	1
Austria	1	0	0
Switzerland	0	0	2
U.S.	0	0	2
Czechoslovakia	0	0	1
CANOE SLALOM			
Germany, East	3	2	4
Czechoslovakia	2	2	2
Poland	1	2	1
Germany, West	1	2	1
U.S.	1	1	1
Switzerland	1	0	0
FLATWATER SPRINT			
U.S.S.R.	6	3	3
Hungary	4	3	5
Germany, East	4	2	1
Italy	2	1	0
Poland	1	0	3
Spain	1	0	1
Norway	1	0	0
Romania	0	6	2
Czechoslovakia	0	1	0
Germany, West	0	1	0
Bulgaria	0	0	2
Yugoslavia	0	0	1

Sandy Satullo in "Copper Kettle" wins the U.S. offshore powerboat racing championship.

being cleared of pollution to improve the environment for such recreation. And each year new canoe trails are being established and artificial slalom courses laid out for canoes and kayaks.

As in other sports, canoeing skills are most evident in international competitions. During 1975 three major championship tournaments were held in Yugoslavia. In the ninth world wildwater competitions, eight of the 16 national teams that took part won at least a bronze medal. In the kayak singles (K1), J.-P. Burny of Belgium won the men's title and G. Grothaus of West Germany the women's. The men's team championship was won by Austria, the women's by Great Britain. In other team championships for men, West Germany won the C1, and France the C2 and the C2 mix.

East German athletes dominated the 14th world championships in canoe slalom, with a total of nine medals (three gold) to runner-up Czechoslovakia's six (two gold). The U.S. won its only medals in the C2 mix, taking all three places.

During the world flatwater sprint championships women took part in three kayak events while the men participated in nine such races (ranging from 500 m. to 10,000 m.) and in six other events involving Canadian canoes. At the completion of 18 separate events, members of seven national teams had won at least one gold medal each, with six going to the Soviet Union.

(JOAN L. MASON)

Water Skiing. The six-member U.S. water ski team finished ahead of 21 other teams in the 14th biennial world water ski championships held in September at Thorpe Water Park, Surrey, England. Its 12,226 points provided a comfortable victory over second place Australia (9,608) and third place Venezuela (9,184). Fourth and fifth places went, respectively, to Canada (8,730) and Great Britain (8,222).

In individual events Venezuela, Italy, and the U.S. shared the honours. Fifteen-year-old Carlos Suarez of Venezuela won the men's overall championship, mainly on the strength of a record 6,260 points in tricks. Roby Zucchi of Italy captured the slalom with a two-round total of $60\frac{1}{4}$ buoys. The jumping competition was won by Wayne Grimditch of the U.S., whose best leaps in two rounds totaled 101.7 m. In the women's competition, Liz Allan Shetter of the U.S. scored an easy overall victory by running a total of 46 buoys in the slalom rounds and by two leaps measuring a total of 71.55 m. Maria Victoria Carrasco of Venezuela set a women's record for tricks with 5,460 points. Water skiing attracted an estimated 20 million participants during 1975, including more than 12 million in the U.S. alone.

(THOMAS C. HARDMAN)

Surfing. Two developments in 1975 would affect surfing for a long time to come. First, an objective scoring system was introduced in Hawaii at the Hang Ten American professional surfing championships. Though somewhat controversial, it replaced a system whereby judges subjectively evaluated a performance on a scale ranging from 0 to 20. Henceforth a specific value would be assigned to each phase of a contestant's maneuver and to the size of the wave. Second, a pro tour also was established with 24 active surfers and 12 alternates representing the three major powers in surfing: Australia, South Africa, and the U.S. The pro-circuit schedule called for four contests in California, plus the Hawaiian Hang Ten, the Duke Classic, the Smirnoff, the South African Durban 500, and the Australian Coke Contest. Winners were expected to share about $65,000 in prize money and perhaps as much as $100,000 in the near future. Amateurs could become professionals by competing in such events as the U.S. surfboard championships and the Makaha international in Oahu.

(J. C. FLANAGAN)

MONTREAL MATIN

Oreste Perri of Italy captured the single kayak championship at the 1975 International Canoeing Competition held in Montreal.

Water Polo. The premier event of 1975 was the second world championship held during July in Cali, Colombia, where 16 teams matched skills in 66 games. In the finals the Soviet Union, displaying superb teamwork, upset favoured Hungary 5–4 before 5,600 excited spectators. Italy nosed out Cuba for third. Having earlier tied the Soviet Union 5–5, Italy then won a protest and a rematch with Cuba after an initial 3–4 loss. Though each team scored four goals in the showdown, the overall record of the Italians lifted them into third place. Because the six top teams in the eight-team finals qualify for the 1976 Olympics, special importance was attached to the fifth through eighth places. Three teams had identical 2–1 records, but on the basis of total goals Romania was awarded fifth, West Germany sixth, and The Netherlands seventh. The Yugoslavian team was the biggest disappointment of the tournament. Forced to forfeit one game on a controversial doping violation, the players lost interest and finished in 13th place.

(WILLIAM ENSIGN FRADY)

U.S.S.R. scores the tying point against Italy in the final minutes of a match in the Water Polo World Championship at Cali, Colombia.

TONY DUFFY

TONY DUFFY

Carlos Suárez of Venezuela won the men's overall tricks championship, held at Surrey, England, in September.

Skin and Scuba Diving. Three U.S. Navy divers and a British Royal Navy petty officer set a new world record in June by descending to a depth of more than 1,100 ft. The Americans, William R. Rhodes, Lowell E. Burwell, and Joseph L. Bennoit, were accompanied in the U.S. Navy diving bell by Victor J. Humphrey of Portsmouth, England. Although all four made open water excursions in the Gulf of Mexico using standard navy umbilical cord breathing gear, Rhodes reached the greatest depth at 1,148 ft. The team spent 11 of their 15 days underwater in decompression after the record descent. The previous world record dive was 1,020 ft. The U.S. Navy's interest in deep diving, which involves the possible need for recovery of "sensitive" military objects from the seafloor, was expected to aid in the exploration of underwater oil and gas reserves.

Another important event in 1975 was the introduction of sophisticated educational programs utilizing videotapes, filmstrips, and texts that would significantly assist the 4,000 to 5,000 certified instructors who teach scuba diving to approximately a quarter-million Americans. (JAMES E. MARTENHOFF)

See also Rowing; Sailing; Swimming.

[452.B.4.a]

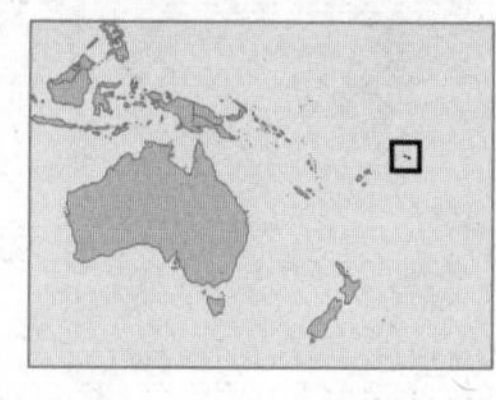

Western Samoa

A constitutional monarchy and member of the Commonwealth of Nations, Western Samoa is an island group in the South Pacific Ocean, about 1,600 mi. E of New Zealand and 2,200 mi. S of Hawaii. Area: 1,133 sq.mi. (2,934 sq.km.), with two major islands, Savai'i (662 sq.mi.) and Upolu (435 sq.mi.), and seven smaller islands. Pop. (1974 est.): 155,000. Cap. and largest city: Apia (pop., 1971, 30,300). Language: Samoan and English. Religion (1971): Congregational 51%, Roman Catholic 22%, Methodist 16%, others 11%. Head of state (*O le Ao o le Malo*) in 1975, Malietoa Tanumafili II; prime ministers, Fiame Mata'afa Faumuina Mulinu'u II to May 20 and, from May 21, Tupua Tamasese Lealofi IV.

Fiame Mata'afa Faumuina Mulinu'u II, prime minister of Western Samoa from 1959 through independence in 1962 to 1970 and again from 1973, died in May 1975. Mata'afa, who was head of one of the four royal families of Western Samoa, was a traditionalist who led his people cautiously into modern ways but was always conscious of the need to preserve *Fa'a Samoa* (the Samoan Way). Mata'afa's wife, Masiofo Fetaui Mata'afa, successfully contested the by-election for the resulting parliamentary vacancy. The new prime minister was Tupua Tamasese Lealofi IV, who had held the post from 1970 to 1973. Shortly after taking office he dismissed the ministers of finance and agriculture for irregularities.

High prices for cocoa and copra exports in 1974 fell in 1975. The government attempted to generate growth by allocating 43% of the gross budget to development projects. Rural development was of particular concern because increasing numbers were leaving the land for an urban existence or for migration to New Zealand. Locally produced foodstuffs were insufficient to meet the urban demand, thus adding expensive foodstuffs to the import bill. The concept of an industrial "free zone" was approved by the government with a view to attracting industries, especially from New Zealand. (BARRIE MACDONALD)

[977.A.3]

Weather:
see Earth Sciences

Weight Lifting:
see Gymnastics and Weight Lifting

Welfare:
see Social and Welfare Services

West Indies:
see Bahamas, The; Barbados; Cuba; Dependent States; Dominican Republic; Grenada; Haiti; Jamaica; Latin-American Affairs; Trinidad and Tobago

Wheat:
see Agriculture and Food Supplies

Wines:
see Industrial Review

Winter Sports

Ice Skating. Expansion of ice skating was significant during 1975 in areas relatively new to the sport, particularly in warm climates where its development has been due to the installation of artificially frozen rinks. The number of rinks in South Africa grew to 11, and the first major international figure-skating competitions in that country were held in Johannesburg on April 2–4. There was increased support for a second annual professional tournament at Jaca, in the Spanish Pyrenees, and the first rink in the Canary Islands opened at Las Palmas. An upsurge of interest in Australia was emphasized by the first victories of Australian figure skaters in contests in Great Britain and Spain.

There was also growth in the established strongholds of the sport. The U.S. had an estimated five million skaters and nearly 2,000 indoor rinks. Canada had approximately 825 figure-skating clubs, with membership near 135,000; these enthusiasts represented only a small part of Canadians who skate. Considerable expansion also took place in most of the other 32 member nations of the International Skating Union (ISU).

Only one of the four titles was retained by the defending champions in what was widely considered the most unpredictable world ice figure and dance championships tournament of recent years, at Colorado Springs, Colo., on March 4–8. The altitude of 6,000 ft. sapped the stamina of many competitors. A total of 105 skaters from 19 nations took part.

The absence of the titleholder, Jan Hoffmann of East Germany, because of an injury threw the men's event wide open. Sergey Volkov, from Moscow, became the new champion and the first Soviet skater to win a solo title. His compatriot, European champion Vladimir Kovalev, finished second and Britain's John Curry third, with Toller Cranston of Canada a disappointing fourth. Though Volkov was an uninspiring free skater, his routine included two triple toe loop jumps and he won because his main rivals, usually better jumpers, made costly errors.

The previous year's Eastern European monopoly of titles was halted by the victory of Dianne de Leeuw of The Netherlands in the women's event. She created a stir by displacing Karin Iten in the compulsory figures. The Swiss girl previously had been the world's best figure tracer since the retirement of Trixi Schuba of Austria. The new champion skated a sensibly careful free performance in the final round, in which she did not need to take undue risks. Her highlight was a brilliant combination of high double lutz and double loop jumps. Dorothy Hamill of the U.S., runner-up for the second straight year, was top scorer in the free skating but could not close the gap that had been caused by her fall from a required flying sit-spin. Christine Errath, the East German title defender, failed to recapture her best form in the compulsory figures, but her spirited late rally well merited a consolatory third-place medal.

The Soviet pairs victory of Aleksandr Zaitsev and Irina Rodnina was their third straight win and a record seventh for the girl, who had previously won four times with Aleksey Ulanov. With their customary panache, the champions—who became husband and wife a few weeks later—were masters of precision whether skating apart or in bodily contact, excelling with an overhead axel lift and well-controlled death spirals. Although Rodnina twice landed awkwardly from double twist lifts, the Moscow team got a six for artistic presentation. The era of Soviet strength in depth was effectively terminated, however, by two East German pairs, Rolf Österreich with Romy Kermer and Uwe Kagelmann with Manuela Gross, second and third, respectively.

The ice dancing outcome was uncertain to the very last, dramatic changes of fortune punctuating the course of the contest. The last-minute withdrawal of Aleksandr Gorshkov and Ludmila Pakhomova prevented the Soviet couple's bid for a record sixth straight win. Four couples stood out above the rest, interchanging their standings frequently until finally Andrey Minenkov and Irina Moiseyeva of the U.S.S.R. defeated the U.S. contenders, Jim Millns and Colleen O'Connor, by a 7–2 verdict from the judges. After getting the only six awarded for artistic presentation, the Americans lost an intriguing tussle of contrasting styles that made judging extremely difficult. Britain's Glyn Watts and Hilary Green overhauled two more Soviet skaters, Gennadi Karponosov and Natalya Linichuk, to take third place.

Harm Kuipers of The Netherlands gained the overall title in the men's world ice speed championship in Oslo, Norway, on February 8–9, but he failed to win any of the four individual events. Two Soviet racers, Vladimir Ivanov and Yuri Kondakov, finished second and third overall. Three Norwegians, Jan Egil Storholt, Åmund Sjøbrend, and Sten Stensen, took the 500 m., 1,500 m., and 5,000 m., respectively. Ivanov won the 10,000 m.

The women's world speed championship at Assen, Neth., on February 22–23, also produced a new overall winner, Karin Kessow of East Germany. Tatjana Averina of the U.S.S.R. was runner-up. Sheila Young of the U.S., overall third, proved the outstanding sprinter, winning both the 500 m. and 1,000 m. Kessow was first in the 1,500 m., and the 3,000 m. went to Sippie Tigchelaar of The Netherlands. Separate world sprint titles for men and women, at Göteborg, Sweden, on February 15–16, were won by Aleksandr Safronov of the U.S.S.R. and Sheila Young.

Four men's and four women's world speed records were broken, all by Soviet skaters at Medeo, U.S.S.R. Yevgeni Kulikov lowered his own sprint time for the 500 m. to 37.00 sec. Valery Muratov lopped 0.31 sec. off the 1,000 m., clocking 1 min. 16.92 sec. Yuri Kondakov covered 5,000 m. in 7 min. 8.92 sec., and Viktor Varlamov, 10,000 m. in 14 min. 52.73 sec. Averina set new women's records for three distances: 500 m. in 41.06 sec., 1,000 m. in 1 min. 23.46 sec., and 1,500 m. in 2 min. 9.9 sec. Tamara Kuznetsova's record time for the 3,000 m. was 4 min. 44.69 sec.

The 36th biennial ISU congress, in Munich, West Germany, on June 9–14, amended the figure-skating scoring system for future championships, allocating 70% of the total marks for free skating and only 30% for compulsory figures, instead of 60–40%. Three newly invented dances, tango romantica, yankee polka, and ravensburger waltz, were added to the ice dancing championship competition.

Skiing. Recreational skiing grew in popularity during 1975, leading to keen competition among equipment manufacturers and mountain resorts. Plastic slopes for pre-snow practice multiplied, with nearly 100 in Great Britain alone, and grass skiing developed both for snow ski training and as a separate sport.

The number of internationally approved alpine ski courses rose to 807, including such climatically unlikely countries as Cyprus, Greece, Great Britain, Lebanon, and Turkey.

TONY DUFFY

Irina Rodnina and Aleksandr Zaitsev won the world pairs championship for 1975 at Colorado Springs, Colorado.

Professional freestyle skiing, with the emphasis on crowd-drawing somersaults and other acrobatic specialties, gained increased support in the U.S., where self-styled men's and women's world titles were won by Scott Brooksbank and Genia Fuller in a predominantly U.S. entry at Snowbird, Utah, on April 4–6. A more representative contest, with men and women competing together, was won by Brooksbank a week later at Cervinia, Italy.

In alpine racing, there were no new winning names in the ninth World Cup series. After finishing runner-up the previous season, Gustavo Thoeni (*see* Biography) of Italy attained his fourth victory in five years, and Annemarie Proell-Moser of Austria gained her fifth straight success. In the tightest men's finish in the history of the competition everything hinged on the final event, a dual slalom on March 23 at Val Gardena, Italy. Before that race Thoeni was even on points with Franz Klammer of Austria and Ingemar Stenmark of Sweden. The cup's destiny depended on a tensely exciting final race between Thoeni

Annemarie Proell-Moser won the women's World Cup for alpine skiing for the fifth consecutive year.

COLORSPORT

WIDE WORLD

Winners in the world two-man bobsled championship at Cervinia, Italy, were Giorgio Alvera and Franco Perruquet in a time of 4:45.38 minutes.

and Stenmark, which Thoeni won when Stenmark slithered too wide of a gate near the finish.

It was the first time a dual slalom had been included in the World Cup, and there was much criticism that it was chosen to end the series. Because it is the only event in which an individual racer can eliminate another at any stage, it was possible for a competitor to assist a better-placed compatriot by not offering the sternest opposition.

Although most at home in slaloms, Thoeni was the first skier since Jean-Claude Killy of France to achieve notable success in all three disciplines (slalom, giant slalom, and downhill). Runner-up Stenmark was top scorer in both the slalom and giant slalom, while Klammer excelled as a downhill specialist, winning eight of those events. Piero Gros, the Italian cup defender who had broken Thoeni's winning sequence the year before, finished fourth overall. A modification of the points system introduced during the year included the adding of alpine combination results in three meetings to encourage versatility. This diminished the value of specialization in any one discipline and spurred Thoeni, previously renowned as a slalomer, to concentrate more on the downhills with fruitful results. Klammer, on the other hand, was unable to match his outstanding downhill ability in the slalom events.

The women's World Cup outcome was resolved quite early in the season through an unassailable lead gained by the dominant Proell-Moser, whose feats included five consecutive giant slalom wins and an unprecedented three victories in three days—two giant slaloms and a downhill. Her familiar hip-swinging style with "egg-shape" stance was typical of her country's technique, her small frame deceptively hiding the courage and stamina essential for downhill mastery. Overall runner-up was Hanni Wenzel of Liechtenstein, with Rosi Mittermaier of West Germany third and Marie-Theres Nadig of Switzerland fourth. Lise-Marie Morerod of Switzerland, the top slalom scorer, failed to take a point for downhill.

The World Cup series was contested over 28 men's and 27 women's events spread through four months at meetings in Austria, Canada, France, Italy, Japan, Switzerland, U.S., West Germany, and Yugoslavia. The Nations' Cup, decided concurrently, was retained by Austria, the country's third consecutive win, with Switzerland and Italy second and third.

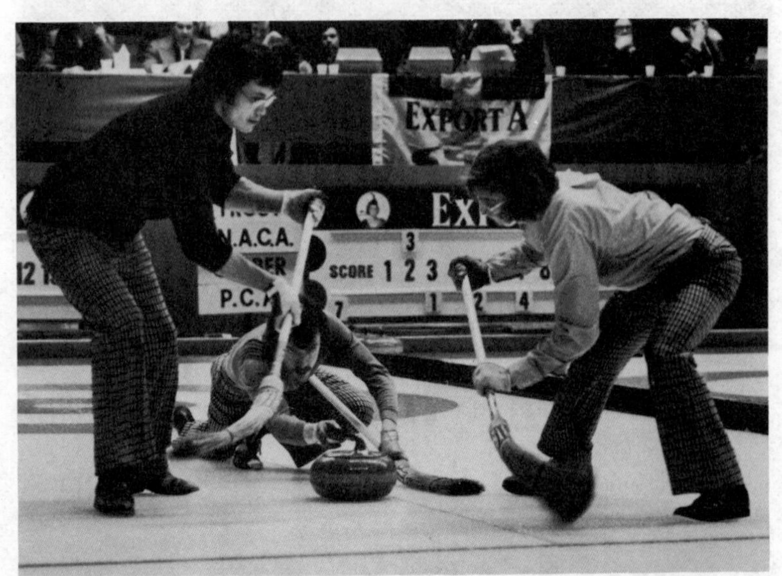

Action at the Alberta curling championship held in Edmonton in February. Tom Reed of St. Albert (throwing) emerged the victor.

EDMONTON JOURNAL

The fifth Can-Am Ski Trophy series, comprising 17 men's and 17 women's events at 11 North American sites, was won by Peter Dodge and Leslie Smith, both of the U.S. Hank Kashiwa of the U.S. was the season's outstanding professional, beating Henri Duvillard of France in a 13-meeting circuit.

The fifth biennial world ski-bob championships, at Val d'Isère, France, on January 26 to February 1, were contested by 35 men and 8 women from nine countries. Alois Fischbauer of Austria became the first bobber to retain the men's title. His compatriot Alexander Kurz was runner-up, with a Swiss, Martin Albrecht, third. The women's title went for a third consecutive time to Gertrude Gebert, the Austrian winner in 1971 and 1973, followed by a Czech, Alana Hrbkova, and another Austrian, Angret Ertler.

The world ski-flying championship, at Kulm, Austria, on March 13–16, was won by Karel Kodejska of Czechoslovakia, followed by an East German, Rainer Schmidt. A new hill record of 495 ft. was achieved by the third-placed Karl Schnabl of Austria.

The 30th biennial International Ski Federation congress, at San Francisco on May 25 to June 1, decided to retain the dual slalom as the first event in future World Cup series, probably influenced by its crowd-drawing potential. New eligibility rules, though still barring prize money or direct payments to racers by equipment manufacturers, went a step nearer professionalism by approving virtually unlimited broken-time payments, *i.e.,* compensation for loss of a regular income while racing and training. The Nordic Committee rejected by one vote a proposal to establish a World Cup in cross-country skiing. A 20-km. event was approved for women in future world championships.

Bobsledding. Fifteen nations took part in the 42nd world bobsledding championships, at Cervinia, Italy, on February 10–23. The two-man event was won by an Italian sled, driven by Giorgio Alvera and braked by Franco Perruquet, in an aggregate time 2.12 sec. better than the West German runners-up, Georg Heibl and Fritz Ohlwärter. Fritz Lüdi and Karl Häseli of Switzerland finished third among the 30 sleds. Erich Scharer steered a Swiss sled, crewed by Werner Camichel, Josef Benz, and brakeman Peter Scharer, to victory in the four-man contest. Wolfgang Zimmerer drove a West German team into second place. An Austrian crew led by Manfred Stengl was third.

The next most interesting meeting of the season was the Nations' Cup event for four-man crews, at Igls, Austria, on March 6–8. It was the first official competition to be held on the new course built for the 1976 Winter Olympics. The run was considered less challenging than most, with fastest starts proving decisive. Scharer and his Swiss world title-winning crew won from an East German sled led by Meinhard Nehmer. Another Swiss quartet, driven by Hans Candrian, finished third.

Tobogganing. Spreading from its most popular areas in Austria, Poland, and East and West Germany, luge tobogganing gained a wider international foothold in 1975. The International Luge Federation increased to 26 member nations, 20 in Europe, 2 in Asia, 3 in North America, and 1 in Africa. The number of regularly active participants rose to approximately 39,000.

East Germans won all three titles in the 21st world championships, at Hammerstrand, Sweden, on February 15–16. In the men's singles, Wolfram Fiedler outpaced the veteran Austrian Manfred Schmid, with another East German, Harald Ehrig, in third place. The doubles went to B. and U. Hahn, with their fellow countrymen Müller and Neumann runners-up and R. Schmid and Schachner of Austria third. In the women's singles, Margit Schumann proved too good for her East German compatriot Ute Rührold. Dana Spalenska of Czechoslovakia finished third.

New weighting regulations were passed, effective as of the 1975–76 winter season. These were instituted because it was realized that the more sophisticated luges and artificially frozen courses consistently favoured the heaviest riders. The new system allowed the lightest competitors to add, on a scale proportionate to the rider's weight, weight belts up to a maximum of 10 kg. (22 lb.) for men and 8 kg. (17.6 lb.) for women.

The skeleton tobogganing season on the Cresta Run at St. Moritz, Switz., was notable for the number of records broken. The outstanding rider was Poldi Birchtold, a Swiss physical-training coach, who set three new best times. He lowered the record from Top to 53.24 sec., from Junction to 42.96 sec., and the flying start from Junction to 34.8 sec. In mostly ideal weather, a record number of 7,749 descents were made during a 65-day season.

Birchtold won the major event, the 66th Grand National, by 0.62 sec. over the runner-up, Ulie Burgerstein of Switzerland. The almost legendary Italian Nino Bibbia, old enough at 52 to be father of most of his rivals, was third on the fearsome course he had dominated for two decades. The 52nd Curzon Cup race from Junction was also won by Birchtold, followed by Bruno Bischofberger of Switzerland.

Curling. More than half a million curlers were playing the game in Canada during 1975, as compared with some 25,000 in Scotland, where it first developed. The game also gained a stronger foothold in New Zealand. The 17th world championship for the Air Canada Silver Broom, watched by 8,000 spectators at Perth, Scotland, on March 17–23, resulted in the first victory for Switzerland since the annual event began in 1959. The winning Swiss rink, from Wallisellen, near Zürich, was skipped by Otto Danieli, son of a former Silver Broom contestant, and included Roland Schneider, Rolf Gautschi, and Ueli Mulli. Canada, 12-time winner of the title, lost 6–5 to the Swiss, and the U.S. beat Sweden 6–4 in the semifinals.

Another form of curling, called Eisschiessen, continued to flourish primarily in Austria and West Germany and, to a lesser extent, in Czechoslovakia, Yugoslavia, the South Tyrol region of Italy, and the Swiss valley of Engadin. The fact that two distinct kinds of curling were drawn to the International Olympic Committee's attention may have hampered the prospects of eventual inclusion of the sport into the Olympics, but renewed efforts to achieve such status gained support, with hopes of acceptance in time for the 1980 Winter Games at Lake Placid, N.Y.

(HOWARD BASS)

See also Ice Hockey.
[452.B.4.g; 452.B.4.h.xxv]

Words and Meanings, New

The satellite Mariner 10 transmitted a **photomosaic** of Venus in its **flyby** past that planet, thus making a valuable contribution to **galactochemistry.** Three new **psi particles,** or **psis,** discovered by subatomic physicists, were provisionally described as **charm quarks,** or **charmsters.** (*See* PHYSICS.) Horizonless **whiteout** acquired heightened significance in Chris Bonington's report on the British Everest expedition.

Autotransfusion marked an advance in heart therapy. Blood was abstracted from a man's body, filtered and cleansed, and returned to the body again. For the first time, the **ballistocardiograph,** recording the vigour of heartbeat, became portable and cheap. In measuring blood pressure the **kilopascal** was reluctantly adopted as the unit in order to conform with European practice. A team of medical engineers at Hemel Hempstead devised a whole range of **telecheiric** machines enabling cripples to move around and work effectively.

On both sides of the Atlantic—at Boston, Mass., and Newcastle upon Tyne, England—the electric **supertram** made a comeback as a light rail vehicle. By the figure of speech known as synecdoche, the **hydrofoil** came to be applied to the boat itself as well as to the metal plates or fins that "foil the water" by forcing the boat above the surface when a certain speed is reached. The year saw the marketing of the perfected electronic piano or **pianotron.**

A team of chemists at Cleveland, Ohio, produced hydrogen from water by **biophotolysis,** and a group of electrical engineers at Schenectady, N.Y., worked on supercooled **cryocables** for transmitting electricity underground into cities. **Olfactronics,** or olfactory electronics, became fashionable as a refined forensic science. The term **proticity** was coined to denote flow of protons on the analogy of electricity denoting flow of electrons. On the whole, the experts grew in power and prestige, and there were serious allusions to **expertocracy.**

Blends continued to appear at all levels. Hooli(gan) football fan(atic)s became **hoolifans,** at least in the daily press. Pessimists, who blamed economic growth for all their troubles, were termed ecological doomsters or **ecodoomsters.** The scientific and technical network operated by the European Economic Community was officially called **Euronet.** At the University of Florida a nuclear pumped or gamma-ray laser was called a **graser.** Some useful blends, like **satnav** and **meteosat,** were not readily distinguishable from syllabic acronyms of the *komsomol* and *Comecon* type. **Satnav** was short for satellite navigation, using one or more of the six U.S. orbiting satellites dominating the whole of the Earth's surface. **Meteosat** would transmit meteorological data for the World Weather Watch program.

Acronyms, both general and particular, continued to multiply. The fourth session of **UNCLOS** (United Nations Conference on the Law of the Sea) met in the summer at Geneva. **RAPID** (Register for the Ascertainment and Prevention of Inherited Diseases) was inaugurated at Edinburgh. **IMOS** denoted that Inadvertent Modification of the Stratosphere by supersonic aircraft which so perturbed the **aeronomists.** Some acronyms ran the risk of ambiguity. It was not always immediately clear whether NEB meant the National Enterprise Board or the New English Bible! Ambiguity also impaired certain functional shifts. Did **expose** (verb into noun) denote "exposure" or "exposition"? On the whole, the British and American varieties of English drew closer together, but one distinction persisted with truly amazing stubbornness: British **envisage** versus American **envision.**

Besides **miniaturization,** several other new derivatives in *-ization* emerged during the year, notably **proportionalization,** embracing any one of a dozen

Wood Products:
see Industrial Review

Wool:
see Agriculture and Food Supplies; Industrial Review

systems of proportional representation (PR) in democratic government. **Statusful,** taken over from the sociologists, had evidently come to stay. **Recency,** an unimpeachable derivative of *recent,* like *frequency* from *frequent,* was inexplicably frowned upon by pundits. Physiologists, in their search for a yearly counterpart of daily or **circadian** rhythms, vacillated between **circannial** and **circannual,** both of which, alas, were morphologically irregular. Australian **walkabout** became popular in Britain and was applied even to the perambulation of the queen herself as she moved about informally among her loyal subjects. Transverse ridges, placed on expressways to discourage speeding, were nicknamed **sleeping policemen.**

Oddly enough, **overview** (perhaps echoing German **Überblick**) tended to replace *survey* altogether, and to **recap** (recapitulate) threatened to oust completely both *sum up* and *summarize.* **Scenario** moved out from theatre and cinema and came to be applied to any plan of action or any setting whatsoever. Whereas hitherto people went through a trying time, they now had a **traumatic experience;** and whereas before they quietly withdrew from public life, they were now said to **keep a low profile.** It seemed strange that so many people deliberately rejected strong Anglo-Saxon monosyllables and said **minimal** for *least,* **maximal** for *most,* and **optimal** for *best.*

Who on earth were these **rising fives**? They were children just under five years of age. Women's Lib fans continued to insist that firemen should be called **firepersons** and **chairperson** used instead of chairman. In a more sinister vein, Orwellian **unperson** was disinterred and used of a public figure who, though living, had lost all significance. At the same time people spoke, more inspiringly, of Joycean **epiphanies** in the romantic sense of "moments of unanticipated vision." (SIMEON POTTER)

[441.C.2.e; 442.B.4]

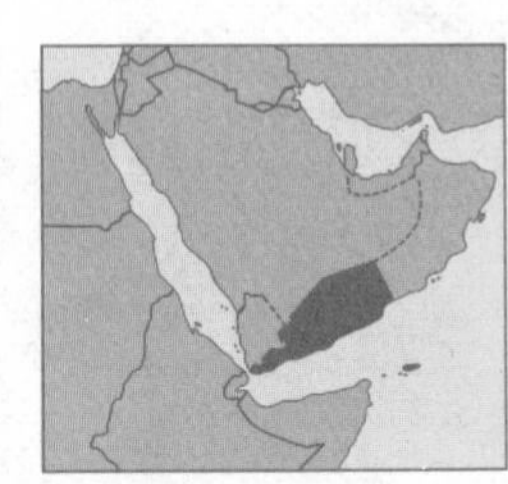

Yemen, People's Democratic Republic of

A people's republic in the southern coastal region of the Arabian Peninsula, Yemen (Aden) is bordered by Yemen (San'a'), Saudi Arabia, and Oman. Area: 111,074 sq.mi. (287,680 sq.km.). Pop. (1974 est.): 1,633,000. Cap. and largest city: Aden (pop., 1973, 132,500). Language: Arabic. Religion: Muslim. Chairman of the Presidential Council in 1975, Salem Ali Rubayyi; prime minister, Ali Nasir Muhammad Husani.

The People's Democratic Republic of Yemen maintained its independent and radical stance in 1975, and relations with its Omani and North Yemeni neighbours remained uneasy. The regime made some attempt to improve its relations with the Arab states of the Persian Gulf, but embassies were not established. The objective of union of the two Yemens was verbally maintained by government spokesmen, and joint commissions of the two countries continued to meet. Relations with San'a' deteriorated sharply in the spring when the Yemen Arab Republic accused the People's Democratic Republic of provocation and sabotage in border areas, but a joint meeting of representatives in Aden in July led to the—possibly premature—announcement that all border issues had been settled.

The country's poor economic condition was alleviated by some aid from Iraq and Kuwait. Future prospects were improved by the reopening of the Suez Canal in June, which offered some hope of restoring the prosperity of Aden port; only 100 ships a month were entering the port, compared with the pre-1967 average of 700. The left-wing regime strengthened its position with the absorption of two smaller groups into the United National Front Political Organization. Pay for all workers in the public sector was increased, and a pensions scheme was introduced. (PETER MANSFIELD)

[978.B.4.b]

World Council of Churches: *see* Religion
Wrestling: *see* Combat Sports
Yachting: *see* Sailing
Yiddish Literature: *see* Literature

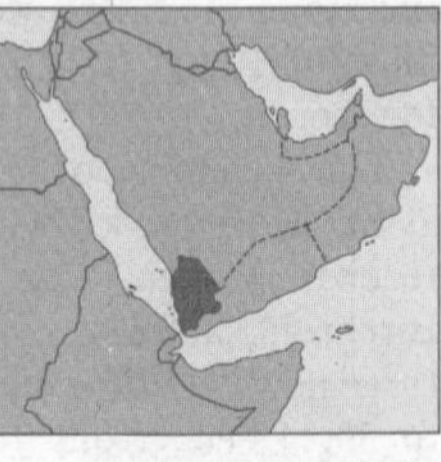

Yemen Arab Republic

A republic situated in the southwestern coastal region of the Arabian Peninsula, Yemen (San'a') is bounded by Yemen (Aden), Saudi Arabia, and the Red Sea. Area: 77,200 sq.mi. (200,000 sq.km.). Pop. (1975): 5,237,900. Cap. and largest city: San'a' (pop., 1975, 134,600). Language: Arabic. Religion: Muslim. Chairman of the Command Council in 1975, Col. Ibrahim al-Hamdi; premiers, Mohsin al-Aini to January 16 and, from January 25, Abdel-Aziz Abdel-Ghani.

A relatively weak central government continued to try to establish political control over the whole country in 1975. On January 16 the premier, Mohsin al-Aini, was dismissed by the ruling military Command Council. The head of the council, strong man Col. Ibrahim al-Hamdi, disapproved of Aini's efforts to strengthen ties with left-wing and moderate Arab states and reduce dependence on Saudi Arabia. A new government was formed on January 25 under the former governor of the Central Bank, Abdel-Aziz Abdel-Ghani, who also joined the Command Council.

Economic aid from Saudi Arabia totaling $273 million was announced after the Yemeni premier's visit to Riyadh in August. Relations with Yemen (Aden) were uneasy throughout the year, despite exchanges of visits between government leaders and meetings of joint economic and military committees. In March San'a' accused Aden of encouraging sabotage on its borders and arrested 11 saboteurs. An announcement that a joint meeting in Aden in July had settled all border differences was not expected to end the dispute. The economic situation remained difficult. The 1975–76 budget, announced at 778 million riyals, showed a deficit of 209 million riyals, to be covered by higher taxes and austerity as well as by foreign aid. (PETER MANSFIELD)

[978.B.4.b]

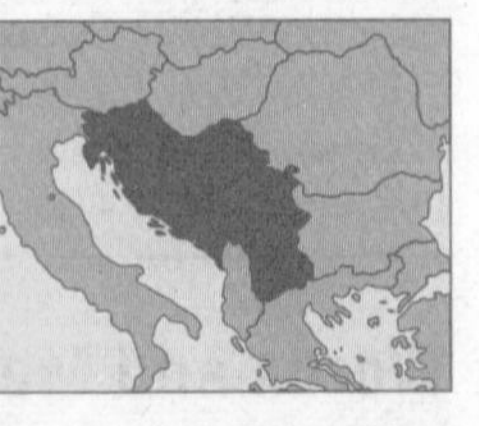

Yugoslavia

A federal socialist republic, Yugoslavia is bordered by Italy, Austria, Hungary, Romania, Bulgaria, Greece, and Albania. Area: 98,766 sq.mi. (255,804 sq.km.). Pop. (1975 est.): 21,322,000. Cap. and largest city: Belgrade (pop., 1971, 746,100). Language: Serbo-Croatian, Slovenian, and Macedonian. Religion (1953): Orthodox 41%; Roman Catholic 32%; Muslim 12%. President of the republic

YUGOSLAVIA

Education. (1973–74) Primary, pupils 2,869,-344, teachers 126,327; secondary, pupils 203,296, teachers 10,164; vocational, pupils 510,861, teachers 9,916; teacher training, students 9,096, teachers 624; higher (including 9 universities), students 328,536, teaching staff 19,197.

Finance. Monetary unit: dinar, with (Sept. 22, 1975) a free rate of 18 dinars to U.S. $1 (37.33 dinars = £1 sterling). Gold, SDRs, and foreign exchange: (June 1975) U.S. $1,136,000,000; (June 1974) U.S. $1,160,000,000. Budget (1973 actual): revenue 60,550,000,000 dinars; expenditure 61.9 billion dinars. Gross material product: (1973) 306 billion dinars; (1972) 245 billion dinars. Money supply: (Nov. 1974) 97.3 billion dinars; (Nov. 1973) 78.2 billion dinars. Cost of living (1970 = 100; May 1975) 244.

Foreign Trade. (1974) Imports 128,220,000,-000 dinars; exports 64,690,000,000 dinars. Import sources: West Germany 18%; Italy 12%; U.S.S.R. 10%; Austria 5%; U.S. 5%. Export destinations: U.S.S.R. 18%; West Germany 10%; U.S. 8%; Czechoslovakia 5%. Main exports: machinery 13%; transport equipment 12%; nonferrous metals 12%; chemicals 10%; food 9%; steel 8%; ships and boats 7%; timber 5%. Tourism (1973): visitors 6,150,000; gross receipts U.S. $631 million.

Agriculture. Production (in 000; metric tons; 1974; 1973 in parentheses): wheat 6,284 (4,-751); barley 794 (676); oats 353 (298); rye 120 (118); corn 8,000 (8,253); potatoes 3,128 (2,974); sunflower seed 298 (*c.* 434); sugar, raw value *c.* 538 (444); dry beans 179 (197); onions 297 (277); tomatoes *c.* 418 (412); cabbages (1973) 665, (1972) 674; watermelons (1973) *c.* 419, (1972) 413; plums (1973) 615, (1972) 972; apples 370 (448); pears 93 (141); wine (1973) 772, (1972) 626; tobacco *c.* 66 (*c.* 66); beef and veal (1973) *c.* 290, (1972) 266; pork (1973) *c.* 345, (1972) 340; timber (cu.m.; 1973) 13,300; fish catch (1973) 48, (1972) 49.

Industry. Fuel and power (in 000; metric tons; 1974): coal 602; lignite 32,982; crude oil 3,458; natural gas (cu.m.) 1,447,000; manufactured gas (cu.m.) 151,000; electricity (kw-hr.) 39,457,000. Production (in 000; metric tons; 1974): cement 6,647; iron ore (35% metal content) 5,035; pig iron 2,315; crude steel 2,791; bauxite 2,353; antimony ore (metal content; 1973) 2.1; chrome ore (oxide content; 1973) 1.1; manganese ore (metal content) 3.3; magnesite (1973) 384; aluminum 147; copper 150; lead 114; zinc 65; gold (troy oz.; 1973) 176; silver (troy oz.; 1973) 4,310; petroleum products (1973) 8,568; sulfuric acid 926; cotton yarn 108; wool yarn 40; rayon, etc., filament yarns and fibres (1973) 67; nylon, etc., filament yarns and fibres (1973) 18; wood pulp (1973) 617; newsprint 79; other paper (1973) 611. Merchant vessels launched (100 gross tons and over; 1974) 777,000 gross tons.

for life and president of the League of Communists in 1975, Marshal Tito (Josip Broz); president of the Federal Executive Council (premier), Dzemal Bijedic.

Relations with the U.S.S.R. deteriorated in 1975, and in the second half of the year Yugoslavia embarked on a near-confrontation course with it and Bulgaria. Internally, the clampdown on dissent was intensified.

On October 15 the Presidium of the League of Communists held a special session on "aspects of enemy activity against Yugoslavia." This ushered in the biggest campaign since 1948–49 against the so-called Cominformists—party members who had opted for the U.S.S.R. in the quarrel between Yugoslavia and the U.S.S.R. in 1948. Speeches by President Tito and other top leaders emphasized the danger from such Stalinist, pro-U.S.S.R. elements, who were said to be actively plotting. Several dozen Cominformists were arrested between August and October. Earlier in the year, on July 2, the seven members of a pro-Soviet Stalinist group of Muslims and Serbs—all former senior officials—had been sentenced to prison terms.

Other dissident groups also came under fire. Eight liberal Marxist academics were suspended from their teaching posts at Belgrade University on January 28, and the magazine of Yugoslavia's dissident Marxists, *Praxis,* of Zagreb, was suppressed in February. Five Albanian nationalists were sentenced in January and more were arrested later. A group of 15 Croat intellectuals and businessmen in Zadar, who had been accused of trying to set up a secret Croat army, were sentenced to up to 13 years on February 17. The campaign against Croat nationalism, touched off by the explosion of a bomb in Zagreb during President Tito's visit there on September 17, was followed later by arrests of Croat intellectuals and students.

Premier Bijedic traveled to the U.S.S.R. in April, and Gen. Stane Potocar, chief of the Yugoslav general staff, visited it in September. Bulgaria's foreign minister, Petr Mladenov, visited Yugoslavia in November, but he failed to "remove obstacles to better relations" and polemics over Macedonia continued. The federal premier also journeyed to China in October. Throughout the year Yugoslavia, together with several other European Communist parties, opposed Soviet attempts to convene a European conference as a prelude to a general attack on China. Yugoslavia's relations with China's ally, Albania, improved dramatically, and in June Albania asked to be connected to the new Yugoslav rail link at Bar in Montenegro close to the Albanian border. Relations with Romania became closer in the defense field with the announcement in April of joint production of the Orao (Eagle) jet fighter, but in August the alleged kidnapping from Bucharest of Col. Vlado Dapcevic, said to be the leader of the Yugoslav Cominformists, caused a temporary strain between the two countries.

On July 9 Austria signed an agreement to return to Yugoslavia archives, historical documents, and cultural objects housed in Vienna since World War I. On November 10 an agreement was signed with Italy formally recognizing the status quo in the former Trieste Free Territory, divided between Yugoslavia and Italy since 1954. In another, signed at the same time, the two countries agreed to set up an industrial free trade zone and to increase economic cooperation in the northern Adriatic. U.S. Pres. Gerald Ford visited Yugoslavia on August 3–4, and resumption of U.S. arms supplies to Yugoslavia was discussed. Arms purchases were also discussed with Sweden, Britain, and France.

Selective import controls were introduced in June, as part of the struggle to contain the country's 30% inflation, and in July all investments for nonmanufacturing purposes were frozen. The foreign trade deficit in the first eight months of 1975 was $2.6 billion, $1.5 billion of which represented a deficit with the EEC. In the first eight months exports to the convertible currency area fell by 21%, while exports to Eastern Europe were 36% above the same period of 1974. The grain harvest of just over four million tons was the worst in ten years. (K. F. CVIIC)

[972.B.3]

Zaire

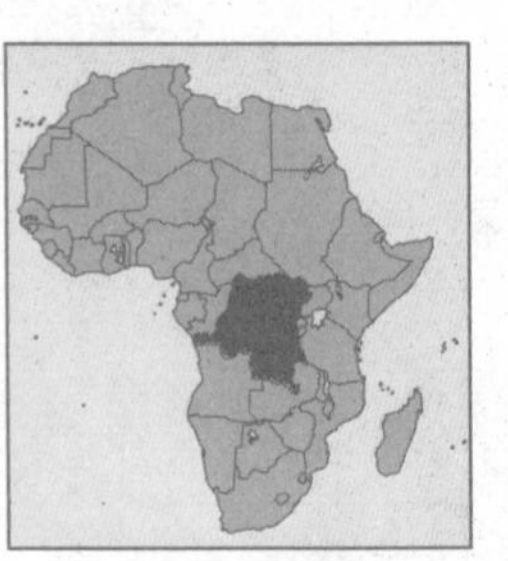

A republic of equatorial Africa, Zaire is bounded by the Central African Republic, Sudan, Uganda, Rwanda, Burundi, Tanzania, Zambia, Angola, Congo, and the Atlantic Ocean. Area: 905,365 sq.mi. (2,344,-885 sq.km.). Pop. (1974): 24,327,100. Cap. and largest city: Kinshasa (pop., 1974, 1,733,800). Language: French; Bantu dialects. Religion: animist approximately 50%; Christian 43%. President in 1975, Mobutu Sese Seko.

The second phase of Pres. Mobutu Sese Seko's authenticity campaign took effect on Jan. 1, 1975. The government took control of the essential sectors of the country's economy and conducted a vigorous drive to check inflation. Education was being reformed to eliminate foreign influences, and religious lessons were

ZAIRE

Education. (1972–73) Primary, pupils 3,292,020, teachers 80,481; secondary, pupils 37,116, teachers 13,792; vocational, pupils 34,687, teachers (1969–70) 3,515; teacher training, students 52,687, teachers (1969–70) 2,643; higher (1973–74), students 19,294, teaching staff 2,550.

Finance. Monetary unit: zaire, with (Sept. 22, 1975) an official exchange rate of 0.50 zaire to U.S. $1 (free rate of 1.04 zaire = £1 sterling). Gold, SDRs, and foreign exchange: (June 1975) U.S. $47,810,000; (June 1974) U.S. $246.6 million. Budget (1972 actual): revenue 336 million zaires; expenditure 506 million zaires.

Foreign Trade. (1973) Imports 377.2 million zaires; exports 502 million zaires. Import sources: Belgium-Luxembourg *c.* 20%; U.S. *c.* 17%; West Germany *c.* 14%; France *c.* 11%; Italy *c.* 8%; Japan *c.* 7%; The Netherlands *c.* 5%. Export destinations: Belgium-Luxembourg *c.* 48%; Italy *c.* 13%; Japan *c.* 7%; France 7%; U.S. 6%; West Germany *c.* 6%; U.K. 5%. Main exports: copper 62%; coffee 7%; diamonds 6%.

Transport and Communications. Roads (1973) *c.* 140,000 km. (including 69,347 km. main regional roads). Motor vehicles in use (1972): passenger 81,384; commercial 54,350. Railways (1972): 5,174 km.; traffic 437 million passenger-km., freight 2,387,000,000 net ton-km. Air traffic (1974): 623.3 million passenger-km.; freight 34,548,000 net ton-km. Shipping (1974): merchant vessels 100 gross tons and over 9; gross tonnage 38,966.

Agriculture. Production (in 000; metric tons; 1974; 1973 in parentheses): rice 250 (227); corn *c.* 524 (477); sweet potatoes (1973) *c.* 250, (1972) 243; cassava (1973) *c.* 10,000, (1972) 9,917; peanuts 308 (280); dry peas *c.* 204 (185); palm kernels *c.* 95 (*c.* 100); palm oil *c.* 190 (*c.* 198); sugar, raw value 64 (*c.* 68); bananas *c.* 76 (69); oranges (1973) *c.* 95, (1972) *c.* 90; coffee *c.* 74 (*c.* 79); rubber *c.* 40 (*c.* 40); cotton, lint *c.* 27 (*c.* 24); timber (cu.m.; 1973) *c.* 14,700, (1972) 14,700; fish catch (1971) 124.

Industry. Production (in 000; metric tons; 1973): coal 115; copper 322; tin 1.2; zinc 68; manganese ore (metal content) 170; gold (troy oz.) 134; silver (troy oz.) 2,200; diamonds (metric carats) 13,097; electricity (kw-hr.) 3,884,000.

to be replaced by political and civic instruction. After an unsuccessful attempt in June to assassinate Mobuto, 7 army officers were condemned to death and 26 others sentenced to imprisonment. The U.S. ambassador was expelled after the U.S. Central Intelligence Agency was accused of complicity.

Zaire took an active interest in the civil war in neighbouring Angola, where it favoured the National Front for the Liberation of Angola (FNLA) in its struggle against the Soviet-backed Popular Movement for the Liberation of Angola. Holden Roberto, head of the FNLA, had lived in Zaire for many years and had directed his guerrilla movement from its territory. Zaire was also concerned with the fate of the oil-rich Angolan enclave of Cabinda. The situation led to some softening of Zaire's attitude toward South Africa and to closer relations with the U.S.

Sales of copper and cobalt in 1974 had been good, and in spite of low copper prices it was decided, with support from the World Bank, the European Investment Bank, and the Libyan government, to increase output of both copper and cobalt as part of the new five-year economic plan. (KENNETH INGHAM)

[978.E.7.a.i]

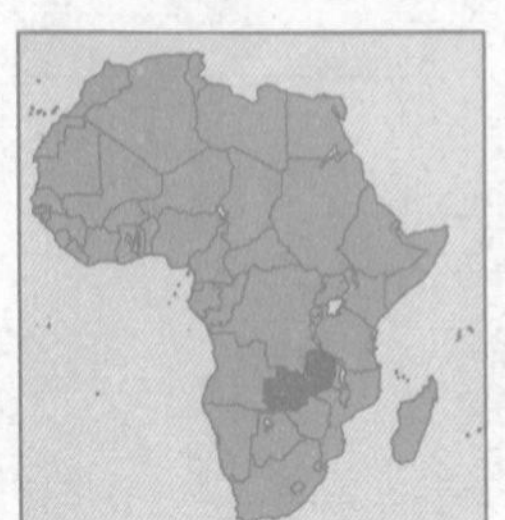

Zambia

A republic and a member of the Commonwealth of Nations, Zambia is bounded by Tanzania, Malawi, Mozambique, Rhodesia, South West Africa, Angola, and Zaire. Area: 290,586 sq.mi. (752,614 sq.km.). Pop. (1974 est.): 4,751,000, about 99% of whom are Africans. Cap. and largest city: Lusaka (pop., 1974 est., 415,000). Language: English and Bantu. Religion: predominantly animist. President in 1975, Kenneth Kaunda; prime ministers, Mainza Chona and, from May 27, Elijah Mudenda.

Zambia's relations with its neighbours, particularly Rhodesia, occupied the government's attention in 1975. In April three of the black Rhodesian independence movements based in Zambia were outlawed because their activities were threatening peace and order. Zambia continued to support the Rhodesian African National Council (ANC) but urged a policy of moderation upon its leaders in the hope of a negotiated settlement with the white Rhodesian government. To this end Kaunda also kept in diplomatic contact with the South African government and was instrumental in bringing the ANC leaders to a meeting with leaders of the white Rhodesian regime at Victoria Falls in August. (*See* AFRICAN AFFAIRS.) In May, and largely in the hope of a peaceful settlement in Angola, Kaunda visited Portugal, and the opening of a Zambian diplomatic mission there was announced. Kaunda was one of the African heads of state who refused to attend the July summit meeting of the Organization of African Unity in Kampala, Uganda, because of his disapproval of the activities of Pres. Idi Amin's government. Relations with Tanzania remained very good, and on October 23 a ceremony was held to mark the completion of the Tanzam railway from Kapiri Mposhi to Dar es Salaam.

The disastrous fall in the price of copper reduced probable earnings to below $500 million in 1975, compared with $900 million in 1974, and there was a serious exodus of white skilled workers from the mines. In June President Kaunda announced a policy of nationalizing resources. All freehold land titles were abolished and state control of cinemas, newspapers, tobacco factories, and privately owned nursing homes and houses for renting was introduced. The resignation of Prime Minister Mainza Chona was announced on May 27; he was succeeded by Elijah Mudenda, a former government minister. (KENNETH INGHAM)

[978.E.8.b.iii]

ZAMBIA

Education. (1973–74) Primary, pupils 810,234, teachers 16,916; secondary, pupils 61,354, teachers 2,880; vocational, pupils 4,609; teacher training, students 2,588, teachers 210; higher, students 2,324, teaching staff (1970) 189.

Finance. Monetary unit: kwacha, with (Sept. 22, 1975) a par value of 0.64 kwacha to U.S. $1 (free rate of 1.34 kwacha = £1 sterling). Gold, SDRs, and foreign exchange: (June 1975) U.S. $118.9 million; (June 1974) U.S. $358.5 million. Budget (1975 est.): revenue 644 million kwachas; expenditure 755 million kwachas. Gross domestic product: (1972) 1,217,000,000 kwachas; (1971) 1,178,000,000 kwachas. Cost of living (1970 = 100): (Feb. 1975) 136; (Feb. 1974) 126.

Foreign Trade. (1974) Imports 581.5 million kwachas; exports 904.7 million kwachas. Import sources (1973): U.K. 22%; South Africa 12%; U.S. 9%; Japan 9%; West Germany 7%; Iran 5%; Italy 5%. Export destinations (1973): Japan 24%; U.K. 20%; Italy 12%; West Germany 10%; France 8%; Brazil 5%. Main export copper 93%.

Agriculture. Production (in 000; metric tons; 1974; 1973 in parentheses): corn *c.* 350 (374); cassava (1973) *c.* 145, (1972) *c.* 145; millet *c.* 63 (*c.* 63); sorghum *c.* 190 (*c.* 190); peanuts (1973) *c.* 100, (1972) *c.* 100; sugar, raw value *c.* 97 (*c.* 65); tobacco *c.* 7 (*c.* 7). Livestock (in 000; 1973–74): cattle *c.* 1,748; sheep *c.* 30; goats (1972–73) *c.* 190; pigs *c.* 121; chickens (1972–73) *c.* 7,500.

Industry. Production (in 000; metric tons; 1974): copper 669; coal (1973) 940; lead 25; zinc 58; electricity (kw-hr.) 5,936,000.

Zoos and Botanical Gardens

Zoos. Throughout the world zoos were realizing more than ever the enormous educational potential of their animals. In the U.K., Edinburgh Zoo undertook to develop a national program of wildlife and environmental education for all sections of the community, and during the year some 25,000 children alone used the zoo's educational centre.

A highly successful International Symposium of Zoo Design and Construction was held at Paignton Zoo, England. Almost every aspect of this complex subject was discussed by 127 delegates, representing most of the world's leading zoos. A second symposium was scheduled for 1976.

Oklahoma City's zoo recorded what was believed to be the first breeding of an aardwolf; it was being hand-reared in the nursery. The Slimbridge Wildfowl Trust, England, bred the African Maccoa duck for the first time in captivity; the two youngsters were hatched in the incubator and reared in the indoor propagation unit. Another "first" for Slimbridge was the rearing of spectacled or Fischer's eider ducks.

The breeding of reptiles is considered more difficult in many ways than that of mammals and birds. Chester Zoo, England, had been very successful in this field, and in 1975 it bred, among other species, Solomon Island prehensile-tailed skinks, believed to have been bred only once or twice in captivity before.

A number of the rarer animal species had studbooks with all the accumulated information about them kept at one particular zoo. Columbia Zoological Park, South Carolina, was accumulating data for a studbook on rare leopard subspecies and the brown hyena, while Chicago's Lincoln Park Zoo was keeping a studbook of the snow leopard. Under the studbook system, one zoo handled all the records for a particular rare species. A zoo actually having an animal received a duplicate record card. When an animal changed hands or died, this duplicate card was returned to the studbook keeper, who was also kept informed of births so that new record cards could be issued. Thus complete records of breeding and life span could be accumulated and mates for single animals could be found by consulting the studbook.

Zoos were playing an increasingly important part in the captive breeding of animals in danger of extinction. A paper circulated by the International Union for Conservation of Nature and Natural Resources listed 112 mammals that had become extinct since the year 1600. The World Wildlife Fund (WWF) recommended a captive breeding program for the pink pigeon and Mauritius parrakeet. The Mauritius kestrel had already laid fertile eggs in captivity. Four Japanese crested ibis were observed in the demilitarized zone in Korea, bringing the total known world population to 11. (*See* ENVIRONMENT.)

Many animals were living longer in zoos than they would in the wild state. Gorillas had long been considered delicate and difficult to keep for any length of time. Generally they were confined in hothouse conditions with very little fresh air, and soon succumbed. In recent years, however, they have bred in captivity and have lived for many years in the more conducive conditions provided for them in modern zoos, where they have spacious enclosures and access to fresh air, even in cold climates. The oldest gorilla in captivity was at the Philadelphia Zoo, where a male animal 44 years old had been at the zoo for 39 years.

KEYSTONE

Mother Maxi and baby Jane, the first camel born at Windsor Safari Park, England.

There were very few zoos in the world that had successfully bred elephants, but the Portland (Ore.) Zoological Gardens had done exceptionally well with these animals. However, they suffered a serious setback with the death of their breeding male, which had sired 15 youngsters since his arrival in 1962. An Asiatic elephant born at Chester Zoo unfortunately died shortly after birth; the mother had been pushed into a ditch before the baby was born, but it was not proved that this contributed toward the death of the youngster. The Dallas (Texas) Zoo reported the uncommon event of the birth of two white leopard cubs. Even more unusual, these youngsters were born to black leopard parents. The black leopard is not a separate species but a melanistic form of the common leopard, and for them to produce the leucistic form was extremely rare.

Cooperation between zoos in various countries was highlighted when a male gorilla was lent to Howlett's Zoo in England by Lincoln Park Zoo, Chicago. The animal sired three youngsters at Howlett's.

To the average visitor, many zoo animals appear very tame and docile. This was often far from the truth, however; even after many generations in captivity animals still retain much of their wild instinct and should always be treated with great respect. This point was illustrated forcibly by the deaths of a manager and his assistant, who were killed by lions at a small commercial zoo in France.

Ziggy, an Indian elephant with a highly publicized reputation as a killer—though it was denied by the keeper he once tried to trample—died at the Chicago Zoological Park in Brookfield, Ill., at the age of about 58. Named after showman Florenz Ziegfeld, who bought him as a calf for his daughter's birthday, Ziggy grew to be one of the largest elephants in captivity. After charging his trainer in 1941, he was sent to Brookfield Zoo, where he was shackled and confined in a solitary compound for nearly 30 years. A Ziggy Fund was established to build a secure enclosure for him, and he was finally freed on July 4, 1973, as an audience of cheering schoolchildren looked on.

(G. S. MOTTERSHEAD)

Zanzibar: *see* Tanzania

Zinc: *see* Mining and Quarrying

Zoology: *see* Life Sciences

Botanical Gardens. The worldwide economic recession, continuing inflation, and soaring fuel prices hit most botanical gardens during 1975. For example, the privately financed Birmingham Botanical Gardens, England, made a vain plea to the City Council for a £10,000 grant, and Scandinavian gardens were restricted in staffing. In order to conserve energy and to relate directly to home gardening, the trend at the Missouri Botanical Garden was away from indoor displays and toward more extensive outdoor displays utilizing the entire 49-ac. area.

In Iran, where financial considerations were not restrictive, a spectacular project, the Aryamehr Botanical Garden, was taking form in the desert about 20 km. from Teheran. Planned in the style of a classical Persian garden, it included the construction of an enormous rock garden and waterfall through a gorge built up to 30 m. high. The 145 ha. were also being laid out with plantings depicting some of the floristic provinces of Iran, including the Caspian forest, Elburz and Zagros mountains, and salt desert.

Another new project was a forest botanical garden of 5.2 ha. at Thessaloniki, Greece, under the department of forestry of the Aristotelian University. Planting had started in 1970, and by early 1975 three-quarters of the 198 species listed had been planted. The garden was intended primarily as an aid for teaching forestry students, but it also offered possibilities for research. In Florida the Marie Selby Botanical Gardens, founded in 1973, were officially opened on July 7, 1975. This nine-acre garden was the only one in the world devoted entirely to the study, research, and display of epiphytic plants.

The role of botanical gardens in plant conservation formed the subject of the two-day meeting of the International Association of Botanical Gardens at Moscow in July. The activities of the 115 gardens in the U.S.S.R. were especially stressed. This conference was complemented by one on the same theme at the Royal Botanic Gardens, Kew, England, where the secretariat of the Threatened Plants Committee of the International Union for Conservation of Nature and Natural Resources was situated from January 1. At Kew provision was being made for special collections such as exotic *Salix, Escallonia, Ceanothus,* and *Yucca.* At Wakehurst Place, Ardingly, Sussex (an annex of the Royal Botanic Gardens), the Sir Henry Price Memorial Garden, designed as a traditional cottage garden, was opened in June.

Construction and layout of the Ericaceae garden at the National Botanic Gardens of South Africa, Kirstenbosch, were completed, and many of the well-established heaths were already flowering. Work had begun on the area selected for the establishment of ornamental trees and shrubs. In these and other areas a complete water reticulation system was installed before any plantings were made.

JOYCE DOPKEEN—THE NEW YORK TIMES

A $2.5 million renovation project at the New York Botanical Garden required the transplanting of more than 8,000 plants, including this 7,000-lb. Mexican desert tree.

A young redshark was successfully hatched in captivity for the first time at Denmark's scientific aquarium in Esbjerg. The egg capsule was just emerging in this view.

NORDISK PRESSEFOTO/PICTORIAL PARADE

Within the Strybing Arboretum, the five-acre collector's garden devoted to plants native to and characteristic of California was dedicated to the former supervisor, Arthur L. Menzies, who died in 1973. Groundbreaking ceremonies were held at South Coast Botanic Garden, Los Angeles, on May 21, 1975, marking the start of construction of the long-awaited administrative centre. The centre was designed to include research and educational activities in the garden, which had been successfully developed after 1960 on an unpromising 87-ac. garbage dump.

Increasing emphasis was being placed on education at the Royal Botanic Gardens, Sydney, Australia, and a variety of themes were being developed in this connection. A new tropical exhibition greenhouse was completed and was being stocked with plants from all over the world. Considerable attention also was being given to a special collection of native Australian orchids. A new succulent garden was being developed, and a rich collection of cacti and other succulents had been accumulated in preparation for planting out.

At the University Botanic Garden, Cambridge, England, the general educational value of the garden was improved by the addition of several demonstrations. Although some of these were of temporary exhibits in the greenhouses, others were more permanent displays on a number of themes, including a European collection of *Saxifraga,* ecotypes of native British *Juniperus communis,* and special displays of bromeliads, orchids, and ferns. A conservation unit with special responsibility for the collection, documentation, and propagation of endangered species, especially in the East Anglian region of England, was established at Cambridge. (FRANK N. HEPPER)

[355.C.6]

ENCYCLOPÆDIA BRITANNICA FILMS. *A Zoo's-Eye View: Dawn to Dark* (1973); *Pandas: A Gift from China* (1974).

CONTRIBUTORS

Names of contributors to the Britannica Book of the Year *with the articles written by them. The arrangement is alphabetical by last name.*

AARSDAL, STENER. Economic Editor, *Børsen,* Copenhagen.
Biography *(in part)*; Denmark

ADAMS, ANDREW M. Correspondent, CBS Radio; *Daily Mail,* London; *San Francisco Chronicle; Black Belt* magazine. Editor and Publisher, *Sumo World.*
Combat Sports *(in part)*

ADHIKARY, MUKUNDA DAS. Secretary, International Society for Krishna Consciousness, United Kingdom.
Biography *(in part)*

AGRELLA, JOSEPH C. Turf Editor, *Chicago Sun-Times.* Co-author of *Ten Commandments for Professional Handicapping; American Race Horses.*
Equestrian Sports *(in part)*

ALEXIOU, CHRISTOS. Lecturer in Modern Greek, School of Hellenic and Roman Studies, University of Birmingham, England.
Literature *(in part)*

ALLABY, MICHAEL. Free-lance Writer and Lecturer. Author of *The Eco-Activists; Who Will Eat?; Ecology; A Blueprint for Survival.* Editor of *The Survival Handbook.*
Environment *(in part)*

ALLAN, J. A. Lecturer in Geography, School of Oriental and African Studies, University of London.
Libya

ALLUM, P. A. Reader in Politics, University of Reading, England; associated with the university's Centre for the Advanced Study of Italian Society. Author of *Politics and Society in Post-War Naples; Italy: Republic Without Government?*
Italy: *Special Report*

ALSTON, REX. Broadcaster and Journalist. Author of *Taking the Air; Over to Rex Alston; Test Commentary; Watching Cricket.*
Cricket

ANTONINI, GUSTAVO. Research Associate Professor, Center for Latin American Studies, University of Florida. Author of *Population and Energy: A Systems Analysis of Resource Utilization in the Dominican Republic.*
Dominican Republic

ARCHIBALD, JOHN J. Feature Writer, *St. Louis Post-Dispatch.* Author of *Bowling for Boys and Girls.*
Bowling *(in part)*

ARNOLD, BRUCE. Free-lance Journalist and Writer, Dublin.
Ireland

ARRINGTON, LEONARD JAMES. Church Historian, Church of Jesus Christ of Latter-day Saints. Author of *Great Basin Kingdom: An Economic History of the Latter-day Saints; Charles C. Rich: Mormon General and Western Frontiersman.*
Religion *(in part)*

ASHBY, PHILIP H. William H. Danforth Professor of Religion, Princeton University. Author of *Modern Trends in Hinduism; The Conflict of Religions.*
Religion *(in part)*

AYTON, CYRIL J. Editor, *Motorcycle Sport,* London.
Motor Sports *(in part)*

BALLARD, MARTIN. Director, Book Development Council, London.
Publishing *(in part)*

BASS, HOWARD. Journalist and Broadcaster. Editor, *Winter Sports,* 1948–69. Winter Sports Correspondent, *Daily Telegraph* and *Sunday Telegraph,* London; *Christian Science Monitor,* Boston; *Canadian Skater,* Vancouver; *Skate,* London; *Skating,* Boston; *Ski Racing,* Denver; *Sportsworld,* London. Author of *The Sense in Sport; This Skating Age; The Magic of Skiing; International Encyclopaedia of Winter Sports; Let's Go Skating.*
Biography *(in part)*; Ice Hockey *(in part)*; Winter Sports

BEALL, JOHN V. Business Development Engineer, Fluor Utah, Inc. Author of sections 1 and 34, *Mining Engineering Handbook.* Frequent Contributor to *Mining Engineering,* New York.
Mining and Quarrying *(in part)*

BEATTY, J. R. Senior Research Associate, B. F. Goodrich Research and Development Center, Brecksville, Ohio. Co-author of *Concepts in Compounding.*
Industrial Review *(in part)*

BECKWITH, DAVID C. Correspondent, *Time* magazine, Washington, D.C.
United States Statistical Supplement: *Developments in the states in 1975*

BERGERRE, MAX. Correspondent ANSA for Vatican Affairs, Rome.
Vatican City State

BICKELHAUPT, DAVID L. Professor of Insurance and Finance, College of Administrative Science, Ohio State University. Author of *Transition to Multiple-Line Insurance Companies; General Insurance* (9th ed.).
Industrial Review *(in part)*

BILEFIELD, LIONEL. Technical Journalist.
Industrial Review *(in part)*

BINSTED, ARTHUR T. E. Chairman, British Bottlers' Institute, London.
Industrial Review *(in part)*

BLYTH, ALAN. Music Critic, *The Times,* London; Assistant Editor, *Opera;* Broadcaster.
Biography *(in part)*; Music *(in part)*

BODDY, WILLIAM C. Editor, *Motor Sport.* Full Member, Guild of Motoring Writers. Author of *The 200 Mile Race; The World's Land Speed Record; Continental Sports Cars; The Sports Car Pocketbook; The Bugatti Story; History of Montlhéry; Vintage Years of the Morgan Threewheeler.*
Motor Sports *(in part)*

BOLT, PETER H. Secretary, British Committee, World Methodist Council. Author of *A Way of Loving.*
Religion *(in part)*

BOONSTRA, DICK. Assistant Professor, Department of Political Science, Free University, Amsterdam.
Netherlands, The; Surinam

BOOTH, JOHN NICHOLLS. Lecturer and Writer; Co-founder, Japan Free Religious Association; Senior Pastor of a number of U.S. churches. Author of *The Quest for Preaching Power; Introducing Unitarian Universalism.*
Religion *(in part)*

BOSWALL, JEFFERY. Producer of Sound and Television Programs, British Broadcasting Corporation Natural History Unit, Bristol, Eng.
Life Sciences *(in part)*

BOYLE, C. L. Lieutenant Colonel, R.A. (retd.). Chairman, Survival Service Commission, International Union for Conservation of Nature and Natural Resources, 1958–63; Secretary, Fauna Preservation Society, London, 1950–63.
Environment *(in part)*

BRACKMAN, ARNOLD C. Asian Affairs Specialist. Author of *Indonesian Communism: A History; Southeast Asia's Second Front: The Power Struggle in the Malay Archipelago; The Communist Collapse in Indonesia; The Last Emperor.*
Indonesia

BRADSHER, HENRY S. Foreign Affairs Specialist, *Washington* (D.C.) *Star.*
Philippines

BRAIDWOOD, ROBERT J. Professor of Old World Prehistory, the Oriental Institute, and Professor of Anthropology, the University of Chicago. Author of *Prehistoric Men* (8th ed.); *Archaeology of the Plain of Antioch.*
Archaeology *(in part)*

BRAZEE, RUTLAGE J. Geophysicist, EDS/NOAA, U.S. Dept. of Commerce, Boulder, Colo.
Earth Sciences *(in part)*

BRECHER, KENNETH. Assistant Professor of Physics, Massachusetts Institute of Technology. Co-author and Co-editor of *High Energy Astrophysics and Its Relation to Elementary Particle Physics.*
Astronomy

BRIERRE, ANNIE. Literary Critic, *La Croix; Histoire Pour Tous; France-Culture; France-U.S.A.* Author of *Ninon de Lenclos.*
Literature *(in part)*

BROWN, WELDON G. Professor Emeritus, University of Chicago.
Chemistry *(in part)*

BRUNO, HAL. Chief Political Correspondent, *Newsweek* magazine.
Biography *(in part)*

BURDIN, JOEL L. Associate Director, American Association of Colleges for Teacher Education; Executive Secretary, Associated Organizations for Teacher Education; Editor, *Journal of Teacher Education,* Washington, D.C. Author of *A Reader's Guide to the Comprehensive Models for Preparing Elementary Teachers.* Co-author of *Elementary School Curriculum and Instruction.*
Education *(in part)*

BURKE, DONALD P. Executive Editor, *Chemical Week.*
Industrial Review *(in part)*

BURKS, ARDATH W. Professor of Political Science and Associate Vice-President for Academic Affairs, Rutgers University, New Brunswick, N.J. Author of *The Government of Japan; East Asia: China, Korea, Japan.*
Japan

BURNETT, LEE. Director, Department of Hematology, National Institute of Cardiology, Mexico City; Bullfight Columnist, *El Redondel.* Translator into English of *El Toreo* by Rafael Vilar.
Arena Sports *(in part)*

BUTLER, DAVID RICHARD. Publications and Information Officer, Institution of Gas Engineers, London.
Energy *(in part)*

BUTLER, FRANK. Sports Editor, *News of the World,* London. Author of *A History of Boxing in Britain.*
Combat Sports *(in part)*

CALASCIONE, JOHN. Press and Publications Officer, International Organization of Consumers Unions, The Hague, Neth.
Consumerism *(in part)*

CALHOUN, DAVID R. Editor, Encyclopædia Britannica, Yearbooks.
Biography *(in part)*; Industrial Review *(in part)*

CAMPBELL, H. C. Chief Librarian, Toronto Public Library, Toronto. Author of *Public Libraries in the Urban Metropolitan Setting.*
Literature *(in part)*

CAMPOS DE ESPAÑA, RAFAEL. Journalist; Chief, Bullfighting Division, Radiotelevisión Española. Author of *Joselito; Filosofía del toreo; Los toros y la radio.*
Arena Sports *(in part)*

LORD CARADON. Formerly U.K. Minister of State for Foreign and Commonwealth Affairs and Permanent Representative at the United Nations.
Dependent States: *Special Report*

CASEMENT, RICHARD. Transport Correspondent, *The Economist,* London. Author of *Urban Traffic: Policies in Congestion.*
Transportation *(in part)*

CASSIDY, VICTOR M. Writer and Editor, currently at work on a biography of Wyndham Lewis.
Biography *(in part)*

CHALMEY, LUCIEN. Honorary Secretary-General, Union Internationale des Producteurs et Distributeurs d'Énergie Électrique, Paris.
Energy *(in part)*

CHAPMAN, KENNETH F. Editor, *Stamp Collecting;* Philatelic Correspondent, *The Times,* London. Author of *Good Stamp Collecting; Commonwealth Stamp Collecting.*
Philately and Numismatics *(in part)*

CHAPPELL, DUNCAN. Director, Law and Justice Study Center, Battelle Memorial Institute, Seattle, Washington. Co-author of *The Police and the Public in Australia and New Zealand; The Australian Criminal Justice System.*
Crime and Law Enforcement

CHOATE, ROGER N. Stockholm Correspondent, *The Times,* London.
Sweden

CHOW, CLAIRE SANDRA. Production Editor, Encyclopædia Britannica.
Biography *(in part)*

CHU, HUNG-TI. Expert in Far Eastern Affairs; Former International Civil Servant and University Professor.
China; Taiwan

CLARKE, R. O. Principal Administrator, Social Affairs and Industrial Relations Division, Organization for Economic Cooperation and Development, Paris. Co-author of *Workers' Participation in Management in Britain.*
Industrial Relations

CLEGG, JERRY S. Professor of Philosophy, Mills College, Oakland, Calif. Author of *The Structure of Plato's Philosophy.*
Philosophy

CLEVELAND, WILLIAM A. Geography Editor, Encyclopædia Britannica.
Mining and Quarrying *(in part)*

CLIFTON, DONALD F. Professor of Metallurgy, University of Idaho.
Materials Sciences *(in part)*

CLOUD, STANLEY WILLS. Political Correspondent, *Time* magazine.
Biography *(in part)*

COCKSEDGE, DAVID. Features Writer, *Athletics Weekly.*
Biography *(in part)*; Track and Field Sports *(in part)*

COGLE, T. C. J. Editor, *Electrical Review,* London.
Industrial Review *(in part)*

COLLINS, L. J. D. Lecturer in Bulgarian History, University of London.
Cyprus

COPELAND, JAMES C. Associate Professor of Microbiology, Ohio State University; Editor, *Microbial Genetics Bulletin.*
Life Sciences *(in part)*

COPPOCK, CHARLES DENNIS. Public Relations Officer, English Lacrosse Union. Author of "Men's Lacrosse" in *The Oxford Companion to Sports and Games.*
Field Hockey and Lacrosse *(in part)*

COSTIN, STANLEY H. British Correspondent, *Australian Tailor and Menswear* and *Herrenjournal International.* Former President, Men's Fashion Writers International.
Fashion and Dress *(in part)*

CRATER, RUFUS W. Chief Correspondent, *Broadcasting,* New York City.
Television and Radio *(in part)*

CROSSLAND, NORMAN. Bonn Correspondent, *The Guardian* and *The Economist,* London.
Biography *(in part)*; German Democratic Republic; Germany, Federal Republic of

CROZIER, BRIAN. Director and Co-founder, Institute for the Study of Conflict, London; Editor, *Conflict Studies.* Author of *Franco; De Gaulle; A Theory of Conflict.*
Crime and Law Enforcement: *Special Report*

CVIIC, K. F. Leader Writer and East European Specialist, *The Economist,* London.
Yugoslavia

CZERWINSKI, EDWARD J. Professor of Slavic Literature, State University of New York, Stony Brook; Artistic Director, Slavic Cultural Center, Inc. Author of *The Soviet Invasion of Czechoslovakia; The Polish Theatre of the Absurd.*
Literature *(in part)*

DAIFUKU, HIROSHI. Chief, Sites and Monuments Division, UNESCO, Paris.
Historic Preservation

DAVID, TUDOR. Managing Editor, *Education,* London.
Education *(in part)*

DAVIS, DONALD A. Editor, *Drug & Cosmetic Industry,* New York. Contributor to *The Science and Technology of Aerosol Packaging.*
Industrial Review *(in part)*

DAWBER, ALFRED. Textile consultant in all aspects of textile production. Specialized writer on textile, engineering, and electrical subjects.
Industrial Review *(in part)*

d'EÇA, RAUL. Retired from foreign service with U.S. Information Service. Co-author of *Latin American History.*
Brazil

DECRAENE, PHILIPPE. Member of editorial staff, *Le Monde,* Paris. Editor in Chief, *Revue française d'Études politiques africaines.* Author of *Le Panafricanisme; Tableau des Partis Politiques Africains.*
Cameroon; Central African Republic; Chad; Comoro Islands; Congo; Dahomey; Dependent States *(in part)*; Gabon; Guinea; Ivory Coast; Malagasy Republic; Mali; Mauritania; Niger; Senegal; Togo; Tunisia; Upper Volta

de la BARRE, KENNETH. Director, Montreal Office, Arctic Institute of North America.
Arctic Regions

DE PUY, NORMAN R. Executive Minister, First Baptist Church of Dearborn, Mich. Author of *The Bible Alive.*
Religion *(in part)*

DESAUTELS, PAUL ERNEST. Curator, Department of Mineral Sciences, National Museum of Natural History, Smithsonian Institution, Washington, D.C. Author of *The Mineral Kingdom; The Gem Kingdom.*
Industrial Review *(in part)*

DIRNBACHER, ELFRIEDE. Austrian Civil Servant.
Austria

DRUCKENBROD, JOHN DAVID. President, Druckenbrod Associates, Silver Spring, Md. Author of *How Trade Associations Are Restoring Order to World Trade.*
Industrial Review *(in part)*

DUHART, JAIME R. Research Officer, Economics Department, Lloyds Bank International Ltd., London.
Argentina; Latin-American Affairs

DUNICAN, PETER. Senior Partner, Ove Arup Partnership, London.
Engineering Projects *(in part)*

EAGLE, HERBERT J. Chairman for Slavic Languages and Literatures, Purdue University, Lafayette, Ind.
Literature *(in part)*

EDLIN, HERBERT L. Publications Officer, Forestry Commission of Great Britain. Author of *Wayside and Woodland Trees; What Wood Is That?; Guide to Tree Planting and Cultivation; Observer's Book of Trees.* Co-author of *Atlas of Plant Life.*
Environment *(in part)*

EISENBERG, WARREN W. Administrative Assistant to Rep. H. John Heinz III, Washington, D.C.
Populations and Areas

EIU. The Economist Intelligence Unit, London.
Economy, World *(in part)*

EMOTO, YOSHINOBU. Staff Writer, *Yomiuri Shimbun*, Tokyo.
Biography (*in part*)

ENGELS, JAN R. Editor, *Vooruitgang* (Quarterly of the Belgian Party for Freedom and Progress), Brussels.
Belgium

ERVIN, SAM J., JR. Retired U.S. Senator from North Carolina. Former Chairman of the Senate Watergate Committee.
Feature Article: *The Bicentennial of the United States*

EWART, W. D. Editor and Director, *Fairplay International Shipping Weekly*, London. Author of *Marine Engines; Atomic Submarines; Hydrofoils and Hovercraft; Building a Ship*. Editor of *World Atlas of Shipping*.
Industrial Review (*in part*); Transportation (*in part*)

FABINYI, ANDREW. Consultant, Pergamon Press, Australia.
Publishing (*in part*)

FARR, D. M. L. Professor of History, Carleton University, Ottawa. Author of *Two Democracies; The Canadian Experience*.
Canada

FENDELL, ROBERT J. New York Editor, *Automotive News*. Author of *The New Era Car Book and Auto Survival Guide*: Co-author of *Encyclopedia of Motor Racing Greats*.
Motor Sports (*in part*)

FERRIER, R. W. Group Historian, British Petroleum Company Ltd., London.
Energy (*in part*)

FIDDICK, PETER. Specialist Writer, *The Guardian*, London.
Biography (*in part*); Publishing (*in part*)

FINK, DIANE J. Director, Division of Cancer Control and Rehabilitation, U.S. National Cancer Institute, Bethesda, Md.
Health and Disease (*in part*)

FIRTH, DAVID. Editor, *The Friend*, London; formerly Editor, *Quaker Monthly*, London.
Religion (*in part*)

FISHER, DAVID. Civil Engineer, Freeman Fox & Partners, London; formerly Executive Editor, *Engineering*, London.
Engineering Projects (*in part*)

FLANAGAN, J. C. Newspaper Columnist.
Water Sports (*in part*)

FOWELL, R. J. Lecturer, Department of Mining Engineering, University of Newcastle upon Tyne, England.
Energy (*in part*)

FRADY, WILLIAM ENSIGN, III. Editor, *Water Polo Scoreboard*, Newport Beach, Calif.
Water Sports (*in part*)

FRANCO, JEAN. Chairperson, Department of Spanish and Portuguese, Stanford University. Author of *The Modern Culture of Latin America; An Introduction to Spanish-American Literature*.
Literature (*in part*)

FRANKLIN, HAROLD. Editor, *English Bridge Quarterly*. Bridge Correspondent, *Yorkshire Post; Yorkshire Evening Post*. Broadcaster. Author of *Best of Bridge on the Air*.
Contract Bridge

FREDRICKSON, DAVID A. Associate Professor of Anthropology and Chairman, Department of Anthropology, California State College, Sonoma, Rohnert Park.
Archaeology (*in part*)

FREEMAN, ARTHUR. Editor in Chief, American Veterinary Medical Association, Schaumburg, Ill.
Veterinary Science

FRIDOVICH, IRWIN. Professor of Biochemistry, Duke University Medical Center, Durham, N.C. Contributor to *Oxidase and Redox Systems; Molecular Mechanisms of Oxygen Activation*.
Life Sciences (*in part*)

FRIEDLY, ROBERT L. Executive Director, Office of Communication, Christian Church (Disciples of Christ), Indianapolis, Ind.
Religion (*in part*)

FROST, DAVID. Rugby Union Correspondent, *The Guardian*, London.
Football (*in part*)

GADDUM, PETER W. Chairman, H. T. Gaddum and Company Ltd., Silk Merchants, Macclesfield, Cheshire, Eng. President, International Silk Association, Lyons. Author of *Silk—How and Where It Is Produced*.
Industrial Review (*in part*)

GALVANO, FABIO. Special Correspondent, *Lo Speciale*, Milan, Italy.
Biography (*in part*); Italy

GANADO, ALBERT. Lawyer, Malta.
Malta

GEORGE, T. J. S. Editor, *Asiaweek*, Hong Kong. Author of *Krishna Menon: A Biography; Lee Kuan Yew's Singapore*.
Biography (*in part*); Cambodia; Korea; Laos; Southeast Asian Affairs; Thailand

GIBNEY, FRANK. President, TBS-Britannica Co., Ltd., Tokyo. Author of *Japan: The Fragile Superpower*.
Feature Article: *The Meiji Restoration: American Democracy in Japan*

GJESTER, FAY. Oslo Correspondent, *Financial Times*, London.
Norway

GOLDSMITH, ARTHUR. Editorial Director, *Popular Photography*, New York City. Author of *The Photography Game*; Co-author of *The Eye of Eisenstaedt*.
Photography

GOLOMBEK, HARRY. British Chess Champion, 1947, 1949, and 1955. Chess Correspondent, *The Times* and *Observer*, London. Author of *Penguin Handbook on the Game of Chess; Modern Opening Chess Strategy*.
Board Games (*in part*)

GOODWIN, R. M. Free-lance Writer, London.
Equestrian Sports (*in part*)

GOULD, DONALD W. Medical Correspondent, *New Statesman*, London.
Drug Abuse; Health and Disease (*in part*)

GREEN, BENNY. Jazz Critic, *Observer*, London; Record Reviewer, British Broadcasting Corporation. Author of *The Reluctant Art; Blame It on My Youth; 58 Minutes to London; Jazz Decade; Drums in My Ears*. Contributor to *Encyclopedia of Jazz*.
Music (*in part*)

GREEN, LARRY. Reporter, *Chicago Daily News*; formerly Head of newspaper's Indochina Bureau.
Vietnam

GRIFFITHS, A. R. G. Senior Lecturer in History, Flinders University of South Australia.
Australia; Biography (*in part*); Nauru; Papua New Guinea

GROSSBERG, ROBERT H. Executive Director, U.S. Jai Alai Players Association, Miami, Fla.; Vice-President, Shearson Hayden Stone Inc.
Court Games (*in part*)

GROVE, ROBERT D. Former Director, Division of Vital Statistics, U.S. Public Health Service. Co-author of *Vital Statistics Rates in the United States, 1900–1940; Vital Statistics Rates in the United States, 1940–1960*.
Demography

HADY, EDMUND CARL. Executive Secretary, American Dart Association. Author and Publisher of *American and English Dart Game Including Tournament Rules*.
Target Sports (*in part*)

HALE, JOHN. Research Officer, Economics Department, Lloyds Bank International Ltd., London.
Bolivia; Guatemala; Uruguay

HALSEY, ASHLEY, JR. Editor, *The American Rifleman*; Director of Publications, National Rifle Association, Washington, D.C.
Target Sports (*in part*)

HANI, GYO. Assistant Managing Editor, *Japan Times*, Tokyo. Author of *Whats and Whatnots About New English*.
Biography (*in part*)

HARDMAN, THOMAS C. Editor and Publisher, *The Water Skier*, American Water Ski Association. Co-author of *Let's Go Water Skiing*.
Water Sports (*in part*)

HARRIES, DAVID A. Director, Kinnear Moodie (1973) Ltd., Peterborough, Eng.
Engineering Projects (*in part*)

HARTER, DONALD H. Professor of Neurology and Microbiology, Columbia University, New York City. Contributor to *Harrison's Principles of Internal Medicine; A Textbook of Neurology; Pharmacotherapeutics of Oral Disease*.
Health and Disease (*in part*)

HASEGAWA, RYUSAKU. Editor, TBS-Britannica Co., Ltd., Tokyo.
Baseball (*in part*)

HAWKLAND, WILLIAM D. Professor of Law, University of Illinois. Author of *Sales Under Uniform Commercial Code; Cases on Bills and Notes; Commercial Paper; Transactional Guide of the Uniform Commercial Code; Cases on Sales and Security*.
Law (*in part*)

HAWLEY, H. B. Specialist, Human Nutrition and Food Science, Switzerland.
Food Processing (*in part*)

HEBBLETHWAITE, PETER. Deputy Editor, *Frontier*, Oxford, England. Author of *Bernanos; The Council Fathers and Atheism; Understanding the Synod; The Runaway Church*.
Religion (*in part*)

HEINDL, L. A. Executive Secretary, U.S. National Committee for the International Hydrological Decade, National Research Council, Washington, D.C. Author of *The Water We Live By*.
Earth Sciences (*in part*)

HENDERSHOTT, MYRL C. Associate Professor of Oceanography, Scripps Institution of Oceanography, La Jolla, Calif.
Earth Sciences (*in part*)

HEPPER, FRANK N. Principal Scientific Officer, Herbarium, Royal Botanic Gardens, Kew, Eng. Co-author of *Plant Collectors in West Africa.* Editor of *Flora of West Tropical Africa* (vol. ii and iii).
Zoos and Botanical Gardens *(in part)*

HERMAN, ROBIN CATHY. Reporter.
Ice Hockey *(in part)*

HERZOG, FREDERICK J. Managing Director, Billiard Congress of America, Chicago.
Billiard Games

HESS, MARVIN G. Executive Vice-President, National Wrestling Coaches Association, Salt Lake City, Utah.
Combat Sports *(in part)*

HILBORNE, BARBARA. Senior Picture Editor, London Office, Encyclopædia Britannica, Yearbooks.
Historic Preservation: *Special Report*

HOLLANDS, R. L. Hockey Correspondent, *Daily Telegraph,* London; Chairman, Hockey Writers Club. Co-author of *Hockey.*
Field Hockey and Lacrosse *(in part)*

HOPE, THOMAS W. President and Publisher, Hope Reports, Inc., Rochester, N.Y. Author of *Hope Reports AV-USA 1972; Hope Reports Education & Media 1972.*
Motion Pictures *(in part)*

HORN, PATRICE DAILY. Editor, *Behavior Today;* Senior Editor, *Psychology Today,* Del Mar, Calif.
Behavioural Sciences

HORRY, JOHN H. Formerly Squash Editor, *British Lawn Tennis and Squash.* Contributor to *The Oxford Companion to Sports and Games.*
Tennis and Rackets *(in part)*

HORSBRUGH-PORTER, SIR ANDREW. Polo Correspondent, *The Times,* London.
Equestrian Sports *(in part)*

HOSKINS, DALMER. Research Officer, International Social Security Association, Geneva.
Social and Welfare Services *(in part)*

HOSOJIMA, IZUMI. Editorial Writer, *Mainichi Shimbun,* Tokyo.
Biography *(in part)*

HOTZ, LOUIS. Former Editorial Writer, the *Johannesburg* (S.Af.) *Star.* Co-author and contributor to *The Jews in South Africa: A History.*
South Africa

HUGHES, TERENCE. Free-lance Writer, London.
Television and Radio *(in part)*

HUNNINGS, NEVILLE MARCH. General Editor, Common Law Reports Ltd., London. Editor of *Common Market Law Reports, European Law Digest,* and *Eurolaw Commercial Intelligence.* Author of *Film Censors and the Law.* Co-editor of *Legal Problems of an Enlarged European Community.*
Law *(in part)*

INGHAM, KENNETH. Professor of History, University of Bristol, Eng. Author of *Reformers in India; A History of East Africa.*
Angola; Cape Verde Islands; Guinea-Bissau; Kenya; Malawi; Mozambique; Rhodesia; São Tomé and Príncipe; Tanzania; Uganda; Zaire; Zambia

IRF. International Road Federation, Geneva.
Engineering Projects *(in part)*

JACQUET, CONSTANT H., JR. Staff Associate for Information Services, Office of Research, Evaluation, and Planning, National Council of Churches. Editor, *Yearbook of American and Canadian Churches.*
United States Statistical Supplement: *Church Membership table*

JARDINE, ADRIAN. Company Director and Public Relations Consultant. Member, Guild of Yachting Writers.
Sailing

JASPERT, W. PINCUS. Technical Editorial Consultant. European Editor, North American Publishing Company, Philadelphia, Pa. Member, Society of Photographic Scientists and Engineers; Member, Comprint International Planning Committee. Editor of *Encyclopaedia of Type Faces.*
Industrial Review *(in part)*

JONES, C. M. Editor, *World Bowls; Lawn Tennis.* Author of *Winning Bowls; How to Become a Champion;* numerous books on tennis. Co-author of *Tackle Bowls My Way; Bryant on Bowls.*
Bowling *(in part)*

JONES, W. GLYN. Professor of Scandinavian Studies, University of Newcastle upon Tyne, Eng. Author of *Johannes Jørgensens modne år; Johannes Jørgensen; Denmark; William Heinesen; Færø og kosmos.*
Literature *(in part)*

JOSEPH, LOU. Manager of Media Relations, Bureau of Public Information, American Dental Association. Author of *A Doctor Discusses Allergy: Facts and Fiction.*
Health and Disease *(in part)*

JUDD, PRUDENCE. Research Officer, Economics Department, Lloyds Bank International Ltd., London.
Ecuador; Peru

KAAN, FREDERIK H. Secretary of the Department of Cooperation and Witness, World Alliance of Reformed Churches (Presbyterian and Congregational), Geneva. Author of *Pilgrim Praise; Break Not the Circle* (hymnals).
Religion *(in part)*

KATZ, MICHAEL. Motor Sports Editor, *New York Times;* formerly Sports Editor, *International Herald Tribune,* Paris.
Gambling

KATZ, WILLIAM A. Professor, School of Library Science, State University of New York, Albany. Author of *Magazines for Libraries* (2nd ed. and supplement).
Publishing *(in part)*

KELLEHER, JOHN A. Editor, *The Dominion,* Wellington, N.Z.
New Zealand

KERRIGAN, ANTHONY. Visiting Professor, State University of New York, Buffalo. Editor and Translator of *Selected Works* of Miguel de Unamuno (10 vol.) and of works of Jorge Luis Borges. Author of *At the Front Door of the Atlantic.*
Literature *(in part)*

KILIAN, MICHAEL D. Columnist and Editorial Writer, *Chicago Tribune;* News Commentator, WTTW Television and WBBM Radio, Chicago.
Aerial Sports

KILLIN, ORLAND B. Professor of Industrial Education and Technology, Eastern Washington State College, Cheney.
Industrial Review *(in part)*

KILNER, PETER. Editor, *Arab Report and Record,* London.
Algeria; Morocco; Sudan

KIMCHE, JON. Editor, *Afro-Asian Affairs,* London. Author of *There Could Have Been Peace: The Untold Story of Why We Failed with Palestine and Again with Israel.*
Israel

KIND, JOSHUA B. Associate Professor of Art History, Northern Illinois University, De Kalb. Author of *Rouault.*
Museums *(in part)*

KITAGAWA, JOSEPH M. Professor of History of Religions and Dean of the Divinity School, the University of Chicago. Author of *Religions of the East; Religion in Japanese History.*
Religion *(in part)*

KLARE, HUGH J. Chairman, Gloucestershire Probation Training Committee, England. Secretary, Howard League for Penal Reform 1950–71. Author of *People in Prison.* Regular Contributor to *Justice of the Peace.*
Prisons and Penology

KNECHT, JEAN. Formerly Assistant Foreign Editor, *Le Monde,* Paris; Formerly Permanent Correspondent in Washington and Vice-President of the Association de la Presse Diplomatique Française.
France

KNORR, N. H. President, Watch Tower Bible and Tract Society of Pennsylvania.
Religion *(in part)*

KOPPER, PHILIP. Free-lance Writer, Washington, D.C.
Biography *(in part)*; **Nobel Prizes**

KOUTCHOUMOW, JOSEPH A. Secretary General, International Publishers Association, Geneva. Author of art and children's books.
Publishing *(in part)*

KOVAN, RICHARD W. Features Editor, *Nuclear Engineering International,* London.
Industrial Review *(in part)*

KRADER, BARBARA. Past President, Society for Ethnomusicology; Executive Secretary, International Folk Music Council, London, 1965–66.
Music *(in part)*

KUBITSCHEK, H. E. Senior Biophysicist, Division of Biological and Medical Research, Argonne National Laboratory. Author of *Introduction to Research with Continuous Cultures.*
Life Sciences *(in part)*

KWAN-TERRY, JOHN. Senior Lecturer, Department of English Language and Literature, University of Singapore. Editor of *The Teaching of Languages in Institutions of Higher Learning in Southeast Asia.*
Literature *(in part)*

LAMB, KEVIN M. Sports Writer, *Chicago Daily News.*
Biography *(in part)*; **Football** *(in part)*

LAPPÉ, MARC. Associate for the Biological Sciences, Institute of Society, Ethics, and the Life Sciences, Hastings-on-Hudson, New York.
Health and Disease: *Special Report*

LEGUM, COLIN. Associate Editor and Commonwealth Correspondent, *Observer,* London. Author of *Must We Lose Africa?; Congo Disaster.* Editor of *Africa Contemporary Record.*
African Affairs; Biography *(in part)*

LEIFER, MICHAEL. Reader in International Relations, London School of Economics and Political Science. Author of *Dilemmas of Statehood in Southeast Asia.*
Malaysia; Singapore

LENNOX-KERR, PETER. European Editor, *Textile Industries*. Author of *Index to Man-Made Fibres of the World; The World Fibres Book*. Editor of *Nonwovens '71*.
Industrial Review (*in part*)

LEVE, MORTON. Executive Director, United States Handball Association, Skokie, Ill.; Founder and Executive Director, National Court Clubs Association. Co-author of *Inside Handball*.
Court Games (*in part*)

LITTELL, FRANKLIN H. Professor of Religion, Temple University, Philadelphia, Pa. Co-editor of *Weltkirchenlexikon*.
Religion (*in part*)

LULING, VIRGINIA R. Social Anthropologist.
Somalia

LUSTIG, LAWRENCE K. Managing Editor, Encyclopædia Britannica, Yearbooks.
Earth Sciences: *Special Report*

McCARTHY, ABIGAIL QUIGLEY. Free-lance Writer; Columnist, *Commonweal* and *New York Times*. Author of *Private Faces/Public Places*.
United Nations: *Special Report*

McCONE, JOHN A. Formerly Director, U.S. Central Intelligence Agency; Retired Chairman of the Board, Hendy International Company.
Defense: *Special Report*

MACDONALD, BARRIE. Lecturer in History, Massey University, Palmerston North, N.Z. Author of several articles on the history and politics of Pacific islands.
Fiji; Tonga; Western Samoa

MacDONALD, M. C. Director, Econtel Research Ltd., London. Editor, *World Series; Business Cycle Series*.
Agriculture and Food Supplies (*in part*); Transportation (*in part*)

MACDONALD, TREVOR J. Manager, International Affairs, British Steel Corporation.
Industrial Review (*in part*)

MACGREGOR-MORRIS, PAMELA. Equestrian Correspondent, *The Times* and *Horse and Hound*, London. Author of books on equestrian topics.
Equestrian Sports (*in part*)

MALLETT, H. M. F. Editor, *Weekly Wool Chart*, Bradford, England.
Industrial Review (*in part*)

MANGO, ANDREW. Orientalist and Broadcaster.
Biography (*in part*); Turkey

MANSFIELD, PETER. Formerly Middle East Correspondent, *Sunday Times*, London. Free-lance Writer on Middle East affairs.
Bahrain; Biography (*in part*); Egypt; Iraq; Jordan; Kuwait; Lebanon; Middle Eastern Affairs; Oman; Qatar; Saudi Arabia; Syria; United Arab Emirates; Yemen, People's Democratic Republic of; Yemen Arab Republic

MARCELLO, ALDO. Civil Engineer.
Engineering Projects (*in part*)

MARSHALL, J. G. SCOTT. Horticultural Consultant.
Gardening (*in part*)

MARTENHOFF, JAMES E. Boating Writer, *Miami* (Fla.) *Herald*. Author of *Handbook of Skin and Scuba Diving; The Powerboat Handbook*.
Water Sports (*in part*)

MARTY, MARTIN E. Professor of the History of Modern Christianity, University of Chicago; Associate Editor, *The Christian Century*.
Religion (*in part*)

MARYLES, DAISY G. News Editor, *Publishers Weekly*, New York City.
Publishing (*in part*)

MASI, ALFONSE T. Professor of Medicine and Director, Division of Connective Tissue Diseases, Department of Medicine, University of Tennessee, Memphis.
Health and Disease (*in part*)

MASON, JOAN L. Executive Secretary, American Canoe Association, Denver, Colo.; Book Editor, *Canoe* magazine.
Water Sports (*in part*)

MATEJA, JAMES L. Automobile Writer and Financial Reporter, *Chicago Tribune*.
Industrial Review (*in part*)

MATTHÍASSON, BJÖRN. Iceland Correspondent, *Financial Times*, London.
Iceland

MAURON, PAUL. Director, International Vine and Wine Office, Paris.
Industrial Review (*in part*)

MAZIE, DAVID M. Associate of Carl T. Rowan, syndicated columnist. Free-lance Writer.
Social and Welfare Services (*in part*)

MAZZE, EDWARD MARK. Dean and Professor of Marketing, W. Paul Stillman School of Business, Seton Hall University, South Orange, N.J. Author of *Personal Selling: Choice Against Chance; Introduction to Marketing: Readings in the Discipline*.
Consumerism (*in part*); Industrial Review (*in part*)

MECHANIC, DAVID. John Bascom Professor of Sociology and Director, Center for Medical Sociology and Health Services Research, University of Wisconsin, Madison. Author of *Medical Sociology; Politics, Medicine and Social Science*.
Health and Disease (*in part*)

MEIJER, REINDER PIETER. Professor of Dutch Language and Literature, University of London. Author of *Literature of the Low Countries; Dutch Grammar and Reader*.
Literature (*in part*)

MERMEL, T. W. Consulting Engineer; Chairman, Committee on World Register of Dams, International Commission on Large Dams; Chairman, U.S. Committee on Dams in the United States. Author of *Register of Dams in the United States; Supervision of Dams by State Authorities*.
Engineering Projects (*in part*)

MEYENDORFF, JOHN. Professor of Church History and Patristics, St. Vladimir's Seminary; Professor of Byzantine History, Fordham University, New York City. Author of *Christ in Eastern Christian Thought; Byzantine Theology*.
Religion (*in part*)

MIHAILOVICH, VASA D. Professor of Slavic Languages and Literatures, University of North Carolina, Chapel Hill.
Literature (*in part*)

MILES, PETER W. Chairman, Department of Entomology, University of Adelaide, Australia.
Life Sciences (*in part*)

MILLAR, THOMAS B. Director, Australian Institute of International Affairs; Professorial Fellow in International Relations, Australian National University, Canberra. Author of *Australia's Defence; Australia's Foreign Policy*.
Australia: *Special Report*

MILLIKIN, SANDRA. Architectural Historian.
Architecture; Art and Art Exhibitions

MITCHELL, K. K. Lecturer, Department of Physical Education, University of Leeds, England. Hon. General Secretary, English Basket Ball Association.
Basketball (*in part*)

MODEAN, ERIK W. Director, News Bureau, Lutheran Council in the U.S.A., New York City.
Religion (*in part*)

MODIANO, MARIO. Athens Correspondent, *The Times*, London.
Greece

MONACO, ALBERT M., JR. Executive Director, United States Volleyball Association, San Francisco, Calif.
Court Games (*in part*)

MORGAN, HAZEL. Production Assistant (Sleevenotes and Covers), E.M.I. Records Ltd., London.
Music (*in part*)

MORRISON, DONALD M. Staff Writer, *Time* magazine.
Publishing (*in part*)

MORTIMER, MOLLY. Commonwealth Correspondent, *The Spectator*, London. Author of *Trusteeship in Practice; Kenya*.
Botswana; Burundi; Commonwealth of Nations; Dependent States (*in part*); Equatorial Guinea; Gambia, The; Ghana; Lesotho; Liberia; Maldives; Mauritius; Nigeria; Rwanda; Sierra Leone; Swaziland

MOSS, ROBERT V. President, United Church of Christ, New York City. Author of *The Life of Paul; We Believe; As Paul Sees Christ*.
Religion (*in part*)

MOTTERSHEAD, G. S. Director-Secretary, Chester Zoo, Chester, England.
Zoos and Botanical Gardens (*in part*)

MULLINS, STEPHANIE. Historian, London.
Biography (*in part*)

NARBOROUGH, COLIN. Reuters Correspondent, Helsinki, Fin.
Finland

NATOLI, SALVATORE J. Educational Affairs Director, Association of American Geographers. Co-author of *Dictionary of Basic Geography; Experiences in Inquiry*.
Geography

NAYLOR, ERNEST. Professor of Marine Biology, University of Liverpool; Director, Marine Biological Laboratory, Port Erin, Isle of Man. Author of *British Marine Isopods*.
Life Sciences (*in part*)

NEILL, JOHN. Chief Chemical Engineer, Submerged Combustion Ltd. Author of Climbers' Club Guides; *Cwm Silyn and Tremadoc, Snowdon South;* Alpine Club Guide: *Selected Climbs in the Pennine Alps*.
Mountaineering

NELSON, BERT D. Editor and Publisher, *Track and Field News*. Author of *Little Red Book; The Decathlon Book*.
Track and Field Sports (*in part*)

NEMOIANU, VIRGIL PETRE. Literary Critic; Professor of Literature, University of Bucharest, Romania. Author of several volumes on English, German, and Romanian literature.
Literature (*in part*)

NETSCHERT, BRUCE C. Vice-President, National Economic Research Associates, Inc., Washington, D.C. Author of *The Future Supply of Oil and Gas.* Co-author of *Energy in the American Economy: 1850–1975.*
Energy (*in part*)

NEUSNER, JACOB. Professor of Religious Studies, Brown University, Providence, R.I. Author of *Invitation to the Talmud; A History of the Mishnaic Law of Purities.*
Religion (*in part*)

NOEL, H. S. Managing Editor, *World Fishing,* London.
Fisheries

NORMAN, GERALDINE. Saleroom Correspondent, *The Times,* London. Author of *The Sale of Works of Art.*
Art Sales

NOVALES, RONALD R. Professor of Biological Sciences, Northwestern University, Evanston, Ill. Contributor to *Handbook of Physiology; Comparative Animal Physiology.*
Life Sciences (*in part*)

NOVICK, JULIUS. Associate Professor of Literature, State University of New York at Purchase; Theater Critic, the *Village Voice* and *The Humanist.* Author of *Beyond Broadway: The Quest for Permanent Theatres.*
Theatre (*in part*)

NOVOSTI. Novosti Press Agency, Moscow.
Literature (*in part*); Publishing (*in part*)

NOZICK, ROBERT. Professor of Philosophy, Harvard University. Author of *Anarchy, State, and Utopia.*
Feature Article: *Free Enterprise in America*

OATES, JEANNETTE. Journalist and Writer.
Biography (*in part*)

OBOLENSKY, ALEXIS. President, World Backgammon Club, Inc. Co-author of *Backgammon: The Action Game.*
Board Games (*in part*)

O'LEARY, JEREMIAH A., JR. Diplomatic Correspondent, *Washington Star.* Author of *Dominican Action—1965; Panama: Canal Issues and Treaty Talks—1967.*
Biography (*in part*); Chile

OSBORNE, KEITH. Editor, *Rowing,* 1961–63; Hon. Editor, *British Rowing Almanack,* 1961– . Author of *Boat Racing in Britain, 1715–1975.*
Rowing

OSTERBIND, CARTER C. Director, Bureau of Economic and Business Research, University of Florida. Editor of *Income in Retirement; Migration, Mobility, and Aging.*
Industrial Review (*in part*)

PAGE, SHEILA A. B. Research Officer, National Institute of Economic and Social Research, London.
Economy, World (*in part*)

PALMER, S. B. Lecturer, Department of Applied Physics, University of Hull, Eng.
Physics

PARKER, SANDY. Fur and Ready-to-Wear News Editor, *Women's Wear Daily.*
Industrial Review (*in part*)

PARNELL, COLIN. Editor, *Wine and Spirit,* London.
Industrial Review (*in part*)

PARSONS, BARRIE H. Executive Editor, *B & T Weekly,* Sydney, Australia.
Television and Radio (*in part*)

PATTERSON, SHEILA. Research Associate, Department of Anthropology, University College, London. Author of *Colour and Culture in South Africa; The Last Trek; Dark Strangers; Immigrants in Industry.*
Bahamas, The; Barbados; Dependent States (*in part*); Grenada; Guyana; Jamaica; Migration, International; Race Relations (*in part*); Trinidad and Tobago

PAUL, CHARLES ROBERT, JR. Staff Member, U.S. Olympic Committee, New York City; Senior Editor, *The Olympian.* Author of *The Olympic Games, 1968.*
Gymnastics and Weight Lifting

PAUL, OGLESBY. Vice-President, Health Sciences, and Professor of Medicine, Northwestern University, Chicago.
Health and Disease (*in part*)

PEARCE, JOAN. Research Officer, Economics Department, Lloyds Bank International, London. Editor of *Latin America: A Broader World Role.*
Colombia; Spain

PENFOLD, ROBIN C. Public Relations Executive, Carl Byoir and Associates Ltd., London. Author of *A Journalist's Guide to Plastics.*
Industrial Review (*in part*)

PERRIG, ALEXANDER. Professor of Art History, University of Hamburg, West Germany.
Art and Art Exhibitions: *Special Report*

PERTILE, LINO. Lecturer in Italian, University of Sussex, England.
Literature (*in part*)

PETHERICK, KARIN. Crown Princess Louise Lecturer in Swedish, University College, London.
Literature (*in part*)

PETTIGREW, THOMAS FRASER. Professor of Social Psychology and Sociology, Harvard University. Author of *Racially Separate or Together?; Racial Discrimination in the United States.*
Race Relations (*in part*)

PFEFFER, IRVING. Professor of Insurance and Finance, Virginia Polytechnic Institute and State University. Author of *Insurance and Economic Theory; The Financing of Small Business; Perspectives on Insurance.*
Stock Exchanges (*in part*)

PICK, OTTO. Professor of International Relations, University of Surrey, Guildford, England; Director, Atlantic Information Centre for Teachers, London and Washington, D.C. Co-author of *Collective Security.*
Union of Soviet Socialist Republics

PIERCE, FRANCIS S. Economist and Free-lance Writer, specializing in questions of public policy.
Economics

PLOTKIN, FREDERICK S. Professor of English Literature and Chairman, Division of Humanities, Stern College, Yeshiva University, New York. Author of *Milton's Inward Jerusalem; Faith and Reason; Judaism and Tragic Theology.*
Literature (*in part*)

POTTER, SIMEON. Emeritus Professor of English Language and Philology, University of Liverpool, England. Author of *Our Language; Language in the Modern World; Modern Linguistics; Changing English.*
Words and Meanings, New

PRAG, DEREK. Consultant on EEC Affairs and Free-lance Journalist; Director, London Information Office of the European Communities, 1965–73. Co-author of *Businessman's Guide to the Common Market.*
European Unity

PRASAD, H. Y. SHARADA. Information Adviser, Prime Minister's Secretariat, New Delhi, India.
India

PREIL, GABRIEL. Free-lance Writer; Hebrew and Yiddish Poet. Author of *Israeli Poetry in Peace and War; Ner Mul Kokhavim* ("Candle Against the Stars"); *Mapat Erev* ("Map of Evening"); *Lieder* ("Poems"); *Haesh Vehadmama* ("The Fire and the Silence"); *Mitoch Zeman Venof* ("Of Time and Place").
Literature (*in part*)

RANGER, ROBIN J. Assistant Professor, Department of Political Science, St. Francis Xavier University, Antigonish, Nova Scotia. Author of *The Politics of Arms Control, 1958–1975.*
Defense

RAPP, GEORGE ROBERT, JR. Dean, College of Letters and Sciences, University of Minnesota, Duluth. Co-author of *Encyclopedia of Minerals; The Evolving Earth.*
Earth Sciences (*in part*)

RAY, G. F. Senior Research Fellow, National Institute of Economic and Social Research, London.
Industrial Review (*in part*)

READ, HARRY. Director, Salvation Army International Information Services, London.
Religion (*in part*)

RECKERT, STEPHEN. Camoens Professor of Portuguese, King's College, University of London. Author of *Do cancioneiro de amigo; Gil Vicente: espíritu y letra.*
Literature (*in part*)

REIBSTEIN, JOAN NATALIE. Free-lance Writer and Editor. Former Staff Writer, *Encyclopædia Britannica.*
Biography (*in part*)

REICHELDERFER, F. W. Consultant on Atmospheric Sciences; Retired Director, Weather Bureau, U.S. Department of Commerce, Washington, D.C.
Earth Sciences (*in part*)

REID, J. H. Senior Lecturer in German, University of Nottingham, England. Author of *Heinrich Böll: Withdrawal and Re-emergence.* Co-author of *Critical Strategies: German Fiction in the 20th Century.*
Literature (*in part*)

REYNOLDS, ARTHUR GUY. Formerly Registrar and Professor of Church History, Emmanuel College, Toronto.
Religion (*in part*)

RICHTER-ALTSCHAFFER, J. H. Economic Consultant; Retired Director for North America, International Federation of Agricultural Producers. Author of *Economic Theory of Public Investment; Agricultural Protection and Trade.*
Agriculture and Food Supplies (*in part*)

RILEY, WALLACE B. Technical Editor, *Computer Design.* Author of *Electronic Computer Memory Technology.*
Computers

RIPLEY, SUZANNE. Assistant Professor, Department of Anthropology, City College, City University of New York. Contributor to *Old World Monkeys.*
Anthropology

ROBERTS, R. L. Editorial Consultant, *Church Times,* London.
Religion *(in part)*

ROBINSON, DAVID. Film Critic, *The Times,* London. Author of *Buster Keaton; Hollywood in the Twenties; The Great Funnies—A History of Screen Comedy; A History of World Cinema.*
Biography *(in part)*; **Motion Pictures** *(in part)*

ROHMER, RICHARD HEATH. Canadian Journalist and Lawyer; Chairman, Royal Commission on Publishing, Ottawa. Author of *The Arctic Imperative; Exodus/U.K.*
Canada: *Special Report*

RUTFORD, ROBERT H. Head, Office of Polar Programs, U.S. National Science Foundation.
Antarctica

SAEKI, SHOICHI. Professor, College of General Education, University of Tokyo. Author of *In Search of Japanese Ego.*
Literature *(in part)*

SAINT-AMOUR, ROBERT. Professor, Department of Literary Studies, University of Quebec at Montreal.
Literature *(in part)*

SAMSON, JACK. Editor, *Field & Stream,* New York City.
Hunting and Fishing

SANDERS, IVAN. Associate Professor of English, Suffolk County (N.Y.) Community College.
Literature *(in part)*

SANDON, HAROLD. Former Professor of Zoology, University of Khartoum, Sudan. Author of *The Protozoan Fauna of the Soil; The Food of Protozoa; An Illustrated Guide to the Fresh-Water Fishes of the Sudan; Essays on Protozoology.*
Life Sciences *(in part)*

SARAHETE, YRJÖ. Secretary, Fédération Internationale des Quilleurs, Helsinki, Fin.
Bowling *(in part)*

SAYERS, RAYMOND S. Professor of Romance Languages, Queens College, and of Comparative Literature, Graduate School, City University of New York. Author of *The Negro in Brazilian Literature; Portugal and Brazil in Transition.*
Literature *(in part)*

SCHOENFIELD, ALBERT. Publisher, *Swimming World.* Contributor to *The Technique of Water Polo; The History of Swimming.*
Swimming

SCHOPFLIN, GEORGE. Specialist in Eastern European Affairs, British Broadcasting Corporation, London. Editor of *The Soviet Union and Eastern Europe: A Handbook.*
Biography *(in part)*; **Czechoslovakia**

SCHULIAN, JOHN. Sportswriter, *Washington* (D.C.) *Post.*
Basketball *(in part)*

SCHULMAN, ELIAS. Associate Professor, Queens College, City College of New York; Professor, Graduate School, Jewish Teachers Seminary. Author of *Israel Tsinberg, His Life and Works; Young Wilno.* Co-editor of *A Biographical Dictionary of Yiddish Literature* (vol. vii).
Literature *(in part)*

SEARS, ROBERT N. Associate Technical Editor, *The American Rifleman.*
Target Sports *(in part)*

SERGEANT, HOWARD. Lecturer and Writer. Editor of *Outposts,* Walton-on-Thames, England. Author of *The Cumberland Wordsworth; Tradition in the Making of Modern Poetry.*
Literature *(in part)*

SHACKLEFORD, PETER. Assistant Director, World Tourism Organization (WTO), Madrid.
Industrial Review *(in part)*

SHAPLEN, ROBERT. Far Eastern Correspondent, *The New Yorker.* Author of *The Lost Revolution: The U.S. in Vietnam; The Road from War.*
Southeast Asian Affairs: *Special Report*

SHARPE, MITCHELL R. Science Writer; Historian, Alabama Space and Rocket Center, Huntsville. Author of *Living in Space: The Environment of the Astronaut; Yuri Gagarin, First Man in Space; "It Is I, Seagull": Valentina Tereshkova, First Woman in Space.* Co-author of *Applied Astronautics; Basic Astronautics.*
Space Exploration

SHAW, T. R. Commander, Royal Navy. Member, British Cave Research Association.
Speleology

SHENK, CLAYTON B. Executive Secretary, U.S. National Archery Association.
Target Sports *(in part)*

SIMPSON, NOEL. Managing Director, Sydney Bloodstock Proprietary Ltd., Sydney, Australia.
Equestrian Sports *(in part)*

SMEDLEY, GLENN B. Member of Board of Governors, American Numismatic Association.
Philately and Numismatics *(in part)*

SMITH, R. W. Dean, Graduate School, University of the Pacific, Stockton, Calif. Editor of *Venture of Islam* by M. G. S. Hodgson.
Religion *(in part)*

SMOGORZEWSKI, K. M. Writer on contemporary history. Founder and Editor, *Free Europe,* London. Author of *The United States and Great Britain; Poland's Access to the Sea.*
Albania; Andorra; Biography *(in part)*; **Bulgaria; Economy, World** *(in part)*; **Hungary; Liechtenstein; Luxembourg; Monaco; Mongolia; Poland; Political Parties; Romania; San Marino**

SNIDER, ARTHUR J. Science Editor, *Chicago Daily News.* Author of *Learning How to Live with Heart Trouble; Learning How to Live with Nervous Tension.*
Health and Disease *(in part)*

SPELMAN, ROBERT A. Administrative Vice-President, U.S. National Association of Furniture Manufacturers.
Industrial Review *(in part)*

STACKS, JOHN F. Correspondent, *Time* magazine, Washington, D.C. Author of *Stripping: The Surface Mining of America.*
Biography *(in part)*

STAERK, MELANIE. Member, Swiss National Commission for UNESCO (Information).
Switzerland

STEEN, LYNN ARTHUR. Professor of Mathematics, St. Olaf College, Northfield, Minn. Author of *Counterexamples in Topology.*
Mathematics

STEVENSON, TOM. Garden Columnist, *Baltimore News American; Washington Post;* Washington Post-Los Angeles Times News Service. Author of *Pruning Guide for Trees, Shrubs and Vines; Lawn Guide; Gardening for the Beginner.*
Gardening *(in part)*

STOKES, J. BUROUGHS. Manager, Committees on Publication, The First Church of Christ, Scientist, Boston.
Religion *(in part)*

STØVERUD, TORBJØRN. W. P. Ker Senior Lecturer in Norwegian, University College, London.
Literature *(in part)*

STRAUSS, MICHAEL. Sports Reporter, *New York Times.* Author of *The New York Times Ski Guide to the United States.*
Combat Sports *(in part)*

SWEETINBURGH, THELMA. Paris Fashion Correspondent for *International Textiles* (Amsterdam) and the British Wool Textile Industry.
Fashion and Dress *(in part)*

SWIFT, RICHARD N. Professor of Politics, New York University, New York City. Author of *International Law: Current and Classic; World Affairs and the College Curriculum.*
United Nations

SYNAN, VINSON. General Secretary, Pentecostal Holiness Church; Chairman, History Department, Oklahoma City Southwestern College. Author of *The Holiness-Pentecostal Movement; The Old Time Power.*
Religion *(in part)*

TAGA, KEIJI. President, Educational Cultural Production, Inc., Tokyo; Television Producer.
Biography *(in part)*

TAISHOFF, SOL J. Chairman and Editor, *Broadcasting,* Washington, D.C.
Television and Radio *(in part)*

TALLAN, NORMAN M. Director, Metallurgy and Ceramics Research Laboratory, Aerospace Research Laboratories, Wright-Patterson Air Fôrce Base, Dayton, Ohio. Editor of *Electrical Properties, Ceramics and Glass.*
Materials Sciences *(in part)*

TATTERSALL, ARTHUR. Textile Trade Expert and Statistician, Manchester, England.
Industrial Review *(in part)*

TAUBERT, SIGFRED. Chairman, International Book Committee, UNESCO; formerly Director, Frankfurt Book Fair.
Publishing *(in part)*

TERRY, WALTER, JR. Dance Critic and Dance Editor, *Saturday Review* magazine, New York. Author of *The Dance in America; The Ballet Companion; Miss Ruth: The "More Living Life" of Ruth St. Denis.*
Dance *(in part)*

THAINE, MARINA. Editor, *Tobacco,* London.
Industrial Review *(in part)*

THOMAS, HARFORD. Retired City and Financial Editor, *The Guardian,* London.
Biography *(in part)*; **Industrial Relations:** *Special Report;* **United Kingdom**

THOMPSON, ANTHONY. European Linguist, College of Librarianship, Aberystwyth, Wales. General Secretary, International Federation of Library Associations, 1962–70. Author of *Vocabularium Bibliothecarii; Library Buildings of Britain and Europe.*
Libraries

TINGAY, LANCE. Lawn Tennis Correspondent, the *Daily Telegraph,* London.
Tennis and Rackets (*in part*)

TRIGG, ROBERT H. Senior Economic Adviser and Manager, Institutional Research, New York Stock Exchange.
Stock Exchanges (*in part*)

TRILLING, OSSIA. Vice-President, International Association of Theatre Critics. Co-editor and contributor, *International Theatre.* Contributor, BBC, the *Financial Times,* London.
Biography (*in part*); **Theatre** (*in part*)

TRUSSELL, TAIT. Administrative Vice-President, American Forest Institute.
Industrial Review (*in part*)

TSUJIMOTO, ICHIRO. Public Relations Officer, Nippon Hoso Kyokai (Japan Broadcasting Corp.), Tokyo.
Television and Radio (*in part*)

TURKEVICH, JOHN. Eugene Higgins Professor of Chemistry, Department of Chemistry, Princeton University. Author of *Chemistry in the Soviet Union; Soviet Men of Science.*
Chemistry (*in part*)

TYPE, MICHAEL. Head of Permanent Secretariat, European Broadcasting Union, Geneva.
Television and Radio (*in part*)

UNHCR. The Office of the United Nations High Commissioner for Refugees, Geneva.
Refugees

UNNY, GOVINDAN. Agence France-Presse Special Correspondent for India, Nepal, and Ceylon.
Bangladesh; Bhutan; Biography (*in part*); **Burma; Dependent States** (*in part*); **Nepal; Sri Lanka**

van PRAAG, JACK H. Chairman, National Badminton News Committee, American Badminton Association, Pasadena, Calif.
Court Games (*in part*)

VERDI, ROBERT WILLIAM. Sportswriter, *Chicago Tribune.*
Baseball (*in part*)

VIANSSON-PONTÉ, PIERRE. Editorial Adviser and Leader Writer, *Le Monde,* Paris. Author of *Les Gaullistes; The King and His Court; Les Politiques; Histoire de la République Gaullienne.*
Biography (*in part*)

VINT, ARTHUR KINGSLEY. Honorary General Secretary, International Table Tennis Federation, Sussex, England.
Table Tennis

WADLEY, J. B. Writer and Broadcaster on cycling. Author of *Tour de France 1970, 1971,* and *1973; Old Roads and New.*
Cycling

WALKER, MARTIN. Journalist, *The Guardian,* London. Author of *The National Front.*
United Kingdom: ***Special Report***

WARD-THOMAS, P. A. Golf Correspondent, *The Guardian,* London.
Golf

WAY, DIANE LOIS. Archivist, Anglican Diocese of Toronto, Ont.
Biography (*in part*)

WEBB, GORDON A. Editor, *Toys International,* London.
Games and Toys

WEBB, HENRY, JR. Retired from U.S. Foreign Service.
El Salvador; Honduras; Nicaragua

WEBB, W. L. Literary Editor, *The Guardian,* London and Manchester.
Literature (*in part*)

WEBSTER, PETER L. Assistant Professor, Department of Botany, University of Massachusetts, Amherst.
Life Sciences (*in part*)

WEEDEN, CYRIL. Assistant Director, Glass Manufacturers' Federation, London.
Industrial Review (*in part*)

WEIGEL, J. TIMOTHY. Sportscaster, NBC Television. Author of *The Buckeyes: Ohio State Football.*
Biography (*in part*)

WEST, RICHARD. Formerly Vietnam Correspondent, *London Daily Mail, New Statesman, Irish Times,* and British Broadcasting Corporation. Author of *Sketches from Vietnam; Victory in Vietnam.*
Refugees: ***Special Report***

WIJNGAARD, BARBARA. Research Officer, Economics Department, Lloyds Bank International Ltd., London.
Costa Rica; Mexico

WILLIAMS, BRIAN. Free-lance Writer, London.
Television and Radio (*in part*)

WILLIAMS, DAVID L. Associate Professor of Government, Ohio University.
Communist Movement

WILLIAMS, L. F. RUSHBROOK. Fellow of All Souls College, Oxford University, 1914–21; Professor of Modern Indian History, Allahabad, India, 1914–19. Author of *The State of Pakistan; Kutch in History and Legend.* Editor of *Handbook to India, Pakistan, Bangladesh, Nepal, and Sri Lanka; Sufi Studies East and West; Pakistan Under Challenge.*
Afghanistan; Iran; Pakistan

WILLIAMS, PETER. Editor, *Dance and Dancers,* London. Chairman, Arts Council, Great Britain's Dance Theatre Committee; Chairman, British Council's Drama Advisory Committee.
Dance (*in part*)

WILLIAMSON, TREVOR. Chief Sports Subeditor, the *Daily Telegraph,* London.
Football (*in part*)

WILSON, MICHAEL. Technical Editor, *Flight International,* London.
Industrial Review (*in part*)

WISE, CONRAD. Editor in Chief, *Museum,* Division of Museums and Standards, UNESCO, Paris.
Museums (*in part*)

WISWELL, TOM. Author; Freestyle World Checkers Champion. Author of *The Science of Checkers; Complete Guide to Checkers.*
Board Games (*in part*)

WITTE, E. RANDALL. News Bureau Director, Professional Rodeo Cowboys Association. Author of annual rodeo reference book.
Arena Sports (*in part*)

WOOD, CHRISTINA MARGARET. Free-lance Sportswriter.
Tennis and Rackets (*in part*)

WOOD, KENNETH H. Editor, *The Advent Review and Sabbath Herald.* Author of *Meditations for Moderns; Relevant Religions.* Co-author of *His Initials Were F. D. N.*
Religion (*in part*)

WOOLLER, MICHAEL. Economic Research Officer, Lloyds Bank International, London.
Biography (*in part*); **Cuba; Haiti; Paraguay; Portugal; Venezuela**

WOOLLEY, DAVID. Editor, *Airports International,* London.
Transportation (*in part*)

WORSNOP, RICHARD L. Associate Editor, Editorial Research Reports, Washington, D.C.
United States (*in part*); **United States:** ***Special Report***

WRIGHT ALMON R. Retired Senior Historian, U.S. Department of State.
Panama

YAGHI, ABDUL RAHMAN. Professor of Modern Arabic Literature, Department of Arabic, University of Jordan. Author of works on modern Arabic literature.
Literature (*in part*)

YAMAMOTO, KIKUO. Associate Professor of Literature, Waseda University, Japan.
Biography (*in part*)

YOUNG, M. NORVEL. Chancellor, Pepperdine University, Malibu, Calif. Editor of *Twentieth Century Christian; Power for Today.* Author of *Preachers of Today; History of Colleges Connected with Churches of Christ.*
Religion (*in part*)

YUFIT, ROBERT I. Project Director, Drug Abuse Program, Department of Psychiatry, University of Chicago; Coordinator, Suicide Assessment Team, Illinois Masonic Hospital.
Health and Disease (*in part*)

Index

The black type entries are article headings in the *Book of the Year*. These black type article entries do not show page notations because they are to be found in their alphabetical position in the body of the book. They show the dates of the issues of the *Book of the Year* in which the articles appear. For example "Archaeology 76, 75, 74" indicates that the article "Archaeology" is to be found in the 1976, 1975, and 1974 *Book of the Year*.

The light type headings that are indented under black type article headings refer to material elsewhere in the text related to the subject under which they are listed. The light type headings that are not indented refer to information in the text not given a special article. Biographies and obituaries are listed as cross references to the articles *"Biography"* and *"Obituaries"* for the year in which they appear. References to illustrations are preceded by the abbreviation "il."

All headings, whether consisting of a single word or more, are treated for the purpose of alphabetization as single complete headings. Names beginning with "Mc" and "Mac" are alphabetized as "Mac"; "St." is treated as "Saint." All references below show the exact quarter of the page by means of the letters *a, b, c* and *d,* signifying, respectively, the upper and lower halves of the first column and the upper and lower halves of the second column. Exceptions to this rule are tables, illustrations, and references from the articles *"Energy"* and *"Industrial Review."*

A

C

D

E

J

M

N

O

P

Q

R

S

T

U

V

W

X

Y

Z